MORNINGSTAR®

Funds500™

Annual Sourcebook
2002 Edition

Introduction by
Don Phillips,
Managing Director,
Morningstar

Morningstar's Accounting, Circulation, and Product Sales and Support departments help bring you *Morningstar Funds 500.*

Morningstar Funds 500 (ISBN # 007-138771-4) is published annually. The subscription rate is $39.95 per year.

Editorial and business communications may be addressed to: *Morningstar Funds 500*, Morningstar, 225 West Wacker Drive, Chicago, IL 60606. While data are gathered from reliable sources, Morningstar, Inc. cannot guarantee accuracy and completeness. Morningstar, Inc. does not have a selling agreement of any kind with the funds listed herein, and no offer or solicitation to sell or buy any of the funds is made.

Table of Contents

What an awful year! On the heels of 2000's tech-stock collapse, investors may well have been thinking that 2001 would bring welcome relief. But unlike the quick stock-market rebounds following the 1987 crash or the 1990 recession, this past year it was not to be. The markets went from bad to worse and the deplorable events of September 11 pushed an already shaky economy into tougher territory still. These are truly the times that try investors' souls.

While the day-to-day news was anything but good, investors were able to take comfort in the time-tested benefits of diversification, dollar-cost averaging, and fundamental analysis. Each of these principles, so disdained during the tech-stock bubble, proved its merit in spades during last year's bear market. Indeed, investors who held on to bond or value funds during the growth-stock mania of recent years got the last laugh. For those investors who had continued to make regular contributions to these out-of-favor areas over the past few years, the rewards were greater. And for those who did solid fundamental analysis to ensure that their portfolios included deep-value funds like First Eagle SoGen Global in addition to less-strict value funds that may have looked better in the recent growth-led years, the rewards were even better still. All of which goes to show once more that while no one can predict the market's near-term direction with any consistency, we can all identify types of behavior that can help investors combat even the toughest of markets.

That sets the stage for the question at hand: What does one do now? Many investors are holding on to once-soaring growth funds in the hope that they will rebound, but not all managers of these funds are buying high-growth stocks today. Indeed, funds like Janus'—which many investors associate with the tech boom—have taken on a most cautious bent of late. Who ever would have thought in 1999 that Berkshire Hathaway would someday grace the list of holdings of the Janus organization as it does today? Such major strategy changes pose a challenge for fund investors. Funds aren't static. Styles evolve; managers come and go. It's more important than ever to know the people, policies, and positioning behind your funds. Without this type of fundamental research, even the best-intentioned portfolio of funds is apt to run afoul of your expectations.

So in rethinking your portfolio for 2002, use tools like our style box to understand the balance of your portfolio committed to large and small, growth or value stocks. Look at the composition scores to get a sense of the embedded cash and bond positions in "stock" mutual funds, and check the international exposure you may have through "domestic" funds. Think also about how market forces have reshaped your portfolio over the past 18 months. Chances are you have much less exposure to stocks relative to cash and bonds now than you did last year. For longer-term investors, it may be time to top up your stock exposure, especially to growth stocks, to re-establish the long-term asset allocation that's right for you.

Finally, take comfort in the examples we've all seen of the rewards of making systematic contributions to funds over an extended period of time. While we all wish to emulate such results, we tend to be too willing to make the contributions at or near market peaks, but too hesitant to step up and make the purchases when prices are depressed. Yet it is those purchases at periods of maximum pessimism that ultimately offer the greatest appreciation potential. Investing may seem a lot less fun these days—certainly CNBC ratings are way down—yet these are far better times to make meaningful progress toward your long-term goals than were the heady days of the late 1990s. As one top fund manager says, "You make your money during markets like this, you just don't know it at the time."

Don Phillips
Managing Director,
Morningstar, Inc.

Technology Disappoints, Bonds Dazzle

It wasn't a good year to take on risk.

As 2000 came to a close, the average specialty-technology fund had posted a 30%-plus loss. Tech-stock investors probably thought things had to get better in 2001.

They were wrong.

Simply put, tech stocks were brutalized again in 2001, as the typical specialty-technology fund fell more than 30% during the year. Telecom-equipment and Internet-related stocks took especially harsh drubbings. Telecom-equipment makers such as **Cisco Systems** CSCO, **JDS Uniphase** JDSU, and **Juniper Networks** JNPR entered the year with sky-high valuations, implying that investors expected them to grow at a sizzling pace for years to come. As debt-laden phone companies pulled back on their capital expenditures, however, all three of those companies' operating fundamentals eroded, and their shares posted enormous losses. Weakening growth rates also took a toll on plenty of Internet companies such as **Homestore.com** HOMS, which restated its financials early in 2002, pushing Net-focused funds like **Amerindo Internet B2B** BTBAX to huge losses.

Specialty-communications funds also posted enormous declines during the year, though the severity of those losses varied enormously. Funds such as **Fidelity Select Multimedia** FBMPX, which focuses on relatively stable cable and media stocks, fared relatively well during the year. But many offerings in the category had a ton of exposure to telecom-equipment, communications-related semiconductor firms, and speculative telecom-service providers like **Global Crossing** GX. Falling long-distance prices, slowing growth in the wireless arena, and declining capital spending on telecom products decimated funds like **Firsthand Communications** TCFOX, which shed more than half its value last year.

Naturally, the stupendous losses in the technology and communications arenas took an enormous toll on the diversified funds that have big stakes in such issues. Morningstar's small-growth, mid-growth, and large-growth categories all posted sizable losses for the year. These funds also tend to have some exposure to risky biotechnology issues, which faltered as investors shifted toward less-speculative fare. Despite rallying furiously in the fourth quarter, some growth funds shed half of their values in a single year, including **Merrill Lynch Focus Twenty** MBFOX and **Invesco Growth** FLRFX.

Investors often turn to overseas markets for diversification, but that didn't help much last year. The flagging Japanese economy continued to weigh on the country's shares, so the typical Japan fund lost more than 20% of its value. Indeed, offerings such as **Fidelity Japan** FJPNX and **Liberty Newport Japan Opportunities** NJOAX, both of which focus on growth stocks, shed 30% of their values during the year. European investors didn't fare much better. With countries on the Continent sliding toward a recession, European markets also posted significant losses in 2001, with growth-focused offerings such as **Invesco European** FEURX posting 35%-plus losses. Despite Argentina's ongoing political and economic problems, diversified emerging-markets funds held up well by comparison. Some markets, including Russia's, actually notched meaningful gains, but the average offering in that category also lost ground during the year.

That said, some funds actually posted robust returns in 2001. With the economy slowing, inflation fears subsiding, and the Federal Reserve aggressively cutting interest rates, most bond funds registered solid gains. Indeed, many long-term Treasury and high-quality corporate offerings, including **Vanguard Long-Term Bond Index** VBLTX and **PIMCO Long-Term U.S. Government** PGOVX, notched double-digit returns. Municipal funds also posted excellent returns, led by offerings such as **Nuveen High Yield Municipal Bond** NHMRX and **PIMCO Municipal Bond** PFMIX. Corporate high-yield funds were the exception to the rule, however, as the slowing economy drove up default rates for the highly leveraged companies that issue junk bonds. Offerings with substantial exposure to telecom junk debt, including **Invesco High-Yield** FHYPX, posted huge losses, as investors soured on upstart telecom-service providers' heavy capital-expenditure needs and significant operating losses. Overall, the high-yield category posted a small gain for the year, but that was the worst showing of any domestic bond-fund group.

Story of 2001: Value Trumps Growth – Again

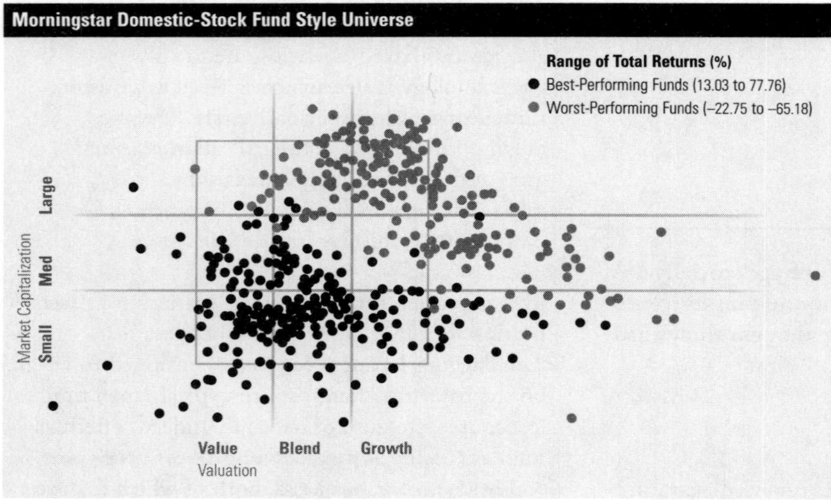

Data through January 8, 2002.

The worst performing funds of 2001 fell in the growth area of the Morningstar style universe, while the best performing funds landed in the small value section.

A number of small-cap value funds prospered, as well. Throughout the year, investors gravitated away from high-P/E stocks and toward those with low valuations—including industrials, banks, and beaten-down retailers—benefiting the small-value category. Indeed, all the small-cap categories outperformed their large-cap counterparts, and a number of small- and mid-cap funds—including *Funds 500* picks such as **Fidelity Low-Priced Stock** FLPSX and **Oakmark Fund** OAKMX—posted healthy double-digit gains. Indeed, the mid-value and small-blend categories also notched healthy, single-digit returns during the year. Precious-metals offerings, which have long been among the worst performers in the entire fund universe, logged a respectable gain in 2001, as political and economic worries drove investors to increase their exposure to hard assets. That allowed **First Eagle SoGen Gold** SGGDX to post a sizzling, 37.3% gain for the year. Real-estate firms also benefited from investors' renewed interest in hard assets, as well as from their ability to put up better operating numbers than most companies did in a difficult economic environment. **Third Avenue Real Estate Value** TAREX and **Cohen & Steers Equity Income** CSEIX logged double-digit gains in 2001. Still, not every class of tangible assets performed well in 2001. The softening global economy, combined with OPEC's temporary inability to implement production cuts, took a toll on oil prices and oil-service companies' shares. **Fidelity Select Energy Service** FSESX, which invests in such firms, lost 21% last year.

Although it may be tempting, investors shouldn't blindly chase funds in the areas that have performed well. The asset classes that posted solid returns in 2001 are now less attractively priced than they have been in some time. For example, the interest rate on long-term Treasuries has fallen below 6%, after dipping below 5% during the year. Such rates are still at very low levels, and based on the historical record, it's arguably more likely that rates will rise than fall. Bond prices move inversely with changes in interest rates, so if rates rise, bond investors may suffer significant losses. If you're buying a high-quality bond fund now, make sure you're doing so because it makes sense in the overall context of your portfolio, not because you expect a repeat of the past year's robust gain. Similarly, although small companies were much more attractively priced than large caps in early 1999, after three years of relatively strong performance, they're no longer as cheap as they once were.

Finally, winning investors typically stick with diversified portfolios, or even adopt mildly contrarian strategies. The investors who have made hay since early 2000 are those who bucked the late-1990s' trend toward putting more and more money in technology and other growth funds. Instead, these savvy investors were looking to beaten-down parts of the market, including small caps and financials, which have handily outperformed growth stocks over the past two years. That's a lesson that the investor of today, who may be contemplating dumping growth exposure, would do well to keep in mind. M

15 Great Funds for the Future

Funds to fit any role in your portfolio, from conservative to aggressive.

If there's anything positive about the terrible market of the past few years, it may be that investors have become acutely aware of the importance of diversification and risk control. Having seen their portfolios decimated by technology stocks and tech-heavy mutual funds, many investors have concluded that they'd rather miss out on the next party if it means they'll also miss the hangover.

But most long-term investors can—and should—make room for some riskier investment types in their portfolios, provided that portfolio is anchored with a group of solid core funds and some more stable, shorter-term investments. Here are some of our favorite ideas within each fund type. We've ranked them by their standard deviations—a measure of volatility—from most conservative to most aggressive. Some are big funds, while others are up-and-comers that we think deserve to be on your radar.

Portfolio Stabilizers

Montgomery Short Duration Govt Bond MNSGX
For investors who are willing to take on a bit more risk than a money-market fund, this fund could fill the bill. Management doesn't make big bets on the direction of interest rates or credit quality—it sticks with Treasury bonds and government-agency and mortgage-backed debt, all of which are rated AAA. Nonetheless, the team here has been consistently able to add value relative to other funds that share its high-quality focus.

Vanguard Total Bond Market Index VBMFX
Like sibling **Vanguard Total Stock Market Index** VTSMX, this fund offers well-diversified exposure to a single asset class—in this case, bonds—in one shot. It holds nearly 7,000 different bonds in an effort to replicate the returns of the Lehman Brothers Aggregate index. Matching the index hasn't meant settling for less, however: returns have been competitive relative to other intermediate-term bond funds, and this fund's ultra-low expenses provide a huge tailwind.

Metropolitan West Total Return Bond MWTRX
This fund doesn't make big credit-quality or interest-rate bets, but its moves around the margins have been enough to help it pull ahead of most other intermediate-term bond funds. Management uses an opportunistic approach, seeking to add value with small duration and yield-curve adjustments, sector rotation, and issue selection. Although this fund's track record is fairly short, the same management team also built strong returns using a similar style at other firms, including PIMCO.

Vanguard Wellesley Income VWINX
This income-oriented fund won't thrive in every market; in 1999's growth-stock heyday, for example, it badly trailed hybrid funds that jumped on the technology-stock bandwagon. But this fund's focus on dividend-paying stocks and high-quality bonds means that it's a sensible diversification tool for a portfolio that's tilted toward growth stocks. When technology stocks tumbled in 2000 and early 2001, this fund came on strong.

Dodge & Cox Balanced DODBX
This fund proves that boring can be beautiful. Management splits the portfolio's assets between cheap stocks and high-quality bonds, and the end result has been a portfolio that hasn't ended a year in the red since 1981. In addition to its low volatility, the fund's returns have been more than competitive with other hybrid funds'. Further, costs are low and management is highly experienced.

Core Stock Funds

Dreyfus Appreciation DGAGX
This fund's unwavering focus on high-quality mega-cap companies—with a particular emphasis on consumer-staple and pharmaceutical stocks—has helped it deliver consistently superb results. The fund's tendency to underweight the technology sector holds it back when that sector rallies, but it has also made for a very smooth ride here.
An added bonus: A glacial turnover rate has led to excellent tax efficiency.

T. Rowe Price Equity-Income PRFDX
This fund might look a little slow when growth stocks rally, but its old-fashioned, value-leaning portfolio will ensure that its investors sleep easy at night. Manager Brian Rogers focuses on dividend-paying securities here, which means that he all but avoids the volatile technology sector in favor of giant energy and industrial names. Lots of large-cap

value funds use a similar strategy, but this one's execution has been better than most.

Fidelity Dividend Growth FDGFX
Fidelity offers a lot of solid funds that fit the core designation, but this offering stands out from the pack. Manager Charles Mangum uses a fairly generic growth-at-a-reasonable price strategy, but the end result has been anything but ho-hum. Being bearish on tech held the fund back during the late 1990s' bubble, but Mangum's attention to stocks' price tags has been vindicated over the past few years. The fund's returns are among the best in the large-blend category.

TIAA-CREF Growth & Income TIGIX
If you can't decide between indexing or active management, here's a way to split the difference. Manager Carlton Martin devotes part of this portfolio to the S&P 500 index, and actively picks stocks with the other portion. Returns have been consistently solid, and low expenses are a gift that keeps on giving. And while this fund hasn't been around very long, TIAA-CREF has long run money in a similar style for teachers and college professors. The fund is also a solid choice for beginning investors, as its minimum is a low $1,500.

Vanguard Total Stock Market Index VTSMX
This offering could be the only domestic-stock fund you'll ever need. It offers exposure to 5,000 U.S. publicly traded companies—large and small, fast-growing and slow-growing—in a single, ultra-cheap package. Over time its returns have been extremely competitive relative to the broad universe of domestic-stock funds, and its returns look equally attractive on an aftertax basis. For investors who'd like to simplify their lives, it doesn't get much better than this.

Aggressive Kickers

Davis Growth Opportunity RPEAX
Managers Chris Davis and Ken Feinberg have long earned our admiration for their great work at two large-cap value funds, **Selected American** SLASX and **Davis New York Venture** NYVTX. For this offering, they turn their attention to faster-growing stocks in the small- and mid-cap realm. That universe of stocks is fraught with potential pitfalls, but Davis and Feinberg aren't likely to throw risk control out the window. Although their firm has been emphasizing technology and health-care names lately, they are patient investors who are keenly sensitive to a stock's valuations.

American Funds Growth Fund of America AGTHX
This is one of the most even-keeled growth funds you're apt to find. It stayed in the game when high-P/E stocks were running hard in the late 1990s, but didn't completely collapse when such stocks went out of vogue. Chalk up that all-weather appeal to this fund's extremely seasoned management team. A sales charge should deter investors who like to invest smaller sums at regular intervals, but this fund has about everything else you could want in a core growth fund.

Vanguard Capital Opportunity VHCOX
This fund requires a steep minimum initial purchase of $25,000, but investors who buy in are gaining access to some of the best investment managers in the business. The team here uses a broad-ranging style that encompasses everything from contrarian plays to fast-growing tech names, large-cap stocks to smaller-cap issues. That flexibility has enabled the fund to thrive in a variety of market conditions, from 1999's go-go market to 2000's valuation correction. Management's phenomenal long-term returns on sibling **Vanguard Primecap** VPMCX mark this as one of the better mid-cap funds around.

Janus Mercury JAMRX
This fund has been badly battered over the past few years, but when growth stocks come on strong, it should be among the funds to beat. Janus has had much success identifying up-and-coming growth stocks over the years, and manager Warren Lammert is among the most senior managers at the firm. It has been plenty volatile, but the fund's long-term returns are spectacular. Further, we don't expect that this fund will be deluged with new cash—as it was in the late 1990s—so Lammert should still have the flexibility to buy a few mid-caps and smaller large caps.

Dresdner RCM Global Technology DRGTX
Like all technology-focused funds, this one is supremely risky. But managers Huachen Chen and Walter Price are among the most seasoned hands in the sector, having run institutional money in a similar style for years before starting this offering. Further, unlike some other technology-fund managers, these two pay at least passing attention to diversification and risk control. Even after this fund's tumble in 2001, when it fell along with the rest of the technology group, the fund's returns are among the best in the entire mutual-fund universe. **M**

Beware of Trendy Funds

Narrowly focused funds are often a recipe for disaster.

Fund companies often chase performance, and their timing isn't any better than anybody else's.

Ryan Jacob boasted in November 1999 that his **Jacob Internet Fund** JAMFX would focus on a new breed of companies that would "revolutionize the global economy." Not much later, Aegis Asset Management touted its new Westcott "Nothing But Net" fund as "the vital missing link in many portfolios" that serious investors couldn't afford to miss. In early 2000, Kinetics Asset Management promised "the future—now" with not one but four new Internet funds. And in March 2000, **Merrill Lynch** MER rolled out its Merrill Lynch Internet Strategies Fund with a pep rally that featured former Merrill Lynch analyst (and Net-stock cheerleader) Henry Blodget and the new fund's manager Paul Meeks. Meeks reportedly growled "Let's get ready to ruuuuumble!" like announcer Michael Buffer.

When fund companies turn up the volume this loud over one kind of new fund or another, it should tell you something: The sector is overheated and due to stall, or worse, crash. That's exactly what happened to the aforementioned Internet funds and dozens of other offerings of their ilk.

Jacob Internet has been more revolting than revolutionary, losing wads of money in nearly every quarter of its existence. Westcott "Nothing But Net" has changed its name to **Westcott Technology** NETAX and abandoned pure dot-com investing. Kinetics' Internet subsector funds actually fared reasonably well in 2001, but only thanks to sizable cash stakes and a dearth of technology stocks. Further, the firm recently announced that it's shuttering two of them for lack of investor interest. And more than a year later, Merrill's exuberant launch of its Internet Strategies fund nine days before the Nasdaq Composite peaked and the Internet bubble burst looks like a flamboyant display of hubris. The offering lost a huge amount of shareholders' money before Merrill threw in the towel and merged it out of existence.

As the halcyon days of the Nasdaq were nearing their end, the fund industry launched more specialty-technology funds than any other type of offering—a total of 259 in 1998, 1999, and 2000. Most of those new tech funds (160) took first flight in 2000 as the category suffered its worst year in the last 30. The average tech fund lost more than 32% in 2000 and was also down a huge amount in 2001. Does this mean new fund launches are a reliable contrarian indicator? To find out, we looked at the domestic-stock fund categories that showed the biggest percentage increases in new funds in each of the past 10 years. We then compared their subsequent performance with both the S&P 500 and the fund groups that had the fewest new launches.

In six of the seven years between 1991 and 1997, the three categories with the most new fund launches, on average, lagged the S&P 500 over the subsequent three-year period. And the least-popular categories for fund launches look pretty good. In five of the years between 1991 and 1997, the groups with the fewest new funds beat the categories with the most fund launches in the ensuing three years. For years in which only shorter-term returns are available, the records of categories with the most fund launches are mixed.

Joining the In-Crowd Can Cost You

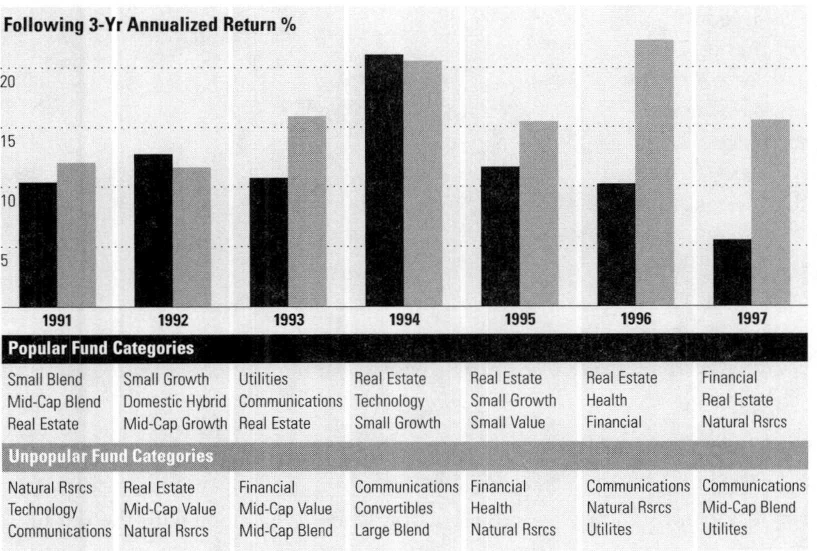

In five of the seven years between 1991 and 1997, the average return of the categories with the most fund launches lagged the categories with the fewest new funds over the next three years.

Specialty-technology funds destroyed the S&P 500, 147% to 21%, in 1999, or one year after 28 new technology funds hit the market. However, tech funds lost scads more than the S&P 500 in 2000, one year after the industry rolled out a plethora of technology offerings. They also badly trailed the benchmark in 2001.

The tech-fund splurge of 2000 may be the most obvious example of poorly timed fund deluges, but not the only one. The industry introduced 30 specialty-real estate funds in 1997, right before the category slid into two money-losing years. The S&P 500, meanwhile, rose more than 28% and 21%, respectively, in 1998 and 1999.

Only one new specialty-communications fund came to market in 1997, just before the communications category went on a tear. The industry took notice and doubled the number of communications funds on the market, only to see communications-related stocks implode in 2000. The specialty-financial fund pipeline swelled in 1996 after the category posted some of the best returns in the business in 1995. Fund companies launched 44 financial sector funds between 1996 and 1998, only to see the sector's once-hot returns cool. The typical specialty-financial fund fell far behind the S&P 500 in 1998 and 1999.

Biotech funds appear to be the latest fund fad. Nearly 46 health-care funds, many of them biotech-focused, came to market in 2000, as the average fund in the category soared 55%. Although the health-care group managed to hold up fairly well in 2001's rough-and-tumble market, brand-new biotech-focused offerings like **GenomicsFund.com** GENEX and **Amerindo Health and Biotech** DNAAX were among the biggest losers.

The track record of funds introduced amid hype and hot performance should arouse skepticism. *Morningstar FundInvestor's* long-running "Buy the Unloved" study offers more cause to be wary. Since 1987, the three fund categories drawing the least new cash in any given year have outperformed that year's best-selling groups over the next three years 90% of the time.

Unless you're a gifted clairvoyant, it's impossible to know when a sector is poised to tumble into a trough. Still, it's best to exercise caution when considering a new fund in a category that has attracted a lot of interest from both performance-chasing investors and asset-hungry fund families. Ask yourself why the firm is launching the fund.

Is it because the manager and firm sincerely believe there are good investment opportunities out there and they have a track record of capitalizing on that area? Is it because they've just hired a talented manager with a specialty in a given area? Or is it because they're trying to exploit the investment style du jour and grab more fee-generating assets?

Which sectors beg these questions now? In 2001, the financial, health, and domestic-hybrid categories had seen the biggest percentage increases in new funds. M

Managers Who Add Value

These skippers get the job done in good times and bad.

From Internet fever to a deep bear market, investors have seen it all over the past few years. Some fund managers have clearly been unable to navigate this changing market environment. Two years ago, investors breathlessly awaited the launch of Ryan Jacob's new fund, **Jacob Internet** JAMFX, after he had racked up triple-digit calendar-year gains at his previous charge, **Kinetics Internet** WWWFX. But since its December 1999 inception, Jacob Internet has lost more than 90% of its value.

Fortunately, not all managers have flamed out the way Jacob did. Indeed, many of them have managed to add significant value throughout the past five years—whatever the market environment.

Meet the Benchmark Crushers

Fund Style-Box Category	Fund Name	5-Year Return%	5-Year Alpha%
Large Blend	**Thompson Plumb Growth** THPGX	18.8	**9.2**
	Thornburg Value TVAFX	16.6	**6.5**
Large Growth	**Smith Barney Aggressive Growth** SHRAX	23.6	**16.3**
	Alger Cap. App. Retirement ALARX	15.6	**8.9**
Large Value	**Clipper** CFIMX	17.5	**7.7**
	Ameristock AMSTX	17.7	**5.6**
Mid Blend	**Parnassus** PARNX	16.6	**8.2**
	Ariel Appreciation CAAPX	15.6	**7.9**
Mid Growth	**Calamos Growth** CVGRX	25.4	**21**
	Bridgeway Aggressive Investors I BRAGX	22.4	**18.5**
Mid Value	**Weitz Partners Value** WPVLX	22.8	**11.6**
	Weitz Value WVALX	20.9	**10.8**
Small Blend	**Meridian Value** MVALX	22.4	**16.8**
	WM Growth Fund of the NW CMNWX	19.5	**15.2**
Small Growth	**Wasatch Micro Cap** WMICX	28.2	**26.9**
	First American Micro Cap FRMPX	21.2	**26.2**
Small Value	**Royce Trust & GiftShares** RGFAX	20.3	**10.2**
	State St Research Aurora SSRAX	19.5	**9.0**

Data through September 30, 2001.

These funds have the highest alphas within their categories, meaning they have beaten a style-specific benchmark (e.g., the Russell 1000 index for large-growth funds) on a risk-adjusted basis over the past five years.

To highlight which fund managers had added the most value for shareholders over the past five years, we relied on a statistic called alpha. In a nutshell, alpha weighs the volatility and returns of a fund versus a benchmark index to determine whether a manager has added value.

Here's how we conducted this study: For funds in each of Morningstar's nine domestic stock-fund categories, we compared a fund's returns and volatility (as measured by beta) versus the performance of a style-specific Russell index, deriving an alpha for each fund. For example, we compared small-growth funds' performance with that of the Russell 2000 Growth index. In our view, if an actively managed fund is to justify its existence, it ought to be able to beat a benchmark index on a risk-adjusted basis. Alpha allows us to measure which managers have been most successful at doing so.

In the table on the left we've listed the top two funds in each category, and we've also explained how some of our favorite managers have been able to add value so consistently.

The Alpha Males and Females

Clipper CFIMX: This has long been one of the favorite funds of Morningstar Managing Director Don Phillips, and it's easy to see why. While some other investors chased hot tech stocks in the late 1990s, this fund's managers patiently stuck to companies that were cheap relative to their intrinsic values. Although stocks such as **Fannie Mae** FNM and **Philip Morris** MO were not market darlings during dot-com mania, they've handily outperformed the broad market over the past year and a half, as investors have again begun to focus on factors such as valuations and earnings. Over time, management's focus on operating fundamentals and price has produced some of the fund world's best risk-adjusted returns.

Bridgeway Aggressive Investors I BRAGX: Computerized stock-picking models have consistently gotten this fund to the right place at the right time. In 2001, stocks such as retailer **Chico's FAS** CHS and savings and loan **New York Community Bancorp** NYCB have propelled the fund to big gains. In the late 1990s, the models homed in on then-surging technology shares and rode them to spectacular gains. In other years, the fund has made successful wagers on energy and retail stocks. Although the fund's sector biases and individual stock picks have tended to change rapidly, one thing has been consistent: terrific returns. The proof is in a five-year return that's the fifth-best in the mid-cap growth category.

Smith Barney Aggressive Growth SHRAX: Simply put, the fund sets the standard for the large-growth category. Manager Richie Freeman looks for companies with good product pipelines, high insider ownership, and positions in dynamic industries. Once he finds these companies, he hangs on to them: The fund's average holding period is nearly 10 years. Some of the fund's biggest long-term winners—**Intel** INTC, **Tyco International** TYC, and **Forest Labs** FRX—have been in the portfolio for well more than a decade. As an added bonus, Freeman's buy-and-hold style has made it extremely tax-efficient. Is there a drawback? Freeman has a big combined stake in technology and health care, and that could hurt the fund in a given year. But long-term investors here have been more than satisfied with their results: The fund's trailing 10-year return is by far the category's best.

Weitz Partners Value WPVLX: Could there be something in the water in Omaha? In addition to being the home of Warren Buffett, Omaha can also claim as a resident Wally Weitz, another Ben Graham disciple with a terrific long-term record. Weitz buys companies that are cheap relative to their cash flows, and he isn't afraid to load up on a particular sector. In the past, he has made big, successful bets on wireless, cable, media, and financials firms, typically buying in when the industry was seriously out of favor with investors. Weitz's willingness to make such large industry bets does carry some risk, but the rewards have been worth it: The fund's trailing three-, five-, and 10-year returns are among the best in the mid-cap value category.

Conclusion

Like any other statistic, alpha has its limitations. It doesn't tell you whether the manager who earned a fund's terrific long-term record is still at the helm. Moreover, even funds that take on a lot of risk can sometimes earn high alphas. For example, **Parnassus Fund** PARNX had the highest alpha in the mid-blend group over the past five years, even though its stake in risky technology shares has sometimes been enormous. In short, knowing even a fund's long-term alpha doesn't relieve investors of the responsibility of doing further fundamental research.

Moreover, some terrific funds didn't make our short list, even though their managers have clearly added a lot of value over time. Funds like **Vanguard Primecap** VPMCX, **Fidelity Dividend Growth** FDGFX, **Legg Mason Value** LMVTX, and **Wasatch Small Cap Growth** WAAEX fell just short of the very upper echelons of their categories, despite having enviable alphas. Obviously, these terrific funds would make welcome additions to most investors' portfolios. **M**

Analyst Picks

Our analysts scrutinized more than 12,000 funds to come up with a handful of favorites for each category.

Analyst Picks

Morningstar Funds 500 Universe

U.S. Equity

Fund Name	Category Name	Page
American Funds Washington Mutual A	Large Value	62
AXP Utilities Income A	Specialty-Utilities	70
Baron Growth	Small Growth	73
Bogle Small Cap Growth Inv	Small Growth	80
Calamos Convertible A	Convertibles	84
Columbia Real Estate Equity	Specialty-Real Estate	90
Davis Convertible Securities A	Convertibles	93
Davis Financial A	Specialty-Financial	94
Davis Growth Opportunity A	Mid-Cap Blend	95
Deutsche Flag Communications A	Specialty-Communications	99
Deutsche Flag Value Builder A	Domestic Hybrid	100
Dodge & Cox Stock	Large Value	105
Dodge & Cox Balanced	Domestic Hybrid	106
Dresdner RCM Global Technology I	Specialty-Technology	108
Eaton Vance Worldwide Health Sci A	Specialty-Health	116
Fidelity Convertible Securities	Convertibles	137
Fidelity	Large Blend	147
Fidelity Low-Priced Stock	Small Value	156
Fidelity Select Health Care	Specialty-Health	166
Fidelity Select Technology	Specialty-Technology	168
Fidelity Utilities	Specialty-Utilities	176
Gabelli Global Telecommunications	Specialty-Communications	201
Gabelli Small Cap Growth	Small Blend	203
Gabelli Westwood Balanced Ret	Domestic Hybrid	205
John Hancock Financial Industries A	Specialty-Financial	208
Harbor Capital Appreciation	Large Growth	213
INVESCO Dynamics Inv	Mid-Cap Growth	225
INVESCO Financial Services Inv	Specialty-Financial	226
INVESCO Telecommunications Inv	Specialty-Communications	229
Janus Enterprise	Mid-Cap Growth	234
Janus Mercury	Large Growth	239
Legg Mason Value Prim	Large Value	253
Longleaf Partners	Mid-Cap Value	262
Managers Special Equity	Small Growth	271
Marsico Focus	Large Growth	273

U.S. Equity

Fund Name	Category Name	Page
MFS Utilities A	Specialty-Utilities	293
Morgan Stanley Inst Mid Cap Growth	Mid-Cap Growth	298
Morgan Stanley Inst Sm Cap Growth	Small Growth	300
Morgan Stanley Inst US Real Estate	Specialty-Real Estate	301
Northern Technology	Specialty-Technology	315
Oak Value	Mid-Cap Blend	317
Oakmark I	Mid-Cap Value	318
Pax World Balanced	Domestic Hybrid	328
T. Rowe Price Blue Chip Growth	Large Blend	337
T. Rowe Price Mid-Cap Growth	Mid-Cap Growth	346
T. Rowe Price Mid-Cap Value	Mid-Cap Value	347
T. Rowe Price New Era	Specialty-Natural Res	350
Royce Total Return	Small Value	377
RS Diversified Growth	Small Growth	378
Security Capital U.S. Real Estate	Specialty-Real Estate	396
Selected American	Large Value	398
T. Rowe Price Small-Cap Stock	Small Blend	353
Third Avenue Value	Small Value	421
TIAA-CREF Growth & Income	Large Blend	425
Tweedy, Browne American Value	Mid-Cap Value	432
Vanguard Capital Opportunity	Mid-Cap Blend	454
Vanguard Energy	Specialty-Natural Res	457
Vanguard 500 Index	Large Blend	462
Vanguard Growth & Income	Large Value	464
Vanguard Growth Equity	Large Growth	465
Vanguard Growth Index	Large Growth	466
Vanguard Health Care	Specialty-Health	467
Vanguard Mid Capitalization Index	Mid-Cap Blend	482
Vanguard Precious Metals	Specialty-Precious Metals	484
Vanguard Primecap	Large Blend	485
Vanguard Wellington	Domestic Hybrid	504
Wasatch Core Growth	Small Blend	510
Weitz Value	Mid-Cap Value	513
Westport Small Cap R	Small Blend	515

Analyst Picks

Morningstar Funds 500 Universe

International

Fund Name	Category Name	Page
American Funds EuroPacific Growth A	Foreign Stock	52
American Funds New Perspective A	World Stock	58
Artisan International	Foreign Stock	65
CS Warburg Pincus Japan Growth Comm	Japan Stock	92
Dreyfus Emerging Markets	Diversified Emerging Mkts	111
Fidelity Pacific Basin	Diversified Pacific/Asia	163
Japan S	Japan Stock	248
Liberty Acorn International Z	Foreign Stock	255
Liberty Newport Tiger A	Pacific/Asia ex-Japan Stk	259
Matthews Pacific Tiger	Pacific/Asia ex-Japan Stk	276
Merrill Lynch Global Allocation B	International Hybrid	280
Merrill Lynch Pacific B	Diversified Pacific/Asia	282
MFS Global Total Return A	International Hybrid	289
Pioneer Emerging Markets A	Diversified Emerging Mkts	335
Scudder Global Discovery A	World Stock	387
Scudder Greater Europe Growth S	Europe Stock	390
Scudder International S	Foreign Stock	392
Scudder Latin America S	Latin America Stock	393
T. Rowe Price New Asia	Pacific/Asia ex-Japan Stk	349
Templeton Developing Markets A	Diversified Emerging Mkts	416
Tweedy, Browne Global Value	Foreign Stock	432
Van Kampen Global Value Equity A	World Stock	446
Van Kampen Latin American A	Latin America Stock	449
Vanguard European Stock Index	Europe Stock	459

Fixed Income

Fund Name	Category Name	Page
Alliance Muni Income National A	Muni National Long	29
BlackRock Intl Bond Svc	International Bond	79
Dodge & Cox Income	Intermediate-Term Bond	104
Eaton Vance Income Fund of Boston A	High Yield Bond	115
Evergreen High Income Municipal Bd B	Muni Short	120
Fidelity Ginnie Mae	Intermediate Government	148
Fidelity High-Income	High Yield Bond	152
Fidelity New Markets Income	Emerging Markets Bond	159
Fidelity Spartan Interm Muni Income	Muni National Interm	172
FPA New Income	Intermediate-Term Bond	183
Franklin Federal Tax-Free Income A	Muni National Long	189
Franklin High Yield Tax-Free Inc A	Muni National Long	191
Fremont Bond	Intermediate-Term Bond	197
John Hancock Strategic Income A	Multisector Bond	211
Metropolitan West Low Duration Bond M	Short-Term Bond	285
Metropolitan West Total Return Bond	Intermediate-Term Bond	286
Montgomery Short Duration Govt Bond R	Short Government	294
Northeast Investors	High Yield Bond	313
PIMCO High Yield A	High Yield Bond	331
T. Rowe Price International Bond	International Bond	344
T. Rowe Price Spectrum Income	Multisector Bond	355
T. Rowe Price Tax-Free Short-Interm	Muni Short	356
T. Rowe Price U.S. Treasury Long-Te	Long Government	357
Principal Government Securities Inc A	Intermediate Government	359
Scudder Medium-Term Tax-Free S	Muni National Interm	394
Sit U.S. Government Securities	Short Government	400
Strong Advantage Inv	Ultrashort Bond	404
Strong Corporate Bond Inv	Long-Term Bond	406
Strong Government Securities Inv	Intermediate Government	407
Strong High-Yield Bond Inv	High Yield Bond	409
Strong Short-Term Bond Inv	Short-Term Bond	412
Strong Short-Term Municipal Bond In	Muni Short	413
USAA Tax-Exempt Intermediate-Term	Muni National Interm	439
USAA Tax-Exempt Short-Term	Muni Short	441
Vanguard GNMA	Intermediate Government	463
Vanguard High-Yield Tax-Exempt	Muni National Long	469
Vanguard Interm-Term Tax-Ex	Muni National Interm	472
Vanguard Long-Term Corporate Bond	Long-Term Bond	479
Vanguard Long-Term Tax-Exempt	Muni National Long	480
Vanguard Long-Term U.S. Treasury	Long Government	481
Vanguard Ltd-Term Tax-Ex	Muni Short	478
Vanguard Short-Term Bond Index	Short-Term Bond	486
Vanguard Short-Term Federal	Short Government	487
Vanguard Total Bond Market Index	Intermediate-Term Bond	497

Review Pages

This section offers a full-page report on each of the 500 funds.

ABN AMRO/Chicago Capital Bond N

Ticker	Load	NAV	Yield	SEC Yield	Total Assets	Mstar Category
CHTBX	12b–1 only	$10.03	6.5%	6.90%	$436.5 mil	Interm–Term Bond

Prospectus Objective: Corp Bond—General

ABN AMRO/Chicago Capital Bond Fund seeks current income consistent with prudent risk of capital.

The fund normally invests at least 65% of assets in fixed-income securities, including corporate debt securities, U.S. government obligations, mortgage- and asset-backed securities, zero-coupon bonds, and convertible debentures. The fund invests primarily in investment-grade debt, though it may invest up to 20% of assets in fixed-income securities rated as low as B. The average weighted maturity generally ranges between three and 10 years.

The fund has gone through several name changes.

Historical Profile
Return Above Avg
Risk Below Avg
Rating ★★★★ Above Avg

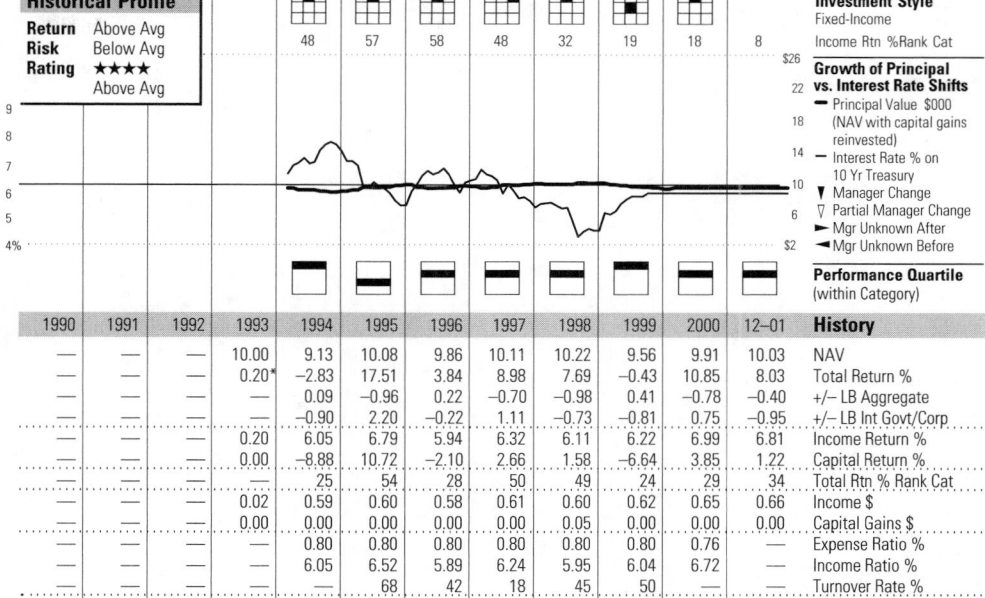

Investment Style: Fixed-Income
Income Rtn %Rank Cat: 48 57 58 48 32 19 18 8

Growth of Principal vs. Interest Rate Shifts
— Principal Value $000 (NAV with capital gains reinvested)
— Interest Rate % on 10 Yr Treasury
▼ Manager Change
▽ Partial Manager Change
► Mgr Unknown After
◄ Mgr Unknown Before

Performance Quartile (within Category)

Portfolio Manager(s)

Thomas J. Marthaler, CFA. Since 12-93. BA'81 U. of St. Thomas; MBA'85 Loyola U. Other funds currently managed: ABN AMRO/Chicago Capital Balanced N, ABN AMRO/Chicago Capital Bond I.

1990	1991	1992	1993	1994	1995	1996	1997	1998	1999	2000	12-01	History
—	—	—	10.00	9.13	10.08	9.86	10.11	10.22	9.56	9.91	10.03	NAV
—	—	—	0.20*	–2.83	17.51	3.84	8.98	7.69	–0.43	10.85	8.03	Total Return %
—	—	—	—	0.09	–0.96	0.22	–0.70	–0.98	0.41	–0.78	–0.40	+/– LB Aggregate
—	—	—	—	–0.90	2.20	–0.22	1.11	–0.73	–0.81	0.75	–0.95	+/– LB Int Govt/Corp
—	—	—	0.20	6.05	6.79	5.94	6.32	6.11	6.22	6.99	6.81	Income Return %
—	—	—	0.00	–8.88	10.72	–2.10	2.66	1.58	–6.64	3.85	1.22	Capital Return %
—	—	—	—	25	54	28	50	49	24	29	34	Total Rtn % Rank Cat
—	—	—	0.02	0.59	0.60	0.58	0.61	0.60	0.62	0.65	0.66	Income $
—	—	—	0.00	0.00	0.00	0.00	0.00	0.05	0.00	0.00	0.00	Capital Gains $
—	—	—	—	0.80	0.80	0.80	0.80	0.80	0.80	0.76	—	Expense Ratio %
—	—	—	—	6.05	6.52	5.89	6.24	5.95	6.04	6.72	—	Income Ratio %
—	—	—	—	—	68	42	18	45	50	—	—	Turnover Rate %
—	—	—	10.0	12.9	73.6	84.3	131.8	157.6	133.4	115.1	358.4	Net Assets $mil

Performance 12-31-01

	1st Qtr	2nd Qtr	3rd Qtr	4th Qtr	Total
1997	–0.43	3.33	3.27	2.56	8.98
1998	1.66	2.06	3.16	0.61	7.69
1999	–0.25	–0.41	0.48	–0.25	–0.43
2000	2.40	1.18	3.09	3.78	10.85
2001	2.95	0.25	4.09	0.56	8.03

Trailing	Total Return%	+/– LB Agg	+/– LB ITGvt/Corp	% Rank All	% Rank Cat	Growth of $10,000
3 Mo	0.56	0.52	0.47	75	17	10,056
6 Mo	4.67	0.02	–0.03	5	23	10,467
1 Yr	8.03	–0.40	–0.95	9	34	10,803
3 Yr Avg	6.04	–0.23	–0.36	22	21	11,924
5 Yr Avg	6.95	–0.47	–0.14	36	22	13,994
10 Yr Avg	—	—	—	—	—	—
15 Yr Avg	—	—	—	—	—	—

Tax Analysis	Tax-Adj Ret%	%Rank Cat	%Pretax Ret	%Rank Cat
3 Yr Avg	3.37	26	55.7	42
5 Yr Avg	4.31	24	62.1	35
10 Yr Avg	—	—	—	—

Potential Capital Gain Exposure: 1% of assets

Risk Analysis

Time Period	Load-Adj Return %	Risk %Rank[1] All	Risk %Rank[1] Cat	Morningstar Return	Morningstar Risk	Morningstar Risk-Adj Rating
1 Yr	8.03					
3 Yr	6.04	10	12	0.24[2]	0.58	★★★★
5 Yr	6.95	14	11	0.44[2]	0.59	★★★★
Incept	6.51	—	—	—	—	

Average Historical Rating (61 months): 3.9★s

[1]1=low, 100=high [2] T-Bill return substituted for category avg.

Category Rating (3 Yr)

1 2 3 4 5
Worst Best

Return Above Avg
Risk Below Avg

Other Measures	Standard Index LB Agg	Best Fit Index LB Agg
Alpha	–0.1	–0.1
Beta	0.90	0.90
R–Squared	94	94

Standard Deviation	3.26
Mean	6.04
Sharpe Ratio	0.39

Portfolio Analysis 11-30-01

Total Fixed-Income: 133	Date of Maturity	Amount $000	Value $000	% Net Assets
US Treasury Bond 7.25%	05-15-16	11,250	13,308	3.01
US Treasury Note 3.375%	01-15-07	11,707	11,870	2.68
GNMA 6.5%	06-20-31	11,480	11,609	2.62
FHLMC 7%	06-01-29	9,747	10,036	2.27
FNMA 7%	08-01-16	9,280	9,654	2.18
FNMA 6.5%	07-01-29	9,120	9,274	2.10
FNMA 6.5%	09-01-16	8,684	8,934	2.02
Conoco 6.95%	04-15-29	8,200	8,306	1.88
FNMA Debenture 5.25%	01-15-09	8,000	8,072	1.83
FNMA 6.5%	10-01-28	7,800	7,939	1.79
Federal Home Loan Bk 4.875%	04-16-04	7,500	7,747	1.75
FNMA 7.5%	09-01-30	6,422	6,695	1.51
US Treasury Note 6.125%	08-15-07	6,000	6,551	1.48
Residential Asset CMO 5.751%	03-25-27	6,225	6,362	1.44
Niagara Mohawk Pwr Step 0%	07-01-10	6,250	5,953	1.35
Federal Home Loan Bk 6.5%	11-15-06	5,075	5,510	1.25
GNMA 7%	01-20-30	5,225	5,380	1.22
CSC Hldgs 7.875%	12-15-07	5,125	5,374	1.21
FNMA Debenture 7%	07-15-05	4,700	5,155	1.17
US Treasury Note 7%	07-15-06	4,500	5,052	1.14

Current Investment Style

Style: Value Blnd Growth; Size: Large Med Small

Avg Eff Duration	—
Avg Eff Maturity	—
Avg Credit Quality	AA
Avg Wtd Coupon	6.54%
Avg Wtd Price	103.73% of par

Special Securities % assets 11-30-01	
Restricted/Illiquid Secs	4
Exotic Mortgage–Backed	0
Emerging–Markets Secs	0
Options/Futures/Warrants	No

Coupon Range	% of Bonds	Rel Cat
0%	1.42	1.14
0% to 7%	53.19	0.98
7% to 8.5%	44.04	1.26
8.5% to 10%	1.36	0.19
More than 10%	0.00	0.00

1.00=Category Average

Credit Analysis % bonds 09-30-01			
US Govt	0	BB	4
AAA	62	B	1
AA	4	Below B	0
A	13	NR/NA	2
BBB	14		

Composition % assets 11-30-01			
Cash	4.1	Bonds	94.4
Stocks	0.0	Other	1.5

Sector Breakdown % bonds 11-30-01			
US Treasuries	7	CMOs	2
GNMA mtgs	8	ARMs	0
FNMA mtgs	20	Other	44
FHLMC mtgs	11		

Analysis by Paul Herbert 11-29-01

ABN AMRO/Chicago Capital Bond Fund remains a solid core bond fund holding.

This fund has had an eventful year. ABN AMRO completed its purchase of the Alleghany Funds in the first quarter, and as a result this fund subsumed ABN AMRO Fixed Income in August. The combined entity's name changed from Alleghany/Chicago Trust Bond Fund in September.

Fortunately, the fund doesn't look much different than it did prior to the deal. Manager Tom Marthaler now manages $200 million more than he did prior to the merger, but he still applies the same strategy. Marthaler focuses his attention on corporate and mortgage-backed paper, but he doesn't make drastic changes to the fund's weightings in either sector. He also eschews interest-rate bets, preferring to keep the fund's duration, a measure of its sensitivity to changing rates, within 10% of the Lehman Brothers Aggregate Bond index's. Instead, Marthaler analyzes company fundamentals and bond structures, so as to pick up bonds that appear inexpensive relative to their sectors or rating agencies' outlooks. These tactics have helped the fund outpace 80% of its intermediate-bond fund peers for the three- and five-year periods.

Marthaler's rigorous analysis has also paid off in 2001. As an example, he identified a favorable provision in AT&T bonds maturing in 2029 and used the opportunity to swap out of poorer-performing AT&T issues expiring in 2009. Thanks to such moves, the fund has topped about two thirds of its peers for the year to date through Dec. 4, 2001.

One concern that we have about the fund is that its analyst staff is small compared with many of its rivals—even after its recent merger. The fund has been able to shine with a lean crew thus far, however, and we see no reason why it couldn't continue to do so with Marthaler at the helm.

Address:	P.O. Box 9765 Providence, RI 02940 800–443–4725 / 800–814–3402
Web Address:	www.abnamrofunds–usa.com
*Inception:	12-13-93
Advisor:	Chicago Trust
Subadvisor:	None
NTF Plans:	Fidelity , Datalynx

Minimum Purchase:	$2500	Add: $50	IRA: $500
Min Auto Inv Plan:	$50	Add: $50	
Sales Fees:	0.25%B		
Management Fee:	.55%, .06%A		
Actual Fees:	Mgt: 0.55%	Dist: 0.25%	
Expense Projections:	3Yr: $282	5Yr: $505	10Yr: $1147
Avg Brok Commission:	—	Income Distrib: Monthly	
Total Cost (relative to category):	Below Avg		

ABN AMRO/Chicago Capital Sm Cap Val N

Ticker	Load	NAV	Yield	Total Assets	Mstar Category
ASCVX	12b–1 only	$12.34	0.1%	$40.7 mil	Small Value

Prospectus Objective: Small Company

ABN AMRO/Chicago Capital Small Cap Value Fund seeks long-term total return.

The fund normally invests at least 65% of assets in small-companies or REITs domiciled in the United States, which have market capitalizations between $50 million and $1 billion. It may invest a portion of assets in cash or U.S. government debt obligations. The fund does not currently intend to engage in futures or options contracts, short-selling activities, leverage, or portfolio hedging techniques.

Historical Profile

Return	Above Avg
Risk	Below Avg
Rating	★★★★ Above Avg

Investment Style
Equity
Average Stock %: 82% (1998), 95% (1999), 96% (2000), 94% (12-01)

▼ Manager Change
▽ Partial Manager Change

Fund Performance vs. Category Average
■ Quarterly Fund Return +/– Category Average
— Category Baseline

Performance Quartile (within Category)

Portfolio Manager(s)

Philip Tasho, CFA. Since 4-01. BA'76 Grinnell College; MBA'79 George Washington U. Other funds currently managed: ABN AMRO/TAMRO Large Cap Value N, ABN AMRO/TAMRO Small Cap N.

History

1990	1991	1992	1993	1994	1995	1996	1997	1998	1999	2000	12-01	History
—	—	—	—	—	—	—	—	10.47	9.61	11.50	12.34	NAV
—	—	—	—	—	—	—	—	4.85*	–7.77	25.85	13.70	Total Return %
—	—	—	—	—	—	—	—	–4.37*	–28.81	34.95	25.57	+/– S&P 500
—	—	—	—	—	—	—	—	—	–6.29	3.04	–0.32	+/– Russell 2000 V
—	—	—	—	—	—	—	—	0.15	0.43	0.69	0.16	Income Return %
—	—	—	—	—	—	—	—	4.70	–8.19	25.16	13.54	Capital Return %
—	—	—	—	—	—	—	—	—	90	22	72	Total Rtn % Rank Cat
—	—	—	—	—	—	—	—	0.01	0.04	0.07	0.02	Income $
—	—	—	—	—	—	—	—	0.00	0.00	0.47	0.70	Capital Gains $
—	—	—	—	—	—	—	—	—	1.40	1.40	—	Expense Ratio %
—	—	—	—	—	—	—	—	—	0.51	0.56	—	Income Ratio %
—	—	—	—	—	—	—	—	—	157	211	—	Turnover Rate %
—	—	—	—	—	—	—	—	31.0	43.9	45.1	40.7	Net Assets $mil

Performance 12-31-01

	1st Qtr	2nd Qtr	3rd Qtr	4th Qtr	Total
1997	—	—	—	—	—
1998	—	—	—	—	4.85 *
1999	–13.28	12.22	–8.05	3.06	–7.77
2000	3.85	1.80	6.79	11.47	25.85
2001	–3.13	11.04	–11.96	20.07	13.70

Trailing	Total Return%	+/– S&P 500	+/– Russ 2000V	% Rank All	% Rank Cat	Growth of $10,000
3 Mo	20.07	9.38	3.35	14	27	12,007
6 Mo	5.70	11.26	4.55	3	16	10,570
1 Yr	13.70	25.57	–0.32	4	72	11,370
3 Yr Avg	9.69	10.71	–1.63	12	70	13,197
5 Yr Avg	—	—	—	—	—	—
10 Yr Avg	—	—	—	—	—	—
15 Yr Avg	—	—	—	—	—	—

Tax Analysis	Tax-Adj Ret%	%Rank Cat	%Pretax Ret	%Rank Cat
3 Yr Avg	8.35	72	86.2	72
5 Yr Avg	—	—	—	—
10 Yr Avg	—	—	—	—

Potential Capital Gain Exposure: 27% of assets

Risk Analysis

Time Period	Load-Adj Return %	Risk %Rank[1] All	Risk %Rank[1] Cat	Morningstar Return	Morningstar Risk	Morningstar Risk-Adj Rating
1 Yr	13.70					
3 Yr	9.69	42	27	1.05[2]	0.58	★★★★
5 Yr	—	—	—	—	—	
Incept	10.89	—	—	—	—	

Average Historical Rating (2 months): 4.0★s

[1] 1=low, 100=high [2] T-Bill return substituted for category avg.

Category Rating (3 Yr)

1 2 **3** 4 5
Worst Best

Return	Below Avg
Risk	Below Avg

Other Measures	Standard Index S&P 500	Best Fit Index SPMid400
Alpha	7.8	1.4
Beta	0.43	0.61
R-Squared	22	59

Standard Deviation	17.00
Mean	9.69
Sharpe Ratio	0.32

Portfolio Analysis 11-30-01

Share change since 10-01 Total Stocks: 56

	Sector	PE	YTD Ret%	% Assets
IKON Office Solutions	Industrials	21.7	377.90	3.48
Pep Boys	Retail	26.8	391.70	3.18
KB Home	Industrials	7.6	20.19	2.84
Ametek	Industrials	14.8	23.96	2.83
CBL & Assoc Properties	Financials	15.9	34.09	2.80
Hughes Sply	Industrials	24.7	75.09	2.72
Entertainment Properties Tr	Financials	11.9	95.65	2.41
Dial	Staples	—	57.57	2.39
Constellation Brands A	Staples	—	—	2.28
United Natural Foods	Retail	35.2	41.84	2.27
☼ Texas Inds	Industrials	NMF	24.18	2.27
Standard Pacific	Industrials	6.2	5.49	2.26
Nash–Finch	Retail	18.9	170.20	2.23
⊖ Ryan's Family Steak House	Services	14.9	129.30	2.22
General Cable	Industrials	81.9	200.10	2.20
MAF Bancorp	Financials	12.6	5.47	2.15
Tractor Sply	Retail	13.8	300.90	2.15
Triad Guaranty	Financials	12.8	9.49	2.05
Core Labs	Services	19.8	–48.60	2.04
☼ Concord Camera	Durables	—	–52.00	2.02
☼ Emmis Broadcstg Cl A	Services	—	–17.60	1.89
meVC Draper Fisher Jurvetson I	N/A	—	—	1.87
Kellwood	Durables	10.4	16.98	1.87
Edwards Lifesciences	Health	—	55.66	1.84
Pioneer Natural Res Canada	Energy	9.3	–2.17	1.78

Current Investment Style

Style: Value Blnd Growth; Size: Large Med Small

	Stock Port Avg	Relative S&P 500 Current	Relative S&P 500 Hist	Rel Cat
Price/Earnings Ratio	21.2	0.69	0.54	0.98
Price/Book Ratio	2.0	0.34	0.33	0.81
Price/Cash Flow	14.8	0.82	0.60	1.16
3 Yr Earnings Growth	5.1	0.35	0.67	0.44
1 Yr Earnings Est%	16.0	—	—	–4.05
Med Mkt Cap $mil	716	0.0	0.0	0.82

Special Securities % assets 11-30-01	
Restricted/Illiquid Secs	0
Emerging–Markets Secs	0
Options/Futures/Warrants	No

Composition % assets 11-30-01	
Cash	3.9
Stocks*	93.1
Bonds	0.0
Other	1.1
*Foreign (% stocks)	2.1

Market Cap	
Giant	0.0
Large	0.0
Medium	20.7
Small	71.7
Micro	5.6

Sector Weightings	% of Stocks	Rel S&P	5-Year High	5-Year Low
Utilities	1.2	0.4	—	—
Energy	4.9	0.7	—	—
Financials	19.1	1.1	—	—
Industrials	20.4	1.8	—	—
Durables	5.5	3.5	—	—
Staples	8.5	1.1	—	—
Services	8.9	0.8	—	—
Retail	16.4	2.4	—	—
Health	6.3	0.4	—	—
Technology	8.8	0.5	—	—

Analysis by Paul Herbert 12-12-01

Things may not turn out as badly as we feared under this fund's new manager, but the fund still doesn't earn a ringing endorsement.

Much has changed for ABN AMRO/Chicago Capital Small Cap Value Fund in 2001. For starters, its manager since inception, Patricia Falkowski, resigned in April. Philip Tasho, the manager of tiny ABN AMRO/TAMRO Small Cap and former boss of Riggs Small Company Stock from late 1995 through mid-2000 took her place. The fund also has a new name, reflecting ABN AMRO's purchase of the former Alleghany funds in the year's first quarter.

We were concerned because the fund has lost a lot in Falkowski. Yet it has gained in other ways under Tasho. In comparing the records of these two stock-pickers, Falkowski's performance here and as the manager of UAM FMA Small Company Fund is slightly superior to Tasho's record. Still, the Riggs fund handily outperformed this fund in 1999, a poor year for small-value funds. Its .2% loss was 7 percentage points higher than this fund's, thanks in no small part to the former's diversification across stocks and sectors.

Still, the fund has its warts. For one, while the fund's portfolios have landed in small-value territory since Tasho took over, the Riggs fund—which he managed in the same style—looked like a small-blend or small-growth fund at times. Such movements can make it difficult for investors to fit the fund in a portfolio. In addition, Tasho holds on to his winners here, which could expose the fund to valuation risk.

In all, investors will find that more-attractive options are available. As an aside, investors shouldn't be surprised if this fund and TAMRO Small Cap fund merge, because Tasho runs each in the same style. This combination makes sense given that cost savings could be realized from merging these two tiny vehicles.

Address:	P.O. Box 9765 Providence, RI 02940 800–443–4725 / 800–814–3402
Web Address:	www.abnamrofunds–usa.com
*Inception:	11-10-98
Advisor:	Chicago Trust
Subadvisor:	None
NTF Plans:	Datalynx , Fidelity Inst.

Minimum Purchase:	$2500	Add: $50	IRA: $500
Min Auto Inv Plan:	$50	Add: $50	
Sales Fees:	0.25%B		
Management Fee:	1.0%, .06%A		
Actual Fees:	Mgt: 1.00%	Dist: 0.25%	
Expense Projections:	3Yr: $57	5Yr: —	10Yr: —
Avg Brok Commission:	—	Income Distrib: Quarterly	
Total Cost (relative to category):	—		

ABN AMRO/Montag & Caldwell Growth N

Ticker	Load	NAV	Yield	Total Assets	Mstar Category
MCGFX	12b–1 only	$24.12	0.0%	$2,130.6 mil	Large Growth

Prospectus Objective: Growth

ABN AMRO/Montag & Caldwell Growth Fund seeks long-term capital appreciation; income is secondary.

The fund invests primarily in common stocks and convertibles. The advisor selects equities that it believes are undervalued based on the issuer's estimated earning potential and ability to produce strong earnings growth over the next 12 to 18 months. These issuers may include established companies with histories of growth as well as companies that the advisor expects are entering periods of earnings growth. It may invest up to 30% of assets in ADRs and EDRs.

Prior to March 1, 1999, the fund was named Montag and Caldwell Growth Fund.

Historical Profile

Return	Above Avg
Risk	Average
Rating	★★★★ Above Avg

Investment Style
Equity
Average Stock %

1994	1995	1996	1997	1998	1999	2000	12–01
90%	96%	96%	97%	95%	97%	97%	

▼ Manager Change
▽ Partial Manager Change

Fund Performance vs. Category Average
■ Quarterly Fund Return +/– Category Average
— Category Baseline

Performance Quartile (within Category)

Portfolio Manager(s)

Ronald E. Canakaris, CFA. Since 11-94. BS U. of Florida; BA'66 U. of Florida. Other funds currently managed: Enterprise Growth A, ABN AMRO/Montag & Caldwell Bal N, Enterprise Growth B.

History

1990	1991	1992	1993	1994	1995	1996	1997	1998	1999	2000	12–01	History
—	—	—	—	9.77	13.52	17.80	23.25	29.65	34.64	27.83	24.12	NAV
—	—	—	—	–2.25*	38.68	32.72	31.85	31.85	22.51	–7.36	–13.33	Total Return %
—	—	—	—	–1.26*	1.15	9.78	–1.51	3.28	1.47	1.74	–1.45	+/– S&P 500
—	—	—	—	—	0.03	7.20	–1.90	–13.25	–7.17	17.16	7.17	+/– Russ Top 200 Grt
—	—	—	—	0.05	0.27	0.04	0.00	0.00	0.00	0.00	0.00	Income Return %
—	—	—	—	–2.30	38.41	32.69	31.85	31.85	22.51	–7.36	–13.33	Capital Return %
—	—	—	—	—	16	2	18	52	85	22	12	Total Rtn % Rank Cat
—	—	—	—	0.01	0.03	0.00	0.00	0.00	0.00	0.00	0.00	Income $
—	—	—	—	0.00	0.00	0.14	0.21	0.94	1.65	4.08	0.00	Capital Gains $
—	—	—	—	—	1.30	1.28	1.23	1.12	1.05	1.03	—	Expense Ratio %
—	—	—	—	—	0.20	–0.06	–0.37	–0.22	–0.16	–0.14	—	Income Ratio %
—	—	—	—	—	—	26	19	30	32	67	—	Turnover Rate %
—	—	—	—	11.2	48.9	196.2	548.6	1,157.2	1,735.9	1,299.2	946.9	Net Assets $mil

Performance 12-31-01

	1st Qtr	2nd Qtr	3rd Qtr	4th Qtr	Total
1997	–0.62	21.25	9.28	0.12	31.85
1998	13.12	7.11	–14.27	26.94	31.85
1999	7.86	1.69	–5.10	17.71	22.51
2000	–2.86	–0.62	–8.52	4.90	–7.36
2001	–15.56	3.62	–9.98	10.04	–13.33

Trailing	Total Return%	+/– S&P 500	+/– Russ Top 200 Grth	% Rank All	% Rank Cat	Growth of $10,000
3 Mo	10.04	–0.65	–2.82	43	87	11,004
6 Mo	–0.94	4.61	6.04	42	3	9,906
1 Yr	–13.33	–1.45	7.17	69	12	8,667
3 Yr Avg	–0.55	0.48	7.47	76	31	9,836
5 Yr Avg	11.32	0.63	2.73	12	24	17,099
10 Yr Avg	—	—	—	—	—	—
15 Yr Avg	—	—	—	—	—	—

Tax Analysis	Tax-Adj Ret%	%Rank Cat	%Pretax Ret	%Rank Cat
3 Yr Avg	–1.74	31	—	—
5 Yr Avg	10.33	16	91.3	11
10 Yr Avg	—	—	—	—

Potential Capital Gain Exposure: 0% of assets

Risk Analysis

Time Period	Load-Adj Return %	Risk %Rank[1] All	Risk %Rank[1] Cat	Morningstar Return	Morningstar Risk	Morningstar Risk-Adj Rating
1 Yr	–13.33					
3 Yr	–0.55	61	4	–1.11[2]	0.86	★★★
5 Yr	11.32	64	7	1.55[2]	0.89	★★★★
Incept	16.98	—	—	—	—	

Average Historical Rating (50 months): 4.5★s

[1] 1=low, 100=high [2] T-Bill return substituted for category avg.

Category Rating (3 Yr)

1 2 3 4 5
Worst Best

Return	Above Avg
Risk	Low

Other Measures	Standard Index S&P 500	Best Fit Index S&P 500
Alpha	–0.9	–0.9
Beta	0.76	0.76
R-Squared	71	71

Standard Deviation	15.20
Mean	–0.55
Sharpe Ratio	–0.42

Portfolio Analysis 11-30-01

Share change since 10–01 Total Stocks: 32	Sector	PE	YTD Ret%	% Assets
Pfizer	Health	34.7	–12.40	5.13
Electronic Data Sys	Technology	25.7	19.83	4.86
Johnson & Johnson	Health	16.6	14.01	4.61
Marsh & McLennan	Financials	27.9	–6.30	4.40
American Intl Grp	Financials	42.0	–19.20	4.26
Coca-Cola	Staples	35.5	–21.40	4.16
PepsiCo	Staples	31.4	–0.54	4.04
Medtronic	Health	76.4	–14.70	4.01
Citigroup	Financials	20.0	0.03	3.89
Procter & Gamble	Staples	38.8	3.12	3.71
Nokia Cl A ADR	Technology	45.8	–43.00	3.65
⊖ Bristol-Myers Squibb	Health	20.2	–26.00	3.19
Colgate-Palmolive	Staples	31.1	–9.45	3.16
Gillette	Staples	56.6	–5.47	3.15
⊕ Amgen	Health	52.8	–11.70	3.12
Costco Wholesale	Retail	34.4	11.12	3.08
Bank of New York	Financials	21.9	–24.80	2.89
Walt Disney	Services	—	–27.70	2.84
⊕ Qualcomm	Technology	—	–38.50	2.40
⊕ Masco	Industrials	98.0	–2.43	2.31
Genentech	Health	NMF	–33.40	2.25
☼ Pharmacia	Health	36.5	–29.30	2.05
Marriott Intl Cl A	Services	20.9	–3.16	1.77
United Parcel Svc B	Services	25.0	–6.09	1.75
Electronic Arts	Technology	90.8	40.65	1.74

Current Investment Style

Style: Value Blnd Growth; Size: Large Med Small

	Stock Port Avg	Relative S&P 500 Current	Relative S&P 500 Hist	Rel Cat
Price/Earnings Ratio	36.4	1.17	1.17	1.02
Price/Book Ratio	8.3	1.45	1.25	1.30
Price/Cash Flow	24.4	1.35	1.20	1.07
3 Yr Earnings Growth	12.3	0.84	0.93	0.57
1 Yr Earnings Est%	7.3	—	—	2.42
Med Mkt Cap $mil	62,275	1.0	1.2	1.32

Special Securities % assets 11-30-01	
Restricted/Illiquid Secs	0
Emerging-Markets Secs	0
Options/Futures/Warrants	No

Composition % assets 11-30-01	
Cash	7.3
Stocks*	92.7
Bonds	0.0
Other	0.0
*Foreign (% stocks)	4.0

Market Cap	
Giant	60.2
Large	37.9
Medium	1.9
Small	0.0
Micro	0.0

Sector Weightings	% of Stocks	Rel S&P	5-Year High	5-Year Low
Utilities	0.0	0.0	0	0
Energy	1.9	0.3	5	0
Financials	16.7	0.9	17	3
Industrials	7.7	0.7	11	0
Durables	0.0	0.0	4	0
Staples	19.7	2.5	27	13
Services	7.9	0.7	20	7
Retail	5.0	0.7	14	3
Health	26.4	1.8	29	11
Technology	14.7	0.8	40	12

Analysis by Brian Portnoy 10-29-01

We continue to be impressed by ABN Amro/Montag & Caldwell Growth.

Among the large-growth set, this fund is holding up quite well. The fund has lost 16.3% for the year to date through Oct. 26, 2001, which is 11 percentage points less than the average rival's decline. Of course, exposure to tech stocks such as Nokia has hamstrung returns, but the fund's substantial exposure to affordable growth stocks has been a source of buoyancy. Generally, the fund's underweight in technology (relative to its peers) and overweight in health care and consumer staples has been the winning recipe lately.

This year's performance highlights the virtues of manager Ron Canakaris' approach. He seeks companies growing faster than the overall market that are trading cheaply relative to his estimates of their intrinsic value. And as a cautious growth investor, he is typically attracted to bellwether food and drug companies such as Coca-Cola; at 20% of assets, the fund's consumer-staples stake is currently five times the category average. Also, Canakaris is not a frenetic trader, but he does add to his favorites on price weakness and sells names with dismal near-term earnings prospects. Thus, he recently purchased more shares of Disney and cut Wells Fargo.

This approach has met with substantial long-term success. Not only does the fund's trailing five-year gain beat 84% of its peers', but Canakaris' 21-year record at near-clone Enterprise Growth beats most of the competition's and the index to boot. And despite owning only about 35 names, the fund has been far less volatile than the average rival over the long haul, thanks in recent years to its aversion to big bets on pricey tech and telecom fare. Its moderation means it won't pace the group in growth rallies, but it's clearly a long-run winner.

Address:	P.O. Box 9765 Providence, RI 02940 800–443–4725 / 800–814–3402
Web Address:	www.abnamrofunds-usa.com
*Inception:	11-02-94
Advisor:	Montag & Caldwell
Subadvisor:	None
NTF Plans:	Fidelity , Datalynx

Minimum Purchase:	$2500	Add: $50	IRA: $500
Min Auto Inv Plan:	$50	Add: $50	
Sales Fees:	0.25%B		
Management Fee:	.80% mx./.60% mn., .06%A		
Actual Fees:	Mgt: 0.67%	Dist: —	
Expense Projections:	3Yr: $36	5Yr: $62	10Yr: $136
Avg Brok Commission:	—	Income Distrib: Quarterly	
Total Cost (relative to category):	—		

AIM Aggressive Growth A

Ticker	Load	NAV	Yield	Total Assets	Mstar Category
AAGFX	NULL	NULL	NULL	$0.0 mil	Mid-Cap Growth

Prospectus Objective: Small Company

AIM Aggressive Growth Fund seeks long-term growth of capital.

The fund invests primarily in equity securities of small- to medium-sized companies that management expects to achieve earnings growth of more than 15% per year. The fund may invest up to 25% of assets in foreign securities.

Class A shares have front loads; Class B have deferred loads and conversion features; Class C have level loads.

Prior to July 1, 1992, the fund was named CIGNA Aggressive Growth Fund.

Historical Profile
Return —
Risk —
Rating Not Rated

Investment Style
Equity
Average Stock %: 87% 95% 98% 95% 96% 97% 96%

▼ Manager Change
▽ Partial Manager Change

Fund Performance vs. Category Average
■ Quarterly Fund Return +/– Category Average
— Category Baseline

Performance Quartile (within Category)

Portfolio Manager(s)

Robert M. Kippes. Since 7-92. BA'88 Stephen F. Austin U. Other funds currently managed: AIM Constellation A, AIM Global Aggressive Growth A, AIM Global Aggressive Growth B.

Ryan E. Crane, CFA. Since 7-99. BS'94 U. of Houston. Other funds currently managed: AIM Constellation A, AIM Global Aggressive Growth A, AIM Global Aggressive Growth B.

Jay K. Rushin, CFA. Since 12-00. BA Florida State U. Other funds currently managed: AIM Constellation A, AIM Global Aggressive Growth A, AIM Global Aggressive Growth B.

1990	1991	1992	1993	1994	1995	1996	1997	1998	1999	2000	12–01	History
2.96	4.02	4.63	6.11	7.16	9.89	10.72	11.55	12.02	15.65	12.77	9.45	NAV
–6.73	64.25	21.19	31.99	17.19	41.60	14.37	12.16	4.99	45.06	2.96	–26.00	Total Return %
–3.61	33.76	13.57	21.94	15.87	4.06	–8.58	–21.19	–23.59	24.02	12.06	–14.12	+/– S&P 500
–1.59	17.21	12.47	20.80	19.35	7.62	–3.11	–10.38	–12.88	–6.25	14.71	–5.84	+/– Russ Midcap Grth
0.68	0.00	0.00	0.01	0.00	0.00	0.00	0.00	0.00	0.00	0.00	0.00	Income Return %
–7.40	64.25	21.18	31.98	17.18	41.60	14.37	12.16	4.99	45.06	2.96	–26.00	Capital Return %
55	28	6	5	1	21	67	76	79	62	35	66	Total Rtn % Rank Cat
0.02	0.00	0.00	0.00	0.00	0.00	0.00	0.00	0.00	0.00	0.00	0.00	Income $
0.12	0.76	0.23	0.00	0.00	0.24	0.57	0.44	0.10	1.61	3.30	0.00	Capital Gains $
1.25	1.25	1.25	1.00	1.07	1.08	1.10	1.06	1.06	1.09	1.04	—	Expense Ratio %
0.62	–0.31	–0.59	–0.24	–0.26	–0.19	–0.76	–0.65	–0.64	–0.69	–0.77	—	Income Ratio %
137	165	164	61	75	52	79	73	69	75	79	—	Turnover Rate %
9.2	16.2	38.2	273.5	714.7	2,304.1	2,723.9	3,679.9	3,069.3	3,424.7	3,891.9	2,685.7	Net Assets $mil

Performance

	1st Qtr	2nd Qtr	3rd Qtr	4th Qtr	Total
1997	–13.90	21.24	19.48	–10.07	12.16
1998	11.08	–2.26	–22.81	25.27	4.99
1999	–6.66	14.62	3.19	31.39	45.06
2000	27.48	–4.76	2.11	–16.94	2.96
2001	–23.88	13.07	–24.66	14.13	–26.00

Trailing	Total Return%	NULL NULL	NULL NULL	% Rank All	% Rank Cat	Growth of $10,000
3 Mo	14.13	3.45	–12.93	26	77	11,413
6 Mo	–14.01	–8.46	–5.75	93	71	8,599
1 Yr	–26.00	–14.12	–5.84	90	66	7,400
3 Yr Avg	3.39	4.42	1.23	49	62	11,053
5 Yr Avg	5.41	–5.29	–3.61	57	70	13,015
10 Yr Avg	14.73	1.80	3.62	6	8	39,507
15 Yr Avg	14.17	0.44	1.36	10	12	73,001

Tax Analysis	Tax-Adj Ret%	%Rank Cat	%Pretax Ret	%Rank Cat
3 Yr Avg	1.24	58	36.6	88
5 Yr Avg	3.89	68	71.9	56
10 Yr Avg	13.48	4	91.6	4

Potential Capital Gain Exposure: –13% of assets

Risk Analysis

Time Period	Load-Adj Return %	Risk %Rank[1] All	Risk %Rank[1] Cat	Morningstar Return	Morningstar Risk	Morningstar Risk-Adj Rating
1 Yr	–30.07					
3 Yr	1.46	91	48	–0.71[2]	1.44	★★★
5 Yr	4.23	92	60	–0.17[2]	1.56	★
10 Yr	14.08	95	69	1.56	1.64	★★★

Average Historical Rating (177 months): 2.7★s

[1]1=low, 100=high [2] T-Bill return substituted for category avg.

Category Rating (3 Yr)

1 2 3 4 5
Worst Best

Return Average
Risk Average

Other Measures	Standard Index S&P 500	Best Fit Index
Alpha	10.1	4.1
Beta	1.23	1.15
R-Squared	36	85

Standard Deviation	38.16
Mean	3.39
Sharpe Ratio	–0.05

Portfolio Analysis

Share change since Total Stocks: NULL	Sector	PE	YTD Ret%	% Assets
⊕ Robert Half Intl	Services	31.1	0.75	1.88
CDW Comp Centers	Retail	28.4	92.68	1.84
Abercrombie & Fitch Cl A	Retail	16.4	32.65	1.83
Tetra Tech	Services	35.1	–21.90	1.73
First Health Grp	Health	25.8	6.26	1.69
Venator Grp	Retail	—	0.97	1.62
Express Scripts	Health	33.6	–8.54	1.61
American Eagle Outfitters	Retail	16.8	–7.09	1.55
⊖ Jack Henry & Assoc	Technology	34.7	–29.30	1.32
Investment Tech Grp	Financials	26.6	40.37	1.31
SEI Investments	Services	43.0	–19.20	1.30
Apollo Grp Cl A	Services	—	—	1.19
OM Grp	Industrials	20.2	22.24	1.18
⊕ Jacobs Engnrg Grp	Services	20.5	42.89	1.15
Apria Healthcare Grp	Health	20.5	–16.00	1.15
⊕ Semtech	Technology	63.7	61.76	1.13
Kinder Morgan	Energy	32.2	7.11	1.09
⊕ Insituform Tech A	Industrials	18.3	–35.80	1.09
Affiliated Managers Grp	Financials	30.6	28.44	1.07
Americredit	Financials	10.6	15.78	1.04
Lincare Hldgs	Health	23.7	0.41	1.03
Citrix Sys	Technology	44.4	0.71	0.99
⊕ Hanover Compressor	Utilities	22.4	–43.30	0.99
CEC Entrtnmt	Services	19.8	27.15	0.98
Investors Finl Svcs	Financials	57.1	–22.90	0.97

Current Investment Style

Style: Value Blnd Growth; Size: Large Med Small

	Stock Port Avg	Relative S&P 500 Current	Relative S&P 500 Hist	Rel Cat
Price/Earnings Ratio	32.0	1.03	1.08	0.92
Price/Book Ratio	5.5	0.96	0.91	0.96
Price/Cash Flow	22.4	1.24	1.20	0.96
3 Yr Earnings Growth	26.8	1.83	1.71	1.14
1 Yr Earnings Est%	10.7	—	—	1.15
Med Mkt Cap $mil	2,132	0.0	0.0	0.38

Analysis by Bridget Hughes 12-10-01

AIM Aggressive Growth Fund continues to struggle, despite some improvements.

In early 2000, this fund made deliberate structural changes. It reduced the stocks in the portfolio to about 150 from almost 400 in 1998 and began to concentrate more on mid-cap territory. In fact, its heft—it had well more than $3 billion in assets at the end of 1999—was getting in the way of its focused small-cap approach. Rather than condemn the fund to a diluted portfolio of too many so-so small-cap ideas, AIM broadened the offering's mandate, and Morningstar therefore moved the fund to the mid-growth category from small growth.

Although these changes make a lot of sense, the fund has been unable to revisit its glory days of the early 1990s. It finished 2000 with a 3% gain—landing just shy of the mid-growth category's top third. But so far in 2001, its 24.8% loss through Dec. 7, 2001, stands below the group's middle. A handful of weak-performing picks, ranging from oil and gas-services firms Hanover Compressor and Cooper Cameron to retailer Talbots, have crimped the fund's returns. That said, the portfolio has been buoyed a bit by some strong retail picks, such as top-10 holding Abercrombie & Fitch.

These retail favorites are the kinds of stocks manager Robert Kippes is sticking with now. He expects major holdings Abercrombie & Fitch and American Eagle Outfitters to do well when consumer spending picks up; he says these two are leaders in the retail realm. He also likes processing firms such as Concord EFS, which takes a piece of each debit-card and credit-card transaction that runs through its network. Kippes likes that company's recurring revenue.

Although there are plenty of mid-growth options that deserve more attention, longtime shareholders should probably give the fund more time to prove itself in its new incarnation.

Special Securities % assets	
Restricted/Illiquid Secs	0
Emerging-Markets Secs	0
Options/Futures/Warrants	No

Sector Weightings	% of Stocks	Rel S&P	5-Year High	5-Year Low
Utilities	1.0	0.3	1	0
Energy	4.9	0.7	9	0
Financials	11.7	0.7	18	1
Industrials	4.9	0.4	17	3
Durables	2.4	1.5	10	0
Staples	0.6	0.1	3	0
Services	19.8	1.8	22	7
Retail	13.0	1.9	18	5
Health	16.0	1.1	29	5
Technology	25.8	1.4	68	14

Composition % assets	
Cash	3.9
Stocks*	96.1
Bonds	0.0
Other	0.0
*Foreign (% stocks)	1.7

Market Cap	
Giant	0.0
Large	3.2
Medium	66.1
Small	30.3
Micro	0.4

Address:	11 Greenway Plaza Suite 1919 Houston, TX 77046–1173 713–626–1919 / 800–959–4246
Web Address:	www.aimfunds.com
Inception:	05-01-84
Advisor:	AIM Adv.
Subadvisor:	None
NTF Plans:	Datalynx , Fidelity Inst.

Minimum Purchase:	$500	Add: $50	IRA: $250
Min Auto Inv Plan:	$50	Add: $50	
Sales Fees:	5.50%L, 0.25%B		
Management Fee:	.80% mx./.63% mn.		
Actual Fees:	Mgt: 0.63%	Dist: 0.25%	
Expense Projections:	3Yr: $869	5Yr: $1103	10Yr: $1773
Avg Brok Commission:	—	Income Distrib: Annually	
Total Cost (relative to category):	—		

AIM Constellation A

Ticker	Load	NAV	Yield	Total Assets	Mstar Category
CSTGX	5.50%	$22.10	0.0%	$11,998.5 mil	Large Growth

Prospectus Objective: Growth

AIM Constellation Fund seeks capital appreciation.

The fund invests primarily in common stocks, emphasizing small- to mid-size emerging-growth companies. Companies in which the fund invests typically fall into two categories: companies that have experienced above-average and consistent long-term earnings growth and exhibit favorable prospects for future growth, and companies that are currently experiencing a dramatic increase in profits.

Class A shares have front loads; B shares have deferred loads, higher 12b-1 fees, and conversion features; C shares have level loads.

Prior to Oct. 1, 1988, the fund was named Constellation Growth Fund.

Historical Profile

Return	Average
Risk	Above Avg
Rating	★★ Below Avg

Investment Style
Equity
Average Stock %: 91% 92% 95% 95% 97% 94% 95%

▼ Manager Change
▽ Partial Manager Change

Fund Performance vs. Category Average
■ Quarterly Fund Return +/– Category Average
— Category Baseline

Performance Quartile (within Category)

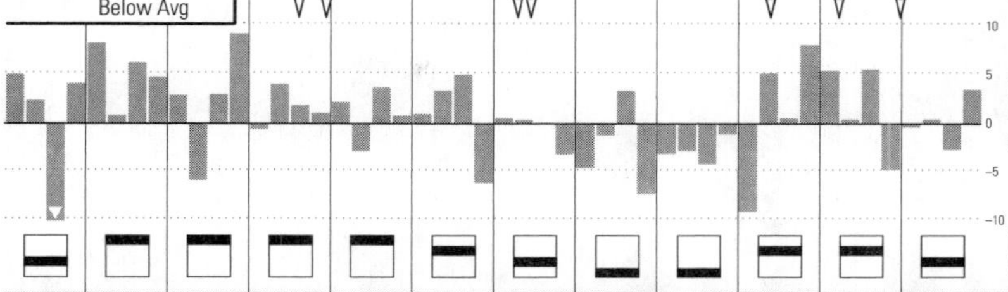

Portfolio Manager(s)

Kenneth Zschappel. Since 4-96.
Robert M. Kippes. Since 8-93.
David P. Barnard. Since 8-90.
Ryan E. Crane, CFA. Since 12-00.
Jay K. Rushin, CFA. Since 12-00.

1990	1991	1992	1993	1994	1995	1996	1997	1998	1999	2000	12-01	History
7.73	12.97	14.92	17.50	17.19	22.51	25.26	26.38	30.52	40.51	28.93	22.10	NAV
–4.09	70.41	15.04	17.29	1.30	35.46	16.27	12.92	18.89	44.38	–10.37	–23.61	Total Return %
–0.98	39.93	7.42	7.24	–0.02	–2.08	–6.68	–20.43	–9.69	23.34	–1.27	–11.73	+/– S&P 500
–5.46	31.01	11.15	17.36	–3.56	–3.20	–9.25	–20.82	–26.21	14.70	14.16	–3.11	+/– Russ Top 200 Grt
0.00	0.00	0.00	0.00	0.00	0.00	0.00	0.00	0.00	0.00	0.00	0.00	Income Return %
–4.09	70.41	15.03	17.29	1.30	35.46	16.27	12.92	18.89	44.38	–10.37	–23.61	Capital Return %
63	4	3	21	19	28	72	93	88	33	31	54	Total Rtn % Rank Cat
0.00	0.00	0.00	0.00	0.00	0.00	0.00	0.00	0.00	0.00	0.00	0.00	Income $
0.00	0.19	0.00	0.00	0.52	0.75	0.89	2.06	0.77	3.28	7.42	0.00	Capital Gains $
1.40	1.40	1.20	1.20	1.20	1.20	1.14	1.11	1.10	1.10	1.08	—	Expense Ratio %
–0.40	–0.40	–0.40	–0.30	–0.20	–0.30	–0.27	–0.40	–0.47	–0.50	–0.61	—	Income Ratio %
192	109	62	70	79	45	58	67	76	62	88	—	Turnover Rate %
108.6	486.9	1,298.7	2,924.8	3,703.5	7,377.4	11,915.2	13,990.8	14,304.0	17,920.4	15,905.3	10,635.5	Net Assets $mil

Performance 12-31-01

	1st Qtr	2nd Qtr	3rd Qtr	4th Qtr	Total
1997	–6.53	15.59	14.44	–8.67	12.92
1998	11.26	1.47	–15.61	24.80	18.89
1999	–1.31	10.16	–2.77	36.59	44.38
2000	14.32	–4.82	5.76	–22.11	–10.37
2001	–21.33	6.94	–23.34	18.44	–23.61

Trailing	Total Return%	+/– S&P 500	+/– Russ Top 200 Grth	% Rank All	% Rank Cat	Growth of $10,000
3 Mo	18.44	7.75	5.58	16	18	11,844
6 Mo	–9.20	–3.65	–2.22	82	53	9,080
1 Yr	–23.61	–11.73	–3.11	86	54	7,639
3 Yr Avg	–0.38	0.64	7.64	75	30	9,886
5 Yr Avg	5.82	–4.88	–2.77	50	73	13,271
10 Yr Avg	11.07	–1.86	–0.02	25	34	28,567
15 Yr Avg	14.59	0.85	1.22	8	14	77,109

Tax Analysis	Tax-Adj Ret%	%Rank Cat	%Pretax Ret	%Rank Cat
3 Yr Avg	–2.28	36	—	—
5 Yr Avg	4.18	70	71.8	63
10 Yr Avg	9.90	22	89.4	9

Potential Capital Gain Exposure: –2% of assets

Risk Analysis

Time Period	Load-Adj Return %	Risk %Rank[1] All	Risk %Rank[1] Cat	Morningstar Return	Morningstar Risk	Morningstar Risk-Adj Rating
1 Yr	–27.81					
3 Yr	–2.24	89	64	–1.42[2]	1.38	★★
5 Yr	4.63	88	74	–0.09[2]	1.38	★★
10 Yr	10.44	92	85	0.81	1.46	★★

Average Historical Rating (193 months): 3.3★s

[1]1=low, 100=high [2] T-Bill return substituted for category avg.

Category Rating (3 Yr)

1 2 **3** 4 5
Worst Best

Return	Above Avg
Risk	Average

Other Measures	Standard Index S&P 500	Best Fit Index Wil 4500
Alpha	5.3	–1.2
Beta	1.40	0.99
R-Squared	67	91
Standard Deviation		30.11
Mean		–0.38
Sharpe Ratio		–0.21

Portfolio Analysis 08-31-01

Share change since 07-01 Total Stocks: 113	Sector	PE	YTD Ret%	% Assets
Microsoft	Technology	57.6	52.78	3.50
Fiserv	Services	40.7	33.82	2.66
American Intl Grp	Financials	42.0	–19.20	2.24
Goldman Sachs Grp	Financials	20.7	–12.80	2.23
⊖ J.P. Morgan Chase & Co.	Financials	27.8	–17.40	2.01
Omnicom Grp	Services	34.5	8.83	1.91
Bed Bath & Beyond	Retail	53.0	51.51	1.89
Pfizer	Health	34.7	–12.40	1.88
⊕ AOL Time Warner	Technology	—	–7.76	1.83
Lowe's	Retail	38.7	109.00	1.82
Analog Devices	Technology	47.7	–13.20	1.82
Morgan Stanley/Dean Witter	Financials	16.6	–28.20	1.74
Merrill Lynch	Financials	18.2	–22.70	1.74
Kohl's	Retail	54.2	15.48	1.56
Intuit	Technology	—	8.42	1.54
Citigroup	Financials	20.0	0.03	1.51
Electronic Data Sys	Technology	25.7	19.83	1.45
TJX	Retail	23.2	44.39	1.43
Celestica	Technology	79.2	–25.50	1.42
⊖ Harley-Davidson	Durables	40.2	36.97	1.39
Cisco Sys	Technology	—	–52.60	1.33
WellPoint Health Networks	Health	19.4	1.39	1.31
Elan ADR	Health	41.0	–3.74	1.27
Microchip Tech	Technology	53.8	76.59	1.24
IBM	Technology	26.9	43.00	1.23

Analysis by Bridget Hughes 11-07-01

AIM Constellation Fund isn't the star it once was, but we think it's still a solid choice.

Lately, performance here has been so-so. After finishing 2000 near the large-growth category's top third, its 28% year-to-date loss through Nov. 5, 2001, is a bit below average. This year, top holdings such as Morgan Stanley and Merrill Lynch have been hurtful: Although both stocks have performed well in the last month or so, they have dropped more than 25% since January. And while the fund has benefited from positive moves in health-care stocks, including UnitedHealth Group and Wellpoint Health Networks, it could have used more in that relatively strong growth area: Its health-care stake is much smaller than the category average.

The fund's middling performance over the past two years is actually an improvement. In the late 1990s, the fund fell behind its peers in a frenzied growth market—an environment in which AIM should have performed well—as a bloated asset base hindered the fund's then-solely mid-cap approach.

AIM has subsequently broadened the fund's mandate—it now invests in both mid-cap and large-cap stocks. Management has also refocused the portfolio: It owns about 100 stocks, down from 400 in the mid-1990s.

Of those 100 stocks, manager Ken Zschappel says about a third of them are longer-term core holdings, versus the earnings-momentum stocks that AIM has a reputation for buying. Harley-Davidson, which Zschappel says has good earnings stability, is one example of a core position. On the momentum side, Zschappel bought Cisco Systems early this year, because he thinks orders for its products may start to pick up.

We expect the fund to perform better when the market rebounds, but we're also impressed that it has been holding its own during this bear market.

Current Investment Style

Style: Value Blnd Growth; Size: Large Med Small

	Stock Port Avg	Relative S&P 500 Current	Relative S&P 500 Hist	Rel Cat
Price/Earnings Ratio	35.2	1.14	1.18	0.99
Price/Book Ratio	5.2	0.91	1.06	0.81
Price/Cash Flow	22.9	1.27	1.26	1.01
3 Yr Earnings Growth	21.3	1.46	1.44	0.99
1 Yr Earnings Est%	4.7	—	—	1.56
Med Mkt Cap $mil	16,802	0.3	0.2	0.35

Special Securities % assets 08-31-01	
Restricted/Illiquid Secs	0
Emerging-Markets Secs	1
Options/Futures/Warrants	No

Composition % assets 08-31-01	
Cash	2.5
Stocks*	97.5
Bonds	0.0
Other	0.0
*Foreign (% stocks)	5.5

Market Cap	
Giant	26.7
Large	41.6
Medium	30.5
Small	0.5
Micro	0.7

Sector Weightings	% of Stocks	Rel S&P	5-Year High	5-Year Low
Utilities	0.0	0.0	1	0
Energy	4.4	0.6	9	0
Financials	20.1	1.1	25	3
Industrials	5.4	0.5	13	2
Durables	2.0	1.3	8	1
Staples	0.7	0.1	6	0
Services	11.6	1.1	21	7
Retail	14.1	2.1	23	6
Health	12.4	0.8	23	5
Technology	29.4	1.6	55	14

Address:	11 Greenway Plaza Suite 1919 Houston, TX 77046–1173 800–959–4246 / 713–626–1919
Web Address:	www.aimfunds.com
Inception:	04-30-76
Advisor:	AIM Adv.
Subadvisor:	AIM Cap. Mgmt.
NTF Plans:	Datalynx , Fidelity Inst.

Minimum Purchase:	$500	Add: $50	IRA: $250
Min Auto Inv Plan:	$50	Add: $50	
Sales Fees:	5.50%L, 0.05%B, 0.25%S		
Management Fee:	.63%		
Actual Fees:	Mgt: 0.63%	Dist: 0.30%	
Expense Projections:	3Yr: $886	5Yr: $1133	10Yr: $1838
Avg Brok Commission:	—	Income Distrib: Annually	
Total Cost (relative to category):		Average	

AIM European Development A

Ticker	Load	NAV	Yield	Total Assets	Mstar Category
AEDAX	5.50%	$17.30	0.0%	$298.0 mil	Europe Stock

Prospectus Objective: Europe Stock

AIM European Development Fund seeks long-term growth of capital.

The fund normally invests at least 80% of assets in equity securities of European companies, typically from at least three countries. It may invest up to 20% of assets in securities that are exchangeable for or convertible into equities of European issuers. The fund may invest up to 65% of assets in securities of European issuers located in developing countries. It may also invest up to 20% of assets in securities of non-European companies.

Class A shares have front loads; B shares have deferred loads and higher 12b-1 fees; C shares have level loads.

Historical Profile

Return	Above Avg
Risk	Average
Rating	★★★★ Above Avg

Investment Style
Equity
Average Stock %: 90% (1998), 97% (1999), 90% (2000), 91% (2001)

▼ Manager Change
▽ Partial Manager Change

Fund Performance vs. Category Average
■ Quarterly Fund Return
+/– Category Average
— Category Baseline

Performance Quartile (within Category)

Portfolio Manager(s)

Jason T. Holzer. Since 4-99. Other funds currently managed: AIM International Equity A, AIM Global Aggressive Growth A, AIM Global Aggressive Growth B.

Clas G. Olsson. Since 11-97. BA'94 U. of Texas at Austin. Other funds currently managed: AIM International Equity A, AIM Global Financial Services A, AIM Global Financial Services B.

1990	1991	1992	1993	1994	1995	1996	1997	1998	1999	2000	12-01	History
—	—	—	—	—	—	—	10.15	14.26	23.76	22.98	17.30	NAV
—	—	—	—	—	—	—	1.50*	40.62	66.62	–3.28	–24.72	Total Return %
—	—	—	—	—	—	—	–2.16*	12.05	45.58	5.82	–12.84	+/– S&P 500
—	—	—	—	—	—	—	—	12.09	50.73	5.11	—	+/– MSCI Europe
—	—	—	—	—	—	—	0.00	0.12	0.00	0.00	0.00	Income Return %
—	—	—	—	—	—	—	1.50	40.50	66.62	–3.28	–24.72	Capital Return %
—	—	—	—	—	—	—	—	2	3	24	65	Total Rtn % Rank Cat
—	—	—	—	—	—	—	0.00	0.01	0.00	0.00	0.00	Income $
—	—	—	—	—	—	—	0.00	0.00	0.00	0.00	0.00	Capital Gains $
—	—	—	—	—	—	—	—	1.98	1.88	1.69	—	Expense Ratio %
—	—	—	—	—	—	—	—	–0.58	–0.69	–0.82	—	Income Ratio %
—	—	—	—	—	—	—	—	—	122	112	—	Turnover Rate %
—	—	—	—	—	—	—	—	93.6	161.0	264.5	157.9	Net Assets $mil

Performance 12-31-01

	1st Qtr	2nd Qtr	3rd Qtr	4th Qtr	Total
1997	—	—	—	—	1.50 *
1998	26.90	13.82	–14.53	13.91	40.62
1999	–3.16	0.94	10.19	54.69	66.62
2000	19.49	–10.46	–0.51	–9.13	–3.28
2001	–21.50	1.83	–12.90	8.13	–24.72

Trailing	Total Return%	+/– S&P 500	+/– MSCI Europe	% Rank All	% Rank Cat	Growth of $10,000
3 Mo	8.13	–2.56	—	51	61	10,813
6 Mo	–5.82	–0.27	—	67	53	9,418
1 Yr	–24.72	–12.84	—	88	65	7,528
3 Yr Avg	6.65	7.68	—	18	10	12,132
5 Yr Avg	—	—	—	—	—	—
10 Yr Avg	—	—	—	—	—	—
15 Yr Avg	—	—	—	—	—	—

Tax Analysis	Tax-Adj Ret%	%Rank Cat	%Pretax Ret	%Rank Cat
3 Yr Avg	6.65	9	100.0	4
5 Yr Avg	—	—	—	—
10 Yr Avg	—	—	—	—

Potential Capital Gain Exposure: 13% of assets

Risk Analysis

Time Period	Load-Adj Return %	Risk %Rank[1] All	Risk %Rank[1] Cat	Morningstar Return	Morningstar Risk	Morningstar Risk-Adj Rating
1 Yr	–28.86					
3 Yr	4.66	81	82	–0.06[2]	1.08	★★★★
5 Yr	—	—	—	—	—	
Incept	12.56	—	—	—	—	

Average Historical Rating (13 months): 4.3★s

[1]1=low, 100=high [2] T-Bill return substituted for category avg.

Category Rating (3 Yr)

1 2 3 4 5
Worst Best

Return	Above Avg
Risk	Above Avg

Other Measures	Standard Index S&P 500	Best Fit Index Wil 4500
Alpha	9.0	5.6
Beta	0.69	0.83
R-Squared	16	63

Standard Deviation	32.36
Mean	6.65
Sharpe Ratio	0.06

Portfolio Analysis 08-31-01

Share change since 07-01 Total Stocks: 93	Sector	Country	% Assets
⊖ Altana	Health	Germany	2.61
Omega Pharma	Technology	Belgium	2.33
⊖ BNP Paribus	Financials	France	2.28
Sanofi–Synthelabo	Health	France	2.28
Bank of Ireland	Financials	Ireland	2.12
Royal Bk of Scotland	Financials	United Kingdom	2.01
Peugeot N/A	N/A	N/A	2.00
Grupo Dragados	Industrials	Spain	1.95
RAS	Financials	Italy	1.89
Nutreco Hldg	Staples	Netherlands	1.86
Aventis Cl A	Health	France	1.81
Ryanair Hldgs ADR	Services	Ireland	1.76
⊖ Man Grp	Financials	United Kingdom	1.75
⊖ Novo–Nordisk	Health	Denmark	1.71
Grupo Ferrovial	Industrials	Spain	1.70
Total Fina Cl B	Energy	France	1.69
Nestle Sa (Reg)istered N/A	N/A	N/A	1.68
BP PLC	N/A	N/A	1.63
Saint James's Place	N/A	N/A	1.58
Anglo Irish Bk	Financials	Ireland	1.56

Current Investment Style

Style: Value Blnd Growth; Size: Large Med Small

	Stock Port Avg	Rel MSCI EAFE Current	Rel MSCI EAFE Hist	Rel Cat
Price/Earnings Ratio	28.4	1.10	1.20	1.20
Price/Cash Flow	18.3	1.43	1.46	1.30
Price/Book Ratio	6.0	1.72	1.89	1.36
3 Yr Earnings Growth	26.2	1.40	1.86	1.09
Med Mkt Cap $mil	4,691	0.2	0.2	0.17

Country Exposure 08-31-01	% assets
France	21
United Kingdom	16
Germany	11
Spain	7
Ireland	6

Hedging History: Never

Special Securities % assets 08-31-01	
Restricted/Illiquid Secs	0
Emerging–Markets Secs	0
Options/Futures/Warrants	No

Composition % assets 08-31-01

Cash	3.5	Bonds	4.3
Stocks	92.2	Other	0.0

Sector Weightings	% of Stocks	Rel Cat	5-Year High	5-Year Low
Utilities	0.0	0.0	—	—
Energy	5.5	0.7	—	—
Financials	22.4	1.0	—	—
Industrials	13.1	1.1	—	—
Durables	6.2	1.4	—	—
Staples	5.6	0.8	—	—
Services	15.0	0.8	—	—
Retail	10.3	2.0	—	—
Health	16.5	1.7	—	—
Technology	5.4	0.7	—	—

Analysis by Emily Hall 11-30-01

Although its recent performance hasn't been great, AIM European Development Fund is a kicky young offering that's worth a look.

In true AIM fashion, this fund is a growth-oriented vehicle. Managers Clas Olsson and Jason Holzer search across Europe and across market caps for firms with strong earnings momentum. Although they would always prefer to buy companies on the cheap, Olsson and Holzer are no value hounds and are willing to pay up for growth when they like a stock. As a result, the portfolio's average price multiple are above the Europe-stock norm.

That affection for growth hasn't been beneficial in 2001, as high-flying names have tumbled from favor. For the year to date through the end of November, the fund is down a bruising 27%.

Until this year, however, the fund had been soaring. It held up quite well in 2000, despite an inhospitable market for growth stocks, thanks in part to some strong picks in the small-cap medical device arena. The fund's longer-term record also remains impressive: For the trailing three years its 7% annualized return is among the best in the group.

The managers' willingness to search across market caps for stocks makes this fund a particularly intriguing diversifier. For instance, Olsson and Holzer have lately been adding to their stake in Spanish construction firms, such as Dragados, because they've found some attractively valued picks with good growth prospects. They've also picked up Swedish security firm Securitas in the wake of the Sept. 11 terrorist attacks.

To be sure, this is an extremely aggressive fund and is best suited for bold investors who'd like to add a streak of European exposure to their portfolios. But for those willing to take the risk, this offering has shaped up to be a fine choice.

Address:	11 Greenway Plaza Suite 1919 Houston, TX 77046–1173 713–626–1919 / 800–959–4246
Web Address:	www.aimfunds.com
*Inception:	11-03-97
Advisor:	AIM Adv.
Subadvisor:	Invesco Asset Mgmt./Invesco Global Asset Mgmt
NTF Plans:	Fidelity Inst.

Minimum Purchase:	$500	Add: $50	IRA: $250
Min Auto Inv Plan:	$50	Add: $50	
Sales Fees:	5.50%L, 0.10%B, 0.25%S		
Management Fee:	.95% mx./.90% mn.		
Actual Fees:	Mgt: 0.95%	Dist: 0.35%	
Expense Projections:	3Yr: $1186	5Yr: $1641	10Yr: $2896
Avg Brok Commission:	—	Income Distrib: Annually	
Total Cost (relative to category):	—		

AIM International Equity A

Ticker	Load	NAV	Yield	Total Assets	Mstar Category
AIIEX	5.50%	$14.90	0.0%	$2,142.9 mil	Foreign Stock

Prospectus Objective: Foreign Stock

AIM International Equity Fund seeks long-term growth of capital.

The fund normally invests at least 70% of assets in foreign equities, including ADRs, issued in at least four countries. It invests in companies that have experienced long-term growth in earnings and that have strong prospects for continued growth. The fund may invest in issuers located in developing countries.

Class A shares have front loads; B shares have deferred loads, higher 12b-1 fees, and conversion features; C shares have level loads.

On October 15, 1993, AIM International Growth merged into this fund. On Feb. 12, 1999, AIM International Growth merged into this fund.

Historical Profile
Return: Average
Risk: Average
Rating: ★★★ Neutral

Investment Style
Equity
Average Stock %: 97% (1993), 97% (1994), 98% (1995), 92% (1996), 96% (1997), 90% (1998), 91% (1999)

▼ Manager Change
▽ Partial Manager Change

Fund Performance vs. Category Average
■ Quarterly Fund Return
+/– Category Average
— Category Baseline

Performance Quartile (within Category)

Portfolio Manager(s)

A. Dale Griffin III, CFA. Since 4-92.
Barrett K. Sides. Since 1-95.
Jason T. Holzer. Since 4-99.
Clas G. Olsson. Since 4-97.

1990	1991	1992	1993	1994	1995	1996	1997	1998	1999	2000	12-01	History
—	—	8.96	13.05	12.12	13.72	15.86	16.70	18.61	27.81	19.19	14.90	NAV
—	—	2.66*	45.78	–3.34	16.41	18.98	5.70	13.42	55.08	–25.70	–22.36	Total Return %
—	—	–9.30*	35.72	–4.65	–21.13	–3.96	–27.65	–15.16	34.04	–16.59	–10.48	+/– S&P 500
—	—	—	13.21	–11.11	5.20	12.93	3.92	–6.58	28.12	–11.53	—	+/– MSCI EAFE
—	—	0.14	0.12	0.32	0.05	0.12	0.39	0.64	0.00	0.00	0.00	Income Return %
—	—	2.52	45.65	–3.65	16.36	18.86	5.30	12.78	55.08	–25.69	–22.36	Capital Return %
—	—	—	18	79	9	21	49	52	26	89	52	Total Rtn % Rank Cat
—	—	0.01	0.01	0.04	0.01	0.02	0.06	0.11	0.00	0.00	0.00	Income $
—	—	0.00	0.00	0.44	0.38	0.43	0.00	0.21	0.93	1.48	0.00	Capital Gains $
—	—	1.80	1.78	1.64	1.67	1.57	1.47	1.45	1.48	1.44	—	Expense Ratio %
—	—	0.30	0.28	0.22	0.10	0.25	0.24	0.28	–0.14	0.30	—	Income Ratio %
—	—	—	62	67	68	66	50	78	86	87	—	Turnover Rate %
—	—	123.9	479.8	653.4	705.5	1,223.4	1,601.7	1,806.2	2,690.7	2,233.4	1,374.5	Net Assets $mil

Performance 12-31-01

	1st Qtr	2nd Qtr	3rd Qtr	4th Qtr	Total
1997	0.06	11.22	3.12	–7.89	5.70
1998	14.73	3.39	–14.64	12.01	13.42
1999	–1.83	5.80	4.35	43.09	55.08
2000	–0.68	–9.67	–7.05	–10.89	–25.70
2001	–16.31	3.05	–14.74	5.60	–22.36

Trailing	Total Return%	+/– S&P 500	+/– MSCI EAFE	% Rank All	% Rank Cat	Growth of $10,000
3 Mo	5.60	–5.09	—	63	80	10,560
6 Mo	–9.97	–4.41	—	85	64	9,003
1 Yr	–22.36	–10.48	—	84	52	7,764
3 Yr Avg	–3.64	–2.61	—	88	59	8,947
5 Yr Avg	1.41	–9.29	—	90	57	10,726
10 Yr Avg	—	—	—	—	—	—
15 Yr Avg	—	—	—	—	—	—

Tax Analysis	Tax-Adj Ret%	%Rank Cat	%Pretax Ret	%Rank Cat
3 Yr Avg	–4.33	54	—	—
5 Yr Avg	0.85	42	60.1	52
10 Yr Avg	—	—	—	—

Potential Capital Gain Exposure: –9% of assets

Risk Analysis

Time Period	Load-Adj Return %	Risk %Rank[1] All	Risk %Rank[1] Cat	Morningstar Return	Morningstar Risk	Morningstar Risk-Adj Rating
1 Yr	–26.63					
3 Yr	–5.44	81	77	–1.99[2]	1.08	★★
5 Yr	0.27	79	73	–0.95[2]	0.92	★★★
Incept	7.55	—	—	—	—	

Average Historical Rating (81 months): 3.6★s

[1]1=low, 100=high [2] T-Bill return substituted for category avg.

Category Rating (3 Yr)

1 Worst — 2 — 3 — 4 — 5 Best (rating: 3)

Return: Average
Risk: Above Avg

Other Measures	Standard Index S&P 500	Best Fit Index Wil 4500
Alpha	–2.1	–6.0
Beta	0.88	0.70
R-Squared	44	77
Standard Deviation		22.17
Mean		–3.64
Sharpe Ratio		–0.45

Analysis by Bridget Hughes 11-28-01

AIM International Equity Fund is finding some signs of improvement, and so are we at this fund.

This offering's recent returns have belied its risky approach. Consider 2001. For the year to date through Nov. 27, its 23.9% loss—painful, to be sure—actually lands around the middle of the foreign-stock pack and looks even better when compared with its growth-oriented peers. That's somewhat surprising considering AIM's penchant for loading up on high-priced stocks in just a couple of sectors. Indeed, its 40% tech stake stung in 2000 and sent the fund to the category's basement that year.

But the managers say they have learned a few hard lessons in the past 18 months or so. First, they are now more cognizant of their sector bets (though they won't be rigidly capping them). Second, rather than focus on earnings alone—particularly when earnings acceleration is sparse—they have begun to consider "second- and third-order effects that may impact earnings," according to comanager Jason Holzer. For example, increased capacity utilization and inventory drawdowns have led the managers to increase their stake in Taiwan Semiconductor Manufacturing, even though its earnings have not yet improved. That kind of thinking might have helped the fund exit many of its high-priced telecom stocks earlier this year, which could have helped the fund avoid a comparatively large 16.3% loss in 2001's first quarter.

That said, we still consider this one of the foreign-stock group's riskier entrants. The managers continue to be more than willing to pay up for faster-growing stocks, giving the portfolio's above-average price multiples. Over the long haul, its bumpy ride has produced rather middling returns. AIM devotees might consider pairing this fund with AIM International Value, which is shaping up to be a decent offering.

Portfolio Analysis 08-31-01

Share change since 07-01 Total Stocks: 89	Sector	Country	% Assets
Teva Pharma Inds ADR	Health	Israel	2.70
⊖ Altana	Health	Germany	2.69
Biovail Corporation Intl	Health	Canada	2.61
⊖ Sanofi-Synthelabo	Health	France	2.53
⊖ BNP Paribus	Financials	France	2.42
Total Fina Cl B	Energy	France	2.35
Bank of Ireland	Financials	Ireland	2.34
Royal Bk of Scotland	Financials	United Kingdom	2.28
Aventis Cl A	Health	France	2.11
Serono	Health	Switzerland	2.10
BP PLC	N/A	N/A	2.10
Peugeot N/A	N/A	N/A	2.02
Bombardier Cl B	Industrials	Canada	1.95
RAS	Financials	Italy	1.93
ENI	Energy	Italy	1.80
Banco Popular Espanol	Financials	Spain	1.79
⊖ Novo-Nordisk	Health	Denmark	1.77
Loblaw	Retail	Canada	1.76
Capita Grp	Services	United Kingdom	1.73
Nestle Sa (Reg)istered N/A	N/A	N/A	1.70

Current Investment Style

Style: Value Blnd Growth; Size: Large Med Small

	Stock Port Avg	Rel MSCI EAFE Current	Rel MSCI EAFE Hist	Rel Cat
Price/Earnings Ratio	31.4	1.21	1.16	1.23
Price/Cash Flow	17.9	1.39	1.32	1.25
Price/Book Ratio	6.0	1.73	1.42	1.54
3 Yr Earnings Growth	25.3	1.35	1.85	1.28
Med Mkt Cap $mil	11,954	0.4	0.5	0.66

Country Exposure 08-31-01	% assets
France	16
Canada	12
United Kingdom	11
Japan	11
Germany	6

Hedging History: Never

Regional Exposure 08-31-01	% assets
Europe	52
Japan	11
Latin America	3
Pacific Rim	4
Other	14

Special Securities % assets 08-31-01	
Restricted/Illiquid Secs	0
Emerging-Markets Secs	9
Options/Futures/Warrants	No

Composition % assets 08-31-01			
Cash	2.7	Bonds	3.8
Stocks	92.4	Other	1.1

Sector Weightings	% of Stocks	Rel Cat	5-Year High	5-Year Low
Utilities	0.0	0.0	6	0
Energy	10.6	1.8	11	0
Financials	19.2	0.9	22	6
Industrials	6.7	0.5	27	5
Durables	5.0	0.7	16	2
Staples	3.9	0.6	20	2
Services	12.5	0.7	43	13
Retail	9.2	1.9	18	1
Health	23.3	2.4	23	1
Technology	9.5	0.9	35	3

Address:	11 Greenway Plaza Suite 1919 Houston, TX 77046-1173 800-959-4246 / 713-626-1919
Web Address:	www.aimfunds.com
*Inception:	04-07-92
Advisor:	AIM Adv.
Subadvisor:	None
NTF Plans:	Datalynx , Fidelity Inst.

Minimum Purchase:	$500	Add: $50	IRA: $250
Min Auto Inv Plan:	$50	Add: $50	
Sales Fees:	5.50%L, 0.05%B, 0.25%S		
Management Fee:	.95% mx./.85% mn.		
Actual Fees:	Mgt: 0.89%	Dist: 0.30%	
Expense Projections:	3Yr: $99*	5Yr: $131*	10Yr: $221*
Avg Brok Commission:	—	Income Distrib: Annually	
Total Cost (relative to category):	—		

AIM Summit

Ticker	Load	NAV	Yield	Total Assets	Mstar Category
SMMIX	3.33%	$10.30	0.0%	$1,947.9 mil	Large Growth

Prospectus Objective: Growth

AIM Summit Fund seeks capital growth. Income is not generally a consideration.

The fund invests primarily in three common-stock areas: core stocks, emerging-growth stocks, and value-oriented stocks. The fund prohibits investment in sin stocks, such as tobacco or liquor companies. It may invest up to 20% of assets in foreign securities.

The fund is available only through Summit Investors Plans, a unit investment trust that calls for fixed monthly investments for 15 years. Shareholders have the option to make additional monthly payments for up to 25 years. The sales charge is contingent upon the plan and monthly investment amounts; the maximum load is 8.50%. The fund offers Class I and II shares.

Past fund names: Aim Summit Fund and AIM Summit Fund - Class I.

Historical Profile

Return Below Avg
Risk Above Avg
Rating ★★ Below Avg

Investment Style
Equity
Average Stock %

1995	1996	1997	1998	1999	2000	12-01
95%	97%	99%	97%	98%	97%	96%

▼ Manager Change
▽ Partial Manager Change

Fund Performance vs. Category Average
■ Quarterly Fund Return +/– Category Average
— Category Baseline

Performance Quartile (within Category)

History

1990	1991	1992	1993	1994	1995	1996	1997	1998	1999	2000	12-01	History
7.56	10.09	9.64	9.70	8.93	11.17	12.15	13.63	17.28	22.48	15.56	10.30	NAV
0.93	43.65	4.50	8.28	−2.82	35.14	19.87	24.22	34.44	50.77	−14.74	−33.80	Total Return %
4.05	13.16	−3.12	−1.78	−4.13	−2.39	−3.07	−9.14	5.87	29.73	−5.64	−21.93	+/– S&P 500
−0.44	4.24	0.61	8.35	−7.67	−3.51	−5.65	−9.53	−10.66	21.09	9.78	−13.31	+/– Russ Top 200 Grt
1.99	1.69	1.02	0.99	1.03	0.29	0.29	0.12	0.25	0.00	0.00	0.00	Income Return %
−1.06	41.95	3.49	7.29	−3.85	34.85	19.59	24.09	34.19	50.76	−14.74	−33.80	Capital Return %
25	42	66	59	59	30	42	57	42	24	50	89	Total Rtn % Rank Cat
0.16	0.13	0.10	0.10	0.10	0.03	0.03	0.02	0.03	0.00	0.00	0.00	Income $
0.15	0.64	0.80	0.64	0.39	0.85	1.17	1.41	0.93	3.17	3.87	0.00	Capital Gains $
0.80	0.75	0.76	0.79	0.72	0.71	0.70	0.68	0.67	0.67	0.72	—	Expense Ratio %
2.02	1.48	1.09	1.13	1.04	0.33	0.29	0.11	0.23	−0.01	−0.11	—	Income Ratio %
143	109	97	116	122	126	118	88	83	92	98	—	Turnover Rate %
316.1	517.8	604.3	712.0	746.4	1,052.8	1,305.6	1,650.2	2,242.0	3,363.8	2,835.3	1,947.9	Net Assets $mil

Portfolio Manager(s)

David P. Barnard. Since 3-95. BBA'73 Western Michigan U.; MBA'76 Western Michigan U. Other funds currently managed: AIM Constellation A, AIM Global Telecom and Technology A, AIM Weingarten A.

Bret W. Stanley, CFA. Since 3-99. BBA'87 U. of Texas; MS'95 U. of Houston. Other funds currently managed: AIM Select Equity A, AIM Select Equity B, AIM Basic Value A.

Robert Lloyd. Since 7-01. Other funds currently managed: AIM Global Telecom and Technology A, AIM Global Telecom and Technology B, AIM Global Telecom and Technology C.

Performance 12-31-01

	1st Qtr	2nd Qtr	3rd Qtr	4th Qtr	Total
1997	−3.05	17.32	14.91	−4.96	24.22
1998	12.77	4.62	−12.25	29.87	34.44
1999	8.56	6.88	−5.24	37.12	50.77
2000	9.16	−4.73	6.37	−22.94	−14.74
2001	−30.33	5.17	−22.28	16.25	−33.81

Trailing	Total Return%	+/– S&P 500	+/– Russ Top 200 Grth	% Rank All	% Rank Cat	Growth of $10,000
3 Mo	16.25	5.57	3.40	21	32	11,625
6 Mo	−9.65	−4.09	−2.66	84	58	9,035
1 Yr	−33.80	−21.93	−13.31	96	89	6,620
3 Yr Avg	−5.24	−4.22	2.78	92	66	8,509
5 Yr Avg	7.28	−3.42	−1.31	34	63	14,210
10 Yr Avg	9.73	−3.20	−1.35	34	65	25,314
15 Yr Avg	11.88	−1.85	−1.49	27	53	53,894

Tax Analysis	Tax-Adj Ret%	%Rank Cat	%Pretax Ret	%Rank Cat
3 Yr Avg	−7.44	71	—	—
5 Yr Avg	5.03	63	69.1	67
10 Yr Avg	7.36	64	75.6	55

Potential Capital Gain Exposure: −21% of assets

Risk Analysis

Time Period	Load-Adj Return %	Risk %Rank[1] All	Risk %Rank[1] Cat	Morningstar Return	Morningstar Risk	Morningstar Risk-Adj Rating
1 Yr	−36.01					
3 Yr	−6.30	93	79	−2.14[2]	1.54	★
5 Yr	6.56	88	78	0.34[2]	1.40	★★
10 Yr	9.36	91	79	0.62	1.40	★★

Average Historical Rating (193 months): 2.6★s

[1] 1=low, 100=high [2] T-Bill return substituted for category avg.

Category Rating (3 Yr)

1 2 3 4 5
Worst Best

Return Average
Risk Above Avg

Other Measures	Standard Index S&P 500	Best Fit Index Wil 4500
Alpha	0.9	−5.5
Beta	1.43	1.04
R-Squared	62	89
Standard Deviation		30.92
Mean		−5.24
Sharpe Ratio		−0.39

Portfolio Analysis 08-31-01

Share change since 06-01 Total Stocks: 101	Sector	PE	YTD Ret%	% Assets
⊕ Microsoft	Technology	57.6	52.78	3.10
Waste Mgmt	Services	52.3	15.03	2.85
⊕ H & R Block	Services	25.5	120.00	2.61
Kroger	Retail	16.3	−22.80	2.55
⊕ Tyco Intl	Industrials	27.1	6.23	2.33
⊖ Genzyme Corporation General Di	Health	—	33.11	2.30
Electronic Data Sys	Technology	25.7	19.83	2.29
⊕ General Elec	Industrials	30.1	−15.00	2.16
Bank of America	Financials	16.7	42.73	1.92
Mattel	Staples	31.9	19.43	1.84
⊕ Gap	Retail	39.8	−45.00	1.79
☼ IDEC Pharmaceuticals	Health	NMF	9.09	1.77
Parker Hannifin	Industrials	19.2	5.77	1.76
First Data	Technology	38.1	49.08	1.74
Ceridian	Technology	27.6	−5.96	1.65
⊖ Computer Assoc Intl	Technology	—	77.28	1.56
UnumProvident	Financials	10.7	0.77	1.55
El Paso	Utilities	NMF	−36.70	1.54
⊖ Health Mgmt Assoc	Health	24.2	−11.30	1.51
⊖ Freddie Mac	Financials	14.0	−3.87	1.40
⊖ UnitedHealth Grp	Financials	26.6	15.37	1.31
⊖ IBM	Technology	26.9	43.00	1.29
⊖ PG & E	Utilities	—	−3.80	1.27
Citigroup	Financials	20.0	0.03	1.25
⊖ McKesson HBOC	Health	—	4.92	1.24

Current Investment Style

Style: Value Blnd Growth; Size: Large Med Small

	Stock Port Avg	Relative S&P 500 Current	Relative S&P 500 Hist	Rel Cat
Price/Earnings Ratio	32.6	1.05	1.16	0.92
Price/Book Ratio	5.9	1.03	1.22	0.92
Price/Cash Flow	20.8	1.16	1.20	0.92
3 Yr Earnings Growth	19.7	1.35	1.43	0.91
1 Yr Earnings Est%	11.5	—	—	3.82
Med Mkt Cap $mil	15,430	0.3	0.3	0.33

Special Securities % assets 08-31-01	
Restricted/Illiquid Secs	0
Emerging-Markets Secs	Trace
Options/Futures/Warrants	No

Composition % assets 08-31-01	
Cash	3.0
Stocks*	97.0
Bonds	0.0
Other	0.0
*Foreign (% stocks)	3.1

Market Cap	
Giant	22.1
Large	42.6
Medium	34.3
Small	1.0
Micro	0.0

Sector Weightings	% of Stocks	Rel S&P	5-Year High	5-Year Low
Utilities	3.6	1.1	5	0
Energy	5.1	0.7	13	1
Financials	15.8	0.9	19	3
Industrials	9.7	0.9	18	3
Durables	1.5	1.0	12	1
Staples	1.9	0.2	19	0
Services	12.1	1.1	19	3
Retail	9.1	1.3	16	2
Health	14.6	1.0	27	4
Technology	26.7	1.5	59	4

Analysis by Bridget Hughes 11-10-01

Performance-hungry investors could do better, but AIM Summit's primary appeal isn't its returns anyway.

This fund is sold as a contractual plan. Investors here commit to make monthly purchases for 15 years. Sign the dotted line and fail to follow through, and hefty monetary penalties are imposed. That sounds harsh, but it encourages shareholders to stick with an investment plan through thick and thin, and it potentially lowers a buyer's average cost of shares (that is, it forces dollar-cost averaging). The plan also benefits the fund: The portfolio managers can count on a steady stream of cash regardless of market climate. That means they're unlikely to be forced to sell losing stocks during a bear market; rather they can use the opportunity to pounce on cheaper stocks.

Although these—along with the fund's comparatively small expense ratio—are favorable characteristics, they don't guarantee success. Indeed, the fund's 10-year return generally hovers around the large-growth category's middle. So far, 2001 isn't helping: Through Nov. 9, its 37% year-to-date loss lands well in the group's bottom quartile. The fund's hefty tech stake has burned: Once-major holdings such as Veritas Software and Nokia have lost more than half their value this year.

Comanager Dave Barnard is optimistic about growth names such as these, though. These days, he is shifting the portfolio—which typically and deliberately invests about 70% of assets in growth stocks and 30% in value names—back into growth fare. He added more Cisco Systems, for example, because he believes its business may be turning positive soon, thanks in part to information from that company's suppliers.

This fund certainly isn't for everyone, but it does have advantages for investors who need help staying the course.

Address:	11 Greenway Plaza Suite 1919 Houston, TX 77046–1173 800–959–4246 / 713–626–1919
Web Address:	www.aimfunds.com
Inception:	11-01-82
Advisor:	AIM Adv.
Subadvisor:	TradeSt. Inv. Assoc.
NTF Plans:	N/A

Minimum Purchase:	$50	Add: $50	IRA: $50
Min Auto Inv Plan:	—	Add: —	
Sales Fees:	3.33%L, 0.30%B		
Management Fee:	1.0% mx./.63% mn., .01%A		
Actual Fees:	Mgt: 0.64%	Dist: —	
Expense Projections:	3Yr: $334	5Yr: $579	10Yr: $1283
Avg Brok Commission:	—	Income Distrib: Annually	
Total Cost (relative to category):		Below Avg	

AIM Value A

Ticker	Load	NAV	Yield	Total Assets	Mstar Category
AVLFX	5.50%	$10.87	0.0%	$18,697.1 mil	Large Blend

Prospectus Objective: Growth

AIM Value Fund seeks long-term growth of capital; income is secondary.

The fund invests in equities. The issuers of these equities may be: out-of-favor cyclical growth companies; established growth companies that are undervalued compared to historical relative valuations; companies with evidence of improving prospects; and companies whose equities are selling at prices that do not reflect the current market value. It may hold up to 25% in foreign securities.

Class A shares have front loads; B shares have deferred loads and higher 12b-1 fees; C shares have level loads.

Past name: CIGNA Value Fund.

Historical Profile

Return: Average
Risk: Average
Rating: ★★★ Neutral

Investment Style: Equity

Average Stock %						71%	92%	99%	94%	95%	92%	91%

▼ Manager Change
▽ Partial Manager Change

Fund Performance vs. Category Average
■ Quarterly Fund Return +/– Category Average
— Category Baseline

Performance Quartile (within Category)

Portfolio Manager(s)

Joel E. Dobberpuhl. Since 7-92. BBA'88 Southern Methodist U. Other funds currently managed: AIM Select Equity A, AIM Select Equity B, AIM Value B.

Robert Shelton. Since 4-97. BS'91 Washington & Lee U. Other funds currently managed: AIM Mid Cap Equity A, AIM Mid Cap Equity B, AIM Value B.

Evan Harrel, CFA. Since 7-98. BA'83 Princeton U.; MBA'87 Harvard U. Other funds currently managed: AIM Value B, AIM Value C, AIM Value II A.

History

1990	1991	1992	1993	1994	1995	1996	1997	1998	1999	2000	12-01	History
4.59	5.85	6.08	6.94	7.05	8.94	9.72	10.81	13.40	16.28	12.51	10.87	NAV
1.89	43.25	16.40	18.70	3.32	34.83	14.52	23.94	32.76	29.94	–14.97	–12.99	Total Return %
5.01	12.77	8.78	8.65	2.01	–2.70	–8.43	–9.41	4.18	8.90	–5.87	–1.11	+/– S&P 500
5.92	10.81	8.75	8.87	2.87	–2.77	–7.65	–9.08	4.12	8.11	–4.01	–0.22	+/– Wilshire Top 750
1.79	1.00	0.68	0.18	0.75	0.42	1.52	0.13	0.27	0.00	0.00	0.00	Income Return %
0.10	42.26	15.72	18.52	2.57	34.41	13.00	23.81	32.48	29.94	–14.97	–12.99	Capital Return %
14	8	7	11	9	41	93	79	6	17	92	51	Total Rtn % Rank Cat
0.09	0.05	0.04	0.01	0.05	0.03	0.14	0.01	0.03	0.00	0.00	0.00	Income $
0.26	0.64	0.66	0.26	0.07	0.53	0.37	1.21	0.87	1.08	1.31	0.01	Capital Gains $
1.21	1.22	1.16	1.09	0.98	1.12	1.11	1.04	1.00	1.00	1.00	—	Expense Ratio %
1.87	0.89	0.75	0.30	0.92	0.74	1.65	0.57	0.26	–0.09	0.11	—	Income Ratio %
131	135	170	177	127	151	126	137	113	66	67	—	Turnover Rate %
86.6	152.1	239.7	763.4	1,358.3	3,397.7	5,128.4	6,736.7	8,836.7	12,686.2	11,259.8	8,560.7	Net Assets $mil

Performance 12-31-01

	1st Qtr	2nd Qtr	3rd Qtr	4th Qtr	Total
1997	–1.54	17.87	8.51	–1.58	23.94
1998	12.30	5.60	–12.09	27.34	32.76
1999	8.88	5.14	–3.65	17.81	29.94
2000	9.03	–8.68	–6.48	–8.69	–14.97
2001	–11.43	6.05	–15.91	10.17	–12.99

Trailing	Total Return%	+/– S&P 500	+/– Wil Top 750	% Rank All	% Rank Cat	Growth of $10,000
3 Mo	10.17	–0.51	–1.15	42	66	11,017
6 Mo	–7.36	–1.81	–1.57	75	75	9,264
1 Yr	–12.99	–1.11	–0.22	68	51	8,701
3 Yr Avg	–1.30	–0.28	0.52	79	52	9,614
5 Yr Avg	9.61	–1.09	–0.51	21	47	15,818
10 Yr Avg	13.30	0.38	0.85	11	17	34,869
15 Yr Avg	15.39	1.66	2.02	6	6	85,603

Tax Analysis	Tax-Adj Ret%	%Rank Cat	%Pretax Ret	%Rank Cat
3 Yr Avg	–2.53	58	—	—
5 Yr Avg	7.79	47	81.1	51
10 Yr Avg	11.36	19	85.4	30

Potential Capital Gain Exposure: –1% of assets

Risk Analysis

Time Period	Load-Adj Return %	Risk %Rank[1] All	Risk %Rank[1] Cat	Morningstar Return	Morningstar Risk	Morningstar Risk-Adj Rating
1 Yr	–17.77					
3 Yr	–3.15	75	79	–1.59[2]	1.03	★★
5 Yr	8.37	73	75	0.78[2]	0.99	★★★
10 Yr	12.66	75	73	1.24	0.98	★★★

Average Historical Rating (177 months): 4.1★s

[1] 1=low, 100=high [2] T-Bill return substituted for category avg.

Category Rating (3 Yr)

1 2 **3** 4 5
Worst — Best

Return: Average
Risk: Above Avg

Other Measures	Standard Index S&P 500	Best Fit Index
Alpha	0.3	4.5
Beta	1.03	1.11
R-Squared	84	84
Standard Deviation		19.06
Mean		–1.30
Sharpe Ratio		–0.38

Portfolio Analysis 08-31-01

Share change since 07-01 Total Stocks: 63

	Sector	PE	YTD Ret%	% Assets
American Intl Grp	Financials	42.0	–19.20	4.04
Pfizer	Health	34.7	–12.40	3.98
⊖ First Data	Technology	38.1	49.08	3.96
⊖ Cox Comms A	Services	31.8	–9.99	3.75
⊖ Comcast	Services	20.3	–13.70	3.47
⊕ General Elec	Industrials	30.1	–15.00	3.24
⊖ Target	Retail	29.8	28.05	3.12
Citigroup	Financials	20.0	0.03	3.03
Omnicom Grp	Services	34.5	8.83	3.00
⊖ Tyco Intl	Industrials	27.1	6.23	2.78
⊖ UnitedHealth Grp	Financials	26.6	15.37	2.76
AOL Time Warner	Technology	—	–7.76	2.38
BP PLC ADR	Energy	14.4	–0.90	2.34
⊖ Freddie Mac	Financials	14.0	–3.87	2.32
J.P. Morgan Chase & Co.	Financials	27.8	–17.40	2.27
⊖ Johnson & Johnson	Health	16.6	14.01	2.25
HCA – The Healthcare Company	Health	24.1	–12.20	2.22
Morgan Stanley/Dean Witter	Financials	16.6	–28.20	2.04
⊖ Analog Devices	Technology	47.7	–13.20	1.91
⊕ ExxonMobil	Energy	15.3	–7.59	1.89
⊖ Safeway	Retail	18.1	–33.20	1.84
⊖ Fannie Mae	Financials	16.2	–6.95	1.75
Nextel Comms Cl A	Services	—	–55.70	1.74
Automatic Data Processing	Services	39.8	–6.27	1.58
Walgreen	Retail	39.1	–19.20	1.58

Current Investment Style

Style: Value Blnd Growth; Size: Large Med Small

	Stock Port Avg	Relative S&P 500 Current	Relative S&P 500 Hist	Rel Cat
Price/Earnings Ratio	29.3	0.95	0.99	0.97
Price/Book Ratio	5.3	0.94	1.00	0.97
Price/Cash Flow	18.5	1.03	1.12	1.00
3 Yr Earnings Growth	23.2	1.59	1.32	1.30
1 Yr Earnings Est%	7.7	—	—	—
Med Mkt Cap $mil	39,141	0.6	0.6	0.75

Special Securities % assets 08-31-01

Restricted/Illiquid Secs	0
Emerging-Markets Secs	Trace
Options/Futures/Warrants	No

Composition % assets 08-31-01

Cash	6.1
Stocks*	93.9
Bonds	0.0
Other	0.0
*Foreign (% stocks)	4.9

Market Cap

Giant	46.1
Large	50.2
Medium	2.7
Small	0.0
Micro	1.0

Sector Weightings	% of Stocks	Rel S&P	5-Year High	5-Year Low
Utilities	3.3	1.1	14	0
Energy	8.1	1.1	9	0
Financials	24.2	1.4	44	0
Industrials	7.7	0.7	24	1
Durables	0.0	0.0	14	0
Staples	1.3	0.2	10	0
Services	16.7	1.5	29	5
Retail	9.2	1.4	16	1
Health	12.5	0.8	26	2
Technology	17.1	0.9	42	4

Analysis by Bridget Hughes 10-29-01

AIM Value Fund is back on the upswing.

Invest in a large-blend fund as growth-oriented as this one, and you're bound to see ups and downs through the years. In 2000, for instance, the fund's 15% loss landed it in the group's bottom decile. Things are looking up—relatively speaking—so far this year: Through Oct. 26, the fund has fallen 16%, but that retreat is smaller than 60% of its large-blend peers'. Of course, growth markets are most favorable to the fund, as its performance in 1998 and 1999 attest. In all, applying a very AIM-like approach to a value mandate has produced inconsistency in returns.

This year, however, comanager Evan Harrel said he had moderated the portfolio a bit. He concedes that it's tougher to find accelerating earnings momentum—AIM's trademark—in the current market, so he's been paying even more attention to valuations and more-qualitative factors. Take recent additions Mirant and Duke, for example, which Harrel said had attractive businesses, but broken-down stocks. And although both Mirant and Duke have had some revenue momentum, Harrel is more encouraged by the potential that electricity deregulation and increasing consumer demand present.

That said, Harrel still favors stocks with stronger growth prospects. For example, because it continues to show increases in its subscriber base and cash flow, Nextel Communications, which has sunk 65% in so far in 2001, remains in the portfolio. The fund's tech weighting is almost double that of its average peer, and its stake in health care—another high-growth, higher-multiple area—is also well above average.

The fund's growth tilt has tended to work well over the long haul—its 10-year return is near the category's top decile—but investors should brace themselves for a bumpy ride.

Address:	11 Greenway Plaza Suite 1919 Houston, TX 77046–1173 800–959–4246 / 713–626–1919
Web Address:	www.aimfunds.com
Inception:	05-01-84
Advisor:	AIM Adv.
Subadvisor:	None
NTF Plans:	Datalynx , Fidelity Inst.

Minimum Purchase:	$500	Add: $50	IRA: $250
Min Auto Inv Plan:	$50	Add: $50	
Sales Fees:	5.50%L, 0.25%B		
Management Fee:	.80% mx./.60% mn., .00%A		
Actual Fees:	Mgt: 0.63%	Dist: 0.25%	
Expense Projections:	3Yr: $857	5Yr: $1082	10Yr: $1729
Avg Brok Commission:	—	Income Distrib: Annually	
Total Cost (relative to category):	Average		

AIM Weingarten A

Ticker	Load	NAV	Yield	Total Assets	Mstar Category
WEINX	5.50%	$13.49	0.0%	$5,213.1 mil	Large Growth

Prospectus Objective: Growth

AIM Weingarten Fund seeks growth of capital.

The fund invests primarily in common stocks. Its investments usually fall into one of the following two categories: companies that management considers to have experienced above-average and consistent growth in earnings and to have potential for significant future growth, and companies that management believes are currently experiencing a dramatic increase in profits. The fund may invest up to 20% of assets in foreign securities.

Class A shares have front loads; B shares have deferred loads and higher 12b-1 fees; C shares have level loads.

Prior to Oct. 1, 1988, the fund was named Weingarten Fund.

Historical Profile
Return Low
Risk Above Avg
Rating ★ Lowest

Investment Style
Equity
Average Stock %

94% 98% 95% 93% 97% 94% 95%

▼ Manager Change
▽ Partial Manager Change

Fund Performance vs. Category Average
■ Quarterly Fund Return +/– Category Average
— Category Baseline

Performance Quartile (within Category)

Portfolio Manager(s)

Jonathan C. Schoolar, CFA. Since 5-87. BA'83 U. of Texas. Other funds currently managed: AIM Select Equity A, AIM Blue Chip A, AIM Select Equity B.

Monika H. Degan, CFA. Since 1-98. BA U. of Houston; MBA U. of Houston. Other funds currently managed: AIM Blue Chip A, AIM Charter A, AIM Global Growth A.

David P. Barnard. Since 3-86. BBA'73 Western Michigan U.; MBA'76 Western Michigan U. Other funds currently managed: AIM Constellation A, AIM Global Telecom and Technology A, AIM Summit.

1990	1991	1992	1993	1994	1995	1996	1997	1998	1999	2000	12-01	History
12.14	17.66	17.33	17.15	15.21	17.73	18.51	19.89	24.82	30.11	20.47	13.49	NAV
5.55	46.86	–1.37	1.53	–0.34	34.76	17.67	25.96	33.05	34.90	–20.37	–34.10	Total Return %
8.66	16.38	–8.99	–8.52	–1.65	–2.78	–5.28	–7.40	4.48	13.86	–11.27	–22.22	+/– S&P 500
4.18	7.46	–5.26	1.61	–5.19	–3.89	–7.85	–7.79	–12.05	5.22	4.15	–13.60	+/– Russ Top 200 Grt
0.76	0.56	0.50	0.63	0.40	0.00	0.34	0.00	0.07	0.00	0.00	0.00	Income Return %
4.78	46.31	–1.87	0.90	–0.74	34.76	17.33	25.95	32.98	34.90	–20.37	–34.10	Capital Return %
5	35	95	89	31	32	58	50	47	53	75	89	Total Rtn % Rank Cat
0.09	0.07	0.09	0.11	0.07	0.00	0.06	0.00	0.01	0.00	0.00	0.00	Income $
0.21	0.09	0.00	0.33	1.78	2.71	2.24	3.35	1.51	3.19	3.54	0.00	Capital Gains $
1.30	1.20	1.10	1.10	1.20	1.20	1.12	1.07	1.04	1.03	1.03	—	Expense Ratio %
0.80	0.70	0.60	0.60	0.40	0.00	0.33	0.07	0.07	–0.38	–4.50	—	Income Ratio %
79	46	37	109	136	139	159	128	125	124	145	—	Turnover Rate %
803.1	3,293.2	5,608.8	4,712.4	3,667.6	4,562.4	5,109.9	5,865.6	7,276.2	9,495.9	7,511.5	4,094.6	Net Assets $mil

Performance 12-31-01

	1st Qtr	2nd Qtr	3rd Qtr	4th Qtr	Total
1997	–1.62	16.80	11.85	–2.00	25.96
1998	12.97	4.81	–12.23	28.03	33.05
1999	6.85	4.86	–2.55	23.55	34.90
2000	13.68	–7.10	–2.61	–22.58	–20.37
2001	–27.65	1.82	–17.57	8.53	–34.10

Trailing	Total Return%	+/– S&P 500	+/– Russ Top 200 Grth	% Rank All	% Rank Cat	Growth of $10,000
3 Mo	8.53	–2.16	–4.33	49	94	10,853
6 Mo	–10.54	–4.99	–3.56	87	66	8,946
1 Yr	–34.10	–22.22	–13.60	96	89	6,590
3 Yr Avg	–10.88	–9.85	–2.85	99	92	7,079
5 Yr Avg	3.48	–7.22	–5.11	83	85	11,864
10 Yr Avg	6.50	–6.43	–4.58	57	87	18,774
15 Yr Avg	11.07	–2.66	–2.30	33	68	48,327

Tax Analysis	Tax-Adj Ret%	%Rank Cat	%Pretax Ret	%Rank Cat
3 Yr Avg	–12.45	91	—	—
5 Yr Avg	1.28	84	36.7	93
10 Yr Avg	4.07	86	62.7	88

Potential Capital Gain Exposure: –36% of assets

Risk Analysis

Time Period	Load-Adj Return %	Risk %Rank[1] All	Risk %Rank[1] Cat	Morningstar Return	Morningstar Risk	Morningstar Risk-Adj Rating
1 Yr	–37.72					
3 Yr	–12.54	91	73	–3.13[2]	1.47	★
5 Yr	2.31	86	63	–0.56[2]	1.30	★
10 Yr	5.90	89	66	0.14	1.32	★

Average Historical Rating (193 months): 3.5★s

[1] 1=low, 100=high [2] T-Bill return substituted for category avg.

Category Rating (3 Yr)

1 2 3 4 5
Worst Best

Return Low
Risk Above Avg

Other Measures	Standard Index S&P 500	Best Fit Index Wil 4500
Alpha	–7.1	–12.2
Beta	1.20	0.86
R-Squared	59	82
Standard Deviation		24.74
Mean		–10.88
Sharpe Ratio		–0.76

Portfolio Analysis 08-31-01

Share change since 06-01 Total Stocks: 79	Sector	PE	YTD Ret%	% Assets
Freddie Mac	Financials	14.0	–3.87	3.07
Fannie Mae	Financials	16.2	–6.95	3.02
HCA – The Healthcare Company	Health	24.1	–12.20	2.62
Lockheed Martin	Industrials	36.8	38.98	2.62
⊖ UnitedHealth Grp	Financials	26.6	15.37	2.46
Johnson & Johnson	Health	16.6	14.01	2.31
Baxter Intl	Health	33.9	22.84	2.20
⊖ Tenet Healthcare	Health	30.1	32.14	2.18
Cendant	Services	20.4	103.70	2.13
⊕ Analog Devices	Technology	47.7	–13.20	2.11
⊕ American Intl Grp	Financials	42.0	–19.20	2.09
⊖ First Data	Technology	38.1	49.08	2.07
⊖ General Elec	Industrials	30.1	–15.00	2.03
⊕ KLA–Tencor	Technology	22.6	47.11	1.96
⊕ Mirant	Utilities	8.3	–43.40	1.95
⊕ Microsoft	Technology	57.6	52.78	1.82
⊕ Lowe's	Retail	38.7	109.00	1.62
United Tech	Industrials	16.3	–16.70	1.61
⊕ Novellus Sys	Technology	25.0	9.77	1.58
Biovail Corporation Intl	Health	NMF	44.82	1.51
☼ Electronic Data Sys	Technology	25.7	19.83	1.51
☼ Bank of America	Financials	16.7	42.73	1.50
☼ Altera	Technology	44.2	–19.30	1.48
Genzyme Corporation General Di	Health	—	33.11	1.45
⊕ Elan ADR	Health	41.0	–3.74	1.45

Current Investment Style

Style: Value Blnd Growth; Size: Large Med Small

	Stock Port Avg	Relative S&P 500 Current	Relative S&P 500 Hist	Rel Cat
Price/Earnings Ratio	33.3	1.08	1.21	0.94
Price/Book Ratio	5.9	1.04	1.20	0.93
Price/Cash Flow	21.9	1.21	1.29	0.96
3 Yr Earnings Growth	25.8	1.76	1.37	1.20
1 Yr Earnings Est%	17.6	—	—	5.85
Med Mkt Cap $mil	17,055	0.3	0.5	0.36

Special Securities % assets 08-31-01	
Restricted/Illiquid Secs	0
Emerging-Markets Secs	1
Options/Futures/Warrants	No

Composition % assets 08-31-01	
Cash	3.8
Stocks*	96.2
Bonds	0.0
Other	0.0
*Foreign (% stocks)	8.0

Market Cap	
Giant	22.0
Large	47.9
Medium	30.1
Small	0.0
Micro	0.0

Sector Weightings	% of Stocks	Rel S&P	5-Year High	5-Year Low
Utilities	3.4	1.1	14	0
Energy	2.5	0.4	21	0
Financials	15.8	0.9	26	3
Industrials	7.5	0.7	23	1
Durables	2.1	1.4	12	0
Staples	0.8	0.1	25	0
Services	5.4	0.5	21	1
Retail	4.6	0.7	16	0
Health	32.5	2.2	35	5
Technology	25.5	1.4	63	4

Analysis by Bridget Hughes 11-10-01

AIM Weingarten Fund's troubled past and recent performance cast doubt on its viability.

Things just keep getting worse for Weingarten. After losing 20% in 2000 and landing just outside the large-growth group's bottom quartile that year, it has dropped more than 36% through Nov. 9, 2001, which is behind almost 90% of its peers. The fund's first quarter, when it lost more than 27%, was particularly hurtful; then, its tech stake burned. As earnings started to deteriorate in those names, the fund dumped them and jumped into steadier growers, such as GE and America Online, that subsequently sank.

Indeed, the fund hasn't made a great case for itself since 1998, when it officially chose its destiny as a large-growth fund. (Previously, the offering had a more flexible mandate.) In 1998's and 1999's growth-frenzied markets, when you might rightfully expect AIM's earnings-momentum growth approach to shame the competition, the fund hovered near the group's middle. (In both years, however, it did boast returns greater than 30%.) And since 1998, the fund has been at least as volatile as its typical peer.

Lead manager Jonathan Schoolar insists his methods work better than the numbers indicate and says he's sticking with the notion that growth-stock prices follow earnings, where his work will continue to focus. He recently bought Cisco Systems (again), because he believes that company's earnings and earnings estimates will improve. Overall, he wants the portfolio's earnings-growth rate to be at least 20%.

It's likely the fund's performance will improve if growth stocks take off, but the offering has another strike against it: AIM's large-cap lineup is tough to distinguish—and the fund family continues to introduce new large-cap funds—making it unclear whether this aggressive fund is necessary.

Address:	11 Greenway Plaza Suite 1919 Houston, TX 77046–1173 800–959–4246 / 713–626–1919
Web Address:	www.aimfunds.com
Inception:	06-17-69
Advisor:	AIM Adv.
Subadvisor:	AIM Cap. Mgmt.
NTF Plans:	Datalynx , Fidelity Inst.

Minimum Purchase:	$500	Add: $50	IRA: $250
Min Auto Inv Plan:	$50	Add: $50	
Sales Fees:	5.50%L, 0.05%B, 0.25%S		
Management Fee:	.63%		
Actual Fees:	Mgt: 0.60%	Dist: 0.30%	
Expense Projections:	3Yr: $875	5Yr: $1113	10Yr: $1795
Avg Brok Commission:	—	Income Distrib: Annually	
Total Cost (relative to category):		Average	

Alliance Muni Income National A

Ticker	Load	NAV	Yield	SEC Yield	Total Assets	Mstar Category
ALTHX	4.25%	$10.12	5.3%	4.87%	$649.9 mil	Muni Natl Long–Term

Prospectus Objective: Muni Bond—National

Alliance Municipal Income Fund National Portfolio seeks current income.

The fund normally invests in investment grade intermediate- to long-term municipal obligations It may invest without limit in AMT-subject bonds. The portfolio's average weighted maturity ranges between 10 and 30 years.

Class A shares have front loads; B shares have deferred loads, higher 12b-1 fees, and conversion features; C shares have no loads and no conversion features. Prior to Sept. 27, 1988, this fund was named Alliance Tax-Free Income High-Income Tax-Free. Equitable Tax-Exempt Front-Load merged into this fund on July 22, 1993.

Historical Profile

Return: Average
Risk: Above Avg
Rating: ★★ Below Avg

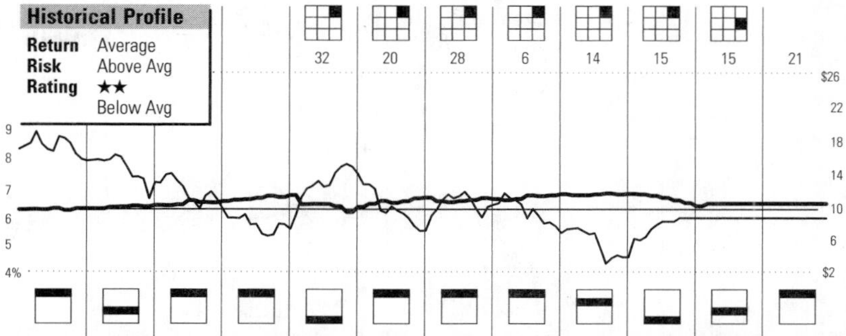

Investment Style rank (Income Rtn %Rank Cat): 32, 20, 28, 6, 14, 15, 15, 21

Investment Style
Fixed-Income
Income Rtn %Rank Cat

Growth of Principal vs. Interest Rate Shifts
- Principal Value $000 (NAV with capital gains reinvested)
- Interest Rate % on 10 Yr Treasury
- Manager Change
- Partial Manager Change
- Mgr Unknown After
- Mgr Unknown Before

Performance Quartile (within Category)

Portfolio Manager(s)

Susan P. Keenan. Since 12-86. BA'80 U. of California-Berkeley. Other funds currently managed: Alliance Muni Income CA A, Alliance Muni Income NY A, Alliance Muni Income Insured CA A.

1990	1991	1992	1993	1994	1995	1996	1997	1998	1999	2000	12-01	History
9.62	10.06	10.43	10.92	9.29	10.73	10.59	11.04	10.98	9.80	10.18	10.12	NAV
7.39	11.84	10.43	13.32	−9.64	22.25	4.33	10.50	5.72	−5.89	9.76	4.68	Total Return %
−1.56	−4.16	3.03	3.58	−6.72	3.78	0.71	0.82	−2.95	−5.06	−1.87	−3.75	+/– LB Aggregate
0.09	−0.30	1.61	1.05	−4.50	4.79	−0.11	1.30	−0.76	−3.82	−1.93	−0.41	+/– LB Muni
7.22	7.10	6.58	6.10	5.61	6.40	5.53	6.08	5.37	5.21	5.76	5.37	Income Return %
0.17	4.75	3.85	7.22	−15.25	15.85	−1.20	4.42	0.35	−11.10	4.01	−0.69	Capital Return %
6	55	10	23	96	2	21	9	31	76	66	24	Total Rtn % Rank Cat
0.67	0.66	0.64	0.62	0.60	0.58	0.58	0.63	0.58	0.56	0.55	0.53	Income $
0.00	0.00	0.00	0.24	0.00	0.00	0.00	0.00	0.10	0.00	0.00	0.00	Capital Gains $
0.60	0.75	0.83	0.65	0.62	0.71	0.69	0.69	0.66	0.66	0.68	—	Expense Ratio %
7.06	6.81	6.35	5.69	5.61	5.84	5.55	5.40	4.98	4.86	5.53	—	Income Ratio %
105	64	86	233	110	118	137	72	56	393	415	—	Turnover Rate %
189.0	211.1	284.3	394.0	318.9	346.4	323.8	336.3	367.6	417.6	404.8	421.3	Net Assets $mil

Performance 12-31-01

	1st Qtr	2nd Qtr	3rd Qtr	4th Qtr	Total
1997	−0.50	4.57	3.33	2.79	10.50
1998	0.61	2.15	2.14	0.72	5.72
1999	0.89	−1.85	−1.64	−3.38	−5.89
2000	2.90	0.69	3.52	2.33	9.76
2001	2.77	1.24	1.32	−0.71	4.68

Trailing	Total Return%	+/– LB Agg	+/– LB Muni	% Rank All	% Rank Cat	Growth of $10,000
3 Mo	−0.71	−0.75	−0.05	88	27	9,929
6 Mo	0.60	−4.05	−1.52	36	90	10,060
1 Yr	4.68	−3.75	−0.41	25	24	10,468
3 Yr Avg	2.64	−3.64	−2.11	58	65	10,813
5 Yr Avg	4.78	−2.64	−1.19	68	44	12,632
10 Yr Avg	6.18	−1.05	−0.45	66	26	18,218
15 Yr Avg	6.98	−1.14	−0.21	67	17	27,523

Tax Analysis	Tax-Adj Ret%	%Rank Cat	%Pretax Ret	%Rank Cat
3 Yr Avg	2.64	65	100.0	1
5 Yr Avg	4.75	40	99.2	43
10 Yr Avg	6.08	21	98.3	36

Potential Capital Gain Exposure: –5% of assets

Risk Analysis

Time Period	Load-Adj Return %	Risk %Rank[1] All	Risk %Rank[1] Cat	Morningstar Return	Morningstar Risk	Morningstar Risk-Adj Rating
1 Yr	0.23					
3 Yr	1.16	22	35	−0.04[2]	1.11	★★
5 Yr	3.88	21	28	0.59[2]	1.07	★★★
10 Yr	5.72	32	58	1.01	1.18	★★

Average Historical Rating (145 months): 3.6★s

[1] 1=low, 100=high [2] T-Bill return substituted for category avg.

Category Rating (3 Yr)

1 2 3 4 5 (Worst … Best): 3

Return: Average
Risk: Average

Other Measures	Standard Index LB Agg	Best Fit Index LB Muni
Alpha	−3.1	−2.0
Beta	0.72	1.00
R–Squared	35	82
Standard Deviation		4.17
Mean		2.64
Sharpe Ratio		−0.65

Portfolio Analysis 09-30-01

Total Fixed-Income: 95	Date of Maturity	Amount $000	Value $000	% Net Assets
OH Hamilton GO 5.25%	12-01-32	51,775	52,259	8.06
SC South GO 6.375%	05-15-28	33,800	35,873	5.53
NY York GO 6.375%	07-15-39	18,925	20,268	3.12
NY Mtg 5.45%	04-01-31	20,000	20,127	3.10
TX Alliance Arpt Spcl Fac Fed Ex 6.375%	04-01-21	18,800	19,174	2.96
MT GO 8%	07-01-20	17,000	18,005	2.78
FL Fiddlers Creek Cmnty Dev Dist 7.5%	05-01-18	15,620	16,729	2.58
TX Houston Arpt 7%	07-01-29	20,000	16,368	2.52
CA Cmnty Dev Spcl Fac Air 5.625%	10-01-34	21,500	15,789	2.43
MA Port Spcl Fac Bosfuel 6%	07-01-36	13,825	14,594	2.25
DC Columbia GO 6.75%	05-15-40	12,900	14,080	2.17
MI Saginaw Hosp Fin St Luke 6.5%	07-01-30	12,475	13,183	2.03
FL Lee GO 7.25%	05-01-12	11,050	11,616	1.79
CT Dev Poll Cntrl Lt/Pwr 5.95%	09-01-28	11,000	11,106	1.71
NY NYC Indl Dev Spcl Fac American 6.9%	08-01-24	12,000	10,681	1.65

Current Investment Style

Not Available

Avg Duration[1]	7.9 Yrs
Avg Nominal Maturity	23.0 Yrs
Avg Credit Quality	—
Avg Wtd Coupon	6.09%
Avg Wtd Price	101.59% of par
Pricing Service	Muller

[1] figure provided by fund

Credit Analysis % bonds 03-31-01			
US Govt	0	BB	0
AAA	32	B	0
AA	13	Below B	0
A	15	NR/NA	18
BBB	22		

Special Securities % assets 09-30-01	
Restricted/Illiquid Secs	0
Inverse Floaters	1
Options/Futures/Warrants	No

Bond Type % assets	
Alternative Minimum Tax (AMT)	N/A
Insured	N/A
Prerefunded	N/A

Top 5 States % bonds			
FL	16.7	TX	8.4
OH	13.2	MI	6.8
NY	11.3		

Composition % assets 09-30-01			
Cash	0.0	Bonds	100.0
Stocks	0.0	Other	0.0

Sector Weightings	% of Bonds	Rel Cat
General Obligation	13.3	0.6
Utilities	1.9	0.2
Health	5.4	0.4
Water/Waste	0.5	0.1
Housing	16.4	2.3
Education	1.8	0.3
Transportation	22.4	1.7
COP/Lease	0.4	0.1
Industrial	7.7	0.6
Misc Revenue	4.1	0.8
Demand	0.8	1.0

Analysis by Eric Jacobson 12-12-01

Alliance Municipal Income National is showing signs of being back on track.

This fund has an aggressive personality for a muni portfolio. Manager Susan Keenan has historically favored long-maturity bonds as an outgrowth of her focus on call protection, and hasn't been afraid to hold large stakes in individual issues when she's been convinced they've been due for quality improvements. The fund's credit profile has been similarly intrepid in that it holds an above-average stake in mid-quality A and BBB credits, as well as an 18% stake in nonrated bonds.

That's not to say Keenan's approach has been misguided. This fund had an excellent record for much of the 1990s, as falling rates and a series of well-executed credit plays helped boost returns. As of early 1999, 12 of the 13 A-share muni funds under Keenan's management—including this one—placed in the best quartiles of their respective categories.

The fund's aggressive tendencies weren't well received by the markets of 1999 and 2000, though. Its long-maturity bonds suffered when interest rates spiked in the former, while the fund's credit-sensitive bonds stumbled along with the economy in the latter. It placed in the muni national long-term category's bottom third during both years.

Things have been looking up in 2001. Keenan purchased several call-protected, yet less-rate-sensitive, issues during the first half of the year, and that appears to have helped the fund avoid some of the pain of 2001's interest-rate hiccups. Mid-quality issues saw a revival this year, as well. As a result, the fund placed in the category's best quartile for the year to date through December 10.

There's no question that this yield-rich fund carries considerable issue-specific and interest-rate risk, but Keenan has shown much skill, and its long record inspires confidence.

Address:	P.O. Box 1520 Secaucus, NJ 07096 800–227–4618 / 201–319–4000
Web Address:	www.alliancecapital.com
Inception:	12-29-86
Advisor:	Alliance Cap. Mgmt. (Bernstein)
Subadvisor:	None
NTF Plans:	Datalynx , Fidelity Inst.

Minimum Purchase:	$250	Add: $50	IRA: —
Min Auto Inv Plan:	$250	Add: $25	
Sales Fees:	4.25%L, 0.05%B, 0.25%S		
Management Fee:	.63%		
Actual Fees:	Mgt: 0.20%	Dist: 0.30%	
Expense Projections:	3Yr: $627	5Yr: $777	10Yr: $1213
Avg Brok Commission:	—	Income Distrib: Monthly	
Total Cost (relative to category):	—		

Alliance North American Govt Income B

Ticker	Load	NAV	Yield	SEC Yield	Total Assets	Mstar Category
ANABX	3.00%d	$6.98	9.6%	9.86%	$2,151.0 mil	International Bond

Prospectus Objective: World Bond

Alliance North American Government Income Trust seeks current income consistent with prudent investment risk.

The fund normally invests at least 65% of assets in investment-grade government securities of the United States, Mexico, and Canada; assets are actively allocated according to market and economic conditions. It may invest the balance of assets in investment-grade government securities of Central and South American countries. The fund may invest up to 25% of total assets in Argentine government securities. The fund is nondiversified.

Class A shares have front loads; B shares have deferred loads, higher 12b-1 fees, and conversion features; C shares have no loads.

Historical Profile

Return High
Risk Above Avg
Rating ★★ Below Avg

Investment Style
Fixed-Income
Income Rtn %Rank Cat: 6, 6, 3, 1, 1, 4, 10, 3

Growth of Principal vs. Interest Rate Shifts
- Principal Value $000 (NAV with capital gains reinvested)
- Interest Rate % on 10 Yr Treasury
- ▼ Manager Change
- ▽ Partial Manager Change
- ► Mgr Unknown After
- ◄ Mgr Unknown Before

Performance Quartile (within Category)

Portfolio Manager(s)

Wayne D. Lyski. Since 3-92. BA Seattle Pacific U.; MBA U. of Pennsylvania - Wharton. Other funds currently managed: Alliance North American Govt Income A, Alliance Bond Corporate Bond A, Alliance Bond Corporate Bond B.

1990	1991	1992	1993	1994	1995	1996	1997	1998	1999	2000	12–01	History
—	—	9.77	10.31	6.42	7.25	7.91	8.08	7.61	7.26	7.72	6.98	NAV
—	—	5.26*	17.81	–30.80	29.57	23.05	15.18	5.72	6.96	17.79	–1.21	Total Return %
—	—	—	8.06	–27.89	11.10	19.43	5.50	–2.95	7.79	6.16	–9.63	+/– LB Aggregate
—	—	—	2.69	–36.79	10.02	18.97	19.44	–12.07	12.03	20.42	2.34	+/– SB World Govt
—	—	7.43	10.76	7.61	14.98	13.14	13.04	11.74	11.79	11.12	9.02	Income Return %
—	—	–2.18	7.05	–38.41	14.59	9.91	2.14	–6.02	–4.83	6.66	–10.23	Capital Return %
—	—	—	26	99	3	4	2	82	7	1	76	Total Rtn % Rank Cat
—	—	0.73	1.00	0.75	0.90	0.90	0.98	0.90	0.85	0.77	0.67	Income $
—	—	0.01	0.12	0.17	0.00	0.00	0.00	0.00	0.00	0.00	0.00	Capital Gains $
—	—	3.13	2.31	2.41	3.33	3.05	2.09	2.07	2.08	2.03	—	Expense Ratio %
—	—	10.16	10.01	10.53	17.31	14.20	12.15	10.44	10.97	9.37	—	Income Ratio %
—	—	—	254	131	180	166	118	175	158	234	—	Turnover Rate %
—	—	256.4	1,475.4	1,152.8	1,199.4	1,309.3	1,393.2	1,302.2	992.5	856.8	870.2	Net Assets $mil

Performance 12-31-01

	1st Qtr	2nd Qtr	3rd Qtr	4th Qtr	Total
1997	0.70	8.06	5.91	–0.06	15.18
1998	2.22	0.42	–3.77	7.03	5.72
1999	3.88	–1.29	2.45	1.82	6.96
2000	7.85	–0.78	5.31	4.53	17.79
2001	1.02	3.58	–1.02	–4.60	–1.21

Trailing	Total Return%	+/– LB Agg	+/– SB World	% Rank All	% Rank Cat	Growth of $10,000
3 Mo	–4.60	–4.64	–0.63	100	100	9,540
6 Mo	–5.58	–10.23	–9.05	65	100	9,442
1 Yr	–1.21	–9.63	2.34	44	76	9,880
3 Yr Avg	7.57	1.29	11.32	16	5	12,447
5 Yr Avg	8.67	1.25	8.56	25	2	15,156
10 Yr Avg	—	—	—	—	—	—
15 Yr Avg	—	—	—	—	—	—

Tax Analysis	Tax-Adj Ret%	%Rank Cat	%Pretax Ret	%Rank Cat
3 Yr Avg	3.35	10	44.2	51
5 Yr Avg	4.14	9	47.7	48
10 Yr Avg	—	—	—	—

Potential Capital Gain Exposure: –14% of assets

Risk Analysis

Time Period	Load-Adj Return %	Risk %Rank[1] All	Risk %Rank[1] Cat	Morningstar Return	Morningstar Risk	Morningstar Risk-Adj Rating
1 Yr	–3.01					
3 Yr	7.57	33	54	0.57[2]	1.64	★★★
5 Yr	8.67	39	72	0.85[2]	1.97	★★
Incept	7.75	—	—	—	—	

Average Historical Rating (82 months): 2.4★s

[1]1=low, 100=high [2] T-Bill return substituted for category avg.

Category Rating (3 Yr)

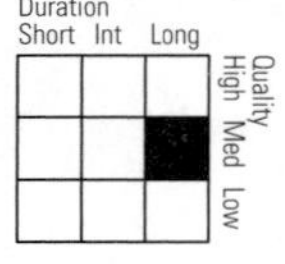

Return High
Risk Average

Other Measures	Standard Index LB Agg	Best Fit Index LB LTTreas
Alpha	1.1	2.8
Beta	1.35	0.65
R–Squared	24	27
Standard Deviation		9.81
Mean		7.57
Sharpe Ratio		0.31

Portfolio Analysis 06-30-01

Total Fixed-Income: 20	Date of Maturity	Value $000	% Net Assets
Republic Argentina 10%	09-19-08	440,552	16.99
US Treasury Bond 8.125%	08-15-19	226,617	8.74
United Mexican States 16%	01-23-03	220,557	8.50
US Treasury Bond 8.875%	08-15-17	204,119	7.87
US Treasury Bond 8.75%	08-15-20	188,039	7.25
US Treasury Bond 12.5%	08-15-14	175,731	6.78
Govt of Canada 6%	06-01-11	128,296	4.95
US Treasury Strip 0%	05-15-13	123,354	4.76
Nacl Financiera Snc 144A 22%	05-20-02	109,596	4.23
US Treasury Strip 0%	02-15-16	108,863	4.20
US Treasury Bond 13.25%	05-15-14	80,628	3.11
US Treasury Bond 5.375%	02-15-31	66,325	2.56
US Treasury Bond 12%	08-15-13	65,390	2.52
United Mexican States FRN	08-25-05	60,048	2.32
Govt of Canada 10.25%	03-15-14	55,734	2.15
Mexico Bonos 5–year 13.5%	03-02-06	54,342	2.10
Govt of Canada 8%	06-01-27	40,184	1.55
Mexico Bonos 14%	01-22-04	37,382	1.44
United Mexican States 14.5%	05-12-05	36,646	1.41
US Treasury Strip 0%	05-15-15	34,194	1.32

Current Investment Style

Duration: Short Int Long; Quality: High Med Low

Avg Eff Duration	—
Avg Eff Maturity	11.0 Yrs
Avg Credit Quality	—
Avg Wtd Coupon	9.56%
Avg Wtd Price	81.72% of par

Special Securities 06-30-01	% assets
Restricted/Illiquid Secs	5
Exotic Mortgage–Backed	0
Emerging–Markets Secs	0
Options/Futures/Warrants	No

Country Exposure % assets

Not Available

Composition % assets 06-30-01

Cash	6.7	Bonds	93.3
Stocks	0.0	Other	0.0

Analysis by William Samuel Rocco 08-09-01 This analysis was written for the A shares.

The advantages of this fund's aggressive approach remain clear.

Alliance North American Government Income Fund is still following its own offbeat and bold itinerary. While most international–bond funds spread their assets across the developed world, this one confines itself to the western hemisphere and pays a lot of attention to a couple of emerging markets in the region: Mexico and Argentina.

Indeed, the fund's stake in Mexican bonds increased from 24% of assets in late 2000 to 26% of assets by the end of June. And though the fund's position in Argentine credits came down over the winter and spring, it was still about 16% of assets at the end of the second quarter. Simply put, manager Wayne Lyski continues to be bullish about the long–term prospects of emerging–markets debt in general and Mexican and Argentine government bonds in particular.

This intrepid positioning has paid off thus far in 2001. Mexican credits have thrived this year, as the economy has fared better than expected and the Fox administration has made some productive moves. U.S government obligations have performed better than their European counterparts, which are the bread and butter of many international–bond funds.

Thus, though many Argentine bonds have struggled along with that nation's economy, the fund has outgained 91% of its peers for the year to date through August 8, 2001.
The fund blew up when the Mexican peso tanked in 1994, and it has suffered more volatility than most of its peers over time. But there's no arguing with its long–term returns:

Thanks to five top–decile showings in the last six calendar years, its long–term record is topnotch. Thus, we think investors who are seeking aggressive exposure to international debt should look here.

Address:	P.O. Box 1520 Secaucus, NJ 07096 800–227–4618 / 201–319–4000
Web Address:	www.alliancecapital.com
*Inception:	03-27-92
Advisor:	Alliance Cap. Mgmt. (Bernstein)
Subadvisor:	None
NTF Plans:	N/A

Minimum Purchase:	$250	Add: $50 IRA: $250
Min Auto Inv Plan:	$250	Add: $25
Sales Fees:	3.00%D, 0.75%B, 0.25%S Conv. in 6 Yrs.	
Management Fee:	.72%	
Actual Fees:	Mgt: 0.73%	Dist: 1.00%
Expense Projections:	3Yr: $953	5Yr: $1454 10Yr: $2754
Avg Brok Commission:	—	Income Distrib: Monthly
Total Cost (relative to category):	—	

Alliance Premier Growth B

Ticker	Load	NAV	Yield	Total Assets	Mstar Category
APGBX	4.00%d	$18.84	0.0%	$11,958.7 mil	Large Growth

Prospectus Objective: Growth

Alliance Premier Growth Fund seeks long-term growth of capital.

The fund normally invests at least 85% of assets in U.S. equities, including common stocks, convertibles, and warrants. The portfolio typically holds 40 stocks, 25 of which usually constitute approximately 70% of assets. It may invest up to 15% in foreign securities. The fund is nondiversified.

Class A shares have front loads; B shares have deferred loads, higher 12b-1 fees, and conversion features; C shares have level loads; Advisor shares are for certain qualified investors.

On March 22, 1996, Alliance Counterpoint Fund merged into the fund.

Historical Profile

Return	Below Avg
Risk	Above Avg
Rating	★★ Below Avg

Investment Style
Equity
Average Stock %: 92% 94% 96% 96% 98% 99% 99%

▼ Manager Change
▽ Partial Manager Change

Fund Performance vs. Category Average
Quarterly Fund Return +/– Category Average
— Category Baseline

Performance Quartile (within Category)

Portfolio Manager(s)

Alfred Harrison, CFA. Since 9-92. BA'61 Cambridge U.; MA'64 Cambridge U. Other funds currently managed: Alliance Premier Growth A, Alliance Premier Growth C, Alliance Premier Growth Adv.

1990	1991	1992	1993	1994	1995	1996	1997	1998	1999	2000	12–01	History
—	—	10.91	11.94	10.52	14.09	16.27	19.97	28.93	34.54	24.96	18.84	NAV
—	—	9.12*	9.44	–6.25	45.89	23.34	31.75	48.34	28.13	–20.39	–24.52	Total Return %
—	—	3.51*	–0.62	–7.56	8.35	0.40	–1.61	19.76	7.09	–11.29	–12.64	+/– S&P 500
—	—	—	9.51	–11.10	7.23	–2.18	–2.00	3.24	–1.55	4.13	–4.02	+/– Russ Top 200 Grt
—	—	0.02	0.00	0.00	0.00	0.00	0.00	0.00	0.00	0.00	0.00	Income Return %
—	—	9.10	9.44	–6.25	45.89	23.34	31.75	48.33	28.13	–20.39	–24.52	Capital Return %
—	—	—	54	82	6	16	19	11	70	75	58	Total Rtn % Rank Cat
—	—	0.00	0.00	0.00	0.00	0.00	0.00	0.00	0.00	0.00	0.00	Income $
—	—	0.00	0.00	0.67	1.27	1.08	1.44	0.63	2.36	2.65	0.00	Capital Gains $
—	—	2.68	2.70	2.47	2.43	2.32	2.25	2.27	2.18	2.13	—	Expense Ratio %
—	—	0.35	–1.14	–1.19	–0.95	–0.94	–1.20	–1.27	–1.53	–1.40	—	Income Ratio %
—	—	—	68	98	114	95	76	82	75	125	—	Turnover Rate %
—	—	38.3	156.3	137.0	239.9	406.9	910.5	3,440.6	9,139.1	8,602.8	5,718.3	Net Assets $mil

Performance 12-31-01

	1st Qtr	2nd Qtr	3rd Qtr	4th Qtr	Total
1997	–1.35	21.31	13.30	–2.83	31.75
1998	20.23	7.50	–12.25	30.79	48.34
1999	9.19	3.32	–5.55	20.23	28.13
2000	6.54	–2.99	–8.24	–16.07	–20.39
2001	–18.39	4.76	–20.01	10.37	–24.52

Trailing	Total Return%	+/– S&P 500	+/– Russ Top 200 Grth	% Rank All	% Rank Cat	Growth of $10,000
3 Mo	10.37	–0.32	–2.49	41	83	11,037
6 Mo	–11.72	–6.16	–4.73	90	75	8,828
1 Yr	–24.52	–12.64	–4.02	87	58	7,548
3 Yr Avg	–8.35	–7.32	–0.33	97	83	7,699
5 Yr Avg	8.51	–2.19	–0.08	26	50	15,046
10 Yr Avg	—	—	—	—	—	—
15 Yr Avg	—	—	—	—	—	—

Tax Analysis	Tax-Adj Ret%	%Rank Cat	%Pretax Ret	%Rank Cat
3 Yr Avg	–9.41	82	—	—
5 Yr Avg	7.30	42	85.7	30
10 Yr Avg	—	—	—	—

Potential Capital Gain Exposure: –52% of assets

Risk Analysis

Time Period	Load-Adj Return %	Risk %Rank[1] All	Risk %Rank[1] Cat	Morningstar Return	Morningstar Risk	Morningstar Risk-Adj Rating
1 Yr	–26.78					
3 Yr	–8.61	89	65	–2.52[2]	1.38	★
5 Yr	8.51	86	62	0.81[2]	1.29	★★★
Incept	12.72	—	—	—	—	

Average Historical Rating (76 months): 3.8★s

[1]1=low, 100=high [2] T-Bill return substituted for category avg.

Category Rating (3 Yr)

1 2 3 4 5
Worst Best

Return	Below Avg
Risk	Average

Other Measures	Standard Index S&P 500	Best Fit Index S&P 500
Alpha	–4.1	–4.1
Beta	1.40	1.40
R-Squared	90	90
Standard Deviation		23.72
Mean		–8.35
Sharpe Ratio		–0.66

Portfolio Analysis 09-30-01

Share change since 06–01 Total Stocks: 51	Sector	PE	YTD Ret%	% Assets
MBNA	Financials	19.6	–3.66	6.59
⊕ Kohl's	Retail	54.2	15.48	6.29
⊖ UnitedHealth Grp	Financials	26.6	15.37	5.78
⊖ Vodafone Airtouch PLC ADR	Services	—	–27.70	5.31
⊕ General Elec	Industrials	30.1	–15.00	4.90
⊕ Tyco Intl	Industrials	27.1	6.23	4.79
⊕ AT&T Wireless Grp	Services	—	–17.00	4.61
⊖ Pfizer	Health	34.7	–12.40	4.49
⊕ Citigroup	Financials	20.0	0.03	4.25
⊕ Enron	Energy	1.6	–99.00	4.10
⊕ Nokia Cl A ADR	Technology	45.8	–43.00	4.02
⊖ Walgreen	Retail	39.1	–19.20	3.38
⊕ AOL Time Warner	Technology	—	–7.76	3.31
⊕ Viacom Cl B	Services	—	—	2.80
⊕ Microsoft	Technology	57.6	52.78	2.57
⊖ Freddie Mac	Financials	14.0	–3.87	2.48
⊕ Goldman Sachs Grp	Financials	20.7	–12.80	2.33
✲ Best Buy	Retail	41.2	151.90	2.17
⊕ Amdocs	Services	NMF	–48.70	1.96
⊕ Electronic Data Sys	Technology	25.7	19.83	1.78
⊕ Sprint (PCS Group)	Services	—	19.43	1.71
⊕ Target	Retail	29.8	28.05	1.43
⊕ Cardinal Health	Health	35.1	–2.51	1.35
⊖ Comcast	Services	20.3	–13.70	1.33
⊕ UAL	Services	—	–64.70	1.22

Current Investment Style

Style: Value Blnd Growth; Size: Large Med Small

	Stock Port Avg	Relative S&P 500 Current	Relative S&P 500 Hist	Rel Cat
Price/Earnings Ratio	31.7	1.02	1.17	0.89
Price/Book Ratio	5.6	0.99	1.19	0.88
Price/Cash Flow	21.7	1.21	1.22	0.96
3 Yr Earnings Growth	29.4	2.01	1.44	1.36
1 Yr Earnings Est%	10.8	—	—	3.61
Med Mkt Cap $mil	39,011	0.6	1.0	0.82

[1]figure is based on 50% or less of stocks

Analysis by Dan Culloton 11-12-01

Times have been tough for Alliance Premier Growth, but there are worse places to ride out a bear market.

The fund has lost more than a quarter of its value so far in 2001 and a third over the last 12 months through Nov. 9, 2001. That hurts, but it could be worse: The fund's losses are still good enough to land in the middle of the large-growth fund pack.

An ill-timed move into technology stocks at the end of 2000 set the offering up for the worst campaign of its life last year. Since then, manager Alfred Harrison, who has been known to jump into stocks and sectors he thinks have been unduly maligned, has grown defensive. His technology weighting is now less than half the fund's three-year historical average, and the offering has bigger slices of its portfolio dedicated to financials and health-care stocks—about 20% each.

The post-Sept. 11 sell-off did not make Harrison any more sanguine about tech. He still thinks many tech stocks are too expensive since estimates of earnings growth have fallen with their stock prices. However, Harrison has been "creeping aggressive" in the weeks since the tragedy, adding to small positions in airlines like Delta and Continental when they tumbled after the attacks. He also bought, and then sold a week later, 5 million shares of General Electric when it dipped. Harrison's sector and stock calls have not always been on the mark. He stuck with Enron, for example, even after an accounting controversy mortally wounded the company.

The fund, however, has solid long-term performance numbers, and Harrison shows no signs of abandoning the strategy that won that record. This fund remains a solid large-growth option.

Special Securities % assets 09-30-01	
Restricted/Illiquid Secs	0
Emerging-Markets Secs	Trace
Options/Futures/Warrants	No

Composition % assets 09-30-01	
Cash	0.8
Stocks*	99.2
Bonds	0.0
Other	0.0
*Foreign (% stocks)	10.0

Market Cap	
Giant	43.2
Large	45.2
Medium	8.2
Small	3.5
Micro	0.0

Sector Weightings	% of Stocks	Rel S&P	5-Year High	5-Year Low
Utilities	0.0	0.0	0	0
Energy	4.2	0.6	8	0
Financials	19.5	1.1	36	10
Industrials	10.3	0.9	11	0
Durables	0.0	0.0	13	0
Staples	0.0	0.0	17	0
Services	24.0	2.2	32	11
Retail	15.4	2.3	20	1
Health	12.1	0.8	17	7
Technology	14.6	0.8	41	11

Address:	P.O. Box 1520 Secaucus, NJ 07096 800–227–4618 / 201–319–4000
Web Address:	www.alliancecapital.com
*Inception:	09-28-92
Advisor:	Alliance Cap. Mgmt. (Bernstein)
Subadvisor:	None
NTF Plans:	N/A

Minimum Purchase:	$250	Add: $50	IRA: $250
Min Auto Inv Plan:	$250	Add: $25	
Sales Fees:	4.00%D, 0.75%B, 0.25%S Conv. in 8 Yrs.		
Management Fee:	1.0%		
Actual Fees:	Mgt: 1.00%	Dist: 1.00%	
Expense Projections:	3Yr: $912	5Yr: $1220	10Yr: $2442
Avg Brok Commission:	—	Income Distrib: Annually	
Total Cost (relative to category):	—		

American Century Equity Growth Inv

Ticker	Load	NAV	Yield	Total Assets	Mstar Category
BEQGX	None	$19.24	0.7%	$1,798.4 mil	Large Blend

Prospectus Objective: Growth and Income

American Century Equity Growth Fund seeks capital appreciation.

The fund primarily invests in common stocks drawn from a universe of the largest 1,500 companies (ranked by market capitalization) traded in the United States. Smaller-capitalization stocks with appropriate growth potential may also be included. The advisor uses a quantitative method to construct a portfolio that may provide a total return greater than that of the S&P 500 index. The fund may invest in foreign securities.

The fund offers Advisor, Institutional, Investor and C shares, all of which vary in fee structure and availability.

Historical Profile

Return Average
Risk Average
Rating ★★★ Neutral

Investment Style
Equity
Average Stock %: 100% 97% 94% 95% 96% 95% 95%

▼ Manager Change
▽ Partial Manager Change

Fund Performance vs. Category Average
■ Quarterly Fund Return +/– Category Average
— Category Baseline

Performance Quartile (within Category)

Portfolio Manager(s)

Management Team

1990	1991	1992	1993	1994	1995	1996	1997	1998	1999	2000	12-01	History
—	11.57	11.68	12.12	11.53	14.24	15.96	19.04	22.71	26.23	21.77	19.24	NAV
—	17.48*	4.14	11.43	–0.23	34.56	27.34	36.06	25.45	18.47	–10.95	–11.01	Total Return %
—	6.17*	–3.48	1.37	–1.55	–2.97	4.40	2.71	–3.13	–2.57	–1.85	0.86	+/– S&P 500
—	—	–3.51	1.59	–0.68	–3.04	5.18	3.04	–3.19	–3.36	0.00	1.75	+/– Wilshire Top 750
—	1.71	2.89	1.99	2.49	1.96	1.85	1.54	1.08	0.83	0.53	0.60	Income Return %
—	15.77	1.26	9.44	–2.72	32.60	25.49	34.53	24.37	17.64	–11.48	–11.61	Capital Return %
—	—	82	38	48	44	7	4	44	65	77	25	Total Rtn % Rank Cat
—	0.16	0.33	0.23	0.30	0.22	0.26	0.24	0.20	0.19	0.14	0.13	Income $
—	0.01	0.02	0.66	0.26	1.01	1.85	2.31	0.88	0.43	1.47	0.00	Capital Gains $
—	0.35	0.75	0.75	0.75	0.71	0.63	0.69	0.69	0.68	0.67	—	Expense Ratio %
—	3.29	2.33	2.04	2.26	1.96	1.74	1.39	1.07	0.77	0.53	—	Income Ratio %
—	—	114	97	94	126	131	161	89	86	79	—	Turnover Rate %
—	38.9	73.4	96.5	97.6	159.3	274.3	770.8	2,018.8	2,317.0	1,912.0	1,477.4	Net Assets $mil

Performance 12-31-01

	1st Qtr	2nd Qtr	3rd Qtr	4th Qtr	Total
1997	1.36	15.33	13.58	2.48	36.06
1998	15.86	2.14	–13.88	23.10	25.45
1999	–0.16	8.28	–3.69	13.78	18.47
2000	2.74	–2.88	–0.88	–9.97	–10.95
2001	–11.84	7.61	–15.43	10.91	–11.01

Trailing	Total Return%	+/– S&P 500	+/– Wil Top 750	% Rank All	% Rank Cat	Growth of $10,000
3 Mo	10.91	0.23	–0.41	38	43	11,091
6 Mo	–6.20	–0.64	–0.41	69	57	9,380
1 Yr	–11.01	0.86	1.75	62	25	8,899
3 Yr Avg	–2.08	–1.06	–0.26	83	67	9,388
5 Yr Avg	9.89	–0.81	–0.23	19	42	16,024
10 Yr Avg	12.26	–0.67	–0.19	17	37	31,786
15 Yr Avg	—	—	—	—	—	—

Tax Analysis	Tax-Adj Ret%	%Rank Cat	%Pretax Ret	%Rank Cat
3 Yr Avg	–2.91	63	—	—
5 Yr Avg	8.05	42	81.4	49
10 Yr Avg	9.97	45	81.3	45

Potential Capital Gain Exposure: 0% of assets

Risk Analysis

Time Period	Load-Adj Return %	Risk %Rank[1] All	Risk %Rank[1] Cat	Morningstar Return	Morningstar Risk	Morningstar Risk-Adj Rating
1 Yr	–11.01					
3 Yr	–2.08	68	52	–1.39[2]	0.93	★★
5 Yr	9.89	68	56	1.17[2]	0.92	★★★
10 Yr	12.26	70	45	1.16	0.90	★★★

Average Historical Rating (92 months): 4.2★s

[1] 1=low, 100=high [2] T-Bill return substituted for category avg.

Category Rating (3 Yr)

1 2 3 4 5 — Worst … Best

Return Average
Risk Average

Other Measures	Standard Index S&P 500	Best Fit Index S&P 500
Alpha	–1.0	–1.0
Beta	1.00	1.00
R-Squared	96	96

Standard Deviation	16.98
Mean	–2.08
Sharpe Ratio	–0.48

Analysis by Peter Di Teresa 10-29-01

American Century Equity Growth Fund remains a solid foundation for a portfolio.

This fund's efforts to beat the S&P 500 index without departing from it by too much make it a good base for a portfolio. Shareholders get exposure to the core of the U.S. market, allowing them to reap the rewards of its long-term strength, and can add other funds for diversification or for an aggressive or conservative tilt.

The fund loosely follows the sector weightings of the S&P 500. It tries to beat the index by using a quantitative model to screen for stocks that have modest valuations and attractive growth characteristics, such as positive earnings momentum. That's similar to sibling American Century Income & Growth's strategy, but this fund puts greater emphasis on the growth component.

The fund's long-term returns don't actually beat those of the index, but they come very close. The fund's 12.5% 10-year return through September 2001 is just 20 basis points shy of the index's return. The difference is less than the fund's expense ratio. That performance is good enough to beat 79% of large-blend funds' for the period.

The fund's style has evolved in recent years, though. Prior to 1999, it made significant sector bets and put less emphasis on growth. It fell behind the index and its peers that year, due to poor sector calls and less growth exposure. The fund struggled again in late 2000, but has been on track since. Its 15% loss for the year to date through Oct. 26 was better than 73% of its category.

Hewing more tightly to the index improves this fund's appeal as a core holding—investors will have a clearer idea of what to expect and should experience less volatility than when the fund made big bets.

Because this fund's tax efficiency has been notably poor in recent years, we think it only makes sense for a tax-sheltered account.

Portfolio Analysis 09-30-01

Share change since 06-01 Total Stocks: 177	Sector	PE	YTD Ret%	% Assets
⊖ General Elec	Industrials	30.1	–15.00	3.74
⊕ Pfizer	Health	34.7	–12.40	3.14
⊖ Citigroup	Financials	20.0	0.03	3.04
⊖ Johnson & Johnson	Health	16.6	14.01	2.71
Microsoft	Technology	57.6	52.78	2.70
⊖ Tyco Intl	Industrials	27.1	6.23	2.49
⊕ ExxonMobil	Energy	15.3	–7.59	2.23
Verizon Comms	Services	29.7	–2.52	2.16
⊕ AOL Time Warner	Technology	—	–7.76	2.12
⊕ Bank of America	Financials	16.7	42.73	1.94
⊖ IBM	Technology	26.9	43.00	1.82
⊕ S&P 500 Index (Fut)	N/A	—	—	1.81
SBC Comms	Services	18.4	–16.00	1.76
⊖ Merck	Health	19.1	–35.90	1.61
PepsiCo	Staples	31.4	–0.54	1.44
⊖ BellSouth	Services	24.9	–5.09	1.37
⊕ Bristol-Myers Squibb	Health	20.2	–26.00	1.35
⊕ Fannie Mae	Financials	16.2	–6.95	1.29
⊖ Wal-Mart Stores	Retail	40.3	8.94	1.26
⊕ Freddie Mac	Financials	14.0	–3.87	1.19
⊕ Occidental Petro	Energy	5.7	13.49	1.17
Chevron	Energy	10.3	9.29	1.05
⊕ Procter & Gamble	Staples	38.8	3.12	1.04
S & P 500 Dep Rec SPDR		—	—	1.02
⊕ Eli Lilly	Health	28.9	–14.40	1.02

Current Investment Style

Style: Value Blnd Growth; Size: Large Med Small

	Stock Port Avg	Relative S&P 500 Current	Relative S&P 500 Hist	Rel Cat
Price/Earnings Ratio	25.5	0.82	0.86	0.84
Price/Book Ratio	5.4	0.94	0.94	0.98
Price/Cash Flow	16.2	0.90	0.90	0.88
3 Yr Earnings Growth	19.2	1.31	1.10	1.08
1 Yr Earnings Est%	6.2	—	—	—
Med Mkt Cap $mil	64,040	1.1	0.7	1.23

Special Securities % assets 09-30-01	
Restricted/Illiquid Secs	0
Emerging-Markets Secs	0
Options/Futures/Warrants	Yes

Composition % assets 09-30-01	
Cash	4.0
Stocks*	94.2
Bonds	0.0
Other	1.8
*Foreign (% stocks)	2.3

Market Cap	
Giant	54.2
Large	24.5
Medium	19.2
Small	2.0
Micro	0.1

Sector Weightings	% of Stocks	Rel S&P	5-Year High	5-Year Low
Utilities	2.8	0.9	14	2
Energy	7.7	1.1	14	2
Financials	19.0	1.1	31	3
Industrials	11.6	1.0	31	9
Durables	1.6	1.0	9	0
Staples	8.0	1.0	18	2
Services	10.1	0.9	22	6
Retail	5.7	0.8	8	1
Health	15.7	1.1	39	7
Technology	17.8	1.0	34	2

Address:	4500 Main Street P.O. Box 419200 Kansas City, MO 64141-6200 415-965-4274 / 800-345-2021
Web Address:	www.americancentury.com
*Inception:	05-09-91
Advisor:	American Century Inv. Mgmt
Subadvisor:	None
NTF Plans:	Datalynx , Fidelity Inst.

Minimum Purchase:	$2500	Add: $50	IRA: $1000
Min Auto Inv Plan:	$2500	Add: $50	
Sales Fees:	No-load		
Management Fee:	.70%		
Actual Fees:	Mgt: 0.68%	Dist: —	
Expense Projections:	3Yr: $217	5Yr: $378	10Yr: $844
Avg Brok Commission:	—	Income Distrib: Quarterly	
Total Cost (relative to category):		Below Avg	

American Century Equity Income Inv

Ticker	Load	NAV	Yield	Total Assets	Mstar Category
TWEIX	None	$7.14	2.4%	$951.9 mil	Mid-Cap Value

Prospectus Objective: Equity–Income

American Century Equity Income Fund seeks current income; capital appreciation is a secondary consideration.

The fund normally invests at least 85% of assets in income-producing securities and at least 65% of assets in U.S. equities. To select investments, the primary consideration is the company's dividend-paying history and potential for increased dividend-paying ability. Management seeks a yield that exceeds that of the S&P 500.

The fund offers Advisor, Institutional, Investor and C shares, all of which vary in fee structure and availability.

Historical Profile
Return High
Risk Low
Rating ★★★★★ Highest

Investment Style Equity
Average Stock %: 80% 81% 79% 75% 77% 75% 69%

▼ Manager Change
▽ Partial Manager Change

Fund Performance vs. Category Average
Quarterly Fund Return +/– Category Average
– Category Baseline

Performance Quartile (within Category)

Portfolio Manager(s)

Phillip N. Davidson, CFA. Since 8-94. BS'78 Illinois State U.; MBA'80 Illinois State U. Other funds currently managed: American Century Value Inv, American Century Strat Alloc: Agg Inv, American Century Strat Alloc: Con Inv.

Scott A. Moore, CFA. Since 2-99. BS Southern Illinois U.; MBA U. of Missouri. Other funds currently managed: American Century Value Inv, American Century Strat Alloc: Agg Inv, American Century Strat Alloc: Con Inv.

History

1990	1991	1992	1993	1994	1995	1996	1997	1998	1999	2000	12-01	History
—	—	—	—	4.96	5.76	6.34	6.66	6.31	5.60	6.62	7.14	NAV
—	—	—	—	0.53*	29.63	23.31	28.26	12.97	–0.18	21.91	11.33	Total Return %
—	—	—	—	–0.40*	–7.91	0.37	–5.09	–15.61	–21.22	31.02	23.21	+/– S&P 500
—	—	—	—	—	–5.31	3.05	–6.10	7.88	–0.07	2.73	8.99	+/– Russ Midcap Val
—	—	—	—	1.03	3.96	3.29	4.14	3.28	3.48	3.24	2.67	Income Return %
—	—	—	—	–0.50	25.66	20.02	24.12	9.68	–3.66	18.67	8.66	Capital Return %
—	—	—	—	—	42	28	35	16	76	33	30	Total Rtn % Rank Cat
—	—	—	—	0.05	0.19	0.19	0.26	0.22	0.22	0.18	0.18	Income $
—	—	—	—	0.02	0.45	0.55	1.16	0.96	0.48	0.00	0.04	Capital Gains $
—	—	—	—	—	1.00	0.98	1.00	1.00	1.00	1.00	1.00	Expense Ratio %
—	—	—	—	—	4.04	3.51	3.46	3.52	3.31	3.41	3.02	Income Ratio %
—	—	—	—	—	—	170	159	158	180	141	169	Turnover Rate %
—	—	—	—	23.8	96.8	187.2	296.8	326.1	327.8	384.9	831.5	Net Assets $mil

Performance 12-31-01

	1st Qtr	2nd Qtr	3rd Qtr	4th Qtr	Total
1997	0.63	13.41	9.35	2.77	28.26
1998	8.11	–2.41	–6.23	14.19	12.97
1999	–4.72	13.39	–5.98	–1.72	–0.18
2000	–0.85	1.06	8.45	12.19	21.91
2001	–1.72	7.14	–3.25	9.28	11.33

Trailing	Total Return%	+/– S&P 500	+/– Russ Midcap Val	% Rank All	% Rank Cat	Growth of $10,000
3 Mo	9.28	–1.41	–2.75	46	79	10,928
6 Mo	5.73	11.29	6.64	3	15	10,573
1 Yr	11.33	23.21	8.99	5	30	11,133
3 Yr Avg	10.65	11.68	3.85	10	49	13,549
5 Yr Avg	14.44	3.74	2.98	5	27	19,631
10 Yr Avg	—	—	—	—	—	—
15 Yr Avg	—	—	—	—	—	—

Tax Analysis	Tax-Adj Ret%	%Rank Cat	%Pretax Ret	%Rank Cat
3 Yr Avg	8.10	51	76.0	63
5 Yr Avg	9.92	41	68.7	86
10 Yr Avg	—	—	—	—

Potential Capital Gain Exposure: 10% of assets

Risk Analysis

Time Period	Load-Adj Return %	Risk %Rank[1] All	Risk %Rank[1] Cat	Morningstar Return	Morningstar Risk	Morningstar Risk-Adj Rating
1 Yr	11.33					
3 Yr	10.65	36	4	1.28[2]	0.46	★★★★
5 Yr	14.44	41	2	2.46[2]	0.50	★★★★★
Incept	16.74	—	—	—	—	

Average Historical Rating (54 months): 4.2★s

[1]1=low, 100=high [2] T-Bill return substituted for category avg.

Category Rating (3 Yr)

1 2 3 4 5 (Worst – Best): 3

Return: Average
Risk: Low

Other Measures	Standard Index S&P 500	Best Fit Index SPMid400
Alpha	8.1	3.5
Beta	0.38	0.38
R-Squared	27	35

Standard Deviation	13.64
Mean	10.65
Sharpe Ratio	0.48

Analysis by Bradley Sweeney 08-17-01

This is an excellent choice for conservative-minded investors.

American Century Equity Income is having another strong year. Management has scored big with a few picks—Student Loan Corporation, for example, has posted a nearly 50% year-to-date gain—but the fund has primarily benefited from the modest contributions of an array of names, including telecom-service providers Sprint and Verizon. The fund has also benefited from its aim to produce a yield that exceeds the S&P 500 index's, though. Management's decision to store about 15% of the fund's assets in convertible bonds to meet that yield objective has certainly lent a hand. Even some convertible issues that haven't seen substantial price appreciation so far this year, such as HCA's, have been contributing a healthy coupon payment, helping the fund past 70% of its mid-cap value rivals for the year to date through August 16, 2001.

It hasn't been unusual for this offering's convertible stake to provide ballast during rocky times for the equity market. When the Russian debt crisis seized the market in 1998's third quarter, for example, the fund's convertible bonds helped cushion the blow—the portfolio lost 9 percentage points less than its typical rival over those three months. Over time these issues have helped to dramatically smooth the fund's trajectory, making it one of the category's least volatile members over the past five years. And it doesn't appear as if shareholders have had to sacrifice much in terms of performance in exchange for this stability: The fund's annualized return for the five years ended August 16, 2001, places it in its category's top quartile.

As with its sibling, American Century Value, nearly our only concern about this fund is its relatively poor tax efficiency. But the fund is a great choice for investors in tax-advantaged accounts.

Portfolio Analysis 09-30-01

Share change since 06-01 Total Stocks: 56	Sector	PE	YTD Ret%	% Assets
⊕ Union Pac Cv Pfd 6.25%	Services	—	—	4.50
⊕ Piedmont Natural Gas	Energy	17.6	–1.86	3.68
⊕ WGL Hldgs	Utilities	16.2	–0.03	3.46
⊕ Cooper Inds	Industrials	11.5	–21.50	3.39
☼ BP PLC ADR	Energy	14.4	–0.90	3.31
⊕ Clorox	Staples	31.1	14.20	2.92
⊖ Hubbell Cl B	Industrials	19.1	16.38	2.69
⊕ AGL Resources	Utilities	16.4	9.39	2.63
Student Loan	Financials	13.6	54.17	2.63
HCA The Healthcare Co Cv 6.75%	N/A	—	—	2.53
⊖ Royal Dutch Petro NY ADR	Energy	12.0	–17.10	2.49
⊕ Sprint	Services	20.5	1.18	2.49
⊖ First Virginia Banks	Financials	14.7	9.39	2.47
⊕ Minnesota Mng & Mfg	Industrials	34.5	0.16	2.17
⊕ FPL Grp	Utilities	13.1	–18.30	2.10
⊕ Campbell Soup	Staples	20.1	–11.20	2.01
⊕ Emerson Elec	Industrials	23.8	–25.60	1.81
⊕ Commerce Bancshares	Financials	14.4	–2.05	1.75
UPS Cv 1.75%	N/A	—	—	1.70
☼ Ryder Sys	Services	29.2	37.06	1.66
Loews Cineplex Cv 3.125%	N/A	—	—	1.65
⊖ Bristol-Myers Squibb	Health	20.2	–26.00	1.48
⊕ CNA Surety	Financials	13.7	13.09	1.48
☼ Air Products and Chemicals	Industrials	22.1	16.61	1.47
⊖ S&P 500 Index (Fut)	N/A	—	—	1.44

Current Investment Style

Style: Value Blnd Growth; Size: Large Med Small

	Stock Port Avg	Relative S&P 500 Current	Relative S&P 500 Hist	Rel Cat
Price/Earnings Ratio	19.6	0.63	0.55	0.83
Price/Book Ratio	3.1	0.55	0.37	1.03
Price/Cash Flow	10.7	0.59	0.47	0.86
3 Yr Earnings Growth	7.2	0.49	0.36	0.61
1 Yr Earnings Est%	–8.1	4.60	—	1.32
Med Mkt Cap $mil	4,920	0.1	0.0	0.69

Special Securities % assets 09-30-01	
Restricted/Illiquid Secs	0
Emerging-Markets Secs	0
Options/Futures/Warrants	Yes

Composition % assets 09-30-01	
Cash	4.6
Stocks*	72.8
Bonds	5.5
Other	17.1
*Foreign (% stocks)	8.5

Market Cap	
Giant	19.2
Large	24.1
Medium	36.4
Small	19.8
Micro	0.5

Sector Weightings	% of Stocks	Rel S&P	5-Year High	5-Year Low
Utilities	13.8	4.3	23	7
Energy	14.2	2.0	16	1
Financials	17.4	1.0	34	15
Industrials	21.1	1.8	37	12
Durables	2.7	1.7	9	0
Staples	9.9	1.3	17	3
Services	12.2	1.1	13	4
Retail	2.8	0.4	15	0
Health	3.1	0.2	5	0
Technology	2.9	0.2	4	0

Address:	4500 Main Street P.O. Box 419200 Kansas City, MO 64141-6200 800-345-2021 / 816-531-5575
Web Address:	www.americancentury.com
*Inception:	08-01-94
Advisor:	American Century Inv. Mgmt
Subadvisor:	None
NTF Plans:	Datalynx , Fidelity Inst.

Minimum Purchase:	$2500	Add: $50	IRA: $1000
Min Auto Inv Plan:	$2500	Add: $50	
Sales Fees:	No-load		
Management Fee:	1.0%		
Actual Fees:	Mgt: 1.00%	Dist: —	
Expense Projections:	3Yr: $318	5Yr: $551	10Yr: $1219
Avg Brok Commission:	—	Income Distrib: Quarterly	
Total Cost (relative to category):	Below Avg		

American Century Ginnie Mae Inv

Ticker	Load	NAV	Yield	SEC Yield	Total Assets	Mstar Category
BGNMX	None	$10.62	6.0%	5.49%	$1,686.5 mil	Intermediate Govt

Prospectus Objective: Government Mortgage

American Century Ginnie Mae Fund seeks current income consistent with safety of principal and liquidity.

The fund invests primarily in mortgage-backed certificates issued by the Government National Mortgage Association. It may invest the balance of assets in other U.S. government securities and its agencies and instrumentalities, including mortgage-backed securities issued by the Federal National Mortgage Association and the Federal Home Loan Mortgage Corporation, among others.

The fund currently offers Investor, Advisor and C shares.

Historical Profile

Return: Above Avg
Risk: Below Avg
Rating: ★★★★ Above Avg

Investment Style Fixed-Income

Income Rtn %Rank Cat: 36, 13, 10, 16, 24, 12, 17, 9

Growth of Principal vs. Interest Rate Shifts
— Principal Value $000 (NAV with capital gains reinvested)
— Interest Rate % on 10 Yr Treasury
▼ Manager Change
▽ Partial Manager Change
► Mgr Unknown After
◄ Mgr Unknown Before

Performance Quartile (within Category)

Portfolio Manager(s)

Management Team

1990	1991	1992	1993	1994	1995	1996	1997	1998	1999	2000	12-01	History
10.15	10.80	10.78	10.76	9.90	10.68	10.49	10.68	10.69	10.14	10.49	10.62	NAV
10.16	15.57	7.67	6.59	−1.67	15.86	5.21	8.79	6.33	0.99	10.35	7.43	Total Return %
1.20	−0.44	0.27	−3.16	1.25	−2.61	1.59	−0.90	−2.35	1.82	−1.28	−1.00	+/– LB Aggregate
1.44	0.25	0.44	−4.06	1.70	−2.48	2.43	−0.79	−3.53	3.23	−2.89	0.19	+/– LB Government
9.25	8.81	7.79	6.69	6.51	7.78	6.94	6.88	6.23	6.28	6.72	6.21	Income Return %
0.90	6.76	−0.12	−0.10	−8.18	8.08	−1.73	1.91	0.09	−5.29	3.63	1.22	Capital Return %
17	28	9	73	16	53	5	40	79	8	64	24	Total Rtn % Rank Cat
0.89	0.86	0.81	0.70	0.68	0.75	0.72	0.70	0.65	0.65	0.66	0.63	Income $
0.00	0.00	0.00	0.01	0.00	0.00	0.00	0.00	0.00	0.00	0.00	0.00	Capital Gains $
0.75	0.72	0.62	0.56	0.54	0.58	0.58	0.55	0.58	0.59	0.59	0.59	Expense Ratio %
9.04	8.85	8.18	7.31	6.12	7.08	6.98	6.84	6.49	5.98	6.42	6.57	Income Ratio %
433	207	97	71	49	120	64	105	133	119	133	143	Turnover Rate %
353.6	702.8	1,006.1	1,257.0	952.3	1,111.4	1,130.8	1,233.6	1,377.1	1,297.9	1,288.3	1,646.4	Net Assets $mil

Performance 12-31-01

	1st Qtr	2nd Qtr	3rd Qtr	4th Qtr	Total
1997	0.08	3.52	2.79	2.17	8.79
1998	1.39	1.60	2.26	0.93	6.33
1999	0.74	−0.84	0.85	0.25	0.99
2000	1.79	1.99	2.69	3.51	10.35
2001	2.94	0.83	3.61	−0.11	7.43

Trailing	Total Return%	+/– LB Agg	+/– LB Govt	% Rank All	% Rank Cat	Growth of $10,000
3 Mo	−0.11	−0.14	0.48	80	20	9,989
6 Mo	3.50	−1.15	−1.35	12	85	10,350
1 Yr	7.43	−1.00	0.19	12	24	10,743
3 Yr Avg	6.18	−0.09	0.30	21	13	11,971
5 Yr Avg	6.73	−0.70	−0.67	39	31	13,847
10 Yr Avg	6.66	−0.57	−0.48	54	16	19,047
15 Yr Avg	7.79	−0.33	−0.10	55	10	30,794

Tax Analysis	Tax-Adj Ret%	%Rank Cat	%Pretax Ret	%Rank Cat
3 Yr Avg	3.61	17	58.5	42
5 Yr Avg	4.12	40	61.3	70
10 Yr Avg	3.98	18	59.7	40

Potential Capital Gain Exposure: −1% of assets

Risk Analysis

Time Period	Load-Adj Return %	Risk %Rank[1] All	Risk %Rank[1] Cat	Morningstar Return	Morningstar Risk	Morningstar Risk-Adj Rating
1 Yr	7.43					
3 Yr	6.18	6	10	0.27[2]	0.49	★★★★
5 Yr	6.73	6	5	0.38[2]	0.45	★★★★
10 Yr	6.66	9	4	0.54[2]	0.64	★★★★

Average Historical Rating (160 months): 4.3★s

[1]1=low, 100=high [2] T-Bill return substituted for category avg.

Category Rating (3 Yr)

1 2 3 4 5 — Worst ... Best

Return: Above Avg
Risk: Low

Other Measures	Standard Index LB Agg	Best Fit Index LB Mtg
Alpha	0.3	−0.7
Beta	0.72	0.94
R-Squared	83	95

Standard Deviation	2.85
Mean	6.18
Sharpe Ratio	0.51

Analysis by Eric Jacobson 12-31-01

Moderation has bred the success of American Century Ginnie Mae.

Comanager Casey Colton keeps things basic. The fund is heavily weighted in Ginnie Mae mortgages, and though he has lately balanced that 80% stake with a 20% slug of inflation-indexed (TIPS) and conventional Treasuries, Colton doesn't usually make large interest-rate or yield-curve bets unless he's got a particularly strong conviction.

Colton's benchmark-focused approach to rate bets has kept the fund's duration (a standard rate-sensitivity measure) somewhat short relative to the average intermediate-term government fund, and that has meant some sluggishness in falling-rate rallies, but also excellent resilience during rising-rate climes. As a result, the fund hasn't had to dig itself out of deep holes in the wake of bear markets, a fact that has helped keep its longer-term returns competitive with more-aggressive rivals. It's no surprise the fund's volatility has been among the lowest of the category.

What has really helped the fund stand out most recently, however, has been Colton's willingness to buy TIPS. He has favored those issues for the bulk of the non-Ginnie Mae portion of the fund for some time, and though they've performed weakly toward the end of 2001—thereby pushing the fund behind the Ginnie Mae indexes for the year—those issues have helped counter the prepayment sensitivity of the fund's mortgages, and have performed well enough to push its three-year return into the best quartile of the category.

To be sure, Colton won't always rely on TIPS to fuel the portfolio. Indeed, he recently cut that stake sharply in favor of conventional Treasuries. He has done an able job of adjusting the fund's sector and yield-curve exposure over the past few years without taking on lots of extra risk, however, and he has got a fine tailwind in the form of a below-average expense ratio.

Portfolio Analysis 09-30-01

Total Fixed-Income: 3049	Date of Maturity	Amount $000	Value $000	% Net Assets
US Treasury Note 3.5%	01-15-11	167,000	175,261	10.62
GNMA 6.5%	07-15-29	145,981	149,444	9.06
US Treasury Note 4.25%	01-15-10	120,000	136,729	8.29
GNMA 7%	12-15-28	103,441	107,250	6.50
GNMA 7%	12-20-29	86,736	89,779	5.44
GNMA 6.5%	12-15-28	82,092	84,077	5.09
GNMA 8%	07-20-30	76,603	80,249	4.86
GNMA 7.5%	03-15-30	70,108	73,156	4.43
GNMA 7%	09-15-31	61,496	63,744	3.86
GNMA 7.5%	12-15-27	48,205	50,396	3.05
GNMA 6%	12-15-28	42,020	42,172	2.56
GNMA 7%	11-15-24	32,833	34,269	2.08
GNMA 7.5%	12-20-23	32,360	33,999	2.06
GNMA 7.5%	02-20-31	28,561	29,689	1.80
GNMA 7%	11-15-26	25,911	26,977	1.63
GNMA 7%	12-15-27	25,378	26,348	1.60
GNMA 7.5%	12-15-26	23,421	24,507	1.49
GNMA 6.5%	11-20-26	20,338	20,896	1.27
GNMA 7.5%	12-15-25	19,749	20,683	1.25
GNMA 6.5%	06-15-31	19,549	19,986	1.21

Current Investment Style

Duration: Short Int Long — Quality: High Med Low

Avg Eff Duration[1]	3.6 Yrs
Avg Eff Maturity	—
Avg Credit Quality	AAA
Avg Wtd Coupon	6.54%
Avg Wtd Price	105.01% of par

[1]figure provided by fund

Special Securities % assets 09-30-01	
Restricted/Illiquid Secs	0
Exotic Mortgage-Backed	0
Emerging-Markets Secs	0
Options/Futures/Warrants	No

Credit Analysis % bonds 06-30-01			
US Govt	23	BB	0
AAA	77	B	0
AA	0	Below B	0
A	0	NR/NA	0
BBB	0		

Sector Breakdown % bonds 09-30-01			
US Treasuries	0	CMOs	0
GNMA mtgs	80	ARMs	0
FNMA mtgs	0	Other	0
FHLMC mtgs	0		

Coupon Range	% of Bonds	Rel Cat
0%	0.00	0.00
0% to 7%	43.04	0.76
7% to 8.5%	50.48	1.51
8.5% to 10%	6.04	1.48
More than 10%	0.44	0.11

1.00=Category Average

Composition % assets 09-30-01			
Cash	5.8	Bonds	94.2
Stocks	0.0	Other	0.0

Address:	4500 Main Street P.O. Box 419200 Kansas City, MO 64141–6200 800–345–2021 / 816–531–5575
Web Address:	www.americancentury.com
Inception:	09-23-85
Advisor:	American Century Inv. Mgmt
Subadvisor:	None
NTF Plans:	Datalynx , Fidelity Inst.

Minimum Purchase:	$2500	Add: $50	IRA: $1000
Min Auto Inv Plan:	$2500	Add: $50	
Sales Fees:	No-load		
Management Fee:	.59%+.31% mx./.00% mn.(G)		
Actual Fees:	Mgt: 0.59%	Dist: —	
Expense Projections:	3Yr: $189	5Yr: $329	10Yr: $736
Avg Brok Commission:	—	Income Distrib: Monthly	
Total Cost (relative to category):	Low		

American Century Global Growth Inv

Ticker	Load	NAV	Yield	Total Assets	Mstar Category
TWGGX	None	$6.32	0.0%	$279.1 mil	World Stock

Prospectus Objective: World Stock

American Century Global Growth Fund seeks capital growth.

The fund normally invests at least 65% of assets in equity securities from developed countries worldwide, including the United States. It may invest in preferred stocks and convertibles. The fund may also invest in debt securities rated BBB or better. Management expects to invest both in companies in developed markets and in issuers in emerging markets. It may invest in futures, options, and repurchase agreements.

The fund currently offers Investor, Advisor and Institutional classes.

Historical Profile

Return Above Avg
Risk Average
Rating ★★★★ Above Avg

Investment Style
Equity
Average Stock %: 94% (1998), 95% (1999), 94% (2000), 96% (12-01)

▼ Manager Change
▽ Partial Manager Change

Fund Performance vs. Category Average
Quarterly Fund Return +/– Category Average
— Category Baseline

Performance Quartile (within Category)

Portfolio Manager(s)

Henrik Strabo. Since 12-98. BA U. of Washington. Other funds currently managed: American Century Intl Growth Inv, American Century Intl Discovery Inv, American Century Strat Alloc: Agg Inv.

Bradley Amoils. Since 12-98. MD U. of Witwaterstrand, Johannesburg; MBA Columbia U. Other funds currently managed: American Century Global Growth Adv, American Century Global Growth Inst.

1990	1991	1992	1993	1994	1995	1996	1997	1998	1999	2000	12-01	History
—	—	—	—	—	—	—	—	5.43	9.81	8.50	6.32	NAV
—	—	—	—	—	—	—	—	8.60*	86.09	–5.77	–25.65	Total Return %
—	—	—	—	—	—	—	—	3.89*	65.05	3.34	–13.77	+/– S&P 500
—	—	—	—	—	—	—	—	—	61.15	7.41	—	+/– MSCI World
—	—	—	—	—	—	—	—	0.00	0.00	0.00	0.00	Income Return %
—	—	—	—	—	—	—	—	8.60	86.09	–5.77	–25.65	Capital Return %
—	—	—	—	—	—	—	—	—	6	33	81	Total Rtn % Rank Cat
—	—	—	—	—	—	—	—	0.00	0.00	0.00	0.00	Income $
—	—	—	—	—	—	—	—	0.00	0.26	0.75	0.00	Capital Gains $
—	—	—	—	—	—	—	—	—	—	1.30	—	Expense Ratio %
—	—	—	—	—	—	—	—	—	—	–0.48	—	Income Ratio %
—	—	—	—	—	—	—	—	—	—	123	—	Turnover Rate %
—	—	—	—	—	—	—	—	72.5	318.0	411.9	274.8	Net Assets $mil

Performance 12-31-01

	1st Qtr	2nd Qtr	3rd Qtr	4th Qtr	Total
1997	—	—	—	—	—
1998	—	—	—	—	8.60 *
1999	7.92	8.19	4.89	51.95	86.09
2000	11.28	–9.42	0.31	–6.79	–5.77
2001	–17.76	–0.72	–14.55	6.58	–25.65

Trailing	Total Return%	+/– S&P 500	+/– MSCI World	% Rank All	% Rank Cat	Growth of $10,000
3 Mo	6.58	–4.11	—	58	89	10,658
6 Mo	–8.93	–3.38	—	81	70	9,107
1 Yr	–25.65	–13.77	—	89	81	7,435
3 Yr Avg	9.25	10.27	—	12	18	13,039
5 Yr Avg	—	—	—	—	—	—
10 Yr Avg	—	—	—	—	—	—
15 Yr Avg	—	—	—	—	—	—

Tax Analysis	Tax-Adj Ret%	%Rank Cat	%Pretax Ret	%Rank Cat
3 Yr Avg	7.97	14	86.2	26
5 Yr Avg	—	—	—	—
10 Yr Avg	—	—	—	—

Potential Capital Gain Exposure: NMF

Risk Analysis

Time Period	Load-Adj Return %	Risk %Rank[1] All	Risk %Rank[1] Cat	Morningstar Return	Morningstar Risk	Morningstar Risk-Adj Rating
1 Yr	–25.65					
3 Yr	9.25	76	60	0.95[2]	0.97	★★★★
5 Yr	—	—	—	—	—	
Incept	11.94	—	—	—	—	

Average Historical Rating (2 months): 4.5★s

[1]1=low, 100=high [2] T-Bill return substituted for category avg.

Category Rating (3 Yr)

1 2 3 4 5 — Worst to Best (4)

Return Above Avg
Risk Average

Other Measures	Standard Index S&P 500	Best Fit Index Wil 4500
Alpha	11.6	7.1
Beta	0.90	0.77
R-Squared	37	72
Standard Deviation		28.11
Mean		9.25
Sharpe Ratio		0.18

Analysis by Bridget Hughes 12-18-01

American Century Global Growth deserves your patience.

A quick glance at this fund's year-to-date performance might disappoint. Its 26.7% year-to-date loss through Dec. 17, 2001, lands well in the world-stock category's bottom quartile. Although the fund rightfully tempered its since-inception commitment to tech stocks at the end of last year, it kept some, such as Cisco Systems, that fell hard and fast earlier this year. And its comparatively small stake in tech at the start of 2001's second quarter kept it from partaking in April's rally. While the average world-stock fund jumped 3.5% in that quarter, this fund fell 0.7%. We might have expected the offering to tank along with most growth funds in 2001's first quarter, but we were disappointed it failed to rebound in the next. In contrast, growthy Janus Worldwide was up 4.1% in 2001's second quarter.

More recently, however, the fund has performed in character. Over the past month, the fund has participated fully in the growth-stock rally, as strong-performing stocks such as top-10 holding Affiliated Computer Services have pushed the fund to a top-quartile return for the period. Although this showing is for a very short time, it does remind us of how well the fund has done in growth-oriented markets: In 1999, the offering jumped 86.1%, dusting the vast majority of its competition. Thanks to that year—and to a respectable performance in 2000's downturn—the fund's trailing three-year return still tops 85% of its peers'.

Also encouraging is the fund's constant strategy. Managers Henrik Strabo and Bradley Amoils continue to seek companies with improving earnings. Lately they've found encouraging news in the telecom area, but the portfolio also still owns a fair share of health-care and financials names.

Portfolio Analysis 09-30-01

Share change since 06-01 Total Stocks: 122	Sector	Country	% Assets
⊕ Washington Mutual	Financials	U.S.	2.86
⊕ Pfizer	Health	U.S.	2.83
⊕ Rite Aid	Retail	U.S.	2.67
⊖ Novo-Nordisk	Health	Denmark	2.45
☼ AmerisourceBergen	N/A	N/A	2.19
☼ Glaxo Wellcome PLC ADR	Health	United Kingdom	2.05
⊕ Affiliated Comp Svcs A	Services	U.S.	1.96
⊕ Aventis Cl A	Health	France	1.94
☼ Procter & Gamble	Staples	U.S.	1.78
⊖ Tyco Intl	Industrials	U.S.	1.67
⊕ Fannie Mae	Financials	U.S.	1.64
⊕ Tenet Healthcare	Health	U.S.	1.59
Baxter Intl	Health	U.S.	1.57
⊕ Philip Morris	Staples	U.S.	1.46
⊕ Nintendo	Durables	Japan	1.41
Arthur J. Gallagher & Co.	Financials	U.S.	1.35
⊕ Laboratory Corp of Amer	Health	U.S.	1.31
Suez Lyon Eaux	Industrials	France	1.29
☼ Reed Intl	Services	United Kingdom	1.25
⊕ Total Fina Cl B	Energy	France	1.20

Current Investment Style

Style: Value Blnd Growth; Size: Large Med Small (Large Growth)

	Stock Port Avg	Rel MSCI EAFE Current	Rel MSCI EAFE Hist	Rel Cat
Price/Earnings Ratio	28.9	1.12	—	1.04
Price/Cash Flow	18.0	1.40	—	1.09
Price/Book Ratio	5.5	1.59	—	1.20
3 Yr Earnings Growth	17.7	0.94	—	0.95
Med Mkt Cap $mil	20,656	0.7	—	0.86

Country Exposure 09-30-01	% assets
U.S.	45
United Kingdom	14
France	5
Denmark	5
Japan	4

Hedging History: —

Regional Exposure 09-30-01	% assets
Europe	36
Pacific Rim	1
Latin America	0
Japan	4
U.S.	45
Other	2

Special Securities % assets 09-30-01	
Restricted/Illiquid Secs	0
Emerging-Markets Secs	1
Options/Futures/Warrants	No

Composition % assets 09-30-01			
Cash	2.0	Bonds	0.0
Stocks	98.0	Other	0.0

Sector Weightings	% of Stocks	Rel Cat	5-Year High	5-Year Low
Utilities	0.8	0.3	—	—
Energy	2.6	0.5	—	—
Financials	24.0	1.3	—	—
Industrials	8.2	0.7	—	—
Durables	3.0	0.8	—	—
Staples	10.2	1.3	—	—
Services	10.9	0.6	—	—
Retail	10.1	1.9	—	—
Health	25.4	1.9	—	—
Technology	4.9	0.3	—	—

Address: 4500 Main Street P.O. Box 419200, Kansas City, MO 64141-6200, 800-345-3533 / 816-531-5575
Web Address: www.americancentury.com
*Inception: 12-01-98
Advisor: American Century Inv. Mgmt
Subadvisor: None
NTF Plans: Fidelity Inst. , Waterhouse

Minimum Purchase: $2500 Add: $250 IRA: $1000
Min Auto Inv Plan: $2500 Add: $50
Sales Fees: No-load
Management Fee: 1.3% mx./1.1% mn.
Actual Fees: Mgt: 1.30% Dist: —
Expense Projections: 3Yr: $410 5Yr: $710 10Yr: $1558
Avg Brok Commission: — Income Distrib: Annually
Total Cost (relative to category): Below Avg

American Century Growth Inv

Ticker	Load	NAV	Yield	Total Assets	Mstar Category
TWCGX	None	$19.52	0.0%	$6,394.5 mil	Large Growth

Prospectus Objective: Growth

American Century Growth Fund seeks capital appreciation.

The fund normally invests substantially all assets in equity securities of large, established companies. However, it may hold up to 10% of assets in cash. The fund may only purchase securities of companies with at least three years of operations. It may invest without limit in foreign securities, including depositary receipts.

The fund offers Advisor, Institutional, and Investor shares, all of which vary in fee structure and availability.

Past names: Twentieth Century Growth Investors and American Century-Twentieth Century Growth Fund.

Historical Profile

Return	Average
Risk	Above Avg
Rating	★★ Below Avg

Investment Style
Equity
Average Stock %

1995	1996	1997	1998	1999	2000	2001
100%	100%	98%	93%	93%	92%	89%

▼ Manager Change
▽ Partial Manager Change

Fund Performance vs. Category Average
Quarterly Fund Return +/– Category Average
— Category Baseline

Performance Quartile (within Category)

Portfolio Manager(s)

C. Kim Goodwin. Since 10-97. BA'81 Princeton U.; MBA'87 U. of Texas, Austin. Other funds currently managed: American Century Select Inv, American Century Select Inst, American Century Select Adv.

Gregory Woodhams, CFA. Since 5-98. BA Rice U.; MA U. of Wisconsin. Other funds currently managed: American Century Strat Alloc: Agg Inv, American Century Strat Alloc: Con Inv, American Century Strat Alloc: Mod Inv.

Prescott LeGard, CFA. Since 5-00. BA DePauw U. Other funds currently managed: American Century Growth Instl, American Century Growth Adv, Principal Inv Ptr Large Gr II AdvPfd.

1990	1991	1992	1993	1994	1995	1996	1997	1998	1999	2000	12-01	History
15.29	25.83	24.36	22.40	18.74	19.39	21.88	24.01	27.16	32.28	24.00	19.52	NAV
–4.22	69.02	–4.29	3.76	–1.49	20.35	15.01	29.28	36.82	34.68	–14.71	–18.67	Total Return %
–1.10	38.54	–11.90	–6.30	–2.80	–17.19	–7.94	–4.07	8.24	13.64	–5.61	–6.79	+/– S&P 500
–5.59	29.62	–8.18	3.83	–6.34	–18.31	–10.51	–4.46	–8.28	5.00	9.81	1.83	+/– Russ Top 200 Grt
0.65	0.09	0.00	0.23	0.23	0.37	0.94	0.00	0.00	0.00	0.00	0.00	Income Return %
–4.87	68.94	–4.29	3.53	–1.71	19.98	14.07	29.28	36.82	34.68	–14.71	–18.67	Capital Return %
65	6	98	75	44	97	79	32	31	54	49	34	Total Rtn % Rank Cat
0.11	0.01	0.00	0.06	0.05	0.07	0.18	0.00	0.00	0.00	0.00	0.00	Income $
0.89	0.00	0.37	2.77	3.22	3.06	0.25	4.17	5.39	4.14	3.58	0.00	Capital Gains $
1.00	1.00	1.00	1.00	1.00	1.00	1.00	1.00	1.00	1.00	1.00	—	Expense Ratio %
0.60	0.20	–0.10	0.20	0.30	0.40	–0.10	0.02	–0.02	–0.24	–0.30	—	Income Ratio %
118	69	53	94	100	141	122	75	126	92	102	—	Turnover Rate %
1,914.7	3,879.1	4,853.4	4,552.5	4,158.0	4,849.0	4,667.2	5,165.9	7,092.9	9,630.8	8,376.3	6,273.0	Net Assets $mil

Performance 12-31-01

	1st Qtr	2nd Qtr	3rd Qtr	4th Qtr	Total
1997	–1.42	19.33	13.52	–3.20	29.28
1998	15.16	7.12	–7.97	20.50	36.82
1999	7.22	3.33	–1.66	23.62	34.68
2000	11.15	–4.07	–3.92	–16.75	–14.71
2001	–19.33	7.13	–17.89	14.62	–18.67

Trailing	Total Return%	+/– S&P 500	+/– Russ Top 200 Grth	% Rank All	% Rank Cat	Growth of $10,000
3 Mo	14.62	3.94	1.77	25	41	11,462
6 Mo	–5.88	–0.33	1.11	68	23	9,412
1 Yr	–18.67	–6.79	1.83	78	34	8,133
3 Yr Avg	–2.24	–1.22	5.78	84	48	9,342
5 Yr Avg	10.57	–0.13	1.98	16	30	16,524
10 Yr Avg	8.39	–4.54	–2.70	41	79	22,375
15 Yr Avg	12.32	–1.41	–1.05	23	44	57,160

Tax Analysis	Tax-Adj Ret%	%Rank Cat	%Pretax Ret	%Rank Cat
3 Yr Avg	–4.07	50	—	—
5 Yr Avg	7.62	39	72.1	62
10 Yr Avg	5.55	80	66.2	82

Potential Capital Gain Exposure: –9% of assets

Risk Analysis

Time Period	Load-Adj Return %	Risk %Rank[1] All	Risk %Rank[1] Cat	Morningstar Return	Morningstar Risk	Morningstar Risk-Adj Rating
1 Yr	–18.67					
3 Yr	–2.24	81	34	–1.42[2]	1.18	★★
5 Yr	10.57	80	34	1.34[2]	1.12	★★★
10 Yr	8.39	89	63	0.47	1.30	★★

Average Historical Rating (193 months): 3.2★s

[1] 1=low, 100=high [2] T-Bill return substituted for category avg.

Category Rating (3 Yr)

1 2 3 4 5 — Worst … Best (rating: 3)

Return	Average
Risk	Average

Other Measures	Standard Index S&P 500	Best Fit Index MSCIACWdFr
Alpha	0.4	5.3
Beta	1.15	1.26
R-Squared	80	84
Standard Deviation		21.78
Mean		–2.24
Sharpe Ratio		–0.38

Portfolio Analysis 09-30-01

Share change since 06-01 Total Stocks: 96	Sector	PE	YTD Ret%	% Assets
⊖ Pfizer	Health	34.7	–12.40	5.80
⊖ PepsiCo	Staples	31.4	–0.54	4.35
⊕ Wal-Mart Stores	Retail	40.3	8.94	3.45
⊕ Intel	Technology	73.1	4.89	3.26
American Intl Grp	Financials	42.0	–19.20	2.86
⊖ Home Depot	Retail	42.9	12.07	2.67
⊖ Microsoft	Technology	57.6	52.78	2.64
⊕ Oracle	Technology	32.1	–52.40	2.61
⊖ Abbott Labs	Health	51.6	17.08	2.54
General Elec	Industrials	30.1	–15.00	2.52
⊕ S & P 500 Dep Rec SPDR		—	—	2.35
⊖ S&P 500 Index (Fut)	N/A	—	—	2.33
⊖ Citigroup	Financials	20.0	0.03	2.19
Nestle	Staples	—	—	1.89
⊖ American Home Products	Health	—	–1.91	1.82
⊖ Amgen	Health	52.8	–11.70	1.76
⊖ IBM	Technology	26.9	43.00	1.64
⊖ NASDAQ 100 Trust Shares	N/A	—	—	1.62
⊖ Texas Instruments	Technology	87.5	–40.70	1.61
⊕ NASDAQ 100 Index (Fut)	N/A	—	—	1.58
⊕ Cisco Sys	Technology	—	–52.60	1.50
⊕ Cardinal Health	Health	35.1	–2.51	1.48
Eli Lilly	Health	28.9	–14.40	1.47
Heineken	Staples	20.6	—	1.39
⊕ Baxter Intl	Health	33.9	22.84	1.39

Current Investment Style

Style: Value Blnd Growth; Size: Large Med Small

	Stock Port Avg	Relative S&P 500 Current	Relative S&P 500 Hist	Rel Cat
Price/Earnings Ratio	37.6	1.21	1.28	1.06
Price/Book Ratio	7.7	1.34	1.33	1.20
Price/Cash Flow	23.8	1.32	1.30	1.05
3 Yr Earnings Growth	16.9	1.15	1.25	0.78
1 Yr Earnings Est%	–0.4	0.20	—	–0.12
Med Mkt Cap $mil	75,536	1.2	1.2	1.60

Analysis by Christopher Davis 10-24-01

American Century Growth Fund remains a respectable, if less than spectacular, core growth option.

This year has been no picnic for large-growth offerings, but this one has fared better than most. Although its 24% loss for the year to date through Oct. 23, 2001, is poor in absolute terms, 66% of its rivals have performed even worse. That showing is better than you'd expect—most offerings with similarly high valuations and tech exposure have lagged the pack by wide margins in 2001.

The fund's strong relative showing owes to its flexible approach. Managers Kim Goodwin, Greg Woodhams, and Prescott LeGard seek firms that are increasing their growth rates, even if the absolute rates of growth aren't all that stellar. So while their picks have much in common with those of other large-growth managers, they will often pick up names that one might not expect to find in growth-oriented portfolios. It has been the latter sorts of names, including PepsiCo and Washington Mutual, that have tempered the enormous losses suffered by top picks like Texas Instruments and Oracle.

The fund's tendency to hold less-aggressive names has resulted in a fairly steady ride. Indeed, its standard deviation, a measure of volatility, is considerably below the category norm. What's more, the fund has posted solid results over the long haul: For the trailing three-year period, it lands in the category's top half.

That said, with a median market cap 80% higher than the category average, the fund may lag its peers when smaller large-cap stocks rule the roost. And it certainly isn't the tamest large-growth offering, either—it once devoted 50% of assets to tech stocks in 2000, and its stake in the sector remains above average. But management has built a solid record here with modest volatility, making this a good choice for core growth exposure.

Special Securities % assets 09-30-01	
Restricted/Illiquid Secs	0
Emerging-Markets Secs	Trace
Options/Futures/Warrants	No

Composition % assets 09-30-01	
Cash	6.2
Stocks*	89.8
Bonds	0.0
Other	4.0
*Foreign (% stocks)	6.0

Market Cap	
Giant	64.9
Large	28.3
Medium	6.6
Small	0.2
Micro	0.0

Sector Weightings	% of Stocks	Rel S&P	5-Year High	5-Year Low
Utilities	0.9	0.3	4	0
Energy	1.3	0.2	10	0
Financials	13.4	0.8	23	5
Industrials	5.3	0.5	26	0
Durables	0.5	0.3	9	0
Staples	13.8	1.8	18	0
Services	2.3	0.2	22	2
Retail	9.4	1.4	20	1
Health	27.6	1.9	39	5
Technology	25.6	1.4	51	19

Address:	4500 Main Street P.O. Box 419200 Kansas City, MO 64141-6200 800-345-2021 / 816-531-5575
Web Address:	www.americancentury.com
Inception:	10-31-58
Advisor:	American Century Inv. Mgmt
Subadvisor:	None
NTF Plans:	Datalynx , Fidelity Inst.

Minimum Purchase:	$2500	Add: $50	IRA: $1000
Min Auto Inv Plan:	$2500	Add: $50	
Sales Fees:	No-load		
Management Fee:	1.0%		
Actual Fees:	Mgt: 1.00%	Dist: —	
Expense Projections:	3Yr: $318	5Yr: $551	10Yr: $1219
Avg Brok Commission:	—	Income Distrib: Annually	
Total Cost (relative to category):		Below Avg	

American Century Income & Growth Inv

Ticker	Load	NAV	Yield	Total Assets	Mstar Category
BIGRX	None	$27.35	1.1%	$5,945.4 mil	Large Value

Prospectus Objective: Growth and Income

American Century Income & Growth Fund seeks capital growth. Income is secondary.

The fund invests primarily in common stocks selected from a universe of the 1,500 largest companies traded in the United States. Management employs optimization models to construct a portfolio that provides a total return and a dividend yield that may exceed those of the S&P 500 index. The fund may also invest in foreign securities.

The fund offers Advisor, Institutional, Investor and C shares, all of which vary in fee structure and availability.

Historical Profile
Return: Above Avg
Risk: Average
Rating: ★★★★ Above Avg

Investment Style
Equity
Average Stock %

1994	1995	1996	1997	1998	1999	2000	12-01
	100%	95%	92%	95%	94%	96%	94%

▼ Manager Change
▽ Partial Manager Change

Fund Performance vs. Category Average
■ Quarterly Fund Return +/– Category Average
— Category Baseline

Performance Quartile (within Category)

Portfolio Manager(s)

John Schniedwind, CFA. Since 6-97.
Kurt Borgwardt, CFA. Since 6-97.
Jeffrey R. Tyler. Since 6-97.
William Martin, CFA. Since 6-97.
Matti von Turk, CFA. Since 5-00.

1990	1991	1992	1993	1994	1995	1996	1997	1998	1999	2000	12-01	History
10.12	13.53	14.11	15.08	13.92	17.81	20.16	24.30	29.25	34.05	30.19	27.35	NAV
1.29*	39.85	7.86	11.32	–0.55	36.88	24.15	34.45	27.67	17.96	–10.54	–8.37	Total Return %
–0.30*	9.37	0.25	1.26	–1.86	–0.66	1.21	1.09	–0.90	–3.08	–1.43	3.50	+/– S&P 500
—	21.70	–1.20	–8.44	1.77	–3.16	1.84	–1.04	6.43	7.00	–12.85	0.42	+/– Russ Top 200 Val
0.09	4.11	3.14	3.03	2.83	3.07	2.52	1.94	1.46	1.15	0.85	1.01	Income Return %
1.20	35.74	4.72	8.29	–3.38	33.81	21.63	32.50	26.21	16.81	–11.39	–9.38	Capital Return %
—	10	65	67	51	16	21	6	4	10	97	68	Total Rtn % Rank Cat
0.01	0.41	0.42	0.42	0.42	0.42	0.44	0.38	0.35	0.33	0.29	0.30	Income $
0.00	0.15	0.03	0.19	0.65	0.75	1.44	2.29	1.30	0.07	0.00	0.00	Capital Gains $
0.00	0.50	0.75	0.75	0.73	0.67	0.62	0.66	0.69	0.68	0.67	—	Expense Ratio %
2.09	4.03	3.16	2.90	2.96	2.61	2.32	1.81	1.31	1.08	0.89	—	Income Ratio %
—	140	63	31	68	70	92	102	86	58	64	—	Turnover Rate %
1.0	59.3	141.2	229.8	224.8	373.7	715.1	1,786.2	4,284.7	6,346.8	5,417.3	4,474.9	Net Assets $mil

Performance 12-31-01

	1st Qtr	2nd Qtr	3rd Qtr	4th Qtr	Total
1997	1.76	15.74	11.25	2.61	34.45
1998	15.17	2.27	–11.29	22.18	27.67
1999	1.91	7.64	–5.53	13.82	17.96
2000	0.65	–4.17	–0.28	–6.98	–10.54
2001	–10.47	7.17	–13.43	10.30	–8.37

Trailing	Total Return%	+/– S&P 500	+/– Russ Top 200 Val	% Rank All	% Rank Cat	Growth of $10,000
3 Mo	10.30	–0.38	4.79	41	32	11,030
6 Mo	–4.51	1.05	1.27	59	58	9,549
1 Yr	–8.37	3.50	0.42	57	68	9,163
3 Yr Avg	–1.12	–0.09	–2.28	78	81	9,669
5 Yr Avg	10.66	–0.04	–0.54	15	30	16,597
10 Yr Avg	12.91	–0.02	–1.12	13	33	33,680
15 Yr Avg	—	—	—	—	—	—

Tax Analysis	Tax-Adj Ret%	%Rank Cat	%Pretax Ret	%Rank Cat
3 Yr Avg	–1.54	73	—	—
5 Yr Avg	9.21	21	86.3	16
10 Yr Avg	11.01	20	85.3	15

Potential Capital Gain Exposure: 9% of assets

Risk Analysis

Time Period	Load-Adj Return %	Risk %Rank[1] All	Risk %Rank[1] Cat	Morningstar Return	Morningstar Risk	Morningstar Risk-Adj Rating
1 Yr	–8.37					
3 Yr	–1.12	63	89	–1.21[2]	0.89	★★★
5 Yr	10.66	64	82	1.37[2]	0.87	★★★★
10 Yr	12.91	65	74	1.29	0.84	★★★★

Average Historical Rating (97 months): 4.3★s

[1]1=low, 100=high [2] T-Bill return substituted for category avg.

Category Rating (3 Yr)

1 2 3 4 5
Worst Best

Return: Below Avg
Risk: Above Avg

Other Measures	Standard Index S&P 500	Best Fit Index S&P 500
Alpha	–0.4	–0.4
Beta	0.96	0.96
R-Squared	97	97

Standard Deviation	16.30
Mean	–1.12
Sharpe Ratio	–0.43

Portfolio Analysis 09-30-01

Share change since 06-01 Total Stocks: 244

	Sector	PE	YTD Ret%	% Assets
Citigroup	Financials	20.0	0.03	3.26
General Elec	Industrials	30.1	–15.00	3.12
⊖ Pfizer	Health	34.7	–12.40	2.97
⊕ Verizon Comms	Services	29.7	–2.52	2.86
⊕ ExxonMobil	Energy	15.3	–7.59	2.81
⊕ Bank of America	Financials	16.7	42.73	2.38
⊕ Microsoft	Technology	57.6	52.78	2.31
⊖ Johnson & Johnson	Health	16.6	14.01	2.23
⊕ SBC Comms	Services	18.4	–16.00	2.04
⊖ S&P 500 Index (Fut)	N/A	—	—	2.02
⊕ IBM	Technology	26.9	43.00	1.88
⊖ Merck	Health	19.1	–35.90	1.78
⊕ AOL Time Warner	Technology	—	–7.76	1.72
⊖ Tyco Intl	Industrials	27.1	6.23	1.50
⊕ BellSouth	Services	24.9	–5.09	1.48
Chevron	Energy	10.3	9.29	1.44
⊖ Occidental Petro	Energy	5.7	13.49	1.43
Fannie Mae	Financials	16.2	–6.95	1.40
⊕ Procter & Gamble	Staples	38.8	3.12	1.34
⊖ Sears Roebuck	Retail	23.4	40.12	1.29
⊕ Royal Dutch Petro NY ADR	Energy	12.0	–17.10	1.20
⊕ Intel	Technology	73.1	4.89	1.10
⊖ Wal-Mart Stores	Retail	40.3	8.94	1.10
Bristol-Myers Squibb	Health	20.2	–26.00	1.08
⊖ FleetBoston Finl	Financials	16.2	0.55	1.05

Current Investment Style

Style: Value Blnd Growth
Size: Large Med Small

	Stock Port Avg	Relative S&P 500 Current	Relative S&P 500 Hist	Rel Cat
Price/Earnings Ratio	23.3	0.75	0.84	0.93
Price/Book Ratio	4.7	0.83	0.89	1.15
Price/Cash Flow	13.8	0.77	0.85	1.00
3 Yr Earnings Growth	17.2	1.18	1.02	1.16
1 Yr Earnings Est%	2.1	—	—	–0.63
Med Mkt Cap $mil	51,919	0.9	0.8	1.63

Analysis by Peter Di Teresa 10-16-01

This fund can serve as a solid core investment, but don't mistake it for a typical value offering.

American Century Income & Growth has earned fine long-term returns. Its five- and 10-year returns through Oct. 15, 2001, are at least in the large-value group's top 29%.

The fund's returns are also competitive with those of the S&P 500 index. That, in fact, is the idea, as the fund strives to beat the S&P with a value angle. Its grasp extends beyond the index, as quantitative models analyze the 1,500 largest U.S. stocks for earnings momentum and value characteristics, but the fund won't drift far from the index's sector weightings.

In fact, even though this fund's price multiples plant it in the value column of Morningstar's style box, the index is a better comparison than is the large-value category. The fund's correlation with the index, as indicated by its R-squared versus the index, is 98—perfect correlation would be 100. The average R-squared against the S&P for large-value funds is 63. While its long-term returns are competitive with the index's, the fund's value bent has helped in this bear market. Its 16.5% loss for the year ended Oct. 15, 2001, is 3.2 percentage points better than the S&P's return.

The bear market has also reinforced the point that this fund is very different from other value offerings. Despite beating the index, its one-year return lands in the category's worst 8%. The problem has been shadowing the S&P. For example, the fund's 16.7% stake in the struggling tech sector is 6 percentage points more than the category average, while its 19.2% stake in the steadier financials area is 6 percentage points less than the average.

This fund can do a fine job as a core holding, but investors shouldn't pick it to fill the value slot in their portfolios.

Special Securities % assets 09-30-01	
Restricted/Illiquid Secs	0
Emerging-Markets Secs	0
Options/Futures/Warrants	Yes

Composition % assets 09-30-01	
Cash	2.6
Stocks*	95.5
Bonds	0.0
Other	2.0
*Foreign (% stocks)	2.3

Market Cap	
Giant	50.9
Large	25.0
Medium	21.8
Small	2.3
Micro	0.1

Sector Weightings	% of Stocks	Rel S&P	5-Year High	5-Year Low
Utilities	4.6	1.5	21	2
Energy	9.0	1.3	11	3
Financials	21.4	1.2	25	7
Industrials	14.5	1.3	26	10
Durables	1.8	1.1	8	0
Staples	5.2	0.7	13	4
Services	13.2	1.2	16	6
Retail	4.7	0.7	7	2
Health	11.8	0.8	23	9
Technology	14.0	0.8	32	2

Address:	4500 Main Street P.O. Box 419200 Kansas City, MO 64141-6200 415-965-4274 / 800-345-2021
Web Address:	www.americancentury.com
*Inception:	12-17-90
Advisor:	American Century Inv. Mgmt
Subadvisor:	None
NTF Plans:	Datalynx , Fidelity Inst.

Minimum Purchase:	$2500	Add: $50	IRA: $1000
Min Auto Inv Plan:	$2500	Add: $50	
Sales Fees:	No-load		
Management Fee:	.52% mx./.34% mn.+.31% mx./.29% mn.(G)		
Actual Fees:	Mgt: 0.68%	Dist: —	
Expense Projections:	3Yr: $217	5Yr: $378	10Yr: $844
Avg Brok Commission:	—	Income Distrib: Quarterly	
Total Cost (relative to category):		Low	

American Century Intl Discovery Inv

Ticker	Load	NAV	Yield	Total Assets	Mstar Category
TWEGX	Closed	$10.24	0.0%	$1,203.5 mil	Foreign Stock

Prospectus Objective: Foreign Stock

American Century International Discovery Fund seeks capital growth.

The fund normally invests at least 65% of assets in equities of at least three countries, not including the U.S. It typically invests in developed markets that have market capitalizations of less than $1 billion, and emerging-markets companies of any size. The fund may invest no more than 50% of assets in emerging markets. It may invest in debt, up to 35% of which may be rated below investment-grade.

The fund offers Advisor, Institutional, and Investor shares, all of which vary in fee structure and availability. The fund has gone through several name changes.

Historical Profile

Return High
Risk Average
Rating ★★★★★ Highest

Investment Style
Equity
Average Stock %: 92% (1995), 94% (1996), 99% (1997), 91% (1998), 97% (1999), 89% (2000), 90% (12-01)

▼ Manager Change
▽ Partial Manager Change

Fund Performance vs. Category Average
Quarterly Fund Return
+/– Category Average
— Category Baseline

Performance Quartile (within Category)

Portfolio Manager(s)

Henrik Strabo. Since 4-94. BA U. of Washington. Other funds currently managed: American Century Intl Growth Inv, American Century Strat Alloc: Agg Inv, American Century Strat Alloc: Con Inv.

Mark S. Kopinski. Since 1-98. BA'79 Monmouth C.; MA'81 U. of Illinois. Other funds currently managed: American Century Intl Growth Inv, American Century Strat Alloc: Agg Inv, American Century Strat Alloc: Con Inv.

Brian Brady. Since 11-98. BA Georgetown U.; MBA Columbia U. Other funds currently managed: American Century Intl Discovery Instl, American Century Intl Discovery Adv.

History

1990	1991	1992	1993	1994	1995	1996	1997	1998	1999	2000	12-01	History
—	—	—	—	5.38	5.88	7.36	8.15	9.57	17.16	13.09	10.24	NAV
—	—	—	—	7.60*	9.89	31.18	17.48	17.86	88.54	−14.21	−21.77	Total Return %
—	—	—	—	2.30*	−27.64	8.23	−15.87	−10.71	67.50	−5.11	−9.90	+/– S&P 500
—	—	—	—	—	−1.32	25.13	15.71	−2.13	61.58	−0.04	—	+/– MSCI EAFE
—	—	—	—	0.00	0.60	0.29	0.28	0.00	0.00	0.00	0.00	Income Return %
—	—	—	—	7.60	9.30	30.88	17.20	17.86	88.54	−14.21	−21.77	Capital Return %
—	—	—	—	—	53	2	8	25	9	39	46	Total Rtn % Rank Cat
—	—	—	—	0.00	0.03	0.02	0.02	0.00	0.00	0.00	0.00	Income $
—	—	—	—	0.00	0.00	0.32	0.47	0.03	0.81	1.64	0.00	Capital Gains $
—	—	—	—	2.00	2.00	1.88	1.70	1.64	1.55	1.36	—	Expense Ratio %
—	—	—	—	−0.48	0.27	−0.31	−0.37	−0.36	−0.65	−0.64	—	Income Ratio %
—	—	—	—	—	168	130	146	178	110	113	—	Turnover Rate %
—	—	—	—	111.9	121.2	390.0	622.1	799.2	1,722.9	1,576.2	1,016.0	Net Assets $mil

Performance 12-31-01

	1st Qtr	2nd Qtr	3rd Qtr	4th Qtr	Total
1997	7.74	9.46	8.18	−7.92	17.48
1998	20.49	7.43	−19.91	13.68	17.86
1999	5.75	13.64	4.00	50.87	88.54
2000	20.46	−15.62	1.15	−16.55	−14.21
2001	−14.67	1.88	−19.07	11.18	−21.77

Trailing	Total Return%	+/– S&P 500	+/– MSCI EAFE	% Rank All	% Rank Cat	Growth of $10,000
3 Mo	11.18	0.50	—	36	24	11,118
6 Mo	−10.02	−4.46	—	85	64	8,998
1 Yr	−21.77	−9.90	—	83	46	7,823
3 Yr Avg	8.16	9.19	—	14	8	12,654
5 Yr Avg	11.87	1.17	—	11	5	17,521
10 Yr Avg	—	—	—	—	—	—
15 Yr Avg	—	—	—	—	—	—

Tax Analysis	Tax-Adj Ret%	%Rank Cat	%Pretax Ret	%Rank Cat
3 Yr Avg	6.89	8	84.5	38
5 Yr Avg	10.64	4	89.6	8
10 Yr Avg	—	—	—	—

Potential Capital Gain Exposure: 3% of assets

Risk Analysis

Time Period	Load-Adj Return %	Risk %Rank[1] All	Risk %Rank[1] Cat	Morningstar Return	Morningstar Risk	Morningstar Risk-Adj Rating
1 Yr	−21.77					
3 Yr	8.16	83	83	0.70[2]	1.13	★★★★
5 Yr	11.87	82	82	1.70[2]	0.97	★★★★★
Incept	13.76	—	—	—	—	

Average Historical Rating (58 months): 5.0★s

[1] 1=low, 100=high [2] T-Bill return substituted for category avg.

Category Rating (3 Yr)

1 2 3 4 5 — Worst … Best

Return: High
Risk: Above Avg

Other Measures	Standard Index S&P 500	Best Fit Index Wil 4500
Alpha	11.8	7.4
Beta	0.88	0.94
R-Squared	25	77

Standard Deviation	33.74
Mean	8.16
Sharpe Ratio	0.11

Portfolio Analysis 09-30-01

Share change since 06-01 Total Stocks: 148	Sector	Country	% Assets
☆ Biovail Intl	Health	Canada	3.47
⊕ Man Grp	Financials	United Kingdom	2.74
⊖ Tandberg	Durables	Norway	1.98
⊕ Amec (UK)	Industrials	United Kingdom	1.97
⊕ Nutreco Hldg	Staples	Netherlands	1.75
⊕ Fugro	Services	Netherlands	1.74
☆ MLP	Financials	Germany	1.66
⊕ Grupo Dragados	Industrials	Spain	1.58
⊖ Tomra Sys	Industrials	Norway	1.54
⊕ Molson Cl A	Staples	Canada	1.43
⊕ CSL	Health	Australia	1.40
⊕ Pilkington	Industrials	United Kingdom	1.27
⊕ Southcorp	Staples	Australia	1.20
⊖ Shire Pharma Grp	Health	United Kingdom	1.13
⊕ Actividades Cons y Serv	Industrials	Spain	1.12
⊕ IHC Caland	Industrials	Netherlands	1.12
⊕ Matalan	Retail	United Kingdom	1.10
⊕ Kyorin Pharmaceutical	Technology	Japan	1.07
⊕ Givaudan	Technology	Switzerland	1.06
⊕ FirstGroup	Services	United Kingdom	1.06

Current Investment Style

Style: Value Blnd Growth; Size: Large Med Small

	Stock Port Avg	Rel MSCI EAFE Current	Rel MSCI EAFE Hist	Rel Cat
Price/Earnings Ratio	27.3	1.05	1.17	1.07
Price/Cash Flow	17.9	1.39	1.57	1.25
Price/Book Ratio	6.4	1.84	1.91	1.63
3 Yr Earnings Growth	22.6	1.21	2.12	1.15
Med Mkt Cap $mil	1,774	0.1	0.1	0.10

Country Exposure 09-30-01	% assets
United Kingdom	20
Canada	8
Japan	7
Australia	6
Netherlands	6

Hedging History: Frequent

Regional Exposure 09-30-01	% assets
Europe	55
Japan	7
Latin America	0
Pacific Rim	10
Other	9

Special Securities % assets 09-30-01	
Restricted/Illiquid Secs	0
Emerging-Markets Secs	7
Options/Futures/Warrants	No

Composition % assets 09-30-01

Cash	12.7	Bonds	0.0
Stocks	87.3	Other	0.0

Sector Weightings	% of Stocks	Rel Cat	5-Year High	5-Year Low
Utilities	0.6	0.2	3	0
Energy	1.8	0.3	7	0
Financials	17.2	0.8	33	4
Industrials	26.6	2.0	36	5
Durables	5.0	0.7	19	2
Staples	10.8	1.5	11	0
Services	14.8	0.8	39	12
Retail	5.3	1.1	12	2
Health	14.3	1.5	14	0
Technology	3.6	0.4	39	4

Analysis by Bridget Hughes 12-10-01

American Century International Discovery isn't exactly the fund it used to be, but we still think it's a compelling option.

This fund has settled on some new digs. After posting stunning returns as a small-cap fund for most of its life, the portfolio attracted loads of new investors and drifted into mid-cap territory in 2000. Recognizing the havoc a huge asset base could wreak on the fund, it closed to new investors and allowed investment in medium-size companies as well as small ones. But after launching American Century International Opportunities in June 2001, the fund family decided to leave the small (and micro-) caps to the new kid on the block. Going forward, this fund plans to focus on mid-cap stocks: those with market caps between $1 billion and $3 billion.

Not only does this modification depart from the guidelines of this fund's early days, but also the portfolio is currently unfamiliar. Continuing to apply its earnings-momentum approach to mid-cap stocks, managers Mark Kopinski and Brian Brady have invested heavily in industrial cyclicals, particularly in the United Kingdom, while limiting the fund's exposure to technology and telecom—two staple areas here through the years. Kopinski and Brady simply haven't seen enough improvement in tech and telecom firms' earnings to warrant investment there, however.

Although the mid-cap focus is fairly new, the fund has given reason to believe it can outperform. So far in 2001—a tough market for growth funds overall—its 21% loss through Dec. 7, 2001, though painful, ranks in the foreign-stock category's top half. And its older sibling American Century International Growth, which has always bought some mid-caps, has proved impressive over the long haul.

Shareholders here ought to sit tight, though they should consider International Opportunities if they want small-cap exposure.

Address:	4500 Main Street P.O. Box 419200 Kansas City, MO 64141-6200 800-345-2021 / 816-531-5575
Web Address:	www.americancentury.com
*Inception:	04-01-94
Advisor:	American Century Inv. Mgmt
Subadvisor:	None
NTF Plans:	Waterhouse , Schwab

Minimum Purchase:	Closed	Add: $250 IRA: —
Min Auto Inv Plan:	Closed	Add: $50
Sales Fees:	No-load, 2.00%R within 6 months	
Management Fee:	1.8% mx./1.2% mn.	
Actual Fees:	Mgt: 1.55%	Dist: —
Expense Projections:	3Yr: $487	5Yr: $840 10Yr: $1832
Avg Brok Commission:	—	Income Distrib: Annually
Total Cost (relative to category):		Average

American Century Intl Growth Inv

Ticker	Load	NAV	Yield	Total Assets	Mstar Category
TWIEX	None	$7.97	0.4%	$3,869.4 mil	Foreign Stock

Prospectus Objective: Foreign Stock

American Century International Growth Fund seeks capital growth.

The fund invests primarily in common stocks of foreign companies that meet certain fundamental and technical standards and have potential for capital appreciation. Management looks for companies whose earnings and revenues are not only growing, but growing at a successively faster, or accelerating, pace. The fund usually invests in issuers from at least three countries outside the United States.

The fund offers C, Advisor, Investor, Institutional and Institutional Service shares. Past fund names: Twentieth Century International Equity Fund and American Century-Twentieth Century International Growth Fund.

Historical Profile

Return Above Avg
Risk Average
Rating ★★★★ Above Avg

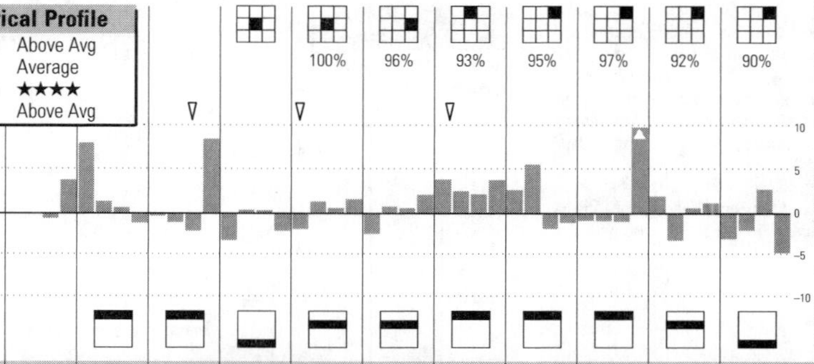

100%
96%
93%
95%
97%
92%
90%
10
5
0
-5
-10

Investment Style
Equity
Average Stock %

▼ Manager Change
▽ Partial Manager Change

Fund Performance vs. Category Average
■ Quarterly Fund Return
+/– Category Average
— Category Baseline

Performance Quartile (within Category)

Portfolio Manager(s)

Mark S. Kopinski. Since 3-97. BA'79 Monmouth C.; MA'81 U. of Illinois. Other funds currently managed: American Century Intl Discovery Inv, American Century Strat Alloc: Agg Inv, American Century Strat Alloc: Con Inv.

Henrik Strabo. Since 8-93. BA U. of Washington. Other funds currently managed: American Century Intl Discovery Inv, American Century Strat Alloc: Agg Inv, American Century Strat Alloc: Con Inv.

1990	1991	1992	1993	1994	1995	1996	1997	1998	1999	2000	12-01	History
—	5.61	5.69	7.70	6.96	7.78	7.96	8.19	9.58	14.97	10.93	7.97	NAV
—	10.14*	4.83	42.65	–4.76	11.89	14.43	19.72	19.01	64.44	–15.01	–26.79	Total Return %
—	–1.18*	–2.79	32.59	–6.07	–25.65	–8.52	–13.63	–9.57	43.41	–5.91	–14.91	+/– S&P 500
—	—	17.00	10.09	–12.54	0.68	8.38	17.94	–0.99	37.48	–0.84	—	+/– MSCI EAFE
—	0.14	3.40	0.00	0.00	0.10	0.00	0.35	0.20	0.06	0.00	0.28	Income Return %
—	10.00	1.42	42.65	–4.76	11.78	14.43	19.37	18.81	64.39	–15.01	–27.07	Capital Return %
—	—	1	25	81	31	42	4	21	17	43	79	Total Rtn % Rank Cat
—	0.01	0.19	0.00	0.00	0.01	0.00	0.03	0.02	0.01	0.00	0.03	Income $
—	0.00	0.00	0.40	0.37	0.00	0.92	1.28	0.14	0.69	1.75	0.00	Capital Gains $
—	1.87	1.91	1.90	1.84	1.77	1.65	1.38	1.33	1.27	1.20	—	Expense Ratio %
—	0.43	0.95	–0.34	–0.53	0.25	–0.07	0.04	0.33	–0.06	–0.16	—	Income Ratio %
—	113	180	255	242	169	158	163	190	117	116	—	Turnover Rate %
—	48.8	222.8	944.5	1,272.4	1,258.4	1,364.8	1,784.3	2,640.0	4,521.0	391.9	3,311.0	Net Assets $mil

Performance 12-31-01

	1st Qtr	2nd Qtr	3rd Qtr	4th Qtr	Total
1997	5.53	13.57	3.77	–3.74	19.72
1998	17.95	6.73	–17.94	15.21	19.01
1999	1.26	5.77	3.61	48.19	64.44
2000	4.49	–8.96	–6.40	–4.55	–15.01
2001	–17.38	–1.77	–13.42	4.19	–26.79

Trailing	Total Return%	+/– S&P 500	+/– MSCI EAFE	% Rank All	% Rank Cat	Growth of $10,000
3 Mo	4.19	–6.49	—	67	89	10,419
6 Mo	–9.79	–4.23	—	84	63	9,021
1 Yr	–26.79	–14.91	—	90	79	7,321
3 Yr Avg	0.77	1.79	—	69	26	10,232
5 Yr Avg	7.83	–2.87	—	30	11	14,579
10 Yr Avg	10.27	–2.66	—	31	6	26,584
15 Yr Avg	—	—	—	—	—	—

Tax Analysis	Tax-Adj Ret%	%Rank Cat	%Pretax Ret	%Rank Cat
3 Yr Avg	–0.82	28	—	—
5 Yr Avg	5.71	12	72.9	34
10 Yr Avg	8.26	9	80.4	33

Potential Capital Gain Exposure: –1% of assets

Risk Analysis

Time Period	Load-Adj Return %	Risk %Rank[1] All	Risk %Rank[1] Cat	Morningstar Return	Morningstar Risk	Morningstar Risk-Adj Rating
1 Yr	–26.79					
3 Yr	0.77	78	72	–0.85[2]	1.03	★★★
5 Yr	7.83	78	70	0.65[2]	0.90	★★★★
10 Yr	10.27	81	58	1.82[2]	0.85	★★★★

Average Historical Rating (92 months): 4.1★s

[1] 1=low, 100=high [2] T-Bill return substituted for category avg.

Category Rating (3 Yr)

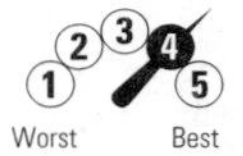

1
2
3
4
5
Worst
Best

Return Above Avg
Risk Above Avg

Other Measures	Standard Index S&P 500	Best Fit Index Wil 4500
Alpha	2.0	–1.5
Beta	0.76	0.69
R-Squared	30	67
Standard Deviation		24.52
Mean		0.77
Sharpe Ratio		–0.20

Analysis by Bridget Hughes 12-10-01

Keep the faith.

Only the truest believers are likely comfortable with this fund's year-to-date return. Through Dec. 7, 2001, the offering has lost 26.3%, landing in the foreign-stock category's bottom quartile. Early this year, although managers Henrik Strabo and Mark Kopinski had slashed the portfolio's longtime commitment to European telecoms, some stocks they kept in that sector stung. Nokia, for example, fell hard and fast, while Vodafone also languished. Strabo and Kopinski sought refuge in the relative safety of pharmaceuticals, and though that helped earlier this year, it has been a drag more recently. Top holding Novo Nordisk, for example, has dropped 10.5% in the past three months.

But such struggles are unusual for this fund. In just one other calendar year (1994) since its 1991 inception has the fund finished in the group's bottom quartile. In almost all the other years, in fact, it has placed well in the group's top half. To be sure, the fund is strongest in growth-oriented markets, when the managers' tolerance of high price multiples is shared by the masses. Consider 1997, 1998, and 1999, when the fund ended each year ahead of more than three fourths of its peers. In those years, the portfolio was chock-full of European tech and telecom, many of which sported rich valuations.

Ever so slowly, Strabo and Kopinski have been moving back into some of these names. They recently added Finland's biggest cellular provider Sonera, for example, which was a favorite here in 2000. They're also upbeat on Vodafone and China Mobile. They have cut some consumer-staples firms, such as Cadbury Schweppes and Danone.

Clearly the fund is a growth-market darling, and it has performed well enough in favorable times to give it long-term appeal.

Portfolio Analysis 09-30-01

Share change since 06-01 Total Stocks: 112

Share change	Sector	Country	% Assets
⊕ Novo-Nordisk	Health	Denmark	3.30
⊕ Aventis Cl A	Health	France	3.21
⊕ Ahold	Retail	Netherlands	3.10
⊕ Glaxo Wellcome PLC ADR	Health	United Kingdom	3.04
⊕ Reed Intl	Services	United Kingdom	2.34
⊕ Diageo	Staples	United Kingdom	2.12
⊕ Suez Lyon Eaux	Industrials	France	1.97
⊖ Nintendo	Durables	Japan	1.85
⊕ ING Groep	Financials	Netherlands	1.83
⊕ Barclays	Financials	United Kingdom	1.74
⊕ Reckitt Benckiser	Staples	United Kingdom	1.63
⊕ British Amer Tobacco	Staples	United Kingdom	1.56
⊕ Tesco UK	Retail	United Kingdom	1.52
⊕ Allianz (Reg)	Financials	Germany	1.50
⊕ Royal Bk of Scotland	Financials	United Kingdom	1.49
⊖ Nestle	Staples	Switzerland	1.45
⊖ Tyco Intl	Industrials	U.S.	1.44
⊖ Sanofi-Synthelabo	Health	France	1.24
⊕ Next	Retail	United Kingdom	1.23
⊕ Compass Grp	Services	United Kingdom	1.22

Current Investment Style

Style: Value Blnd Growth; Size: Large Med Small

	Stock Port Avg	Rel MSCI EAFE Current	Rel MSCI EAFE Hist	Rel Cat
Price/Earnings Ratio	27.6	1.07	1.18	1.08
Price/Cash Flow	16.1	1.25	1.34	1.12
Price/Book Ratio	4.8	1.37	1.46	1.22
3 Yr Earnings Growth	16.4	0.87	1.83	0.83
Med Mkt Cap $mil	19,712	0.7	0.7	1.09

Country Exposure 09-30-01	% assets
United Kingdom	32
France	12
Japan	9
Netherlands	7
Germany	6

Hedging History: Frequent

Regional Exposure 09-30-01	% assets
Europe	72
Japan	9
Latin America	0
Pacific Rim	1
Other	5

Special Securities % assets 09-30-01	
Restricted/Illiquid Secs	0
Emerging-Markets Secs	1
Options/Futures/Warrants	No

Composition % assets 09-30-01

Cash	10.0	Bonds	0.0
Stocks	90.1	Other	0.0

Sector Weightings	% of Stocks	Rel Cat	5-Year High	5-Year Low
Utilities	1.9	0.7	12	0
Energy	3.6	0.6	13	0
Financials	23.8	1.1	33	4
Industrials	9.5	0.7	42	4
Durables	4.8	0.7	24	0
Staples	12.5	1.8	18	0
Services	15.8	0.9	41	9
Retail	9.2	1.9	19	1
Health	17.8	1.8	19	0
Technology	1.2	0.1	26	1

Address:	4500 Main Street P.O. Box 419200 Kansas City, MO 64141-6200 800-345-2021 / 816-531-5575
Web Address:	www.americancentury.com
*Inception:	05-09-91
Advisor:	American Century Inv. Mgmt
Subadvisor:	None
NTF Plans:	Datalynx , Fidelity Inst.

Minimum Purchase:	$2500	Add: $250 IRA: $1000
Min Auto Inv Plan:	$2500	Add: $50
Sales Fees:	No-load	
Management Fee:	1.5% mx./1.1% mn.	
Actual Fees:	Mgt: 1.27%	Dist: —
Expense Projections:	3Yr: $401	5Yr: $694 10Yr: $1525
Avg Brok Commission:	—	Income Distrib: Annually
Total Cost (relative to category):		Below Avg

American Century Government Bond Inv

Ticker	Load	NAV	Yield	SEC Yield	Total Assets	Mstar Category
BLAGX	None	$10.27	5.2%	5.08%	$123.9 mil	Long Government

Prospectus Objective: Government General

American Century Government Bond Fund seeks current income exempt from state taxes, consistent with preservation of capital.

The fund invests primarily in securities issued or guaranteed by the U.S. Treasury and agencies or instrumentalities of the U.S. government. The fund invests primarily in securities with remaining maturities of 10 years or more. The average maturity typically ranges between 20 and 30 years.

The fund currently offers Investor and Advisor shares.

Past names: Benham Long-Term Treasury and Agency Fund and American Century-Benham Long-Term Treasury Fund.

Historical Profile

Return: Above Avg
Risk: Above Avg
Rating: ★★ Below Avg

Investment Style Fixed-Income

Income Rtn %Rank Cat: 39 23 34 17 26 30 35 42

Growth of Principal vs. Interest Rate Shifts
- Principal Value $000 (NAV with capital gains reinvested)
- Interest Rate % on 10 Yr Treasury
- Manager Change
- Partial Manager Change
- Mgr Unknown After
- Mgr Unknown Before

Performance Quartile (within Category)

Portfolio Manager(s)

Management Team

History

1990	1991	1992	1993	1994	1995	1996	1997	1998	1999	2000	12-01	History
—	—	9.78	10.22	8.69	10.55	9.78	10.56	10.70	9.23	10.41	10.27	NAV
—	—	-0.21*	17.64	-9.25	29.26	-1.37	14.76	12.76	-8.68	19.28	3.81	Total Return %
—	—	—	7.89	-6.33	10.79	-4.98	5.07	4.09	-7.85	7.65	-4.61	+/– LB Aggregate
—	—	—	0.46	-1.66	-1.65	-0.54	-0.36	-0.56	-0.43	-1.00	-0.53	+/– LB LT Government
—	—	1.99	6.94	5.98	7.17	5.86	6.34	5.86	5.35	6.16	5.23	Income Return %
—	—	-2.20	10.69	-15.23	22.09	-7.23	8.41	6.90	-14.03	13.12	-1.41	Capital Return %
—	—	—	13	84	16	82	15	26	76	21	83	Total Rtn % Rank Cat
—	—	0.20	0.66	0.59	0.60	0.60	0.60	0.60	0.56	0.55	0.53	Income $
—	—	0.00	0.59	0.00	0.00	0.00	0.00	0.57	0.00	0.00	0.00	Capital Gains $
—	—	—	0.00	0.57	0.67	0.67	0.60	0.54	0.51	0.51	0.51	Expense Ratio %
—	—	—	7.18	5.89	6.84	5.93	6.28	6.00	5.37	5.84	5.58	Income Ratio %
—	—	—	—	200	147	112	40	57	105	182	107	Turnover Rate %
—	—	—	23.2	28.7	104.2	121.1	129.4	163.0	97.7	108.4	119.0	Net Assets $mil

Performance 12-31-01

	1st Qtr	2nd Qtr	3rd Qtr	4th Qtr	Total
1997	-3.29	5.44	5.82	6.35	14.76
1998	1.55	4.31	7.22	-0.72	12.76
1999	-4.25	-2.38	-0.16	-2.14	-8.68
2000	7.89	1.02	2.53	6.75	19.28
2001	1.09	-1.47	6.48	-2.12	3.81

Trailing	Total Return%	+/– LB Agg	+/– LB LT Govt	% Rank All	% Rank Cat	Growth of $10,000
3 Mo	-2.12	-2.15	—	99	86	9,788
6 Mo	4.22	-0.43	—	7	47	10,422
1 Yr	3.81	-4.61	—	32	83	10,381
3 Yr Avg	4.18	-2.09	—	38	54	11,308
5 Yr Avg	7.91	0.49	—	30	15	14,633
10 Yr Avg	—	—	—	—	—	—
15 Yr Avg	—	—	—	—	—	—

Tax Analysis	Tax-Adj Ret%	%Rank Cat	%Pretax Ret	%Rank Cat
3 Yr Avg	1.96	60	47.0	59
5 Yr Avg	5.32	21	67.3	28
10 Yr Avg	—	—	—	—

Potential Capital Gain Exposure: 0% of assets

Risk Analysis

Time Period	Load-Adj Return %	Risk %Rank[1] All	Risk %Rank[1] Cat	Morningstar Return	Morningstar Risk	Morningstar Risk-Adj Rating
1 Yr	3.81					
3 Yr	4.18	32	75	-0.16[2]	1.48	★★
5 Yr	7.91	37	78	0.67[2]	1.50	★★
Incept	7.65	—	—	—	—	

Average Historical Rating (76 months): 1.9★s

[1]1=low, 100=high [2] T-Bill return substituted for category avg.

Category Rating (3 Yr)

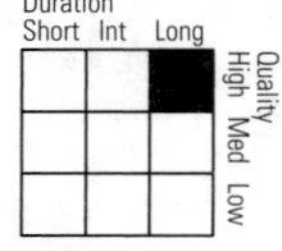

Return: Average
Risk: Above Avg

Other Measures	Standard Index LB Agg	Best Fit Index LB LTTreas
Alpha	-2.9	-0.6
Beta	1.88	0.98
R-Squared	75	99

Standard Deviation	7.51
Mean	4.18
Sharpe Ratio	-0.12

Portfolio Analysis 09-30-01

Total Fixed-Income: 8	Date of Maturity	Amount $000	Value $000	% Net Assets
US Treasury Bond 10.625%	08-15-15	15,000	23,114	17.92
US Treasury Bond 8.75%	08-15-20	16,500	22,997	17.82
US Treasury Bond 6.125%	11-15-27	16,800	18,261	14.15
US Treasury Bond 6.875%	08-15-25	13,500	15,971	12.38
US Treasury Bond 8.125%	08-15-19	12,000	15,751	12.21
US Treasury Bond 8.875%	02-15-19	8,000	11,154	8.65
US Treasury Bond 5.25%	02-15-29	6,000	5,792	4.49
US Treasury Strip 0%	11-15-27	25,120	5,692	4.41

Analysis by Christine Benz 12-12-01

With its newly broadened mandate, American Century Government Bond Fund is more attractive than before.

This fund recently changed its name, mandate, and manager. Formerly called American Century Long-Term Treasury, the fund was a focused play on its namesake securities. But in response to its shrinking investable universe (earlier this fall, the Treasury announced that it would stop issuing new 30-year Treasury bonds), the fund broadened its charter in early December. Though it will still focus on longer-duration government securities, management now has the latitude to scoop up mortgage-backed and agency bonds in addition to Treasuries. American Century also changed managers on this fund in December, with Jeremy Fletcher taking over for longtime manager Dave Schroeder.

We think these developments are generally for the better. Although the fund's previous focus on Treasuries made it an easy way to play declining interest rates (Treasuries are highly sensitive to changes in rates), the fund's increased flexibility could help improve its risk/reward profile overall. Government-agency and mortgage-backed bonds boast higher yields than Treasuries, and because they're less sensitive to changes in rates, they're also less volatile. So far this year, for example, funds that have focused on mortgage-backeds have fared far better than Treasury-only funds, as investors have grown concerned that the latest round of rate cuts is nearing an end. And though the fund will still play the long end of the yield curve, and may still be volatile, it stands to be less of a roller-coaster ride than it was in the past.

In all, we find a lot to like here. American Century has a capable bond team, and this fund's relatively low expenses should provide a consistent tailwind. This is a solid choice for exposure to long-duration government bonds.

Current Investment Style

Duration: Short Int Long; Quality: High Med Low

Avg Eff Duration[1]	10.7 Yrs
Avg Eff Maturity	19.6 Yrs
Avg Credit Quality	AAA
Avg Wtd Coupon	7.80%
Avg Wtd Price	119.12% of par

[1]figure provided by fund

Special Securities % assets 09-30-01

Restricted/Illiquid Secs	0
Exotic Mortgage-Backed	0
Emerging-Markets Secs	0
Options/Futures/Warrants	No

Credit Analysis % bonds 06-30-01

US Govt	99	BB	0
AAA	1	B	0
AA	0	Below B	0
A	0	NR/NA	0
BBB	0		

Sector Breakdown % bonds 09-30-01

US Treasuries	100	CMOs	0
GNMA mtgs	0	ARMs	0
FNMA mtgs	0	Other	0
FHLMC mtgs	0		

Coupon Range	% of Bonds	Rel Cat
0%	4.79	0.36
0% to 7%	33.71	0.65
7% to 8.5%	13.27	0.54
8.5% to 10%	28.76	3.38
More than 10%	19.47	8.25

1.00=Category Average

Composition % assets 09-30-01

Cash	7.3	Bonds	92.7
Stocks	0.0	Other	0.0

Address:	4500 Main Street P.O. Box 419200, Kansas City, MO 64141-6200, 415-965-4274 / 800-345-2021
Web Address:	www.americancentury.com
*Inception:	09-08-92
Advisor:	American Century Inv. Mgmt
Subadvisor:	None
NTF Plans:	Datalynx , Fidelity Inst.

Minimum Purchase:	$2500	Add: $50	IRA: $1000
Min Auto Inv Plan:	$2500	Add: $50	
Sales Fees:	No-load		
Management Fee:	.51%		
Actual Fees:	Mgt: 0.51%	Dist: —	
Expense Projections:	3Yr: $163	5Yr: $285	10Yr: $640
Avg Brok Commission:	—	Income Distrib: Monthly	
Total Cost (relative to category):	Low		

American Century Select Inv

Ticker	Load	NAV	Yield	Total Assets	Mstar Category
TWCIX	None	$37.00	0.2%	$5,190.0 mil	Large Growth

Prospectus Objective: Growth

American Century Select Fund seeks capital growth; income is a secondary consideration.

The fund normally invests at least 80% of assets in dividend-paying common stocks; however, these securities are chosen primarily for their growth potential. It intends to remain fully invested in stocks, regardless of the movement of stock prices generally. The fund may also invest without limit in foreign securities, including depositary receipts.

The fund offers Advisor, Institutional, and Investor shares, all of which vary in fee structure and availability. Past names: Twentieth Century Select Investors and American Century-Twentieth Century Select Fund.

Historical Profile
Return: Average
Risk: Average
Rating: ★★★ Neutral

Investment Style
Equity
Average Stock %: 99% 100% 98% 94% 97% 94% 96%

▼ Manager Change
▽ Partial Manager Change

Fund Performance vs. Category Average
■ Quarterly Fund Return +/– Category Average
— Category Baseline

Performance Quartile (within Category)

Portfolio Manager(s)

Kenneth Crawford. Since 6-99. BA U. of Wisconsin; MA U. of Wisconsin. Other funds currently managed: American Century Select Inst, American Century Select Adv.

Timothy Reynolds. Since 8-01. BA Texas A&M U.; MS Texas Tech UI. Other funds currently managed: American Century Select Inst, American Century Select Adv.

C. Kim Goodwin. Since 8-01. BA'81 Princeton U.; MBA'87 U. of Texas, Austin. Other funds currently managed: American Century Growth Inv, American Century Select Inst, American Century Select Adv.

History

1990	1991	1992	1993	1994	1995	1996	1997	1998	1999	2000	12-01	History
34.14	42.40	38.72	39.46	33.10	35.62	38.53	42.59	47.39	52.68	45.29	37.00	NAV
–0.78	31.17	–4.43	14.67	–8.04	22.67	19.22	32.19	35.72	22.23	–8.71	–18.16	Total Return %
2.33	0.68	–12.05	4.62	–9.35	–14.87	–3.73	–1.16	7.14	1.19	0.39	–6.29	+/– S&P 500
–2.15	–8.24	–8.32	14.75	–12.89	–15.99	–6.30	–1.55	–9.38	–7.45	15.81	2.34	+/– Russ Top 200 Grt
1.79	1.91	1.17	1.12	0.71	0.81	0.91	0.51	0.40	0.00	0.00	0.14	Income Return %
–2.57	29.25	–5.60	13.56	–8.75	21.85	18.31	31.68	35.32	22.23	–8.71	–18.30	Capital Return %
37	78	99	30	92	95	47	17	36	85	27	31	Total Rtn % Rank Cat
0.65	0.65	0.50	0.43	0.28	0.27	0.32	0.20	0.17	0.00	0.00	0.06	Income $
1.55	1.82	1.33	4.47	2.87	4.66	3.68	7.93	9.79	5.10	2.79	0.00	Capital Gains $
1.00	1.00	1.00	1.00	1.00	1.00	1.00	1.00	1.00	1.00	1.00	—	Expense Ratio %
1.80	1.70	1.40	1.10	1.00	0.90	0.50	0.33	0.25	0.03	–0.11	—	Income Ratio %
83	84	95	82	126	106	105	94	165	130	67	—	Turnover Rate %
3,196.7	4,634.1	4,691.9	4,976.0	3,995.2	3,982.8	4,060.5	5,006.3	6,498.2	7,674.4	6,474.5	4,972.8	Net Assets $mil

Performance 12-31-01

	1st Qtr	2nd Qtr	3rd Qtr	4th Qtr	Total
1997	1.51	19.43	6.66	2.23	32.19
1998	13.76	5.33	–7.43	22.36	35.72
1999	8.50	2.47	–4.82	15.50	22.23
2000	5.18	–3.05	–0.73	–9.83	–8.71
2001	–14.64	3.60	–13.91	7.49	–18.16

Trailing	Total Return%	+/– S&P 500	+/– Russ Top 200 Grth	% Rank All	% Rank Cat	Growth of $10,000
3 Mo	7.49	–3.19	–5.36	54	96	10,749
6 Mo	–7.46	–1.90	–0.47	76	35	9,254
1 Yr	–18.16	–6.29	2.34	78	31	8,184
3 Yr Avg	–2.98	–1.96	5.04	86	53	9,131
5 Yr Avg	10.38	–0.32	1.78	17	32	16,382
10 Yr Avg	9.21	–3.71	–1.87	37	72	24,144
15 Yr Avg	10.84	–2.90	–2.54	35	74	46,793

Tax Analysis	Tax-Adj Ret%	%Rank Cat	%Pretax Ret	%Rank Cat
3 Yr Avg	–4.34	52	—	—
5 Yr Avg	7.49	40	72.2	62
10 Yr Avg	6.32	77	68.6	78

Potential Capital Gain Exposure: 8% of assets

Risk Analysis

Time Period	Load-Adj Return %	Risk %Rank[1] All	Risk %Rank[1] Cat	Morningstar Return	Morningstar Risk	Morningstar Risk-Adj Rating
1 Yr	–18.16					
3 Yr	–2.98	66	11	–1.56[2]	0.92	★★
5 Yr	10.38	66	8	1.29[2]	0.89	★★★★
10 Yr	9.21	77	16	0.60	1.01	★★

Average Historical Rating (193 months): 3.4★s

[1]1=low, 100=high [2] T-Bill return substituted for category avg.

Category Rating (3 Yr)

1 2 **3** 4 5
Worst — Best

Return: Average
Risk: Below Avg

Other Measures	Standard Index S&P 500	Best Fit Index S&P 500
Alpha	–2.3	–2.3
Beta	0.95	0.95
R-Squared	94	94
Standard Deviation		16.17
Mean		–2.98
Sharpe Ratio		–0.57

Portfolio Analysis 09-30-01

Share change since 06-01 Total Stocks: 81	Sector	PE	YTD Ret%	% Assets
⊖ Pfizer	Health	34.7	–12.40	3.78
☼ S&P 500 Index (Fut)	N/A	—	—	3.75
⊕ PepsiCo	Staples	31.4	–0.54	3.47
⊖ American Intl Grp	Financials	42.0	–19.20	3.39
⊖ General Elec	Industrials	30.1	–15.00	3.14
⊖ Citigroup	Financials	20.0	0.03	3.03
⊕ Wal-Mart Stores	Retail	40.3	8.94	2.94
Abbott Labs	Health	51.6	17.08	2.91
⊕ ExxonMobil	Energy	15.3	–7.59	2.86
⊕ Verizon Comms	Services	29.7	–2.52	2.84
⊖ Microsoft	Technology	57.6	52.78	2.42
⊕ Johnson & Johnson	Health	16.6	14.01	2.11
⊕ Philip Morris	Staples	12.1	9.12	2.07
⊕ Intel	Technology	73.1	4.89	1.88
⊕ AT&T	Services	7.8	40.59	1.79
Freddie Mac	Financials	14.0	–3.87	1.65
☼ Lockheed Martin	Industrials	36.8	38.98	1.60
☼ American Home Products	Health	—	–1.91	1.55
☼ Bank of America	Financials	16.7	42.73	1.51
⊕ BellSouth	Services	24.9	–5.09	1.46
⊕ Home Depot	Retail	42.9	12.07	1.45
⊖ Fannie Mae	Financials	16.2	–6.95	1.36
⊕ Cisco Sys	Technology	—	–52.60	1.36
☼ Kimberly-Clark	Industrials	18.5	–13.80	1.32
Amgen	Health	52.8	–11.70	1.31

Current Investment Style

Style: Value Blnd Growth; Size: Large Med Small

	Stock Port Avg	Relative S&P 500 Current	Relative S&P 500 Hist	Rel Cat
Price/Earnings Ratio	31.1	1.01	1.12	0.88
Price/Book Ratio	6.7	1.17	1.20	1.05
Price/Cash Flow	19.2	1.07	1.15	0.85
3 Yr Earnings Growth	16.8	1.15	1.10	0.78
1 Yr Earnings Est%	3.1	—	—	1.03
Med Mkt Cap $mil	86,838	1.4	1.4	1.83

Special Securities % assets 09-30-01	
Restricted/Illiquid Secs	0
Emerging-Markets Secs	0
Options/Futures/Warrants	Yes

Composition % assets 09-30-01	
Cash	6.0
Stocks*	90.4
Bonds	0.0
Other	3.6
*Foreign (% stocks)	0.7

Market Cap	
Giant	70.1
Large	25.8
Medium	4.1
Small	0.0
Micro	0.0

Sector Weightings	% of Stocks	Rel S&P	5-Year High	5-Year Low
Utilities	0.0	0.0	6	0
Energy	5.4	0.8	18	0
Financials	18.2	1.0	20	3
Industrials	9.8	0.9	25	5
Durables	0.0	0.0	18	0
Staples	12.8	1.6	23	1
Services	8.9	0.8	23	2
Retail	8.2	1.2	16	1
Health	21.0	1.4	23	1
Technology	15.7	0.9	37	1

Analysis by Christopher Davis 10-25-01

Wait until the dust settles before choosing American Century Select Fund.

This offering certainly has been no stranger to change in recent years. Nearly its entire management team jumped ship in mid-1999, so Ken Crawford was elevated from analyst to comanager. Jerry Sullivan, who had joined Crawford in early 2000, left earlier this year to help run behemoth sibling American Century Ultra Fund. American Century then enlisted one of the fund's analysts, Tim Reynolds, to replace Sullivan in July 2001. Amid these changes, the fund ditched a mandate that required it to place at least 80% of assets in dividend-paying stocks.

Throughout it all, the fund's fairly conservative growth style hasn't changed much, though. The dividend policy change could have led it to load up on pricey, nondividend-paying tech stocks, but that didn't happen. Indeed, management has kept the fund's price multiples and sector weightings in line with its bogy, the S&P 500 index, which placed it in the large-blend slot of the Morningstar style box in June. And because management looks for companies that are increasing their growth rates—regardless of the absolute rate of that growth—the fund owns a slug of names that one wouldn't ordinarily associate with a growth offering, including Freddie Mac and Philip Morris. Because such stocks tend to fare relatively well in a rough-and-tumble market, the fund has outpaced 81% of its large-growth rivals for the year to date through Oct. 24, 2001.

Nonetheless, the high level of manager turnover leaves question marks surrounding the fund's long-term prospects. Reynolds hasn't been here all that long, and Crawford's record here and elsewhere is much too brief to be very meaningful. While that's no reason for current shareholders to jump ship, we think prospective investors will find more-proven offerings elsewhere.

Address:	4500 Main Street P.O. Box 419200 Kansas City, MO 64141-6200 800-345-2021 / 816-531-5575
Web Address:	www.americancentury.com
Inception:	10-31-58
Advisor:	American Century Inv. Mgmt
Subadvisor:	None
NTF Plans:	Datalynx , Fidelity Inst.

Minimum Purchase:	$2500	Add: $50	IRA: $1000
Min Auto Inv Plan:	$2500	Add: $50	
Sales Fees:	No-load		
Management Fee:	1.0%		
Actual Fees:	Mgt: 1.00%	Dist: —	
Expense Projections:	3Yr: $318	5Yr: $551	10Yr: $1219
Avg Brok Commission:	—	Income Distrib: Annually	
Total Cost (relative to category):		Below Avg	

American Century Small Cap Value Inv

Ticker	Load	NAV	Yield	Total Assets	Mstar Category
ASVIX	Closed	$8.02	0.5%	$1,225.5 mil	Small Value

Prospectus Objective: Small Company

American Century Small Cap Value Fund seeks long-term capital growth; income is a secondary objective.

The fund normally invests at least 65% of assets in equity securities of U.S. companies with small market capitalizations. It may invest in foreign securities, covertible securities, corporate and government debt, and non-leveraged stock index futures contracts. The fund invests in companies that the advisor believes are undervalued by the market.

The fund currently offers C, Advisor, Institutional and Investor shares, all of which differ in fee structure and availability.

Historical Profile
Return High
Risk Low
Rating ★★★★★ Highest

Investment Style
Equity
Average Stock %: 93% 95% 90% 92%

▼ Manager Change
▽ Partial Manager Change

Fund Performance vs. Category Average
■ Quarterly Fund Return +/– Category Average
– Category Baseline

Performance Quartile (within Category)

Portfolio Manager(s)

Management Team

History

	1990	1991	1992	1993	1994	1995	1996	1997	1998	1999	2000	12-01
NAV	—	—	—	—	—	—	—	—	5.12	4.73	6.32	8.02
Total Return %	—	—	—	—	—	—	—	—	3.31*	–0.86	39.42	30.52
+/– S&P 500	—	—	—	—	—	—	—	—	–5.07*	–21.90	48.52	42.39
+/– Russell 2000 V	—	—	—	—	—	—	—	—	—	0.62	16.60	16.50
Income Return %	—	—	—	—	—	—	—	—	0.00	1.06	1.08	0.59
Capital Return %	—	—	—	—	—	—	—	—	3.31	–1.93	38.34	29.93
Total Rtn % Rank Cat	—	—	—	—	—	—	—	—	—	58	2	7
Income $	—	—	—	—	—	—	—	—	0.00	0.05	0.05	0.04
Capital Gains $	—	—	—	—	—	—	—	—	0.04	0.28	0.20	0.18
Expense Ratio %	—	—	—	—	—	—	—	—	—	1.25	1.25	1.25
Income Ratio %	—	—	—	—	—	—	—	—	—	1.02	1.04	1.10
Turnover Rate %	—	—	—	—	—	—	—	—	—	153	178	144
Net Assets $mil	—	—	—	—	—	—	—	—	12.2	19.5	66.4	1,090.1

Performance 12-31-01

	1st Qtr	2nd Qtr	3rd Qtr	4th Qtr	Total
1997	—	—	—	—	—
1998	—	—	—	14.53	3.31 *
1999	–7.31	15.80	–7.88	0.25	–0.86
2000	6.94	3.85	9.37	14.79	39.42
2001	4.71	16.48	–9.24	17.91	30.52

Trailing	Total Return%	+/– S&P 500	+/– Russ 2000V	% Rank All	% Rank Cat	Growth of $10,000
3 Mo	17.91	7.22	1.19	17	43	11,791
6 Mo	7.01	12.56	5.85	2	9	10,701
1 Yr	30.52	42.39	16.50	1	7	13,052
3 Yr Avg	21.73	22.76	10.41	2	11	18,039
5 Yr Avg	—	—	—	—	—	—
10 Yr Avg	—	—	—	—	—	—
15 Yr Avg	—	—	—	—	—	—

Tax Analysis	Tax-Adj Ret%	%Rank Cat	%Pretax Ret	%Rank Cat
3 Yr Avg	19.58	11	90.1	57
5 Yr Avg	—	—	—	—
10 Yr Avg	—	—	—	—

Potential Capital Gain Exposure: 12% of assets

Risk Analysis

Time Period	Load-Adj Return %	Risk %Rank[1] All	Risk %Rank[1] Cat	Morningstar Return	Morningstar Risk	Morningstar Risk-Adj Rating
1 Yr	30.52					
3 Yr	21.73	36	6	4.16[2]	0.46	★★★★★
5 Yr	—	—	—	—	—	
Incept	19.93	—	—	—	—	

Average Historical Rating (6 months): 5.0★s

[1]1=low, 100=high [2] T-Bill return substituted for category avg.

Category Rating (3 Yr)

1 2 3 4 5
Worst Best

Return: Above Avg
Risk: Low

Other Measures	Standard Index S&P 500	Best Fit Index SPMid400
Alpha	19.9	12.9
Beta	0.48	0.59
R-Squared	27	55

Standard Deviation	18.67
Mean	21.73
Sharpe Ratio	1.01

Portfolio Analysis 09-30-01

Share change since 06-01 Total Stocks: 108

	Sector	PE	YTD Ret%	% Assets
⊕ Wisconsin Energy	Utilities	12.7	3.65	2.44
⊕ PMI Grp	Financials	10.4	–0.76	2.05
⊕ Sensient Tech	Staples	17.2	–5.99	1.87
⊕ Georgia Gulf	Industrials	—	10.41	1.87
⊕ Owens & Minor	Health	28.9	5.81	1.85
⊕ Littelfuse	Technology	41.7	–8.33	1.69
⊕ G & K Svcs A	Services	19.9	15.17	1.66
⊕ Kellwood	Durables	10.4	16.98	1.63
⊕ Wausau–Mosinee Paper Mills	Industrials	NMF	22.90	1.62
⊕ Sybron Dental Tech	Health	—	27.88	1.61
⊕ Westport Resources	Energy	—	–20.90	1.58
⊕ Intl Multifoods	Staples	24.4	17.66	1.56
⊖ Jack In The Box	Services	13.4	–6.45	1.55
⊕ Valassis Comms	Services	18.9	12.85	1.49
⊖ Methode Electncs A	Technology	28.6	1.78	1.49
⊕ Anixter Intl	Technology	27.1	34.15	1.48
⊕ Avnet	Technology	—	19.93	1.47
⊕ Casey's General Stores	Retail	24.0	0.39	1.47
⊕ Regal–Beloit	Industrials	20.6	31.09	1.42
Advo	Services	17.4	–3.10	1.41
⊕ The Phoenix Companies	Financials	—	—	1.39
⊖ Northwest Natural Gas	Utilities	14.6	1.38	1.30
⊕ Claire's Stores	Retail	21.6	–15.00	1.27
⊕ AGL Resources	Utilities	16.4	9.39	1.21
⊕ Sappi ADR	Industrials	—	—	1.20

Current Investment Style

Style: Value Blnd Growth; Size: Large Med Small

	Stock Port Avg	Relative S&P 500 Current	Relative S&P 500 Hist	Rel Cat
Price/Earnings Ratio	23.2	0.75	0.56	1.07
Price/Book Ratio	2.4	0.43	0.32	1.01
Price/Cash Flow	11.4	0.63	0.44	0.89
3 Yr Earnings Growth	6.7	0.46	0.63	0.58
1 Yr Earnings Est%	–14.0	7.90	—	3.54
Med Mkt Cap $mil	729	0.0	0.0	0.84

Special Securities % assets 09-30-01

Restricted/Illiquid Secs	0
Emerging–Markets Secs	1
Options/Futures/Warrants	No

Composition % assets 09-30-01

Cash	6.4
Stocks*	93.4
Bonds	0.2
Other	0.0
*Foreign (% stocks)	2.8

Market Cap

Giant	0.0
Large	0.0
Medium	22.6
Small	68.9
Micro	8.4

Sector Weightings	% of Stocks	Rel S&P	5-Year High	5-Year Low
Utilities	8.5	2.7	—	—
Energy	5.1	0.7	—	—
Financials	13.3	0.7	—	—
Industrials	19.4	1.7	—	—
Durables	4.8	3.1	—	—
Staples	6.1	0.8	—	—
Services	15.5	1.4	—	—
Retail	6.9	1.0	—	—
Health	7.6	0.5	—	—
Technology	12.8	0.7	—	—

Analysis by Christopher Davis 12-13-01

We like what we see at American Century Small Cap Value Fund.

This young offering recently shut its doors to new investors to prevent asset bloat from cramping its style. With assets soaring to $1 billion in November—up from just more than $100 million at the start of 2001—the fund certainly had attracted a lot of attention.

It's not hard to see why. The fund's record is impressive, if somewhat brief: Its annualized 21% gain for the trailing three years ending Dec. 11, 2001, lands just outside the small-value category's top decile. The fund posted these results while suffering less volatility than its typical peer. Indeed, it has been a bear-market standout, smoking its rivals with an eye-catching 24% return for the year to date and a category-topping 39% gain in 2000. Other small-value offerings boast similar records, but unlike some of those funds, this one has put up strong numbers without betting heavily on individual names or sectors.

So, what's behind that success? As investors turned their attention away from pricey, big-cap stocks to relatively inexpensive small caps in 2000 and 2001, the fund's emphasis on smaller, cheaper names has undoubtedly been a boon to returns. While that focus has helped, the stock-picking here has been on the mark as well. By looking for firms that are cheap based on at least two of five valuation measures, managers Todd Vingers and Ben Giele have homed in on a smattering of traditional value names, including regional bank Hibernia and mortgage insurer Radian Group, which have fared relatively well. But the fund has also benefited from strong-performing picks in not-so-traditional value sectors, such as software maker Structural Dynamics.

This offering doesn't own a particularly lengthy track record, but we think investors who bought this fund before it closed have every reason to stay the course.

Address:	4500 Main Street P.O. Box 419200 Kansas City, MO 64141–6200 800–345–2021
Web Address:	www.americancentury.com
*Inception:	07-30-98
Advisor:	American Century Inv. Mgmt
Subadvisor:	None
NTF Plans:	Fidelity Inst. , Waterhouse

Minimum Purchase:	Closed	Add: $50	IRA: —
Min Auto Inv Plan:	Closed	Add: $50	
Sales Fees:	No–load		
Management Fee:	1.3%		
Actual Fees:	Mgt: 1.25%	Dist: —	
Expense Projections:	3Yr: $395	5Yr: —	10Yr: —
Avg Brok Commission:	—	Income Distrib: Quarterly	
Total Cost (relative to category):	—		

American Century Tax Managed Val Inv

Ticker	Load	NAV	Yield	Total Assets	Mstar Category
ACTIX	None	$5.80	1.0%	$53.1 mil	Large Value

Prospectus Objective: Growth

American Century Tax Managed Value Fund seeks capital growth while attempting to minimize the impact of federal taxes on shareholder returns.

The fund primarily invests in common stocks. It may invest in preferred stocks, foreign securities, convertibles, notes, bonds, and other debt securities. The fund may seeks to minimize realized capital gains by keeping portfolio turnover low and generally holding its investments for long periods.

The fund offers Advisor, Institutional, and Investor shares, all of which vary in fee structure and availability.

Historical Profile
Return —
Risk —
Rating Not Rated

Investment Style
Equity
Average Stock %: 98% (1999), 96% (2000), 96% (12-01)

▼ Manager Change
▽ Partial Manager Change

Fund Performance vs. Category Average
■ Quarterly Fund Return +/– Category Average
— Category Baseline

Performance Quartile (within Category)

Portfolio Manager(s)

Mark L. Mallon, CFA. Since 3-99. BA Westminster C.; MBA Cornell U. Other funds currently managed: American Century Strat Alloc: Agg Inv, American Century Strat Alloc: Con Inv, American Century Strat Alloc: Mod Inv.

Charles A. Ritter, CFA. Since 3-99. MBA'74 U. of Chicago; MS'82 Carnegie Mellon U. Other funds currently managed: American Century Strat Alloc: Agg Inv, American Century Strat Alloc: Con Inv, American Century Strat Alloc: Mod Inv.

History

1990	1991	1992	1993	1994	1995	1996	1997	1998	1999	2000	12-01	History
—	—	—	—	—	—	—	—	—	5.08	5.49	5.80	NAV
—	—	—	—	—	—	—	—	—	2.60*	9.75	6.78	Total Return %
—	—	—	—	—	—	—	—	—	–12.69*	18.86	18.66	+/– S&P 500
—	—	—	—	—	—	—	—	—	—	7.44	15.58	+/– Russ Top 200 Val
—	—	—	—	—	—	—	—	—	1.00	1.60	1.10	Income Return %
—	—	—	—	—	—	—	—	—	1.60	8.15	5.68	Capital Return %
—	—	—	—	—	—	—	—	—	—	35	4	Total Rtn % Rank Cat
—	—	—	—	—	—	—	—	—	0.05	0.08	0.06	Income $
—	—	—	—	—	—	—	—	—	0.00	0.00	0.00	Capital Gains $
—	—	—	—	—	—	—	—	—	1.10	1.10	—	Expense Ratio %
—	—	—	—	—	—	—	—	—	1.14	1.56	—	Income Ratio %
—	—	—	—	—	—	—	—	—	—	73	—	Turnover Rate %
—	—	—	—	—	—	—	—	—	44.8	39.8	53.1	Net Assets $mil

Performance 12-31-01

	1st Qtr	2nd Qtr	3rd Qtr	4th Qtr	Total
1997	—	—	—	—	—
1998	—	—	—	—	—
1999	—	13.00	–12.21	3.43	2.60 *
2000	–0.59	–2.18	6.48	6.00	9.75
2001	1.28	7.37	–9.72	8.77	6.78

Trailing	Total Return%	+/– S&P 500	+/– Russ Top 200 Val	% Rank All	% Rank Cat	Growth of $10,000
3 Mo	8.77	–1.92	—	48	52	10,877
6 Mo	–1.80	3.75	—	46	20	9,820
1 Yr	6.78	18.66	—	15	4	10,678
3 Yr Avg	—	—	—	—	—	—
5 Yr Avg	—	—	—	—	—	—
10 Yr Avg	—	—	—	—	—	—
15 Yr Avg	—	—	—	—	—	—

Tax Analysis	Tax-Adj Ret%	%Rank Cat	%Pretax Ret	%Rank Cat
3 Yr Avg	—	—	—	—
5 Yr Avg	—	—	—	—
10 Yr Avg	—	—	—	—

Potential Capital Gain Exposure: 9% of assets

Risk Analysis

Time Period	Load-Adj Return %	Risk %Rank[1] All	Risk %Rank[1] Cat	Morningstar Return	Morningstar Risk	Morningstar Risk-Adj Rating
1 Yr	6.78					
3 Yr	—	—	—	—	—	
5 Yr	—	—	—	—	—	
Incept	6.92	—	—	—	—	

Average Historical Rating —

[1]1=low, 100=high

Category Rating (3 Yr)

Other Measures	Standard Index S&P 500	Best Fit Index
Alpha	—	—
Beta	—	—
R-Squared	—	—

Return	Standard Deviation	—
Risk	Mean	—
	Sharpe Ratio	—

Portfolio Analysis 09-30-01

Share change since 06-01 Total Stocks: 86	Sector	PE	YTD Ret%	% Assets
⊕ ExxonMobil	Energy	15.3	–7.59	4.87
⊕ S & P 500 Dep Rec SPDR		—	—	4.23
⊕ Citigroup	Financials	20.0	0.03	3.54
⊕ Verizon Comms	Services	29.7	–2.52	2.96
⊕ Bank of America	Financials	16.7	42.73	2.35
⊕ Philip Morris	Staples	12.1	9.12	2.26
⊕ Fannie Mae	Financials	16.2	–6.95	2.24
⊕ Royal Dutch Petro NY ADR	Energy	12.0	–17.10	2.19
⊕ FPL Grp	Utilities	13.1	–18.30	2.18
⊕ Allstate	Financials	17.1	–21.00	2.09
⊕ Merck	Health	19.1	–35.90	1.72
⊕ Computer Assoc Intl	Technology	—	77.28	1.53
⊕ AT&T	Services	7.8	40.59	1.50
⊕ McDonald's	Services	19.2	–21.50	1.46
⊕ FleetBoston Finl	Financials	16.2	0.55	1.35
⊕ Bank One	Financials	29.1	9.13	1.29
⊕ IBM	Technology	26.9	43.00	1.27
⊕ Conoco Cl A	Energy	9.0	1.56	1.26
⊕ US Bancorp	Financials	13.5	–6.14	1.26
☼ Wachovia	Financials	—	23.13	1.24
⊕ Washington Mutual	Financials	10.1	–5.32	1.19
Sprint	Services	20.5	1.18	1.18
⊕ Loews	Financials	—	8.35	1.10
Equity Residential Properties	Financials	22.1	10.14	1.08
⊕ Household Intl	Financials	14.7	6.89	1.08

Current Investment Style

Style: Value Blnd Growth; Size: Large Med Small

	Stock Port Avg	Relative S&P 500 Current	Relative S&P 500 Hist	Rel Cat
Price/Earnings Ratio	21.5	0.69	—	0.85
Price/Book Ratio	3.4	0.60	—	0.83
Price/Cash Flow	10.8	0.60	—	0.79
3 Yr Earnings Growth	14.5	0.99	—	0.98
1 Yr Earnings Est%	–3.7	2.07	—	1.11
Med Mkt Cap $mil	23,046	0.4	—	0.73

Analysis by Emily Hall 12-11-01

American Century Tax Managed Value Fund looks good even before you put taxes into the equation.

This young offering is off to a very impressive start. In the two years since its inception, the fund has delivered an annualized return of more than 6%, beating both the S&P 500 index and its typical large value-rival.

The fund has been especially strong in 2001. Its 6.5% showing through early December is good enough to land it in the top 5% of the category. A solid set of picks across sectors has helped in recent months, with everything from Bank of America to AT&T to IBM boosting returns.

Managers Charles Ritter and Mark Mallon follow a fairly straightforward value approach. They start with a universe of 500 mostly large- and mid-cap companies and screen for firms that are trading below historic levels and appear reasonably-priced relative to their expected returns. The managers then examine the top-ranked picks closely to see if each one is worthy of a spot in the portfolio. The result is a fund that looks not unlike the typical large-value offering—except for a slightly smaller median market cap and slightly lower price multiples.

What sets this fund apart is its tax sensitivity. The managers will harvest tax losses when they can, although they also try to pay attention to portfolio construction at the same time. For instance, Ritter and Mallon report that in 2000 they sold several bank stocks for tax-loss purposes, but they upped their weighting in their remaining bank stocks at the same time to maintain the portfolio's exposure to the sector.

To be sure, two years is not a long record, and it's hard to say how well the fund will hold up in a variety of market conditions. The fund's early performance is certainly encouraging. If the fund can keep this up, it likely will become a compelling tax-managed choice.

Special Securities % assets 09-30-01	
Restricted/Illiquid Secs	0
Emerging-Markets Secs	0
Options/Futures/Warrants	No

Composition % assets 09-30-01	
Cash	3.8
Stocks*	96.2
Bonds	0.0
Other	0.0
*Foreign (% stocks)	2.3

Market Cap	
Giant	34.1
Large	43.7
Medium	21.7
Small	0.5
Micro	0.0

Sector Weightings	% of Stocks	Rel S&P	5-Year High	5-Year Low
Utilities	4.5	1.4	—	—
Energy	12.9	1.8	—	—
Financials	29.7	1.7	—	—
Industrials	10.3	0.9	—	—
Durables	6.5	4.2	—	—
Staples	5.9	0.7	—	—
Services	12.9	1.2	—	—
Retail	4.6	0.7	—	—
Health	5.4	0.4	—	—
Technology	7.4	0.4	—	—

Address:	4500 Main Street P.O. Box 419200 Kansas City, MO 64141–6200 800–345–3533 / 816–531–5575
Web Address:	www.americancentury.com
*Inception:	03-31-99
Advisor:	American Century Inv. Mgmt
Subadvisor:	None
NTF Plans:	N/A

Minimum Purchase:	$10000	Add: $250 IRA: $10000
Min Auto Inv Plan:	$10000	Add: $600
Sales Fees:	No-load, 2.00%R within 12 months	
Management Fee:	1.1% mx./.90% mn.	
Actual Fees:	Mgt: 1.10%	Dist: —
Expense Projections:	3Yr: $349	5Yr: $604 10Yr: $1334
Avg Brok Commission:	—	Income Distrib: Annually
Total Cost (relative to category):		—

American Century Value Inv

Ticker	Load	NAV	Yield	Total Assets	Mstar Category
TWVLX	None	$7.00	1.2%	$2,343.2 mil	Mid-Cap Value

Prospectus Objective: Growth and Income

American Century Value Fund seeks long-term capital appreciation. Income is secondary.

The fund normally invests at least 65% of assets in U.S. equity securities. Although it may invest in companies of all sizes, the fund's overall characteristics are most similar to those in the mid-cap arena. The fund looks for stocks of companies that they believe are undervalued at the time of purchase. To identify these companies, management looks for companies with earnings, cash flows and/or assets that may not be reflected accurately in the companies' stock prices or may be outside the companies' historical ranges.

The fund currently offers C, Advisor, Institutional, and Investor shares.

Historical Profile

Return Above Avg
Risk Below Avg
Rating ★★★★ Above Avg

Investment Style Equity — Average Stock %: 1995 97%, 1996 97%, 1997 97%, 1998 97%, 1999 97%, 2000 89%, 12-01 87%

▼ Manager Change
▽ Partial Manager Change

Fund Performance vs. Category Average
■ Quarterly Fund Return
+/– Category Average
— Category Baseline

Performance Quartile (within Category)

Portfolio Manager(s)

Phillip N. Davidson, CFA. Since 9-93. BS'78 Illinois State U.; MBA'80 Illinois State U. Other funds currently managed: American Century Equity Income Inv, American Century Strat Alloc: Agg Inv, American Century Strat Alloc: Con Inv.

Scott A. Moore, CFA. Since 2-99. BS Southern Illinois U.; MBA U. of Missouri. Other funds currently managed: American Century Equity Income Inv, American Century Strat Alloc: Agg Inv, American Century Strat Alloc: Con Inv.

History

1990	1991	1992	1993	1994	1995	1996	1997	1998	1999	2000	12-01	History
—	—	—	5.12	4.92	5.90	6.59	6.95	6.05	5.49	6.38	7.00	NAV
—	—	—	3.07*	3.99	32.80	24.25	26.01	4.99	–0.80	18.27	12.86	Total Return %
—	—	—	1.45*	2.68	–4.74	1.30	–7.34	–23.59	–21.83	27.37	24.74	+/– S&P 500
—	—	—	—	6.12	–2.14	3.99	–8.35	–0.10	–0.69	–0.92	10.52	+/– Russ Midcap Val
—	—	—	0.87	2.49	2.72	1.89	1.80	1.23	1.49	1.81	1.30	Income Return %
—	—	—	2.20	1.50	30.08	22.36	24.21	3.76	–2.29	16.46	11.56	Capital Return %
—	—	—	—	15	33	25	55	43	80	43	24	Total Rtn % Rank Cat
—	—	—	0.04	0.12	0.13	0.11	0.12	0.08	0.09	0.10	0.08	Income $
—	—	—	0.00	0.27	0.48	0.61	1.20	1.15	0.41	0.00	0.11	Capital Gains $
—	—	—	—	1.00	1.00	0.97	1.00	1.00	1.00	1.00	1.00	Expense Ratio %
—	—	—	—	3.37	2.65	2.17	1.86	1.38	1.19	1.48	1.71	Income Ratio %
—	—	—	—	—	94	145	111	130	130	115	150	Turnover Rate %
—	—	—	61.3	153.1	652.5	1,548.2	2,418.6	2,082.6	1,605.4	1,516.2	1,929.0	Net Assets $mil

Performance 12-31-01

	1st Qtr	2nd Qtr	3rd Qtr	4th Qtr	Total
1997	0.35	12.87	11.82	–0.51	26.01
1998	11.45	–4.88	–10.85	11.10	4.99
1999	–4.33	18.45	–11.00	–1.63	–0.80
2000	–2.20	–1.56	8.70	13.01	18.27
2001	–1.42	8.86	–7.34	13.51	12.86

Trailing	Total Return%	+/– S&P 500	+/– Russ Midcap Val	% Rank All	% Rank Cat	Growth of $10,000
3 Mo	13.51	2.82	1.48	28	41	11,351
6 Mo	5.17	10.73	6.08	3	17	10,517
1 Yr	12.86	24.74	10.52	4	24	11,286
3 Yr Avg	9.81	10.84	3.00	11	55	13,241
5 Yr Avg	11.86	1.17	0.40	11	48	17,517
10 Yr Avg	—	—	—	—	—	—
15 Yr Avg	—	—	—	—	—	—

Tax Analysis	Tax-Adj Ret%	%Rank Cat	%Pretax Ret	%Rank Cat
3 Yr Avg	7.91	53	80.7	44
5 Yr Avg	8.02	63	67.6	88
10 Yr Avg	—	—	—	—

Potential Capital Gain Exposure: 11% of assets

Risk Analysis

Time Period	Load-Adj Return %	Risk %Rank¹ All	Risk %Rank¹ Cat	Morningstar Return	Morningstar Risk	Morningstar Risk-Adj Rating
1 Yr	12.86					
3 Yr	9.81	50	57	1.08²	0.70	★★★★
5 Yr	11.86	55	53	1.70²	0.76	★★★★
Incept	14.53	—	—	—	—	

Average Historical Rating (65 months): 3.6★s

¹1=low, 100=high ² T-Bill return substituted for category avg.

Category Rating (3 Yr)

1 2 **3** 4 5 — Worst ... Best

Return Average
Risk Average

Other Measures	Standard Index S&P 500	Best Fit Index SPMid400
Alpha	9.0	2.7
Beta	0.56	0.51
R-Squared	28	31

Standard Deviation	19.70
Mean	9.81
Sharpe Ratio	0.28

Analysis by Bradley Sweeney 08-16-01

This is a solid option for those looking for a dyed-in-the-wool value offering.

American Century Value has been enjoying the market's renewed interest in valuations. Unlike many of its value-oriented peers, which pursue companies that appear inexpensive relative to other firms in their industries, this offering takes a more orthodox approach. Managers Phil Davidson and Scott Moore focus on stocks that are cheap based on traditional valuation measures, regardless of what industry the firms are in.

Historically that has meant that the fund has held much smaller stakes in less-traditional value sectors, such as technology and health care, than the typical mid-cap value fund. And this year hasn't been any different. With a modest 7% of assets in tech at the year's midpoint, the portfolio has escaped much of that sector's recent woes. But the fund hasn't just benefited from its avoidance of tech shares. Some names that management picked up on the cheap last year, such as telecom-service providers Sprint and Verizon, have recovered somewhat from their drubbing in 2000, helping propel the fund past more than three fourths of its rivals for the year to date through August 16, 2001.

Of course, management's focus on absolute valuations hasn't always served the fund well—the fund badly lagged its average rival in 1999, for example. In that year, the fund lost out to peers that were willing to fold some more richly priced tech stocks into the mix. But it's tough to argue with the fund's long-term results. The fund hasn't exactly blown the competition out of the water, but its annualized return since its 1993 inception bests its typical peer's by more than a full percentage point. One of the few strikes against this fund is its relatively poor tax efficiency, which has made for some less-than-attractive after-tax returns.

Address:	4500 Main Street P.O. Box 419200 Kansas City, MO 64141-6200 800-345-2021 / 816-531-5575
Web Address:	www.americancentury.com
*Inception:	09-01-93
Advisor:	American Century Inv. Mgmt
Subadvisor:	None
NTF Plans:	Datalynx , Fidelity Inst.

Minimum Purchase:	$2500	Add: $50	IRA: $1000
Min Auto Inv Plan:	$2500	Add: $50	
Sales Fees:	No-load		
Management Fee:	1.0%		
Actual Fees:	Mgt: 1.00%	Dist: —	
Expense Projections:	3Yr: $318	5Yr: $551	10Yr: $1219
Avg Brok Commission:	—	Income Distrib: Quarterly	
Total Cost (relative to category):		Below Avg	

Portfolio Analysis 09-30-01

Share change since 06-01 Total Stocks: 86	Sector	PE	YTD Ret%	% Assets
⊕ FPL Grp	Utilities	13.1	–18.30	3.66
☼ BP PLC ADR	Energy	14.4	–0.90	3.63
First Virginia Banks	Financials	14.7	9.39	3.61
⊕ Clorox	Staples	31.1	14.20	3.41
⊖ Royal Dutch Petro NY ADR	Energy	12.0	–17.10	3.28
⊖ Sprint	Services	20.5	1.18	3.27
☼ BellSouth	Services	24.9	–5.09	3.02
⊕ Waste Mgmt	Services	52.3	15.03	2.69
⊕ Martin Marietta Matls	Industrials	22.0	11.56	2.58
⊕ Minnesota Mng & Mfg	Industrials	34.5	0.16	2.56
⊖ S&P 500 Index (Fut)	N/A	—	—	2.44
⊖ Verizon Comms	Services	29.7	–2.52	2.42
⊕ Emerson Elec	Industrials	23.8	–25.60	2.37
⊕ Bristol-Myers Squibb	Health	20.2	–26.00	2.18
⊕ Federated Dept Stores	Retail	16.6	16.86	2.16
⊕ AGL Resources	Utilities	16.4	9.39	2.15
⊕ Campbell Soup	Staples	20.1	–11.20	2.04
⊕ Air Products and Chemicals	Industrials	22.1	16.61	1.93
⊕ WGL Hldgs	Utilities	16.2	–0.03	1.79
⊕ Dover	Industrials	21.1	–7.38	1.66
⊖ Minerals Tech	Industrials	21.5	36.76	1.64
⊖ Chubb	Financials	48.3	–18.60	1.54
⊖ Wisconsin Energy	Utilities	12.7	3.65	1.53
⊖ Marshall & Ilsley	Financials	22.0	27.06	1.51
☼ Allstate	Financials	17.1	–21.00	1.48

Current Investment Style — Style: Value Blnd Growth; Size: Large Med Small

	Stock Port Avg	Relative S&P 500 Current	Relative S&P 500 Hist	Rel Cat
Price/Earnings Ratio	24.0	0.78	0.62	1.02
Price/Book Ratio	4.0	0.70	0.36	1.32
Price/Cash Flow	11.5	0.64	0.45	0.93
3 Yr Earnings Growth	9.4	0.64	0.41	0.80
1 Yr Earnings Est%	–10.4	5.86	—	1.69
Med Mkt Cap $mil	10,349	0.2	0.1	1.46

Special Securities % assets 09-30-01	
Restricted/Illiquid Secs	0
Emerging-Markets Secs	0
Options/Futures/Warrants	Yes

Composition % assets 09-30-01	
Cash	5.1
Stocks*	92.6
Bonds	0.0
Other	2.4
*Foreign (% stocks)	9.0

Market Cap	
Giant	24.1
Large	32.4
Medium	35.2
Small	8.3
Micro	0.0

Sector Weightings	% of Stocks	Rel S&P	5-Year High	5-Year Low
Utilities	9.6	3.0	14	2
Energy	10.6	1.5	19	5
Financials	14.8	0.8	25	8
Industrials	16.7	1.5	32	11
Durables	4.2	2.7	9	0
Staples	8.9	1.1	19	5
Services	20.2	1.9	23	8
Retail	4.5	0.7	16	0
Health	4.3	0.3	11	0
Technology	6.3	0.3	10	0

American Century Veedot Inv

Ticker	Load	NAV	Yield	Total Assets	Mstar Category
AMVIX	None	$4.66	0.0%	$255.9 mil	Mid–Cap Growth

Prospectus Objective: Growth

American Century Veedot Fund seeks capital appreciation.

The fund primarily invests in common stocks, but it may invest in domestic and foreign preferred stocks, convertible securities, and non-leveraged futures, options, notes, bonds, and other debt securities. It may invest in foreign securities. The fund invests in securities that the advisor believes will appreciate in value and whose issuers meet managment's growth requirements. This fund is non-diversified.

Historical Profile
Return —
Risk —
Rating Not Rated

Investment Style
Equity
Average Stock %: 92% (1999), 97% (2000), 90% (12-01)

▼ Manager Change
▽ Partial Manager Change

Fund Performance vs. Category Average
■ Quarterly Fund Return +/– Category Average
— Category Baseline

Performance Quartile (within Category)

Portfolio Manager(s)

James E. Stowers III. Since 11-99. BS'81 Arizona State U. Other funds currently managed: American Century Ultra Inv, American Century Ultra Adv, American Century Ultra Inst.

John Small Jr.. Since 11-99. MS Air Force Inst. of Technology; BS Rockford C. Other fund currently managed: American Century Veedot Instl.

1990	1991	1992	1993	1994	1995	1996	1997	1998	1999	2000	12–01	History
—	—	—	—	—	—	—	—	—	5.92	5.84	4.66	NAV
—	—	—	—	—	—	—	—	—	18.40*	–1.35	–20.21	Total Return %
—	—	—	—	—	—	—	—	—	12.53*	7.75	–8.33	+/– S&P 500
—	—	—	—	—	—	—	—	—	—	10.40	–0.05	+/– Russ Midcap Grth
—	—	—	—	—	—	—	—	—	0.00	0.00	0.00	Income Return %
—	—	—	—	—	—	—	—	—	18.40	–1.35	–20.21	Capital Return %
—	—	—	—	—	—	—	—	—	—	42	45	Total Rtn % Rank Cat
—	—	—	—	—	—	—	—	—	0.00	0.00	0.00	Income $
—	—	—	—	—	—	—	—	—	0.00	0.00	0.00	Capital Gains $
—	—	—	—	—	—	—	—	—	—	1.50	—	Expense Ratio %
—	—	—	—	—	—	—	—	—	—	–0.92	—	Income Ratio %
—	—	—	—	—	—	—	—	—	—	—	—	Turnover Rate %
—	—	—	—	—	—	—	—	—	73.4	342.6	245.5	Net Assets $mil

Performance 12-31-01

	1st Qtr	2nd Qtr	3rd Qtr	4th Qtr	Total
1997	—	—	—	—	—
1998	—	—	—	—	—
1999	—	—	—	—	18.40 *
2000	25.17	–9.85	–0.90	–11.78	–1.35
2001	–17.98	7.93	–15.28	6.39	–20.21

Trailing	Total Return%	+/– S&P 500	+/– Russ Midcap Grth	% Rank All	% Rank Cat	Growth of $10,000
3 Mo	6.39	–4.29	–20.67	59	99	10,639
6 Mo	–9.86	–4.31	–1.61	85	49	9,014
1 Yr	–20.21	–8.33	–0.05	81	45	7,979
3 Yr Avg	—	—	—	—	—	—
5 Yr Avg	—	—	—	—	—	—
10 Yr Avg	—	—	—	—	—	—
15 Yr Avg	—	—	—	—	—	—

Tax Analysis	Tax-Adj Ret%	%Rank Cat	%Pretax Ret	%Rank Cat
3 Yr Avg	—	—	—	—
5 Yr Avg	—	—	—	—
10 Yr Avg	—	—	—	—

Potential Capital Gain Exposure: –44% of assets

Risk Analysis

Time Period	Load-Adj Return %	Risk %Rank[1] All	Risk %Rank[1] Cat	Morningstar Return	Morningstar Risk	Morningstar Risk-Adj Rating
1 Yr	–21.80					
3 Yr	—	—	—	—	—	
5 Yr	—	—	—	—	—	
Incept	–4.25	—	—	—	—	

Average Historical Rating —

[1]1=low, 100=high

Category Rating (3 Yr)

Return
Risk

Other Measures	Standard Index S&P 500	Best Fit Index
Alpha	—	—
Beta	—	—
R–Squared	—	—
Standard Deviation		—
Mean		—
Sharpe Ratio		—

Portfolio Analysis 09-30-01

Share change since 06–01 Total Stocks: 165	Sector	PE	YTD Ret%	% Assets
⊕ Tenet Healthcare	Health	30.1	32.14	1.70
☆ Alliant Techsystems	Industrials	28.6	73.48	1.39
☆ Lockheed Martin	Industrials	36.8	38.98	1.25
First Health Grp	Health	25.8	6.26	1.19
☆ Philip Morris	Staples	12.1	9.12	1.18
☆ Pediatrix Medical Grp	Health	28.0	40.96	1.16
⊕ Intl Flavors & Fragrances	Staples	32.3	49.78	1.13
St. Jude Medical	Health	42.0	26.39	1.11
☆ WellPoint Health Networks	Health	19.4	1.39	1.11
⊕ Elcor	Industrials	55.6	66.46	0.99
☆ AmerisourceBergen	N/A	—	—	0.96
☆ InterActive	Services	—	—	0.96
☆ Homestake Mng	Industrials	—	89.70	0.95
☆ Anheuser–Busch	Staples	24.6	1.01	0.94
Pitney Bowes	Industrials	17.2	19.80	0.93
⊕ Mylan Labs	Health	24.7	49.68	0.93
☆ Baxter Intl	Health	33.9	22.84	0.90
☆ Ultramar Diamond Shamrock	Energy	5.7	62.73	0.88
☆ Frontier Oil	Energy	3.8	144.40	0.87
⊕ Dial	Staples	—	57.57	0.84
⊖ Hibernia	Financials	16.3	44.26	0.83
⊕ Becton Dickinson	Health	22.9	–3.20	0.83
Healthsouth	Health	28.0	–9.15	0.83
☆ Barr Labs	Health	25.0	8.80	0.80
☆ Hershey Foods	Staples	25.4	7.12	0.80

Current Investment Style

Style: Value Blnd Growth; Size: Large Med Small

	Stock Port Avg	Relative S&P 500 Current	Relative S&P 500 Hist	Rel Cat
Price/Earnings Ratio	26.9	0.87	—	0.78
Price/Book Ratio	4.8	0.83	—	0.84
Price/Cash Flow	16.7	0.93	—	0.72
3 Yr Earnings Growth	11.9	0.81	—	0.51
1 Yr Earnings Est%	22.7	—	—	2.43
Med Mkt Cap $mil	2,684	0.0	—	0.48

Special Securities % assets 09-30-01	
Restricted/Illiquid Secs	0
Emerging–Markets Secs	0
Options/Futures/Warrants	No

Composition % assets 09-30-01	
Cash	13.4
Stocks*	86.6
Bonds	0.0
Other	0.0
*Foreign (% stocks)	0.0

Market Cap	
Giant	5.0
Large	20.3
Medium	44.6
Small	28.6
Micro	1.5

Sector Weightings	% of Stocks	Rel S&P	5-Year High	5-Year Low
Utilities	1.1	0.3	—	—
Energy	3.5	0.5	—	—
Financials	24.8	1.4	—	—
Industrials	11.7	1.0	—	—
Durables	1.8	1.1	—	—
Staples	12.9	1.6	—	—
Services	6.2	0.6	—	—
Retail	3.5	0.5	—	—
Health	30.3	2.0	—	—
Technology	4.2	0.2	—	—

Analysis by Bradley Sweeney 08-24-01

The jury is still out.

In an extremely trying year for growth-oriented investors, American Century Veedot is faring better than most. Although managers Jim Stowers III and John Small focus on firms with increasing earnings- and/or revenue-growth rates, they don't rely exclusively on the historical information that is contained in financial statements. But instead of conducting forward-looking analysis, as the firm's other growth-oriented managers do, Stowers and Small study trading patterns, looking for indications that a stock that is declining in value will continue to do so, or that an appreciating issue will continue to follow an upward trajectory.

That focus on trading patterns, which is also called technical analysis, has served the fund extremely well in 2001. After scoring some big gains with some of its energy-related picks last year, management's technical analysis threw up some red flags early this year, as many of those same names began to falter. Management aggressively sold most of its energy holdings, reducing what had been a more than 20% stake in the sector at the end of March 2001 to less than 1% of the fund's assets at the year's midpoint. That move has proven to be a huge boon to performance as most energy stocks have continued to decline in the face of falling energy prices. But the fund has also benefited from its flexibility to roam up and down the market-cap ladder. Strong performances from a diverse set of names, from the giant Microsoft to the tiny Action Performance Companies, haven't prevented the portfolio from posting a loss, but they kept the fund ahead of 55% of its mid-cap growth rivals in 2001.

Of course that sort of flexibility carries a great deal of potential risk, as a sector or market–cap bet might backfire. The fund has put up decent numbers so far, but we'd like to see more before recommending it.

Address:	4500 Main Street P.O. Box 419200 Kansas City, MO 64141–6200 800–345–2021
Web Address:	www.americancentury.com
*Inception:	11-30-99
Advisor:	American Century Inv. Mgmt
Subadvisor:	None
NTF Plans:	N/A

Minimum Purchase:	$10000	Add: $50	IRA: $10000
Min Auto Inv Plan:	$10000	Add: $50	
Sales Fees:	No–load, 2.00%R within 60 months		
Management Fee:	1.5% mx./1.4% mn.		
Actual Fees:	Mgt: 1.50%	Dist: —	
Expense Projections:	3Yr: $693	5Yr: —	10Yr: —
Avg Brok Commission:	—	Income Distrib: Annually	
Total Cost (relative to category):	—		

American Funds Amcap A

Ticker	Load	NAV	Yield	Total Assets	Mstar Category
AMCPX	5.75%	$16.12	0.5%	$7,706.0 mil	Large Growth

Prospectus Objective: Growth

American Funds Amcap Fund seeks long-term growth of capital. Current income is incidental.

The fund invests primarily in common stocks of issuers located in the U.S., though it may also purchase convertible securities and high-quality fixed-income obligations. It does not maintain strict percentages of any particular type of investment. The fund seeks issues that display fundamental value characteristics.

Class A shares have front loads: B shares have deferred loads, higher 12b-1 fees, and conversion features.

Historical Profile

Return	Above Avg
Risk	Average
Rating	★★★★ Above Avg

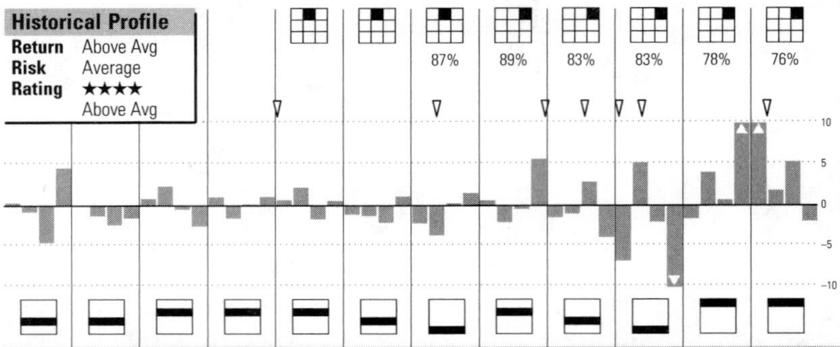

Investment Style
Equity
Average Stock %: 87% 89% 83% 83% 78% 76%

▼ Manager Change
▽ Partial Manager Change

Fund Performance vs. Category Average
▮ Quarterly Fund Return +/– Category Average
— Category Baseline

Performance Quartile (within Category)

Portfolio Manager(s)

R. Michael Shanahan. Since 1-86.
Timothy D. Armour. Since 5-96.
Claudia P. Huntington. Since 5-96.
C. Ross Sappenfield. Since 1-99.

1990	1991	1992	1993	1994	1995	1996	1997	1998	1999	2000	12-01	History
9.97	12.96	13.40	12.83	11.71	13.67	14.16	15.65	17.71	18.78	17.78	16.12	NAV
–3.98	36.88	7.19	11.01	–0.24	28.71	14.16	30.55	30.02	21.78	7.50	–5.01	Total Return %
–0.87	6.39	–0.43	0.95	–1.55	–8.83	–8.78	–2.80	1.44	0.74	16.60	6.86	+/– S&P 500
–5.35	–2.53	3.30	11.08	–5.09	–9.95	–11.36	–3.19	–15.08	–7.90	32.02	15.49	+/– Russ Top 200 Grt
2.24	1.53	1.17	0.93	1.05	1.47	0.90	0.73	0.85	0.58	0.59	0.49	Income Return %
–6.23	35.35	6.02	10.08	–1.29	27.24	13.26	29.82	29.17	21.19	6.91	–5.51	Capital Return %
62	62	42	45	29	70	81	26	57	86	2	3	Total Rtn % Rank Cat
0.25	0.15	0.15	0.12	0.13	0.17	0.12	0.10	0.13	0.10	0.11	0.09	Income $
0.71	0.46	0.32	1.82	0.95	1.19	1.31	2.47	2.29	2.48	2.26	0.71	Capital Gains $
0.72	0.79	0.75	0.73	0.72	0.71	0.71	0.69	0.68	0.67	0.68	0.67	Expense Ratio %
2.33	2.08	1.37	1.02	0.89	1.16	1.16	0.81	0.62	0.70	0.72	1.18	Income Ratio %
18	16	8	15	22	18	35	24	31	36	34	39	Turnover Rate %
1,897.3	2,734.2	2,939.9	3,078.8	2,877.2	3,532.7	3,784.1	4,536.6	5,830.0	7,188.0	7,654.9	7,436.7	Net Assets $mil

Performance 12-31-01

	1st Qtr	2nd Qtr	3rd Qtr	4th Qtr	Total
1997	–1.41	14.73	10.74	4.23	30.55
1998	12.91	3.29	–8.62	22.00	30.02
1999	0.96	10.27	–5.25	15.45	21.78
2000	7.35	–1.24	0.85	0.54	7.50
2001	–8.38	8.37	–15.40	13.08	–5.01

Trailing	Total Return%	+/– S&P 500	+/– Russ Top 200 Grth	% Rank All	% Rank Cat	Growth of $10,000
3 Mo	13.08	2.39	0.22	29	57	11,308
6 Mo	–4.33	1.22	2.65	58	15	9,567
1 Yr	–5.01	6.86	15.49	51	3	9,499
3 Yr Avg	7.53	8.56	15.56	16	3	12,434
5 Yr Avg	16.11	5.41	7.52	3	3	21,106
10 Yr Avg	13.92	0.99	2.84	9	8	36,812
15 Yr Avg	14.35	0.61	0.98	9	16	74,694

Tax Analysis	Tax-Adj Ret%	%Rank Cat	%Pretax Ret	%Rank Cat
3 Yr Avg	5.27	4	69.9	54
5 Yr Avg	13.23	7	82.1	41
10 Yr Avg	11.00	10	79.0	44

Potential Capital Gain Exposure: 20% of assets

Risk Analysis

Time Period	Load-Adj Return %	Risk %Rank[1] All	Risk %Rank[1] Cat	Morningstar Return	Morningstar Risk	Morningstar Risk-Adj Rating
1 Yr	–10.47					
3 Yr	5.43	48	1	0.10[2]	0.67	★★★★
5 Yr	14.75	50	1	2.56[2]	0.69	★★★★★
10 Yr	13.25	62	2	1.37	0.80	★★★★

Average Historical Rating (193 months): 3.3★s

[1]1=low, 100=high [2] T-Bill return substituted for category avg.

Category Rating (3 Yr)

1 2 3 4 5 (Worst … Best)

Return	High
Risk	Low

Other Measures	Standard Index S&P 500	Best Fit Index S&P 500
Alpha	7.5	7.5
Beta	0.83	0.83
R-Squared	84	84

Standard Deviation	16.40
Mean	7.53
Sharpe Ratio	0.18

Portfolio Analysis 09-30-01

Share change since 06-01 Total Stocks: 107	Sector	PE	YTD Ret%	% Assets
FNMA N/A	N/A	—	—	6.06
Medtronic	Health	76.4	–14.70	2.50
Fannie Mae	Financials	16.2	–6.95	2.45
⊖ USA Educ	Financials	68.9	24.74	2.39
Viacom Cl B	Services	—	—	2.24
AOL Time Warner	Technology	—	–7.76	2.05
Philip Morris	Staples	12.1	9.12	1.80
⊖ Concord EFS	Financials	86.3	49.21	1.79
⊕ Western Wireless Cl A	Services	—	–27.90	1.64
Robert Half Intl	Services	31.1	0.75	1.49
⊖ AutoZone	Retail	39.0	151.90	1.47
⊕ Lowe's	Retail	38.7	109.00	1.40
⊖ Centurytel	Services	13.3	–7.66	1.37
⊕ Interpublic Grp	Services	—	–29.80	1.29
American Intl Grp	Financials	42.0	–19.20	1.28
Kohl's	Retail	54.2	15.48	1.25
Microsoft	Technology	57.6	52.78	1.17
Texas Instruments	Technology	87.5	–40.70	1.14
Wells Fargo	Financials	22.4	–20.20	1.13
Avon Products	Staples	21.6	–1.21	1.08
M & T Bk	Financials	20.8	8.63	1.06
Dollar General	Retail	19.4	–20.40	1.04
⊕ Clear Channel Comms	Services	—	5.10	1.00
FHLMC N/A	N/A	—	—	0.94
Cisco Sys	Technology	—	–52.60	0.93

Current Investment Style

Style: Value Blnd Growth; Size: Large Med Small

	Stock Port Avg	Relative S&P 500 Current	Relative S&P 500 Hist	Rel Cat
Price/Earnings Ratio	35.3	1.14	1.10	0.99
Price/Book Ratio	5.6	0.99	0.98	0.88
Price/Cash Flow	21.4	1.19	1.16	0.94
3 Yr Earnings Growth	17.4	1.19	1.20	0.81
1 Yr Earnings Est%	–5.5	3.11	—	–1.83
Med Mkt Cap $mil	14,217	0.2	0.3	0.30

[1]figure is based on 50% or less of stocks

Analysis by William Harding 10-24-01

This is a good fund, but it isn't as good as its sibling.

Amcap Fund's cautious tendencies have been a virtue amid the market's severe retreat. Although the fund has still lost 12% for the year to date through October 23, 2001, that showing compares quite favorably with its peers. Indeed, the average large-growth offering has shed 29% of its value so far this year. The fund's hefty cash stake—25% of assets as of September 30, 2001—is fairly typical here, and has helped offset its stock losses.

In addition to leaving a lot of cash in the coffers, management further dampens volatility by keeping its stock selection fairly tame by growth standards. The team invests in some up-and-comers, such as PMC Sierra, but financially strong, stable firms dominate the portfolio. In fact, a look at the fund's top-25 holdings reveals many names that aren't all that common in growth funds, including Philip Morris and Fannie Mae. Further, the fund has generally avoided many speculative tech and telecom names that have been the hardest hit during the market's correction.

The fund's conservative approach to growth investing, however, can lead to middling results in markets that favor go-go growth stocks. For instance, the fund's 21.8% gain in 1999 lagged 85% of its peers'. Thus, investors in search of outsized gains won't be happy here. Still, the fund's long-term record is appealing. Its trailing five- and 10-year returns land in the category's top decile.

But one offering that tops that record—and limits this fund's appeal—is sibling Growth Fund of America. Though both funds hold cash, that offering is not quite as defensive as this one, leading to better performance in bull markets. That fund also boasts a deeper and somewhat more-seasoned management team.

Despite its standout sibling, this is a decent choice for investors who value security in the growth portion of their portfolio.

Special Securities % assets 09-30-01	
Restricted/Illiquid Secs	0
Emerging-Markets Secs	0
Options/Futures/Warrants	No

Composition % assets 09-30-01	
Cash	15.2
Stocks*	73.5
Bonds	11.3
Other	0.0
*Foreign (% stocks)	0.0

Market Cap	
Giant	27.8
Large	34.3
Medium	31.5
Small	6.4
Micro	0.0

Sector Weightings	% of Stocks	Rel S&P	5-Year High	5-Year Low
Utilities	0.0	0.0	1	0
Energy	0.9	0.1	1	0
Financials	19.4	1.1	21	13
Industrials	4.4	0.4	12	2
Durables	1.0	0.6	3	0
Staples	4.5	0.6	11	4
Services	25.2	2.3	36	21
Retail	10.6	1.6	11	1
Health	10.0	0.7	16	5
Technology	24.1	1.3	31	16

Address:	333 S. Hope Street Los Angeles, CA 90071 800–421–4120 / 213–486–9200
Web Address:	www.americanfunds.com
Inception:	05-01-67
Advisor:	Cap. Research & Mgmt.
Subadvisor:	None
NTF Plans:	N/A

Minimum Purchase:	$250	Add: $50	IRA: $250
Min Auto Inv Plan:	$250	Add: $50	
Sales Fees:	5.75%L, 0.25%B		
Management Fee:	.49% mx./.31% mn.		
Actual Fees:	Mgt: 0.37%	Dist: 0.23%	
Expense Projections:	3Yr: $780	5Yr: $932	10Yr: $1373
Avg Brok Commission:	—	Income Distrib: Semi–Ann.	
Total Cost (relative to category):		Below Avg	

American Funds American Balanced A

Ticker	Load	NAV	Yield	Total Assets	Mstar Category
ABALX	5.75%	$15.85	3.47%	$9,459.9 mil	Domestic Hybrid

Prospectus Objective: Balanced

American Funds American Balanced Fund seeks capital preservation, current income, and long-term growth of capital and income.

The fund normally invests in a broad range of equities, debt, and cash instruments. It typically maintains at least 50% of assets in equities and at least 25% in bonds. Fixed-income securities must be rated investment-grade at the time of purchase. The fund may invest up to 10% of assets in foreign securities. Management primarily seeks securities that it believes are undervalued and provide long-term opportunities.

Historical Profile

Return —
Risk —
Rating
Not Rated

Investment Style
Equity
Average Stock %

55% 52% 53% 54% 54% 56% 58%

▼ Manager Change
▽ Partial Manager Change

Fund Performance vs. Category Average
Quarterly Fund Return +/– Category Average
— Category Baseline

Performance Quartile (within Category)

Portfolio Manager(s)

Abner D. Goldstine. Since 9-75.
Robert G. O'Donnell. Since 4-86.
J. Dale Harvey. Since 9-96.
John H. Smet. Since 3-97.
Hilda L. Applbaum, CFA. Since 3-00.

1990	1991	1992	1993	1994	1995	1996	1997	1998	1999	2000	12-01	History
10.32	12.05	12.28	12.57	12.00	14.15	14.55	15.68	15.76	14.42	15.47	15.85	NAV
–1.57	24.69	9.48	11.27	0.34	27.13	13.17	21.04	11.13	3.47	15.86	8.19	Total Return %
1.55	–5.79	1.86	1.22	–0.98	–10.41	–9.78	–12.32	–17.44	–17.57	24.96	20.06	+/- S&P 500
–10.53	8.69	2.08	1.52	3.25	8.66	9.55	11.35	2.46	4.30	4.22	–0.24	+/- LB Aggregate
5.68	6.14	5.10	4.97	4.54	4.74	4.03	3.93	3.63	3.63	3.94	3.68	Income Return %
–7.24	18.55	4.38	6.30	–4.20	22.38	9.13	17.10	7.50	–0.17	11.91	4.51	Capital Return %
66	39	33	56	17	32	51	29	60	77	6	4	Total Rtn % Rank Cat
0.63	0.62	0.60	0.60	0.56	0.56	0.56	0.56	0.56	0.56	0.56	0.56	Income $
0.27	0.13	0.27	0.46	0.05	0.47	0.85	1.30	1.05	1.30	0.58	0.30	Capital Gains $
0.84	0.82	0.74	0.71	0.68	0.67	0.67	0.65	0.63	0.66	0.69	—	Expense Ratio %
5.95	5.56	5.19	4.74	4.76	4.38	4.01	3.74	3.57	3.59	3.93	—	Income Ratio %
26	25	17	28	32	39	44	44	54	48	51	—	Turnover Rate %
370.4	642.0	1,066.5	1,709.5	2,081.9	3,047.5	3,941.3	5,035.8	5,881.4	5,981.0	6,042.1	8,511.9	Net Assets $mil

Performance

	1st Qtr	2nd Qtr	3rd Qtr	4th Qtr	Total
1997	2.49	10.01	5.86	1.40	21.04
1998	6.63	–0.43	–3.63	8.62	11.13
1999	1.20	7.63	–5.19	0.20	3.47
2000	0.69	2.30	3.36	8.81	15.86
2001	1.23	4.77	–4.65	6.99	8.19

Trailing	Total Return%	+/– S&P 500	+/–LB Agg	% Rank All	% Rank Cat	Growth of $10,000
3 Mo	6.99	–3.70	6.95	56	35	10,699
6 Mo	2.01	7.57	–2.64	22	7	10,201
1 Yr	8.19	20.06	–0.24	9	4	10,819
3 Yr Avg	9.05	10.08	2.78	13	4	12,968
5 Yr Avg	11.77	1.07	4.34	11	6	17,444
10 Yr Avg	11.86	–1.07	4.63	19	8	30,675
15 Yr Avg	11.86	–1.87	3.74	27	7	53,721

Tax Analysis	Tax-Adj Ret%	%Rank Cat	%Pretax Ret	%Rank Cat
3 Yr Avg	6.50	3	71.8	15
5 Yr Avg	8.91	8	75.7	24
10 Yr Avg	9.02	11	76.0	26

Potential Capital Gain Exposure: 8% of assets

Risk Analysis

Time Period	Load-Adj Return %	Risk %Rank[1] All	Risk %Rank[1] Cat	Morningstar Return	Morningstar Risk	Morningstar Risk-Adj Rating
1 Yr	1.97					
3 Yr	6.92	32	11	0.43[2]	0.34	★★★★
5 Yr	10.45	38	13	1.31[2]	0.38	★★★★
10 Yr	11.20	44	9	0.95	0.41	★★★★

Average Historical Rating (193 months): 3.5★s

[1]1=low, 100=high [2] T-Bill return substituted for category avg.

Category Rating (3 Yr)

1 2 3 4 5
Worst Best

Return High
Risk Below Avg

Other Measures	Standard Index S&P 500	Best Fit Index S&P500
Alpha	6.0	6.0
Beta	0.35	0.35
R-Squared	41	41

Standard Deviation	9.89
Mean	9.05
Sharpe Ratio	0.48

Analysis by William Harding 09-14-01

American Balanced Fund is a solid option for conservative investors.

After returning a splendid 15% in 2000's rough market—thereby beating the vast majority of its domestic-hybrid peers during the year—this fund is again leading the pack. Although its 4% gain for the year to date through mid-September may look modest, it's better than 95% of its competitors'. More important, the fund's long-term record is topnotch as well. It ranks in the category's top 10% for the trailing three- and five-year periods.

Management's disciplined, slightly contrarian approach has been key to the fund's success. It keeps its bond exposure at a fairly conservative level, and is broadly diversified across industries and individual names. In addition, management steers clear of stocks with lofty price tags, instead buying stocks when they are out of favor. For example, picks JC Penney and IKON Office Solutions have rebounded hugely this year, gaining more than 100% and 240%, respectively, in 2001.

Management's willingness to go against the grain is a hallmark here. Recently, the fund has picked up shares in some beaten-down tech names such as Motorola. Although this line of attack may cause the fund to lag at times—such as in 1999's growth-at-any-price market—it has paid off more often than not.

More aggressive investors will want to look elsewhere, but those who are transitioning into or are in retirement should find its sensible, even-keeled approach to their liking.

Portfolio Analysis

Total Stocks: Share change since	Sector	PE Ratio	YTD Return %	% Net Assets
⊕ AT & T	Services	7.8	40.59	1.85
⊖ Bristol-Myers Squibb	Health	20.2	–26.00	1.79
⊕ Allstate	Financials	17.1	–21.00	1.66
Texaco	Energy	—	6.76	1.47
⊕ Philip Morris	Staples	12.1	9.12	1.27
Genuine Parts	Durables	16.8	45.48	1.24
McDonald's	Services	19.2	–21.50	1.23
⊕ Heinz HJ	Staples	29.6	–9.86	1.12
⊕ Phillips Petro	Energy	7.1	8.56	1.10
⊕ Schering-Plough	Health	22.2	–35.90	1.04

Total Fixed-Income:	Date of Maturity	Amount $000	Value $000	% Net Assets
US Treasury Note 3.625%	01-15-08	100,000	114,057	1.62
FNMA N/A		84,700	84,359	1.20
FHLMC N/A		70,400	70,202	1.00
GNMA 7.5%	10-15-30	62,589	65,347	0.93
FNMA Debenture 5.25%	06-15-06	49,250	51,220	0.73
FHLMC 5.5%	07-15-06	44,250	46,504	0.66
US Treasury Note 3.375%	01-15-07	36,250	41,804	0.59
US Treasury Bond 8.875%	08-15-17	29,425	40,712	0.58
Federal Home Ln Bk 4.875%	04-16-04	38,750	40,009	0.57
US Treasury Note 5%	02-15-11	35,000	35,973	0.51

Equity Style
Style: Value
Size: Large-Cap

Fixed-Income Style
Duration: Intermediate
Quality: High

	Portfolio Avg	Rel S&P
Price/Earnings Ratio	24.9	0.80
Price/Book Ratio	3.8	0.67
Price/Cash Flow	13.7	0.76
3 Yr Earnings Growth	10.6	0.72
1 Yr Earnings Est%	–8.2	4.63
Debt % Total Cap	38.2	1.24
Med Mkt Cap $mil	18,204	0.30

Avg Eff Duration[1]	4.5 Yrs
Avg Eff Maturity	—
Avg Credit Quality	AA
Avg Wtd Coupon	6.36%

Special Securities % assets	
Restricted/Illiquid Secs	5
Emerging-Markets Secs	Trace
Options/Futures/Warrants	No

Composition % of assets	
Cash	6.1
Stocks*	57.4
Bonds	35.8
Other	0.7
*Foreign (% of stocks)	4.7

Market Cap	
Giant	29.3
Large	48.0
Medium	18.6
Small	4.1
Micro	0.0

Sector Weightings	% of Stocks	Rel S&P	5-Year High	5-Year Low
Utilities	4.7	1.5	16	3
Energy	7.5	1.1	16	7
Financials	17.9	1.0	25	14
Industrials	17.1	1.5	26	15
Durables	6.9	4.4	9	0
Staples	6.0	0.8	12	4
Services	15.6	1.4	20	7
Retail	5.5	0.8	9	2
Health	10.6	0.7	16	5
Technology	8.2	0.5	10	1

Address:	333 S. Hope Street Los Angeles, CA 90071 415-421-9360 / 800-421-4120
Web Address:	www.americanfunds.com
Inception:	01-01-33
Advisor:	Cap. Research & Mgmt.
Subadvisor:	None
NTF Plans:	N/A

Minimum Purchase:	$250	Add: $50	IRA: $250
Min Auto Inv Plan:	$50	Add: $50	
Sales Fees:	5.75%L, 0.25%B		
Management Fee:	.42% mx./.26% mn.		
Actual Fees:	Mgt: 0.29%	Dist: 0.25%	
Expense Projections:	3Yr: $783	5Yr: $937	10Yr: $1384
Avg Brok Commission:	—	Income Distrib: Quarterly	
Total Cost (relative to category):		Below Avg	

American Funds American Mutual A

Ticker	Load	NAV	Yield	Total Assets	Mstar Category
AMRMX	5.75%	$24.05	2.9%	$8,954.7 mil	Large Value

Prospectus Objective: Growth and Income

American Funds American Mutual Fund seeks a balance of three objectives: current income, capital growth, and conservation of principal.

The fund invests chiefly in equity securities, including common stocks and preferred stocks. It invests primarily in securities issued by companies domiciled in the United States and/or listed on the S&P 500. The fund may also invest in high-quality convertible and debt obligations. Its purchases are limited to a list of securities preapproved by the board of directors.

Historical Profile

Return Average
Risk Low
Rating ★★★★ Above Avg

Investment Style
Equity
Average Stock %: 99%, 78%, 80%, 72%, 70%, 73%, 77%

▼ Manager Change
▽ Partial Manager Change

Fund Performance vs. Category Average
■ Quarterly Fund Return +/– Category Average
— Category Baseline

Performance Quartile (within Category)

Portfolio Manager(s)

Jon B. Lovelace Jr.. Since 1-58.
Robert G. O'Donnell. Since 1-77.
R. Michael Shanahan. Since 1-86.
Alan N. Berro. Since 1-99.
J. Dale Harvey. Since 1-99.

History

1990	1991	1992	1993	1994	1995	1996	1997	1998	1999	2000	12-01	History
18.67	21.05	20.79	21.77	20.11	24.33	25.76	29.21	29.65	23.83	23.87	24.05	NAV
–1.62	21.72	7.83	14.28	0.33	31.38	16.22	26.39	14.76	–0.12	9.12	6.67	Total Return %
1.50	–8.76	0.22	4.23	–0.98	–6.15	–6.73	–6.96	–13.82	–21.16	18.23	18.55	+/– S&P 500
2.05	3.57	–1.23	–5.48	2.65	–8.65	–6.10	–9.10	–6.48	–11.07	6.81	15.46	+/– Russ Top 200 Val
4.99	4.79	4.25	4.10	3.92	4.24	3.50	3.14	2.77	2.52	3.14	3.05	Income Return %
–6.62	16.93	3.59	10.18	–3.58	27.15	12.72	23.25	12.00	–2.64	5.98	3.62	Capital Return %
19	85	66	45	40	64	86	57	41	79	39	4	Total Rtn % Rank Cat
0.99	0.88	0.88	0.84	0.84	0.84	0.84	0.80	0.80	0.74	0.74	0.72	Income $
0.20	0.66	0.97	1.11	0.87	1.15	1.61	2.48	2.93	5.05	1.26	0.65	Capital Gains $
0.60	0.63	0.60	0.59	0.60	0.59	0.59	0.58	0.56	0.57	0.59	0.59	Expense Ratio %
5.00	4.47	4.15	3.83	4.07	3.92	3.36	2.95	2.75	2.67	3.29	3.29	Income Ratio %
12	24	37	22	18	23	24	19	29	42	29	29	Turnover Rate %
3,426.4	4,328.9	4,709.6	5,194.3	5,278.6	6,945.8	7,981.7	9,738.6	10,629.5	9,652.0	8,515.4	8,836.3	Net Assets $mil

Performance 12-31-01

	1st Qtr	2nd Qtr	3rd Qtr	4th Qtr	Total
1997	1.90	11.87	6.72	3.90	26.39
1998	9.31	–0.98	–5.71	12.44	14.76
1999	–0.22	9.14	–7.60	–0.74	–0.12
2000	–1.94	–2.02	6.30	6.86	9.12
2001	–0.20	5.29	–5.30	7.20	6.67

Trailing	Total Return%	+/– S&P 500	+/– Russ Top 200 Val	% Rank All	% Rank Cat	Growth of $10,000
3 Mo	7.20	–3.48	1.69	55	74	10,720
6 Mo	1.52	7.07	7.30	29	4	10,152
1 Yr	6.67	18.55	15.46	16	4	10,667
3 Yr Avg	5.15	6.18	3.99	30	25	11,627
5 Yr Avg	11.02	0.32	–0.19	14	26	16,864
10 Yr Avg	12.28	–0.65	–1.75	17	47	31,839
15 Yr Avg	12.21	–1.52	–1.29	25	45	56,291

Tax Analysis	Tax-Adj Ret%	%Rank Cat	%Pretax Ret	%Rank Cat
3 Yr Avg	2.20	32	42.6	76
5 Yr Avg	7.93	33	72.0	59
10 Yr Avg	9.19	49	74.8	64

Potential Capital Gain Exposure: 15% of assets

Risk Analysis

Time Period	Load-Adj Return %	Risk %Rank[1] All	Risk %Rank[1] Cat	Morningstar Return	Morningstar Risk	Morningstar Risk-Adj Rating
1 Yr	0.54					
3 Yr	3.10	40	3	–0.38[2]	0.55	★★★
5 Yr	9.71	44	2	1.12[2]	0.55	★★★★
10 Yr	11.62	50	2	1.03	0.58	★★★★

Average Historical Rating (193 months): 3.7★s

[1] 1=low, 100=high [2] T-Bill return substituted for category avg.

Category Rating (3 Yr)

1 2 3 4 5
Worst Best

Return: Above Avg
Risk: Low

Other Measures	Standard Index S&P 500	Best Fit Index S&P 500
Alpha	2.8	2.8
Beta	0.43	0.43
R-Squared	36	36

Standard Deviation	12.62
Mean	5.15
Sharpe Ratio	0.02

Portfolio Analysis 09-30-01

Share change since 06-01 Total Stocks: 115	Sector	PE	YTD Ret%	% Assets
☼ Bank of America	Financials	16.7	42.73	2.87
⊕ Allstate	Financials	17.1	–21.00	1.71
Royal Dutch Petro NY ADR	Energy	12.0	–17.10	1.68
⊕ AT & T	N/A	—	—	1.66
Xcel Energy	Utilities	12.2	0.57	1.60
⊖ Texaco	Energy	—	6.76	1.45
⊖ Centurytel	Services	13.3	–7.66	1.43
⊕ Norfolk Southern	Services	27.0	39.54	1.38
⊖ Household Intl	Financials	14.7	6.89	1.38
US Treasury Note FRN	N/A	—	—	1.35
IBM	Technology	26.9	43.00	1.27
Bank One	Financials	29.1	9.13	1.25
⊖ Verizon Comms	Services	29.7	–2.52	1.21
⊕ J.P. Morgan Chase & Co.	Financials	27.8	–17.40	1.19
⊕ ALLTEL	Services	17.7	1.14	1.16
⊕ Honeywell Intl	Durables	NMF	–27.00	1.16
⊖ Bristol-Myers Squibb	Health	20.2	–26.00	1.16
⊖ Pitney Bowes	Industrials	17.2	19.80	1.06
Westvaco	Industrials	32.7	0.58	1.04
⊕ Comerica	Financials	14.2	–0.47	1.01
⊕ Heinz HJ	Staples	29.6	–9.86	1.00
⊕ Johnson & Johnson	Health	16.6	14.01	0.97
Duke Energy	Utilities	15.5	–6.04	0.94
⊕ May Dept Stores	Retail	15.2	15.97	0.91
⊖ Albertson's	Retail	29.7	22.01	0.91

Current Investment Style

Style: Value Blnd Growth
Size: Large Med Small

	Stock Port Avg	Relative S&P 500 Current	Relative S&P 500 Hist	Rel Cat
Price/Earnings Ratio	23.8	0.77	0.69	0.94
Price/Book Ratio	3.5	0.61	0.58	0.84
Price/Cash Flow	12.0	0.67	0.63	0.87
3 Yr Earnings Growth	8.4	0.57	0.49	0.57
1 Yr Earnings Est%	1.2	—	—	–0.36
Med Mkt Cap $mil	17,159	0.3	0.4	0.54

Analysis by William Harding 10-02-01

This isn't the best offering in American's stable of funds, but it's a decent pick for risk-averse investors.

American Mutual Fund's conservative nature has proven its worth during the market's recent slump. Its 0.49% loss for the year to date ended Sept. 28, 2001 is a significant feat considering that the S&P 500 has declined more than 20% this year. Further, this showing bests nearly all of its competitors in the large-value camp.

This fund is the tamest of all the dedicated equity offerings in American's lineup. It tends to maintain a large cash stake (currently about 20% of assets are on ice) and invests in stocks that pay rich dividends. This generally leads the fund to carry a small stake in technology stocks and to favor traditionally defensive areas of the market such as utilities and financial services.

The fund's mild approach has produced decent, if not spectacular, returns over time, with remarkably low volatility relative to other large-value funds. It has significantly trailed the broad market indexes when stocks rally big, such as in 1998 and 1999, but its long-term record should appeal to conservative investors.

Nonetheless, we think investors considering buying here should check out this fund's siblings first. American Funds offers one of the best lineups of core large-cap funds around. Offerings such as Fundamental Investors, Investment Company of America, and Washington Mutual have posted superior performance over time without taking on a heck of a lot more risk than this fund. And American Balanced Fund is a terrific domestic-hybrid option for conservative investors.

Special Securities % assets 09-30-01	
Restricted/Illiquid Secs	0
Emerging-Markets Secs	0
Options/Futures/Warrants	No

Composition % assets 09-30-01	
Cash	21.4
Stocks*	76.5
Bonds	2.1
Other	0.0
*Foreign (% stocks)	2.4

Market Cap	
Giant	24.7
Large	52.0
Medium	22.4
Small	0.8
Micro	0.0

Sector Weightings	% of Stocks	Rel S&P	5-Year High	5-Year Low
Utilities	10.8	3.4	19	2
Energy	9.2	1.3	12	5
Financials	23.4	1.3	28	10
Industrials	12.7	1.1	22	12
Durables	5.9	3.8	6	1
Staples	3.8	0.5	4	1
Services	14.0	1.3	28	14
Retail	6.5	1.0	7	1
Health	8.0	0.5	13	5
Technology	5.8	0.3	8	3

Address:	333 S. Hope Street Los Angeles, CA 90071 800-421-4120 / 213-486-9200
Web Address:	www.americanfunds.com
Inception:	02-21-50
Advisor:	Cap. Research & Mgmt.
Subadvisor:	None
NTF Plans:	N/A

Minimum Purchase:	$250	Add: $50	IRA: $25
Min Auto Inv Plan:	$50	Add: $50	
Sales Fees:	5.75%L, 0.25%B		
Management Fee:	.38% mx./.24% mn.		
Actual Fees:	Mgt: 0.28%	Dist: 0.21%	
Expense Projections:	3Yr: $753	5Yr: $885	10Yr: $1270
Avg Brok Commission:	—	Income Distrib: Quarterly	
Total Cost (relative to category):		Below Avg	

American Funds Capital Inc Builder A

Ticker	Load	NAV	Yield	Total Assets	Mstar Category
CAIBX	5.75%	$43.59	4.7%	$8,842.1 mil	International Hybrid

Prospectus Objective: Equity–Income

American Funds Capital Income Builder seeks current income and growth of income.

The fund normally invests at least 50% of assets in common stocks, and at least 90% in income-producing securities. It may also invest up to 40% of assets in foreign securities. Management selects securities that it believes are undervalued and represent solid long-term investment opportunities.

Class A shares have front loads; B shares have deferred loads, higher 12b-1 fees, and conversion features.

Historical Profile
Return Above Avg
Risk Low
Rating ★★★★★ Highest

Investment Style
Equity
Average Stock %: 60% 72% 64% 63% 62% 63% 63%

▼ Manager Change
▽ Partial Manager Change

Fund Performance vs. Category Average
■ Quarterly Fund Return +/– Category Average
— Category Baseline

Performance Quartile (within Category)

Portfolio Manager(s)

Jon B. Lovelace Jr.. Since 7-87.
James B. Lovelace, CFA. Since 1-88.
Janet A. McKinley. Since 7-87.
Steven T. Watson. Since 1-00.
Joyce E. Gordon. Since 1-99.

1990	1991	1992	1993	1994	1995	1996	1997	1998	1999	2000	12-01	History
25.31	30.00	31.31	34.30	31.72	37.23	41.03	46.90	47.47	42.67	44.82	43.59	NAV
3.89	25.70	10.00	15.29	−2.26	25.05	17.64	23.33	11.75	−2.76	12.52	4.74	Total Return %
20.91	7.41	15.23	−7.22	−7.33	4.33	4.16	7.57	−12.58	−27.70	25.70	—	+/– MSCI World
−7.86	10.25	5.45	3.02	−3.54	5.74	13.20	21.97	−3.56	2.32	10.18	5.54	+/– JPM World Govt
5.36	5.76	5.13	5.17	4.97	5.63	5.01	4.68	4.22	4.18	4.80	4.73	Income Return %
−1.46	19.94	4.87	10.12	−7.22	19.43	12.63	18.65	7.53	−6.95	7.72	0.01	Capital Return %
1	33	33	62	30	12	15	1	45	98	1	6	Total Rtn % Rank Cat
1.35	1.43	1.51	1.59	1.67	1.75	1.83	1.89	1.95	1.96	2.01	2.09	Income $
0.00	0.23	0.11	0.12	0.10	0.50	0.73	1.61	2.81	1.54	0.94	1.17	Capital Gains $
1.01	0.98	0.81	0.72	0.73	0.72	0.71	0.65	0.64	0.64	0.67	—	Expense Ratio %
5.70	5.09	4.71	4.69	5.29	4.96	5.19	4.04	4.35	4.15	4.67	—	Income Ratio %
25	14	17	11	36	18	28	28	24	21	41	—	Turnover Rate %
236.4	656.8	1,452.8	3,040.2	3,596.5	4,809.0	5,809.2	7,803.4	9,238.7	8,392.0	7,707.6	8234.4	Net Assets $mil

Performance 12-31-01

	1st Qtr	2nd Qtr	3rd Qtr	4th Qtr	Total
1997	1.25	8.85	7.51	4.08	23.33
1998	7.72	−0.11	−4.07	8.27	11.75
1999	−1.55	3.40	−5.39	0.97	−2.76
2000	−0.53	1.20	5.81	5.64	12.52
2001	−0.64	4.41	−2.66	3.73	4.74

Trailing	Total Return%	+/– MSCI World	+/– JPM World Govt	% Rank All	% Rank Cat	Growth of $10,000
3 Mo	3.73	1,002.73	6.92	68	79	10,373
6 Mo	0.97	999.97	−2.76	34	11	10,097
1 Yr	4.74	1,003.74	5.54	25	6	10,474
3 Yr Avg	4.65	1,003.65	5.87	34	20	11,460
5 Yr Avg	9.57	1,008.57	7.16	21	7	15,794
10 Yr Avg	11.16	1,010.16	5.90	24	16	28,800
15 Yr Avg	—	—	—	—	—	—

Tax Analysis	Tax-Adj Ret%	%Rank Cat	%Pretax Ret	%Rank Cat
3 Yr Avg	2.22	20	47.8	62
5 Yr Avg	6.96	5	72.7	7
10 Yr Avg	8.68	1	77.8	1

Potential Capital Gain Exposure: 17% of assets

Risk Analysis

Time Period	Load-Adj Return %	Risk %Rank[1] All	Risk %Rank[1] Cat	Morningstar Return	Morningstar Risk	Morningstar Risk-Adj Rating
1 Yr	−1.28					
3 Yr	2.60	33	7	−0.49[2]	0.33	★★★★
5 Yr	8.28	39	3	0.76[2]	0.33	★★★★★
10 Yr	10.50	45	40	1.92[2]	0.35	★★★★★

Average Historical Rating (138 months): 3.7★s

[1] 1=low, 100=high [2] T-Bill return substituted for category avg.

Category Rating (3 Yr)

1 2 3 4 5
Worst Best

Return Above Avg
Risk Low

Other Measures	Standard Index S&P 500	Best Fit Index SPMid400
Alpha	1.0	−1.6
Beta	0.23	0.25
R–Squared	26	38

Standard Deviation	8.04
Mean	4.65
Sharpe Ratio	−0.04

Portfolio Analysis 09-30-01

Total Stocks: 114 Share change since 06–01	Sector	PE Ratio	YTD Return %	% Net Assets
⊕ Philip Morris	Staples	12.1	9.12	2.13
⊕ Nisource	Utilities	33.4	−21.60	1.64
Bank of America	Financials	—	—	1.51
Archstone Communities Tr	N/A	—	—	1.48
Bank of Nova Scotia	Financials	11.9	—	1.48
⊕ Wachovia	Financials	—	23.13	1.47
Powergen	Utilities	17.1	—	1.40
XL Cap Cl A	Financials	22.8	5.82	1.40
Pinnacle West Cap	Utilities	12.5	−9.06	1.39
Royal Bk Canada	Financials	19.5	0.51	1.32

Total Fixed-Income: 139	Date of Maturity	Amount $000	Value $000	% Net Assets
FHLMC N/A		184,444	183,918	2.19
FNMA N/A		178,759	178,099	2.12
US Treasury Bond 10.75%	05-15-03	150,000	168,962	2.01
US Treasury Bond 11.875%	11-15-03	110,000	130,006	1.55
US Treasury Bond 8.75%	11-15-08	100,000	111,469	1.32
US Treasury Bond 11.125%	08-15-03	90,000	103,415	1.23
US Treasury Bond 8.375%	08-15-08	43,000	47,125	0.56
FNMA 6%	10-01-16	40,000	40,650	0.48
WCG 144A 8.25%	03-15-04	38,000	39,029	0.46
Fed Nat Mtg Disc N/A		36,000	35,878	0.43

Equity Style
Style: Blend
Size: Large–Cap

Fixed-Income Style
Duration: —
Quality: —
NA

	Portfolio Avg	Rel S&P
Price/Earnings Ratio	19.3	0.74
Price/Cash Flow	10.3	0.80
Price/Book Ratio	3.0	0.86
3 Yr Earnings Growth	6.6	0.35
Med Mkt Cap $mil	9,692	0.35
Med Mkt Cap $mil	8,145	0.10

Avg Eff Duration	—
Avg Eff Maturity	—
Avg Credit Quality	—
Avg Wtd Coupon	6.35%

Analysis by Emily Hall 09-21-01

In all sorts of weather, American Funds Capital Income Builder Fund just keeps on truckin'.

Like nearly every one of its peers, this offering has lost money in the vicious mid-September market downturn. But the fund has lost less than its typical international-hybrid peer. And its long-term record is consistently strong.

To be sure, the fund is never going to win any prizes for most exciting or most popular. Its strategy is downright boring. Given the fund's emphasis on income, management loads up on lots of North American and European stocks that pay hefty dividends. Not surprisingly, the equity portfolio is heavily tilted toward utilities, financials firms, and REITs. This focus on stodgy names tempers the fund's above-average stake in stocks relative to its international hybrid peers. Management also usually carries a sizable chunk of cash in the portfolio, which helps moderate the effects of market swings.

The stock market's ugly tumble during the past year is a reminder that boring can be attractive. The fund's 2.3% loss for the year to date through Sept. 20, 2001, is among the very best in the category. And over the long term, the fund has been equally solid: Its 10-year annualized return is 12%—a top-quintile showing—while its volatility over the same period has been right in line with the international-hybrid group.

Of course, the fund does look weak in go-go growth markets. Indeed, its performance in the heady days of 1999 was downright pitiful. But the fund's management team—which is made up of several American Funds' veterans—stayed its conservative course and is looking a lot wiser these days.

For those who don't like to stay up nights worrying about their funds, this offering remains a fine choice.

Special Securities % assets 09-30-01	
Restricted/Illiquid Secs	4
Emerging–Markets Secs	1
Options/Futures/Warrants	Yes

Country Exposure % of Assets

Composition % assets 09-30-01	
Cash	9.4
U.S. Stocks	43.1
Foreign Stocks	21.7
U.S. Bonds	24.9
Foreign Bonds	0.1
Other	0.8

Address:	333 S. Hope Street Los Angeles, CA 90071 800–421–4120 / 213–486–9200
Web Address:	www.americanfunds.com
Inception:	07-30-87
Advisor:	Cap. Research & Mgmt.
Subadvisor:	None
NTF Plans:	N/A

Minimum Purchase:	$250	Add: $50	IRA: $250
Min Auto Inv Plan:	$250	Add: $50	
Sales Fees:	5.75%L, 0.30%B		
Management Fee:	.24% mx./.15% mn.		
Actual Fees:	Mgt: 0.34%	Dist: 0.23%	
Expense Projections:	3Yr: $777	5Yr: $927	10Yr: $1362
Avg Brok Commission:	—	Income Distrib: Quarterly	
Total Cost (relative to category):		Below Avg	

American Funds Capital World Bond A

Ticker	Load	NAV	Yield	SEC Yield	Total Assets	Mstar Category
CWBFX	3.75%	$14.53	2.2%	4.52%	$402.8 mil	International Bond

Prospectus Objective: World Bond

American Funds Capital World Bond Fund seeks total return consistent with prudent investment management.

The fund normally invests at least 65% of assets in bonds denominated in various currencies, including U.S. dollars, or in multinational currency units. It typically maintains investments in at least three countries, primarily developed countries. Issuers located in any one country may not represent more than 40% of assets. The fund may use currency futures and options. It may also invest up to 25% of assets in lower quality, higher yielding debt securities. This fund is non-diversified.

Class A shares have front loads; B shares have deferred loads, higher 12b-1 fees, and conversion features.

Historical Profile

Return Below Avg
Risk Above Avg
Rating ★★ Below Avg

Investment Style
Fixed-Income

Income Rtn %Rank Cat: 20, 46, 70, 61, 51, 53, 75, 76

Growth of Principal vs. Interest Rate Shifts
- Principal Value $000 (NAV with capital gains reinvested)
- Interest Rate % on 10 Yr Treasury
- ▼ Manager Change
- ∇ Partial Manager Change
- ► Mgr Unknown After
- ◄ Mgr Unknown Before

Performance Quartile (within Category)

Portfolio Manager(s)

James R. Mulally. Since 8-87.
Mark H. Dalzell. Since 4-91.
Thomas H. Hogh. Since 2-96.
Robert H. Neithart. Since 1-99.
Susan M. Tolson. Since 1-99.

1990	1991	1992	1993	1994	1995	1996	1997	1998	1999	2000	12–01	History
14.81	15.89	14.94	16.33	15.12	17.09	16.95	15.75	16.18	14.96	14.63	14.53	NAV
11.65	15.28	0.82	16.73	–1.43	21.41	6.35	–0.36	10.09	–2.16	1.47	1.53	Total Return %
2.69	–0.72	–6.59	6.98	1.49	2.94	2.73	–10.05	1.41	–1.33	–10.17	–6.90	+/– LB Aggregate
–3.64	–0.94	–3.95	1.61	–7.42	1.86	2.27	3.90	–7.70	2.91	4.10	5.07	+/– SB World Govt
8.38	7.57	5.96	6.71	6.02	8.14	5.67	5.17	5.18	5.05	3.59	2.21	Income Return %
3.27	7.71	–5.14	10.02	–7.45	13.27	0.68	–5.54	4.91	–7.21	–2.13	–0.68	Capital Return %
83	16	75	31	20	17	68	75	47	43	59	50	Total Rtn % Rank Cat
1.18	1.10	0.93	0.98	0.96	1.20	0.95	0.86	0.80	0.80	0.53	0.32	Income $
0.00	0.00	0.16	0.08	0.00	0.00	0.23	0.28	0.32	0.07	0.00	0.00	Capital Gains $
1.52	1.42	1.38	1.19	1.11	1.12	1.09	1.07	1.06	1.08	1.12	—	Expense Ratio %
8.40	7.54	6.88	6.25	6.88	6.83	6.07	5.21	5.15	4.66	4.66	—	Income Ratio %
76	81	95	28	77	105	91	79	101	129	52	—	Turnover Rate %
50.7	94.0	255.0	525.5	563.2	698.4	815.3	710.0	625.7	515.0	416.8	392.1	Net Assets $mil

Performance 12-31-01

	1st Qtr	2nd Qtr	3rd Qtr	4th Qtr	Total
1997	–2.71	2.27	1.23	–1.07	–0.36
1998	1.39	1.72	4.30	2.34	10.09
1999	–2.17	–2.25	2.86	–0.54	–2.16
2000	–1.34	–0.20	–1.87	5.01	1.47
2001	–1.99	–0.15	3.32	0.41	1.53

Trailing	Total Return%	+/– LB Agg	+/– SB World	% Rank All	% Rank Cat	Growth of $10,000
3 Mo	0.41	0.37	4.38	76	25	10,041
6 Mo	3.74	–0.91	0.27	11	38	10,374
1 Yr	1.53	–6.90	5.07	40	50	10,153
3 Yr Avg	0.26	–6.01	4.01	72	52	10,078
5 Yr Avg	2.03	–5.40	1.92	88	53	11,055
10 Yr Avg	5.17	–2.06	0.36	90	31	16,557
15 Yr Avg	—	—	—	—	—	—

Tax Analysis	Tax-Adj Ret%	%Rank Cat	%Pretax Ret	%Rank Cat
3 Yr Avg	–1.25	48	—	—
5 Yr Avg	0.09	52	4.3	99
10 Yr Avg	2.85	27	55.2	33

Potential Capital Gain Exposure: 21% of assets

Risk Analysis

Time Period	Load-Adj Return %	Risk %Rank[1] All	Risk %Rank[1] Cat	Morningstar Return	Morningstar Risk	Morningstar Risk-Adj Rating
1 Yr	–2.28					
3 Yr	–1.01	33	46	–1.19[2]	1.52	★★
5 Yr	1.25	37	42	–0.77[2]	1.48	★★
10 Yr	4.77	43	43	0.01[2]	1.41	★

Average Historical Rating (137 months): 2.1★s

[1] 1=low, 100=high [2] T–Bill return substituted for category avg.

Category Rating (3 Yr)

1 2 3 4 5
Worst Best

Return Average
Risk Average

Other Measures	Standard Index LB Agg	Best Fit Index SB World
Alpha	–5.7	1.1
Beta	1.08	0.66
R–Squared	37	78
Standard Deviation		5.83
Mean		0.26
Sharpe Ratio		–0.93

Portfolio Analysis 09-30-01

Total Fixed-Income: 252	Date of Maturity	Value $000	% Net Assets
Hellenic Republic 8.8%	06-19-07	10,631	2.59
Ford Motor Credit 5.25%	06-16-08	9,431	2.29
Bayerische Vereinsbank 5.5%	01-15-08	8,750	2.13
Republic of Germany 6.5%	10-14-05	7,961	1.94
Govt of New Zealand 4.954%	02-15-16	7,114	1.73
Nykredit 6%	10-01-29	6,663	1.62
Republic of Germany 5.25%	01-04-08	6,403	1.56
Republic of Germany 8%	07-22-02	6,255	1.52
Hellenic Republic 8.6%	03-26-08	6,225	1.51
Bundesobl 12 5%	11-12-02	6,012	1.46
Republic of Germany 7.25%	10-21-02	5,528	1.34
Kingdom of Spain 3.1%	09-20-06	5,274	1.28
Govt of France N/A		5,108	1.24
Govt of Japan 0.9%	12-22-08	5,071	1.23
Republic of Germany 6.875%	05-12-05	4,983	1.21
Republic of Germany 6.25%	01-04-30	4,750	1.16
Treuhandan 7.5%	09-09-04	4,721	1.15
Treuhandan Gtd 7.125%	01-29-03	4,669	1.14
News Amer Hldgs 8.625%	02-07-14	4,572	1.11
KFW Intl Fin FRN	12-20-04	4,477	1.09

Current Investment Style

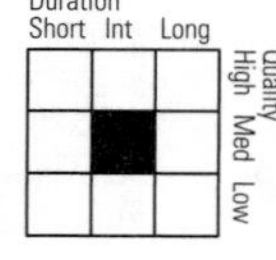

Avg Eff Duration[1]	4.5 Yrs
Avg Eff Maturity	—
Avg Credit Quality	A
Avg Wtd Coupon	6.71%
Avg Wtd Price	77.67% of par

[1] figure provided by fund

Special Securities 09-30-01	% assets
Restricted/Illiquid Secs	4
Exotic Mortgage–Backed	0
Emerging–Markets Secs	Trace
Options/Futures/Warrants	Yes

Country Exposure % assets

Not Available

Composition % assets 09-30-01			
Cash	5.9	Bonds	87.1
Stocks	0.0	Other	7.0

Analysis by Kunal Kapoor 08-08-01

Capital World Bond Fund doesn't get too cute.

In a category littered with failed offerings, this fund has managed to get the job done by walking the middle road. Unlike its more aggressive international-bond rivals, the fund doesn't make massive—or frequent—regional, currency, and sector bets. Instead, the fund tends to invest methodically in undervalued securities around the globe, often making opportunistic purchases in hard-hit markets.

And while the fund has recently increased its appetite for risk—it can now put as much as a fourth of its assets in junk bonds—it remains comparatively restrained. For example, the fund is a cautious player when it comes to emerging markets. In those regions, the fund tends to limit the size of exposure to individual markets, instead choosing to spread its bets.

This tendency to play it safe has generally kept the fund near the middle of the pack. For the year to date through August 10, 2001, for instance, the fund ranks exactly in the category's middle. And its returns over the three- and five-year periods also hug the category average. But the fund is less volatile than its peers, has lower expenses, and boasts experienced managers.

That experience was on display recently in Turkey. Prior to the lira's devaluation, the fund had no exposure to that country. Soon after, however, the managers bought heavily discounted Turkish T-bills with durations of less than a year. More-inexperienced managers may not have done that kind of bargain-hunting, especially because it came so soon after the devaluation. Moreover, the managers didn't get caught up in the telecom euphoria of early 2000, thus avoiding a brutal sell-off in the high-yield market during the summer and fall of that year.

All told, this fund gives investors an opportunity to gain access to an asset class without some of the heartache that comes with rival funds.

Address:	333 S. Hope Street Los Angeles, CA 90071 800–421–4120 / 213–486–9200
Web Address:	www.americanfunds.com
Inception:	08-04-87
Advisor:	Cap. Research & Mgmt.
Subadvisor:	None
NTF Plans:	N/A

Minimum Purchase:	$250	Add: $50	IRA: $250
Min Auto Inv Plan:	$50	Add: $50	
Sales Fees:	3.75%L, 0.30%B		
Management Fee:	.70% mx./.50% mn.		
Actual Fees:	Mgt: 0.65%	Dist: 0.23%	
Expense Projections:	3Yr: $718	5Yr: $969	10Yr: $1687
Avg Brok Commission:	—	Income Distrib: Quarterly	
Total Cost (relative to category):		Average	

American Funds Capital World Gr&Inc A

Ticker	Load	NAV	Yield	Total Assets	Mstar Category
CWGIX	5.75%	$24.50	2.0%	$10,569.7 mil	World Stock

Prospectus Objective: World Stock

American Funds Capital World Growth & Income Fund seeks long-term capital growth and current income.

The fund invests in foreign and domestic equities, debt obligations, and money-market instruments. Management allocates assets according to long-term economic and market trends. The fund invests principally in equity securities. The debt portion concentrates on intermediate- and long-term fixed-income securities; foreign debt consists mostly of governmental obligations. It cannot invest more than 40% of assets in any one country. The fund may invest up to 10% of assets in developing countries.

Class A share have front loads; B shares have deferred loads, higher 12b-1 fees, and conversion features.

Historical Profile
Return: High
Risk: Low
Rating: ★★★★★ Highest

Investment Style
Equity
Average Stock %: 78% 87% 83% 82% 87% 82% 81%

▼ Manager Change
▽ Partial Manager Change

Fund Performance vs. Category Average
■ Quarterly Fund Return +/– Category Average
— Category Baseline

Performance Quartile (within Category)

Portfolio Manager(s)

Stephen E. Bepler, CFA. Since 3-93.
Mark E. Denning. Since 3-93.
Gregg E. Ireland. Since 3-93.
Carl M. Kawaja. Since 2-98.
Steven T. Watson. Since 1-99.
Timothy P. Dunn. Since 1-98.

History

1990	1991	1992	1993	1994	1995	1996	1997	1998	1999	2000	12-01	History
—	—	—	18.07	17.47	20.26	22.97	24.51	25.42	29.83	26.47	24.50	NAV
—	—	—	22.22*	1.22	21.39	21.55	17.99	16.20	27.30	1.38	–4.96	Total Return %
—	—	—	15.60*	–0.09	–16.14	–1.40	–15.36	–12.37	6.26	10.48	6.92	+/– S&P 500
—	—	—	—	–3.85	0.67	8.07	2.23	–8.14	2.37	14.56	—	+/– MSCI World
—	—	—	2.39	2.91	3.59	3.50	2.83	2.31	2.00	1.78	1.91	Income Return %
—	—	—	19.83	–1.69	17.80	18.05	15.16	13.89	25.30	–0.40	–6.87	Capital Return %
—	—	—	—	38	29	14	25	45	64	18	9	Total Rtn % Rank Cat
—	—	—	0.32	0.52	0.62	0.70	0.64	0.56	0.51	0.53	0.50	Income $
—	—	—	0.00	0.29	0.27	0.85	1.87	2.37	1.81	3.20	0.16	Capital Gains $
—	—	—	—	0.87	0.88	0.85	0.82	0.78	0.79	0.79	—	Expense Ratio %
—	—	—	—	3.11	3.24	3.28	2.53	2.25	1.93	2.08	—	Income Ratio %
—	—	—	—	19	26	30	32	39	34	41	—	Turnover Rate %
—	—	—	1,761.6	2,827.1	3,723.4	5,213.0	7,358.8	8,696.9	10,964.0	11,122.2	10,345.8	Net Assets $mil

Performance 12-31-01

	1st Qtr	2nd Qtr	3rd Qtr	4th Qtr	Total
1997	2.64	11.44	5.87	–2.56	17.99
1998	12.98	–1.03	–9.65	15.02	16.20
1999	2.52	7.35	–0.65	16.43	27.30
2000	4.32	–1.09	–2.09	0.35	1.38
2001	–3.73	3.88	–11.20	7.02	–4.96

Trailing	Total Return%	+/– S&P 500	+/– MSCI World	% Rank All	% Rank Cat	Growth of $10,000
3 Mo	7.02	–3.66	—	56	86	10,702
6 Mo	–4.97	0.59	—	62	23	9,503
1 Yr	–4.96	6.92	—	51	9	9,504
3 Yr Avg	7.04	8.07	—	17	20	12,266
5 Yr Avg	10.96	0.26	—	14	14	16,817
10 Yr Avg	—	—	—	—	—	—
15 Yr Avg	—	—	—	—	—	—

Tax Analysis	Tax-Adj Ret%	%Rank Cat	%Pretax Ret	%Rank Cat
3 Yr Avg	5.00	18	71.0	53
5 Yr Avg	8.49	16	77.5	37
10 Yr Avg	—	—	—	—

Potential Capital Gain Exposure: 9% of assets

Risk Analysis

Time Period	Load-Adj Return %	Risk %Rank[1] All	Risk %Rank[1] Cat	Morningstar Return	Morningstar Risk	Morningstar Risk-Adj Rating
1 Yr	–10.42					
3 Yr	4.95	42	8	0.0[2]	0.54	★★★★
5 Yr	9.65	46	3	1.10[2]	0.52	★★★★★
Incept	12.87	—	—	—	—	

Average Historical Rating (70 months): 4.7★s

[1] 1=low, 100=high [2] T-Bill return substituted for category avg.

Category Rating (3 Yr)

1 2 3 4 5
Worst Best

Return: Above Avg
Risk: Low

Other Measures	Standard Index S&P 500	Best Fit Index MSACWorld
Alpha	5.7	8.9
Beta	0.62	0.73
R-Squared	69	84
Standard Deviation		13.46
Mean		7.04
Sharpe Ratio		0.18

Analysis by Kunal Kapoor 07-05-01

Capital World Growth & Income Fund doesn't make for good cocktail party chatter, but we think you could retire on it.

This fund's strategy has put it in the market's sweet spot of late. Indeed, with investors suddenly rediscovering dividends and value stocks, this fund has been outshining its world-stock rivals. It posted a small gain in 2000, and is at the breakeven point for the year to date through July 4, 2001. Meanwhile, the majority of its rivals have posted double-digit losses during those periods.

Patience has been key to the fund's recent—and considerable past—success. Its managers, like many good buy-and-hold investors, will accept some temporary problems and endure short-term pain if confident about a holding's long-term prospects. For example, when many rivals gave up tobacco stocks in the late 1990s, this offering stuck with those stocks; it has since been rewarded for its patience. More recently, the managers have been very patient while evaluating the fund's substantial telecom holdings. For example, they've stuck with Vodafone, despite its near-term woes. And such patience isn't very dangerous; with more than 300 names in the portfolio, the damage any one holding can do is limited.

Indeed, the fund has been far less volatile than most of its peers over time, so it looks good from a risk perspective as well as from a reward perspective. Thus, we continue to be impressed with this fund. In fact, we think it and sibling New Perspective are two of the best world-stock options, with this one being the better choice for conservative investors.

Portfolio Analysis 09-30-01

Share change since 06-01 Total Stocks: 287	Sector	Country	% Assets
Philip Morris	Staples	U.S.	4.54
⊕ Astrazeneca (Swe)	Health	United Kingdom	1.79
Elan ADR	Health	Ireland	1.49
Shell Canada Cl A	Energy	Canada	1.39
⊕ ING Groep (Cert)	Financials	Netherlands	1.24
RJ Reynolds Tobacco Hldgs	Staples	U.S.	1.13
⊕ Imperial Tobacco Grp	Staples	United Kingdom	1.11
Washington Mutual	Financials	U.S.	1.10
⊕ Norske Skogindustrier Cl A	Industrials	Norway	0.92
⊕ Lloyds TSB Grp	Financials	United Kingdom	0.84
Vodafone Airtouch	Services	United Kingdom	0.80
CSX	Services	U.S.	0.79
⊖ Lockheed Martin	Industrials	U.S.	0.77
⊖ Williams Companies	Utilities	U.S.	0.76
Samsung SDI	Technology	South Korea	0.76
⊕ Shionogi	Health	Japan	0.74
⊕ Nestle (Reg)	Staples	Switzerland	0.72
Barrick Gold	Industrials	Canada	0.70
AT & T	Services	U.S.	0.68
Gallaher Grp	Staples	United Kingdom	0.68

Current Investment Style

Style: Value Blnd Growth; Size: Large Med Small

	Stock Port Avg	Rel MSCI EAFE Current	Rel MSCI EAFE Hist	Rel Cat
Price/Earnings Ratio	23.2	0.90	0.88	0.84
Price/Cash Flow	13.8	1.07	1.02	0.84
Price/Book Ratio	3.1	0.89	0.94	0.67
3 Yr Earnings Growth	14.2	0.76	1.10	0.76
Med Mkt Cap $mil	11,595	0.4	0.4	0.48

Country Exposure 09-30-01	% assets
U.S.	28
United Kingdom	8
Japan	5
Canada	4
Hong Kong	3

Hedging History: Rare

Regional Exposure 09-30-01	% assets
Europe	19
Japan	5
Latin America	1
Pacific Rim	9
U.S.	28
Other	4

Special Securities % assets 09-30-01	
Restricted/Illiquid Secs	2
Emerging-Markets Secs	9
Options/Futures/Warrants	Yes

Sector Weightings	% of Stocks	Rel Cat	5-Year High	5-Year Low
Utilities	6.8	2.8	13	5
Energy	3.4	0.6	7	3
Financials	23.3	1.3	29	14
Industrials	16.7	1.5	22	13
Durables	2.7	0.7	9	3
Staples	15.7	2.0	16	5
Services	10.5	0.6	26	11
Retail	2.1	0.4	5	2
Health	10.8	0.8	11	4
Technology	8.0	0.5	12	0

Composition % assets 09-30-01

Cash	13.7	Bonds	1.4
Stocks	82.2	Other	2.8

Address: 333 S. Hope Street, Los Angeles, CA 90071, 800–421–4120 / 213–486–9200
Web Address: www.americanfunds.com
*Inception: 03-26-93
Advisor: Cap. Research & Mgmt.
Subadvisor: None
NTF Plans: N/A

Minimum Purchase: $1000 Add: $50 IRA: $250
Min Auto Inv Plan: $50 Add: $50
Sales Fees: 5.75%L, 0.05%B, 0.25%S
Management Fee: .60% mx./.40% mn.
Actual Fees: Mgt: 0.43% Dist: 0.23%
Expense Projections: 3Yr: $810 5Yr: $983 10Yr: $1486
Avg Brok Commission: — Income Distrib: Quarterly
Total Cost (relative to category): —

American Funds EuroPacific Growth A

Ticker	Load	NAV	Yield	Total Assets	Mstar Category
AEPGX	5.75%	$26.87	2.4%	$27,356.7 mil	Foreign Stock

Prospectus Objective: Foreign Stock

American Funds EuroPacific Growth Fund seeks long-term growth of capital.

The fund normally invests at least 65% of assets in equity securities of issuers domiciled in Europe or the Pacific Basin. It may invest up to 20% of assets in securities issued in developing countries. In addition to direct foreign investment, the fund may purchase American Depositary Receipts. It may also invest in convertible securities and straight debt securities; no more than 5% of assets may be invested in debt securities rated below investment-grade.

The fund currently offers Class A, B, C, and F shares, all of which differ in fee structure and availability.

Historical Profile

Return Above Avg
Risk Below Avg
Rating ★★★★ Above Avg

Investment Style
Equity
Average Stock %: 79% 83% 84% 85% 88% 82% 79%

▼ Manager Change
▽ Partial Manager Change

Fund Performance vs. Category Average
■ Quarterly Fund Return +/– Category Average
— Category Baseline

Performance Quartile (within Category)

1990	1991	1992	1993	1994	1995	1996	1997	1998	1999	2000	12–01	History
14.12	16.43	16.55	22.11	21.13	23.13	26.04	26.02	28.40	42.66	31.35	26.87	NAV
–0.11	18.55	2.30	35.60	1.13	12.87	18.64	9.19	15.54	56.97	–17.84	–12.18	Total Return %
3.01	–11.94	–5.32	25.55	–0.19	–24.66	–4.31	–24.17	–13.04	35.94	–8.74	–0.30	+/– S&P 500
23.34	6.42	14.47	3.04	–6.65	1.66	12.59	7.41	–4.46	30.01	–3.67	—	+/– MSCI EAFE
2.24	2.09	1.55	1.45	1.49	2.33	1.90	1.78	1.40	1.03	0.50	2.09	Income Return %
–2.36	16.45	0.75	34.15	–0.37	10.54	16.74	7.41	14.14	55.95	–18.33	–14.26	Capital Return %
1	14	8	51	43	24	22	33	36	25	59	8	Total Rtn % Rank Cat
0.33	0.30	0.26	0.24	0.32	0.49	0.43	0.45	0.36	0.29	0.19	0.66	Income $
0.18	0.00	0.00	0.07	0.90	0.21	0.89	1.93	1.26	1.39	3.74	0.00	Capital Gains $
1.24	1.28	1.24	1.10	0.99	0.97	0.95	0.90	0.86	0.84	0.84	0.84	Expense Ratio %
2.29	2.23	1.85	1.40	1.13	1.80	2.09	1.77	1.64	1.45	0.93	1.89	Income Ratio %
26	9	10	10	21	16	22	26	31	32	29	37	Turnover Rate %
929.9	1,716.7	2,623.4	5,803.0	8,269.5	10,922.3	15,726.6	18,853.5	20,797.9	34,782.7	31,496.1	26,819.2	Net Assets $mil

Portfolio Manager(s)

Stephen E. Bepler, CFA. Since 4-84.
Mark E. Denning. Since 1-90.
Martial Chaillet. Since 6-94.
Alwyn Heong. Since 6-99.
Thierry Vandeventer. Since 4-84.
Robert W. Lovelace, CFA. Since 6-94.

Performance 12-31-01

	1st Qtr	2nd Qtr	3rd Qtr	4th Qtr	Total
1997	2.53	12.21	2.59	–7.49	9.19
1998	13.60	–0.19	–13.57	17.89	15.54
1999	6.37	8.10	5.74	29.10	56.97
2000	4.57	–6.70	–8.53	–7.93	–17.84
2001	–8.39	1.85	–14.02	9.48	–12.18

Trailing	Total Return%	+/– S&P 500	+/– MSCI EAFE	% Rank All	% Rank Cat	Growth of $10,000
3 Mo	9.48	–1.21	—	45	34	10,948
6 Mo	–5.87	–0.31	—	67	15	9,413
1 Yr	–12.18	–0.30	—	65	8	8,783
3 Yr Avg	4.24	5.27	—	38	14	11,327
5 Yr Avg	7.40	–3.30	—	33	12	14,289
10 Yr Avg	10.38	–2.55	—	30	5	26,843
15 Yr Avg	11.53	–2.21	—	29	4	51,362

Tax Analysis	Tax-Adj Ret%	%Rank Cat	%Pretax Ret	%Rank Cat
3 Yr Avg	2.77	15	65.4	71
5 Yr Avg	5.72	12	77.4	27
10 Yr Avg	8.89	6	85.7	12

Potential Capital Gain Exposure: 0% of assets

Risk Analysis

Time Period	Load-Adj Return %	Risk %Rank[1] All	Risk %Rank[1] Cat	Morningstar Return	Morningstar Risk	Morningstar Risk-Adj Rating
1 Yr	–17.22					
3 Yr	2.20	59	21	–0.57[2]	0.77	★★★★
5 Yr	6.13	61	16	0.25[2]	0.70	★★★★
10 Yr	9.73	69	9	1.60[2]	0.68	★★★★

Average Historical Rating (177 months): 4.2★s

[1] 1=low, 100=high [2] T-Bill return substituted for category avg.

Category Rating (3 Yr)

1 2 3 4 5
Worst Best

Return Above Avg
Risk Below Avg

Other Measures	Standard Index S&P 500	Best Fit Index MSCIWaxUSN
Alpha	4.2	9.5
Beta	0.77	1.01
R-Squared	58	86
Standard Deviation		17.81
Mean		4.24
Sharpe Ratio		–0.05

Portfolio Analysis 09-30-01

Share change since 06–01 Total Stocks: 252	Sector	Country	% Assets
Astrazeneca (Swe)	Health	United Kingdom	3.58
Elan ADR	Health	Ireland	2.20
⊕ ING Groep (Cert)	Financials	Netherlands	1.64
⊕ Nestle (Reg)	Staples	Switzerland	1.63
⊖ Vodafone Airtouch	Services	United Kingdom	1.63
⊕ Aventis	Health	France	1.46
Bank of Nova Scotia	Financials	Canada	1.38
⊕ Petroleo Brasil ADR	N/A	N/A	1.35
Taiwan Semicon	Technology	Taiwan	1.30
⊕ Vivendi Universal	N/A	N/A	1.19
⊖ Nintendo	Durables	Japan	1.15
⊖ Samsung Electncs	Technology	South Korea	1.08
⊕ Unilever	Staples	United Kingdom	1.01
⊕ Groupe Danone	Staples	France	0.98
⊕ Novartis	N/A	N/A	0.93
Astrazeneca	Health	United Kingdom	0.91
⊕ Hon Hai Precision Inds	N/A	N/A	0.89
Telefonos de Mexico ADR L	Services	Mexico	0.89
☼ Hbos	N/A	N/A	0.87
UPM–Kymmene	Industrials	Finland	0.86

Current Investment Style

Style: Value Blnd Growth; Size: Large Med Small

	Stock Port Avg	Rel MSCI EAFE Current	Rel MSCI EAFE Hist	Rel Cat
Price/Earnings Ratio	27.9	1.08	0.98	1.09
Price/Cash Flow	16.1	1.25	1.14	1.12
Price/Book Ratio	3.5	1.00	1.08	0.89
3 Yr Earnings Growth	13.4[1]	0.72	1.44	0.68
Med Mkt Cap $mil	13,551	0.5	0.7	0.75

[1] figure is based on 50% or less of stocks

Country Exposure 09-30-01	% assets
United Kingdom	15
Japan	13
Netherlands	4
France	4
Canada	3

Hedging History: Rare

Regional Exposure 09-30-01	% assets
Europe	37
Japan	13
Latin America	2
Pacific Rim	9
Other	4

Special Securities % assets 09-30-01	
Restricted/Illiquid Secs	3
Emerging–Markets Secs	10
Options/Futures/Warrants	Yes

Composition % assets 09-30-01			
Cash	17.8	Bonds	0.3
Stocks	80.3	Other	1.6

Sector Weightings	% of Stocks	Rel Cat	5-Year High	5-Year Low
Utilities	2.2	0.8	16	2
Energy	4.2	0.7	5	1
Financials	17.7	0.8	22	7
Industrials	14.8	1.1	27	9
Durables	6.8	1.0	17	6
Staples	8.9	1.3	11	2
Services	16.2	0.9	32	12
Retail	1.4	0.3	8	1
Health	17.9	1.8	18	1
Technology	10.0	1.0	27	1

Analysis by Emily Hall 12-05-01

There is good reason to believe American Funds EuroPacific Growth can shake off its current slump.

Longtime shareholders used to this fund's stellar results got an unpleasant surprise in 2000: Caught with a slug of pricey technology and telecom stocks, the fund tumbled nearly 18%. It was not only the fund's first below-average showing in years, it was also only the second loss in the fund's history. (The first time was in 1991, when the fund dropped 0.11%.)

The fund's 13% loss through early December 2001 probably doesn't feel much better. The good news for shareholders, though, is that it could have been worse. It has been a nasty year overseas, and this offering's year-to-date performance is actually among the top 20% of the foreign-stock group.

The fund's no-nonsense strategy has helped staunch the bleeding. The managers, finding a dearth of opportunities, raised cash to nearly 20% in early 2001 from a more typical 10% to 15%. Additionally, some of the fund's technology and telecom names, such as Vodafone and Taiwan Semiconductor have bounced back nicely in recent months.

Moreover, the fund's recent troubles do little to tarnish its fabulous long-term record. Its five-, 10-, and 15-year returns still rank in the category's top quintile. Add to the package low volatility, long-tenured management, low expenses, and low turnover, and this offering still looks mighty appealing.

To be sure, this fund is no nimble young thing. Its $27 billion asset base is one of the biggest of all funds, foreign or domestic, and that limits its ability to venture into the smaller-cap regions of Asia and Europe. But for those interested in a straightforward, large-cap foreign fund this offering remains a fantastic choice.

Address:	333 S. Hope Street Los Angeles, CA 90071 800–421–4120 / 213–486–9200
Web Address:	www.americanfunds.com
Inception:	04-16-84
Advisor:	Cap. Research & Mgmt.
Subadvisor:	None
NTF Plans:	N/A

Minimum Purchase:	$250	Add: $25	IRA: $250
Min Auto Inv Plan:	$50	Add: $50	
Sales Fees:	5.75%L, 0.25%B		
Management Fee:	.69% mx./.46% mn.		
Actual Fees:	Mgt: 0.46%	Dist: 0.25%	
Expense Projections:	3Yr: $828	5Yr: $1014	10Yr: $1553
Avg Brok Commission:	—	Income Distrib: Annually	
Total Cost (relative to category):		Below Avg	

American Funds Fundamental Invs A

Ticker	Load	NAV	Yield	Total Assets	Mstar Category
ANCFX	5.75%	$27.45	1.4%	$20,053.2 mil	Large Value

Prospectus Objective: Growth and Income

American Funds Fundamental Investors Fund seeks growth of capital and income.

The fund primarily invests in common stocks and convertibles. It may also invest in fixed-income securities and cash equivalents. The fund primarily invests in debt securities that are rated BBB or better, but it may also invest up to 5% of assets in debt rated below investment-grade. The fund may invest up to 15% of assets in foreign securities.

Historical Profile
Return Above Avg
Risk Below Avg
Rating ★★★★ Above Avg

Investment Style
Equity
Average Stock %: 97% 92% 91% 88% 90% 88% 88%

▼ Manager Change
▽ Partial Manager Change

Fund Performance vs. Category Average
▆ Quarterly Fund Return +/– Category Average
— Category Baseline

Performance Quartile (within Category)

Portfolio Manager(s)

James E. Drasdo. Since 8-78.
Gordon Crawford. Since 8-91.
Dina N. Perry. Since 1-93.
Michael T. Kerr. Since 1-99.

1990	1991	1992	1993	1994	1995	1996	1997	1998	1999	2000	12-01	History
14.32	17.47	17.52	18.15	17.50	22.29	24.54	27.40	28.92	32.59	31.16	27.45	NAV
–6.24	30.34	10.19	18.16	1.33	34.21	19.99	26.67	16.72	24.58	4.27	–9.55	Total Return %
–3.12	–0.14	2.57	8.10	0.01	–3.33	–2.96	–6.68	–11.86	3.54	13.37	2.33	+/– S&P 500
–2.57	12.19	1.12	–1.61	3.64	–5.82	–2.33	–8.82	–4.52	13.63	1.96	–0.76	+/– Russ Top 200 Val
3.02	2.83	2.44	2.48	2.45	2.32	1.82	1.74	1.47	1.41	1.25	1.30	Income Return %
–9.26	27.51	7.75	15.67	–1.13	31.88	18.17	24.93	15.24	23.17	3.02	–10.85	Capital Return %
53	29	39	19	24	40	53	53	26	5	59	75	Total Rtn % Rank Cat
0.49	0.40	0.42	0.43	0.44	0.40	0.40	0.42	0.40	0.40	0.40	0.40	Income $
0.58	0.68	1.24	2.03	0.45	0.68	1.76	3.13	2.59	2.79	2.36	0.38	Capital Gains $
0.70	0.69	0.65	0.65	0.68	0.70	0.66	0.63	0.63	0.63	0.64	—	Expense Ratio %
3.15	2.50	2.56	2.43	2.45	2.08	1.78	1.54	1.47	1.33	1.28	—	Income Ratio %
12	17	24	29	23	25	39	45	53	46	43	—	Turnover Rate %
823.5	1,155.6	1,439.7	1,979.3	2,611.1	4,754.5	7,165.4	10,464.6	12,712.9	16,603.0	19,871.7	19,099.6	Net Assets $mil

Performance 12-31-01

	1st Qtr	2nd Qtr	3rd Qtr	4th Qtr	Total
1997	2.43	13.98	9.93	–1.30	26.67
1998	11.10	1.56	–10.41	15.46	16.72
1999	6.55	9.75	–4.93	12.07	24.58
2000	7.03	–1.08	0.88	–2.38	4.27
2001	–8.47	4.61	–15.48	11.77	–9.55

Trailing	Total Return%	+/– S&P 500	+/– Russ Top 200 Val	% Rank All	% Rank Cat	Growth of $10,000
3 Mo	11.77	1.09	6.26	34	17	11,177
6 Mo	–5.53	0.02	0.24	65	73	9,447
1 Yr	–9.55	2.33	–0.76	60	75	9,045
3 Yr Avg	5.52	6.55	4.36	27	22	11,750
5 Yr Avg	11.68	0.98	0.47	11	19	17,372
10 Yr Avg	13.95	1.02	–0.08	9	18	36,905
15 Yr Avg	13.83	0.09	0.33	12	13	69,774

Tax Analysis	Tax-Adj Ret%	%Rank Cat	%Pretax Ret	%Rank Cat
3 Yr Avg	3.80	24	68.8	46
5 Yr Avg	9.45	19	80.9	29
10 Yr Avg	11.39	14	81.7	30

Potential Capital Gain Exposure: 6% of assets

Risk Analysis

Time Period	Load-Adj Return %	Risk %Rank[1] All	Risk %Rank[1] Cat	Morningstar Return	Morningstar Risk	Morningstar Risk-Adj Rating
1 Yr	–14.75					
3 Yr	3.46	49	24	–0.31[2]	0.69	★★★
5 Yr	10.36	51	20	1.29[2]	0.71	★★★★
10 Yr	13.28	56	23	1.37	0.72	★★★★

Average Historical Rating (193 months): 3.9★s

[1] 1=low, 100=high [2] T-Bill return substituted for category avg.

Category Rating (3 Yr)

1 2 3 4 5
Worst — Best

Return: Above Avg
Risk: Below Avg

Other Measures	Standard Index S&P 500	Best Fit Index S&P 500
Alpha	5.6	5.6
Beta	0.86	0.86
R-Squared	92	92
Standard Deviation		15.94
Mean		5.52
Sharpe Ratio		0.04

Portfolio Analysis 09-30-01

Share change since 06-01 Total Stocks: 178	Sector	PE	YTD Ret%	% Assets
Dow Chemical	Industrials	NMF	–4.43	2.19
AOL Time Warner	Technology	—	–7.76	2.13
Canadian Pacific	Services	5.2	48.86	1.85
Astrazeneca (Swe)	Health	—	—	1.68
⊕ Microsoft	Technology	57.6	52.78	1.57
⊕ American Intl Grp	Financials	42.0	–19.20	1.57
⊖ AT & T	N/A	—	—	1.55
SBC Comms	Services	18.4	–16.00	1.52
Texas Instruments	Technology	87.5	–40.70	1.47
Viacom Cl B	Services	—	—	1.42
Suncor Energy	Energy	58.1	29.23	1.38
☼ Bank of America	Financials	16.7	42.73	1.37
⊕ TXU	Utilities	13.7	12.17	1.14
⊕ Eli Lilly	Health	28.9	–14.40	1.12
Minnesota Mng & Mfg	Industrials	34.5	0.16	1.04
⊕ Unilever (NY)	Staples	59.1	–6.32	1.03
Pharmacia	Health	36.5	–29.30	1.00
Colgate-Palmolive	Staples	31.1	–9.45	0.97
ALCOA	Industrials	21.4	7.86	0.95
⊕ Allstate	Financials	17.1	–21.00	0.94
⊕ Bristol-Myers Squibb	Health	20.2	–26.00	0.93
⊕ Lowe's	Retail	38.7	109.00	0.93
⊕ Berkshire Hathaway Cl A	Financials	—	—	0.92
Coca-Cola	Staples	35.5	–21.40	0.91
American Home Products	Health	—	–1.91	0.89

Current Investment Style

Style: Value Blnd Growth; Size: Large Med Small

	Stock Port Avg	Relative S&P 500 Current	Relative S&P 500 Hist	Rel Cat
Price/Earnings Ratio	31.4	1.01	0.95	1.25
Price/Book Ratio	5.0	0.88	0.72	1.22
Price/Cash Flow	16.3	0.90	0.83	1.18
3 Yr Earnings Growth	9.6	0.66	0.56	0.65
1 Yr Earnings Est%	–7.4	4.20	—	2.24
Med Mkt Cap $mil	26,513	0.4	0.4	0.83

Special Securities % assets 09-30-01	
Restricted/Illiquid Secs	Trace
Emerging-Markets Secs	0
Options/Futures/Warrants	Yes

Composition % assets 09-30-01	
Cash	6.8
Stocks*	88.8
Bonds	2.4
Other	2.0
*Foreign (% stocks)	15.2

Market Cap	
Giant	30.5
Large	50.1
Medium	18.6
Small	0.8
Micro	0.0

Sector Weightings	% of Stocks	Rel S&P	5-Year High	5-Year Low
Utilities	4.2	1.3	10	2
Energy	8.1	1.1	18	2
Financials	12.4	0.7	22	7
Industrials	15.8	1.4	28	8
Durables	2.3	1.5	10	1
Staples	8.2	1.0	10	1
Services	16.9	1.6	37	14
Retail	2.9	0.4	6	1
Health	10.4	0.7	16	4
Technology	18.8	1.0	22	7

Analysis by William Harding 12-03-01

This is a good choice for investors looking for a core holding that dabbles in growth stocks.

Fundamental Investors Fund is down this year, but that doesn't limit its appeal. This fund has lost 10.5% through the first 11 months of 2001, placing it in the bottom third of the large-value group. Management's tendency to shop the bargain bins for beaten-down growth names explains much of the divergence.

This year, the team has scooped up shares of a number of leading tech companies, such as Cisco Systems and EMC. Consequently, the fund had about 19% of assets devoted to technology at the end of September, compared with less than 10% for its average large-value peer. That line of attack has generally been a drag on performance this year. Not surprisingly, cheap stocks in defensive areas of the market have held up better than high-P/E fare, especially racy tech stocks, during the market's downturn.

Though management may have been a tad early moving into technology, this approach has proven its merit over time. The fund's long-term returns all rank in the category's top quintile and also outpace those of the S&P 500 index. Meanwhile, the fund hasn't been any more volatile than the average fund in the large-value camp, even though it courts more price risk than the typical large-value offering. Each of the fund's experienced managers invest his or her share of the fund's assets independently. As a result, the fund is broadly diversified across 200 holdings in various industries, limiting issue-specific risk.

Investors who want a more typical value offering should check out sibling Washington Mutual, while growth enthusiasts should consider Growth Fund of America. But this is a worthwhile option for those looking for broad exposure to large-cap stocks, including a healthy dose of foreign-stock exposure. It also boasts a decent yield for income-oriented investors.

Address:	333 S. Hope Street Los Angeles, CA 90071 415-421-9360 / 800-421-4120
Web Address:	www.americanfunds.com
Inception:	01-01-33
Advisor:	Cap. Research & Mgmt.
Subadvisor:	None
NTF Plans:	N/A

Minimum Purchase:	$250	Add: $50	IRA: $25
Min Auto Inv Plan:	$50	Add: $50	
Sales Fees:	5.75%L, 0.25%B		
Management Fee:	.39% mx./.28% mn.		
Actual Fees:	Mgt: 0.27%	Dist: 0.25%	
Expense Projections:	3Yr: $768	5Yr: $911	10Yr: $1327
Avg Brok Commission:	—	Income Distrib: Quarterly	
Total Cost (relative to category):	Below Avg		

American Funds Growth Fund of Amer A

Ticker	Load	NAV	Yield	Total Assets	Mstar Category
AGTHX	5.75%	$23.71	0.2%	$38,428.7 mil	Large Growth

Prospectus Objective: Growth

American Funds Growth Fund of America seeks capital growth.

The fund normally invests at least 65% of assets in common stocks and convertible securities. It may invest in a wide range of companies, including growing and profitable companies, turnaround situations, and unseasoned companies. The fund may invest up to 15% of assets in foreign securities. It may also invest up to 10% of assets in debt securities rated below investment-grade.

Historical Profile

Return Above Avg
Risk Average
Rating ★★★★ Above Avg

Investment Style
Equity
Average Stock %

		98%	82%	89%	87%	87%	83%	83%

▼ Manager Change
▽ Partial Manager Change

Fund Performance vs. Category Average
■ Quarterly Fund Return +/– Category Average
— Category Baseline

Performance Quartile (within Category)

Portfolio Manager(s)

James E. Drasdo. Since 1-86.
R. Michael Shanahan. Since 1-86.
Gordon Crawford. Since 1-91.
James F. Rothenberg, CFA. Since 1-88.
Don D. O'Neal. Since 1-94.
Michael T. Kerr. Since 1-98.

1990	1991	1992	1993	1994	1995	1996	1997	1998	1999	2000	12-01	History
9.01	11.47	12.17	13.38	12.77	15.27	16.57	18.78	22.40	29.14	27.08	23.71	NAV
–4.18	35.85	7.35	14.54	0.02	29.75	14.84	26.86	31.78	45.70	7.49	–12.28	Total Return %
–1.06	5.36	–0.26	4.48	–1.29	–7.79	–8.11	–6.50	3.21	24.66	16.59	–0.40	+/– S&P 500
–5.54	–3.56	3.46	14.61	–4.83	–8.91	–10.68	–6.89	–13.32	16.02	32.01	8.22	+/– Russ Top 200 Grt
2.38	1.94	0.83	0.49	0.64	1.14	0.72	0.78	0.48	0.20	0.50	0.17	Income Return %
–6.55	33.90	6.53	14.04	–0.61	28.61	14.12	26.07	31.30	45.50	6.99	–12.44	Capital Return %
64	66	41	31	26	64	79	45	52	31	2	9	Total Rtn % Rank Cat
0.24	0.18	0.10	0.06	0.09	0.15	0.11	0.13	0.09	0.05	0.15	0.05	Income $
0.41	0.54	0.05	0.49	0.52	1.14	0.86	2.06	2.21	3.20	4.10	0.00	Capital Gains $
0.79	0.83	0.79	0.77	0.78	0.75	0.75	0.72	0.70	0.70	0.70	0.71	Expense Ratio %
2.67	2.13	1.11	0.56	0.49	0.90	0.90	0.73	0.48	0.28	0.58	0.76	Income Ratio %
18	19	11	25	25	27	27	34	39	46	47	36	Turnover Rate %
2,060.6	3,457.7	4,332.9	5,062.5	5,274.2	7,891.2	9,675.3	12,247.7	16,246.9	27,407.0	37,005.8	35,402.0	Net Assets $mil

Performance 12-31-01

	1st Qtr	2nd Qtr	3rd Qtr	4th Qtr	Total
1997	0.54	11.88	14.00	–1.08	26.86
1998	11.77	2.43	–9.49	27.17	31.78
1999	6.03	12.29	–2.17	25.09	45.70
2000	17.64	–1.34	1.89	–9.11	7.49
2001	–14.11	9.54	–20.60	17.43	–12.28

Trailing	Total Return%	+/– S&P 500	+/– Russ Top 200 Grth	% Rank All	% Rank Cat	Growth of $10,000
3 Mo	17.43	6.74	4.57	19	23	11,743
6 Mo	–6.77	–1.21	0.22	73	31	9,323
1 Yr	–12.28	–0.40	8.22	66	9	8,772
3 Yr Avg	11.17	12.19	19.19	9	2	13,738
5 Yr Avg	18.09	7.39	9.50	2	2	22,966
10 Yr Avg	15.46	2.53	4.37	4	3	42,087
15 Yr Avg	15.83	2.09	2.46	4	8	90,603

Tax Analysis	Tax-Adj Ret%	%Rank Cat	%Pretax Ret	%Rank Cat
3 Yr Avg	9.29	1	83.2	38
5 Yr Avg	15.79	2	87.3	26
10 Yr Avg	13.51	2	87.4	13

Potential Capital Gain Exposure: 2% of assets

Risk Analysis

Time Period	Load-Adj Return %	Risk %Rank[1] All	Risk %Rank[1] Cat	Morningstar Return	Morningstar Risk	Morningstar Risk-Adj Rating
1 Yr	–17.32					
3 Yr	8.99	64	8	0.89[2]	0.89	★★★★
5 Yr	16.70	64	6	3.19[2]	0.88	★★★★★
10 Yr	14.77	73	10	1.73	0.95	★★★★

Average Historical Rating (193 months): 3.6★s

[1] 1=low, 100=high [2] T-Bill return substituted for category avg.

Category Rating (3 Yr)

1 2 3 4 5
Worst Best

Return High
Risk Low

Other Measures	Standard Index S&P 500	Best Fit Index Wil 4500
Alpha	13.7	8.3
Beta	1.07	0.71
R-Squared	69	82

Standard Deviation	24.60
Mean	11.17
Sharpe Ratio	0.29

Portfolio Analysis 09-30-01

Share change since 06-01 Total Stocks: 198	Sector	PE	YTD Ret%	% Assets
⊕ AOL Time Warner	Technology	—	–7.76	2.65
⊕ Viacom Cl B	Services	—	—	2.59
⊕ Lowe's	Retail	38.7	109.00	2.53
⊕ Berkshire Hathaway Cl A	Financials	—	—	2.39
American Intl Grp	Financials	42.0	–19.20	2.15
Philip Morris	Staples	12.1	9.12	2.04
Forest Labs	Health	52.2	23.35	1.80
⊕ Texas Instruments	Technology	87.5	–40.70	1.72
Fannie Mae	Financials	16.2	–6.95	1.71
⊕ Clear Channel Comms	Services	—	5.10	1.70
⊕ Comcast	Services	20.3	–13.70	1.30
⊕ Eli Lilly	Health	28.9	–14.40	1.23
⊕ Microsoft	Technology	57.6	52.78	1.18
⊖ HCA – The Healthcare Company	Health	24.1	–12.20	1.11
Minnesota Mng & Mfg	Industrials	34.5	0.16	0.93
United Parcel Svc B	Services	25.0	–6.09	0.89
⊕ Southwest Air	Services	25.0	–17.20	0.88
Starbucks	Retail	41.4	–13.90	0.87
Progressive	Financials	33.4	44.40	0.85
⊖ Marsh & McLennan	Financials	27.9	–6.30	0.84
XL Cap Cl A	Financials	22.8	5.82	0.81
⊕ Astrazeneca (Swe)	Health	—	—	0.81
⊕ Taiwan Semicon	Technology	—	—	0.73
⊕ Applied Matls	Technology	66.8	5.01	0.73
⊖ Walt Disney	Services	—	–27.70	0.73

Current Investment Style

Style: Value Blnd Growth
Size: Large Med Small

	Stock Port Avg	Relative S&P 500 Current	Relative S&P 500 Hist	Rel Cat
Price/Earnings Ratio	34.5	1.11	1.19	0.97
Price/Book Ratio	5.0	0.88	0.92	0.79
Price/Cash Flow	21.4	1.19	1.16	0.94
3 Yr Earnings Growth	18.0	1.23	0.99	0.84
1 Yr Earnings Est%	–3.2	1.80	—	–1.06
Med Mkt Cap $mil	23,593	0.4	0.4	0.50

[1] figure is based on 50% or less of stocks

Analysis by William Harding 12-19-01

This fund's relatively steady nature makes it an appealing large-growth option.

Growth Fund of America's attention to risk control kept it from leading the pack in go-go growth years like 1998 and 1999. But by the same token, it has helped the fund weather 2001's slumping market for growth equities better than its average rival. The fund's 12% loss for the year to date through Dec. 17 is poor on an absolute basis, but 90% of funds in the large-growth camp have lost even more.

That sturdiness is one of the fund's best features. Each manager on its six-member team picks stocks independently of the others. The resulting portfolio is well diversified across industries and issues, which keeps a lid on risk. Further, the managers are more valuation-sensitive than their typical rival. The fund thus has little exposure to the type of speculative technology issues that have led the market down over the past 20 months. A frequently large cash stake also cushions the fund against downturns in growth stocks.

The market's downdraft gave management the opportunity to put some of that cash to work in the third quarter. A number of beaten-down tech names got cheap enough to attract the managers' attention, and they added to names such as Broadcom and JDS Uniphase. The team also boosted the fund's position in retailer Lowe's, which has chipped in with big gains this year. Nevertheless, the fund still ended the quarter with 17% of assets in cash.

Some investors may cringe at the thought of so much money sitting idle, but the fund's approach has worked well over time. As one would expect, it has fared much better than its typical peer in down markets. It doesn't shine in the headiest bull markets, but it's almost always competitive, and its long-term returns land in the large-growth category's upper echelons. Strong returns, below-average risk relative to its peers, and experienced managers make this a superb growth offering.

Special Securities % assets 09-30-01	
Restricted/Illiquid Secs	Trace
Emerging-Markets Secs	2
Options/Futures/Warrants	Yes

Composition % assets 09-30-01	
Cash	17.9
Stocks*	81.5
Bonds	0.0
Other	0.6
*Foreign (% stocks)	9.9

Market Cap	
Giant	31.3
Large	40.7
Medium	25.9
Small	2.2
Micro	0.0

Sector Weightings	% of Stocks	Rel S&P	5-Year High	5-Year Low
Utilities	0.7	0.2	2	0
Energy	3.1	0.4	6	1
Financials	15.4	0.9	17	5
Industrials	4.8	0.4	8	1
Durables	0.0	0.0	3	0
Staples	4.5	0.6	10	3
Services	23.2	2.1	47	23
Retail	5.5	0.8	6	1
Health	16.7	1.1	19	4
Technology	26.2	1.4	47	18

Address:	333 S. Hope Street Los Angeles, CA 90071 800–421–4120 / 415–421–9360
Web Address:	www.americanfunds.com
Inception:	01-01-59
Advisor:	Cap. Research & Mgmt.
Subadvisor:	None
NTF Plans:	N/A

Minimum Purchase:	$250	Add: $50	IRA: $250
Min Auto Inv Plan:	$50	Add: $50	
Sales Fees:	5.75%L, 0.25%B		
Management Fee:	.50% mx./.33% mn.		
Actual Fees:	Mgt: 0.32%	Dist: 0.25%	
Expense Projections:	3Yr: $859	5Yr: $992	10Yr: $1531
Avg Brok Commission:	—	Income Distrib: Annually	
Total Cost (relative to category):		Below Avg	

American Funds Income Fund of Amer A

Ticker	Load	NAV	Yield	Total Assets	Mstar Category
AMECX	5.75%	$15.82	5.0%	$20,433.6 mil	Domestic Hybrid

Prospectus Objective: Asset Allocation

American Funds Income Fund of America seeks current income; capital appreciation is secondary.

The fund allocates assets among common and preferred stocks, straight debt securities, convertibles, and cash equivalents. The relative percentages vary according to market conditions. The fund normally maintains at least 65% of assets in income-producing securities. It may also invest in dollar-denominated foreign fixed-income securities. The fund may purchase straight debt securities rated as low as CC, though it may invest no more than 20% of assets in securities rated below BBB.

The fund offers A, B, C & F shares, all which differ in fee structure and availability.

Historical Profile
Return: Average
Risk: Low
Rating: ★★★★ Above Avg

Investment Style
Equity
Average Stock %: 51% 54% 49% 49% 52% 53%

▼ Manager Change
▽ Partial Manager Change

Fund Performance vs. Category Average
■ Quarterly Fund Return +/– Category Average
— Category Baseline

Performance Quartile (within Category)

Portfolio Manager(s)

Stephen E. Bepler, CFA. Since 1-84.
Abner D. Goldstine. Since 11-73.
Dina N. Perry. Since 1-92.
Janet A. McKinley. Since 1-91.
John H. Smet. Since 1-92.
David C. Barclay. Since 6-98.
Hilda L. Applbaum, CFA. Since 1-98.

History

1990	1991	1992	1993	1994	1995	1996	1997	1998	1999	2000	12-01	History
11.46	13.19	13.68	14.39	13.14	15.87	16.52	17.77	17.34	15.74	15.94	15.82	NAV
−2.95	23.78	12.03	14.01	−2.50	29.08	15.23	22.16	9.47	0.52	9.98	5.41	Total Return %
0.17	−6.70	4.41	3.95	−3.82	−8.46	−7.72	−11.19	−19.11	−20.52	19.09	17.29	+/– S&P 500
−11.91	7.78	4.63	4.26	0.41	10.61	11.61	12.48	0.79	1.35	−1.65	−3.01	+/– LB Aggregate
7.07	7.61	6.52	6.20	5.90	6.45	5.79	5.17	5.04	5.11	5.18	5.11	Income Return %
−10.02	16.17	5.51	7.81	−8.40	22.62	9.44	16.99	4.42	−4.60	4.80	0.30	Capital Return %
75	50	16	34	51	16	34	22	70	86	12	6	Total Rtn % Rank Cat
0.88	0.85	0.84	0.83	0.83	0.83	0.90	0.82	0.88	0.87	0.80	0.80	Income $
0.07	0.08	0.22	0.35	0.06	0.18	0.81	1.48	1.19	0.81	0.48	0.16	Capital Gains $
0.67	0.73	0.66	0.62	0.63	0.65	0.62	0.61	0.59	0.59	0.63	0.62	Expense Ratio %
7.36	7.23	6.40	6.05	5.92	6.12	5.56	5.09	4.75	4.99	5.52	5.18	Income Ratio %
19	23	23	29	26	26	38	41	35	44	35	44	Turnover Rate %
2,171.2	3,525.3	6,501.5	10,338.9	10,502.7	13,777.5	16,192.2	20,220.8	22,909.0	21,450.0	18,567.7	19,745.6	Net Assets $mil

Performance 12-31-01

	1st Qtr	2nd Qtr	3rd Qtr	4th Qtr	Total
1997	1.86	7.99	7.61	3.21	22.16
1998	6.86	−0.47	−4.91	8.24	9.47
1999	−0.23	4.50	−4.44	0.89	0.52
2000	−0.44	−0.42	4.67	5.99	9.98
2001	0.44	4.62	−3.91	4.40	5.41

Trailing	Total Return%	+/– S&P 500	+/– LB Agg	% Rank All	% Rank Cat	Growth of $10,000
3 Mo	4.40	−6.29	4.36	67	76	10,440
6 Mo	0.32	5.87	−4.34	38	19	10,032
1 Yr	5.41	17.29	−3.01	21	6	10,541
3 Yr Avg	5.23	6.26	−1.04	29	18	11,653
5 Yr Avg	9.28	−1.42	1.85	22	23	15,583
10 Yr Avg	11.18	−1.75	3.95	24	15	28,862
15 Yr Avg	11.23	−2.51	3.11	32	17	49,325

Tax Analysis	Tax-Adj Ret%	%Rank Cat	%Pretax Ret	%Rank Cat
3 Yr Avg	2.53	25	48.4	59
5 Yr Avg	6.18	29	66.6	57
10 Yr Avg	8.10	22	72.5	49

Potential Capital Gain Exposure: 4% of assets

Risk Analysis

Time Period	Load-Adj Return %	Risk %Rank[1] All	Risk %Rank[1] Cat	Morningstar Return	Morningstar Risk	Morningstar Risk-Adj Rating
1 Yr	−0.65					
3 Yr	3.18	33	13	−0.37[2]	0.36	★★★★
5 Yr	7.99	38	15	0.68[2]	0.39	★★★
10 Yr	10.53	43	7	0.82	0.40	★★★★

Average Historical Rating (193 months): 3.7★s

[1] 1=low, 100=high [2] T-Bill return substituted for category avg.

Category Rating (3 Yr): 1 2 3 4 5 (Worst – Best)

Return: Above Avg
Risk: Below Avg

Other Measures	Standard Index S&P 500	Best Fit Index SPMid400
Alpha	2.0	−1.4
Beta	0.30	0.29
R-Squared	41	51

Standard Deviation	8.39
Mean	5.23
Sharpe Ratio	0.04

Portfolio Analysis 09-30-01

Total Stocks: 171
Share change since 06-01

Stock	Sector	PE Ratio	YTD Return %	% Net Assets
Philip Morris	Staples	12.1	9.12	2.25
RJ Reynolds Tobacco Hldgs	Staples	3.1	22.37	1.47
Consolid Edison	Utilities	14.3	10.91	1.35
⊕ Dow Chemical	Industrials	NMF	−4.43	1.24
☼ Wachovia	Financials	—	23.13	1.23
⊕ J.P. Morgan Chase & Co.	Financials	27.8	−17.40	1.18
⊕ Weyerhaeuser	Industrials	21.0	9.73	1.12
Albertson's	Retail	29.7	22.01	1.00
Georgia-Pacific Timber Grp	Industrials	—	23.76	0.98
Paccar	Industrials	27.0	36.79	0.93

Total Fixed-Income: 585	Date of Maturity	Amount $000	Value $000	% Net Assets
SB Treasury 144A Reset 9.4%	12-29-49	124,750	123,503	0.61
US Treasury Note 3.625%	01-15-08	65,000	74,137	0.37
Nextel Comm Step 0%	02-15-08	145,775	72,888	0.36
US Treasury Bond 8.875%	08-15-17	52,275	72,327	0.36
US Treasury Note 6.75%	05-15-05	65,000	71,825	0.36
Solectron FRN	12-31-20	131,200	66,269	0.33
Charter Comm 144A N/A	05-15-11	124,750	66,118	0.33
Celestica Cv N/A		181,000	65,359	0.32
GNMA 7.5%	10-15-29	61,739	64,460	0.32
RC Trust Cv Pfd 8.25%		1,054	63,315	0.31

Equity Style
Style: Value
Size: Large-Cap

	Portfolio Avg	Rel S&P
Price/Earnings Ratio	21.1	0.68
Price/Book Ratio	3.1	0.55
Price/Cash Flow	11.1	0.61
3 Yr Earnings Growth	9.1	0.62
1 Yr Earnings Est%	−4.7	2.64
Debt % Total Cap	40.8	1.32
Med Mkt Cap $mil	10,856	0.18

Fixed-Income Style
Duration: Intermediate
Quality: Medium

Avg Eff Duration[1]	4.6 Yrs
Avg Eff Maturity	—
Avg Credit Quality	BBB
Avg Wtd Coupon	6.65%

[1] figure provided by fund as of 06-30-01

Special Securities % assets 09-30-01	
Restricted/Illiquid Secs	6
Emerging-Markets Secs	1
Options/Futures/Warrants	Yes

Composition % of assets 09-30-01	
Cash	13.1
Stocks*	52.1
Bonds	29.6
Other	5.2
*Foreign (% of stocks)	19.0

Market Cap	
Giant	21.3
Large	40.5
Medium	35.8
Small	2.3
Micro	0.0

Sector Weightings	% of Stocks	Rel S&P	5-Year High	5-Year Low
Utilities	15.4	4.8	33	7
Energy	9.7	1.4	21	3
Financials	22.4	1.3	31	20
Industrials	21.2	1.9	24	7
Durables	1.9	1.2	9	0
Staples	15.4	1.9	15	0
Services	5.4	0.5	14	5
Retail	5.6	0.8	8	1
Health	2.7	0.2	19	0
Technology	0.3	0.0	7	0

Analysis by William Harding 01-03-02

This fund is a solid pick for investors in search of a balanced fund that offers a smooth ride.

Income Fund of America has performed true to form amid the stock market's recent troubles. Typical of many offerings in the American Funds lineup, this fund follows a more staid path than its typical rival. The fund's asset mix is moderate compared with many of its peers'—it typically devotes 40% to 50% of assets to stocks and often has a good chunk of cash on sidelines. In picking stocks for the portfolio, management emphasizes large-cap names with high dividend yields.

This penchant for income leads the fund to hold big stakes in financial and utility stocks and little exposure to tech names. Though this conservatism can hold the fund back at times, as in 1999, it has been a boon in down markets. The fund's 5.4% gain in 2001 outpaced 94% of its peers, and its 10% return in 2000 landed near the category's top decile.

This fund's cautious nature shines when stocks tank, but its superb track record signals that it has held its own in various market environments. The fund has consistently earned above-average returns relative to its peers over the past 15 years, thanks in large part to savvy management. Investors will have a tough time finding more experienced managers—the average tenure of the fund's portfolio counselors is 18 years. Further, American Funds boasts tremendous research capabilities around the globe.

Finally, the fund's low expense ratio, which is half that of the typical front-load domestic hybrid offering's, ensures that the fund will enjoy a leg up on the competition in the future, and helps the fund pay out a healthy income stream relative to its rival. All told, this offering should appeal to risk-averse, income-minded investors.

Address:	333 S. Hope Street Los Angeles, CA 90071 415-421-9360 / 800-421-4120
Web Address:	www.americanfunds.com
Inception:	01-01-71
Advisor:	Cap. Research & Mgmt.
Subadvisor:	None
NTF Plans:	N/A

Minimum Purchase:	$250	Add: $50	IRA: $250
Min Auto Inv Plan:	$50	Add: $50	
Sales Fees:	5.75%L, 0.25%B		
Management Fee:	.24% mx./.15% mn.		
Actual Fees:	Mgt: 0.30%	Dist: 0.23%	
Expense Projections:	3Yr: $765	5Yr: $906	10Yr: $1316
Avg Brok Commission:	—	Income Distrib: Quarterly	
Total Cost (relative to category):		Below Avg	

American Funds Investment Co Amer A

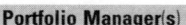

Ticker	Load	NAV	Yield	Total Assets	Mstar Category
AIVSX	5.75%	$28.53	1.8%	$55,785.4 mil	Large Value

Prospectus Objective: Growth and Income

American Funds Investment Company of America seeks long-term growth of capital and income.

The fund invests primarily in common stocks, but it may also invest in high-quality convertibles and debt securities. When choosing securities, management gives the possibility of appreciation and potential dividends more weight than current yield. Stocks are chosen from a list prepared by the fund's directors. The fund may invest up to 10% of assets in foreign issues.

Historical Profile
Return Above Avg
Risk Below Avg
Rating ★★★★ Above Avg

Investment Style
Equity
Average Stock %

90% 85% 90% 84% 85% 83% 81%

▼ Manager Change
▽ Partial Manager Change

Fund Performance vs. Category Average
■ Quarterly Fund Return +/– Category Average
— Category Baseline

Performance Quartile (within Category)

Portfolio Manager(s)

Jon B. Lovelace Jr.. Since 4-58.
Gregg E. Ireland. Since 1-92.
James B. Lovelace, CFA. Since 1-91.
Don D. O'Neal. Since 1-91.
R. Michael Shanahan. Since 1-90.
Dina N. Perry. Since 1-94.
James F. Rothenberg, CFA. Since 1-94.
James E. Drasdo. Since 1-87.
C. Ross Sappenfield. Since 1-99.

1990	1991	1992	1993	1994	1995	1996	1997	1998	1999	2000	12-01	History
14.52	17.48	17.89	18.72	17.67	21.61	24.23	28.25	31.07	32.46	31.06	28.53	NAV
0.68	26.54	6.99	11.62	0.15	30.63	19.35	29.81	22.94	16.56	3.84	–4.59	Total Return %
3.80	–3.94	–0.63	1.56	–1.16	–6.91	–3.60	–3.55	–5.64	–4.48	12.94	7.29	+/– S&P 500
4.35	8.39	–2.08	–8.14	2.47	–9.41	–2.96	–5.68	1.70	5.60	1.53	4.20	+/– Russ Top 200 Val
3.93	3.08	2.72	2.66	2.59	2.86	2.33	2.08	1.83	1.66	1.63	1.70	Income Return %
–3.25	23.46	4.27	8.96	–2.44	27.77	17.02	27.73	21.10	14.89	2.21	–6.28	Capital Return %
8	53	77	64	42	68	59	28	10	15	61	42	Total Rtn % Rank Cat
0.59	0.44	0.47	0.47	0.48	0.50	0.50	0.50	0.51	0.51	0.52	0.52	Income $
0.22	0.38	0.32	0.75	0.60	0.91	1.03	2.60	2.94	3.04	2.08	0.59	Capital Gains $
0.55	0.59	0.58	0.59	0.60	0.60	0.59	0.56	0.55	0.55	0.56	—	Expense Ratio %
3.95	3.29	3.06	3.03	2.83	2.70	2.17	1.90	1.65	1.54	1.74	—	Income Ratio %
11	6	10	18	31	21	17	26	25	28	25	—	Turnover Rate %
5,922.8	10,525.9	15,428.4	19,005.0	19,279.6	25,678.3	30,875.5	39,717.7	48,497.6	56,095.0	56,212.0	54,008.1	Net Assets $mil

Performance 12-31-01

	1st Qtr	2nd Qtr	3rd Qtr	4th Qtr	Total
1997	2.78	14.86	8.05	1.76	29.81
1998	11.35	1.58	–7.38	17.34	22.94
1999	2.83	9.21	–6.46	10.96	16.56
2000	3.63	–1.10	0.45	0.86	3.84
2001	–5.77	4.62	–10.24	7.82	–4.59

Trailing	Total Return%	+/– S&P 500	+/– Russ Top 200 Val	% Rank All	% Rank Cat	Growth of $10,000
3 Mo	7.82	–2.86	2.31	52	66	10,782
6 Mo	–3.22	2.34	2.56	52	36	9,678
1 Yr	–4.59	7.29	4.20	50	42	9,541
3 Yr Avg	4.91	5.94	3.75	32	26	11,547
5 Yr Avg	13.00	2.30	1.80	8	11	18,427
10 Yr Avg	13.14	0.21	–0.89	12	29	34,359
15 Yr Avg	13.60	–0.13	0.10	13	15	67,739

Tax Analysis	Tax-Adj Ret%	%Rank Cat	%Pretax Ret	%Rank Cat
3 Yr Avg	3.03	28	61.6	59
5 Yr Avg	10.68	12	82.1	23
10 Yr Avg	10.91	23	83.1	20

Potential Capital Gain Exposure: 26% of assets

Risk Analysis

Time Period	Load-Adj Return %	Risk %Rank[1] All	Risk %Rank[1] Cat	Morningstar Return	Morningstar Risk	Morningstar Risk-Adj Rating
1 Yr	–10.07					
3 Yr	2.86	43	6	–0.43[2]	0.59	★★★
5 Yr	11.67	47	6	1.65[2]	0.63	★★★★
10 Yr	12.47	53	12	1.20	0.67	★★★★

Average Historical Rating (193 months): 4.0★s

[1] 1=low, 100=high [2] T-Bill return substituted for category avg.

Category Rating (3 Yr)

1 2 3 4 5
Worst Best

Return Above Avg
Risk Low

Other Measures	Standard Index S&P 500	Best Fit Index S&P 500
Alpha	3.9	3.9
Beta	0.69	0.69
R-Squared	90	90

Standard Deviation	12.95
Mean	4.91
Sharpe Ratio	0.00

Analysis by William Harding 12-13-01

Investment Company of America is the fund industry's answer to Cal Ripken.

One of the fund world's most impressive winning streaks is in danger of ending. This offering has gone 24 years without posting a negative calendar-year return. But 2001 has been especially troubling for large caps and growth stocks—two areas the fund favors more than its typical large-value peer. The fund has thus lost 6.3% for the year to date ended Dec. 14, 2001. That's still pretty good relative to its average rival, however: Indeed, it ranks on the cusp of the category's best third for the period.

The fund's biases flow from a strategy that's disciplined, but far from dogmatic. For the most part, management favors established blue-chip companies that pay dividends. To limit risk, the team also keeps the fund well-diversified across sectors, and keeps individual position sizes fairly small. However, the team will snap up depressed growth names if they get cheap enough. For example, the fund bought shares in wireless names Nokia and Ericsson Telephone in the third quarter of 2001. As a result, the portfolio often has a bit more of a growth flavor than its typical rival.

That bias can cause the fund to lag more-dedicated value offerings when that style is in favor. Such was the case in 2000, as the fund's 4% gain trailed the majority of large-value funds. That said, the fund's performance over time has been more even keeled than most of its value peers because it doesn't fall as far behind during growth rallies. Further, management's attention to diversifying the fund across issues and sectors and its willingness to hold sizable cash stakes have helped make the fund significantly less volatile than the category norm.

Investors who are looking for a more typical value option should consider sibling Washington Mutual. But those simply looking for a solid, core holding will find a nice home here.

Portfolio Analysis 09-30-01

Share change since 06-01 Total Stocks: 184	Sector	PE	YTD Ret%	% Assets
Philip Morris	Staples	12.1	9.12	3.19
⊖ Fannie Mae	Financials	16.2	–6.95	2.88
Pfizer	Health	34.7	–12.40	2.34
⊖ Viacom Cl B	Services	—	—	1.97
⊕ Pharmacia	Health	36.5	–29.30	1.77
⊕ AOL Time Warner	Technology	—	–7.76	1.70
Royal Dutch Petro NY ADR	Energy	12.0	–17.10	1.59
⊖ Bank of America	Financials	16.7	42.73	1.53
⊕ Lowe's	Retail	38.7	109.00	1.40
⊕ AT&T	N/A	—	—	1.39
⊕ American Intl Grp	Financials	42.0	–19.20	1.19
⊕ Dow Chemical	Industrials	NMF	–4.43	1.17
⊖ PepsiCo	Staples	31.4	–0.54	1.14
IBM	Technology	26.9	43.00	1.06
Wells Fargo	Financials	22.4	–20.20	1.03
⊕ Texas Instruments	Technology	87.5	–40.70	0.98
⊖ USA Educ	Financials	68.9	24.74	0.91
☼ Chevron Texaco	N/A	—	—	0.90
⊖ Bristol-Myers Squibb	Health	20.2	–26.00	0.89
Household Intl	Financials	14.7	6.89	0.88
⊕ Allstate	Financials	17.1	–21.00	0.84
Washington Mutual	Financials	10.1	–5.32	0.84
ALCOA	Industrials	21.4	7.86	0.84
⊕ Raytheon	Industrials	—	7.27	0.77
SBC Comms	Services	18.4	–16.00	0.76

Current Investment Style

Style: Value Blnd Growth; Size: Large Med Small

	Stock Port Avg	Relative S&P 500 Current	Relative S&P 500 Hist	Rel Cat
Price/Earnings Ratio	28.3	0.91	0.91	1.12
Price/Book Ratio	4.9	0.87	0.80	1.20
Price/Cash Flow	16.9	0.94	0.85	1.23
3 Yr Earnings Growth	12.6	0.86	0.75	0.85
1 Yr Earnings Est%	1.4	—	—	–0.42
Med Mkt Cap $mil	37,173	0.6	0.6	1.17

Special Securities % assets 09-30-01	
Restricted/Illiquid Secs	0
Emerging-Markets Secs	0
Options/Futures/Warrants	No

Composition % assets 09-30-01	
Cash	18.7
Stocks*	81.3
Bonds	0.0
Other	0.0
*Foreign (% stocks)	9.0

Market Cap	
Giant	44.7
Large	45.3
Medium	10.0
Small	0.0
Micro	0.0

Sector Weightings	% of Stocks	Rel S&P	5-Year High	5-Year Low
Utilities	2.7	0.8	11	1
Energy	7.4	1.1	12	5
Financials	19.4	1.1	23	13
Industrials	12.2	1.1	21	11
Durables	3.1	2.0	5	1
Staples	10.7	1.4	13	5
Services	12.8	1.2	27	13
Retail	5.3	0.8	6	2
Health	13.8	0.9	15	6
Technology	12.7	0.7	18	5

Address:	333 S. Hope Street Los Angeles, CA 90071 800-421-4120 / 213-486-9200
Web Address:	www.americanfunds.com
Inception:	01-01-34
Advisor:	Cap. Research & Mgmt.
Subadvisor:	None
NTF Plans:	N/A

Minimum Purchase:	$250	Add: $50	IRA: $250
Min Auto Inv Plan:	$50	Add: $50	
Sales Fees:	5.75%L, 0.25%B		
Management Fee:	.39% mx./.23% mn.		
Actual Fees:	Mgt: 0.24%	Dist: 0.23%	
Expense Projections:	3Yr: $744	5Yr: $870	10Yr: $1236
Avg Brok Commission:	—	Income Distrib: Quarterly	
Total Cost (relative to category):		Below Avg	

American Funds New Economy A

Ticker	Load	NAV	Yield	Total Assets	Mstar Category
ANEFX	5.75%	$18.30	0.0%	$8,219.0 mil	Large Blend

Prospectus Objective: Growth

American Funds New Economy Fund seeks long-term growth of capital; current income is secondary.

The fund normally invests at least 75% of assets in equity securities of companies involved in, or with future prospects that are closely tied to, the services sector; it may invest the balance outside the service sector. Prospective issuers include companies in the following fields: telecommunications, computer systems, broadcasting and publishing, health care, advertising, leisure, tourism, financial services, distribution, and transportation. The fund may invest up to 40% of assets in securities of foreign issuers. It may also invest up to 10% of assets in debt rated below investment-grade.

Historical Profile
Return: Average
Risk: Average
Rating: ★★★ Neutral

Investment Style
Equity
Average Stock %

1996	1997	1998	1999	2000	12-01
85%	88%	85%	84%	85%	91%

▼ Manager Change
▽ Partial Manager Change

Fund Performance vs. Category Average
■ Quarterly Fund Return +/– Category Average
— Category Baseline

Performance Quartile (within Category)

Portfolio Manager(s)

Gordon Crawford. Since 1-94.
Claudia P. Huntington. Since 1-95.
Timothy D. Armour. Since 1-91.
Alwyn Heong. Since 1-00.

1990	1991	1992	1993	1994	1995	1996	1997	1998	1999	2000	12-01	History
9.45	11.84	13.23	15.89	13.74	16.18	16.98	19.97	22.95	29.82	22.14	18.30	NAV
–10.10	29.16	16.82	30.99	–8.14	24.37	12.89	28.85	28.84	45.88	–16.20	–17.34	Total Return %
–6.98	–1.32	9.21	20.93	–9.45	–13.17	–10.06	–4.50	0.26	24.84	–7.09	–5.47	+/– S&P 500
–6.07	–3.28	9.17	21.15	–8.59	–13.24	–9.27	–4.17	0.20	24.05	–5.24	–4.58	+/– Wilshire Top 750
2.29	1.54	0.68	0.83	1.07	1.39	0.87	0.77	0.70	0.79	0.00	0.00	Income Return %
–12.38	27.63	16.15	30.15	–9.21	22.98	12.02	28.09	28.14	45.09	–16.20	–17.34	Capital Return %
89	69	5	2	97	92	96	53	17	3	94	78	Total Rtn % Rank Cat
0.26	0.15	0.08	0.11	0.17	0.19	0.14	0.13	0.14	0.18	0.00	0.00	Income $
0.96	0.20	0.49	1.28	0.68	0.69	1.13	1.72	2.54	3.18	2.93	0.00	Capital Gains $
0.92	0.92	0.89	0.85	0.85	0.88	0.84	0.81	0.79	0.78	0.81	—	Expense Ratio %
2.50	1.33	0.67	0.76	1.25	1.33	0.85	0.66	0.60	0.42	0.42	—	Income Ratio %
17	19	19	27	26	27	30	32	39	48	54	—	Turnover Rate %
795.9	1,006.5	1,172.1	2,117.2	2,594.4	3,545.9	4,132.4	4,985.0	6,530.6	10,865.0	10,437.5	8,086.4	Net Assets $mil

Performance 12-31-01

	1st Qtr	2nd Qtr	3rd Qtr	4th Qtr	Total
1997	–1.59	15.16	9.54	3.80	28.85
1998	16.07	1.86	–10.78	22.13	28.84
1999	3.27	12.49	–1.24	27.15	45.88
2000	8.18	–8.21	–5.17	–11.00	–16.20
2001	–13.10	8.16	–25.23	17.61	–17.34

Trailing	Total Return%	+/– S&P 500	+/– Wil Top 750	% Rank All	% Rank Cat	Growth of $10,000
3 Mo	17.61	6.92	6.29	18	5	11,761
6 Mo	–12.06	–6.51	–6.27	90	97	8,794
1 Yr	–17.34	–5.47	–4.58	76	78	8,266
3 Yr Avg	0.35	1.37	2.17	71	33	10,105
5 Yr Avg	10.90	0.20	0.78	14	21	16,775
10 Yr Avg	12.72	–0.21	0.27	14	23	33,108
15 Yr Avg	12.89	–0.84	–0.48	18	37	61,634

Tax Analysis	Tax-Adj Ret%	%Rank Cat	%Pretax Ret	%Rank Cat
3 Yr Avg	–1.19	35	—	—
5 Yr Avg	8.96	30	82.2	46
10 Yr Avg	10.66	33	83.8	34

Potential Capital Gain Exposure: –7% of assets

Risk Analysis

Time Period	Load-Adj Return %	Risk %Rank[1] All	Risk %Rank[1] Cat	Morningstar Return	Morningstar Risk	Morningstar Risk-Adj Rating
1 Yr	–22.10					
3 Yr	–1.61	79	90	–1.31[2]	1.13	★★
5 Yr	9.59	75	84	1.09[2]	1.03	★★★
10 Yr	12.05	78	83	1.11	1.03	★★★

Average Historical Rating (182 months): 3.5★s

[1]1=low, 100=high [2] T-Bill return substituted for category avg.

Category Rating (3 Yr)

1 2 **3** 4 5
Worst Best

Return: Above Avg
Risk: High

Other Measures	Standard Index S&P 500	Best Fit Index Wil 4500
Alpha	3.3	–1.9
Beta	1.14	0.74
R-Squared	69	80

Standard Deviation	23.89
Mean	0.35
Sharpe Ratio	–0.22

Portfolio Analysis 09-30-01

Share change since 06-01 Total Stocks: 191	Sector	PE	YTD Ret%	% Assets
Berkshire Hathaway Cl A	Financials	—	—	4.39
Viacom Cl B	Services	—	—	4.01
AOL Time Warner	Technology	—	–7.76	3.72
⊕ American Intl Grp	Financials	42.0	–19.20	3.18
Clear Channel Comms	Services	—	5.10	2.66
Wells Fargo	Financials	22.4	–20.20	1.95
⊖ Concord EFS	Financials	86.3	49.21	1.77
Carnival	Services	16.4	–7.54	1.69
Freddie Mac	Financials	14.0	–3.87	1.61
⊕ USA Networks	Services	58.1	40.50	1.34
⊕ XL Cap Cl A	Financials	22.8	5.82	1.26
Texas Instruments	Technology	87.5	–40.70	1.25
⊕ ING Groep (Cert)	Financials	—	—	1.24
Dollar General	Retail	19.4	–20.40	1.22
Comcast	Services	20.3	–13.70	1.14
⊕ Applied Matls	Technology	66.8	5.01	1.10
⊕ Western Wireless Cl A	Services	—	–27.90	1.04
Allied Waste Inds	Services	NMF	–3.45	1.04
⊕ AT & T	N/A	—	—	1.02
Kirch Media 144A	N/A	—	—	0.99
⊕ Kohl's	Retail	54.2	15.48	0.96
Microsoft	Technology	57.6	52.78	0.96
MGM Mirage	Services	21.9	2.42	0.94
Manulife Finl	Financials	17.9	—	0.91
Service Corp Intl	Services	—	185.10	0.90

Current Investment Style

Style: Value Blnd Growth; Size: Large Med Small

	Stock Port Avg	Relative S&P 500 Current	Relative S&P 500 Hist	Rel Cat
Price/Earnings Ratio	36.3	1.17	1.11	1.20
Price/Book Ratio	4.1	0.72	0.78	0.74
Price/Cash Flow	21.7	1.20	1.02	1.18
3 Yr Earnings Growth	18.3[1]	1.25	0.98	1.02
1 Yr Earnings Est%	–16.4[1]	9.24	—	—
Med Mkt Cap $mil	15,473	0.3	0.3	0.30

[1]figure is based on 50% or less of stocks

Special Securities % assets 09-30-01	
Restricted/Illiquid Secs	3
Emerging-Markets Secs	3
Options/Futures/Warrants	No

Composition % assets 09-30-01	
Cash	9.9
Stocks*	89.1
Bonds	0.0
Other	1.0
*Foreign (% stocks)	16.2

Market Cap	
Giant	24.5
Large	36.6
Medium	30.8
Small	7.6
Micro	0.5

Sector Weightings	% of Stocks	Rel S&P	5-Year High	5-Year Low
Utilities	0.8	0.3	10	0
Energy	0.6	0.1	3	0
Financials	27.3	1.5	39	13
Industrials	0.4	0.0	4	0
Durables	0.5	0.3	2	0
Staples	0.1	0.0	1	0
Services	35.1	3.2	57	31
Retail	7.3	1.1	17	4
Health	0.0	0.0	9	0
Technology	27.9	1.5	37	6

Analysis by William Harding 12-17-01

New Economy Fund's fairly narrow mandate detracts from its appeal a bit.

Despite its name, this fund doesn't fish solely in the choppy surf of the technology sector. The fund was conceived in 1983 to invest in stocks whose prospects are tied to the service and information-related areas of the global economy. It has substantial exposure to tech—it devoted about 28% of its equity portfolio to the sector at the end of the third quarter. However, the fund is also heavily weighted in media and insurance stocks like Berkshire Hathaway.

Still, the fund's heavy weighting in tech and communications companies makes it especially susceptible to downturns in those industries. That has been all too apparent in 2001. The fund has come back strong as tech has rallied over the past two months, but the sector's slide earlier in the year has left this offering with a 19% loss for the year to date through Dec. 13. The loss is worse than three fourths of its large-blend peers' and is well behind the S&P 500 index for the period.

Despite the risks of its style, the fund has its virtues. Its bias toward tech and telecom names led to superb returns in 1998 and 1999. Moreover, even after its recent tumble, the fund's trailing five- and 10-year returns land in the top third of the large-blend group. It also features experienced management. Comanager Gordon Crawford, for example, has covered media stocks for more than two decades.

The fund's risks make it unappealing as a core holding, but its strengths make it worth a look for those seeking an aggressive growth fund. Even so, American Funds fans should beware of the potential for overlap: This offering shares a number of holdings in common with some of the firm's other options, including Growth Fund of America and Amcap.

Address:	333 S. Hope Street Los Angeles, CA 90071 800–421–4120 / 213–486–9200
Web Address:	www.americanfunds.com
Inception:	12-01-83
Advisor:	Cap. Research & Mgmt.
Subadvisor:	None
NTF Plans:	N/A

Minimum Purchase:	$250	Add: $50	IRA: $250
Min Auto Inv Plan:	$50	Add: $50	
Sales Fees:	5.75%L, 0.25%B		
Management Fee:	.60%		
Actual Fees:	Mgt: 0.40%	Dist: 0.24%	
Expense Projections:	3Yr: $819	5Yr: $999	10Yr: $1519
Avg Brok Commission:	—	Income Distrib: Annually	
Total Cost (relative to category):		Average	

American Funds New Perspective A

Ticker	Load	NAV	Yield	Total Assets	Mstar Category
ANWPX	5.75%	$21.69	1.7%	$28,153.3 mil	World Stock

Prospectus Objective: World Stock

American Funds New Perspective Fund seeks long-term growth of capital; potential for income is a secondary consideration.

The fund invests primarily in common stocks of foreign and U.S. companies. The advisor looks for worldwide changes in international-trade patterns and economic and political relationships. It then searches for companies that may benefit from the new opportunities created by such changes. The advisor closely follows securities, industries, governments, and currency-exchange markets worldwide.

The fund currently offers Class A, B, C, and F shares, all of which differ in fee structure and availability.

Historical Profile

Return High
Risk Low
Rating ★★★★★ Highest

Investment Style
Equity
Average Stock %: 99% 85% 86% 86% 86% 86% 87%

▼ Manager Change
▽ Partial Manager Change

Fund Performance vs. Category Average
■ Quarterly Fund Return +/– Category Average
— Category Baseline

Performance Quartile (within Category)

Portfolio Manager(s)

Thierry Vandeventer. Since 1-78.
Mark E. Denning. Since 1-92.
Gregg E. Ireland. Since 1-92.
Carl M. Kawaja. Since 1-88.
Don D. O'Neal. Since 12-99.
Dina N. Perry. Since 12-97.
Timothy P. Dunn. Since 1-97.

1990	1991	1992	1993	1994	1995	1996	1997	1998	1999	2000	12–01	History
10.24	12.07	12.30	15.01	14.37	16.38	18.17	19.36	22.95	29.44	24.05	21.69	NAV
–2.08	22.64	3.98	26.98	2.97	20.43	17.28	14.98	28.53	40.07	–7.24	–8.30	Total Return %
1.04	–7.85	–3.64	16.92	1.65	–17.10	–5.67	–18.37	–0.05	19.03	1.86	3.58	+/– S&P 500
14.94	4.36	9.20	4.47	–2.11	–0.29	3.80	–0.78	4.19	15.14	5.94	—	+/– MSCI World
2.70	2.55	1.66	1.71	1.54	2.17	1.98	1.60	1.35	0.74	0.66	1.54	Income Return %
–4.78	20.09	2.31	25.26	1.43	18.27	15.30	13.38	27.18	39.33	–7.90	–9.84	Capital Return %
9	42	33	71	14	33	42	37	12	46	37	15	Total Rtn % Rank Cat
0.30	0.26	0.20	0.21	0.23	0.31	0.32	0.29	0.26	0.17	0.20	0.37	Income $
0.43	0.20	0.05	0.37	0.84	0.60	0.69	1.21	1.57	2.34	3.10	0.00	Capital Gains $
0.82	0.86	0.85	0.87	0.84	0.83	0.82	0.79	0.77	0.77	0.79	—	Expense Ratio %
2.55	2.80	1.82	1.40	1.48	2.12	2.00	1.56	1.27	1.06	1.00	—	Income Ratio %
14	8	6	15	25	22	18	26	30	29	34	—	Turnover Rate %
1,569.7	2,457.8	3,320.4	5,086.0	6,540.2	9,292.3	12,895.0	16,202.7	21,257.0	32,173.0	31,304.3	27,393.8	Net Assets $mil

Performance 12-31-01

	1st Qtr	2nd Qtr	3rd Qtr	4th Qtr	Total
1997	2.86	11.96	5.00	–4.90	14.98
1998	15.50	2.64	–10.21	20.74	28.53
1999	5.97	6.92	1.20	22.17	40.07
2000	6.69	–1.50	–7.34	–4.75	–7.24
2001	–7.11	4.37	–14.99	11.26	–8.30

Trailing	Total Return%	+/– S&P 500	+/– MSCI World	% Rank All	% Rank Cat	Growth of $10,000
3 Mo	11.26	0.57	—	36	48	11,126
6 Mo	–5.42	0.14	—	64	30	9,459
1 Yr	–8.30	3.58	—	57	15	9,170
3 Yr Avg	6.01	7.04	—	22	21	11,914
5 Yr Avg	11.98	1.28	—	10	10	17,608
10 Yr Avg	12.95	0.03	—	13	6	33,808
15 Yr Avg	13.19	–0.54	—	16	6	64,137

Tax Analysis	Tax-Adj Ret%	%Rank Cat	%Pretax Ret	%Rank Cat
3 Yr Avg	4.25	23	70.7	55
5 Yr Avg	10.04	10	83.8	22
10 Yr Avg	11.12	6	85.8	12

Potential Capital Gain Exposure: 12% of assets

Risk Analysis

Time Period	Load-Adj Return %	Risk %Rank[1] All	Risk %Rank[1] Cat	Morningstar Return	Morningstar Risk	Morningstar Risk-Adj Rating
1 Yr	–13.57					
3 Yr	3.94	55	24	–0.21[2]	0.72	★★★★
5 Yr	10.66	55	16	1.37[2]	0.64	★★★★★
10 Yr	12.29	62	10	2.72[2]	0.62	★★★★★

Average Historical Rating (193 months): 4.1★s

[1] 1=low, 100=high [2] T–Bill return substituted for category avg.

Category Rating (3 Yr)

1 2 3 4 5
Worst Best

Return Above Avg
Risk Below Avg

Other Measures	Standard Index S&P 500	Best Fit Index MSCIACWrdFre
Alpha	6.1	10.3
Beta	0.82	0.95
R–Squared	77	90

Standard Deviation	16.88
Mean	6.01
Sharpe Ratio	0.07

Portfolio Analysis 09-30-01

Share change since 06–01 Total Stocks: 247	Sector	Country	% Assets
⊖ Astrazeneca (Swe)	Health	United Kingdom	3.21
⊕ Philip Morris	Staples	U.S.	3.04
⊖ Pfizer	Health	U.S.	2.45
⊕ American Intl Grp	Financials	U.S.	1.46
⊕ ING Groep (Cert)	Financials	Netherlands	1.36
⊕ AT & T	Services	U.S.	1.35
⊕ Nestle (Reg)	Staples	Switzerland	1.32
⊖ Viacom Cl B	Services	U.S.	1.26
⊕ Shionogi	Health	Japan	1.26
AOL Time Warner	Technology	U.S.	1.26
Intl Paper	Industrials	U.S.	1.22
⊖ Vodafone Airtouch	Services	United Kingdom	1.20
Coca–Cola	Staples	U.S.	1.17
⊖ Bank of America	Financials	U.S.	1.15
⊕ Taiwan Semicon	Technology	Taiwan	1.08
⊖ ENI	Energy	Italy	1.05
Royal Bk Canada	Financials	Canada	1.04
⊕ Dow Chemical	Industrials	U.S.	1.01
Elan ADR	Health	Ireland	1.00
⊕ Groupe Danone	Staples	France	0.90

Current Investment Style

Style: Value Blnd Growth; Size: Large Med Small

	Stock Port Avg	Rel MSCI EAFE Current	Rel MSCI EAFE Hist	Rel Cat
Price/Earnings Ratio	29.2	1.13	1.12	1.06
Price/Cash Flow	16.5	1.29	1.31	1.00
Price/Book Ratio	4.1	1.19	1.31	0.90
3 Yr Earnings Growth	15.6	0.83	1.82	0.84
Med Mkt Cap $mil	26,864	1.0	1.1	1.12

Country Exposure 09-30-01	% assets
U.S.	43
United Kingdom	8
Japan	8
Canada	5
Netherlands	3

Hedging History: Never

Regional Exposure 09-30-01	% assets
Europe	23
Japan	8
Latin America	1
Pacific Rim	4
U.S.	43
Other	5

Special Securities % assets 09-30-01	
Restricted/Illiquid Secs	Trace
Emerging–Markets Secs	4
Options/Futures/Warrants	Yes

Composition % assets 09-30-01			
Cash	10.5	Bonds	0.1
Stocks	88.6	Other	0.8

Sector Weightings	% of Stocks	Rel Cat	5-Year High	5-Year Low
Utilities	1.2	0.5	8	0
Energy	6.4	1.2	9	2
Financials	13.8	0.8	15	7
Industrials	16.6	1.5	24	11
Durables	3.6	0.9	14	4
Staples	11.9	1.5	16	4
Services	15.8	0.9	33	12
Retail	1.9	0.4	3	1
Health	14.8	1.1	15	4
Technology	14.2	0.9	28	5

Analysis by Emily Hall 12-05-01

American Funds New Perspective defies expectations.

At more than $25 billion in assets, this is one of the largest funds in the Morningstar universe. Such girth could have rendered the fund unable to respond to changing market conditions. But with its steady-as-you-go style, size hasn't been much of a problem, and this offering has managed to deliver impressive results year-in and year-out. Most astonishing is that the fund managed above-average results in the go-go growth market of 1999 but also managed to keep a lid on losses in the ugly markets of 2000 and 2001.

Moreover, given its size, this fund isn't able to make its way by ferreting out lots of unusual small-cap companies. Indeed, the fund's mammoth portfolio of more than 200 names is stuffed full of well-known European, American, and Asian giants.

Boring as it may seem, though, there's a lot to like about this portfolio. The managers don't place big bets on any individual name and they usually keep cash around 10% to 15% of assets. The result is not only solid performance but also a fairly smooth ride: The fund's volatility is well below that of its typical peer.

This year has been no exception. Although the fund's 9% loss for the year through early December may not seem that impressive, it's still good enough to land the fund in the top quintile of the world-stock category. Strong picks across sectors, including Bank of America and Alcoa, have held up quite well in recent months.

The fund isn't for those who are interested in a smaller-cap offering, but for most other investors searching for a straightforward world-stock option, it remains an excellent choice.

Address:	333 S. Hope Street Los Angeles, CA 90071 800–421–4120 / 213–486–9200
Web Address:	www.americanfunds.com
Inception:	03-13-73
Advisor:	Cap. Research & Mgmt.
Subadvisor:	None
NTF Plans:	N/A

Minimum Purchase:	$250	Add: $50	IRA: $250
Min Auto Inv Plan:	$50	Add: $50	
Sales Fees:	5.75%L, 0.25%B		
Management Fee:	.60% mx./.40% mn.		
Actual Fees:	Mgt: 0.40%	Dist: 0.25%	
Expense Projections:	3Yr: $813	5Yr: $989	10Yr: $1497
Avg Brok Commission:	—	Income Distrib: Annually	
Total Cost (relative to category):		Below Avg	

American Funds New World A

Ticker	Load	NAV	Yield	Total Assets	Mstar Category
NEWFX	5.75%	$20.58	2.6%	$1,146.6 mil	Div Emerging Mkts

Prospectus Objective: World Stock

American Funds New World Fund seeks long-term capital appreciation.

The fund primarily invests in equity securities. It normally invests at least 35% of assets in equity an debt securities of issuers in qualified countries that have developing economies and/or markets. In determining whether a country is qualified, the fund will consider factors such as the country's per capita gross domestic product, the percentage of the country's economy that is industrialized, and the overall regulatory environment.

Historical Profile
Return —
Risk —
Rating Not Rated

Investment Style
Equity
Average Stock %: 70% (1999), 75% (2000), 75% (12-01)

▼ Manager Change
▽ Partial Manager Change

Fund Performance vs. Category Average
Quarterly Fund Return +/– Category Average
— Category Baseline

Performance Quartile (within Category)

Portfolio Manager(s)

Robert W. Lovelace, CFA. Since 6-99.
Mark E. Denning. Since 6-99.
David C. Barclay. Since 6-99.
Carl M. Kawaja. Since 6-99.
Alwyn Heong. Since 6-99.

1990	1991	1992	1993	1994	1995	1996	1997	1998	1999	2000	12-01	History
—	—	—	—	—	—	—	—	—	28.29	22.01	20.58	NAV
—	—	—	—	—	—	—	—	—	20.97*	–20.90	–3.96	Total Return %
—	—	—	—	—	—	—	—	—	10.52*	–11.80	7.91	+/– S&P 500
—	—	—	—	—	—	—	—	—	—	9.10	—	+/– MSCI Emerging
—	—	—	—	—	—	—	—	—	0.90	1.31	2.48	Income Return %
—	—	—	—	—	—	—	—	—	20.08	–22.21	–6.44	Capital Return %
—	—	—	—	—	—	—	—	—	—	3	49	Total Rtn % Rank Cat
—	—	—	—	—	—	—	—	—	0.20	0.37	0.55	Income $
—	—	—	—	—	—	—	—	—	0.00	0.00	0.00	Capital Gains $
—	—	—	—	—	—	—	—	—	1.44	1.35	—	Expense Ratio %
—	—	—	—	—	—	—	—	—	1.83	1.61	—	Income Ratio %
—	—	—	—	—	—	—	—	—	—	30	—	Turnover Rate %
—	—	—	—	—	—	—	—	—	1,050.1	1,221.9	1,117.9	Net Assets $mil

Performance 12-31-01

	1st Qtr	2nd Qtr	3rd Qtr	4th Qtr	Total
1997	—	—	—	—	—
1998	—	—	—	—	—
1999	—	—	–3.44	25.17	20.97 *
2000	4.10	–9.44	–8.62	–8.18	–20.90
2001	–5.22	7.53	–18.32	15.38	–3.96

Trailing	Total Return%	+/– S&P 500	+/– MSCI Emerging	% Rank All	% Rank Cat	Growth of $10,000
3 Mo	15.38	4.69	—	23	94	11,538
6 Mo	–5.76	–0.21	—	66	86	9,424
1 Yr	–3.96	7.91	—	49	49	9,604
3 Yr Avg	—	—	—	—	—	—
5 Yr Avg	—	—	—	—	—	—
10 Yr Avg	—	—	—	—	—	—
15 Yr Avg	—	—	—	—	—	—

Tax Analysis	Tax-Adj Ret%	%Rank Cat	%Pretax Ret	%Rank Cat
3 Yr Avg	—	—	—	—
5 Yr Avg	—	—	—	—
10 Yr Avg	—	—	—	—

Potential Capital Gain Exposure: –25% of assets

Risk Analysis

Time Period	Load-Adj Return %	Risk %Rank[1] All	Risk %Rank[1] Cat	Morningstar Return	Morningstar Risk	Morningstar Risk-Adj Rating
1 Yr	–9.49					
3 Yr	—	—	—	—	—	
5 Yr	—	—	—	—	—	
Incept	–5.50	—	—	—	—	

Average Historical Rating —

[1]1=low, 100=high

Category Rating (3 Yr)

Other Measures	Standard Index S&P 500	Best Fit Index
Alpha	—	—
Beta	—	—
R-Squared	—	—

	Standard Deviation	—
Return	Mean	—
Risk	Sharpe Ratio	—

Portfolio Analysis 09-30-01

Share change since 06-01 Total Stocks: 119	Sector	Country	% Assets
⊕ Petroleo Brasil ADR	N/A	N/A	2.01
Samsung SDI	Technology	South Korea	1.70
Sappi	Industrials	South Africa	1.68
⊖ Samsung Electncs	Technology	South Korea	1.60
⊕ Aventis	Health	France	1.58
Housing Dev Fin	Financials	India	1.55
⊖ PepsiCo	Staples	U.S.	1.41
Coca-Cola	Staples	U.S.	1.40
Avon Products	Staples	U.S.	1.32
Govt of Russia 144A FRN	N/A	N/A	1.28
China Unicom	Services	China	1.22
⊕ Telefonos de Mexico ADR L	Services	Mexico	1.17
Astrazeneca (Swe)	Health	United Kingdom	1.15
⊕ Unibanco Unit	N/A	N/A	1.13
Sasol	Industrials	South Africa	1.11
Fomento Economico Mex	Staples	Mexico	1.11
Suzuki Motor	Durables	Japan	1.06
⊕ Votorantim Celulose e Papel (A	Industrials	Brazil	1.05
Hankuk Elec Glass		South Korea	1.05
Orkla Cl A	Staples	Norway	1.00

Current Investment Style

Style: Value Blnd Growth; Size: Large Med Small

	Stock Port Avg	Rel MSCI EAFE Current	Rel MSCI EAFE Hist	Rel Cat
Price/Earnings Ratio	19.1	0.74	—	1.10
Price/Cash Flow	11.6	0.90	—	1.16
Price/Book Ratio	3.6	1.02	—	1.11
3 Yr Earnings Growth	21.4[1]	1.14	—	0.82
Med Mkt Cap $mil	6,045	0.2	—	1.44

[1]figure is based on 50% or less of stocks

Country Exposure 09-30-01	% assets
U.S.	10
South Korea	7
Mexico	5
Japan	5
Hong Kong	3

Hedging History: —

Regional Exposure 09-30-01	% assets
Europe	12
Africa/Mid East	5
Pacific/Asia	19
Latin America	7
Other	10

Special Securities % assets 09-30-01	
Restricted/Illiquid Secs	3
Emerging-Markets Secs	32
Options/Futures/Warrants	Yes

Composition % assets 09-30-01

Cash	12.3	Bonds	12.2
Stocks	74.2	Other	1.4

Sector Weightings	% of Stocks	Rel Cat	5-Year High	5-Year Low
Utilities	1.3	0.2	—	—
Energy	2.2	0.3	—	—
Financials	12.3	0.6	—	—
Industrials	21.8	1.3	—	—
Durables	5.0	1.5	—	—
Staples	18.0	2.4	—	—
Services	14.8	0.8	—	—
Retail	2.9	0.9	—	—
Health	9.3	2.4	—	—
Technology	12.5	0.9	—	—

Analysis by Kunal Kapoor 07-06-01

We think that New World Fund's chances of succeeding in emerging markets are as good as anyone's.

Yes, we know that this isn't your pure-bred emerging-markets fund, but for those looking to get exposure to the world's developing markets, this fund is worth looking at. Indeed, despite investing mostly in multinationals, the fund has a chunk of its assets in firms that are domiciled in Asia and Latin America. (The fund must keep 35% of its assets in emerging markets, and the remainder is invested in companies that earn a large portion of their revenues in those markets.) It fell hard in 2000 as emerging markets tumbled, for example, and it has held its own so far in 2001 as those markets have done relatively well.

The fund's positioning aside, it's an intriguing pick as a small portion of a portfolio. For one, the fund's managers are an experienced and talented bunch who have succeeded at standout offerings, including EuroPacific Growth. Moreover, for most folks, the fund is a legitimate source of exposure to emerging-market stocks. But because it isn't immersed entirely in them, this fund sidesteps a fear that comes with a pure emerging-markets offering—that of getting burned as badly as is possible with such a fund.

To be sure, the fund isn't likely to be easy to own. Aside from its potential volatility, the fund does have some sector biases brought on by the fact that some of the developing world's best-known companies tend to be concentrated in areas such as energy and telecom. Indeed, the fund is carrying a large telecom stake (even though it has come down a little), and the recent sell-off in that sector has only emboldened management to add to long-term favorites such as China Unicom.

Overall, we think the fund has what it takes to succeed in the long run.

Address:	333 S. Hope Street Los Angeles, CA 90071 800-421-4120
Web Address:	www.americanfunds.com
*Inception:	06-17-99
Advisor:	Cap. Research & Mgmt.
Subadvisor:	None
NTF Plans:	N/A

Minimum Purchase:	$250	Add: $50	IRA: $250
Min Auto Inv Plan:	$50	Add: $50	
Sales Fees:	5.75%L, 0.25%B, 0.05%S		
Management Fee:	.85%		
Actual Fees:	Mgt: 0.80%	Dist: 0.26%	
Expense Projections:	3Yr: $978	5Yr: $1272	10Yr: $2105
Avg Brok Commission:	—	Income Distrib: Annually	

Total Cost (relative to category): —

American Funds Smallcap World A

Ticker	Load	NAV	Yield	Total Assets	Mstar Category
SMCWX	5.75%	$22.92	0.2%	$8,571.6 mil	Small Growth

Prospectus Objective: World Stock

American Funds Smallcap World Fund seeks long-term growth of capital.

The fund normally invests at least 65% of assets in equity securities of companies with market capitalizations ranging from $50 million to $1.5 billion, and that are domiciled in at least three countries. It may also invest in convertible securities, government obligations, preferred stocks, repurchase agreements, and corporate debt securities.

Historical Profile

Return Below Avg
Risk Above Avg
Rating ★★ Below Avg

Investment Style
Equity
Average Stock %

97% 85% 89% 89% 90% 89% 87%

▼ Manager Change
▽ Partial Manager Change

Fund Performance vs. Category Average
▦ Quarterly Fund Return +/– Category Average
— Category Baseline

Performance Quartile (within Category)

Portfolio Manager(s)

Gordon Crawford. Since 4-90.
Mark E. Denning. Since 1-91.
Greg Wendt. Since 12-97.
Claudia P. Huntington. Since 12-95.
Martial Chaillet. Since 12-98.
J. Blair Frank. Since 12-99.
Jonathan Knowles. Since 1-99.

1990	1991	1992	1993	1994	1995	1996	1997	1998	1999	2000	12-01	History
14.16	18.70	18.95	23.58	21.41	23.50	25.61	25.98	24.63	39.14	27.78	22.92	NAV
–3.76*	32.89	6.69	30.04	–2.85	22.70	19.75	11.83	0.38	61.64	–15.56	–17.35	Total Return %
–6.21*	2.41	–0.93	19.98	–4.17	–14.83	–3.20	–21.52	–28.19	40.60	–6.45	–5.47	+/– S&P 500
—	–18.29	–1.08	16.68	–0.42	–8.34	8.49	–1.12	–0.85	18.55	6.88	–8.12	+/– Russ 2000 Grth
2.34	0.78	0.70	0.32	0.47	1.08	0.51	0.39	0.35	0.06	0.00	0.14	Income Return %
–6.10	32.12	5.99	29.72	–3.32	21.63	19.24	11.44	0.04	61.58	–15.56	–17.49	Capital Return %
—	94	71	7	59	80	47	75	63	40	79	75	Total Rtn % Rank Cat
0.35	0.11	0.13	0.06	0.11	0.23	0.12	0.10	0.09	0.02	0.00	0.04	Income $
0.00	0.00	0.83	0.97	1.35	2.45	2.35	2.50	1.29	0.61	5.29	0.00	Capital Gains $
0.49	1.31	1.21	1.15	1.12	1.13	1.09	1.07	1.06	1.09	1.10	1.10	Expense Ratio %
1.70	1.11	0.85	0.33	0.38	0.97	0.68	0.40	0.27	0.12	—	0.00	Income Ratio %
—	19	23	25	29	46	43	42	44	50	63	63	Turnover Rate %
610.3	1,350.6	1,481.9	2,712.9	3,482.7	4,765.7	7,073.4	8,667.0	8,108.8	12,374.0	11,329.0	8,421.8	Net Assets $mil

Performance 12-31-01

	1st Qtr	2nd Qtr	3rd Qtr	4th Qtr	Total
1997	–3.48	12.84	10.34	–6.95	11.83
1998	11.16	–4.29	–19.90	17.79	0.38
1999	–0.49	17.54	2.64	34.64	61.64
2000	16.07	–9.91	–1.69	–17.86	–15.56
2001	–18.79	10.37	–25.22	23.31	–17.35

Trailing	Total Return%	+/– S&P 500	+/– Russ 2000 Grth	% Rank All	% Rank Cat	Growth of $10,000
3 Mo	23.31	12.62	–2.86	9	51	12,331
6 Mo	–7.79	–2.24	1.47	77	62	9,221
1 Yr	–17.35	–5.47	–8.12	76	75	8,265
3 Yr Avg	4.10	5.13	3.85	39	74	11,281
5 Yr Avg	4.84	–5.86	1.97	68	74	12,664
10 Yr Avg	9.63	–3.30	2.44	35	71	25,080
15 Yr Avg	—	—	—	—	—	—

Tax Analysis	Tax-Adj Ret%	%Rank Cat	%Pretax Ret	%Rank Cat
3 Yr Avg	2.84	67	69.3	70
5 Yr Avg	3.34	69	69.1	71
10 Yr Avg	7.64	55	79.3	48

Potential Capital Gain Exposure: –13% of assets

Risk Analysis

Time Period	Load-Adj Return %	Risk %Rank[1] All	Risk %Rank[1] Cat	Morningstar Return	Morningstar Risk	Morningstar Risk-Adj Rating
1 Yr	–22.10					
3 Yr	2.07	88	40	–0.59[2]	1.34	★★★
5 Yr	3.60	86	26	–0.30[2]	1.29	★★
10 Yr	8.98	86	14	0.56	1.23	★★

Average Historical Rating (105 months): 2.7★s

[1]1=low, 100=high [2] T-Bill return substituted for category avg.

Category Rating (3 Yr)

1 2 3 4 5
Worst Best

Return Below Avg
Risk Average

Other Measures	Standard Index S&P 500	Best Fit Index Wil 4500
Alpha	8.6	3.2
Beta	1.11	1.00
R-Squared	42	92
Standard Deviation		31.61
Mean		4.10
Sharpe Ratio		–0.03

Portfolio Analysis 09-30-01

Share change since 06-01 Total Stocks: 560	Sector	PE	YTD Ret%	% Assets
⊖ Arthur J. Gallagher & Co.	Financials	26.3	10.31	1.38
Triad Hospitals	Health	—	–9.87	1.23
⊖ Semtech	Technology	63.7	61.76	1.23
Extended Stay Amer	Services	24.5	27.63	1.21
✵ Earthlink	Technology	—	141.90	1.17
Michaels Stores	Retail	29.3	148.60	1.10
Westwood One	Services	77.1	55.59	1.01
⊕ OM Grp	Industrials	20.2	22.24	1.01
⊕ JJB Sports	Retail	19.1	—	0.94
Cheesecake Factory	Services	46.4	35.91	0.78
⊖ Service Corp Intl	Services	—	185.10	0.77
Imclone Sys	Health	—	5.59	0.77
✵ Triquint Semicon	Technology	26.7	–71.90	0.73
Idexx Labs	Health	25.9	29.59	0.69
⊕ Cambrex	Industrials	23.6	–3.39	0.67
✵ Education Mgmt	Services	39.0	1.40	0.67
Wetherspoon Jd	N/A	—	—	0.65
⊖ Black Box	Technology	16.3	9.45	0.62
Exar	Technology	54.9	–32.60	0.59
Scios	Health	—	6.83	0.57
Performance Food Grp	Staples	33.5	37.25	0.56
BRL Hardy	Staples	23.8	—	0.53
HNC Software	Technology	—	–30.60	0.53
CIMA Labs	Health	39.3	–44.40	0.51
Choicepoint	Services	70.4	15.97	0.51

Current Investment Style

Style: Value Blnd Growth; Size: Large Med Small

	Stock Port Avg	Relative S&P 500 Current	Relative S&P 500 Hist	Rel Cat
Price/Earnings Ratio	29.7	0.96	1.03	0.92
Price/Book Ratio	4.3	0.75	1.22	0.88
Price/Cash Flow	20.4	1.13	1.46	0.92
3 Yr Earnings Growth	24.8[1]	1.70	—	0.99
1 Yr Earnings Est%	–8.0[1]	4.54	—	–1.03
Med Mkt Cap $mil	935	0.0	0.0	0.90

[1]figure is based on 50% or less of stocks

Special Securities % assets 09-30-01	
Restricted/Illiquid Secs	4
Emerging-Markets Secs	5
Options/Futures/Warrants	Yes

Composition % assets 09-30-01	
Cash	11.2
Stocks*	87.6
Bonds	0.2
Other	1.1
*Foreign (% stocks)	26.7

Market Cap	
Giant	0.0
Large	0.6
Medium	31.4
Small	60.5
Micro	7.6

Sector Weightings	% of Stocks	Rel S&P	5-Year High	5-Year Low
Utilities	0.0	0.0	5	0
Energy	2.2	0.3	10	2
Financials	6.7	0.4	14	6
Industrials	11.0	1.0	23	9
Durables	1.8	1.1	6	2
Staples	4.2	0.5	6	2
Services	24.5	2.3	37	20
Retail	7.7	1.1	13	5
Health	14.2	1.0	15	3
Technology	27.8	1.5	32	9

Analysis by William Harding 12-10-01

This fund isn't without strong points, but its appeal is limited.

Smallcap World Fund is fairly distinctive. It's the sole small-cap offering in American Funds' lineup, and it's also one of the only domestically focused small-growth funds that also buys foreign stocks. Currently about 30% of the fund's assets are devoted to foreign equities, mostly in Europe and Asia. Over time, the fund's foreign stake has typically been in the 30% to 45% range.

This line of attack has been a mixed blessing for shareholders. The fund's global flavor has been a drain on performance in recent years as domestic stocks have generally outpaced their international counterparts. As a result, the fund's trailing five- and 10-year returns lag more than 70% of its small-growth rivals'. On the other hand, foreign and small-cap stocks are good diversifiers for a large-cap-dominated portfolio. Moreover, management's picks are spread across more than 500 holdings, which tempers volatility.

That said, this fund could be a tough fit for many portfolios. Most investors might instead look to a fund like EuroPacific Growth for foreign exposure, then look outside American Funds for a small- or mid-cap option. The shop's bread and butter is running large-cap portfolios, and this offering's large asset may hinder its ability to maneuver in the small-cap arena.

But investors who want the convenience of a one-stop option for small-cap and foreign stocks should be fine here. Investors will be hard-pressed to find more-experienced and savvy managers than those at American Funds, and the team in charge here has had tremendous success over the long haul on a number of offerings, such as Growth Fund of America and EuroPacific Growth. Further, like all of the firm's funds, this one offers below-average expenses.

Address:	333 S. Hope Street Los Angeles, CA 90071 800–421–4120 / 213–486–9200
Web Address:	www.americanfunds.com
*Inception:	04-30-90
Advisor:	Cap. Research & Mgmt.
Subadvisor:	None
NTF Plans:	N/A

Minimum Purchase:	$250	Add: $50	IRA: $250
Min Auto Inv Plan:	$50	Add: $50	
Sales Fees:	5.75%L, 0.05%B, 0.25%S		
Management Fee:	.80%		
Actual Fees:	Mgt: 0.66%	Dist: 0.27%	
Expense Projections:	3Yr: $979	5Yr: $1195	10Yr: $1965
Avg Brok Commission:	—	Income Distrib: Annually	
Total Cost (relative to category):		Average	

American Funds Tax–Exempt Bond Fd A

Ticker	Load	NAV	Yield	SEC Yield	Total Assets	Mstar Category
AFTEX	3.75%	$12.01	4.9%	3.91%	$2,336.4 mil	Muni Natl Interm–Term

Prospectus Objective: Muni Bond—National

American Funds Tax-Exempt Bond Fund seeks current income exempt from federal income taxes, consistent with the preservation of capital.

The fund normally invests at least 65% of assets in tax-exempt securities rated A or higher. It may invest up to 20% of assets in bonds rated below BBB. If market conditions warrant, the fund may make investments in short-term taxable obligations. The fund may not invest in private-activity bonds subject to the Alternative Minimum Tax.

Historical Profile
Return Average
Risk Below Avg
Rating ★★★★ Above Avg

Investment Style
Fixed-Income
Income Rtn %Rank Cat: 13, 6, 10, 8, 12, 16, 10, 12

Growth of Principal vs. Interest Rate Shifts
— Principal Value $000 (NAV with capital gains reinvested)
— Interest Rate % on 10 Yr Treasury
▼ Manager Change
▽ Partial Manager Change
► Mgr Unknown After
◄ Mgr Unknown Before

Performance Quartile (within Category)

Portfolio Manager(s)

Neil L. Langberg. Since 10-79.
Rebecca L. Ford. Since 1-86.
Mark R. MacDonald. Since 1-94.
Brenda S. Ellerin. Since 12-98.
David A. Hoag. Since 12-98.

History

1990	1991	1992	1993	1994	1995	1996	1997	1998	1999	2000	12-01	History
11.06	11.56	11.79	12.37	11.11	12.23	12.09	12.47	12.41	11.50	11.97	12.01	NAV
6.17	11.17	9.04	11.71	–4.81	17.28	4.57	8.98	6.07	–2.32	9.67	5.57	Total Return %
–2.78	–4.84	1.64	1.97	–1.89	–1.19	0.96	–0.70	–2.60	–1.49	–1.96	–2.85	+/– LB Aggregate
–1.13	–0.98	0.22	–0.56	0.34	–0.18	0.14	–0.22	–0.41	–0.25	–2.02	0.49	+/– LB Muni
6.79	6.46	6.22	5.93	5.60	6.20	5.38	5.40	5.04	4.87	5.43	5.01	Income Return %
–0.62	4.71	2.82	5.79	–10.40	11.08	–0.80	3.59	1.04	–7.19	4.24	0.56	Capital Return %
61	40	21	32	80	16	14	11	20	63	33	5	Total Rtn % Rank Cat
0.73	0.69	0.70	0.68	0.67	0.67	0.64	0.64	0.61	0.59	0.61	0.59	Income $
0.00	0.00	0.08	0.09	0.00	0.09	0.04	0.04	0.19	0.04	0.00	0.03	Capital Gains $
0.70	0.72	0.71	0.71	0.69	0.66	0.68	0.68	0.66	0.65	0.67	—	Expense Ratio %
6.65	6.33	6.04	5.62	5.53	5.87	5.35	5.27	4.98	4.78	5.22	—	Income Ratio %
40	25	17	16	22	49	27	14	23	15	29	—	Turnover Rate %
602.8	769.4	1,022.0	1,404.5	1,253.1	1,501.6	1,513.0	1,666.0	1,862.9	1,816.0	1,898.0	2,260.2	Net Assets $mil

Performance 12-31-01

	1st Qtr	2nd Qtr	3rd Qtr	4th Qtr	Total
1997	–0.01	3.29	2.96	2.49	8.98
1998	1.33	1.24	2.94	0.44	6.07
1999	0.54	–1.59	–0.35	–0.93	–2.32
2000	2.19	1.07	2.63	3.46	9.67
2001	2.35	1.16	2.94	–0.95	5.57

Trailing	Total Return%	+/– LB Agg	+/– LB Muni	% Rank All	% Rank Cat	Growth of $10,000
3 Mo	–0.95	–0.98	–0.28	92	54	9,905
6 Mo	1.96	–2.69	–0.16	23	22	10,196
1 Yr	5.57	–2.85	0.49	20	5	10,557
3 Yr Avg	4.19	–2.09	–0.56	38	21	11,310
5 Yr Avg	5.51	–1.92	–0.47	55	10	13,074
10 Yr Avg	6.40	–0.83	–0.23	59	5	18,594
15 Yr Avg	6.66	–1.46	–0.53	74	32	26,287

Tax Analysis	Tax-Adj Ret%	%Rank Cat	%Pretax Ret	%Rank Cat
3 Yr Avg	4.14	22	98.9	72
5 Yr Avg	5.40	9	98.1	77
10 Yr Avg	6.27	5	98.0	56

Potential Capital Gain Exposure: 3% of assets

Risk Analysis

Time Period	Load-Adj Return %	Risk %Rank[1] All	Risk %Rank[1] Cat	Morningstar Return	Morningstar Risk	Morningstar Risk-Adj Rating
1 Yr	1.61					
3 Yr	2.87	9	43	0.29[2]	0.80	★★★★
5 Yr	4.70	9	41	0.73[2]	0.80	★★★★
10 Yr	5.99	12	64	1.03	0.86	★★★★

Average Historical Rating (193 months): 2.9★s

[1] 1=low, 100=high [2] T-Bill return substituted for category avg.

Category Rating (3 Yr)

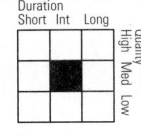

1 2 3 4 5
Worst Best

Return Above Avg
Risk Average

Other Measures	Standard Index LB Agg	Best Fit Index LB Muni
Alpha	–1.6	–0.6
Beta	0.74	0.88
R-Squared	56	97

Standard Deviation	3.46
Mean	4.19
Sharpe Ratio	–0.26

Portfolio Analysis 09-30-01

Total Fixed-Income: 673	Date of Maturity	Amount $000	Value $000	% Net Assets
LA Lake Charles Harbor/Term Dist 7.75%	08-15-22	24,000	25,616	1.13
WA Pub Pwr Sply Sys Proj #2 6%	07-01-07	19,900	22,138	0.97
TX Transp 3.75%	08-29-02	20,700	21,004	0.92
CO Arapahoe Cap Impr Tr Hwy 6.95%	08-31-20	17,500	20,533	0.90
WA Central Puget Sound Regl Trans 4.75%	02-01-28	21,940	20,250	0.89
PA Philadelphia Hosp/Higher Educ 6.5%	11-15-08	15,500	16,297	0.72
PA Montgomery Indl Dev Retiremt 5.25%	11-15-28	17,500	16,295	0.72
VA Fairfax Econ Dev Natl Cable 7.5%	10-01-29	15,500	16,289	0.72
IN Hlth Fac Fin Daughters Charity 5%	11-01-26	15,010	15,867	0.70
CO Denver Arpt Sys 7.25%	11-15-25	14,210	15,266	0.67
KY Transp 0%	06-26-02	15,000	15,198	0.67
NV Clark GO Impr Dist #91/92 7.5%	12-01-19	14,000	14,991	0.66
CO Harris Hlth 6.375%	06-01-29	13,900	14,727	0.65
IL Chicago Skyway Toll Brdg 6.5%	01-01-10	13,250	14,593	0.64
CA Long Beach Aquarium of Pacific 6.125%	07-01-23	12,500	14,080	0.62

Current Investment Style

Duration: Short Int Long
Quality: High Med Low

Avg Duration[1]	6.6 Yrs
Avg Nominal Maturity	11.4 Yrs
Avg Credit Quality	A
Avg Wtd Coupon	5.69%
Avg Wtd Price	103.44% of par
Pricing Service	J.J. Kenny

[1] figure provided by fund

Credit Analysis % bonds 06-30-01

US Govt	0	BB	13
AAA	44	B	5
AA	15	Below B	0
A	10	NR/NA	0
BBB	14		

Special Securities % assets 09-30-01

Restricted/Illiquid Secs	Trace
Inverse Floaters	Trace
Options/Futures/Warrants	No

Bond Type % assets

Alternative Minimum Tax (AMT)	N/A
Insured	N/A
Prerefunded	N/A

Top 5 States % bonds

IL	11.4	WA	6.8
TX	8.5	PA	5.8
CO	7.5		

Composition % assets 09-30-01

Cash	1.8	Bonds	98.2
Stocks	0.0	Other	0.0

Sector Weightings	% of Bonds	Rel Cat
General Obligation	18.3	0.7
Utilities	9.0	1.0
Health	32.4	2.6
Water/Waste	2.8	0.5
Housing	3.3	0.5
Education	5.8	0.7
Transportation	9.3	0.8
COP/Lease	1.4	0.6
Industrial	9.2	1.2
Misc Revenue	7.4	1.5
Demand	1.2	1.3

Analysis by Eric Jacobson 12-11-01

American Funds Tax Exempt Bond Fund of America has shown that it's deserving of investor confidence.

Not that that there was cause for major worry. True, this fund has long held a larger-than-average stake in credit-sensitive municipals, and has run the risk of getting stung by weakness in that subset of the market. It hasn't gone overboard, though, and the fund's well-reputed research staff has been reassuring. Indeed, over the past several years, the only notable weakness displayed by this fund has come during periods of rising rates, such as 1994 and 1999, when it easily outlegged its longer rivals, but suffered relative to the intermediate-term peer group that it qualifies for under Morningstar guidelines.

The credit markets have been a big problem over the past couple of years, but they've been banner years for this fund. Despite a general distaste for credit risk in the marketplace, as well as a series of individual bond blowups across that spectrum, the portfolio has come through quite nicely. And though there's been softness among hospitals and life-care centers, the fund earned a top-third finish in 2000.

More recently, the fund's multiple managers have been shifting into some mid-maturity, callable bonds, and upgrading their health-care stake to higher-quality issuers as older, lower-quality positions have risen in value. The team has also drawn in its rate sensitivity. And thanks in large part to the fund's avoidance of bonds subject to the alternative minimum tax (AMT), it had very light exposure to the airline credits that saw trouble late in 2001. The net result has been a 5.4% year-to-date return that places in the muni national intermediate-term group's best decile.

No fund is perfect, and this one's bound to have rocky days again. It has passed a major test over the past couple of years, though, inspiring much confidence in its management.

Address:	333 S. Hope Street Los Angeles, CA 90071 213–486–9200 / 800–421–4120
Web Address:	www.americanfunds.com
Inception:	10-03-79
Advisor:	Cap. Research & Mgmt.
Subadvisor:	None
NTF Plans:	N/A

Minimum Purchase:	$250	Add: $50 IRA: —
Min Auto Inv Plan:	$50	Add: $50
Sales Fees:	3.75%L, 0.25%B	
Management Fee:	.30% mx./.16% mn.	
Actual Fees:	Mgt: 0.34%	Dist: 0.25%
Expense Projections:	3Yr: $575	5Yr: $724 10Yr: $1155
Avg Brok Commission:	—	Income Distrib: Monthly
Total Cost (relative to category):		Average

American Funds Washington Mutual A

Ticker	Load	NAV	Yield	Total Assets	Mstar Category
AWSHX	5.75%	$28.25	1.9%	$49,297.6 mil	Large Value

Prospectus Objective: Growth and Income

American Funds Washington Mutual Fund seeks income and the opportunity for growth of principal.

The fund invests in common stocks or equivalent securities that are legal for the investment of trust funds in the District of Columbia. It intends to be fully invested and well diversified. Management tries to select a portfolio that an investor with fiduciary responsibility might select under the Prudent Investor Rule of the Superior Court of the District of Columbia.

Historical Profile

Return Above Avg
Risk Below Avg
Rating ★★★★ Above Avg

Investment Style
Equity
Average Stock %: 100% 97% 97% 96% 97% 96% 96%

▼ Manager Change
▽ Partial Manager Change

Fund Performance vs. Category Average
■ Quarterly Fund Return +/– Category Average
— Category Baseline

Performance Quartile (within Category)

Portfolio Manager(s)

Stephen E. Bepler, CFA. Since 1-81.
James K. Dunton, CFA. Since 1-78.
Timothy D. Armour. Since 1-90.
Gregg E. Ireland. Since 1-90.
Robert G. O'Donnell. Since 1-93.
James B. Lovelace, CFA. Since 1-90.
James F. Rothenberg, CFA. Since 1-93.
Alan N. Berro. Since 1-98.
J. Dale Harvey. Since 1-97.

1990	1991	1992	1993	1994	1995	1996	1997	1998	1999	2000	12-01	History
13.63	15.90	16.58	17.78	16.84	21.97	24.54	30.35	32.91	29.56	29.03	28.25	NAV
–3.82	23.50	9.10	13.05	0.49	41.22	20.18	33.29	19.37	1.16	9.06	1.51	Total Return %
–0.70	–6.99	1.48	3.00	–0.83	3.68	–2.77	–0.06	–9.21	–19.88	18.16	13.39	+/– S&P 500
–0.15	5.34	0.03	–6.71	2.80	1.19	–2.14	–2.20	–1.87	–9.80	6.75	10.31	+/– Russ Top 200 Val
4.24	4.17	3.57	3.42	3.53	3.73	2.85	2.55	2.02	1.77	1.98	1.91	Income Return %
–8.06	19.33	5.53	9.63	–3.05	37.49	17.33	30.74	17.35	–0.62	7.08	–0.39	Capital Return %
35	75	54	54	38	4	52	9	14	72	39	14	Total Rtn % Rank Cat
0.62	0.56	0.56	0.56	0.62	0.62	0.62	0.62	0.61	0.58	0.58	0.55	Income $
0.06	0.30	0.18	0.39	0.41	1.09	1.20	1.66	2.60	3.11	2.50	0.64	Capital Gains $
0.69	0.77	0.74	0.70	0.69	0.69	0.66	0.64	0.62	0.61	0.63	0.65	Expense Ratio %
4.01	4.24	3.58	3.33	3.29	3.57	2.98	2.56	2.08	1.84	1.91	1.95	Income Ratio %
7	11	10	19	24	26	23	20	18	28	26	25	Turnover Rate %
5,606.9	8,215.4	10,100.4	12,638.5	12,668.3	18,786.1	25,374.5	38,246.0	51,773.8	53,136.0	47,413.8	48,135.1	Net Assets $mil

Performance 12-31-01

	1st Qtr	2nd Qtr	3rd Qtr	4th Qtr	Total
1997	3.10	14.44	7.62	4.97	33.29
1998	12.24	0.34	–7.01	13.98	19.37
1999	0.22	9.39	–9.39	1.83	1.16
2000	–0.82	–3.05	6.50	6.51	9.06
2001	–1.53	4.17	–7.41	6.89	1.51

Trailing	Total Return%	+/– S&P 500	+/– Russ Top 200 Val	% Rank All	% Rank Cat	Growth of $10,000
3 Mo	6.89	–3.79	1.38	57	78	10,689
6 Mo	–1.03	4.53	4.75	43	13	9,897
1 Yr	1.51	13.39	10.31	40	14	10,151
3 Yr Avg	3.85	4.87	2.68	43	33	11,199
5 Yr Avg	12.25	1.55	1.04	9	14	17,819
10 Yr Avg	14.12	1.20	0.10	8	15	37,480
15 Yr Avg	13.69	–0.05	0.19	12	14	68,505

Tax Analysis	Tax-Adj Ret%	%Rank Cat	%Pretax Ret	%Rank Cat
3 Yr Avg	1.70	37	44.2	75
5 Yr Avg	9.94	15	81.2	28
10 Yr Avg	11.81	9	83.6	18

Potential Capital Gain Exposure: 20% of assets

Risk Analysis

Time Period	Load-Adj Return %	Risk %Rank[1] All	Risk %Rank[1] Cat	Morningstar Return	Morningstar Risk	Morningstar Risk-Adj Rating
1 Yr	–4.32					
3 Yr	1.82	49	24	–0.64[2]	0.69	★★★
5 Yr	10.93	50	15	1.44[2]	0.69	★★★★
10 Yr	13.45	55	21	1.41	0.70	★★★★

Average Historical Rating (193 months): 3.9★s

[1] 1=low, 100=high [2] T-Bill return substituted for category avg.

Category Rating (3 Yr)

1 2 3 4 5
Worst Best

Return Above Avg
Risk Below Avg

Other Measures	Standard Index S&P 500	Best Fit Index S&P 500
Alpha	2.5	2.5
Beta	0.55	0.55
R-Squared	41	41

Standard Deviation	15.08
Mean	3.85
Sharpe Ratio	–0.08

Portfolio Analysis 09-30-01

Share change since 06-01 Total Stocks: 152	Sector	PE	YTD Ret%	% Assets
⊖ Bank of America	Financials	16.7	42.73	3.28
⊖ Texaco	Energy	—	6.76	2.58
⊕ AT & T	N/A	—	—	2.21
⊕ Wells Fargo	Financials	22.4	–20.20	1.77
⊕ J.P. Morgan Chase & Co.	Financials	27.8	–17.40	1.75
⊕ Allstate	Financials	17.1	–21.00	1.68
☼ Chevron Texaco	N/A	—	—	1.68
⊕ ExxonMobil	Energy	15.3	–7.59	1.67
⊕ Wachovia	Financials	—	23.13	1.65
⊖ Verizon Comms	Services	29.7	–2.52	1.64
⊖ Household Intl	Financials	14.7	6.89	1.59
⊖ Bank One	Financials	29.1	9.13	1.45
⊕ Pfizer	Health	34.7	–12.40	1.42
⊕ Kimberly-Clark	Industrials	18.5	–13.80	1.40
⊕ Pharmacia	Health	36.5	–29.30	1.39
⊖ Bristol-Myers Squibb	Health	20.2	–26.00	1.38
Sara Lee	Staples	8.4	–6.95	1.34
⊕ Eli Lilly	Health	28.9	–14.40	1.32
Intl Paper	Industrials	—	1.43	1.29
SBC Comms	Services	18.4	–16.00	1.28
⊖ Albertson's	Retail	29.7	22.01	1.07
⊖ McDonald's	Services	19.2	–21.50	1.06
⊕ American Elec Pwr	Utilities	20.2	–1.28	1.05
⊕ Hewlett-Packard	Technology	97.8	–33.90	1.03
⊕ Heinz HJ	Staples	29.6	–9.86	1.02

Current Investment Style

Style: Value Blnd Growth
Size: Large Med Small

	Stock Port Avg	Relative S&P 500 Current	Relative S&P 500 Hist	Rel Cat
Price/Earnings Ratio	24.3	0.78	0.74	0.96
Price/Book Ratio	4.5	0.79	0.64	1.09
Price/Cash Flow	13.9	0.77	0.67	1.01
3 Yr Earnings Growth	11.1	0.76	0.48	0.75
1 Yr Earnings Est%	–1.0	0.58	—	0.31
Med Mkt Cap $mil	24,646	0.4	0.4	0.78

Special Securities % assets 09-30-01	
Restricted/Illiquid Secs	0
Emerging-Markets Secs	0
Options/Futures/Warrants	No

Composition % assets 09-30-01	
Cash	5.0
Stocks*	95.0
Bonds	0.0
Other	0.0
*Foreign (% stocks)	0.3

Market Cap	
Giant	30.9
Large	55.7
Medium	13.2
Small	0.3
Micro	0.0

Sector Weightings	% of Stocks	Rel S&P	5-Year High	5-Year Low
Utilities	10.2	3.2	18	4
Energy	7.4	1.1	14	4
Financials	24.7	1.4	28	19
Industrials	14.4	1.3	21	11
Durables	4.5	2.9	7	1
Staples	7.3	0.9	7	1
Services	10.1	0.9	24	9
Retail	6.0	0.9	7	1
Health	10.3	0.7	20	5
Technology	5.2	0.3	9	1

Analysis by William Harding 10-04-01

This all-weather offering is an excellent pick for risk-averse investors.

American Funds Washington Mutual Fund's recent showing demonstrates why it should anchor an investor's portfolio. The fund has held up admirably amid the market's steep slide this year. It is down only 4% for the year to date ended October 2, 2001, besting the S&P 500 index by 15 percentage points and outpacing more than 90% of its large-value rivals.

The fund's strong relative showing isn't a product of any fancy portfolio maneuvering; rather, it owes to its managers' commitment to their conservative, value-oriented strategy. The team only invests in cheaply priced, established blue-chip companies—most of which pay dividends. Generally speaking, this approach has led the fund to overweight the financial and utilities sectors, which have been relative bright spots in the market over the past year.

The fund's strict value discipline can be a hindrance at times. Such was the case in 1999's roaring market, when the fund gained a meager 1%. As a result, the fund witnessed significant outflows in 2000 as investors flocked to more aggressive offerings. That's too bad: The fund's strength over time has more than made up for its occasional shortfalls, and its long-term record is solid.

The fund has adhered to the same basic investment criteria since 1952 with only a few tweaks. One adjustment is that the fund is now allowed to make limited investments in companies that do not pay dividends. This has enabled management to nibble on some beaten-down tech names, including Dell and Oracle. These new positions represent a tiny percentage of assets, however, so the fund's profile hasn't changed markedly.

This fund has it all: above-average returns, low volatility, and a sound approach that is well executed by experienced managers.

Address:	333 S. Hope Street Los Angeles, CA 90071 800-421-4120 / 202-842-5665
Web Address:	www.americanfunds.com
Inception:	07-31-52
Advisor:	Cap. Research & Mgmt.
Subadvisor:	None
NTF Plans:	N/A

Minimum Purchase:	$250	Add: $50	IRA: $250
Min Auto Inv Plan:	$50	Add: $50	
Sales Fees:	5.75%L, 0.25%S		
Management Fee:	.23% mx./.20% mn., .18%A		
Actual Fees:	Mgt: 0.29%	Dist: 0.24%	
Expense Projections:	3Yr: $765	5Yr: $906	10Yr: $1316
Avg Brok Commission:	—	Income Distrib: Quarterly	
Total Cost (relative to category):	Below Avg		

Ameristock

Ticker	Load	NAV	Yield	Total Assets	Mstar Category
AMSTX	None	$40.40	0.7%	$863.4 mil	Large Value

Prospectus Objective: Equity–Income

Ameristock Fund seeks capital appreciation and current income.

The fund normally invests at least 80% of assets in common stocks. Management emphasizes large-cap companies that it judges to have low P/E ratios and high dividend yields. The fund may invest in foreign securities only through American depositary receipts. It may also invest in high-quality fixed-income securities and may engage in options and futures transactions.

Historical Profile
- **Return** High
- **Risk** Below Avg
- **Rating** ★★★★★ Highest

Investment Style
Equity
Average Stock %: 93% (1996), 94% (1997), 95% (1998), 95% (1999), 99% (2000), 97% (12-01)

▼ Manager Change
▽ Partial Manager Change

Fund Performance vs. Category Average
■ Quarterly Fund Return +/– Category Average
— Category Baseline

Performance Quartile (within Category)

Portfolio Manager(s)

Nicholas D. Gerber. Since 8-95. BA Skidmore C;; MBA U. of San Francisco. Other fund currently managed: Ameristock Focused Value.

Andrew Ngim. Since 1-00. Other funds currently managed: Ameristock Focused Value, Ameristock Large Company Growth.

1990	1991	1992	1993	1994	1995	1996	1997	1998	1999	2000	12-01	History
—	—	—	—	—	16.96	21.18	26.81	34.91	35.11	40.22	40.40	NAV
—	—	—	—	—	14.29*	27.69	32.86	31.98	2.73	20.70	1.25	Total Return %
—	—	—	—	—	3.80*	4.74	–0.49	3.40	–18.31	29.80	13.13	+/– S&P 500
—	—	—	—	—	—	5.37	–2.63	10.74	–8.23	18.39	10.05	+/– Russ Top 200 Val
—	—	—	—	—	1.22	2.31	2.02	0.90	1.19	1.28	0.71	Income Return %
—	—	—	—	—	13.07	25.37	30.84	31.08	1.53	19.41	0.54	Capital Return %
—	—	—	—	—	—	8	11	2	65	6	15	Total Rtn % Rank Cat
—	—	—	—	—	0.18	0.39	0.42	0.24	0.42	0.45	0.29	Income $
—	—	—	—	—	0.00	0.04	0.83	0.22	0.34	1.63	0.04	Capital Gains $
—	—	—	—	—	—	0.00	0.56	0.90	0.94	0.99	0.83	Expense Ratio %
—	—	—	—	—	—	2.40	2.40	1.48	1.22	1.51	1.50	Income Ratio %
—	—	—	—	—	—	—	22	12	9	31	6	Turnover Rate %
—	—	—	—	—	0.2	4.8	7.3	35.6	109.7	164.1	—	Net Assets $mil

Performance 12-31-01

	1st Qtr	2nd Qtr	3rd Qtr	4th Qtr	Total
1997	3.54	14.27	5.91	6.02	32.86
1998	13.13	3.79	–5.62	19.10	31.98
1999	2.84	8.33	–8.18	0.42	2.73
2000	1.05	–2.03	14.41	6.55	20.70
2001	0.32	4.51	–10.10	7.42	1.25

Trailing	Total Return%	+/– S&P 500	+/– Russ Top 200 Val	% Rank All	% Rank Cat	Growth of $10,000
3 Mo	7.42	–3.26	1.91	54	72	10,742
6 Mo	–3.43	2.13	2.35	53	39	9,657
1 Yr	1.25	13.13	10.05	40	15	10,125
3 Yr Avg	7.88	8.90	6.71	15	8	12,554
5 Yr Avg	17.09	6.40	5.89	3	1	22,013
10 Yr Avg	—	—	—	—	—	—
15 Yr Avg	—	—	—	—	—	—

Tax Analysis	Tax-Adj Ret%	%Rank Cat	%Pretax Ret	%Rank Cat
3 Yr Avg	6.94	6	88.2	13
5 Yr Avg	16.10	1	94.2	3
10 Yr Avg	—	—	—	—

Potential Capital Gain Exposure: –1% of assets

Risk Analysis

Time Period	Load-Adj Return %	Risk %Rank[1] All	Risk %Rank[1] Cat	Morningstar Return	Morningstar Risk	Morningstar Risk-Adj Rating
1 Yr	1.25					
3 Yr	7.88	48	19	0.64[2]	0.67	★★★★
5 Yr	17.09	49	12	3.32[2]	0.67	★★★★★
Incept	20.21	—	—	—	—	

Average Historical Rating (41 months): 4.6★s

[1] 1=low, 100=high [2] T-Bill return substituted for category avg.

Category Rating (3 Yr)

1 2 3 4 5 (Worst → Best): 5

Return: High
Risk: Below Avg

Other Measures	Standard Index S&P 500	Best Fit Index S&P 500
Alpha	6.6	6.6
Beta	0.55	0.55
R-Squared	36	36
Standard Deviation		16.80
Mean		7.88
Sharpe Ratio		0.20

Portfolio Analysis 07-31-01

Share change since 03-01 Total Stocks: 47

Stock	Sector	PE	YTD Ret%	% Assets
⊕ Dell Comp	Technology	61.8	55.87	4.03
⊕ Bristol-Myers Squibb	Health	20.2	–26.00	3.92
⊕ IBM	Technology	26.9	43.00	3.83
⊕ American Home Products	Health	—	–1.91	3.81
☼ First Union	Financials	21.5	16.12	3.80
⊕ Sears Roebuck	Retail	23.4	40.12	3.78
☼ Texas Instruments	Technology	87.5	–40.70	3.78
⊕ Sara Lee	Staples	8.4	–6.95	3.74
⊕ McDonald's	Services	19.2	–21.50	3.68
⊕ Ford Motor	Durables	43.7	–30.00	3.64
⊕ Boeing	Industrials	10.2	–40.40	3.58
⊕ Verizon Comms	Services	29.7	–2.52	3.24
⊕ General Motors	Durables	NMF	–0.97	3.06
☼ Bank of America	Financials	16.7	42.73	2.88
⊕ Intel	Technology	73.1	4.89	2.80
⊖ Fannie Mae	Financials	16.2	–6.95	2.59
⊕ SBC Comms	Services	18.4	–16.00	2.10
⊕ Merrill Lynch	Financials	18.2	–22.70	1.98
⊕ Procter & Gamble	Staples	38.8	3.12	1.97
⊕ Dow Chemical	Industrials	NMF	–4.43	1.97
⊕ Johnson & Johnson	Health	16.6	14.01	1.83
⊕ Merck	Health	19.1	–35.90	1.83
⊕ ExxonMobil	Energy	15.3	–7.59	1.81
⊕ BellSouth	Services	24.9	–5.09	1.77
⊕ Agilent Tech	Technology	58.2	–47.90	1.74

Current Investment Style

Style: Value Blnd Growth; Size: Large Med Small

	Stock Port Avg	Relative S&P 500 Current	Relative S&P 500 Hist	Rel Cat
Price/Earnings Ratio	31.0	1.00	0.67	1.23
Price/Book Ratio	6.0	1.05	0.70	1.46
Price/Cash Flow	13.9	0.77	0.64	1.01
3 Yr Earnings Growth	7.1	0.49	0.90	0.48
1 Yr Earnings Est%	–18.0	10.18	—	5.44
Med Mkt Cap $mil	58,989	1.0	1.0	1.86

Special Securities % assets 07-31-01	
Restricted/Illiquid Secs	0
Emerging-Markets Secs	0
Options/Futures/Warrants	No

Composition % assets 07-31-01	
Cash	10.1
Stocks*	89.9
Bonds	0.0
Other	0.0
*Foreign (% stocks)	1.6

Market Cap	
Giant	60.0
Large	39.9
Medium	0.1
Small	0.0
Micro	0.0

Sector Weightings	% of Stocks	Rel S&P	5-Year High	5-Year Low
Utilities	0.0	0.0	0	0
Energy	4.9	0.7	12	2
Financials	18.4	1.0	37	10
Industrials	10.8	1.0	18	8
Durables	7.2	4.6	14	6
Staples	6.6	0.8	14	5
Services	12.2	1.1	23	11
Retail	6.2	0.9	9	2
Health	13.9	0.9	14	7
Technology	19.7	1.1	20	5

Analysis by Catherine Hickey 11-27-01

This little-known fund continues to show why it deserves to be on investors' radar.

Once again, Ameristock Fund is knocking 'em dead. It's on top of the large-value category so far in 2001, and its three- and five-year returns are topnotch, landing in the group's top decile. The fund owes its success to manager Nick Gerber's patient, deliberate approach. Even after the dramatic turns in the market after the Sept. 11 terrorist attacks, Gerber is standing pat with many picks. Perhaps his bravest bet is on Boeing, a stock that has fallen sharply this year as slowing airline traffic has dimmed the prospects for new airplane orders. Gerber believes that even though the firm's near-term outlook is tough, Boeing's satellite division will benefit from increased defense spending.

Gerber's convictions have been right more often than not, as the fund's mix of fallen growth stocks and true-blue value names has helped it keep pace in a variety of markets. In 2001, for example, the fund has gotten a boost from names as disparate as First Union and Dell Computer. Gerber shrewdly added a position in the latter late in 2000, reasoning that he always liked the company's "direct" business model. That stock has snapped back with a vengeance this year. The fund's double-digit cash position (now 10% of assets) has also helped, as cash has bested most stocks this year.

The fund's slow-going approach has made for low volatility and superb tax efficiency, factors that should appeal to investors looking for a core value holding. It can lag when growth vastly outperforms value (as in 1999), but for the most part, its returns have been consistently strong. What's more, though the fund is still fairly small, its expenses are reasonable. Gerber's tiny shop lacks the research muscle of a larger organization, but for exposure to large, liquid stocks, this fund has made a pretty compelling case for itself.

Address:	1301 East Ninth Street – 36th Floor Cleveland, OH 44114 800-394-5064
Web Address:	www.ameristock.com
*Inception:	08-31-95
Advisor:	Ameristock
Subadvisor:	None
NTF Plans:	Datalynx, Fidelity Inst.

Minimum Purchase:	$1000	Add: $100 IRA: $1000
Min Auto Inv Plan:	—	Add: —
Sales Fees:	No-load	
Management Fee:	1.0% mx./.75% mn.	
Actual Fees:	Mgt: 1.00%	Dist: —
Expense Projections:	3Yr: $33*	5Yr: $58* 10Yr: $132*
Avg Brok Commission:	—	Income Distrib: Semi-Ann.
Total Cost (relative to category):	—	

Ariel Appreciation

Ticker	Load	NAV	Yield	Total Assets	Mstar Category
CAAPX	12b–1 only	$37.02	0.2%	$771.3 mil	Mid–Cap Blend

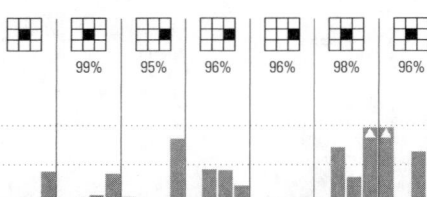

Prospectus Objective: Growth

Ariel Appreciation Fund seeks long-term capital appreciation.

The fund normally invests 80% of assets in equities with market capitalizations between $200 million and $5 billion. It may invest the balance of assets in debt. The fund seeks environmentally responsible companies; it may not invest in issuers primarily involved in the manufacture of weapons systems, nuclear energy, or tobacco.

Calvert-Ariel Appreciation Fund. Merged funds: Washington Area Growth Fund on Sept. 16, 1991; Calvert Capital Value Fund on June 12, 1992; and Ariel Appreciation Fund C on Dec. 8, 1994.

Historical Profile

Return Above Avg
Risk Below Avg
Rating ★★★★ Above Avg

Investment Style
Equity
Average Stock %: 99% 95% 96% 96% 98% 96%

▼ Manager Change
▽ Partial Manager Change

Fund Performance vs. Category Average
■ Quarterly Fund Return +/– Category Average
— Category Baseline

Performance Quartile (within Category)

Portfolio Manager(s)

Eric T. McKissack, CFA. Since 12-89. BS'76 MIT; MBA'81 U. of California-Berkeley. Other funds currently managed: PaineWebber Pace Sm/Med Co Val Eq P, PaineWebber Pace Sm/Med Co Val Eq B, PaineWebber Pace Sm/Med Co Val Eq C.

1990	1991	1992	1993	1994	1995	1996	1997	1998	1999	2000	12-01	History
14.53	19.15	21.60	22.89	19.51	22.24	26.07	32.82	35.69	30.97	32.53	37.02	NAV
–1.51	33.16	13.24	7.95	–8.39	24.17	23.72	37.95	19.55	–3.79	18.82	16.23	Total Return %
1.61	2.68	5.62	–2.10	–9.71	–13.37	0.77	4.59	–9.03	–24.83	27.93	28.11	+/– S&P 500
3.61	–16.91	1.34	–5.98	–4.80	–6.75	4.53	5.70	0.43	–18.51	1.33	16.83	+/– S&P Mid 400
1.11	1.16	0.44	0.24	0.27	1.02	0.33	0.26	0.11	0.12	0.38	0.20	Income Return %
–2.63	32.00	12.80	7.71	–8.66	23.14	23.38	37.69	19.44	–3.91	18.45	16.03	Capital Return %
10	60	54	75	85	66	29	5	12	98	11	2	Total Rtn % Rank Cat
0.17	0.17	0.08	0.05	0.06	0.20	0.07	0.07	0.04	0.04	0.12	0.06	Income $
0.08	0.02	0.00	0.35	1.40	1.77	1.37	3.07	3.46	3.15	3.95	0.71	Capital Gains $
0.70	1.50	1.44	1.37	1.35	1.36	1.36	1.33	1.26	1.26	1.31	—	Expense Ratio %
2.23	1.61	0.57	0.33	0.17	0.61	0.50	0.07	0.25	0.13	0.25	—	Income Ratio %
4	20	2	56	12	18	26	19	20	24	31	—	Turnover Rate %
26.2	90.1	179.3	219.3	128.5	139.3	146.3	204.4	283.8	334.6	339.8	771.3	Net Assets $mil

Performance 12-31-01

	1st Qtr	2nd Qtr	3rd Qtr	4th Qtr	Total
1997	–0.35	14.59	13.20	6.71	37.95
1998	9.11	1.98	–12.92	23.38	19.55
1999	–0.76	8.27	–11.76	1.47	–3.79
2000	–3.71	4.56	8.02	9.26	18.82
2001	1.84	8.66	–10.00	16.70	16.23

Trailing	Total Return%	+/– S&P 500	+/– S&P Mid 400	% Rank All	% Rank Cat	Growth of $10,000
3 Mo	16.70	6.01	–1.29	20	48	11,670
6 Mo	5.03	10.58	6.58	4	4	10,503
1 Yr	16.23	28.11	16.83	3	2	11,623
3 Yr Avg	9.94	10.96	–0.30	11	21	13,288
5 Yr Avg	16.99	6.29	0.88	3	5	21,913
10 Yr Avg	14.19	1.26	–0.81	8	32	37,697
15 Yr Avg	—	—	—	—	—	—

Tax Analysis	Tax-Adj Ret%	%Rank Cat	%Pretax Ret	%Rank Cat
3 Yr Avg	7.92	21	79.7	42
5 Yr Avg	14.85	5	87.4	21
10 Yr Avg	12.39	19	87.3	12

Potential Capital Gain Exposure: 23% of assets

Risk Analysis

Time Period	Load-Adj Return %	Risk %Rank[1] All	Risk %Rank[1] Cat	Morningstar Return	Morningstar Risk	Morningstar Risk-Adj Rating
1 Yr	16.23					
3 Yr	9.94	43	10	1.11[2]	0.60	★★★★
5 Yr	16.99	47	5	3.28[2]	0.64	★★★★★
10 Yr	14.19	56	10	1.59	0.73	★★★★

Average Historical Rating (110 months): 3.0★s

[1] 1=low, 100=high [2] T-Bill return substituted for category avg.

Category Rating (3 Yr)

1 2 3 **4** 5
Worst — Best

Return: Above Avg
Risk: Low

Other Measures	Standard Index S&P 500	Best Fit Index SPMid400
Alpha	8.7	2.8
Beta	0.54	0.47
R-Squared	31	31
Standard Deviation		18.00
Mean		9.94
Sharpe Ratio		0.32

Portfolio Analysis 09-30-01

Share change since 06-01 Total Stocks: 38	Sector	PE	YTD Ret%	% Assets
⊕ McCormick	Staples	20.2	18.62	4.71
⊕ MBIA	Financials	14.6	9.88	4.62
⊕ H & R Block	Services	25.5	120.00	4.26
⊕ Centurytel	Services	13.3	–7.66	4.16
⊕ XL Cap Cl A	Financials	22.8	5.82	3.87
⊕ MBNA	Financials	19.6	–3.66	3.73
⊕ Rouse	Financials	19.3	20.91	3.73
⊕ Apogent Tech	Health	29.0	25.85	3.66
⊕ Lee Enterprises	Services	5.1	24.50	3.56
⊕ SunGard Data Sys	Technology	33.3	22.78	3.49
⊖ Hasbro	Durables	—	54.09	3.19
⊕ Pitney Bowes	Industrials	17.2	19.80	3.17
⊕ McClatchy Cl A	Services	33.6	11.32	3.04
⊕ Avery Dennison	Industrials	22.1	5.37	2.91
⊕ Herman Miller	Durables	17.4	–17.20	2.87
⊕ Clorox	Staples	31.1	14.20	2.86
⊕ Equifax	Services	18.3	43.78	2.83
⊕ Dun & Bradstreet	Services	41.1	36.43	2.83
⊕ Harte-Hanks Comms	Services	22.9	19.51	2.62
⊕ Cendant	Services	20.4	103.70	2.52
⊕ Carnival	Services	16.4	–7.54	2.42
⊕ Franklin Resources	Financials	18.5	–6.78	2.37
⊕ ServiceMaster	Services	22.3	24.29	2.23
⊕ Tribune	Services	NMF	–10.40	2.22
⊕ Interpublic Grp	Services	—	–29.80	2.14

Current Investment Style

Style: Value Blnd Growth; Size: Large Med Small

	Stock Port Avg	Relative S&P 500 Current	Relative S&P 500 Hist	Rel Cat
Price/Earnings Ratio	23.7	0.76	0.65	0.87
Price/Book Ratio	4.3	0.75	0.61	0.99
Price/Cash Flow	14.4	0.80	0.63	0.83
3 Yr Earnings Growth	6.1	0.42	0.82	0.37
1 Yr Earnings Est%	–9.7	5.46	—	–4.26
Med Mkt Cap $mil	4,631	0.1	0.1	0.51

Special Securities % assets 09-30-01	
Restricted/Illiquid Secs	0
Emerging-Markets Secs	0
Options/Futures/Warrants	No

Composition % assets 09-30-01	
Cash	2.8
Stocks*	97.2
Bonds	0.0
Other	0.0
*Foreign (% stocks)	4.0

Market Cap	
Giant	0.0
Large	26.4
Medium	72.5
Small	1.2
Micro	0.0

Sector Weightings	% of Stocks	Rel S&P	5-Year High	5-Year Low
Utilities	0.0	0.0	0	0
Energy	0.0	0.0	0	0
Financials	20.7	1.2	25	0
Industrials	6.4	0.6	25	6
Durables	12.4	7.9	19	0
Staples	9.8	1.2	17	4
Services	36.5	3.4	38	20
Retail	3.9	0.6	17	2
Health	6.9	0.5	17	2
Technology	3.6	0.2	6	0

Analysis by Peter Di Teresa 11-28-01

Ariel Appreciation Fund's unabated dedication to the American consumer is still paying off.

There may be a recession on and consumer confidence may be declining, but this fund's emphasis on consumer stocks hasn't done it any harm. The fund boasted a 12.1% return for the year to date ending Nov. 26, 2001, topping 98% of its mid-cap blend peers. The fund has benefited from strength throughout its portfolio, with holdings such as H & R Block and Hasbro posting notably large gains. That comes on top of an 18.8% return in 2000, 15 percentage points better than the category average.

The fund also has a competitive 10-year return and topnotch three- and five-year numbers. On top of that, shareholders have had to endure less volatility than the mid-blend average to reap those rewards.

Manager Eric McKissack targets stocks trading for no more than 60% of their intrinsic values and emphasizes free cash flow in his analysis. Hence his preference for consumer-related issues, which often produce lots of cash.

In keeping with his value discipline and liking for consumer issues, McKissack notes that he has recently found buying opportunities in the area. During the third quarter, he added stocks such as Black & Decker and Jones Apparel Group, and purchased more shares of Nieman Marcus Group. Along with attractive fundamentals, these companies stand to benefit from tax and interest-rate cuts intended to stimulate the economy.

Such picks don't always pay off. For example, the fund landed in the category's depths in 1999 when it was hampered by its usual minimal tech stake and hurt by some blowups. Nonetheless, the fund's overall stability and solid returns merit a look from mid-cap investors.

Address:	200 E. Randolph St. Suite 2900 Chicago, IL 60601 800–292–7435 / 312–726–0140
Web Address:	www.arielmutualfunds.com
Inception:	12-01-89
Advisor:	Ariel Cap. Mgmt.
Subadvisor:	None
NTF Plans:	Fidelity , Datalynx

Minimum Purchase:	$1000	Add: $50	IRA: $250
Min Auto Inv Plan:	$50	Add: $50	
Sales Fees:	0.25%B		
Management Fee:	.75% mx./.65% mn.		
Actual Fees:	Mgt: 0.75%	Dist: 0.25%	
Expense Projections:	3Yr: $400	5Yr: $692	10Yr: $1523
Avg Brok Commission:	—	Income Distrib: Annually	
Total Cost (relative to category):	—		

Artisan International

Ticker	Load	NAV	Yield	Total Assets	Mstar Category
ARTIX	None	$18.36	0.4%	$6,170.7 mil	Foreign Stock

Prospectus Objective: Foreign Stock

Artisan International Fund seeks long-term capital growth.

The fund ordinarily invests at least 65% of assets in equities of foreign issuers; it normally maintains investments in at least three foreign countries. When selecting investments, management places equal emphasis on country selection and stock selection; it avoids countries that it believes have overvalued markets, and focuses on companies that have dominant or increasing market share in strong industries. The fund typically invests no more than 5% of assets in convertibles or in debt rated below BBB. It may invest in emerging markets.

The fund offers Institutional and International shares.

Historical Profile

Return: High
Risk: Average
Rating: ★★★★★ Highest

Investment Style
Equity
Average Stock %: 97% (1996), 94% (1997), 91% (1998), 97% (1999), 93% (2000), 94% (12-01)

▼ Manager Change
▽ Partial Manager Change

Fund Performance vs. Category Average
▇ Quarterly Fund Return +/– Category Average
— Category Baseline

Performance Quartile (within Category)

10
5
0
–5
–10

Portfolio Manager(s)

Mark L. Yockey, CFA. Since 12-95. BA'79 Michigan State U.; MBA'84 Michigan State U. Other funds currently managed: Masters' Select International, Artisan International Instl.

1990	1991	1992	1993	1994	1995	1996	1997	1998	1999	2000	12-01	History
—	—	—	—	—	10.00	13.32	12.46	16.12	28.50	21.90	18.36	NAV
—	—	—	—	—	—	34.37	3.46	32.18	81.29	–10.59	–15.86	Total Return %
—	—	—	—	—	–0.47*	11.43	–29.89	3.60	60.25	–1.48	–3.98	+/– S&P 500
—	—	—	—	—	—	28.33	1.68	12.18	54.33	3.58	—	+/– MSCI EAFE
—	—	—	—	—	0.00	0.00	1.48	0.28	0.15	0.00	0.30	Income Return %
—	—	—	—	—	0.00	34.37	1.98	31.89	81.14	–10.59	–16.16	Capital Return %
—	—	—	—	—	—	1	65	2	11	29	16	Total Rtn % Rank Cat
—	—	—	—	—	0.00	0.00	0.20	0.04	0.02	0.00	0.07	Income $
—	—	—	—	—	0.00	0.11	1.13	0.24	0.54	3.55	0.00	Capital Gains $
—	—	—	—	—	—	2.50	1.61	1.45	1.38	1.27	1.22	Expense Ratio %
—	—	—	—	—	—	1.60	1.07	0.37	0.59	–0.10	0.45	Income Ratio %
—	—	—	—	—	—	—	104	109	79	99	72	Turnover Rate %
—	—	—	—	—	—	191.5	300.8	504.6	2,240.0	3,664.0	—	Net Assets $mil

Performance 12-31-01

	1st Qtr	2nd Qtr	3rd Qtr	4th Qtr	Total
1997	5.33	3.21	1.59	–6.31	3.46
1998	20.22	8.48	–18.83	24.86	32.18
1999	11.23	4.13	4.98	49.10	81.29
2000	17.61	–10.02	–11.11	–4.95	–10.59
2001	–12.83	2.30	–14.08	9.82	–15.86

Trailing	Total Return%	+/– S&P 500	+/– MSCI EAFE	% Rank All	% Rank Cat	Growth of $10,000
3 Mo	9.82	–0.87	—	44	32	10,982
6 Mo	–5.65	–0.09	—	65	13	9,435
1 Yr	–15.86	–3.98	—	74	16	8,414
3 Yr Avg	10.90	11.93	—	10	5	13,639
5 Yr Avg	13.28	2.58	—	7	3	18,652
10 Yr Avg	—	—	—	—	—	—
15 Yr Avg	—	—	—	—	—	—

Tax Analysis	Tax-Adj Ret%	%Rank Cat	%Pretax Ret	%Rank Cat
3 Yr Avg	8.80	5	80.8	51
5 Yr Avg	11.06	4	83.3	19
10 Yr Avg	—	—	—	—

Potential Capital Gain Exposure: –20% of assets

Risk Analysis

Time Period	Load-Adj Return %	Risk %Rank[1] All	Risk %Rank[1] Cat	Morningstar Return	Morningstar Risk	Morningstar Risk-Adj Rating
1 Yr	–15.86					
3 Yr	10.90	68	37	1.34[2]	0.87	★★★★★
5 Yr	13.28	75	54	2.11[2]	0.85	★★★★★
Incept	16.51	—	—	—	—	

Average Historical Rating (37 months): 5.0★s

[1] 1=low, 100=high [2] T-Bill return substituted for category avg.

Category Rating (3 Yr)

1 2 3 4 5
Worst Best

Return: High
Risk: Average

Other Measures	Standard Index S&P 500	Best Fit Index Wil 4500
Alpha	12.8	8.7
Beta	0.81	0.74
R-Squared	30	68

Standard Deviation	28.25
Mean	10.90
Sharpe Ratio	0.24

Portfolio Analysis 11-30-01

Share change since 10-01 Total Stocks: 82	Sector	Country	% Assets
⊕ Diageo	Staples	United Kingdom	3.96
⊕ Compass Grp	Services	United Kingdom	3.62
Lloyds TSB Grp	Financials	United Kingdom	3.44
⊕ Fortis (NL)	N/A	N/A	3.43
⊕ Muenchener Rueckvers (Reg)	Financials	Germany	3.37
UBS (Reg)	Financials	Switzerland	3.28
⊕ Allianz (Reg)	Financials	Germany	3.17
⊕ Honda Motor	Durables	Japan	2.92
Unilever (Cert)	Staples	United Kingdom	2.73
Assicurazioni Generali	Financials	Italy	2.62
Wolters Kluwer	Services	Netherlands	2.58
⊕ Interbrew	Staples	Belgium	2.34
⊕ British Amer Tobacco	Staples	United Kingdom	2.25
⊕ Novartis (Reg)	Health	Switzerland	2.04
Suez Lyon Eaux	Industrials	France	1.83
⊕ Telefonos de Mexico ADR L	Services	Mexico	1.78
Rolo Banca 1473	Financials	Italy	1.73
Promise	Financials	Japan	1.72
⊕ Marks & Spencer	Retail	United Kingdom	1.64
Bank of Ireland	Financials	Ireland	1.53

Current Investment Style

Style: Value Blnd Growth
Size: Large Med Small

	Stock Port Avg	Rel MSCI EAFE Current	Rel MSCI EAFE Hist	Rel Cat
Price/Earnings Ratio	21.4	0.83	1.00	0.84
Price/Cash Flow	11.6	0.90	1.17	0.81
Price/Book Ratio	3.6	1.03	1.20	0.92
3 Yr Earnings Growth	18.8	1.01	1.13	0.96
Med Mkt Cap $mil	24,171	0.9	0.4	1.34

Country Exposure 11-30-01	% assets
United Kingdom	20
Italy	12
Germany	8
Switzerland	8
Japan	7

Hedging History: Never

Regional Exposure 11-30-01	% assets
Europe	67
Japan	7
Latin America	6
Pacific Rim	4
Other	2

Special Securities % assets 11-30-01	
Restricted/Illiquid Secs	0
Emerging-Markets Secs	8
Options/Futures/Warrants	No

Composition % assets 11-30-01

Cash	1.7	Bonds	0.0
Stocks	98.2	Other	0.1

Sector Weightings	% of Stocks	Rel Cat	5-Year High	5-Year Low
Utilities	0.0	0.0	5	0
Energy	3.2	0.5	4	0
Financials	37.0	1.7	40	10
Industrials	5.9	0.4	12	3
Durables	5.5	0.8	11	0
Staples	17.0	2.4	17	1
Services	21.1	1.2	57	21
Retail	4.2	0.9	7	0
Health	4.9	0.5	13	1
Technology	1.3	0.1	21	0

Analysis by William Samuel Rocco 12-11-01

Little has changed at Artisan International, and that's good news.

Manager Mark Yockey hasn't made any notable new purchases lately, and he hasn't done any significant selling, either. But he hasn't been totally subdued. He added to his stakes in Munich Re, Allianz, and some other insurers right after the Sept. 11 attacks because he thought they were oversold.

Yockey also added to his positions in this Swiss financial power UBS and the British catering firm Compass Group on weakness earlier this fall. He also has added to Diageo and Telmex, which have been strong performers of late, because he remains confident about their prospects and their managements.

The fund hasn't suffered for Yockey's recent reserve. Munich Re and the fund's other insurers have rebounded sharply this fall, while UBS has also bounced back. And Compass Group jumped 9% yesterday after it announced better-than-expected numbers.

Meanwhile, several of Yockey's other picks have posted strong gains in 2001. For example, Telmex has continued to prosper in recent months, and British American Tobacco and some of his consumer-staples stocks have also posted nice gains. And the Spanish retailer Inditex, which Yockey likes for its innovative and broad roster of stores, as well as for its growth rates and strong finances, is up 35% since its late-spring purchase. Thus, the fund has lost less than 80% of its peers for the year to date through Dec. 11, 2001.

Top-quartile performances are nothing new here. And the fund hasn't suffered significantly more volatility than its average peer. Toss in a relatively low expense ratio, and it's easy to see why this fund remains one of our favorite foreign options.

Address:	PO Box 8412 Boston, MA 02266–8412 800–344–1770
Web Address:	www.artisanfunds.com
*Inception:	12-28-95
Advisor:	Artisan Partners
Subadvisor:	None
NTF Plans:	Fidelity , Fidelity Inst.

Minimum Purchase:	$1000	Add: $50	IRA: $1000
Min Auto Inv Plan:	$50	Add: $50	
Sales Fees:	No-load		
Management Fee:	1.0% mx./.93% mn.		
Actual Fees:	Mgt: 0.99%	Dist: —	
Expense Projections:	3Yr: $437	5Yr: $755	10Yr: $1657
Avg Brok Commission:	—	Income Distrib: Annually	
Total Cost (relative to category):		Below Avg	

Artisan Small Cap Value

Ticker	Load	NAV	Yield	Total Assets	Mstar Category
ARTVX	Closed	$12.68	0.1%	$438.0 mil	Small Value

Prospectus Objective: Small Company

Artisan Small Cap Value Fund seeks long-term capital growth.

The fund invests primarily in common stocks issued by companies with market capitalizations of less than $1 billion, and that are judged by the advisor to appear undervalued relative to earnings, book value, cash flows, or potential earnings growth. The advisor emphasizes investments in businesses that have positive cash flows, strong balance sheets, and business strategies that are economically sound. The fund may, at times, invest up to 10% of assets in foreign securities.

Historical Profile

Return High
Risk Low
Rating ★★★★★ Highest

Investment Style
Equity
Average Stock %

1997	1998	1999	2000	12-01
92%	91%	94%	90%	90%

▼ Manager Change
▽ Partial Manager Change

Fund Performance vs. Category Average
■ Quarterly Fund Return +/– Category Average
— Category Baseline

Performance Quartile (within Category)

Portfolio Manager(s)

James C. Kieffer, CFA. Since 7-00. BA'87 Emroy U.

Scott C. Satterwhite, CFA. Since 9-97. BA'79 The University of the South; MBA'81 Tulane U. Other funds currently managed: SEI Instl Mgd Small Cap Value A, SEI Instl Invmt Small Cap.

1990	1991	1992	1993	1994	1995	1996	1997	1998	1999	2000	12-01	History
—	—	—	—	—	—	—	10.31	9.14	10.16	11.70	12.68	NAV
—	—	—	—	—	—	—	3.10*	–5.76	15.42	20.83	15.04	Total Return %
—	—	—	—	—	—	—	0.73*	–34.33	–5.62	29.93	26.92	+/– S&P 500
—	—	—	—	—	—	—	—	0.67	16.90	–1.98	1.03	+/– Russell 2000 V
—	—	—	—	—	—	—	0.00	0.00	0.30	0.52	0.14	Income Return %
—	—	—	—	—	—	—	3.10	–5.76	15.12	20.31	14.90	Capital Return %
—	—	—	—	—	—	—	—	41	18	43	64	Total Rtn % Rank Cat
—	—	—	—	—	—	—	0.00	0.00	0.03	0.05	0.02	Income $
—	—	—	—	—	—	—	0.00	0.54	0.35	0.49	0.71	Capital Gains $
—	—	—	—	—	—	—	—	1.93	1.66	1.35	1.20	Expense Ratio %
—	—	—	—	—	—	—	—	–0.50	–0.45	0.60	0.45	Income Ratio %
—	—	—	—	—	—	—	—	53	49	38	41	Turnover Rate %
—	—	—	—	—	—	—	24.0	54.1	143.1	335.0	—	Net Assets $mil

Performance 12-31-01

	1st Qtr	2nd Qtr	3rd Qtr	4th Qtr	Total
1997	—	—	—	3.20	3.10 *
1998	8.83	1.34	–20.15	7.03	–5.76
1999	–4.60	21.45	–4.15	3.93	15.42
2000	1.57	3.00	6.68	8.26	20.83
2001	1.79	9.57	–11.80	16.94	15.05

Trailing	Total Return%	+/– S&P 500	+/– Russ 2000V	% Rank All	% Rank Cat	Growth of $10,000
3 Mo	16.94	6.26	0.22	20	50	11,694
6 Mo	3.14	8.70	1.99	14	39	10,314
1 Yr	15.04	26.92	1.03	3	64	11,504
3 Yr Avg	17.07	18.09	5.75	3	20	16,044
5 Yr Avg	—	—	—	—	—	—
10 Yr Avg	—	—	—	—	—	—
15 Yr Avg	—	—	—	—	—	—

Tax Analysis	Tax-Adj Ret%	%Rank Cat	%Pretax Ret	%Rank Cat
3 Yr Avg	15.10	24	88.5	62
5 Yr Avg	—	—	—	—
10 Yr Avg	—	—	—	—

Potential Capital Gain Exposure: 15% of assets

Risk Analysis

Time Period	Load-Adj Return %	Risk %Rank[1] All	Risk %Rank[1] Cat	Morningstar Return	Morningstar Risk	Morningstar Risk-Adj Rating
1 Yr	15.04					
3 Yr	17.07	34	1	2.88[2]	0.41	★★★★★
5 Yr	—	—	—	—	—	
Incept	10.99	—	—	—	—	

Average Historical Rating (16 months): 4.0★s

[1] 1=low, 100=high [2] T-Bill return substituted for category avg.

Category Rating (3 Yr)

Worst 1 2 3 4 5 Best

Return Above Avg
Risk Low

Other Measures	Standard Index S&P 500	Best Fit Index SPMid400
Alpha	15.0	8.5
Beta	0.47	0.55
R-Squared	33	60

Standard Deviation	16.06
Mean	17.07
Sharpe Ratio	0.85

Portfolio Analysis 11-30-01

Share change since 10-01 Total Stocks: 86	Sector	PE	YTD Ret%	% Assets
Zale	Retail	12.5	44.10	2.96
Mueller Inds	Industrials	21.7	24.01	2.56
Borg Warner	Durables	19.3	32.37	2.55
Briggs & Stratton	Industrials	25.3	–0.78	2.52
Kellwood	Durables	10.4	16.98	2.49
Advo	Services	17.4	–3.10	2.36
Emcor Grp	Industrials	13.8	78.04	2.21
⊕ Centex Const Prods	Industrials	18.1	18.15	2.10
Lincoln Elec Hldgs	Industrials	14.5	27.77	2.09
Clarcor	Industrials	16.0	33.91	2.01
USFreightways	Services	15.9	5.74	1.97
Minerals Tech	Industrials	21.5	36.76	1.96
John Hancock Bank & Thrift	N/A	—	—	1.93
⊕ Forest Oil	Energy	7.4	–23.50	1.86
Footstar	Retail	—	–36.70	1.85
Genlyte Grp	Industrials	10.9	25.31	1.82
Stone Energy	Energy	—	–38.80	1.81
Regal-Beloit	Industrials	20.6	31.09	1.79
Stewart Info Svcs	Financials	9.8	–10.90	1.78
⊖ Tecumseh Products A	Industrials	18.3	23.91	1.78
Carlisle	Industrials	40.2	–11.80	1.77
AK Steel Hldg	Industrials	27.1	31.55	1.73
Kaydon	Industrials	NMF	–7.01	1.66
Superior Inds Intl	Durables	17.0	29.10	1.59
Kirby	Services	17.6	31.19	1.57

Current Investment Style

Style: Value Blnd Growth; Size: Large Med Small

	Stock Port Avg	Relative S&P 500 Current	Relative S&P 500 Hist	Rel Cat
Price/Earnings Ratio	19.2	0.62	0.52	0.89
Price/Book Ratio	1.8	0.31	0.24	0.72
Price/Cash Flow	8.7	0.48	0.41	0.69
3 Yr Earnings Growth	3.4	0.23	0.62	0.29
1 Yr Earnings Est%	–18.3	10.31	—	4.62
Med Mkt Cap $mil	705	0.0	0.0	0.81

Special Securities % assets 11-30-01	
Restricted/Illiquid Secs	Trace
Emerging-Markets Secs	1
Options/Futures/Warrants	No

Composition % assets 11-30-01	
Cash	8.3
Stocks*	91.7
Bonds	0.0
Other	0.0
*Foreign (% stocks)	4.3

Market Cap	
Giant	0.3
Large	0.6
Medium	3.8
Small	85.5
Micro	9.8

Sector Weightings	% of Stocks	Rel S&P	5-Year High	5-Year Low
Utilities	1.6	0.5	—	—
Energy	11.7	1.7	—	—
Financials	17.5	1.0	—	—
Industrials	37.7	3.3	—	—
Durables	11.2	7.2	—	—
Staples	1.5	0.2	—	—
Services	10.7	1.0	—	—
Retail	7.0	1.0	—	—
Health	0.8	0.1	—	—
Technology	0.3	0.0	—	—

Analysis by William Samuel Rocco 12-27-01

This patient value shopper's subpar returns in 2001 should be kept in perspective.

Artisan Small Cap Value has continued to move at a measured pace in recent months. Lead manager Scott Satterwhite has maintained the fund's hefty stake in industrial stocks. While he did trim a few cyclical names on strength in late summer, he added to others on weakness, and recently beefed up his stake in Centex Construction Products. Thus, the fund now has 37% of its assets in industrial stocks, whereas its average peer has 20%.

Satterwhite has also kept the fund heavy on energy stocks. He has added to several oil- and gas-service companies and producers in recent months, because he likes their prices as well as their prospects. He has increased his stake in Forest Oil, for example, due to optimism about its potential reserves and cheap valuations. And he picked up the reinsurer IPC Holdings right after the September attacks.

This value discipline has had a mixed effect in 2001. Most of Satterwhite's industrial picks have earned nice gains for the year. Centex Construction Products is up 17% in 2001, for example. However, despite some recent strength, Forest Oil and many of his other energy stocks are down big for the year. Therefore, this fund has returned 14.5% for the year to date through Dec. 26, 2001, while the typical small-value offering has gained 16.7%. The fund has outpaced its average peer by a wide margin since opening in late 1997, as Satterwhite's stock selection has usually been on the mark. And it has suffered limited volatility along the way. Thus, we still think this closed fund is one of its group's best.

Address:	PO Box 8412 Boston, MA 02266-8412 800-344-1770
Web Address:	www.artisanfunds.com
*Inception:	09-29-97
Advisor:	Artisan Partners
Subadvisor:	None
NTF Plans:	Fidelity , Fidelity Inst.

Minimum Purchase:	Closed	Add: $50 IRA: —
Min Auto Inv Plan:	Closed	Add: $50
Sales Fees:	No-load	
Management Fee:	1.0% mx./.93% mn.	
Actual Fees:	Mgt: 1.00%	Dist: —
Expense Projections:	3Yr: $523	5Yr: $902 10Yr: $1965
Avg Brok Commission:	—	Income Distrib: Annually
Total Cost (relative to category):		Average

AXP Global Bond A

Ticker	Load	NAV	Yield	SEC Yield	Total Assets	Mstar Category
IGBFX	4.75%	$5.57	3.4%	4.34%	$339.8 mil	International Bond

Prospectus Objective: World Bond

AXP Global Bond Fund seeks total return through income and growth of capital.

The fund invests primarily in fixed-income debt obligations of U.S. and foreign issuers. It normally invests at least 80% of assets investment-grade corporate or government debt obligations including money market instruments of issuers located in at least three different countries. It may invest the balance of assets in debt rated as low as B. This fund is non-diversified.

Class A shares have front loads; B shares have deferred loads, 12b-1 fees, and conversion features; C shares have level loads; and Y shares are designed for institutional investors. Past name: IDS Global Bond Fund.

Historical Profile

Return Below Avg
Risk Above Avg
Rating ★★ Below Avg

Investment Style
Fixed-Income
Income Rtn %Rank Cat: 48, 52, 79, 80, 62, 73, 71, 66

Growth of Principal vs. Interest Rate Shifts
— Principal Value $000 (NAV with capital gains reinvested)
— Interest Rate % on 10 Yr Treasury
▼ Manager Change
▽ Partial Manager Change
► Mgr Unknown After
◄ Mgr Unknown Before

Performance Quartile (within Category)

Portfolio Manager(s)

Nicholas Pifer. Since 6-00. Other funds currently managed: AXP Global Bond B, AXP Global Bond Y, AXP Global Bond C.

1990	1991	1992	1993	1994	1995	1996	1997	1998	1999	2000	12-01	History
5.49	5.82	5.71	6.18	5.58	6.22	6.31	6.11	6.27	5.71	5.68	5.57	NAV
12.96	15.35	8.09	17.87	–4.93	19.43	7.70	3.13	8.10	–4.88	3.35	1.43	Total Return %
4.00	–0.66	0.68	8.12	–2.02	0.97	4.08	–6.55	–0.58	–4.05	–8.28	–7.00	+/– LB Aggregate
–2.34	–0.87	3.32	2.75	–10.92	–0.12	3.62	7.40	–9.69	0.19	5.99	4.97	+/– SB World Govt
9.86	7.64	8.18	8.30	4.55	7.79	5.42	4.41	4.78	4.17	3.83	3.39	Income Return %
3.09	7.71	–0.09	9.57	–9.49	11.65	2.28	–1.28	3.32	–9.05	–0.48	–1.96	Capital Return %
58	11	3	23	55	33	55	46	69	65	47	52	Total Rtn % Rank Cat
0.51	0.41	0.46	0.46	0.28	0.42	0.33	0.27	0.29	0.26	0.22	0.19	Income $
0.00	0.07	0.11	0.07	0.02	0.00	0.04	0.12	0.04	0.00	0.00	0.00	Capital Gains $
1.73	1.34	1.39	1.31	1.26	1.25	1.20	1.16	1.16	1.21	1.30	—	Expense Ratio %
10.60	7.15	6.50	5.11	5.56	6.15	5.72	5.74	5.86	5.49	5.49	—	Income Ratio %
130	123	160	90	64	92	49	56	27	48	48	—	Turnover Rate %
36.0	56.7	103.6	320.0	449.8	583.6	714.3	742.6	734.6	550.9	391.0	339.8	Net Assets $mil

Performance 12-31-01

	1st Qtr	2nd Qtr	3rd Qtr	4th Qtr	Total
1997	–3.13	4.03	2.07	0.26	3.13
1998	2.69	0.23	1.85	3.11	8.10
1999	–2.17	–2.21	1.41	–1.97	–4.88
2000	0.58	–0.30	–1.97	5.13	3.35
2001	–1.76	–1.39	5.38	–0.65	1.43

Trailing	Total Return%	+/– LB Agg	+/– SB World	% Rank All	% Rank Cat	Growth of $10,000
3 Mo	–0.65	–0.68	3.33	87	54	9,935
6 Mo	4.70	0.05	1.23	5	22	10,470
1 Yr	1.43	–7.00	4.97	40	52	10,143
3 Yr Avg	–0.10	–6.37	3.66	73	55	9,971
5 Yr Avg	2.14	–5.29	2.03	87	51	11,116
10 Yr Avg	5.64	–1.58	0.84	81	27	17,317
15 Yr Avg	—	—	—	—	—	—

Tax Analysis	Tax-Adj Ret%	%Rank Cat	%Pretax Ret	%Rank Cat
3 Yr Avg	–1.60	52	—	—
5 Yr Avg	0.35	46	16.2	87
10 Yr Avg	3.34	20	59.1	18

Potential Capital Gain Exposure: –14% of assets

Risk Analysis

Time Period	Load-Adj Return %	Risk %Rank[1] All	Risk %Rank[1] Cat	Morningstar Return	Morningstar Risk	Morningstar Risk-Adj Rating
1 Yr	–3.39					
3 Yr	–1.70	34	56	–1.32[2]	1.68	★★
5 Yr	1.15	38	52	–0.79[2]	1.69	★★
10 Yr	5.13	45	61	0.10[2]	1.61	★

Average Historical Rating (118 months): 2.3★s

[1]1=low, 100=high [2] T-Bill return substituted for category avg.

Category Rating (3 Yr)

1 2 3 4 5
Worst Best

Return Average
Risk Average

Other Measures	Standard Index LB Agg	Best Fit Index SB World
Alpha	–6.3	0.9
Beta	1.31	0.67
R-Squared	51	76
Standard Deviation		6.05
Mean		–0.10
Sharpe Ratio		–0.97

Portfolio Analysis 11-30-01

Total Fixed-Income: 63	Date of Maturity	Value $000	% Net Assets
US Treasury Bond 7.5%	11-15-16	43,163	8.76
Republic of Italy 8.5%	01-01-04	31,779	6.45
Republic of Germany 7.5%	11-11-04	29,212	5.93
Republic of Germany 6.5%	07-04-27	20,149	4.09
Kingdom of Belgium 7.25%	04-29-04	19,733	4.01
Republic of Germany 8%	07-22-02	17,012	3.45
Govt of Canada 7.5%	12-01-03	14,540	2.95
United Kingdom Treasury 8%	06-10-03	12,616	2.56
US Treasury Note (Fut)	12-19-01	11,908	2.42
US Treasury Note 6.5%	10-15-06	10,708	2.17
AHB Pfandbrief 5%	09-02-09	9,722	1.97
FNMA Debenture 5.75%	02-15-08	9,414	1.91
Govt of France 6.5%	04-25-11	9,186	1.86
Inter-American Dev Bk 1.9%	07-08-09	8,993	1.83
Buoni Poliennali Del Tesoro 7.25%	11-01-26	8,930	1.81
Govt of France 7.5%	04-25-05	8,689	1.76
Treuhandanstalt 3.98%	01-29-03	8,675	1.76
Kingdom of Denmark 8%	05-15-03	8,656	1.76
Govt of Canada 1.9%	03-23-09	8,569	1.74
Ford Motor Credit FRN	02-07-05	7,990	1.62

Current Investment Style

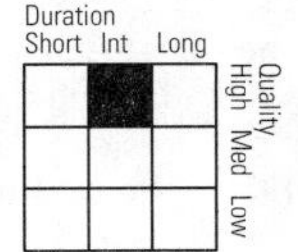

Avg Eff Duration[1]	4.7 Yrs
Avg Eff Maturity	—
Avg Credit Quality	AA
Avg Wtd Coupon	7.05%
Avg Wtd Price	86.54% of par

[1]figure provided by fund

Special Securities 11-30-01	% assets
Restricted/Illiquid Secs	2
Exotic Mortgage-Backed	0
Emerging-Markets Secs	4
Options/Futures/Warrants	Yes

Country Exposure % assets

Not Available

Composition % assets 11-30-01

Cash	5.7	Bonds	92.0
Stocks	0.0	Other	2.4

Analysis by Gabriel Presler 12-07-01

In a category of extremes, AXP Global Bond beats a moderate path to moderate returns.

Managers in the international-bond category face an array of options. Some concentrate only on foreign markets to provide diversification. Others, like this fund, often stake up to 50% of assets stateside. Some choose to run fully hedged or unhedged portfolios. Others adjust currency exposure depending on their macroeconomic outlooks, as this fund does. Generally, these broad decisions dictate each fund's relative performance. In the last two years of dollar strength, for example, it has been rare to find a foreign-focused, unhedged fund that has been able to squeeze into the top half of the category.

This fund's middle-of-the-road approach means it almost always winds up in the middle third of the category, and 2001 has been no exception. Broad exposure to U.S. bonds helped the fund, particularly because manager Nicholas Pifer tilted the fund's domestic exposure to short- and intermediate-term Treasury issues. Hedging much of the fund's yen exposure also proved wise, as the Japanese currency fell against the greenback and Japan's depressed yields rose slightly on concerns about its slow restructuring. But exposure to the euro dragged on performance. And the fund's relatively small position in emerging markets—one of the fixed-income world's most successful asset classes this year—also hurt. Thus, the fund's 1.3% gain for the year to date through Dec. 6, 2001, again ranks in the middle third of its group.

Despite its decent relative performance over time, this fund's structure can make it a tough fit for most portfolios. With its U.S. stake, it doesn't offer as much diversification as its foreign-only rivals, and its opportunistic hedging policies haven't always paid off. Other offerings have more appeal.

Address:	IDS Tower 10 Minneapolis, MN 55440–0010 800–328–8300 / 612–671–3733
Web Address:	www.americanexpress.com/advisors
Inception:	03-20-89
Advisor:	American Express Financial
Subadvisor:	None
NTF Plans:	N/A

Minimum Purchase:	$2000	Add: $100	IRA: None
Min Auto Inv Plan:	$2000	Add: $100	
Sales Fees:	4.75%L, 0.25%B		
Management Fee:	.77% mx./.67% mn., .06%A		
Actual Fees:	Mgt: 0.74%	Dist: 0.25%	
Expense Projections:	3Yr: $850	5Yr: $1107	10Yr: $1843
Avg Brok Commission:	—	Income Distrib: Quarterly	
Total Cost (relative to category):	—		

AXP High–Yield Tax–Exempt A

Ticker	Load	NAV	Yield	SEC Yield	Total Assets	Mstar Category
INHYX	4.75%	$4.35	5.8%	4.56%	$4,625.8 mil	Muni Natl Long–Term

Prospectus Objective: Muni Bond—National

AXP High-Yield Tax-Exempt Fund seeks a high yield exempt from federal income taxes.

The fund normally invests at least 80% of net assets in bonds and in other debt obligations issued by or on behalf of state or local governmental units whose interest is exempt from federal income tax and is not subject to the alternative minimum tax. It invests primarily in medium and lower quality bonds and other debt obligations. The fund may invest up to 20% of assets in Alternative Minimum Tax-subject bonds.

Class A shares have front loads; B shares have deferred loads, 12b-1 fees, and conversion features; C shares have level loads; and Y shares are available only to institutional investors.

Historical Profile

Return: Average
Risk: Below Avg
Rating: ★★★ Neutral

Investment Style: Fixed-Income

Income Rtn %Rank Cat: 8, 10, 9, 7, 6, 1, 8, 9

Growth of Principal vs. Interest Rate Shifts
— Principal Value $000 (NAV with capital gains reinvested)
— Interest Rate % on 10 Yr Treasury
▼ Manager Change
▽ Partial Manager Change
► Mgr Unknown After
◄ Mgr Unknown Before

Performance Quartile (within Category)

1990	1991	1992	1993	1994	1995	1996	1997	1998	1999	2000	12–01	History
4.44	4.61	4.66	4.78	4.25	4.69	4.54	4.68	4.67	4.29	4.43	4.35	NAV
5.20	11.99	8.70	9.69	–5.05	17.39	2.81	9.27	5.41	–2.29	9.52	3.91	Total Return %
–3.76	–4.01	1.30	–0.06	–2.13	–1.08	–0.81	–0.41	–3.26	–1.46	–2.11	–4.51	+/– LB Aggregate
–2.11	–0.15	–0.12	–2.59	0.10	–0.08	–1.63	0.07	–1.07	–0.22	–2.18	–1.17	+/– LB Muni
7.65	7.53	7.05	6.60	6.32	6.76	5.98	6.03	5.63	6.12	6.04	5.81	Income Return %
–2.45	4.46	1.65	3.09	–11.36	10.62	–3.18	3.24	–0.22	–8.41	3.47	–1.90	Capital Return %
78	49	61	94	24	36	70	45	48	3	68	51	Total Rtn % Rank Cat
0.34	0.32	0.32	0.30	0.29	0.28	0.27	0.27	0.26	0.28	0.25	0.25	Income $
0.02	0.02	0.02	0.02	0.00	0.00	0.00	0.00	0.00	0.00	0.00	0.00	Capital Gains $
0.60	0.60	0.62	0.61	0.59	0.68	0.70	0.70	0.70	0.74	0.79	—	Expense Ratio %
7.62	7.26	6.86	6.32	6.50	6.31	6.02	5.85	5.56	5.73	5.93	—	Income Ratio %
22	10	12	10	17	14	9	4	14	16	15	—	Turnover Rate %
4,749.9	5,435.8	6,116.3	6,845.7	5,604.9	6,363.4	5,927.8	5,773.0	5,728.2	4,963.3	4,618.8	4,625.8	Net Assets $mil

Portfolio Manager(s)

Terrence M. Fettig, CFA. Since 1-01. BA'71 Illinois Benedictine C.; MBA'78 U. of Notre Dame. Other funds currently managed: AXP High-Yield Tax-Exempt B, AXP High-Yield Tax-Exempt Y, AXP High-Yield Tax-Exempt C.

Performance 12-31-01

	1st Qtr	2nd Qtr	3rd Qtr	4th Qtr	Total
1997	–0.07	3.33	2.99	2.75	9.27
1998	1.19	1.38	2.67	0.07	5.41
1999	0.78	–1.39	–1.03	–0.65	–2.29
2000	2.23	1.49	1.91	3.58	9.52
2001	1.74	0.52	2.53	–0.91	3.91

Trailing	Total Return%	+/– LB Agg	+/– LB Muni	% Rank All	% Rank Cat	Growth of $10,000
3 Mo	–0.91	–0.94	–0.24	92	41	9,909
6 Mo	1.60	–3.05	–0.52	28	43	10,160
1 Yr	3.91	–4.51	–1.17	31	51	10,391
3 Yr Avg	3.60	–2.67	–1.15	47	29	11,120
5 Yr Avg	5.07	–2.35	–0.90	63	30	12,808
10 Yr Avg	5.76	–1.47	–0.88	78	57	17,499
15 Yr Avg	6.38	–1.74	–0.81	80	46	25,292

Tax Analysis	Tax-Adj Ret%	%Rank Cat	%Pretax Ret	%Rank Cat
3 Yr Avg	3.59	28	99.8	57
5 Yr Avg	5.07	25	99.9	25
10 Yr Avg	5.73	51	99.5	14

Potential Capital Gain Exposure: 2% of assets

Risk Analysis

Time Period	Load-Adj Return %	Risk %Rank[1] All	Risk %Rank[1] Cat	Morningstar Return	Morningstar Risk	Morningstar Risk-Adj Rating
1 Yr	–1.02					
3 Yr	1.93	12	7	0.21[2]	0.88	★★★
5 Yr	4.06	10	8	0.70[2]	0.83	★★★★
10 Yr	5.24	12	9	0.97	0.86	★★★

Average Historical Rating (193 months): 4.1★s

[1] 1=low, 100=high [2] T-Bill return substituted for category avg.

Category Rating (3 Yr)

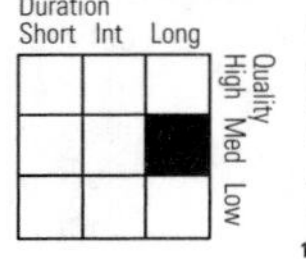

Return: High
Risk: Low

Other Measures	Standard Index LB Agg	Best Fit Index LB Muni
Alpha	–2.2	–1.1
Beta	0.73	0.95
R–Squared	46	94

Standard Deviation	3.75
Mean	3.60
Sharpe Ratio	–0.42

Portfolio Analysis 11-30-01

Total Fixed-Income: 651	Date of Maturity	Amount $000	Value $000	% Net Assets
NC East Muni Pwr Sys 5.75%	01-01-19	55,000	54,878	1.10
NH Indl Dev Poll Cntrl Pub Svc 7.5%	05-01-21	51,485	52,588	1.06
CA COP Community Development 5.	10-01-11	44,800	49,809	1.00
WA Pub Pwr Sply Sys Proj #1 5.75%	07-01-11	40,000	43,931	0.88
NC East Muni Pwr Sys 5.5%	01-01-11	37,800	37,808	0.76
CA North Pwr Geotherm Proj #3 5%	07-01-09	33,535	36,248	0.73
MA GO 7.96%	01-01-21	36,455	36,078	0.72
TX Alliance Arpt Spcl Fac American 7.5%	12-01-29	37,400	35,125	0.70
NE Pub Pwr Dist 5.25%	01-01-14	30,610	31,820	0.64
NM Farmington Poll Cntrl Pub Svc 0%	08-15-23	30,650	31,049	0.62
CA Foothill/Eastern Transp 5%	01-01-35	31,070	30,805	0.62
IL Chicago O'Hare Intl Arpt 6%	01-01-18	29,000	29,006	0.58
NJ Econ Dev Indl Dev 5%	07-01-08	27,000	28,645	0.57
MA GO 6%	11-01-13	25,000	28,504	0.57
NY Dorm State Univ Educ Fac 5.5%	05-15-13	24,530	26,753	0.54

Current Investment Style

Duration: Short Int Long; Quality: High Med Low

Avg Duration[1]	9.1 Yrs
Avg Nominal Maturity	19.1 Yrs
Avg Credit Quality	A
Avg Wtd Coupon	6.25%
Avg Wtd Price	97.99% of par
Pricing Service	J.J. Kenny

[1] figure provided by fund

Credit Analysis % bonds 09-30-01

US Govt	0	BB	4
AAA	36	B	1
AA	7	Below B	0
A	10	NR/NA	29
BBB	13		

Special Securities % assets 11-30-01

Restricted/Illiquid Secs	0
Inverse Floaters	1
Options/Futures/Warrants	No

Bond Type % assets 03-31-01

Alternative Minimum Tax (AMT)	14.9
Insured	—
Prerefunded	—

Top 5 States % bonds

CA	9.3	CO	6.6
TX	7.5	FL	5.6
IL	7.3		

Composition % assets 11-30-01

Cash	1.1	Bonds	98.9
Stocks	0.0	Other	0.0

Sector Weightings	% of Bonds	Rel Cat
General Obligation	21.3	1.0
Utilities	15.4	1.9
Health	12.0	0.8
Water/Waste	3.7	0.6
Housing	5.2	0.7
Education	2.7	0.4
Transportation	10.9	0.8
COP/Lease	4.0	1.4
Industrial	18.9	1.5
Misc Revenue	5.0	1.0
Demand	0.9	1.1

Analysis by Bradley Sweeney 08-10-01

Shareholders should shrug off the management change here; this remains a respectable choice.

AXP High-Yield Tax-Exempt Fund lost its longtime manager at the end of 2000 when Kurt Larson, who had managed the fund for more than 20 years, stepped down. Larson had amassed an impressive long-term record here by typically storing about a fourth of the fund's assets in low-quality, nonrated municipal debt. As the fund became more popular—it was home to more than $6 billion in total assets in the early 1990s—he took to holding an enormous number of bonds to keep the fund fully invested. Although a new face is at the helm, shareholders shouldn't expect dramatic changes. Terry Fettig, who took over at the beginning of 2001, worked with Larson at AXP for more than 10 years and is planning to employ a nearly identical approach.

Although the fund has gotten off to a slow start in 2001, it's much too early to judge how successful Fettig will be at employing this strategy. With Fettig stating that the portfolio has been relatively free of credit-quality problems, it seems that the bulk of the blame for this year's underperformance rests with his decision to keep the portfolio's duration—a measure of interest-rate sensitivity—below his average peer's. As a result, the fund is trailing 64% of its peers in the muni-national-long -term category for the year to date through August 9, 2001.

We think that shareholders have been adequately compensated over time for this offering's allocation to below-investment-grade debt. And we have been favorably impressed with the low level of volatility that has been a product of such a massive portfolio. We don't expect these features to change substantially under the fund's new management. This remains a respectable choice for income-hungry investors who aren't afraid of taking on a bit of credit risk.

Address:	IDS Tower 10 Minneapolis, MN 55440–0010 800–328–8300 / 612–671–3733
Web Address:	www.americanexpress.com/advisors
Inception:	05-07-79
Advisor:	American Express Financial
Subadvisor:	None
NTF Plans:	N/A

Minimum Purchase:	$2000	Add: $100 IRA: —
Min Auto Inv Plan:	$2000	Add: $100
Sales Fees:	4.75%L, 0.25%B	
Management Fee:	.49% mx./.36% mn., .04%A	
Actual Fees:	Mgt: 0.44%	Dist: 0.25%
Expense Projections:	3Yr: $713	5Yr: $871 10Yr: $1331
Avg Brok Commission:	—	Income Distrib: Monthly
Total Cost (relative to category):	—	

AXP New Dimensions A

Ticker	Load	NAV	Yield	Total Assets	Mstar Category
INNDX	5.75%	$24.49	0.0%	$12,946.8 mil	Large Blend

Prospectus Objective: Growth

AXP New Dimensions Fund seeks long-term capital appreciation.

The fund invests primarily in common stocks of U.S. companies. These companies usually operate in areas where dynamic economic and technological changes are occurring. They may also exhibit excellence in technology, marketing, or management. The fund may invest up to 30% of assets in foreign securities. The fund will not invest more than 5% of net assets in bonds below investment grade.

Class A shares have front loads; B shares have deferred loads, 12b-1 fees, and conversion features; C shares have level loads; and Y shares are for institutional investors. Past name: IDS New Dimensions Fund.

Historical Profile
Return: Average
Risk: Average
Rating: ★★★ Neutral

Investment Style
Equity
Average Stock %: 88% (1995), 89% (1996), 90% (1997), 93% (1998), 91% (1999), 91% (2000), 95% (12-01)

▼ Manager Change
▽ Partial Manager Change

Fund Performance vs. Category Average
■ Quarterly Fund Return +/– Category Average
— Category Baseline

Performance Quartile (within Category)

Portfolio Manager(s)

Gordon Fines. Since 4-91. Other funds currently managed: AXP New Dimensions Y, AXP New Dimensions B, AXP Growth Dimensions A.

Douglas Guffy. Since 9-00. Other funds currently managed: AXP New Dimensions Y, AXP New Dimensions B, AXP Growth Dimensions A.

Anne Obermeyer. Since 9-00. Other funds currently managed: AXP New Dimensions Y, AXP New Dimensions B, AXP Growth Dimensions A.

History

1990	1991	1992	1993	1994	1995	1996	1997	1998	1999	2000	12-01	History
9.23	13.28	13.21	14.34	13.29	17.27	20.70	23.85	28.83	35.78	29.00	24.49	NAV
5.40	50.67	5.27	14.03	–2.98	35.57	24.41	24.63	28.31	31.54	–8.82	–15.50	Total Return %
8.52	20.19	–2.35	3.97	–4.29	–1.97	1.47	–8.73	–0.26	10.50	0.28	–3.62	+/– S&P 500
9.43	18.23	–2.38	4.19	–3.43	–2.04	2.25	–8.40	–0.32	9.71	2.14	–2.73	+/– Wilshire Top 750
2.23	1.54	0.30	0.54	0.82	1.10	0.73	0.82	0.25	0.20	0.07	0.00	Income Return %
3.18	49.13	4.97	13.49	–3.80	34.47	23.69	23.81	28.07	31.34	–8.89	–15.49	Capital Return %
4	5	77	26	76	36	16	76	23	15	52	70	Total Rtn % Rank Cat
0.22	0.14	0.04	0.07	0.12	0.15	0.13	0.17	0.06	0.06	0.03	0.00	Income $
0.96	0.49	0.73	0.65	0.51	0.60	0.67	1.74	1.69	2.06	3.46	0.02	Capital Gains $
0.88	0.90	0.95	0.92	0.90	0.90	0.94	0.91	0.82	0.86	0.90	1.00	Expense Ratio %
2.43	1.65	0.57	0.51	0.75	1.07	0.78	0.73	0.55	0.24	0.19	0.12	Income Ratio %
91	81	75	60	48	54	—	32	38	34	34	29	Turnover Rate %
929.2	1,948.1	2,668.5	3,739.8	4,458.4	4,865.9	6,784.8	8,887.2	11,919.6	16,911.4	15,947.1	12,946.8	Net Assets $mil

Performance 12-31-01

	1st Qtr	2nd Qtr	3rd Qtr	4th Qtr	Total
1997	–1.69	15.53	7.95	1.65	24.63
1998	12.83	3.42	–11.50	24.25	28.31
1999	6.07	5.79	–4.61	22.88	31.54
2000	7.77	–4.56	–1.96	–9.58	–8.82
2001	–15.41	5.38	–15.74	12.52	–15.50

Trailing	Total Return%	+/– S&P 500	+/–Wil Top 750	% Rank All	% Rank Cat	Growth of $10,000
3 Mo	12.52	1.83	1.19	31	24	11,252
6 Mo	–5.20	0.36	0.60	63	30	9,480
1 Yr	–15.50	–3.62	–2.73	73	70	8,451
3 Yr Avg	0.45	1.47	2.27	71	31	10,135
5 Yr Avg	10.14	–0.56	0.02	18	37	16,207
10 Yr Avg	12.28	–0.65	–0.17	17	37	31,836
15 Yr Avg	15.16	1.42	1.79	6	7	83,033

Tax Analysis	Tax-Adj Ret%	%Rank Cat	%Pretax Ret	%Rank Cat
3 Yr Avg	–0.70	30	—	—
5 Yr Avg	8.71	34	85.9	31
10 Yr Avg	10.80	28	88.0	25

Potential Capital Gain Exposure: 16% of assets

Risk Analysis

Time Period	Load-Adj Return %	Risk %Rank[1] All	Risk %Rank[1] Cat	Morningstar Return	Morningstar Risk	Morningstar Risk-Adj Rating
1 Yr	–20.35					
3 Yr	–1.51	72	68	–1.29[2]	0.99	★★
5 Yr	8.84	72	75	0.90[2]	0.98	★★★
10 Yr	11.61	78	83	1.03	1.02	★★★

Average Historical Rating (193 months): 4.3★s

[1]1=low, 100=high [2] T-Bill return substituted for category avg.

Category Rating (3 Yr)

Worst 1 2 3 4 5 Best

Return: Above Avg
Risk: Above Avg

Other Measures	Standard Index S&P 500	Best Fit Index MSCIACWdFr
Alpha	2.2	6.7
Beta	1.06	1.15
R-Squared	89	92
Standard Deviation		19.34
Mean		0.45
Sharpe Ratio		–0.27

Analysis by William Harding 10-29-01

This fund is a respectable choice for investors looking for a core holding with a growth bent.

Investors need to look past AXP New Dimensions Fund's showing this year to see its appeal, though. The stock market's severe retreat this year has taken its toll on this fund. It has lost nearly 19% for the year to date ended Oct. 26, 2001, lagging two thirds of funds in the large-blend category and the S&P 500 by more than 3 percentage points. But this fund isn't your typical large-blend offering. Rather, it tends to walk the line between the large-growth and large-blend categories and is best described as a mild-mannered growth option.

Against that backdrop, the fund's showing looks brighter. The fund hasn't fallen as far the large-growth category average of 27.5% this year, thanks to prudent moves of lead manager Gordon Fines. For instance, he began scaling back the fund's tech stake in the spring of 2000 after riding some names to big gains in 1998 and 1999. Fines has further cut the fund's tech stake this year to 15% of assets (small by growth-fund standards) as he reckons capital spending is still depressed.

Fines is spying compelling growth picks outside of tech, however. In particular, he has added to positions in health-care, financials, and consumer-related stocks such as Philip Morris. But that's not to suggest that there have been wholesale changes to the portfolio. Indeed, the fund's turnover rate is a modest 34%, and its top picks are peppered with longtime holdings like Pfizer and Citigroup.

Fines' strategy of buying quality companies at attractive valuations and holding on for a while has produced respectable results. The fund's long-term returns best the large-blend and large-growth averages, and it hasn't been much more volatile than the typical large-blend fund. Although this isn't your mainstream S&P 500-like blend offering, it's a suitable core holding nonetheless.

Portfolio Analysis 11-30-01

Share change since 10-01 Total Stocks: 72	Sector	PE	YTD Ret%	% Assets
⊖ Citigroup	Financials	20.0	0.03	4.88
Microsoft	Technology	57.6	52.78	3.49
General Elec	Industrials	30.1	–15.00	3.49
⊖ ExxonMobil	Energy	15.3	–7.59	3.39
IBM	Technology	26.9	43.00	3.14
Pfizer	Health	34.7	–12.40	2.98
American Intl Grp	Financials	42.0	–19.20	2.84
Wal-Mart Stores	Retail	40.3	8.94	2.75
Viacom Cl B	Services	—	—	2.37
Morgan Stanley/Dean Witter	Financials	16.6	–28.20	2.26
⊕ Intel	Technology	73.1	4.89	2.22
Cardinal Health	Health	35.1	–2.51	2.17
ChevronTexaco	Energy	10.3	9.29	2.12
AOL Time Warner	Technology	—	–7.76	2.02
Minnesota Mng & Mfg	Industrials	34.5	0.16	1.97
Bank of America	Financials	16.7	42.73	1.95
Texas Instruments	Technology	87.5	–40.70	1.89
Automatic Data Processing	Services	39.8	–6.27	1.88
Tyco Intl	Industrials	27.1	6.23	1.86
⊕ Philip Morris	Staples	12.1	9.12	1.83
Johnson & Johnson	Health	16.6	14.01	1.71
Target	Retail	29.8	28.05	1.70
Cisco Sys	Technology	—	–52.60	1.57
⊖ Southwest Air	Services	25.0	–17.20	1.57
⊕ Verizon Comms	Services	29.7	–2.52	1.53

Current Investment Style

Style: Value Blnd Growth; Size: Large Med Small

	Stock Port Avg	Relative S&P 500 Current	Relative S&P 500 Hist	Rel Cat
Price/Earnings Ratio	32.2	1.04	1.10	1.06
Price/Book Ratio	5.7	0.99	1.07	1.03
Price/Cash Flow	18.9	1.05	1.14	1.03
3 Yr Earnings Growth	17.8	1.22	1.18	1.00
1 Yr Earnings Est%	0.5	—	—	–5.22
Med Mkt Cap $mil	83,660	1.4	1.2	1.60

Special Securities % assets 11-30-01	
Restricted/Illiquid Secs	0
Emerging-Markets Secs	0
Options/Futures/Warrants	No

Composition % assets 11-30-01	
Cash	3.0
Stocks*	96.0
Bonds	0.0
Other	1.0
*Foreign (% stocks)	0.3

Market Cap	
Giant	63.8
Large	34.6
Medium	1.6
Small	0.0
Micro	0.0

Sector Weightings	% of Stocks	Rel S&P	5-Year High	5-Year Low
Utilities	2.6	0.8	5	0
Energy	7.0	1.0	11	1
Financials	22.3	1.2	23	5
Industrials	11.0	1.0	24	3
Durables	0.0	0.0	9	0
Staples	4.2	0.5	12	1
Services	12.0	1.1	38	5
Retail	9.8	1.5	26	2
Health	13.3	0.9	24	1
Technology	17.9	1.0	41	13

Address: IDS Tower 10, Minneapolis, MN 55440–0010, 800–328–8300 / 612–671–3733
Web Address: www.americanexpress.com/advisors
Inception: 07-30-68
Advisor: American Express Financial
Subadvisor: None
NTF Plans: N/A

Minimum Purchase: $2000 Add: $100 IRA: None
Min Auto Inv Plan: $2000 Add: $100
Sales Fees: 5.75%L, 0.25%B
Management Fee: .60% mx./.50% mn.+(–).12%P, .05%A
Actual Fees: Mgt: 0.56% Dist: 0.25%
Expense Projections: 3Yr: $78* 5Yr: $98* 10Yr: $157*
Avg Brok Commission: — Income Distrib: Annually
Total Cost (relative to category): —

AXP Utilities Income A

Ticker	Load	NAV	Yield	Total Assets	Mstar Category
INUTX	5.75%	$7.54	5.7%	$2,081.0 mil	Spec Utilities

Prospectus Objective: Specialty—Utilities

AXP Utilities Income Fund seeks current income; growth of income and capital appreciation are secondary considerations.

The fund normally invests at least 65% of assets in securities of companies in the utilities industry. These include companies that produce or supply electric power, natural gas, water, sanitary services, or telecommunication and other communication services (excluding radio or television broadcasts) for public use. The fund may invest up to 25% of its total assets in foreign investments

Class A shares have front loads; B shares have deferred loads and 12b-1 fees; C shares have level loads; and Y shares are available only to institutional investors.

Historical Profile
Return: Average
Risk: Below Avg
Rating: ★★★ Neutral

Investment Style
Equity
Average Stock %: 83% 88% 85% 90% 88% 91% 90%

▼ Manager Change
▽ Partial Manager Change

Fund Performance vs. Category Average
■ Quarterly Fund Return +/– Category Average
— Category Baseline

Performance Quartile (within Category)

Portfolio Manager(s)

Bern Fleming, CFA. Since 1-95. BS'61 U.S. Naval Academy; MBA U. of Illinois. Other funds currently managed: AXP Utilities Income B, AXP Utilities Income Y, AXP Utilities Income C.

1990	1991	1992	1993	1994	1995	1996	1997	1998	1999	2000	12-01	History
5.52	6.30	6.42	6.90	5.94	7.00	7.54	8.42	9.48	9.35	10.36	7.54	NAV
–1.80	21.97	10.34	18.77	–7.07	23.47	14.42	29.04	22.75	8.73	17.02	–20.10	Total Return %
1.32	–8.52	2.72	8.71	–8.38	–14.07	–8.52	–4.32	–5.83	–12.31	26.13	–8.23	+/– S&P 500
1.87	3.81	1.27	–0.99	–4.75	–16.56	–7.89	–6.45	1.51	–2.23	14.71	–11.31	+/– Russ Top 200 Val
6.43	6.27	5.33	4.35	4.63	5.11	3.38	3.41	2.65	2.12	1.72	4.32	Income Return %
–8.23	15.69	5.01	14.42	–11.70	18.35	11.05	25.63	20.10	6.60	15.31	–24.43	Capital Return %
53	41	33	17	24	81	24	27	35	70	30	45	Total Rtn % Rank Cat
0.38	0.34	0.33	0.28	0.31	0.30	0.23	0.25	0.22	0.20	0.16	0.44	Income $
0.05	0.06	0.18	0.44	0.16	0.00	0.22	1.00	0.59	0.73	0.39	0.29	Capital Gains $
0.96	0.90	0.92	0.86	0.82	0.89	0.90	0.89	0.86	0.86	0.99	1.03	Expense Ratio %
6.65	6.37	5.37	4.78	4.55	4.84	4.03	3.42	2.81	2.23	1.97	1.62	Income Ratio %
53	57	49	64	102	68	84	90	83	71	89	85	Turnover Rate %
218.0	327.5	509.6	796.4	585.9	672.4	694.3	862.7	1,180.1	1,493.7	1,824.1	1,383.5	Net Assets $mil

Performance 12-31-01

	1st Qtr	2nd Qtr	3rd Qtr	4th Qtr	Total
1997	–0.82	9.35	4.62	13.73	29.04
1998	10.37	–2.17	0.84	12.73	22.75
1999	–3.49	9.48	–5.25	8.61	8.73
2000	3.45	–4.67	17.85	0.68	17.02
2001	–6.30	–4.29	–10.75	–0.18	–20.10

Trailing	Total Return%	+/– S&P 500	+/– Russ Top 200 Val	% Rank All	% Rank Cat	Growth of $10,000
3 Mo	–0.18	–10.86	–5.69	80	47	9,982
6 Mo	–10.91	–5.35	–5.13	88	27	8,909
1 Yr	–20.10	–8.23	–11.31	80	45	7,990
3 Yr Avg	0.55	1.57	–0.62	70	39	10,165
5 Yr Avg	9.99	–0.71	–1.21	19	30	16,100
10 Yr Avg	10.73	–2.20	–3.30	28	16	27,702
15 Yr Avg	—	—	—	—	—	—

Tax Analysis	Tax-Adj Ret%	%Rank Cat	%Pretax Ret	%Rank Cat
3 Yr Avg	–1.73	39	—	—
5 Yr Avg	7.02	27	70.3	39
10 Yr Avg	7.86	22	73.3	22

Potential Capital Gain Exposure: –9% of assets

Risk Analysis

Time Period	Load-Adj Return %	Risk %Rank[1] All	Risk %Rank[1] Cat	Morningstar Return	Morningstar Risk	Morningstar Risk-Adj Rating
1 Yr	–24.70					
3 Yr	–1.42	53	37	–1.27[2]	0.75	★★★
5 Yr	8.70	50	34	0.86[2]	0.70	★★★
10 Yr	10.07	56	18	0.74	0.72	★★★

Average Historical Rating (126 months): 3.3★s

[1] 1=low, 100=high [2] T-Bill return substituted for category avg.

Category Rating (3 Yr)

1 2 3 4 5 — Worst … Best (rating: 3)

Return: Average
Risk: Average

Other Measures	Standard Index S&P 500	Best Fit Index SPMid400
Alpha	–1.8	–6.0
Beta	0.32	0.43
R-Squared	14	34
Standard Deviation		14.54
Mean		0.55
Sharpe Ratio		–0.35

Portfolio Analysis 11-30-01

Share chng since 10-01 Total Stocks: 50	Subsector	PE	YTD Ret%	% Assets
⊕ BellSouth	Phone Services	24.9	–5.09	6.00
⊖ Verizon Comms	Phone Services	29.7	–2.52	5.77
⊖ Dominion Resources	Electric	19.3	–6.59	4.42
Duke Energy	Electric	15.5	–6.04	4.27
ALLTEL	Phone Services	17.7	1.14	3.38
El Paso	Utilities	NMF	–36.70	3.15
Xcel Energy	Electric	12.2	0.57	3.10
⊕ Sprint	Phone Services	20.5	1.18	3.09
⊖ SBC Comms	Phone Services	18.4	–16.00	3.00
⊖ DTE Energy	Electric	24.2	13.12	2.93
⊖ Mirant	Utilities	8.3	–43.40	2.88
Keyspan	Energy	20.2	–14.10	2.72
FirstEnergy	Electric	12.8	16.42	2.55
⊖ Entergy	Electric	11.7	–4.50	2.44
Public Svc Entpr	Electric	11.3	–8.99	2.30
Williams Companies	Utilities	17.9	–29.10	2.15
⊖ Allegheny Energy	Electric	10.0	–21.70	1.98
⊖ TXU	Electric	13.7	12.17	1.70
BCE	Phone Services	3.8	–18.70	1.63
Equitable Resources	Energy	14.8	3.98	1.54
NRG Energy	Utilities	—	–43.80	1.52
⊖ Dynegy	Energy	12.8	–54.20	1.43
⊖ AT & T	N/A	—	—	1.40
Nisource	Electric	33.4	–21.60	1.38
Questar	Energy	11.8	–14.40	1.32

Current Investment Style

Style: Value Blnd Growth; Size: Large Med Small

	Stock Port Avg	Relative S&P 500 Current	Relative S&P 500 Hist	Rel Cat
Price/Earnings Ratio	18.7	0.60	0.74	0.97
Price/Book Ratio	2.2	0.39	0.51	0.95
Price/Cash Flow	8.7	0.48	0.62	0.95
3 Yr Earnings Growth	16.1	1.10	0.58	1.02
1 Yr Earnings Est%	12.0	—	—	1.49
Med Mkt Cap $mil	11,603	0.2	0.2	0.95

Special Securities % assets 11-30-01	
Restricted/Illiquid Secs	0
Emerging-Markets Secs	0
Options/Futures/Warrants	No

Composition % assets 11-30-01	
Cash	9.5
Stocks*	86.6
Bonds	0.0
Other	3.9
*Foreign (% stocks)	4.6

Market Cap	
Giant	19.6
Large	36.0
Medium	41.8
Small	2.6
Micro	0.0

Subsector Weightings	% of Stocks	Rel Cat
Electric	40.0	1.0
Gas	4.1	1.1
Phone Services	27.1	1.4
Phone Equip.	0.0	0.0
Energy	4.7	1.0
Energy Services	0.0	0.0
Water	1.2	2.0
Other	23.0	0.9

Analysis by Bradley Sweeney 08-06-01

This offering is one of our favorites in the utility group.

Despite its fairly conservative leanings, AXP Utilities Income isn't having a banner year. The fund has been stung in 2001 by its exposure to independent energy producers such as Calpine and Dynegy, which have sold off sharply following a great run in 2000. Consequently, the fund has barely edged out its average rival for the year to date through August 1, 2001. The fund's record since the tech wreck began in March 2000 is exceptional, however. Unlike many of its peers in the specialty-utilities category, it has kept its telecommunications exposure to a minimum and has tended to avoid that sector's more-speculative concerns. That fairly conservative stance has been a huge boon to performance over the last 12 months, as the market has punished the more-speculative subset of the telecom sector, including telecom-equipment makers and competitive local exchange carriers (those firms that are attempting to compete with the Baby Bells for both data and voice traffic).

Manager Bern Fleming's fairly conservative approach may have held the fund back in 1999's telecom-crazy market, but it hasn't been a drag on performance over the long haul. Indeed, the fund has beat out 70% of its rivals over the five years ended Aug. 1, 2001. And when Fleming has dabbled in more-speculative names, he has generally chosen to hold their convertible bonds, a less risky way to gain equity-like exposure to such firms. These tactics have also helped make this one of the least volatile offerings in the utilities category.

This offering's yield, which is slightly less than the category average, isn't likely to appeal to income-hungry investors. But those who are interested in the relative safety of a portfolio that is laden with dividend-paying names will find a respectable home here.

Address:	IDS Tower 10 Minneapolis, MN 55440–0010 800–328–8300 / 612–671–3733
Web Address:	www.americanexpress.com/advisors
Inception:	08-01-88
Advisor:	American Express Financial
Subadvisor:	None
NTF Plans:	N/A

Minimum Purchase:	$2000	Add: $100	IRA: None
Min Auto Inv Plan:	$2000	Add: $100	
Sales Fees:	5.75%L, 0.25%B		
Management Fee:	.53% mx./.40% mn., .04%A		
Actual Fees:	Mgt: 0.52%	Dist: 0.25%	
Expense Projections:	3Yr: $76*	5Yr: $95*	10Yr: $151*
Avg Brok Commission:	—	Income Distrib: Quarterly	
Total Cost (relative to category):	—		

Babson Growth

Ticker	Load	NAV	Yield	Total Assets	Mstar Category
BABSX	None	$11.07	0.0%	$292.8 mil	Large Growth

Prospectus Objective: Growth

Babson Growth Fund seeks long-term growth of capital and dividend income; current yield is secondary.

The fund invests primarily in common stocks. In selecting investments, management looks for progressive, well-managed companies in growing industries. These companies must, in management's opinion, have demonstrated a consistent and above-average ability to increase their earnings and dividends and must have favorable prospects of sustaining such growth. The fund may also invest in convertible securities, preferred stocks, and high-grade bonds.

Historical Profile
Return Average
Risk Above Avg
Rating ★★
Below Avg

Investment Style
Equity
Average Stock %: 97% 100% 98% 98% 98% 96% 97%

▼ Manager Change
▽ Partial Manager Change

Fund Performance vs. Category Average
■ Quarterly Fund Return +/– Category Average
— Category Baseline

Performance Quartile (within Category)

Portfolio Manager(s)

James B. Gribbell, CFA. Since 1-96. BS'89 U. of Pennsylvania. Other fund currently managed: DLB Core Growth.

1990	1991	1992	1993	1994	1995	1996	1997	1998	1999	2000	12-01	History
9.75	12.02	12.58	13.08	11.97	14.66	15.43	18.08	20.64	20.71	14.23	11.07	NAV
–9.44	26.06	9.10	10.27	–0.56	31.43	21.80	27.99	32.24	12.57	–7.85	–20.47	Total Return %
–6.32	–4.43	1.48	0.22	–1.88	–6.11	–1.14	–5.36	3.67	–8.47	1.25	–8.60	+/– S&P 500
–10.81	–13.35	5.21	10.35	–5.41	–7.22	–3.72	–5.75	–12.86	–17.11	16.68	0.03	+/– Russ Top 200 Grt
2.36	2.22	1.67	1.55	1.59	1.28	0.78	0.60	0.22	0.00	0.00	0.00	Income Return %
–11.80	23.84	7.43	8.72	–2.15	30.15	21.02	27.39	32.02	12.57	–7.85	–20.47	Capital Return %
91	94	24	51	32	57	28	37	49	96	23	41	Total Rtn % Rank Cat
0.27	0.22	0.20	0.19	0.20	0.15	0.11	0.09	0.04	0.00	0.00	0.00	Income $
0.55	0.04	0.33	0.55	0.81	0.85	2.13	1.50	3.05	2.30	5.01	0.25	Capital Gains $
0.86	0.86	0.86	0.86	0.86	0.85	0.85	0.83	0.80	0.79	0.79	0.80	Expense Ratio %
2.28	2.26	1.69	1.54	1.54	1.42	0.82	0.61	0.30	0.09	–0.18	–0.16	Income Ratio %
23	22	12	13	10	17	33	20	35	39	62	64	Turnover Rate %
221.3	256.8	244.6	245.3	226.5	271.1	311.1	395.8	512.1	500.3	415.7	292.8	Net Assets $mil

Performance 12-31-01

	1st Qtr	2nd Qtr	3rd Qtr	4th Qtr	Total
1997	0.97	15.82	7.58	1.73	27.99
1998	12.67	2.78	–9.53	26.23	32.24
1999	–0.48	2.99	–6.90	17.97	12.57
2000	15.84	–5.15	–0.14	–16.01	–7.85
2001	–18.06	7.29	–20.46	13.74	–20.47

Trailing	Total Return%	+/– S&P 500	+/– Russ Top 200 Grth	% Rank All	% Rank Cat	Growth of $10,000
3 Mo	13.74	3.05	0.88	27	48	11,374
6 Mo	–9.54	–3.98	–2.55	84	56	9,046
1 Yr	–20.47	–8.60	0.03	81	41	7,953
3 Yr Avg	–6.21	–5.19	1.81	94	72	8,250
5 Yr Avg	6.90	–3.79	–1.69	37	66	13,963
10 Yr Avg	10.34	–2.59	–0.75	30	53	26,742
15 Yr Avg	10.50	–3.23	–2.87	38	80	44,717

Tax Analysis	Tax-Adj Ret%	%Rank Cat	%Pretax Ret	%Rank Cat
3 Yr Avg	–9.12	80	—	—
5 Yr Avg	3.83	73	55.5	84
10 Yr Avg	7.49	62	72.5	65

Potential Capital Gain Exposure: –2% of assets

Risk Analysis

Time Period	Load-Adj Return %	Risk %Rank[1] All	Risk %Rank[1] Cat	Morningstar Return	Morningstar Risk	Morningstar Risk-Adj Rating
1 Yr	–20.47					
3 Yr	–6.21	86	51	–2.12[2]	1.30	★
5 Yr	6.90	82	44	0.42[2]	1.17	★★
10 Yr	10.34	80	21	0.79	1.07	★★★

Average Historical Rating (193 months): 3.0★s

[1]1=low, 100=high [2] T-Bill return substituted for category avg.

Category Rating (3 Yr)

1 2 3 4 5
Worst Best

Return: Below Avg
Risk: Average

Other Measures	Standard Index S&P 500	Best Fit Index MSCIACWdFr
Alpha	–3.3	1.7
Beta	1.18	1.30
R-Squared	75	80
Standard Deviation		22.20
Mean		–6.21
Sharpe Ratio		–0.59

Portfolio Analysis 09-30-01

Share change since 06-01 Total Stocks: 49	Sector	PE	YTD Ret%	% Assets
⊖ Freddie Mac	Financials	14.0	–3.87	5.27
⊖ Pfizer	Health	34.7	–12.40	5.09
⊕ Kinder Morgan	Energy	32.2	7.11	4.19
American Intl Grp	Financials	42.0	–19.20	4.11
☼ Liberty Media Cor	N/A	—	—	3.80
Citigroup	Financials	20.0	0.03	3.61
⊕ ExxonMobil	Energy	15.3	–7.59	3.37
Medtronic	Health	76.4	–14.70	3.23
Paychex	Services	49.4	–27.10	2.79
⊖ Microsoft	Technology	57.6	52.78	2.53
American Home Products	Health	—	–1.91	2.25
⊖ Bristol-Myers Squibb	Health	20.2	–26.00	2.24
☼ Ascential Softwar	N/A	—	—	2.23
Automatic Data Processing	Services	39.8	–6.27	2.18
Clear Channel Comms	Services	—	5.10	2.16
☼ Fifth Third Bancorp	Financials	38.3	4.53	2.12
Pharmacia	Health	36.5	–29.30	2.12
☼ Merck	Health	19.1	–35.90	2.08
AOL Time Warner	Technology	—	–7.76	2.02
⊕ Fiserv	Services	40.7	33.82	2.01
Johnson & Johnson	Health	16.6	14.01	1.96
⊖ Symantec	Technology	—	98.74	1.92
☼ Philip Morris	Staples	12.1	9.12	1.90
☼ Washington Mutual	Financials	10.1	–5.32	1.90
⊕ Linear Tech	Technology	34.9	–15.30	1.88

Current Investment Style

Style: Value Blnd Growth; Size: Large Med Small

	Stock Port Avg	Relative S&P 500 Current	Relative S&P 500 Hist	Rel Cat
Price/Earnings Ratio	32.0	1.03	1.21	0.90
Price/Book Ratio	6.7	1.17	1.15	1.04
Price/Cash Flow	21.4	1.19	1.29	0.94
3 Yr Earnings Growth	19.5	1.33	1.29	0.90
1 Yr Earnings Est%	8.5	—	—	2.83
Med Mkt Cap $mil	53,698	0.9	0.6	1.13

Special Securities % assets 09-30-01	
Restricted/Illiquid Secs	0
Emerging-Markets Secs	0
Options/Futures/Warrants	No

Composition % assets 09-30-01	
Cash	0.0
Stocks*	100.0
Bonds	0.0
Other	0.0
*Foreign (% stocks)	0.7

Market Cap	
Giant	55.6
Large	32.6
Medium	11.9
Small	0.0
Micro	0.0

Sector Weightings	% of Stocks	Rel S&P	5-Year High	5-Year Low
Utilities	0.0	0.0	6	0
Energy	10.1	1.4	11	1
Financials	23.3	1.3	23	6
Industrials	2.0	0.2	30	2
Durables	0.0	0.0	9	0
Staples	5.8	0.7	22	1
Services	14.9	1.4	19	6
Retail	2.3	0.3	11	2
Health	20.6	1.4	31	6
Technology	21.0	1.1	50	2

Analysis by Bridget Hughes 11-12-01

Babson Growth Fund isn't a returns powerhouse, but it's still a solid choice.

More often than not, this fund lands in the large-growth category's middle third. Sure, it has had its moments: In 2000, the fund's 7.8% loss ranked in the group's top quartile. And it has also disappointed; most recently, its lack of high-flying tech names kept its 12.6% 1999 return in the category's cellar. But 2001 is thus far looking more typical. Through Nov. 12, the fund has dropped 23.6%. That's jarring, but still ahead of its median peer.

The fund's middling performance isn't surprising, considering its stereotypical portfolio. Indeed, manager Jim Gribbell has invested primarily in sectors he thinks will gather most corporate profits over the next five years. Since he joined the fund five years ago, that's translated into a portfolio filled with technology, financial-services, health-care, and media and communications stocks—all regular stomping grounds for large-growth managers.

Around the edges of the portfolio, Gribbell also invests in other, shorter-term ideas: He recently added natural-gas producer Kinder Morgan, for example, because acquisitions the firm made eight months ago have contributed to growth. Gribbell also likes the fact that 95% of the company's revenue recurs every quarter.

That said, Gribbell has been spending most of his time lately readjusting the portfolio's tech and telecom picks. He moved out of some telecom names, because he thinks he'll have plenty of time to buy them back at cheaper valuations before they come back into favor. (Gribbell thinks that will take two or three years.) Instead, he's focusing on companies with recurring revenues, such as top-10 holding Paychex. He also thinks the semiconductor cycle is turning soon, so he has increased some existing positions there, such as Linear Technology and Analog Devices.

Although the fund isn't a standout, it is competitive and an easy fit for a portfolio.

Address:	PO Box 219757 Kansas City, MO 64121-9757 800-422-2766 / 816-751-5900
Web Address:	www.babsonfunds.com
Inception:	04-20-60
Advisor:	Jones & Babson
Subadvisor:	David L. Babson & Co.
NTF Plans:	Fidelity , Fidelity Inst.

Minimum Purchase:	$1000	Add: $100	IRA: $250
Min Auto Inv Plan:	$100	Add: $50	
Sales Fees:	No-load		
Management Fee:	.85% mx./.70% mn.		
Actual Fees:	Mgt: 0.78%	Dist: —	
Expense Projections:	3Yr: $252	5Yr: $439	10Yr: $978
Avg Brok Commission:	—	Income Distrib: Semi-Ann.	
Total Cost (relative to category):	Low		

Baron Asset

Ticker	Load	NAV	Yield	Total Assets	Mstar Category
BARAX	12b–1 only	$44.46	0.0%	$3,361.1 mil	Mid–Cap Growth

Prospectus Objective: Small Company

Baron Asset Fund seeks capital appreciation.

The fund invests in companies with market capitalizations between $100 million and $2 billion that the advisor believes have undervalued assets or favorable growth prospects. To determine favorable value relative to price, the advisor looks for fundamentals such as strong balance sheets, undervalued and unrecognized assets, low multiples of free cash flow and income, perceived management skills, unit growth, and the potential to capitalize on anticipated economic trends. The fund may engage in short-term trading and invest in special situations. It may also invest without limit in domestically traded depositary receipts.

Historical Profile
Return Above Avg
Risk Above Avg
Rating ★★★ Neutral

Investment Style
Equity
Average Stock %: 96% 89% 94% 94% 98% 100% 99%

▼ Manager Change
▽ Partial Manager Change

Fund Performance vs. Category Average
■ Quarterly Fund Return +/– Category Average
— Category Baseline

Performance Quartile (within Category)

Portfolio Manager(s)

Ronald Baron. Since 6-87. BA'65 Bucknell U. Other funds currently managed: Baron Growth, Baron Capital Asset Ins.

History

1990	1991	1992	1993	1994	1995	1996	1997	1998	1999	2000	12-01	History
11.75	15.71	17.73	21.11	22.01	29.74	36.23	48.51	50.54	58.77	54.39	44.46	NAV
–18.49	34.00	13.90	23.48	7.42	35.28	21.96	33.90	4.27	16.28	0.36	–10.12	Total Return %
–15.37	3.52	6.29	13.43	6.11	–2.26	–0.99	0.54	–24.31	–4.75	9.46	1.76	+/– S&P 500
–13.36	–13.03	5.19	12.29	9.58	1.30	4.48	11.35	–13.60	–35.02	12.10	10.04	+/– Russ Midcap Grth
1.35	0.30	0.00	0.00	0.00	0.00	0.00	0.00	0.08	0.00	0.00	0.00	Income Return %
–19.84	33.70	13.90	23.48	7.42	35.28	21.96	33.89	4.18	16.28	0.36	–10.12	Capital Return %
90	88	17	15	10	45	25	3	80	88	38	21	Total Rtn % Rank Cat
0.20	0.04	0.00	0.00	0.00	0.00	0.00	0.00	0.04	0.00	0.00	0.00	Income $
0.00	0.00	0.16	0.77	0.66	0.03	0.04	0.00	0.00	0.00	4.61	4.07	Capital Gains $
1.80	1.70	1.70	1.80	1.60	1.40	1.40	1.30	1.32	1.31	1.33	—	Expense Ratio %
1.50	0.50	–0.50	–0.70	–0.70	–0.50	–0.30	–0.50	0.11	–0.57	–1.09	—	Income Ratio %
98	143	96	108	56	35	19	13	23	16	3	—	Turnover Rate %
42.3	46.0	48.0	64.1	87.1	353.1	1,326.3	3,793.0	5,672.3	6,147.0	4,257.1	3,361.1	Net Assets $mil

Performance 12-31-01

	1st Qtr	2nd Qtr	3rd Qtr	4th Qtr	Total
1997	–3.45	19.33	13.63	2.28	33.90
1998	10.66	–2.76	–23.45	26.58	4.27
1999	7.18	11.93	–14.94	13.96	16.28
2000	10.24	–10.46	9.21	–6.90	0.36
2001	–16.57	9.30	–18.91	21.55	–10.12

Trailing	Total Return%	+/– S&P 500	+/– Russ Midcap Grth	% Rank All	% Rank Cat	Growth of $10,000
3 Mo	21.55	10.86	–5.52	11	34	12,155
6 Mo	–1.44	4.12	6.82	44	8	9,856
1 Yr	–10.12	1.76	10.04	61	21	8,988
3 Yr Avg	1.60	2.63	–0.56	65	67	10,489
5 Yr Avg	7.93	–2.77	–1.09	30	57	14,644
10 Yr Avg	13.82	0.90	2.72	9	14	36,501
15 Yr Avg	—	—	—	—	—	—

Tax Analysis	Tax-Adj Ret%	%Rank Cat	%Pretax Ret	%Rank Cat
3 Yr Avg	0.46	62	28.7	93
5 Yr Avg	7.19	44	90.7	11
10 Yr Avg	13.17	5	95.3	1

Potential Capital Gain Exposure: 24% of assets

Risk Analysis

Time Period	Load-Adj Return %	Risk %Rank[1] All	Risk %Rank[1] Cat	Morningstar Return	Morningstar Risk	Morningstar Risk-Adj Rating
1 Yr	–10.12					
3 Yr	1.60	83	33	–0.69[2]	1.23	★★★
5 Yr	7.93	85	30	0.67[2]	1.26	★★
10 Yr	13.82	87	17	1.50	1.25	★★★

Average Historical Rating (139 months): 3.2★s

[1] 1=low, 100=high [2] T-Bill return substituted for category avg.

Category Rating (3 Yr)

1 2 3 4 5 — Worst … Best

Return: Average
Risk: Below Avg

Other Measures	Standard Index S&P 500	Best Fit Index SPMid400
Alpha	5.2	–7.4
Beta	1.20	1.09
R-Squared	69	75
Standard Deviation		25.54
Mean		1.60
Sharpe Ratio		–0.15

Analysis by Christopher Traulsen 11-18-01

Baron Asset Fund refuses to follow the herd, and for the most part, that's for the best.

Other managers may trip lemminglike over one another as they attempt to avoid missing out on the latest trend, but Ron Baron sticks resolutely to what he knows. He buys companies with strong long-term growth prospects and talented managers, at discounts to his estimates of their true values. When the market tanked following the September attacks, for example, he waded in and bought names he thought still had strong long-term potential at bargain prices, including HMOs Anthem and Trigon Healthcare.

Baron's criteria largely keep him out of technology stocks—the product cycles are too short and the valuations too rich. Even in 1998 and 1999, when tech stocks soared, Baron stayed the course—it cost the fund dearly, but it has also helped it fare much better than its typical mid-growth peer in 2001's difficult market. The fund is down 18% for the year to date through Nov. 16, but 75% of its peers have lost even more for the period.

Over time, Baron's style has served investors well. The fund's poor 1998 and 1999 showings have left it with a mediocre five-year return, but its 10-year showing ranks in the category's best quartile. Still, the fund's recent returns would have been much better were it not for huge positions in slumping stocks such as Charles Schwab. This is one significant risk of Baron's style: He's so sure he knows his companies better than anyone else that he'll risk a lot of money on relatively few stocks.

The fund's dearth of tech and attention to valuation help offset its issue-specific risk, but investors still need to be prepared for significant bumps along the way. Baron has been right more often than not, however, and has shown a marked ability to unearth strong growth stories at reasonable prices. For investors with the patience to ride out some lean times, we think this fund is a solid choice.

Portfolio Analysis 06-30-01

Share change since 03-01 Total Stocks: 46	Sector	PE	YTD Ret%	% Assets
Sotheby's Hldgs	Services	—	–28.30	8.78
⊖ Robert Half Intl	Services	31.1	0.75	7.05
Charles Schwab	Financials	61.9	–45.30	7.02
Choicepoint	Services	70.4	15.97	5.88
⊖ Polo Ralph Lauren	Durables	14.7	19.93	5.57
⊖ Apollo Grp Cl A	Services	—	—	5.31
DeVRY	Services	33.5	–24.60	4.75
OM Grp	Industrials	20.2	22.24	3.61
⊖ Choice Hotels Intl	Services	27.7	61.82	3.27
⊖ Manor Care	Health	22.6	14.96	3.09
Vail Resorts	Services	34.1	–24.30	3.08
⊖ Libbey	Staples	11.5	8.49	2.96
Dollar Tree Stores	Retail	30.9	26.16	2.90
Principal Cash	N/A	—	—	2.66
Saga Comms	Services	38.3	39.16	2.37
⊖ Citizens Comms	Services	—	–18.70	2.19
⊖ Education Mgmt	Services	39.0	1.40	2.18
⊕ SEACOR SMIT	Services	15.3	–11.80	2.00
☼ Vail Resorts 144A	Services	—	—	1.93
⊖ American Tower Cl A	Services	—	–75.00	1.91
⊖ Ethan Allen Interiors	Durables	22.1	24.76	1.88
⊕ Sun Intl Hotels	Services	14.9	6.74	1.77
Southern Union	Utilities	27.7	–25.20	1.61
⊖ Hispanic Brdcstg Cl A	Services	85.0	0.00	1.17
⊖ NTL	Services	—	–96.00	1.15

Current Investment Style

Style: Value Blnd Growth; Size: Large Med Small

	Stock Port Avg	Relative S&P 500 Current	Relative S&P 500 Hist	Rel Cat
Price/Earnings Ratio	33.1	1.07	1.15	0.96
Price/Book Ratio	4.5	0.80	0.88	0.80
Price/Cash Flow	17.4	0.97	1.07	0.75
3 Yr Earnings Growth	14.9	1.02	1.64	0.64
1 Yr Earnings Est%	–3.7	2.07	—	–0.39
Med Mkt Cap $mil	1,957	0.0	0.0	0.35

Special Securities % assets 06-30-01	
Restricted/Illiquid Secs	2
Emerging-Markets Secs	0
Options/Futures/Warrants	Yes

Composition % assets 06-30-01	
Cash	0.1
Stocks*	99.2
Bonds	0.0
Other	0.7
*Foreign (% stocks)	3.9

Market Cap	
Giant	0.0
Large	8.5
Medium	50.3
Small	41.1
Micro	0.2

Sector Weightings	% of Stocks	Rel S&P	5-Year High	5-Year Low
Utilities	1.8	0.6	5	0
Energy	0.0	0.0	3	0
Financials	9.1	0.5	25	0
Industrials	4.0	0.4	6	0
Durables	9.2	5.9	10	0
Staples	3.3	0.4	28	0
Services	64.9	6.0	65	35
Retail	4.1	0.6	20	3
Health	3.7	0.3	24	2
Technology	0.0	0.0	14	0

Address: 767 Fifth Avenue – 49th Floor, New York, NY 10153, 212–583–2000 / 800–992–2766
Web Address: www.baronfunds.com
Inception: 06-12-87
Advisor: BAMCO
Subadvisor: None
NTF Plans: Fidelity , Datalynx

Minimum Purchase: $2000 Add: None IRA: $2000
Min Auto Inv Plan: $500 Add: $50
Sales Fees: 0.25%B
Management Fee: 1.0%
Actual Fees: Mgt: 1.00% Dist: 0.25%
Expense Projections: 3Yr: $415 5Yr: $718 10Yr: $1579
Avg Brok Commission: — Income Distrib: Annually
Total Cost (relative to category): Below Avg

Baron Growth

Ticker	Load	NAV	Yield	Total Assets	Mstar Category
BGRFX	12b–1 only	$30.67	0.0%	$586.9 mil	Small Growth

Prospectus Objective: Growth

Baron Growth Fund seeks capital appreciation; income is a secondary consideration.

The fund invests in both equity and debt securities; the percentage allocated to each asset class varies depending on the advisor's view of investment opportunities and economic conditions. The equity portion consists mainly of common stocks and stock-related investments issued by companies with market capitalizations between $100 million and $2 billion. The fund may invest up to 25% of assets in debt rated below investment-grade. It may invest up to 10% of assets directly in foreign securities, and may invest without limit in ADRs.

Past name: Baron Growth and Income Fund.

Historical Profile
Return High
Risk Average
Rating ★★★★★ Highest

Investment Style
Equity
Average Stock %: 86% 88% 99% 97% 92% 99% 88%

▼ Manager Change
▽ Partial Manager Change

Fund Performance vs. Category Average
■ Quarterly Fund Return +/– Category Average
— Category Baseline

Performance Quartile (within Category)

Portfolio Manager(s)

Ronald Baron. Since 12-94. BA'65 Bucknell U. Other funds currently managed: Baron Asset, Baron Capital Asset Ins.

1990	1991	1992	1993	1994	1995	1996	1997	1998	1999	2000	12-01	History
—	—	—	—	10.00	15.11	19.04	24.88	24.87	33.68	28.82	30.67	NAV
—	—	—	—	—	52.54	27.73	31.07	0.10	44.71	–4.59	12.67	Total Return %
—	—	—	—	—	15.01	4.78	–2.29	–28.47	23.68	4.52	24.55	+/– S&P 500
—	—	—	—	—	21.50	16.46	18.12	–1.13	1.63	17.85	21.90	+/– Russ 2000 Grth
—	—	—	—	—	0.37	0.60	0.09	0.14	0.00	0.00	0.00	Income Return %
—	—	—	—	—	52.17	27.12	30.98	–0.04	44.71	–4.59	12.67	Capital Return %
—	—	—	—	—	8	19	9	65	58	45	7	Total Rtn % Rank Cat
—	—	—	—	0.00	0.04	0.09	0.02	0.04	0.00	0.00	0.00	Income $
—	—	—	—	0.00	0.11	0.16	0.06	0.00	1.88	3.19	1.64	Capital Gains $
—	—	—	—	—	2.00	1.50	1.40	1.37	1.37	1.36	—	Expense Ratio %
—	—	—	—	—	1.10	1.20	0.40	0.20	–0.20	–0.78	—	Income Ratio %
—	—	—	—	—	—	40	25	40	53	39	—	Turnover Rate %
—	—	—	—	—	41.0	244.0	415.1	343.7	620.0	500.5	586.9	Net Assets $mil

Performance 12-31-01

	1st Qtr	2nd Qtr	3rd Qtr	4th Qtr	Total
1997	–2.47	17.50	14.07	0.26	31.07
1998	9.65	–4.44	–22.06	22.56	0.10
1999	7.56	17.46	–7.51	23.85	44.71
2000	1.37	–6.80	1.38	–0.39	–4.59
2001	–7.77	18.66	–13.82	19.47	12.67

Trailing	Total Return%	+/– S&P 500	+/– Russ 2000 Grth	% Rank All	% Rank Cat	Growth of $10,000
3 Mo	19.47	8.78	–6.71	15	72	11,947
6 Mo	2.95	8.51	12.22	15	7	10,295
1 Yr	12.67	24.55	21.90	4	7	11,267
3 Yr Avg	15.87	16.90	15.62	4	21	15,557
5 Yr Avg	15.34	4.64	12.47	4	18	20,411
10 Yr Avg	—	—	—	—	—	—
15 Yr Avg	—	—	—	—	—	—

Tax Analysis	Tax-Adj Ret%	%Rank Cat	%Pretax Ret	%Rank Cat
3 Yr Avg	14.08	17	88.7	26
5 Yr Avg	14.23	13	92.8	10
10 Yr Avg	—	—	—	—

Potential Capital Gain Exposure: 28% of assets

Risk Analysis

Time Period	Load-Adj Return %	Risk %Rank[1] All	Risk %Rank[1] Cat	Morningstar Return	Morningstar Risk	Morningstar Risk-Adj Rating
1 Yr	12.67					
3 Yr	15.87	66	9	2.57[2]	0.92	★★★★★
5 Yr	15.34	77	9	2.74[2]	1.05	★★★★★
Incept	21.78	—	—	—	—	

Average Historical Rating (49 months): 3.4★s

[1] 1=low, 100=high [2] T-Bill return substituted for category avg.

Category Rating (3 Yr)

1 2 3 4 5 — Worst ... Best (rating: 4)

Return: Above Avg
Risk: Low

Other Measures	Standard Index S&P 500	Best Fit Index Wil 4500
Alpha	18.5	13.0
Beta	1.05	0.68
R–Squared	64	73
Standard Deviation		25.85
Mean		15.87
Sharpe Ratio		0.48

Portfolio Analysis 09-30-01

Share change since 06-01 Total Stocks: 60	Sector	PE	YTD Ret%	% Assets
⊖ Choicepoint	Services	70.4	15.97	5.96
⊕ Southern Union	Utilities	27.7	–25.20	5.54
⊕ Extended Stay Amer	Services	24.5	27.63	4.44
OM Grp	Industrials	20.2	22.24	3.88
⊖ Ethan Allen Interiors	Durables	22.1	24.76	3.59
Blackrock	Financials	—	–0.71	2.95
⊖ Choice Hotels Intl	Services	27.7	61.82	2.67
⊕ Sun Intl Hotels	Services	14.9	6.74	2.66
⊖ Apollo Grp Cl A	Services	—	—	2.47
Krispy Kreme Doughnut	Retail	67.0	113.00	2.47
Kronos	Technology	56.7	134.50	2.32
Gabelli Asset Mgmt Cl A	Financials	21.3	30.17	2.16
Saga Comms	Services	38.3	39.16	2.11
⊖ Univ of Phoenix	Services	—	—	1.83
⊕ Millipore	Industrials	63.9	–2.89	1.76
DeVRY	Services	33.5	–24.60	1.76
SEACOR SMIT	Services	15.3	–11.80	1.75
⊕ Dollar Tree Stores	Retail	30.9	26.16	1.75
Libbey	Staples	11.5	8.49	1.74
☼ Charles River Labs	Health	—	22.30	1.73
⊕ Smart & Final	Retail	22.2	22.82	1.71
Robert Half Intl	Services	31.1	0.75	1.67
⊖ Education Mgmt	Services	39.0	1.40	1.67
⊖ Radio One Cl D	Services	—	—	1.49
⊕ Harte–Hanks Comms	Services	22.9	19.51	1.49

Current Investment Style

Style: Value Blnd Growth; Size: Large Med Small

	Stock Port Avg	Relative S&P 500 Current	Relative S&P 500 Hist	Rel Cat
Price/Earnings Ratio	32.6	1.05	0.99	1.01
Price/Book Ratio	4.8	0.84	0.87	0.99
Price/Cash Flow	19.1	1.06	1.00	0.86
3 Yr Earnings Growth	19.8	1.35	—	0.79
1 Yr Earnings Est%	3.9	—	—	0.51
Med Mkt Cap $mil	1,345	0.0	0.0	1.29

Analysis by Christopher Traulsen 11-29-01

Baron Growth Fund is well worth the considerable patience it can require.

Not long ago, some investors didn't want anything to do with this fund. Its asset base shrunk from $620 million in 1999 to $500 million at the end of 2000. We're pretty sure some folks are regretting that move. The fund owns one of the small-growth category's best returns this year and is in positive territory in this difficult period for growth investing.

The fund hasn't always had it so easy. It looked thoroughly mediocre relative to its peer group in 1998 and 1999, making manager Ron Baron's almost total avoidance of the technology sector seem like a titanic mistake. Baron's shockingly old-fashioned approach is to buy only companies he thinks could double in value in four to five years, meaning that he has to buy them at about half what he thinks they're worth. And unlike other growth managers, Baron isn't interested in speculating that richly valued shares will go higher, which generally keeps him out of tech stocks.

This year, that stance has held the fund in good stead, but Baron's nose for uncovering strong growth stories at reasonable prices has also played a big role. Doughnut-maker Krispy Kreme, for example, is up 85% in 2001. And when some of Baron's favorite hotel stocks—such as Sun International—got hammered in September, he waded in and bought more of them. He was able to do so because he's a long-term investor who knows his companies well enough to see when something is truly wrong, and when they're being oversold on short-term concerns.

This fund's performance will diverge significantly from its peer group's at times, and it will lag in tech-driven rallies. However, Baron has been right often enough to have delivered great long-term returns here, with much less volatility than his typical rival. For investors who share his long-term perspective, this is an appealing choice.

Special Securities % assets 09-30-01	
Restricted/Illiquid Secs	0
Emerging–Markets Secs	0
Options/Futures/Warrants	No

Composition % assets 09-30-01	
Cash	12.8
Stocks*	87.2
Bonds	0.0
Other	0.0
*Foreign (% stocks)	7.5

Market Cap	
Giant	0.0
Large	0.0
Medium	49.0
Small	49.3
Micro	1.7

Sector Weightings	% of Stocks	Rel S&P	5-Year High	5-Year Low
Utilities	6.4	2.0	7	2
Energy	1.4	0.2	3	0
Financials	8.7	0.5	40	8
Industrials	6.5	0.6	7	1
Durables	6.6	4.2	8	0
Staples	2.4	0.3	4	0
Services	48.3	4.5	67	27
Retail	8.5	1.3	10	3
Health	7.3	0.5	17	0
Technology	4.0	0.2	9	1

Address:	767 Fifth Avenue – 49th Floor New York, NY 10153 212–583–2000 / 800–992–2766
Web Address:	www.baronfunds.com
*Inception:	12-31-94
Advisor:	BAMCO
Subadvisor:	None
NTF Plans:	Fidelity , Fidelity Inst.

Minimum Purchase:	$2000	Add: None IRA: $2000
Min Auto Inv Plan:	$500	Add: $50
Sales Fees:	0.25%B	
Management Fee:	1.0%	
Actual Fees:	Mgt: 1.00%	Dist: 0.25%
Expense Projections:	3Yr: $443	5Yr: $766 10Yr: $1680
Avg Brok Commission:	—	Income Distrib: Annually
Total Cost (relative to category):		Below Avg

Baron Small Cap

Ticker	Load	NAV	Yield	Total Assets	Mstar Category
BSCFX	12b–1 only	$15.21	0.0%	$704.1 mil	Small Growth

Prospectus Objective: Small Company

Baron Small Cap Fund seeks capital appreciation.

The fund primarily invests in common stocks of companies with market capitalizations under $1 billion. It may invest up to 35% of assets in securities of larger companies. The advisor looks for companies that it believes have strong balance sheets, undervalued and unrecognized assets, low multiples of free cash flow and income, perceived management skills, unit growth, and the potential to capitalize on anticipated economic trends. The fund may also invest in convertibles, preferred stocks, and warrants. It may invest up to 35% of assets in debt rated below investment-grade, and up to 10% in foreign securities.

Historical Profile

Return High
Risk Above Avg
Rating ★★★★★ Highest

Investment Style
Equity
Average Stock %: 96% 98% 92% 100% 99%

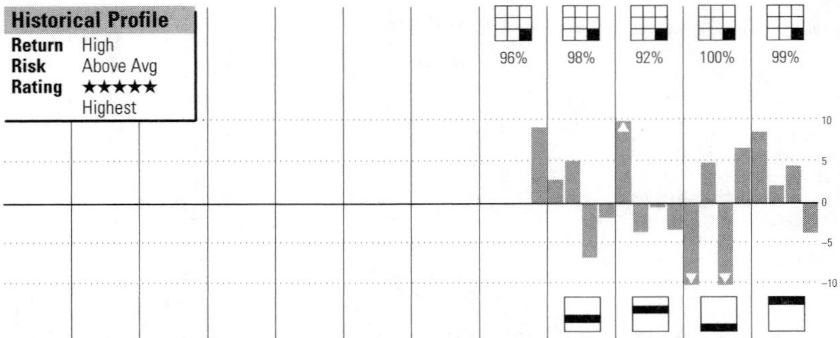

▼ Manager Change
▽ Partial Manager Change

Fund Performance vs. Category Average
■ Quarterly Fund Return +/– Category Average
— Category Baseline

Performance Quartile (within Category)

Portfolio Manager(s)

Clifford Greenberg. Since 9-97.

History

1990	1991	1992	1993	1994	1995	1996	1997	1998	1999	2000	12-01	History
—	—	—	—	—	—	—	10.31	10.54	18.00	14.46	15.21	NAV
—	—	—	—	—	—	—	3.10*	2.23	70.78	–17.53	5.19	Total Return %
—	—	—	—	—	—	—	0.23*	–26.34	49.74	–8.43	17.06	+/– S&P 500
—	—	—	—	—	—	—	—	1.00	27.69	4.90	14.42	+/– Russ 2000 Grth
—	—	—	—	—	—	—	0.00	0.00	0.00	0.00	0.00	Income Return %
—	—	—	—	—	—	—	3.10	2.23	70.78	–17.53	5.19	Capital Return %
—	—	—	—	—	—	—	—	52	31	83	15	Total Rtn % Rank Cat
—	—	—	—	—	—	—	0.00	0.00	0.00	0.00	0.00	Income $
—	—	—	—	—	—	—	0.00	0.00	0.00	0.38	0.00	Capital Gains $
—	—	—	—	—	—	—	—	1.39	1.34	1.33	—	Expense Ratio %
—	—	—	—	—	—	—	—	–0.20	–0.99	–0.90	—	Income Ratio %
—	—	—	—	—	—	—	—	—	43	53	—	Turnover Rate %
—	—	—	—	—	—	—	285.3	470.0	1,089.0	746.2	704.1	Net Assets $mil

Performance 12-31-01

	1st Qtr	2nd Qtr	3rd Qtr	4th Qtr	Total
1997	—	—	—	3.10	3.10 *
1998	14.84	1.10	–28.07	22.42	2.23
1999	12.81	12.36	0.07	34.63	70.78
2000	–0.89	0.28	–10.29	–7.51	–17.53
2001	–8.78	19.41	–19.43	19.86	5.19

Trailing	Total Return%	+/– S&P 500	+/– Russ 2000 Grth	% Rank All	% Rank Cat	Growth of $10,000
3 Mo	19.86	9.17	–6.31	14	68	11,986
6 Mo	–3.43	2.13	5.84	53	33	9,657
1 Yr	5.19	17.06	14.42	22	15	10,519
3 Yr Avg	14.00	15.02	13.75	6	26	14,814
5 Yr Avg	—	—	—	—	—	—
10 Yr Avg	—	—	—	—	—	—
15 Yr Avg	—	—	—	—	—	—

Tax Analysis	Tax-Adj Ret%	%Rank Cat	%Pretax Ret	%Rank Cat
3 Yr Avg	13.80	18	98.6	6
5 Yr Avg	—	—	—	—
10 Yr Avg	—	—	—	—

Potential Capital Gain Exposure: 35% of assets

Risk Analysis

Time Period	Load-Adj Return %	Risk %Rank[1] All	Risk %Rank[1] Cat	Morningstar Return	Morningstar Risk	Morningstar Risk-Adj Rating
1 Yr	5.19					
3 Yr	14.00	77	20	2.09[2]	1.08	★★★★★
5 Yr	—	—	—	—	—	
Incept	11.04	—	—	—	—	

Average Historical Rating (16 months): 3.8★s

[1] 1=low, 100=high [2] T-Bill return substituted for category avg.

Category Rating (3 Yr)

1 2 3 4 5
Worst Best

Return: Above Avg
Risk: Below Avg

Other Measures	Standard Index S&P 500	Best Fit Index Wil 4500
Alpha	17.7	12.0
Beta	1.10	0.77
R-Squared	53	71
Standard Deviation		29.64
Mean		14.00
Sharpe Ratio		0.35

Portfolio Analysis 09-30-01

Share change since 12-00 Total Stocks: 57	Sector	PE	YTD Ret%	% Assets
⊖ Career Educ	Services	47.6	75.23	12.19
⊖ Iron Mountain	Services	—	17.98	5.85
⊕ Choicepoint	Services	70.4	15.97	5.46
☼ United Surgical Partners	Health	—	—	4.14
⊖ Radio One Cl D	Services	—	—	3.93
⊕ Community Health Sys	Health	—	–27.10	3.75
⊖ Apollo Grp Cl A	Services	—	—	3.39
⊕ Province Healthcare	Health	37.6	–21.60	2.96
☼ Ventas	Financials	—	123.10	2.73
☼ California Pizza Kitchen	Retail	—	–12.30	2.72
⊖ Westwood One	Services	77.1	55.59	2.69
☼ Amsurg Cl A	Health	40.0	11.51	2.52
☼ Dollar Tree Stores	Retail	30.9	26.16	2.46
⊕ Viad	Services	36.4	4.48	2.32
☼ LNR Ppty	Financials	8.5	41.97	2.26
☼ AMC Entrtnmt	Services	—	200.00	2.25
Gabelli Asset Mgmt Cl A	Financials	21.3	30.17	2.22
☼ Premier Parks	Services	—	–10.50	2.10
☼ Charles River Labs	Health	—	22.30	2.04
☼ Catalina Mktg	Services	37.7	–10.80	1.98
⊖ Kenneth Cole Productions A	Staples	14.8	–56.00	1.66
☼ FTI Consult	Services	52.9	220.00	1.63
⊖ Casella Waste Sys Cl A	Services	—	70.47	1.63
⊖ SBA Comm	Services	—	–68.20	1.48
☼ Ross Stores	Retail	17.3	91.38	1.47

Current Investment Style

Style: Value Blnd Growth; Size: Large Med Small

	Stock Port Avg	Relative S&P 500 Current	Relative S&P 500 Hist	Rel Cat
Price/Earnings Ratio	39.9	1.29	1.11	1.24
Price/Book Ratio	4.4	0.77	0.68	0.91
Price/Cash Flow	21.7	1.20	1.00	0.98
3 Yr Earnings Growth	—	—	—	—
1 Yr Earnings Est%	9.6[1]	—	—	1.24
Med Mkt Cap $mil	1,451	0.0	0.0	1.39

[1] figure is based on 50% or less of stocks

Analysis by Christopher Traulsen 11-17-01

Baron Small Cap Fund can require patience, but it's worth the wait.

Manager Cliff Greenberg doesn't just buy the most rapidly growing companies at just any price. He wants to buy companies he thinks can double in price in three to four years. To do that, he needs to buy them relatively cheaply. Some of his buys are growth plays whose prospects Greenberg thinks the market has underestimated. Others are fallen angels that he thinks are due for a turnaround. Still others are special situations, companies undergoing management changes, restructuring, or other events that could make for a brighter future.

The resulting portfolio doesn't look much like the typical small-growth fund. That's partly because Greenberg avoids technology companies, most of which he thinks are too difficult to value accurately to deserve a spot in the portfolio. As tech stocks have tanked in 2001, that trait has worked in the fund's favor. Greenberg has also helped the fund's cause with smart picks such as Career Education and Krispy Kreme Doughnuts (he has since trimmed the latter on valuation concerns). As a result, the fund has just a 6.7% loss for the year to date through Nov. 15, 2001—which bests nearly 80% of the fund's peers.

Greenberg has had enough such picks to propel the fund to a top-third three-year return (the fund has only been around since late 1997). His long-term focus has also made the fund very tax-efficient. There are a couple of caveats, though. For one, the fund's bet against tech can work against it—when tech rebounds, this offering won't participate much. Further, Greenberg has a penchant for letting his winners run, so individual positions can grow quite large, exposing the fund to significant risk.

Nevertheless, Greenberg has shown himself to be a talented stock-picker, and has delivered excellent results here over time. We think this fund is an excellent choice.

Special Securities % assets 09-30-01	
Restricted/Illiquid Secs	0
Emerging-Markets Secs	0
Options/Futures/Warrants	No

Composition % assets 09-30-01	
Cash	0.0
Stocks*	98.7
Bonds	0.0
Other	1.3
*Foreign (% stocks)	2.5

Market Cap	
Giant	0.0
Large	0.0
Medium	39.9
Small	55.7
Micro	4.4

Sector Weightings	% of Stocks	Rel S&P	5-Year High	5-Year Low
Utilities	0.0	0.0	—	—
Energy	0.0	0.0	—	—
Financials	8.9	0.5	—	—
Industrials	1.3	0.1	—	—
Durables	2.1	1.3	—	—
Staples	1.3	0.2	—	—
Services	61.0	5.6	—	—
Retail	8.3	1.2	—	—
Health	16.8	1.1	—	—
Technology	0.3	0.0	—	—

Address: 767 Fifth Avenue – 49th Floor, New York, NY 10153, 212-583-2000 / 800-992-2766
Web Address: www.baronfunds.com
*Inception: 09-30-97
Advisor: BAMCO
Subadvisor: None
NTF Plans: Fidelity , Fidelity Inst.

Minimum Purchase: $2000 Add: None IRA: $2000
Min Auto Inv Plan: $500 Add: $50
Sales Fees: 0.25%B
Management Fee: 1.0%
Actual Fees: Mgt: 1.00% Dist: 0.25%
Expense Projections: 3Yr: $425 5Yr: $734 10Yr: $1613
Avg Brok Commission: — Income Distrib: Annually

Total Cost (relative to category): Below Avg

Berger Small Cap Value Instl

Ticker	Load	NAV	Yield	Total Assets	Mstar Category
BSVIX	Closed	$28.15	0.8%	$3,229.1 mil	Small Value

Prospectus Objective: Small Company

Berger Small Cap Value Fund seeks capital appreciation.

The fund normally invests at least 65% of assets in equities of small companies whose market capitalization is less than the 12-month average of the maximum market capitalization for companies included in the Russell 2000 index. It may invest in special situations, such as companies experiencing reorganizations, mergers, new products, or particular tax advantages. It is nondiversified.

Prior to May 18, 1990, the fund was reorganized from a Delaware Corporation into a newly formed Massachusetts business trust. Prior to Oct. 20, 1987, fund shares were not publicly offered. Past fund name: Omni Investment Fund.

Historical Profile
Return High
Risk Below Avg
Rating ★★★★★ Highest

Investment Style
Equity
Average Stock %: 81% 86% 87% 89% 89% 91% 89%

▼ Manager Change
▽ Partial Manager Change

Fund Performance vs. Category Average
■ Quarterly Fund Return +/– Category Average
— Category Baseline

Performance Quartile (within Category)

Portfolio Manager(s)

Robert H. Perkins, CFA. Since 2-85. BA'62 Miami U. Other funds currently managed: Berger Small Cap Value Inv, SunAmSty-Sel Small-Cap Value A, SunAmStySel Small-Cap Value B.

Thomas H. Perkins. Since 1-99. Other funds currently managed: Berger Small Cap Value Inv, Berger Mid Cap Value.

1990	1991	1992	1993	1994	1995	1996	1997	1998	1999	2000	12-01	History
9.23	11.38	13.39	13.99	12.75	14.57	16.48	19.94	19.32	21.67	25.47	28.15	NAV
–21.92	24.86	19.72	16.09	6.70	26.09	25.60	36.93	1.83	14.69	27.16	20.42	Total Return %
–18.81	–5.63	12.10	6.04	5.39	–11.45	2.66	3.58	–26.75	–6.35	36.26	32.30	+/– S&P 500
–0.15	–16.84	–9.42	–7.75	8.25	0.34	4.23	5.24	8.26	16.17	4.35	6.40	+/– Russell 2000 V
2.36	1.52	1.24	0.02	0.00	0.86	0.72	1.59	0.74	1.25	1.78	0.96	Income Return %
–24.28	23.34	18.48	16.07	6.70	25.23	24.88	35.35	1.08	13.44	25.38	19.46	Capital Return %
86	92	58	61	6	36	35	20	13	19	18	31	Total Rtn % Rank Cat
0.29	0.14	0.14	0.00	0.00	0.11	0.11	0.23	0.14	0.24	0.39	0.24	Income $
0.00	0.00	0.09	1.54	2.14	1.39	1.72	2.37	0.81	0.23	1.60	2.25	Capital Gains $
1.84	1.52	1.41	1.31	1.43	1.64	1.48	1.33	1.19	1.01	0.88	—	Expense Ratio %
2.34	1.24	0.73	0.18	–0.04	0.64	0.69	0.63	1.26	1.69	1.99	—	Income Ratio %
146	130	105	108	125	90	69	81	69	66	72	—	Turnover Rate %
9.9	11.9	14.0	16.3	18.3	31.8	36.0	61.2	143.6	524.8	1,003.1	1,517.4	Net Assets $mil

Performance 12-31-01

	1st Qtr	2nd Qtr	3rd Qtr	4th Qtr	Total
1997	3.03	12.13	17.28	1.06	36.93
1998	8.63	–2.45	–16.56	15.17	1.83
1999	–5.33	22.14	–6.00	5.51	14.69
2000	3.78	0.22	10.34	10.80	27.16
2001	1.73	13.89	–16.71	24.78	20.42

Trailing	Total Return%	+/– S&P 500	+/– Russ 2000V	% Rank All	% Rank Cat	Growth of $10,000
3 Mo	24.78	14.09	8.06	8	5	12,478
6 Mo	3.93	9.49	2.78	9	32	10,393
1 Yr	20.42	32.30	6.40	2	31	12,042
3 Yr Avg	20.65	21.67	9.33	2	13	17,562
5 Yr Avg	19.62	8.92	8.42	2	7	24,487
10 Yr Avg	19.12	6.19	4.01	1	1	57,509
15 Yr Avg	15.97	2.24	3.13	4	7	92,320

Tax Analysis	Tax-Adj Ret%	%Rank Cat	%Pretax Ret	%Rank Cat
3 Yr Avg	18.14	13	87.9	63
5 Yr Avg	17.17	7	87.5	43
10 Yr Avg	16.14	1	84.4	34

Potential Capital Gain Exposure: 18% of assets

Risk Analysis

Time Period	Load-Adj Return %	Risk %Rank[1] All	Risk %Rank[1] Cat	Morningstar Return	Morningstar Risk	Morningstar Risk-Adj Rating
1 Yr	20.42					
3 Yr	20.65	44	31	3.85[2]	0.61	★★★★★
5 Yr	19.62	51	22	4.21[2]	0.70	★★★★★
10 Yr	19.12	60	43	3.03	0.78	★★★★★

Average Historical Rating (167 months): 3.5★s

[1] 1=low, 100=high [2] T-Bill return substituted for category avg.

Category Rating (3 Yr)

1 2 3 4 5
Worst Best

Return: Above Avg
Risk: Below Avg

Other Measures	Standard Index S&P 500	Best Fit Index SPMid400
Alpha	20.5	11.1
Beta	0.69	0.76
R-Squared	41	65
Standard Deviation		21.94
Mean		20.65
Sharpe Ratio		0.81

Portfolio Analysis 09-30-01

Share change since 06-01 Total Stocks: 72	Sector	PE	YTD Ret%	% Assets
Ross Stores	Retail	17.3	91.38	2.74
Briggs & Stratton	Industrials	25.3	–0.78	2.56
Trinity Inds	Industrials	—	12.40	2.45
Rayonier	Industrials	22.1	30.83	2.37
⊕ La-Z-Boy	Durables	31.6	41.17	2.33
CNF	Services	—	0.56	2.23
Home Properties of New York	Financials	16.5	22.39	2.22
⊕ Manitowoc	Industrials	16.1	8.39	2.17
Tecumseh Products A	Industrials	18.3	23.91	2.13
⊕ Noble Affiliates	Energy	8.7	–22.90	2.06
⊕ Greater Bay Bancorp	Financials	15.3	–29.00	2.00
⊕ Newfield Explor	Energy	8.2	–25.10	1.99
⊕ Alpharma Cl A	Health	16.9	–39.30	1.91
⊕ Key Energy Svcs	Energy	11.5	–11.80	1.90
⊕ Wolverine World Wide	Staples	14.8	–0.25	1.70
IPC Hldgs	Financials	17.1	40.95	1.64
⊕ Kaydon	Industrials	NMF	–7.01	1.60
☼ Stone Energy	Energy	—	–38.80	1.57
⊕ Dycom Inds	Services	14.8	–53.50	1.56
Brandywine Realty Tr	Financials	29.7	10.52	1.50
⊖ Manor Care	Health	22.6	14.96	1.42
⊕ Advanced Digital Info	Technology	—	–30.20	1.41
Prentiss Properties Tr	Financials	11.2	10.26	1.39
⊖ Longview Fibre	Industrials	24.6	–9.60	1.38
⊖ Fleetwood Enterprises	Durables	—	9.47	1.33

Current Investment Style

Style: Value Blnd Growth; Size: Large Med Small

	Stock Port Avg	Relative S&P 500 Current	Relative S&P 500 Hist	Rel Cat
Price/Earnings Ratio	21.8	0.71	0.56	1.01
Price/Book Ratio	2.0	0.36	0.26	0.84
Price/Cash Flow	10.9	0.61	0.57	0.86
3 Yr Earnings Growth	5.2	0.36	0.79	0.45
1 Yr Earnings Est%	–2.8	1.58	—	0.71
Med Mkt Cap $mil	858	0.0	0.0	0.98

Analysis by Alan Papier 01-02-02

This fund's shareholders should consider themselves fortunate.

Berger Small Cap Value Fund is closed to new investors. And given its successful track record, it's unlikely that assets will dwindle to such an extent that manager Bob Perkins will feel comfortable reopening the fund anytime soon. To be sure, the fund closed at roughly $1 billion in assets in early 2000, and currently contains more than $1.4 billion.

Still, the portfolio's size hasn't hampered Perkins' ability to select small, downtrodden companies that appear poised for a rebound. In fact, the fund gained 20.4% in 2001, and ranked in the top third of the small-cap value category for the fifth consecutive year. Perkins' nose for value led him to make nursing home operator Manor Care and generic drugmaker Perrigo top-25 holdings coming in to the year, and both stocks rebounded smartly in 2001. The fund also benefited from a slew of takeovers, as its focus on companies with little or no debt, lots of free cash flow, and low stock prices relative to underlying asset values means that its holdings are often acquisition targets. For example, Structural Dynamics Research was gobbled up by Electronic Data Systems, and Mitchell Energy was acquired by Devon Energy in 2001.

That said, however, Perkins' willingness to load up in specific sectors when he finds a cache of underpriced stocks can cause the fund to lag its peers if the sectors' weakness persists. For instance, the fund's energy stake—which stood at nearly 10% of assets as of Sept. 30, 2001, and was among the highest in the category throughout 2001—held it back for most of the year.

All in all, we think the fund's spectacular long-term returns, moderate volatility, and proven management make it one of the best small-value offerings.

Special Securities % assets 09-30-01	
Restricted/Illiquid Secs	0
Emerging-Markets Secs	0
Options/Futures/Warrants	No

Composition % assets 09-30-01	
Cash	9.3
Stocks*	90.7
Bonds	0.0
Other	0.0
*Foreign (% stocks)	1.8

Market Cap	
Giant	0.0
Large	0.0
Medium	19.1
Small	79.8
Micro	1.1

Sector Weightings	% of Stocks	Rel S&P	5-Year High	5-Year Low
Utilities	0.0	0.0	6	0
Energy	9.6	1.4	12	1
Financials	20.8	1.2	61	19
Industrials	28.2	2.5	28	2
Durables	7.4	4.8	13	0
Staples	0.0	0.0	5	0
Services	8.5	0.8	35	6
Retail	6.1	0.9	13	0
Health	3.7	0.3	17	0
Technology	15.7	0.9	23	0

Address:	210 University Boulevard Suite 900 Denver, CO 80206 303-329-0200 / 800-333-1001
Web Address:	www.bergerfunds.com
Inception:	02-14-85
Advisor:	Berger Assoc.
Subadvisor:	Perkins Wolf McDonnell
NTF Plans:	N/A

Minimum Purchase:	Closed	Add: None IRA: —
Min Auto Inv Plan:	Closed	Add: $100
Sales Fees:	No-load	
Management Fee:	.85% mx./.75% mn.	
Actual Fees:	Mgt: 0.85%	Dist: —
Expense Projections:	3Yr: $303	5Yr: $526 10Yr: $1166
Avg Brok Commission:	—	Income Distrib: Annually
Total Cost (relative to category):	Low	

Bernstein International Value II

Ticker	Load	NAV	Yield	Total Assets	Mstar Category
SIMTX	None	$14.53	3.1%	$1,541.2 mil	Foreign Stock

Prospectus Objective: Foreign Stock

Bernstein International Value Portfolio II Fund seeks capital growth on a total-return basis.

The fund normally invests at least 65% of assets in foreign equity securities of at least three foreign countries. It may invest in common and preferred stocks, warrants, convertibles, American Depositary Receipts, and Global Depositary Receipts. The fund typically invests in countries that comprise the EAFE index (Europe, Australia and the Far East) and Canada. It may invest in emerging markets. The fund may enter into futures contracts and options.

Historical Profile
Return —
Risk —
Rating
Not Rated

Investment Style
Equity
Average Stock %: 91% (1999), 95% (12-01)

▼ Manager Change
▽ Partial Manager Change

Fund Performance vs. Category Average
■ Quarterly Fund Return +/– Category Average
— Category Baseline

Performance Quartile (within Category)

Portfolio Manager(s)

Management Team

History

	1990	1991	1992	1993	1994	1995	1996	1997	1998	1999	2000	12-01
NAV	—	—	—	—	—	—	—	—	—	21.25	17.20	14.53
Total Return %	—	—	—	—	—	—	—	—	—	10.54*	–3.25	–12.92
+/– S&P 500	—	—	—	—	—	—	—	—	—	1.14*	5.85	–1.05
+/– MSCI EAFE	—	—	—	—	—	—	—	—	—	—	10.92	—
Income Return %	—	—	—	—	—	—	—	—	—	1.04	3.69	2.62
Capital Return %	—	—	—	—	—	—	—	—	—	9.50	–6.94	–15.54
Total Rtn % Rank Cat	—	—	—	—	—	—	—	—	—	—	11	10
Income $	—	—	—	—	—	—	—	—	—	0.19	0.79	0.45
Capital Gains $	—	—	—	—	—	—	—	—	—	0.02	2.56	0.00
Expense Ratio %	—	—	—	—	—	—	—	—	—	1.26	—	—
Income Ratio %	—	—	—	—	—	—	—	—	—	2.23	—	—
Turnover Rate %	—	—	—	—	—	—	—	—	—	—	—	—
Net Assets $mil	—	—	—	—	—	—	—	—	—	2,519.5	1,782.1	1,541.2

Performance 12-31-01

	1st Qtr	2nd Qtr	3rd Qtr	4th Qtr	Total
1997	—	—	—	—	—
1998	—	—	—	—	—
1999	—	—	2.39	6.80	10.54 *
2000	–0.89	2.37	–5.19	0.59	–3.25
2001	–6.05	2.41	–14.44	5.77	–12.92

Trailing	Total Return%	+/– S&P 500	+/– MSCI EAFE	% Rank All	% Rank Cat	Growth of $10,000
3 Mo	5.77	–4.91	—	62	78	10,577
6 Mo	–9.50	–3.95	—	84	60	9,050
1 Yr	–12.92	–1.05	—	68	10	8,708
3 Yr Avg	—	—	—	—	—	—
5 Yr Avg	—	—	—	—	—	—
10 Yr Avg	—	—	—	—	—	—
15 Yr Avg	—	—	—	—	—	—

Tax Analysis	Tax-Adj Ret%	%Rank Cat	%Pretax Ret	%Rank Cat
3 Yr Avg	—	—	—	—
5 Yr Avg	—	—	—	—
10 Yr Avg	—	—	—	—

Potential Capital Gain Exposure: NMF

Risk Analysis

Time Period	Load-Adj Return %	Risk %Rank[1] All	Risk %Rank[1] Cat	Morningstar Return	Morningstar Risk	Morningstar Risk-Adj Rating
1 Yr	–12.92					
3 Yr	—	—	—	—	—	
5 Yr	—	—	—	—	—	
Incept	–2.63	—	—	—	—	

Average Historical Rating —

[1]1=low, 100=high

Category Rating (3 Yr)

Return
Risk

Other Measures	Standard Index S&P 500	Best Fit Index
Alpha	—	—
Beta	—	—
R-Squared	—	—
Standard Deviation		—
Mean		—
Sharpe Ratio		—

Portfolio Analysis 09-30-01

Share change since 03-99 Total Stocks: 143	Sector	Country	% Assets
☆ Eni Eur1	N/A	N/A	3.06
⊖ BASF	Industrials	Germany	2.69
☆ Daiwa House Ind	Industrials	Japan	2.05
⊖ E.On AG ADR	Services	Germany	2.00
☆ Takefuji	Financials	Japan	1.75
☆ Honda Motor	Durables	Japan	1.66
☆ Fuji Heavy Inds	Durables	Japan	1.64
☆ Peugeot Sa Eur1	N/A	N/A	1.58
⊖ Tokyo Style	Durables	Japan	1.50
☆ Royal Bk of Scotland	Financials	United Kingdom	1.47
☆ Bank of Montreal	Financials	Canada	1.43
☆ OJI Paper	Industrials	Japan	1.41
☆ Ufj Hldgs Jpy50000	N/A	N/A	1.39
⊖ Siemens	Industrials	Germany	1.37
☆ British Amer Tobacco	Staples	United Kingdom	1.36
☆ Volkswagen	Durables	Germany	1.32
☆ Talisman Energy	Energy	Canada	1.27
☆ Swiss Reinsurance Chf0.1	N/A	N/A	1.27
⊖ Kyushu Elec Pwr	Utilities	Japan	1.24
⊖ CGNU	Financials	United Kingdom	1.23

Current Investment Style

Style: Value Blnd Growth; Size: Large Med Small

	Stock Port Avg	Rel MSCI EAFE Current	Rel MSCI EAFE Hist	Rel Cat
Price/Earnings Ratio	21.0	0.81	—	0.82
Price/Cash Flow	8.7	0.68	—	0.61
Price/Book Ratio	1.8	0.51	—	0.46
3 Yr Earnings Growth	11.1	0.59	—	0.57
Med Mkt Cap $mil	8,292	0.3	—	0.46

Country Exposure 09-30-01	% assets
Japan	30
United Kingdom	13
Germany	12
France	5
Canada	5

Hedging History: —

Regional Exposure 09-30-01	% assets
Europe	44
Pacific Rim	4
Latin America	0
Japan	30
Other	5

Special Securities % assets 09-30-01	
Restricted/Illiquid Secs	0
Emerging–Markets Secs	1
Options/Futures/Warrants	Yes

Composition % assets 09-30-01			
Cash	1.0	Bonds	0.0
Stocks	95.3	Other	3.8

Sector Weightings	% of Stocks	Rel Cat	5-Year High	5-Year Low
Utilities	4.3	1.5	—	—
Energy	6.4	1.1	—	—
Financials	28.4	1.3	—	—
Industrials	23.5	1.7	—	—
Durables	12.9	1.9	—	—
Staples	3.1	0.4	—	—
Services	11.2	0.6	—	—
Retail	2.5	0.5	—	—
Health	2.5	0.3	—	—
Technology	5.2	0.5	—	—

Analysis by Gabriel Presler 12-10-01

Despite its short record, Bernstein International Value II is part of a winning tradition.

In mid-1999, Bernstein decided to split its value-oriented foreign-stock fund into two offerings, one of which would cater to taxable accounts. That fund became Bernstein Tax-Managed International Value and retained the original fund's strong long-term record. This fund, on the other hand, launched as a separate offering, so its successful pedigree is hard to discern.

Not that investors need convincing of this fund's merits. Since global markets soured a year and a half ago, this offering has led the foreign-stock category, thanks to its deep-value style. While the managers here don't veer too far from the MSCI index's regional weightings, they're willing to drastically underweight any sector they consider overpriced. This flexibility has helped performance in a jittery market. For example, the fund held few of the European telecom and Asian technology companies that plagued its rivals in 2000. Instead, it got a boost from broad exposure to European financials firms and consumer-related stocks.

The fund's tendency to go its own way has worked equally well in 2001. Extensive exposure to automakers, such as Peugeot, has boosted returns. And strong stock-picking in Japan has also helped results; positions in Takefugi and a few other lending firms have been resilient, despite the Japanese market's wretched overall performance. Thus, the fund's loss of 15% for the year to date through Dec. 8, 2001, while poor on an absolute basis, actually outpaces more than 80% of its peers.

Its sibling's record indicates that the fund's value style won't always pay off; Tax-Managed International Value lags in growth rallies. Still, this fund is likely to be a solid bet for conservative shareholders able to afford its hefty minimum investment fee.

Address:	767 Fifth Avenue New York, NY 10153 212–756–4097
Web Address:	www.Bernstein.com
*Inception:	05-03-99
Advisor:	Sanford C. Bernstein & Co.
Subadvisor:	None
NTF Plans:	N/A

Minimum Purchase:	$25000	Add: $5000	IRA: —
Min Auto Inv Plan:	—	Add: —	
Sales Fees:	No-load		
Management Fee:	1.0% mx./.90% mn., .25%A		
Actual Fees:	Mgt: 0.95%	Dist: —	
Expense Projections:	3Yr: $41*	5Yr: —	10Yr: —
Avg Brok Commission:	—	Income Distrib: Annually	
Total Cost (relative to category):	—		

Bernstein Tax–Managed Intl Value

Ticker	Load	NAV	Yield	Total Assets	Mstar Category
SNIVX	None	$15.90	1.8%	$2,586.7 mil	Foreign Stock

Prospectus Objective: Foreign Stock

Bernstein Tax-Managed International Value Portfolio seeks total return.

The fund normally invests at least 65% of assets in at least three foreign countries. It expects, however, to be invested in as many as 20 countries that compose the EAFE index. The fund intends to primarily purchase equities, either ADRs and EDRs or direct foreign obligations. It may invest uncommitted cash balances in fixed-income securities. To select securities, the advisor uses a bottom-up approach, seeking undervalued securities as evidenced by low P/E and price/book ratios. The fund seeks to control currency risk through techniques such as forward currency transactions.

Past name: Bernstein International Value Portfolio.

Historical Profile
Return: Above Avg
Risk: Low
Rating: ★★★★ Above Avg

Investment Style
Equity
Average Stock %: 94% 95% 94% 94% 94% 97%

▼ Manager Change
▽ Partial Manager Change

Fund Performance vs. Category Average
■ Quarterly Fund Return +/– Category Average
— Category Baseline

Performance Quartile (within Category)

Portfolio Manager(s)

Andrew S. Adelson, et al. Since 6-92. BS'77 U. of Pennsylvania; MBA'78 U. of Pennsylvania.

1990	1991	1992	1993	1994	1995	1996	1997	1998	1999	2000	12-01	History
—	—	11.68	15.59	15.43	16.24	17.85	17.72	17.81	21.54	18.50	15.90	NAV
—	—	–5.14*	34.63	3.84	8.03	17.45	9.31	10.95	22.73	–5.05	–12.52	Total Return %
—	—	–15.03*	24.57	2.52	–29.51	–5.49	–24.05	–17.63	1.69	4.05	–0.65	+/– S&P 500
—	—	—	2.07	–3.94	–3.18	11.41	7.53	–9.05	–4.23	9.12	—	+/– MSCI EAFE
—	—	0.42	0.14	0.77	0.67	6.11	6.22	5.25	0.00	0.75	1.54	Income Return %
—	—	–5.56	34.49	3.07	7.36	11.34	3.08	5.70	22.73	–5.80	–14.06	Capital Return %
—	—	—	55	25	68	28	32	66	90	16	8	Total Rtn % Rank Cat
—	—	0.05	0.02	0.11	0.10	0.99	1.11	0.93	0.00	0.16	0.29	Income $
—	—	0.13	0.12	0.63	0.33	0.22	0.71	0.87	0.30	1.79	0.00	Capital Gains $
—	—	2.00	1.53	1.39	1.35	1.31	1.27	1.26	1.24	1.24	—	Expense Ratio %
—	—	0.59	1.27	1.13	1.17	1.37	1.37	0.98	0.80	40.62	—	Income Ratio %
—	—	—	21	24	30	22	26	30	32	—	—	Turnover Rate %
—	—	100.9	705.1	1,429.1	2,169.3	3,495.2	4,697.8	5,457.7	3,886.4	2,867.6	2,586.7	Net Assets $mil

Performance 12-31-01

	1st Qtr	2nd Qtr	3rd Qtr	4th Qtr	Total
1997	3.53	8.39	4.44	–6.73	9.31
1998	18.62	2.00	–17.72	11.45	10.95
1999	3.65	6.77	1.62	9.13	22.73
2000	–1.62	2.03	–5.50	0.11	–5.05
2001	–6.97	3.49	–14.54	6.33	–12.52

Trailing	Total Return%	+/– S&P 500	+/– MSCI EAFE	% Rank All	% Rank Cat	Growth of $10,000
3 Mo	6.33	–4.35	—	59	72	10,633
6 Mo	–9.13	–3.58	—	82	54	9,087
1 Yr	–12.52	–0.65	—	67	8	8,748
3 Yr Avg	0.64	1.67	—	70	27	10,194
5 Yr Avg	4.33	–6.37	—	75	24	12,363
10 Yr Avg	—	—	—	—	—	—
15 Yr Avg	—	—	—	—	—	—

Tax Analysis	Tax-Adj Ret%	%Rank Cat	%Pretax Ret	%Rank Cat
3 Yr Avg	–0.38	25	—	—
5 Yr Avg	2.46	26	56.8	59
10 Yr Avg	—	—	—	—

Potential Capital Gain Exposure: –1% of assets

Risk Analysis

Time Period	Load-Adj Return %	Risk %Rank[1] All	Risk %Rank[1] Cat	Morningstar Return	Morningstar Risk	Morningstar Risk-Adj Rating
1 Yr	–12.52					
3 Yr	0.64	47	2	–0.88[2]	0.61	★★★★
5 Yr	4.33	54	3	–0.15[2]	0.62	★★★★
Incept	7.99	—	—	—	—	

Average Historical Rating (79 months): 3.6★s

[1] 1=low, 100=high [2] T-Bill return substituted for category avg.

Category Rating (3 Yr)

1 2 3 4 5
Worst Best

Return: Above Avg
Risk: Low

Other Measures	Standard Index S&P 500	Best Fit Index MSCIWdxUSN
Alpha	–0.7	3.2
Beta	0.59	0.78
R-Squared	57	84
Standard Deviation		13.40
Mean		0.64
Sharpe Ratio		–0.37

Portfolio Analysis 09-30-01

Share change since 03-99 Total Stocks: 138

Stock	Sector	Country	% Assets
⊖ ENI	Energy	Italy	2.71
⊖ BASF	Industrials	Germany	2.54
☼ Volkswagen	Durables	Germany	2.20
☼ E.On AG	N/A	N/A	2.19
☼ Takefuji	Financials	Japan	1.70
☼ Peugeot Sa–ADR	Technology	France	1.66
☼ British Amer Tobacco	Staples	United Kingdom	1.60
☼ Honda Motor	Durables	Japan	1.55
☼ Banca Intesa	Financials	Italy	1.53
☼ UFJ Hldgs	N/A	N/A	1.42
☼ Bank of Montreal	Financials	Canada	1.42
☼ Canon	Industrials	Japan	1.39
☼ Fuji Heavy Inds	Durables	Japan	1.39
⊕ Daiichi Pharma	Health	Japan	1.39
☼ ANZ Bkg Grp	Financials	Australia	1.38
⊖ Shell Transp & Trad	Energy	United Kingdom	1.36
⊖ Royal & Sun Alliance Ins	Financials	United Kingdom	1.27
☼ Talisman Energy	Energy	Canada	1.26
☼ OJI Paper	Industrials	Japan	1.25
☼ Swiss Reinsurance	Financials	Switzerland	1.24

Current Investment Style

Style: Value Blnd Growth; Size: Large Med Small

	Stock Port Avg	Rel MSCI EAFE Current	Rel MSCI EAFE Hist	Rel Cat
Price/Earnings Ratio	20.6	0.80	0.87	0.81
Price/Cash Flow	8.2	0.64	0.72	0.57
Price/Book Ratio	2.0	0.57	0.39	0.50
3 Yr Earnings Growth	14.4	0.77	0.19	0.73
Med Mkt Cap $mil	9,427	0.3	0.2	0.52

Country Exposure 09-30-01	% assets
Japan	27
United Kingdom	13
Germany	9
France	8
Italy	7

Hedging History: Frequent

Regional Exposure 09-30-01	% assets
Europe	51
Japan	27
Latin America	0
Pacific Rim	5
Other	6

Special Securities % assets 09-30-01	
Restricted/Illiquid Secs	0
Emerging–Markets Secs	Trace
Options/Futures/Warrants	No

Composition % assets 09-30-01

Cash	0.0	Bonds	0.0
Stocks	96.7	Other	3.3

Sector Weightings	% of Stocks	Rel Cat	5-Year High	5-Year Low
Utilities	3.3	1.2	7	3
Energy	9.9	1.7	10	4
Financials	27.6	1.3	32	27
Industrials	24.3	1.8	26	20
Durables	11.3	1.7	18	9
Staples	3.8	0.5	7	2
Services	6.7	0.4	16	7
Retail	3.5	0.7	6	2
Health	2.7	0.3	5	3
Technology	6.8	0.7	7	0

Analysis by Gabriel Presler 12-10-01

Bernstein Tax-Managed International Value's mix of orthodoxy and rebellion results in strong performances.

This fund's two-pronged approach is fairly unusual in the foreign-stock category. It pays close attention to the regional weighting of the MSCI-EAFE index and is thus forced to build extensive positions in markets that its peers avoid, such as Japan. But it goes its own way when it comes to sector exposure. The managers drastically underweight industries they consider overvalued and the fund usually devotes the bulk of its assets to cyclical and industrial companies. The portfolio's valuations are thus lower than category norms.

Since global markets soured a year and a half ago, this strategy has protected the fund. In 2000, for example, it helped performance in a jittery market, as the fund held few of the European telecom and Asian tech companies that plagued its rivals. Instead, it got a boost from broad exposure to European financials firms and relatively resilient Japanese consumer-related stocks. Although it lost more than 5% of its value, it bested 80% of its peers.

In 2001's increasingly volatile market, the fund has continued to hold up relatively well. That's pretty admirable; after all, its 30% stake in Japan, one of the developed world's more miserable markets, has been something of a liability. But strong stock-picking, particularly in Japan's auto industry (such as a substantial stake in Honda) has been helpful. And the fund's flexibility with sector exposure has also been helpful; a heavy stake in consumer-cyclical firms in Europe has proved relatively resilient. Thus the fund's loss of 13% for the year to date through Dec. 10, 2001, while ugly, actually outpaces 90% of its peers.

Of course, the fund's value style doesn't always pay off, especially during growth rallies. But overall, this has been a fairly strong choice for shareholders with the means to pay its high minimum investment fees.

Address:	767 Fifth Avenue New York, NY 10153 212–756–4097
Web Address:	www.Bernstein.com
*Inception:	06-22-92
Advisor:	Sanford C. Bernstein & Co.
Subadvisor:	None
NTF Plans:	N/A

Minimum Purchase:	$25000	Add: $5000	IRA: —
Min Auto Inv Plan:	—	Add: —	
Sales Fees:	No-load		
Management Fee:	1.0% mx./.90% mn., .25%A		
Actual Fees:	Mgt: 0.94%	Dist: —	
Expense Projections:	3Yr: $40*	5Yr: $69*	10Yr: $152*
Avg Brok Commission:	—	Income Distrib: Annually	
Total Cost (relative to category):	—		

Black Oak Emerging Technology

Ticker	Load	NAV	Yield	Total Assets	Mstar Category
BOGSX	None	$3.95	0.0%	$154.3 mil	Spec Technology

Prospectus Objective: Specialty—Technology

Black Oak Emerging Technology Fund seeks long term capital growth.

The fund primarily invests at least 80% of assets in common stocks of technology companies. The type of companies that advisor considers to be emerging technology companies can be expected to change over time as developments in technology occur. The fund may invest in stocks of small to medium capitalization size companies. Additionally, the fund invests in companies with relatively short operating histories. The advisor buys and holds companies for the long-term and seeks to keep portfolio turnover to a minimum. This fund is non-diversified.

Historical Profile

Return —
Risk —
Rating Not Rated

Investment Style
Equity
Average Stock % 91%

▼ Manager Change
▽ Partial Manager Change

Fund Performance vs. Category Average
■ Quarterly Fund Return +/– Category Average
— Category Baseline

Performance Quartile (within Category)

Portfolio Manager(s)

James D. Oelschlager. Since 12-00. BA'64 Denison U.; JD'67 Northwestern U. Other funds currently managed: Pin Oak Aggressive Stock, Target Large Capitalization Growth, White Oak Growth Stock.

Thomas H. Hipp. Since 12-00.

History

1990	1991	1992	1993	1994	1995	1996	1997	1998	1999	2000	12-01	History
—	—	—	—	—	—	—	—	—	—	10.00	3.95	NAV
—	—	—	—	—	—	—	—	—	—	—	–60.50	Total Return %
—	—	—	—	—	—	—	—	—	—	—	–48.62	+/– S&P 500
—	—	—	—	—	—	—	—	—	—	—	–44.91	+/– PSE Tech 100
—	—	—	—	—	—	—	—	—	—	0.00	0.00	Income Return %
—	—	—	—	—	—	—	—	—	—	0.00	–60.50	Capital Return %
—	—	—	—	—	—	—	—	—	—	—	97	Total Rtn % Rank Cat
—	—	—	—	—	—	—	—	—	—	0.00	0.00	Income $
—	—	—	—	—	—	—	—	—	—	0.00	0.00	Capital Gains $
—	—	—	—	—	—	—	—	—	—	—	—	Expense Ratio %
—	—	—	—	—	—	—	—	—	—	—	—	Income Ratio %
—	—	—	—	—	—	—	—	—	—	—	—	Turnover Rate %
—	—	—	—	—	—	—	—	—	—	0.0	154.3	Net Assets $mil

Performance 12-31-01

	1st Qtr	2nd Qtr	3rd Qtr	4th Qtr	Total
1997	—	—	—	—	—
1998	—	—	—	—	—
1999	—	—	—	—	—
2000	—	—	—	—	0.00 *
2001	–48.50	19.42	–59.67	59.27	–60.50

Trailing	Total Return%	+/– S&P 500	+/– PSE Tech 100	% Rank All	% Rank Cat	Growth of $10,000
3 Mo	59.27	48.59	26.36	1	3	15,927
6 Mo	–35.77	–30.22	–30.49	100	99	6,423
1 Yr	–60.50	–48.62	–44.91	100	97	3,950
3 Yr Avg	—	—	—	—	—	—
5 Yr Avg	—	—	—	—	—	—
10 Yr Avg	—	—	—	—	—	—
15 Yr Avg	—	—	—	—	—	—

Tax Analysis	Tax-Adj Ret%	%Rank Cat	%Pretax Ret	%Rank Cat
3 Yr Avg	—	—	—	—
5 Yr Avg	—	—	—	—
10 Yr Avg	—	—	—	—

Potential Capital Gain Exposure: NMF

Risk Analysis

Time Period	Load-Adj Return %	Risk %Rank[1] All	Risk %Rank[1] Cat	Morningstar Return	Morningstar Risk	Morningstar Risk-Adj Rating
1 Yr	–60.50					
3 Yr	—	—	—	—	—	
5 Yr	—	—	—	—	—	
Incept	–60.30	—	—	—	—	

Average Historical Rating —

[1]1=low, 100=high

Category Rating (3 Yr)

Other Measures	Standard Index S&P 500	Best Fit Index
Alpha	—	—
Beta	—	—
R-Squared	—	—
Standard Deviation		—
Mean		—
Sharpe Ratio		—

Return
Risk

Portfolio Analysis 09-30-01

Share chng since 06-01 Total Stocks: 25	Subsector	PE	YTD Ret%	% Assets
Cree	Technology	79.6	–17.00	8.49
Microtune	Technology	—	41.64	8.20
Rudolph Tech	Technology	27.9	13.69	7.13
Marvell Tech	Technology	—	63.28	6.43
Amkor Tech	Technology	—	3.42	6.26
Research in Motion	Technology	—	–70.30	6.06
Openwave Sys	Technology	—	–79.50	5.53
⊕ StorageNetworks	Technology	—	–75.00	4.85
Aether Sys	Technology	—	–76.40	4.52
AXT	Technology	13.4	–56.30	4.08
DMC Stratex Networks	Technology	—	–48.10	3.56
OTG Software	Technology	—	–37.90	3.52
Packeteer	Technology	—	–40.40	3.29
⊕ Micromuse	Technology	51.7	–75.10	2.87
Finisar	Technology	—	–64.90	2.66
CIENA	Telecom	NMF	–82.30	2.25
⊕ Stanford Microdevices	Technology	—	–83.00	2.10
Stratos Lightwave	Technology	—	–63.90	2.08
Akamai Tech	Technology	—	–71.80	1.97
ONI Sys	Technology	—	–84.10	1.82
Cacheflow	Technology	—	–84.20	1.21
New Focus	Technology	—	–89.00	1.18
Redback Net	Technology	—	–90.30	1.07
Transmeta	Technology	—	–90.20	0.71
⊖ Avici Sys	Technology	—	–88.10	0.55

Current Investment Style

Style: Value Blnd Growth; Size: Large Med Small

	Stock Port Avg	Relative S&P 500 Current	Relative S&P 500 Hist	Rel Cat
Price/Earnings Ratio	42.2[1]	1.36	—	0.91
Price/Book Ratio	2.9	0.50	—	0.46
Price/Cash Flow	26.9	1.49	—	1.04
3 Yr Earnings Growth	—	—	—	—
1 Yr Earnings Est%	—	—	—	—
Med Mkt Cap $mil	897	0.0	—	0.06

[1]figure is based on 50% or less of stocks

Analysis by William Harding 09-12-01

This fund's recent trials and tribulations illustrate why it isn't suitable for most investors.

A more fitting moniker for this fund might be Black & Blue Oak. All technology funds have struggled amid the sector's recent crash, but Black Oak Emerging Technology Fund's showing has been terrible. Suffering shareholders have seen about 67% of their investment evaporate so far this year. Nearly all of the fund's holdings have posted steep losses, with a few declining more than 90%.

Put simply, this is one risky fund. Not only does it operate in one of the market's most volatile sectors, but it's highly concentrated in a small number of holdings, and it emphasizes smaller, more-speculative names than most other tech offerings. Investing in these types of stocks can be a big gamble—some may hit it big, but others could well fail. The risks become more pronounced during economic slumps (such as the current one). Indeed, the fund had a stake in now-defunct Winstar Communications (it sold the position before the company filed for bankruptcy).

The fund's approach leads to extreme fluctuations in returns. The fund got a jolt from a rebound in technology shares right out of the gates, gaining a category-leading 30% in January 2001. That rally proved short-lived, however, and its holdings in formerly high-flying networking and wireless infrastructure have been especially hard hit since than.

It's hard to find a silver lining amid the fund's recent troubles, but investors can take some solace in management's experience in picking tech stocks—comanager Jim Oelschlager has built a superior long-term record at tech-heavy White Oak Growth Stock. The fund also boasts relatively low expenses. Still, it's only appropriate for the most aggressive investors, and even they should only put a tiny part of their portfolios here.

Address:	P.O. Box 219441 Kansas City, MO 64121–9441 888–462–5386
Web Address:	www.oakassociates.com
*Inception:	12-29-00
Advisor:	Oak Assoc.
Subadvisor:	None
NTF Plans:	Fidelity Inst., Waterhouse

Minimum Purchase:	$2000	Add: $50	IRA: $2000
Min Auto Inv Plan:	$2000	Add: $25	
Sales Fees:	No-load		
Management Fee:	.74%		
Actual Fees:	Mgt: 0.74%	Dist: —	
Expense Projections:	3Yr: $361	5Yr: —	10Yr: —
Avg Brok Commission:	—	Income Distrib: Annually	
Total Cost (relative to category):	—		

Special Securities % assets 09-30-01

Restricted/Illiquid Secs	0
Emerging-Markets Secs	0
Options/Futures/Warrants	No

Composition % assets 09-30-01

Cash	6.8
Stocks*	93.2
Bonds	0.0
Other	0.0
*Foreign (% stocks)	6.6

Market Cap

Giant	0.0
Large	0.0
Medium	22.2
Small	65.5
Micro	12.3

Subsector Weightings	% of Stocks	Rel Cat
Computers	0.0	0.0
Semiconductors	0.0	0.0
Semi Equipment	0.0	0.0
Networking	0.0	0.0
Periph/Hardware	0.0	0.0
Software	0.0	0.0
Computer Svs	0.0	0.0
Telecom	2.4	0.3
Health Care	0.0	0.0
Other	97.6	2.6

BlackRock Intl Bond Svc

Ticker	Load	NAV	Yield	SEC Yield	Total Assets	Mstar Category
CIFIX	12b–1 only	$10.43	5.2%	5.28%	$127.3 mil	International Bond

Prospectus Objective: World Bond

BlackRock International Bond Portfolio Fund seeks current income consistent with preservation of capital.

The fund normally invests at least 65% of assets in debt issued in at least three foreign countries. These securities may include debt issued by foreign sovereign governments, supranational organizations, foreign banks and bank holding companies, and foreign corporations.

Investor A, B, and C shares are offered by the fund, all of which differ in fee structure; Institutional and Service shares are for institutional investors. On April 1, 1996, PNC International Fixed-Income Portfolio merged into this fund. The fund has gone through several name changes.

Historical Profile

Return High
Risk Below Avg
Rating ★★★★★ Highest

Investment Style
Fixed-Income

Income Rtn %Rank Cat: 83 | 37 | 94 | 62 | 52 | 23 | 2 | 23

Growth of Principal vs. Interest Rate Shifts
— Principal Value $000 (NAV with capital gains reinvested)
— Interest Rate % on 10 Yr Treasury
▼ Manager Change
▽ Partial Manager Change
► Mgr Unknown After
◄ Mgr Unknown Before

9 8 7 6 5 4% | $26 22 18 14 10 6 $2

Performance Quartile (within Category)

Portfolio Manager(s)

Andrew Gordon. Since 1-97. BA'81 U. of Pennsylvania; MBA'86 U. of Pennsylvania. Other funds currently managed: BlackRock Intl Bond Inv B, BlackRock Intl Bond Inv A, BlackRock Intl Bond Instl.

Keith T. Anderson. Since 7-99. BS'81 Nichols C.; MBA'83 Rice U. Other funds currently managed: Smith Barney Adjustable Rate Govt A, BlackRock Low Duration Bd Instl, BlackRock Interm Govt Instl.

1990	1991	1992	1993	1994	1995	1996	1997	1998	1999	2000	12-01	History
—	10.54	10.44	10.90	10.12	11.26	10.58	10.64	11.20	10.43	10.20	10.43	NAV
—	6.11*	6.17	15.31	–3.71	20.02	10.39	9.93	11.14	0.18	11.36	7.68	Total Return %
—	—	–1.24	5.56	–0.79	1.55	6.78	0.24	2.47	1.01	–0.28	–0.74	+/– LB Aggregate
—	—	1.40	0.19	–9.70	0.47	6.31	14.19	–6.65	5.25	13.99	11.23	+/– SB World Govt
—	0.00	5.73	8.91	1.25	8.75	3.94	5.17	5.15	6.20	13.75	5.44	Income Return %
—	6.11	0.44	6.40	–4.96	11.28	6.45	4.76	5.99	–6.03	–2.40	2.25	Capital Return %
—	—	20	44	44	27	33	9	31	28	5	10	Total Rtn % Rank Cat
—	0.00	0.59	0.90	0.14	0.88	0.43	0.53	0.54	0.67	1.38	0.54	Income $
—	0.06	0.14	0.22	0.24	0.00	1.39	0.42	0.06	0.12	0.00	0.00	Capital Gains $
—	—	1.33	1.30	1.38	1.24	1.09	1.29	1.31	1.33	1.22	—	Expense Ratio %
—	—	6.79	6.31	6.00	5.96	3.82	5.02	3.79	3.50	4.36	—	Income Ratio %
—	—	—	115	128	131	—	272	225	317	266	—	Turnover Rate %
—	20.8	37.5	43.7	44.6	42.4	7.9	1.3	2.3	3.7	4.1	12.0	Net Assets $mil

Performance 12-31-01

	1st Qtr	2nd Qtr	3rd Qtr	4th Qtr	Total
1997	0.95	3.33	2.94	2.37	9.93
1998	2.56	1.70	5.05	1.43	11.14
1999	1.41	–0.93	–0.30	0.01	0.18
2000	2.02	2.56	1.98	4.36	11.36
2001	3.45	0.82	2.87	0.36	7.68

Trailing	Total Return%	+/– LB Agg	+/– SB World	% Rank All	% Rank Cat	Growth of $10,000
3 Mo	0.36	0.32	4.33	76	28	10,036
6 Mo	3.24	–1.41	–0.23	14	49	10,324
1 Yr	7.68	–0.74	11.23	11	10	10,768
3 Yr Avg	6.30	0.03	10.06	20	11	12,012
5 Yr Avg	7.97	0.55	7.87	29	6	14,676
10 Yr Avg	8.65	1.42	3.84	40	3	22,923
15 Yr Avg	—	—	—	—	—	—

Tax Analysis	Tax-Adj Ret%	%Rank Cat	%Pretax Ret	%Rank Cat
3 Yr Avg	2.87	20	45.5	46
5 Yr Avg	4.72	3	59.1	17
10 Yr Avg	5.34	1	61.7	11

Potential Capital Gain Exposure: –3% of assets

Risk Analysis

Time Period	Load-Adj Return %	Risk %Rank[1] All	Risk %Rank[1] Cat	Morningstar Return	Morningstar Risk	Morningstar Risk-Adj Rating
1 Yr	7.68					
3 Yr	6.30	7	10	0.29[2]	0.52	★★★★
5 Yr	7.97	6	10	0.68[2]	0.45	★★★★★
10 Yr	8.65	7	8	1.20[2]	0.59	★★★★★

Average Historical Rating (90 months): 4.8★s

[1] 1=low, 100=high [2] T-Bill return substituted for category avg.

Category Rating (3 Yr)

1 2 3 4 5
Worst Best

Return Above Avg
Risk Low

Other Measures	Standard Index LB Agg	Best Fit Index LB Agg
Alpha	0.5	0.5
Beta	0.63	0.63
R-Squared	53	53

Standard Deviation	3.08
Mean	6.30
Sharpe Ratio	0.52

Portfolio Analysis 11-30-01

Total Fixed-Income: 42	Date of Maturity	Value $000	% Net Assets
Eur Borrow Bond 3.15%	12-28-01	19,800	12.99
Republic of Italy 6.75%	02-01-07	10,948	7.18
Republic of Germany 6.5%	10-14-05	9,130	5.99
Dec 30 Yr Bond Long (Fut)		8,909	5.84
Republic of Germany 4.5%	02-18-03	6,680	4.38
Republic Of Austria 3.9%	10-20-05	5,981	3.92
Inter-American Dev Bk 5.75%	04-15-04	5,823	3.82
Kingdom of Spain 8%	05-30-04	5,811	3.81
Hellenic Republic 5.95%	03-24-05	5,692	3.73
Province Of Ontario 6.375%	06-10-04	4,710	3.09
Statens Bostadsfinansier 6.5%	09-18-02	4,053	2.66
AB Spintab 6.25%	09-18-02	4,045	2.65
Republic of Italy 0%	11-01-26	3,628	2.38
Realkredit Danmark 7%	10-01-32	3,608	2.37
Chase CC Master Tr FRN	09-15-04	3,503	2.30
Govt of Canada 6%	09-01-05	3,392	2.23
First Union Commrcl 6.65%	12-18-07	3,273	2.15
Toyota Auto Rcvbls Tr 6.8%	04-15-07	3,169	2.08
Dec 30 Yr Bond Long (Fut)		3,143	2.06
European Invest Bk 5.625%	02-03-05	3,139	2.06

Current Investment Style

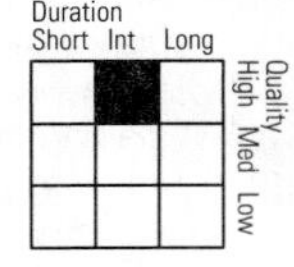

Avg Eff Duration[1]	5.7 Yrs
Avg Eff Maturity	—
Avg Credit Quality	AA
Avg Wtd Coupon	5.44%
Avg Wtd Price	83.53% of par

[1] figure provided by fund

Special Securities 11-30-01	% assets
Restricted/Illiquid Secs	1
Exotic Mortgage-Backed	0
Emerging-Markets Secs	0
Options/Futures/Warrants	Yes

Country Exposure % assets

Not Available

Composition % assets 11-30-01

Cash	2.7	Bonds	88.7
Stocks	0.0	Other	8.7

Analysis by Gabriel Presler 07-25-01

BlackRock International Bond Fund's legacy of small, sound decisions has resulted in an excellent record.

Unlike many of its peers in the international-bond category, this fund doesn't make a lot of drastic shifts in its currency, regional, and sector allocations. Instead, the managers hedge the fund's portfolio into the dollar, and they stick close to the Salomon Brothers World index when it comes to the regional allocation. They also steer clear of high-yield debt and prefer investment-grade bonds when dabbling in emerging markets.

Playing it safe has certainly worked well in 2001. The fund's overweight position in high-quality shorter-term corporate bonds in the U.S. and in Europe boosted performance as short-term rates fell. Exposure to high-quality emerging-markets debt from Greece and Mexico has also been a boon throughout the year. These positions have helped to balance the fund's decision to underweight Japan, the world's best-performing bond market this year. Thus, the offering has been able to post a gain of almost 5% for the year to date through July 23, 2001, outpacing 95% of its peers.

While this moderate approach has worked in the past, the fund isn't for everyone. First of all, its exposure to the dollar and its hefty U.S. stake mean that it doesn't offer as much diversification away from the domestic market as some of its more daring rivals. Moreover, its approach could hold it back in the case of a faltering dollar or high-yield rally.

For more-cautious investors, though, this fund is hard to beat. The fund has generally managed to steer clear of the volatility that can plague its rivals; in 1998, for example, its avoidance of lower-quality emerging-markets and corporate bonds helped it avoid the group's meltdown. Its excellent long-term record and proven managers make this a good choice.

Address:	Four Falls Corporate Center 6th Floor West Conshohocken, PA 19428–2961 800–441–7762
Web Address:	www.blackrock.com
*Inception:	07-01-91
Advisor:	BlackRock
Subadvisor:	BlackRock Financial Mgmt.
NTF Plans:	N/A

Minimum Purchase:	$5000	Add: None IRA: —
Min Auto Inv Plan:	$5000	Add: $50
Sales Fees:	0.15%B, 0.15%S	
Management Fee:	.55% mx./.45% mn., .23%A	
Actual Fees:	Mgt: 0.23%	Dist: 0.30%
Expense Projections:	3Yr: $449	5Yr: $785 10Yr: $1735
Avg Brok Commission:	—	Income Distrib: Monthly
Total Cost (relative to category):	—	

Bogle Small Cap Growth Inv

Ticker	Load	NAV	Yield	Total Assets	Mstar Category
BOGLX	None	$20.10	0.0%	$112.1 mil	Small Growth

Prospectus Objective: Growth

Bogle Small Cap Growth Fund seeks capital appreciation.

The fund normally seeks its objective by taking long positions in the stocks of U.S. companies with market capitalization under 2 billion that the advisor has identified as likely to appreciate more than the index as defined below. The fund attempts to achieve a total return greater than the total return of the Russell 2000 index.

The fund offers Investor and Institutional classes. The Institutional class is available only to institutional investors.

Historical Profile
Return —
Risk —
Rating Not Rated

Investment Style
Equity
Average Stock %: 87% (1999), 97% (2000), 99% (12-01)

▼ Manager Change
▽ Partial Manager Change

Fund Performance vs. Category Average
■ Quarterly Fund Return +/– Category Average
— Category Baseline

Performance Quartile (within Category)

Portfolio Manager(s)

John C. Bogle Jr., CFA. Since 9-99. BS'82 Vanderbilt U.; MBA'83 Vanderbilt U. Other fund currently managed: Bogle Small Cap Growth Instl.

1990	1991	1992	1993	1994	1995	1996	1997	1998	1999	2000	12-01	History
—	—	—	—	—	—	—	—	—	15.61	19.13	20.10	NAV
—	—	—	—	—	—	—	—	—	30.08*	26.83	5.07	Total Return %
—	—	—	—	—	—	—	—	—	15.21*	35.93	16.95	+/– S&P 500
—	—	—	—	—	—	—	—	—	—	49.26	14.30	+/– Russ 2000 Grth
—	—	—	—	—	—	—	—	—	0.00	0.00	0.00	Income Return %
—	—	—	—	—	—	—	—	—	30.08	26.83	5.07	Capital Return %
—	—	—	—	—	—	—	—	—	—	4	16	Total Rtn % Rank Cat
—	—	—	—	—	—	—	—	—	0.00	0.00	0.00	Income $
—	—	—	—	—	—	—	—	—	0.00	0.66	0.00	Capital Gains $
—	—	—	—	—	—	—	—	—	—	1.35	—	Expense Ratio %
—	—	—	—	—	—	—	—	—	—	–0.68	—	Income Ratio %
—	—	—	—	—	—	—	—	—	—	94	—	Turnover Rate %
—	—	—	—	—	—	—	—	—	6.5	27.1	68.6	Net Assets $mil

Performance 12-31-01

	1st Qtr	2nd Qtr	3rd Qtr	4th Qtr	Total
1997	—	—	—	—	—
1998	—	—	—	—	—
1999	—	—	—	30.08	30.08 *
2000	16.08	5.46	7.38	–3.52	26.83
2001	–8.73	16.38	–13.44	14.27	5.07

Trailing	Total Return%	+/– S&P 500	+/– Russ 2000 Grth	% Rank All	% Rank Cat	Growth of $10,000
3 Mo	14.27	3.58	–11.90	26	95	11,427
6 Mo	–1.08	4.47	8.18	43	19	9,892
1 Yr	5.07	16.95	14.30	22	16	10,507
3 Yr Avg	—	—	—	—	—	—
5 Yr Avg	—	—	—	—	—	—
10 Yr Avg	—	—	—	—	—	—
15 Yr Avg	—	—	—	—	—	—

Tax Analysis	Tax-Adj Ret%	%Rank Cat	%Pretax Ret	%Rank Cat
3 Yr Avg	—	—	—	—
5 Yr Avg	—	—	—	—
10 Yr Avg	—	—	—	—

Potential Capital Gain Exposure: 5% of assets

Risk Analysis

Time Period	Load-Adj Return %	Risk %Rank[1] All	Risk %Rank[1] Cat	Morningstar Return	Morningstar Risk	Morningstar Risk-Adj Rating
1 Yr	5.07					
3 Yr	—	—	—	—	—	
5 Yr	—	—	—	—	—	
Incept	27.63	—	—	—	—	

Average Historical Rating —

[1]1=low, 100=high

Category Rating (3 Yr)

Return
Risk

Other Measures	Standard Index S&P 500	Best Fit Index
Alpha	—	—
Beta	—	—
R-Squared	—	—
Standard Deviation		—
Mean		—
Sharpe Ratio		—

Portfolio Analysis 11-30-01

Share change since 10-01 Total Stocks: 195	Sector	PE	YTD Ret%	% Assets
Standard Commrcl	Staples	7.1	145.30	0.86
⊕ Independence Cmnty Bk	Financials	16.7	45.40	0.82
Circuit City–CARMAX Grp	Retail	54.1	477.40	0.80
⊕ UCBH Hldgs	Financials	22.9	22.68	0.78
Emcor Grp	Industrials	13.8	78.04	0.76
⊕ Wintrust Finl	Financials	16.7	92.94	0.75
Administaff	Services	46.5	0.77	0.74
McAfee.com	Services	—	578.20	0.74
⊕ BOK Finl	Financials	16.2	52.73	0.74
⊕ Doral Finl	Financials	12.1	30.92	0.73
Alliance Gaming	Services	34.6	566.80	0.72
ITT Inds	Durables	16.2	32.06	0.72
⊕ Farmer Mac Cl C	Financials	38.2	73.26	0.72
⊕ Aztar	Services	14.3	41.44	0.71
Varian Medical Sys	Technology	34.3	4.89	0.71
Network Assoc	Technology	—	517.20	0.71
⊕ BankUnited Finl A	Financials	17.1	74.71	0.71
Commerce Grp (Inc)	Financials	10.6	43.58	0.70
Itron	Industrials	56.1	735.80	0.70
Storage Tech	Technology	36.9	129.60	0.69
Tech Data	Technology	19.2	60.11	0.67
☼ Foot Locker	N/A	—	—	0.67
Action Performance	Durables	—	1,188.00	0.66
Western Gas Resources	Energy	12.1	–3.42	0.66
Office Depot	Retail	NMF	160.20	0.66

Current Investment Style

Style: Value Blnd Growth; Size: Large Med Small

	Stock Port Avg	Relative S&P 500 Current	Relative S&P 500 Hist	Rel Cat
Price/Earnings Ratio	27.4	0.88	—	0.85
Price/Book Ratio	4.0	0.69	—	0.81
Price/Cash Flow	15.2	0.84	—	0.69
3 Yr Earnings Growth	11.4[1]	0.78	—	0.45
1 Yr Earnings Est%	32.1	—	—	4.14
Med Mkt Cap $mil	699	0.0	—	0.67

[1]figure is based on 50% or less of stocks

Analysis by Kelli Stebel 07-18-01

Investors would be remiss to pass this fund by before it closes.

Bogle Small Cap Growth is the real thing. In its short life, this fund has put up spectacular numbers. Since its inception in October 1999 through June 2001, the fund has gained more than 75%, three times the return of its average small-growth rival. And the fund didn't achieve that record by betting the farm on one particular sector. Indeed, while many of its more-aggressive peers, who were loaded up with tech stocks, fell on their faces during 2000's harsh market, this fund gained 26%.

The fund's outstanding success owes to the strength of manager John Bogle's quantitative modeling system. Bogle keeps a keen eye on balance sheet items, like inventory trends, and looks for stocks with lots of free cash flow. That approach has helped the fund sidestep a lot of the market's potholes during the last 18 months. As many speculative and financially unstable companies blew up, hurting many of the fund's more-aggressive peers, this offering has been insulated.

Bogle isn't sitting on his laurels and admiring the fund's record, though. These days, for example, Bogle is concerned about the quality of earnings estimates trends. Given all the economic turmoil, Bogle said he was even starting to look at companies with falling earnings and would rely more on his quality screens, which focus on a firm's fundamentals. One of his new holdings, for example, is Business Object, which preannounced an upcoming earnings disappointment. Despite that, Bogle thinks the company's strong free cash flow and decent profit margins make its shares a steal at their current prices.

Investors should note that Bogle plans to close this fund when assets reach $150 million to maintain its small-cap focus. Assets are about $80 million, so prospective shareholders shouldn't dally. This offering would be excellent for a portfolio's small-cap slot.

Special Securities % assets 11-30-01	
Restricted/Illiquid Secs	0
Emerging-Markets Secs	1
Options/Futures/Warrants	No

Composition % assets 11-30-01	
Cash	0.0
Stocks*	100.0
Bonds	0.0
Other	0.0
*Foreign (% stocks)	1.0

Market Cap	
Giant	0.0
Large	0.9
Medium	27.3
Small	62.1
Micro	9.7

Sector Weightings	% of Stocks	Rel S&P	5-Year High	5-Year Low
Utilities	0.9	0.3	—	—
Energy	3.4	0.5	—	—
Financials	15.8	0.9	—	—
Industrials	15.4	1.3	—	—
Durables	4.1	2.6	—	—
Staples	3.4	0.4	—	—
Services	12.9	1.2	—	—
Retail	8.7	1.3	—	—
Health	16.2	1.1	—	—
Technology	19.1	1.0	—	—

Address: c/o PFPC PO Box 8713, Wilmington, DE 19899, 877-264-5346
Web Address: —
*Inception: 09-30-99
Advisor: Bogle Inv. Mgmt.
Subadvisor: None
NTF Plans: N/A

Minimum Purchase: $10000 Add: $250 IRA: $2000
Min Auto Inv Plan: — Add: —
Sales Fees: No-load
Management Fee: 1.0%
Actual Fees: Mgt: 1.00% Dist: —c
Expense Projections: 3Yr: $428 5Yr: — 10Yr: —
Avg Brok Commission: — Income Distrib: Annually
Total Cost (relative to category): —

Brandywine

Ticker	Load	NAV	Yield	Total Assets	Mstar Category
BRWIX	None	$23.35	0.0%	$4,223.9 mil	Mid-Cap Growth

Prospectus Objective: Growth

Brandywine Fund seeks long-term capital appreciation; current income is secondary.

The fund invests principally in common stocks of well-financed companies that have proven records of profitability and strong earnings momentum. These stocks are likely to be issues of smaller, lesser-known companies moving from a lower to a higher market share within their industry group. The fund may also invest, however, in stocks of larger, better-researched companies. It may invest up to 15% of assets in foreign securities, including American depositary receipts.

Historical Profile
Return Above Avg
Risk Above Avg
Rating ★★★ Neutral

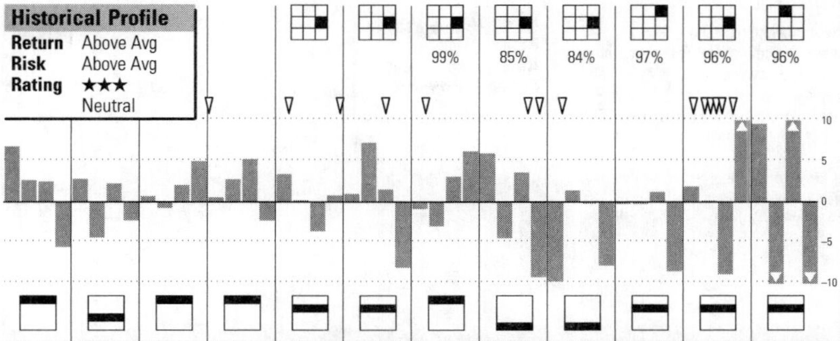

Investment Style
Equity
Average Stock %: 99% 85% 84% 97% 96% 96%

▼ Manager Change
▽ Partial Manager Change

Fund Performance vs. Category Average
Quarterly Fund Return +/– Category Average
— Category Baseline

Performance Quartile (within Category)

Portfolio Manager(s)

Foster S. Friess, CFA. Since 12-85.
William F. D'Alonzo. Since 12-85.
Carl S. Gates. Since 1-88.
John Ragard, CFA. Since 1-93.
William Dugdale. Since 8-95.
Jonathan Fenn. Since 3-94.

1990	1991	1992	1993	1994	1995	1996	1997	1998	1999	2000	12-01	History
15.17	20.17	22.74	24.97	23.50	28.08	33.69	30.89	30.28	42.88	29.39	23.35	NAV
0.56	49.18	15.68	22.58	0.02	35.75	24.92	12.02	–0.65	53.50	7.10	–20.55	Total Return %
3.68	18.69	8.06	12.52	–1.30	–1.79	1.98	–21.33	–29.23	32.46	16.20	–8.68	+/– S&P 500
5.69	2.15	6.97	11.39	2.18	1.77	7.44	–10.52	–18.52	2.20	18.85	–0.40	+/– Russ Midcap Grth
1.79	0.86	0.05	0.00	0.00	0.00	0.00	0.00	0.86	0.00	0.00	0.00	Income Return %
–1.23	48.32	15.63	22.58	0.02	35.75	24.92	12.02	–1.51	53.50	7.10	–20.55	Capital Return %
19	60	15	18	42	43	13	76	90	50	27	47	Total Rtn % Rank Cat
0.28	0.13	0.01	0.00	0.00	0.00	0.00	0.00	0.26	0.00	0.00	0.00	Income $
1.00	2.12	0.54	2.87	1.45	3.84	1.35	7.02	0.07	3.12	16.11	0.00	Capital Gains $
1.12	1.09	1.10	1.10	1.10	1.07	1.06	1.04	1.04	1.05	1.04	1.06	Expense Ratio %
0.93	1.50	0.20	–0.10	0.10	–0.40	–0.40	–0.30	0.60	–0.70	–0.60	–0.30	Income Ratio %
158	188	189	150	190	194	203	192	264	209	244	284	Turnover Rate %
312.1	623.6	839.7	1,527.5	2,299.3	4,210.5	6,546.9	8,414.5	4,890.0	5,515.0	5,770.7	4,223.9	Net Assets $mil

Performance 12-31-01

	1st Qtr	2nd Qtr	3rd Qtr	4th Qtr	Total
1997	–2.08	11.88	18.97	–14.05	12.02
1998	2.85	0.85	–18.88	18.08	–0.65
1999	2.61	11.39	1.39	32.46	53.50
2000	18.14	–5.21	–3.77	–0.62	7.10
2001	–12.39	1.98	–12.68	1.83	–20.55

Trailing	Total Return%	+/– S&P 500	+/– Russ Midcap Grth	% Rank All	% Rank Cat	Growth of $10,000
3 Mo	1.83	–8.85	–25.23	72	100	10,183
6 Mo	–11.08	–5.53	–2.82	88	54	8,892
1 Yr	–20.55	–8.68	–0.40	81	47	7,945
3 Yr Avg	9.31	10.34	7.15	12	28	13,061
5 Yr Avg	7.77	–2.93	–1.25	30	58	14,536
10 Yr Avg	13.33	0.41	2.23	11	19	34,960
15 Yr Avg	15.26	1.53	2.45	6	7	84,213

Tax Analysis	Tax-Adj Ret%	%Rank Cat	%Pretax Ret	%Rank Cat
3 Yr Avg	4.92	37	52.9	75
5 Yr Avg	3.98	67	51.3	86
10 Yr Avg	10.02	28	75.2	46

Potential Capital Gain Exposure: 3% of assets

Risk Analysis

Time Period	Load-Adj Return %	Risk %Rank[1] All	Risk %Rank[1] Cat	Morningstar Return	Morningstar Risk	Morningstar Risk-Adj Rating
1 Yr	–20.55					
3 Yr	9.31	68	12	0.96[2]	0.93	★★★★
5 Yr	7.77	79	15	0.63[2]	1.10	★★★
10 Yr	13.33	86	16	1.39	1.23	★★★

Average Historical Rating (157 months): 3.8★s

[1] 1=low, 100=high [2] T-Bill return substituted for category avg.

Category Rating (3 Yr)

1 2 3 4 5
Worst Best

Return: Above Avg
Risk: Below Avg

Other Measures	Standard Index S&P 500	Best Fit Index Wil 4500
Alpha	10.5	6.3
Beta	0.84	0.56
R-Squared	45	55
Standard Deviation		23.38
Mean		9.31
Sharpe Ratio		0.21

Portfolio Analysis 06-30-01

Share change since 04-01 Total Stocks: 173	Sector	PE	YTD Ret%	% Assets
⊕ Tyco Intl	Industrials	27.1	6.23	4.89
⊕ UnitedHealth Grp	Financials	26.6	15.37	4.37
⊖ Tenet Healthcare	Health	30.1	32.14	3.92
⊕ SPX	Durables	30.0	26.54	3.18
Microsoft	Technology	57.6	52.78	3.07
⊖ Boeing	Industrials	10.2	–40.40	3.02
✲ Raytheon	Industrials	—	7.27	2.89
⊖ Kroger	Retail	16.3	–22.80	2.88
Cendant	Services	20.4	103.70	2.84
⊕ ACE	Financials	17.4	–5.39	2.67
✲ Progressive	Financials	33.4	44.40	2.38
⊖ Duke Energy	Utilities	15.5	–6.04	2.37
✲ Washington Mutual	Financials	10.1	–5.32	2.22
⊕ Ivax	Health	17.5	–34.20	2.07
St. Jude Medical	Health	42.0	26.39	2.02
⊖ Nabors Inds	Energy	15.8	–41.90	1.79
⊕ Universal Health Svcs B	Health	12.7	–23.40	1.76
Fannie Mae	Financials	16.2	–6.95	1.73
Caremark Rx	Health	46.6	20.25	1.39
Diamond Offshore Drilling	Energy	25.8	–22.80	1.30
✲ Talbots	Retail	18.2	–19.80	1.29
✲ Cooper Cameron	Industrials	38.8	–38.90	1.06
✲ BMC Software	Technology	—	16.93	0.98
✲ Americredit	Financials	10.6	15.78	0.97
✲ Ocean Energy	Energy	10.6	11.58	0.96

Current Investment Style

Style: Value Blnd Growth; Size: Large Med Small

	Stock Port Avg	Relative S&P 500 Current	Relative S&P 500 Hist	Rel Cat
Price/Earnings Ratio	25.0	0.81	1.11	0.72
Price/Book Ratio	3.7	0.65	0.91	0.65
Price/Cash Flow	16.3	0.91	1.08	0.70
3 Yr Earnings Growth	14.3	0.98	1.03	0.61
1 Yr Earnings Est%	22.8	—	—	2.44
Med Mkt Cap $mil	5,793	0.1	0.1	1.03

Analysis by Bridget Hughes 11-13-01

Seemingly in perpetual motion, Brandywine Fund makes a fine, albeit aggressive, core growth holding.

This is one busy fund. With a turnover ratio regularly north of 200% per year, today's portfolio can quickly fade from memory. In 2001, the fund has been in and out of a slew of energy names. More recently, it added to its small stake in defense-related stocks, such as Alliant Technologies and Flir Systems. After the September tragedy, it also bought (and then sold) several insurance brokers, including Brown & Brown and Hilb Rogal and Hamilton.

The energy, defense, and insurance areas may seem like unusual places for growth funds to invest, but Brandywine pays little attention to stereotypes. It seeks firms with rapidly increasing earnings whose stocks are trading at reasonable valuations. Consider supermarket operator Kroger, which has actually been part of the portfolio for more than one year. Comanager Bill D'Alonzo sees its operating margins expanding as the grocer sells more of its own brands. The managers believe its earnings can increase 18% to 20% this year and next, giving it a forward P/E ratio in the mid- to upper teens.

The fund's approach has generally worked well. For most of 2001, its dearth of tech stocks has helped, as have its investments in health-care names. Top-five holding Tenet Healthcare, for example, is up more than 25%. D'Alonzo says that the fund also made a profit in the insurance brokers it traded and that it benefited from its energy picks. Although the fund has dropped almost 24% through Nov. 12, that loss ranks in the mid-growth category's top half.

The fund's short-term record hasn't always been as solid—a 1997 and 1998 asset-allocation debacle hurt in those years, and it has missed out on tech's rally in the past month—but long-term results are superb.

Special Securities % assets 06-30-01	
Restricted/Illiquid Secs	0
Emerging-Markets Secs	1
Options/Futures/Warrants	No

Composition % assets 06-30-01	
Cash	2.4
Stocks*	97.6
Bonds	0.0
Other	0.0
*Foreign (% stocks)	6.7

Market Cap	
Giant	13.7
Large	26.9
Medium	45.2
Small	13.7
Micro	0.6

Sector Weightings	% of Stocks	Rel S&P	5-Year High	5-Year Low
Utilities	3.6	1.1	18	0
Energy	9.8	1.4	19	0
Financials	14.5	0.8	20	1
Industrials	16.4	1.4	22	3
Durables	4.0	2.5	15	0
Staples	1.1	0.1	6	0
Services	8.6	0.8	22	3
Retail	8.5	1.3	36	4
Health	26.8	1.8	29	3
Technology	6.8	0.4	68	4

Address:	P.O. Box 4166 Greenville, DE 19807 800-656-3017
Web Address:	www.brandywinefunds.com
Inception:	12-12-85
Advisor:	Friess Assoc.
Subadvisor:	None
NTF Plans:	N/A

Minimum Purchase:	$25000	Add: $1000 IRA: $25000
Min Auto Inv Plan:	—	Add: —
Sales Fees:	No-load	
Management Fee:	1.0%	
Actual Fees:	Mgt: 1.00%	Dist: —
Expense Projections:	3Yr: $33*	5Yr: $57* 10Yr: $130*
Avg Brok Commission:	—	Income Distrib: Annually
Total Cost (relative to category):	—	

Brazos Micro Cap Y

Ticker	Load	NAV	Yield	Total Assets	Mstar Category
BJMIX	Closed	$19.62	0.0%	$357.8 mil	Small Growth

Prospectus Objective: Small Company

Brazos Micro Cap Fund seeks capital appreciation.

The fund normally invests in common stocks and securities convertible into common stocks that have potential for capital appreciation. It invests in companies with market capitalization of $600 million or lower, or companies represented in the lower 50% of the Russell 2000 Index. The fund may invest in securities of foreign issuers.

Class A and II shares have front loads; Class B has deferred loads and conversion features. Previous Names: Brazos/JMIC Micro Cap Growth and Brazos Micro Cap Growth.

Historical Profile
Return High
Risk Above Avg
Rating ★★★★★ Highest

Investment Style
Equity
Average Stock %

	1997	1998	1999	2000	12-01
Average Stock %		75%	86%	92%	87%

▼ Manager Change
▽ Partial Manager Change

Fund Performance vs. Category Average
Quarterly Fund Return +/– Category Average
— Category Baseline

Performance Quartile (within Category)

Portfolio Manager(s)

Management Team

1990	1991	1992	1993	1994	1995	1996	1997	1998	1999	2000	12-01	History
—	—	—	—	—	—	—	10.00	13.28	20.86	18.74	19.62	NAV
—	—	—	—	—	—	—	—	32.80	80.84	18.90	4.70	Total Return %
—	—	—	—	—	—	—	—	4.23	59.80	28.00	16.57	+/– S&P 500
—	—	—	—	—	—	—	—	31.57	37.76	41.33	13.93	+/– Russ 2000 Grth
—	—	—	—	—	—	—	—	0.00	0.00	0.00	0.00	Income Return %
—	—	—	—	—	—	—	—	32.80	80.84	18.90	4.70	Capital Return %
—	—	—	—	—	—	—	—	3	25	8	17	Total Rtn % Rank Cat
—	—	—	—	—	—	—	0.00	0.00	0.00	0.00	0.00	Income $
—	—	—	—	—	—	—	0.00	0.00	2.71	6.27	0.00	Capital Gains $
—	—	—	—	—	—	—	—	1.60	1.54	1.46	—	Expense Ratio %
—	—	—	—	—	—	—	—	–0.46	–0.95	–0.77	—	Income Ratio %
—	—	—	—	—	—	—	—	—	150	159	—	Turnover Rate %
—	—	—	—	—	—	—	—	58.2	146.7	185.5	302.6	Net Assets $mil

Performance 12-31-01

	1st Qtr	2nd Qtr	3rd Qtr	4th Qtr	Total
1997	—	—	—	—	—
1998	27.70	3.05	–16.26	20.51	32.80
1999	4.82	27.51	–0.94	36.58	80.84
2000	12.99	3.73	12.31	–9.68	18.90
2001	–8.48	20.93	–23.43	23.55	4.70

Trailing	Total Return%	+/– S&P 500	+/– Russ 2000 Grth	% Rank All	% Rank Cat	Growth of $10,000
3 Mo	23.55	12.87	–2.62	9	50	12,355
6 Mo	–5.40	0.15	3.87	64	45	9,460
1 Yr	4.70	16.57	13.93	25	17	10,470
3 Yr Avg	31.06	32.08	30.81	1	5	22,511
5 Yr Avg	—	—	—	—	—	—
10 Yr Avg	—	—	—	—	—	—
15 Yr Avg	—	—	—	—	—	—

Tax Analysis	Tax-Adj Ret%	%Rank Cat	%Pretax Ret	%Rank Cat
3 Yr Avg	25.08	5	80.7	47
5 Yr Avg	—	—	—	—
10 Yr Avg	—	—	—	—

Potential Capital Gain Exposure: 14% of assets

Risk Analysis

Time Period	Load-Adj Return %	Risk %Rank[1] All	Risk %Rank[1] Cat	Morningstar Return	Morningstar Risk	Morningstar Risk-Adj Rating
1 Yr	4.70					
3 Yr	31.06	77	20	7.03[2]	1.08	★★★★★
5 Yr	—	—	—	—	—	
Incept	31.47	—	—	—	—	

Average Historical Rating (13 months): 5.0★s

[1]1=low, 100=high [2] T-Bill return substituted for category avg.

Category Rating (3 Yr)

1 2 3 4 5 — Worst … Best (5)

Return High
Risk Below Avg

Other Measures	Standard Index S&P 500	Best Fit Index Wil 4500
Alpha	37.6	30.8
Beta	1.12	1.03
R-Squared	36	81

Standard Deviation	43.09
Mean	31.06
Sharpe Ratio	0.68

Analysis by Bridget Hughes 11-14-01

Spreading its bets has helped the closed Brazos Micro Cap Portfolio become one of the premier micro-cap growth choices.

Unlike some of its even more-aggressive peers, this fund doesn't easily get swept off its feet by just one area. First, it has rules. The fund's position sizes are limited to no more than 4% of assets, and it caps its allocation to any one sector at about 30%. Second, each of its eight portfolio managers covers a different industry. To build the fund, they force themselves to share the portfolio. These guidelines have typically led to a diversified portfolio with a tech stake more modest than its peers'.

To be sure, that smaller tech stake has helped this year, but good stock-picking has keyed the fund's relatively solid return. Take top holding Mobil Mini. That storage-container and leasing company has jumped 38% through Nov. 13, 2001. Comanager Brian Gerber (who covers part of the technology sector) says that company, though small with a market cap of $450 million, is the market leader in its industry. It also has a fairly healthy balance sheet and good growth rates, two characteristics that Gerber and his colleagues prize. Other winners include Maximus (up 23%) and Alloy Online (up 76%). The fund has still gotten hurt by the tech downdraft, but its 8.2% loss for the year to date through Nov. 13 puts it near the small-growth category's top quartile.

The fund's top-notch returns are certainly appealing, and its strong stock-picking has helped smooth volatility over the years, but the fund still isn't for conservative investors. Micro-cap stocks by nature tend to be riskier investments. Also, with just 65 to 100 names, this fund is vulnerable to blow-ups in just a few stocks.

Portfolio Analysis 11-30-01

Share change since 10-01 Total Stocks: 51	Sector	PE	YTD Ret%	% Assets
⊖ Websense	Technology	—	121.10	3.59
⊖ Mobile Mini	Industrials	30.8	70.09	3.51
Education Mgmt	Services	39.0	1.40	3.44
General Comm A	Services	NMF	21.86	3.25
Triad Guaranty	Financials	12.8	9.49	3.17
TALX	Technology	89.2	3.53	2.94
Alloy Online	Services	—	180.00	2.82
Ryland Grp	Industrials	8.8	80.25	2.65
Caminus	Technology	—	–1.08	2.40
Endocare	Health	—	40.63	2.34
Finl Federal	Financials	17.2	30.89	2.32
Beazer Homes USA	Industrials	9.0	82.93	2.29
Witness Sys	Technology	—	–1.33	2.28
AstroPower	Technology	NMF	28.86	2.23
Allegiance Telecom	Services	—	–62.70	2.20
SkillSoft	Technology	—	38.24	2.18
SeaChange Intl	Technology	—	67.97	2.12
First Horizon	Health	—	43.37	2.07
⊖ Electronics Boutique Hldgs	Retail	71.3	128.20	2.07
United Surgical Partners	Health	—	—	2.00
P F Chang's China Bistro	Services	41.9	50.45	1.86
Accredo Health	Health	53.7	18.65	1.82
FirstService	Services	22.9	—	1.81
Speechworks Intl	Technology	—	–77.00	1.77
Harvard Bioscience	Technology	—	0.66	1.71

Current Investment Style

Style: Value Blnd Growth; Size: Large Med Small

	Stock Port Avg	Relative S&P 500 Current	Relative S&P 500 Hist	Rel Cat
Price/Earnings Ratio	33.8	1.09	0.98	1.05
Price/Book Ratio	5.4	0.95	0.72	1.12
Price/Cash Flow	24.6	1.37	1.11	1.12
3 Yr Earnings Growth	—	—	—	—
1 Yr Earnings Est%	24.2[1]	—	—	3.11
Med Mkt Cap $mil	517	0.0	0.0	0.50

[1]figure is based on 50% or less of stocks

Special Securities % assets 11-30-01	
Restricted/Illiquid Secs	0
Emerging-Markets Secs	0
Options/Futures/Warrants	No

Composition % assets 11-30-01	
Cash	8.8
Stocks*	91.2
Bonds	0.0
Other	0.0
*Foreign (% stocks)	5.7

Market Cap	
Giant	0.0
Large	0.0
Medium	1.1
Small	90.7
Micro	8.2

Sector Weightings	% of Stocks	Rel S&P	5-Year High	5-Year Low
Utilities	0.0	0.0	—	—
Energy	2.6	0.4	—	—
Financials	7.9	0.4	—	—
Industrials	14.0	1.2	—	—
Durables	1.3	0.8	—	—
Staples	0.0	0.0	—	—
Services	24.0	2.2	—	—
Retail	4.0	0.6	—	—
Health	18.9	1.3	—	—
Technology	27.3	1.5	—	—

Address:	733 3rd Avenue 3rd Floor New York, NY 10017 800–426–9157
Web Address:	www.brazosfund.com
*Inception:	12-31-97
Advisor:	John McStay Inv. Counsel
Subadvisor:	None
NTF Plans:	N/A

Minimum Purchase:	Closed	Add: $1000 IRA: —
Min Auto Inv Plan:	Closed	Add: $50
Sales Fees:	No-load	
Management Fee:	1.2%, .15%A	
Actual Fees:	Mgt: 1.20%	Dist: —
Expense Projections:	3Yr: $461	5Yr: $797 10Yr: $1746
Avg Brok Commission:	—	Income Distrib: Annually
Total Cost (relative to category):		Below Avg

Buffalo Small Cap

Ticker	Load	NAV	Yield	Total Assets	Mstar Category
BUFSX	None	$19.96	0.0%	$536.5 mil	Small Growth

Prospectus Objective: Growth

Buffalo Small Cap Fund seeks long-term growth of capital.

The fund normally invests at least 65% of its assets in equity securities issued by small capitalization companies. It targets a mix of value and growth companies with average market caps of $1 billion or less. The fund may not purchase any securities that would cause 25% or more of the assets of the fund at the time of purchase to be invested in any one industry.

Historical Profile
Return High
Risk Below Avg
Rating ★★★★★ Highest

Investment Style
Equity
Average Stock %: 68% 93% 92% 93%

▼ Manager Change
▽ Partial Manager Change

Fund Performance vs. Category Average
Quarterly Fund Return
+/– Category Average
— Category Baseline

Performance Quartile (within Category)

Portfolio Manager(s)

Tom Laming. Since 4-98. BS U. of Kansas; MBA Indiana U. Other funds currently managed: Buffalo Equity, Buffalo USA Global, AFBA Five Star Equity.

Kent Gasaway, CFA. Since 4-98. BS'82 Kansas State U. Other funds currently managed: Buffalo Balanced, Buffalo Equity, Buffalo USA Global.

Bob Male, CFA. Since 4-98. BS U. of Kansas; MBA Southern Methodist U. Other funds currently managed: AFBA Five Star Equity, AFBA Five Star Balanced, AFBA Five Star USA Global.

History

1990	1991	1992	1993	1994	1995	1996	1997	1998	1999	2000	12-01	History
—	—	—	—	—	—	—	—	9.63	12.76	15.24	19.96	NAV
—	—	—	—	—	—	—	—	–3.28*	34.79	33.69	31.18	Total Return %
—	—	—	—	—	—	—	—	–15.34*	13.76	42.80	43.05	+/– S&P 500
—	—	—	—	—	—	—	—	—	–8.29	56.13	40.41	+/– Russ 2000 Grth
—	—	—	—	—	—	—	—	0.42	0.00	0.00	0.00	Income Return %
—	—	—	—	—	—	—	—	–3.70	34.79	33.69	31.18	Capital Return %
—	—	—	—	—	—	—	—	—	67	2	1	Total Rtn % Rank Cat
—	—	—	—	—	—	—	—	0.04	0.00	0.00	0.00	Income $
—	—	—	—	—	—	—	—	0.00	0.21	1.67	0.03	Capital Gains $
—	—	—	—	—	—	—	—	—	—	1.12	1.04	Expense Ratio %
—	—	—	—	—	—	—	—	—	—	–0.27	–0.12	Income Ratio %
—	—	—	—	—	—	—	—	—	—	42	31	Turnover Rate %
—	—	—	—	—	—	—	—	—	23.5	49.2	536.5	Net Assets $mil

Performance 12-31-01

	1st Qtr	2nd Qtr	3rd Qtr	4th Qtr	Total
1997	—	—	—	—	—
1998	—	—	–11.70	15.41	–3.28*
1999	–1.45	15.70	–0.64	18.98	34.79
2000	20.53	1.89	10.08	–1.11	33.69
2001	–1.77	23.45	–16.18	29.06	31.18

Trailing	Total Return%	+/– S&P 500	+/– Russ 2000 Grth	% Rank All	% Rank Cat	Growth of $10,000
3 Mo	29.06	18.38	2.89	5	18	12,906
6 Mo	8.18	13.73	17.44	1	1	10,818
1 Yr	31.18	43.05	40.41	1	1	13,118
3 Yr Avg	33.21	34.24	32.97	1	4	23,639
5 Yr Avg	—	—	—	—	—	—
10 Yr Avg	—	—	—	—	—	—
15 Yr Avg	—	—	—	—	—	—

Tax Analysis	Tax-Adj Ret%	%Rank Cat	%Pretax Ret	%Rank Cat
3 Yr Avg	31.82	2	95.8	13
5 Yr Avg	—	—	—	—
10 Yr Avg	—	—	—	—

Potential Capital Gain Exposure: 16% of assets

Risk Analysis

Time Period	Load-Adj Return %	Risk %Rank[1] All	Risk %Rank[1] Cat	Morningstar Return	Morningstar Risk	Morningstar Risk-Adj Rating
1 Yr	31.18					
3 Yr	33.21	52	4	7.76[2]	0.73	★★★★★
5 Yr	—	—	—	—	—	
Incept	24.91	—	—	—	—	

Average Historical Rating (9 months): 5.0★s

[1]1=low, 100=high [2] T-Bill return substituted for category avg.

Category Rating (3 Yr)

1 2 3 4 5
Worst Best

Return High
Risk Low

Other Measures	Standard Index S&P 500	Best Fit Index Russ 2000
Alpha	34.6	25.7
Beta	0.69	0.96
R-Squared	23	86
Standard Deviation		32.35
Mean		33.21
Sharpe Ratio		0.97

Portfolio Analysis 09-30-01

Share change since 03-01 Total Stocks: 63

	Sector	PE	YTD Ret%	% Assets
⊕ Argosy Gaming	Services	16.5	69.48	4.48
⊕ Elcor	Industrials	55.6	66.46	3.17
⊕ Galen Hldgs ADR	Health	82.0	—	3.01
⊕ Strayer Educ	Services	31.6	91.97	2.90
⊕ ITT Educational Svcs	Services	28.6	67.59	2.85
⊕ Ethan Allen Interiors	Durables	22.1	24.76	2.75
☆ Performance Food Grp	Staples	33.5	37.25	2.58
☆ First Horizon	Health	—	43.37	2.33
☆ Medicis Pharma Cl A	Health	38.0	9.24	2.17
⊕ Zale	Retail	12.5	44.10	2.10
⊕ Education Mgmt	Services	39.0	1.40	2.05
☆ Borders Grp	Retail	53.6	69.75	2.02
⊕ Brunswick	Industrials	15.2	35.60	1.96
⊕ Frontier Oil	Energy	3.8	144.40	1.95
☆ Monaco Coach	Durables	24.6	85.46	1.90
⊕ FirstService	Services	22.9	—	1.88
☆ Four Seasons Hotels	Services	27.7	–26.40	1.85
☆ Ultimate Electrncs	Retail	23.3	36.75	1.82
☆ Boston Private Finl Hldgs	Financials	25.7	11.85	1.82
☆ Legg Mason	Financials	23.6	–7.53	1.80
☆ Raymond James Finl	Financials	18.0	3.36	1.80
☆ Wind River Sys	Technology	—	–47.50	1.79
⊕ Gentex	Durables	30.7	43.52	1.75
⊕ MKS Instrs	Industrials	NMF	74.39	1.68
⊕ Advent Software	Technology	61.7	24.68	1.68

Current Investment Style

Style: Value Blnd Growth; Size: Large Med Small

	Stock Port Avg	Relative S&P 500 Current	Relative S&P 500 Hist	Rel Cat
Price/Earnings Ratio	30.7	0.99	—	0.96
Price/Book Ratio	4.6	0.81	—	0.94
Price/Cash Flow	18.7	1.04	—	0.85
3 Yr Earnings Growth	14.8	1.01	—	0.59
1 Yr Earnings Est%	4.1	—	—	0.52
Med Mkt Cap $mil	1,389	0.0	—	1.33

[1]figure is based on 50% or less of stocks

Analysis by Brian Portnoy 11-09-01

Buffalo Small Cap is simply blowing away the competition.

In an anemic market, this offering could hardly look healthier. Out of 235 small-growth competitors, its 14.2% gain for the year to date through Nov. 8, 2001, ranks as the category's second best. By comparison, its average rival has lost 18.3%.

Such staggering outperformance owes to management's theme-based stock-picking approach, which zeroes in on industries with strong long-term growth stories. Those include education, casino gaming, specialty-pharmaceutical, and retail firms. (Many of their themes stem from the macro-trend toward an older, richer population.) Strayer Education and Ethan Allen Interiors are among the fund's long-term winners. Conversely, energy isn't a theme, so the fund avoided the recent sell-off of energy-service stocks that hurt so many rivals.

The fund's moderation has also been a source of strength since its 1998 inception. For management to consider it, a stock must be relatively affordable according to standard criteria such as P/E and P/B and have a clean balance sheet (most of the firms in the portfolio have little or no debt). Thus, the fund avoided the pricey, leveraged tech and telecom fare that has been shellacked since the market's sell-off began in early 2000. While it didn't keep up with its racier peers during 1999's growth heyday, the fund's 27.2%, annualized gain over the past three years puts it in the top 2% of all domestic-equity funds.

It's likely that the gap between this fund and its rivals will eventually narrow, and the portfolio certainly isn't positioned to outperform if tech roars back. But overall, it's hard to find a single red flag here. With an asset base of $350 million that has grown seven-fold since January, investors have finally begun to notice that this is one of the best small-cap choices available.

Special Securities % assets 09-30-01

Restricted/Illiquid Secs	0
Emerging-Markets Secs	0
Options/Futures/Warrants	No

Composition % assets 09-30-01

Cash	9.4
Stocks*	90.6
Bonds	0.0
Other	0.0
*Foreign (% stocks)	9.3

Market Cap

Giant	0.0
Large	1.5
Medium	39.6
Small	55.8
Micro	3.1

Sector Weightings	% of Stocks	Rel S&P	5-Year High	5-Year Low
Utilities	0.0	0.0	—	—
Energy	2.2	0.3	—	—
Financials	14.3	0.8	—	—
Industrials	7.9	0.7	—	—
Durables	8.1	5.2	—	—
Staples	2.9	0.4	—	—
Services	28.8	2.7	—	—
Retail	8.0	1.2	—	—
Health	13.1	0.9	—	—
Technology	14.7	0.8	—	—

Address:	PO Box 219757 Kansas City, MO 64121–9757 800–492–8332
Web Address:	www.buffalofunds.com
*Inception:	04-14-98
Advisor:	Jones & Babson
Subadvisor:	Kornitzer Cap. Mgmt.
NTF Plans:	Fidelity Inst. , Waterhouse

Minimum Purchase:	$2500	Add: $100	IRA: $250
Min Auto Inv Plan:	$2500	Add: $100	
Sales Fees:	No-load		
Management Fee:	1.0%		
Actual Fees:	Mgt: 1.00%	Dist: —	
Expense Projections:	3Yr: $325	5Yr: $563	10Yr: $1248
Avg Brok Commission:	—	Income Distrib: Semi-Ann.	
Total Cost (relative to category):		Low	

Calamos Convertible A

Ticker	Load	NAV	Yield	Total Assets	Mstar Category
CCVIX	4.75%	$18.56	3.3%	$523.5 mil	Convertible

Prospectus Objective: Convertible Bond

Calamos Convertible Fund seeks current income. Capital appreciation is secondary.

The fund normally invests at least 65% of assets in a diversified portfolio of convertible securities that are generally rated BBB or higher. It may, however, invest in convertibles rated BB or lower. The fund may also write covered call options, and invest up to 15% of assets in warrants.

Class A shares have front loads; C shares are no-load and have higher 12b-1 fees. Prior to Sept. 1, 1987, the fund was named Noddings-Calamos Convertible Income Fund. From that date until May 1, 1992, it was named Calamos Convertible Income Fund.

Historical Profile

Return: Above Avg
Risk: Below Avg
Rating: ★★★★ Above Avg

Investment Style Equity — Average Stock %

▼ Manager Change
▽ Partial Manager Change

Fund Performance vs. Category Average
■ Quarterly Fund Return +/– Category Average
— Category Baseline

Performance Quartile (within Category)

History

1990	1991	1992	1993	1994	1995	1996	1997	1998	1999	2000	12-01	History
				83	85	68	68	72	62	61	51	Average Stock %
9.91	12.93	13.40	13.80	11.82	13.85	14.41	15.87	16.87	21.80	20.38	18.56	NAV
–3.56	36.75	7.62	17.55	–7.04	29.25	16.70	20.42	11.64	35.11	7.11	–4.14	Total Return %
–0.44	6.27	—	7.50	–8.35	–8.28	–6.24	–12.93	–16.94	14.07	16.21	7.73	+/– S&P 500
3.31	7.62	–9.97	–1.01	–2.32	6.06	4.80	3.77	–0.02	1.60	13.27	1.73	+/– Conv.Bond Idx
5.19	4.24	2.78	3.98	2.52	3.16	3.53	3.21	2.71	2.96	2.58	3.13	Income Return %
–8.75	32.51	4.84	13.57	–9.56	26.09	13.17	17.21	8.93	32.15	4.54	–7.28	Capital Return %
31	31	88	31	79	3	48	31	20	38	20	33	Total Rtn % Rank Cat
0.56	0.41	0.36	0.52	0.34	0.37	0.47	0.45	0.43	0.50	0.53	0.63	Income $
0.12	0.14	0.14	1.35	0.68	1.00	1.18	1.05	0.38	0.37	2.42	0.33	Capital Gains $
1.10	1.20	1.20	1.70	1.60	1.60	1.50	1.50	1.40	1.40	1.40	1.20	Expense Ratio %
5.50	4.30	3.40	3.20	2.80	3.30	3.00	2.80	3.30	2.60	2.30	2.50	Income Ratio %
93	63	84	73	73	42	65	52	76	78	91	93	Turnover Rate %
12.7	16.4	17.2	17.5	16.0	21.2	31.6	51.8	68.3	85.9	129.2	249.9	Net Assets $mil

Portfolio Manager(s)

John P. Calamos. Since 6-85. BS'63 Illinois Institute of Technology; MBA'65 Illinois Institute of Technology. Other funds currently managed: Calamos Growth A, Calamos Market Neutral A, Calamos Convertible Growth & Inc A.

Nick P. Calamos, CFA. Since 9-88. BA'83 Southern Illinois U.; MS'89 Northern Illinois U. Other funds currently managed: Calamos Convertible Growth & Inc A, Calamos Convertible C, Calamos Convertible Growth & Inc C.

Performance 12-31-01

	1st Qtr	2nd Qtr	3rd Qtr	4th Qtr	Total
1997	2.08	10.47	6.45	0.32	20.42
1998	10.84	1.21	–10.54	11.24	11.64
1999	2.43	5.78	–0.72	25.61	35.11
2000	4.71	–2.39	7.52	–2.53	7.11
2001	–5.53	2.44	–7.37	6.93	–4.14

Trailing	Total Return%	+/– S&P 500	+/– Conv Bond Index	% Rank All	% Rank Cat	Growth of $10,000
3 Mo	6.93	–3.75	–1.22	56	72	10,693
6 Mo	–0.95	4.60	1.71	42	8	9,905
1 Yr	–4.14	7.73	1.73	49	33	9,586
3 Yr Avg	11.53	12.55	5.88	9	10	13,873
5 Yr Avg	13.28	2.58	4.31	7	7	18,650
10 Yr Avg	12.71	–0.22	1.81	14	17	33,083
15 Yr Avg	11.51	–2.22	1.21	29	1	51,276

Tax Analysis	Tax-Adj Ret%	%Rank Cat	%Pretax Ret	%Rank Cat
3 Yr Avg	8.88	10	77.0	23
5 Yr Avg	10.69	9	80.5	12
10 Yr Avg	9.76	17	76.8	17

Potential Capital Gain Exposure: 2% of assets

Risk Analysis

Time Period	Load-Adj Return %	Risk %Rank[1] All	Risk %Rank[1] Cat	Morningstar Return	Morningstar Risk	Morningstar Risk-Adj Rating
1 Yr	–8.70					
3 Yr	9.73	40	12	1.06[2]	0.53	★★★★
5 Yr	12.18	44	15	1.79[2]	0.55	★★★★
10 Yr	12.16	52	31	1.14	0.64	★★★★

Average Historical Rating (163 months): 2.7★s

[1] 1=low, 100=high [2] T-Bill return substituted for category avg.

Category Rating (3 Yr)

1 2 3 4 5
Worst Best

Return: Above Avg
Risk: Below Avg

Other Measures	Standard Index S&P 500	Best Fit Index Wil 4500
Alpha	9.9	7.3
Beta	0.54	0.45
R-Squared	40	78

Standard Deviation	15.98
Mean	11.53
Sharpe Ratio	0.47

Analysis by William Harding 09-12-01

Simply put, this is one of the best offerings in the convertible category.

Looking for an attractive risk/reward profile? Calamos Convertible Fund has delivered long-term returns that are better than the S&P 500's, with less volatility than the index. The fund's record compared with its peers is equally impressive: Its annual returns have landed in the category's top half in each of the past six years, and it's on track to accomplish that task again this year.

The fund's success owes to its talented, experienced management. Calamos' founder, John Calamos, has been investing in convertibles for more than 20 years, and his nephew Nick adds another 15 years of experience. The pair aim to invest in convertibles with moderate conversion premiums, meaning that they offer most of the upside potential of stocks but limit downside risk. That line of attack has kept the fund clear of many of the more equity-sensitive convertibles—those that have high correlation to stock-price movements—that have gotten crushed amid the stock market's retreat over the past year.

The Calamoses also deserve kudos for savvy issue selection. Management uses detailed quantitative models to identify attractively valued issues and then follows that with fundamental research. The fund reaped big gains from tech issues in 1999 and early 2000, but the team's models began souring on that sector in the second quarter of 2000. Consequently, the pair pared tech in favor of more-defensive sectors of the market, helping the fund sidestep much of tech's collapse over the past year.

Investors will be hard-pressed to find a convertible fund that's more attractive than this one. We think investors looking for strong return potential with below-average downside risk will find a nice home here.

Address:	1111 E. Warrenville Road Naperville, IL 60563–1448 800–823–7386 / 630–245–7200
Web Address:	www.calamos.com
Inception:	06-21-85
Advisor:	Calamos Asset Mgmt.
Subadvisor:	None
NTF Plans:	Fidelity Inst.

Minimum Purchase:	$500	Add: $50	IRA: $500
Min Auto Inv Plan:	—	Add: —	
Sales Fees:	4.75%L, 0.25%S, 1.00%R within 6 months		
Management Fee:	.75% mx./.50% mn.		
Actual Fees:	Mgt: 0.75%	Dist: 0.25%	
Expense Projections:	3Yr: $823	5Yr: $1078	10Yr: $1806
Avg Brok Commission:	—	Income Distrib: Quarterly	
Total Cost (relative to category):	Average		

Portfolio Analysis 09-30-01

Total Fixed-Income: 108	Date of Maturity	Amount $000	Value $000	% Net Assets
Boeing		266	8,911	2.24
Starwood Hotels 144A Cv N/A	05-25-21	11,000	8,635	2.17
Wash Mutual 144A 5.375%	05-01-41	133	7,437	1.87
Lucent Tech 144A N/A	08-01-31	7	7,272	1.82
Diamond Offshore 144A Cv 1.5%	04-15-31	8,400	7,098	1.78
Electra Data Sys Cv 3.81%	08-17-04	139	7,069	1.77
Morgan Stan Dean Witter Cv 0.5%	03-30-08	8,220	6,930	1.74
Goldman Sachs Grp Cv FRN	12-12-07	7,100	6,415	1.61
Metlife Cap Tr Cv 4%	04-07-03	64	5,963	1.50
Masco Cv N/A	07-20-31	15,000	5,944	1.49
Givaudan Cv 1%	06-07-06	5,500	5,933	1.49
Lennar Cv N/A	04-04-21	16,000	5,740	1.44
Cendant 144A Cv N/A	02-13-21	9,350	5,587	1.40
Kellogg		186	5,580	1.40
Amazon.com Cv 4.75%	02-01-09	13,830	5,532	1.39
Loews Cv N/A	02-16-21	8,000	5,480	1.37
Sealed Air A Cv Pfd $2.00		137	5,419	1.36
Suiza Cap Tr Cv Pfd 5.5%		115	5,290	1.33
Jones Apparel Grp 144A Cv N/A	02-01-21	10,650	5,205	1.31
First Data Cv 2%	03-01-08	5,000	5,125	1.29
News Amer Hldgs 144A Cv N/A	02-28-21	11,000	5,033	1.26
Newell Finl Cv Pfd 5.25%		138	5,027	1.26
US Treasury Strip 0%	11-15-18	13,000	4,943	1.24
Reebok Intl 144A Cv 4.25%	03-01-21	5,300	4,883	1.23
Arrow Electronics Cv N/A	02-21-21	12,200	4,880	1.22

Investment Style

Avg Eff Maturity	4.8 Yrs
Avg Credit Quality	BBB
Avg Wtd Coupon	3.56%
Avg Wtd Price	75.96% of par
Avg Conversion Premium	18%

Coupon Range	% of Bonds	Rel Cat
0%	13.1	1.30
0% to 7%	79.0	.97
7% to 8.5%	7.9	1.01
8.5% to 10%	0.0	0.00
More than 10%	0.0	0.00

1.00 = Category Average

Special Securities % of assets 09-30-01	
Restricted/Illiquid Secs	29
Emerging-Markets Secs	0
Options/Futures/Warrants	Yes

Composition % assets 09-30-01	
Cash	0.9
Stocks	12.1
Bonds	14.2
Convertibles	72.5
Other	0.3

Credit Breakdown % bonds 09-30-01			
US Govt	0	BB	15
AAA	2	B	11
AA	0	Below B	3
A	26	NR/NA	4
BBB	39		

Country Exposure % assets

NA

Sector Breakdown % bonds 09-30-01			
US Treasuries	2	CMOs	0
GNMA mtgs	0	ARMs	0
FNMA mtgs	0	Other	96
FHLMC mtgs	0		

Calvert Social Investment Tech A

Ticker	Load	NAV	Yield	Total Assets	Mstar Category
CTHAX	4.75%	$5.56	0.0%	$4.5 mil	Spec Technology

Prospectus Objective: Specialty—Technology

Calvert Social Investment Technology Fund seeks growth of capital

The Fund invests at least 65% of assets in the stocks of U.S. and non-U.S. companies principally engaged in research, development, and manufacture of technology and in the stocks of companies that should benefit from the commercialization of technological advances. It may also invest up to 10% in private equity. Additionally, the fund may engage in short selling. The Fund uses an active trading strategy, which may cause the fund to have a relatively high amount of short-term capital gains, which are taxable at the ordinary income tax rate. "This fund is non-diversified."

Historical Profile
Return —
Risk —
Rating Not Rated

Investment Style
Equity
Average Stock %: 100% (2000), 100% (12-01)

▼ Manager Change
▽ Partial Manager Change

Fund Performance vs. Category Average
■ Quarterly Fund Return +/– Category Average
— Category Baseline

Performance Quartile (within Category)

Portfolio Manager(s)

Robert E. Turner, CFA. Since 10-00. BS'77 Bradley U.; MBA'78 Bradley U. Other funds currently managed: Vanguard Growth Equity, Turner Midcap Growth, Turner Top 20 Instl.

1990	1991	1992	1993	1994	1995	1996	1997	1998	1999	2000	12-01	History
—	—	—	—	—	—	—	—	—	—	9.99	5.56	NAV
—	—	—	—	—	—	—	—	—	—	-33.40*	-44.34	Total Return %
—	—	—	—	—	—	—	—	—	—	-25.97*	-32.47	+/- S&P 500
—	—	—	—	—	—	—	—	—	—	—	-28.75	+/- PSE Tech 100
—	—	—	—	—	—	—	—	—	—	0.00	0.00	Income Return %
—	—	—	—	—	—	—	—	—	—	-33.40	-44.34	Capital Return %
—	—	—	—	—	—	—	—	—	—	—	62	Total Rtn % Rank Cat
—	—	—	—	—	—	—	—	—	—	0.00	0.00	Income $
—	—	—	—	—	—	—	—	—	—	0.00	0.00	Capital Gains $
—	—	—	—	—	—	—	—	—	—	—	—	Expense Ratio %
—	—	—	—	—	—	—	—	—	—	—	—	Income Ratio %
—	—	—	—	—	—	—	—	—	—	—	—	Turnover Rate %
—	—	—	—	—	—	—	—	—	—	1.2	2.8	Net Assets $mil

Performance 12-31-01

	1st Qtr	2nd Qtr	3rd Qtr	4th Qtr	Total
1997	—	—	—	—	—
1998	—	—	—	—	—
1999	—	—	—	—	—
2000	—	—	—	—	-33.40 *
2001	-41.24	20.44	-44.84	42.56	-44.34

Trailing	Total Return%	+/– S&P 500	+/– PSE Tech 100	% Rank All	% Rank Cat	Growth of $10,000
3 Mo	42.56	31.88	—	1	25	14,256
6 Mo	-21.36	-15.80	—	99	68	7,864
1 Yr	-44.34	-32.47	—	99	62	5,566
3 Yr Avg	—	—	—	—	—	—
5 Yr Avg	—	—	—	—	—	—
10 Yr Avg	—	—	—	—	—	—
15 Yr Avg	—	—	—	—	—	—

Tax Analysis	Tax-Adj Ret%	%Rank Cat	%Pretax Ret	%Rank Cat
3 Yr Avg	—	—	—	—
5 Yr Avg	—	—	—	—
10 Yr Avg	—	—	—	—

Potential Capital Gain Exposure: NMF

Risk Analysis

Time Period	Load-Adj Return %	Risk %Rank[1] All	Risk %Rank[1] Cat	Morningstar Return	Morningstar Risk	Morningstar Risk-Adj Rating
1 Yr	-46.99					
3 Yr	—	—	—	—	—	
5 Yr	—	—	—	—	—	
Incept	-59.02	—	—	—	—	

Average Historical Rating —

[1]1=low, 100=high

Category Rating (3 Yr)

Return
Risk

Other Measures	Standard Index S&P 500	Best Fit Index
Alpha	—	—
Beta	—	—
R-Squared	—	—
Standard Deviation		—
Mean		—
Sharpe Ratio		—

Analysis by Heather Haynos 12-10-01

Calvert Social Investment Technology Fund hasn't had an auspicious beginning, but it does have some things going for it.

This fund chose a lousy time to come on the market. Since its inception in October 2000, the fast-growing technology stocks it favors have largely been in the dumps. Since inception through the end of October, it has lost more than six percentage points more than its typical specialty-technology rival.

Still, Calvert Group chose wisely when it selected its subadvisor. The fund is managed by Bob Turner and comanagers Christopher McHugh and Robb Parlanti of Turner Funds. Turner and his team have compiled impressive long-term records at high-octane funds such as Vanguard Growth Equity. Moreover, Turner's ability to position the portfolio for a comeback is evident, even in these troubled times. During the sector's brief rally in April 2001, for example, the fund returned 30%, 10 percentage points more than its typical peer.

Because this is a Calvert fund, it also has a social bent. Turner eschews firms with poor labor records, as well as ones such as Motorola, which derive a significant portion of their revenues from defense contracts. Currently, the team is positioning the fund for the early stages of a recovery in the tech arena. Thus, the trio has been adding to top holdings Intel and Texas Instruments, as well as to stocks in the storage area such as Qlogic and Brocade Communications. Such firms are getting a boost from the perceived need for greater backup after the September 11 attacks, says Turner.

Given its socially conscious and pure-tech mandates, this fund isn't right for everyone. Still, in light of Turner's strong record elsewhere, those in search of such an offering would do well to keep it on their radar screens.

Portfolio Analysis 11-30-01

Share chng since 10-01 Total Stocks: 25	Subsector	PE	YTD Ret%	% Assets
Intel	Semiconductors	73.1	4.89	6.21
⊕ Cisco Sys	Networking	—	-52.60	6.14
☼ Nokia Cl A ADR	Telecom	45.8	-43.00	4.69
Broadcom	Technology	—	-51.20	4.52
Texas Instruments	Semiconductors	87.5	-40.70	4.37
⊕ Dell Comp	Computers	61.8	55.87	3.95
⊕ Genentech	Health Care	NMF	-33.40	3.80
Finisar	Technology	—	-64.90	3.70
Sanmina	Technology	NMF	-48.00	3.59
CDW Comp Centers	Retail	28.4	92.68	3.33
Altera	Semiconductors	44.2	-19.30	3.25
☼ Qlogic	Semi Equipment	49.5	-42.10	3.24
⊕ Brocade Comm Sys	Technology	—	-63.90	3.15
Millennium Pharma	Health Care	—	-60.30	3.15
Polycom	Technology	67.5	6.87	3.10
☼ Nextel Comms Cl A	Telecom	—	-55.70	3.04
SunGard Data Sys	Computer Svs	33.3	22.78	2.91
☼ EMC	Software	NMF	-79.40	2.84
☼ Taiwan Semicon ADR	Technology	26.4	39.36	2.83
GlobeSpan	Technology	—	-52.90	2.70
☼ Gilead Sciences	Health Care	—	58.48	2.62
Internet Sec Sys	Technology	—	-59.10	2.50
☼ IDEC Pharmaceuticals	Health Care	NMF	9.09	2.52
☼ Marvell Tech	Technology	—	63.28	2.47
☼ Siebel Sys	Software	54.9	-58.60	2.23

Current Investment Style

Style: Value Blnd Growth; Size: Large Med Small

	Stock Port Avg	Relative S&P 500 Current	Relative S&P 500 Hist	Rel Cat
Price/Earnings Ratio	52.2	1.69	—	1.13
Price/Book Ratio	7.1	1.24	—	1.14
Price/Cash Flow	26.9	1.50	—	1.04
3 Yr Earnings Growth	37.2[1]	2.54	—	1.24
1 Yr Earnings Est%	-27.2	15.37	—	1.64
Med Mkt Cap $mil	9,905	0.2	—	0.62

[1]figure is based on 50% or less of stocks

Special Securities % assets 11-30-01	
Restricted/Illiquid Secs	0
Emerging-Markets Secs	3
Options/Futures/Warrants	No

Composition % assets 11-30-01	
Cash	0.0
Stocks*	100.0
Bonds	0.0
Other	0.0
*Foreign (% stocks)	7.7

Market Cap	
Giant	28.7
Large	30.3
Medium	38.2
Small	2.8
Micro	0.0

Subsector Weightings	% of Stocks	Rel Cat
Computers	4.0	0.7
Semiconductors	14.1	1.3
Semi Equipment	5.0	1.3
Networking	8.1	2.3
Periph/Hardware	0.0	0.0
Software	7.4	0.6
Computer Svs	3.0	0.5
Telecom	7.9	1.0
Health Care	13.9	3.5
Other	36.6	1.0

Address:	4550 Montgomery Avenue Suite 1000N Bethesda, MD 20814 800-368-2748 / 301-951-4820
Web Address:	www.calvertgroup.com
*Inception:	10-31-00
Advisor:	Calvert Asset Mgmt.
Subadvisor:	None
NTF Plans:	Fidelity Inst.

Minimum Purchase:	$2000	Add: $250	IRA: $1000
Min Auto Inv Plan:	$2000	Add: $250	
Sales Fees:	4.75%L, 0.25%B		
Management Fee:	1.5%		
Actual Fees:	Mgt: 1.25%	Dist: 0.25%	
Expense Projections:	3Yr: $1165	5Yr: —	10Yr: —
Avg Brok Commission:	—	Income Distrib: Annually	
Total Cost (relative to category):	—		

Calvert Tax–Free Reserv Limited–Trm A

Ticker	Load	NAV	Yield	SEC Yield	Total Assets	Mstar Category
CTFLX	1.00%	$10.69	4.1%	3.15%	$668.5 mil	Muni Short–Term

Prospectus Objective: Muni Bond—National

Calvert Tax-Free Reserves Limited-Term Portfolio seeks interest income exempt from federal taxes consistent with prudent investment management and preservation of capital.

The fund invests primarily in a diversified portfolio of investment-grade municipal obligations. It limits fixed-rate investments to obligations with remaining maturities of three or fewer years; variable-rate investments may have longer maturities. The average-weighted maturity typically ranges between one and two years.

Class A shares have front loads. The fund's Class C shares merged into Class A shares on Oct. 30, 1996.

Historical Profile

Return: Low
Risk: Low
Rating: ★★★★★ Highest

Investment Style
Fixed-Income

Income Rtn %Rank Cat: 80, 59, 47, 66, 77, 78, 36, 28

Growth of Principal vs. Interest Rate Shifts
- Principal Value $000 (NAV with capital gains reinvested)
- Interest Rate % on 10 Yr Treasury
- ▼ Manager Change
- ▽ Partial Manager Change
- ► Mgr Unknown After
- ◄ Mgr Unknown Before

Performance Quartile (within Category)

Portfolio Manager(s)

David R. Rochat. Since 3-81. BA'59 Middlebury C. Other funds currently managed: Calvert Tax-Free Reserv VT Muni A, Calvert Tax-Free Reserv Long-Term A.

Reno J. Martini. Since 1-83. Indiana U. of Pennsylvania. Other funds currently managed: Calvert Tax-Free Reserv VT Muni A, Calvert Tax-Free Reserv Long-Term A, Calvert CA Municipal Intermediate A.

Thomas Dailey. Since 1-99. BS LaRoche C.

History

1990	1991	1992	1993	1994	1995	1996	1997	1998	1999	2000	12-01	History
10.61	10.65	10.68	10.72	10.59	10.72	10.69	10.70	10.71	10.64	10.66	10.69	NAV
6.50	6.46	5.08	4.02	2.42	5.55	3.94	4.08	3.87	2.86	4.53	4.46	Total Return %
–2.45	–9.54	–2.32	–5.73	5.34	–12.92	0.32	–5.61	–4.80	3.69	–7.11	–3.96	+/– LB Aggregate
–0.80	–5.68	–3.74	–8.25	7.56	–11.91	–0.50	–5.13	–2.61	4.93	–7.17	–0.62	+/– LB Muni
6.49	6.07	4.79	3.64	3.66	4.30	4.22	3.98	3.76	3.52	4.33	4.18	Income Return %
0.02	0.39	0.29	0.38	–1.23	1.25	–0.28	0.10	0.11	–0.66	0.20	0.28	Capital Return %
50	94	90	90	2	98	34	87	88	2	94	63	Total Rtn % Rank Cat
0.67	0.63	0.50	0.38	0.39	0.45	0.44	0.42	0.40	0.37	0.45	0.44	Income $
0.00	0.00	0.00	0.00	0.00	0.00	0.00	0.00	0.00	0.00	0.00	0.00	Capital Gains $
0.77	0.73	0.71	0.67	0.66	0.70	0.70	0.69	0.71	0.71	0.70	—	Expense Ratio %
6.35	5.99	4.58	3.59	3.60	4.21	4.17	3.91	3.70	3.47	4.22	—	Income Ratio %
12	1	5	14	27	33	45	52	45	78	82	—	Turnover Rate %
151.5	291.3	567.0	653.8	547.6	457.9	512.1	566.2	543.1	523.8	463.8	668.5	Net Assets $mil

Performance 12-31-01

	1st Qtr	2nd Qtr	3rd Qtr	4th Qtr	Total
1997	0.78	1.20	0.97	1.06	4.08
1998	0.93	0.86	1.11	0.92	3.87
1999	0.75	0.50	0.81	0.77	2.86
2000	0.98	1.10	1.16	1.21	4.53
2001	1.39	1.11	1.10	0.78	4.46

Trailing	Total Return%	+/– LB Agg	+/– LB Muni	% Rank All	% Rank Cat	Growth of $10,000
3 Mo	0.78	0.75	1.45	74	1	10,078
6 Mo	1.89	–2.76	–0.23	24	45	10,189
1 Yr	4.46	–3.96	–0.62	27	63	10,446
3 Yr Avg	3.95	–2.33	–0.81	41	34	11,231
5 Yr Avg	3.96	–3.47	–2.02	80	75	12,141
10 Yr Avg	4.08	–3.15	–2.55	96	90	14,912
15 Yr Avg	4.73	–3.39	–2.45	97	66	20,015

Tax Analysis	Tax-Adj Ret%	%Rank Cat	%Pretax Ret	%Rank Cat
3 Yr Avg	3.95	33	100.0	58
5 Yr Avg	3.96	74	100.0	46
10 Yr Avg	4.08	90	100.0	23

Potential Capital Gain Exposure: 0% of assets

Risk Analysis

Time Period	Load-Adj Return %	Risk %Rank[1] All	Risk %Rank[1] Cat	Morningstar Return	Morningstar Risk	Morningstar Risk-Adj Rating
1 Yr	3.41					
3 Yr	3.60	1	1	0.29[2]	0.03	★★★★★
5 Yr	3.75	1	1	0.31[2]	0.04	★★★★★
10 Yr	3.97	1	1	0.35	0.03	★★★★

Average Historical Rating (193 months): 4.5★s

[1]1=low, 100=high [2] T-Bill return substituted for category avg.

Category Rating (3 Yr)

1 2 3 4 5 — Worst / Best

Return: Average
Risk: Low

Other Measures	Standard Index LB Agg	Best Fit Index LB Corp
Alpha	–1.0	–1.0
Beta	0.06	0.07
R–Squared	17	28

Standard Deviation	0.44
Mean	3.95
Sharpe Ratio	–2.26

Portfolio Analysis 11-30-01

Total Fixed-Income: 137	Date of Maturity	Amount $000	Value $000	% Net Assets
WV Econ Dev Commcl Dev 8%	04-01-25	23,000	22,351	3.36
NY NYC Indl Dev Nippon Cargo Dmd	11-01-15	18,000	18,000	2.71
CA Hsg 6.25%	01-01-37	16,750	16,785	2.53
LA Orleans GO 4.15%	10-01-17	16,000	16,000	2.41
CA Hsg 6.25%	08-01-31	15,385	15,385	2.32
VA Louisa Pwr 4.9%	09-01-30	15,000	15,103	2.27
CO Denver Arpt Sys 4.5%	11-15-02	12,000	12,238	1.84
TX GO 3.75%	08-29-02	10,500	10,640	1.60
KY Hlth 5.85%	11-15-05	10,000	10,334	1.56
WI De Pere Indl Dev 4.2%	06-01-29	10,000	10,008	1.51
CO Burke Pwr 4.53%	09-01-30	8,500	8,552	1.29
HI Honolulu Multi–Fam Hsg 3.6%	06-01-20	8,355	8,355	1.26
WI Solid Waste 4.55%	03-01-28	8,200	8,200	1.23
AR GO FRN	03-01-10	8,000	8,000	1.20
IL Indl Dev 4.55%	12-01-09	8,000	8,000	1.20

Current Investment Style

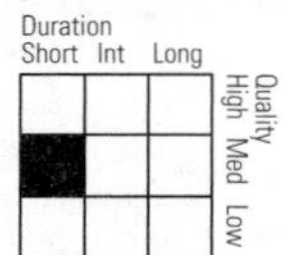

Avg Duration[1]	0.8 Yrs
Avg Nominal Maturity	0.7 Yrs
Avg Credit Quality	A
Avg Wtd Coupon	4.94%
Avg Wtd Price	100.29% of par
Pricing Service	J.J. Kenny

[1]figure provided by fund

Credit Analysis % bonds 09-30-01

US Govt	0	BB	0
AAA	26	B	0
AA	5	Below B	0
A	30	NR/NA	11
BBB	28		

Special Securities % assets 11-30-01

Restricted/Illiquid Secs	0
Inverse Floaters	0
Options/Futures/Warrants	No

Bond Type % assets

Alternative Minimum Tax (AMT)	N/A
Insured	N/A
Prerefunded	N/A

Top 5 States % bonds

CA	12.7	AL	6.1
CO	6.5	IL	6.0
TX	6.5		

Composition % assets 11-30-01

Cash	21.1	Bonds	78.9
Stocks	0.0	Other	0.0

Sector Weightings	% of Bonds	Rel Cat
General Obligation	16.0	0.6
Utilities	8.6	1.1
Health	9.4	0.8
Water/Waste	0.6	0.1
Housing	23.7	3.2
Education	1.6	0.3
Transportation	5.1	0.6
COP/Lease	1.2	0.4
Industrial	23.1	2.3
Misc Revenue	2.6	0.4
Demand	8.2	2.5

Analysis by Alan Papier 11-21-01

Calvert Tax-Free Reserves Limited-Term Portfolio's long-term record belies its appeal.

Investors may take one look at this fund's seemingly unimpressive trailing returns and dismiss it out of hand. Indeed, the fund lands in the bottom half of the muni short-term category over all longer-term periods measured by Morningstar.

But we think investors willing to look past the fund's relative performance record will discover its appeal. For one thing, it has been the least volatile muni-short offering over all time periods measured. What's more, the fund's above-average stake of A and BBB rated bonds has helped it maintain a competitive yield without taking on much interest-rate risk.

To be sure, the fund's stability over time is a function of its close-to-maturity holdings. As a bond nears the time at which its principal is to be repaid, its price is less susceptible to fluctuations due to interest-rate changes or other factors. And because the fund's duration is usually at the extreme low end of the category, it is less sensitive to interest-rate movements than almost all of its peers. Recently, its duration stood at 0.8 years, while the category average was 2.8 years. That orientation may help to minimize capital losses and stabilize the NAV, but it also limits the fund's upside when interest rates fall, as has been the case in 2001.

While this fund may make sense for investors seeking some respite from anemic yields elsewhere, it isn't a perfect money-market substitute. For instance, its willingness to take on more credit risk than its average peer can dent the NAV in difficult years like 1994.

But we don't think that's much of a concern: Management has a good grasp of the borrower's ability to repay, given that its holdings are so close to maturity. All in all, we think conservative muni-bond investors will be hard-pressed to find a more-tranquil option.

Address:	4550 Montgomery Avenue Suite 1000N Bethesda, MD 20814 800–368–2748 / 301–951–4820
Web Address:	www.calvertgroup.com
Inception:	03-04-81
Advisor:	Calvert Asset Mgmt.
Subadvisor:	None
NTF Plans:	Fidelity Inst.

Minimum Purchase:	$2000	Add: $250 IRA: —
Min Auto Inv Plan:	$2000	Add: $50
Sales Fees:	1.00%L	
Management Fee:	.61%	
Actual Fees:	Mgt: 0.61%	Dist: —
Expense Projections:	3Yr: $331	5Yr: $502 10Yr: $997
Avg Brok Commission:	—	Income Distrib: Monthly
Total Cost (relative to category):	—	

Clipper

Ticker	Load	NAV	Yield	Total Assets	Mstar Category
CFIMX	None	$83.53	1.2%	$2,468.0 mil	Large Value

Prospectus Objective: Growth

Clipper Fund seeks long-term growth of capital.

The fund primarily invests in undervalued equity securities, including common stocks, convertible debt, convertible preferred stocks, and warrants. It typically purchases shares when the market price appears to be lower than the fundamental worth of the securities, and sells securities when their share price reaches intrinsic value. The fund normally consists of between 15 and 35 stocks. It may also invest up to 25% of assets in debt rated below investment-grade. This fund is non-diversified.

Historical Profile
Return High
Risk Low
Rating ★★★★★ Highest

Investment Style
Equity
Average Stock %: 77% (1996), 62% (1997), 62% (1998), 70% (1999), 82% (2000), 63% (12-01)

▼ Manager Change
▽ Partial Manager Change

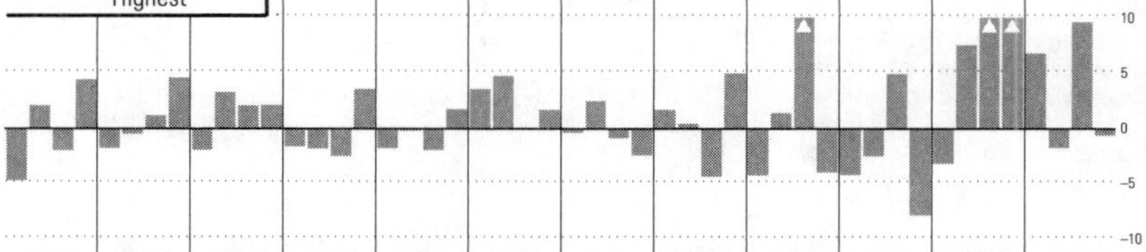

Fund Performance vs. Category Average
■ Quarterly Fund Return +/– Category Average
— Category Baseline

Performance Quartile (within Category)

Portfolio Manager(s)

James H. Gipson. Since 2-84.
Michael C. Sandler. Since 2-84.
Bruce Veaco. Since 1-86.
Peter Quinn. Since 8-87.
Douglas Grey. Since 1-86.

1990	1991	1992	1993	1994	1995	1996	1997	1998	1999	2000	12-01	History
38.80	48.10	51.74	50.05	46.09	60.74	67.57	76.86	75.37	65.28	79.25	83.53	NAV
–7.57	32.57	15.90	11.26	–2.51	45.22	19.43	30.44	19.20	–2.02	37.40	10.26	Total Return %
–4.45	2.09	8.28	1.21	–3.82	7.68	–3.52	–2.91	–9.38	–23.06	46.50	22.14	+/– S&P 500
–3.90	14.42	6.83	–8.50	–0.19	5.18	–2.88	–5.05	–2.04	–12.97	35.09	19.05	+/– Russ Top 200 Val
2.63	3.05	1.99	1.46	1.41	1.64	1.37	2.01	2.26	2.98	2.86	1.36	Income Return %
–10.20	29.52	13.92	9.81	–3.92	43.58	18.05	28.43	16.94	–5.00	34.53	8.90	Capital Return %
62	20	12	68	76	1	58	23	15	86	1	1	Total Rtn % Rank Cat
1.14	1.18	0.96	0.75	0.71	0.76	0.83	1.36	1.63	2.25	1.87	1.08	Income $
0.21	1.97	3.02	6.73	2.00	5.42	4.27	9.83	12.86	6.16	8.38	2.75	Capital Gains $
1.15	1.15	1.12	1.11	1.11	1.11	1.08	1.08	1.06	1.10	1.09	—	Expense Ratio %
2.71	2.67	2.02	1.41	1.41	1.39	1.32	1.84	2.13	2.54	2.88	—	Income Ratio %
23	42	46	64	45	31	24	31	65	63	46	—	Turnover Rate %
125.1	161.3	209.9	239.8	247.1	403.5	542.8	824.1	1,234.2	960.6	1,366.3	2,468.0	Net Assets $mil

Performance 12-31-01

	1st Qtr	2nd Qtr	3rd Qtr	4th Qtr	Total
1997	3.27	14.19	4.44	5.91	30.44
1998	7.12	0.83	–1.74	12.32	19.20
1999	–3.34	7.37	–4.31	–1.34	–2.02
2000	–3.03	5.55	16.20	15.54	37.40
2001	1.03	3.02	–2.52	8.67	10.26

Trailing	Total Return%	+/– S&P 500	+/– Russ Top 200 Val	% Rank All	% Rank Cat	Growth of $10,000
3 Mo	8.67	–2.01	3.16	49	53	10,867
6 Mo	5.93	11.49	11.71	2	1	10,593
1 Yr	10.26	22.14	19.05	6	1	11,026
3 Yr Avg	14.07	15.10	12.91	6	2	14,844
5 Yr Avg	18.21	7.51	7.00	2	1	23,079
10 Yr Avg	17.54	4.61	3.51	2	1	50,323
15 Yr Avg	16.04	2.31	2.54	4	2	93,180

Tax Analysis	Tax-Adj Ret%	%Rank Cat	%Pretax Ret	%Rank Cat
3 Yr Avg	11.14	2	79.2	24
5 Yr Avg	14.60	2	80.2	32
10 Yr Avg	14.23	4	81.2	31

Potential Capital Gain Exposure: 17% of assets

Risk Analysis

Time Period	Load-Adj Return %	Risk %Rank[1] All	Risk %Rank[1] Cat	Morningstar Return	Morningstar Risk	Morningstar Risk-Adj Rating
1 Yr	10.26					
3 Yr	14.07	33	1	2.11[2]	0.37	★★★★★
5 Yr	18.21	39	1	3.70[2]	0.41	★★★★★
10 Yr	17.54	50	3	2.50	0.58	★★★★★

Average Historical Rating (179 months): 4.0★s

[1]1=low, 100=high [2] T-Bill return substituted for category avg.

Category Rating (3 Yr)

1 Worst — 5 Best

Return High
Risk Low

Other Measures	Standard Index S&P 500	Best Fit Index Wil REIT
Alpha	10.3	5.7
Beta	0.18	0.43
R-Squared	8	26
Standard Deviation		12.87
Mean		14.07
Sharpe Ratio		0.81

Portfolio Analysis 06-30-01

Share change since 03-01 Total Stocks: 27	Sector	PE	YTD Ret%	% Assets
⊕ Freddie Mac	Financials	14.0	–3.87	7.88
⊖ Philip Morris	Staples	12.1	9.12	5.76
⊕ McDonald's	Services	19.2	–21.50	4.07
⊕ Fannie Mae	Financials	16.2	–6.95	3.64
⊕ Staples	Retail	77.9	58.30	3.64
⊕ Equity Residential Properties	Financials	22.1	10.14	3.45
⊕ Newell Rubbermaid	Durables	25.5	25.20	2.71
⊕ UST, Inc.	Staples	12.3	32.23	2.64
⊕ RR Donnelley & Sons	Services	26.8	13.72	2.64
⊕ Manpower	Services	17.0	–10.70	2.45
⊕ Sara Lee	Staples	8.4	–6.95	2.24
⊕ American Express	Financials	28.3	–34.40	2.09
⊕ Equity Office Properties Tr	Financials	18.7	–1.76	2.01
⊕ Security Cap Grp Cl B	Financials	11.3	26.45	1.94
☼ Computer Sciences	Technology	57.6	–18.50	1.92
☼ Interpublic Grp	Services	—	–29.80	1.86
⊕ Archstone Communities Tr	Financials	14.8	9.11	1.71
⊕ Apartment Invest & Mgmt	Financials	NMF	–1.80	1.58
⊕ Pitney Bowes	Industrials	17.2	19.80	1.33
⊕ Office Depot	Retail	NMF	160.20	1.32
⊕ Target	Retail	29.8	28.05	1.29
⊕ Mack-Cali Realty	Financials	13.3	18.32	1.05
⊕ Golden West Finl	Financials	12.9	–12.40	0.98
⊕ Old Republic Intl	Financials	9.7	–10.50	0.93
⊖ Tyson Foods Cl A	Staples	28.9	–8.17	0.32

Current Investment Style

Style: Value Blnd Growth; Size: Large Med Small

	Stock Port Avg	Relative S&P 500 Current	Relative S&P 500 Hist	Rel Cat
Price/Earnings Ratio	23.1	0.75	0.60	0.92
Price/Book Ratio	4.2	0.73	0.58	1.01
Price/Cash Flow	10.8	0.60	0.54	0.78
3 Yr Earnings Growth	12.3	0.84	0.61	0.83
1 Yr Earnings Est%	13.0	—	—	—
Med Mkt Cap $mil	11,368	0.2	0.4	0.36

Analysis by Christopher Traulsen 12-28-01

Clipper Fund is one of the best at what it does; just don't buy it for the wrong reasons.

This fund's recent performance is remarkable. For the year to date through Dec. 27, 2001, it has returned 6%, besting 95% of its large-value rivals. In 2000, it soared 37%, besting nearly all of its peers.

The key to the fund's strength is the managers' strict value discipline. The team only buys dominant companies trading at discounts of at least 30% to their intrinsic values. When they can't find enough high-quality, cheap names to flesh out the portfolio, they hold bonds or cash. Indeed, it's not uncommon for the fund to have more than 30% of its assets in cash, as it now does.

The managers' value discipline keeps them out of pricey technology and telecom names and overweight in stodgy financials issues. That dearth of exposure to sinking growth names has held the fund in good stead over the past two years, and the managers have also homed in on strong, once-unloved picks such as H&R Block and Philip Morris.

Still, investors who buy the fund now expecting it to reprise its recent dominance in the near future may be disappointed. The fund's lack of growth exposure and big cash stakes can badly dent its returns in growth-led markets. Given that value stocks have handily beaten growth issues over the last two years, growth may be due for a rally. When that happens, this fund could easily look sluggish.

For long-term investors with the patience to ride out some dry spells, however, the fund's disciplined process, experienced and successful managers, reasonable expenses, and sterling long-term returns give it much appeal. Its concentration in relatively few names and sectors does expose it to significant risk, but the managers' attention to valuation and willingness to hold cash has still made it less volatile than most rivals. It's also a good diversifier for growth-heavy portfolios.

Special Securities % assets 06-30-01	
Restricted/Illiquid Secs	0
Emerging-Markets Secs	0
Options/Futures/Warrants	No

Composition % assets 06-30-01	
Cash	38.2
Stocks*	61.8
Bonds	0.0
Other	0.0
*Foreign (% stocks)	0.0

Market Cap	
Giant	31.4
Large	19.3
Medium	49.1
Small	0.3
Micro	0.0

Sector Weightings	% of Stocks	Rel S&P	5-Year High	5-Year Low
Utilities	0.0	0.0	0	0
Energy	0.0	0.0	0	0
Financials	44.1	2.5	56	10
Industrials	2.7	0.2	17	0
Durables	4.4	2.8	7	0
Staples	17.7	2.2	48	12
Services	17.8	1.6	45	0
Retail	10.1	1.5	27	0
Health	0.0	0.0	20	0
Technology	3.1	0.2	3	0

Address: 9601 Wilshire Boulevard Suite 828, Beverly Hills, CA 90210, 800-776-5033 / 310-247-3940
Web Address: www.clipperfund.com
Inception: 02-29-84
Advisor: Pacific Financial Research
Subadvisor: None
NTF Plans: Fidelity , Fidelity Inst.

Minimum Purchase: $5000 — Add: $1000 — IRA: $2000
Min Auto Inv Plan: $5000 — Add: $150
Sales Fees: No-load
Management Fee: 1.0%
Actual Fees: Mgt: 1.00% — Dist: —
Expense Projections: 3Yr: $350 — 5Yr: $606 — 10Yr: $1340
Avg Brok Commission: — — Income Distrib: Annually
Total Cost (relative to category): Below Avg

Columbia Balanced

Ticker	Load	NAV	Yield	Total Assets	Mstar Category
CBALX	None	$20.67	2.8%	$951.9 mil	Domestic Hybrid

Prospectus Objective: Balanced

Columbia Balanced Fund seeks total return.

The fund invests primarily in common stocks and investment-grade fixed-income securities. It allocates assets between these types of securities using a top-down approach. The fund normally invests 35% to 65% of assets in common stocks, and 35% to 65% of assets in fixed-income securities. There is no limit on the average maturity of the bond portion of the portfolio. It primarily invests in debt securities rated BBB or higher, or their unrated equivalents, including corporate debt securities, asset-backed securities, collateralized bonds, and loan and mortgage obligations.

Historical Profile
Return Average
Risk Low
Rating ★★★ Neutral

Investment Style
Equity
Average Stock %: 52% 55% 52% 53% 57% 60%

▼ Manager Change
▽ Partial Manager Change

Fund Performance vs. Category Average
▀ Quarterly Fund Return +/– Category Average
— Category Baseline

Performance Quartile (within Category)

Portfolio Manager(s)

Leonard A. Aplet, CFA. Since 9-97. BS'76 Oregon State U.; MBA'87 U. of California-Berkeley. Other funds currently managed: Columbia Fixed-Income Securities, CMC Fixed Income Securities.

Guy Pope, CFA. Since 2-98. BA'88 Colorado C.; MBA'93 Northwestern U.

Jeffrey L. Rippey, CFA. Since 9-97. BA'78 Pacific Lutheran U. Other funds currently managed: Columbia Fixed-Income Securities, Columbia Short Term Bond, Columbia High-Yield.

1990	1991	1992	1993	1994	1995	1996	1997	1998	1999	2000	12-01	History
—	16.05	16.80	17.91	17.28	20.08	20.32	21.42	23.17	24.72	22.96	20.67	NAV
—	7.87*	8.89	13.65	0.10	25.05	11.84	18.76	20.07	12.70	0.82	–7.40	Total Return %
—	–0.93*	1.27	3.59	–1.21	–12.49	–11.10	–14.60	–8.51	–8.34	9.92	4.48	+/– S&P 500
—	—	1.49	3.90	3.02	6.58	8.23	9.07	11.40	13.53	–10.81	–15.82	+/– LB Aggregate
—	0.59	3.60	3.46	3.62	4.29	3.84	4.14	3.45	3.01	2.82	2.57	Income Return %
—	7.28	5.29	10.18	–3.52	20.76	8.00	14.61	16.62	9.69	–2.00	–9.97	Capital Return %
—	—	39	38	17	52	64	48	14	32	52	75	Total Rtn % Rank Cat
—	0.09	0.57	0.57	0.64	0.73	0.76	0.83	0.73	0.69	0.68	0.59	Income $
—	0.04	0.08	0.59	0.00	0.74	1.34	1.83	1.76	0.66	1.34	0.00	Capital Gains $
—	0.62	0.81	0.73	0.72	0.69	0.66	0.68	0.67	0.66	0.65	—	Expense Ratio %
—	3.41	4.08	3.32	3.82	4.05	3.82	3.83	3.22	2.85	2.73	—	Income Ratio %
—	180	138	108	98	108	133	149	128	133	105	—	Turnover Rate %
—	13.0	90.2	186.6	249.7	486.8	672.6	792.4	975.4	1,040.9	1,126.9	—	Net Assets $mil

Performance 12-31-01

	1st Qtr	2nd Qtr	3rd Qtr	4th Qtr	Total
1997	1.23	9.42	5.38	1.73	18.76
1998	7.94	3.49	–4.76	12.86	20.07
1999	3.84	2.38	–3.58	9.94	12.70
2000	6.92	–1.37	–0.43	–3.98	0.82
2001	–7.84	3.33	–8.72	6.53	–7.40

Trailing	Total Return%	+/– S&P 500	+/– LB Agg	% Rank All	% Rank Cat	Growth of $10,000
3 Mo	6.53	–4.16	6.49	58	44	10,653
6 Mo	–2.76	2.80	–7.41	50	69	9,724
1 Yr	–7.40	4.48	–15.82	56	75	9,260
3 Yr Avg	1.71	2.74	–4.56	64	58	10,522
5 Yr Avg	8.45	–2.25	1.03	27	31	15,003
10 Yr Avg	10.02	–2.90	2.79	32	36	25,993
15 Yr Avg	—	—	—	—	—	—

Tax Analysis	Tax-Adj Ret%	%Rank Cat	%Pretax Ret	%Rank Cat
3 Yr Avg	–0.14	57	—	—
5 Yr Avg	5.92	34	70.0	43
10 Yr Avg	7.52	36	75.1	36

Potential Capital Gain Exposure: 2% of assets

Risk Analysis

Time Period	Load-Adj Return %	Risk %Rank[1] All	Risk %Rank[1] Cat	Morningstar Return	Morningstar Risk	Morningstar Risk-Adj Rating
1 Yr	–7.40					
3 Yr	1.71	43	64	–0.67[2]	0.60	★★★
5 Yr	8.45	43	48	0.80[2]	0.54	★★★
10 Yr	10.02	48	40	0.74	0.54	★★★

Average Historical Rating (88 months): 3.5★s

[1]1=low, 100=high [2] T-Bill return substituted for category avg.

Category Rating (3 Yr)

1 2 **3** 4 5
Worst Best

Return Average
Risk Average

Other Measures	Standard Index S&P 500	Best Fit Index S&P 500
Alpha	0.2	0.2
Beta	0.61	0.61
R-Squared	90	90

Standard Deviation	11.00
Mean	1.71
Sharpe Ratio	–0.34

Portfolio Analysis 11-30-01

Total Stocks: 105 Share change since 10-01	Sector	PE Ratio	YTD Return %	% Net Assets
Pfizer	Health	34.7	–12.40	3.01
Citigroup	Financials	20.0	0.03	2.58
General Elec	Industrials	30.1	–15.00	2.45
Tyco Intl	Industrials	27.1	6.23	1.83
⊕ Intel	Technology	73.1	4.89	1.77
Baxter Intl	Health	33.9	22.84	1.65
Microsoft	Technology	57.6	52.78	1.61
ExxonMobil	Energy	15.3	–7.59	1.55
Wal-Mart Stores	Retail	40.3	8.94	1.46
⊕ Bristol-Myers Squibb	Health	20.2	–26.00	1.43

Total Fixed-Income: 155	Date of Maturity	Amount $000	Value $000	% Net Assets
FNMA 6%	11-01-16	27,032	27,370	2.85
US Treasury Bond 8.875%	08-15-17	15,920	21,636	2.25
FNMA 6.5%	11-01-31	19,889	20,110	2.09
GNMA 7%	02-15-31	10,174	10,486	1.09
Federal Home Loan Bk 4.5%	07-07-03	8,070	8,276	0.86
US Treasury Note 3.375%	01-15-07	7,764	7,869	0.82
CMC Secs CMO 7.25%	11-25-27	7,235	7,581	0.79
Comml Cap Access 144A 6.615%	11-15-28	6,460	6,738	0.70
FNMA Debenture 7.13%	01-15-30	5,385	6,114	0.64
GNMA 7.5%	04-20-17	5,652	6,014	0.63

Equity Style
Style: Blend
Size: Large-Cap

	Portfolio Avg	Rel S&P
Price/Earnings Ratio	32.6	1.05
Price/Book Ratio	5.5	0.96
Price/Cash Flow	19.2	1.07
3 Yr Earnings Growth	15.5	1.06
1 Yr Earnings Est%	–1.9	1.08
Debt % Total Cap	29.5	0.96
Med Mkt Cap $mil	66,575	1.10

Fixed-Income Style
Duration: Intermediate
Quality: High

Avg Eff Duration[1]	4.5 Yrs
Avg Eff Maturity	5.3 Yrs
Avg Credit Quality	AA
Avg Wtd Coupon	6.94%

[1]figure provided by fund as of 09-30-01

Analysis by Kelli Stebel 07-31-01

Shareholders shouldn't worry about this fund's recent misstep.

Columbia Balanced's aggressive nature has come back to haunt it during 2001. This fund typically has 60% of assets dedicated to equities, compared with just 50% for its typical peer. And while most domestic-hybrid funds fill their equity portfolios with moderate blue chips, this fund prefers growthier companies, like health-care and technology stocks. The fund's penchant for pricey stocks has hurt returns this year, as tech has been decimated and earnings at giant pharmaceuticals have slowed in recent months.

These days, encouraged by the recent Fed easing, comanager Guy Pope reports that he and the team are a bit more aggressive. The team has picked up shares of Washington Mutual, thinking that its future earnings growth looks particularly strong in a low-interest-rate environment. Pope says they also favor stocks related to home building, like Home Depot and Masco, arguing that a stronger economy will spur new-home construction.

Despite this year's subpar showing, the fund's returns have been consistently solid over the long haul. Its above-average equity weighting and penchant for growth stocks were big pluses throughout growth-dominated years like 1998 and 1999. And on the bond side, an emphasis on high-quality corporate bonds and mortgage-backed securities kept the fund from falling to the bottom of the pack during 2000's rough market. Since the current management team took over in September 1997, the fund has outpaced its typical peer by 2 percentage points.

This fund remains a good pick for investors looking for a more aggressive hybrid fund.

Special Securities % assets 11-30-01	
Restricted/Illiquid Secs	2
Emerging-Markets Secs	Trace
Options/Futures/Warrants	No

Composition % of assets 11-30-01	
Cash	0.0
Stocks*	59.2
Bonds	40.8
Other	0.0
*Foreign (% of stocks)	2.3

Market Cap	
Giant	61.4
Large	26.1
Medium	12.5
Small	0.0
Micro	0.0

Sector Weightings	% of Stocks	Rel S&P	5-Year High	5-Year Low
Utilities	0.4	0.1	6	0
Energy	4.9	0.7	13	4
Financials	19.4	1.1	25	10
Industrials	13.6	1.2	22	7
Durables	3.0	1.9	9	0
Staples	3.5	0.5	19	0
Services	12.7	1.2	25	7
Retail	6.6	1.0	13	3
Health	17.5	1.2	21	5
Technology	18.2	1.0	39	4

Address:	1301 SW Fifth Avenue P.O. Box 1350 Portland, OR 97207-1350 800-547-1707 / 503-222-3606
Web Address:	www.columbiafunds.com
*Inception:	09-12-91
Advisor:	Columbia Funds Mgmt.
Subadvisor:	None
NTF Plans:	Fidelity Inst. , Waterhouse

Minimum Purchase:	$1000	Add: $100 IRA: $1000
Min Auto Inv Plan:	$50	Add: $50
Sales Fees:	No-load	
Management Fee:	.50%	
Actual Fees:	Mgt: 0.50%	Dist: —
Expense Projections:	3Yr: $214	5Yr: $373 10Yr: $835
Avg Brok Commission:	—	Income Distrib: Quarterly
Total Cost (relative to category):	—	

Columbia Growth

Ticker	Load	NAV	Yield	Total Assets	Mstar Category
CLMBX	None	$31.35	0.0%	$1,219.4 mil	Large Growth

Prospectus Objective: Growth

Columbia Growth Fund seeks capital appreciation.

The fund invests primarily in common stocks. When selecting investments, management considers sales trends, earnings, profit margins, the potential for new-product development, the company's competitive position within its industry, the ability of management, and investment in research and facilities. These fundamental factors are judged within the framework of general economic conditions and market action to finalize investment decisions. The fund may invest up to 10% of assets in foreign common stocks issued by companies located in developed countries.

Historical Profile
Return: Average
Risk: Above Avg
Rating: ★★★ Neutral

Investment Style Equity — Average Stock %: 100% | 100% | 100% | 100% | 99% | 99% | 100%

▼ Manager Change
▽ Partial Manager Change

Fund Performance vs. Category Average
■ Quarterly Fund Return +/– Category Average
— Category Baseline

Performance Quartile (within Category)

Portfolio Manager(s)

Alexander S. Macmillan III, CFA et al.Since 1-92. BA'74 Harvard U.; MBA'80 Dartmouth C.

1990	1991	1992	1993	1994	1995	1996	1997	1998	1999	2000	12-01	History
21.68	26.26	26.18	26.38	24.84	29.84	30.74	34.34	42.51	48.91	40.07	31.35	NAV
–3.28	34.42	11.91	13.09	–0.63	32.89	20.88	26.32	30.34	26.02	–7.94	–21.40	Total Return %
–0.16	3.93	4.29	3.03	–1.94	–4.64	–2.07	–7.03	1.77	4.98	1.16	–9.52	+/– S&P 500
–4.65	–4.99	8.02	13.16	–5.48	–5.76	–4.64	–7.42	–14.76	–3.66	16.59	–0.90	+/– Russ Top 200 Grt
2.10	1.97	0.85	0.77	0.99	1.17	0.57	0.55	0.23	0.00	0.00	0.00	Income Return %
–5.37	32.45	11.06	12.32	–1.61	31.72	20.31	25.76	30.11	26.02	–7.94	–21.40	Capital Return %
59	70	10	38	33	45	36	48	56	75	24	45	Total Rtn % Rank Cat
0.48	0.39	0.20	0.18	0.26	0.29	0.17	0.17	0.08	0.00	0.00	0.00	Income $
0.46	2.44	2.98	3.02	1.11	2.88	5.16	4.32	2.17	4.66	5.27	0.15	Capital Gains $
0.96	0.90	0.86	0.82	0.81	0.75	0.71	0.71	0.68	0.65	0.65	—	Expense Ratio %
2.08	1.50	0.77	0.66	1.12	1.14	0.63	0.55	0.21	–0.07	–0.18	—	Income Ratio %
172	164	116	106	79	95	75	96	105	118	114	—	Turnover Rate %
270.7	431.5	518.4	605.4	591.7	848.7	1,064.1	1,324.9	1,753.0	2,160.7	1,919.2	—	Net Assets $mil

Performance 12-31-01

	1st Qtr	2nd Qtr	3rd Qtr	4th Qtr	Total
1997	–1.66	16.77	9.04	0.88	26.32
1998	15.43	5.30	–14.61	25.59	30.34
1999	9.01	5.09	–7.89	19.42	26.02
2000	12.88	–2.16	–1.93	–15.01	–7.94
2001	–20.86	8.89	–22.01	16.95	–21.40

Trailing	Total Return%	+/– S&P 500	+/– Russ Top 200 Grth	% Rank All	% Rank Cat	Growth of $10,000
3 Mo	16.95	6.27	4.10	20	27	11,695
6 Mo	–8.79	–3.23	–1.80	81	49	9,121
1 Yr	–21.40	–9.52	–0.90	82	45	7,860
3 Yr Avg	–3.03	–2.00	4.99	87	53	9,119
5 Yr Avg	8.47	–2.23	–0.12	27	51	15,014
10 Yr Avg	11.73	–1.19	0.65	21	24	30,329
15 Yr Avg	13.29	–0.45	–0.09	15	29	64,952

Tax Analysis	Tax-Adj Ret%	%Rank Cat	%Pretax Ret	%Rank Cat
3 Yr Avg	–4.69	55	—	—
5 Yr Avg	6.45	50	76.2	55
10 Yr Avg	8.85	38	75.5	56

Potential Capital Gain Exposure: 5% of assets

Risk Analysis

Time Period	Load-Adj Return %	Risk %Rank[1] All	Risk %Rank[1] Cat	Morningstar Return	Morningstar Risk	Morningstar Risk-Adj Rating
1 Yr	–21.40					
3 Yr	–3.03	87	57	–1.57[2]	1.33	★★
5 Yr	8.47	83	46	0.80[2]	1.19	★★★
10 Yr	11.73	84	38	1.05	1.17	★★★

Average Historical Rating (193 months): 3.8★s

[1] 1=low, 100=high [2] T-Bill return substituted for category avg.

Category Rating (3 Yr): 3 (scale 1 Worst – 5 Best)
Return: Average
Risk: Average

Other Measures	Standard Index S&P 500	Best Fit Index MSCIACWdFr
Alpha	1.3	6.9
Beta	1.37	1.46
R-Squared	86	86

Standard Deviation	25.02
Mean	–3.03
Sharpe Ratio	–0.37

Portfolio Analysis 11-30-01

Share change since 10-01 Total Stocks: 89	Sector	PE	YTD Ret%	% Assets
⊖ Pfizer	Health	34.7	–12.40	5.77
⊖ Microsoft	Technology	57.6	52.78	5.11
General Elec	Industrials	30.1	–15.00	4.84
⊖ Tyco Intl	Industrials	27.1	6.23	4.72
⊕ Intel	Technology	73.1	4.89	3.92
⊖ Baxter Intl	Health	33.9	22.84	2.72
Wal-Mart Stores	Retail	40.3	8.94	2.61
IBM	Technology	26.9	43.00	2.37
⊖ American Intl Grp	Financials	42.0	–19.20	2.33
⊕ AOL Time Warner	Technology	—	–7.76	2.31
⊕ Bristol-Myers Squibb	Health	20.2	–26.00	2.26
Abbott Labs	Health	51.6	17.08	1.92
⊖ Lowe's	Retail	38.7	109.00	1.84
Pharmacia	Health	36.5	–29.30	1.80
⊖ Johnson & Johnson	Health	16.6	14.01	1.77
⊖ Citigroup	Financials	20.0	0.03	1.74
⊕ Amgen	Health	52.8	–11.70	1.51
Fannie Mae	Financials	16.2	–6.95	1.50
⊕ Gillette	Staples	56.6	–5.47	1.48
⊕ Lucent Tech	Technology	—	–53.20	1.43
⊖ Flextronics Intl	Technology	—	–15.80	1.43
⊖ Celestica	Technology	79.2	–25.50	1.31
Dell Comp	Technology	61.8	55.87	1.28
⊕ Clear Channel Comms	Services	—	5.10	1.26
Texas Instruments	Technology	87.5	–40.70	1.25

Current Investment Style

Style: Value Blnd Growth; Size: Large Med Small

	Stock Port Avg	Relative S&P 500 Current	Relative S&P 500 Hist	Rel Cat
Price/Earnings Ratio	37.7	1.22	1.22	1.06
Price/Book Ratio	6.9	1.21	1.17	1.08
Price/Cash Flow	23.3	1.29	1.28	1.02
3 Yr Earnings Growth	19.1	1.31	1.34	0.89
1 Yr Earnings Est%	0.1	—	—	0.02
Med Mkt Cap $mil	72,221	1.2	1.0	1.53

Special Securities % assets 11-30-01	
Restricted/Illiquid Secs	0
Emerging-Markets Secs	0
Options/Futures/Warrants	No

Sector Weightings	% of Stocks	Rel S&P	5-Year High	5-Year Low
Utilities	0.0	0.0	5	0
Energy	2.1	0.3	9	0
Financials	9.5	0.5	25	7
Industrials	11.7	1.0	22	5
Durables	0.3	0.2	10	0
Staples	3.3	0.4	18	0
Services	8.2	0.8	22	6
Retail	8.6	1.3	18	5
Health	24.3	1.6	27	6
Technology	32.2	1.8	44	8

Composition % assets 11-30-01	
Cash	0.0
Stocks*	100.0
Bonds	0.0
Other	0.0
*Foreign (% stocks)	1.6

Market Cap	
Giant	60.4
Large	29.1
Medium	10.5
Small	0.0
Micro	0.0

Analysis by Kunal Kapoor 08-02-01

Columbia Growth Fund rarely heats up like some of its rivals do, but you won't catch it playing with fire, either.

This fund has never emerged as a standout, but it keeps getting the job done. Since current manager Alex Macmillan took the helm in 1992, the fund has placed in its category's top quartile just once, but it has landed in the second quartile on six other occasions, and has made an appearance in the third quartile on only two occasions. (It's never fallen into the category's bottom echelons under Macmillan's watch.) All this has produced a top-half trailing 10-year record through July 2001. (The offering trails the S&P 500 index by 0.57% annually over that stretch, which is attributable to its reasonable 0.65% annual fee.)

Like other large-growth funds, this offering currently finds itself in a tough situation. With the market gravitating away from both aggressive-growth areas such as technology and defensive growth areas such as health care, the offering has had few places to hide. Indeed, its greater than 17% loss for the year to date is emblematic of its group's misfortunes (the fund just edges past its typical rival over that stretch.)

Despite these losses and a greater focus on stock valuations, Macmillan hasn't fiddled excessively with the portfolio's makeup since the beginning of the year. Indeed, he says that the Federal Reserve's interest-rate cuts should lift the economy, so he's banking on rebounds in areas such as retail, media, and technology. And while he says that some retail and media stocks such as Kohl's and Clear Channel Communications are beginning to look expensive after running up, he thinks that value opportunities still exist in other areas, such as semiconductors.

Overall, investors will find this to be a decent growth fund. The offering is steady and bankable, although not a category killer.

Address:	1301 SW Fifth Avenue P.O. Box 1350 Portland, OR 97207-1350 800-547-1707 / 503-222-3606
Web Address:	www.columbiafunds.com
Inception:	06-16-67
Advisor:	Columbia Funds Mgmt.
Subadvisor:	None
NTF Plans:	Fidelity Inst. , Waterhouse

Minimum Purchase:	$1000	Add: $100 IRA: $1000
Min Auto Inv Plan:	$50	Add: $50
Sales Fees:	No-load	
Management Fee:	.75% mx./.50% mn.	
Actual Fees:	Mgt: 0.56%	Dist: —
Expense Projections:	3Yr: $218	5Yr: $379 10Yr: $847
Avg Brok Commission:	—	Income Distrib: Annually
Total Cost (relative to category):	—	

Columbia Real Estate Equity

Ticker	Load	NAV	Yield	Total Assets	Mstar Category
CREEX	None	$18.04	4.4%	$500.3 mil	Spec Real Estate

Prospectus Objective: Specialty—Real Estate

Columbia Real Estate Equity Fund seeks capital appreciation and current income.

The fund normally invests at least 65% of assets in equity securities issued by companies engaged in the real estate industry. These companies may include real estate investment trusts, mortgage real estate investment trusts, and real estate brokers or developers. It may invest the balance of assets in equity securities of other types of companies and in investment-grade debt securities. The fund may invest up to 20% of assets in securities of foreign real estate companies.

Historical Profile

Return Average
Risk Below Avg
Rating ★★★ Neutral

Investment Style
Equity

	1994	1995	1996	1997	1998	1999	2000	12-01
Average Stock %			100%	100%	97%	93%	96%	100%

▼ Manager Change
▽ Partial Manager Change

Fund Performance vs. Category Average
■ Quarterly Fund Return +/– Category Average
— Category Baseline

Performance Quartile (within Category)

Portfolio Manager(s)

David W. Jellison, CFA. Since 4-94. BBA'80 U. of Michigan; MBA'84 Northwestern U.

1990	1991	1992	1993	1994	1995	1996	1997	1998	1999	2000	12–01	History
—	—	—	—	11.72	12.71	16.16	18.80	15.76	14.57	17.89	18.04	NAV
—	—	—	—	1.77*	16.86	40.19	25.89	–11.85	–1.74	29.32	5.41	Total Return %
—	—	—	—	–5.17*	–20.67	17.25	–7.46	–40.42	–22.77	38.42	17.28	+/– S&P 500
—	—	—	—	—	4.62	3.15	6.22	5.16	0.84	–1.73	–6.95	+/– Wilshire REIT
—	—	—	—	2.70	4.65	6.21	4.98	4.08	5.30	5.65	4.49	Income Return %
—	—	—	—	–0.93	12.21	33.98	20.91	–15.93	–7.03	23.67	0.92	Capital Return %
—	—	—	—	—	33	10	17	9	32	37	88	Total Rtn % Rank Cat
—	—	—	—	0.31	0.53	0.77	0.79	0.75	0.82	0.81	0.79	Income $
—	—	—	—	0.18	0.38	0.70	0.68	0.09	0.11	0.06	0.00	Capital Gains $
—	—	—	—	1.14	1.18	1.06	1.02	1.01	0.99	0.96	—	Expense Ratio %
—	—	—	—	6.28	6.71	6.23	4.87	4.60	5.66	5.16	—	Income Ratio %
—	—	—	—	8	54	46	34	6	29	25	—	Turnover Rate %
—	—	—	—	17.4	21.6	68.1	151.6	164.2	241.7	437.5	—	Net Assets $mil

Performance 12-31-01

	1st Qtr	2nd Qtr	3rd Qtr	4th Qtr	Total
1997	4.13	4.29	13.66	1.99	25.89
1998	1.14	–5.21	–8.13	0.08	–11.85
1999	–2.90	9.17	–7.88	0.62	–1.74
2000	3.11	10.95	8.71	3.98	29.32
2001	–4.02	10.35	–5.05	4.82	5.41

Trailing	Total Return%	+/– S&P 500	+/– Wil REIT	% Rank All	% Rank Cat	Growth of $10,000
3 Mo	4.82	–5.86	–0.06	65	32	10,482
6 Mo	–0.47	5.08	–2.84	41	85	9,953
1 Yr	5.41	17.28	–6.95	21	88	10,541
3 Yr Avg	10.23	11.26	–2.55	11	59	13,394
5 Yr Avg	8.25	–2.45	0.91	28	14	14,864
10 Yr Avg	—	—	—	—	—	—
15 Yr Avg	—	—	—	—	—	—

Tax Analysis	Tax-Adj Ret%	%Rank Cat	%Pretax Ret	%Rank Cat
3 Yr Avg	8.14	57	79.6	55
5 Yr Avg	6.09	12	73.8	11
10 Yr Avg	—	—	—	—

Potential Capital Gain Exposure: 10% of assets

Risk Analysis

Time Period	Load-Adj Return %	Risk %Rank[1] All	Risk %Rank[1] Cat	Morningstar Return	Morningstar Risk	Morningstar Risk-Adj Rating
1 Yr	5.41					
3 Yr	10.23	41	54	1.18[2]	0.57	★★★★
5 Yr	8.25	49	28	0.85[2]	0.67	★★★
Incept	12.43	—	—	—	—	

Average Historical Rating (58 months): 3.3★s

[1] 1=low, 100=high [2] T-Bill return substituted for category avg.

Category Rating (3 Yr)

1 2 **3** 4 5
Worst Best

Return Average
Risk Average

Other Measures	Standard Index S&P 500	Best Fit Index Wil REIT
Alpha	6.6	–2.0
Beta	0.13	0.96
R-Squared	3	95

Standard Deviation	14.48
Mean	10.23
Sharpe Ratio	0.42

Portfolio Analysis 11-30-01

Share chng since 10–01 Total Stocks: 28	Subsector	PE	YTD Ret%	% Assets
Equity Office Properties Tr	Industrial/Office	18.7	–1.76	11.77
⊕ Cousins Properties	Diversified	17.0	–7.98	6.87
⊕ Equity Residential Properties	Apartment	22.1	10.14	5.79
⊕ Vornado Realty Tr	Retail	17.6	16.25	5.71
⊕ AvalonBay Communities	Apartment	15.9	–0.38	5.66
⊕ Simon Ppty Grp	Retail	27.9	31.72	5.62
⊖ General Growth Properties	Retail	29.2	13.92	5.61
⊕ iStar Finl	Diversified	8.8	39.61	5.60
⊕ TrizecHahn	Diversified	28.0	5.92	5.14
⊕ Plum Creek Timber	Industrials	18.4	20.75	5.12
Security Cap Grp Cl B	Diversified	11.3	26.45	3.76
⊕ Reckson Assoc Realty	Industrial/Office	—	0.15	3.43
✲ Archstone Smith Tr	N/A	—	—	3.33
⊖ Host Marriott	Hotel	6.2	–24.80	2.97
⊕ Public Storage	Self Storage	22.6	44.92	2.95
Kimco Realty	Retail	15.6	18.16	2.55
⊕ Boston Properties	Industrial/Office	17.8	–7.37	2.55
⊖ Starwood Hotels & Resorts	Hotel	18.7	–12.90	2.31
Camden Ppty Tr	Apartment	23.4	17.32	2.12
Alexandria Real Est Eq	Industrial/Office	25.4	15.87	2.12
Prologis Tr	Industrial/Office	20.3	3.19	2.09
⊕ CarrAmerica Realty	Industrial/Office	21.5	2.32	1.47
Liberty Ppty Tr	Industrial/Office	13.5	13.22	1.37
Prentiss Properties Tr	Industrial/Office	11.2	10.26	1.33
First Indl Realty Tr	Industrial/Office	14.3	–0.38	0.80

Current Investment Style

Style: Value Blnd Growth; Size: Large Med Small

	Stock Port Avg	Relative S&P 500 Current	Relative S&P 500 Hist	Rel Cat
Price/Earnings Ratio	19.0	0.62	0.63	0.97
Price/Book Ratio	1.8	0.31	0.24	1.02
Price/Cash Flow	—	—	—	—
3 Yr Earnings Growth	26.3	1.80	0.98	1.29
1 Yr Earnings Est%	59.8	—	—	0.99
Med Mkt Cap $mil	2,770	0.1	0.0	1.21

Analysis by Kunal Kapoor 08-02-01

Plain and simple, we think that Columbia Real Estate Equity Fund is a solid pick.

With only three funds making the cut for our real-estate Fund Analyst Picks, we clearly like this one enough to include it. That's because manager David Jellison has churned out consistently strong performance. The fund has ranked in the category's top half in every calendar year since its 1994 inception, and thus owns a top quintile five-year return for the trailing period through August 1, 2001. What's more, the fund has been less volatile than its typical rival over that stretch.

To be sure, the fund isn't bulletproof, and it will lag its peers from time to time. So far this year, for instance, its near-5% gain puts it in the category's bottom half. Indeed, despite a prescient weighting in lodging and retail-related REITs, the fund has been hurt somewhat by its 28% stake in office REITs. A lack of exposure to the relatively small health-care subsector, which has had a strong run, also hasn't helped.

Jellison isn't fiddling much with the portfolio's makeup to jazz up returns. Because he expects the economy to recover sooner rather than later, he says he'll keep the portfolio positioned to benefit from an upturn. Thus, he's used price drops in favorites, such as Equity Office Properties, to add to the fund's position in those stocks. (Jellison says that EOP is cheap relative to its peers and trades for less than its net asset value.) Jellison is also keeping the fund's combined 32% stake in hotels and retail REITs, which typically benefit in the early stages of a recovery.

Overall, we like this fund's long-term prospects. However, we continue to carefully watch how the fund handles its added girth, as it has doubled in size in less than two years.

Special Securities % assets 11-30-01	
Restricted/Illiquid Secs	0
Emerging-Markets Secs	0
Options/Futures/Warrants	No

Subsector Weightings	% of Stocks	Rel Cat
Diversified	22.1	2.2
Health Care	0.0	0.0
Industrial/Office	28.4	0.9
Mortgage Backed	0.0	0.0
Apartment	14.8	0.8
Retail	20.9	1.1
Dvlp./Man. Home	0.0	0.0
Self Storage	3.1	0.9
Hotel	5.5	1.2
Other	5.3	0.7

Composition % assets 11-30-01	
Cash	0.0
Stocks*	100.0
Bonds	0.0
Other	0.0
*Foreign (% stocks)	5.1

Market Cap	
Giant	0.0
Large	12.2
Medium	75.1
Small	12.8
Micro	0.0

Address:	1301 SW Fifth Avenue P.O. Box 1350 Portland, OR 97207–1350 800–547–1707 / 503–222–3606
Web Address:	www.columbiafunds.com
*Inception:	04-04-94
Advisor:	Columbia Funds Mgmt.
Subadvisor:	None
NTF Plans:	Fidelity Inst. , Waterhouse

Minimum Purchase:	$1000	Add: $100 IRA: $1000
Min Auto Inv Plan:	$50	Add: $50
Sales Fees:	No–load	
Management Fee:	.75%	
Actual Fees:	Mgt: 0.75%	Dist: —
Expense Projections:	3Yr: $322	5Yr: $558 10Yr: $1236
Avg Brok Commission:	—	Income Distrib: Quarterly
Total Cost (relative to category):		—

Columbia Small Cap

Ticker	Load	NAV	Yield	Total Assets	Mstar Category
CMSCX	None	$22.20	0.0%	$488.6 mil	Small Growth

Prospectus Objective: Small Company

Columbia Small Cap Fund seeks capital appreciation.

The fund normally invests at least 65% of assets in common stocks or securities convertible into common stocks issued by companies with market capitalizations of less than $1 billion. It may invest the balance in securities issued by larger companies. The fund may also invest in preferred stocks and debt securities that are convertible or exchangeable into small-cap stocks. It may purchase up to 25% of assets in foreign securities, including American depositary receipts.

Historical Profile
Return High
Risk Above Avg
Rating ★★★★ Above Avg

Investment Style Equity — Average Stock %: 99% (1996), 100% (1997), 93% (1998), 93% (1999), 90% (2000), 100% (12-01)

▼ Manager Change
▽ Partial Manager Change

Fund Performance vs. Category Average
■ Quarterly Fund Return +/– Category Average
— Category Baseline

Performance Quartile (within Category)

Portfolio Manager(s)

Richard J. Johnson, CFA. Since 10-96. MBA UCLA; '80 Occidental C. Other funds currently managed: Columbia Special, CMC Small Cap, CMC Small/Mid Cap.

1990	1991	1992	1993	1994	1995	1996	1997	1998	1999	2000	12-01	History
—	—	—	—	—	—	12.99	16.65	17.43	27.26	25.87	22.20	NAV
—	—	—	—	—	—	7.62*	34.10	4.69	59.32	5.85	–14.19	Total Return %
—	—	—	—	—	—	–0.43*	0.75	–23.88	38.28	14.96	–2.31	+/– S&P 500
—	—	—	—	—	—	—	21.16	3.46	16.24	28.29	–4.95	+/– Russ 2000 Grth
—	—	—	—	—	—	0.00	0.00	0.00	0.00	0.00	0.00	Income Return %
—	—	—	—	—	—	7.62	34.10	4.69	59.32	5.85	–14.19	Capital Return %
—	—	—	—	—	—	—	5	41	41	27	63	Total Rtn % Rank Cat
—	—	—	—	—	—	0.00	0.00	0.00	0.00	0.00	0.00	Income $
—	—	—	—	—	—	0.00	0.77	0.00	0.50	3.04	0.00	Capital Gains $
—	—	—	—	—	—	1.61	1.46	1.34	1.30	1.22	—	Expense Ratio %
—	—	—	—	—	—	0.00	–0.81	–0.68	–0.84	–0.44	—	Income Ratio %
—	—	—	—	—	—	33	172	158	188	145	—	Turnover Rate %
—	—	—	—	—	—	21.1	96.4	160.5	290.4	519.0	—	Net Assets $mil

Performance 12-31-01

	1st Qtr	2nd Qtr	3rd Qtr	4th Qtr	Total
1997	–5.00	19.77	22.67	–3.92	34.10
1998	12.67	–3.36	–18.20	17.54	4.69
1999	–9.47	14.64	2.05	50.43	59.32
2000	22.93	–3.97	–1.12	–9.32	5.85
2001	–17.51	14.25	–25.64	22.45	–14.19

Trailing	Total Return%	+/– S&P 500	+/– Russ 2000 Grth	% Rank All	% Rank Cat	Growth of $10,000
3 Mo	22.45	11.76	–3.72	10	56	12,245
6 Mo	–8.94	–3.39	0.32	81	68	9,106
1 Yr	–14.19	–2.31	–4.95	70	63	8,581
3 Yr Avg	13.11	14.14	12.87	7	29	14,472
5 Yr Avg	15.23	4.53	12.37	4	18	20,319
10 Yr Avg	—	—	—	—	—	—
15 Yr Avg	—	—	—	—	—	—

Tax Analysis	Tax-Adj Ret%	%Rank Cat	%Pretax Ret	%Rank Cat
3 Yr Avg	11.52	25	87.8	28
5 Yr Avg	13.85	14	90.9	15
10 Yr Avg	—	—	—	—

Potential Capital Gain Exposure: 1% of assets

Risk Analysis

Time Period	Load-Adj Return %	Risk %Rank[1] All	Risk %Rank[1] Cat	Morningstar Return	Morningstar Risk	Morningstar Risk-Adj Rating
1 Yr	–14.19					
3 Yr	13.11	87	38	1.87[2]	1.32	★★★★
5 Yr	15.23	87	29	2.71[2]	1.37	★★★★
Incept	16.06	—	—	—	—	

Average Historical Rating (28 months): 4.0★s

[1]1=low, 100=high [2] T-Bill return substituted for category avg.

Category Rating (3 Yr): 4 (1 Worst – 5 Best)

Return Above Avg
Risk Average

Other Measures	Standard Index S&P 500	Best Fit Index Wil 4500
Alpha	19.4	13.3
Beta	1.17	1.10
R–Squared	36	87
Standard Deviation		39.20
Mean		13.11
Sharpe Ratio		0.24

Portfolio Analysis 11-30-01

Share change since 10-01 Total Stocks: 128

Holding	Sector	PE	YTD Ret%	% Assets
⊕ Davita	Health	18.3	42.77	2.58
⊕ Stericycle	Services	60.3	59.69	2.30
⊕ Sepracor	Health	—	–28.70	2.28
⊕ Zale	Retail	12.5	44.10	1.85
⊕ Sylvan Learning Sys	Services	39.4	48.99	1.83
⊕ First Health Grp	Health	25.8	6.26	1.80
⊕ Biovail Corporation Intl	Health	NMF	44.82	1.79
⊕ Retek	Technology	—	22.54	1.69
⊕ Caremark Rx	Health	46.6	20.25	1.67
⊕ Outback Steakhouse	Services	20.4	32.37	1.62
⊕ Lamar Advertising Cl A	Services	—	9.71	1.59
⊕ Priority Healthcare Cl B	Health	61.7	–13.70	1.53
⊕ Entercom Comms	Services	NMF	45.19	1.45
⊕ Michaels Stores	Retail	29.3	148.60	1.39
⊕ Lattice Semicon	Technology	—	11.95	1.33
⊕ Transkaryotic Therapies	Health	—	17.46	1.33
⊖ Precise Software Solutions	Technology	—	–16.50	1.29
⊕ Amphenol	Technology	20.5	22.61	1.20
⊕ Neurocrine Biosciences	Health	—	54.90	1.17
⊕ Quintiles Transnational	Health	—	–23.20	1.15
⊕ Education Mgmt	Services	39.0	1.40	1.14
⊕ Pharmaceutical Resources	Health	NMF	387.10	1.12
⊕ Wilson Greatbatch Tech	Durables	—	27.79	1.09
⊕ Alkermes	Health	—	–15.90	1.08
⊕ Radio One Cl D	Services	—	—	1.08

Current Investment Style — Style: Value Blnd Growth; Size: Large Med Small (Small Growth)

	Stock Port Avg	Relative S&P 500 Current	Relative S&P 500 Hist	Rel Cat
Price/Earnings Ratio	34.9	1.13	1.12	1.09
Price/Book Ratio	5.9	1.04	0.84	1.22
Price/Cash Flow	24.8	1.38	1.16	1.12
3 Yr Earnings Growth	26.3[1]	1.80	—	1.04
1 Yr Earnings Est%	11.5[1]	—	—	1.49
Med Mkt Cap $mil	1,386	0.0	0.0	1.33

[1]figure is based on 50% or less of stocks

Special Securities % assets 11-30-01	
Restricted/Illiquid Secs	0
Emerging–Markets Secs	1
Options/Futures/Warrants	No

Composition % assets 11-30-01	
Cash	0.0
Stocks*	100.0
Bonds	0.0
Other	0.0
*Foreign (% stocks)	7.5

Market Cap	
Giant	0.0
Large	0.0
Medium	48.6
Small	50.3
Micro	1.1

Sector Weightings	% of Stocks	Rel S&P	5-Year High	5-Year Low
Utilities	0.5	0.2	—	—
Energy	0.7	0.1	—	—
Financials	3.2	0.2	—	—
Industrials	3.8	0.3	—	—
Durables	1.9	1.2	—	—
Staples	0.0	0.0	—	—
Services	24.9	2.3	—	—
Retail	5.3	0.8	—	—
Health	32.2	2.2	—	—
Technology	27.5	1.5	—	—

Analysis by Kelli Stebel 12-10-01

This fund deserves more attention that it has gotten.

Columbia Small Cap isn't as well-known as some of the entrants in the small-cap growth category. Its solid record should turn investors' heads, though. Since its inception in October 1996, the fund has outpaced its average peer by more than 5 percentage points annually. Manager Rick Johnson's moderate approach focuses on firms with solid fundamentals, and that's helped him avoid many landmines during the past 20 uncertain months, as the past 20 months have made or broken most funds.

It's worth noting that the fund hasn't been completely immune to blowups recently. It's still down 16% for the year to date through Dec. 7, which is a bit more than its typical peer's 10% drop. Stock picks like Wind River Systems dropped precipitously after Johnson purchased them. When he finally cut the ties at Wind River, the stock jumped during the recent growth rally. Wary of valuations, Johnson has also been holding about 10% in cash these days. That's been a hindrance lately as growth stocks rebounded smartly during October and November.

Even with growth stocks showing signs of life, Johnson says he's not making any big moves these days. That's not altogether surprising, as Johnson strictly adheres to his valuation-conscious approach. He's added a few biotech stocks, like Sepracor, which he likes for its solid revenue stream. But while many of his competitors are adding tech stocks, Johnson has been trimming tech holdings like software-maker Retek, thinking that tech stocks have run up too fast given their shaky outlooks recently.

Given Johnson's attention to valuation, the fund's solid risk/reward profile makes it a good choice for those who want to avoid some of this category's dicier options.

Address:	1301 SW Fifth Avenue P.O. Box 1350 Portland, OR 97207–1350 800–547–1707 / 503–222–3606
Web Address:	www.columbiafunds.com
*Inception:	10-01-96
Advisor:	Columbia Funds Mgmt.
Subadvisor:	None
NTF Plans:	Fidelity Inst. , Waterhouse

Minimum Purchase:	$2000	Add: $100 IRA: $2000
Min Auto Inv Plan:	$50	Add: $50
Sales Fees:	No–load	
Management Fee:	1.0%	
Actual Fees:	Mgt: 1.00%	Dist: —
Expense Projections:	3Yr: $425	5Yr: $734 10Yr: $1613
Avg Brok Commission:	—	Income Distrib: Annually
Total Cost (relative to category):	—	

CS Warburg Pincus Japan Growth Comm

Ticker	Load	NAV	Yield	Total Assets	Mstar Category
WPJGX	12b–1 only	$5.21	0.0%	$53.5 mil	Japan Stock

Prospectus Objective: Pacific Stock

Credit Suisse Warburg Pincus Japan Growth Fund seeks long-term capital growth.

The fund invests at least 65% of assets in common and preferred stocks, convertible securities, and American depositary receipts of Japanese issuers. It may invest in companies of any size that management believes present attractive opportunities for growth. The fund may invest the remaining assets only in securities of other Asian issuers. It may hedge part or all of its exposure to the Japanese yen. This fund is non-diversified.

Advisor shares are designed for institutional investors; Common shares may be purchased directly by individuals. Past fund names: Warburg Pincus Advisor Japan Growth Fund and CS Warburg Pincus Japan Growth.

Historical Profile

Return: Below Avg
Risk: High
Rating: ★★ Below Avg

Investment Style
Equity
Average Stock %: 97% 90% 98% 95% 100% 97%

▼ Manager Change
▽ Partial Manager Change

Fund Performance vs. Category Average
■ Quarterly Fund Return +/– Category Average
— Category Baseline

Performance Quartile (within Category)

Portfolio Manager(s)

Management Team

1990	1991	1992	1993	1994	1995	1996	1997	1998	1999	2000	12-01	History
—	—	—	—	—	10.00	9.21	9.35	9.47	34.53	6.96	5.21	NAV
—	—	—	—	—	—	–5.49	1.52	1.28	266.10	–68.70	–25.14	Total Return %
—	—	—	—	—	—	–28.44	–31.83	–27.29	245.06	–59.60	–13.27	+/– S&P 500
—	—	—	—	—	—	10.01	25.19	–3.77	204.57	–40.54	—	+/– MSCI Japan
—	—	—	—	—	0.00	2.45	0.00	0.00	0.00	0.00	0.00	Income Return %
—	—	—	—	—	0.00	–7.95	1.52	1.28	266.10	–68.70	–25.14	Capital Return %
—	—	—	—	—	—	18	4	80	5	91	19	Total Rtn % Rank Cat
—	—	—	—	—	0.00	0.25	0.00	0.00	0.00	0.00	0.00	Income $
—	—	—	—	—	0.00	0.00	0.00	0.00	0.11	5.65	0.00	Capital Gains $
—	—	—	—	—	—	1.75	1.75	1.75	1.76	1.38	—	Expense Ratio %
—	—	—	—	—	—	–1.03	–1.03	–0.76	–1.32	–1.41	—	Income Ratio %
—	—	—	—	—	—	—	94	76	171	118	—	Turnover Rate %
—	—	—	—	—	—	17.5	26.6	52.8	835.9	104.2	52.5	Net Assets $mil

Performance 12-31-01

	1st Qtr	2nd Qtr	3rd Qtr	4th Qtr	Total
1997	–1.74	21.99	–3.53	–12.21	1.52
1998	5.56	1.62	–9.07	3.84	1.28
1999	27.35	40.46	34.77	51.86	266.10
2000	–17.84	–29.50	–13.94	–37.21	–68.70
2001	2.87	–6.98	–35.59	21.45	–25.14

Trailing	Total Return%	+/– S&P 500	+/– MSCI Japan	% Rank All	% Rank Cat	Growth of $10,000
3 Mo	21.45	10.76	—	11	4	12,145
6 Mo	–21.77	–16.22	—	99	23	7,823
1 Yr	–25.14	–13.27	—	88	19	7,486
3 Yr Avg	–4.99	–3.96	—	92	62	8,577
5 Yr Avg	–2.48	–13.18	—	96	28	8,819
10 Yr Avg	—	—	—	—	—	—
15 Yr Avg	—	—	—	—	—	—

Tax Analysis	Tax-Adj Ret%	%Rank Cat	%Pretax Ret	%Rank Cat
3 Yr Avg	–8.85	77	—	—
5 Yr Avg	–4.88	42	—	—
10 Yr Avg	—	—	—	—

Potential Capital Gain Exposure: –79% of assets

Risk Analysis

Time Period	Load-Adj Return %	Risk %Rank[1] All	Risk %Rank[1] Cat	Morningstar Return	Morningstar Risk	Morningstar Risk-Adj Rating
1 Yr	–25.14					
3 Yr	–4.99	99	92	–1.91[2]	2.24	★
5 Yr	–2.48	98	85	–1.42[2]	1.77	★★
Incept	–2.99	—	—	—	—	

Average Historical Rating (37 months): 3.3★s

[1] 1=low, 100=high [2] T-Bill return substituted for category avg.

Category Rating (3 Yr)

1 2 3 4 5
Worst Best

Return: Average
Risk: Above Avg

Other Measures	Standard Index S&P 500	Best Fit Index MSCIPacNdD
Alpha	7.5	14.1
Beta	1.50	1.73
R-Squared	30	57

Standard Deviation	50.66
Mean	–4.99
Sharpe Ratio	–0.23

Portfolio Analysis 11-30-01

Share change since 10-01 Total Stocks: 34	Sector	Country	% Assets
Intelligent Wave	N/A	N/A	5.26
Orix	Financials	Japan	4.98
Kyocera	Technology	Japan	4.15
Nintendo	Durables	Japan	4.14
Tokyo Electron	Technology	Japan	4.14
Sony	Durables	Japan	4.12
Disco Japan	Industrials	Japan	4.08
Sega Enterprises	Durables	Japan	4.05
Trans Cosmos	Technology	Japan	3.91
Konami	Technology	Japan	3.80
Rohm	Technology	Japan	3.78
Nomura Secs	Financials	Japan	3.76
Softbank	Financials	Japan	3.69
Trend Micro	Technology	Japan	3.15
⊕ NTT DoCoMo	Services	Japan	3.11
Tokyo Seimitsu	Durables	Japan	3.09
Daiwa Secs Grp	Financials	Japan	3.06
Murata Mfg	Technology	Japan	2.99
Furukawa Elec	Industrials	Japan	2.96
☼ Dentsu Tec	Services	Japan	2.75

Current Investment Style

Style: Value Blnd Growth; Size: Large Med Small

	Stock Port Avg	Rel MSCI EAFE Current	Rel MSCI EAFE Hist	Rel Cat
Price/Earnings Ratio	32.9	1.27	1.45	1.02
Price/Cash Flow	17.0	1.33	1.61	1.22
Price/Book Ratio	3.8	1.09	0.93	1.48
3 Yr Earnings Growth	28.4	1.52	0.42	1.66
Med Mkt Cap $mil	4,996	0.2	0.4	0.67

Country Exposure 11-30-01	% assets
Japan	90
Hong Kong	1

Hedging History: —

Sector Weightings	% of Stocks	Rel Cat	5-Year High	5-Year Low
Utilities	0.0	0.0	2	0
Energy	0.0	0.0	1	0
Financials	20.4	1.4	36	12
Industrials	17.1	0.8	34	0
Durables	19.7	1.4	28	7
Staples	2.6	0.8	4	0
Services	10.2	0.9	13	0
Retail	0.0	0.0	12	0
Health	0.0	0.0	14	0
Technology	30.0	1.7	52	21

Special Securities % assets 11-30-01	
Restricted/Illiquid Secs	0
Emerging-Markets Secs	1
Options/Futures/Warrants	No

Composition % assets 11-30-01			
Cash	3.6	Bonds	0.0
Stocks	96.1	Other	0.3

Analysis by Gregg Wolper 12-01-01

With Credit Suisse Warburg Pincus Japan Growth Fund, the potential risks, as well as the possible rewards, are right out front.

This fund not only concentrates on just one market—a risky mandate even when that market is a big one—but consistently targets the more growth-oriented areas of that market, which has led to large weightings in technology and Internet-related shares. That makeup has made the fund extraordinarily volatile, for better and for worse. When its favorite stocks are climbing, it can reach incredible heights, as its 266% gain in 1999 clearly demonstrated. But when Japan's Internet and technology shares collapsed beginning in early 2000; this fund was crushed. It lost 69% that year and another 31% in the first 10 months of 2001 (landing in the category's bottom decile for both periods), before rebounding a bit in recent weeks.

Manager Nick Edwards freely concedes that he and comanager Todd Jacobson were too optimistic about the prospects for a rebound in the tech sector, and were also overly positive on the chances for fairly rapid passage of needed legislative reforms. But Edwards remains confident that tech is the place to be. He says that the field still has strong long-term growth prospects and that a disproportionate number of the high-quality companies in Japan lie in the technology area. Thus, when prices fell further after Sept. 11, he and Jacobson bought shares of tech firms Tokyo Electron and Murata Manufacturing, as well as of automakers Honda and Toyota. These picks have jumped in the past two months, helping the fund's year-to-date return through Nov. 30 get near the category's middle.

This fund is thus the best choice for those wishing to play Japan's technology sector and other growth-oriented names—with high risk coming as part of the bargain. It's not an appropriate fund for anyone else.

Address:	466 Lexington Avenue New York, NY 10017–3147 800–927–2874 / 800–927–2874
Web Address:	www.csam.com
*Inception:	12-29-95
Advisor:	Credit Suisse Asset Mgmt.
Subadvisor:	None
NTF Plans:	Fidelity , Datalynx

Minimum Purchase:	$2500	Add: $100 IRA: $500
Min Auto Inv Plan:	$2500	Add: $50
Sales Fees:	0.25%B, 2.00%R within 6 months	
Management Fee:	1.3%, .22%A	
Actual Fees:	Mgt: 0.82%	Dist: 0.25%
Expense Projections:	3Yr: $685	5Yr: $1175 10Yr: $2524
Avg Brok Commission:	—	Income Distrib: Annually
Total Cost (relative to category):	Average	

Davis Convertible Securities A

Ticker	Load	NAV	Yield	Total Assets	Mstar Category
RPFCX	4.75%	$21.36	3.7%	$180.3 mil	Convertible

Prospectus Objective: Convertible Bond

Davis Convertible Securities Fund seeks current income and capital appreciation.

The fund normally invests at least 65% of assets in convertible securities. It may invest the balance of assets in other securities, including common and preferred stocks, corporate and U.S. government debt securities, and money-market instruments. The fund may invest up to 35% of assets in debt securities rated below investment-grade.

Class A shares have front loads; B shares have deferred loads, higher 12b-1 fees, and conversion features; C shares have level loads. Prior to Oct. 1, 1995, the fund was named Retirement Planning Funds of America Convertible Securities Fund.

Historical Profile
Return: Below Avg
Risk: Below Avg
Rating: ★★ Below Avg

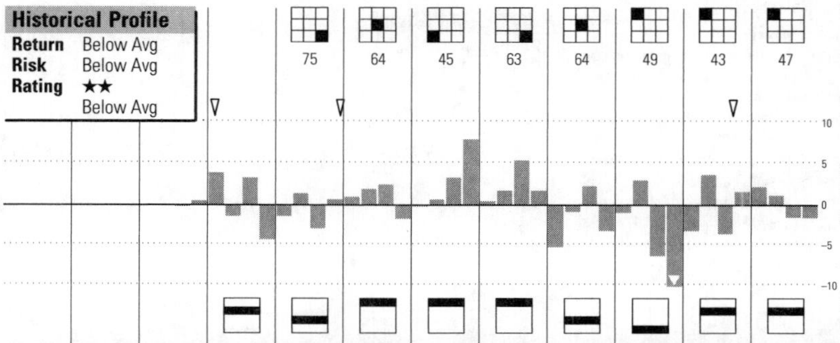

Investment Style
Equity
Average Stock %

1993	1994	1995	1996	1997	1998	1999	2000	12-01
75	64	45	63	64	49	43	47	

▼ Manager Change
▽ Partial Manager Change

Fund Performance vs. Category Average
■ Quarterly Fund Return +/– Category Average
— Category Baseline

Performance Quartile (within Category)

Portfolio Manager(s)

Andrew A. Davis. Since 2-93. BA Colby C. Other funds currently managed: Davis Real Estate A, Davis Convertible Securities B, Davis Real Estate B.

Jason Voss, CFA. Since 9-00. MBA U. of Colorado. Other funds currently managed: Davis Convertible Securities B, Davis Convertible Securities Y, Davis Convertible Securities C.

1990	1991	1992	1993	1994	1995	1996	1997	1998	1999	2000	12-01	History
—	—	15.73	17.45	15.57	18.22	21.22	25.26	23.76	25.21	23.96	21.36	NAV
—	—	12.98*	17.26	–6.72	26.68	29.46	28.69	–1.80	12.97	–0.97	–7.56	Total Return %
—	—	5.10*	7.20	–8.03	–10.85	6.51	–4.67	–30.37	–8.07	8.13	4.32	+/– S&P 500
—	—	5.10	–1.30	–2.00	3.49	17.55	12.03	–13.46	–20.54	5.19	–1.68	+/– Conv.Bond Idx
—	—	2.91	4.32	3.33	4.30	4.06	3.53	3.08	3.30	3.42	3.34	Income Return %
—	—	10.08	12.94	–10.05	22.38	25.39	25.15	–4.88	9.67	–4.39	–10.90	Capital Return %
—	—	—	36	70	10	1	2	72	86	46	44	Total Rtn % Rank Cat
—	—	0.40	0.67	0.57	0.66	0.73	0.74	0.77	0.77	0.85	0.79	Income $
—	—	0.00	0.30	0.15	0.78	1.54	1.22	0.27	0.77	0.19	0.00	Capital Gains $
—	—	1.35	1.21	1.20	1.14	1.05	1.07	1.16	1.12	1.07	—	Expense Ratio %
—	—	4.94	3.89	4.06	3.87	3.34	3.00	3.27	2.99	3.02	—	Income Ratio %
—	—	—	62	45	54	43	24	14	33	25	—	Turnover Rate %
—	—	24.3	44.7	47.8	59.8	42.8	89.8	133.6	117.3	102.7	89.1	Net Assets $mil

Performance 12-31-01

	1st Qtr	2nd Qtr	3rd Qtr	4th Qtr	Total
1997	1.27	10.71	14.33	0.39	28.69
1998	2.30	–1.99	–9.15	7.82	–1.80
1999	1.73	11.23	–7.98	8.50	12.97
2000	6.90	0.74	–0.90	–7.21	–0.97
2001	–5.38	4.77	–13.20	7.43	–7.56

Trailing	Total Return%	+/– S&P 500	+/– Conv Bond Index	% Rank All	% Rank Cat	Growth of $10,000
3 Mo	7.43	–3.25	–0.72	54	64	10,743
6 Mo	–6.75	–1.19	–4.09	73	82	9,325
1 Yr	–7.56	4.32	–1.68	56	44	9,244
3 Yr Avg	1.13	2.15	–4.52	67	86	10,342
5 Yr Avg	5.50	–5.20	–3.46	55	75	13,069
10 Yr Avg	—	—	—	—	—	—
15 Yr Avg	—	—	—	—	—	—

Tax Analysis	Tax-Adj Ret%	%Rank Cat	%Pretax Ret	%Rank Cat
3 Yr Avg	–0.66	82	—	—
5 Yr Avg	3.39	68	61.7	57
10 Yr Avg	—	—	—	—

Potential Capital Gain Exposure: –3% of assets

Risk Analysis

Time Period	Load-Adj Return %	Risk %Rank[1] All	Risk %Rank[1] Cat	Morningstar Return	Morningstar Risk	Morningstar Risk-Adj Rating
1 Yr	–11.95					
3 Yr	–0.50	51	47	–1.10[2]	0.71	★★★
5 Yr	4.48	50	52	–0.12[2]	0.69	★★
Incept	10.04	—	—	—	—	

Average Historical Rating (81 months): 2.9★s

[1] 1=low, 100=high [2] T-Bill return substituted for category avg.

Category Rating (3 Yr)

1 2 3 4 5
Worst Best

Return: Below Avg
Risk: Average

Other Measures	Standard Index S&P 500	Best Fit Index SPMid400
Alpha	0.2	–6.8
Beta	0.66	0.64
R-Squared	61	75

Standard Deviation	14.38
Mean	1.13
Sharpe Ratio	–0.31

Portfolio Analysis 08-31-01

Total Fixed-Income: 22	Date of Maturity	Amount $000	Value $000	% Net Assets
Vornado Realty Tr		305	12,242	6.24
Kerr–McGee FRN	12-31-04	264	11,670	5.94
EOP Operating 7.25%		9,500	10,284	5.24
Sealed Air A Cv Pfd $2.00		243	10,277	5.24
General Growth Cv Pfd 7.25%		400	10,200	5.20
Exchangeable Ctfs		10,600	9,408	4.79
SL Green Rlty Cv Pfd 8%		240	7,591	3.87
American Tower Cl A		7,800	7,274	3.71
Citigroup		152	6,937	3.53
American Intl Grp FRN	05-15-07	6,095	5,958	3.04
Equity Residentl E Cv Pfd 7%		172	5,617	2.86
Reckson Assoc Cv Pfd 7.625%		230	5,197	2.65
Six Flags		201	5,025	2.56
News ADR		152	4,961	2.53
AES Tr Cv FRN	12-31-29	85	4,669	2.38
Hewlett–Packard Cv 0%	10-14-17	8,199	4,151	2.11
Texas Instruments		120	3,957	2.02
Costco Cv 0%	08-19-17	4,500	3,949	2.01
Kmart Financing Cv Pfd 7.75%		89	3,914	1.99
Premier Parks		231	3,837	1.95
Burr–Brown		3,400	3,812	1.94
Can Natl Railway Cv Pfd 5.25%		63	3,783	1.93
SAP ADR		103	3,552	1.81
Crown Castle Intl		145	3,452	1.76
CenterPoint Properties		58	2,835	1.44

Investment Style

Avg Eff Maturity	—
Avg Credit Quality	BBB
Avg Wtd Coupon	3.88%
Avg Wtd Price	86.75% of par
Avg Conversion Premium	20%

Coupon Range	% of Bonds	Rel Cat
0%	36.5	3.62
0% to 7%	25.2	.31
7% to 8.5%	38.3	4.89
8.5% to 10%	0.0	0.00
More than 10%	0.0	0.00

1.00 = Category Average

Special Securities of assets 08-31-01

Restricted/Illiquid Secs	1
Emerging–Markets Secs	0
Options/Futures/Warrants	No

Composition % assets 08-31-01

Cash	4.6
Stocks	39.0
Bonds	16.6
Convertibles	38.8
Other	1.1

Credit Breakdown % bonds 09-30-01

US Govt	0	BB	1
AAA	29	B	24
AA	0	Below B	3
A	21	NR/NA	3
BBB	19		

Country Exposure % assets

NA

Sector Breakdown % bonds 08-31-01

US Treasuries	0	CMOs	0
GNMA mtgs	0	ARMs	0
FNMA mtgs	0	Other	100
FHLMC mtgs	0		

Analysis by William Harding 09-06-01

Investors need to look under the hood to see Davis Convertible Securities Fund's real appeal.

Some convertible investors might be put off at first by the fund's unorthodox makeup. About 30% of the fund's assets are devoted to common stocks, with the remainder in preferred stocks and convertible bonds. That equity weighting, however, isn't as gutsy as it appears. Most of it is dedicated to REITs, which offer high yields and are generally less volatile than stocks. (The fund's fondness for REITs isn't shocking since lead manager Andrew Davis also runs Davis Real Estate.) Indeed, the fund's volatility has been well below the group's norm.

The fund's strategy has worked fairly well for it this year: Its 5% loss for the year to date ended Sept. 3, 2001, compares favorably with other convertible funds and to the equity market in general. The fund has had a couple of disappointments, such as top-10 holding American Tower, but its value-oriented picks in the real estate, energy, and financials areas have held up fairly well. Furthermore, management's valuation discipline led it to steer clear of the racy tech and biotech issues that flooded the convertible market in 1999 and 2000 and have since crashed.

The fund's value-based approach will cause it to lag in growth rallies. It thus trailed its typical peer by significant margins in 1998 and 1999's tech-dominated markets. Still, the fund's trailing three-year return is slightly above the category's average, and it posted some of the best returns in the group from 1995 through 1997. In Davis, it also has a seasoned manager at the helm who owns a big stake of the fund and, as a member of the family that owns the advisor, is likely to be on board for years to come. Put that together with its solid returns and reasonable volatility, and you have an attractive package for convertibles investors.

Address:	2949 E. Elvira Rd. Ste 101 Tucson, AZ 85706 800–279–0279 / 800–279–0279
Web Address:	www.davisfunds.com
*Inception:	05-01-92
Advisor:	Davis Selected Advisers
Subadvisor:	Davis Selected Advisers – NY
NTF Plans:	Datalynx , Fidelity Inst.

Minimum Purchase:	$1000	Add: $25	IRA: $250
Min Auto Inv Plan:	$1000	Add: $25	
Sales Fees:	4.75%L, 0.25%B		
Management Fee:	.75% mx./.55% mn.		
Actual Fees:	Mgt: 0.75%	Dist: 0.14%	
Expense Projections:	3Yr: $799	5Yr: $1037	10Yr: $1719
Avg Brok Commission:	—	Income Distrib: Quarterly	
Total Cost (relative to category):		Average	

Davis Financial A

Ticker	Load	NAV	Yield	Total Assets	Mstar Category
RPFGX	4.75%	$32.98	0.0%	$1,184.8 mil	Spec Financials

Prospectus Objective: Specialty—Financial

Davis Financial Fund seeks capital growth.

The fund invests primarily in common stocks and other equity securities concentrated in the banking and financial-services industries. It generally invests a minimum of 25% of assets in each of these two industries. It may also invest in securities of foreign issuers.

Class A shares have front loads; B shares have deferred loads, higher 12b-1 fees, and conversion features; C shares have level loads. Prior to Dec. 1, 1994, the fund was named Retirement Planning Funds of America Global Value Fund. After Oct. 1, 1995, it was named Retirement Planning Funds of America Financial Value Fund.

Historical Profile

Return Above Avg
Risk Average
Rating ★★★★ Above Avg

Investment Style
Equity
Average Stock %: 98% 97% 87% 97% 100% 99% 99%

▼ Manager Change
▽ Partial Manager Change

Fund Performance vs. Category Average
■ Quarterly Fund Return +/– Category Average
— Category Baseline

Performance Quartile (within Category)

1990	1991	1992	1993	1994	1995	1996	1997	1998	1999	2000	12-01	History
—	8.76	11.20	11.73	10.68	14.50	18.06	25.68	29.32	29.07	36.30	32.98	NAV
—	23.31*	32.60	15.17	–4.80	50.51	31.50	44.53	14.17	–0.85	32.16	–9.13	Total Return %
—	11.13*	24.98	5.11	–6.11	12.98	8.55	11.18	–14.40	–21.89	41.26	2.74	+/– S&P 500
—	—	23.63	3.89	–4.73	14.06	10.30	13.24	–9.25	–24.41	43.09	1.76	+/– Wilshire 5000
—	0.25	0.57	0.72	0.77	0.66	1.03	0.69	0.00	0.00	0.00	0.01	Income Return %
—	23.05	32.03	14.45	–5.56	49.85	30.46	43.84	14.17	–0.85	32.16	–9.15	Capital Return %
—	—	61	40	80	5	27	51	13	41	22	79	Total Rtn % Rank Cat
—	0.02	0.05	0.08	0.09	0.07	0.15	0.13	0.00	0.00	0.00	0.00	Income $
—	0.04	0.35	1.08	0.40	1.50	0.87	0.30	0.00	0.00	1.93	0.00	Capital Gains $
—	2.49	1.68	1.32	1.24	1.18	1.15	1.07	1.06	1.04	1.05	—	Expense Ratio %
—	0.51	0.43	0.57	0.67	0.53	0.92	0.77	0.34	0.36	–0.21	—	Income Ratio %
—	—	50	70	44	42	26	6	11	18	35	—	Turnover Rate %
—	9.2	31.6	50.8	57.6	79.9	107.6	287.8	460.7	425.2	632.8	600.4	Net Assets $mil

Portfolio Manager(s)

Christopher C. Davis. Since 5-91. MA'87 U. of St. Andrews. Other funds currently managed: Davis NY Venture A, Davis Growth Opportunity B, Selected American.

Kenneth C. Feinberg. Since 5-97. BA'79 Johns Hopkins U.; MBA'85 Columbia U. Other funds currently managed: Davis NY Venture A, Davis Growth Opportunity B, Selected American.

Performance 12-31-01

	1st Qtr	2nd Qtr	3rd Qtr	4th Qtr	Total
1997	4.21	17.11	10.89	6.80	44.53
1998	8.22	4.50	–15.94	20.11	14.17
1999	2.76	6.24	–13.31	4.76	–0.85
2000	4.30	2.97	18.16	4.14	32.16
2001	–10.66	9.31	–16.30	11.17	–9.13

Trailing	Total Return%	+/– S&P 500	+/– Wil 5000	% Rank All	% Rank Cat	Growth of $10,000
3 Mo	11.17	0.49	–1.20	36	12	11,117
6 Mo	–6.95	–1.40	–1.47	74	83	9,305
1 Yr	–9.13	2.74	1.76	59	79	9,087
3 Yr Avg	5.99	7.01	6.64	22	46	11,906
5 Yr Avg	14.46	3.76	4.76	5	25	19,647
10 Yr Avg	18.91	5.99	6.63	1	30	56,534
15 Yr Avg	—	—	—	—	—	—

Tax Analysis	Tax-Adj Ret%	%Rank Cat	%Pretax Ret	%Rank Cat
3 Yr Avg	5.60	42	93.4	29
5 Yr Avg	14.06	18	97.2	3
10 Yr Avg	17.22	15	91.0	7

Potential Capital Gain Exposure: 26% of assets

Risk Analysis

Time Period	Load-Adj Return %	Risk %Rank[1] All	Risk %Rank[1] Cat	Morningstar Return	Morningstar Risk	Morningstar Risk-Adj Rating
1 Yr	–13.45					
3 Yr	4.28	71	62	–0.14[2]	0.97	★★★
5 Yr	13.35	71	23	2.13[2]	0.96	★★★★
10 Yr	18.34	74	25	2.76	0.96	★★★★★

Average Historical Rating (93 months): 4.4★s

[1]1=low, 100=high [2] T-Bill return substituted for category avg.

Category Rating (3 Yr)

1 2 3 4 5
Worst Best

Return Average
Risk Average

Other Measures	Standard Index S&P 500	Best Fit Index S&P 500
Alpha	7.7	7.7
Beta	0.92	0.92
R-Squared	51	51
Standard Deviation		23.73
Mean		5.99
Sharpe Ratio		0.05

Analysis by Brian Portnoy 12-04-01

Davis Financial has long benefited from its convictions, but 2001's a different story.

This just isn't managers Ken Feinberg and Chris Davis' year. Their sizable commitment to American Express, which they have owned since 1995 and still consider to be one of the best-managed financial-services firms in the industry, has stung badly. Its credit-card, asset-management, and travel businesses have taken their lumps, and the stock is off 40% so far this year. Even more damaging has been the fund's big stake in Providian Financial, whose stock has been decimated due to its focus on the subprime-lending market in a recessionary economy and a number of poor management decisions. Some nonfinancial holdings, especially Tellabs, have also hurt badly. For the year to date through Dec. 3, 2001, the fund has lost nearly 13% of its value and trails three fourths of its specialty-financial rivals.

The contrast between this year's performance and the fund's historical showing is striking. Indeed, Feinberg and Davis have earned—and still maintain—one of the group's best records. Not only do the fund's long-term gains best most of the competition, but also its risk scores are very good. Such a record owes to the strength of management's stock selection more than to a tame portfolio. After all, the fund's compact portfolio of fewer than 40 names and a willingness to park more than 50% of assets in the top-10 holdings invite a lot of volatility. But over time, the fund has found plenty of winners, frequently from the consumer-finance industry, and relatively few dogs.

This year, of course, for once shows how a big devotion to a few issues, such as American Express, can take its toll. But the fund's solid risk/reward profile, low expenses, and high tax efficiency still recommend it as one of the category's finer choices.

Portfolio Analysis 08-31-01

Share chng since 07-01 Total Stocks: 38

	Subsector	PE	YTD Ret%	% Assets
Transatlantic Hldgs	Insurance	75.8	29.55	7.06
American Express	Finance/Mortg.	28.3	–34.40	7.05
Philip Morris	Staples	12.1	9.12	5.83
Tyco Intl	Industrials	27.1	6.23	5.56
Household Intl	Finance/Mortg.	14.7	6.89	5.18
Moody's	Services	33.5	56.04	4.93
⊕ Julius Baer Hldg	Foreign Banks	—	—	4.81
Dun & Bradstreet	Services	41.1	36.43	4.55
Providian Finl	Finance/Mortg.	1.4	–93.80	4.23
Berkshire Hathaway Cl A	Financials	—	—	3.49
Capital One Finl	Finance/Mortg.	19.8	–17.80	3.37
Citigroup	Insurance	20.0	0.03	3.29
Stilwell Finl	Financials	—	–30.80	3.12
Cincinnati Finl	Insurance	53.0	–1.43	3.02
Sealed Air	Industrials	27.4	33.84	2.70
Costco Wholesale	Retail	34.4	11.12	2.54
Golden West Finl	Thrifts	12.9	–12.40	2.46
Sun Life Finl Svcs	Financials	—	–17.60	2.16
American Intl Grp	Insurance	42.0	–19.20	2.09
First Data	Technology	38.1	49.08	2.08
Everest Re Grp	Insurance	17.6	–1.29	2.07
Aon	Insurance	46.1	6.32	1.86
Lexmark Intl	Technology	26.9	33.14	1.86
Loews	Financials	—	8.35	1.71
Tellabs	Phone Equip.	41.6	–73.50	1.69

Current Investment Style

Style: Value Blnd Growth; Size: Large Med Small

	Stock Port Avg	Relative S&P 500 Current	Relative S&P 500 Hist	Rel Cat
Price/Earnings Ratio	29.7	0.96	0.73	1.40
Price/Book Ratio	3.3	0.59	0.57	1.10
Price/Cash Flow	20.4[1]	1.13	0.73	1.29
3 Yr Earnings Growth	18.2	1.24	1.07	1.12
1 Yr Earnings Est%	–8.3	4.67	—	–2.66
Med Mkt Cap $mil	10,058	0.2	0.3	0.46

[1]figure is based on 50% or less of stocks

Special Securities % assets 08-31-01	
Restricted/Illiquid Secs	0
Emerging-Markets Secs	0
Options/Futures/Warrants	No

Composition % assets 08-31-01	
Cash	0.2
Stocks*	99.8
Bonds	0.0
Other	0.0
*Foreign (% stocks)	7.4

Market Cap	
Giant	28.2
Large	22.2
Medium	43.0
Small	6.2
Micro	0.4

Subsector Weightings	% of Stocks	Rel Cat
Money Ctr. Banks	0.0	0.0
Other U.S. Banks	1.5	0.1
Foreign Banks	4.8	1.3
Thrifts	2.5	0.4
Insurance	21.2	1.1
Finance/Mortg.	21.3	2.1
Broker/Inv Bank	1.6	0.3
Money Mgmt	0.0	0.0
Other	47.1	1.9

Address:	2949 E. Elvira Rd. Ste 101 Tucson, AZ 85706 800-279-0279 / 800-279-0279
Web Address:	www.davisfunds.com
*Inception:	05-01-91
Advisor:	Davis Selected Advisers
Subadvisor:	Davis Selected Advisers – NY
NTF Plans:	Datalynx , Fidelity Inst.

Minimum Purchase:	$1000	Add: $25	IRA: $250
Min Auto Inv Plan:	$1000	Add: $25	
Sales Fees:	4.75%L, 0.25%B		
Management Fee:	.75% mx./.55% mn.		
Actual Fees:	Mgt: 0.63%	Dist: 0.18%	
Expense Projections:	3Yr: $793	5Yr: $1027	10Yr: $1697
Avg Brok Commission:	—	Income Distrib: Semi-Ann.	
Total Cost (relative to category):		Below Avg	

Davis Growth Opportunity A

Ticker	Load	NAV	Yield	Total Assets	Mstar Category
RPEAX	4.75%	$16.81	0.0%	$204.3 mil	Mid-Cap Blend

Prospectus Objective: Growth

Davis Growth Opportunity Fund seeks growth of capital.

The fund invests primarily in common stocks and other equity securities. It emphasizes long-term investment, as opposed to short-term profits, when making portfolio changes, although the fund may realize short-term profits or losses.

Class A shares have front loads; B shares have deferred loads, higher 12b-1 fees, and conversion features; C shares have level loads; Y shares are for institutional investors. Prior to May 1, 1993, the fund was named Retirement Plannings Funds of America Equity Fund. After Oct. 1, 1995, the fund was named Retirement Planning Funds of America Growth Fund.

Historical Profile

Return Above Avg
Risk Above Avg
Rating ★★★ Neutral

Investment Style
Equity
Average Stock %

99% 95% 95% 93% 99% 97% 95%

▼ Manager Change
▽ Partial Manager Change

Fund Performance vs. Category Average
Quarterly Fund Return +/– Category Average
— Category Baseline

Performance Quartile (within Category)

Portfolio Manager(s)

Christopher C. Davis. Since 1-99. MA'87 U. of St. Andrews. Other funds currently managed: Davis NY Venture A, Davis Growth Opportunity B, Davis Financial A.

Kenneth C. Feinberg. Since 1-99. BA'79 Johns Hopkins U.; MBA'85 Columbia U. Other funds currently managed: Davis NY Venture A, Davis Growth Opportunity B, Davis Financial A.

1990	1991	1992	1993	1994	1995	1996	1997	1998	1999	2000	12-01	History
—	—	—	—	12.84	17.25	18.93	22.49	21.96	22.17	18.60	16.81	NAV
—	—	—	—	-2.70*	46.54	18.73	27.70	2.32	31.45	11.49	-8.06	Total Return %
—	—	—	—	-5.26*	9.00	-4.22	-5.65	-26.25	10.41	20.59	3.81	+/- S&P 500
—	—	—	—	—	15.62	-0.45	-4.55	-16.79	16.73	-6.00	-7.46	+/- S&P Mid 400
—	—	—	—	0.00	0.00	0.00	0.00	0.00	0.00	0.00	0.00	Income Return %
—	—	—	—	-2.70	46.54	18.73	27.70	2.32	31.45	11.49	-8.06	Capital Return %
—	—	—	—	—	4	60	51	65	20	35	62	Total Rtn % Rank Cat
—	—	—	—	0.00	0.00	0.00	0.00	0.00	0.00	0.00	0.00	Income $
—	—	—	—	0.57	1.55	1.56	1.68	1.03	5.65	5.68	0.28	Capital Gains $
—	—	—	—	1.42	1.51	1.48	1.27	1.32	1.29	1.19	—	Expense Ratio %
—	—	—	—	-0.08	-0.71	-0.76	-0.58	-0.38	-0.50	-0.59	—	Income Ratio %
—	—	—	—	—	30	31	19	18	100	60	—	Turnover Rate %
—	—	—	—	6.1	22.9	27.2	48.2	52.7	68.1	84.2	100.7	Net Assets $mil

Performance 12-31-01

	1st Qtr	2nd Qtr	3rd Qtr	4th Qtr	Total
1997	-0.69	18.19	25.70	-13.45	27.70
1998	13.83	-6.17	-20.44	20.42	2.32
1999	0.32	9.49	-5.38	26.48	31.45
2000	9.83	-1.97	2.18	1.34	11.49
2001	-9.03	8.10	-18.21	14.30	-8.06

Trailing	Total Return%	+/- S&P 500	+/- S&P Mid 400	% Rank All	% Rank Cat	Growth of $10,000
3 Mo	14.30	3.62	-3.68	25	66	11,430
6 Mo	-6.51	-0.95	-4.95	71	75	9,349
1 Yr	-8.06	3.81	-7.46	57	62	9,194
3 Yr Avg	10.45	11.47	0.21	10	17	13,473
5 Yr Avg	11.98	1.28	-4.14	10	32	17,605
10 Yr Avg	—	—	—	—	—	—
15 Yr Avg	—	—	—	—	—	—

Tax Analysis	Tax-Adj Ret%	%Rank Cat	%Pretax Ret	%Rank Cat
3 Yr Avg	4.32	48	41.3	91
5 Yr Avg	7.21	56	60.2	87
10 Yr Avg	—	—	—	—

Potential Capital Gain Exposure: -1% of assets

Risk Analysis

Time Period	Load-Adj Return %	Risk %Rank[1] All	Risk %Rank[1] Cat	Morningstar Return	Morningstar Risk	Morningstar Risk-Adj Rating
1 Yr	-12.43					
3 Yr	8.67	69	60	0.82[2]	0.95	★★★★
5 Yr	10.89	82	81	1.43[2]	1.17	★★★
Incept	15.86	—	—	—	—	

Average Historical Rating (50 months): 2.2★s

[1]1=low, 100=high [2] T-Bill return substituted for category avg.

Category Rating (3 Yr)

1 2 3 4 5
Worst Best

Return Above Avg
Risk Average

Other Measures	Standard Index S&P 500	Best Fit Index
Alpha	12.8	18.2
Beta	1.05	1.19
R-Squared	67	76
Standard Deviation		24.27
Mean		10.45
Sharpe Ratio		0.26

Portfolio Analysis 08-31-01

Share change since 07-01 Total Stocks: 57	Sector	PE	YTD Ret%	% Assets
Apogent Tech	Health	29.0	25.85	4.11
Golden West Finl	Financials	12.9	-12.40	3.58
Transatlantic Hldgs	Financials	75.8	29.55	3.56
Stilwell Finl	Financials	—	-30.80	3.48
Sigma-Aldrich	Industrials	20.3	1.02	3.37
Capital One Finl	Financials	19.8	-17.80	3.25
Kinder Morgan	Energy	32.2	7.11	3.16
Eli Lilly	Health	28.9	-14.40	3.09
Wm. Wrigley Jr.	Staples	32.9	8.93	2.85
WPP Grp	Services	23.2	—	2.84
Merck	Health	19.1	-35.90	2.48
Speedway Motor Sports	Services	20.9	5.33	2.36
Symantec	Technology	—	98.74	2.32
Sealed Air	Industrials	27.4	33.84	2.28
Providian Finl	Financials	1.4	-93.80	2.22
IMS Health	Technology	22.4	-27.50	2.12
Bristol-Myers Squibb	Health	20.2	-26.00	2.01
Marriott Intl Cl A	Services	20.9	-3.16	1.99
Moody's	Services	33.5	56.04	1.86
⊕ Agilent Tech	Technology	58.2	-47.90	1.81
Phillips Petro	Energy	7.1	8.56	1.80
Everest Re Grp	Financials	17.6	-1.29	1.55
Advent Software	Technology	61.7	24.68	1.54
⊕ Tellabs	Technology	41.6	-73.50	1.49
☼ Applied Matls	Technology	66.8	5.01	1.49

Current Investment Style

Style: Value Blnd Growth; Size: Large Med Small

	Stock Port Avg	Relative S&P 500 Current	Relative S&P 500 Hist	Rel Cat
Price/Earnings Ratio	28.2	0.91	0.87	1.04
Price/Book Ratio	4.3	0.75	0.82	1.00
Price/Cash Flow	18.4	1.02	0.95	1.06
3 Yr Earnings Growth	17.7	1.21	1.05	1.06
1 Yr Earnings Est%	-1.6	0.92	—	-0.71
Med Mkt Cap $mil	5,776	0.1	0.1	0.64

[1]figure is based on 50% or less of stocks

Special Securities % assets 08-31-01	
Restricted/Illiquid Secs	0
Emerging-Markets Secs	1
Options/Futures/Warrants	No

Composition % assets 08-31-01	
Cash	6.3
Stocks*	93.0
Bonds	0.5
Other	0.2
*Foreign (% stocks)	5.1

Market Cap	
Giant	10.5
Large	21.6
Medium	59.9
Small	7.6
Micro	0.4

Sector Weightings	% of Stocks	Rel S&P	5-Year High	5-Year Low
Utilities	0.0	0.0	0	0
Energy	6.8	1.0	17	0
Financials	25.8	1.4	37	12
Industrials	8.0	0.7	16	0
Durables	1.0	0.6	2	0
Staples	4.2	0.5	7	0
Services	17.2	1.6	22	7
Retail	2.2	0.3	10	0
Health	13.9	0.9	25	2
Technology	21.0	1.1	51	17

Analysis by Russel Kinnel 11-20-01

Davis Growth Opportunity is a cut above most mid-cap funds.

Investing skill and a long-term focus set this fund apart. Ken Feinberg and Chris Davis vigorously analyze balance sheets and look for companies that can consistently generate strong cash flows. In addition, they get to know the management at the fund's holdings thoroughly. Their willingness to hold a stock for the long term enables them to develop good information sources within a company.

Solid results at Davis New York Venture and Davis Financial bear out the managers' skill. And a strong team of analysts helps execute the pair's strategy. Analysts here have a fair amount of stock-picking authority—one reason that the fund spans such a range of industries. Though nearly everything the team buys has a modest valuation versus the firm's estimated future earnings, the fund usually has at least one third of assets in the growth bastions of tech and health care.

Thus, we have confidence that performance will usually be better than it's been so far in 2001. The fund has taken hits on almost every front. The biggest mistake this year has been subprime lender Providian Financial. The company's stock has lost more than 90% of its value in 2001 as defaults have soared and its lenders have raised the firm's cost of capital. In addition, the fund suffered through two communications debacles: Tellabs and Agilent Technologies. Most of its peers have a disaster or two, though, and the fund's losses are only a bit worse than the average mid-blend fund's.

The good news is that the fund's returns have been double the mid-blend category average since Davis and Feinberg took the helm in 1999. We're optimistic that their team's stock picks will eventually win the day.

Address:	2949 E. Elvira Rd. Ste 101 Tucson, AZ 85706 800-279-0279 / 800-279-0279
Web Address:	www.davisfunds.com
*Inception:	12-01-94
Advisor:	Davis Selected Advisers
Subadvisor:	Davis Selected Advisers – NY
NTF Plans:	Datalynx , Fidelity Inst.

Minimum Purchase:	$1000	Add: $25	IRA: $250
Min Auto Inv Plan:	$1000	Add: $25	
Sales Fees:	4.75%L, 0.25%B		
Management Fee:	.75% mx./.55% mn.		
Actual Fees:	Mgt: 0.75%	Dist: 0.25%	
Expense Projections:	3Yr: $865	5Yr: $1149	10Yr: $1958
Avg Brok Commission:	—	Income Distrib: Annually	
Total Cost (relative to category):		Average	

Davis NY Venture A

Ticker	Load	NAV	Yield	Total Assets	Mstar Category
NYVTX	4.75%	$25.43	0.1%	$21,789.0 mil	Large Value

Prospectus Objective: Growth

Davis New York Venture Fund seeks growth of capital.

The fund invests primarily in equities issued by companies with market capitalizations of at least $5 billion, though it may also hold securities of smaller companies. It may invest in securities of foreign issuers.

Class A shares have front loads; B shares have deferred loads, higher 12b-1 fees, and conversion features; C shares have level loads; Y shares are designed for institutional investors. Prior to Oct. 1, 1995, the fund was named New York Venture Fund.

Historical Profile

Return Above Avg
Risk Average
Rating ★★★★ Above Avg

Investment Style
Equity
Average Stock %: 89% 90% 92% 94% 92% 94%

▼ Manager Change
▽ Partial Manager Change

Fund Performance vs. Category Average
■ Quarterly Fund Return +/– Category Average
— Category Baseline

Performance Quartile (within Category)

Portfolio Manager(s)

Christopher C. Davis. Since 10-95. MA'87 U. of St. Andrews. Other funds currently managed: Davis Growth Opportunity B, Davis Financial A, Selected American.

Kenneth C. Feinberg. Since 5-98. BA'79 Johns Hopkins U.; MBA'85 Columbia U. Other funds currently managed: Davis Growth Opportunity B, Davis Financial A, Selected American.

1990	1991	1992	1993	1994	1995	1996	1997	1998	1999	2000	12-01	History
8.16	10.51	11.06	11.97	11.16	14.52	17.50	22.33	25.01	28.76	28.74	25.43	NAV
–2.90	40.55	12.18	16.09	–1.93	40.56	26.54	33.68	14.73	17.59	9.92	–11.41	Total Return %
0.22	10.07	4.56	6.03	–3.24	3.03	3.59	0.33	–13.85	–3.45	19.02	0.47	+/– S&P 500
0.77	22.39	3.11	–3.67	0.39	0.53	4.22	–1.81	–6.51	6.64	7.61	–2.62	+/– Russ Top 200 Val
1.87	2.34	1.62	2.36	1.00	1.34	1.24	1.31	0.47	0.01	0.19	0.10	Income Return %
–4.77	38.21	10.55	13.73	–2.93	39.22	25.30	32.36	14.26	17.58	9.73	–11.51	Capital Return %
27	8	25	32	71	6	10	8	41	11	34	83	Total Rtn % Rank Cat
0.17	0.19	0.17	0.26	0.12	0.15	0.18	0.23	0.11	0.00	0.05	0.03	Income $
0.54	0.65	0.53	0.58	0.45	1.01	0.70	0.83	0.48	0.62	2.64	0.00	Capital Gains $
0.97	0.97	0.91	0.89	0.87	0.90	0.87	0.89	0.91	0.90	0.88	0.89	Expense Ratio %
3.78	1.84	1.36	0.85	1.19	1.11	1.30	0.98	0.80	0.56	0.31	0.50	Income Ratio %
47	52	26	24	13	15	19	24	11	25	29	15	Turnover Rate %
341.9	459.0	547.9	937.7	1,090.5	1,798.2	2,658.8	4,655.5	6,820.3	8,139.4	10,599.6	10,463.3	Net Assets $mil

Performance 12-31-01

	1st Qtr	2nd Qtr	3rd Qtr	4th Qtr	Total
1997	1.94	16.70	11.91	0.40	33.68
1998	8.11	2.20	–14.43	21.36	14.73
1999	3.20	11.97	–9.00	11.83	17.59
2000	9.84	–2.31	1.30	1.13	9.92
2001	–10.19	3.22	–14.19	11.38	–11.41

Trailing	Total Return%	+/– S&P 500	+/– Russ Top 200 Val	% Rank All	% Rank Cat	Growth of $10,000
3 Mo	11.38	0.69	5.86	35	20	11,138
6 Mo	–4.43	1.13	1.35	59	57	9,557
1 Yr	–11.41	0.47	–2.62	63	83	8,859
3 Yr Avg	4.62	5.65	3.46	34	28	11,451
5 Yr Avg	11.92	1.22	0.72	10	18	17,562
10 Yr Avg	14.84	1.91	0.81	5	8	39,893
15 Yr Avg	15.57	1.84	2.07	5	3	87,641

Tax Analysis	Tax-Adj Ret%	%Rank Cat	%Pretax Ret	%Rank Cat
3 Yr Avg	3.60	25	77.8	28
5 Yr Avg	10.65	12	89.3	10
10 Yr Avg	12.89	7	86.8	9

Potential Capital Gain Exposure: 11% of assets

Risk Analysis

Time Period	Load-Adj Return %	Risk %Rank[1] All	Risk %Rank[1] Cat	Morningstar Return	Morningstar Risk	Morningstar Risk-Adj Rating
1 Yr	–15.62					
3 Yr	2.94	54	49	–0.42[2]	0.75	★★★
5 Yr	10.84	60	63	1.42[2]	0.82	★★★★
10 Yr	14.28	70	86	1.61	0.90	★★★★

Average Historical Rating (193 months): 4.6★s

[1]1=low, 100=high [2] T-Bill return substituted for category avg.

Category Rating (3 Yr)

1 2 3 4 5
Worst Best

Return Above Avg
Risk Average

Other Measures	Standard Index S&P 500	Best Fit Index S&P 500
Alpha	4.8	4.8
Beta	0.85	0.85
R-Squared	84	84
Standard Deviation		16.54
Mean		4.62
Sharpe Ratio		–0.02

Portfolio Analysis 08-31-01

Share change since 07-01 Total Stocks: 75	Sector	PE	YTD Ret%	% Assets
Tyco Intl	Industrials	27.1	6.23	6.23
American Express	Financials	28.3	–34.40	5.30
Household Intl	Financials	14.7	6.89	4.76
Philip Morris	Staples	12.1	9.12	4.37
Merck	Health	19.1	–35.90	3.97
Citigroup	Financials	20.0	0.03	3.69
Wells Fargo	Financials	22.4	–20.20	3.44
Costco Wholesale	Retail	34.4	11.12	2.97
United Parcel Svc B	Services	25.0	–6.09	2.81
Berkshire Hathaway Cl A	Financials	—	—	2.78
Masco	Industrials	98.0	–2.43	2.68
Bristol-Myers Squibb	Health	20.2	–26.00	2.44
Eli Lilly	Health	28.9	–14.40	2.33
American Home Products	Health	—	–1.91	2.26
McDonald's	Services	19.2	–21.50	2.20
Sealed Air	Industrials	27.4	33.84	1.99
Lexmark Intl	Technology	26.9	33.14	1.96
Golden West Finl	Financials	12.9	–12.40	1.91
American Intl Grp	Financials	42.0	–19.20	1.90
⊕ Phillips Petro	Energy	7.1	8.56	1.87
Hewlett-Packard	Technology	97.8	–33.90	1.78
Transatlantic Hldgs	Financials	75.8	29.55	1.71
Morgan Stanley/Dean Witter	Financials	16.6	–28.20	1.52
Tellabs	Technology	41.6	–73.50	1.50
Minnesota Mng & Mfg	Industrials	34.5	0.16	1.47

Current Investment Style

Style: Value Blnd Growth; Size: Large Med Small

	Stock Port Avg	Relative S&P 500 Current	Relative S&P 500 Hist	Rel Cat
Price/Earnings Ratio	26.6	0.86	0.82	1.06
Price/Book Ratio	5.1	0.89	0.75	1.24
Price/Cash Flow	16.6	0.92	0.91	1.20
3 Yr Earnings Growth	16.4	1.12	0.96	1.11
1 Yr Earnings Est%	–3.7	2.11	—	1.13
Med Mkt Cap $mil	38,585	0.6	0.9	1.21

Analysis by Russel Kinnel 10-17-01

We expect Davis New York Venture Fund to come back strong.

The fund's poor year-to-date performance is due to weakness in individual issues and a growing bet on pharmaceutical shares. Shares of American Express and Tellabs have taken a drubbing that far surpasses that suffered by the average stock in their industries. American Express was dealt the double blow of poor investments and a steep drop in travel following the September terrorist attacks. Tellabs, meanwhile, has lost three fourths of its value as telecom-equipment spending has plummeted.

Management's increased investment in big drug companies has also been a drag. Merck has fallen 25% because a promising new drug, Vioxx, hasn't lived up to expectations. In addition, some of the fund's other top drug stocks have fallen as much as the S&P 500, which has done significantly worse than the average large-value fund. Despite that weakness, comanagers Chris Davis and Ken Feinberg still like key traits of their big pharmaceutical purchases. They cite strong growth potential, "honest accounting," share buybacks, and low prices relative to owner earnings as the key attractions.

Those criteria are the same they've looked for in the past, even though the addition of drug stocks takes them a bit more into growth territory than before. Thus, the fund may track the S&P 500 a bit more closely than the large-value averages, but its long-term prospects are intact. All of the most important elements still remain: The Davis family has a large sum invested in this fund; management's analysis is more thorough than competitors'; and the core strategy continues to be buying strong companies with good growth potential whose shares trade at modest valuations.

Special Securities % assets 08-31-01	
Restricted/Illiquid Secs	0
Emerging-Markets Secs	0
Options/Futures/Warrants	No

Sector Weightings	% of Stocks	Rel S&P	5-Year High	5-Year Low
Utilities	0.0	0.0	8	0
Energy	5.6	0.8	13	1
Financials	39.3	2.2	62	37
Industrials	15.6	1.4	16	1
Durables	0.4	0.3	4	0
Staples	6.3	0.8	16	1
Services	8.7	0.8	14	5
Retail	3.6	0.5	7	0
Health	11.8	0.8	15	3
Technology	8.7	0.5	34	6

Composition % assets 08-31-01	
Cash	3.6
Stocks*	96.2
Bonds	0.0
Other	0.2
*Foreign (% stocks)	2.9

Market Cap	
Giant	48.8
Large	26.7
Medium	23.0
Small	1.5
Micro	0.0

Address: 2949 E. Elvira Rd. Ste 101
Tucson, AZ 85706
800-279-0279 / 800-279-0279
Web Address: www.davisfunds.com

Inception: 02-17-69
Advisor: Davis Selected Advisers
Subadvisor: Davis Selected Advisers – NY
NTF Plans: Datalynx , Fidelity Inst.

Minimum Purchase: $1000 Add: $25 IRA: $250
Min Auto Inv Plan: $1000 Add: $25
Sales Fees: 4.75%L, 0.25%S
Management Fee: .75% mx./.50% mn.
Actual Fees: Mgt: 0.54% Dist: 0.23%
Expense Projections: 3Yr: $751 5Yr: $955 10Yr: $1541
Avg Brok Commission: — Income Distrib: Annually
Total Cost (relative to category): —

Delaware Trend A

Ticker	Load	NAV	Yield	Total Assets	Mstar Category
DELTX	5.75%	$17.73	0.0%	$1,258.3 mil	Mid-Cap Growth

Prospectus Objective: Aggressive Growth

Delaware Trend Fund seeks long-term capital appreciation.

The fund invests primarily in common stocks and convertibles of companies that management believes have the fundamental characteristics to support growth. Management purchases securities of companies that it expects to benefit from trends within the economy, the political arena, and society at large. The fund may invest in foreign securities.

Class A shares have front loads; B shares have deferred loads, higher 12b-1 fees, and conversion features; C shares have level loads; Institutional shares are intended for institutions. Prior to June 15, 1988, the fund was named Delta Trend Fund.

Historical Profile

Return: Above Avg
Risk: Above Avg
Rating: ★★★ Neutral

Investment Style: Equity
Average Stock %: 95% | 91% | 92% | 97% | 97% | 97% | 93%

▼ Manager Change
▽ Partial Manager Change

Fund Performance vs. Category Average
Quarterly Fund Return +/– Category Average
— Category Baseline

Performance Quartile (within Category)

Portfolio Manager(s)

Gerald S. Frey. Since 6-96.
Marshall T. Bassett. Since 8-99.
John A. Heffern. Since 8-99.
Jeffrey W. Hynoski. Since 8-99.
Stephen T. Lampe. Since 8-99.
Lori P. Wachs, CFA. Since 8-99.

1990	1991	1992	1993	1994	1995	1996	1997	1998	1999	2000	12-01	History
6.86	11.81	13.13	13.95	11.75	15.79	15.84	16.91	16.29	24.13	20.83	17.73	NAV
−24.61	74.49	22.40	22.37	−9.97	42.51	10.71	19.43	13.57	71.33	−6.79	−14.88	Total Return %
−21.49	44.01	14.78	12.31	−11.28	4.98	−12.24	−13.92	−15.00	50.29	2.31	−3.01	+/– S&P 500
−19.48	27.46	13.69	11.17	−7.81	8.54	−6.78	−3.11	−4.30	20.03	4.96	5.27	+/– Russ Midcap Grth
0.52	0.00	0.00	0.00	0.00	0.00	0.00	0.00	0.00	0.00	0.00	0.00	Income Return %
−25.13	74.49	22.40	22.37	−9.97	42.51	10.71	19.43	13.57	71.33	−6.79	−14.88	Capital Return %
94	9	5	19	95	19	82	41	54	34	53	32	Total Rtn % Rank Cat
0.05	0.00	0.00	0.00	0.00	0.00	0.00	0.00	0.00	0.00	0.00	0.00	Income $
0.52	0.16	1.15	1.94	0.79	0.90	1.51	1.94	2.60	2.98	2.12	0.00	Capital Gains $
1.27	1.29	1.18	1.33	1.37	1.36	1.31	1.34	1.34	1.45	1.29	1.34	Expense Ratio %
0.82	−0.24	−0.43	−0.61	−0.72	−0.58	−0.79	−0.47	−0.70	−0.87	−0.80	−0.68	Income Ratio %
80	67	76	75	67	64	90	115	114	86	77	50	Turnover Rate %
63.5	104.0	169.6	277.6	268.0	399.3	481.3	499.5	446.8	722.9	800.3	—	Net Assets $mil

Performance 12-31-01

	1st Qtr	2nd Qtr	3rd Qtr	4th Qtr	Total
1997	−5.93	12.35	20.20	−5.98	19.43
1998	9.88	−0.16	−15.79	22.94	13.57
1999	2.03	18.11	5.32	35.00	71.33
2000	22.92	−6.24	5.84	−23.59	−6.79
2001	−25.16	23.54	−26.43	25.12	−14.88

Trailing	Total Return%	+/– S&P 500	+/– Russ Midcap Grth	% Rank All	% Rank Cat	Growth of $10,000
3 Mo	25.12	14.44	−1.94	8	18	12,512
6 Mo	−7.94	−2.39	0.32	78	39	9,206
1 Yr	−14.88	−3.01	5.27	72	32	8,512
3 Yr Avg	10.77	11.80	8.61	10	22	13,593
5 Yr Avg	13.02	2.32	4.00	8	23	18,438
10 Yr Avg	14.65	1.72	3.54	6	10	39,224
15 Yr Avg	15.80	2.07	2.99	5	2	90,319

Tax Analysis	Tax-Adj Ret%	%Rank Cat	%Pretax Ret	%Rank Cat
3 Yr Avg	9.07	19	84.2	34
5 Yr Avg	10.80	20	82.9	30
10 Yr Avg	11.98	10	81.8	22

Potential Capital Gain Exposure: 15% of assets

Risk Analysis

Time Period	Load-Adj Return %	Risk %Rank[1] All	Risk %Rank[1] Cat	Morningstar Return	Morningstar Risk	Morningstar Risk-Adj Rating
1 Yr	−19.78					
3 Yr	8.61	91	53	0.80[2]	1.47	★★★★
5 Yr	11.69	90	49	1.65[2]	1.47	★★★
10 Yr	13.97	93	49	1.53	1.53	★★★

Average Historical Rating (193 months): 2.8★s

[1] 1=low, 100=high [2] T-Bill return substituted for category avg.

Category Rating (3 Yr)

1 2 3 4 5
Worst Best

Return: Above Avg
Risk: Average

Other Measures	Standard Index S&P 500	Best Fit Index Wil 4500
Alpha	19.5	12.1
Beta	1.40	1.21
R-Squared	44	89
Standard Deviation		42.24
Mean		10.77
Sharpe Ratio		0.16

Portfolio Analysis 09-30-01

Share change since 06-01 Total Stocks: 74	Sector	PE	YTD Ret%	% Assets
⊕ PartnerRe	Financials	22.4	−10.50	4.06
⊕ Everest Re Grp	Financials	17.6	−1.29	3.84
⊕ Radian Grp	Financials	11.6	14.64	3.72
⊖ Jack Henry & Assoc	Technology	34.7	−29.30	3.56
⊖ Sonic	Services	25.7	54.42	2.99
⊖ Mettler-Toledo Intl	Industrials	34.1	−4.64	2.33
⊕ Trimeris	Health	—	−18.00	2.32
⊕ Krispy Kreme Doughnut	Retail	67.0	113.00	2.25
⊖ CEC Entrtnmt	Services	19.8	27.15	2.21
⊖ CIMA Labs	Health	39.3	−44.40	2.18
⊕ Neurocrine Biosciences	Health	—	54.90	2.09
⊕ Cheesecake Factory	Services	46.4	35.91	2.05
⊖ WebEx Comms	Services	—	19.04	1.91
⊕ KB Home	Industrials	7.6	20.19	1.88
⊖ American Italian Pasta	Staples	29.0	56.75	1.84
⊕ Dollar Tree Stores	Retail	30.9	26.16	1.82
⊕ West	Services	22.7	−11.30	1.82
⊕ Advanced Fibre Comm	Technology	7.4	−2.18	1.80
⊕ DR Horton	Industrials	9.7	48.67	1.67
⊕ Cullen/Frost Bankers	Financials	17.2	−24.20	1.65
⊕ Mediacom Comms	Services	—	6.24	1.63
⊕ Micrel	Technology	84.6	−22.10	1.60
⊖ Extended Stay Amer	Services	24.5	27.63	1.60
⊕ Tekelec	Technology	—	−39.60	1.57
⊖ Bisys Grp	Services	42.7	22.76	1.54

Current Investment Style

Style: Value Blnd Growth; Size: Large Med Small

	Stock Port Avg	Relative S&P 500 Current	Relative S&P 500 Hist	Rel Cat
Price/Earnings Ratio	27.5	0.89	1.17	0.79
Price/Book Ratio	4.7	0.83	1.12	0.83
Price/Cash Flow	22.7	1.26	1.34	0.98
3 Yr Earnings Growth	25.5	1.74	—	1.09
1 Yr Earnings Est%	−8.5	4.78	—	−0.91
Med Mkt Cap $mil	1,612	0.0	0.0	0.29

[1] figure is based on 50% or less of stocks

Analysis by Dan McNeela 12-03-01

Delaware Trend is showing some durability.

Consistency hasn't always been the strong suit of this fund, but that was before manager Gerry Frey took over the top spot in 1997. Prior to Frey's arrival, the theme-based portfolio was filled with small- and micro-cap stocks. That led to multiple finishes in both the top and bottom deciles of the small-growth category.

Frey performed major surgery on the fund once he assumed control. He instituted a bottom-up approach, dedicated his analysts to one of four broadly defined stock categories instead of having a pool of generalists, and cut way back on the number of micro-cap stocks. These changes steadied the portfolio, as many of the smaller stock were less financially sound. Frey has also been willing to let his successes remain in the fund even if they've grown in size. That prompted the fund's move into Morningstar's mid-cap growth category, even though it still has a decidedly small-cap flavor.

The overall results have been much more solid than they had been prior to Frey's arrival. Frey and his team hit on a bunch of winners among data storage and semiconductor companies in 1999, racking up a 71% gain. And the ensuing collapse in the tech sector hasn't sunk the fund on a relative basis. It fell behind in the first quarter of 2001, when it shed 25% of its value, but since then, the fund has made a comeback of sorts. Its 19.8% year-to-date loss through November ranks near the top third of the hard-hit mid-growth category. Food stocks have been the best performers, with nice gains from fast-food restaurant chain Sonic and Krispy Kreme Doughnut.

Investors won't get pure mid-cap exposure here, but Frey's team has made enough good picks to make this fund worth considering for the more-aggressive portion of a portfolio.

Special Securities % assets 09-30-01	
Restricted/Illiquid Secs	0
Emerging-Markets Secs	0
Options/Futures/Warrants	No

Composition % assets 09-30-01	
Cash	4.5
Stocks*	95.5
Bonds	0.0
Other	0.0
*Foreign (% stocks)	7.5

Market Cap	
Giant	0.0
Large	0.0
Medium	59.5
Small	40.2
Micro	0.4

Sector Weightings	% of Stocks	Rel S&P	5-Year High	5-Year Low
Utilities	0.0	0.0	2	0
Energy	0.0	0.0	6	0
Financials	22.1	1.2	22	0
Industrials	6.8	0.6	8	1
Durables	1.1	0.7	14	0
Staples	3.4	0.4	5	0
Services	29.2	2.7	41	27
Retail	11.3	1.7	31	8
Health	11.4	0.8	20	3
Technology	14.8	0.8	43	12

Address: 1818 Market Street, Philadelphia, PA 19103–3682, 800–523–4640 / 215–255–1241
Web Address: www.delawarefunds.com
Inception: 10-03-68
Advisor: Delaware Mgmt.
Subadvisor: None
NTF Plans: Fidelity Inst.

Minimum Purchase: $1000 Add: $100 IRA: $250
Min Auto Inv Plan: $1000 Add: $25
Sales Fees: 5.75%L, 0.30%B
Management Fee: .75%
Actual Fees: Mgt: 0.75% Dist: 0.28%
Expense Projections: 3Yr: $1007 5Yr: $1322 10Yr: $2210
Avg Brok Commission: — Income Distrib: Semi–Ann.
Total Cost (relative to category): Average

Delphi Value Retail

Ticker	Load	NAV	Yield	Total Assets	Mstar Category
KDVRX	12b–1 only	$13.18	0.0%	$72.7 mil	Mid–Cap Value

Prospectus Objective: Growth

Delphi Value Fund seeks capital growth.

The fund normally invests at least 65% of assets in equity securities. This may include common and preferred stocks, warrants, rights, convertible debt securities, trust certificates, partnership interests, and equity participations. It may also invest up to 35% of assets in foreign securities. Management measures value of companies using price/earning multiples, cash flow multiples and price-to-liquidationvalues.

Retail shares are subject to 12b-1 fees; Institutional shares are for institutional investors only. Prior to May 1, 2000, the fund was named Kobren Delphi Value Fund.

Historical Profile

Return: Above Avg
Risk: Below Avg
Rating: ★★★★ Above Avg

Investment Style
Equity
Average Stock %: 35% (1998), 95% (1999), 94% (2000), 93% (12-01)

▼ Manager Change
▽ Partial Manager Change

Fund Performance vs. Category Average
■ Quarterly Fund Return +/– Category Average
— Category Baseline

Performance Quartile (within Category)

Portfolio Manager(s)

Scott M. Black. Since 12-98. BA Johns Hopkins U.; MBA Harvard U. Other fund currently managed: Delphi Value Instl.

1990	1991	1992	1993	1994	1995	1996	1997	1998	1999	2000	12-01	History
—	—	—	—	—	—	—	—	10.12	11.19	13.00	13.18	NAV
—	—	—	—	—	—	—	—	1.20*	11.30	17.30	1.90	Total Return %
—	—	—	—	—	—	—	—	–3.09*	–9.74	26.40	13.78	+/– S&P 500
—	—	—	—	—	—	—	—	—	11.40	–1.89	–0.44	+/– Russ Midcap Val
—	—	—	—	—	—	—	—	0.00	0.02	0.00	0.00	Income Return %
—	—	—	—	—	—	—	—	1.20	11.28	17.30	1.90	Capital Return %
—	—	—	—	—	—	—	—	—	40	48	60	Total Rtn % Rank Cat
—	—	—	—	—	—	—	—	0.00	0.00	0.00	0.00	Income $
—	—	—	—	—	—	—	—	0.00	0.07	0.12	0.07	Capital Gains $
—	—	—	—	—	—	—	—	1.75	1.75	—	—	Expense Ratio %
—	—	—	—	—	—	—	—	0.82	0.00	—	—	Income Ratio %
—	—	—	—	—	—	—	—	—	17	—	—	Turnover Rate %
—	—	—	—	—	—	—	—	4.8	31.0	45.3	44.8	Net Assets $mil

Performance 12-31-01

	1st Qtr	2nd Qtr	3rd Qtr	4th Qtr	Total
1997	—	—	—	—	—
1998	—	—	—	—	1.20 *
1999	1.19	11.82	–9.69	8.93	11.30
2000	10.01	–2.19	5.90	2.95	17.30
2001	–2.38	6.54	–15.01	15.29	1.90

Trailing	Total Return%	+/– S&P 500	+/– Russ Midcap Val	% Rank All	% Rank Cat	Growth of $10,000
3 Mo	15.29	4.61	3.26	23	33	11,529
6 Mo	–2.02	3.54	–1.11	47	64	9,798
1 Yr	1.90	13.78	–0.44	39	60	10,190
3 Yr Avg	9.98	11.01	3.17	11	55	13,304
5 Yr Avg	—	—	—	—	—	—
10 Yr Avg	—	—	—	—	—	—
15 Yr Avg	—	—	—	—	—	—

Tax Analysis	Tax-Adj Ret%	%Rank Cat	%Pretax Ret	%Rank Cat
3 Yr Avg	9.68	38	96.9	8
5 Yr Avg	—	—	—	—
10 Yr Avg	—	—	—	—

Potential Capital Gain Exposure: 18% of assets

Risk Analysis

Time Period	Load-Adj Return %	Risk %Rank[1] All	Risk %Rank[1] Cat	Morningstar Return	Morningstar Risk	Morningstar Risk-Adj Rating
1 Yr	1.90					
3 Yr	9.98	47	47	1.12[2]	0.66	★★★★
5 Yr	—	—	—	—	—	
Incept	10.27	—	—	—	—	

Average Historical Rating (1 month): 4.0★s

[1]1=low, 100=high [2] T–Bill return substituted for category avg.

Category Rating (3 Yr)

1 Worst — 2 — 3 — 4 — 5 Best

Return: Average
Risk: Average

Other Measures	Standard Index S&P 500	Best Fit Index SPMid400
Alpha	9.9	0.8
Beta	0.78	0.76
R–Squared	66	83
Standard Deviation	17.88	
Mean	9.98	
Sharpe Ratio	0.32	

Portfolio Analysis 11-30-01

Share change since 10–01 Total Stocks: 80	Sector	PE	YTD Ret%	% Assets
⊕ Berkshire Hathaway Cl B	Financials	64.8	7.26	1.93
☼ Global Santa Fe	N/A	—	—	1.84
Gannett	Services	20.3	8.10	1.74
Comcast	Services	20.3	–13.70	1.72
DR Horton	Industrials	9.7	48.67	1.66
RenaissanceRe Hldgs	Financials	14.7	23.16	1.65
XL Cap Cl A	Financials	22.8	5.82	1.59
Saint Joe	Financials	25.7	26.62	1.59
USA Networks	Services	58.1	40.50	1.55
Fedex	Services	29.3	29.83	1.53
Viacom Cl B	Services	—	—	1.52
Harte–Hanks Comms	Services	22.9	19.51	1.50
First Essex Bancorp	Financials	13.3	45.30	1.50
General Dynamics	Industrials	17.6	3.63	1.49
IPC Hldgs	Financials	17.1	40.95	1.48
Morgan Stanley/Dean Witter	Financials	16.6	–28.20	1.47
⊖ McClatchy Cl A	Services	33.6	11.32	1.44
⊕ Wells Fargo	Financials	22.4	–20.20	1.44
AFC Enterprises	Retail	—	—	1.42
North Fork Bancorp	Financials	16.5	34.11	1.38
McGraw–Hill	Services	24.7	5.70	1.38
Goldman Sachs Grp	Financials	20.7	–12.80	1.36
Cox Comms A	Services	31.8	–9.99	1.33
Bear Stearns	Financials	12.9	16.96	1.33
Pepsi Bottling Grp	Staples	23.6	17.90	1.32

Current Investment Style

Style: Value Blnd Growth; Size: Large Med Small

	Stock Port Avg	Relative S&P 500 Current	Relative S&P 500 Hist	Rel Cat
Price/Earnings Ratio	23.2	0.75	—	0.98
Price/Book Ratio	2.8	0.49	—	0.93
Price/Cash Flow	12.0	0.66	—	0.97
3 Yr Earnings Growth	12.7	0.87	—	1.07
1 Yr Earnings Est%	–10.8	6.12	—	1.76
Med Mkt Cap $mil	3,918	0.1	—	0.55

[1]figure is based on 50% or less of stocks

Analysis by Bridget Hughes 11-29-01

Delphi Value Fund is stronger than it looks.

A quick glance at this fund's performance might cause you to dismiss it. After all, for the year to date through Nov. 28, 2001, it ranks in the mid-value category's bottom quartile. Hurt by a 9% energy stake, which was a source of gains in earlier years, and its perpetual devotion to media names—such as Comcast, which is down 7.7% in 2001, Cox Communications (down 15.3%), and Charter Communications (down 33.7%)—the fund has shed 5.2% of its value. In contrast, about half of its peers have produced gains. Just shy of its three-year anniversary, the fund's return since its mid-December 1998 inception lags the average mid-value offering's.

But it would be premature at least—and probably just plain wrong—to dismiss manager Scott Black and his staid approach. For one thing, in 1999 and 2000, the fund produced competitive results. More important, however, Black's audited record (which spans more than 20 years) with his company's private accounts is decidedly better than most in the mid-value camp. In short, Black is a manager with a great long-term record who has experienced some short-term performance problems.

To be sure, shareholders here need to be patient. As the fund's low turnover suggests, even Black may expect some of his picks to take some time to pan out. In fact, he's hanging on to most of the fund's energy names, because he believes they're the "best of breed" and will rebound when oil prices do. In general, his strategy runs in the same vein as those of Mario Gabelli; Tweedy, Browne; and Warren Buffett—all of whom have suffered bouts of weak returns over shorter intervals.

One concern is the hefty expense ratio, which Kobren Insight Funds (which distributes this offering) has capped at 1.75%. As the fund grows, that should fall, but these economies of scale are realized gradually. Still, we think this fund's pedigree bodes well for its future.

Special Securities % assets 11-30-01	
Restricted/Illiquid Secs	0
Emerging–Markets Secs	0
Options/Futures/Warrants	No

Composition % assets 11-30-01	
Cash	5.2
Stocks*	94.9
Bonds	0.0
Other	0.0
*Foreign (% stocks)	8.4

Market Cap	
Giant	6.7
Large	24.4
Medium	48.5
Small	18.8
Micro	1.7

Sector Weightings	% of Stocks	Rel S&P	5-Year High	5-Year Low
Utilities	2.1	0.7	—	—
Energy	6.2	0.9	—	—
Financials	33.5	1.9	—	—
Industrials	12.3	1.1	—	—
Durables	2.6	1.7	—	—
Staples	2.7	0.3	—	—
Services	28.7	2.6	—	—
Retail	4.2	0.6	—	—
Health	0.0	0.0	—	—
Technology	7.7	0.4	—	—

Address:	P.O. Box 5146 Westborough, MA 01581 800–895–9936
Web Address:	www.kobren.com
*Inception:	12-17-98
Advisor:	Kobren Insight Mgmt.
Subadvisor:	Delphi Mgmt.
NTF Plans:	Fidelity Inst. , Waterhouse

Minimum Purchase:	$2500	Add: $500 IRA: $2000
Min Auto Inv Plan:	$2500	Add: $500
Sales Fees:	0.25%B	
Management Fee:	1.0%	
Actual Fees:	Mgt: 1.00%	Dist: 0.25%
Expense Projections:	3Yr: $468	5Yr: — 10Yr: —
Avg Brok Commission:	—	Income Distrib: Annually
Total Cost (relative to category):	—	

Deutsche Flag Communications A

Ticker	Load	NAV	Yield	Total Assets	Mstar Category
TISHX	5.50%	$18.58	0.0%	$1,006.1 mil	Spec Communications

Prospectus Objective: Specialty—Communications

Deutsche Flag Communications Fund seeks current income and capital growth.

The fund normally invests at least 65% of assets in common stocks, convertibles, and debt of companies in the communications industry. These companies may include those offering products and services that facilitate new information-based applications. This fund is non-diversified.

Class A shares have front loads; B shares have deferred loads, higher 12b-1 fees, and conversion features; D shares are closed to investment; Institutional Shares are for institutional investors. Prior to May 1, 1998, the fund was named Flag Investors Telephone Income Trust. Past fund names: Flag Investors Communications Fund and Flag Investors Telephone Income Fund.

Historical Profile
Return: Average
Risk: Above Avg
Rating: ★★★ Neutral

Investment Style
Equity
Average Stock %: 95% 97% 98% 96% 92% 93% 96%

▼ Manager Change
▽ Partial Manager Change

Fund Performance vs. Category Average
■ Quarterly Fund Return +/– Category Average
— Category Baseline

Performance Quartile (within Category)

Portfolio Manager(s)

Bruce E. Behrens, CFA. Since 1-84. BA'66 Denison U.; MBA'68 U. of Michigan. Other funds currently managed: Deutsche Flag Communications B, Deutsche Flag Communications Instl, Deutsche Flag Communications C.

Liam Burke. Since 4-97. Georgetown U. Other funds currently managed: Deutsche Flag Communications B, Deutsche Flag Communications Instl, Deutsche Flag Communications C.

History

1990	1991	1992	1993	1994	1995	1996	1997	1998	1999	2000	12-01	History
9.61	11.31	12.24	13.73	12.33	14.87	15.60	19.37	34.23	43.65	26.37	18.58	NAV
–7.52	23.19	12.40	18.09	–6.57	33.44	13.46	37.36	85.30	45.47	–34.52	–29.54	Total Return %
–4.41	–7.29	4.79	8.03	–7.88	–4.10	–9.49	4.01	56.72	24.43	–25.42	–17.67	+/– S&P 500
–1.34	–11.01	3.43	6.81	–6.50	–3.01	–7.74	6.07	61.87	21.91	–23.58	–18.65	+/– Wilshire 5000
4.13	4.90	3.78	3.49	2.61	3.65	2.58	2.62	0.65	0.64	0.11	0.00	Income Return %
–11.65	18.30	8.62	14.60	–9.18	29.79	10.87	34.74	84.65	44.83	–34.63	–29.54	Capital Return %
25	60	60	66	66	27	33	14	1	68	43	34	Total Rtn % Rank Cat
0.45	0.46	0.42	0.42	0.35	0.44	0.38	0.40	0.13	0.21	0.05	0.00	Income $
0.13	0.02	0.01	0.28	0.15	1.01	0.84	1.50	1.18	5.43	2.50	0.00	Capital Gains $
0.92	0.92	0.92	0.92	0.92	0.93	1.14	1.11	1.05	0.96	1.05	—	Expense Ratio %
4.54	4.38	3.81	3.12	3.14	2.85	1.74	1.07	0.48	0.62	0.09	—	Income Ratio %
2	7	6	14	23	24	20	26	14	17	—	—	Turnover Rate %
177.9	238.6	307.6	468.9	436.2	492.4	506.0	622.8	1,250.8	2,115.5	1,434.6	729.7	Net Assets $mil

Performance 12-31-01

	1st Qtr	2nd Qtr	3rd Qtr	4th Qtr	Total
1997	–2.69	19.56	10.22	7.12	37.36
1998	24.06	3.13	–4.21	51.19	85.30
1999	16.62	5.01	–6.62	27.21	45.47
2000	–0.41	–13.63	–3.60	–21.03	–34.52
2001	–16.31	1.31	–21.96	6.48	–29.54

Trailing	Total Return%	+/– S&P 500	+/– Wil 5000	% Rank All	% Rank Cat	Growth of $10,000
3 Mo	6.48	–4.21	–5.90	59	56	10,648
6 Mo	–16.91	–11.35	–11.42	96	43	8,309
1 Yr	–29.54	–17.67	–18.65	93	34	7,046
3 Yr Avg	–12.45	–11.42	–11.80	99	73	6,712
5 Yr Avg	11.30	0.60	1.60	13	42	17,083
10 Yr Avg	12.36	–0.57	0.08	16	40	32,074
15 Yr Avg	13.45	–0.29	0.45	14	50	66,344

Tax Analysis	Tax-Adj Ret%	%Rank Cat	%Pretax Ret	%Rank Cat
3 Yr Avg	–13.70	73	—	—
5 Yr Avg	9.54	35	84.4	33
10 Yr Avg	10.35	40	83.8	20

Potential Capital Gain Exposure: –21% of assets

Risk Analysis

Time Period	Load-Adj Return %	Risk %Rank[1] All	Risk %Rank[1] Cat	Morningstar Return	Morningstar Risk	Morningstar Risk-Adj Rating
1 Yr	–33.42					
3 Yr	–14.08	94	50	–3.35[2]	1.61	★
5 Yr	10.05	88	46	1.21[2]	1.39	★★★
10 Yr	11.73	89	50	1.05	1.31	★★★

Average Historical Rating (180 months): 4.3★s

[1]1=low, 100=high [2] T-Bill return substituted for category avg.

Category Rating (3 Yr)

1 2 3 4 5
Worst Best

Return: Below Avg
Risk: Average

Other Measures	Standard Index S&P 500	Best Fit Index MSCIACWdFr
Alpha	–7.9	–2.6
Beta	1.33	1.45
R-Squared	64	67

Standard Deviation	25.92
Mean	–12.45
Sharpe Ratio	–0.80

Analysis by William Harding 08-17-01

We think this fund remains one of the better options in a struggling sector of the economy.

The meltdown in communication stocks has exacted a sizable toll on Deutsche Flag Communications Fund, but it has fared better than most of its rivals. It has lost roughly 39% of its value over the trailing 12 months ended August 15, 2001, compared with a 51% decline for the average communications offering. The fund benefited, at least in relative terms, from its focus on large service providers such as Verizon, which held up relatively well. In addition, top holding AOL Time Warner (management began picking up shares of AOL back in 1996) has gained 14% so far this year.

That's not to suggest managers Bruce Behrens and Liam Burke are pleased with the fund's slide of late. In fact, they're disappointed that they didn't better manage its risks. One clear misstep was the fund's investment in Winstar Communications, which recently filed for bankruptcy protection under Chapter 11. But to management's credit, its emphasis on companies with strong cash flows steered it clear of many other speculative companies with shaky business models. For example, the fund has had much less exposure than its typical peer to cash-strapped emerging telecom-service carriers.

The communications sector is far from out of the woods yet, but we think investors who want exposure to the sector have good reason to stick by this offering. Behrens and Burke have guided the fund to a respectable long-term record, and investors will have a tough time finding more qualified managers in this sector. Behrens has been on board since the fund's 1984 inception (it is the oldest offering in the category) and Burke has been covering the industry for several years.

Like most sector funds, this offering will experience wild gyrations in its returns at times, so investors would be wise to limit it to a small portion of their portfolios.

Portfolio Analysis 11-30-01

Share chng since 08-01 Total Stocks: 31

Holding	Subsector	PE	YTD Ret%	% Assets
⊖ AOL Time Warner	Technology	—	–7.76	11.84
⊖ Alltel	Phone Services	17.7	1.14	9.60
⊖ SBC Comms	Phone Services	18.4	–16.00	9.01
⊖ Verizon Comms	Phone Services	29.7	–2.52	8.43
⊖ BCE	Phone Services	3.8	–18.70	4.86
Qwest Comms Intl	Phone Equip.	—	–65.40	4.72
Convergys	Services	41.2	–17.20	3.78
Celestica	Technology	79.2	–25.50	3.50
Sun Microsystems	Technology	NMF	–55.80	3.50
Black Box	Phone Equip.	16.3	9.45	3.42
Vodafone Airtouch PLC ADR	Wireless	—	–27.70	3.15
Charter Comms	Services	—	–27.50	3.15
⊖ General Motors Cl H	Technology	42.9	–32.80	2.70
Qualcomm	Phone Equip.	—	–38.50	2.57
Novell	Technology	—	–12.00	2.15
Mediacom Comms	Services	—	6.24	2.11
Telefonos de Mexico ADR L	Phone Services	9.9	29.75	1.86
☼ Liberty Livewire	Services	—	—	1.86
News ADR	Broadcasting	—	–1.28	1.79
Telefonica ADR	Phone Services	22.4	–16.60	1.65
Agilent Tech	Technology	58.2	–47.90	1.59
⊕ Lucent Tech	Phone Equip.	—	–53.20	1.47
Solectron	Technology	—	–66.70	1.43
Avaya	Services	—	17.81	1.08
Dobson Comms	Services	—	–41.60	0.73

Current Investment Style

Style: Value Blnd Growth; Size: Large Med Small

	Stock Port Avg	Relative S&P 500 Current	Relative S&P 500 Hist	Rel Cat
Price/Earnings Ratio	28.2	0.91	1.01	0.92
Price/Book Ratio	2.7	0.48	0.96	0.61
Price/Cash Flow	14.5	0.81	0.90	0.86
3 Yr Earnings Growth	33.4[1]	2.28	1.36	1.14
1 Yr Earnings Est%	–9.1[1]	5.16	—	0.44
Med Mkt Cap $mil	26,044	0.4	1.0	0.96

[1]figure is based on 50% or less of stocks

Special Securities % assets 11-30-01	
Restricted/Illiquid Secs	0
Emerging-Markets Secs	2
Options/Futures/Warrants	No

Composition % assets 11-30-01	
Cash	5.0
Stocks*	94.8
Bonds	0.0
Other	0.1
*Foreign (% stocks)	17.7

Market Cap	
Giant	43.2
Large	36.1
Medium	13.8
Small	6.7
Micro	0.3

Subsector Weightings	% of Stocks	Rel Cat
Phone Services	37.9	1.3
Phone Equip.	13.4	1.3
Wireless	3.3	0.4
Broadcasting	1.9	1.2
Cable	0.0	0.0
Publishing	0.0	0.0
Media	0.0	0.0
Technology	18.5	1.6
Other	25.1	0.7

Address:	1 South Street Baltimore, MD 21202 800–730–1313
Web Address:	www.deam–us.com
Inception:	01-18-84
Advisor:	Inv. Co. Cap.
Subadvisor:	Alex. Brown Inv. Mgmt.
NTF Plans:	Fidelity Inst.

Minimum Purchase:	$2000	Add: $100	IRA: $1000
Min Auto Inv Plan:	$250	Add: $100	
Sales Fees:	5.50%L, 0.25%B		
Management Fee:	.85%		
Actual Fees:	Mgt: 0.58%	Dist: 0.25%	
Expense Projections:	3Yr: $839	5Yr: $1052	10Yr: $1663
Avg Brok Commission:	—	Income Distrib: Quarterly	
Total Cost (relative to category):	Average		

Deutsche Flag Value Builder A

Ticker	Load	NAV	Yield	Total Assets	Mstar Category
FLVBX	5.50%	$22.36	1.7%	$889.8 mil	Domestic Hybrid

Prospectus Objective: Balanced

Deutsche Flag Value Builder Fund seeks long-term capital appreciation and current income.

The fund normally invests between 40% and 75% of assets in equities, focusing on common stocks that are judged to be undervalued. Fixed-income securities constitute at least 25% of assets; the average weighted maturity ranges from two to 10 years. The fund may invest up to 10% of assets in debt rated BB or lower.

Class A shares have front loads; B shares have deferred loads, higher 12b-1 fees, and conversion features; C shares have level loads; D shares are closed to investment. Prior to May 7, 2001, the fund was named Flag Investors Value Builder Fund.

Historical Profile

Return	Average
Risk	Below Avg
Rating	★★★★ Above Avg

Investment Style Equity — Average Stock %

1996	1997	1998	1999	2000	12-01
67%	60%	59%	69%	71%	70%

▼ Manager Change
▽ Partial Manager Change

Fund Performance vs. Category Average
■ Quarterly Fund Return +/– Category Average
— Category Baseline

Performance Quartile (within Category)

Portfolio Manager(s)

Hobart C. Buppert. Since 6-92. BS'70 Loyola C.; MBA'75 Loyola C. Other funds currently managed: Deutsche Flag Value Builder B, Deutsche Flag Value Builder Instl, Deutsche Flag Value Builder C.

History

1990	1991	1992	1993	1994	1995	1996	1997	1998	1999	2000	12-01	History
—	—	10.66	11.53	11.12	13.99	16.98	20.06	22.82	24.75	22.09	22.36	NAV
—	—	7.76*	11.76	–0.37	32.75	24.64	22.67	18.52	13.81	–0.49	3.20	Total Return %
—	—	–0.28*	1.70	–1.69	–4.79	1.69	–10.68	–10.05	–7.22	8.62	15.07	+/– S&P 500
—	—	—	2.01	2.54	14.28	21.02	12.98	9.85	14.64	–12.12	–5.22	+/– LB Aggregate
—	—	1.16	3.08	3.03	3.42	2.60	2.67	2.86	2.32	2.12	1.69	Income Return %
—	—	6.60	8.67	–3.40	29.33	22.04	19.99	15.66	11.50	–2.61	1.51	Capital Return %
—	—	—	51	22	4	2	18	20	24	61	11	Total Rtn % Rank Cat
—	—	0.11	0.33	0.35	0.37	0.36	0.45	0.57	0.52	0.51	0.37	Income $
—	—	0.00	0.05	0.02	0.36	0.06	0.28	0.33	0.65	1.97	0.05	Capital Gains $
—	—	—	1.35	1.35	1.35	1.31	1.27	1.14	1.12	1.09	1.11	Expense Ratio %
—	—	—	2.88	3.14	3.07	2.72	2.51	2.49	2.64	2.06	2.13	Income Ratio %
—	—	—	—	8	18	15	13	7	10	26	8	Turnover Rate %
—	—	59.1	119.7	136.1	183.8	250.6	408.4	610.3	716.2	569.3	571.8	Net Assets $mil

Performance 12-31-01

	1st Qtr	2nd Qtr	3rd Qtr	4th Qtr	Total
1997	0.94	10.45	8.12	1.76	22.67
1998	10.12	1.04	–9.66	17.91	18.52
1999	5.83	5.07	–8.29	11.61	13.81
2000	–5.98	–2.41	5.42	2.88	–0.49
2001	–1.40	9.94	–15.08	12.12	3.20

Trailing	Total Return%	+/– S&P 500	+/–LB Agg	% Rank All	% Rank Cat	Growth of $10,000
3 Mo	12.12	1.43	12.08	33	6	11,212
6 Mo	–4.79	0.76	–9.45	61	91	9,521
1 Yr	3.20	15.07	–5.22	36	11	10,320
3 Yr Avg	5.34	6.36	–0.94	28	17	11,688
5 Yr Avg	11.19	0.49	3.76	13	9	16,994
10 Yr Avg	—	—	—	—	—	—
15 Yr Avg	—	—	—	—	—	—

Tax Analysis	Tax-Adj Ret%	%Rank Cat	%Pretax Ret	%Rank Cat
3 Yr Avg	3.58	14	67.1	25
5 Yr Avg	9.51	6	85.0	5
10 Yr Avg	—	—	—	—

Potential Capital Gain Exposure: 24% of assets

Risk Analysis

Time Period	Load-Adj Return %	Risk %Rank¹ All	Risk %Rank¹ Cat	Morningstar Return	Morningstar Risk	Morningstar Risk-Adj Rating
1 Yr	–2.48					
3 Yr	3.37	52	87	–0.33²	0.72	★★★
5 Yr	9.94	51	87	1.18²	0.70	★★★★
Incept	12.91	—	—	—	—	

Average Historical Rating (79 months): 3.7★s

¹1=low, 100=high ² T-Bill return substituted for category avg.

Category Rating (3 Yr)

1 2 **3** 4 5 — Worst … Best

Return	Above Avg
Risk	Above Avg

Other Measures	Standard Index S&P 500	Best Fit Index S&P 500
Alpha	5.3	5.3
Beta	0.80	0.80
R-Squared	73	73

Standard Deviation	16.67
Mean	5.34
Sharpe Ratio	0.03

Analysis by Brian Portnoy 12-06-01

Deutsche Flag Value Builder is certainly a winner, but it's not a conservative choice.

Relative to its more-staid domestic-hybrid peers, this fund has been anything but a smooth ride lately. It suffered outsized losses in the early autumn sell-off, but has climbed upward during the past month's market rally. The reason behind this volatility is plain to see: The fund has substantially more equity exposure than average (currently, 70% versus the category norm of 52%). Generally, the fund's longtime overweight in stocks has made it relatively vulnerable to the market's gyrations. Moreover, its bond stake doesn't play it safe, composed mostly of mid-grade and high-yield corporate paper.

For long-run investors, the ride has certainly been worth it. Manager Hoby Buppert has built one of the category's best records. Since inception, its annualized gain of 12.5% beats most of the competition's and includes six consecutive top-quartile calendar-year finishes in the mid- to late-1990s. Its performance since the equity market began its tumble in early 2000 has also been good. Last year, for example, the fund suffered some due to holdings such as Cendant and Novell, but trailed the pack by only a few percentage points.

And, on the whole, this year counts as another feather in Buppert's cap. Even as equities have suffered dearly, both in absolute terms and relative to the bond market, the fund's 1.4% gain for year to date through Dec. 5, 2001, beats 82% of the competition's. With an ultra-low turnover of 8%, the fund has benefited from longtime holdings, including Cendant, IBM, and Concord EFS. Exposure to mid-grade bonds has also been a boon this year.

Slow and steady isn't this fund's game, but those willing to endure some ups and downs will likely be pleased here.

Portfolio Analysis 11-30-01

Total Stocks: 42 Share change since 08-01	Sector	PE Ratio	YTD Return %	% Net Assets
AOL Time Warner	Technology	—	–7.76	4.95
Tyco Intl	Industrials	27.1	6.23	4.62
XL Cap Cl A	Financials	22.8	5.82	4.55
Cendant	Services	20.4	103.70	4.38
SEI Investments	Services	43.0	–19.20	4.12
⊕ Concord EFS	Financials	86.3	49.21	3.78
Allied Waste Inds	Services	NMF	–3.45	3.18
Citigroup	Financials	20.0	0.03	2.86
Cardinal Health	Health	35.1	–2.51	2.75
Blyth	Staples	17.1	–2.71	2.33

Total Fixed-Income: 64	Date of Maturity	Amount $000	Value $000	% Net Assets
Allied Waste Inds 10%	08-01-09	11,000	11,330	1.31
Marriott Intl 6.625%	11-15-03	10,000	10,437	1.20
US Resturant Ppty Cv Pfd 7.72%		524	9,818	1.13
Millipore 7.5%	04-01-07	9,050	9,186	1.06
Cendant 7.75%	12-01-03	8,000	8,121	0.94
Central Parking Cv Pfd 5.25%		544	7,820	0.90
Amazon.com Step 0%	05-01-08	9,230	6,553	0.76
Ford Motor Credit 6.7%	07-16-04	6,150	6,323	0.73
Marriott Intl 7.875%	09-15-09	5,700	5,964	0.69
Crown Castle Intl 9%	05-15-11	6,000	5,640	0.65

Equity Style
Style: Value
Size: Large-Cap

	Portfolio Avg	Rel S&P
Price/Earnings Ratio	28.8	0.93
Price/Book Ratio	4.9	0.86
Price/Cash Flow	15.5	0.86
3 Yr Earnings Growth	25.0	1.71
1 Yr Earnings Est%	–8.1	4.59
Debt % Total Cap	39.2¹	1.27
Med Mkt Cap $mil	18,591	0.31

¹figure is based on 50% or less of stocks

Fixed-Income Style NA
Duration: —
Quality: —

Avg Eff Duration	—
Avg Eff Maturity	—
Avg Credit Quality	BBB
Avg Wtd Coupon	7.33%

Special Securities % assets 11-30-01	
Restricted/Illiquid Secs	0
Emerging-Markets Secs	0
Options/Futures/Warrants	No

Composition % of assets 11-30-01	
Cash	4.0
Stocks*	69.5
Bonds	23.2
Other	3.2
*Foreign (% of stocks)	7.5

Market Cap	
Giant	30.9
Large	32.8
Medium	24.5
Small	9.3
Micro	2.6

Sector Weightings	% of Stocks	Rel S&P	5-Year High	5-Year Low
Utilities	0.0	0.0	3	0
Energy	1.7	0.2	9	0
Financials	30.7	1.7	39	19
Industrials	12.1	1.1	24	9
Durables	1.5	1.0	8	0
Staples	5.8	0.7	12	2
Services	23.6	2.2	31	10
Retail	1.4	0.2	7	0
Health	9.1	0.6	13	5
Technology	14.1	0.8	31	3

Address:	1 South Street Baltimore, MD 21202 800-730-1313
Web Address:	www.deam-us.com
*Inception:	06-15-92
Advisor:	Inv. Co. Cap.
Subadvisor:	Alex. Brown Inv. Mgmt.
NTF Plans:	Fidelity Inst.

Minimum Purchase:	$2000 Add: $100 IRA: $1000
Min Auto Inv Plan:	$250 Add: $100
Sales Fees:	5.50%L, 0.25%B
Management Fee:	1.0% mx./.70% mn.
Actual Fees:	Mgt: 0.75% Dist: 0.25%
Expense Projections:	3Yr: $790 5Yr: $1039 10Yr: $1752
Avg Brok Commission:	— Income Distrib: Quarterly
Total Cost (relative to category):	Average

Deutsche International Equity Invm

Ticker	Load	NAV	Yield	Total Assets	Mstar Category
BTEQX	None	$18.87	0.1%	$767.3 mil	Foreign Stock

Prospectus Objective: Foreign Stock

Deutsche Institutional International Equity Fund - Investment class seeks long-term growth of capital.

The fund normally invests at least 65% of assets in equity securities issued by companies domiciled outside of the United States. It diversifies investments by issuer and does not concentrate in any one industry, geographic region, or individual country. The fund usually invests in issues that make up the EAFE index, plus Canada. The fund may invest up to 15% of assets in companies located in emerging markets.

Historical Profile
Return Average
Risk Average
Rating ★★★ Neutral

Investment Style: Equity — Average Stock %: 96% 93% 90% 93% 98% 93% 93%

▼ Manager Change
▽ Partial Manager Change

Fund Performance vs. Category Average
■ Quarterly Fund Return +/– Category Average
— Category Baseline

Performance Quartile (within Category)

	1990	1991	1992	1993	1994	1995	1996	1997	1998	1999	2000	12-01	History
	—	—	9.75	13.18	13.37	14.87	17.61	20.06	24.18	31.97	25.31	18.87	NAV
	—	—	–2.50*	37.38	4.11	16.10	21.32	17.37	20.82	32.22	–20.17	–25.39	Total Return %
	—	—	–6.55*	27.32	2.79	–21.43	–1.63	–15.99	–7.75	11.18	–11.06	–13.52	+/– S&P 500
	—	—	—	4.82	–3.67	4.89	15.27	15.59	0.83	5.25	–6.00	—	+/– MSCI EAFE
	—	—	0.00	1.49	0.68	2.33	0.10	0.08	0.27	0.00	0.66	0.05	Income Return %
	—	—	–2.50	35.88	3.42	13.77	21.22	17.28	20.55	32.22	–20.82	–25.44	Capital Return %
	—	—	—	42	22	10	8	8	14	60	71	72	Total Rtn % Rank Cat
	—	—	0.00	0.15	0.09	0.31	0.01	0.01	0.06	0.00	0.21	0.01	Income $
	—	—	0.00	0.07	0.26	0.33	0.40	0.59	0.00	0.00	0.00	0.00	Capital Gains $
	—	—	1.50	1.50	1.50	1.50	1.50	1.50	1.50	1.50	1.50	—	Expense Ratio %
	—	—	0.97	0.79	0.84	1.55	0.91	0.53	0.61	0.19	–0.07	—	Income Ratio %
	—	—	—	17	15	21	68	63	65	106	140	—	Turnover Rate %
	—	—	—	33.8	56.1	85.7	210.3	573.8	1,643.4	2,414.6	2,019.4	767.3	Net Assets $mil

Portfolio Manager(s)

Michael Levy. Since 3-93. BA'68 U. of Michigan; MS'71 U. of Michigan. Other funds currently managed: Deutsche International Eq A {23781}, Deutsche European Equity Instl, BT Advisor International Equity.

Robert Reiner. Since 8-94. MA'79 U. of Southern California; MA'81 Harvard U. Other funds currently managed: Deutsche International Eq A {23781}, BT Advisor International Equity, SunAmerica International Equity A.

Julie Wang, CFA. Since 3-93. MBA U. of Pennsylvania; BA Yale U. Other funds currently managed: Deutsche International Eq A {23781}, BT Advisor International Equity, Deutsche Instl International Eq I.

Performance 12-31-01

	1st Qtr	2nd Qtr	3rd Qtr	4th Qtr	Total
1997	3.92	15.30	4.89	–6.62	17.37
1998	19.44	3.46	–16.58	17.20	20.82
1999	–4.51	4.16	0.67	32.05	32.22
2000	0.34	–7.51	–8.39	–6.10	–20.17
2001	–13.39	–1.60	–18.08	6.87	–25.39

Trailing	Total Return%	+/– S&P 500	+/– MSCI EAFE	% Rank All	% Rank Cat	Growth of $10,000
3 Mo	6.87	–3.82	—	57	65	10,687
6 Mo	–12.46	–6.90	—	91	86	8,754
1 Yr	–25.39	–13.52	—	89	72	7,461
3 Yr Avg	–7.65	–6.63	—	96	90	7,875
5 Yr Avg	2.23	–8.47	—	87	44	11,167
10 Yr Avg	—	—	—	—	—	—
15 Yr Avg	—	—	—	—	—	—

Tax Analysis	Tax-Adj Ret%	%Rank Cat	%Pretax Ret	%Rank Cat
3 Yr Avg	–7.76	83	—	—
5 Yr Avg	1.95	31	87.4	13
10 Yr Avg	—	—	—	—

Potential Capital Gain Exposure: –40% of assets

Risk Analysis

Time Period	Load-Adj Return %	Risk %Rank[1] All	Risk %Rank[1] Cat	Morningstar Return	Morningstar Risk	Morningstar Risk-Adj Rating
1 Yr	–25.39					
3 Yr	–7.65	79	73	–2.36[2]	1.04	★★
5 Yr	2.23	77	66	–0.58[2]	0.88	★★★
Incept	8.70	—	—	—	—	

Average Historical Rating (77 months): 4.5★s

[1] 1=low, 100=high [2] T-Bill return substituted for category avg.

Category Rating (3 Yr)

1 2 3 4 5 — Worst … Best

Return Below Avg
Risk Above Avg

Other Measures	Standard Index S&P 500	Best Fit Index MSCIEasNdD
Alpha	–7.5	–1.9
Beta	0.71	1.08
R-Squared	38	76

Standard Deviation	18.42
Mean	–7.65
Sharpe Ratio	–0.81

Portfolio Analysis 11-30-01

Share change since 08-01 Total Stocks: 87	Sector	Country	% Assets
☼ Vodafone Airtouch	Services	United Kingdom	2.67
⊖ Tyco Intl	Industrials	U.S.	2.33
⊖ Elan ADR	Health	Ireland	2.08
⊖ Total Fina Cl B	Energy	France	2.00
⊖ Muenchener Rueckvers (Reg)	Financials	Germany	1.88
⊖ Banco Popular Espanol	Financials	Spain	1.84
⊖ Aventis Cl A	Health	France	1.84
⊖ Eni–ente Nazionale	N/A	N/A	1.82
⊖ Ahold	Retail	Netherlands	1.81
⊖ UniCredito Italiano	Financials	Italy	1.71
⊖ E.ON Cl B	Services	Germany	1.70
⊖ Reckitt Benckiser	Staples	United Kingdom	1.69
⊖ Bank of Ireland	Financials	Ireland	1.66
⊖ Interbrew	Staples	Belgium	1.64
⊖ Philips Electrics (NV)	Durables	Netherlands	1.62
⊖ CRH	Industrials	Ireland	1.59
⊕ Allianz (Reg)	Financials	Germany	1.59
⊖ Royal Bk Canada	Financials	Canada	1.58
⊖ Suez Lyon Eaux	Industrials	France	1.57
⊕ Glaxosmithkline	Technology	United Kingdom	1.43

Current Investment Style

Style: Value Blnd Growth; Size: Large Med Small

	Stock Port Avg	Rel MSCI EAFE Current	Rel MSCI EAFE Hist	Rel Cat
Price/Earnings Ratio	23.9	0.92	0.98	0.94
Price/Cash Flow	13.2	1.02	1.09	0.92
Price/Book Ratio	3.6	1.03	1.10	0.91
3 Yr Earnings Growth	25.5	1.37	0.78	1.30
Med Mkt Cap $mil	19,214	0.7	0.8	1.07

Country Exposure 11-30-01	% assets
United Kingdom	13
France	11
Japan	8
Germany	8
Netherlands	7

Hedging History: Frequent

Regional Exposure 11-30-01	% assets
Europe	61
Japan	8
Latin America	2
Pacific Rim	3
Other	9

Special Securities % assets 11-30-01	
Restricted/Illiquid Secs	Trace
Emerging–Markets Secs	7
Options/Futures/Warrants	No

Composition % assets 11-30-01			
Cash	9.8	Bonds	0.0
Stocks	89.7	Other	0.6

Sector Weightings	% of Stocks	Rel Cat	5-Year High	5-Year Low
Utilities	2.6	0.9	11	0
Energy	5.5	0.9	10	1
Financials	26.1	1.2	34	10
Industrials	15.4	1.1	26	8
Durables	5.7	0.8	18	3
Staples	7.0	1.0	7	1
Services	15.5	0.9	33	7
Retail	4.5	0.9	19	1
Health	12.4	1.3	15	3
Technology	5.2	0.5	25	3

Analysis by Gregg Wolper 12-14-01

Deutsche International Equity Fund is having trouble finding its footing on unfamiliar turf.

This fund was one of the finest foreign-stock funds for most of the 1990s. From 1994 through 1998, it enjoyed five straight calendar years in the category's top quartile. But since then, the fund has struggled. Indeed, its trailing three-year loss of 7.3% through Dec. 13, 2001, puts it in the group's bottom decile. And 2001 itself has been no picnic: It has lost 28% so far this year, landing in the bottom quartile in a tough year for global markets.

Comanager Rob Reiner, who was also around for the good years, says that the main reason for the fund's weak performance in recent years is that the managers' growth-at-a-reasonable-price philosophy has been out of step with the markets. In 1999 through early 2000, aggressive-growth strategies were in favor, and since then, value-oriented stock-picking has led to success. Because this fund doesn't use either method, Reiner says, it has been left out in the cold. He's not second-guessing the fund's strategy: For example, he criticizes the current swing back toward high valuations for firms with doubtful earnings prospects, and says the fund will recover when investors regain their senses.

There's some truth in that outline, but shareholders also have reason to expect the fund to be able to handle various market climates better than it has. After all, the market winds weren't always perfectly in its favor during the mid- to late-1990s, but it was able to succeed consistently nonetheless.

Reiner and his team are still trying. They've added to the fund's insurance and reinsurance stake, for example, thinking that such stocks were unjustly punished in September. And they've bought a few beaten-down stocks in emerging markets. Investors are best advised to wait until this fund has shown persuasive signs of recovery, though, before jumping in.

Address:	1 South Street Baltimore, MD 21202 800–730–1313
Web Address:	www.deam–us.com
*Inception:	08-04-92
Advisor:	Bankers Trust
Subadvisor:	None
NTF Plans:	Fidelity , Datalynx

Minimum Purchase:	$2500	Add: $250 IRA: $500
Min Auto Inv Plan:	$1000	Add: $100
Sales Fees:	No–load	
Management Fee:	.65%, 1.0%A	
Actual Fees:	Mgt: 0.65%	Dist: —
Expense Projections:	3Yr: $503	5Yr: $882 10Yr: $1948
Avg Brok Commission:	—	Income Distrib: Annually
Total Cost (relative to category):		Average

DFA One–Year Fixed–Income

Ticker	Load	NAV	Yield	SEC Yield	Total Assets	Mstar Category
DFIHX	None	$10.27	4.5%	—	$726.8 mil	Ultrashort Bond

Prospectus Objective: Corp Bond—High Quality

DFA One-Year Fixed-Income Portfolio seeks a stable real value of capital with a minimum of risk.

The fund invests in high-quality debt obligations with maturities no longer than two years from the date of purchase. It invests principally in certificates of deposit, commercial paper, bankers' acceptances, and bonds issued by both domestic and foreign entities, but denominated in U.S. dollars. The average weighted maturity may not exceed one year.

The fund is only offered to institutional investors or clients of registered investment advisors. Prior to April 10, 1989, the fund was named DFA Fixed-Income Portfolio.

Historical Profile

Return Average
Risk Low
Rating ★★★★★ Highest

Investment Style
Fixed-Income
Income Rtn %Rank Cat: 66 53 76 66 73 68 70 81

Growth of Principal vs. Interest Rate Shifts
— Principal Value $000 (NAV with capital gains reinvested)
— Interest Rate % on 10 Yr Treasury
▼ Manager Change
▽ Partial Manager Change
► Mgr Unknown After
◄ Mgr Unknown Before

Performance Quartile (within Category)

Portfolio Manager(s)

Jeanne C. Sinquefield. Since 7-83. PhD U. of Chicago; MBA U. of Chicago. Other funds currently managed: DFA Continental Small Company, DFA Five-Year Government, DFA Five Year Global Fixed-Income.

David A. Plecha. Since 5-89. BS'83 U. of Michigan; MBA'87 U. of California-Los Angeles. Other funds currently managed: DFA Five-Year Government, DFA Five Year Global Fixed-Income, DFA Intermediate Govt Fixed-Income.

Judith A. Jonas. Since 1-92. BA'77 U. of California-Berkeley; MBA'83 U. of California-Los Angeles. Other funds currently managed: DFA Five-Year Government, DFA Five Year Global Fixed-Income, DFA Intermediate Govt Fixed-Income.

1990	1991	1992	1993	1994	1995	1996	1997	1998	1999	2000	12-01	History
10.14	10.29	10.18	10.20	9.98	10.16	10.17	10.17	10.18	10.11	10.16	10.27	NAV
9.10	8.68	5.20	4.46	2.43	8.00	5.75	6.00	5.70	4.60	6.73	5.76	Total Return %
0.14	–7.33	–2.20	–5.29	5.34	–10.47	2.14	–3.69	–2.97	5.43	–4.91	–2.66	+/– LB Aggregate
0.92	2.73	1.44	1.18	–2.58	2.02	0.67	0.43	0.33	–0.55	0.40	2.28	+/– 6 Month CD
8.69	6.86	4.78	4.10	4.55	6.18	5.65	5.94	5.53	5.31	6.21	4.65	Income Return %
0.41	1.82	0.42	0.36	–2.13	1.82	0.10	0.05	0.17	–0.71	0.52	1.11	Capital Return %
33	16	43	55	57	25	66	70	33	68	40	34	Total Rtn % Rank Cat
0.85	0.68	0.48	0.41	0.46	0.60	0.56	0.59	0.55	0.53	0.61	0.46	Income $
0.00	0.03	0.15	0.02	0.01	0.00	0.00	0.01	0.01	0.00	0.00	0.00	Capital Gains $
0.21	0.21	0.21	0.21	0.21	0.20	0.21	0.22	0.21	0.21	0.20	—	Expense Ratio %
8.27	6.75	4.81	3.38	4.47	5.86	5.39	5.79	5.51	5.07	5.90	—	Income Ratio %
96	82	126	62	141	81	96	83	24	58	35	—	Turnover Rate %
416.0	470.0	530.2	599.0	573.0	696.1	746.3	725.2	743.3	691.5	714.9	—	Net Assets $mil

Performance 12-31-01

	1st Qtr	2nd Qtr	3rd Qtr	4th Qtr	Total
1997	1.07	1.74	1.57	1.48	6.00
1998	1.43	1.31	1.49	1.35	5.70
1999	1.13	1.06	1.02	1.31	4.60
2000	1.34	1.48	2.04	1.70	6.73
2001	1.59	1.15	2.05	0.85	5.76

Trailing	Total Return%	+/– LB Agg	+/– 6 Month CD	% Rank All	% Rank Cat	Growth of $10,000
3 Mo	0.85	0.81	0.36	73	38	10,085
6 Mo	2.92	–1.73	1.66	16	20	10,292
1 Yr	5.76	–2.66	2.28	19	34	10,576
3 Yr Avg	5.69	–0.58	0.71	25	44	11,807
5 Yr Avg	5.76	–1.67	0.58	51	46	13,228
10 Yr Avg	5.45	–1.78	0.56	86	50	17,006
15 Yr Avg	6.37	–1.75	0.58	81	1	25,267

Tax Analysis	Tax-Adj Ret%	%Rank Cat	%Pretax Ret	%Rank Cat
3 Yr Avg	3.53	38	62.1	19
5 Yr Avg	3.53	26	61.3	16
10 Yr Avg	3.32	37	60.8	12

Potential Capital Gain Exposure: 2% of assets

Risk Analysis

Time Period	Load-Adj Return %	Risk %Rank[1] All	Risk %Rank[1] Cat	Morningstar Return	Morningstar Risk	Morningstar Risk-Adj Rating
1 Yr	5.76					
3 Yr	5.69	1	35	0.16[2]	0.07	★★★★★
5 Yr	5.76	1	24	0.16[2]	0.08	★★★★★
10 Yr	5.45	1	27	0.19[2]	0.13	★★★★★

Average Historical Rating (186 months): 4.6★s

[1]1=low, 100=high [2] T-Bill return substituted for category avg.

Category Rating (3 Yr)

1 2 **3** 4 5
Worst Best

Return Average
Risk Average

Other Measures	Standard Index LB Agg	Best Fit Index LB Int
Alpha	0.5	0.5
Beta	0.13	0.18
R-Squared	44	54

Standard Deviation	0.69
Mean	5.69
Sharpe Ratio	1.27

Portfolio Analysis 06-30-01

Total Fixed-Income: 44	Date of Maturity	Amount $000	Value $000	% Net Assets
FHLMC Debenture 7.375%	05-15-03	42	44,425	6.31
Bank of America 6.05%	07-19-01	27	27,755	3.94
Wal-Mart Stores 6.15%	08-10-01	26	26,688	3.79
Credit Agricole Indosuez Na 7.14%	07-03-01	25	26,259	3.73
Chase Manhattan 4.141%	09-06-02	22	22,074	3.14
Federal Farm Credit Bk 5%	02-03-03	21	21,595	3.07
FNMA Debenture 4.625%	05-15-03	21	21,532	3.06
Federal Home Loan Bk 4.5%	04-25-03	21	21,518	3.06
Panasonic Fin Amer N/A	07-02-01	22	21,500	3.06
Abbott Labs N/A	07-05-01	21	21,393	3.04
Corporate Asset Fdg N/A	07-03-01	21	20,998	2.98
Cba (delaware) Fin N/A	07-05-01	21	20,993	2.98
Eksportfinans N/A	07-02-01	20	20,000	2.84
Bp Amoco Cap N/A	07-02-01	20	20,000	2.84
Ciesco L.p N/A	07-02-01	20	20,000	2.84
United Parcel Svc N/A	07-06-01	20	19,991	2.84
Nestle Fin France N/A	07-06-01	20	19,991	2.84
Koch Inds N/A	07-06-01	20	19,991	2.84
Export Dev N/A	07-13-01	20	19,977	2.84
Paccar Finl 5.97%	07-12-01	17	17,304	2.46

Current Investment Style

Maturity: Short Int Long; Quality: High Med Low

Avg Eff Duration[1]	0.9 Yrs
Avg Eff Maturity	0.9 Yrs
Avg Credit Quality	AAA
Avg Wtd Coupon	2.82%
Avg Wtd Price	—

[1]figure provided by fund

Special Securities % assets 06-30-01	
Restricted/Illiquid Secs	0
Exotic Mortgage–Backed	0
Emerging–Markets Secs	0
Options/Futures/Warrants	No

Credit Analysis % bonds 09-30-01			
US Govt	0	BB	0
AAA	97	B	0
AA	3	Below B	0
A	0	NR/NA	0
BBB	0		

Sector Breakdown % bonds 06-30-01			
US Treasuries	0	CMOs	0
GNMA mtgs	0	ARMs	0
FNMA mtgs	3	Other	82
FHLMC mtgs	15		

Coupon Range	% of Bonds	Rel Cat
0%	0.00	0.00
0% to 7%	62.37	1.13
7% to 8.5%	37.63	1.60
8.5% to 10%	0.00	0.00
More than 10%	0.00	0.00

1.00=Category Average

Composition % assets 06-30-01			
Cash	3.0	Bonds	97.0
Stocks	0.0	Other	0.0

Analysis by Langdon Healy 12-11-01

This is a decent choice for conservative investors looking for somewhere to park cash on a short-term basis.

DFA One-Year Fixed-Income Fund is a straightforward, conservatively positioned, ultrashort bond fund. The managers only buy high-quality bonds that will mature in two years or less from the date the fund purchases them. Its average weighted maturity must remain below one year.

While these constraints limit the fund's return potential relative to more flexible ultrashort bond funds, they also keep volatility to a minimum. The fund's 10-year annualized return of 5.53% is average, but it has been less volatile than two thirds of the ultrashort-bond group with 10-year records. So far this year, the fund is performing a bit better, as its 5.45% return through December 10, 2001 bests two thirds of its rivals.

Part of the fund's relative success owes to its low expense ratio. At 0.20% annually, the fund charges investors 66 basis points less than the average ultrashort fund. This difference is huge in a category where the spread between a top-performing fund and a laggard is sometimes only a few basis points. Over time, this expense advantage has helped produce a favorable risk/reward profile.

While the fund might not be exciting, it does provide a fairly safe short-term haven for cash. Its NAV isn't pegged to stay in place over time (as a money market's is), but its fluctuations usually aren't dramatic. Thus, this fund may be an appropriate alternative for money-market investors willing to take on some interest-rate risk in exchange for a slightly higher yield.

Though the fund has a steep $2 million initial investment hurdle, it can be purchased through select fund supermarkets for an initial investment of only $2500.

Address:	1299 Ocean Avenue 11th Floor Santa Monica, CA 90401 310–395–8005
Web Address:	www.dfafunds.com
Inception:	07-27-83
Advisor:	Dimensional Fund Adv.
Subadvisor:	None
NTF Plans:	N/A

Minimum Purchase:	$2.00 mil	Add: None IRA: —
Min Auto Inv Plan:	—	Add: —
Sales Fees:	No–load	
Management Fee:	.15%, .10%A	
Actual Fees:	Mgt: 0.15%	Dist: —
Expense Projections:	3Yr: $68	5Yr: $118 10Yr: $268
Avg Brok Commission:	—	Income Distrib: Monthly
Total Cost (relative to category):		Below Avg

DFA U.S. Micro Cap

Ticker	Load	NAV	Yield	Total Assets	Mstar Category
DFSCX	None	$10.01	0.4%	$1,512.7 mil	Small Blend

Prospectus Objective: Small Company

DFA U.S. 9-10 Small Company Portfolio seeks long-term capital appreciation.

The fund invests in a diverse group of small companies with readily marketable securities. These companies may be traded on the NYSE, the AMEX, or the over-the-counter market, but their market capitalizations must be comparable with those in the smallest quintile of the NYSE. The portfolio is rebalanced at least semiannually.

The fund is designed primarily for institutional investors. Prior to April 10, 1989, the fund was named DFA Investment Dimensions Small Company. Prior to 1983, the fund was named DFA Small Company.

Historical Profile
Return High
Risk Above Avg
Rating ★★★★ Above Avg

Investment Style
Equity
Average Stock %: 100% 99% 98% 97% 98% 98%

▼ Manager Change
▽ Partial Manager Change

Fund Performance vs. Category Average
Quarterly Fund Return +/– Category Average
— Category Baseline

Performance Quartile (within Category)

Portfolio Manager(s)

Jeanne C. Sinquefield. Since 4-83.
Robert T. Deere. Since 11-91.
Art Barlow. Since 8-90.
Carl Snyder. Since 7-91.
Scott Thornton. Since 7-92.
Karen McGinley, CFA. Since 7-93.

1990	1991	1992	1993	1994	1995	1996	1997	1998	1999	2000	12-01	History
4.64	6.55	7.36	8.25	8.49	10.53	11.20	11.78	10.76	12.61	9.64	10.01	NAV
–21.56	44.26	23.48	20.97	3.09	34.48	17.65	22.78	–7.32	29.79	–3.60	22.77	Total Return %
–18.45	13.78	15.86	10.91	1.78	–3.06	–5.30	–10.57	–35.89	8.75	5.50	34.65	+/– S&P 500
–2.06	–1.79	5.07	2.06	4.92	6.04	1.11	0.41	–4.77	8.53	–0.57	20.28	+/– Russell 2000
1.15	0.97	0.61	0.25	0.18	0.51	0.26	0.23	1.28	3.49	3.89	0.51	Income Return %
–22.72	43.29	22.87	20.72	2.91	33.97	17.39	22.55	–8.60	26.29	–7.49	22.26	Capital Return %
83	40	6	30	19	19	65	78	68	17	88	7	Total Rtn % Rank Cat
0.08	0.05	0.04	0.02	0.02	0.04	0.03	0.03	0.15	0.38	0.49	0.05	Income $
0.72	0.09	0.67	0.62	0.00	0.84	1.16	1.89	0.00	0.89	1.99	1.71	Capital Gains $
0.62	0.64	0.68	0.70	0.65	0.62	0.61	0.60	0.59	0.61	0.56	—	Expense Ratio %
0.99	0.75	0.53	0.26	0.16	0.45	0.22	0.21	0.18	0.30	0.34	—	Income Ratio %
4	10	10	10	17	25	24	28	26	23	37	—	Turnover Rate %
566.0	730.0	671.8	643.0	663.0	946.1	1,186.6	1,437.3	1,360.2	1,451.5	1,378.0	—	Net Assets $mil

Performance 12-31-01

	1st Qtr	2nd Qtr	3rd Qtr	4th Qtr	Total
1997	–2.95	12.51	20.85	–6.96	22.78
1998	10.95	–5.36	–22.72	14.20	–7.32
1999	–7.90	20.18	–3.19	21.12	29.79
2000	21.09	–8.58	3.44	–15.82	–3.60
2001	0.73	21.83	–17.50	21.26	22.77

Trailing	Total Return%	+/– S&P 500	+/– Russ 2000	% Rank All	% Rank Cat	Growth of $10,000
3 Mo	21.26	10.58	0.18	12	22	12,126
6 Mo	0.04	5.60	4.13	39	42	10,004
1 Yr	22.77	34.65	20.28	2	7	12,277
3 Yr Avg	15.38	16.41	8.96	5	21	15,360
5 Yr Avg	11.82	1.12	4.29	11	41	17,479
10 Yr Avg	15.59	2.66	4.08	4	15	42,583
15 Yr Avg	12.57	–1.16	1.82	21	47	59,094

Tax Analysis	Tax-Adj Ret%	%Rank Cat	%Pretax Ret	%Rank Cat
3 Yr Avg	11.29	29	73.4	81
5 Yr Avg	8.65	52	73.2	85
10 Yr Avg	12.83	18	82.3	34

Potential Capital Gain Exposure: 2% of assets

Risk Analysis

Time Period	Load-Adj Return %	Risk %Rank[1] All	Risk %Rank[1] Cat	Morningstar Return	Morningstar Risk	Morningstar Risk-Adj Rating
1 Yr	22.77					
3 Yr	15.38	82	92	2.44[2]	1.19	★★★★★
5 Yr	11.82	85	92	1.69[2]	1.26	★★★★
10 Yr	15.59	87	90	1.94	1.26	★★★★

Average Historical Rating (193 months): 2.4★s

[1]1=low, 100=high [2] T-Bill return substituted for category avg.

Category Rating (3 Yr)

1 2 3 4 5
Worst Best

Return Above Avg
Risk High

Other Measures	Standard Index S&P 500	Best Fit Index Russ 2000
Alpha	18.4	9.3
Beta	0.79	1.12
R-Squared	22	83
Standard Deviation		34.18
Mean		15.38
Sharpe Ratio		0.35

Portfolio Analysis 12-31-00

Share change since 11-00 Total Stocks: 2738

	Sector	PE	YTD Ret%	% Assets
⊖ Scios	Health	—	6.83	0.50
Inverness Medical Tech	Health	—	–1.77	0.48
⊖ Carreker	Technology	—	–83.00	0.41
CIMA Labs	Health	39.3	–44.40	0.41
Impath	Health	65.5	–33.00	0.37
⊕ Cryolife	Health	61.2	–0.83	0.35
⊖ Ameripath	Health	56.2	28.04	0.30
RehabCare Grp	Health	17.8	–42.30	0.29
⊖ ArQule	Health	—	–46.80	0.29
⊖ Boston Comms Grp	Technology	35.5	–59.20	0.28
NeoPharm	Health	—	–27.20	0.28
⊖ Key Prodtn	Energy	6.3	–49.30	0.28
⊖ Meridian Resources	Energy	3.6	–53.70	0.27
Unit	Energy	6.8	–31.80	0.26
⊖ Sterling Bancorp	Financials	16.7	50.58	0.26
NPS Pharmaceuticals	Health	—	–20.20	0.25
⊖ Woodhead Inds	Durables	19.1	–17.30	0.25
⊖ Regent Comm	Services	—	13.67	0.24
MapInfo	Technology	87.2	–66.70	0.24
⊖ Gymboree	Retail	—	–14.00	0.23
Noven Pharmaceuticals	Health	22.2	–52.50	0.23
⊖ Bel Fuse Cl B	Technology	—	—	0.23
⊖ Comstock Resources	Energy	4.4	–52.50	0.23
⊖ Penn Engnrg & Mfg	Industrials	14.7	–3.26	0.23
☼ Queens County Bancorp	Financials	26.6	43.38	0.23

Current Investment Style

Style: Value Blnd Growth; Size: Large Med Small

	Stock Port Avg	Relative S&P 500 Current	Relative S&P 500 Hist	Rel Cat
Price/Earnings Ratio	23.3	0.75	0.64	0.94
Price/Book Ratio	2.7	0.47	0.43	0.84
Price/Cash Flow	14.0	0.78	0.67	0.90
3 Yr Earnings Growth	14.5[1]	0.99	0.80	0.85
1 Yr Earnings Est%	–5.4[1]	3.07	—	–6.31
Med Mkt Cap $mil	166	0.0	—	0.17

[1]figure is based on 50% or less of stocks

Special Securities % assets 12-31-00	
Restricted/Illiquid Secs	0
Emerging-Markets Secs	Trace
Options/Futures/Warrants	Yes

Composition % assets 12-31-00	
Cash	0.6
Stocks*	99.4
Bonds	0.0
Other	0.0
*Foreign (% stocks)	0.1

Market Cap	
Giant	0.0
Large	0.1
Medium	0.1
Small	26.9
Micro	72.9

Sector Weightings	% of Stocks	Rel S&P	5-Year High	5-Year Low
Utilities	1.3	0.4	4	1
Energy	5.7	0.8	6	2
Financials	14.0	0.8	14	8
Industrials	17.2	1.5	29	16
Durables	5.2	3.3	8	4
Staples	2.4	0.3	4	2
Services	14.3	1.3	17	11
Retail	5.3	0.8	8	4
Health	17.0	1.1	23	7
Technology	17.7	1.0	29	16

Analysis by Heather Haynos 12-18-01

For those who can handle its risks, DFA U.S. Micro Cap Fund's rewards can be great.

In a tough market for stocks, this fund is putting the competition to shame. For the year to date through Dec. 17, 2001, its more than 18% return was better than that of 92% of its small-blend peers.

The fund has been spurred on by a couple of factors. For one, it invests in tiny stocks, which have generally fared better than large caps in 2001's dicey markets. What's more, this portfolio features particularly small issues. Its median market cap, for example, is less than $200 million, which is a fraction of the category average. Such stocks, while considerably riskier than larger fare, often have the potential for the greatest returns. The fund has also been buoyed by its value leanings. Although its average P/E ratio approximates that of the small-blend average, the fund has fallen into the small-value style box over the past four years. And value fare has definitely beaten out growth over the past two years.

The fund's longer-term record is also strong. Its 10- and 15-year trailing returns place it well into the small-blend group's top half. Still, these results haven't come without cost. The fund is also one of the group's riskiest. It trailed more than three fourths of its peers in 2000, for example, and endured a disappointing stretch from 1996 through 1998, when large caps held center stage.

The fund's premise is inherently risky. It maintains that broad exposure to the smallest 20% of stocks will reward investors with higher returns in exchange for assuming higher risks. While the fund has generally lived up to its promise, its ultra-small-cap focus makes it riskier than most and not as versatile as a more mainstream small-cap offering.

Address: 1299 Ocean Avenue 11th Floor
Santa Monica, CA 90401
310-395-8005
Web Address: www.dfafunds.com

Inception: 12-22-81
Advisor: Dimensional Fund Adv.
Subadvisor: None
NTF Plans: N/A

Minimum Purchase:	$2.00 mil	Add: None	IRA: —
Min Auto Inv Plan:	—	Add: —	
Sales Fees:	No-load		
Management Fee:	.50%		
Actual Fees:	Mgt: 0.50%	Dist: —	
Expense Projections:	3Yr: $195	5Yr: $340	10Yr: $762
Avg Brok Commission:	—	Income Distrib: Annually	
Total Cost (relative to category):	Low		

Dodge & Cox Income

Ticker	Load	NAV	Yield	SEC Yield	Total Assets	Mstar Category
DODIX	None	$12.20	6.0%	—	$1,226.7 mil	Interm–Term Bond

Prospectus Objective: Corp Bond—High Quality

Dodge & Cox Income Fund seeks income consistent with long-term preservation of capital; capital appreciation is a secondary consideration.

The fund normally invests at least 80% of assets in the following: debt obligations issued or guaranteed by the U.S. government, its agencies, or instrumentalities; investment-grade debt securities, including U.S. dollar-denominated foreign issues; unrated securities deemed to be of investment-grade quality; bankers' acceptances, bank certificates of deposit, repurchase agreements, and commercial paper. At least 65% of assets are held in the first two categories. The fund may invest up to 25% of assets in dollar-denominated foreign securities.

Historical Profile

Return High
Risk Average
Rating ★★★★★ Highest

Investment Style
Fixed-Income

Income Rtn %Rank Cat: 25 13 38 42 33 35 17 18

Growth of Principal vs. Interest Rate Shifts
— Principal Value $000 (NAV with capital gains reinvested)
— Interest Rate % on 10 Yr Treasury
▼ Manager Change
▽ Partial Manager Change
► Mgr Unknown After
◄ Mgr Unknown Before

Performance Quartile (within Category)

Portfolio Manager(s)

Management Team

History

1990	1991	1992	1993	1994	1995	1996	1997	1998	1999	2000	12-01	History
10.61	11.59	11.55	11.89	10.74	12.02	11.68	12.08	12.25	11.40	11.80	12.20	NAV
7.42	17.94	7.80	11.34	−2.89	20.21	3.62	10.00	8.08	−0.81	10.70	10.32	Total Return %
−1.54	1.94	0.40	1.60	0.03	1.74	—	0.32	−0.60	0.02	−0.93	1.90	+/– LB Aggregate
−1.75	3.31	0.63	2.56	−0.96	4.90	−0.44	2.14	−0.34	−1.20	0.60	1.34	+/– LB Int Govt/Corp
7.81	7.85	7.27	6.92	6.58	7.74	6.31	6.40	6.11	5.94	7.02	6.42	Income Return %
−0.39	10.09	0.53	4.42	−9.47	12.47	−2.69	3.60	1.97	−6.75	3.68	3.90	Capital Return %
52	29	33	32	26	14	33	15	37	35	34	4	Total Rtn % Rank Cat
0.81	0.81	0.82	0.78	0.76	0.81	0.74	0.73	0.72	0.71	0.78	0.74	Income $
0.01	0.04	0.09	0.17	0.05	0.03	0.00	0.00	0.06	0.04	0.00	0.06	Capital Gains $
0.69	0.64	0.62	0.60	0.54	0.54	0.50	0.49	0.47	0.46	0.46	—	Expense Ratio %
7.99	7.63	7.14	6.50	6.90	6.85	6.65	6.32	6.00	6.10	6.67	—	Income Ratio %
13	15	12	26	55	53	37	28	35	24	34	—	Turnover Rate %
52.1	96.2	136.3	180.0	195.4	303.3	532.8	705.5	952.0	974.0	1,020.8	—	Net Assets $mil

Performance 12-31-01

	1st Qtr	2nd Qtr	3rd Qtr	4th Qtr	Total
1997	−0.77	3.68	3.69	3.12	10.00
1998	1.41	2.41	3.14	0.90	8.08
1999	−0.33	−0.99	0.43	0.09	−0.81
2000	2.11	1.32	2.72	4.17	10.70
2001	3.82	1.32	4.24	0.61	10.32

Trailing	Total Return%	+/– LB Agg	+/– LB ITGvt/Corp	% Rank All	% Rank Cat	Growth of $10,000
3 Mo	0.61	0.58	0.52	74	16	10,061
6 Mo	4.88	0.23	0.18	4	14	10,488
1 Yr	10.32	1.90	1.34	6	4	11,032
3 Yr Avg	6.60	0.33	0.20	19	8	12,114
5 Yr Avg	7.57	0.14	0.48	32	5	14,402
10 Yr Avg	7.65	0.43	0.85	45	9	20,908
15 Yr Avg	—	—	—	—	—	—

Tax Analysis	Tax-Adj Ret%	%Rank Cat	%Pretax Ret	%Rank Cat
3 Yr Avg	3.94	8	59.7	14
5 Yr Avg	4.92	3	65.0	7
10 Yr Avg	4.90	4	64.1	1

Potential Capital Gain Exposure: NMF

Risk Analysis

Time Period	Load-Adj Return %	Risk %Rank[1] All	Risk %Rank[1] Cat	Morningstar Return	Morningstar Risk	Morningstar Risk-Adj Rating
1 Yr	10.32					
3 Yr	6.60	10	12	0.36[2]	0.58	★★★★
5 Yr	7.57	16	18	0.58[2]	0.62	★★★★★
10 Yr	7.65	27	46	0.86[2]	0.92	★★★★★

Average Historical Rating (121 months): 4.0★s

[1]1=low, 100=high [2] T-Bill return substituted for category avg.

Category Rating (3 Yr)

1 2 3 4 5
Worst Best

Return High
Risk Below Avg

Other Measures	Standard Index LB Agg	Best Fit Index LB Corp
Alpha	0.4	0.9
Beta	0.95	0.80
R–Squared	92	93

Standard Deviation	3.51
Mean	6.60
Sharpe Ratio	0.55

Portfolio Analysis 06-30-01

Total Fixed-Income: 126	Date of Maturity	Amount $000	Value $000	% Net Assets
FHLMC CMO PAC 6%	11-15-08	40,000	40,650	3.27
US Treasury Note 3.875%	01-15-09	32,145	33,200	2.67
FNMA CMO 7%	03-25-21	31,250	31,943	2.57
Federal Natl Mtge Assn 7.5%	07-25-28	30,427	31,434	2.53
US Treasury Note 6.75%	05-15-05	28,000	29,811	2.40
GMAC 8.875%	06-01-10	23,075	25,922	2.09
American Home Products 6.7%	03-15-11	25,000	24,733	1.99
Ford Motor Credit 6.875%	02-01-06	22,500	22,936	1.85
EOP Operating 8.375%	03-16-06	21,000	22,557	1.81
US Treasury Note 3.5%	01-15-11	21,789	21,871	1.76
FHLMC CMO PAC 6.5%	04-15-22	20,000	20,275	1.63
Raychem 7.2%	10-15-08	20,000	20,167	1.62
FHLMC CMO PAC 6%	10-15-08	20,100	20,050	1.61
Time Warner Entertnmnt 8.375%	07-15-33	17,250	18,588	1.50
FHLMC 6.5%	06-01-12	17,746	18,029	1.45
Union Pacific 6.7%	02-23-19	17,829	17,546	1.41
Eastman Chemical 7.25%	01-15-24	20,650	17,313	1.39
FNMA CMO PAC 6.25%	03-25-23	17,000	17,239	1.39
FHLMC 7.9%	02-01-21	15,950	16,689	1.34
California Infrastruct 6.42%	09-25-08	16,220	16,570	1.33

Current Investment Style

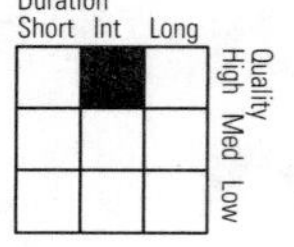

Avg Eff Duration[1]	4.4 Yrs
Avg Eff Maturity	10.0 Yrs
Avg Credit Quality	—
Avg Wtd Coupon	6.89%
Avg Wtd Price	101.24% of par

[1]figure provided by fund

Special Securities % assets 06-30-01

Restricted/Illiquid Secs	0
Exotic Mortgage–Backed	0
Emerging–Markets Secs	0
Options/Futures/Warrants	No

Credit Analysis % bonds 03-31-01

US Govt	55	BB	2
AAA	3	B	0
AA	0	Below B	0
A	18	NR/NA	0
BBB	21		

Sector Breakdown % bonds 06-30-01

US Treasuries	2	CMOs	3
GNMA mtgs	4	ARMs	1
FNMA mtgs	15	Other	50
FHLMC mtgs	18		

Coupon Range	% of Bonds	Rel Cat
0%	0.00	0.00
0% to 7%	46.43	0.86
7% to 8.5%	45.50	1.31
8.5% to 10%	6.67	0.93
More than 10%	1.41	0.52

1.00=Category Average

Composition % assets 06-30-01

Cash	5.7	Bonds	94.3
Stocks	0.0	Other	0.0

Analysis by Alan Papier 11-21-01

It shouldn't come as a surprise that Dodge & Cox Income Fund is chalking up another exceptional year.

This fund's gain of 9.9% for the year to date through Nov. 20, 2001, ranked in the top decile of the intermediate-term bond category. Similarly, all of the fund's longer-term returns rank in the group's top 10%. And unlike some offerings that shoot the lights out during rallies or make a habit of being defensive, this fund has been a consistent performer regardless of market environment. Indeed, the fund's streak of top-40% finishes is at 10 calendar years (and counting), a span that includes several bond market cycles.

The fund's long-term success is predicated on management's ability to unearth cheap bonds. Rather than actively rotate among bond market sectors, or position the portfolio based on expected interest-rate or yield-curve shifts, management focuses on security selection. The team targets corporate and mortgage-related bonds, because those typically throw off current income streams in excess of the market average. Additionally, the team emphasizes noncallable bonds, or those with call and prepayment protection, to keep the holdings it has diligently identified and researched. Such an approach has kept portfolio turnover low, and trading costs and taxable distributions to a minimum.

The fund's issue-selection proficiency has been on display in 2001. Some of the fund's mid-quality (A and BBB rated) corporates have rebounded sharply this year after the segment lagged in 2000. In addition, the fund's focus on collateralized mortgage obligations (CMOs)—which have better prepayment protection than other mortgage bonds—has been a boon, given the recent refinancing boom.

This fund's well-executed strategy, low expenses, and consistent, long-term record speak volumes.

Address:	One Sansome Street 35th Floor San Francisco, CA 94104 800–621–3979
Web Address:	www.dodgeandcox.com
Inception:	01-03-89
Advisor:	Dodge & Cox
Subadvisor:	None
NTF Plans:	N/A

Minimum Purchase:	$2500	Add: $100	IRA: $1000
Min Auto Inv Plan:	$2500	Add: $100	
Sales Fees:	No–load		
Management Fee:	.50% mx./.40% mn.		
Actual Fees:	Mgt: 0.41%	Dist: —	
Expense Projections:	3Yr: $151	5Yr: $263	10Yr: $591
Avg Brok Commission:	—	Income Distrib: Quarterly	
Total Cost (relative to category):	—		

Dodge & Cox Stock

Ticker	Load	NAV	Yield	Total Assets	Mstar Category
DODGX	None	$100.51	1.7%	$6,308.7 mil	Large Value

Prospectus Objective: Growth and Income

Dodge & Cox Stock Fund seeks long-term growth of principal and income; current income is a secondary consideration.

The fund intends to remain fully invested in equities with at least 65% of assets in common stocks. It may invest in preferred stocks and convertibles. The fund may invest up to 20% of assets in American Depositary Receipts. Management seeks companies with financial strength and a sound economic background.

Historical Profile
Return High
Risk Below Avg
Rating ★★★★★ Highest

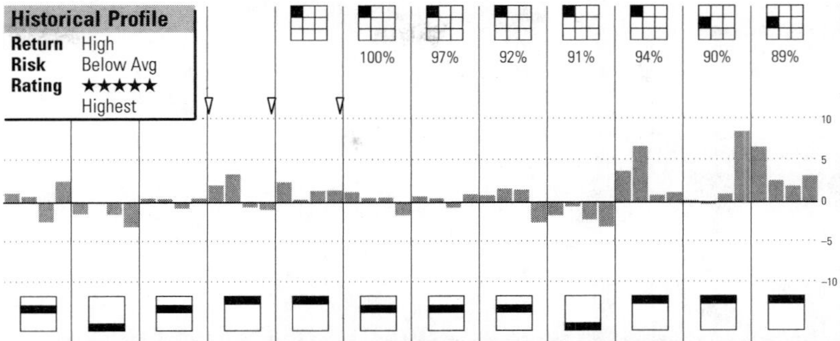

Investment Style
Equity
Average Stock %: 100% 97% 92% 91% 94% 90% 89%

▼ Manager Change
▽ Partial Manager Change

Fund Performance vs. Category Average
Quarterly Fund Return +/– Category Average
— Category Baseline

Performance Quartile (within Category)

Portfolio Manager(s)

Management Team

1990	1991	1992	1993	1994	1995	1996	1997	1998	1999	2000	12-01	History
38.79	44.85	48.37	53.23	53.94	67.83	79.81	94.57	90.70	100.52	96.67	100.51	NAV
–5.09	21.47	10.82	18.31	5.17	33.38	22.27	28.40	5.40	20.21	16.31	9.33	Total Return %
–1.97	–9.01	3.20	8.26	3.85	–4.16	–0.68	–4.95	–23.18	–0.83	25.41	21.21	+/– S&P 500
–1.42	3.32	1.75	–1.45	7.48	–6.66	–0.05	–7.09	–15.84	9.25	14.00	18.12	+/– Russ Top 200 Val
3.21	3.23	2.50	2.18	2.19	2.62	1.92	1.89	1.68	1.66	2.18	1.82	Income Return %
–8.30	18.24	8.32	16.13	2.98	30.75	20.35	26.51	3.72	18.55	14.13	7.51	Capital Return %
43	87	36	17	5	46	28	38	88	7	12	2	Total Rtn % Rank Cat
1.35	1.24	1.11	1.04	1.15	1.40	1.29	1.49	1.56	1.48	2.09	1.73	Income $
0.28	0.87	0.16	2.84	0.89	2.52	1.68	6.09	7.42	6.70	17.10	3.20	Capital Gains $
0.65	0.64	0.64	0.62	0.61	0.60	0.59	0.57	0.57	0.55	0.54	—	Expense Ratio %
3.47	2.87	2.43	1.95	2.16	2.07	1.79	1.67	1.63	1.46	2.13	—	Income Ratio %
7	5	7	15	7	13	10	19	19	18	32	—	Turnover Rate %
173.0	281.3	335.9	435.9	543.5	1,227.9	2,252.0	4,087.0	4,355.3	4,624.5	5,728.5	—	Net Assets $mil

Performance 12-31-01

	1st Qtr	2nd Qtr	3rd Qtr	4th Qtr	Total
1997	2.45	15.42	10.23	–1.50	28.40
1998	9.73	–1.05	–14.30	13.26	5.40
1999	4.53	16.64	–8.39	7.61	20.21
2000	0.27	–2.22	6.24	11.66	16.31
2001	0.95	7.30	–10.23	12.44	9.33

Trailing	Total Return%	+/– S&P 500	+/– Russ Top 200 Val	% Rank All	% Rank Cat	Growth of $10,000
3 Mo	12.44	1.75	6.92	31	14	11,244
6 Mo	0.94	6.49	6.71	34	6	10,094
1 Yr	9.33	21.21	18.12	7	2	10,933
3 Yr Avg	15.19	16.22	14.03	5	2	15,285
5 Yr Avg	15.65	4.95	4.44	4	3	20,686
10 Yr Avg	16.62	3.69	2.59	3	2	46,514
15 Yr Avg	15.49	1.75	1.99	5	4	86,692

Tax Analysis	Tax-Adj Ret%	%Rank Cat	%Pretax Ret	%Rank Cat
3 Yr Avg	12.28	2	80.9	21
5 Yr Avg	12.93	3	82.6	21
10 Yr Avg	14.38	3	86.5	11

Potential Capital Gain Exposure: 21% of assets

Risk Analysis

Time Period	Load-Adj Return %	Risk %Rank[1] All	Risk %Rank[1] Cat	Morningstar Return	Morningstar Risk	Morningstar Risk-Adj Rating
1 Yr	9.33					
3 Yr	15.19	40	3	2.39[2]	0.54	★★★★★
5 Yr	15.65	47	9	2.84[2]	0.64	★★★★★
10 Yr	16.62	55	18	2.23	0.70	★★★★★

Average Historical Rating (193 months): 4.2★s

[1] 1=low, 100=high [2] T-Bill return substituted for category avg.

Category Rating (3 Yr)
1 Worst — 5 Best

Return High
Risk Low

Other Measures	Standard Index S&P 500	Best Fit Index SPMid400
Alpha	14.3	7.1
Beta	0.63	0.55
R-Squared	45	46
Standard Deviation		18.27
Mean		15.19
Sharpe Ratio		0.64

Analysis by William Samuel Rocco 10-16-01

It's business as usual at Dodge & Cox Stock, and that's great.

This fund hasn't deviated one bit from its hard-core value discipline in the aftermath of the Sept. 11, 2001, terrorist attack. Its managers have always been quite patient—turnover is normally less than half the group norm here—and they have remained so lately. In particular, they've stuck with the insurers Chubb and St. Paul—which have exposure to last month's tragedy—and they've continued adding to consumer as well as other names on weakness.

Meanwhile, the managers, who began to find good bargains in the tech sector over the summer, have continued to find attractive opportunities there. Thus, they've been putting a good portion of incoming cash into computer-related stocks. Their tech stake—which includes consumer-electronic and office-equipment issues, as well as software and hardware-names—is up to 11%. (While still less than the 15% the S&P 500 index has in such stocks, it's higher than the 8% the fund had this summer.)

It's encouraging that the managers are staying the course. They're looking prescient about Chubb and St. Paul, which are up 22% and 35%, respectively, over the past month. Thanks to nice gains from Xerox, Kmart, Whirlpool and various other holdings, the fund is up 1% and leads 96% of its peers for the year to date through October 15, 2001.

What's more, the fund's strict bargain-hunting has delivered similarly impressive returns over the long term while keeping volatility well under control. The fund also boasts a low expense ratio. For all these reasons, we think this fund remains one of the best large-value offerings around.

Portfolio Analysis 06-30-01

Share change since 03-01 Total Stocks: 80	Sector	PE	YTD Ret%	% Assets
⊕ Bank One	Financials	29.1	9.13	2.65
⊕ Golden West Finl	Financials	12.9	–12.40	2.63
⊕ Dow Chemical	Industrials	NMF	–4.43	2.59
⊕ Phillips Petro	Energy	7.1	8.56	2.45
⊕ Xerox	Technology	—	127.10	2.38
⊖ Union Pacific	Services	17.1	13.96	2.23
⊕ AT & T	N/A	—	—	2.22
⊕ Fedex	Services	29.3	29.83	2.20
⊕ May Dept Stores	Retail	15.2	15.97	2.15
⊕ News ADR Pfd	Services	—	—	2.13
⊕ Unocal	Energy	10.9	–4.58	2.05
⊖ Loews	Financials	—	8.35	1.92
⊕ Genuine Parts	Durables	16.8	45.48	1.89
⊕ Kmart	Retail	—	2.77	1.89
⊕ Occidental Petro	Energy	5.7	13.49	1.84
⊕ Lockheed Martin	Industrials	36.8	38.98	1.79
⊕ Chevron	Energy	10.3	9.29	1.70
⊕ Whirlpool	Durables	71.9	57.27	1.63
⊕ Amerada Hess	Energy	4.7	–13.00	1.54
⊕ Equity Office Properties Tr	Financials	18.7	–1.76	1.52
⊕ Bank of America	Financials	16.7	42.73	1.49
⊖ ALCOA	Industrials	21.4	7.86	1.45
⊕ WellPoint Health Networks	Health	19.4	1.39	1.42
⊕ Deere	Industrials	—	–2.52	1.41
⊕ Rio Tinto UK ADR	Industrials	20.9	8.78	1.38

Current Investment Style

Style: Value Blnd Growth; Size: Large Med Small

	Stock Port Avg	Relative S&P 500 Current	Relative S&P 500 Hist	Rel Cat
Price/Earnings Ratio	25.2	0.82	0.73	1.00
Price/Book Ratio	2.4	0.43	0.37	0.59
Price/Cash Flow	10.0	0.56	0.47	0.73
3 Yr Earnings Growth	13.7	0.94	0.45	0.93
1 Yr Earnings Est%	–2.8	1.59	—	0.85
Med Mkt Cap $mil	10,133	0.2	0.2	0.32

Special Securities % assets 06-30-01	
Restricted/Illiquid Secs	0
Emerging-Markets Secs	0
Options/Futures/Warrants	No

Composition % assets 06-30-01	
Cash	9.6
Stocks*	88.3
Bonds	0.0
Other	2.1
*Foreign (% stocks)	4.5

Market Cap	
Giant	7.7
Large	53.5
Medium	37.1
Small	1.7
Micro	0.0

Sector Weightings	% of Stocks	Rel S&P	5-Year High	5-Year Low
Utilities	4.3	1.4	9	3
Energy	12.0	1.7	14	7
Financials	19.5	1.1	22	14
Industrials	23.5	2.1	27	17
Durables	9.0	5.8	13	4
Staples	2.0	0.3	6	2
Services	8.9	0.8	13	7
Retail	7.6	1.1	12	4
Health	7.3	0.5	9	2
Technology	6.0	0.3	17	5

Address: One Sansome Street 35th Floor, San Francisco, CA 94104, 800-621-3979
Web Address: www.dodgeandcox.com
Inception: 01-04-65
Advisor: Dodge & Cox
Subadvisor: None
NTF Plans: N/A

Minimum Purchase: $2500 Add: $100 IRA: $1000
Min Auto Inv Plan: $2500 Add: $100
Sales Fees: No-load
Management Fee: .50%
Actual Fees: Mgt: 0.50% Dist: —
Expense Projections: 3Yr: $183 5Yr: $318 10Yr: $714
Avg Brok Commission: — Income Distrib: Quarterly
Total Cost (relative to category): —

Dodge & Cox Balanced

Ticker	Load	NAV	Yield	Total Assets	Mstar Category
DODBX	None	$65.42	3.2%	$4,997.5 mil	Domestic Hybrid

Prospectus Objective: Balanced

Dodge & Cox Balanced Fund seeks income, conservation of principal, and long-term growth of principal and income.

The fund may invest up to 75% of assets in common stocks and convertible securities. It may invest up to 20% of assets in American Depositary Receipts. The fund typically invests in investment-grade debt securities. It may invest in government obligations, mortgage- and asset-backed securities, CMOs, and corporate bonds. When selecting securities, management may consider yield to maturity, quality, liquidity, and current yield.

Historical Profile
Return: Above Avg
Risk: Low
Rating: ★★★★★ Highest

Investment Style
Equity
Average Stock %: 60% 57% 58% 57% 59% 60% 59%

▼ Manager Change
▽ Partial Manager Change

Fund Performance vs. Category Average
■ Quarterly Fund Return +/– Category Average
— Category Baseline

Performance Quartile (within Category)

Portfolio Manager(s)

Management Team

1990	1991	1992	1993	1994	1995	1996	1997	1998	1999	2000	12-01	History
35.03	40.09	42.44	46.40	45.21	54.60	59.82	66.78	65.22	65.71	63.42	65.42	NAV
0.94	20.72	10.57	15.95	1.99	28.02	14.76	21.19	6.70	12.06	15.14	10.05	Total Return %
4.06	–9.76	2.95	5.89	0.68	–9.52	–8.19	–12.16	–21.88	–8.98	24.24	21.93	+/– S&P 500
–8.02	4.72	3.16	6.20	4.91	9.55	11.14	11.51	–1.98	12.89	3.51	1.63	+/– LB Aggregate
5.01	5.11	4.36	3.97	3.85	4.90	3.70	3.77	3.41	3.47	3.91	3.44	Income Return %
–4.07	15.61	6.21	11.98	–1.86	23.11	11.06	17.42	3.29	8.58	11.23	6.61	Capital Return %
41	72	23	16	10	24	36	28	82	35	7	3	Total Rtn % Rank Cat
1.81	1.76	1.72	1.66	1.76	2.18	1.99	2.22	2.23	2.22	2.47	2.14	Income $
0.33	0.29	0.08	1.07	0.36	0.91	0.69	3.27	3.74	4.98	9.22	2.05	Capital Gains $
0.70	0.65	0.63	0.60	0.58	0.57	0.56	0.55	0.54	0.53	0.53	—	Expense Ratio %
5.24	4.78	4.27	3.67	3.94	3.85	3.60	3.39	3.29	3.18	3.70	—	Income Ratio %
10	10	6	15	20	20	17	32	26	17	23	—	Turnover Rate %
82.6	179.4	268.8	486.8	725.3	1,800.3	3,629.8	5,076.6	5,693.0	5,138.0	4,909.1	—	Net Assets $mil

Performance 12-31-01

	1st Qtr	2nd Qtr	3rd Qtr	4th Qtr	Total
1997	1.11	10.96	7.86	0.15	21.19
1998	6.55	0.23	–7.93	8.51	6.70
1999	2.81	9.92	–5.29	4.69	12.06
2000	1.25	–1.09	5.16	9.33	15.14
2001	1.95	5.19	–5.22	8.27	10.05

Trailing	Total Return%	+/– S&P 500	+/– LB Agg	% Rank All	% Rank Cat	Growth of $10,000
3 Mo	8.27	–2.42	8.23	51	21	10,827
6 Mo	2.62	8.17	–2.04	17	6	10,262
1 Yr	10.05	21.93	1.63	6	3	11,005
3 Yr Avg	12.39	13.42	6.12	7	2	14,198
5 Yr Avg	12.92	2.22	5.49	8	3	18,359
10 Yr Avg	13.43	0.50	6.20	11	3	35,266
15 Yr Avg	13.08	–0.66	4.96	16	1	63,199

Tax Analysis	Tax-Adj Ret%	%Rank Cat	%Pretax Ret	%Rank Cat
3 Yr Avg	9.01	2	72.7	13
5 Yr Avg	9.82	4	76.0	23
10 Yr Avg	10.87	1	81.0	12

Potential Capital Gain Exposure: 16% of assets

Risk Analysis

Time Period	Load-Adj Return %	Risk %Rank¹ All	Risk %Rank¹ Cat	Morningstar Return	Morningstar Risk	Morningstar Risk-Adj Rating
1 Yr	10.05					
3 Yr	12.39	33	11	1.69[2]	0.34	★★★★★
5 Yr	12.92	39	17	2.00[2]	0.41	★★★★★
10 Yr	13.43	45	16	1.41	0.46	★★★★★

Average Historical Rating (193 months): 4.0★s

¹1=low, 100=high ² T-Bill return substituted for category avg.

Category Rating (3 Yr)

1 Worst — 5 Best

Return: High
Risk: Below Avg

Other Measures	Standard Index S&P 500	Best Fit Index SPMid400
Alpha	9.6	5.1
Beta	0.40	0.35
R-Squared	44	46

Standard Deviation	11.31
Mean	12.39
Sharpe Ratio	0.75

Portfolio Analysis 06-30-01

Total Stocks: 80 Share change since 03-01	Sector	PE Ratio	YTD Return %	% Net Assets
Golden West Finl	Financials	12.9	–12.40	1.97
Kmart	Retail	—	2.77	1.69
Dow Chemical	Industrials	NMF	–4.43	1.65
Bank One	Financials	29.1	9.13	1.63
⊕ Phillips Petro	Energy	7.1	8.56	1.57
⊖ Union Pacific	Services	17.1	13.96	1.49
Xerox	Technology	—	127.10	1.40
⊕ AT & T	Services	7.8	40.59	1.36
Genuine Parts	Durables	16.8	45.48	1.35
⊖ Loews	Financials	—	8.35	1.33

Total Fixed-Income: 127	Date of Maturity	Amount $000	Value $000	% Net Assets
US Treasury Note 3.875%	01-15-09	116,900	120,735	2.30
News ADR Pfd		2,148	69,589	1.32
Union Pacific 6.33%	01-02-20	46,290	44,199	0.84
FHLMC CMO PAC 6.5%	10-15-07	41,500	42,524	0.81
EOP Operating 8.375%	03-16-06	35,000	37,596	0.72
California Infrastruct 6.38%	09-25-08	35,775	36,323	0.69
Federal Natl Mtge Assn 7.5%	02-25-41	35,000	35,700	0.68
Ford Motor Credit 6.875%	02-01-06	35,000	35,678	0.68
Raychem 7.2%	10-15-08	34,560	34,848	0.66
American Home Products 6.7%	03-15-11	35,000	34,627	0.66

Equity Style
Style: Value
Size: Large-Cap

Fixed-Income Style
Duration: Intermediate
Quality: High

	Portfolio Avg	Rel S&P
Price/Earnings Ratio	24.5	0.79
Price/Book Ratio	2.4	0.42
Price/Cash Flow	9.9	0.55
3 Yr Earnings Growth	13.2	0.90
1 Yr Earnings Est%	–4.3	2.45
Debt % Total Cap	40.4	1.31
Med Mkt Cap $mil	10,129	0.17

Avg Eff Duration¹	4.2 Yrs
Avg Eff Maturity	10.4 Yrs
Avg Credit Quality	—
Avg Wtd Coupon	6.81%

¹figure provided by fund as of 03-31-01

Analysis by William Samuel Rocco 10-31-01

Dodge & Cox Balanced Fund remains both steady and outstanding.

This fund's managers have always been slow-moving value hounds—turnover is usually below 30% per year here—and they've stuck to their discipline since the Sept. 11 attack. They've continued to nibble at bargains in the tech sector in recent weeks, and they've continued to add to selective holdings on weakness. They haven't done much buying other than that, though.

Overall, the fund, which has received some inflows, has seen its cash stake decrease to roughly 3% of assets over the past few months, while its equity stake has increased a bit to 61% of assets. About 35% of the fund remains in a mix of mid-quality corporate and intermediate-term government bonds.

This patient, value-oriented discipline has really come through this year. For starters, the managers' stock selection has been first-rate. Indeed, top-10 names Genuine Parts and Xerox are up 29% and 48%, respectively, in 2001. And several of their energy picks, including Occidental Petroleum and Chevron Texaco, have posted solid gains. Meanwhile, their fixed-income holdings, particularly their corporate bonds, have been strong performers. As a result, the fund has returned 3% for the year to date through Oct. 30 and leads 95% of its rivals.

The long-term returns are similarly impressive here. What's more, the fund has been far less volatile than most of its peers. And its expense ratio is quite low. For all these reasons, we think this fund remains one of the best domestic-hybrid offerings around.

Special Securities % assets 06-30-01	
Restricted/Illiquid Secs	0
Emerging-Markets Secs	0
Options/Futures/Warrants	No

Composition % of assets 06-30-01	
Cash	7.0
Stocks*	59.1
Bonds	32.7
Other	1.3
*Foreign (% of stocks)	4.5

Market Cap	
Giant	9.4
Large	51.4
Medium	37.3
Small	1.9
Micro	0.0

Sector Weightings	% of Stocks	Rel S&P	5-Year High	5-Year Low
Utilities	4.4	1.4	8	3
Energy	11.2	1.6	14	7
Financials	19.0	1.1	22	15
Industrials	22.9	2.0	27	17
Durables	8.2	5.3	13	3
Staples	3.5	0.5	4	2
Services	10.9	1.0	12	8
Retail	7.7	1.1	11	4
Health	6.4	0.4	9	2
Technology	5.8	0.3	17	5

Address:	One Sansome Street 35th Floor San Francisco, CA 94104 800-621-3979
Web Address:	www.dodgeandcox.com
Inception:	06-26-31
Advisor:	Dodge & Cox
Subadvisor:	None
NTF Plans:	N/A

Minimum Purchase:	$2500	Add: $100 IRA: $1000
Min Auto Inv Plan:	$2500	Add: $100
Sales Fees:	No-load	
Management Fee:	.50%	
Actual Fees:	Mgt: 0.50%	Dist: —c
Expense Projections:	3Yr: $173	5Yr: $302 10Yr: $677
Avg Brok Commission:	—	Income Distrib: Quarterly
Total Cost (relative to category):	—	

Domini Social Equity

Ticker	Load	NAV	Yield	Total Assets	Mstar Category
DSEFX	12b–1 only	$27.37	0.2%	$1,207.1 mil	Large Blend

Prospectus Objective: Growth and Income

Domini Social Equity Fund seeks long-term total return that corresponds with the performance of the Domini Social index, which consists of approximately 400 companies that meet certain social criteria.

The fund invests substantially all assets in stocks in the index. To construct the index, the advisor selects companies in the S&P 500 based on social responsibility and on its requirements for industrydiversification, financial solvency, market capitalization, and minimal portfolio turnover. The index also includes companies not included in theS&P 500.

Prior to Oct. 26, 1993, the fund was named Domini Social IndexTrust.

Historical Profile
Return: Above Avg
Risk: Average
Rating: ★★★ Neutral

Investment Style
Equity
Average Stock %: 100% 100% 100% 100% 100% 100%

▼ Manager Change
▽ Partial Manager Change

Fund Performance vs. Category Average
■ Quarterly Fund Return +/– Category Average
— Category Baseline

Performance Quartile (within Category)

Portfolio Manager(s)

John O'Toole. Since 12-94. BA U. of Pennsylvania; MBA U. of Chicago. Other funds currently managed: Dreyfus Premier Midcap Stock R, Dreyfus Premier Midcap Stock A, Domini Instl Social Equity.

History

1990	1991	1992	1993	1994	1995	1996	1997	1998	1999	2000	12–01	History
—	10.72	11.87	12.43	12.10	16.11	19.35	26.22	34.40	41.89	34.57	27.37	NAV
—	8.37*	12.10	6.53	−0.36	35.17	21.84	36.02	32.99	22.63	−15.05	−12.76	Total Return %
—	−1.08*	4.49	−3.52	−1.67	−2.36	−1.10	2.67	4.41	1.59	−5.95	−0.89	+/– S&P 500
—	—	4.45	−3.31	−0.81	−2.43	−0.32	3.00	4.35	0.80	−4.10	0.00	+/– Wilshire Top 750
—	0.63	1.17	1.18	1.62	1.25	0.95	0.31	0.06	0.04	0.00	0.14	Income Return %
—	7.74	10.93	5.35	−1.97	33.92	20.89	35.72	32.93	22.58	−15.05	−12.90	Capital Return %
—	—	17	79	51	40	44	5	6	34	92	49	Total Rtn % Rank Cat
—	0.06	0.13	0.14	0.20	0.15	0.15	0.06	0.02	0.01	0.00	0.05	Income $
—	0.00	0.02	0.07	0.08	0.08	0.12	0.03	0.45	0.27	0.98	2.75	Capital Gains $
—	0.75	0.75	0.75	0.75	0.90	0.98	0.98	1.17	0.98	0.96	0.93	Expense Ratio %
—	1.49	1.53	1.41	1.67	1.38	1.01	0.62	0.07	0.06	−0.05	0.06	Income Ratio %
—	—	3	4	8	6	5	1	5	8	9	19	Turnover Rate %
—	3.6	10.3	27.0	33.7	69.4	115.3	301.4	715.8	1,343.8	1,329.0	1,207.1	Net Assets $mil

Performance 12-31-01

	1st Qtr	2nd Qtr	3rd Qtr	4th Qtr	Total
1997	3.20	17.31	7.70	4.32	36.02
1998	14.07	3.75	−9.83	24.62	32.99
1999	4.71	6.47	−6.36	17.47	22.63
2000	2.72	−5.28	−4.96	−8.15	−15.05
2001	−12.24	5.17	−14.26	10.24	−12.76

Trailing	Total Return%	+/– S&P 500	+/– Wil Top 750	% Rank All	% Rank Cat	Growth of $10,000
3 Mo	10.24	−0.45	−1.09	42	64	11,024
6 Mo	−5.49	0.07	0.30	65	34	9,451
1 Yr	−12.76	−0.89	0.00	67	49	8,724
3 Yr Avg	−3.14	−2.11	−1.32	87	78	9,087
5 Yr Avg	10.45	−0.25	0.33	16	28	16,438
10 Yr Avg	12.41	−0.52	−0.04	16	32	32,217
15 Yr Avg	—	—	—	—	—	—

Tax Analysis	Tax-Adj Ret%	%Rank Cat	%Pretax Ret	%Rank Cat
3 Yr Avg	−4.00	75	—	—
5 Yr Avg	9.77	17	93.5	12
10 Yr Avg	11.74	10	94.6	4

Potential Capital Gain Exposure: –12% of assets

Risk Analysis

Time Period	Load-Adj Return %	Risk %Rank[1] All	Risk %Rank[1] Cat	Morningstar Return	Morningstar Risk	Morningstar Risk-Adj Rating
1 Yr	−12.76					
3 Yr	−3.14	72	69	−1.59[2]	0.99	★★
5 Yr	10.45	70	64	1.31[2]	0.95	★★★★
10 Yr	12.41	71	54	1.19	0.92	★★★

Average Historical Rating (92 months): 4.0★s

[1] 1=low, 100=high [2] T-Bill return substituted for category avg.

Category Rating (3 Yr)

1 2 3 4 5 (Worst – Best)

Return: Below Avg
Risk: Above Avg

Other Measures	Standard Index S&P 500	Best Fit Index S&P 500
Alpha	−1.8	−1.8
Beta	1.04	1.04
R-Squared	96	96

Standard Deviation	17.58
Mean	−3.14
Sharpe Ratio	−0.54

Portfolio Analysis 10-31-01

Share change since 09–01 Total Stocks: 400	Sector	PE	YTD Ret%	% Assets
⊕ Microsoft	Technology	57.6	52.78	6.19
⊕ American Intl Grp	Financials	42.0	−19.20	4.10
⊕ Johnson & Johnson	Health	16.6	14.01	3.49
⊕ Intel	Technology	73.1	4.89	3.29
⊕ Merck	Health	19.1	−35.90	2.94
⊕ Verizon Comms	Services	29.7	−2.52	2.69
⊕ AOL Time Warner	Technology	—	−7.76	2.66
⊕ SBC Comms	Services	18.4	−16.00	2.58
⊕ Cisco Sys	Technology	—	−52.60	2.46
⊕ Coca-Cola	Staples	35.5	−21.40	2.39
⊕ Procter & Gamble	Staples	38.8	3.12	1.93
⊕ Home Depot	Retail	42.9	12.07	1.78
⊕ PepsiCo	Staples	31.4	−0.54	1.73
⊕ Fannie Mae	Financials	16.2	−6.95	1.65
⊕ J.P. Morgan Chase & Co.	Financials	27.8	−17.40	1.40
⊕ BellSouth	Services	24.9	−5.09	1.38
⊕ Wells Fargo	Financials	22.4	−20.20	1.34
⊕ Dell Comp	Technology	61.8	55.87	1.25
⊕ Amgen	Health	52.8	−11.70	1.18
⊕ Schering-Plough	Health	22.2	−35.90	1.08
⊕ AT&T	Services	7.8	40.59	1.07
⊕ Medtronic	Health	76.4	−14.70	0.97
⊕ Texas Instruments	Technology	87.5	−40.70	0.97
⊕ Freddie Mac	Financials	14.0	−3.87	0.94
⊕ Minnesota Mng & Mfg	Industrials	34.5	0.16	0.82

Current Investment Style

Style: Value Blnd Growth; Size: Large Med Small

	Stock Port Avg	Relative S&P 500 Current	Relative S&P 500 Hist	Rel Cat
Price/Earnings Ratio	33.4	1.08	1.06	1.10
Price/Book Ratio	5.6	0.98	1.05	1.02
Price/Cash Flow	19.6	1.09	1.06	1.06
3 Yr Earnings Growth	16.0	1.09	1.13	0.89
1 Yr Earnings Est%	−4.3	2.44	—	—
Med Mkt Cap $mil	56,116	0.9	1.1	1.07

Special Securities % assets 10-31-01	
Restricted/Illiquid Secs	0
Emerging-Markets Secs	0
Options/Futures/Warrants	No

Composition % assets 10-31-01	
Cash	0.0
Stocks*	100.0
Bonds	0.0
Other	0.0
*Foreign (% stocks)	0.0

Market Cap	
Giant	55.6
Large	32.0
Medium	11.3
Small	1.1
Micro	0.1

Sector Weightings	% of Stocks	Rel S&P	5-Year High	5-Year Low
Utilities	1.0	0.3	4	1
Energy	1.3	0.2	6	1
Financials	22.1	1.2	24	12
Industrials	5.0	0.4	8	3
Durables	1.1	0.7	4	1
Staples	10.1	1.3	17	6
Services	14.4	1.3	23	12
Retail	7.1	1.0	19	7
Health	12.7	0.9	13	5
Technology	25.2	1.4	44	6

Analysis by Catherine Hickey 09-22-01

This fund remains a fine social index option.

Domini Social Equity Fund's solid showing during this year's continued growth downturn demonstrates why it's still a solid core holding. It's down 23% for the year to date through Sept. 21, 2001, but in this year's rough-and-tumble market, that ranks squarely in the large-blend category's top half.

Like other socially screened funds, this one carries an above-average weighting in tech stocks (those companies tend to pass screens on pollution and workplace diversity more easily than manufacturers or energy companies). However, while Domini's overweight in tech is sizable, it isn't gigantic. Further, the fund has a big stake in Microsoft, which is one of the few tech stocks in positive territory this year, and another in AOL Time Warner, which has held up fairly well.

This fund's solid showing under tough conditions should indicate its standing on the risk spectrum for social index funds. So far, TIAA-CREF Social Choice Equity, whose screens allow for larger stakes in utilities and energy and hence seems a bit more moderate than this offering, isn't outperforming Domini by much this year. However, because of its bigger allocations to value sectors, it courts less volatility from price risk than Domini does. By contrast, funds such as Citizens Core Growth and Vanguard Calvert Social Index are quite a bit heavier in tech and telecom and skimp more on value sectors than Domini. Both of these funds are having a rougher year than both Domini and TIAA-CREF. Thus, investors who want a socially screened option that will give some cushion when growth tanks might look here.

This fund isn't the cheapest social fund, so if expenses are your greatest worry, look at TIAA-CREF or Vanguard. Other investors will find a comfortable home here.

Address:	P.O. Box 60494, King of Prussia, PA 19406–0494, 800–762–6814
Web Address:	http://www.domini.com
*Inception:	06-03-91
Advisor:	Domini Social Inv.s
Subadvisor:	Mellon Equity
NTF Plans:	Waterhouse , Schwab

Minimum Purchase:	$1000	Add: $50 IRA: $250
Min Auto Inv Plan:	$500	Add: $25
Sales Fees:	0.25%B	
Management Fee:	.20%, .50%A	
Actual Fees:	Mgt: 0.20%	Dist: 0.25%
Expense Projections:	3Yr: $328	5Yr: $578 10Yr: $1295
Avg Brok Commission:	—	Income Distrib: Semi–Ann.
Total Cost (relative to category):	Below Avg	

Dresdner RCM Global Technology I

Ticker	Load	NAV	Yield	Total Assets	Mstar Category
DRGTX	None	$30.54	0.0%	$432.0 mil	Spec Technology

Prospectus Objective: Specialty—Technology

Dresdner RCM Global Technology Fund seeks capital appreciation.

The fund normally invests at least 65% of assets in equities issued by technology companies located in at least three countries, including the U.S. The advisor seeks companies that exhibit one or more of the following qualities: superior management, strong balance sheets, new or superior products or services, potential for revenue growth, and a commitment to research and development. It may invest up to 50% in foreign securities. The fund is nondiversified.

After Dec. 31, 1998, the fund changed to a multi-class structure.

Past fund name: RCM Global Technology Fund.

Historical Profile
Return High
Risk High
Rating ★★★★★ Highest

Investment Style
Equity
Average Stock %: 92% 87% 92% 90% 89% 86%

▼ Manager Change
▽ Partial Manager Change

Fund Performance vs. Category Average
■ Quarterly Fund Return +/– Category Average
— Category Baseline

Performance Quartile (within Category)

Portfolio Manager(s)

Huachen Chen, CFA. Since 12-95. BS'83 Cornell U.; MS'85 Northwestern U. Other funds currently managed: Dresdner RCM Global Technology N, SunAmerica Focused TechNet A, SunAmerica Focused TechNet B.

Walter C. Price, Jr., CFA. Since 12-95. BS'72 M.I.T; MS'72 M.I.T. Other funds currently managed: Dresdner RCM Global Technology N, SunAmerica Focused TechNet A, SunAmerica Focused TechNet B.

1990	1991	1992	1993	1994	1995	1996	1997	1998	1999	2000	12-01	History
—	—	—	—	—	10.04	12.60	13.69	21.47	59.21	50.32	30.54	NAV
—	—	—	—	—	0.40*	26.41	27.08	61.06	182.95	–14.33	–39.31	Total Return %
—	—	—	—	—	–0.01*	3.47	–6.27	32.49	161.92	–5.23	–27.43	+/– S&P 500
—	—	—	—	—	—	6.38	7.11	6.46	66.56	1.89	–23.72	+/– PSE Tech 100
—	—	—	—	—	0.00	0.90	0.00	0.00	0.00	0.00	0.00	Income Return %
—	—	—	—	—	0.40	25.52	27.08	61.06	182.95	–14.33	–39.31	Capital Return %
—	—	—	—	—	—	14	4	36	14	10	48	Total Rtn % Rank Cat
—	—	—	—	—	0.00	0.09	0.00	0.00	0.00	0.00	0.00	Income $
—	—	—	—	—	0.00	0.00	2.21	0.57	1.38	0.43	0.00	Capital Gains $
—	—	—	—	—	—	1.73	1.75	1.75	1.50	1.21	—	Expense Ratio %
—	—	—	—	—	—	–1.34	–1.15	–0.99	–1.02	–0.26	—	Income Ratio %
—	—	—	—	—	—	156	189	266	119	451	—	Turnover Rate %
—	—	—	—	—	1.0	5.1	6.9	18.2	197.1	366.3	199.7	Net Assets $mil

Performance 12-31-01

	1st Qtr	2nd Qtr	3rd Qtr	4th Qtr	Total
1997	–8.89	19.86	23.33	–5.65	27.08
1998	16.80	11.88	–15.60	46.02	61.06
1999	16.30	13.10	17.67	82.82	182.95
2000	26.79	–6.99	10.83	–34.45	–14.33
2001	–34.12	–1.48	–33.31	40.22	–39.31

Trailing	Total Return%	+/– S&P 500	+/– PSE Tech 100	% Rank All	% Rank Cat	Growth of $10,000
3 Mo	40.22	29.54	7.31	2	35	14,022
6 Mo	–6.49	–0.94	–1.21	71	8	9,351
1 Yr	–39.31	–27.43	–23.72	98	48	6,069
3 Yr Avg	13.73	14.76	–1.50	6	8	14,712
5 Yr Avg	24.67	13.97	1.46	1	2	30,112
10 Yr Avg	—	—	—	—	—	—
15 Yr Avg	—	—	—	—	—	—

Tax Analysis	Tax-Adj Ret%	%Rank Cat	%Pretax Ret	%Rank Cat
3 Yr Avg	13.26	5	96.5	18
5 Yr Avg	22.83	2	92.6	4
10 Yr Avg	—	—	—	—

Potential Capital Gain Exposure: –32% of assets

Risk Analysis

Time Period	Load-Adj Return %	Risk %Rank[1] All	Risk %Rank[1] Cat	Morningstar Return	Morningstar Risk	Morningstar Risk-Adj Rating
1 Yr	–39.31					
3 Yr	13.73	98	29	2.02[2]	2.13	★★★★
5 Yr	24.67	97	26	6.23[2]	1.89	★★★★★
Incept	24.96	—	—	—	—	

Average Historical Rating (37 months): 5.0★s

[1] 1=low, 100=high [2] T-Bill return substituted for category avg.

Category Rating (3 Yr)

1 2 3 4 5 — Worst ... Best (rating: 5)

Return High
Risk Below Avg

Other Measures	Standard Index S&P 500	Best Fit Index Wil 4500
Alpha	32.1	21.6
Beta	1.83	1.56
R-Squared	38	76
Standard Deviation		65.39
Mean		13.73
Sharpe Ratio		0.15

Portfolio Analysis 11-30-01

Share chng since 10-01 Total Stocks: 72	Subsector	PE	YTD Ret%	% Assets
EBAY	Services	NMF	102.70	4.24
Utstarcom	Technology	—	83.87	3.72
Brocade Comm Sys	Technology	—	–63.90	3.66
⊖ Affiliated Comp Svcs A	Computer Svs	39.9	74.88	3.41
⊕ NVIDIA	Technology	84.2	308.50	3.01
Veritas Software	Software	—	–48.70	2.71
Check Point Software Tech	Software	32.0	–55.20	2.68
Yahoo Japan	Technology	NMF	—	2.52
Concurrent Comp	Technology	—	176.20	2.52
⊕ Siebel Sys	Software	54.9	–58.60	2.44
Taiwan Semicon ADR	Technology	26.4	39.36	2.38
⊕ Finisar	Technology	—	–64.90	2.31
⊕ Juniper Net	Technology	NMF	–84.90	2.27
⊖ Emulex	Technology	—	–50.50	2.27
☼ McDATA	Technology	NMF	—	2.20
Flextronics Intl	Technology	—	–15.80	2.11
⊕ Marvell Tech	Technology	—	63.28	2.11
⊕ SeaChange Intl	Technology	—	67.97	2.08
Tyco Intl	Industrials	27.1	6.23	1.96
⊕ Maxim Integrated Products	Semiconductors	68.2	9.82	1.93
Softbank	Financials	7.5	–38.40	1.82
Nokia Cl A ADR	Telecom	45.8	–43.00	1.80
⊕ Samsung Electncs GDR	Technology	—	—	1.79
Nintendo	Durables	32.2	—	1.74
⊕ NetIQ	Technology	—	–59.60	1.73

Current Investment Style

Style: Value Blnd Growth; Size: Large Med Small

	Stock Port Avg	Relative S&P 500 Current	Relative S&P 500 Hist	Rel Cat
Price/Earnings Ratio	48.3	1.56	1.51	1.05
Price/Book Ratio	8.5	1.49	1.62	1.38
Price/Cash Flow	31.9	1.77	1.47	1.23
3 Yr Earnings Growth	39.5[1]	2.70	1.93	1.32
1 Yr Earnings Est%	14.5[1]	—	—	–0.87
Med Mkt Cap $mil	6,010	0.1	0.2	0.38

[1] figure is based on 50% or less of stocks

Analysis by Kelli Stebel 07-30-01

Despite a recent hiccup, this offering remains one of the best tech funds.

Dresdner RCM Global Technology looks a little green around the gills so far in 2001. For the year to date through July 30, the fund has already lost more than 41%, placing in the technology category's bottom quartile. And while many tech funds got a boost in the second quarter, when an interest-rate cut sparked a rally, this fund has missed most of that pop.

The main problem recently has been the fund's big cash stake. Although comanager Walter Price said that he and comanager Huachen Chen had been putting the cash to work, the fund's cash stake was as high as 30% earlier this year. In addition, the duo hasn't been bulking up on semiconductors and semi-equipment makers, a source of strength for some other tech funds so far this year. Price said that he and Chen don't see demand growing for chips, especially with a slowdown in PC and communication sales.

Despite the fund's recent blip, it remains a strong choice. That's because Chen and Price have several advantages over their competition. Compared with many of their upstart peers, this duo is very seasoned, having run institutional tech money for Dresdner since the mid-1980s. They are also backed by an enormous research staff. Price said that 10 analysts work exclusively on this fund and that more than 300 "grass-roots" researchers are at their disposal. The fund's long-term record shows the payoff. Though this year's performance has made a slight dent in its longer-term results, the fund's three- and five-year annualized returns still place in its category's top decile.

Quite simply, if you're looking for a tech fund, this is the kind of experienced, well-diversified offering to buy.

Special Securities % assets 11-30-01	
Restricted/Illiquid Secs	2
Emerging-Markets Secs	7
Options/Futures/Warrants	No

Composition % assets 11-30-01	
Cash	2.9
Stocks*	97.1
Bonds	0.0
Other	0.0
*Foreign (% stocks)	17.2

Market Cap	
Giant	9.2
Large	28.8
Medium	48.2
Small	13.8
Micro	0.0

Subsector Weightings	% of Stocks	Rel Cat
Computers	0.4	0.1
Semiconductors	3.5	0.3
Semi Equipment	0.2	0.0
Networking	2.6	0.7
Periph/Hardware	0.0	0.0
Software	15.6	1.2
Computer Svs	6.4	1.1
Telecom	4.9	0.6
Health Care	1.9	0.5
Other	64.7	1.7

Address: Four Embarcadero Center Suite 3000, San Francisco, CA 94111, 800-726-7240 / 415-954-5400
Web Address: www.dresdnerrcm.com
*Inception: 12-27-95
Advisor: Dresdner RCM Global Investors
Subadvisor: None
NTF Plans: Fidelity

Minimum Purchase: $250000 Add: $250 IRA: $2000
Min Auto Inv Plan: — Add: —
Sales Fees: No-load
Management Fee: 1.0%
Actual Fees: Mgt: 1.00% Dist: —
Expense Projections: 3Yr: $55* 5Yr: $95* 10Yr: $206*
Avg Brok Commission: — Income Distrib: Annually
Total Cost (relative to category): —

Dreyfus Disciplined Stock

Ticker	Load	NAV	Yield	Total Assets	Mstar Category
DDSTX	12b-1 only	$31.97	0.3%	$2,510.2 mil	Large Blend

Prospectus Objective: Growth and Income

Dreyfus Disciplined Stock Fund seeks capital appreciation and income.

The fund normally invests at least 65% of assets in equities, primarily dividend-paying stocks. The fund's economic sector and industry exposure is similar to that of the S&P 500 index.

Investor shares have a 0.25% 12b-1 fee and are sold primarily to retail investors; R shares are sold primarily to bank trust departments and other financial-service providers. Prior to Oct. 17, 1994, the fund was named Laurel Stock Portfolio - Trust Shares. On Dec. 15, 1997, Dreyfus Disciplined Stock Fund - Investor Shares merged into the fund. On that same day, the fund dropped its R share class designation.

Historical Profile
Return Average
Risk Average
Rating ★★★
Neutral

Investment Style
Equity
Average Stock %
100% 98% 98% 99% 100% 99% 99%

▼ Manager Change
▽ Partial Manager Change

Fund Performance vs. Category Average
Quarterly Fund Return
+/– Category Average
— Category Baseline

Performance Quartile (within Category)

Portfolio Manager(s)

Bert J. Mullins, et al. Since 12-87. BS'65 Indiana U.

1990	1991	1992	1993	1994	1995	1996	1997	1998	1999	2000	12-01	History
13.34	17.00	16.94	18.26	17.31	22.78	26.40	31.12	37.46	42.76	36.97	31.97	NAV
0.23	33.64	7.58	11.83	–1.06	36.86	24.88	31.94	26.62	18.21	–9.23	–13.31	Total Return %
3.35	3.15	–0.04	1.77	–2.37	–0.68	1.93	–1.41	–1.95	–2.83	–0.13	–1.43	+/– S&P 500
4.26	1.20	–0.07	1.99	–1.51	–0.75	2.72	–1.08	–2.01	–3.62	1.72	–0.54	+/– Wilshire Top 750
2.10	1.92	1.59	1.61	1.57	1.84	1.19	0.89	0.71	0.19	0.02	0.22	Income Return %
–1.87	31.72	5.99	10.22	–2.63	35.02	23.69	31.06	25.91	18.02	–9.25	–13.53	Capital Return %
27	36	43	36	57	21	14	31	39	66	57	54	Total Rtn % Rank Cat
0.28	0.25	0.27	0.27	0.28	0.32	0.27	0.23	0.22	0.07	0.01	0.08	Income $
0.05	0.52	1.07	0.40	0.47	0.56	1.78	3.37	1.65	1.39	1.92	0.00	Capital Gains $
0.82	0.90	0.90	0.90	0.90	0.90	0.90	0.90	0.99	1.00	1.00	—	Expense Ratio %
2.22	1.92	1.73	1.82	1.54	1.61	1.23	0.87	0.61	0.28	0.02	—	Income Ratio %
76	69	84	64	106	60	64	69	54	57	50	—	Turnover Rate %
11.0	31.6	48.8	201.9	219.8	438.8	874.9	1,645.5	2,817.6	3,523.4	3,183.1	2,510.2	Net Assets $mil

Performance 12-31-01

	1st Qtr	2nd Qtr	3rd Qtr	4th Qtr	Total
1997	0.64	17.30	9.32	2.24	31.94
1998	14.49	2.82	–12.24	22.56	26.62
1999	3.10	6.98	–6.47	14.59	18.21
2000	3.77	–3.32	0.82	–10.25	–9.23
2001	–12.15	5.34	–15.40	10.73	–13.31

Trailing	Total Return%	+/– S&P 500	+/– Wil Top 750	% Rank All	% Rank Cat	Growth of $10,000
3 Mo	10.73	0.04	–0.60	38	46	11,073
6 Mo	–6.33	–0.77	–0.54	70	60	9,367
1 Yr	–13.31	–1.43	–0.54	69	54	8,669
3 Yr Avg	–2.39	–1.36	–0.56	84	71	9,301
5 Yr Avg	9.22	–1.48	–0.90	23	53	15,540
10 Yr Avg	12.20	–0.73	–0.25	17	38	31,614
15 Yr Avg	—	—	—	—	—	—

Tax Analysis	Tax-Adj Ret%	%Rank Cat	%Pretax Ret	%Rank Cat
3 Yr Avg	–2.97	63	—	—
5 Yr Avg	7.91	45	85.9	31
10 Yr Avg	10.59	35	86.8	27

Potential Capital Gain Exposure: 12% of assets

Risk Analysis

Time Period	Load-Adj Return %	Risk %Rank[1] All	Risk %Rank[1] Cat	Morningstar Return	Morningstar Risk	Morningstar Risk-Adj Rating
1 Yr	–13.31					
3 Yr	–2.39	70	61	–1.45[2]	0.96	★★
5 Yr	9.22	70	63	0.99[2]	0.95	★★★
10 Yr	12.20	71	53	1.14	0.91	★★★

Average Historical Rating (133 months): 4.3★s

[1]1=low, 100=high [2] T-Bill return substituted for category avg.

Category Rating (3 Yr)

1 2 3 4 5
Worst Best

Return Below Avg
Risk Average

Other Measures	Standard Index S&P 500	Best Fit Index S&P 500
Alpha	–1.2	–1.2
Beta	1.02	1.02
R-Squared	98	98
Standard Deviation		17.15
Mean		–2.39
Sharpe Ratio		–0.50

Analysis by Brian Portnoy 10-12-01

Is there a case to be made for Dreyfus Disciplined Stock?

Yes, there is. Most importantly, the fund's returns are solid: Over the past decade ended Sept. 30, 2001, its 12.2% annualized gain trails its bogy by only 51 basis points (or 0.51%) per year, which is less than its annual expense ratio. Additionally, such gains owe to manager Bert Mullins' consistent approach for almost 15 years. The fund's quantitative model screens for stocks that are both undervalued and exhibit higher-than-expected earnings momentum. The model is sector-neutral to the S&P 500, but it will mildly under- or overweight specific stocks to add value. Mullins frequently tweaks the process to emphasize variables that have been strongly correlated with recent stock-price movements.

Does that mean we think it's a good choice to serve as an investor's core holding? No, we don't. Several factors should give investors pause before buying this enchanced-index offering. First, its good marks are due mostly to strong performance in the early 1990s; in the past few years, it has struggled to keep up with its bogy. Second, the fund's 1% expense ratio puts it at a disadvantage, sometimes upwards of 80 basis points per year, against cheaper S&P 500 index options. Finally, the fund is less tax-efficient than well-managed index funds.

In short, our bottom line remains the same: There's little reason to own this fund over a cheaper index option with relatively little tracking error and better tax efficiency.

Portfolio Analysis 09-30-01

Share change since 06-01 Total Stocks: 137

	Sector	PE	YTD Ret%	% Assets
⊖ General Elec	Industrials	30.1	–15.00	3.70
⊕ Pfizer	Health	34.7	–12.40	3.57
⊕ ExxonMobil	Energy	15.3	–7.59	3.26
⊖ Microsoft	Technology	57.6	52.78	3.21
⊕ Citigroup	Financials	20.0	0.03	2.70
⊕ Wal-Mart Stores	Retail	40.3	8.94	2.62
⊕ AOL Time Warner	Technology	—	–7.76	2.19
⊕ American Intl Grp	Financials	42.0	–19.20	2.16
⊖ IBM	Technology	26.9	43.00	2.01
⊖ SBC Comms	Services	18.4	–16.00	2.01
⊕ Fannie Mae	Financials	16.2	–6.95	1.82
⊕ Verizon Comms	Services	29.7	–2.52	1.76
⊖ Tyco Intl	Industrials	27.1	6.23	1.72
⊖ Texaco	Energy	—	6.76	1.66
⊖ Bank of America	Financials	16.7	42.73	1.63
⊖ Intel	Technology	73.1	4.89	1.56
⊕ PepsiCo	Staples	31.4	–0.54	1.54
⊖ Abbott Labs	Health	51.6	17.08	1.53
⊕ Philip Morris	Staples	12.1	9.12	1.45
⊖ American Home Products	Health	—	–1.91	1.36
⊕ Home Depot	Retail	42.9	12.07	1.35
⊕ Washington Mutual	Financials	10.1	–5.32	1.24
⊖ FleetBoston Finl	Financials	16.2	0.55	1.18
⊕ US Bancorp	Financials	13.5	–6.14	1.13
⊕ Pharmacia	Health	36.5	–29.30	1.08

Current Investment Style

Style: Value Blnd Growth; Size: Large Med Small

	Stock Port Avg	Relative S&P 500 Current	Relative S&P 500 Hist	Rel Cat
Price/Earnings Ratio	30.0	0.97	1.00	0.99
Price/Book Ratio	5.8	1.02	1.05	1.06
Price/Cash Flow	18.5	1.03	1.03	1.00
3 Yr Earnings Growth	18.0	1.23	1.14	1.01
1 Yr Earnings Est%	5.1	—	—	—
Med Mkt Cap $mil	67,955	1.1	0.9	1.30

Special Securities % assets 09-30-01	
Restricted/Illiquid Secs	0
Emerging-Markets Secs	Trace
Options/Futures/Warrants	No

Composition % assets 09-30-01	
Cash	0.5
Stocks*	99.5
Bonds	0.0
Other	0.0
*Foreign (% stocks)	2.7

Market Cap	
Giant	57.1
Large	31.6
Medium	11.2
Small	0.0
Micro	0.0

Sector Weightings	% of Stocks	Rel S&P	5-Year High	5-Year Low
Utilities	2.8	0.9	12	1
Energy	7.4	1.1	12	6
Financials	18.6	1.0	19	6
Industrials	12.2	1.1	19	10
Durables	0.5	0.3	6	0
Staples	8.6	1.1	16	4
Services	9.8	0.9	17	8
Retail	8.6	1.3	10	4
Health	14.4	1.0	14	8
Technology	17.1	0.9	32	5

Address:	144 Glenn Curtiss Blvd Uniondale, NY 11556–0144 800–373–9387 / 718–895–1206
Web Address:	www.dreyfus.com/funds
Inception:	12-31-87
Advisor:	Dreyfus
Subadvisor:	None
NTF Plans:	Fidelity Inst. , Waterhouse

Minimum Purchase:	$2500	Add: $100	IRA: $750
Min Auto Inv Plan:	$100	Add: $100	
Sales Fees:	0.10%B		
Management Fee:	.90%		
Actual Fees:	Mgt: 0.90%	Dist: 0.10%	
Expense Projections:	3Yr: $318	5Yr: $552	10Yr: $1225
Avg Brok Commission:	—	Income Distrib: Quarterly	
Total Cost (relative to category):		Below Avg	

Dreyfus Emerging Leaders

Ticker	Load	NAV	Yield	Total Assets	Mstar Category
DRELX	Closed	$34.77	0.0%	$1,361.6 mil	Small Growth

Prospectus Objective: Small Company

Dreyfus Emerging Leaders Fund seeks capital growth.

The fund generally invests at least 65% of assets in equities issued by companies with market capitalizations of less than $1.5 billion. It emphasizes growth companies, which the advisor believes have above-average earnings or sales growth, above-average retention of earnings, and relatively high P/E ratios. To select investments, the advisor pays particular attention to companies it considers to be new leaders, which it defines as emerging companies that it believes offer new or innovative products, services, or processes that may boost earnings growth. The fund may invest up to 25% of assets in foreign securities.

Historical Profile
Return High
Risk Average
Rating ★★★★★ Highest

Investment Style
Equity
Average Stock %: 91% 95% 94% 94% 94% 95%

▼ Manager Change
▽ Partial Manager Change

Fund Performance vs. Category Average
■ Quarterly Fund Return +/– Category Average
— Category Baseline

Performance Quartile (within Category)

Portfolio Manager(s)

Paul Kandel. Since 10-96. BA Haverford C.; MBA Columbia U. Other funds currently managed: Dreyfus New Leaders, Dreyfus Growth Opportunity, Dreyfus Premier Future Leaders A.

Hilary R. Woods, CFA. Since 10-96. BS Franklin & Marshall C. Other funds currently managed: Dreyfus New Leaders, Dreyfus, Dreyfus Premier Future Leaders A.

History

1990	1991	1992	1993	1994	1995	1996	1997	1998	1999	2000	12-01	History
—	—	—	—	—	15.90	20.39	24.57	26.62	36.73	39.59	34.77	NAV
—	—	—	—	—	27.40*	37.40	33.91	8.56	38.26	9.49	–9.91	Total Return %
—	—	—	—	—	21.44*	14.46	0.56	–20.02	17.22	18.59	1.97	+/– S&P 500
—	—	—	—	—	—	26.14	20.96	7.33	–4.83	31.92	–0.68	+/– Russ 2000 Grth
—	—	—	—	—	0.20	0.00	0.00	0.00	0.00	0.00	0.00	Income Return %
—	—	—	—	—	27.20	37.40	33.91	8.56	38.25	9.49	–9.91	Capital Return %
—	—	—	—	—	—	5	5	25	63	21	49	Total Rtn % Rank Cat
—	—	—	—	—	0.03	0.00	0.00	0.00	0.00	0.00	0.00	Income $
—	—	—	—	—	0.00	1.41	2.67	0.05	0.07	0.59	0.84	Capital Gains $
—	—	—	—	—	—	1.16	1.39	1.39	1.38	1.26	—	Expense Ratio %
—	—	—	—	—	—	0.09	–0.62	–0.63	–0.49	–0.37	—	Income Ratio %
—	—	—	—	—	—	204	198	199	100	76	—	Turnover Rate %
—	—	—	—	—	17.4	61.4	129.0	155.8	612.4	1,417.0	1,361.6	Net Assets $mil

Performance 12-31-01

	1st Qtr	2nd Qtr	3rd Qtr	4th Qtr	Total
1997	–3.24	17.79	18.46	–0.82	33.91
1998	12.13	–4.97	–17.84	24.00	8.56
1999	0.49	17.12	–3.99	22.35	38.26
2000	11.92	–3.72	–1.09	2.72	9.49
2001	–13.92	11.44	–18.40	15.09	–9.91

Trailing	Total Return%	+/– S&P 500	+/– Russ 2000 Grth	% Rank All	% Rank Cat	Growth of $10,000
3 Mo	15.09	4.41	–11.08	24	94	11,509
6 Mo	–6.09	–0.53	3.18	69	50	9,391
1 Yr	–9.91	1.97	–0.68	60	49	9,009
3 Yr Avg	10.90	11.92	10.65	10	35	13,638
5 Yr Avg	14.67	3.97	11.80	5	19	19,825
10 Yr Avg	—	—	—	—	—	—
15 Yr Avg	—	—	—	—	—	—

Tax Analysis	Tax-Adj Ret%	%Rank Cat	%Pretax Ret	%Rank Cat
3 Yr Avg	10.57	30	97.0	10
5 Yr Avg	13.60	15	92.7	11
10 Yr Avg	—	—	—	—

Potential Capital Gain Exposure: 4% of assets

Risk Analysis

Time Period	Load-Adj Return %	Risk %Rank[1] All	Risk %Rank[1] Cat	Morningstar Return	Morningstar Risk	Morningstar Risk-Adj Rating
1 Yr	–9.91					
3 Yr	10.90	69	12	1.34[2]	0.95	★★★★
5 Yr	14.67	75	8	2.53[2]	1.03	★★★★★
Incept	21.98	—	—	—	—	

Average Historical Rating (40 months): 4.3★s

[1] 1=low, 100=high [2] T-Bill return substituted for category avg.

Category Rating (3 Yr)

1 2 3 4 5
Worst Best

Return Average
Risk Below Avg

Other Measures	Standard Index S&P 500	Best Fit Index Russ 2000
Alpha	12.7	4.5
Beta	0.89	0.91
R-Squared	44	88

Standard Deviation	25.57
Mean	10.90
Sharpe Ratio	0.27

Portfolio Analysis 11-30-01

Share change since 10-01 Total Stocks: 80	Sector	PE	YTD Ret%	% Assets
Commerce Bancorp NJ	Financials	27.5	17.01	2.16
⊖ Pactiv	Industrials	18.3	43.43	2.09
First Midwest Bancorp	Financials	18.5	30.24	1.94
Davita	Health	18.3	42.77	1.92
☼ NDC health	N/A	—	—	1.91
Church & Dwight	Staples	21.0	21.11	1.90
Humana	Financials	18.1	–22.60	1.87
Valspar	Industrials	35.0	25.05	1.83
Network Assoc	Technology	—	517.20	1.77
Mercury General	Financials	21.7	2.38	1.67
Valassis Comms	Services	18.9	12.85	1.66
Aeroflex	Technology	75.7	–34.30	1.63
Dreyer's Grand Ice Cream	Staples	NMF	20.39	1.62
First Virginia Banks	Financials	14.7	9.39	1.60
American Eagle Outfitters	Retail	16.8	–7.09	1.59
⊖ Elantec Semicon	Technology	41.7	38.38	1.58
Protective Life	Financials	13.7	–8.65	1.57
⊖ Forward Air	Services	34.6	–9.09	1.57
Global Payments	Services	—	—	1.55
SkyWest	Services	27.1	–11.10	1.53
Idex	Industrials	25.4	6.08	1.53
Annuity and Life Re Hldgs	Financials	16.9	–20.80	1.51
Westamerica Bancorp	Financials	17.2	–5.98	1.51
City Natl	Financials	16.4	22.90	1.50
Harte-Hanks Comms	Services	22.9	19.51	1.50

Current Investment Style

Style: Value Blnd Growth; Size: Large Med Small

	Stock Port Avg	Relative S&P 500 Current	Relative S&P 500 Hist	Rel Cat
Price/Earnings Ratio	28.2	0.91	0.87	0.88
Price/Book Ratio	3.2	0.56	0.63	0.65
Price/Cash Flow	16.5	0.92	0.88	0.75
3 Yr Earnings Growth	11.0	0.75	1.47	0.44
1 Yr Earnings Est%	–3.3	1.84	—	–0.42
Med Mkt Cap $mil	1,285	0.0	0.0	1.23

[1] figure is based on 50% or less of stocks

Special Securities % assets 11-30-01	
Restricted/Illiquid Secs	0
Emerging-Markets Secs	1
Options/Futures/Warrants	Yes

Composition % assets 11-30-01	
Cash	5.5
Stocks*	94.5
Bonds	0.0
Other	0.0
*Foreign (% stocks)	4.4

Market Cap	
Giant	0.0
Large	0.0
Medium	45.7
Small	52.0
Micro	2.3

Sector Weightings	% of Stocks	Rel S&P	5-Year High	5-Year Low
Utilities	2.6	0.8	8	0
Energy	6.7	0.9	11	4
Financials	20.3	1.1	24	9
Industrials	17.5	1.5	24	10
Durables	0.4	0.3	8	0
Staples	5.3	0.7	6	0
Services	11.9	1.1	22	6
Retail	4.3	0.6	10	3
Health	9.8	0.7	19	7
Technology	21.3	1.2	30	11

Analysis by Brian Portnoy 10-24-01

Dreyfus Emerging Leaders has gone through some growing pains, but it retains its attractive long-term marks.

This fund, which remains closed to new investors, is having a so-so year. For the year to date through Oct. 25, 2001, it has shed 18.1% of its value, which is 1 percentage point less than the average small-growth rival has lost. The fund's tech stake, though underweight relative to its peers', has caused problems. Software firm Dendrite International has fallen 56% this year, for example. Energy-service stocks, which sunk as oil and gas prices fell, have hurt returns, as has a passel of retail and radio stocks. On the other hand, the fund's health-care and financials stakes have been relatively buoyant.

Over the long haul, performance has been far more impressive. Its five-year return ranks among the category's elite thanks to smart stock selection based on management's consistently executed moderate growth strategy. The one dent in its rock-solid record occurred in 1999 when more-aggressive peers shot ahead by betting the farm on pricey tech and telecom fare. That said, an aversion to large sector bets and attention to valuation have mitigated losses during the protracted market correction, producing one of the category's better risk profiles.

Our one concern here is the fund's sizable asset base of nearly $1.2 billion. (Out of 238 small-growth funds, only five have more assets.) Small-cap funds with asset bases as large as this have difficulty building significant positions in smaller, less-liquid stocks (or at least take on extra risk in doing so). Not surprisingly, the fund now owns a sizable slug of mid-caps and has benefited less from this year's smaller-cap rally. Even so, the fund's outstanding performance over time for now trumps any worries about management's marginal loss in flexibility.

Address:	144 Glenn Curtiss Blvd Uniondale, NY 11556–0144 800–373–9387 / 718–895–1206
Web Address:	www.dreyfus.com/funds
*Inception:	09-28-95
Advisor:	Dreyfus
Subadvisor:	None
NTF Plans:	Fidelity , Datalynx

Minimum Purchase:	Closed	Add: $100 IRA: —
Min Auto Inv Plan:	Closed	Add: $100
Sales Fees:	No-load, 1.00%R within 1 month	
Management Fee:	.90%	
Actual Fees:	Mgt: 0.90%	Dist: —
Expense Projections:	3Yr: $400	5Yr: $692 10Yr: $1523
Avg Brok Commission:	—	Income Distrib: Annually
Total Cost (relative to category):		Below Avg

Dreyfus Emerging Markets

Ticker	Load	NAV	Yield	Total Assets	Mstar Category
DRFMX	None	$11.34	1.4%	$287.1 mil	Div Emerging Mkts

Prospectus Objective: Diversified Emg Markets—Stock

Dreyfus Emerging Markets Fund seeks long-term capital appreciation.

The fund normally invests at least 65% of assets in equities issued by foreign issuers in at least three countries having emerging-markets. It ordinarily invests in at least three emerging-market countries. Management takes a value-oriented and research-driven approach to security selection. It seeks companies with low price/book, price/earnings, and price/cash-flow ratios, or higher than average dividend payments in relation to price. Management also considers broader measures of value, including operating return characteristics, overall financial health, and positive changes in business momentum. The fund is nondiversified.

Historical Profile
- **Return** Above Avg
- **Risk** Average
- **Rating** ★★★★ Above Avg

Investment Style
Equity
Average Stock %: 76% 91% 89% 92% 96% 98%

▼ Manager Change
▽ Partial Manager Change

Fund Performance vs. Category Average
■ Quarterly Fund Return +/– Category Average
— Category Baseline

Performance Quartile (within Category)

Portfolio Manager(s)

D. Kirk Henry, CFA. Since 6-96. BA Stanford U.; MBA U. of Chicago. Other funds currently managed: Dreyfus Premier Emerging Markets A, Dreyfus Premier Emerging Markets B, Dreyfus Premier Emerging Markets C.

1990	1991	1992	1993	1994	1995	1996	1997	1998	1999	2000	12-01	History
—	—	—	—	—	—	12.42	11.76	9.53	15.50	10.68	11.34	NAV
—	—	—	—	—	—	–0.30*	–1.53	–18.01	74.93	–20.30	7.70	Total Return %
—	—	—	—	—	—	–11.98*	–34.88	–46.59	53.89	–11.20	19.58	+/– S&P 500
—	—	—	—	—	—	—	13.59	7.29	8.74	9.70	—	+/– MSCI Emerging
—	—	—	—	—	—	0.16	0.14	0.77	1.15	0.86	1.50	Income Return %
—	—	—	—	—	—	–0.46	–1.68	–18.78	73.77	–21.17	6.21	Capital Return %
—	—	—	—	—	—	—	36	8	40	2	3	Total Rtn % Rank Cat
—	—	—	—	—	—	0.02	0.02	0.09	0.11	0.13	0.16	Income $
—	—	—	—	—	—	0.02	0.44	0.02	1.01	1.59	0.00	Capital Gains $
—	—	—	—	—	—	—	—	1.94	1.88	1.85	—	Expense Ratio %
—	—	—	—	—	—	—	—	0.54	1.42	1.48	—	Income Ratio %
—	—	—	—	—	—	—	—	87	88	106	—	Turnover Rate %
—	—	—	—	—	—	16.0	63.2	57.7	190.8	218.2	287.1	Net Assets $mil

Performance 12-31-01

	1st Qtr	2nd Qtr	3rd Qtr	4th Qtr	Total
1997	8.29	11.67	–5.39	–13.94	–1.53
1998	6.29	–18.64	–19.47	17.73	–18.01
1999	11.33	32.71	–4.33	23.76	74.93
2000	–1.23	–5.23	–8.82	–6.63	–20.30
2001	–1.31	9.01	–18.54	22.89	7.71

Trailing	Total Return%	+/– S&P 500	+/– MSCI Emerging	% Rank All	% Rank Cat	Growth of $10,000
3 Mo	22.89	12.21	—	10	62	12,289
6 Mo	0.11	5.67	—	39	12	10,011
1 Yr	7.70	19.58	—	11	3	10,770
3 Yr Avg	14.51	15.54	—	5	3	15,015
5 Yr Avg	3.92	–6.78	—	80	4	12,122
10 Yr Avg	—	—	—	—	—	—
15 Yr Avg	—	—	—	—	—	—

Tax Analysis	Tax-Adj Ret%	%Rank Cat	%Pretax Ret	%Rank Cat
3 Yr Avg	11.28	6	77.7	97
5 Yr Avg	1.75	4	44.7	75
10 Yr Avg	—	—	—	—

Potential Capital Gain Exposure: –21% of assets

Risk Analysis

Time Period	Load-Adj Return %	Risk %Rank[1] All	Risk %Rank[1] Cat	Morningstar Return	Morningstar Risk	Morningstar Risk-Adj Rating
1 Yr	7.70					
3 Yr	14.51	68	1	2.22[2]	0.87	★★★★★
5 Yr	3.92	86	2	–0.24[2]	1.10	★★★
Incept	3.50	—	—	—	—	

Average Historical Rating (31 months): 2.9★s

[1]1=low, 100=high [2] T-Bill return substituted for category avg.

Category Rating (3 Yr)

1 Worst — 5 Best (rating: 5)

Return: High
Risk: Low

Other Measures	Standard Index S&P 500	Best Fit Index MSCIPcxIND
Alpha	17.2	11.8
Beta	0.99	0.94
R-Squared	47	79
Standard Deviation		28.12
Mean		14.51
Sharpe Ratio		0.39

Portfolio Analysis 09-30-01

Share change since 06-01 Total Stocks: 148	Sector	Country	% Assets
Korea Elec Pwr	Utilities	South Korea	2.46
⊕ Mahanager Tele 144A GDR	Services	India	2.31
⊕ Videsh Sanchar Nigam I	Services	India	2.19
⊕ Bank Hapoalim	Financials	Israel	2.02
⊕ SK (For)	Energy	South Korea	1.96
⊖ Kimberly-Clark	Industrials	U.S.	1.91
⊕ CEMIG	Utilities	Brazil	1.51
⊖ Telefonos de Mexico ADR L	Services	Mexico	1.39
⊕ Telebras ADR OTC	Services	Brazil	1.37
⊕ Pohang Iron & Steel ADR	Industrials	South Korea	1.30
☼ Old Mutual	Financials	United Kingdom	1.29
⊕ Pliva 144A GDR	Health	Croatia	1.27
⊕ Manila Elec Cl B	Utilities	Philippines	1.26
⊕ Nampak	Industrials	South Africa	1.25
⊕ Nedcor	Financials	South Africa	1.21
⊖ Gas Authority India 144A GDR	Utilities	India	1.21
⊕ Companhia Vale do Rio Doce	Industrials	Brazil	1.15
☼ Sime Darby Malaysia	Durables	Malaysia	1.13
⊕ Commrcl Intl Bk 144A GDR	Financials	Egypt	1.13
⊕ Banco Latinoamer Export E	Financials	Panama	1.08

Current Investment Style

Style: Value Blnd Growth; Size: Large Med Small

	Stock Port Avg	Rel MSCI EAFE Current	Rel MSCI EAFE Hist	Rel Cat
Price/Earnings Ratio	12.9	0.50	0.50	0.74
Price/Cash Flow	8.1	0.63	0.53	0.81
Price/Book Ratio	1.7	0.47	0.39	0.51
3 Yr Earnings Growth	16.4[1]	0.87	—	0.63
Med Mkt Cap $mil	1,559	0.1	0.1	0.37

[1]figure is based on 50% or less of stocks

Country Exposure 09-30-01	% assets
South Korea	12
India	12
Brazil	10
Mexico	7
South Africa	6

Hedging History: —

Regional Exposure 09-30-01	% assets
Europe	10
Africa/Mid East	13
Pacific/Asia	47
Latin America	20
Other	2

Special Securities % assets 09-30-01	
Restricted/Illiquid Secs	13
Emerging-Markets Secs	89
Options/Futures/Warrants	No

Composition % assets 09-30-01

Cash	1.1	Bonds	0.0
Stocks	98.9	Other	0.0

Sector Weightings	% of Stocks	Rel Cat	5-Year High	5-Year Low
Utilities	11.3	1.7	—	—
Energy	7.5	1.1	—	—
Financials	16.2	0.8	—	—
Industrials	19.7	1.2	—	—
Durables	9.2	2.8	—	—
Staples	6.6	0.9	—	—
Services	19.3	1.1	—	—
Retail	2.3	0.8	—	—
Health	2.4	0.6	—	—
Technology	5.5	0.4	—	—

Analysis by William Samuel Rocco 10-17-01

This value hound still ranks among the best in its wild breed.

Dreyfus Emerging Markets continues to be much more price-conscious than most of its rivals. Manager Kirk Henry sold China's Qingling Motors this summer and Greece's Hellenic Telecommunications this fall, in fact, because both were looking a bit rich after posting strong gains in the first part of 2001.

Meanwhile, Henry has sniffed out fetching bargains lately. He has bought back Qingling Motors, which plunged due to poor numbers shortly after he sold it. He also has purchased China Mobil, the Indian petro-chemical giant Reliance, and a few other large caps. These names, which had been too expensive for his tastes, dropped significantly in recent weeks. And he has just initiated small positions in a handful of tech companies for similar reasons. Overall, the fund's price multiples range from one half to three fourths of the category averages.

This penurious approach has served the fund well this year. Henry's China plays have paid off. Qingling Motors has been a big contributor, as have Shandong International Power and Guanshen Railroad. Moreover, Hellenic Telecom, which was the fund's top holding for most of the year, has posted double-digit gains, as have a couple of Mexican names. As a result, the fund has lost 9% for the year to date through Oct. 16, 2001, whereas its average peer has lost 19%.

Henry has also executed his bargain-basement style deftly in past emerging-markets storms—the fund posted top-decile results in 1998 and 2000—and he has managed to earn above-average results in rallies. All told, the fund has earned the best five-year returns in the category, while suffering much less volatility than the norm. Given all that, we think this fund remains a great choice for emerging-markets fans.

Address:	144 Glenn Curtiss Blvd Uniondale, NY 11556–0144 718–895–1206 / 800–373–9387
Web Address:	www.dreyfus.com/funds
*Inception:	06-28-96
Advisor:	Dreyfus
Subadvisor:	None
NTF Plans:	Fidelity , Datalynx

Minimum Purchase:	$2500	Add: $100 IRA: $750
Min Auto Inv Plan:	$100	Add: $100
Sales Fees:	No-load, 1.00%R within 6 months	
Management Fee:	1.3%	
Actual Fees:	Mgt: 1.25%	Dist: —
Expense Projections:	3Yr: $582	5Yr: $1001 10Yr: $2169
Avg Brok Commission:	—	Income Distrib: Annually
Total Cost (relative to category):		Below Avg

Dreyfus Intermediate Municipal Bond

Ticker	Load	NAV	Yield	SEC Yield	Total Assets	Mstar Category
DITEX	None	$13.34	4.9%	3.65%	$1,056.8 mil	Muni Natl Interm–Term

Prospectus Objective: Muni Bond—National

Dreyfus Intermediate Municipal Bond Fund seeks current income exempt from federal income tax, consistent with preservation of capital.

The fund normally invests at least 80% of assets in high-quality municipal obligations; it may invest the balance in lower-rated obligations. The average weighted maturity typically ranges between three and 10 years. The fund may invest up to 5% of assets in zero-coupon or payment-in-kind bonds, and may invest an unlimited amount in bonds subject to the Alternative Minimum Tax.

Prior to Sept. 12, 1990, the fund was named Dreyfus Intermediate Tax-Exempt Bond Fund.

Historical Profile

Return: Average
Risk: Below Avg
Rating: ★★★★ Above Avg

Investment Style
Fixed-Income
Income Rtn %Rank Cat: 22, 20, 18, 24, 18, 17, 25, 17

Growth of Principal vs. Interest Rate Shifts
— Principal Value $000 (NAV with capital gains reinvested)
— Interest Rate % on 10 Yr Treasury
▼ Manager Change
▽ Partial Manager Change
► Mgr Unknown After
◄ Mgr Unknown Before

Performance Quartile (within Category)

Portfolio Manager(s)

Monica S. Wieboldt. Since 5-85. BA SUNY-New Paltz. Other funds currently managed: Dreyfus CA Intermediate Muni Bond, Dreyfus FL Intermediate Muni Bond, Dreyfus MA Intermediate Muni Bond.

History

1990	1991	1992	1993	1994	1995	1996	1997	1998	1999	2000	12-01	History
13.48	13.95	13.97	14.61	13.14	14.22	13.91	14.12	14.08	13.12	13.46	13.34	NAV
6.75	11.13	8.71	11.56	−4.57	14.23	3.82	7.62	5.52	−1.54	7.73	3.98	Total Return %
−2.21	−4.87	1.31	1.81	−1.65	−4.24	0.21	−2.07	−3.15	−0.71	−3.90	−4.45	+/– LB Aggregate
−0.55	−1.01	−0.11	−0.72	0.58	−3.23	−0.62	−1.58	−0.96	0.53	−3.96	−1.10	+/– LB Muni
7.15	6.92	6.25	5.68	5.27	5.69	5.20	5.14	4.90	4.81	5.04	4.95	Income Return %
−0.40	4.22	2.47	5.87	−9.84	8.55	−1.37	2.48	0.62	−6.35	2.69	−0.97	Capital Return %
35	45	32	36	75	39	51	47	46	41	80	71	Total Rtn % Rank Cat
0.94	0.90	0.85	0.77	0.75	0.73	0.72	0.70	0.68	0.66	0.65	0.65	Income $
0.00	0.08	0.31	0.16	0.06	0.03	0.11	0.12	0.13	0.09	0.00	0.00	Capital Gains $
0.71	0.69	0.70	0.71	0.70	0.73	0.71	0.73	0.74	0.75	0.75	—	Expense Ratio %
7.01	6.84	6.47	5.68	5.22	5.52	5.14	5.10	4.91	4.75	4.97	—	Income Ratio %
40	31	48	60	36	42	49	47	40	20	21	—	Turnover Rate %
1,143.5	1,379.0	1,570.6	1,832.8	1,447.6	1,550.3	1,430.3	1,372.4	1,320.5	1,133.3	1,066.0	1,056.8	Net Assets $mil

Performance 12-31-01

	1st Qtr	2nd Qtr	3rd Qtr	4th Qtr	Total
1997	−0.13	2.66	2.58	2.33	7.62
1998	1.04	1.28	2.71	0.39	5.52
1999	0.45	−1.69	−0.03	−0.27	−1.54
2000	1.56	1.18	2.36	2.42	7.73
2001	2.39	0.62	2.17	−1.22	3.98

Trailing	Total Return%	+/– LB Agg	+/– LB Muni	% Rank All	% Rank Cat	Growth of $10,000
3 Mo	−1.22	−1.26	−0.56	96	80	9,878
6 Mo	0.92	−3.73	−1.20	34	92	10,092
1 Yr	3.98	−4.45	−1.10	31	71	10,398
3 Yr Avg	3.32	−2.96	−1.43	50	75	11,029
5 Yr Avg	4.61	−2.82	−1.37	71	68	12,525
10 Yr Avg	5.57	−1.66	−1.06	84	62	17,192
15 Yr Avg	6.08	−2.04	−1.11	88	80	24,231

Tax Analysis	Tax-Adj Ret%	%Rank Cat	%Pretax Ret	%Rank Cat
3 Yr Avg	3.27	77	98.5	73
5 Yr Avg	4.48	70	97.2	88
10 Yr Avg	5.35	72	96.2	83

Potential Capital Gain Exposure: 1% of assets

Risk Analysis

Time Period	Load-Adj Return %	Risk %Rank[1] All	Risk %Rank[1] Cat	Morningstar Return	Morningstar Risk	Morningstar Risk-Adj Rating
1 Yr	3.98					
3 Yr	3.32	7	21	0.37[2]	0.74	★★★★
5 Yr	4.61	8	29	0.68[2]	0.76	★★★★
10 Yr	5.57	10	47	0.89	0.82	★★★

Average Historical Rating (185 months): 4.2★s

[1] 1=low, 100=high [2] T-Bill return substituted for category avg.

Category Rating (3 Yr)

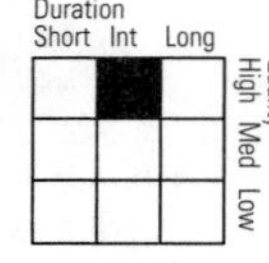

Worst Best

Return: Average
Risk: Below Avg

Other Measures	Standard Index LB Agg	Best Fit Index LB Muni
Alpha	−2.3	−1.4
Beta	0.62	0.75
R–Squared	53	93

Standard Deviation	2.98
Mean	3.32
Sharpe Ratio	−0.65

Portfolio Analysis 09-30-01

Total Fixed-Income: 239	Date of Maturity	Amount $000	Value $000	% Net Assets
NY NYC GO 6.375%	08-15-09	19,750	22,141	2.06
CO E–470 Pub Hwy 0%	09-01-10	30,000	20,379	1.90
MI Detroit Res Rec 6.25%	12-13-08	11,000	12,652	1.18
MI Hosp Fin Genesys Hlth Sys 8.1%	10-01-13	10,000	12,088	1.13
MI Hosp Fin Daughters Charity 5.375%	11-15-07	11,500	12,045	1.12
WA Pub Pwr Sply Sys Proj #1 6%	07-01-07	9,720	10,866	1.01
AZ Maricopa Indl Dev Hosp Fac 7.15%	12-01-04	9,835	10,728	1.00
NC Muni Pwr #1 5.5%	01-01-10	10,000	10,715	1.00
IL Hoffman Estates Tax Increment 5.25%	11-15-09	10,000	10,508	0.98
IN Muni Pwr Sply Sys 5.7%	01-01-06	8,400	9,165	0.85
MD GO FRN	05-01-35	9,000	9,000	0.84
TX Harris Hlth Fac Dev Meml Hosp 5.5%	06-01-12	8,295	8,980	0.84
MI Detroit Res Rec 6.25%	12-13-08	7,755	8,919	0.83
TX Tarrant Hlth Fac Dev Methodist Sys 6%	09-01-10	7,725	8,824	0.82
SC Charleston Hosp Fac Med Society 5.5%	10-01-05	7,945	8,542	0.80

Current Investment Style

Duration: Short Int Long; Quality: High Med Low

Avg Duration[1]	4.7 Yrs
Avg Nominal Maturity	8.1 Yrs
Avg Credit Quality	AA
Avg Wtd Coupon	5.81%
Avg Wtd Price	105.05% of par
Pricing Service	J.J. Kenny

[1] figure provided by fund

Credit Analysis % bonds 06-30-01

US Govt	0	BB	3
AAA	48	B	1
AA	19	Below B	1
A	17	NR/NA	0
BBB	11		

Special Securities % assets 09-30-01

Restricted/Illiquid Secs	1
Inverse Floaters	Trace
Options/Futures/Warrants	No

Bond Type % assets 03-31-99

Alternative Minimum Tax (AMT)	15.2
Insured	—
Prerefunded	—

Top 5 States % bonds

IN	8.2	MI	6.5
TX	7.6	WA	5.3
NY	7.4		

Composition % assets 09-30-01

Cash	0.8	Bonds	99.2
Stocks	0.0	Other	0.0

Sector Weightings	% of Bonds	Rel Cat
General Obligation	20.3	0.7
Utilities	7.9	0.9
Health	19.6	1.6
Water/Waste	0.6	0.1
Housing	6.7	0.9
Education	10.5	1.3
Transportation	10.0	0.9
COP/Lease	2.4	1.1
Industrial	15.6	2.0
Misc Revenue	5.9	1.2
Demand	0.6	0.6

Analysis by Dan McNeela 07-27-01

Look for Dreyfus Intermediate Municipal Bond to bounce back.

Despite a total return of 7.7% in 2000, the fund didn't have a great year on a relative basis. In fact, more than three fourths of the funds in the muni-national intermediate-term category finished ahead of this fund that year. Most of that shortcoming resulted from the fund's stance on duration. Manager Monica Wieboldt allowed the fund's duration, a measure of interest-rate sensitivity, to fall to just 5.1 years. That left the fund shorter than it has been in recent years, and significantly below the 5.9-year average for the category.

Those results were so weak that three-, five-, and 10-year returns have fallen into the category's bottom half. But we feel there are enough reasons for investors to hold on. Wieboldt is very experienced, having managed muni funds since 1985, and underperformance here is rare. The fund has finished in the bottom half of its category just twice in the past 10 years. Further, below-average expenses still give this fund an advantage over most rivals. Most important, however, may be the fund's lower-than-average volatility. The fund's risk scores rank it in the category's best quartile over the past three- and five-year periods.

Performance has picked up lately. As of July 26, 2001, the fund is back near the top third of the rankings with a gain of 3.8%. Wieboldt hasn't been tempted to take on additional credit risk, and she's also kept interest-rate risk in check. Those factors should continue to keep the fund among the less volatile in the category.

Even though the fund's poor showing in 2000 has pushed long-term returns to the middle of the category, the fund remains a solid choice.

Address:	144 Glenn Curtiss Blvd Uniondale, NY 11556–0144 800–373–9387 / 718–895–1206
Web Address:	www.dreyfus.com/funds
Inception:	08-11-83
Advisor:	Dreyfus
Subadvisor:	None
NTF Plans:	Fidelity , Datalynx

Minimum Purchase:	$2500	Add: $100 IRA: $750
Min Auto Inv Plan:	$100	Add: $100
Sales Fees:	No–load	
Management Fee:	.60%	
Actual Fees:	Mgt: 0.58%	Dist: —
Expense Projections:	3Yr: $246	5Yr: $428 10Yr: $954
Avg Brok Commission:	—	Income Distrib: Monthly
Total Cost (relative to category):		Below Avg

Dreyfus Midcap Value

Ticker	Load	NAV	Yield	Total Assets	Mstar Category
DMCVX	None	$26.29	0.0%	$1,346.3 mil	Mid-Cap Value

Prospectus Objective: Growth and Income

Dreyfus MidCap Value Fund seeks investment results that exceed the performance of the Russell Midcap index.

The fund normally invests at least 65% of assets in common stocks issued by companies with market capitalizations between $400 million and $4 billion. Investments may also include preferred stocks and convertible securities of both domestic and foreign issuers. Management focuses investments in companies that it believes are undervalued, have overall business efficiency and profitability, and strong business momentum.

Historical Profile

Return: High
Risk: Above Avg
Rating: ★★★★★ Highest

Investment Style: Equity
Average Stock %: 95% 96% 99% 100% 98% 100%

▼ Manager Change
▽ Partial Manager Change

Fund Performance vs. Category Average
■ Quarterly Fund Return +/– Category Average
— Category Baseline

Performance Quartile (within Category)

Portfolio Manager(s)

Peter I. Higgins, CFA. Since 9-95. MBA U. of Pennsylvania; BA/BS U. of Pennsylvania. Other fund currently managed: Dreyfus Small Company Value.

William Goldenberg. Since 3-01.

Brian Ferguson. Since 3-01.

1990	1991	1992	1993	1994	1995	1996	1997	1998	1999	2000	12-01	History
—	—	—	—	—	13.54	16.83	20.52	17.80	21.46	23.94	26.29	NAV
—	—	—	—	—	8.73*	37.33	28.00	–4.21	28.06	27.46	17.10	Total Return %
—	—	—	—	—	2.72*	14.39	–5.35	–32.78	7.02	36.56	28.97	+/– S&P 500
—	—	—	—	—	—	17.07	–6.36	–9.29	28.16	8.27	14.76	+/– Russ Midcap Val
—	—	—	—	—	0.28	0.30	0.00	0.00	0.00	0.00	0.00	Income Return %
—	—	—	—	—	8.45	37.04	28.00	–4.21	28.06	27.46	17.10	Capital Return %
—	—	—	—	—	—	1	39	85	6	21	16	Total Rtn % Rank Cat
—	—	—	—	—	0.04	0.04	0.00	0.00	0.00	0.00	0.00	Income $
—	—	—	—	—	0.02	1.75	1.05	1.78	1.24	3.28	1.71	Capital Gains $
—	—	—	—	—	—	—	1.25	1.29	1.34	1.27	1.15	Expense Ratio %
—	—	—	—	—	—	—	–0.14	–0.25	–0.89	–0.38	–0.20	Income Ratio %
—	—	—	—	—	—	—	155	169	257	242	192	Turnover Rate %
—	—	—	—	—	2.4	8.4	124.0	94.5	85.8	288.3	1,346.3	Net Assets $mil

Performance 12-31-01

	1st Qtr	2nd Qtr	3rd Qtr	4th Qtr	Total
1997	2.91	17.38	13.03	–6.26	28.00
1998	13.45	–4.77	–27.65	22.55	–4.21
1999	–0.11	28.57	–9.06	9.64	28.06
2000	12.95	2.93	8.66	0.89	27.46
2001	9.57	6.94	–22.82	29.48	17.10

Trailing	Total Return%	+/– S&P 500	+/– Russ Midcap Val	% Rank All	% Rank Cat	Growth of $10,000
3 Mo	29.48	18.80	17.45	5	1	12,948
6 Mo	–0.06	5.49	0.85	39	42	9,994
1 Yr	17.10	28.97	14.76	3	16	11,710
3 Yr Avg	24.10	25.13	17.29	2	2	19,113
5 Yr Avg	18.57	7.87	7.11	2	8	23,435
10 Yr Avg	—	—	—	—	—	—
15 Yr Avg	—	—	—	—	—	—

Tax Analysis	Tax-Adj Ret%	%Rank Cat	%Pretax Ret	%Rank Cat
3 Yr Avg	20.20	2	83.8	38
5 Yr Avg	15.02	11	80.9	39
10 Yr Avg	—	—	—	—

Potential Capital Gain Exposure: –3% of assets

Risk Analysis

Time Period	Load-Adj Return %	Risk %Rank[1] All	Risk %Rank[1] Cat	Morningstar Return	Morningstar Risk	Morningstar Risk-Adj Rating
1 Yr	17.10					
3 Yr	24.10	70	94	4.85[2]	0.96	★★★★★
5 Yr	18.57	78	97	3.83[2]	1.08	★★★★★
Incept	22.15	—	—	—	—	

Average Historical Rating (40 months): 3.6★s

[1]1=low, 100=high [2] T-Bill return substituted for category avg.

Category Rating (3 Yr)

1 2 3 4 5 — Worst / Best

Return: High
Risk: High

Other Measures	Standard Index S&P 500	Best Fit Index S&P 500
Alpha	30.5	30.5
Beta	1.35	1.35
R-Squared	63	63

Standard Deviation	36.60
Mean	24.10
Sharpe Ratio	0.59

Portfolio Analysis 09-30-01

Share change since 06-01 Total Stocks: 138	Sector	PE	YTD Ret%	% Assets
⊖ ICN Pharmaceuticals	Health	NMF	10.39	2.87
⊕ RadioShack	Retail	21.5	–29.20	2.29
⊕ Conexant Sys	Technology	—	–6.60	2.28
☼ Scientific-Atlanta	Technology	15.5	–26.30	2.14
⊖ Stilwell Finl	Financials	—	–30.80	2.12
⊕ Sunoco	Energy	5.8	13.95	1.83
⊖ Mirant	Utilities	8.3	–43.40	1.74
⊖ Bausch & Lomb	Health	81.9	–4.42	1.74
⊕ Valero Energy (New)	Energy	4.0	3.39	1.72
⊖ NCR	Technology	15.5	–24.90	1.65
⊖ Tyson Foods Cl A	Staples	28.9	–8.17	1.59
⊕ FleetBoston Finl	Financials	16.2	0.55	1.49
⊕ CVS	Retail	16.2	–50.30	1.44
⊕ Cendant	Services	20.4	103.70	1.42
⊕ Solectron	Technology	—	–66.70	1.40
⊕ Gap	Retail	39.8	–45.00	1.32
⊖ Guidant	Health	42.6	–7.67	1.27
⊖ Ingersoll-Rand	Industrials	27.0	1.41	1.26
☼ Transocean Sedco Forex	Energy	58.3	–26.20	1.22
⊕ E*Trade Grp	Financials	—	38.98	1.19
⊕ Park Place Entrtnmt	Services	—	–23.10	1.17
⊕ Devon Energy	Energy	5.6	–36.30	1.13
⊕ Nextel Comms Cl A	Services	—	–55.70	1.13
⊕ Santa Fe Intl	Energy	31.0	–11.00	1.13
⊕ Interpublic Grp	Services	—	–29.80	1.12

Current Investment Style

Style: Value Blnd Growth; Size: Large Med Small

	Stock Port Avg	Relative S&P 500 Current	Relative S&P 500 Hist	Rel Cat
Price/Earnings Ratio	28.0	0.91	0.71	1.19
Price/Book Ratio	2.9	0.52	0.33	0.97
Price/Cash Flow	12.9	0.72	0.57	1.04
3 Yr Earnings Growth	18.3	1.25	0.81	1.54
1 Yr Earnings Est%	–8.2	4.63	—	1.33
Med Mkt Cap $mil	4,771	0.1	0.0	0.67

[1]figure is based on 50% or less of stocks

Analysis by Brian Portnoy 11-28-01

For those who can hang on tight, Dreyfus Midcap Value is well worth the ride.

It comes as no surprise that this fund has climbed back into the category's upper echelon for the year to date. Propelled by the recent market rally, the fund's 14% gain over the month through Nov. 27, 2001, is the category's best, thanks to a snap back in some of the fund's beaten-down growth fare. For example, Conexant Systems is up 54% over the past month, while new acquistion Scientific-Atlanta has grown by a third. Such a strong run counterbalances the fund's awful summer, when sagging energy and tech stocks took a large chunk out of the fund's gains and pushed it toward the rear of the mid-value pack. But now, the fund's 10.9% gain for the year to date ended Nov. 27, ranks in the group's top quintile.

Long-term investors should get used to this sort of bumpy ride. It's part and parcel of Peter Higgins' maverick approach to mid-value investing, which involves buying beaten-down growth-stocks and staying relatively light on traditional value fare such as industrials and consumer staples. That has produced one of the category's most volatile records, but also one of its best. Over the past five years, the fund's return ranks among the category's elite.

The fund is not an appropriate choice for those looking for a tame offering. But we think investors seeking a mid-value choice should give this one a close look. Despite its volatility, the fund sticks to its valuation discipline by quickly selling its winners before their price multiples expand too far. And though the fund has dipped into some large-cap stocks due to its growing asset base, its median market cap remains well below the category norm. The fund will close when it reaches $1.4 billion in assets, so interested investors should get in while they can.

Special Securities % assets 09-30-01	
Restricted/Illiquid Secs	0
Emerging-Markets Secs	0
Options/Futures/Warrants	No

Sector Weightings	% of Stocks	Rel S&P	5-Year High	5-Year Low
Utilities	3.3	1.1	4	0
Energy	15.3	2.2	15	2
Financials	14.0	0.8	17	4
Industrials	11.2	1.0	25	11
Durables	2.1	1.4	13	1
Staples	2.1	0.3	4	0
Services	12.9	1.2	21	8
Retail	9.6	1.4	17	6
Health	6.8	0.5	14	3
Technology	22.7	1.2	32	12

Composition % assets 09-30-01	
Cash	0.0
Stocks*	99.5
Bonds	0.0
Other	0.5
*Foreign (% stocks)	4.6

Market Cap	
Giant	2.5
Large	22.4
Medium	67.1
Small	7.4
Micro	0.0

Address: 144 Glenn Curtiss Blvd
Uniondale, NY 11556-0144
800-373-9387 / 718-895-1206
Web Address: www.dreyfus.com/funds

*Inception: 09-29-95
Advisor: Dreyfus
Subadvisor: None
NTF Plans: Fidelity , Datalynx

Minimum Purchase: $2500 Add: $100 IRA: $750
Min Auto Inv Plan: $100 Add: $100
Sales Fees: No-load, 1.00%R within 1 month
Management Fee: .75%
Actual Fees: Mgt: 0.75% Dist: —
Expense Projections: 3Yr: $415 5Yr: $718 10Yr: $1579
Avg Brok Commission: — Income Distrib: Annually
Total Cost (relative to category): Below Avg

Dreyfus Small Company Value

Ticker	Load	NAV	Yield	Total Assets	Mstar Category
DSCVX	Closed	$20.80	0.0%	$332.8 mil	Small Value

Prospectus Objective: Small Company

Dreyfus Small Company Value Fund seeks capital appreciation.

The fund normally invests at least 65% of assets in equity securities issued by companies with market capitalizations between $90 million and $900 million. To select investments, management seeks companies with low P/E and P/B ratios and that pay higher-than-average dividends. The fund may invest in foreign equities and in money-market instruments. It may also engage in various investment techniques, such as leveraging, lending of portfolio securities, foreign-currency transactions, futures and options transactions, and short-selling to increase returns.

Prior to Sept. 29, 1995, the fund was named Dreyfus Focus Small Company Value Fund.

Historical Profile
Return High
Risk Above Avg
Rating ★★★★ Above Avg

Investment Style
Equity
Average Stock %: 90% 89% 91% 99% 100% 100% 100%

▼ Manager Change
▽ Partial Manager Change

Fund Performance vs. Category Average
Quarterly Fund Return +/– Category Average
— Category Baseline

Performance Quartile (within Category)

Portfolio Manager(s)

Peter I. Higgins, CFA. Since 11-97. MBA U. of Pennsylvania; BA/BS U. of Pennsylvania. Other fund currently managed: Dreyfus Midcap Value.

1990	1991	1992	1993	1994	1995	1996	1997	1998	1999	2000	12-01	History
—	—	—	12.37	11.35	14.33	17.04	21.07	19.75	22.44	21.90	20.80	NAV
—	—	—	–1.04*	–1.19	36.11	34.15	26.05	–6.27	21.26	5.40	28.60	Total Return %
—	—	—	–0.36*	–2.50	–1.42	11.21	–7.30	–34.84	0.22	14.51	40.47	+/– S&P 500
—	—	—	—	0.36	10.36	12.78	–5.64	0.17	22.74	–17.41	14.58	+/– Russell 2000 V
—	—	—	0.00	2.67	0.79	0.28	0.18	0.00	0.00	0.00	0.00	Income Return %
—	—	—	–1.04	–3.86	35.32	33.87	25.87	–6.26	21.26	5.40	28.60	Capital Return %
—	—	—	—	53	8	10	76	44	16	89	10	Total Rtn % Rank Cat
—	—	—	0.00	0.33	0.09	0.04	0.03	0.00	0.00	0.00	0.00	Income $
—	—	—	0.00	0.53	1.01	2.10	0.39	0.00	1.41	1.61	7.06	Capital Gains $
—	—	—	—	—	0.91	1.27	1.23	1.21	1.23	1.16	—	Expense Ratio %
—	—	—	—	—	0.79	0.62	0.22	–0.44	–0.78	–0.57	—	Income Ratio %
—	—	—	—	—	161	184	76	132	170	169	—	Turnover Rate %
—	—	—	5.0	5.1	7.1	23.8	402.3	327.4	304.6	296.3	332.8	Net Assets $mil

Performance 12-31-01

	1st Qtr	2nd Qtr	3rd Qtr	4th Qtr	Total
1997	2.23	14.01	14.35	–5.42	26.05
1998	11.01	–6.93	–27.19	24.61	–6.27
1999	–8.10	29.42	–6.05	8.51	21.26
2000	11.01	–3.45	1.00	–2.62	5.40
2001	15.39	14.68	–31.09	41.02	28.60

Trailing	Total Return%	+/– S&P 500	+/– Russ 2000V	% Rank All	% Rank Cat	Growth of $10,000
3 Mo	41.02	30.34	24.30	2	1	14,102
6 Mo	–2.82	2.73	–3.97	51	87	9,718
1 Yr	28.60	40.47	14.58	1	10	12,860
3 Yr Avg	18.01	19.04	6.69	3	17	16,436
5 Yr Avg	14.20	3.50	3.00	5	17	19,420
10 Yr Avg	—	—	—	—	—	—
15 Yr Avg	—	—	—	—	—	—

Tax Analysis	Tax-Adj Ret%	%Rank Cat	%Pretax Ret	%Rank Cat
3 Yr Avg	12.05	40	66.9	98
5 Yr Avg	10.54	38	74.2	92
10 Yr Avg	—	—	—	—

Potential Capital Gain Exposure: –5% of assets

Risk Analysis

Time Period	Load-Adj Return %	Risk %Rank[1] All	Risk %Rank[1] Cat	Morningstar Return	Morningstar Risk	Morningstar Risk-Adj Rating
1 Yr	28.60					
3 Yr	18.01	81	96	3.13[2]	1.16	★★★★★
5 Yr	14.20	84	94	2.39[2]	1.22	★★★★
Incept	16.79	—	—	—	—	

Average Historical Rating (61 months): 3.7★s

[1]1=low, 100=high [2] T-Bill return substituted for category avg.

Category Rating (3 Yr)

1 2 3 4 5
Worst Best

Return Above Avg
Risk High

Other Measures	Standard Index S&P 500	Best Fit Index SPMid400
Alpha	24.4	8.4
Beta	1.25	1.22
R-Squared	47	60

Standard Deviation	37.59
Mean	18.01
Sharpe Ratio	0.39

Analysis by Brian Portnoy 01-02-02

Dreyfus Small Company Value has wrapped up another year with pizzazz.

This fund shot the lights out in 2001, when it gained 28.6% and beat 90% of its small-value rivals. It has been anything but a smooth ride, though. In fact, in summer 2001, the fund was worst-performing small-value fund on a year-to-date basis; its impressive year-end numbers stem in large part from a category-best, fourth-quarter rally of 41%.

Manager Peter Higgins' stake in Arch Coal exemplifies 2001's wild ride. The company, which owns coal mines throughout the U.S., saw its stock price triple early in the year on positive energy news, but fell back to earth mid-year, alongside many of Higgins' other energy-related holdings. It then rallied 50% from its September low and, all told, was up 62% in 2001. Though not as volatile, Midway Games, Varian Semiconductor Equipment, and funeral-home operator Service Corp International were also major contributors. The fund's oversized tech stake (28% versus the category average of 11%) was the primary factor behind the fund's late-year surge.

Investors in this now-closed fund who aren't dizzy from the fund's roller-coaster ride would be smart to hang on. Higgins is one of the most unconventional—and most successful—value managers in the industry. His other charge, Dreyfus Midcap Value, is a top performer, and this small-cap offering, over the long haul, has impressed as well. Over the past three years, its annualized gain of 18% lands in the category's top quintile and beats the broad market by a country mile. What's more, his unusual approach in no way indicates a lack of value discipline. A propensity to sell winners quickly keeps the fund's price multiples and market cap in line with its peers'.

In short, the fund's a keeper.

Portfolio Analysis 09-30-01

Share change since 06-01 Total Stocks: 119	Sector	PE	YTD Ret%	% Assets
⊖ Regis	Services	19.5	78.94	2.33
⊕ Arch Coal	Industrials	—	62.38	2.30
⊕ Midway Games	Technology	—	111.40	2.24
⊕ Tesoro Petro	Energy	5.1	12.77	2.02
⊕ Credence Sys	Technology	—	–19.20	1.88
⊖ Gartner Grp A	Services	—	69.42	1.76
⊖ Massey Energy Company	Industrials	—	63.97	1.67
⊕ Varian Semicond Equip	Technology	11.1	45.64	1.62
⊖ Agrium	Industrials	17.1	–27.10	1.62
⊖ Key Energy Svcs	Energy	11.5	–11.80	1.61
⊕ Foster Wheeler	Industrials	9.3	–2.02	1.59
⊖ Trimble Nav	Technology	—	–32.40	1.54
⊕ Seitel	Energy	28.9	–26.20	1.52
⊖ Premier Parks	Services	—	–10.50	1.51
⊕ Teledyne Tech	Industrials	60.3	–31.00	1.37
⊕ CTS	Industrials	NMF	–56.00	1.36
⊕ Allen Telecom	Technology	44.7	–52.60	1.35
☼ MCSI	Technology	18.5	9.71	1.34
⊖ PolyOne	Industrials	—	71.42	1.33
⊖ Stolt Nielsen S.A. (ADR) Cl B	Services	—	—	1.32
Service Corp Intl	Services	—	185.10	1.32
☼ Emmis Broadcstg Cl A	Services	—	–17.60	1.30
☼ American Eagle Outfitters	Retail	16.8	–7.09	1.25
OfficeMax	Retail	—	56.52	1.19
⊖ York Intl	Industrials	23.5	26.51	1.18

Current Investment Style

Style: Value Blnd Growth; Size: Large Med Small

	Stock Port Avg	Relative S&P 500 Current	Relative S&P 500 Hist	Rel Cat
Price/Earnings Ratio	24.8	0.80	0.67	1.14
Price/Book Ratio	2.2	0.39	0.28	0.92
Price/Cash Flow	12.7	0.71	0.58	1.00
3 Yr Earnings Growth	9.5[1]	0.65	—	0.82
1 Yr Earnings Est%	–7.3[1]	4.15	—	1.86
Med Mkt Cap $mil	672	0.0	0.0	0.77

[1]figure is based on 50% or less of stocks

Special Securities % assets 09-30-01	
Restricted/Illiquid Secs	0
Emerging-Markets Secs	0
Options/Futures/Warrants	No

Composition % assets 09-30-01	
Cash	0.0
Stocks*	100.0
Bonds	0.0
Other	0.0
*Foreign (% stocks)	3.9

Market Cap	
Giant	0.0
Large	0.0
Medium	5.0
Small	81.5
Micro	13.5

Sector Weightings	% of Stocks	Rel S&P	5-Year High	5-Year Low
Utilities	0.0	0.0	1	0
Energy	11.5	1.6	12	3
Financials	1.1	0.1	18	0
Industrials	25.6	2.2	29	13
Durables	3.7	2.4	13	3
Staples	0.0	0.0	5	0
Services	22.1	2.0	23	10
Retail	8.5	1.3	17	4
Health	0.0	0.0	10	0
Technology	27.6	1.5	31	8

Address:	144 Glenn Curtiss Blvd Uniondale, NY 11556–0144 800–373–9387 / 718–895–1206
Web Address:	www.dreyfus.com/funds
*Inception:	12-29-93
Advisor:	Dreyfus
Subadvisor:	None
NTF Plans:	Fidelity , Datalynx

Minimum Purchase:	Closed	Add: $100 IRA: —
Min Auto Inv Plan:	Closed	Add: $100
Sales Fees:	No-load, 1.00%R within 1 month	
Management Fee:	.75%	
Actual Fees:	Mgt: 0.75%	Dist: —
Expense Projections:	3Yr: $381	5Yr: $660 10Yr: $1455
Avg Brok Commission:	—	Income Distrib: Annually
Total Cost (relative to category):		Below Avg

Eaton Vance Income Fund of Boston A

Ticker	Load	NAV	Yield	SEC Yield	Total Assets	Mstar Category
EVIBX	4.75%	$6.08	13.0%	—	$780.0 mil	High–Yield Bond

Prospectus Objective: Corp Bond—High Yield

Eaton Vance Income Fund of Boston seeks to maximize current income.

The fund will typically invest a substantial portion of its assets in bonds issued in connection with mergers, acquisitions and other highly leveraged transactions. It may invest in a wide variety of other income-producing debt securities, including senior secured floating-rate loans, as well as preferred stocks that pay dividends. Some debt securities acquired by the fund do not pay current income or do not make regular interest payments, while others may pay interest in the form of additional debt securities. The fund may invest in foreign debt securities and may invest up to 20% of its net assets in common stocks and other equity investments.

Historical Profile

Return Above Avg
Risk Above Avg
Rating ★★★ Neutral

Investment Style
Fixed-Income
Income Rtn %Rank Cat: 8, 14, 7, 7, 29, 19, 20, 14

Growth of Principal vs. Interest Rate Shifts
— Principal Value $000 (NAV with capital gains reinvested)
— Interest Rate % on 10 Yr Treasury
▼ Manager Change
▽ Partial Manager Change
► Mgr Unknown After
◄ Mgr Unknown Before

Performance Quartile (within Category)

Portfolio Manager(s)

Michael W. Weilheimer, CFA. Since 1-96. BS'83 State U. of New York; MBA'87 U. of Chicago. Other funds currently managed: Eaton Vance High-Income B, Eaton Vance High-Income C, Diversified Inv High Yield Bond.

Tom Huggins. Since 1-00. Other funds currently managed: Eaton Vance High-Income B, Eaton Vance High-Income C, Eaton Vance Income Fund of Boston I.

1990	1991	1992	1993	1994	1995	1996	1997	1998	1999	2000	12-01	History
6.25	7.71	8.12	8.60	7.66	7.96	8.20	8.70	8.16	8.31	6.87	6.08	NAV
–15.42	42.84	18.28	17.97	–1.29	15.29	13.74	16.43	2.69	12.19	–7.62	–0.14	Total Return %
–24.38	26.83	10.88	8.22	1.63	–3.18	10.13	6.75	–5.99	13.02	–19.25	–8.56	+/– LB Aggregate
–9.04	–0.92	1.62	–0.94	–0.31	–2.10	1.32	3.80	2.10	8.91	–2.41	–5.92	+/– FB High–Yield
14.39	18.10	13.07	11.84	10.21	11.28	10.52	10.01	9.28	10.39	10.95	12.11	Income Return %
–29.81	24.74	5.21	6.13	–11.50	4.01	3.22	6.42	–6.59	1.81	–18.58	–12.25	Capital Return %
81	24	33	61	24	75	36	6	26	6	54	70	Total Rtn % Rank Cat
1.16	1.05	0.95	0.91	0.84	0.82	0.80	0.79	0.77	0.81	0.87	0.79	Income $
0.00	0.00	0.00	0.00	0.00	0.00	0.00	0.00	0.00	0.00	0.00	0.00	Capital Gains $
1.05	1.15	1.08	1.03	1.04	1.09	1.07	1.05	1.04	1.01	1.04	—	Expense Ratio %
14.26	15.36	12.02	11.01	9.75	10.50	9.96	9.32	9.22	9.97	10.18	—	Income Ratio %
67	80	90	102	70	84	81	105	141	132	98	—	Turnover Rate %
57.8	72.6	83.2	102.7	97.9	113.3	154.0	209.2	247.9	384.6	638.1	—	Net Assets $mil

Performance 12-31-01

	1st Qtr	2nd Qtr	3rd Qtr	4th Qtr	Total
1997	0.91	6.14	6.17	2.39	16.43
1998	5.57	0.76	–7.36	4.20	2.69
1999	6.03	1.77	–0.41	4.41	12.19
2000	2.69	–0.18	–1.87	–8.16	–7.62
2001	3.21	–4.08	–5.89	7.17	–0.14

Trailing	Total Return%	+/– LB Agg	+/– FB High–Yield	% Rank All	% Rank Cat	Growth of $10,000
3 Mo	7.17	7.14	1.53	55	18	10,717
6 Mo	0.87	–3.79	–0.57	35	46	10,087
1 Yr	–0.14	–8.56	–5.92	43	70	9,986
3 Yr Avg	1.15	–5.12	–0.02	67	32	10,350
5 Yr Avg	4.35	–3.08	1.11	75	11	12,373
10 Yr Avg	8.37	1.14	0.54	41	6	22,349
15 Yr Avg	8.40	0.28	–0.26	50	2	33,536

Tax Analysis	Tax-Adj Ret%	%Rank Cat	%Pretax Ret	%Rank Cat
3 Yr Avg	–3.11	35	—	—
5 Yr Avg	0.23	13	5.2	86
10 Yr Avg	4.12	20	49.2	28

Potential Capital Gain Exposure: –31% of assets

Risk Analysis

Time Period	Load-Adj Return %	Risk %Rank[1] All	Risk %Rank[1] Cat	Morningstar Return	Morningstar Risk	Morningstar Risk-Adj Rating
1 Yr	–4.88					
3 Yr	–0.48	37	57	–1.09[2]	2.12	★★
5 Yr	3.34	40	38	–0.36[2]	2.06	★★
10 Yr	7.85	43	35	0.92[2]	1.46	★★★

Average Historical Rating (193 months): 3.9★s

[1]1=low, 100=high [2] T-Bill return substituted for category avg.

Category Rating (3 Yr)

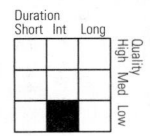

1 2 **3** 4 5
Worst Best

Return Above Avg
Risk Average

Other Measures	Standard Index LB Agg	Best Fit Index FB HY
Alpha	–3.2	1.0
Beta	0.06	1.24
R–Squared	0	86
Standard Deviation		9.97
Mean		1.15
Sharpe Ratio		–0.44

Analysis by Eric Jacobson 12-12-01

Eaton Vance Income Fund of Boston is struggling but not necessarily sinking.

This fund's difficulties shouldn't come as a huge surprise. Any fund that has performed as well in bull markets as this one should be expected to have a bumpy ride when things get tough. And it's true the fund has emphasized high-yield sectors that have bumped around a bit, including cable and wireless issuers, which together consumed roughly 20% of assets in late September. As a result, the portfolio's nearly flat total return placed it in the high-yield category's bottom third for the year to date through Dec. 10, 2001.

That showing could have been a lot worse, however, were it not for the fund's return-steadying cash stake, which has fluctuated over the course of the year, but clocked in at more than 9.5% in the third quarter. That clearly owes to the caution of comanagers Michael Weilheimer and Thomas Huggins, who have been concerned about the market's health since early 2000. The pair also wisely cut back on wireline telecom issuers, which have performed disastrously this year, while beefing up the fund's exposure to the BB slice of the market—an area that's thrived. By comparison, sibling fund Eaton Vance High Income typically holds less cash, and trails this one by more than 100 basis points, even when its higher expenses are taken into account.

If there's one lesson to take away from the past couple of years, it's that avoiding drastic losses may be as much or more important than pumping out high returns when the bulls are running. So far, this portfolio—which sports a terrific long-term record—appears to be showing some ability to thrive in hot markets without crashing when the high-yield sector stumbles. Investors who can tolerate its typically aggressive, more credit-sensitive approach should find this a profitable long-term holding.

Address:	255 State Street Boston, MA 02109 800–225–6265 / 617–482–8260
Web Address:	www.eatonvance.com
Inception:	06-30-72
Advisor:	Eaton Vance Mgmt.
Subadvisor:	None
NTF Plans:	Datalynx , Fidelity Inst.

Minimum Purchase:	$1000	Add: $50	IRA: $50
Min Auto Inv Plan:	$1000	Add: $50	
Sales Fees:	4.75%L, 0.25%B		
Management Fee:	.63%		
Actual Fees:	Mgt: 0.63%	Dist: 0.12%	
Expense Projections:	3Yr: $79*	5Yr: $103*	10Yr: $170*
Avg Brok Commission:	—	Income Distrib: Monthly	
Total Cost (relative to category):	—		

Portfolio Analysis 06-30-01

Total Fixed-Income: 274	Date of Maturity	Amount $000	Value $000	% Net Assets
Allied Waste Inds 10%	08-01-09	18,780	19,390	2.53
Charter Comm 10.75%	10-01-09	15,925	16,841	2.19
Chesapeake Energy 8.125%	04-01-11	13,130	12,342	1.61
TeleWest Step 0%	10-01-07	13,105	11,106	1.45
Waterford Gaming 144A 9.5%	03-15-10	10,939	10,789	1.41
Calpine 8.625%	08-15-10	10,550	10,225	1.33
Mandalay Resort Grp 10.25%	08-01-07	9,630	10,136	1.32
Dresser Inds 144A 9.375%	04-15-11	9,295	9,458	1.23
AFC Enterprises 10.25%	05-15-07	8,800	9,196	1.20
NTL Comms 11.875%	10-01-10	13,040	8,737	1.14
NWA 8.875%	06-01-06	8,960	8,665	1.13
William Carter 10.375%	12-01-06	8,350	8,642	1.13
Intermedia Comm Step 0%	07-15-07	9,227	8,166	1.06
Tritel PCS 10.375%	01-15-11	8,745	8,045	1.05
Allied Waste Inds 8.875%	04-01-08	7,800	8,044	1.05
Hollywood Casino 13%	05-01-06	7,345	7,749	1.01
Penn Natl Gaming 11.125%	03-01-08	7,255	7,581	0.99
Abraxas Petro 11.5%	11-01-04	7,803	7,296	0.95
AES 9.375%	09-15-10	6,650	6,750	0.88
MGM Grand 8.5%	09-15-10	6,250	6,494	0.85

Current Investment Style

Duration: Short Int Long
Quality: High Med Low

Avg Eff Duration[1]	4.4 Yrs
Avg Eff Maturity	—
Avg Credit Quality	B
Avg Wtd Coupon	9.18%
Avg Wtd Price	90.57% of par

[1]figure provided by fund

Special Securities % assets 06-30-01	
Restricted/Illiquid Secs	5
Exotic Mortgage–Backed	0
Emerging–Markets Secs	0
Options/Futures/Warrants	Yes

Coupon Range	% of Bonds	Rel Cat
0%, PIK	8.77	1.40
0% to 9%	21.72	0.72
9% to 12%	56.22	1.06
12% to 14%	11.56	1.31
More than 14%	1.74	1.25

1.00=Category Average

Credit Analysis % bonds 06-30-01			
US Govt	0	BB	20
AAA	3	B	58
AA	0	Below B	13
A	0	NR/NA	4
BBB	2		

Composition % assets 06-30-01			
Cash	4.7	Bonds	89.3
Stocks	0.4	Other	5.6

Sector Breakdown % bonds 06-30-01			
US Treasuries	0	CMOs	0
GNMA mtgs	0	ARMs	0
FNMA mtgs	0	Other	100
FHLMC mtgs	0		

Eaton Vance Worldwide Health Sci A

Ticker	Load	NAV	Yield	Total Assets	Mstar Category
ETHSX	5.75%	$10.33	0.0%	$947.6 mil	Spec Health Care

Prospectus Objective: Specialty—Health

Eaton Vance Worldwide Health Sciences Fund seeks long-term capital growth.

The fund normally invests in common stocks issued by U.S. and foreign health-science companies engaged in the development, production, or distribution of products or services related to scientific advances in health care. Selected companies may be active in biotechnology, diagnostics, managed health care, medical equipment and supplies, and pharmaceuticals. The fund concentrates at least 25% of its assets in the medical research and health care industry.

Class A shares have front loads; B shares have deferred loads and higher 12b-1 fees; C shares have level loads.

Historical Profile

Return: High
Risk: Average
Rating: ★★★★★ Highest

Investment Style
Equity
Average Stock %: 100% (1993), 97% (1994), 100% (1995), 96% (1996), 92% (1997), 94% (1998), 98% (1999)

▼ Manager Change
▽ Partial Manager Change

Fund Performance vs. Category Average
■ Quarterly Fund Return +/– Category Average
— Category Baseline

Performance Quartile (within Category)

1990	1991	1992	1993	1994	1995	1996	1997	1998	1999	2000	12-01	History
2.31	3.07	2.78	3.25	2.82	4.01	4.53	4.91	5.83	6.68	11.63	10.33	NAV
5.12	42.35	2.32	26.40	–6.32	61.11	18.25	10.50	23.53	23.98	81.56	–6.63	Total Return %
8.24	11.87	–5.30	16.34	–7.64	23.57	–4.70	–22.85	–5.05	2.94	90.67	5.25	+/– S&P 500
11.30	8.14	–6.65	15.12	–6.25	24.66	–2.95	–20.80	0.10	0.42	92.50	4.27	+/– Wilshire 5000
0.00	0.00	0.00	0.00	0.00	0.00	0.00	0.00	0.00	0.00	0.00	0.00	Income Return %
5.12	42.35	2.32	26.40	–6.32	61.11	18.25	10.50	23.53	23.98	81.56	–6.63	Capital Return %
70	90	18	1	76	10	18	75	41	25	17	23	Total Rtn % Rank Cat
0.00	0.00	0.00	0.00	0.00	0.00	0.00	0.00	0.00	0.00	0.00	0.00	Income $
0.27	0.21	0.35	0.25	0.23	0.47	0.20	0.10	0.22	0.47	0.51	0.45	Capital Gains $
3.51	2.50	2.48	2.50	2.50	2.44	2.21	2.22	1.83	1.69	1.79	1.71	Expense Ratio %
–2.26	–1.47	–1.45	–1.53	–1.65	–1.82	–1.81	–1.82	–1.21	–1.11	–1.29	–0.89	Income Ratio %
143	81	71	77	49	45	66	14	34	41	31	24	Turnover Rate %
4.4	10.7	9.8	12.0	12.5	35.0	56.7	93.7	97.3	104.7	591.7	947.6	Net Assets $mil

Portfolio Manager(s)

Samuel D. Isaly. Since 8-89. BA'67 Princeton U.; M.SC.'68 London School of Economics. Other funds currently managed: Eaton Vance Worldwide Health Sci B, Eaton Vance Worldwide Health Sci C, Eaton Vance Worldwide Health Sci D.

Performance 12-31-01

	1st Qtr	2nd Qtr	3rd Qtr	4th Qtr	Total
1997	3.09	8.57	11.20	–11.21	10.50
1998	6.72	–6.11	–3.05	27.16	23.53
1999	–5.66	0.55	9.95	18.88	23.98
2000	36.53	19.96	13.74	–2.53	81.56
2001	–19.26	13.42	–8.10	10.96	–6.63

Trailing	Total Return%	+/– S&P 500	+/– Wil 5000	% Rank All	% Rank Cat	Growth of $10,000
3 Mo	10.96	0.27	–1.42	37	36	11,096
6 Mo	1.97	7.52	7.45	23	18	10,197
1 Yr	–6.63	5.25	4.27	54	23	9,337
3 Yr Avg	28.09	29.12	28.74	1	4	21,018
5 Yr Avg	23.46	12.77	13.76	1	6	28,689
10 Yr Avg	20.81	7.88	8.53	1	1	66,214
15 Yr Avg	19.40	5.67	6.40	1	12	142,923

Tax Analysis	Tax-Adj Ret%	%Rank Cat	%Pretax Ret	%Rank Cat
3 Yr Avg	26.63	10	94.8	30
5 Yr Avg	22.31	3	95.1	9
10 Yr Avg	18.74	1	90.1	9

Potential Capital Gain Exposure: 4% of assets

Risk Analysis

Time Period	Load-Adj Return %	Risk %Rank[1] All	Risk %Rank[1] Cat	Morningstar Return	Morningstar Risk	Morningstar Risk-Adj Rating
1 Yr	–11.99					
3 Yr	25.59	51	25	5.30[2]	0.71	★★★★★
5 Yr	22.01	64	44	5.12[2]	0.88	★★★★★
10 Yr	20.09	78	40	3.38	1.03	★★★★★

Average Historical Rating (162 months): 3.4★s

[1] 1=low, 100=high [2] T-Bill return substituted for category avg.

Category Rating (3 Yr)

1 2 3 4 5 (Worst … Best): 5

Return: High
Risk: Below Avg

Other Measures	Standard Index S&P 500	Best Fit Index Wil 4500
Alpha	28.7	26.0
Beta	0.46	0.67
R-Squared	9	49

Standard Deviation	34.91
Mean	28.09
Sharpe Ratio	0.74

Portfolio Analysis 11-30-01

Share chng since 09-01 Total Stocks: 46

	Subsector	PE	YTD Ret%	% Assets
Pfizer	Gen Pharm/Bio	34.7	–12.40	5.64
⊕ Amgen	Gen Pharm/Bio	52.8	–11.70	5.19
Altana	Gen Pharm/Bio	32.6	—	4.70
⊕ Pharmacia	Chemicals	36.5	–29.30	4.63
Immunex	Gen Pharm/Bio	89.4	–31.70	4.50
Genentech	Gen Pharm/Bio	NMF	–33.40	4.49
⊕ Serono	Health	68.5	—	4.31
Eli Lilly	Gen Pharm/Bio	28.9	–14.40	4.31
Sanofi-Synthelabo	Health	50.5	—	4.15
⊕ American Home Products	Gen Pharm/Bio	—	–1.91	4.07
☼ Novartis ADR	Gen Pharm/Bio	22.3	–17.40	3.85
Gilead Sciences	Emg. Pharm/Bio	—	58.48	3.76
Sepracor	Emg. Pharm/Bio	—	–28.70	3.51
⊕ Genzyme Corporation General Di	Emg. Pharm/Bio	—	33.11	3.41
Abgenix	Health	—	–43.00	3.00
Fujisawa Pharma	Gen Pharm/Bio	39.6	—	2.98
Schering-Plough	Gen Pharm/Bio	22.2	–35.90	2.98
Abbott Labs	Gen Pharm/Bio	51.6	17.08	2.86
⊕ Incyte Genomics	Gen Pharm/Bio	—	–21.30	2.48
⊕ Enzon	Health	NMF	–9.32	2.44
Forest Labs	Gen Pharm/Bio	52.2	23.35	1.84
⊕ COR Therapeutics	Emg. Pharm/Bio	NMF	–31.90	1.75
Banyu Pharma	Gen Pharm/Bio	26.9	—	1.48
Chugai Pharma	Gen Pharm/Bio	26.7	—	1.43
⊕ Molecular Devices	Diagnostics	—	–69.50	1.41

Current Investment Style

Style: Value Blnd Growth; Size: Large Med Small

	Stock Port Avg	Relative S&P 500 Current	Relative S&P 500 Hist	Rel Cat
Price/Earnings Ratio	43.3	1.40	1.30	1.07
Price/Book Ratio	9.3	1.62	1.03	1.02
Price/Cash Flow	30.6	1.70	1.35	1.07
3 Yr Earnings Growth	21.0[1]	1.43	0.83	0.97
1 Yr Earnings Est%	19.3[1]	—	—	0.85
Med Mkt Cap $mil	17,409	0.3	0.1	0.79

[1] figure is based on 50% or less of stocks

Special Securities % assets 11-30-01

Restricted/Illiquid Secs	Trace
Emerging-Markets Secs	Trace
Options/Futures/Warrants	Yes

Composition % assets 11-30-01

Cash	5.9
Stocks*	93.4
Bonds	0.0
Other	0.7
*Foreign (% stocks)	26.7

Market Cap

Giant	40.0
Large	19.7
Medium	27.8
Small	11.5
Micro	1.0

Subsector Weightings	% of Stocks	Rel Cat
Gen Pharm/Bio	57.5	1.3
Medical Devices	0.0	0.0
Hospitals	0.0	0.0
Other Providers	0.0	0.0
HMOs/PPOs	0.0	0.0
Emg. Pharm/Bio	16.0	0.9
Diagnostics	1.5	1.0
Tech/Bus Svs	0.0	0.0
Other	25.0	1.1

Analysis by Peter Di Teresa 08-17-01

Eaton Vance Worldwide Health Sciences Fund distinctiveness makes it an appealing pick.

Investors going for growth have found this fund is one of the most rewarding offerings in the specialty-health category. Through August 16, 2001, its returns for three years and longer were among the very best in the group.

That comes from the strategy of manager Sam Isaly and his team at Orbimed (the fund's subadvisor) of buying growing companies at attractive prices. There's nothing uncommon about that approach, but Isaly doesn't end up with the same old stocks as his peers. Sure, this fund has a slug of the big-cap drug companies that grace many health-care funds, but it puts an equal amount in biotech, which is decidedly atypical.

In fact, from pretty much any perspective, this fund looks distinctive. It puts more in small and mid-cap stocks than the norm, and it doesn't hesitate to venture overseas. The fund's current 28% foreign stake is nearly four times the category average, yet that's actually on the low side for this offering. Isaly also keeps turnover modest—with its 31% ratio, this fund moves more deliberately than all but one of its peers.

The fund's giant-cap drug holdings generally afford some stability, and its foreign stocks add diversification, but Isaly acknowledges that its bent toward smaller companies and significant biotech stake put it on the risky side. That said, the fund's riskier ventures aren't merely speculative. When Isaly buys biotechs, for example, he focuses on companies that are either making money or close to it.

In fact, the fund lost less than most peers when health stocks collapsed in this year's first quarter and is in the top third for the year to date. While the fund's predilections could well spell greater volatility than in the past, we think this is an appealing investment for more aggressive health-care investors.

Address:	255 State Street Boston, MA 02109 617-482-8260 / 800-225-6265
Web Address:	www.eatonvance.com
Inception:	07-26-85
Advisor:	OrbiMed Adv., Inc.
Subadvisor:	None
NTF Plans:	Datalynx , Fidelity Inst.

Minimum Purchase:	$1000	Add: $50 IRA: $50
Min Auto Inv Plan:	$50	Add: $50
Sales Fees:	5.75%L, 0.25%B	
Management Fee:	.25% mx./.17% mn.+(–).25%P, .50%A	
Actual Fees:	Mgt: 1.11%	Dist: 0.25%
Expense Projections:	3Yr: $1080	5Yr: $1445 10Yr: $2468
Avg Brok Commission:	—	Income Distrib: Annually
Total Cost (relative to category):	Average	

Enterprise Internet A

Ticker	Load	NAV	Yield	Total Assets	Mstar Category
EIFAX	4.75%	$10.22	0.0%	$122.0 mil	Spec Technology

Prospectus Objective: Specialty—Technology

Enterprise Internet Fund seeks long-term capital appreciation.

The fund normally invests at least 65% of assets in the equity securities of companies in the Internet, Intranet and "high tech" sectors. It may invest in equity securities including common stocks, preferred stocks, warrents and other securities convertible into common stock. The fund may also invest in non-investment grade securities, foreign securities, as well as illiquid or restricted securities.

The fund offers A, B, C, and Y shares all of which vary in fee structure and availability.

Historical Profile
Return —
Risk —
Rating Not Rated

Investment Style
Equity
Average Stock %: 97% (2000), 92% (12-01)

▼ Manager Change
▽ Partial Manager Change

Fund Performance vs. Category Average
■ Quarterly Fund Return +/– Category Average
— Category Baseline

Performance Quartile (within Category)

Portfolio Manager(s)

Dan Chung, CFA. Since 9-00. BA'84 Stanford U.; JD'87 Harvard Law School. Other funds currently managed: Alger LargeCap Growth B, Alger Balanced B, Alger MidCap Growth B.

1990	1991	1992	1993	1994	1995	1996	1997	1998	1999	2000	12–01	History
—	—	—	—	—	—	—	—	—	31.72	15.47	10.22	NAV
—	—	—	—	—	—	—	—	—	220.79*	–51.10	–33.94	Total Return %
—	—	—	—	—	—	—	—	—	213.73*	–42.00	–22.06	+/– S&P 500
—	—	—	—	—	—	—	—	—	—	–34.88	–18.35	+/– PSE Tech 100
—	—	—	—	—	—	—	—	—	0.00	0.00	0.00	Income Return %
—	—	—	—	—	—	—	—	—	220.79	–51.10	–33.94	Capital Return %
—	—	—	—	—	—	—	—	—	—	87	33	Total Rtn % Rank Cat
—	—	—	—	—	—	—	—	—	0.00	0.00	0.00	Income $
—	—	—	—	—	—	—	—	—	0.35	0.10	0.00	Capital Gains $
—	—	—	—	—	—	—	—	—	1.90	1.86	—	Expense Ratio %
—	—	—	—	—	—	—	—	—	–1.28	–1.64	—	Income Ratio %
—	—	—	—	—	—	—	—	—	—	256	—	Turnover Rate %
—	—	—	—	—	—	—	—	—	118.8	92.7	49.1	Net Assets $mil

Performance 12-31-01

	1st Qtr	2nd Qtr	3rd Qtr	4th Qtr	Total
1997	—	—	—	—	—
1998	—	—	—	—	—
1999	—	—	83.00	75.30	220.79 *
2000	12.94	–21.69	5.04	–47.36	–51.10
2001	–29.67	24.17	–41.38	29.04	–33.94

Trailing	Total Return%	+/– S&P 500	+/– PSE Tech 100	% Rank All	% Rank Cat	Growth of $10,000
3 Mo	29.04	18.36	–3.87	5	78	12,904
6 Mo	–24.35	–18.80	–19.07	100	84	7,565
1 Yr	–33.94	–22.06	–18.35	96	33	6,606
3 Yr Avg	—	—	—	—	—	—
5 Yr Avg	—	—	—	—	—	—
10 Yr Avg	—	—	—	—	—	—
15 Yr Avg	—	—	—	—	—	—

Tax Analysis	Tax-Adj Ret%	%Rank Cat	%Pretax Ret	%Rank Cat
3 Yr Avg	—	—	—	—
5 Yr Avg	—	—	—	—
10 Yr Avg	—	—	—	—

Potential Capital Gain Exposure: –108% of assets

Risk Analysis

Time Period	Load-Adj Return %	Risk %Rank¹ All	Risk %Rank¹ Cat	Morningstar Return	Morningstar Risk	Morningstar Risk-Adj Rating
1 Yr	–37.07					
3 Yr	—	—	—	—	—	
5 Yr	—	—	—	—	—	
Incept	–0.52	—	—	—	—	

Average Historical Rating —

¹1=low, 100=high

Category Rating (3 Yr)

Return
Risk

Other Measures	Standard Index S&P 500	Best Fit Index
Alpha	—	—
Beta	—	—
R–Squared	—	—
Standard Deviation		—
Mean		—
Sharpe Ratio		—

Portfolio Analysis 11-30-01

Share chng since 10–01 Total Stocks: 42	Subsector	PE	YTD Ret%	% Assets
Tyco Intl	Industrials	27.1	6.23	6.40
Amdocs	Services	NMF	–48.70	5.22
⊖ Microsoft	Software	57.6	52.78	4.83
Freemarkets	Retail	—	26.16	4.61
Bisys Grp	Services	42.7	22.76	4.50
EBAY	Services	NMF	102.70	4.16
Nokia Cl A ADR	Telecom	45.8	–43.00	3.71
⊖ Synopsys	Software	67.1	24.52	3.67
Sun Microsystems	Computers	NMF	–55.80	3.29
Microchip Tech	Semiconductors	53.8	76.59	3.26
First Data	Computer Svs	38.1	49.08	2.95
Dell Comp	Computers	61.8	55.87	2.93
Overture Svcs	N/A	—	—	2.74
Qualcomm	Telecom	—	–38.50	2.63
⊕ VeriSign	Technology	—	–48.70	2.50
Charter Comms	Services	—	–27.50	2.48
Oracle	Software	32.1	–52.40	2.26
⊖ AOL Time Warner	Computer Svs	—	–7.76	2.04
Comcast	Cable	20.3	–13.70	1.92
Sprint (PCS Group)	Services	—	19.43	1.87
Fiserv	Services	40.7	33.82	1.81
Dupont Photomasks	Industrials	NMF	–17.70	1.64
Integrated Device Tech	Semiconductors	8.9	–19.70	1.54
☼ Brocade Comm Sys	Technology	—	–63.90	1.54
Intel	Semiconductors	73.1	4.89	1.53

Current Investment Style

Style: Value Blnd Growth; Size: Large Med Small

	Stock Port Avg	Relative S&P 500 Current	Relative S&P 500 Hist	Rel Cat
Price/Earnings Ratio	47.2	1.53	—	1.02
Price/Book Ratio	6.7	1.18	—	1.09
Price/Cash Flow	25.7	1.43	—	0.99
3 Yr Earnings Growth	28.6	1.96	—	0.96
1 Yr Earnings Est%	–14.7¹	8.30	—	0.88
Med Mkt Cap $mil	13,400	0.2	—	0.84

¹figure is based on 50% or less of stocks

Special Securities % assets 11-30-01	
Restricted/Illiquid Secs	0
Emerging–Markets Secs	2
Options/Futures/Warrants	No

Composition % assets 11-30-01	
Cash	7.7
Stocks*	92.3
Bonds	0.0
Other	0.0
*Foreign (% stocks)	6.1

Market Cap	
Giant	33.5
Large	19.8
Medium	37.7
Small	9.1
Micro	0.0

Subsector Weightings	% of Stocks	Rel Cat
Computers	6.9	1.3
Semiconductors	8.6	0.8
Semi Equipment	0.0	0.0
Networking	0.0	0.0
Periph/Hardware	0.0	0.0
Software	14.8	1.1
Computer Svs	5.6	0.9
Telecom	7.9	1.0
Health Care	0.0	0.0
Other	56.2	1.5

Analysis by Christopher Traulsen 12-12-01

Enterprise Internet Fund's chief attraction has been diminished, but there's reason to stay the course.

Generally speaking, we don't think much of Internet funds. Most are extremely volatile, and the definition of an Internet company has become so fuzzy, it's nearly meaningless. Finally, most Net funds are run by managers with little or no prior experience managing retail offerings.

Before Sept. 11, however, this fund offered something that most of its Net-focused rivals didn't. It was comanaged by David Alger and Dan Chung, and backed by the research team at Fred Alger management—a shop with an excellent reputation for growth investing. That, as well as the fund's strong performance compared with other Internet offerings, gave us reason to think it was more appealing than the vast bulk of its rivals.

However, Fred Alger's main office was destroyed in the terrorist attack of Sept. 11. Sadly, much of the firm's staff—including comanager and Alger president David Alger—lost their lives. The firm relocated to a facility it operates in New Jersey and immediately began rebuilding. Founder Fred Alger returned from retirement and will now comanage this fund with Dan Chung.

The blow to Alger was big, but it doesn't eliminate this fund's appeal. For one, Chung already handled most of the management duties here, so his continued presence should help keep the fund on course. The firm has also begun to hire a number of experienced analysts, including former Alger tech analyst David Hyun. Finally, there just aren't many other Net funds with much appeal at all.

We still think most investors will be better off with a general tech fund than with this or any other Internet offering, and we'd hold off buying here until Alger's new look comes into focus. That said, we don't think the shakeup at Alger is in itself cause to sell this fund.

Address:	3343 Peachtree Road Suite 450 Atlanta, GA 30326 404–261–1116 / 800–368–3527
Web Address:	www.enterprisefunds.com
*Inception:	07-01-99
Advisor:	Enterprise Cap. Mgmt.
Subadvisor:	None
NTF Plans:	Datalynx

Minimum Purchase:	$1000	Add: $50	IRA: $250
Min Auto Inv Plan:	$1000	Add: $25	
Sales Fees:	4.75%L, 0.20%B, 0.25%S		
Management Fee:	1.0%		
Actual Fees:	Mgt: 1.00%	Dist: 0.45%	
Expense Projections:	3Yr: $1054	5Yr: —	10Yr: —
Avg Brok Commission:	—	Income Distrib: Annually	
Total Cost (relative to category):	—		

Evergreen Equity Income I

Ticker	Load	NAV	Yield	Total Assets	Mstar Category
EVTRX	None	$20.35	3.9%	$885.1 mil	Mid-Cap Value

Prospectus Objective: Equity-Income

Evergreen Equity Income Fund - Class I seeks current income and capital appreciation.

The fund normally invests at least 75% of assets in equities; it may invest the balance in debt. The percentage invested in each asset class varies according to market conditions. The fund invests primarily in income-producing stocks.

Class A shares have front loads; B shares have deferred loads; C shares have level loads; Y shares sold to shareholders of record in any Evergreen fund prior to Dec. 30, 1994, and to institutional investors.

Past fund names: Evergreen Total Return Fund, Income & Growth Fund and Evergreen Equity Income Fund.

Historical Profile

Return: Average
Risk: Below Avg
Rating: ★★★ Neutral

Investment Style: Equity

Average Stock %: 74% · 75% · 73% · 67% · 71% · 64% · 62%

▼ Manager Change
▽ Partial Manager Change

Fund Performance vs. Category Average
■ Quarterly Fund Return +/– Category Average
– Category Baseline

Performance Quartile (within Category)

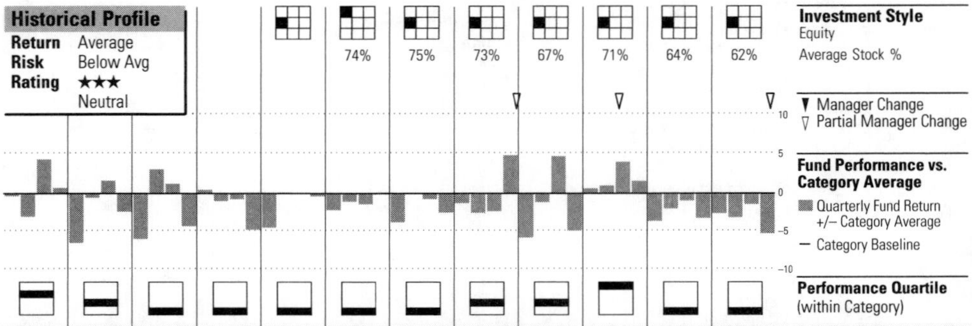

Portfolio Manager(s)

Sujatha Avutu. Since 11-01. Other funds currently managed: Evergreen Equity Income A, Evergreen Equity Income B, Evergreen Equity Income C.

1990	1991	1992	1993	1994	1995	1996	1997	1998	1999	2000	12-01	History
16.49	19.12	19.43	19.62	17.03	19.92	21.33	23.93	20.59	22.38	22.44	20.35	NAV
–6.30	22.99	10.03	12.93	–6.42	23.87	12.89	25.58	–0.79	16.37	7.16	–5.37	Total Return %
–3.18	–7.49	2.41	2.87	–7.74	–13.67	–10.05	–7.77	–29.37	–4.67	16.27	6.50	+/- S&P 500
9.78	–14.93	–11.65	–2.70	–4.29	–11.07	–7.37	–8.78	–5.88	16.47	–12.02	–7.71	+/- Russ Midcap Val
5.89	6.70	5.77	5.75	5.64	6.54	5.60	5.25	4.41	5.37	4.43	3.64	Income Return %
–12.19	16.29	4.25	7.18	–12.06	17.32	7.29	20.34	–5.20	11.00	2.73	–9.02	Capital Return %
30	75	80	76	82	78	86	61	67	19	83	95	Total Rtn % Rank Cat
1.08	1.08	1.08	1.08	1.08	1.09	1.09	1.08	1.02	1.08	0.97	0.81	Income $
0.00	0.00	0.46	1.20	0.25	0.00	0.00	1.59	2.13	0.40	0.47	0.06	Capital Gains $
1.18	1.23	1.21	1.18	1.18	1.24	1.19	1.18	1.25	1.21	1.23	—	Expense Ratio %
5.64	5.90	5.73	5.65	5.29	5.70	5.70	5.14	4.46	4.61	4.29	—	Income Ratio %
89	137	137	164	106	151	138	168	133	124	115	—	Turnover Rate %
1,101.5	1,122.1	1,077.9	1,195.4	943.7	916.9	856.6	937.0	826.1	835.5	760.1	648.3	Net Assets $mil

Performance 12-31-01

	1st Qtr	2nd Qtr	3rd Qtr	4th Qtr	Total
1997	–0.02	10.65	9.13	4.03	25.58
1998	5.61	–3.43	–11.55	9.97	–0.79
1999	–0.17	14.50	–5.76	8.02	16.37
2000	–0.80	–2.59	7.34	3.32	7.16
2001	–4.02	4.70	–13.18	8.46	–5.37

Trailing	Total Return%	+/– S&P 500	+/– Russ Midcap Val	% Rank All	% Rank Cat	Growth of $10,000
3 Mo	8.46	–2.22	–3.57	50	83	10,846
6 Mo	–5.83	–0.28	–4.92	67	94	9,417
1 Yr	–5.37	6.50	–7.71	52	95	9,463
3 Yr Avg	5.67	6.70	–1.14	25	80	11,800
5 Yr Avg	8.01	–2.69	–3.45	29	80	14,701
10 Yr Avg	9.10	–3.82	–5.31	38	91	23,902
15 Yr Avg	8.56	–5.18	–4.91	50	87	34,260

Tax Analysis	Tax-Adj Ret%	%Rank Cat	%Pretax Ret	%Rank Cat
3 Yr Avg	3.53	81	62.3	91
5 Yr Avg	4.91	87	61.3	94
10 Yr Avg	6.06	91	66.6	91

Potential Capital Gain Exposure: 3% of assets

Risk Analysis

Time Period	Load-Adj Return %	Risk %Rank[1] All	Risk %Rank[1] Cat	Morningstar Return	Morningstar Risk	Morningstar Risk-Adj Rating
1 Yr	–5.37					
3 Yr	5.67	41	18	0.16[2]	0.56	★★★★
5 Yr	8.01	47	13	0.69[2]	0.63	★★★
10 Yr	9.10	53	12	0.58	0.66	★★★

Average Historical Rating (193 months): 3.2★s

[1]1=low, 100=high [2] T-Bill return substituted for category avg.

Category Rating (3 Yr)

1 2 **3** 4 5
Worst — Best

Return: Below Avg
Risk: Below Avg

Other Measures	Standard Index S&P 500	Best Fit Index SPMid400
Alpha	4.3	–2.2
Beta	0.60	0.55
R-Squared	62	70

Standard Deviation	13.53
Mean	5.67
Sharpe Ratio	0.06

Analysis by Christopher Davis 11-30-01

Investors should expect much of the same from Evergreen Equity Income Fund, and that's not a good thing.

Evergreen recently enlisted Sujatha Avutu to take charge of this offering after giving former managers Irene O'Neill and Phil Foreman the boot. Avutu, the firm's financials sector analyst prior to taking the reins here, hasn't run a mutual fund before.

Avutu certainly hasn't inherited a powerhouse. Shareholders have endured years of simply woeful returns: It landed in the mid-value group's bottom half in nine of the past 10 years, and it is on pace to do so again in 2001. Indeed, the fund's 7% loss for the year to date through Nov. 29, 2001, lands in the category's bottom decile.

Unfortunately, the yield-oriented approach that produced those dismal results is likely to remain intact under Avutu. The fund has long boasted the category's highest yield, but its pursuit of income has usually led it to concentrate in just a handful of dividend-rich sectors, such as financials and utilities (Avutu says the fund's stake in the latter won't be as large as before, though). What's more, the fund owns a slew of income-generating preferred stocks and convertible bonds. That mix has been especially troublesome in rising interest-rate environments. When rates ticked upward in 1994 and 2000, for instance, the fund landed in the category's bottom quartile.

So, is there any reason at all to own this fund? Its plump yield gives it enough cushion to make it one of the category's least volatile offerings, and the fund may appeal to income-oriented investors who don't want to own a bond fund. However, most intermediate-term bond offerings own better long-term records, feature higher yields, and are far less volatile than this fund.

New manager or not, we think investors won't have to look far to find a more-compelling option than this one.

Portfolio Analysis 09-30-01

Share change since 06-01 Total Stocks: 122

Holding	Sector	PE	YTD Ret%	% Assets
American Home Products	Health	—	–1.91	2.09
⊖ J.C. Penney	Retail	—	154.60	1.77
XL Cap Cl A	Financials	22.8	5.82	1.61
⊖ Verizon Comms	Services	29.7	–2.52	1.55
Gables Residential Tr	Financials	15.8	14.43	1.54
North Fork Bancorp	Financials	16.5	34.11	1.53
⊖ Raytheon (Units)	N/A	—	—	1.44
Abbott Labs	Health	51.6	17.08	1.37
⊖ CMS Energy (Acts) Pfd	Utilities	—	—	1.28
Estee Lauder (Traces) Pfd	Retail	—	—	1.27
⊕ General Elec	Industrials	30.1	–15.00	1.25
Qwest Trends Tr 144A Pfd 5.75%	Utilities	—	—	1.24
Dominion Resources	Utilities	19.3	–6.59	1.23
Bristol-Myers Squibb	Health	20.2	–26.00	1.20
Union Pac Cv Pfd 6.25%	Services	—	—	1.17
EchoStar Comm 4.875%	N/A	—	—	1.15
Dana	Durables	—	–4.89	1.12
⊕ Cummins Cap Pfd Cv	N/A	—	—	1.11
Duke Energy (Unit)	N/A	—	—	1.07
FNMA Debenture 7.125%	N/A	—	—	1.05
⊕ May Dept Stores	Retail	15.2	15.97	1.04
Equity Residential Properties	Financials	22.1	10.14	1.03
⊖ Qualcomm	Technology	—	–38.50	1.02
Nisource Cv Pfd 7.75%	Utilities	—	—	0.98
Williams Companies	Utilities	17.9	–29.10	0.98

Current Investment Style

Style: Value Blnd Growth; Size: Large Med Small

	Stock Port Avg	Relative S&P 500 Current	Relative S&P 500 Hist	Rel Cat
Price/Earnings Ratio	23.1	0.75	0.65	0.98
Price/Book Ratio	4.1	0.72	0.46	1.36
Price/Cash Flow	13.9	0.77	0.64	1.12
3 Yr Earnings Growth	12.2	0.83	0.45	1.03
1 Yr Earnings Est%	–3.4	1.91	—	0.55
Med Mkt Cap $mil	9,570	0.2	0.1	1.35

[1]figure is based on 50% or less of stocks

Special Securities % assets 09-30-01	
Restricted/Illiquid Secs	3
Emerging-Markets Secs	0
Options/Futures/Warrants	No

Composition % assets 09-30-01	
Cash	2.0
Stocks*	66.0
Bonds	12.2
Other	19.8
*Foreign (% stocks)	5.5

Market Cap	
Giant	25.7
Large	29.4
Medium	37.3
Small	5.5
Micro	2.2

Sector Weightings	% of Stocks	Rel S&P	5-Year High	5-Year Low
Utilities	7.1	2.2	37	7
Energy	5.0	0.7	14	2
Financials	35.8	2.0	53	17
Industrials	10.1	0.9	15	4
Durables	7.0	4.5	8	0
Staples	1.5	0.2	6	0
Services	5.3	0.5	27	3
Retail	11.4	1.7	11	0
Health	10.6	0.7	15	2
Technology	6.3	0.3	8	0

Address: 401 South Tryon Street Suite 500, Charlotte, NC 28288-1195, 800-343-2898
Web Address: www.evergreeninvestments.com

Inception: 08-31-78
Advisor: Evergreen Inv. Mgmt.
Subadvisor: Lieber & Co.
NTF Plans: Waterhouse

Minimum Purchase: $1000 — Add: None — IRA: $250
Min Auto Inv Plan: $1000 — Add: $25
Sales Fees: No-load
Management Fee: 1.0% mx./.80% mn.
Actual Fees: Mgt: 0.75% — Dist: —
Expense Projections: 3Yr: $368 — 5Yr: $638 — 10Yr: $1409
Avg Brok Commission: — — Income Distrib: Quarterly
Total Cost (relative to category): Below Avg

Evergreen Health Care A

Ticker	Load	NAV	Yield	Total Assets	Mstar Category
EHABX	5.75%	$16.21	0.0%	$135.0 mil	Spec Health Care

Prospectus Objective: Specialty—Health

Evergreen Health Care seeks long-term capital growth.

The fund normally invests at least 65% of assets in the equity securities of healthcare companies. This includes companies that develop, produce or distribute products or services related to the healthcare or medical industries and derive more than 50% of their sales from products and services in healthcare. The fund may invest in securities of relatively well-known and large companies as well as small and medium sized companies. It may invest in securities of both domestic and foreign issuers. The fund is nondiversified.

The fund offers Class A, B, C, and Y shares, all of which differ in fee structure and availability.

Historical Profile
Return —
Risk —
Rating Not Rated

Investment Style
Equity
Average Stock %: 98% (2000), 98% (12-01)

▼ Manager Change
▽ Partial Manager Change

Fund Performance vs. Category Average
■ Quarterly Fund Return
+/– Category Average
— Category Baseline

Performance Quartile (within Category)

Portfolio Manager(s)

Liu-Er Chen, CFA. Since 12-99. Other funds currently managed: Evergreen Global Opportunities A, Evergreen Global Opportunities B, Evergreen Global Opportunities C.

1990	1991	1992	1993	1994	1995	1996	1997	1998	1999	2000	12-01	History
—	—	—	—	—	—	—	—	—	10.48	15.87	16.21	NAV
—	—	—	—	—	—	—	—	—	4.80*	119.05	2.14	Total Return %
—	—	—	—	—	—	—	—	—	2.39*	128.15	14.02	+/– S&P 500
—	—	—	—	—	—	—	—	—	—	129.98	13.03	+/– Wilshire 5000
—	—	—	—	—	—	—	—	—	0.00	0.00	0.00	Income Return %
—	—	—	—	—	—	—	—	—	4.80	119.05	2.14	Capital Return %
—	—	—	—	—	—	—	—	—	—	2	5	Total Rtn % Rank Cat
—	—	—	—	—	—	—	—	—	0.00	0.00	0.00	Income $
—	—	—	—	—	—	—	—	—	0.00	6.09	0.00	Capital Gains $
—	—	—	—	—	—	—	—	—	—	1.75	—	Expense Ratio %
—	—	—	—	—	—	—	—	—	—	–1.10	—	Income Ratio %
—	—	—	—	—	—	—	—	—	—	—	—	Turnover Rate %
—	—	—	—	—	—	—	—	—	—	16.6	32.3	Net Assets $mil

Performance 12-31-01

	1st Qtr	2nd Qtr	3rd Qtr	4th Qtr	Total
1997	—	—	—	—	—
1998	—	—	—	—	—
1999	—	—	—	—	4.80 *
2000	53.63	21.12	16.29	1.23	119.05
2001	–21.30	24.50	–8.87	14.40	2.14

Trailing	Total Return%	+/– S&P 500	+/– Wil 5000	% Rank All	% Rank Cat	Growth of $10,000
3 Mo	14.40	3.71	2.03	25	29	11,440
6 Mo	4.24	9.80	9.73	7	4	10,424
1 Yr	2.14	14.02	13.03	39	5	10,214
3 Yr Avg	—	—	—	—	—	—
5 Yr Avg	—	—	—	—	—	—
10 Yr Avg	—	—	—	—	—	—
15 Yr Avg	—	—	—	—	—	—

Tax Analysis	Tax-Adj Ret%	%Rank Cat	%Pretax Ret	%Rank Cat
3 Yr Avg	—	—	—	—
5 Yr Avg	—	—	—	—
10 Yr Avg	—	—	—	—

Potential Capital Gain Exposure: 5% of assets

Risk Analysis

Time Period	Load-Adj Return %	Risk %Rank[1] All	Risk %Rank[1] Cat	Morningstar Return	Morningstar Risk	Morningstar Risk-Adj Rating
1 Yr	–3.73					
3 Yr	—	—	—	—	—	
5 Yr	—	—	—	—	—	
Incept	47.87	—	—	—	—	
Average Historical Rating						—

[1]1=low, 100=high

Category Rating (3 Yr)

Return
Risk

Other Measures	Standard Index S&P 500	Best Fit Index
Alpha	—	—
Beta	—	—
R-Squared	—	—
Standard Deviation		—
Mean		—
Sharpe Ratio		—

Portfolio Analysis 09-30-01

Share chng since 06-01 Total Stocks: 114	Subsector	PE	YTD Ret%	% Assets
⊕ Pfizer	Gen Pharm/Bio	34.7	–12.40	4.80
⊕ Merck	Gen Pharm/Bio	19.1	–35.90	3.32
⊕ Genentech	Gen Pharm/Bio	NMF	–33.40	3.29
⊕ Aventis S.A. ADR	Gen Pharm/Bio	—	–15.30	2.99
☼ Akzo Nobel NV	Industrials	18.5	—	2.85
⊖ Abbott Labs	Gen Pharm/Bio	51.6	17.08	2.59
⊕ Pharmacia	Chemicals	36.5	–29.30	2.43
☼ Bristol-Myers Squibb	Gen Pharm/Bio	20.2	–26.00	2.22
⊖ ILEX Onocology	Health	—	2.76	2.09
☼ Cigna	Insurance	13.2	–29.00	2.07
⊕ Amgen	Gen Pharm/Bio	52.8	–11.70	2.05
⊕ Quintiles Transnational	Health	—	–23.20	2.04
Glaxo Wellcome PLC ADR	Gen Pharm/Bio	24.2	–9.77	1.96
⊕ Bausch & Lomb	Medical Devices	81.9	–4.42	1.83
☼ Wilson Greatbatch Tech	Durables	—	27.79	1.75
Novartis ADR	Gen Pharm/Bio	22.3	–17.40	1.75
☼ Medtronic	Medical Devices	76.4	–14.70	1.73
⊕ CVS	Retail	16.2	–50.30	1.72
☼ Ivax	Gen Pharm/Bio	17.5	–34.20	1.55
⊕ Quest Diagnostics	Diagnostics	51.2	1.00	1.54
⊕ Medarex	Emg. Pharm/Bio	61.9	–55.90	1.36
Scios	Emg. Pharm/Bio	—	6.83	1.33
Roche Hldgs (Gen)	Gen Pharm/Bio	0.3	—	1.29
☼ Wright Medical Grp	Health	—	—	1.27
Cyberonics	Medical Devices	—	14.11	1.26

Current Investment Style

Style: Value Blnd Growth; Size: Large Med Small

	Stock Port Avg	Relative S&P 500 Current	Relative S&P 500 Hist	Rel Cat
Price/Earnings Ratio	35.9	1.16	—	0.89
Price/Book Ratio	6.6	1.16	—	0.74
Price/Cash Flow	24.6	1.37	—	0.86
3 Yr Earnings Growth	16.5[1]	1.12	—	0.76
1 Yr Earnings Est%	18.4[1]	—	—	0.81
Med Mkt Cap $mil	7,182	0.1	—	0.33

[1]figure is based on 50% or less of stocks

Analysis by Peter Di Teresa 09-25-01

This young fund has the makings of an appealing pick.

Evergreen Health Care Fund made a stunning debut in 2000, racking up a 119% return. No other health-care fund did better. In fact, only one fund of any stripe did.

That was undoubtedly an impressive start, but plenty of funds come out strong and then stumble. This fund earns attention because it has so far avoided the classic sophomore slump.

After reaping 2000's strength, this fund has weathered 2001's fallback better than most. Its 19.7% loss for the year to date through Sept. 21, 2001, was in the category's best quintile. When the group fell 22% in the first quarter, this fund lost fractionally less, and when health care climbed 14.4% in the second quarter, the fund gained 10 percentage points more. And during the dramatic market sell-off of the week of Sept. 17, 2001, the fund's 11.1% loss was right around the median.

The key to the fund's strength has been diversifying among market caps and sectors. Manager Liu-Er Chen has committed as much of the portfolio to large caps as to small caps, with 25% in mid-size stocks. He has staked roughly 40% of the portfolio on drug companies and 30% on biotech (that's a bit light on drugs and heavier on biotech than most peers), putting the remainder in a variety of subsectors.

Chen uses quantitative screens specific to each subsector to sift stocks. He examines appealing prospects to determine a fair market price for them and buys the attractive ones. For drug companies and biotech firms, his research focuses on new products and their likely contributions to revenue.

Although this fund is still young, its ability to stay competitive in very different markets is encouraging.

Special Securities % assets 09-30-01	
Restricted/Illiquid Secs	0
Emerging-Markets Secs	2
Options/Futures/Warrants	No

Composition % assets 09-30-01	
Cash	0.0
Stocks*	100.0
Bonds	0.0
Other	0.0
*Foreign (% stocks)	21.1

Market Cap	
Giant	28.5
Large	17.8
Medium	23.9
Small	26.7
Micro	3.1

Subsector Weightings	% of Stocks	Rel Cat
Gen Pharm/Bio	43.7	1.0
Medical Devices	8.0	1.4
Hospitals	0.0	0.0
Other Providers	1.1	1.0
HMOs/PPOs	0.3	0.1
Emg. Pharm/Bio	13.0	0.7
Diagnostics	2.3	1.6
Tech/Bus Svs	0.8	0.4
Other	31.0	1.4

Address: 401 South Tryon Street Suite 500
Charlotte, NC 28288–1195
800–343–2898 / 800–343–2898
Web Address: www.evergreeninvestments.com

*Inception: 12-22-99
Advisor: Evergreen Inv. Mgmt.
Subadvisor: None
NTF Plans: N/A

Minimum Purchase: $1000 Add: None IRA: $250
Min Auto Inv Plan: $50 Add: $25
Sales Fees: 5.75%L, 0.25%B
Management Fee: .95%
Actual Fees: Mgt: 0.95% Dist: 0.25%
Expense Projections: 3Yr: $1109 5Yr: $1494 10Yr: $2569
Avg Brok Commission: — Income Distrib: Annually
Total Cost (relative to category): —

Evergreen High Income Municipal Bd B

Ticker	Load	NAV	Yield	SEC Yield	Total Assets	Mstar Category
VMPIX	4.00%d	$8.62	4.2%	5.26%	$616.4 mil	Muni Short–Term

Prospectus Objective: Muni Bond—National

Evergreen High Income Municipal Bond Fund seeks current income exempt from federal income tax.

The fund normally invests at least 80% of assets in municipal bonds without limitation as to quality ratings, maturity ranges, or types of issuers. The fund may invest without limit in high-yield securities. A significant portion of the portfolio may be invested in obligations with maturities of 20 or more years.

Class A shares have front loads; B shares have deferred loads, higher 12b-1 fees, and conversion features; C shares have level loads; Y shares are for institutions. The fund has gone through several name changes.

Historical Profile
Return Below Avg
Risk Low
Rating ★★★★ Above Avg

Investment Style: Fixed-Income — Income Rtn %Rank Cat: 1, 3, 3, 2, 4, 9, 3, 16

Growth of Principal vs. Interest Rate Shifts
— Principal Value $000 (NAV with capital gains reinvested)
— Interest Rate % on 10 Yr Treasury
▼ Manager Change
▽ Partial Manager Change
► Mgr Unknown After
◄ Mgr Unknown Before

Performance Quartile (within Category)

Portfolio Manager(s)

B. Clark Stamper. Since 6-90. BS'79 San Diego State U.; MBA'83 San Diego State U. Other funds currently managed: Evergreen High Income Municipal Bd A, Evergreen High Income Municipal Bd C, Evergreen High Income Municipal Bd I.

1990	1991	1992	1993	1994	1995	1996	1997	1998	1999	2000	12-01	History
9.20	9.46	9.51	9.41	9.02	9.17	9.16	9.19	9.08	8.42	8.61	8.62	NAV
2.81	11.73	8.36	8.32	2.29	7.85	5.54	6.95	3.86	−2.84	8.02	4.42	Total Return %
−6.15	−4.28	0.96	−1.43	5.20	−10.62	1.93	−2.73	−4.82	−2.01	−3.61	−4.00	+/− LB Aggregate
−4.49	−0.41	−0.46	−3.96	7.43	−9.62	1.10	−2.25	−2.62	−0.78	−3.67	−0.66	+/− LB Muni
7.50	8.70	6.85	6.92	6.51	5.45	5.43	6.06	5.06	4.63	5.66	4.32	Income Return %
−4.69	3.03	1.51	1.40	−4.23	2.39	0.12	0.89	−1.21	−7.47	2.36	0.10	Capital Return %
93	1	14	24	4	58	3	4	90	98	6	65	Total Rtn % Rank Cat
0.70	0.77	0.63	0.64	0.60	0.48	0.49	0.54	0.45	0.41	0.46	0.37	Income $
0.08	0.00	0.08	0.23	0.00	0.06	0.02	0.05	0.00	0.00	0.00	0.00	Capital Gains $
2.44	2.41	2.41	2.26	2.07	2.14	2.10	2.02	1.80	1.82	1.79	—	Expense Ratio %
6.08	7.13	5.53	5.50	4.59	5.37	5.89	5.87	4.62	4.54	5.01	—	Income Ratio %
29	55	47	108	113	128	107	113	126	73	30	—	Turnover Rate %
80.2	97.9	131.4	183.1	143.2	123.9	108.7	179.7	257.2	205.4	180.5	205.3	Net Assets $mil

Performance 12-31-01

	1st Qtr	2nd Qtr	3rd Qtr	4th Qtr	Total
1997	1.08	1.86	1.78	2.06	6.95
1998	0.86	1.02	1.69	0.24	3.86
1999	0.58	−0.98	−1.22	−1.24	−2.84
2000	2.67	0.61	2.02	2.51	8.02
2001	1.60	0.98	1.85	−0.06	4.42

Trailing	Total Return%	+/− LB Agg	+/− LB Muni	% Rank All	% Rank Cat	Growth of $10,000
3 Mo	−0.06	−0.10	0.60	79	56	9,994
6 Mo	1.78	−2.87	−0.34	26	61	10,178
1 Yr	4.42	−4.00	−0.66	27	65	10,442
3 Yr Avg	3.10	−3.17	−1.65	53	83	10,959
5 Yr Avg	4.01	−3.42	−1.96	79	71	12,173
10 Yr Avg	5.22	−2.01	−1.41	89	19	16,634
15 Yr Avg	5.88	−2.24	−1.31	91	1	23,563

Tax Analysis	Tax-Adj Ret%	%Rank Cat	%Pretax Ret	%Rank Cat
3 Yr Avg	3.10	83	100.0	13
5 Yr Avg	3.99	71	99.5	70
10 Yr Avg	5.11	19	97.8	90

Potential Capital Gain Exposure: −2% of assets

Risk Analysis

Time Period	Load-Adj Return %	Risk %Rank[1] All	Risk %Rank[1] Cat	Morningstar Return	Morningstar Risk	Morningstar Risk-Adj Rating
1 Yr	1.42					
3 Yr	2.50	8	98	0.19[2]	0.75	★★★
5 Yr	3.85	5	91	0.53[2]	0.65	★★★★
10 Yr	5.22	2	70	0.87	0.40	★★★★★

Average Historical Rating (165 months): 4.6★s

[1] 1=low, 100=high [2] T-Bill return substituted for category avg.

Category Rating (3 Yr)

Return Average
Risk High

Other Measures	Standard Index LB Agg	Best Fit Index LB Muni
Alpha	−2.4	−1.6
Beta	0.53	0.75
R-Squared	35	85

Standard Deviation	3.07
Mean	3.10
Sharpe Ratio	−0.70

Analysis by Scott Berry 12-06-01

Despite its added volatility, we're fans of Evergreen High Income Municipal Bond.

This fund is not the tamest short-term municipal-bond fund. Unlike its average peer, which holds a portfolio of plain-vanilla, high-quality municipal bonds, this fund is not averse to investing heavily in zero-coupon bonds and lower-quality, nonrated issues. In fact, in years past the fund's nonrated stake has been as high as 45% of assets. But while the fund's aggressive approach has made it one of the most volatile muni short funds, it has also helped the fund deliver impressive long-term returns.

The fund's success owes much to manager Clark Stamper's ability to exploit market inefficiencies. His bread and butter has been callable bonds. Specifically, he buys issues that are priced as though they will be called but that he believes are unlikely to be called for various reasons, such as a municipality's inability to refinance a particular issue. As these bonds trade past their call dates, the fund is able to soak up the added yield they provide.

Stamper has also contributed to the fund's success by making timely adjustments to the fund's interest-rate sensitivity. For example, he bulked up on zero-coupon bonds and other rate-sensitive issues in 2000, and the fund soared as interest rates fell. More recently, he has taken a decidedly defensive posture. In fact, Stamper has reined in the fund's interest-rate risk and has bumped up the fund's average credit quality in an effort to insulate the fund from what he predicts will be a volatile period for the municipal bond market.

To be sure, this fund is no money-market alternative. For one thing, interest-rate forecasting can be difficult to pull off consistently. But we think long-term investors will continue to do well here. And while the fund's expense ratio has long been a concern, it has come down about 10% over the last year.

Address:	401 South Tryon Street Suite 500 Charlotte, NC 28288–1195 505–983–4335 / 800–343–2898
Web Address:	www.evergreeninvestments.com
Inception:	03-29-85
Advisor:	Evergreen Inv. Mgmt.
Subadvisor:	Stamper Cap. & Inv.s
NTF Plans:	N/A

Minimum Purchase:	$1000	Add: $25 IRA: —
Min Auto Inv Plan:	$1000	Add: $25
Sales Fees:	4.00%D, 0.75%B, 0.25%S Conv. in 8 Yrs.	
Management Fee:	.65% mx./.55% mn.	
Actual Fees:	Mgt: 0.54%	Dist: 1.00%
Expense Projections:	3Yr: $874	5Yr: $1198 10Yr: $1891
Avg Brok Commission:	—	Income Distrib: Monthly
Total Cost (relative to category):		Above Avg

Portfolio Analysis 06-30-01

Total Fixed-Income: 377	Date of Maturity	Amount $000	Value $000	% Net Assets
PA Allegheny Hosp Dev 9.25%	11-15-30	18,500	18,574	3.79
LA West Feliciana Poll Cntrl Util 9%	05-01-15	15,450	15,979	3.26
RI Hsg/Mtg Fin Homeownshp 6.75%	10-01-25	10,000	10,327	2.10
HI Arpt Sys 7%	07-01-18	10,100	10,304	2.10
DE Econ Dev Poll Cntrl Pwr/Lt 7.15%	07-01-18	8,640	8,815	1.80
CA Poll Cntrl Fin South Edison 6.4%	12-01-24	6,750	6,929	1.41
CA Poll Cntrl Fin South Edison 6.4%	12-01-24	6,000	6,202	1.26
IL Chicago Pub Bldg Com 7.125%	01-01-15	6,115	6,177	1.26
DC Columbia GO 5.375%	05-15-10	6,000	6,074	1.24
HI Arpt Sys 7%	07-01-18	5,915	6,035	1.23
TX State GO 6.5%	12-01-21	5,800	5,989	1.22
TN Nashville Metro Arpt 6.6%	07-01-15	5,400	5,509	1.12
CO Denver Arpt 7.25%	11-15-23	5,075	5,418	1.10
FL Dade Indl Dev Solid Waste Disp 7.15%	02-01-23	5,250	5,370	1.09
LA Pub Fac Alton Ochsner Med Foundn 6.5%	05-15-22	5,000	5,197	1.06

Current Investment Style

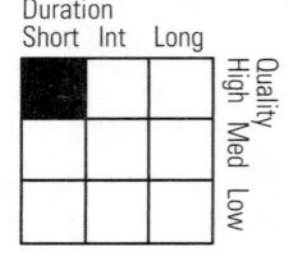

Avg Duration[1]	3.0 Yrs
Avg Nominal Maturity	16.5 Yrs
Avg Credit Quality	AA
Avg Wtd Coupon	6.18%
Avg Wtd Price	91.87% of par
Pricing Service	—

[1] figure provided by fund

Credit Analysis % bonds 09-30-01

US Govt	0	BB	4
AAA	50	B	6
AA	10	Below B	1
A	14	NR/NA	11
BBB	4		

Special Securities % assets 06-30-01

Restricted/Illiquid Secs	0
Inverse Floaters	0
Options/Futures/Warrants	No

Bond Type % assets 12-31-00

Alternative Minimum Tax (AMT)	9.6
Insured	—
Prerefunded	—

Top 5 States % bonds

PA	8.7	TX	7.5
CA	8.7	FL	6.8
LA	8.2		

Composition % assets 06-30-01

Cash	4.9	Bonds	95.1
Stocks	0.0	Other	0.0

Sector Weightings	% of Bonds	Rel Cat
General Obligation	10.8	0.4
Utilities	3.6	0.5
Health	21.7	1.8
Water/Waste	1.2	0.2
Housing	14.2	1.9
Education	2.3	0.4
Transportation	13.3	1.4
COP/Lease	1.1	0.4
Industrial	24.9	2.5
Misc Revenue	5.2	0.9
Demand	0.0	0.0

Excelsior Value & Restructuring

Ticker	Load	NAV	Yield	Total Assets	Mstar Category
UMBIX	None	$32.06	0.3%	$2,221.3 mil	Large Value

Prospectus Objective: Growth

Excelsior Value & Restructuring Fund seeks long-term capital appreciation.

The fund normally invests at least 65% of assets in common and preferred stocks, and convertibles issued by companies management expects to benefit from restructuring or redeployment of assets. These may include companies involved in mergers, consolidations, liquidations, spin-offs, financial restructurings, and reorganizations. The fund may invest in investment-grade debt.

Past names: UST Master Business & Industrial Restructuring Fund and Excelsior Business & Industrial Restructuring Fund.

Historical Profile
Return High
Risk Average
Rating ★★★★★ Highest

Investment Style
Equity
Average Stock %: 95% 93% 96% 97% 98% 97% 97%

▼ Manager Change
▽ Partial Manager Change

Fund Performance vs. Category Average
■ Quarterly Fund Return +/– Category Average
— Category Baseline

Performance Quartile (within Category)

Portfolio Manager(s)

David J. Williams, CFA. Since 12-92. BA Yale U.; MBA Harvard U.

1990	1991	1992	1993	1994	1995	1996	1997	1998	1999	2000	12-01	History
—	—	7.00	9.69	9.76	13.20	15.87	20.82	22.71	32.14	33.82	32.06	NAV
—	—	—	39.95	2.59	38.81	25.05	33.58	10.32	41.98	7.22	–4.96	Total Return %
—	—	—	29.90	1.28	1.28	2.10	0.23	–18.25	20.94	16.32	6.92	+/– S&P 500
—	—	—	20.19	4.90	–1.22	2.74	–1.91	–10.92	31.03	4.91	3.83	+/– Russ Top 200 Val
—	—	—	1.08	0.64	0.98	0.96	0.59	0.55	0.38	1.85	0.24	Income Return %
—	—	—	38.88	1.95	37.83	24.08	32.98	9.78	41.60	5.37	–5.19	Capital Return %
—	—	—	1	16	8	19	9	65	1	47	45	Total Rtn % Rank Cat
—	—	0.00	0.08	0.06	0.09	0.12	0.09	0.11	0.09	0.59	0.08	Income $
—	—	0.00	0.02	0.12	0.24	0.47	0.27	0.14	0.00	0.00	0.00	Capital Gains $
—	—	—	0.99	0.99	0.98	0.91	0.91	0.89	0.93	0.90	—	Expense Ratio %
—	—	—	2.48	0.77	0.83	0.88	0.90	0.54	0.59	0.25	—	Income Ratio %
—	—	—	9	75	82	56	62	30	43	20	—	Turnover Rate %
—	—	—	7.4	25.9	57.8	113.1	230.0	597.1	943.1	1,730.7	2,221.3	Net Assets $mil

Performance 12-31-01

	1st Qtr	2nd Qtr	3rd Qtr	4th Qtr	Total
1997	0.38	18.70	15.68	–3.08	33.58
1998	14.27	–1.21	–20.46	22.87	10.32
1999	5.20	16.27	–9.34	28.03	41.98
2000	5.48	–5.81	5.74	2.06	7.22
2001	–9.25	8.63	–16.82	15.91	–4.96

Trailing	Total Return%	+/– S&P 500	+/– Russ Top 200 Val	% Rank All	% Rank Cat	Growth of $10,000
3 Mo	15.91	5.22	10.39	22	5	11,591
6 Mo	–3.59	1.97	2.19	54	42	9,641
1 Yr	–4.96	6.92	3.83	51	45	9,504
3 Yr Avg	13.10	14.13	11.94	7	2	14,468
5 Yr Avg	16.35	5.65	5.14	3	2	21,320
10 Yr Avg	—	—	—	—	—	—
15 Yr Avg	—	—	—	—	—	—

Tax Analysis	Tax-Adj Ret%	%Rank Cat	%Pretax Ret	%Rank Cat
3 Yr Avg	12.74	1	97.2	5
5 Yr Avg	15.94	1	97.5	1
10 Yr Avg	—	—	—	—

Potential Capital Gain Exposure: 14% of assets

Risk Analysis

Time Period	Load-Adj Return %	Risk %Rank[1] All	Risk %Rank[1] Cat	Morningstar Return	Morningstar Risk	Morningstar Risk-Adj Rating
1 Yr	–4.96					
3 Yr	13.10	62	83	1.87[2]	0.87	★★★★★
5 Yr	16.35	67	91	3.07[2]	0.91	★★★★★
Incept	20.38	—	—	—	—	

Average Historical Rating (73 months): 4.8★s

[1] 1=low, 100=high [2] T-Bill return substituted for category avg.

Category Rating (3 Yr)

1 2 3 4 5 — Worst … Best (5)

Return High
Risk Above Avg

Other Measures	Standard Index S&P 500	Best Fit Index MSCIACWdFr
Alpha	15.5	20.8
Beta	1.09	1.19
R-Squared	79	82
Standard Deviation		23.66
Mean		13.10
Sharpe Ratio		0.39

Portfolio Analysis 04-30-01

Share change since 03-01 Total Stocks: 75

	Sector	PE	YTD Ret%	% Assets
⊖ Viacom Cl B	Services	—	—	2.30
AmeriSource Health Cl A	Health	30.3	25.90	2.15
IBM	Technology	26.9	43.00	2.14
⊕ Texas Instruments	Technology	87.5	–40.70	2.11
⊕ Black & Decker	Durables	17.6	–2.67	2.08
☼ J.P. Morgan Chase & Co.	Financials	27.8	–17.40	2.03
⊕ Vishay Intertechnology	Technology	13.7	28.93	2.01
Union Pacific	Services	17.1	13.96	1.98
Citigroup	Financials	20.0	0.03	1.95
⊕ General Motors Cl H	Technology	42.9	–32.80	1.82
⊕ Nokia Cl A ADR	Technology	45.8	–43.00	1.78
⊕ Avon Products	Staples	21.6	–1.21	1.73
Suiza Foods	Staples	—	25.44	1.73
News ADR	Services	—	–1.28	1.72
Centex	Industrials	10.2	52.56	1.71
☼ BF Goodrich	Industrials	6.7	–24.30	1.66
Morgan Stanley/Dean Witter	Financials	16.6	–28.20	1.65
American Home Products	Health	—	–1.91	1.65
⊕ Stilwell Finl	Financials	—	–30.80	1.65
AOL Time Warner	Technology	—	–7.76	1.63
⊕ AT & T Liberty Media Cl A	Services	—	3.22	1.63
Dynegy	Energy	12.8	–54.20	1.58
⊕ Harris	Technology	28.0	0.33	1.57
United Tech	Industrials	16.3	–16.70	1.55
⊕ Bristol-Myers Squibb	Health	20.2	–26.00	1.53

Current Investment Style

Style: Value Blnd Growth; Size: Large Med Small

	Stock Port Avg	Relative S&P 500 Current	Relative S&P 500 Hist	Rel Cat
Price/Earnings Ratio	24.4	0.79	0.82	0.97
Price/Book Ratio	3.9	0.69	0.78	0.95
Price/Cash Flow	13.9	0.77	0.81	1.01
3 Yr Earnings Growth	15.0	1.03	1.34	1.02
1 Yr Earnings Est%	–15.0	8.48	—	4.53
Med Mkt Cap $mil	9,371	0.2	0.3	0.30

Analysis by Gabriel Presler 12-12-01

A petulant market has illustrated the perils of Excelsior Value & Restructuring, but we're not about to dismiss this offering.

Manager David Williams seeks companies that have disappointed Wall Street analysts by missing quarterly earnings estimates. He buys stocks with low valuations that have the potential to improve their bottom line through consolidation, reorganization, or management changes. In recent years, this has meant that the fund looks different from its large-value rivals. It often holds fallen-growth heroes; its tech exposure, for example, is double the category average.

While this strategy has generally paid off since the fund's inception in 1992, it certainly doesn't guarantee success. In jittery years like 2001, it's often companies in flux that suffer first and worst. Thus many of the fund's top picks hit the skids this year. Large positions in financials firms such as Stilwell Financial and a few technology companies were particularly painful, and the fund declined relative to its peers throughout the year. In the wake of Sept. 11, though, the fund's sector bets have helped it; some of its tech- and communications-related stocks, such as Harris, have helped prop up returns. Thus, its loss of 7% for the year to date through Dec. 11, 2001, is about average for the category.

But that's about as bad as it gets here. True, the fund is one of the more volatile offerings in the group because Williams' sector bets don't always pay off. And it's not the right choice for cautious investors looking for a staid value fund. But the fund has consistently put up solid returns, with three- and five-year marks in the top decile of the category. It's an admirable choice for investors seeking a fund with a little spice.

Special Securities % assets 04-30-01	
Restricted/Illiquid Secs	Trace
Emerging-Markets Secs	0
Options/Futures/Warrants	No

Composition % assets 04-30-01	
Cash	0.7
Stocks*	99.0
Bonds	0.0
Other	0.3
*Foreign (% stocks)	7.0

Market Cap	
Giant	19.9
Large	31.5
Medium	36.8
Small	11.8
Micro	0.0

Sector Weightings	% of Stocks	Rel S&P	5-Year High	5-Year Low
Utilities	2.7	0.9	3	0
Energy	5.8	0.8	8	2
Financials	19.2	1.1	24	16
Industrials	13.9	1.2	31	7
Durables	6.2	4.0	12	5
Staples	4.6	0.6	11	4
Services	18.5	1.7	25	6
Retail	2.6	0.4	8	0
Health	5.4	0.4	14	2
Technology	21.1	1.2	31	5

Address: 114 W. 47th Street, New York, NY 10036–1532, 800–446–1012 / 800–446–1012
Web Address: www.excelsiorfunds.com
*Inception: 12-31-92
Advisor: U.S. Trust of New York/U.S. Trust Co. N.A.
Subadvisor: None
NTF Plans: Fidelity , Datalynx

Minimum Purchase:	$500	Add: $50	IRA: $250
Min Auto Inv Plan:	$500	Add: $50	
Sales Fees:	No-load		
Management Fee:	.60%		
Actual Fees:	Mgt: 0.48%	Dist: —	
Expense Projections:	3Yr: $421	5Yr: $729	10Yr: $1601
Avg Brok Commission:	—	Income Distrib: Quarterly	
Total Cost (relative to category):	Average		

FAM Value

Ticker	Load	NAV	Yield	Total Assets	Mstar Category
FAMVX	None	$36.17	0.5%	$501.4 mil	Small Value

Prospectus Objective: Small Company

FAM Value Fund seeks to maximize total return.

The fund invests primarily in common stocks and securities convertible into common stocks. It may only purchase convertible securities rated A or higher. Management seeks to identify well-managed, financially sound companies that it considers to be undervalued. It may invest the balance of assets in investment-grade fixed-income securities, such as U.S. Treasury obligations, securities issued by agencies of the U.S. government, bank certificates, or corporate debt.

Historical Profile
Return: Above Avg
Risk: Below Avg
Rating: ★★★★ Above Avg

Investment Style
Equity
Average Stock %: 93% 100% 98% 94% 87% 92% 93%

▼ Manager Change
▽ Partial Manager Change

Fund Performance vs. Category Average
■ Quarterly Fund Return +/– Category Average
— Category Baseline

Performance Quartile (within Category)

Portfolio Manager(s)

Thomas O. Putnam. Since 1-87. BA'66 U. of Rochester; MBA'68 Tulane U. Other fund currently managed: FAM Equity-Income.

John C. Fox, CFA. Since 5-00.

1990	1991	1992	1993	1994	1995	1996	1997	1998	1999	2000	12-01	History
12.06	16.87	20.50	20.40	21.04	24.58	26.53	35.76	34.44	31.35	32.70	36.17	NAV
–5.39	47.63	25.04	0.21	6.83	19.73	11.22	39.06	6.19	–4.84	19.21	15.09	Total Return %
–2.28	17.15	17.42	–9.85	5.52	–17.80	–11.73	5.71	–22.39	–25.88	28.31	26.96	+/– S&P 500
16.38	5.93	–4.10	–23.64	8.38	–6.02	–10.15	7.37	12.62	–3.36	–3.61	1.07	+/– Russell 2000 V
0.61	0.70	0.56	0.44	0.60	0.99	0.72	0.28	0.57	0.85	1.16	0.53	Income Return %
–6.00	46.93	24.47	–0.24	6.24	18.74	10.49	38.78	5.62	–5.69	18.05	14.55	Capital Return %
13	20	17	94	4	72	99	15	4	73	51	64	Total Rtn % Rank Cat
0.08	0.08	0.10	0.09	0.12	0.21	0.18	0.08	0.20	0.29	0.36	0.17	Income $
0.02	0.82	0.48	0.05	0.63	0.40	0.63	1.06	3.26	1.09	4.03	1.30	Capital Gains $
1.53	1.49	1.50	1.39	1.39	1.25	1.27	1.24	1.19	1.23	1.26	—	Expense Ratio %
0.72	0.66	0.81	0.57	0.58	0.92	0.64	0.25	0.57	0.86	1.08	—	Income Ratio %
9	14	10	5	2	10	12	9	17	16	10	—	Turnover Rate %
6.5	13.9	42.0	220.0	210.3	266.3	253.6	331.8	376.2	373.0	367.3	501.4	Net Assets $mil

Performance 12-31-01

	1st Qtr	2nd Qtr	3rd Qtr	4th Qtr	Total
1997	–1.24	14.85	16.98	4.81	39.06
1998	8.14	1.01	–15.18	14.62	6.19
1999	–7.14	9.76	–10.80	4.67	–4.84
2000	–2.49	3.40	9.59	7.88	19.21
2001	–1.04	13.04	–6.45	9.97	15.09

Trailing	Total Return%	+/– S&P 500	+/– Russ 2000V	% Rank All	% Rank Cat	Growth of $10,000
3 Mo	9.97	–0.71	–6.75	43	98	10,997
6 Mo	2.88	8.43	1.73	16	40	10,288
1 Yr	15.09	26.96	1.07	3	64	11,509
3 Yr Avg	9.29	10.32	–2.03	12	73	13,055
5 Yr Avg	14.03	3.33	2.83	6	20	19,277
10 Yr Avg	13.14	0.21	–1.98	12	48	34,359
15 Yr Avg	13.26	–0.47	0.43	15	23	64,777

Tax Analysis	Tax-Adj Ret%	%Rank Cat	%Pretax Ret	%Rank Cat
3 Yr Avg	7.61	74	81.9	83
5 Yr Avg	12.37	17	88.2	35
10 Yr Avg	11.86	41	90.3	3

Potential Capital Gain Exposure: 35% of assets

Risk Analysis

Time Period	Load-Adj Return %	Risk %Rank[1] All	Risk %Rank[1] Cat	Morningstar Return	Morningstar Risk	Morningstar Risk-Adj Rating
1 Yr	15.09					
3 Yr	9.29	44	32	0.96[2]	0.61	★★★★
5 Yr	14.03	47	9	2.33[2]	0.64	★★★★★
10 Yr	13.14	55	29	1.34	0.71	★★★★

Average Historical Rating (145 months): 3.8★s

[1]1=low, 100=high [2] T-Bill return substituted for category avg.

Category Rating (3 Yr)

1 2 3 4 5 — Worst ... Best (rating: 3)

Return: Below Avg
Risk: Below Avg

Other Measures	Standard Index S&P 500	Best Fit Index SPMid400
Alpha	7.3	2.1
Beta	0.42	0.45
R-Squared	23	34

Standard Deviation	16.37
Mean	9.29
Sharpe Ratio	0.30

Analysis by Laura Pavlenko Lutton 12-31-01

This fund is a tough fit for most portfolios.

FAM Value Fund has returned 15.7% for the year to date through December 27, 2001, which puts it in the middle of the surging small-value pack. That showing is better than it looks, however, as the fund's lofty median market cap lands it in mid-cap territory. In 2001, the smallest stocks have led the way, putting this offering at a distinct disadvantage. Relative to the mid-value group, its year-to-date showing is well above average.

Big gains from top holdings such as H&R Block have helped lift the fund. But much of the fund's performance is explained by its financials stocks—more than 45% of the fund's equities are in the sector. Stakes in large- and mid-cap financials such as top holding White Mountains Insurance and Citigroup were sluggish, and they held the fund back relative to its small-cap peers. There were some bright spots, however, as picks like Brown & Brown and North Fork Bancorporation delivered top-flight returns.

The fund's large financials stake flows from the strategy used by managers Tom Putnam and John Fox. The pair looks for companies that trade cheaply and have solid growth in earnings and sales, high margins, and healthy balance sheets—traits that are often found in the financials sector.

The team's style has delivered respectable long-term returns, but the fund's appeal is still pretty limited. In addition to concentrating the fund in financials, the managers will let individual positions get quite large. When financials or one or two favored picks stumble, the fund can take a real hit, and its year-to-year performance has been extremely uneven. Investors with the patience to ride out some lean times may still want to give it a look, but other funds offer better, more consistent returns without as much sector risk.

Address:	111 N. Grand Street P.O. Box 399 Cobleskill, NY 12043 800-932-3271 / 518-234-7400
Web Address:	www.famfunds.com
Inception:	01-01-87
Advisor:	Fenimore Asset Mgmt.
Subadvisor:	None
NTF Plans:	Fidelity , Fidelity Inst.

Minimum Purchase:	$2000	Add: $50	IRA: $100
Min Auto Inv Plan:	$2000	Add: $50	
Sales Fees:	No-load		
Management Fee:	1.0%		
Actual Fees:	Mgt: 1.00%	Dist: —	
Expense Projections:	3Yr: $39*	5Yr: $68*	10Yr: $150*
Avg Brok Commission:	—	Income Distrib: Annually	
Total Cost (relative to category):	—		

Portfolio Analysis 06-30-01

Share change since 09-00 Total Stocks: 44	Sector	PE	YTD Ret%	% Assets
White Mountains Ins Grp	Financials	—	9.45	9.03
⊖ Brown & Brown	Financials	35.9	57.09	4.72
⊕ H & R Block	Services	25.5	120.00	4.26
Kaydon	Industrials	NMF	–7.01	4.08
Protective Life	Financials	13.7	–8.65	4.03
Watson Pharmaceuticals	Health	51.5	–38.60	3.78
Berkshire Hathaway Cl A	Financials	—	—	3.57
⊕ ServiceMaster	Services	22.3	24.29	3.50
⊕ Reynolds & Reynolds	Services	18.2	22.02	3.39
⊕ M & T Bk	Financials	20.8	8.63	3.13
⊖ Conmed	Health	21.2	74.83	3.12
Idex	Industrials	25.4	6.08	2.79
Allied Cap	Financials	11.6	35.33	2.71
⊕ New England Busn Svc	Services	14.0	9.45	2.65
⊕ Southtrust	Financials	15.9	24.18	2.65
⊕ Zebra Tech	Technology	27.0	36.12	2.46
⊖ Banknorth Grp	Financials	13.3	15.81	2.43
North Fork Bancorp	Financials	16.5	34.11	2.35
⊖ Franklin Resources	Financials	18.5	–6.78	2.11
Tennant	Industrials	27.5	–21.10	1.93
⊕ American Pwr Conversion	Technology	23.3	16.85	1.73
⊕ Waddell & Reed Finl Cl A	Financials	23.3	–13.40	1.64
☼ C-COR.net	Technology	—	49.91	1.44
⊕ Whole Foods Market	Retail	36.0	42.53	1.41
⊕ TrustCo Bk Corporation of NY	Financials	20.6	24.38	1.37

Current Investment Style

Style: Value Blnd Growth; Size: Large Med Small

	Stock Port Avg	Relative S&P 500 Current	Relative S&P 500 Hist	Rel Cat
Price/Earnings Ratio	25.5	0.82	0.53	1.18
Price/Book Ratio	3.8	0.66	0.35	1.56
Price/Cash Flow	17.4[1]	0.96	0.66	1.36
3 Yr Earnings Growth	8.3	0.57	0.90	0.71
1 Yr Earnings Est%	0.7	—	—	–0.17
Med Mkt Cap $mil	2,388	0.0	0.0	2.74

[1]figure is based on 50% or less of stocks

Special Securities % assets 06-30-01	
Restricted/Illiquid Secs	0
Emerging-Markets Secs	0
Options/Futures/Warrants	No

Composition % assets 06-30-01	
Cash	7.4
Stocks*	92.7
Bonds	0.0
Other	0.0
*Foreign (% stocks)	0.0

Market Cap	
Giant	2.1
Large	3.3
Medium	64.6
Small	24.3
Micro	5.7

Sector Weightings	% of Stocks	Rel S&P	5-Year High	5-Year Low
Utilities	0.0	0.0	0	0
Energy	0.0	0.0	1	0
Financials	47.5	2.7	60	32
Industrials	13.4	1.2	35	13
Durables	0.0	0.0	11	0
Staples	0.0	0.0	4	0
Services	20.2	1.9	20	2
Retail	1.8	0.3	8	0
Health	9.1	0.6	20	6
Technology	8.1	0.4	10	1

Fidelity Advisor Balanced T

Ticker	Load	NAV	Yield	Total Assets	Mstar Category
FAIGX	3.50%	$15.53	2.5%	$2,026.1 mil	Domestic Hybrid

Prospectus Objective: Balanced

Fidelity Advisor Balanced Fund - Class T seeks income and capital growth.

The fund normally invests at least 60% of assets in equities, and the remaining assets in fixed-income securities. It must invest at least 25% of assets in fixed-income senior securities. It may invest in foreign securities.

Class A shares have front loads; B shares have deferred loads, higher 12b-1 fees, and conversion features; C shares have level loads and higher 12b-1 fees; T shares have lower front loads and higher 12b-1 fees than A shares; Institutional shares are for institutional investors. Past names: Plymouth Income & Growth Portfolio and Fidelity Advisor Income and Growth Fund - Class T.

Historical Profile
Return Below Avg
Risk Below Avg
Rating ★★★ Neutral

Investment Style
Equity
Average Stock %: 38% 59% 61% 61% 61% 56% 56%

▼ Manager Change
▽ Partial Manager Change

Fund Performance vs. Category Average
■ Quarterly Fund Return +/– Category Average
— Category Baseline

Performance Quartile (within Category)

Portfolio Manager(s)

John D. Avery, et al. Since 1-98. BA'86 Harvard U.; MBA'93 U. of Pennsylvania.

1990	1991	1992	1993	1994	1995	1996	1997	1998	1999	2000	12-01	History
11.04	13.68	13.78	15.47	14.36	15.71	16.38	18.20	18.69	18.25	16.24	15.53	NAV
–2.94	34.48	9.20	19.66	–5.09	14.06	8.43	22.33	15.45	4.50	–5.71	–1.91	Total Return %
0.17	4.00	1.58	9.60	–6.41	–23.47	–14.52	–11.02	–13.12	–16.54	3.39	9.96	+/– S&P 500
–11.90	18.48	1.80	9.91	–2.18	–4.41	4.81	12.65	6.78	5.33	–17.34	–10.33	+/– LB Aggregate
5.02	4.41	4.00	3.67	1.88	4.31	3.29	3.40	2.83	2.44	2.61	2.42	Income Return %
–7.96	30.07	5.20	15.98	–6.98	9.75	5.14	18.94	12.62	2.06	–8.32	–4.34	Capital Return %
74	11	39	7	80	96	87	20	34	72	92	31	Total Rtn % Rank Cat
0.59	0.48	0.54	0.50	0.29	0.61	0.51	0.55	0.51	0.45	0.47	0.39	Income $
0.00	0.61	0.60	0.48	0.04	0.03	0.11	1.26	1.73	0.81	0.51	0.00	Capital Gains $
1.85	1.71	1.60	1.51	1.58	1.46	1.25	1.17	1.15	1.14	1.15	—	Expense Ratio %
5.29	4.19	3.97	3.24	3.79	3.99	3.32	2.98	2.68	2.45	2.57	—	Income Ratio %
297	220	389	200	202	297	223	70	85	93	120	—	Turnover Rate %
66.9	158.6	476.5	1,961.4	3,160.0	3,488.5	2,877.6	2,995.2	3,063.8	2,809.7	2,021.9	1,678.8	Net Assets $mil

Performance 12-31-01

	1st Qtr	2nd Qtr	3rd Qtr	4th Qtr	Total
1997	1.37	12.56	4.89	2.21	22.33
1998	8.31	2.67	–5.86	10.28	15.45
1999	1.76	3.20	–5.40	5.19	4.50
2000	0.30	–0.88	–0.23	–4.94	–5.71
2001	–5.25	4.04	–8.20	8.39	–1.91

Trailing	Total Return%	+/– S&P 500	+/– LB Agg	% Rank All	% Rank Cat	Growth of $10,000
3 Mo	8.39	–2.29	8.36	50	20	10,839
6 Mo	–0.49	5.06	–5.15	41	28	9,951
1 Yr	–1.91	9.96	–10.33	45	31	9,809
3 Yr Avg	–1.13	–0.10	–7.40	78	86	9,665
5 Yr Avg	6.42	–4.28	–1.01	42	65	13,650
10 Yr Avg	7.67	–5.26	0.44	45	78	20,935
15 Yr Avg	—	—	—	—	—	—

Tax Analysis	Tax-Adj Ret%	%Rank Cat	%Pretax Ret	%Rank Cat
3 Yr Avg	–2.60	85	—	—
5 Yr Avg	4.21	64	65.5	62
10 Yr Avg	5.61	69	73.2	42

Potential Capital Gain Exposure: 6% of assets

Risk Analysis

Time Period	Load-Adj Return %	Risk %Rank[1] All	Risk %Rank[1] Cat	Morningstar Return	Morningstar Risk	Morningstar Risk-Adj Rating
1 Yr	–5.34					
3 Yr	–2.30	45	75	–1.43[2]	0.63	★★★
5 Yr	5.67	46	71	0.14[2]	0.62	★★★
10 Yr	7.29	52	72	0.31	0.63	★★

Average Historical Rating (144 months): 3.4★s

[1] 1=low, 100=high [2] T-Bill return substituted for category avg.

Category Rating (3 Yr)

1 2 3 4 5
Worst Best

Return Below Avg
Risk Above Avg

Other Measures	Standard Index S&P 500	Best Fit Index S&P 500
Alpha	–2.8	–2.8
Beta	0.58	0.58
R-Squared	92	92
Standard Deviation		10.09
Mean		–1.13
Sharpe Ratio		–0.70

Portfolio Analysis 05-31-01

Total Stocks: 161 Share change since 11–00	Sector	PE Ratio	YTD Return %	% Net Assets
⊖ General Elec	Industrials	30.1	–15.00	3.46
⊖ Microsoft	Technology	57.6	52.78	2.17
☼ S&P 500 Index (Fut)	N/A	—	—	2.06
⊕ Philip Morris	Staples	12.1	9.12	1.75
⊕ Pfizer	Health	34.7	–12.40	1.56
⊖ ExxonMobil	Energy	15.3	–7.59	1.44
⊕ Citigroup	Financials	20.0	0.03	1.43
⊖ American Intl Grp	Financials	42.0	–19.20	1.43
⊕ AOL Time Warner	Technology	—	–7.76	0.86
⊖ Viacom Cl B	Services	—	—	0.82

Total Fixed-Income: 366	Date of Maturity	Amount $000	Value $000	% Net Assets
FNMA 6.5%	02-01-24	104	116,004	5.32
FNMA 7.5%	10-01-26	227	37,346	1.71
US Treasury Bond 6.125%	08-15-29	25,390	26,199	1.20
US Treasury Note 6.5%	02-15-10	24,130	25,910	1.19
FNMA 6%	11-01-23	222	25,672	1.18
GNMA 7.5%	06-15-23	496	25,390	1.16
US Treasury Note 7%	07-15-06	21,200	23,032	1.06
GNMA 6.5%	01-15-29	859	22,656	1.04
US Treasury Note N/A	05-31-03	13,530	13,538	0.62
FNMA Debenture N/A	01-15-10	12,080	13,052	0.60

Analysis by Scott Cooley 12-17-01

It's too early to say whether Fidelity Advisor Balanced Fund has turned the corner.

To be sure, this fund has put up relatively good returns so far in 2001. For the year to date through Dec. 14, the fund has lost 3.6%. In 2001's difficult market, that's good enough to put the fund in the top third of the domestic-hybrid category. Given that the fund has more of a growth bias than its typical category rival, and that value issues have paced the market, that performance is particularly strong.

Several factors have helped the fund in 2001. Lead manager John Avery has done a good job of picking stocks. He avoided entirely several of the hardest-hit networking-equipment stocks, including JDS Uniphase, while scoring big with plays on moderately valued issues such as Philip Morris, Microsoft, IBM, and Bank of America. Although Avery's market-sensitive issues, including Bank of New York, have tumbled along with the market, several industrial-cyclical and semiconductor issues have registered solid returns. Avery picked up shares in several chipmakers in the wake of the Sept. 11 terrorist attacks, and they have since rebounded sharply.

Finally, on the bond side manager Kevin Grant sticks mostly to high-quality issues, which have outperformed junk in 2001.Despite this relatively strong recent performance, the fund's longer-term returns are far from stellar. Indeed, during Avery's four-year tenure, the fund has posted mixed results, including two years, 1999 and 2000, when its cumulative return lagged the category average by 12 percentage points. In short, the fund was light on tech in 1999, when it would have helped, and had too much exposure to the sector in 2000, when tech tumbled.

In light of Avery's subpar overall record, we think it's tough to make a strong case for this fund.

Equity Style
Style: Growth
Size: Large–Cap

Fixed-Income Style
Duration: —
Quality: —
NA

	Portfolio Avg	Rel S&P
Price/Earnings Ratio	31.8	1.03
Price/Book Ratio	5.6	0.99
Price/Cash Flow	17.6	0.98
3 Yr Earnings Growth	15.3	1.05
1 Yr Earnings Est%	–5.6	3.14
Debt % Total Cap	33.9	1.10
Med Mkt Cap $mil	56,371	0.93

Avg Eff Duration	—
Avg Eff Maturity	—
Avg Credit Quality	—
Avg Wtd Coupon	7.07%

Special Securities % assets 05-31-01	
Restricted/Illiquid Secs	3
Emerging–Markets Secs	Trace
Options/Futures/Warrants	Yes

Composition % of assets 05-31-01	
Cash	6.1
Stocks*	56.3
Bonds	35.0
Other	2.6
*Foreign (% of stocks)	1.1

Market Cap	
Giant	54.6
Large	26.7
Medium	17.1
Small	1.6
Micro	0.0

Sector Weightings	% of Stocks	Rel S&P	5-Year High	5-Year Low
Utilities	0.7	0.2	7	0
Energy	7.4	1.0	28	6
Financials	17.7	1.0	30	2
Industrials	17.8	1.6	53	11
Durables	1.8	1.2	16	0
Staples	7.1	0.9	14	0
Services	9.6	0.9	19	1
Retail	5.6	0.8	11	1
Health	13.7	0.9	15	0
Technology	18.8	1.0	31	0

Address:	82 Devonshire Street Boston, MA 02109 800–522–7297 / 617–439–6793
Web Address:	www.fidelity.com
Inception:	01-06-87
Advisor:	Fidelity Mgmt. & Research
Subadvisor:	FMR (U.K.)/FMR (Far East)
NTF Plans:	Datalynx , Fidelity Inst.

Minimum Purchase:	$2500	Add: $100	IRA: $500
Min Auto Inv Plan:	$100	Add: $100	
Sales Fees:	3.50%L, 0.50%B		
Management Fee:	.15%+.52% mx./.27% mn.(G)		
Actual Fees:	Mgt: 0.43%	Dist: 0.50%	
Expense Projections:	3Yr: $706	5Yr: $966	10Yr: $1710
Avg Brok Commission:	—	Income Distrib: Quarterly	
Total Cost (relative to category):		Average	

Fidelity Advisor Equity Growth T

Ticker	Load	NAV	Yield	Total Assets	Mstar Category
FAEGX	3.50%	$48.69	0.0%	$12,324.7 mil	Large Growth

Prospectus Objective: Growth

Fidelity Advisor Equity Growth Fund seeks capital appreciation.

The fund invests primarily in common and preferred stocks and convertibles of companies with above-average growth characteristics. Generally, it will be invested in the securities of smaller, lesser- known companies. It may also purchase high-yield, high-risk securities.

This fund offers multiple shareclasses, all of which differ in fee structure and availability. Prior to January 29, 1992, the fund was named Equity Portfolio: Growth.

Historical Profile

Return Average
Risk Above Avg
Rating ★★★ Neutral

Investment Style
Equity
Average Stock %

1994	1995	1996	1997	1998	1999	2000	12-01
	84%	86%	99%	95%	97%	97%	97%

▼ Manager Change
▽ Partial Manager Change

Fund Performance vs. Category Average
■ Quarterly Fund Return +/– Category Average
— Category Baseline

Performance Quartile (within Category)

Portfolio Manager(s)

Jennifer S. Uhrig. Since 1-97. BA'83 Harvard U.; MBA'87 Dartmouth C. Other funds currently managed: Fidelity Advisor Equity Growth Instl, Fidelity Advisor Equity Growth A, Fidelity Advisor Equity Growth B.

1990	1991	1992	1993	1994	1995	1996	1997	1998	1999	2000	12–01	History
—	—	26.55	29.02	28.36	37.51	42.01	46.24	57.09	71.61	59.57	48.69	NAV
—	—	13.69*	14.85	–0.89	39.14	16.24	23.93	38.72	36.27	–11.48	–18.19	Total Return %
—	—	8.92*	4.80	–2.20	1.61	–6.70	–9.42	10.14	15.23	–2.38	–6.32	+/– S&P 500
—	—	—	14.93	–5.74	0.49	–9.28	–9.81	–6.38	6.59	13.04	2.31	+/– Russ Top 200 Grt
—	—	0.31	0.00	0.28	0.21	0.46	0.00	0.00	0.00	0.00	0.00	Income Return %
—	—	13.38	14.85	–1.16	38.93	15.79	23.93	38.72	36.27	–11.48	–18.19	Capital Return %
—	—	—	29	35	14	72	58	27	48	35	31	Total Rtn % Rank Cat
—	—	0.08	0.00	0.08	0.06	0.17	0.00	0.00	0.00	0.00	0.00	Income $
—	—	0.40	1.44	0.32	1.88	1.40	5.65	6.61	5.70	3.84	0.05	Capital Gains $
—	—	1.47	1.84	1.70	1.54	1.34	1.29	1.27	1.28	1.26	—	Expense Ratio %
—	—	0.25	–0.24	0.15	0.21	0.54	–0.08	–0.41	–0.43	–0.57	—	Income Ratio %
—	—	—	160	137	97	76	108	122	82	99	—	Turnover Rate %
—	—	38.7	427.1	908.2	2,099.8	3,439.5	4,160.2	5,622.5	9,059.9	9,126.4	7,152.7	Net Assets $mil

Performance 12-31-01

	1st Qtr	2nd Qtr	3rd Qtr	4th Qtr	Total
1997	–2.19	17.17	9.25	–1.02	23.93
1998	12.72	5.44	–5.95	24.10	38.72
1999	8.28	5.24	–2.89	23.15	36.27
2000	8.46	–3.41	–3.55	–12.39	–11.48
2001	–16.75	8.19	–22.07	16.54	–18.19

Trailing	Total Return%	+/– S&P 500	+/– Russ Top 200 Grth	% Rank All	% Rank Cat	Growth of $10,000
3 Mo	16.54	5.85	3.68	20	30	11,654
6 Mo	–9.18	–3.62	–2.19	82	53	9,082
1 Yr	–18.19	–6.32	2.31	78	31	8,181
3 Yr Avg	–0.44	0.58	7.58	75	30	9,868
5 Yr Avg	11.15	0.45	2.56	13	26	16,964
10 Yr Avg	—	—	—	—	—	—
15 Yr Avg	—	—	—	—	—	—

Tax Analysis	Tax-Adj Ret%	%Rank Cat	%Pretax Ret	%Rank Cat
3 Yr Avg	–1.65	30	—	—
5 Yr Avg	8.99	26	80.6	44
10 Yr Avg	—	—	—	—

Potential Capital Gain Exposure: –8% of assets

Risk Analysis

Time Period	Load-Adj Return %	Risk %Rank[1] All	Risk %Rank[1] Cat	Morningstar Return	Morningstar Risk	Morningstar Risk-Adj Rating
1 Yr	–21.06					
3 Yr	–1.62	80	30	–1.31[2]	1.15	★★
5 Yr	10.36	79	28	1.29[2]	1.09	★★★
Incept	14.14	—	—	—	—	

Average Historical Rating (76 months): 3.7★s

[1]1=low, 100=high [2] T–Bill return substituted for category avg.

Category Rating (3 Yr)

1 2 3 4 5
Worst Best

Return Above Avg
Risk Below Avg

Other Measures	Standard Index S&P 500	Best Fit Index MSCIACWdFr
Alpha	2.5	7.8
Beta	1.18	1.30
R–Squared	79	84

Standard Deviation	22.85
Mean	–0.44
Sharpe Ratio	–0.27

Analysis by Scott Cooley 11-15-01

There's no reason for investors to give up on Fidelity Advisor Equity Growth Fund.

The fund has already begun bouncing back from a tough third quarter. Anticipating an economic recovery, manager Jennifer Uhrig built big stakes in retail and cyclical tech issues, such as semiconductor stocks. In the wake of the September terrorist attacks, those economically sensitive issues fell sharply, and the fund suffered a steep, 22% loss during the quarter. But Uhrig stuck to her guns, picking up more beaten-down chip shares at discount prices. With fears of a deep, prolonged economic slowdown ebbing a bit, those issues have subsequently rebounded sharply. During the trailing month through Nov. 14, 2001, the fund has posted an 8.4% gain, leading nearly two thirds of its peers.

There's nothing wrong with the fund's returns over longer periods, either. As 2001 dawned, the valuation-conscious Uhrig had less exposure to speculative tech shares than her peers had. When those stocks crumbled, this fund held up better than most of its rivals. She also had smaller stakes in flagging networkers than many of her peers and scored with some nontraditional growth picks such as Philip Morris and a handful of regional telephone companies. That kind of stock-picking has generated a well-below average loss here so far in 2001, and a five-year return that lands in the category's top quartile.

An economic recovery would help Uhrig extend that record. She says the fund still has plenty of exposure to retailers and cyclical tech shares, arguing that fiscal and monetary stimulus, among other factors, should help produce an economic recovery. Within financials, she likes the brokerages, which should benefit from a stock-market rebound.

Given Uhrig's excellent longer-term risk/reward profile, don't be surprised if those bets work out, too.

Portfolio Analysis 05-31-01

Share change since 11–00 Total Stocks: 198	Sector	PE	YTD Ret%	% Assets
⊕ Microsoft	Technology	57.6	52.78	5.87
⊕ General Elec	Industrials	30.1	–15.00	4.43
⊖ Pfizer	Health	34.7	–12.40	4.20
⊕ Intel	Technology	73.1	4.89	3.72
⊕ AOL Time Warner	Technology	—	–7.76	2.78
⊕ Eli Lilly	Health	28.9	–14.40	2.49
⊖ IBM	Technology	26.9	43.00	1.75
⊖ Cisco Sys	Technology	—	–52.60	1.70
⊕ Merck	Health	19.1	–35.90	1.68
⊕ Home Depot	Retail	42.9	12.07	1.53
⊖ Bank One	Financials	29.1	9.13	1.45
⊕ Dell Comp	Technology	61.8	55.87	1.41
⊕ Wal–Mart Stores	Retail	40.3	8.94	1.38
⊖ Philip Morris	Staples	12.1	9.12	1.35
⊖ Bristol–Myers Squibb	Health	20.2	–26.00	1.24
⊖ Coca–Cola	Staples	35.5	–21.40	1.11
⊕ American Home Products	Health	—	–1.91	1.06
⊕ Viacom Cl B	Services	—	—	1.05
⊕ American Express	Financials	28.3	–34.40	1.03
⊕ Citigroup	Financials	20.0	0.03	1.02
⊕ American Intl Grp	Financials	42.0	–19.20	0.94
⊖ Texas Instruments	Technology	87.5	–40.70	0.91
⊕ Gillette	Staples	56.6	–5.47	0.84
⊕ Qualcomm	Technology	—	–38.50	0.77
⊕ McKesson HBOC	Health	—	4.92	0.72

Current Investment Style

Style: Value Blnd Growth
Size: Large Med Small

	Stock Port Avg	Relative S&P 500 Current	Relative S&P 500 Hist	Rel Cat
Price/Earnings Ratio	36.2	1.17	1.13	1.02
Price/Book Ratio	6.1	1.08	1.11	0.96
Price/Cash Flow	21.0	1.16	1.13	0.92
3 Yr Earnings Growth	15.5	1.06	1.14	0.72
1 Yr Earnings Est%	–3.7	2.11	—	–1.25
Med Mkt Cap $mil	54,764	0.9	0.7	1.16

Special Securities % assets 05-31-01	
Restricted/Illiquid Secs	Trace
Emerging–Markets Secs	1
Options/Futures/Warrants	No

Composition % assets 05-31-01	
Cash	2.6
Stocks*	97.4
Bonds	0.0
Other	0.0
*Foreign (% stocks)	6.1

Market Cap	
Giant	52.2
Large	26.6
Medium	20.1
Small	1.1
Micro	0.0

Sector Weightings	% of Stocks	Rel S&P	5-Year High	5-Year Low
Utilities	0.3	0.1	2	0
Energy	2.9	0.4	7	1
Financials	12.7	0.7	16	8
Industrials	8.3	0.7	12	4
Durables	1.3	0.8	6	1
Staples	5.5	0.7	10	0
Services	9.9	0.9	21	9
Retail	8.0	1.2	18	4
Health	19.4	1.3	20	7
Technology	31.7	1.7	49	19

Address:	82 Devonshire Street Boston, MA 02109 800–522–7297 / 617–439–6793
Web Address:	www.fidelity.com
*Inception:	09-10-92
Advisor:	Fidelity Mgmt. & Research
Subadvisor:	FMR (U.K.)/FMR (Far East)
NTF Plans:	Datalynx , Fidelity Inst.

Minimum Purchase:	$2500	Add: $100	IRA: $500
Min Auto Inv Plan:	$100	Add: $100	
Sales Fees:	3.50%L, 0.25%B, 0.25%S		
Management Fee:	.30%+.52% mx./.27% mn.(G)		
Actual Fees:	Mgt: 0.58%	Dist: 0.50%	
Expense Projections:	3Yr: $745	5Yr: $1033	10Yr: $1852
Avg Brok Commission:	—	Income Distrib: Semi–Ann.	
Total Cost (relative to category):		Average	

Fidelity Advisor Growth Opport T

Ticker	Load	NAV	Yield	Total Assets	Mstar Category
FAGOX	3.50%	$28.76	0.7%	$9,711.4 mil	Large Blend

Prospectus Objective: Growth

Fidelity Advisor Growth Opportunities Fund seeks capital growth.

The fund normally invests in equity securities of companies that management believes have long-term growth potential. It may also purchase fixed-income securities. The fund may invest up to 35% of assets in debt securities rated below BBB. It also may invest without limit in foreign securities.

This fund offers shares A,B,C, and T, all of which differ in fee structure and availability.

Historical Profile
Return: Below Avg
Risk: Average
Rating: ★★ Below Avg

Investment Style
Equity
Average Stock %: 74% 77% 80% 85% 88% 94% 98%

▼ Manager Change
▽ Partial Manager Change

Fund Performance vs. Category Average
Quarterly Fund Return +/– Category Average
– Category Baseline

Performance Quartile (within Category)

Portfolio Manager(s)

Bettina Doulton. Since 2-00. BA'86 Boston C. Other funds currently managed: Fidelity Advisor Growth Opport Instl, Fidelity Advisor Growth Opport A, Fidelity Advisor Growth Opport B.

History

1990	1991	1992	1993	1994	1995	1996	1997	1998	1999	2000	12–01	History
15.12	19.77	21.32	25.12	24.40	31.64	35.30	42.45	50.24	46.66	34.15	28.76	NAV
–1.65	42.68	15.03	22.17	2.86	33.04	17.73	28.56	23.98	3.88	–18.25	–15.14	Total Return %
1.47	12.20	7.41	12.12	1.54	–4.50	–5.21	–4.79	–4.59	–17.16	–9.15	–3.26	+/– S&P 500
2.38	10.24	7.38	12.33	2.41	–4.57	–4.43	–4.47	–4.65	–17.95	–7.29	–2.37	+/– Wilshire Top 750
1.09	0.60	0.66	0.33	1.07	1.68	1.71	1.33	0.83	0.74	0.00	0.56	Income Return %
–2.74	42.09	14.37	21.84	1.78	31.36	16.02	27.23	23.15	3.14	–18.25	–15.69	Capital Return %
35	9	11	5	11	53	77	55	51	96	97	68	Total Rtn % Rank Cat
0.17	0.09	0.13	0.07	0.27	0.41	0.54	0.47	0.35	0.37	0.00	0.19	Income $
0.00	1.53	1.26	0.84	1.16	0.40	1.44	2.39	1.87	5.05	4.02	0.03	Capital Gains $
2.00	1.73	1.60	1.64	1.62	1.58	1.34	1.27	1.13	1.11	1.03	—	Expense Ratio %
1.49	0.47	0.80	0.43	1.12	1.56	1.88	1.03	0.92	0.73	–0.01	—	Income Ratio %
136	142	94	69	43	39	33	33	25	43	110	—	Turnover Rate %
69.5	264.4	715.5	2,340.6	4,826.6	10,946.2	15,105.1	21,012.0	26,122.7	24,245.9	13,847.9	8,055.8	Net Assets $mil

Performance 12-31-01

	1st Qtr	2nd Qtr	3rd Qtr	4th Qtr	Total
1997	0.57	14.42	7.56	3.87	28.56
1998	10.11	1.23	–7.67	20.48	23.98
1999	–1.16	7.86	–8.20	6.14	3.88
2000	–0.58	–3.91	–3.44	–11.38	–18.25
2001	–15.56	7.60	–16.58	11.97	–15.14

Trailing	Total Return%	+/– S&P 500	+/– Wil Top 750	% Rank All	% Rank Cat	Growth of $10,000
3 Mo	11.97	1.28	0.64	33	30	11,197
6 Mo	–6.60	–1.04	–0.80	72	65	9,340
1 Yr	–15.14	–3.26	–2.37	73	68	8,486
3 Yr Avg	–10.34	–9.32	–8.52	99	97	7,207
5 Yr Avg	2.81	–7.89	–7.31	86	96	11,487
10 Yr Avg	10.03	–2.90	–2.42	32	73	26,007
15 Yr Avg	—	—	—	—	—	—

Tax Analysis	Tax-Adj Ret%	%Rank Cat	%Pretax Ret	%Rank Cat
3 Yr Avg	–11.75	98	—	—
5 Yr Avg	1.21	96	43.1	97
10 Yr Avg	8.32	66	83.0	39

Potential Capital Gain Exposure: 0% of assets

Risk Analysis

Time Period	Load-Adj Return %	Risk %Rank[1] All	Risk %Rank[1] Cat	Morningstar Return	Morningstar Risk	Morningstar Risk-Adj Rating
1 Yr	–18.11					
3 Yr	–11.40	78	87	–2.95[2]	1.09	★
5 Yr	2.08	72	72	–0.61[2]	0.97	★★
10 Yr	9.64	70	50	0.67	0.90	★★★

Average Historical Rating (134 months): 4.1★s

[1] 1=low, 100=high [2] T-Bill return substituted for category avg.

Category Rating (3 Yr)

1 2 3 4 5
Worst Best

Return: Low
Risk: Above Avg

Other Measures	Standard Index S&P 500	Best Fit Index S&P 500
Alpha	–9.6	–9.6
Beta	0.95	0.95
R-Squared	88	88
Standard Deviation		15.54
Mean		–10.34
Sharpe Ratio		–1.16

Analysis by Scott Cooley 11-28-01

We're not quite ready to throw in the towel on Fidelity Advisor Growth Opportunities Fund.

To be sure, this fund has posted disappointing numbers so far in 2001. For the year to date through Nov. 27, it has lost 15.1%, leaving it behind two thirds of its large-blend peers—and 3 percentage points below the S&P 500. Manager Bettina Doulton's affinity for moderately valued drugmakers, including Schering-Ploughand Bristol-Myers Squibb, was a big negative, as patent-expiration issues plagued both stocks. Some brokerage stocks, such as Merrill Lynch, also performed poorly, offsetting the gains on Doulton's better picks, including (perhaps surprisingly, given the market environment) several tech stocks and Tyco International.

As shareholders well know, this year's thus-far disapointing results follow on the heels of an even worse year in 2000. When Doulton took over the portfolio that year, she tilted it toward growth issues, especially tech stocks, and sold or trimmed predecessor George Vanderheiden's value-oriented picks, ranging from hospitals and regional banks to tobacco. We can't criticize Doulton for managing with a growth-oriented approach—that's what she had done for years before taking over here—but when value trumped growth later in the year, this fund suffered.

We're still inclined to give Doulton a bit more time to right this ship. In her stints as a diversified manager prior to taking over here, stretching back to the early 1990s, she beat her average peer at every fund she managed. We still think her long-term record is more indicative of her money-management skills than her recent results have been.

That said, we'll be keeping a close eye on the fund in the near term. Doulton needs to improve this fund's performance—and soon—or it will be time for shareholders to look elsewhere.

Portfolio Analysis 05-31-01

Share change since 11–00 Total Stocks: 150	Sector	PE	YTD Ret%	% Assets
⊖ General Elec	Industrials	30.1	–15.00	5.75
⊕ Citigroup	Financials	20.0	0.03	3.99
⊖ Microsoft	Technology	57.6	52.78	3.78
⊕ Pfizer	Health	34.7	–12.40	2.87
⊖ Fannie Mae	Financials	16.2	–6.95	2.62
⊖ Bristol–Myers Squibb	Health	20.2	–26.00	2.42
⊕ American Intl Grp	Financials	42.0	–19.20	2.29
⊖ Freddie Mac	Financials	14.0	–3.87	2.26
⊕ J.P. Morgan Chase & Co.	Financials	27.8	–17.40	2.26
⊖ ExxonMobil	Energy	15.3	–7.59	2.21
⊕ AOL Time Warner	Technology	—	–7.76	2.15
⊕ Tyco Intl	Industrials	27.1	6.23	1.96
⊖ Viacom Cl B	Services	—	—	1.94
⊕ Merrill Lynch	Financials	18.2	–22.70	1.88
⊖ Eli Lilly	Health	28.9	–14.40	1.72
⊕ Coca–Cola	Staples	35.5	–21.40	1.61
⊕ Intel	Technology	73.1	4.89	1.57
⊕ Philip Morris	Staples	12.1	9.12	1.56
⊕ Gillette	Staples	56.6	–5.47	1.41
⊕ Morgan Stanley/Dean Witter	Financials	16.6	–28.20	1.29
⊕ American Home Products	Health	—	–1.91	1.24
⊕ Halliburton	Energy	8.3	–63.20	1.21
⊕ Bank of America	Financials	16.7	42.73	1.16
⊕ Univision Comms A	Services	96.3	–1.17	1.12
⊕ PeopleSoft	Technology	73.1	8.10	1.05

Current Investment Style

Style: Value Blnd Growth; Size: Large Med Small

	Stock Port Avg	Relative S&P 500 Current	Relative S&P 500 Hist	Rel Cat
Price/Earnings Ratio	31.4	1.01	0.97	1.03
Price/Book Ratio	5.8	1.02	0.94	1.05
Price/Cash Flow	18.8	1.04	0.92	1.02
3 Yr Earnings Growth	14.5	0.99	1.09	0.81
1 Yr Earnings Est%	–3.0	1.67	—	—
Med Mkt Cap $mil	73,392	1.2	1.5	1.40

Special Securities % assets 05-31-01	
Restricted/Illiquid Secs	Trace
Emerging–Markets Secs	0
Options/Futures/Warrants	No

Composition % assets 05-31-01	
Cash	2.0
Stocks*	97.9
Bonds	0.0
Other	0.1
*Foreign (% stocks)	1.9

Market Cap	
Giant	62.8
Large	25.5
Medium	11.7
Small	0.0
Micro	0.0

Sector Weightings	% of Stocks	Rel S&P	5-Year High	5-Year Low
Utilities	0.0	0.0	7	0
Energy	7.4	1.1	16	6
Financials	21.7	1.2	24	14
Industrials	16.0	1.4	23	6
Durables	0.5	0.3	14	0
Staples	6.2	0.8	11	1
Services	12.3	1.1	16	6
Retail	3.9	0.6	11	3
Health	13.0	0.9	17	2
Technology	19.0	1.0	43	7

Address:	82 Devonshire Street Boston, MA 02109 800–522–7297 / 617–439–6793
Web Address:	www.fidelity.com
Inception:	11-18-87
Advisor:	Fidelity Mgmt. & Research
Subadvisor:	FMR (U.K.)/FMR (Far East)
NTF Plans:	Datalynx , Fidelity Inst.

Minimum Purchase:	$2500	Add: $100 IRA: $500
Min Auto Inv Plan:	$100	Add: $100
Sales Fees:	3.50%L, 0.50%B	
Management Fee:	.30%+.52% mx./.27% mn.(G)+(–).20%P	
Actual Fees:	Mgt: 0.43%	Dist: 0.50%
Expense Projections:	3Yr: $694	5Yr: $945 10Yr: $1665
Avg Brok Commission:	—	Income Distrib: Annually
Total Cost (relative to category):		Average

Fidelity Advisor High–Yield T

Ticker	Load	NAV	Yield	SEC Yield	Total Assets	Mstar Category
FAHYX	3.50%	$8.37	9.7%	—	$2,705.6 mil	High–Yield Bond

Prospectus Objective: Corp Bond—High Yield

Fidelity Advisor High-Yield Fund seeks income and capital appreciation.

The fund normally invests at least 65% of assets in lower quality debt securities, preferred stocks, convertibles, and zero coupon bonds. It may invest the balance of assets in equities.

This fund offers multiple shareclasses, all of which differ in fee structure and availability. Past names: Plymouth Aggressive Income Portfolio, Plymouth High-Yield Portfolio, and Fidelity Advisor High-Yield Fund.

Historical Profile

Return: Average
Risk: High
Rating: ★★ Below Avg

Investment Style
Fixed-Income

Income Rtn %Rank Cat: 98, 77, 29, 34, 43, 97, 95, 79

Growth of Principal vs. Interest Rate Shifts
— Principal Value $000 (NAV with capital gains reinvested)
— Interest Rate % on 10 Yr Treasury
▼ Manager Change
▽ Partial Manager Change
► Mgr Unknown After
◄ Mgr Unknown Before

Performance Quartile (within Category)

Portfolio Manager(s)

Thomas T. Soviero, CFA. Since 6-00. BS Boston C. Other funds currently managed: Fidelity Advisor High-Yield B, Fidelity Advisor High-Yield Instl, Fidelity Advisor High-Yield A.

1990	1991	1992	1993	1994	1995	1996	1997	1998	1999	2000	12-01	History
8.40	10.00	10.91	11.83	10.84	11.87	12.20	12.58	11.33	11.37	9.27	8.37	NAV
7.30	34.95	23.09	20.45	–1.50	19.27	13.26	15.09	–0.44	8.47	–11.39	–1.16	Total Return %
–1.66	18.94	15.69	10.70	1.42	0.80	9.65	5.40	–9.12	9.30	–23.02	–9.58	+/– LB Aggregate
13.68	–8.81	6.43	1.54	–0.52	1.89	0.84	2.46	–1.02	5.19	–6.18	–6.93	+/– FB High–Yield
12.77	15.24	11.51	9.33	7.18	9.58	9.89	9.36	8.92	7.14	7.85	9.07	Income Return %
–5.47	19.71	11.58	11.12	–8.67	9.70	3.37	5.73	–9.36	1.33	–19.24	–10.23	Capital Return %
1	52	4	30	25	13	46	15	61	17	80	78	Total Rtn % Rank Cat
1.07	1.21	1.10	0.98	0.82	1.00	1.13	1.09	1.08	0.78	0.86	0.81	Income $
0.00	0.00	0.23	0.26	0.00	0.00	0.06	0.30	0.13	0.12	0.00	0.00	Capital Gains $
1.10	1.10	1.10	1.11	1.20	1.15	1.11	1.08	1.07	1.04	1.03	—	Expense Ratio %
12.72	12.20	9.95	8.09	6.92	8.32	9.20	8.72	8.91	8.80	9.76	—	Income Ratio %
90	103	100	79	118	112	121	105	75	61	63	—	Turnover Rate %
17.2	43.8	161.8	549.5	682.8	1,267.6	1,775.8	2,268.1	2,397.8	2,431.9	1,657.2	1,501.1	Net Assets $mil

Performance 12-31-01

	1st Qtr	2nd Qtr	3rd Qtr	4th Qtr	Total
1997	0.13	5.59	7.58	1.19	15.09
1998	6.02	–0.59	–9.74	4.65	–0.44
1999	5.72	1.36	–2.50	3.82	8.47
2000	–0.88	–3.25	–1.23	–6.45	–11.39
2001	2.37	–2.87	–6.28	6.06	–1.16

Trailing	Total Return%	+/– LB Agg	+/– FB High–Yield	% Rank All	% Rank Cat	Growth of $10,000
3 Mo	6.06	6.03	0.42	61	40	10,606
6 Mo	–0.60	–5.25	–2.04	41	71	9,940
1 Yr	–1.16	–9.58	–6.93	44	78	9,884
3 Yr Avg	–1.69	–7.97	–2.86	81	61	9,501
5 Yr Avg	1.71	–5.71	–1.53	89	45	10,886
10 Yr Avg	7.94	0.71	0.11	43	16	21,477
15 Yr Avg	—	—	—	—	—	—

Tax Analysis	Tax-Adj Ret%	%Rank Cat	%Pretax Ret	%Rank Cat
3 Yr Avg	–4.79	54	—	—
5 Yr Avg	–1.77	38	—	—
10 Yr Avg	4.21	16	53.0	18

Potential Capital Gain Exposure: –43% of assets

Risk Analysis

Time Period	Load-Adj Return %	Risk %Rank[1] All	Risk %Rank[1] Cat	Morningstar Return	Morningstar Risk	Morningstar Risk-Adj Rating
1 Yr	–4.62					
3 Yr	–2.85	42	82	–1.53[2]	2.54	★
5 Yr	0.99	44	80	–0.82[2]	2.54	★
10 Yr	7.56	46	68	0.82[2]	1.75	★★

Average Historical Rating (144 months): 4.1★s

[1]1=low, 100=high [2] T-Bill return substituted for category avg.

Category Rating (3 Yr)

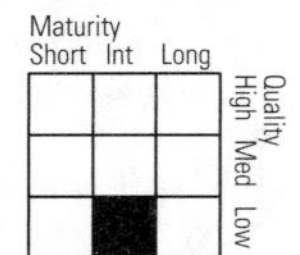

Worst Best

Return: Average
Risk: Above Avg

Other Measures	Standard Index LB Agg	Best Fit Index FB HY
Alpha	–6.2	–1.5
Beta	0.30	1.31
R–Squared	1	84

Standard Deviation	10.38
Mean	–1.69
Sharpe Ratio	–0.74

Portfolio Analysis 04-30-01

Total Fixed-Income: 222	Date of Maturity	Amount $000	Value $000	% Net Assets
Laboratory Corp of Amer		800	112,842	3.70
Nextel Comm Pfd PIK 13%		109	84,663	2.77
CSC Hldgs Pfd PIK 11.125%		599	65,294	2.14
Pathmark Stores		2,969	56,418	1.85
Allied Waste Inds 10%	08-01-09	52,445	54,149	1.77
Quest Diagnostics		438	53,900	1.77
Rite Aid 144A 10.5%	09-15-02	47,775	46,820	1.53
Total Renal Care 7%	05-15-09	46,350	42,179	1.38
EchoStar Comms Cl A		1,400	41,944	1.37
EchoStar DBS 9.375%	02-01-09	40,895	41,917	1.37
AMC Entrtnmt 9.5%	02-01-11	47,215	40,133	1.31
Rite Aid 144A 6%	12-15-05	52,990	38,683	1.27
Owens–Illinois 7.15%	05-15-05	45,450	38,292	1.25
Rite Aid 7.125%	01-15-07	48,750	34,613	1.13
Telecorp 11.625%	04-15-09	51,970	33,391	1.09
Intermedia Pfd PIK 13.5%		37	32,817	1.08
Tritel PCS 12.75%	05-15-09	50,540	32,598	1.07
Millicom Intl Step 0%	06-01-06	38,725	32,529	1.07
AMC Entrtnmt 9.5%	03-15-09	36,359	31,269	1.02
NTL Pfd PIK 13%		42	31,241	1.02

Current Investment Style

Maturity: Short Int Long
Quality: High Med Low

Avg Eff Duration	—
Avg Eff Maturity	6.9 Yrs
Avg Credit Quality	B
Avg Wtd Coupon	8.76%
Avg Wtd Price	82.16% of par

Special Securities % assets 04-30-01	
Restricted/Illiquid Secs	8
Exotic Mortgage–Backed	0
Emerging–Markets Secs	2
Options/Futures/Warrants	Yes

Credit Analysis % bonds 06-30-01			
US Govt	0	BB	7
AAA	0	B	43
AA	0	Below B	5
A	0	NR/NA	40
BBB	5		

Sector Breakdown % bonds 04-30-01			
US Treasuries	0	CMOs	0
GNMA mtgs	0	ARMs	0
FNMA mtgs	0	Other	99
FHLMC mtgs	0		

Coupon Range	% of Bonds	Rel Cat
0%, PIK	12.40	1.98
0% to 9%	25.00	0.83
9% to 12%	40.91	0.77
12% to 14%	21.38	2.43
More than 14%	0.28	0.20

1.00=Category Average

Composition % assets 04-30-01			
Cash	8.9	Bonds	69.1
Stocks	10.8	Other	11.3

Analysis by Scott Berry 12-07-01

Despite its lackluster near-term returns, Fidelity Advisor High-Yield should not be dismissed.

This fund has struggled over the last two years, but its difficulties have been more a result of its aggressive approach than missteps by management. Specifically, the fund's exposure to the telecommunications sector, and to B rated bonds in general, has cost it some ground. Telecom was all the rage in the late 1990s, and helped fuel the fund's top-tier returns in 1999. But as the economy cooled, mountains of debt overwhelmed many of the sector's bigger names and forced a number of them to default on their obligations.

To its credit, this fund has stuck to its guns, which is starting to be of benefit. While its loss of 1.1% for the year to date through Dec. 5, 2001, still ranks in the category's bottom 20%, signs of an economic recovery have helped the fund gain ground on its average peer over the last two months. Manager Tom Soviero has stuck with telecom, for example, though he has shifted some of the fund's exposure to telecom bank debt. He argues that bank debt is more secure than high-yield paper and that current yields on bank debt are quite compelling.

While Soviero still focuses on the single-B area of the market, the fund does hold close to 20% of its assets in what he considers more-defensive issues. He views Owens-Illinois, which has a relatively stable financial situation and which recently reported increased earnings, as an example. And while this group of holdings may not juice the fund's returns, it provides added liquidity to the portfolio and can help smooth out some of the bumps caused by the fund's riskier holdings.

The fund's added credit risk and its recent middling returns may turn off potential investors, but we think the fund's success and Fidelity's reputation for solid credit research make it worth a look.

Address:	82 Devonshire Street Boston, MA 02109 800–522–7297 / 617–439–6793
Web Address:	www.fidelity.com
Inception:	01-05-87
Advisor:	Fidelity Mgmt. & Research
Subadvisor:	FMR (U.K.)/FMR (Far East)
NTF Plans:	Datalynx , Fidelity Inst.

Minimum Purchase:	$2500	Add: $100	IRA: $500
Min Auto Inv Plan:	$100	Add: $100	
Sales Fees:	3.50%L, 0.25%B		
Management Fee:	.45%+.37% mx./.12% mn.(G)		
Actual Fees:	Mgt: 0.58%	Dist: 0.25%	
Expense Projections:	3Yr: $669	5Yr: $904	10Yr: $1577
Avg Brok Commission:	—	Income Distrib: Monthly	
Total Cost (relative to category):	Average		

Fidelity Advisor Small Cap T

Ticker	Load	NAV	Yield	Total Assets	Mstar Category
FSCTX	3.50%	$18.00	0.0%	$1,371.7 mil	Small Growth

Prospectus Objective: Small Company

Fidelity Advisor Small Cap Fund seeks long-term growth of capital.

The fund normally invests at least 65% of assets in equity securities issued by companies with small market capitalizations. The fund has the flexibility, however, to invest in other market capitalizations and security types as the advisor deems suitable. Management may also purchase debt securities of various credit qualities and foreign securities as well.

This fund offers multiple shareclasses, all of which differ in fee structure and availability.

Historical Profile

Return	Above Avg
Risk	Above Avg
Rating	★★★★ Above Avg

Investment Style
Equity
Average Stock %: 87% (1998), 92% (1999), 92% (2000), 91% (12-01)

▼ Manager Change
▽ Partial Manager Change

Fund Performance vs. Category Average
■ Quarterly Fund Return +/– Category Average
— Category Baseline

Performance Quartile (within Category)

Portfolio Manager(s)

Harry Lange, CFA. Since 9-98. BS'75 General Motors Institute; MBA'83 Harvard U. Other funds currently managed: Fidelity Capital Appreciation, Fidelity Advisor Small Cap A, Fidelity Advisor Small Cap B.

1990	1991	1992	1993	1994	1995	1996	1997	1998	1999	2000	12-01	History
—	—	—	—	—	—	—	—	13.88	22.80	18.73	18.00	NAV
—	—	—	—	—	—	—	—	38.80*	68.46	–17.55	–3.90	Total Return %
—	—	—	—	—	—	—	—	16.02*	47.42	–8.44	7.98	+/– S&P 500
—	—	—	—	—	—	—	—	—	25.38	4.89	5.33	+/– Russ 2000 Grth
—	—	—	—	—	—	—	—	0.00	0.00	0.00	0.00	Income Return %
—	—	—	—	—	—	—	—	38.80	68.46	–17.55	–3.90	Capital Return %
—	—	—	—	—	—	—	—	—	33	84	34	Total Rtn % Rank Cat
—	—	—	—	—	—	—	—	0.00	0.00	0.00	0.00	Income $
—	—	—	—	—	—	—	—	0.00	0.51	0.08	0.00	Capital Gains $
—	—	—	—	—	—	—	—	1.93	1.56	1.53	—	Expense Ratio %
—	—	—	—	—	—	—	—	–0.63	–0.77	–0.80	—	Income Ratio %
—	—	—	—	—	—	—	—	204	62	64	—	Turnover Rate %
—	—	—	—	—	—	—	—	100.2	602.9	668.4	668.7	Net Assets $mil

Performance 12-31-01

	1st Qtr	2nd Qtr	3rd Qtr	4th Qtr	Total
1997	—	—	—	—	—
1998	—	—	—	36.35	38.80 *
1999	7.71	14.90	3.27	31.81	68.46
2000	–0.64	–2.39	–0.73	–14.36	–17.55
2001	–9.88	13.21	–22.29	21.21	–3.90

Trailing	Total Return%	+/– S&P 500	+/– Russ 2000 Grth	% Rank All	% Rank Cat	Growth of $10,000
3 Mo	21.21	10.53	–4.96	12	61	12,121
6 Mo	–5.81	–0.25	3.46	67	48	9,419
1 Yr	–3.90	7.98	5.33	49	34	9,610
3 Yr Avg	10.11	11.13	9.86	11	40	13,349
5 Yr Avg	—	—	—	—	—	—
10 Yr Avg	—	—	—	—	—	—
15 Yr Avg	—	—	—	—	—	—

Tax Analysis	Tax-Adj Ret%	%Rank Cat	%Pretax Ret	%Rank Cat
3 Yr Avg	9.71	34	96.1	12
5 Yr Avg	—	—	—	—
10 Yr Avg	—	—	—	—

Potential Capital Gain Exposure: 6% of assets

Risk Analysis

Time Period	Load-Adj Return %	Risk %Rank[1] All	Risk %Rank[1] Cat	Morningstar Return	Morningstar Risk	Morningstar Risk-Adj Rating
1 Yr	–7.26					
3 Yr	8.81	84	32	0.85[2]	1.26	★★★★
5 Yr	—	—	—	—	—	
Incept	19.18	—	—	—	—	

Average Historical Rating (4 months): 4.0★s

[1]1=low, 100=high [2] T-Bill return substituted for category avg.

Category Rating (3 Yr)

1 2 **3** 4 5 — Worst … Best

Return	Average
Risk	Below Avg

Other Measures	Standard Index S&P 500	Best Fit Index Wil 4500
Alpha	15.0	9.1
Beta	1.16	0.96
R-Squared	47	87
Standard Deviation		32.83
Mean		10.11
Sharpe Ratio		0.18

Portfolio Analysis 05-31-01

Share change since 11-00 Total Stocks: 147	Sector	PE	YTD Ret%	% Assets
⊕ American Italian Pasta	Staples	29.0	56.75	4.01
⊕ WMS Inds	Durables	19.8	–0.62	3.48
Copart	Services	43.8	69.16	3.22
⊕ Brunswick	Industrials	15.2	35.60	3.21
⊕ Robert Mondavi Cl A	Staples	20.1	–29.70	2.68
Expeditors Intl of WA	Services	32.7	6.46	2.68
☼ LNR Ppty	Financials	8.5	41.97	2.58
⊖ Lennar	Industrials	8.8	29.32	2.42
☼ CIMA Labs	Health	39.3	–44.40	2.25
⊖ Teekay Shipping	Energy	3.3	–7.24	2.21
⊕ Anchor Gaming	Services	—	56.15	2.20
☼ Mettler-Toledo Intl	Industrials	34.1	–4.64	2.18
⊕ Callaway Golf	Durables	19.3	4.30	2.04
⊖ Millipore	Industrials	63.9	–2.89	1.93
Human Genome Sciences	Health	—	–51.30	1.84
⊕ Korn/Ferry Intl	Services	—	–49.80	1.72
⊕ Martin Marietta Matls	Industrials	22.0	11.56	1.71
Cable Design Tech	Industrials	62.2	–18.60	1.53
⊕ Liz Claiborne	Durables	13.7	20.58	1.47
⊖ BJ Svcs	Energy	15.5	–5.77	1.45
Frontline	Services	0.9	—	1.42
Florida Rock Inds	Industrials	15.1	41.77	1.41
⊕ FactSet Rsrch Sys	Technology	35.3	–5.26	1.40
⊕ Forward Air	Services	34.6	–9.09	1.33
⊕ Handleman	Services	9.2	98.00	1.28

Current Investment Style

Style: Value Blnd Growth; Size: Large Med Small

	Stock Port Avg	Relative S&P 500 Current	Relative S&P 500 Hist	Rel Cat
Price/Earnings Ratio	25.4	0.82	—	0.79
Price/Book Ratio	3.7	0.64	—	0.75
Price/Cash Flow	20.0	1.11	—	0.91
3 Yr Earnings Growth	22.7[1]	1.55	—	0.90
1 Yr Earnings Est%	4.0	—	—	0.51
Med Mkt Cap $mil	1,157	0.0	—	1.11

[1]figure is based on 50% or less of stocks

Analysis by Scott Cooley 11-12-01

Even in a difficult year, Fidelity Advisor Small Cap Fund is getting the job done.

Shareholders might not be rejoicing about this fund's return this year, but it has held up better than its typical small-growth peer. For the year to date through Nov. 9, 2001, the fund has declined 14.1%, leaving it ahead of 65% of its rivals. Manager Harry Lange has stashed less in the hard-hit technology sector than most rivals, which has been a plus. Lange's willingness to buy stocks that may seem more suited for value portfolios—including homebuilder Lennar, real-estate firm LNR Property, and vehicle auctioneer Copart—has helped the fund immeasurably in this year's growth-stock sell-off.

Lange isn't a bandwagon-hopper, though. Indeed, he prefers to go against the grain. In 2001's third quarter, for example, Lange scooped up shares of fallen semiconductor firms. Lange says he thinks there are faint signs of a revival in the PC industry, which he thinks will recover well before some other tech areas, including networking equipment. Indeed, according to figures provided by Fidelity, the fund's tech stake was slightly above 20% on Sept. 30, up from the low double digits earlier this year. Meanwhile, Lange has trimmed his exposure to real-estate companies, which have been relatively strong performers, because their share prices have risen even though their near-term fundamentals are likely to erode.

Lange's longer-term numbers here are solid, too. Over the past three years, Lange has made enough good picks in a variety of areas to top the average fund in the small-growth and small-blend categories. (One might argue that because of Lange's valuation consciousness, the latter is a more-appropriate basis for comparison.)

This fund offers a decent performance record and an experienced manager. It's well worth investors' consideration.

Special Securities % assets 05-31-01	
Restricted/Illiquid Secs	Trace
Emerging-Markets Secs	2
Options/Futures/Warrants	No

Composition % assets 05-31-01	
Cash	8.7
Stocks*	91.3
Bonds	0.0
Other	0.0
*Foreign (% stocks)	8.6

Market Cap	
Giant	0.0
Large	0.1
Medium	38.6
Small	56.1
Micro	5.2

Sector Weightings	% of Stocks	Rel S&P	5-Year High	5-Year Low
Utilities	1.0	0.3	—	—
Energy	5.4	0.8	—	—
Financials	5.9	0.3	—	—
Industrials	21.6	1.9	—	—
Durables	8.8	5.7	—	—
Staples	7.4	0.9	—	—
Services	25.9	2.4	—	—
Retail	3.7	0.5	—	—
Health	7.3	0.5	—	—
Technology	12.9	0.7	—	—

Address:	82 Devonshire Street Boston, MA 02109 800–522–7297 / 800–522–7297
Web Address:	www.fidelity.com
*Inception:	09-09-98
Advisor:	Fidelity Mgmt. & Research
Subadvisor:	FMR (U.K.)/FMR (Far East)
NTF Plans:	Fidelity Inst.

Minimum Purchase:	$2500	Add: $100 IRA: $500
Min Auto Inv Plan:	$100	Add: $100
Sales Fees:	3.50%L, 0.25%B, 0.25%S	
Management Fee:	.45%+.52% mx./.00% mn.(G)	
Actual Fees:	Mgt: 0.73%	Dist: 0.50%
Expense Projections:	3Yr: $834	5Yr: $1185 10Yr: $2173
Avg Brok Commission:	—	Income Distrib: Annually
Total Cost (relative to category):		Average

Fidelity Advisor Value Strat T

Ticker	Load	NAV	Yield	Total Assets	Mstar Category
FASPX	3.50%	$26.88	0.0%	$1,136.4 mil	Small Blend

Prospectus Objective: Growth

Fidelity Advisor Value Strategies Fund seeks capital appreciation.

The fund normally invests at least 65% of assets in equities of companies believed by management to involve a special situation; such as a technological advance, a new product, or new management. It may invest in debt securities of all types and quality. It may invest up to 30% of assets in foreign securities.

Class A, B, C, T, Initial, and Institutional shares are offered by the fund, all of which differ in fee structure and availability. The fund has gone through several name changes.

Historical Profile
Return Above Avg
Risk Average
Rating ★★★★ Above Avg

Investment Style
Equity
Average Stock %

	1995	1996	1997	1998	1999	2000	12-01
Average Stock %	68%	94%	94%	96%	99%	98%	95%

▼ Manager Change
▽ Partial Manager Change

Fund Performance vs. Category Average
▪ Quarterly Fund Return +/– Category Average
— Category Baseline

Performance Quartile (within Category)

Portfolio Manager(s)

Harris B. Leviton. Since 3-96. BA'83 Johns Hopkins U.; MBA'87 Stanford U. Other funds currently managed: Fidelity Advisor Value Strat Initial, Fidelity Advisor Value Strat B, Fidelity Advisor Value Strat Instl.

1990	1991	1992	1993	1994	1995	1996	1997	1998	1999	2000	12-01	History
17.65	18.49	19.05	20.80	18.71	24.88	22.69	25.27	24.81	23.07	24.16	26.88	NAV
–7.12	23.01	12.87	20.44	–7.12	38.09	1.53	26.01	0.84	18.78	11.24	12.11	Total Return %
–4.00	–7.47	5.26	10.38	–8.44	0.55	–21.42	–7.34	–27.74	–2.26	20.34	23.98	+/– S&P 500
12.39	–23.04	–5.54	1.53	–5.30	9.64	–15.01	3.65	3.39	–2.49	14.26	9.62	+/– Russell 2000
3.79	3.51	3.08	2.26	1.68	2.08	0.78	0.00	0.00	0.00	0.00	0.00	Income Return %
–10.90	19.50	9.79	18.18	–8.80	36.00	0.75	26.01	0.84	18.78	11.24	12.11	Capital Return %
29	84	60	35	95	13	98	45	20	32	53	30	Total Rtn % Rank Cat
0.75	0.62	0.57	0.43	0.35	0.39	0.19	0.00	0.00	0.00	0.00	0.00	Income $
0.00	2.42	1.21	1.71	0.26	0.55	2.35	3.04	0.65	6.01	1.41	0.19	Capital Gains $
1.59	1.56	1.46	1.57	1.84	1.61	1.27	1.23	1.15	1.16	1.14	—	Expense Ratio %
3.70	3.61	3.22	2.06	1.89	1.90	0.70	–0.29	–0.53	–0.48	–0.40	—	Income Ratio %
114	223	211	183	159	142	151	—	64	60	48	—	Turnover Rate %
178.6	197.6	205.4	310.0	376.7	615.0	563.2	520.6	453.5	407.8	402.5	740.0	Net Assets $mil

Performance 12-31-01

	1st Qtr	2nd Qtr	3rd Qtr	4th Qtr	Total
1997	–4.16	17.86	18.07	–5.52	26.01
1998	13.62	–8.27	–17.99	17.98	0.84
1999	–5.96	23.88	–2.38	4.45	18.78
2000	12.22	–9.63	12.61	–2.59	11.24
2001	2.91	17.45	–28.69	30.06	12.11

Trailing	Total Return%	+/– S&P 500	+/– Russ 2000	% Rank All	% Rank Cat	Growth of $10,000
3 Mo	30.06	19.38	8.98	5	6	13,006
6 Mo	–7.25	–1.70	–3.17	75	92	9,275
1 Yr	12.11	23.98	9.62	5	30	11,211
3 Yr Avg	13.99	15.02	7.57	6	27	14,812
5 Yr Avg	13.48	2.78	5.96	7	27	18,821
10 Yr Avg	12.79	–0.14	1.28	13	68	33,314
15 Yr Avg	12.41	–1.33	1.65	22	52	57,792

Tax Analysis	Tax-Adj Ret%	%Rank Cat	%Pretax Ret	%Rank Cat
3 Yr Avg	10.95	32	78.3	68
5 Yr Avg	10.66	33	79.1	62
10 Yr Avg	10.05	71	78.6	65

Potential Capital Gain Exposure: 15% of assets

Risk Analysis

Time Period	Load-Adj Return %	Risk %Rank[1] All	Risk %Rank[1] Cat	Morningstar Return	Morningstar Risk	Morningstar Risk-Adj Rating
1 Yr	8.18					
3 Yr	12.64	67	64	1.76[2]	0.93	★★★★
5 Yr	12.68	76	64	1.93[2]	1.03	★★★★
10 Yr	12.39	78	61	1.18	1.02	★★★

Average Historical Rating (149 months): 3.1★s

[1] 1=low, 100=high [2] T-Bill return substituted for category avg.

Category Rating (3 Yr)

1 2 3 4 5
Worst Best

Return Above Avg
Risk Average

Other Measures	Standard Index S&P 500	Best Fit Index SPMid400
Alpha	17.3	4.3
Beta	1.06	1.05
R-Squared	53	70
Standard Deviation	28.33	
Mean	13.99	
Sharpe Ratio	0.36	

Portfolio Analysis 05-31-01

Share change since 11-00 Total Stocks: 118

	Sector	PE	YTD Ret%	% Assets
⊕ WMS Inds	Durables	19.8	–0.62	7.24
⊕ Jack In The Box	Services	13.4	–6.45	4.53
☼ Nintendo	Durables	32.2	—	3.40
⊕ Cable Design Tech	Industrials	62.2	–18.60	3.22
Borders Grp	Retail	53.6	69.75	2.75
⊕ Legato Sys	Technology	—	74.37	2.60
⊕ Anchor Gaming	Services	—	56.15	2.49
☼ Kmart	Retail	—	2.77	2.32
⊕ Performance Tech	Technology	29.6	–2.24	2.03
Beazer Homes USA	Industrials	9.0	82.93	2.02
⊕ Burlington Northern Santa Fe	Services	13.9	2.46	2.02
Fossil	Durables	14.4	45.14	1.98
Metropolitan Life Ins	Financials	—	–8.82	1.87
⊕ Midway Games	Technology	—	111.40	1.86
⊕ i-Stat	Health	—	–70.10	1.83
☼ Clarent	Technology	—	–52.70	1.77
⊖ Wet Seal A	Retail	16.2	71.78	1.74
⊕ Navistar Intl	Durables	—	50.88	1.72
Maxwell Shoe	Staples	11.7	31.16	1.69
⊖ Jones Apparel Grp	Durables	15.8	3.05	1.68
⊕ Cygnus	Health	—	7.69	1.65
☼ Vignette	Technology	—	–70.10	1.63
Pentair	Industrials	38.0	54.40	1.50
⊕ American Standard	Industrials	14.9	38.36	1.49
Lennar	Industrials	8.8	29.32	1.42

Current Investment Style

Style: Value Blnd Growth; Size: Large Med Small

	Stock Port Avg	Relative S&P 500 Current	Relative S&P 500 Hist	Rel Cat
Price/Earnings Ratio	25.1	0.81	0.56	1.01
Price/Book Ratio	2.6	0.46	0.46	0.82
Price/Cash Flow	12.9	0.72	0.61	0.83
3 Yr Earnings Growth	14.2	0.97	1.41	0.84
1 Yr Earnings Est%	–10.4	5.86	—	–12.07
Med Mkt Cap $mil	889	0.0	0.0	0.91

[1]figure is based on 50% or less of stocks

Analysis by Christopher Traulsen 10-25-01

Fidelity Advisor Value Strategies isn't having a great year, but it remains a solid choice.

This fund certainly hasn't fared badly in 2001. For the year to date through Oct. 24, it's down 7%. Nobody likes losing money, but the loss is actually a bit better than the small-blend norm.

The fund hasn't fared particularly well, however, considering it usually has a notable value-tilt that should have helped it outdo its peers by a large margin this year. But manager Harris Leviton thought he saw compelling valuations among technology stocks early in 2001. He thus took the fund's tech stake from 8% of equities in late 2000 to 18% by May 2001. Some picks, including cable-modem maker Terayon Communications, have soared, but other tech buys, including Vignette and Clarent, have continued to slide.

Leviton is sticking by his picks, however. Indeed, he added to some as they skidded following the World Trade Center attack (he also bought regional airlines and hotels). One new buy is Yahoo. Although he favors small caps, Leviton said he had been foraging more among larger-cap fare recently. He thinks that even with the risks inherent in Yahoo's ad-driven business model, it was extremely cheap at roughly two times cash and securities.

We think there's ample reason to think Leviton knows what he's doing. He has a history of uncovering out of favor niche businesses that go on to deliver strong gains for the fund. Leviton has had past successes with video-game, apparel, gaming, and restaurant stocks in his tenure. He's guided the fund to a top-third three-year return, and the fund's five-year return is solidly above the norm (Leviton came on board in March 1996).

This fund's forays into larger caps make it unsuitable for small-cap purists. However, we think it's a good pick for investors seeking a moderate take on small- and mid-cap stocks.

Special Securities % assets 05-31-01	
Restricted/Illiquid Secs	1
Emerging-Markets Secs	0
Options/Futures/Warrants	Yes

Sector Weightings	% of Stocks	Rel S&P	5-Year High	5-Year Low
Utilities	0.0	0.0	37	0
Energy	0.1	0.0	18	0
Financials	2.0	0.1	50	0
Industrials	23.3	2.0	36	2
Durables	23.9	15.3	24	0
Staples	0.3	0.0	14	0
Services	15.5	1.4	54	11
Retail	11.6	1.7	20	0
Health	5.4	0.4	16	0
Technology	17.9	1.0	18	0

Composition % assets 05-31-01	
Cash	2.5
Stocks*	95.2
Bonds	0.8
Other	1.5
*Foreign (% stocks)	6.1

Market Cap	
Giant	0.0
Large	12.7
Medium	22.6
Small	46.2
Micro	18.5

Address: 82 Devonshire Street, Boston, MA 02109, 800–522–7297 / 617–439–6793
Web Address: www.fidelity.com
Inception: 08-20-86
Advisor: Fidelity Mgmt. & Research
Subadvisor: FMR (U.K.)/FMR (Far East)
NTF Plans: Datalynx , Fidelity Inst.

Minimum Purchase: $2500 Add: $100 IRA: $500
Min Auto Inv Plan: $100 Add: $100
Sales Fees: 3.50%L, 0.50%B
Management Fee: .30%+.52% mx./.27% mn.(G)+(–).20%P
Actual Fees: Mgt: 0.35% Dist: 0.50%
Expense Projections: 3Yr: $712 5Yr: $976 10Yr: $1732
Avg Brok Commission: — Income Distrib: Annually
Total Cost (relative to category): Average

Fidelity Aggressive Growth

Ticker	Load	NAV	Yield	Total Assets	Mstar Category
FDEGX	None	$19.02	0.0%	$7,410.2 mil	Large Growth

Prospectus Objective: Aggressive Growth

Fidelity Aggressive Growth Fund seeks capital appreciation.

The fund normally invests at least 65% of assets in equity securities issued by companies that are in development stages and that management believes may achieve rapid growth in earnings and/or revenues. The fund invests in both small companies and large established companies with strong growth prospects. It may also invest in debt securities and foreign securities, enter into currency-exchange contracts, and invest in stock-index futures and options.

Prior to Jan. 29, 1999, the fund was named Fidelity Emerging Growth Fund.

Historical Profile
Return: Below Avg
Risk: High
Rating: ★ Lowest

Investment Style
Equity
Average Stock %: 90% 95% 95% 96% 97% 97% 97%

▼ Manager Change
▽ Partial Manager Change

Fund Performance vs. Category Average
Quarterly Fund Return
+/– Category Average
— Category Baseline

Performance Quartile (within Category)

Portfolio Manager(s)

Robert C. Bertelson. Since 2-00. BA'82 Stanford U.; MBA'86 Harvard U.

1990	1991	1992	1993	1994	1995	1996	1997	1998	1999	2000	12-01	History
10.06	16.38	17.58	17.33	16.99	22.32	25.19	23.75	31.77	59.63	36.17	19.02	NAV
0.60*	67.10	8.36	19.88	–0.18	35.94	15.80	19.45	43.28	103.02	–27.14	–47.27	Total Return %
–0.16*	36.62	0.74	9.82	–1.49	–1.59	–7.15	–13.90	14.71	81.99	–18.04	–35.39	+/– S&P 500
—	27.69	4.47	19.95	–5.03	–2.71	–9.72	–14.29	–1.82	73.35	–2.62	–26.77	+/– Russ Top 200 Grt
0.00	0.00	0.12	0.00	0.00	0.00	0.00	0.00	0.00	0.00	0.00	0.00	Income Return %
0.60	67.10	8.23	19.88	–0.18	35.94	15.80	19.45	43.28	103.02	–27.14	–47.27	Capital Return %
—	11	29	14	28	25	76	79	16	2	92	97	Total Rtn % Rank Cat
0.00	0.00	0.02	0.00	0.00	0.00	0.00	0.00	0.00	0.00	0.00	0.00	Income $
0.00	0.39	0.14	3.57	0.31	0.80	0.60	6.00	2.08	3.92	7.58	0.09	Capital Gains $
—	1.31	1.09	1.19	1.02	1.09	1.09	1.05	1.05	0.97	0.89	—	Expense Ratio %
—	–0.10	0.56	–0.20	–0.41	–0.66	–0.31	–0.60	–0.67	–0.58	–0.55	—	Income Ratio %
—	326	531	332	180	102	105	212	199	186	176	—	Turnover Rate %
2.3	724.3	641.3	652.6	635.2	1,249.9	1,854.0	1,981.5	2,897.0	15,199.3	15,220.4	7,410.2	Net Assets $mil

Performance 12-31-01

	1st Qtr	2nd Qtr	3rd Qtr	4th Qtr	Total
1997	–5.08	14.97	15.68	–5.38	19.45
1998	15.09	7.78	–8.38	26.07	43.28
1999	19.53	12.12	2.14	48.33	103.02
2000	14.42	–10.31	–1.94	–27.60	–27.14
2001	–35.40	5.32	–40.34	29.92	–47.27

Trailing	Total Return%	+/– S&P 500	+/–Russ Top 200 Grth	% Rank All	% Rank Cat	Growth of $10,000
3 Mo	29.92	19.23	17.06	5	5	12,992
6 Mo	–22.49	–16.94	–15.51	99	98	7,751
1 Yr	–47.27	–35.39	–26.77	99	97	5,273
3 Yr Avg	–7.95	–6.92	0.07	97	81	7,800
5 Yr Avg	5.95	–4.75	–2.64	49	72	13,349
10 Yr Avg	10.54	–2.38	–0.54	29	48	27,247
15 Yr Avg	—	—	—	—	—	—

Tax Analysis	Tax-Adj Ret%	%Rank Cat	%Pretax Ret	%Rank Cat
3 Yr Avg	–9.94	85	—	—
5 Yr Avg	2.93	78	49.3	88
10 Yr Avg	7.85	54	74.5	58

Potential Capital Gain Exposure: –136% of assets

Risk Analysis

Time Period	Load-Adj Return %	Risk %Rank[1] All	Risk %Rank[1] Cat	Morningstar Return	Morningstar Risk	Morningstar Risk-Adj Rating
1 Yr	–47.27					
3 Yr	–7.95	98	97	–2.41[2]	2.31	★
5 Yr	5.95	98	98	0.20[2]	1.96	★
10 Yr	10.54	97	98	0.83	1.92	★

Average Historical Rating (97 months): 3.4★s

[1] 1=low, 100=high [2] T-Bill return substituted for category avg.

Category Rating (3 Yr)

1 2 3 4 5
Worst Best

Return: Below Avg
Risk: High

Other Measures	Standard Index S&P 500	Best Fit Index Wil 4500
Alpha	6.4	–3.2
Beta	2.07	1.48
R-Squared	60	84

Standard Deviation	47.26
Mean	–7.95
Sharpe Ratio	–0.32

Analysis by William Harding 12-31-01

Investors shouldn't be fooled by the fund's recent big jump—it still has problems.

A fourth-quarter rally in beaten-down technology shares was a major boon to returns for Fidelity Aggressive Growth Fund. To be sure, the fund has gained a solid 32% over the past three months through Dec. 28. Unfortunately, the fund still has a massive climb back. Its 46% loss for the year to date lags 98% of funds in the large-growth camp and trails its benchmark, the Russell Mid Cap Growth index, by 27 percentage points. Further, the fund has lost considerably more than its benchmark and large-growth rivals since Bob Bertelson replaced former manager Erin Sullivan in February 2000.

Part of the fund's troubles owes to the high-octane portfolio that Bertelson inherited. A big stake in racy tech and biotech names produced mammoth gains in 1999 but was a liability as those stocks headed south beginning in the spring of 2000. Some growth skippers responded by keeping cash on the sidelines or favoring steadier growth names, but Bertelson has stuck to the fund's aggressive knitting. Most of the fund's assets are concentrated in three sectors of the economy that have generally had a rough go of it over the past 20 months—technology, health care, and energy.

This strategy has potential for big gains, as evidenced by the fund's showing in 2001's fourth quarter, but too many blemishes remain. Bertelson's record on Fidelity OTC was merely middling relative to its bogy, the Nasdaq Composite index. Further, he will likely be hampered by this fund's girth. For example, with more than 15 million shares invested in Ciena as of May 31, 2001, it's likely difficult for Bertelson to act swiftly amid signs of trouble without driving the price down.

Suffering shareholders should consider replacing this offering with a more nimble option.

Portfolio Analysis 05-31-01

Share change since 11-00 Total Stocks: 97	Sector	PE	YTD Ret%	% Assets
⊕ CIENA	Technology	NMF	–82.30	7.55
⊕ BEA Sys	Technology	—	–77.10	5.74
⊖ BJ Svcs	Energy	15.5	–5.77	4.11
⊕ Schlumberger	Energy	55.0	–30.30	3.41
⊕ Gemstar–TV Guide Intl	Services	—	–39.90	3.22
⊕ Noble Drilling	Energy	18.3	–21.60	3.09
⊕ Weatherford Intl	Energy	66.5	–21.10	2.63
☼ Baker Hughes	Energy	45.0	–11.10	2.58
⊕ IDEC Pharmaceuticals	Health	NMF	9.09	2.57
⊕ Human Genome Sciences	Health	—	–51.30	2.52
⊖ Scientific–Atlanta	Technology	15.5	–26.30	2.34
⊕ Transocean Sedco Forex	Energy	58.3	–26.20	2.19
⊕ Comverse Tech	Technology	22.2	–79.40	2.15
☼ Openwave Sys	Technology	—	–79.50	2.00
⊖ Medtronic	Health	76.4	–14.70	1.88
⊕ Tidewater	Energy	15.1	–22.30	1.83
⊕ Allergan	Health	48.7	–22.10	1.83
⊕ Juniper Net	Technology	NMF	–84.90	1.81
⊕ Cephalon	Health	—	19.38	1.71
⊕ Smith Intl	Industrials	19.3	–28.00	1.70
⊕ Peregrine Sys	Technology	—	–24.90	1.60
⊕ Millennium Pharma	Health	—	–60.30	1.59
⊕ Cooper Cameron	Industrials	38.8	–38.90	1.49
☼ Amgen	Health	52.8	–11.70	1.47
⊕ Applera Corporation	Industrials	38.1	–58.00	1.38

Current Investment Style

Style: Value Blnd Growth; Size: Large Med Small

	Stock Port Avg	Relative S&P 500 Current	Relative S&P 500 Hist	Rel Cat
Price/Earnings Ratio	41.4	1.34	1.48	1.17
Price/Book Ratio	5.2	0.91	1.44	0.81
Price/Cash Flow	26.0	1.45	1.38	1.15
3 Yr Earnings Growth	2.5[1]	0.17	1.05	0.12
1 Yr Earnings Est%	12.7	—	—	4.24
Med Mkt Cap $mil	5,199	0.1	0.3	0.11

[1] figure is based on 50% or less of stocks

Special Securities % assets 05-31-01

Restricted/Illiquid Secs	Trace
Emerging–Markets Secs	Trace
Options/Futures/Warrants	No

Composition % assets 05-31-01

Cash	2.0
Stocks*	97.5
Bonds	0.0
Other	0.6
*Foreign (% stocks)	1.7

Market Cap

Giant	4.9
Large	27.3
Medium	62.9
Small	4.4
Micro	0.5

Sector Weightings	% of Stocks	Rel S&P	5-Year High	5-Year Low
Utilities	0.8	0.2	2	0
Energy	26.8	3.8	27	0
Financials	0.4	0.0	10	0
Industrials	5.4	0.5	11	1
Durables	0.5	0.3	8	0
Staples	0.0	0.0	5	0
Services	5.3	0.5	30	5
Retail	0.5	0.1	26	0
Health	22.6	1.5	31	2
Technology	37.6	2.1	67	18

Address:	82 Devonshire Street, Boston, MA 02109, 800–544–8888
Web Address:	www.fidelity.com
*Inception:	12-28-90
Advisor:	Fidelity Mgmt. & Research
Subadvisor:	FMR (U.K.)/FMR (Far East)
NTF Plans:	Fidelity Inst.

Minimum Purchase:	$2500	Add: $250 IRA: $500
Min Auto Inv Plan:	$2500	Add: $100
Sales Fees:	No-load, 1.50%R within 3 months	
Management Fee:	.35%+.52% mx./.27% mn.(G)+(–).20%P	
Actual Fees:	Mgt: 0.72%	Dist: —
Expense Projections:	3Yr: $315	5Yr: $547 10Yr: $1213
Avg Brok Commission:	—	Income Distrib: Annually
Total Cost (relative to category):		Below Avg

Fidelity Asset Manager

Ticker	Load	NAV	Yield	Total Assets	Mstar Category
FASMX	None	$15.50	4.2%	$11,923.7 mil	Domestic Hybrid

Prospectus Objective: Multiasset—Global

Fidelity Asset Manager seeks total return with reduced risk over the long term.

The fund normally allocates assets within the following investment parameters: 30% to 70% in stocks, 20% to 60% in bonds, and 0% to 50% in short-term fixed-income instruments. A neutral mix consists of 50% stocks, 40% bonds, and 10% money-market instruments. The bond portion consists of debt of varying quality with maturities of more than three years. A single reallocation may not involve more than 10% of assets. The fund may purchase foreign issues.

Historical Profile

Return Average
Risk Low
Rating ★★★ Neutral

Investment Style
Equity
Average Stock %: 45% 55% 50% 54% 52% 46%

▼ Manager Change
▽ Partial Manager Change

Fund Performance vs. Category Average
Quarterly Fund Return +/– Category Average
— Category Baseline

Performance Quartile (within Category)

Portfolio Manager(s)

Dick Habermann, et al. Since 3-96. BA'62 Yale U.; MBA'68 Harvard U.

1990	1991	1992	1993	1994	1995	1996	1997	1998	1999	2000	12-01	History
10.87	12.46	13.37	15.40	13.83	15.85	16.47	18.35	17.39	18.38	16.82	15.50	NAV
5.38	23.64	12.75	23.29	–6.60	18.16	12.73	22.28	16.09	13.59	2.38	–3.93	Total Return %
8.50	–6.85	5.13	13.23	–7.92	–19.38	–10.22	–11.08	–12.48	–7.45	11.49	7.95	+/– S&P 500
–3.58	7.63	5.34	13.54	–3.68	–0.31	9.11	12.59	7.42	14.42	–9.25	–12.35	+/– LB Aggregate
5.94	4.14	3.85	4.48	2.62	3.36	3.97	3.75	3.31	3.26	3.58	3.92	Income Return %
–0.56	19.49	8.89	18.81	–9.22	14.79	8.76	18.52	12.78	10.33	–1.20	–7.85	Capital Return %
12	52	12	1	91	92	55	21	30	26	43	47	Total Rtn % Rank Cat
0.65	0.45	0.48	0.59	0.40	0.46	0.62	0.61	0.60	0.56	0.65	0.65	Income $
0.00	0.50	0.19	0.43	0.17	0.00	0.75	1.11	3.15	0.74	1.34	0.00	Capital Gains $
1.17	1.17	1.17	1.09	1.04	0.97	0.93	0.78	0.74	0.73	0.71	—	Expense Ratio %
5.89	5.74	5.58	4.28	3.63	4.27	3.64	3.39	3.19	3.01	3.32	—	Income Ratio %
105	134	134	98	109	137	131	79	136	104	109	—	Turnover Rate %
372.0	1,016.3	3,392.7	9,094.4	11,075.6	11,165.4	10,971.9	12,099.0	12,879.2	13,253.9	12,961.4	11,923.7	Net Assets $mil

Performance 12-31-01

	1st Qtr	2nd Qtr	3rd Qtr	4th Qtr	Total
1997	–0.04	11.28	6.22	3.48	22.28
1998	7.53	0.52	–5.83	14.05	16.09
1999	1.73	3.91	–3.67	11.56	13.59
2000	4.43	–0.51	2.44	–3.80	2.38
2001	–5.86	3.42	–7.79	7.00	–3.93

Trailing	Total Return%	+/– S&P 500	+/– LB Agg	% Rank All	% Rank Cat	Growth of $10,000
3 Mo	7.00	–3.68	6.97	56	34	10,700
6 Mo	–1.33	4.23	–5.98	44	42	9,867
1 Yr	–3.93	7.95	–12.35	49	47	9,607
3 Yr Avg	3.77	4.79	–2.51	44	31	11,173
5 Yr Avg	9.66	–1.04	2.24	20	18	15,860
10 Yr Avg	10.62	–2.31	3.39	29	23	27,426
15 Yr Avg	—	—	—	—	—	—

Tax Analysis	Tax-Adj Ret%	%Rank Cat	%Pretax Ret	%Rank Cat
3 Yr Avg	1.44	37	38.3	72
5 Yr Avg	6.58	24	68.1	52
10 Yr Avg	8.02	22	75.6	30

Potential Capital Gain Exposure: 3% of assets

Risk Analysis

Time Period	Load-Adj Return %	Risk %Rank[1] All	Risk %Rank[1] Cat	Morningstar Return	Morningstar Risk	Morningstar Risk-Adj Rating
1 Yr	–3.93					
3 Yr	3.77	40	49	–0.25[2]	0.53	★★★
5 Yr	9.66	43	47	1.11[2]	0.54	★★★★
10 Yr	10.62	49	46	0.84	0.55	★★★

Average Historical Rating (121 months): 3.9★s

[1]1=low, 100=high [2] T-Bill return substituted for category avg.

Category Rating (3 Yr)

1 2 3 4 5
Worst Best

Return Above Avg
Risk Average

Other Measures	Standard Index S&P 500	Best Fit Index MSCIACWdFr
Alpha	1.9	4.2
Beta	0.55	0.59
R-Squared	85	87

Standard Deviation	10.42
Mean	3.77
Sharpe Ratio	–0.13

Analysis by Scott Cooley 09-08-01

Fidelity Asset Manager Fund's recent middling returns aren't much cause for concern.

With a 7.4% loss for the year to date through Sept. 7, 2001, this fund lands smack-dab in the middle of the domestic-hybrid pack. So far in 2001, funds with small equity stakes, pronounced value tilts, or smaller-cap biases have produced the category's best returns. This fund has none of those. Charles Mangum, who has run the fund's equity subportfolio since February, is more of a growth-at-a-reasonable-price than a value investor, and he places most of his bets on large-cap issues. Lead manager Dick Habermann, who sets the fund's asset allocations, typically keeps the portfolio's stock weight near 50%, and in fact, this summer, he ramped it up to a bullish 58.7%, according to Fidelity. In the short term, at least, that moves looks like a loser.

But this fund still has a lot to recommend it. Over the past few years, Mangum has built one of the large-cap world's best records at Fidelity Dividend Growth. Even here in 2001, Mangum has made enough good picks like Cardinal Health and Microsoft to keep the fund's returns competitive. There's also little reason for concern about the fund's mostly high-quality bond portfolio. Fidelity has shown an ability to add value at its bond funds by emphasizing individual issue selection over interest-rate bets. And while Habermann's recent decision to boost the fund's stock weighting has backfired, to some extent, he keeps those wagers small, so they are unlikely to harm returns too much.

With moderate costs and prudent management, the fund's longer-term record is pretty solid. Over the past five years, a period that roughly coincides with Habermann's tenure, the fund has beaten more than 80% of its rivals. The fund isn't having a great 2001, but we think it's still a terrific core holding.

Portfolio Analysis 09-30-01

Total Stocks: 148 Share change since 03-01	Sector	PE Ratio	YTD Return %	% Net Assets
⊕ S&P 500 Index (Fut)	N/A	—	—	7.64
⊕ Cardinal Health	Health	35.1	–2.51	3.51
⊕ Bristol-Myers Squibb	Health	20.2	–26.00	2.87
⊕ Clear Channel Comms	Services	—	5.10	2.30
⊕ Citigroup	Financials	20.0	0.03	1.93
⊕ Conoco Cl B	Energy	—	—	1.65
⊖ General Elec	Industrials	30.1	–15.00	1.63
⊕ Microsoft	Technology	57.6	52.78	1.58
⊖ Schering-Plough	Health	22.2	–35.90	1.25
⊕ Philip Morris	Staples	12.1	9.12	1.22

Total Fixed-Income: 537	Date of Maturity	Amount $000	Value $000	% Net Assets
FNMA 6.5%	05-01-23	348	346,561	3.10
FNMA 7%	06-01-22	200	174,386	1.56
FNMA 7.5%	02-01-22	14	142,725	1.28
FNMA 6%	11-01-23	247	126,583	1.13
US Treasury Bond 8.125%	08-15-19	65,920	86,592	0.78
GNMA 6.5%	12-15-23	110	65,185	0.58
US Treasury Bond 11.75%	02-15-10	42,750	53,665	0.48
US Treasury Bond 5.25%	02-15-29	48,200	46,528	0.42
US Treasury Bond 6.875%	08-15-25	38,900	46,060	0.41
FHLMC 7.5%	08-01-26	674	44,459	0.40

Equity Style
Style: Blend
Size: Large-Cap

	Portfolio Avg	Rel S&P
Price/Earnings Ratio	28.4	0.92
Price/Book Ratio	5.4	0.94
Price/Cash Flow	20.6	1.14
3 Yr Earnings Growth	17.7	1.21
1 Yr Earnings Est%	–3.5	1.99
Debt % Total Cap	31.1[1]	1.01
Med Mkt Cap $mil	49,419	0.81

[1]figure is based on 50% or less of stocks

Fixed-Income Style
Duration: —
Quality: —
NA

Avg Eff Duration	—
Avg Eff Maturity	—
Avg Credit Quality	—
Avg Wtd Coupon	7.39%

Special Securities % assets 09-30-01	
Restricted/Illiquid Secs	4
Emerging-Markets Secs	1
Options/Futures/Warrants	Yes

Composition % of assets 09-30-01	
Cash	11.7
Stocks*	45.3
Bonds	34.4
Other	8.7
*Foreign (% of stocks)	0.9

Market Cap	
Giant	52.5
Large	35.9
Medium	11.2
Small	0.1
Micro	0.3

Sector Weightings	% of Stocks	Rel S&P	5-Year High	5-Year Low
Utilities	0.0	0.0	9	0
Energy	5.6	0.8	12	5
Financials	23.7	1.3	26	11
Industrials	9.2	0.8	29	7
Durables	0.9	0.6	13	1
Staples	6.8	0.9	10	2
Services	15.7	1.4	18	8
Retail	3.7	0.6	11	3
Health	19.3	1.3	19	3
Technology	15.1	0.8	34	4

Address:	82 Devonshire Street Boston, MA 02109 800–544–8888
Web Address:	www.fidelity.com
Inception:	12-28-88
Advisor:	Fidelity Mgmt. & Research
Subadvisor:	FMR (U.K.)/FMR (Far East)
NTF Plans:	Fidelity , Fidelity Inst.

Minimum Purchase:	$2500	Add: $250 IRA: $500
Min Auto Inv Plan:	$2500	Add: $100
Sales Fees:	No-load	
Management Fee:	.25%+.52% mx./.27% mn.(G)	
Actual Fees:	Mgt: 0.53%	Dist: —
Expense Projections:	3Yr: $240	5Yr: $417 10Yr: $930
Avg Brok Commission:	—	Income Distrib: Quarterly
Total Cost (relative to category):		Low

Fidelity Asset Manager: Growth

Ticker	Load	NAV	Yield	Total Assets	Mstar Category
FASGX	None	$14.34	2.9%	$4,234.2 mil	Large Blend

Prospectus Objective: Multiasset—Global

Fidelity Asset Manager: Growth seeks total return.

The fund allocates assets among domestic and foreign stocks, bonds, and short-term instruments. Management considers a neutral asset mix to consist of roughly 70% stocks, 25% bonds, and 5% short-term instruments. Management regularly reviews asset allocations and reallocations are gradual; a single reallocation does not involve more than 20% of assets. It may invest up to 35% of assets in debt securities rated below investment-grade. The fund may engage in various options and futures strategies.

Historical Profile

Return Average
Risk Below Avg
Rating ★★★ Neutral

Investment Style Equity — Average Stock %: 66% (1996), 73% (1997), 70% (1998), 71% (1999), 69% (2000), 65% (12-01)

▼ Manager Change
▽ Partial Manager Change

Fund Performance vs. Category Average
Quarterly Fund Return +/– Category Average
– Category Baseline

Performance Quartile (within Category)

Portfolio Manager(s)

Dick Habermann, et al. Since 3-96. BA'62 Yale U.; MBA'68 Harvard U.

1990	1991	1992	1993	1994	1995	1996	1997	1998	1999	2000	12–01	History
—	10.00	11.77	14.25	12.84	15.17	16.35	18.48	18.68	19.67	15.91	14.34	NAV
—	—	20.03	26.32	–7.39	19.95	17.59	26.46	18.08	13.97	–3.55	–7.22	Total Return %
—	–0.72*	12.41	16.26	–8.70	–17.58	–5.36	–6.89	–10.50	–7.07	5.56	4.66	+/– S&P 500
—	—	12.38	16.48	–7.84	–17.65	–4.58	–6.56	–10.56	–7.86	7.41	5.55	+/– Wilshire Top 750
—	0.00	1.50	0.76	1.33	1.79	2.83	2.45	1.89	2.41	2.34	2.64	Income Return %
—	0.00	18.53	25.55	–8.72	18.16	14.75	24.01	16.18	11.56	–5.89	–9.86	Capital Return %
—	—	3	3	93	96	78	65	74	81	28	9	Total Rtn % Rank Cat
—	0.00	0.15	0.09	0.19	0.23	0.43	0.40	0.35	0.45	0.46	0.42	Income $
—	0.00	0.08	0.51	0.17	0.00	1.07	1.75	2.68	1.10	2.56	0.00	Capital Gains $
—	—	1.64	1.19	1.15	1.02	1.01	0.86	0.80	0.80	0.77	—	Expense Ratio %
—	—	3.50	3.02	2.64	3.16	2.51	2.36	2.49	2.38	2.46	—	Income Ratio %
—	—	693	97	104	119	138	70	150	101	197	—	Turnover Rate %
—	9.0	236.7	1,795.0	2,852.9	2,894.6	3,377.8	4,662.9	5,119.9	5,490.4	4,826.8	4,234.2	Net Assets $mil

Performance 12-31-01

	1st Qtr	2nd Qtr	3rd Qtr	4th Qtr	Total
1997	0.18	13.74	7.19	3.54	26.46
1998	9.52	1.19	–8.20	16.07	18.08
1999	4.02	2.57	–4.42	11.75	13.97
2000	2.24	–1.34	2.47	–6.68	–3.55
2001	–8.99	4.77	–11.14	9.51	–7.22

Trailing	Total Return%	+/– S&P 500	+/– Wil Top 750	% Rank All	% Rank Cat	Growth of $10,000
3 Mo	9.51	–1.18	–1.81	45	76	10,951
6 Mo	–2.69	2.86	3.10	50	8	9,731
1 Yr	–7.22	4.66	5.55	55	9	9,278
3 Yr Avg	0.66	1.68	2.48	70	29	10,199
5 Yr Avg	8.78	–1.92	–1.34	25	59	15,230
10 Yr Avg	11.67	–1.26	–0.78	21	50	30,164
15 Yr Avg	—	—	—	—	—	—

Tax Analysis	Tax-Adj Ret%	%Rank Cat	%Pretax Ret	%Rank Cat
3 Yr Avg	–1.72	42	—	—
5 Yr Avg	5.83	68	66.4	84
10 Yr Avg	9.43	51	80.8	46

Potential Capital Gain Exposure: –13% of assets

Risk Analysis

Time Period	Load-Adj Return %	Risk %Rank[1] All	Risk %Rank[1] Cat	Morningstar Return	Morningstar Risk	Morningstar Risk-Adj Rating
1 Yr	–7.22					
3 Yr	0.66	53	9	–0.87[2]	0.74	★★★
5 Yr	8.78	52	7	0.88[2]	0.72	★★★
10 Yr	11.67	58	5	1.04	0.75	★★★

Average Historical Rating (85 months): 3.0★s

[1] 1=low, 100=high [2] T–Bill return substituted for category avg.

Category Rating (3 Yr)

1 2 3 4 5
Worst Best

Return Above Avg
Risk Low

Other Measures	Standard Index S&P 500	Best Fit Index S&P 500
Alpha	0.1	0.1
Beta	0.76	0.76
R–Squared	87	87
Standard Deviation		13.79
Mean		0.66
Sharpe Ratio		–0.36

Analysis by Scott Cooley 10-22-01

Fidelity Asset Manager: Growth could be having an even better year, but our enthusiasm for it remains undiminished.

Despite this fund's top-decile return for the year to date through Oct. 19, 2001, it could have performed better. Lead manager Dick Habermann pushed the fund's equity stake to about 75% early in the third quarter, in the belief that Federal Reserve easings would give the economy and the market a lift. Stocks continued to fall, however, so the fund would have been better off with its neutral equity allocation of 70%. Still, because the fund's combined bond and cash stake totaled 25% of assets, it held up much better than its typical peer during the quarter, falling 4 percentage points less than the group average.

The fund still boasts significant long-term advantages over its peers, too. Charles Mangum, who runs the equity subportfolio of the fund, has built an outstanding longer-term record at Fidelity Dividend Growth. His stock-picking this year has been characteristically solid. He built relatively little exposure to mega-cap issues, which have faltered, and several of his picks, including Cardinal Health and Computer Associates International, have registered solid gains—no mean feat in this market environment. We typically aren't fans of asset-allocation bets, but there's no question that Habermann has gotten most of them right over the years, consistently overweighting equities during the late-1990s bull market. And the fund's substantial bond and cash holdings give it an above-average yield.

This clearly isn't an appropriate holding for an investor seeking pure-stock exposure—the fund will likely lag the group in a bull market—but Mangum's record elsewhere suggests this offering will deliver competitive risk-adjusted returns.

Portfolio Analysis 09-30-01

Share change since 03–01 Total Stocks: 148	Sector	PE	YTD Ret%	% Assets
⊕ Cardinal Health	Health	35.1	–2.51	4.81
⊕ Bristol–Myers Squibb	Health	20.2	–26.00	3.93
⊕ S&P 500 Index (Fut)	N/A	—	—	3.70
⊕ Clear Channel Comms	Services	—	5.10	3.17
⊕ Citigroup	Financials	20.0	0.03	2.64
⊕ Conoco Cl B	Energy	—	—	2.26
⊖ General Elec	Industrials	30.1	–15.00	2.24
⊕ Microsoft	Technology	57.6	52.78	2.16
⊖ Schering–Plough	Health	22.2	–35.90	1.77
⊕ Philip Morris	Staples	12.1	9.12	1.73
⊖ Freddie Mac	Financials	14.0	–3.87	1.49
⊖ Fannie Mae	Financials	16.2	–6.95	1.49
⊖ PNC Finl Svcs Grp	Financials	13.5	–20.70	1.42
⊕ Verizon Comms	Services	29.7	–2.52	1.15
FNMA 6.5%	N/A	—	—	1.03
⊕ BellSouth	Services	24.9	–5.09	0.98
⊕ American Intl Grp	Financials	42.0	–19.20	0.93
⊕ Dell Comp	Technology	61.8	55.87	0.92
⊕ J.P. Morgan Chase & Co.	Financials	27.8	–17.40	0.89
⊕ AT&T	Services	7.8	40.59	0.86
⊖ SBC Comms	Services	18.4	–16.00	0.84
⊕ Coca–Cola	Staples	35.5	–21.40	0.83
⊕ Cisco Sys	Technology	—	–52.60	0.78
⊕ American Express	Financials	28.3	–34.40	0.75
⊕ Household Intl	Financials	14.7	6.89	0.73

Current Investment Style

Style: Value Blnd Growth; Size: Large Med Small

	Stock Port Avg	Relative S&P 500 Current	Relative S&P 500 Hist	Rel Cat
Price/Earnings Ratio	28.4	0.92	1.03	0.94
Price/Book Ratio	5.4	0.94	1.07	0.98
Price/Cash Flow	20.5	1.14	1.03	1.11
3 Yr Earnings Growth	17.7	1.21	1.27	0.99
1 Yr Earnings Est%	–3.6	2.01	—	—
Med Mkt Cap $mil	49,095	0.8	1.0	0.94

[1] figure is based on 50% or less of stocks

Special Securities % assets 09-30-01	
Restricted/Illiquid Secs	3
Emerging–Markets Secs	Trace
Options/Futures/Warrants	Yes

Composition % assets 09-30-01	
Cash	6.6
Stocks*	65.5
Bonds	22.1
Other	5.7
*Foreign (% stocks)	1.0

Market Cap	
Giant	52.4
Large	36.0
Medium	11.3
Small	0.1
Micro	0.3

Sector Weightings	% of Stocks	Rel S&P	5-Year High	5-Year Low
Utilities	0.0	0.0	11	0
Energy	5.6	0.8	16	3
Financials	23.7	1.3	26	11
Industrials	9.2	0.8	20	5
Durables	0.9	0.6	12	1
Staples	6.9	0.9	11	2
Services	15.6	1.4	17	3
Retail	3.7	0.6	13	3
Health	19.2	1.3	19	3
Technology	15.1	0.8	39	8

Address:	82 Devonshire Street Boston, MA 02109 800–544–8888
Web Address:	www.fidelity.com
*Inception:	12-30-91
Advisor:	Fidelity Mgmt. & Research
Subadvisor:	FMR (U.K.)/FMR (Far East)
NTF Plans:	Fidelity , Fidelity Inst.

Minimum Purchase:	$2500	Add: $250 IRA: $500
Min Auto Inv Plan:	$2500	Add: $100
Sales Fees:	No–load	
Management Fee:	.30%+.52% mx./.27% mn.(G)	
Actual Fees:	Mgt: 0.58%	Dist: —
Expense Projections:	3Yr: $265	5Yr: $460 10Yr: $1025
Avg Brok Commission:	—	Income Distrib: Annually
Total Cost (relative to category):		Below Avg

Fidelity Balanced

Ticker	Load	NAV	Yield	Total Assets	Mstar Category
FBALX	None	$14.90	3.0%	$7,005.1 mil	Domestic Hybrid

Prospectus Objective: Balanced

Fidelity Balanced Fund seeks income consistent with preservation of capital.

The fund invests in a broadly diversified portfolio of high-yielding securities, including common and preferred stocks, and bonds. It usually invests at least 25% of assets in fixed-income senior securities rated BBB or higher. The fund may write covered call options and buy put options.

Historical Profile
Return Above Avg
Risk Low
Rating ★★★★ Above Avg

Investment Style
Equity
Average Stock %: 48% 59% 55% 62% 56% 55%

▼ Manager Change
▽ Partial Manager Change

Fund Performance vs. Category Average
Quarterly Fund Return +/– Category Average
— Category Baseline

Performance Quartile (within Category)

Portfolio Manager(s)

Kevin E. Grant, CFA. Since 2-97. BA'82 U. of Hartford; MBA'86 U. of Hartford. Other funds currently managed: Fidelity Investment Grade Bond, Fidelity Puritan, Fidelity Spartan Investment Gr Bond.

Robert D. Ewing, CFA. Since 2-00. BS Boston C.

1990	1991	1992	1993	1994	1995	1996	1997	1998	1999	2000	12-01	History
10.63	12.35	12.29	13.39	12.29	13.52	14.08	15.27	16.36	15.36	15.19	14.90	NAV
–0.47	26.78	7.95	19.28	–5.31	14.90	9.34	23.45	20.22	8.86	5.32	2.25	Total Return %
2.65	–3.70	0.33	9.22	–6.63	–22.63	–13.61	–9.90	–8.36	–12.18	14.42	14.12	+/– S&P 500
–9.42	10.78	0.54	9.53	–2.40	–3.57	5.72	13.76	11.54	9.69	–6.31	–6.18	+/– LB Aggregate
6.12	5.79	5.49	5.01	3.02	4.72	4.90	4.07	3.10	2.94	3.18	3.00	Income Return %
–6.58	20.99	2.46	14.27	–8.34	10.19	4.44	19.37	17.12	5.92	2.14	–0.76	Capital Return %
54	29	47	9	81	95	83	14	14	54	29	13	Total Rtn % Rank Cat
0.68	0.60	0.66	0.60	0.40	0.57	0.65	0.56	0.46	0.46	0.48	0.45	Income $
0.00	0.45	0.36	0.64	0.00	0.00	0.00	1.46	1.27	1.98	0.49	0.17	Capital Gains $
0.97	0.98	0.96	0.93	1.01	0.90	0.79	0.74	0.67	0.65	0.67	—	Expense Ratio %
6.74	5.93	5.68	5.07	4.09	5.33	4.12	3.58	2.97	2.67	2.98	—	Income Ratio %
223	238	242	162	157	269	247	70	135	157	139	—	Turnover Rate %
293.1	725.2	1,754.5	4,684.5	4,999.1	4,880.1	3,919.2	4,283.9	5,316.4	6,122.6	6,096.0	7,005.1	Net Assets $mil

Performance 12-31-01

	1st Qtr	2nd Qtr	3rd Qtr	4th Qtr	Total
1997	1.23	11.29	7.82	1.63	23.45
1998	9.00	2.31	–4.37	12.73	20.22
1999	5.26	4.86	–4.35	3.11	8.86
2000	2.25	–0.97	2.96	1.01	5.32
2001	–2.13	4.87	–6.83	6.92	2.25

Trailing	Total Return%	+/– S&P 500	+/– LB Agg	% Rank All	% Rank Cat	Growth of $10,000
3 Mo	6.92	–3.76	6.89	56	36	10,692
6 Mo	–0.38	5.18	–5.03	40	27	9,962
1 Yr	2.25	14.12	–6.18	39	13	10,225
3 Yr Avg	5.44	6.47	–0.83	27	16	11,723
5 Yr Avg	11.71	1.01	4.28	11	6	17,397
10 Yr Avg	10.30	–2.63	3.07	31	31	26,646
15 Yr Avg	10.95	–2.78	2.83	34	22	47,521

Tax Analysis	Tax-Adj Ret%	%Rank Cat	%Pretax Ret	%Rank Cat
3 Yr Avg	2.71	23	49.8	56
5 Yr Avg	8.46	9	72.2	33
10 Yr Avg	7.51	36	72.9	45

Potential Capital Gain Exposure: 4% of assets

Risk Analysis

Time Period	Load-Adj Return %	Risk %Rank[1] All	Risk %Rank[1] Cat	Morningstar Return	Morningstar Risk	Morningstar Risk-Adj Rating
1 Yr	2.25					
3 Yr	5.44	36	25	0.11[2]	0.44	★★★★
5 Yr	11.71	40	25	1.66[2]	0.46	★★★★
10 Yr	10.30	47	28	0.78	0.51	★★★

Average Historical Rating (146 months): 3.7★s

[1] 1=low, 100=high [2] T-Bill return substituted for category avg.

Category Rating (3 Yr)

1 Worst ... 5 Best (rating: 4)

Return Above Avg
Risk Below Avg

Other Measures	Standard Index S&P 500	Best Fit Index S&P 500
Alpha	3.1	3.1
Beta	0.50	0.50
R-Squared	81	81
Standard Deviation		9.69
Mean		5.44
Sharpe Ratio		0.06

Portfolio Analysis 07-31-01

Total Stocks: 199 Share change since 01-01	Sector	PE Ratio	YTD Return %	% Net Assets
⊕ ExxonMobil	Energy	15.3	–7.59	1.53
⊖ Bristol-Myers Squibb	Health	20.2	–26.00	1.32
⊕ Citigroup	Financials	20.0	0.03	1.31
⊕ Bank of America	Financials	16.7	42.73	1.17
⊖ Freddie Mac	Financials	14.0	–3.87	1.17
⊕ Philip Morris	Staples	12.1	9.12	1.09
⊕ Microsoft	Technology	57.6	52.78	0.86
⊕ American Intl Grp	Financials	42.0	–19.20	0.83
⊕ BellSouth	Services	24.9	–5.09	0.80
⊕ PNC Finl Svcs Grp	Financials	13.5	–20.70	0.77

Total Fixed-Income: 468	Date of Maturity	Amount $000	Value $000	% Net Assets
FNMA 6.5%	01-01-24	1,519	373,476	5.44
FNMA N/A	08-01-31	210,280	209,196	3.05
GNMA 6.5%	06-15-29	508	154,142	2.25
US Treasury Note N/A	06-30-03	110,115	110,304	1.61
US Treasury Note 7%	07-15-06	85,340	94,261	1.37
FNMA 6%	12-01-23	3,379	74,923	1.09
FNMA 7.5%	04-01-27	19	73,646	1.07
FNMA 7%	12-01-08	21	73,042	1.06
GNMA 7%	12-15-25	551	69,257	1.01
US Treasury Bond 11.25%	02-15-15	41,000	63,999	0.93

Equity Style
Style: Value
Size: Large-Cap

	Portfolio Avg	Rel S&P
Price/Earnings Ratio	28.0	0.91
Price/Book Ratio	4.4	0.78
Price/Cash Flow	14.7	0.82
3 Yr Earnings Growth	13.4	0.92
1 Yr Earnings Est%	–8.5	4.82
Debt % Total Cap	34.2	1.11
Med Mkt Cap $mil	28,925	0.48

Fixed-Income Style
Duration: —
Quality: —
NA

Avg Eff Duration	—
Avg Eff Maturity	—
Avg Credit Quality	—
Avg Wtd Coupon	7.14%

Special Securities % assets 07-31-01	
Restricted/Illiquid Secs	3
Emerging-Markets Secs	Trace
Options/Futures/Warrants	Yes

Composition % of assets 07-31-01	
Cash	7.6
Stocks*	53.9
Bonds	38.3
Other	0.3
*Foreign (% of stocks)	1.5

Market Cap	
Giant	37.7
Large	36.1
Medium	23.6
Small	2.5
Micro	0.0

Sector Weightings	% of Stocks	Rel S&P	5-Year High	5-Year Low
Utilities	1.3	0.4	7	0
Energy	7.2	1.0	34	6
Financials	23.2	1.3	36	3
Industrials	12.7	1.1	64	8
Durables	4.4	2.8	11	1
Staples	7.0	0.9	8	0
Services	17.8	1.6	29	1
Retail	5.5	0.8	11	0
Health	8.9	0.6	10	0
Technology	12.3	0.7	17	0

Analysis by Catherine Hickey 11-28-01

This fund continues to prove that boring can be beautiful.

Fidelity Balanced Fund plays the straight-and-narrow course. Its asset allocation rarely deviates from a 60/40 split between stocks and bonds. The fund avoids big bets with its bond stake, and equity-portfolio manager Bob Ewing also uses a fairly cautious style on the stock side. His strategy rides the line between value and growth-at-a-reasonable-price, as he focuses on solidly profitable companies that are trading cheaply relative to industry peers.

Ewing says that lately he is emphasizing valuations even more than usual. Growth stocks have snapped back sharply since the September terrorist attacks, and Ewing believes that, absent improved earnings news, many of these issues are fairly valued. Thus, he has cut tech names and put more money into economically sensitive stocks like industrials, which are trading more cheaply and will benefit from an economic recovery. Ewing has also added marginally to gaming and lodging issues in recent months.

Ewing has only been on board here since March 2000, when he took the reins from Stephen DuFour. DuFour racked up a strong record, but the fund hasn't skipped a beat under Ewing's watch. It notched a solid return in 2000, and its tiny gain for the year to date through Nov. 27, 2001, is good enough to place in the domestic-hybrid group's top quartile. Its value-leaning stock portfolio, as well as its high overall credit quality on the bond side, has worked to its favor so far this year.

In a growth rally, this fund may not look that hot; its so-so performance over the last three months shows that it can lag when the Nasdaq snaps back. However, hybrid funds are built for stability, not flashy returns. So far, solid results and moderate volatility are just what Ewing has delivered.

Address:	82 Devonshire Street Boston, MA 02109 800–544–8888
Web Address:	www.fidelity.com
Inception:	11-06-86
Advisor:	Fidelity Mgmt. & Research
Subadvisor:	FMR (Far East)/FMR (U.K.)
NTF Plans:	Fidelity , Fidelity Inst.

Minimum Purchase:	$2500	Add: $250 IRA: $500
Min Auto Inv Plan:	$2500	Add: $100
Sales Fees:	No-load	
Management Fee:	.15%+.52% mx./.27% mn.(G)	
Actual Fees:	Mgt: 0.44%	Dist: —
Expense Projections:	3Yr: $218	5Yr: $379 10Yr: $847
Avg Brok Commission:	—	Income Distrib: Quarterly
Total Cost (relative to category):	Low	

Fidelity Blue Chip Growth

Ticker	Load	NAV	Yield	Total Assets	Mstar Category
FBGRX	None	$42.94	0.1%	$21,958.6 mil	Large Growth

Prospectus Objective: Growth

Fidelity Blue Chip Growth Fund seeks long-term capital appreciation.

The fund normally invests at least 65% of assets in common stocks issued by blue-chip companies. It defines these as companies with market capitalizations of at least $200 million, if the company's stock is included in the S&P 500 or the Dow Jones Industrial Average, or $1 billion if not included in either index. Management selects companies that it expects to achieve high long-term earnings growth.

Historical Profile

Return	Average
Risk	Average
Rating	★★★ Neutral

Investment Style
Equity
Average Stock %: 85% 97% 96% 96% 97% 97%

▼ Manager Change
▽ Partial Manager Change

Fund Performance vs. Category Average
■ Quarterly Fund Return +/– Category Average
— Category Baseline

Performance Quartile (within Category)

Portfolio Manager(s)

John McDowell, CFA. Since 3-96. BA'80 Williams C.; MBA'85 Harvard U. Other funds currently managed: MassMutual Instl Blue Chip Growth S, MassMutual Instl Blue Chip Growth Y, MassMutual Instl Blue Chip Growth L.

1990	1991	1992	1993	1994	1995	1996	1997	1998	1999	2000	12-01	History
14.43	22.25	22.83	24.17	25.95	30.77	32.69	39.46	50.39	60.11	51.53	42.94	NAV
3.50	54.81	6.17	24.50	9.85	28.38	15.38	27.02	34.76	24.26	–10.54	–16.55	Total Return %
6.62	24.33	–1.45	14.45	8.54	–9.16	–7.57	–6.33	6.18	3.22	–1.44	–4.68	+/– S&P 500
2.14	15.40	2.28	24.58	5.00	–10.28	–10.14	–6.72	–10.34	–5.42	13.98	3.95	+/– Russ Top 200 Grt
1.07	0.55	0.64	0.04	0.00	0.48	0.93	0.81	0.25	0.28	0.00	0.12	Income Return %
2.43	54.25	5.53	24.46	9.85	27.90	14.44	26.22	34.51	23.98	–10.54	–16.67	Capital Return %
13	25	52	6	1	73	77	43	41	81	31	25	Total Rtn % Rank Cat
0.15	0.08	0.14	0.01	0.00	0.12	0.28	0.26	0.10	0.14	0.00	0.06	Income $
0.00	0.00	0.62	4.12	0.58	2.47	2.25	1.75	2.06	2.07	2.52	0.00	Capital Gains $
1.26	1.26	1.27	1.25	1.22	1.02	0.95	0.78	0.70	0.70	0.86	0.87	Expense Ratio %
1.14	0.80	0.55	0.46	0.21	0.25	1.10	0.81	0.52	0.32	–0.02	0.01	Income Ratio %
68	99	71	319	271	182	206	51	49	38	40	46	Turnover Rate %
131.4	390.0	567.4	1,094.7	3,287.0	7,801.9	9,569.7	13,428.4	19,904.1	27,876.3	26,646.7	21,958.6	Net Assets $mil

Performance 12-31-01

	1st Qtr	2nd Qtr	3rd Qtr	4th Qtr	Total
1997	0.00	16.73	7.70	1.03	27.02
1998	13.99	4.22	–8.05	23.35	34.76
1999	5.72	2.57	–4.53	20.03	24.26
2000	5.82	–2.09	–1.51	–12.33	–10.54
2001	–16.67	8.29	–18.41	13.34	–16.55

Trailing	Total Return%	+/– S&P 500	+/– Russ Top 200 Grth	% Rank All	% Rank Cat	Growth of $10,000
3 Mo	13.34	2.66	0.48	28	54	11,334
6 Mo	–7.53	–1.97	–0.54	76	37	9,247
1 Yr	–16.55	–4.68	3.95	75	25	8,345
3 Yr Avg	–2.47	–1.45	5.55	85	49	9,276
5 Yr Avg	9.69	–1.01	1.10	20	37	15,878
10 Yr Avg	13.07	0.14	1.99	12	14	34,151
15 Yr Avg	—	—	—	—	—	—

Tax Analysis	Tax-Adj Ret%	%Rank Cat	%Pretax Ret	%Rank Cat
3 Yr Avg	–3.09	41	—	—
5 Yr Avg	8.65	28	89.3	19
10 Yr Avg	11.08	10	84.8	21

Potential Capital Gain Exposure: 14% of assets

Risk Analysis

Time Period	Load-Adj Return %	Risk %Rank[1] All	Risk %Rank[1] Cat	Morningstar Return	Morningstar Risk	Morningstar Risk-Adj Rating
1 Yr	–16.55					
3 Yr	–2.47	77	23	–1.46[2]	1.08	★★
5 Yr	9.69	74	16	1.11[2]	1.01	★★★
10 Yr	13.07	76	14	1.33	0.99	★★★★

Average Historical Rating (133 months): 4.8★s

[1]1=low, 100=high [2] T-Bill return substituted for category avg.

Category Rating (3 Yr)

1 2 3 4 5
Worst Best

Return	Average
Risk	Below Avg

Other Measures	Standard Index S&P 500	Best Fit Index MSCIACWdFr
Alpha	–0.4	4.1
Beta	1.11	1.19
R-Squared	89	89

Standard Deviation	19.83
Mean	–2.47
Sharpe Ratio	–0.44

Portfolio Analysis 07-31-01

Share change since 01-01 Total Stocks: 188	Sector	PE	YTD Ret%	% Assets
⊖ General Elec	Industrials	30.1	–15.00	5.24
⊕ Microsoft	Technology	57.6	52.78	4.68
⊕ Pfizer	Health	34.7	–12.40	4.08
⊕ Intel	Technology	73.1	4.89	3.47
⊕ AOL Time Warner	Technology	—	–7.76	2.86
⊕ Wal-Mart Stores	Retail	40.3	8.94	2.22
⊖ Bristol-Myers Squibb	Health	20.2	–26.00	1.87
⊖ Philip Morris	Staples	12.1	9.12	1.87
⊕ Citigroup	Financials	20.0	0.03	1.83
⊕ American Intl Grp	Financials	42.0	–19.20	1.76
⊖ IBM	Technology	26.9	43.00	1.66
⊕ Home Depot	Retail	42.9	12.07	1.57
⊖ Cisco Sys	Technology	—	–52.60	1.54
⊖ Merck	Health	19.1	–35.90	1.38
⊖ Freddie Mac	Financials	14.0	–3.87	1.37
⊕ Coca-Cola	Staples	35.5	–21.40	1.37
⊕ American Home Products	Health	—	–1.91	1.29
⊖ Fannie Mae	Financials	16.2	–6.95	1.27
⊕ Medtronic	Health	76.4	–14.70	1.13
⊕ ExxonMobil	Energy	15.3	–7.59	1.03
⊕ Chevron	Energy	10.3	9.29	1.02
⊖ Viacom Cl B	Services	—	—	1.01
⊕ Amgen	Health	52.8	–11.70	1.00
⊖ Omnicom Grp	Services	34.5	8.83	0.97
⊖ Dell Comp	Technology	61.8	55.87	0.95

Current Investment Style

Style: Value Blnd Growth; Size: Large Med Small

	Stock Port Avg	Relative S&P 500 Current	Relative S&P 500 Hist	Rel Cat
Price/Earnings Ratio	34.9	1.13	1.12	0.98
Price/Book Ratio	6.6	1.16	1.19	1.04
Price/Cash Flow	21.1	1.17	1.16	0.93
3 Yr Earnings Growth	17.7	1.21	1.14	0.82
1 Yr Earnings Est%	–3.0	1.70	—	–1.00
Med Mkt Cap $mil	72,317	1.2	1.0	1.53

Special Securities % assets 07-31-01	
Restricted/Illiquid Secs	0
Emerging-Markets Secs	Trace
Options/Futures/Warrants	No

Composition % assets 07-31-01	
Cash	2.6
Stocks*	97.4
Bonds	0.0
Other	0.0
*Foreign (% stocks)	1.9

Market Cap	
Giant	59.2
Large	29.2
Medium	11.5
Small	0.2
Micro	0.0

Sector Weightings	% of Stocks	Rel S&P	5-Year High	5-Year Low
Utilities	0.3	0.1	10	0
Energy	4.1	0.6	21	1
Financials	11.2	0.6	23	0
Industrials	10.6	0.9	29	8
Durables	0.6	0.4	16	0
Staples	8.3	1.1	17	0
Services	8.5	0.8	24	2
Retail	7.4	1.1	16	2
Health	19.2	1.3	27	3
Technology	29.9	1.6	41	4

Analysis by Scott Cooley 11-25-01

Moderation has been a virtue for Fidelity Blue Chip Growth Fund.

Although manager John McDowell likes companies with strong short- and long-term earnings growth, he isn't willing to pay just any price for them. Thus, the fund has consistently had a bit more of a conservative streak than its average large-growth peer. Not only has the fund's tech stake been lower than its average peer's—McDowell devoted just 20.2% of assets there on Sept. 30, according to Fidelity—but it tends to own steadier companies within the group. Indeed, issues such as Microsoft and IBM are featured prominently in the portfolio. Thus, during the technology bloodbath of 2000 and 2001, the fund has held up better than the typical large-growth fund. For the year to date through Nov. 23, the fund had lost 16.5%, leaving it ahead of three fourths of its rivals.

That said, McDowell modestly increased the portfolio's aggressiveness in the wake of the Sept. 11 terrorist attacks. For example, he said he has added to his holdings in several retailers, which got pummeled in the third quarter. McDowell thought they offered attractive valuations relative to their growth rates. And he has stuck with significant bets on two tech stocks, Microsoft and Intel, which were both among the fund's top-four holdings as of Sept. 30. McDowell says Microsoft should benefit from a product-upgrade cycle, as well as improved PC demand, while Intel has re-established "clear dominance" over top rival Advanced Micro Devices.

Although McDowell's strategy has a drawback—the fund tends to lag in tech-driven markets—he has capably executed it. The fund's five-year return tops nearly two thirds of its rivals', even though it got left in the dust in 1999, when go-go growth funds led the pack. This fund will likely get left behind again in the next big tech rally, but for moderate, large-growth exposure, it's tough to beat.

Address:	82 Devonshire Street Boston, MA 02109 800-544-8888
Web Address:	www.fidelity.com
Inception:	12-31-87
Advisor:	Fidelity Mgmt. & Research
Subadvisor:	FMR (U.K.)/FMR (Far East)
NTF Plans:	Fidelity Inst.

Minimum Purchase:	$2500	Add: $250 IRA: $500
Min Auto Inv Plan:	$2500	Add: $100
Sales Fees:	No-load	
Management Fee:	.30%+.52% mx./.27% mn.(G)+(–).20%P	
Actual Fees:	Mgt: 0.47%	Dist: —
Expense Projections:	3Yr: $227	5Yr: $395 10Yr: $883
Avg Brok Commission:	—	Income Distrib: Semi-Ann.
Total Cost (relative to category):	Low	

Fidelity Capital Appreciation

Ticker	Load	NAV	Yield	Total Assets	Mstar Category
FDCAX	None	$20.55	0.0%	$2,311.1 mil	Large Blend

Prospectus Objective: Aggressive Growth

Fidelity Capital Appreciation Fund seeks capital appreciation.

The fund invests primarily in domestic or foreign common stocks issued by well-known and established companies and by smaller, lesser-known companies. The fund seeks investment opportunities in companies involved in prospective acquisitions, reorganizations, spin-offs, consolidations, and liquidations. It does not maintain strict limitations on the amount that may be invested in foreign securities or in any one foreign country. The fund may use hedging techniques if market conditions warrant.

Historical Profile
Return Above Avg
Risk Above Avg
Rating ★★★★ Above Avg

Investment Style
Equity
Average Stock %: 90% 92% 96% 95% 95% 97% 94%

▼ Manager Change
▽ Partial Manager Change

Fund Performance vs. Category Average
■ Quarterly Fund Return +/– Category Average
— Category Baseline

Performance Quartile (within Category)

Portfolio Manager(s)

Harry Lange, CFA. Since 3-96. BS'75 General Motors Institute; MBA'83 Harvard U. Other funds currently managed: Fidelity Advisor Small Cap A, Fidelity Advisor Small Cap B, Fidelity Advisor Small Cap C.

History	1990	1991	1992	1993	1994	1995	1996	1997	1998	1999	2000	12-01
NAV	13.84	12.34	13.57	16.92	15.31	16.78	17.64	19.38	22.07	29.87	22.23	20.55
Total Return %	–15.69	9.99	16.37	33.41	2.52	18.77	15.12	26.52	16.95	45.84	–18.10	–7.56
+/– S&P 500	–12.57	–20.49	8.75	23.36	1.21	–18.77	–7.83	–6.83	–11.63	24.81	–9.00	4.32
+/– Wilshire Top 750	–11.66	–22.45	8.72	23.58	2.07	–18.84	–7.04	–6.51	–11.69	24.02	–7.14	5.21
Income Return %	1.02	4.48	1.46	0.74	1.03	2.61	0.72	0.45	0.52	2.58	0.50	0.00
Capital Return %	–16.71	5.51	14.91	32.68	1.49	16.16	14.40	26.06	16.43	43.26	–18.60	–7.56
Total Rtn % Rank Cat	97	100	8	1	13	98	91	64	78	3	97	10
Income $	0.17	0.62	0.18	0.10	0.17	0.40	0.12	0.08	0.10	0.57	0.15	0.00
Capital Gains $	0.01	2.13	0.60	1.06	1.85	1.00	1.54	2.85	0.45	1.49	2.13	0.00
Expense Ratio %	1.14	0.83	0.71	0.86	1.17	1.06	0.80	0.66	0.67	0.65	0.83	—
Income Ratio %	1.61	3.87	1.63	0.93	1.22	2.31	1.24	0.43	0.46	0.56	0.15	—
Turnover Rate %	56	72	99	120	124	87	205	176	121	78	85	—
Net Assets $mil	1,414.6	992.7	983.4	1,428.2	1,623.2	1,669.1	1,642.0	2,109.6	2,602.3	3,686.4	2,707.3	2,311.1

Performance 12-31-01

	1st Qtr	2nd Qtr	3rd Qtr	4th Qtr	Total
1997	–0.85	17.50	12.41	–3.39	26.52
1998	10.42	0.75	–15.77	24.81	16.95
1999	6.07	10.68	–4.32	29.84	45.84
2000	6.43	–9.34	–3.47	–12.07	–18.10
2001	–10.71	12.64	–21.38	16.89	–7.56

Trailing	Total Return%	+/– S&P 500	+/– Wil Top 750	% Rank All	% Rank Cat	Growth of $10,000
3 Mo	16.89	6.21	5.57	20	6	11,689
6 Mo	–8.09	–2.54	–2.30	78	82	9,191
1 Yr	–7.56	4.32	5.21	56	10	9,244
3 Yr Avg	3.36	4.38	5.18	50	14	11,042
5 Yr Avg	10.32	–0.38	0.20	17	33	16,337
10 Yr Avg	13.52	0.60	1.07	10	16	35,552
15 Yr Avg	13.71	–0.03	0.34	12	20	68,676

Tax Analysis	Tax-Adj Ret%	%Rank Cat	%Pretax Ret	%Rank Cat
3 Yr Avg	1.80	13	53.7	62
5 Yr Avg	8.17	40	79.2	59
10 Yr Avg	10.91	27	80.7	46

Potential Capital Gain Exposure: 10% of assets

Risk Analysis

Time Period	Load-Adj Return %	Risk %Rank[1] All	Risk %Rank[1] Cat	Morningstar Return	Morningstar Risk	Morningstar Risk-Adj Rating
1 Yr	–7.56					
3 Yr	3.36	85	96	–0.33[2]	1.28	★★★
5 Yr	10.32	84	98	1.28[2]	1.23	★★★
10 Yr	13.52	82	92	1.43	1.11	★★★★

Average Historical Rating (146 months): 3.2★s

[1] 1=low, 100=high [2] T-Bill return substituted for category avg.

Category Rating (3 Yr)

1 Worst 2 3 4 5 Best

Return Above Avg
Risk High

Other Measures	Standard Index S&P 500	Best Fit Index Wil 4500
Alpha	7.6	1.6
Beta	1.27	0.85
R-Squared	69	85

Standard Deviation	27.49
Mean	3.36
Sharpe Ratio	–0.07

Portfolio Analysis 04-30-01

Share change since 10-00 Total Stocks: 171

	Sector	PE	YTD Ret%	% Assets
⊖ Lennar	Industrials	8.8	29.32	3.72
☼ Philip Morris	Staples	12.1	9.12	3.46
☼ IBM	Technology	26.9	43.00	2.59
⊕ General Elec	Industrials	30.1	–15.00	2.52
☼ AT&T	Services	7.8	40.59	2.23
⊕ Tech Data	Technology	19.2	60.11	2.17
☼ Nokia Cl A ADR	Technology	45.8	–43.00	2.13
Daiwa Secs Grp	Financials	—	—	2.08
Nomura Secs	Financials	14.6	—	2.05
⊕ Fannie Mae	Financials	16.2	–6.95	1.94
⊖ Dell Comp	Technology	61.8	55.87	1.81
⊕ Microsoft	Technology	57.6	52.78	1.69
⊖ Noble Drilling	Energy	18.3	–21.60	1.68
⊕ Intel	Technology	73.1	4.89	1.65
⊕ Freddie Mac	Financials	14.0	–3.87	1.59
⊖ Equity Office Properties Tr	Financials	18.7	–1.76	1.53
⊕ Callaway Golf	Durables	19.3	4.30	1.53
⊕ Eli Lilly	Health	28.9	–14.40	1.47
⊖ Ensco Intl	Energy	15.7	–26.70	1.43
⊕ ALCOA	Industrials	21.4	7.86	1.43
⊕ BEA Sys	Technology	—	–77.10	1.41
☼ Bristol-Myers Squibb	Health	20.2	–26.00	1.35
⊖ KLA-Tencor	Technology	22.6	47.11	1.34
⊕ Praxair	Industrials	28.6	26.22	1.31
⊕ CIENA	Technology	NMF	–82.30	1.25

Current Investment Style

Style: Value Blnd Growth; Size: Large Med Small

	Stock Port Avg	Relative S&P 500 Current	Relative S&P 500 Hist	Rel Cat
Price/Earnings Ratio	28.4	0.92	1.08	0.94
Price/Book Ratio	4.6	0.80	0.87	0.83
Price/Cash Flow	16.3	0.91	0.99	0.88
3 Yr Earnings Growth	16.7	1.14	1.54	0.93
1 Yr Earnings Est%	–2.3	1.29	—	—
Med Mkt Cap $mil	10,633	0.2	0.3	0.20

Analysis by Scott Cooley 11-01-01

No one will accuse Harry Lange of being a closet indexer.

Although some Fidelity large-blend funds bear more than a passing resemblance to the S&P 500 index, this one does not. As of Sept. 30, 2001, its top-10 holdings included names such as homebuilder Lennar, technology-equipment wholesaler Tech Data, and online real-estate firm Homestore.com. More strikingly, the fund's tech weight stood at 30.4%, which is twice the S&P 500 index's exposure to the sector, according to Fidelity. Meanwhile, the fund's 2.8% energy stake was less than half the S&P 500's.

Changes in the tech stake have driven the fund's return in 2001. In March, Lange thought tech stocks had hit rock bottom, so he loaded up on the sector, pushing the portfolio's weight to 47%. Tech rallied sharply in April, and Lange sold into that strength. It appears that Lange did some buying again in September, and the fund has prospered during the past month's tech rebound. During October, the fund beat 96% of its large-blend peers, and for the year to date through Oct. 31, its 16.5% loss is better than more than 80% of its rivals'.

Lange's willingness to deviate from the pack has often paid off, but it does expose shareholders to considerable risks. For example, in 2000 a number of Lange's atypical picks, such as Tumbleweed Communications, posted enormous share-price declines. The fund consequently stumbled to a bottom-decile, 18.1% loss. If tech stocks were to tumble now, this fund would almost certainly lag its peers.

Over time, however, Lange has used this strategy to good effect, besting three fifths of his peers during the trailing five years. This fund bounces around too much to be considered a core holding, but it makes a nice addition to a well-diversified portfolio.

Special Securities % assets 04-30-01	
Restricted/Illiquid Secs	Trace
Emerging-Markets Secs	Trace
Options/Futures/Warrants	Yes

Composition % assets 04-30-01	
Cash	6.1
Stocks*	93.9
Bonds	0.0
Other	0.0
*Foreign (% stocks)	12.0

Market Cap	
Giant	31.0
Large	25.9
Medium	35.7
Small	7.0
Micro	0.5

Sector Weightings	% of Stocks	Rel S&P	5-Year High	5-Year Low
Utilities	0.3	0.1	34	0
Energy	5.6	0.8	21	0
Financials	15.5	0.9	31	8
Industrials	15.7	1.4	35	7
Durables	2.9	1.8	18	0
Staples	5.5	0.7	16	0
Services	12.3	1.1	36	12
Retail	1.4	0.2	13	0
Health	8.0	0.5	13	0
Technology	33.0	1.8	35	0

Address:	82 Devonshire Street Boston, MA 02109 800-544-8888
Web Address:	www.fidelity.com
Inception:	11-26-86
Advisor:	Fidelity Mgmt. & Research
Subadvisor:	FMR (U.K.)/FMR (Far East)
NTF Plans:	Fidelity , Fidelity Inst.

Minimum Purchase:	$2500	Add: $250 IRA: $500
Min Auto Inv Plan:	$2500	Add: $100
Sales Fees:	No-load	
Management Fee:	.30%+.52% mx./.27% mn.(G)+(–).20%P	
Actual Fees:	Mgt: 0.43%	Dist: —
Expense Projections:	3Yr: $214	5Yr: $373 10Yr: $835
Avg Brok Commission:	—	Income Distrib: Annually
Total Cost (relative to category):		Below Avg

Fidelity Contrafund

Ticker	Load	NAV	Yield	Total Assets	Mstar Category
FCNTX	3.00%	$42.77	0.5%	$32,320.9 mil	Large Blend

Prospectus Objective: Growth

Fidelity Contrafund seeks capital appreciation.

The fund invests primarily in common stocks and convertible securities that management judges to be undervalued. It may also invest in preferred stocks, warrants, and debt securities. Management seeks companies that are currently out of favor with the investing public and that may have favorable long-term outlooks because of termination of unprofitable operations; changes in management, industry, or products; or a possible merger or acquisition. The fund may invest up to 5% of assets in lower-quality debt obligations. It may also invest in foreign securities.

Historical Profile
Return: Above Avg
Risk: Average
Rating: ★★★★ Above Avg

Investment Style Equity

Average Stock %: 83% | 85% | 91% | 89% | 92% | 90% | 90%

▼ Manager Change
▽ Partial Manager Change

Fund Performance vs. Category Average
■ Quarterly Fund Return +/– Category Average
— Category Baseline

Performance Quartile (within Category)

Portfolio Manager(s)

William Danoff. Since 9-90. BA'82 Harvard U.; MBA'86 U. of Pennsylvania.

1990	1991	1992	1993	1994	1995	1996	1997	1998	1999	2000	12–01	History
17.35	25.60	27.47	30.84	30.28	38.02	42.15	46.63	56.81	60.02	49.18	42.77	NAV
3.94	54.92	15.89	21.43	–1.12	36.28	21.94	23.00	31.57	25.03	–6.80	–12.59	Total Return %
7.05	24.44	8.28	11.37	–2.44	–1.25	–1.01	–10.35	2.99	3.99	2.30	–0.71	+/– S&P 500
7.96	22.48	8.24	11.59	–1.57	–1.32	–0.23	–10.03	2.93	3.21	4.15	0.18	+/– Wilshire Top 750
0.54	0.63	0.80	0.66	0.00	0.30	1.05	0.84	0.64	0.50	0.41	0.45	Income Return %
3.40	54.28	15.09	20.76	–1.12	35.98	20.88	22.15	30.92	24.54	–7.21	–13.04	Capital Return %
8	3	9	7	59	28	43	82	9	26	41	47	Total Rtn % Rank Cat
0.09	0.11	0.20	0.18	0.00	0.09	0.38	0.35	0.30	0.28	0.24	0.22	Income $
0.00	1.06	1.92	2.25	0.22	3.13	3.45	4.56	4.22	10.22	6.62	0.00	Capital Gains $
1.06	0.89	0.87	1.06	1.00	0.96	0.79	0.67	0.61	0.62	0.84	—	Expense Ratio %
3.02	1.01	1.19	0.46	0.59	0.44	1.28	0.91	0.70	0.48	0.45	—	Income Ratio %
320	217	297	255	235	223	159	144	197	177	166	—	Turnover Rate %
332.1	1,002.4	1,958.3	6,193.3	8,682.4	14,831.7	23,797.9	30,808.5	38,821.3	46,927.0	40,284.8	32,320.9	Net Assets $mil

Performance 12-31-01

	1st Qtr	2nd Qtr	3rd Qtr	4th Qtr	Total
1997	–1.47	12.88	11.93	–1.20	23.00
1998	12.28	4.48	–9.36	23.73	31.57
1999	5.79	5.51	–4.66	17.50	25.03
2000	5.56	–6.58	1.13	–6.54	–6.80
2001	–13.18	3.47	–8.80	6.70	–12.59

Trailing	Total Return%	+/– S&P 500	+/– Wil Top 750	% Rank All	% Rank Cat	Growth of $10,000
3 Mo	6.70	–3.99	–4.62	57	95	10,670
6 Mo	–2.70	2.86	3.10	50	8	9,730
1 Yr	–12.59	–0.71	0.18	67	47	8,741
3 Yr Avg	0.62	1.64	2.44	70	29	10,186
5 Yr Avg	10.51	–0.19	0.39	16	26	16,483
10 Yr Avg	14.32	1.39	1.87	7	8	38,113
15 Yr Avg	16.92	3.19	3.55	2	1	104,298

Tax Analysis	Tax-Adj Ret%	%Rank Cat	%Pretax Ret	%Rank Cat
3 Yr Avg	–1.65	40	—	—
5 Yr Avg	7.93	44	75.4	69
10 Yr Avg	11.68	12	81.6	44

Potential Capital Gain Exposure: 4% of assets

Risk Analysis

Time Period	Load-Adj Return %	Risk %Rank[1] All	Risk %Rank[1] Cat	Morningstar Return	Morningstar Risk	Morningstar Risk-Adj Rating
1 Yr	–15.21					
3 Yr	–0.40	58	18	–1.08[2]	0.81	★★★
5 Yr	9.84	59	19	1.15[2]	0.81	★★★
10 Yr	13.97	64	17	1.53	0.83	★★★★

Average Historical Rating (193 months): 4.2★s

[1] 1=low, 100=high [2] T-Bill return substituted for category avg.

Category Rating (3 Yr)

1 2 3 4 5 — Worst … Best

Return: Above Avg
Risk: Below Avg

Other Measures	Standard Index S&P 500	Best Fit Index MSCIACWdFr
Alpha	–0.1	3.0
Beta	0.69	0.78
R-Squared	67	75

Standard Deviation	14.48
Mean	0.62
Sharpe Ratio	–0.35

Portfolio Analysis 06-30-01

Share change since 12–00 Total Stocks: 409	Sector	PE	YTD Ret%	% Assets
⊖ ExxonMobil	Energy	15.3	–7.59	2.75
⊕ Fannie Mae	Financials	16.2	–6.95	2.23
⊖ Pfizer	Health	34.7	–12.40	2.09
⊖ Berkshire Hathaway Cl A	Financials	—	—	2.06
⊕ Minnesota Mng & Mfg	Industrials	34.5	0.16	1.89
⊕ Colgate–Palmolive	Staples	31.1	–9.45	1.88
⊖ BP PLC ADR	Energy	14.4	–0.90	1.52
⊕ Household Intl	Financials	14.7	6.89	1.39
⊕ Avon Products	Staples	21.6	–1.21	1.35
⊖ American Intl Grp	Financials	42.0	–19.20	1.33
⊖ Metropolitan Life Ins	Financials	—	–8.82	1.31
⊕ Bank One	Financials	29.1	9.13	1.29
⊕ Alberta Energy	Energy	43.9	–20.80	1.27
⊕ Automatic Data Processing	Services	39.8	–6.27	1.16
⊕ PepsiCo	Staples	31.4	–0.54	1.09
☼ Microsoft	Technology	57.6	52.78	1.02
⊖ McDonald's	Services	19.2	–21.50	0.99
⊕ Lockheed Martin	Industrials	36.8	38.98	0.98
⊖ Elan ADR	Health	41.0	–3.74	0.92
⊖ CVS	Retail	16.2	–50.30	0.88
⊕ Allstate	Financials	17.1	–21.00	0.79
⊕ HCA – The Healthcare Company	Health	24.1	–12.20	0.75
⊖ Viacom Cl B	Services	—	—	0.71
⊕ First Data	Technology	38.1	49.08	0.71
⊕ Fifth Third Bancorp	Financials	38.3	4.53	0.69

Current Investment Style

Style: Value Blnd Growth; Size: Large Med Small

	Stock Port Avg	Relative S&P 500 Current	Relative S&P 500 Hist	Rel Cat
Price/Earnings Ratio	27.4	0.88	1.08	0.90
Price/Book Ratio	5.2	0.91	1.00	0.94
Price/Cash Flow	16.9	0.94	1.10	0.92
3 Yr Earnings Growth	13.9	0.95	1.01	0.78
1 Yr Earnings Est%	7.9	—	—	—
Med Mkt Cap $mil	18,539	0.3	0.4	0.35

Analysis by Christopher Traulsen 10-30-01

Fidelity Contrafund keeps beating the odds.

We recently moved this fund back to the large-blend category after it had briefly resided in the large-growth group. The move reflects the fact that over the past three years, the fund's portfolio has had more in common with a blend style than a pure growth style of investing. Indeed, its current valuations are all either in line with or below large-blend norms.

Manager Will Danoff's frugal side has been on full display this year. After riding technology stocks up in the late 1990s, Danoff cut the fund's tech stake sharply early in 2001, keeping it in the low single digits for most of the year. Instead, he has focused on defensive areas, adding consumer staples such as Avon Products. He's also continued to buy mid-caps, which he thinks offer attractive valuations. As of June 30, 30% of the fund was in mid-caps.

Danoff's bets have been on the mark: Tech has been awful and smaller-cap fare has outperformed large caps by a wide margin in 2001. The fund is down 16% for the year to date through Oct. 29, but that beats 75% of its peers. That's nothing new—the fund's longer-term returns also rank in the category's best quartile, and Danoff's tendency to spread the fund over hundreds of names has helped limit its volatility.

That success is hard-won, however. The fund's massive asset base means that Danoff's fast-trading style and attempts to buy mid-caps run up the fund's trading costs. Its big asset base also means that the fund can't turn on a dime. Thus, although Danoff still thinks tech is overvalued, it's going to take him a while to build the fund's weighting back up when he decides it's attractive. That could leave the fund high and dry in a tech rally.

But even though we wish Danoff's challenge was smaller, there's no denying that he's continued to deliver the goods. For investors seeking a core holding, his talents make this a solid choice.

Address:	82 Devonshire Street Boston, MA 02109 800–544–8888
Web Address:	www.fidelity.com
Inception:	05-17-67
Advisor:	Fidelity Mgmt. & Research
Subadvisor:	FMR (Far East)/FMR (U.K.)
NTF Plans:	Fidelity Inst.

Minimum Purchase:	$2500	Add: $250	IRA: $500
Min Auto Inv Plan:	$2500	Add: $250	
Sales Fees:	3.00%L		
Management Fee:	.30%+.52% mx./.27% mn.(G)+(–).20%P		
Actual Fees:	Mgt: 0.45%	Dist: —	
Expense Projections:	3Yr: $502	5Yr: $651	10Yr: $1086
Avg Brok Commission:	—	Income Distrib: Annually	
Total Cost (relative to category):		Below Avg	

Special Securities % assets 06-30-01	
Restricted/Illiquid Secs	0
Emerging–Markets Secs	Trace
Options/Futures/Warrants	No

Composition % assets 06-30-01	
Cash	8.5
Stocks*	90.2
Bonds	1.4
Other	0.0
*Foreign (% stocks)	18.9

Market Cap	
Giant	27.3
Large	39.6
Medium	29.5
Small	3.4
Micro	0.3

Sector Weightings	% of Stocks	Rel S&P	5-Year High	5-Year Low
Utilities	0.9	0.3	9	0
Energy	14.4	2.0	28	1
Financials	23.9	1.3	29	4
Industrials	10.4	0.9	25	5
Durables	3.6	2.3	11	1
Staples	10.3	1.3	10	1
Services	13.1	1.2	37	9
Retail	6.2	0.9	13	3
Health	12.3	0.8	22	2
Technology	5.1	0.3	39	4

Fidelity Contrafund II

Ticker	Load	NAV	Yield	Total Assets	Mstar Category
FCONX	3.00%	$10.35	0.4%	$1,031.7 mil	Large Blend

Prospectus Objective: Growth

Fidelity Contrafund II seeks capital appreciation.

The fund invests primarily in common stocks and securities convertible into common stocks issued by companies that management judges to be undervalued by the public. Types of companies the fund may purchase include those experiencing positive fundamental change, such as new management or a product launch; companies whose earnings potential has increased or is expected to increase; or companies that are undervalued in relation to securities of other companies in the same industry. The fund may invest in issuers regardless of market capitalization.

Historical Profile

Return Average
Risk Average
Rating ★★★
Neutral

Investment Style
Equity
Average Stock %: 94% (1998), 95% (1999), 97% (2000), 93% (12-01)

▼ Manager Change
▽ Partial Manager Change

Fund Performance vs. Category Average
■ Quarterly Fund Return +/– Category Average
— Category Baseline

Performance Quartile (within Category)

Portfolio Manager(s)

Adam Hetnarski. Since 2-00. Other funds currently managed: Fidelity Destiny II, Fidelity Destiny II N.

History

1990	1991	1992	1993	1994	1995	1996	1997	1998	1999	2000	12-01	History
—	—	—	—	—	—	—	—	11.14	14.91	11.49	10.35	NAV
—	—	—	—	—	—	—	—	11.40*	42.52	–8.35	–9.59	Total Return %
—	—	—	—	—	—	—	—	–0.79*	21.49	0.76	2.29	+/– S&P 500
—	—	—	—	—	—	—	—	—	20.70	2.61	3.18	+/– Wilshire Top 750
—	—	—	—	—	—	—	—	0.00	0.00	0.00	0.35	Income Return %
—	—	—	—	—	—	—	—	11.40	42.52	–8.35	–9.93	Capital Return %
—	—	—	—	—	—	—	—	—	4	49	17	Total Rtn % Rank Cat
—	—	—	—	—	—	—	—	0.00	0.00	0.00	0.04	Income $
—	—	—	—	—	—	—	—	0.00	0.72	2.45	0.00	Capital Gains $
—	—	—	—	—	—	—	—	1.23	0.87	0.86	0.91	Expense Ratio %
—	—	—	—	—	—	—	—	–0.28	–0.01	–0.08	0.19	Income Ratio %
—	—	—	—	—	—	—	—	141	293	291	168	Turnover Rate %
—	—	—	—	—	—	—	—	595.8	1,374.1	1,451.1	1,031.7	Net Assets $mil

Performance 12-31-01

	1st Qtr	2nd Qtr	3rd Qtr	4th Qtr	Total
1997	—	—	—	—	—
1998	—	3.60	–13.51	24.33	11.40*
1999	7.63	5.09	–5.85	33.84	42.52
2000	7.58	–1.25	0.35	–14.03	–8.35
2001	–11.23	11.37	–15.96	8.81	–9.59

Trailing	Total Return%	+/– S&P 500	+/– Wil Top 750	% Rank All	% Rank Cat	Growth of $10,000
3 Mo	8.81	–1.87	–2.51	48	83	10,881
6 Mo	–8.55	–3.00	–2.76	80	85	9,145
1 Yr	–9.59	2.29	3.18	60	17	9,041
3 Yr Avg	5.70	6.73	7.53	25	7	11,811
5 Yr Avg	—	—	—	—	—	—
10 Yr Avg	—	—	—	—	—	—
15 Yr Avg	—	—	—	—	—	—

Tax Analysis	Tax-Adj Ret%	%Rank Cat	%Pretax Ret	%Rank Cat
3 Yr Avg	2.94	10	51.6	65
5 Yr Avg	—	—	—	—
10 Yr Avg	—	—	—	—

Potential Capital Gain Exposure: –20% of assets

Risk Analysis

Time Period	Load-Adj Return %	Risk %Rank[1] All	Risk %Rank[1] Cat	Morningstar Return	Morningstar Risk	Morningstar Risk-Adj Rating
1 Yr	–12.30					
3 Yr	4.64	73	72	–0.07[2]	1.00	★★★
5 Yr	—	—	—	—	—	
Incept	6.71	—	—	—	—	

Average Historical Rating (10 months): 3.9★s

[1]1=low, 100=high [2] T-Bill return substituted for category avg.

Category Rating (3 Yr)

1 2 3 4 5
Worst Best

Return High
Risk Above Avg

Other Measures	Standard Index S&P 500	Best Fit Index MSCIACWdFr
Alpha	8.3	13.7
Beta	1.12	1.25
R-Squared	76	83
Standard Deviation		23.40
Mean		5.70
Sharpe Ratio		0.04

Analysis by Scott Cooley 10-27-01

Fidelity Contrafund II is again dusting the competition.

Although the fund's tech stake has been above the S&P 500's this year, that hasn't kept manager Adam Hetnarski from recording relatively strong returns. The fund entered the year with an enormous tech weight, but soon thereafter Hetnarski cut back on it, when he realized tech firms' operations wouldn't improve as quickly as he had hoped. While Hetnarski still devoted more to tech than most of his peers, he has emphasized the right areas, favoring PC-related stocks such as Dell Computer and Microsoft over networking companies, which have been especially hard-hit in the downturn. Hetnarski also steered clear of most financials with a lot of market sensitivity, which has been a plus this year.

Hetnarski said he had continued to tilt the fund away from telecom-equipment makers and toward PC-related companies. He reasons that the latter could benefit from an upgrade cycle, as many companies will need to replace computers purchased well in advance of Y2K. Meanwhile, he said the demise of many smaller telecom-service firms would depress infrastructure spending for some time, so telecom-equipment companies have only small weights in the portfolio. However, as small telecom-service providers go out of business, that should improve the pricing power of larger firms. By Sept. 30, Hetnarski had raised the fund's telecom-service stake to 9.5%, 3 percentage points above the weight of his S&P 500 benchmark.

For the year to date through Oct. 26, Hetnarski's moves have produced an 11% loss, beating the S&P 500 by more than 4 percentage points. In addition to putting up solid numbers during the recent bear market, Hetnarski also made hay in 1999, when he managed Fidelity Export & Multinational. He is clearly one of Fidelity's most-promising young managers.

Portfolio Analysis 06-30-01

Share change since 12-00 Total Stocks: 123	Sector	PE	YTD Ret%	% Assets
⊕ Microsoft	Technology	57.6	52.78	7.11
⊕ American Intl Grp	Financials	42.0	–19.20	4.11
⊖ General Elec	Industrials	30.1	–15.00	3.87
Philip Morris	Staples	12.1	9.12	3.10
⊕ Bristol-Myers Squibb	Health	20.2	–26.00	3.10
☼ Pfizer	Health	34.7	–12.40	2.82
⊖ Fannie Mae	Financials	16.2	–6.95	2.78
⊖ Freddie Mac	Financials	14.0	–3.87	2.56
⊖ ExxonMobil	Energy	15.3	–7.59	2.07
⊕ Viacom Cl B	Services	—	—	1.73
☼ AT&T	Services	7.8	40.59	1.63
⊕ Coca-Cola	Staples	35.5	–21.40	1.62
⊕ Guidant	Health	42.6	–7.67	1.60
☼ ALCOA	Industrials	21.4	7.86	1.59
☼ Alcan Aluminium	Industrials	29.2	6.78	1.41
⊕ BellSouth	Services	24.9	–5.09	1.40
⊕ Ingram Micro Cl A	Technology	43.3	53.96	1.40
☼ Intel	Technology	73.1	4.89	1.24
⊕ Cardinal Health	Health	35.1	–2.51	1.21
☼ FleetBoston Finl	Financials	16.2	0.55	1.21
⊖ Lexmark Intl	Technology	26.9	33.14	1.20
⊖ Dell Comp	Technology	61.8	55.87	1.16
⊕ Intl Paper	Industrials	—	1.43	1.14
⊕ Bowater	Industrials	22.0	–14.00	1.11
☼ Daiwa Secs Grp	Financials	—	—	1.09

Current Investment Style

Style: Value Blnd Growth; Size: Large Med Small

	Stock Port Avg	Relative S&P 500 Current	Relative S&P 500 Hist	Rel Cat
Price/Earnings Ratio	32.8	1.06	1.04	1.08
Price/Book Ratio	5.6	0.97	1.07	1.01
Price/Cash Flow	19.5	1.08	1.09	1.06
3 Yr Earnings Growth	16.8	1.15	1.23	0.94
1 Yr Earnings Est%	–8.2	4.64	—	—
Med Mkt Cap $mil	45,284	0.8	0.4	0.87

Special Securities % assets 06-30-01	
Restricted/Illiquid Secs	Trace
Emerging-Markets Secs	1
Options/Futures/Warrants	No

Composition % assets 06-30-01	
Cash	6.1
Stocks*	93.4
Bonds	0.2
Other	0.3
*Foreign (% stocks)	7.5

Market Cap	
Giant	50.5
Large	24.7
Medium	20.3
Small	4.4
Micro	0.2

Sector Weightings	% of Stocks	Rel S&P	5-Year High	5-Year Low
Utilities	0.0	0.0	—	—
Energy	2.5	0.4	—	—
Financials	18.2	1.0	—	—
Industrials	14.1	1.2	—	—
Durables	2.2	1.4	—	—
Staples	8.4	1.1	—	—
Services	8.5	0.8	—	—
Retail	1.2	0.2	—	—
Health	17.6	1.2	—	—
Technology	27.3	1.5	—	—

Address:	82 Devonshire Street Boston, MA 02109 800-544-8888 / 617-439-0547
Web Address:	www.fidelity.com
*Inception:	04-01-98
Advisor:	Fidelity Mgmt. & Research
Subadvisor:	FMR (Far East)/FMR (U.K.)
NTF Plans:	Fidelity Inst.

Minimum Purchase:	$2500	Add: $250 IRA: $500
Min Auto Inv Plan:	$2500	Add: $100
Sales Fees:	3.00%L	
Management Fee:	.59%+.52% mx./.27% mn.(G)+(–).20%P	
Actual Fees:	Mgt: 0.59%	Dist: —
Expense Projections:	3Yr: $588	5Yr: $799 10Yr: $1409
Avg Brok Commission:	—	Income Distrib: Semi-Ann.
Total Cost (relative to category):		Average

Fidelity Convertible Securities

Ticker	Load	NAV	Yield	Total Assets	Mstar Category
FCVSX	None	$19.90	4.7%	$1,828.8 mil	Convertible

Prospectus Objective: Convertible Bond

Fidelity Convertible Securities Fund seeks current income and capital appreciation.

The fund normally invests at least 65% of assets in convertible securities. It may invest the balance of assets in corporate or U.S. government debt securities, common stocks, preferred stocks, and money-market instruments. The fund may invest in securities rated below investment-grade. It may also invest a substantial portion of assets in unrated securities. The fund may purchase foreign securities.

Historical Profile

Return High
Risk Average
Rating ★★★★★ Highest

Investment Style
Equity
Average Stock %: 16, 39, 22, 51, 52, 54, 58, 11

▼ Manager Change
▽ Partial Manager Change

Fund Performance vs. Category Average
Quarterly Fund Return +/– Category Average
— Category Baseline

Performance Quartile (within Category)

Portfolio Manager(s)

Lawrence Rakers. Since 6-01. MS'87 U. of Illinois; MBA'93 U. of Illinois.

1990	1991	1992	1993	1994	1995	1996	1997	1998	1999	2000	12-01	History
10.65	13.67	15.55	16.45	15.36	16.77	17.56	17.51	18.49	24.28	20.78	19.90	NAV
–2.89	38.74	22.02	17.79	–1.76	19.38	15.05	14.46	16.28	44.08	7.21	0.50	Total Return %
0.22	8.25	14.40	7.73	–3.07	–18.15	–7.90	–18.89	–12.29	23.05	16.31	12.38	+/– S&P 500
3.97	9.61	4.43	–0.77	2.96	–3.81	3.14	–2.20	4.62	10.57	13.37	6.38	+/– Conv.Bond Idx
5.46	6.12	4.98	4.77	4.96	5.03	4.70	4.04	3.60	3.18	2.90	4.55	Income Return %
–8.35	32.61	17.04	13.02	–6.71	14.35	10.35	10.41	12.68	40.90	4.31	–4.05	Capital Return %
18	18	5	26	16	82	60	85	14	26	17	7	Total Rtn % Rank Cat
0.62	0.64	0.67	0.73	0.80	0.76	0.77	0.70	0.62	0.58	0.69	0.93	Income $
0.00	0.37	0.40	1.09	0.00	0.76	0.89	1.77	1.16	1.50	4.57	0.02	Capital Gains $
1.31	1.17	0.96	0.92	0.85	0.70	0.83	0.73	0.77	0.82	0.77	—	Expense Ratio %
5.63	4.99	4.82	4.62	4.61	4.59	4.48	3.46	3.21	2.85	2.96	—	Income Ratio %
223	152	258	312	318	203	175	212	223	246	262	—	Turnover Rate %
59.7	133.4	480.4	1,063.9	891.3	1,045.7	1,119.6	1,002.5	1,035.6	1,422.7	1,901.7	1,828.8	Net Assets $mil

Performance 12-31-01

	1st Qtr	2nd Qtr	3rd Qtr	4th Qtr	Total
1997	–2.21	10.51	11.56	–5.06	14.46
1998	15.70	0.66	–13.84	15.88	16.28
1999	4.35	9.77	–3.04	29.73	44.08
2000	13.40	–0.01	3.37	–8.53	7.21
2001	–6.93	9.64	–15.95	17.19	0.50

Trailing	Total Return%	+/– S&P 500	+/– Conv Bond Index	% Rank All	% Rank Cat	Growth of $10,000
3 Mo	17.19	6.50	9.03	19	4	11,719
6 Mo	–1.50	4.05	1.15	45	14	9,850
1 Yr	0.50	12.38	6.38	42	7	10,050
3 Yr Avg	15.79	16.81	10.14	4	4	15,524
5 Yr Avg	15.62	4.92	6.66	4	4	20,661
10 Yr Avg	14.89	1.96	3.99	5	5	40,069
15 Yr Avg	—	—	—	—	—	—

Tax Analysis	Tax-Adj Ret%	%Rank Cat	%Pretax Ret	%Rank Cat
3 Yr Avg	11.03	4	69.9	30
5 Yr Avg	11.00	4	70.4	22
10 Yr Avg	10.86	5	73.0	35

Potential Capital Gain Exposure: –4% of assets

Risk Analysis

Time Period	Load-Adj Return %	Risk %Rank[1] All	Risk %Rank[1] Cat	Morningstar Return	Morningstar Risk	Morningstar Risk-Adj Rating
1 Yr	0.50					
3 Yr	15.79	62	68	2.55[2]	0.88	★★★★★
5 Yr	15.62	63	75	2.83[2]	0.87	★★★★★
10 Yr	14.89	63	75	1.76	0.83	★★★★★

Average Historical Rating (144 months): 4.4★s

[1]1=low, 100=high [2] T-Bill return substituted for category avg.

Category Rating (3 Yr)

1 2 3 4 5
Worst Best

Return High
Risk Average

Other Measures	Standard Index S&P 500	Best Fit Index Wil 4500
Alpha	18.0	13.0
Beta	0.96	0.79
R-Squared	51	94

Standard Deviation	26.47
Mean	15.79
Sharpe Ratio	0.46

Analysis by William Harding 09-13-01

This fund remains a suitable pick for investors who don't mind some uncertainty.

The merry-go-round of manager changes has continued at Fidelity Convertible Securities Fund. In the latest round, Larry Rakers, who had managed Fidelity Select Technology since February 2000, became the fund's ninth skipper in 11 years when he replaced Peter Saperstone in June 2001. This fund appears to be a stopover destination for Fidelity sector-fund managers who are on their way to running diversified portfolios. Saperstone has moved on to Advisor Mid Cap Stock, and his predecessor here, Beso Sikharulidze, recently took charge of Mid-Cap Stock.

It's too soon to tell what line of attack Rakers will take at the fund's helm. But previous managers often made substantial alterations to the fund's sector and asset mix. Within the past few years, for example, management generally emphasized equity-sensitive tech and telecom issues. Such issues racked up big gains prior to spring 2000—and helped the fund build a superb long-term record—but have also contributed to above-average volatility here.

Although frequent manager turnover is generally a red flag for fund investors, this offering has generally made the best of its lot. Fidelity's strong stock research, as well as the fact that the fund has had some good stock-pickers at the helm in the past, has played an important role in the fund's superior long-term performance compared with its peers. Successful Fidelity managers Stephen DuFour (Fidelity Equity Income II), Charles Mangum (Fidelity Dividend Growth), and David Felman (who ran Mid-Cap Stock before leaving the firm for a hedge fund) have all had tours of duty here.

Portfolio Analysis 05-31-01

Total Fixed-Income: 102	Date of Maturity	Amount $000	Value $000	% Net Assets
Healthsouth		5,226	66,374	3.34
Reliant Energy FRN	09-15-29	749	59,452	2.99
McKesson Fin Tr Cv Pfd 5%		1,152	58,737	2.95
Tyco Cv N/A	11-17-20	65,000	51,622	2.60
Georgia Pac Cv Pfd 3.75%		1,203	46,837	2.35
Harrah's Entrtnmt		1,256	45,932	2.31
Adelphia Comms		1,043	39,922	2.01
Rite Aid		4,253	35,596	1.79
Adelphia Comm N/A	02-15-06	36,409	34,760	1.75
Continental Air Cv Pfd 3%		668	33,812	1.70
Omnicon Grp N/A	02-07-31	28,800	29,860	1.50
Perkinelmer		431	29,775	1.50
Terayon Comm Cv 5%	08-01-07	75,230	28,587	1.44
Amazon.com Cv 4.75%	02-01-09	56,000	28,420	1.43
Alcan Aluminium		604	27,047	1.36
Metlife Cap Tr Cv Pfd 4%		255	25,519	1.28
Redback Net 5%	04-01-07	39,880	25,349	1.27
Reebok Intl 144A N/A	03-01-21	23,250	24,514	1.23
Omnicon Grp Cv 2.25%	01-06-13	10,500	20,102	1.01
Avon Products Cv N/A	07-12-20	38,450	19,379	0.97
Ace Cv Pfd 4.125%		245	19,359	0.97
Enron		351	18,556	0.93
Tribune Cv Pfd		155	18,406	0.93
Cor Therapeutic Cv 5%	03-01-07	14,600	17,602	0.88
Radio One Cv Pfd		16	17,521	0.88

Investment Style

Avg Eff Maturity	—
Avg Credit Quality	—
Avg Wtd Coupon	3.57%
Avg Wtd Price	77.43% of par
Avg Conversion Premium	—

Coupon Range	% of Bonds	Rel Cat
0%	17.5	1.73
0% to 7%	80.1	.98
7% to 8.5%	2.5	.31
8.5% to 10%	0.0	0.00
More than 10%	0.0	0.00

1.00 = Category Average

Special Securities of assets 05-31-01	
Restricted/Illiquid Secs	12
Emerging-Markets Secs	0
Options/Futures/Warrants	No

Composition % assets 05-31-01	
Cash	7.9
Stocks	24.1
Bonds	18.9
Convertibles	49.1
Other	0.0

Credit Breakdown % bonds 11-30-98			
US Govt	0	BB	13
AAA	0	B	32
AA	5	Below B	18
A	5	NR/NA	21
BBB	6		

Country Exposure % assets

NA

Sector Breakdown % bonds 05-31-01			
US Treasuries	0	CMOs	0
GNMA mtgs	0	ARMs	0
FNMA mtgs	0	Other	100
FHLMC mtgs	0		

Address:	82 Devonshire Street Boston, MA 02109 800–544–8888
Web Address:	www.fidelity.com
Inception:	01-05-87
Advisor:	Fidelity Mgmt. & Research
Subadvisor:	FMR (Far East)/FMR (U.K.)
NTF Plans:	Fidelity , Fidelity Inst.

Minimum Purchase:	$2500	Add: $250 IRA: $500
Min Auto Inv Plan:	$2500	Add: $100
Sales Fees:	No-load	
Management Fee:	.20%+.52% mx./.27% mn.(G)+(–).15%P	
Actual Fees:	Mgt: 0.60%	Dist: —
Expense Projections:	3Yr: $271	5Yr: $471 10Yr: $1049
Avg Brok Commission:	—	Income Distrib: Annually
Total Cost (relative to category):		Low

Fidelity Destiny I

Ticker	Load	NAV	Yield	Total Assets	Mstar Category
FDESX	8.67%	$12.74	0.9%	$3,978.3 mil	Large Growth

Prospectus Objective: Growth

Fidelity Destiny I seeks capital appreciation.

The fund invests in domestic, foreign and preferred stocks as well as warrants, futures, and options. It may invest in fixed income securities, including debt rated below investment-grade.

Historical Profile
Return: Below Avg
Risk: Average
Rating: ★★ Below Avg

Investment Style
Equity
Average Stock %: 85% 81% 83% 84% 87% 97% 94%

▼ Manager Change
▽ Partial Manager Change

Fund Performance vs. Category Average
■ Quarterly Fund Return +/– Category Average
– Category Baseline

Performance Quartile (within Category)

Portfolio Manager(s)

Karen Firestone. Since 2-00. BA'77 Harvard U.; MBA'83 Harvard U. Other funds currently managed: Fidelity Large Cap Stock, Fidelity Advisor Large Cap T, Fidelity Advisor Large Cap B.

1990	1991	1992	1993	1994	1995	1996	1997	1998	1999	2000	12-01	History
12.53	15.74	15.22	16.81	14.61	18.74	20.03	23.64	26.95	24.33	15.55	12.74	NAV
–3.15	39.01	15.08	26.42	4.43	36.95	18.55	30.92	25.63	4.96	–20.07	–17.29	Total Return %
–0.03	8.53	7.46	16.36	3.11	–0.58	–4.40	–2.43	–2.94	–16.08	–10.97	–5.41	+/– S&P 500
–4.52	–0.40	11.19	26.49	–0.42	–1.70	–6.97	–2.82	–19.47	–24.72	4.46	3.21	+/– Russ Top 200 Grt
0.74	3.97	2.02	1.69	2.02	2.94	2.40	2.35	1.78	1.63	0.53	0.77	Income Return %
–3.89	35.04	13.06	24.73	2.41	34.01	16.14	28.58	23.85	3.33	–20.60	–18.06	Capital Return %
58	54	2	4	7	21	51	25	73	99	74	27	Total Rtn % Rank Cat
0.10	0.49	0.30	0.25	0.34	0.43	0.45	0.47	0.42	0.44	0.13	0.12	Income $
0.49	1.06	2.44	2.05	2.53	0.81	1.73	2.03	2.17	3.44	3.78	0.00	Capital Gains $
0.53	0.50	0.61	0.66	0.70	0.68	0.65	0.38	0.33	0.31	0.25	—	Expense Ratio %
3.37	2.45	2.00	1.83	1.69	2.35	2.40	2.20	1.71	1.55	0.85	—	Income Ratio %
75	84	75	75	77	55	42	32	27	36	145	—	Turnover Rate %
1,690.4	2,293.0	2,573.8	3,153.8	3,207.8	4,278.7	4,903.2	6,140.0	7,365.3	7,222.6	5,126.0	3,969.2	Net Assets $mil

Performance 12-31-01

	1st Qtr	2nd Qtr	3rd Qtr	4th Qtr	Total
1997	0.40	15.37	8.10	4.56	30.92
1998	10.32	1.50	–7.14	20.83	25.63
1999	–1.22	8.23	–7.88	6.58	4.96
2000	–3.41	–3.23	–2.86	–11.96	–20.07
2001	–14.15	6.52	–18.71	11.26	–17.29

Trailing	Total Return%	+/– S&P 500	+/– Russ Top 200 Grth	% Rank All	% Rank Cat	Growth of $10,000
3 Mo	11.26	0.58	–1.59	36	76	11,126
6 Mo	–9.55	–4.00	–2.56	84	56	9,045
1 Yr	–17.29	–5.41	3.21	76	27	8,271
3 Yr Avg	–11.47	–10.44	–3.44	99	93	6,939
5 Yr Avg	2.68	–8.02	–5.91	86	90	11,414
10 Yr Avg	10.91	–2.02	–0.18	26	39	28,152
15 Yr Avg	12.73	–1.01	–0.64	19	36	60,317

Tax Analysis	Tax-Adj Ret%	%Rank Cat	%Pretax Ret	%Rank Cat
3 Yr Avg	–13.76	94	—	—
5 Yr Avg	0.04	90	1.7	100
10 Yr Avg	7.31	66	67.1	81

Potential Capital Gain Exposure: –26% of assets

Risk Analysis

Time Period	Load-Adj Return %	Risk %Rank[1] All	Risk %Rank[1] Cat	Morningstar Return	Morningstar Risk	Morningstar Risk-Adj Rating
1 Yr	–24.46					
3 Yr	–14.10	79	26	–3.35[2]	1.13	★
5 Yr	0.83	73	13	–0.85[2]	0.99	★
10 Yr	9.90	71	10	0.71	0.92	★★★

Average Historical Rating (193 months): 4.2★s

[1] 1=low, 100=high [2] T-Bill return substituted for category avg.

Category Rating (3 Yr)

1 2 3 4 5
Worst Best

Return: Low
Risk: Below Avg

Other Measures	Standard Index S&P 500	Best Fit Index MSCIACWdFr
Alpha	–10.7	–7.3
Beta	0.94	1.00
R-Squared	83	83

Standard Deviation	15.70
Mean	–11.47
Sharpe Ratio	–1.24

Analysis by Scott Cooley 11-02-01

Don't be too quick to dismiss Fidelity Destiny I Portfolio.

To be sure, this fund's trailing returns are downright ugly. Growth-oriented Karen Firestone took over the portfolio from value-biased George Vanderheiden in early 2000. If Fidelity had tried to sabotage the fund, it couldn't have made the switch at a worse time. As shareholders are painfully aware, the fund switched from a value to a growth strategy just before tech crumbled and value areas like financials and tobacco, which were Vanderheiden favorites, caught fire. Understandably, many investors who had counted on the fund for value exposure have redeemed their shares.

For investors seeking a growth-oriented large-cap fund, however, this fund has a few things in its favor. Firestone's overall record as a manager is solid; she has beaten the large-blend and large-growth category averages during her 3.5-year tenure at Fidelity Large Cap Stock. (That fund's portfolio, which is nearly identical to this one, has bounced between blend and growth over the years.) And for investors who can tolerate this fund's mammoth upfront load—and can stick to the required 10-year program of dollar-cost averaging—the overall cost of ownership is lower than at most load offerings.

In 2001, this fund has put up a solid return relative to the large-growth group. The valuation-conscious Firestone stashed less in tech than her average rival early in the year, and that—combined with a few good picks—has allowed the fund to post a 20.9% loss, which bests 83% of its rivals. That said, Firestone moved to increase the fund's aggressiveness in September, trimming cash and adding to tech during the sector's brutal sell-off.

Those contrarian moves have allowed Firestone to build a good record elsewhere. This fund isn't a sell candidate yet.

Portfolio Analysis 09-30-01

Share change since 03-01 Total Stocks: 176

Sector		PE	YTD Ret%	% Assets
⊕ Microsoft	Technology	57.6	52.78	4.81
⊕ Pfizer	Health	34.7	–12.40	3.72
⊖ General Elec	Industrials	30.1	–15.00	2.99
⊕ Philip Morris	Staples	12.1	9.12	2.95
⊕ ExxonMobil	Energy	15.3	–7.59	2.42
⊕ Bristol-Myers Squibb	Health	20.2	–26.00	2.38
⊕ Wal-Mart Stores	Retail	40.3	8.94	2.15
⊖ AOL Time Warner	Technology	—	–7.76	2.11
⊖ Fannie Mae	Financials	16.2	–6.95	2.09
⊖ Merck	Health	19.1	–35.90	2.04
⊕ IBM	Technology	26.9	43.00	2.00
⊕ Coca-Cola	Staples	35.5	–21.40	1.84
⊖ Intel	Technology	73.1	4.89	1.63
⊖ Citigroup	Financials	20.0	0.03	1.53
☼ Verizon Comms	Services	29.7	–2.52	1.48
⊖ American Intl Grp	Financials	42.0	–19.20	1.38
☼ American Home Products	Health	—	–1.91	1.35
⊕ Amgen	Health	52.8	–11.70	1.25
⊕ Bank of America	Financials	16.7	42.73	1.23
SBC Comms	Services	18.4	–16.00	1.19
⊕ McDonald's	Services	19.2	–21.50	1.18
⊕ Anheuser-Busch	Staples	24.6	1.01	1.09
⊕ Medtronic	Health	76.4	–14.70	1.06
⊕ PepsiCo	Staples	31.4	–0.54	0.99
⊖ Procter & Gamble	Staples	38.8	3.12	0.94

Current Investment Style

Style: Value Blnd Growth; Size: Large Med Small

	Stock Port Avg	Relative S&P 500 Current	Relative S&P 500 Hist	Rel Cat
Price/Earnings Ratio	30.9	1.00	1.00	0.87
Price/Book Ratio	6.2	1.09	0.90	0.98
Price/Cash Flow	18.1	1.01	0.98	0.80
3 Yr Earnings Growth	14.9	1.02	1.00	0.69
1 Yr Earnings Est%	–1.7	0.98	—	–0.58
Med Mkt Cap $mil	70,533	1.2	0.8	1.49

Special Securities % assets 09-30-01

Restricted/Illiquid Secs	Trace
Emerging-Markets Secs	1
Options/Futures/Warrants	No

Composition % assets 09-30-01	
Cash	6.2
Stocks*	93.8
Bonds	0.0
Other	0.0
*Foreign (% stocks)	4.6

Market Cap	
Giant	58.4
Large	22.0
Medium	16.3
Small	3.1
Micro	0.3

Sector Weightings	% of Stocks	Rel S&P	5-Year High	5-Year Low
Utilities	0.4	0.1	7	0
Energy	6.7	0.9	13	2
Financials	14.9	0.8	25	10
Industrials	9.3	0.8	22	6
Durables	1.5	1.0	14	1
Staples	11.9	1.5	12	2
Services	10.7	1.0	17	7
Retail	5.0	0.7	11	4
Health	20.0	1.3	20	3
Technology	19.7	1.1	41	7

Address:	82 Devonshire Street Boston, MA 02109 800-544-8888 / 617-439-0547
Web Address:	www.fidelity.com
Inception:	07-10-70
Advisor:	Fidelity Mgmt. & Research
Subadvisor:	FMR (Far East)/FMR (U.K.)
NTF Plans:	N/A

Minimum Purchase:	$50	Add: $50	IRA: $50
Min Auto Inv Plan:	$50	Add: $50	
Sales Fees:	8.67%L, 0.25%S		
Management Fee:	.17%+.52% mx./.27% mn.(G)+(–).24%P		
Actual Fees:	Mgt: 0.31%	Dist: 0.25%	
Expense Projections:	3Yr: $38*	5Yr: $67*	10Yr: $147*
Avg Brok Commission:	—	Income Distrib: Annually	
Total Cost (relative to category):	—		

Fidelity Destiny II

Ticker	Load	NAV	Yield	Total Assets	Mstar Category
FDETX	8.67%	$10.93	0.9%	$4,988.1 mil	Large Blend

Prospectus Objective: Growth

Fidelity Destiny Portfolios: Destiny II seeks capital appreciation.

The fund invests in domestic and foreign common and preferred stocks (including foreign stocks), warrants, and futures, and options. It may invest in fixed income securities, including debt rated below investment-grade.

Historical Profile
Return Average
Risk Average
Rating ★★★
Neutral

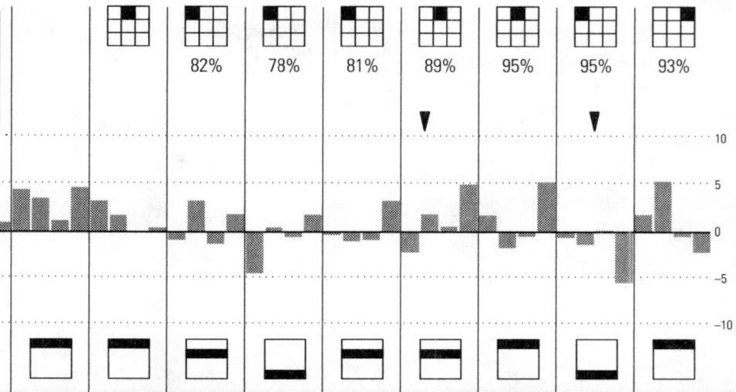

Investment Style
Equity
Average Stock %: 82% 78% 81% 89% 95% 95% 93%

▼ Manager Change
▽ Partial Manager Change

Fund Performance vs. Category Average
■ Quarterly Fund Return +/– Category Average
— Category Baseline

Performance Quartile (within Category)

Portfolio Manager(s)

Adam Hetnarski. Since 6-00. Other funds currently managed: Fidelity Contrafund II, Fidelity Destiny II N.

1990	1991	1992	1993	1994	1995	1996	1997	1998	1999	2000	12-01	History
6.32	7.79	7.82	9.05	8.27	10.70	11.61	13.79	14.25	16.24	12.17	10.93	NAV
–2.52	41.55	15.44	26.80	4.44	36.02	17.86	29.64	28.11	25.40	–13.75	–9.35	Total Return %
0.59	11.07	7.82	16.75	3.13	–1.52	–5.09	–3.71	–0.46	4.36	–4.64	2.52	+/– S&P 500
1.50	9.11	7.79	16.96	3.99	–1.59	–4.31	–3.39	–0.52	3.57	–2.79	3.41	+/– Wilshire Top 750
1.77	1.87	1.61	1.13	1.84	2.70	2.34	2.15	0.87	0.77	0.49	0.82	Income Return %
–4.29	39.68	13.83	25.67	2.60	33.32	15.52	27.49	27.24	24.63	–14.24	–10.18	Capital Return %
43	12	10	2	6	29	76	48	27	25	89	16	Total Rtn % Rank Cat
0.12	0.11	0.12	0.09	0.17	0.22	0.25	0.25	0.12	0.11	0.08	0.10	Income $
0.05	0.96	0.99	0.73	0.99	0.31	0.75	0.97	3.04	1.43	1.80	0.00	Capital Gains $
0.87	0.84	0.88	0.84	0.80	0.80	0.78	0.53	0.48	0.47	0.56	—	Expense Ratio %
3.07	1.70	1.60	1.41	1.56	2.33	2.38	2.11	1.23	0.79	0.37	—	Income Ratio %
112	129	113	81	72	52	37	35	106	77	113	—	Turnover Rate %
236.0	413.2	567.0	1,260.1	1,468.2	2,207.5	2,797.2	3,808.0	4,997.0	6,329.1	5,494.7	4,937.6	Net Assets $mil

Performance 12-31-01

	1st Qtr	2nd Qtr	3rd Qtr	4th Qtr	Total
1997	0.52	14.57	7.70	4.52	29.64
1998	10.44	3.68	–10.89	25.56	28.11
1999	5.33	5.13	–6.46	21.07	25.40
2000	3.51	–4.10	0.06	–13.16	–13.75
2001	–10.76	10.68	–15.64	8.79	–9.35

Trailing	Total Return%	+/– S&P 500	+/– Wil Top 750	% Rank All	% Rank Cat	Growth of $10,000
3 Mo	8.79	–1.89	–2.53	48	83	10,879
6 Mo	–8.22	–2.67	–2.43	79	83	9,178
1 Yr	–9.35	2.52	3.41	59	16	9,065
3 Yr Avg	–0.66	0.37	1.17	76	43	9,804
5 Yr Avg	10.24	–0.46	0.12	18	35	16,283
10 Yr Avg	14.84	1.91	2.39	5	5	39,907
15 Yr Avg	15.91	2.18	2.54	4	2	91,580

Tax Analysis	Tax-Adj Ret%	%Rank Cat	%Pretax Ret	%Rank Cat
3 Yr Avg	–2.33	54	—	—
5 Yr Avg	7.68	49	75.0	70
10 Yr Avg	11.73	10	79.0	59

Potential Capital Gain Exposure: –3% of assets

Risk Analysis

Time Period	Load-Adj Return %	Risk %Rank[1] All	Risk %Rank[1] Cat	Morningstar Return	Morningstar Risk	Morningstar Risk-Adj Rating
1 Yr	–17.21					
3 Yr	–3.61	73	74	–1.67[2]	1.01	★★
5 Yr	8.26	69	61	0.75[2]	0.94	★★★
10 Yr	13.81	69	40	1.50	0.88	★★★★

Average Historical Rating (157 months): 4.3★s

[1] 1=low, 100=high [2] T-Bill return substituted for category avg.

Category Rating (3 Yr)

1 2 **3** 4 5
Worst Best

Return: Average
Risk: Above Avg

Other Measures	Standard Index S&P 500	Best Fit Index MSCIACWdFr
Alpha	0.9	5.3
Beta	1.03	1.12
R-Squared	83	86
Standard Deviation		19.25
Mean		–0.66
Sharpe Ratio		–0.34

Portfolio Analysis 09-30-01

Share change since 03-01 Total Stocks: 115

	Sector	PE	YTD Ret%	% Assets
⊕ Microsoft	Technology	57.6	52.78	7.89
⊕ Bristol-Myers Squibb	Health	20.2	–26.00	4.93
⊕ Pfizer	Health	34.7	–12.40	4.90
⊕ Philip Morris	Staples	12.1	9.12	4.17
⊕ Coca-Cola	Staples	35.5	–21.40	3.47
⊕ AT&T	Services	7.8	40.59	3.33
⊕ BellSouth	Services	24.9	–5.09	2.52
⊕ Cardinal Health	Health	35.1	–2.51	2.43
⊕ SBC Comms	Services	18.4	–16.00	2.24
☼ Johnson & Johnson	Health	16.6	14.01	1.99
⊕ Amgen	Health	52.8	–11.70	1.88
⊖ Freddie Mac	Financials	14.0	–3.87	1.88
☼ Chevron	N/A	—	—	1.76
⊖ General Elec	Industrials	30.1	–15.00	1.73
⊕ ExxonMobil	Energy	15.3	–7.59	1.62
⊕ Intl Paper	Industrials	—	1.43	1.58
⊕ Ingram Micro Cl A	Technology	43.3	53.96	1.55
☼ Honeywell Intl	Durables	NMF	–27.00	1.43
⊕ Bowater	Industrials	22.0	–14.00	1.27
⊕ Arrow Electncs	Technology	NMF	4.45	1.23
☼ Barr Labs	Health	25.0	8.80	1.20
☼ Morgan Stanley/Dean Witter	Financials	16.6	–28.20	1.18
⊕ Alcan Aluminium	Industrials	29.2	6.78	1.17
⊖ Fannie Mae	Financials	16.2	–6.95	1.16
⊖ ALCOA	Industrials	21.4	7.86	1.01

Current Investment Style

Style: Value Blnd Growth; Size: Large Med Small

	Stock Port Avg	Relative S&P 500 Current	Relative S&P 500 Hist	Rel Cat
Price/Earnings Ratio	31.4	1.01	1.08	1.03
Price/Book Ratio	6.0	1.05	1.07	1.09
Price/Cash Flow	18.8	1.05	1.07	1.02
3 Yr Earnings Growth	17.0	1.16	1.01	0.95
1 Yr Earnings Est%	–4.0	2.26	—	—
Med Mkt Cap $mil	61,072	1.0	1.8	1.17

Special Securities % assets 09-30-01	
Restricted/Illiquid Secs	Trace
Emerging-Markets Secs	Trace
Options/Futures/Warrants	No

Composition % assets 09-30-01	
Cash	7.2
Stocks*	92.4
Bonds	0.1
Other	0.3
*Foreign (% stocks)	7.8

Market Cap	
Giant	57.2
Large	20.0
Medium	18.3
Small	3.9
Micro	0.8

Sector Weightings	% of Stocks	Rel S&P	5-Year High	5-Year Low
Utilities	0.0	0.0	7	0
Energy	2.8	0.4	16	2
Financials	8.6	0.5	25	9
Industrials	13.0	1.1	22	6
Durables	2.5	1.6	14	1
Staples	10.8	1.4	11	1
Services	13.6	1.3	26	7
Retail	4.4	0.6	12	3
Health	24.5	1.7	25	2
Technology	19.8	1.1	39	8

Analysis by Scott Cooley 12-11-01

Fidelity Destiny II continues to impress.

Since taking over, manager Adam Hetnarski has gotten a lot more right than wrong. After a misstep—in which he added to the fund's technology stake in late 2000, a move that he quickly reversed—he's had only moderate exposure to the sector in 2001. And within that space, he has favored the right stocks. PC-related issues such as Dell Computer, which have held up well, occupied prominent positions in the portfolio earlier this year, and Hetnarski has maintained a large wager on Microsoft. That stock has gained more than 50% for the year to date through December 10. Hetnarski has largely missed the runup of regional-bank stocks, but he has scored big gains on Philip Morris, UST, Alcoa, and AT&T. So far in 2001, the fund has declined 9.9%, a return that is better than 86% of its large-blend rivals'.

For Hetnarski to continue to beat his peers, he'll probably need the help of drug stocks and a PC-upgrade cycle. Hetnarski contends that pharmaceuticals offer above-market long-term earnings-growth rates but trade at a discount to the S&P 500. And he argues that Microsoft, which consumed 8% of assets as of September 30, should benefit from a "surge of personal computer buying" and the rollout of its new operating system, Windows XP. Hetnarski notes in a recent shareholder report that in the past, the introduction of a new operating system has "prompted a wave of hardware purchases."

Hetnarski is by no means a closet indexer—giant GE was not even in the portfolio's top 10 on September 30—so the fund may experience some bigs ups and downs. But Hetnarski is building a good record here, and has also put up solid numbers in stints at Fidelity Contrafund II and Fidelity Export & Multinational. Therefore, the fund has the look of a solid core holding.

Address:	82 Devonshire Street Boston, MA 02109 800–544–8888 / 617–439–0547
Web Address:	www.fidelity.com
Inception:	12-30-85
Advisor:	Fidelity Mgmt. & Research
Subadvisor:	FMR (U.K.)/FMR (Far East)
NTF Plans:	N/A

Minimum Purchase:	$50	Add: $50	IRA: $50
Min Auto Inv Plan:	$50	Add: $50	
Sales Fees:	8.67%L, 0.25%S		
Management Fee:	.30%+.52% mx./.27% mn.(G)+(–).24%P		
Actual Fees:	Mgt: 0.45%	Dist: 0.25%	
Expense Projections:	3Yr: $43*	5Yr: $74*	10Yr: $164*
Avg Brok Commission:	—	Income Distrib: Annually	
Total Cost (relative to category):	—		

Fidelity Diversified International

Ticker	Load	NAV	Yield	Total Assets	Mstar Category
FDIVX	None	$19.08	0.1%	$6,378.9 mil	Foreign Stock

Prospectus Objective: Foreign Stock

Fidelity Diversified International Fund seeks capital appreciation.

The fund invests primarily in equities of companies located outside of the United States. The majority of investments are made in companies with capitalizations of $100 million or more. The fund may also invest in debt securities of any quality. To select securities, the fund utilizes a computer-aided quantitative analysis in conjunction with fundamental research. The computer model reviews historical earnings, dividend yields, and earnings-per-share.

Historical Profile

Return Above Avg
Risk Below Avg
Rating ★★★★ Above Avg

Investment Style
Equity
Average Stock %

1995	1996	1997	1998	1999	2000	12-01
91%	91%	82%	89%	90%	90%	98%

▼ Manager Change
▽ Partial Manager Change

Fund Performance vs. Category Average
■ Quarterly Fund Return +/– Category Average
— Category Baseline

Performance Quartile (within Category)

Portfolio Manager(s)

William Bower. Since 4-01. MBA U. of Michigan. Other funds currently managed: Fidelity Advisor Diversified Intl A, Fidelity Advisor Diversified Intl B, Fidelity Advisor Diversified Intl C.

1990	1991	1992	1993	1994	1995	1996	1997	1998	1999	2000	12-01	History
—	10.06	8.57	11.60	11.30	12.69	14.71	16.13	17.72	25.62	21.94	19.08	NAV
—	0.60*	−13.81	36.67	1.09	17.97	20.02	13.73	14.39	50.65	−8.96	−12.99	Total Return %
—	−2.27*	−21.43	26.61	−0.23	−19.56	−2.93	−19.63	−14.18	29.61	0.15	−1.11	+/– S&P 500
—	—	−1.63	4.11	−6.69	6.76	13.97	11.95	−5.61	23.68	5.21	—	+/– MSCI EAFE
—	0.00	0.99	0.12	0.26	1.95	1.18	1.29	1.43	1.41	2.15	0.05	Income Return %
—	0.60	−14.80	36.55	0.83	16.02	18.84	12.43	12.97	49.24	−11.10	−13.03	Capital Return %
—	—	98	45	44	7	16	16	46	31	22	10	Total Rtn % Rank Cat
—	0.00	0.10	0.01	0.03	0.22	0.15	0.19	0.23	0.25	0.55	0.01	Income $
—	0.00	0.00	0.10	0.39	0.41	0.36	0.41	0.47	0.70	0.81	0.00	Capital Gains $
—	—	2.00	1.47	1.25	1.12	1.27	1.23	1.19	1.18	1.12	—	Expense Ratio %
—	—	1.38	0.84	0.96	1.55	1.53	1.49	1.46	0.94	1.62	—	Income Ratio %
—	—	56	56	89	101	94	81	95	73	94	—	Turnover Rate %
—	—	37.5	238.8	306.0	340.7	754.1	1,536.4	2,156.9	4,908.5	6,579.7	6,378.9	Net Assets $mil

Performance 12-31-01

	1st Qtr	2nd Qtr	3rd Qtr	4th Qtr	Total
1997	2.52	12.07	3.43	−4.30	13.73
1998	13.33	2.41	−14.48	15.25	14.39
1999	2.71	6.76	5.35	30.41	50.65
2000	0.27	−4.05	−3.16	−2.28	−8.96
2001	−11.76	2.53	−12.04	9.34	−12.99

Trailing	Total Return%	+/– S&P 500	+/– MSCI EAFE	% Rank All	% Rank Cat	Growth of $10,000
3 Mo	9.34	−1.35	—	46	35	10,934
6 Mo	−3.83	1.73	—	55	5	9,617
1 Yr	−12.99	−1.11	—	68	10	8,701
3 Yr Avg	6.07	7.10	—	22	12	11,934
5 Yr Avg	9.20	−1.50	—	23	9	15,525
10 Yr Avg	10.10	−2.83	—	32	8	26,176
15 Yr Avg	—	—	—	—	—	—

Tax Analysis	Tax-Adj Ret%	%Rank Cat	%Pretax Ret	%Rank Cat
3 Yr Avg	5.03	11	82.9	43
5 Yr Avg	8.05	7	87.5	13
10 Yr Avg	9.00	5	89.1	5

Potential Capital Gain Exposure: –7% of assets

Risk Analysis

Time Period	Load-Adj Return %	Risk %Rank[1] All	Risk %Rank[1] Cat	Morningstar Return	Morningstar Risk	Morningstar Risk-Adj Rating
1 Yr	−12.99					
3 Yr	6.07	56	16	0.24[2]	0.72	★★★★
5 Yr	9.20	57	8	0.99[2]	0.65	★★★★★
10 Yr	10.10	73	20	1.75[2]	0.73	★★★★

Average Historical Rating (85 months): 4.3★s

[1] 1=low, 100=high [2] T-Bill return substituted for category avg.

Category Rating (3 Yr)

1 2 3 4 5
Worst Best

Return Above Avg
Risk Below Avg

Other Measures	Standard Index S&P 500	Best Fit Index MSCIWdxUSN
Alpha	5.8	11.5
Beta	0.70	1.03
R-Squared	47	86

Standard Deviation	18.37
Mean	6.07
Sharpe Ratio	0.07

Portfolio Analysis 04-30-01

Share change since 10-00 Total Stocks: 498

	Sector	Country	% Assets
☼ Fid Cash Central Fund	N/A	N/A	11.45
⊕ Nestle (Reg)	Staples	Switzerland	1.38
⊕ Glaxo Wellcome PLC ADR	Health	United Kingdom	1.31
⊕ Novartis (Reg)	Health	Switzerland	1.30
⊖ Shell Transp & Trad (Reg)	Energy	United Kingdom	1.27
☼ ING Groep	Financials	Netherlands	0.93
⊖ Nippon Telegraph & Tele	Services	Japan	0.89
⊕ Telefonica ADR	Services	Spain	0.88
⊕ Nomura Secs	Financials	Japan	0.87
☼ Total Fina Elf ADR	Energy	France	0.77
☼ Canadian Pacific (New)	Services	Canada	0.77
⊕ BNP Paribus	Financials	France	0.74
⊕ Telefonos de Mexico ADR L	Services	Mexico	0.74
☼ Ahold	Retail	Netherlands	0.74
⊕ Norsk Hydro	Industrials	Norway	0.67
☼ Bp ADR	N/A	N/A	0.66
⊕ Nikko Secs	Financials	Japan	0.65
☼ Suncor Energy (Can)	Energy	Canada	0.64
⊕ Lloyds TSB Grp	Financials	United Kingdom	0.63
⊖ Nokia Cl A ADR	Technology	Finland	0.63

Analysis by Emily Hall 11-30-01

It's hard trying to live up to a legend, but Fidelity Diversified International Fund's new manager is off to a good start.

Bill Bower took the reins at this fund in April after longtime manager Greg Fraser left Fidelity to start his own firm. Fraser's departure was a blow—over his 10 years at the helm, he amassed one of the best records in the foreign-stock category.

Bower has been on the job about six months now, and thus far the fund has held up just fine. For the year to date through Nov. 29, 2001, the fund is down 15%—placing it in the top decile of the foreign-stock group. Much of the fund's recent strength owes to its lack of technology, media, and telecom names. During the first three quarters of the year, these former market darlings were pummeled. Moreover, the fund had a smaller stake in Japan than its typical rival, which also helped.

One could argue that Bower's early success is largely a result of the portfolio he inherited from Fraser. It's true that Bower hasn't made massive changes to the fund's makeup (apart from trimming the fund's mammoth 550-stock portfolio to about 400 names). But Bower is starting to make some shifts of his own now, which will give investors a better idea of how the fund will perform under his watch. Bower reports that he started to add to the fund's stake in technology and telecom in the late summer, and continued after the vicious mid-September sell-off. Such a move proved prescient, as many technology and telecom names have enjoyed an impressive rally lately.

Six months is not a lot to go on, but Bower amassed a decent record at his former charge, Fidelity International Growth & Income. Certainly, though, we'll continue to watch the fund's progress carefully.

Current Investment Style

Style: Value Blnd Growth
Size: Large Med Small

	Stock Port Avg	Rel MSCI EAFE Current	Rel MSCI EAFE Hist	Rel Cat
Price/Earnings Ratio	21.4	0.83	1.02	0.84
Price/Cash Flow	11.4	0.89	1.03	0.80
Price/Book Ratio	3.4	0.97	1.09	0.86
3 Yr Earnings Growth	21.4	1.14	0.97	1.09
Med Mkt Cap $mil	9,273	0.3	0.5	0.51

Country Exposure 04-30-01	% assets
Canada	11
Japan	11
United Kingdom	10
France	7
Netherlands	6

Hedging History: Never

Regional Exposure 04-30-01	% assets
Europe	48
Japan	11
Latin America	2
Pacific Rim	5
Other	12

Special Securities % assets 04-30-01	
Restricted/Illiquid Secs	Trace
Emerging-Markets Secs	5
Options/Futures/Warrants	Yes

Composition % assets 04-30-01

Cash	0.0	Bonds	1.4
Stocks	98.4	Other	0.2

Sector Weightings	% of Stocks	Rel Cat	5-Year High	5-Year Low
Utilities	2.1	0.8	11	1
Energy	9.8	1.7	11	4
Financials	25.5	1.2	29	11
Industrials	16.9	1.3	24	13
Durables	4.1	0.6	17	4
Staples	9.5	1.3	12	4
Services	14.2	0.8	24	8
Retail	2.5	0.5	5	1
Health	11.7	1.2	12	6
Technology	3.6	0.4	17	3

Address:	82 Devonshire Street Boston, MA 02109 800-544-8888
Web Address:	www.fidelity.com
*Inception:	12-27-91
Advisor:	Fidelity Mgmt. & Research
Subadvisor:	FMR (U.K.)/FMR (Far East)
NTF Plans:	Fidelity , Fidelity Inst.

Minimum Purchase:	$2500	Add: $250	IRA: $500
Min Auto Inv Plan:	$2500	Add: $100	
Sales Fees:	No-load		
Management Fee:	.45%+.52% mx./.27% mn.(G)+(–).20%P		
Actual Fees:	Mgt: 0.83%	Dist: —	
Expense Projections:	3Yr: $384	5Yr: $665	10Yr: $1466
Avg Brok Commission:	—	Income Distrib: Annually	
Total Cost (relative to category):		Below Avg	

Fidelity Dividend Growth

Ticker	Load	NAV	Yield	Total Assets	Mstar Category
FDGFX	None	$28.33	0.5%	$15,210.3 mil	Large Blend

Prospectus Objective: Growth

Fidelity Dividend Growth Fund seeks capital appreciation.

The fund normally invests at least 65% of assets in equities issued by companies that exhibit potential for dividend growth. It may invest in companies of any size. The fund uses fundamental analyses of companies and industries to determine a company's soundness and future prospects. It may invest up to 35% of assets in debt securities rated below investment-grade. The fund may also invest in foreign securities.

Historical Profile
Return High
Risk Below Avg
Rating ★★★★★ Highest

Investment Style
Equity
Average Stock %: 99% 93% 93% 95% 97% 96% 93%

▼ Manager Change
▽ Partial Manager Change

Fund Performance vs. Category Average
Quarterly Fund Return +/– Category Average
— Category Baseline

Performance Quartile (within Category)

Portfolio Manager(s)

Charles Mangum. Since 1-97. BA'86 Southern Methodist U.; MBA'90 U. of Chicago. Other funds currently managed: Fidelity Advisor Dividend Growth T, Fidelity Advisor Dividend Growth Inst, Fidelity Advisor Dividend Growth B.

1990	1991	1992	1993	1994	1995	1996	1997	1998	1999	2000	12-01	History
—	—	—	12.11	12.37	15.84	20.09	23.27	28.73	28.99	29.96	28.33	NAV
—	—	—	21.72*	4.27	37.53	30.14	27.90	35.85	8.81	12.25	–3.74	Total Return %
—	—	—	12.97*	2.95	—	7.20	–5.45	7.28	–12.23	21.36	8.13	+/– S&P 500
—	—	—	—	3.82	–0.07	7.98	–5.13	7.22	–13.02	23.21	9.02	+/– Wilshire Top 750
—	—	—	0.09	0.08	0.74	0.58	0.76	0.58	0.50	0.63	0.50	Income Return %
—	—	—	21.63	4.19	36.80	29.56	27.14	35.28	8.31	11.62	–4.25	Capital Return %
—	—	—	—	7	10	4	58	3	92	3	5	Total Rtn % Rank Cat
—	—	—	0.01	0.01	0.09	0.09	0.15	0.13	0.14	0.18	0.15	Income $
—	—	—	0.05	0.24	1.07	0.37	2.19	2.19	2.14	2.40	0.33	Capital Gains $
—	—	—	2.50	1.40	1.19	0.99	0.92	0.86	0.84	0.74	—	Expense Ratio %
—	—	—	–0.73	0.13	0.78	0.86	0.99	0.64	0.58	0.52	—	Income Ratio %
—	—	—	90	291	162	129	141	109	104	86	—	Turnover Rate %
—	—	—	88.7	102.4	528.8	2,345.2	4,480.4	10,368.6	12,623.9	11,781.4	15,210.3	Net Assets $mil

Performance 12-31-01

	1st Qtr	2nd Qtr	3rd Qtr	4th Qtr	Total
1997	–1.19	16.47	9.37	1.62	27.90
1998	16.29	4.14	–6.15	19.53	35.85
1999	5.15	6.45	–9.56	7.48	8.81
2000	1.79	5.96	3.36	0.68	12.25
2001	–8.28	7.68	–12.70	11.64	–3.74

Trailing	Total Return%	+/– S&P 500	+/– Wil Top 750	% Rank All	% Rank Cat	Growth of $10,000
3 Mo	11.64	0.96	0.32	34	33	11,164
6 Mo	–2.54	3.01	3.25	49	7	9,746
1 Yr	–3.74	8.13	9.02	49	5	9,626
3 Yr Avg	5.54	6.57	7.37	26	7	11,757
5 Yr Avg	15.36	4.66	5.24	4	2	20,429
10 Yr Avg	—	—	—	—	—	—
15 Yr Avg	—	—	—	—	—	—

Tax Analysis	Tax-Adj Ret%	%Rank Cat	%Pretax Ret	%Rank Cat
3 Yr Avg	3.92	7	70.8	42
5 Yr Avg	12.81	3	83.4	41
10 Yr Avg	—	—	—	—

Potential Capital Gain Exposure: 9% of assets

Risk Analysis

Time Period	Load-Adj Return %	Risk %Rank[1] All	Risk %Rank[1] Cat	Morningstar Return	Morningstar Risk	Morningstar Risk-Adj Rating
1 Yr	–3.74					
3 Yr	5.54	51	7	0.13[2]	0.71	★★★★
5 Yr	15.36	51	6	2.75[2]	0.71	★★★★★
Incept	19.33	—	—	—	—	

Average Historical Rating (69 months): 4.9★s

[1] 1=low, 100=high [2] T-Bill return substituted for category avg.

Category Rating (3 Yr)

1 2 3 4 5 (5)
Worst Best

Return High
Risk Low

Other Measures	Standard Index S&P 500	Best Fit Index S&P 500
Alpha	5.6	5.6
Beta	0.84	0.84
R-Squared	84	84
Standard Deviation		16.32
Mean		5.54
Sharpe Ratio		0.04

Portfolio Analysis 07-31-01

Share change since 01-01 Total Stocks: 163	Sector	PE	YTD Ret%	% Assets
⊕ Cardinal Health	Health	35.1	–2.51	6.93
⊕ Bristol-Myers Squibb	Health	20.2	–26.00	5.47
⊕ Clear Channel Comms	Services	—	5.10	4.42
⊕ Conoco Cl B	Energy	—	—	3.47
⊖ Fannie Mae	Financials	16.2	–6.95	3.05
⊖ Schering-Plough	Health	22.2	–35.90	2.36
⊕ Microsoft	Technology	57.6	52.78	2.31
⊖ Comerica	Financials	14.2	–0.47	2.26
⊕ General Elec	Industrials	30.1	–15.00	2.17
⊕ Philip Morris	Staples	12.1	9.12	2.03
⊕ PNC Finl Svcs Grp	Financials	13.5	–20.70	1.98
⊕ Citigroup	Financials	20.0	0.03	1.73
⊕ Coca-Cola	Staples	35.5	–21.40	1.52
⊕ Dell Comp	Technology	61.8	55.87	1.45
⊕ BellSouth	Services	24.9	–5.09	1.38
⊕ Verizon Comms	Services	29.7	–2.52	1.38
⊖ SBC Comms	Services	18.4	–16.00	1.34
⊖ IBM	Technology	26.9	43.00	1.30
⊕ Eli Lilly	Health	28.9	–14.40	1.27
⊕ Bank of America	Financials	16.7	42.73	1.21
⊕ J.P. Morgan Chase & Co.	Financials	27.8	–17.40	1.18
⊕ Cisco Sys	Technology	—	–52.60	1.14
⊕ AT&T	Services	7.8	40.59	1.11
⊕ Computer Assoc Intl	Technology	—	77.28	1.06
Alberto-Culver Cl A	Staples	—	—	1.05

Current Investment Style

Style: Value Blnd Growth; Size: Large Med Small

	Stock Port Avg	Relative S&P 500 Current	Relative S&P 500 Hist	Rel Cat
Price/Earnings Ratio	28.3	0.91	0.91	0.93
Price/Book Ratio	5.2	0.92	0.86	0.95
Price/Cash Flow	20.3	1.13	0.98	1.10
3 Yr Earnings Growth	15.3	1.05	1.01	0.86
1 Yr Earnings Est%	–7.3	4.14	—	—
Med Mkt Cap $mil	45,915	0.8	0.8	0.88

Analysis by Scott Cooley 10-22-01

Fidelity Dividend Growth Fund still looks like a winner.

Manager Charles Mangum seemingly has the Midas touch. Strong picks such as Cardinal Health have allowed the fund to hold up better than its rivals so far this year. He also recently picked up shares in battered tech firms following the Sept. 11 terrorist attacks. By Sept. 30, the fund, which 18 months ago had a tiny tech stake relative to the S&P 500, had an overweight in the sector of three percentage points. Of course, it's far too soon to say how this shift will play out over the long haul, but so far, it has been a plus, as the Nasdaq Composite index has rebounded to pre-Sept. 11 levels.

Given the tech bounceback, Mangum says the best stock picks are outside the sector. He believes many oil-services firms are now attractively priced, arguing that their current share prices reflect the view that oil and natural-gas prices will go much lower, which he doubts. He still sees value in drug stocks, thanks to their above-market long-term growth rates and moderate valuations. And with expansionary monetary and fiscal policies in place, he says he has slowly shifted some money into media and brokerage stocks, which should benefit from the resulting rebound of the economy and the stock market.

Mangum's long-term record suggests investors shouldn't bet against these areas. The fund's five-year return, which roughly coincides with Mangum's tenure, beats 99% of the large-blend competition. Moreover, Mangum has crushed his S&P 500 benchmark by more than five percentage points on an annualized basis, thanks to strong picks in financials and technology, among other sectors. Mangum's willingness to make big sector and individual-issue bets has occasionally produced poor short-term results, but truly long-term investors would be hard-pressed to find a better core holding.

Special Securities % assets 07-31-01	
Restricted/Illiquid Secs	Trace
Emerging-Markets Secs	Trace
Options/Futures/Warrants	No

Composition % assets 07-31-01	
Cash	3.2
Stocks*	93.2
Bonds	0.9
Other	2.7
*Foreign (% stocks)	1.1

Market Cap	
Giant	48.7
Large	37.9
Medium	12.5
Small	0.9
Micro	0.0

Sector Weightings	% of Stocks	Rel S&P	5-Year High	5-Year Low
Utilities	0.0	0.0	2	0
Energy	5.4	0.8	11	2
Financials	21.1	1.2	21	7
Industrials	8.6	0.8	23	7
Durables	1.5	1.0	12	1
Staples	7.2	0.9	16	3
Services	16.3	1.5	26	10
Retail	3.6	0.5	11	2
Health	19.7	1.3	22	3
Technology	16.6	0.9	24	5

Address: 82 Devonshire Street, Boston, MA 02109, 800-544-8888
Web Address: www.fidelity.com
*Inception: 04-27-93
Advisor: Fidelity Mgmt. & Research
Subadvisor: FMR (U.K.)/FMR (Far East)
NTF Plans: Fidelity , Fidelity Inst.

Minimum Purchase: $2500 Add: $250 IRA: $500
Min Auto Inv Plan: $2500 Add: $100
Sales Fees: No-load
Management Fee: .30%+.52% mx./.27% mn.(G)+(–).20%P
Actual Fees: Mgt: 0.64% Dist: —
Expense Projections: 3Yr: $246 5Yr: $428 10Yr: $954
Avg Brok Commission: — Income Distrib: Annually
Total Cost (relative to category): Below Avg

Fidelity Equity–Income

Ticker	Load	NAV	Yield	Total Assets	Mstar Category
FEQIX	None	$48.77	1.5%	$21,831.5 mil	Large Value

Prospectus Objective: Equity–Income

Fidelity Equity-Income Fund seeks income; potential for capital appreciation is also a consideration.

The fund normally invests at least 65% of assets in income-producing equity securities that have a demonstrated yield higher than the composite yield on the stocks in the S&P 500 index. It may invest the balance of its assets in all types of domestic and foreign securities, including bonds and convertibles. The fund may invest up to 20% of assets in debt securities rated below investment-grade. It does not intend to invest in debt securities of companies without proven earnings or credit.

Historical Profile
Return: Above Avg
Risk: Below Avg
Rating: ★★★★ Above Avg

Investment Style
Equity
Average Stock %: 84% (1996), 87% (1997), 92% (1998), 94% (1999), 93% (2000), 93% (12-01)

▼ Manager Change
▽ Partial Manager Change

Fund Performance vs. Category Average
■ Quarterly Fund Return +/– Category Average
— Category Baseline

Performance Quartile (within Category)

Portfolio Manager(s)

Stephen R. Petersen, CFA. Since 8-93. BA U. of Wisconsin; MS U. of Wisconsin. Other fund currently managed: Fidelity Puritan.

History

1990	1991	1992	1993	1994	1995	1996	1997	1998	1999	2000	12-01	History
21.34	26.31	29.01	33.84	30.70	37.93	42.83	52.41	55.55	53.48	53.43	48.77	NAV
–14.02	29.40	14.68	21.31	0.24	31.81	21.03	29.98	12.52	7.15	8.54	–5.02	Total Return %
–10.90	–1.08	7.06	11.25	–1.07	–5.72	–1.92	–3.37	–16.05	–13.88	17.64	6.86	+/– S&P 500
–10.35	11.25	5.61	1.55	2.56	–8.22	–1.29	–5.51	–8.72	–3.80	6.23	3.77	+/– Russ Top 200 Val
5.89	5.73	4.17	4.02	3.00	3.18	2.74	2.28	1.64	1.48	1.67	1.44	Income Return %
–19.91	23.68	10.51	17.29	–2.75	28.63	18.28	27.71	10.88	5.67	6.87	–6.45	Capital Return %
93	35	15	6	41	61	42	27	54	47	43	46	Total Rtn % Rank Cat
1.55	1.20	1.08	1.15	0.98	0.96	1.02	0.96	0.85	0.81	0.87	0.76	Income $
0.30	0.00	0.00	0.12	2.22	1.36	1.84	2.04	2.39	5.14	3.32	1.18	Capital Gains $
0.71	0.70	0.68	0.67	0.66	0.69	0.67	0.66	0.65	0.66	0.67	0.67	Expense Ratio %
6.10	6.21	4.81	4.02	3.55	3.37	2.86	2.46	1.90	1.54	1.42	1.63	Income Ratio %
92	107	111	84	70	50	39	30	23	30	26	25	Turnover Rate %
3,925.5	4,413.7	4,976.0	6,641.9	7,412.8	10,492.1	14,258.9	21,177.7	23,707.4	22,828.6	22,352.9	21,831.5	Net Assets $mil

Performance 12-31-01

	1st Qtr	2nd Qtr	3rd Qtr	4th Qtr	Total
1997	2.24	14.80	8.33	2.22	29.98
1998	11.39	–0.12	–12.93	16.16	12.52
1999	2.40	10.58	–8.78	3.74	7.15
2000	–2.36	–0.07	7.09	3.88	8.54
2001	–5.99	5.25	–12.22	9.35	–5.02

Trailing	Total Return%	+/– S&P 500	+/– Russ Top 200 Val	% Rank All	% Rank Cat	Growth of $10,000
3 Mo	9.35	–1.33	3.84	46	45	10,935
6 Mo	–4.01	1.55	1.77	56	49	9,599
1 Yr	–5.02	6.86	3.77	51	46	9,498
3 Yr Avg	3.37	4.40	2.21	50	36	11,047
5 Yr Avg	10.07	–0.63	–1.13	18	36	16,157
10 Yr Avg	13.65	0.72	–0.38	10	22	35,943
15 Yr Avg	12.33	–1.41	–1.17	23	40	57,179

Tax Analysis	Tax-Adj Ret%	%Rank Cat	%Pretax Ret	%Rank Cat
3 Yr Avg	1.49	39	44.0	75
5 Yr Avg	8.14	31	80.8	29
10 Yr Avg	11.48	12	84.1	17

Potential Capital Gain Exposure: 23% of assets

Risk Analysis

Time Period	Load-Adj Return %	Risk %Rank[1] All	Risk %Rank[1] Cat	Morningstar Return	Morningstar Risk	Morningstar Risk-Adj Rating
1 Yr	–5.02					
3 Yr	3.37	51	35	–0.33[2]	0.72	★★★
5 Yr	10.07	55	38	1.21[2]	0.76	★★★★
10 Yr	13.65	57	32	1.46	0.74	★★★★

Average Historical Rating (193 months): 4.0★s

[1] 1=low, 100=high [2] T-Bill return substituted for category avg.

Category Rating (3 Yr)

1 2 **3** 4 5
Worst — Best

Return: Average
Risk: Average

Other Measures	Standard Index S&P 500	Best Fit Index S&P 500
Alpha	2.7	2.7
Beta	0.68	0.68
R-Squared	58	58
Standard Deviation		15.60
Mean		3.37
Sharpe Ratio		–0.12

Analysis by Christopher Traulsen 09-29-01

Fidelity Equity-Income Fund is doing about what you'd expect, and that's a big part of its appeal.

All things considered, this offering isn't faring too badly. It's down about 15% for the year to date through Sept. 27, 2001. That's a large absolute loss, but it ranks smack in the middle of the large-value category and is well ahead of the S&P 500 index for the period. Financials such as Citigroup and Bank of New York have hurt the fund, as has an overweighting in energy. On the flip side, strong picks such as Verizon and Bank of America, and an underweighting in technology have limited losses.

Such a showing is pretty typical for this fund. Year in and year out, with few exceptions, it tends to do a bit better than the category average. That's partly because the fund's equity-income mandate forces manager Stephen Petersen to focus on companies that pay healthy dividends and doesn't leave him much room to edge into smaller companies (which generally pay less in the way of dividends) or fallen growth issues that might promise strength. The fund's asset base also forces Petersen to load up on giant-cap names, which holds it back when smaller-cap names lead, as they have in 2001.

Still, even if its year-to-year performance looks a bit bland, the fund holds plenty of appeal. Petersen has added just enough value each year to help the fund beat its average rival by a comfy margin over the longer term. Recently, he's added a bit to the Regional Bells, which has likely helped performance. Further, the fund boasts a nice yield, which helps keep its volatility moderate. It has an experienced manager in Petersen, who's guided the fund since 1993, and also boasts low expenses.

For investors looking for a core holding that doesn't take too many chances, we think this fund remains an excellent choice.

Portfolio Analysis 07-31-01

Share change since 01-01 Total Stocks: 215

Holding	Sector	PE	YTD Ret%	% Assets
⊖ Citigroup	Financials	20.0	0.03	3.66
Fannie Mae	Financials	16.2	–6.95	3.51
⊕ ExxonMobil	Energy	15.3	–7.59	3.29
⊕ SBC Comms	Services	18.4	–16.00	2.32
⊖ General Elec	Industrials	30.1	–15.00	2.01
⊕ Total Fina Elf ADR	Energy	15.5	–1.76	1.91
⊕ BellSouth	Services	24.9	–5.09	1.79
⊕ J.P. Morgan Chase & Co.	Financials	27.8	–17.40	1.55
⊕ Viacom Cl B	Services	—	—	1.53
Wells Fargo	Financials	22.4	–20.20	1.51
⊖ BP PLC ADR	Energy	14.4	–0.90	1.50
⊖ Philip Morris	Staples	12.1	9.12	1.49
Tyco Intl	Industrials	27.1	6.23	1.46
Bristol–Myers Squibb	Health	20.2	–26.00	1.43
⊖ Bank of America	Financials	16.7	42.73	1.43
⊖ Household Intl	Financials	14.7	6.89	1.39
⊖ Eli Lilly	Health	28.9	–14.40	1.31
Bank of New York	Financials	21.9	–24.80	1.26
Verizon Comms	Services	29.7	–2.52	1.22
⊕ American Express	Financials	28.3	–34.40	1.04
⊕ Gillette	Staples	56.6	–5.47	1.00
Merck	Health	19.1	–35.90	0.98
Royal Dutch Petro NY ADR	Energy	12.0	–17.10	0.97
Halliburton	Energy	8.3	–63.20	0.93
⊖ Hartford Finl Svcs Grp	Financials	23.2	–9.63	0.91

Current Investment Style

Style: Value Blnd Growth; Size: Large Med Small

	Stock Port Avg	Relative S&P 500 Current	Relative S&P 500 Hist	Rel Cat
Price/Earnings Ratio	24.7	0.80	0.76	0.98
Price/Book Ratio	4.0	0.70	0.65	0.97
Price/Cash Flow	12.4	0.69	0.73	0.90
3 Yr Earnings Growth	13.5	0.92	0.80	0.91
1 Yr Earnings Est%	–5.7	3.20	—	1.71
Med Mkt Cap $mil	43,759	0.7	1.0	1.38

Special Securities % assets 07-31-01	
Restricted/Illiquid Secs	1
Emerging–Markets Secs	Trace
Options/Futures/Warrants	No

Composition % assets 07-31-01	
Cash	3.0
Stocks*	94.0
Bonds	0.7
Other	2.3
*Foreign (% stocks)	6.7

Market Cap	
Giant	48.6
Large	33.7
Medium	15.7
Small	2.0
Micro	0.0

Sector Weightings	% of Stocks	Rel S&P	5-Year High	5-Year Low
Utilities	2.0	0.6	14	2
Energy	13.0	1.8	16	9
Financials	28.0	1.6	29	17
Industrials	19.0	1.7	28	19
Durables	2.6	1.7	10	2
Staples	5.2	0.7	8	2
Services	14.5	1.3	18	10
Retail	3.5	0.5	10	3
Health	6.4	0.4	8	1
Technology	5.8	0.3	6	1

Address: 82 Devonshire Street, Boston, MA 02109, 800–544–8888
Web Address: www.fidelity.com
Inception: 05-16-66
Advisor: Fidelity Mgmt. & Research
Subadvisor: FMR (U.K.)/FMR (Far East)
NTF Plans: Fidelity , Fidelity Inst.

Minimum Purchase: $2500 Add: $250 IRA: $500
Min Auto Inv Plan: $2500 Add: $100
Sales Fees: No–load
Management Fee: .20%+.52% mx./.27% mn.(G)
Actual Fees: Mgt: 0.48% Dist: —
Expense Projections: 3Yr: $221 5Yr: $384 10Yr: $859
Avg Brok Commission: — Income Distrib: Quarterly
Total Cost (relative to category): Low

Fidelity Equity–Income II

Ticker	Load	NAV	Yield	Total Assets	Mstar Category
FEQTX	None	$21.03	1.5%	$12,211.7 mil	Large Value

Prospectus Objective: Equity–Income

Fidelity Equity-Income II Fund seeks income; potential for capital appreciation is also a consideration.

The fund normally invests at least 65% of assets in income-producing equity securities. It may invest the balance of assets in debt securities of any type or credit quality. The fund may also invest in foreign securities, enter into currency-exchange contracts, and invest in stock-index futures and options.

Historical Profile

Return: Above Avg
Risk: Below Avg
Rating: ★★★★ Above Avg

Investment Style
Equity
Average Stock %: 81% 85% 91% 94% 93% 83% 92%

▼ Manager Change
▽ Partial Manager Change

Fund Performance vs. Category Average
■ Quarterly Fund Return +/– Category Average
— Category Baseline

Performance Quartile (within Category)

Portfolio Manager(s)

Stephen DuFour. Since 2-00. BA'88 U. of Notre Dame; MBA'92 U. of Chicago. Other funds currently managed: Fidelity Advisor Equity Value A, Fidelity Advisor Equity Value B, Fidelity Advisor Equity Value C.

History

1990	1991	1992	1993	1994	1995	1996	1997	1998	1999	2000	12-01	History
10.39	14.52	16.51	18.41	17.72	21.43	23.75	27.01	30.01	27.37	23.86	21.03	NAV
4.51*	46.60	19.06	18.89	3.16	26.39	18.71	27.17	22.98	4.37	7.46	–7.16	Total Return %
0.18*	16.11	11.44	8.83	1.85	–11.14	–4.24	–6.18	–5.60	–16.67	16.56	4.72	+/– S&P 500
—	28.44	9.99	–0.88	5.48	–13.64	–3.60	–8.32	1.74	–6.58	5.15	1.63	+/– Russ Top 200 Val
0.61	4.50	2.65	2.76	2.14	2.10	2.41	1.83	1.25	1.21	1.55	1.40	Income Return %
3.90	42.10	16.41	16.13	1.02	24.29	16.30	25.34	21.73	3.16	5.91	–8.56	Capital Return %
—	4	6	13	13	89	66	50	9	57	46	61	Total Rtn % Rank Cat
0.06	0.46	0.38	0.45	0.39	0.37	0.51	0.43	0.33	0.36	0.42	0.33	Income $
0.00	0.17	0.36	0.73	0.88	0.55	1.14	2.63	2.65	3.50	4.98	0.79	Capital Gains $
2.50	1.52	1.01	0.88	0.81	0.75	0.72	0.68	0.66	0.64	0.63	—	Expense Ratio %
3.89	3.83	3.09	2.69	2.36	2.37	2.13	1.58	1.20	1.19	1.47	—	Income Ratio %
167	206	89	55	75	45	46	77	62	71	151	—	Turnover Rate %
6.2	370.9	2,169.8	5,021.9	7,697.5	11,977.0	15,238.4	16,977.5	19,453.7	17,579.9	13,914.9	12,211.7	Net Assets $mil

Performance 12-31-01

	1st Qtr	2nd Qtr	3rd Qtr	4th Qtr	Total
1997	0.18	15.93	6.01	3.30	27.17
1998	12.46	3.12	–12.03	20.55	22.98
1999	2.66	5.12	–7.64	4.71	4.37
2000	–0.63	–3.97	9.05	3.27	7.46
2001	–7.48	4.75	–13.40	10.61	–7.16

Trailing	Total Return%	+/– S&P 500	+/– Russ Top 200 Val	% Rank All	% Rank Cat	Growth of $10,000
3 Mo	10.61	–0.07	5.10	39	29	11,061
6 Mo	–4.21	1.34	1.57	57	53	9,579
1 Yr	–7.16	4.72	1.63	55	61	9,284
3 Yr Avg	1.36	2.38	0.19	66	58	10,412
5 Yr Avg	10.24	–0.45	–0.96	17	34	16,285
10 Yr Avg	13.56	0.64	–0.47	10	24	35,676
15 Yr Avg	—	—	—	—	—	—

Tax Analysis	Tax-Adj Ret%	%Rank Cat	%Pretax Ret	%Rank Cat
3 Yr Avg	–1.43	72	—	—
5 Yr Avg	7.26	43	70.9	64
10 Yr Avg	10.89	24	80.3	36

Potential Capital Gain Exposure: 9% of assets

Risk Analysis

Time Period	Load-Adj Return %	Risk %Rank[1] All	Risk %Rank[1] Cat	Morningstar Return	Morningstar Risk	Morningstar Risk-Adj Rating
1 Yr	–7.16					
3 Yr	1.36	51	36	–0.74[2]	0.72	★★★
5 Yr	10.24	54	34	1.26[2]	0.75	★★★★
10 Yr	13.56	57	28	1.44	0.73	★★★★

Average Historical Rating (101 months): 4.3★s

[1] 1=low, 100=high [2] T-Bill return substituted for category avg.

Category Rating (3 Yr)

1 2 **3** 4 5
Worst Best

Return: Average
Risk: Average

Other Measures	Standard Index S&P 500	Best Fit Index S&P 500
Alpha	0.4	0.4
Beta	0.67	0.67
R-Squared	69	69
Standard Deviation		13.76
Mean		1.36
Sharpe Ratio		–0.30

Analysis by Christopher Traulsen 10-09-01

Fidelity Equity-Income II is better than it looks right now.

This fund is down 14.2% for the year to date through Oct. 4, 2001—a bottom-third showing in the large-value category. The fund's large asset base has forced manager Stephen DuFour to emphasize larger-cap names, so the fund hasn't benefited as much as its peers from the relative strength of smaller-cap stocks in 2001. Also, DuFour bought a passel of financials with substantial transactional exposure in late 2000, including Charles Schwab and Morgan Stanley Dean Witter. In the rough market environment of the past year, those firms' businesses have slowed markedly.

Nevertheless, we think investors should look beyond the fund's recent woes. The period over which it has fared poorly is far too short to be very meaningful. Of greater import is the fact that DuFour built a solid record running the equity portion of Fidelity Balanced before coming here in early 2000. Also, while DuFour is clearly willing to make contrarian bets, the fund aims to pay a dividend above the S&P 500's, so he keeps a core of steadier, yield-rich stocks in the fund.

DuFour remains confident. He sees the downturn in his financials picks as a cyclical event that it will pay to look beyond. He has also added a few beaten-down technology stocks, such as Cisco Systems, in 2001. Indeed, DuFour has found so many attractively valued names in different sectors that he has brought the number of names in the fund up to 250 to accommodate all of them.

Good value managers have the confidence and the knowledge to buy in areas that others are fleeing. Maybe some of DuFour's picks won't pan out, but his past record suggests that he has been right enough to add considerable value. Add in this fund's low expenses and Fidelity's expert research staff, and we think this offering holds considerable appeal.

Portfolio Analysis 05-31-01

Share change since 11-00 Total Stocks: 262	Sector	PE	YTD Ret%	% Assets
⊖ ExxonMobil	Energy	15.3	–7.59	4.95
⊕ BellSouth	Services	24.9	–5.09	4.67
⊕ PNC Finl Svcs Grp	Financials	13.5	–20.70	3.40
⊕ Mellon Finl	Financials	23.8	–21.90	3.27
⊕ Charles Schwab	Financials	61.9	–45.30	2.81
⊕ Morgan Stanley/Dean Witter	Financials	16.6	–28.20	2.12
⊕ Coca-Cola	Staples	35.5	–21.40	2.04
⊖ Fannie Mae	Financials	16.2	–6.95	1.95
⊕ Citigroup	Financials	20.0	0.03	1.70
⊕ AT & T Liberty Media Cl A	Services	—	3.22	1.65
⊕ Kimberly-Clark	Industrials	18.5	–13.80	1.60
☼ Chevron	Energy	10.3	9.29	1.51
⊖ Philip Morris	Staples	12.1	9.12	1.50
⊕ DuPont De Nemours E.I.	Industrials	65.4	–9.14	1.47
⊕ FleetBoston Finl	Financials	16.2	0.55	1.46
⊕ Bristol-Myers Squibb	Health	20.2	–26.00	1.37
⊕ Schlumberger	Energy	55.0	–30.30	1.34
⊖ J.P. Morgan Chase & Co.	Financials	27.8	–17.40	1.33
⊖ Merck	Health	19.1	–35.90	1.21
⊕ ALCOA	Industrials	21.4	7.86	1.17
⊕ McDonald's	Services	19.2	–21.50	1.00
⊕ American Intl Grp	Financials	42.0	–19.20	0.94
⊖ Gannett	Services	20.3	8.10	0.86
⊕ Tribune Cv Pfd	Industrials	—	—	0.85
⊖ Johnson & Johnson	Health	16.6	14.01	0.79

Current Investment Style

Style: Value Blnd Growth; Size: Large Med Small

	Stock Port Avg	Relative S&P 500 Current	Relative S&P 500 Hist	Rel Cat
Price/Earnings Ratio	26.0	0.84	0.85	1.03
Price/Book Ratio	4.2	0.74	0.80	1.02
Price/Cash Flow	14.6	0.81	0.81	1.06
3 Yr Earnings Growth	12.1	0.82	0.85	0.82
1 Yr Earnings Est%	–8.1	4.56	—	2.44
Med Mkt Cap $mil	29,673	0.5	1.0	0.93

Special Securities % assets 05-31-01	
Restricted/Illiquid Secs	Trace
Emerging-Markets Secs	0
Options/Futures/Warrants	No

Composition % assets 05-31-01	
Cash	3.2
Stocks*	92.0
Bonds	1.6
Other	3.2
*Foreign (% stocks)	1.8

Market Cap	
Giant	34.6
Large	44.3
Medium	19.9
Small	1.2
Micro	0.0

Sector Weightings	% of Stocks	Rel S&P	5-Year High	5-Year Low
Utilities	1.2	0.4	10	0
Energy	10.6	1.5	19	7
Financials	29.3	1.6	34	16
Industrials	17.2	1.5	35	10
Durables	3.5	2.2	9	0
Staples	6.1	0.8	15	1
Services	17.6	1.6	18	7
Retail	3.0	0.4	12	1
Health	6.2	0.4	15	1
Technology	5.5	0.3	7	0

Address: 82 Devonshire Street, Boston, MA 02109, 800-544-8888
Web Address: www.fidelity.com
*Inception: 08-21-90
Advisor: Fidelity Mgmt. & Research
Subadvisor: FMR (Far East)/FMR (U.K.)
NTF Plans: Fidelity , Fidelity Inst.

Minimum Purchase: $2500 Add: $250 IRA: $500
Min Auto Inv Plan: $2500 Add: $100
Sales Fees: No-load
Management Fee: .20%+.52% mx./.27% mn.(G)
Actual Fees: Mgt: 0.48% Dist: —
Expense Projections: 3Yr: $211 5Yr: $368 10Yr: $822
Avg Brok Commission: — Income Distrib: Quarterly
Total Cost (relative to category): Low

Fidelity Europe

Ticker	Load	NAV	Yield	Total Assets	Mstar Category
FIEUX	None	$24.76	1.0%	$1,152.8 mil	Europe Stock

Prospectus Objective: Europe Stock

Fidelity Europe Fund seeks growth of capital.

The fund normally invests at least 65% of assets in companies that have their principal activities in Europe. Managmenet intends to diversify assets among several countries, and will take into consideration the size of the market in each country relative to the size of the markets in Europe as a whole when determining geographic allocation. The fund may invest in eastern European countries that are considered to be emerging markets. It may also invest up to 35% of assets in debt securities rated below investment-grade.

Historical Profile
Return Above Avg
Risk Average
Rating ★★★★ Above Avg

Investment Style
Equity
Average Stock %: 91% 90% 93% 92% 95% 90% 99%

▼ Manager Change
▽ Partial Manager Change

Fund Performance vs. Category Average
Quarterly Fund Return +/– Category Average
— Category Baseline

Performance Quartile (within Category)

Portfolio Manager(s)

Thierry Serero. Since 10-98. BS Israel Institute of Technology; MBA European Institute of Business.

1990	1991	1992	1993	1994	1995	1996	1997	1998	1999	2000	12-01	History
15.67	15.79	15.10	19.12	20.00	22.82	26.61	29.94	33.48	37.47	29.77	24.76	NAV
–4.59	4.16	–2.52	27.17	6.26	18.84	25.63	22.89	20.77	18.69	–9.14	–16.03	Total Return %
–1.47	–26.32	–10.14	17.11	4.94	–18.70	2.68	–10.46	–7.80	–2.35	–0.04	–4.15	+/– S&P 500
–0.75	–8.95	2.19	–2.12	3.97	–2.79	4.54	–0.92	–7.76	2.79	–0.75	—	+/– MSCI Europe
2.26	3.25	1.84	0.53	1.05	0.60	1.05	1.47	0.94	0.54	0.32	0.81	Income Return %
–6.85	0.91	–4.36	26.64	5.21	18.24	24.58	21.42	19.84	18.15	–9.46	–16.83	Capital Return %
44	64	26	60	20	32	39	22	69	73	62	18	Total Rtn % Rank Cat
0.38	0.51	0.29	0.08	0.20	0.12	0.24	0.39	0.28	0.18	0.12	0.24	Income $
0.00	0.00	0.00	0.00	0.11	0.81	1.73	2.35	2.25	1.94	4.09	0.00	Capital Gains $
1.45	1.31	1.22	1.25	1.35	1.18	1.27	1.18	1.09	0.89	1.05	—	Expense Ratio %
2.87	2.83	2.38	1.44	0.85	1.12	1.20	1.53	1.15	0.76	0.54	—	Income Ratio %
148	80	95	76	49	38	45	57	114	106	144	—	Turnover Rate %
366.0	291.1	436.8	494.9	478.9	500.9	773.2	951.5	1,622.6	1,477.7	1,406.8	1,152.8	Net Assets $mil

Performance 12-31-01

	1st Qtr	2nd Qtr	3rd Qtr	4th Qtr	Total
1997	3.65	9.35	7.46	0.90	22.89
1998	18.97	4.46	–17.36	17.59	20.77
1999	–2.48	–0.55	0.55	21.70	18.69
2000	7.05	–5.98	–2.92	–7.00	–9.14
2001	–14.01	–1.41	–18.19	21.06	–16.03

Trailing	Total Return%	+/– S&P 500	+/– MSCI Europe	% Rank All	% Rank Cat	Growth of $10,000
3 Mo	21.06	10.37	—	12	5	12,106
6 Mo	–0.96	4.60	—	42	11	9,904
1 Yr	–16.03	–4.15	—	74	18	8,397
3 Yr Avg	–3.25	–2.23	—	87	49	9,056
5 Yr Avg	6.09	–4.61	—	46	34	13,440
10 Yr Avg	10.21	–2.72	—	31	26	26,426
15 Yr Avg	10.09	–3.65	—	41	1	42,264

Tax Analysis	Tax-Adj Ret%	%Rank Cat	%Pretax Ret	%Rank Cat
3 Yr Avg	–4.61	52	—	—
5 Yr Avg	4.35	34	71.5	34
10 Yr Avg	8.79	21	86.2	15

Potential Capital Gain Exposure: –28% of assets

Risk Analysis

Time Period	Load-Adj Return %	Risk %Rank[1] All	Risk %Rank[1] Cat	Morningstar Return	Morningstar Risk	Morningstar Risk-Adj Rating
1 Yr	–16.03					
3 Yr	–3.25	76	69	–1.61[2]	0.98	★★★
5 Yr	6.09	72	58	0.24[2]	0.81	★★★★
10 Yr	10.21	77	45	1.79[2]	0.78	★★★★

Average Historical Rating (148 months): 3.7★s

[1] 1=low, 100=high [2] T-Bill return substituted for category avg.

Category Rating (3 Yr)

1 2 **3** 4 5
Worst — Best

Return: Average
Risk: Above Avg

Other Measures	Standard Index S&P 500	Best Fit Index MSCIEasNdD
Alpha	–2.1	3.7
Beta	0.90	1.17
R-Squared	57	85

Standard Deviation	19.80
Mean	–3.25
Sharpe Ratio	–0.48

Portfolio Analysis 04-30-01

Share change since 10–00 Total Stocks: 101	Sector	Country	% Assets
☼ Marschollek, Lautenschlaeger	Financials	Germany	4.25
☼ Vodafone Grp	N/A	N/A	3.61
⊕ BP Amoco	Energy	United Kingdom	3.42
☼ Fid Cash Central Fund	N/A	N/A	3.16
⊕ Nokia	Technology	Finland	2.92
⊕ Business Objects	Services	France	2.84
⊕ Luxottica Grp ADR	Retail	Italy	2.56
⊖ Bayer	Health	Germany	2.28
⊖ Total Fina Cl B	Energy	France	2.28
☼ SAP ADR	Technology	Germany	2.23
⊖ Royal Dutch Petro	Energy	Netherlands	2.21
⊖ Unibail	Financials	France	2.10
⊖ Dresdner Bk	Financials	Germany	2.00
⊕ BNP Paribus	Financials	France	1.99
☼ Asm Lithography Hldg	Technology	Netherlands	1.95
☼ Centros Comerciales Pryca	Retail	Spain	1.95
☼ Deutsche Telekom (Reg)	Services	Germany	1.88
⊕ NH Hoteles	Financials	Spain	1.85
⊕ Technip	Industrials	France	1.84
⊕ Saipem	Industrials	Italy	1.76

Current Investment Style

Style: Value Blnd Growth; Size: Large Med Small

	Stock Port Avg	Rel MSCI EAFE Current	Rel MSCI EAFE Hist	Rel Cat
Price/Earnings Ratio	30.4	1.17	1.16	1.28
Price/Cash Flow	18.7	1.45	1.25	1.33
Price/Book Ratio	5.5	1.57	1.84	1.24
3 Yr Earnings Growth	26.5	1.42	1.01	1.11
Med Mkt Cap $mil	6,113	0.2	0.7	0.22

Country Exposure 04-30-01	% assets
France	20
United Kingdom	16
Germany	15
Switzerland	7
Italy	7

Hedging History: Never

Special Securities % assets 04-30-01	
Restricted/Illiquid Secs	1
Emerging-Markets Secs	1
Options/Futures/Warrants	No

Composition % assets 04-30-01

Cash	0.0	Bonds	0.1
Stocks	98.8	Other	1.1

Sector Weightings	% of Stocks	Rel Cat	5-Year High	5-Year Low
Utilities	0.3	0.1	16	0
Energy	10.2	1.2	11	0
Financials	23.9	1.0	34	10
Industrials	15.1	1.2	27	6
Durables	0.3	0.1	12	0
Staples	3.1	0.5	15	2
Services	14.4	0.8	32	13
Retail	8.7	1.7	10	3
Health	8.9	0.9	17	4
Technology	15.2	1.8	22	0

Analysis by Emily Hall 10-09-01

Fidelity Europe is looking awfully mediocre these days, but don't count it out just yet.

Like nearly every other Europe-focused fund, this offering has wilted badly in recent months. For the year to date through Oct. 8, 2001, the fund is down about 27.5%, right in line with the group average. The fund's trailing three-year return at 0.27% trails its typical peer as well.

The main culprit behind the fund's lackluster results has been its focus on growth stocks. Manager Thierry Serero prefers companies that are growing faster than the market average. Although that generally leads him to industries with strong growth opportunities, he isn't averse to picking up a front-runner in a pokier industry or a company with an impressive restructuring plan. Of course, such a strategy hasn't helped much in recent months, when an above-average stake in tech stocks and dearth of safe-haven consumer staples have left the fund looking anemic.

Serero isn't backing down from his strategy, though. He continues to find tech picks that he likes, especially in the software arena. Serero has also peppered the portfolio with some large and mid-cap health-care names, such as Swiss orthopedic device maker Synthes-Stratec, which is now a top-10 holding.

Investors who got into this offering because they wanted a growth-oriented European fund should be pleased to know that Serero has stayed the course. They can also take solace in the fact that the fund—backed by Fidelity's large army of analysts—has delivered decent risk-adjusted returns over the long run.

This will probably never be the most thrilling fund in the group, but it will rarely be the worst either.

Address:	82 Devonshire Street Boston, MA 02109 800–544–8888
Web Address:	www.fidelity.com
Inception:	10-01-86
Advisor:	Fidelity Mgmt. & Research
Subadvisor:	FMR (U.K.)/FMR (Far East)
NTF Plans:	Fidelity Inst.

Minimum Purchase:	$2500	Add: $250	IRA: $500
Min Auto Inv Plan:	$2500	Add: $100	
Sales Fees:	No–load, 1.00%R within 1 month		
Management Fee:	.45%+.52% mx./.27% mn.(G)+(–).20%P		
Actual Fees:	Mgt: 0.60%	Dist: —	
Expense Projections:	3Yr: $306	5Yr: $531	10Yr: $1178
Avg Brok Commission:	—	Income Distrib: Annually	
Total Cost (relative to category):		Low	

Fidelity Four–in–One Index

Ticker	Load	NAV	Yield	Total Assets	Mstar Category
FFNOX	None	$21.93	2.0%	$289.2 mil	Large Blend

Prospectus Objective: Asset Allocation

Fidelity Four-in-One Index Fund seeks high total return.

The fund invests primarily in four Fidelity stock and bond index funds. Its targeted asset allocation is as follows: approximately 55% of assets in the Spartan Market Index Fund, 15% in the Spartan International Index Fund, 15% in the Spartan Extended Market Index Fund and 15% in the Fidelity U.S. Bond Index Fund. The advisors intend the fund to remain close to its target asset allocation, but may modify the underlying funds and asset allocation strategy from time to time.

Historical Profile
Return —
Risk —
Rating Not Rated

Investment Style
Equity
Average Stock %: 79% (2000), 80% (12-01)

▼ Manager Change
▽ Partial Manager Change

Fund Performance vs. Category Average
Quarterly Fund Return +/– Category Average
— Category Baseline

Performance Quartile (within Category)

Portfolio Manager(s)

Jennifer Farrelly, CFA. Since 6-99. BA'85 Middlebury C.

History

1990	1991	1992	1993	1994	1995	1996	1997	1998	1999	2000	12-01	History
—	—	—	—	—	—	—	—	—	27.69	24.91	21.93	NAV
—	—	—	—	—	—	—	—	—	11.74*	-7.65	-10.04	Total Return %
—	—	—	—	—	—	—	—	—	2.24*	1.45	1.84	+/– S&P 500
—	—	—	—	—	—	—	—	—	—	3.31	2.73	+/– Wilshire Top 750
—	—	—	—	—	—	—	—	—	0.98	2.06	1.81	Income Return %
—	—	—	—	—	—	—	—	—	10.76	-9.72	-11.85	Capital Return %
—	—	—	—	—	—	—	—	—	—	45	19	Total Rtn % Rank Cat
—	—	—	—	—	—	—	—	—	0.24	0.57	0.45	Income $
—	—	—	—	—	—	—	—	—	0.00	0.10	0.03	Capital Gains $
—	—	—	—	—	—	—	—	—	—	0.08	0.08	Expense Ratio %
—	—	—	—	—	—	—	—	—	—	2.20	1.77	Income Ratio %
—	—	—	—	—	—	—	—	—	—	4	23	Turnover Rate %
—	—	—	—	—	—	—	—	—	231.0	324.6	289.2	Net Assets $mil

Performance 12-31-01

	1st Qtr	2nd Qtr	3rd Qtr	4th Qtr	Total
1997	—	—	—	—	—
1998	—	—	—	—	—
1999	—	—	-3.72	14.68	11.74*
2000	3.25	-3.19	-0.80	-6.87	-7.65
2001	-10.68	5.37	-12.89	9.72	-10.04

Trailing	Total Return%	+/– S&P 500	+/– Wil Top 750	% Rank All	% Rank Cat	Growth of $10,000
3 Mo	9.72	-0.97	-1.61	44	73	10,972
6 Mo	-4.42	1.13	1.37	59	21	9,558
1 Yr	-10.04	1.84	2.73	61	19	8,996
3 Yr Avg	—	—	—	—	—	—
5 Yr Avg	—	—	—	—	—	—
10 Yr Avg	—	—	—	—	—	—
15 Yr Avg	—	—	—	—	—	—

Tax Analysis	Tax-Adj Ret%	%Rank Cat	%Pretax Ret	%Rank Cat
3 Yr Avg	—	—	—	—
5 Yr Avg	—	—	—	—
10 Yr Avg	—	—	—	—

Potential Capital Gain Exposure: -20% of assets

Risk Analysis

Time Period	Load-Adj Return %	Risk %Rank[1] All	Risk %Rank[1] Cat	Morningstar Return	Morningstar Risk	Morningstar Risk-Adj Rating
1 Yr	-10.04					
3 Yr	—	—	—	—	—	
5 Yr	—	—	—	—	—	
Incept	-2.92	—	—	—	—	

Average Historical Rating —

[1]1=low, 100=high

Category Rating (3 Yr)

Other Measures	Standard Index S&P 500	Best Fit Index
Alpha	—	—
Beta	—	—
R-Squared	—	—
Standard Deviation		—
Mean		—
Sharpe Ratio		—

Return
Risk

Portfolio Analysis 08-31-01

Share change since 02-01 Total Stocks: 4	Sector	PE	YTD Ret%	% Assets
⊖ Fidelity Spartan 500 Index	N/A	—	—	53.86
⊖ Fidelity U.S. Bond Index	N/A	—	—	15.86
⊕ Fidelity Spartan International Index	N/A	—	—	15.32
⊕ Fidelity Spartan Extended Mkt Index	N/A	—	—	14.90

Analysis by Gregg Wolper 12-11-01

If you dread the prospect of assembling your own diversified portfolio, Fidelity Four-in-One Index Fund provides a reasonable solution.

By including large and small U.S. stocks, foreign stocks, and bonds all in one package—and by relying on index funds for all the components, eliminating worries about manager changes—this fund can legitimately claim to serve as an all-in-one investment package. The question is whether the particular mix and structure is appropriate.

In general, the answer is yes. To begin with, this fund puts about 55% of assets in Fidelity Spartan 500 Index. That's a good decision, because the S&P 500 focuses on big, well-established U.S. companies, and Spartan 500 does a sound job of tracking that index. The rest of the portfolio is divided almost equally among Fidelity funds tracking bond, foreign, and small- to mid-cap indexes. These are solid choices, too. One shortcoming of this lineup is that Fidelity International Index tracks the MSCI EAFE index, which most active managers have been able to beat during the past decade. However, that index goes very light on emerging markets, which dampens volatility.

Investors wishing to take a hands-off approach should note that this fund does not adjust its portfolio weightings over time, as do "lifestyle" funds-of-funds such as those in the Fidelity Freedom series. So holding this as your only fund forever might not be the right course; you might, for example, want more bonds in your portfolio at some point.

So far, this young fund has held up relatively well. Its 13.2% trailing one-year loss through Dec. 10, 2001, lands in the large-blend category's top quartile. Of course, when stock markets are stronger, this fund's bond stake will hold it back. For the most part, though, this straightforward offering will serve more-passive investors well.

Current Investment Style

Not Available

	Stock Port Avg	Relative S&P 500 Current	Relative S&P 500 Hist	Rel Cat
Price/Earnings Ratio	24.4	0.79	—	0.81
Price/Book Ratio	4.5	0.78	—	0.81
Price/Cash Flow	15.5	0.86	—	0.84
3 Yr Earnings Growth	18.1	1.24	—	1.02
1 Yr Earnings Est%	-1.7	0.95	—	18.78
Med Mkt Cap $mil	52,380	0.9	—	1.00

Special Securities % assets
Restricted/Illiquid Secs
Emerging–Markets Secs
Options/Futures/Warrants

Composition % assets 08-31-01	
Cash	2.4
Stocks*	80.4
Bonds	15.2
Other	2.0
*Foreign (% stocks)	14.4

Market Cap	
Giant	—
Large	—
Medium	—
Small	—
Micro	—

Sector Weightings	% of Stocks	Rel S&P	5-Year High	5-Year Low
Utilities	3.4	1.1	—	—
Energy	7.2	1.0	—	—
Financials	19.7	1.1	—	—
Industrials	11.2	1.0	—	—
Durables	3.2	2.1	—	—
Staples	5.6	0.7	—	—
Services	14.1	1.3	—	—
Retail	5.5	0.8	—	—
Health	11.7	0.8	—	—
Technology	18.6	1.0	—	—

Address:	82 Devonshire Street Boston, MA 02109 800–544–8888
Web Address:	www.fidelity.com
*Inception:	06-29-99
Advisor:	Strategic Advisers
Subadvisor:	Deutsche Asset Mgmt.
NTF Plans:	Fidelity Inst.

Minimum Purchase:	$10000	Add: $1000 IRA: $500
Min Auto Inv Plan:	$10000	Add: $500
Sales Fees:	No-load, 0.50%R within 3 months	
Management Fee:	.10%, .08%A	
Actual Fees:	Mgt: 0.10%	Dist: —
Expense Projections:	3Yr: $211	5Yr: — 10Yr: —
Avg Brok Commission:	—	Income Distrib: Semi–Ann.
Total Cost (relative to category):	—	

Fidelity Freedom 2040

Ticker	Load	NAV	Yield	Total Assets	Mstar Category
FFFFX	None	$7.39	0.9%	$161.3 mil	Large Blend

Prospectus Objective: Asset Allocation

Fidelity Freedom 2040 Fund seeks high total return.

The fund invests in a combination of Fidelity equity, fixed-income, and money-market funds using a moderate asset allocation strategy designed for investors expecting to retire around the year 2040. The fund allocates assets among the underlying Fidelity funds according to an asset allocation strategy that becomes increasingly conservative until it reaches 20% in domestic equity funds, 40% in investment-grade fixed-income funds, and 40% in money market funds. The fund currently allocates 75 % of assets to domestic equity funds, 15% to international equity funds, and 10% to high yield fixed-income funds.

Historical Profile
Return —
Risk —
Rating
Not Rated

Investment Style
Equity
Average Stock %
85%

▼ Manager Change
▽ Partial Manager Change

Fund Performance vs. Category Average
■ Quarterly Fund Return +/– Category Average
— Category Baseline

Performance Quartile (within Category)

Portfolio Manager(s)

Ren Y. Cheng. Since 9-00. BA'79 National Taiwan U. Other funds currently managed: Fidelity Freedom Income, Fidelity Freedom 2000, Fidelity Freedom 2010.

1990	1991	1992	1993	1994	1995	1996	1997	1998	1999	2000	12-01	History
—	—	—	—	—	—	—	—	—	—	8.75	7.39	NAV
—	—	—	—	—	—	—	—	—	—	–11.90*	–13.50	Total Return %
—	—	—	—	—	—	—	—	—	—	–0.70*	–1.62	+/– S&P 500
—	—	—	—	—	—	—	—	—	—	—	–0.73	+/– Wilshire Top 750
—	—	—	—	—	—	—	—	—	—	0.60	0.81	Income Return %
—	—	—	—	—	—	—	—	—	—	–12.50	–14.31	Capital Return %
—	—	—	—	—	—	—	—	—	—	—	57	Total Rtn % Rank Cat
—	—	—	—	—	—	—	—	—	—	0.06	0.07	Income $
—	—	—	—	—	—	—	—	—	—	0.00	0.12	Capital Gains $
—	—	—	—	—	—	—	—	—	—	—	0.08	Expense Ratio %
—	—	—	—	—	—	—	—	—	—	—	1.46	Income Ratio %
—	—	—	—	—	—	—	—	—	—	—	38	Turnover Rate %
—	—	—	—	—	—	—	—	—	—	25.5	161.3	Net Assets $mil

Performance 12-31-01

	1st Qtr	2nd Qtr	3rd Qtr	4th Qtr	Total
1997	—	—	—	—	—
1998	—	—	—	—	—
1999	—	—	—	—	—
2000	—	—	—	–9.18	–11.90 *
2001	–12.91	6.26	–16.92	12.51	–13.50

Trailing	Total Return%	+/– S&P 500	+/– Wil Top 750	% Rank All	% Rank Cat	Growth of $10,000
3 Mo	12.51	1.83	1.19	31	24	11,251
6 Mo	–6.52	–0.97	–0.73	71	63	9,348
1 Yr	–13.50	–1.62	–0.73	69	57	8,650
3 Yr Avg	—	—	—	—	—	—
5 Yr Avg	—	—	—	—	—	—
10 Yr Avg	—	—	—	—	—	—
15 Yr Avg	—	—	—	—	—	—

Tax Analysis	Tax-Adj Ret%	%Rank Cat	%Pretax Ret	%Rank Cat
3 Yr Avg	—	—	—	—
5 Yr Avg	—	—	—	—
10 Yr Avg	—	—	—	—

Potential Capital Gain Exposure: NMF

Risk Analysis

Time Period	Load-Adj Return %	Risk %Rank[1] All	Risk %Rank[1] Cat	Morningstar Return	Morningstar Risk	Morningstar Risk-Adj Rating
1 Yr	–13.50					
3 Yr	—	—	—	—	—	
5 Yr	—	—	—	—	—	
Incept	–18.63	—	—	—	—	

Average Historical Rating —

[1]1=low, 100=high

Category Rating (3 Yr)

Return
Risk

Other Measures	Standard Index S&P 500	Best Fit Index
Alpha	—	—
Beta	—	—
R–Squared	—	—
Standard Deviation		—
Mean		—
Sharpe Ratio		—

Portfolio Analysis 09-30-01

Share change since 03-01 Total Stocks: 15	Sector	PE	YTD Ret%	% Assets
⊕ Fidelity Growth & Income	N/A	—	—	12.08
⊕ Fidelity Equity–Income	N/A	—	—	11.71
⊕ Fidelity Disciplined Equity	N/A	—	—	11.58
⊕ Fidelity	N/A	—	—	11.31
⊕ Fidelity Blue Chip Growth	N/A	—	—	11.22
⊕ Fidelity Capital & Income	N/A	—	—	9.83
⊕ Fidelity Growth Company	N/A	—	—	6.29
⊕ Fidelity Mid–Cap Stock	N/A	—	—	6.06
⊕ Fidelity Europe	N/A	—	—	5.27
⊕ Fidelity OTC	N/A	—	—	4.72
⊕ Fidelity Diversified International	N/A	—	—	3.98
⊕ Fidelity Overseas	N/A	—	—	3.79
⊕ Fidelity Japan	N/A	—	—	1.39
⊕ Fidelity Southeast Asia	N/A	—	—	0.72
☼ Fidelity Government Income	N/A	—	—	0.00

Analysis by Gregg Wolper 09-08-01

We think Fidelity Freedom 2040 Fund is a solid option for certain investors.

This fund has a complicated structure but provides simplicity for its owners. It is a fund of funds that holds stakes in 14 other Fidelity funds and adjusts those stakes over time. Thus, with one purchase, a shareholder can gain access to a variety of stocks and bonds and can also rest assured that, without having to make any changes oneself, the asset mix will become tamer as time goes by.

The other main benefit of this fund is the strength of its holdings. Ten of this offering's 13 stock-fund holdings boast three-year trailing returns through Sept. 7, 2001, that land well into the top half of their categories, as does its only bond fund. For its Fidelity Freedom siblings, the results are three-year rankings in the top quartile of their category. This fund, which came out in September 2000, doesn't have a three-year record itself as yet.

So far in its history—a rough 12-month stretch in the markets—the fund has middling returns compared with the large-blend category as a whole. Although its stock funds have generally held up well, it has suffered from a 10% allocation to its high-yield bond component, Fidelity Capital & Income, which has been hit hard by troubles in the telecom sector. That offering is in the bottom decile of its category for the year to date through Sept. 7. Fidelity Disciplined Equity, a quantitative offering, has also been below par in 2001.

It's worth noting that this fund is substantially bolder than its Fidelity Freedom siblings with shorter maturity dates, and not just because it allocates more of its assets to equities. For example, it currently has no money allocated to higher-quality bond funds, while its siblings have significant amounts in such funds, and it has about 15% of assets invested abroad, compared with only about 6% for Fidelity Freedom 2010.

Current Investment Style	Stock Port Avg	Relative S&P 500 Current	Relative S&P 500 Hist	Rel Cat
Price/Earnings Ratio	31.1	1.00	—	1.02
Price/Book Ratio	5.0	0.88	—	0.91
Price/Cash Flow	18.1	1.00	—	0.98
3 Yr Earnings Growth	22.0	1.51	—	1.23
1 Yr Earnings Est%	–0.4	0.21	—	4.11
Med Mkt Cap $mil	37,409	0.6	—	0.72

Not Available

Special Securities % assets 09-30-01	
Restricted/Illiquid Secs	1
Emerging–Markets Secs	2
Options/Futures/Warrants	No

Composition % assets 09-30-01	
Cash	6.3
Stocks*	86.3
Bonds	5.8
Other	1.6
*Foreign (% stocks)	16.1

Market Cap	
Giant	37.8
Large	28.6
Medium	21.7
Small	4.5
Micro	7.5

Sector Weightings	% of Stocks	Rel S&P	5-Year High	5-Year Low
Utilities	1.6	0.5	—	—
Energy	6.4	0.9	—	—
Financials	18.9	1.1	—	—
Industrials	11.7	1.0	—	—
Durables	2.2	1.4	—	—
Staples	5.5	0.7	—	—
Services	12.4	1.1	—	—
Retail	7.7	1.1	—	—
Health	12.8	0.9	—	—
Technology	21.0	1.1	—	—

Address:	82 Devonshire Street Boston, MA 02109 800–544–8888
Web Address:	www.fidelity.com
*Inception:	09-06-00
Advisor:	Strategic Advisers
Subadvisor:	None
NTF Plans:	Fidelity Inst.

Minimum Purchase:	$2500	Add: $250	IRA: $500
Min Auto Inv Plan:	$2500	Add: $100	
Sales Fees:	No–load		
Management Fee:	.10%		
Actual Fees:	Mgt: 0.08%	Dist: —	
Expense Projections:	3Yr: $278	5Yr: —	10Yr: —
Avg Brok Commission:	—	Income Distrib: Quarterly	
Total Cost (relative to category):	—		

Fidelity

Ticker	Load	NAV	Yield	Total Assets	Mstar Category
FFIDX	None	$28.88	0.7%	$12,452.3 mil	Large Blend

Prospectus Objective: Growth and Income

Fidelity Fund seeks long-term capital growth. Current return is also a consideration.

The fund invests primarily in common stocks and convertible securities. It may also purchase debt securities for current income. The percentage of assets in any one type of security may vary. The fund diversifies its portfolio among various securities and industries. It intends to invest less than 35% of assets in lower-quality debt; it may also purchase restricted securities. In addition, the fund may invest in foreign securities, and use options and futures contracts.

Historical Profile
Return: Above Avg
Risk: Average
Rating: ★★★★ Above Avg

Investment Style
Equity
Average Stock %: 87% 93% 94% 93% 93% 95% 99%

▼ Manager Change
▽ Partial Manager Change

Fund Performance vs. Category Average
Quarterly Fund Return
+/– Category Average
— Category Baseline

Performance Quartile (within Category)

Portfolio Manager(s)

Nicholas Thakore. Since 6-00. BBA'89 U. of Michigan; MBA'93 U. of Pennsylvania.

1990	1991	1992	1993	1994	1995	1996	1997	1998	1999	2000	12–01	History
16.29	18.46	18.94	19.27	18.48	22.61	24.70	29.81	36.69	42.61	32.77	28.88	NAV
–5.10	24.15	8.46	18.36	2.58	32.85	19.82	32.06	31.00	24.22	–10.97	–11.22	Total Return %
–1.98	–6.34	0.84	8.31	1.27	–4.69	–3.12	–1.29	2.43	3.18	–1.87	0.65	+/– S&P 500
–1.07	–8.30	0.81	8.52	2.13	–4.76	–2.34	–0.97	2.37	2.39	–0.01	1.54	+/– Wilshire Top 750
4.18	3.10	2.62	2.44	1.77	2.32	1.70	1.32	1.03	0.82	0.57	0.64	Income Return %
–9.28	21.05	5.84	15.92	0.82	30.53	18.13	30.74	29.97	23.40	–11.54	–11.87	Capital Return %
74	87	35	12	12	54	65	29	10	29	78	27	Total Rtn % Rank Cat
0.74	0.50	0.48	0.44	0.33	0.42	0.37	0.32	0.30	0.29	0.23	0.21	Income $
0.00	1.15	0.58	2.55	0.94	1.40	1.82	2.35	1.81	2.21	5.20	0.00	Capital Gains $
0.66	0.68	0.67	0.66	0.65	0.64	0.60	0.59	0.56	0.55	0.56	0.56	Expense Ratio %
4.04	2.84	2.37	2.94	1.85	2.18	1.71	1.34	1.01	0.87	0.57	0.55	Income Ratio %
259	267	151	261	207	157	150	107	65	71	113	217	Turnover Rate %
1,065.9	1,309.7	1,353.2	1,546.2	1,886.1	3,213.7	4,450.8	6,529.6	10,563.2	16,114.3	15,082.3	12,452.3	Net Assets $mil

Performance 12-31-01

	1st Qtr	2nd Qtr	3rd Qtr	4th Qtr	Total
1997	0.02	17.38	8.32	3.84	32.06
1998	13.06	5.00	–10.84	23.77	31.00
1999	5.78	4.48	–6.55	20.27	24.22
2000	3.29	–4.84	–0.81	–8.68	–10.97
2001	–14.08	13.37	–18.30	11.55	–11.22

Trailing	Total Return%	+/– S&P 500	+/–Wil Top 750	% Rank All	% Rank Cat	Growth of $10,000
3 Mo	11.55	0.87	0.23	35	34	11,155
6 Mo	–8.86	–3.31	–3.07	81	87	9,114
1 Yr	–11.22	0.65	1.54	63	27	8,878
3 Yr Avg	–0.61	0.41	1.21	76	42	9,818
5 Yr Avg	11.18	0.48	1.06	13	18	16,985
10 Yr Avg	13.54	0.61	1.09	10	15	35,604
15 Yr Avg	13.38	–0.36	0.01	15	30	65,761

Tax Analysis	Tax-Adj Ret%	%Rank Cat	%Pretax Ret	%Rank Cat
3 Yr Avg	–2.25	53	—	—
5 Yr Avg	9.10	26	81.4	50
10 Yr Avg	10.70	32	79.0	58

Potential Capital Gain Exposure: –119% of assets

Risk Analysis

Time Period	Load-Adj Return %	Risk %Rank[1] All	Risk %Rank[1] Cat	Morningstar Return	Morningstar Risk	Morningstar Risk-Adj Rating
1 Yr	–11.22					
3 Yr	–0.61	74	75	–1.12[2]	1.02	★★★
5 Yr	11.18	70	62	1.51[2]	0.94	★★★★
10 Yr	13.54	70	46	1.43	0.90	★★★★

Average Historical Rating (193 months): 3.8★s

[1] 1=low, 100=high [2] T-Bill return substituted for category avg.

Category Rating (3 Yr)

1 2 **3** 4 5
Worst — Best

Return: Average
Risk: Above Avg

Other Measures	Standard Index S&P 500	Best Fit Index MSCIACWdFr
Alpha	1.1	5.7
Beta	1.05	1.15
R-Squared	83	88
Standard Deviation		19.63
Mean		–0.61
Sharpe Ratio		–0.33

Portfolio Analysis 06-30-01

Share change since 12–00 Total Stocks: 264	Sector	PE	YTD Ret%	% Assets
⊖ Philip Morris	Staples	12.1	9.12	3.45
⊖ General Elec	Industrials	30.1	–15.00	3.38
⊕ Microsoft	Technology	57.6	52.78	2.97
⊕ Pfizer	Health	34.7	–12.40	2.88
⊖ Bristol–Myers Squibb	Health	20.2	–26.00	2.45
⊕ Citigroup	Financials	20.0	0.03	2.22
⊕ AOL Time Warner	Technology	—	–7.76	2.07
⊕ Intel	Technology	73.1	4.89	1.97
⊖ Fannie Mae	Financials	16.2	–6.95	1.80
⊕ Sun Microsystems	Technology	NMF	–55.80	1.74
⊕ Cisco Sys	Technology	—	–52.60	1.66
⊕ Computer Assoc Intl	Technology	—	77.28	1.62
⊕ AT&T	Services	7.8	40.59	1.56
⊕ Tyco Intl	Industrials	27.1	6.23	1.51
⊖ Freddie Mac	Financials	14.0	–3.87	1.47
⊕ EMC	Technology	NMF	–79.40	1.45
⊕ Union Pacific	Services	17.1	13.96	1.23
⊖ Coca–Cola	Staples	35.5	–21.40	1.20
⊕ Merrill Lynch	Financials	18.2	–22.70	1.13
⊖ NVIDIA	Technology	84.2	308.50	1.07
⊕ Bank of America	Financials	16.7	42.73	0.97
⊕ General Motors Cl H	Technology	42.9	–32.80	0.93
⊕ Novartis ADR	Health	22.3	–17.40	0.90
✲ Sanofi–Synthelabo	Health	50.5	—	0.89
⊕ Nextel Comms Cl A	Services	—	–55.70	0.85

Current Investment Style

Style: Value Blnd Growth; Size: Large Med Small

	Stock Port Avg	Relative S&P 500 Current	Relative S&P 500 Hist	Rel Cat
Price/Earnings Ratio	31.7	1.03	1.01	1.05
Price/Book Ratio	5.3	0.94	0.97	0.97
Price/Cash Flow	19.0	1.06	1.03	1.03
3 Yr Earnings Growth	16.1	1.10	1.00	0.90
1 Yr Earnings Est%	–7.6	4.32	—	—
Med Mkt Cap $mil	33,347	0.6	0.8	0.64

Analysis by Scott Cooley 12-24-01

There's still a lot to like about Fidelity Fund.

Although shareholders probably aren't thrilled about the fund's 11.75% loss through Dec. 21, 2001, that showing is not too bad. The average large-blend fund has lost 14.2% during the period, and the S&P 500 index has declined more than 12%. Although manager Nick Thakore got burned in July, after adding tech shares on weakness—a decision he quickly reversed—the portfolio's positioning has been spot-on this year. For the most part, the portfolio has been defensively positioned, with scant exposure to hard-hit areas such as communications equipment and large stakes in more-resilient fare such as Philip Morris.

There are no signs Thakore has gotten more bullish on technology stocks. As of Oct. 31, the date when Fidelity last released sector weights for the fund, the portfolio's tech stake stood at 13.9%, which is more than 2 percentage points lower than the sector's weight in the index. And even a few months ago, when tech shares were much cheaper than they are now, Thakore said the sector's fundamentals were eroding so quickly that he was turning up few bargains in that area. Therefore, he continued to make defensive names such as Philip Morris, Coca-Cola, and Pfizer top positions in the fund. That defensiveness hurt returns in November, when tech shares rallied sharply, but it has helped the fund in December, as other sectors have paced the market.

There's reason for long-term optimism at this fund, too. Thakore has done a good job here since taking over in mid-2000. Although the fund posted a weak return last year, the carnage would have been far worse if Thakore hadn't sold off much of the fund's speculative fare soon after arriving. Moreover, he posted a strong gain in his previous stint at Fidelity Trend. In short, Thakore is developing a very good track record as a diversified-fund manager.

Special Securities % assets 06-30-01	
Restricted/Illiquid Secs	1
Emerging-Markets Secs	1
Options/Futures/Warrants	No

Sector Weightings	% of Stocks	Rel S&P	5-Year High	5-Year Low
Utilities	0.8	0.3	7	0
Energy	2.9	0.4	17	3
Financials	16.2	0.9	23	9
Industrials	12.0	1.1	29	11
Durables	1.6	1.0	11	1
Staples	6.0	0.8	11	1
Services	13.5	1.2	21	7
Retail	3.7	0.5	14	2
Health	14.1	1.0	18	1
Technology	29.4	1.6	31	4

Composition % assets 06-30-01	
Cash	0.3
Stocks*	98.5
Bonds	0.9
Other	0.3
*Foreign (% stocks)	6.6

Market Cap	
Giant	43.2
Large	28.7
Medium	25.8
Small	2.2
Micro	0.1

Address:	82 Devonshire Street Boston, MA 02109 800–544–8888
Web Address:	www.fidelity.com
Inception:	04-30-30
Advisor:	Fidelity Mgmt. & Research
Subadvisor:	FMR (U.K.)/FMR (Far East)
NTF Plans:	Fidelity , Fidelity Inst.

Minimum Purchase:	$2500	Add: $250 IRA: $500
Min Auto Inv Plan:	$2500	Add: $100
Sales Fees:	No-load	
Management Fee:	.09%+.52% mx./.27% mn.(G)	
Actual Fees:	Mgt: 0.38%	Dist: —
Expense Projections:	3Yr: $183	5Yr: $318 10Yr: $714
Avg Brok Commission:	—	Income Distrib: Quarterly
Total Cost (relative to category):		Below Avg

Fidelity Ginnie Mae

Ticker	Load	NAV	Yield	SEC Yield	Total Assets	Mstar Category
FGMNX	None	$10.86	5.8%	—	$3,901.4 mil	Intermediate Govt

Prospectus Objective: Government Mortgage

Fidelity Ginnie Mae Portfolio seeks current income consistent with prudent investment risk.

The fund normally invests at least 65% of assets in mortgage-backed securities issued by the Government National Mortgage Association. It may also invest in other obligations backed by the U.S. government, including U.S. Treasury bonds, notes, and bills, as well as repurchase agreements involving those obligations. The fund may also invest a portion of assets in other types of domestic and foreign debt securities.

On May 27, 1999, Fidelity Spartan Ginnie Mae Fund merged into the fund.

Historical Profile

Return Above Avg
Risk Below Avg
Rating ★★★★ Above Avg

Investment Style
Fixed-Income
Income Rtn %Rank Cat: 55, 30, 26, 18, 16, 13, 7, 17

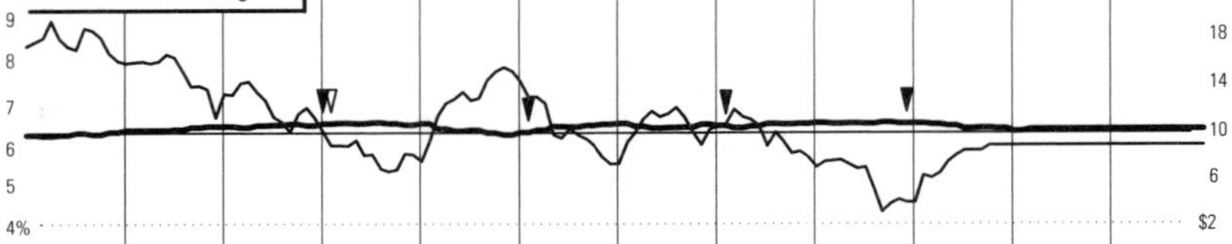

Growth of Principal vs. Interest Rate Shifts
- Principal Value $000 (NAV with capital gains reinvested)
- Interest Rate % on 10 Yr Treasury
- ▼ Manager Change
- ▽ Partial Manager Change
- ► Mgr Unknown After
- ◄ Mgr Unknown Before

Performance Quartile (within Category)

1990	1991	1992	1993	1994	1995	1996	1997	1998	1999	2000	12–01	History
10.56	11.10	11.07	10.86	9.99	10.89	10.70	10.89	10.89	10.36	10.73	10.86	NAV
10.50	13.57	6.70	6.11	−2.00	16.61	4.86	8.70	6.39	1.25	10.74	7.24	Total Return %
1.55	−2.44	−0.70	−3.64	0.92	−1.86	1.24	−0.98	−2.29	2.08	−0.90	−1.18	+/– LB Aggregate
1.79	−1.75	−0.53	−4.54	1.38	−1.73	2.09	−0.88	−3.47	3.50	−2.50	0.01	+/– LB Government
8.53	8.17	6.93	5.81	6.00	7.38	6.57	6.84	6.39	6.25	6.99	6.05	Income Return %
1.97	5.39	−0.23	0.30	−8.00	9.22	−1.71	1.87	0.00	−5.00	3.75	1.20	Capital Return %
5	77	32	83	21	40	8	45	76	7	49	31	Total Rtn % Rank Cat
0.85	0.83	0.75	0.62	0.63	0.71	0.69	0.71	0.68	0.66	0.70	0.63	Income $
0.00	0.00	0.00	0.25	0.02	0.00	0.00	0.00	0.00	0.00	0.00	0.00	Capital Gains $
0.83	0.83	0.80	0.80	0.82	0.75	0.75	0.75	0.72	0.64	0.63	0.62	Expense Ratio %
8.71	8.24	7.73	7.26	7.03	7.24	6.69	6.75	6.58	6.43	6.67	6.40	Income Ratio %
96	125	114	259	303	210	107	—	172	73	75	120	Turnover Rate %
719.7	891.1	947.4	887.4	704.5	805.6	793.1	862.5	1,093.5	1,757.6	1,890.2	3,901.4	Net Assets $mil

Portfolio Manager(s)

Thomas Silvia. Since 12-98. BS'83 U. of Rhode Island; MBA'87 Columbia U. Other funds currently managed: Fidelity Advisor Govt Investment T, Fidelity U.S. Bond Index, Fidelity Government Income.

Performance 12-31-01

	1st Qtr	2nd Qtr	3rd Qtr	4th Qtr	Total
1997	−0.11	3.72	2.79	2.08	8.70
1998	1.44	1.60	2.56	0.65	6.39
1999	0.79	−0.95	1.10	0.31	1.25
2000	2.03	1.94	2.91	3.45	10.74
2001	2.49	0.99	3.76	−0.14	7.24

Trailing	Total Return%	+/– LB Agg	+/– LB Govt	% Rank All	% Rank Cat	Growth of $10,000
3 Mo	−0.14	−0.18	0.45	80	22	9,986
6 Mo	3.61	−1.04	−1.24	12	80	10,361
1 Yr	7.24	−1.18	0.01	13	31	10,724
3 Yr Avg	6.34	0.06	0.45	20	10	12,024
5 Yr Avg	6.82	−0.61	−0.58	38	22	13,905
10 Yr Avg	6.55	−0.68	−0.58	56	22	18,865
15 Yr Avg	7.41	−0.71	−0.47	60	34	29,219

Tax Analysis	Tax-Adj Ret%	%Rank Cat	%Pretax Ret	%Rank Cat
3 Yr Avg	3.76	13	59.3	32
5 Yr Avg	4.20	33	61.6	66
10 Yr Avg	3.90	24	59.5	41

Potential Capital Gain Exposure: −1% of assets

Risk Analysis

Time Period	Load-Adj Return %	Risk %Rank[1] All	Risk %Rank[1] Cat	Morningstar Return	Morningstar Risk	Morningstar Risk-Adj Rating
1 Yr	7.24					
3 Yr	6.34	5	7	0.30[2]	0.48	★★★★
5 Yr	6.82	7	8	0.40[2]	0.47	★★★★
10 Yr	6.55	9	6	0.51[2]	0.65	★★★★

Average Historical Rating (158 months): 3.9★s

[1] 1=low, 100=high [2] T-Bill return substituted for category avg.

Category Rating (3 Yr)

1 2 3 4 5 — Worst ... Best

Return High
Risk Low

Other Measures	Standard Index LB Agg	Best Fit Index LB Mtg
Alpha	0.4	−0.5
Beta	0.72	0.94
R-Squared	81	95

Standard Deviation	2.86
Mean	6.34
Sharpe Ratio	0.58

Portfolio Analysis 07-31-01

Total Fixed-Income: 254	Date of Maturity	Amount $000	Value $000	% Net Assets
GNMA 7%	09-15-29	83	617,685	21.98
GNMA 6.5%	10-15-23	36	546,229	19.43
GNMA 7.5%	05-15-03	1	467,088	16.62
GNMA 8%	07-15-24	15	454,889	16.18
GNMA N/A	08-01-31	284,789	289,136	10.29
GNMA 6%	12-20-23	13	91,071	3.24
GNMA 8.5%	03-15-05	72	74,157	2.64
GNMA 7.5%	07-15-31	40,695	42,106	1.50
GNMA 7.5%	12-15-30	26,769	27,512	0.98
GNMA 9%	11-15-04	8	21,163	0.75
GNMA 6.5%	12-15-28	18,841	18,990	0.68
GNMA N/A	12-15-30	13,837	14,317	0.51
GNMA CMO N/A	04-01-29	12,800	13,376	0.48
GNMA N/A	12-15-28	10,618	10,701	0.38
GNMA N/A	12-15-29	10,094	10,445	0.37
GNMA 6.5%	07-15-31	9,999	10,071	0.36
GNMA 7%	07-20-23	8,874	9,001	0.32
GNMO CMO 6.5%	10-20-26	7,319	7,277	0.26
GNMA 7.25%	04-15-05	1	7,087	0.25
FNMA CMO N/A	08-20-24	5,758	5,880	0.21

Current Investment Style

Not Available

Avg Eff Duration[1]	3.0 Yrs
Avg Eff Maturity	—
Avg Credit Quality	—
Avg Wtd Coupon	0.00%
Avg Wtd Price	102.00% of par

[1] figure provided by fund

Special Securities % assets 07-31-01	
Restricted/Illiquid Secs	0
Exotic Mortgage–Backed	0
Emerging–Markets Secs	0
Options/Futures/Warrants	No

Credit Analysis % bonds 03-31-01			
US Govt	0	BB	0
AAA	97	B	0
AA	0	Below B	0
A	0	NR/NA	3
BBB	0		

Sector Breakdown % bonds 07-31-01			
US Treasuries	0	CMOs	0
GNMA mtgs	99	ARMs	0
FNMA mtgs	0	Other	0
FHLMC mtgs	1		

Coupon Range	% of Bonds	Rel Cat
0%	0.00	0.00
0% to 7%	27.76	0.49
7% to 8.5%	67.02	2.01
8.5% to 10%	4.72	1.16
More than 10%	0.49	0.13

1.00=Category Average

Composition % assets 07-31-01			
Cash	7.3	Bonds	92.7
Stocks	0.0	Other	0.0

Analysis by Scott Berry 10-12-01

Like a thoroughbred with champion bloodlines, Fidelity Ginnie Mae Fund is a good bet.

This fund puts Fidelity's conservative bond investing approach to good use. Rather than try to add value with risky bets on the overall direction of interest rates, manager Tom Silvia shifts the fund's assets between higher- and lower-coupon mortgages and looks for select opportunities in adjustable-rate mortgages and CMOs. This approach has kept volatility to a minimum while helping the fund deliver solid long-term returns. Indeed, the fund's long-term trailing returns all rank in the intermediate-term bond category's top third and compare favorably with those of other mortgage-focused offerings.

Relative to its average category peer, the fund has struggled a bit recently. The Federal Reserve's aggressive interest-rate cuts have prompted homeowners to refinance mortgages at lower rates, which has stifled the performance of mortgage-focused funds. Moreover, investors have flocked to the relative safety of Treasury bonds in the wake of the recent terrorist attacks. This increased demand has driven Treasury prices higher, which in turn has fueled the performance of the fund's Treasury-focused peers.

Nevertheless, we think this fund is a good choice for conservative investors in search of a core bond holding. It sports one of the more attractive risk/reward profiles in the intermediate-term government category, and its expense ratio checks in at a reasonable 62 basis points. All in all, we think this a solid mortgage fund that should continue to serve investors well.

Address:	82 Devonshire Street Boston, MA 02109 800–544–8888
Web Address:	www.fidelity.com
Inception:	11-08-85
Advisor:	Fidelity Mgmt. & Research
Subadvisor:	FMR (Far East)/FMR (U.K.)
NTF Plans:	Fidelity , Fidelity Inst.

Minimum Purchase:	$2500	Add: $250 IRA: $500
Min Auto Inv Plan:	$2500	Add: $100
Sales Fees:	No–load	
Management Fee:	.30%+.37% mx./.13% mn.(G)	
Actual Fees:	Mgt: 0.43%	Dist: —
Expense Projections:	3Yr: $227	5Yr: $395 10Yr: $883
Avg Brok Commission:	—	Income Distrib: Monthly
Total Cost (relative to category):		Below Avg

Fidelity Growth & Income

Ticker	Load	NAV	Yield	Total Assets	Mstar Category
FGRIX	None	$37.38	1.0%	$34,255.1 mil	Large Blend

Prospectus Objective: Growth and Income

Fidelity Growth and Income Portfolio seeks long-term growth, current income, and growth of income, consistent with reasonable investment risk.

The fund invests primarily in dividend-paying common stocks with growth potential. Generally, the fund sells securities with dividends that fall below the yield of the S&P 500 index. Some common-stock selections, however, may be made in securities not paying dividends, but offering prospects for capital growth or future income. The fund's fixed-income investments generally consist of corporate bonds.

Historical Profile

Return: Above Avg
Risk: Below Avg
Rating: ★★★★ Above Avg

Investment Style
Equity
Average Stock %: 89% 94% 94% 93% 95% 86%

▼ Manager Change
▽ Partial Manager Change

Fund Performance vs. Category Average
■ Quarterly Fund Return +/– Category Average
— Category Baseline

Performance Quartile (within Category)

Portfolio Manager(s)

Steven Kaye. Since 1-93. BA Johns Hopkins U.; MBA U. of Pennsylvania-Wharton.

1990	1991	1992	1993	1994	1995	1996	1997	1998	1999	2000	12-01	History
15.22	20.49	19.71	22.22	21.09	27.05	30.73	38.10	45.84	47.16	42.10	37.38	NAV
–6.80	41.84	11.54	19.53	2.27	35.38	20.02	30.17	28.31	10.42	–1.98	–9.35	Total Return %
–3.68	11.36	3.92	9.47	0.95	–2.15	–2.92	–3.18	–0.27	–10.62	7.12	2.53	+/– S&P 500
–2.77	9.40	3.89	9.69	1.82	–2.22	–2.14	–2.85	–0.33	–11.41	8.98	3.42	+/– Wilshire Top 750
3.44	2.53	2.95	2.68	1.83	2.31	1.73	1.42	1.04	0.87	0.80	0.93	Income Return %
–10.23	39.31	8.59	16.85	0.44	33.07	18.29	28.76	27.27	9.55	–2.78	–10.28	Capital Return %
84	12	18	9	14	38	63	45	24	89	22	15	Total Rtn % Rank Cat
0.58	0.38	0.57	0.52	0.40	0.48	0.46	0.43	0.39	0.39	0.37	0.39	Income $
0.22	0.64	2.40	0.77	1.24	0.90	1.12	1.36	2.16	2.90	3.91	0.38	Capital Gains $
0.87	0.87	0.86	0.83	0.82	0.77	0.74	0.71	0.68	0.66	0.66	—	Expense Ratio %
3.43	2.62	2.49	2.67	2.09	2.21	1.82	1.43	1.02	0.88	0.82	—	Income Ratio %
108	215	221	87	92	67	41	38	32	35	41	—	Turnover Rate %
1,729.5	3,355.5	4,828.6	7,684.0	9,344.9	14,818.6	23,896.5	36,656.8	48,639.8	48,528.3	39,761.7	34,255.1	Net Assets $mil

Performance 12-31-01

	1st Qtr	2nd Qtr	3rd Qtr	4th Qtr	Total
1997	1.12	16.75	6.42	3.60	30.17
1998	12.69	2.99	–8.27	20.52	28.31
1999	1.94	4.73	–6.60	10.73	10.42
2000	0.52	0.21	1.31	–3.96	–1.98
2001	–10.91	5.80	–9.64	6.45	–9.35

Trailing	Total Return%	+/– S&P 500	+/– Wil Top 750	% Rank All	% Rank Cat	Growth of $10,000
3 Mo	6.45	–4.24	–4.88	59	96	10,645
6 Mo	–3.82	1.74	1.97	55	14	9,618
1 Yr	–9.35	2.53	3.42	59	15	9,065
3 Yr Avg	–0.63	0.39	1.19	76	43	9,811
5 Yr Avg	10.38	–0.32	0.26	17	30	16,387
10 Yr Avg	13.76	0.83	1.31	9	12	36,303
15 Yr Avg	14.96	1.22	1.59	6	8	80,909

Tax Analysis	Tax-Adj Ret%	%Rank Cat	%Pretax Ret	%Rank Cat
3 Yr Avg	–2.00	48	—	—
5 Yr Avg	8.82	32	85.0	34
10 Yr Avg	11.55	15	83.9	33

Potential Capital Gain Exposure: 35% of assets

Risk Analysis

Time Period	Load-Adj Return %	Risk %Rank[1] All	Risk %Rank[1] Cat	Morningstar Return	Morningstar Risk	Morningstar Risk-Adj Rating
1 Yr	–9.35					
3 Yr	–0.63	49	5	–1.12[2]	0.69	★★★
5 Yr	10.38	52	6	1.30[2]	0.72	★★★★
10 Yr	13.76	54	3	1.49	0.69	★★★★

Average Historical Rating (157 months): 4.7★s

[1]1=low, 100=high [2] T-Bill return substituted for category avg.

Category Rating (3 Yr)

1 Worst, 2, 3, 4, 5 Best

Return: Average
Risk: Low

Other Measures	Standard Index S&P 500	Best Fit Index S&P 500
Alpha	–1.6	–1.6
Beta	0.69	0.69
R-Squared	91	91
Standard Deviation		12.18
Mean		–0.63
Sharpe Ratio		–0.53

Portfolio Analysis 07-31-01

Share change since 01-01 Total Stocks: 216	Sector	PE	YTD Ret%	% Assets
⊖ General Elec	Industrials	30.1	–15.00	4.47
⊕ ExxonMobil	Energy	15.3	–7.59	3.74
⊕ Microsoft	Technology	57.6	52.78	3.72
⊕ Pfizer	Health	34.7	–12.40	3.39
⊖ Fannie Mae	Financials	16.2	–6.95	3.34
⊖ S&P 500 Index (Fut)	N/A	—	—	2.91
⊕ USA Educ	Financials	68.9	24.74	2.87
⊕ Wal-Mart Stores	Retail	40.3	8.94	2.50
⊕ Philip Morris	Staples	12.1	9.12	2.33
⊖ American Intl Grp	Financials	42.0	–19.20	1.88
⊖ Citigroup	Financials	20.0	0.03	1.85
⊖ Freddie Mac	Financials	14.0	–3.87	1.83
⊕ Tyco Intl	Industrials	27.1	6.23	1.56
⊕ IBM	Technology	26.9	43.00	1.43
⊖ SBC Comms	Services	18.4	–16.00	1.38
⊖ Bristol-Myers Squibb	Health	20.2	–26.00	1.35
⊕ Verizon Comms	Services	29.7	–2.52	1.11
⊕ AOL Time Warner	Technology	—	–7.76	1.07
⊖ Eli Lilly	Health	28.9	–14.40	1.04
⊕ American Home Products	Health	—	–1.91	1.02
⊖ UnitedHealth Grp	Financials	26.6	15.37	1.00
⊕ BellSouth	Services	24.9	–5.09	1.00
⊕ AT&T	Services	7.8	40.59	0.94
⊕ Amgen	Health	52.8	–11.70	0.94
⊕ MBIA	Financials	14.6	9.88	0.91

Current Investment Style

Style: Value Blnd Growth; Size: Large Med Small

	Stock Port Avg	Relative S&P 500 Current	Relative S&P 500 Hist	Rel Cat
Price/Earnings Ratio	30.9	1.00	0.97	1.02
Price/Book Ratio	6.3	1.11	1.00	1.15
Price/Cash Flow	17.9	1.00	1.01	0.97
3 Yr Earnings Growth	15.6	1.06	0.97	0.87
1 Yr Earnings Est%	4.0	—	—	—
Med Mkt Cap $mil	74,819	1.2	1.0	1.43

Analysis by Scott Cooley 12-13-01

Although it won't lead the pack in a technology bull market, Fidelity Growth & Income Fund has a lot to recommend it.

As tech shares have bounced strongly off their post-Sept. 11 lows, this fund has fallen behind the pack. Even at the end of September, with tech stocks much cheaper than they are now, manager Steve Kaye said he found few compelling values in the sector. Thus, the fund had less in tech than its average large-blend rival and the S&P 500. With tech leading the market higher between late September and November, this fund understandably lagged its peer group during that period. For the trailing three months through Dec. 12, 2001, the fund's 2.6% gain was more than 1.5 percentage points behind that of the S&P 500 and the average category offering.

Overall, however, Kaye's avoidance of richly valued tech shares has been the right call. For the year to date, the fund's 10.6% decline leaves it well ahead of the S&P 500 and its average rival. Although Kaye's decision to underweight tech hurt in 1999, it also allowed the fund to hold up well during 2000's tech bloodbath. Moreover, over time Kaye has executed this cautious, risk-conscious approach with distinction: Thanks to strong picks in a variety of areas, especially health care, the funds' longer-term returns all land in the category's upper echelons.

Kaye is sticking with this approach. As of Oct. 31, the fund's tech weight of 8.4% was only about half the S&P 500's, according to Fidelity. Meanwhile, Kaye has continued to favor moderately valued issues with decent growth prospects, including top-10 holdings Philip Morris, USA Education, Freddie Mac, and Fannie Mae.

This fund won't keep up with more-growth-oriented peers in a big rally, but given Kaye's strong long-term record, as well as the fund's moderate risk profile and low costs, it still makes an excellent core holding.

Special Securities % assets 07-31-01	
Restricted/Illiquid Secs	Trace
Emerging-Markets Secs	Trace
Options/Futures/Warrants	Yes

Sector Weightings	% of Stocks	Rel S&P	5-Year High	5-Year Low
Utilities	0.4	0.1	13	0
Energy	6.6	0.9	15	4
Financials	21.9	1.2	23	10
Industrials	12.0	1.1	23	11
Durables	1.3	0.8	9	1
Staples	8.3	1.1	15	0
Services	11.2	1.0	18	9
Retail	5.6	0.8	11	5
Health	18.9	1.3	20	4
Technology	13.9	0.8	28	4

Composition % assets 07-31-01	
Cash	10.6
Stocks*	86.0
Bonds	0.0
Other	3.4
*Foreign (% stocks)	1.8

Market Cap	
Giant	60.9
Large	29.8
Medium	9.0
Small	0.4
Micro	0.0

Address: 82 Devonshire Street
Boston, MA 02109
800-544-8888
Web Address: www.fidelity.com

Inception: 12-30-85
Advisor: Fidelity Mgmt. & Research
Subadvisor: FMR (Far East)/FMR (U.K.)
NTF Plans: Fidelity, Fidelity Inst.

Minimum Purchase: $2500 — Add: $250 — IRA: $500
Min Auto Inv Plan: $2500 — Add: $100
Sales Fees: No-load
Management Fee: .20%+.52% mx./.27% mn.(G)
Actual Fees: Mgt: 0.49% — Dist: —
Expense Projections: 3Yr: $218 — 5Yr: $379 — 10Yr: $847
Avg Brok Commission: — — Income Distrib: Quarterly
Total Cost (relative to category): Below Avg

Fidelity Growth & Income II

Ticker	Load	NAV	Yield	Total Assets	Mstar Category
FGRTX	None	$9.23	1.0%	$160.2 mil	Large Blend

Prospectus Objective: Growth and Income

Fidelity Growth and Income Fund II seeks total return.

The fund primarily invests in equity securities that pay current dividends. It may invest in common and preferred stocks, convertible securities, warrants, debt securities, foreign securities, asset-backed securities, mortgage securities, and repurchase agreements. The fund typically invests less than 35% of assets in non-investment grade debt securities.

The fund is designed for institutional investors.

Historical Profile

Return Below Avg
Risk Below Avg
Rating ★★★ Neutral

Investment Style
Equity
Average Stock %: 92% (1999), 83% (2000), 83% (12-01)

▼ Manager Change
▽ Partial Manager Change

Fund Performance vs. Category Average
■ Quarterly Fund Return +/– Category Average
– Category Baseline

Performance Quartile (within Category)

Portfolio Manager(s)

Louis Salemy. Since 12-98. BA'84 Boston C.; MBA'89 New York U.

History

1990	1991	1992	1993	1994	1995	1996	1997	1998	1999	2000	12-01	History
—	—	—	—	—	—	—	—	10.10	10.79	10.26	9.23	NAV
—	—	—	—	—	—	—	—	1.00*	8.09	–3.89	–9.15	Total Return %
—	—	—	—	—	—	—	—	0.58*	–12.95	5.21	2.73	+/– S&P 500
—	—	—	—	—	—	—	—	—	–13.74	7.07	3.62	+/– Wilshire Top 750
—	—	—	—	—	—	—	—	0.00	0.70	1.02	0.88	Income Return %
—	—	—	—	—	—	—	—	1.00	7.39	–4.91	–10.03	Capital Return %
—	—	—	—	—	—	—	—	—	93	29	15	Total Rtn % Rank Cat
—	—	—	—	—	—	—	—	0.00	0.07	0.11	0.09	Income $
—	—	—	—	—	—	—	—	0.00	0.05	0.00	0.00	Capital Gains $
—	—	—	—	—	—	—	—	—	1.12	0.84	0.86	Expense Ratio %
—	—	—	—	—	—	—	—	—	0.62	0.83	1.12	Income Ratio %
—	—	—	—	—	—	—	—	—	59	59	79	Turnover Rate %
—	—	—	—	—	—	—	—	1.0	217.9	170.8	160.2	Net Assets $mil

Performance 12-31-01

	1st Qtr	2nd Qtr	3rd Qtr	4th Qtr	Total
1997	—	—	—	—	—
1998	—	—	—	—	1.00 *
1999	2.57	4.07	–6.43	8.21	8.09
2000	–0.45	–1.96	3.43	–4.79	–3.89
2001	–10.24	5.00	–12.24	9.85	–9.15

Trailing	Total Return%	+/– S&P 500	+/– Wil Top 750	% Rank All	% Rank Cat	Growth of $10,000
3 Mo	9.85	–0.84	–1.48	43	71	10,985
6 Mo	–3.60	1.96	2.19	54	12	9,640
1 Yr	–9.15	2.73	3.62	59	15	9,086
3 Yr Avg	–1.91	–0.88	–0.08	82	64	9,438
5 Yr Avg	—	—	—	—	—	—
10 Yr Avg	—	—	—	—	—	—
15 Yr Avg	—	—	—	—	—	—

Tax Analysis	Tax-Adj Ret%	%Rank Cat	%Pretax Ret	%Rank Cat
3 Yr Avg	–2.32	54	—	—
5 Yr Avg	—	—	—	—
10 Yr Avg	—	—	—	—

Potential Capital Gain Exposure: –5% of assets

Risk Analysis

Time Period	Load-Adj Return %	Risk %Rank[1] All	Risk %Rank[1] Cat	Morningstar Return	Morningstar Risk	Morningstar Risk-Adj Rating
1 Yr	–9.15					
3 Yr	–1.91	53	9	–1.36[2]	0.74	★★★
5 Yr	—	—	—	—	—	
Incept	–1.58	—	—	—	—	

Average Historical Rating (1 month): 3.0★s

[1] 1=low, 100=high [2] T–Bill return substituted for category avg.

Category Rating (3 Yr)

1 2 **3** 4 5
Worst Best

Return Average
Risk Low

Other Measures	Standard Index S&P 500	Best Fit Index S&P 500
Alpha	–2.7	–2.7
Beta	0.71	0.71
R–Squared	89	89
Standard Deviation		12.55
Mean		–1.91
Sharpe Ratio		–0.63

Analysis by Kelli Stebel 10-31-01

Don't be dismayed by this fund's poor absolute returns.

Fidelity Growth & Income II's record since its inception in late 1998 might look a little disappointing. Though the fund's relative showing during 2000 was decent, it still lost nearly 4%. And so far this year, it is still in the red. For the year to date through Oct. 30, 2001, the fund is down about 15%.

Upon closer inspection, though, investors will find that this fund's moderate strategy has produced exactly the sort of results shareholders should have expected. Manager Louis Salemy uses the S&P 500 as his benchmark, but he prefers companies with steady earnings, keeping him away from most of the market's high-flying tech stocks. So when momentum stocks paced the market in 1999, the fund couldn't keep up with its more-aggressive peers. And though the fund's losses in 2000 and so far in 2001 might be disappointing, they've still been better than the broader market's, as well as the vast majority of large-blend offerings'. Most of the fund's rivals have been hit harder by the tech implosion.

Salemy says he hasn't been making any wholesale changes to the fund these days, mostly because he wants to avoid flipping the portfolio in this year's volatile market. He has moderately cut mortgage lender Fannie Mae, while adding to brokerage houses like Merrill Lynch, which he likes for their low credit risk—a plus in an environment of weak economic growth.

Shareholders should also feel confident that Salemy can deliver. He is backed by Fidelity's deep research staff and has managed several of Fidelity's sector funds. Most notably, Salemy had a successful four-year run at Fidelity Select Financial Services. Given that backdrop, investors should stay put.

Portfolio Analysis 06-30-01

Share change since 12–00 Total Stocks: 74	Sector	PE	YTD Ret%	% Assets
ExxonMobil	Energy	15.3	–7.59	5.26
⊖ Freddie Mac	Financials	14.0	–3.87	4.79
⊕ Microsoft	Technology	57.6	52.78	4.47
Philip Morris	Staples	12.1	9.12	4.35
General Elec	Industrials	30.1	–15.00	4.07
⊖ Fannie Mae	Financials	16.2	–6.95	3.54
⊕ Morgan Stanley/Dean Witter	Financials	16.6	–28.20	3.06
⊕ EchoStar Comms	Technology	—	20.75	2.48
Wal–Mart Stores	Retail	40.3	8.94	2.24
⊕ Merrill Lynch	Financials	18.2	–22.70	2.23
☼ Amgen	Health	52.8	–11.70	2.18
⊕ Omnicom Grp	Services	34.5	8.83	2.17
⊕ Gillette	Staples	56.6	–5.47	1.91
American Intl Grp	Financials	42.0	–19.20	1.91
⊕ Pfizer	Health	34.7	–12.40	1.79
⊖ S&P 500 Index (Fut)	N/A	—	—	1.75
⊕ Nextel Comms Cl A	Services	—	–55.70	1.71
EchoStar Comm 144A N/A	N/A	—	—	1.68
⊕ Adobe Sys	Technology	37.4	–46.50	1.15
McGraw–Hill	Services	24.7	5.70	1.15
⊕ Pegasus Comms Cl A	Services	—	–59.50	1.14
⊕ General Motors Cl H	Technology	42.9	–32.80	1.10
⊖ SBC Comms	Services	18.4	–16.00	1.09
⊕ Coca–Cola	Staples	35.5	–21.40	1.06
Home Depot	Retail	42.9	12.07	1.04

Current Investment Style

Style: Value Blnd Growth; Size: Large Med Small

	Stock Port Avg	Relative S&P 500 Current	Relative S&P 500 Hist	Rel Cat
Price/Earnings Ratio	30.0	0.97	—	0.99
Price/Book Ratio	6.3	1.10	—	1.14
Price/Cash Flow	18.5	1.03	—	1.00
3 Yr Earnings Growth	16.1	1.10	—	0.90
1 Yr Earnings Est%	3.3	—	—	—
Med Mkt Cap $mil	55,433	0.9	—	1.06

Special Securities % assets 06-30-01	
Restricted/Illiquid Secs	2
Emerging–Markets Secs	Trace
Options/Futures/Warrants	Yes

Composition % assets 06-30-01	
Cash	13.4
Stocks*	83.3
Bonds	1.7
Other	1.7
*Foreign (% stocks)	1.2

Market Cap	
Giant	56.9
Large	32.3
Medium	9.1
Small	1.4
Micro	0.3

Sector Weightings	% of Stocks	Rel S&P	5-Year High	5-Year Low
Utilities	0.6	0.2	—	—
Energy	6.2	0.9	—	—
Financials	24.2	1.4	—	—
Industrials	12.8	1.1	—	—
Durables	0.5	0.3	—	—
Staples	10.4	1.3	—	—
Services	17.2	1.6	—	—
Retail	6.2	0.9	—	—
Health	9.4	0.6	—	—
Technology	12.5	0.7	—	—

Address:	82 Devonshire Street Boston, MA 02109 800–544–8888
Web Address:	www.fidelity.com
*Inception:	12-28-98
Advisor:	Fidelity Mgmt. & Research
Subadvisor:	FMR (Far East)/FMR (U.K.)
NTF Plans:	Fidelity Inst.

Minimum Purchase:	$2500	Add: $250 IRA: $500
Min Auto Inv Plan:	$2500	Add: $100
Sales Fees:	No-load	
Management Fee:	.20%+.52% mx./.25% mn.(G)	
Actual Fees:	Mgt: 0.48%	Dist: —
Expense Projections:	3Yr: $362	5Yr: $628 10Yr: $1386
Avg Brok Commission:	—	Income Distrib: Quarterly
Total Cost (relative to category):		Average

Fidelity Growth Company

Ticker	Load	NAV	Yield	Total Assets	Mstar Category
FDGRX	None	$53.22	0.0%	$22,741.6 mil	Large Growth

Prospectus Objective: Growth

Fidelity Growth Company Fund seeks capital appreciation.

The fund invests primarily in various common stocks including preferreds, convertibles, and warrants issued by companies that the advisor believes have above-average growth potential, measured by earnings or gross sales. To select investments, the advisor focuses mainly on smaller, lesser-known companies in emerging areas of the economy. It may also seek investment opportunities in revitalized or well-positioned larger companies in mature industries.

The fund was formerly named Fidelity Mercury Fund.

Historical Profile
Return Above Avg
Risk Above Avg
Rating ★★★ Neutral

Investment Style
Equity
Average Stock %: 86% 88% 95% 96% 98% 98% 99%

▼ Manager Change
▽ Partial Manager Change

Fund Performance vs. Category Average
■ Quarterly Fund Return +/– Category Average
— Category Baseline

Performance Quartile (within Category)

Portfolio Manager(s)

Steven S. Wymer. Since 1-97. BS'85 U. of Illinois; MBA'89 U. of Chicago.

1990	1991	1992	1993	1994	1995	1996	1997	1998	1999	2000	12-01	History
19.60	27.09	27.64	29.06	27.26	36.29	40.46	43.32	51.02	84.30	71.43	53.22	NAV
3.59	48.33	7.94	16.19	−2.22	39.61	16.81	18.91	27.23	79.48	−6.32	−25.31	Total Return %
6.71	17.85	0.33	6.13	−3.54	2.08	−6.14	−14.44	−1.35	58.44	2.78	−13.44	+/– S&P 500
2.23	8.93	4.05	16.26	−7.08	0.96	−8.71	−14.83	−17.87	49.80	18.21	−4.81	+/– Russ Top 200 Grt
0.00	0.41	0.34	0.25	0.76	0.59	0.78	0.54	0.21	0.00	0.00	0.00	Income Return %
3.59	47.92	7.61	15.94	−2.98	39.03	16.03	18.36	27.02	79.48	−6.32	−25.31	Capital Return %
12	31	33	23	52	13	67	82	68	8	19	63	Total Rtn % Rank Cat
0.00	0.08	0.09	0.07	0.22	0.16	0.28	0.22	0.09	0.00	0.00	0.00	Income $
0.00	1.73	1.48	2.92	0.92	1.57	1.60	4.35	3.73	6.29	7.50	0.16	Capital Gains $
1.14	1.07	1.09	1.07	1.05	0.95	0.85	0.68	0.63	0.72	0.85	—	Expense Ratio %
1.51	0.75	0.52	0.43	0.64	0.76	0.96	0.54	0.24	−0.11	−0.31	—	Income Ratio %
189	174	250	159	135	97	78	93	76	86	69	—	Turnover Rate %
601.7	1,376.4	1,810.7	2,542.7	2,993.4	6,278.8	9,272.6	10,509.4	11,440.4	24,337.2	30,397.4	22,741.6	Net Assets $mil

Performance 12-31-01

	1st Qtr	2nd Qtr	3rd Qtr	4th Qtr	Total
1997	−2.72	15.70	9.57	−3.58	18.91
1998	12.80	1.57	−8.34	21.16	27.23
1999	9.00	9.56	3.99	44.52	79.48
2000	18.78	−8.18	2.71	−16.37	−6.32
2001	−26.49	12.01	−26.04	22.66	−25.31

Trailing	Total Return%	+/– S&P 500	+/– Russ Top 200 Grth	% Rank All	% Rank Cat	Growth of $10,000
3 Mo	22.66	11.97	9.80	10	10	12,266
6 Mo	−9.29	−3.73	−2.30	83	53	9,071
1 Yr	−25.31	−13.44	−4.81	89	63	7,469
3 Yr Avg	7.89	8.91	15.91	15	3	12,558
5 Yr Avg	13.70	3.00	5.10	6	11	18,998
10 Yr Avg	14.28	1.35	3.20	7	5	37,992
15 Yr Avg	16.14	2.41	2.77	4	7	94,335

Tax Analysis	Tax-Adj Ret%	%Rank Cat	%Pretax Ret	%Rank Cat
3 Yr Avg	6.41	3	81.3	41
5 Yr Avg	11.77	11	86.0	29
10 Yr Avg	12.21	6	85.5	20

Potential Capital Gain Exposure: −7% of assets

Risk Analysis

Time Period	Load-Adj Return %	Risk %Rank[1] All	Risk %Rank[1] Cat	Morningstar Return	Morningstar Risk	Morningstar Risk-Adj Rating
1 Yr	−25.31					
3 Yr	7.89	91	72	0.64[2]	1.46	★★★
5 Yr	13.70	87	67	2.23[2]	1.34	★★★★
10 Yr	14.28	89	65	1.61	1.31	★★★

Average Historical Rating (192 months): 4.0★s

[1]1=low, 100=high [2] T-Bill return substituted for category avg.

Category Rating (3 Yr)

1 2 3 4 5 — Worst / Best

Return: High
Risk: Above Avg

Other Measures	Standard Index S&P 500	Best Fit Index Wil 4500
Alpha	15.0	8.7
Beta	1.24	1.14
R-Squared	37	84

Standard Deviation	39.71
Mean	7.89
Sharpe Ratio	0.08

Portfolio Analysis 05-31-01

Share change since 11-00 Total Stocks: 265	Sector	PE	YTD Ret%	% Assets
⊕ Microsoft	Technology	57.6	52.78	5.26
⊕ PeopleSoft	Technology	73.1	8.10	2.68
⊕ BEA Sys	Technology	—	−77.10	2.36
⊕ AOL Time Warner	Technology	—	−7.76	2.14
⊕ Home Depot	Retail	42.9	12.07	2.14
⊕ Qualcomm	Technology	—	−38.50	2.14
⊕ Xilinx	Technology	—	−15.30	1.87
⊕ Intel	Technology	73.1	4.89	1.82
⊖ General Elec	Industrials	30.1	−15.00	1.74
⊕ Amgen	Health	52.8	−11.70	1.63
⊕ Dell Comp	Technology	61.8	55.87	1.43
⊕ Minnesota Mng & Mfg	Industrials	34.5	0.16	1.42
⊕ J.C. Penney	Retail	—	154.60	1.34
⊕ Gillette	Staples	56.6	−5.47	1.29
⊖ Wal-Mart Stores	Retail	40.3	8.94	1.29
⊕ Texas Instruments	Technology	87.5	−40.70	1.29
⊖ McKesson HBOC	Health	—	4.92	1.21
⊕ Deere	Industrials	—	−2.52	1.11
⊕ Sepracor	Health	—	−28.70	1.03
⊕ Natl Semicon	Technology	—	52.99	1.01
⊕ Sonus Networks	Technology	—	−81.70	1.01
⊖ Pfizer	Health	34.7	−12.40	0.99
⊖ Coca-Cola	Staples	35.5	−21.40	0.99
⊖ Network Appliance	Technology	NMF	−65.90	0.96
☼ Goodyear Tire & Rubber	Durables	—	7.97	0.96

Current Investment Style

Style: Value Blnd Growth; Size: Large Med Small

	Stock Port Avg	Relative S&P 500 Current	Relative S&P 500 Hist	Rel Cat
Price/Earnings Ratio	40.2	1.30	1.27	1.13
Price/Book Ratio	6.1	1.07	1.29	0.96
Price/Cash Flow	23.1	1.28	1.16	1.02
3 Yr Earnings Growth	15.9	1.09	1.27	0.74
1 Yr Earnings Est%	−0.5	0.29	—	−0.17
Med Mkt Cap $mil	16,478	0.3	0.4	0.35

[1]figure is based on 50% or less of stocks

Analysis by Scott Cooley 11-16-01

Fidelity Growth Company has toned down its act a bit, but it still packs plenty of punch.

Manager Steve Wymer has continued to position this portfolio fairly aggressively, though perhaps less so than a year ago. According to the most-recent figures provided by Fidelity, the fund's combined tech and health-care stakes topped 50% of assets. That's above the group norm. However, fewer speculative stocks dot the fund's top-10 holdings now. A year ago, issues such as Sepracor and Applera were among the fund's largest holdings; now, brand-name companies such as McKesson and Gillette have replaced them. And Wymer's second-largest holding, J.C. Penney, is a turnaround play that hardly any other large-growth funds own.

Despite that somewhat more-defensive mien, the fund still exhibits greater-than-average volatility. Its technology shares and 18% stake in consumer-discretionary issues, including media and retail names, got whacked during the third quarter, when the fund's 26% loss was five percentage points worse than its average large-growth peer's. But the fund's biotech, tech, and consumer-discretionary holdings have rebounded sharply over the past month. Although the fund's year-to-date loss through November 15 is worse than the group average, its return during the past month's market rally beats 90% of its peers'.

Over the long term, Wymer has built an admirable record here. This is one of the few funds that put up a breathtaking gain in 1999 and also held up relatively well in 2000. Thanks to early bets on areas such as biotech, as well as good stock-picking, Wymer has built an exceptional five-year record here.

Given Wymer's record and the fund's pleasingly moderate expense ratio, we think this is still a solid choice for aggressive investors.

Special Securities % assets 05-31-01	
Restricted/Illiquid Secs	Trace
Emerging-Markets Secs	Trace
Options/Futures/Warrants	No

Composition % assets 05-31-01	
Cash	0.4
Stocks*	99.5
Bonds	0.0
Other	0.2
*Foreign (% stocks)	2.3

Market Cap	
Giant	32.3
Large	30.4
Medium	32.6
Small	4.3
Micro	0.4

Sector Weightings	% of Stocks	Rel S&P	5-Year High	5-Year Low
Utilities	0.0	0.0	3	0
Energy	2.5	0.4	7	1
Financials	4.0	0.2	18	4
Industrials	8.9	0.8	18	4
Durables	3.0	1.9	7	0
Staples	5.2	0.7	11	0
Services	9.8	0.9	17	6
Retail	9.1	1.3	17	4
Health	21.7	1.5	27	7
Technology	35.9	2.0	48	16

Address:	82 Devonshire Street Boston, MA 02109 800-544-8888
Web Address:	www.fidelity.com
Inception:	01-17-83
Advisor:	Fidelity Mgmt. & Research
Subadvisor:	FMR (U.K.)/FMR (Far East)
NTF Plans:	Fidelity , Fidelity Inst.

Minimum Purchase:	$2500	Add: $250 IRA: $500
Min Auto Inv Plan:	$2500	Add: $100
Sales Fees:	No-load	
Management Fee:	.30%+.52% mx./.27% mn.(G)+(–).20%P	
Actual Fees:	Mgt: 0.51%	Dist: —
Expense Projections:	3Yr: $237	5Yr: $411 10Yr: $918
Avg Brok Commission:	—	Income Distrib: Annually
Total Cost (relative to category):		Low

Fidelity High–Income

Ticker	Load	NAV	Yield	SEC Yield	Total Assets	Mstar Category
SPHIX	None	$8.13	11.0%	—	$1,551.1 mil	High–Yield Bond

Prospectus Objective: Corp Bond—High Yield

Fidelity High-Income Fund seeks current income; growth of capital may also be considered.

The fund invests at least 65% of assets in high-yielding fixed-income securities of all types; these higher yields are usually derived from low-rated and long-term securities. It may also invest a portion of assets in debt securities not paying current income in anticipation of possible future income. The fund may invest up to 10% of assets in illiquid securities, and up to 20% in equity securities, when consistent with the fund's primary objective.

Prior to June 27, 1998, the fund was named Fidelity Spartan High-Income Fund.

Historical Profile

Return: Average
Risk: High
Rating: ★★ Below Avg

Investment Style
Fixed-Income

Income Rtn %Rank Cat: 71, 28, 67, 36, 65, 64, 100, 63

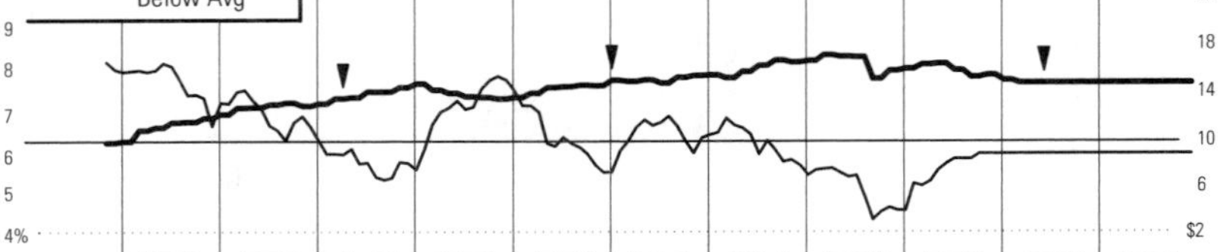

Growth of Principal vs. Interest Rate Shifts
— Principal Value $000 (NAV with capital gains reinvested)
— Interest Rate % on 10 Yr Treasury
▼ Manager Change
▽ Partial Manager Change
► Mgr Unknown After
◄ Mgr Unknown Before

Performance Quartile (within Category)

1990	1991	1992	1993	1994	1995	1996	1997	1998	1999	2000	12–01	History
9.51	11.00	11.65	12.17	11.46	12.21	12.54	13.03	12.11	12.00	9.45	8.13	NAV
–0.56*	34.34	21.50	21.86	3.21	18.53	14.16	15.92	3.30	8.89	–14.20	–4.84	Total Return %
—	18.34	14.10	12.12	6.12	0.06	10.55	6.24	–5.37	9.72	–25.83	–13.27	+/– LB Aggregate
—	–9.41	4.84	2.95	4.18	1.15	1.74	3.30	2.72	5.61	–8.99	–10.62	+/– FB High–Yield
4.34	14.62	12.16	10.30	8.56	10.73	9.21	9.33	8.58	8.97	7.27	9.88	Income Return %
–4.90	19.72	9.34	11.56	–5.35	7.80	4.95	6.59	–5.28	–0.08	–21.47	–14.72	Capital Return %
—	58	8	13	1	21	30	8	21	14	87	89	Total Rtn % Rank Cat
0.43	1.30	1.26	1.13	1.00	1.17	1.07	1.11	1.06	1.04	0.84	0.89	Income $
0.00	0.32	0.37	0.79	0.08	0.12	0.25	0.31	0.30	0.13	0.09	0.00	Capital Gains $
—	0.70	0.70	0.70	0.75	0.80	0.79	0.80	0.80	0.80	0.74	0.74	Expense Ratio %
—	11.98	11.43	9.57	8.07	8.41	8.85	8.51	8.57	9.20	9.85	10.68	Income Ratio %
—	72	99	136	213	172	170	102	85	68	50	68	Turnover Rate %
2,659.1	201.8	434.7	664.6	617.5	1,080.6	1,717.3	2,446.9	2,861.9	3,261.7	2,130.9	1,551.1	Net Assets $mil

Portfolio Manager(s)

Fred Hoff. Since 6-00.

Performance 12-31-01

	1st Qtr	2nd Qtr	3rd Qtr	4th Qtr	Total
1997	0.97	6.18	7.08	0.98	15.92
1998	6.25	0.69	–8.34	5.35	3.30
1999	6.87	1.60	–2.20	2.54	8.89
2000	–1.88	–3.06	–0.86	–9.02	–14.20
2001	3.30	–5.81	–6.96	5.11	–4.84

Trailing	Total Return%	+/– LB Agg	+/– FB High–Yield	% Rank All	% Rank Cat	Growth of $10,000
3 Mo	5.11	5.08	–0.53	64	65	10,511
6 Mo	–2.20	–6.86	–3.65	48	84	9,780
1 Yr	–4.84	–13.27	–10.62	51	89	9,516
3 Yr Avg	–3.84	–10.12	–5.01	89	85	8,890
5 Yr Avg	1.26	–6.17	–1.98	90	56	10,647
10 Yr Avg	8.21	0.98	0.38	42	12	22,016
15 Yr Avg	—	—	—	—	—	—

Tax Analysis	Tax-Adj Ret%	%Rank Cat	%Pretax Ret	%Rank Cat
3 Yr Avg	–7.15	81	—	—
5 Yr Avg	–2.43	54	—	—
10 Yr Avg	3.91	26	47.7	32

Potential Capital Gain Exposure: –76% of assets

Risk Analysis

Time Period	Load-Adj Return %	Risk %Rank[1] All	Risk %Rank[1] Cat	Morningstar Return	Morningstar Risk	Morningstar Risk-Adj Rating
1 Yr	–4.84					
3 Yr	–3.84	43	85	–1.71[2]	2.61	★
5 Yr	1.26	44	79	–0.77[2]	2.52	★
10 Yr	8.21	45	63	1.04[2]	1.68	★★★

Average Historical Rating (101 months): 4.5★s

[1] 1=low, 100=high [2] T-Bill return substituted for category avg.

Category Rating (3 Yr)

1 2 3 4 5 — Worst … Best

Return: Below Avg
Risk: Above Avg

Other Measures	Standard Index LB Agg	Best Fit Index FB HY
Alpha	–8.1	–3.4
Beta	0.16	1.37
R–Squared	0	87
Standard Deviation		10.54
Mean		–3.84
Sharpe Ratio		–0.97

Portfolio Analysis 04-30-01

Total Fixed-Income: 189	Date of Maturity	Amount $000	Value $000	% Net Assets
CSC Hldgs Pfd PIK 11.125%		747	81,425	3.79
Nextel Comm FRN	/ /	101	68,978	3.21
CSC Hldgs H Pfd PIK 11.75%		422	46,086	2.15
NTL Step 0%	02-01-06	54,295	45,608	2.12
Nextel Comm Pfd PIK 13%		52	40,496	1.89
McCaw Intl Step 0%	04-15-07	65,360	35,948	1.67
Broadwing Pikp 12.5%		35	35,000	1.63
Millicom Intl Step 0%	06-01-06	39,424	33,116	1.54
Frontiervision Step 0%	09-15-07	29,990	30,515	1.42
HMH Properties 7.875%	08-01-08	30,815	29,891	1.39
EchoStar Comms Cl A		946	28,329	1.32
Bally's Total Fitness 9.875%	10-15-07	26,810	26,207	1.22
Echostar 10.375%	10-01-07	24,800	25,668	1.20
Charter Comm 8.625%	04-01-09	26,000	25,285	1.18
AES 8.875%	02-15-11	25,000	25,125	1.17
GS Escrow 7%	08-01-03	25,000	24,815	1.16
Gothic Prodtn 11.125%	05-01-05	21,858	24,372	1.14
Chesapeake Energy 144A 8.125%	04-01-11	25,000	24,313	1.13
NTL Step 0%	04-01-08	44,265	23,903	1.11
Intermedia Comm 8.6%	06-01-08	25,850	23,782	1.11

Current Investment Style

Not Available

Avg Eff Duration	—
Avg Eff Maturity	—
Avg Credit Quality	—
Avg Wtd Coupon	0.00%
Avg Wtd Price	86.62% of par

Special Securities % assets 04-30-01	
Restricted/Illiquid Secs	10
Exotic Mortgage–Backed	0
Emerging–Markets Secs	1
Options/Futures/Warrants	Yes

Credit Analysis % bonds 03-31-01

US Govt	0	BB	6
AAA	0	B	42
AA	0	Below B	7
A	0	NR/NA	44
BBB	1		

Sector Breakdown % bonds 04-30-01

US Treasuries	0	CMOs	0
GNMA mtgs	2	ARMs	0
FNMA mtgs	0	Other	99
FHLMC mtgs	0		

Coupon Range	% of Bonds	Rel Cat
0%, PIK	20.31	3.24
0% to 9%	30.35	1.00
9% to 12%	34.52	0.65
12% to 14%	14.77	1.68
More than 14%	0.06	0.04

1.00=Category Average

Composition % assets 04-30-01

Cash	6.3	Bonds	76.1
Stocks	3.4	Other	14.2

Analysis by Scott Berry 10-23-01

We're close to throwing in the towel on Fidelity High-Income, but we haven't given up hope yet.

This fund just can't seem to get out of its rut. While the majority of high-yield funds have struggled over the past few years, this fund has performed worse than most. Indeed, it dropped 14.2% in 2000 and another 8.8% for the year to date through Oct. 22, 2001, while its average peer lost just 8.4% in 2000 and just 1.8% for the year to date.

The fund's woes have stemmed largely from its oversized telecom stake. While manager Fred Hoff has tried to position the fund more defensively in recent months, picking up utility and health-care names, the telecom sector still weighs heavily on its year-to-date return. High-profile blowups such as PSINet and Winstar hit the fund hard, and even well-financed telecom companies, such as Nextel, have been knocked down in recent months.

The fund's below-average credit quality has also contributed to its slide. With the economy teetering on the edge of recession, investors have shunned lower-rated bonds, which in years past were this fund's bread and butter. Indeed, this fund has historically devoted a larger percentage of its assets to bonds rated B and below than the overwhelming majority of its category peers. Though this added credit risk wasn't a factor for much of the 1990s, it has been over the last 18 months.

A longtime Morningstar favorite, this fund has started to try our patience. That the fund hasn't kept pace with its average peer is not surprising given its added credit risk and the current economic environment, but the degree to which it has underperformed is a concern. We're still confident in this fund's long-term potential, but we think it's only suitable for experienced high-yield investors comfortable with its obvious risks.

Address:	82 Devonshire Street Boston, MA 02109 800–544–8888
Web Address:	www.fidelity.com
*Inception:	08-29-90
Advisor:	Fidelity Mgmt. & Research
Subadvisor:	FMR (U.K.)/FMR (Far East)
NTF Plans:	Fidelity , Fidelity Inst.

Minimum Purchase:	$2500	Add: $250	IRA: $500
Min Auto Inv Plan:	$2500	Add: $100	
Sales Fees:	No-load, 1.00%R within 9 months		
Management Fee:	.58%		
Actual Fees:	Mgt: 0.58%	Dist: —	
Expense Projections:	3Yr: $240	5Yr: $417	10Yr: $930
Avg Brok Commission:	—	Income Distrib: Monthly	
Total Cost (relative to category):		Low	

Fidelity Independence

Ticker	Load	NAV	Yield	Total Assets	Mstar Category
FDFFX	None	$15.77	1.3%	$5,485.6 mil	Large Growth

Prospectus Objective: Growth

Fidelity Independence Fund seeks capital appreciation.

The fund invests primarily in common stocks of domestic or foreign companies of any size. The fund is designed for tax-advantaged accounts (e.g., IRAs or similar retirement plans) that can tolerate fluctuations in the stock market. Therefore, the fund does not generally consider the length of holding when trading securities.

Past fund names: Fidelity Freedom Fund and Fidelity Retirement Growth Fund.

Historical Profile

Return: Average
Risk: Above Avg
Rating: ★★★ Neutral

Investment Style
Equity
Average Stock %: 82% 89% 98% 97% 97% 96% 90%

▼ Manager Change
▽ Partial Manager Change

Fund Performance vs. Category Average
■ Quarterly Fund Return +/– Category Average
— Category Baseline

Performance Quartile (within Category)

Portfolio Manager(s)

J. Fergus Shiel. Since 6-96. BA'80 U. of Virginia; MBA'89 Columbia U. Other funds currently managed: Fidelity Advisor Dynamic Cap App A, Fidelity Advisor Dynamic Cap App T, Fidelity Advisor Dynamic Cap App B.

1990	1991	1992	1993	1994	1995	1996	1997	1998	1999	2000	12-01	History
13.45	18.23	16.44	18.14	16.24	18.19	17.29	16.85	20.51	25.85	22.01	15.77	NAV
–10.16	45.59	10.60	22.13	0.06	24.28	8.34	18.54	35.89	47.03	1.70	–27.22	Total Return %
–7.04	15.10	2.98	12.07	–1.25	–13.25	–14.61	–14.81	7.32	25.99	10.81	–15.35	+/– S&P 500
–11.52	6.18	6.71	22.20	–4.79	–14.37	–17.19	–15.20	–9.21	17.35	26.23	–6.72	+/– Russ Top 200 Grt
0.73	1.49	0.88	0.85	1.22	2.18	1.44	0.75	0.83	0.25	0.31	0.91	Income Return %
–10.88	44.10	9.72	21.28	–1.16	22.10	6.90	17.79	35.06	46.78	1.39	–28.13	Capital Return %
93	39	16	10	25	89	97	82	35	30	5	69	Total Rtn % Rank Cat
0.11	0.20	0.16	0.14	0.22	0.35	0.26	0.13	0.14	0.05	0.08	0.20	Income $
0.57	1.04	3.53	1.75	1.68	1.58	2.15	3.41	2.13	3.66	4.19	0.06	Capital Gains $
0.98	0.83	1.02	1.05	1.07	0.99	0.70	0.59	0.57	0.58	0.85	—	Expense Ratio %
2.34	1.56	1.01	0.80	1.13	1.92	1.26	0.66	0.68	0.25	0.19	—	Income Ratio %
127	119	138	101	72	108	230	205	266	310	249	—	Turnover Rate %
1,317.8	1,835.2	2,211.6	2,848.2	3,184.9	4,071.6	4,045.9	3,932.2	4,946.1	7,268.5	8,474.2	5,485.6	Net Assets $mil

Performance 12-31-01

	1st Qtr	2nd Qtr	3rd Qtr	4th Qtr	Total
1997	–1.91	15.27	10.79	–5.37	18.54
1998	18.58	4.00	–9.53	21.80	35.89
1999	7.16	6.23	–4.81	35.68	47.03
2000	17.53	–2.52	0.54	–11.71	1.70
2001	–24.86	7.46	–21.28	14.50	–27.22

Trailing	Total Return%	+/– S&P 500	+/– Russ Top 200 Grth	% Rank All	% Rank Cat	Growth of $10,000
3 Mo	14.50	3.81	1.64	25	42	11,450
6 Mo	–9.86	–4.31	–2.88	85	60	9,014
1 Yr	–27.22	–15.35	–6.72	91	69	7,278
3 Yr Avg	2.86	3.89	10.88	56	12	10,883
5 Yr Avg	11.88	1.18	3.29	10	18	17,531
10 Yr Avg	12.30	–0.63	1.22	17	19	31,901
15 Yr Avg	13.71	–0.02	0.34	12	25	68,724

Tax Analysis	Tax-Adj Ret%	%Rank Cat	%Pretax Ret	%Rank Cat
3 Yr Avg	–0.59	22	—	—
5 Yr Avg	7.64	38	64.3	75
10 Yr Avg	8.02	52	65.2	84

Potential Capital Gain Exposure: –20% of assets

Risk Analysis

Time Period	Load-Adj Return %	Risk %Rank[1] All	Risk %Rank[1] Cat	Morningstar Return	Morningstar Risk	Morningstar Risk-Adj Rating
1 Yr	–27.22					
3 Yr	2.86	92	75	–0.43[2]	1.50	★★★
5 Yr	11.88	87	71	1.71[2]	1.36	★★★
10 Yr	12.30	87	51	1.16	1.25	★★★

Average Historical Rating (190 months): 3.8★s

[1]1=low, 100=high [2] T-Bill return substituted for category avg.

Category Rating (3 Yr)

1 2 3 **4** 5
Worst — Best

Return: Above Avg
Risk: Above Avg

Other Measures	Standard Index S&P 500	Best Fit Index Wil 4500
Alpha	9.8	3.4
Beta	1.30	1.14
R-Squared	41	85
Standard Deviation		37.77
Mean		2.86
Sharpe Ratio		–0.06

Portfolio Analysis 05-31-01

Share change since 11-00 Total Stocks: 130	Sector	PE	YTD Ret%	% Assets
Philip Morris	Staples	12.1	9.12	16.83
RJ Reynolds Tobacco Hldgs	Staples	3.1	22.37	8.99
⊕ EchoStar Comms	Technology	—	20.75	5.05
⊕ BEA Sys	Technology	—	–77.10	4.55
⊕ CIENA	Technology	NMF	–82.30	2.86
⊖ Nokia Cl A ADR	Technology	45.8	–43.00	2.73
⊕ Merrill Lynch	Financials	18.2	–22.70	2.62
⊖ Immunex	Health	89.4	–31.70	1.66
⊕ Bristol-Myers Squibb	Health	20.2	–26.00	1.63
⊕ Lehman Brothers Hldgs	Financials	12.4	–0.84	1.52
☼ Minnesota Mng & Mfg	Industrials	34.5	0.16	1.51
Global Marine	Energy	—	–43.20	1.50
⊕ Charles Schwab	Financials	61.9	–45.30	1.41
⊖ PeopleSoft	Technology	73.1	8.10	1.33
⊕ Juniper Net	Technology	NMF	–84.90	1.26
☼ Peregrine Sys	Technology	—	–24.90	1.24
⊕ UST, Inc.	Staples	12.3	32.23	1.09
☼ Dollar General	Retail	19.4	–20.40	1.05
⊖ Staples	Retail	77.9	58.30	0.94
⊕ Perkinelmer	Services	29.9	–32.70	0.94
⊖ Safeway	Retail	18.1	–33.20	0.89
☼ Computer Assoc Intl	Technology	—	77.28	0.88
Ensco Intl	Energy	15.7	–26.70	0.86
⊖ Walgreen	Retail	39.1	–19.20	0.85
☼ Best Buy	Retail	41.2	151.90	0.82

Current Investment Style

Style: Value Blnd Growth; Size: Large Med Small

	Stock Port Avg	Relative S&P 500 Current	Relative S&P 500 Hist	Rel Cat
Price/Earnings Ratio	26.6	0.86	1.18	0.75
Price/Book Ratio	5.2	0.91	1.40	0.81
Price/Cash Flow	20.4	1.14	1.13	0.90
3 Yr Earnings Growth	16.8	1.15	1.39	0.78
1 Yr Earnings Est%	–0.1	0.06	—	–0.03
Med Mkt Cap $mil	12,308	0.2	0.5	0.26

Special Securities % assets 05-31-01	
Restricted/Illiquid Secs	0
Emerging-Markets Secs	Trace
Options/Futures/Warrants	Yes

Composition % assets 05-31-01	
Cash	9.6
Stocks*	90.2
Bonds	0.0
Other	0.2
*Foreign (% stocks)	7.0

Market Cap	
Giant	27.5
Large	29.8
Medium	39.2
Small	3.3
Micro	0.3

Sector Weightings	% of Stocks	Rel S&P	5-Year High	5-Year Low
Utilities	0.0	0.0	5	0
Energy	4.6	0.7	23	0
Financials	8.3	0.5	17	1
Industrials	8.7	0.8	26	3
Durables	0.7	0.5	13	0
Staples	33.8	4.3	34	1
Services	4.0	0.4	26	4
Retail	6.7	1.0	13	4
Health	5.4	0.4	26	4
Technology	27.8	1.5	63	7

Analysis by William Harding 11-13-01

This fund doesn't fit neatly into a box, but it's a decent choice for tax-deferred accounts.

Fidelity Independence manager Fergus Shiel marches to the beat of his own drummer by investing in everything from high-flying tech names to depressed cyclicals. The portfolio's price multiples land it in the large-growth category, but it doesn't resemble many of its peers. In fact, the fund's 41% R-squared (a measure of correlation) relative to the S&P 500 index is one of the lowest in the group.

Shiel's frequent maneuvering drives the fund's performance. In 2001, he has rotated heavily into consumer staples, leaving the fund with 40% of assets there at the end of September. Many of his staples picks, particularly Philip Morris and RJ Reynolds, have performed well during this year's economic slump. But Shiel's moves don't always work out. He slashed the fund's tech weighting to 14% of assets as of Sept. 30, 2001, from more than 40% a year earlier. But that proved too little too late to stem losses in holdings such as Ciena and Juniper Networks. Thus, the fund has lost more than 30% for the year through Nov. 8, 2001.

Shiel's eclectic mix of stocks and frequent sector shifts have generally worked fairly well over the long haul, however. His growth-oriented holdings fueled strong gains in 1998 and 1999 and his stodgier stocks picked up the slack in 2000. All told, the fund's returns easily best the average large-growth fund since Shiel took the helm in 1996 but trail the S&P 500 by a slight margin.

Despite its good long-term record, this fund is not for conservative investors or those in taxable accounts. Because of Shiel's frequent trading, this fund has been a tax nightmare. In addition, big bets on sectors and individual holdings—the fund's top-10 names soak up 50% of assets—will lead to severe swings in performance.

Address:	82 Devonshire Street Boston, MA 02109 800-544-8888
Web Address:	www.fidelity.com
Inception:	03-25-83
Advisor:	Fidelity Mgmt. & Research
Subadvisor:	FMR (U.K.)/FMR (Far East)
NTF Plans:	Fidelity , Fidelity Inst.

Minimum Purchase:	$2500	Add: $250	IRA: $500
Min Auto Inv Plan:	$2500	Add: $100	
Sales Fees:	No-load		
Management Fee:	.30%+.52% mx./.27% mn.(G)+(–).20%P		
Actual Fees:	Mgt: 0.43%	Dist: —	
Expense Projections:	3Yr: $202	5Yr: $351	10Yr: $786
Avg Brok Commission:	—	Income Distrib: Annually	
Total Cost (relative to category):	Low		

Fidelity Latin America

Ticker	Load	NAV	Yield	Total Assets	Mstar Category
FLATX	3.00%	$12.01	2.1%	$209.6 mil	Latin America Stock

Prospectus Objective: Foreign Stock

Fidelity Latin America Fund seeks total return through income and capital appreciation.

The fund normally invests at least 65% of assets in Latin American securities. It focuses on equity securities, but may invest in any combination of equity and debt securities. Equities may include common stocks, preferred stocks, and convertibles. The fund may invest up to 35% of assets in debt securities rated below investment-grade. It may invest up to 35% of assets in a single industy.

Historical Profile

Return Average
Risk High
Rating ★★★ Neutral

Investment Style
Equity
Average Stock %: 66% 77% 66% 80% 87% 88% 82%

▼ Manager Change
▽ Partial Manager Change

Fund Performance vs. Category Average
■ Quarterly Fund Return +/– Category Average
— Category Baseline

Performance Quartile (within Category)

Portfolio Manager(s)

Margaret Reynolds. Since 6-01. Other funds currently managed: Fidelity Advisor Latin America A, Fidelity Advisor Latin America T, Fidelity Advisor Latin America B.

1990	1991	1992	1993	1994	1995	1996	1997	1998	1999	2000	12-01	History
—	—	—	16.10	12.37	10.21	13.11	17.22	10.37	15.91	13.06	12.01	NAV
—	—	—	62.08*	–23.17	–16.47	30.72	32.89	–38.35	54.90	–17.47	–6.04	Total Return %
—	—	—	55.07*	–24.48	–54.00	7.78	–0.46	–66.92	33.86	–8.36	5.84	+/– S&P 500
—	—	—	—	–17.89	–0.69	11.99	4.50	–0.15	–6.91	–1.54	—	+/– MSCI Latin Am
—	—	—	0.44	0.00	0.97	2.25	1.53	1.45	1.35	0.44	1.91	Income Return %
—	—	—	61.65	–23.17	–17.44	28.47	31.36	–39.80	53.55	–17.91	–7.95	Capital Return %
—	—	—	—	80	35	26	27	38	75	59	60	Total Rtn % Rank Cat
—	—	—	0.05	0.00	0.12	0.23	0.20	0.25	0.14	0.07	0.25	Income $
—	—	—	0.05	0.00	0.00	0.00	0.00	0.00	0.00	0.00	0.00	Capital Gains $
—	—	—	1.94	1.48	1.41	1.32	1.29	1.33	1.30	1.23	—	Expense Ratio %
—	—	—	1.21	0.47	0.97	1.48	1.19	1.49	1.55	0.44	—	Income Ratio %
—	—	—	72	77	57	70	64	31	49	51	—	Turnover Rate %
—	—	—	798.9	616.1	473.8	535.1	860.6	307.0	409.9	267.6	209.6	Net Assets $mil

Performance 12-31-01

	1st Qtr	2nd Qtr	3rd Qtr	4th Qtr	Total
1997	13.96	22.09	4.71	–8.79	32.89
1998	0.29	–18.88	–30.76	9.45	–38.35
1999	11.96	16.28	–12.30	35.67	54.90
2000	4.53	–7.46	–6.24	–9.00	–17.47
2001	–7.12	8.00	–22.75	21.26	–6.04

Trailing	Total Return%	+/– S&P 500	+/– MSCI Latin Am	% Rank All	% Rank Cat	Growth of $10,000
3 Mo	21.26	10.57	—	12	63	12,126
6 Mo	–6.33	–0.77	—	70	11	9,367
1 Yr	–6.04	5.84	—	53	60	9,396
3 Yr Avg	6.30	7.33	—	20	65	12,013
5 Yr Avg	–0.32	–11.02	—	93	72	9,842
10 Yr Avg	—	—	—	—	—	—
15 Yr Avg	—	—	—	—	—	—

Tax Analysis	Tax-Adj Ret%	%Rank Cat	%Pretax Ret	%Rank Cat
3 Yr Avg	5.80	71	92.0	84
5 Yr Avg	–0.88	72	—	—
10 Yr Avg	—	—	—	—

Potential Capital Gain Exposure: –42% of assets

Risk Analysis

Time Period	Load-Adj Return %	Risk %Rank[1] All	Risk %Rank[1] Cat	Morningstar Return	Morningstar Risk	Morningstar Risk-Adj Rating
1 Yr	–8.86					
3 Yr	5.23	92	58	0.06[2]	1.41	★★★★
5 Yr	–0.92	97	81	–1.16[2]	1.58	★★
Incept	3.04	—	—	—	—	

Average Historical Rating (69 months): 1.9★s

[1] 1=low, 100=high [2] T-Bill return substituted for category avg.

Category Rating (3 Yr)

1 Worst … 5 Best

Return: Below Avg
Risk: Average

Other Measures	Standard Index S&P 500	Best Fit Index Wil 4500
Alpha	12.3	6.3
Beta	1.20	0.93
R-Squared	40	65

Standard Deviation	35.98
Mean	6.30
Sharpe Ratio	0.04

Portfolio Analysis 04-30-01

Share change since 10–00 Total Stocks: 37	Sector	Country	% Assets
⊖ Telefonos de Mexico ADR L	Services	Mexico	10.05
☼ Bebidas Das America ADR Pfd	N/A	N/A	8.38
⊕ Petrobras Pfd	Energy	Brazil	6.46
☼ Wal-Mart de Mexico Cl C	Retail	Mexico	6.07
☼ Fomento Economico Mex	Staples	Mexico	4.97
⊕ Grupo Televisa (Part) ADR	Services	Mexico	4.41
⊕ Telesp Celular Part ADR	Services	Brazil	4.25
⊖ Banacci	N/A	N/A	4.25
⊕ Unibanco GDR	Financials	Brazil	4.00
⊕ Vale do Rio Doce A	Industrials	Brazil	3.96
⊕ Brasileira de Distrib ADR	Retail	Brazil	3.46
☼ Pecom Energia S.A.	Energy	Argentina	2.51
⊖ Itaubanco Pn Pfd	N/A	N/A	2.30
☼ Distribucion Svc D&S	Retail	Chile	2.17
⊕ Grupo Carso Cl A1	Staples	Mexico	2.05
☼ America Movil Ser L ADR	N/A	N/A	2.00
⊖ TV Azteca ADR	Services	Mexico	2.00
⊕ Panamerican Beverages Cl A	Staples	Mexico	1.93
☼ Embraer ADR	Industrials	Brazil	1.79
⊕ Grupo Iusacell Cl V ADR	Technology	Mexico	1.61

Current Investment Style

Style: Value Blnd Growth; Size: Large Med Small

	Stock Port Avg	Rel MSCI EAFE Current	Rel MSCI EAFE Hist	Rel Cat
Price/Earnings Ratio	17.7[1]	0.68	0.59	1.19
Price/Cash Flow	6.8[1]	0.53	1.08	0.97
Price/Book Ratio	3.1[1]	0.88	0.52	1.18
3 Yr Earnings Growth	27.8[1]	1.48	—	1.23
Med Mkt Cap $mil	10,229[1]	0.4	0.3	1.89

[1] figure is based on 50% or less of stocks

Country Exposure 04-30-01	% assets
Mexico	33
Brazil	27
Chile	5
Argentina	4
Peru	2

Hedging History: Never

Special Securities % assets 04-30-01	
Restricted/Illiquid Secs	0
Emerging-Markets Secs	73
Options/Futures/Warrants	Yes

Composition % assets 04-30-01

Cash	5.8	Bonds	0.0
Stocks	82.0	Other	12.2

Sector Weightings	% of Stocks	Rel Cat	5-Year High	5-Year Low
Utilities	2.0	0.3	19	1
Energy	12.2	1.2	12	4
Financials	7.7	0.6	19	1
Industrials	12.2	0.7	29	6
Durables	0.0	0.0	9	0
Staples	16.1	1.2	27	11
Services	31.8	1.1	59	11
Retail	15.9	1.8	16	2
Health	0.0	0.0	0	0
Technology	2.2	5.7	3	0

Analysis by William Samuel Rocco 09-21-01

This fund's new manager has taken over in tough conditions.

Margaret Reynolds replaced longtime manager Patti Satterthwaite at the end of June. Unfortunately, Reynolds arrived just in time for the latest big sell-off south of the border. Indeed, after posting a 3% gain in the first six months of the year, the typical Latin America offering has plunged 24% since June, burdened by everything from worries about an Argentine debt default to fears of a global recession.

This fund hasn't suffered quite as much as its typical peer lately. Its minimal exposure to Argentina has paid off, as has its moderate overweighting in Mexico (which has held up a little better than most of its neighbors this summer). Indeed, a few of the fund's Mexican picks have incurred relatively limited losses, including top holding Telmex. As a result, this fund has lost 1 percentage point less than the average Latin America offering during the three months ending Sept. 20, 2001.

The fact that the fund has plunged a bit less than the group norm this summer is no reason to celebrate Reynolds' arrival, of course. However, there are reasons to be sanguine about her presence. She worked as an analyst on this fund—and as an associate manager on other Latin America offerings—for years before taking charge here, so she knows the region and this fund's strategy well. Meanwhile, she is maintaining that strategy, which focuses on blue chips with strong cash flows and balance sheets and has produced four top-third showings in the past six years. Finally, Fidelity's ample international resources remain in place and at her disposal.

Thus, we think this fund is still a solid option for investors who are bold enough to venture south of the border.

Address:	82 Devonshire Street Boston, MA 02109 800–544–8888
Web Address:	www.fidelity.com
*Inception:	04-20-93
Advisor:	Fidelity Mgmt. & Research
Subadvisor:	FMR (U.K.)/FMR (Far East)
NTF Plans:	Fidelity Inst.

Minimum Purchase:	$2500	Add: $250 IRA: $500
Min Auto Inv Plan:	$2500	Add: $100
Sales Fees:	3.00%L, 1.50%R within 3 months	
Management Fee:	.45%+.52% mx./.27% mn.(G)	
Actual Fees:	Mgt: 0.73%	Dist: —
Expense Projections:	3Yr: $706	5Yr: $1002 10Yr: $1843
Avg Brok Commission:	—	Income Distrib: Annually
Total Cost (relative to category):	Low	

Fidelity Leveraged Company Stock

Ticker	Load	NAV	Yield	Total Assets	Mstar Category
FLVCX	None	$10.18	2.0%	$119.5 mil	Mid–Cap Blend

Prospectus Objective: Growth

Fidelity Leveraged Company Stock Fund seeks capital appreciation.

The fund normally invests at least 65% in stocks. It generally invests in common stocks of leveraged companies (companies that issue lower-quality debt and other companies with leverage capital structures). These companies may be in troubled or uncertain financial conditions, and may be involved in bankruptcy proceedings, reorganizations, or financial restructuring. The fund can invest in domestic and foreign issuers and in growth or value stocks. The fund is considered non-diversified.

Historical Profile
Return —
Risk —
Rating Not Rated

Investment Style Equity
Average Stock % 75%

▼ Manager Change
▽ Partial Manager Change

Fund Performance vs. Category Average
■ Quarterly Fund Return +/– Category Average
— Category Baseline

Performance Quartile (within Category)

Portfolio Manager(s)

David Glancy, CFA. Since 12-00. BA'83 Tulane U.; MBA'85 Emory U. Other funds currently managed: Fidelity Capital & Income, Fidelity Advisor Leveraged Co Stk A, Fidelity Advisor Leveraged Co Stk B.

History

1990	1991	1992	1993	1994	1995	1996	1997	1998	1999	2000	12-01	History
—	—	—	—	—	—	—	—	—	—	10.07	10.18	NAV
—	—	—	—	—	—	—	—	—	—	0.70*	3.23	Total Return %
—	—	—	—	—	—	—	—	—	—	–0.51*	15.11	+/– S&P 500
—	—	—	—	—	—	—	—	—	—	—	3.83	+/– S&P Mid 400
—	—	—	—	—	—	—	—	—	—	0.00	2.00	Income Return %
—	—	—	—	—	—	—	—	—	—	0.70	1.23	Capital Return %
—	—	—	—	—	—	—	—	—	—	—	19	Total Rtn % Rank Cat
—	—	—	—	—	—	—	—	—	—	0.00	0.20	Income $
—	—	—	—	—	—	—	—	—	—	0.00	0.00	Capital Gains $
—	—	—	—	—	—	—	—	—	—	—	—	Expense Ratio %
—	—	—	—	—	—	—	—	—	—	—	—	Income Ratio %
—	—	—	—	—	—	—	—	—	—	—	—	Turnover Rate %
—	—	—	—	—	—	—	—	—	—	—	—	Net Assets $mil

Performance 12-31-01

	1st Qtr	2nd Qtr	3rd Qtr	4th Qtr	Total
1997	—	—	—	—	—
1998	—	—	—	—	—
1999	—	—	—	—	—
2000	—	—	—	—	0.70 *
2001	–1.59	8.98	–21.10	22.00	3.23

Trailing	Total Return%	+/– S&P 500	+/– S&P Mid 400	% Rank All	% Rank Cat	Growth of $10,000
3 Mo	22.00	11.32	4.02	11	13	12,200
6 Mo	–3.75	1.81	–2.19	55	56	9,625
1 Yr	3.23	15.11	3.83	36	19	10,323
3 Yr Avg	—	—	—	—	—	—
5 Yr Avg	—	—	—	—	—	—
10 Yr Avg	—	—	—	—	—	—
15 Yr Avg	—	—	—	—	—	—

Tax Analysis	Tax-Adj Ret%	%Rank Cat	%Pretax Ret	%Rank Cat
3 Yr Avg	—	—	—	—
5 Yr Avg	—	—	—	—
10 Yr Avg	—	—	—	—

Potential Capital Gain Exposure: NMF

Risk Analysis

Time Period	Load-Adj Return %	Risk %Rank[1] All	Risk %Rank[1] Cat	Morningstar Return	Morningstar Risk	Morningstar Risk-Adj Rating
1 Yr	3.23					
3 Yr	—	—	—	—	—	
5 Yr	—	—	—	—	—	
Incept	3.83	—	—	—	—	

Average Historical Rating —

[1]1=low, 100=high

Category Rating (3 Yr)

Other Measures	Standard Index S&P 500	Best Fit Index
Alpha	—	—
Beta	—	—
R–Squared	—	—
Standard Deviation		—
Mean (Return)		—
Sharpe Ratio (Risk)		—

Portfolio Analysis 07-31-01

Share change since 01-01 Total Stocks: 118	Sector	PE	YTD Ret%	% Assets
⊕ EchoStar Comms	Technology	—	20.75	9.96
⊕ AMC Entrtnmt	Services	—	200.00	3.63
⊕ Conoco Cl A	Energy	9.0	1.56	3.22
⊕ General Motors Cl H	Technology	42.9	–32.80	2.75
⊕ American Standard	Industrials	14.9	38.36	2.73
☼ Rite Aid	Retail	—	113.00	2.45
⊕ Pathmark Stores	Retail	—	49.45	2.21
⊕ CMS Energy	Utilities	—	–19.80	2.11
⊕ Markel	Financials	—	–0.75	1.79
⊕ Davita	Health	18.3	42.77	1.60
⊕ Pegasus Comms Cl A	Services	—	–59.50	1.50
⊕ American Finl Grp	Financials	—	–3.81	1.48
☼ General Dynamics	Industrials	17.6	3.63	1.35
⊕ Vesta Ins Grp	Financials	—	57.80	1.32
⊕ Tricon Global Restaurants	Services	16.3	49.09	1.16
⊕ Mattel	Staples	31.9	19.43	1.15
⊕ Nextel Comms Cl A	Services	—	–55.70	1.01
⊕ AT & T Liberty Media Cl A	Services	—	3.22	0.99
☼ Kansas City Southern Inds	Services	47.1	39.56	0.96
⊕ Midway Games	Technology	—	111.40	0.95
⊕ Western Gas Resources	Energy	12.1	–3.42	0.95
⊕ Lyondell Chemical	Energy	—	–0.75	0.95
⊕ Lockheed Martin	Industrials	36.8	38.98	0.88
☼ 7–Eleven	Retail	16.3	33.83	0.87
☼ Alliant Techsystems	Industrials	28.6	73.48	0.85

Current Investment Style

Style: Value Blnd Growth; Size: Large Med Small

	Stock Port Avg	Relative S&P 500 Current	Relative S&P 500 Hist	Rel Cat
Price/Earnings Ratio	21.7[1]	0.70	—	0.80
Price/Book Ratio	3.6	0.63	—	0.84
Price/Cash Flow	14.5	0.81	—	0.84
3 Yr Earnings Growth	—	—	—	—
1 Yr Earnings Est%	2.1[1]	—	—	0.90
Med Mkt Cap $mil	2,906	0.1	—	0.32

[1]figure is based on 50% or less of stocks

Special Securities % assets 07-31-01	
Restricted/Illiquid Secs	1
Emerging–Markets Secs	0
Options/Futures/Warrants	Yes

Composition % assets 07-31-01	
Cash	16.2
Stocks*	76.9
Bonds	6.8
Other	0.1
*Foreign (% stocks)	1.2

Market Cap	
Giant	1.8
Large	30.1
Medium	34.3
Small	28.5
Micro	5.4

Sector Weightings	% of Stocks	Rel S&P	5-Year High	5-Year Low
Utilities	2.8	0.9	—	—
Energy	10.6	1.5	—	—
Financials	10.2	0.6	—	—
Industrials	28.8	2.5	—	—
Durables	0.4	0.2	—	—
Staples	2.8	0.4	—	—
Services	20.6	1.9	—	—
Retail	9.1	1.3	—	—
Health	4.5	0.3	—	—
Technology	10.2	0.6	—	—

Analysis by Christopher Traulsen 10-25-01

Fidelity Leveraged Company Stock Fund's risks are starting to show, but we still think it's an intriguing offering.

Clearly, this is not a fund you want at the heart of your portfolio. In keeping with its name, it invests in companies that borrow heavily to finance their operations. (The fund itself is not leveraged.) In good times, such companies can earn huge returns using very little of their own capital. In an economic slowdown, however, they can quickly slump. Their debt obligations remain large, but their revenues slow, putting a big drag on cash flow. Thus, the risks here are high, to say the least.

That has been illustrated recently, as the fund's debt-laden holdings have faced a slowing economy and tight capital markets. One such company is former top-10 holding Focal Communications. Fund manager David Glancy said the local exchange carrier was growing its business as expected. However, because it needed additional funding and was already heavily in debt, it got squeezed in the current funding crunch, sending it down sharply. The fund on the whole has also suffered recently—although it started strong in 2001, it has lost 13% over the trailing three months, earning a bottom-decile showing in the mid-blend category.

Still, we think there's reason to like this fund. For one, although its risks are relatively high, it gives individuals the ability to profit from companies that use leverage smartly. Glancy also has plenty of experience finding those types of names, as he has run high-yield bond fund Fidelity Capital & Income with considerable success since 1996. He's also already had some notably strong picks here, including AMC Entertainment and Rite Aid, helping the fund limit its losses to 10.8% for the year to date through Oct. 24—a top-third showing relative to its category peers.

For investors who candle handle its risks, we think the fund merits consideration.

Address:	82 Devonshire Street Boston, MA 02109 800–544–8888
Web Address:	www.fidelity.com
*Inception:	12-19-00
Advisor:	Fidelity Mgmt. & Research
Subadvisor:	None
NTF Plans:	Fidelity Inst.

Minimum Purchase:	$10000	Add: $500	IRA: $500
Min Auto Inv Plan:	$10000	Add: $500	
Sales Fees:	No-load, 1.50%R within 3 months		
Management Fee:	.65%		
Actual Fees:	Mgt: 0.65%	Dist: —	
Expense Projections:	3Yr: $362	5Yr: —	10Yr: —
Avg Brok Commission:	—	Income Distrib: Semi–Ann.	
Total Cost (relative to category):	—		

Fidelity Low–Priced Stock

Ticker	Load	NAV	Yield	Total Assets	Mstar Category
FLPSX	3.00%	$27.42	0.55%	$10,453.9 mil	Small Value

Prospectus Objective: Small Company

Fidelity Low-Priced Stock Fund seeks capital appreciation.

The fund normally invests at least 65% of assets in equity securities that are priced at $35 per share or less. It may hold securities that have appreciated beyond that level and still satisfy the 65% requirement. The low-priced stocks purchased are considered to be undervalued. Often the issuing companies have market capitalizations of less than $100 million, and some have a negative net worth. The fund reserves the right to invest without limitation in preferred stocks and investment-grade debt for temporary, defensive purposes.

Historical Profile
Return High
Risk Low
Rating ★★★★★

Investment Style
Equity
Average Stock %

1994	1995	1996	1997	1998	1999	2000	12-01
		76%	79%	84%	96%	97%	84%

▼ Manager Change
▽ Partial Manager Change

Fund Performance vs. Category Average
■ Quarterly Fund Return +/– Category Average
— Category Baseline

Performance Quartile (within Category)

1990	1991	1992	1993	1994	1995	1996	1997	1998	1999	2000	12–01	History
9.47	13.05	15.96	17.30	16.00	18.50	21.35	25.13	22.85	22.64	23.12	27.42	NAV
–0.08	46.26	28.95	20.21	4.81	24.89	26.89	26.73	0.53	5.08	18.83	26.71	Total Return %
3.04	15.78	21.33	10.16	3.49	–12.64	3.95	–6.62	–28.04	–15.96	27.93	38.58	+/– S&P 500
21.70	4.56	–0.18	–3.63	6.36	–0.86	5.52	–4.96	6.96	6.56	–3.98	12.69	+/– Russell 2000 V
1.42	1.60	0.78	1.02	0.55	1.46	1.33	1.34	0.81	0.67	0.75	0.70	Income Return %
–1.49	44.66	28.18	19.19	4.25	23.43	25.56	25.39	–0.28	4.41	18.08	26.00	Capital Return %
1	28	13	25	12	41	29	73	16	40	55	13	Total Rtn % Rank Cat
0.14	0.15	0.10	0.16	0.09	0.23	0.24	0.28	0.20	0.15	0.16	0.16	Income $
0.26	0.60	0.69	1.62	2.05	1.24	1.66	1.58	1.94	1.19	3.43	1.54	Capital Gains $
1.92	1.36	1.20	1.12	1.13	1.11	1.04	1.01	0.95	1.08	0.80	1.00	Expense Ratio %
3.77	2.14	1.27	1.00	0.51	1.31	1.46	1.36	1.10	0.52	0.58	0.92	Income Ratio %
126	84	82	47	54	65	79	45	47	24	15	44	Turnover Rate %
88.8	375.3	2,240.4	2,060.1	2,354.5	3,349.9	5,664.3	10,691.1	9,194.8	6,646.3	6,363.5	10,439.9	Net Assets $mil

Portfolio Manager(s)

Joel C. Tillinghast, CFA. Since 12-89. BA'80 Wesleyan U.; MBA'83 Northwestern U.

Performance

	1st Qtr	2nd Qtr	3rd Qtr	4th Qtr	Total
1997	0.42	11.71	13.02	–0.04	26.73
1998	9.43	–1.38	–16.77	11.92	0.53
1999	–7.05	15.54	–7.50	5.78	5.08
2000	4.46	0.89	6.64	5.73	18.83
2001	3.94	12.90	–7.30	16.48	26.71

Trailing	Total Return%	+/– S&P 500	+/– Russ 2000	% Rank All	% Rank Cat	Growth of $10,000
3 Mo	16.48	5.79	–0.24	21	56	11,648
6 Mo	7.98	13.53	6.83	1	5	10,798
1 Yr	26.71	38.58	12.69	1	13	12,671
3 Yr Avg	16.52	17.55	5.20	4	23	15,821
5 Yr Avg	15.05	4.35	3.85	4	14	20,157
10 Yr Avg	17.90	4.97	2.79	2	6	51,900
15 Yr Avg	—	—	—	—	—	—

Tax Analysis	Tax-Adj Ret%	%Rank Cat	%Pretax Ret	%Rank Cat
3 Yr Avg	14.18	29	85.8	73
5 Yr Avg	12.54	16	83.3	65
10 Yr Avg	14.91	6	83.3	44

Potential Capital Gain Exposure: 24% of assets

Risk Analysis

Time Period	Load-Adj Return %	Risk %Rank[1] All	Risk %Rank[1] Cat	Morningstar Return	Morningstar Risk	Morningstar Risk-Adj Rating
1 Yr	22.90					
3 Yr	15.35	36	4	2.43[2]	0.44	★★★★★
5 Yr	14.35	43	2	2.43[2]	0.54	★★★★★
10 Yr	17.54	50	8	2.51	0.58	★★★★★

Average Historical Rating (109 months): 4.5★s

[1] 1=low, 100=high [2] T-Bill return substituted for category avg.

Category Rating (3 Yr)

1 2 3 4 5
Worst Best

Return Above Avg
Risk Low

Other Measures	Standard Index S&P 500	Best Fit Index S&PMdcap400
Alpha	14.3	7.8
Beta	0.47	0.56
R-Squared	40	73
Standard Deviation		14.56
Mean		16.52
Sharpe Ratio		0.90

Portfolio Analysis

Share change since Total Stocks: NULL	Sector	PE	YTD Ret%	% Assets
⊕ DR Horton	Industrials	9.7	48.67	1.51
⊕ Outback Steakhouse	Services	20.4	32.37	1.24
✲ Computer Sciences	Technology	57.6	–18.50	1.14
⊕ AutoZone	Retail	39.0	151.90	1.11
⊕ Applebee's Intl	Services	19.2	63.55	1.09
⊖ Biomet	Health	40.7	17.13	1.04
⊖ BJ's Whlse Club	Retail	40.5	14.92	0.96
⊕ Doral Finl	Financials	12.1	30.92	0.85
⊕ PMI Grp	Financials	10.4	–0.76	0.84
⊖ Sonic	Services	25.7	54.42	0.84
⊖ Affiliated Comp Svcs A	Services	39.9	74.88	0.83
⊕ Ross Stores	Retail	17.3	91.38	0.80
⊕ C & D Tech	Industrials	12.8	–47.00	0.80
⊕ USX–Marathon Grp	Energy	9.6	11.58	0.80
⊕ Black Box	Technology	16.3	9.45	0.79
⊖ CDW Comp Centers	Retail	28.4	92.68	0.78
⊕ Universal Health Svcs B	Health	12.7	–23.40	0.77
⊕ Tech Data	Technology	19.2	60.11	0.76
⊖ Firstbank	Financials	11.6	23.10	0.75
⊖ Gallaher Grp ADR	Staples	12.9	15.31	0.70
⊕ USEC	Industrials	7.4	78.52	0.67
Reynolds & Reynolds	Services	18.2	22.02	0.66
⊕ RenaissanceRe Hldgs	Financials	14.7	23.16	0.66
Metro Cl A	Staples	14.4	—	0.63
⊕ USFreightways	Services	15.9	5.74	0.59

Current Investment Style

Style: Value Blnd Growth; Size: Large Med Small

	Stock Port Avg	Relative S&P 500 Current	Relative S&P 500 Hist	Rel Cat
Price/Earnings Ratio	19.1	0.62	0.54	0.88
Price/Book Ratio	2.6	0.46	0.36	1.09
Price/Cash Flow	12.1	0.67	0.60	0.95
3 Yr Earnings Growth	17.4	1.19	1.04	1.50
1 Yr Earnings Est%	–1.8	0.99	—	0.44
Med Mkt Cap $mil	775	0.0	0.0	0.89

Analysis by Scott Cooley 11-12-01

Fidelity Low-Priced Stock's bet on the American consumer has helped the fund post yet another strong gain.

There's a bear market going on, but you wouldn't know it from looking at this fund's 2001 performance. Throughout the year, manager Joel Tillinghast has maintained considerable exposure to restaurants and retailers—both areas that depend on consumers' willingness to spend. Tillinghast was attracted to these stocks because he believed they offered solid growth prospects at modest to moderate valuations. Those sorts of stocks—companies with reasonable P/Es and good earnings visibility—have performed especially well in this year's turbulent market environment, with issues such as Ross Stores, Applebee's International, and Autozone among the stocks that have posted robust gains. For the year to date through Nov. 9, 2001, the fund had gained 15.8%, putting it ahead of 90% of its small-value rivals.

The fund has experienced much long-term success, too. Although the portfolio is diffuse, with more than 700 individual holdings, Tillinghast has added considerable value with his stock selection, picking winners in areas ranging from insurance and health care to homebuilding and semiconductors. Despite frequently holding a lot of cash, the fund has still generated a 10-year return that tops more than 90% of its rivals'. And thanks to that cash and the portfolio's diversification, the fund has exhibited below-average volatility.

Although we've expressed concern that the fund's cash stake was getting too high—it topped 20% of assets in August—the September sell-off gave Tillinghast the opportunity to buy beaten-down stocks. By Sept. 30, the fund's cash stake was 16%, according to Fidelity. With cash falling and Tillinghast's terrific long-term record to bank on, this still looks to us like an outstanding small-value option.

Special Securities % assets	
Restricted/Illiquid Secs	Trace
Emerging–Markets Secs	1
Options/Futures/Warrants	No

Composition % assets	
Cash	19.2
Stocks*	80.4
Bonds	0.0
Other	0.5
*Foreign (% stocks)	16.2

Market Cap	
Giant	0.0
Large	4.3
Medium	30.8
Small	45.2
Micro	19.7

Sector Weightings	% of Stocks	Rel S&P	5-Year High	5-Year Low
Utilities	0.3	0.1	12	0
Energy	4.9	0.7	9	2
Financials	17.3	1.0	25	10
Industrials	19.4	1.7	27	13
Durables	5.5	3.5	10	4
Staples	4.9	0.6	8	3
Services	16.9	1.6	21	8
Retail	11.5	1.7	12	5
Health	9.4	0.6	13	4
Technology	10.0	0.5	20	8

Address:	82 Devonshire Street Boston, MA 02109 800–544–8888
Web Address:	www.fidelity.com
Inception:	12-27-89
Advisor:	Fidelity Mgmt. & Research
Subadvisor:	FMR (U.K.)/FMR (Far East)
NTF Plans:	Fidelity Inst.

Minimum Purchase:	$2500	Add: $250 IRA: $500
Min Auto Inv Plan:	$2500	Add: $100
Sales Fees:	3.00%L, 1.50%R within 3 months	
Management Fee:	.35%+.52% mx./.27% mn.(G)+(–).20%P	
Actual Fees:	Mgt: 0.82%	Dist: —
Expense Projections:	3Yr: $636	5Yr: $883 10Yr: $1589
Avg Brok Commission:	—	Income Distrib: Semi–Ann.

Total Cost (relative to category): Below Avg

Fidelity Magellan

Ticker	Load	NAV	Yield	Total Assets	Mstar Category
FMAGX	Closed	$104.22	0.4%	$79,515.2 mil	Large Blend

Prospectus Objective: Growth

Fidelity Magellan Fund seeks capital appreciation.

The fund invests primarily in common stocks and convertible securities. It features domestic corporations operating primarily in the United States, domestic corporations that have significant activities and interests outside the U.S., and foreign companies. No limitations are placed on total foreign investment, but no more than 40% of assets may be invested in companies operating exclusively in one foreign country.

The fund closed to new investment in 1965 and reopened in 1981. It closed again in 1997.

Historical Profile

Return Above Avg
Risk Average
Rating ★★★ Neutral

Investment Style
Equity
Average Stock %

1996	1997	1998	1999	2000	2001
79%	96%	95%	93%	97%	94%

▼ Manager Change
▽ Partial Manager Change

Fund Performance vs. Category Average
Quarterly Fund Return +/– Category Average
— Category Baseline

Performance Quartile (within Category)

Portfolio Manager(s)

Robert E. Stansky, CFA. Since 6-96. BA'78 Nichols C.; MBA'83 New York U.

1990	1991	1992	1993	1994	1995	1996	1997	1998	1999	2000	12-01	History
53.93	68.61	63.01	70.85	66.80	85.98	80.65	95.27	120.82	136.63	119.30	104.22	NAV
–4.51	41.03	7.02	24.66	–1.81	36.82	11.69	26.59	33.63	24.05	–9.29	–11.65	Total Return %
–1.39	10.54	–0.60	14.60	–3.13	–0.71	–11.26	–6.76	5.05	3.01	–0.19	0.22	+/– S&P 500
–0.48	8.59	–0.64	14.82	–2.26	–0.78	–10.48	–6.43	4.99	2.22	1.66	1.11	+/– Wilshire Top 750
1.42	2.46	1.93	1.22	0.18	0.88	1.41	1.57	0.72	0.63	0.20	0.39	Income Return %
–5.93	38.57	5.09	23.43	–1.99	35.94	10.28	25.03	32.91	23.42	–9.49	–12.04	Capital Return %
65	14	56	5	66	21	97	63	5	29	58	31	Total Rtn % Rank Cat
0.83	1.30	1.25	0.75	0.13	0.59	1.10	1.25	0.67	0.73	0.27	0.46	Income $
2.42	5.43	8.82	6.50	2.64	4.69	12.85	5.21	5.15	11.39	4.69	0.80	Capital Gains $
1.03	1.06	1.05	1.00	0.99	0.96	0.92	0.64	0.61	0.60	0.74	0.88	Expense Ratio %
2.54	2.47	1.57	2.11	1.07	0.39	0.95	1.75	0.77	0.66	0.46	0.29	Income Ratio %
82	135	172	155	132	120	155	67	34	37	28	24	Turnover Rate %
12,325.7	19,257.1	22,268.9	31,705.1	36,441.5	53,702.3	53,988.7	63,766.2	83,552.1	105,938.5	93,066.9	79,515.2	Net Assets $mil

Performance 12-31-01

	1st Qtr	2nd Qtr	3rd Qtr	4th Qtr	Total
1997	–0.56	16.55	9.67	–0.40	26.59
1998	14.22	3.37	–11.05	27.22	33.63
1999	7.39	5.93	–5.97	15.97	24.05
2000	4.85	–3.96	–0.58	–9.40	–9.29
2001	–12.41	7.18	–15.36	11.18	–11.65

Trailing	Total Return%	+/– S&P 500	+/– Wil Top 750	% Rank All	% Rank Cat	Growth of $10,000
3 Mo	11.18	0.49	–0.15	36	39	11,118
6 Mo	–5.90	–0.34	–0.10	68	49	9,410
1 Yr	–11.65	0.22	1.11	64	31	8,835
3 Yr Avg	–0.20	0.83	1.63	74	38	9,941
5 Yr Avg	10.95	0.25	0.83	14	20	16,816
10 Yr Avg	12.90	–0.02	0.45	13	21	33,659
15 Yr Avg	14.44	0.71	1.07	8	14	75,642

Tax Analysis	Tax-Adj Ret%	%Rank Cat	%Pretax Ret	%Rank Cat
3 Yr Avg	–1.34	37	—	—
5 Yr Avg	9.50	21	86.7	28
10 Yr Avg	10.36	38	80.3	51

Potential Capital Gain Exposure: 28% of assets

Risk Analysis

Time Period	Load-Adj Return %	Risk %Rank[1] All	Risk %Rank[1] Cat	Morningstar Return	Morningstar Risk	Morningstar Risk-Adj Rating
1 Yr	–14.30					
3 Yr	–1.21	69	58	–1.23[2]	0.95	★★
5 Yr	10.28	68	57	1.27[2]	0.92	★★★
10 Yr	12.56	72	59	1.22	0.94	★★★

Average Historical Rating (193 months): 4.6★s

[1]1=low, 100=high [2] T-Bill return substituted for category avg.

Category Rating (3 Yr)

1 2 3 4 5
Worst Best

Return Average
Risk Average

Other Measures	Standard Index S&P 500	Best Fit Index S&P 500
Alpha	1.1	1.1
Beta	1.04	1.04
R-Squared	97	97
Standard Deviation		17.90
Mean		–0.20
Sharpe Ratio		–0.33

Portfolio Analysis 09-30-01

Share change since 03-01 Total Stocks: 257	Sector	PE	YTD Ret%	% Assets
⊖ General Elec	Industrials	30.1	–15.00	4.76
⊖ Citigroup	Financials	20.0	0.03	3.95
⊕ American Intl Grp	Financials	42.0	–19.20	3.00
⊕ ExxonMobil	Energy	15.3	–7.59	2.83
⊕ Tyco Intl	Industrials	27.1	6.23	2.69
⊕ Pfizer	Health	34.7	–12.40	2.65
⊕ Microsoft	Technology	57.6	52.78	2.64
⊕ Viacom Cl B	Services	—	—	2.18
⊕ Wal-Mart Stores	Retail	40.3	8.94	2.00
⊖ Fannie Mae	Financials	16.2	–6.95	1.88
⊕ AOL Time Warner	Technology	—	–7.76	1.77
⊖ Philip Morris	Staples	12.1	9.12	1.77
⊕ Bristol-Myers Squibb	Health	20.2	–26.00	1.65
⊕ IBM	Technology	26.9	43.00	1.57
⊖ Home Depot	Retail	42.9	12.07	1.55
⊖ Wells Fargo	Financials	22.4	–20.20	1.55
⊕ Cardinal Health	Health	35.1	–2.51	1.39
⊕ SBC Comms	Services	18.4	–16.00	1.36
⊕ Verizon Comms	Services	29.7	–2.52	1.33
Bank of America	Financials	16.7	42.73	1.30
Freddie Mac	Financials	14.0	–3.87	1.22
Coca-Cola	Staples	35.5	–21.40	1.21
⊕ Intel	Technology	73.1	4.89	1.14
⊖ Morgan Stanley/Dean Witter	Financials	16.6	–28.20	1.10
⊖ Eli Lilly	Health	28.9	–14.40	1.08

Current Investment Style

Style: Value Blnd Growth; Size: Large Med Small

	Stock Port Avg	Relative S&P 500 Current	Relative S&P 500 Hist	Rel Cat
Price/Earnings Ratio	29.8	0.96	1.10	0.98
Price/Book Ratio	5.6	0.98	1.12	1.02
Price/Cash Flow	18.6	1.03	1.10	1.01
3 Yr Earnings Growth	17.3	1.18	1.34	0.97
1 Yr Earnings Est%	1.1	—	—	—
Med Mkt Cap $mil	89,209	1.5	1.9	1.71

Analysis by Scott Cooley 10-16-01

Fidelity Magellan is well on its way toward putting up another respectable calendar-year return.

The fund is sitting on an ugly year-to-date loss, but it's holding up better than its average large-blend peer. With technology firms' business prospects eroding, manager Bob Stansky has underweighted that sector relative to the fund's large-blend peer group and its S&P 500 benchmark. That has been a plus for the fund, as tech shares have underperformed the broad market. But this fund's returns have been highly correlated with the index's over the past few years, so when the market falls, it takes this offering with it. Although the fund has beaten the index and more than three fourths of its peers through Oct. 15, 2001, it nevertheless has lost 16.5%.

Although the market was extremely turbulent during the third quarter, it appears that Stansky made few changes to the portfolio. As of Sept. 30, the fund still had less in tech shares than the index, according to figures provided by Fidelity. That's significant, because Stansky has sometimes loaded up on a sector when it's out of favor. His decision not to do so with tech stocks, which were extremely poor performers during the third quarter, suggests he thinks the sector's fundamentals are eroding at least as fast as its share prices. Most of the fund's other sector weights were roughly in line with the index's, though the portfolio continued to have a bias toward financials.

As the fund is currently positioned, it's hard to imagine its returns deviating much from the index's in the short term. However, Stansky has proven that he can add significant value on a stock-by-stock basis. Indeed, during his five-year tenure the fund has outpaced more than three fourths of its rivals. A fund of this size is unlikely to put up spectacular returns in a given year, but we think it's still a fine long-term core holding.

Special Securities % assets 09-30-01	
Restricted/Illiquid Secs	Trace
Emerging-Markets Secs	0
Options/Futures/Warrants	No

Composition % assets 09-30-01	
Cash	5.6
Stocks*	94.4
Bonds	0.0
Other	0.0
*Foreign (% stocks)	2.9

Market Cap	
Giant	67.4
Large	26.1
Medium	6.3
Small	0.1
Micro	0.1

Sector Weightings	% of Stocks	Rel S&P	5-Year High	5-Year Low
Utilities	0.3	0.1	9	0
Energy	7.6	1.1	25	1
Financials	21.7	1.2	22	7
Industrials	12.9	1.1	31	10
Durables	1.3	0.9	16	1
Staples	5.9	0.7	10	0
Services	13.7	1.3	17	10
Retail	7.5	1.1	11	2
Health	15.5	1.0	15	2
Technology	13.7	0.8	42	4

Address:	82 Devonshire Street Boston, MA 02109 800-544-8888
Web Address:	www.fidelity.com
Inception:	05-02-63
Advisor:	Fidelity Mgmt. & Research
Subadvisor:	FMR (U.K.)/FMR (Far East)
NTF Plans:	Fidelity Inst.

Minimum Purchase:	Closed	Add: $250 IRA: —
Min Auto Inv Plan:	Closed	Add: $100
Sales Fees:	3.00%L	
Management Fee:	.57%+.52% mx./.27% mn.(G)+(–).20%P	
Actual Fees:	Mgt: 0.57%	Dist: —
Expense Projections:	3Yr: $532	5Yr: $704 10Yr: $1202
Avg Brok Commission:	—	Income Distrib: Semi-Ann.
Total Cost (relative to category):		Below Avg

Fidelity Mid–Cap Stock

Ticker	Load	NAV	Yield	Total Assets	Mstar Category
FMCSX	None	$22.57	0.7%	$6,546.7 mil	Mid–Cap Growth

Prospectus Objective: Growth

Fidelity Mid-Cap Stock Fund seeks long-term growth of capital.

The fund normally invests at least 65% of assets in equity securities issued by companies with medium-size market capitalizations. Companies that fall within the capitalization range of the S&P MidCap 400 are considered for investment. The fund's equity investments may include common and preferred stocks, convertible securities, and warrants. It may invest up to 35% of assets in debt securities, including those rated below investment-grade. The fund may also invest in foreign securities.

Historical Profile
Return High
Risk Average
Rating ★★★★★ Highest

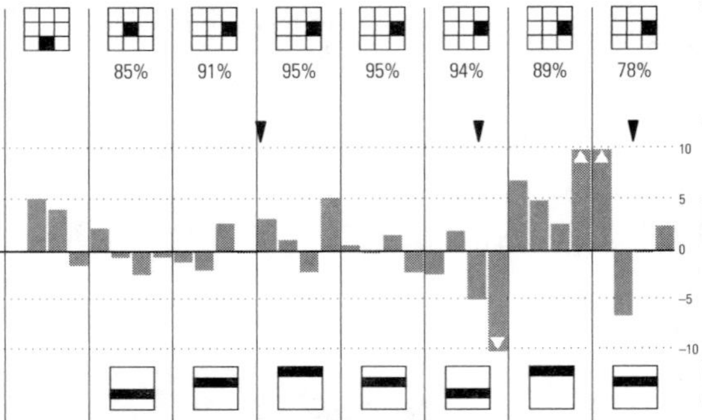

Investment Style
Equity
Average Stock %: 85% (1995), 91% (1996), 95% (1997), 95% (1998), 94% (1999), 89% (2000), 78% (12-01)

▼ Manager Change
▽ Partial Manager Change

Fund Performance vs. Category Average
■ Quarterly Fund Return +/– Category Average
— Category Baseline

Performance Quartile (within Category)

Portfolio Manager(s)

Beso Sikharulidze. Since 6-01. BS'86 Georgia Tech. U., Repub. of Georgia; MBA'92 Harvard U.

1990	1991	1992	1993	1994	1995	1996	1997	1998	1999	2000	12-01	History
—	—	—	—	10.70	13.50	14.64	16.69	17.88	21.87	26.06	22.57	NAV
—	—	—	—	8.46*	33.93	18.12	27.08	15.18	39.83	32.07	–12.80	Total Return %
—	—	—	—	4.48*	–3.61	–4.83	–6.27	–13.39	18.79	41.18	–0.93	+/– S&P 500
—	—	—	—	—	–0.05	0.64	4.54	–2.68	–11.48	43.82	7.35	+/– Russ Midcap Grth
—	—	—	—	0.00	0.57	0.23	0.07	0.00	0.06	0.49	0.61	Income Return %
—	—	—	—	8.46	33.36	17.89	27.01	15.18	39.77	31.58	–13.42	Capital Return %
—	—	—	—	—	52	44	15	48	66	1	27	Total Rtn % Rank Cat
—	—	—	—	0.00	0.06	0.03	0.01	0.00	0.01	0.10	0.16	Income $
—	—	—	—	0.14	0.74	1.26	1.77	1.28	2.59	2.50	0.00	Capital Gains $
—	—	—	—	—	1.22	1.00	0.96	0.86	0.74	0.86	0.84	Expense Ratio %
—	—	—	—	—	0.95	1.01	0.17	–0.10	0.08	–0.20	0.81	Income Ratio %
—	—	—	—	—	163	179	155	132	121	205	218	Turnover Rate %
—	—	—	—	126.1	1,160.2	1,695.1	1,763.1	1,784.5	2,286.2	7,011.3	6,546.7	Net Assets $mil

Performance 12-31-01

	1st Qtr	2nd Qtr	3rd Qtr	4th Qtr	Total
1997	–4.85	17.37	13.28	0.46	27.08
1998	13.12	–0.71	–17.16	23.79	15.18
1999	0.50	13.56	–4.63	28.47	39.83
2000	23.27	–0.37	7.71	–0.16	32.07
2001	–10.05	5.54	–24.66	21.91	–12.80

Trailing	Total Return%	+/– S&P 500	+/– Russ Midcap Grth	% Rank All	% Rank Cat	Growth of $10,000
3 Mo	21.91	11.22	–5.16	11	33	12,191
6 Mo	–8.15	–2.60	0.11	79	40	9,185
1 Yr	–12.80	–0.93	7.35	67	27	8,720
3 Yr Avg	17.21	18.24	15.05	3	7	16,103
5 Yr Avg	18.71	8.01	9.69	2	6	23,571
10 Yr Avg	—	—	—	—	—	—
15 Yr Avg	—	—	—	—	—	—

Tax Analysis	Tax-Adj Ret%	%Rank Cat	%Pretax Ret	%Rank Cat
3 Yr Avg	14.52	9	84.4	34
5 Yr Avg	15.72	6	84.0	28
10 Yr Avg	—	—	—	—

Potential Capital Gain Exposure: 1% of assets

Risk Analysis

Time Period	Load-Adj Return %	Risk %Rank[1] All	Risk %Rank[1] Cat	Morningstar Return	Morningstar Risk	Morningstar Risk-Adj Rating
1 Yr	–12.80					
3 Yr	17.21	67	12	2.92[2]	0.93	★★★★★
5 Yr	18.71	72	7	3.88[2]	0.97	★★★★★
Incept	19.72	—	—	—	—	

Average Historical Rating (58 months): 3.8★s

[1] 1=low, 100=high [2] T-Bill return substituted for category avg.

Category Rating (3 Yr)
1 2 3 4 5 (Worst – Best): 5
Return High
Risk Below Avg

Other Measures	Standard Index S&P 500	Best Fit Index Russ 2000
Alpha	19.3	11.0
Beta	0.71	1.01
R–Squared	19	75
Standard Deviation		32.75
Mean		17.21
Sharpe Ratio		0.42

Analysis by William Harding 10-25-01

Despite this fund's management change, we think investors should stay the course here.

The departure of successful stock-picker David Felman from the helm of Fidelity Mid-Cap Stock Fund in June 2001 was certainly cause for concern. But Beso Sikharulidze seems to be a capable replacement. He has earned good results at his other Fidelity charges, albeit over shorter time periods, and he is off to a respectable start here. The fund's 21% loss for the year to date ended Oct. 30, 2001, is tough to take, but nearly three fourths of its mid-growth peers have lost even more for the period.

Investors have seen major changes to the portfolio under Sikharulidze. His fundamental research drives the fund's sector biases, whereas Felman was more willing to make big, top-down sector bets. Its current positioning is thus more typical of a mid-growth offering than it was under Felman. Sikharulidze erased Felman's anti-tech bet by ratcheting up the fund's tech weighting to 30% of assets by the end of September, from 2% in March. In addition, the fund's health-care stake nearly doubled over that period, while financials were cut by about a third.

Some of those moves have hurt the fund in the near term, but Sikharulidze is scooping up shares at fairly cheap prices and is sticking with what he knows. For instance, his work on Select Health Care has helped him ferret out picks in that sector. Further, he has drawn on his experience managing Fidelity Convertible Securities by investing about 10% of assets in convertibles. These are hybrid securities that offer more downside protection than stocks.

With only six months on the job, it's too soon to give Sikharulidze a complete evaluation. However, we don't think investors should sell their shares. Also, despite the changes to the portfolio, Fidelity estimates that the fund will distribute only $.05 per share in capital gains this December.

Portfolio Analysis 04-30-01

Share change since 10-00 Total Stocks: 266	Sector	PE	YTD Ret%	% Assets
⊕ Freddie Mac	Financials	14.0	–3.87	4.41
⊕ Fannie Mae	Financials	16.2	–6.95	2.19
⊕ USA Educ	Financials	68.9	24.74	2.13
⊕ Ambac Finl Grp	Financials	15.2	–0.16	1.11
⊕ Newmont Mng	Industrials	—	12.69	1.08
⊕ Philip Morris	Staples	12.1	9.12	1.07
⊕ IDEC Pharmaceuticals	Health	NMF	9.09	0.98
⊕ RJ Reynolds Tobacco Hldgs	Staples	3.1	22.37	0.96
☼ Fidelity Natl Finl	Financials	8.5	–25.00	0.92
⊖ Genzyme Corporation General Di	Health	—	33.11	0.89
⊕ Tosco	Energy	—	37.22	0.85
⊕ Affiliated Comp Svcs A	Services	39.9	74.88	0.83
☼ Berkshire Hathaway Cl A	Financials	—	—	0.80
⊕ Barrick Gold	Industrials	—	–1.28	0.71
US Treasury Note 6.5%	N/A	—	—	0.68
⊕ Sysco	Staples	28.8	–11.70	0.68
⊕ SunGard Data Sys	Technology	33.3	22.78	0.67
⊕ Praxair	Industrials	28.6	26.22	0.67
US Treasury Bond 5.25%	N/A	—	—	0.67
⊕ Sigma–Aldrich	Industrials	20.3	1.02	0.67
⊕ American Standard	Industrials	14.9	38.36	0.66
⊖ Cigna	Financials	13.2	–29.00	0.64
US Treasury Bond 6.125%	N/A	—	—	0.63
⊕ MBIA	Financials	14.6	9.88	0.62
☼ St. Jude Medical	Health	42.0	26.39	0.62

Current Investment Style

Style: Value Blnd Growth; Size: Large Med Small (Growth/Med highlighted)

	Stock Port Avg	Relative S&P 500 Current	Relative S&P 500 Hist	Rel Cat
Price/Earnings Ratio	24.6	0.80	1.04	0.71
Price/Book Ratio	4.2	0.73	0.92	0.73
Price/Cash Flow	15.9	0.88	1.02	0.69
3 Yr Earnings Growth	12.7	0.87	1.23	0.54
1 Yr Earnings Est%	13.8	—	—	1.48
Med Mkt Cap $mil	6,760	0.1	0.1	1.20

[1] figure is based on 50% or less of stocks

Special Securities % assets 04-30-01

Restricted/Illiquid Secs	0
Emerging–Markets Secs	Trace
Options/Futures/Warrants	No

Composition % assets 04-30-01

Cash	18.0
Stocks*	78.1
Bonds	3.8
Other	0.0
*Foreign (% stocks)	9.8

Market Cap

Giant	7.1
Large	27.9
Medium	56.3
Small	8.8
Micro	0.0

Sector Weightings	% of Stocks	Rel S&P	5-Year High	5-Year Low
Utilities	6.0	1.9	9	0
Energy	7.8	1.1	13	1
Financials	29.7	1.7	30	7
Industrials	17.7	1.6	23	6
Durables	2.1	1.4	13	1
Staples	8.6	1.1	9	2
Services	8.4	0.8	22	8
Retail	2.2	0.3	13	1
Health	15.5	1.1	25	4
Technology	1.9	0.1	41	2

Address:	82 Devonshire Street Boston, MA 02109 800–544–8888
Web Address:	www.fidelity.com
*Inception:	03-29-94
Advisor:	Fidelity Mgmt. & Research
Subadvisor:	FMR (U.K.)/FMR (Far East)
NTF Plans:	Fidelity , Fidelity Inst.

Minimum Purchase:	$2500	Add: $250	IRA: $500
Min Auto Inv Plan:	$2500	Add: $100	
Sales Fees:	No–load		
Management Fee:	.30%+.52% mx./.27% mn.(G)+(–).20%P		
Actual Fees:	Mgt: 0.50%	Dist: —	
Expense Projections:	3Yr: $246	5Yr: $428	10Yr: $954
Avg Brok Commission:	—	Income Distrib: Semi–Ann.	
Total Cost (relative to category):	Low		

Fidelity New Markets Income

Ticker	Load	NAV	Yield	SEC Yield	Total Assets	Mstar Category
FNMIX	None	$10.91	11.1%	—	$293.2 mil	Emerging Markets

Prospectus Objective: World Bond

Fidelity New Markets Income Fund seeks current income; capital appreciation is a secondary objective.

The fund normally invests at least 65% of assets in debt securities issued by companies and governments in emerging markets. The fund expects to emphasize investment in Latin America, and, to a lesser extent, Asia, Africa, and emerging European nations. The debt securities held by the fund may be below investment-grade; some securities may be in default. The fund invests in at least three countries, and it manages the asset allocation with regard to geographic region and currency denomination. The fund is nondiversified.

Historical Profile

Return High
Risk High
Rating ★★★ Neutral

Investment Style
Fixed-Income

Income Rtn %Rank Cat: 80 78 64 11 51 44 26 42

Growth of Principal vs. Interest Rate Shifts
- Principal Value $000 (NAV with capital gains reinvested)
- Interest Rate % on 10 Yr Treasury
- ▼ Manager Change
- ▽ Partial Manager Change
- ► Mgr Unknown After
- ◄ Mgr Unknown Before

Performance Quartile (within Category)

Portfolio Manager(s)

John H. Carlson. Since 6-95. BS'73 Wayne State U.; MS'75 U. of Michigan. Other funds currently managed: Fidelity International Bond, Fidelity Emerging Markets, Fidelity Advisor Emerg Mkts Inc T.

1990	1991	1992	1993	1994	1995	1996	1997	1998	1999	2000	12–01	History
—	—	—	13.07	10.19	9.95	12.96	12.97	8.99	11.13	11.39	10.91	NAV
—	—	—	38.84*	–16.55	7.97	41.39	17.52	–22.38	36.69	14.38	6.64	Total Return %
—	—	—	—	–13.63	–10.50	37.78	7.84	–31.05	37.52	2.75	–1.78	+/– LB Aggregate
—	—	—	—	2.38	–18.80	2.08	4.50	–8.03	10.72	–1.28	—	+/– JP Emg Mkts Bd
—	—	—	6.05	4.50	9.43	9.75	10.81	8.25	11.76	12.20	11.12	Income Return %
—	—	—	32.79	–21.05	–1.45	31.65	6.71	–30.63	24.93	2.18	–4.48	Capital Return %
—	—	—	—	60	84	20	11	48	5	18	57	Total Rtn % Rank Cat
—	—	—	0.55	0.57	0.92	0.93	1.32	1.02	1.01	1.30	1.21	Income $
—	—	—	0.17	0.20	0.00	0.00	0.87	0.20	0.00	0.00	0.00	Capital Gains $
—	—	—	1.24	1.28	1.17	1.09	1.08	1.13	1.07	0.99	—	Expense Ratio %
—	—	—	6.29	5.87	9.51	7.68	7.56	10.50	9.88	9.41	—	Income Ratio %
—	—	—	324	409	306	405	656	488	273	278	—	Turnover Rate %
—	—	—	283.9	179.5	173.5	305.8	371.3	206.9	214.4	257.6	293.2	Net Assets $mil

Performance 12-31-01

	1st Qtr	2nd Qtr	3rd Qtr	4th Qtr	Total
1997	1.85	11.52	7.10	–3.40	17.52
1998	5.76	–7.10	–29.19	11.56	–22.38
1999	7.76	9.94	–0.29	15.73	36.69
2000	9.15	–0.56	4.53	0.82	14.38
2001	1.82	5.13	–4.63	4.47	6.64

Trailing	Total Return%	+/– LB Agg	+/– JP Emg Mkts Bd	% Rank All	% Rank Cat	Growth of $10,000
3 Mo	4.47	4.43	—	66	80	10,447
6 Mo	–0.37	–5.02	—	40	57	9,963
1 Yr	6.64	–1.78	—	16	57	10,664
3 Yr Avg	18.58	12.31	—	3	21	16,674
5 Yr Avg	8.75	1.32	—	25	3	15,210
10 Yr Avg	—	—	—	—	—	—
15 Yr Avg	—	—	—	—	—	—

Tax Analysis	Tax-Adj Ret%	%Rank Cat	%Pretax Ret	%Rank Cat
3 Yr Avg	13.75	18	74.0	5
5 Yr Avg	3.97	11	45.4	20
10 Yr Avg	—	—	—	—

Potential Capital Gain Exposure: –17% of assets

Risk Analysis

Time Period	Load-Adj Return %	Risk %Rank[1] All	Risk %Rank[1] Cat	Morningstar Return	Morningstar Risk	Morningstar Risk-Adj Rating
1 Yr	6.64					
3 Yr	18.58	36	43	3.28[2]	1.96	★★★★★
5 Yr	8.75	59	24	0.87[2]	3.67	★★
Incept	12.10	—	—	—	—	

Average Historical Rating (68 months): 2.2★s

[1] 1=low, 100=high [2] T-Bill return substituted for category avg.

Category Rating (3 Yr)

1 2 3 **4** 5
Worst Best

Return Above Avg
Risk Average

Other Measures	Standard Index LB Agg	Best Fit Index Wil 4500
Alpha	13.6	13.9
Beta	0.24	0.31
R-Squared	0	43
Standard Deviation		15.51
Mean		18.58
Sharpe Ratio		1.00

Portfolio Analysis 06-30-01

Total Fixed-Income: 112	Date of Maturity	Value $000	% Net Assets
Govt of Mexico Opt (Call)		10,921	3.70
Govt of Russia 144A N/A	03-31-30	9,462	3.20
Govt of Russia N/A	03-31-30	9,132	3.09
Republic of Brazil N/A	04-15-24	8,978	3.04
Govt of Russia N/A	06-24-28	8,209	2.78
Govt of Russia N/A	06-26-07	7,387	2.50
Govt of Mexico 11.375%	09-15-16	6,865	2.32
Republic of Brazil FRN	04-15-12	6,637	2.25
Republic of Brazil 11%	08-17-40	5,928	2.01
Govt of Mexico Opt (Call)		5,481	1.86
Republic of Argentina 12%	06-19-31	5,429	1.84
United Mexican States N/A	12-30-19	5,335	1.81
Republic of Bulgaria FRN	07-28-12	5,123	1.73
Republic of Brazil 0%	10-15-09	4,846	1.64
Republic of Turkey 0%	06-15-09	4,743	1.61
Republic of Argentina 12.25%	06-19-18	4,564	1.55
Republic of Turkey N/A	06-15-10	4,418	1.50
Govt of Russia N/A	07-24-05	4,323	1.46
Republic of Argentina 12.375%	02-21-12	4,267	1.45
Republic of Brazil N/A	04-15-14	4,239	1.44

Current Investment Style

Not Available

Avg Eff Duration	—
Avg Eff Maturity	—
Avg Credit Quality	—
Avg Wtd Coupon	0.00%
Avg Wtd Price	81.28% of par

Analysis by Gabriel Presler 07-25-01

In a savage category, Fidelity New Markets Income Fund's sober approach has generally met with success.

There's nothing safe about investing in emerging-markets debt, but this fund is about as close as it gets. Manager John Carlson doesn't make big bets against the relative country and duration weightings of the J.P. Morgan Emerging Markets Bond index. The fund generally sticks with sovereign debt, often holds more issues than its peers, and steers clear of local currencies, preferring dollar-denominated Brady Bonds instead. Over time, this staid approach has led to one of the best long-term records in the group.

Carlson tends to make only minor adjustments to the portfolio's country weightings, but his recent alterations have had mixed results in 2001. He built the fund's already-large stake in Russian debt, for example, optimistic about that country's oil companies and current account surplus. Carlson also broadened the fund's exposure to Mexico, one of the category's strongest bond markets this year. The performance of both regions, combined with Carlson's habitual loyalty to dollar-denominated Brady bonds, has boosted performance lately.

His moves haven't been foolproof, though. Like his rivals, Carlson tends to underweight Argentina—its huge national debt takes up a large portion of the index. Still, the fund's 14% stake in that country is a bit broader than group norms, so when Argentina hit the skids in the early spring of this year, the fund's relative performance suffered. In fact, its 3% gain for the year to date through August 9, 2001, lags the category average slightly.

The fund may struggle from time to time—in 1998, it lost 28% in the third quarter alone—but over time it has proven itself to be one of the best offerings in the category.

Special Securities % of assets 06-30-01	
Restricted/Illiquid Secs	8
Exotic Mortgage-Backed	0
Emerging-Markets Secs	3
Options/Futures/Warrants	Yes

Country Exposure % of assets

Not Available

Composition % assets 06-30-01

Cash	10.8	Bonds	82.8
Stocks	0.8	Other	5.5

Address:	82 Devonshire Street Boston, MA 02109 800–544–8888
Web Address:	www.fidelity.com
*Inception:	05-04-93
Advisor:	Fidelity Mgmt. & Research
Subadvisor:	FMR (U.K.)/FMR (Far East)
NTF Plans:	Fidelity , Fidelity Inst.

Minimum Purchase:	$2500	Add: $250	IRA: $500
Min Auto Inv Plan:	$2500	Add: $100	
Sales Fees:	No-load, 1.00%R within 6 months		
Management Fee:	.55%+.37% mx./.13% mn.(G)		
Actual Fees:	Mgt: 0.69%	Dist: —	
Expense Projections:	3Yr: $359	5Yr: $622	10Yr: $1375
Avg Brok Commission:	—	Income Distrib: Monthly	
Total Cost (relative to category):	—		

Fidelity New Millennium

Ticker	Load	NAV	Yield	Total Assets	Mstar Category
FMILX	Closed	$27.63	0.0%	$2,939.4 mil	Mid-Cap Growth

Prospectus Objective: Aggressive Growth

Fidelity New Millennium Fund seeks capital appreciation.

The fund invests in all types of foreign and domestic equity securities, including common and preferred stock and securities that are convertible into common or preferred stock. Management seeks undervalued stocks that may benefit from social and economic trends. The fund may also invest in indexed securities, illiquid investments, restricted securities, repurchase agreements, securities loans, and interfund loans. The fund may purchase lower-rated, higher-yielding bonds.

Historical Profile
Return High
Risk High
Rating ★★★★★ Highest

Investment Style
Equity
Average Stock %: 89% 94% 94% 95% 96% 94% 96%

▼ Manager Change
▽ Partial Manager Change

Fund Performance vs. Category Average
■ Quarterly Fund Return +/– Category Average
— Category Baseline

Performance Quartile (within Category)

Portfolio Manager(s)

Neal P. Miller. Since 12-92. BA'65 Carleton C.; MBA'67 U. of Michigan. Other fund currently managed: Vantagepoint Growth.

1990	1991	1992	1993	1994	1995	1996	1997	1998	1999	2000	12-01	History
—	—	10.08	12.30	12.11	16.96	20.25	22.19	26.27	47.46	34.33	27.63	NAV
—	—	0.80*	24.67	0.83	52.14	23.15	24.63	27.70	108.78	–6.03	–18.15	Total Return %
—	—	1.38*	14.62	–0.49	14.61	0.20	–8.72	–0.88	87.74	3.07	–6.28	+/– S&P 500
—	—	—	13.48	2.99	18.16	5.67	2.09	9.83	57.48	5.72	2.00	+/– Russ Midcap Grth
—	—	0.00	0.10	0.00	0.00	0.00	0.00	0.00	0.00	0.00	0.00	Income Return %
—	—	0.80	24.57	0.83	52.14	23.15	24.63	27.70	108.78	–6.03	–18.15	Capital Return %
—	—	—	13	34	5	22	20	16	13	52	40	Total Rtn % Rank Cat
—	—	0.00	0.01	0.00	0.00	0.00	0.00	0.00	0.00	0.00	0.00	Income $
—	—	0.00	0.25	0.28	1.40	0.60	2.89	1.94	6.37	10.11	0.53	Capital Gains $
—	—	—	1.32	1.29	1.18	1.03	0.94	0.83	0.93	0.89	—	Expense Ratio %
—	—	—	–0.10	–0.05	–0.15	–0.17	–0.13	–0.13	–0.36	–0.36	—	Income Ratio %
—	—	—	204	199	176	158	142	121	116	97	—	Turnover Rate %
—	—	1.8	276.0	319.7	594.2	1,252.9	1,564.2	1,683.7	3,772.4	3,572.4	2,939.4	Net Assets $mil

Performance 12-31-01

	1st Qtr	2nd Qtr	3rd Qtr	4th Qtr	Total
1997	–2.72	17.65	19.41	–8.80	24.63
1998	13.61	–0.60	–14.65	32.49	27.70
1999	24.54	12.25	–2.81	53.66	108.78
2000	17.54	–10.82	5.97	–15.40	–6.03
2001	–26.06	17.35	–28.30	31.57	–18.15

Trailing	Total Return%	+/– S&P 500	+/– Russ Midcap Grth	% Rank All	% Rank Cat	Growth of $10,000
3 Mo	31.57	20.89	4.51	4	6	13,157
6 Mo	–5.67	–0.11	2.59	66	26	9,433
1 Yr	–18.15	–6.28	2.00	77	40	8,185
3 Yr Avg	17.10	18.13	14.94	3	7	16,058
5 Yr Avg	20.64	9.94	11.62	1	4	25,556
10 Yr Avg	—	—	—	—	—	—
15 Yr Avg	—	—	—	—	—	—

Tax Analysis	Tax-Adj Ret%	%Rank Cat	%Pretax Ret	%Rank Cat
3 Yr Avg	13.47	11	78.8	44
5 Yr Avg	17.04	5	82.5	32
10 Yr Avg	—	—	—	—

Potential Capital Gain Exposure: 10% of assets

Risk Analysis

Time Period	Load-Adj Return %	Risk %Rank[1] All	Risk %Rank[1] Cat	Morningstar Return	Morningstar Risk	Morningstar Risk-Adj Rating
1 Yr	–20.61					
3 Yr	15.92	96	76	2.58[2]	1.74	★★★★
5 Yr	19.91	93	72	4.32[2]	1.65	★★★★★
Incept	21.73	—	—	—	—	

Average Historical Rating (73 months): 4.7★s

[1] 1=low, 100=high [2] T-Bill return substituted for category avg.

Category Rating (3 Yr)

1 Worst — 5 Best (rating: 5)

Return: High
Risk: Above Avg

Other Measures	Standard Index S&P 500	Best Fit Index Wil 4500
Alpha	31.7	21.4
Beta	1.81	1.44
R-Squared	51	87

Standard Deviation	55.19
Mean	17.10
Sharpe Ratio	0.25

Portfolio Analysis 05-31-01

Share change since 11-00 Total Stocks: 295

	Sector	PE	YTD Ret%	% Assets
⊕ Qlogic	Technology	49.5	–42.10	6.45
⊕ Emulex	Technology	—	–50.50	3.91
⊕ IBM	Technology	26.9	43.00	3.30
⊕ Microsoft	Technology	57.6	52.78	2.96
⊖ Stanley Works	Industrials	20.4	52.96	2.77
⊖ Micron Tech	Technology	—	–12.60	2.73
⊕ McKesson HBOC	Health	—	4.92	2.37
⊖ Global Marine	Energy	—	–43.20	2.33
⊖ Ensco Intl	Energy	15.7	–26.70	2.04
⊕ Andrew	Technology	28.8	0.64	1.97
Smith Intl	Industrials	19.3	–28.00	1.93
⊕ Daiwa Secs Grp	Financials	—	—	1.82
⊕ Medtronic	Health	76.4	–14.70	1.76
⊖ Nomura Secs	Financials	14.6	—	1.76
⊕ CR Bard	Health	29.7	40.91	1.62
⊕ Brocade Comm Sys	Technology	—	–63.90	1.51
⊕ Cadence Design Sys	Technology	5.3	–20.20	1.42
⊖ HCA – The Healthcare Company	Health	24.1	–12.20	1.26
⊕ Sun Microsystems	Technology	NMF	–55.80	1.13
⊖ Nikko Secs	Financials	—	—	1.04
⊕ Hillenbrand Inds	Durables	22.5	9.08	1.01
⊖ Tenet Healthcare	Health	30.1	32.14	1.00
⊕ CIENA	Technology	NMF	–82.30	0.98
⊕ UnitedHealth Grp	Financials	26.6	15.37	0.95
☼ Intel	Technology	73.1	4.89	0.95

Current Investment Style

Style: Value Blnd Growth; Size: Large Med Small

	Stock Port Avg	Relative S&P 500 Current	Relative S&P 500 Hist	Rel Cat
Price/Earnings Ratio	33.4	1.08	1.18	0.96
Price/Book Ratio	4.9	0.87	1.11	0.87
Price/Cash Flow	21.3	1.19	1.06	0.92
3 Yr Earnings Growth	18.8	1.29	1.68	0.80
1 Yr Earnings Est%	3.9	—	—	0.42
Med Mkt Cap $mil	5,085	0.1	0.1	0.90

[1] figure is based on 50% or less of stocks

Analysis by Christopher Traulsen 12-14-01

Fidelity New Millennium Fund is still one of the best growth offerings out there.

This fund, which remains closed to new investors, has not had the easiest time in 2001. Indeed, until the recent tech-led rally, it was faring even worse than its typical mid-growth rival. But a strong past three months has boosted its relative rankings. Although it's still down 18% for the year to date through Dec. 11, two thirds of its rivals have lost even more.

That pattern is typical. Never one to shrink from making a bet and always on the lookout for rapid growth, manager Neal Miller runs an aggressive portfolio. In keeping with his style, he has kept in place—and even increased—his wagers on some technology stocks. As of Oct. 31, the fund had 38% of its assets in the sector. Specifically, Miller has stuck with his storage theme, adding to top-10 holdings such as Qlogic during the year. Storage stocks have taken a beating, but Miller thinks demand for networked storage was strong to start with and will be increased by the rush to create new facilities after the events of Sept. 11.

Miller is more flexible than his tech bet might suggest, however. His thematic approach also led him to hospital companies such as Tenet Healthcare and HCA, which have fared relatively well in 2001. Further, the fund's top holding as of Sept. 30 was toolmaker Stanley Works. Far from a glamour stock, the company is a turnaround play that's part of Miller's bet that baby boomers will start to spend more money on home improvement. Stanley Works is up 49% thus far in 2001.

Miller's style clearly has risks, but also the potential for glittering rewards. The fund notched six top-quartile returns in seven years from 1993 through 1999, and its long-term returns are outstanding. It also closed in time to keep it reasonably nimble. Investors here have every reason to count themselves lucky.

Special Securities % assets 05-31-01	
Restricted/Illiquid Secs	Trace
Emerging-Markets Secs	Trace
Options/Futures/Warrants	No

Composition % assets 05-31-01	
Cash	4.4
Stocks*	95.6
Bonds	0.0
Other	0.0
*Foreign (% stocks)	5.1

Market Cap	
Giant	15.3
Large	25.1
Medium	50.0
Small	9.5
Micro	0.2

Sector Weightings	% of Stocks	Rel S&P	5-Year High	5-Year Low
Utilities	0.3	0.1	3	0
Energy	7.2	1.0	15	3
Financials	7.9	0.4	12	1
Industrials	11.2	1.0	25	6
Durables	3.1	2.0	11	0
Staples	1.7	0.2	5	0
Services	12.8	1.2	36	9
Retail	3.2	0.5	13	1
Health	13.6	0.9	18	3
Technology	39.0	2.1	58	19

Address:	82 Devonshire Street Boston, MA 02109 800-544-8888
Web Address:	www.fidelity.com
*Inception:	12-28-92
Advisor:	Fidelity Mgmt. & Research
Subadvisor:	FMR (U.K.)/FMR (Far East)
NTF Plans:	Fidelity Inst.

Minimum Purchase:	Closed	Add: $250 IRA: —
Min Auto Inv Plan:	Closed	Add: $100
Sales Fees:	3.00%L	
Management Fee:	.35%+.52% mx./.27% mn.(G)+(–).20%P	
Actual Fees:	Mgt: 0.74%	Dist: —
Expense Projections:	3Yr: $594	5Yr: $810 10Yr: $1431
Avg Brok Commission:	—	Income Distrib: Annually

Total Cost (relative to category): Below Avg

Fidelity OTC

Ticker	Load	NAV	Yield	Total Assets	Mstar Category
FOCPX	None	$31.17	0.0%	$8,069.7 mil	Large Growth

Prospectus Objective: Growth

Fidelity OTC Portfolio seeks capital appreciation.

The fund normally invests at least 65% of assets in equity securities principally traded on the over-the-counter (OTC) market. It may continue to hold securities purchased on the OTC market that subsequently begin to trade on the NYSE, AMEX, or foreign exchanges. Investments may include common and preferred stocks, convertible securities, and warrants. The fund may invest up to 5% of assets in debt securities rated below investment-grade. It may also invest in securities of foreign issuers.

Historical Profile

Return Average
Risk High
Rating ★★ Below Avg

Investment Style
Equity
Average Stock %: 87% 95% 96% 94% 96% 91%

▼ Manager Change
▽ Partial Manager Change

Fund Performance vs. Category Average
Quarterly Fund Return +/– Category Average
— Category Baseline

Performance Quartile (within Category)

Portfolio Manager(s)

Jason Weiner. Since 2-00. BA Swarthmore C.

1990	1991	1992	1993	1994	1995	1996	1997	1998	1999	2000	12-01	History
18.54	24.78	25.65	24.14	23.27	30.33	32.71	33.45	43.63	67.97	41.05	31.17	NAV
–4.75	49.16	14.94	8.33	–2.70	38.23	23.74	9.91	40.38	72.53	–26.81	–24.07	Total Return %
–1.63	18.68	7.32	–1.72	–4.01	0.69	0.79	–23.44	11.81	51.49	–17.70	–12.19	+/– S&P 500
–6.12	9.75	11.05	8.41	–7.55	–0.43	–1.79	–23.83	–4.72	42.85	–2.28	–3.57	+/– Russ Top 200 Grt
0.25	0.67	1.08	0.42	0.87	0.09	0.26	0.00	0.00	0.00	0.00	0.00	Income Return %
–5.00	48.49	13.86	7.91	–3.57	38.14	23.47	9.91	40.38	72.53	–26.81	–24.07	Capital Return %
72	30	4	58	58	17	13	95	22	10	91	55	Total Rtn % Rank Cat
0.05	0.12	0.25	0.10	0.21	0.02	0.08	0.00	0.00	0.00	0.00	0.00	Income $
0.58	2.51	2.24	3.42	0.00	1.80	4.32	2.52	2.38	5.51	12.66	0.00	Capital Gains $
1.35	1.29	1.17	1.08	0.88	0.81	0.82	0.84	0.75	0.74	0.75	0.94	Expense Ratio %
2.30	1.00	0.59	0.53	0.48	0.35	0.42	–0.15	–0.32	–0.16	–0.43	–0.40	Income Ratio %
212	198	245	213	222	62	133	147	125	117	196	219	Turnover Rate %
618.7	1,070.2	1,243.6	1,343.0	1,381.3	2,350.1	3,387.2	3,858.1	5,476.4	11,705.4	10,979.4	8,069.7	Net Assets $mil

Performance 12-31-01

	1st Qtr	2nd Qtr	3rd Qtr	4th Qtr	Total
1997	–8.59	16.42	16.09	–11.03	9.91
1998	18.57	0.13	–8.23	28.85	40.38
1999	9.81	7.70	–0.19	46.16	72.53
2000	16.20	–8.39	–3.45	–28.78	–26.81
2001	–28.06	19.40	–31.96	29.93	–24.07

Trailing	Total Return%	+/– S&P 500	+/– Russ Top 200 Grth	% Rank All	% Rank Cat	Growth of $10,000
3 Mo	29.93	19.24	17.07	5	5	12,993
6 Mo	–11.60	–6.04	–4.61	89	74	8,840
1 Yr	–24.07	–12.19	–3.57	87	55	7,593
3 Yr Avg	–1.39	–0.36	6.63	80	39	9,589
5 Yr Avg	8.15	–2.55	–0.44	28	54	14,795
10 Yr Avg	11.86	–1.07	0.77	20	21	30,660
15 Yr Avg	13.95	0.21	0.58	11	22	70,892

Tax Analysis	Tax-Adj Ret%	%Rank Cat	%Pretax Ret	%Rank Cat
3 Yr Avg	–3.99	50	—	—
5 Yr Avg	5.54	59	68.0	68
10 Yr Avg	8.95	35	75.5	56

Potential Capital Gain Exposure: –60% of assets

Risk Analysis

Time Period	Load-Adj Return %	Risk %Rank[1] All	Risk %Rank[1] Cat	Morningstar Return	Morningstar Risk	Morningstar Risk-Adj Rating
1 Yr	–24.07					
3 Yr	–1.39	96	94	–1.26[2]	1.79	★★
5 Yr	8.15	94	95	0.72[2]	1.68	★★
10 Yr	11.86	93	90	1.07	1.54	★★

Average Historical Rating (169 months): 4.0★s

[1] 1=low, 100=high [2] T-Bill return substituted for category avg.

Category Rating (3 Yr)

1 2 3 4 5
Worst Best

Return Average
Risk High

Other Measures	Standard Index S&P 500	Best Fit Index Wil 4500
Alpha	9.1	1.0
Beta	1.71	1.28
R-Squared	55	84

Standard Deviation	41.90
Mean	–1.39
Sharpe Ratio	–0.18

Portfolio Analysis 07-31-01

Share change since 01-01 Total Stocks: 149	Sector	PE	YTD Ret%	% Assets
⊕ Microsoft	Technology	57.6	52.78	16.00
☼ Intel	Technology	73.1	4.89	4.89
⊕ Altera	Technology	44.2	–19.30	2.83
⊕ Brocade Comm Sys	Technology	—	–63.90	2.35
☼ ASML Hldg (Reg)	N/A	—	—	2.34
⊕ Amgen	Health	52.8	–11.70	2.08
⊕ Check Point Software Tech	Technology	32.0	–55.20	1.94
☼ Broadcom	Technology	—	–51.20	1.91
⊕ Qualcomm	Technology	—	–38.50	1.51
⊕ Fifth Third Bancorp	Financials	38.3	4.53	1.50
⊖ Cisco Sys	Technology	—	–52.60	1.49
⊕ Dell Comp	Technology	61.8	55.87	1.39
☼ Sanmina	Technology	NMF	–48.00	1.36
⊖ Expeditors Intl of WA	Services	32.7	6.46	1.27
⊕ Dollar Tree Stores	Retail	30.9	26.16	1.24
⊕ Intersil Hldg	Technology	NMF	40.60	1.20
⊕ Vignette	Technology	—	–70.10	1.19
☼ Chartered Semicon Mfg ADR	Technology	—	—	1.12
⊖ IDEC Pharmaceuticals	Health	NMF	9.09	0.96
⊕ Cintas	Services	36.1	–9.33	0.94
⊕ Lam Rsrch	Technology	21.5	60.14	0.90
☼ Marvell Tech	Technology	—	63.28	0.89
☼ Electronic Arts	Technology	90.8	40.65	0.89
⊕ Comcast	Services	20.3	–13.70	0.88
⊖ Concord EFS	Financials	86.3	49.21	0.88

Current Investment Style

Style: Value Blnd Growth; Size: Large Med Small

	Stock Port Avg	Relative S&P 500 Current	Relative S&P 500 Hist	Rel Cat
Price/Earnings Ratio	46.8	1.51	1.27	1.32
Price/Book Ratio	6.6	1.16	1.25	1.04
Price/Cash Flow	26.8	1.49	1.29	1.18
3 Yr Earnings Growth	25.2	1.72	1.69	1.17
1 Yr Earnings Est%	–8.5	4.80	—	–2.83
Med Mkt Cap $mil	9,363	0.2	0.2	0.20

[1]figure is based on 50% or less of stocks

Analysis by Scott Cooley 11-14-01

Unless you're in the market for a tech fund, you probably won't be interested in Fidelity OTC Portfolio.

When tech stocks are in the dumps, this fund will be, too. By prospectus, manager Jason Weiner must put a solid majority of the fund's assets in Nasdaq-listed stocks, and that means the fund will always have big stakes in risky tech and biotech stocks. Indeed, tech stocks alone have regularly consumed two thirds or more of the fund's assets in recent years—an aggressive sector bet even by the standards of the risky large-growth category.

Given the fund's composition, it should be no surprise that it has offered a wild ride in 2001. The fund's enormous tech stake has been a huge negative, given the sector's weakness this year, and Weiner's preference for cyclical tech stocks took a toll on the fund during the third quarter. Its whopping 32% loss during that period was worse than that of its benchmark Nasdaq Composite index, thanks to the weakness of semiconductor-related issues. But those stocks have bounced back strongly more recently. For the trailing month through Nov. 13, the fund has soared 15.4%, beating 95% of its large-growth rivals.

It's still difficult to make a call about this fund's longer-term prospects. To Weiner's credit: During his overall tenure here, which began in February 2000, he has beaten his Nasdaq Composite benchmark. But he also has posted returns that are wretched both in absolute terms and in comparison with the large-growth category. Before taking over here, he put up decent numbers in two brief stints as a diversified-fund manager, but while those results are encouraging, his tenures were too short to be very meaningful. For those who bought this fund because they wanted an aggressive play on tech stocks, Weiner hasn't done anything that should provoke them to sell. But he hasn't yet made a strong case for this fund, either.

Special Securities % assets 07-31-01	
Restricted/Illiquid Secs	Trace
Emerging-Markets Secs	4
Options/Futures/Warrants	No

Composition % assets 07-31-01	
Cash	6.9
Stocks*	93.1
Bonds	0.1
Other	0.0
*Foreign (% stocks)	6.4

Market Cap	
Giant	31.3
Large	12.9
Medium	39.6
Small	16.2
Micro	0.0

Sector Weightings	% of Stocks	Rel S&P	5-Year High	5-Year Low
Utilities	0.0	0.0	2	0
Energy	0.0	0.0	7	0
Financials	4.6	0.3	39	0
Industrials	1.2	0.1	15	0
Durables	0.2	0.1	7	0
Staples	1.1	0.1	3	0
Services	8.9	0.8	29	7
Retail	4.1	0.6	10	1
Health	11.5	0.8	26	2
Technology	68.4	3.7	81	12

Address:	82 Devonshire Street Boston, MA 02109 800-544-8888
Web Address:	www.fidelity.com
Inception:	12-31-84
Advisor:	Fidelity Mgmt. & Research
Subadvisor:	FMR (U.K.)/FMR (Far East)
NTF Plans:	Fidelity Inst.

Minimum Purchase:	$2500	Add: $250	IRA: $500
Min Auto Inv Plan:	$2500	Add: $100	
Sales Fees:	No-load		
Management Fee:	.35%+.52% mx./.27% mn.(G)+(–).20%P		
Actual Fees:	Mgt: 0.50%	Dist: —	
Expense Projections:	3Yr: $240	5Yr: $417	10Yr: $930
Avg Brok Commission:	—	Income Distrib: Semi-Ann.	
Total Cost (relative to category):		Low	

Fidelity Overseas

Ticker	Load	NAV	Yield	Total Assets	Mstar Category
FOSFX	None	$27.42	0.0%	$3,481.2 mil	Foreign Stock

Prospectus Objective: Foreign Stock

Fidelity Overseas Fund seeks long-term growth of capital.

The fund invests in equities issued by companies, whose principal business activities are outside of the United States. It invests at least 65% of assets in at least three different countries outside of North America. While the fund may invest up to 35% of assets in Canada, Mexico, and the U.S., it does not expect to allocate a significant portion to U.S. securities. The fund may also invest in debt securities of any quality.

Historical Profile
Return Average
Risk Average
Rating ★★★ Neutral

Investment Style
Equity
Average Stock %: 86% (1995), 82% (1996), 88% (1997), 88% (1998), 89% (1999), 94% (2000), 92% (12-01)

▼ Manager Change
▽ Partial Manager Change

Fund Performance vs. Category Average
■ Quarterly Fund Return +/– Category Average
— Category Baseline

Performance Quartile (within Category)

Portfolio Manager(s)

Richard Mace, Jr.. Since 3-96. BA'85 U. of Virginia; MBA'88 U. of Pennsylvania. Other funds currently managed: Fidelity Advisor Overseas T, Fidelity Worldwide, Fidelity Global Balanced.

1990	1991	1992	1993	1994	1995	1996	1997	1998	1999	2000	12-01	History
24.79	25.26	19.90	27.43	27.30	29.07	30.84	32.54	35.98	48.01	34.37	27.42	NAV
–6.60	8.61	–11.46	40.05	1.27	9.06	13.10	10.92	12.84	42.89	–18.33	–20.22	Total Return %
–3.49	–21.87	–19.07	30.00	–0.04	–28.48	–9.85	–22.43	–15.74	21.85	–9.23	–8.35	+/– S&P 500
16.85	–3.52	0.72	7.49	–6.51	–2.15	7.05	9.14	–7.16	15.92	–4.16	—	+/– MSCI EAFE
2.41	1.77	1.46	2.16	0.00	1.25	1.27	1.10	0.61	1.22	1.79	0.00	Income Return %
–9.01	6.84	–12.92	37.89	1.27	7.81	11.83	9.82	12.22	41.66	–20.12	–20.22	Capital Return %
21	80	92	31	42	60	46	25	55	39	62	37	Total Rtn % Rank Cat
0.68	0.44	0.37	0.43	0.00	0.34	0.37	0.34	0.20	0.44	0.86	0.00	Income $
0.86	1.16	2.10	0.00	0.47	0.35	1.63	1.34	0.51	2.64	4.12	0.00	Capital Gains $
1.26	1.53	1.52	1.27	1.24	1.05	1.12	1.20	1.24	1.23	1.16	—	Expense Ratio %
1.34	2.19	1.78	1.00	0.90	1.78	1.74	1.28	0.82	0.85	0.55	—	Income Ratio %
96	132	122	64	49	49	82	68	69	85	132	—	Turnover Rate %
974.9	958.1	781.9	1,519.6	2,194.1	2,409.9	3,247.1	3,704.9	3,846.5	5,403.7	4,652.6	3,481.2	Net Assets $mil

Performance 12-31-01

	1st Qtr	2nd Qtr	3rd Qtr	4th Qtr	Total
1997	3.21	12.47	2.49	–6.77	10.92
1998	13.98	1.64	–17.40	17.91	12.84
1999	2.81	5.11	5.74	25.06	42.89
2000	0.54	–5.26	–7.24	–7.57	–18.33
2001	–11.26	0.00	–18.39	10.16	–20.22

Trailing	Total Return%	+/– S&P 500	+/– MSCI EAFE	% Rank All	% Rank Cat	Growth of $10,000
3 Mo	10.16	–0.52	—	42	30	11,016
6 Mo	–10.10	–4.54	—	85	65	8,990
1 Yr	–20.22	–8.35	—	81	37	7,978
3 Yr Avg	–2.35	–1.33	—	84	50	9,310
5 Yr Avg	3.11	–7.59	—	85	36	11,652
10 Yr Avg	6.08	–6.85	—	69	52	18,049
15 Yr Avg	6.96	–6.77	—	68	48	27,435

Tax Analysis	Tax-Adj Ret%	%Rank Cat	%Pretax Ret	%Rank Cat
3 Yr Avg	–3.88	50	—	—
5 Yr Avg	1.71	33	55.2	61
10 Yr Avg	4.62	49	75.9	49

Potential Capital Gain Exposure: –21% of assets

Risk Analysis

Time Period	Load-Adj Return %	Risk %Rank[1] All	Risk %Rank[1] Cat	Morningstar Return	Morningstar Risk	Morningstar Risk-Adj Rating
1 Yr	–20.22					
3 Yr	–2.35	73	51	–1.44[2]	0.94	★★★
5 Yr	3.11	73	46	–0.41[2]	0.82	★★★
10 Yr	6.08	82	63	0.37[2]	0.86	★★★

Average Historical Rating (169 months): 3.4★s

[1] 1=low, 100=high [2] T-Bill return substituted for category avg.

Category Rating (3 Yr)

1 2 **3** 4 5
Worst Best

Return Average
Risk Average

Other Measures	Standard Index S&P 500	Best Fit Index MSCIWdxUSN
Alpha	–1.8	3.6
Beta	0.84	1.12
R-Squared	62	92
Standard Deviation		17.91
Mean		–2.35
Sharpe Ratio		–0.47

Portfolio Analysis 04-30-01

Share change since 10–00 Total Stocks: 135	Sector	Country	% Assets
☼ Fid Cash Central Fund	N/A	N/A	14.39
⊖ Total Fina Cl B	Energy	France	3.94
☼ Vodafone Grp	N/A	N/A	2.98
⊕ Nikko Secs	Financials	Japan	2.53
⊕ Nomura Secs	Financials	Japan	2.48
⊕ Sony	Durables	Japan	2.44
☼ Glaxosmithkline	Technology	United Kingdom	2.08
⊖ Nestle (Reg)	Staples	Switzerland	2.04
⊕ Lloyds TSB Grp	Financials	United Kingdom	1.79
⊕ Royal Dutch Petro	Energy	Netherlands	1.58
☼ Topix Index (Fut)	N/A	N/A	1.55
☼ CAC 40 Index (Fut)	N/A	N/A	1.53
⊕ Telefonica	Services	Spain	1.52
☼ FTSE 100 Index (Fut)	N/A	N/A	1.46
☼ DJ Eurostoxx Index 50 (Fut)	N/A	N/A	1.44
☼ DAX Index (Fut)	N/A	N/A	1.43
⊖ Nippon Telegraph & Tele	Services	Japan	1.43
⊕ Sanofi–Synthelabo	Health	France	1.40
⊕ Daiwa Secs Grp	Financials	Japan	1.33
☼ ING Groep	Financials	Netherlands	1.27

Current Investment Style

Style: Value Blnd Growth; Size: Large Med Small

	Stock Port Avg	Rel MSCI EAFE Current	Rel MSCI EAFE Hist	Rel Cat
Price/Earnings Ratio	27.8	1.08	1.10	1.09
Price/Cash Flow	13.7	1.06	1.06	0.95
Price/Book Ratio	4.1	1.18	1.33	1.05
3 Yr Earnings Growth	24.8	1.32	1.13	1.26
Med Mkt Cap $mil	36,604	1.3	1.1	2.03

Country Exposure 04-30-01	% assets
Japan	25
France	10
United Kingdom	7
Netherlands	6
Switzerland	6

Hedging History: Never

Regional Exposure 04-30-01	% assets
Europe	41
Japan	25
Latin America	0
Pacific Rim	7
Other	5

Special Securities % assets 04-30-01	
Restricted/Illiquid Secs	0
Emerging–Markets Secs	6
Options/Futures/Warrants	Yes

Composition % assets 04-30-01			
Cash	1.4	Bonds	0.0
Stocks	92.3	Other	6.4

Sector Weightings	% of Stocks	Rel Cat	5-Year High	5-Year Low
Utilities	1.3	0.5	18	0
Energy	9.4	1.6	13	2
Financials	28.2	1.3	44	12
Industrials	8.7	0.6	35	9
Durables	7.3	1.1	21	5
Staples	4.0	0.6	10	0
Services	12.9	0.7	25	5
Retail	4.8	1.0	8	2
Health	9.1	0.9	11	2
Technology	14.4	1.4	21	2

Analysis by Emily Hall 11-28-01

Fidelity Overseas is a good fund for those who don't like surprises.

Manager Rick Mace's strategy is about as straightforward as they come. He buys well-known large-cap names and keeps the fund's country and sector weightings fairly close to those of his benchmark, the MSCI EAFE index. Any moves that Mace makes to overweight or underweight a sector or country tend to be fairly modest. The result is an offering that looks a lot like its bogy.

Such an approach also means that this offering delivers solid results but rarely tops the foreign-stock group. Its three- and five-year returns both land in the category's top half. The fund's results relative to its bogy, by contrast, are quite mixed. In years such as 1997 and 1999, the fund has sped past its benchmark, but it struggled to keep pace in 1998 and 2000.

This year, the fund has actually held up quite well. The fund's year-to-date loss of 19% through late November probably isn't tickling investors. But that showing is actually good enough to place the fund among the category's top third and has helped the fund eke past its benchmark. Although the fund has its share of technology and telecom stocks, its lack of racy growth names has left it in fairly good shape.

Given the weak economy, Mace has also made some moves to focus on his stronger picks by paring down the portfolio's holdings in recent months. He has shaved the fund's once-enormous set of more than 300 names to about 150. Even with such a dramatic reduction, though, the fund is still quite diversified. Moreover, Mace doesn't stuff lots of assets into any one name, which helps the fund limit its individual security risk.

This offering will probably never be a barnburner, but more-conservative investors who'd like a predictable foreign-stock choice might find this offering appealing.

Address:	82 Devonshire Street Boston, MA 02109 800–544–8888
Web Address:	www.fidelity.com
Inception:	12-04-84
Advisor:	Fidelity Mgmt. & Research
Subadvisor:	FMR (U.K.)/FMR (Far East)
NTF Plans:	Fidelity , Fidelity Inst.

Minimum Purchase:	$2500	Add: $250	IRA: $500
Min Auto Inv Plan:	$2500	Add: $100	
Sales Fees:	No–load		
Management Fee:	.45%+.52% mx./.27% mn.(G)+(–).20%P		
Actual Fees:	Mgt: 0.92%	Dist: —	
Expense Projections:	3Yr: $403	5Yr: $697	10Yr: $1534
Avg Brok Commission:	—	Income Distrib: Annually	
Total Cost (relative to category):		Below Avg	

Fidelity Pacific Basin

Ticker	Load	NAV	Yield	Total Assets	Mstar Category
FPBFX	3.00%	$13.85	0.0%	$330.9 mil	Div Pacific Stock

Prospectus Objective: Pacific Stock

Fidelity Pacific Basin Fund seeks long-term growth of capital.

The fund normally invests at least 65% of assets in companies that have their principal business activities in the Pacific Basin. It invests the balance in securities of issuers in other Asian countries. It normally invests a significant percentage of assets in Japan. The fund may invest up to 35% of assets in debt securities rated below investment-grade.

Historical Profile

Return: Average
Risk: Above Avg
Rating: ★★★ Neutral

Investment Style
Equity
Average Stock %

	1994	1995	1996	1997	1998	1999	2000	12-01
Average Stock %		91%	94%	94%	94%	96%	94%	100%

▼ Manager Change
▽ Partial Manager Change

Fund Performance vs. Category Average
■ Quarterly Fund Return +/– Category Average
— Category Baseline

Performance Quartile (within Category)

Portfolio Manager(s)

William J. Kennedy. Since 12-98. Other funds currently managed: Fidelity Advisor Japan A, Fidelity Advisor Japan T, Fidelity Advisor Japan B.

1990	1991	1992	1993	1994	1995	1996	1997	1998	1999	2000	12-01	History
11.40	12.83	11.74	18.80	16.19	15.20	14.70	12.23	13.22	28.74	17.29	13.85	NAV
–27.21	12.54	–7.62	63.91	–2.81	–6.12	–2.76	–15.10	8.26	119.61	–35.32	–19.90	Total Return %
–24.10	–17.94	–15.24	53.85	–4.13	–43.65	–25.71	–48.45	–20.31	98.57	–26.22	–8.02	+/– S&P 500
7.21	1.24	10.78	28.22	–15.64	–8.90	5.81	10.39	5.82	61.98	–9.53	—	+/– MSCI Pacific
1.01	0.00	0.86	1.11	0.11	0.00	0.53	1.70	0.16	1.97	3.90	0.00	Income Return %
–28.22	12.54	–8.48	62.80	–2.92	–6.11	–3.29	–16.80	8.10	117.64	–39.22	–19.90	Capital Return %
83	75	60	53	37	95	96	16	5	25	54	37	Total Rtn % Rank Cat
0.16	0.00	0.11	0.13	0.02	0.00	0.08	0.25	0.02	0.26	1.12	0.00	Income $
0.00	0.00	0.00	0.27	2.02	0.00	0.00	0.00	0.00	0.00	0.23	0.00	Capital Gains $
1.59	1.88	1.84	1.59	1.54	1.32	1.24	1.31	1.72	1.36	1.22	—	Expense Ratio %
0.88	0.12	0.65	0.15	0.04	0.44	0.30	–0.04	–0.16	–0.24	–0.42	—	Income Ratio %
118	143	105	77	88	65	85	42	57	101	144	—	Turnover Rate %
71.2	93.4	112.5	526.7	475.5	469.2	446.9	213.6	227.4	989.0	446.7	330.9	Net Assets $mil

Performance 12-31-01

	1st Qtr	2nd Qtr	3rd Qtr	4th Qtr	Total
1997	–6.80	19.12	–7.66	–17.18	–15.10
1998	0.00	–4.01	–7.24	21.58	8.26
1999	12.41	17.97	20.42	37.53	119.61
2000	–4.91	–9.44	–11.16	–15.45	–35.32
2001	–10.64	3.62	–21.42	10.10	–19.90

Trailing	Total Return%	+/– S&P 500	+/– MSCI Pacific	% Rank All	% Rank Cat	Growth of $10,000
3 Mo	10.10	–0.59	—	42	49	11,010
6 Mo	–13.49	–7.94	—	92	65	8,651
1 Yr	–19.90	–8.02	—	80	37	8,010
3 Yr Avg	4.40	5.42	—	36	20	11,379
5 Yr Avg	0.90	–9.80	—	91	12	10,459
10 Yr Avg	3.46	–9.47	—	97	20	14,051
15 Yr Avg	3.88	–9.85	—	98	33	17,708

Tax Analysis	Tax-Adj Ret%	%Rank Cat	%Pretax Ret	%Rank Cat
3 Yr Avg	3.37	15	76.6	35
5 Yr Avg	0.13	6	14.6	33
10 Yr Avg	2.50	20	72.2	16

Potential Capital Gain Exposure: –32% of assets

Risk Analysis

Time Period	Load-Adj Return %	Risk %Rank[1] All	Risk %Rank[1] Cat	Morningstar Return	Morningstar Risk	Morningstar Risk-Adj Rating
1 Yr	–22.30					
3 Yr	3.35	84	40	–0.33[2]	1.15	★★★★
5 Yr	0.29	87	17	–0.95[2]	1.15	★★★
10 Yr	3.14	94	45	–0.38[2]	1.20	★★

Average Historical Rating (148 months): 2.3★s

[1] 1=low, 100=high [2] T-Bill return substituted for category avg.

Category Rating (3 Yr)

1 2 3 4 5
Worst Best

Return	Above Avg
Risk	Average

Other Measures	Standard Index S&P 500	Best Fit Index MSCIPacNdD
Alpha	7.6	12.2
Beta	1.03	1.19
R-Squared	45	87
Standard Deviation		27.96
Mean		4.40
Sharpe Ratio		–0.02

Portfolio Analysis 04-30-01

Share change since 10-00 Total Stocks: 163	Sector	Country	% Assets
⊖ Toyota Motor	Durables	Japan	4.26
⊖ Sony	Durables	Japan	3.50
✲ Fid Cash Central Fund	N/A	N/A	3.14
⊕ Nomura Secs	Financials	Japan	3.13
✲ Nissan Motor	Durables	Japan	2.53
⊕ Sun Hung Kai Properties	Financials	Hong Kong	2.17
⊖ Takeda Chem Inds	Health	Japan	1.91
⊖ News	Services	Australia	1.80
⊖ Canon	Industrials	Japan	1.76
⊕ Samsung Electncs	Technology	South Korea	1.62
⊖ Hutchison Whampoa	Financials	Hong Kong	1.58
⊕ Sumitomo Mitsui Bk	Financials	Japan	1.57
BHP	Industrials	Australia	1.48
✲ JAFCO Company	Financials	Japan	1.33
✲ China Telecom HK	Services	Hong Kong	1.31
⊖ NEC	Technology	Japan	1.26
⊖ Honda Motor	Durables	Japan	1.23
⊕ Ricoh	Technology	Japan	1.23
⊕ Cheung Kong Hldgs	Financials	Hong Kong	1.14
⊖ Natl Australia Bk	Financials	Australia	1.11

Current Investment Style

Style: Value Blnd Growth; Size: Large Med Small

	Stock Port Avg	Rel MSCI EAFE Current	Rel MSCI EAFE Hist	Rel Cat
Price/Earnings Ratio	27.3	1.05	1.20	1.01
Price/Cash Flow	14.6	1.14	1.16	1.02
Price/Book Ratio	3.0	0.87	0.86	1.04
3 Yr Earnings Growth	18.0	0.96	1.62	0.98
Med Mkt Cap $mil	13,816	0.5	0.5	1.52

Country Exposure 04-30-01	% assets
Japan	54
Hong Kong	14
Australia	10
South Korea	5
Taiwan	4

Hedging History: Never

Special Securities % assets 04-30-01	
Restricted/Illiquid Secs	0
Emerging–Markets Secs	24
Options/Futures/Warrants	No

Composition % assets 04-30-01

Cash	0.0	Bonds	0.0
Stocks	100.0	Other	0.0

Sector Weightings	% of Stocks	Rel Cat	5-Year High	5-Year Low
Utilities	0.6	0.2	6	0
Energy	0.4	0.2	6	0
Financials	32.3	1.4	35	13
Industrials	8.5	0.7	40	8
Durables	17.7	1.4	20	11
Staples	2.4	0.4	6	1
Services	10.3	0.7	17	6
Retail	3.2	0.7	9	2
Health	4.9	1.0	8	0
Technology	19.8	1.3	30	2

Analysis by Emily Hall 11-06-01

Fidelity Pacific Basin is probably best for those who'd like a Japan fund with some bite.

This offering isn't exactly what it appears to be. While manager William Kennedy does invest a chunk of money in such countries as China, Malaysia and Australia, most of his attention is focused on Japan. As of Sept. 30, 2001, the fund had nearly 60% of its assets in Japanese stocks, including many multinational blue chips. Such a monstrous stake in Japan is not uncommon here. Indeed, the fund has held as much as 70% in Japanese stocks from time to time during the past six years.

Kennedy's affection for Japanese stocks isn't driven by some sort of macroeconomic call, though. Rather, he looks for companies with solid free cash flows, decent growth prospects, and reasonable prices. It just so happens that the majority of names that meet his criteria are from Japan.

Of course, Kennedy does nibble around the margins elsewhere. For instance, the fund's second largest stake currently is in Australia, where Kennedy says he has been able to find some picks with acceptable earnings growth, good disclosure, and solid management teams.

This approach has worked well during Kennedy's nearly three-year tenure. For the trailing three years through Nov. 6, this offering has returned 5.2%, noticeably better than the 2.4% return of its typical peer. Interestingly, the fund has also bested the Japan fund average over the same period by about 5 percentage points, indicating that his Japan-with-a- dash-of-everything-else strategy—not to mention decent stock-picking—has worked pretty well.

To be sure, investors should be aware of the risks: The fund's fortunes are closely tied to the strength of the Japanese market. But for those investors who are comfortable with such an approach, this has developed into a solid choice.

Address:	82 Devonshire Street Boston, MA 02109 800–544–8888
Web Address:	www.fidelity.com
Inception:	10-01-86
Advisor:	Fidelity Mgmt. & Research
Subadvisor:	FMR (Far East)/FMR (U.K.)
NTF Plans:	Fidelity Inst.

Minimum Purchase:	$2500	Add: $250 IRA: $500
Min Auto Inv Plan:	$2500	Add: $100
Sales Fees:	3.00%L, 1.50%R within 3 months	
Management Fee:	.45%+.52% mx./.27% mn.(G)+(–).20%P	
Actual Fees:	Mgt: 0.92%	Dist: —
Expense Projections:	3Yr: $721	5Yr: $1027 10Yr: $1897
Avg Brok Commission:	—	Income Distrib: Annually
Total Cost (relative to category):		Below Avg

Fidelity Puritan

Ticker	Load	NAV	Yield	Total Assets	Mstar Category
FPURX	None	$17.67	3.3%	$20,314.8 mil	Domestic Hybrid

Prospectus Objective: Balanced

Fidelity Puritan Fund seeks income and capital growth consistent with reasonable risk.

The fund invests in a diversified array of high-yielding securities such as common stocks, preferred stocks, and bonds. The relative holdings vary in response to changing market conditions. The bonds may have any quality rating or maturity; the fund may invest in lower-quality, higher-yielding assets. The fund may purchase foreign securities, zero-coupon bonds, and indexed securities. It may also engage in futures contracts, short sales, and swap agreements.

Historical Profile

Return Average
Risk Low
Rating ★★★★ Above Avg

Investment Style: Equity — Average Stock %: 61% 62% 59% 63% 62% 61%

▼ Manager Change
▽ Partial Manager Change

Fund Performance vs. Category Average
■ Quarterly Fund Return +/– Category Average
— Category Baseline

Performance Quartile (within Category)

Portfolio Manager(s)

Kevin E. Grant, CFA. Since 3-96. BA'82 U. of Hartford; MBA'86 U. of Hartford. Other funds currently managed: Fidelity Balanced, Fidelity Investment Grade Bond, Fidelity Spartan Investment Gr Bond.

Stephen R. Petersen, CFA. Since 2-00. BA U. of Wisconsin; MS U. of Wisconsin. Other fund currently managed: Fidelity Equity-Income.

History

1990	1991	1992	1993	1994	1995	1996	1997	1998	1999	2000	12-01	History
12.05	14.14	14.74	15.75	14.81	17.01	17.24	19.38	20.07	19.03	18.83	17.67	NAV
–6.35	24.46	15.43	21.45	1.78	21.46	15.15	22.35	16.60	2.86	7.77	–1.05	Total Return %
–3.23	–6.03	7.81	11.39	0.47	–16.07	–7.79	–11.00	–11.98	–18.18	16.88	10.82	+/– S&P 500
–15.31	8.45	8.03	11.70	4.70	2.99	11.54	12.67	7.92	3.69	–3.86	–9.48	+/– LB Aggregate
5.98	6.79	5.99	5.05	3.50	3.36	3.80	4.03	3.57	3.26	3.28	3.24	Income Return %
–12.33	17.67	9.44	16.40	–1.72	18.10	11.36	18.32	13.02	–0.40	4.49	–4.30	Capital Return %
89	42	5	5	10	81	35	20	27	80	19	27	Total Rtn % Rank Cat
0.80	0.80	0.82	0.72	0.54	0.49	0.62	0.68	0.67	0.64	0.61	0.60	Income $
0.00	0.00	0.69	1.36	0.71	0.44	1.54	0.96	1.56	0.97	1.01	0.35	Capital Gains $
0.65	0.66	0.64	0.74	0.79	0.77	0.72	0.66	0.63	0.63	0.64	0.63	Expense Ratio %
6.30	5.94	6.23	4.89	4.00	3.50	3.44	3.69	3.40	3.23	3.24	3.23	Income Ratio %
58	108	102	76	74	76	139	80	84	80	62	67	Turnover Rate %
4,356.7	5,108.9	5,911.8	8,988.2	11,769.4	15,628.3	18,501.7	22,821.8	25,682.3	24,370.6	21,368.7	20,314.8	Net Assets $mil

Performance 12-31-01

	1st Qtr	2nd Qtr	3rd Qtr	4th Qtr	Total
1997	1.48	12.34	4.83	2.38	22.35
1998	8.07	2.56	–6.66	12.71	16.60
1999	1.38	3.30	–5.45	3.87	2.86
2000	–0.07	0.58	4.39	2.72	7.77
2001	–3.32	3.64	–6.80	5.96	–1.06

Trailing	Total Return%	+/– S&P 500	+/– LB Agg	% Rank All	% Rank Cat	Growth of $10,000
3 Mo	5.96	–4.73	5.92	61	59	10,596
6 Mo	–1.25	4.31	–5.90	43	41	9,875
1 Yr	–1.05	10.82	–9.48	44	27	9,895
3 Yr Avg	3.13	4.15	–3.14	53	38	10,969
5 Yr Avg	9.37	–1.33	1.94	22	22	15,647
10 Yr Avg	12.06	–0.87	4.83	18	5	31,227
15 Yr Avg	11.45	–2.29	3.33	30	16	50,824

Tax Analysis	Tax-Adj Ret%	%Rank Cat	%Pretax Ret	%Rank Cat
3 Yr Avg	0.97	42	30.9	84
5 Yr Avg	6.72	22	71.8	35
10 Yr Avg	8.92	12	74.0	40

Potential Capital Gain Exposure: 11% of assets

Risk Analysis

Time Period	Load-Adj Return %	Risk %Rank[1] All	Risk %Rank[1] Cat	Morningstar Return	Morningstar Risk	Morningstar Risk-Adj Rating
1 Yr	–1.05					
3 Yr	3.13	35	24	–0.38[2]	0.43	★★★
5 Yr	9.37	41	27	1.03[2]	0.47	★★★★
10 Yr	12.06	47	23	1.12	0.50	★★★★

Average Historical Rating (193 months): 4.3★s

[1] 1=low, 100=high [2] T-Bill return substituted for category avg.

Category Rating (3 Yr): 3 (1 Worst – 5 Best)

Return Average
Risk Below Avg

Other Measures	Standard Index S&P 500	Best Fit Index S&P 500
Alpha	0.5	0.5
Beta	0.42	0.42
R-Squared	71	71

Standard Deviation	8.56
Mean	3.13
Sharpe Ratio	–0.25

Portfolio Analysis 07-31-01

Total Stocks: 220 (Share change since 01-01)	Sector	PE Ratio	YTD Return %	% Net Assets
⊕ ExxonMobil	Energy	15.3	–7.59	3.47
⊖ Freddie Mac	Financials	14.0	–3.87	2.65
⊖ Fannie Mae	Financials	16.2	–6.95	2.59
Citigroup	Financials	20.0	0.03	2.31
J.P. Morgan Chase & Co.	Financials	27.8	–17.40	1.76
⊖ SBC Comms	Services	18.4	–16.00	1.47
⊖ General Elec	Industrials	30.1	–15.00	1.29
⊕ BellSouth	Services	24.9	–5.09	1.14
Bristol-Myers Squibb	Health	20.2	–26.00	1.13
Tyco Intl	Industrials	27.1	6.23	1.02

Total Fixed-Income: 521	Date of Maturity	Amount $000	Value $000	% Net Assets
FNMA 6.5%	04-01-24	15	873,257	4.17
FNMA N/A	08-01-31	433,525	432,996	2.07
US Treasury Note N/A	06-30-03	252,170	252,604	1.21
FNMA 7%	11-01-27	60	211,022	1.01
FNMA 6%	12-01-23	2,027	195,552	0.93
FNMA 7.5%	07-01-27	2,177	167,440	0.80
US Treasury Bond 11.25%	02-15-15	103,090	160,917	0.77
FNMA 5.5%	05-01-11	337	143,006	0.68
US Treasury Bond 6.125%	08-15-29	120,650	129,472	0.62
GNMA 7.5%	04-15-23	614	114,896	0.55

Equity Style
Style: Value
Size: Large-Cap

Fixed-Income Style NA
Duration: —
Quality: —

	Portfolio Avg	Rel S&P
Price/Earnings Ratio	24.5	0.79
Price/Book Ratio	4.1	0.72
Price/Cash Flow	12.6	0.70
3 Yr Earnings Growth	13.3	0.91
1 Yr Earnings Est%	–4.2	2.39
Debt % Total Cap	33.7	1.09
Med Mkt Cap $mil	47,650	0.78

Avg Eff Duration	—
Avg Eff Maturity	—
Avg Credit Quality	AA
Avg Wtd Coupon	0.00%

Special Securities % assets 07-31-01	
Restricted/Illiquid Secs	3
Emerging-Markets Secs	Trace
Options/Futures/Warrants	Yes

Composition % of assets 07-31-01	
Cash	4.4
Stocks*	60.6
Bonds	33.6
Other	1.5
*Foreign (% of stocks)	6.2

Market Cap	
Giant	53.1
Large	32.0
Medium	13.5
Small	1.4
Micro	0.0

Sector Weightings	% of Stocks	Rel S&P	5-Year High	5-Year Low
Utilities	1.3	0.4	8	0
Energy	14.8	2.1	19	7
Financials	28.7	1.6	30	9
Industrials	19.2	1.7	47	16
Durables	2.4	1.5	11	0
Staples	4.8	0.6	13	1
Services	13.0	1.2	18	4
Retail	3.4	0.5	14	2
Health	6.3	0.4	15	0
Technology	6.2	0.3	11	1

Analysis by Christopher Traulsen 09-29-01

Fidelity Puritan is showing why it's a good choice for conservative investors.

This fund is down 7.8% for the year to date through Sept. 27, 2001. That's certainly not an insignificant loss, but it's pretty good considering how far equity markets are down. Indeed, fully two thirds of the fund's domestic-hybrid peers have lost even more in the period.

Although its 63% equity weighting is a bit on the high side for the category, the fund has benefited from its value bias. Equity manager Stephen Petersen tries to buy big, dividend-paying blue chips on the cheap. That leads him to focus on areas such as financials and energy instead of expensive arenas like technology. As growth rates have come in sharply in 2001, the priciest stocks (which had the highest growth rates implied in their valuations) have fallen the hardest, and the type of fare Petersen favors has held up relatively well.

Petersen hasn't gotten everything right. Certain financials, such as Citigroup and American Express, have gotten clobbered amid the slowdown. And, although bond manager Kevin Grant favors a relatively staid portfolio of agency-backed debt, Treasuries, and corporates, a small high-yield stake has detracted from the fund's returns recently. Thus, even though the fund has outperformed its overall peer group, other large value-oriented hybrid offerings have fared better.

Nonetheless, we think this fund is a solid choice for conservative investors. Petersen only took the helm here in early 2000, but he has run all-equity Fidelity Equity-Income in the same style for years and has put up solid numbers there with few surprises. His value style will cause the fund to lag in growth-led rallies, but it should make the offering steadier than many of its peers—just what most investors want in a hybrid fund.

Address:	82 Devonshire Street, Boston, MA 02109, 800–544–8888
Web Address:	www.fidelity.com
Inception:	04-16-47
Advisor:	Fidelity Mgmt. & Research
Subadvisor:	FMR (Far East)/FMR (U.K.)
NTF Plans:	Fidelity , Fidelity Inst.

Minimum Purchase:	$2500	Add: $250	IRA: $500
Min Auto Inv Plan:	$2500	Add: $100	
Sales Fees:	No-load		
Management Fee:	.15%+.52% mx./.27% mn.(G)		
Actual Fees:	Mgt: 0.44%	Dist: —	
Expense Projections:	3Yr: $205	5Yr: $357	10Yr: $798
Avg Brok Commission:	—	Income Distrib: Quarterly	
Total Cost (relative to category):	Low		

Fidelity Select Biotechnology

Ticker	Load	NAV	Yield	Total Assets	Mstar Category
FBIOX	3.00%	$65.12	0.0%	$3,002.1 mil	Spec Health Care

Prospectus Objective: Specialty—Health

Fidelity Select Biotechnology seeks capital appreciation.

The fund normally invests at least 80% of assets in the securities of companies principally engaged in the research and development of biotechnological or biomedical products, services, and processes. Securities of related manufacturing or distributing companies may also be considered for purchase. The fund may invest up to 25% of assets in one issuer; it may invest up to 5% in low-quality debt. The fund is nondiversified.

The fund waives sales charges on shares purchased through portfolio advisory services.

Historical Profile
Return Above Avg
Risk High
Rating ★★★★ Above Avg

Investment Style
Equity
Average Stock %: 66% 87% 96% 88% 92% 91% 93%

▼ Manager Change
▽ Partial Manager Change

Fund Performance vs. Category Average
■ Quarterly Fund Return +/– Category Average
— Category Baseline

Performance Quartile (within Category)

Portfolio Manager(s)

Brian Younger. Since 9-00. BA'98 Harvard U. Other funds currently managed: Fidelity Advisor Biotechnology A, Fidelity Advisor Biotechnology B, Fidelity Advisor Biotechnology C.

1990	1991	1992	1993	1994	1995	1996	1997	1998	1999	2000	12-01	History
19.94	36.42	28.41	28.61	23.41	34.83	32.51	32.54	39.77	67.13	86.80	65.12	NAV
44.35	99.05	–10.34	0.70	–18.18	49.10	5.56	15.38	30.90	77.72	32.79	–24.98	Total Return %
47.47	68.56	–17.96	–9.35	–19.49	11.57	–17.38	–17.97	2.33	56.68	41.89	–13.10	+/– S&P 500
50.53	64.84	–19.31	–10.58	–18.11	12.65	–15.63	–15.91	7.47	54.16	43.72	–14.08	+/– Wilshire 5000
0.00	0.10	0.00	0.00	0.00	0.30	0.09	0.00	0.00	0.00	0.00	0.00	Income Return %
44.35	98.94	–10.34	0.70	–18.18	48.80	5.48	15.38	30.90	77.72	32.79	–24.98	Capital Return %
1	1	45	57	88	35	90	69	30	8	85	89	Total Rtn % Rank Cat
0.00	0.02	0.00	0.00	0.00	0.07	0.03	0.00	0.00	0.00	0.00	0.00	Income $
0.67	2.52	3.89	0.00	0.00	0.00	4.06	4.71	2.41	2.82	2.11	0.00	Capital Gains $
2.07	1.63	1.50	1.50	1.61	1.59	1.43	1.56	1.47	1.30	1.15	1.00	Expense Ratio %
–0.31	0.24	–0.34	–0.37	–0.69	–0.27	0.35	–0.59	–0.81	–0.75	–0.51	–0.37	Income Ratio %
290	166	160	79	51	77	67	41	162	86	72	74	Turnover Rate %
223.9	1,146.5	796.0	557.2	396.1	846.5	635.0	551.0	704.4	1,622.8	4,117.8	3,002.1	Net Assets $mil

Performance 12-31-01

	1st Qtr	2nd Qtr	3rd Qtr	4th Qtr	Total
1997	–5.54	10.58	14.62	–3.63	15.38
1998	10.42	–6.31	0.32	26.13	30.90
1999	9.08	3.42	12.00	40.66	77.72
2000	12.66	21.25	10.34	–11.90	32.79
2001	–34.80	21.19	–19.85	18.46	–24.98

Trailing	Total Return%	+/– S&P 500	+/– Wil 5000	% Rank All	% Rank Cat	Growth of $10,000
3 Mo	18.46	7.78	6.09	16	24	11,846
6 Mo	–5.05	0.51	0.44	62	73	9,495
1 Yr	–24.98	–13.10	–14.08	88	89	7,502
3 Yr Avg	20.98	22.00	21.63	2	25	17,705
5 Yr Avg	21.74	11.04	12.03	1	12	26,741
10 Yr Avg	12.01	–0.92	–0.27	19	63	31,095
15 Yr Avg	18.61	4.88	5.61	1	25	129,378

Tax Analysis	Tax-Adj Ret%	%Rank Cat	%Pretax Ret	%Rank Cat
3 Yr Avg	20.07	26	95.7	26
5 Yr Avg	20.01	12	92.0	27
10 Yr Avg	10.37	63	86.3	36

Potential Capital Gain Exposure: –1% of assets

Risk Analysis

Time Period	Load-Adj Return %	Risk %Rank¹ All	Risk %Rank¹ Cat	Morningstar Return	Morningstar Risk	Morningstar Risk-Adj Rating
1 Yr	–27.23					
3 Yr	19.75	96	92	3.60²	1.80	★★★★★
5 Yr	21.00	93	100	4.73²	1.60	★★★★★
10 Yr	11.67	97	100	1.04	1.86	★★

Average Historical Rating (157 months): 3.3★s

¹1=low, 100=high ² T-Bill return substituted for category avg.

Category Rating (3 Yr)

1 2 **3** 4 5
Worst Best

Return Above Avg
Risk High

Other Measures	Standard Index S&P 500	Best Fit Index Wil 4500
Alpha	33.1	28.4
Beta	0.78	1.23
R-Squared	7	51
Standard Deviation		66.00
Mean		20.98
Sharpe Ratio		0.27

Portfolio Analysis 08-31-01

Share chng since 02-01 Total Stocks: 64	Subsector	PE	YTD Ret%	% Assets
⊕ Amgen	Gen Pharm/Bio	52.8	–11.70	11.14
⊕ IDEC Pharmaceuticals	Gen Pharm/Bio	NMF	9.09	6.66
⊕ Gilead Sciences	Emg. Pharm/Bio	—	58.48	5.94
⊕ MedImmune	Gen Pharm/Bio	78.6	–2.81	5.09
⊕ Millennium Pharma	Emg. Pharm/Bio	—	–60.30	4.78
⊕ Imclone Sys	Emg. Pharm/Bio	—	5.59	4.59
⊕ Biogen	Gen Pharm/Bio	30.5	–4.52	4.46
Human Genome Sciences	Emg. Pharm/Bio	—	–51.30	4.03
⊕ Genzyme Corporation General Di	Emg. Pharm/Bio	—	33.11	3.54
⊕ Cephalon	Emg. Pharm/Bio	—	19.38	2.90
⊕ Bristol-Myers Squibb	Gen Pharm/Bio	20.2	–26.00	2.74
⊕ Invitrogen	Health	—	–28.30	2.70
Protein Design Labs	Emg. Pharm/Bio	NMF	–24.10	2.25
⊖ Immunex	Gen Pharm/Bio	89.4	–31.70	2.11
⊖ Pfizer	Gen Pharm/Bio	34.7	–12.40	2.06
COR Therapeutics	Emg. Pharm/Bio	NMF	–31.90	2.03
Sepracor	Emg. Pharm/Bio	—	–28.70	1.97
⊕ CV Therapeutics	Emg. Pharm/Bio	—	–26.40	1.95
⊕ Vertex Pharmaceuticals	Emg. Pharm/Bio	—	–65.60	1.94
⊕ Celgene	Emg. Pharm/Bio	—	–1.78	1.71
Celera Genomics Grp	Health	—	–25.70	1.40
⊖ Alkermes	Emg. Pharm/Bio	—	–15.90	1.31
⊖ Abgenix	Health	—	–43.00	1.28
⊖ Enzon	Health	NMF	–9.32	1.17
⊖ ICOS	Emg. Pharm/Bio	—	10.59	1.11

Current Investment Style

Style: Value Blnd Growth; Size: Large Med Small

	Stock Port Avg	Relative S&P 500 Current	Relative S&P 500 Hist	Rel Cat
Price/Earnings Ratio	50.8¹	1.64	1.32	1.26
Price/Book Ratio	10.7	1.88	1.65	1.18
Price/Cash Flow	35.2	1.96	1.54	1.23
3 Yr Earnings Growth	—	—	—	—
1 Yr Earnings Est%	23.8¹	—	—	1.05
Med Mkt Cap $mil	5,704	0.1	0.1	0.26

¹figure is based on 50% or less of stocks

Analysis by Peter Di Teresa 08-31-01

Fidelity Select Biotechnology is still one of the better biotech plays.

Investors should note, however, what a risky proposition a relatively pure subsector play can be. For the year to date through August 30, 2001, this fund was 27% in the red and lagging 87% of all health-care funds. And that's despite a 21% gain in the second quarter—the fund lost more than a third of its value in the first three months of the year.

With that kind of vulnerability, it might be hard to see why this fund has any appeal. The fact of the matter is, most of its biotech peers have been suffering a lot more. This fund's volatility is also lower—at 72, its three-year standard deviation is the lowest of any biotech fund. (To put that figure in perspective, it's still nearly twice the health-care average.) The fund's returns are also competitive with the biotech group's.

This fund tends to hold up better in ugly markets than its biotech peers because it focuses on bigger companies. (In part, that's a concession to its $3 billion asset base, which makes it the fourth-largest in the specialty-health group and by far the largest biotech fund.) Like his predecessors, manager Brian Younger focuses on established biotechs with multiple products in their pipelines, preferring them to smaller firms that have everything staked on just one product. Big biotech names such as Amgen and MedImmune tend, therefore, to figure prominently in the portfolio. Unlike most biotech peers, the fund also typically keeps from 12% to 18% of its assets in large-cap drug companies such as Pfizer, lending the portfolio some additional stability.

Although the fund is steadier than most biotech offerings, it's clearly just for investors who don't worry about losses.

Special Securities % assets 08-31-01	
Restricted/Illiquid Secs	1
Emerging-Markets Secs	0
Options/Futures/Warrants	No

Composition % assets 08-31-01	
Cash	7.3
Stocks*	92.2
Bonds	0.5
Other	0.0
*Foreign (% stocks)	0.4

Market Cap	
Giant	17.3
Large	17.1
Medium	53.6
Small	11.5
Micro	0.5

Subsector Weightings	% of Stocks	Rel Cat
Gen Pharm/Bio	39.1	0.9
Medical Devices	0.0	0.0
Hospitals	0.0	0.0
Other Providers	0.0	0.0
HMOs/PPOs	0.0	0.0
Emg. Pharm/Bio	48.4	2.7
Diagnostics	0.2	0.1
Tech/Bus Svs	0.0	0.0
Other	12.2	0.5

Address:	82 Devonshire Street Boston, MA 02109 800-544-8888
Web Address:	www.fidelity.com
Inception:	12-16-85
Advisor:	Fidelity Mgmt. & Research
Subadvisor:	FMR (U.K.)/FMR (Far East)
NTF Plans:	Fidelity Inst.

Minimum Purchase:	$2500	Add: $250 IRA: $500
Min Auto Inv Plan:	$2500	Add: $100
Sales Fees:	3.00%L, 0.75%R within 1 month	
Management Fee:	.30%+.52% mx./.27% mn.(G)	
Actual Fees:	Mgt: 0.59%	Dist: —
Expense Projections:	3Yr: $665	5Yr: $927 10Yr: $1674
Avg Brok Commission:	—	Income Distrib: Semi-Ann.
Total Cost (relative to category):	Below Avg	

Fidelity Select Health Care

Ticker	Load	NAV	Yield	Total Assets	Mstar Category
FSPHX	3.00%	$127.26	0.1%	$2,511.2 mil	Spec Health Care

Prospectus Objective: Specialty—Health

Fidelity Select Health Care Portfolio seeks capital appreciation.

The fund invests at least 80% of assets in equity securities of companies in the health-care industry. These may include companies engaged in the design, manufacture, or sale of products or services used for or in connection with health care or medicine. The fund may invest up to 25% of assets in securities of one issuer and up to 5% of assets in lower-quality bonds. The fund is nondiversified.

The fund waives sales charges on shares purchased through portfolio advisory services.

Historical Profile
Return Above Avg
Risk Average
Rating ★★★★ Above Avg

Investment Style
Equity
Average Stock %: 82% 86% 90% 87% 94% 94% 94%

▼ Manager Change
▽ Partial Manager Change

Fund Performance vs. Category Average
■ Quarterly Fund Return +/– Category Average
— Category Baseline

Performance Quartile (within Category)

Portfolio Manager(s)

Yolanda S. Strock. Since 6-00. MBA Duke U. Other funds currently managed: Fidelity Advisor Health Care A, Fidelity Advisor Health Care Instl, Fidelity Advisor Health Care T.

1990	1991	1992	1993	1994	1995	1996	1997	1998	1999	2000	12-01	History
52.98	85.95	62.19	63.62	70.80	97.57	95.40	101.87	136.77	124.82	150.13	127.26	NAV
24.32	83.69	–17.43	2.42	21.43	45.88	15.40	31.14	41.24	–2.89	36.68	–15.01	Total Return %
27.43	53.21	–25.05	–7.64	20.11	8.34	–7.55	–2.21	12.67	–23.93	45.78	–3.13	+/– S&P 500
30.50	49.49	–26.40	–8.87	21.50	9.43	–5.80	–0.15	17.81	–26.45	47.62	–4.12	+/– Wilshire 5000
0.42	0.64	0.20	0.11	0.98	0.84	0.68	0.27	0.19	0.06	0.20	0.09	Income Return %
23.90	83.05	–17.64	2.30	20.45	45.04	14.71	30.87	41.05	–2.95	36.48	–15.10	Capital Return %
20	20	90	42	1	60	27	12	2	88	76	58	Total Rtn % Rank Cat
0.20	0.34	0.16	0.07	0.62	0.59	0.65	0.25	0.19	0.08	0.24	0.13	Income $
5.67	8.81	8.51	0.00	5.74	4.92	15.95	20.73	6.17	7.85	18.63	0.19	Capital Gains $
1.74	1.53	1.44	1.46	1.55	1.36	1.30	1.32	1.18	1.05	1.05	0.97	Expense Ratio %
1.61	1.28	–0.02	0.24	0.26	1.08	1.06	0.52	0.31	0.14	0.12	0.21	Income Ratio %
126	159	154	112	213	151	54	59	79	66	70	78	Turnover Rate %
373.2	1,169.8	753.9	573.0	796.1	1,448.7	1,242.3	1,631.5	3,032.1	2,427.4	3,123.6	2,511.2	Net Assets $mil

Performance 12-31-01

	1st Qtr	2nd Qtr	3rd Qtr	4th Qtr	Total
1997	1.50	21.26	2.50	3.96	31.14
1998	15.73	7.29	0.31	13.41	41.24
1999	1.99	–3.17	–9.13	8.22	–2.89
2000	3.29	20.87	3.48	5.80	36.68
2001	–18.22	1.64	0.28	1.96	–15.01

Trailing	Total Return%	+/– S&P 500	+/– Wil 5000	% Rank All	% Rank Cat	Growth of $10,000
3 Mo	1.96	–8.72	–10.41	71	86	10,196
6 Mo	2.25	7.81	7.73	20	16	10,225
1 Yr	–15.01	–3.13	–4.12	72	58	8,499
3 Yr Avg	4.10	5.12	4.75	39	86	11,281
5 Yr Avg	15.88	5.18	6.17	3	51	20,896
10 Yr Avg	13.70	0.77	1.42	10	45	36,117
15 Yr Avg	18.47	4.74	5.47	1	37	127,078

Tax Analysis	Tax-Adj Ret%	%Rank Cat	%Pretax Ret	%Rank Cat
3 Yr Avg	2.63	86	64.1	95
5 Yr Avg	13.39	45	84.3	54
10 Yr Avg	10.91	36	79.6	54

Potential Capital Gain Exposure: 26% of assets

Risk Analysis

Time Period	Load-Adj Return %	Risk %Rank[1] All	Risk %Rank[1] Cat	Morningstar Return	Morningstar Risk	Morningstar Risk-Adj Rating
1 Yr	–17.56					
3 Yr	3.05	51	27	–0.39[2]	0.71	★★★
5 Yr	15.18	50	25	2.69[2]	0.70	★★★★★
10 Yr	13.36	74	10	1.39	0.96	★★★★

Average Historical Rating (193 months): 4.2★s

[1] 1=low, 100=high [2] T-Bill return substituted for category avg.

Category Rating (3 Yr)

1 2 3 4 5 (Worst — Best)

Return Below Avg
Risk Below Avg

Other Measures	Standard Index S&P 500	Best Fit Index S&P 500
Alpha	1.3	1.3
Beta	0.21	0.21
R-Squared	5	5
Standard Deviation		16.26
Mean		4.10
Sharpe Ratio		–0.06

Portfolio Analysis 08-31-01

Share chng since 02-01 Total Stocks: 72	Subsector	PE	YTD Ret%	% Assets
⊖ Bristol-Myers Squibb	Gen Pharm/Bio	20.2	–26.00	8.27
⊖ Pfizer	Gen Pharm/Bio	34.7	–12.40	7.57
⊕ Amgen	Gen Pharm/Bio	52.8	–11.70	6.56
⊕ Merck	Gen Pharm/Bio	19.1	–35.90	5.86
⊖ American Home Products	Gen Pharm/Bio	—	–1.91	5.21
⊕ Abbott Labs	Gen Pharm/Bio	51.6	17.08	4.73
⊕ Johnson & Johnson	Gen Pharm/Bio	16.6	14.01	4.70
⊕ Medtronic	Medical Devices	76.4	–14.70	4.43
⊖ Eli Lilly	Gen Pharm/Bio	28.9	–14.40	4.33
⊕ Cardinal Health	Health	35.1	–2.51	3.38
⊕ Forest Labs	Gen Pharm/Bio	52.2	23.35	2.91
⊕ Guidant	Medical Devices	42.6	–7.67	2.22
⊕ Baxter Intl	Gen Pharm/Bio	33.9	22.84	2.12
⊕ Pharmacia	Chemicals	36.5	–29.30	2.01
⊕ Tenet Healthcare	Hospitals	30.1	32.14	1.98
⊕ HCA – The Healthcare Company	Hospitals	24.1	–12.20	1.89
⊕ IDEC Pharmaceuticals	Gen Pharm/Bio	NMF	9.09	1.70
⊕ McKesson HBOC	Health	—	4.92	1.49
☼ Gilead Sciences	Emg. Pharm/Bio	—	58.48	1.45
⊕ Allergan	Gen Pharm/Bio	48.7	–22.10	1.21
⊖ Schering-Plough	Gen Pharm/Bio	22.2	–35.90	1.14
⊖ Biogen	Gen Pharm/Bio	30.5	–4.52	0.94
☼ Healthsouth	Other Providers	28.0	–9.15	0.90
⊖ Becton Dickinson	Medical Devices	22.9	–3.20	0.78
⊕ Biomet	Medical Devices	40.7	17.13	0.76

Current Investment Style

Style: Value Blnd Growth; Size: Large Med Small

	Stock Port Avg	Relative S&P 500 Current	Relative S&P 500 Hist	Rel Cat
Price/Earnings Ratio	35.9	1.16	1.19	0.89
Price/Book Ratio	10.5	1.84	1.55	1.16
Price/Cash Flow	26.5	1.47	1.36	0.92
3 Yr Earnings Growth	21.5	1.47	0.91	0.99
1 Yr Earnings Est%	19.3	—	—	0.85
Med Mkt Cap $mil	64,353	1.1	1.0	2.93

Analysis by Peter Di Teresa 08-27-01

Investors seeking mainstream health-care exposure will find this fund a solid pick.

Fidelity Select Health Care invests in a wider variety of health-care issues than do many of its peers. Large-cap pharmaceutical companies are the core of its portfolio, while about one third is dedicated to other subsectors. Of those, services such as hospitals and HMOs and medical technology take up the largest portions.

Like her numerous predecessors, current manager Yolanda Strock takes something of a value approach to this growth sector. She seeks stocks that look relatively cheap and boast improving fundamentals.

That style has suffered in recent years. Underweighting biotech was a drawback and large-cap drug stocks were done in by slowing earnings in 1999, resulting in the fund's worst relative performance since 1992. In 2000, biotechs zoomed early in the year, then HMOs and other providers came to the fore as the fund's heavy drug stake still lumbered. The fund gained 37%, a poor job in a year when its peers romped, and landed in the group's bottom quartile. For the year to date through August 22, the fund's broad portfolio has resulted in just average losses versus its peers.

Because this fund, like other Fidelity Select offerings, is a training ground, don't expect Strock or any manager to be here too long. What counts for the Select funds are strategy and Fidelity's research talent. That this fund's five- and 10-year returns and even its volatility still look good despite 1999 and 2000 is a testament to the fund's strategy and Fidelity's research. This fund remains a sound choice for long-term health-care investing.

Special Securities % assets 08-31-01	
Restricted/Illiquid Secs	Trace
Emerging-Markets Secs	0
Options/Futures/Warrants	No

Composition % assets 08-31-01	
Cash	7.7
Stocks*	92.3
Bonds	0.0
Other	0.0
*Foreign (% stocks)	0.8

Market Cap	
Giant	60.3
Large	23.6
Medium	15.2
Small	0.8
Micro	0.0

Subsector Weightings	% of Stocks	Rel Cat
Gen Pharm/Bio	66.3	1.5
Medical Devices	10.7	1.9
Hospitals	4.3	1.5
Other Providers	1.3	1.2
HMOs/PPOs	0.2	0.1
Emg. Pharm/Bio	5.0	0.3
Diagnostics	0.4	0.3
Tech/Bus Svs	0.0	0.0
Other	11.8	0.5

Address:	82 Devonshire Street Boston, MA 02109 800-544-8888
Web Address:	www.fidelity.com
Inception:	07-14-81
Advisor:	Fidelity Mgmt. & Research
Subadvisor:	FMR (U.K.)/FMR (Far East)
NTF Plans:	Fidelity Inst.

Minimum Purchase:	$2500	Add: $250 IRA: $500
Min Auto Inv Plan:	$2500	Add: $100
Sales Fees:	3.00%L, 0.75%R within 1 month	
Management Fee:	.30%+.52% mx./.27% mn.(G)	
Actual Fees:	Mgt: 0.58%	Dist: —
Expense Projections:	3Yr: $638	5Yr: $880 10Yr: $1574
Avg Brok Commission:	—	Income Distrib: Semi-Ann.
Total Cost (relative to category):		Below Avg

Fidelity Select Network & Infrastruct

Ticker	Load	NAV	Yield	Total Assets	Mstar Category
FNINX	3.00%	$2.95	0.0%	$145.8 mil	Spec Technology

Prospectus Objective: Specialty—Technology

Fidelity Networking and Infrastructure Fund seeks capital appreciation.

The fund primarily invests in common stock. The fund normally invests at least 80% of assets in securities of companies principally engaged in the development, manufacture, sale or distribution of products, services, or technologies that support the flow of electronic information, including voice, data, images, and commercial transactions. The fund's management uses fundamental analysis of each issuer's financial condition and industry position and market and economic conditions to select investments. It invests in both domestic and foreign issuers. The fund is nondiversified.

Historical Profile
Return —
Risk —
Rating Not Rated

Investment Style Equity
Average Stock % 91%

▼ Manager Change
▽ Partial Manager Change

Fund Performance vs. Category Average
Quarterly Fund Return
+/– Category Average
— Category Baseline

Performance Quartile (within Category)

Portfolio Manager(s)

Sonu Kalra. Since 1-02..

History

1990	1991	1992	1993	1994	1995	1996	1997	1998	1999	2000	12-01	History
—	—	—	—	—	—	—	—	—	—	5.93	2.95	NAV
—	—	—	—	—	—	—	—	—	—	–40.70*	–50.25	Total Return %
—	—	—	—	—	—	—	—	—	—	–32.15*	–38.38	+/– S&P 500
—	—	—	—	—	—	—	—	—	—	—	–34.66	+/– PSE Tech 100
—	—	—	—	—	—	—	—	—	—	0.00	0.00	Income Return %
—	—	—	—	—	—	—	—	—	—	–40.70	–50.25	Capital Return %
—	—	—	—	—	—	—	—	—	—	—	81	Total Rtn % Rank Cat
—	—	—	—	—	—	—	—	—	—	0.00	0.00	Income $
—	—	—	—	—	—	—	—	—	—	0.00	0.00	Capital Gains $
—	—	—	—	—	—	—	—	—	—	—	—	Expense Ratio %
—	—	—	—	—	—	—	—	—	—	—	—	Income Ratio %
—	—	—	—	—	—	—	—	—	—	—	—	Turnover Rate %
—	—	—	—	—	—	—	—	—	—	137.8	145.8	Net Assets $mil

Performance 12-31-01

	1st Qtr	2nd Qtr	3rd Qtr	4th Qtr	Total
1997	—	—	—	—	—
1998	—	—	—	—	—
1999	—	—	—	—	—
2000	—	—	—	–41.05	–40.70 *
2001	–44.01	7.83	–43.85	46.77	–50.25

Trailing	Total Return%	+/– S&P 500	+/– PSE Tech 100	% Rank All	% Rank Cat	Growth of $10,000
3 Mo	46.77	36.08	13.85	1	16	14,677
6 Mo	–17.60	–12.04	–12.32	97	52	8,240
1 Yr	–50.25	–38.38	–34.66	100	81	4,975
3 Yr Avg	—	—	—	—	—	—
5 Yr Avg	—	—	—	—	—	—
10 Yr Avg	—	—	—	—	—	—
15 Yr Avg	—	—	—	—	—	—

Tax Analysis	Tax-Adj Ret%	%Rank Cat	%Pretax Ret	%Rank Cat
3 Yr Avg	—	—	—	—
5 Yr Avg	—	—	—	—
10 Yr Avg	—	—	—	—

Potential Capital Gain Exposure: NMF

Risk Analysis

Time Period	Load-Adj Return %	Risk %Rank[1] All	Risk %Rank[1] Cat	Morningstar Return	Morningstar Risk	Morningstar Risk-Adj Rating
1 Yr	–51.75					
3 Yr	—	—	—	—	—	
5 Yr	—	—	—	—	—	
Incept	–62.47	—	—	—	—	

Average Historical Rating —

[1]1=low, 100=high

Category Rating (3 Yr)

Other Measures	Standard Index S&P 500	Best Fit Index
Alpha	—	—
Beta	—	—
R-Squared	—	—
Standard Deviation		—
Return Mean		—
Risk Sharpe Ratio		—

Portfolio Analysis 08-31-01

Share chng since 02-01 Total Stocks: 96

	Subsector	PE	YTD Ret%	% Assets
⊕ Cisco Sys	Networking	—	–52.60	8.03
⊕ Sun Microsystems	Computers	NMF	–55.80	5.11
⊕ BellSouth	Telecom	24.9	–5.09	3.31
⊕ SBC Comms	Telecom	18.4	–16.00	3.29
⊕ Brocade Comm Sys	Technology	—	–63.90	3.21
⊕ Microsoft	Software	57.6	52.78	3.14
⊕ CIENA	Telecom	NMF	–82.30	3.06
⊕ Veritas Software	Software	—	–48.70	2.99
⊕ EMC	Software	NMF	–79.40	2.60
⊕ Marvell Tech	Technology	—	63.28	2.45
⊖ Check Point Software Tech	Software	32.0	–55.20	2.44
⊕ Agilent Tech	Technology	58.2	–47.90	2.25
⊖ STMicroelectronics (NY)	Semiconductors	29.1	–25.90	2.12
⊕ Flextronics Intl	Technology	—	–15.80	2.06
⊖ VeriSign	Technology	—	–48.70	1.77
☆ Tellium	Technology	—	—	1.65
⊕ Vitesse Semicon	Semi Equipment	—	–77.50	1.55
⊕ NVIDIA	Technology	84.2	308.50	1.50
⊕ JDS Uniphase	Technology	—	–79.00	1.44
☆ SunGard Data Sys	Computer Svs	33.3	22.78	1.43
⊕ BEA Sys	Technology	—	–77.10	1.42
⊕ Lucent Tech	Telecom	—	–53.20	1.30
⊕ Qlogic	Semi Equipment	49.5	–42.10	1.25
⊕ Micron Tech	Semiconductors	—	–12.60	1.18
⊕ Network Assoc	Networking	—	517.20	1.11

Current Investment Style

Style: Value Blnd Growth; Size: Large Med Small

	Stock Port Avg	Relative S&P 500 Current	Relative S&P 500 Hist	Rel Cat
Price/Earnings Ratio	46.9[1]	1.51	—	1.01
Price/Book Ratio	5.4	0.95	—	0.88
Price/Cash Flow	25.7	1.43	—	0.99
3 Yr Earnings Growth	28.9[1]	1.97	—	0.97
1 Yr Earnings Est%	–33.3[1]	18.81	—	2.00
Med Mkt Cap $mil	10,298	0.2	—	0.65

[1]figure is based on 50% or less of stocks

Analysis by Christopher Traulsen 12-12-01

Fidelity Select Networking & Infrastructure Portfolio's problems this year highlight its limitations.

This fund has done little to impress thus far in its young life. It's down 47% for the year to date through Dec. 11, 2001, landing in the worst quartile of the specialty-technology category. In 2000, it dropped 41% over the last three months of the year (the fund launched in late September 2000).

The fund's limited mandate is the bulk of the problem. Although manager Jed Weiss has some latitude to decide what falls within the fund's purview, the fund is naturally exposed to companies that sell the capital goods, software, and services that fuel global computer networks. The problem is, spending on such things has dropped dramatically amid the economic slowdown, and the appearance, of all things, of a bandwidth glut.

Weiss can and has taken steps to reduce the fund's exposure to the spending crunch. Earlier in the year, for example, he ramped up the fund's exposure to Regional Bells such as SBC Communications, and cut the fund's exposure to competitive local exchange carriers and companies that sell equipment to telecom carriers. As the year has moved on, though, he's gotten a bit more aggressive, buying beaten-down names such as JDS Uniphase and moving into storage networking with picks such as Brocade Communications.

Some of Weiss' recent moves have worked out nicely, and the fund has fared well over the past three months. Fidelity's superior research capabilities also lend it appeal. Still, we have trouble seeing who it's right for. It's too narrow to serve as one's only tech holding, yet it will overlap extensively with broader tech funds. Further, its narrow focus may cause volatile inflows and outflows—an added challenge to overcome. We think most investors will be better served by a general tech fund.

Special Securities % assets 08-31-01	
Restricted/Illiquid Secs	0
Emerging-Markets Secs	4
Options/Futures/Warrants	No

Composition % assets 08-31-01	
Cash	9.3
Stocks*	90.7
Bonds	0.0
Other	0.0
*Foreign (% stocks)	8.6

Market Cap	
Giant	21.1
Large	23.1
Medium	42.6
Small	13.0
Micro	0.2

Subsector Weightings	% of Stocks	Rel Cat
Computers	6.5	1.2
Semiconductors	7.4	0.7
Semi Equipment	4.1	1.0
Networking	11.1	3.1
Periph/Hardware	0.0	0.0
Software	14.0	1.1
Computer Svs	2.8	0.5
Telecom	12.7	1.6
Health Care	0.0	0.0
Other	41.5	1.1

Address: 82 Devonshire Street, Boston, MA 02109, 800-544-8888
Web Address: www.fidelity.com
*Inception: 09-21-00
Advisor: Fidelity Mgmt. & Research
Subadvisor: FMR (Far East)/FMR (U.K.)
NTF Plans: Fidelity Inst.

Minimum Purchase: $2500 Add: $250 IRA: $500
Min Auto Inv Plan: $100 Add: $100
Sales Fees: 3.00%L
Management Fee: .57%+.52% mx./.00% mn.(G)
Actual Fees: Mgt: 0.57% Dist: —
Expense Projections: 3Yr: $639 5Yr: — 10Yr: —
Avg Brok Commission: — Income Distrib: Semi-Ann.
Total Cost (relative to category): —

Fidelity Select Technology

Ticker	Load	NAV	Yield	Total Assets	Mstar Category
FSPTX	3.00%	$60.60	0.0%	$2,714.8 mil	Spec Technology

Prospectus Objective: Specialty—Technology

Fidelity Select Technology Portfolio seeks capital appreciation.

The fund normally invests at least 80% of assets in companies that may benefit from technological advances. It has a broadly defined scope and may invest in securities of any company eligible for purchase by any of Fidelity's other technology-related portfolios. The fund may invest up to 25% of assets in one issuer, and up to 5% in low-quality debt. The fund is nondiversified.

The fund waives sales charges on shares purchased through portfolio-advisory services.

Historical Profile

Return High
Risk High
Rating ★★★★ Above Avg

Investment Style
Equity
Average Stock %: 82% 88% 84% 87% 87% 94% 91%

▼ Manager Change
▽ Partial Manager Change

Fund Performance vs. Category Average
■ Quarterly Fund Return +/– Category Average
— Category Baseline

Performance Quartile (within Category)

Portfolio Manager(s)

Christopher F. Zepf. Since 6-01. MBA Dartmouth C. Other funds currently managed: Fidelity Advisor Technology A, Fidelity Advisor Technology Instl, Fidelity Advisor Technology T.

1990	1991	1992	1993	1994	1995	1996	1997	1998	1999	2000	12-01	History
21.46	33.92	33.79	38.73	41.36	51.31	55.68	45.28	78.86	152.39	88.72	60.60	NAV
10.51	58.97	8.72	28.65	11.13	43.67	15.63	10.37	74.16	131.67	–32.50	–31.70	Total Return %
13.62	28.49	1.11	18.59	9.81	6.14	–7.31	–22.98	45.59	110.63	–23.39	–19.82	+/– S&P 500
10.96	11.59	3.16	9.61	–9.75	–4.04	–4.40	–9.60	19.56	15.27	–16.28	–16.10	+/– PSE Tech 100
0.00	0.75	0.00	0.38	0.00	0.00	0.00	0.00	0.00	0.00	0.00	0.00	Income Return %
10.50	58.23	8.72	28.27	11.13	43.67	15.63	10.37	74.16	131.67	–32.50	–31.70	Capital Return %
9	27	63	50	52	57	61	40	18	48	54	29	Total Rtn % Rank Cat
0.00	0.16	0.00	0.13	0.00	0.00	0.00	0.00	0.00	0.00	0.00	0.00	Income $
0.00	0.00	2.75	3.70	1.50	8.05	3.68	15.69	0.00	19.80	20.73	0.00	Capital Gains $
2.09	1.83	1.72	1.64	1.54	1.56	1.39	1.44	1.30	1.20	1.04	0.94	Expense Ratio %
–0.76	0.61	–0.84	0.52	–0.65	–0.98	–0.52	–0.72	–0.45	–0.54	–0.34	–0.46	Income Ratio %
327	442	353	259	213	102	112	549	556	339	210	114	Turnover Rate %
96.2	124.8	130.2	229.8	227.4	400.6	491.3	526.5	1,061.3	5,208.6	4,287.3	2,714.8	Net Assets $mil

Performance 12-31-01

	1st Qtr	2nd Qtr	3rd Qtr	4th Qtr	Total
1997	–3.23	19.47	19.19	–19.90	10.37
1998	17.76	4.28	–2.82	45.96	74.16
1999	18.63	14.73	4.92	62.22	131.67
2000	25.29	–9.59	–6.16	–36.50	–32.50
2001	–34.06	21.01	–38.25	38.64	–31.70

Trailing	Total Return%	+/– S&P 500	+/– PSE Tech 100	% Rank All	% Rank Cat	Growth of $10,000
3 Mo	38.64	27.96	5.73	2	42	13,864
6 Mo	–14.39	–8.84	–9.11	94	32	8,561
1 Yr	–31.70	–19.82	–16.10	95	29	6,830
3 Yr Avg	2.22	3.25	–13.02	61	31	10,682
5 Yr Avg	15.48	4.78	–7.73	4	16	20,533
10 Yr Avg	18.15	5.23	–4.40	2	36	53,022
15 Yr Avg	16.07	2.34	–2.14	4	70	93,541

Tax Analysis	Tax-Adj Ret%	%Rank Cat	%Pretax Ret	%Rank Cat
3 Yr Avg	–1.20	37	—	—
5 Yr Avg	10.62	23	68.6	90
10 Yr Avg	13.97	54	77.0	81

Potential Capital Gain Exposure: –93% of assets

Risk Analysis

Time Period	Load-Adj Return %	Risk %Rank[1] All	Risk %Rank[1] Cat	Morningstar Return	Morningstar Risk	Morningstar Risk-Adj Rating
1 Yr	–33.74					
3 Yr	1.19	98	52	–0.77[2]	2.33	★★
5 Yr	14.77	98	55	2.56[2]	2.10	★★★★
10 Yr	17.79	98	70	2.59	2.06	★★★★

Average Historical Rating (193 months): 2.5★s

[1] 1=low, 100=high [2] T-Bill return substituted for category avg.

Category Rating (3 Yr)

1 2 3 4 5
Worst Best

Return Above Avg
Risk Average

Other Measures	Standard Index S&P 500	Best Fit Index Wil 4500
Alpha	23.4	11.1
Beta	2.32	1.71
R-Squared	56	82

Standard Deviation	63.58
Mean	2.22
Sharpe Ratio	–0.05

Portfolio Analysis 08-31-01

Share chng since 02-01 Total Stocks: 137	Subsector	PE	YTD Ret%	% Assets
⊕ Microsoft	Software	57.6	52.78	11.69
⊕ Intel	Semiconductors	73.1	4.89	7.58
⊕ Cisco Sys	Networking	—	–52.60	6.29
⊕ Oracle	Software	32.1	–52.40	2.84
⊕ Computer Assoc Intl	Software	—	77.28	2.46
⊖ Dell Comp	Computers	61.8	55.87	2.40
⊕ Brocade Comm Sys	Technology	—	–63.90	2.30
⊕ IBM	Computers	26.9	43.00	2.02
⊕ Adobe Sys	Software	37.4	–46.50	1.95
⊖ Flextronics Intl	Technology	—	–15.80	1.85
⊖ Sun Microsystems	Computers	NMF	–55.80	1.80
⊕ Analog Devices	Periph/Hardware	47.7	–13.20	1.76
⊕ CIENA	Telecom	NMF	–82.30	1.67
⊖ NVIDIA	Technology	84.2	308.50	1.63
☆ ASM Lithography Hldg (Reg)	Semi Equipment	23.0	–24.40	1.37
First Data	Computer Svs	38.1	49.08	1.31
⊕ Micron Tech	Semiconductors	—	–12.60	1.31
⊕ PeopleSoft	Software	73.1	8.10	1.24
⊕ Intersil Hldg	Technology	NMF	40.60	1.24
⊕ KLA-Tencor	Semiconductors	22.6	47.11	1.13
⊕ Gemstar–TV Guide Intl	Services	—	–39.90	1.12
☆ Motorola	Telecom	—	–25.00	1.01
⊖ Texas Instruments	Semiconductors	87.5	–40.70	0.99
☆ AOL Time Warner	Computer Svs	—	–7.76	0.98
☆ Advanced Micro Devices	Semiconductors	40.7	14.82	0.89

Current Investment Style

Style: Value Blnd Growth; Size: Large Med Small

	Stock Port Avg	Relative S&P 500 Current	Relative S&P 500 Hist	Rel Cat
Price/Earnings Ratio	48.3	1.56	1.44	1.05
Price/Book Ratio	6.3	1.10	1.42	1.02
Price/Cash Flow	23.9	1.33	1.44	0.92
3 Yr Earnings Growth	23.1	1.58	2.00	0.77
1 Yr Earnings Est%	–27.3	15.41	—	1.64
Med Mkt Cap $mil	19,178	0.3	0.5	1.21

[1] figure is based on 50% or less of stocks

Special Securities % assets 08-31-01	
Restricted/Illiquid Secs	1
Emerging-Markets Secs	1
Options/Futures/Warrants	Yes

Composition % assets 08-31-01	
Cash	7.1
Stocks*	92.5
Bonds	0.1
Other	0.4
*Foreign (% stocks)	2.4

Market Cap	
Giant	37.7
Large	20.7
Medium	32.4
Small	8.4
Micro	0.8

Subsector Weightings	% of Stocks	Rel Cat
Computers	7.9	1.5
Semiconductors	18.1	1.6
Semi Equipment	3.7	0.9
Networking	7.4	2.1
Periph/Hardware	2.3	1.5
Software	24.9	1.9
Computer Svs	5.0	0.8
Telecom	5.4	0.7
Health Care	0.0	0.0
Other	25.3	0.7

Analysis by Christopher Traulsen 10-14-01

Its frequent manager changes notwithstanding, Fidelity Select Technology Portfolio is a solid choice.

This fund got yet another new manager in June 2001, when Christopher Zepf replaced Larry Rakers. Zepf, who started covering networking stocks for Fidelity in 2000, ran Advisor Developing Communications before taking the reins here. Zepf declined to reveal specific changes he's made since coming aboard, but he said he cut the number of names in the fund from more than 150 to roughly 100. He also noted that he thinks semiconductor stocks are due for an improvement as the chip inventory glut is gradually being reduced.

Whatever Zepf has done, investors shouldn't get too attached to his style—he'll probably be gone in a year or two. Frequent manager changes are typical here, as they are at all Fidelity sector offerings. While such changes would be unsettling at most shops, at Fidelity, they seem to have relatively little impact. In part, that's because the managers are backed by a research operation that's one of the deepest in the industry. Fidelity has 18 tech analysts working out of the U.S., and many more overseas.

Despite the fund's frequent manager changes, it has put up solid numbers over the past decade and has a top-quartile five-year return. More impressive, it has not once landed in the category's bottom quartile in the last 10 years. The fund has fared about as well as can be expected in 2001. Its loss of 40% for the year to date through Oct. 11, 2001, is horrible in absolute terms, but three fourths of its rivals have fallen even further.

This offering rarely outperforms its peers in big rallies, as its huge asset base and diversified approach limit its ability to benefit from hot subsectors. However, we think its low costs, superior research staff, and sturdy longer-term results make it a good choice.

Address:	82 Devonshire Street Boston, MA 02109 800–544–8888
Web Address:	www.fidelity.com
Inception:	07-14-81
Advisor:	Fidelity Mgmt. & Research
Subadvisor:	FMR (U.K.)/FMR (Far East)
NTF Plans:	Fidelity Inst.

Minimum Purchase:	$2500	Add: $250 IRA: $500
Min Auto Inv Plan:	$2500	Add: $100
Sales Fees:	3.00%L, 0.75%R within 1 month	
Management Fee:	.30%+.52% mx./.27% mn.(G)	
Actual Fees:	Mgt: 0.59%	Dist: —
Expense Projections:	3Yr: $632	5Yr: $869 10Yr: $1552
Avg Brok Commission:	—	Income Distrib: Semi-Ann.
Total Cost (relative to category):		Below Avg

Fidelity Short–Term Bond

Ticker	Load	NAV	Yield	SEC Yield	Total Assets	Mstar Category
FSHBX	None	$8.80	5.3%	—	$3,338.6 mil	Short–Term Bond

Prospectus Objective: Corp Bond—General

Fidelity Short-Term Bond Portfolio seeks to obtain a high level of current income consistent with preservation of capital.

The fund invests primarily in a broad range of investment-grade fixed-income securities. It may also invest a portion of assets in lower-rated securities. The dollar-weighted average maturity may not exceed three years. The fund may buy and sell futures contracts and options with respect to 25% of assets.

On Oct. 31, 1996, Fidelity Short-Term World Bond Fund merged into the fund. On June 24, 1999, Fidelity Spartan Short-Term Bond Fund merged into the fund.

Historical Profile
Return Above Avg
Risk Below Avg
Rating ★★★★★ Highest

Investment Style
Fixed-Income
Income Rtn %Rank Cat

17 | 95 | 48 | 27 | 28 | 41 | 41 | 54

Growth of Principal vs. Interest Rate Shifts
— Principal Value $000 (NAV with capital gains reinvested)
— Interest Rate % on 10 Yr Treasury
▼ Manager Change
▽ Partial Manager Change
► Mgr Unknown After
◄ Mgr Unknown Before

9 8 7 6 5 4% · $26 22 18 14 10 6 $2

Performance Quartile (within Category)

Portfolio Manager(s)

Andrew J. Dudley, CFA. Since 2-97. BA Yale U.; MBA U. of Chicago. Other funds currently managed: Fidelity Advisor Interm Bond Instl, Fidelity Advisor Short Fix-Inc T, Fidelity Instl Short-Interm Govt.

1990	1991	1992	1993	1994	1995	1996	1997	1998	1999	2000	12-01	History
9.05	9.45	9.38	9.55	8.60	8.88	8.72	8.70	8.71	8.50	8.62	8.80	NAV
5.78	14.03	7.39	9.13	–4.09	9.82	4.78	6.21	6.15	3.29	7.85	7.63	Total Return %
–3.17	–1.98	–0.01	–0.62	–1.17	–8.65	1.16	–3.48	–2.53	4.12	–3.78	–0.79	+/– LB Aggregate
–4.00	2.35	1.14	3.72	–4.59	–0.14	–0.48	–0.44	–0.83	0.33	–0.32	–0.90	+/– LB 1–3 Govt
9.02	9.38	8.20	7.30	6.15	4.96	5.93	6.37	6.04	5.77	6.35	5.52	Income Return %
–3.23	4.64	–0.81	1.83	–10.25	4.86	–1.16	–0.17	0.11	–2.48	1.50	2.10	Capital Return %
84	32	9	12	98	79	36	62	55	20	46	45	Total Rtn % Rank Cat
0.81	0.82	0.75	0.66	0.57	0.41	0.51	0.54	0.51	0.49	0.53	0.46	Income $
0.00	0.00	0.00	0.00	0.00	0.13	0.06	0.00	0.00	0.00	0.00	0.00	Capital Gains $
0.83	0.83	0.86	0.77	0.80	0.69	0.68	0.70	0.70	0.65	0.62	0.58	Expense Ratio %
8.28	8.65	8.23	7.68	6.70	6.37	6.37	6.41	6.26	5.83	5.96	6.23	Income Ratio %
148	164	87	63	73	113	151	104	117	133	126	84	Turnover Rate %
224.3	568.8	1,659.4	2,469.5	1,514.8	1,196.6	995.6	875.2	841.7	1,333.1	1,773.3	3,338.6	Net Assets $mil

Performance 12-31-01

	1st Qtr	2nd Qtr	3rd Qtr	4th Qtr	Total
1997	0.52	2.17	1.94	1.44	6.21
1998	1.52	1.50	2.51	0.49	6.15
1999	1.05	0.46	0.97	0.77	3.29
2000	1.16	1.78	2.29	2.40	7.85
2001	2.93	1.17	3.10	0.26	7.63

Trailing	Total Return%	+/– LB Agg	+/– LB 1–3 Yr Govt	% Rank All	% Rank Cat	Growth of $10,000
3 Mo	0.26	0.22	–0.52	76	45	10,026
6 Mo	3.36	–1.29	–0.95	13	54	10,336
1 Yr	7.63	–0.79	–0.90	11	45	10,763
3 Yr Avg	6.24	–0.04	–0.29	21	21	11,990
5 Yr Avg	6.21	–1.21	–0.43	45	34	13,517
10 Yr Avg	5.74	–1.49	–0.29	79	53	17,481
15 Yr Avg	6.47	–1.65	–0.53	78	61	25,612

Tax Analysis	Tax-Adj Ret%	%Rank Cat	%Pretax Ret	%Rank Cat
3 Yr Avg	3.88	21	62.1	34
5 Yr Avg	3.80	38	61.1	56
10 Yr Avg	3.31	68	57.6	60

Potential Capital Gain Exposure: –6% of assets

Risk Analysis

Time Period	Load-Adj Return %	Risk %Rank[1] All	Risk %Rank[1] Cat	Morningstar Return	Morningstar Risk	Morningstar Risk-Adj Rating
1 Yr	7.63					
3 Yr	6.24	2	27	0.28[2]	0.25	★★★★★
5 Yr	6.21	3	24	0.26[2]	0.26	★★★★★
10 Yr	5.74	4	37	0.27[2]	0.43	★★★★

Average Historical Rating (148 months): 3.9★s

[1]1=low, 100=high [2] T–Bill return substituted for category avg.

Category Rating (3 Yr)

1 2 3 4 5
Worst Best

Return Above Avg
Risk Below Avg

Other Measures	Standard Index LB Agg	Best Fit Index LB Int
Alpha	0.7	0.6
Beta	0.42	0.52
R–Squared	80	80
Standard Deviation		1.70
Mean		6.24
Sharpe Ratio		0.90

Portfolio Analysis 04-30-01

Total Fixed-Income: 260	Date of Maturity	Amount $000	Value $000	% Net Assets
US Treasury Note 6.5%	05-31-02	115,000	117,893	5.73
FHLMC 5.25%	02-15-04	79,300	79,907	3.88
US Treasury Bond 11.75%	02-15-10	55,000	67,753	3.29
Federal Home Loan Bk 6.375%	11-15-02	56,700	58,206	2.83
FHLMC 6.375%	11-15-03	31,100	32,203	1.56
Province of Ontario 7.75%	06-04-02	23,900	24,684	1.20
FHLMC 6.5%	12-15-23	12,366	23,321	1.13
GNMA 8.5%	11-15-28	20,492	21,370	1.04
US Treasury Bond 10.75%	05-15-03	16,000	17,945	0.87
Discover CC Master Tr FRN	07-18-05	17,119	17,132	0.83
General Elec Cap 6.65%	09-03-02	16,700	17,077	0.83
AmeriCredit Auto Ln Tr 7.02%	12-12-05	16,000	16,538	0.80
Sears Credit Account Tr 7%	07-15-08	15,700	16,289	0.79
FHLMC CMO 6.5%	12-15-24	15,944	16,168	0.79
DaimlerChrysler N/A	11-06-05	15,000	15,605	0.76
US Treasury Note 5.625%	11-30-02	15,000	15,307	0.74
FNMA Debenture 5.375%	03-15-02	15,000	15,131	0.74
Associates North Amer 5.75%	11-01-03	14,800	14,976	0.73
DaimlerChrysler N/A	06-08-03	14,700	14,891	0.72
Asset Securitization 7.1%	08-13-29	14,031	14,586	0.71

Current Investment Style

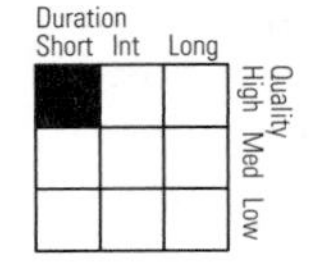

Avg Eff Duration[1]	1.8 Yrs
Avg Eff Maturity	—
Avg Credit Quality	—
Avg Wtd Coupon	0.00%
Avg Wtd Price	102.50% of par

[1]figure provided by fund

Special Securities % assets 04-30-01	
Restricted/Illiquid Secs	6
Exotic Mortgage–Backed	0
Emerging–Markets Secs	Trace
Options/Futures/Warrants	No

Credit Analysis % bonds 03-31-01

US Govt	0	BB	0
AAA	51	B	0
AA	7	Below B	0
A	16	NR/NA	5
BBB	20		

Coupon Range	% of Bonds	Rel Cat
0%	0.48	0.40
0% to 7%	60.09	0.94
7% to 8.5%	29.32	1.02
8.5% to 10%	4.66	1.14
More than 10%	5.44	3.18

1.00=Category Average

Composition % assets 04-30-01

Cash	8.8	Bonds	91.2
Stocks	0.0	Other	0.0

Analysis by Scott Berry 10-23-01

For Fidelity Short-Term Bond the best offense is a good defense.

In the tame universe of short-term bond funds, this fund's conservative approach stands out. Its duration is tied to that of the Lehman Brothers 1-3 Year Government/Corporate index and tends to be about half a year shorter than the category average. The fund's relatively short duration makes it less sensitive to changing interest rates and therefore less volatile than its average peer. The fund also takes on very little credit risk by sticking with high-quality corporate bonds.

In recent months, the fund's conservative tilt has held it back a bit. While the fund has benefited from the Federal Reserve's aggressive interest-rate cuts, the fund's longer-duration peers have gotten a bigger lift. So while the fund's 7.7% gain for the year to date through Oct. 22, 2001, may seem impressive on an absolute basis, it doesn't stand out from its short-term rivals'.

However, the fund's long-term record is more impressive. In rising interest-rate environments, such as 1999, the fund's relatively short duration has helped it hold up much better than its average peer. And in falling rate environments, such as 2001, the fund has stayed within striking distance thanks in part to the added yield of its BBB holdings. Altogether, the fund's three- and five-year trailing returns rank solidly in the short-term bond category's top half.

So while investors won't be blown away by this fund's performance, we think its above-average returns and low volatility make it a good choice for conservative investors. Its below-average expense ratio simply adds to its appeal.

Address:	82 Devonshire Street Boston, MA 02109 800–544–8888
Web Address:	www.fidelity.com
Inception:	09-15-86
Advisor:	Fidelity Mgmt. & Research
Subadvisor:	FMR (U.K.)/FMR (Far East)
NTF Plans:	Fidelity , Fidelity Inst.

Minimum Purchase:	$2500	Add: $250	IRA: $500
Min Auto Inv Plan:	$2500	Add: $100	
Sales Fees:	No–load		
Management Fee:	.30%+.37% mx./.13% mn.(G)		
Actual Fees:	Mgt: 0.43%	Dist: —	
Expense Projections:	3Yr: $218	5Yr: $379	10Yr: $847
Avg Brok Commission:	—	Income Distrib: Monthly	
Total Cost (relative to category):	Below Avg		

Fidelity Small Cap Independence

Ticker	Load	NAV	Yield	Total Assets	Mstar Category
FDSCX	None	$16.80	0.0%	$958.0 mil	Small Blend

Prospectus Objective: Small Company

Fidelity Small Cap Independence Fund seeks capital appreciation.

The fund normally invests at least 65% of assets in common and preferred stock issued by companies with market capitalizations of $1 billion or less. The fund may also invest a portion of assets in larger, more-established companies. To select securities, the advisor relies on computer-aided quantitative analysis supported by fundamental research. This model examines historical earnings, dividend yield, earnings per share, payout ratio, financial leverage, and other factors.

Past fund names: Fidelity Small Cap Stock Fund and Fidelity Small Cap Stock Selector Fund.

Historical Profile

Return Average
Risk Average
Rating ★★★ Neutral

Investment Style
Equity
Average Stock %: 78% 85% 89% 91% 93% 92% 94%

▼ Manager Change
▽ Partial Manager Change

Fund Performance vs. Category Average
■ Quarterly Fund Return +/– Category Average
— Category Baseline

Performance Quartile (within Category)

1990	1991	1992	1993	1994	1995	1996	1997	1998	1999	2000	12–01	History
—	—	—	10.82	10.45	12.39	13.56	15.93	14.19	16.09	16.23	16.80	NAV
—	—	—	8.82*	–3.33	26.63	13.63	27.25	–7.39	14.10	5.76	6.29	Total Return %
—	—	—	3.95*	–4.64	–10.91	–9.31	–6.10	–35.97	–6.93	14.86	18.17	+/– S&P 500
—	—	—	—	–1.50	–1.81	–2.90	4.89	–4.84	–7.16	8.78	3.80	+/– Russell 2000
—	—	—	0.20	0.09	0.77	0.08	0.97	0.19	0.63	0.19	0.00	Income Return %
—	—	—	8.62	–3.42	25.86	13.55	26.28	–7.58	13.47	5.57	6.29	Capital Return %
—	—	—	—	82	46	82	41	70	44	67	52	Total Rtn % Rank Cat
—	—	—	0.02	0.01	0.08	0.01	0.13	0.03	0.09	0.03	0.00	Income $
—	—	—	0.04	0.00	0.77	0.51	1.14	0.62	0.00	0.74	0.44	Capital Gains $
—	—	—	—	1.18	0.90	0.99	0.90	0.97	0.82	0.84	—	Expense Ratio %
—	—	—	—	0.03	0.40	0.39	0.41	0.63	0.15	0.20	—	Income Ratio %
—	—	—	—	210	182	192	176	88	173	159	—	Turnover Rate %
—	—	—	666.3	664.8	488.2	538.0	824.8	748.0	612.2	688.6	958.0	Net Assets $mil

Portfolio Manager(s)

James M. Harmon. Since 4-01. BA'94 Harvard U. Other fund currently managed: Fidelity Small Cap Retirement.

Performance 12-31-01

	1st Qtr	2nd Qtr	3rd Qtr	4th Qtr	Total
1997	–4.65	17.36	14.67	–0.83	27.25
1998	11.86	–3.85	–24.51	14.07	–7.39
1999	–8.39	12.17	–1.93	13.22	14.10
2000	11.87	–1.22	1.57	–5.78	5.76
2001	–13.25	11.29	–5.87	16.96	6.29

Trailing	Total Return%	+/– S&P 500	+/– Russ 2000	% Rank All	% Rank Cat	Growth of $10,000
3 Mo	16.96	6.27	–4.12	20	64	11,696
6 Mo	10.09	15.65	14.18	1	1	11,009
1 Yr	6.29	18.17	3.80	17	52	10,629
3 Yr Avg	8.65	9.68	2.23	14	63	12,826
5 Yr Avg	8.61	–2.09	1.09	26	70	15,115
10 Yr Avg	—	—	—	—	—	—
15 Yr Avg	—	—	—	—	—	—

Tax Analysis	Tax-Adj Ret%	%Rank Cat	%Pretax Ret	%Rank Cat
3 Yr Avg	8.02	56	92.8	28
5 Yr Avg	7.51	67	87.2	37
10 Yr Avg	—	—	—	—

Potential Capital Gain Exposure: 16% of assets

Risk Analysis

Time Period	Load-Adj Return %	Risk %Rank[1] All	Risk %Rank[1] Cat	Morningstar Return	Morningstar Risk	Morningstar Risk-Adj Rating
1 Yr	6.29					
3 Yr	8.65	61	52	0.81[2]	0.86	★★★★
5 Yr	8.61	71	49	0.84[2]	0.96	★★★
Incept	10.21	—	—	—	—	

Average Historical Rating (67 months): 1.7★s

[1] 1=low, 100=high [2] T–Bill return substituted for category avg.

Category Rating (3 Yr)

1 2 **3** 4 5
Worst Best

Return Average
Risk Average

Other Measures	Standard Index S&P 500	Best Fit Index Russ 2000
Alpha	8.2	2.6
Beta	0.61	0.65
R–Squared	30	65

Standard Deviation	20.54
Mean	8.65
Sharpe Ratio	0.21

Analysis by Scott Cooley 10-27-01

Right now, most shareholders' primary complaint about Fidelity Small Cap Independence Fund may be that James Harmon didn't take it over sooner.

Harmon has managed this fund only since April 2001, but he is off to a fast start. He has already made several deft moves. He was bullish on energy-service stocks earlier this year, but turned negative by mid-year, avoiding much of the industry's recent malaise. He had exposure to the security industry before the Sept. 11 terrorist attacks, increased his stakes there when the markets reopened, and then watched those stocks soar thereafter. One security holding, Kroll, has gained more than 100% since Sept. 10. Moreover, late in the third quarter, Harmon had devoted less of the fund to hard-hit tech issues than most of its rivals had, and that was a plus. Over the trailing three months, the fund's 4.2% gain is among the best of any small-cap offering.

Increasing the fund's exposure to security firms wasn't Harmon's only recent move. He continued to trim the fund's energy stake in September, on worries that declining exploration would pinch oil-services firms' profits. He also increased the fund's exposure to property-and-casualty insurers after the attacks, on the belief that those firms will now have a greater ability to raise prices.

Although these moves seem sensible, it's worth keeping in mind this fund's risks. Harmon's frenetic trading—the fund's turnover rate may top 300% or 400%—and willingness to make huge industry bets are likely to backfire at some point. And by trading that frequently, Harmon will likely recognize plenty of short-term gains, which means his picks will have to be truly outstanding to produce excellent, long-term after-tax returns.

That said, there's no denying that Harmon is off to a good start here and at his other charge, Fidelity Small Cap Retirement. This is a portfolio worth keeping an eye on.

Portfolio Analysis 04-30-01

Share change since 10–00 Total Stocks: 236	Sector	PE	YTD Ret%	% Assets
☼ Caremark Rx	Health	46.6	20.25	2.06
⊕ Patterson–UTI Energy	Energy	10.2	–37.40	1.95
⊕ UTI Energy	Energy	—	4.64	1.85
☼ National–Oilwell	Energy	20.6	–46.70	1.77
☼ Spinnaker Explor	Energy	13.6	–3.15	1.72
⊕ Manor Care	Health	22.6	14.96	1.65
☼ Marine Drilling	Energy	—	–51.70	1.65
☼ Healthsouth	Health	28.0	–9.15	1.65
☼ TETRA Technologies	Industrials	45.5	35.16	1.57
⊕ Corinthian Colleges	Services	32.5	7.78	1.37
⊕ CIMA Labs	Health	39.3	–44.40	1.35
☼ eFunds	Services	—	49.65	1.34
☼ Conseco	Financials	—	–66.10	1.33
☼ AmeriSource Health Cl A	Health	30.3	25.90	1.28
☼ Corvel	Financials	27.1	41.88	1.16
☼ Trigon Healthcare	Health	27.5	–10.70	1.15
☼ Offshore Logistics	Energy	11.1	–17.50	1.14
⊕ Syncor Intl	Health	21.7	–21.20	1.13
☼ Berkshire Hathaway Cl A	Financials	—	—	1.12
☼ Lincare Hldgs	Health	23.7	0.41	1.09
☼ Horizon Offshore	Services	14.5	–61.80	1.09
⊕ Valero Energy (New)	Energy	4.0	3.39	1.08
⊖ Unisource Energy Hldg	Utilities	10.1	–1.28	1.07
⊕ Affiliated Comp Svcs A	Services	39.9	74.88	1.03
☼ Renal Care Grp	Health	22.8	17.13	1.01

Current Investment Style

Style: Value Blnd Growth; Size: Large Med Small

	Stock Port Avg	Relative S&P 500 Current	Relative S&P 500 Hist	Rel Cat
Price/Earnings Ratio	27.0	0.87	0.70	1.08
Price/Book Ratio	3.4	0.59	0.54	1.06
Price/Cash Flow	17.6	0.98	0.78	1.13
3 Yr Earnings Growth	14.5[1]	0.99	1.18	0.85
1 Yr Earnings Est%	25.9	—	—	—
Med Mkt Cap $mil	976	0.0	0.0	1.00

[1] figure is based on 50% or less of stocks

Special Securities % assets 04-30-01	
Restricted/Illiquid Secs	0
Emerging–Markets Secs	Trace
Options/Futures/Warrants	No

Composition % assets 04-30-01	
Cash	6.0
Stocks*	94.0
Bonds	0.0
Other	0.0
*Foreign (% stocks)	0.4

Market Cap	
Giant	0.0
Large	0.8
Medium	33.7
Small	57.2
Micro	8.3

Sector Weightings	% of Stocks	Rel S&P	5-Year High	5-Year Low
Utilities	3.5	1.1	5	0
Energy	20.2	2.9	20	0
Financials	8.0	0.4	28	4
Industrials	6.8	0.6	21	7
Durables	0.9	0.6	13	1
Staples	1.1	0.1	4	0
Services	17.6	1.6	26	7
Retail	2.9	0.4	16	3
Health	26.3	1.8	26	4
Technology	12.8	0.7	53	7

Address:	82 Devonshire Street Boston, MA 02109 800–544–8888
Web Address:	www.fidelity.com
*Inception:	06-28-93
Advisor:	Fidelity Mgmt. & Research
Subadvisor:	FMR (Far East)/FMR (U.K.)
NTF Plans:	Fidelity Inst.

Minimum Purchase:	$2500	Add: $250	IRA: $500
Min Auto Inv Plan:	$100	Add: $100	
Sales Fees:	No–load, 1.50%R within 3 months		
Management Fee:	.35%+.52% mx./.27% mn.(G)+(–).20%P		
Actual Fees:	Mgt: 0.42%	Dist: —	
Expense Projections:	3Yr: $274	5Yr: $477	10Yr: $1061
Avg Brok Commission:	—	Income Distrib: Semi–Ann.	
Total Cost (relative to category):		Below Avg	

Fidelity Small Cap Stock

Ticker	Load	NAV	Yield	Total Assets	Mstar Category
FSLCX	None	$14.36	0.1%	$1,354.2 mil	Small Growth

Prospectus Objective: Small Company

Fidelity Small Cap Stock Fund seeks long-term growth of capital.

The fund normally invests at least 65% of assets in equity securities of companies with small market capitalizations. Management considers companies with market capitalizations similar to those in the Russell 2000 index to be in the small range. The fund may invest without limit in preferred stocks and investment-grade debt for temporary purposes. It may invest up to 35% of assets in securities rated below investment-grade.

Historical Profile
Return High
Risk Average
Rating ★★★★★ Highest

Investment Style
Equity
Average Stock %: 92% (1997), 83% (1998), 90% (1999), 92% (2000), 89% (12-01)

▼ Manager Change
▽ Partial Manager Change

Fund Performance vs. Category Average
■ Quarterly Fund Return +/– Category Average
— Category Baseline

Performance Quartile (within Category)

Portfolio Manager(s)

Paul L. Antico. Since 3-98. BS'91 MIT.

1990	1991	1992	1993	1994	1995	1996	1997	1998	1999	2000	12-01	History
—	—	—	—	—	—	—	—	8.91	12.71	13.51	14.36	NAV
—	—	—	—	—	—	—	—	–10.69*	42.65	11.85	6.44	Total Return %
—	—	—	—	—	—	—	—	–27.03*	21.61	20.95	18.32	+/– S&P 500
—	—	—	—	—	—	—	—	—	–0.44	34.28	15.67	+/– Russ 2000 Grth
—	—	—	—	—	—	—	—	0.21	0.00	0.32	0.15	Income Return %
—	—	—	—	—	—	—	—	–10.90	42.65	11.52	6.29	Capital Return %
—	—	—	—	—	—	—	—	—	60	15	13	Total Rtn % Rank Cat
—	—	—	—	—	—	—	—	0.02	0.00	0.04	0.02	Income $
—	—	—	—	—	—	—	—	0.00	0.00	0.65	0.00	Capital Gains $
—	—	—	—	—	—	—	—	1.48	0.99	1.13	1.05	Expense Ratio %
—	—	—	—	—	—	—	—	0.67	0.01	–0.01	0.36	Income Ratio %
—	—	—	—	—	—	—	—	75	170	120	126	Turnover Rate %
—	—	—	—	—	—	—	—	552.4	688.3	1,141.9	1,354.2	Net Assets $mil

Performance 12-31-01

	1st Qtr	2nd Qtr	3rd Qtr	4th Qtr	Total
1997	—	—	—	—	—
1998	—	–6.12	–26.48	21.85	–10.69*
1999	–1.68	18.38	2.31	19.79	42.65
2000	12.59	3.28	1.11	–4.86	11.85
2001	–8.51	12.54	–14.88	21.46	6.44

Trailing	Total Return%	+/– S&P 500	+/– Russ 2000 Grth	% Rank All	% Rank Cat	Growth of $10,000
3 Mo	21.46	10.77	–4.72	11	60	12,146
6 Mo	3.38	8.94	12.65	13	7	10,338
1 Yr	6.44	18.32	15.67	17	13	10,644
3 Yr Avg	19.31	20.33	19.06	3	13	16,982
5 Yr Avg	—	—	—	—	—	—
10 Yr Avg	—	—	—	—	—	—
15 Yr Avg	—	—	—	—	—	—

Tax Analysis	Tax-Adj Ret%	%Rank Cat	%Pretax Ret	%Rank Cat
3 Yr Avg	18.76	12	97.2	9
5 Yr Avg	—	—	—	—
10 Yr Avg	—	—	—	—

Potential Capital Gain Exposure: 11% of assets

Risk Analysis

Time Period	Load-Adj Return %	Risk %Rank[1] All	Risk %Rank[1] Cat	Morningstar Return	Morningstar Risk	Morningstar Risk-Adj Rating
1 Yr	4.31					
3 Yr	19.31	58	4	3.48[2]	0.81	★★★★★
5 Yr	—	—	—	—	—	
Incept	11.56	—	—	—	—	

Average Historical Rating (10 months): 4.7★s

[1]1=low, 100=high [2] T-Bill return substituted for category avg.

Category Rating (3 Yr)

1 2 3 4 5
Worst Best

Return: Above Avg
Risk: Low

Other Measures	Standard Index S&P 500	Best Fit Index Russ 2000
Alpha	20.1	12.2
Beta	0.73	0.89
R-Squared	32	93

Standard Deviation	25.88
Mean	19.31
Sharpe Ratio	0.63

Portfolio Analysis 04-30-01

Share change since 10-00 Total Stocks: 198	Sector	PE	YTD Ret%	% Assets
⊕ Venator Grp	Retail	—	0.97	4.54
⊖ CEC Entrtnmt	Services	19.8	27.15	3.24
Papa John's Intl	Services	19.1	23.51	2.91
⊕ Insight Enterprises	Retail	21.6	37.14	2.71
⊕ Coinstar	Industrials	—	63.93	2.50
⊕ Apartment Invest & Mgmt	Financials	NMF	–1.80	2.27
⊕ Alexandria Real Est Eq	Financials	25.4	15.87	2.11
⊕ eFunds	Services	—	49.65	2.04
⊕ CIMA Labs	Health	39.3	–44.40	1.81
⊖ Hibbett Sporting Goods	Retail	17.9	–15.80	1.75
⊕ Human Genome Sciences	Health	—	–51.30	1.55
⊕ Outback Steakhouse	Services	20.4	32.37	1.49
⊖ i-Stat	Health	—	–70.10	1.45
⊖ Myriad Genetics	Health	—	–36.30	1.34
⊕ York Intl	Industrials	23.5	26.51	1.31
⊖ MapInfo	Technology	87.2	–66.70	1.21
⊖ Ultimate Electncs	Retail	23.3	36.75	1.20
☼ Tech Data	Technology	19.2	60.11	1.20
⊕ New Horizons Worldwide	Services	13.4	–17.10	1.09
⊖ Pinnacle Sys	Technology	—	7.66	0.99
☼ Martin Marietta Matls	Industrials	22.0	11.56	0.93
☼ Texas Inds	Industrials	NMF	24.18	0.89
⊕ Kingsway Finl Svcs	Financials	16.6	—	0.86
⊕ Fleming Companies	Retail	—	57.07	0.75
Cornell Corrections	Services	26.7	228.30	0.73

Current Investment Style

Style: Value Blnd Growth; Size: Large Med Small

	Stock Port Avg	Relative S&P 500 Current	Relative S&P 500 Hist	Rel Cat
Price/Earnings Ratio	27.2	0.88	0.87	0.85
Price/Book Ratio	3.4	0.59	0.65	0.70
Price/Cash Flow	15.2	0.84	0.89	0.69
3 Yr Earnings Growth	16.8[1]	1.15	—	0.67
1 Yr Earnings Est%	13.0[1]	—	—	1.67
Med Mkt Cap $mil	732	0.0	0.0	0.70

[1]figure is based on 50% or less of stocks

Special Securities % assets 04-30-01	
Restricted/Illiquid Secs	Trace
Emerging-Markets Secs	0
Options/Futures/Warrants	Yes

Composition % assets 04-30-01	
Cash	10.8
Stocks*	88.6
Bonds	0.0
Other	0.6
*Foreign (% stocks)	12.1

Market Cap	
Giant	0.0
Large	0.0
Medium	22.2
Small	59.9
Micro	18.0

Sector Weightings	% of Stocks	Rel S&P	5-Year High	5-Year Low
Utilities	0.0	0.0	—	—
Energy	1.8	0.3	—	—
Financials	11.3	0.6	—	—
Industrials	16.1	1.4	—	—
Durables	1.6	1.0	—	—
Staples	0.7	0.1	—	—
Services	23.3	2.1	—	—
Retail	17.9	2.6	—	—
Health	11.7	0.8	—	—
Technology	15.6	0.9	—	—

Analysis by Christopher Traulsen 12-11-01

Fidelity Small Cap Stock Fund takes a pleasingly well-rounded approach to small-growth investing.

This young fund is putting the finishing touches on its second straight year of solid relative performance. It's up 4.4% for the year to date through December 7, putting it near the small-growth category's top decile for the period. The fund ended 2000 with a 12% return, better than 85% of its rivals'.

That type of strength in tough periods for growth investing has been, and in our opinion should continue to be, typical of this offering. Manager Paul Antico likes stocks that have strong growth prospects, but he also aims to purchase them well before that growth is priced in. That has usually led him to limit the fund's exposure to the technology sector, and to spread his bets around less-glamorous areas such as restaurants and retail.

Antico doesn't ignore traditional growth areas—he just waits until they're cheap enough before buying in. He bought technology distributors and semiconductor capital-equipment companies when they fell earlier in 2001, for example, including top-10 holding Tech Data. He also found many buying opportunities in the aftermath of September 11. With the recent rally, however, he has sold some of his picks into strength, bringing the fund's cash stake back up to 10%.

This fund hasn't been around long, but it has outperformed the vast bulk of its peers over the past three years. Thanks to Antico's attention to valuation, the fund has also been far less volatile than its typical rival over that period. As its subpar 1999 return shows, the fund is likely to lag when the priciest stocks lead the way. But we think Antico's ability to find strong picks in a variety of industries, as well as the backing of Fidelity's top-flight research staff, makes it a strong choice for investors seeking a moderate approach to small-growth investing.

Address:	82 Devonshire Street Boston, MA 02109 617-330-0586 / 800-544-8888
Web Address:	www.fidelity.com
*Inception:	03-12-98
Advisor:	Fidelity Mgmt. & Research
Subadvisor:	FMR (U.K.)/FMR (Far East)
NTF Plans:	Fidelity , Fidelity Inst.

Minimum Purchase:	$2500	Add: $250 IRA: $500
Min Auto Inv Plan:	$2500	Add: $100
Sales Fees:	No-load, 2.00%R within 36 months	
Management Fee:	.45%+.52% mx./.27% mn.(G)+(–).20%P	
Actual Fees:	Mgt: 0.73%	Dist: —
Expense Projections:	3Yr: $331	5Yr: $574 10Yr: $1271
Avg Brok Commission:	—	Income Distrib: Semi-Ann.
Total Cost (relative to category):	Low	

Fidelity Spartan Interm Muni Income

Ticker	Load	NAV	Yield	SEC Yield	Total Assets	Mstar Category
FLTMX	None	$9.84	4.7%	—	$1,487.0 mil	Muni Natl Interm–Term

Prospectus Objective: Muni Bond—National

Fidelity Spartan Intermediate Municipal Income Fund seeks income exempt from federal income taxes, consistent with preservation of capital.

The fund normally invests at least 80% of assets in tax-exempt obligations. It may purchase only investment-grade obligations. The average weighted maturity is usually 10 or fewer years and is adjusted within these parameters depending on interest-rate changes. The fund may invest in Alternative Minimum Tax-subject securities.

Past names: Fidelity Limited-Term Municipals Fund and Fidelity Limited-Term Municipal Income Fund. On March 19, 1998, Fidelity Spartan Intermediate Municipal Income Fund merged into the fund.

Historical Profile

Return Above Avg
Risk Below Avg
Rating ★★★★★ Highest

Investment Style: Fixed-Income — Income Rtn %Rank Cat: 24, 22, 25, 24, 20, 19, 20, 21

Growth of Principal vs. Interest Rate Shifts
- Principal Value $000 (NAV with capital gains reinvested)
- Interest Rate % on 10 Yr Treasury
- ▼ Manager Change
- ▽ Partial Manager Change
- ► Mgr Unknown After
- ◄ Mgr Unknown Before

Performance Quartile (within Category)

Portfolio Manager(s)

Christine Jones Thompson, CFA. Since 7-00. BA'80 Tufts U.; MBA'85 U. of Pennsylvania. Other funds currently managed: Fidelity Advisor Municipal Inc T, Fidelity Spartan CA Municipal Income, Fidelity Spartan MA Municipal Income.

History

	1990	1991	1992	1993	1994	1995	1996	1997	1998	1999	2000	12-01
NAV	9.27	9.52	9.60	9.99	8.99	9.80	9.70	9.94	9.98	9.41	9.78	9.84
Total Return %	6.97	11.19	8.17	12.24	–4.76	14.84	4.44	8.23	5.89	–1.06	9.26	5.37
+/– LB Aggregate	–1.99	–4.82	0.77	2.49	–1.85	–3.63	0.82	–1.45	–2.79	–0.23	–2.38	–3.05
+/– LB Muni	–0.34	–0.96	–0.65	–0.04	0.38	–2.62	0.00	–0.97	–0.59	1.01	–2.44	0.29
Income Return %	6.79	6.71	6.19	5.53	5.26	5.67	5.10	5.13	4.88	4.77	5.18	4.79
Capital Return %	0.17	4.48	1.97	6.71	–10.02	9.17	–0.67	3.10	1.00	–5.83	4.07	0.58
Total Rtn % Rank Cat	23	37	54	22	77	29	21	26	27	22	40	10
Income $	0.61	0.60	0.57	0.52	0.51	0.50	0.49	0.49	0.47	0.47	0.48	0.46
Capital Gains $	0.05	0.15	0.10	0.24	0.02	0.00	0.03	0.05	0.06	0.00	0.00	0.00
Expense Ratio %	0.67	0.68	0.64	0.57	0.56	0.57	0.56	0.55	0.50	0.48	0.49	—
Income Ratio %	6.63	6.41	5.94	5.19	5.42	5.25	5.06	4.97	4.58	4.72	5.03	—
Turnover Rate %	72	42	50	111	30	31	27	22	18	21	19	—
Net Assets $mil	466.3	692.7	964.7	1,195.2	881.3	941.1	901.0	911.8	1,146.0	1,061.2	1,209.8	1,487.0

Performance 12-31-01

	1st Qtr	2nd Qtr	3rd Qtr	4th Qtr	Total
1997	0.00	2.98	2.69	2.35	8.23
1998	0.95	1.41	2.83	0.58	5.89
1999	0.79	–1.66	0.28	–0.45	–1.06
2000	2.00	1.37	2.00	3.58	9.26
2001	2.33	0.90	2.78	–0.71	5.37

Trailing	Total Return%	+/– LB Agg	+/– LB Muni	% Rank All	% Rank Cat	Growth of $10,000
3 Mo	–0.71	–0.75	–0.05	88	26	9,929
6 Mo	2.05	–2.60	–0.07	22	14	10,205
1 Yr	5.37	–3.05	0.29	21	10	10,537
3 Yr Avg	4.44	–1.84	–0.32	36	12	11,391
5 Yr Avg	5.48	–1.95	–0.50	56	11	13,054
10 Yr Avg	6.11	–1.11	–0.52	67	24	18,103
15 Yr Avg	6.41	–1.71	–0.77	79	48	25,410

Tax Analysis	Tax-Adj Ret%	%Rank Cat	%Pretax Ret	%Rank Cat
3 Yr Avg	4.43	11	100.0	39
5 Yr Avg	5.42	8	99.0	55
10 Yr Avg	5.94	27	97.2	72

Potential Capital Gain Exposure: 3% of assets

Risk Analysis

Time Period	Load-Adj Return %	Risk %Rank[1] All	Risk %Rank[1] Cat	Morningstar Return	Morningstar Risk	Morningstar Risk-Adj Rating
1 Yr	4.84					
3 Yr	4.26	6	6	0.61[2]	0.68	★★★★★
5 Yr	5.37	6	9	0.90[2]	0.69	★★★★★
10 Yr	6.06	9	42	1.02	0.79	★★★★

Average Historical Rating (193 months): 4.0★s

[1]1=low, 100=high [2] T-Bill return substituted for category avg.

Category Rating (3 Yr)

1 2 3 4 5 — Worst ... Best

Return Above Avg
Risk Low

Other Measures	Standard Index LB Agg	Best Fit Index LB Muni
Alpha	–1.3	–0.3
Beta	0.69	0.80
R-Squared	59	97

Standard Deviation	3.15
Mean	4.44
Sharpe Ratio	–0.19

Portfolio Analysis 06-30-01

Total Fixed-Income: 389	Date of Maturity	Amount $000	Value $000	% Net Assets
MA New England Educ Ln Mktg 6.5%	09-01-02	34,215	35,539	2.53
MI Detroit Conv Fac Cobo Hall 5.25%	09-30-12	22,300	22,422	1.60
NY Metro Transp Commuter Fac 6%	07-01-24	19,915	21,297	1.52
UT Intermountain Pwr Sply 0%	07-01-12	17,000	18,745	1.33
WA Seattle Pwr 4.5%	03-28-03	15,000	15,231	1.08
WA King GO 5.85%	12-01-13	13,480	14,512	1.03
TX Harris GO Toll Rd 0%	08-01-05	16,275	13,847	0.99
IL Chicago Wtr 5.5%	12-01-13	11,990	12,748	0.91
AK North Slope GO 0%	06-30-01	12,000	12,000	0.85
MN Rochester Hlth Care Fac Mayo 5.5%	11-15-27	11,750	11,926	0.85
TX Harris GO Toll Rd 0%	08-01-03	12,570	11,705	0.83
WA Pub Pwr Sply Sys Proj #3 0%	07-01-07	15,130	11,592	0.82
DC Hosp 6.875%	08-15-31	11,000	11,515	0.82
LA New Orleans GO 0%	09-01-05	13,500	11,407	0.81
AR Brazos GO 0%	04-01-33	11,000	11,144	0.79

Current Investment Style

Not Available

Avg Duration[1]	5.0 Yrs
Avg Nominal Maturity	8.3 Yrs
Avg Credit Quality	—
Avg Wtd Coupon	2.10%
Avg Wtd Price	98.91% of par
Pricing Service	Muller

[1]figure provided by fund

Analysis by Eric Jacobson 08-26-01

Just call Fidelity Spartan Intermediate Municipal Income 'Old Faithful'.

A brief look at this fund's annual rankings shows an incredibly consistent record. This portfolio has placed in the best half of its muni-national intermediate peer group during 10 of the past 11 calendar years. The fund offers something for yield-focused investors, too. Its income returns have placed in the category's best quartile for several years running. As if that weren't enough, the fund sports low Morningstar risk scores.

That's all the more impressive given that the fund has had a few manager changes in recent years, the latest about 12 months ago when Christine Thompson took the reins. That's a testament to just how strong a system Fidelity has put in place for managing munis, though. Like her colleagues, Thompson ties this fund's interest-rate sensitivity to that of an index (in this case the Lehman Brothers 1-17 Year Municipal Bond index) and focuses almost all of her attention on rotating among various bond structures and parts of the maturity spectrum (or yield curve, in bondspeak).

Despite the fact that such moves tend to be fairly modest, Thompson and her predecessors have shown that they can really help create a good, consistent record. Although the competition was fierce in 2000, for example, as more-aggressive funds strove to capitalize on last year's rallying market, this fund managed to best its average rival as Thompson swapped back and forth between discount and premium bonds. The fund has managed to outperform its rivals thus far in 2001, as well, in part because it lost less when the market hiccuped in April and because it holds few embattled California bonds. Add in this fund's diminutive expense ratio, and you have one of the best intermediate muni funds around.

Credit Analysis % bonds 03-31-01

US Govt	0	BB	0
AAA	58	B	0
AA	17	Below B	0
A	7	NR/NA	10
BBB	7		

Special Securities % assets 06-30-01

Restricted/Illiquid Secs	0
Inverse Floaters	0
Options/Futures/Warrants	No

Bond Type % assets 03-31-00

Alternative Minimum Tax (AMT)	9.0
Insured	—
Prerefunded	—

Top 5 States % bonds

TX	15.9	NY	8.6
WA	10.3	IL	6.7
MA	8.8		

Composition % assets 06-30-01

Cash	2.8	Bonds	97.2
Stocks	0.0	Other	0.0

Sector Weightings	% of Bonds	Rel Cat
General Obligation	39.3	1.4
Utilities	15.2	1.7
Health	8.1	0.7
Water/Waste	2.2	0.4
Housing	1.4	0.2
Education	8.1	1.0
Transportation	15.3	1.3
COP/Lease	0.5	0.2
Industrial	7.2	0.9
Misc Revenue	2.6	0.5
Demand	0.0	0.0

Address:	82 Devonshire Street Boston, MA 02109 800–544–8888
Web Address:	www.fidelity.com
Inception:	04-15-77
Advisor:	Fidelity Mgmt. & Research
Subadvisor:	Fidelity Inv.s Money Mgmt
NTF Plans:	Fidelity , Fidelity Inst.

Minimum Purchase:	$10000	Add: $1000 IRA: —
Min Auto Inv Plan:	$500	Add: $500
Sales Fees:	No-load, 0.50%R	
Management Fee:	.10%+.37% mx./.13% mn.(G)	
Actual Fees:	Mgt: 0.36%	Dist: —
Expense Projections:	3Yr: $154	5Yr: $269 10Yr: $604
Avg Brok Commission:	—	Income Distrib: Monthly
Total Cost (relative to category):	Low	

Fidelity Spartan Municipal Income

Ticker	Load	NAV	Yield	SEC Yield	Total Assets	Mstar Category
FHIGX	None	$12.68	4.8%	—	$4,513.9 mil	Muni Natl Interm–Term

Prospectus Objective: Muni Bond—National

Fidelity Spartan Municipal Income Fund seeks high current yield exempt from federal income tax.

The fund normally invests at least 80% of assets in investment-grade tax-exempt debt.

This fund has gone through several mergers and name changes.

Historical Profile

Return: High
Risk: Average
Rating: ★★★★ Above Avg

Investment Style
Fixed-Income
Income Rtn %Rank Cat: 3, 13, 9, 25, 21, 22, 11, 17

Growth of Principal vs. Interest Rate Shifts
- Principal Value $000 (NAV with capital gains reinvested)
- Interest Rate % on 10 Yr Treasury
- ▼ Manager Change
- ▽ Partial Manager Change
- ► Mgr Unknown After
- ◄ Mgr Unknown Before

Chart scales: 9, 8, 7, 6, 5, 4% (interest rate); $26, 22, 18, 14, 10, 6, $2 (principal value)

Performance Quartile (within Category)

Portfolio Manager(s)

George A. Fischer. Since 1-98. BA'83 Boston C.; MBA'89 U. of Pennsylvania-Wharton. Other funds currently managed: Fidelity Spartan CT Municipal Income, Fidelity Spartan MI Municipal Income, Fidelity Spartan NJ Municipal Income.

History	1990	1991	1992	1993	1994	1995	1996	1997	1998	1999	2000	12-01
NAV	12.36	12.58	12.60	12.95	11.25	12.36	12.27	12.68	12.82	11.91	12.70	12.68
Total Return %	8.47	10.18	8.36	13.11	−7.45	16.18	4.95	9.23	6.04	−2.48	12.30	5.00
+/– LB Aggregate	−0.48	−5.83	0.96	3.36	−4.53	−2.29	1.33	−0.46	−2.63	−1.65	0.67	−3.42
+/– LB Muni	1.17	−1.97	−0.46	0.84	−2.31	−1.28	0.51	0.02	−0.44	−0.42	0.60	−0.08
Income Return %	7.11	7.02	6.63	6.22	6.00	6.07	5.38	5.09	4.85	4.75	5.41	4.94
Capital Return %	1.36	3.16	1.73	6.89	−13.45	10.11	−0.43	4.13	1.19	−7.24	6.89	0.06
Total Rtn % Rank Cat	1	68	45	8	95	18	7	7	21	68	2	21
Income $	0.86	0.84	0.81	0.76	0.76	0.67	0.65	0.61	0.60	0.60	0.63	0.61
Capital Gains $	0.23	0.16	0.19	0.50	0.00	0.00	0.03	0.08	0.01	0.01	0.00	0.04
Expense Ratio %	0.57	0.56	0.56	0.56	0.56	0.57	0.56	0.55	0.53	0.49	0.42	—
Income Ratio %	6.96	6.72	6.40	5.85	6.21	5.69	5.32	4.92	4.75	4.77	4.98	—
Turnover Rate %	58	44	47	53	48	50	53	31	25	28	4	—
Net Assets $mil	1,767.5	1,991.8	2,060.2	2,108.6	1,671.3	1,794.4	1,796.2	2,347.1	4,638.9	4,062.7	4,452.1	4,513.9

Performance 12-31-01

	1st Qtr	2nd Qtr	3rd Qtr	4th Qtr	Total
1997	−0.34	3.51	3.02	2.78	9.23
1998	1.02	1.36	3.11	0.44	6.04
1999	0.69	−1.99	−0.33	−0.85	−2.48
2000	3.18	1.39	2.38	4.85	12.30
2001	2.17	0.75	3.01	−0.97	5.00

Trailing	Total Return%	+/– LB Agg	+/– LB Muni	% Rank All	% Rank Cat	Growth of $10,000
3 Mo	−0.97	−1.01	−0.31	93	58	9,903
6 Mo	2.01	−2.65	−0.12	22	18	10,201
1 Yr	5.00	−3.42	−0.08	23	21	10,500
3 Yr Avg	4.76	−1.51	0.01	33	8	11,499
5 Yr Avg	5.90	−1.53	−0.08	49	5	13,318
10 Yr Avg	6.30	−0.93	−0.33	62	10	18,420
15 Yr Avg	6.78	−1.34	−0.41	71	20	26,740

Tax Analysis	Tax-Adj Ret%	%Rank Cat	%Pretax Ret	%Rank Cat
3 Yr Avg	4.74	6	99.5	52
5 Yr Avg	5.85	2	99.2	48
10 Yr Avg	6.09	16	96.6	81

Potential Capital Gain Exposure: 4% of assets

Risk Analysis

Time Period	Load-Adj Return %	Risk %Rank[1] All	Risk %Rank[1] Cat	Morningstar Return	Morningstar Risk	Morningstar Risk-Adj Rating
1 Yr	4.48					
3 Yr	4.59	14	74	0.71[2]	0.94	★★★★
5 Yr	5.79	15	80	1.02[2]	0.96	★★★★
10 Yr	6.25	21	78	1.12	1.02	★★★

Average Historical Rating (193 months): 4.2★s

[1]1=low, 100=high [2] T-Bill return substituted for category avg.

Category Rating (3 Yr)

1 2 3 4 5 — Worst ... Best

Return: High
Risk: Above Avg

Other Measures	Standard Index LB Agg	Best Fit Index LB Muni
Alpha	−1.3	0.0
Beta	0.90	1.08
R-Squared	56	99
Standard Deviation		4.18
Mean		4.76
Sharpe Ratio		−0.05

Portfolio Analysis 06-30-01

Total Fixed-Income: 824	Date of Maturity	Amount $000	Value $000	% Net Assets
AR GO 5.75%	05-15-33	65,000	67,961	1.49
WA Pub Pwr Sply Sys Proj #2 5.4%	07-01-12	56,550	59,040	1.29
NY NYC Muni Wtr Fin Swr Sys 5.75%	06-15-29	56,120	58,159	1.27
IL Chicago GO Brd Educ Sch Reform 5.75%	12-01-27	47,250	49,005	1.07
MA Wtr Res 5.75%	08-01-39	33,000	34,513	0.75
WA Pub Pwr Sply Sys Proj #2 5.55%	07-01-10	31,000	31,882	0.70
UT Intermountain Pwr Sply 5.75%	07-01-16	30,260	31,824	0.70
UT Intermountain Pwr Sply 6%	07-01-16	29,500	31,428	0.69
ND Mercer Poll Cntrl Antelope Vlly 7.2%	06-30-13	26,000	31,393	0.69
NY Dorm City Univ Sys 7.5%	07-01-10	24,650	29,102	0.64
AK Valdez Marine Term BP Pipeline 5.5%	10-01-28	28,205	27,974	0.61
MO Hlth/Educ Fac N/A	03-01-30	26,050	27,827	0.61
MA Indl Fin Biomed Rsrch 0%	08-01-03	29,600	27,519	0.60
CO Hlth 6.625%	02-01-13	26,700	27,513	0.60
NY Metro Transp Commuter Fac 6.125%	07-01-29	25,000	26,854	0.59

Current Investment Style

Not Available

Avg Duration[1]	7.0 Yrs
Avg Nominal Maturity	12.6 Yrs
Avg Credit Quality	—
Avg Wtd Coupon	2.63%
Avg Wtd Price	100.89% of par
Pricing Service	Muller

[1]figure provided by fund

Credit Analysis % bonds 03-31-01

US Govt	0	BB	0
AAA	61	B	0
AA	19	Below B	0
A	6	NR/NA	8
BBB	6		

Special Securities % assets 06-30-01

Restricted/Illiquid Secs	0
Inverse Floaters	0
Options/Futures/Warrants	No

Bond Type % assets 03-31-00

Alternative Minimum Tax (AMT)	10.1
Insured	—
Prerefunded	—

Top 5 States % bonds

NY	13.9	TX	8.8
MA	10.0	WA	5.5
IL	9.1		

Composition % assets 06-30-01

Cash	1.0	Bonds	99.0
Stocks	0.0	Other	0.0

Sector Weightings	% of Bonds	Rel Cat
General Obligation	31.5	1.1
Utilities	14.9	1.7
Health	10.4	0.9
Water/Waste	7.1	1.1
Housing	1.5	0.2
Education	4.7	0.6
Transportation	18.0	1.6
COP/Lease	1.6	0.7
Industrial	7.4	0.9
Misc Revenue	2.8	0.6
Demand	0.1	0.1

Analysis by Eric Jacobson 08-17-01

This fund makes a terrific core holding.

For starters, Fidelity Spartan Municipal Income focuses mostly on high-quality bonds, which are appropriate building blocks for the fixed-income portion of a portfolio. Beyond that, Fidelity's moderate approach to interest-rate sensitivity also makes a lot of sense. For the past several years, all of the firm's bond funds have pegged their durations (a standard measure of rate sensitivity) to those of appropriate indexes. That usually gives this fund (and other Fidelity offerings) a marketlike response to rate movements, and means that it's very unlikely to be whipsawed by an ill-timed interest-rate bet. By virtue of its chosen index, meanwhile, the fund sits almost exactly astride Morningstar's intermediate- and long-term muni categories. (The fund's history has been such that it just squeaks into the intermediate-term group.)

What's particularly impressive about this fund, however, is that even with a high-quality bent and no interest-rate bets, manager George Fischer has managed to produce a record that's the envy of most rivals. That can be attributed in large part to Fischer's adept sector, yield-curve and bond-structure plays. Most recently, Fischer has avoided big concentrations in California bonds, which have underperformed thanks to concerns about the state's handling of its power crisis. The fund also got some help from its modest health-care stake as hospitals rebounded during the first part of 2001.

Rounding out the picture here is a modest expense ratio of 0.49%. That gives the fund a big advantage over its more expensive rivals, and allows its fairly moderate strategy to produce great results.

Address:	82 Devonshire Street Boston, MA 02109 800–544–8888
Web Address:	www.fidelity.com
Inception:	12-01-77
Advisor:	Fidelity Mgmt. & Research
Subadvisor:	Fidelity Inv.s Money Mgmt
NTF Plans:	Fidelity , Fidelity Inst.

Minimum Purchase:	$10000	Add: $1000 IRA: —
Min Auto Inv Plan:	$500	Add: $500
Sales Fees:	No–load, 0.50%R	
Management Fee:	.25%+.37% mx./.13% mn.(G)	
Actual Fees:	Mgt: 0.38%	Dist: —
Expense Projections:	3Yr: $157	5Yr: $274 10Yr: $616
Avg Brok Commission:	—	Income Distrib: Monthly
Total Cost (relative to category):		Low

Fidelity Spartan Short–Int Muni Inc

Ticker	Load	NAV	Yield	SEC Yield	Total Assets	Mstar Category
FSTFX	None	$10.27	3.8%	—	$1,188.6 mil	Muni Short–Term

Prospectus Objective: Muni Bond—National

Fidelity Spartan Short-Intermediate Municipal Income Fund seeks current income exempt from federal income tax, consistent with preservation of capital.

The fund normally invests at least 80% of assets in securities exempt from federal income tax. It usually invests in high-quality short-term municipal obligations with maturities of five or fewer years; the dollar-weighted average maturity typically ranges between two and five years.

The fund was named Fidelity Short-Term Tax-Free Portfolio prior to Oct. 1, 1990. From that date until Feb. 20, 1996, it was named Fidelity Spartan Short-Intermediate Municipal Fund.

Historical Profile

Return: Below Avg
Risk: Low
Rating: ★★★★★ Highest

Investment Style
Fixed-Income

Income Rtn %Rank Cat: 26 | 40 | 41 | 35 | 37 | 45 | 49 | 44

Growth of Principal vs. Interest Rate Shifts
- Principal Value $000 (NAV with capital gains reinvested)
- Interest Rate % on 10 Yr Treasury
- ▼ Manager Change
- ▽ Partial Manager Change
- ► Mgr Unknown After
- ◄ Mgr Unknown Before

Performance Quartile (within Category)

Portfolio Manager(s)

Christine Jones Thompson, CFA. Since 7-00. BA'80 Tufts U.; MBA'85 U. of Pennsylvania. Other funds currently managed: Fidelity Advisor Municipal Inc T, Fidelity Spartan CA Municipal Income, Fidelity Spartan MA Municipal Income.

1990	1991	1992	1993	1994	1995	1996	1997	1998	1999	2000	12-01	History
9.52	9.78	9.88	10.11	9.66	10.04	10.00	10.11	10.16	9.93	10.12	10.27	NAV
6.42	8.85	6.18	7.12	–0.08	8.47	3.88	5.45	4.69	1.61	6.20	5.70	Total Return %
–2.54	–7.15	–1.22	–2.63	2.83	–10.00	0.26	–4.23	–3.99	2.44	–5.43	–2.73	+/– LB Aggregate
–0.88	–3.29	–2.63	–5.16	5.06	–8.99	–0.56	–3.75	–1.79	3.68	–5.49	0.61	+/– LB Muni
6.07	6.03	5.13	4.66	4.44	4.48	4.27	4.32	4.18	3.90	4.21	3.98	Income Return %
0.35	2.83	1.06	2.46	–4.52	3.99	–0.39	1.14	0.51	–2.28	1.99	1.71	Capital Return %
62	38	66	39	42	39	41	32	48	19	38	1	Total Rtn % Rank Cat
0.56	0.56	0.49	0.45	0.44	0.42	0.42	0.42	0.41	0.39	0.41	0.40	Income $
0.00	0.00	0.00	0.01	0.00	0.00	0.00	0.00	0.00	0.00	0.00	0.02	Capital Gains $
0.60	0.55	0.55	0.55	0.47	0.55	0.54	0.55	0.55	0.55	0.54	—	Expense Ratio %
5.90	5.68	4.95	4.55	4.45	4.38	4.17	4.25	4.15	3.89	4.02	—	Income Ratio %
75	59	28	56	44	51	78	32	33	66	53	—	Turnover Rate %
58.7	242.3	655.8	1,188.2	913.1	904.9	737.2	699.5	639.0	765.1	958.4	1,188.6	Net Assets $mil

Performance 12-31-01

	1st Qtr	2nd Qtr	3rd Qtr	4th Qtr	Total
1997	0.35	1.88	1.67	1.45	5.45
1998	0.93	0.95	2.03	0.71	4.69
1999	0.96	–0.43	0.76	0.31	1.61
2000	1.02	1.22	1.55	2.28	6.20
2001	2.22	1.11	2.32	–0.05	5.70

Trailing	Total Return%	+/– LB Agg	+/– LB Muni	% Rank All	% Rank Cat	Growth of $10,000
3 Mo	–0.05	–0.09	0.61	79	53	9,995
6 Mo	2.27	–2.39	0.14	20	4	10,227
1 Yr	5.70	–2.73	0.61	20	1	10,570
3 Yr Avg	4.48	–1.79	–0.27	35	3	11,406
5 Yr Avg	4.72	–2.71	–1.26	70	15	12,592
10 Yr Avg	4.89	–2.34	–1.74	93	38	16,124
15 Yr Avg	5.03	–3.09	–2.16	96	44	20,882

Tax Analysis	Tax-Adj Ret%	%Rank Cat	%Pretax Ret	%Rank Cat
3 Yr Avg	4.46	3	99.5	73
5 Yr Avg	4.70	14	99.7	63
10 Yr Avg	4.88	38	99.8	47

Potential Capital Gain Exposure: 2% of assets

Risk Analysis

Time Period	Load-Adj Return %	Risk %Rank[1] All	Risk %Rank[1] Cat	Morningstar Return	Morningstar Risk	Morningstar Risk-Adj Rating
1 Yr	5.17					
3 Yr	4.31	1	31	0.49[2]	0.27	★★★★★
5 Yr	4.61	2	34	0.57[2]	0.31	★★★★★
10 Yr	4.84	2	40	0.59	0.31	★★★★

Average Historical Rating (145 months): 4.5★s

[1] 1=low, 100=high [2] T-Bill return substituted for category avg.

Category Rating (3 Yr)

1 2 3 4 5 — Worst … Best (4)

Return: Above Avg
Risk: Below Avg

Other Measures	Standard Index LB Agg	Best Fit Index LB Muni
Alpha	–0.9	–0.4
Beta	0.36	0.38
R-Squared	56	76

Standard Deviation	1.69
Mean	4.48
Sharpe Ratio	–0.32

Portfolio Analysis 06-30-01

Total Fixed-Income: 282	Date of Maturity	Amount $000	Value $000	% Net Assets
TX Austin GO 5%	09-01-03	20,990	21,743	2.09
PR GO 5%	07-01-05	20,890	21,739	2.09
CA GO 5.5%	06-01-03	20,000	20,809	2.00
TX State GO 6.25%	10-01-04	16,210	17,604	1.69
NJ GO 5.5%	05-01-07	15,835	17,114	1.65
WA Pierce GO 5%	12-01-02	11,295	11,610	1.12
TX Houston Wtr/Swr Sys 0%	12-01-03	12,000	11,039	1.06
TX Muni Pwr 5.25%	09-01-06	10,000	10,607	1.02
AZ Transp Brd 5.25%	07-01-05	10,000	10,600	1.02
NJ Transp Cap Grant N/A	02-01-04	10,000	10,434	1.00
NC Muni Pwr #1 Catawba Elec 6%	01-01-05	9,750	10,284	0.99
WA Seattle Pwr 4.5%	03-28-03	10,000	10,154	0.98
TN Shelby GO 0%	05-01-10	15,750	10,112	0.97
NC East Muni Pwr Sys 6.25%	01-01-02	9,255	9,458	0.91
DC Hosp 6.875%	08-15-31	9,000	9,421	0.91

Current Investment Style

Not Available

Avg Duration[1]	2.8 Yrs
Avg Nominal Maturity	2.8 Yrs
Avg Credit Quality	—
Avg Wtd Coupon	1.48%
Avg Wtd Price	102.41% of par
Pricing Service	Muller

[1] figure provided by fund

Credit Analysis % bonds 03-31-01

US Govt	0	BB	0
AAA	63	B	0
AA	18	Below B	0
A	5	NR/NA	10
BBB	5		

Special Securities % assets 06-30-01

Restricted/Illiquid Secs	0
Inverse Floaters	0
Options/Futures/Warrants	No

Bond Type % assets 03-31-00

Alternative Minimum Tax (AMT)	6.8
Insured	—
Prerefunded	—

Top 5 States % bonds

TX	17.1	NJ	5.4
GA	8.0	CO	4.4
WA	7.8		

Composition % assets 06-30-01

Cash	5.6	Bonds	94.4
Stocks	0.0	Other	0.0

Sector Weightings	% of Bonds	Rel Cat
General Obligation	53.8	1.9
Utilities	10.4	1.3
Health	3.1	0.3
Water/Waste	3.4	0.6
Housing	0.0	0.0
Education	7.1	1.1
Transportation	14.4	1.6
COP/Lease	0.6	0.2
Industrial	2.8	0.3
Misc Revenue	4.4	0.8
Demand	0.0	0.0

Analysis by Eric Jacobson 09-30-01

The good just get better.

This fund has already made a name for itself. Its long-term returns are terrific, and its month-to-month volatility is moderate, even for the muni short-term category in which it resides. Impressively, that's all been done without taking on excess credit risk. Like her predecessors, manager Christine Thompson generally keeps the fund concentrated in the highest tiers of the credit spectrum.

Management has earned its record without risky interest-rate plays. In keeping with Fidelity policy, Thompson locks the fund's duration (a measure of rate sensitivity) in line with its benchmark index's.

Thompson is an active manager, though, which has gone a long way toward bolstering the fund's record. Like her colleagues, Thompson focuses mostly on yield-curve positioning, coupon and call structures, as well as sector positioning and tax issues. Most recently, the fund benefited from a dearth of issues in California, which has been plagued by deregulation troubles (though that held it back slightly as those rallied in 2000). The fund's high-quality short-maturity focus has also been a big plus as the Fed has cut interest rates, and investors have flocked to high-quality issues, particularly in the wake of the Sept. 11 terrorist attacks.

What makes that proven package even better has been that Fidelity lets the efficiencies of its scale flow down to investors. This fund's expenses are quite reasonable at less than a half a percentage point—a huge advantage over its average peer. Indeed, few places exist where costs matter more than in the muni short-term group. Add in that municipals in this maturity range have become particularly cheap relative to taxable bonds, and we think this fund makes an absolutely terrific choice.

Address:	82 Devonshire Street Boston, MA 02109 800–544–8888
Web Address:	www.fidelity.com
Inception:	12-24-86
Advisor:	Fidelity Mgmt. & Research
Subadvisor:	None
NTF Plans:	Fidelity , Fidelity Inst.

Minimum Purchase:	$10000	Add: $1000 IRA: —
Min Auto Inv Plan:	$10000	Add: $500
Sales Fees:	No–load, 0.50%R	
Management Fee:	.55%	
Actual Fees:	Mgt: 0.55%	Dist: —
Expense Projections:	3Yr: $176	5Yr: $307 10Yr: $689
Avg Brok Commission:	—	Income Distrib: Monthly
Total Cost (relative to category):		Below Avg

Fidelity Tax–Managed Stock

Ticker	Load	NAV	Yield	Total Assets	Mstar Category
FTXMX	None	$10.60	0.3%	$97.7 mil	Large Blend

Prospectus Objective: Growth

Fidelity Tax-Managed Stock Fund seeks long-term growth of capital.

The fund normally invests at least 65% of assets in common stocks and securities convertible into common stocks. It is managed using an investment strategy that is sensistive to the potential impact of federal income tax on shareholders' returns. Management uses fundamental analysis and quantitative research to identify securities for investment.

Historical Profile

Return	Below Avg
Risk	Average
Rating	★★ Below Avg

Investment Style
Equity
Average Stock %: 99% (1999), 96% (2000), 97% (12-01)

▼ Manager Change
▽ Partial Manager Change

Fund Performance vs. Category Average
■ Quarterly Fund Return +/– Category Average
— Category Baseline

Performance Quartile (within Category)

Portfolio Manager(s)

Timothy E. Heffernan, CFA. Since 11-98. BBA'84 Northeastern U. Other funds currently managed: Fidelity Congress Street, Fidelity Exchange, Fidelity Advisor Tax Managed A.

1990	1991	1992	1993	1994	1995	1996	1997	1998	1999	2000	12-01	History
—	—	—	—	—	—	—	—	11.13	13.33	12.14	10.60	NAV
—	—	—	—	—	—	—	—	11.30*	19.95	–8.93	–12.40	Total Return %
—	—	—	—	—	—	—	—	0.44*	–1.09	0.18	–0.52	+/– S&P 500
—	—	—	—	—	—	—	—	—	–1.87	2.03	0.37	+/– Wilshire Top 750
—	—	—	—	—	—	—	—	0.00	0.18	0.00	0.29	Income Return %
—	—	—	—	—	—	—	—	11.30	19.77	–8.93	–12.69	Capital Return %
—	—	—	—	—	—	—	—	—	55	53	44	Total Rtn % Rank Cat
—	—	—	—	—	—	—	—	0.00	0.02	0.00	0.04	Income $
—	—	—	—	—	—	—	—	0.00	0.00	0.00	0.00	Capital Gains $
—	—	—	—	—	—	—	—	—	1.10	0.96	—	Expense Ratio %
—	—	—	—	—	—	—	—	—	0.14	0.00	—	Income Ratio %
—	—	—	—	—	—	—	—	—	32	58	—	Turnover Rate %
—	—	—	—	—	—	—	—	21.7	78.7	105.6	97.7	Net Assets $mil

Performance 12-31-01

	1st Qtr	2nd Qtr	3rd Qtr	4th Qtr	Total
1997	—	—	—	—	—
1998	—	—	—	—	11.30 *
1999	3.23	5.66	–5.93	16.91	19.95
2000	3.00	–2.99	–1.50	–7.47	–8.93
2001	–13.18	7.40	–16.17	12.06	–12.40

Trailing	Total Return%	+/– S&P 500	+/–Wil Top 750	% Rank All	% Rank Cat	Growth of $10,000
3 Mo	12.06	1.38	0.74	33	28	11,206
6 Mo	–6.05	–0.50	–0.26	68	52	9,395
1 Yr	–12.40	–0.52	0.37	66	44	8,760
3 Yr Avg	–1.45	–0.43	0.37	80	55	9,570
5 Yr Avg	—	—	—	—	—	—
10 Yr Avg	—	—	—	—	—	—
15 Yr Avg	—	—	—	—	—	—

Tax Analysis	Tax-Adj Ret%	%Rank Cat	%Pretax Ret	%Rank Cat
3 Yr Avg	–1.52	39	—	—
5 Yr Avg	—	—	—	—
10 Yr Avg	—	—	—	—

Potential Capital Gain Exposure: –10% of assets

Risk Analysis

Time Period	Load-Adj Return %	Risk %Rank[1] All	Risk %Rank[1] Cat	Morningstar Return	Morningstar Risk	Morningstar Risk-Adj Rating
1 Yr	–13.27					
3 Yr	–1.45	65	37	–1.28[2]	0.91	★★
5 Yr	—	—	—	—	—	
Incept	2.01	—	—	—	—	

Average Historical Rating (3 months): 2.0★s

[1]1=low, 100=high [2] T–Bill return substituted for category avg.

Category Rating (3 Yr)

1 2 **3** 4 5
Worst Best

Return	Average
Risk	Average

Other Measures	Standard Index S&P 500	Best Fit Index S&P 500
Alpha	–0.5	–0.5
Beta	0.98	0.98
R–Squared	96	96
Standard Deviation		16.79
Mean		–1.45
Sharpe Ratio		–0.44

Portfolio Analysis 04-30-01

Share change since 10–00 Total Stocks: 161	Sector	PE	YTD Ret%	% Assets
⊕ General Elec	Industrials	30.1	–15.00	4.53
⊖ Microsoft	Technology	57.6	52.78	3.37
⊕ Pfizer	Health	34.7	–12.40	2.81
⊕ Citigroup	Financials	20.0	0.03	2.77
⊕ Viacom Cl B	Services	—	—	2.26
⊕ Bristol–Myers Squibb	Health	20.2	–26.00	2.26
⊕ BellSouth	Services	24.9	–5.09	2.20
American Intl Grp	Financials	42.0	–19.20	2.09
⊕ Intel	Technology	73.1	4.89	2.03
⊖ ExxonMobil	Energy	15.3	–7.59	1.99
⊕ AOL Time Warner	Technology	—	–7.76	1.90
⊕ SBC Comms	Services	18.4	–16.00	1.87
⊕ Merck	Health	19.1	–35.90	1.65
⊕ S&P 500 Index (Fut)	N/A	—	—	1.60
⊖ Procter & Gamble	Staples	38.8	3.12	1.58
⊕ Clear Channel Comms	Services	—	5.10	1.55
⊖ Fannie Mae	Financials	16.2	–6.95	1.54
☼ Verizon Comms	Services	29.7	–2.52	1.53
⊕ Coca–Cola	Staples	35.5	–21.40	1.45
⊕ Cardinal Health	Health	35.1	–2.51	1.34
⊕ Tyco Intl	Industrials	27.1	6.23	1.30
⊖ Philip Morris	Staples	12.1	9.12	1.30
⊕ Wells Fargo	Financials	22.4	–20.20	1.25
⊕ Thermo Electron	Industrials	—	–7.03	1.22
⊖ IBM	Technology	26.9	43.00	1.20

Current Investment Style

Style: Value Blnd Growth; Size: Large Med Small

	Stock Port Avg	Relative S&P 500 Current	Relative S&P 500 Hist	Rel Cat
Price/Earnings Ratio	30.0	0.97	—	0.99
Price/Book Ratio	5.6	0.98	—	1.02
Price/Cash Flow	18.3	1.02	—	0.99
3 Yr Earnings Growth	15.8	1.08	—	0.88
1 Yr Earnings Est%	–0.7	0.41	—	8.00
Med Mkt Cap $mil	71,915	1.2	—	1.38

Analysis by Scott Cooley 11-01-01

Fidelity Tax-Managed Stock Fund has achieved only part of its objective.

There's no doubt this fund has kept the tax collector at bay. It hasn't paid out a capital gain in the past, and manager Tim Heffernan says it won't this year, either. The bear market of the past 18 months has given him an opportunity to improve the fund's tax position. He has frequently sold losing picks, producing a net realized loss of $17 million, which is equal to nearly 20% of fund assets. Those losses may be used to offset gains Heffernan records in the future, so the fund should continue to be highly tax-efficient for some time to come.

So far, Heffernan hasn't done as good a job on the return front. Over the trailing three years through October 31, the fund has lost 0.9% per year, which puts it in the bottom third of the large-blend category. On an after-tax basis its returns are better, but they're still only a little above middling. And the fund lags its S&P 500 benchmark by nearly the amount of its expense ratio. We expected more value-added here, especially given that Heffernan enjoys the support of a large, talented analyst staff.

Heffernan may have more opportunities to add value in the future. With a chunk of net realized losses in the bank, he can now afford to trade more, which means he may be more comfortable building large positions in cyclical areas that may eventually have to be sold. Right now, for example, Heffernan reports increasing the fund's exposure to cyclical semiconductor issues, which offer attractive valuations and strong longer-term growth prospects.

This hasn't been a bad fund. But until Heffernan proves he can pick stocks as well as he can manage the tax situation, we can't make a strong case for it.

Special Securities % assets 04-30-01	
Restricted/Illiquid Secs	0
Emerging–Markets Secs	0
Options/Futures/Warrants	Yes

Composition % assets 04-30-01	
Cash	1.3
Stocks*	97.1
Bonds	0.0
Other	1.6
*Foreign (% stocks)	2.0

Market Cap	
Giant	57.8
Large	23.6
Medium	15.6
Small	3.0
Micro	0.0

Sector Weightings	% of Stocks	Rel S&P	5-Year High	5-Year Low
Utilities	0.7	0.2	—	—
Energy	7.7	1.1	—	—
Financials	15.0	0.8	—	—
Industrials	16.9	1.5	—	—
Durables	0.6	0.4	—	—
Staples	7.0	0.9	—	—
Services	15.5	1.4	—	—
Retail	4.6	0.7	—	—
Health	12.9	0.9	—	—
Technology	19.2	1.0	—	—

Address:	82 Devonshire Street Boston, MA 02109 800–544–8888 / 617–563–6414
Web Address:	www.fidelity.com
*Inception:	11-02-98
Advisor:	Fidelity Mgmt. & Research
Subadvisor:	FMR (Far East)/FMR (U.K.)
NTF Plans:	Fidelity Inst.

Minimum Purchase:	$10000	Add: $1000 IRA: $10000
Min Auto Inv Plan:	$10000	Add: $500
Sales Fees:	No–load, 1.00%R within 24 months	
Management Fee:	.59%+.52% mx./.27% mn.(G)	
Actual Fees:	Mgt: 0.58%	Dist: —
Expense Projections:	3Yr: $353	5Yr: $612 10Yr: $1352
Avg Brok Commission:	—	Income Distrib: Annually
Total Cost (relative to category):	Average	

Fidelity Utilities

Ticker	Load	NAV	Yield	Total Assets	Mstar Category
FIUIX	None	$13.49	1.2%	$1,427.1 mil	Spec Utilities

Prospectus Objective: Specialty—Utilities

Fidelity Utilities Fund seeks current income and capital appreciation.

The fund normally invests at least 65% of assets in public utilities; these companies include providers of electricity, natural gas, water, sanitary services, telephone or telegraph services, or other communication services.

On Oct. 1, 1991, Fidelity Qualified Dividend Fund merged into this fund. On Dec. 31, 1991, Fidelity Corporate Trust Adjustable-Rate Preferred merged into this fund. Prior to Sept. 8, 1994, the fund was named Fidelity Utilities Income Fund.

Historical Profile
Return Average
Risk Average
Rating ★★★ Neutral

Investment Style
Equity
Average Stock %

93% 98% 83% 87% 91% 88%

▼ Manager Change
▽ Partial Manager Change

Fund Performance vs. Category Average
■ Quarterly Fund Return +/– Category Average
— Category Baseline

Performance Quartile (within Category)

Portfolio Manager(s)

Timothy J. Cohen. Since 9-00. MBA U. of Pennsylvania-Wharton. Other funds currently managed: Fidelity Select Telecommunications, Fidelity Advisor Telecomm&Util Gr A, Fidelity Advisor Telecomm&Util Gr Ins.

1990	1991	1992	1993	1994	1995	1996	1997	1998	1999	2000	12-01	History
11.79	13.38	13.79	15.18	13.06	16.16	16.91	19.46	23.18	25.77	16.09	13.49	NAV
1.85	21.18	10.90	15.61	–5.29	30.62	11.44	31.60	28.54	26.75	–20.46	–15.19	Total Return %
4.96	–9.30	3.28	5.55	–6.60	–6.91	–11.51	–1.76	–0.04	5.71	–11.36	–3.31	+/– S&P 500
5.51	3.03	1.83	–4.15	–2.97	–9.41	–10.87	–3.89	7.30	15.80	–22.77	–6.40	+/– Russ Top 200 Val
5.65	5.47	4.58	3.84	3.67	4.20	3.02	2.65	1.83	0.81	0.36	1.00	Income Return %
–3.81	15.71	6.32	11.77	–8.95	26.43	8.42	28.95	26.71	25.94	–20.82	–16.19	Capital Return %
15	47	11	30	9	33	51	5	13	28	94	21	Total Rtn % Rank Cat
0.69	0.63	0.60	0.52	0.54	0.54	0.48	0.44	0.35	0.18	0.09	0.16	Income $
0.30	0.18	0.38	0.22	0.80	0.28	0.54	2.20	1.29	3.05	4.73	0.00	Capital Gains $
1.02	0.94	0.95	0.87	0.86	0.87	0.77	0.81	0.85	0.83	0.79	—	Expense Ratio %
6.19	5.93	5.11	4.57	3.39	3.87	3.69	2.96	2.34	1.63	0.61	—	Income Ratio %
61	43	39	73	47	98	98	56	57	55	50	—	Turnover Rate %
215.0	620.4	960.8	1,456.0	1,079.6	1,510.7	1,267.9	1,708.7	2,128.5	2,885.0	2,125.2	1,427.1	Net Assets $mil

Performance 12-31-01

	1st Qtr	2nd Qtr	3rd Qtr	4th Qtr	Total
1997	–1.31	10.53	7.45	12.26	31.60
1998	12.66	–0.79	–2.94	18.49	28.54
1999	3.58	11.38	–4.98	15.62	26.75
2000	11.39	–8.71	–4.26	–18.30	–20.46
2001	–5.04	1.04	–11.11	–0.56	–15.19

Trailing	Total Return%	+/– S&P 500	+/– Russ Top 200 Val	% Rank All	% Rank Cat	Growth of $10,000
3 Mo	–0.56	–11.25	–6.08	85	51	9,944
6 Mo	–11.61	–6.06	–5.83	89	32	8,839
1 Yr	–15.19	–3.31	–6.40	73	21	8,481
3 Yr Avg	–5.09	–4.06	–6.25	92	84	8,550
5 Yr Avg	7.66	–3.04	–3.55	31	59	14,462
10 Yr Avg	9.84	–3.09	–4.19	34	38	25,564
15 Yr Avg	—	—	—	—	—	—

Tax Analysis	Tax-Adj Ret%	%Rank Cat	%Pretax Ret	%Rank Cat
3 Yr Avg	–7.66	90	—	—
5 Yr Avg	4.72	59	61.7	73
10 Yr Avg	7.10	38	72.2	38

Potential Capital Gain Exposure: –11% of assets

Risk Analysis

Time Period	Load-Adj Return %	Risk %Rank[1] All	Risk %Rank[1] Cat	Morningstar Return	Morningstar Risk	Morningstar Risk-Adj Rating
1 Yr	–15.19					
3 Yr	–5.09	73	81	–1.93[2]	1.00	★★
5 Yr	7.66	64	79	0.60[2]	0.88	★★★
10 Yr	9.84	67	82	0.70	0.87	★★★

Average Historical Rating (134 months): 3.8★s

[1]1=low, 100=high [2] T-Bill return substituted for category avg.

Category Rating (3 Yr)

1 2 3 4 5
Worst Best

Return Below Avg
Risk Above Avg

Other Measures	Standard Index S&P 500	Best Fit Index Wil 4500
Alpha	–5.0	–8.3
Beta	0.76	0.46
R-Squared	55	56

Standard Deviation	16.68
Mean	–5.09
Sharpe Ratio	–0.70

Analysis by Paul Herbert 08-11-01

Fidelity Utilities Fund may lack broad appeal, but it has plenty of other marks in its favor.

Specialty-utilities funds typically fall into one of three camps—telecom heavy, gas- and electric-utilities heavy, or somewhere in between. For the better part of this fund's history, it has been the poster child for the first camp, as its managers have favored the higher growth rates that telecom service and equipment stocks, and even satellite plays have offered. As a result the fund has been more volatile than its typical category peer and has also had a higher correlation with the S&P 500 index, suggesting that it has less appeal as a diversifier than its typical rival.

While these harsh realities put quite a damper on the fund's overall attractiveness, some investors may find its other features to their liking. For one, as telecom stocks ran up in price during most of the 1990s, the fund was able to build a 10-year return that places in the category's top third. Its utilities-light portfolio has also made it a standout in 2001. Investors bid up the prices of independent power producers in 2000 and have become skittish about lower commodity prices and plant overbuilding. Manager Tim Cohen has mostly avoided this area, and instead stuck with regional telephone companies like Verizon, which stand to benefit as they take share from long-distance companies. The fund has lost 6.7% for so far in 2001, but that ranks ahead of 90% of its peers for the year to date through August 14.

There are a few other reasons to like the fund. For one, Fidelity boasts a deep bench of analysts covering the telecom and utilities areas, which should give the fund a leg up on its rivals. In addition, its 80-basis-point expense ratio is among the category's lowest.

Still, given that the fund offers little value as a diversifier or income vehicle, only those betting on its ability to keep offering solid returns need apply.

Address:	82 Devonshire Street Boston, MA 02109 800–544–8888
Web Address:	www.fidelity.com
Inception:	11-27-87
Advisor:	Fidelity Mgmt. & Research
Subadvisor:	FMR (U.K.)/FMR (Far East)
NTF Plans:	Fidelity , Fidelity Inst.

Minimum Purchase:	$2500	Add: $250 IRA: $500
Min Auto Inv Plan:	$2500	Add: $100
Sales Fees:	No-load	
Management Fee:	.20%+.52% mx./.27% mn.(G)+(–).15%P	
Actual Fees:	Mgt: 0.58%	Dist: —
Expense Projections:	3Yr: $255	5Yr: $444 10Yr: $990
Avg Brok Commission:	—	Income Distrib: Quarterly
Total Cost (relative to category):		Low

Portfolio Analysis 07-31-01

Share chng since 01–01 Total Stocks: 37	Subsector	PE	YTD Ret%	% Assets
Verizon Comms	Phone Services	29.7	–2.52	9.02
BellSouth	Phone Services	24.9	–5.09	8.93
SBC Comms	Phone Services	18.4	–16.00	7.16
Citizens Comms	Electric	—	–18.70	6.59
AT&T	Phone Services	7.8	40.59	6.53
⊕ AES	Electric	24.8	–70.40	5.37
⊕ Alltel	Phone Services	17.7	1.14	4.75
⊕ Southern	Electric	14.0	33.19	3.97
⊖ EchoStar Comms	Cable	—	20.75	3.73
⊕ American Elec Pwr	Electric	20.2	–1.28	3.30
Enron	Energy	1.6	–99.00	3.17
⊕ Niagara Mohawk Hldgs	Electric	—	6.24	2.96
⊕ Comcast	Cable	20.3	–13.70	2.59
☼ Vodafone Airtouch PLC ADR	Wireless	—	–27.70	2.56
☼ Northeast Utilities	Electric	NMF	–25.50	2.40
☼ Tyco Intl	Industrials	27.1	6.23	1.77
☼ DPL	Electric	9.0	–24.80	1.77
⊕ Nisource	Electric	33.4	–21.60	1.75
⊖ Kinder Morgan	Energy	32.2	7.11	1.70
☼ Nextel Comms Cl A	Wireless	—	–55.70	1.63
Qwest Comms Intl	Phone Equip.	—	–65.40	1.50
⊕ Keyspan	Energy	20.2	–14.10	1.11
General Motors Cl H	Technology	42.9	–32.80	1.08
Centurytel	Phone Services	13.3	–7.66	1.07
☼ Entergy	Electric	11.7	–4.50	0.92

Current Investment Style

Style: Value Blnd Growth; Size: Large Med Small

	Stock Port Avg	Relative S&P 500 Current	Relative S&P 500 Hist	Rel Cat
Price/Earnings Ratio	22.2	0.72	0.92	1.15
Price/Book Ratio	2.6	0.45	0.65	1.09
Price/Cash Flow	9.8	0.54	0.81	1.08
3 Yr Earnings Growth	22.1	1.51	0.64	1.40
1 Yr Earnings Est%	–6.4	3.63	—	–0.80
Med Mkt Cap $mil	22,574	0.4	0.5	1.85

Special Securities % assets 07-31-01	
Restricted/Illiquid Secs	0
Emerging-Markets Secs	1
Options/Futures/Warrants	No

Composition % assets 07-31-01	
Cash	10.0
Stocks*	90.0
Bonds	0.0
Other	0.0
*Foreign (% stocks)	4.3

Market Cap	
Giant	40.8
Large	29.2
Medium	29.8
Small	0.1
Micro	0.2

Subsector Weightings	% of Stocks	Rel Cat
Electric	32.3	0.8
Gas	0.0	0.0
Phone Services	41.6	2.1
Phone Equip.	1.7	1.0
Energy	1.9	0.4
Energy Services	0.0	0.0
Water	0.0	0.0
Other	22.5	0.8

Fidelity Value

Ticker	Load	NAV	Yield	Total Assets	Mstar Category
FDVLX	None	$51.51	1.0%	$5,237.5 mil	Mid-Cap Value

Prospectus Objective: Growth

Fidelity Value Fund seeks capital appreciation.

The fund invests primarily in equity securities issued by companies that management believes are undervalued or that possess valuable fixed assets. Valuable assets may include equipment, natural resources, and real estate, as well as intangible assets such as trademarks, franchises, and transportation routes. The fund may invest in securities of foreign issuers.

Prior to July 1986, the fund was called Fidelity Discoverer Fund.

Historical Profile

Return Above Avg
Risk Average
Rating ★★★★ Above Avg

Investment Style
Equity
Average Stock %: 86% 93% 96% 95% 91% 93% 92%

▼ Manager Change
▽ Partial Manager Change

Fund Performance vs. Category Average
■ Quarterly Fund Return +/– Category Average
— Category Baseline

Performance Quartile (within Category)

Portfolio Manager(s)

Richard B. Fentin. Since 3-96. BA'76 Emory U.; MBA'80 Harvard U.

1990	1991	1992	1993	1994	1995	1996	1997	1998	1999	2000	12-01	History
24.10	29.50	35.35	40.23	40.81	49.64	51.54	54.04	46.35	43.81	46.35	51.51	NAV
–12.82	26.20	21.15	22.94	7.63	27.13	16.85	21.08	0.18	8.55	8.10	12.25	Total Return %
–9.71	–4.29	13.53	12.88	6.31	–10.40	–6.09	–12.27	–28.39	–12.49	17.21	24.12	+/– S&P 500
3.26	–11.73	–0.53	7.31	9.76	–7.80	–3.41	–13.28	–4.91	8.66	–11.08	9.91	+/– Russ Midcap Val
4.04	3.53	0.78	0.96	0.42	1.18	1.07	0.93	1.02	1.57	2.17	1.10	Income Return %
–16.86	22.67	20.37	21.98	7.21	25.96	15.78	20.15	–0.83	6.98	5.94	11.15	Capital Return %
76	70	19	28	4	63	73	84	63	49	81	27	Total Rtn % Rank Cat
1.17	0.85	0.23	0.34	0.17	0.48	0.53	0.48	0.55	0.73	0.95	0.51	Income $
0.00	0.00	0.15	2.80	2.28	1.73	5.92	7.95	7.15	5.62	0.00	0.00	Capital Gains $
1.06	0.98	1.00	1.11	1.08	0.96	0.88	0.66	0.61	0.54	0.48	—	Expense Ratio %
4.55	2.93	2.01	1.43	1.29	1.58	1.34	1.01	1.06	1.50	1.87	—	Income Ratio %
165	137	81	117	112	125	112	56	36	50	48	—	Turnover Rate %
97.9	123.4	667.5	1,716.1	3,720.4	5,745.8	7,080.1	7,913.7	5,522.6	4,383.1	3,522.1	5,237.5	Net Assets $mil

Performance 12-31-01

	1st Qtr	2nd Qtr	3rd Qtr	4th Qtr	Total
1997	2.06	13.67	8.91	–4.17	21.08
1998	11.53	–2.07	–20.06	14.75	0.18
1999	–2.31	25.60	–11.18	–0.39	8.55
2000	–6.05	0.66	1.98	12.10	8.10
2001	2.91	8.70	–12.02	14.04	12.25

Trailing	Total Return%	+/– S&P 500	+/– Russ Midcap Val	% Rank All	% Rank Cat	Growth of $10,000
3 Mo	14.04	3.36	2.01	26	38	11,404
6 Mo	0.34	5.90	1.25	37	38	10,034
1 Yr	12.25	24.12	9.91	5	27	11,225
3 Yr Avg	9.62	10.64	2.81	12	56	13,172
5 Yr Avg	9.83	–0.87	–1.64	19	68	15,978
10 Yr Avg	14.30	1.37	–0.12	7	52	38,049
15 Yr Avg	12.78	–0.96	–0.69	19	54	60,716

Tax Analysis	Tax-Adj Ret%	%Rank Cat	%Pretax Ret	%Rank Cat
3 Yr Avg	8.01	51	83.2	40
5 Yr Avg	7.22	69	73.5	76
10 Yr Avg	11.71	50	81.9	43

Potential Capital Gain Exposure: 2% of assets

Risk Analysis

Time Period	Load-Adj Return %	Risk %Rank[1] All	Risk %Rank[1] Cat	Morningstar Return	Morningstar Risk	Morningstar Risk-Adj Rating
1 Yr	12.25					
3 Yr	9.62	54	70	1.04[2]	0.75	★★★★
5 Yr	9.83	60	65	1.15[2]	0.83	★★★
10 Yr	14.30	60	49	1.61	0.79	★★★★

Average Historical Rating (193 months): 3.2★s

[1]1=low, 100=high [2] T-Bill return substituted for category avg.

Category Rating (3 Yr)

Worst 1 2 3 4 5 Best

Return Average
Risk Above Avg

Other Measures	Standard Index S&P 500	Best Fit Index SPMid400
Alpha	9.2	2.2
Beta	0.59	0.59
R-Squared	26	34
Standard Deviation		21.68
Mean		9.62
Sharpe Ratio		0.25

Analysis by Kelli Stebel 11-29-01

This fund is finally strutting its stuff, but that's not enough to give it a ringing endorsement.

In this year's turbulent market, Fidelity Value Fund is excelling. The fund's paper and chemical companies, such as Deluxe and PolyOne, which hurt performance in previous years, have rebounded smartly recently, as investors have bid up cyclical names in anticipation of an economic recovery. That's led to an 8% gain for the year to date through November 27, which places the fund in the mid-cap value category's top third.

With the Fed continuing to cut rates, manager Richard Fentin turned a bit more offensive this summer. Fentin trimmed some financial holdings such as Freddie Mac and Fannie Mae, instead bulking up on retail names such as Tricon Global Restaurants, which he thought was trading at an attractive valuation.

Despite its strong performance this year, investors should approach this fund with caution. Throughout Fentin's five-year tenure, this fund's performance has been mediocre to subpar. Even compared with portfolios with similarly low P/E ratios, returns here have been lackluster. Part of the problem has been the portfolio's huge industrial-cyclical stake. The fund has typically held between 30% and 40% of assets in such names, more than three times the weighting of its typical peer. Although such stocks have helped the fund this year, they generally detracted from the fund's returns throughout the late 1990s, as financials dominated value investing's few rallies.

In order to merit investor consideration, this fund will need to produce strong returns consistently. But until then, shareholders can find more-fetching value offerings elsewhere, particularly among our Analyst Picks.

Portfolio Analysis 04-30-01

Share change since 10-00 Total Stocks: 223	Sector	PE	YTD Ret%	% Assets
⊖ American Standard	Industrials	14.9	38.36	2.80
⊖ Republic Svcs Cl A	Services	15.6	16.19	2.51
⊖ Waste Mgmt	Services	52.3	15.03	1.65
⊖ Harsco	Industrials	15.7	43.96	1.64
⊖ Freddie Mac	Financials	14.0	–3.87	1.16
John H Harland	Industrials	24.8	58.79	1.14
⊖ Fannie Mae	Financials	16.2	–6.95	1.12
⊖ CNF	Services	—	0.56	1.04
⊖ Consolid Stores	N/A	—	—	1.03
⊖ Snap-On	Industrials	39.1	24.81	1.03
⊖ Ametek	Industrials	14.8	23.96	1.01
⊖ Autonation	Services	14.2	105.50	0.99
⊕ Eaton	Industrials	22.8	17.90	0.91
⊖ RR Donnelley & Sons	Services	26.8	13.72	0.88
⊕ Ingersoll-Rand	Industrials	27.0	1.41	0.86
⊕ CSX	Services	26.6	38.21	0.85
⊖ Black & Decker	Durables	17.6	–2.67	0.83
⊕ Conoco Cl B	Energy	—	—	0.81
⊕ PNC Finl Svcs Grp	Financials	13.5	–20.70	0.81
⊕ Textron	Industrials	—	–8.47	0.79
Regis	Services	19.5	78.94	0.79
⊖ Ferro	Industrials	19.7	15.11	0.79
⊖ Deluxe	Industrials	17.1	116.30	0.77
⊖ Halliburton	Energy	8.3	–63.20	0.77
GenCorp	Industrials	19.1	48.08	0.77

Current Investment Style

Style: Value Blnd Growth; Size: Large Med Small

	Stock Port Avg	Relative S&P 500 Current	Relative S&P 500 Hist	Rel Cat
Price/Earnings Ratio	23.6	0.76	0.65	1.00
Price/Book Ratio	2.8	0.49	0.37	0.92
Price/Cash Flow	10.7	0.60	0.50	0.86
3 Yr Earnings Growth	8.9	0.61	0.69	0.75
1 Yr Earnings Est%	–2.7	1.53	—	0.44
Med Mkt Cap $mil	4,183	0.1	0.1	0.59

Special Securities % assets 04-30-01	
Restricted/Illiquid Secs	Trace
Emerging-Markets Secs	0
Options/Futures/Warrants	No

Composition % assets 04-30-01	
Cash	7.5
Stocks*	91.9
Bonds	0.0
Other	0.7
*Foreign (% stocks)	0.7

Market Cap	
Giant	4.4
Large	20.8
Medium	55.1
Small	19.7
Micro	0.1

Sector Weightings	% of Stocks	Rel S&P	5-Year High	5-Year Low
Utilities	5.4	1.7	7	0
Energy	8.4	1.2	15	6
Financials	16.2	0.9	25	0
Industrials	30.7	2.7	45	22
Durables	4.1	2.7	13	2
Staples	0.9	0.1	9	1
Services	25.7	2.4	26	8
Retail	2.6	0.4	18	3
Health	1.7	0.1	7	0
Technology	4.4	0.2	12	1

Address:	82 Devonshire Street Boston, MA 02109 800-544-8888
Web Address:	www.fidelity.com
Inception:	12-01-78
Advisor:	Fidelity Mgmt. & Research
Subadvisor:	FMR (U.K.)/FMR (Far East)
NTF Plans:	Fidelity , Fidelity Inst.

Minimum Purchase:	$2500	Add: $250 IRA: $500
Min Auto Inv Plan:	$2500	Add: $100
Sales Fees:	No-load	
Management Fee:	.30%+.52% mx./.25% mn.(G)+(–).20%P	
Actual Fees:	Mgt: 0.32%	Dist: —
Expense Projections:	3Yr: $179	5Yr: $313 10Yr: $701
Avg Brok Commission:	—	Income Distrib: Annually
Total Cost (relative to category):	Low	

Fidelity Worldwide

Ticker	Load	NAV	Yield	Total Assets	Mstar Category
FWWFX	None	$14.66	0.0%	$807.5 mil	World Stock

Prospectus Objective: World Stock

Fidelity Worldwide Fund seeks growth of capital.

The fund usually invests in securities of issuers from anywhere in the world; it normally maintains investments in at least three countries, including the United States. Its equity investments may include established companies and new or small-capitalization companies. Although it may invest anywhere in the world, the fund mainly purchases securities of issuers in developed countries in North America, the Pacific Basin, and Europe. It may invest in debt securities of any rating. The fund may also invest in closed-end investment companies.

Historical Profile
Return Above Avg
Risk Below Avg
Rating ★★★★ Above Avg

Investment Style
Equity
Average Stock %: 76% 85% 86% 89% 95% 93% 100%

▼ Manager Change
▽ Partial Manager Change

Fund Performance vs. Category Average
■ Quarterly Fund Return +/– Category Average
— Category Baseline

Performance Quartile (within Category)

Portfolio Manager(s)

Douglas Chase. Since 9-99. MBA'93 U. of Michigan. Other fund currently managed: Fidelity Export & Multinational.

Richard Mace, Jr.. Since 4-01. BA'85 U. of Virginia; MBA'88 U. of Pennsylvania. Other funds currently managed: Fidelity Advisor Overseas T, Fidelity Overseas, Fidelity Global Balanced.

1990	1991	1992	1993	1994	1995	1996	1997	1998	1999	2000	12-01	History
8.82	9.41	9.73	13.03	12.68	13.44	15.39	15.95	16.53	19.90	15.63	14.66	NAV
–11.02*	7.88	6.21	36.55	2.96	7.19	18.72	12.08	7.18	30.80	–8.01	–6.21	Total Return %
–4.93*	–22.61	–1.41	26.49	1.65	–30.35	–4.22	–21.28	–21.39	9.76	1.09	5.67	+/– S&P 500
—	–10.41	11.43	14.04	–2.12	–13.53	5.24	–3.69	–17.16	5.87	5.17	—	+/– MSCI World
0.78	1.13	2.76	1.03	0.54	1.18	1.26	0.71	0.63	0.60	2.01	0.00	Income Return %
–11.80	6.74	3.44	35.52	2.42	6.01	17.46	11.36	6.56	30.19	–10.02	–6.21	Capital Return %
—	92	18	33	15	93	31	54	72	57	42	11	Total Rtn % Rank Cat
0.08	0.10	0.26	0.10	0.07	0.15	0.17	0.11	0.10	0.10	0.40	0.00	Income $
0.00	0.00	0.00	0.15	0.66	0.00	0.38	1.16	0.44	1.52	2.25	0.00	Capital Gains $
2.00	1.69	1.51	1.40	1.32	1.16	1.18	1.16	1.12	1.07	1.04	—	Expense Ratio %
2.09	2.19	2.02	1.99	1.40	2.05	1.71	1.24	0.91	0.47	0.48	—	Income Ratio %
123	129	130	57	69	70	49	85	100	164	235	—	Turnover Rate %
94.4	100.9	99.0	339.6	703.9	654.1	925.5	1,145.3	1,013.6	1,125.4	928.3	807.5	Net Assets $mil

Performance 12-31-01

	1st Qtr	2nd Qtr	3rd Qtr	4th Qtr	Total
1997	2.66	11.27	6.31	–7.71	12.08
1998	15.61	0.71	–21.22	16.85	7.18
1999	1.15	7.12	0.28	20.39	30.80
2000	2.31	–1.08	–4.82	–4.51	–8.01
2001	–9.28	6.56	–15.16	14.35	–6.21

Trailing	Total Return%	+/– S&P 500	+/– MSCI World	% Rank All	% Rank Cat	Growth of $10,000
3 Mo	14.35	3.67	—	25	20	11,435
6 Mo	–2.98	2.58	—	51	11	9,702
1 Yr	–6.21	5.67	—	54	11	9,379
3 Yr Avg	4.11	5.14	—	39	29	11,285
5 Yr Avg	6.27	–4.42	—	44	46	13,557
10 Yr Avg	9.92	–3.00	—	33	36	25,759
15 Yr Avg	—	—	—	—	—	—

Tax Analysis	Tax-Adj Ret%	%Rank Cat	%Pretax Ret	%Rank Cat
3 Yr Avg	2.10	31	51.0	80
5 Yr Avg	4.38	45	69.8	49
10 Yr Avg	8.38	27	84.4	15

Potential Capital Gain Exposure: –6% of assets

Risk Analysis

Time Period	Load-Adj Return %	Risk %Rank[1] All	Risk %Rank[1] Cat	Morningstar Return	Morningstar Risk	Morningstar Risk-Adj Rating
1 Yr	–6.21					
3 Yr	4.11	54	23	–0.18[2]	0.71	★★★★
5 Yr	6.27	64	31	0.28[2]	0.73	★★★★
10 Yr	9.92	70	22	1.68[2]	0.69	★★★★

Average Historical Rating (104 months): 4.0★s

[1]1=low, 100=high [2] T-Bill return substituted for category avg.

Category Rating (3 Yr)

1 2 3 4 5 (Worst – Best)

Return Above Avg
Risk Below Avg

Other Measures	Standard Index S&P 500	Best Fit Index MSACWorld
Alpha	4.1	8.1
Beta	0.80	0.94
R-Squared	75	89

Standard Deviation	16.33
Mean	4.11
Sharpe Ratio	–0.06

Portfolio Analysis 04-30-01

Share change since 10-00 Total Stocks: 269	Sector	Country	% Assets
☆ Fid Cash Central Fund	N/A	N/A	8.51
⊕ Cardinal Health	Health	U.S.	3.73
⊕ Pfizer	Health	U.S.	3.32
⊕ Avon Products	Staples	U.S.	2.89
⊕ Autonation	Services	U.S.	2.69
⊕ Bristol-Myers Squibb	Health	U.S.	2.41
☆ Guidant	Health	U.S.	1.80
⊕ Total Fina Cl B	Energy	France	1.80
⊕ Computer Assoc Intl	Technology	U.S.	1.70
⊕ Freddie Mac	Financials	U.S.	1.67
⊕ Tyco Intl	Industrials	U.S.	1.50
⊕ Fannie Mae	Financials	U.S.	1.15
⊖ General Elec	Industrials	U.S.	1.13
⊕ Affiliated Comp Svcs A	Services	U.S.	1.08
⊕ Intel	Technology	U.S.	1.03
⊕ Merrill Lynch	Financials	U.S.	0.99
⊕ Clear Channel Comms	Services	U.S.	0.92
☆ SBC Comms	Services	U.S.	0.91
Telecom Italia	Services	Italy	0.89
☆ ACE	Financials	Bermuda	0.89

Current Investment Style

Style: Value Blnd Growth; Size: Large Med Small

	Stock Port Avg	Rel MSCI EAFE Current	Rel MSCI EAFE Hist	Rel Cat
Price/Earnings Ratio	27.4	1.06	0.94	0.99
Price/Cash Flow	17.0	1.32	1.17	1.03
Price/Book Ratio	4.8	1.39	1.08	1.05
3 Yr Earnings Growth	17.4	0.93	1.02	0.93
Med Mkt Cap $mil	22,345	0.8	0.5	0.93

Country Exposure 04-30-01	% assets
U.S.	57
Japan	7
France	5
United Kingdom	4
Netherlands	2

Hedging History: Never

Regional Exposure 04-30-01	% assets
Europe	19
Japan	7
Latin America	0
Pacific Rim	4
U.S.	57
Other	1

Special Securities % assets 04-30-01	
Restricted/Illiquid Secs	0
Emerging-Markets Secs	4
Options/Futures/Warrants	No

Composition % assets 04-30-01

Cash	0.0	Bonds	0.0
Stocks	100.0	Other	0.0

Sector Weightings	% of Stocks	Rel Cat	5-Year High	5-Year Low
Utilities	0.6	0.2	8	0
Energy	4.5	0.8	16	0
Financials	16.3	0.9	32	10
Industrials	10.8	1.0	36	9
Durables	3.1	0.8	13	3
Staples	8.3	1.0	10	2
Services	21.3	1.3	21	4
Retail	3.0	0.6	15	3
Health	16.5	1.3	17	1
Technology	15.6	1.0	23	1

Analysis by Emily Hall 11-30-01

Fidelity Worldwide Fund has undergone a smooth management transition and remains a decent, if unexciting, choice.

In April of this year Rick Mace replaced Penelope Dobkin as lead manager here. (Doug Chase, who has been picking U.S. stocks for the fund since 1999, remains.) The shift from Dobkin to Mace wasn't particularly worrisome. Mace is head of Fidelity's international team and has steered his other charges, Fidelity Overseas and Fidelity Global Balanced, to decent results.

Mace has continued this fund's move toward conservatism, which began in the late 1990s. In her early years as manager, Dobkin was something of a contrarian who was willing to make fairly significant bets on sectors and countries. She also tended to underweight the fund's stake in U.S. stocks. But a couple of stumbles led her to change the fund's tune, and it became a much more typical world-stock offering. The fund now follows a growth-at-a-reasonable-price approach, makes few outsized bets, and holds loads of U.S. stocks.

Indeed, it could be argued that the fund is now dominated by U.S. stocks. At the end of September, nearly two thirds of the fund's assets were stuffed into American names. Moreover, not a single one of the fund's top-10 picks came from overseas.

That emphasis on the U.S. has been a boon lately. Through the end of November 2001, the fund has lost much less than its typical peer. Although the U.S. market has struggled in 2001, many European and Asian bourses have been even worse. The fund has also benefited from some good stock picks, including Autonation.

The fund is a decent, moderately conservative choice. However, investors should be aware that they are getting a lot of U.S. exposure here.

Address:	82 Devonshire Street Boston, MA 02109 800-544-8888
Web Address:	www.fidelity.com
*Inception:	05-30-90
Advisor:	Fidelity Mgmt. & Research
Subadvisor:	FMR (U.K.)/FMR (Far East)
NTF Plans:	Fidelity , Fidelity Inst.

Minimum Purchase:	$2500	Add: $250 IRA: $500
Min Auto Inv Plan:	$2500	Add: $100
Sales Fees:	No-load	
Management Fee:	.45%+.52% mx./.27% mn.(G)	
Actual Fees:	Mgt: 0.73%	Dist: —
Expense Projections:	3Yr: $356	5Yr: $617 10Yr: $1363
Avg Brok Commission:	—	Income Distrib: Annually
Total Cost (relative to category):		Below Avg

First Eagle Fund of America Y

Ticker	Load	NAV	Yield	Total Assets	Mstar Category
FEAFX	None	$21.58	0.0%	$429.7 mil	Mid-Cap Blend

Prospectus Objective: Growth

First Eagle Fund of America seeks capital appreciation.

The fund normally invests at least 65% of assets in equity securities, including common stocks, preferred stocks, convertibles, and warrants. The advisor seeks securities that are undervalued in their respective trading markets relative to the issuers' overall financial and managerial strength. The fund may invest in special situations, such as companies involved in mergers, liquidations, or reorganizations. It may invest up to 10% of assets in foreign securities. The fund may also invest in debt rated as low as D. The fund is nondiversified.

The fund offers Class A, C and Y shares.

Historical Profile
Return: High
Risk: Below Avg
Rating: ★★★★★ Highest

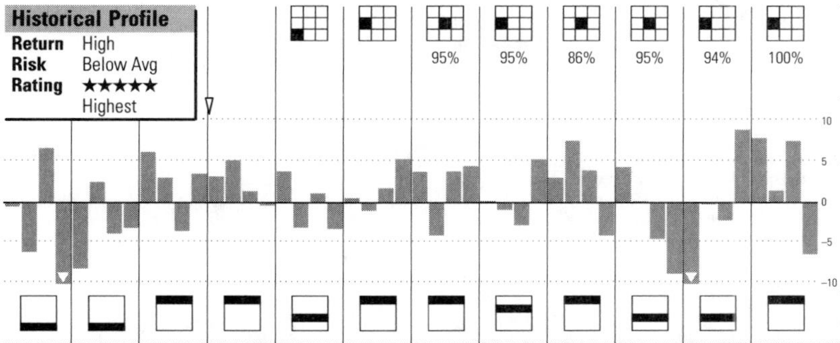

Investment Style
Equity
Average Stock %: 95% | 95% | 86% | 95% | 94% | 100%

▼ Manager Change
▽ Partial Manager Change

Fund Performance vs. Category Average
■ Quarterly Fund Return +/- Category Average
— Category Baseline

Performance Quartile (within Category)

Portfolio Manager(s)

Harold J. Levy. Since 4-87. BA'75 Wesleyan U.; MBA'79 U. of Chicago. Other funds currently managed: First Eagle Fund of America C, First Eagle Fund of America A.

David L. Cohen. Since 10-89. MBA'78 New York U.; JD'81 U. of Miami. Other funds currently managed: First Eagle Fund of America C, First Eagle Fund of America A.

History

1990	1991	1992	1993	1994	1995	1996	1997	1998	1999	2000	12-01	History
10.51	11.85	13.48	15.04	12.70	16.96	18.30	19.33	21.43	20.56	20.47	21.58	NAV
-17.59	20.91	24.31	23.85	-2.60	36.40	29.34	29.46	20.99	12.09	0.32	8.25	Total Return %
-14.47	-9.58	16.69	13.80	-3.91	-1.14	6.39	-3.89	-7.58	-8.95	9.43	20.13	+/- S&P 500
-12.47	-29.16	12.41	9.92	0.99	5.48	10.15	-2.78	1.88	-2.63	-17.17	8.85	+/- S&P Mid 400
2.21	0.82	0.00	0.00	0.00	0.00	0.00	0.00	0.00	0.00	0.00	0.00	Income Return %
-19.80	20.09	24.31	23.85	-2.60	36.40	29.34	29.46	20.99	12.09	0.32	8.25	Capital Return %
78	85	18	18	52	11	5	41	11	74	58	11	Total Rtn % Rank Cat
0.29	0.08	0.00	0.00	0.00	0.00	0.00	0.00	0.00	0.00	0.00	0.00	Income $
0.00	0.74	1.17	1.62	2.00	0.35	3.13	4.10	1.84	3.29	0.15	0.57	Capital Gains $
1.10	2.00	3.00	2.90	1.90	1.90	1.80	1.70	1.50	1.40	1.40	—	Expense Ratio %
1.30	0.80	-1.00	-1.50	-0.70	-0.30	-0.20	-0.30	-0.40	-0.20	-0.20	—	Income Ratio %
72	92	145	141	110	81	93	98	83	55	89	—	Turnover Rate %
63.3	74.4	85.6	108.3	105.1	136.2	171.4	268.9	456.5	528.5	375.4	422.0	Net Assets $mil

Performance 12-31-01

	1st Qtr	2nd Qtr	3rd Qtr	4th Qtr	Total
1997	-1.20	14.21	10.90	3.45	29.46
1998	14.02	4.99	-13.48	16.82	20.99
1999	3.87	11.28	-10.48	8.33	12.09
2000	-3.11	-3.06	2.23	4.49	0.32
2001	-1.51	10.57	-9.29	9.59	8.25

Trailing	Total Return%	+/- S&P 500	+/- S&P Mid 400	% Rank All	% Rank Cat	Growth of $10,000
3 Mo	9.59	-1.10	-8.40	45	86	10,959
6 Mo	-0.59	4.97	0.97	41	21	9,941
1 Yr	8.25	20.13	8.85	9	11	10,825
3 Yr Avg	6.77	7.80	-3.47	18	48	12,173
5 Yr Avg	13.78	3.08	-2.33	6	23	19,067
10 Yr Avg	17.57	4.64	2.56	2	3	50,443
15 Yr Avg	—	—	—	—	—	—

Tax Analysis	Tax-Adj Ret%	%Rank Cat	%Pretax Ret	%Rank Cat
3 Yr Avg	5.47	37	80.7	39
5 Yr Avg	11.51	23	83.6	31
10 Yr Avg	14.50	6	82.6	38

Potential Capital Gain Exposure: 15% of assets

Risk Analysis

Time Period	Load-Adj Return %	Risk %Rank[1] All	Risk %Rank[1] Cat	Morningstar Return	Morningstar Risk	Morningstar Risk-Adj Rating
1 Yr	8.25					
3 Yr	6.77	41	4	0.39[2]	0.57	★★★★
5 Yr	13.78	49	6	2.26[2]	0.66	★★★★★
10 Yr	17.57	57	14	2.51	0.74	★★★★★

Average Historical Rating (141 months): 3.9★s

[1]1=low, 100=high [2] T-Bill return substituted for category avg.

Category Rating (3 Yr)

1 2 3 4 5
Worst Best

Return: Average
Risk: Low

Other Measures	Standard Index S&P 500	Best Fit Index MSCIACWdFr
Alpha	5.3	7.9
Beta	0.58	0.63
R-Squared	56	58
Standard Deviation		13.95
Mean		6.77
Sharpe Ratio		0.15

Analysis by Dan McNeela 10-22-01

Despite some near-term turbulence, First Eagle Fund of America is likely to remain dependable.

Managers Harold Levy and David Cohen have built a strong record by buying stocks when there is a good deal of uncertainty surrounding some aspect of the company, whether it's a new management team or recent merger and acquisition activity. But during the past two years this steady fund has taken a couple sizable hits. Investments in Loral Space & Communications and Comdisco have been pretty major misses for a fund that rarely disappoints.

By investing before the dust has settled, management can step into situations that are just beginning to erode. Loral's 40% stake in satellite-based mobile phone company Globalstar Telecommunications became nearly worthless in 2000. And Comdisco is nearly bankrupt after a failed attempt to enter the telecom market.

But the long-term picture for the fund is still very positive. The fund's 10-year annualized returns easily rank in the mid-blend category's top decile. And management's eye for value has helped it achieve that position with mild volatility, proving that this fund is not taking big gambles on unproven companies. Further, most of the fund's holdings have held up well in 2001. The fund's small gain of 2% year to date through Oct. 19 is enough to rank it in the category's top decile in what has been a rough year for the market.

Levy and Cohen's experience and proven track record suggest that they're likely to emerge from the recent market turmoil in good shape. After all, this is the same pair that delivered seven years of 20%-plus gains in the 1990s. The fund has been successful by looking beyond short-term uncertainty to find great buys. We think that shareholders will find that the strategy will work for them too.

Address:	1345 Avenue of the Americas New York, NY 10105-4300 212-698-3000 / 800-451-3623
Web Address:	www.firsteaglefunds.com
Inception:	04-10-87
Advisor:	Arnhold & S. Bleichroeder
Subadvisor:	None
NTF Plans:	Fidelity , Datalynx

Minimum Purchase:	$2500	Add: $100 IRA: $500
Min Auto Inv Plan:	$2500	Add: $100
Sales Fees:	No-load	
Management Fee:	1.0%	
Actual Fees:	Mgt: 1.00%	Dist: —
Expense Projections:	3Yr: $474	5Yr: $818 10Yr: $1791
Avg Brok Commission:	—	Income Distrib: Annually
Total Cost (relative to category):		—

Portfolio Analysis 10-31-01

Share change since 09-01 Total Stocks: 45	Sector	PE	YTD Ret%	% Assets
⊖ Biogen	Health	30.5	-4.52	5.59
⊕ General Dynamics	Industrials	17.6	3.63	5.50
Thermo Electron	Industrials	—	-7.03	3.97
American Standard	Industrials	14.9	38.36	3.82
L-3 Comms Hldgs	Technology	33.0	16.88	3.81
Cephalon	Health	—	19.38	3.54
Aon	Financials	46.1	6.32	3.36
Tricon Global Restaurants	Services	16.3	49.09	3.35
Packaging Corporation	Industrials	11.9	12.56	3.31
⊖ Storage Tech	Technology	36.9	129.60	3.28
USA Educ	Financials	68.9	24.74	3.25
Millipore	Industrials	63.9	-2.89	2.96
Tenet Healthcare	Health	30.1	32.14	2.82
Amphenol	Technology	20.5	22.61	2.82
Equifax	Services	18.3	43.78	2.78
Dun & Bradstreet	Services	41.1	36.43	2.58
TJX	Retail	23.2	44.39	2.58
Intl Game Tech	Durables	24.4	42.29	2.45
Cadence Design Sys	Technology	5.3	-20.20	2.34
Waste Mgmt	Services	52.3	15.03	2.33
Celgene	Health	—	-1.78	2.30
⊖ Harris	Technology	28.0	0.33	2.25
⊖ Mandalay Resort Grp	Services	15.3	-2.45	2.23
Clorox	Staples	31.1	14.20	2.16
Alliant Techsystems	Industrials	28.6	73.48	2.09

Current Investment Style

Style: Value Blnd Growth; Size: Large Med Small

	Stock Port Avg	Relative S&P 500 Current	Relative S&P 500 Hist	Rel Cat
Price/Earnings Ratio	28.2	0.91	0.82	1.04
Price/Book Ratio	6.5	1.14	0.70	1.51
Price/Cash Flow	16.0	0.89	0.77	0.92
3 Yr Earnings Growth	19.3	1.32	0.85	1.16
1 Yr Earnings Est%	5.8	—	—	2.55
Med Mkt Cap $mil	4,589	0.1	0.1	0.51

Special Securities % assets 10-31-01	
Restricted/Illiquid Secs	2
Emerging-Markets Secs	0
Options/Futures/Warrants	No

Composition % assets 10-31-01	
Cash	0.0
Stocks*	99.8
Bonds	0.0
Other	0.2
*Foreign (% stocks)	0.0

Market Cap	
Giant	0.0
Large	36.5
Medium	62.1
Small	1.4
Micro	0.0

Sector Weightings	% of Stocks	Rel S&P	5-Year High	5-Year Low
Utilities	0.0	0.0	10	0
Energy	1.8	0.3	4	0
Financials	11.5	0.6	33	6
Industrials	26.7	2.3	43	8
Durables	2.6	1.7	17	0
Staples	3.7	0.5	13	0
Services	14.8	1.4	34	0
Retail	3.8	0.6	19	0
Health	16.9	1.1	23	0
Technology	18.4	1.0	32	1

First Eagle SoGen Global A

Ticker	Load	NAV	Yield	Total Assets	Mstar Category
SGENX	5.00%	$23.82	2.6%	$1,671.0 mil	International Hybrid

Prospectus Objective: Multiasset—Global

First Eagle SoGen Global Fund seeks long-term capital growth.

The fund invests primarily in foreign and domestic common stocks and convertible securities. It may also purchase fixed-income instruments if they provide a potential for capital appreciation. With regard to debt, the fund maintains no restrictions on credit quality; it may purchase debt upon which the issuer has defaulted. The fund normally invests in at least three countries. It may invest up to 10% of assets in illiquid or restricted securities.

The fund currently offers Class A, C, and I shares, all of which differ in fee structure and availability. Prior to January 3, 2000, the fund was named SoGen International Fund.

Historical Profile
Return Above Avg
Risk Low
Rating ★★★★★ Highest

Investment Style
Equity
Average Stock %: 65% 58% 60% 63% 72% 75% 80%

▼ Manager Change
▽ Partial Manager Change

Fund Performance vs. Category Average
■ Quarterly Fund Return +/– Category Average
— Category Baseline

Performance Quartile (within Category)

Portfolio Manager(s)

Jean-Marie Eveillard. Since 1-79. BA'57 Lycee Descartes; MBA'62 Ecole des Hautes Etudes Commerciale. Other funds currently managed: First Eagle SoGen Gold, First Eagle SoGen Overseas A, First Eagle SoGen Global I.

Charles de Vaulx. Since 3-87. BA'81 Institute Friley; MBA'84 E.S.C. Rouen. Other funds currently managed: First Eagle SoGen Gold, First Eagle SoGen Overseas A, First Eagle SoGen Global I.

History

	1990	1991	1992	1993	1994	1995	1996	1997	1998	1999	2000	12-01
NAV	16.41	18.11	18.65	22.82	22.68	24.58	26.09	25.45	23.03	24.65	22.29	23.82
Total Return %	–1.27	17.93	8.41	26.17	2.53	15.24	13.64	8.54	–0.26	19.56	9.73	10.21
+/– MSCI World	15.74	–0.36	13.64	3.67	–2.55	–5.48	0.16	–7.23	–24.60	–5.37	22.90	—
+/– JPM World Govt	–13.03	2.48	3.86	13.90	1.25	–4.08	9.20	7.18	–15.58	24.64	7.39	11.00
Income Return %	4.01	5.12	3.53	2.54	0.66	3.58	4.43	5.21	4.20	4.65	5.64	2.83
Capital Return %	–5.28	12.81	4.88	23.63	1.87	11.66	9.21	3.32	–4.47	14.92	4.09	7.38
Total Rtn % Rank Cat	60	83	50	1	1	87	76	87	93	34	4	2
Income $	0.71	0.84	0.64	0.47	0.15	0.81	1.09	1.36	1.07	1.07	1.39	0.63
Capital Gains $	0.47	0.37	0.34	0.23	0.56	0.73	0.74	1.47	1.35	1.73	3.19	0.09
Expense Ratio %	1.38	1.30	1.37	1.31	1.28	1.26	1.25	1.21	1.19	1.23	1.32	—
Income Ratio %	4.32	4.84	4.00	3.69	2.34	2.70	3.71	3.08	2.80	2.75	2.68	—
Turnover Rate %	31	24	24	18	24	13	10	13	21	10	16	—
Net Assets $mil	209.4	313.2	531.3	1,427.4	1,822.5	2,613.3	3,776.7	3,997.9	2,633.7	1,905.4	1,651.1	1,610.6

Performance 12-31-01

	1st Qtr	2nd Qtr	3rd Qtr	4th Qtr	Total
1997	2.26	7.61	3.90	–5.07	8.54
1998	7.74	–1.46	–10.97	5.52	–0.26
1999	–0.56	9.17	3.08	6.85	19.56
2000	1.62	0.72	2.93	4.15	9.73
2001	1.79	6.13	–7.64	10.45	10.21

Trailing	Total Return%	+/– MSCI World	+/– JPM World Govt	% Rank All	% Rank Cat	Growth of $10,000
3 Mo	10.45	1,009.45	13.64	40	4	11,045
6 Mo	2.01	1,001.01	–1.71	22	8	10,201
1 Yr	10.21	1,009.21	11.00	6	2	11,021
3 Yr Avg	13.08	1,012.08	14.30	7	2	14,458
5 Yr Avg	9.37	1,008.37	6.96	22	12	15,651
10 Yr Avg	11.14	1,010.14	5.88	24	33	28,743
15 Yr Avg	11.47	1,010.47	—	30	1	50,980

Tax Analysis	Tax-Adj Ret%	%Rank Cat	%Pretax Ret	%Rank Cat
3 Yr Avg	9.63	2	73.7	12
5 Yr Avg	6.11	7	65.2	23
10 Yr Avg	8.59	16	77.1	16

Potential Capital Gain Exposure: 9% of assets

Risk Analysis

Time Period	Load-Adj Return %	Risk %Rank¹ All	Risk %Rank¹ Cat	Morningstar Return	Morningstar Risk	Morningstar Risk-Adj Rating
1 Yr	2.60					
3 Yr	10.41	31	3	1.40²	0.29	★★★★★
5 Yr	7.82	39	8	0.75²	0.35	★★★★★
10 Yr	10.34	44	1	1.94²	0.32	★★★★★

Average Historical Rating (193 months): 4.2★s

¹1=low, 100=high ² T-Bill return substituted for category avg.

Category Rating (3 Yr)

1 2 3 4 5 (5)
Worst — Best

Return High
Risk Low

Other Measures	Standard Index S&P 500	Best Fit Index MSCIPCExJND
Alpha	10.1	8.1
Beta	0.38	0.35
R-Squared	46	70

Standard Deviation	10.52
Mean	13.08
Sharpe Ratio	0.88

Portfolio Analysis 11-30-01

Total Stocks: 148 Share change since 10-01	Sector	PE Ratio	YTD Return %	% Net Assets
Buderus	Industrials	21.7	—	5.85
Rayonier	Industrials	22.1	30.83	5.61
⊕ Financiera Alba	Financials	17.5	—	2.72
⊖ Manpower	Services	17.0	–10.70	2.39
⊕ Shimano	Durables	23.8	—	1.80
Security Cap Grp Cl B	Financials	11.3	26.45	1.35
IMI	Industrials	8.9	—	1.32
⊕ Eurafrance	Financials	2.5	—	1.32
⊖ Dae Duck Electncs	Technology	12.4	—	1.26
Shaw Brothers (Hong Kong)	Financials	13.5	—	1.15

Total Fixed-Income: 55	Date of Maturity	Amount $000	Value $000	% Net Assets
US Treasury Note 3.375%	01-15-07	40,000	45,628	2.91
Hornbach Hldg Pfd		385	18,631	1.19
Freeport McMoRan Cl Gold ARP		700	16,800	1.07
Riverwood Hldg 10.25%	04-01-06	10,000	10,425	0.66
Sealed Air A Cv Pfd $2.00		210	9,608	0.61
CalEnergy Cap Cv Pfd 6.5%		250	9,188	0.59
Christiana Bank FRN	11-29-49	10,000	8,163	0.52
Bangkok Bk 144A 9.025%	03-15-29	10,000	8,050	0.51
Sagem Pfd		185	7,883	0.50
US Treasury Note 4.25%	01-15-10	7,415	7,859	0.50

Equity Style
Style: Value
Size: Medium-Cap

Fixed-Income Style
Duration: —
Quality: —
NA

	Portfolio Avg	Rel S&P
Price/Earnings Ratio	19.4	0.75
Price/Cash Flow	14.0	1.09
Price/Book Ratio	2.3	0.66
3 Yr Earnings Growth	12.1	0.65
Med Mkt Cap $mil	1,548	0.06

Avg Eff Duration	—
Avg Eff Maturity	—
Avg Credit Quality	—
Avg Wtd Coupon	6.44%

Special Securities % assets 11-30-01	
Restricted/Illiquid Secs	1
Emerging-Markets Secs	8
Options/Futures/Warrants	No

Composition % assets 11-30-01	
Cash	0.1
U.S. Stocks	32.3
Foreign Stocks	47.5
U.S. Bonds	12.4
Foreign Bonds	0.6
Other	7.2

Country Exposure 05-28-99	% of Assets
U.S.	23.2
Japan	10.4
France	7.9

Analysis by Gregg Wolper 12-18-01

By taking what other investors don't want, First Eagle SoGen Global Fund has amassed a record many investors would envy.

To say that managers Jean-Marie Eveillard and Charles de Vaulx don't follow the crowd is an understatement. This portfolio shows few household names, and many of its favorites barely show up on rival managers' radar screens. For example, top holding Buderus, a German maker of heating systems, takes up 6.5% of assets here; only two other managers devote as much as 1% to that firm.

The managers' strict-value approach doesn't always yield quick results. But they're willing to wait; the fund's turnover rate is miniscule. In some years, that means the fund lags more-growth-oriented rivals. Indeed, for much of the mid-1990s, this fund's performance was unimpressive. But over time, this strategy has resulted in fine returns with remarkably low volatility.

In 2001, the fund succeeded on several fronts. First, several of its larger holdings, including Buderus, Canadian Pacific, and Legrand (a French maker of electrical components), rose sharply after takeover bids or internal reorganizations. In addition, the managers hedged most of their yen and some of their euro exposure into the dollar, which helped as the dollar rose. Third, the fund's small stake in gold-related assets—Eveillard says he considers gold a perennial insurance policy—helped out as that asset enjoyed a rare good year. Thus, through Dec. 17, 2001, the fund has topped the international-hybrid category with a year-to-date gain of 7.9%.

Don't expect this portfolio to change much anytime soon: Eveillard says he's recently had trouble finding good stocks selling at prices cheap enough to interest him, so he'll stick with what he's got. That mixture of stinginess and patience has rewarded shareholders well over time—and is likely to continue doing so.

Address:	1345 Avenue of the Americas New York, NY 10105 212–698–3000 / 800–334–2143
Web Address:	www.firsteaglesogen.com
Inception:	04-28-70
Advisor:	Arnhold & S. Bleichroeder
Subadvisor:	None
NTF Plans:	Datalynx , Fidelity Inst.

Minimum Purchase:	$1000	Add: $100	IRA: $1000
Min Auto Inv Plan:	$100	Add: $100	
Sales Fees:	5.00%L, 0.25%B, 2.00%R		
Management Fee:	1.0% mx./.75% mn.		
Actual Fees:	Mgt: 0.75%	Dist: 0.25%	
Expense Projections:	3Yr: $871	5Yr: $1142	10Yr: $1914
Avg Brok Commission:	—	Income Distrib: Annually	
Total Cost (relative to category):		Average	

Forward Hoover Small Cap Equity

Ticker	Load	NAV	Yield	Total Assets	Mstar Category
FFSCX	12b–1 only	$14.78	0.0%	$85.4 mil	Small Growth

Prospectus Objective: Small Company

Forward Hoover Small Capitalization Equity Fund seeks total return.

The fund normally invests at least 65% of assets in equity securities of companies with market capitalizations no larger than the largest market capitalization of the companies included in the Russell 2000 Index. It typically expects that the weighted average market capitalization is less than $1 billion. The fund may invest in all types of equity and debt securities, including common and preferred stocks, convertibles, warrants, options, restricted securities, trust units or certificates, bonds, notes, commercial paper, and various types of depositary receipts.

Prior to March 2, 2000, the fund was named Forward Small Capitalization Equity Fund.

Historical Profile

Return	Above Avg
Risk	Average
Rating	★★★★ Above Avg

Investment Style
Equity
Average Stock %: 100% (1999), 100% (2000), 98% (12-01)

▼ Manager Change
▽ Partial Manager Change

Fund Performance vs. Category Average
■ Quarterly Fund Return +/– Category Average
— Category Baseline

Performance Quartile (within Category)

Portfolio Manager(s)

Irene Hoover, CFA. Since 10-98. BA'63 Stanford U.; MA'65 Northwestern U.

1990	1991	1992	1993	1994	1995	1996	1997	1998	1999	2000	12-01	History
—	—	—	—	—	—	—	—	11.39	12.19	14.26	14.78	NAV
—	—	—	—	—	—	—	—	13.99*	7.03	17.88	4.27	Total Return %
—	—	—	—	—	—	—	—	–7.29*	–14.01	26.98	16.14	+/– S&P 500
—	—	—	—	—	—	—	—	—	–36.06	40.31	13.50	+/– Russ 2000 Grth
—	—	—	—	—	—	—	—	0.09	0.01	0.00	0.00	Income Return %
—	—	—	—	—	—	—	—	13.90	7.02	17.88	4.27	Capital Return %
—	—	—	—	—	—	—	—	—	95	9	18	Total Rtn % Rank Cat
—	—	—	—	—	—	—	—	0.01	0.00	0.00	0.00	Income $
—	—	—	—	—	—	—	—	0.00	0.00	0.11	0.09	Capital Gains $
—	—	—	—	—	—	—	—	1.45	1.45	1.64	—	Expense Ratio %
—	—	—	—	—	—	—	—	0.21	–0.54	1.99	—	Income Ratio %
—	—	—	—	—	—	—	—	23	134	183	—	Turnover Rate %
—	—	—	—	—	—	—	—	29.6	46.8	85.4	—	Net Assets $mil

Performance 12-31-01

	1st Qtr	2nd Qtr	3rd Qtr	4th Qtr	Total
1997	—	—	—	—	—
1998	—	—	—	13.99	13.99 *
1999	–4.21	15.12	–8.92	6.56	7.03
2000	19.36	3.57	1.26	–5.84	17.88
2001	–5.47	8.53	–16.75	22.07	4.27

Trailing	Total Return%	+/– S&P 500	+/– Russ 2000 Grth	% Rank All	% Rank Cat	Growth of $10,000
3 Mo	22.07	11.39	–4.10	11	58	12,207
6 Mo	1.63	7.19	10.90	28	10	10,163
1 Yr	4.27	16.14	13.50	28	18	10,427
3 Yr Avg	9.57	10.60	9.32	12	43	13,155
5 Yr Avg	—	—	—	—	—	—
10 Yr Avg	—	—	—	—	—	—
15 Yr Avg	—	—	—	—	—	—

Tax Analysis	Tax-Adj Ret%	%Rank Cat	%Pretax Ret	%Rank Cat
3 Yr Avg	9.47	35	99.0	4
5 Yr Avg	—	—	—	—
10 Yr Avg	—	—	—	—

Potential Capital Gain Exposure: 19% of assets

Risk Analysis

Time Period	Load-Adj Return %	Risk %Rank[1] All	Risk %Rank[1] Cat	Morningstar Return	Morningstar Risk	Morningstar Risk-Adj Rating
1 Yr	4.27					
3 Yr	9.57	76	17	1.03[2]	1.05	★★★★
5 Yr	—	—	—	—	—	
Incept	13.26	—	—	—	—	

Average Historical Rating (4 months): 3.8★s

[1] 1=low, 100=high [2] T-Bill return substituted for category avg.

Category Rating (3 Yr)

1 2 3 4 5 (Worst → Best): 3

Return	Average
Risk	Below Avg

Other Measures	Standard Index S&P 500	Best Fit Index SPMid400
Alpha	12.1	–0.1
Beta	0.98	1.06
R-Squared	49	75
Standard Deviation		26.57
Mean		9.57
Sharpe Ratio		0.20

Portfolio Analysis 10-31-01

Share change since 08-01 Total Stocks: 74	Sector	PE	YTD Ret%	% Assets
Tractor Sply	Retail	13.8	300.90	3.07
⊖ Investment Tech Grp	Financials	26.6	40.37	2.79
⊕ ITT Educational Svcs	Services	28.6	67.59	2.09
⊖ Maximus	Services	22.6	20.38	2.06
Massey Energy Company	Industrials	—	63.97	1.96
⊖ Polycom	Technology	67.5	6.87	1.95
⊕ Florida Rock Inds	Industrials	15.1	41.77	1.95
Mid Atlantic Medical Svcs	Health	18.8	14.57	1.94
Gabelli Asset Mgmt Cl A	Financials	21.3	30.17	1.83
Legg Mason	Financials	23.6	–7.53	1.81
Whirlpool	Durables	71.9	57.27	1.79
First Health Grp	Health	25.8	6.26	1.77
⊕ SkyWest	Services	27.1	–11.10	1.69
Whole Foods Market	Retail	36.0	42.53	1.67
Waddell & Reed Finl Cl A	Financials	23.3	–13.40	1.67
⊕ Sylvan Learning Sys	Services	39.4	48.99	1.64
⊖ American Italian Pasta	Staples	29.0	56.75	1.54
⊕ Riverstone Networks	Technology	—	—	1.53
Msc.Software	Technology	21.4	98.73	1.49
Scottish Annuity & Life Hldg	Financials	—	63.15	1.48
Varian	Technology	22.2	–4.24	1.48
Swift Transp	Services	71.7	8.57	1.43
⊖ H & R Block	Services	25.5	120.00	1.38
☼ Exar	Technology	54.9	–32.60	1.38
Gentex	Durables	30.7	43.52	1.37

Current Investment Style

Style: Value Blnd Growth; Size: Large Med Small (Small Growth)

	Stock Port Avg	Relative S&P 500 Current	Relative S&P 500 Hist	Rel Cat
Price/Earnings Ratio	28.1	0.91	—	0.87
Price/Book Ratio	4.6	0.81	—	0.94
Price/Cash Flow	18.4	1.02	—	0.84
3 Yr Earnings Growth	19.6	1.34	—	0.78
1 Yr Earnings Est%	9.0	—	—	1.15
Med Mkt Cap $mil	1,360	0.0	—	1.30

Analysis by Kelli Stebel 12-10-01

This solid, moderate offering is worth a long look.

Forward Hoover Small Cap Equity isn't topping the charts. Its three-year record, in fact, looks fairly middling. But that doesn't tell the whole story here. Manager Irene Hoover's valuation-conscious strategy keeps the fund at arm's length from the small-cap arena's dicier names. That approach holds this offering back during momentum-led markets, like 1999, when the fund finished in the small-growth category's bottom decile. But when the market became more discerning about valuations, this fund shines. Indeed, in the past 20 months, the fund has easily topped its peers. From March 2000, when the current correction began, through November 2001, the fund is up 2%, while its average peer has lost more than 20%.

Hoover has made several savvy moves of late, giving the fund an edge over its peers. For starters, she came into 2001 with a huge overweight in energy. That could have been disastrous as energy sold off dramatically in April, but Hoover began trimming her positions early in the first quarter, avoiding much of that sector's wrath. In addition, Hoover moved into some tech names in early October. She added holdings like software developer MoldFlow, which have helped the fund participate in the recent growth rally.

This isn't the first time Hoover has succeeded running retail mutual funds. Hoover built an excellent record at Jurika & Voyles Small-Cap during her three-year tenure, and has brought the same mix of value and growth investing to this offering. It's worth noting that this fund isn't apt to rally as much when growth comes back into style, but its well-diversified portfolio, experienced management, and moderate approach make it an easy choice for an investor's small-cap slot.

Special Securities % assets 10-31-01	
Restricted/Illiquid Secs	0
Emerging-Markets Secs	2
Options/Futures/Warrants	No

Composition % assets 10-31-01	
Cash	17.0
Stocks*	83.0
Bonds	0.0
Other	0.0
*Foreign (% stocks)	6.4

Market Cap	
Giant	0.0
Large	0.0
Medium	49.9
Small	47.2
Micro	3.0

Sector Weightings	% of Stocks	Rel S&P	5-Year High	5-Year Low
Utilities	1.0	0.3	—	—
Energy	10.2	1.4	—	—
Financials	17.5	1.0	—	—
Industrials	10.3	0.9	—	—
Durables	4.7	3.0	—	—
Staples	2.7	0.3	—	—
Services	16.2	1.5	—	—
Retail	11.9	1.8	—	—
Health	6.6	0.4	—	—
Technology	19.0	1.0	—	—

Address:	433 California Street Ste 1010 San Francisco, CA 94104 800–999–6809 / 800–999–6809
Web Address:	www.forwardfunds.com
*Inception:	09-30-98
Advisor:	Webster Inv. Mgmt.
Subadvisor:	Hoover Cap. Mgmt.
NTF Plans:	Fidelity Inst. , Waterhouse

Minimum Purchase:	$2500	Add: $250 IRA: $250
Min Auto Inv Plan:	—	Add: —
Sales Fees:	0.25%B	
Management Fee:	1.1%, .35%A	
Actual Fees:	Mgt: 0.90%	Dist: —
Expense Projections:	3Yr: $32*	5Yr: $47* 10Yr: —
Avg Brok Commission:	—	Income Distrib: Annually
Total Cost (relative to category):	—	

FPA Capital

Ticker	Load	NAV	Yield	Total Assets	Mstar Category
FPPTX	5.25%	$28.26	0.1%	$551.6 mil	Small Value

Prospectus Objective: Small Company

FPA Capital Fund seeks long-term growth of capital. Current income is secondary.

The fund invests primarily in common stocks of medium and small companies that the advisor believes have above-average ability to increase market value. It may also invest in U.S. government and government agency obligations, corporate debt securities, preferred stocks, and convertibles. In selecting investments, the advisor considers a company's profitability, book value, replacement cost of assets, and free cash flow. The fund may invest up to 10% of assets in foreign issues.

Historical Profile

Return High
Risk Above Avg
Rating ★★★★★ Highest

Investment Style
Equity
Average Stock %: 71% 75% 80% 74% 96% 95% 95%

▼ Manager Change
▽ Partial Manager Change

Fund Performance vs. Category Average
■ Quarterly Fund Return +/– Category Average
– Category Baseline

Performance Quartile (within Category)

Portfolio Manager(s)

Robert L. Rodriguez, CFA. Since 7-84. BS'71 U. of Southern California; MBA'75 U. of Southern California. Other fund currently managed: FPA New Income.

1990	1991	1992	1993	1994	1995	1996	1997	1998	1999	2000	12-01	History
10.91	16.96	18.89	20.06	20.61	27.50	34.01	36.28	31.04	31.02	22.29	28.26	NAV
–13.80	64.51	21.57	16.74	10.37	38.39	37.76	17.70	–0.42	14.24	–3.08	38.13	Total Return %
–10.68	34.03	13.95	6.68	9.06	0.86	14.82	–15.65	–29.00	–6.80	6.02	50.01	+/– S&P 500
7.98	22.81	–7.57	–7.10	11.92	12.64	16.39	–13.99	6.01	15.71	–25.89	24.11	+/– Russell 2000 V
1.56	1.39	0.42	0.27	0.21	0.68	1.29	1.27	1.89	0.71	0.49	0.13	Income Return %
–15.35	63.12	21.15	16.47	10.17	37.71	36.47	16.43	–2.31	13.52	–3.57	38.00	Capital Return %
59	1	37	55	1	6	7	98	17	20	97	3	Total Rtn % Rank Cat
0.21	0.15	0.07	0.05	0.04	0.14	0.34	0.42	0.65	0.22	0.14	0.03	Income $
1.06	0.58	1.34	1.70	1.34	0.73	2.60	2.84	4.79	4.03	7.76	2.39	Capital Gains $
1.17	1.21	1.08	1.06	1.03	0.95	0.87	0.84	0.83	0.86	0.86	—	Expense Ratio %
1.37	1.32	0.55	0.29	0.20	0.48	1.28	1.27	1.38	1.20	0.35	—	Income Ratio %
21	12	13	19	16	11	21	21	24	19	18	—	Turnover Rate %
66.1	98.9	125.1	153.7	191.8	353.0	568.0	730.9	673.7	538.8	384.1	551.6	Net Assets $mil

Performance 12-31-01

	1st Qtr	2nd Qtr	3rd Qtr	4th Qtr	Total
1997	0.58	6.35	12.12	–1.87	17.70
1998	11.18	0.18	–23.61	17.04	–0.42
1999	–2.26	21.00	–9.58	6.82	14.24
2000	7.29	–7.87	6.97	–8.34	–3.08
2001	3.23	21.77	–15.96	30.75	38.13

Trailing	Total Return%	+/– S&P 500	+/– Russ 2000V	% Rank All	% Rank Cat	Growth of $10,000
3 Mo	30.75	20.07	14.03	4	2	13,075
6 Mo	9.88	15.44	8.73	1	3	10,988
1 Yr	38.13	50.01	24.11	1	3	13,813
3 Yr Avg	15.21	16.24	3.89	5	29	15,293
5 Yr Avg	12.38	1.68	1.19	9	40	17,925
10 Yr Avg	18.27	5.34	3.16	1	3	53,534
15 Yr Avg	18.24	4.51	5.40	1	1	123,436

Tax Analysis	Tax-Adj Ret%	%Rank Cat	%Pretax Ret	%Rank Cat
3 Yr Avg	10.56	53	69.4	94
5 Yr Avg	8.35	57	67.5	98
10 Yr Avg	14.83	10	81.2	65

Potential Capital Gain Exposure: 15% of assets

Risk Analysis

Time Period	Load-Adj Return %	Risk %Rank[1] All	Risk %Rank[1] Cat	Morningstar Return	Morningstar Risk	Morningstar Risk-Adj Rating
1 Yr	30.88					
3 Yr	13.16	74	92	1.88[2]	1.03	★★★★
5 Yr	11.18	75	90	1.51[2]	1.03	★★★★
10 Yr	17.63	82	96	2.53	1.11	★★★★★

Average Historical Rating (193 months): 3.3★s

[1] 1=low, 100=high [2] T-Bill return substituted for category avg.

Category Rating (3 Yr)

1 2 3 4 5
Worst Best

Return Above Avg
Risk High

Other Measures	Standard Index S&P 500	Best Fit Index SPMid400
Alpha	19.4	5.2
Beta	1.16	1.12
R-Squared	55	69

Standard Deviation	30.92
Mean	15.21
Sharpe Ratio	0.38

Portfolio Analysis 09-30-01

Share change since 06-01 Total Stocks: 34	Sector	PE	YTD Ret%	% Assets
⊖ Ross Stores	Retail	17.3	91.38	8.82
⊖ Michaels Stores	Retail	29.3	148.60	8.72
Avnet	Technology	—	19.93	6.90
Arrow Electncs	Technology	NMF	4.45	6.81
Storage Tech	Technology	36.9	129.60	5.49
US Treasury Note 3.38%	N/A	—	—	5.32
⊕ Conseco	Financials	—	–66.10	4.38
Thor Inds	Industrials	17.7	88.14	3.81
Countrywide Credit Ind	Financials	10.6	–17.70	3.59
Big Lots	Retail	17.1	–2.02	3.35
Champion Enterprises	Industrials	—	347.60	3.32
Celanese AG	Industrials	19.5	—	3.08
⊕ Centex	Industrials	10.2	52.56	2.83
Hutchinson Tech	Technology	—	68.87	2.79
⊕ Fleetwood Enterprises	Durables	—	9.47	2.67
☼ Ensco Intl	Energy	15.7	–26.70	2.51
Belden	Industrials	14.3	–6.40	2.38
☼ National-Oilwell	Energy	20.6	–46.70	2.38
☼ Patterson-UTI Energy	Energy	10.2	–37.40	2.37
Horace Mann Educators	Financials	NMF	1.49	2.22
Recoton	Durables	—	78.36	1.96
Coachmen Inds	Durables	—	16.43	1.90
Westcorp	Financials	10.2	27.46	1.57
⊖ Reebok Intl	Staples	16.0	–3.07	1.45
Oregon Steel Mills	Industrials	—	365.60	1.35

Current Investment Style

Style: Value Blnd Growth; Size: Large Med Small

	Stock Port Avg	Relative S&P 500 Current	Relative S&P 500 Hist	Rel Cat
Price/Earnings Ratio	25.6	0.83	0.65	1.18
Price/Book Ratio	2.0	0.35	0.26	0.83
Price/Cash Flow	14.6	0.81	0.57	1.15
3 Yr Earnings Growth	8.5	0.58	0.65	0.73
1 Yr Earnings Est%	9.3	—	—	–2.35
Med Mkt Cap $mil	1,914	0.0	0.0	2.20

Analysis by Christopher Davis 07-31-01

Again and again, FPA Capital Fund's against-the-grain approach makes a compelling case for itself.

Former shareholders who dismissed this offering's contrarian approach as hopelessly old-fashioned in 2000 have probably removed their feet from their mouths by now. After suffering an atypical bottom-decile showing in 2000, the fund has staged a strong rebound in 2001. Indeed, its 27% gain for the year to date through July 30, 2001, is among the best in the small-value group. Top picks, such as retailer Ross Stores and network storage manufacturer Electronic Storage, hurt performance in 2000, but they have snapped back nicely this year.

Such turnarounds flow from manager Bob Rodriguez's strategy. He is drawn to firms that have stumbled and that have bargain-basement price multiples to show for it. As the fund's glacial turnover rate suggests, he is patient—often waiting years for companies to sort out their problems. Rodriguez bought Oregon Steel Mills in late 1997, for example, only to see its share price plunge over the next three years. The maker of steel for natural-gas pipelines is on the rebound in 2001, however, and Rodriguez is hopeful that demand for its product will continue to increase.

That kind of patience may pay off over the long haul, but the fund can stumble when Rodriguez's picks don't recover as quickly as he thinks they will. The fund can also get burned by its concentrated approach—nearly 60% of assets were stuffed into its top-10 names in June 2001. Consequently, the fund is much more volatile than its typical peer.

But shareholders have been handsomely rewarded for the bumpy ride through time: The fund's trailing 10-year return, all earned under Rodriguez, is one of the best in Morningstar's database. Those who can stomach its volatility will find this offering an appealing choice. But given its poor tax efficiency, investors may want to hold the fund in a nontaxable account.

Special Securities % assets 09-30-01	
Restricted/Illiquid Secs	0
Emerging-Markets Secs	0
Options/Futures/Warrants	No

Composition % assets 09-30-01	
Cash	0.0
Stocks*	94.5
Bonds	5.5
Other	0.0
*Foreign (% stocks)	3.4

Market Cap	
Giant	0.0
Large	0.0
Medium	59.9
Small	30.1
Micro	10.0

Sector Weightings	% of Stocks	Rel S&P	5-Year High	5-Year Low
Utilities	0.0	0.0	0	0
Energy	7.9	1.1	8	0
Financials	12.8	0.7	33	9
Industrials	19.6	1.7	26	7
Durables	9.2	5.9	21	7
Staples	0.0	0.0	0	0
Services	2.4	0.2	12	0
Retail	23.7	3.5	28	0
Health	0.0	0.0	14	0
Technology	24.4	1.3	35	18

Address:	11400 W. Olympic Boulevard Suite 1200, Los Angeles, CA 90064, 800–982–4372 / 310–473–0225
Web Address:	—
Inception:	02-01-68
Advisor:	First Pacific Adv.
Subadvisor:	None
NTF Plans:	N/A

Minimum Purchase:	$1500	Add: $100	IRA: $100
Min Auto Inv Plan:	$1500	Add: $100	
Sales Fees:	5.25%L		
Management Fee:	.75% mx./.65% mn.		
Actual Fees:	Mgt: 0.65%	Dist: —	
Expense Projections:	3Yr: $90*	5Yr: $108*	10Yr: $161*
Avg Brok Commission:	—	Income Distrib: Semi-Ann.	
Total Cost (relative to category):	—		

FPA New Income

Ticker	Load	NAV	Yield	SEC Yield	Total Assets	Mstar Category
FPNIX	3.50%	$10.93	5.8%	—	$705.3 mil	Interm–Term Bond

Prospectus Objective: Corp Bond—High Quality

FPA New Income seeks current income and long-term total return.

The fund invests at least 75% of assets in U.S. government obligations, nonconvertible debt securities rated at least AA, bank obligations, repurchase agreements, and commercial paper. It may invest the balance of assets in securities rated below AA, convertible securities, and preferred stocks. The fund may invest up to 10% of assets in foreign securities. The portfolio's average maturity may vary substantially over time.

Prior to January 1982, the fund purchased mainly equities.

Prior to July 1984, it was named Transamerica New Income.

Historical Profile

Return: High
Risk: Below Avg
Rating: ★★★★★ Highest

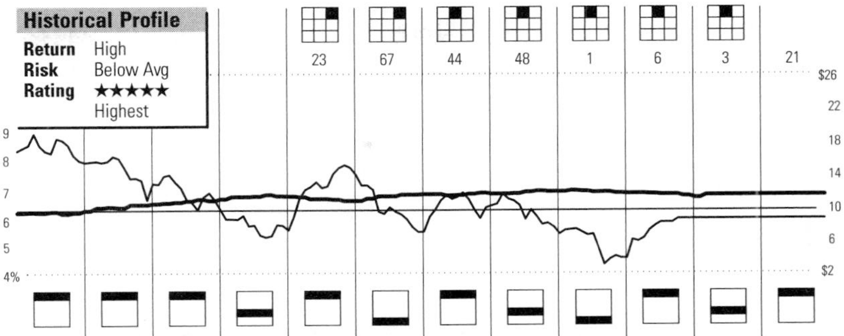

Investment Style: Fixed-Income

Income Rtn %Rank Cat: 23 | 67 | 44 | 48 | 1 | 6 | 3 | 21

Growth of Principal vs. Interest Rate Shifts
— Principal Value $000 (NAV with capital gains reinvested)
— Interest Rate % on 10 Yr Treasury
▼ Manager Change
▽ Partial Manager Change
► Mgr Unknown After
◄ Mgr Unknown Before

Performance Quartile (within Category)

Portfolio Manager(s)

Robert L. Rodriguez, CFA. Since 7-84. BS'71 U. of Southern California; MBA'75 U. of Southern California. Other fund currently managed: FPA Capital.

1990	1991	1992	1993	1994	1995	1996	1997	1998	1999	2000	12-01	History
9.84	10.72	10.92	11.23	10.40	11.17	11.09	11.24	10.74	10.30	10.38	10.93	NAV
8.38	18.80	11.12	10.17	1.46	14.36	7.12	8.31	3.86	3.39	9.32	12.33	Total Return %
–0.58	2.80	3.72	0.42	4.38	–4.11	3.51	–1.37	–4.82	4.22	–2.31	3.91	+/– LB Aggregate
–0.79	4.18	3.95	1.39	3.39	–0.95	3.07	0.44	–4.56	3.00	–0.79	3.35	+/– LB Int Govt/Corp
8.15	9.04	6.99	6.50	6.60	6.60	6.21	6.30	7.71	6.78	7.69	6.30	Income Return %
0.23	9.76	4.13	3.67	–5.14	7.76	0.91	2.01	–3.86	–3.39	1.63	6.03	Capital Return %
20	17	3	57	1	90	2	70	98	2	65	2	Total Rtn % Rank Cat
0.78	0.86	0.72	0.69	0.71	0.67	0.67	0.68	0.84	0.71	0.77	0.64	Income $
0.07	0.01	0.20	0.07	0.27	0.00	0.16	0.05	0.08	0.09	0.08	0.07	Capital Gains $
0.94	0.87	0.78	0.73	0.74	0.68	0.63	0.59	0.59	0.60	0.61	—	Expense Ratio %
8.48	8.46	7.17	6.48	6.41	6.50	6.44	6.37	6.06	6.43	7.31	—	Income Ratio %
29	26	22	41	39	31	16	69	47	24	21	—	Turnover Rate %
38.3	54.9	87.7	114.8	129.9	233.6	375.5	563.2	582.2	515.3	486.1	705.3	Net Assets $mil

Performance 12-31-01

	1st Qtr	2nd Qtr	3rd Qtr	4th Qtr	Total
1997	0.56	3.16	2.83	1.53	8.31
1998	1.99	0.90	0.72	0.20	3.86
1999	1.30	2.14	0.19	–0.27	3.39
2000	3.01	–0.67	4.43	2.31	9.32
2001	5.68	1.76	3.23	1.19	12.33

Trailing	Total Return%	+/– LB Agg	+/– LB ITGvt/Corp	% Rank All	% Rank Cat	Growth of $10,000
3 Mo	1.19	1.15	1.10	73	7	10,119
6 Mo	4.45	–0.20	–0.25	6	32	10,445
1 Yr	12.33	3.91	3.35	4	2	11,233
3 Yr Avg	8.28	2.01	1.88	14	1	12,696
5 Yr Avg	7.39	–0.04	0.29	33	8	14,281
10 Yr Avg	8.07	0.84	1.26	43	2	21,731
15 Yr Avg	9.06	0.94	1.43	47	1	36,748

Tax Analysis	Tax-Adj Ret%	%Rank Cat	%Pretax Ret	%Rank Cat
3 Yr Avg	5.27	1	63.6	3
5 Yr Avg	4.38	18	59.4	62
10 Yr Avg	5.08	1	63.0	8

Potential Capital Gain Exposure: 0% of assets

Risk Analysis

Time Period	Load-Adj Return %	Risk %Rank[1] All	Risk %Rank[1] Cat	Morningstar Return	Morningstar Risk	Morningstar Risk-Adj Rating
1 Yr	8.40					
3 Yr	7.00	4	1	0.44[2]	0.36	★★★★★
5 Yr	6.62	5	1	0.36[2]	0.40	★★★★★
10 Yr	7.69	4	1	0.87[2]	0.41	★★★★★

Average Historical Rating (193 months): 4.3★s

[1]1=low, 100=high [2] T-Bill return substituted for category avg.

Category Rating (3 Yr)

1 2 3 4 5 — Worst … Best

Return: High
Risk: Low

Other Measures	Standard Index LB Agg	Best Fit Index LB Corp
Alpha	2.5	2.8
Beta	0.54	0.52
R–Squared	32	42

Standard Deviation	3.39
Mean	8.28
Sharpe Ratio	1.13

Portfolio Analysis 06-30-01

Total Fixed-Income: 69	Date of Maturity	Amount $000	Value $000	% Net Assets
US Treasury Note 3.375%	01-15-07	222,722	225,575	37.52
FHLMC CMO 6%	03-15-09	22,316	22,190	3.69
GNMA 7%	09-20-28	21,127	21,348	3.55
FNMA CMO Z 7%	11-25-19	15,249	15,240	2.53
FNMA 7%	01-01-30	13,803	13,924	2.32
Oregon Steel Mills 11%	06-15-03	15,100	13,590	2.26
FNMA CMO Z 7%	04-25-24	13,481	13,447	2.24
FHLMC CMO 6%	08-15-08	11,250	11,152	1.85
FHLMC CMO 6%	09-15-08	10,817	10,729	1.78
GNMA CMO 7.5%	12-20-29	10,538	10,422	1.73
CKE Restaurants Cv 4.25%	03-15-04	19,000	9,500	1.58
Charming Shoppes Cv 7.5%	07-15-06	9,600	9,096	1.51
FNMA 7%	01-01-31	7,377	7,425	1.24
Riviera Hldgs 10%	08-15-04	8,000	6,800	1.13
Advantica Restrnt 11.25%	01-15-08	11,428	6,628	1.10
FNMA Debenture 7.25%	01-15-10	6,000	6,440	1.07
Green Tree Finl 7.3%	03-15-27	9,967	6,217	1.03
FHLMC CMO 8.5%	03-15-26	5,655	5,950	0.99
GNMA 7%	05-20-24	5,870	5,895	0.98
GNMA 7.5%	10-20-27	5,609	5,756	0.96

Current Investment Style

Not Available

Avg Eff Duration	—
Avg Eff Maturity	—
Avg Credit Quality	—
Avg Wtd Coupon	5.63%
Avg Wtd Price	96.23% of par

Special Securities % assets 06-30-01	
Restricted/Illiquid Secs	0
Exotic Mortgage–Backed	3
Emerging–Markets Secs	0
Options/Futures/Warrants	No

Coupon Range	% of Bonds	Rel Cat
0%	0.00	0.00
0% to 7%	58.12	1.08
7% to 8.5%	31.56	0.91
8.5% to 10%	3.08	0.43
More than 10%	7.26	2.67

1.00=Category Average

Credit Analysis % bonds 12-31-00			
US Govt	77	BB	6
AAA	0	B	10
AA	1	Below B	0
A	0	NR/NA	5
BBB	2		

Composition % assets 06-30-01			
Cash	13.9	Bonds	81.1
Stocks	0.0	Other	5.0

Sector Breakdown % bonds 06-30-01			
US Treasuries	0	CMOs	0
GNMA mtgs	12	ARMs	0
FNMA mtgs	14	Other	17
FHLMC mtgs	13		

Analysis by Alan Papier 11-08-01

FPA New Income Fund remains vigilant against bonds' sworn enemies.

This fund's strategy is predicated on the notion that rising interest rates can destroy the value of bonds. While that paradigm can explain much about bond market performance, this fund's exceptional long-term risk/reward profile shows that it has guarded against rising rates better than most peers. In 1994, for example, when rates climbed quickly, the fund led its category with a 1.5% gain and was one of only two intermediate-term bond offerings to finish in the black.

With the Federal Reserve aggressively slashing rates throughout 2001, several interest-rate benchmarks have hit all-time lows. Thus, despite the still-weak economy, management is worried that interest rates can only rise and has shortened the fund's duration (a measure of interest-rate sensitivity) from 4.1 years at 2001's start to about 2.5 in mid-October. The fund's duration is typically below average, but now it's among the shortest in the category.

That defensive posture has kept the fund from rallying as hard as its peers over the past couple months. Indeed, the Fed has continued to push down short-term rates, and long-term rates plummeted after the Treasury announced that it would cease 30-year bond issuance.

Still, the fund continues to impress. It ranked in the top 15% of the category for the year to date through Nov. 7, 2001, and had been one of the top performers in the group through the end of September. Inflation-indexed Treasuries, or TIPS, which have consumed at least one third of the fund's assets throughout the year, have topped the performance charts for the broad bond market. Like rising rates, inflation, too, can take a big bite out of bond investors' returns.

This fund should appeal to investors willing to give their core bond fund room to roam. We think it's one of the best in its class.

Address:	11400 W. Olympic Boulevard Suite 1200 Los Angeles, CA 90064 800–982–4372 / 310–473–0225
Web Address:	—
Inception:	04-01-69
Advisor:	First Pacific Adv.
Subadvisor:	None
NTF Plans:	N/A

Minimum Purchase:	$1500	Add: $100 IRA: $100
Min Auto Inv Plan:	$1500	Add: $100
Sales Fees:	3.50%L	
Management Fee:	.50%	
Actual Fees:	Mgt: 0.50%	Dist: —
Expense Projections:	3Yr: $63*	5Yr: $76* 10Yr: $115*
Avg Brok Commission:	—	Income Distrib: Quarterly
Total Cost (relative to category):	—	

FPA Perennial

Ticker	Load	NAV	Yield	Total Assets	Mstar Category
FPPFX	5.25%	$23.15	0.0%	$51.9 mil	Small Blend

Prospectus Objective: Growth and Income

FPA Perennial Fund seeks long-term growth of capital; current income is a secondary concern.

The fund invests in common stocks chosen for their attractive value, growth prospects, and quality of management. The advisor generally seeks companies with consistently high returns on invested capital and substantial reinvestment in the business. The fund may invest up to 25% of assets in foreign securities; it may not invest more than 10% of assets in foreign issues that are not ADRs.

The fund serves primarily as an investment vehicle for individual, partnership, and corporate retirement plans.

Historical Profile
Return High
Risk Average
Rating ★★★★★ Highest

Investment Style
Equity
Average Stock %: 94% 98% 99% 93% 99% 100% 97%

▼ Manager Change
▽ Partial Manager Change

Fund Performance vs. Category Average
■ Quarterly Fund Return +/– Category Average
— Category Baseline

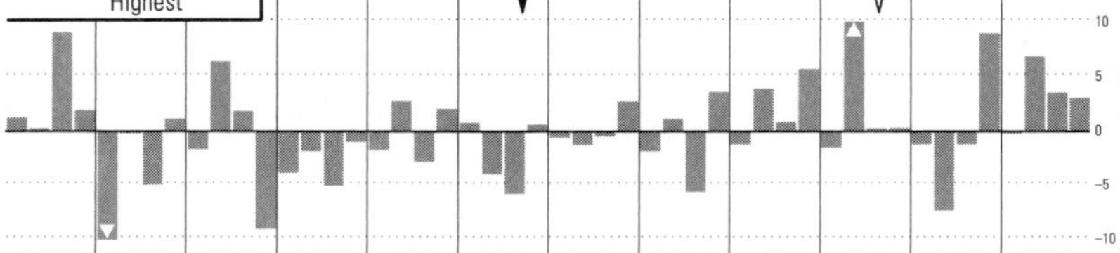

Performance Quartile (within Category)

Portfolio Manager(s)

Eric S. Ende. Since 9-95. MBA New York U.; MA Oxford U. Other fund currently managed: FPA Paramount.

Steven R. Geist, CFA. Since 8-99. BS New York U.; MS Purdue U. Other fund currently managed: FPA Paramount.

1990	1991	1992	1993	1994	1995	1996	1997	1998	1999	2000	12-01	History
19.82	22.40	23.94	23.76	21.97	22.36	22.58	24.00	20.15	20.45	20.59	23.15	NAV
0.97	21.69	13.07	4.64	–0.04	17.27	20.39	24.30	4.80	25.31	10.16	22.73	Total Return %
4.08	–8.79	5.45	–5.42	–1.35	–20.26	–2.55	–9.05	–23.78	4.27	19.27	34.61	+/– S&P 500
20.47	–24.36	–5.34	–14.27	1.79	–11.17	3.86	1.93	7.35	4.05	13.19	20.24	+/– Russell 2000
5.28	3.78	2.60	2.00	2.00	2.13	1.03	0.22	0.48	0.00	0.00	0.00	Income Return %
–4.31	17.91	10.47	2.64	–2.03	15.15	19.37	24.08	4.31	25.31	10.16	22.73	Capital Return %
16	88	57	90	41	84	49	58	10	20	57	8	Total Rtn % Rank Cat
1.15	0.73	0.57	0.47	0.46	0.44	0.22	0.05	0.11	0.00	0.00	0.00	Income $
1.85	0.71	0.67	0.76	1.31	2.48	3.41	3.19	4.63	4.56	1.81	2.07	Capital Gains $
1.14	1.10	1.08	1.02	1.13	1.19	1.19	1.16	1.16	1.30	—	—	Expense Ratio %
3.78	3.11	2.37	2.03	1.95	1.63	0.48	0.21	1.47	–0.15	—	—	Income Ratio %
29	33	30	43	31	58	30	19	34	16	—	—	Turnover Rate %
51.5	62.4	76.3	88.3	52.0	47.4	45.8	50.2	45.5	43.1	40.1	51.9	Net Assets $mil

Performance 12-31-01

	1st Qtr	2nd Qtr	3rd Qtr	4th Qtr	Total
1997	–3.56	16.49	9.96	0.63	24.30
1998	9.32	–0.84	–20.28	21.27	4.80
1999	–9.98	29.16	–4.46	12.80	25.31
2000	7.04	–7.90	2.97	8.52	10.16
2001	–4.76	21.52	–13.40	22.45	22.73

Trailing	Total Return%	+/– S&P 500	+/– Russ 2000	% Rank All	% Rank Cat	Growth of $10,000
3 Mo	22.45	11.76	1.37	10	21	12,245
6 Mo	6.05	11.60	10.13	2	5	10,605
1 Yr	22.73	34.61	20.24	2	8	12,273
3 Yr Avg	19.21	20.24	12.80	3	11	16,943
5 Yr Avg	17.16	6.46	9.63	3	10	22,070
10 Yr Avg	13.93	1.01	2.42	9	40	36,856
15 Yr Avg	13.55	–0.18	2.79	13	23	67,260

Tax Analysis	Tax-Adj Ret%	%Rank Cat	%Pretax Ret	%Rank Cat
3 Yr Avg	16.14	13	84.0	49
5 Yr Avg	13.37	13	77.9	72
10 Yr Avg	10.44	56	74.9	81

Potential Capital Gain Exposure: 40% of assets

Risk Analysis

Time Period	Load-Adj Return %	Risk %Rank[1] All	Risk %Rank[1] Cat	Morningstar Return	Morningstar Risk	Morningstar Risk-Adj Rating
1 Yr	16.29					
3 Yr	17.09	58	45	2.89[2]	0.81	★★★★★
5 Yr	15.90	63	34	2.92[2]	0.86	★★★★★
10 Yr	13.32	62	20	1.38	0.81	★★★★

Average Historical Rating (178 months): 3.1★s

[1] 1=low, 100=high [2] T-Bill return substituted for category avg.

Category Rating (3 Yr)

1 2 3 4 5
Worst Best

Return Above Avg
Risk Average

Other Measures	Standard Index S&P 500	Best Fit Index SPMid400
Alpha	20.0	9.4
Beta	0.77	0.87
R-Squared	40	67

Standard Deviation	24.66
Mean	19.21
Sharpe Ratio	0.65

Portfolio Analysis 09-30-01

Share change since 06-01 Total Stocks: 34

	Sector	PE	YTD Ret%	% Assets
⊖ O'Reilly Automotive	Retail	33.8	36.34	5.16
⊖ Graco	Industrials	18.3	43.32	4.90
Landauer	Services	21.2	95.24	4.64
Ocular Sciences	Durables	19.6	100.40	3.88
Clayton Homes	Industrials	22.8	49.60	3.79
OM Grp	Industrials	20.2	22.24	3.69
Office Depot	Retail	NMF	160.20	3.38
☼ Triquint Semicon	Technology	26.7	–71.90	3.37
⊖ Idex	Industrials	25.4	6.08	3.35
Brown & Brown	Financials	35.9	57.09	3.24
HON Inds	Durables	21.9	10.51	3.22
☼ Noble Drilling	Energy	18.3	–21.60	3.13
☼ Tidewater	Energy	15.1	–22.30	2.98
Natl Commerce	Financials	32.4	3.99	2.95
⊖ Manitowoc	Industrials	16.1	8.39	2.91
Black Box	Technology	16.3	9.45	2.82
Zebra Tech	Technology	27.0	36.12	2.80
⊖ Donaldson	Industrials	22.6	40.99	2.80
Denison Intl ADR	Industrials	11.3	11.33	2.70
⊕ SanDisk	Technology	—	–48.10	2.45
Belden	Industrials	14.3	–6.40	2.29
Manpower	Services	17.0	–10.70	2.16
☼ Cal Dive Intl	Energy	25.2	–7.31	2.15
⊖ Crane	Industrials	15.7	–8.48	2.15
Arrow Electncs	Technology	NMF	4.45	2.13

Current Investment Style

Style: Value Blnd Growth; Size: Large Med Small

	Stock Port Avg	Relative S&P 500 Current	Relative S&P 500 Hist	Rel Cat
Price/Earnings Ratio	25.5	0.82	0.58	1.02
Price/Book Ratio	3.8	0.66	0.45	1.18
Price/Cash Flow	16.0	0.89	0.70	1.03
3 Yr Earnings Growth	10.3	0.70	0.87	0.61
1 Yr Earnings Est%	–1.2	0.69	—	–1.42
Med Mkt Cap $mil	1,591	0.0	0.0	1.62

Analysis by Christopher Davis 12-31-01

We continue to think FPA Perennial Fund is an appealing choice.

Management's preferences here are clear: Eric Ende and Steve Geist look for companies with high returns on equity, solid balance sheets, and modest valuations. Their preference for such firms usually leads them to companies whose main lines of business rarely change, such as industrial cyclicals (the fund's stake in the sector is more than twice the small-blend norm). That tendency has often kept them from delving into more-dynamic areas, but they still will pick up tech stocks when those names are selling on the cheap.

That fairly temperate approach has been a boon to returns in 2001. The fund's outsized stake in industrial cyclicals paid off, with names like Graco and Clayton Homes posting handsome gains. And retailers such as Circuit City Group and Office Depot have surged, as prospects for the economy improve. What's more, tech picks such as Kemet have rebounded sharply after getting hammered in 2001's first quarter. All told, the fund gained 23% in 2001, placing it in the small-blend group's best decile. It has fared about as well over the long haul, too: The fund's trailing five-year return, all of which was earned under Ende, lands just outside the category's top decile.

Nonetheless, the fund comes with a couple caveats. For one, its compact portfolio of 34 stocks makes it vulnerable to blowups in individual names. And the fund's huge cyclical stake can be a liability when growth stocks rule the roost or if the economy heads south again.

Even so, we think the fund's experienced management and fine long-term record make it a compelling option for small-cap exposure.

Special Securities % assets 09-30-01	
Restricted/Illiquid Secs	0
Emerging-Markets Secs	0
Options/Futures/Warrants	No

Composition % assets 09-30-01	
Cash	0.0
Stocks*	100.0
Bonds	0.0
Other	0.0
*Foreign (% stocks)	3.0

Market Cap	
Giant	0.0
Large	0.0
Medium	57.3
Small	39.7
Micro	3.0

Sector Weightings	% of Stocks	Rel S&P	5-Year High	5-Year Low
Utilities	0.0	0.0	0	0
Energy	9.0	1.3	9	0
Financials	6.8	0.4	28	3
Industrials	37.0	3.2	46	21
Durables	7.8	5.0	15	2
Staples	0.0	0.0	7	0
Services	7.4	0.7	19	6
Retail	11.0	1.6	21	6
Health	2.0	0.1	17	2
Technology	19.1	1.0	30	0

Address:	11400 W. Olympic Boulevard Suite 1200 Los Angeles, CA 90064 800–982–4372 / 310–473–0225
Web Address:	—
Inception:	04-02-84
Advisor:	First Pacific Adv.
Subadvisor:	None
NTF Plans:	N/A

Minimum Purchase:	$1500	Add: $100 IRA: $100
Min Auto Inv Plan:	$1500	Add: $100
Sales Fees:	5.25%L	
Management Fee:	.75% mx./.65% mn.	
Actual Fees:	Mgt: 0.75%	Dist: —
Expense Projections:	3Yr: $995	5Yr: $1247 10Yr: $1967
Avg Brok Commission:	—	Income Distrib: Semi–Ann.
Total Cost (relative to category):	—	

Franklin AGE High Income A

Ticker	Load	NAV	Yield	SEC Yield	Total Assets	Mstar Category
AGEFX	4.25%	$1.92	11.6%	1.70%	$2,549.8 mil	High-Yield Bond

Prospectus Objective: Corp Bond—High Yield

Franklin AGE High Income Fund seeks high current income; capital appreciation is secondary.

The fund invests in both fixed-income debt securities and dividend-paying stocks. It attempts to invest in the highest-yielding securities currently available without excessive risk. The fund may invest in securities rated as low as CCC.

The fund offers Class A, B, C, and Advisor shares, all of which differ in fee structure and availability.

Prior to 1981, the fund was named AGE Fund. On June 30, 1992, Franklin Pennsylvania Investors Fund High-Income Portfolio merged into this fund.

Historical Profile
Return: Average
Risk: Above Avg
Rating: ★★ Below Avg

Investment Style
Fixed-Income
Income Rtn %Rank Cat: 30 31 31 29 32 34 26 32

Growth of Principal vs. Interest Rate Shifts
- Principal Value $000 (NAV with capital gains reinvested)
- Interest Rate % on 10 Yr Treasury
- ▼ Manager Change
- ▽ Partial Manager Change
- ► Mgr Unknown After
- ◄ Mgr Unknown Before

Performance Quartile (within Category)

Portfolio Manager(s)

Christopher J. Molumphy, CFA. Since 1-91. BA Stanford U.; MBA U. of Chicago. Other funds currently managed: Franklin Income A, Franklin Strategic Income A, Franklin Income C.

R. Martin Wiskemann. Since 1-72. BA'47 Handelsschule of Zurich. Other funds currently managed: Franklin AGE High Income C, Franklin AGE High Income Adv, Franklin AGE High Income B.

History

1990	1991	1992	1993	1994	1995	1996	1997	1998	1999	2000	12-01	History
2.01	2.58	2.72	2.91	2.60	2.80	2.91	2.98	2.76	2.51	2.08	1.92	NAV
−14.45	48.27	16.65	17.64	−1.55	18.67	14.21	12.09	1.52	0.48	−7.37	2.92	Total Return %
−23.40	32.27	9.24	7.89	1.37	0.20	10.59	2.41	−7.16	1.31	−19.00	−5.50	+/– LB Aggregate
−8.07	4.52	−0.02	−1.27	−0.57	1.28	1.79	−0.54	0.94	−2.80	−2.16	−2.86	+/– FB High-Yield
15.37	17.94	11.05	10.26	9.48	10.63	9.85	9.46	9.23	10.01	10.81	11.21	Income Return %
−29.82	30.34	5.59	7.38	−11.03	8.04	4.36	2.63	−7.72	−9.52	−18.18	−8.29	Capital Return %
75	10	58	66	28	18	29	65	34	88	49	48	Total Rtn % Rank Cat
0.40	0.34	0.27	0.27	0.26	0.26	0.26	0.26	0.26	0.26	0.26	0.22	Income $
0.00	0.00	0.00	0.00	0.00	0.00	0.00	0.00	0.00	0.00	0.00	0.00	Capital Gains $
0.56	0.59	0.58	0.56	0.59	0.66	0.70	0.71	0.70	0.72	0.74	0.76	Expense Ratio %
14.47	14.87	12.18	10.78	9.61	9.71	9.07	9.31	0.90	9.40	10.28	10.30	Income Ratio %
18	29	44	38	42	29	20	20	30	28	19	21	Turnover Rate %
1,253.6	1,753.0	1,829.5	2,600.0	1,719.6	2,075.9	2,487.4	3,003.3	3,172.0	2,825.7	2,131.4	2,029.4	Net Assets $mil

Performance 12-31-01

	1st Qtr	2nd Qtr	3rd Qtr	4th Qtr	Total
1997	0.19	5.21	4.71	1.56	12.09
1998	3.27	0.54	−6.31	4.36	1.52
1999	1.68	−0.16	−2.83	1.86	0.48
2000	−2.60	1.14	−0.20	−5.78	−7.37
2001	4.80	−2.42	−5.09	6.04	2.92

Trailing	Total Return%	+/– LB Agg	+/– FB High-Yield	% Rank All	% Rank Cat	Growth of $10,000
3 Mo	6.04	6.00	0.39	61	41	10,604
6 Mo	0.64	−4.01	−0.80	36	51	10,064
1 Yr	2.92	−5.50	−2.86	37	48	10,292
3 Yr Avg	−1.42	−7.70	−2.59	80	58	9,580
5 Yr Avg	1.74	−5.69	−1.50	89	44	10,901
10 Yr Avg	7.15	−0.07	−0.68	49	37	19,958
15 Yr Avg	7.15	−0.97	−1.51	65	43	28,183

Tax Analysis	Tax-Adj Ret%	%Rank Cat	%Pretax Ret	%Rank Cat
3 Yr Avg	−5.47	63	—	—
5 Yr Avg	−2.21	47	—	—
10 Yr Avg	3.15	35	44.1	40

Potential Capital Gain Exposure: −53% of assets

Risk Analysis

Time Period	Load-Adj Return %	Risk %Rank[1] All	Risk %Rank[1] Cat	Morningstar Return	Morningstar Risk	Morningstar Risk-Adj Rating
1 Yr	−1.45					
3 Yr	−2.84	38	60	−1.53[2]	2.18	★
5 Yr	0.86	40	42	−0.84[2]	2.10	★
10 Yr	6.69	44	37	0.55[2]	1.47	★★

Average Historical Rating (193 months): 2.8★s

[1]1=low, 100=high [2] T-Bill return substituted for category avg.

Category Rating (3 Yr)

1 2 3 4 5 — Worst … Best

Return: Average
Risk: Average

Other Measures	Standard Index LB Agg	Best Fit Index FB HY
Alpha	−6.3	−1.9
Beta	0.44	1.17
R-Squared	3	97

Standard Deviation	8.66
Mean	−1.42
Sharpe Ratio	−0.85

Portfolio Analysis 09-30-01

Total Fixed-Income: 200	Date of Maturity	Amount $000	Value $000	% Net Assets
Intermedia Comm Step 0%	07-15-07	37,500	37,125	1.53
Dobson/Sygnet Comm 12.25%	12-15-08	34,250	35,534	1.47
Key Energy Grp 14%	01-15-09	27,939	32,270	1.33
Willis Corroon FRN	/ /	30,000	31,200	1.29
Avecia Grp 11%	07-01-09	33,000	31,185	1.29
EchoStar 10.375%	10-01-07	30,000	30,450	1.26
Crown Castle Intl N/A	08-01-11	51,000	29,835	1.23
Horseshoe Gaming 8.625%	05-15-09	30,200	29,747	1.23
Ultrapetrol 10.5%	04-01-08	34,000	29,070	1.20
At&t Wireless Grp 7.875%	03-01-11	27,000	28,990	1.20
Charter Comm 9.92%	04-01-11	44,000	28,490	1.18
Univ Compression Step 0%	02-15-08	31,800	28,461	1.17
P&L Coal Hldgs 9.625%	05-15-08	26,600	27,731	1.14
GS Superhwy Hldgs 10.25%	08-15-07	26,000	25,935	1.07
Conproca 144A 12%	06-16-10	23,300	25,688	1.06
Office Depot 10%	07-15-08	25,000	25,375	1.05
Voicestream Wire 0%	11-15-09	29,750	25,139	1.04
Sovereign Bancorp 10.5%	11-15-06	23,000	24,840	1.02
Adelphia Comm 10.875%	10-01-10	27,500	24,613	1.02
Chancellor Media 144A 8%	11-01-08	23,500	24,499	1.01

Current Investment Style

Maturity: Short Int Long; Quality: High Med Low

Avg Eff Duration	—
Avg Eff Maturity	7.2 Yrs
Avg Credit Quality	B
Avg Wtd Coupon	7.85%
Avg Wtd Price	84.05% of par

Special Securities % assets 09-30-01	
Restricted/Illiquid Secs	3
Exotic Mortgage-Backed	0
Emerging-Markets Secs	3
Options/Futures/Warrants	Yes

Credit Analysis % bonds 09-30-01			
US Govt	0	BB	20
AAA	0	B	53
AA	0	Below B	8
A	1	NR/NA	11
BBB	7		

Sector Breakdown % bonds 09-30-01			
US Treasuries	0	CMOs	0
GNMA mtgs	0	ARMs	0
FNMA mtgs	0	Other	100
FHLMC mtgs	0		

Coupon Range	% of Bonds	Rel Cat
0%, PIK	15.16	2.42
0% to 9%	20.48	0.68
9% to 12%	54.53	1.02
12% to 14%	7.76	0.88
More than 14%	2.07	1.49

1.00=Category Average

Composition % assets 09-30-01			
Cash	4.2	Bonds	92.3
Stocks	2.2	Other	1.3

Analysis by Scott Berry 12-07-01

Franklin AGE High Income should appeal to less-intrepid junk bond investors.

This fund has a reputation for being a bit more defensive than its average high-yield peer. In recent years, for example, it has shied away from risky telecom bonds and focused on less-cyclical sectors of the market, such as cable and health care. The fund's caution held it back a bit in 1999, but has paid off over the last two years, as a number of high-profile defaults and a slew of earnings disappointments have weighed on the telecom sector and lower-rated bonds in general.

The fund's defensive positioning continued for much of 2001, but in the weeks following the Sept. 11 terrorist attacks, management took advantage of select opportunities in lower-quality issues. Lead manager Chris Molumphy argues that the flight to quality following the attacks led to extremely cheap valuations for lower-quality bonds. Specifically, he targeted the gaming and lodging sectors, two of the high-yield market's hardest-hit areas.

For the most part, these moves have paid off. The fund gained 4.0% for the year to date through Dec. 6, 2001, versus 2.0% for its average peer. And while the fund's recent shift into lower-quality issues could add to its volatility, we don't think investors should be overly concerned. Indeed, the fund's risk profile is simply more aligned with the category norm than it has been in recent years.

Overall, this fund has gotten the job done. Its five- and 10-year trailing returns both rank solidly in the category's top half and its returns have come with less volatility than those of its average peer. And while it may not be the top-performing high-yield fund, we think its steady performance and below-average expense ratio make it worth considering.

Address:	One Franklin Parkway San Mateo, CA 94403 650-312-2000 / 800-342-5236
Web Address:	—
Inception:	12-31-69
Advisor:	Franklin Advisers
Subadvisor:	None
NTF Plans:	Datalynx

Minimum Purchase:	$1000	Add: $50	IRA: $250
Min Auto Inv Plan:	$1000	Add: $50	
Sales Fees:	4.25%L, 0.15%B		
Management Fee:	.63% mx./.45% mn.		
Actual Fees:	Mgt: 0.46%	Dist: 0.13%	
Expense Projections:	3Yr: $647	5Yr: $811	10Yr: $1287
Avg Brok Commission:	—	Income Distrib: Monthly	
Total Cost (relative to category):	—		

Franklin Balance Sheet Investment A

Ticker	Load	NAV	Yield	Total Assets	Mstar Category
FRBSX	5.75%	$40.02	1.7%	$1,864.3 mil	Small Value

Prospectus Objective: Small Company

Franklin Balance Sheet Investment Fund seeks total return.

The fund invests primarily in equities it judges to be undervalued; these typically include common and preferred stocks, bonds, and commercial paper that may be purchased at prices below the book value of the company. Other factors considered in selecting securities include valuable franchises, ownership of valuable trademarks or trade names, control of distribution networks or of market share for particular products, and excess cash. The fund also invests in closed-end funds trading at a discount or otherwise believed to be undervalued. The fund is nondiversified.

Historical Profile
Return: Above Avg
Risk: Low
Rating: ★★★★★ Highest

Investment Style
Equity
Average Stock %

	1996	1997	1998	1999	2000	12-01
Average Stock %	72%	87%	80%	90%	96%	88%

▼ Manager Change
▽ Partial Manager Change

Fund Performance vs. Category Average
■ Quarterly Fund Return +/– Category Average
— Category Baseline

Performance Quartile (within Category)

Portfolio Manager(s)

Bruce C. Baughman. Since 4-90. BA'70 Stanford U.; MS'79 New York U. Other funds currently managed: Franklin MicroCap Value A, Franklin Small Cap Value A, Franklin Small Cap Value C.

William J. Lippman. Since 4-90. BBA City C. of New York; MBA New York U. Other funds currently managed: Franklin Rising Dividends A, Franklin Rising Dividends C, Franklin MicroCap Value A.

Margaret McGee. Since 4-90. BA William Paterson C. Other funds currently managed: Franklin Rising Dividends A, Franklin Rising Dividends C, Franklin MicroCap Value A.

History

1990	1991	1992	1993	1994	1995	1996	1997	1998	1999	2000	12-01	History
12.27	15.94	18.32	21.85	21.62	26.68	28.49	33.54	31.60	30.47	35.67	40.02	NAV
–15.51*	34.96	22.03	25.58	1.50	30.05	17.51	25.98	–0.61	–1.53	20.47	17.70	Total Return %
–15.75*	4.48	14.41	15.53	0.19	–7.49	–5.44	–7.38	–29.18	–22.57	29.57	29.58	+/– S&P 500
—	–6.74	–7.11	1.74	3.05	4.29	–3.87	–5.72	5.82	–0.06	–2.34	3.68	+/– Russell 2000 V
2.69	4.87	2.91	1.90	0.96	1.59	1.65	1.67	1.60	1.14	1.19	1.94	Income Return %
–18.20	30.09	19.12	23.68	0.54	28.46	15.85	24.30	–2.21	–2.67	19.28	15.77	Capital Return %
—	60	34	2	31	16	89	78	18	61	45	46	Total Rtn % Rank Cat
0.41	0.59	0.46	0.35	0.21	0.34	0.44	0.47	0.53	0.36	0.36	0.69	Income $
0.00	0.00	0.62	0.77	0.35	1.06	2.36	1.80	1.16	0.28	0.61	1.17	Capital Gains $
0.00	0.00	0.00	0.00	1.19	1.17	1.08	1.08	0.93	0.93	1.06	—	Expense Ratio %
2.31	3.79	3.16	1.89	0.99	1.30	1.69	1.59	1.47	1.19	1.00	—	Income Ratio %
—	32	31	31	25	29	35	25	12	18	9	—	Turnover Rate %
1.6	3.8	5.9	32.1	143.7	450.1	710.8	1,285.8	1,516.6	1,136.1	1,112.8	1,777.9	Net Assets $mil

Performance 12-31-01

	1st Qtr	2nd Qtr	3rd Qtr	4th Qtr	Total
1997	3.40	11.52	11.47	–1.99	25.98
1998	9.77	–0.74	–13.56	5.53	–0.61
1999	–9.85	17.59	–8.85	1.90	–1.53
2000	0.83	2.81	8.81	6.81	20.47
2001	1.96	12.61	–10.35	14.34	17.70

Trailing	Total Return%	+/– S&P 500	+/– Russ 2000V	% Rank All	% Rank Cat	Growth of $10,000
3 Mo	14.34	3.66	–2.38	25	79	11,434
6 Mo	2.51	8.07	1.36	18	42	10,251
1 Yr	17.70	29.58	3.68	3	46	11,770
3 Yr Avg	11.77	12.79	0.44	8	56	13,962
5 Yr Avg	11.82	1.12	0.62	11	46	17,481
10 Yr Avg	15.31	2.38	0.20	5	24	41,551
15 Yr Avg	—	—	—	—	—	—

Tax Analysis	Tax-Adj Ret%	%Rank Cat	%Pretax Ret	%Rank Cat
3 Yr Avg	10.72	51	91.1	53
5 Yr Avg	10.42	43	88.2	36
10 Yr Avg	13.51	24	88.3	6

Potential Capital Gain Exposure: 26% of assets

Risk Analysis

Time Period	Load-Adj Return %	Risk %Rank[1] All	Risk %Rank[1] Cat	Morningstar Return	Morningstar Risk	Morningstar Risk-Adj Rating
1 Yr	10.93					
3 Yr	9.58	38	14	1.03[2]	0.51	★★★★
5 Yr	10.50	44	6	1.33[2]	0.57	★★★★
10 Yr	14.63	50	1	1.69	0.57	★★★★★

Average Historical Rating (106 months): 4.2★s

[1] 1=low, 100=high [2] T-Bill return substituted for category avg.

Category Rating (3 Yr)

1 2 **3** 4 5
Worst — Best

Return: Average
Risk: Below Avg

Other Measures	Standard Index S&P 500	Best Fit Index SPMid400
Alpha	9.3	3.8
Beta	0.38	0.50
R-Squared	24	56

Standard Deviation	14.58
Mean	11.77
Sharpe Ratio	0.53

Analysis by Dan Culloton 12-31-01

If the managers of Franklin Balance Sheet Investment witnessed Aesop's famous road race, they would have bet on the turtle.

The fund 's lead manager, Bruce Baughman, keeps things relatively simple. He buys stocks that are trading at discounts to book value and hangs on to them. He prefers debt-light firms with conservative, workaday management to highly leveraged businesses with visionary superstar executives. Baughman, who has managed this fund since inception, couldn't give a hoot about whether a company has a potentially stock-boosting catalyst.

A good example is Dillard's, which Baughman was buying last quarter. He admits the company, whose stock rose 39% this year after falling steeply for three straight years, has been operationally challenged. But it was still trading at half of its book value late last year, and Baughman thinks management can get the stock to book value if it runs business in a workman-like way.

This faith in plodding stocks requires patience, but it has helped the fund plug along. It has finished seven of its 11 years in the top half of its category and just two in the bottom quarter of the group. Though its penchant for small, cheap issues has lead to a couple lagging years here and there, absolute returns have been fairly steady. The fund lost money in back-to-back years in 1998 and 1999, but the 2% loss for that period looks small after gains of more than 20% and nearly 18% in the last two years.

Managment has also built an impressive long-term record. Over its lifetime, its annualized returns have been about three basis points higher than the average small-cap value fund's, and nearly 30 basis points better than the Russell 2000 Value index's. Overall, this is a good option for investors seeking exposure to small, unloved stocks.

Portfolio Analysis 09-30-01

Share change since 06-01 Total Stocks: 102	Sector	PE	YTD Ret%	% Assets
⊕ Sierra Pacific Resources	Utilities	—	–2.25	3.58
⊕ American Natl Ins	Financials	15.9	19.75	3.12
Aztar	Services	14.3	41.44	2.56
Niagara Mohawk Hldgs	Utilities	—	6.24	2.42
⊕ Overseas Shipholding Grp	Services	8.1	0.30	2.35
Northeast Utilities	Utilities	NMF	–25.50	2.25
⊕ Tommy Hilfiger	Retail	9.4	40.12	2.12
Corn Products Intl	Staples	21.0	22.93	2.07
St. Paul	Financials	—	–16.90	1.99
Entergy	Utilities	11.7	–4.50	1.96
☆ Bunge	Staples	—	—	1.87
⊖ Handleman	Services	9.2	98.00	1.83
⊕ Stancorp Finl Grp	Financials	15.4	–0.38	1.78
Hasbro	Durables	—	54.09	1.73
Charming Shoppes	Retail	18.3	–11.50	1.72
⊖ Fred's	Retail	36.9	144.60	1.61
⊖ Nash–finch	Retail	18.9	170.20	1.58
⊕ Reliance Steel & Aluminum	Industrials	15.4	7.01	1.51
⊕ Tecumseh Products A	Industrials	18.3	23.91	1.48
⊕ Federated Dept Stores	Retail	16.6	16.86	1.23
⊕ Timken	Industrials	—	11.51	1.23
⊕ Hutchinson Tech	Technology	—	68.87	1.22
Esco Tech	Technology	14.8	66.72	1.15
⊕ Alaska Air Grp	Services	—	–2.18	1.10
☆ Dillard's	Retail	NMF	36.82	1.10

Current Investment Style

Style: Value Blnd Growth; Size: Large Med Small

	Stock Port Avg	Relative S&P 500 Current	Relative S&P 500 Hist	Rel Cat
Price/Earnings Ratio	20.0	0.64	0.51	0.92
Price/Book Ratio	1.4	0.25	0.16	0.58
Price/Cash Flow	10.1	0.56	0.43	0.79
3 Yr Earnings Growth	19.4	1.32	0.53	1.67
1 Yr Earnings Est%	–1.2	0.70	—	0.31
Med Mkt Cap $mil	1,066	0.0	0.0	1.22

Special Securities % assets 09-30-01	
Restricted/Illiquid Secs	Trace
Emerging–Markets Secs	1
Options/Futures/Warrants	Yes

Composition % assets 09-30-01	
Cash	15.6
Stocks*	82.9
Bonds	0.9
Other	0.7
*Foreign (% stocks)	3.9

Market Cap	
Giant	1.4
Large	5.2
Medium	32.3
Small	53.1
Micro	8.0

Sector Weightings	% of Stocks	Rel S&P	5-Year High	5-Year Low
Utilities	13.5	4.2	14	0
Energy	0.6	0.1	13	0
Financials	25.9	1.5	72	25
Industrials	17.5	1.5	22	4
Durables	3.2	2.0	13	3
Staples	6.6	0.8	8	0
Services	12.8	1.2	18	0
Retail	15.0	2.2	27	3
Health	0.0	0.0	3	0
Technology	4.8	0.3	8	0

Address:	One Franklin Parkway San Mateo, CA 94403 650–312–2000 / 800–342–5236
Web Address:	www.franklintempleton.com
*Inception:	04-02-90
Advisor:	Franklin Advisory Services
Subadvisor:	None
NTF Plans:	Datalynx , Fidelity Inst.

Minimum Purchase:	$1000	Add: $50	IRA: $250
Min Auto Inv Plan:	$50	Add: $50	
Sales Fees:	5.75%L, 0.25%B, 0.25%S		
Management Fee:	.63% mx./.40% mn., .15%A		
Actual Fees:	Mgt: 0.48%	Dist: 0.25%	
Expense Projections:	3Yr: $893	5Yr: $1126	10Yr: $1795
Avg Brok Commission:	—	Income Distrib: Quarterly	
Total Cost (relative to category):	Below Avg		

Franklin CA Growth A

Ticker	Load	NAV	Yield	Total Assets	Mstar Category
FKCGX	5.75%	$31.76	0.0%	$1,894.0 mil	Mid-Cap Growth

Prospectus Objective: Growth

Franklin California Growth Fund seeks capital appreciation.

The fund normally invests at least 65% of assets in companies that maintain their headquarters or conduct a majority of their operations in California. It primarily invests in small- and mid-cap companies with market capitalizations up to $2.5 billion. The fund may invest up to 35% of assets in companies located outside of California. It is nondiversified.

The fund currently offers class A, B, and C shares, all of which differ in fee structure and availability.

Prior to July 12, 1993, it was named Franklin California 250 Growth Fund and followed a different objective.

Historical Profile

Return: High
Risk: Above Avg
Rating: ★★★★ Above Avg

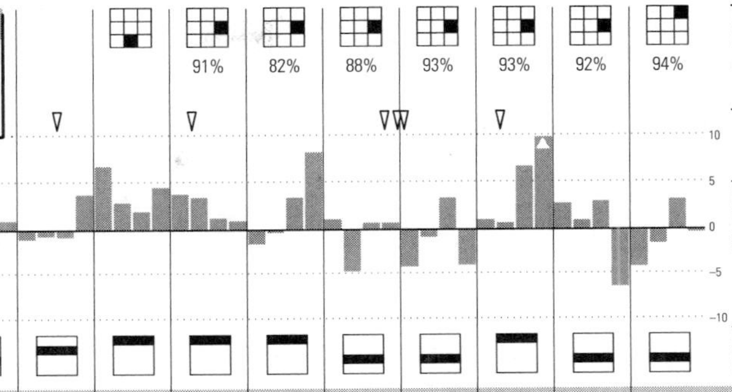

Investment Style
Equity
Average Stock %

1995	1996	1997	1998	1999	2000	12-01
91%	82%	88%	93%	93%	92%	94%

▼ Manager Change
▽ Partial Manager Change

Fund Performance vs. Category Average
■ Quarterly Fund Return +/– Category Average
— Category Baseline

Performance Quartile (within Category)

Portfolio Manager(s)

Conrad B. Herrmann, CFA. Since 7-93. BA'82 Brown U.; MBA'89 Harvard U. Other funds currently managed: Franklin Growth A, Franklin Growth and Income A, Franklin Growth and Income C.

Canyon Chan. Since 4-99. BA'91 Stanford U. Other funds currently managed: Franklin CA Growth C, Franklin CA Growth B.

History

1990	1991	1992	1993	1994	1995	1996	1997	1998	1999	2000	12-01	History
—	10.21	10.64	11.76	12.36	16.11	20.44	22.61	24.31	47.30	41.37	31.76	NAV
—	2.11*	4.87	17.62	16.53	47.63	30.43	15.71	10.72	95.17	–7.04	–23.23	Total Return %
—	–4.84*	–2.75	7.57	15.21	10.10	7.49	–17.65	–17.86	74.13	2.06	–11.35	+/– S&P 500
—	—	–3.84	6.43	18.69	13.66	12.95	–6.84	–7.15	43.86	4.71	–3.07	+/– Russ Midcap Grth
—	0.72	0.64	1.37	1.09	1.87	0.76	0.69	0.65	0.32	0.40	0.00	Income Return %
—	1.39	4.23	16.25	15.44	45.76	29.68	15.02	10.07	94.84	–7.44	–23.23	Capital Return %
—	—	72	37	1	11	6	57	65	19	54	57	Total Rtn % Rank Cat
—	0.07	0.07	0.15	0.12	0.23	0.12	0.14	0.15	0.08	0.19	0.00	Income $
—	0.00	0.00	0.58	1.10	1.78	0.43	0.86	0.53	0.00	2.44	0.00	Capital Gains $
—	—	0.00	0.00	0.09	0.25	0.71	1.08	0.99	1.00	0.88	0.88	Expense Ratio %
—	—	1.27	1.23	1.16	1.63	1.42	0.84	0.67	0.41	0.11	—	Income Ratio %
—	—	—	38	135	80	62	45	49	53	61	35	Turnover Rate %
—	—	3.5	4.2	8.2	46.5	188.3	573.3	754.8	1,603.9	2,074.0	1,464.9	Net Assets $mil

Performance 12-31-01

	1st Qtr	2nd Qtr	3rd Qtr	4th Qtr	Total
1997	–6.95	11.74	16.05	–4.12	15.71
1998	8.54	–1.32	–15.27	22.00	10.72
1999	3.83	12.27	7.08	56.36	95.17
2000	19.07	–4.37	8.11	–24.49	–7.04
2001	–25.99	10.55	–21.27	19.17	–23.23

Trailing	Total Return%	+/– S&P 500	+/– Russ Midcap Grth	% Rank All	% Rank Cat	Growth of $10,000
3 Mo	19.17	8.49	–7.89	15	50	11,917
6 Mo	–6.17	–0.62	2.09	69	29	9,383
1 Yr	–23.23	–11.35	–3.07	86	57	7,677
3 Yr Avg	11.68	12.70	9.52	8	18	13,928
5 Yr Avg	12.28	1.58	3.26	9	27	17,843
10 Yr Avg	17.32	4.39	6.21	2	2	49,385
15 Yr Avg	—	—	—	—	—	—

Tax Analysis	Tax-Adj Ret%	%Rank Cat	%Pretax Ret	%Rank Cat
3 Yr Avg	11.07	15	94.8	13
5 Yr Avg	11.36	16	92.6	7
10 Yr Avg	15.52	2	89.6	8

Potential Capital Gain Exposure: 5% of assets

Risk Analysis

Time Period	Load-Adj Return %	Risk %Rank[1] All	Risk %Rank[1] Cat	Morningstar Return	Morningstar Risk	Morningstar Risk-Adj Rating
1 Yr	–27.64					
3 Yr	9.49	91	48	1.01[2]	1.44	★★★★
5 Yr	10.96	87	33	1.45[2]	1.36	★★★
10 Yr	16.62	88	23	2.23	1.30	★★★★★

Average Historical Rating (87 months): 4.4★s

[1] 1=low, 100=high [2] T-Bill return substituted for category avg.

Category Rating (3 Yr)

1 Worst — 5 Best (rating: 4)

Return: Above Avg
Risk: Average

Other Measures	Standard Index S&P 500	Best Fit Index Wil 4500
Alpha	20.8	13.2
Beta	1.43	1.23
R-Squared	44	90
Standard Deviation		43.25
Mean		11.68
Sharpe Ratio		0.18

Portfolio Analysis 09-30-01

Share change since 06-01 Total Stocks: 105

	Sector	PE	YTD Ret%	% Assets
⊖ Mattel	Staples	31.9	19.43	3.14
⊖ Tenet Healthcare	Health	30.1	32.14	2.95
Amgen	Health	52.8	–11.70	2.72
Wellpoint Health Networks	Health	19.4	1.39	2.70
⊖ Pmi Grp	Financials	10.4	–0.76	2.33
Chevron	Energy	10.3	9.29	2.09
⊕ Safeway	Retail	18.1	–33.20	2.08
⊖ Wells Fargo	Financials	22.4	–20.20	2.06
Watson Pharmaceuticals	Health	51.5	–38.60	2.03
⊕ Calpine	Utilities	8.9	–62.70	1.88
⊖ Golden State Bancorp	Financials	9.6	–15.60	1.88
Genentech	Health	NMF	–33.40	1.77
Expeditors Intl Of Wa	Services	32.7	6.46	1.75
⊖ Mckesson Hboc	Health	—	4.92	1.75
⊖ Clorox	Staples	31.1	14.20	1.60
City Natl	Financials	16.4	22.90	1.60
Fox Entrtnmt Grp Cl A	Services	NMF	48.42	1.59
⊕ Varian	Technology	22.2	–4.24	1.57
⊖ Univision Comms A	Services	96.3	–1.17	1.42
Silicon Valley Bancshare	Financials	12.1	–22.60	1.38
Semtech	Technology	63.7	61.76	1.31
Catellus Dev	Financials	21.2	5.14	1.30
Robert Half Intl	Services	31.1	0.75	1.24
☼ Idec Pharmaceuticals	Health	NMF	9.09	1.22
⊖ Essex Ppty Tr	Financials	20.9	–4.44	1.21

Current Investment Style

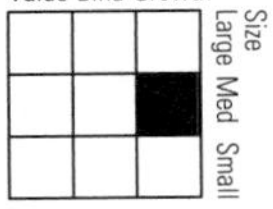

Style: Value Blnd Growth; Size: Large Med Small

	Stock Port Avg	Relative S&P 500 Current	Relative S&P 500 Hist	Rel Cat
Price/Earnings Ratio	33.0	1.06	1.12	0.95
Price/Book Ratio	4.7	0.82	1.06	0.82
Price/Cash Flow	22.5	1.25	1.21	0.97
3 Yr Earnings Growth	23.8	1.63	1.47	1.01
1 Yr Earnings Est%	8.1	—	—	0.87
Med Mkt Cap $mil	5,215	0.1	0.1	0.93

Special Securities % assets 09-30-01	
Restricted/Illiquid Secs	0
Emerging-Markets Secs	0
Options/Futures/Warrants	No

Composition % assets 09-30-01	
Cash	3.1
Stocks*	96.0
Bonds	0.4
Other	0.6
*Foreign (% stocks)	0.0

Market Cap	
Giant	9.0
Large	29.4
Medium	43.8
Small	17.8
Micro	0.0

Sector Weightings	% of Stocks	Rel S&P	5-Year High	5-Year Low
Utilities	2.7	0.9	7	1
Energy	2.2	0.3	12	1
Financials	19.7	1.1	22	5
Industrials	2.5	0.2	10	2
Durables	0.0	0.0	8	0
Staples	5.0	0.6	5	0
Services	13.1	1.2	19	7
Retail	4.7	0.7	9	3
Health	26.0	1.8	26	6
Technology	24.2	1.3	66	24

Analysis by Dan Culloton 12-04-01

Franklin California Growth is a provincial but potentially profitable fund.

This offering has amassed an attractive long-term record by investing primarily in companies that keep their headquarters or do most of their business in California. Such narrow regional restrictions would normally hamstring a mutual fund, but they haven't hampered this one. The world's fifth-largest economy is its playground and the managers have found plenty of opportunities among California's 1,400 publicly traded companies over the years.

Indeed the fund's 10-year annualized return of 16.3% through the end of November was better than 98% of its mid-cap growth peers'. Even when this fund has suffered, as it has this year and did in 2000, it has never fallen into the category's bottom quartile.

Managers Conrad Herrmann and Canyon Chan have kept the fund in a relatively defensive position for most of this year. They've reduced the portfolio's tech stake to well below its three-year average of 44% by selling names like Cisco Systems and favoring health-care holdings like Wellpoint Health Networks and Tenet Healthcare. They've also liked consumer-staple and retail stocks like household products maker Clorox and grocer Safeway.

Safeway hasn't helped much this year, but the other aforementioned holdings have provided some buoyancy. For the year to date through Dec. 3, it was down about 25%, with gains on issues such as Tenet Healthcare offset by losses on stocks like generic drugmaker Watson Pharmaceuticals and power generator Calpine. The fund, however, was still in the middle of the mid-growth pack for the year.

This fund is no shrinking violet. It has a shown a propensity for risky, high P/E stocks in the past. It has compensated investors for that risk, though, so we still think it's a solid growth fund.

Address:	One Franklin Parkway San Mateo, CA 94403 650-312-2000 / 800-342-5236
Web Address:	www.franklintempleton.com
*Inception:	10-31-91
Advisor:	Franklin Advisers
Subadvisor:	None
NTF Plans:	Datalynx , Fidelity Inst.

Minimum Purchase:	$1000	Add: $50 IRA: $250
Min Auto Inv Plan:	$50	Add: $50
Sales Fees:	5.75%L, 0.25%B	
Management Fee:	.63% mx./.40% mn.	
Actual Fees:	Mgt: 0.44%	Dist: 0.25%
Expense Projections:	3Yr: $840	5Yr: $1035 10Yr: $1597
Avg Brok Commission:	—	Income Distrib: Semi-Ann.
Total Cost (relative to category):		Below Avg

Franklin DynaTech A

Ticker	Load	NAV	Yield	Total Assets	Mstar Category
FKDNX	5.75%	$20.38	1.5%	$657.6 mil	Large Growth

Prospectus Objective: Growth

Franklin DynaTech Fund seeks capital appreciation.

The fund invests primarily in companies that emphasize technological development in fast-growing industries or in undervalued securities. It primarily purchases common stocks, but it may also hold utility debt securities and preferred stocks. The fund typically invests in high-quality debt; a B rating is its lowest parameter. In certain circumstances, investments may be made for short-term trading profits.

Class A shares have front loads; C shares have level loads. Prior to Jan. 1, 1999, Class A and C shares were called Class I and II shares.

Historical Profile

Return Average
Risk Average
Rating ★★★ Neutral

Investment Style
Equity
Average Stock %

1991	1992	1993	1994	1995	1996	1997	1998
			90%	81%	78%	85%	51%

Average Stock %: 90% 81% 78% 85% 51% 53% 42%

▼ Manager Change
▽ Partial Manager Change

Fund Performance vs. Category Average
▮ Quarterly Fund Return +/– Category Average
— Category Baseline

Performance Quartile (within Category)

1990	1991	1992	1993	1994	1995	1996	1997	1998	1999	2000	12-01	History
7.06	9.44	9.60	9.59	9.91	12.16	15.21	16.33	20.54	27.77	23.81	20.38	NAV
3.25	35.43	4.14	7.47	5.22	26.13	28.79	14.62	27.34	37.19	–12.24	–13.11	Total Return %
6.37	4.94	–3.48	–2.59	3.91	–11.41	5.85	–18.73	–1.23	16.15	–3.14	–1.24	+/– S&P 500
1.88	–3.98	0.25	7.54	0.37	–12.53	3.27	–19.12	–17.76	7.51	12.29	7.39	+/– Russ Top 200 Grt
2.39	1.59	1.24	1.29	0.51	1.19	0.45	1.12	1.49	1.80	2.07	1.30	Income Return %
0.86	33.84	2.90	6.18	4.71	24.94	28.34	13.51	25.85	35.39	–14.31	–14.41	Capital Return %
16	67	69	63	5	85	4	91	68	45	39	12	Total Rtn % Rank Cat
0.17	0.11	0.12	0.12	0.05	0.12	0.06	0.17	0.24	0.37	0.58	0.31	Income $
0.00	0.00	0.11	0.60	0.13	0.23	0.40	0.97	0.00	0.00	0.00	0.00	Capital Gains $
0.79	0.93	0.81	0.81	1.00	1.01	1.05	1.04	1.02	1.00	0.94	—	Expense Ratio %
2.09	1.57	1.42	1.03	0.69	1.11	0.43	0.75	1.55	1.70	1.98	—	Income Ratio %
11	7	11	27	10	10	12	6	11	6	5	—	Turnover Rate %
36.3	56.0	69.9	69.5	69.6	91.0	120.9	180.5	287.5	666.2	690.9	575.8	Net Assets $mil

Portfolio Manager(s)

Rupert H. Johnson, Jr.. Since 1-68. BA'62 Washington & Lee U. Other funds currently managed: Franklin Global Health Care A, Franklin Global Health Care C, Franklin DynaTech C.

Robert Dean, CFA. Since 3-00. BA U. of San Diego. Other funds currently managed: Franklin DynaTech C, Franklin Technology A, Franklin Technology Adv.

Performance 12-31-01

	1st Qtr	2nd Qtr	3rd Qtr	4th Qtr	Total
1997	–1.18	11.31	10.46	–5.66	14.62
1998	8.51	3.10	–2.35	16.56	27.34
1999	6.18	3.67	2.21	21.93	37.19
2000	11.02	–4.41	–2.95	–14.78	–12.24
2001	–13.06	4.11	–12.95	10.28	–13.11

Trailing	Total Return%	+/– S&P 500	+/– Russ Top 200 Grth	% Rank All	% Rank Cat	Growth of $10,000
3 Mo	10.28	–0.41	–2.58	41	85	11,028
6 Mo	–4.00	1.56	2.99	56	12	9,600
1 Yr	–13.11	–1.24	7.39	68	12	8,689
3 Yr Avg	1.51	2.54	9.54	65	18	10,461
5 Yr Avg	8.83	–1.87	0.24	25	46	15,270
10 Yr Avg	11.31	–1.61	0.23	24	31	29,210
15 Yr Avg	13.77	0.04	0.40	12	24	69,262

Tax Analysis	Tax-Adj Ret%	%Rank Cat	%Pretax Ret	%Rank Cat
3 Yr Avg	0.81	14	53.8	73
5 Yr Avg	7.96	35	90.1	15
10 Yr Avg	10.30	16	91.0	7

Potential Capital Gain Exposure: 14% of assets

Risk Analysis

Time Period	Load-Adj Return %	Risk %Rank[1] All	Risk %Rank[1] Cat	Morningstar Return	Morningstar Risk	Morningstar Risk-Adj Rating
1 Yr	–18.11					
3 Yr	–0.47	70	13	–1.09[2]	0.96	★★★
5 Yr	7.55	68	8	0.58[2]	0.92	★★★
10 Yr	10.66	75	11	0.85	0.97	★★★

Average Historical Rating (193 months): 2.7★s

[1]1=low, 100=high [2] T-Bill return substituted for category avg.

Category Rating (3 Yr)

1 2 3 4 5
Worst Best

Return Above Avg
Risk Below Avg

Other Measures	Standard Index S&P 500	Best Fit Index Wil 4500
Alpha	2.5	–1.6
Beta	0.90	0.60
R-Squared	62	77

Standard Deviation	19.73
Mean	1.51
Sharpe Ratio	–0.20

Analysis by Kelli Stebel 11-09-01

Don't let Franklin Dynatech's record fool you—this fund isn't worth buying.

All of this offering's annualized returns of one year or more land in the large-growth category's top third. What's more, the fund has posted decent results in market rallies and downturns alike. And the fund has had the same lead manager, Rupert Johnson, at the helm since its inception in 1968.

That record doesn't tell the whole story, though. The fund carries an enormous cash position, with the rest of the assets divided between technology and health-care stocks. In the past few years, that cash stake has hovered at about 50% of assets, but comanager Robert Dean reports that the fund has about 60% of assets in cash these days. There's little doubt that cash cushion has helped the fund in less-certain times, particularly this year's topsy-turvy market. The fund has lost about 15% of its value for the year to date through Nov. 9, 2001, compared with a 26% drop by the typical large-growth fund.

Investors could have put this kind of portfolio together on their own, however, and achieved better results at the same time. A similar portfolio, combining the average technology and health-care offering in Morningstar's database with a 60% cash stake, would have yielded better results over the past three- and five-year periods, and it certainly would be cheaper.

Given that backdrop, there's really no reason to own this fund. For a fund consisting primarily of T-bills, shareholders don't need to pay this offering's nearly 1% price tag. And its odd mix of holdings and cash make it a tough fit for most investors' portfolios. Shareholders seeking downside protection can find more-appropriate options.

Portfolio Analysis 09-30-01

Share change since 06-01 Total Stocks: 75	Sector	PE	YTD Ret%	% Assets
Intel	Technology	73.1	4.89	3.76
Microsoft	Technology	57.6	52.78	3.45
Pfizer	Health	34.7	–12.40	2.62
Genentech	Health	NMF	–33.40	1.76
IBM	Technology	26.9	43.00	1.67
Motorola	Technology	—	–25.00	1.48
Cisco Sys	Technology	—	–52.60	1.20
AOL Time Warner	Technology	—	–7.76	1.09
Check Point Software Tech	Technology	32.0	–55.20	1.09
Amgen	Health	52.8	–11.70	0.97
First Data	Technology	38.1	49.08	0.86
Medtronic	Health	76.4	–14.70	0.79
Linear Tech	Technology	34.9	–15.30	0.70
UnitedHealth Grp	Financials	26.6	15.37	0.66
Applied Matls	Technology	66.8	5.01	0.66
Nokia Cl A ADR	Technology	45.8	–43.00	0.64
Bristol-Myers Squibb	Health	20.2	–26.00	0.64
Schering-Plough	Health	22.2	–35.90	0.61
Hewlett-Packard	Technology	97.8	–33.90	0.58
Agilent Tech	Technology	58.2	–47.90	0.57
Sony ADR	Durables	NMF	–35.10	0.55
✲ Liberty Media Group A	N/A	—	—	0.54
Intuit	Technology	—	8.42	0.53
WorldCom	Services	24.3	3.12	0.50
Electronic Arts	Technology	90.8	40.65	0.45

Current Investment Style

Style: Value Blnd Growth; Size: Large Med Small

	Stock Port Avg	Relative S&P 500 Current	Relative S&P 500 Hist	Rel Cat
Price/Earnings Ratio	45.5	1.47	1.35	1.28
Price/Book Ratio	6.5	1.14	1.28	1.02
Price/Cash Flow	25.3	1.40	1.31	1.11
3 Yr Earnings Growth	20.2	1.38	1.48	0.94
1 Yr Earnings Est%	–9.0	5.06	—	–2.99
Med Mkt Cap $mil	58,289	1.0	1.1	1.23

Special Securities % assets 09-30-01	
Restricted/Illiquid Secs	0
Emerging-Markets Secs	1
Options/Futures/Warrants	No

Composition % assets 09-30-01	
Cash	62.0
Stocks*	38.0
Bonds	0.0
Other	0.0
*Foreign (% stocks)	7.4

Market Cap	
Giant	53.6
Large	35.8
Medium	9.9
Small	0.8
Micro	0.1

Sector Weightings	% of Stocks	Rel S&P	5-Year High	5-Year Low
Utilities	0.0	0.0	4	0
Energy	0.7	0.1	2	0
Financials	2.9	0.2	3	0
Industrials	1.0	0.1	7	1
Durables	1.5	0.9	3	0
Staples	0.6	0.1	3	0
Services	7.3	0.7	20	6
Retail	0.0	0.0	12	0
Health	23.3	1.6	37	9
Technology	62.7	3.4	72	32

Address:	One Franklin Parkway San Mateo, CA 94403 650-312-2000 / 800-342-5236
Web Address:	www.franklintempleton.com
Inception:	01-01-68
Advisor:	Franklin Advisers
Subadvisor:	None
NTF Plans:	Datalynx , Fidelity Inst.

Minimum Purchase:	$1000	Add: $50	IRA: $250
Min Auto Inv Plan:	$50	Add: $50	
Sales Fees:	5.75%L, 0.25%B		
Management Fee:	.60% mx./.40% mn.		
Actual Fees:	Mgt: 0.52%	Dist: 0.25%	
Expense Projections:	3Yr: $875	5Yr: $1096	10Yr: $1729
Avg Brok Commission:	—	Income Distrib: Annually	
Total Cost (relative to category):		Average	

Franklin Federal Tax–Free Income A

Ticker	Load	NAV	Yield	SEC Yield	Total Assets	Mstar Category
FKTIX	4.25%	$11.76	5.4%	5.10%	$7,060.5 mil	Muni Natl Long–Term

Prospectus Objective: Muni Bond—National

Franklin Federal Tax-Free Income Fund seeks interest income exempt from federal income taxes, consistent with capital preservation.

The fund normally invests at least 80% of assets in investment-grade securities that generate income exempt from federal taxes. It may invest up to 20% of assets in taxable or AMT-subject bonds.

Class A shares have front loads; B shares have deferred loads, 12b-1 fees, and conversion features; C shares have level loads.

Past name include: Franklin Cash Management Fund, Franklin Hawaii Municipal Bond Fund, Franklin Indiana Tax-Free Income Fund

Historical Profile
Return Above Avg
Risk Below Avg
Rating ★★★★★ Highest

Investment Style: Fixed-Income — Income Rtn %Rank Cat: 5, 7, 6, 8, 7, 7, 11, 18

Growth of Principal vs. Interest Rate Shifts
— Principal Value $000 (NAV with capital gains reinvested)
— Interest Rate % on 10 Yr Treasury
▼ Manager Change
▽ Partial Manager Change
► Mgr Unknown After
◄ Mgr Unknown Before

Performance Quartile (within Category)

1990	1991	1992	1993	1994	1995	1996	1997	1998	1999	2000	12–01	History
11.19	11.76	12.01	12.53	11.29	12.19	12.01	12.35	12.39	11.39	11.85	11.76	NAV
5.53	13.23	9.56	11.25	−3.73	15.10	4.70	8.97	5.94	−2.79	10.14	4.63	Total Return %
−3.43	−2.77	2.16	1.50	−0.82	−3.37	1.09	−0.71	−2.74	−1.96	−1.49	−3.79	+/– LB Aggregate
−1.78	1.09	0.74	−1.02	1.41	−2.36	0.27	−0.23	−0.55	−0.72	−1.55	−0.45	+/– LB Muni
7.71	7.86	7.27	6.77	6.41	6.87	6.12	5.98	5.58	5.49	5.90	5.45	Income Return %
−2.19	5.37	2.28	4.48	−10.15	8.23	−1.42	2.99	0.36	−8.28	4.25	−0.81	Capital Return %
72	15	23	76	13	82	12	55	24	7	59	27	Total Rtn % Rank Cat
0.85	0.85	0.83	0.79	0.78	0.75	0.73	0.70	0.67	0.66	0.65	0.63	Income $
0.00	0.00	0.00	0.00	0.00	0.00	0.00	0.00	0.00	0.01	0.00	0.00	Capital Gains $
0.50	0.50	0.51	0.51	0.52	0.59	0.57	0.58	0.59	0.60	0.60	—	Expense Ratio %
7.39	7.34	7.07	6.68	6.27	6.47	6.20	6.00	5.70	5.41	5.64	—	Income Ratio %
18	29	15	13	25	20	25	16	15	10	17	—	Turnover Rate %
4,086.1	4,986.5	5,959.5	7,060.4	6,561.4	7,210.6	7,032.0	7,096.2	7,189.4	6,570.1	6,430.3	6,576.4	Net Assets $mil

Portfolio Manager(s)

Sheila Amoroso. Since 1-87. BS San Francisco State U. Other funds currently managed: Franklin LA Tax-Free Income A, Franklin CA Tax-Free Income A, Franklin MD Tax-Free Income A.

Francisco Rivera. Since 6-00. Other funds currently managed: Franklin LA Tax-Free Income A, Franklin MA Insured Tax-Free Inc A, Franklin GA Tax-Free Income A.

John Wiley. Since 6-00. BS U. of California-Berkeley; MBA Saint Mary's C. Other funds currently managed: Franklin LA Tax-Free Income A, Franklin CA Tax-Free Income A, Franklin CA Insured Tax-Free Inc A.

Performance 12-31-01

	1st Qtr	2nd Qtr	3rd Qtr	4th Qtr	Total
1997	0.22	3.10	2.88	2.51	8.97
1998	1.12	1.62	2.44	0.63	5.94
1999	0.96	−1.45	−0.88	−1.42	−2.79
2000	2.62	1.27	2.39	3.51	10.14
2001	1.97	0.82	2.34	−0.55	4.63

Trailing	Total Return%	+/– LB Agg	+/– LB Muni	% Rank All	% Rank Cat	Growth of $10,000
3 Mo	−0.55	−0.59	0.11	85	15	9,945
6 Mo	1.78	−2.88	−0.35	26	30	10,178
1 Yr	4.63	−3.79	−0.45	25	27	10,463
3 Yr Avg	3.86	−2.42	−0.89	43	17	11,203
5 Yr Avg	5.28	−2.15	−0.70	59	20	12,933
10 Yr Avg	6.22	−1.01	−0.41	64	24	18,288
15 Yr Avg	6.69	−1.43	−0.50	73	28	26,418

Tax Analysis	Tax-Adj Ret%	%Rank Cat	%Pretax Ret	%Rank Cat
3 Yr Avg	3.85	15	99.9	50
5 Yr Avg	5.28	16	100.0	22
10 Yr Avg	6.22	16	100.0	4

Potential Capital Gain Exposure: 3% of assets

Risk Analysis

Time Period	Load-Adj Return %	Risk %Rank[1] All	Risk %Rank[1] Cat	Morningstar Return	Morningstar Risk	Morningstar Risk-Adj Rating
1 Yr	0.18					
3 Yr	2.37	9	3	0.25[2]	0.81	★★★★
5 Yr	4.37	7	3	0.74[2]	0.74	★★★★
10 Yr	5.76	7	5	1.10	0.71	★★★★★

Average Historical Rating (183 months): 4.4★s

[1]1=low, 100=high [2] T-Bill return substituted for category avg.

Category Rating (3 Yr)

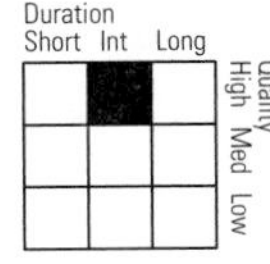

Return High
Risk Low

Other Measures	Standard Index LB Agg	Best Fit Index LB Muni
Alpha	−1.9	−0.9
Beta	0.71	0.90
R–Squared	49	97

Standard Deviation	3.52
Mean	3.86
Sharpe Ratio	−0.36

Portfolio Analysis 09-30-01

Total Fixed-Income: 994	Date of Maturity	Amount $000	Value $000	% Net Assets
Ma Tpk Metro Hwy Sys 5%	01-01-37	77,130	74,282	1.04
Ny Nyc Go 6.125%	08-01-25	65,785	69,769	0.98
Ca Foothill/eastern Transp Corridor 6.5%	01-01-32	59,240	68,761	0.97
NC East Muni Pwr Sys 5%		65,350	65,259	0.92
Nv Clark Indl Dev Sw Gas 7.5%	09-01-32	62,470	65,069	0.92
Ar Pope Poll Cntrl Pwr/lt 6.3%	11-01-20	60,500	60,727	0.85
Pr Hwy/transp 5%	07-01-36	59,000	58,229	0.82
NY NYC Muni Wtr Fin Swr Sys 5%		55,000	56,790	0.80
Nh Indl Dev Poll Cntrl Pub Svc 7.5%	05-01-21	50,690	51,751	0.73
Co Denver Arpt Sys 5.125%	11-15-23	43,000	43,252	0.61
Nc East Muni Pwr Sys 6.25%	01-01-23	39,030	41,801	0.59
Co Denver Spcl Fac Arpt United 6.875%	10-01-32	47,980	41,010	0.58
IL Metro Pier/Expo 5%		39,580	39,577	0.56
MS Busn Fin Wtr Poll Cntrl Pwr 5%		40,000	39,138	0.55
DC Columbia GO 6.5%		35,000	38,857	0.55

Current Investment Style

Duration: Short Int Long; Quality: High Med Low

Avg Duration[1]	5.9 Yrs
Avg Nominal Maturity	19.8 Yrs
Avg Credit Quality	AA
Avg Wtd Coupon	5.87%
Avg Wtd Price	102.10% of par
Pricing Service	Muller

[1]figure provided by fund

Credit Analysis % bonds 09-30-01

US Govt	0	BB	3
AAA	45	B	0
AA	17	Below B	0
A	15	NR/NA	1
BBB	19		

Special Securities % assets 09-30-01

Restricted/Illiquid Secs	0
Inverse Floaters	0
Options/Futures/Warrants	No

Bond Type % assets 03-31-01

Alternative Minimum Tax (AMT)	12.2
Insured	—
Prerefunded	14.2

Top 5 States % bonds

NY	18.3	MA	4.5
IL	7.1	NC	4.2
CA	5.8		

Composition % assets 09-30-01

Cash	1.9	Bonds	98.1
Stocks	0.0	Other	0.0

Sector Weightings	% of Bonds	Rel Cat
General Obligation	16.6	0.8
Utilities	9.3	1.2
Health	13.4	0.9
Water/Waste	4.5	0.8
Housing	10.0	1.4
Education	3.5	0.5
Transportation	15.8	1.2
COP/Lease	3.2	1.1
Industrial	19.0	1.5
Misc Revenue	2.9	0.6
Demand	1.9	2.3

Analysis by Scott Berry 11-01-01

Investors can't go wrong with Franklin Federal Tax-Free Income.

It's hard to find fault with this fund. It's a solid performer, keeps volatility to a minimum, offers an above-average yield, and charges below-average expenses. With these characteristics, it's no surprise that this is the largest fund in the muni national long-term category.

The fund's long-term success owes much to Franklin's buy-and-hold approach. Indeed, management is content to buy what it considers attractively priced bonds and clip their coupons until they mature or get called away. This approach has paid off particularly well in rising interest-rate environments, such as 1994 and 1999. During those years, the fund's stash of older, higher-yielding bonds, which are less sensitive to interest-rate changes, helped limit its losses. In fact, in each of those years the fund's total returns ranked in the category's top 15%.

The fund's performance hasn't stood out in recent months, but it still ranks in the category's top half for the year to date through Oct. 31, 2001. The fund's stash of insured health-care bonds gave it a lift in early 2001, as those issues benefited from increased Medicare payments. More recently, however, the fund's relatively short duration has held it back, as falling interest rates have given longer-duration funds an added lift. Even so, the fund has managed to gain more than 6% for the year to date, which isn't too shabby given its low-risk profile.

This Morningstar Analyst Pick has a lot going for it. We like its approach and we like its results. Investors looking for a reliable tax-free income fund have found one here.

Address:	One Franklin Parkway San Mateo, CA 94403 650–312–2000 / 800–342–5236
Web Address:	www.franklintempleton.com
Inception:	10-07-83
Advisor:	Franklin Advisers
Subadvisor:	None
NTF Plans:	Fidelity Inst.

Minimum Purchase:	$1000	Add: $50	IRA: $250
Min Auto Inv Plan:	$50	Add: $50	
Sales Fees:	4.25%L, 0.10%B		
Management Fee:	.63% mx./.45% mn.		
Actual Fees:	Mgt: 0.45%	Dist: 0.08%	
Expense Projections:	3Yr: $609	5Yr: $746	10Yr: $1143
Avg Brok Commission:	—	Income Distrib: Monthly	
Total Cost (relative to category):		Below Avg	

Franklin Growth A

Ticker	Load	NAV	Yield	Total Assets	Mstar Category
FKGRX	5.75%	$31.51	0.5%	$2,361.8 mil	Large Blend

Prospectus Objective: Growth

Franklin Growth Series seeks capital appreciation; current income is a secondary consideration.

The fund will normally invest in equity securities of compnaies that are leaders in their industries. It may invest up to 40% of assets in smaller companies, as well as in new and emerging industries where growth is expected to be above average. The fund may invest in any shares traded on any national securities exchange. The fund may also write covered call options.

The fund currently offers Class A, B, C, and Advisor shares, all of which differ in fee structure and availability. Prior to Jan. 1, 1999, Class A and C shares were called Class I and II shares.

Historical Profile

Return Average
Risk Below Avg
Rating ★★★ Neutral

Investment Style
Equity
Average Stock %

1994	1995	1996	1997	1998	1999	2000	12-01
	100%	84%	79%	78%	77%	95%	98%

▼ Manager Change
▽ Partial Manager Change

Fund Performance vs. Category Average
■ Quarterly Fund Return +/– Category Average
— Category Baseline

Performance Quartile (within Category)

Portfolio Manager(s)

V. Jerry Palmieri. Since 3-65. BA Williams C. Other funds currently managed: Franklin Growth C, Franklin Growth Adv, Franklin Growth B.

Conrad B. Herrmann, CFA. Since 7-91. BA'82 Brown U.; MBA'89 Harvard U. Other funds currently managed: Franklin Growth and Income A, Franklin CA Growth A, Franklin Growth and Income C.

1990	1991	1992	1993	1994	1995	1996	1997	1998	1999	2000	12-01	History
11.46	13.98	14.13	14.75	15.00	20.44	23.43	27.09	31.45	34.54	35.03	31.51	NAV
2.07	26.75	2.93	7.13	2.93	38.41	16.68	18.60	18.52	12.19	7.53	–9.47	Total Return %
5.19	–3.73	–4.69	–2.93	1.61	0.87	–6.26	–14.75	–10.05	–8.85	16.63	2.41	+/– S&P 500
6.10	–5.69	–4.73	–2.71	2.48	0.80	–5.48	–14.42	–10.11	–9.64	18.49	3.30	+/– Wilshire Top 750
2.33	3.08	1.35	2.10	0.92	1.09	1.11	1.99	1.62	1.44	1.16	0.44	Income Return %
–0.25	23.67	1.57	5.03	2.01	37.31	15.57	16.62	16.90	10.74	6.37	–9.91	Capital Return %
13	81	86	76	11	6	84	91	73	85	7	16	Total Rtn % Rank Cat
0.27	0.35	0.19	0.30	0.14	0.16	0.23	0.47	0.44	0.45	0.40	0.16	Income $
0.00	0.15	0.07	0.08	0.04	0.15	0.20	0.24	0.21	0.26	1.67	0.05	Capital Gains $
0.73	0.70	0.66	0.64	0.77	0.90	0.87	0.89	0.88	0.89	0.93	—	Expense Ratio %
2.74	2.58	2.06	1.64	1.23	1.08	1.16	1.60	1.78	1.19	1.27	—	Income Ratio %
0	8	1	2	7	1	2	2	1	4	8	—	Turnover Rate %
195.9	407.8	589.9	566.9	538.0	803.3	1,110.1	1,508.8	1,898.6	2,194.2	2,139.1	1,884.4	Net Assets $mil

Performance 12-31-01

	1st Qtr	2nd Qtr	3rd Qtr	4th Qtr	Total
1997	0.17	11.33	3.67	2.58	18.60
1998	7.57	1.78	–3.64	12.34	18.52
1999	3.40	6.27	–3.91	6.24	12.19
2000	5.27	3.03	–1.47	0.62	7.53
2001	–10.39	4.68	–15.37	14.03	–9.47

Trailing	Total Return%	+/– S&P 500	+/– Wil Top 750	% Rank All	% Rank Cat	Growth of $10,000
3 Mo	14.03	3.35	2.71	26	14	11,403
6 Mo	–3.49	2.06	2.30	53	11	9,651
1 Yr	–9.47	2.41	3.30	59	16	9,053
3 Yr Avg	2.98	4.01	4.80	54	16	10,921
5 Yr Avg	8.95	–1.75	–1.17	24	56	15,352
10 Yr Avg	10.90	–2.03	–1.55	26	64	28,139
15 Yr Avg	12.56	–1.17	–0.81	21	46	58,995

Tax Analysis	Tax-Adj Ret%	%Rank Cat	%Pretax Ret	%Rank Cat
3 Yr Avg	2.19	12	73.5	38
5 Yr Avg	8.11	42	90.6	20
10 Yr Avg	10.13	42	92.9	7

Potential Capital Gain Exposure: 41% of assets

Risk Analysis

Time Period	Load-Adj Return %	Risk %Rank[1] All	Risk %Rank[1] Cat	Morningstar Return	Morningstar Risk	Morningstar Risk-Adj Rating
1 Yr	–14.67					
3 Yr	0.97	47	3	–0.81[2]	0.65	★★★
5 Yr	7.67	46	1	0.61[2]	0.60	★★★
10 Yr	10.25	54	2	0.77	0.69	★★★

Average Historical Rating (193 months): 3.3★s

[1] 1=low, 100=high [2] T-Bill return substituted for category avg.

Category Rating (3 Yr)

① ② ③ ❹ ⑤
Worst Best

Return Above Avg
Risk Low

Other Measures	Standard Index S&P 500	Best Fit Index S&P 500
Alpha	2.6	2.6
Beta	0.77	0.77
R-Squared	80	80
Standard Deviation	14.94	
Mean	2.98	
Sharpe Ratio	–0.15	

Portfolio Analysis 09-30-01

Share change since 06-01 Total Stocks: 136	Sector	PE	YTD Ret%	% Assets
FNMA N/A	N/A	—	—	4.35
Pfizer	Health	34.7	–12.40	3.73
Tyco Intl	Industrials	27.1	6.23	3.41
Schering-plough	Health	22.2	–35.90	3.23
Johnson & Johnson	Health	16.6	14.01	2.67
Ibm	Technology	26.9	43.00	2.50
Northrop Grumman	Industrials	19.2	23.67	2.44
Amgen	Health	52.8	–11.70	2.28
Aol Time Warner	Technology	—	–7.76	2.16
General Dynamics	Industrials	17.6	3.63	2.14
Minnesota Mng & Mfg	Industrials	34.5	0.16	1.90
Automatic Data Processing	Services	39.8	–6.27	1.82
Bristol-myers Squibb	Health	20.2	–26.00	1.72
American Home Products	Health	—	–1.91	1.69
⊕ Boeing	Industrials	10.2	–40.40	1.62
⊕ El Paso	Utilities	NMF	–36.70	1.61
⊕ Computer Sciences	Technology	57.6	–18.50	1.61
Eli Lilly	Health	28.9	–14.40	1.56
Baxter Intl	Health	33.9	22.84	1.33
⊕ Illinois Tool Works	Industrials	25.4	15.31	1.31
Merck	Health	19.1	–35.90	1.29
Allergan	Health	48.7	–22.10	1.28
Delta Air Lines	Services	—	–41.50	1.28
⊕ Microsoft	Technology	57.6	52.78	1.24
Emerson Elec	Industrials	23.8	–25.60	1.14

Current Investment Style

Style: Value Blnd Growth; Size: Large Med Small

	Stock Port Avg	Relative S&P 500 Current	Relative S&P 500 Hist	Rel Cat
Price/Earnings Ratio	31.2	1.01	0.98	1.03
Price/Book Ratio	5.8	1.01	0.98	1.05
Price/Cash Flow	17.5	0.97	0.91	0.95
3 Yr Earnings Growth	13.9	0.95	1.10	0.78
1 Yr Earnings Est%	–2.1	1.19	—	—
Med Mkt Cap $mil	23,936	0.4	0.5	0.46

Special Securities % assets 09-30-01	
Restricted/Illiquid Secs	0
Emerging-Markets Secs	0
Options/Futures/Warrants	No

Composition % assets 09-30-01	
Cash	0.0
Stocks*	95.6
Bonds	4.4
Other	0.0
*Foreign (% stocks)	3.7

Market Cap	
Giant	37.7
Large	31.6
Medium	24.3
Small	6.2
Micro	0.2

Sector Weightings	% of Stocks	Rel S&P	5-Year High	5-Year Low
Utilities	1.7	0.5	2	0
Energy	2.6	0.4	6	3
Financials	0.0	0.0	0	0
Industrials	31.6	2.8	32	17
Durables	1.6	1.0	2	0
Staples	2.4	0.3	4	1
Services	16.2	1.5	36	16
Retail	1.8	0.3	5	0
Health	24.5	1.7	34	19
Technology	17.5	1.0	25	7

Analysis by Dan Culloton 11-01-01

Low volatility has been this fund's saving grace, but that could change now that it has jettisoned its cash cushion.

A big cash stake, sometimes approaching a third of its assets, kept Franklin Growth far away from the punch bowl during the roaring '90s. The fund spent four straight years eating the dust of its category and the S&P 500 as veteran manager Jerry Palmieri refused to pay for stocks with stratospheric multiples. Since the bear market started, however, the fund has vaulted to the top of its category and ahead of its benchmark. For the year to date through Oct. 30, 2001, the fund was down 18%, but still about a percentage point in front of the S&P 500 and better than 75% of other large-blend funds. In 2000, the fund's 7.5% gain put it ahead of more than 90% of its peers.

Palmieri, a conservative, buy-and-hold investor who focuses on industry leaders with proven earnings, has used the market sell-off as an opportunity to put cash to work. He has been buying stocks as they have fallen this year, and the thick buffer of cash that used to smooth returns is all but gone. For the first time in a long time, the fund is nearly fully invested, with 95% of its assets in stocks. Palmieri has picked up leading but severely beaten-down tech stocks like JDS Uniphase. He's also added to holdings, such as AMR and Boeing, that he thinks will appreciate when the economy recovers and Americans resume flying at a more-normal rate.

This fund hasn't beaten its peers or benchmark often, but it hasn't lost money often either. Palmieri's experience and conservative approach have made it suitable for risk-averse investors, but shareholders who prized its modest volatility in the past should know that it's now considerably more vulnerable to market fluctuations.

Address:	One Franklin Parkway San Mateo, CA 94403 650-312-2000 / 800-342-5236
Web Address:	www.franklintempleton.com
Inception:	03-31-48
Advisor:	Franklin Inv. Advisory Svcs
Subadvisor:	None
NTF Plans:	Datalynx , Fidelity Inst.

Minimum Purchase:	$1000	Add: $50 IRA: $250
Min Auto Inv Plan:	$50	Add: $50
Sales Fees:	5.75%L, 0.25%B	
Management Fee:	.63% mx./.40% mn.	
Actual Fees:	Mgt: 0.46%	Dist: 0.24%
Expense Projections:	3Yr: $843	5Yr: $1040 10Yr: $1608
Avg Brok Commission:	—	Income Distrib: Annually
Total Cost (relative to category):		Average

Franklin High Yield Tax–Free Inc A

Ticker	Load	NAV	Yield	SEC Yield	Total Assets	Mstar Category
FRHIX	4.25%	$10.49	5.6%	4.95%	$5,272.3 mil	Muni Natl Long–Term

Prospectus Objective: Muni Bond—National

Franklin High Yield Tax-Free Income Fund seeks a high current yield exempt from federal income taxes.

The fund normally invests at least 80% of assets in securities that pay interest exempt from federal income tax, including the Alternative Minimum Tax. It invests primarily in municipal securities rated below investment-grade or unrated; it may invest no more than 10% of assets, however, in defaulted debt. The fund maintains no restrictions on average maturity.

Class A shares have front loads; C shares have level loads.

Historical Profile

Return: Average
Risk: Below Avg
Rating: ★★★★ Above Avg

Investment Style
Fixed-Income
Income Rtn %Rank Cat: 3, 3, 2, 2, 3, 3, 5, 10

Growth of Principal vs. Interest Rate Shifts
— Principal Value $000 (NAV with capital gains reinvested)
— Interest Rate % on 10 Yr Treasury
▼ Manager Change
▽ Partial Manager Change
► Mgr Unknown After
◄ Mgr Unknown Before

Performance Quartile (within Category)

Portfolio Manager(s)

Sheila Amoroso. Since 1-87. BS San Francisco State U. Other funds currently managed: Franklin LA Tax-Free Income A, Franklin CA Tax-Free Income A, Franklin Federal Tax-Free Income A.

John Hopp. Since 1-93. Other funds currently managed: Franklin High Yield Tax-Free Inc C, Franklin High Yield Tax-Free Inc B.

John Wiley. Since 12-00. BS U. of California-Berkeley; MBA Saint Mary's C. Other funds currently managed: Franklin LA Tax-Free Income A, Franklin CA Tax-Free Income A, Franklin Federal Tax-Free Income A.

History

1990	1991	1992	1993	1994	1995	1996	1997	1998	1999	2000	12-01	History
10.28	10.66	10.77	11.38	10.35	11.26	11.19	11.64	11.51	10.51	10.47	10.49	NAV
5.12	12.40	9.06	13.27	–2.56	16.31	6.15	10.65	4.81	–3.24	5.86	5.89	Total Return %
–3.84	–3.61	1.65	3.52	0.36	–2.16	2.53	0.97	–3.87	–2.41	–5.77	–2.54	+/– LB Aggregate
–2.19	0.25	0.24	0.99	2.58	–1.15	1.71	1.45	–1.68	–1.17	–5.83	0.81	+/– LB Muni
8.22	8.48	7.82	7.44	6.76	7.30	6.70	6.44	5.85	5.78	6.23	5.74	Income Return %
–3.11	3.91	1.23	5.83	–9.33	9.01	–0.55	4.21	–1.04	–9.02	–0.37	0.15	Capital Return %
81	32	41	26	7	59	2	8	77	12	88	7	Total Rtn % Rank Cat
0.84	0.84	0.81	0.78	0.75	0.73	0.73	0.70	0.66	0.65	0.64	0.59	Income $
0.00	0.00	0.01	0.00	0.00	0.00	0.00	0.00	0.02	0.00	0.00	0.00	Capital Gains $
0.54	0.52	0.53	0.54	0.53	0.60	0.61	0.62	0.61	0.62	0.61	0.62	Expense Ratio %
7.52	7.90	7.73	7.45	6.79	6.92	6.68	6.41	5.98	5.64	5.92	5.90	Income Ratio %
23	71	103	33	16	16	9	7	16	19	25	11	Turnover Rate %
1,683.4	2,044.1	2,568.2	3,327.3	3,124.5	3,694.1	4,309.6	5,226.5	5,897.3	5,154.5	4,733.2	4,604.9	Net Assets $mil

Performance 12-31-01

	1st Qtr	2nd Qtr	3rd Qtr	4th Qtr	Total
1997	0.38	3.33	3.67	2.91	10.65
1998	1.37	1.70	1.94	–0.28	4.81
1999	1.06	–1.13	–0.71	–2.47	–3.24
2000	2.14	–0.16	2.22	1.56	5.86
2001	2.16	1.39	2.34	–0.11	5.89

Trailing	Total Return%	+/– LB Agg	+/– LB Muni	% Rank All	% Rank Cat	Growth of $10,000
3 Mo	–0.11	–0.15	0.55	80	4	9,989
6 Mo	2.22	–2.43	0.10	20	10	10,222
1 Yr	5.89	–2.54	0.81	19	7	10,589
3 Yr Avg	2.75	–3.53	–2.01	57	62	10,847
5 Yr Avg	4.70	–2.73	–1.28	70	48	12,579
10 Yr Avg	6.46	–0.77	–0.18	58	13	18,692
15 Yr Avg	7.32	–0.80	0.13	62	6	28,841

Tax Analysis	Tax-Adj Ret%	%Rank Cat	%Pretax Ret	%Rank Cat
3 Yr Avg	2.75	61	100.0	5
5 Yr Avg	4.69	44	99.9	27
10 Yr Avg	6.45	6	99.9	8

Potential Capital Gain Exposure: –4% of assets

Risk Analysis

Time Period	Load-Adj Return %	Risk %Rank[1] All	Risk %Rank[1] Cat	Morningstar Return	Morningstar Risk	Morningstar Risk-Adj Rating
1 Yr	1.39					
3 Yr	1.27	10	4	0.05[2]	0.83	★★★
5 Yr	3.79	8	3	0.65[2]	0.77	★★★★
10 Yr	5.99	6	3	1.23	0.64	★★★★★

Average Historical Rating (154 months): 4.9★s

[1] 1=low, 100=high [2] T-Bill return substituted for category avg.

Category Rating (3 Yr)

1 Worst — 5 Best

Return: Average
Risk: Low

Other Measures	Standard Index LB Agg	Best Fit Index LB Muni
Alpha	–2.8	–2.0
Beta	0.54	0.77
R–Squared	31	77
Standard Deviation		3.27
Mean		2.75
Sharpe Ratio		–0.78

Portfolio Analysis 09-30-01

Total Fixed-Income: 741	Date of Maturity	Amount $000	Value $000	% Net Assets
Az Pima Indl Dev Tucson Elec Pwr 6%	09-01-29	94,690	92,677	1.73
Nm Farmington Poll Cntrl Pub Svc 6.375%	04-01-22	66,125	67,285	1.26
OR Klamath Falls Elec 6%		61,060	61,096	1.14
NJ Econ Dev Continental Airline 6%		73,030	58,802	1.10
Nm Farmington Poll Cntrl Pub Svc 0%	08-15-23	58,250	58,362	1.09
Ct Dev Poll Cntrl Lt/pwr 5.85%	09-01-28	57,075	57,907	1.08
Az Pima Indl Dev Tucson Elec Pwr 6%	09-01-29	53,500	52,363	0.98
Az Apache Indl Dev Poll Cntrl 5.85%	03-01-28	53,150	51,078	0.96
NV Henderson GO Loc Impt Dist 7%		46,925	49,832	0.93
CO Eagle Sports/Hsg Fac 6.95%		41,200	43,949	0.82
NJ Econ Dev Continental Airline 6%		54,420	43,882	0.82
Ca Foothill/eastern Transp Corridor 6.5%	01-01-32	37,675	43,730	0.82
CA Bay Area Govt Assn Impr Brd 7%		38,610	41,086	0.77
Nm Farmington Poll Cntrl Tucson 6.95%	10-01-20	37,000	38,469	0.72
Ca San Joaquin Hills Transp Corridor 0%	01-01-26	131,900	37,726	0.71

Current Investment Style

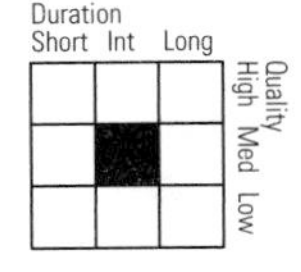

Avg Duration[1]	6.7 Yrs
Avg Nominal Maturity	19.6 Yrs
Avg Credit Quality	BBB
Avg Wtd Coupon	6.21%
Avg Wtd Price	98.85% of par
Pricing Service	Muller

[1] figure provided by fund

Credit Analysis % bonds 09-30-01

US Govt	0	BB	14
AAA	21	B	2
AA	4	Below B	1
A	9	NR/NA	28
BBB	20		

Special Securities % assets 09-30-01

Restricted/Illiquid Secs	0
Inverse Floaters	0
Options/Futures/Warrants	Yes

Bond Type % assets 03-31-01

Alternative Minimum Tax (AMT)	19.6
Insured	—
Prerefunded	14.9

Top 5 States % bonds

CA	13.1	AZ	7.1
FL	10.9	PA	6.2
NY	9.7		

Composition % assets 09-30-01

Cash	1.7	Bonds	98.3
Stocks	0.0	Other	0.1

Sector Weightings	% of Bonds	Rel Cat
General Obligation	14.0	0.7
Utilities	7.8	1.0
Health	13.1	0.9
Water/Waste	3.1	0.5
Housing	4.4	0.6
Education	0.7	0.1
Transportation	13.8	1.0
COP/Lease	3.6	1.3
Industrial	31.1	2.4
Misc Revenue	7.6	1.5
Demand	0.9	1.0

Analysis by Scott Berry 12-07-01

Franklin High Yield Tax-Free Income does a lot of things right.

This fund is one of the largest municipal bond funds and one of the most diversified. In fact, it recently held more than 750 different issues and its top-10 holdings accounted for just 12% of its net assets. That level of diversification serves the fund well by limiting the damage caused by individual defaults and blowups, which are a nearly unavoidable side effect of investing in lower-quality municipal bonds.

The fund's relatively conservative approach has also served it well. While the fund's 30% stake in nonrated bonds is evidence that it doesn't shy away from credit risk, lead manager John Wiley avoids duration bets and keeps portfolio turnover to a minimum. Instead, he simply looks to buy attractively valued, high-coupon bonds and is content to soak up their yield until their maturity or call date. In years past, that approach has resulted in the fund owning a collection of older, higher-yielding issues, which tend to be less sensitive to interest-rate changes than more recently issued bonds.

For the year to date through Dec. 5, 2001, the fund gained a solid 6.4% and ranked in the muni national long-term category's top 10%. The fund has benefited in recent months from its exposure to utilities and land-secured bonds, which according to Wiley have outperformed the market as a whole. He also credits increased retail demand for the fund's recent success. With interest rates at historically low levels, retail investors have chased the higher yields being offered by lower-quality bonds, pushing prices higher.

This fund is certainly riskier than its investment-grade peers and is sure to hit some bumps in the road, but we think it makes a good complement to a portfolio of higher-quality municipal bonds.

Address:	One Franklin Parkway San Mateo, CA 94403 650–312–2000 / 800–342–5236
Web Address:	www.franklintempleton.com
Inception:	03-18-86
Advisor:	Franklin Advisers
Subadvisor:	None
NTF Plans:	N/A

Minimum Purchase:	$1000	Add: $50	IRA: $250
Min Auto Inv Plan:	$1000	Add: $50	
Sales Fees:	4.25%L, 0.10%B		
Management Fee:	.63% mx./.45% mn.		
Actual Fees:	Mgt: 0.46%	Dist: 0.09%	
Expense Projections:	3Yr: $615	5Yr: $756	10Yr: $1166
Avg Brok Commission:	—	Income Distrib: Monthly	
Total Cost (relative to category):		Below Avg	

Franklin Income A

Ticker	Load	NAV	Yield	Total Assets	Mstar Category
FKINX	4.25%	$2.18	8.2%	$8,019.9 mil	Domestic Hybrid

Prospectus Objective: Balanced

Franklin Income Series seeks income while maintaining prospects for capital appreciation.

The fund invests in a diversified portfolio of income-producing securities; there are no restrictions as to the proportion of any particular type of security. The fund may also invest in securities of any rating or unrated securities.

Class A shares have front loads; B shares have deferred loads; C shares have level loads; Advisor shares are designed for institutional investors and certain qualified investors. Prior to Jan. 1, 1999, Class A and C shares were called Class I and II shares.

Historical Profile

Return Below Avg
Risk Low
Rating ★★★ Neutral

Investment Style
Equity
Average Stock %: 28% 29% 29% 35% 32% 38% 35%

▼ Manager Change
▽ Partial Manager Change

Fund Performance vs. Category Average
Quarterly Fund Return +/– Category Average
— Category Baseline

Performance Quartile (within Category)

Portfolio Manager(s)

Charles B. Johnson. Since 3-57. BA'54 Yale U. Other funds currently managed: Franklin Income C, Franklin Income Adv, Franklin Income B.

Fred Fromm. Since 1-98. BA'92 U. of California. Other funds currently managed: Franklin Income C, Franklin Income Adv, Franklin Income B.

Christopher J. Molumphy, CFA. Since 6-00. BA Stanford U.; MBA U. of Chicago. Other funds currently managed: Franklin AGE High Income A, Franklin Strategic Income A, Franklin Income C.

History

1990	1991	1992	1993	1994	1995	1996	1997	1998	1999	2000	12–01	History
1.68	2.11	2.21	2.46	2.10	2.32	2.36	2.53	2.36	2.15	2.36	2.18	NAV
–8.76	41.15	15.26	21.54	–6.37	21.29	10.45	16.85	0.95	–0.74	20.58	0.65	Total Return %
–5.64	10.67	7.65	11.48	–7.68	–16.24	–12.50	–16.50	–27.62	–21.78	29.68	12.53	+/– S&P 500
–17.71	25.15	7.86	11.79	–3.45	2.83	6.83	7.16	–7.72	0.09	8.94	–7.77	+/– LB Aggregate
11.09	13.70	9.81	8.43	7.58	8.91	8.04	7.90	7.36	7.91	8.70	7.91	Income Return %
–19.84	27.46	5.45	13.11	–13.95	12.39	2.40	8.95	–6.40	–8.65	11.88	–7.25	Capital Return %
97	5	6	5	89	83	77	63	96	90	3	20	Total Rtn % Rank Cat
0.22	0.22	0.20	0.18	0.18	0.18	0.18	0.18	0.18	0.18	0.18	0.18	Income $
0.00	0.01	0.01	0.03	0.03	0.03	0.01	0.03	0.01	0.01	0.03	0.02	Capital Gains $
0.55	0.56	0.55	0.54	0.64	0.71	0.70	0.72	0.72	—	0.76	—	Expense Ratio %
10.73	10.17	9.11	7.84	7.37	8.26	8.27	7.45	6.83	—	8.01	—	Income Ratio %
12	34	23	25	23	59	25	16	22	—	24	—	Turnover Rate %
1,252.9	1,796.4	2,739.8	4,327.8	4,789.3	6,216.8	7,081.7	8,043.7	7,783.9	6,284.8	6,136.4	6,242.6	Net Assets $mil

Performance 12-31-01

	1st Qtr	2nd Qtr	3rd Qtr	4th Qtr	Total
1997	0.19	5.90	5.25	4.64	16.85
1998	3.42	–2.16	–3.45	3.33	0.95
1999	–2.77	5.59	–1.96	–1.39	–0.74
2000	0.71	5.95	8.98	3.69	20.58
2001	0.21	1.50	–4.63	3.76	0.65

Trailing	Total Return%	+/– S&P 500	+/– LB Agg	% Rank All	% Rank Cat	Growth of $10,000
3 Mo	3.76	–6.92	3.72	68	83	10,376
6 Mo	–1.05	4.51	–5.70	43	37	9,895
1 Yr	0.65	12.53	–7.77	41	20	10,065
3 Yr Avg	6.40	7.43	0.13	20	10	12,046
5 Yr Avg	7.28	–3.42	–0.15	34	50	14,210
10 Yr Avg	9.58	–3.35	2.35	35	43	24,969
15 Yr Avg	9.93	–3.81	1.81	42	47	41,354

Tax Analysis	Tax-Adj Ret%	%Rank Cat	%Pretax Ret	%Rank Cat
3 Yr Avg	2.93	20	45.8	61
5 Yr Avg	3.87	70	53.2	88
10 Yr Avg	6.05	62	63.2	85

Potential Capital Gain Exposure: –3% of assets

Risk Analysis

Time Period	Load-Adj Return %	Risk %Rank[1] All	Risk %Rank[1] Cat	Morningstar Return	Morningstar Risk	Morningstar Risk-Adj Rating
1 Yr	–3.63					
3 Yr	4.87	32	9	–0.01[2]	0.32	★★★★
5 Yr	6.35	38	13	0.30[2]	0.38	★★★
10 Yr	9.11	44	8	0.58	0.41	★★★

Average Historical Rating (193 months): 3.6★s

[1] 1=low, 100=high [2] T–Bill return substituted for category avg.

Category Rating (3 Yr)

1 2 3 4 5
Worst Best

Return High
Risk Low

Other Measures	Standard Index S&P 500	Best Fit Index SPMid400
Alpha	2.4	0.1
Beta	0.15	0.23
R–Squared	11	33

Standard Deviation	8.24
Mean	6.40
Sharpe Ratio	0.21

Portfolio Analysis 09-30-01

Total Stocks: 47 Share change since 06–01	Sector	PE Ratio	YTD Return %	% Net Assets
Philip Morris	Staples	12.1	9.12	7.17
✵ Canadian Oil Sands Tr	N/A	—	—	1.62
TXU	Utilities	13.7	12.17	1.56
Xcel Energy	Utilities	12.2	0.57	1.48
American Elec Pwr	Utilities	20.2	–1.28	1.46
⊕ General Motors	Durables	NMF	–0.97	1.45
Public Svc Entpr	Utilities	11.3	–8.99	1.35
Entergy	Utilities	11.7	–4.50	1.20
⊕ Dominion Resources	Utilities	19.3	–6.59	1.00
GPU	Utilities	—	13.38	0.93

Total Fixed-Income: 201	Date of Maturity	Amount $000	Value $000	% Net Assets
FNMA 6.5%		274,087	279,023	3.77
US Treasury Note 5.875%	11-15-04	173,000	185,570	2.51
FNMA N/A		148,000	147,824	2.00
Conproca 144A 12%	06-16-10	90,000	99,225	1.34
FHLMC Debenture 6%		90,000	98,610	1.33
Republic of Brazil FRN	04-15-06	96,560	80,447	1.09
Glenborough Rlty Cv Pfd 7.75%		3,400	65,416	0.88
Lone Cypress 11%		65,930	65,271	0.88
Macerich 144A Cv 7.25%	12-15-02	65,000	62,644	0.85
Republic of Argentina 5.75%	03-31-23	98,000	59,780	0.81

Equity Style
Style: Value
Size: Large–Cap

Fixed-Income Style
Duration: Intermediate
Quality: Low

	Portfolio Avg	Rel S&P
Price/Earnings Ratio	16.7	0.54
Price/Book Ratio	2.6	0.45
Price/Cash Flow	7.9	0.44
3 Yr Earnings Growth	8.2	0.56
1 Yr Earnings Est%	5.5	—
Debt % Total Cap	55.0	1.78
Med Mkt Cap $mil	11,119	0.18

Avg Eff Duration	—
Avg Eff Maturity	7.0 Yrs
Avg Credit Quality	BB
Avg Wtd Coupon	8.27%

Analysis by Scott Berry 11-27-01

Franklin Income isn't for everyone, but those looking to diversify a growth-oriented portfolio may find it to their liking.

This fund's unique mix of high-yield bonds, emerging-markets debt, and dividend-paying stocks has limited its volatility while helping it deliver surprisingly competitive long-term returns. The fund tends to lag other domestic-hybrid funds during stock market rallies, as it typically holds just 40% of its assets in stocks versus its average peer's 50%. But, when the stock market sours, as it has over the last couple of years, this fund can make up a lot of ground in a hurry.

The fund has gained more than 5% over the trailing 12 months through Nov. 26, 2001, while its average peer has lost 4%. The strong performance of the fund's fixed-income holdings has helped drive its recent returns, but the fund's exposure to riskier sectors of the bond market, including high-yield and emerging-markets debt, could certainly have a negative influence on the fund's future performance should those sectors fall on hard times. Indeed, the fund recently held a 26% stake in high-yield bonds, while its average peer held less than 5%.

The fund's current positioning reflects management's contrarian approach. As emerging-markets bonds rallied in early 2001, management took profits and funneled them to the high-yield sector, which has struggled the last few years. On the stock side, management has recently found opportunities in beaten-down automotive stocks such as GM and Ford, but has continued to focus mainly on the utility and consumer-staples sectors, which recently accounted for more than half of the fund's equity exposure.

The fund's quirky porfolio can provide diversification for growth-stock-heavy portfolios. But investors looking for a more traditional balanced fund will want to look elsewhere.

Address:	One Franklin Parkway San Mateo, CA 94403 650–312–2000 / 800–342–5236
Web Address:	www.franklintempleton.com
Inception:	08-31-48
Advisor:	Franklin Advisers
Subadvisor:	None
NTF Plans:	N/A

Minimum Purchase:	$1000	Add: $50	IRA: $250
Min Auto Inv Plan:	$50	Add: $50	
Sales Fees:	4.25%L, 0.15%B		
Management Fee:	.63% mx./.40% mn.		
Actual Fees:	Mgt: 0.45%	Dist: 0.15%	
Expense Projections:	3Yr: $648	5Yr: $814	10Yr: $1293
Avg Brok Commission:	—	Income Distrib: Monthly	
Total Cost (relative to category):		Below Avg	

Special Securities % assets 09-30-01	
Restricted/Illiquid Secs	2
Emerging–Markets Secs	7
Options/Futures/Warrants	No

Composition % of assets 09-30-01	
Cash	7.7
Stocks*	36.8
Bonds	42.2
Other	13.4
*Foreign (% of stocks)	7.2

Market Cap	
Giant	23.3
Large	42.0
Medium	29.6
Small	5.1
Micro	0.0

Sector Weightings	% of Stocks	Rel S&P	5-Year High	5-Year Low
Utilities	51.3	16.1	78	51
Energy	3.5	0.5	10	1
Financials	4.5	0.3	16	0
Industrials	7.6	0.7	17	3
Durables	5.7	3.6	6	0
Staples	26.4	3.3	27	0
Services	1.1	0.1	9	0
Retail	0.0	0.0	1	0
Health	0.0	0.0	19	0
Technology	0.0	0.0	6	0

Franklin Insured Tax-Free Income A

Ticker	Load	NAV	Yield	SEC Yield	Total Assets	Mstar Category
FTFIX	4.25%	$11.91	5.0%	5.05%	$1,633.6 mil	Muni Natl Long-Term

Prospectus Objective: Muni Bond—National

Franklin Insured Tax-Free Income Fund seeks current income exempt from federal income taxes, consistent with preservation of capital.

The fund invests at least 80% of assets in securities that generate interest exempt from federal income taxes. It may not invest more than 25% of assets in the municipal securities of a single state or territory. The fund's municipal securities are typically insured by the issuer or by an independent insurance agency.

Class A shares have front loads; C shares have level loads.

Historical Profile

Return: Average
Risk: Below Avg
Rating: ★★★★ Above Avg

Investment Style Fixed-Income

Income Rtn %Rank Cat: 24 | 26 | 17 | 16 | 13 | 21 | 27 | 29

Growth of Principal vs. Interest Rate Shifts
- Principal Value $000 (NAV with capital gains reinvested)
- Interest Rate % on 10 Yr Treasury
- ▼ Manager Change
- ▽ Partial Manager Change
- ► Mgr Unknown After
- ◄ Mgr Unknown Before

Performance Quartile (within Category)

Portfolio Manager(s)

Sheila Amoroso. Since 2-87. BS San Francisco State U. Other funds currently managed: Franklin LA Tax-Free Income A, Franklin CA Tax-Free Income A, Franklin Federal Tax-Free Income A.

John Pomeroy. Since 8-89. BS'86 San Francisco State U. Other funds currently managed: Franklin MD Tax-Free Income A, Franklin MN Insured Tax-Free Inc A, Franklin MA Insured Tax-Free Inc A.

1990	1991	1992	1993	1994	1995	1996	1997	1998	1999	2000	12-01	History
11.28	11.75	12.04	12.70	11.54	12.37	12.16	12.32	12.30	11.26	11.97	11.91	NAV
6.57	11.35	9.20	11.84	−3.58	13.63	4.11	8.15	6.05	−3.46	12.08	4.57	Total Return %
−2.39	−4.66	1.79	2.09	−0.67	−4.84	0.50	−1.53	−2.63	−2.63	0.45	−3.85	+/– LB Aggregate
−0.74	−0.80	0.38	−0.44	1.56	−3.83	−0.33	−1.05	−0.44	−1.39	0.39	−0.51	+/– LB Muni
7.20	7.02	6.63	6.23	5.76	6.29	5.79	5.70	5.37	5.08	5.53	5.12	Income Return %
−0.64	4.32	2.57	5.61	−9.34	7.35	−1.67	2.45	0.67	−8.54	6.55	−0.55	Capital Return %
33	72	38	62	12	94	25	85	17	18	23	28	Total Rtn % Rank Cat
0.79	0.77	0.76	0.73	0.71	0.71	0.70	0.68	0.65	0.61	0.61	0.60	Income $
0.00	0.00	0.00	0.00	0.00	0.00	0.00	0.12	0.10	0.02	0.00	0.00	Capital Gains $
0.54	0.53	0.53	0.53	0.52	0.59	0.60	0.60	0.61	0.62	0.62	0.62	Expense Ratio %
6.92	6.95	6.55	6.22	5.79	6.00	5.81	5.68	5.44	5.11	5.23	5.23	Income Ratio %
12	10	6	8	7	14	14	19	28	13	13	10	Turnover Rate %
819.1	1,072.2	1,432.5	1,807.3	1,621.4	1,722.7	1,666.5	1,683.4	1,731.0	1,504.8	1,469.7	1,519.1	Net Assets $mil

Performance 12-31-01

	1st Qtr	2nd Qtr	3rd Qtr	4th Qtr	Total
1997	−0.08	2.78	2.55	2.70	8.15
1998	1.01	1.65	2.78	0.49	6.05
1999	0.77	−1.62	−1.26	−1.38	−3.46
2000	3.15	1.26	2.38	4.81	12.08
2001	1.68	0.68	2.51	−0.35	4.57

Trailing	Total Return%	+/– LB Agg	+/– LB Muni	% Rank All	% Rank Cat	Growth of $10,000
3 Mo	−0.35	−0.39	0.31	82	8	9,965
6 Mo	2.15	−2.50	0.03	21	13	10,215
1 Yr	4.57	−3.85	−0.51	26	28	10,457
3 Yr Avg	4.20	−2.07	−0.55	38	7	11,315
5 Yr Avg	5.35	−2.08	−0.62	58	16	12,977
10 Yr Avg	6.10	−1.13	−0.53	68	32	18,077
15 Yr Avg	6.52	−1.60	−0.67	77	39	25,794

Tax Analysis	Tax-Adj Ret%	%Rank Cat	%Pretax Ret	%Rank Cat
3 Yr Avg	4.19	6	99.7	58
5 Yr Avg	5.27	16	98.4	59
10 Yr Avg	6.06	24	99.3	16

Potential Capital Gain Exposure: 3% of assets

Risk Analysis

Time Period	Load-Adj Return %	Risk %Rank[1] All	Risk %Rank[1] Cat	Morningstar Return	Morningstar Risk	Morningstar Risk-Adj Rating
1 Yr	0.13					
3 Yr	2.71	14	10	0.27[2]	0.93	★★★
5 Yr	4.44	12	9	0.70[2]	0.87	★★★
10 Yr	5.64	10	7	0.98	0.81	★★★★

Average Historical Rating (165 months): 3.5★s

[1] 1=low, 100=high [2] T-Bill return substituted for category avg.

Category Rating (3 Yr)

1 2 3 4 5 — Worst … Best

Return: High
Risk: Low

Other Measures	Standard Index LB Agg	Best Fit Index LB Muni
Alpha	−1.7	−0.5
Beta	0.82	1.04
R-Squared	50	98
Standard Deviation		4.04
Mean		4.20
Sharpe Ratio		−0.22

Portfolio Analysis 09-30-01

Total Fixed-Income: 467	Date of Maturity	Amount $000	Value $000	% Net Assets
TX Harris Hlth Fac Dev 5%		22,000	21,701	1.34
Ca Corona Cop 7%	09-01-20	15,000	20,914	1.29
AZ Mesa Indl Dev 5%		18,000	19,029	1.17
Ny Dorm St Johns Univ 5.7%	07-01-26	15,000	15,611	0.96
GA M/C Hosp Columbus Regl Hlth 5%		15,000	15,587	0.96
Oh Tpk Com 5.5%	02-15-26	14,000	15,540	0.96
TX Austin Hotel Occupancy Tax 5%		13,750	14,382	0.89
GA Atlanta Arpt 5%		13,750	14,172	0.87
AZ Mesa Indl Dev 5%		12,655	13,234	0.82
Wa Hlth Care Fac Swedish Sys 5.5%	11-15-28	13,000	13,195	0.81
Tx Matagorda Navig Dist #1 Poll 6.1%	07-01-28	12,850	13,166	0.81
Tx Coastal Bend Hlth Fac Dev 6.3%	01-01-17	12,230	12,970	0.80
Mn Agric/econ Dev Brd Fairview 5.75%	11-15-26	12,280	12,863	0.79
Wv Harrison Com Solid Waste 6.75%	08-01-24	11,560	12,719	0.78
MN Sauk Rapids GO 5%		11,850	12,505	0.77

Current Investment Style

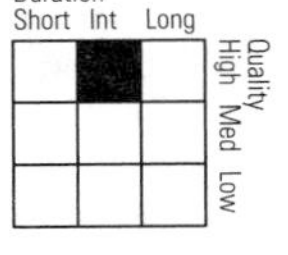

Avg Duration[1]	5.9 Yrs
Avg Nominal Maturity	19.8 Yrs
Avg Credit Quality	AAA
Avg Wtd Coupon	5.67%
Avg Wtd Price	104.59% of par
Pricing Service	Muller

[1] figure provided by fund

Credit Analysis % bonds 09-30-01

US Govt	0	BB	0
AAA	100	B	0
AA	0	Below B	0
A	0	NR/NA	0
BBB	0		

Special Securities % assets 09-30-01

Restricted/Illiquid Secs	0
Inverse Floaters	0
Options/Futures/Warrants	No

Bond Type % assets 03-31-01

Alternative Minimum Tax (AMT)	7.9
Insured	98.0
Prerefunded	17.7

Top 5 States % bonds

TX	13.1	CO	5.2
MA	6.6	WA	5.1
NY	6.6		

Composition % assets 09-30-01

Cash	0.0	Bonds	100.0
Stocks	0.0	Other	0.0

Sector Weightings	% of Bonds	Rel Cat
General Obligation	11.2	0.5
Utilities	5.3	0.7
Health	27.3	1.8
Water/Waste	12.7	2.1
Housing	2.9	0.4
Education	8.3	1.3
Transportation	9.8	0.7
COP/Lease	8.0	2.8
Industrial	11.4	0.9
Misc Revenue	2.8	0.6
Demand	0.2	0.2

Analysis by Scott Berry 11-28-01

Franklin Insured Tax-Free Income is more than just a face in the crowd.

Much like Treasury bonds, insured municipal bonds are a somewhat homogeneous asset class. The yields on various issues fall in a very narrow range and credit risk is not a concern. That makes it difficult for muni-insured bond funds to distinguish themselves from one another. However, this is one fund that has stood out.

The fund has delivered solid total returns, but its low volatility is what has set it apart from its average muni-insured peer. Insured muni-bond funds tend to be more sensitive to interest-rate changes, and thus more volatile than more-diversified offerings, but this offering has bucked the trend. Not only has it been far less volatile than its average insured peer, but it has also been less volatile than the average muni-national fund, which holds a diverse mix of insured and noninsured bonds.

The fund's low volatility owes much to Franklin's buy-and-hold approach. Bonds that the fund purchased years ago, when interest rates were much higher, have served to mute its sensitivity to changing interest rates. A number of these bonds have matured or been called away in recent years, so the fund's volatility could pick up a bit. But its buy-and-hold strategy should continue to pay off over the long term.

For the year to date through Nov. 27, 2001, the fund has gained a respectable 5.4%. Falling interest rates have given the fund a small lift, but its relatively short duration has kept it from keeping pace with a number of its muni-insured peers.

Even so, this fund has proven its worth over the long term. We think investors looking to own a portfolio of insured municipal bonds will be hard-pressed to find a better broker-sold option.

Address:	One Franklin Parkway San Mateo, CA 94403 650-312-2000 / 800-342-5236
Web Address:	www.franklintempleton.com
Inception:	04-03-85
Advisor:	Franklin Advisers
Subadvisor:	None
NTF Plans:	N/A

Minimum Purchase:	$1000	Add: $50	IRA: —
Min Auto Inv Plan:	$1000	Add: $50	
Sales Fees:	4.25%L, 0.10%B		
Management Fee:	.52% mx./.38% mn.		
Actual Fees:	Mgt: —	Dist: —	
Expense Projections:	3Yr: $615	5Yr: $756	10Yr: $1166
Avg Brok Commission:	—	Income Distrib: Monthly	
Total Cost (relative to category):	—		

Franklin Small–Mid Cap Growth A

Ticker	Load	NAV	Yield	Total Assets	Mstar Category
FRSGX	5.75%	$31.17	0.3%	$9,884.2 mil	Mid–Cap Growth

Prospectus Objective: Small Company

Franklin Small-Mid Cap Growth Fund seeks long-term capital growth.

The fund normally invests at least 65% of assets in equity securities of companies that have market capitalization of less than $1.5 billion, or less than the highest market value in the Russell 2000 Index, whichever is greater. It may invest the balance of assets in equity securities of larger companies. The fund may also invest in IPOs, and can invest a very small portion of assets in private or illiquid securities.

Class A shares have front loads; C shares have level loads; Advisor shares are for qualified investors.

The fund has gone through several name changes.

Historical Profile

Return Average
Risk High
Rating ★★★ Neutral

Investment Style: Equity — Average Stock %: 92% (1994), 90% (1995), 95% (1996), 92% (1997), 94% (1998), 94% (1999)

▼ Manager Change
▽ Partial Manager Change

Fund Performance vs. Category Average
■ Quarterly Fund Return +/– Category Average
— Category Baseline

Performance Quartile (within Category)

Portfolio Manager(s)

Michael McCarthy. Since 3-93. BA U. of California-Los Angeles. Other funds currently managed: Franklin Small-Mid Cap Growth C, Franklin Small-Mid Cap Growth Adv, Strategic Partners High Growth A.

Edward B. Jamieson. Since 2-92. BA'70 Bucknell U.; MBA'75 U. of Chicago. Other funds currently managed: Franklin Convertible Securities A, Franklin Convertible Securities C, Franklin Small-Mid Cap Growth C.

Aidan O'Connell. Since 9-98. BA'90 Dartmouth C.; MBA'96 Wharton School of Business. Other funds currently managed: Franklin Small-Mid Cap Growth C, Franklin Small-Mid Cap Growth Adv, Strategic Partners High Growth A.

History

1990	1991	1992	1993	1994	1995	1996	1997	1998	1999	2000	12-01	History
—	—	11.01	12.94	13.00	17.01	20.72	22.93	22.57	44.13	39.33	31.17	NAV
—	—	11.11*	21.77	9.02	42.20	27.07	15.79	–0.02	97.08	–9.80	–20.53	Total Return %
—	—	2.43*	11.71	7.71	4.67	4.12	–17.57	–28.60	76.04	–0.70	–8.65	+/– S&P 500
—	—	—	10.58	11.19	8.23	9.59	–6.76	–17.89	45.78	1.95	–0.37	+/– Russ Midcap Grth
—	—	1.01	0.39	0.17	0.11	0.40	0.44	0.63	0.19	0.55	0.21	Income Return %
—	—	10.10	21.38	8.86	42.10	26.67	15.34	–0.65	96.89	–10.35	–20.74	Capital Return %
—	—	—	21	7	20	9	56	89	17	61	47	Total Rtn % Rank Cat
—	—	0.09	0.04	0.02	0.01	0.07	0.09	0.14	0.04	0.24	0.08	Income $
—	—	0.00	0.40	1.00	1.38	0.80	0.93	0.18	0.26	0.23	0.00	Capital Gains $
—	—	0.00	0.00	0.30	0.69	0.97	0.92	0.89	0.94	0.85	0.86	Expense Ratio %
—	—	2.45	0.84	0.24	0.25	0.09	0.10	0.32	0.30	0.24	0.29	Income Ratio %
—	—	—	63	90	105	88	55	43	47	25	27	Turnover Rate %
—	—	4.6	14.8	39.9	245.7	800.0	2,756.1	3,960.9	8,819.7	10,956.0	8,526.2	Net Assets $mil

Performance 12-31-01

	1st Qtr	2nd Qtr	3rd Qtr	4th Qtr	Total
1997	–9.12	18.69	16.82	–8.12	15.79
1998	11.16	–4.59	–23.56	23.32	–0.02
1999	1.82	15.75	4.66	59.78	97.08
2000	13.71	–2.21	3.28	–21.46	–9.80
2001	–24.10	12.19	–25.14	24.68	–20.53

Trailing	Total Return%	+/– S&P 500	+/– Russ Midcap Grth	% Rank All	% Rank Cat	Growth of $10,000
3 Mo	24.68	13.99	–2.39	8	20	12,468
6 Mo	–6.67	–1.11	1.59	72	33	9,333
1 Yr	–20.53	–8.65	–0.37	81	47	7,947
3 Yr Avg	12.21	13.23	10.05	8	17	14,128
5 Yr Avg	10.34	–0.36	1.32	17	40	16,354
10 Yr Avg	—	—	—	—	—	—
15 Yr Avg	—	—	—	—	—	—

Tax Analysis	Tax-Adj Ret%	%Rank Cat	%Pretax Ret	%Rank Cat
3 Yr Avg	11.95	13	97.8	9
5 Yr Avg	9.87	25	95.5	3
10 Yr Avg	—	—	—	—

Potential Capital Gain Exposure: 5% of assets

Risk Analysis

Time Period	Load-Adj Return %	Risk %Rank[1] All	Risk %Rank[1] Cat	Morningstar Return	Morningstar Risk	Morningstar Risk-Adj Rating
1 Yr	–25.10					
3 Yr	10.01	94	64	1.13[2]	1.60	★★★★
5 Yr	9.04	93	67	0.95[2]	1.60	★★
Incept	15.37	—	—	—	—	

Average Historical Rating (83 months): 3.6★s

[1] 1=low, 100=high [2] T-Bill return substituted for category avg.

Category Rating (3 Yr)

1 2 3 **4** 5
Worst — Best

Return: Above Avg
Risk: Average

Other Measures	Standard Index S&P 500	Best Fit Index Wil 4500
Alpha	22.7	14.5
Beta	1.51	1.32
R–Squared	45	93
Standard Deviation		46.34
Mean		12.21
Sharpe Ratio		0.18

Analysis by Dan Culloton 12-11-01

Reopening this fund hasn't hindered it yet, but the risk of asset bloat still lingers.

Franklin Small-Mid Cap Growth reopened in September, when it changed its name and augmented its investment universe. We had mixed feelings about the changes then, and we're still wary. At one time, the offering couldn't buy anything larger than the largest stock in the Russell 2000. That stricture became onerous after Russell rebalanced the index this past summer and the biggest market cap in the benchmark dropped from $4 billion to $1.8 billion. So Franklin opted to let the fund consider stocks with market caps up to $8.5 billion. That helped manager Ed Jamieson and his team, who had been deploying its large asset base in larger issues before the change.

Jamieson says reopening hasn't hurt, because a tough market and weak fund flows have reduced assets by $3 billion this last year. Moreover, management found plenty of buying opportunities during the market's post-Sept. 11 swoon. It bought beat-up stocks like airline Skywest and Starwood Hotels.

Since then, stocks have rallied and the fund has trimmed winners like network chipmaker PMC-Sierra. The fund has redirected some of that money to health-care issues, but its cash stake still is 14% of assets. This has more to do with the lack of attractively priced growth stocks than a lack of liquidity, Jamieson said. But it's still disconcerting for the biggest fund in the mid-cap growth category. We worry it could find itself in a bind if assets increase significantly.

Jamieson and his staff have amassed an admirable record at this fund, and it's worth holding as long as you recognize it no longer provides pure small-cap exposure. Prospective investors might be better off looking for a fund with a smaller asset base and more flexibility.

Portfolio Analysis 09-30-01

Share change since 06-01 Total Stocks: 334	Sector	PE	YTD Ret%	% Assets
FNMA N/A	N/A	—	—	3.09
Affiliated Comp Svcs A	Services	39.9	74.88	2.81
Expeditors Intl Of Wa	Services	32.7	6.46	1.73
Mettler–toledo Intl	Industrials	34.1	–4.64	1.54
Tcf Finl	Financials	18.2	10.24	1.26
Federated Investors B	Financials	23.3	10.11	1.25
⊕ Waters	Industrials	32.0	–53.50	1.25
Tektronix	Technology	26.3	–23.40	1.19
Natl Commerce	Financials	32.4	3.99	1.18
⊖ Concord Efs	Financials	86.3	49.21	1.04
⊕ Synopsys	Technology	67.1	24.52	0.96
Ch Robinson Worldwide	Services	30.1	–7.37	0.92
⊕ Micrel	Technology	84.6	–22.10	0.90
⊕ Adolph Coors Cl B	Staples	16.8	–32.50	0.90
Varco Intl	Energy	20.5	–31.10	0.86
⊕ Novellus Sys	Technology	25.0	9.77	0.85
⊕ Radian Grp	Financials	11.6	14.64	0.82
Polycom	Technology	67.5	6.87	0.79
⊕ Hispanic Brdcstg Cl A	Services	85.0	0.00	0.78
Golden State Bancorp	Financials	9.6	–15.60	0.76
Varian Medical Sys	Technology	34.3	4.89	0.76
Silicon Valley Bancshare	Financials	12.1	–22.60	0.72
Reinsurance Grp Of Amer	Financials	23.6	–5.61	0.72
⊖ L–3 Comms Hldgs	Technology	33.0	16.88	0.70
Security Cap Grp Cl B	Financials	11.3	26.45	0.70

Current Investment Style

Style: Value Blnd Growth; Size: Large Med Small

	Stock Port Avg	Relative S&P 500 Current	Relative S&P 500 Hist	Rel Cat
Price/Earnings Ratio	30.7	0.99	1.05	0.89
Price/Book Ratio	5.2	0.90	1.03	0.91
Price/Cash Flow	22.1	1.23	1.20	0.95
3 Yr Earnings Growth	21.8[1]	1.49	—	0.93
1 Yr Earnings Est%	4.2	—	—	0.45
Med Mkt Cap $mil	2,198	0.0	0.0	0.39

[1] figure is based on 50% or less of stocks

Special Securities % assets 09-30-01	
Restricted/Illiquid Secs	0
Emerging–Markets Secs	1
Options/Futures/Warrants	No

Composition % assets 09-30-01	
Cash	0.0
Stocks*	96.4
Bonds	3.6
Other	0.0
*Foreign (% stocks)	4.3

Market Cap	
Giant	0.0
Large	4.5
Medium	64.8
Small	29.4
Micro	1.4

Sector Weightings	% of Stocks	Rel S&P	5-Year High	5-Year Low
Utilities	1.7	0.5	2	0
Energy	4.7	0.7	11	0
Financials	18.8	1.1	19	3
Industrials	6.4	0.6	16	3
Durables	1.7	1.1	6	0
Staples	1.8	0.2	4	0
Services	23.8	2.2	26	10
Retail	2.6	0.4	32	1
Health	9.7	0.7	25	0
Technology	28.9	1.6	59	11

Address:	One Franklin Parkway San Mateo, CA 94403 650–312–2000 / 800–342–5236
Web Address:	www.franklintempleton.com
*Inception:	02-14-92
Advisor:	Franklin Advisers
Subadvisor:	None
NTF Plans:	Datalynx , Fidelity Inst.

Minimum Purchase:	$1000	Add: $50 IRA: $250
Min Auto Inv Plan:	$1000	Add: $50
Sales Fees:	5.75%L, 0.25%B	
Management Fee:	.63% mx./.40% mn.	
Actual Fees:	Mgt: 0.46%	Dist: 0.25%
Expense Projections:	3Yr: $843	5Yr: $1040 10Yr: $1608
Avg Brok Commission:	—	Income Distrib: Semi–Ann.
Total Cost (relative to category):	—	

Franklin Strategic Income A

Ticker	Load	NAV	Yield	SEC Yield	Total Assets	Mstar Category
FRSTX	4.25%	$9.36	8.5%	6.60%	$367.4 mil	Multisector Bond

Prospectus Objective: Multisector Bond

Franklin Strategic Income Fund seeks current income. Capital appreciation is secondary.

The fund actively allocates at least 65% of assets among foreign debt, domestic and foreign high-yield debt, U.S. government obligations, mortgage-related securites, and convertibles. To select specific issues, management uses both a top-down macroeconomic analysis and bottom-up fundamental sector, industry, and issuer analysis. This fund is non-diversified.

The fund currently offers Class A, B, C, and Advisor shares, all of which differ in fee structure and availability.

On Aug. 12, 1999, Franklin Investment Grade Income Fund merged into the fund.

Historical Profile
Return Below Avg
Risk Above Avg
Rating ★★ Below Avg

Investment Style
Fixed-Income
Income Rtn %Rank Cat: 27 (1995), 12 (1996), 18 (1997), 26 (1998), 43 (1999), 44 (2000), 28 (12-01)

Growth of Principal vs. Interest Rate Shifts
— Principal Value $000 (NAV with capital gains reinvested)
— Interest Rate % on 10 Yr Treasury
▼ Manager Change
▽ Partial Manager Change
► Mgr Unknown After
◄ Mgr Unknown Before

Performance Quartile (within Category)

Portfolio Manager(s)

Christopher J. Molumphy, CFA. Since 6-94. BA Stanford U.; MBA U. of Chicago. Other funds currently managed: Franklin AGE High Income A, Franklin Income A, Franklin Income C.

Eric G. Takaha, CFA. Since 10-97. BS U. of California, Berkeley; MBA Stanford U. Other funds currently managed: Franklin Strategic Income B, Franklin Strategic Income C, Franklin Strategic Income Adv.

1990	1991	1992	1993	1994	1995	1996	1997	1998	1999	2000	12–01	History
—	—	—	—	9.77	10.59	11.12	11.19	10.76	10.18	9.65	9.36	NAV
—	—	—	—	1.74*	18.68	17.05	10.00	4.05	2.33	2.60	5.40	Total Return %
—	—	—	—	—	0.21	13.44	0.32	–4.63	3.16	–9.03	–3.02	+/– LB Aggregate
—	—	—	—	—	1.29	4.63	–2.63	3.47	–0.95	7.81	–0.37	+/– FB High–Yield
—	—	—	—	4.04	8.75	9.07	8.40	7.95	7.86	7.90	8.52	Income Return %
—	—	—	—	–2.30	9.93	7.98	1.59	–3.90	–5.53	–5.30	–3.12	Capital Return %
—	—	—	—	—	41	4	34	34	49	36	35	Total Rtn % Rank Cat
—	—	—	—	0.41	0.82	0.92	0.90	0.86	0.82	0.78	0.79	Income $
—	—	—	—	0.00	0.11	0.27	0.09	0.00	0.00	0.00	0.00	Capital Gains $
—	—	—	—	—	0.25	0.25	0.23	0.25	0.58	0.75	0.75	Expense Ratio %
—	—	—	—	—	7.93	8.53	8.60	7.65	7.99	8.10	8.18	Income Ratio %
—	—	—	—	—	—	74	114	47	49	44	36	Turnover Rate %
—	—	—	—	5.9	9.7	22.9	102.0	233.1	275.8	244.8	250.4	Net Assets $mil

Performance 12-31-01

	1st Qtr	2nd Qtr	3rd Qtr	4th Qtr	Total
1997	–0.70	5.02	4.33	1.11	10.00
1998	2.76	–0.50	–4.18	6.20	4.05
1999	0.60	0.50	–1.50	2.76	2.33
2000	–0.16	0.95	1.57	0.23	2.60
2001	2.04	–0.13	–1.67	5.20	5.41

Trailing	Total Return%	+/– LB Agg	+/– FB High–Yield	% Rank All	% Rank Cat	Growth of $10,000
3 Mo	5.20	5.16	–0.45	64	6	10,520
6 Mo	3.44	–1.22	2.00	13	20	10,344
1 Yr	5.40	–3.02	–0.37	21	35	10,540
3 Yr Avg	3.43	–2.84	2.26	49	41	11,066
5 Yr Avg	4.84	–2.59	1.60	67	32	12,666
10 Yr Avg	—	—	—	—	—	—
15 Yr Avg	—	—	—	—	—	—

Tax Analysis	Tax-Adj Ret%	%Rank Cat	%Pretax Ret	%Rank Cat
3 Yr Avg	0.22	38	6.4	89
5 Yr Avg	1.52	32	31.4	48
10 Yr Avg	—	—	—	—

Potential Capital Gain Exposure: –15% of assets

Risk Analysis

Time Period	Load-Adj Return %	Risk %Rank[1] All	Risk %Rank[1] Cat	Morningstar Return	Morningstar Risk	Morningstar Risk-Adj Rating
1 Yr	0.93					
3 Yr	1.95	32	60	–0.62[2]	1.40	★★
5 Yr	3.93	37	68	–0.24[2]	1.59	★★
Incept	7.36	—	—	—	—	

Average Historical Rating (56 months): 3.3★s

[1] 1=low, 100=high [2] T-Bill return substituted for category avg.

Category Rating (3 Yr)

1 Worst — 2 — 3 — 4 — 5 Best

Return Average
Risk Average

Other Measures	Standard Index LB Agg	Best Fit Index FB HY
Alpha	–2.2	1.3
Beta	0.73	0.75
R–Squared	14	76
Standard Deviation		6.52
Mean		3.43
Sharpe Ratio		–0.27

Portfolio Analysis 09-30-01

Total Fixed-Income: 253	Date of Maturity	Amount $000	Value $000	% Net Assets
Republic of Brazil 14.5%	10-15-09	10,895	10,298	2.97
United Mexican States 11.375%	09-15-16	7,250	8,394	2.42
Republic of Bulgaria FRN	07-28-24	8,145	6,282	1.81
Federal Home Loan Bk 5%		6,000	6,180	1.78
Govt of France 4%		5,839	5,043	1.45
FHLMC 6%		4,550	4,797	1.38
Republic of Germany 4%		4,674	4,225	1.22
Republic of Brazil 11%		6,600	4,214	1.21
Republic of Panama 9.375%	04-01-29	3,530	3,618	1.04
Govt of Russia 10%	06-26-07	4,000	3,558	1.03
Russian Federation 11%		4,000	3,553	1.02
United Kingdom Treasury 7%		2,081	3,418	0.98
Sovereign Bancorp 10.5%	11-15-06	3,000	3,240	0.93
Pioneer Natural 9.625%	04-01-10	3,000	3,238	0.93
United Mexican States 10.375%	02-17-09	2,930	3,227	0.93
Republic of Venezuela 9.25%	09-15-27	4,758	3,175	0.91
Kroger 6.8%		3,000	3,114	0.90
Iron Mountain 144A 8.625%		3,000	3,079	0.89
Govt of France 6.75%	10-25-03	3,178	3,073	0.89
AOL Time Warner 6.75%		3,000	3,064	0.88

Current Investment Style

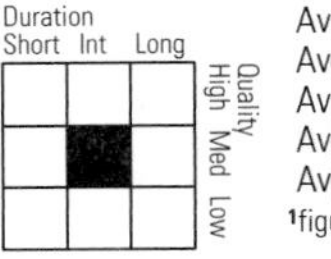

Avg Eff Duration[1]	4.8 Yrs
Avg Eff Maturity	—
Avg Credit Quality	BBB
Avg Wtd Coupon	7.91%
Avg Wtd Price	91.12% of par

[1] figure provided by fund

Special Securities % assets 09-30-01	
Restricted/Illiquid Secs	3
Exotic Mortgage–Backed	0
Emerging–Markets Secs	10
Options/Futures/Warrants	No

Coupon Range	% of Bonds	Rel Cat
0%	5.99	1.37
0% to 7%	29.22	0.87
7% to 8.5%	13.57	0.54
8.5% to 10%	25.56	1.42
More than 10%	25.65	1.35

1.00=Category Average

Credit Analysis % bonds 09-30-01			
US Govt	0	BB	22
AAA	26	B	32
AA	2	Below B	7
A	2	NR/NA	0
BBB	9		

Composition % assets 09-30-01			
Cash	1.8	Bonds	90.9
Stocks	1.9	Other	5.5

Country Exp % assets
Not Available

Sector Breakdown % bonds 09-30-01			
US Treasuries	0	CMOs	0
GNMA mtgs	2	ARMs	0
FNMA mtgs	8	Other	84
FHLMC mtgs	5		

Analysis by Scott Berry 12-07-01

Aggressive bond investors should like what they find at Franklin Strategic Income.

Given that this fund invests heavily in two of the bond market's riskiest sectors, emerging-markets debt and domestic high-yield bonds, its returns have been remarkably consistent. In fact, since its inception in 1994, the fund's calendar-year returns have all ranked in the multisector bond category's top half. That feat is even more impressive considering that both sectors have experienced periods of extreme volatility during that time frame.

The fund's success owes much to its approach. In addition to his own credit research, manager Chris Molumphy cherrypicks his favorite ideas from other Franklin funds, including Franklin AGE High Income and Templeton Global Bond, while rotating the fund's assets among the high-yield, emerging markets, and government-bond sectors. For example, in recent months he reduced the fund's government bond exposure, and as government bond prices fell on hopes of an economic recovery, the fund's limited exposure minimized the damage.

Thanks to that timely move and the recently improved performance of the high-yield sector, the fund gained 5.9% for the year to date through Dec. 6, 2001 and ranked in the top third of the group. Molumphy also credits stakes in convertible securities and real-estate investment trusts, both of which have performed well in 2001, for the fund's recent success.

Despite its consistent performance, the fund's added credit risk should not be overlooked. A misstep by management could certainly negatively affect the fund's relative performance.

But that said, we think this fund has a lot to offer aggressive investors and we think its solid returns have thus far compensated for its added risk.

Address:	One Franklin Parkway San Mateo, CA 94403 650–312–2000 / 800–342–5236
Web Address:	www.franklintempleton.com
*Inception:	06-01-94
Advisor:	Franklin Advisers
Subadvisor:	Templeton Inv. Counsel
NTF Plans:	Datalynx , Fidelity Inst.

Minimum Purchase:	$1000	Add: $50	IRA: $250
Min Auto Inv Plan:	$1000	Add: $50	
Sales Fees:	4.25%L, 0.25%B		
Management Fee:	.63% mx./.45% mn.		
Actual Fees:	Mgt: 0.55%	Dist: 0.25%	
Expense Projections:	3Yr: $727	5Yr: $949	10Yr: $1586
Avg Brok Commission:	—	Income Distrib: Monthly	
Total Cost (relative to category):		Below Avg	

Franklin U.S. Government Secs A

Ticker	Load	NAV	Yield	SEC Yield	Total Assets	Mstar Category
FKUSX	4.25%	$6.83	6.4%	3.53%	$7,963.1 mil	Intermediate Govt

Prospectus Objective: Government Mortgage

Franklin U.S. Government Securities Series seeks income.

The fund invests in a portfolio limited to U.S. government securities. These include U.S. treasury bonds, notes and bills, and securities issued by U.S. government agencies. A substantial portion the fund's investments are usually held in obligations of the Government National Mortgage Association(GNMA).

The fund currently offers Class A, B, C, and Advisor shares, all of which differ in fee structure and availability. Prior to Jan. 1, 1999, Class A and C shares were called Class I and II shares. On Sept. 9, 1993, Franklin Pennsylvania Investors U.S. Government Securities Fund merged into this fund.

Historical Profile

Return: Average
Risk: Below Avg
Rating: ★★★★ Above Avg

Investment Style: Fixed-Income

Income Rtn %Rank Cat: 8, 9, 4, 7, 6, 6, 14, 2

Growth of Principal vs. Interest Rate Shifts
- Principal Value $000 (NAV with capital gains reinvested)
- Interest Rate % on 10 Yr Treasury
- ▼ Manager Change
- ▽ Partial Manager Change
- ► Mgr Unknown After
- ◄ Mgr Unknown Before

Performance Quartile (within Category)

Portfolio Manager(s)

Jack Lemein. Since 3-84. BS'67 U. of Illinois. Other funds currently managed: Franklin Adjustable U.S. Govt Secs, Franklin Short-Interm U.S. Govt A, Franklin U.S. Government Secs C.

T. Anthony Coffey, CFA. Since 8-89. BA'84 Harvard U.; MBA'89 U. of California-Los Angeles. Other funds currently managed: Franklin Adjustable U.S. Govt Secs, Franklin Short-Interm U.S. Govt A, Franklin Strategic Mortgage.

Roger Bayston, CFA. Since 9-93. BS'86 U. of Virginia; MBA'91 U. of California-Los Angeles. Other funds currently managed: Franklin Adjustable U.S. Govt Secs, Franklin Short-Interm U.S. Govt A, Franklin Strategic Mortgage.

History

1990	1991	1992	1993	1994	1995	1996	1997	1998	1999	2000	12-01	History
6.99	7.25	7.18	7.11	6.42	6.97	6.78	6.92	6.91	6.53	6.76	6.83	NAV
10.78	13.71	7.40	6.91	−2.68	16.73	4.60	9.46	6.61	0.82	10.56	7.67	Total Return %
1.82	−2.29	—	−2.84	0.24	−1.74	0.98	−0.23	−2.07	1.65	−1.07	−0.75	+/− LB Aggregate
2.06	−1.61	0.17	−3.74	0.69	−1.60	1.83	−0.12	−3.25	3.07	−2.67	0.43	+/− LB Government
10.25	9.67	8.31	7.96	7.27	7.86	7.30	7.25	6.73	6.47	6.80	6.62	Income Return %
0.53	4.04	−0.91	−1.05	−9.96	8.87	−2.70	2.21	−0.13	−5.65	3.76	1.05	Capital Return %
2	72	14	67	37	39	11	14	69	11	56	16	Total Rtn % Rank Cat
0.68	0.65	0.58	0.55	0.50	0.49	0.49	0.48	0.45	0.43	0.43	0.43	Income $
0.00	0.00	0.00	0.00	0.00	0.00	0.00	0.00	0.00	0.00	0.00	0.00	Capital Gains $
0.52	0.52	0.53	0.52	0.55	0.61	0.61	0.64	0.65	0.67	0.70	—	Expense Ratio %
9.72	9.26	8.46	7.71	7.37	7.50	7.18	7.01	6.67	6.43	6.62	—	Income Ratio %
18	22	39	43	18	5	8	2	26	15	4	—	Turnover Rate %
11,388.2	13,028.3	13,631.9	13,857.1	10,984.6	11,105.9	10,001.8	9,287.8	8,901.4	7,530.3	6,918.2	7,159.8	Net Assets $mil

Performance 12-31-01

	1st Qtr	2nd Qtr	3rd Qtr	4th Qtr	Total
1997	0.63	3.61	2.77	2.16	9.46
1998	1.41	1.80	2.80	0.45	6.61
1999	0.60	−0.87	0.88	0.23	0.82
2000	1.79	1.82	2.92	3.66	10.56
2001	2.53	1.03	3.87	0.08	7.67

Trailing	Total Return%	+/− LB Agg	+/− LB Govt	% Rank All	% Rank Cat	Growth of $10,000
3 Mo	0.08	0.04	0.67	78	9	10,008
6 Mo	3.95	−0.71	−0.91	9	56	10,395
1 Yr	7.67	−0.75	0.43	11	16	10,767
3 Yr Avg	6.27	0.00	0.39	20	11	12,002
5 Yr Avg	6.97	−0.46	−0.43	36	14	14,005
10 Yr Avg	6.69	−0.54	−0.45	54	14	19,108
15 Yr Avg	7.72	−0.40	−0.16	57	17	30,514

Tax Analysis	Tax-Adj Ret%	%Rank Cat	%Pretax Ret	%Rank Cat
3 Yr Avg	3.60	20	57.4	50
5 Yr Avg	4.22	29	60.6	77
10 Yr Avg	3.82	31	57.2	70

Potential Capital Gain Exposure: −2% of assets

Risk Analysis

Time Period	Load-Adj Return %	Risk %Rank[1] All	Risk %Rank[1] Cat	Morningstar Return	Morningstar Risk	Morningstar Risk-Adj Rating
1 Yr	3.09					
3 Yr	4.74	6	10	−0.04[2]	0.49	★★★
5 Yr	6.04	6	6	0.23[2]	0.46	★★★★
10 Yr	6.23	9	5	0.41[2]	0.65	★★★★

Average Historical Rating (193 months): 3.5★s

[1] 1=low, 100=high [2] T-Bill return substituted for category avg.

Category Rating (3 Yr)

1 2 3 4 5 — Worst … Best

Return: Above Avg
Risk: Low

Other Measures	Standard Index LB Agg	Best Fit Index LB Mtg
Alpha	0.3	−0.6
Beta	0.77	0.98
R-Squared	88	96
Standard Deviation		2.94
Mean		6.27
Sharpe Ratio		0.53

Portfolio Analysis 09-30-01

Total Fixed-Income: 20379	Date of Maturity	Amount $000	Value $000	% Net Assets
GNMA 6.5%	12-15-28	815,461	834,567	10.57
GNMA 7%	12-15-23	780,565	815,091	10.33
GNMA 6.5%	12-15-23	467,487	482,055	6.11
GNMA 6%	12-20-28	480,429	480,127	6.08
GNMA 7%	11-15-28	434,905	450,758	5.71
GNMA 6.5%	09-15-29	422,158	432,174	5.48
GNMA 6%	04-20-31	286,652	286,000	3.62
GNMA 7.5%	12-15-22	250,219	263,134	3.33
GNMA 8%	12-15-22	243,954	259,474	3.29
GNMA 7%	12-15-22	196,145	204,924	2.60
GNMA 7.5%	12-15-23	190,987	200,666	2.54
GNMA 7%	07-15-31	184,089	190,818	2.42
GNMA 7.5%	12-15-30	175,094	182,710	2.31
GNMA 6.5%	11-20-24	172,092	177,366	2.25
GNMA 7%	12-20-30	134,487	139,637	1.77
GNMA 8%	12-15-17	124,244	132,905	1.68
GNMA 8%	10-15-30	105,377	110,699	1.40
GNMA 6.5%	12-20-27	108,182	110,531	1.40
GNMA 7.5%	12-15-29	90,336	94,282	1.19
GNMA 7.5%	11-15-17	76,674	81,301	1.03

Current Investment Style

Duration: Short Int Long; Quality: High Med Low

Avg Eff Duration[1]	1.9 Yrs
Avg Eff Maturity	—
Avg Credit Quality	AAA
Avg Wtd Coupon	7.18%
Avg Wtd Price	104.14% of par

[1] figure provided by fund

Special Securities % assets 09-30-01	
Restricted/Illiquid Secs	0
Exotic Mortgage-Backed	0
Emerging-Markets Secs	0
Options/Futures/Warrants	No

Coupon Range	% of Bonds	Rel Cat
0%	0.00	0.00
0% to 7%	41.80	0.74
7% to 8.5%	49.43	1.48
8.5% to 10%	3.90	0.96
More than 10%	4.88	1.25

1.00=Category Average

Credit Analysis % bonds 09-30-01			
US Govt	0	BB	0
AAA	100	B	0
AA	0	Below B	0
A	0	NR/NA	0
BBB	0		

Composition % assets 09-30-01			
Cash	3.4	Bonds	96.6
Stocks	0.0	Other	0.0

Sector Breakdown % bonds 09-30-01			
US Treasuries	0	CMOs	0
GNMA mtgs	100	ARMs	0
FNMA mtgs	0	Other	0
FHLMC mtgs	0		

Analysis by Scott Berry 12-05-01

Franklin U.S. Government Securities' narrow focus serves it, and investors, quite well.

This fund is not as diversified as its name implies. In fact, it invests almost exclusively in GNMA (Ginnie Mae) mortgages. The fund isn't required to have such a narrow focus, but managers Roger Bayston and Jack Lemein argue that their research has shown that Ginnie Mae mortgages boast one of the most attractive risk/return profiles of any investment alternative. And as a result, they've chosen to focus the fund on that area of the market.

The fund's long-term success helps make their case. Indeed, the fund outperformed more than 80% of its intermediate-term rivals over the five-year period ended Nov. 30, 2001, and outperformed more than 70% of its peers over the trailing 10 years. Importantly, the fund's performance during that span also compares favorably with those of its mortgage-focused competitors, ranking in that group's top third over the long term.

For the year to date through Dec. 3, 2001, the fund gained a solid 8.3%, while its average intermediate-term government peer gained 7.9%. The fund's stash of seasoned Ginnie Maes helped insulate the portfolio from the negative effects of prepayments, but its relatively short duration—a result of management's buy-and-hold approach—prevented the fund from keeping pace with a number of its longer-duration peers.

This fund follows the standard Franklin formula. It avoids duration bets, keeps turnover to a minimum, and charges below-average expenses. And as with many other Franklin offerings, the result has been solid total returns without undue volatility.

All in all, we think it makes a fine choice for government bond investors.

Address:	One Franklin Parkway San Mateo, CA 94403 650-312-2000 / 800-342-5236
Web Address:	www.franklintempleton.com
Inception:	05-31-70
Advisor:	Franklin Advisers
Subadvisor:	None
NTF Plans:	Fidelity Inst.

Minimum Purchase:	$1000	Add: $50	IRA: $250
Min Auto Inv Plan:	$50	Add: $50	
Sales Fees:	4.25%L, 0.50%B, 0.15%S		
Management Fee:	.63% mx./.40% mn.		
Actual Fees:	Mgt: 0.45%	Dist: 0.10%	
Expense Projections:	3Yr: $630	5Yr: $782	10Yr: $1224
Avg Brok Commission:	—	Income Distrib: Monthly	
Total Cost (relative to category):		Below Avg	

Fremont Bond

Ticker	Load	NAV	Yield	SEC Yield	Total Assets	Mstar Category
FBDFX	None	$10.10	5.2%	4.18%	$783.0 mil	Interm–Term Bond

Prospectus Objective: Corp Bond—General

Fremont Bond Fund seeks total return consistent with preservation of capital.

The fund ordinarily invests at least 65% of assets in debt securities, such as U.S. and foreign government obligations, domestic and foreign corporate debt, and mortgage- and asset-backed securities. The average maturity typically ranges between five and 15 years. The fund invests primarily in investment-grade securities; it may invest up to 10% of assets in debt rated B or BB. The fund may invest up to 40% of assets in securities of foreign issuers, but no more than 20% of assets in issues denominated in foreign currencies.

Prior to March 18, 1994, the fund was named Fremont Income Fund.

Historical Profile

Return High
Risk Average
Rating ★★★★★ Highest

Investment Style
Fixed-Income
Income Rtn %Rank Cat: 70 15 8 17 2 41 3 58

Growth of Principal vs. Interest Rate Shifts
— Principal Value $000 (NAV with capital gains reinvested)
— Interest Rate % on 10 Yr Treasury
▼ Manager Change
▽ Partial Manager Change
► Mgr Unknown After
◄ Mgr Unknown Before

Performance Quartile (within Category)

Portfolio Manager(s)

William H. Gross, CFA. Since 3-94. BA'66 Duke U.; MBA'71 U. of California-Los Angeles. Other funds currently managed: Harbor Bond, PIMCO Total Return II Instl, PIMCO Low Duration II Instl.

History

1990	1991	1992	1993	1994	1995	1996	1997	1998	1999	2000	12-01	History
—	—	—	10.10	9.15	10.14	9.95	10.13	10.22	9.51	9.97	10.10	NAV
—	—	—	4.37*	–4.02	21.25	5.22	9.72	10.00	–1.24	12.75	9.42	Total Return %
—	—	—	—	–1.10	2.78	1.61	0.03	1.32	–0.41	1.12	1.00	+/– LB Aggregate
—	—	—	—	–2.08	5.94	1.17	1.85	1.58	–1.63	2.65	0.44	+/– LB Int Govt/Corp
—	—	—	3.70	5.60	7.66	6.99	6.86	7.23	5.87	7.70	5.59	Income Return %
—	—	—	0.66	–9.61	13.59	–1.77	2.86	2.76	–7.11	5.05	3.83	Capital Return %
—	—	—	—	56	7	8	21	3	48	4	8	Total Rtn % Rank Cat
—	—	—	0.37	0.55	0.68	0.69	0.66	0.71	0.58	0.71	0.54	Income $
—	—	—	0.01	0.00	0.22	0.00	0.09	0.18	0.00	0.00	0.25	Capital Gains $
—	—	—	0.50	0.66	0.60	0.68	0.61	0.60	0.60	0.62	—	Expense Ratio %
—	—	—	5.35	5.76	6.69	6.82	6.40	5.92	6.01	6.44	—	Income Ratio %
—	—	—	13	205	21	154	191	256	298	176	—	Turnover Rate %
—	—	—	12.0	59.8	93.0	72.7	109.4	216.0	174.7	297.5	783.0	Net Assets $mil

Performance 12-31-01

	1st Qtr	2nd Qtr	3rd Qtr	4th Qtr	Total
1997	–0.65	4.33	3.38	2.39	9.72
1998	1.54	2.30	5.25	0.61	10.00
1999	–0.28	–1.51	0.54	0.02	–1.24
2000	2.93	1.93	2.91	4.44	12.75
2001	3.05	–0.07	6.37	–0.09	9.42

Trailing	Total Return%	+/– LB Agg	+/– LB ITGvt/Corp	% Rank All	% Rank Cat	Growth of $10,000
3 Mo	–0.09	–0.13	–0.18	79	49	9,991
6 Mo	6.27	1.61	1.57	2	2	10,627
1 Yr	9.42	1.00	0.44	6	8	10,942
3 Yr Avg	6.81	0.53	0.41	18	4	12,184
5 Yr Avg	8.02	0.59	0.92	29	2	14,704
10 Yr Avg	—	—	—	—	—	—
15 Yr Avg	—	—	—	—	—	—

Tax Analysis	Tax-Adj Ret%	%Rank Cat	%Pretax Ret	%Rank Cat
3 Yr Avg	3.99	7	58.6	21
5 Yr Avg	5.03	2	62.8	27
10 Yr Avg	—	—	—	—

Potential Capital Gain Exposure: 0% of assets

Risk Analysis

Time Period	Load-Adj Return %	Risk %Rank[1] All	Risk %Rank[1] Cat	Morningstar Return	Morningstar Risk	Morningstar Risk-Adj Rating
1 Yr	9.42					
3 Yr	6.81	17	49	0.40[2]	0.70	★★★★
5 Yr	8.02	21	40	0.69[2]	0.69	★★★★★
Incept	7.54	—	—	—	—	

Average Historical Rating (69 months): 4.1★s

[1] 1=low, 100=high [2] T-Bill return substituted for category avg.

Category Rating (3 Yr)

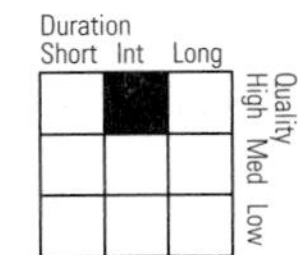

Return High
Risk Average

Other Measures	Standard Index LB Agg	Best Fit Index LB Agg
Alpha	0.3	0.3
Beta	1.15	1.15
R–Squared	93	93
Standard Deviation		4.21
Mean		6.81
Sharpe Ratio		0.51

Analysis by Eric Jacobson 12-31-01

Fremont Bond finally seems to be getting some well-deserved recognition.

Despite its inherent advantages, this fund grew at a snail's pace since its 1993 inception. That seemed odd because the fund has such an excellent record and is managed under a subadvisory agreement by PIMCO's legendary bond manager, Bill Gross. Making the phenomenon more confounding is that this fund is far and away an easier, less-costly choice for do-it-yourselfers. To be sure, it carries no load and charges roughly 20% less than the comparable share class of Gross' PIMCO Total Return that's available in fund supermarkets.

The fund came out of obscurity in 2001, though, nearly tripling in assets before the end of the year. That growth mirrored (to some extent) the continued growth of PIMCO Total Return, one of the year's best-selling funds.

Gross' 2001 performance gives a glimpse as to why investors have become enamored with his funds. After badly lagging the intermediate-term bond category average at midyear (thanks to a hefty overweight in underperforming mortgages), Gross made a very bold call on the direction of interest rates—that they would fall further—and extended his funds' durations to their limit of 20% longer than the Lehman Brothers Aggregate. The move paid off in spades, and his portfolios ended the year in the category's top decile.

There are more interesting things on tap. Gross is shedding some of the caution he's displayed in recent years, building up modest stakes in corporates and emerging-markets debt. He's also declared a willingness to buy previously shunned high-yield issues under the right circumstances. That could heighten volatility here, but overall we think this is one of the most attractive core bonds funds around.

Portfolio Analysis 10-31-01

Total Fixed-Income: 314	Date of Maturity	Amount $000	Value $000	% Net Assets
GNMA TBA 6%		104,500	106,264	9.51
GNMA 6.5%		65,000	67,844	6.07
GNMA 8%	12-15-30	57,258	60,626	5.42
Bundesobligation 5%	08-19-05	28,400	26,814	2.40
CS First Boston 3.011%	08-25-31	23,411	23,470	2.10
US Treasury Note 3.875%	01-15-09	19,373	20,554	1.84
FNT 4.21%	09-25-31	19,212	19,255	1.72
Ford Motor Credit 3.303%	06-23-03	19,500	19,210	1.72
Asset Servicing & Securitizing 3.828%	10-25-30	17,000	17,036	1.52
First Nationwide Tr 4.26%	09-25-31	16,159	16,426	1.47
FHLMC 6.5%	08-15-31	16,087	15,610	1.40
EMC 144A Cv 3.25%	05-25-40	14,044	14,044	1.26
FNMA ARM	05-01-36	13,360	13,629	1.22
France Telecom 144A 6.32%	03-14-03	12,300	12,308	1.10
Bear Stearns ARM	12-25-30	11,615	11,804	1.06
FNMA CMO PAC 8%	01-25-22	11,197	11,392	1.02
FNMA CMO Z 7.2%	05-25-23	9,925	10,502	0.94
Resident Fdg CMO 7%	11-25-27	10,000	10,409	0.93
FNMA Debenture 7.125%	06-15-10	8,900	10,336	0.92
GMAC 5.75%	11-10-03	10,000	10,214	0.91

Current Investment Style

Duration: Short Int Long; Quality: High Med Low

Avg Eff Duration[1]	5.4 Yrs
Avg Eff Maturity	6.8 Yrs
Avg Credit Quality	AAA
Avg Wtd Coupon	5.80%
Avg Wtd Price	102.13% of par

[1] figure provided by fund

Special Securities % assets 10-31-01	
Restricted/Illiquid Secs	4
Exotic Mortgage–Backed	1
Emerging–Markets Secs	0
Options/Futures/Warrants	No

Coupon Range	% of Bonds	Rel Cat
0%	0.00	0.00
0% to 7%	79.20	1.47
7% to 8.5%	18.22	0.52
8.5% to 10%	2.08	0.29
More than 10%	0.50	0.18

1.00=Category Average

Credit Analysis % bonds 06-30-01			
US Govt	0	BB	0
AAA	78	B	0
AA	3	Below B	0
A	14	NR/NA	0
BBB	5		

Composition % assets 10-31-01			
Cash	20.5	Bonds	78.3
Stocks	0.0	Other	1.3

Sector Breakdown % bonds 10-31-01			
US Treasuries	1	CMOs	5
GNMA mtgs	34	ARMs	3
FNMA mtgs	5	Other	44
FHLMC mtgs	5		

Address:	50 Beale Street Suite 100 San Francisco, CA 94105 800–548–4539 /
Web Address:	www.fremontfunds
*Inception:	04-30-93
Advisor:	Fremont Inv. Adv.
Subadvisor:	Pacific Inv. Mgmt.
NTF Plans:	N/A

Minimum Purchase:	$2000	Add: $100 IRA: $1000
Min Auto Inv Plan:	$50	Add: $50
Sales Fees:	No–load	
Management Fee:	.40%, .15%A	
Actual Fees:	Mgt: 0.40%	Dist: —
Expense Projections:	3Yr: $209	5Yr: $368 10Yr: $830
Avg Brok Commission:	—	Income Distrib: Monthly
Total Cost (relative to category):		Below Avg

Fremont U.S. Micro–Cap

Ticker	Load	NAV	Yield	Total Assets	Mstar Category
FUSMX	None	$28.29	0.0%	$712.1 mil	Small Growth

Prospectus Objective: Small Company

Fremont U.S. Micro-Cap Fund seeks long-term capital appreciation.

The fund ordinarily invests at least 65% of assets in common stocks and convertible securities issued by micro-cap companies: companies that fall within the smallest 10% of market capitalization of U.S. companies. The fund aims to invest in companies that are in the early stages of an emerging-growth cycle. It may invest up to 5% of assets in nonconvertible bonds and preferred stocks rated in the top two categories. The fund may invest up to 25% of assets in securities of small companies domiciled in foreign countries.

Historical Profile
Return High
Risk High
Rating ★★★★★ Highest

Investment Style
Equity
Average Stock %: 85% 72% 81% 86% 83% 76% 73%

▼ Manager Change
▽ Partial Manager Change

Fund Performance vs. Category Average
■ Quarterly Fund Return +/– Category Average
— Category Baseline

Performance Quartile (within Category)

Portfolio Manager(s)

Robert E. Kern, et al. Since 6-94. BSME Purdue U.

1990	1991	1992	1993	1994	1995	1996	1997	1998	1999	2000	12-01	History
—	—	—	—	10.13	15.10	21.50	20.28	20.86	39.35	26.87	28.29	NAV
—	—	—	—	1.50*	54.04	48.70	6.99	2.86	129.50	–10.62	5.28	Total Return %
—	—	—	—	–3.36*	16.51	25.76	–26.37	–25.72	108.47	–1.52	17.16	+/– S&P 500
—	—	—	—	—	23.00	37.44	–5.96	1.63	86.42	11.81	14.52	+/– Russ 2000 Grth
—	—	—	—	0.20	0.00	0.00	0.00	0.00	0.00	0.06	0.00	Income Return %
—	—	—	—	1.30	54.04	48.70	6.99	2.86	129.50	–10.69	5.28	Capital Return %
—	—	—	—	—	6	2	89	50	9	64	15	Total Rtn % Rank Cat
—	—	—	—	0.02	0.00	0.00	0.00	0.00	0.00	0.02	0.00	Income $
—	—	—	—	0.00	0.50	0.92	2.76	0.00	5.86	9.23	0.00	Capital Gains $
—	—	—	—	2.50	2.04	1.96	1.88	1.94	1.82	1.57	—	Expense Ratio %
—	—	—	—	0.68	–0.67	–0.51	–0.67	–1.22	–0.97	0.06	—	Income Ratio %
—	—	—	—	129	144	81	125	170	164	117	—	Turnover Rate %
—	—	—	—	2.1	10.0	142.9	166.9	164.8	574.1	628.5	712.1	Net Assets $mil

Performance 12-31-01

	1st Qtr	2nd Qtr	3rd Qtr	4th Qtr	Total
1997	–9.63	16.83	16.34	–12.90	6.99
1998	8.73	–7.48	–29.02	44.06	2.86
1999	4.65	31.10	11.74	49.70	129.50
2000	20.99	2.29	–7.25	–22.14	–10.62
2001	–13.66	25.17	–23.21	26.86	5.29

Trailing	Total Return%	+/– S&P 500	+/– Russ 2000 Grth	% Rank All	% Rank Cat	Growth of $10,000
3 Mo	26.86	16.18	0.69	6	27	12,686
6 Mo	–2.58	2.97	6.68	50	26	9,742
1 Yr	5.28	17.16	14.52	21	15	10,528
3 Yr Avg	29.26	30.28	29.01	1	5	21,596
5 Yr Avg	18.90	8.20	16.03	2	9	23,766
10 Yr Avg	—	—	—	—	—	—
15 Yr Avg	—	—	—	—	—	—

Tax Analysis	Tax-Adj Ret%	%Rank Cat	%Pretax Ret	%Rank Cat
3 Yr Avg	22.73	7	77.7	55
5 Yr Avg	14.40	12	76.2	53
10 Yr Avg	—	—	—	—

Potential Capital Gain Exposure: –1% of assets

Risk Analysis

Time Period	Load-Adj Return %	Risk %Rank[1] All	Risk %Rank[1] Cat	Morningstar Return	Morningstar Risk	Morningstar Risk-Adj Rating
1 Yr	5.28					
3 Yr	29.26	91	50	6.44[2]	1.44	★★★★★
5 Yr	18.90	93	58	3.95[2]	1.62	★★★★★
Incept	25.56	—	—	—	—	

Average Historical Rating (55 months): 3.8★s

[1]1=low, 100=high [2] T-Bill return substituted for category avg.

Category Rating (3 Yr)

1 2 3 4 5 — Worst / Best (5)

Return High
Risk Average

Other Measures	Standard Index S&P 500	Best Fit Index Wil 4500
Alpha	39.0	31.6
Beta	1.22	1.24
R-Squared	30	83

Standard Deviation	51.90
Mean	29.26
Sharpe Ratio	0.52

Analysis by Bridget Hughes 09-25-01

Fremont U.S. Micro-Cap Fund is winning the battle against the bulge.

Conventional logic said this fund should be suffering from its heft. With it and its institutional clone sporting a combined total of more than $900 million in assets, it is by far the largest micro-cap offering, and upon reopening its doors in January 2001, it invited more inflows. Investing in micro-caps is easier with a smaller amount of money, though, because it's less likely that buying or selling those wee stocks will move their prices to shareholders' detriment.

There have been no signs of performance slippage here, however. Lead manager Bob Kern says his investment universe—the bottom 5% of stocks in terms of market cap—gives him a menu of more than 4,000 stocks with market caps between $10 million and $700 million. The portfolio isn't spread over hundreds of holdings—it typically buys about 80 names—and its median market cap is still a tiny $280 million. Despite a meager 1997 and subpar 2000, the fund's trailing three- and five-year returns through Sept. 24, 2001, land in the small-growth category's best decile. And it has delivered those returns with no more volatility than its average peer.

Lately, the fund's perennial double-digit cash stake—currently about 25% of assets—has helped as stocks have plummeted, but more often than not, its stock picks have been winners and have been able to compensate for the fund's cash hoard during up markets. (Kern said he has always kept a hefty cash balance so he can pounce on ideas without having to sell something else in the portfolio.)

Although a smaller asset base would make this fund even more attractive, its record is so good that it is still a solid choice.

Portfolio Analysis 06-30-01

Share change since 05-01 Total Stocks: 77	Sector	PE	YTD Ret%	% Assets
Gene Logic	Health	—	2.53	3.75
Arthrocare	Health	43.7	–8.05	3.04
Endocare	Health	—	40.63	2.49
⊖ Microsemi	Technology	51.2	113.50	2.23
⊕ Zygo	Technology	33.8	–43.70	2.20
Anaren Microwave	Technology	42.2	–74.20	1.99
ATMI	Technology	NMF	22.31	1.87
⊕ Intermagnetics General	Industrials	35.5	57.72	1.81
⊖ Sage	Technology	—	151.30	1.78
⊕ Eclipsys	Technology	—	–31.60	1.57
⊖ Genesis Microchip	Technology	NMF	614.80	1.56
⊕ Oshkosh Truck Cl B	Industrials	16.4	11.75	1.53
Championship Auto Racing Tm	Services	NMF	–23.30	1.52
⊕ Costar Grp	Technology	—	1.63	1.47
ASM Intl ADR	Technology	—	—	1.46
Take-Two Interact Software	Technology	37.6	40.61	1.42
Cadiz	Financials	—	–10.20	1.41
⊕ Bei Tech	Technology	21.5	50.31	1.36
⊖ Cash Amer Intl	Retail	—	95.60	1.36
⊖ AAON	Industrials	16.0	107.50	1.36
⊕ IXYS	Industrials	31.1	–44.60	1.19
Bright Horizons Family Sol	Services	35.0	7.14	1.18
Electronics Boutique Hldgs	Retail	71.3	128.20	1.15
II-VI	Industrials	25.3	13.44	1.11
Fusion Medical Tech	Health	—	43.25	1.10

Current Investment Style

Style: Value Blnd Growth; Size: Large Med Small

	Stock Port Avg	Relative S&P 500 Current	Relative S&P 500 Hist	Rel Cat
Price/Earnings Ratio	36.4	1.17	0.97	1.13
Price/Book Ratio	3.8	0.67	0.74	0.79
Price/Cash Flow	23.4	1.30	1.09	1.06
3 Yr Earnings Growth	27.3[1]	1.87	—	1.09
1 Yr Earnings Est%	–33.8[1]	19.09	—	–4.35
Med Mkt Cap $mil	315	0.0	0.0	0.30

[1]figure is based on 50% or less of stocks

Special Securities % assets 06-30-01	
Restricted/Illiquid Secs	0
Emerging-Markets Secs	0
Options/Futures/Warrants	No

Composition % assets 06-30-01	
Cash	26.8
Stocks*	73.2
Bonds	0.0
Other	0.0
*Foreign (% stocks)	2.4

Market Cap	
Giant	0.0
Large	0.0
Medium	0.0
Small	59.2
Micro	40.8

Sector Weightings	% of Stocks	Rel S&P	5-Year High	5-Year Low
Utilities	0.0	0.0	0	0
Energy	0.0	0.0	8	0
Financials	2.0	0.1	15	0
Industrials	11.6	1.0	18	6
Durables	4.3	2.7	11	0
Staples	0.3	0.0	3	0
Services	12.0	1.1	29	9
Retail	3.9	0.6	16	4
Health	17.4	1.2	17	6
Technology	48.4	2.6	59	28

Address: 50 Beale Street Suite 100, San Francisco, CA 94105, 800-548-4539 /
Web Address: www.fremontfunds
*Inception: 06-30-94
Advisor: Fremont Inv. Adv.
Subadvisor: Kern Cap. Mgmt.
NTF Plans: Fidelity , Datalynx

Minimum Purchase: $2000 Add: $100 IRA: $1000
Min Auto Inv Plan: $50 Add: $50
Sales Fees: No-load
Management Fee: 2.5% mx./1.5% mn.
Actual Fees: Mgt: 1.82% Dist: —
Expense Projections: 3Yr: $573 5Yr: $985 10Yr: $2137
Avg Brok Commission: — Income Distrib: Annually
Total Cost (relative to category): Average

Gabelli Asset

Ticker	Load	NAV	Yield	Total Assets	Mstar Category
GABAX	12b–1 only	$32.97	0.0%	$1,911.0 mil	Mid-Cap Blend

Prospectus Objective: Growth

Gabelli Asset Fund seeks capital growth; current income is a secondary consideration.

The fund invests primarily in equity securities. At least 80% of its holdings are listed on nationally recognized securities exchanges or included in the Nasdaq National Market System. The advisor generally selects securities that it believes have favorable value-to-price characteristics; it considers such factors as earnings expectations, earnings and price histories, balance sheet characteristics, and perceived management skills. The fund may invest up to 25% of assets in foreign securities. It may invest in convertible securities rated B or higher.

Historical Profile

Return Above Avg
Risk Below Avg
Rating ★★★★★ Highest

Investment Style
Equity
Average Stock %: 95% 95% 98% 94% 93% 93% 91%

▼ Manager Change
▽ Partial Manager Change

Fund Performance vs. Category Average
Quarterly Fund Return
+/– Category Average
– Category Baseline

Performance Quartile (within Category)

Portfolio Manager(s)

Mario J. Gabelli, CFA. Since 3-86. BS'65 Fordham U.; MBA'67 Columbia U. Other funds currently managed: Gabelli Equity-Income, Gabelli Small Cap Growth, Gabelli Value.

1990	1991	1992	1993	1994	1995	1996	1997	1998	1999	2000	12–01	History
15.63	17.96	19.88	23.30	22.21	25.75	26.42	31.85	35.47	40.84	33.90	32.97	NAV
–5.80	18.14	14.89	21.84	–0.15	24.94	13.36	38.07	15.93	28.49	–2.37	0.16	Total Return %
–2.68	–12.35	7.28	11.78	–1.46	–12.59	–9.59	4.72	–12.64	7.46	6.74	12.03	+/– S&P 500
–0.68	–31.93	2.99	7.91	3.44	–5.97	–5.83	5.82	–3.18	13.78	–19.86	0.76	+/– S&P Mid 400
4.42	2.46	1.41	0.83	1.12	1.14	0.59	0.26	0.06	0.00	0.75	0.00	Income Return %
–10.22	15.67	13.48	21.01	–1.27	23.80	12.77	37.80	15.87	28.49	–3.12	0.16	Capital Return %
39	89	39	21	30	62	91	4	20	31	69	27	Total Rtn % Rank Cat
0.77	0.39	0.25	0.17	0.26	0.25	0.15	0.07	0.02	0.00	0.31	0.00	Income $
0.00	0.12	0.50	0.76	0.79	1.75	2.62	4.54	1.40	4.63	5.57	0.98	Capital Gains $
1.20	1.30	1.31	1.31	1.28	1.33	1.34	1.38	1.36	1.37	0.77	—	Expense Ratio %
4.51	2.34	1.42	0.82	1.10	0.95	0.52	0.22	0.06	–0.10	1.36	—	Income Ratio %
56	20	14	16	19	26	15	22	21	32	48	—	Turnover Rate %
342.7	485.4	631.8	948.0	981.8	1,090.4	1,081.6	1,334.2	1,593.6	1,994.0	1,908.6	1,911.0	Net Assets $mil

Performance 12-31-01

	1st Qtr	2nd Qtr	3rd Qtr	4th Qtr	Total
1997	2.20	16.48	11.26	4.25	38.07
1998	13.03	1.14	–14.20	18.20	15.93
1999	4.82	11.30	–4.49	15.33	28.49
2000	0.22	–1.83	–0.10	–0.66	–2.37
2001	–2.57	7.33	–13.40	10.60	0.16

Trailing	Total Return%	+/– S&P 500	+/– S&P Mid 400	% Rank All	% Rank Cat	Growth of $10,000
3 Mo	10.60	–0.09	–7.39	39	81	11,060
6 Mo	–4.22	1.33	–2.67	57	58	9,578
1 Yr	0.16	12.03	0.76	42	27	10,016
3 Yr Avg	7.91	8.93	–2.33	15	42	12,565
5 Yr Avg	15.00	4.30	–1.11	4	18	20,112
10 Yr Avg	14.82	1.89	–0.19	6	22	39,817
15 Yr Avg	15.41	1.68	–0.57	5	15	85,882

Tax Analysis	Tax-Adj Ret%	%Rank Cat	%Pretax Ret	%Rank Cat
3 Yr Avg	5.61	36	71.0	59
5 Yr Avg	12.73	12	84.9	26
10 Yr Avg	12.69	12	85.6	25

Potential Capital Gain Exposure: 29% of assets

Risk Analysis

Time Period	Load-Adj Return %	Risk %Rank[1] All	Risk %Rank[1] Cat	Morningstar Return	Morningstar Risk	Morningstar Risk-Adj Rating
1 Yr	0.16					
3 Yr	7.91	42	5	0.65[2]	0.58	★★★★
5 Yr	15.00	46	4	2.63[2]	0.62	★★★★★
10 Yr	14.82	53	4	1.74	0.66	★★★★★

Average Historical Rating (155 months): 4.3★s

[1] 1=low, 100=high [2] T-Bill return substituted for category avg.

Category Rating (3 Yr)

1 2 3 4 5
Worst Best

Return Average
Risk Low

Other Measures	Standard Index S&P 500	Best Fit Index
Alpha	7.1	10.2
Beta	0.71	0.76
R-Squared	78	79
Standard Deviation		14.60
Mean		7.91
Sharpe Ratio		0.23

Analysis by Gabriel Presler 11-30-01

Gabelli Asset suffers a few missteps from time to time, but we think it's a solid option for investors who can tolerate a few quirks.

When growth stocks fell from favor in 2000, this fund—one of the older offerings from a shop known for its value approach—was supposed to shine. But shareholders here suffered a rude shock: Heavy exposure to media-related companies dragged on the fund's returns. It lost 2% of its value and ended the year in the mid-blend category's bottom half.

This poor relative performance hasn't lasted, though. Some of manager Mario Gabelli's bold sector bets have paid off in 2001. After suffering ugly losses last year, media-related stocks, including Media General and Viacom, posted nice gains in the early part of the year. While the group's share prices have declined lately—due to a weakening advertising market—some of Gabelli's other favorites have hoisted the baton. Performance has gotten a nice boost from longtime positions in defense firms, such as Northrop Grumman, for example. The fund's exposure to staple firms, such as Ralston Purina, has also been a boon. While its 3.5% loss for the year to date through Nov. 29, 2001, may not look good on an absolute basis, it has outpaced 75% of its rivals.

Despite its strong performance in 2001, this isn't the right choice for investors interested in staid performance. Gabelli's penchant for making broad sector bets can backfire from time to time; heavy telecom stakes dragged down the fund's relative performance in 1996 and 2000. Still, the fund's unusual moves have generally paid off. Its 10-year return is in the top third of the category and it has been one of the least volatile offerings in the category. This combination makes it one of the group's better offerings.

Portfolio Analysis 11-30-01

Share change since 10–01 Total Stocks: 387	Sector	PE	YTD Ret%	% Assets
News ADR Pfd	Services	—	—	3.52
Telephone and Data Sys	Services	—	0.29	3.39
AT & T Liberty Media Cl A	Services	—	3.22	3.18
Viacom Cl A	Services	—	–5.85	2.02
Ralston Purina	Staples	—	27.94	2.01
USA Networks	Services	58.1	40.50	1.86
Cablevision Sys A	Services	5.6	–34.20	1.51
AOL Time Warner	Technology	—	–7.76	1.35
Navistar Intl	Durables	—	50.88	1.19
PepsiCo	Staples	31.4	–0.54	1.06
Media General Cl A	Services	36.9	38.79	1.03
Neiman–Marcus Grp Cl B		—	—	1.01
Centurytel	Services	13.3	–7.66	1.01
ITT Inds	Durables	16.2	32.06	0.98
⊕ AT&T	Services	7.8	40.59	0.95
Willamette Inds	Industrials	19.8	13.20	0.94
Genuine Parts	Durables	16.8	45.48	0.91
Deere	Industrials	—	–2.52	0.87
Procter & Gamble	Staples	38.8	3.12	0.86
Berkshire Hathaway Cl A	Financials	—	—	0.84
Northrop Grumman	Industrials	19.2	23.67	0.82
⊖ Commonwealth Tele Entrp	Services	—	30.00	0.81
Waste Mgmt	Services	52.3	15.03	0.76
Gillette	Staples	56.6	–5.47	0.76
Idex	Industrials	25.4	6.08	0.76

Current Investment Style

Style: Value Blnd Growth; Size: Large Med Small

	Stock Port Avg	Relative S&P 500 Current	Relative S&P 500 Hist	Rel Cat
Price/Earnings Ratio	25.8	0.83	0.83	0.95
Price/Book Ratio	3.5	0.62	0.57	0.82
Price/Cash Flow	13.8	0.77	0.76	0.79
3 Yr Earnings Growth	13.2[1]	0.90	0.65	0.80
1 Yr Earnings Est%	–13.8[1]	7.77	—	–6.06
Med Mkt Cap $mil	6,760	0.1	0.1	0.75

[1] figure is based on 50% or less of stocks

Special Securities % assets 11-30-01	
Restricted/Illiquid Secs	0
Emerging-Markets Secs	1
Options/Futures/Warrants	Yes

Composition % assets 11-30-01	
Cash	7.0
Stocks*	89.4
Bonds	0.0
Other	3.6
*Foreign (% stocks)	8.9

Market Cap	
Giant	17.5
Large	26.7
Medium	33.6
Small	20.0
Micro	2.2

Sector Weightings	% of Stocks	Rel S&P	5-Year High	5-Year Low
Utilities	2.6	0.8	9	0
Energy	3.0	0.4	5	0
Financials	6.3	0.4	9	4
Industrials	19.0	1.7	26	12
Durables	7.2	4.6	14	4
Staples	15.9	2.0	17	9
Services	38.8	3.6	54	26
Retail	1.1	0.2	5	1
Health	2.7	0.2	8	3
Technology	3.6	0.2	6	2

Address:	One Corporate Center Rye, NY 10580–1434 800–422–3554 / 914–921–5100
Web Address:	www.gabelli.com
Inception:	03-03-86
Advisor:	Gabelli Funds
Subadvisor:	None
NTF Plans:	Fidelity , Datalynx

Minimum Purchase:	$1000	Add: None IRA: $1000
Min Auto Inv Plan:	$100	Add: $100
Sales Fees:	0.25%B	
Management Fee:	1.0%, .10%A	
Actual Fees:	Mgt: 1.00%	Dist: 0.25%
Expense Projections:	3Yr: $434	5Yr: $750 10Yr: $1646
Avg Brok Commission:	—	Income Distrib: —
Total Cost (relative to category):		Average

Gabelli Blue Chip Value AAA

Ticker	Load	NAV	Yield	Total Assets	Mstar Category
GABBX	12b–1 only	$10.71	0.0%	$42.5 mil	Large Value

Prospectus Objective: Growth

Gabelli Blue Chip Value Fund seeks capital appreciation.

The fund will primarily invest at least 65% of assets in large, well-known companies with market capitalizations greater than $5 billion. "Blue Chip" companies are generally identified by their substantial capitalization, established history of earnings and dividends, ample liquidity, and easy access to credit. The fund will focus on companies that seem to be undervalued and seem to have the potential to achieve signicant capital appreciation. It may also invest in preferred stocks and investment-grade debt securities.

Class AAA shares are the only shares offered on this fund.

Historical Profile

Return —
Risk —
Rating Not Rated

Investment Style: Equity — Average Stock %: 92% (2000), 95% (12-01)

▼ Manager Change
▽ Partial Manager Change

Fund Performance vs. Category Average
■ Quarterly Fund Return +/– Category Average
— Category Baseline

Performance Quartile (within Category)

Portfolio Manager(s)

Barbara G. Marcin, CFA. Since 8-99.

1990	1991	1992	1993	1994	1995	1996	1997	1998	1999	2000	12-01	History
—	—	—	—	—	—	—	—	—	11.65	12.17	10.71	NAV
—	—	—	—	—	—	—	—	—	17.79*	11.08	–11.77	Total Return %
—	—	—	—	—	—	—	—	—	9.33*	20.18	0.11	+/– S&P 500
—	—	—	—	—	—	—	—	—	—	8.77	–2.98	+/– Russ Top 200 Val
—	—	—	—	—	—	—	—	—	0.00	0.00	0.00	Income Return %
—	—	—	—	—	—	—	—	—	17.79	11.08	–11.77	Capital Return %
—	—	—	—	—	—	—	—	—	—	29	85	Total Rtn % Rank Cat
—	—	—	—	—	—	—	—	—	0.00	0.00	0.00	Income $
—	—	—	—	—	—	—	—	—	0.13	0.77	0.03	Capital Gains $
—	—	—	—	—	—	—	—	—	2.00	—	—	Expense Ratio %
—	—	—	—	—	—	—	—	—	0.50	—	—	Income Ratio %
—	—	—	—	—	—	—	—	—	71	—	—	Turnover Rate %
—	—	—	—	—	—	—	—	—	—	25.5	42.5	Net Assets $mil

Performance 12-31-01

	1st Qtr	2nd Qtr	3rd Qtr	4th Qtr	Total
1997	—	—	—	—	—
1998	—	—	—	—	—
1999	—	—	—	23.46	17.79*
2000	6.44	–1.94	8.80	–2.19	11.08
2001	1.31	–0.16	–20.07	9.13	–11.77

Trailing	Total Return%	+/– S&P 500	+/– Russ Top 200 Val	% Rank All	% Rank Cat	Growth of $10,000
3 Mo	9.13	–1.56	3.61	47	49	10,913
6 Mo	–12.77	–7.22	–6.99	91	100	8,723
1 Yr	–11.77	0.11	–2.98	64	85	8,823
3 Yr Avg	—	—	—	—	—	—
5 Yr Avg	—	—	—	—	—	—
10 Yr Avg	—	—	—	—	—	—
15 Yr Avg	—	—	—	—	—	—

Tax Analysis	Tax-Adj Ret%	%Rank Cat	%Pretax Ret	%Rank Cat
3 Yr Avg	—	—	—	—
5 Yr Avg	—	—	—	—
10 Yr Avg	—	—	—	—

Potential Capital Gain Exposure: –2% of assets

Risk Analysis

Time Period	Load-Adj Return %	Risk %Rank¹ All	Risk %Rank¹ Cat	Morningstar Return	Morningstar Risk	Morningstar Risk-Adj Rating
1 Yr	–11.77					
3 Yr	—	—	—	—	—	
5 Yr	—	—	—	—	—	
Incept	6.30	—	—	—	—	

Average Historical Rating —

[1]1=low, 100=high

Category Rating (3 Yr)

Return
Risk

Other Measures	Standard Index S&P 500	Best Fit Index
Alpha	—	—
Beta	—	—
R–Squared	—	—
Standard Deviation		—
Mean		—
Sharpe Ratio		—

Portfolio Analysis 11-30-01

Share change since 10–01 Total Stocks: 44	Sector	PE	YTD Ret%	% Assets
⊖ Lucent Tech	Technology	—	–53.20	6.81
Cendant	Services	20.4	103.70	6.23
American Home Products	Health	—	–1.91	5.48
Sprint	Services	20.5	1.18	5.33
⊖ Compaq Comp	Technology	—	–34.50	4.38
Baker Hughes	Energy	45.0	–11.10	3.80
Philip Morris	Staples	12.1	9.12	3.58
WorldCom	Services	24.3	3.12	3.13
Conoco Cl A	Energy	9.0	1.56	3.04
⊖ Motorola	Technology	—	–25.00	2.61
⊕ Walt Disney	Services	—	–27.70	2.45
⊕ Cablevision Sys A	Services	5.6	–34.20	2.32
Lehman Brothers Hldgs	Financials	12.4	–0.84	2.28
Intl Paper	Industrials	—	1.43	2.24
AT&T Wireless Grp	Services	—	–17.00	2.23
Nextel Comms Cl A	Services	—	–55.70	2.06
Honeywell Intl	Durables	NMF	–27.00	2.05
⊖ Verizon Comms	Services	29.7	–2.52	1.98
Agere Sys	Technology	—	—	1.86
Schering–Plough	Health	22.2	–35.90	1.85
Analog Devices	Technology	47.7	–13.20	1.80
EOG Resources	Energy	8.1	–28.10	1.71
⊖ Williams Companies	Utilities	17.9	–29.10	1.61
Ryder Sys	Services	29.2	37.06	1.55
Mattel	Staples	31.9	19.43	1.48

Current Investment Style

Style: Value Blnd Growth; Size: Large Med Small

	Stock Port Avg	Relative S&P 500 Current	Relative S&P 500 Hist	Rel Cat
Price/Earnings Ratio	24.3	0.79	—	0.97
Price/Book Ratio	4.4	0.76	—	1.06
Price/Cash Flow	11.8	0.65	—	0.85
3 Yr Earnings Growth	26.1¹	1.79	—	1.77
1 Yr Earnings Est%	–3.3	1.88	—	1.01
Med Mkt Cap $mil	19,686	0.3	—	0.62

¹figure is based on 50% or less of stocks

Analysis by Bridget Hughes 08-23-01

We think that Gabelli Blue Chip Value AAA Fund is worth checking out, but only if you can ignore its short-term performance swings.

This two-year-old fund hasn't been a model of consistency. Indeed, compared with the rest of the large-value group, its returns have been all over the map. It posted a stunning 23.5% return in 1999's fourth quarter, for example, while its average peer gained just 6.3%. More recently, it gained 1.3% in 2001's first quarter as the average large-value fund fell 5.5%. In this year's second quarter, however, it sank 0.2%; the typical large-value offering jumped 4.9%. Since its inception through August 17, 1999, however, it has bested the category norm by more than 11 percentage points.

The fund's schizophrenia stems from its concentrated portfolio. With just 43 stocks and 46% of assets in its top-10 holdings, the fund is one of the category's more-focused. It currently socks more than 6.5% of assets in top holding Lucent Technologies, more than double the stake of any other large-value fund. Cendant, Compaq Computer, and American Home Products are other 5%-plus positions.

Manager Barbara Marcin is comfortable with her style. She looks for stocks with "a lot of negatives priced into them," that she thinks will rebound in the next year or two. Lucent fits that bill: Most telecom stocks been crushed as the industry suffers through a capital-spending crunch, and the company was also scorned for engaging in questionable accounting practices that effectively inflated sales figures. But Marcin likes the firm's relationships with its customers and notes that Lucent has continued to win business from companies such as Verizon Communications and Qualcomm. Meanwhile, though, the stock's performance has weighed on the fund.

Marcin doesn't have much of a public performance record, so investing here is something of a leap of faith.

Special Securities % assets 11-30-01	
Restricted/Illiquid Secs	0
Emerging–Markets Secs	0
Options/Futures/Warrants	No

Composition % assets 11-30-01	
Cash	11.2
Stocks*	88.9
Bonds	0.0
Other	0.0
*Foreign (% stocks)	1.4

Market Cap	
Giant	18.4
Large	70.3
Medium	9.5
Small	1.7
Micro	0.0

Sector Weightings	% of Stocks	Rel S&P	5-Year High	5-Year Low
Utilities	1.8	0.6	—	—
Energy	13.0	1.8	—	—
Financials	4.0	0.2	—	—
Industrials	4.5	0.4	—	—
Durables	2.3	1.5	—	—
Staples	5.7	0.7	—	—
Services	36.2	3.3	—	—
Retail	0.0	0.0	—	—
Health	8.2	0.6	—	—
Technology	24.3	1.3	—	—

Address: One Corporate Center, Rye, NY 10580–1434, 800–422–3554 / 914–921–5100
Web Address: www.gabelli.com
*Inception: 08-26-99
Advisor: Gabelli Funds
Subadvisor: None
NTF Plans: Datalynx , Fidelity Inst.

Minimum Purchase: $1000 — Add: None — IRA: $1000
Min Auto Inv Plan: $100 — Add: $100
Sales Fees: 0.25%B
Management Fee: 1.0%
Actual Fees: Mgt: 1.00% — Dist: 0.25%
Expense Projections: 3Yr: $551 — 5Yr: — — 10Yr: —
Avg Brok Commission: — — Income Distrib: Annually
Total Cost (relative to category): —

Gabelli Global Telecommunications

Ticker	Load	NAV	Yield	Total Assets	Mstar Category
GABTX	12b–1 only	$13.96	0.0%	$235.5 mil	Spec Communications

Prospectus Objective: Specialty—Communications

Gabelli Global Telecommunications Fund seeks capital appreciation. Current income is a secondary objective.

The fund invests at least 65% of assets in securities issued by companies in the telecommunications industry. These companies may be domiciled in the United States or elsewhere. These companies may provide service and/or equipment for telephone systems, wireless communications, computer hardware and software for communications, and television and radio broadcasting. This fund is non-diversified.

Historical Profile
Return Above Avg
Risk Average
Rating ★★★★ Above Avg

Investment Style
Equity
Average Stock %: 91% 94% 93% 87% 75% 86% 98%

▼ Manager Change
▽ Partial Manager Change

Fund Performance vs. Category Average
■ Quarterly Fund Return +/– Category Average
— Category Baseline

Performance Quartile (within Category)

Portfolio Manager(s)

Mario J. Gabelli, CFA et al.Since 2-95. BS'65 Fordham U.; MBA'67 Columbia U.

Marc Gabelli. Since 1–93. BA'90 Boston C.

1990	1991	1992	1993	1994	1995	1996	1997	1998	1999	2000	12-01	History
—	—	—	10.20	9.73	11.12	11.28	13.32	16.62	26.95	17.63	13.96	NAV
—	—	—	5.45*	–3.68	16.16	8.99	31.87	34.75	80.27	–24.08	–20.73	Total Return %
—	—	—	5.47*	–4.99	–21.38	–13.95	–1.48	6.18	59.24	–14.98	–8.85	+/– S&P 500
—	—	—	—	–3.61	–20.29	–12.20	0.57	11.33	56.71	–13.15	–9.84	+/– Wilshire 5000
—	—	—	1.04	0.64	0.66	0.41	0.00	0.08	0.27	2.34	0.00	Income Return %
—	—	—	4.40	–4.31	15.50	8.58	31.87	34.67	80.00	–26.42	–20.73	Capital Return %
—	—	—	—	55	90	50	35	66	31	13	6	Total Rtn % Rank Cat
—	—	—	0.10	0.07	0.06	0.05	0.00	0.01	0.05	0.63	0.00	Income $
—	—	—	0.00	0.03	0.12	0.79	1.55	1.30	2.90	2.15	0.02	Capital Gains $
—	—	—	2.54	1.80	1.75	1.72	1.74	1.60	1.48	1.46	—	Expense Ratio %
—	—	—	1.28	0.74	0.53	0.34	0.01	0.08	0.28	2.36	—	Income Ratio %
—	—	—	—	14	24	7	9	20	60	49	—	Turnover Rate %
—	—	—	44.4	137.8	122.8	108.6	117.9	170.1	459.3	331.7	234.5	Net Assets $mil

Performance 12-31-01

	1st Qtr	2nd Qtr	3rd Qtr	4th Qtr	Total
1997	0.09	16.65	8.05	4.53	31.87
1998	19.44	1.95	–10.73	23.96	34.75
1999	15.40	14.44	4.24	30.95	80.27
2000	4.94	–10.15	–6.18	–14.18	–24.08
2001	–10.89	3.50	–19.86	7.25	–20.73

Trailing	Total Return%	+/– S&P 500	+/– Wil 5000	% Rank All	% Rank Cat	Growth of $10,000
3 Mo	7.25	–3.43	–5.12	55	51	10,725
6 Mo	–14.05	–8.50	–8.57	93	23	8,595
1 Yr	–20.73	–8.85	–9.84	81	6	7,927
3 Yr Avg	2.75	3.78	3.40	57	15	10,849
5 Yr Avg	14.03	3.33	4.32	6	21	19,278
10 Yr Avg	—	—	—	—	—	—
15 Yr Avg	—	—	—	—	—	—

Tax Analysis	Tax-Adj Ret%	%Rank Cat	%Pretax Ret	%Rank Cat
3 Yr Avg	0.56	15	20.2	75
5 Yr Avg	11.73	21	83.6	50
10 Yr Avg	—	—	—	—

Potential Capital Gain Exposure: 2% of assets

Risk Analysis

Time Period	Load-Adj Return %	Risk %Rank[1] All	Risk %Rank[1] Cat	Morningstar Return	Morningstar Risk	Morningstar Risk-Adj Rating
1 Yr	–20.73					
3 Yr	2.75	77	12	–0.46[2]	1.08	★★★
5 Yr	14.03	73	1	2.33[2]	0.99	★★★★
Incept	11.75	—	—	—	—	

Average Historical Rating (62 months): 3.8★s

[1]1=low, 100=high [2] T-Bill return substituted for category avg.

Category Rating (3 Yr)

1 2 3 4 5
Worst Best

Return Above Avg
Risk Below Avg

Other Measures	Standard Index S&P 500	Best Fit Index MSCIACWdFr
Alpha	5.4	10.4
Beta	1.06	1.20
R-Squared	61	68
Standard Deviation		24.19
Mean		2.75
Sharpe Ratio		–0.10

Analysis by Gabriel Presler 11-30-01

A streak of orthodoxy has helped Gabelli Global Telecommunications Fund outpace its rivals.

In the communications category, where extensive globe-trotting, daring strategies, and high price tags are the norm, this fund's staid nature stands out. First of all, managers Marc and Mario Gabelli buy on the cheap, so the fund's portfolio valuations are much lower than the category average. What's more, they stick to communications-related stocks, rather than dipping into the tech firms that often drive returns (and volatility) for their peers. Finally, the fund doesn't travel much, preferring to stake the bulk of its portfolio in the U.S. and Canadian markets.

In 2001's nasty conditions, this staid approach has helped contain loss. The fund's value orientation helped it sidestep the dramatic declines that some of the sector's more-expensive firms suffered. So did its tendency to stick close to home: European and Asian telecom firms have suffered more than their domestic rivals this year. More important, though, has been the management team's stock-picking prowess. For example, large positions in Commonwealth Telephone and AT&T have worked nicely in 2001. Thus, while the fund has lost more than 21% of its value for the year to date through Nov. 29, 2001, it has easily outpaced more than 90% of its rivals.

Would-be investors won't always enjoy such strong relative performance, though. The fund's caution can often hold it back, especially during growth rallies. The Gabelli duo is also willing to devote up to 8% of assets to individual positions, so the portfolio can court some serious issue-specific risk. Still, solid stock-picking and attention to valuation has resulted in a strong long-term record and very low relative volatility, making this one of the better options in the category.

Portfolio Analysis 11-30-01

Share chng since 10-01 Total Stocks: 231	Subsector	PE	YTD Ret%	% Assets
⊖ Telephone and Data Sys	Wireless	—	0.29	7.31
Centurytel	Phone Services	13.3	–7.66	3.90
Deutsche Telekom ADR	Services	9.3	–41.10	3.17
Verizon Comms	Phone Services	29.7	–2.52	2.61
Liberty Mint		—	—	2.58
Commonwealth Tele Entrp	Services	—	30.00	2.45
TIM	Wireless	10.9	—	2.42
Nextel Comms Cl A	Wireless	—	–55.70	2.38
BCE	Phone Services	3.8	–18.70	2.36
AT&T Wireless Grp	Services	—	–17.00	2.26
Telefonica ADR	Phone Services	22.4	–16.60	2.18
AT&T	Phone Services	7.8	40.59	2.03
Alltel	Phone Services	17.7	1.14	2.00
Swisscom ADR	Phone Services	10.9	12.72	1.84
NTT DoCoMo	Services	60.1	—	1.83
⊖ Sprint (PCS Group)	Services	—	19.43	1.81
Rogers Wireless Comm B	Services	—	–17.70	1.75
SBC Comms	Phone Services	18.4	–16.00	1.73
Cable & Wireless Comm ADR	Phone Services	8.0	–61.40	1.63
Rogers Comms Cl B	Wireless	6.4	–1.18	1.58
United States Cellular	Wireless	22.9	–24.90	1.52
BellSouth	Phone Services	24.9	–5.09	1.48
SK Telecom ADR	Services	20.0	–8.04	1.41
⊕ Telus	Phone Services	—	—	1.41
Sprint	Phone Services	20.5	1.18	1.40

Current Investment Style

Style: Value Blnd Growth; Size: Large Med Small

	Stock Port Avg	Relative S&P 500 Current	Relative S&P 500 Hist	Rel Cat
Price/Earnings Ratio	21.6	0.70	0.84	0.71
Price/Book Ratio	3.7	0.64	0.64	0.82
Price/Cash Flow	10.4	0.58	0.67	0.62
3 Yr Earnings Growth	25.1[1]	1.71	—	0.85
1 Yr Earnings Est%	–16.5[1]	9.29	—	0.79
Med Mkt Cap $mil	9,704	0.2	0.3	0.36

[1]figure is based on 50% or less of stocks

Special Securities % assets 11-30-01	
Restricted/Illiquid Secs	1
Emerging-Markets Secs	6
Options/Futures/Warrants	Yes

Composition % assets 11-30-01	
Cash	0.9
Stocks*	98.4
Bonds	0.0
Other	0.7
*Foreign (% stocks)	37.9

Market Cap	
Giant	23.0
Large	29.4
Medium	34.4
Small	12.5
Micro	0.8

Subsector Weightings	% of Stocks	Rel Cat
Phone Services	33.5	1.1
Phone Equip.	3.4	0.3
Wireless	19.1	2.3
Broadcasting	0.6	0.4
Cable	3.0	1.1
Publishing	0.5	1.3
Media	0.0	0.0
Technology	0.1	0.0
Other	39.8	1.2

Address:	One Corporate Center Rye, NY 10580–1434 800–422–3554 / 914–921–5100
Web Address:	www.gabelli.com
*Inception:	11-01-93
Advisor:	Gabelli Funds
Subadvisor:	None
NTF Plans:	Fidelity , Datalynx

Minimum Purchase:	$1000	Add: None IRA: $1000
Min Auto Inv Plan:	$100	Add: $100
Sales Fees:	0.25%B	
Management Fee:	1.0%, .06%A	
Actual Fees:	Mgt: 1.00%	Dist: 0.25%
Expense Projections:	3Yr: $490	5Yr: $845 10Yr: $1845
Avg Brok Commission:	—	Income Distrib: Annually
Total Cost (relative to category):	—	

Gabelli Growth

Ticker	Load	NAV	Yield	Total Assets	Mstar Category
GABGX	12b–1 only	$28.68	0.0%	$2,957.8 mil	Large Blend

Prospectus Objective: Growth

Gabelli Growth Fund seeks capital appreciation; current income is a secondary consideration.

The fund invests in a diversified portfolio of readily marketable common stocks and convertibles. It invests primarily in securities that management believes to be undervalued and to have favorable prospects for earnings growth. Other desired characteristics include above-average or expanding market shares, profit margins, and returns on equity. The fund may invest up to 25% of assets in foreign securities.

Historical Profile

Return Above Avg
Risk Above Avg
Rating ★★★ Neutral

Investment Style
Equity
Average Stock %

99% 97% 99% 96% 99% 98% 99%

▼ Manager Change
▽ Partial Manager Change

Fund Performance vs. Category Average
Quarterly Fund Return +/– Category Average
— Category Baseline

Performance Quartile (within Category)

Portfolio Manager(s)

Howard F. Ward, CFA. Since 1-95. BA'78 Northwestern U. Other funds currently managed: MainStay Blue Chip Growth A, MainStay Blue Chip Growth B, MainStay Blue Chip Growth C.

1990	1991	1992	1993	1994	1995	1996	1997	1998	1999	2000	12–01	History
16.27	21.28	21.59	23.26	19.68	22.16	24.14	28.63	35.40	46.51	37.79	28.68	NAV
–1.99	34.32	4.49	11.26	–3.40	32.72	19.42	42.63	29.79	46.26	–10.57	–24.10	Total Return %
1.13	3.83	–3.13	1.20	–4.71	–4.81	–3.52	9.28	1.21	25.22	–1.47	–12.22	+/– S&P 500
2.04	1.87	–3.16	1.42	–3.85	–4.88	–2.74	9.60	1.15	24.43	0.39	–11.33	+/– Wilshire Top 750
2.28	0.95	0.40	0.42	0.37	0.28	0.11	0.01	0.00	0.00	0.00	0.00	Income Return %
–4.28	33.37	4.09	10.84	–3.77	32.44	19.31	42.62	29.78	46.25	–10.57	–24.10	Capital Return %
39	32	80	39	80	56	68	1	13	2	75	95	Total Rtn % Rank Cat
0.39	0.15	0.09	0.09	0.09	0.06	0.02	0.00	0.00	0.00	0.00	0.00	Income $
0.07	0.42	0.56	0.67	2.70	3.91	2.30	5.79	1.75	5.16	3.85	0.00	Capital Gains $
1.50	1.45	1.41	1.41	1.36	1.44	1.43	1.43	1.41	1.37	1.38	—	Expense Ratio %
2.67	0.97	0.46	0.22	0.31	0.22	0.12	–0.23	–0.33	–0.68	–0.63	—	Income Ratio %
75	50	46	81	40	140	88	83	40	52	55	—	Turnover Rate %
203.0	420.9	624.4	695.9	483.6	526.4	623.4	951.5	1,864.0	3,155.2	3,835.4	2,957.8	Net Assets $mil

Performance 12-31-01

	1st Qtr	2nd Qtr	3rd Qtr	4th Qtr	Total
1997	1.49	19.39	14.22	3.05	42.63
1998	12.89	3.25	–14.47	30.19	29.79
1999	8.84	7.40	–0.75	26.06	46.26
2000	7.72	–0.74	–5.73	–11.27	–10.57
2001	–20.19	3.38	–22.26	18.33	–24.10

Trailing	Total Return%	+/– S&P 500	+/– Wil Top 750	% Rank All	% Rank Cat	Growth of $10,000
3 Mo	18.33	7.65	7.01	17	4	11,833
6 Mo	–8.00	–2.45	–2.21	78	81	9,200
1 Yr	–24.10	–12.22	–11.33	87	95	7,590
3 Yr Avg	–0.24	0.79	1.58	74	38	9,928
5 Yr Avg	12.94	2.24	2.82	8	7	18,378
10 Yr Avg	12.58	–0.35	0.13	15	27	32,713
15 Yr Avg	—	—	—	—	—	—

Tax Analysis	Tax-Adj Ret%	%Rank Cat	%Pretax Ret	%Rank Cat
3 Yr Avg	–1.72	42	—	—
5 Yr Avg	10.96	8	84.7	36
10 Yr Avg	10.10	43	80.3	50

Potential Capital Gain Exposure: –13% of assets

Risk Analysis

Time Period	Load-Adj Return %	Risk %Rank[1] All	Risk %Rank[1] Cat	Morningstar Return	Morningstar Risk	Morningstar Risk-Adj Rating
1 Yr	–24.10					
3 Yr	–0.24	79	90	–1.05[2]	1.13	★★
5 Yr	12.94	78	92	2.01[2]	1.07	★★★★
10 Yr	12.58	80	87	1.22	1.07	★★★

Average Historical Rating (141 months): 4.1★s

[1] 1=low, 100=high [2] T–Bill return substituted for category avg.

Category Rating (3 Yr)

1 2 3 4 5
Worst Best

Return Average
Risk High

Other Measures	Standard Index S&P 500	Best Fit Index S&P 500
Alpha	3.8	3.8
Beta	1.33	1.33
R–Squared	89	89
Standard Deviation		24.51
Mean		–0.24
Sharpe Ratio		–0.25

Portfolio Analysis 11-30-01

Share change since 10–01 Total Stocks: 41	Sector	PE	YTD Ret%	% Assets
⊖ State Street	Financials	28.6	–15.10	5.90
⊖ Pfizer	Health	34.7	–12.40	5.50
⊕ Viacom Cl B	Services	—	—	4.85
AOL Time Warner	Technology	—	–7.76	4.68
⊕ Clear Channel Comms	Services	—	5.10	4.65
⊖ Mellon Finl	Financials	23.8	–21.90	4.34
⊕ Home Depot	Retail	42.9	12.07	4.27
Johnson & Johnson	Health	16.6	14.01	4.02
⊕ Northern Tr	Financials	27.4	–25.40	3.21
⊖ Qualcomm	Technology	—	–38.50	3.02
Automatic Data Processing	Services	39.8	–6.27	2.99
⊕ American Home Products	Health	—	–1.91	2.80
Texas Instruments	Technology	87.5	–40.70	2.64
Omnicom Grp	Services	34.5	8.83	2.64
Intel	Technology	73.1	4.89	2.64
⊖ Marsh & McLennan	Financials	27.9	–6.30	2.30
⊖ Interpublic Grp	Services	—	–29.80	2.19
⊖ Analog Devices	Technology	47.7	–13.20	2.17
Cisco Sys	Technology	—	–52.60	2.03
⊖ Motorola	Technology	—	–25.00	1.99
Tellabs	Technology	41.6	–73.50	1.91
⊕ Tiffany	Retail	27.1	0.09	1.88
⊕ Nokia Cl A ADR	Technology	45.8	–43.00	1.83
⊕ Sun Microsystems	Technology	NMF	–55.80	1.81
⊕ EMC	Technology	NMF	–79.40	1.78

Current Investment Style

Style: Value Blnd Growth; Size: Large Med Small

	Stock Port Avg	Relative S&P 500 Current	Relative S&P 500 Hist	Rel Cat
Price/Earnings Ratio	36.7	1.19	1.14	1.21
Price/Book Ratio	6.4	1.12	1.09	1.16
Price/Cash Flow	25.9	1.44	1.29	1.41
3 Yr Earnings Growth	24.0	1.64	1.28	1.34
1 Yr Earnings Est%	–13.6	7.70	—	—
Med Mkt Cap $mil	36,307	0.6	0.6	0.69

[1] figure is based on 50% or less of stocks

Analysis by Gabriel Presler 11-30-01

Gabelli Growth has fallen on hard times, but we're not dismissing it yet.

After enjoying three years of category-topping returns, this fund's investors are staring at some pretty ugly losses. The fund dropped 10% in 2000, lagging 75% of its peers. The pain didn't stop there; in 2001, it has given back 25% of its value for the year to date through Nov. 30, 2001, trailing 95% of its large-blend rivals.

It's not hard to figure out what's going on. This fund has always been one of the more aggressive in the category, but in 2001 it has looked downright brazen. While many of his peers have gone on the defensive, manager Howard Ward has stayed true to his favorite firms. That means that the fund is heavily exposed to big, blue-chip tech and networking stocks, many of which have been brutalized in 2001. And although some of the fund's top health-care picks have done well, there haven't been too many bright spots. Ward runs a concentrated portfolio—he holds 46 firms—and he's willing to virtually ignore sectors in which he doesn't see impressive growth potential. Thus the fund has had little exposure to the industrial and consumer-related stocks that have propped up returns for its peers.

Signing on here takes guts. Given the fund's miserable performance recently, would-be investors have to believe in the eventual recovery of large, blue-chip growth stocks and they must share Ward's conviction that this portfolio is filled with resilient industry leaders. It's worth noting that such faith has been rewarded in the near term at least, as some beleaguered tech stocks have staged mini-rallies, helping the fund outpace 90% of its rivals over the last three months. Ward's history is also a point in the fund's favor; he has displayed deft timing and solid stock-picking in the past and has guided the fund to a top-decile five-year record. There's reason to believe this offering can rise again.

Special Securities % assets 11-30-01	
Restricted/Illiquid Secs	0
Emerging–Markets Secs	0
Options/Futures/Warrants	No

Composition % assets 11-30-01	
Cash	0.3
Stocks*	99.7
Bonds	0.0
Other	0.0
*Foreign (% stocks)	4.2

Market Cap	
Giant	44.9
Large	49.5
Medium	5.6
Small	0.0
Micro	0.0

Sector Weightings	% of Stocks	Rel S&P	5-Year High	5-Year Low
Utilities	0.0	0.0	5	0
Energy	0.0	0.0	10	0
Financials	22.4	1.3	25	3
Industrials	0.7	0.1	28	0
Durables	0.0	0.0	6	0
Staples	0.0	0.0	25	0
Services	23.1	2.1	29	6
Retail	6.2	0.9	14	3
Health	16.0	1.1	21	8
Technology	31.8	1.7	35	2

Address: One Corporate Center
Rye, NY 10580–1434
800–422–3554 / 914–921–5100
Web Address: www.gabelli.com
Inception: 04-10-87
Advisor: Gabelli Funds
Subadvisor: None
NTF Plans: Fidelity , Datalynx

Minimum Purchase: $1000 Add: None IRA: $1000
Min Auto Inv Plan: $100 Add: $100
Sales Fees: 0.25%B
Management Fee: 1.0%, .10%A
Actual Fees: Mgt: 1.00% Dist: 0.25%
Expense Projections: 3Yr: $434 5Yr: $750 10Yr: $1646
Avg Brok Commission: — Income Distrib: —
Total Cost (relative to category): Average

Gabelli Small Cap Growth

Ticker	Load	NAV	Yield	Total Assets	Mstar Category
GABSX	12b–1 only	$19.21	0.1%	$440.2 mil	Small Blend

Prospectus Objective: Small Company

Gabelli Small Cap Growth Fund seeks capital appreciation.

The fund normally invests at least 65% of assets in the equity securities of companies with market capitalizations of less than $500 million, that are likely to have rapid growth in revenue and/or earnings and above-average capital appreciation. It may invest the balance of assets in nonconvertible-debt securities of any credit rating, but no more than 5% in those rated D. The fund may invest up to 35% of assets in foreign securities.

Historical Profile
Return: Above Avg
Risk: Below Avg
Rating: ★★★★ Above Avg

Investment Style
Equity
Average Stock %: 99% (1996), 91% (1997), 96% (1998), 97% (1999), 93% (2000), 90% (12-01)

▼ Manager Change
▽ Partial Manager Change

Fund Performance vs. Category Average
■ Quarterly Fund Return +/– Category Average
— Category Baseline

Performance Quartile (within Category)

Portfolio Manager(s)

Mario J. Gabelli, CFA. Since 10-91. BS'65 Fordham U.; MBA'67 Columbia U. Other funds currently managed: Gabelli Asset, Gabelli Equity-Income, Gabelli Value.

1990	1991	1992	1993	1994	1995	1996	1997	1998	1999	2000	12-01	History
—	12.21	14.50	17.38	15.84	18.50	18.53	21.58	21.01	21.43	18.71	19.21	NAV
—	22.78*	20.27	22.76	−2.93	25.25	11.88	36.47	−0.02	14.21	11.30	4.65	Total Return %
—	14.39*	12.65	12.70	−4.25	−12.28	−11.06	3.12	−28.59	−6.83	20.40	16.53	+/– S&P 500
—	—	1.86	3.85	−1.11	−3.19	−4.66	14.11	2.54	−7.05	14.33	2.17	+/– Russell 2000
—	0.12	0.20	0.00	0.00	0.00	0.00	0.00	0.00	0.00	0.26	0.07	Income Return %
—	22.66	20.07	22.76	−2.93	25.25	11.88	36.47	−0.02	14.21	11.05	4.58	Capital Return %
—	—	21	12	78	55	91	10	23	43	52	64	Total Rtn % Rank Cat
—	0.01	0.03	0.00	0.00	0.00	0.00	0.00	0.00	0.00	0.06	0.01	Income $
—	0.07	0.16	0.42	1.03	1.34	2.16	3.66	0.53	2.46	4.73	0.35	Capital Gains $
—	—	1.97	1.64	1.54	1.54	1.58	1.62	1.44	1.56	1.49	—	Expense Ratio %
—	—	0.32	0.03	−0.28	−0.24	−0.42	−0.36	−0.14	−0.34	0.26	—	Income Ratio %
—	—	—	14	19	17	11	14	20	24	47	—	Turnover Rate %
—	25.7	123.9	215.0	196.2	228.6	216.7	293.0	321.3	338.2	374.4	440.2	Net Assets $mil

Performance 12-31-01

	1st Qtr	2nd Qtr	3rd Qtr	4th Qtr	Total
1997	3.13	16.33	14.66	−0.79	36.47
1998	10.89	−1.42	−20.26	14.71	−0.02
1999	−6.76	17.10	−4.80	9.87	14.21
2000	3.78	2.38	3.65	1.07	11.30
2001	−1.39	10.73	−16.15	14.31	4.65

Trailing	Total Return%	+/– S&P 500	+/– Russ 2000	% Rank All	% Rank Cat	Growth of $10,000
3 Mo	14.31	3.62	−6.77	25	88	11,431
6 Mo	−4.16	1.40	−0.07	57	75	9,584
1 Yr	4.65	16.53	2.17	25	64	10,465
3 Yr Avg	9.98	11.01	3.56	11	52	13,303
5 Yr Avg	12.66	1.97	5.14	8	33	18,152
10 Yr Avg	13.81	0.88	2.30	9	43	36,455
15 Yr Avg	—	—	—	—	—	—

Tax Analysis	Tax-Adj Ret%	%Rank Cat	%Pretax Ret	%Rank Cat
3 Yr Avg	7.24	61	72.6	82
5 Yr Avg	10.19	38	80.5	56
10 Yr Avg	11.68	34	84.6	21

Potential Capital Gain Exposure: 14% of assets

Risk Analysis

Time Period	Load-Adj Return %	Risk %Rank¹ All	Risk %Rank¹ Cat	Morningstar Return	Morningstar Risk	Morningstar Risk-Adj Rating
1 Yr	4.65					
3 Yr	9.98	44	11	1.12²	0.61	★★★★
5 Yr	12.66	49	6	1.93²	0.66	★★★★
10 Yr	13.81	56	4	1.50	0.73	★★★★

Average Historical Rating (87 months): 3.5★s

¹1=low, 100=high ² T-Bill return substituted for category avg.

Category Rating (3 Yr)

1 2 **3** 4 5
Worst — Best

Return: Average
Risk: Below Avg

Other Measures	Standard Index S&P 500	Best Fit Index SPMid400
Alpha	9.0	1.3
Beta	0.62	0.67
R-Squared	47	74

Standard Deviation	16.62
Mean	9.98
Sharpe Ratio	0.35

Analysis by Gabriel Presler 10-05-01

Gabelli Small Cap Growth may not provide the excitement its name suggests, but it's a solid choice.

This fund's staid nature is in keeping with its familial ties, but not category norms. Manager Mario Gabelli has made a name for himself buying firms trading at discounts to their private-market values, often targeting companies well-positioned for consolidation or takeover. He's willing to make considerable sector bets in his search for cheap companies, so this offering often looks very different from its rivals in the small-blend group. The fund's stakes in communications- and consumer-staples firms, for example, are double the group average; its exposure to financials companies is miniscule relative to its peers'. Gabelli's a patient man, too; the fund's turnover rate is about a third of the category average.

This approach hasn't saved the fund from losses in 2001's wretched market, but it has helped its relative performance. After steep drops in 2000, some of the Gabelli's top media picks, including Ackerley Group, have rallied this year. And the recoveries of a few old industrial firms, including Modine Manufacturing, Roper Industries, and Thomas & Betts—all of which suffered significant losses in 2000—have propped up performance. Thus the fund's loss of more than 9% for the year to date through Oct. 5, 2001, while ugly on an absolute basis, is slightly better than the group average.

Strong relative performance is no surprise here, but this offering comes with a few caveats: First of all, Gabelli funds tend to be pricey, and the fund's expense ratio is higher than the category average. What's more, this fund isn't as tax-efficient as some of its peers. Overall, though, the fund has provided shareholders with strong long-term returns and has shielded them from volatility, making it a good choice for conservative investors.

Portfolio Analysis 11-30-01

Share change since 10-01 Total Stocks: 390	Sector	PE	YTD Ret%	% Assets
⊕ Liberty	Services	37.1	3.36	1.74
⊖ Aztar	Services	14.3	41.44	1.60
Thomas Inds	Industrials	13.9	8.91	1.45
Clarcor	Industrials	16.0	33.91	1.44
Flowers Foods	Staples	—	—	1.32
⊕ CH Energy Grp	Utilities	17.1	2.22	1.32
Sensient Tech	Staples	17.2	−5.99	1.30
Roper Inds	Industrials	29.0	50.94	1.20
Ackerley Grp	Services	11.8	94.44	1.19
News ADR Pfd	Services	—	—	1.19
Thomas & Betts	Industrials	—	34.36	1.17
⊕ Kaman A	Industrials	25.6	−4.80	1.15
RPC	Energy	14.1	56.70	1.10
⊖ Wolverine World Wide	Staples	14.8	−0.25	1.08
⊕ Baldor Elec	Industrials	24.9	1.34	1.06
⊖ Flowserve	Industrials	—	24.49	1.05
Crane	Industrials	15.7	−8.48	1.04
⊖ Franklin Elec	Industrials	18.9	21.30	0.97
⊖ Ametek	Industrials	14.8	23.96	0.91
⊕ J.M. Smucker	Staples	28.3	29.50	0.90
⊕ Baker Cap Grp	Financials	—	—	0.90
Greif Brothers Cl A	Industrials	4.2	17.89	0.90
PepsiAmericas	Staples	26.0	−15.50	0.89
⊕ HB Fuller	Industrials	17.6	48.69	0.83
Gaylord Entrtnmt	Services	—	17.84	0.82

Current Investment Style

Style: Value Blnd Growth; Size: Large Med Small

	Stock Port Avg	Relative S&P 500 Current	Relative S&P 500 Hist	Rel Cat
Price/Earnings Ratio	23.2	0.75	0.67	0.93
Price/Book Ratio	2.4	0.42	0.37	0.76
Price/Cash Flow	12.7	0.71	0.65	0.82
3 Yr Earnings Growth	12.2	0.83	0.64	0.72
1 Yr Earnings Est%	−11.4¹	6.42	—	−13.21
Med Mkt Cap $mil	668	0.0	0.0	0.68

¹figure is based on 50% or less of stocks

Special Securities % assets 11-30-01	
Restricted/Illiquid Secs	Trace
Emerging–Markets Secs	Trace
Options/Futures/Warrants	No

Composition % assets 11-30-01	
Cash	8.9
Stocks*	89.8
Bonds	0.0
Other	1.3
*Foreign (% stocks)	2.8

Market Cap	
Giant	0.1
Large	0.9
Medium	13.8
Small	68.9
Micro	16.2

Sector Weightings	% of Stocks	Rel S&P	5-Year High	5-Year Low
Utilities	4.8	1.5	5	0
Energy	1.5	0.2	2	0
Financials	4.8	0.3	8	2
Industrials	36.9	3.2	43	29
Durables	4.1	2.6	16	4
Staples	9.8	1.2	10	3
Services	28.9	2.7	34	20
Retail	2.4	0.4	9	2
Health	3.3	0.2	6	0
Technology	3.5	0.2	12	3

Address:	One Corporate Center Rye, NY 10580–1434 800–422–3554 / 914–921–5100
Web Address:	www.gabelli.com
*Inception:	10-22-91
Advisor:	Gabelli Funds
Subadvisor:	None
NTF Plans:	Fidelity , Datalynx

Minimum Purchase:	$1000	Add: None IRA: $1000
Min Auto Inv Plan:	$100	Add: $100
Sales Fees:	0.25%B	
Management Fee:	1.0%, .06%A	
Actual Fees:	Mgt: 1.00%	Dist: 0.25%
Expense Projections:	3Yr: $48*	5Yr: $83* 10Yr: $182*
Avg Brok Commission:	—	Income Distrib: Annually
Total Cost (relative to category):		—

Gabelli Value

Ticker	Load	NAV	Yield	Total Assets	Mstar Category
GABVX	5.50%	$16.43	0.3%	$1,270.4 mil	Mid–Cap Value

Prospectus Objective: Growth

Gabelli Value Fund seeks long-term capital appreciation.

The fund invests primarily in common stocks, preferred stocks, and convertibles of companies that management judges to be undervalued. When selecting investments, the advisor considers such factors as the market price of the issuer's securities, balance sheet characteristics, and strength of management. The fund may invest up to 50% of assets in companies that have announced a merger, consolidation, liquidation, or similar reorganization. It may invest up to 25% of assets in foreign securities. This fund is non-diversified.

Historical Profile
Return: High
Risk: Average
Rating: ★★★★★ Highest

Investment Style
Equity
Average Stock %: 93% 98% 98% 97% 96% 93% 91%

▼ Manager Change
▽ Partial Manager Change

Fund Performance vs. Category Average
■ Quarterly Fund Return +/– Category Average
– Category Baseline

Performance Quartile (within Category)

Portfolio Manager(s)

Mario J. Gabelli, CFA. Since 9-89. BS'65 Fordham U.; MBA'67 Columbia U. Other funds currently managed: Gabelli Asset, Gabelli Equity-Income, Gabelli Small Cap Growth.

1990	1991	1992	1993	1994	1995	1996	1997	1998	1999	2000	12–01	History
8.51	9.48	10.13	12.09	10.49	11.62	11.52	14.30	16.08	19.45	16.13	16.43	NAV
–5.59	15.32	12.69	39.45	—	22.56	8.65	48.23	23.23	31.92	–7.85	5.36	Total Return %
–2.48	–15.16	5.07	29.39	–1.32	–14.98	–14.29	14.88	–5.35	10.88	1.25	17.23	+/– S&P 500
10.49	–22.60	–8.99	23.82	2.13	–12.38	–11.61	13.87	18.14	32.02	–27.04	3.02	+/– Russ Midcap Val
5.69	2.20	0.97	0.49	0.75	0.48	0.00	0.00	0.00	0.00	0.00	0.32	Income Return %
–11.29	13.13	11.72	38.95	–0.75	22.08	8.65	48.23	23.23	31.92	–7.85	5.04	Capital Return %
23	93	65	1	45	85	98	1	4	4	99	47	Total Rtn % Rank Cat
0.54	0.19	0.09	0.05	0.09	0.05	0.00	0.00	0.00	0.00	0.00	0.05	Income $
0.00	0.15	0.46	1.99	1.51	1.18	1.11	2.72	1.49	1.72	1.75	0.52	Capital Gains $
1.39	1.45	1.52	1.53	1.50	1.50	1.40	1.42	1.40	1.38	1.37	—	Expense Ratio %
4.45	1.43	0.75	0.38	0.73	0.42	–0.12	–0.45	–0.41	–0.40	–0.14	—	Income Ratio %
59	16	10	21	67	65	37	44	46	59	66	—	Turnover Rate %
850.7	576.3	423.6	496.2	438.4	486.4	461.1	596.7	797.6	1,204.4	1,157.9	1,270.4	Net Assets $mil

Performance 12-31-01

	1st Qtr	2nd Qtr	3rd Qtr	4th Qtr	Total
1997	0.95	21.32	11.48	8.56	48.23
1998	14.90	3.10	–13.16	19.79	23.23
1999	7.52	13.24	–3.32	12.06	31.92
2000	–3.86	1.02	–2.38	–2.80	–7.85
2001	0.68	8.56	–14.58	12.84	5.36

Trailing	Total Return%	+/– S&P 500	+/– Russ Midcap Val	% Rank All	% Rank Cat	Growth of $10,000
3 Mo	12.84	2.16	0.81	30	47	11,284
6 Mo	–3.61	1.95	–2.70	54	77	9,639
1 Yr	5.36	17.23	3.02	21	47	10,536
3 Yr Avg	8.60	9.62	1.79	14	60	12,807
5 Yr Avg	18.53	7.83	7.07	2	9	23,394
10 Yr Avg	17.21	4.29	2.80	2	13	48,953
15 Yr Avg	—	—	—	—	—	—

Tax Analysis	Tax-Adj Ret%	%Rank Cat	%Pretax Ret	%Rank Cat
3 Yr Avg	6.62	59	77.0	61
5 Yr Avg	15.86	6	85.6	20
10 Yr Avg	14.13	15	82.1	39

Potential Capital Gain Exposure: 19% of assets

Risk Analysis

Time Period	Load-Adj Return %	Risk %Rank[1] All	Risk %Rank[1] Cat	Morningstar Return	Morningstar Risk	Morningstar Risk-Adj Rating
1 Yr	–0.44					
3 Yr	6.57	45	38	0.35[2]	0.63	★★★★
5 Yr	17.19	47	14	3.35[2]	0.64	★★★★★
10 Yr	16.55	62	56	2.21	0.81	★★★★★

Average Historical Rating (112 months): 3.6★s

[1] 1=low, 100=high [2] T-Bill return substituted for category avg.

Category Rating (3 Yr)

1 2 3 4 5
Worst — Best

Return: Average
Risk: Average

Other Measures	Standard Index S&P 500	Best Fit Index S&P 500
Alpha	8.4	8.4
Beta	0.76	0.76
R-Squared	68	68

Standard Deviation	16.99
Mean	8.60
Sharpe Ratio	0.25

Portfolio Analysis 11-30-01

Share change since 10–01 Total Stocks: 144	Sector	PE	YTD Ret%	% Assets
⊖ Viacom Cl A	Services	—	–5.85	7.21
Media General Cl A	Services	36.9	38.79	6.07
Telephone and Data Sys	Services	—	0.29	5.18
⊕ Cablevision Sys A	Services	5.6	–34.20	3.57
Ralston Purina	Staples	—	27.94	3.28
⊕ AT & T Liberty Media Cl A	Services	—	3.22	2.98
⊖ Navistar Intl	Durables	—	50.88	2.43
Liberty	Services	37.1	3.36	2.43
USA Networks	Services	58.1	40.50	2.38
⊕ AT&T	Services	7.8	40.59	2.09
Willamette Inds	Industrials	19.8	13.20	1.91
⊖ Cendant	Services	20.4	103.70	1.88
⊕ Vivendi ADR	Services	17.0	–16.70	1.50
PepsiAmericas	Staples	26.0	–15.50	1.46
⊖ Honeywell Intl	Durables	NMF	–27.00	1.42
Sprint	Services	20.5	1.18	1.35
⊖ Autonation	Services	14.2	105.50	1.30
⊖ Archer Daniels Midland	Staples	24.7	1.91	1.21
⊖ Waste Mgmt	Services	52.3	15.03	1.18
⊖ Flowers Foods	Staples	—	—	1.06
⊖ News ADR Pfd	Services	—	—	1.05
⊕ Hercules	Industrials	—	–47.50	1.02
⊕ American Express	Financials	28.3	–34.40	1.00
⊕ Thomas & Betts	Industrials	—	34.36	0.95
⊖ Catellus Dev	Financials	21.2	5.14	0.94

Current Investment Style

Style: Value Blnd Growth; Size: Large Med Small

	Stock Port Avg	Relative S&P 500 Current	Relative S&P 500 Hist	Rel Cat
Price/Earnings Ratio	27.7	0.89	0.87	1.17
Price/Book Ratio	2.4	0.42	0.40	0.79
Price/Cash Flow	13.8	0.77	0.80	1.12
3 Yr Earnings Growth	17.5[1]	1.19	0.65	1.47
1 Yr Earnings Est%	–27.4[1]	15.47	—	4.45
Med Mkt Cap $mil	5,690	0.1	0.1	0.80

[1] figure is based on 50% or less of stocks

Special Securities % assets 11-30-01	
Restricted/Illiquid Secs	0
Emerging–Markets Secs	Trace
Options/Futures/Warrants	No

Composition % assets 11-30-01	
Cash	8.4
Stocks*	90.6
Bonds	0.0
Other	1.1
*Foreign (% stocks)	6.4

Market Cap	
Giant	15.0
Large	27.5
Medium	32.7
Small	23.6
Micro	1.1

Sector Weightings	% of Stocks	Rel S&P	5-Year High	5-Year Low
Utilities	1.3	0.4	5	0
Energy	0.2	0.0	2	0
Financials	2.7	0.2	10	1
Industrials	14.9	1.3	18	6
Durables	7.0	4.5	11	0
Staples	12.4	1.6	17	5
Services	58.0	5.3	80	46
Retail	0.7	0.1	5	0
Health	0.5	0.0	9	0
Technology	2.3	0.1	5	1

Analysis by Gabriel Presler 10-18-01

Gabelli Value Fund's new category doesn't indicate a shift in strategy—and that's good for investors.

This offering has always bounced around the style box a bit—but not because manager Mario Gabelli is a capricious investor. Instead, this offering's shifting identity has a lot to do with his taste for communications-related firms. The fund has generally devoted half of its portfolio to such firms. In 1998 and 1999, it sat firmly in the mid-blend group as its valuations grew, thanks to appreciating telecom and media stocks. Since 2000, Gabelli's favorite firms have struggled, and the fund has settled back into the mid-value group.

This new home hasn't helped the fund's looks. Some of Gabelli's old favorites, including Cablevision and Liberty Media, have posted heavy losses in 2001. What's more, the fund suffered for its lack of exposure to the fairly resilient consumer-cyclical and health-care sectors, which have been popular among mid-value funds in 2001. The fund's loss of 6% for the year to date through Oct. 18, 2001, lags half its rivals.

Nonetheless, Gabelli's patience and bargain-hunting style have generally paid off. In 2000, for example, he bought ailing Cendant and Sprint, both of which have staged nice recoveries this year. Such success is common here; the fund's 10-year record is admirable relative to both the mid-blend and the mid-value groups.

Although the fund is no more volatile than its peers, it isn't right for cautious investors. Gabelli's tendency to buy beaten-up growth stocks and make big sector bets can result in some sharp drops from time to time. What's more, this portfolio rarely offers exposure to traditional "value" companies. But those who understand and can tolerate the fund's characteristics are getting a solid holding.

Address:	One Corporate Center Rye, NY 10580–1434 800–422–3554 / 914–921–5100
Web Address:	www.gabelli.com
Inception:	09-29-89
Advisor:	Gabelli Funds
Subadvisor:	None
NTF Plans:	Datalynx , Fidelity Inst.

Minimum Purchase:	$1000	Add: None IRA: $250
Min Auto Inv Plan:	$100	Add: $100
Sales Fees:	5.50%L, 0.25%B	
Management Fee:	1.0%, .10%A	
Actual Fees:	Mgt: 1.00%	Dist: 0.25%
Expense Projections:	3Yr: $987	5Yr: $1287 10Yr: $2137
Avg Brok Commission:	—	Income Distrib: Annually
Total Cost (relative to category):	Average	

Gabelli Westwood Balanced Ret

Ticker	Load	NAV	Yield	Total Assets	Mstar Category
WEBAX	12b–1 only	$10.99	2.2%	$170.1 mil	Domestic Hybrid

Prospectus Objective: Balanced

Gabelli Westwood Balanced Fund seeks capital appreciation and current income.

The fund invests between 30% and 70% of assets in common stocks or convertibles issued by seasoned companies with above-average historical earnings growth, or by smaller companies with outstanding potential for capital appreciation. It may invest the balance in investment-grade U.S. dollar- or foreign currency-denominated debt. The fund invests at least 25% in fixed-income senior securities and up to 25% in foreign securities.

Service and Retail shares are sold by the fund.

The previous name was the Westwood Balanced Fund.

Historical Profile
Return Average
Risk Low
Rating ★★★★ Above Avg

Investment Style
Equity
Average Stock %: 65% 60% 59% 60% 62% 62% 65%

▼ Manager Change
▽ Partial Manager Change

Fund Performance vs. Category Average
■ Quarterly Fund Return +/– Category Average
— Category Baseline

Performance Quartile (within Category)

Portfolio Manager(s)

Susan M. Byrne. Since 10-91. BA U. of California-Berkeley. Other funds currently managed: Gabelli Westwood Balanced Svc, Gabelli Westwood Equity Svc, Gabelli Westwood Equity Ret.

Mark Freeman, CFA. Since 12-00. MS Louisiana State U. Other funds currently managed: Gabelli Westwood Balanced Svc, Gabelli Westwood Intermediate Bd Ret.

1990	1991	1992	1993	1994	1995	1996	1997	1998	1999	2000	12-01	History
—	10.56	9.96	7.23	7.05	8.89	9.68	11.00	11.88	11.71	11.62	10.99	NAV
—	7.34*	5.86	18.60	0.05	31.16	18.11	22.45	11.51	7.75	11.49	–3.26	Total Return %
—	–0.67*	–1.76	8.55	–1.27	–6.37	–4.84	–10.90	–17.07	–13.29	20.59	8.61	+/– S&P 500
—	—	–1.54	8.86	2.96	12.69	14.49	12.76	2.84	8.58	–0.14	–11.69	+/– LB Aggregate
—	1.03	2.37	2.87	2.53	2.88	2.57	2.77	2.27	2.13	2.45	2.13	Income Return %
—	6.31	3.49	15.74	–2.49	28.28	15.54	19.68	9.24	5.62	9.04	–5.39	Capital Return %
—	—	72	10	18	9	10	19	57	59	9	40	Total Rtn % Rank Cat
—	0.10	0.25	0.28	0.18	0.20	0.23	0.27	0.25	0.25	0.28	0.25	Income $
—	0.04	0.96	4.27	0.00	0.13	0.58	0.56	0.12	0.81	1.10	0.00	Capital Gains $
—	—	1.44	1.82	1.68	1.25	1.32	1.25	1.17	1.20	1.19	—	Expense Ratio %
—	—	3.13	1.90	1.55	2.47	2.62	2.60	2.37	2.06	2.21	—	Income Ratio %
—	—	178	192	168	133	111	110	77	86	65	—	Turnover Rate %
—	9.1	4.1	1.4	3.5	9.5	30.8	80.6	141.8	160.0	147.8	163.2	Net Assets $mil

Performance 12-31-01

	1st Qtr	2nd Qtr	3rd Qtr	4th Qtr	Total
1997	1.37	11.43	6.91	1.40	22.45
1998	6.90	–0.48	–4.69	9.98	11.51
1999	0.06	7.23	–4.61	5.28	7.75
2000	3.18	1.64	2.70	3.51	11.49
2001	–1.34	0.33	–8.03	6.27	–3.26

Trailing	Total Return%	+/– S&P 500	+/– LB Agg	% Rank All	% Rank Cat	Growth of $10,000
3 Mo	6.27	–4.42	6.23	60	51	10,627
6 Mo	–2.27	3.29	–6.92	48	62	9,773
1 Yr	–3.26	8.61	–11.69	48	40	9,674
3 Yr Avg	5.14	6.16	–1.14	30	19	11,621
5 Yr Avg	9.67	–1.03	2.25	20	18	15,868
10 Yr Avg	11.93	–0.99	4.71	19	7	30,878
15 Yr Avg	—	—	—	—	—	—

Tax Analysis	Tax-Adj Ret%	%Rank Cat	%Pretax Ret	%Rank Cat
3 Yr Avg	2.90	20	56.5	43
5 Yr Avg	7.61	13	78.7	15
10 Yr Avg	8.34	17	69.9	60

Potential Capital Gain Exposure: 5% of assets

Risk Analysis

Time Period	Load-Adj Return %	Risk %Rank[1] All	Risk %Rank[1] Cat	Morningstar Return	Morningstar Risk	Morningstar Risk-Adj Rating
1 Yr	–3.26					
3 Yr	5.14	34	20	0.04[2]	0.41	★★★★
5 Yr	9.67	39	19	1.11[2]	0.44	★★★★
10 Yr	11.93	46	18	1.09	0.47	★★★★

Average Historical Rating (88 months): 4.2★s

[1]1=low, 100=high [2] T-Bill return substituted for category avg.

Category Rating (3 Yr)

1 2 3 4 5
Worst Best

Return Above Avg
Risk Below Avg

Other Measures	Standard Index S&P 500	Best Fit Index S&P 500
Alpha	2.5	2.5
Beta	0.42	0.42
R-Squared	63	63
Standard Deviation		9.43
Mean		5.14
Sharpe Ratio		0.02

Portfolio Analysis 11-30-01

Total Stocks: 46 Share change since 10-01	Sector	PE Ratio	YTD Return %	% Net Assets
WellPoint Health Networks	Health	19.4	1.39	2.12
Sears Roebuck	Retail	23.4	40.12	1.91
ALCOA	Industrials	21.4	7.86	1.87
IBM	Technology	26.9	43.00	1.86
Pfizer	Health	34.7	–12.40	1.83
Hewlett-Packard	Technology	97.8	–33.90	1.78
Union Pacific	Services	17.1	13.96	1.77
General Motors	Durables	NMF	–0.97	1.77
⊖ Apple Comp	Technology	—	47.23	1.74
Georgia-Pacific	Industrials	—	–9.87	1.73

Total Fixed-Income: 38	Date of Maturity	Amount $000	Value $000	% Net Assets
US Treasury Note 7.25%	05-15-04	3,000	3,290	1.95
US Treasury Note 6.125%	08-15-07	2,800	3,057	1.81
US Treasury Note 7.5%	02-15-05	2,550	2,855	1.69
US Treasury Note 6%	08-15-09	2,220	2,412	1.43
US Treasury Note 7%	07-15-06	2,100	2,357	1.40
FNMA Debenture 6.5%	08-15-04	1,625	1,748	1.04
General Electric Capital 7.5%	05-15-05	1,500	1,653	0.98
GTE 6.46%	04-15-08	1,585	1,636	0.97
US Treasury Note 6.625%	05-15-07	1,445	1,611	0.95
Archstone Communities Tr 7%	03-01-13	1,600	1,606	0.95

Equity Style
Style: Value
Size: Large-Cap

Fixed-Income Style
Duration: —
Quality: —
NA

	Portfolio Avg	Rel S&P
Price/Earnings Ratio	21.6	0.70
Price/Book Ratio	3.2	0.55
Price/Cash Flow	12.2	0.68
3 Yr Earnings Growth	16.1	1.10
1 Yr Earnings Est%	1.0	—
Debt % Total Cap	43.6	1.41
Med Mkt Cap $mil	24,878	0.41

Avg Eff Duration	—
Avg Eff Maturity	—
Avg Credit Quality	—
Avg Wtd Coupon	6.66%

Special Securities % assets 11-30-01	
Restricted/Illiquid Secs	0
Emerging-Markets Secs	0
Options/Futures/Warrants	No

Composition % of assets 11-30-01	
Cash	1.8
Stocks*	67.1
Bonds	31.1
Other	0.0
*Foreign (% of stocks)	0.0

Market Cap	
Giant	29.9
Large	52.7
Medium	17.4
Small	0.0
Micro	0.0

Sector Weightings	% of Stocks	Rel S&P	5-Year High	5-Year Low
Utilities	10.4	3.3	13	0
Energy	11.4	1.6	16	6
Financials	24.8	1.4	26	5
Industrials	13.6	1.2	39	4
Durables	2.8	1.8	17	0
Staples	9.0	1.1	9	0
Services	7.5	0.7	23	5
Retail	3.0	0.5	14	0
Health	6.3	0.4	11	0
Technology	11.2	0.6	20	5

Analysis by Gabriel Presler 11-30-01

Gabelli Westwood Balanced Fund's asset-allocation moves paint a rosy picture of the future.

Just as many domestic-hybrid funds went on the defensive, ramping up their cash exposure or fixed-income stakes, this fund got more aggressive, building its equity exposure from 55% to 65% of assets. Manager Susan Byrne and Mark Freeman are positioning the portfolio for stronger equity markets in 2002.

That doesn't mean the fund has left its caution behind, though. Byrne, who runs the offering's equity portfolio, buys 45 companies trading at a discount to her estimate of their long-term growth prospects, and she's not afraid to make significant sector bets in her search for value. Lately, for example, she has loaded up on higher-yielding energy firms and a few fallen-growth tech stocks—a move that has dragged on returns, as investors fled the energy sector and companies such as Compaq have continued to struggle.

Meanwhile, fixed-income manager Mark Freeman continues to run a conservative portfolio, tilting the fund toward short- and intermediate-term Treasuries and mortgage-backed paper. He will occasionally venture into corporate paper, but the fund rarely buys high-yield issues, preferring bonds from the likes of IBM and GE. This staid profile has worked nicely this year, especially since shorter-term Treasuries have outperformed. Thus, despite volatility in the fund's equity portfolio, its loss of 4% for the year to date through Nov. 29 looks decent compared with the group.

Of course, hybrid investors aren't likely pleased with a loss, no matter how small, but the fund's longer-term record indicates ample reason for hope. Since Byrne introduced the fund in 1991, it has outpaced 90% of its peers, and while it doesn't shine in growth rallies, its returns are rarely worse than middling. It continues to be a strong choice.

Address:	One Corporate Center Rye, NY 10580–1434 800–937–8966
Web Address:	www.gabelli.com
*Inception:	10-01-91
Advisor:	Gabelli Adv.
Subadvisor:	Westwood Mgmt.
NTF Plans:	Fidelity , Datalynx

Minimum Purchase:	$1000	Add: None IRA: $250
Min Auto Inv Plan:	None	Add: None
Sales Fees:	0.25%B	
Management Fee:	.75%	
Actual Fees:	Mgt: 0.75%	Dist: 0.25%
Expense Projections:	3Yr: $381	5Yr: $660 10Yr: $1445
Avg Brok Commission:	—	Income Distrib: Quarterly
Total Cost (relative to category):	Below Avg	

Galaxy II U.S. Treasury Index Ret

Ticker	Load	NAV	Yield	SEC Yield	Total Assets	Mstar Category
IUTIX	None	$10.64	5.6%	3.82%	$163.0 mil	Intermediate Govt

Prospectus Objective: Government Treasury

Galaxy II U.S. Treasury Index Fund seeks to replicate the performance of the U.S. Treasury index, a proprietary index maintained by the advisor.

The fund invests at least 80% of assets in securities included in the index, which consists of U.S. Treasury notes and bonds with remaining maturities of at least one year and outstanding principal of at least $25 million. The fund does not hold all of the issues in the index because of the costs involved and the illiquidity of some of the securities. Rather, it selects securities through statistical portfolio optimization.

Prior to July 1, 1994, the fund was named IBM U.S. Treasury Index Fund.

Historical Profile

Return Above Avg
Risk Average
Rating ★★★
Neutral

Investment Style
Fixed-Income
Income Rtn %Rank Cat: 58 46 48 40 33 18 38 32

Growth of Principal vs. Interest Rate Shifts
— Principal Value $000 (NAV with capital gains reinvested)
— Interest Rate % on 10 Yr Treasury
▼ Manager Change
▽ Partial Manager Change
► Mgr Unknown After
◄ Mgr Unknown Before

Performance Quartile (within Category)

Portfolio Manager(s)

David Lindsay, CFA. Since 7-94. BA'64 Yale U.; MBA'66 Harvard U. Other funds currently managed: Galaxy Asset Allocation Ret A, Galaxy Asset Allocation Tr, Galaxy Corporate Bond Tr.

1990	1991	1992	1993	1994	1995	1996	1997	1998	1999	2000	12–01	History
—	10.74	10.68	10.83	9.63	10.66	10.23	10.51	10.88	9.93	10.58	10.64	NAV
—	11.07*	6.77	10.22	–3.69	18.06	2.21	9.27	9.76	–2.85	13.11	6.28	Total Return %
—	—	–0.63	0.47	–0.77	–0.41	–1.41	–0.41	1.09	–2.02	1.48	–2.14	+/– LB Aggregate
—	—	–0.46	–0.44	–0.32	–0.28	–0.57	–0.30	–0.09	–0.61	–0.13	–0.96	+/– LB Government
—	3.66	6.04	5.66	5.92	7.07	6.23	6.38	6.14	6.09	6.31	5.74	Income Return %
—	7.41	0.74	4.56	–9.61	10.99	–4.03	2.90	3.62	–8.94	6.79	0.55	Capital Return %
—	—	26	16	64	18	73	20	6	80	3	74	Total Rtn % Rank Cat
—	0.35	0.63	0.59	0.62	0.66	0.65	0.63	0.63	0.64	0.61	0.59	Income $
—	0.00	0.13	0.34	0.18	0.00	0.00	0.00	0.00	0.00	0.00	0.00	Capital Gains $
—	—	0.40	0.40	0.40	0.40	0.40	0.40	0.40	0.41	0.41	—	Expense Ratio %
—	—	6.40	5.87	5.21	6.43	6.35	6.31	6.12	5.77	5.95	—	Income Ratio %
—	—	—	35	75	50	35	39	79	70	56	—	Turnover Rate %
—	—	142.0	152.8	104.8	128.1	114.3	115.5	190.6	165.9	167.5	163.0	Net Assets $mil

Performance 12-31-01

	1st Qtr	2nd Qtr	3rd Qtr	4th Qtr	Total
1997	–0.82	3.20	3.36	3.29	9.27
1998	1.40	2.57	5.57	–0.03	9.76
1999	–1.73	–1.13	0.70	–0.71	–2.85
2000	3.57	1.43	2.60	4.95	13.11
2001	2.17	–0.46	5.45	–0.89	6.28

Trailing	Total Return%	+/– LB Agg	+/– LB Govt	% Rank All	% Rank Cat	Growth of $10,000
3 Mo	–0.89	–0.93	—	91	82	9,911
6 Mo	4.51	–0.15	—	6	19	10,451
1 Yr	6.28	–2.14	—	18	74	10,628
3 Yr Avg	5.31	–0.97	—	29	52	11,678
5 Yr Avg	6.97	–0.45	—	36	13	14,007
10 Yr Avg	6.72	–0.51	—	53	13	19,157
15 Yr Avg	—	—	—	—	—	—

Tax Analysis	Tax-Adj Ret%	%Rank Cat	%Pretax Ret	%Rank Cat
3 Yr Avg	2.88	64	54.3	75
5 Yr Avg	4.49	10	64.4	26
10 Yr Avg	4.08	14	60.8	23

Potential Capital Gain Exposure: 0% of assets

Risk Analysis

Time Period	Load-Adj Return %	Risk %Rank[1] All	Risk %Rank[1] Cat	Morningstar Return	Morningstar Risk	Morningstar Risk-Adj Rating
1 Yr	6.28					
3 Yr	5.31	22	82	0.08[2]	0.78	★★★
5 Yr	6.97	27	76	0.44[2]	0.77	★★★★
10 Yr	6.72	34	74	0.56[2]	1.00	★★★

Average Historical Rating (91 months): 3.1★s

[1] 1=low, 100=high [2] T-Bill return substituted for category avg.

Category Rating (3 Yr)

1 2 3 4 5
Worst Best

Return Average
Risk Above Avg

Other Measures	Standard Index LB Agg	Best Fit Index LB Govt
Alpha	–1.1	–0.6
Beta	1.17	1.05
R-Squared	89	99

Standard Deviation	4.36
Mean	5.31
Sharpe Ratio	0.10

Analysis by Scott Cooley 12-10-01

Galaxy II U.S. Treasury Index Fund has both finer and less-attractive features.

This fund does have positive attributes. Its 41-basis-point (or 0.41%) expense ratio is pleasingly low. Indeed, it's lower than all but a handful of intermediate-government funds'. Over time, manager David Lindsay has capably tracked his benchmark, the Salomon Smith Barney U.S. Treasury index. And some investors will appreciate the ease of reinvesting dividends, which can be done automatically with a mutual fund.

Like any fund, this one has drawbacks, too. Some investors would be comfortable investing directly in Treasuries, which for many would be even cheaper than buying this fund. Moreover, in certain circumstances one might take on less reinvestment risk by purchasing Treasuries on their own. For example, a person who's saving for a 10-year period could buy a zero-coupon Treasury with that maturity and know precisely how much money he or she will have a decade hence. However, the fund's benchmark changes constantly, as new issues come to market, old issues are retired and interest rates change.

This portfolio has mostly performed well over the past couple of years, and that's both a boon and a curse to investors. Despite a recent uptick in longer-term interest rates, the fund has returned 5.1% for the year to date through Dec. 7, 2001. That follows a gain of 13.1% in 2000, as falling interest rates gave a boost to this fund's net asset value. However, the interest rates of intermediate- and long-term Treasuries, which dominate this index, have fallen sharply over the past couple of decades. Thus, this fund's payout is much lower than it was in the early 1990s.

Still, this fund clearly is a decent way to gain broad-based Treasury exposure.

Portfolio Analysis 09-30-01

Total Fixed-Income: 26	Date of Maturity	Amount $000	Value $000	% Net Assets
US Treasury Bond 7.5%	11-15-24	11,350	14,342	8.55
US Treasury Note 7.25%	08-15-04	12,900	14,301	8.52
US Treasury Bond 6.125%	11-15-27	11,900	12,935	7.71
US Treasury Note 5.75%	08-15-03	11,600	12,219	7.28
US Treasury Note 5.625%	05-15-08	9,865	10,617	6.33
US Treasury Note 5.5%	02-28-03	7,950	8,264	4.93
US Treasury Bond 12%	08-15-13	5,675	8,184	4.88
US Treasury Note 3.875%	06-30-03	8,000	8,152	4.86
US Treasury Bond 7.5%	11-15-16	5,700	7,008	4.18
US Treasury Note 6%	08-15-09	6,000	6,600	3.93
US Treasury Note 5.75%	08-15-10	6,000	6,503	3.88
US Treasury Note 5.25%	08-15-03	6,000	6,267	3.74
US Treasury Note 7%	07-15-06	4,425	5,014	2.99
US Treasury Note 6.5%	10-15-06	4,450	4,957	2.95
US Treasury Bond 8.5%	02-15-20	3,521	4,789	2.85
US Treasury Note 6.5%	08-15-05	4,250	4,685	2.79
US Treasury Note 5.5%	05-15-19	4,100	4,381	2.61
US Treasury Bond 8.125%	08-15-21	3,200	4,242	2.53
US Treasury Note 5.625%	12-31-02	3,200	3,320	1.98
US Treasury Bond 10.75%	08-15-05	2,650	3,319	1.98

Current Investment Style

Duration: Short Int Long — Quality: High Med Low

Avg Eff Duration[1]	6.1 Yrs
Avg Eff Maturity	9.8 Yrs
Avg Credit Quality	AAA
Avg Wtd Coupon	6.76%
Avg Wtd Price	114.40% of par

[1] figure provided by fund

Special Securities % assets 09-30-01	
Restricted/Illiquid Secs	0
Exotic Mortgage–Backed	0
Emerging–Markets Secs	0
Options/Futures/Warrants	No

Credit Analysis % bonds 09-30-01			
US Govt	100	BB	0
AAA	0	B	0
AA	0	Below B	0
A	0	NR/NA	0
BBB	0		

Coupon Range	% of Bonds	Rel Cat
0%	0.00	0.00
0% to 7%	56.50	0.99
7% to 8.5%	31.67	0.95
8.5% to 10%	4.84	1.19
More than 10%	6.98	1.79

1.00=Category Average

Composition % assets 09-30-01			
Cash	1.0	Bonds	99.0
Stocks	0.0	Other	0.0

Address:	290 Donald Lynch Boulevard Marlboro, MA 01752 800–628–0414
Web Address:	www.galaxyfunds.com
*Inception:	06-04-91
Advisor:	Fleet Inv. Adv.
Subadvisor:	None
NTF Plans:	N/A

Minimum Purchase:	$2500	Add: $100 IRA: $500
Min Auto Inv Plan:	$2500	Add: None
Sales Fees:	No–load	
Management Fee:	.10%, .30%A	
Actual Fees:	Mgt: 0.40%	Dist: —
Expense Projections:	3Yr: $13*	5Yr: $23* 10Yr: $51*
Avg Brok Commission:	—	Income Distrib: Monthly
Total Cost (relative to category):	—	

Galaxy Small Cap Value Ret A

Ticker	Load	NAV	Yield	Total Assets	Mstar Category
SSCEX	5.75%	$14.33	0.1%	$567.4 mil	Small Blend

Prospectus Objective: Small Company

Galaxy Small Capitalization Equity Fund seeks long-term capital appreciation.

The fund normally invests at least 65% of assets in equity securities issued by companies with market capitalizations under $1 billion. In addition to common stocks, the fund may invest in convertible securities rated at least BB, preferred stocks, and investment-grade corporate debt securities. It may also invest up to 20% of assets in foreign securities that are in the form of depositary receipts.

Retail shares have front loads; Trust shares are for institutional and certain qualified investors. Prior to Dec. 6, 1995, the fund was named Shawmut Small Capitalization Equity Fund.

Historical Profile
Return: Above Avg
Risk: Below Avg
Rating: ★★★★ Above Avg

Investment Style
Equity
Average Stock %: 89% 89% 89% 93% 91% 90%

▼ Manager Change
▽ Partial Manager Change

Fund Performance vs. Category Average
■ Quarterly Fund Return
+/– Category Average
— Category Baseline

Performance Quartile (within Category)

Portfolio Manager(s)

Peter C. Larson. Since 2-93. BA U. of Connecticut. Other funds currently managed: Galaxy Small Cap Value Tr, Galaxy Small Cap Value Prime A, Galaxy Small Cap Value Prime B.

1990	1991	1992	1993	1994	1995	1996	1997	1998	1999	2000	12-01	History
—	—	—	10.86	10.30	12.64	13.82	15.37	13.16	13.06	13.25	14.33	NAV
—	—	—	6.35*	0.32	31.38	26.84	31.23	–5.66	10.45	16.61	18.29	Total Return %
—	—	—	–0.41*	–1.00	–6.15	3.89	–2.13	–34.24	–10.59	25.71	30.17	+/– S&P 500
—	—	—	—	2.14	2.94	10.30	8.86	–3.11	–10.81	19.64	15.81	+/– Russell 2000
—	—	—	0.00	0.00	0.00	0.19	0.29	0.23	0.26	0.04	0.08	Income Return %
—	—	—	6.35	0.32	31.38	26.65	30.94	–5.89	10.19	16.57	18.21	Capital Return %
—	—	—	—	38	29	17	28	55	57	29	12	Total Rtn % Rank Cat
—	—	—	0.00	0.00	0.00	0.02	0.04	0.04	0.03	0.00	0.01	Income $
—	—	—	0.32	0.57	0.87	2.14	2.68	1.27	1.36	1.87	1.31	Capital Gains $
—	—	—	1.33	1.31	1.35	1.40	1.30	1.31	1.31	1.44	—	Expense Ratio %
—	—	—	–0.19	–0.10	–0.19	0.08	–0.25	0.38	0.13	0.08	—	Income Ratio %
—	—	—	—	29	32	39	52	33	42	43	—	Turnover Rate %
—	—	—	16.5	19.6	29.6	37.8	69.9	93.4	87.5	92.6	114.3	Net Assets $mil

Performance 12-31-01

	1st Qtr	2nd Qtr	3rd Qtr	4th Qtr	Total
1997	–2.24	16.58	18.67	–2.97	31.23
1998	10.53	–7.37	–15.93	9.60	–5.66
1999	–7.83	16.50	–4.27	7.45	10.45
2000	4.21	0.90	6.05	4.58	16.61
2001	2.27	12.26	–10.79	15.50	18.29

Trailing	Total Return%	+/– S&P 500	+/– Russ 2000	% Rank All	% Rank Cat	Growth of $10,000
3 Mo	15.50	4.82	—	23	76	11,550
6 Mo	3.04	8.59	—	15	18	10,304
1 Yr	18.29	30.17	—	2	12	11,829
3 Yr Avg	15.07	16.09	—	5	24	15,236
5 Yr Avg	13.53	2.83	—	7	27	18,862
10 Yr Avg	—	—	—	—	—	—
15 Yr Avg	—	—	—	—	—	—

Tax Analysis	Tax-Adj Ret%	%Rank Cat	%Pretax Ret	%Rank Cat
3 Yr Avg	11.87	24	78.8	65
5 Yr Avg	10.37	37	76.7	77
10 Yr Avg	—	—	—	—

Potential Capital Gain Exposure: 9% of assets

Risk Analysis

Time Period	Load-Adj Return %	Risk %Rank[1] All	Risk %Rank[1] Cat	Morningstar Return	Morningstar Risk	Morningstar Risk-Adj Rating
1 Yr	11.49					
3 Yr	12.82	38	3	1.80[2]	0.50	★★★★★
5 Yr	12.19	49	9	1.80[2]	0.68	★★★★
Incept	13.82	—	—	—	—	

Average Historical Rating (71 months): 3.3★s

[1]1=low, 100=high [2] T-Bill return substituted for category avg.

Category Rating (3 Yr)

1 2 3 **4** 5
Worst Best

Return: Above Avg
Risk: Low

Other Measures	Standard Index S&P 500	Best Fit Index SPMid400
Alpha	12.8	6.7
Beta	0.43	0.55
R-Squared	27	60
Standard Deviation		15.84
Mean		15.07
Sharpe Ratio		0.72

Analysis by Heather Haynos 12-05-01

Galaxy Small Cap Value Fund has a lot going for it.

With the exception of 1998 and 1999, when growth stocks held center stage, this fund has trounced its small-blend competition in every calendar year since its 1993 inception. Its three- and five-year trailing returns land in the category's top third. What's more, thanks to its value leanings, the fund has been one of the group's least-volatile offerings over time. A lower-than-average turnover rate has also made the offering relatively tax-efficient.

The fund's solid track record owes much to manager Peter Larson's eye for value. Larson tends to be a bit of a contrarian, buying in some beaten-down names when he thinks earnings have hit rock bottom. For example, he purchased top-five holding Albany International, a maker of paper-making supplies, in the latter half of 2000, when its stock was trading at all-time lows. But new management with an eye for cost-cutting provided the necessary catalyst, says Larson, and the stock is now up more than 50% for the year to date through Dec. 4, 2001.

The fund's strengths have been on full display in 2001. It has delivered a 12% return for the year to date through Dec. 4, a top-quintile showing relative to category peers. Larson's attention to value and consequent tech underweighting have helped considerably. He also favors smaller-cap stocks more than his typical rival, which has helped the fund in this year's small-cap-led market. Finally, he's made a bevy of very good picks. Top-10 holding Res-Care, a health-services firm, for example, returned 85% for the year to date through Dec. 4. Garment-services provider UniFirst was up 96% for the period.

This offering isn't for investors who want a fund that outpaces its peers in growth-led markets such as 1999's. But for those seeking a solid performer that takes fewer chances than many of its rivals, it's a good choice.

Portfolio Analysis 11-30-01

Share change since 10-01 Total Stocks: 197	Sector	PE	YTD Ret%	% Assets
Invacare	Health	16.1	–1.45	1.88
ICN Pharmaceuticals	Health	NMF	10.39	1.80
Benchmark Electrncs	Technology	—	–15.90	1.45
UniFirst	Services	18.8	122.00	1.36
LSI Inds	Industrials	26.0	29.69	1.35
Albany Intl	Industrials	16.6	61.87	1.26
Proquest	N/A	—	—	1.24
Res-Care	Health	26.0	96.67	1.17
Scios	Health	—	6.83	1.16
Pentair	Industrials	38.0	54.40	1.11
United Natural Foods	Retail	35.2	41.84	1.10
Applebee's Intl	Services	19.2	63.55	1.10
O'Charley's	Services	19.3	3.91	1.08
Analogic	Technology	NMF	–12.90	1.07
⊖ G & K Svcs A	Services	19.9	15.17	1.07
Jack In The Box	Services	13.4	–6.45	1.07
Greif Brothers Cl A	Industrials	4.2	17.89	1.06
Advo	Services	17.4	–3.10	1.02
Oshkosh Truck Cl B	Industrials	16.4	11.75	1.00
Progress Software	Technology	32.0	19.68	1.00
Datascope	Health	16.7	–0.44	0.99
Southwest Gas	Utilities	18.3	6.07	0.94
Delta and Pine Land	Industrials	27.9	8.91	0.91
Flowserve	Industrials	—	24.49	0.90
West Pharma Svc	Industrials	NMF	11.55	0.88

Current Investment Style

Style: Value Blnd Growth; Size: Large Med Small

	Stock Port Avg	Relative S&P 500 Current	Relative S&P 500 Hist	Rel Cat
Price/Earnings Ratio	23.2	0.75	0.66	0.93
Price/Book Ratio	2.3	0.41	0.37	0.72
Price/Cash Flow	13.4	0.74	0.61	0.86
3 Yr Earnings Growth	13.1	0.89	0.73	0.77
1 Yr Earnings Est%	0.9	—	—	1.03
Med Mkt Cap $mil	597	0.0	0.0	0.61

Special Securities % assets 11-30-01	
Restricted/Illiquid Secs	1
Emerging-Markets Secs	Trace
Options/Futures/Warrants	No

Composition % assets 11-30-01	
Cash	7.8
Stocks*	91.8
Bonds	0.0
Other	0.3
*Foreign (% stocks)	1.2

Market Cap	
Giant	0.0
Large	0.0
Medium	10.2
Small	71.3
Micro	18.5

Sector Weightings	% of Stocks	Rel S&P	5-Year High	5-Year Low
Utilities	4.7	1.5	6	1
Energy	6.0	0.8	13	4
Financials	14.0	0.8	17	6
Industrials	22.2	1.9	22	10
Durables	2.2	1.4	11	2
Staples	2.0	0.3	5	2
Services	22.5	2.1	23	14
Retail	3.8	0.6	12	1
Health	11.3	0.8	13	6
Technology	11.6	0.6	24	9

Address: 290 Donald Lynch Boulevard, Marlboro, MA 01752, 800–628–0414
Web Address: www.galaxyfunds.com
*Inception: 02-12-93
Advisor: Fleet Inv. Adv.
Subadvisor: None
NTF Plans: N/A

Minimum Purchase: $2500 Add: $100 IRA: $500
Min Auto Inv Plan: None Add: $50
Sales Fees: 5.75%L
Management Fee: .75%, .09%A
Actual Fees: Mgt: 0.75% Dist: —
Expense Projections: 3Yr: $852 5Yr: $1198 10Yr: $2172
Avg Brok Commission: — Income Distrib: Quarterly
Total Cost (relative to category): Average

John Hancock Financial Industries A

Ticker	Load	NAV	Yield	Total Assets	Mstar Category
FIDAX	5.00%	$16.52	0.0%	$2,098.5 mil	Spec Financials

Prospectus Objective: Specialty—Financial

John Hancock Financial Industries Fund seeks capital appreciation.

The fund normally invests at least 65% of assets in U.S. and foreign financial-services companies. These companies may include banks, thrifts, finance companies, brokerage and advisory firms, real-estate-related firms, and insurance companies. The fund may also purchase up to 5% of assets in bonds rated below investment-grade. It may also invest up to 15% of assets in investment-grade short-term securities.

The fund currently offers Class A, B, C, and I shares, all of which differ in fee structure and availability.

Historical Profile
Return: Average
Risk: Average
Rating: ★★★ Neutral

Investment Style: Equity

Average Stock %: 100% (1997), 94% (1998), 96% (1999), 99% (2000), 99% (12-01)

▼ Manager Change
▽ Partial Manager Change

Fund Performance vs. Category Average
■ Quarterly Fund Return +/– Category Average
— Category Baseline

Performance Quartile (within Category)

1990	1991	1992	1993	1994	1995	1996	1997	1998	1999	2000	12-01	History
—	—	—	—	—	—	11.23	15.34	15.93	15.76	20.55	16.52	NAV
—	—	—	—	—	—	40.19*	37.76	4.93	–1.07	30.39	–17.86	Total Return %
—	—	—	—	—	—	22.47*	4.40	–23.65	–22.11	39.50	–5.98	+/– S&P 500
—	—	—	—	—	—	—	6.46	–18.50	–24.63	41.33	–6.97	+/– Wilshire 5000
—	—	—	—	—	—	0.26	0.99	1.02	0.00	0.00	0.00	Income Return %
—	—	—	—	—	—	39.93	36.76	3.91	–1.07	30.39	–17.86	Capital Return %
—	—	—	—	—	—	—	88	60	42	31	97	Total Rtn % Rank Cat
—	—	—	—	—	—	0.03	0.11	0.16	0.00	0.00	0.00	Income $
—	—	—	—	—	—	0.65	0.02	0.00	0.00	0.00	0.36	Capital Gains $
—	—	—	—	—	—	1.20	1.20	1.37	1.39	1.40	—	Expense Ratio %
—	—	—	—	—	—	0.37	1.10	0.92	0.62	0.21	—	Income Ratio %
—	—	—	—	—	—	31	6	30	40	48	—	Turnover Rate %
—	—	—	—	—	—	—	534.7	906.3	622.8	709.7	501.0	Net Assets $mil

Portfolio Manager(s)

James K. Schmidt, CFA. Since 3-96. BS'72 Brown U.; MBA'74 MIT. Other funds currently managed: John Hancock Regional Bank A, John Hancock Regional Bank B, John Hancock Financial Industries B.

Thomas C. Goggins. Since 2-98. BBA'81 U. of Wisconsin; MBA'87 Northwestern U. Other funds currently managed: John Hancock Regional Bank A, John Hancock Regional Bank B, John Hancock Financial Industries B.

Thomas Finucane. Since 3-96. BA C. of the Holy Cross; MBA Babson Graduate School of Bus. Other funds currently managed: John Hancock Regional Bank A, John Hancock Regional Bank B, John Hancock Financial Industries B.

Performance 12-31-01

	1st Qtr	2nd Qtr	3rd Qtr	4th Qtr	Total
1997	–2.32	16.86	14.51	5.38	37.76
1998	10.37	1.59	–20.12	17.15	4.93
1999	0.88	4.48	–14.77	10.13	–1.07
2000	4.00	0.79	22.94	1.18	30.39
2001	–13.97	5.77	–15.67	7.04	–17.86

Trailing	Total Return%	+/– S&P 500	+/– Wil 5000	% Rank All	% Rank Cat	Growth of $10,000
3 Mo	7.04	–3.64	–5.33	56	43	10,704
6 Mo	–9.73	–4.18	–4.25	84	95	9,027
1 Yr	–17.86	–5.98	–6.97	77	97	8,214
3 Yr Avg	1.95	2.98	2.60	63	75	10,597
5 Yr Avg	8.90	–1.80	–0.81	24	85	15,317
10 Yr Avg	—	—	—	—	—	—
15 Yr Avg	—	—	—	—	—	—

Tax Analysis	Tax-Adj Ret%	%Rank Cat	%Pretax Ret	%Rank Cat
3 Yr Avg	1.80	67	92.6	31
5 Yr Avg	8.65	66	97.2	7
10 Yr Avg	—	—	—	—

Potential Capital Gain Exposure: 32% of assets

Risk Analysis

Time Period	Load-Adj Return %	Risk %Rank[1] All	Risk %Rank[1] Cat	Morningstar Return	Morningstar Risk	Morningstar Risk-Adj Rating
1 Yr	–21.96					
3 Yr	0.22	75	82	–0.96[2]	1.04	★★★
5 Yr	7.79	76	69	0.64[2]	1.04	★★★
Incept	13.07	—	—	—	—	

Average Historical Rating (34 months): 2.6★s

[1] 1=low, 100=high [2] T-Bill return substituted for category avg.

Category Rating (3 Yr)

1 Worst – 5 Best

Return: Below Avg
Risk: Above Avg

Other Measures	Standard Index S&P 500	Best Fit Index S&P 500
Alpha	3.1	3.1
Beta	0.85	0.85
R-Squared	46	46
Standard Deviation		21.95
Mean		1.95
Sharpe Ratio		–0.16

Analysis by Scott Cooley 12-31-01

Investors should keep John Hancock Financial Industries Fund on a short leash.

This has long been one of our favorite specialty-financials funds. Lead manager Jim Schmidt is one of the most-experienced skippers of any specialty-financials fund, and he has built a solid long-term record at sibling Regional Bank. Moreover, he receives the support of two experienced comanagers, Tom Finucane and Tom Goggins, and three other dedicated financial-services analysts.

But the fund had posted so-so long-term numbers before 2001, and it tanked this year. For the year to date through Dec. 28, the fund has dropped 17.5% and lags 96% of its peers. Management made an ill-timed bet on brokerage stocks, and although they trimmed it significantly at midyear, issues such as Charles Schwab and Merrill Lynch still stung. Several banks with exposure to the stock market, including State Street, also faltered. And the fund had less exposure to regional banks than many of its rivals; those issues got a boost from falling short-term interest rates. This fund should not be compared with many of the group's 2001 leaders, as they have much narrower, subsector-specific mandates, but this fund also lagged more-diversified offerings.

Schmidt and company are sticking to their guns. They believe that hard-hit, growth-oriented financials such as Wells Fargo are now very attractively valued, so they're keeping a bet on them. They're also sticking with a smaller wager on brokerages, though they've emphasized firms such as Goldman Sachs that have large institutional businesses. Management believes that slice of the brokerage business will recover before individuals return to the market.

Given Schmidt's long-term record elsewhere and wealth of experience, we're inclined to give him the benefit of the doubt. But if he doesn't right this ship soon, investors will have good reason to look elsewhere.

Portfolio Analysis 10-31-01

Share chng since 09-01 Total Stocks: 50	Subsector	PE	YTD Ret%	% Assets
Citigroup	Insurance	20.0	0.03	5.93
⊖ American Intl Grp	Insurance	42.0	–19.20	5.63
Fannie Mae	Finance/Mortg.	16.2	–6.95	5.23
⊖ Fifth Third Bancorp	Other U.S. Banks	38.3	4.53	5.03
Wells Fargo	Other U.S. Banks	22.4	–20.20	4.54
⊖ Freddie Mac	Finance/Mortg.	14.0	–3.87	3.98
⊕ Goldman Sachs Grp	Financials	20.7	–12.80	3.87
⊖ Bank of America	Other U.S. Banks	16.7	42.73	3.64
⊕ State Street	Other U.S. Banks	28.6	–15.10	3.51
⊕ Mellon Finl	Other U.S. Banks	23.8	–21.90	3.20
Household Intl	Finance/Mortg.	14.7	6.89	2.69
⊖ FleetBoston Finl	Other U.S. Banks	16.2	0.55	2.63
⊕ Marsh & McLennan	Insurance	27.9	–6.30	2.61
⊕ PNC Finl Svcs Grp	Other U.S. Banks	13.5	–20.70	2.59
⊖ BB&T	Other U.S. Banks	17.7	–0.49	2.40
✵ Credit Suisse Grp	Foreign Banks	—	—	2.12
⊕ American Express	Finance/Mortg.	28.3	–34.40	2.07
✵ Berkshire Hathaway Cl B	Financials	64.8	7.26	2.04
General Elec	Industrials	30.1	–15.00	1.92
⊕ Merrill Lynch	Broker/Inv Bank	18.2	–22.70	1.91
MBNA	Finance/Mortg.	19.6	–3.66	1.83
Capital One Finl	Finance/Mortg.	19.8	–17.80	1.73
Tyco Intl	Industrials	27.1	6.23	1.73
Charles Schwab	Broker/Inv Bank	61.9	–45.30	1.69
✵ UBS AG REG	Financials	13.2	–8.20	1.66

Current Investment Style

Style: Value Blnd Growth; Size: Large Med Small

	Stock Port Avg	Relative S&P 500 Current	Relative S&P 500 Hist	Rel Cat
Price/Earnings Ratio	24.5	0.79	0.70	1.15
Price/Book Ratio	3.7	0.65	0.53	1.22
Price/Cash Flow	—	—	—	—
3 Yr Earnings Growth	18.1	1.24	1.03	1.11
1 Yr Earnings Est%	3.8	—	—	1.21
Med Mkt Cap $mil	40,276	0.7	0.3	1.83

Special Securities % assets 10-31-01	
Restricted/Illiquid Secs	0
Emerging-Markets Secs	0
Options/Futures/Warrants	No

Composition % assets 10-31-01	
Cash	0.0
Stocks*	99.7
Bonds	0.0
Other	0.3
*Foreign (% stocks)	10.9

Market Cap	
Giant	44.0
Large	46.3
Medium	9.7
Small	0.0
Micro	0.0

Subsector Weightings	% of Stocks	Rel Cat
Money Ctr. Banks	1.6	0.6
Other U.S. Banks	33.2	1.2
Foreign Banks	2.1	0.6
Thrifts	1.4	0.2
Insurance	15.8	0.8
Finance/Mortg.	18.5	1.8
Broker/Inv Bank	6.0	1.2
Money Mgmt	0.0	0.0
Other	21.5	0.9

Address: 101 Huntington Avenue
Boston, MA 02199–7603
800–225–5291
Web Address: www.jhancock.com

*Inception: 03-14-96
Advisor: John Hancock Advisers
Subadvisor: None
NTF Plans: Fidelity Inst.

Minimum Purchase:	$1000	Add: None IRA: $250
Min Auto Inv Plan:	$1000	Add: $25
Sales Fees:	5.00%L, 0.05%B, 0.25%S	
Management Fee:	.80% mx./.70% mn.	
Actual Fees:	Mgt: 0.76%	Dist: 0.30%
Expense Projections:	3Yr: $912	5Yr: $1212 10Yr: $2064
Avg Brok Commission:	—	Income Distrib: Annually
Total Cost (relative to category):	—	

John Hancock Small Cap Growth B

Ticker	Load	NAV	Yield	Total Assets	Mstar Category
TSEGX	5.00%d	$8.77	0.0%	$1,355.9 mil	Small Growth

Prospectus Objective: Small Company

John Hancock Focused Small Cap Growth Fund seeks long-term capital growth.

The fund normally invests at least 80% of assets in common stocks of small companies with market capitalizations of no more than $1 billion.

This fund offers multiple shareclasses, all of which differ in fee structure and availability. In August and September 1991, Transamerica Special Global Growth and Transamerica Sunbelt Growth merged into this fund. The fund has gone through several name changes.

Historical Profile
Return: Average
Risk: High
Rating: ★★ Below Avg

Investment Style
Equity
Average Stock %: 100% 99% 97% 99% 99% 98% 97%

▼ Manager Change
▽ Partial Manager Change

Fund Performance vs. Category Average
■ Quarterly Fund Return +/– Category Average
— Category Baseline

Performance Quartile (within Category)

Portfolio Manager(s)

Bernice S. Behar, CFA. Since 4-96. BA'83 U. of California-Berkeley. Other funds currently managed: John Hancock Small Cap Growth A, John Hancock Focused Small Cap Gr I, John Hancock Small Cap Growth C.

Anurag Pandit, CFA. Since 1-96. U. of Delhi, India; MA MIT. Other funds currently managed: John Hancock Small Cap Growth A, John Hancock Focused Small Cap Gr I, John Hancock Small Cap Growth C.

History

1990	1991	1992	1993	1994	1995	1996	1997	1998	1999	2000	12-01	History
3.22	5.09	5.71	6.39	6.29	8.94	9.88	8.85	9.60	13.83	10.30	8.77	NAV
–1.23	60.26	12.18	11.91	–1.57	42.13	20.12	14.55	11.59	63.62	–22.04	–14.85	Total Return %
1.89	29.78	4.56	1.85	–2.88	4.60	–2.83	–18.80	–16.99	42.58	–12.93	–2.98	+/– S&P 500
16.18	9.08	4.41	–1.45	0.87	11.09	8.86	1.61	10.35	20.53	0.40	–5.62	+/– Russ 2000 Grth
0.00	0.00	0.00	0.00	0.00	0.00	0.00	0.00	0.00	0.00	0.00	0.00	Income Return %
–1.23	60.26	12.18	11.91	–1.56	42.13	20.12	14.55	11.59	63.62	–22.04	–14.85	Capital Return %
34	27	51	69	47	23	44	66	20	38	91	67	Total Rtn % Rank Cat
0.00	0.00	0.00	0.00	0.00	0.00	0.00	0.00	0.00	0.00	0.00	0.00	Income $
0.00	0.06	0.00	0.00	0.00	0.00	0.85	2.52	0.23	1.51	0.56	0.00	Capital Gains $
3.11	2.85	2.64	2.28	2.19	2.11	2.05	2.02	2.07	2.03	2.03	2.16	Expense Ratio %
–1.64	–1.83	–1.99	–1.58	–1.46	–1.55	–1.59	–1.30	–1.73	–1.87	–1.62	–1.59	Income Ratio %
82	66	48	29	25	23	44	96	103	104	104	82	Turnover Rate %
18.2	65.9	107.0	243.1	289.0	411.5	454.5	448.3	435.0	1,050.3	811.6	510.9	Net Assets $mil

Performance 12-31-01

	1st Qtr	2nd Qtr	3rd Qtr	4th Qtr	Total
1997	–9.72	16.93	21.09	–10.39	14.55
1998	10.73	–2.96	–21.77	32.73	11.59
1999	1.25	11.42	1.02	43.58	63.62
2000	14.03	–9.45	–2.73	–22.37	–22.04
2001	–20.58	15.16	–26.65	26.92	–14.85

Trailing	Total Return%	+/– S&P 500	+/– Russ 2000 Grth	% Rank All	% Rank Cat	Growth of $10,000
3 Mo	26.92	16.23	0.74	6	26	12,692
6 Mo	–6.90	–1.35	2.37	73	57	9,310
1 Yr	–14.85	–2.98	–5.62	72	67	8,515
3 Yr Avg	2.79	3.82	2.55	57	77	10,861
5 Yr Avg	6.78	–3.92	3.91	38	62	13,884
10 Yr Avg	11.35	–1.58	4.16	23	42	29,290
15 Yr Avg	—	—	—	—	—	—

Tax Analysis	Tax-Adj Ret%	%Rank Cat	%Pretax Ret	%Rank Cat
3 Yr Avg	1.66	72	59.5	79
5 Yr Avg	5.02	61	74.0	63
10 Yr Avg	10.17	28	89.7	6

Potential Capital Gain Exposure: –7% of assets

Risk Analysis

Time Period	Load-Adj Return %	Risk %Rank[1] All	Risk %Rank[1] Cat	Morningstar Return	Morningstar Risk	Morningstar Risk-Adj Rating
1 Yr	–18.26					
3 Yr	1.92	96	74	–0.62[2]	1.76	★★
5 Yr	6.65	95	71	0.36[2]	1.75	★★
10 Yr	11.35	96	79	0.98	1.78	★★

Average Historical Rating (135 months): 3.4★s

[1] 1=low, 100=high [2] T-Bill return substituted for category avg.

Category Rating (3 Yr)

1 2 3 4 5
Worst Best

Return: Below Avg
Risk: Above Avg

Other Measures	Standard Index S&P 500	Best Fit Index Wil 4500
Alpha	12.0	5.3
Beta	1.36	1.35
R-Squared	34	92
Standard Deviation		44.20
Mean		2.79
Sharpe Ratio		–0.06

Analysis by Kelli Stebel 07-23-01

John Hancock Small Cap Growth has thrown some gutter balls lately, but its overall game is still appealing.

There's little doubt that this fund has disappointed shareholders lately. For a fund that typically holds up well during market downdrafts, this fund got pummeled in 2000, losing more than 22% and finishing in its category's bottom quintile. And things haven't gotten any better so far this year. The fund has already shed about 14% of its value for the year to date through July 20, 2001.

Though lead manager Bernice Behar spreads this fund's assets across about 175 holdings and usually stays away from sector bets, the fund got caught with big positions in struggling media and telecom stocks over the past year. Behar admitted that she held on to some media companies too long last fall, after their fundamentals had begun to decline. And more recently, the fund was stung by a big overweight in biotech stocks in early 2001. But Behar was quick to pull the trigger there and sold off the fund's slug of sliding biotech holdings before they did too much damage.

The fund's poor performance over the past 15 months has taken a toll on its long-term record, but that's probably not enough reason for shareholders to cut the strings. Despite the fund's recent debacle, Behar has typically put up consistent numbers here using a fairly moderate approach. And Behar, who isn't looking to make any more big bets these days, has been refocusing the portfolio away from formerly high-flying technology stocks. In place of technology, Behar has added retail holdings, such as Ethan Allen Interiors.

Shareholders are likely, and rightfully, frustrated with the fund's performance recently, considering that one of its main attributes had been solid downside performance. But missing the mark once shouldn't completely negate the fund's fine overall record.

Portfolio Analysis 11-30-01

Share change since 10-01 Total Stocks: 161

	Sector	PE	YTD Ret%	% Assets
⊖ Secure Computing	Technology	—	108.10	1.43
⊖ LTX	Technology	—	61.85	1.31
⊖ Macromedia	Technology	—	–70.70	1.31
Corporate Executive Board	Services	66.7	–7.67	1.28
⊖ Whole Foods Market	Retail	36.0	42.53	1.23
⊖ Performance Food Grp	Staples	33.5	37.25	1.22
⊖ Wilson Greatbatch Tech	Durables	—	27.79	1.21
⊖ Semtech	Technology	63.7	61.76	1.19
☼ McDATA	Technology	NMF	—	1.19
⊖ Affiliated Managers Grp	Financials	30.6	28.44	1.19
⊖ Microsemi	Technology	51.2	113.50	1.15
⊖ NPS Pharmaceuticals	Health	—	–20.20	1.15
99 Cents Only Stores	Retail	43.8	108.70	1.13
Rudolph Tech	Technology	27.9	13.69	1.08
⊖ Scholastic	Services	NMF	13.58	1.07
⊖ Accredo Health	Health	53.7	18.65	1.04
Overture Svcs	N/A	—	—	1.03
⊖ CV Therapeutics	Health	—	–26.40	1.00
⊕ Tweeter Home Entertmnt Grp	Retail	33.3	137.90	0.98
PLX Tech	Technology	—	51.69	0.97
⊖ Cerner	Services	—	7.96	0.96
⊖ Spinnaker Explor	Energy	13.6	–3.15	0.95
⊖ Cytyc	Health	49.3	25.16	0.95
⊖ Waste Connections	Services	28.7	–6.27	0.94
AirGate PCS	Services	—	28.31	0.93

Current Investment Style

Style: Value Blnd Growth; Size: Large Med Small

	Stock Port Avg	Relative S&P 500 Current	Relative S&P 500 Hist	Rel Cat
Price/Earnings Ratio	36.8	1.19	1.13	1.14
Price/Book Ratio	5.4	0.94	1.02	1.10
Price/Cash Flow	25.0	1.39	1.24	1.13
3 Yr Earnings Growth	22.7[1]	1.55	—	0.90
1 Yr Earnings Est%	0.3	—	—	0.04
Med Mkt Cap $mil	1,036	0.0	0.0	0.99

[1] figure is based on 50% or less of stocks

Special Securities % assets 11-30-01	
Restricted/Illiquid Secs	0
Emerging-Markets Secs	1
Options/Futures/Warrants	No

Composition % assets 11-30-01	
Cash	0.3
Stocks*	99.7
Bonds	0.0
Other	0.0
*Foreign (% stocks)	3.1

Market Cap	
Giant	0.0
Large	0.0
Medium	31.1
Small	65.9
Micro	2.9

Sector Weightings	% of Stocks	Rel S&P	5-Year High	5-Year Low
Utilities	0.7	0.2	1	0
Energy	5.3	0.8	10	1
Financials	7.3	0.4	20	1
Industrials	6.6	0.6	11	3
Durables	2.6	1.7	5	0
Staples	3.3	0.4	4	0
Services	20.6	1.9	39	13
Retail	7.6	1.1	19	3
Health	16.3	1.1	26	5
Technology	29.8	1.6	44	16

Address: 101 Huntington Avenue, Boston, MA 02199–7603, 800–225–5291
Web Address: www.jhancock.com
Inception: 10-26-87
Advisor: John Hancock Advisers
Subadvisor: None
NTF Plans: N/A

Minimum Purchase: $1000 Add: None IRA: $250
Min Auto Inv Plan: $1000 Add: $25
Sales Fees: 5.00%D, 0.75%B, 0.25%S Conv. in 8 Yrs.
Management Fee: .75%
Actual Fees: Mgt: 0.74% Dist: 1.00%
Expense Projections: 3Yr: $937 5Yr: $1293 10Yr: $2166
Avg Brok Commission: — Income Distrib: Annually
Total Cost (relative to category): Average

John Hancock Small Cap Value B

Ticker	Load	NAV	Yield	Total Assets	Mstar Category
SPVBX	5.00%d	$19.90	0.0%	$980.7 mil	Small Growth

Prospectus Objective: Growth

John Hancock Small Cap Value Fund seeks capital appreciation; income is secondary.

The fund normally invests in undervalued equities with below-average market/book value ratios. To select securities, the advisor considers issuers' financial strength, competitive positions, projected earnings and dividends. It also seeks companies with limited downside risk; these companies have high relative value, high instrinsic value, going concern value, and favorable net asset value and replacement book value.

Class A shares have front loads; B shares have deferred loads, higher 12b-1 fees, and conversion features; C shares are for institutional investors.

The previous name was the John Hancock Special Value Fund.

Historical Profile
Return: High
Risk: Above Avg
Rating: ★★★★★ Highest

Investment Style: Equity — Average Stock %: 97% 86% 94% 93% 95% 92% 99%

▼ Manager Change
▽ Partial Manager Change

Fund Performance vs. Category Average
■ Quarterly Fund Return +/– Category Average
— Category Baseline

Performance Quartile (within Category)

Portfolio Manager(s)

James S Yu, CFA. Since 12-00. MBA Columbia University; BS Rutgers College & School of Bus. Other funds currently managed: John Hancock Small Cap Value A, John Hancock Small Cap Equity, John Hancock Small Cap Value C.

1990	1991	1992	1993	1994	1995	1996	1997	1998	1999	2000	12-01	History
—	—	—	8.50	8.83	10.38	10.31	12.21	11.74	21.43	18.24	19.90	NAV
—	—	—	—	5.13*	21.40	12.14	24.41	–2.77	97.03	–6.95	10.20	Total Return %
—	—	—	—	3.59*	–16.13	–10.81	–8.94	–31.34	75.99	2.15	22.07	+/– S&P 500
—	—	—	—	—	–9.64	0.88	11.46	–4.00	53.94	15.49	19.43	+/– Russ 2000 Grth
—	—	—	—	1.24	1.38	0.63	0.00	0.00	0.00	0.00	0.00	Income Return %
—	—	—	—	3.88	20.02	11.50	24.41	–2.77	97.03	–6.95	10.20	Capital Return %
—	—	—	—	—	68	90	56	38	2	94	40	Total Rtn % Rank Cat
—	—	—	—	0.11	0.12	0.07	0.00	0.00	0.00	0.00	0.00	Income $
—	—	—	—	0.00	0.21	1.24	0.60	0.13	1.37	1.81	0.17	Capital Gains $
—	—	—	—	1.72	1.73	1.69	1.69	1.71	2.06	2.06	2.05	Expense Ratio %
—	—	—	—	1.53	1.21	0.60	–0.24	–0.45	–1.34	–1.38	–1.65	Income Ratio %
—	—	—	—	—	9	72	140	—	140	36	66	Turnover Rate %
—	—	—	—	3.3	17.0	22.1	35.0	33.0	130.4	234.5	382.8	Net Assets $mil

Performance 12-31-01

	1st Qtr	2nd Qtr	3rd Qtr	4th Qtr	Total
1997	–3.69	19.94	16.54	–7.59	24.41
1998	9.66	–6.72	–21.54	21.15	–2.77
1999	0.68	27.33	4.19	47.52	97.03
2000	10.55	1.22	–3.09	–14.20	–6.95
2001	–2.63	25.23	–33.81	36.55	10.20

Trailing	Total Return%	+/– S&P 500	+/– Russ 2000 Grth	% Rank All	% Rank Cat	Growth of $10,000
3 Mo	36.55	25.86	10.37	2	4	13,655
6 Mo	–9.62	–4.07	–0.36	84	95	9,038
1 Yr	10.20	22.07	19.43	6	40	11,020
3 Yr Avg	26.42	27.44	26.17	1	5	20,203
5 Yr Avg	19.57	8.87	16.70	2	6	24,439
10 Yr Avg	—	—	—	—	—	—
15 Yr Avg	—	—	—	—	—	—

Tax Analysis	Tax-Adj Ret%	%Rank Cat	%Pretax Ret	%Rank Cat
3 Yr Avg	24.08	5	91.2	35
5 Yr Avg	17.79	5	90.9	26
10 Yr Avg	—	—	—	—

Potential Capital Gain Exposure: 2% of assets

Risk Analysis

Time Period	Load-Adj Return %	Risk %Rank¹ All	Risk %Rank¹ Cat	Morningstar Return	Morningstar Risk	Morningstar Risk-Adj Rating
1 Yr	6.20					
3 Yr	25.79	86	96	5.36²	1.30	★★★★★
5 Yr	19.47	86	97	4.15²	1.31	★★★★★
Incept	16.95	—	—	—	—	

Average Historical Rating (61 months): 3.1★s

¹1=low, 100=high ² T-Bill return substituted for category avg.

Category Rating (3 Yr)

1 2 3 4 5 — Worst … Best

Return: High
Risk: High

Other Measures	Standard Index S&P 500	Best Fit Index Russ 2000
Alpha	34.8	20.9
Beta	1.33	1.28
R-Squared	45	81

Standard Deviation	43.77
Mean	26.42
Sharpe Ratio	0.55

Analysis by Kelli Stebel 11-19-01

A management shakeup at John Hancock Small Cap Value leaves its future uncertain.

Lead manager Tim Quinlisk is leaving this offering, effective Dec. 21, 2001, to join a hedge fund. Comanager Scott Mayo resigned as of Nov. 6, 2001, and the duo will join Mayo's father, Richard Mayo, in running a hedge fund. Quinlisk and Mayo had run this fund together since May 2000, but Quinlisk also served as a comanager with Tim Keefe from January 1998 until January 2000.

Hancock announced that comanager James Yu, who joined this fund in December 2000, will take the reins here. Yu will also run Quinlisk's other former charge, John Hancock Large Cap Value. A Hancock spokesperson reports that Yu plans on following the same approach that Quinlisk had used effectively during his tenure here. Still, that's not altogether comforting for shareholders. Yu worked as an analyst at Merrill Lynch before joining John Hancock in late 2000, but this will be his first stint running a retail mutual fund solo. Ultimately, the fund's success will come down to Yu's stock-picking ability. And without a previous record to examine, it's difficult to predict how Yu will fare.

As a family, Hancock has had trouble with frequent manager turnover at its largest funds in the past. Current CIO William Braman, who joined Hancock in June 2000, is making strides to reorganize the firm's research staff. That said, the departure of an experienced manager like Quinlisk is a blow. This fund's future looks uncertain, and until the dust settles, we would advise shareholders to hold off investing any more money.

Portfolio Analysis 11-30-01

Share change since 10-01 Total Stocks: 60	Sector	PE	YTD Ret%	% Assets
⊖ Hain Celestial Grp	Staples	42.3	–15.50	5.21
Pegasus Comms Cl A	Services	—	–59.50	5.18
⊕ Cumulus Media Cl A	Services	—	346.30	4.47
Covance	Health	34.9	111.10	3.87
⊖ ProQuest	N/A	—	—	3.52
⊖ Pathmark Stores	Retail	—	49.45	3.32
⊖ XM Satellite Radio Hldgs	Services	—	14.30	3.09
Alpha Inds	Technology	NMF	–41.00	2.77
Vicor	Technology	73.6	–46.60	2.73
Wind River Sys	Technology	—	–47.50	2.61
Alpharma Cl A	Health	16.9	–39.30	2.57
Ntelos	Services	—	–12.10	2.52
Pittston Brink's Grp	Services	—	11.74	2.50
⊕ i-Stat	Health	—	–70.10	2.36
Casella Waste Sys Cl A	Services	—	70.47	2.35
Three-Five Sys	Technology	—	–11.60	2.35
RailAmerica	Services	16.3	84.34	2.27
UNOVA	Industrials	—	60.00	2.12
Aspen Tech	Technology	—	–49.40	2.03
⊖ Concord Comms	Technology	—	136.00	2.02
☼ Arrisystems	Technology	—	—	1.93
MKS Instrs	Industrials	NMF	74.39	1.91
⊕ Cyberonics	Health	—	14.11	1.85
Nextel Partners A	Services	—	–28.60	1.83
CTC Comms Grp	Services	—	11.35	1.68

Current Investment Style

Style: Value Blnd Growth; Size: Large Med Small

	Stock Port Avg	Relative S&P 500 Current	Relative S&P 500 Hist	Rel Cat
Price/Earnings Ratio	37.1¹	1.20	0.93	1.15
Price/Book Ratio	3.0	0.52	0.52	0.61
Price/Cash Flow	21.1	1.17	0.94	0.96
3 Yr Earnings Growth	14.5¹	0.99	—	0.58
1 Yr Earnings Est%	–4.9¹	2.77	—	–0.63
Med Mkt Cap $mil	745	0.0	0.0	0.71

¹figure is based on 50% or less of stocks

Special Securities % assets 11-30-01	
Restricted/Illiquid Secs	1
Emerging-Markets Secs	0
Options/Futures/Warrants	No

Composition % assets 11-30-01	
Cash	3.9
Stocks*	96.1
Bonds	0.0
Other	0.0
*Foreign (% stocks)	1.8

Market Cap	
Giant	0.0
Large	0.0
Medium	13.3
Small	72.6
Micro	14.1

Sector Weightings	% of Stocks	Rel S&P	5-Year High	5-Year Low
Utilities	0.0	0.0	6	0
Energy	4.2	0.6	6	0
Financials	5.3	0.3	36	0
Industrials	4.4	0.4	42	4
Durables	0.0	0.0	22	0
Staples	6.1	0.8	19	0
Services	34.9	3.2	45	8
Retail	4.5	0.7	9	1
Health	11.6	0.8	13	0
Technology	29.0	1.6	37	0

Address:	101 Huntington Avenue Boston, MA 02199–7603 800–225–5291
Web Address:	www.jhancock.com
*Inception:	01-03-94
Advisor:	John Hancock Advisers
Subadvisor:	None
NTF Plans:	N/A

Minimum Purchase:	$1000	Add: None IRA: $250
Min Auto Inv Plan:	$1000	Add: $25
Sales Fees:	5.00%D, 0.75%B, 0.25%S Conv. in 8 Yrs.	
Management Fee:	.70%	
Actual Fees:	Mgt: 0.70%	Dist: 1.00%
Expense Projections:	3Yr: $946	5Yr: $1308 10Yr: $2210
Avg Brok Commission:	—	Income Distrib: Annually
Total Cost (relative to category):		Above Avg

John Hancock Strategic Income A

Ticker	Load	NAV	Yield	SEC Yield	Total Assets	Mstar Category
JHFIX	4.50%	$6.51	8.3%	8.24%	$1,161.1 mil	Multisector Bond

Prospectus Objective: Multisector Bond

John Hancock Strategic Income Fund seeks current income.

The fund invests primarily in the following three fixed-income sectors: foreign government and corporate debt, U.S. government securities, and debt securities of U.S. issuers rated as low as CC. It does not maintain a fixed allocation among the types of securities; the fund may invest without limit in any one sector.

Class A shares have front loads; B shares have deferred loads, higher 12b-1 fees, and conversion features; C shares have level loads.

The previous name was the John Hancock High-Income Trust Fixed-Income Portfolio. On Feb. 22, 1999, John Hancock World Bond Fund merged into the fund.

Historical Profile

Return: Average
Risk: Above Avg
Rating: ★★★ Neutral

Investment Style
Fixed-Income
Income Rtn %Rank Cat: 1 | 4 | 11 | 6 | 19 | 41 | 26 | 34

Growth of Principal vs. Interest Rate Shifts
- Principal Value $000 (NAV with capital gains reinvested)
- Interest Rate % on 10 Yr Treasury
- ▼ Manager Change
- ▽ Partial Manager Change
- ► Mgr Unknown After
- ◄ Mgr Unknown Before

Performance Quartile (within Category)

Portfolio Manager(s)

Frederick L. Cavanaugh Jr.. Since 8-86.
Arthur N Calavritinos, CFA. Since 1-95.
Janet L. Clay. Since 6-98.
Daniel S. Janis III. Since 10-99.

1990	1991	1992	1993	1994	1995	1996	1997	1998	1999	2000	12-01	History
6.37	7.56	7.38	7.69	6.81	7.37	7.54	7.77	7.57	7.24	6.73	6.51	NAV
–9.77	33.55	7.54	13.74	–3.05	18.71	11.68	12.69	5.41	3.35	1.14	4.92	Total Return %
–18.73	17.55	0.14	3.99	–0.13	0.24	8.06	3.00	–3.26	4.18	–10.50	–3.50	+/– LB Aggregate
–3.39	–10.20	–9.12	–5.18	–2.08	1.33	–0.74	0.06	4.83	0.07	6.35	–0.86	+/– FB High–Yield
12.57	14.33	10.20	9.39	8.79	10.14	9.15	8.92	8.12	7.86	8.47	8.33	Income Return %
–22.34	19.22	–2.66	4.35	–11.84	8.57	2.53	3.76	–2.71	–4.51	–7.33	–3.41	Capital Return %
78	12	50	64	22	40	35	6	14	40	55	46	Total Rtn % Rank Cat
0.96	0.86	0.74	0.67	0.65	0.66	0.65	0.65	0.61	0.57	0.59	0.54	Income $
0.00	0.00	0.00	0.00	0.00	0.00	0.00	0.04	0.00	0.00	0.00	0.00	Capital Gains $
1.53	1.75	1.69	1.58	1.32	1.09	1.03	1.00	0.92	0.89	0.91	0.93	Expense Ratio %
12.60	13.46	10.64	9.63	8.71	9.24	9.13	8.61	8.20	7.71	8.09	8.40	Income Ratio %
81	60	80	97	91	55	78	132	112	55	36	48	Turnover Rate %
67.5	114.5	219.7	339.4	317.9	354.2	407.3	444.9	511.8	549.0	506.7	504.6	Net Assets $mil

Performance 12-31-01

	1st Qtr	2nd Qtr	3rd Qtr	4th Qtr	Total
1997	–0.40	5.66	5.80	1.20	12.69
1998	3.70	0.83	–1.39	2.23	5.41
1999	1.66	0.08	–0.63	2.23	3.35
2000	1.20	0.29	–0.21	–0.14	1.14
2001	1.46	0.57	–0.31	3.14	4.92

Trailing	Total Return%	+/– LB Agg	+/– FB High–Yield	% Rank All	% Rank Cat	Growth of $10,000
3 Mo	3.14	3.11	–2.50	70	36	10,314
6 Mo	2.82	–1.83	1.38	16	38	10,282
1 Yr	4.92	–3.50	–0.86	23	46	10,492
3 Yr Avg	3.12	–3.15	1.95	53	46	10,967
5 Yr Avg	5.43	–2.00	2.19	57	23	13,027
10 Yr Avg	7.43	0.20	–0.41	47	25	20,478
15 Yr Avg	7.36	–0.76	–1.30	61	50	29,029

Tax Analysis	Tax-Adj Ret%	%Rank Cat	%Pretax Ret	%Rank Cat
3 Yr Avg	–0.11	46	—	—
5 Yr Avg	2.07	27	38.1	41
10 Yr Avg	3.91	25	52.6	26

Potential Capital Gain Exposure: –14% of assets

Risk Analysis

Time Period	Load-Adj Return %	Risk %Rank[1] All	Risk %Rank[1] Cat	Morningstar Return	Morningstar Risk	Morningstar Risk-Adj Rating
1 Yr	0.20					
3 Yr	1.55	30	25	–0.70[2]	1.05	★★
5 Yr	4.46	35	22	–0.12[2]	1.12	★★
10 Yr	6.94	32	27	0.63[2]	0.97	★★★

Average Historical Rating (148 months): 2.7★s

[1] 1=low, 100=high [2] T–Bill return substituted for category avg.

Category Rating (3 Yr)

1 2 **3** 4 5
Worst — Best

Return: Average
Risk: Below Avg

Other Measures	Standard Index LB Agg	Best Fit Index FB HY
Alpha	–2.5	0.0
Beta	0.65	0.48
R–Squared	24	64

Standard Deviation	4.49
Mean	3.12
Sharpe Ratio	–0.46

Analysis by Scott Berry 11-08-01

John Hancock Strategic Income Fund is a good option for bond investors looking to cover a lot of ground with one fund.

This fund's diversified mix of U.S. government bonds, high-yield corporate issues, and foreign debt has produced solid long-term returns without undue volatility. During the 1990s, the fund's high-yield stake fueled its returns, as a booming economy kept defaults to a minimum. And in recent years, the strong performance of the fund's Treasury and emerging-markets positions has kept it comfortably ahead of its average multisector-bond peer.

Specifically, the fund got a big lift when long-term Treasury bonds rallied hard in the wake of the Treasury's announcement that it wouldn't issue additional 30-year bonds. In an effort to take advantage of the yield discrepancy between short- and long-term Treasuries, manager Fred Cavanaugh had shifted assets into longer-term issues earlier in the year. The fund has also gotten a lift in recent months from its exposure to Russia, which has been one of the best-performing emerging markets.

Cavanaugh's timely adjustments to the fund's allocations have contributed to the fund's long-term success as well. For example, he has placed less of an emphasis on high yield in recent years, which has helped the fund avoid a lot of that sector's trouble. Given their historically low valuation, Cavanaugh has taken a closer look at the high-yield bond market in recent months, but he argues that a lack of liquidity continues to make it less attractive than other areas.

Overall, we like what this fund brings to the table. Its solid management, steady performance, and added diversification make it one of the better multisector bond offerings available.

Portfolio Analysis 11-30-01

Total Fixed-Income: 152	Date of Maturity	Amount $000	Value $000	% Net Assets
US Treasury Bond 8.125%	08-15-19	60,500	78,319	6.69
US Treasury Bond 10.75%	08-15-05	33,000	40,853	3.49
Russia Government 8.25%	03-31-10	48,280	40,845	3.49
US Treasury Bond 9.25%	02-15-16	27,600	38,166	3.26
Canada Government 5.5%	06-01-09	49,000	31,974	2.73
US Treasury Bond 6.25%	08-15-23	29,215	31,739	2.71
Govt of Canada 7%	12-01-06	45,000	31,654	2.70
Republic of Panama 9.625%	02-08-11	28,150	28,995	2.48
US Treasury Note 6.125%	08-15-07	23,600	25,750	2.20
Govt of New Zealand 6%	11-15-11	59,650	23,973	2.05
Govt of Canada 5.75%	06-01-29	35,525	23,444	2.00
US Treasury Bond 5.25%	11-15-28	24,000	23,115	1.97
Govt of Canada 8.75%	12-01-05	30,000	22,202	1.90
Govt of Canada 5.50%	06-01-10	33,425	21,729	1.86
US Treasury Note 6.5%	08-15-05	19,300	21,121	1.80
US Treasury Note 7.25%	08-15-04	17,100	18,837	1.61
Bonos Y Oblig Del Estado 5.4%	07-30-11	20,025	18,702	1.60
Buoni Poliennali Del Tes 5.25%	08-01-11	20,025	18,156	1.55
US Treasury Note 5%	02-15-11	17,000	17,329	1.48
Govt of Russia 12.75%	06-24-28	11,400	12,113	1.03

Current Investment Style

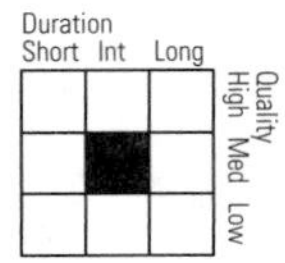

Avg Eff Duration[1]	5.8 Yrs
Avg Eff Maturity	9.4 Yrs
Avg Credit Quality	A
Avg Wtd Coupon	8.26%
Avg Wtd Price	95.34% of par

[1] figure provided by fund

Special Securities % assets 11-30-01	
Restricted/Illiquid Secs	2
Exotic Mortgage–Backed	0
Emerging–Markets Secs	2
Options/Futures/Warrants	Yes

Credit Analysis % bonds 09-30-01			
US Govt	64	BB	11
AAA	1	B	17
AA	0	Below B	1
A	0	NR/NA	0
BBB	6		

Sector Breakdown % bonds 11-30-01			
US Treasuries	21	CMOs	0
GNMA mtgs	0	ARMs	0
FNMA mtgs	0	Other	70
FHLMC mtgs	0		

Coupon Range	% of Bonds	Rel Cat
0%	3.19	0.73
0% to 7%	30.13	0.90
7% to 8.5%	21.90	0.87
8.5% to 10%	20.07	1.12
More than 10%	24.72	1.30

1.00=Category Average

Composition % assets 11-30-01			
Cash	9.8	Bonds	85.6
Stocks	0.7	Other	3.9

Country Exp % assets

Not Available

Address:	101 Huntington Avenue Boston, MA 02199–7603 800–225–5291
Web Address:	www.jhancock.com
Inception:	08-18-86
Advisor:	John Hancock Advisers
Subadvisor:	None
NTF Plans:	Fidelity Inst.

Minimum Purchase:	$1000	Add: None IRA: $250
Min Auto Inv Plan:	$1000	Add: $25
Sales Fees:	4.50%L, 0.05%B, 0.25%S	
Management Fee:	.60% mx./.30% mn.	
Actual Fees:	Mgt: 0.37%	Dist: 0.30%
Expense Projections:	3Yr: $727	5Yr: $931 10Yr: $1519
Avg Brok Commission:	—	Income Distrib: Monthly
Total Cost (relative to category):		Below Avg

Harbor Bond

Ticker	Load	NAV	Yield	SEC Yield	Total Assets	Mstar Category
HABDX	None	$11.42	4.6%	—	$1,005.7 mil	Interm–Term Bond

Prospectus Objective: Corp Bond—General

Harbor Bond Fund seeks total return consistent with preservation of capital.

The fund invests at least 65% of assets in high-quality domestic or foreign obligations, including those issued by governments, supranational organizations, and corporations, as well as mortgage-related and other asset-backed securities. It may invest up to 10% of assets in debt rated as low as B. Normally, it invests at least 60% of assets in domestic issues and at least 80% in issues denominated in U.S. dollars. The average maturity typically ranges between eight and 15 years; the fund intends to maintain a duration equal to that of the market, plus or minus 1.5 years.

Historical Profile

Return	High
Risk	Average
Rating	★★★★★ Highest

Investment Style: Fixed-Income

Income Rtn %Rank Cat: 81 10 40 70 64 84 93 87

Growth of Principal vs. Interest Rate Shifts
- Principal Value $000 (NAV with capital gains reinvested)
- Interest Rate % on 10 Yr Treasury
- ▼ Manager Change
- ▽ Partial Manager Change
- ► Mgr Unknown After
- ◄ Mgr Unknown Before

Performance Quartile (within Category)

Portfolio Manager(s)

William H. Gross, CFA. Since 12-87. BA'66 Duke U.; MBA'71 U. of California-Los Angeles. Other funds currently managed: PIMCO Total Return II Instl, PIMCO Low Duration II Instl, PIMCO Low Duration Instl.

1990	1991	1992	1993	1994	1995	1996	1997	1998	1999	2000	12-01	History
10.29	11.11	11.10	11.31	10.28	11.41	11.24	11.37	11.28	10.68	11.23	11.42	NAV
7.94	19.65	9.11	12.41	−3.76	19.15	4.94	9.39	9.56	−0.33	11.34	9.03	Total Return %
−1.02	3.65	1.70	2.66	−0.84	0.68	1.32	−0.29	0.89	0.50	−0.29	0.61	+/– LB Aggregate
−1.23	5.03	1.94	3.63	−1.82	3.84	0.88	1.52	1.15	−0.72	1.24	0.05	+/– LB Int Govt/Corp
8.45	8.63	6.86	5.96	5.49	7.84	6.29	6.04	5.74	5.07	5.34	4.88	Income Return %
−0.51	11.02	2.25	6.46	−9.25	11.31	−1.36	3.36	3.82	−5.40	6.00	4.16	Capital Return %
40	9	10	19	50	27	10	34	5	21	18	12	Total Rtn % Rank Cat
0.85	0.86	0.74	0.65	0.61	0.78	0.70	0.66	0.64	0.56	0.56	0.54	Income $
0.00	0.26	0.25	0.50	0.00	0.00	0.00	0.23	0.51	0.00	0.07	0.27	Capital Gains $
1.22	0.86	0.77	0.72	0.77	0.70	0.70	0.67	0.65	0.61	0.60	—	Expense Ratio %
8.30	8.12	7.30	6.19	6.29	7.11	6.40	6.04	5.41	5.35	6.16	—	Income Ratio %
91	58	53	120	151	89	193	252	278	271	494	—	Turnover Rate %
26.0	41.1	76.6	171.8	167.0	233.4	288.3	384.6	494.4	618.4	787.2	1,005.7	Net Assets $mil

Performance 12-31-01

	1st Qtr	2nd Qtr	3rd Qtr	4th Qtr	Total
1997	−0.70	3.86	3.32	2.66	9.39
1998	1.50	2.49	4.93	0.38	9.56
1999	0.11	−1.13	0.71	−0.02	−0.33
2000	2.17	1.74	2.54	4.46	11.34
2001	2.69	0.24	4.74	1.13	9.03

Trailing	Total Return%	+/– LB Agg	+/– LB ITGvt/Corp	% Rank All	% Rank Cat	Growth of $10,000
3 Mo	1.13	1.10	1.04	73	8	10,113
6 Mo	5.92	1.27	1.22	2	3	10,592
1 Yr	9.03	0.61	0.05	7	12	10,903
3 Yr Avg	6.56	0.29	0.16	19	9	12,100
5 Yr Avg	7.72	0.29	0.62	31	4	14,503
10 Yr Avg	7.91	0.68	1.10	44	6	21,404
15 Yr Avg	—	—	—	—	—	—

Tax Analysis	Tax-Adj Ret%	%Rank Cat	%Pretax Ret	%Rank Cat
3 Yr Avg	4.15	4	63.3	4
5 Yr Avg	4.94	3	64.0	15
10 Yr Avg	5.04	1	63.8	2

Potential Capital Gain Exposure: 1% of assets

Risk Analysis

Time Period	Load-Adj Return %	Risk %Rank[1] All	Risk %Rank[1] Cat	Morningstar Return	Morningstar Risk	Morningstar Risk-Adj Rating
1 Yr	9.03					
3 Yr	6.56	12	25	0.35[2]	0.64	★★★★
5 Yr	7.72	18	26	0.62[2]	0.65	★★★★★
10 Yr	7.91	22	27	0.94[2]	0.86	★★★★★

Average Historical Rating (133 months): 4.5★s

[1] 1=low, 100=high [2] T-Bill return substituted for category avg.

Category Rating (3 Yr)

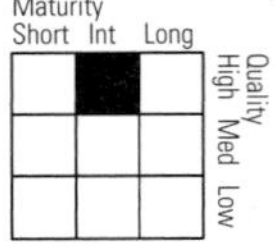

Return High
Risk Below Avg

Other Measures	Standard Index LB Agg	Best Fit Index LB Agg
Alpha	0.2	0.2
Beta	1.06	1.06
R-Squared	92	92

Standard Deviation	3.88
Mean	6.56
Sharpe Ratio	0.48

Portfolio Analysis 06-30-01

Total Fixed-Income: 275	Date of Maturity	Amount $000	Value $000	% Net Assets
GNMA TBA 6.5%		155,100	153,356	7.08
GNMA TBA 7%		138,000	139,185	6.43
US Treasury Note 3.875%	01-15-09	37,599	38,844	1.79
Republic of Germany (Fut)	09-06-01	39,700	35,588	1.64
GNMA 6%	11-15-29	34,007	32,957	1.52
GNMA TBA 6%		34,000	32,827	1.52
US Treasury Note 3.625%	07-15-02	24,821	25,294	1.17
Int Rate S Swaption	06-06-15	23,000	23,431	1.08
Euribor s Mar02 (Fut)	03-18-02	28,500	23,146	1.07
Int Rt S Swaption	02-02-04	−14,700	20,702	0.96
FHLMC 7%	10-15-30	20,953	20,533	0.95
FNMA 7.468%	10-01-40	19,806	20,058	0.93
Ford Motor Credit FRN	06-20-03	20,000	19,930	0.92
FHLMC CMO FRN	03-15-25	19,020	19,072	0.88
Txu Elec 144A 4.31%	06-15-03	19,000	19,000	0.88
Texas Utilities Elec 4.31%	06-15-08	19,000	19,000	0.88
Int Rate S Swaption	06-15-06	18,200	18,541	0.86
PNC Mortgage CMO 6.5%	02-25-29	17,633	17,095	0.79
CS First Boston 6.8%	12-15-30	16,998	17,017	0.79
Providian Gateway 6.9%	03-16-09	16,800	16,871	0.78

Current Investment Style

Maturity: Short Int Long; Quality: High Med Low

Avg Eff Duration[1]	4.4 Yrs
Avg Eff Maturity	7.0 Yrs
Avg Credit Quality	AA
Avg Wtd Coupon	6.30%
Avg Wtd Price	98.83% of par

[1] figure provided by fund

Special Securities % assets 06-30-01	
Restricted/Illiquid Secs	3
Exotic Mortgage-Backed	1
Emerging-Markets Secs	1
Options/Futures/Warrants	Yes

Coupon Range	% of Bonds	Rel Cat
0%	0.62	0.50
0% to 7%	60.24	1.11
7% to 8.5%	36.79	1.06
8.5% to 10%	2.34	0.33
More than 10%	0.01	0.00

1.00=Category Average

Credit Analysis % bonds 09-30-01

US Govt	0	BB	2
AAA	66	B	0
AA	8	Below B	0
A	19	NR/NA	0
BBB	5		

Composition % assets 06-30-01

Cash	11.8	Bonds	51.4
Stocks	0.0	Other	36.5

Sector Breakdown % bonds 06-30-01

US Treasuries	2	CMOs	9
GNMA mtgs	32	ARMs	1
FNMA mtgs	3	Other	40
FHLMC mtgs	7		

Analysis by Eric Jacobson 12-31-01

To watch Harbor Bond, you might think this fund management stuff was easy.

One need only look at the fund's annual returns over the past 10 years: It's never placed any lower than the best half of the intermediate-term bond category. Of course, the fund has hit speedbumps now and then, but manager Bill Gross (the PIMCO legend who runs this portfolio under a subadvisory arrangement with Harbor) has been consistently able to claw himself back up to the top of the pack, time after time. The fund's long-term returns are all stellar.

The most recent example of Gross' resilience came in 2001. Though his concentration in mortgages proved a mistake as the sector lagged during the year's first half, Gross anticipated that rates would fall as the year progressed. He therefore extended the fund's duration (a measure of rate sensitivity) at midyear, which helped prop the fund back up. He also began building a larger stake in corporates toward the end of the year, thereby giving the fund a boost in the fourth quarter, as credit-sensitive bonds generally outperformed the broader market. By the end of 2001, the fund's gain of 9% placed in the top 15% of the category.

It's worth keeping an eye on how Gross' sector calls develop. He's already stashed more than 23% in corporates, a significant departure from his credit-conscious focus on GNMA mortgages over the past couple of years, and the fund also has roughly 10% of assets invested in asset-backeds. What's more, Gross has hinted that he may purchase larger stakes in emerging markets and high-yield credits if he sees value there. So while this is clearly a terrific portfolio with a terrific manager, investors ought to assume that the potential for a higher level of volatility now exists. That's no reason to shy away from the fund, but it does suggest that a bit more attention to its makeup might be worthwhile.

Address:	One SeaGate Toledo, OH 43666 800–422–1050 / 419–247–2477
Web Address:	www.harborfunds.com
Inception:	12-29-87
Advisor:	Harbor Cap. Adv.
Subadvisor:	Pacific Inv. Mgmt.
NTF Plans:	N/A

Minimum Purchase:	$1000	Add: $500	IRA: $500
Min Auto Inv Plan:	$500	Add: $100	
Sales Fees:	No-load		
Management Fee:	.70%		
Actual Fees:	Mgt: 0.49%	Dist: —	
Expense Projections:	3Yr: $281	5Yr: $493	10Yr: $1122
Avg Brok Commission:	—	Income Distrib: Quarterly	

Total Cost (relative to category): —

Harbor Capital Appreciation

Ticker	Load	NAV	Yield	Total Assets	Mstar Category
HACAX	None	$29.23	0.1%	$6,792.2 mil	Large Growth

Prospectus Objective: Growth

Harbor Capital Appreciation Fund seeks long-term growth of capital; dividend income is secondary.

The fund normally invests at least 65% of assets in equity securities of established companies, typically those with market capitalizations of at least $1 billion. To select securities, the advisor seeks companies exhibiting superior sales growth, high returns on equity, strong balance sheets, excellent management capability, strong R&D, and unique marketing competence. The fund may also invest in short-term obligations and foreign securities in the form of depositary receipts.

Prior to May 1, 1990, the fund was named Harbor U.S. Equities Fund.

Historical Profile
Return: Above Avg
Risk: Above Avg
Rating: ★★★★ Above Avg

Investment Style Equity — Average Stock %

1994	1995	1996	1997	1998	1999	2000	12-01
	100%	98%	97%	96%	98%	96%	96%

▼ Manager Change
▽ Partial Manager Change

Fund Performance vs. Category Average
■ Quarterly Fund Return +/– Category Average
— Category Baseline

Performance Quartile (within Category)

Portfolio Manager(s)

Spiros Segalas. Since 5-90. BA'55 Princeton U. Other funds currently managed: Scudder Focus Value+Growth A, Scudder Focus Value+Growth B, Scudder Focus Value+Growth C.

History

	1990	1991	1992	1993	1994	1995	1996	1997	1998	1999	2000	12-01
NAV	11.09	16.11	15.65	16.37	16.71	22.69	26.33	29.47	37.99	50.65	35.58	29.23
Total Return %	–1.81	54.79	9.98	12.12	3.37	37.82	19.85	31.46	36.80	45.81	–17.00	–17.74
+/– S&P 500	1.31	24.30	2.36	2.06	2.06	0.29	–3.10	–1.90	8.23	24.77	–7.90	–5.86
+/– Russ Top 200 Grt	–3.18	15.38	6.09	12.19	–1.48	–0.83	–5.67	–2.29	–8.30	16.13	7.52	2.76
Income Return %	1.14	0.39	0.12	0.22	0.23	0.15	0.09	0.25	0.22	0.00	0.00	0.11
Capital Return %	–2.95	54.40	9.86	11.90	3.14	37.67	19.76	31.20	36.58	45.81	–17.00	–17.85
Total Rtn % Rank Cat	45	26	21	40	9	18	43	22	32	31	60	29
Income $	0.14	0.04	0.02	0.03	0.04	0.03	0.02	0.07	0.07	0.00	0.00	0.04
Capital Gains $	0.86	0.98	2.04	1.13	0.17	0.31	0.86	4.85	2.28	4.60	6.17	0.00
Expense Ratio %	0.88	0.89	0.91	0.86	0.81	0.75	0.75	0.70	0.68	0.66	0.64	—
Income Ratio %	1.18	0.47	0.12	0.24	0.24	0.23	0.11	0.23	0.24	–0.05	–0.07	—
Turnover Rate %	162	90	69	93	73	52	74	73	70	68	86	—
Net Assets $mil	62.1	90.9	105.0	149.9	239.1	989.3	1,681.7	2,906.3	4,696.7	7,947.1	7,786.0	6,792.2

Performance 12-31-01

	1st Qtr	2nd Qtr	3rd Qtr	4th Qtr	Total
1997	–1.44	19.81	14.63	–2.88	31.46
1998	15.27	5.12	–13.16	30.01	36.80
1999	12.08	4.86	–3.29	28.28	45.81
2000	12.81	–7.68	–4.28	–16.74	–17.00
2001	–16.33	4.40	–19.53	17.03	–17.74

Trailing	Total Return%	+/– S&P 500	+/– Russ Top 200 Grth	% Rank All	% Rank Cat	Growth of $10,000
3 Mo	17.03	6.34	4.17	19	27	11,703
6 Mo	–5.83	–0.27	1.16	67	23	9,417
1 Yr	–17.74	–5.86	2.76	77	29	8,226
3 Yr Avg	–0.15	0.88	7.87	74	28	9,955
5 Yr Avg	12.35	1.65	3.76	9	15	17,903
10 Yr Avg	14.19	1.26	3.11	8	5	37,696
15 Yr Avg	—	—	—	—	—	—

Tax Analysis	Tax-Adj Ret%	%Rank Cat	%Pretax Ret	%Rank Cat
3 Yr Avg	–1.78	32	—	—
5 Yr Avg	10.31	17	83.4	37
10 Yr Avg	12.36	5	87.1	17

Potential Capital Gain Exposure: –25% of assets

Risk Analysis

Time Period	Load-Adj Return %	Risk %Rank[1] All	Risk %Rank[1] Cat	Morningstar Return	Morningstar Risk	Morningstar Risk-Adj Rating
1 Yr	–17.74					
3 Yr	–0.15	86	50	–1.03[2]	1.29	★★
5 Yr	12.35	84	52	1.84[2]	1.22	★★★★
10 Yr	14.19	88	60	1.59	1.28	★★★★

Average Historical Rating (133 months): 4.2★s

[1] 1=low, 100=high [2] T-Bill return substituted for category avg.

Category Rating (3 Yr)

1 2 3 4 5 — Worst … Best

Return: Above Avg
Risk: Average

Other Measures	Standard Index S&P 500	Best Fit Index MSCIACWdFr
Alpha	4.2	10.2
Beta	1.34	1.46
R-Squared	80	83
Standard Deviation		26.05
Mean		–0.15
Sharpe Ratio		–0.23

Portfolio Analysis 09-30-01

Share change since 06-01 Total Stocks: 68

Share change	Sector	PE	YTD Ret%	% Assets
⊖ Citigroup	Financials	20.0	0.03	3.84
⊕ American Intl Grp	Financials	42.0	–19.20	3.59
⊖ American Home Products	Health	—	–1.91	3.55
⊕ PepsiCo	Staples	31.4	–0.54	3.39
⊖ Microsoft	Technology	57.6	52.78	3.33
⊕ Johnson & Johnson	Health	16.6	14.01	2.91
⊕ Pfizer	Health	34.7	–12.40	2.90
⊖ General Elec	Industrials	30.1	–15.00	2.77
⊖ Home Depot	Retail	42.9	12.07	2.67
⊖ Amgen	Health	52.8	–11.70	2.51
⊕ IBM	Technology	26.9	43.00	2.43
⊖ Schlumberger	Energy	55.0	–30.30	2.34
⊖ Kohl's	Retail	54.2	15.48	2.31
⊕ Abbott Labs	Health	51.6	17.08	2.26
⊖ Viacom Cl B	Services	—	—	2.22
⊕ Tyco Intl	Industrials	27.1	6.23	2.16
☼ Liberty Media Grp	N/A	—	—	1.96
⊖ Pharmacia	Health	36.5	–29.30	1.95
☼ S & P 500 Dep Rec SPDR		—	—	1.82
⊕ Baxter Intl	Health	33.9	22.84	1.81
⊖ Wal-Mart Stores	Retail	40.3	8.94	1.79
⊖ Halliburton	Energy	8.3	–63.20	1.58
⊕ Household Intl	Financials	14.7	6.89	1.58
☼ Sprint (PCS Group)	Services	—	19.43	1.56
⊖ Genentech	Health	NMF	–33.40	1.47

Current Investment Style

Style: Value Blnd Growth; Size: Large Med Small

	Stock Port Avg	Relative S&P 500 Current	Relative S&P 500 Hist	Rel Cat
Price/Earnings Ratio	36.4	1.18	1.28	1.02
Price/Book Ratio	7.4	1.30	1.24	1.16
Price/Cash Flow	24.3	1.35	1.37	1.07
3 Yr Earnings Growth	17.1	1.17	1.29	0.79
1 Yr Earnings Est%	0.7	—	—	0.22
Med Mkt Cap $mil	75,062	1.2	1.0	1.59

Special Securities % assets 09-30-01

Restricted/Illiquid Secs	0
Emerging-Markets Secs	0
Options/Futures/Warrants	No

Composition % assets 09-30-01

Cash	3.7
Stocks*	96.4
Bonds	0.0
Other	0.0
*Foreign (% stocks)	4.8

Market Cap

Giant	63.5
Large	30.1
Medium	6.5
Small	0.0
Micro	0.0

Sector Weightings	% of Stocks	Rel S&P	5-Year High	5-Year Low
Utilities	0.0	0.0	4	0
Energy	4.2	0.6	6	0
Financials	20.9	1.2	22	3
Industrials	8.4	0.7	10	0
Durables	0.0	0.0	7	0
Staples	5.6	0.7	10	0
Services	9.2	0.9	31	9
Retail	10.2	1.5	17	4
Health	22.5	1.5	26	5
Technology	19.0	1.0	47	16

Analysis by Christopher Traulsen 11-11-01

Harbor Capital Appreciation Fund is even more appealing than usual at the moment.

It's no secret that this is one of the better large-growth funds. Sig Segalas is one of the most experienced, successful managers in the business, and he's backed by a well-oiled research machine at Jennison Associates Capital, the firm he cofounded in 1969. The fund has failed to beat the large-growth category average in only one calendar year since Segalas took the helm in 1990, and its three-, five-, and 10-year returns all rank in the category's best quartile. Finally, with a 0.64% expense ratio, the fund is dirt cheap.

Like most large-growth offerings, it's having a tough year in absolute terms: For the year to date through Nov. 9, 2001, it has lost 21%. Nevertheless, in this extremely difficult year for key growth sectors such as technology, more than two thirds of the fund's rivals have registered even bigger losses. Segalas helped the fund's cause by trimming its tech exposure early, and by maintaining sizable weightings in pharmaceutical and financials stocks, which have generally fared much better than tech thus far in 2001. Retail picks such as Kohl's, Home Depot, and Wal-Mart Stores have also held up reasonably well. In the third quarter, Segalas continued to take a measured approach, adding new positions in relatively mundane names such as Fannie Mae, Freddie Mac, and Gillette.

The fund's recent losses have a silver lining—namely, this offering now has a big stash of unrealized losses that should make it more tax-efficient in future years. Segalas has always kept an eye on tax efficiency, but the fund paid out sizable gains in the late 1990s as he trimmed holdings on valuation concerns. Investors who buy now are getting a top-flight fund that's likely to be tax-efficient for some time, just when growth stocks are the cheapest they've been in a long while.

Address:	One SeaGate Toledo, OH 43666 800-422-1050 / 419-247-2477
Web Address:	www.harborfunds.com
Inception:	12-29-87
Advisor:	Harbor Cap. Adv.
Subadvisor:	Jennison Assoc. Cap.
NTF Plans:	N/A

Minimum Purchase:	$1000	Add: $500 IRA: $500
Min Auto Inv Plan:	$500	Add: $100
Sales Fees:	No-load	
Management Fee:	.60%	
Actual Fees:	Mgt: 0.60%	Dist: —
Expense Projections:	3Yr: $220	5Yr: $385 10Yr: $877
Avg Brok Commission:	—	Income Distrib: Annually
Total Cost (relative to category):	—	

Harbor International

Ticker	Load	NAV	Yield	Total Assets	Mstar Category
HAINX	None	$29.63	0.9%	$3,655.5 mil	Foreign Stock

Prospectus Objective: Foreign Stock

Harbor International Fund seeks long-term capital growth. Current income is a secondary consideration.

The fund normally invests at least 65% of assets in common stocks or comparable equity securities of issuers that do business primarily outside of the United States. It normally maintains investments in a minimum of three countries, emphasizing Europe, the Pacific Basin, and the more-industrialized emerging markets. The fund may also invest in depositary receipts, investment-grade fixed-income securities, and currency contracts.

Historical Profile

Return: Above Avg
Risk: Below Avg
Rating: ★★★★ Above Avg

Investment Style
Equity
Average Stock %: 92% (1996), 91% (1997), 92% (1998), 93% (1999), 95% (2000), 95% (12-01)

▼ Manager Change
▽ Partial Manager Change

Fund Performance vs. Category Average
Quarterly Fund Return +/– Category Average
— Category Baseline

Performance Quartile (within Category)

Portfolio Manager(s)

Hakan Castegren. Since 12-87. MBA'57 Stockholm School of Econ.

1990	1991	1992	1993	1994	1995	1996	1997	1998	1999	2000	12-01	History
14.42	17.30	16.87	24.32	24.45	27.84	32.20	35.86	36.72	41.86	35.09	29.63	NAV
–9.76	21.46	–0.20	45.42	5.43	16.06	20.12	15.49	10.36	23.89	–4.97	–12.25	Total Return %
–6.64	–9.02	–7.82	35.36	4.11	–21.47	–2.83	–17.86	–18.21	2.85	4.14	–0.38	+/– S&P 500
13.69	9.33	11.97	12.86	–2.35	4.85	14.07	13.71	–9.63	–3.08	9.20	—	+/– MSCI EAFE
2.02	1.46	1.26	1.26	1.01	1.66	1.50	1.25	1.61	1.77	1.69	0.76	Income Return %
–11.78	20.00	–1.46	44.16	4.41	14.40	18.62	14.24	8.75	22.12	–6.66	–13.01	Capital Return %
53	2	20	21	13	10	14	12	69	88	16	8	Total Rtn % Rank Cat
0.34	0.21	0.22	0.21	0.25	0.41	0.42	0.40	0.58	0.65	0.71	0.27	Income $
0.34	0.00	0.18	0.00	0.94	0.13	0.80	0.90	2.30	2.86	3.79	0.88	Capital Gains $
1.40	1.35	1.28	1.20	1.10	1.04	0.99	0.97	0.94	0.92	0.92	—	Expense Ratio %
2.82	1.76	1.98	1.28	1.09	1.53	1.42	1.20	1.27	0.78	1.40	—	Income Ratio %
28	19	25	16	29	14	10	6	14	48	10	—	Turnover Rate %
61.6	220.8	761.9	2,537.9	2,953.1	3,460.2	4,318.6	5,276.6	5,373.9	5,842.6	4,829.0	3,655.5	Net Assets $mil

Performance 12-31-01

	1st Qtr	2nd Qtr	3rd Qtr	4th Qtr	Total
1997	5.06	13.36	2.06	–4.99	15.49
1998	13.66	–1.52	–16.64	18.28	10.36
1999	3.00	4.63	0.94	13.90	23.89
2000	–2.22	1.93	–5.13	0.51	–4.97
2001	–10.74	2.59	–13.17	10.36	–12.25

Trailing	Total Return%	+/– S&P 500	+/– MSCI EAFE	% Rank All	% Rank Cat	Growth of $10,000
3 Mo	10.36	–0.32	—	41	29	11,036
6 Mo	–4.17	1.39	—	57	7	9,583
1 Yr	–12.25	–0.38	—	66	8	8,775
3 Yr Avg	1.09	2.12	—	67	24	10,331
5 Yr Avg	5.66	–5.04	—	53	17	13,168
10 Yr Avg	10.88	–2.05	—	27	3	28,088
15 Yr Avg	—	—	—	—	—	—

Tax Analysis	Tax-Adj Ret%	%Rank Cat	%Pretax Ret	%Rank Cat
3 Yr Avg	–0.81	28	—	—
5 Yr Avg	3.83	16	67.7	39
10 Yr Avg	9.42	3	86.6	6

Potential Capital Gain Exposure: 31% of assets

Risk Analysis

Time Period	Load-Adj Return %	Risk %Rank[1] All	Risk %Rank[1] Cat	Morningstar Return	Morningstar Risk	Morningstar Risk-Adj Rating
1 Yr	–12.25					
3 Yr	1.09	52	10	–0.79[2]	0.68	★★★★
5 Yr	5.66	61	15	0.14[2]	0.70	★★★★
10 Yr	10.88	73	18	2.08[2]	0.73	★★★★

Average Historical Rating (133 months): 4.7★s

[1]1=low, 100=high [2] T–Bill return substituted for category avg.

Category Rating (3 Yr)

1 2 3 4 5
Worst Best

Return: Above Avg
Risk: Low

Other Measures	Standard Index S&P 500	Best Fit Index MSCIEasNdD
Alpha	0.3	4.7
Beta	0.66	0.88
R–Squared	56	89

Standard Deviation	14.98
Mean	1.09
Sharpe Ratio	–0.30

Analysis by William Samuel Rocco 12-17-01

Harbor International Fund continues to shine while keeping things pretty simple.

This value fan has fared much better than most of its peers throughout 2001. Manager Hakan Castegren's value bias was advantageous during the first part of the year, and a handful of his picks thrived. BP Amoco and some of his other commodity-related holdings posted small gains over the first 8.5 months of the year, while Imperial Tobacco and Swedish Match earned big gains.

Further, the fund has returned nearly 2% over the past three months, whereas its typical peer has returned just 50 basis points. Diageo and a few other consumer-staples and drug stocks have posted small but significant gains this fall. And Ericsson, Sony, and Canon have bounced back sharply. For the year to date through Dec. 14, the fund is ahead of 90% of its rivals.

The positioning and positions that have helped the fund this year are nothing new. Castegren has always focused on undervalued blue chips, particularly consumer staples, and moved quite slowly while doing so. Imperial Tobacco, Swedish Match, Diageo, Canon, Sony, and Ericsson have been in the portfolio for years. And Castegren has made only a few portfolio moves in 2001, buying Danish drugmaker Novo-Nordisk and the French steelmaker Usinor earlier this year and adjusting his stake in selected issues this fall.

Castegren's reserved value strategy has also delivered topnotch returns over the long term, while keeping volatility under control. Thus, we think this fund remains an excellent core international holding, though it might work better in a tax-deferred account. The fund will make a significant capital-gains distribution this year, as it did in 1998, 1999, and 2000.

Portfolio Analysis 06-30-01

Share change since 03-01 Total Stocks: 72	Sector	Country	% Assets
⊕ Richemont Cl A (Unit)	N/A	N/A	3.45
Canon	Industrials	Japan	3.19
Imperial Tobacco Grp	Staples	United Kingdom	3.14
Billiton ADR	Industrials	United Kingdom	3.01
⊕ BP Amoco	Energy	United Kingdom	2.87
⊕ Petrobras Pfd	Energy	Brazil	2.71
⊕ Sony	Durables	Japan	2.55
⊕ ING Groep	Financials	Netherlands	2.55
⊕ LM Ericsson Tele B	Technology	Sweden	2.54
☼ Novo–Nordisk	Health	Denmark	2.40
⊕ Nestle (Reg)	Staples	Switzerland	2.32
⊕ Novartis (Reg)	Health	Switzerland	2.30
⊕ Total Fina Cl B	Energy	France	2.15
⊕ News ADR	Services	Australia	2.12
⊕ Diageo	Staples	United Kingdom	2.10
Royal Dutch Petro NY ADR	Energy	Netherlands	2.03
⊕ ABN Amro Hldgs	Financials	Netherlands	2.02
Swedish Match	Staples	Sweden	2.01
⊕ Peugeot Citroen	Durables	France	1.97
⊕ Assicurazioni Generali	Financials	Italy	1.76

Current Investment Style

Style: Value Blnd Growth; Size: Large Med Small

	Stock Port Avg	Rel MSCI EAFE Current	Rel MSCI EAFE Hist	Rel Cat
Price/Earnings Ratio	17.2	0.67	0.81	0.67
Price/Cash Flow	10.7	0.83	0.86	0.74
Price/Book Ratio	2.6	0.76	0.75	0.68
3 Yr Earnings Growth	23.3	1.25	1.33	1.19
Med Mkt Cap $mil	22,812	0.8	0.9	1.26

Country Exposure 06-30-01	% assets
United Kingdom	18
France	15
Switzerland	13
Netherlands	7
Sweden	7

Hedging History: Rare

Regional Exposure 06-30-01	% assets
Europe	74
Japan	7
Latin America	3
Pacific Rim	7
Other	0

Special Securities % assets 06-30-01	
Restricted/Illiquid Secs	0
Emerging–Markets Secs	8
Options/Futures/Warrants	Yes

Composition % assets 06-30-01

Cash	6.8	Bonds	0.0
Stocks	92.5	Other	0.7

Sector Weightings	% of Stocks	Rel Cat	5-Year High	5-Year Low
Utilities	0.0	0.0	10	0
Energy	10.9	1.9	18	5
Financials	26.4	1.2	40	16
Industrials	21.4	1.6	36	14
Durables	7.2	1.1	17	7
Staples	16.2	2.3	16	3
Services	6.5	0.4	13	3
Retail	0.0	0.0	5	0
Health	8.3	0.9	14	0
Technology	3.2	0.3	12	0

Address:	One SeaGate Toledo, OH 43666 800–422–1050 / 419–247–2477
Web Address:	www.harborfunds.com
Inception:	12-29-87
Advisor:	Harbor Cap. Adv.
Subadvisor:	Northern Cross Inv.s
NTF Plans:	N/A

Minimum Purchase:	$1000	Add: $500 IRA: $500
Min Auto Inv Plan:	$500	Add: $100
Sales Fees:	No–load	
Management Fee:	.85%	
Actual Fees:	Mgt: 0.79%	Dist: —
Expense Projections:	3Yr: $323	5Yr: $566 10Yr: $1289
Avg Brok Commission:	—	Income Distrib: Annually

Total Cost (relative to category): —

Harbor Large Cap Value

Ticker	Load	NAV	Yield	Total Assets	Mstar Category
HAVLX	None	$14.39	1.4%	$159.9 mil	Large Value

Prospectus Objective: Equity–Income

Harbor Large Cap Value Fund seeks maximum long-term total return from a combination of capital growth and income.

The fund ordinarily invests at least 80% of assets in a diversified portfolio of large cap equity securities. It primarily invests in common stocks, preferred stocks, rights and depositary receipts, of U.S. companies with market capitalizations of at least $5 billion at the time of initial investment.

Historical Profile

Return: Above Avg
Risk: Average
Rating: ★★★★ Above Avg

Investment Style
Equity
Average Stock %: 97% (1996), 97% (1997), 98% (1998), 98% (1999), 98% (2000), 99% (12-01)

▼ Manager Change
▽ Partial Manager Change

Fund Performance vs. Category Average
Quarterly Fund Return +/– Category Average
— Category Baseline

Performance Quartile (within Category)

Portfolio Manager(s)

Jeff Shaw. Since 9-01. Other fund currently managed: Managers Value.

1990	1991	1992	1993	1994	1995	1996	1997	1998	1999	2000	12-01	History
11.46	13.06	13.50	13.21	11.88	14.34	14.79	15.20	14.34	13.55	14.03	14.39	NAV
–5.60	21.27	7.46	8.38	0.70	35.37	20.02	34.14	6.92	7.59	7.16	4.10	Total Return %
–2.49	–9.22	–0.16	–1.68	–0.62	–2.16	–2.92	0.79	–21.65	–13.45	16.27	15.98	+/– S&P 500
–1.94	3.11	–1.61	–11.38	3.01	–4.66	–2.29	–1.35	–14.32	–3.37	4.85	12.89	+/– Russ Top 200 Val
4.00	4.10	2.91	2.43	2.74	3.47	2.83	2.23	1.80	1.81	2.02	1.44	Income Return %
–9.60	17.16	4.55	5.95	–2.04	31.90	17.19	31.91	5.12	5.78	5.14	2.66	Capital Return %
47	89	69	84	35	30	53	6	83	44	48	7	Total Rtn % Rank Cat
0.52	0.46	0.38	0.33	0.36	0.41	0.40	0.33	0.27	0.26	0.27	0.20	Income $
0.43	0.35	0.15	1.10	1.07	1.27	2.00	4.16	1.63	1.57	0.19	0.00	Capital Gains $
1.01	0.93	0.84	0.88	1.04	0.90	0.83	0.83	0.79	0.76	0.80	—	Expense Ratio %
3.96	3.61	3.11	2.48	2.66	3.00	2.65	1.98	1.67	1.65	2.05	—	Income Ratio %
31	33	20	50	151	136	132	146	114	110	106	—	Turnover Rate %
26.4	42.0	66.9	60.0	57.0	91.7	116.8	174.8	176.6	155.3	142.3	159.9	Net Assets $mil

Performance 12-31-01

	1st Qtr	2nd Qtr	3rd Qtr	4th Qtr	Total
1997	2.37	13.93	10.81	3.79	34.14
1998	12.09	–4.11	–13.68	15.24	6.92
1999	1.63	14.70	–11.03	3.73	7.59
2000	–1.33	–2.43	4.87	6.15	7.16
2001	–3.31	8.15	–11.39	12.34	4.10

Trailing	Total Return%	+/– S&P 500	+/– Russ Top 200 Val	% Rank All	% Rank Cat	Growth of $10,000
3 Mo	12.34	1.66	6.83	32	14	11,234
6 Mo	–0.45	5.11	5.33	41	11	9,955
1 Yr	4.10	15.98	12.89	30	7	10,410
3 Yr Avg	6.27	7.30	5.11	20	18	12,002
5 Yr Avg	11.47	0.78	0.27	12	20	17,214
10 Yr Avg	12.61	–0.32	–1.42	15	40	32,801
15 Yr Avg	—	—	—	—	—	—

Tax Analysis	Tax-Adj Ret%	%Rank Cat	%Pretax Ret	%Rank Cat
3 Yr Avg	3.95	23	63.1	57
5 Yr Avg	7.36	41	64.1	79
10 Yr Avg	8.56	61	67.9	90

Potential Capital Gain Exposure: 5% of assets

Risk Analysis

Time Period	Load-Adj Return %	Risk %Rank[1] All	Risk %Rank[1] Cat	Morningstar Return	Morningstar Risk	Morningstar Risk-Adj Rating
1 Yr	4.10					
3 Yr	6.27	54	52	0.29[2]	0.76	★★★★
5 Yr	11.47	58	55	1.59[2]	0.80	★★★★
10 Yr	12.61	63	64	1.23	0.82	★★★★

Average Historical Rating (133 months): 3.0★s

[1] 1=low, 100=high [2] T-Bill return substituted for category avg.

Category Rating (3 Yr)

1 Worst — 2 — 3 — 4 — 5 Best

Return: Above Avg
Risk: Average

Other Measures	Standard Index S&P 500	Best Fit Index S&P 500
Alpha	6.3	6.3
Beta	0.76	0.76
R-Squared	55	55
Standard Deviation		18.55
Mean		6.27
Sharpe Ratio		0.08

Portfolio Analysis 06-30-01

Share change since 12-00 Total Stocks: 187	Sector	PE	YTD Ret%	% Assets
⊕ SBC Comms	Services	18.4	–16.00	2.53
⊖ Citigroup	Financials	20.0	0.03	2.47
⊖ ExxonMobil	Energy	15.3	–7.59	2.45
⊖ Verizon Comms	Services	29.7	–2.52	2.17
⊖ Bank of America	Financials	16.7	42.73	2.01
⊖ J.P. Morgan Chase & Co.	Financials	27.8	–17.40	1.92
⊕ Chubb	Financials	48.3	–18.60	1.91
American Intl Grp	Financials	42.0	–19.20	1.82
☼ Schering–Plough	Health	22.2	–35.90	1.68
⊕ Emerson Elec	Industrials	23.8	–25.60	1.65
⊖ Alltel	Services	17.7	1.14	1.64
⊖ Pall	Industrials	25.3	16.26	1.59
⊕ Glaxo Wellcome PLC ADR	Health	24.2	–9.77	1.54
⊕ Bristol–Myers Squibb	Health	20.2	–26.00	1.52
⊖ Diebold	Technology	34.3	23.51	1.50
⊕ Rohm and Haas	Industrials	17.9	–2.45	1.48
⊕ US Bancorp	Financials	13.5	–6.14	1.44
⊖ Bemis	Industrials	19.4	50.19	1.43
⊕ SunTrust Banks	Financials	13.7	2.01	1.42
⊕ May Dept Stores	Retail	15.2	15.97	1.41
☼ Sprint	Services	20.5	1.18	1.36
⊖ Torchmark	Financials	13.5	3.29	1.36
☼ Schlumberger	Energy	55.0	–30.30	1.33
☼ FPL Grp	Utilities	13.1	–18.30	1.32
⊕ Parker Hannifin	Industrials	19.2	5.77	1.32

Current Investment Style

Style: Value Blnd Growth; Size: Large Med Small

	Stock Port Avg	Relative S&P 500 Current	Relative S&P 500 Hist	Rel Cat
Price/Earnings Ratio	24.1	0.78	0.65	0.96
Price/Book Ratio	3.8	0.66	0.43	0.92
Price/Cash Flow	12.1	0.67	0.60	0.87
3 Yr Earnings Growth	11.7	0.80	0.59	0.79
1 Yr Earnings Est%	–9.0	5.07	—	2.71
Med Mkt Cap $mil	17,133	0.3	0.2	0.54

Analysis by Christopher Traulsen 09-23-01

Harbor Large Cap Value Fund's changes weren't needed, but they don't merit much concern.

Effective Sept. 20, 2001, Harbor fired this fund's two longtime subabvisors: DePrince Race & Zollo Inc., which ran 70% of the fund using a value-based style; and Richards & Tierney Inc., which ran the rest of the portfolio using an enhanced-index strategy. The fund is now managed by Jeff Shaw of Armstrong Shaw Associates. In keeping with his firm's focus on large caps, Harbor has changed the fund's name to Harbor Large Cap Value. The change in management will not affect the fund's expense ratio. (Shareholders will have a chance to vote on the new subadvisory agreement on Dec. 5, 2001, but the other changes do not require a vote).

The fund had fared well under DePrince and Tierney. However, Harbor president James Williams said DePrince's focus on securities that paid dividends well in excess of the S&P 500 index average was too limiting. In contrast, Shaw has no such requirement. Instead, the firm seeks to buy companies trading at discounts of 30% or more from their intrinsic values. To estimate a company's value, Shaw uses discounted cash-flow analysis and evaluates comparable transactions and historic valuations.

Given the fund's strong previous results, we don't think the change was necessary. However, Shaw has been running private accounts in this style for years, and uses a conservative, disciplined approach. Further, Harbor has an excellent record of selecting subadvisors at its funds. There are no guarantees, but Shaw's style likely will make the fund more tax-efficient than it was under DePrince and Tierney (tax efficiency was the fund's glaring weakness under the former managers). We would take a wait-and-see approach for now, but we suspect that the change will ultimately yield strong results.

Special Securities % assets 06-30-01	
Restricted/Illiquid Secs	0
Emerging–Markets Secs	0
Options/Futures/Warrants	No

Composition % assets 06-30-01	
Cash	3.2
Stocks*	96.8
Bonds	0.0
Other	0.0
*Foreign (% stocks)	3.4

Market Cap	
Giant	31.4
Large	29.3
Medium	37.5
Small	1.7
Micro	0.0

Sector Weightings	% of Stocks	Rel S&P	5-Year High	5-Year Low
Utilities	3.6	1.1	13	0
Energy	7.2	1.0	20	3
Financials	28.3	1.6	34	7
Industrials	23.0	2.0	39	6
Durables	2.6	1.7	11	0
Staples	4.9	0.6	14	3
Services	12.9	1.2	22	0
Retail	6.4	1.0	13	2
Health	7.5	0.5	9	2
Technology	3.5	0.2	8	0

Address: One SeaGate, Toledo, OH 43666, 800–422–1050 / 419–247–2477
Web Address: www.harborfunds.com
Inception: 12-29-87
Advisor: Harbor Cap. Adv.
Subadvisor: Armstrong Shaw Assoc.
NTF Plans: N/A

Minimum Purchase: $1000 — Add: $500 — IRA: $500
Min Auto Inv Plan: $500 — Add: $100
Sales Fees: No–load
Management Fee: .60%
Actual Fees: Mgt: 0.60% — Dist: —
Expense Projections: 3Yr: $255 — 5Yr: $447 — 10Yr: $1018
Avg Brok Commission: — — Income Distrib: Quarterly
Total Cost (relative to category): —

Hartford Global Leaders A

Ticker	Load	NAV	Yield	Total Assets	Mstar Category
HALAX	5.50%	$14.00	0.0%	$421.5 mil	World Stock

Prospectus Objective: World Stock

Hartford Global Leaders seeks capital growth.

The fund normally invests at least 65% of assets in equities of issuers in at least five countries, including the U.S. It may invest up to 25% of assets in emerging countries. The fund uses a two-tiered investment approach. First, under the "top-down" approach, management analyzes the global macro economic and investment environments, including an evaluation of demographic trends and investor sentiment. Second, it is followed by a "bottom up" approach emphasizing characteristics such as a strong balance sheet and a high return on equity.

The fund currently offers Class A, B, C, and Y shares.

Historical Profile

Return	Above Avg
Risk	Average
Rating	★★★★ Above Avg

Investment Style
Equity
Average Stock %: 1999 90%; 2000 93%; 12-01 96%

▼ Manager Change
▽ Partial Manager Change

Fund Performance vs. Category Average
■ Quarterly Fund Return +/– Category Average
— Category Baseline

Performance Quartile (within Category)

Portfolio Manager(s)

Andrew S. Offit. Since 9-98. BBA'82 Emory U.; MBA'87 U. of Pennsylvania-Wharton. Other funds currently managed: First Investors Global A, Fortis Global Growth A, Fortis Global Growth B.

History

1990	1991	1992	1993	1994	1995	1996	1997	1998	1999	2000	12-01	History
—	—	—	—	—	—	—	—	12.67	18.56	16.97	14.00	NAV
—	—	—	—	—	—	—	—	30.34*	47.68	–7.27	–17.33	Total Return %
—	—	—	—	—	—	—	—	9.06*	26.64	1.84	–5.46	+/– S&P 500
—	—	—	—	—	—	—	—	—	22.74	5.91	—	+/– MSCI World
—	—	—	—	—	—	—	—	0.00	0.00	0.00	0.00	Income Return %
—	—	—	—	—	—	—	—	30.34	47.68	–7.26	–17.33	Capital Return %
—	—	—	—	—	—	—	—	—	36	37	51	Total Rtn % Rank Cat
—	—	—	—	—	—	—	—	0.00	0.00	0.00	0.00	Income $
—	—	—	—	—	—	—	—	0.35	0.12	0.25	0.03	Capital Gains $
—	—	—	—	—	—	—	—	1.65	1.57	—	—	Expense Ratio %
—	—	—	—	—	—	—	—	–0.19	–0.15	—	—	Income Ratio %
—	—	—	—	—	—	—	—	—	204	—	—	Turnover Rate %
—	—	—	—	—	—	—	—	3.8	84.2	270.8	—	Net Assets $mil

Performance 12-31-01

	1st Qtr	2nd Qtr	3rd Qtr	4th Qtr	Total
1997	—	—	—	—	—
1998	—	—	—	30.34	30.34 *
1999	6.95	5.32	–0.56	31.85	47.68
2000	6.57	–3.22	–2.26	–8.02	–7.27
2001	–15.44	3.49	–15.92	12.36	–17.33

Trailing	Total Return%	+/– S&P 500	+/– MSCI World	% Rank All	% Rank Cat	Growth of $10,000
3 Mo	12.36	1.67	—	32	32	11,236
6 Mo	–5.53	0.02	—	65	33	9,447
1 Yr	–17.33	–5.46	—	76	51	8,267
3 Yr Avg	4.22	5.25	—	38	28	11,321
5 Yr Avg	—	—	—	—	—	—
10 Yr Avg	—	—	—	—	—	—
15 Yr Avg	—	—	—	—	—	—

Tax Analysis	Tax-Adj Ret%	%Rank Cat	%Pretax Ret	%Rank Cat
3 Yr Avg	3.92	24	92.8	14
5 Yr Avg	—	—	—	—
10 Yr Avg	—	—	—	—

Potential Capital Gain Exposure: –14% of assets

Risk Analysis

Time Period	Load-Adj Return %	Risk %Rank[1] All	Risk %Rank[1] Cat	Morningstar Return	Morningstar Risk	Morningstar Risk-Adj Rating
1 Yr	–21.88					
3 Yr	2.28	70	52	–0.55[2]	0.90	★★★★
5 Yr	—	—	—	—	—	
Incept	10.76	—	—	—	—	

Average Historical Rating (4 months): 4.0★s

[1]1=low, 100=high [2] T-Bill return substituted for category avg.

Category Rating (3 Yr)

1 2 3 4 5 — Worst ... Best

Return	Above Avg
Risk	Average

Other Measures	Standard Index S&P 500	Best Fit Index MSCIWorldxUS
Alpha	5.4	11.3
Beta	0.91	1.15
R-Squared	59	80
Standard Deviation		21.16
Mean		4.22
Sharpe Ratio		–0.04

Portfolio Analysis 06-30-01

Share change since 03-01 Total Stocks: 78	Sector	Country	% Assets
⊕ Microsoft	Technology	U.S.	2.77
Staples	Retail	U.S.	2.43
⊕ Bank of America	Financials	U.S.	2.28
⊕ DuPont De Nemours E.I.	Industrials	U.S.	2.15
⊖ Reed Intl	Services	United Kingdom	2.11
⊕ Citigroup	Financials	U.S.	2.10
☼ VeriSign	Technology	U.S.	2.03
⊕ USA Networks	Services	U.S.	1.99
ExxonMobil	Energy	U.S.	1.95
☼ Fannie Mae	Financials	U.S.	1.92
Lloyds TSB Grp	Financials	United Kingdom	1.89
⊕ Unilever (NY)	Staples	Netherlands	1.85
⊕ Waste Mgmt	Services	U.S.	1.76
⊕ Vivendi	Services	France	1.74
Samsung Electr 144A GDR	N/A	N/A	1.73
☼ COLT Telecom Grp	Services	United Kingdom	1.72
⊕ American Home Products	Health	U.S.	1.65
☼ American Intl Grp	Financials	U.S.	1.56
⊕ Bank One	Financials	U.S.	1.49
☼ IBM	Technology	U.S.	1.49

Current Investment Style

Style: Value Blnd Growth; Size: Large Med Small

	Stock Port Avg	Rel MSCI EAFE Current	Rel MSCI EAFE Hist	Rel Cat
Price/Earnings Ratio	33.7	1.30	—	1.22
Price/Cash Flow	19.3	1.50	—	1.17
Price/Book Ratio	5.3	1.52	—	1.15
3 Yr Earnings Growth	13.8	0.74	—	0.74
Med Mkt Cap $mil	41,873	1.5	—	1.74

Country Exposure 06-30-01	% assets
U.S.	56
United Kingdom	16
Germany	4
France	3
Netherlands	3

Hedging History: —

Regional Exposure 06-30-01	% assets
Europe	32
Pacific Rim	3
Latin America	0
Japan	1
U.S.	56
Other	1

Special Securities % assets 06-30-01	
Restricted/Illiquid Secs	2
Emerging-Markets Secs	3
Options/Futures/Warrants	No

Composition % assets 06-30-01			
Cash	4.5	Bonds	0.0
Stocks	95.5	Other	0.0

Sector Weightings	% of Stocks	Rel Cat	5-Year High	5-Year Low
Utilities	1.9	0.8	—	—
Energy	4.9	0.9	—	—
Financials	18.0	1.0	—	—
Industrials	12.0	1.1	—	—
Durables	3.3	0.8	—	—
Staples	5.5	0.7	—	—
Services	18.2	1.1	—	—
Retail	6.3	1.2	—	—
Health	9.1	0.7	—	—
Technology	20.9	1.4	—	—

Analysis by Brian Portnoy 11-12-01

Just by hanging in there, Hartford Global Leaders is proving its mettle.

Considering how lousy the global market for large-cap growth fare has been in 2001, this offering is putting in a decent showing. Though painful on an absolute basis, its 19.2% loss for the year to date through Nov. 9, 2001, is not only a tad better than the category norm, but it's also well above average for the subgroup of world-stock funds that focus on large-growth stocks.

The fund's median market cap is nearly double the category average and its P/E multiple is above the norm for even large-growth peers, so it has been fighting an uphill battle in a market paced by smaller value fare. While some of managers Andy Offit's picks, such as Colt Telecom Group, have hurt badly, solid stock-picking and a focus on global market leaders has generally been a source of buoyancy not only this year but in previous years as well. For example, the fund beat the category norm in both 1999 and 2000—markets that rewarded very different styles of investing. Thus, its longer-term marks are solid: Over the trailing three-year period, its 7.5% gain lands in the group's top quartile.

With virtually no exposure to the Japanese market, this fund is a good choice for investors seeking exposure to big-cap American and European market leaders. It's consistently focused on growth stocks, even more so lately since Offit argues that valuations, especially in telecom, are increasingly attractive. Ericsson and Korean telecom giant SK Telecom are recent acquisitions, for example. But as shown in the past, such as in early 2000, the fund will move into more defensive fare when the risks of holding higher-priced stocks become too steep. Overall, therefore, above-average gains with attention to risk management make this an attractive option.

Address:	P.O. Box 219054 Kansas City, MO 64121-9054 888-843-7824
Web Address:	www.thehartford.com
*Inception:	09-30-98
Advisor:	Hartford Inv. Financial Svcs
Subadvisor:	Wellington Mgmt.
NTF Plans:	Datalynx , Fidelity Inst.

Minimum Purchase:	$500	Add: $25	IRA: $250
Min Auto Inv Plan:	$500	Add: $25	
Sales Fees:	5.50%L, 0.10%B, 0.25%S		
Management Fee:	.85% mx./.70% mn.		
Actual Fees:	Mgt: 0.85%	Dist: 0.30%	
Expense Projections:	3Yr: $1032	5Yr: $1384	10Yr: $2373
Avg Brok Commission:	—	Income Distrib: Annually	
Total Cost (relative to category):	Average		

Heartland Value

Ticker	Load	NAV	Yield	Total Assets	Mstar Category
HRTVX	12b–1 only	$37.25	0.0%	$1,093.2 mil	Small Value

Prospectus Objective: Small Company

Heartland Value Fund seeks long-term capital appreciation.

The fund normally invests at least 65% of assets in equities of companies with market capitalizations of less than $750 million. It emphasizes securities that are underpriced relative to price/earnings, price/book, and price/cash-flow ratios; earnings growth, long-term debt/capital; dividend stability, and undervalued assets; among other factors. The fund may invest up to 5% of assets in both convertibles and warrants. It may also invest up to 15% of assets in foreign securities; this limitation does not include ADRs.

On Nov. 6, 1998, Heartland Small Cap Contrarian Fund merged into the fund.

Historical Profile

Return High
Risk Average
Rating ★★★★★ Highest

Investment Style
Equity
Average Stock %: 88% 86% 88% 100% 98% 96%

▼ Manager Change
∇ Partial Manager Change

Fund Performance vs. Category Average
■ Quarterly Fund Return +/– Category Average
— Category Baseline

Performance Quartile (within Category)

Portfolio Manager(s)

William J. Nasgovitz. Since 12-84. BA'66 U. of Wisconsin. Other funds currently managed: Heartland Value Plus, Heartland Select Value.

Eric J. Miller. Since 7-97. BA'75 Dartmouth C.; MBA'79 Amos Tuck School. Other fund currently managed: Heartland Select Value.

1990	1991	1992	1993	1994	1995	1996	1997	1998	1999	2000	12–01	History
11.32	16.06	20.41	23.22	22.72	27.95	31.65	33.87	29.29	36.50	32.98	37.25	NAV
–17.09	49.35	42.48	18.77	1.71	29.80	20.99	23.19	–11.46	25.01	2.03	29.45	Total Return %
–13.97	18.87	34.86	8.71	0.40	–7.73	–1.96	–10.16	–40.04	3.97	11.13	41.33	+/– S&P 500
4.69	7.65	13.34	–5.08	3.26	4.05	–0.38	–8.50	–5.03	26.49	–20.78	15.43	+/– Russell 2000 V
0.00	0.00	0.00	0.00	0.00	0.57	0.23	0.55	0.17	0.00	0.00	0.00	Income Return %
–17.09	49.35	42.48	18.77	1.71	29.23	20.75	22.64	–11.63	25.01	2.03	29.45	Capital Return %
77	8	1	44	29	18	74	84	76	14	92	9	Total Rtn % Rank Cat
0.00	0.00	0.00	0.00	0.00	0.13	0.07	0.17	0.06	0.00	0.00	0.00	Income $
0.14	0.85	2.47	1.02	0.88	1.40	2.08	4.87	0.63	0.10	4.03	5.19	Capital Gains $
1.70	1.70	1.50	1.51	1.39	1.29	1.23	1.12	1.15	1.34	1.22	—	Expense Ratio %
0.10	–0.50	–0.50	–0.71	–0.52	0.61	0.22	0.49	0.22	–0.70	–0.46	—	Income Ratio %
76	79	76	51	35	31	31	55	36	23	48	—	Turnover Rate %
19.9	29.9	49.2	186.5	338.9	1,190.9	1,627.0	2,126.7	1,545.5	1,195.5	895.6	1,093.2	Net Assets $mil

Performance 12-31-01

	1st Qtr	2nd Qtr	3rd Qtr	4th Qtr	Total
1997	0.32	13.70	14.76	–5.89	23.19
1998	9.65	–5.25	–18.57	4.64	–11.46
1999	–8.26	21.73	–7.46	20.96	25.01
2000	–2.02	–4.77	8.14	1.12	2.03
2001	8.44	17.23	–14.75	19.45	29.45

Trailing	Total Return%	+/– S&P 500	+/– Russ 2000V	% Rank All	% Rank Cat	Growth of $10,000
3 Mo	19.45	8.76	2.73	15	29	11,945
6 Mo	1.83	7.39	0.68	25	54	10,183
1 Yr	29.45	41.33	15.43	1	9	12,945
3 Yr Avg	18.19	19.22	6.87	3	16	16,511
5 Yr Avg	12.49	1.79	1.29	9	37	18,009
10 Yr Avg	17.15	4.22	2.04	2	10	48,676
15 Yr Avg	14.35	0.61	1.51	9	15	74,725

Tax Analysis	Tax-Adj Ret%	%Rank Cat	%Pretax Ret	%Rank Cat
3 Yr Avg	15.93	20	87.6	65
5 Yr Avg	10.46	41	83.8	64
10 Yr Avg	14.96	3	87.2	24

Potential Capital Gain Exposure: 32% of assets

Risk Analysis

Time Period	Load-Adj Return %	Risk %Rank[1] All	Risk %Rank[1] Cat	Morningstar Return	Morningstar Risk	Morningstar Risk-Adj Rating
1 Yr	28.16					
3 Yr	17.80	46	38	3.18[2]	0.65	★★★★★
5 Yr	12.26	59	45	1.88[2]	0.81	★★★★
10 Yr	17.03	65	57	2.38	0.84	★★★★★

Average Historical Rating (169 months): 3.4★s

[1]1=low, 100=high [2] T-Bill return substituted for category avg.

Category Rating (3 Yr)

1 2 3 4 5
Worst Best

Return Above Avg
Risk Average

Other Measures	Standard Index S&P 500	Best Fit Index Russ 2000
Alpha	18.2	11.8
Beta	0.66	0.64
R-Squared	31	57
Standard Deviation		23.46
Mean		18.19
Sharpe Ratio		0.64

Portfolio Analysis 10-31-01

Share change since 08–01 Total Stocks: 184	Sector	PE	YTD Ret%	% Assets
ICN Pharmaceuticals	Health	NMF	10.39	4.54
⊕ US Oncology	Health	—	19.44	2.32
URS	Services	11.8	86.61	2.17
NABI	Health	4.3	123.10	2.15
Presidential Life	Financials	18.9	40.58	1.92
⊖ Henry Schein	Health	22.0	6.95	1.86
Republic Svcs Cl A	Services	15.6	16.19	1.81
⊕ Humana	Financials	18.1	–22.60	1.78
Associated Banc-Corp	Financials	13.6	20.35	1.67
InterDigital Comms	Technology	—	79.43	1.50
⊕ Aphton	Health	—	–18.80	1.50
Patterson-UTI Energy	Energy	10.2	–37.40	1.39
Wackenhut Corrections	Services	15.6	87.93	1.24
⊕ Navigant Consult	Services	—	44.24	1.24
⊖ Fukuda Denshi	Technology	10.3	—	1.23
Lufkin Inds	Industrials	9.9	53.62	1.19
BTG	Technology	—	121.40	1.16
Republic Bancorp	Financials	16.3	44.54	1.15
M/I Schottenstein Homes	Industrials	7.4	106.80	1.12
⊕ Wackenhut Cl B	Services	—	—	1.06
⊕ Cinar Cl A	Services	—	–68.20	1.03
⊖ AMERCO	Services	—	–4.10	1.01
⊖ LifeCore Biomedical	Health	—	140.80	1.00
Regis	Services	19.5	78.94	0.97
Orthologic	Health	—	70.09	0.97

Current Investment Style

Style: Value Blnd Growth; Size: Large Med Small

	Stock Port Avg	Relative S&P 500 Current	Relative S&P 500 Hist	Rel Cat
Price/Earnings Ratio	19.5	0.63	0.56	0.90
Price/Book Ratio	2.2	0.39	0.26	0.92
Price/Cash Flow	12.6	0.70	0.55	0.99
3 Yr Earnings Growth	5.7	0.39	0.49	0.49
1 Yr Earnings Est%	5.7[1]	—	—	–1.43
Med Mkt Cap $mil	362	0.0	0.0	0.42

[1]figure is based on 50% or less of stocks

Analysis by Laura Pavlenko Lutton 12-31-01

Despite its recent strength, Heartland Value Fund isn't quite a compelling choice.

Small-value funds have had a great year in 2001, and in absolute terms, the same is true for this fund. Holdings such as engineering-services firm URS, and plasma-center operator NABI helped drive the fund to a 29.5% return in 2001. However, a good deal of the fund's strength came from its heavy emphasis on micro-cap stocks—by far the best-performing area of the market in 2001. Indeed, its 2001 return ranks in the small-value category's top decile, but it's somewhat less impressive relative to other micro-cap offerings in the category.

Further, the fund's recent performance doesn't tell the whole story. After putting up stellar numbers in the early 1990s, the fund stumbled in the latter half of the decade and fared badly in 2000. Part of the problem was asset bloat: Money flooded into the fund in 1995, tripling its size to $1.2 billion. Bulk is a liability for small-cap funds because liquidity constraints can force managers to hold positions they would rather not, impairing the ability to take advantage of buying opportunities. The performance disparity is telling: The fund finished in the category's top half in every year but one from 1990 through 1995. From 1996 through 2000, the fund ranked in the category's worst third in four of five years.

Manager Bill Nasgovitz is a seasoned veteran who has been picking stocks for longer than most small-value funds have been around. However, he has a considerable challenge to maneuver this fund successfully among the tiny companies he favors. Thus far, he hasn't met it convincingly. We're encouraged by the fund's recent results, but not enough to wholeheartedly recommend it.

Special Securities % assets 10-31-01	
Restricted/Illiquid Secs	0
Emerging-Markets Secs	Trace
Options/Futures/Warrants	No

Composition % assets 10-31-01	
Cash	4.1
Stocks*	95.7
Bonds	0.2
Other	0.0
*Foreign (% stocks)	8.5

Market Cap	
Giant	0.0
Large	0.0
Medium	16.3
Small	43.0
Micro	40.7

Sector Weightings	% of Stocks	Rel S&P	5-Year High	5-Year Low
Utilities	0.9	0.3	3	0
Energy	6.7	0.9	11	2
Financials	16.1	0.9	31	7
Industrials	11.6	1.0	24	12
Durables	4.2	2.7	5	2
Staples	3.3	0.4	8	1
Services	20.4	1.9	26	11
Retail	1.8	0.3	16	2
Health	24.1	1.6	34	7
Technology	11.0	0.6	24	2

Address: 789 N. Water Street, Milwaukee, WI 53202, 414–347–7777 / 800–432–7856
Web Address: www.heartlandfunds.com

Inception: 12-28-84
Advisor: Heartland Adv.
Subadvisor: None
NTF Plans: Fidelity , Fidelity Inst.

Minimum Purchase: $5000 Add: $100 IRA: $500
Min Auto Inv Plan: $1000 Add: $50
Sales Fees: 0.25%B, 1.00%R
Management Fee: .75%
Actual Fees: Mgt: 0.75% Dist: 0.25%
Expense Projections: 3Yr: $425 5Yr: $734 10Yr: $1613
Avg Brok Commission: — Income Distrib: Annually
Total Cost (relative to category): Below Avg

Homestead Value

Ticker	Load	NAV	Yield	Total Assets	Mstar Category
HOVLX	None	$25.50	1.2%	$320.0 mil	Mid–Cap Value

Prospectus Objective: Growth and Income

Homestead Value Fund seeks long-term growth of capital and income; current income is secondary.

The fund normally invests at least 80% of assets in common stocks. It may invest the balance in other equity securities and high-grade debt. The fund primarily selects established companies that may be undervalued or overlooked (i.e., selling at a discount to their fundamental value). This screening process looks at earnings potential, price/earnings ratios, dividend income, competitive advantages, and price/book ratios. The fund may invest up to 10% of assets in ADRs.

Historical Profile

Return	Above Avg
Risk	Below Avg
Rating	★★★★ Above Avg

Investment Style
Equity
Average Stock %: 85% 89% 92% 94% 95% 97% 92%

▼ Manager Change
▽ Partial Manager Change

Fund Performance vs. Category Average
■ Quarterly Fund Return +/– Category Average
— Category Baseline

Performance Quartile (within Category)

Portfolio Manager(s)

Stuart E. Teach, CFA. Since 11-90. BS'68 Ohio State U.; MBA'72 Miami U. Other fund currently managed: Homestead Small Company Stock.

Peter R. Morris. Since 11-90. BA'71 Coe C. Other fund currently managed: Homestead Small Company Stock.

1990	1991	1992	1993	1994	1995	1996	1997	1998	1999	2000	12-01	History
10.15	11.48	12.49	14.54	14.50	18.44	20.99	25.50	26.50	23.53	25.38	25.50	NAV
0.59*	17.16	11.66	18.83	2.50	33.78	17.94	26.70	8.31	–3.21	9.64	5.90	Total Return %
–3.58*	–13.32	4.04	8.77	1.18	–3.75	–5.00	–6.65	–20.26	–24.25	18.75	17.78	+/– S&P 500
—	–20.76	–10.02	3.20	4.63	–1.15	–2.32	–7.66	3.23	–3.10	–9.54	3.57	+/– Russ Midcap Val
0.39	3.87	2.15	1.79	1.99	2.82	2.10	1.76	1.57	1.56	1.65	1.30	Income Return %
0.20	13.29	9.51	17.03	0.51	30.97	15.84	24.94	6.74	–4.77	7.99	4.60	Capital Return %
—	90	70	56	25	30	69	49	30	88	78	45	Total Rtn % Rank Cat
0.04	0.39	0.25	0.22	0.29	0.41	0.39	0.37	0.40	0.41	0.39	0.33	Income $
0.00	0.01	0.08	0.07	0.11	0.53	0.36	0.71	0.72	1.74	0.00	1.05	Capital Gains $
1.25	1.25	1.25	1.25	1.15	0.84	0.73	0.79	0.72	0.74	0.85	—	Expense Ratio %
6.09	3.80	2.33	1.92	2.19	2.50	2.08	1.59	1.52	1.47	1.58	—	Income Ratio %
—	26	5	2	4	10	5	6	10	17	18	—	Turnover Rate %
0.0	10.2	19.4	52.8	90.1	147.6	232.4	367.0	445.6	375.7	335.2	320.0	Net Assets $mil

Performance 12-31-01

	1st Qtr	2nd Qtr	3rd Qtr	4th Qtr	Total
1997	3.05	13.45	9.65	–1.16	26.70
1998	10.82	–1.27	–11.58	11.96	8.31
1999	0.49	14.71	–14.66	–1.60	–3.21
2000	–0.89	–4.25	5.83	9.18	9.64
2001	–1.30	6.30	–8.92	10.83	5.91

Trailing	Total Return%	+/– S&P 500	+/– Russ Midcap Val	% Rank All	% Rank Cat	Growth of $10,000
3 Mo	10.83	0.14	–1.21	38	72	11,083
6 Mo	0.94	6.50	1.85	34	35	10,094
1 Yr	5.90	17.78	3.57	19	45	10,590
3 Yr Avg	3.97	5.00	–2.84	41	88	11,239
5 Yr Avg	9.05	–1.65	–2.41	24	72	15,424
10 Yr Avg	12.71	–0.21	–1.70	14	63	33,098
15 Yr Avg	—	—	—	—	—	—

Tax Analysis	Tax-Adj Ret%	%Rank Cat	%Pretax Ret	%Rank Cat
3 Yr Avg	2.51	90	63.3	89
5 Yr Avg	7.65	66	84.5	24
10 Yr Avg	11.38	58	89.5	4

Potential Capital Gain Exposure: 30% of assets

Risk Analysis

Time Period	Load-Adj Return %	Risk %Rank[1] All	Risk %Rank[1] Cat	Morningstar Return	Morningstar Risk	Morningstar Risk-Adj Rating
1 Yr	5.90					
3 Yr	3.97	52	64	–0.20[2]	0.73	★★★
5 Yr	9.05	52	38	0.95[2]	0.72	★★★
10 Yr	12.71	57	38	1.25	0.73	★★★★

Average Historical Rating (98 months): 3.7★s

[1]1=low, 100=high [2] T-Bill return substituted for category avg.

Category Rating (3 Yr)

1 2 3 4 5
Worst Best

Return	Below Avg
Risk	Average

Other Measures	Standard Index S&P 500	Best Fit Index SPMid400
Alpha	2.9	–3.2
Beta	0.56	0.53
R–Squared	33	39

Standard Deviation	17.10
Mean	3.97
Sharpe Ratio	–0.07

Analysis by Peter Di Teresa 09-25-01

Homestead Value Fund goes its own way, but that has proved a mixed blessing.

Comanagers Stuart Teach and Peter Morris characterize themselves as traditional value investors. Indeed, they scan out-of-favor sectors and stocks for profitable companies with appealing valuations. They particularly like companies they think Wall Street has misunderstood. Eastman Kodak and Office Depot are two such firms. The managers think that the Street hasn't given due credit for how the companies are positioning for the future.

That style, while not unusual, has led to atypical results. Top holdings such as Southwest Airlines and natural-gas firm Questar appear in few peers' portfolios. And as indicated by its R-Squared of 31 versus the S&P 500 index, the fund has lower correlation with large caps than does its typical peer, which has an R-Squared of 43 with the index. The fund has equally low correlation with mid-cap indexes. Overall, it can add greater variety to a portfolio than can many other mid-cap value offerings.

The catch has been that the fund's returns haven't been compelling. The fund has been solid lately—its returns for the year to date through Sept. 21, 2001, are in the category's best 39%. But the fund hasn't had enough stretches like that to deliver competitive long-term returns—all of its longer-term returns are well below the average. Poor relative returns in 1999 and 2000 didn't help as the fund was first held back by minimal exposure to growth issues, but was unable to capitalize on that in 2000 as a number of holdings disappointed. Yet the fund's longer-term returns were subpar prior to those years.

We love a fund that sets its own course, but we need to see its recent strength continue to recommend this offering.

Portfolio Analysis 10-31-01

Share change since 09-00 Total Stocks: 39	Sector	PE	YTD Ret%	% Assets
Wendy's Intl	Services	18.9	12.16	4.23
⊕ Genuine Parts	Durables	16.8	45.48	4.23
⊕ Bank of America	Financials	16.7	42.73	3.93
⊕ May Dept Stores	Retail	15.2	15.97	3.79
⊖ Bemis	Industrials	19.4	50.19	3.75
⊕ Southwest Air	Services	25.0	–17.20	3.62
⊕ Abbott Labs	Health	51.6	17.08	3.39
⊕ J.P. Morgan Chase & Co.	Financials	27.8	–17.40	3.31
⊖ Allstate	Financials	17.1	–21.00	3.28
☼ Transocean Sedco Forex	Energy	58.3	–26.20	3.12
Citigroup	Financials	20.0	0.03	3.11
BP PLC ADR	Energy	14.4	–0.90	2.88
American Home Products	Health	—	–1.91	2.69
☼ Phillips Petro	Energy	7.1	8.56	2.65
⊕ BellSouth	Services	24.9	–5.09	2.49
☼ Schering–Plough	Health	22.2	–35.90	2.48
Chubb I	Financials	48.3	–18.60	2.46
⊕ Maytag	Durables	19.8	–1.75	2.46
⊖ Avery Dennison	Industrials	22.1	5.37	2.45
☼ ChevronTexaco	N/A	—	—	2.45
⊖ Questar	Energy	11.8	–14.40	2.43
⊕ Longs Drug Stores	Retail	26.0	–0.93	2.33
⊖ Ruddick	Retail	—	43.13	2.32
⊖ Hughes Sply	Industrials	24.7	75.09	1.97
⊕ Kmart	Retail	—	2.77	1.95

Current Investment Style

Style: Value Blnd Growth; Size: Large Med Small

	Stock Port Avg	Relative S&P 500 Current	Relative S&P 500 Hist	Rel Cat
Price/Earnings Ratio	24.0	0.78	0.64	1.02
Price/Book Ratio	3.8	0.66	0.42	1.24
Price/Cash Flow	11.5	0.64	0.55	0.92
3 Yr Earnings Growth	8.0	0.55	0.58	0.68
1 Yr Earnings Est%	–5.3	3.01	—	0.87
Med Mkt Cap $mil	10,398	0.2	0.1	1.46

Special Securities % assets 10-31-01	
Restricted/Illiquid Secs	0
Emerging–Markets Secs	0
Options/Futures/Warrants	No

Composition % assets 10-31-01	
Cash	7.6
Stocks*	92.1
Bonds	0.0
Other	0.3
*Foreign (% stocks)	3.1

Market Cap	
Giant	28.3
Large	22.9
Medium	36.9
Small	11.8
Micro	0.2

Sector Weightings	% of Stocks	Rel S&P	5-Year High	5-Year Low
Utilities	0.0	0.0	4	0
Energy	15.9	2.2	17	8
Financials	22.1	1.2	25	11
Industrials	15.6	1.4	38	16
Durables	7.5	4.8	13	4
Staples	1.9	0.2	3	0
Services	13.8	1.3	16	10
Retail	13.7	2.0	14	8
Health	9.5	0.6	10	2
Technology	0.0	0.0	7	0

Address:	4301 Wilson Boulevard Arlington, VA 22203 800–258–3030
Web Address:	www.nreca.org
*Inception:	11-19-90
Advisor:	RE Advisers
Subadvisor:	None
NTF Plans:	Waterhouse

Minimum Purchase:	$500	Add: None IRA: $200
Min Auto Inv Plan:	None	Add: None
Sales Fees:	No–load	
Management Fee:	.65% mx./.40% mn.	
Actual Fees:	Mgt: 0.55%	Dist: —
Expense Projections:	3Yr: $234	5Yr: $408 10Yr: $911
Avg Brok Commission:	—	Income Distrib: Semi–Ann.
Total Cost (relative to category):	Low	

Wayne Hummer Growth

Ticker	Load	NAV	Yield	Total Assets	Mstar Category
WHGRX	2.00%	$36.56	0.2%	$156.4 mil	Large Growth

Prospectus Objective: Growth

Wayne Hummer Growth Fund seeks long-term capital growth; current income is secondary.

The fund invests primarily in common stocks of domestic corporations. It may invest to a limited extent in investment-grade preferred stocks, bonds, or convertible debentures when such securities are believed to offer good opportunities for capital growth. For defensive purposes, the fund may invest in fixed-income securities or retain cash. It usually intends to hold securities at least six months.

Historical Profile

Return: Above Avg
Risk: Below Avg
Rating: ★★★★ Above Avg

Investment Style: Equity
Average Stock %: 99% 98% 97% 98% 98% 96%

▼ Manager Change
▽ Partial Manager Change

Fund Performance vs. Category Average
Quarterly Fund Return +/– Category Average
— Category Baseline

Performance Quartile (within Category)

Portfolio Manager(s)

Thomas J. Rowland, CFA. Since 3-87. BBA'67 U. of Notre Dame; MBA'72 Northwestern U. Other fund currently managed: Wayne Hummer CorePortfolio.

1990	1991	1992	1993	1994	1995	1996	1997	1998	1999	2000	12-01	History
16.00	20.02	21.64	22.06	21.34	25.81	27.50	32.80	36.81	45.97	40.09	36.56	NAV
5.01	28.86	10.36	3.26	–0.91	24.81	11.87	30.27	17.55	38.04	–3.73	–6.78	Total Return %
8.13	–1.63	2.74	–6.80	–2.22	–12.72	–11.08	–3.08	–11.02	17.00	5.37	5.09	+/– S&P 500
3.64	–10.55	6.47	3.33	–5.76	–13.84	–13.65	–3.47	–27.55	8.36	20.80	13.71	+/– Russ Top 200 Grt
2.75	2.44	1.46	0.98	1.39	1.46	1.55	1.28	0.50	0.19	0.04	0.15	Income Return %
2.26	26.42	8.90	2.28	–2.30	23.35	10.31	28.99	17.05	37.85	–3.77	–6.93	Capital Return %
6	83	19	79	36	88	91	27	90	43	13	3	Total Rtn % Rank Cat
0.44	0.39	0.29	0.21	0.31	0.31	0.39	0.34	0.16	0.07	0.02	0.06	Income $
0.75	0.17	0.14	0.07	0.21	0.48	0.90	2.37	1.51	3.99	4.17	0.74	Capital Gains $
1.50	1.36	1.23	1.12	1.07	1.07	1.06	0.99	0.96	0.94	0.95	0.91	Expense Ratio %
1.91	2.87	2.01	1.41	1.33	1.44	1.29	0.97	0.58	0.41	0.15	0.13	Income Ratio %
3	13	3	1	2	3	6	9	7	12	10	9	Turnover Rate %
26.4	50.3	79.2	99.0	87.7	100.2	104.6	128.5	128.9	183.4	170.1	156.4	Net Assets $mil

Performance 12-31-01

	1st Qtr	2nd Qtr	3rd Qtr	4th Qtr	Total
1997	1.93	14.54	9.21	2.17	30.27
1998	10.06	0.03	–12.28	21.72	17.55
1999	–0.41	12.08	–5.83	31.33	38.04
2000	1.87	–5.48	0.97	–0.98	–3.73
2001	–10.30	5.73	–11.97	11.65	–6.78

Trailing	Total Return%	+/– S&P 500	+/– Russ Top 200 Grth	% Rank All	% Rank Cat	Growth of $10,000
3 Mo	11.65	0.97	–1.20	34	74	11,165
6 Mo	–1.71	3.84	5.28	46	4	9,829
1 Yr	–6.78	5.09	13.71	55	3	9,322
3 Yr Avg	7.40	8.42	15.42	16	4	12,388
5 Yr Avg	13.66	2.96	5.07	6	11	18,969
10 Yr Avg	11.58	–1.35	0.50	22	24	29,908
15 Yr Avg	12.56	–1.17	–0.81	21	38	59,017

Tax Analysis	Tax-Adj Ret%	%Rank Cat	%Pretax Ret	%Rank Cat
3 Yr Avg	5.55	4	75.1	51
5 Yr Avg	11.76	11	86.1	29
10 Yr Avg	10.14	20	87.6	11

Potential Capital Gain Exposure: 48% of assets

Risk Analysis

Time Period	Load-Adj Return %	Risk %Rank[1] All	Risk %Rank[1] Cat	Morningstar Return	Morningstar Risk	Morningstar Risk-Adj Rating
1 Yr	–8.65					
3 Yr	6.68	55	3	0.37[2]	0.77	★★★★
5 Yr	13.20	55	3	2.09[2]	0.76	★★★★
10 Yr	11.35	60	1	0.98	0.78	★★★

Average Historical Rating (181 months): 3.3★s

[1]1=low, 100=high [2] T-Bill return substituted for category avg.

Category Rating (3 Yr)

1 2 3 4 5 — Worst ... Best

Return: High
Risk: Low

Other Measures	Standard Index S&P 500	Best Fit Index MSCIACWdFr
Alpha	8.3	12.7
Beta	0.89	1.01
R-Squared	63	72

Standard Deviation	20.39
Mean	7.40
Sharpe Ratio	0.14

Portfolio Analysis 09-30-01

Share change since 06-01 Total Stocks: 44

	Sector	PE	YTD Ret%	% Assets
Cardinal Health	Health	35.1	–2.51	7.86
Northern Tr	Financials	27.4	–25.40	5.20
Qualcomm	Technology	—	–38.50	5.05
Patterson Dental	Health	33.0	20.83	3.92
Illinois Tool Works	Industrials	25.4	15.31	3.83
⊕ H & R Block	Services	25.5	120.00	3.28
McCormick	Staples	20.2	18.62	3.24
Applied Matls	Technology	66.8	5.01	3.22
Avery Dennison	Industrials	22.1	5.37	3.18
Fastenal	Retail	33.2	21.25	2.83
Old Republic Intl	Financials	9.7	–10.50	2.78
Interpublic Grp	Services	—	–29.80	2.67
Cincinnati Finl	Financials	53.0	–1.43	2.65
⊕ Apogent Tech	Health	29.0	25.85	2.37
CVS	Retail	16.2	–50.30	2.35
⊕ Health Mgmt Assoc	Health	24.2	–11.30	2.21
Cooper	Health	20.5	25.61	2.09
Concord EFS	Financials	86.3	49.21	2.08
Aon	Financials	46.1	6.32	2.01
Sonoco Products	Industrials	25.8	27.00	1.83
⊕ Fiserv	Services	40.7	33.82	1.81
Kronos	Technology	56.7	134.50	1.74
⊖ PepsiCo	Staples	31.4	–0.54	1.72
Cintas	Services	36.1	–9.33	1.71
Emerson Elec	Industrials	23.8	–25.60	1.67

Current Investment Style

Style: Value Blnd Growth; Size: Large Med Small

	Stock Port Avg	Relative S&P 500 Current	Relative S&P 500 Hist	Rel Cat
Price/Earnings Ratio	32.8	1.06	1.02	0.92
Price/Book Ratio	4.7	0.82	0.84	0.74
Price/Cash Flow	21.4	1.19	1.06	0.94
3 Yr Earnings Growth	13.9	0.95	1.07	0.64
1 Yr Earnings Est%	–2.7	1.52	—	–0.90
Med Mkt Cap $mil	7,141	0.1	0.2	0.15

Analysis by Peter Di Teresa 11-13-01

Its transformation has been successful so far, but it's hard to know what to do with this fund.

Back in 1999, Wayne Hummer Growth Fund manager Tom Rowland decided to put a growth spin on what had been a blend offering with little exposure to growth sectors. Paying greater attention to growth issues paid off, as the fund posted a 38% gain in 1999, its best absolute return in years. For that transitional year, the fund beat most of its old mid-blend competitors and its new large-growth peers. (The portfolio edged into large-cap territory because many holdings made substantial gains.)

While opening up the fund to more growth investments, Rowland didn't alter his basic strategy. He focuses on stocks trading at reasonable price multiples that boast high returns on equity and strong balance sheets. Thus, even in 1999's heady market, this fund didn't get caught up in the bidding for overheated stocks with doubtful fundamentals.

That relative conservatism has been a source of strength in this bear market. While the large-growth category fell 14.8% last year, this fund suffered a relatively mild 3.7% drop. Its 13% loss for the year to date through Nov. 9, 2001, is less than half the average loss for the category. The fund has gotten a boost from an eclectic mix of picks, such as dental distributor Patterson Dental, H&R Block, and seasonings company McCormick.

As that mix suggests, this fund doesn't play a clear role. It holds substantial mid- and large-cap positions, so it won't fill either slot. Investors who find it an appealing growth pick based on its recent performance may be surprised in an up market. When growth revived in April and October of 2001, this fund lagged the competition significantly.

That said, investors who have made room for this offering have been rewarded with both good returns and moderate volatility.

Special Securities % assets 09-30-01

Restricted/Illiquid Secs	0
Emerging–Markets Secs	0
Options/Futures/Warrants	No

Composition % assets 09-30-01	
Cash	4.4
Stocks*	95.7
Bonds	0.0
Other	0.0
*Foreign (% stocks)	0.5

Market Cap	
Giant	1.8
Large	40.5
Medium	48.2
Small	9.4
Micro	0.0

Sector Weightings	% of Stocks	Rel S&P	5-Year High	5-Year Low
Utilities	0.0	0.0	3	0
Energy	1.5	0.2	7	1
Financials	15.4	0.9	19	9
Industrials	16.0	1.4	45	14
Durables	1.8	1.1	5	1
Staples	5.2	0.7	13	4
Services	14.7	1.4	19	7
Retail	7.8	1.2	12	1
Health	21.6	1.5	22	4
Technology	16.0	0.9	39	2

Address:	300 S. Wacker Drive 14th Floor Chicago, IL 60606 800–621–4477 / 312–431–1700
Web Address:	www.whummer.com
Inception:	12-30-83
Advisor:	Wayne Hummer Mgmt.
Subadvisor:	None
NTF Plans:	Waterhouse

Minimum Purchase:	$1000	Add: $500	IRA: $500
Min Auto Inv Plan:	$1000	Add: $100	
Sales Fees:	2.00%L		
Management Fee:	.80% mx./.50% mn.		
Actual Fees:	Mgt: 0.76%	Dist: —	
Expense Projections:	3Yr: $30	5Yr: $52	10Yr: $115
Avg Brok Commission:	—	Income Distrib: Quarterly	
Total Cost (relative to category):		Low	

ICAP Equity

Ticker	Load	NAV	Yield	Total Assets	Mstar Category
ICAEX	None	$43.01	0.9%	$1,189.5 mil	Large Value

Prospectus Objective: Growth and Income

ICAP Equity Portfolio seeks total return with moderate risk.

Management attempts to achieve a total return greater than the S&P 500 with an equal or lesser degree of risk by investing in domestic equities with market capitalizations of at least $500 million. Investments are decided by interest rates, inflation, business cycle outlook, and strategic economic and/or industry themes. Management employs computer models to search for issuers possessing best relative value based on P/E projections and earnings momentum. The advisor establishes an upside price target and a downside risk potential for each investment.

Historical Profile
Return Above Avg
Risk Below Avg
Rating ★★★★ Above Avg

Investment Style
Equity
Average Stock %: 94% (1995), 98% (1996), 95% (1997), 92% (1998), 94% (1999), 94% (2000), 95% (12-01)

▼ Manager Change
▽ Partial Manager Change

Fund Performance vs. Category Average
■ Quarterly Fund Return +/– Category Average
— Category Baseline

Performance Quartile (within Category)

Portfolio Manager(s)

Robert H. Lyon. Since 12-94. BA Northwestern U.; MBA U. of Pennsylvania-Wharton. Other funds currently managed: ICAP Discretionary Equity, HSBC Investor Equity A, Nuveen Large-Cap Value A.

Donald D. Niemann, CFA. Since 12-94. BA Princeton U.; MBA Harvard U. Other funds currently managed: ICAP Discretionary Equity, Nuveen Large-Cap Value A, Nuveen Large-Cap Value B.

Jerrold K. Senser, CFA. Since 12-94. BA U. of Michigan; MBA U. of Chicago. Other funds currently managed: ICAP Discretionary Equity, Nuveen Large-Cap Value A, Nuveen Large-Cap Value B.

History

1990	1991	1992	1993	1994	1995	1996	1997	1998	1999	2000	12-01	History
—	—	—	—	20.00	26.03	31.16	35.12	38.63	43.14	43.66	43.01	NAV
—	—	—	—	—	38.85	26.26	29.09	11.42	16.28	7.86	–0.61	Total Return %
—	—	—	—	—	1.32	3.31	–4.27	–17.15	–4.76	16.96	11.27	+/– S&P 500
—	—	—	—	—	–1.18	3.95	–6.40	–9.82	5.33	5.55	8.18	+/– Russ Top 200 Val
—	—	—	—	—	1.40	1.15	1.22	1.43	1.33	1.13	0.85	Income Return %
—	—	—	—	—	37.45	25.11	27.86	9.99	14.95	6.73	–1.46	Capital Return %
—	—	—	—	—	7	13	33	60	16	45	22	Total Rtn % Rank Cat
—	—	—	—	0.00	0.28	0.30	0.38	0.50	0.51	0.48	0.37	Income $
—	—	—	—	0.00	1.42	1.37	4.60	0.00	1.24	2.35	0.00	Capital Gains $
—	—	—	—	—	0.80	0.80	0.80	0.80	0.80	0.80	—	Expense Ratio %
—	—	—	—	—	1.49	1.15	1.06	1.39	1.22	1.13	—	Income Ratio %
—	—	—	—	—	105	125	121	133	118	116	—	Turnover Rate %
—	—	—	—	—	46.8	149.1	371.4	717.3	959.5	1,050.2	1,189.5	Net Assets $mil

Performance 12-31-01

	1st Qtr	2nd Qtr	3rd Qtr	4th Qtr	Total
1997	3.82	17.23	8.60	–2.34	29.09
1998	12.06	3.45	–17.48	16.48	11.42
1999	4.11	12.33	–9.72	10.13	16.28
2000	1.34	–4.85	5.79	5.74	7.86
2001	–3.77	3.73	–10.18	10.85	–0.61

Trailing	Total Return%	+/– S&P 500	+/– Russ Top 200 Val	% Rank All	% Rank Cat	Growth of $10,000
3 Mo	10.85	0.16	5.33	38	26	11,085
6 Mo	–0.43	5.12	5.34	40	10	9,957
1 Yr	–0.61	11.27	8.18	43	22	9,939
3 Yr Avg	7.62	8.65	6.46	15	10	12,466
5 Yr Avg	12.39	1.69	1.18	9	13	17,929
10 Yr Avg	—	—	—	—	—	—
15 Yr Avg	—	—	—	—	—	—

Tax Analysis	Tax-Adj Ret%	%Rank Cat	%Pretax Ret	%Rank Cat
3 Yr Avg	6.50	7	85.3	17
5 Yr Avg	10.95	10	88.4	12
10 Yr Avg	—	—	—	—

Potential Capital Gain Exposure: 15% of assets

Risk Analysis

Time Period	Load-Adj Return %	Risk %Rank[1] All	Risk %Rank[1] Cat	Morningstar Return	Morningstar Risk	Morningstar Risk-Adj Rating
1 Yr	–0.61					
3 Yr	7.62	45	10	0.58[2]	0.63	★★★★
5 Yr	12.39	51	20	1.85[2]	0.71	★★★★
Incept	17.76	—	—	—	—	

Average Historical Rating (49 months): 4.1★s

[1] 1=low, 100=high [2] T-Bill return substituted for category avg.

Category Rating (3 Yr)

1 Worst — 5 Best (rating: 5)

Return High
Risk Low

Other Measures	Standard Index S&P 500	Best Fit Index S&P 500
Alpha	6.4	6.4
Beta	0.63	0.63
R-Squared	64	64
Standard Deviation		14.34
Mean		7.62
Sharpe Ratio		0.21

Analysis by Paul Herbert 12-09-01

ICAP Equity Fund continues to be one of the best large-value offerings around.

It's not easy to catch ICAP Equity's managers sitting on their hands. Following the Sept. 11 terrorist attacks, manager Rob Lyon and his team added to their holdings in beaten-down stocks such as Target and News Corporation. More recently, they've picked up several beaten-down names, including travel-services firm Cendant as a play on the recovery of the travel sector, and personal-products maker Estee Lauder. They have also sold off their stake in Allstate because they're skeptical about the health of the company's homeowners' insurance unit.

Interested investors will have to be comfortable with high turnover, as the fund's typically greater-than-100% turnover rate suggests, but the fund hasn't suffered for this frequent trading. Lyon and his crew seek cheap stocks with catalysts for future earnings growth, and they aren't shy about selling off a stock when they think its longer-term prospects have dimmed. Their willingness to cut stocks loose hasn't hurt the fund's after-tax returns or its tax efficiency over the trailing three- and five-year periods, which rank in the large-value category's top quintile.

Great returns for taxable and nontaxable investors aren't the only reasons to own the fund, though. It has also shown the ability to post category-beating returns in years when value investing is out of favor, such as 1999, thanks to the team's willingness to look for cheap stocks in growth areas such as technology and telecom. In addition, the managers have tons of experience, both with ICAP and elsewhere. Finally, expenses are low at 80 basis points, and ICAP recently cut the fund's minimum initial investment to $1,000 from $10,000.

All told, this is a great core large-value holding.

Portfolio Analysis 10-31-01

Share change since 09-01 Total Stocks: 45

	Sector	PE	YTD Ret%	% Assets
⊕ Citigroup	Financials	20.0	0.03	4.62
⊕ Fannie Mae	Financials	16.2	–6.95	3.88
⊖ Loews	Financials	—	8.35	3.82
⊕ Metropolitan Life Ins	Financials	—	–8.82	3.46
⊕ Tyco Intl	Industrials	27.1	6.23	3.20
⊕ Household Intl	Financials	14.7	6.89	2.94
⊕ Abbott Labs	Health	51.6	17.08	2.92
⊕ Electronic Data Sys	Technology	25.7	19.83	2.84
⊕ Phillips Petro	Energy	7.1	8.56	2.80
⊕ Philips Electncs NV ADR	Durables	4.3	–18.70	2.77
⊕ Bank One	Financials	29.1	9.13	2.75
Kimberly-Clark	Industrials	18.5	–13.80	2.71
⊖ Northrop Grumman	Industrials	19.2	23.67	2.70
⊕ FleetBoston Finl	Financials	16.2	0.55	2.52
⊕ Gannett	Services	20.3	8.10	2.48
⊖ Weyerhaeuser	Industrials	21.0	9.73	2.41
⊖ Bristol-Myers Squibb	Health	20.2	–26.00	2.41
⊕ American Elec Pwr	Utilities	20.2	–1.28	2.41
⊕ Target	Retail	29.8	28.05	2.39
⊕ Verizon Comms	Services	29.7	–2.52	2.37
⊕ Entergy	Utilities	11.7	–4.50	2.33
⊖ Sears Roebuck	Retail	23.4	40.12	2.27
⊖ IBM	Technology	26.9	43.00	2.17
⊕ Liberty Media Group A	N/A	—	—	2.16
⊕ Wells Fargo	Financials	22.4	–20.20	1.98

Current Investment Style

Style: Value Blnd Growth; Size: Large Med Small

	Stock Port Avg	Relative S&P 500 Current	Relative S&P 500 Hist	Rel Cat
Price/Earnings Ratio	22.3	0.72	0.72	0.88
Price/Book Ratio	3.8	0.66	0.54	0.92
Price/Cash Flow	13.9	0.77	0.68	1.01
3 Yr Earnings Growth	17.6	1.20	0.75	1.19
1 Yr Earnings Est%	–5.0	2.80	—	1.50
Med Mkt Cap $mil	30,504	0.5	0.6	0.96

Special Securities % assets 10-31-01	
Restricted/Illiquid Secs	0
Emerging-Markets Secs	0
Options/Futures/Warrants	No

Composition % assets 10-31-01	
Cash	3.3
Stocks*	95.2
Bonds	0.0
Other	1.6
*Foreign (% stocks)	4.8

Market Cap	
Giant	34.2
Large	53.4
Medium	12.4
Small	0.0
Micro	0.0

Sector Weightings	% of Stocks	Rel S&P	5-Year High	5-Year Low
Utilities	5.4	1.7	8	0
Energy	6.9	1.0	12	1
Financials	31.6	1.8	32	11
Industrials	16.8	1.5	24	11
Durables	3.8	2.4	14	1
Staples	2.8	0.4	11	0
Services	10.9	1.0	27	11
Retail	5.3	0.8	7	2
Health	9.6	0.7	15	7
Technology	6.9	0.4	16	2

Address: 225 W. Wacker Drive Suite 2400
Chicago, IL 60606
888-221-4227
Web Address: www.icapfunds.com/contents.html
*Inception: 12-31-94
Advisor: Institutional Cap.
Subadvisor: None
NTF Plans: N/A

Minimum Purchase: $1000 Add: $1000 IRA: $1000
Min Auto Inv Plan: $1000 Add: $250
Sales Fees: No-load
Management Fee: .80%, .18%A
Actual Fees: Mgt: 0.80% Dist: —
Expense Projections: 3Yr: $274 5Yr: $475 10Yr: $1066
Avg Brok Commission: — Income Distrib: Quarterly
Total Cost (relative to category): Below Avg

ICAP Select Equity

Ticker	Load	NAV	Yield	Total Assets	Mstar Category
ICSLX	None	$28.50	0.5%	$53.7 mil	Large Value

Prospectus Objective: Growth

ICAP Select Equity Portfolio seeks a total return greater than that of the S&P 500 index.

The fund normally invests at least 65% of assets in dollar-denominated equity securities of at least 15 companies with market capitalizations of $500 million or more. Investments may include common and preferred stocks, ADRs, warrants, and convertibles rated at least investment-grade. The fund may invest the remaining 35% of assets in cash and short-term fixed-income securities. This fund is non-diversified.

Historical Profile

Return	Above Avg
Risk	Below Avg
Rating	★★★★ Above Avg

Investment Style
Equity
Average Stock %: 89% (1998), 91% (1999), 93% (2000), 95% (12-01)

▼ Manager Change
▽ Partial Manager Change

Fund Performance vs. Category Average
■ Quarterly Fund Return +/– Category Average
— Category Baseline

Performance Quartile (within Category)

Portfolio Manager(s)

Robert H. Lyon. Since 12-97. BA Northwestern U.; MBA U. of Pennsylvania-Wharton. Other funds currently managed: ICAP Discretionary Equity, ICAP Equity, HSBC Investor Equity A.

1990	1991	1992	1993	1994	1995	1996	1997	1998	1999	2000	12-01	History
—	—	—	—	—	—	—	20.00	22.77	27.91	29.50	28.50	NAV
—	—	—	—	—	—	—	—	15.33	27.17	9.49	–1.66	Total Return %
—	—	—	—	—	—	—	—	–13.25	6.13	18.59	10.22	+/– S&P 500
—	—	—	—	—	—	—	—	–5.91	16.22	7.18	7.13	+/– Russ Top 200 Val
—	—	—	—	—	—	—	—	1.45	1.70	1.15	0.47	Income Return %
—	—	—	—	—	—	—	—	13.88	25.46	8.34	–2.13	Capital Return %
—	—	—	—	—	—	—	—	37	3	36	26	Total Rtn % Rank Cat
—	—	—	—	—	—	—	0.00	0.29	0.39	0.32	0.14	Income $
—	—	—	—	—	—	—	0.00	0.00	0.63	0.72	0.37	Capital Gains $
—	—	—	—	—	—	—	—	0.80	0.80	0.80	—	Expense Ratio %
—	—	—	—	—	—	—	—	1.82	1.63	1.24	—	Income Ratio %
—	—	—	—	—	—	—	—	250	375	400	—	Turnover Rate %
—	—	—	—	—	—	—	—	9.6	23.8	38.2	53.7	Net Assets $mil

Performance 12-31-01

	1st Qtr	2nd Qtr	3rd Qtr	4th Qtr	Total
1997	—	—	—	—	—
1998	13.66	2.92	–16.91	18.66	15.33
1999	10.06	11.54	–10.85	16.20	27.17
2000	5.78	–3.27	2.85	4.04	9.49
2001	–2.08	5.73	–14.55	11.16	–1.66

Trailing	Total Return%	+/– S&P 500	+/– Russ Top 200 Val	% Rank All	% Rank Cat	Growth of $10,000
3 Mo	11.16	0.48	5.65	37	23	11,116
6 Mo	–5.02	0.54	0.76	62	65	9,498
1 Yr	–1.66	10.22	7.13	45	26	9,834
3 Yr Avg	11.04	12.07	9.88	9	3	13,693
5 Yr Avg	—	—	—	—	—	—
10 Yr Avg	—	—	—	—	—	—
15 Yr Avg	—	—	—	—	—	—

Tax Analysis	Tax-Adj Ret%	%Rank Cat	%Pretax Ret	%Rank Cat
3 Yr Avg	10.00	3	90.5	10
5 Yr Avg	—	—	—	—
10 Yr Avg	—	—	—	—

Potential Capital Gain Exposure: –11% of assets

Risk Analysis

Time Period	Load-Adj Return %	Risk %Rank[1] All	Risk %Rank[1] Cat	Morningstar Return	Morningstar Risk	Morningstar Risk-Adj Rating
1 Yr	–1.66					
3 Yr	11.04	46	13	1.37[2]	0.64	★★★★
5 Yr	—	—	—	—	—	
Incept	12.09	—	—	—	—	

Average Historical Rating (13 months): 4.5★s

[1]1=low, 100=high [2] T-Bill return substituted for category avg.

Category Rating (3 Yr)

1 2 3 4 5 — Worst … Best (5)

Return	High
Risk	Below Avg

Other Measures	Standard Index S&P 500	Best Fit Index S&P 500
Alpha	10.4	10.4
Beta	0.70	0.70
R-Squared	61	61
Standard Deviation		16.82
Mean		11.04
Sharpe Ratio		0.41

Portfolio Analysis 10-31-01

Share change since 09-01 Total Stocks: 22	Sector	PE	YTD Ret%	% Assets
⊕ Metropolitan Life Ins	Financials	—	–8.82	8.21
⊕ Tyco Intl	Industrials	27.1	6.23	8.00
⊕ Citigroup	Financials	20.0	0.03	7.88
⊕ Fannie Mae	Financials	16.2	–6.95	7.62
⊕ Loews	Financials	—	8.35	5.91
☼ Target	Retail	29.8	28.05	4.67
⊕ Schering-Plough	Health	22.2	–35.90	4.67
⊖ American Elec Pwr	Utilities	20.2	–1.28	4.62
☼ Nestle (Reg) ADR	Staples	24.2	–5.97	4.57
☼ Pancanadian Energy	N/A	—	—	4.26
☼ Kerr-McGee	Energy	6.9	–15.70	4.14
☼ Diageo ADR (New)	Staples	—	—	4.09
⊖ Northrop Grumman	Industrials	19.2	23.67	4.05
⊖ Phillips Petro	Energy	7.1	8.56	3.90
⊕ News ADR Pfd	Services	—	—	3.89
⊖ Electronic Data Sys	Technology	25.7	19.83	3.74
⊖ Gannett	Services	20.3	8.10	3.52
⊖ Household Intl	Financials	14.7	6.89	3.46
⊖ Republic Svcs Cl A	Services	15.6	16.19	2.38
⊖ Allstate	Financials	17.1	–21.00	1.83
⊖ Orient Express Hotels	Services	—	–16.00	1.60
☼ Fording	N/A	—	—	0.00

Current Investment Style

Style: Value Blnd Growth; Size: Large Med Small

	Stock Port Avg	Relative S&P 500 Current	Relative S&P 500 Hist	Rel Cat
Price/Earnings Ratio	19.8	0.64	0.67	0.79
Price/Book Ratio	3.0	0.52	0.43	0.72
Price/Cash Flow	13.6	0.75	0.66	0.98
3 Yr Earnings Growth	18.6	1.27	0.70	1.26
1 Yr Earnings Est%	–0.1	0.05	—	0.03
Med Mkt Cap $mil	28,825	0.5	0.5	0.91

[1]figure is based on 50% or less of stocks

Special Securities % assets 10-31-01

Restricted/Illiquid Secs	0
Emerging-Markets Secs	0
Options/Futures/Warrants	No

Composition % assets 10-31-01

Cash	5.0
Stocks*	91.2
Bonds	0.0
Other	3.8
*Foreign (% stocks)	9.3

Market Cap

Giant	38.6
Large	47.0
Medium	12.5
Small	1.9
Micro	0.0

Sector Weightings	% of Stocks	Rel S&P	5-Year High	5-Year Low
Utilities	5.2	1.6	—	—
Energy	9.0	1.3	—	—
Financials	39.3	2.2	—	—
Industrials	13.6	1.2	—	—
Durables	0.0	0.0	—	—
Staples	9.7	1.2	—	—
Services	8.4	0.8	—	—
Retail	5.3	0.8	—	—
Health	5.3	0.4	—	—
Technology	4.2	0.2	—	—

Analysis by Paul Herbert 12-31-01

ICAP Select Equity Fund continues to impress, but it's not for all investors.

This fund didn't seem to have much trouble posting a category-beating return in 2001. Much of its success has come in the past few months, as manager Rob Lyon picked up stocks that were beaten down following the September tragedies. Target has been one of the fund's biggest winners, as the stock has rallied off of its September low. Picks such as this have helped the fund to outpace 75% of its peers during 2001.

Such performances are beginning to seem old hat for the fund. Indeed, it has topped its typical peer in each of the past four calendar years, thanks in large part to its adaptability. Like many value managers, Lyon seeks cheap stocks with near-term catalysts for earnings growth. He's willing to buy stocks in any sector, however, not just the traditional value areas. This helped the fund in 1999, when Lyon held technology stocks like Motorola, which posted a triple-digit gain in that year. His rapid-trading style has also been beneficial, as a timely shift into defensive names lead to peer-beating results in 2000 and 2001.

We still have a few reservations about the fund, despite its fine performance. For one, it's quite top-heavy, with the largest five positions typically taking up about 40% of assets, and Lyon pays little attention to sector weightings. These factors make it more likely that the fund will be hurt if one of its favorite names or areas struggles. What's more, the fund's high-turnover style increases the chance that investors will be hit with a large capital-gains distribution.

So far, the fund hasn't been much more volatile than its diversified sibling ICAP Equity, and it has been very tax-efficient. Nonetheless, we don't recommend it for taxable accounts or for those investors who can't handle a few bumps in the road.

Address:	225 W. Wacker Drive Suite 2400 Chicago, IL 60606 888-221-4227
Web Address:	www.icapfunds.com/contents.html
*Inception:	12-31-97
Advisor:	Institutional Cap.
Subadvisor:	None
NTF Plans:	N/A

Minimum Purchase:	$1000	Add: $1000 IRA: $1000
Min Auto Inv Plan:	$1000	Add: $250
Sales Fees:	No-load	
Management Fee:	.80%, .18%A	
Actual Fees:	Mgt: 0.80%	Dist: —
Expense Projections:	3Yr: $412	5Yr: $765 10Yr: $1761
Avg Brok Commission:	—	Income Distrib: Quarterly
Total Cost (relative to category):		Average

ICM/Isabelle Small Cap Value Invmt

Ticker	Load	NAV	Yield	Total Assets	Mstar Category
IZZYX	12b–1 only	$11.83	0.0%	$99.6 mil	Small Value

Prospectus Objective: Small Company

ICM/Isabelle Small Cap Value Fund seeks capital appreciation.

The fund normally invests at least 80% of assets in common stocks of companies with market capitalizations of less than $1 billion. It may invest the balance in companies of other market capitalizations. The fund may also invest no more than 25% of assets in any one industry.

The fund offers Institutional and Investment share classes.

Historical Profile

Return	High
Risk	Average
Rating	★★★★★ Highest

Investment Style
Equity
Average Stock %: 85% (1998), 100% (1999), 99% (2000), 100% (12-01)

▼ Manager Change
▽ Partial Manager Change

Fund Performance vs. Category Average
■ Quarterly Fund Return +/– Category Average
— Category Baseline

Performance Quartile (within Category)

Portfolio Manager(s)

Warren J. Isabelle, CFA. Since 3-98. MS'80 U. of Massachusetts; MBA'81 U. of Pennsylvania. Other funds currently managed: ICM/Isabelle Small Cap Value Instl, IDEX Isabelle Small Cap Value A, IDEX Isabelle Small Cap Value B.

1990	1991	1992	1993	1994	1995	1996	1997	1998	1999	2000	12–01	History
—	—	—	—	—	—	—	—	6.91	10.33	10.87	11.83	NAV
—	—	—	—	—	—	—	—	–30.62*	49.49	7.73	8.83	Total Return %
—	—	—	—	—	—	—	—	–46.96*	28.46	16.84	20.71	+/– S&P 500
—	—	—	—	—	—	—	—	—	50.97	–15.08	–5.19	+/– Russell 2000 V
—	—	—	—	—	—	—	—	0.00	0.00	0.00	0.00	Income Return %
—	—	—	—	—	—	—	—	–30.62	49.49	7.73	8.83	Capital Return %
—	—	—	—	—	—	—	—	—	2	87	86	Total Rtn % Rank Cat
—	—	—	—	—	—	—	—	0.00	0.00	0.00	0.00	Income $
—	—	—	—	—	—	—	—	0.00	0.00	0.25	0.00	Capital Gains $
—	—	—	—	—	—	—	—	1.95	1.95	1.82	—	Expense Ratio %
—	—	—	—	—	—	—	—	–1.31	–1.39	–0.43	—	Income Ratio %
—	—	—	—	—	—	—	—	—	84	54	—	Turnover Rate %
—	—	—	—	—	—	—	—	1.1	9.5	75.2	—	Net Assets $mil

Performance 12-31-01

	1st Qtr	2nd Qtr	3rd Qtr	4th Qtr	Total
1997	—	—	—	—	—
1998	—	–9.60	–32.41	13.09	–30.62 *
1999	–3.18	25.41	–1.67	25.21	49.49
2000	15.00	–1.60	3.08	–7.64	7.73
2001	5.98	19.27	–29.11	21.46	8.83

Trailing	Total Return%	+/– S&P 500	+/– Russ 2000V	% Rank All	% Rank Cat	Growth of $10,000
3 Mo	21.46	10.77	4.74	11	15	12,146
6 Mo	–13.90	–8.35	–15.05	93	100	8,610
1 Yr	8.83	20.71	–5.19	7	86	10,883
3 Yr Avg	20.57	21.60	9.25	2	14	17,528
5 Yr Avg	—	—	—	—	—	—
10 Yr Avg	—	—	—	—	—	—
15 Yr Avg	—	—	—	—	—	—

Tax Analysis	Tax-Adj Ret%	%Rank Cat	%Pretax Ret	%Rank Cat
3 Yr Avg	20.27	10	98.5	20
5 Yr Avg	—	—	—	—
10 Yr Avg	—	—	—	—

Potential Capital Gain Exposure: 11% of assets

Risk Analysis

Time Period	Load-Adj Return %	Risk %Rank[1] All	Risk %Rank[1] Cat	Morningstar Return	Morningstar Risk	Morningstar Risk-Adj Rating
1 Yr	8.83					
3 Yr	20.57	54	70	3.83[2]	0.76	★★★★★
5 Yr	—	—	—	—	—	
Incept	5.27	—	—	—	—	

Average Historical Rating (10 months): 4.7★s

[1]1=low, 100=high [2] T-Bill return substituted for category avg.

Category Rating (3 Yr)

1 2 3 4 5
Worst Best

Return	Above Avg
Risk	Above Avg

Other Measures	Standard Index S&P 500	Best Fit Index Russ 2000
Alpha	20.8	14.3
Beta	0.59	0.72
R-Squared	21	60
Standard Deviation		26.60
Mean		20.57
Sharpe Ratio		0.66

Portfolio Analysis 04-30-01

Share change since 09–00 Total Stocks: 53	Sector	PE	YTD Ret%	% Assets
⊖ Scios	Health	—	6.83	6.31
⊕ Consolid Freightways	Services	—	21.54	4.27
⊕ PolyOne	Industrials	—	71.42	3.58
⊕ Crompton	Industrials	—	–12.40	3.48
⊖ Stancorp Finl Grp	Financials	15.4	–0.38	3.47
⊕ InterTAN	Retail	17.7	8.04	3.23
⊕ AK Steel Hldg	Industrials	27.1	31.55	3.16
⊕ Signal Tech	Industrials	—	–42.70	3.10
☼ Bns Cl A	N/A	—	—	2.86
⊖ Wausau–Mosinee Paper Mills	Industrials	NMF	22.90	2.77
☼ 4 Kids Entrtnmt	Durables	14.3	124.10	2.57
⊕ Magnetek	Industrials	50.1	–30.60	2.40
⊕ Pioneer–Standard Electncs	Technology	14.9	16.72	2.37
⊕ JLG Inds	Industrials	19.0	0.54	2.23
⊕ Ariad Pharmaceuticals	Health	—	12.21	2.02
⊕ Bellwether Explor	Energy	1.5	–58.80	1.99
☼ Nacco Inds	Industrials	7.2	31.87	1.98
☼ Auspex Sys	Technology	—	–74.20	1.93
⊕ Presidential Life	Financials	18.9	40.58	1.89
Intergraph	Technology	26.9	129.00	1.88
⊕ DT Inds	Industrials	—	54.36	1.87
⊕ Material Sciences	Industrials	—	31.63	1.85
⊖ Woodhead Inds	Durables	19.1	–17.30	1.82
⊕ Commonwealth Inds	Industrials	—	8.60	1.80
☼ SilverStream Software	Technology	—	–66.90	1.77

Current Investment Style

Style: Value Blnd Growth; Size: Large Med Small

	Stock Port Avg	Relative S&P 500 Current	Relative S&P 500 Hist	Rel Cat
Price/Earnings Ratio	25.3[1]	0.82	—	1.17
Price/Book Ratio	2.4	0.42	—	0.99
Price/Cash Flow	8.9[1]	0.49	—	0.70
3 Yr Earnings Growth	–6.2[1]	—	—	–0.54
1 Yr Earnings Est%	–39.7[1]	22.44	—	10.05
Med Mkt Cap $mil	271	0.0	—	0.31

[1]figure is based on 50% or less of stocks

Analysis by Christopher Davis 09-05-01

ICM/Isabelle Small Cap Value Fund's offbeat approach can lead to appealing, if uneven, results.

You'd be hard-pressed to pigeonhole manager Warren Isabelle. It's tempting to typecast him as a stodgy value hound. After all, the fund's stake in staid industrial cyclical stocks is twice the small-value norm. But Isabelle isn't afraid to deviate from the well-trod path of other value investors: The fund boasts relatively small utilities, energy, and financials stakes, and devotes more to the tech and health-care sectors than its typical peer. Not only is the fund's blend of industrial, health-care and technology names rather unconventional, it is laden with tiny, out-of-favor names that few of his rivals even own. And it is much more concentrated than most of its peers, with just roughly 50 names.

That mix is volatile. Indeed, the fund's standard deviation, a measure of volatility, is substantially above the category average. Not unexpectedly, the fund has subjected shareholders to an exceedingly bumpy ride this year. The fund led the small-value pack by a wide margin through June, gaining 26% over the stretch. But then it plunged 13% during the next two months, as top picks like Crompton and Scios took it on the chin. All told, the fund's 5% gain for the year to date through Sept. 9, 2001, lands in the category's bottom third.

The fund's risky style can yield exceptional gains, too. Its 50% return in 1999, for instance, left most of its rivals in the dust. Prior to taking charge here, Isabelle built a superb record using the same style at Pioneer Mid-Cap Value Fund. While that offering eventually struggled under the weight of a swelling asset base, he has pledged to close this fund once its assets reach $500 million.

Aggressive investors in search of a small-value offering will do well to consider this one.

Special Securities % assets 04-30-01	
Restricted/Illiquid Secs	0
Emerging–Markets Secs	0
Options/Futures/Warrants	No

Composition % assets 04-30-01	
Cash	0.0
Stocks*	100.0
Bonds	0.0
Other	0.0
*Foreign (% stocks)	1.2

Market Cap	
Giant	0.0
Large	0.0
Medium	3.9
Small	46.1
Micro	50.0

Sector Weightings	% of Stocks	Rel S&P	5-Year High	5-Year Low
Utilities	0.0	0.0	—	—
Energy	2.7	0.4	—	—
Financials	7.2	0.4	—	—
Industrials	41.8	3.7	—	—
Durables	7.4	4.7	—	—
Staples	0.0	0.0	—	—
Services	7.9	0.7	—	—
Retail	5.4	0.8	—	—
Health	12.2	0.8	—	—
Technology	15.4	0.8	—	—

Address:	150 Motor Pkwy Hauppauge, NY 11788–0132 800–472–6114
Web Address:	www.icmfunds.com
*Inception:	03-12-98
Advisor:	Ironwood Cap. Mgmt.
Subadvisor:	None
NTF Plans:	Fidelity Inst. , Waterhouse

Minimum Purchase:	$1000	Add: $100 IRA: $1000
Min Auto Inv Plan:	$1000	Add: $100
Sales Fees:	0.25%B	
Management Fee:	1.0%, .15%A	
Actual Fees:	Mgt: 1.00%	Dist: 0.25%
Expense Projections:	3Yr: $612*	5Yr: $1052* 10Yr: $2275*
Avg Brok Commission:	—	Income Distrib: Annually
Total Cost (relative to category):	—	

IDEX Janus Global A

Ticker	Load	NAV	Yield	Total Assets	Mstar Category
IGLBX	Closed	$25.73	0.0%	$942.9 mil	World Stock

Prospectus Objective: World Stock

IDEX Janus Global Fund seeks long-term growth of capital.

The fund invests principally in common stocks of foreign and domestic issuers and depositary receipts including ADRs, GDRs, and EDRs. When evaluating foreign investments the fund manager considers such factors as: expected level of inflation in various countries; government policies that might affect business conditions; the outlook for currency relationships; and prospects for economic growth among countries, regions or geographic areas.

The fund currently offers Class A, B, C, M and T shares, all of which differ in fee structure and availability. The fund has gone through several name changes.

Historical Profile

Return Above Avg
Risk Average
Rating ★★★★ Above Avg

Investment Style
Equity
Average Stock %: 92% 89% 91% 89% 95% 92% 90%

▼ Manager Change
▽ Partial Manager Change

Fund Performance vs. Category Average
■ Quarterly Fund Return +/– Category Average
— Category Baseline

Performance Quartile (within Category)

Portfolio Manager(s)

Helen Young Hayes, CFA. Since 10-92. BA'84 Yale U. Other funds currently managed: Janus Worldwide, IDEX Janus Global M, Janus Overseas.

Laurence J. Chang, CFA. Since 1-00. Dartmouth C.; MS Stanford U. Other funds currently managed: Janus Worldwide, IDEX Janus Global M, IDEX Janus Global B.

History

1990	1991	1992	1993	1994	1995	1996	1997	1998	1999	2000	12–01	History
—	—	11.87	15.54	15.11	17.50	20.07	22.04	27.52	43.71	33.65	25.73	NAV
—	—	18.70*	30.92	0.88	19.99	26.81	20.39	24.86	63.31	–17.71	–23.54	Total Return %
—	—	13.30*	20.86	–0.44	–17.54	3.87	–12.96	–3.71	42.27	–8.61	–11.66	+/– S&P 500
—	—	—	8.42	–4.20	–0.73	13.33	4.63	0.53	38.38	–4.53	—	+/– MSCI World
—	—	0.00	0.00	0.00	0.00	0.00	0.00	0.00	0.00	0.00	0.00	Income Return %
—	—	18.70	30.92	0.88	19.99	26.81	20.39	24.86	63.31	–17.71	–23.54	Capital Return %
—	—	—	57	41	35	2	21	20	19	74	74	Total Rtn % Rank Cat
—	—	0.00	0.00	0.00	0.00	0.00	0.00	0.00	0.00	0.00	0.00	Income $
—	—	0.00	0.00	0.56	0.62	2.10	2.07	0.00	1.13	2.47	0.00	Capital Gains $
—	—	—	2.84	2.14	1.97	2.06	1.91	1.82	1.73	1.64	—	Expense Ratio %
—	—	—	–0.87	–0.55	–0.43	–0.67	–0.50	–0.45	–0.22	–0.56	—	Income Ratio %
—	—	—	117	148	161	98	91	88	145	53	—	Turnover Rate %
—	—	—	34.9	85.4	90.5	147.6	227.0	350.2	657.3	640.3	396.5	Net Assets $mil

Performance 12-31-01

	1st Qtr	2nd Qtr	3rd Qtr	4th Qtr	Total
1997	5.58	12.13	5.39	–3.51	20.39
1998	16.42	7.76	–16.02	18.52	24.86
1999	6.00	5.25	2.15	43.31	63.31
2000	11.83	–9.31	–5.82	–13.85	–17.71
2001	–17.47	4.29	–20.96	12.41	–23.54

Trailing	Total Return%	+/– S&P 500	+/– MSCI World	% Rank All	% Rank Cat	Growth of $10,000
3 Mo	12.41	1.72	—	31	30	11,241
6 Mo	–11.15	–5.60	—	88	89	8,885
1 Yr	–23.54	–11.66	—	86	74	7,646
3 Yr Avg	0.91	1.94	—	68	45	10,276
5 Yr Avg	9.09	–1.61	—	23	23	15,447
10 Yr Avg	—	—	—	—	—	—
15 Yr Avg	—	—	—	—	—	—

Tax Analysis	Tax-Adj Ret%	%Rank Cat	%Pretax Ret	%Rank Cat
3 Yr Avg	0.29	37	32.0	90
5 Yr Avg	8.07	18	88.8	13
10 Yr Avg	—	—	—	—

Potential Capital Gain Exposure: –21% of assets

Risk Analysis

Time Period	Load-Adj Return %	Risk %Rank[1] All	Risk %Rank[1] Cat	Morningstar Return	Morningstar Risk	Morningstar Risk-Adj Rating
1 Yr	–27.74					
3 Yr	–0.97	82	74	–1.19[2]	1.12	★★★
5 Yr	7.86	79	59	0.65[2]	0.90	★★★★
Incept	14.43	—	—	—	—	

Average Historical Rating (76 months): 4.8★s

[1] 1=low, 100=high [2] T-Bill return substituted for category avg.

Category Rating (3 Yr): 3 (scale 1 Worst – 5 Best)

Return: Average
Risk: Above Avg

Other Measures	Standard Index S&P 500	Best Fit Index Wil 4500
Alpha	3.9	–1.0
Beta	1.06	0.80
R-Squared	51	80

Standard Deviation	26.00
Mean	0.91
Sharpe Ratio	–0.18

Portfolio Analysis 10-31-01

Share change since 09–01 Total Stocks: 128	Sector	Country	% Assets
⊖ Tyco Intl	Industrials	U.S.	4.58
Citigroup	Financials	U.S.	2.96
⊖ NTT DoCoMo	Services	Japan	2.66
Pfizer	Health	U.S.	2.47
⊕ Petrobras ADR	Energy	Brazil	2.21
General Elec	Industrials	U.S.	2.06
Total Fina Cl B	Energy	France	2.01
⊖ Takeda Chem Inds	Health	Japan	1.79
⊖ Banco Bilbao Vizcaya Arg	Financials	Spain	1.74
⊕ Clear Channel Comms	Services	U.S.	1.70
Ahold	Retail	Netherlands	1.70
Unilever (Cert)	Staples	United Kingdom	1.66
⊕ Viacom Cl B	Services	U.S.	1.39
Comcast	Services	U.S.	1.37
⊖ Telefonos de Mexico ADR L	Services	Mexico	1.36
⊖ STMicroelectronics	Technology	France	1.24
⊖ Wal-Mart Stores	Retail	U.S.	1.24
⊕ Microsoft	Technology	U.S.	1.12
⊖ Diageo	Staples	United Kingdom	1.09
⊖ Securitas Cl B	Services	Sweden	1.08

Current Investment Style (Style: Value Blnd Growth; Size: Large Med Small)

	Stock Port Avg	Rel MSCI EAFE Current	Rel MSCI EAFE Hist	Rel Cat
Price/Earnings Ratio	31.3	1.21	1.36	1.13
Price/Cash Flow	19.0	1.48	1.66	1.15
Price/Book Ratio	5.3	1.53	1.82	1.15
3 Yr Earnings Growth	21.8	1.16	1.59	1.17
Med Mkt Cap $mil	43,268	1.5	1.7	1.80

Country Exposure 10-31-01	% assets
U.S.	42
United Kingdom	9
Japan	7
France	6
Netherlands	4

Hedging History: Always

Regional Exposure 10-31-01	% assets
Europe	29
Japan	7
Latin America	5
Pacific Rim	1
U.S.	42
Other	0

Special Securities % assets 10-31-01	
Restricted/Illiquid Secs	0
Emerging–Markets Secs	7
Options/Futures/Warrants	No

Sector Weightings	% of Stocks	Rel Cat	5-Year High	5-Year Low
Utilities	0.0	0.0	2	0
Energy	10.2	1.9	11	0
Financials	15.2	0.8	23	4
Industrials	10.5	0.9	17	1
Durables	2.9	0.7	17	3
Staples	5.3	0.7	22	0
Services	22.0	1.3	42	13
Retail	5.2	1.0	21	0
Health	17.8	1.4	19	5
Technology	10.9	0.7	36	1

Composition % assets 10-31-01

Cash	4.0	Bonds	0.0
Stocks	96.0	Other	0.0

Analysis by Emily Hall 10-31-01

Idex Janus Global Fund is looking bruised, but shareholders have reason to stay the course.

It's been a pretty unpleasant couple of years for this offering and its shareholders. The growth-stock rout of 2000 and 2001 has not been kind to this portfolio, which entered the new century with loads of high-flying technology and telecom names. Managers Helen Young Hayes and Laurence Chang have acknowledged the weakening economy, and have been trimming many of their picks in the tech and telecom arenas. Moreover, they have diversified the portfolio by adding names in areas such as health care and energy. But these moves haven't been enough to save the fund from dismal performance. For the year to date through Oct. 30, this offering has lost a bruising 30%, placing it in the worst quartile of the world stock group.

All is not lost, though. Until the market turned sour in the spring of 2000, this offering had consistently outperformed its peers year in and year out. Indeed, the fund's recent troubles haven't put too much of a dent in its long-term record: For the trailing five years, the fund's return still ranks in the category's top third.

The managers' willingness to load up on particular sectors is certainly a reminder, though, that investors need to expect volatility. Currently, the fund is looking fairly diversified, but Janus' firmwide taste for growth probably means that this offering could again sport large overweightings when market conditions for growth stocks improve.

Still, for those who can handle the heat, there is plenty of reason to stay with this closed offering.

Address:	570 Carillon Pkwy St. Petersburg, FL 33716 888–233–4339 / 888–233–4339
Web Address:	www.idexfunds.com
*Inception:	10-01-92
Advisor:	Idex Mgmt.
Subadvisor:	Janus Cap. Corporation
NTF Plans:	N/A

Minimum Purchase:	Closed	Add: $50	IRA: —
Min Auto Inv Plan:	Closed	Add: $50	
Sales Fees:	5.50%L, 0.10%B, 0.25%S		
Management Fee:	1.0% mx./.85% mn.		
Actual Fees:	Mgt: 1.00%	Dist: 0.35%	
Expense Projections:	3Yr: $1091	5Yr: $1481	10Yr: $2570
Avg Brok Commission:	—	Income Distrib: Annually	
Total Cost (relative to category):	—		

INVESCO Balanced Inv

Ticker	Load	NAV	Yield	Total Assets	Mstar Category
IMABX	12b–1 only	$14.63	2.0%	$1,143.4 mil	Domestic Hybrid

Prospectus Objective: Balanced

INVESCO Balanced Fund seeks capital appreciation.

The fund invests primarily in a combination of common stocks and fixed income securities, including preferred stocks, convertible securities and bonds. The fund invests the majority of its total assets in common stocks and approximately one-quarter of assets in investment grade debt securities.

The fund currently offers Class C, K, Institutional and Investor shares, all of which differ in fee structure and availability. On June 11, 1999, Invesco Multi-Asset Allocation Fund merged into the fund. Prior to Feb. 29, 2000 the fund was named INVESCO Balanced.

Historical Profile

Return Average
Risk Below Avg
Rating ★★★ Neutral

Investment Style
Equity
Average Stock %

	1994	1995	1996	1997	1998	1999	2000	12-01
Average Stock %		65%	59%	61%	63%	64%	66%	63%

▼ Manager Change
▽ Partial Manager Change

Fund Performance vs. Category Average
■ Quarterly Fund Return +/– Category Average
– Category Baseline

Performance Quartile (within Category)

Portfolio Manager(s)

Peter Lovell. Since 10-98. BA Colorado State U.; MBA Regis U. Other funds currently managed: North American Balanced C, North American Balanced A, North American Balanced B.

Charles P. Mayer. Since 6-96. BA St. Peter's C.; MBA St. John's U. Other funds currently managed: INVESCO Equity Income Inv, INVESCO Value Equity Inv, INVESCO Total Return Inv.

Richard Hinderlie. Since 9–01.

1990	1991	1992	1993	1994	1995	1996	1997	1998	1999	2000	12–01	History
—	—	—	10.06	10.54	13.19	13.82	14.48	16.01	17.80	16.86	14.63	NAV
—	—	—	0.72*	9.44	36.46	14.66	19.54	17.33	16.83	–1.85	–11.54	Total Return %
—	—	—	–0.47*	8.12	–1.08	–8.29	–13.82	–11.25	–4.21	7.25	0.34	+/– S&P 500
—	—	—	—	12.35	17.99	11.04	9.85	8.66	17.66	–13.48	–19.96	+/– LB Aggregate
—	—	—	0.12	2.17	2.91	3.04	2.58	1.81	2.11	2.04	1.75	Income Return %
—	—	—	0.60	7.26	33.54	11.62	16.95	15.52	14.72	–3.89	–13.29	Capital Return %
—	—	—	—	1	1	37	42	24	15	71	92	Total Rtn % Rank Cat
—	—	—	0.01	0.22	0.30	0.39	0.35	0.26	0.34	0.36	0.29	Income $
—	—	—	0.00	0.25	0.84	0.87	1.63	0.66	0.52	0.25	0.00	Capital Gains $
—	—	—	—	1.25	1.25	1.29	1.29	1.22	1.21	1.15	1.07	Expense Ratio %
—	—	—	—	2.87	3.12	3.03	2.46	2.18	1.94	1.98	2.07	Income Ratio %
—	—	—	—	—	255	259	155	108	—	89	67	Turnover Rate %
—	—	—	0.6	12.5	87.5	134.2	167.7	260.3	487.0	1,007.2	916.9	Net Assets $mil

Performance 12-31-01

	1st Qtr	2nd Qtr	3rd Qtr	4th Qtr	Total
1997	–0.29	9.81	7.84	1.24	19.54
1998	9.42	1.01	–6.61	13.67	17.33
1999	4.57	5.76	–4.20	10.28	16.83
2000	2.89	–2.22	4.92	–7.01	–1.85
2001	–9.97	3.31	–12.52	8.73	–11.54

Trailing	Total Return%	+/– S&P 500	+/– LB Agg	% Rank All	% Rank Cat	Growth of $10,000
3 Mo	8.73	–1.96	8.69	48	17	10,873
6 Mo	–4.89	0.67	–9.54	61	92	9,511
1 Yr	–11.54	0.34	–19.96	64	92	8,846
3 Yr Avg	0.48	1.50	–5.80	71	73	10,144
5 Yr Avg	7.31	–3.39	–0.12	33	50	14,227
10 Yr Avg	—	—	—	—	—	—
15 Yr Avg	—	—	—	—	—	—

Tax Analysis	Tax-Adj Ret%	%Rank Cat	%Pretax Ret	%Rank Cat
3 Yr Avg	–0.64	65	—	—
5 Yr Avg	5.18	46	70.9	39
10 Yr Avg	—	—	—	—

Potential Capital Gain Exposure: –4% of assets

Risk Analysis

Time Period	Load-Adj Return %	Risk %Rank[1] All	Risk %Rank[1] Cat	Morningstar Return	Morningstar Risk	Morningstar Risk-Adj Rating
1 Yr	–11.54					
3 Yr	0.48	51	87	–0.91[2]	0.72	★★★
5 Yr	7.31	48	79	0.52[2]	0.65	★★★
Incept	11.74	—	—	—	—	

Average Historical Rating (62 months): 4.0★s

[1] 1=low, 100=high [2] T-Bill return substituted for category avg.

Category Rating (3 Yr)

1 2 3 4 5
Worst Best

Return Below Avg
Risk Above Avg

Other Measures	Standard Index S&P 500	Best Fit Index S&P 500
Alpha	–0.2	–0.2
Beta	0.74	0.74
R-Squared	90	90
Standard Deviation		13.15
Mean		0.48
Sharpe Ratio		–0.39

Portfolio Analysis 09-30-01

Total Stocks: 56 Share change since 06–01	Sector	PE Ratio	YTD Return %	% Net Assets
⊕ Wells Fargo	Financials	22.4	–20.20	1.79
⊕ Pfizer	Health	34.7	–12.40	1.77
⊖ American Home Products	Health	—	–1.91	1.76
⊕ General Elec	Industrials	30.1	–15.00	1.67
⊕ Citigroup	Financials	20.0	0.03	1.66
⊕ Bank of New York	Financials	21.9	–24.80	1.66
⊕ ExxonMobil	Energy	15.3	–7.59	1.66
⊕ Forest Labs	Health	52.2	23.35	1.56
⊕ J.P. Morgan Chase & Co.	Financials	27.8	–17.40	1.51
⊕ Genentech	Health	NMF	–33.40	1.46

Total Fixed-Income: 59	Date of Maturity	Amount $000	Value $000	% Net Assets
US Treasury Note 5.75%	08-15-10	42,500	46,046	4.31
US Treasury Note 4%	04-30-03	30,500	31,106	2.91
US Treasury Note 5.25%	05-15-04	19,000	20,015	1.87
US Treasury Note 5.625%	05-15-08	16,355	17,596	1.65
US Treasury Note 5.625%	11-30-02	17,000	17,589	1.65
US Treasury Note 5.875%	11-15-04	9,600	10,295	0.96
US Treasury Note 6.75%	05-15-05	9,000	9,948	0.93
FHLMC 6.5%	09-01-11	8,336	8,670	0.81
US Treasury Note 6%	08-15-09	7,500	8,248	0.77
Niagara Mohawk Pwr 8.75%	04-01-22	7,000	7,305	0.68

Analysis by William Harding 09-26-01

We still think it's a solid choice, but our enthusiasm for Invesco Balanced Fund has waned a bit.

We recently dropped this fund from our Fund Analyst Picks in the domestic-hybrid category for a couple of reasons. First, all-star fixed-income manager Jerry Paul was recently replaced by Richard Hinderlie, who runs Invesco U.S. Government Securities. That choice is logical because the fund tends to keep a large portion of its bond assets in Treasuries, but it may lose its edge on the corporate bond side. Paul is best known for his prowess in picking high-yield securities, which this fund avoids, but he has been astute at picking investment-grade corporates as well.

The fund's recent performance has also been dreadful. It has lost nearly 25% for the year to date ended Sept. 25, 2001, which lands in the domestic-hybrid category's bottom 10%. We typically don't give short-term numbers much weight, but such a large loss is troubling for investors who look to a balanced fund for safety. The fund's bullish equity stake (it devotes 61% of asset to stocks, compared with 50% for the average hybrid fund) has been a detriment this year as stocks have generally underperformed bonds. Moreover, this fund has tilted toward large-growth names, which have taken it on the chin this year. Its tech holdings have been hit especially hard, and its more-defensive financials picks have also suffered.

There could well be light at the end of the tunnel for this fund. Management's bullish stance on stocks and its growth bent was generally a boon through much of the 1990s, and we think the fund could easily rebound when growth stocks return to favor. Thus, with its equity management intact, it's a reasonable choice for investors who can stomach its risks. However, it's clearly inappropriate for cautious investors, and with Paul's departure, it's not the compelling choice that it was.

Equity Style
Style: Blend
Size: Large-Cap

	Portfolio Avg	Rel S&P
Price/Earnings Ratio	35.8	1.16
Price/Book Ratio	6.4	1.12
Price/Cash Flow	20.8	1.15
3 Yr Earnings Growth	16.1	1.10
1 Yr Earnings Est%	–0.7	0.37
Debt % Total Cap	29.0	0.94
Med Mkt Cap $mil	43,046	0.71

Fixed-Income Style
Duration: Intermediate
Quality: High

Avg Eff Duration	—
Avg Eff Maturity	6.5 Yrs
Avg Credit Quality	AA
Avg Wtd Coupon	6.25%

Special Securities % assets 09-30-01	
Restricted/Illiquid Secs	1
Emerging-Markets Secs	1
Options/Futures/Warrants	No

Composition % of assets 09-30-01	
Cash	6.5
Stocks*	62.5
Bonds	31.0
Other	0.0
*Foreign (% of stocks)	3.7

Market Cap	
Giant	46.9
Large	43.8
Medium	9.2
Small	0.0
Micro	0.0

Sector Weightings	% of Stocks	Rel S&P	5-Year High	5-Year Low
Utilities	3.7	1.2	16	0
Energy	5.8	0.8	24	1
Financials	20.1	1.1	27	1
Industrials	11.5	1.0	47	6
Durables	0.0	0.0	13	0
Staples	7.3	0.9	15	1
Services	12.3	1.1	25	7
Retail	6.0	0.9	16	0
Health	16.7	1.1	18	0
Technology	16.6	0.9	28	1

Address:	P.O. Box 173706 Denver, CO 80217–3706 800–525–8085 / 303–930–6300
Web Address:	www.invescofunds.com
*Inception:	12-01-93
Advisor:	Invesco Funds Grp.
Subadvisor:	None
NTF Plans:	Fidelity , Datalynx

Minimum Purchase:	$1000	Add: $50	IRA: $250
Min Auto Inv Plan:	$50	Add: $50	
Sales Fees:	0.25%B		
Management Fee:	.60% mx./.50% mn., .03%A		
Actual Fees:	Mgt: 0.60%	Dist: 0.25%	
Expense Projections:	3Yr: $40*	5Yr: $69*	10Yr: $152*
Avg Brok Commission:	—	Income Distrib: Quarterly	
Total Cost (relative to category):	—		

INVESCO Dynamics Inv

Ticker	Load	NAV	Yield	Total Assets	Mstar Category
FIDYX	12b–1 only	$15.93	0.0%	$6,267.6 mil	Mid–Cap Growth

Prospectus Objective: Aggressive Growth

INVESCO Dynamics Fund seeks capital appreciation.

The fund invests primarily in common stocks of mid-sized U.S. companies with market capitalizations between $2 billion and $15 billion at the time of purchase. The core of the fund's portfolio is invested in securities of established companies that are leaders in attractive growth markets with a history of strong returns. The remainder is invested in securities that show accelerating growth, driven by product cycles, favorable industry or sector conditions and other factors that management believes will lead to rapid sales or earnings growth.

The fund currently offers C, K, Investor and Institutional shares.

Historical Profile

Return Above Avg
Risk Above Avg
Rating ★★★ Neutral

Investment Style
Equity
Average Stock %: 85% 94% 98% 96% 93% 94% 94%

▼ Manager Change
▽ Partial Manager Change

Fund Performance vs. Category Average
■ Quarterly Fund Return +/– Category Average
— Category Baseline

Performance Quartile (within Category)

Portfolio Manager(s)

Timothy J. Miller, CFA. Since 12-93. BS St. Louis U.; MBA U. of Missouri-St. Louis. Other funds currently managed: North American Mid Cap Growth A, North American Mid Cap Growth B, North American Mid Cap Growth C.

Thomas R. Wald, CFA. Since 10-97. BA Tulane U.; MBA U. of Pennsylvania. Other funds currently managed: INVESCO Health Sciences Inv, INVESCO Dynamics Instl, INVESCO Dynamics C.

1990	1991	1992	1993	1994	1995	1996	1997	1998	1999	2000	12–01	History
7.09	10.47	11.50	12.83	10.24	12.34	12.85	13.96	15.75	25.86	23.77	15.93	NAV
–6.27	67.00	13.18	19.12	–1.95	37.55	15.29	24.47	23.25	71.80	–7.76	–32.89	Total Return %
–3.16	36.52	5.57	9.06	–3.26	0.02	–7.65	–8.88	–5.32	50.76	1.34	–21.01	+/– S&P 500
–1.14	19.97	4.47	7.92	0.22	3.57	–2.19	1.93	5.38	20.49	3.98	–12.73	+/– Russ Midcap Grth
1.57	0.00	0.03	0.00	0.00	0.29	0.14	0.00	0.00	0.00	0.00	0.00	Income Return %
–7.84	67.00	13.15	19.12	–1.95	37.26	15.15	24.47	23.25	71.80	–7.76	–32.89	Capital Return %
50	23	20	28	57	34	63	21	20	33	56	81	Total Rtn % Rank Cat
0.12	0.00	0.00	0.00	0.00	0.03	0.02	0.00	0.00	0.00	0.00	0.00	Income $
0.00	1.20	0.29	0.80	2.30	1.71	1.36	1.95	1.30	1.04	0.08	0.02	Capital Gains $
0.98	1.15	1.18	1.20	1.17	1.20	1.14	1.16	1.08	1.03	0.89	1.00	Expense Ratio %
1.47	0.59	–0.17	–0.38	–0.37	0.33	0.16	–0.31	–0.43	–0.32	–0.34	–0.49	Income Ratio %
225	243	174	144	169	176	196	204	178	—	75	55	Turnover Rate %
57.6	141.3	273.6	319.2	338.8	624.8	856.2	1,120.5	1,549.6	4,609.8	8,258.9	6,146.4	Net Assets $mil

Performance 12-31-01

	1st Qtr	2nd Qtr	3rd Qtr	4th Qtr	Total
1997	–7.94	16.48	17.05	–0.84	24.47
1998	15.47	2.48	–17.80	26.70	23.25
1999	9.08	14.78	–1.17	38.83	71.80
2000	15.12	–2.96	10.42	–25.23	–7.76
2001	–29.79	12.58	–35.02	30.65	–32.89

Trailing	Total Return%	+/– S&P 500	+/– Russ Midcap Grth	% Rank All	% Rank Cat	Growth of $10,000
3 Mo	30.65	19.97	3.59	4	8	13,065
6 Mo	–15.10	–9.54	–6.84	95	81	8,490
1 Yr	–32.89	–21.01	–12.73	95	81	6,711
3 Yr Avg	2.07	3.10	–0.09	62	66	10,635
5 Yr Avg	10.29	–0.41	1.27	17	41	16,315
10 Yr Avg	13.09	0.16	1.98	12	20	34,203
15 Yr Avg	13.89	0.16	1.08	11	17	70,370

Tax Analysis	Tax-Adj Ret%	%Rank Cat	%Pretax Ret	%Rank Cat
3 Yr Avg	1.66	56	80.2	42
5 Yr Avg	8.51	33	82.7	32
10 Yr Avg	10.20	25	78.0	29

Potential Capital Gain Exposure: –29% of assets

Risk Analysis

Time Period	Load-Adj Return %	Risk %Rank[1] All	Risk %Rank[1] Cat	Morningstar Return	Morningstar Risk	Morningstar Risk-Adj Rating
1 Yr	–32.89					
3 Yr	2.07	96	74	–0.59[2]	1.73	★★
5 Yr	10.29	92	62	1.27[2]	1.57	★★★
10 Yr	13.09	93	45	1.33	1.52	★★★

Average Historical Rating (193 months): 2.9★s

[1] 1=low, 100=high [2] T-Bill return substituted for category avg.

Category Rating (3 Yr)

1 2 3 4 5
Worst Best

Return Average
Risk Above Avg

Other Measures	Standard Index S&P 500	Best Fit Index Wil 4500
Alpha	12.7	4.4
Beta	1.68	1.31
R–Squared	55	92
Standard Deviation		42.60
Mean		2.07
Sharpe Ratio		–0.08

Analysis by Peter Di Teresa 11-30-01

This fund can still soar in a rising market, and that's why aggressive investors shouldn't rule it out.

With its 34.7% loss for the year to date through Nov. 29, 2001—worse than four fifths of its mid-cap growth peers—no one would mistake Invesco Dynamics Fund for a safe harbor. But that downside shouldn't come as a surprise—managers Tim Miller and Tom Wald are dedicated growth investors who are willing to stake a lot on areas they like.

Despite their tendency to load up on sectors—even now the fund has 40% in tech—Miller points out that sector plays haven't been the problem this year. Rather, the fund has suffered more from too-rosy expectations from the economy. The fund holds a mix of core stocks that are market leaders with histories of high growth and more-speculative issues that have the potential to become dominant. The fund was positioned for the Fed to deliver a soft landing and recovery, so it had more in noncore holdings than it would have otherwise. As the economy continued to sour, the fund suffered accordingly. The managers culled the portfolio, shifting assets into core issues. Miller noted that they added in particular to semiconductor firms such as Novellus, Altera, and Linear Technology.

It isn't clear what effect that shift will have (the fund still has about 40% of its stock assets in noncore issues), but investors can take some reassurance from the fund's recent performance. It came on strong with the market's rebound, gaining nearly 11% in October and 12% in the 30 days ending Nov. 29. Very few peers did better.

The ability to make the most of favorable environments has certainly made this fund a rewarding long-term investment, but it's only for those who can hang on during the downturns.

Portfolio Analysis 06-30-01

Share change since 03–01 Total Stocks: 147	Sector	PE	YTD Ret%	% Assets
⊖ Forest Labs	Health	52.2	23.35	2.37
Harrah's Entrtnmt	Services	—	40.32	1.90
⊖ EBAY	Services	NMF	102.70	1.56
⊕ Genzyme Corporation General	Health	—	33.11	1.54
⊕ VeriSign	Technology	—	–48.70	1.38
⊕ Time Warner Telecom Cl A	Services	—	–72.10	1.20
⊕ Waddell & Reed Finl Cl A	Financials	23.3	–13.40	1.20
Paychex	Services	49.4	–27.10	1.16
USA Ntwks	Services	58.1	40.50	1.14
⊖ King Pharmaceuticals	Health	45.8	8.68	1.13
Andrx	Health	66.4	21.66	1.13
Kohl's	Retail	54.2	15.48	1.12
NVIDIA	Technology	84.2	308.50	1.10
⊕ Rational Software	Technology	—	–49.90	1.10
TMP Worldwide	Services	71.5	–22.00	1.07
Omnicom Grp	Services	34.5	8.83	1.05
⊕ Xilinx	Technology	—	–15.30	1.05
Teva Pharma Inds ADR	Health	48.9	–15.50	1.03
USA Educ	Financials	68.9	24.74	1.02
⊕ Novellus Sys	Technology	25.0	9.77	1.00
Adobe Sys	Technology	37.4	–46.50	0.96
⊕ Brocade Comm Sys	Technology	—	–63.90	0.95
Entercom Comms	Services	NMF	45.19	0.95
⊖ John Hancock Finl Svcs	Financials	—	10.66	0.94
⊕ Quest Software	Technology	—	–21.20	0.94

Current Investment Style

Style: Value Blnd Growth; Size: Large Med Small

	Stock Port Avg	Relative S&P 500 Current	Relative S&P 500 Hist	Rel Cat
Price/Earnings Ratio	39.4	1.27	1.25	1.14
Price/Book Ratio	5.8	1.02	1.25	1.02
Price/Cash Flow	27.8	1.55	1.25	1.20
3 Yr Earnings Growth	28.4[1]	1.94	1.44	1.21
1 Yr Earnings Est%	6.9	—	—	0.74
Med Mkt Cap $mil	5,420	0.1	0.1	0.96

[1] figure is based on 50% or less of stocks

Special Securities % assets 06-30-01	
Restricted/Illiquid Secs	0
Emerging–Markets Secs	2
Options/Futures/Warrants	No

Composition % assets 06-30-01	
Cash	6.1
Stocks*	93.9
Bonds	0.0
Other	0.0
*Foreign (% stocks)	5.4

Market Cap	
Giant	0.0
Large	34.6
Medium	60.7
Small	4.6
Micro	0.1

Sector Weightings	% of Stocks	Rel S&P	5-Year High	5-Year Low
Utilities	0.0	0.0	6	0
Energy	3.4	0.5	16	0
Financials	12.7	0.7	18	0
Industrials	2.8	0.2	22	2
Durables	0.0	0.0	8	0
Staples	0.0	0.0	8	0
Services	23.1	2.1	38	9
Retail	2.4	0.4	28	2
Health	15.2	1.0	22	3
Technology	40.5	2.2	49	11

Address:	P.O. Box 173706 Denver, CO 80217–3706 800–525–8085 / 303–930–6300
Web Address:	www.invescofunds.com
Inception:	09-15-67
Advisor:	Invesco Funds Grp.
Subadvisor:	None
NTF Plans:	Fidelity , Datalynx

Minimum Purchase:	$1000	Add: $50	IRA: $250
Min Auto Inv Plan:	$50	Add: $50	
Sales Fees:	0.25%B		
Management Fee:	.60% mx./.50% mn., .02%A		
Actual Fees:	Mgt: —	Dist: —	
Expense Projections:	3Yr: —	5Yr: —	10Yr: —
Avg Brok Commission:	—	Income Distrib: Annually	
Total Cost (relative to category):	—		

INVESCO Financial Services Inv

Ticker	Load	NAV	Yield	Total Assets	Mstar Category
FSFSX	12b–1 only	$27.27	0.4%	$1,265.9 mil	Spec Financials

Prospectus Objective: Specialty—Financial

INVESCO Financial Services Fund seeks growth.

The fund will primarily invest in equity securities of companies involved in the financial services sector. The fund will keep the portfolio holdings well-diversified across the entire financial services sector. It may invest up to 25% of assets in securities of foreign companies.

The fund currently offers Class C, K and Investor shares, all of which differ in fee structure and availability. The fund has experienced several name changes.

Historical Profile

Return Above Avg
Risk Average
Rating ★★★★ Above Avg

Investment Style
Equity
Average Stock %: 95% | 97% | 94% | 95% | 94% | 92% | 94%

▼ Manager Change
▽ Partial Manager Change

Fund Performance vs. Category Average
■ Quarterly Fund Return +/– Category Average
— Category Baseline

Performance Quartile (within Category)

1990	1991	1992	1993	1994	1995	1996	1997	1998	1999	2000	12–01	History
8.50	14.57	17.24	15.91	14.64	19.02	22.22	28.11	29.18	26.62	32.29	27.27	NAV
–7.16	74.00	26.78	18.50	–5.89	39.81	30.29	44.79	13.45	0.73	26.69	–10.17	Total Return %
–4.04	43.51	19.16	8.44	–7.20	2.27	7.35	11.44	–15.12	–20.31	35.79	1.71	+/– S&P 500
–0.97	39.79	17.81	7.21	–5.82	3.36	9.09	13.49	–9.98	–22.83	37.63	0.72	+/– Wilshire 5000
0.08	1.41	1.30	1.22	2.18	1.97	2.82	1.12	0.89	0.27	0.31	0.33	Income Return %
–7.23	72.59	25.48	17.28	–8.06	37.84	27.47	43.67	12.57	0.46	26.38	–10.50	Capital Return %
1	9	76	26	86	66	33	44	17	38	50	87	Total Rtn % Rank Cat
0.01	0.12	0.19	0.21	0.35	0.29	0.53	0.25	0.25	0.08	0.08	0.10	Income $
0.02	0.10	0.91	4.31	0.00	1.14	1.94	3.70	2.24	2.65	1.22	1.60	Capital Gains $
2.50	1.13	1.07	1.03	1.18	1.26	1.11	0.99	1.05	1.26	1.29	1.25	Expense Ratio %
–0.16	1.76	1.28	1.16	1.66	2.10	2.48	1.19	0.85	0.25	0.25	0.36	Income Ratio %
528	249	208	236	88	171	141	96	52	83	—	99	Turnover Rate %
3.9	91.0	246.6	339.2	236.4	432.5	622.2	1,307.2	1,522.9	1,123.2	1,592.4	1,250.3	Net Assets $mil

Portfolio Manager(s)

Jeffrey G. Morris, CFA. Since 3-97. BS Colorado State U.; MS U. of Colorado. Other funds currently managed: INVESCO Financial Services C, INVESCO Financial Services K.

Joseph W. Skornicka, CFA. Since 7-01. MBA U of Michigan; BA Michigan State U. Other funds currently managed: INVESCO Financial Services C, INVESCO Financial Services K.

Performance 12-31-01

	1st Qtr	2nd Qtr	3rd Qtr	4th Qtr	Total
1997	2.03	18.79	11.25	7.38	44.79
1998	11.03	4.23	–18.20	19.85	13.45
1999	3.63	1.29	–15.18	13.14	0.73
2000	2.02	–1.70	22.76	2.90	26.69
2001	–10.41	6.86	–12.64	7.41	–10.17

Trailing	Total Return%	+/– S&P 500	+/– Wil 5000	% Rank All	% Rank Cat	Growth of $10,000
3 Mo	7.41	–3.27	–4.96	54	39	10,741
6 Mo	–6.16	–0.61	–0.68	69	69	9,384
1 Yr	–10.17	1.71	0.72	61	87	8,983
3 Yr Avg	4.66	5.69	5.31	34	57	11,464
5 Yr Avg	13.49	2.80	3.79	7	40	18,831
10 Yr Avg	17.10	4.18	4.82	3	61	48,498
15 Yr Avg	17.46	3.73	4.46	2	18	111,810

Tax Analysis	Tax-Adj Ret%	%Rank Cat	%Pretax Ret	%Rank Cat
3 Yr Avg	3.10	59	66.6	70
5 Yr Avg	11.16	51	82.7	55
10 Yr Avg	13.81	61	80.7	92

Potential Capital Gain Exposure: –1% of assets

Risk Analysis

Time Period	Load-Adj Return %	Risk %Rank[1] All	Risk %Rank[1] Cat	Morningstar Return	Morningstar Risk	Morningstar Risk-Adj Rating
1 Yr	–10.17					
3 Yr	4.66	74	74	–0.06[2]	1.02	★★★
5 Yr	13.49	76	73	2.17[2]	1.04	★★★★
10 Yr	17.10	79	67	2.37	1.04	★★★★★

Average Historical Rating (152 months): 4.5★s

[1] 1=low, 100=high [2] T-Bill return substituted for category avg.

Category Rating (3 Yr)

1 2 **3** 4 5
Worst Best

Return: Average
Risk: Above Avg

Other Measures	Standard Index S&P 500	Best Fit Index S&P 500
Alpha	5.9	5.9
Beta	0.83	0.83
R–Squared	40	40

Standard Deviation	23.53
Mean	4.66
Sharpe Ratio	–0.01

Portfolio Analysis 09-30-01

Share chng since 06–01 Total Stocks: 44

Stock	Subsector	PE	YTD Ret%	% Assets
Citigroup	Insurance	20.0	0.03	5.04
⊖ Wells Fargo	Other U.S. Banks	22.4	–20.20	5.02
⊕ American Intl Grp	Insurance	42.0	–19.20	4.46
⊕ Fifth Third Bancorp	Other U.S. Banks	38.3	4.53	4.44
⊖ FleetBoston Finl	Other U.S. Banks	16.2	0.55	4.33
⊕ Lehman Brothers Hldgs	Broker/Inv Bank	12.4	–0.84	4.03
⊖ Bank of New York	Other U.S. Banks	21.9	–24.80	3.80
⊕ J.P. Morgan Chase & Co.	Money Ctr. Banks	27.8	–17.40	3.79
⊕ Bank of America	Other U.S. Banks	16.7	42.73	3.70
⊕ Goldman Sachs Grp	Financials	20.7	–12.80	3.62
⊕ Everest Re Grp	Insurance	17.6	–1.29	3.59
⊕ Ambac Finl Grp	Insurance	15.2	–0.16	2.96
⊕ TCF Finl	Other U.S. Banks	18.2	10.24	2.77
⊕ Golden West Finl	Thrifts	12.9	–12.40	2.75
Freddie Mac	Finance/Mortg.	14.0	–3.87	2.65
Radian Grp	Insurance	11.6	14.64	2.63
Northern Tr	Other U.S. Banks	27.4	–25.40	2.50
Marsh & McLennan	Insurance	27.9	–6.30	2.36
Fannie Mae	Finance/Mortg.	16.2	–6.95	2.34
✵ Household Intl	Finance/Mortg.	14.7	6.89	2.01
⊕ State Street	Other U.S. Banks	28.6	–15.10	1.80
⊕ AFLAC	Insurance	19.3	–31.40	1.77
✵ UBS (Reg)	Foreign Banks	20.1	—	1.71
⊕ Arthur J. Gallagher & Co.	Financials	26.3	10.31	1.56
⊕ Natl Commerce	Other U.S. Banks	32.4	3.99	1.39

Current Investment Style

Style: Value Blnd Growth; Size: Large Med Small

	Stock Port Avg	Relative S&P 500 Current	Relative S&P 500 Hist	Rel Cat
Price/Earnings Ratio	22.3	0.72	0.68	1.05
Price/Book Ratio	3.7	0.64	0.55	1.20
Price/Cash Flow	—	—	—	—
3 Yr Earnings Growth	18.1	1.24	0.99	1.11
1 Yr Earnings Est%	5.7	—	—	1.83
Med Mkt Cap $mil	27,382	0.5	0.3	1.25

Special Securities % assets 09-30-01	
Restricted/Illiquid Secs	0
Emerging–Markets Secs	0
Options/Futures/Warrants	No

Composition % assets 09-30-01	
Cash	6.0
Stocks*	94.0
Bonds	0.0
Other	0.0
*Foreign (% stocks)	3.3

Market Cap	
Giant	35.5
Large	37.1
Medium	26.5
Small	1.0
Micro	0.0

Subsector Weightings	% of Stocks	Rel Cat
Money Ctr. Banks	4.1	1.6
Other U.S. Banks	36.5	1.4
Foreign Banks	1.8	0.5
Thrifts	3.0	0.5
Insurance	26.0	1.3
Finance/Mortg.	9.8	1.0
Broker/Inv Bank	6.3	1.2
Money Mgmt	0.6	0.8
Other	12.0	0.5

Analysis by Scott Cooley 11-27-01

Invesco Financial Services Fund's appeal has dimmed a bit.

The fund's return so far in 2001 isn't anything to brag about. For the year to date through Nov. 26, it has lost 10.2%, and lags four fifths of its specialty-financial peers. Comanagers Jeff Morris and Joe Skornicka lean toward growth-oriented financials such as Wells Fargo and American International Group. Those issues have been decidedly out of favor this year. The fund's diversification across financial subsectors has also worked against it. Several of its brokerage and insurance holdings have struggled. The category's top-returning funds this year have been narrowly focused offerings with considerable exposure to smaller-cap thrifts and regional banks, which have benefited from the Federal Reserve's interest-rate cuts. Those issues typically don't get much play here.

The managers are sticking to their guns. Morris and Skornicka argue that growth financials are now very attractively valued, so they have stuck with most of their favorites from early in the year. Indeed, they bought shares of insurers RenaissanceRe Holdings and Swiss Reinsurance in the wake of the Sept. 11 terrorist attacks. Management thought those issues were attractively priced and should benefit from an improved pricing environment. They've also added to their stakes in brokerages that focus on institutional accounts, including Goldman Sachs, because the managers think institutions will return to the stock market before individual investors do.

Although the fund sports respectable long–term numbers, we can't give it a wholehearted recommendation. Morris has announced plans to leave the fund in early 2002, and Skornicka lacks a long managerial record. There's no reason to sell this fund, but we're not as bullish as we once were, either.

Address:	P.O. Box 173706 Denver, CO 80217–3706 800–525–8085 / 303–930–6300
Web Address:	www.invescofunds.com
Inception:	06-02-86
Advisor:	Invesco Funds Grp.
Subadvisor:	None
NTF Plans:	Fidelity , Datalynx

Minimum Purchase:	$1000	Add: $50	IRA: $250
Min Auto Inv Plan:	$50	Add: $50	
Sales Fees:	0.25%B		
Management Fee:	.75% mx./.55% mn., .02%A		
Actual Fees:	Mgt: —	Dist: —	
Expense Projections:	3Yr: $421	5Yr: $729	10Yr: $1601
Avg Brok Commission:	—	Income Distrib: Annually	
Total Cost (relative to category):	Below Avg		

INVESCO Growth Inv

Ticker	Load	NAV	Yield	Total Assets	Mstar Category
FLRFX	12b–1 only	$2.60	0.0%	$928.5 mil	Large Growth

Prospectus Objective: Growth

INVESCO Growth Fund seeks long-term capital appreciation and current income.

The fund invests primarily in common stocks of large companies that have market capitalizations of more than $15 billion and that have a history of consistent earnings growth regardless of business cycles. It may invest in preferred stocks and debt instruments that are convertible into common stocks.

The fund currently offers C, K and Investor shares, all of which differ in fee structure and availability. Past names: Financial Industrial Fund and Invesco Growth Fund.

Historical Profile
Return: Low
Risk: High
Rating: ★ Lowest

Investment Style
Equity
Average Stock %: 97% 97% 100% 98% 100% 99% 100%

▼ Manager Change
▽ Partial Manager Change

Fund Performance vs. Category Average
■ Quarterly Fund Return +/– Category Average
— Category Baseline

Performance Quartile (within Category)

Portfolio Manager(s)

Trent E. May, CFA. Since 10-96. BS'86 The Florida Inst. of Tech.; MBA'92 Rollins C. Other funds currently managed: INVESCO Growth & Income Inv, INVESCO Endeavor Inv, INVESCO Growth C.

Douglas J. McEldowney, CFA. Since 4-99. BA U. of Kentucky; MBA Rollins C. Other funds currently managed: INVESCO Growth C, INVESCO Growth K.

History

1990	1991	1992	1993	1994	1995	1996	1997	1998	1999	2000	12-01	History
4.36	5.59	5.12	5.54	4.52	4.95	5.19	4.96	6.46	8.11	5.15	2.60	NAV
–1.25	42.15	2.91	17.95	–8.80	29.54	20.97	27.23	41.72	38.49	–23.92	–49.07	Total Return %
1.87	11.67	–4.70	7.89	–10.12	–8.00	–1.98	–6.13	13.14	17.45	–14.82	–37.19	+/– S&P 500
–2.62	2.75	–0.98	18.02	–13.65	–9.12	–4.56	–6.52	–3.38	8.81	0.60	–28.57	+/– Russ Top 200 Grt
2.44	1.69	0.77	0.63	0.62	1.18	0.57	0.15	0.40	0.01	0.00	0.00	Income Return %
–3.69	40.46	2.14	17.32	–9.42	28.36	20.40	27.07	41.31	38.48	–23.92	–49.07	Capital Return %
40	46	77	17	94	65	34	42	19	42	84	98	Total Rtn % Rank Cat
0.11	0.07	0.04	0.03	0.03	0.05	0.03	0.01	0.02	0.00	0.00	0.00	Income $
0.02	0.48	0.54	0.44	0.50	0.84	0.77	1.60	0.51	0.76	1.07	0.02	Capital Gains $
0.78	1.00	1.04	1.04	1.03	1.06	1.05	1.07	1.04	1.03	1.02	1.16	Expense Ratio %
2.17	1.52	0.93	0.72	0.47	1.07	0.64	0.22	0.37	–0.08	–0.63	–0.96	Income Ratio %
86	69	77	77	63	111	207	286	153	—	168	129	Turnover Rate %
340.3	455.0	449.0	510.2	444.5	535.5	651.3	753.3	1,220.1	1,637.4	2,122.8	917.4	Net Assets $mil

Performance 12-31-01

	1st Qtr	2nd Qtr	3rd Qtr	4th Qtr	Total
1997	–1.54	18.40	6.75	2.24	27.23
1998	12.90	5.18	–5.92	26.85	41.72
1999	6.04	3.07	–3.39	31.17	38.49
2000	7.77	–0.11	6.76	–33.80	–23.92
2001	–40.19	11.36	–43.15	34.51	–49.07

Trailing	Total Return%	+/– S&P 500	+/– Russ Top 200 Grth	% Rank All	% Rank Cat	Growth of $10,000
3 Mo	34.51	23.82	21.65	3	2	13,451
6 Mo	–23.53	–17.98	–16.54	99	99	7,647
1 Yr	–49.07	–37.19	–28.57	100	98	5,093
3 Yr Avg	–18.74	–17.71	–10.72	100	100	5,366
5 Yr Avg	–0.66	–11.36	–9.25	94	96	9,675
10 Yr Avg	5.31	–7.61	–5.77	88	95	16,782
15 Yr Avg	8.22	–5.51	–5.15	51	92	32,716

Tax Analysis	Tax-Adj Ret%	%Rank Cat	%Pretax Ret	%Rank Cat
3 Yr Avg	–20.87	100	—	—
5 Yr Avg	–4.49	98	—	—
10 Yr Avg	1.35	97	25.3	100

Potential Capital Gain Exposure: –62% of assets

Risk Analysis

Time Period	Load-Adj Return %	Risk %Rank[1] All	Risk %Rank[1] Cat	Morningstar Return	Morningstar Risk	Morningstar Risk-Adj Rating
1 Yr	–49.07					
3 Yr	–18.74	99	97	–3.97[2]	2.33	★
5 Yr	–0.66	97	98	–1.12[2]	1.90	★
10 Yr	5.31	95	96	0.07	1.71	★

Average Historical Rating (193 months): 2.8★s

[1]1=low, 100=high [2] T-Bill return substituted for category avg.

Category Rating (3 Yr)

1 2 3 4 5 — Worst … Best

Return: Low
Risk: High

Other Measures	Standard Index S&P 500	Best Fit Index MSCIACWdFr
Alpha	–5.2	3.9
Beta	2.23	2.41
R-Squared	72	74
Standard Deviation		41.81
Mean		–18.74
Sharpe Ratio		–0.69

Analysis by Peter Di Teresa 10-22-01

Even investors with a taste for danger may find Invesco Growth Fund hard to swallow.

Since late 2000, this fund (formerly named Invesco Blue Chip Growth) has been paying a heavy price for its daring style. Manager Trent May focuses on just 30 to 50 names. Those stocks are companies that are leaders in industries fueling the U.S. economy's growth. Naturally, the fund tends to load up on tech, health-care, and services stocks.

That style courted risk, but it also garnered strong returns. The fund's three-year annualized return through August 2000 was a remarkable 9 percentage points better than the large-growth group's 28.4% average.

The fund ran into a brick wall in the fourth quarter of 2000, though. It plummeted 33.8%, twice the category average. A hefty tech stake hurt, and May notes that networking and optical issues, which had actually held up for most of the year, were especially injurious. The fund's miseries haven't lightened much in 2001. For the year to date through Oct. 19, 2001, it had lost 56.5%. Its three-year return was a dreadful 17.6% per-year loss—only four large-growth funds lost more.

In spite of that beating, the fund still has an aggressive stance, with 56% of its portfolio in tech issues—the idea is to be positioned for the early stages of a market recovery, which can be sudden. When the market rallied in April, that bent paid off and the fund skyrocketed 25%, while the group settled for a 10% surge. Although April showed that the fund could still deliver the goods in a favorable market, it's impossible to downplay the disastrous months preceding and following it.

With numerous large-growth funds featuring less-dramatic downsides and stronger long-term returns, even investors who can stomach this fund's volatility could do a lot better.

Portfolio Analysis 09-30-01

Share change since 06-01 Total Stocks: 48

	Sector	PE	YTD Ret%	% Assets
⊖ AOL Time Warner	Technology	—	–7.76	5.44
⊕ JDS Uniphase	Technology	—	–79.00	4.46
⊖ Maxim Integrated Products	Technology	68.2	9.82	4.46
⊕ Cisco Sys	Technology	—	–52.60	4.40
⊕ Pfizer	Health	34.7	–12.40	4.32
⊕ Citigroup	Financials	20.0	0.03	4.27
⊕ EBAY	Services	NMF	102.70	3.98
⊕ Analog Devices	Technology	47.7	–13.20	3.95
⊕ Genentech	Health	NMF	–33.40	3.47
☼ Liberty Media Cl A	N/A	—	—	3.45
⊕ Qwest Comms Intl	Services	—	–65.40	3.37
⊕ Applied Micro Circuits	Technology	—	–84.90	3.37
⊕ Brocade Comm Sys	Technology	—	–63.90	3.06
⊕ Charles Schwab	Financials	61.9	–45.30	2.83
⊖ Nextel Comms Cl A	Services	—	–55.70	2.76
⊕ Sun Microsystems	Technology	NMF	–55.80	2.65
⊕ Xilinx	Technology	—	–15.30	2.46
⊖ VeriSign	Technology	—	–48.70	2.05
Merrill Lynch	Financials	18.2	–22.70	2.01
⊕ Vitesse Semicon	Technology	—	–77.50	1.96
⊕ Goldman Sachs Grp	Financials	20.7	–12.80	1.89
⊕ Oracle	Technology	32.1	–52.40	1.62
⊖ EMC	Technology	NMF	–79.40	1.59
⊖ Microsoft	Technology	57.6	52.78	1.53
⊕ Applied Matls	Technology	66.8	5.01	1.53

Current Investment Style

Style: Value Blnd Growth; Size: Large Med Small

	Stock Port Avg	Relative S&P 500 Current	Relative S&P 500 Hist	Rel Cat
Price/Earnings Ratio	47.4	1.53	1.35	1.33
Price/Book Ratio	6.0	1.05	1.41	0.93
Price/Cash Flow	25.8	1.43	1.35	1.14
3 Yr Earnings Growth	23.0[1]	1.57	1.38	1.07
1 Yr Earnings Est%	–12.8	7.21	—	–4.25
Med Mkt Cap $mil	23,910	0.4	1.1	0.51

[1]figure is based on 50% or less of stocks

Special Securities % assets 09-30-01	
Restricted/Illiquid Secs	0
Emerging-Markets Secs	1
Options/Futures/Warrants	No

Composition % assets 09-30-01	
Cash	0.0
Stocks*	100.0
Bonds	0.0
Other	0.0
*Foreign (% stocks)	3.8

Market Cap	
Giant	29.2
Large	54.2
Medium	16.7
Small	0.0
Micro	0.0

Sector Weightings	% of Stocks	Rel S&P	5-Year High	5-Year Low
Utilities	1.4	0.4	12	0
Energy	0.6	0.1	12	0
Financials	11.5	0.6	18	4
Industrials	4.4	0.4	20	3
Durables	0.0	0.0	14	0
Staples	1.1	0.1	18	0
Services	12.9	1.2	30	6
Retail	1.7	0.3	22	1
Health	10.1	0.7	28	5
Technology	56.4	3.1	71	6

Address: P.O. Box 173706, Denver, CO 80217–3706, 800–525–8085 / 303–930–6300
Web Address: www.invescofunds.com
Inception: 11-25-35
Advisor: Invesco Funds Grp.
Subadvisor: None
NTF Plans: Fidelity , Datalynx

Minimum Purchase: $1000 Add: $50 IRA: $250
Min Auto Inv Plan: $50 Add: $50
Sales Fees: 0.25%B
Management Fee: .60% mx./.50% mn., .02%A
Actual Fees: Mgt: — Dist: 0.25%
Expense Projections: 3Yr: $331 5Yr: $574 10Yr: $1271
Avg Brok Commission: — Income Distrib: Quarterly
Total Cost (relative to category): Below Avg

INVESCO Small Company Growth Inv

Ticker	Load	NAV	Yield	Total Assets	Mstar Category
FIEGX	Closed	$12.14	0.0%	$1,239.2 mil	Small Growth

Prospectus Objective: Small Company

INVESCO Small Company Growth Fund seeks long-term growth of capital.

The fund normally invests at least 65% of assets in equities of companies with market capitalizations of less than $1 billion. Management typically selects undervalued companies it judges to have the potential for accelerating earnings growth resulting from management changes, rapid sales growth, or new products. The fund may invest up to 25% of assets in foreign securities; ADRs are not subject to this limitation.

The fund offers C shares which are available to qualified investors and Investor shares. The fund has gone through several name changes. On June 4, 1999, Invesco Small Company Value Fund merged into the fund.

Historical Profile

Return Above Avg
Risk High
Rating ★★★ Neutral

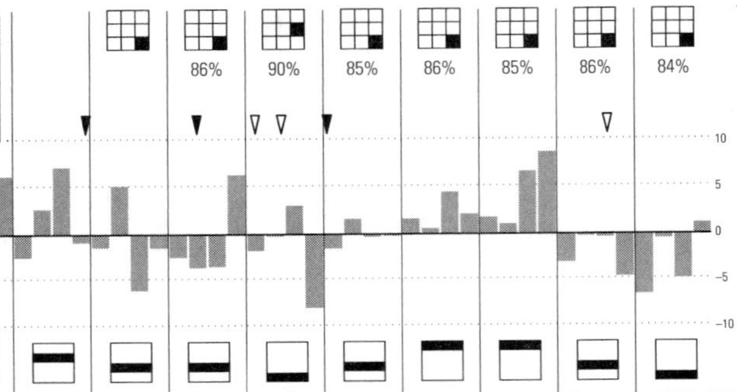

Investment Style
Equity
Average Stock %: 86% 90% 85% 86% 85% 86% 84%

▼ Manager Change
▽ Partial Manager Change

Fund Performance vs. Category Average
■ Quarterly Fund Return +/– Category Average
— Category Baseline

Performance Quartile (within Category)

Portfolio Manager(s)

Stacie A. Cowell, CFA. Since 1-97. MA U. of Colorado-Denver; BA Colgate U. Other funds currently managed: Maxim INVESCO SmallCap Growth, INVESCO Small Company Growth C, AXP Small Cap Growth A.

History

1990	1991	1992	1993	1994	1995	1996	1997	1998	1999	2000	12-01	History
—	7.81	9.82	12.11	9.17	11.69	12.52	11.21	11.58	18.62	15.35	12.14	NAV
—	–2.38*	25.74	23.39	–3.74	30.02	11.62	18.31	14.90	81.64	–12.19	–20.91	Total Return %
—	–5.25*	18.12	13.33	–5.06	–7.51	–11.32	–15.04	–13.68	60.60	–3.09	–9.04	+/– S&P 500
—	—	17.97	10.03	–1.31	–1.02	0.36	5.36	13.67	38.55	10.24	–11.68	+/– Russ 2000 Grth
—	0.00	0.00	0.00	0.00	0.49	0.00	0.00	0.00	0.00	0.00	0.00	Income Return %
—	–2.38	25.74	23.39	–3.74	29.53	11.62	18.31	14.90	81.64	–12.19	–20.91	Capital Return %
—	—	4	27	69	62	78	52	14	25	66	82	Total Rtn % Rank Cat
—	0.00	0.00	0.00	0.00	0.05	0.00	0.00	0.00	0.00	0.00	0.00	Income $
—	0.00	0.00	0.01	2.49	0.18	0.53	3.42	1.17	1.99	0.93	0.00	Capital Gains $
—	—	1.93	1.54	1.37	1.49	1.48	1.52	1.48	1.51	1.20	1.29	Expense Ratio %
—	—	–0.95	–0.70	–0.26	0.41	–0.78	–0.55	–0.42	–0.58	–0.34	–0.28	Income Ratio %
—	—	—	153	196	228	221	216	158	203	186	112	Turnover Rate %
—	1.0	123.0	223.0	179.2	212.7	267.9	313.6	316.8	876.0	1,616.2	1,234.6	Net Assets $mil

Performance 12-31-01

	1st Qtr	2nd Qtr	3rd Qtr	4th Qtr	Total
1997	–10.38	19.96	17.53	–6.37	18.31
1998	13.56	–3.54	–16.94	26.27	14.90
1999	–1.21	16.87	7.26	46.68	81.64
2000	12.89	–4.80	0.55	–18.74	–12.19
2001	–23.84	16.85	–28.70	24.64	–20.91

Trailing	Total Return%	+/– S&P 500	+/– Russ 2000 Grth	% Rank All	% Rank Cat	Growth of $10,000
3 Mo	24.64	13.96	–1.53	8	43	12,464
6 Mo	–11.13	–5.57	–1.86	88	82	8,887
1 Yr	–20.91	–9.04	–11.68	82	82	7,909
3 Yr Avg	8.05	9.08	7.80	15	52	12,615
5 Yr Avg	11.39	0.69	8.52	12	34	17,147
10 Yr Avg	14.03	1.10	6.84	8	8	37,166
15 Yr Avg	—	—	—	—	—	—

Tax Analysis	Tax-Adj Ret%	%Rank Cat	%Pretax Ret	%Rank Cat
3 Yr Avg	5.62	51	69.8	69
5 Yr Avg	7.26	45	63.7	76
10 Yr Avg	10.87	20	77.5	53

Potential Capital Gain Exposure: –26% of assets

Risk Analysis

Time Period	Load-Adj Return %	Risk %Rank[1] All	Risk %Rank[1] Cat	Morningstar Return	Morningstar Risk	Morningstar Risk-Adj Rating
1 Yr	–20.91					
3 Yr	8.05	95	70	0.68[2]	1.68	★★★
5 Yr	11.39	93	60	1.57[2]	1.64	★★★
10 Yr	14.03	95	55	1.55	1.69	★★★

Average Historical Rating (85 months): 2.7★s

[1] 1=low, 100=high [2] T-Bill return substituted for category avg.

Category Rating (3 Yr)

1 2 **3** 4 5
Worst — Best

Return: Average
Risk: Above Avg

Other Measures	Standard Index S&P 500	Best Fit Index Wil 4500
Alpha	18.0	10.4
Beta	1.46	1.33
R-Squared	41	92

Standard Deviation	45.41
Mean	8.05
Sharpe Ratio	0.08

Analysis by Peter Di Teresa 12-31-01

We still think this fund is worth keeping, but we're also keeping an eye on it.

After losing 12% and lagging two thirds of its peers in 2000, Invesco Small Company Growth Fund has had a downright miserable 2001. For the year to date through Dec. 28, it was down 20.9% and trailing four fifths of its competitors.

We think there are reasons for sticking with this fund, though. Its bear-market woes are no surprise, and manager Stacie Cowell has led it to topnotch returns in friendlier markets. Cowell focuses on high-growth industries such as tech and health care and prefers firms that can outpace their industry peers. Such stocks often command high prices, so the fund typically sports greater price risk than most small-growth offerings. Cowell also has made sector bets of 40% of assets. In such an uncertain market, it's no wonder that this portfolio has suffered.

Cowell gets credit for turning this offering around, though. When she took the helm in early 1997, the fund had just completed three years of ever-worsening relative performance. During her first three years, the fund delivered a 35% annualized return, nearly 11 percentage points better than the category average. Despite its recent mauling, the fund's five-year return through Dec. 28, 2001, ranked in the group's top third.

The fund did gain 28% as the market revived during the past three months, but that was only slightly above average. We would expect it to do better, but a 14% cash stake (9 percentage points more than the average) and a 38% mid-cap stake have probably hindered the fund lately. (The strongest-performing small-growth funds of late have much smaller market caps.)

Three months is too short a period to determine if this fund can still deliver good bull-market returns. We'll be closely monitoring its progress in market advances.

Portfolio Analysis 09-30-01

Share change since 06-01 Total Stocks: 131	Sector	PE	YTD Ret%	% Assets
⊕ Province Healthcare	Health	37.6	–21.60	2.31
City Natl	Financials	16.4	22.90	1.87
⊕ Commerce Bancorp NJ	Financials	27.5	17.01	1.83
⊖ Accredo Health	Health	53.7	18.65	1.49
⊕ Aeroflex	Technology	75.7	–34.30	1.47
⊕ Waddell & Reed Finl Cl A	Financials	23.3	–13.40	1.44
⊕ Investors Finl Svcs	Financials	57.1	–22.90	1.42
⊖ Jack Henry & Assoc	Technology	34.7	–29.30	1.41
⊕ Waste Connections	Services	28.7	–6.27	1.37
⊕ Raymond James Finl	Financials	18.0	3.36	1.32
⊕ First Health Grp	Health	25.8	6.26	1.14
⊖ Stericycle	Services	60.3	59.69	1.12
⊕ Arthur J. Gallagher & Co.	Financials	26.3	10.31	1.10
⊕ First Horizon	Health	—	43.37	1.08
⊖ Barr Labs	Health	25.0	8.80	1.03
☼ Earthlink	Technology	—	141.90	1.01
⊕ Pharmaceutical Resources	Health	NMF	387.10	0.99
⊕ Radio One Cl D	Services	—	—	0.97
⊕ Anaren Microwave	Technology	42.2	–74.20	0.97
⊕ United Surgical Partners	Health	—	—	0.97
⊕ Insight Enterprises	Retail	21.6	37.14	0.95
⊖ Advance Paradigm	Health	43.2	29.01	0.90
⊕ Career Educ	Services	47.6	75.23	0.89
☼ Pharmaceutical Product Dev	Services	36.3	30.05	0.89
⊖ Cephalon	Health	—	19.38	0.88

Current Investment Style

Style: Value Blnd Growth; Size: Large Med Small

	Stock Port Avg	Relative S&P 500 Current	Relative S&P 500 Hist	Rel Cat
Price/Earnings Ratio	37.7	1.22	1.17	1.17
Price/Book Ratio	5.8	1.01	0.93	1.19
Price/Cash Flow	24.8	1.38	1.23	1.13
3 Yr Earnings Growth	28.4[1]	1.94	—	1.13
1 Yr Earnings Est%	8.4	—	—	1.08
Med Mkt Cap $mil	1,112	0.0	0.0	1.06

[1] figure is based on 50% or less of stocks

Special Securities % assets 09-30-01	
Restricted/Illiquid Secs	0
Emerging-Markets Secs	0
Options/Futures/Warrants	No

Composition % assets 09-30-01	
Cash	14.4
Stocks*	85.6
Bonds	0.0
Other	0.0
*Foreign (% stocks)	2.3

Market Cap	
Giant	0.0
Large	0.0
Medium	38.1
Small	59.5
Micro	2.4

Sector Weightings	% of Stocks	Rel S&P	5-Year High	5-Year Low
Utilities	0.0	0.0	2	0
Energy	4.2	0.6	13	0
Financials	13.7	0.8	19	1
Industrials	3.9	0.3	33	0
Durables	0.2	0.1	7	0
Staples	2.8	0.4	6	0
Services	16.1	1.5	31	9
Retail	6.9	1.0	32	2
Health	24.5	1.7	34	2
Technology	27.8	1.5	54	11

Address:	P.O. Box 173706 Denver, CO 80217–3706 800–525–8085 / 303–930–6300
Web Address:	www.invescofunds.com
*Inception:	12-27-91
Advisor:	Invesco Funds Grp.
Subadvisor:	None
NTF Plans:	Fidelity , Datalynx

Minimum Purchase:	Closed	Add: $50	IRA: —
Min Auto Inv Plan:	Closed	Add: $50	
Sales Fees:	0.25%B		
Management Fee:	.75% mx./.55% mn., .02%A		
Actual Fees:	Mgt: 0.75%	Dist: 0.25%	
Expense Projections:	3Yr: $47*	5Yr: $81*	10Yr: $178*
Avg Brok Commission:	—	Income Distrib: Annually	
Total Cost (relative to category):	—		

INVESCO Telecommunications Inv

Ticker	Load	NAV	Yield	Total Assets	Mstar Category
ISWCX	12b–1 only	$16.62	0.0%	$866.0 mil	Spec Communications

Prospectus Objective: Specialty—Communications

INVESCO Telecommunications Fund seeks total return.

The fund invests primarily in the equity securities of companies engaged in the design, development, manufacture, distribution, or sale of communications services and equipment and companies that are involved in supplying equipment or services to such companies. It typically invests in at least three countries; although U.S. issuers will often dominate the portfolio. The fund's portfolio emphasizes strongly managed market leaders.

The fund offers C, K and Investor shares, all of which differ in fee structure and availability. The fund has gone through several name changes.

Historical Profile
Return Below Avg
Risk High
Rating ★★ Below Avg

Investment Style Equity
Average Stock %: 79% 90% 94% 90% 92% 85%

▼ Manager Change
▽ Partial Manager Change

Fund Performance vs. Category Average
■ Quarterly Fund Return +/– Category Average
— Category Baseline

Performance Quartile (within Category)

Portfolio Manager(s)

Brian B. Hayward, CFA. Since 7-97. BA U. of Missouri; MA U. of Missouri. Other funds currently managed: INVESCO Utilities Inv, INVESCO Utilities C, INVESCO Telecommunications C.

1990	1991	1992	1993	1994	1995	1996	1997	1998	1999	2000	12-01	History
—	—	—	—	10.40	11.83	12.63	15.34	21.21	51.63	36.28	16.62	NAV
—	—	—	—	5.02*	27.37	16.81	30.29	40.99	144.28	–26.91	–54.19	Total Return %
—	—	—	—	4.09*	–10.17	–6.14	–3.07	12.41	123.25	–17.81	–42.31	+/– S&P 500
—	—	—	—	—	–9.08	–4.39	–1.01	17.56	120.72	–15.97	–43.30	+/– Wilshire 5000
—	—	—	—	0.48	1.56	1.11	0.41	0.00	0.00	0.00	0.00	Income Return %
—	—	—	—	4.54	25.81	15.69	29.87	40.99	144.28	–26.91	–54.19	Capital Return %
—	—	—	—	—	63	1	50	46	5	21	91	Total Rtn % Rank Cat
—	—	—	—	0.05	0.16	0.13	0.05	0.00	0.00	0.00	0.00	Income $
—	—	—	—	0.05	1.25	1.02	1.04	0.37	0.15	1.46	0.00	Capital Gains $
—	—	—	—	—	1.95	1.66	1.69	1.32	1.24	0.99	1.10	Expense Ratio %
—	—	—	—	—	1.43	1.78	0.56	–0.16	–0.49	–0.32	–0.32	Income Ratio %
—	—	—	—	—	215	157	96	55	62	—	61	Turnover Rate %
—	—	—	—	15.8	31.9	54.1	83.6	323.5	2,373.0	2,779.0	851.0	Net Assets $mil

Performance 12-31-01

	1st Qtr	2nd Qtr	3rd Qtr	4th Qtr	Total
1997	–4.51	20.73	13.85	–0.73	30.29
1998	25.16	2.40	–21.72	40.53	40.99
1999	28.48	17.91	–0.59	62.22	144.28
2000	24.75	–12.93	–0.98	–32.04	–26.91
2001	–34.15	–0.42	–41.40	19.23	–54.19

Trailing	Total Return%	+/– S&P 500	+/– Wil 5000	% Rank All	% Rank Cat	Growth of $10,000
3 Mo	19.23	8.54	6.85	15	28	11,923
6 Mo	–30.14	–24.58	–24.66	100	93	6,986
1 Yr	–54.19	–42.31	–43.30	100	91	4,581
3 Yr Avg	–6.48	–5.45	–5.83	95	36	8,179
5 Yr Avg	8.48	–2.22	–1.22	27	64	15,024
10 Yr Avg	—	—	—	—	—	—
15 Yr Avg	—	—	—	—	—	—

Tax Analysis	Tax-Adj Ret%	%Rank Cat	%Pretax Ret	%Rank Cat
3 Yr Avg	–6.89	36	—	—
5 Yr Avg	7.59	57	89.5	16
10 Yr Avg	—	—	—	—

Potential Capital Gain Exposure: –65% of assets

Risk Analysis

Time Period	Load-Adj Return %	Risk %Rank[1] All	Risk %Rank[1] Cat	Morningstar Return	Morningstar Risk	Morningstar Risk-Adj Rating
1 Yr	–54.19					
3 Yr	–6.48	98	100	–2.17[2]	2.25	★
5 Yr	8.48	97	100	0.81[2]	1.92	★★
Incept	12.18	—	—	—	—	

Average Historical Rating (54 months): 4.3★s

[1]1=low, 100=high [2] T-Bill return substituted for category avg.

Category Rating (3 Yr)

1 2 **3** 4 5
Worst Best

Return Average
Risk High

Other Measures	Standard Index S&P 500	Best Fit Index Wil 4500
Alpha	9.7	–0.6
Beta	2.17	1.52
R-Squared	61	82
Standard Deviation		50.83
Mean		–6.48
Sharpe Ratio		–0.26

Analysis by William Harding 08-21-01

Invesco Telecommunications Fund has earned the benefit of the doubt, but barely.

To say that this fund has had a rough go of it lately would be an understatement. Communications stocks in general have taken it on the chin this year as companies have drastically cut spending on telecom gear amid the economic slump and overcapacity in the sector. This fund has struggled more than most, however. It has lost roughly 50% for the year to date ended August 17, 2001, which is worse than 90% of its peers.

Much of the problem owes to manager Brian Hayward's affinity for the riskier, potentially higher-growth areas of the telecom sector, such as telecom equipment and local exchange carriers (CLECs). He simply refuses to load up on stodgy old-line service companies, even when that's what's working best. In effect, this is more a telecom technology and emerging carrier fund than a broad communications fund.

That bias has been a recipe for disaster in 2001. Hayward has cut back on equipment names, such as JDS Uniphase, and added to steadier Regional Bells, but his moves were too little, too late to stop the bleeding. Further, in a questionable move, Hayward added to his stake in some CLECs in late 2000, which have been punished this year as funding concerns have plagued the group.

The fund's huge loss is hard to take, and Hayward has made some serious missteps. Nevertheless, he has guided the fund to superb returns in better times, and even after its recent slide, its five-year return still ranks near the middle of the communications pack (Hayward started in mid-1997). We therefore think that current investors will want to give him a bit of time to turn things around. But those considering this offering should ask themselves if they can afford to lose half their money in the span of several months. If the answer is no, then steer clear of it.

Portfolio Analysis 09-30-01

Share chng since 06-01 Total Stocks: 62

Share chng	Stock	Subsector	PE	YTD Ret%	% Assets
⊖	BellSouth	Phone Services	24.9	–5.09	3.90
☆	Liberty Media Cl A	N/A	—	—	3.67
	EchoStar Comms	Cable	—	20.75	3.08
⊕	WorldCom	Phone Services	24.3	3.12	2.92
⊕	Amdocs	Services	NMF	–48.70	2.67
⊖	SBC Comms	Phone Services	18.4	–16.00	2.60
⊖	Nokia Cl A ADR	Phone Equip.	45.8	–43.00	2.36
⊖	AOL Time Warner	Technology	—	–7.76	2.34
⊕	Nextel Comms Cl A	Wireless	—	–55.70	2.22
⊖	Tekelec	Phone Equip.	—	–39.60	2.03
⊖	Flextronics Intl	Technology	—	–15.80	2.00
	AT & T Canada Cl B Dep Rec	Phone Services	—	3.43	1.96
	Vodafone Airtouch	Wireless	—	—	1.89
⊖	Comcast	Cable	20.3	–13.70	1.82
⊕	Time Warner Telecom Cl A	Services	—	–72.10	1.80
	Cisco Sys	Technology	—	–52.60	1.79
⊖	Qwest Comms Intl	Phone Equip.	—	–65.40	1.73
⊖	Celestica	Technology	79.2	–25.50	1.71
⊕	Utstarcom	Technology	—	83.87	1.67
	TIM	Wireless	10.9	—	1.65
⊕	Comverse Tech	Phone Equip.	22.2	–79.40	1.57
	Gemstar–TV Guide Intl	Services	—	–39.90	1.55
⊖	El Paso	Utilities	NMF	–36.70	1.41
⊕	Allegiance Telecom	Phone Services	—	–62.70	1.39
⊖	Qualcomm	Phone Equip.	—	–38.50	1.35

Current Investment Style

Style: Value Blnd Growth; Size: Large Med Small

	Stock Port Avg	Relative S&P 500 Current	Relative S&P 500 Hist	Rel Cat
Price/Earnings Ratio	34.9[1]	1.13	1.44	1.14
Price/Book Ratio	4.1	0.71	1.46	0.90
Price/Cash Flow	19.0	1.06	1.36	1.13
3 Yr Earnings Growth	—	—	—	—
1 Yr Earnings Est%	–19.5[1]	11.02	—	0.93
Med Mkt Cap $mil	13,403	0.2	0.3	0.50

[1]figure is based on 50% or less of stocks

Special Securities % assets 09-30-01	
Restricted/Illiquid Secs	Trace
Emerging-Markets Secs	2
Options/Futures/Warrants	No

Composition % assets 09-30-01	
Cash	16.8
Stocks*	81.0
Bonds	1.4
Other	0.8
*Foreign (% stocks)	17.6

Market Cap	
Giant	29.6
Large	22.7
Medium	35.0
Small	11.9
Micro	0.8

Subsector Weightings	% of Stocks	Rel Cat
Phone Services	21.5	0.7
Phone Equip.	15.7	1.5
Wireless	9.3	1.1
Broadcasting	0.0	0.0
Cable	7.2	2.8
Publishing	0.0	0.0
Media	0.0	0.0
Technology	7.8	0.7
Other	38.5	1.1

Address: P.O. Box 173706
Denver, CO 80217–3706
800–525–8085 / 303–930–6300
Web Address: www.invescofunds.com
*Inception: 08-01-94
Advisor: Invesco Funds Grp.
Subadvisor: None
NTF Plans: Fidelity , Datalynx

Minimum Purchase: $1000 Add: $50 IRA: $250
Min Auto Inv Plan: $50 Add: $50
Sales Fees: 0.25%B
Management Fee: .65% mx./.45% mn., .02%A
Actual Fees: Mgt: 0.51% Dist: 0.25%
Expense Projections: 3Yr: $322 5Yr: $558 10Yr: $1236
Avg Brok Commission: — Income Distrib: Annually
Total Cost (relative to category): Below Avg

INVESCO Total Return Inv

Ticker	Load	NAV	Yield	Total Assets	Mstar Category
FSFLX	12b–1 only	$25.01	1.7%	$1,250.0 mil	Domestic Hybrid

Prospectus Objective: Balanced

INVESCO Total Return Fund seeks capital appreciation and current income.

The fund invests in a combination of equities and investment-grade fixed-income securities. It maintains at least 30% of assets in equities, and at least 30% in fixed- and variable-rate debt securities. The dollar-weighted average maturity of the fund's fixed-income component normally varies between three and 15 years. The fund may invest up to 25% of assets in foreign securities.

The fund offers C shares which are available to qualified investors and Investor shares. The fund has gone through several name changes.

Historical Profile
Return Below Avg
Risk Below Avg
Rating ★★★ Neutral

Investment Style
Equity
Average Stock %: 66% 64% 65% 68% 65% 65%

▼ Manager Change
▽ Partial Manager Change

Fund Performance vs. Category Average
■ Quarterly Fund Return +/– Category Average
– Category Baseline

Performance Quartile (within Category)

Portfolio Manager(s)

Charles P. Mayer. Since 12-00. BA St. Peter's C.; MBA St. John's U. Other funds currently managed: INVESCO Equity Income Inv, INVESCO Value Equity Inv, North American Balanced C.

Richard R. Hinderlie. Since 12-00. BA Pacific Lutheran U.; MBA Arizona State U. Other funds currently managed: INVESCO U.S. Government Secs Inv, INVESCO Select Income Inv, INVESCO Select Income C.

1990	1991	1992	1993	1994	1995	1996	1997	1998	1999	2000	12-01	History
14.21	16.43	17.18	18.26	18.10	22.34	24.30	29.09	31.36	28.96	26.43	25.01	NAV
–0.34	24.94	9.85	12.36	2.52	28.64	13.07	25.04	13.63	–1.36	–3.65	–0.93	Total Return %
2.78	–5.54	2.23	2.31	1.21	–8.90	–9.88	–8.31	–14.95	–22.40	5.45	10.95	+/– S&P 500
–9.30	8.94	2.44	2.61	5.44	10.17	9.45	15.36	4.95	–0.53	–15.28	–9.35	+/– LB Aggregate
5.06	5.14	4.01	4.07	3.15	4.11	3.74	3.09	2.77	2.64	2.59	1.68	Income Return %
–5.40	19.80	5.83	8.29	–0.63	24.53	9.33	21.95	10.85	–3.99	–6.24	–2.61	Capital Return %
53	38	31	46	9	20	51	7	42	91	83	27	Total Rtn % Rank Cat
0.75	0.72	0.65	0.69	0.57	0.73	0.82	0.74	0.80	0.82	0.74	0.44	Income $
0.06	0.55	0.19	0.32	0.05	0.13	0.09	0.48	0.82	1.16	0.70	0.73	Capital Gains $
1.00	0.92	0.88	0.93	0.96	0.95	0.89	0.86	0.79	0.83	1.00	1.27	Expense Ratio %
5.22	4.62	4.06	3.51	3.31	3.97	3.44	3.11	2.82	2.61	2.60	1.98	Income Ratio %
24	49	13	19	12	30	10	4	17	—	49	76	Turnover Rate %
55.0	82.2	137.2	240.6	293.7	768.3	1,227.4	2,160.7	3,040.8	2,934.7	1,827.2	1,249.5	Net Assets $mil

Performance 12-31-01

	1st Qtr	2nd Qtr	3rd Qtr	4th Qtr	Total
1997	1.87	11.86	6.70	2.85	25.04
1998	8.59	0.44	–5.28	9.99	13.63
1999	–1.66	8.39	–8.41	1.03	–1.36
2000	–3.41	–1.70	0.68	0.78	–3.65
2001	–3.66	4.42	–7.45	6.42	–0.93

Trailing	Total Return%	+/– S&P 500	+/– LB Agg	% Rank All	% Rank Cat	Growth of $10,000
3 Mo	6.42	–4.27	6.38	59	47	10,642
6 Mo	–1.51	4.04	–6.17	45	47	9,849
1 Yr	–0.93	10.95	–9.35	44	27	9,907
3 Yr Avg	–1.99	–0.96	–8.26	83	92	9,416
5 Yr Avg	5.99	–4.71	–1.43	48	72	13,377
10 Yr Avg	9.43	–3.50	2.20	36	48	24,620
15 Yr Avg	—	—	—	—	—	—

Tax Analysis	Tax-Adj Ret%	%Rank Cat	%Pretax Ret	%Rank Cat
3 Yr Avg	–3.54	91	—	—
5 Yr Avg	4.35	60	72.7	32
10 Yr Avg	7.72	29	81.9	11

Potential Capital Gain Exposure: –7% of assets

Risk Analysis

Time Period	Load-Adj Return %	Risk %Rank[1] All	Risk %Rank[1] Cat	Morningstar Return	Morningstar Risk	Morningstar Risk-Adj Rating
1 Yr	–0.93					
3 Yr	–1.99	44	70	–1.38[2]	0.61	★★★
5 Yr	5.99	45	58	0.21[2]	0.58	★★★
10 Yr	9.43	49	50	0.64	0.57	★★★

Average Historical Rating (136 months): 3.7★s

[1] 1=low, 100=high [2] T-Bill return substituted for category avg.

Category Rating (3 Yr)

1 2 3 4 5
Worst Best

Return Low
Risk Above Avg

Other Measures	Standard Index S&P 500	Best Fit Index S&P 500
Alpha	–4.0	–4.0
Beta	0.49	0.49
R-Squared	64	64

Standard Deviation	10.22
Mean	–1.99
Sharpe Ratio	–0.79

Analysis by William Harding 09-27-01

Recent developments are encouraging for shareholders who have stuck it out here.

Management changes are usually cause for concern, but this one seems to be paying dividends. Charlie Mayer and Richard Hinderlie took charge of Invesco Total Return Fund in December 2000. The former management team had erred badly by breaking away from its value discipline and drifting into expensive tech stocks in 2000. As a result, the fund got whipsawed when value stocks staged a rally and the tech sector tumbled.

Upon taking the fund's helm, Mayer refocused the portfolio on value-oriented stocks and jettisoned pricey tech names, such as Sun Microsystems and Oracle. Those moves have helped the fund weather this year's storm relatively well. Its 9% loss for the year to date ended Sept. 25, 2001, bests nearly two thirds of its domestic-hybrid rivals. The fund's emphasis on cheaper fare and high-quality bonds, such as Treasury and government agency issues, provides some ballast.

Investors can find solace in the fact that this fund's strategy will be consistent going forward with Mayer at the helm. He has more than 30 years of experience, and he has stayed committed to his value bent during his years of running the stock portion of Invesco Equity Income. (In addition, Mayer was named manager of Invesco Value Equity and comanager of Invesco Balanced in December 2000.) Because he picks stocks for so many funds, investors should be on the lookout for stock overlap, as these offerings share a large number of holdings in common.

There are certainly other worthwhile balanced funds to consider, but we think this offering is heading in the right direction.

Portfolio Analysis 09-30-01

Total Stocks: 59 Share change since 06-01	Sector	PE Ratio	YTD Return %	% Net Assets
⊖ Citigroup	Financials	20.0	0.03	2.90
⊕ ExxonMobil	Energy	15.3	–7.59	2.85
FleetBoston Finl	Financials	16.2	0.55	2.02
Bank of America	Financials	16.7	42.73	1.97
Verizon Comms	Services	29.7	–2.52	1.92
General Elec	Industrials	30.1	–15.00	1.77
SBC Comms	Services	18.4	–16.00	1.77
Chevron	Energy	10.3	9.29	1.62
Marsh & McLennan	Financials	27.9	–6.30	1.54
Philip Morris	Staples	12.1	9.12	1.54

Total Fixed-Income: 25	Date of Maturity	Amount $000	Value $000	% Net Assets
GNMA 6%	04-15-29	68,510	68,748	5.46
FHLMC 6%	06-01-16	57,170	58,344	4.64
FNMA Debenture 5.125%	02-13-04	37,949	39,425	3.13
US Treasury Bond 7.5%	11-15-16	25,000	30,730	2.44
FHLMC 6%	05-01-14	22,866	23,450	1.86
US Treasury Note 5%	02-15-11	15,000	15,422	1.23
FHLMC 6%	05-01-31	14,831	14,811	1.18
MBNA CC Master Tr 7.35%	07-16-07	12,000	13,149	1.05
US Treasury Bond 8.125%	08-15-19	10,000	13,123	1.04
US Treasury Bond 7.25%	08-15-22	10,000	12,220	0.97

Equity Style
Style: Value
Size: Large-Cap

Fixed-Income Style
Duration: Long
Quality: High

	Portfolio Avg	Rel S&P
Price/Earnings Ratio	26.2	0.85
Price/Book Ratio	4.5	0.79
Price/Cash Flow	14.2	0.79
3 Yr Earnings Growth	16.2	1.10
1 Yr Earnings Est%	–6.6	3.72
Debt % Total Cap	34.8	1.13
Med Mkt Cap $mil	65,420	1.08

Avg Eff Duration	—
Avg Eff Maturity	13.3 Yrs
Avg Credit Quality	AAA
Avg Wtd Coupon	6.22%

Special Securities % assets 09-30-01	
Restricted/Illiquid Secs	0
Emerging-Markets Secs	0
Options/Futures/Warrants	No

Composition % of assets 09-30-01	
Cash	6.3
Stocks*	63.7
Bonds	29.9
Other	0.0
*Foreign (% of stocks)	5.0

Market Cap	
Giant	62.4
Large	28.0
Medium	9.6
Small	0.0
Micro	0.0

Sector Weightings	% of Stocks	Rel S&P	5-Year High	5-Year Low
Utilities	1.2	0.4	8	1
Energy	11.0	1.6	11	2
Financials	32.0	1.8	37	8
Industrials	12.8	1.1	33	11
Durables	5.2	3.3	7	2
Staples	6.4	0.8	11	4
Services	10.8	1.0	14	5
Retail	3.9	0.6	13	3
Health	8.6	0.6	14	7
Technology	8.1	0.4	16	7

Address:	P.O. Box 173706 Denver, CO 80217–3706 800–525–8085 / 303–930–6300
Web Address:	www.invescofunds.com
Inception:	09-22-87
Advisor:	Invesco Funds Grp.
Subadvisor:	Invesco Cap. Mgmt.
NTF Plans:	Fidelity , Datalynx

Minimum Purchase:	$1000	Add: $50	IRA: $250
Min Auto Inv Plan:	$50	Add: $50	
Sales Fees:	0.25%B		
Management Fee:	.75% mx./.50% mn., .02%A		
Actual Fees:	Mgt: 0.58%	Dist: 0.25%	
Expense Projections:	3Yr: $33*	5Yr: $51*	10Yr: $126*
Avg Brok Commission:	—	Income Distrib: Quarterly	
Total Cost (relative to category):	—		

Janus

Ticker	Load	NAV	Yield	Total Assets	Mstar Category
JANSX	Closed	$24.60	0.0%	$25,621.8 mil	Large Growth

Prospectus Objective: Growth

Janus Fund seeks long-term capital growth consistent with preservation of capital.

The fund invests primarily in common stocks of larger, more-established companies, though it may invest in a large number of issuers of any size. The advisor uses a bottom-up approach to choosing investments, emphasizing companies with earnings-growth potential. It may invest without limit in foreign securities. The fund may also invest in preferred stocks, warrants, government securities, and corporate debt. It may use derivatives for hedging purposes or as a means of enhancing return.

Historical Profile
Return Average
Risk Above Avg
Rating ★★★ Neutral

Investment Style
Equity
Average Stock %: 88% 92% 95% 93% 95% 98%

▼ Manager Change
▽ Partial Manager Change

Fund Performance vs. Category Average
■ Quarterly Fund Return
+/– Category Average
– Category Baseline

Performance Quartile (within Category)

Portfolio Manager(s)

Blaine P. Rollins, CFA. Since 1-00. BS'89 U. of Colorado. Other funds currently managed: Janus Adviser Growth, Janus Aspen Growth Instl.

1990	1991	1992	1993	1994	1995	1996	1997	1998	1999	2000	12-01	History
13.79	18.60	18.68	19.39	18.78	23.04	24.45	24.90	33.65	44.05	33.29	24.60	NAV
–0.74	42.80	6.87	10.92	–1.10	29.43	19.61	22.72	38.89	47.13	–14.91	–26.10	Total Return %
2.38	12.31	–0.75	0.86	–2.42	–8.10	–3.33	–10.64	10.31	26.09	–5.81	–14.23	+/– S&P 500
–2.11	3.39	2.98	10.99	–5.96	–9.22	–5.91	–11.03	–6.21	17.45	9.61	–5.60	+/– Russ Top 200 Grt
2.18	1.35	1.57	2.08	0.04	4.13	0.91	0.95	0.34	0.00	1.26	0.00	Income Return %
–2.92	41.45	5.29	8.84	–1.15	25.30	18.71	21.77	38.55	47.13	–16.17	–26.10	Capital Return %
35	43	44	47	39	66	45	68	26	29	50	65	Total Rtn % Rank Cat
0.31	0.19	0.29	0.39	0.01	0.78	0.21	0.23	0.08	0.00	0.55	0.00	Income $
0.01	0.91	0.90	0.94	0.39	0.49	2.92	4.75	0.82	5.22	3.84	0.00	Capital Gains $
1.02	0.98	0.97	0.92	0.91	0.86	0.85	0.86	0.87	0.84	0.84	—	Expense Ratio %
2.11	1.77	1.54	1.55	1.12	1.25	0.91	0.85	0.00	–0.14	–0.19	—	Income Ratio %
307	132	153	127	139	118	104	132	70	63	65	—	Turnover Rate %
1,156.1	2,993.0	5,831.9	9,199.6	9,400.6	12,466.2	15,890.3	19,280.2	25,490.6	42,330.2	39,174.4	25,621.8	Net Assets $mil

Performance 12-31-01

	1st Qtr	2nd Qtr	3rd Qtr	4th Qtr	Total
1997	–0.25	13.24	9.12	–0.45	22.72
1998	14.50	6.12	–11.00	28.44	38.89
1999	11.35	7.29	–1.57	25.12	47.13
2000	10.44	–6.70	0.73	–18.02	–14.91
2001	–18.02	7.00	–25.82	13.57	–26.10

Trailing	Total Return%	+/– S&P 500	+/– Russ Top 200 Grth	% Rank All	% Rank Cat	Growth of $10,000
3 Mo	13.57	2.89	0.72	28	51	11,357
6 Mo	–15.75	–10.20	–8.77	96	93	8,425
1 Yr	–26.10	–14.23	–5.60	90	65	7,390
3 Yr Avg	–2.56	–1.54	5.46	85	50	9,251
5 Yr Avg	9.53	–1.16	0.94	21	39	15,767
10 Yr Avg	11.09	–1.84	0.00	25	34	28,615
15 Yr Avg	14.08	0.34	0.70	10	21	72,090

Tax Analysis	Tax-Adj Ret%	%Rank Cat	%Pretax Ret	%Rank Cat
3 Yr Avg	–4.15	51	—	—
5 Yr Avg	7.29	42	76.4	54
10 Yr Avg	8.83	39	79.7	41

Potential Capital Gain Exposure: –9% of assets

Risk Analysis

Time Period	Load-Adj Return %	Risk %Rank[1] All	Risk %Rank[1] Cat	Morningstar Return	Morningstar Risk	Morningstar Risk-Adj Rating
1 Yr	–26.10					
3 Yr	–2.56	87	57	–1.48[2]	1.33	★★
5 Yr	9.53	83	45	1.07[2]	1.18	★★★
10 Yr	11.09	80	22	0.93	1.09	★★★

Average Historical Rating (193 months): 4.5★s

[1]1=low, 100=high [2] T-Bill return substituted for category avg.

Category Rating (3 Yr)

1 2 3 4 5
Worst Best

Return Average
Risk Average

Other Measures	Standard Index S&P 500	Best Fit Index MSCIACWdFr
Alpha	2.1	8.0
Beta	1.38	1.49
R-Squared	81	82

Standard Deviation	26.25
Mean	–2.56
Sharpe Ratio	–0.33

Analysis by Christine Benz 11-15-01

It probably doesn't fit the "core fund" designation, but we still like Janus Fund.

Although it held up fairly well throughout 2000 and for much of this year, this fund recently fell hard. Media-related holdings like AOL Time Warner and Viacom dropped sharply in the third quarter, as the Sept. 11 attacks took a toll on their ad revenues. Bank of New York also fell hard, as investors fretted that its securities-processing business would slow down with the market. In all, the fund's third-quarter return was among the worst in the large-growth category.

The fund's 12-month return isn't all that bad—at least in relative terms. But the fact that it's a 34% loss—and trails the S&P 500 index by 18 percentage points—might come as a rude awakening to investors who had been relying on the fund as a core holding.

The fact is, this fund has changed radically over the past several years. Blaine Rollins took the reins in early 2000, but the alterations here date back to his predecessor, Jim Craig, who ramped up the portfolio's aggressiveness in the mid- to late 1990s. That bold positioning—including large stakes in individual stocks and bigger allocations to technology and telecom shares—helped the fund generate phenomenal returns in the late 1990s. But predictably, it has also introduced more volatility.

For investors looking for a straight-ahead growth fund, however, we think this closed fund is still a fine option. Rollins is still pretty new here, but he generated strong returns at Janus Balanced and Janus Equity-Income before taking over. We're also impressed that despite the fund's girth, Rollins isn't running this like a closet index fund. Some may prefer a more nimble offering, but we think this fund will continue to get the job done.

Portfolio Analysis 10-31-01

Share change since 04-01 Total Stocks: 97	Sector	PE	YTD Ret%	% Assets
⊖ AOL Time Warner	Technology	—	–7.76	9.15
⊖ Comcast	Services	20.3	–13.70	6.61
⊖ Linear Tech	Technology	34.9	–15.30	4.45
⊖ Viacom Cl B	Services	—	—	4.26
⊖ Maxim Integrated Products	Technology	68.2	9.82	4.17
⊖ Boeing	Industrials	10.2	–40.40	3.69
⊕ Colgate-Palmolive	Staples	31.1	–9.45	3.47
⊕ Tenet Healthcare	Health	30.1	32.14	2.45
⊖ Bank of New York	Financials	21.9	–24.80	2.44
⊕ Tyco Intl	Industrials	27.1	6.23	2.02
⊕ Walgreen	Retail	39.1	–19.20	1.98
⊖ Charles Schwab	Financials	61.9	–45.30	1.84
⊖ General Elec	Industrials	30.1	–15.00	1.65
☼ Coca-Cola	Staples	35.5	–21.40	1.57
⊖ Clear Channel Comms	Services	—	5.10	1.56
⊕ General Dynamics	Industrials	17.6	3.63	1.51
☼ ACE	Financials	17.4	–5.39	1.47
☼ XL Cap Cl A	Financials	22.8	5.82	1.46
⊕ MGIC Invest	Financials	10.9	–8.33	1.44
United Parcel Svc B	Services	25.0	–6.09	1.42
⊖ Cisco Sys	Technology	—	–52.60	1.35
⊖ Univision Comms A	Services	96.3	–1.17	1.31
⊖ Merrill Lynch	Financials	18.2	–22.70	1.27
⊖ Applied Matls	Technology	66.8	5.01	1.24
⊖ Nokia Cl A ADR	Technology	45.8	–43.00	1.15

Current Investment Style

Style: Value Blnd Growth; Size: Large Med Small

	Stock Port Avg	Relative S&P 500 Current	Relative S&P 500 Hist	Rel Cat
Price/Earnings Ratio	32.2	1.04	1.28	0.91
Price/Book Ratio	5.7	1.00	1.20	0.89
Price/Cash Flow	20.6	1.14	1.30	0.91
3 Yr Earnings Growth	18.2	1.24	1.35	0.84
1 Yr Earnings Est%	–12.0	6.79	—	–4.01
Med Mkt Cap $mil	27,156	0.5	0.7	0.57

[1]figure is based on 50% or less of stocks

Special Securities % assets 10-31-01	
Restricted/Illiquid Secs	Trace
Emerging-Markets Secs	Trace
Options/Futures/Warrants	No

Composition % assets 10-31-01	
Cash	0.7
Stocks*	99.0
Bonds	0.3
Other	0.0
*Foreign (% stocks)	7.6

Market Cap	
Giant	24.9
Large	59.0
Medium	15.1
Small	0.3
Micro	0.7

Sector Weightings	% of Stocks	Rel S&P	5-Year High	5-Year Low
Utilities	0.5	0.1	10	0
Energy	0.7	0.1	19	0
Financials	17.8	1.0	30	2
Industrials	12.9	1.1	25	2
Durables	0.6	0.4	13	0
Staples	6.5	0.8	12	0
Services	24.9	2.3	45	7
Retail	3.4	0.5	25	0
Health	6.7	0.5	30	0
Technology	26.0	1.4	36	0

Address:	100 Fillmore Street Suite 300 Denver, CO 80206-4923 800-525-8983
Web Address:	www.janus.com
Inception:	02-05-70
Advisor:	Janus Cap. Corporation
Subadvisor:	None
NTF Plans:	Fidelity , Datalynx

Minimum Purchase:	Closed	Add: $100 IRA: —
Min Auto Inv Plan:	Closed	Add: $100
Sales Fees:	No-load	
Management Fee:	.65%	
Actual Fees:	Mgt: 0.65%	Dist: —
Expense Projections:	3Yr: $271	5Yr: $471 10Yr: $1049
Avg Brok Commission:	—	Income Distrib: Annually
Total Cost (relative to category):		Low

Janus 2

Ticker	Load	NAV	Yield	Total Assets	Mstar Category
JTWOX	None	$7.45	0.0%	$406.0 mil	Large Growth

Prospectus Objective: Growth

Janus 2 Fund seeks long-term growth of capital in a manner consistent with the preservation of capital.

The Fund typically invests in common stocks selected for their growth potential. The Fund may invest in companies of any size, from larger, well-established companies to smaller, emerging growth companies. It may invest without limit in foreign equity and debt securities. The Fund normally limits investment in high-yield/high-risk bonds to less than 35% of its net assets. The portfolio manager applies a "bottom up" approach in choosing investments by looking at companies one at a time to determine if a company is an attractive investment opportunity.

Historical Profile
Return —
Risk —
Rating
Not Rated

Investment Style
Equity
Average Stock %
93%

▼ Manager Change
▽ Partial Manager Change

Fund Performance vs. Category Average
■ Quarterly Fund Return +/– Category Average
— Category Baseline

Performance Quartile (within Category)

Portfolio Manager(s)

John H. Schreiber, CFA. Since 12-00. BS U. of Washington; MBA Harvard U. Other funds currently managed: Janus Adviser Growth, Janus Aspen Growth Instl.

1990	1991	1992	1993	1994	1995	1996	1997	1998	1999	2000	12-01	History
—	—	—	—	—	—	—	—	—	—	10.00	7.45	NAV
—	—	—	—	—	—	—	—	—	—	—	–25.50	Total Return %
—	—	—	—	—	—	—	—	—	—	—	–13.62	+/– S&P 500
—	—	—	—	—	—	—	—	—	—	—	–5.00	+/– Russ Top 200 Grt
—	—	—	—	—	—	—	—	—	—	0.00	0.00	Income Return %
—	—	—	—	—	—	—	—	—	—	0.00	–25.50	Capital Return %
—	—	—	—	—	—	—	—	—	—	—	64	Total Rtn % Rank Cat
—	—	—	—	—	—	—	—	—	—	0.00	0.00	Income $
—	—	—	—	—	—	—	—	—	—	0.00	0.00	Capital Gains $
—	—	—	—	—	—	—	—	—	—	—	—	Expense Ratio %
—	—	—	—	—	—	—	—	—	—	—	—	Income Ratio %
—	—	—	—	—	—	—	—	—	—	—	—	Turnover Rate %
—	—	—	—	—	—	—	—	—	—	—	406.0	Net Assets $mil

Performance 12-31-01

	1st Qtr	2nd Qtr	3rd Qtr	4th Qtr	Total
1997	—	—	—	—	—
1998	—	—	—	—	—
1999	—	—	—	—	—
2000	—	—	—	—	0.00 *
2001	–14.90	8.23	–27.58	11.69	–25.50

Trailing	Total Return%	+/– S&P 500	+/– Russ Top 200 Grth	% Rank All	% Rank Cat	Growth of $10,000
3 Mo	11.69	1.01	–1.16	34	73	11,169
6 Mo	–19.11	–13.55	–12.12	97	96	8,089
1 Yr	–25.50	–13.62	–5.00	89	64	7,450
3 Yr Avg	—	—	—	—	—	—
5 Yr Avg	—	—	—	—	—	—
10 Yr Avg	—	—	—	—	—	—
15 Yr Avg	—	—	—	—	—	—

Tax Analysis	Tax-Adj Ret%	%Rank Cat	%Pretax Ret	%Rank Cat
3 Yr Avg	—	—	—	—
5 Yr Avg	—	—	—	—
10 Yr Avg	—	—	—	—

Potential Capital Gain Exposure: NMF

Risk Analysis

Time Period	Load-Adj Return %	Risk %Rank[1] All	Risk %Rank[1] Cat	Morningstar Return	Morningstar Risk	Morningstar Risk-Adj Rating
1 Yr	–25.50					
3 Yr	—	—	—	—	—	
5 Yr	—	—	—	—	—	
Incept	–25.38	—	—	—	—	

Average Historical Rating —

[1]1=low, 100=high

Category Rating (3 Yr)

Other Measures	Standard Index S&P 500	Best Fit Index
Alpha	—	—
Beta	—	—
R–Squared	—	—
Standard Deviation		—
Return — Mean		—
Risk — Sharpe Ratio		—

Portfolio Analysis 10-31-01

Share change since 04–01 Total Stocks: 39	Sector	PE	YTD Ret%	% Assets
☼ Liberty Media Group A	N/A	—	—	12.46
AOL Time Warner	Technology	—	–7.76	8.42
⊕ Enzon	Health	NMF	–9.32	5.01
☼ Laboratory Corp of Amer	Health	21.0	–8.13	4.88
⊕ Coca-Cola	Staples	35.5	–21.40	4.78
☼ Triquint Semicon	Technology	26.7	–71.90	4.77
⊖ Microsoft	Technology	57.6	52.78	4.71
☼ Motorola	Technology	—	–25.00	4.42
⊕ Lehman Brothers Hldgs	Financials	12.4	–0.84	3.79
⊕ Bank of Ireland	Financials	14.4	—	3.62
⊕ Washington Mutual	Financials	10.1	–5.32	3.26
⊕ Tyco Intl	Industrials	27.1	6.23	2.98
⊖ Pfizer	Health	34.7	–12.40	2.54
⊕ Capital One Finl	Financials	19.8	–17.80	2.51
⊖ Citigroup	Financials	20.0	0.03	2.46
☼ ARM Hldgs	Technology	NMF	—	2.05
⊖ Viacom Cl B	Services	—	—	1.97
⊕ MGM Mirage	Services	21.9	2.42	1.50
☼ Fannie Mae	Financials	16.2	–6.95	1.31
⊖ Colgate-Palmolive	Staples	31.1	–9.45	1.24
☼ Coach	Staples	—	35.58	1.13
⊖ Insight Enterprises	Retail	21.6	37.14	1.10
☼ Medtronic	Health	76.4	–14.70	1.09
☼ Sprint (PCS Group)	Services	—	19.43	1.05
☼ Stryker	Health	46.0	15.38	0.91

Current Investment Style

Style: Value Blnd Growth; Size: Large Med Small

	Stock Port Avg	Relative S&P 500 Current	Relative S&P 500 Hist	Rel Cat
Price/Earnings Ratio	31.0	1.00	—	0.87
Price/Book Ratio	6.6	1.15	—	1.03
Price/Cash Flow	24.4	1.36	—	1.08
3 Yr Earnings Growth	24.2	1.65	—	1.12
1 Yr Earnings Est%	14.3	—	—	4.78
Med Mkt Cap $mil	27,188	0.5	—	0.57

[1]figure is based on 50% or less of stocks

Analysis by Christine Benz 11-11-01

Janus Fund 2's ho-hum debut may be a blessing in disguise.

This offering has underwhelmed since its launch in late 2000. The ongoing valuation correction has hit it hard, and the fund has lost more than a fourth of its value since its launch—a middling showing within the large-cap growth camp. As a result, this is a rare new Janus fund that hasn't attracted much interest: Its assets stand at less than $500 million. That contrasts sharply with funds like Janus Global Technology and Janus Global Life Sciences. Both offerings quickly hit $1 billion in assets, arguably weighing on their managers' maneuverability and prompting early closings.

Manager John Schreiber has faced no such challenges here. With new money flowing in at a deliberate pace, he has been able to pop non-mega-cap holdings like Insight Enterprises, a solid-performing computer-equipment retailer, in among his top holdings. Further, he has readily been able to reposition the portfolio. This summer, for example, he had the fund positioned for an economic rebound, with big positions in brokerage, media, and semiconductor-related stocks. More recently, however, he pulled in his horns, reducing the semiconductor names and adding defensive stocks like Coca-Cola. Such moves would probably be more complicated with big asset inflows (or outflows) to contend with.

Such flexibility, combined with Schreiber's background (he's an assistant portoflio manager on Janus Fund) and Janus' research muscle, make this an appealing alternative to bigger Janus funds. Those with significant exposure to other big-cap Janus funds will want to steer clear, however, because the funds have a fair amount of overlap.

Special Securities % assets 10-31-01	
Restricted/Illiquid Secs	0
Emerging-Markets Secs	0
Options/Futures/Warrants	No

Composition % assets 10-31-01	
Cash	7.3
Stocks*	92.7
Bonds	0.0
Other	0.0
*Foreign (% stocks)	6.1

Market Cap	
Giant	39.4
Large	26.6
Medium	29.6
Small	3.2
Micro	1.2

Sector Weightings	% of Stocks	Rel S&P	5-Year High	5-Year Low
Utilities	0.0	0.0	—	—
Energy	0.0	0.0	—	—
Financials	25.5	1.4	—	—
Industrials	3.7	0.3	—	—
Durables	0.8	0.5	—	—
Staples	8.9	1.1	—	—
Services	7.5	0.7	—	—
Retail	2.0	0.3	—	—
Health	18.8	1.3	—	—
Technology	32.9	1.8	—	—

Address:	100 Fillmore Street Suite 300 Denver, CO 80206–4923 800–525–8983 / 800–525–3713
Web Address:	www.janus.com
*Inception:	12-29-00
Advisor:	Janus Cap. Corporation
Subadvisor:	None
NTF Plans:	Fidelity Inst. , Waterhouse

Minimum Purchase:	$2500	Add: $100	IRA: —
Min Auto Inv Plan:	—	Add: —	
Sales Fees:	0.00%S		
Management Fee:	.65%		
Actual Fees:	Mgt: 0.65%	Dist: —	
Expense Projections:	3Yr: $281	5Yr: —	10Yr: —
Avg Brok Commission:	—	Income Distrib: Annually	
Total Cost (relative to category):	—		

Janus Balanced

Ticker	Load	NAV	Yield	Total Assets	Mstar Category
JABAX	None	$19.63	2.7%	$4,472.3 mil	Domestic Hybrid

Prospectus Objective: Balanced

Janus Balanced Fund seeks long-term growth of capital, consistent with capital preservation and balanced by current income.

The fund invests in both equity and debt securities, normally allocating 40% to 60% of assets to each type. Equity investments consist primarily of common stocks chosen for their growth potential and income-producing common and preferred stocks. Fixed-income investments consist primarily of investment-grade corporate and U.S. government securities. At least 25% of assets are invested in fixed-income senior securities at all times.

Historical Profile
Return: Above Avg
Risk: Low
Rating: ★★★★★ Highest

Investment Style
Equity
Average Stock %: 55% 58% 43% 34% 45% 45%

▼ Manager Change
▽ Partial Manager Change

Fund Performance vs. Category Average
■ Quarterly Fund Return
+/– Category Average
— Category Baseline

Performance Quartile (within Category)

Portfolio Manager(s)

Karen L. Reidy, CFA. Since 1-00. BA'89 U. of Colorado. Other funds currently managed: IDEX Janus Balanced A, IDEX Janus Balanced M, IDEX Janus Balanced B.

1990	1991	1992	1993	1994	1995	1996	1997	1998	1999	2000	12-01	History
—	—	11.23	12.19	11.63	13.72	14.14	15.33	19.61	23.39	21.24	19.63	NAV
—	—	12.53*	10.56	0.02	27.32	15.31	21.81	31.20	23.51	–2.16	–5.04	Total Return %
—	—	6.78*	0.50	–1.29	–10.22	–7.64	–11.55	2.62	2.47	6.94	6.83	+/– S&P 500
—	—	—	0.81	2.94	8.85	11.69	12.12	22.52	24.34	–13.79	–13.47	+/– LB Aggregate
—	—	0.23	1.98	4.66	9.26	1.91	2.54	2.32	2.35	4.17	2.52	Income Return %
—	—	12.30	8.58	–4.64	18.06	13.40	19.26	28.88	21.16	–6.34	–7.56	Capital Return %
—	—	—	66	18	30	33	24	2	5	73	57	Total Rtn % Rank Cat
—	—	0.02	0.22	0.56	1.06	0.26	0.36	0.35	0.46	0.96	0.53	Income $
—	—	0.00	0.00	0.00	0.00	1.41	1.49	0.11	0.32	0.69	0.00	Capital Gains $
—	—	2.50	1.70	1.42	1.32	1.21	1.10	1.03	0.91	0.85	—	Expense Ratio %
—	—	–0.12	2.15	2.28	2.52	2.35	2.63	2.34	2.37	2.92	—	Income Ratio %
—	—	130	131	167	185	151	139	73	64	87	—	Turnover Rate %
—	—	12.9	77.4	93.4	138.9	219.7	389.4	1,136.6	3,420.4	4,739.2	4,472.3	Net Assets $mil

Performance 12-31-01

	1st Qtr	2nd Qtr	3rd Qtr	4th Qtr	Total
1997	1.56	10.59	6.23	2.09	21.81
1998	9.92	5.24	–4.49	18.75	31.20
1999	7.39	3.00	–3.35	15.52	23.51
2000	4.10	–2.97	–0.60	–2.56	–2.16
2001	–5.74	2.16	–5.94	4.84	–5.04

Trailing	Total Return%	+/– S&P 500	+/–LB Agg	% Rank All	% Rank Cat	Growth of $10,000
3 Mo	4.84	–5.84	4.81	65	72	10,484
6 Mo	–1.39	4.17	–6.04	44	43	9,861
1 Yr	–5.04	6.83	–13.47	51	57	9,496
3 Yr Avg	4.69	5.72	–1.58	34	23	11,474
5 Yr Avg	12.89	2.19	5.46	8	3	18,336
10 Yr Avg	—	—	—	—	—	—
15 Yr Avg	—	—	—	—	—	—

Tax Analysis	Tax-Adj Ret%	%Rank Cat	%Pretax Ret	%Rank Cat
3 Yr Avg	3.15	17	67.1	25
5 Yr Avg	10.84	2	84.1	7
10 Yr Avg	—	—	—	—

Potential Capital Gain Exposure: –5% of assets

Risk Analysis

Time Period	Load-Adj Return %	Risk %Rank[1] All	Risk %Rank[1] Cat	Morningstar Return	Morningstar Risk	Morningstar Risk-Adj Rating
1 Yr	–5.04					
3 Yr	4.69	41	53	–0.05[2]	0.55	★★★★
5 Yr	12.89	43	48	2.00[2]	0.54	★★★★★
Incept	13.82	—	—	—	—	

Average Historical Rating (77 months): 4.1★s

[1]1=low, 100=high [2] T-Bill return substituted for category avg.

Category Rating (3 Yr)

1 2 3 4 5
Worst Best

Return: Above Avg
Risk: Average

Other Measures	Standard Index S&P 500	Best Fit Index MSCIACWdFr
Alpha	2.8	5.3
Beta	0.54	0.61
R-Squared	68	77

Standard Deviation	11.46
Mean	4.69
Sharpe Ratio	–0.03

Portfolio Analysis 10-31-01

Total Stocks: 62 Share change since 04-01	Sector	PE Ratio	YTD Return %	% Net Assets
⊖ Citigroup	Financials	20.0	0.03	2.66
⊖ General Elec	Industrials	30.1	–15.00	1.97
⊕ Tenet Healthcare	Health	30.1	32.14	1.80
⊕ ExxonMobil	Energy	15.3	–7.59	1.78
⊕ Marsh & McLennan	Financials	27.9	–6.30	1.37
⊕ Automatic Data Processing	Services	39.8	–6.27	1.25
⊕ El Paso	Utilities	NMF	–36.70	1.23
⊕ American Intl Grp	Financials	42.0	–19.20	1.16
☼ AT&T Wireless	N/A	—	—	1.14
⊕ Minnesota Mng & Mfg	Industrials	34.5	0.16	1.09

Total Fixed-Income: 103	Date of Maturity	Amount $000	Value $000	% Net Assets
FNMA Debenture 4.75%	11-14-03	123,570	128,542	2.91
US Treasury Bond 6.125%	08-15-29	73,500	85,467	1.94
US Treasury Note 5.875%	11-15-04	75,665	81,996	1.86
Federal Home Loan Bk 4.875%	05-14-04	76,790	80,150	1.82
FNMA Debenture 6.625%	09-15-09	62,100	70,018	1.59
US Treasury Note 6.5%	10-15-06	46,630	52,619	1.19
FNMA Debenture 5.5%	03-15-11	47,000	49,233	1.12
US Treasury Bond 7.25%	05-15-16	35,800	44,523	1.01
Federal Home Loan Bk 6.5%	11-15-05	38,900	42,644	0.97
US Treasury Bond 5.25%	02-15-29	41,010	42,269	0.96

Equity Style
Style: Blend
Size: Large-Cap

	Portfolio Avg	Rel S&P
Price/Earnings Ratio	31.5	1.02
Price/Book Ratio	5.1	0.89
Price/Cash Flow	15.4	0.86
3 Yr Earnings Growth	14.3	0.98
1 Yr Earnings Est%	–4.6	2.58
Debt % Total Cap	33.5	1.08
Med Mkt Cap $mil	35,784	0.59

Fixed-Income Style
Duration: Intermediate
Quality: High

Avg Eff Duration[1]	4.7 Yrs
Avg Eff Maturity	7.1 Yrs
Avg Credit Quality	AA
Avg Wtd Coupon	6.22%

[1]figure provided by fund as of 06-30-01

Special Securities % assets 10-31-01	
Restricted/Illiquid Secs	0
Emerging-Markets Secs	0
Options/Futures/Warrants	No

Composition % of assets 10-31-01	
Cash	11.6
Stocks*	45.0
Bonds	42.8
Other	0.7
*Foreign (% of stocks)	5.9

Market Cap	
Giant	41.7
Large	46.1
Medium	11.7
Small	0.0
Micro	0.6

Sector Weightings	% of Stocks	Rel S&P	5-Year High	5-Year Low
Utilities	2.9	0.9	9	0
Energy	10.3	1.5	17	0
Financials	27.5	1.5	50	11
Industrials	11.0	1.0	34	0
Durables	7.9	5.1	9	0
Staples	7.0	0.9	25	0
Services	10.3	1.0	40	5
Retail	3.2	0.5	12	0
Health	11.2	0.8	25	2
Technology	8.8	0.5	39	0

Analysis by Catherine Hickey 09-27-01

The reasons for Janus investors to like this fund have never been more apparent.

It hasn't been one of Janus' greatest years. Some of the firm's funds, including Enterprise and Mercury, have taken a beating as investors continue to punish tech and telecom stocks, two sectors that have historically been mainstays of Janus portfolios.

Janus Balanced Fund has been a different story, though. It has held up nicely in these tough market conditions thanks to its moderate approach, which has been made even more cautious than usual by current skipper Karen Reidy. Like her predecessor, Blaine Rollins, she limits the fund's stock stake to between 40% and 50% of assets and invests the rest in converts, bonds and cash. Having less than half the fund's assets in stocks has helped lately, as bonds have generally outperformed stocks in 2001.

Also, Reidy's stock picks have not been dominated as much by fast-growing tech shares as Rollins' were. Instead, her search for well-managed companies with strong returns on capital has led her to make energy names like ExxonMobil top holdings. Because those names have held up well relative to tech, the fund is doing well versus some of its growth-leaning peers.

A caveat: Although this is one of the mildest offerings in the Janus stable, it's still a Janus fund. That means it probably won't ever totally abandon a taste for high-growth stocks. Thus, investors who want a value-driven hybrid fund or one that sticks with an S&P 500-like stock portfolio should look elsewhere. However, Reidy's record here and at her other charge, Janus Core Equity, shows she is a talented manager with a knack for positioning her funds well for challenging market conditions. As a Janus fund that walks on the mild side, it's a solid choice.

Address:	100 Fillmore Street Suite 300 Denver, CO 80206-4923 800-525-8983
Web Address:	www.janus.com
*Inception:	09-01-92
Advisor:	Janus Cap. Corporation
Subadvisor:	None
NTF Plans:	Fidelity, Datalynx

Minimum Purchase:	$2500	Add: $100	IRA: $500
Min Auto Inv Plan:	$500	Add: $100	
Sales Fees:	No-load		
Management Fee:	.65%		
Actual Fees:	Mgt: 0.65%	Dist: —	
Expense Projections:	3Yr: $287	5Yr: $498	10Yr: $1108
Avg Brok Commission:	—	Income Distrib: Quarterly	
Total Cost (relative to category):		Below Avg	

Janus Enterprise

Ticker	Load	NAV	Yield	Total Assets	Mstar Category
JAENX	None	$32.00	0.0%	$3,209.2 mil	Mid-Cap Growth

Prospectus Objective: Growth

Janus Enterprise Fund seeks long-term capital growth.

The fund invests primarily in common stocks of companies with market capitalizations that fall within the range of companies included in the S&P MidCap 400 index. It may also invest in larger or smaller companies. It may also invest in preferred stock, American depositary receipts, convertibles, corporate and government debt, and cash equivalents. The fund may invest in special situations from time to time. It may invest without limit in foreign securities. This fund is non-diversified.

Historical Profile

Return Below Avg
Risk High
Rating ★★ Below Avg

Investment Style
Equity
Average Stock %: 99% 96% 97% 98% 97% 97% 92%

▼ Manager Change
▽ Partial Manager Change

Fund Performance vs. Category Average
■ Quarterly Fund Return +/– Category Average
— Category Baseline

Performance Quartile (within Category)

Portfolio Manager(s)

James P. Goff, CFA. Since 9-92. BA'86 Yale U. Other funds currently managed: IDEX Janus Capital Appreciation A, IDEX Janus Capital Appreciation M, IDEX Janus Capital Appreciation B.

1990	1991	1992	1993	1994	1995	1996	1997	1998	1999	2000	12-01	History
—	—	19.44	21.92	22.98	27.44	29.34	30.48	36.22	76.67	53.27	32.00	NAV
—	—	29.73*	15.67	8.92	27.25	11.65	10.82	33.75	121.90	–30.52	–39.93	Total Return %
—	—	23.98*	5.62	7.60	–10.28	–11.30	–22.53	5.17	100.86	–21.42	–28.05	+/– S&P 500
—	—	—	4.48	11.08	–6.73	–5.84	–11.72	15.88	70.60	–18.77	–19.77	+/– Russ Midcap Grth
—	—	0.13	0.09	2.36	7.13	0.00	0.00	0.00	0.00	0.00	0.00	Income Return %
—	—	29.60	15.59	6.56	20.12	11.65	10.82	33.75	121.90	–30.52	–39.93	Capital Return %
—	—	—	48	8	80	79	81	9	9	92	93	Total Rtn % Rank Cat
—	—	0.02	0.02	0.52	1.64	0.00	0.00	0.00	0.00	0.00	0.00	Income $
—	—	0.00	0.55	0.38	0.16	1.28	1.96	4.30	3.33	0.00	0.00	Capital Gains $
—	—	2.50	1.36	1.25	1.23	1.12	1.04	1.08	0.95	0.88	—	Expense Ratio %
—	—	–0.81	0.14	–0.32	0.02	–0.78	–0.61	–0.67	–0.67	–0.65	—	Income Ratio %
—	—	53	201	193	194	93	111	134	98	80	—	Turnover Rate %
—	—	98.9	258.6	354.1	498.9	721.8	573.1	728.0	4,434.5	6,267.1	3,209.2	Net Assets $mil

Performance 12-31-01

	1st Qtr	2nd Qtr	3rd Qtr	4th Qtr	Total
1997	–13.50	16.63	8.04	1.67	10.82
1998	11.32	4.92	–14.63	34.15	33.75
1999	16.15	11.77	8.23	57.93	121.90
2000	11.57	–7.42	–1.54	–31.68	–30.52
2001	–32.66	8.42	–27.80	13.96	–39.93

Trailing	Total Return%	+/– S&P 500	+/– Russ Midcap Grth	% Rank All	% Rank Cat	Growth of $10,000
3 Mo	13.96	3.28	–13.10	26	78	11,396
6 Mo	–17.72	–12.16	–9.46	97	89	8,228
1 Yr	–39.93	–28.05	–19.77	98	93	6,007
3 Yr Avg	–2.52	–1.50	–4.68	85	82	9,261
5 Yr Avg	6.54	–4.16	–2.48	41	66	13,727
10 Yr Avg	—	—	—	—	—	—
15 Yr Avg	—	—	—	—	—	—

Tax Analysis	Tax-Adj Ret%	%Rank Cat	%Pretax Ret	%Rank Cat
3 Yr Avg	–3.02	75	—	—
5 Yr Avg	5.47	55	83.6	29
10 Yr Avg	—	—	—	—

Potential Capital Gain Exposure: –112% of assets

Risk Analysis

Time Period	Load-Adj Return %	Risk %Rank[1] All	Risk %Rank[1] Cat	Morningstar Return	Morningstar Risk	Morningstar Risk-Adj Rating
1 Yr	–39.93					
3 Yr	–2.52	97	88	–1.47[2]	1.97	★
5 Yr	6.54	95	80	0.34[2]	1.76	★★
Incept	13.22	—	—	—	—	

Average Historical Rating (77 months): 3.2★s

[1] 1=low, 100=high [2] T-Bill return substituted for category avg.

Category Rating (3 Yr)

1 2 3 4 5
Worst Best

Return Below Avg
Risk Above Avg

Other Measures	Standard Index S&P 500	Best Fit Index Wil 4500
Alpha	8.9	1.0
Beta	1.64	1.40
R-Squared	45	88

Standard Deviation	45.15
Mean	–2.52
Sharpe Ratio	–0.19

Analysis by Catherine Hickey 11-09-01

This fund has shown just how low it can go, but shareholders with long time horizons would do well to hang on.

The story of Janus Enterprise Fund mirrors the recent fortunes of Janus as a whole. The Denver-based fund company rode to glory on fantastic returns during the growth-fueled late 1990s, but many of its funds have taken a turn for the worse as growth stocks have tanked since March 2000. Enterprise is one Janus fund that soared in 1998 and 1999. However, since March 2000, the fund has registered steep losses, and its year-to-date loss of 40.2% lands in the mid-growth category's bottom decile.

This fund has demonstrated just how far it can fall. But perhaps a bigger danger lurking on its horizon is that it may not bounce back as rapidly as investors might expect it to during a growth rally. Manager Jim Goff has recently made a nod toward moderation by taking down his earnings-growth expectations for companies; he now looks for 15% growth rates instead of 20% or more. Nowadays, steady-growing firms such as Walgreen rub shoulders with racier issues such as Human Genome Sciences. A more moderate approach may have hampered the fund's returns somewhat during the tech rally of the last several weeks; its performance was below average during that time.

Nevertheless, we still think this fund holds appeal. Goff has shown that he can deliver the goods when his style is in favor, and he is still backed by Janus' topnotch research staff. What's more, a more moderate approach may help the fund stave off such sharp losses during another tough market for growth stocks. However, we still think this fund is best used as part of a well-diversified portfolio.

Portfolio Analysis 10-31-01

Share change since 04-01 Total Stocks: 71	Sector	PE	YTD Ret%	% Assets
⊕ EBAY	Services	NMF	102.70	5.07
⊖ Paychex	Services	49.4	–27.10	4.55
⊖ Apollo Grp Cl A	Services	—	—	3.67
⊖ Crown Castle Intl	Services	—	–60.50	3.39
⊖ Human Genome Sciences	Health	—	–51.30	3.26
☼ Bank Amer	N/A	—	—	3.26
☼ Kinder Morgan	Energy	32.2	7.11	3.17
⊕ Walgreen	Retail	39.1	–19.20	2.79
⊕ Enzon	Health	NMF	–9.32	2.78
⊕ Concord EFS	Financials	86.3	49.21	2.76
⊖ Andrx	Health	66.4	21.66	2.53
⊖ Cree	Technology	79.6	–17.00	2.41
⊖ Western Wireless Cl A	Services	—	–27.90	2.39
⊕ Laboratory Corp of Amer	Health	21.0	–8.13	2.34
☼ Charter Comms	Services	—	–27.50	2.12
⊕ Berkshire Hathaway Cl B	Financials	64.8	7.26	2.05
⊕ Cendant	Services	20.4	103.70	1.99
⊖ Sepracor	Health	—	–28.70	1.81
☼ Invitrogen	Health	—	–28.30	1.70
⊖ Millennium Pharma	Health	—	–60.30	1.69
☼ Calpine	Utilities	8.9	–62.70	1.68
⊖ Lamar Advertising Cl A	Services	—	9.71	1.59
⊖ Integrated Device Tech	Technology	8.9	–19.70	1.58
⊕ Hanover Compressor	Utilities	22.4	–43.30	1.51
⊖ Cardinal Health	Health	35.1	–2.51	1.47

Current Investment Style

Style: Value Blnd Growth; Size: Large Med Small

	Stock Port Avg	Relative S&P 500 Current	Relative S&P 500 Hist	Rel Cat
Price/Earnings Ratio	41.7	1.35	1.52	1.20
Price/Book Ratio	5.9	1.03	1.58	1.03
Price/Cash Flow	23.8	1.32	1.52	1.03
3 Yr Earnings Growth	27.8[1]	1.90	—	1.18
1 Yr Earnings Est%	21.8	—	—	2.34
Med Mkt Cap $mil	5,194	0.1	0.1	0.92

[1] figure is based on 50% or less of stocks

Special Securities % assets 10-31-01

Restricted/Illiquid Secs	1
Emerging-Markets Secs	0
Options/Futures/Warrants	No

Composition % assets 10-31-01	
Cash	2.6
Stocks*	97.2
Bonds	0.2
Other	0.0
*Foreign (% stocks)	0.0

Market Cap	
Giant	2.4
Large	30.2
Medium	65.2
Small	2.2
Micro	0.0

Sector Weightings	% of Stocks	Rel S&P	5-Year High	5-Year Low
Utilities	4.5	1.4	8	0
Energy	5.2	0.7	5	0
Financials	10.4	0.6	35	0
Industrials	1.3	0.1	34	0
Durables	0.0	0.0	11	0
Staples	0.0	0.0	23	0
Services	36.5	3.4	60	5
Retail	3.2	0.5	29	0
Health	31.7	2.1	32	3
Technology	7.3	0.4	43	0

Address:	100 Fillmore Street Suite 300, Denver, CO 80206-4923, 800-525-8983
Web Address:	www.janus.com
*Inception:	09-01-92
Advisor:	Janus Cap. Corporation
Subadvisor:	None
NTF Plans:	Fidelity , Datalynx

Minimum Purchase:	$2500	Add: $100	IRA: $500
Min Auto Inv Plan:	$500	Add: $100	
Sales Fees:	No-load		
Management Fee:	.65%		
Actual Fees:	Mgt: 0.65%	Dist: —	
Expense Projections:	3Yr: $300	5Yr: $520	10Yr: $1155
Avg Brok Commission:	—	Income Distrib: Annually	
Total Cost (relative to category):		Low	

Janus Global Life Sciences

Ticker	Load	NAV	Yield	Total Assets	Mstar Category
JAGLX	Closed	$17.57	0.0%	$2,418.0 mil	Spec Health Care

Prospectus Objective: Specialty—Health

Janus Global Life Sciences Fund seeks long-term growth of capital.

The fund normally invests at least 65% of assets in foreign and domestic securities of companies the manager believes have a life science orientation. These securities generally consist of companies that relate to maintaining or improving the quality of life, such as health care, nutrition, personal hygiene, medical diagnostics, and nuclear and biochemical research. Management utilizes a bottom-up investment approach and looks at companies without regard to size, country allocation, place of principal business activity, or other similar criteria.

Historical Profile
Return High
Risk Above Avg
Rating ★★★★★ Highest

Investment Style
Equity
Average Stock % — 96% 86% 92%

▼ Manager Change
▽ Partial Manager Change

Fund Performance vs. Category Average
■ Quarterly Fund Return +/– Category Average
— Category Baseline

Performance Quartile (within Category)

Portfolio Manager(s)

Thomas R. Malley, CFA. Since 1-99. BS Stanford U. Other funds currently managed: Janus Aspen Global Life Sciences Inst, Janus Aspen Global Life Sciences Svc.

1990	1991	1992	1993	1994	1995	1996	1997	1998	1999	2000	12-01	History
—	—	—	—	—	—	—	—	10.00	16.10	21.45	17.57	NAV
—	—	—	—	—	—	—	—	—	61.00	33.34	–18.09	Total Return %
—	—	—	—	—	—	—	—	—	39.96	42.44	–6.21	+/– S&P 500
—	—	—	—	—	—	—	—	—	37.44	44.27	–7.20	+/– Wilshire 5000
—	—	—	—	—	—	—	—	—	0.00	0.10	0.00	Income Return %
—	—	—	—	—	—	—	—	—	61.00	33.24	–18.09	Capital Return %
—	—	—	—	—	—	—	—	—	10	84	71	Total Rtn % Rank Cat
—	—	—	—	—	—	—	—	0.00	0.00	0.02	0.00	Income $
—	—	—	—	—	—	—	—	0.00	0.00	0.00	0.00	Capital Gains $
—	—	—	—	—	—	—	—	—	1.19	0.94	—	Expense Ratio %
—	—	—	—	—	—	—	—	—	–0.41	0.14	—	Income Ratio %
—	—	—	—	—	—	—	—	—	235	147	—	Turnover Rate %
—	—	—	—	—	—	—	—	—	601.1	3,992.2	2,418.0	Net Assets $mil

Performance 12-31-01

	1st Qtr	2nd Qtr	3rd Qtr	4th Qtr	Total
1997	—	—	—	—	—
1998	—	—	—	—	—
1999	4.20	11.90	5.15	31.32	61.00
2000	17.58	7.08	12.73	–6.05	33.34
2001	–26.25	12.83	–7.51	6.42	–18.09

Trailing	Total Return%	+/– S&P 500	+/– Wil 5000	% Rank All	% Rank Cat	Growth of $10,000
3 Mo	6.42	–4.26	–5.95	59	66	10,642
6 Mo	–1.57	3.99	3.92	45	56	9,843
1 Yr	–18.09	–6.21	–7.20	77	71	8,191
3 Yr Avg	20.70	21.73	21.35	2	26	17,584
5 Yr Avg	—	—	—	—	—	—
10 Yr Avg	—	—	—	—	—	—
15 Yr Avg	—	—	—	—	—	—

Tax Analysis	Tax-Adj Ret%	%Rank Cat	%Pretax Ret	%Rank Cat
3 Yr Avg	20.69	25	99.9	2
5 Yr Avg	—	—	—	—
10 Yr Avg	—	—	—	—

Potential Capital Gain Exposure: –18% of assets

Risk Analysis

Time Period	Load-Adj Return %	Risk %Rank[1] All	Risk %Rank[1] Cat	Morningstar Return	Morningstar Risk	Morningstar Risk-Adj Rating
1 Yr	–18.09					
3 Yr	20.70	83	75	3.87[2]	1.24	★★★★★
5 Yr	—	—	—	—	—	
Incept	20.68	—	—	—	—	

Average Historical Rating (1 month): 5.0★s

[1]1=low, 100=high [2] T-Bill return substituted for category avg.

Category Rating (3 Yr)

1 2 **3** 4 5
Worst Best

Return Above Avg
Risk Above Avg

Other Measures	Standard Index S&P 500	Best Fit Index Russ 2000
Alpha	25.4	18.4
Beta	0.24	1.16
R-Squared	1	45
Standard Deviation		52.52
Mean		20.70
Sharpe Ratio		0.34

Analysis by Peter Di Teresa 08-29-01

Janus Global Life Sciences Fund is more moderate than it was, but it's still for aggressive health-care investors.

This fund got off to a flying start in 1999 when it gained 61% and trounced almost all of its rivals for the year. Credit that to a bold portfolio. Manager Tom Malley embraced the high-growth style common to Janus funds, loading more than half of assets into biotech stocks and holding lots of smaller caps.

Accordingly, the fund was hammered in 2000, losing more than most of its peers from March through May as it plummeted 37%. It was hit with a double whammy, as redemptions forced Malley to sell tanking stocks and lock in losses. Health-care funds posted strong gains during the remainder of the year, but this offering lagged as biotech issues suffered.

Malley has since adopted a less daring style. He isn't putting much in small caps (with roughly $4 billion in this and clone funds, he doesn't have much choice) and has broadened subsector exposure. The fund currently has about 20% in biotech, 25% in big drug companies, 12% in generic drugmakers, and the rest in medical-device manufacturers, HMOs, and drug distributors.

Malley's style is still aggressive, though. For example, the fund has less in drug firms, typically the most stable subsector, than do most peers. Malley says he won't throw half the fund into one subsector again, but he will boost stakes where he sees good opportunities. He hasn't abandoned his growth bent, either.

The fund's 18.5% loss for the year to date through August 28 leaves it behind nearly three fourths of its peers. That said, Malley's changes have likely stanched the fund's losses—notably aggressive offerings are doing much worse.

We think shareholders in this closed fund should wait to see how it does in a friendlier market.

Portfolio Analysis 10-31-01

Share chng since 04-01 Total Stocks: 61

	Subsector	PE	YTD Ret%	% Assets
⊖ Sanofi-Synthelabo	Health	50.5	—	4.26
⊕ Baxter Intl	Gen Pharm/Bio	33.9	22.84	3.90
⊖ Biovail Corporation Intl	Health	NMF	44.82	3.83
⊖ Teva Pharma Inds ADR	Gen Pharm/Bio	48.9	–15.50	3.82
⊕ Laboratory Corp of Amer	Tech/Bus Svs	21.0	–8.13	3.66
⊖ American Home Products	Gen Pharm/Bio	—	–1.91	3.06
⊖ Pfizer	Gen Pharm/Bio	34.7	–12.40	2.87
⊕ St. Jude Medical	Medical Devices	42.0	26.39	2.78
⊖ Cytyc	Diagnostics	49.3	25.16	2.74
☼ Shire Pharma Grp	Gen Pharm/Bio	—	–20.50	2.42
⊕ Tenet Healthcare	Hospitals	30.1	32.14	2.38
☼ Pharmaceutical Resources 144A	N/A	—	—	2.37
⊖ WellPoint Health Networks	HMOs/PPOs	19.4	1.39	2.30
⊕ Cell Therapeutics	Health	—	–46.40	2.20
⊖ Andrx	Emg. Pharm/Bio	66.4	21.66	2.16
☼ Sepracor	Emg. Pharm/Bio	—	–28.70	2.16
⊖ Cardinal Health	Health	35.1	–2.51	2.16
⊕ HCA – The Healthcare Company	Hospitals	24.1	–12.20	2.08
⊕ Genzyme Corporation General Di	Emg. Pharm/Bio	—	33.11	2.04
☼ Health Mgmt Assoc	Hospitals	24.2	–11.30	2.03
⊕ Oxford Health Plans	HMOs/PPOs	11.5	–23.70	1.99
⊖ UnitedHealth Grp	HMOs/PPOs	26.6	15.37	1.94
⊖ Aventis Cl A	Gen Pharm/Bio	NMF	—	1.93
☼ Biomet	Medical Devices	40.7	17.13	1.89
⊕ Protein Design Labs	Emg. Pharm/Bio	NMF	–24.10	1.85

Current Investment Style

Style: Value Blnd Growth; Size: Large Med Small

	Stock Port Avg	Relative S&P 500 Current	Relative S&P 500 Hist	Rel Cat
Price/Earnings Ratio	39.1	1.26	—	0.97
Price/Book Ratio	8.8	1.54	—	0.97
Price/Cash Flow	29.2	1.62	—	1.02
3 Yr Earnings Growth	25.8[1]	1.77	—	1.19
1 Yr Earnings Est%	31.9	—	—	1.41
Med Mkt Cap $mil	8,104	0.1	—	0.37

[1]figure is based on 50% or less of stocks

Special Securities % assets 10-31-01	
Restricted/Illiquid Secs	7
Emerging-Markets Secs	4
Options/Futures/Warrants	No

Composition % assets 10-31-01	
Cash	0.4
Stocks*	99.6
Bonds	0.0
Other	0.0
*Foreign (% stocks)	24.1

Market Cap	
Giant	18.6
Large	26.2
Medium	46.0
Small	9.2
Micro	0.0

Subsector Weightings	% of Stocks	Rel Cat
Gen Pharm/Bio	31.3	0.7
Medical Devices	8.0	1.4
Hospitals	7.2	2.5
Other Providers	0.0	0.0
HMOs/PPOs	6.9	3.3
Emg. Pharm/Bio	12.9	0.7
Diagnostics	3.1	2.1
Tech/Bus Svs	4.1	1.9
Other	26.5	1.2

Address:	100 Fillmore Street Suite 300 Denver, CO 80206–4923 800–525–8983
Web Address:	www.janus.com
*Inception:	12-31-98
Advisor:	Janus Cap. Corporation
Subadvisor:	None
NTF Plans:	Fidelity Inst. , Waterhouse

Minimum Purchase:	Closed	Add: $100 IRA: —
Min Auto Inv Plan:	Closed	Add: $100
Sales Fees:	No-load	
Management Fee:	.65%	
Actual Fees:	Mgt: 0.65%	Dist: —
Expense Projections:	3Yr: $353	5Yr: $612 10Yr: $1352
Avg Brok Commission:	—	Income Distrib: Annually
Total Cost (relative to category):	—	

Janus Global Technology

Ticker	Load	NAV	Yield	Total Assets	Mstar Category
JAGTX	Closed	$12.14	0.0%	$2,518.4 mil	Spec Technology

Prospectus Objective: Specialty—Technology

Janus Global Technology Fund seeks long-term growth of capital.

The fund normally invests at least 65% of assets in foreign and domestic securities of companies the manager believes will benefit significantly from advances or improvements in technology. These companies either have or will develop products, processes, or services to enhance technology, or rely extensively on technology in connection with their operations or services. Management utilizes a bottom-up investment approach and looks at companies without regard to size, country allocation, place of principal business activity, or other similar criteria.

Historical Profile

Return	Above Avg
Risk	High
Rating	★★★ Neutral

Investment Style
Equity
Average Stock %: 82% (1999), 91% (2000), 76% (12-01)

▼ Manager Change
▽ Partial Manager Change

Fund Performance vs. Category Average
■ Quarterly Fund Return +/– Category Average
— Category Baseline

Performance Quartile (within Category)

Portfolio Manager(s)

C. Mike Lu, CFA. Since 1-99. BA Yale. U. Other funds currently managed: Janus Aspen Global Technology Instl, Janus Aspen Global Technology Svc.

1990	1991	1992	1993	1994	1995	1996	1997	1998	1999	2000	12-01	History
—	—	—	—	—	—	—	—	10.00	30.93	20.22	12.14	NAV
—	—	—	—	—	—	—	—	—	213.54	–33.67	–39.96	Total Return %
—	—	—	—	—	—	—	—	—	192.51	–24.57	–28.08	+/– S&P 500
—	—	—	—	—	—	—	—	—	97.15	–17.45	–24.37	+/– PSE Tech 100
—	—	—	—	—	—	—	—	—	1.98	1.05	0.00	Income Return %
—	—	—	—	—	—	—	—	—	211.57	–34.72	–39.96	Capital Return %
—	—	—	—	—	—	—	—	—	7	57	52	Total Rtn % Rank Cat
—	—	—	—	—	—	—	—	0.00	0.20	0.33	0.00	Income $
—	—	—	—	—	—	—	—	0.00	0.18	0.00	0.00	Capital Gains $
—	—	—	—	—	—	—	—	—	1.02	0.90	—	Expense Ratio %
—	—	—	—	—	—	—	—	—	–0.11	0.17	—	Income Ratio %
—	—	—	—	—	—	—	—	—	31	47	—	Turnover Rate %
—	—	—	—	—	—	—	—	—	7,409.3	5,309.2	2,518.4	Net Assets $mil

Performance 12-31-01

	1st Qtr	2nd Qtr	3rd Qtr	4th Qtr	Total
1997	—	—	—	—	—
1998	—	—	—	—	—
1999	29.90	21.40	13.57	75.07	213.54
2000	19.24	–11.01	–6.40	–33.22	–33.67
2001	–30.46	3.56	–36.20	30.68	–39.96

Trailing	Total Return%	+/– S&P 500	+/– PSE Tech 100	% Rank All	% Rank Cat	Growth of $10,000
3 Mo	30.68	19.99	–2.23	4	74	13,068
6 Mo	–16.62	–11.07	–11.34	96	48	8,338
1 Yr	–39.96	–28.08	–24.37	98	52	6,004
3 Yr Avg	7.68	8.71	–7.55	15	17	12,487
5 Yr Avg	—	—	—	—	—	—
10 Yr Avg	—	—	—	—	—	—
15 Yr Avg	—	—	—	—	—	—

Tax Analysis	Tax-Adj Ret%	%Rank Cat	%Pretax Ret	%Rank Cat
3 Yr Avg	7.29	17	94.8	21
5 Yr Avg	—	—	—	—
10 Yr Avg	—	—	—	—

Potential Capital Gain Exposure: –73% of assets

Risk Analysis

Time Period	Load-Adj Return %	Risk %Rank[1] All	Risk %Rank[1] Cat	Morningstar Return	Morningstar Risk	Morningstar Risk-Adj Rating
1 Yr	–39.96					
3 Yr	7.68	98	28	0.60[2]	2.10	★★★
5 Yr	—	—	—	—	—	
Incept	7.68	—	—	—	—	

Average Historical Rating (1 month): 3.0★s

[1] 1=low, 100=high [2] T-Bill return substituted for category avg.

Category Rating (3 Yr)

1 2 3 4 5 — Worst … Best

Return	Above Avg
Risk	Below Avg

Other Measures	Standard Index S&P 500	Best Fit Index Wil 4500
Alpha	25.1	14.1
Beta	2.04	1.49
R-Squared	54	78

Standard Deviation	57.59
Mean	7.68
Sharpe Ratio	0.05

Portfolio Analysis 10-31-01

Share chng since 04-01 Total Stocks: 67	Subsector	PE	YTD Ret%	% Assets
⊕ Microsoft	Software	57.6	52.78	6.00
⊕ Nokia Cl A ADR	Telecom	45.8	–43.00	5.06
⊕ Cadence Design Sys	Software	5.3	–20.20	2.68
⊕ NVIDIA	Technology	84.2	308.50	2.54
⊖ Veritas Software	Software	—	–48.70	2.32
⊖ Applied Matls	Semi Equipment	66.8	5.01	2.30
☼ Intuit	Software	—	8.42	2.10
⊕ Electronic Arts	Software	90.8	40.65	2.06
⊖ NTT DoCoMo	Services	60.1	—	1.99
☼ PeopleSoft	Software	73.1	8.10	1.87
⊕ ARM Hldgs	Technology	NMF	—	1.70
⊕ Walt Disney	Media	—	–27.70	1.67
⊖ China Mobile ADR	N/A	—	—	1.65
☼ Electro Data Sys	N/A	—	—	1.43
⊖ Teradyne	Semi Equipment	NMF	–19.00	1.40
⊖ Maxim Integrated Products	Semiconductors	68.2	9.82	1.36
⊖ ASM Lithography Hldg	Semi Equipment	—	—	1.34
⊕ Integrated Device Tech	Semiconductors	8.9	–19.70	1.30
⊖ Celestica	Technology	79.2	–25.50	1.29
⊕ VeriSign	Technology	—	–48.70	1.28
⊕ Logica	Technology	30.9	—	1.27
⊖ Xilinx	Semiconductors	—	–15.30	1.23
⊖ Cisco Sys	Networking	—	–52.60	1.14
Electronic Data Sys	Computer Svs	25.7	19.83	1.12
⊖ Sun Microsystems	Computers	NMF	–55.80	1.12

Current Investment Style

Style: Value Blnd Growth; Size: Large Med Small

	Stock Port Avg	Relative S&P 500 Current	Relative S&P 500 Hist	Rel Cat
Price/Earnings Ratio	45.1	1.46	—	0.98
Price/Book Ratio	7.0	1.22	—	1.13
Price/Cash Flow	25.7	1.43	—	0.99
3 Yr Earnings Growth	27.4	1.87	—	0.92
1 Yr Earnings Est%	–6.0	3.39	—	0.36
Med Mkt Cap $mil	15,906	0.3	—	1.00

Special Securities % assets 10-31-01	
Restricted/Illiquid Secs	1
Emerging-Markets Secs	6
Options/Futures/Warrants	No

Composition % assets 10-31-01	
Cash	20.0
Stocks*	76.6
Bonds	3.4
Other	0.0
*Foreign (% stocks)	32.4

Market Cap	
Giant	31.1
Large	32.3
Medium	32.2
Small	4.4
Micro	0.0

Subsector Weightings	% of Stocks	Rel Cat
Computers	3.7	0.7
Semiconductors	8.8	0.8
Semi Equipment	6.8	1.7
Networking	1.5	0.4
Periph/Hardware	0.0	0.0
Software	27.5	2.1
Computer Svs	2.7	0.4
Telecom	11.2	1.4
Health Care	0.0	0.0
Other	37.8	1.0

Analysis by Catherine Hickey 10-29-01

This remains an attractive technology offering.

Like most tech funds, Janus Global Technology Fund has been hit hard by the tech sector's drubbing in 2001. Through Oct. 25, 2001, this closed fund had lost a brutal 43%. However, though that steep loss has to be tough to swallow under any circumstances, shareholders can take heart that the fund is running a bit above the category average this year.

Manager Mike Lu has limited the damage to this fund's returns through his attention to diversification. Lu spreads the fund's assets widely across tech subsectors and doesn't take enormous positions in individual names. Even though Lu owns shares of some companies that have shed much of their value this year (Ciena comes to mind), healthy stakes in blue-chip firms like Microsoft have stanched the fund's losses somewhat.

In a recent fund update on Janus' website, Lu said he thinks many tech firms will continue to suffer as corporate IT spending keeps slowing. For this reason, he prefers tech firms that provide essential services to corporations over more-glamorous fare. He likes PeopleSoft, for example, which makes back-office software that companies rely on to help automate core business tasks.

Shareholders of this fund would do well to stick with it. Lu has admirably navigated the extremely volatile tech area and has produced solid results. Janus' technology research staff is also one of the best in the fund industry. In addition, it's one global tech fund that actually offers global exposure; at last count, about 24% of the fund was in foreign issues. Our concerns about the fund's girth have been allayed, too, as depreciation has lopped billions off its asset base, and it remains closed. Those who own shares of this fund will still find it a solid way to gain tech exposure.

Address:	100 Fillmore Street Suite 300 Denver, CO 80206–4923 800–525–8983
Web Address:	www.janus.com
*Inception:	12-31-98
Advisor:	Janus Cap. Corporation
Subadvisor:	None
NTF Plans:	Fidelity Inst. , Waterhouse

Minimum Purchase:	Closed	Add: $100 IRA: —
Min Auto Inv Plan:	Closed	Add: $100
Sales Fees:	No-load	
Management Fee:	.65%	
Actual Fees:	Mgt: 0.65%	Dist: —
Expense Projections:	3Yr: $322	5Yr: $558 10Yr: $1236
Avg Brok Commission:	—	Income Distrib: Annually
Total Cost (relative to category):	Low	

Janus Growth & Income

Ticker	Load	NAV	Yield	Total Assets	Mstar Category
JAGIX	None	$29.97	1.0%	$7,147.9 mil	Large Growth

Prospectus Objective: Growth and Income

Janus Growth and Income Fund seeks long-term growth of capital and current income.

The fund invests in any combination of equity and fixed-income securities, provided that at least 25% of assets are maintained in securities selected for their growth potential, and at least 25% of assets are invested in securities selected for current income. The fixed-income portion consists primarily of investment-grade debt, though it may hold up to 35% of assets in debt rated below BBB. The fund may invest without limit in foreign securities. It may engage in options and futures strategies.

Historical Profile
Return: Above Avg
Risk: Average
Rating: ★★★★ Above Avg

Investment Style
Equity
Average Stock %: 90% 93% 93% 86% 82% 83% 80%

▼ Manager Change
▽ Partial Manager Change

Fund Performance vs. Category Average
■ Quarterly Fund Return
+/– Category Average
— Category Baseline

Performance Quartile (within Category)

Portfolio Manager(s)

David J. Corkins. Since 8-97. BA Dartmouth C.; MBA'93 Columbia U. Other funds currently managed: Janus Adviser Growth & Income, Janus Aspen Growth & Income Instl, IDEX Janus Growth & Income A.

History

1990	1991	1992	1993	1994	1995	1996	1997	1998	1999	2000	12-01	History
—	13.68	14.24	14.69	13.88	16.67	19.05	23.15	29.10	41.94	35.35	29.97	NAV
—	37.14*	5.35	6.70	–4.87	36.35	26.03	34.66	34.87	51.18	–11.41	–14.36	Total Return %
—	21.39*	–2.27	–3.36	–6.19	–1.18	3.09	1.31	6.29	30.14	–2.31	–2.49	+/– S&P 500
—	—	1.46	6.77	–9.73	–2.30	0.51	0.92	–10.23	21.50	13.11	6.13	+/– Russ Top 200 Grt
—	0.34	1.14	1.17	0.65	7.33	0.58	0.37	0.34	0.34	0.55	0.85	Income Return %
—	36.80	4.21	5.52	–5.52	29.02	25.45	34.29	34.53	50.85	–11.96	–15.22	Capital Return %
—	—	59	66	76	23	8	10	40	23	35	16	Total Rtn % Rank Cat
—	0.03	0.15	0.17	0.09	1.01	0.10	0.07	0.08	0.10	0.23	0.30	Income $
—	0.00	0.00	0.33	0.00	1.23	1.89	2.38	2.02	1.84	1.62	0.00	Capital Gains $
—	2.33	1.52	1.28	1.22	1.17	1.03	0.96	0.96	0.90	0.88	—	Expense Ratio %
—	0.76	1.61	1.13	1.26	1.11	0.70	0.30	0.33	0.37	0.49	—	Income Ratio %
—	—	120	138	123	195	153	127	95	43	41	—	Turnover Rate %
—	93.3	311.0	513.8	456.5	632.4	1,100.5	2,004.5	3,504.1	7,492.6	8,349.1	7,147.9	Net Assets $mil

Performance 12-31-01

	1st Qtr	2nd Qtr	3rd Qtr	4th Qtr	Total
1997	0.47	18.91	10.63	1.89	34.66
1998	14.88	6.15	–8.97	21.49	34.87
1999	12.58	4.09	–0.15	29.20	51.18
2000	9.04	–8.29	0.24	–11.62	–11.41
2001	–11.82	5.24	–15.86	9.68	–14.37

Trailing	Total Return%	+/– S&P 500	+/– Russ Top 200 Grth	% Rank All	% Rank Cat	Growth of $10,000
3 Mo	9.68	–1.01	–3.18	44	88	10,968
6 Mo	–7.72	–2.16	–0.73	77	39	9,228
1 Yr	–14.36	–2.49	6.13	71	16	8,564
3 Yr Avg	4.67	5.70	12.70	34	8	11,469
5 Yr Avg	15.81	5.11	7.22	3	4	20,829
10 Yr Avg	14.36	1.44	3.28	7	4	38,274
15 Yr Avg	—	—	—	—	—	—

Tax Analysis	Tax-Adj Ret%	%Rank Cat	%Pretax Ret	%Rank Cat
3 Yr Avg	3.81	6	81.5	40
5 Yr Avg	14.25	4	90.2	15
10 Yr Avg	12.55	4	87.3	14

Potential Capital Gain Exposure: 1% of assets

Risk Analysis

Time Period	Load-Adj Return %	Risk %Rank[1] All	Risk %Rank[1] Cat	Morningstar Return	Morningstar Risk	Morningstar Risk-Adj Rating
1 Yr	–14.36					
3 Yr	4.67	69	12	–0.06[2]	0.94	★★★
5 Yr	15.81	68	9	2.89[2]	0.92	★★★★★
10 Yr	14.36	77	15	1.63	1.00	★★★★

Average Historical Rating (92 months): 3.9★s

[1] 1=low, 100=high [2] T-Bill return substituted for category avg.

Category Rating (3 Yr)

1 2 3 4 5 — Worst … Best (5)

Return: High
Risk: Below Avg

Other Measures	Standard Index S&P 500	Best Fit Index MSCIACWdFr
Alpha	6.1	10.8
Beta	0.98	1.10
R-Squared	72	80

Standard Deviation	20.65
Mean	4.67
Sharpe Ratio	–0.02

Portfolio Analysis 10-31-01

Share change since 04-01 Total Stocks: 72	Sector	PE	YTD Ret%	% Assets
⊕ Citigroup	Financials	20.0	0.03	4.47
⊕ American Intl Grp	Financials	42.0	–19.20	3.90
US Treasury Note 5.25%	N/A	—	—	3.07
⊕ Pfizer	Health	34.7	–12.40	2.86
⊖ Comcast	Services	20.3	–13.70	2.67
⊕ ExxonMobil	Energy	15.3	–7.59	2.60
☼ Liberty Media Group A	N/A	—	—	2.39
☼ Microsoft	Technology	57.6	52.78	2.17
⊕ US Bancorp	Financials	13.5	–6.14	2.07
⊕ Marsh & McLennan	Financials	27.9	–6.30	2.05
⊕ El Paso	Utilities	NMF	–36.70	1.96
⊖ General Elec	Industrials	30.1	–15.00	1.91
⊕ Viacom Cl B	Services	—	—	1.88
⊕ PepsiCo	Staples	31.4	–0.54	1.82
⊖ Maxim Integrated Products	Technology	68.2	9.82	1.75
⊕ DuPont De Nemours E.I.	Industrials	65.4	–9.14	1.62
⊕ Honeywell Intl	Durables	NMF	–27.00	1.60
US Treasury Note 5.25%	N/A	—	—	1.57
⊕ J.P. Morgan Chase & Co.	Financials	27.8	–17.40	1.52
☼ Tyco Intl	Industrials	27.1	6.23	1.46
⊕ Cox Comms A	Services	31.8	–9.99	1.43
⊕ Anheuser-Busch	Staples	24.6	1.01	1.40
⊖ Household Intl	Financials	14.7	6.89	1.28
⊕ Goldman Sachs Grp	Financials	20.7	–12.80	1.24
⊖ Medtronic	Health	76.4	–14.70	1.24

Current Investment Style

Style: Value Blnd Growth; Size: Large Med Small

	Stock Port Avg	Relative S&P 500 Current	Relative S&P 500 Hist	Rel Cat
Price/Earnings Ratio	34.4	1.11	1.26	0.97
Price/Book Ratio	5.3	0.92	1.25	0.82
Price/Cash Flow	18.6	1.03	1.27	0.82
3 Yr Earnings Growth	16.7	1.14	1.37	0.78
1 Yr Earnings Est%	–6.7	3.80	—	–2.24
Med Mkt Cap $mil	40,798	0.7	0.9	0.86

[1] figure is based on 50% or less of stocks

Analysis by Catherine Hickey 11-27-01

This low-key fund is becoming one of Janus' star offerings.

Janus Growth & Income Fund was never the Denver-based firm's golden child. Indeed, this fund was often overlooked during the shop's go-go times during the late 1990s. Back then, funds like Janus Mercury and Janus Enterprise got most of the attention because of their tech-fueled gains. However, as those offerings have been clobbered during tech's downturn since March 2000, this fund has continued to build a great record. It lost 3 percentage points less than its average large-growth peer in 2000, and its 16% loss for the year to date through Nov. 30, 2001 (though poor in absolute terms) ranks in the category's best quintile.

In part, the fund has benefited from its bond stake, which soaks up roughly 8% of assets. Manager David Corkins uses the bonds to help meet the income portion of the fund's mandate. But Corkins' commitment to diversification and his solid stock-picking have also helped separate the fund from its peers. He doesn't bet the farm on any one sector or stock, and he has steered clear of many of the high-risk issues that have hurt other Janus funds. Though Corkins does own racier issues such as EMC, the fund's top holdings are populated with more-cautious fare such as Citigroup and General Electric. Solid picks like Maxim Integrated Products have also helped the fund best its peers in 2001.

To be sure, this is still a Janus fund, and investors should note that it courts more risk than an S&P 500 index offering. However, over time, it has delivered excellent returns relative to its large-growth peer group, and has proved more durable than other Janus funds. We think investors seeking a large-growth pick that isn't wildly aggressive would do well to look here.

Special Securities % assets 10-31-01	
Restricted/Illiquid Secs	0
Emerging-Markets Secs	0
Options/Futures/Warrants	No

Composition % assets 10-31-01	
Cash	11.3
Stocks*	78.8
Bonds	7.7
Other	2.2
*Foreign (% stocks)	4.9

Market Cap	
Giant	45.1
Large	37.7
Medium	16.1
Small	0.2
Micro	0.9

Sector Weightings	% of Stocks	Rel S&P	5-Year High	5-Year Low
Utilities	3.3	1.0	5	0
Energy	7.3	1.0	12	0
Financials	30.7	1.7	52	8
Industrials	7.9	0.7	21	0
Durables	5.0	3.2	17	0
Staples	8.4	1.1	16	0
Services	15.0	1.4	34	3
Retail	0.6	0.1	22	0
Health	8.5	0.6	30	0
Technology	13.5	0.7	39	0

Address:	100 Fillmore Street Suite 300 Denver, CO 80206–4923 800–525–8983
Web Address:	www.janus.com
*Inception:	05-15-91
Advisor:	Janus Cap. Corporation
Subadvisor:	None
NTF Plans:	Fidelity , Datalynx

Minimum Purchase:	$2500	Add: $100	IRA: $500
Min Auto Inv Plan:	$500	Add: $100	
Sales Fees:	No-load		
Management Fee:	.65%		
Actual Fees:	Mgt: 0.65%	Dist: —	
Expense Projections:	3Yr: $290	5Yr: $504	10Yr: $1120
Avg Brok Commission:	—	Income Distrib: Quarterly	
Total Cost (relative to category):	Below Avg		

Janus High–Yield

Ticker	Load	NAV	Yield	SEC Yield	Total Assets	Mstar Category
JAHYX	None	$9.37	8.0%	7.76%	$433.1 mil	High–Yield Bond

Prospectus Objective: Corp Bond—High Yield

Janus High-Yield Fund seeks high current income; capital appreciation is a secondary consideration.

The fund normally invests at least 65% of assets in fixed-income securities rated below investment-grade. Potential investments may include corporate bonds and notes, government securities, preferred stocks, and convertible securities. The fund may purchase defaulted debt securities if the advisor believes that the issuer is likely to resume interest payments in the near future. It may invest without limit in foreign securities.

Historical Profile

Return Average
Risk Above Avg
Rating ★★
Below Avg

Investment Style
Fixed-Income
Income Rtn %Rank Cat: 20 (1996), 70 (1997), 75 (1998), 68 (1999), 85 (2000), 95 (12-01)

Growth of Principal vs. Interest Rate Shifts
- Principal Value $000 (NAV with capital gains reinvested)
- Interest Rate % on 10 Yr Treasury
- ▼ Manager Change
- ▽ Partial Manager Change
- ► Mgr Unknown After
- ◄ Mgr Unknown Before

Performance Quartile (within Category)

Portfolio Manager(s)

Sandy R. Rufenacht. Since 7-96. BA U. of Northern Colorado. Other funds currently managed: Janus Short-Term Bond, Janus Aspen High Yield Instl.

History

1990	1991	1992	1993	1994	1995	1996	1997	1998	1999	2000	12-01	History
—	—	—	—	—	10.00	11.23	11.39	10.61	10.28	9.69	9.37	NAV
—	—	—	—	—	—	23.99	15.47	0.97	5.54	2.49	4.52	Total Return %
—	—	—	—	—	—	20.37	5.79	–7.71	6.37	–9.14	–3.90	+/– LB Aggregate
—	—	—	—	—	—	11.57	2.85	0.39	2.26	7.70	–1.25	+/– FB High–Yield
—	—	—	—	—	0.00	10.11	8.80	8.21	8.76	8.57	8.01	Income Return %
—	—	—	—	—	0.00	13.87	6.67	–7.24	–3.22	–6.07	–3.49	Capital Return %
—	—	—	—	—	—	1	13	41	39	5	34	Total Rtn % Rank Cat
—	—	—	—	—	0.00	0.97	0.95	0.90	0.89	0.85	0.75	Income $
—	—	—	—	—	0.00	0.11	0.56	0.00	0.00	0.00	0.00	Capital Gains $
—	—	—	—	—	—	1.00	1.00	0.96	1.00	1.00	—	Expense Ratio %
—	—	—	—	—	—	9.00	8.45	7.85	8.48	8.43	—	Income Ratio %
—	—	—	—	—	—	324	404	336	310	295	—	Turnover Rate %
—	—	—	—	—	—	238.2	357.4	295.2	275.2	300.8	433.1	Net Assets $mil

Performance 12-31-01

	1st Qtr	2nd Qtr	3rd Qtr	4th Qtr	Total
1997	1.65	4.23	6.33	2.51	15.47
1998	4.86	0.88	–5.76	1.28	0.97
1999	3.14	–0.08	–1.89	4.38	5.54
2000	1.84	1.73	1.24	–2.28	2.49
2001	3.35	–1.61	–2.53	5.46	4.52

Trailing	Total Return%	+/– LB Agg	+/– FB High-Yield	% Rank All	% Rank Cat	Growth of $10,000
3 Mo	5.46	5.42	–0.19	63	57	10,546
6 Mo	2.79	–1.86	1.35	16	13	10,279
1 Yr	4.52	–3.90	–1.25	26	34	10,452
3 Yr Avg	4.18	–2.10	3.01	38	7	11,306
5 Yr Avg	5.68	–1.75	2.44	53	5	13,182
10 Yr Avg	—	—	—	—	—	—
15 Yr Avg	—	—	—	—	—	—

Tax Analysis	Tax-Adj Ret%	%Rank Cat	%Pretax Ret	%Rank Cat
3 Yr Avg	0.85	6	20.5	53
5 Yr Avg	1.95	5	34.3	27
10 Yr Avg	—	—	—	—

Potential Capital Gain Exposure: –12% of assets

Risk Analysis

Time Period	Load-Adj Return %	Risk %Rank[1] All	Risk %Rank[1] Cat	Morningstar Return	Morningstar Risk	Morningstar Risk-Adj Rating
1 Yr	4.52					
3 Yr	4.18	31	5	–0.16[2]	1.33	★★
5 Yr	5.68	37	7	0.14[2]	1.46	★★
Incept	8.52	—	—	—	—	

Average Historical Rating (37 months): 3.1★s

[1] 1=low, 100=high [2] T-Bill return substituted for category avg.

Category Rating (3 Yr)

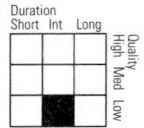

1 2 3 4 **5**
Worst Best

Return High
Risk Low

Other Measures	Standard Index LB Agg	Best Fit Index FB HY
Alpha	–1.0	2.2
Beta	0.34	0.79
R–Squared	3	86
Standard Deviation		6.54
Mean		4.18
Sharpe Ratio		–0.14

Analysis by Scott Berry 11-29-01

Janus High-Yield is making a name for itself.

This fund is becoming a fixture near the top of the high-yield performance charts. In fact, it is one of only two high-yield offerings to rank in the category's top half in each of the last five years. The fund's success is also reflected in its three- and five-year trailing returns, which rank solidly in the category's top decile.

The fund's recent success owes much to manager Sandy Rufenacht's distaste for telecommunications bonds, which have gotten crushed over the last few years. Rufenacht typically favors bonds that are issued by companies with hard assets and positive cash flow. Most telecommuncations companies don't fit that mold, so Rufenacht has largely avoided the sector. Instead, he has held large stakes in the energy, casino, and cable sectors, which have been among the more stable areas of the high-yield market.

For much of 2001, the fund's approach has kept it well ahead of its average peer. The fund's casino holdings got hit hard in the weeks following the September terrorist attacks, but Rufenacht bought on that weakness and prices have since rebounded to near pre-attack levels. The fund has gained 4.6% for the year to date through Nov. 28, 2001, while its average peer has gained 1.7%.

One potential drawback for the fund is its cash stake, which is typically double the size of its average peer's, and which at times has ballooned to more than 30% of the fund's assets. Such a large cash stake can pay off when the market falters, as it did when the high-yield market stumbled in September 2001, but could hold the fund back during market rallies.

Nevertheless, we like what this fund has done and think it makes a solid choice for high-yield investors.

Portfolio Analysis 10-31-01

Total Fixed-Income: 128	Date of Maturity	Amount $000	Value $000	% Net Assets
Isle of Capri Cap 13%	08-31-04	6,000	6,390	1.57
Bergen Brunswig 7.375%	01-15-03	6,000	6,135	1.51
Mediacom Cap 9.5%	01-15-13	6,000	6,120	1.50
CSC Hldgs 7.625%	04-01-11	6,000	6,068	1.49
Venetian Casino 12.25%	11-15-04	6,000	5,445	1.34
Price Comm Wireless 11.75%	07-15-07	5,000	5,375	1.32
Hard Rock Hotel 9.25%	04-01-05	6,000	5,340	1.31
Frontiervision 11%	10-15-06	5,000	5,125	1.26
L-3 Comms Hldgs 4%	11-15-11	5,000	5,100	1.25
Forest Oil 8%	06-15-08	5,000	5,050	1.24
Calpine Canada Energy Fin 8.5%	05-01-08	5,000	5,006	1.23
Winn–dixie Stores 8.875%	04-01-08	5,000	4,788	1.17
Voicestream Wire 10.375%	11-15-09	4,000	4,560	1.12
Avis Rent–A–Car 11%	05-01-09	4,000	4,280	1.05
Magellan Health Svcs 144A 9.375%	11-15-07	4,000	4,200	1.03
Charter Comm 10.25%	01-15-10	4,000	4,080	1.00
Station Casinos 8.875%	12-01-08	4,000	3,700	0.91
Tritel PCS 10.375%	01-15-11	3,000	3,443	0.84
Venetian Casino 10%	11-15-05	4,000	3,340	0.82
Labranche & Co 12%	03-01-07	3,000	3,240	0.80

Current Investment Style

Duration: Short Int Long
Quality: High Med Low

Avg Eff Duration[1]	4.3 Yrs
Avg Eff Maturity	6.0 Yrs
Avg Credit Quality	BB
Avg Wtd Coupon	9.34%
Avg Wtd Price	98.64% of par

[1] figure provided by fund

Special Securities % assets 10-31-01	
Restricted/Illiquid Secs	3
Exotic Mortgage–Backed	0
Emerging–Markets Secs	0
Options/Futures/Warrants	No

Coupon Range	% of Bonds	Rel Cat
0%, PIK	1.37	0.22
0% to 9%	37.86	1.25
9% to 12%	52.25	0.98
12% to 14%	8.52	0.97
More than 14%	0.00	0.00

1.00=Category Average

Credit Analysis % bonds 06-30-01

US Govt	0	BB	24
AAA	0	B	52
AA	4	Below B	4
A	1	NR/NA	7
BBB	8		

Composition % assets 10-31-01

Cash	23.2	Bonds	76.4
Stocks	0.0	Other	0.4

Sector Breakdown % bonds 10-31-01

US Treasuries	0	CMOs	0
GNMA mtgs	0	ARMs	0
FNMA mtgs	0	Other	100
FHLMC mtgs	0		

Address:	100 Fillmore Street Suite 300 Denver, CO 80206–4923 800–525–8983
Web Address:	www.janus.com
*Inception:	12-29-95
Advisor:	Janus Cap. Corporation
Subadvisor:	None
NTF Plans:	Fidelity , Datalynx

Minimum Purchase:	$2500	Add: $100 IRA: $500
Min Auto Inv Plan:	$500	Add: $100
Sales Fees:	No-load, 1.00%R within 3 months	
Management Fee:	.75% mx./.65% mn.	
Actual Fees:	Mgt: 0.72%	Dist: —
Expense Projections:	3Yr: $384	5Yr: $579 10Yr: $1283
Avg Brok Commission:	—	Income Distrib: Monthly
Total Cost (relative to category):	Below Avg	

Janus Mercury

Ticker	Load	NAV	Yield	Total Assets	Mstar Category
JAMRX	None	$20.79	0.2%	$8,437.7 mil	Large Growth

Prospectus Objective: Growth

Janus Mercury Fund seeks long-term growth of capital.

The fund invests primarily in common stocks issued by companies of any size. The advisor uses a bottom-up approach to choosing investments, emphasizing companies with earnings-growth potential. It may invest without limit in foreign securities. The fund may also invest in preferred stocks, warrants, government securities, and corporate debt. It may use derivatives for hedging purposes or as a means of enhancing return. This fund is non-diversified.

Historical Profile

Return Above Avg
Risk Above Avg
Rating ★★★★ Above Avg

Investment Style
Equity
Average Stock %: 89% 91% 94% 95% 86% 92%

▼ Manager Change
▽ Partial Manager Change

Fund Performance vs. Category Average
■ Quarterly Fund Return +/– Category Average
— Category Baseline

Performance Quartile (within Category)

Portfolio Manager(s)

Warren B. Lammert III, CFA. Since 5-93. BA'84 Yale U.; MS'89 London School of Economics. Other funds currently managed: WM Growth A, WM Growth B, WM Growth I.

1990	1991	1992	1993	1994	1995	1996	1997	1998	1999	2000	12-01	History
—	—	—	11.98	13.61	16.04	16.52	16.50	24.11	43.81	29.67	20.79	NAV
—	—	—	19.80*	15.86	33.01	17.67	11.88	58.41	96.23	–22.75	–29.78	Total Return %
—	—	—	12.29*	14.54	–4.53	–5.28	–21.47	29.83	75.19	–13.65	–17.90	+/– S&P 500
—	—	—	—	11.00	–5.65	–7.85	–21.86	13.31	66.55	1.77	–9.28	+/– Russ Top 200 Grt
—	—	—	0.00	1.37	12.91	0.47	0.25	0.00	0.00	3.80	0.15	Income Return %
—	—	—	19.80	14.48	20.09	17.20	11.63	58.41	96.23	–26.55	–29.93	Capital Return %
—	—	—	—	1	43	57	93	6	5	81	77	Total Rtn % Rank Cat
—	—	—	0.00	0.16	1.76	0.08	0.04	0.00	0.00	1.66	0.04	Income $
—	—	—	0.00	0.11	0.30	2.28	1.90	2.01	3.27	2.78	0.00	Capital Gains $
—	—	—	1.75	1.33	1.12	1.00	0.96	0.97	0.91	0.88	—	Expense Ratio %
—	—	—	–0.40	0.25	0.50	0.45	0.21	–0.33	–0.39	0.08	—	Income Ratio %
—	—	—	151	283	201	177	157	105	89	71	—	Turnover Rate %
—	—	—	126.9	690.1	1,596.4	2,061.3	1,911.4	3,111.5	13,543.1	13,345.0	8,437.7	Net Assets $mil

Performance 12-31-01

	1st Qtr	2nd Qtr	3rd Qtr	4th Qtr	Total
1997	–5.81	13.37	8.73	–3.64	11.88
1998	18.67	10.32	–6.94	30.04	58.41
1999	23.68	7.51	3.40	42.72	96.23
2000	12.83	–14.46	0.64	–20.47	–22.75
2001	–24.30	9.39	–23.12	10.30	–29.78

Trailing	Total Return%	+/– S&P 500	+/–Russ Top 200 Grth	% Rank All	% Rank Cat	Growth of $10,000
3 Mo	10.30	–0.39	–2.56	41	85	11,030
6 Mo	–15.20	–9.65	–8.21	95	92	8,480
1 Yr	–29.78	–17.90	–9.28	93	77	7,022
3 Yr Avg	2.10	3.13	10.13	62	16	10,644
5 Yr Avg	13.54	2.84	4.94	7	11	18,865
10 Yr Avg	—	—	—	—	—	—
15 Yr Avg	—	—	—	—	—	—

Tax Analysis	Tax-Adj Ret%	%Rank Cat	%Pretax Ret	%Rank Cat
3 Yr Avg	0.10	17	4.6	98
5 Yr Avg	10.95	13	80.9	43
10 Yr Avg	—	—	—	—

Potential Capital Gain Exposure: –53% of assets

Risk Analysis

Time Period	Load-Adj Return %	Risk %Rank¹ All	Risk %Rank¹ Cat	Morningstar Return	Morningstar Risk	Morningstar Risk-Adj Rating
1 Yr	–29.78					
3 Yr	2.10	91	72	–0.59²	1.45	★★★
5 Yr	13.54	87	68	2.19²	1.35	★★★★
Incept	17.67	—	—	—	—	

Average Historical Rating (69 months): 4.2★s

¹1=low, 100=high ² T-Bill return substituted for category avg.

Category Rating (3 Yr)

1 2 3 4 5
Worst Best

Return Above Avg
Risk Above Avg

Other Measures	Standard Index S&P 500	Best Fit Index Wil 4500
Alpha	8.9	1.9
Beta	1.46	0.96
R-Squared	63	73

Standard Deviation	33.62
Mean	2.10
Sharpe Ratio	–0.10

Portfolio Analysis 10-31-01

Share change since 04-01 Total Stocks: 61	Sector	PE	YTD Ret%	% Assets
⊖ Nokia Cl A ADR	Technology	45.8	–43.00	6.58
⊕ Comcast	Services	20.3	–13.70	4.47
⊕ Pfizer	Health	34.7	–12.40	4.46
⊕ Citigroup	Financials	20.0	0.03	4.32
⊖ AOL Time Warner	Technology	—	–7.76	4.32
☼ Liberty Media Group A	N/A	—	—	3.72
⊖ Analog Devices	Technology	47.7	–13.20	3.35
☼ Raytheon	Industrials	—	7.27	2.70
☼ Berkshire Hathaway Cl B	Financials	64.8	7.26	2.48
☼ HCA – The Healthcare Company	Health	24.1	–12.20	2.25
⊕ Cablevision Sys A	Services	5.6	–34.20	2.25
⊕ Celestica	Technology	79.2	–25.50	2.10
Tenet Healthcare	Health	30.1	32.14	2.06
☼ AT&T Wireless	N/A	—	—	1.91
⊖ Electronic Arts	Technology	90.8	40.65	1.84
☼ Laboratory Corp of Amer	Health	21.0	–8.13	1.72
Cox Comms A	Services	31.8	–9.99	1.62
☼ Waters	Industrials	32.0	–53.50	1.61
⊕ J.P. Morgan Chase & Co.	Financials	27.8	–17.40	1.60
☼ Fannie Mae	Financials	16.2	–6.95	1.59
☼ American Home Products	Health	—	–1.91	1.58
⊖ Flextronics Intl	Technology	—	–15.80	1.56
☼ McKesson HBOC	Health	—	4.92	1.54
⊖ Dominion Resources	Utilities	19.3	–6.59	1.41
⊖ Petroleo Brasileiro ADR	N/A	—	—	1.39

Current Investment Style

Style: Value Blnd Growth; Size: Large Med Small

	Stock Port Avg	Relative S&P 500 Current	Relative S&P 500 Hist	Rel Cat
Price/Earnings Ratio	33.0	1.07	1.34	0.93
Price/Book Ratio	5.4	0.95	1.49	0.85
Price/Cash Flow	21.8	1.21	1.41	0.96
3 Yr Earnings Growth	24.5¹	1.67	1.39	1.14
1 Yr Earnings Est%	4.1	—	—	1.38
Med Mkt Cap $mil	26,267	0.4	0.5	0.55

¹figure is based on 50% or less of stocks

Special Securities % assets 10-31-01	
Restricted/Illiquid Secs	0
Emerging-Markets Secs	1
Options/Futures/Warrants	No

Composition % assets 10-31-01	
Cash	6.8
Stocks*	93.2
Bonds	0.0
Other	0.0
*Foreign (% stocks)	14.9

Market Cap	
Giant	37.8
Large	46.6
Medium	14.8
Small	0.0
Micro	0.8

Sector Weightings	% of Stocks	Rel S&P	5-Year High	5-Year Low
Utilities	3.1	1.0	5	0
Energy	2.8	0.4	12	0
Financials	20.1	1.1	24	4
Industrials	6.7	0.6	20	1
Durables	1.2	0.8	25	0
Staples	2.0	0.3	13	0
Services	17.0	1.6	38	5
Retail	0.8	0.1	17	0
Health	19.3	1.3	27	3
Technology	27.0	1.5	49	23

Analysis by Christine Benz 11-11-01

Looking to upgrade your growth-fund holdings? We submit Janus Mercury.

Although investors might want to ignore the havoc that has been wrought on the growth portion of their portfolios over the past year and a half, there's reason to give it some attention. With many holding growth funds at NAV levels far below their purchase prices, it could be a good time to take a tax loss on your lesser funds (thereby gaining ammunition to offset gains down the road) and swap into some better-quality offerings. In the latter camp, this fund more than fits the bill.

Like many aggressive offerings, Mercury has been badly battered over the past year and a half; its 12-month trailing return through Nov. 8, 2001, lands in the large-growth category's bottom quartile. And Enron appears to have weighed on the fund's recent returns, even as growth stocks have bounced back over the past month. Yet manager Warren Lammert's record of success here stretches back to the early 1990s, and since its inception, the fund has more than doubled the return of the typical large-growth fund. While tech and telecom-equipment stocks fueled the fund's gains in the late 1990s, Lammert has had success in other areas as well, including drugmakers and cable stocks. In 1998's blue-chip-fueled rally, for example, the fund trumped the typical large-growth fund, thanks to a sizable dose of pharmaceutical stocks.

Owning this fund will never be easy, because it has always been concentrated and fairly streaky. And shareholders will want to make sure that its weak return in October—a strong month overall for growth funds—was just an anomaly. That said, we still maintain that this is a solid choice for those who can endure some volatility.

Address:	100 Fillmore Street Suite 300 Denver, CO 80206–4923 800–525–8983
Web Address:	www.janus.com
*Inception:	05-03-93
Advisor:	Janus Cap. Corporation
Subadvisor:	None
NTF Plans:	Fidelity , Datalynx

Minimum Purchase:	$2500	Add: $100 IRA: $500
Min Auto Inv Plan:	$500	Add: $100
Sales Fees:	No-load	
Management Fee:	.65%	
Actual Fees:	Mgt: 0.65%	Dist: —
Expense Projections:	3Yr: $293	5Yr: $509 10Yr: $1131
Avg Brok Commission:	—	Income Distrib: Annually
Total Cost (relative to category):		Below Avg

Janus Olympus

Ticker	Load	NAV	Yield	Total Assets	Mstar Category
JAOLX	Closed	$27.85	0.4%	$3,437.4 mil	Large Growth

Prospectus Objective: Aggressive Growth

Janus Olympus Fund seeks long-term growth of capital.

The fund invests primarily in common stocks. It may also invest in preferred stocks, warrants, convertible securities, and debt securities. Management typically selects stocks issued by companies that it believes have earnings-growth potential that is not recognized by the market. The fund may invest without limit in equity and debt securities of foreign issuers. This fund is non-diversified.

Historical Profile

Return: Above Avg
Risk: Above Avg
Rating: ★★★★ Above Avg

Investment Style
Equity
Average Stock %: 90% 94% 92% 86% 79% 89%

▼ Manager Change
▽ Partial Manager Change

Fund Performance vs. Category Average
■ Quarterly Fund Return +/– Category Average
— Category Baseline

Performance Quartile (within Category)

Portfolio Manager(s)

Claire Young, CFA. Since 9-97. BS Yale U. Other funds currently managed: MassMutual Instl Agg Growth Equity S, MassMutual Instl Agg Growth Equity A, MassMutual Instl Agg Growth Equity Y.

1990	1991	1992	1993	1994	1995	1996	1997	1998	1999	2000	12-01	History
—	—	—	—	—	12.00	14.48	17.58	27.58	53.26	41.15	27.85	NAV
—	—	—	—	—	—	21.73	26.73	56.97	100.12	–21.63	–32.05	Total Return %
—	—	—	—	—	—	–1.21	–6.63	28.40	79.08	–12.53	–20.17	+/– S&P 500
—	—	—	—	—	—	–3.79	–7.02	11.88	70.45	2.89	–11.55	+/– Russ Top 200 Grt
—	—	—	—	—	0.00	1.08	0.28	0.07	0.05	0.44	0.26	Income Return %
—	—	—	—	—	0.00	20.66	26.45	56.90	100.07	–22.07	–32.31	Capital Return %
—	—	—	—	—	—	28	45	8	4	77	84	Total Rtn % Rank Cat
—	—	—	—	—	0.00	0.13	0.04	0.01	0.01	0.23	0.11	Income $
—	—	—	—	—	0.00	0.00	0.71	0.00	1.78	0.39	0.00	Capital Gains $
—	—	—	—	—	—	1.15	1.03	1.01	0.93	0.90	—	Expense Ratio %
—	—	—	—	—	—	1.64	0.26	–0.21	0.06	0.51	—	Income Ratio %
—	—	—	—	—	—	303	244	123	91	96	—	Turnover Rate %
—	—	—	—	—	—	412.9	629.2	1,288.1	6,174.4	6,165.4	3,437.4	Net Assets $mil

Performance 12-31-01

	1st Qtr	2nd Qtr	3rd Qtr	4th Qtr	Total
1997	–4.63	22.45	10.41	–1.71	26.73
1998	16.33	10.48	–7.93	32.66	56.97
1999	23.39	3.03	3.79	51.67	100.12
2000	11.10	–8.74	–0.02	–22.69	–21.63
2001	–26.29	3.46	–25.84	20.16	–32.05

Trailing	Total Return%	+/– S&P 500	+/– Russ Top 200 Grth	% Rank All	% Rank Cat	Growth of $10,000
3 Mo	20.16	9.47	7.30	13	14	12,016
6 Mo	–10.90	–5.34	–3.91	88	69	8,910
1 Yr	–32.05	–20.17	–11.55	95	84	6,795
3 Yr Avg	2.14	3.17	10.16	62	16	10,656
5 Yr Avg	16.21	5.51	7.62	3	3	21,198
10 Yr Avg	—	—	—	—	—	—
15 Yr Avg	—	—	—	—	—	—

Tax Analysis	Tax-Adj Ret%	%Rank Cat	%Pretax Ret	%Rank Cat
3 Yr Avg	1.67	12	77.8	47
5 Yr Avg	15.54	2	95.8	5
10 Yr Avg	—	—	—	—

Potential Capital Gain Exposure: –31% of assets

Risk Analysis

Time Period	Load-Adj Return %	Risk %Rank[1] All	Risk %Rank[1] Cat	Morningstar Return	Morningstar Risk	Morningstar Risk-Adj Rating
1 Yr	–32.05					
3 Yr	2.14	94	82	–0.58[2]	1.59	★★★
5 Yr	16.21	89	81	3.02[2]	1.43	★★★★★
Incept	17.08	—	—	—	—	

Average Historical Rating (37 months): 4.8★s

[1] 1=low, 100=high [2] T-Bill return substituted for category avg.

Category Rating (3 Yr)

① ② ③ ❹ ⑤
Worst — Best

Return: Above Avg
Risk: Above Avg

Other Measures	Standard Index S&P 500	Best Fit Index Wil 4500
Alpha	9.3	2.7
Beta	1.38	1.08
R-Squared	47	79
Standard Deviation		36.82
Mean		2.14
Sharpe Ratio		–0.09

Analysis by Christine Benz 11-11-01

Among the now-humbled bull-market babies, we like Janus Olympus Fund's prospects better than most.

Like most funds that posted big returns during growth stocks' heyday in the late 1990s, this offering's recent results have been predictably awful. This fund came into 2000 with more in technology and telecommunications-equipment stocks than many of its peers, and these issues have been among the hardest hit in the ongoing valuation correction. Manager Claire Young also downplayed a few pockets of decent performance in these areas—notably, AOL Time Warner and Microsoft. Finally, Young's attempts to stabilize the portfolio have mostly fallen flat. Walgreen, Kroger, and Safeway, purveyors of goods people need in good times and bad, have all been disappointing performers of late. In all, the fund is sitting on a near-50% loss for the trailing 12 months, a bottom-quartile showing in the hard-hit large-growth group.

Yet we still believe that in moderation, this fund could make a great kicker for a well-diversified portfolio. For one thing, it closed with a lot less in assets than most of the other Janus funds, and Olympus also appears to have fewer "clones" on the institutional side than some of its siblings; both factors should make the fund a lot more maneuverable than some other Janus funds. And Young has shown that when growth stocks are running hard, Olympus is a fund to beat. The fund's returns on her watch are topnotch in the large-cap growth camp.

Although Young has taken steps to rein in the portfolio's aggressiveness over the past year, all but the most intrepid investors should steer clear. Nonetheless, we still think it's a worthwhile choice for investors who can tolerate ups and downs.

Portfolio Analysis 10-31-01

Share change since 04-01 Total Stocks: 65	Sector	PE	YTD Ret%	% Assets
⊕ Goldman Sachs Grp	Financials	20.7	–12.80	4.01
⊕ Maxim Integrated Products	Technology	68.2	9.82	3.89
Citigroup	Financials	20.0	0.03	3.73
⊕ NVIDIA	Technology	84.2	308.50	3.17
⊖ Walgreen	Retail	39.1	–19.20	3.01
Pfizer	Health	34.7	–12.40	2.99
⊕ Veritas Software	Technology	—	–48.70	2.65
⊕ Safeway	Retail	18.1	–33.20	2.52
Tenet Healthcare	Health	30.1	32.14	2.46
⊖ Comcast	Services	20.3	–13.70	2.43
⊕ AOL Time Warner	Technology	—	–7.76	2.32
⊖ Tiffany	Retail	27.1	0.09	2.13
⊖ Fannie Mae	Financials	16.2	–6.95	1.99
⊕ Applied Matls	Technology	66.8	5.01	1.90
⊕ MGIC Invest	Financials	10.9	–8.33	1.88
⊕ Clear Channel Comms	Services	—	5.10	1.87
☼ Nike	Staples	26.5	1.86	1.86
⊖ General Elec	Industrials	30.1	–15.00	1.83
☼ Medtronic	Health	76.4	–14.70	1.74
⊕ Microsoft	Technology	57.6	52.78	1.74
☼ MGM Mirage	Services	21.9	2.42	1.66
⊕ Fiserv	Services	40.7	33.82	1.66
⊖ Genentech	Health	NMF	–33.40	1.65
⊕ Bank of New York	Financials	21.9	–24.80	1.59
⊖ Wal-Mart Stores	Retail	40.3	8.94	1.57

Current Investment Style

Style: Value Blnd Growth; Size: Large Med Small

	Stock Port Avg	Relative S&P 500 Current	Relative S&P 500 Hist	Rel Cat
Price/Earnings Ratio	34.3	1.11	1.43	0.97
Price/Book Ratio	6.3	1.10	1.68	0.98
Price/Cash Flow	24.3	1.35	1.48	1.07
3 Yr Earnings Growth	19.8	1.35	1.70	0.92
1 Yr Earnings Est%	5.2	—	—	1.74
Med Mkt Cap $mil	24,506	0.4	0.5	0.52

Special Securities % assets 10-31-01	
Restricted/Illiquid Secs	0
Emerging-Markets Secs	0
Options/Futures/Warrants	No

Composition % assets 10-31-01	
Cash	3.4
Stocks*	94.5
Bonds	2.1
Other	0.0
*Foreign (% stocks)	3.4

Market Cap	
Giant	25.9
Large	51.6
Medium	22.3
Small	0.2
Micro	0.0

Sector Weightings	% of Stocks	Rel S&P	5-Year High	5-Year Low
Utilities	0.0	0.0	2	0
Energy	2.7	0.4	9	0
Financials	18.7	1.0	28	2
Industrials	5.8	0.5	7	0
Durables	1.7	1.1	13	0
Staples	5.8	0.7	6	0
Services	19.6	1.8	29	3
Retail	10.9	1.6	16	0
Health	12.9	0.9	32	4
Technology	22.0	1.2	66	22

Address: 100 Fillmore Street Suite 300, Denver, CO 80206-4923, 800-525-8983
Web Address: www.janus.com
*Inception: 12-29-95
Advisor: Janus Cap. Corporation
Subadvisor: None
NTF Plans: Fidelity , Datalynx

Minimum Purchase: Closed — Add: $100 — IRA: —
Min Auto Inv Plan: Closed — Add: $100
Sales Fees: No-load
Management Fee: .65%
Actual Fees: Mgt: 0.65% — Dist: —
Expense Projections: 3Yr: $296 — 5Yr: $515 — 10Yr: $1143
Avg Brok Commission: — — Income Distrib: Annually
Total Cost (relative to category): Below Avg

Janus Orion

Ticker	Load	NAV	Yield	Total Assets	Mstar Category
JORNX	None	$5.98	0.0%	$688.4 mil	Mid-Cap Growth

Prospectus Objective: Aggressive Growth

Janus Orion seeks long-term growth of capital.

The fund may invest in companies of any size from larger, well-established companies to smaller emerging growth companies. The fund usually invests no more than 35% of assets in high-yield/high-risk bonds. The fund may invest without limit in foreign equity and debt securities. It may also typically invest up to 15% in illiquid securities. The fund normally concentrates its investments in a core group of twenty to thirty common stocks. This fund is non-diversified.

Historical Profile

Return —
Risk —
Rating Not Rated

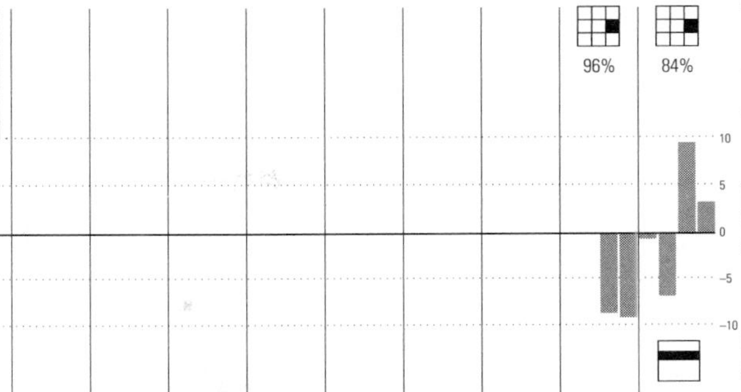

Investment Style
Equity
Average Stock %
96% 84%

▼ Manager Change
▽ Partial Manager Change

Fund Performance vs. Category Average
■ Quarterly Fund Return +/– Category Average
— Category Baseline

Performance Quartile (within Category)

Portfolio Manager(s)

Ron Sachs, CFA. Since 6-00. JD U. of Michigan; BA Princeton U.

1990	1991	1992	1993	1994	1995	1996	1997	1998	1999	2000	12-01	History
—	—	—	—	—	—	—	—	—	—	7.01	5.98	NAV
—	—	—	—	—	—	—	—	—	—	-29.69*	-14.69	Total Return %
—	—	—	—	—	—	—	—	—	—	-20.98*	-2.82	+/– S&P 500
—	—	—	—	—	—	—	—	—	—	—	5.46	+/– Russ Midcap Grth
—	—	—	—	—	—	—	—	—	—	0.21	0.00	Income Return %
—	—	—	—	—	—	—	—	—	—	-29.90	-14.69	Capital Return %
—	—	—	—	—	—	—	—	—	—	—	31	Total Rtn % Rank Cat
—	—	—	—	—	—	—	—	—	—	0.02	0.00	Income $
—	—	—	—	—	—	—	—	—	—	0.00	0.00	Capital Gains $
—	—	—	—	—	—	—	—	—	—	1.12	—	Expense Ratio %
—	—	—	—	—	—	—	—	—	—	0.82	—	Income Ratio %
—	—	—	—	—	—	—	—	—	—	35	—	Turnover Rate %
—	—	—	—	—	—	—	—	—	—	878.6	688.4	Net Assets $mil

Performance 12-31-01

	1st Qtr	2nd Qtr	3rd Qtr	4th Qtr	Total
1997	—	—	—	—	—
1998	—	—	—	—	—
1999	—	—	—	—	—
2000	—	—	-3.40	-27.22	-29.69 *
2001	-22.54	5.34	-14.86	22.79	-14.69

Trailing	Total Return%	+/– S&P 500	+/– Russ Midcap Grth	% Rank All	% Rank Cat	Growth of $10,000
3 Mo	22.79	12.11	-4.27	10	28	12,279
6 Mo	4.55	10.10	12.81	5	1	10,455
1 Yr	-14.69	-2.82	5.46	72	31	8,531
3 Yr Avg	—	—	—	—	—	—
5 Yr Avg	—	—	—	—	—	—
10 Yr Avg	—	—	—	—	—	—
15 Yr Avg	—	—	—	—	—	—

Tax Analysis	Tax-Adj Ret%	%Rank Cat	%Pretax Ret	%Rank Cat
3 Yr Avg	—	—	—	—
5 Yr Avg	—	—	—	—
10 Yr Avg	—	—	—	—

Potential Capital Gain Exposure: NMF

Risk Analysis

Time Period	Load-Adj Return %	Risk %Rank[1] All	Risk %Rank[1] Cat	Morningstar Return	Morningstar Risk	Morningstar Risk-Adj Rating
1 Yr	-14.69					
3 Yr	—	—	—	—	—	
5 Yr	—	—	—	—	—	
Incept	-28.81	—	—	—	—	

Average Historical Rating —

[1]1=low, 100=high

Category Rating (3 Yr)

Return
Risk

Other Measures	Standard Index S&P 500	Best Fit Index
Alpha	—	—
Beta	—	—
R-Squared	—	—
Standard Deviation		—
Mean		—
Sharpe Ratio		—

Analysis by Emily Hall 11-27-01

Janus Orion is still finding its feet.

It wasn't exactly an auspicious beginning: This young fund has gone the way of most Janus offerings lately—way down. Launched in 2000, the fund was full of racy technology and telecom names that quickly hit the skids. In the fourth quarter of 2000—its second full quarter of existence—the fund lost a wrenching 27%.

Manager Ron Sachs hasn't stood still, though. Taking the fund's go-anywhere-for-growth mandate seriously, he has opted for decidedly staid but steady fare lately: As of the end of September, the fund had more than a 6% stake in Berkshire Hathaway. That migration toward larger, more-mature companies has been something of a boon. Although the fund is still bleeding, its 29% loss for the trailing 12 months through mid-November is actually right around the mid-growth category average.

But the shift also makes it difficult to recommend this offering. The fund seems to be making decisions that are awfully similar to those of its siblings. If there are investors out there who already owned a large-cap Janus fund but were looking to this offering to act as a smaller-cap diversifier, then they should probably think about going elsewhere.

Moreover, this is Sachs' first turn as a lead manager and he doesn't have much of a public record yet to support his fund's case. True, he's backed by Janus' team of analysts, but that isn't always a benefit—as the last 18 months have demonstrated.

It could be that when the market finally starts to favor growth again, this offering will shine. But there's so much uncertainty surrounding this hyper-aggressive offering that the Janus pedigree isn't enough to make it a wildly compelling choice. Contrarian investors who are willing to take a flier might want to jump in now, but most other investors might be just as happy with one of the more proven mid-cap growth options out there.

Portfolio Analysis 10-31-01

Share change since 04-01 Total Stocks: 35	Sector	PE	YTD Ret%	% Assets
Berkshire Hathaway Cl B	Financials	64.8	7.26	5.80
☼ Clear Channel Comms	Services	—	5.10	4.88
☼ Bank of New York	Financials	21.9	-24.80	4.30
☼ Embraer ADR	Industrials	11.6	-41.70	3.96
⊕ Hispanic Brdcstg Cl A	Services	85.0	0.00	3.84
⊕ Sepracor	Health	—	-28.70	3.75
☼ E*Trade Grp	Financials	—	38.98	3.31
☼ Community Health Sys	Health	—	-27.10	3.15
☼ Starwood Hotels & Resorts	Services	18.7	-12.90	3.14
☼ Redback Net	Technology	—	-90.30	2.99
☼ Atlas Air	Services	—	-55.10	2.98
☼ Cendant	Services	20.4	103.70	2.85
☼ XL Cap Cl A	Financials	22.8	5.82	2.68
☼ Smith & Nephew	Technology	27.9	—	2.56
☼ Ticketmaster Online-City B	Services	—	95.70	2.52
⊖ Goldman Sachs Grp	Financials	20.7	-12.80	2.41
☼ Anadarko Petro	Energy	11.1	-19.70	2.40
⊕ Vitesse Semicon	Technology	—	-77.50	2.39
⊖ Tenet Healthcare	Health	30.1	32.14	2.23
Costco Wholesale	Retail	34.4	11.12	1.91
Ceridian	Technology	27.6	-5.96	1.83
☼ Liberty Media Group A	N/A	—	—	1.80
☼ OSI Pharmaceuticals	Health	—	-42.90	1.69
☼ Barnes & Noble	Retail	—	11.70	1.57
☼ Halliburton	Energy	8.3	-63.20	1.52

Current Investment Style

Style: Value Blnd Growth; Size: Large Med Small

	Stock Port Avg	Relative S&P 500 Current	Relative S&P 500 Hist	Rel Cat
Price/Earnings Ratio	29.9	0.96	—	0.86
Price/Book Ratio	3.6	0.63	—	0.63
Price/Cash Flow	20.3[1]	1.13	—	0.87
3 Yr Earnings Growth	17.5[1]	1.20	—	0.75
1 Yr Earnings Est%	-15.0[1]	8.45	—	-1.60
Med Mkt Cap $mil	4,467	0.1	—	0.79

[1]figure is based on 50% or less of stocks

Special Securities % assets 10-31-01

Restricted/Illiquid Secs	0
Emerging-Markets Secs	4
Options/Futures/Warrants	No

Composition % assets 10-31-01

Cash	19.5
Stocks*	80.5
Bonds	0.0
Other	0.0
*Foreign (% stocks)	11.2

Market Cap

Giant	7.3
Large	31.8
Medium	46.0
Small	14.9
Micro	0.0

Sector Weightings	% of Stocks	Rel S&P	5-Year High	5-Year Low
Utilities	0.0	0.0	—	—
Energy	4.9	0.7	—	—
Financials	27.1	1.5	—	—
Industrials	5.0	0.4	—	—
Durables	0.0	0.0	—	—
Staples	0.9	0.1	—	—
Services	27.4	2.5	—	—
Retail	4.4	0.7	—	—
Health	16.5	1.1	—	—
Technology	13.8	0.8	—	—

Address: 100 Fillmore Street Suite 300
Denver, CO 80206-4923
800-295-2687 / 800-504-4440
Web Address: www.janus.com
*Inception: 06-30-00
Advisor: Janus Cap. Corporation
Subadvisor: None
NTF Plans: Fidelity Inst. , Waterhouse

Minimum Purchase: $2500 Add: $100 IRA: $500
Min Auto Inv Plan: $500 Add: $100
Sales Fees: No-load
Management Fee: .65%
Actual Fees: Mgt: 0.65% Dist: —
Expense Projections: 3Yr: $397 5Yr: — 10Yr: —
Avg Brok Commission: — Income Distrib: Annually
Total Cost (relative to category): —

Janus Overseas

Ticker	Load	NAV	Yield	Total Assets	Mstar Category
JAOSX	Closed	$20.30	0.5%	$5,278.5 mil	Foreign Stock

Prospectus Objective: Foreign Stock

Janus Overseas Fund seeks long-term growth of capital.

The fund normally invests at least 65% of assets in common stocks of issuers located in at least five foreign countries. The fund may at times invest a portion of or all assets in stocks of U.S. companies. The fund may invest in companies of any size, regardless of country of origin. In addition to common stocks, the fund may invest in preferred stocks, warrants, foreign-government obligations, corporate bonds and debentures, and short-term instruments.

Historical Profile

Return: High
Risk: Average
Rating: ★★★★★ Highest

Investment Style
Equity
Average Stock %: 82% 85% 88% 92% 95% 90% 88%

▼ Manager Change
▽ Partial Manager Change

Fund Performance vs. Category Average
■ Quarterly Fund Return +/– Category Average
— Category Baseline

Performance Quartile (within Category)

Portfolio Manager(s)

Helen Young Hayes, CFA. Since 5-94. BA'84 Yale U. Other funds currently managed: Janus Worldwide, IDEX Janus Global A, IDEX Janus Global M.

Brent A. Lynn, CFA. Since 12-00. BA Stanford U; MBA Stanford U. Other funds currently managed: ASAF Janus Overseas Growth X, ASAF Janus Overseas Growth A, ASAF Janus Overseas Growth B.

History

1990	1991	1992	1993	1994	1995	1996	1997	1998	1999	2000	12-01	History
—	—	—	—	10.05	12.05	15.22	17.39	20.08	37.20	26.54	20.30	NAV
—	—	—	—	0.50*	22.06	28.83	18.23	16.03	86.07	–18.57	–23.11	Total Return %
—	—	—	—	–2.98*	–15.48	5.89	–15.13	–12.54	65.03	–9.46	–11.23	+/– S&P 500
—	—	—	—	—	10.85	22.79	16.45	–3.97	59.11	–4.40	—	+/– MSCI EAFE
—	—	—	—	0.00	1.65	0.35	0.63	0.56	0.00	2.12	0.38	Income Return %
—	—	—	—	0.50	20.41	28.48	17.59	15.47	86.07	–20.68	–23.49	Capital Return %
—	—	—	—	—	3	3	5	32	10	64	58	Total Rtn % Rank Cat
—	—	—	—	0.00	0.17	0.04	0.10	0.10	0.00	0.79	0.10	Income $
—	—	—	—	0.00	0.05	0.26	0.50	0.00	0.14	3.06	0.00	Capital Gains $
—	—	—	—	2.16	1.73	1.23	1.01	0.96	0.91	0.88	—	Expense Ratio %
—	—	—	—	–0.64	0.36	0.73	0.81	0.58	–0.03	0.22	—	Income Ratio %
—	—	—	—	181	188	71	72	105	92	62	—	Turnover Rate %
—	—	—	—	65.4	129.4	955.4	3,240.9	4,329.0	8,765.4	8,156.8	5,278.5	Net Assets $mil

Performance 12-31-01

	1st Qtr	2nd Qtr	3rd Qtr	4th Qtr	Total
1997	7.36	10.65	5.48	–5.64	18.23
1998	14.95	6.58	–19.58	17.77	16.03
1999	4.28	6.30	4.49	60.63	86.07
2000	14.62	–11.42	–7.02	–13.74	–18.57
2001	–16.99	1.59	–20.82	15.16	–23.11

Trailing	Total Return%	+/– S&P 500	+/– MSCI EAFE	% Rank All	% Rank Cat	Growth of $10,000
3 Mo	15.16	4.48	—	23	8	11,516
6 Mo	–8.82	–3.26	—	81	49	9,118
1 Yr	–23.11	–11.23	—	85	58	7,689
3 Yr Avg	5.23	6.25	—	29	12	11,651
5 Yr Avg	9.83	–0.87	—	19	7	15,982
10 Yr Avg	—	—	—	—	—	—
15 Yr Avg	—	—	—	—	—	—

Tax Analysis	Tax-Adj Ret%	%Rank Cat	%Pretax Ret	%Rank Cat
3 Yr Avg	4.07	12	77.9	58
5 Yr Avg	8.80	6	89.5	8
10 Yr Avg	—	—	—	—

Potential Capital Gain Exposure: –10% of assets

Risk Analysis

Time Period	Load-Adj Return %	Risk %Rank[1] All	Risk %Rank[1] Cat	Morningstar Return	Morningstar Risk	Morningstar Risk-Adj Rating
1 Yr	–23.11					
3 Yr	5.23	85	90	0.06[2]	1.19	★★★★
5 Yr	9.83	83	84	1.15[2]	0.99	★★★★★
Incept	12.84	—	—	—	—	

Average Historical Rating (57 months): 4.9★s

[1] 1=low, 100=high [2] T-Bill return substituted for category avg.

Category Rating (3 Yr)

① ② ③ ④ ⑤
Worst — Best

Return: Above Avg
Risk: Above Avg

Other Measures	Standard Index S&P 500	Best Fit Index Wil 4500
Alpha	9.5	4.3
Beta	1.05	0.92
R-Squared	36	76

Standard Deviation	32.54
Mean	5.23
Sharpe Ratio	0.01

Analysis by Emily Hall 10-26-01

Janus Overseas may no longer look like a foreign fund superstar, but shareholders have reason to wait for a comeback.

Faced with a worsening economic environment, managers Helen Young Hayes and Brent Lynn have been tending to their ailing portfolio. Even before the horrible events of Sept. 11, 2001, Hayes and Lynn were working to increase the variety of stocks in the fund, adding around the margins to areas like healthvcare and energy.

In the days following the World Trade Center attack, the fund suffered its share of nasty surprises. Exposure to companies like aircraft-maker Bombardier and carmaker Porsche whacked performance. But Hayes and Lynn have continued their efforts to reshape the portfolio. They grabbed up names that looked unbearably cheap in the wake of the market's September sell-off, such as French pharmaceutical firm Sanofi-Synthelabo.

It's too soon to tell if such moves will boost results, but investors here are surely smarting from the last year-and-a-half of dismal performance. The fund entered 2000 with big stakes in technology and telecom stocks, which hurt it badly when the bottom fell out of the go-go growth market. Hayes and Lynn have been lightening their tech and telecom stakes for a while now, but that hasn't been enough to aid returns. For the trailing year through Oct. 25, the fund lost a bruising 35%, placing in the bottom decile of the foreign-fund category.

Investors reaching for their parachutes should think long and hard before bailing, though. Until its recent troubles, this offering proved itself a formidable competitor year in and year out. Indeed, it's a testament to management that despite such a miserable showing in recent months, the fund's three- and five-year records are still among the best in the group.

Portfolio Analysis 10-31-01

Share change since 04-01 Total Stocks: 112	Sector	Country	% Assets
⊖ Tyco Intl	Industrials	U.S.	4.64
⊖ NTT DoCoMo	Services	Japan	3.51
⊖ Total Fina Cl B	Energy	France	2.82
⊕ Reckitt Benckiser	Staples	United Kingdom	2.57
⊖ Telefonos de Mexico ADR L	Services	Mexico	2.18
⊕ Ahold	Retail	Netherlands	1.95
⊖ Banco Bilbao Vizcaya Arg	Financials	Spain	1.92
✲ Takeda Chem Inds	Health	Japan	1.80
✲ Reliance Inds ADR	Durables	India	1.78
Grupo Televisa (Part) ADR	Services	Mexico	1.63
⊕ Unilever (Cert)	Staples	United Kingdom	1.62
⊖ Porsche Pfd	N/A	N/A	1.57
⊖ Petrobras ADR	Energy	Brazil	1.53
⊕ Schlumberger	Energy	U.S.	1.49
✲ Roche Hldgs ADR	Health	Switzerland	1.40
⊕ STMicroelectronics	Technology	France	1.38
⊖ AEGON NV (Ams)	Financials	Netherlands	1.37
⊖ Shaw Comms Cl B (Canada)	Services	Canada	1.33
⊖ Serono	Health	Switzerland	1.20
⊖ Securitas Cl B	Services	Sweden	1.14

Current Investment Style

Style: Value Blnd Growth; Size: Large Med Small

	Stock Port Avg	Rel MSCI EAFE Current	Rel MSCI EAFE Hist	Rel Cat
Price/Earnings Ratio	31.5	1.22	1.34	1.24
Price/Cash Flow	16.6	1.29	1.62	1.16
Price/Book Ratio	4.8	1.38	1.88	1.23
3 Yr Earnings Growth	24.3	1.30	1.72	1.24
Med Mkt Cap $mil	20,269	0.7	0.9	1.12

Country Exposure 10-31-01	% assets
United Kingdom	14
Japan	10
U.S.	8
France	7
Netherlands	7

Hedging History: Frequent

Regional Exposure 10-31-01	% assets
Europe	44
Japan	10
Latin America	6
Pacific Rim	7
Other	12

Special Securities % assets 10-31-01	
Restricted/Illiquid Secs	0
Emerging-Markets Secs	14
Options/Futures/Warrants	No

Composition % assets 10-31-01			
Cash	13.0	Bonds	1.5
Stocks	84.0	Other	1.6

Sector Weightings	% of Stocks	Rel Cat	5-Year High	5-Year Low
Utilities	0.0	0.0	3	0
Energy	10.0	1.7	10	0
Financials	8.6	0.4	25	2
Industrials	9.6	0.7	16	1
Durables	5.9	0.9	21	6
Staples	11.1	1.6	11	0
Services	25.0	1.4	49	17
Retail	3.7	0.8	13	0
Health	11.2	1.2	18	2
Technology	14.8	1.5	36	0

Address:	100 Fillmore Street Suite 300, Denver, CO 80206-4923, 800-525-8983
Web Address:	www.janus.com
*Inception:	05-02-94
Advisor:	Janus Cap. Corporation
Subadvisor:	None
NTF Plans:	Fidelity, Datalynx

Minimum Purchase:	Closed	Add: $100	IRA: —
Min Auto Inv Plan:	Closed	Add: $100	
Sales Fees:	No-load		
Management Fee:	.65%		
Actual Fees:	Mgt: 0.65%	Dist: —	
Expense Projections:	3Yr: $290	5Yr: $504	10Yr: $1120
Avg Brok Commission:	—	Income Distrib: Annually	
Total Cost (relative to category):	Low		

Janus Special Situations

Ticker	Load	NAV	Yield	Total Assets	Mstar Category
JASSX	None	$14.85	0.1%	$1,037.7 mil	Mid–Cap Blend

Prospectus Objective: Growth

Janus Special Situations Fund seeks capital appreciation.

The fund invests primarily in common stocks issued by domestic and foreign companies. It may also invest, to a lesser extent, in other types of securities, including preferred stocks, warrants, convertibles, and debt obligations. For the debt portion, the fund may invest no more than 35% of assets in high-yield securities, no more than 25% in mortgage- and asset-backed securities, and no more than 10% in zero-coupon bonds. This fund is non-diversified.

Historical Profile
Return Above Avg
Risk Above Avg
Rating ★★★★ Above Avg

Investment Style
Equity
Average Stock %: 98% 98% 97% 98% 99%

▼ Manager Change
▽ Partial Manager Change

Fund Performance vs. Category Average
■ Quarterly Fund Return +/– Category Average
— Category Baseline

Performance Quartile (within Category)

Portfolio Manager(s)

David C. Decker, CFA. Since 12-96. BA Tufts U.; MBA'92 Duke U. Other funds currently managed: Janus Strategic Value, Janus Adviser Strategic Value, Janus Aspen Strategic Value Instl.

1990	1991	1992	1993	1994	1995	1996	1997	1998	1999	2000	12–01	History
—	—	—	—	—	—	10.00	13.93	17.41	23.05	17.69	14.85	NAV
—	—	—	—	—	—	—	46.04	25.31	52.46	–17.54	–16.00	Total Return %
—	—	—	—	—	—	—	12.69	–3.27	31.42	–8.44	–4.12	+/– S&P 500
—	—	—	—	—	—	—	13.79	6.19	37.74	–35.03	–15.40	+/– S&P Mid 400
—	—	—	—	—	—	—	0.00	0.01	0.00	0.88	0.06	Income Return %
—	—	—	—	—	—	—	46.04	25.30	52.46	–18.42	–16.05	Capital Return %
—	—	—	—	—	—	—	1	5	7	93	88	Total Rtn % Rank Cat
—	—	—	—	—	—	0.00	0.00	0.00	0.00	0.20	0.01	Income $
—	—	—	—	—	—	0.00	0.66	0.04	3.31	1.11	0.00	Capital Gains $
—	—	—	—	—	—	—	1.18	1.08	0.98	0.94	—	Expense Ratio %
—	—	—	—	—	—	—	–0.08	–0.49	–0.76	–0.58	—	Income Ratio %
—	—	—	—	—	—	—	—	117	104	58	—	Turnover Rate %
—	—	—	—	—	—	80.7	389.4	893.7	1,420.6	1,436.4	1,037.7	Net Assets $mil

Performance 12-31-01

	1st Qtr	2nd Qtr	3rd Qtr	4th Qtr	Total
1997	5.60	17.52	17.41	0.23	46.04
1998	17.37	3.25	–19.55	28.53	25.31
1999	8.16	17.74	0.18	19.51	52.46
2000	14.53	–6.10	–10.85	–14.00	–17.54
2001	–8.31	3.39	–25.64	19.17	–16.00

Trailing	Total Return%	+/– S&P 500	+/– S&P Mid 400	% Rank All	% Rank Cat	Growth of $10,000
3 Mo	19.17	8.48	1.19	15	26	11,917
6 Mo	–11.39	–5.83	–9.83	89	93	8,861
1 Yr	–16.00	–4.12	–15.40	74	88	8,400
3 Yr Avg	1.84	2.86	–8.41	63	68	10,561
5 Yr Avg	14.08	3.39	–2.03	6	21	19,326
10 Yr Avg	—	—	—	—	—	—
15 Yr Avg	—	—	—	—	—	—

Tax Analysis	Tax-Adj Ret%	%Rank Cat	%Pretax Ret	%Rank Cat
3 Yr Avg	–0.13	66	—	—
5 Yr Avg	12.33	18	87.6	20
10 Yr Avg	—	—	—	—

Potential Capital Gain Exposure: –19% of assets

Risk Analysis

Time Period	Load-Adj Return %	Risk %Rank[1] All	Risk %Rank[1] Cat	Morningstar Return	Morningstar Risk	Morningstar Risk-Adj Rating
1 Yr	–16.00					
3 Yr	1.84	83	87	–0.64[2]	1.22	★★★
5 Yr	14.08	80	79	2.35[2]	1.12	★★★★
Incept	14.08	—	—	—	—	

Average Historical Rating (25 months): 4.1★s

[1]1=low, 100=high [2] T-Bill return substituted for category avg.

Category Rating (3 Yr)

1 2 3 4 5
Worst Best

Return	Below Avg
Risk	Above Avg

Other Measures	Standard Index S&P 500	Best Fit Index MSCIACWdFr
Alpha	5.7	11.5
Beta	1.22	1.37
R–Squared	68	75
Standard Deviation		26.26
Mean		1.84
Sharpe Ratio		–0.14

Portfolio Analysis 10-31-01

Share change since 04–01 Total Stocks: 37	Sector	PE	YTD Ret%	% Assets
⊕ Viacom Cl B	Services	—	—	6.66
⊕ Cadence Design Sys	Technology	5.3	–20.20	6.27
⊕ El Paso	Utilities	NMF	–36.70	6.18
⊕ Ceridian	Technology	27.6	–5.96	4.90
⊕ Earthlink	Technology	—	141.90	4.68
☼ Clear Channel Comms	Services	—	5.10	4.42
⊕ Becton Dickinson	Health	22.9	–3.20	4.26
☼ SK	Energy	9.1	—	4.07
⊕ Apple Comp	Technology	—	47.23	4.00
⊕ Arbitron	Services	—	—	3.63
⊕ Moody's	Services	33.5	56.04	3.60
⊕ Anadarko Petro	Energy	11.1	–19.70	3.55
⊖ Mattel	Staples	31.9	19.43	3.34
⊖ Citigroup	Financials	20.0	0.03	3.33
⊖ Bally Total Fitness Hldg	Services	8.4	–36.30	3.32
⊖ Symantec	Technology	—	98.74	3.23
☼ Reliance Inds ADR	Durables	—	—	2.95
⊕ Toys "R" Us	Retail	28.8	24.28	2.80
⊕ Intl Flavors & Fragrances	Staples	32.3	49.78	2.49
⊖ Advanced Micro Devices	Technology	40.7	14.82	2.22
☼ Westwood One	Services	77.1	55.59	2.08
⊖ SBS Broadcstg	Services	—	–30.80	1.85
⊕ E*Trade Grp	Financials	—	38.98	1.77
Magnum Hunter Resources	Energy	10.5	–23.60	1.76
⊖ Delphi Automotive Sys	Durables	—	23.78	1.69

Current Investment Style

Style: Value Blnd Growth; Size: Large Med Small

	Stock Port Avg	Relative S&P 500 Current	Relative S&P 500 Hist	Rel Cat
Price/Earnings Ratio	26.0	0.84	1.06	0.96
Price/Book Ratio	3.8	0.67	0.68	0.89
Price/Cash Flow	15.8	0.88	0.95	0.91
3 Yr Earnings Growth	11.5[1]	0.79	—	0.69
1 Yr Earnings Est%	7.9	—	—	3.49
Med Mkt Cap $mil	5,128	0.1	0.1	0.57

[1]figure is based on 50% or less of stocks

Analysis by Catherine Hickey 11-12-01

Its recent struggles may be tough to withstand, but there are valid reasons to stick with this fund.

Janus Special Situations Fund continues to get roughed up. Its 21.4% loss for the year through Nov. 8, 2001, falls near the mid-blend group's bottom decile. Manager David Decker searches for companies with lots of free cash flow that he thinks are trading at attractive valuations. This approach often leads him to buy cable and telecom stocks, and many of those companies have been punished this year. However, wayward stock picks, such as Winstar and Enron, that the fund held earlier this year, have also likely hurt performance.

Despite the fund's lackluster recent returns, we still think this fund has its charms. When the market favors Decker's style, the fund can dust its peers (as it did from 1997 to 1999). Decker's stock picks during those years were right on target. Janus also boasts an excellent research staff to feed Decker's ideas. Further, despite its recent slump, the fund still boasts a better return from its 1997 inception through Oct. 31 than its typical mid-blend rival.

That said, it's clear that those who can't handle some significant down periods should look elsewhere. This fund takes on considerable price risk, and a preponderance of cable and telecom picks expose it disproportionately to the ups and downs of those industries. What's more, Decker will devote large chunks of assets to top holdings, and if just one or two such names slide, it can really hurt performance.

Investors who have long time horizons would do well to give Decker time to turn things around here. This is no all-weather fund, though, and is best used along with an old-fashioned value fund for diversification purposes.

Special Securities % assets 10-31-01	
Restricted/Illiquid Secs	0
Emerging–Markets Secs	8
Options/Futures/Warrants	No

Sector Weightings	% of Stocks	Rel S&P	5-Year High	5-Year Low
Utilities	6.2	1.9	—	—
Energy	10.6	1.5	—	—
Financials	7.7	0.4	—	—
Industrials	1.5	0.1	—	—
Durables	7.3	4.7	—	—
Staples	5.8	0.7	—	—
Services	28.8	2.7	—	—
Retail	2.8	0.4	—	—
Health	4.2	0.3	—	—
Technology	25.2	1.4	—	—

Composition % assets 10-31-01	
Cash	0.7
Stocks*	99.3
Bonds	0.0
Other	0.0
*Foreign (% stocks)	9.5

Market Cap	
Giant	4.8
Large	22.8
Medium	57.1
Small	15.3
Micro	0.0

Address:	100 Fillmore Street Suite 300 Denver, CO 80206–4923 800–525–8983
Web Address:	www.janus.com
*Inception:	12-31-96
Advisor:	Janus Cap. Corporation
Subadvisor:	None
NTF Plans:	Fidelity , Datalynx

Minimum Purchase:	$2500	Add: $100 IRA: $500
Min Auto Inv Plan:	$500	Add: $100
Sales Fees:	No–load	
Management Fee:	.65%	
Actual Fees:	Mgt: 0.65%	Dist: —
Expense Projections:	3Yr: $306	5Yr: $531 10Yr: $1178
Avg Brok Commission:	—	Income Distrib: Annually
Total Cost (relative to category):	Below Avg	

Janus Strategic Value

Ticker	Load	NAV	Yield	Total Assets	Mstar Category
JSVAX	None	$9.26	0.3%	$2,079.2 mil	Large Value

Prospectus Objective: Growth

Janus Strategic Value Fund seeks long-term capital appreciation.

The fund invests primarily in common stocks that the portfolio manager believes are undervalued relative to their intrinsic worth. The portfolio manager will evaluate securities based on price/earnings (P/E) ratios and price/free cash flow. The fund may invest in preferred securities, convertibles, options and futures. It may also invest up to 35% of assets in high-yield debt securities. This fund is non-diversified.

Historical Profile
Return —
Risk —
Rating
Not Rated

Investment Style
Equity
Average Stock %
98% 98%

▼ Manager Change
▽ Partial Manager Change

Fund Performance vs. Category Average
Quarterly Fund Return +/– Category Average
— Category Baseline

Performance Quartile (within Category)

Portfolio Manager(s)

David C. Decker, CFA. Since 2-00. BA Tufts U.; MBA'92 Duke U. Other funds currently managed: Janus Special Situations, Janus Adviser Strategic Value, Janus Aspen Strategic Value Instl.

1990	1991	1992	1993	1994	1995	1996	1997	1998	1999	2000	12-01	History
—	—	—	—	—	—	—	—	—	—	10.52	9.26	NAV
—	—	—	—	—	—	—	—	—	—	7.75*	–11.74	Total Return %
—	—	—	—	—	—	—	—	—	—	10.20*	0.14	+/– S&P 500
—	—	—	—	—	—	—	—	—	—	—	–2.95	+/– Russ Top 200 Val
—	—	—	—	—	—	—	—	—	—	2.55	0.23	Income Return %
—	—	—	—	—	—	—	—	—	—	5.20	–11.97	Capital Return %
—	—	—	—	—	—	—	—	—	—	—	85	Total Rtn % Rank Cat
—	—	—	—	—	—	—	—	—	—	0.25	0.02	Income $
—	—	—	—	—	—	—	—	—	—	0.00	0.00	Capital Gains $
—	—	—	—	—	—	—	—	—	—	0.99	—	Expense Ratio %
—	—	—	—	—	—	—	—	—	—	0.14	—	Income Ratio %
—	—	—	—	—	—	—	—	—	—	72	—	Turnover Rate %
—	—	—	—	—	—	—	—	—	—	2,940.3	2,079.2	Net Assets $mil

Performance 12-31-01

	1st Qtr	2nd Qtr	3rd Qtr	4th Qtr	Total
1997	—	—	—	—	—
1998	—	—	—	—	—
1999	—	—	—	—	—
2000	—	3.70	–1.78	–2.22	7.75 *
2001	–6.46	3.86	–22.31	16.94	–11.74

Trailing	Total Return%	+/– S&P 500	+/– Russ Top 200 Val	% Rank All	% Rank Cat	Growth of $10,000
3 Mo	16.94	6.26	11.42	20	4	11,694
6 Mo	–9.15	–3.59	–3.37	82	94	9,085
1 Yr	–11.74	0.14	–2.95	64	85	8,826
3 Yr Avg	—	—	—	—	—	—
5 Yr Avg	—	—	—	—	—	—
10 Yr Avg	—	—	—	—	—	—
15 Yr Avg	—	—	—	—	—	—

Tax Analysis	Tax-Adj Ret%	%Rank Cat	%Pretax Ret	%Rank Cat
3 Yr Avg	—	—	—	—
5 Yr Avg	—	—	—	—
10 Yr Avg	—	—	—	—

Potential Capital Gain Exposure: –15% of assets

Risk Analysis

Time Period	Load-Adj Return %	Risk %Rank[1] All	Risk %Rank[1] Cat	Morningstar Return	Morningstar Risk	Morningstar Risk-Adj Rating
1 Yr	–11.74					
3 Yr	—	—	—	—	—	
5 Yr	—	—	—	—	—	
Incept	–2.69	—	—	—	—	

Average Historical Rating —

[1]1=low, 100=high

Category Rating (3 Yr)

Other Measures	Standard Index S&P 500	Best Fit Index
Alpha	—	—
Beta	—	—
R-Squared	—	—

	Standard Deviation	—
Return	Mean	—
Risk	Sharpe Ratio	—

Portfolio Analysis 10-31-01

Share change since 04-01 Total Stocks: 47	Sector	PE	YTD Ret%	% Assets
⊖ El Paso	Utilities	NMF	–36.70	7.80
⊕ Cemex (Part) ADR	Industrials	—	—	4.83
⊕ Cadence Design Sys	Technology	5.3	–20.20	4.44
☼ Viacom Cl B	Services	—	—	4.02
☼ Lehman Brothers Hldgs	Financials	12.4	–0.84	3.95
⊕ Becton Dickinson	Health	22.9	–3.20	3.90
⊖ Citigroup	Financials	20.0	0.03	3.88
⊕ Packaging Corporation	Industrials	11.9	12.56	3.77
⊕ Ceridian	Technology	27.6	–5.96	3.72
⊕ Apple Comp	Technology	—	47.23	3.71
⊖ Mattel	Staples	31.9	19.43	3.60
⊕ Anadarko Petro	Energy	11.1	–19.70	3.42
Kinder Morgan	Energy	32.2	7.11	2.85
☼ SK	Energy	9.1	—	2.79
Moody's	Services	33.5	56.04	2.61
⊕ Valassis Comms	Services	18.9	12.85	2.61
☼ Berkshire Hathaway Cl B	Financials	64.8	7.26	2.22
☼ Apache	Energy	8.0	–21.20	2.14
⊖ Delphi Automotive Sys	Durables	—	23.78	1.98
☼ Clear Channel Comms	Services	—	5.10	1.95
⊕ Burlington Resources	Energy	8.4	–24.60	1.89
☼ Reliance Inds ADR	Durables	—	—	1.74
⊖ Lear	Durables	16.8	53.71	1.70
⊖ Advanced Micro Devices	Technology	40.7	14.82	1.69
Iron Mountain	Services	—	17.98	1.60

Current Investment Style

Style: Value Blnd Growth; Size: Large Med Small

	Stock Port Avg	Relative S&P 500 Current	Relative S&P 500 Hist	Rel Cat
Price/Earnings Ratio	24.7	0.80	—	0.98
Price/Book Ratio	3.1	0.54	—	0.75
Price/Cash Flow	14.0	0.78	—	1.01
3 Yr Earnings Growth	20.4	1.40	—	1.38
1 Yr Earnings Est%	4.8	—	—	–1.46
Med Mkt Cap $mil	6,921	0.1	—	0.22

Special Securities % assets 10-31-01	
Restricted/Illiquid Secs	0
Emerging-Markets Secs	11
Options/Futures/Warrants	No

Sector Weightings	% of Stocks	Rel S&P	5-Year High	5-Year Low
Utilities	7.9	2.5	—	—
Energy	16.1	2.3	—	—
Financials	12.2	0.7	—	—
Industrials	11.4	1.0	—	—
Durables	9.1	5.8	—	—
Staples	4.6	0.6	—	—
Services	19.5	1.8	—	—
Retail	1.5	0.2	—	—
Health	4.0	0.3	—	—
Technology	13.8	0.8	—	—

Composition % assets 10-31-01	
Cash	1.2
Stocks*	98.1
Bonds	0.7
Other	0.0
*Foreign (% stocks)	14.4

Market Cap	
Giant	7.1
Large	29.2
Medium	55.9
Small	7.9
Micro	0.0

Analysis by Catherine Hickey 11-09-01

This fund still could turn things around, but shareholders would do well to give it time.

Janus Strategic Value Fund still hasn't found its footing. The fund's atypical and somewhat growthy approach is partially to blame. Manager David Decker looks for companies with solid cash flow and sound franchises that he thinks are trading at valuations below their intrinsic values. This strategy leads him to invest sizable portions of assets in technology, cable, and media issues. And as growth stocks continue to tumble, the fund is at a disadvantage to peers that specialize in dividend-rich, old-economy plays.

However, poor timing wasn't the only reason for this fund's subpar performance since inception. Wayward stock picks such as Winstar and Enron have burned it, too. Decker sold Winstar and declined to talk about Enron back in August, but such holdings have stung the fund in its short life.

Though the news overall has been grim here, the fund's strong performance in October shows that it may be poised to rebound when growth returns to favor. Its one-month return as of Nov. 7, 2001, lands in the top third of the category. The fund has been helped along by tech stocks' recent bounce. For example, Advanced Micro Devices is struggling on the year, but it has gained 45% in the last month.

The fund's potential in better times for growth is why we still think current shareholders should give Decker a chance to turn things around here. His record at his other charge, Janus Special Situations, shows that he can trounce the competition when his style is in favor. However, investors shouldn't expect this to be an all-weather vehicle, nor has it demonstrated that it can provide the ballast that more conservative value funds offer.

Address:	100 Fillmore Street Suite 300 Denver, CO 80206–4923 800–525–1068 / 800–504–4440
Web Address:	www.janus.com
*Inception:	02-29-00
Advisor:	Janus Cap. Corporation
Subadvisor:	None
NTF Plans:	Fidelity Inst. , Waterhouse

Minimum Purchase:	$2500	Add: $100	IRA: $500
Min Auto Inv Plan:	$500	Add: $100	
Sales Fees:	No-load		
Management Fee:	.65%		
Actual Fees:	Mgt: 0.65%	Dist: —	
Expense Projections:	3Yr: $397	5Yr: —	10Yr: —
Avg Brok Commission:	—	Income Distrib: Annually	
Total Cost (relative to category):	—		

Janus Twenty

Ticker	Load	NAV	Yield	Total Assets	Mstar Category
JAVLX	Closed	$38.46	0.9%	$15,082.3 mil	Large Growth

Prospectus Objective: Growth

Janus Twenty Fund seeks capital appreciation consistent with preservation of capital.

The fund invests primarily in a concentrated portfolio of between 20 and 30 common stocks. To select investments, the advisor evaluates improvement in profit margins, earnings, and unit growth; these factors indicate the fundamental investment value of the security. The advisor also seeks stocks with strong current financial positions and the potential for future growth. It may invest without limit in foreign securities. This fund is non-diversified.

Prior to May 22, 1989, the fund was named Janus Value Fund. As of April 16, 1999 this fund was closed to new investors.

Historical Profile

Return Average
Risk Above Avg
Rating ★★ Below Avg

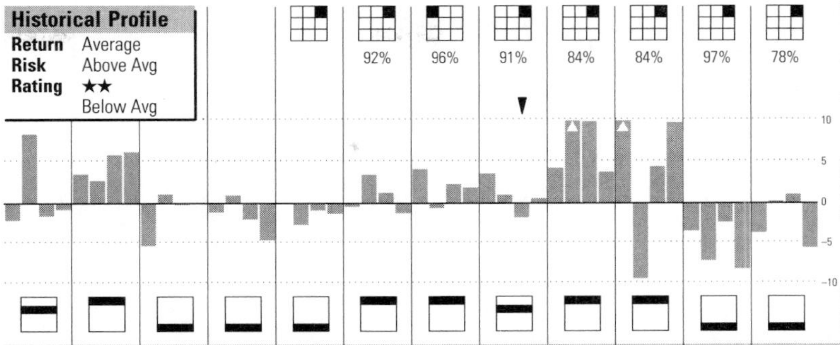

Investment Style
Equity
Average Stock %

	1994	1995	1996	1997	1998	1999	2000	12-01
Average Stock %		92%	96%	91%	84%	84%	97%	78%

▼ Manager Change
▽ Partial Manager Change

Fund Performance vs. Category Average
Quarterly Fund Return +/– Category Average
— Category Baseline

Performance Quartile (within Category)

Portfolio Manager(s)

Scott W. Schoelzel. Since 8-97. BA'80 Colorado C. Other funds currently managed: SunAmStySel Multi-Cap Growth A, SunAmStySel Multi-Cap Growth B, SunAmStySel Multi-Cap Growth II.

1990	1991	1992	1993	1994	1995	1996	1997	1998	1999	2000	12-01	History
14.56	24.19	24.29	24.42	22.71	25.67	27.47	30.99	53.30	83.43	54.80	38.46	NAV
0.59	69.21	1.97	3.43	–6.73	36.22	27.86	29.70	73.39	64.90	–32.42	–29.20	Total Return %
3.71	38.73	–5.65	–6.62	–8.04	–1.31	4.91	–3.66	44.82	43.86	–23.31	–17.33	+/– S&P 500
–0.78	29.81	–1.92	3.51	–11.58	–2.43	2.34	–4.05	28.30	35.23	–7.89	–8.70	+/– Russ Top 200 Grt
1.27	0.16	0.76	1.04	0.28	10.04	0.71	0.36	0.45	0.35	0.00	0.61	Income Return %
–0.68	69.05	1.21	2.39	–7.00	26.18	27.15	29.34	72.95	64.55	–32.42	–29.81	Capital Return %
27	5	81	78	87	24	5	30	2	14	98	76	Total Rtn % Rank Cat
0.19	0.02	0.18	0.25	0.07	2.28	0.18	0.10	0.14	0.19	0.00	0.34	Income $
0.00	0.42	0.19	0.45	0.00	2.99	5.32	4.46	0.30	4.08	1.75	0.00	Capital Gains $
1.32	1.07	1.12	1.05	1.02	0.99	0.92	0.91	0.91	0.87	0.85	—	Expense Ratio %
1.28	1.30	1.27	0.87	0.57	0.62	0.67	0.33	0.39	0.40	–0.13	—	Income Ratio %
228	163	79	99	102	147	137	123	54	40	27	—	Turnover Rate %
243.9	1,348.4	3,137.2	3,515.9	2,504.3	3,057.4	4,070.7	6,003.6	15,797.2	36,909.4	24,253.5	15,082.3	Net Assets $mil

Performance 12-31-01

	1st Qtr	2nd Qtr	3rd Qtr	4th Qtr	Total
1997	1.60	17.77	9.37	–0.90	29.70
1998	18.59	14.53	–1.54	29.67	73.39
1999	23.04	–4.25	1.18	38.35	64.90
2000	5.51	–12.28	–2.10	–25.42	–32.42
2001	–24.60	6.75	–19.68	9.51	–29.20

Trailing	Total Return%	+/– S&P 500	+/– Russ Top 200 Grth	% Rank All	% Rank Cat	Growth of $10,000
3 Mo	9.51	–1.18	–3.35	45	90	10,951
6 Mo	–12.04	–6.49	–5.06	90	77	8,796
1 Yr	–29.20	–17.33	–8.70	93	76	7,080
3 Yr Avg	–7.59	–6.57	0.43	96	80	7,890
5 Yr Avg	12.15	1.45	3.56	10	17	17,744
10 Yr Avg	11.76	–1.17	0.68	20	22	30,403
15 Yr Avg	15.07	1.34	1.70	6	9	82,109

Tax Analysis	Tax-Adj Ret%	%Rank Cat	%Pretax Ret	%Rank Cat
3 Yr Avg	–8.20	76	—	—
5 Yr Avg	10.79	13	88.8	21
10 Yr Avg	9.65	24	82.1	36

Potential Capital Gain Exposure: –5% of assets

Risk Analysis

Time Period	Load-Adj Return %	Risk %Rank[1] All	Risk %Rank[1] Cat	Morningstar Return	Morningstar Risk	Morningstar Risk-Adj Rating
1 Yr	–29.20					
3 Yr	–7.59	94	86	–2.35[2]	1.63	★
5 Yr	12.15	88	78	1.78[2]	1.40	★★★★
10 Yr	11.76	91	82	1.06	1.43	★★

Average Historical Rating (165 months): 3.9★s

[1] 1=low, 100=high [2] T–Bill return substituted for category avg.

Category Rating (3 Yr)

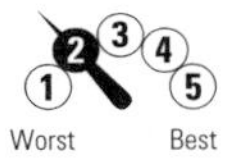

1 2 3 4 5
Worst Best

Return Below Avg
Risk Above Avg

Other Measures	Standard Index S&P 500	Best Fit Index MSCIACWdFr
Alpha	–1.7	4.7
Beta	1.46	1.62
R–Squared	68	73
Standard Deviation		29.38
Mean		–7.59
Sharpe Ratio		–0.50

Portfolio Analysis 10-31-01

Share change since 04–01 Total Stocks: 20	Sector	PE	YTD Ret%	% Assets
⊖ AOL Time Warner	Technology	—	–7.76	13.06
⊖ Nokia Cl A ADR	Technology	45.8	–43.00	8.39
⊕ Microsoft	Technology	57.6	52.78	6.90
⊕ American Intl Grp	Financials	42.0	–19.20	6.02
⊖ General Elec	Industrials	30.1	–15.00	5.79
⊕ ExxonMobil	Energy	15.3	–7.59	5.26
☼ Eli Lilly	Health	28.9	–14.40	4.51
⊕ Viacom Cl B	Services	—	—	4.13
⊕ Pfizer	Health	34.7	–12.40	3.75
⊖ Goldman Sachs Grp	Financials	20.7	–12.80	3.66
☼ Citigroup	Financials	20.0	0.03	3.47
⊕ Home Depot	Retail	42.9	12.07	2.83
☼ Bank Amer	N/A	—	—	2.74
⊖ Telefonos de Mexico ADR L	Services	9.9	29.75	2.29
⊖ Merrill Lynch	Financials	18.2	–22.70	1.75
⊕ BP PLC ADR	Energy	14.4	–0.90	1.31
Charter Comm 8.625%	N/A	—	—	1.25
☼ Texas Instruments	Technology	87.5	–40.70	0.81
☼ Wells Fargo	Financials	22.4	–20.20	0.79
Level 3 Comm 9.125%	N/A	—	—	0.58
⊖ Human Genome Sciences	Health	—	–51.30	0.48
⊖ Millennium Pharma	Health	—	–60.30	0.27

Analysis by Christine Benz 10-27-01

In its current guise, Janus Twenty could have a hard time doing what its shareholders need it to do.

This fund, once the poster child for Janus' spectacular ascendance in the late 1990s, has fallen from grace in an equally dramatic fashion over the past year and a half. It has lost 57% of its value since March 2000, and it has also far underperformed other large-cap growth funds. The culprits behind this reversal of fortune are clear. Coming into early 2000, this fund was aggressively positioned even by the standards of the generally bold Janus family. With more than 60% of its portfolio in technology stocks in early 2000 and most of the rest in telecom and media names, the fund couldn't help but tumble in the recent valuation correction. Complicating manager Scott Schoelzel's task was the fund's big asset base and concentrated setup; in repositioning the fund, Schoelzel would have to dump huge volumes of certain stocks into the market, further depressing their share prices.

But reposition he did. Schoelzel still has sizable commitments to AOL Time Warner, Nokia, Viacom, and Microsoft, but most of the rest of the fund's aggressive holdings are gone, supplanted by blue-chip financials and drug stocks. Additionally, the fund has a large cash position—some 25% of assets as of mid-October—as Schoelzel was selling stocks such as Sun Microsystems and Cisco more quickly than he could put money to work.

That relatively defensive positioning has been a boon in the rough-and-tumble market of the past three months, but it could also make it tough to deliver the kind of huge upside that shareholders may be expecting to compensate for its woeful recent returns. One could certainly do worse than own a huge fund run by a talented manager, but investors here shouldn't expect miracles.

Current Investment Style

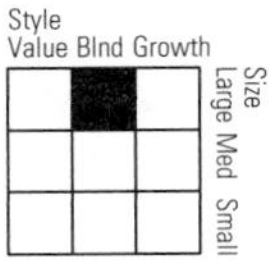

Style: Value Blnd Growth; Size: Large Med Small (Large Blend)

	Stock Port Avg	Relative S&P 500 Current	Relative S&P 500 Hist	Rel Cat
Price/Earnings Ratio	34.0	1.10	1.45	0.96
Price/Book Ratio	5.8	1.01	1.78	0.90
Price/Cash Flow	20.1	1.12	1.41	0.89
3 Yr Earnings Growth	23.4	1.60	2.05	1.09
1 Yr Earnings Est%	1.1	—	—	0.35
Med Mkt Cap $mil	153,262	2.5	1.7	3.24

[1] figure is based on 50% or less of stocks

Special Securities % assets 10-31-01	
Restricted/Illiquid Secs	0
Emerging–Markets Secs	2
Options/Futures/Warrants	No

Composition % assets 10-31-01	
Cash	20.0
Stocks*	78.2
Bonds	1.8
Other	0.0
*Foreign (% stocks)	15.3

Market Cap	
Giant	88.2
Large	10.8
Medium	1.1
Small	0.0
Micro	0.0

Sector Weightings	% of Stocks	Rel S&P	5-Year High	5-Year Low
Utilities	0.0	0.0	7	0
Energy	8.7	1.2	9	0
Financials	20.8	1.2	40	3
Industrials	7.7	0.7	26	0
Durables	0.0	0.0	18	0
Staples	0.0	0.0	13	0
Services	8.5	0.8	27	5
Retail	3.8	0.6	24	0
Health	11.9	0.8	36	0
Technology	38.6	2.1	61	0

Address:	100 Fillmore Street Suite 300 Denver, CO 80206–4923 800–525–8983
Web Address:	www.janus.com
Inception:	04-26-85
Advisor:	Janus Cap. Corporation
Subadvisor:	None
NTF Plans:	Fidelity , Datalynx

Minimum Purchase:	Closed	Add: $100	IRA: —
Min Auto Inv Plan:	Closed	Add: $100	
Sales Fees:	No–load		
Management Fee:	.65%		
Actual Fees:	Mgt: 0.65%	Dist: —	
Expense Projections:	3Yr: $281	5Yr: $488	10Yr: $1084
Avg Brok Commission:	—	Income Distrib: Annually	
Total Cost (relative to category):		Low	

Janus Venture

Ticker	Load	NAV	Yield	Total Assets	Mstar Category
JAVTX	Closed	$43.98	0.0%	$1,174.9 mil	Small Growth

Prospectus Objective: Small Company

Janus Venture Fund seeks capital appreciation.

The fund emphasizes investments in common stocks of small companies. It may also invest in large or well-known companies with potential for capital appreciation. The fund may invest a portion of assets in preferred stocks, warrants, convertibles, and debt securities. It may invest up to 25% of assets in mortgage- and asset-backed securities, and without limit in foreign-equity and debt securities. This fund is non-diversified.

Historical Profile

Return Average
Risk High
Rating ★★ Below Avg

Investment Style
Equity
Average Stock %

96% 85% 91% 96% 95% 95%

▼ Manager Change
▽ Partial Manager Change

Fund Performance vs. Category Average
Quarterly Fund Return +/– Category Average
— Category Baseline

Performance Quartile (within Category)

Portfolio Manager(s)

William H. Bales. Since 2-97. BA U. of Colorado; MBA U. of Colorado.

1990	1991	1992	1993	1994	1995	1996	1997	1998	1999	2000	12–01	History
34.71	47.63	49.30	48.88	48.68	54.10	53.06	50.05	57.14	121.67	49.94	43.98	NAV
–0.40	47.82	7.44	9.08	5.46	26.46	8.02	12.61	23.22	140.71	–45.77	–11.93	Total Return %
2.72	17.34	–0.18	–0.98	4.15	–11.08	–14.92	–20.74	–5.36	119.68	–36.67	–0.06	+/– S&P 500
17.01	–3.37	–0.33	–4.28	7.89	–4.58	–3.24	–0.33	21.99	97.63	–23.34	–2.70	+/– Russ 2000 Grth
0.29	0.71	2.44	1.07	0.06	7.41	0.00	0.14	0.01	0.00	0.00	0.00	Income Return %
–0.69	47.11	5.00	8.01	5.40	19.05	8.02	12.48	23.21	140.71	–45.77	–11.93	Capital Return %
27	72	68	78	16	72	87	74	4	5	99	53	Total Rtn % Rank Cat
0.11	0.25	1.16	0.53	0.03	3.61	0.00	0.07	0.00	0.00	0.00	0.00	Income $
0.89	3.43	0.71	4.37	2.84	3.85	5.28	9.29	4.41	14.26	16.38	0.00	Capital Gains $
1.16	1.04	1.07	0.97	0.96	0.91	0.88	0.92	0.94	0.92	0.86	—	Expense Ratio %
1.24	2.10	1.32	1.29	0.27	0.29	–0.33	0.11	–0.29	–0.55	–0.35	—	Income Ratio %
184	167	124	139	114	113	136	146	90	104	87	—	Turnover Rate %
276.9	1,464.1	1,706.4	1,778.7	1,496.1	1,790.4	1,705.5	1,234.3	1,246.2	2,876.1	1,486.6	1,174.9	Net Assets $mil

Performance 12-31-01

	1st Qtr	2nd Qtr	3rd Qtr	4th Qtr	Total
1997	–11.99	12.66	13.99	–0.36	12.61
1998	12.31	2.23	–14.13	24.98	23.22
1999	10.19	15.53	3.46	82.76	140.71
2000	–0.74	–16.10	–6.75	–30.17	–45.77
2001	–22.69	25.54	–27.67	25.44	–11.93

Trailing	Total Return%	+/– S&P 500	+/– Russ 2000 Grth	% Rank All	% Rank Cat	Growth of $10,000
3 Mo	25.44	14.76	–0.73	7	34	12,544
6 Mo	–9.26	–3.71	0.00	83	70	9,074
1 Yr	–11.93	–0.06	–2.70	65	53	8,807
3 Yr Avg	4.76	5.78	4.51	33	72	11,496
5 Yr Avg	9.79	–0.91	6.92	20	42	15,952
10 Yr Avg	10.41	–2.51	3.23	30	57	26,933
15 Yr Avg	13.77	0.03	5.62	12	25	69,210

Tax Analysis	Tax-Adj Ret%	%Rank Cat	%Pretax Ret	%Rank Cat
3 Yr Avg	1.91	72	40.3	90
5 Yr Avg	6.70	49	68.5	72
10 Yr Avg	7.47	64	71.8	73

Potential Capital Gain Exposure: –10% of assets

Risk Analysis

Time Period	Load-Adj Return %	Risk %Rank[1] All	Risk %Rank[1] Cat	Morningstar Return	Morningstar Risk	Morningstar Risk-Adj Rating
1 Yr	–11.93					
3 Yr	4.76	98	96	–0.04[2]	2.14	★★
5 Yr	9.79	97	84	1.14[2]	1.88	★★
10 Yr	10.41	95	59	0.80	1.72	★★

Average Historical Rating (165 months): 4.0★s

[1] 1=low, 100=high [2] T-Bill return substituted for category avg.

Category Rating (3 Yr)

1 2 3 4 5
Worst Best

Return Below Avg
Risk High

Other Measures	Standard Index S&P 500	Best Fit Index Wil 4500
Alpha	19.8	10.6
Beta	1.76	1.55
R-Squared	41	87
Standard Deviation		54.99
Mean		4.76
Sharpe Ratio		0.00

Portfolio Analysis 10-31-01

Share change since 04–01 Total Stocks: 88	Sector	PE	YTD Ret%	% Assets
⊖ Enzon	Health	NMF	–9.32	4.22
☼ Ball	Industrials	—	55.31	3.17
Insight Enterprises	Retail	21.6	37.14	2.87
School Speciality	Industrials	21.0	14.04	2.82
⊕ Province Healthcare	Health	37.6	–21.60	2.48
⊕ Accredo Health	Health	53.7	18.65	2.39
⊕ First Health Grp	Health	25.8	6.26	2.28
⊕ Lifepoint Hosps	Health	43.1	–32.00	2.28
⊕ HCC Ins Hldgs	Financials	81.0	3.26	2.26
Apria Healthcare Grp	Health	20.5	–16.00	2.05
⊖ Valassis Comms	Services	18.9	12.85	1.93
⊕ Career Educ	Services	47.6	75.23	1.92
⊕ Microtune	Technology	—	41.64	1.91
Lamar Advertising Cl A	Services	—	9.71	1.87
⊖ Cerus 144A	N/A	—	—	1.84
Radio One Cl D	Services	—	—	1.75
☼ Stellent	N/A	—	—	1.74
☼ Brown & Brown	Financials	35.9	57.09	1.57
⊖ Alpha Inds	Technology	NMF	–41.00	1.57
⊕ Retek	Technology	—	22.54	1.51
Cox Radio Cl A	Services	—	12.93	1.49
☼ SkillSoft	Technology	—	38.24	1.47
☼ InterCept Grp	Technology	—	53.25	1.46
☼ TALX	Technology	89.2	3.53	1.46
⊕ Westwood One	Services	77.1	55.59	1.45

Current Investment Style

Style: Value Blnd Growth; Size: Large Med Small

	Stock Port Avg	Relative S&P 500 Current	Relative S&P 500 Hist	Rel Cat
Price/Earnings Ratio	39.7	1.28	1.24	1.24
Price/Book Ratio	5.0	0.88	1.27	1.03
Price/Cash Flow	25.7	1.43	1.29	1.17
3 Yr Earnings Growth	—	—	—	—
1 Yr Earnings Est%	14.0[1]	—	—	1.80
Med Mkt Cap $mil	1,312	0.0	0.0	1.26

[1] figure is based on 50% or less of stocks

Analysis by Catherine Hickey 07-24-01

This fund isn't out of the woods, but those who have held on here would do well to stay put.

Meet the more moderate Janus Venture Fund. In the aftermath of this fund's abysmal 2000 performance, when the fund lost more than 45%, manager Will Bales is toning things down to make sure that such enormous downswings are a thing of the past. To this end, Bales said he was quicker to sell a stock these days than he was; for example, he dumped Williams-Sonoma late in the first quarter of this year after the stock had a big runup. This tighter sell discipline is a departure from years past, when Bales and former comanager Jonathan Coleman let positions in many of their aggressive-growth stocks ride. Also, look for more-balanced sector representation in the portfolio. Thrifts like American Financial are now among Bales' favorites.

These moves have helped give performance a boost, though it still has ground to make up. The fund has lost just more than 12% so far in 2001, which is below average for the small-growth category but is a far cry from 2000's debacle. A number of Bales' less-aggressive picks have buoyed performance; for instance, retailers like Insight Enterprises have been big winners. However, some of Bales' remaining biotech and tech picks have dragged down the fund.

Those high-growth laggards address an important point: This fund remains aggressive. At last count, its price multiples were still above the small-growth average, and Bales isn't abandoning pricey, fast-growing companies if he still thinks their prospects are sunny. Thus, investors who want a very cautious small-growth offering should look elsewhere.

However, positives do exist. Bales is making progress toward making this a more durable fund, he's backed by Janus' crack analyst staff, and Janus is throwing more weight behind its small-cap team.

Special Securities % assets 10-31-01	
Restricted/Illiquid Secs	2
Emerging-Markets Secs	0
Options/Futures/Warrants	No

Composition % assets 10-31-01	
Cash	4.7
Stocks*	94.1
Bonds	1.2
Other	0.0
*Foreign (% stocks)	3.6

Market Cap	
Giant	0.0
Large	0.0
Medium	45.7
Small	52.7
Micro	1.7

Sector Weightings	% of Stocks	Rel S&P	5-Year High	5-Year Low
Utilities	0.0	0.0	5	0
Energy	0.0	0.0	8	0
Financials	8.4	0.5	36	1
Industrials	9.6	0.8	29	2
Durables	0.0	0.0	9	0
Staples	0.0	0.0	6	0
Services	27.8	2.6	42	13
Retail	5.8	0.9	29	2
Health	26.4	1.8	26	2
Technology	22.0	1.2	53	2

Address: 100 Fillmore Street Suite 300, Denver, CO 80206–4923, 800–525–8983
Web Address: www.janus.com

Inception: 04-30-85
Advisor: Janus Cap. Corporation
Subadvisor: None
NTF Plans: Fidelity , Fidelity Inst.

Minimum Purchase: Closed — Add: $100 — IRA: —
Min Auto Inv Plan: Closed — Add: $100
Sales Fees: No–load
Management Fee: .65%
Actual Fees: Mgt: 0.65% — Dist: —
Expense Projections: 3Yr: $287 — 5Yr: $498 — 10Yr: $1108
Avg Brok Commission: — — Income Distrib: Annually
Total Cost (relative to category): Low

Janus Worldwide

Ticker	Load	NAV	Yield	Total Assets	Mstar Category
JAWWX	Closed	$43.84	0.0%	$21,678.6 mil	World Stock

Prospectus Objective: World Stock

Janus Worldwide Fund seeks long-term growth of capital consistent with preservation of capital.

The fund invests primarily in foreign and domestic common stocks. Investments are usually spread across at least five different countries, including the United States, though it may at times invest in a single country. The fund may also invest in preferred stocks, warrants, government securities, and corporate debt. It may use derivatives for hedging purposes or as a means of enhancing return.

Historical Profile
Return: High
Risk: Average
Rating: ★★★★★ Highest

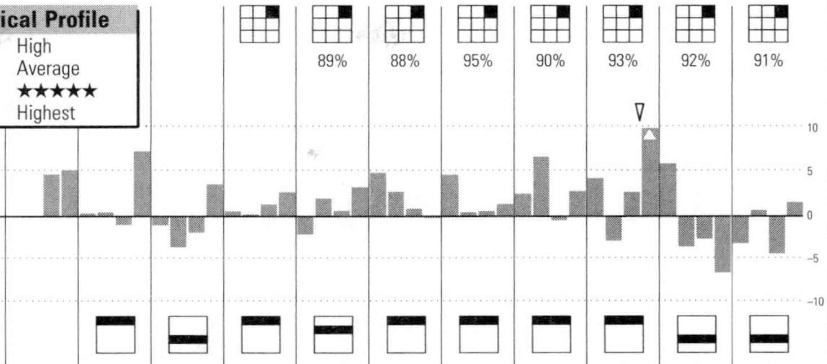

Investment Style
Equity
Average Stock %: 89% 88% 95% 90% 93% 92% 91%

▼ Manager Change
▽ Partial Manager Change

Fund Performance vs. Category Average
■ Quarterly Fund Return +/– Category Average
— Category Baseline

Performance Quartile (within Category)

Portfolio Manager(s)

Helen Young Hayes, CFA. Since 10-92. BA'84 Yale U. Other funds currently managed: IDEX Janus Global A, IDEX Janus Global M, Janus Overseas.

Laurence J. Chang, CFA. Since 9-99. Dartmouth C.; MS Stanford U. Other funds currently managed: IDEX Janus Global A, IDEX Janus Global M, IDEX Janus Global B.

History

	1990	1991	1992	1993	1994	1995	1996	1997	1998	1999	2000	12-01
NAV	—	18.55	20.00	25.03	24.39	28.40	33.69	37.78	47.36	76.43	56.86	43.84
Total Return %	—	24.00*	9.01	28.41	3.61	21.90	26.41	20.48	25.87	64.37	–16.87	–22.88
+/– S&P 500	—	8.25*	1.39	18.35	2.30	–15.64	3.46	–12.87	–2.71	43.33	–7.77	–11.00
+/– MSCI World	—	—	14.23	5.91	–1.47	1.18	12.93	4.72	1.53	39.43	–3.69	—
Income Return %	—	0.01	1.19	1.38	2.15	1.07	0.54	0.58	0.51	0.06	0.99	0.02
Capital Return %	—	23.99	7.82	27.03	1.47	20.82	25.86	19.90	25.36	64.31	–17.86	–22.90
Total Rtn % Rank Cat	—	—	6	69	10	27	4	20	18	16	71	72
Income $	—	0.00	0.22	0.28	0.54	0.26	0.15	0.20	0.19	0.03	0.75	0.01
Capital Gains $	—	0.05	0.00	0.38	1.01	1.07	2.04	2.60	0.00	1.28	6.17	0.00
Expense Ratio %	—	2.50	1.73	1.32	1.12	1.23	1.01	0.95	0.92	0.88	0.86	—
Income Ratio %	—	0.02	1.74	0.92	0.42	0.99	0.73	0.65	0.47	0.07	0.13	—
Turnover Rate %	—	—	147	124	158	142	80	79	86	68	58	—
Net Assets $mil	—	29.1	208.3	935.2	1,542.6	1,975.5	5,046.3	10,567.8	16,322.7	33,802.9	33,144.3	21,678.6

Performance 12-31-01

	1st Qtr	2nd Qtr	3rd Qtr	4th Qtr	Total
1997	5.67	12.58	5.74	–4.23	20.48
1998	16.41	7.19	–16.10	20.24	25.87
1999	6.76	5.68	2.53	42.11	64.37
2000	11.81	–8.45	–5.73	–13.86	–16.87
2001	–17.17	4.12	–20.80	12.91	–22.88

Trailing	Total Return%	+/– S&P 500	+/– MSCI World	% Rank All	% Rank Cat	Growth of $10,000
3 Mo	12.91	2.22	—	30	24	11,291
6 Mo	–10.58	–5.02	—	87	86	8,942
1 Yr	–22.88	–11.00	—	85	72	7,712
3 Yr Avg	1.76	2.79	—	64	39	10,538
5 Yr Avg	9.83	–0.87	—	19	20	15,980
10 Yr Avg	13.57	0.65	—	10	3	35,710
15 Yr Avg	—	—	—	—	—	—

Tax Analysis	Tax-Adj Ret%	%Rank Cat	%Pretax Ret	%Rank Cat
3 Yr Avg	0.84	34	47.6	83
5 Yr Avg	8.71	13	88.6	14
10 Yr Avg	12.24	1	90.2	3

Potential Capital Gain Exposure: –10% of assets

Risk Analysis

Time Period	Load-Adj Return %	Risk %Rank[1] All	Risk %Rank[1] Cat	Morningstar Return	Morningstar Risk	Morningstar Risk-Adj Rating
1 Yr	–22.88					
3 Yr	1.76	81	73	–0.65[2]	1.10	★★★
5 Yr	9.83	78	57	1.15[2]	0.89	★★★★★
10 Yr	13.57	79	47	3.37[2]	0.80	★★★★★

Average Historical Rating (92 months): 5.0★s

[1] 1=low, 100=high [2] T-Bill return substituted for category avg.

Category Rating (3 Yr)

1 2 3 4 5 (Worst — Best): 3

Return: Average
Risk: Above Avg

Other Measures	Standard Index S&P 500	Best Fit Index Wil 4500
Alpha	4.7	–0.3
Beta	1.07	0.79
R-Squared	54	80
Standard Deviation		25.75
Mean		1.76
Sharpe Ratio		–0.14

Portfolio Analysis 10-31-01

Share change since 04-01 Total Stocks: 126

	Sector	Country	% Assets
⊖ Tyco Intl	Industrials	U.S.	4.58
⊕ Citigroup	Financials	U.S.	2.91
⊖ NTT DoCoMo	Services	Japan	2.66
☼ Bank Amer	Financials	U.S.	2.46
⊖ Pfizer	Health	U.S.	2.42
⊖ General Elec	Industrials	U.S.	2.03
⊖ Total Fina Cl B	Energy	France	1.98
☼ Takeda Chem Inds	Health	Japan	1.78
⊖ Banco Bilbao Vizcaya Arg	Financials	Spain	1.74
⊕ Ahold	Retail	Netherlands	1.70
⊕ Clear Channel Comms	Services	U.S.	1.70
⊕ Unilever (Cert)	Staples	United Kingdom	1.59
⊖ Petrobras ADR	Energy	Brazil	1.43
⊖ Viacom Cl B	Services	U.S.	1.38
⊖ Comcast	Services	U.S.	1.34
⊖ Telefonos de Mexico ADR L	Services	Mexico	1.34
⊖ Wal-Mart Stores	Retail	U.S.	1.27
⊖ STMicroelectronics	Technology	France	1.25
☼ Microsoft	Technology	U.S.	1.12
⊕ Diageo	Staples	United Kingdom	1.09

Current Investment Style

Style: Value Blnd Growth; Size: Large Med Small

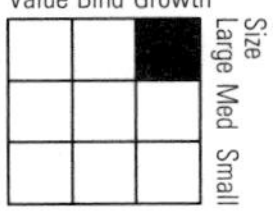

	Stock Port Avg	Rel MSCI EAFE Current	Rel MSCI EAFE Hist	Rel Cat
Price/Earnings Ratio	30.8	1.19	1.39	1.11
Price/Cash Flow	18.5	1.44	1.74	1.13
Price/Book Ratio	5.2	1.50	2.06	1.13
3 Yr Earnings Growth	21.7	1.16	2.24	1.16
Med Mkt Cap $mil	43,439	1.6	1.8	1.81

Country Exposure 10-31-01	% assets
U.S.	42
United Kingdom	8
Japan	6
France	6
Netherlands	5

Hedging History: Always

Regional Exposure 10-31-01	% assets
Europe	29
Japan	6
Latin America	4
Pacific Rim	2
U.S.	42
Other	0

Special Securities % assets 10-31-01	
Restricted/Illiquid Secs	0
Emerging-Markets Secs	8
Options/Futures/Warrants	No

Composition % assets 10-31-01

Cash	8.8	Bonds	0.2
Stocks	90.5	Other	0.5

Sector Weightings	% of Stocks	Rel Cat	5-Year High	5-Year Low
Utilities	0.0	0.0	8	0
Energy	9.1	1.7	9	0
Financials	16.9	0.9	31	3
Industrials	10.7	1.0	23	2
Durables	3.0	0.8	19	0
Staples	5.0	0.6	24	0
Services	21.6	1.3	49	7
Retail	5.2	1.0	17	0
Health	17.5	1.3	21	0
Technology	11.0	0.7	39	1

Analysis by Emily Hall 10-30-01

Janus Worldwide Fund is not flawless, but for those who can stand the turbulence, there is reason to stay put.

It's been a pretty unpleasant couple of years for this offering and its shareholders. The growth-stock rout of 2000 and 2001 has not been kind to this portfolio, which entered the new century with loads of high-flying technology and telecom names. Managers Helen Young Hayes and Laurence Chang have acknowledged the weakening economy and have been trimming many of their picks in the tech and telecom arenas. Moreover, they have diversified the portfolio by adding names in areas such as health care and energy. But these moves haven't been enough to save the fund from dismal performance. For the year to date through Oct. 29, this offering has lost a bruising 31%, placing it in the worst quartile of the world stock group.

All is not lost, though. Until the market turned sour in the spring of 2000, this offering had consistently outperformed peers year in and year out. Indeed, the fund's recent troubles haven't put too much of a dent in its long-term record: For the trailing five years, the fund's return still ranks in the category's top quartile. Moreover, the fund's 10-year trailing return is still the best in the group. (Although to be fair, there are less than three dozen world-stock funds with at least a 10-year record, so its competition is rather limited.)

The managers' willingness to load up on particular sectors is certainly a reminder, though, that investors need to expect volatility. Currently, the fund is looking fairly diversified, but Janus' firmwide taste for growth probably means that this offering could again sport large overweightings when market conditions for growth stocks improve.

Still, for those who can handle the heat, there is plenty of reason to stay with this closed offering.

Address:	100 Fillmore Street Suite 300 Denver, CO 80206-4923 800-525-8983
Web Address:	www.janus.com
*Inception:	05-15-91
Advisor:	Janus Cap. Corporation
Subadvisor:	None
NTF Plans:	Fidelity , Datalynx

Minimum Purchase:	Closed	Add: $100	IRA: —
Min Auto Inv Plan:	Closed	Add: $100	
Sales Fees:	No-load		
Management Fee:	.65%		
Actual Fees:	Mgt: 0.65%	Dist: —	
Expense Projections:	3Yr: $284	5Yr: $493	10Yr: $1096
Avg Brok Commission:	—	Income Distrib: Annually	
Total Cost (relative to category):	Low		

Japan S

Ticker	Load	NAV	Yield	Total Assets	Mstar Category
SJPNX	None	$6.63	0.0%	$325.9 mil	Japan Stock

Prospectus Objective: Pacific Stock

Japan Fund seeks long-term capital appreciation.

The fund normally invests at least 80% of assets in Japanese securities. It may invest in stocks of any size, including up to 30% of net assets in smaller companies that are traded over-the-counter. To select investments, the advisor considers an issuer's size, quality of management, product line, business strategy or competitive industry position, marketing and technical strengths, research and development efforts, financial strength, growth potential, P/E ratios, and other stock valuation measures.

The fund currently offers A, B, C S and AARP shares, all of which differ in fee structure and availability.

Historical Profile

Return: Average
Risk: Above Avg
Rating: ★★★ Neutral

Investment Style
Equity
Average Stock %: 91% 89% 87% 92% 91% 97% 96%

▼ Manager Change
▽ Partial Manager Change

Fund Performance vs. Category Average
■ Quarterly Fund Return +/– Category Average
— Category Baseline

Performance Quartile (within Category)

Portfolio Manager(s)

Seung Kwak, CFA. Since 9-88. BA'83 Middlebury C.; MA'85 Yale U. Other funds currently managed: Japan A, Japan B, Japan C.

Sean Lenihan. Since 5-01. Other funds currently managed: Japan A, Japan B, Japan C.

History

1990	1991	1992	1993	1994	1995	1996	1997	1998	1999	2000	12-01	History
10.76	10.69	8.90	10.33	10.51	9.44	8.33	6.77	8.33	16.41	9.99	6.63	NAV
–16.36	3.11	–16.75	23.64	10.03	–9.07	–10.93	–14.40	24.34	119.88	–27.28	–33.63	Total Return %
–13.24	–27.37	–24.36	13.58	8.72	–46.60	–33.87	–47.75	–4.23	98.84	–18.18	–21.76	+/– S&P 500
19.74	–5.81	4.71	–1.84	–11.40	–9.76	4.58	9.28	19.29	58.35	0.88	—	+/– MSCI Japan
1.50	0.00	0.00	3.15	0.00	0.00	0.87	4.43	1.11	0.96	3.53	0.00	Income Return %
–17.86	3.11	–16.74	20.49	10.03	–9.07	–11.80	–18.82	23.23	118.92	–30.81	–33.63	Capital Return %
1	50	20	33	83	90	37	57	7	42	33	78	Total Rtn % Rank Cat
0.20	0.00	0.00	0.28	0.00	0.00	0.08	0.37	0.08	0.08	0.58	0.00	Income $
0.99	0.41	0.00	0.39	0.85	0.11	0.00	0.00	0.00	1.77	1.83	0.00	Capital Gains $
1.05	1.26	1.42	1.25	1.08	1.21	1.16	1.21	1.26	0.98	1.08	—	Expense Ratio %
0.72	–0.15	–0.31	–0.47	–0.40	–0.24	–0.34	–0.38	–0.14	–0.20	–0.40	—	Income Ratio %
53	46	47	82	74	70	73	96	90	114	74	—	Turnover Rate %
313.5	334.9	409.1	471.1	586.0	550.3	383.7	270.8	348.3	1,089.9	624.1	323.5	Net Assets $mil

Performance 12-31-01

	1st Qtr	2nd Qtr	3rd Qtr	4th Qtr	Total
1997	–6.67	25.59	–10.81	–18.12	–14.40
1998	5.98	0.70	–8.25	26.98	24.34
1999	15.73	16.29	29.53	26.14	119.88
2000	5.87	–9.56	–8.12	–17.34	–27.28
2001	–12.41	0.69	–19.86	–6.09	–33.63

Trailing	Total Return%	+/– S&P 500	+/– MSCI Japan	% Rank All	% Rank Cat	Growth of $10,000
3 Mo	–6.09	–16.78	—	100	69	9,391
6 Mo	–24.74	–19.19	—	100	65	7,526
1 Yr	–33.63	–21.76	—	96	78	6,637
3 Yr Avg	2.00	3.02	—	63	10	10,612
5 Yr Avg	2.47	–8.23	—	87	4	11,296
10 Yr Avg	0.36	–12.57	—	99	1	10,363
15 Yr Avg	3.13	–10.61	—	98	1	15,867

Tax Analysis	Tax-Adj Ret%	%Rank Cat	%Pretax Ret	%Rank Cat
3 Yr Avg	–1.09	25	—	—
5 Yr Avg	0.10	4	4.1	50
10 Yr Avg	–1.29	1	—	—

Potential Capital Gain Exposure: –45% of assets

Risk Analysis

Time Period	Load-Adj Return %	Risk %Rank[1] All	Risk %Rank[1] Cat	Morningstar Return	Morningstar Risk	Morningstar Risk-Adj Rating
1 Yr	–33.63					
3 Yr	2.00	86	46	–0.61[2]	1.21	★★★
5 Yr	2.47	88	15	–0.53[2]	1.17	★★★
10 Yr	0.36	97	50	–0.94[2]	1.43	★★

Average Historical Rating (193 months): 3.2★s

[1]1=low, 100=high [2] T-Bill return substituted for category avg.

Category Rating (3 Yr)

1 (Worst) 2 3 4 5 (Best)

Return: Above Avg
Risk: Average

Other Measures	Standard Index S&P 500	Best Fit Index MSCIPacND
Alpha	4.6	9.7
Beta	0.92	1.21
R-Squared	36	89

Standard Deviation	27.44
Mean	2.00
Sharpe Ratio	–0.12

Portfolio Analysis 09-30-01

Share change since 06-01 Total Stocks: 59

	Sector	Country	% Assets
⊕ Mitsubishi	Retail	Japan	4.08
⊕ Toyota Motor	Durables	Japan	3.96
⊖ NTT DoCoMo	Services	Japan	3.92
⊖ Nomura Secs	Financials	Japan	3.27
⊕ Fuji Photo Film	Industrials	Japan	3.26
⊕ Mitsui	Industrials	Japan	3.26
⊕ Ajinomoto	Staples	Japan	3.25
⊕ Daikin Inds	Industrials	Japan	3.12
⊕ Bank of Yokohama	Financials	Japan	3.00
⊖ Chiba Bk	Financials	Japan	2.79
⊖ Canon	Industrials	Japan	2.51
⊕ Mizuho Hldgs	Technology	Japan	2.32
⊖ Yokogawa Elec	Technology	Japan	2.11
⊖ Sharp	Technology	Japan	2.08
⊕ Sumitomo Tr & Bkg	Financials	Japan	2.03
⊖ Takeda Chem Inds	Health	Japan	2.03
✲ Nippon Unipac Hldg	N/A	N/A	1.89
✲ OJI Paper	Industrials	Japan	1.87
⊖ Daiwa Secs Grp	Financials	Japan	1.85
⊖ Nikko Secs	Financials	Japan	1.78

Current Investment Style

Style: Value Blnd Growth; Size: Large Med Small

	Stock Port Avg	Rel MSCI EAFE Current	Rel MSCI EAFE Hist	Rel Cat
Price/Earnings Ratio	31.7	1.23	1.31	0.98
Price/Cash Flow	13.5	1.05	1.06	0.97
Price/Book Ratio	2.1	0.61	0.59	0.83
3 Yr Earnings Growth	17.4	0.93	1.16	1.01
Med Mkt Cap $mil	7,896	0.3	0.3	1.05

Country Exposure 09-30-01	% assets
Japan	86

Hedging History: Frequent

Sector Weightings	% of Stocks	Rel Cat	5-Year High	5-Year Low
Utilities	0.0	0.0	5	0
Energy	0.0	0.0	2	0
Financials	19.6	1.3	21	3
Industrials	31.8	1.5	49	15
Durables	7.8	0.5	21	8
Staples	4.7	1.4	9	0
Services	11.6	1.0	22	3
Retail	6.1	1.0	16	3
Health	5.2	0.8	8	0
Technology	13.2	0.8	22	5

Special Securities % assets 09-30-01	
Restricted/Illiquid Secs	0
Emerging-Markets Secs	0
Options/Futures/Warrants	Yes

Composition % assets 09-30-01			
Cash	2.9	Bonds	0.0
Stocks	92.6	Other	4.6

Analysis by Gregg Wolper 11-26-01

Although Japan Fund has struggled more than usual in 2001, it remains a sound choice in an iffy market.

Over the years, this fund has proven itself among the best vehicles for investing in Japan. Through Nov. 23, 2001, its trailing returns for the three-, five-, and 10-year periods (the 10-year includes only four funds) are all in the top decile of the category. Its volatility level, average in the group over the past three years, is better than that over longer stretches. Also encouraging is its consistency from year to year, with a few exceptions. Adding to the fund's appeal is its flexible mandate—it can own companies of all sizes.

That background makes the fund's poor performance so far in 2001 a bit of a surprise. Through Nov. 23, the fund's 28.3% loss sits in the bottom quartile of the category. One reason is that small stocks have outperformed in Japan this year. That meant rivals that focus solely on smaller fare, such as DFA Japanese Small Company, would have surpassed this fund no matter what it did. And this offering didn't do itself any favors in that regard; its stake in small caps is near its lowest ebb—just a few percent of assets— in years.

In assessing blame for this year's showing, management also cites an overweight in certain financials stocks, particularly securities companies, as well as an underweight in electric utilities, which have held up relatively well. The managers state, however, that they won't get more defensive because they'd risk missing out on an overall market rebound. Plus, they remain confident in most of their picks, such as the securities firms.

Whether that specific tack works out, it's reassuring to know that management isn't making wholesale changes in response to this year's woes. The fund's approach has worked for a long time, so we're willing to stay confident in it, and this fund, for now.

Address:	PO Box 21969 Kansas City, MO 64121 800-535-2726 / 800-535-2726
Web Address:	www.scudderfunds.com
Inception:	04-01-62
Advisor:	Zurich Scudder Inv.s
Subadvisor:	None
NTF Plans:	Fidelity , Datalynx

Minimum Purchase:	$2500	Add: $100	IRA: $1000
Min Auto Inv Plan:	$2500	Add: $50	
Sales Fees:	No-load, 2.00%R		
Management Fee:	.78%		
Actual Fees:	Mgt: 0.78%	Dist: —	
Expense Projections:	3Yr: $400	5Yr: $692	10Yr: $1523
Avg Brok Commission:	—	Income Distrib: Annually	
Total Cost (relative to category):	—		

Lazard International Equity Instl

Ticker	Load	NAV	Yield	Total Assets	Mstar Category
LZIEX	None	$10.01	0.0%	$2,371.5 mil	Foreign Stock

Prospectus Objective: Foreign Stock

Lazard International Equity Portfolio seeks capital appreciation.

The fund usually invests at least 80% of assets in equity securities issued by companies located in at least three foreign countries. The fund may invest the balance of assets in fixed-income securities and money-market instruments. The fund invests primarily in common stocks of foreign companies, but may also invest in both American and global depositary receipts. This fund is non-diversified.

Institutional shares are designed for institutional investors; Open shares are for individual investors, are subject to 12b-1 fees, and have lower minimum initial purchase requirements.

Historical Profile

Return Average
Risk Below Avg
Rating ★★★ Neutral

Investment Style
Equity
Average Stock %

1994	1995	1996	1997	1998	1999	2000	12-01
	93%	95%	97%	95%	98%	97%	98%

▼ Manager Change
▽ Partial Manager Change

Fund Performance vs. Category Average
■ Quarterly Fund Return +/– Category Average
— Category Baseline

Performance Quartile (within Category)

Portfolio Manager(s)

John R. Reinsberg, et al. Since 1-92. BA'78 U. of Pennsylvania; MBA'82 Columbia U.

1990	1991	1992	1993	1994	1995	1996	1997	1998	1999	2000	12–01	History
—	10.30	9.48	12.32	11.23	12.50	13.62	13.97	15.23	17.29	13.46	10.01	NAV
—	3.19*	–6.62	31.05	0.24	13.14	15.64	11.84	16.04	24.07	–10.55	–24.85	Total Return %
—	–4.19*	–14.24	20.99	–1.08	–24.39	–7.30	–21.51	–12.53	3.04	–1.45	–12.98	+/– S&P 500
—	—	5.55	–1.51	–7.54	1.93	9.60	10.07	–3.95	–2.89	3.62	—	+/– MSCI EAFE
—	0.19	1.34	0.44	0.00	0.81	1.54	2.48	1.03	3.54	1.00	0.00	Income Return %
—	3.00	–7.96	30.61	0.24	12.33	14.10	9.36	15.01	20.54	–11.55	–24.86	Capital Return %
—	—	71	72	52	22	36	21	32	88	28	69	Total Rtn % Rank Cat
—	0.02	0.14	0.04	0.00	0.09	0.19	0.34	0.14	0.54	0.17	0.00	Income $
—	0.00	0.00	0.06	1.12	0.11	0.62	0.93	0.81	0.99	1.80	0.11	Capital Gains $
—	1.05	1.05	0.99	0.94	0.95	0.90	0.89	0.90	0.88	0.88	—	Expense Ratio %
—	2.19	2.13	1.13	0.75	1.82	1.93	1.18	1.37	2.09	0.97	—	Income Ratio %
—	—	60	87	106	63	39	37	41	35	51	—	Turnover Rate %
—	5.0	176.0	589.6	831.9	1,299.5	1,815.4	2,099.5	2,876.8	3,583.1	3,010.3	2,249.0	Net Assets $mil

Performance 12-31-01

	1st Qtr	2nd Qtr	3rd Qtr	4th Qtr	Total
1997	2.28	9.88	3.95	–4.26	11.84
1998	14.96	3.24	–17.11	17.96	16.04
1999	0.20	5.18	5.11	12.01	24.07
2000	–3.12	–1.43	–6.47	0.15	–10.55
2001	–13.45	–0.43	–16.38	4.27	–24.86

Trailing	Total Return%	+/– S&P 500	+/– MSCI EAFE	% Rank All	% Rank Cat	Growth of $10,000
3 Mo	4.27	–6.41	—	67	88	10,427
6 Mo	–12.81	–7.25	—	91	88	8,719
1 Yr	–24.85	–12.98	—	88	69	7,515
3 Yr Avg	–5.87	–4.85	—	93	78	8,340
5 Yr Avg	1.60	–9.10	—	89	55	10,824
10 Yr Avg	5.68	–7.25	—	81	56	17,371
15 Yr Avg	—	—	—	—	—	—

Tax Analysis	Tax-Adj Ret%	%Rank Cat	%Pretax Ret	%Rank Cat
3 Yr Avg	–7.75	82	—	—
5 Yr Avg	–0.39	59	—	—
10 Yr Avg	3.97	58	69.9	64

Potential Capital Gain Exposure: –28% of assets

Risk Analysis

Time Period	Load-Adj Return %	Risk %Rank[1] All	Risk %Rank[1] Cat	Morningstar Return	Morningstar Risk	Morningstar Risk-Adj Rating
1 Yr	–24.85					
3 Yr	–5.87	61	24	–2.07[2]	0.79	★★
5 Yr	1.60	66	25	–0.70[2]	0.74	★★★
10 Yr	5.68	78	32	0.25[2]	0.80	★★★

Average Historical Rating (87 months): 3.4★s

[1]1=low, 100=high [2] T-Bill return substituted for category avg.

Category Rating (3 Yr)

1 2 3 4 5
Worst Best

Return Below Avg
Risk Below Avg

Other Measures	Standard Index S&P 500	Best Fit Index MSCIWdxUSN
Alpha	–6.7	–2.6
Beta	0.66	0.88
R-Squared	60	91

Standard Deviation	13.63
Mean	–5.87
Sharpe Ratio	–0.93

Portfolio Analysis 11-30-01

Share change since 10–01 Total Stocks: 64	Sector	Country	% Assets
⊖ Philips Electncs (NV)	Durables	Netherlands	2.99
⊖ HSBC Hldgs (UK) (2nd)	Financials	United Kingdom	2.93
⊕ Novartis (Reg)	Health	Switzerland	2.68
ABN Amro Hldgs	Financials	Netherlands	2.58
⊕ ENI	Energy	Italy	2.53
⊖ Total Fina Cl B	Energy	France	2.43
⊖ Vivendi	Services	France	2.39
Royal Dutch Petro	Energy	Netherlands	2.35
⊖ Alcatel	Durables	France	2.27
Diageo	Staples	United Kingdom	2.27
⊖ Toyota Motor	Durables	Japan	2.15
⊖ Telecom Italia	Services	Italy	2.08
⊕ BP Amoco	Energy	United Kingdom	2.03
Suez Lyon Eaux	Industrials	France	2.03
Endesa	Utilities	Spain	1.97
East Japan Railway	Services	Japan	1.94
Akzo Nobel NV	Industrials	Netherlands	1.89
⊖ AXA Finl	Financials	U.S.	1.83
Investor Cl B	N/A	N/A	1.77
Banque Nationale de Paris	Financials	France	1.76

Current Investment Style

Style: Value Blnd Growth; Size: Large Med Small

	Stock Port Avg	Rel MSCI EAFE Current	Rel MSCI EAFE Hist	Rel Cat
Price/Earnings Ratio	21.2	0.82	0.86	0.83
Price/Cash Flow	11.4	0.88	0.79	0.79
Price/Book Ratio	2.9	0.84	0.77	0.75
3 Yr Earnings Growth	22.4	1.20	1.09	1.14
Med Mkt Cap $mil	30,201	1.1	1.8	1.67

Country Exposure 11-30-01	% assets
Japan	19
Netherlands	16
United Kingdom	16
France	14
Italy	7

Hedging History: Never

Regional Exposure 11-30-01	% assets
Europe	69
Japan	19
Latin America	0
Pacific Rim	6
Other	2

Special Securities % assets 11-30-01	
Restricted/Illiquid Secs	0
Emerging-Markets Secs	2
Options/Futures/Warrants	No

Composition % assets 11-30-01			
Cash	1.1	Bonds	0.0
Stocks	98.8	Other	0.1

Sector Weightings	% of Stocks	Rel Cat	5-Year High	5-Year Low
Utilities	3.0	1.1	8	1
Energy	9.8	1.7	11	3
Financials	29.9	1.4	33	10
Industrials	8.9	0.7	25	9
Durables	14.6	2.1	21	10
Staples	7.1	1.0	13	3
Services	15.2	0.9	23	6
Retail	1.7	0.4	4	0
Health	6.8	0.7	9	3
Technology	3.1	0.3	9	3

Analysis by Gregg Wolper 12-22-01

Lazard International Equity Fund is struggling through an uncharacteristically weak stretch, but there's good reason to stick with it.

This fund's showing in 2001 has not been impressive. Through Dec. 21, its year-to-date loss of 26.5% lags two thirds of the funds in the foreign-stock category. What's worse, this offering takes a value-oriented approach, and that style has been in favor for most of 2001. Some other foreign funds with value strategies have much narrower losses—or even gains. So one could have expected much better performance from this fund even considering the slide in the market indexes.

Lead manager John Reinsberg cites several reasons why that didn't happen. He says he sold a number of pharmaceutical stocks that had performed well since early 2000 because they'd gotten too expensive. He cut the fund's weighting in that sector by half to below 6%, much less than the weightings of most rivals. That hurt after Sept. 11, when investors favored such comforting names. Also hurting the fund in 2001 was its affection for financials, some of which have plunged. Finally, the fund was stung by a few Japanese holdings that haven't followed through on restructuring plans as Reinsberg had expected.

The fund has no plans to deviate from its style, though. For example, Reinsberg says he'll stay overweighted in financials. He says European institutions such as BNP, Fortis, and others with significant asset-management operations have a great opportunity to profit from the increasing public interest in equities, yet they trade at reasonable valuations.

Even though the fund—which tilts more toward growth than some value rivals do—hasn't shined in 2001, it has over time; prior to 2001, it had finished five of the previous six calendar years well in the category's top half, with growth-crazed 1999 the only exception. This fund will likely find its way again.

Address:	30 Rockefeller Plaza New York, NY 10112 212–632–6000 / 800–823–6300
Web Address:	www.lazardfunds.com/
*Inception:	10-29-91
Advisor:	Lazard Asset Mgmt.
Subadvisor:	None
NTF Plans:	N/A

Minimum Purchase:	$1000000	Add: None IRA: —
Min Auto Inv Plan:	$1000000	Add: None
Sales Fees:	No-load	
Management Fee:	.75%, .02%A	
Actual Fees:	Mgt: 0.75%	Dist: —
Expense Projections:	3Yr: $287	5Yr: $498 10Yr: $1108
Avg Brok Commission:	—	Income Distrib: Semi-Ann.

Total Cost (relative to category): —

Legg Mason American Leading Co Prim

Ticker	Load	NAV	Yield	Total Assets	Mstar Category
LMALX	12b–1 only	$18.49	0.0%	$581.7 mil	Large Value

Prospectus Objective: Growth and Income

Legg Mason American Leading Company Trust seeks long-term capital appreciation and current income, consistent with low risk.

The fund normally invests at least 75% of assets in dividend-paying common stocks issued by leading companies with market capitalization of at least $2 billion; most are in the top half of the S&P 500. These companies have a major market share, and possess financial and management strengths that may enable them to maintain or increase their market shares. The fund may invest up to 25% of assets in foreign securities and up to 25% of assets in high-quality debt instruments.

Primary shares have level loads; Navigator shares are designed for institutional investors.

Historical Profile
Return Average
Risk Average
Rating ★★★ Neutral

Investment Style
Equity
Average Stock %: 1996 96%, 1997 92%, 1998 94%, 1999 94%, 2000 98%, 12-01 100%

▼ Manager Change
▽ Partial Manager Change

Fund Performance vs. Category Average
Quarterly Fund Return +/– Category Average
— Category Baseline

Performance Quartile (within Category)

Portfolio Manager(s)

David E. Nelson, CFA. Since 4-98. BA'69 Wesleyan U.; MBA'76 Washington U.

1990	1991	1992	1993	1994	1995	1996	1997	1998	1999	2000	12-01	History
—	—	—	10.06	9.53	11.61	14.40	15.90	18.50	19.13	19.12	18.49	NAV
—	—	—	0.85*	–4.19	22.94	28.36	23.75	21.33	5.26	0.51	–3.30	Total Return %
—	—	—	–0.77*	–5.51	–14.59	5.42	–9.61	–7.25	–15.78	9.61	8.58	+/– S&P 500
—	—	—	—	–1.88	–17.09	6.05	–11.74	0.09	–5.70	–1.81	5.50	+/– Russ Top 200 Val
—	—	—	0.25	1.10	1.05	0.19	0.00	0.00	0.00	0.00	0.00	Income Return %
—	—	—	0.60	–5.29	21.89	28.17	23.75	21.33	5.25	0.51	–3.29	Capital Return %
—	—	—	—	89	96	7	77	11	54	76	35	Total Rtn % Rank Cat
—	—	—	0.03	0.11	0.10	0.02	0.00	0.00	0.00	0.00	0.00	Income $
—	—	—	0.00	0.00	0.00	0.48	1.85	0.72	0.36	0.11	0.00	Capital Gains $
—	—	—	—	1.95	1.95	1.95	1.95	1.95	1.93	1.90	—	Expense Ratio %
—	—	—	—	1.14	1.21	0.69	0.05	–0.28	–0.37	–0.58	—	Income Ratio %
—	—	—	—	21	31	43	56	51	48	44	—	Turnover Rate %
—	—	—	51.8	56.0	71.7	91.0	172.0	238.8	328.0	295.0	571.8	Net Assets $mil

Performance 12-31-01

	1st Qtr	2nd Qtr	3rd Qtr	4th Qtr	Total
1997	2.36	15.19	4.72	0.22	23.75
1998	11.82	–0.62	–11.92	23.95	21.33
1999	10.16	3.49	–14.67	8.20	5.26
2000	–2.30	–0.57	2.54	0.90	0.51
2001	–4.39	7.39	–15.03	10.85	–3.30

Trailing	Total Return%	+/– S&P 500	+/– Russ Top 200 Val	% Rank All	% Rank Cat	Growth of $10,000
3 Mo	10.85	0.17	5.33	38	26	11,085
6 Mo	–5.81	–0.25	–0.03	67	77	9,419
1 Yr	–3.30	8.58	5.50	48	35	9,671
3 Yr Avg	0.76	1.79	–0.40	69	64	10,230
5 Yr Avg	8.96	–1.74	–2.24	24	49	15,359
10 Yr Avg	—	—	—	—	—	—
15 Yr Avg	—	—	—	—	—	—

Tax Analysis	Tax-Adj Ret%	%Rank Cat	%Pretax Ret	%Rank Cat
3 Yr Avg	0.61	48	79.6	23
5 Yr Avg	8.16	31	91.1	7
10 Yr Avg	—	—	—	—

Potential Capital Gain Exposure: 11% of assets

Risk Analysis

Time Period	Load-Adj Return %	Risk %Rank[1] All	Risk %Rank[1] Cat	Morningstar Return	Morningstar Risk	Morningstar Risk-Adj Rating
1 Yr	–3.30					
3 Yr	0.76	61	82	–0.85[2]	0.86	★★★
5 Yr	8.96	63	82	0.93[2]	0.87	★★★
Incept	10.75	—	—	—	—	

Average Historical Rating (65 months): 3.3★s

[1] 1=low, 100=high [2] T-Bill return substituted for category avg.

Category Rating (3 Yr)

1 2 3 4 5
Worst Best

Return Average
Risk Above Avg

Other Measures	Standard Index S&P 500	Best Fit Index S&P 500
Alpha	1.2	1.2
Beta	0.88	0.88
R-Squared	79	79

Standard Deviation	16.96
Mean	0.76
Sharpe Ratio	–0.29

Portfolio Analysis 09-30-01

Share change since 06-01 Total Stocks: 57	Sector	PE	YTD Ret%	% Assets
⊖ Lloyds TSB Grp	Financials	16.3	—	5.76
⊕ Washington Mutual	Financials	10.1	–5.32	5.54
IBM	Technology	26.9	43.00	5.46
⊖ TJX	Retail	23.2	44.39	4.55
Citigroup	Financials	20.0	0.03	3.99
⊖ Waste Mgmt	Services	52.3	15.03	3.89
Albertson's	Retail	29.7	22.01	3.84
UnitedHealth Grp	Financials	26.6	15.37	3.67
⊖ Bank One	Financials	29.1	9.13	3.65
Health Net	Health	35.7	–16.80	3.55
AOL Time Warner	Technology	—	–7.76	3.55
⊖ May Dept Stores	Retail	15.2	15.97	3.40
⊖ Eastman Kodak	Industrials	17.8	–21.90	3.22
⊖ J.P. Morgan Chase & Co.	Financials	27.8	–17.40	3.20
Dell Comp	Technology	61.8	55.87	3.11
⊕ MGIC Invest	Financials	10.9	–8.33	2.92
Bank of America	Financials	16.7	42.73	2.58
FleetBoston Finl	Financials	16.2	0.55	2.46
⊕ Alltel	Services	17.7	1.14	2.39
UnumProvident	Financials	10.7	0.77	2.25
Sprint	Services	20.5	1.18	2.25
Fannie Mae	Financials	16.2	–6.95	2.22
⊕ Circuit City Grp	Retail	99.8	126.70	2.19
⊖ Lexmark Intl	Technology	26.9	33.14	2.16
Kroger	Retail	16.3	–22.80	2.09

Current Investment Style

Style: Value Blnd Growth; Size: Large Med Small

	Stock Port Avg	Relative S&P 500 Current	Relative S&P 500 Hist	Rel Cat
Price/Earnings Ratio	26.3	0.85	0.78	1.04
Price/Book Ratio	4.3	0.75	0.76	1.03
Price/Cash Flow	12.7	0.71	0.81	0.92
3 Yr Earnings Growth	19.8	1.35	1.26	1.34
1 Yr Earnings Est%	–1.4	0.81	—	0.44
Med Mkt Cap $mil	28,515	0.5	0.7	0.90

Special Securities % assets 09-30-01

Restricted/Illiquid Secs	0
Emerging-Markets Secs	0
Options/Futures/Warrants	No

Composition % assets 09-30-01

Cash	0.8
Stocks*	99.2
Bonds	0.0
Other	0.0
*Foreign (% stocks)	6.2

Market Cap

Giant	40.9
Large	38.7
Medium	20.4
Small	0.0
Micro	0.0

Sector Weightings	% of Stocks	Rel S&P	5-Year High	5-Year Low
Utilities	0.0	0.0	2	0
Energy	0.0	0.0	10	0
Financials	32.3	1.8	35	10
Industrials	4.8	0.4	26	2
Durables	2.0	1.3	8	0
Staples	0.4	0.1	21	0
Services	13.7	1.3	19	4
Retail	15.4	2.3	15	0
Health	13.1	0.9	21	7
Technology	18.3	1.0	25	5

Analysis by Alan Papier 10-15-01

It's too bad Legg Mason American Leading Companies Trust isn't priced to be more successful.

This fund is swimming with iron weights tied to its wrists and ankles in the form of its 1.90% annual expense ratio, which is 50 basis points higher than its average peer's. To be sure, the fund is among the most expensive offerings in the large-value category, and that structural disadvantage adds up over time. For example, the fund posted an annualized gain of 9.57% for the five-year period ended Oct. 10, 2001. But an investment of $10,000 at the beginning of that period would have netted $364 more if the fund carried just average-size expenses.

In spite of that handicap, manager David Nelson has done a respectable job since taking over here in 1998. Indeed, the fund's after-tax three-year return ranked in the top third of the category. What's more, he successfully navigated a potential pothole when the fund absorbed Legg Mason Total Return in June 2001. Since the merger, Nelson has tweaked various positions based on his particular investment criteria. For instance, he bought additional shares of Washington Mutual to keep it among the fund's top holdings. Nelson thinks that the company exemplifies the type of investment he seeks—an industry leader (of financial services and mortgage lending) with strong management that trades cheaply based on a comparison of various valuation ratios.

That pursuit of value means that the fund can load up on specific sectors at times, and that it can be vulnerable when those market segments fall out of favor. Thus, it has been more volatile than most of its peers over time. Yet we think the fund's tax efficiency and sound strategy would still make it a decent option if only it weren't prohibitively expensive.

Address:	100 Light St. P.O. Box 1476 Baltimore, MD 21203–1476 800–577–8589 / 410–539–0000
Web Address:	www.leggmason.com
*Inception:	09-01-93
Advisor:	Legg Mason Funds Mgmt.
Subadvisor:	Legg Mason Cap. Mgmt.
NTF Plans:	Datalynx

Minimum Purchase:	$1000	Add: $100 IRA: $1000
Min Auto Inv Plan:	$1000	Add: $50
Sales Fees:	0.75%B, 0.25%S	
Management Fee:	.75%	
Actual Fees:	Mgt: 0.75%	Dist: 1.00%
Expense Projections:	3Yr: $597	5Yr: $1026 10Yr: $2222
Avg Brok Commission:	—	Income Distrib: Annually
Total Cost (relative to category):		Above Avg

Legg Mason Opportunity Prim

Ticker	Load	NAV	Yield	Total Assets	Mstar Category
LMOPX	1.00%d	$9.80	0.4%	$1,713.6 mil	Mid-Cap Blend

Prospectus Objective: Growth

Legg Mason Opportunity Fund - Primary shares seek capital appreciation.

The fund typically invests in equity securities. It normally invests in equity securities that the adviser believes are trading at a price below their intrinsic worth. The fund's management seeks securities that they feel have strong prospects for future growth. The adviser also considers securities undergoing restructurings and aquisitions as well as in securities that may benefit from economic and regulatory changes. The fund may invest in foreign securities. It may invest convertible securities and debt rated below investment-grade. The fund engage in derivative trading and short selling. The fund is nondiversified.

Historical Profile
Return —
Risk —
Rating Not Rated

Investment Style
Equity
Average Stock %: 85% (2000), 89% (12-01)

▼ Manager Change
▽ Partial Manager Change

Fund Performance vs. Category Average
■ Quarterly Fund Return +/– Category Average
— Category Baseline

Performance Quartile (within Category)

Portfolio Manager(s)

William H. Miller III, CFA. Since 12-99. BA'72 Washington & Lee U. Other funds currently managed: Legg Mason Value Prim, Legg Mason Value Instl, Masters' Select Equity.

History

	1990	1991	1992	1993	1994	1995	1996	1997	1998	1999	2000	12-01
NAV	—	—	—	—	—	—	—	—	—	10.00	9.65	9.80
Total Return %	—	—	—	—	—	—	—	—	—	—	–1.68	1.94
+/– S&P 500	—	—	—	—	—	—	—	—	—	–0.42*	7.42	13.82
+/– S&P Mid 400	—	—	—	—	—	—	—	—	—	—	–19.18	2.54
Income Return %	—	—	—	—	—	—	—	—	—	0.00	0.40	0.37
Capital Return %	—	—	—	—	—	—	—	—	—	0.00	–2.08	1.57
Total Rtn % Rank Cat	—	—	—	—	—	—	—	—	—	—	67	21
Income $	—	—	—	—	—	—	—	—	—	0.00	0.04	0.04
Capital Gains $	—	—	—	—	—	—	—	—	—	0.00	0.14	0.00
Expense Ratio %	—	—	—	—	—	—	—	—	—	1.99	—	—
Income Ratio %	—	—	—	—	—	—	—	—	—	—	—	—
Turnover Rate %	—	—	—	—	—	—	—	—	—	—	—	—
Net Assets $mil	—	—	—	—	—	—	—	—	—	—	1,112.1	1,713.6

Performance 12-31-01

	1st Qtr	2nd Qtr	3rd Qtr	4th Qtr	Total
1997	—	—	—	—	—
1998	—	—	—	—	—
1999	—	—	—	—	0.00 *
2000	6.70	–2.72	5.78	–10.46	–1.68
2001	5.60	11.48	–29.49	22.81	1.94

Trailing	Total Return%	+/– S&P 500	+/– S&P Mid 400	% Rank All	% Rank Cat	Growth of $10,000
3 Mo	22.81	12.13	4.83	10	11	12,281
6 Mo	–13.40	–7.85	–11.85	92	97	8,660
1 Yr	1.94	13.82	2.54	39	21	10,194
3 Yr Avg	—	—	—	—	—	—
5 Yr Avg	—	—	—	—	—	—
10 Yr Avg	—	—	—	—	—	—
15 Yr Avg	—	—	—	—	—	—

Tax Analysis	Tax-Adj Ret%	%Rank Cat	%Pretax Ret	%Rank Cat
3 Yr Avg	—	—	—	—
5 Yr Avg	—	—	—	—
10 Yr Avg	—	—	—	—

Potential Capital Gain Exposure: NMF

Risk Analysis

Time Period	Load-Adj Return %	Risk %Rank¹ All	Risk %Rank¹ Cat	Morningstar Return	Morningstar Risk	Morningstar Risk-Adj Rating
1 Yr	1.94					
3 Yr	—	—	—	—	—	
5 Yr	—	—	—	—	—	
Incept	0.11	—	—	—	—	

Average Historical Rating —

¹1=low, 100=high

Category Rating (3 Yr)

Other Measures	Standard Index S&P 500	Best Fit Index
Alpha	—	—
Beta	—	—
R-Squared	—	—
Standard Deviation		—
Return — Mean		—
Risk — Sharpe Ratio		—

Portfolio Analysis 09-30-01

Share change since 06-01 Total Stocks: 34	Sector	PE	YTD Ret%	% Assets
⊖ Republic Svcs Cl A	Services	15.6	16.19	6.04
⊖ Cott	Staples	—	108.50	5.23
☼ Level 3 Comms	Services	—	–84.70	5.03
UnumProvident	Financials	10.7	0.77	4.42
Level 3 Comm 9.125%	N/A	—	—	4.41
⊕ Oxford Health Plans	Health	11.5	–23.70	4.10
⊕ Nextel Comms Cl A	Services	—	–55.70	3.92
Amazon.com Cv 4.75%	N/A	—	—	3.78
Pentair	Industrials	38.0	54.40	3.74
⊕ Abercrombie & Fitch Cl A	Retail	16.4	32.65	3.48
☼ Entercom Comms	Services	NMF	45.19	3.43
☼ Providian Finl	Financials	1.4	–93.80	3.37
⊕ Viad	Services	36.4	4.48	3.11
Symantec	Technology	—	98.74	2.93
⊖ Washington Mutual	Financials	10.1	–5.32	2.93
⊖ Tricon Global Restaurants	Services	16.3	49.09	2.87
⊕ Unisys	Technology	28.5	–14.20	2.70
⊕ AOL Time Warner	Technology	—	–7.76	2.52
☼ Conseco	Financials	—	–66.10	2.48
Mandalay Resort Grp	Services	15.3	–2.45	2.47
⊕ Amazon.com	Retail	—	–30.40	2.34
Omnicare	Health	38.3	15.52	2.32
⊕ Gateway Inc	Technology	—	–55.30	2.32
⊕ Acxiom	Technology	—	–55.10	2.29
⊖ Hollywood Entrtnmt	Retail	—	1,244.00	2.28

Current Investment Style

Style: Value Blnd Growth; Size: Large Med Small

	Stock Port Avg	Relative S&P 500 Current	Relative S&P 500 Hist	Rel Cat
Price/Earnings Ratio	22.2	0.72	—	0.82
Price/Book Ratio	3.5	0.62	—	0.82
Price/Cash Flow	12.0	0.67	—	0.69
3 Yr Earnings Growth	17.8¹	1.22	—	1.07
1 Yr Earnings Est%	–4.3	2.41	—	–1.88
Med Mkt Cap $mil	2,555	0.0	—	0.28

¹figure is based on 50% or less of stocks

Analysis by Christopher Traulsen 12-03-01

Legg Mason Opportunity Trust has a good shot at being worth its risks—just don't put it at the heart of your portfolio.

Bill Miller has repeatedly called this fund an experiment, and he isn't kidding. While he uses the same wide-ranging stock-picking strategy here that he does at Value Trust, the fund is otherwise quite different. It's much more concentrated than Value Trust, with anywhere from 20 to 35 names in its portfolio at any given time. Its smaller asset base also allows Miller to take sizable positions in small- and mid-cap stocks if he chooses—which Value Trust is too large to do. Finally, Miller expects to employ strategies here that aren't common at mutual funds, including shorting securities and making currency bets.

What all of this means is that the fund is risky. To see why, one needs look no further than this year. Miller has, at various points, loaded up on troubled telecom and networking names such as Level 3 Communications and Exodus, and has also delved into badly hurt financials such as Providian and Conseco. He's also shorted the Nasdaq 100 index at various points during the year, albeit with good results.

While the fund has delivered a top-quartile year-to-date return of 0.2%, its performance has been anything but smooth. It gained 21% in 2001's first five months, fell 31% from June through September, then soared 18% in November. Picks such as Level 3 are a big part of the reason why. The fund had over 9% of its assets in the common stock and debt of Level 3 at the end of September, and the stock was up 61% over the trailing month, after losing 31% in the third quarter.

Bill Miller is one of the most talented investors there is, period. If you're going to buy a souped-up, focused fund, he's exactly who you want at the helm. But take this fund for what it is—an experiment that should be at the fringe of your portfolio, not the core.

Special Securities % assets 09-30-01	
Restricted/Illiquid Secs	1
Emerging-Markets Secs	0
Options/Futures/Warrants	No

Sector Weightings	% of Stocks	Rel S&P	5-Year High	5-Year Low
Utilities	0.0	0.0	—	—
Energy	2.4	0.3	—	—
Financials	17.5	1.0	—	—
Industrials	4.2	0.4	—	—
Durables	0.0	0.0	—	—
Staples	5.9	0.7	—	—
Services	34.0	3.1	—	—
Retail	9.1	1.3	—	—
Health	7.2	0.5	—	—
Technology	19.8	1.1	—	—

Composition % assets 09-30-01	
Cash	1.0
Stocks*	88.2
Bonds	6.5
Other	4.4
*Foreign (% stocks)	8.4

Market Cap	
Giant	4.1
Large	3.3
Medium	74.2
Small	16.8
Micro	1.7

Address: 100 Light St. P.O. Box 1476, Baltimore, MD 21203–1476, 410–539–0000 / 800–577–8589
Web Address: www.leggmason.com
*Inception: 12-30-99
Advisor: LMM
Subadvisor: Legg Mason Fund Adviser
NTF Plans: N/A

Minimum Purchase: $1000 Add: $100 IRA: $1000
Min Auto Inv Plan: $1000 Add: $50
Sales Fees: 1.00%D, 0.75%B, 0.25%S
Management Fee: 1.0% mx./.75% mn.
Actual Fees: Mgt: 1.00% Dist: 1.00%
Expense Projections: 3Yr: $707 5Yr: — 10Yr: —
Avg Brok Commission: — Income Distrib: Annually
Total Cost (relative to category): —

Legg Mason Special Investment Prim

Ticker	Load	NAV	Yield	Total Assets	Mstar Category
LMASX	12b–1 only	$33.73	0.0%	$2,251.0 mil	Mid–Cap Blend

Prospectus Objective: Small Company

Legg Mason Special Investment Trust seeks capital appreciation.

The fund invests primarily in equity securities issued by companies with market capitalizations of less than $2.5 billion, emphasizing securities that appear to be undervalued in relation to their long-term earning power or asset values. The fund also seeks firms involved in special situations that may prompt a price increase in their securities. The fund may invest up to 20% of assets in companies involved in actual or anticipated reorganizations or restructurings.

Primary shares have level loads; Navigator shares are designed for institutional investors.

Historical Profile

Return Above Avg
Risk Above Avg
Rating ★★★★ Above Avg

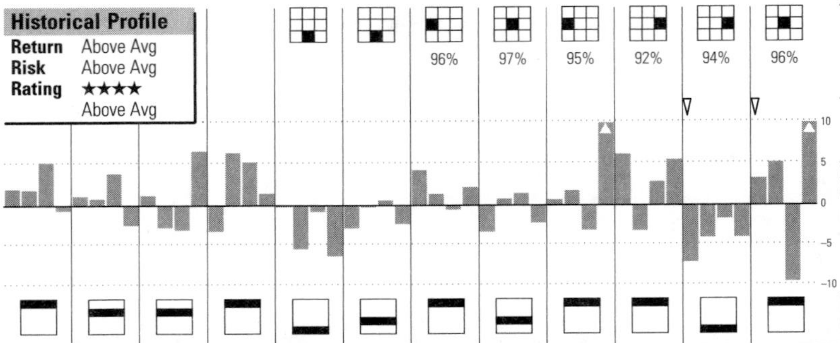

Investment Style
Equity
Average Stock %

1996	1997	1998	1999	2000	2001
96%	97%	95%	92%	94%	96%

▼ Manager Change
▽ Partial Manager Change

Fund Performance vs. Category Average
Quarterly Fund Return +/– Category Average
— Category Baseline

Performance Quartile (within Category)

Portfolio Manager(s)

Lisa O. Rapuano, CFA. Since 1-00. BA Yale U. Other fund currently managed: Legg Mason Special Investment Instl.

History

1990	1991	1992	1993	1994	1995	1996	1997	1998	1999	2000	12–01	History
12.12	16.78	17.98	22.14	19.03	22.81	27.83	32.27	36.70	40.15	33.94	33.73	NAV
0.52	39.44	15.36	24.13	–13.07	22.50	28.65	22.12	23.31	35.54	–12.00	2.26	Total Return %
3.64	8.96	7.74	14.07	–14.39	–15.03	5.70	–11.23	–5.27	14.50	–2.90	14.14	+/– S&P 500
5.64	–10.62	3.46	10.20	–9.48	–8.42	9.47	–10.13	4.19	20.82	–29.50	2.86	+/– S&P Mid 400
2.01	0.25	0.66	0.17	0.00	0.16	0.00	0.00	0.00	0.00	0.00	0.00	Income Return %
–1.49	39.20	14.71	23.96	–13.07	22.34	28.65	22.12	23.31	35.54	–12.00	2.26	Capital Return %
7	39	36	10	92	71	8	74	9	14	87	20	Total Rtn % Rank Cat
0.27	0.03	0.11	0.03	0.00	0.03	0.00	0.00	0.00	0.00	0.00	0.00	Income $
1.32	0.08	1.10	0.14	0.23	0.44	1.41	1.50	2.66	8.04	1.52	1.00	Capital Gains $
2.30	2.30	2.10	2.00	1.94	1.93	1.96	1.92	1.86	1.84	1.80	1.79	Expense Ratio %
1.00	1.40	0.80	0.20	0.00	–0.20	0.00	–0.90	–1.10	–1.00	–1.20	–0.90	Income Ratio %
116	76	57	33	17	28	36	29	30	48	29	37	Turnover Rate %
76.2	163.6	287.4	510.0	581.6	713.4	964.4	1,366.8	1,730.2	2,567.4	2,281.1	2,241.9	Net Assets $mil

Performance 12-31-01

	1st Qtr	2nd Qtr	3rd Qtr	4th Qtr	Total
1997	–4.60	15.84	15.12	–4.01	22.12
1998	11.62	–0.86	–20.49	40.13	23.31
1999	5.69	7.99	–3.18	22.64	35.54
2000	0.32	–6.86	2.77	–8.37	–12.00
2001	–6.22	14.34	–26.29	29.38	2.26

Trailing	Total Return%	+/– S&P 500	+/– S&P Mid 400	% Rank All	% Rank Cat	Growth of $10,000
3 Mo	29.38	18.70	11.40	5	3	12,938
6 Mo	–4.64	0.92	–3.08	60	62	9,536
1 Yr	2.26	14.14	2.86	39	20	10,226
3 Yr Avg	6.84	7.87	–3.40	17	47	12,197
5 Yr Avg	12.93	2.23	–3.18	8	28	18,367
10 Yr Avg	13.68	0.75	–1.33	10	38	36,030
15 Yr Avg	14.02	0.28	–1.97	10	25	71,551

Tax Analysis	Tax-Adj Ret%	%Rank Cat	%Pretax Ret	%Rank Cat
3 Yr Avg	4.94	44	72.2	56
5 Yr Avg	11.12	24	86.0	24
10 Yr Avg	12.18	29	89.1	3

Potential Capital Gain Exposure: 26% of assets

Risk Analysis

Time Period	Load-Adj Return %	Risk %Rank[1] All	Risk %Rank[1] Cat	Morningstar Return	Morningstar Risk	Morningstar Risk-Adj Rating
1 Yr	2.26					
3 Yr	6.84	74	71	0.41[2]	1.02	★★★★
5 Yr	12.93	79	76	2.01[2]	1.11	★★★★
10 Yr	13.68	87	83	1.47	1.24	★★★

Average Historical Rating (157 months): 3.2★s

[1] 1=low, 100=high [2] T-Bill return substituted for category avg.

Category Rating (3 Yr)

1 2 **3** 4 5
Worst Best

Return Average
Risk Above Avg

Other Measures	Standard Index S&P 500	Best Fit Index Wil 4500
Alpha	10.0	4.6
Beta	1.12	0.70
R-Squared	64	68
Standard Deviation		25.86
Mean		6.84
Sharpe Ratio		0.08

Analysis by Christopher Traulsen 12-02-01

Legg Mason Special Investment Trust requires a mountain of patience and a strong stomach, but it's probably worth the wait.

This fund's 3.4% loss for the year to date through November 30, 2001 is a smaller drop than three fourths of its mid-blend peers', but it has taken a roller-coaster ride to get there. From April 1 through May 31, it logged a 17% increase, only to plunge nearly 30% from June through September, followed by a 15% runup in the past month.

Such ups and downs are the norm here. Manager Lisa Rapuano has only been flying solo at this fund since January 2001, but even when Bill Miller was comanager, the portfolio was extremely volatile. In August 1998, for example, it lost 25%, only to sprint to a 62% gain over the ensuing five months.

The reasons for the fund's gut-wrenching performances are pretty clear. First, it is concentrated, with more than half its assets in its top-10 holdings at the end of the third quarter. Second, Rapuano, like Miller, is willing to bet big on stocks in some high-risk industries, including some that traditional value managers would find quite pricey. At the end of September, for example, 25% of the fund's stock portfolio was devoted to the tech sector, including emerging names such as wireless-email concern Research in Motion.

A few missteps can badly dent returns, but when Rapuano's picks work, the fund can soar. Anti-virus software maker Symantec, for example, is up 95% thus far in 2001. Rapuano is off to a strong start here overall, and has exhibited considerable savvy over the years as the shop's lead tech and media analyst. This is a risky pick, but we think Rapuano has the skills to reward investors who have the time and risk tolerance to ride out some sizable bumps.

Portfolio Analysis 09-30-01

Share change since 06–01 Total Stocks: 33	Sector	PE	YTD Ret%	% Assets
⊖ Republic Svcs Cl A	Services	15.6	16.19	7.74
⊖ Radian Grp	Financials	11.6	14.64	6.89
Symantec	Technology	—	98.74	5.75
⊖ WellPoint Health Networks	Health	19.4	1.39	5.71
⊖ Caremark Rx	Health	46.6	20.25	5.61
UnumProvident	Financials	10.7	0.77	4.87
Mandalay Resort Grp	Services	15.3	–2.45	3.76
UnionBanCal	Financials	16.7	62.76	3.73
⊖ TJX	Retail	23.2	44.39	3.62
AOL Time Warner	Technology	—	–7.76	3.46
WPP Grp	Services	23.2	—	3.22
⊕ Level 3 Comms	Services	—	–84.70	3.12
☼ Entercom Comms	Services	NMF	45.19	2.93
⊕ Sybase	Technology	NMF	–20.40	2.77
Manpower	Services	17.0	–10.70	2.62
Amazon.com Cv 4.75%	N/A	—	—	2.60
Acxiom	Technology	—	–55.10	2.59
⊖ Ceridian	Technology	27.6	–5.96	2.40
Big Lots	Retail	17.1	–2.02	2.28
⊕ Research in Motion	Technology	—	–70.30	2.18
⊖ Cadence Design Sys	Technology	5.3	–20.20	2.12
⊖ Proquest Company	N/A	—	—	1.98
Banknorth Grp	Financials	13.3	15.81	1.97
Sovereign Bancorp	Financials	76.5	52.19	1.88
⊕ Cell Genesys	Health	89.4	1.87	1.85

Current Investment Style

Style: Value Blnd Growth; Size: Large Med Small

	Stock Port Avg	Relative S&P 500 Current	Relative S&P 500 Hist	Rel Cat
Price/Earnings Ratio	24.7	0.80	0.86	0.91
Price/Book Ratio	3.4	0.59	0.86	0.79
Price/Cash Flow	13.4	0.74	0.81	0.77
3 Yr Earnings Growth	13.5[1]	0.92	1.56	0.81
1 Yr Earnings Est%	–24.8	14.01	—	–10.92
Med Mkt Cap $mil	3,658	0.1	0.1	0.41

[1] figure is based on 50% or less of stocks

Special Securities % assets 09-30-01	
Restricted/Illiquid Secs	0
Emerging–Markets Secs	0
Options/Futures/Warrants	No

Composition % assets 09-30-01	
Cash	0.5
Stocks*	96.9
Bonds	0.0
Other	2.6
*Foreign (% stocks)	5.6

Market Cap	
Giant	3.7
Large	7.2
Medium	73.1
Small	16.1
Micro	0.0

Sector Weightings	% of Stocks	Rel S&P	5-Year High	5-Year Low
Utilities	0.0	0.0	9	0
Energy	0.0	0.0	1	0
Financials	22.9	1.3	48	9
Industrials	0.0	0.0	8	0
Durables	0.0	0.0	15	0
Staples	0.0	0.0	7	0
Services	29.5	2.7	38	11
Retail	8.1	1.2	17	4
Health	13.9	0.9	17	3
Technology	25.7	1.4	55	1

Address: 100 Light St. P.O. Box 1476
Baltimore, MD 21203–1476
800–577–8589 / 410–539–0000
Web Address: www.leggmason.com
Inception: 12-30-85
Advisor: Legg Mason Fund Adviser
Subadvisor: None
NTF Plans: Datalynx

Minimum Purchase: $1000 Add: $100 IRA: $1000
Min Auto Inv Plan: $1000 Add: $50
Sales Fees: 0.75%B, 0.25%S
Management Fee: 1.0% mx./.65% mn.
Actual Fees: Mgt: 0.70% Dist: 1.00%
Expense Projections: 3Yr: $566 5Yr: $975 10Yr: $2116
Avg Brok Commission: — Income Distrib: Annually
Total Cost (relative to category): Average

Legg Mason Value Prim

Ticker	Load	NAV	Yield	Total Assets	Mstar Category
LMVTX	12b–1 only	$50.06	0.0%	$11,758.2 mil	Large Value

Prospectus Objective: Growth

Legg Mason Value Trust seeks long-term growth of capital.

The fund invests primarily in equity securities that are undervalued in relation to the long-term earning power or asset value of their issuers. It generally invests in companies with market capitalizations in excess of $5 billion, but may invest in companies of any size. The fund may invest up to 25% of assets long-term debt securities. Up to 10% of assets may be invested in debt securities rated below investment-grade.

Primary shares have level loads; Institutional, Financial Intermediary & Navigator shares are designed for institutional investors.

Historical Profile
Return High
Risk Average
Rating ★★★★★ Highest

Investment Style
Equity
Average Stock %: 91% 91% 92% 94% 98% 99%

▼ Manager Change
▽ Partial Manager Change

Fund Performance vs. Category Average
■ Quarterly Fund Return +/– Category Average
— Category Baseline

Performance Quartile (within Category)

Portfolio Manager(s)

William H. Miller III, CFA. Since 4-82. BA'72 Washington & Lee U. Other funds currently managed: Legg Mason Value Instl, Masters' Select Equity, Legg Mason Opportunity Prim.

1990	1991	1992	1993	1994	1995	1996	1997	1998	1999	2000	12–01	History
11.84	15.70	17.32	18.87	19.04	25.19	32.99	42.74	61.58	75.27	55.44	50.06	NAV
–16.96	34.73	11.44	11.26	1.39	40.76	38.43	37.05	48.04	26.71	–7.14	–9.29	Total Return %
–13.84	4.25	3.82	1.20	0.07	3.23	15.49	3.70	19.47	5.67	1.97	2.59	+/– S&P 500
–13.29	16.57	2.37	–8.50	3.70	0.73	16.12	1.56	26.80	15.76	–9.45	–0.50	+/– Russ Top 200 Val
2.48	1.91	1.02	1.04	0.27	0.93	0.66	0.11	0.00	0.00	0.00	0.00	Income Return %
–19.43	32.82	10.42	10.22	1.12	39.83	37.77	36.94	48.04	26.71	–7.14	–9.29	Capital Return %
97	15	32	69	23	5	2	2	1	3	95	74	Total Rtn % Rank Cat
0.36	0.23	0.16	0.18	0.05	0.17	0.16	0.04	0.00	0.00	0.00	0.00	Income $
0.04	0.00	0.00	0.20	0.04	1.24	1.53	2.32	1.41	2.46	14.47	0.26	Capital Gains $
1.86	1.90	1.90	1.86	1.82	1.81	1.82	1.77	1.73	1.69	1.68	1.69	Expense Ratio %
2.20	2.50	1.70	1.10	0.50	0.50	0.80	0.40	–0.10	–0.40	–0.60	–0.50	Income Ratio %
31	39	39	22	26	20	20	11	13	19	20	27	Turnover Rate %
636.2	747.9	842.0	913.9	932.5	1,340.4	1,976.1	3,683.1	8,079.2	12,540.1	10,596.8	9,788.5	Net Assets $mil

Performance 12-31-01

	1st Qtr	2nd Qtr	3rd Qtr	4th Qtr	Total
1997	3.40	18.05	16.49	–3.62	37.05
1998	17.20	5.23	–11.64	35.86	48.04
1999	18.69	–0.58	–9.70	18.91	26.71
2000	–0.01	–3.31	1.78	–5.63	–7.14
2001	–3.08	7.33	–20.01	9.02	–9.29

Trailing	Total Return%	+/– S&P 500	+/– Russ Top 200 Val	% Rank All	% Rank Cat	Growth of $10,000
3 Mo	9.02	–1.67	3.50	47	50	10,902
6 Mo	–12.80	–7.24	–7.02	91	100	8,720
1 Yr	–9.29	2.59	–0.50	59	74	9,071
3 Yr Avg	2.20	3.22	1.03	61	48	10,673
5 Yr Avg	16.71	6.01	5.51	3	1	21,655
10 Yr Avg	18.16	5.23	4.13	1	1	53,045
15 Yr Avg	15.16	1.43	1.66	6	5	83,093

Tax Analysis	Tax-Adj Ret%	%Rank Cat	%Pretax Ret	%Rank Cat
3 Yr Avg	0.43	50	19.7	90
5 Yr Avg	15.10	1	90.3	8
10 Yr Avg	16.78	1	92.4	4

Potential Capital Gain Exposure: 9% of assets

Risk Analysis

Time Period	Load-Adj Return %	Risk %Rank[1] All	Risk %Rank[1] Cat	Morningstar Return	Morningstar Risk	Morningstar Risk-Adj Rating
1 Yr	–9.29					
3 Yr	2.20	71	97	–0.57[2]	0.98	★★★
5 Yr	16.71	70	96	3.19[2]	0.95	★★★★★
10 Yr	18.16	75	94	2.70	0.97	★★★★★

Average Historical Rating (193 months): 3.6★s

[1] 1=low, 100=high [2] T-Bill return substituted for category avg.

Category Rating (3 Yr)

1 2 **3** 4 5
Worst Best

Return Average
Risk High

Other Measures	Standard Index S&P 500	Best Fit Index S&P 500
Alpha	4.5	4.5
Beta	1.11	1.11
R-Squared	82	82
Standard Deviation		21.62
Mean		2.20
Sharpe Ratio		–0.15

Portfolio Analysis 09-30-01

Share change since 06–01 Total Stocks: 36	Sector	PE	YTD Ret%	% Assets
⊖ UnitedHealth Grp	Financials	26.6	15.37	7.02
⊖ Waste Mgmt	Services	52.3	15.03	6.90
⊖ Washington Mutual	Financials	10.1	–5.32	5.75
⊖ Albertson's	Retail	29.7	22.01	5.16
AOL Time Warner	Technology	—	–7.76	4.95
MGIC Invest	Financials	10.9	–8.33	4.88
Bank One	Financials	29.1	9.13	3.82
⊕ Citigroup	Financials	20.0	0.03	3.78
⊖ McKesson HBOC	Health	—	4.92	3.53
⊕ Kroger	Retail	16.3	–22.80	3.38
⊖ Fannie Mae	Financials	16.2	–6.95	3.36
⊕ Eastman Kodak	Industrials	17.8	–21.90	3.35
FleetBoston Finl	Financials	16.2	0.55	3.26
Lloyds TSB Grp	Financials	16.3	—	3.08
IBM	Technology	26.9	43.00	2.93
J.P. Morgan Chase & Co.	Financials	27.8	–17.40	2.71
☼ Qwest Comms Intl	Services	—	–65.40	2.18
⊖ Dell Comp	Technology	61.8	55.87	2.16
⊕ WPP Grp	Services	23.2	—	2.14
⊖ Toys "R" Us	Retail	28.8	24.28	2.11
⊖ Health Net	Health	35.7	–16.80	1.99
⊕ Nextel Comms Cl A	Services	—	–55.70	1.94
⊖ Starwood Hotels & Resorts	Services	18.7	–12.90	1.85
⊖ Berkshire Hathaway Cl A	Financials	—	—	1.77
Amazon.com	Retail	—	–30.40	1.67

Current Investment Style

Style: Value Blnd Growth; Size: Large Med Small

	Stock Port Avg	Relative S&P 500 Current	Relative S&P 500 Hist	Rel Cat
Price/Earnings Ratio	25.8	0.83	0.86	1.03
Price/Book Ratio	3.4	0.60	1.05	0.83
Price/Cash Flow	10.5	0.58	0.89	0.76
3 Yr Earnings Growth	20.6	1.41	1.48	1.40
1 Yr Earnings Est%	4.1	—	—	–1.24
Med Mkt Cap $mil	20,860	0.3	0.5	0.66

[1] figure is based on 50% or less of stocks

Special Securities % assets 09-30-01	
Restricted/Illiquid Secs	0
Emerging–Markets Secs	0
Options/Futures/Warrants	No

Composition % assets 09-30-01	
Cash	2.2
Stocks*	97.8
Bonds	0.0
Other	0.0
*Foreign (% stocks)	5.3

Market Cap	
Giant	27.2
Large	49.6
Medium	23.3
Small	0.0
Micro	0.0

Sector Weightings	% of Stocks	Rel S&P	5-Year High	5-Year Low
Utilities	1.1	0.4	13	0
Energy	0.0	0.0	4	0
Financials	36.2	2.0	54	25
Industrials	4.4	0.4	9	0
Durables	1.5	0.9	19	1
Staples	0.0	0.0	12	0
Services	17.3	1.6	27	3
Retail	12.5	1.9	13	1
Health	12.8	0.9	14	2
Technology	14.2	0.8	41	0

Analysis by Christopher Traulsen 10-14-01

Legg Mason Value Trust remains a great choice for the right investor.

This fund has recently endured a considerable rough patch. Over the past three months ended Oct. 12, 2001, it has lost 16%—6 percentage points more than the S&P 500 index and a much greater loss than the average large-value fund. In 2000, although it beat the S&P 500 index for a tenth straight year, it lagged its average peer by a huge amount.

The reasons for its underperformance are clear. In addition to shopping traditional value arenas such as financials, manager Bill Miller plies beaten-down growth areas looking to pick up companies he thinks are mispriced. In 2001, for example, he has bought telecom-equipment companies such as Tellabs and Corning and added substantially to a position in e-tailer Amazon.com. As the economy has slowed and the technology and telecom sectors in particular have come under pressure, this fund has been hit far harder than its average rival.

Miller still thinks these companies are worth significantly more than their market values. He even took advantage of their continued slide in the third quarter to add to some positions. He also bought a new stake in Lucent. It's cheap, and Miller thinks its balance sheet and growth rate are improving.

While some quibble about Miller's definition of value, the debate seems fruitless. The fact is, Miller has been extremely adept at identifying enough mispriced securities to outperform the market on a fairly regular basis. In that regard, this offering's spectacular record speaks for itself. The cost of his style is that the fund ventures into areas where there is considerable business risk and added volatility imparted by herd-like trading patterns.

Clearly, this fund is a poor fit for investors seeking to diversify a growth-heavy portfolio. For others, though, we continue to think it's among the best there is.

Address:	100 Light St. P.O. Box 1476 Baltimore, MD 21203–1476 800–577–8589 / 410–539–0000
Web Address:	www.leggmason.com
Inception:	04-16-82
Advisor:	Legg Mason Fund Adviser
Subadvisor:	None
NTF Plans:	Datalynx

Minimum Purchase:	$1000	Add: $100	IRA: $1000
Min Auto Inv Plan:	$1000	Add: $50	
Sales Fees:	0.70%B, 0.25%S		
Management Fee:	1.0% mx./.65% mn.		
Actual Fees:	Mgt: 0.66%	Dist: 0.95%	
Expense Projections:	3Yr: $530	5Yr: $913	10Yr: $1987
Avg Brok Commission:	—	Income Distrib: Quarterly	
Total Cost (relative to category):		Average	

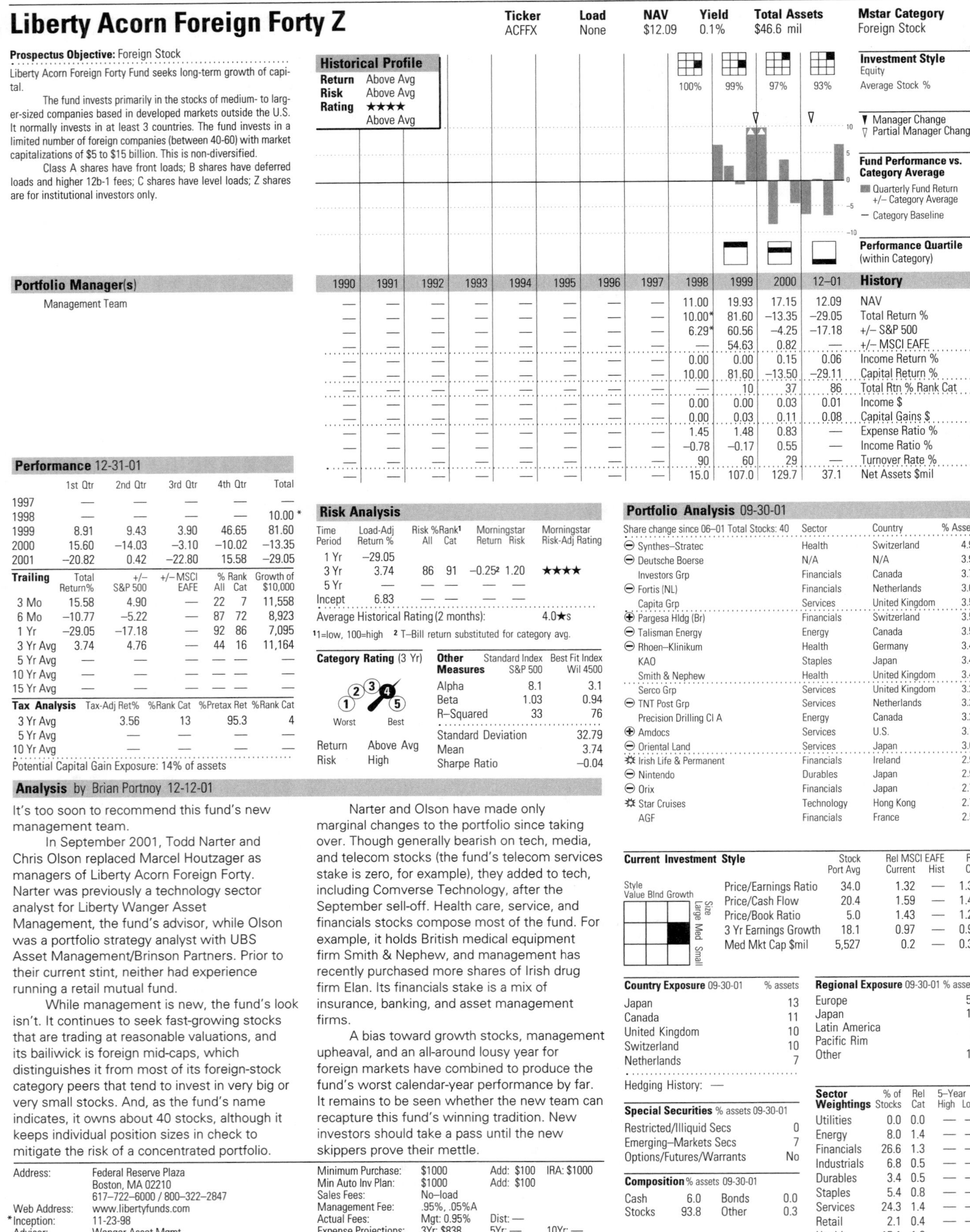

Liberty Acorn Foreign Forty Z

Ticker	Load	NAV	Yield	Total Assets	Mstar Category
ACFFX	None	$12.09	0.1%	$46.6 mil	Foreign Stock

Prospectus Objective: Foreign Stock

Liberty Acorn Foreign Forty Fund seeks long-term growth of capital.

The fund invests primarily in the stocks of medium- to larger-sized companies based in developed markets outside the U.S. It normally invests in at least 3 countries. The fund invests in a limited number of foreign companies (between 40-60) with market capitalizations of $5 to $15 billion. This is non-diversified.

Class A shares have front loads; B shares have deferred loads and higher 12b-1 fees; C shares have level loads; Z shares are for institutional investors only.

Historical Profile

Return: Above Avg
Risk: Above Avg
Rating: ★★★★ Above Avg

Investment Style
Equity
Average Stock %: 100% (1998), 99% (1999), 97% (2000), 93% (12-01)

▼ Manager Change
▽ Partial Manager Change

Fund Performance vs. Category Average
■ Quarterly Fund Return +/– Category Average
— Category Baseline

Performance Quartile (within Category)

Portfolio Manager(s)

Management Team

History

1990	1991	1992	1993	1994	1995	1996	1997	1998	1999	2000	12-01	History
—	—	—	—	—	—	—	—	11.00	19.93	17.15	12.09	NAV
—	—	—	—	—	—	—	—	10.00*	81.60	–13.35	–29.05	Total Return %
—	—	—	—	—	—	—	—	6.29*	60.56	–4.25	–17.18	+/– S&P 500
—	—	—	—	—	—	—	—	—	54.63	0.82	—	+/– MSCI EAFE
—	—	—	—	—	—	—	—	0.00	0.00	0.15	0.06	Income Return %
—	—	—	—	—	—	—	—	10.00	81.60	–13.50	–29.11	Capital Return %
—	—	—	—	—	—	—	—	—	10	37	86	Total Rtn % Rank Cat
—	—	—	—	—	—	—	—	0.00	0.00	0.03	0.01	Income $
—	—	—	—	—	—	—	—	0.00	0.03	0.11	0.08	Capital Gains $
—	—	—	—	—	—	—	—	1.45	1.48	0.83	—	Expense Ratio %
—	—	—	—	—	—	—	—	–0.78	–0.17	0.55	—	Income Ratio %
—	—	—	—	—	—	—	—	90	60	29	—	Turnover Rate %
—	—	—	—	—	—	—	—	15.0	107.0	129.7	37.1	Net Assets $mil

Performance 12-31-01

	1st Qtr	2nd Qtr	3rd Qtr	4th Qtr	Total
1997	—	—	—	—	—
1998	—	—	—	—	10.00 *
1999	8.91	9.43	3.90	46.65	81.60
2000	15.60	–14.03	–3.10	–10.02	–13.35
2001	–20.82	0.42	–22.80	15.58	–29.05

Trailing	Total Return%	+/– S&P 500	+/– MSCI EAFE	% Rank All	% Rank Cat	Growth of $10,000
3 Mo	15.58	4.90	—	22	7	11,558
6 Mo	–10.77	–5.22	—	87	72	8,923
1 Yr	–29.05	–17.18	—	92	86	7,095
3 Yr Avg	3.74	4.76	—	44	16	11,164
5 Yr Avg	—	—	—	—	—	—
10 Yr Avg	—	—	—	—	—	—
15 Yr Avg	—	—	—	—	—	—

Tax Analysis	Tax-Adj Ret%	%Rank Cat	%Pretax Ret	%Rank Cat
3 Yr Avg	3.56	13	95.3	4
5 Yr Avg	—	—	—	—
10 Yr Avg	—	—	—	—

Potential Capital Gain Exposure: 14% of assets

Risk Analysis

Time Period	Load-Adj Return %	Risk %Rank[1] All	Risk %Rank[1] Cat	Morningstar Return	Morningstar Risk	Morningstar Risk-Adj Rating
1 Yr	–29.05					
3 Yr	3.74	86	91	–0.25[2]	1.20	★★★★
5 Yr	—	—	—	—	—	
Incept	6.83	—	—	—	—	

Average Historical Rating (2 months): 4.0★s

[1]1=low, 100=high [2] T-Bill return substituted for category avg.

Category Rating (3 Yr)

1 2 3 4 5
Worst Best

Return: Above Avg
Risk: High

Other Measures	Standard Index S&P 500	Best Fit Index Wil 4500
Alpha	8.1	3.1
Beta	1.03	0.94
R–Squared	33	76

Standard Deviation	32.79
Mean	3.74
Sharpe Ratio	–0.04

Portfolio Analysis 09-30-01

Share change since 06–01 Total Stocks: 40

	Sector	Country	% Assets
⊖ Synthes–Stratec	Health	Switzerland	4.94
⊖ Deutsche Boerse	N/A	N/A	3.92
Investors Grp	Financials	Canada	3.78
⊖ Fortis (NL)	Financials	Netherlands	3.69
Capita Grp	Services	United Kingdom	3.59
⊕ Pargesa Hldg (Br)	Financials	Switzerland	3.59
⊖ Talisman Energy	Energy	Canada	3.55
⊖ Rhoen–Klinikum	Health	Germany	3.48
KAO	Staples	Japan	3.48
Smith & Nephew	Health	United Kingdom	3.45
Serco Grp	Services	United Kingdom	3.27
⊖ TNT Post Grp	Services	Netherlands	3.25
Precision Drilling Cl A	Energy	Canada	3.20
⊕ Amdocs	Services	U.S.	3.12
⊖ Oriental Land	Services	Japan	3.07
☼ Irish Life & Permanent	Financials	Ireland	2.97
⊖ Nintendo	Durables	Japan	2.92
⊖ Orix	Financials	Japan	2.75
☼ Star Cruises	Technology	Hong Kong	2.72
AGF	Financials	France	2.59

Current Investment Style

Style: Value Blnd Growth; Size: Large Med Small

	Stock Port Avg	Rel MSCI EAFE Current	Rel MSCI EAFE Hist	Rel Cat
Price/Earnings Ratio	34.0	1.32	—	1.33
Price/Cash Flow	20.4	1.59	—	1.42
Price/Book Ratio	5.0	1.43	—	1.27
3 Yr Earnings Growth	18.1	0.97	—	0.92
Med Mkt Cap $mil	5,527	0.2	—	0.31

Country Exposure 09-30-01	% assets
Japan	13
Canada	11
United Kingdom	10
Switzerland	10
Netherlands	7

Hedging History: —

Regional Exposure 09-30-01	% assets
Europe	50
Japan	13
Latin America	0
Pacific Rim	9
Other	15

Special Securities % assets 09-30-01	
Restricted/Illiquid Secs	0
Emerging–Markets Secs	7
Options/Futures/Warrants	No

Composition % assets 09-30-01			
Cash	6.0	Bonds	0.0
Stocks	93.8	Other	0.3

Sector Weightings	% of Stocks	Rel Cat	5-Year High	5-Year Low
Utilities	0.0	0.0	—	—
Energy	8.0	1.4	—	—
Financials	26.6	1.3	—	—
Industrials	6.8	0.5	—	—
Durables	3.4	0.5	—	—
Staples	5.4	0.8	—	—
Services	24.3	1.4	—	—
Retail	2.1	0.4	—	—
Health	15.1	1.6	—	—
Technology	8.4	0.8	—	—

Analysis by Brian Portnoy 12-12-01

It's too soon to recommend this fund's new management team.

In September 2001, Todd Narter and Chris Olson replaced Marcel Houtzager as managers of Liberty Acorn Foreign Forty. Narter was previously a technology sector analyst for Liberty Wanger Asset Management, the fund's advisor, while Olson was a portfolio strategy analyst with UBS Asset Management/Brinson Partners. Prior to their current stint, neither had experience running a retail mutual fund.

While management is new, the fund's look isn't. It continues to seek fast-growing stocks that are trading at reasonable valuations, and its bailiwick is foreign mid-caps, which distinguishes it from most of its foreign-stock category peers that tend to invest in very big or very small stocks. And, as the fund's name indicates, it owns about 40 stocks, although it keeps individual position sizes in check to mitigate the risk of a concentrated portfolio.

Narter and Olson have made only marginal changes to the portfolio since taking over. Though generally bearish on tech, media, and telecom stocks (the fund's telecom services stake is zero, for example), they added to tech, including Comverse Technology, after the September sell-off. Health care, service, and financials stocks compose most of the fund. For example, it holds British medical equipment firm Smith & Nephew, and management has recently purchased more shares of Irish drug firm Elan. Its financials stake is a mix of insurance, banking, and asset management firms.

A bias toward growth stocks, management upheaval, and an all-around lousy year for foreign markets have combined to produce the fund's worst calendar-year performance by far. It remains to be seen whether the new team can recapture this fund's winning tradition. New investors should take a pass until the new skippers prove their mettle.

Address:	Federal Reserve Plaza Boston, MA 02210 617–722–6000 / 800–322–2847
Web Address:	www.libertyfunds.com
*Inception:	11-23-98
Advisor:	Wanger Asset Mgmt.
Subadvisor:	None
NTF Plans:	Fidelity Inst. , Waterhouse

Minimum Purchase:	$1000	Add: $100	IRA: $1000
Min Auto Inv Plan:	$1000	Add: $100	
Sales Fees:	No–load		
Management Fee:	.95%, .05%A		
Actual Fees:	Mgt: 0.95%	Dist: —	
Expense Projections:	3Yr: $838	5Yr: —	10Yr: —
Avg Brok Commission:	—	Income Distrib: Semi–Ann.	
Total Cost (relative to category):	—		

Liberty Acorn Z

Ticker	Load	NAV	Yield	Total Assets	Mstar Category
ACRNX	None	$17.88	0.2%	$4,960.8 mil	Small Growth

Prospectus Objective: Small Company

Libery Acorn Fund seeks long-term growth of capital.

The fund invests primarily in the stocks of small- and medium-sized companies. The fund generally invests in the stocks of companies with capitalizations of less than $2 billion. It will usually invest the majority of its assets in U.S. companies, but it may invest up to 33% of assets in companies outside the U.S. in developed markets and emerging markets.

Class A shares have front loads; B shares have deferred loads, higher 12b-1 fees, and conversion features; C shares have level loads; Z shares are for institutional investors only.

Historical Profile

Return	High
Risk	Average
Rating	★★★★★ Highest

Investment Style
Equity
Average Stock %

1996	1997	1998	1999	2000	12-01
94%	90%	93%	93%	91%	92%

▼ Manager Change
▽ Partial Manager Change

Fund Performance vs. Category Average
■ Quarterly Fund Return
+/– Category Average
— Category Baseline

Performance Quartile (within Category)

Portfolio Manager(s)

Ralph Wanger, CFA. Since 6-70. BS'55 Massachusetts Inst. of Tech; MS'58 Massachusetts Inst. of Tech. Other funds currently managed: Liberty Acorn A, Liberty Acorn B, Liberty Acorn C.

Charles P. McQuaid, CFA. Since 5-95. BBA'74 U. of Massachusetts; MBA'76 U. of Chicago. Other funds currently managed: Liberty Acorn A, Liberty Acorn B, Liberty Acorn C.

1990	1991	1992	1993	1994	1995	1996	1997	1998	1999	2000	12-01	History
6.51	9.32	11.06	13.95	12.24	13.60	15.04	16.99	16.85	18.53	17.21	17.88	NAV
–17.56	47.41	24.23	32.35	–7.45	20.80	22.55	24.98	6.02	33.38	10.06	6.14	Total Return %
–14.44	16.92	16.62	22.29	–8.76	–16.73	–0.40	–8.37	–22.56	12.34	19.16	18.01	+/– S&P 500
–0.15	–3.78	16.46	18.99	–5.02	–10.24	11.29	12.04	4.79	–9.71	32.49	15.37	+/– Russ 2000 Grth
1.52	1.57	1.49	0.56	0.79	0.74	0.81	1.07	0.18	0.54	0.61	0.23	Income Return %
–19.08	45.84	22.74	31.78	–8.24	20.06	21.74	23.91	5.84	32.84	9.44	5.90	Capital Return %
86	75	6	4	87	86	32	28	36	68	20	14	Total Rtn % Rank Cat
0.13	0.10	0.14	0.06	0.11	0.09	0.11	0.16	0.03	0.09	0.11	0.04	Income $
0.44	0.15	0.35	0.59	0.56	1.08	1.47	1.61	1.06	3.54	2.86	0.35	Capital Gains $
0.82	0.72	0.67	0.65	0.62	0.57	0.57	0.56	0.84	0.85	0.83	—	Expense Ratio %
1.60	1.30	0.72	0.30	0.55	0.89	0.53	0.75	0.30	0.49	0.55	—	Income Ratio %
36	25	25	20	18	29	33	32	24	34	29	—	Turnover Rate %
769.5	1,150.3	1,449.0	2,042.6	1,982.8	2,399.3	2,853.7	3,687.1	3,585.0	3,919.8	3,986.3	4,222.5	Net Assets $mil

Performance 12-31-01

	1st Qtr	2nd Qtr	3rd Qtr	4th Qtr	Total
1997	–2.46	13.50	13.71	–0.72	24.98
1998	12.01	–0.28	–19.51	17.92	6.02
1999	–3.56	15.78	–2.04	21.94	33.38
2000	0.43	–1.83	9.52	1.92	10.06
2001	–5.17	15.03	–18.57	19.49	6.14

Trailing	Total Return%	+/– S&P 500	+/– Russ 2000 Grth	% Rank All	% Rank Cat	Growth of $10,000
3 Mo	19.49	8.81	–6.68	15	72	11,949
6 Mo	–2.70	2.86	6.57	50	27	9,730
1 Yr	6.14	18.01	15.37	18	14	10,614
3 Yr Avg	15.93	16.95	15.68	4	21	15,580
5 Yr Avg	15.60	4.90	12.73	4	16	20,643
10 Yr Avg	16.61	3.69	9.43	3	2	46,505
15 Yr Avg	15.95	2.22	7.80	4	5	92,047

Tax Analysis	Tax-Adj Ret%	%Rank Cat	%Pretax Ret	%Rank Cat
3 Yr Avg	12.99	21	81.6	42
5 Yr Avg	13.04	17	83.6	35
10 Yr Avg	14.21	2	85.6	17

Potential Capital Gain Exposure: 37% of assets

Risk Analysis

Time Period	Load-Adj Return %	Risk %Rank[1] All	Risk %Rank[1] Cat	Morningstar Return	Morningstar Risk	Morningstar Risk-Adj Rating
1 Yr	6.14					
3 Yr	15.93	49	3	2.58[2]	0.69	★★★★★
5 Yr	15.60	58	4	2.83[2]	0.80	★★★★★
10 Yr	16.61	69	3	2.23	0.88	★★★★★

Average Historical Rating (193 months): 4.2★s

[1]1=low, 100=high [2] T-Bill return substituted for category avg.

Category Rating (3 Yr)

1 2 3 4 5
Worst Best

Return	Above Avg
Risk	Low

Other Measures	Standard Index S&P 500	Best Fit Index Russ 2000
Alpha	15.8	9.1
Beta	0.68	0.72
R-Squared	39	84

Standard Deviation	21.27
Mean	15.93
Sharpe Ratio	0.59

Portfolio Analysis 09-30-01

Share change since 06-01 Total Stocks: 249	Sector	PE	YTD Ret%	% Assets
⊕ Americredit	Financials	10.6	15.78	3.21
Intl Game Tech	Durables	24.4	42.29	2.28
First Health Grp	Health	25.8	6.26	2.25
XTO Energy	N/A	—	—	1.98
SEI Investments	Services	43.0	–19.20	1.77
Expeditors Intl of WA	Services	32.7	6.46	1.69
Natl Data	Services	38.4	54.53	1.66
Affiliated Managers Grp	Financials	30.6	28.44	1.59
Harley-Davidson	Durables	40.2	36.97	1.55
TCF Finl	Financials	18.2	10.24	1.21
Dynegy	Energy	12.8	–54.20	1.20
Telephone and Data Sys	Services	—	0.29	1.08
Equitable Resources	Energy	14.8	3.98	1.07
Global Payments	Services	—	—	1.07
ITT Educational Svcs	Services	28.6	67.59	1.06
⊕ Neuberger Berman	Financials	23.6	–18.20	0.93
Borders Grp	Retail	53.6	69.75	0.83
⊖ Anchor Gaming	Services	—	56.15	0.83
Bally Total Fitness Hldg	Services	8.4	–36.30	0.82
☼ Liberty Media Group A	N/A	—	—	0.81
Jones Apparel Grp	Durables	15.8	3.05	0.80
Clarcor	Industrials	16.0	33.91	0.79
Carnival	Services	16.4	–7.54	0.79
THQ	Technology	36.2	98.85	0.77
⊖ People's Bk	Financials	11.7	–13.00	0.76

Current Investment Style

Style: Value Blnd Growth; Size: Large Med Small

	Stock Port Avg	Relative S&P 500 Current	Relative S&P 500 Hist	Rel Cat
Price/Earnings Ratio	26.3	0.85	0.84	0.82
Price/Book Ratio	4.8	0.84	0.70	0.98
Price/Cash Flow	17.9	1.00	0.89	0.81
3 Yr Earnings Growth	20.2	1.38	1.35	0.80
1 Yr Earnings Est%	14.3	—	—	1.84
Med Mkt Cap $mil	1,313	0.0	0.0	1.26

[1]figure is based on 50% or less of stocks

Special Securities % assets 09-30-01

Restricted/Illiquid Secs	Trace
Emerging-Markets Secs	1
Options/Futures/Warrants	No

Composition % assets 09-30-01

Cash	7.6
Stocks*	91.9
Bonds	0.0
Other	0.5
*Foreign (% stocks)	8.3

Market Cap

Giant	0.0
Large	5.3
Medium	45.1
Small	43.0
Micro	6.7

Sector Weightings	% of Stocks	Rel S&P	5-Year High	5-Year Low
Utilities	2.1	0.7	6	1
Energy	6.3	0.9	11	3
Financials	25.5	1.4	26	16
Industrials	7.6	0.7	15	6
Durables	9.1	5.9	16	4
Staples	0.9	0.1	5	0
Services	24.2	2.2	37	23
Retail	4.6	0.7	9	2
Health	9.5	0.6	12	5
Technology	10.2	0.6	14	7

Analysis by Christopher Traulsen 11-30-01

Liberty Acorn Fund remains an appealing choice for investors seeking a moderate approach to growth investing.

In our last analysis, we said the sale of this fund's advisor to FleetBoston wasn't reason for much concern. We still think that's the case. Moreover, the fund continues to prove its worth. For the year to date through Nov. 29, 2001, it's down just 0.4%. That ranks in the small-growth category's best quintile in this difficult year for growth investing.

The fund's strength flows directly from management's commitment to buying companies that are undervalued relative to their growth prospects—based on fundamentals, not the hope that speculative valuations will rise even higher. This generally leads the managers to underweight the pricey technology sector and favor niche companies that trade at more-favorable valuations.

That bent has helped the fund a great deal in 2001: Despite their recent rebound, for most of the year the tech sector and expensive growth stocks in general have plummeted in the face of a slowing economy. With scant exposure to such names, the fund has avoided much of that downdraft. Management has also owned its share of winners, with names such as International Game Tech and Harley-Davidson contributing double-digit returns.

That said, no one name has much of an impact on this fund's returns. Its portfolio is spread across roughly 250 stocks, and the largest position rarely exceeds 3% of assets. Given that diversification and the fund's emphasis on valuation, it usually lags in growth-led markets such as 1999's, but over time it has delivered sturdy returns with far less volatility than its typical rival. Given that strength, and the advisor's time-tested, disciplined approach, we think it's a very good choice. True small-cap investors may want to look elsewhere, however, as the fund holds many mid-caps.

Address:	Federal Reserve Plaza Boston, MA 02210 617-722-6000 / 800-322-2847
Web Address:	www.libertyfunds.com
Inception:	06-10-70
Advisor:	Wanger Asset Mgmt.
Subadvisor:	None
NTF Plans:	Fidelity Inst. , Waterhouse

Minimum Purchase:	$1000	Add: $100	IRA: $1000
Min Auto Inv Plan:	$1000	Add: $100	
Sales Fees:	No-load		
Management Fee:	.75% mx./.65% mn., .05%A		
Actual Fees:	Mgt: 0.69%	Dist: —	
Expense Projections:	3Yr: $268	5Yr: $466	10Yr: $1037
Avg Brok Commission:	—	Income Distrib: Semi-Ann.	
Total Cost (relative to category):	—		

Liberty Acorn International Z

Ticker	Load	NAV	Yield	Total Assets	Mstar Category
ACINX	None	$18.47	0.0%	$1,679.5 mil	Foreign Stock

Prospectus Objective: Foreign Stock

Liberty Acorn International Fund seeks long-term growth of capital.

The fund normally invests at least 75% of assets in stocks of foreign companies based in developed and emerging markets. It invests primarily in stocks of companies based outside the U.S. with capitalizations of less than $5 billion. The fund advisor believes that smaller companies - particularly outside the U.S. - that are not as well known by financial analysts may offer higher return potential.

Class A shares have front loads; B shares have deferred loads, higher 12b-1 fees, and conversion features; C shares have level loads; Z shares are for institutional investors only.

Historical Profile
Return: Above Avg
Risk: Average
Rating: ★★★★ Above Avg

Investment Style: Equity
Average Stock %: 96% 90% 87% 86% 93% 88% 81%

▼ Manager Change
▽ Partial Manager Change

Fund Performance vs. Category Average
■ Quarterly Fund Return +/– Category Average
— Category Baseline

Performance Quartile (within Category)

Portfolio Manager(s)

Leah Zell, CFA. Since 9-92. BA'72 Radcliffe C.; PhD'79 Harvard U. Other funds currently managed: Liberty Acorn International A, Liberty Acorn International B, Liberty Acorn International C.

1990	1991	1992	1993	1994	1995	1996	1997	1998	1999	2000	12-01	History
—	—	10.69	15.94	15.24	16.59	19.61	18.39	20.82	35.33	23.86	18.47	NAV
—	—	6.90*	49.11	–3.80	8.95	20.66	0.19	15.43	79.20	–19.98	–21.15	Total Return %
—	—	1.51*	39.05	–5.11	–28.59	–2.29	–33.17	–13.15	58.16	–10.88	–9.27	+/– S&P 500
—	—	—	16.55	–11.58	–2.26	14.61	–1.59	–4.57	52.23	–5.81	—	+/– MSCI EAFE
—	—	0.00	0.00	0.56	0.00	0.72	1.95	0.82	1.06	1.87	0.00	Income Return %
—	—	6.90	49.11	–4.36	8.94	19.93	–1.77	14.61	78.14	–21.85	–21.15	Capital Return %
—	—	—	11	79	62	11	83	38	12	70	41	Total Rtn % Rank Cat
—	—	0.00	0.00	0.09	0.00	0.12	0.38	0.15	0.22	0.66	0.00	Income $
—	—	0.00	0.00	0.01	0.01	0.28	0.90	0.27	1.55	4.10	0.39	Capital Gains $
—	—	2.40	1.20	1.20	1.20	1.17	1.19	1.12	1.11	1.05	—	Expense Ratio %
—	—	–1.40	0.10	0.50	0.90	0.51	0.58	0.86	0.12	0.02	—	Income Ratio %
—	—	20	19	20	26	34	39	37	46	63	—	Turnover Rate %
—	—	29.6	901.4	1,364.8	1,276.8	1,771.7	1,628.3	1,726.1	2,868.2	2,461.1	1,620.3	Net Assets $mil

Performance 12-31-01

	1st Qtr	2nd Qtr	3rd Qtr	4th Qtr	Total
1997	2.14	5.94	–0.67	–6.79	0.19
1998	18.16	2.00	–16.05	14.08	15.43
1999	1.15	15.48	8.32	41.63	79.20
2000	12.09	–14.18	–4.17	–13.19	–19.98
2001	–12.36	–1.84	–18.76	12.83	–21.15

Trailing	Total Return%	+/– S&P 500	+/– MSCI EAFE	% Rank All	% Rank Cat	Growth of $10,000
3 Mo	12.83	2.14	—	30	15	11,283
6 Mo	–8.34	–2.78	—	79	43	9,166
1 Yr	–21.15	–9.27	—	82	41	7,885
3 Yr Avg	4.18	5.20	—	38	14	11,307
5 Yr Avg	5.51	–5.19	—	55	17	13,075
10 Yr Avg	—	—	—	—	—	—
15 Yr Avg	—	—	—	—	—	—

Tax Analysis	Tax-Adj Ret%	%Rank Cat	%Pretax Ret	%Rank Cat
3 Yr Avg	2.33	16	55.9	76
5 Yr Avg	3.93	16	71.3	35
10 Yr Avg	—	—	—	—

Potential Capital Gain Exposure: –3% of assets

Risk Analysis

Time Period	Load-Adj Return %	Risk %Rank[1] All	Risk %Rank[1] Cat	Morningstar Return	Morningstar Risk	Morningstar Risk-Adj Rating
1 Yr	–21.15					
3 Yr	4.18	78	69	–0.16[2]	1.02	★★★★
5 Yr	5.51	77	66	0.11[2]	0.88	★★★★
Incept	11.01	—	—	—	—	

Average Historical Rating (76 months): 4.0★s

[1] 1=low, 100=high [2] T-Bill return substituted for category avg.

Category Rating (3 Yr): 4 (1 Worst – 5 Best)

Return: Above Avg
Risk: Above Avg

Other Measures	Standard Index S&P 500	Best Fit Index Wil 4500
Alpha	6.3	2.1
Beta	0.86	0.78
R-Squared	34	76

Standard Deviation	26.59
Mean	4.18
Sharpe Ratio	–0.03

Portfolio Analysis 09-30-01

Share change since 06-01 Total Stocks: 162

Share change	Stock	Sector	Country	% Assets
⊖	Serco Grp	Services	United Kingdom	1.92
☼	Smith & Nephew	Health	United Kingdom	1.71
	Capita Grp	Services	United Kingdom	1.70
⊖	Irish Life & Permanent	Financials	Ireland	1.60
	Power Finl	Financials	Canada	1.58
⊕	Rhoen-Klinikum	Health	Germany	1.48
	Richemont Cl A (Unit)	Staples	Switzerland	1.47
⊖	Orix	Financials	Japan	1.46
	SSL Intl	Health	United Kingdom	1.38
⊖	Autogrill	Services	Italy	1.29
	Rhoen-Klinikum	Health	Germany	1.28
⊖	Li & Fung	Retail	Hong Kong	1.19
	Givaudan-Lavirotte	Industrials	France	1.13
	Stinnes	Services	Germany	1.09
⊖	Nintendo	Durables	Japan	1.07
⊕	Saipem	Industrials	Italy	1.02
	Television Broadcasts	Services	Hong Kong	1.02
⊕	Anglo Irish Bk	Financials	Ireland	0.99
	Bellsystem 24	Services	Japan	0.95
☼	Star Cruises	Technology	Hong Kong	0.94

Current Investment Style

Style: Value Blnd Growth; Size: Large Med Small

	Stock Port Avg	Rel MSCI EAFE Current	Rel MSCI EAFE Hist	Rel Cat
Price/Earnings Ratio	27.1	1.05	1.11	1.06
Price/Cash Flow	15.5	1.20	1.48	1.08
Price/Book Ratio	5.0	1.43	1.60	1.27
3 Yr Earnings Growth	16.9	0.90	1.79	0.86
Med Mkt Cap $mil	1,564	0.1	0.1	0.09

Country Exposure 09-30-01	% assets
United Kingdom	13
Japan	10
Germany	8
Canada	6
France	5

Hedging History: Frequent

Regional Exposure 09-30-01	% assets
Europe	51
Japan	10
Latin America	1
Pacific Rim	8
Other	7

Special Securities % assets 09-30-01	
Restricted/Illiquid Secs	0
Emerging-Markets Secs	7
Options/Futures/Warrants	Yes

Composition % assets 09-30-01			
Cash	5.6	Bonds	0.0
Stocks	80.1	Other	14.3

Sector Weightings	% of Stocks	Rel Cat	5-Year High	5-Year Low
Utilities	1.4	0.5	6	0
Energy	4.2	0.7	8	1
Financials	14.4	0.7	21	7
Industrials	16.0	1.2	16	3
Durables	4.3	0.6	13	2
Staples	4.0	0.6	11	3
Services	32.7	1.8	41	18
Retail	3.2	0.7	15	3
Health	12.4	1.3	14	2
Technology	7.5	0.7	33	0

Analysis by Brian Portnoy 12-11-01

Liberty Acorn International is a fine choice for foreign small-cap exposure, despite its recent struggles.

Like many of its rivals, this fund has taken an up-and-down ride over the past couple years. Contrary to its growth-at-a-reasonable-price roots, the fund was swept away in the growth-stock frenzy of the late 1990s. It gained 79% in 1999, for example, but has fallen sharply from its perch, shedding approximately 45% of its value from March 2000, when the prolonged market correction began, through mid-December 2001. Unlike last year, this year's losses, though substantial, have been in line with its peers'.

Manager Leah Zell admits to letting the fund drift from its moorings as a sober growth offering specializing in relatively unknown foreign companies, but she and her team of analysts have refocused the fund in recent months. As a result, its median market cap has come down (and not only through price depreciation), giving it more of a small-cap profile than it has had recently. Still, the fund features a mix of small and mid-caps, as letting winners ride is central to Zell's strategy.

The fund now sports a relatively diversified portfolio as well. Its tech stake is less than 10%, while business service, health care, and industrial firms attract a lot of the fund's assets. Zell likes service companies because they're typically not capital intensive and can generate ample cash flows; Serco Group, a British facilities management firm, and Rhoen-Klinikum, a German hospital management company, are two of her favorites. The fund has also shifted its slim Japanese assets into smaller stocks and has snapped up a mix of property, food, bank, and media stocks from Hong Kong and Singapore.

There's no denying that the fund has looked much better, but its long-term record and Zell's extensive experience suggest that the fund is ripe for a turnaround.

Address:	Federal Reserve Plaza Boston, MA 02210 617-722-6000 / 800-322-2847
Web Address:	www.libertyfunds.com
*Inception:	09-23-92
Advisor:	Wanger Asset Mgmt.
Subadvisor:	None
NTF Plans:	Fidelity Inst., Waterhouse

Minimum Purchase:	$1000	Add: $100 IRA: $1000
Min Auto Inv Plan:	$1000	Add: $100
Sales Fees:	No-load	
Management Fee:	1.2% mx./.75% mn., .05%A	
Actual Fees:	Mgt: 0.82%	Dist: —
Expense Projections:	3Yr: $356	5Yr: $617 10Yr: $1363
Avg Brok Commission:	—	Income Distrib: Semi-Ann.
Total Cost (relative to category):	—	

Liberty Acorn Twenty Z

Ticker	Load	NAV	Yield	Total Assets	Mstar Category
ACTWX	None	$15.23	0.0%	$99.2 mil	Mid-Cap Growth

Prospectus Objective: Growth

Liberty Acorn Twenty Fund seeks long-term capital growth.

The fund normally invests in the stocks of medium- to larger-sized U.S. companies. It usually invests in a limited number of companies (between 20-25) with market capitalizations of $2 billion to $12 billion. This fund is non-diversified.

Class A shares have front loads; B shares have deferred loads, higher 12b-1 fees, and conversion features; C shares have level loads; Z shares are for institutional investors only.

Historical Profile
Return High
Risk Below Avg
Rating ★★★★★ Highest

Investment Style
Equity
Average Stock %: 100% (1998), 94% (1999), 96% (2000), 91% (12-01)

▼ Manager Change
▽ Partial Manager Change

Fund Performance vs. Category Average
■ Quarterly Fund Return +/– Category Average
— Category Baseline

Performance Quartile (within Category)

Portfolio Manager(s)

John H. Park, CFA. Since 11-98. Other funds currently managed: Liberty Acorn Twenty A, Liberty Acorn Twenty B, Liberty Acorn Twenty C.

1990	1991	1992	1993	1994	1995	1996	1997	1998	1999	2000	12-01	History
—	—	—	—	—	—	—	—	10.71	13.70	14.13	15.23	NAV
—	—	—	—	—	—	—	—	7.10*	29.30	11.68	8.00	Total Return %
—	—	—	—	—	—	—	—	3.39*	8.26	20.78	19.88	+/– S&P 500
—	—	—	—	—	—	—	—	—	–22.01	23.42	28.16	+/– Russ Midcap Grth
—	—	—	—	—	—	—	—	0.00	0.00	0.00	0.00	Income Return %
—	—	—	—	—	—	—	—	7.10	29.30	11.68	8.00	Capital Return %
—	—	—	—	—	—	—	—	—	78	18	1	Total Rtn % Rank Cat
—	—	—	—	—	—	—	—	0.00	0.00	0.00	0.00	Income $
—	—	—	—	—	—	—	—	0.00	0.14	1.09	0.03	Capital Gains $
—	—	—	—	—	—	—	—	1.35	1.37	1.34	—	Expense Ratio %
—	—	—	—	—	—	—	—	0.22	–0.62	–0.52	—	Income Ratio %
—	—	—	—	—	—	—	—	173	101	116	—	Turnover Rate %
—	—	—	—	—	—	—	—	33.0	68.3	66.5	69.4	Net Assets $mil

Performance 12-31-01

	1st Qtr	2nd Qtr	3rd Qtr	4th Qtr	Total
1997	—	—	—	—	—
1998	—	—	—	—	7.10*
1999	7.19	13.59	–7.13	14.35	29.30
2000	2.34	1.05	10.32	–2.11	11.68
2001	–6.86	11.25	–11.34	17.57	8.00

Trailing	Total Return%	+/– S&P 500	+/– Russ Midcap Grth	% Rank All	% Rank Cat	Growth of $10,000
3 Mo	17.57	6.88	–9.49	18	60	11,757
6 Mo	4.24	9.79	12.50	7	1	10,424
1 Yr	8.00	19.88	28.16	9	1	10,800
3 Yr Avg	15.97	16.99	13.81	4	10	15,595
5 Yr Avg	—	—	—	—	—	—
10 Yr Avg	—	—	—	—	—	—
15 Yr Avg	—	—	—	—	—	—

Tax Analysis	Tax-Adj Ret%	%Rank Cat	%Pretax Ret	%Rank Cat
3 Yr Avg	15.04	7	94.2	14
5 Yr Avg	—	—	—	—
10 Yr Avg	—	—	—	—

Potential Capital Gain Exposure: 33% of assets

Risk Analysis

Time Period	Load-Adj Return %	Risk %Rank¹ All	Risk %Rank¹ Cat	Morningstar Return	Morningstar Risk	Morningstar Risk-Adj Rating
1 Yr	8.00					
3 Yr	15.97	51	2	2.59²	0.71	★★★★★
5 Yr	—	—	—	—	—	
Incept	17.95	—	—	—	—	

Average Historical Rating (2 months): 5.0★s

¹1=low, 100=high ² T-Bill return substituted for category avg.

Category Rating (3 Yr)

① ② ③ ④ ⑤
Worst — Best

Return High
Risk Low

Other Measures	Standard Index S&P 500	Best Fit Index SPMid400
Alpha	16.9	6.7
Beta	0.88	0.78
R-Squared	63	65
Standard Deviation		21.72
Mean		15.97
Sharpe Ratio		0.57

Portfolio Analysis 09-30-01

Share change since 06-01 Total Stocks: 21

	Sector	PE	YTD Ret%	% Assets
Boston Scientific	Health	—	76.21	10.40
⊕ H & R Block	Services	25.5	120.00	8.07
Associated Banc-Corp	Financials	13.6	20.35	6.44
First Health Grp	Health	25.8	6.26	5.59
⊕ Expeditors Intl of WA	Services	32.7	6.46	5.10
☼ Liberty Media Group A	N/A	—	—	4.43
☼ Immunex	Health	89.4	–31.70	4.37
⊕ Harley-Davidson	Durables	40.2	36.97	4.36
TCF Finl	Financials	18.2	10.24	4.09
Herman Miller	Durables	17.4	–17.20	3.95
⊕ Waters	Industrials	32.0	–53.50	3.40
Jones Apparel Grp	Durables	15.8	3.05	3.39
⊕ Techne	Health	44.9	2.18	3.13
☼ Dynegy	Energy	12.8	–54.20	2.94
⊕ Callaway Golf	Durables	19.3	4.30	2.92
☼ Intl Game Tech	Durables	24.4	42.29	2.69
☼ Americredit	Financials	10.6	15.78	2.41
Telephone and Data Sys	Services	—	0.29	2.39
☼ Choicepoint	Services	70.4	15.97	2.38
⊕ Tektronix	Technology	26.3	–23.40	2.11
⊖ SEI Investments	Services	43.0	–19.20	1.70

Analysis by Christopher Traulsen 11-20-01

The sale of Liberty Acorn Twenty Fund's advisor doesn't diminish its appeal.

This fund's advisor was acquired last year by Liberty Financial, which has itself just been acquired by FleetBoston Financial. Such sales are cause for concern, as they can lead to the loss of key personnel or a change to the fund's style. Purchasers also often increase the funds' expense ratios, to recoup their investments that much more quickly.

In this case, however, we don't see much reason for concern. Manager John Park and the other Acorn managers have contracted to stay on board through 2005. Fleet has also agreed to preserve Acorn's autonomy. While Fleet could raise the fund's marketing and administrative fees, the new advisory agreement retains the same management fee as before, and Fleet has agreed to consult with the Board before changing the fund's 1.35% expense ratio cap.

The fund itself holds much appeal. It only holds 20 to 25 names, so it carries significant issue-specific risk. However, unlike many mid-growth managers, skipper John Park isn't willing to play the growth-at-any-price game. Instead, he tries to buy companies that have solid growth prospects at reasonable prices. Thus, the fund tends to hold less tech and take on less valuation risk than its average peer. Park has also proved a strong stock-picker. Backed by Acorn's very capable research staff, he has found such gems as top holding Boston Scientific, which is up 83% this year. In all, the fund is up 3% for the year to date through Nov. 16—a top-percentile return in the category.

The fund isn't for everyone—Park's discipline can hold it back in growth-led markets, and its concentrated portfolio will lead to the occasional stumble. Nevertheless, given the shop's superior research abilities and Park's strong record here, we think it's one of the better focused funds around.

Current Investment Style

Style: Value Blnd Growth; Size: Large Med Small

	Stock Port Avg	Relative S&P 500 Current	Relative S&P 500 Hist	Rel Cat
Price/Earnings Ratio	28.2	0.91	—	0.81
Price/Book Ratio	6.3	1.11	—	1.12
Price/Cash Flow	23.6	1.31	—	1.02
3 Yr Earnings Growth	26.4	1.81	—	1.13
1 Yr Earnings Est%	13.3	—	—	1.43
Med Mkt Cap $mil	4,396	0.1	—	0.78

¹figure is based on 50% or less of stocks

Special Securities % assets 09-30-01	
Restricted/Illiquid Secs	0
Emerging-Markets Secs	0
Options/Futures/Warrants	No

Composition % assets 09-30-01	
Cash	13.5
Stocks*	86.5
Bonds	0.0
Other	0.0
*Foreign (% stocks)	0.0

Market Cap	
Giant	0.0
Large	27.0
Medium	69.5
Small	3.6
Micro	0.0

Sector Weightings	% of Stocks	Rel S&P	5-Year High	5-Year Low
Utilities	0.0	0.0	—	—
Energy	3.6	0.5	—	—
Financials	15.8	0.9	—	—
Industrials	4.2	0.4	—	—
Durables	21.2	13.6	—	—
Staples	0.0	0.0	—	—
Services	24.0	2.2	—	—
Retail	0.0	0.0	—	—
Health	28.7	1.9	—	—
Technology	2.6	0.1	—	—

Address:	Federal Reserve Plaza Boston, MA 02210 617-722-6000 / 800-322-2847
Web Address:	www.libertyfunds.com
*Inception:	11-23-98
Advisor:	Wanger Asset Mgmt.
Subadvisor:	None
NTF Plans:	Fidelity Inst. , Waterhouse

Minimum Purchase:	$1000	Add: $100 IRA: $1000
Min Auto Inv Plan:	$1000	Add: $100
Sales Fees:	No-load	
Management Fee:	.90%, .05%A	
Actual Fees:	Mgt: 0.90%	Dist: —
Expense Projections:	3Yr: $576	5Yr: — 10Yr: —
Avg Brok Commission:	—	Income Distrib: Semi-Ann.
Total Cost (relative to category):	—	

Liberty Acorn USA Z

Ticker	Load	NAV	Yield	Total Assets	Mstar Category
AUSAX	None	$17.52	0.0%	$289.9 mil	Small Blend

Prospectus Objective: Small Company

Liberty Acorn USA Fund seeks long-term growth of capital.

The fund normally invests at least 65% in U.S. companies. It may invest primarily in stocks of small- and medium-sized U.S. companies. It generally invests in the stocks of U.S. companies with capitalizations of less than $2 billion. The fund can invest in foreign securities and options or futures.

Class A shares have front loads; B shares have deferred loads, higher 12b-1 fees, and conversion features; C shares have level loads; Z shares are for institutional investors only.

Historical Profile

Return Above Avg
Risk Average
Rating ★★★★ Above Avg

Investment Style
Equity
Average Stock %: 95% 93% 92% 91% 94% 93%

▼ Manager Change
▽ Partial Manager Change

Fund Performance vs. Category Average
Quarterly Fund Return +/– Category Average
— Category Baseline

Performance Quartile (within Category)

Portfolio Manager(s)

Robert A. Mohn, CFA et al.Since 9-96. BS'83 Stanford U.; MBA'92 U. of Chicago.

1990	1991	1992	1993	1994	1995	1996	1997	1998	1999	2000	12–01	History
—	—	—	—	—	—	11.65	15.12	14.80	16.75	14.90	17.52	NAV
—	—	—	—	—	—	16.50*	32.30	5.79	23.02	–8.99	19.25	Total Return %
—	—	—	—	—	—	2.71*	–1.05	–22.79	1.99	0.11	31.13	+/– S&P 500
—	—	—	—	—	—	—	9.93	8.34	1.76	–5.96	16.77	+/– Russell 2000
—	—	—	—	—	—	0.00	0.00	0.00	0.00	0.00	0.00	Income Return %
—	—	—	—	—	—	16.50	32.30	5.79	23.02	–8.99	19.25	Capital Return %
—	—	—	—	—	—	—	22	8	23	97	10	Total Rtn % Rank Cat
—	—	—	—	—	—	0.00	0.00	0.00	0.00	0.00	0.00	Income $
—	—	—	—	—	—	0.00	0.29	1.12	1.37	0.32	0.24	Capital Gains $
—	—	—	—	—	—	1.79	1.35	1.20	1.15	1.15	—	Expense Ratio %
—	—	—	—	—	—	–0.99	–0.49	–0.42	0.00	–0.32	—	Income Ratio %
—	—	—	—	—	—	20	33	42	49	45	—	Turnover Rate %
—	—	—	—	—	—	52.7	184.4	281.5	371.5	222.5	229.2	Net Assets $mil

Performance 12-31-01

	1st Qtr	2nd Qtr	3rd Qtr	4th Qtr	Total
1997	–1.46	16.03	15.17	0.48	32.30
1998	12.90	0.71	–19.25	15.22	5.79
1999	–7.91	17.54	–4.44	18.93	23.02
2000	–1.19	–15.06	4.80	3.47	–8.99
2001	3.56	21.71	–15.92	12.53	19.26

Trailing	Total Return%	+/– S&P 500	+/– Russ 2000	% Rank All	% Rank Cat	Growth of $10,000
3 Mo	12.53	1.85	–8.55	31	94	11,253
6 Mo	–5.38	0.17	–1.30	64	83	9,462
1 Yr	19.25	31.13	16.77	2	10	11,925
3 Yr Avg	10.12	11.14	3.70	11	50	13,352
5 Yr Avg	13.32	2.62	5.80	7	29	18,687
10 Yr Avg	—	—	—	—	—	—
15 Yr Avg	—	—	—	—	—	—

Tax Analysis	Tax-Adj Ret%	%Rank Cat	%Pretax Ret	%Rank Cat
3 Yr Avg	9.19	46	90.8	37
5 Yr Avg	12.18	21	91.5	22
10 Yr Avg	—	—	—	—

Potential Capital Gain Exposure: 29% of assets

Risk Analysis

Time Period	Load-Adj Return %	Risk %Rank[1] All	Risk %Rank[1] Cat	Morningstar Return	Morningstar Risk	Morningstar Risk-Adj Rating
1 Yr	19.25					
3 Yr	10.12	58	47	1.15[2]	0.82	★★★★
5 Yr	13.32	63	35	2.12[2]	0.87	★★★★
Incept	15.73	—	—	—	—	

Average Historical Rating (28 months): 3.0★s

[1]1=low, 100=high [2] T-Bill return substituted for category avg.

Category Rating (3 Yr)

1 2 **3** 4 5
Worst — Best

Return: Average
Risk: Average

Other Measures	Standard Index S&P 500	Best Fit Index SPMid400
Alpha	10.6	1.1
Beta	0.73	0.84
R-Squared	38	68
Standard Deviation		22.09
Mean		10.12
Sharpe Ratio		0.27

Portfolio Analysis 09-30-01

Share change since 06–01 Total Stocks: 64

Stock	Sector	PE	YTD Ret%	% Assets
Americredit	Financials	10.6	15.78	5.85
⊖ Conectiv	Utilities	4.6	27.17	4.80
⊕ ITT Educational Svcs	Services	28.6	67.59	4.37
⊖ Telephone and Data Sys	Services	—	0.29	4.06
Magellan Health Svcs	Health	11.0	43.08	4.03
Natl Data	Services	38.4	54.53	3.96
Micros Sys	Technology	NMF	37.53	3.85
Wackenhut Cl B	Services	—	—	3.21
JDA Software Grp	Technology	77.1	71.09	3.12
Lincare Hldgs	Health	23.7	0.41	2.69
Salem Comm Cl A	Technology	—	53.97	2.67
Global Payments	Services	—	—	2.59
Edwards Lifesciences	Health	—	55.66	2.52
First Health Grp	Health	25.8	6.26	2.22
Tesoro Petro	Energy	5.1	12.77	2.05
Gadzooks	Retail	14.9	–6.85	1.96
Atmos Energy	Utilities	14.5	–8.21	1.71
World Acceptance	Financials	8.4	32.73	1.69
⊕ Beverly Enterprises	Health	—	5.03	1.65
⊕ Chittenden	Financials	15.4	17.37	1.65
⊕ Callaway Golf	Durables	19.3	4.30	1.63
⊕ Serologicals	Health	30.3	42.73	1.55
Mediacom Comms	Services	—	6.24	1.52
⊖ Equitable Resources	Energy	14.8	3.98	1.51
Hub Grp Cl A	Services	NMF	16.44	1.51

Current Investment Style

Style: Value Blnd Growth; Size: Large Med Small

	Stock Port Avg	Relative S&P 500 Current	Relative S&P 500 Hist	Rel Cat
Price/Earnings Ratio	24.8	0.80	0.73	1.00
Price/Book Ratio	3.3	0.59	0.50	1.04
Price/Cash Flow	15.6	0.86	0.77	1.00
3 Yr Earnings Growth	16.7[1]	1.14	1.29	0.99
1 Yr Earnings Est%	13.0	—	—	15.16
Med Mkt Cap $mil	963	0.0	0.0	0.98

[1]figure is based on 50% or less of stocks

Special Securities % assets 09-30-01	
Restricted/Illiquid Secs	0
Emerging-Markets Secs	1
Options/Futures/Warrants	No

Composition % assets 09-30-01	
Cash	6.7
Stocks*	92.0
Bonds	0.0
Other	1.3
*Foreign (% stocks)	1.1

Market Cap	
Giant	0.0
Large	1.3
Medium	38.6
Small	47.4
Micro	12.7

Sector Weightings	% of Stocks	Rel S&P	5-Year High	5-Year Low
Utilities	7.2	2.2	14	2
Energy	5.2	0.7	19	4
Financials	12.9	0.7	20	10
Industrials	1.5	0.1	19	0
Durables	2.7	1.7	4	0
Staples	0.4	0.1	1	0
Services	30.2	2.8	34	20
Retail	4.6	0.7	6	0
Health	18.5	1.2	18	8
Technology	17.0	0.9	38	5

Analysis by Christopher Traulsen 11-16-01

FleetBoston's acquisition of Liberty Acorn USA Fund's advisor isn't cause for alarm.

This fund's advisor was sold to Liberty last year, and Liberty has now been acquired by FleetBoston Financial. Such sales should give investors pause. For one, key personnel often depart following a sale. For another, the purchaser usually has an incentive to raise fund expenses in order to recoup its investment.

With regard to personnel, we don't see much risk of immediate change. The principals of Acorn all signed contracts when Liberty bought the firm, and those contracts remain in effect. Further, the surest way for Fleet to squander its investment would be to scare off talent, and the Acorn funds hold a big chunk of the assets Fleet bought. There's no way to know whether Fleet will ultimately raise the funds' expenses, but the new advisory agreement doesn't change the fund's management fee, or the no-load status of holders of the fund's Z-shares.

The fund itself remains an attractive offering. It's headed by Rob Mohn but draws heavily on the research of the whole Acorn team. The idea is to offer investors a more concentrated take on Liberty Acorn fund's time-tested style. Like Liberty Acorn, it focuses on stocks with strong growth potential that are trading at discounts to the team's estimates of their true worths. Over time, including in 2001, the fund has delivered very good returns relative to its peers. It has also been quite volatile, however, in part because it takes large positions in individual names.

In fact, sibling Liberty Acorn has delivered a better return than this offering during this fund's lifetime, with far less volatility. Acorn USA does offer the potential for greater upside gains in more-favorable conditions and is a fine fund in its own right, but investors in search of a smoother ride will prefer Liberty Acorn.

Address:	Federal Reserve Plaza Boston, MA 02210 617–722–6000 / 800–322–2847
Web Address:	www.libertyfunds.com
*Inception:	09-04-96
Advisor:	Wanger Asset Mgmt.
Subadvisor:	None
NTF Plans:	Fidelity Inst. , Waterhouse

Minimum Purchase:	$1000	Add: $100 IRA: $1000
Min Auto Inv Plan:	$1000	Add: $100
Sales Fees:	No-load	
Management Fee:	.95% mx./.90% mn., .05%A	
Actual Fees:	Mgt: 0.94%	Dist: —
Expense Projections:	3Yr: $381	5Yr: $660 10Yr: $1455
Avg Brok Commission:	—	Income Distrib: Semi-Ann.
Total Cost (relative to category):	—	

Liberty Newport Tiger A

Ticker	Load	NAV	Yield	Total Assets	Mstar Category
CNTAX	5.75%	$9.38	0.9%	$538.7 mil	Pacific ex–Japan

Prospectus Objective: Pacific Stock

Liberty-Newport Tiger Fund seeks capital appreciation.

The fund invests primarily in equity securities issued in the ten Tigers of Asia: Hong Kong, Singapore, South Korea, Taiwan, Malaysia, Thailand, Indonesia, China, the Philippines, and India. It may invest in companies of any size. Management emphasizes companies that are able to adapt to changing markets and technologies.

Class A shares have front loads; B shares have deferred loads, 12b-1 fees, and conversion features; C shares have level loads; T and Z shares are closed to new investors. Past names include: Colonial Newport Tiger Fund and Newport Tiger Fund.

Historical Profile

Return	Below Avg
Risk	High
Rating	★★ Below Avg

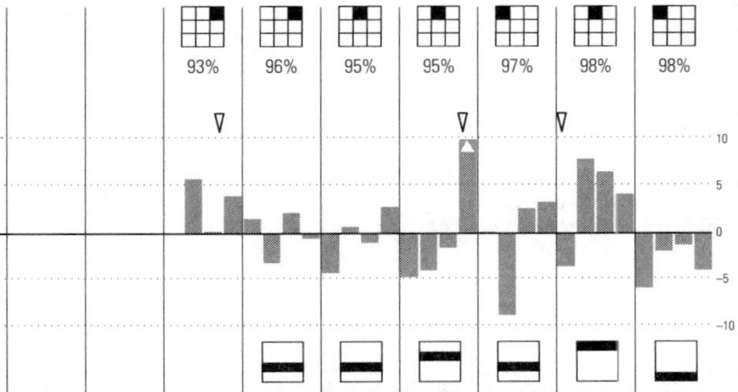

Investment Style
Equity
Average Stock %: 93% 96% 95% 95% 97% 98% 98%

▼ Manager Change
▽ Partial Manager Change

Fund Performance vs. Category Average
Quarterly Fund Return +/– Category Average
— Category Baseline

Performance Quartile (within Category)

Portfolio Manager(s)

Christopher Legallet. Since 10-98. BA U. of California-Los Angeles; MBA U. of California-Los Angeles. Other funds currently managed: Liberty Newport Tiger T, Liberty Newport Tiger Z, Liberty Newport Tiger B.

1990	1991	1992	1993	1994	1995	1996	1997	1998	1999	2000	12–01	History
—	—	—	—	—	12.46	13.75	9.02	7.78	13.47	11.34	9.38	NAV
—	—	—	—	—	17.47*	10.94	–33.95	–12.08	73.14	–15.81	–16.55	Total Return %
—	—	—	—	—	–7.59*	–12.01	–67.31	–40.65	52.10	–6.71	–4.67	+/– S&P 500
—	—	—	—	—	—	2.71	8.11	–4.92	7.90	19.18	—	+/– MSCI FE ex Jpn
—	—	—	—	—	0.55	0.57	0.25	1.67	0.00	0.00	0.75	Income Return %
—	—	—	—	—	16.92	10.36	–34.20	–13.75	73.14	–15.81	–17.30	Capital Return %
—	—	—	—	—	—	54	51	47	54	17	88	Total Rtn % Rank Cat
—	—	—	—	—	0.06	0.07	0.03	0.15	0.00	0.00	0.09	Income $
—	—	—	—	—	0.02	0.00	0.04	0.00	0.00	0.00	0.00	Capital Gains $
—	—	—	—	—	—	1.74	1.73	1.78	1.77	1.71	—	Expense Ratio %
—	—	—	—	—	—	0.62	0.64	2.02	0.97	0.07	—	Income Ratio %
—	—	—	—	—	—	6	12	15	14	25	—	Turnover Rate %
—	—	—	—	—	195.7	576.8	330.5	252.6	404.5	297.2	187.5	Net Assets $mil

Performance 12-31-01

	1st Qtr	2nd Qtr	3rd Qtr	4th Qtr	Total
1997	–6.91	11.42	–12.59	–27.16	–33.95
1998	0.67	–31.27	–7.70	37.69	–12.08
1999	2.31	28.64	–3.71	36.61	73.14
2000	2.45	–4.20	–7.11	–7.65	–15.81
2001	–11.64	0.60	–23.02	21.95	–16.55

Trailing	Total Return%	+/– S&P 500	+/– MSCI FE ex Jpn	% Rank All	% Rank Cat	Growth of $10,000
3 Mo	21.95	11.27	—	11	64	12,195
6 Mo	–6.12	–0.56	—	69	72	9,388
1 Yr	–16.55	–4.67	—	75	88	8,345
3 Yr Avg	6.75	7.77	—	18	35	12,164
5 Yr Avg	–6.72	–17.42	—	98	42	7,063
10 Yr Avg	—	—	—	—	—	—
15 Yr Avg	—	—	—	—	—	—

Tax Analysis	Tax-Adj Ret%	%Rank Cat	%Pretax Ret	%Rank Cat
3 Yr Avg	6.62	35	98.2	51
5 Yr Avg	–6.96	38	—	—
10 Yr Avg	—	—	—	—

Potential Capital Gain Exposure: –43% of assets

Risk Analysis

Time Period	Load-Adj Return %	Risk %Rank[1] All	Risk %Rank[1] Cat	Morningstar Return	Morningstar Risk	Morningstar Risk-Adj Rating
1 Yr	–21.35					
3 Yr	4.66	84	23	–0.06[2]	1.16	★★★★
5 Yr	–7.82	97	55	–2.20[2]	1.61	★
Incept	–2.08	—	—	—	—	

Average Historical Rating (46 months): 1.6★s

[1] 1=low, 100=high [2] T-Bill return substituted for category avg.

Category Rating (3 Yr)

1 2 **3** 4 5
Worst Best

Return	Average
Risk	Below Avg

Other Measures	Standard Index S&P 500	Best Fit Index MSCIPcxIND
Alpha	11.5	5.1
Beta	1.22	1.15
R–Squared	53	87
Standard Deviation		31.24
Mean		6.75
Sharpe Ratio		0.07

Portfolio Analysis 09-30-01

Share change since 06–01 Total Stocks: 35	Sector	Country	% Assets
⊖ Hong Kong & China Gas	Energy	Hong Kong	7.37
Hutchison Whampoa	Financials	Hong Kong	5.56
DBS Grp Hldgs	Financials	Singapore	5.53
China Telecom HK	Services	Hong Kong	5.34
⊖ Singapore Tech Engnrg	Industrials	Singapore	4.93
⊖ Huaneng Pwr Intl Cl H	Utilities	China	4.78
⊖ Sun Hung Kai Properties	Financials	Hong Kong	4.65
⊖ Cheung Kong Hldgs	Financials	Hong Kong	4.30
⊖ HSBC Hldgs (HK)	Financials	Hong Kong	4.27
Hang Seng Bk	Financials	Hong Kong	4.23
✲ Taiwan Semicon	Technology	Taiwan	4.16
⊖ Singapore Press Hldgs	Services	Singapore	4.04
⊖ Li & Fung	Retail	Hong Kong	3.73
Giordano Intl	Retail	Hong Kong	3.69
Samsung Electncs	Technology	South Korea	3.03
Citic Pacific	Durables	Hong Kong	2.96
Johnson Elec Hldgs	Durables	Hong Kong	2.80
Housing Dev Fin	Financials	India	2.79
Infosys Tech	Technology	India	2.55
Datacraft Asia	Technology	Singapore	1.69

Analysis by William Samuel Rocco 11-09-01 This analysis was written for the T shares.

Here's another reminder that one bad year doesn't ruin a good fund's appeal.

Liberty Newport Tiger Fund has really struggled thus far in 2001 despite helpful moves by manager Chris Legallet. Hong Kong has fared worse than most of its neighbors this year, and Legallet has reduced his stake in that market, selling Citic Pacific and other issues in recent months. But the fund still has more exposure to Hong Kong than most of its peers. Similarly, while Legallet has decreased his stake in hard–hit Singapore, the fund remains significantly overweighted there as well.

Meanwhile, Korea has been emerging Asia's best market by far in 2001—it's currently up about 10% for the year to date—and Legallet has continued to beef up his position in that market. However, though he has added to Kookmin Bank and other names recently, the fund is still slightly underweight in Korea, and it was markedly so for most of the year.

Thus, the fund has plunged 27% and lags 90% of its peers for the year to date through Nov. 8, 2001.

That smarts, of course, but it's important to note that the fund's blue–chip strategy has always led to oversized stakes in Hong Kong and Singapore, and while Legallet has begun to find more high–quality large caps elsewhere in the region, the fund is likely to stay overweighted in the region's two most–liquid markets. What's more, though the fund's elitist strategy has backfired thus far in 2001, it has worked relatively well though time. The fund has outpaced the majority of its peers over the long term, and it has been no more volatile than most members of its wild group.

Due to that risk/reward profile, as well as Newport's Asian expertise, we think this fund remains one of the best options in its chaotic category.

Current Investment Style

Style: Value Blnd Growth; Size: Large Med Small

	Stock Port Avg	Rel MSCI EAFE Current	Rel MSCI EAFE Hist	Rel Cat
Price/Earnings Ratio	21.0	0.81	0.82	1.08
Price/Cash Flow	17.8	1.38	1.15	1.21
Price/Book Ratio	3.9	1.12	0.66	1.20
3 Yr Earnings Growth	24.3	1.30	0.64	0.92
Med Mkt Cap $mil	8,619	0.3	0.4	1.13

Country Exposure 09-30-01	% assets
Hong Kong	50
Singapore	19
China	7
Taiwan	7
India	7

Hedging History: —

Special Securities % assets 09-30-01	
Restricted/Illiquid Secs	0
Emerging–Markets Secs	77
Options/Futures/Warrants	Yes

Composition % assets 09-30-01			
Cash	3.5	Bonds	0.0
Stocks	96.5	Other	0.0

Sector Weightings	% of Stocks	Rel Cat	5–Year High	5–Year Low
Utilities	4.9	1.0	12	1
Energy	7.6	2.4	10	0
Financials	34.6	1.1	61	31
Industrials	7.0	0.9	12	1
Durables	6.0	1.0	9	3
Staples	1.4	0.4	2	0
Services	14.7	0.8	26	14
Retail	8.7	1.9	10	0
Health	0.0	0.0	1	0
Technology	15.2	0.8	15	0

Address:	Federal Reserve Plaza Boston, MA 02210 617–722–6000 / 800–322–2847
Web Address:	www.libertyfunds.com
*Inception:	04-03-95
Advisor:	Newport Fund Mgmt.
Subadvisor:	None
NTF Plans:	Datalynx , Fidelity Inst.

Minimum Purchase:	$1000	Add: $250	IRA: $25
Min Auto Inv Plan:	$1000	Add: $50	
Sales Fees:	5.75%L, 0.25%S		
Management Fee:	1.0% mx./.75% mn., .25%A		
Actual Fees:	Mgt: 1.02%	Dist: 0.25%	
Expense Projections:	3Yr: $1099	5Yr: $1477	10Yr: $2534
Avg Brok Commission:	—	Income Distrib: Annually	
Total Cost (relative to category):		Below Avg	

LKCM Small Cap Equity

Ticker	Load	NAV	Yield	Total Assets	Mstar Category
LKSCX	None	$17.29	0.4%	$220.6 mil	Small Blend

Prospectus Objective: Small Company

LKCM Small Cap Equity Portfolio seeks capital appreciation.

The fund ordinarily invests at least 65% of its assets in equity securities of companies that have market capitalizations of less than $1 billion. It invests in companies believed to have potential for above-average growth in earnings and/or revenues. The fund may invest up to 5% of its assets in convertible debt securities rated below investment grade. It may also invest in U.S. government obligations, investment-grade corporate debt securities, and short-term instruments. The fund may invest to a limited extent in securities of foreign issuers.

Historical Profile

Return Average
Risk Average
Rating ★★★★ Above Avg

Investment Style
Equity
Average Stock %: 100% 90% 97% 84% 87% 82% 79%

▼ Manager Change
▽ Partial Manager Change

Fund Performance vs. Category Average
▒ Quarterly Fund Return +/– Category Average
— Category Baseline

Performance Quartile (within Category)

Portfolio Manager(s)

J. Luther King Jr., CFA. Since 7-94. BS'62 Texas Christian U.; MBA'65 Texas Christian U. Other funds currently managed: IDEX LKCM Strategic Total Return A, IDEX LKCM Strategic Total Return M, IDEX LKCM Strategic Total Return B.

1990	1991	1992	1993	1994	1995	1996	1997	1998	1999	2000	12–01	History
—	—	—	—	10.50	13.84	16.20	16.89	15.72	18.08	17.00	17.29	NAV
—	—	—	—	5.00*	33.23	26.95	23.07	–6.26	16.83	11.37	7.50	Total Return %
—	—	—	—	2.25*	–4.31	4.00	–10.28	–34.84	–4.21	20.47	19.38	+/– S&P 500
—	—	—	—	—	4.79	10.41	0.71	–3.71	–4.44	14.40	5.01	+/– Russell 2000
—	—	—	—	0.00	1.33	0.49	0.45	0.39	0.18	0.28	0.44	Income Return %
—	—	—	—	5.00	31.89	26.46	22.62	–6.65	16.64	11.10	7.06	Capital Return %
—	—	—	—	—	22	16	74	60	34	51	46	Total Rtn % Rank Cat
—	—	—	—	0.00	0.14	0.07	0.07	0.07	0.03	0.05	0.07	Income $
—	—	—	—	0.00	0.00	1.02	2.64	0.05	0.25	3.10	0.92	Capital Gains $
—	—	—	—	—	1.00	1.00	0.95	0.91	0.90	0.93	—	Expense Ratio %
—	—	—	—	—	1.15	0.39	0.22	0.35	0.16	0.32	—	Income Ratio %
—	—	—	—	—	—	66	34	35	48	79	—	Turnover Rate %
—	—	—	—	—	122.8	199.1	255.3	246.4	230.2	211.0	220.6	Net Assets $mil

Performance 12-31-01

	1st Qtr	2nd Qtr	3rd Qtr	4th Qtr	Total
1997	–1.97	14.52	15.87	–5.39	23.07
1998	9.35	–5.58	–18.98	12.05	–6.26
1999	–2.42	12.58	–3.53	10.23	16.83
2000	6.42	–0.05	–2.24	7.11	11.37
2001	–4.59	8.51	–7.33	12.05	7.50

Trailing	Total Return%	+/– S&P 500	+/– Russ 2000	% Rank All	% Rank Cat	Growth of $10,000
3 Mo	12.05	1.36	–9.03	33	96	11,205
6 Mo	3.84	9.39	7.92	10	14	10,384
1 Yr	7.50	19.38	5.01	12	46	10,750
3 Yr Avg	11.83	12.86	5.42	8	38	13,987
5 Yr Avg	10.04	–0.66	2.52	18	58	16,137
10 Yr Avg	—	—	—	—	—	—
15 Yr Avg	—	—	—	—	—	—

Tax Analysis	Tax-Adj Ret%	%Rank Cat	%Pretax Ret	%Rank Cat
3 Yr Avg	9.85	39	83.3	50
5 Yr Avg	7.96	61	79.3	61
10 Yr Avg	—	—	—	—

Potential Capital Gain Exposure: 29% of assets

Risk Analysis

Time Period	Load-Adj Return %	Risk %Rank[1] All	Risk %Rank[1] Cat	Morningstar Return	Morningstar Risk	Morningstar Risk-Adj Rating
1 Yr	7.50					
3 Yr	11.83	43	10	1.56[2]	0.60	★★★★
5 Yr	10.04	57	20	1.21[2]	0.78	★★★★
Incept	15.13	—	—	—	—	

Average Historical Rating (54 months): 2.9★s

[1] 1=low, 100=high [2] T-Bill return substituted for category avg.

Category Rating (3 Yr)

1 2 3 4 5
Worst Best

Return Average
Risk Low

Other Measures	Standard Index S&P 500	Best Fit Index Russ 2000
Alpha	10.0	5.4
Beta	0.47	0.55
R-Squared	29	74

Standard Deviation	16.51
Mean	11.83
Sharpe Ratio	0.47

Analysis by Peter Di Teresa 12-28-01

Small-cap investors who get queasy from volatility will want to take a look at this fund.

Relative to most small-cap offerings, LKCM Small Cap Equity Fund is a model of tranquility. Its three-year standard deviation of 16.57 is 27% lower than the small-blend average, and its five-year number is comparably mild. And when the category fell 17% in 2001's third quarter, this fund dropped less than half as much. (The fund did lose 19% in 1998's third quarter, its worst-ever quarter, but that was still less than most peers lost.)

The fund has benefited from focusing on steady companies going for cheap prices. Manager Luther King and his team look for companies with high returns on equity that dominate their businesses. Such firms usually have good growth potential and are better able to weather difficult times. Buying stocks that are cheaper than their fair market values also affords some protection.

The fund has been helped particularly in this tumultuous market by King's reluctance to overpay for investments. He let cash build up to roughly one fifth of assets in 1999's overheated market and has been slow to deploy it. That has given the fund a cushion against volatility.

Even though 2001 has been a rough year, the fund's 7.6% return for the year to date through Dec. 27 is only a bit better than average. That's because the fund's style can also dull its ability to exploit a favorable market. As the market has come on strong in the past three months, the fund is in its category's depths for the period, despite a 14% gain.

The fund's trade-off between volatility and returns won't appeal to investors who want to shoot out the lights. That said, the fund's returns since its mid-1994 inception are above average, so shareholders haven't been shortchanged here.

Portfolio Analysis 09-30-01

Share change since 06–01 Total Stocks: 76	Sector	PE	YTD Ret%	% Assets
Kirby	Services	17.6	31.19	3.03
RailAmerica	Services	16.3	84.34	3.01
Texas Regl Bancshares	Financials	15.9	18.42	2.50
Mobile Mini	Industrials	30.8	70.09	2.39
⊖ Cott	Staples	—	108.50	2.17
Lindsay Mfg	Industrials	28.9	–13.80	1.92
Sylvan Learning Sys	Services	39.4	48.99	1.65
⊕ InterTAN	Retail	17.7	8.04	1.62
⊕ Roper Inds	Industrials	29.0	50.94	1.56
Reliance Steel & Aluminum	Industrials	15.4	7.01	1.50
⊖ Henry Schein	Health	22.0	6.95	1.39
☼ Landstar Sys	Services	13.3	30.79	1.39
CNA Surety	Financials	13.7	13.09	1.36
⊕ Dal–Tile Intl	Industrials	16.0	63.87	1.33
⊕ King Pharmaceuticals	Health	45.8	8.68	1.33
☼ P F Chang's China Bistro	Services	41.9	50.45	1.30
Swift Transp	Services	71.7	8.57	1.28
⊕ Tetra Tech	Services	35.1	–21.90	1.28
Tom Brown	Energy	10.8	–17.80	1.26
Triad Hospitals	Health	—	–9.87	1.24
Patterson Dental	Health	33.0	20.83	1.24
Brandywine Realty Tr	Financials	29.7	10.52	1.23
Harris	Technology	28.0	0.33	1.22
⊕ Cohu	Industrials	—	43.29	1.22
☼ Wright Medical Grp	Health	—	—	1.22

Current Investment Style

Style: Value Blnd Growth; Size: Large Med Small

	Stock Port Avg	Relative S&P 500 Current	Relative S&P 500 Hist	Rel Cat
Price/Earnings Ratio	23.6	0.76	0.73	0.95
Price/Book Ratio	3.0	0.52	0.44	0.93
Price/Cash Flow	15.1	0.84	0.77	0.97
3 Yr Earnings Growth	20.3	1.39	1.22	1.20
1 Yr Earnings Est%	18.9	—	—	22.01
Med Mkt Cap $mil	867	0.0	0.0	0.88

[1]figure is based on 50% or less of stocks

Special Securities % assets 09-30-01	
Restricted/Illiquid Secs	0
Emerging–Markets Secs	0
Options/Futures/Warrants	Yes

Composition % assets 09-30-01	
Cash	18.5
Stocks*	81.5
Bonds	0.0
Other	0.0
*Foreign (% stocks)	3.5

Market Cap	
Giant	0.0
Large	2.1
Medium	28.4
Small	66.9
Micro	2.6

Sector Weightings	% of Stocks	Rel S&P	5-Year High	5-Year Low
Utilities	0.0	0.0	2	0
Energy	5.7	0.8	16	6
Financials	16.6	0.9	22	7
Industrials	27.2	2.4	29	13
Durables	2.1	1.4	2	0
Staples	2.8	0.4	6	1
Services	25.9	2.4	35	15
Retail	4.2	0.6	8	1
Health	10.9	0.7	17	10
Technology	4.6	0.3	24	2

Address: 301 Commerce Street Suite 1600, Fort Worth, TX 76102, 817–332–3235
Web Address: www.lkcm.com
*Inception: 07-14-94
Advisor: PricewaterhouseCoopers
Subadvisor: None
NTF Plans: N/A

Minimum Purchase: $10000 Add: $1000 IRA: $10000
Min Auto Inv Plan: $10000 Add: $100
Sales Fees: No–load
Management Fee: .75%, .06%A
Actual Fees: Mgt: 0.75% Dist: —
Expense Projections: 3Yr: $288 5Yr: $500 10Yr: $1100
Avg Brok Commission: — Income Distrib: Annually
Total Cost (relative to category): Below Avg

Longleaf Partners

Ticker	Load	NAV	Yield	Total Assets	Mstar Category
LLPFX	None	$24.51	0.8%	$4,534.9 mil	Mid–Cap Value

Prospectus Objective: Growth

Longleaf Partners Fund seeks long-term capital growth.

The fund invests primarily in common stocks; at least 75% of the equity portion consists of common stocks issued by companies with market capitalizations greater than $1 billion. The advisor typically selects stocks of companies that it believes have unrecognized intrinsic value. The fund may invest the balance of assets in equities of smaller companies, debt securities, options, warrants, and money market instruments. It may also invest up to 30% of assets in foreign securities.

Prior to July 22, 1994, the fund was named Southeastern Asset Management Value Trust.

Historical Profile

Return	High
Risk	Below Avg
Rating	★★★★★ Highest

Investment Style Equity — Average Stock %: 93% 95% 92% 92% 99% 90%

▼ Manager Change ▽ Partial Manager Change

Fund Performance vs. Category Average — Quarterly Fund Return +/– Category Average; — Category Baseline

Performance Quartile (within Category)

Portfolio Manager(s)

O. Mason Hawkins, CFA. Since 4-87. BA'70 U. of Florida; MBA'71 U. of Georgia. Other funds currently managed: Longleaf Partners Small-Cap, Longleaf Partners Realty, Masters' Select Equity.

G. Staley Cates, CFA. Since 4-94. BBA'86 U. of Texas. Other funds currently managed: Longleaf Partners Small-Cap, Longleaf Partners Realty, Masters' Select Equity.

John B. Buford, CFA. Since 1-99. BBA'85 U. of Texas. Other fund currently managed: Longleaf Partners Small-Cap.

1990	1991	1992	1993	1994	1995	1996	1997	1998	1999	2000	12–01	History
10.21	13.34	14.70	16.92	17.13	21.15	22.85	25.98	24.39	20.49	22.71	24.51	NAV
–16.37	39.17	20.50	22.23	8.97	27.48	21.02	28.25	14.28	2.19	20.60	10.34	Total Return %
–13.26	8.69	12.88	12.17	7.65	–10.06	–1.93	–5.10	–14.29	–18.85	29.70	22.22	+/– S&P 500
–0.29	1.25	–1.18	6.60	11.10	–7.46	0.76	–6.11	9.19	2.29	1.42	8.01	+/– Russ Midcap Val
1.17	0.54	0.53	0.64	0.95	1.40	1.81	0.94	1.15	1.42	0.80	0.87	Income Return %
–17.54	38.63	19.97	21.59	8.02	26.08	19.20	27.31	13.14	0.77	19.80	9.47	Capital Return %
87	13	21	36	2	60	42	36	14	68	37	32	Total Rtn % Rank Cat
0.15	0.06	0.07	0.09	0.16	0.24	0.38	0.21	0.25	0.29	0.15	0.20	Income $
0.23	0.79	1.29	0.95	1.14	0.44	2.38	3.11	4.81	4.23	1.72	0.33	Capital Gains $
1.32	1.30	1.29	1.26	1.17	1.01	0.95	0.94	0.93	0.92	0.93	—	Expense Ratio %
1.13	0.42	0.50	0.63	1.18	1.45	1.61	0.81	1.12	1.16	0.75	—	Income Ratio %
52	45	29	19	27	13	33	38	44	50	20	—	Turnover Rate %
129.6	177.9	243.7	397.3	753.5	1,876.5	2,300.1	2,605.1	3,688.0	3,630.7	3,757.0	4,534.9	Net Assets $mil

Performance 12-31-01

	1st Qtr	2nd Qtr	3rd Qtr	4th Qtr	Total
1997	2.14	12.38	14.75	–2.64	28.25
1998	13.59	3.96	–18.35	18.52	14.28
1999	6.23	14.16	–15.31	–0.51	2.19
2000	–5.42	8.46	4.85	12.12	20.60
2001	–0.40	11.32	–13.62	15.22	10.35

Trailing	Total Return%	+/– S&P 500	+/– Russ Midcap Val	% Rank All	% Rank Cat	Growth of $10,000
3 Mo	15.22	4.53	3.18	23	33	11,522
6 Mo	–0.48	5.08	0.43	41	45	9,952
1 Yr	10.34	22.22	8.01	6	32	11,034
3 Yr Avg	10.79	11.81	3.98	10	48	13,598
5 Yr Avg	14.79	4.09	3.33	5	24	19,931
10 Yr Avg	17.31	4.38	2.89	2	10	49,343
15 Yr Avg	—	—	—	—	—	—

Tax Analysis	Tax-Adj Ret%	%Rank Cat	%Pretax Ret	%Rank Cat
3 Yr Avg	8.41	46	77.9	55
5 Yr Avg	11.84	26	80.0	42
10 Yr Avg	14.56	10	84.1	30

Potential Capital Gain Exposure: 13% of assets

Risk Analysis

Time Period	Load-Adj Return %	Risk %Rank[1] All	Risk %Rank[1] Cat	Morningstar Return	Morningstar Risk	Morningstar Risk-Adj Rating
1 Yr	10.34					
3 Yr	10.79	49	55	1.31[2]	0.69	★★★★
5 Yr	14.79	52	39	2.57[2]	0.72	★★★★★
10 Yr	17.31	54	20	2.43	0.69	★★★★★

Average Historical Rating (141 months): 4.3★s

[1] 1=low, 100=high [2] T-Bill return substituted for category avg.

Category Rating (3 Yr): 3 (1 Worst – 5 Best)

Return: Average
Risk: Average

Other Measures	Standard Index S&P 500	Best Fit Index Wil REIT
Alpha	10.0	1.2
Beta	0.57	0.72
R–Squared	29	30

Standard Deviation	19.80
Mean	10.79
Sharpe Ratio	0.34

Portfolio Analysis 09-30-01

Share change since 06–01 Total Stocks: 24	Sector	PE	YTD Ret%	% Assets
Marriott Intl Cl A	Services	20.9	–3.16	7.36
⊖ Waste Mgmt	Services	52.3	15.03	5.93
Georgia–Pacific Timber Grp	Industrials	—	23.76	5.05
Tricon Global Restaurants	Services	16.3	49.09	4.97
General Motors	Durables	NMF	–0.97	4.77
Fedex	Services	29.3	29.83	4.59
⊕ Nippon Fire & Marine Ins	Financials	37.0	—	4.41
⊕ Telephone and Data Sys	Services	—	0.29	4.37
⊕ AT&T	Services	7.8	40.59	4.05
⊕ General Motors Cl H	Technology	42.9	–32.80	4.01
Knight Ridder	Services	59.0	16.13	3.70
⊕ TrizecHahn	Financials	28.0	5.92	3.69
Pioneer Natural Res Canada	Energy	9.3	–2.17	3.55
Diageo	Staples	21.7	—	3.41
☼ Walt Disney	Services	—	–27.70	2.91
⊕ Hilton Hotels	Services	17.9	4.72	2.87
Rayonier	Industrials	22.1	30.83	2.61
Host Marriott	Financials	6.2	–24.80	1.84
Coca–Cola Enterprises	Staples	NMF	0.60	1.37
Aetna (Old)	Health	—	22.34	1.04
☼ AT&T Wireless Grp	Services	—	–17.00	0.96
Ucar Intl	Industrials	—	9.74	0.88
Diageo ADR (New)	Staples	—	—	0.57
⊖ Allied Waste Inds	Services	NMF	–3.45	0.53

Current Investment Style

Style: Value Blnd Growth; Size: Large Med Small

	Stock Port Avg	Relative S&P 500 Current	Relative S&P 500 Hist	Rel Cat
Price/Earnings Ratio	31.3	1.01	0.61	1.33
Price/Book Ratio	2.3	0.40	0.44	0.75
Price/Cash Flow	10.6	0.59	0.46	0.85
3 Yr Earnings Growth	11.7[1]	0.80	0.75	0.99
1 Yr Earnings Est%	–18.1	10.22	—	2.94
Med Mkt Cap $mil	9,495	0.2	0.1	1.33

[1] figure is based on 50% or less of stocks

Special Securities % assets 09-30-01	
Restricted/Illiquid Secs	0
Emerging–Markets Secs	0
Options/Futures/Warrants	No

Composition % assets 09-30-01	
Cash	7.1
Stocks*	92.9
Bonds	0.0
Other	0.0
*Foreign (% stocks)	15.2

Market Cap	
Giant	5.2
Large	42.4
Medium	47.9
Small	4.5
Micro	0.0

Sector Weightings	% of Stocks	Rel S&P	5-Year High	5-Year Low
Utilities	0.0	0.0	1	0
Energy	4.5	0.6	6	0
Financials	12.5	0.7	33	3
Industrials	10.8	0.9	17	0
Durables	6.0	3.9	14	0
Staples	6.7	0.9	29	0
Services	53.2	4.9	67	27
Retail	0.0	0.0	16	0
Health	1.3	0.1	14	0
Technology	5.1	0.3	5	0

Analysis by Christopher Traulsen 10-31-01

Now is the time when Longleaf Partners Fund earns its keep.

With the markets slumping and a seemingly endless stream of disappointing economic data reported daily, investors may rightly feel a bit pessimistic. Not the comanagers of this mid-value fund. For them, now is the time to recheck the value of their current holdings, and then go bargain-hunting.

The former is an important task—the fund had about 18% of its assets in the hotel industry at mid-year, spread across Marriott International, Host Marriott, and Hilton Hotels. All took big hits after the terrorist attacks, hurting the fund. Staley Cates is quick to point out that these are three of the strongest firms in the industry and that as weaker rivals scale back they will benefit from the dwindling supply of rooms.

That observation illustrates a key point about this fund's approach—because the managers focus on the long term, they're able to ignore, or better yet, take advantage of short-term shifts in market prices. Two of their biggest recent buys were GM Hughes, which owns DirecTV, and Walt Disney. The former sold off due to a slowdown in its growth rate, but the managers see that as a near-term phenomenon, and the company is currently a takeover target. Disney was put under immense pressure in the third quarter, in part due to forced selling by the Bass family to meet margin calls in the wake of the terrorist attacks.

Such buys bode well for this fund. The comanagers have a lengthy record of discovering gems among the market's refuse, and they have guided the fund to top-quintile long-term returns. The fund can lag at times because the managers run a concentrated portfolio and their picks may remain out of favor, but over time their focus on value has kept volatility moderate. For investors who share the managers' long-term orientation, the fund is one of the best there is.

Address:	6410 Poplar Avenue Suite 900 Memphis, TN 38119 800–445–9469 / 901–761–2474
Web Address:	www.LongleafPartners.com
Inception:	04-08-87
Advisor:	Southeastern Asset Mgmt.
Subadvisor:	None
NTF Plans:	N/A

Minimum Purchase:	$10000	Add: None	IRA: $10000
Min Auto Inv Plan:	$10000	Add: $100	
Sales Fees:	No–load		
Management Fee:	1.0% mx./.75% mn., .10%A		
Actual Fees:	Mgt: 0.78%	Dist: —	
Expense Projections:	3Yr: $305	5Yr: $529	10Yr: $1174
Avg Brok Commission:	—	Income Distrib: Annually	
Total Cost (relative to category):		Below Avg	

Longleaf Partners International

Ticker	Load	NAV	Yield	Total Assets	Mstar Category
LLINX	None	$12.34	1.0%	$834.4 mil	Foreign Stock

Prospectus Objective: Foreign Stock

Longleaf Partners International Fund seeks long-term capital growth.

The fund normally invests at least 65% of assets in foreign equity securities. It typically invests in at least three countries outside of the United States. On occasion, the fund may invest a significant portion of assets in a single country. This fund is non-diversified.

Historical Profile
Return High
Risk Low
Rating ★★★★★ Highest

Investment Style
Equity
Average Stock %: 70% (1998), 88% (1999), 96% (2000), 82% (12-01)

▼ Manager Change
▽ Partial Manager Change

Fund Performance vs. Category Average
■ Quarterly Fund Return +/– Category Average
— Category Baseline

Performance Quartile (within Category)

Portfolio Manager(s)

O. Mason Hawkins, CFA. Since 10-98. BA'70 U. of Florida; MBA'71 U. of Georgia. Other funds currently managed: Longleaf Partners Small-Cap, Longleaf Partners, Longleaf Partners Realty.

G. Staley Cates, CFA. Since 10-98. BBA'86 U. of Texas. Other funds currently managed: Longleaf Partners Small-Cap, Longleaf Partners, Longleaf Partners Realty.

Eugene Andrew McDermott. Since 10-98. BA'92 Princeton U.

1990	1991	1992	1993	1994	1995	1996	1997	1998	1999	2000	12-01	History
—	—	—	—	—	—	—	—	9.97	12.02	12.06	12.34	NAV
—	—	—	—	—	—	—	—	9.02*	24.37	25.93	10.47	Total Return %
—	—	—	—	—	—	—	—	–6.01*	3.33	35.04	22.35	+/– S&P 500
—	—	—	—	—	—	—	—	—	–2.60	40.10	—	+/– MSCI EAFE
—	—	—	—	—	—	—	—	0.06	0.57	3.80	1.15	Income Return %
—	—	—	—	—	—	—	—	8.96	23.80	22.14	9.32	Capital Return %
—	—	—	—	—	—	—	—	—	87	1	1	Total Rtn % Rank Cat
—	—	—	—	—	—	—	—	0.01	0.06	0.38	0.13	Income $
—	—	—	—	—	—	—	—	0.00	0.33	2.63	0.85	Capital Gains $
—	—	—	—	—	—	—	—	1.75	1.75	1.79	—	Expense Ratio %
—	—	—	—	—	—	—	—	0.10	0.60	3.36	—	Income Ratio %
—	—	—	—	—	—	—	—	—	50	69	—	Turnover Rate %
—	—	—	—	—	—	—	—	75.1	294.1	402.5	834.4	Net Assets $mil

Performance 12-31-01

	1st Qtr	2nd Qtr	3rd Qtr	4th Qtr	Total
1997	—	—	—	—	—
1998	—	—	—	—	9.02 *
1999	5.92	15.72	1.80	–0.33	24.37
2000	2.08	10.11	9.62	2.21	25.93
2001	9.12	6.00	–7.67	3.44	10.47

Trailing	Total Return%	+/– S&P 500	+/– MSCI EAFE	% Rank All	% Rank Cat	Growth of $10,000
3 Mo	3.44	–7.24	—	69	95	10,344
6 Mo	–4.49	1.06	—	59	8	9,551
1 Yr	10.47	22.35	—	5	1	11,047
3 Yr Avg	20.05	21.08	—	2	2	17,303
5 Yr Avg	—	—	—	—	—	—
10 Yr Avg	—	—	—	—	—	—
15 Yr Avg	—	—	—	—	—	—

Tax Analysis	Tax-Adj Ret%	%Rank Cat	%Pretax Ret	%Rank Cat
3 Yr Avg	15.88	2	79.2	53
5 Yr Avg	—	—	—	—
10 Yr Avg	—	—	—	—

Potential Capital Gain Exposure: 3% of assets

Risk Analysis

Time Period	Load-Adj Return %	Risk %Rank[1] All	Risk %Rank[1] Cat	Morningstar Return	Morningstar Risk	Morningstar Risk-Adj Rating
1 Yr	10.47					
3 Yr	20.05	35	1	3.69[2]	0.41	★★★★★
5 Yr	—	—	—	—	—	
Incept	22.06	—	—	—	—	

Average Historical Rating (3 months): 5.0★s

[1]1=low, 100=high [2] T-Bill return substituted for category avg.

Category Rating (3 Yr)

1 2 3 4 5 (5 indicated)
Worst Best

Return High
Risk Low

Other Measures	Standard Index S&P 500	Best Fit Index MSCIPcxIND
Alpha	17.6	15.5
Beta	0.39	0.32
R-Squared	20	26
Standard Deviation		17.41
Mean		20.05
Sharpe Ratio		0.98

Portfolio Analysis 09-30-01

Share change since 06-01 Total Stocks: 29	Sector	Country	% Assets
Nippon Fire & Marine Ins	Financials	Japan	9.44
⊕ Fairfax Finl Hldgs	Financials	Canada	7.08
☼ Fiat	Durables	Italy	6.10
⊕ Nissan Fire & Marine Ins	Financials	Japan	5.35
TrizecHahn	Financials	Canada	5.34
⊕ Nippon Broadcstg Sys	Services	Japan	5.29
⊕ Renault	Durables	France	5.00
Tricon Global Restaurants	Services	U.S.	4.50
⊕ Ezaki Glico	Staples	Japan	4.35
⊕ Hollinger Intl	Services	U.S.	4.22
☼ Sky Perfect Comms	N/A	N/A	4.05
⊕ Taisho Pharma	Health	Japan	3.65
⊕ Molson Cl A	Staples	Canada	3.56
☼ Philips Electncs (NV)	Durables	Netherlands	3.47
☼ News	Services	Australia	3.43
Brascan	Industrials	Canada	2.99
⊕ Brierley Investments	Services	New Zealand	2.62
☼ Philips Electncs NV ADR	Durables	Netherlands	2.28
O&Y Properties	Financials	Canada	2.22
Diageo ADR (New)	Staples	United Kingdom	1.91

Current Investment Style

Style: Value Blnd Growth; Size: Large Med Small

	Stock Port Avg	Rel MSCI EAFE Current	Rel MSCI EAFE Hist	Rel Cat
Price/Earnings Ratio	21.4	0.83	0.77	0.84
Price/Cash Flow	12.2	0.95	0.84	0.85
Price/Book Ratio	1.2	0.35	0.30	0.31
3 Yr Earnings Growth	13.1	0.70	—	0.67
Med Mkt Cap $mil	2,236	0.1	0.1	0.12

Country Exposure 09-30-01	% assets
Japan	31
Canada	22
U.S.	9
Italy	6
Netherlands	6

Hedging History: Always

Regional Exposure 09-30-01	% assets
Europe	21
Japan	31
Latin America	0
Pacific Rim	7
Other	31

Special Securities % assets 09-30-01	
Restricted/Illiquid Secs	0
Emerging–Markets Secs	0
Options/Futures/Warrants	No

Composition % assets 09-30-01

Cash	9.3	Bonds	0.0
Stocks	90.7	Other	0.0

Sector Weightings	% of Stocks	Rel Cat	5-Year High	5-Year Low
Utilities	0.0	0.0	—	—
Energy	0.5	0.1	—	—
Financials	33.7	1.6	—	—
Industrials	3.4	0.3	—	—
Durables	19.7	2.9	—	—
Staples	11.8	1.7	—	—
Services	24.7	1.4	—	—
Retail	2.1	0.4	—	—
Health	4.1	0.4	—	—
Technology	0.0	0.0	—	—

Analysis by Christopher Traulsen 10-31-01

Longleaf Partners International Fund is very good at what it does—just don't buy it for the wrong reasons.

This fund is just plain embarrassing the competition. The average foreign stock fund is down 26% for the year to date through Oct. 30, 2001, and this fund is up 9.5%. Over the trailing three years, it has beaten its typical peer by an average of 20 percentage points a year.

Part of that owes to the fund's strict value approach. The foreign-stock category has a decided growth tilt, but this fund's managers only buy companies trading at discounts of at least 40% to their intrinsic values. In 2000 and 2001, the fund's stance has been a recipe for success as growth stocks have tanked.

But the fund's strengths go beyond just its value bias: In both 2000 and 2001, it has beaten every foreign-stock fund there is by a huge margin, including other value offerings. Issue selection has been the real key. The fund only holds 20 to 25 stocks, and the managers have done an excellent job ferreting out bargains: DeBeers soared this year as it was taken private, and top holding Nippon Fire and Marine has been a strong performer. The fund also boasts experienced managers: Staley Cates and Mason Hawkins have used this style with great success at the firm's domestic funds for over a decade, and Andrew McDermott has been at this fund since its inception.

Investors shouldn't jump in here expecting the fund to always do so well, though. In growth-led years, it is likely to lag badly, as it did in 1999. Also, its concentrated format will lead to occasional bumps in the road; and it's fully hedged, which will hurt when the dollar weakens. Finally, the team will hold cash when it can't find stocks that meet its criteria (though a big chunk of money was put to work in the third quarter with buys such as Fiat and Phillips Electronics). But for investors seeking a value-oriented foreign offering, we think this is a strong choice.

Address:	6410 Poplar Avenue Suite 900 Memphis, TN 38119 800–445–9469 / 901–761–2474
Web Address:	www.LongleafPartners.com
*Inception:	10-26-98
Advisor:	Southeastern Asset Mgmt.
Subadvisor:	None
NTF Plans:	N/A

Minimum Purchase:	$10000	Add: None IRA: $10000
Min Auto Inv Plan:	$10000	Add: $100
Sales Fees:	No-load	
Management Fee:	1.5%, .10%A	
Actual Fees:	Mgt: 1.50%	Dist: —
Expense Projections:	3Yr: $582	5Yr: — 10Yr: —
Avg Brok Commission:	—	Income Distrib: Annually
Total Cost (relative to category):	—	

Longleaf Partners Small–Cap

Ticker	Load	NAV	Yield	Total Assets	Mstar Category
LLSCX	Closed	$21.68	1.0%	$1,635.0 mil	Small Value

Prospectus Objective: Small Company

Longleaf Partners Small-Cap Fund seeks long-term capital growth.

The fund normally invests in companies of the size included in the Russell 2000 index. It may invest the remainder in larger-cap companies. The advisor selects issuers on the basis of unrecognized intrinsic worth, indications of a shareholder-oriented management, evidence of financial strength, attractive future prospects, and limited institutional ownership.

Prior to July 22, 1994, the fund was named Southeastern Asset Management Small-Cap Fund. The fund closed to new investors on Sept. 1, 1997.

Historical Profile

Return Above Avg
Risk Below Avg
Rating ★★★★★ Highest

Investment Style: Equity — Average Stock %: 98% 85% 85% 97% 97% 76%

▼ Manager Change
▽ Partial Manager Change

Fund Performance vs. Category Average
■ Quarterly Fund Return +/– Category Average
— Category Baseline

Performance Quartile (within Category)

Portfolio Manager(s)

O. Mason Hawkins, CFA. Since 3-91. BA'70 U. of Florida; MBA'71 U. of Georgia. Other funds currently managed: Longleaf Partners, Longleaf Partners Realty, Masters' Select Equity.

G. Staley Cates, CFA. Since 3-91. BBA'86 U. of Texas. Other funds currently managed: Longleaf Partners, Longleaf Partners Realty, Masters' Select Equity.

John B. Buford, CFA. Since 1-99. BBA'85 U. of Texas. Other fund currently managed: Longleaf Partners.

1990	1991	1992	1993	1994	1995	1996	1997	1998	1999	2000	12-01	History
8.50	10.67	11.40	13.49	13.28	14.46	17.86	22.18	21.95	20.20	22.62	21.68	NAV
–30.01	26.26	6.84	19.84	3.70	18.57	30.64	29.04	12.71	4.05	12.80	5.45	Total Return %
–26.89	–4.22	–0.78	9.78	2.39	–18.96	7.70	–4.31	–15.87	–16.99	21.90	17.32	+/– S&P 500
–8.23	–15.44	–22.29	–4.01	5.25	–7.18	9.27	–2.65	19.14	5.53	–10.02	–8.57	+/– Russell 2000 V
2.87	0.71	0.00	0.00	0.00	0.89	0.16	1.01	0.84	0.40	0.24	1.15	Income Return %
–32.88	25.56	6.84	19.84	3.70	17.69	30.48	28.03	11.87	3.65	12.55	4.29	Capital Return %
95	88	89	30	19	85	13	65	3	43	75	92	Total Rtn % Rank Cat
0.36	0.06	0.00	0.00	0.00	0.12	0.02	0.18	0.17	0.08	0.05	0.24	Income $
0.23	0.00	0.00	0.17	0.70	1.17	1.01	0.69	2.77	2.54	0.11	1.84	Capital Gains $
1.43	1.43	1.45	1.45	1.38	1.30	1.23	1.09	1.01	0.97	0.98	—	Expense Ratio %
3.48	0.60	–0.03	–0.45	–0.22	0.84	0.18	1.18	0.87	0.38	0.24	—	Income Ratio %
15	65	26	14	20	33	28	17	53	47	22	—	Turnover Rate %
47.9	60.4	62.2	85.1	99.6	136.0	252.2	915.3	1,351.0	1,431.1	1,477.2	1,635.0	Net Assets $mil

Performance 12-31-01

	1st Qtr	2nd Qtr	3rd Qtr	4th Qtr	Total
1997	6.89	9.74	7.83	2.02	29.04
1998	12.40	1.16	–13.40	14.46	12.71
1999	–2.82	13.83	–5.56	–0.40	4.05
2000	–4.95	6.77	4.93	5.93	12.80
2001	0.35	9.16	–9.28	6.10	5.45

Trailing	Total Return%	+/– S&P 500	+/– Russ 2000V	% Rank All	% Rank Cat	Growth of $10,000
3 Mo	6.10	–4.58	–10.61	60	100	10,610
6 Mo	–3.74	1.81	–4.90	55	90	9,626
1 Yr	5.45	17.32	–8.57	21	92	10,545
3 Yr Avg	7.36	8.39	–3.96	16	79	12,375
5 Yr Avg	12.47	1.77	1.28	9	39	17,998
10 Yr Avg	13.98	1.06	–1.13	8	37	37,020
15 Yr Avg	—	—	—	—	—	—

Tax Analysis	Tax-Adj Ret%	%Rank Cat	%Pretax Ret	%Rank Cat
3 Yr Avg	5.60	84	76.1	91
5 Yr Avg	10.49	40	84.1	61
10 Yr Avg	12.33	31	88.2	10

Potential Capital Gain Exposure: 6% of assets

Risk Analysis

Time Period	Load-Adj Return %	Risk %Rank[1] All	Risk %Rank[1] Cat	Morningstar Return	Morningstar Risk	Morningstar Risk-Adj Rating
1 Yr	5.45					
3 Yr	7.36	46	37	0.52[2]	0.64	★★★★
5 Yr	12.47	46	8	1.87[2]	0.60	★★★★
10 Yr	13.98	53	18	1.54	0.67	★★★★★

Average Historical Rating (121 months): 3.0★s

[1] 1=low, 100=high [2] T-Bill return substituted for category avg.

Category Rating (3 Yr)

① ❷ ③ ④ ⑤
Worst Best

Return Below Avg
Risk Average

Other Measures	Standard Index S&P 500	Best Fit Index SPMid400
Alpha	5.4	0.0
Beta	0.43	0.50
R-Squared	23	42
Standard Deviation		16.15
Mean		7.36
Sharpe Ratio		0.17

Analysis by Christopher Traulsen 10-31-01

Longleaf Partners Small-Cap Fund is better than it looks right now.

This fund, which remains closed to new investors, has had a tough run lately. Blowups at prominent holdings such as Safety-Kleen, USG, and U.S. Industries have caused it to lag its peers badly in 2000 and thus far in 2001. As a result, its three-year return now ranks in the small-value category's bottom third. Longleaf also estimates the fund will distribute $1.83 per share in capital gains, or 8% of the fund's Oct. 31 NAV, on Nov. 14.

Nevertheless, we think investors should look beyond the fund's recent woes. Its managers are among the best value investors around. They've made some mistakes here lately, but over the years, they've had tremendous success using their disciplined style at this fund and its siblings. They also have a lot of their own money tied up here, so their interests are aligned with shareholders'.

The managers operate on the principle that if you buy something for significantly less than it's worth, you should earn a decent return. One recent buy is the debt of networker Level 3 Communications. The firm has been badly beaten down, but the managers think the value of its network and its liquid assets make its debt very attractive, particularly since they were able to get the bonds at fire-sale prices.

Of course, the strategy only works if a manager is smart enough to figure out what a company is worth, and at that, the managers have generally excelled: Despite the fund's near-term glitches, they've had enough success over the years to power it to a top-third 10-year return. Even this year, the strength of holdings such as Fleming Companies and Genlyte Group showcase their ability to find gems amid the market's refuse.

Investors here have a fund with a good record, superior, shareholder friendly management, and reasonable expenses. To us, that still seems like a pretty good combination.

Portfolio Analysis 09-30-01

Share change since 06-01 Total Stocks: 24	Sector	PE	YTD Ret%	% Assets
⊖ Fleming Companies	Retail	—	57.07	6.00
⊕ Fairfax Finl Hldgs	Financials	—	—	5.66
⊕ Alleghany	Financials	7.3	–4.48	4.47
Level 3 Comm 9.125%	N/A	—	—	4.41
⊕ Texas Inds	Industrials	NMF	24.18	4.23
Genlyte Grp	Industrials	10.9	25.31	4.17
MONY Grp	Financials	50.1	–29.00	4.13
⊕ Hollinger Intl	Services	—	–22.90	3.92
☼ Forest City Enterprises Cl A	Financials	19.0	48.90	3.75
Catellus Dev	Financials	21.2	5.14	3.54
Ralcorp Hldgs	Staples	17.1	38.63	3.45
Neiman–Marcus Grp Cl B		—	—	3.30
TimberWest Forest	Financials	—	—	3.06
Brascan	Industrials	27.5	32.06	2.97
IHOP	Services	16.0	35.10	2.85
PepsiAmericas	Staples	26.0	–15.50	2.72
⊖ Hilb Rogal & Hamilton	Financials	28.7	42.84	2.62
Thomas Inds	Industrials	13.9	8.91	2.18
Hilton Hotels	Services	17.9	4.72	1.33
Deltic Timber	Industrials	37.5	15.89	1.28
US Inds	Durables	—	–68.00	1.12
USG	Industrials	—	–74.50	0.68
⊖ Wyndham Intl Cl A	Services	—	–68.00	0.45
☼ Macerich	Financials	22.9	51.81	0.44
☼ Neiman–Marcus Grp	Retail	18.4	–12.60	0.28

Current Investment Style

Style: Value Blnd Growth; Size: Large Med Small

	Stock Port Avg	Relative S&P 500 Current	Relative S&P 500 Hist	Rel Cat
Price/Earnings Ratio	25.6	0.83	0.59	1.18
Price/Book Ratio	1.8	0.31	0.28	0.73
Price/Cash Flow	8.2[1]	0.46	0.50	0.64
3 Yr Earnings Growth	11.8	0.81	1.07	1.02
1 Yr Earnings Est%	3.7[1]	—	—	–0.93
Med Mkt Cap $mil	1,130	0.0	0.0	1.30

[1] figure is based on 50% or less of stocks

Special Securities % assets 09-30-01	
Restricted/Illiquid Secs	0
Emerging–Markets Secs	0
Options/Futures/Warrants	No

Composition % assets 09-30-01	
Cash	18.9
Stocks*	76.2
Bonds	4.9
Other	0.0
*Foreign (% stocks)	17.1

Market Cap	
Giant	0.0
Large	0.0
Medium	56.0
Small	40.4
Micro	3.6

Sector Weightings	% of Stocks	Rel S&P	5-Year High	5-Year Low
Utilities	0.0	0.0	6	0
Energy	0.0	0.0	11	0
Financials	42.4	2.4	54	18
Industrials	23.8	2.1	24	4
Durables	1.7	1.1	9	0
Staples	9.5	1.2	25	0
Services	13.1	1.2	53	10
Retail	9.6	1.4	23	0
Health	0.0	0.0	8	0
Technology	0.0	0.0	10	0

Address:	6410 Poplar Avenue Suite 900 Memphis, TN 38119 800–445–9469 / 901–761–2474
Web Address:	www.LongleafPartners.com
Inception:	12-28-88
Advisor:	Southeastern Asset Mgmt.
Subadvisor:	None
NTF Plans:	N/A

Minimum Purchase:	Closed	Add: None	IRA: —
Min Auto Inv Plan:	Closed	Add: $100	
Sales Fees:	No-load		
Management Fee:	1.0% mx./.75% mn., .10%A		
Actual Fees:	Mgt: 0.83%	Dist: —	
Expense Projections:	3Yr: $321	5Yr: $557	10Yr: $1234
Avg Brok Commission:	—	Income Distrib: Annually	
Total Cost (relative to category):		Below Avg	

Loomis Sayles Bond Instl

Ticker	Load	NAV	Yield	SEC Yield	Total Assets	Mstar Category
LSBDX	None	$10.44	8.6%	8.71%	$1,414.4 mil	Multisector Bond

Prospectus Objective: Corp Bond—General

Loomis Sayles Bond Fund seeks total return through a combination of current income and capital appreciation.

The fund invests primarily in investment-grade securities, although it may invest up to 35% of its assets in lower fixed income securities and up to 20% of its assets in preferred stocks. The fund may invest in fixed income securities of any maturity. It may invest without limit in Canadian issues, and may invest up to 20% of assets in securities issued in other foreign countries, including emerging markets securities.

The fund offers Institutional, Retail and Administrative share classes.

Historical Profile

Return Above Avg
Risk Above Avg
Rating ★★★★ Above Avg

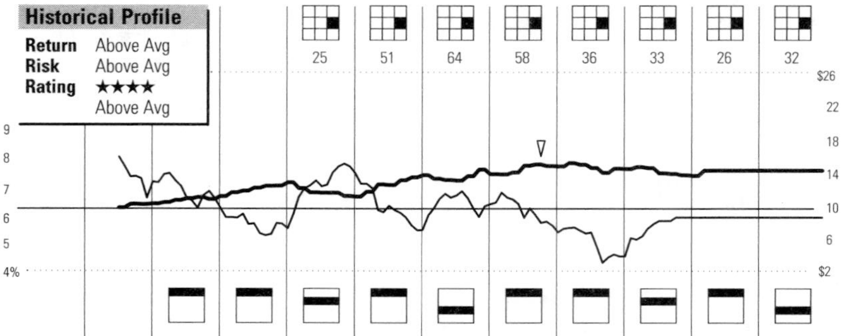

Investment Style
Fixed-Income
Income Rtn %Rank Cat: 25, 51, 64, 58, 36, 33, 26, 32

Growth of Principal vs. Interest Rate Shifts
— Principal Value $000 (NAV with capital gains reinvested)
— Interest Rate % on 10 Yr Treasury
▼ Manager Change
▽ Partial Manager Change
► Mgr Unknown After
◄ Mgr Unknown Before

Performance Quartile (within Category)

1990	1991	1992	1993	1994	1995	1996	1997	1998	1999	2000	12-01	History
—	10.23	10.36	11.37	10.05	12.29	12.38	12.83	11.95	11.52	11.06	10.44	NAV
—	8.83*	14.29	22.22	–4.07	31.96	10.29	12.70	4.70	4.50	4.36	2.66	Total Return %
—	—	6.89	12.47	–1.15	13.49	6.68	3.01	–3.98	5.33	–7.27	–5.76	+/– LB Aggregate
—	—	–2.37	3.31	–3.10	14.58	–2.13	0.07	4.12	1.22	9.57	–3.12	+/– FB High–Yield
—	5.25	7.63	7.98	7.79	8.43	7.21	7.14	7.63	8.27	8.49	8.39	Income Return %
—	3.58	6.66	14.24	–11.86	23.53	3.09	5.56	–2.94	–3.77	–4.14	–5.73	Capital Return %
—	—	10	10	42	1	56	5	21	31	22	73	Total Rtn % Rank Cat
—	0.52	0.76	0.81	0.86	0.83	0.86	0.86	0.95	0.96	0.95	0.90	Income $
—	0.12	0.54	0.46	0.00	0.08	0.26	0.22	0.52	0.00	0.00	0.00	Capital Gains $
—	1.00	1.00	0.94	0.84	0.79	0.75	0.75	0.75	0.75	0.75	—	Expense Ratio %
—	8.97	7.50	8.26	7.92	8.34	7.93	7.36	7.34	8.15	8.32	—	Income Ratio %
—	—	101	170	87	35	42	41	—	33	17	—	Turnover Rate %
—	9.7	18.4	64.2	82.5	252.4	538.2	1,258.5	1,495.6	1,536.9	1,577.3	1,346.1	Net Assets $mil

Portfolio Manager(s)

Daniel J. Fuss, CFA. Since 5-91. BS'55 Marquette U.; MBA'65 Marquette U. Other funds currently managed: Managers Bond, CDC Nvest Strategic Income A, CDC Nvest Strategic Income B.

Kathleen C. Gaffney, CFA. Since 10-97. BA'83 U. of Massachusetts. Other funds currently managed: CDC Nvest Strategic Income A, CDC Nvest Strategic Income B, CDC Nvest Strategic Income C.

Performance 12-31-01

	1st Qtr	2nd Qtr	3rd Qtr	4th Qtr	Total
1997	–0.24	5.84	6.18	0.52	12.70
1998	3.82	0.45	–5.01	5.68	4.70
1999	3.60	0.40	–2.10	2.63	4.50
2000	4.25	–1.00	0.78	0.34	4.36
2001	0.44	–0.53	0.06	2.69	2.66

Trailing	Total Return%	+/– LB Agg	+/– FB High–Yield	% Rank All	% Rank Cat	Growth of $10,000
3 Mo	2.69	2.66	–2.95	70	47	10,269
6 Mo	2.75	–1.90	1.31	17	42	10,275
1 Yr	2.66	–5.76	–3.12	38	73	10,266
3 Yr Avg	3.84	–2.44	2.67	43	31	11,196
5 Yr Avg	5.72	–1.70	2.48	52	13	13,210
10 Yr Avg	9.92	2.70	2.09	33	1	25,761
15 Yr Avg	—	—	—	—	—	—

Tax Analysis	Tax-Adj Ret%	%Rank Cat	%Pretax Ret	%Rank Cat
3 Yr Avg	0.53	33	13.7	77
5 Yr Avg	2.20	25	38.4	40
10 Yr Avg	6.26	1	63.1	5

Potential Capital Gain Exposure: –24% of assets

Risk Analysis

Time Period	Load-Adj Return %	Risk %Rank[1] All	Risk %Rank[1] Cat	Morningstar Return	Morningstar Risk	Morningstar Risk-Adj Rating
1 Yr	2.66					
3 Yr	3.84	33	84	–0.23[2]	1.60	★★
5 Yr	5.72	38	85	0.15[2]	1.74	★★
10 Yr	9.92	44	79	1.68[2]	1.53	★★★★★

Average Historical Rating (92 months): 4.3★s

[1]1=low, 100=high [2] T-Bill return substituted for category avg.

Category Rating (3 Yr)

1 2 **3** 4 5
Worst Best

Return Above Avg
Risk Above Avg

Other Measures	Standard Index LB Agg	Best Fit Index FB HY
Alpha	–2.2	1.5
Beta	1.05	0.68
R-Squared	25	53

Standard Deviation	7.16
Mean	3.84
Sharpe Ratio	–0.18

Portfolio Analysis 09-30-01

Total Fixed-Income: 313	Date of Maturity	Amount $000	Value $000	% Net Assets
Loews Cv 3.125%	09-15-07	81,700	69,576	4.73
Philip Morris 7.75%	01-15-27	50,235	51,905	3.53
Govt of Canada 0%	06-01-25	273,160	43,045	2.92
Intl Bk Reconstr/Dev 0%	08-20-07	152,375	42,120	2.86
Analog Devices 4.75%	10-01-05	44,835	41,192	2.80
Bangkok Bk 144A 9.025%	03-15-29	48,910	37,416	2.54
Republic of Brazil 8%	04-15-14	47,963	32,255	2.19
Time Warner 6.95%	01-15-28	33,900	32,119	2.18
FNMA Debenture 6.25%	05-15-29	28,750	29,114	1.98
Province of Manitoba 7.75%	12-22-25	39,245	28,677	1.95
FNMA N/A	10-29-07	103,925	27,919	1.90
Ontario Hydro 0%	10-15-21	146,050	25,059	1.70
Republic of Brazil 10.125%	05-15-27	36,181	22,749	1.55
Provinve of Manitoba 6.5%	09-22-17	34,300	22,506	1.53
Republic of Venezuela 9.25%	09-15-27	31,350	21,005	1.43
Province of Alberta 5.93%	09-16-16	28,339	18,353	1.25
R&B Falcon 7.375%	04-15-18	18,000	17,678	1.20
Province Brit Columbia 0%	08-23-24	122,250	17,639	1.20
First Indl 7.6%	07-15-28	18,750	17,601	1.20
FHLMC 5.625%	03-15-11	16,150	16,549	1.12

Current Investment Style

Duration: Short Int Long
Quality: High Med Low

Avg Eff Duration[1]	9.3 Yrs
Avg Eff Maturity	17.0 Yrs
Avg Credit Quality	BBB
Avg Wtd Coupon	5.74%
Avg Wtd Price	71.72% of par

[1]figure provided by fund

Special Securities % assets 09-30-01	
Restricted/Illiquid Secs	7
Exotic Mortgage–Backed	0
Emerging–Markets Secs	14
Options/Futures/Warrants	Yes

Credit Analysis % bonds 06-30-01			
US Govt	6	BB	18
AAA	9	B	10
AA	12	Below B	3
A	13	NR/NA	0
BBB	30		

Sector Breakdown % bonds 09-30-01			
US Treasuries	0	CMOs	0
GNMA mtgs	0	ARMs	0
FNMA mtgs	5	Other	94
FHLMC mtgs	2		

Coupon Range	% of Bonds	Rel Cat
0%	18.60	4.25
0% to 7%	34.00	1.01
7% to 8.5%	33.54	1.34
8.5% to 10%	7.77	0.43
More than 10%	6.06	0.32

1.00=Category Average

Composition % assets 09-30-01			
Cash	1.7	Bonds	85.3
Stocks	0.3	Other	12.7

Country Exp % assets

Not Available

Analysis by Eric Jacobson 12-12-01

It would be surprising to see Loomis Sayles Bond's current slump last much longer.

It's true enough that the fund is lagging in 2001. Comanagers Dan Fuss and Kathleen Gaffney almost always focus on long-maturity bonds to minimize reinvestment risk. And despite a general drop in interest rates, those issues have been knocked down by a few unexpected long-term yield spikes. The pair has also been willing to load up on lower-quality debt when it has looked cheap, and some high-yield telecom and Internet holdings proved troublesome over the past several months. Some exposure to what appeared to be undervalued foreign currencies also proved a liability as the greenback stayed strong. Overall, the fund's 1.8% return through Dec. 10, 2001, lands it just inside the multisector-bond category's bottom quartile.

The fund's history, however, is replete with examples of successes canceling out missteps. In 1999, for example, one might have expected its rate-sensitive profile to cause a bad spill. Emerging-markets bonds and technology converts both thrived in that year, though, and the fund's stakes in those sectors compensated for the rising-rate pain. And though some telecom holdings have caused problems this year, Fuss and Gaffney's choices were much less affected by the carnage that sector wrought on rivals in 2000.

Ultimately, buying this fund requires a long time horizon and some faith in Fuss and Gaffney's bottom-up, value-driven approach. The pair has been known to jump on beaten-down sectors a bit early at times, and owing to its rate sensitivity, the fund clearly courts much short-term volatility. Their value plays have worked more often than not, however, and the fund's long-term record remains stellar. This team's skill and history suggest a strong recovery is somewhere in the cards.

Address:	One Financial Center Boston, MA 02111 800–633–3330 / 617–482–2450
Web Address:	www.loomissayles.com/
*Inception:	05-16-91
Advisor:	Loomis Sayles
Subadvisor:	None
NTF Plans:	Datalynx , Fidelity Inst.

Minimum Purchase:	$25000	Add: $50	IRA: $25000
Min Auto Inv Plan:	$25000	Add: $50	
Sales Fees:	No-load		
Management Fee:	.60%		
Actual Fees:	Mgt: 0.60%	Dist: —	
Expense Projections:	3Yr: $24*	5Yr: $42*	10Yr: $93*
Avg Brok Commission:	—	Income Distrib: Quarterly	
Total Cost (relative to category):	—		

Lord Abbett Affiliated A

Ticker	Load	NAV	Yield	Total Assets	Mstar Category
LAFFX	5.75%	$13.69	1.7%	$11,071.4 mil	Large Value

Prospectus Objective: Growth and Income

Lord Abbett Affiliated Fund seeks long-term growth of capital and income, consistent with low volatility.

The fund normally invests in equities of large, seasoned companies. The advisor may sell stocks it judges to be overpriced relative to risks assumed. The fund may write covered call options with respect to no more than 10% of assets. It may also invest up to 10% in foreign securities.

The fund currently has Class A, B, C, P, and Y shares.

Prior to March 1, 1996, the fund was named Affiliated Fund.

Historical Profile

Return Above Avg
Risk Below Avg
Rating ★★★★ Above Avg

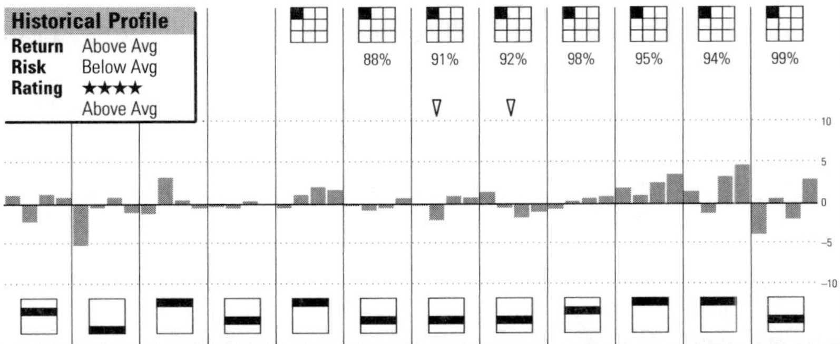

Investment Style Equity — Average Stock %: 88% 91% 92% 98% 95% 94% 99%

▼ Manager Change ▽ Partial Manager Change

Fund Performance vs. Category Average — Quarterly Fund Return +/– Category Average; — Category Baseline

Performance Quartile (within Category)

Portfolio Manager(s)

W. Thomas Hudson Jr., CFA. Since 6-82. BS'64 St. Mary's C. Other funds currently managed: Lord Abbett Large-Cap Research A, Lord Abbett All Value C, Lord Abbett Balanced A.

Robert G. Morris. Since 6-91. Other funds currently managed: Lord Abbett Large-Cap Research A, Lord Abbett All Value C, Lord Abbett Balanced A.

Eli Salzman. Since 6-97. Other funds currently managed: Lord Abbett Large-Cap Research A, Lord Abbett All Value C, Lord Abbett Balanced A.

1990	1991	1992	1993	1994	1995	1996	1997	1998	1999	2000	12-01	History
8.95	10.13	10.27	10.67	9.99	11.59	12.58	13.97	14.74	15.20	15.76	13.69	NAV
–5.29	22.00	12.38	13.23	3.95	31.70	20.14	25.16	14.42	16.88	15.24	–7.94	Total Return %
–2.18	–8.48	4.76	3.18	2.63	–5.83	–2.81	–8.19	–14.16	–4.16	24.34	3.93	+/– S&P 500
–1.63	3.85	3.31	–6.53	6.26	–8.33	–2.17	–10.33	–6.82	5.93	12.93	0.85	+/– Russ Top 200 Val
4.20	4.56	3.94	3.27	3.02	3.08	2.64	2.44	1.74	1.66	1.61	1.54	Income Return %
–9.49	17.44	8.44	9.96	0.93	28.62	17.50	22.72	12.67	15.22	13.63	–9.48	Capital Return %
46	83	23	51	9	62	53	68	43	14	15	66	Total Rtn % Rank Cat
0.43	0.40	0.39	0.33	0.32	0.30	0.30	0.30	0.24	0.24	0.24	0.24	Income $
0.53	0.33	0.68	0.60	0.77	1.19	1.03	1.39	0.95	1.76	1.39	0.57	Capital Gains $
0.50	0.58	0.60	0.63	0.63	0.63	0.66	0.65	0.63	0.74	0.79	—	Expense Ratio %
4.37	4.22	3.73	2.95	2.91	2.90	2.61	2.15	1.64	1.36	1.62	—	Income Ratio %
32	56	42	45	51	54	47	46	56	62	52	—	Turnover Rate %
3,210.5	3,605.2	3,805.8	4,156.6	4,081.6	5,306.6	6,292.2	7,729.7	8,593.6	9,704.2	10,658.0	—	Net Assets $mil

Performance 12-31-01

	1st Qtr	2nd Qtr	3rd Qtr	4th Qtr	Total
1997	3.05	13.38	7.12	0.01	25.16
1998	10.75	–0.26	–11.55	17.10	14.42
1999	2.72	10.79	–6.67	10.04	16.88
2000	1.59	–3.13	8.61	7.82	15.24
2001	–9.47	5.32	–13.97	12.22	–7.94

Trailing	Total Return%	+/– S&P 500	+/– Russ Top 200 Val	% Rank All	% Rank Cat	Growth of $10,000
3 Mo	12.22	1.54	6.70	32	15	11,222
6 Mo	–3.46	2.10	2.32	53	40	9,654
1 Yr	–7.94	3.93	0.85	57	66	9,206
3 Yr Avg	7.43	8.46	6.27	16	11	12,399
5 Yr Avg	12.17	1.47	0.96	9	15	17,756
10 Yr Avg	14.03	1.10	0.00	8	17	37,162
15 Yr Avg	12.87	–0.86	–0.63	18	26	61,503

Tax Analysis	Tax-Adj Ret%	%Rank Cat	%Pretax Ret	%Rank Cat
3 Yr Avg	5.11	14	68.7	47
5 Yr Avg	9.64	17	79.3	35
10 Yr Avg	10.98	21	78.3	45

Potential Capital Gain Exposure: 19% of assets

Risk Analysis

Time Period	Load-Adj Return %	Risk %Rank[1] All	Risk %Rank[1] Cat	Morningstar Return	Morningstar Risk	Morningstar Risk-Adj Rating
1 Yr	–13.24					
3 Yr	5.33	47	17	0.08[2]	0.66	★★★★
5 Yr	10.85	52	24	1.42[2]	0.72	★★★★
10 Yr	13.35	56	24	1.39	0.72	★★★★

Average Historical Rating (193 months): 3.3★s

[1]1=low, 100=high [2] T-Bill return substituted for category avg.

Category Rating (3 Yr)

1 2 3 4 5 — Worst / Best

Return Above Avg
Risk Below Avg

Other Measures	Standard Index S&P 500	Best Fit Index S&P 500
Alpha	6.8	6.8
Beta	0.70	0.70
R-Squared	63	63

Standard Deviation	16.00
Mean	7.43
Sharpe Ratio	0.18

Portfolio Analysis 10-31-01

Share change since 08-01 Total Stocks: 91	Sector	PE	YTD Ret%	% Assets
⊕ ExxonMobil	Energy	15.3	–7.59	4.28
⊕ Mellon Finl	Financials	23.8	–21.90	2.64
⊕ Verizon Comms	Services	29.7	–2.52	2.56
⊕ American Intl Grp	Financials	42.0	–19.20	2.27
⊕ Target	Retail	29.8	28.05	2.17
⊕ United Parcel Svc B	Services	25.0	–6.09	2.17
⊕ Wells Fargo	Financials	22.4	–20.20	2.10
⊕ Viacom Cl B	Services	—	—	2.09
⊕ ALCOA	Industrials	21.4	7.86	2.04
⊕ Minnesota Mng & Mfg	Industrials	34.5	0.16	1.89
⊕ Wachovia	Financials	—	23.13	1.86
⊕ Apple Comp	Technology	—	47.23	1.86
☼ Gannett	Services	20.3	8.10	1.84
⊕ Walt Disney	Services	—	–27.70	1.80
⊕ First Data	Technology	38.1	49.08	1.77
⊖ American Home Products	Health	—	–1.91	1.71
☼ Amex Finl		—	—	1.69
⊖ PepsiCo	Staples	31.4	–0.54	1.67
⊕ Deere	Industrials	—	–2.52	1.57
⊖ Waste Mgmt	Services	52.3	15.03	1.55
⊕ United Tech	Industrials	16.3	–16.70	1.53
⊕ PeopleSoft	Technology	73.1	8.10	1.52
⊖ Dominion Resources	Utilities	19.3	–6.59	1.49
Total Fina Elf ADR	Energy	15.5	–1.76	1.39
⊖ Schering-Plough	Health	22.2	–35.90	1.38

Current Investment Style

Style: Value Blnd Growth; Size: Large Med Small

	Stock Port Avg	Relative S&P 500 Current	Relative S&P 500 Hist	Rel Cat
Price/Earnings Ratio	28.0	0.90	0.86	1.11
Price/Book Ratio	4.2	0.74	0.69	1.02
Price/Cash Flow	14.5	0.81	0.74	1.05
3 Yr Earnings Growth	14.6	1.00	0.61	0.99
1 Yr Earnings Est%	–1.9	1.10	—	0.59
Med Mkt Cap $mil	28,220	0.5	0.6	0.89

Analysis by Langdon Healy 10-16-01

This fund's poor performance this year shouldn't be taken out of context.

Lord Abbett Affiliated Fund's 17.4% year-to-date loss ended Oct. 9, 2001 places it in the bottom quintile of the large-cap value category. But the fund has had only two other bottom-quartile results in the past 15 years, and its overall return during that period is in the category's top quartile. Moreover, the fund hasn't incurred excessive volatility over time.

The fund's reliance on accurate macro-economic projections helps explain its recent stumble. A team of managers evaluates near-term macro-economic factors to determine sector weightings for the fund. They then zero in on the cheapest one third of firms in each sector, buying the ones that they think offer the best combination of value and strong fundamentals.

Recent developments have demonstrated the risks of the top-down elements in the fund's style, however. The managers decided in the summer of 2001 to shift the fund out of defensive stocks (such as utilities) that helped it achieve a top-quintile category ranking in 2000. A more bullish view of the economy led them to stocks that they thought would be early beneficiaries of a recovery, including those in the transportation industry. In the wake of the Sept. 11 terrorist attacks, these stocks have been battered, and the fund fell nearly 14% in the third quarter.

Even though management made unfortunate sector calls this year, these bets have traditionally been fairly mild. Management typically doesn't stash more than a third of net assets in any one sector and spreads its picks across 100 names. Additionally, the fund's value orientation helps keep a lid on risk.

Despite the mixed results generated from the fund's sector moves, we recommend that investors stay the course—it has proved to be a solid long-term offering.

Special Securities % assets 10-31-01	
Restricted/Illiquid Secs	0
Emerging-Markets Secs	0
Options/Futures/Warrants	No

Composition % assets 10-31-01	
Cash	0.0
Stocks*	99.7
Bonds	0.0
Other	0.4
*Foreign (% stocks)	4.5

Market Cap	
Giant	36.2
Large	48.8
Medium	15.0
Small	0.0
Micro	0.0

Sector Weightings	% of Stocks	Rel S&P	5-Year High	5-Year Low
Utilities	7.3	2.3	19	4
Energy	8.5	1.2	15	6
Financials	18.9	1.1	28	11
Industrials	15.4	1.4	33	10
Durables	0.8	0.5	9	0
Staples	5.0	0.6	12	1
Services	18.8	1.7	19	3
Retail	7.0	1.0	7	1
Health	5.9	0.4	11	3
Technology	12.3	0.7	17	6

Address:	90 Hudson Street, Jersey City, NJ 07302, 800-201-6984
Web Address:	www.lordabbett.com
Inception:	05-01-34
Advisor:	Lord Abbett & Co.
Subadvisor:	None
NTF Plans:	N/A

Minimum Purchase:	$250	Add: None IRA: $250
Min Auto Inv Plan:	$250	Add: $50
Sales Fees:	5.75%L, 0.25%B, 0.25%S	
Management Fee:	.50% mx./.30% mn.	
Actual Fees:	Mgt: 0.31%	Dist: 0.35%
Expense Projections:	3Yr: $801	5Yr: $968 10Yr: $1454
Avg Brok Commission:	—	Income Distrib: Quarterly
Total Cost (relative to category):	—	

Lord Abbett Growth Opportunities A

Ticker	Load	NAV	Yield	Total Assets	Mstar Category
LMGAX	5.75%	$18.22	0.0%	$302.3 mil	Mid-Cap Growth

Prospectus Objective: Growth

Lord Abbett Growth Opportunities Fund seeks capital appreciation.

The fund normally invests at least 65% of assets in common stocks of companies with market capitalizations between $1 billion and $6 billion. It may invest up to 35% of assets in foreign securities. The fund may use forwards and options for hedging purposes. It may invest in rights, warrants, and repurchase agreements.

The fund currently offers Class A, B, C, and Y shares.

Historical Profile

Return: Above Avg
Risk: Average
Rating: ★★★★ Above Avg

Investment Style
Equity
Average Stock %: 92% (1998), 97% (2000), 100% (12-01)

▼ Manager Change
▽ Partial Manager Change

Fund Performance vs. Category Average
■ Quarterly Fund Return +/– Category Average
— Category Baseline

Performance Quartile (within Category)

Portfolio Manager(s)

Stephen J. McGruder, CFA. Since 10-98. BA'66 Claremont McKenna C.; BS'66 Stanford U. Other funds currently managed: Lord Abbett Developing Growth A, Lord Abbett Developing Growth C, Lord Abbett Developing Growth B.

Frederic D. Ohr. Since 10-98. Other funds currently managed: Lord Abbett Growth Opportunities B, Lord Abbett Growth Opportunities C, Lord Abbett Growth Opportunities Y.

History

1990	1991	1992	1993	1994	1995	1996	1997	1998	1999	2000	12-01	History
—	—	—	—	—	10.49	12.68	14.25	13.85	21.66	20.83	18.22	NAV
—	—	—	—	—	6.30*	23.65	30.90	13.36	58.03	−3.83	−12.53	Total Return %
—	—	—	—	—	−4.94*	0.71	−2.46	−15.22	36.99	5.27	−0.65	+/– S&P 500
—	—	—	—	—	—	6.17	8.35	−4.51	6.73	7.91	7.63	+/– Russ Midcap Grth
—	—	—	—	—	1.19	2.67	1.74	1.05	0.09	0.00	0.00	Income Return %
—	—	—	—	—	5.11	20.98	29.16	12.30	57.94	−3.83	−12.53	Capital Return %
—	—	—	—	—	—	20	7	54	45	46	26	Total Rtn % Rank Cat
—	—	—	—	—	0.12	0.28	0.22	0.15	0.01	0.00	0.00	Income $
—	—	—	—	—	0.02	0.00	2.06	1.41	0.19	0.00	0.00	Capital Gains $
—	—	—	—	—	—	—	—	0.02	0.41	1.49	—	Expense Ratio %
—	—	—	—	—	—	—	—	1.14	0.25	−1.18	—	Income Ratio %
—	—	—	—	—	—	—	—	137	105	113	—	Turnover Rate %
—	—	—	—	—	—	—	—	5.6	65.1	195.1	—	Net Assets $mil

Performance 12-31-01

	1st Qtr	2nd Qtr	3rd Qtr	4th Qtr	Total
1997	0.79	14.48	12.78	0.59	30.90
1998	8.98	1.09	−20.70	29.75	13.36
1999	−3.83	12.76	−0.33	46.21	58.03
2000	9.42	−8.90	1.67	−5.10	−3.83
2001	−16.71	14.12	−20.71	16.05	−12.53

Trailing	Total Return%	+/– S&P 500	+/– Russ Midcap Grth	% Rank All	% Rank Cat	Growth of $10,000
3 Mo	16.05	5.37	—	22	69	11,605
6 Mo	−7.98	−2.42	—	78	39	9,202
1 Yr	−12.53	−0.65	—	67	26	8,747
3 Yr Avg	9.95	10.98	—	11	25	13,293
5 Yr Avg	14.55	3.85	—	5	15	19,724
10 Yr Avg	—	—	—	—	—	—
15 Yr Avg	—	—	—	—	—	—

Tax Analysis	Tax-Adj Ret%	%Rank Cat	%Pretax Ret	%Rank Cat
3 Yr Avg	9.81	17	98.5	7
5 Yr Avg	13.02	10	89.5	15
10 Yr Avg	—	—	—	—

Potential Capital Gain Exposure: −10% of assets

Risk Analysis

Time Period	Load-Adj Return %	Risk %Rank[1] All	Risk %Rank[1] Cat	Morningstar Return	Morningstar Risk	Morningstar Risk-Adj Rating
1 Yr	−17.56					
3 Yr	7.80	77	22	0.62[2]	1.09	★★★★
5 Yr	13.20	76	11	2.09[2]	1.04	★★★★
Incept	14.93	—	—	—	—	

Average Historical Rating (31 months): 4.3★s

[1] 1=low, 100=high [2] T-Bill return substituted for category avg.

Category Rating (3 Yr)

1 2 3 4 5 — Worst … Best (rating: 4)

Return: Above Avg
Risk: Below Avg

Other Measures	Standard Index S&P 500	Best Fit Index Wil 4500
Alpha	13.3	8.0
Beta	1.06	0.82
R-Squared	49	80

Standard Deviation	28.84
Mean	9.95
Sharpe Ratio	0.20

Portfolio Analysis 10-31-01

Share change since 09-01 Total Stocks: 94	Sector	PE	YTD Ret%	% Assets
Laboratory Corp of Amer	Health	21.0	−8.13	2.83
Caremark Rx	Health	46.6	20.25	2.46
XL Cap Cl A	Financials	22.8	5.82	2.36
HCC Ins Hldgs	Financials	81.0	3.26	2.34
Amerisource Bergen	N/A	—	—	2.22
Barnes & Noble	Retail	—	11.70	2.03
Michaels Stores	Retail	29.3	148.60	1.95
Arthur J. Gallagher & Co.	Financials	26.3	10.31	1.88
⊕ RenaissanceRe Hldgs	Financials	14.7	23.16	1.85
Teva Pharma Inds ADR	Health	48.9	−15.50	1.84
McKesson HBOC	Health	—	4.92	1.83
⊖ Whole Foods Market	Retail	36.0	42.53	1.80
L-3 Comms Hldgs	Technology	33.0	16.88	1.80
Kinder Morgan	Energy	32.2	7.11	1.78
⊕ Ivax	Health	17.5	−34.20	1.76
⊕ Sicor	Health	47.5	8.60	1.66
⊖ UnitedHealth Grp	Financials	26.6	15.37	1.63
Barr Labs	Health	25.0	8.80	1.59
⊕ Enzon	Health	NMF	−9.32	1.56
⊕ Concord EFS	Financials	86.3	49.21	1.53
Intuit	Technology	—	8.42	1.50
Dynegy	Energy	12.8	−54.20	1.47
⊕ Xto Enerrgy	N/A	—	—	1.32
SunGard Data Sys	Technology	33.3	22.78	1.31
Cytyc	Health	49.3	25.16	1.30

Current Investment Style

Style: Value Blnd Growth; Size: Large Med Small

	Stock Port Avg	Relative S&P 500 Current	Relative S&P 500 Hist	Rel Cat
Price/Earnings Ratio	36.2	1.17	—	1.05
Price/Book Ratio	5.4	0.95	—	0.95
Price/Cash Flow	22.4	1.24	—	0.97
3 Yr Earnings Growth	15.9[1]	1.09	—	0.68
1 Yr Earnings Est%	23.8	—	—	2.55
Med Mkt Cap $mil	4,114	0.1	—	0.73

[1] figure is based on 50% or less of stocks

Analysis by Heather Haynos 12-10-01

Lord Abbett Growth Opportunities Fund continues to look strong.

Relatively speaking, this fund is standing taller than ever. Its 13.8% loss for the year to date through Dec. 7, 2001, places in the mid-cap growth category's top third. That's the best relative performance the fund has seen in three years. Still, its overall record is pretty impressive. Its five-year trailing return, for example, stands in the group's top quintile.

Shifts into defensive growth areas have helped curb losses during a rocky period for stocks. Managers Stephen McGruder and Frederic Ohr beefed up the portfolio's health-care weighting in the fall, for instance, emphasizing management-services firms such as top holding Caremark RX, which have generally been strong. Consumer-staples stocks have also had a hand in buoying the portfolio. Whole Foods Market, for example, is up 50% for the year to date through Dec. 7. The duo continues to emphasize those sectors, which they believe will be more resilient in the current downturn.

Although the fund's price multiples are considerably higher than the category norm, McGruder and Ohr have done a decent job of curbing volatility during their tenure. That's largely because the two have tended to avoid huge sector bets (particularly in technology) which have caused considerable pain for some of the fund's peers.Although McGruder and Ohr can only take partial credit for this fund's fine record, the two have had ample time to prove themselves here. And while its expenses are a little steep, this fund's consistent record and low volatility are strong draws.

Special Securities % assets 10-31-01	
Restricted/Illiquid Secs	0
Emerging-Markets Secs	2
Options/Futures/Warrants	No

Composition % assets 10-31-01	
Cash	0.0
Stocks*	100.0
Bonds	0.0
Other	0.0
*Foreign (% stocks)	8.2

Market Cap	
Giant	0.0
Large	17.8
Medium	75.8
Small	6.4
Micro	0.0

Sector Weightings	% of Stocks	Rel S&P	5-Year High	5-Year Low
Utilities	1.0	0.3	—	—
Energy	7.2	1.0	—	—
Financials	16.6	0.9	—	—
Industrials	1.7	0.2	—	—
Durables	1.5	1.0	—	—
Staples	0.5	0.1	—	—
Services	12.5	1.2	—	—
Retail	9.0	1.3	—	—
Health	29.2	2.0	—	—
Technology	20.7	1.1	—	—

Address: 90 Hudson Street, Jersey City, NJ 07302, 800-201-6984
Web Address: www.lordabbett.com
*Inception: 08-01-95
Advisor: Lord Abbett & Co.
Subadvisor: None
NTF Plans: N/A

Minimum Purchase: $1000 Add: $50 IRA: $250
Min Auto Inv Plan: $1000 Add: $50
Sales Fees: 5.75%L, 0.10%B, 0.25%S
Management Fee: .90%
Actual Fees: Mgt: 0.90% Dist: 0.35%
Expense Projections: 3Yr: $1183 5Yr: $1619 10Yr: $2829
Avg Brok Commission: — Income Distrib: Annually
Total Cost (relative to category): —

MainStay Convertible B

Ticker	Load	NAV	Yield	Total Assets	Mstar Category
MCSVX	5.00%d	$11.59	2.4%	$649.5 mil	Convertible

Prospectus Objective: Convertible Bond

MainStay Convertible Fund seeks capital appreciation and current income.

The fund normally invests at least 65% of assets in investment-grade convertible securities. It may also invest in nonconvertible corporate debt, equity securities, U.S. government securities, and/or cash or cash equivalents.

Class A shares have front loads; B shares have deferred loads, higher 12b-1 fees, and conversion features; C shares have level loads.

Historical Profile
Return: Average
Risk: Below Avg
Rating: ★★★★ Above Avg

Investment Style
Equity
Average Stock %

	1994	1995	1996	1997	1998	1999	2000	12-01
Average Stock %	54	67	48	56	54	45	46	84

▼ Manager Change
▽ Partial Manager Change

Fund Performance vs. Category Average
■ Quarterly Fund Return +/– Category Average
— Category Baseline

Performance Quartile (within Category)

Portfolio Manager(s)

Thomas Wynn, CFA. Since 9-97. BA'83 U. of Notre Dame; MBA'88 New York U. Other funds currently managed: MainStay Convertible A, MainStay Strategic Value A, MainStay Strategic Value B.

Edmund C. Spelman. Since 8-99. BA'79 U. of Pennsylvania; MS'79 U. of Pennsylvania. Other funds currently managed: MainStay Capital Appreciation B, MainStay Total Return B, Eclipse Growth Equity.

1990	1991	1992	1993	1994	1995	1996	1997	1998	1999	2000	12-01	History
7.90	11.43	12.06	12.69	11.67	13.45	13.80	13.52	12.49	14.54	12.46	11.59	NAV
–6.70	48.47	13.11	24.47	–1.34	23.02	11.39	10.67	0.53	32.99	6.44	–4.76	Total Return %
–3.58	17.99	5.49	14.41	–2.66	–14.51	–11.55	–22.68	–28.05	11.95	15.54	7.12	+/– S&P 500
0.17	19.34	–4.48	5.91	3.38	–0.17	–0.51	–5.98	–11.14	–0.52	12.60	1.12	+/– Conv.Bond Idx
3.87	3.19	3.05	3.90	3.85	4.12	4.04	3.76	3.45	3.35	3.16	2.21	Income Return %
–10.57	45.28	10.06	20.56	–5.19	18.90	7.35	6.92	–2.93	29.64	3.27	–6.96	Capital Return %
62	1	47	1	8	35	71	92	62	45	25	37	Total Rtn % Rank Cat
0.34	0.25	0.34	0.47	0.48	0.47	0.54	0.51	0.46	0.41	0.46	0.27	Income $
0.00	0.00	0.49	1.79	0.38	0.40	0.63	1.22	0.64	1.54	2.50	0.00	Capital Gains $
2.50	2.70	2.30	1.90	1.90	2.10	2.10	2.08	2.15	2.02	1.99	—	Expense Ratio %
4.70	2.80	2.90	3.40	3.50	4.30	3.80	3.47	2.99	3.09	2.88	—	Income Ratio %
204	283	291	370	269	243	296	273	347	374	245	—	Turnover Rate %
16.9	23.3	35.3	77.4	180.3	426.0	796.8	841.5	657.7	658.3	655.4	563.0	Net Assets $mil

Performance 12-31-01

	1st Qtr	2nd Qtr	3rd Qtr	4th Qtr	Total
1997	0.20	5.93	9.03	–4.37	10.67
1998	8.29	–1.33	–9.82	4.32	0.53
1999	4.02	8.07	1.20	16.89	32.99
2000	9.19	0.26	1.74	–4.43	6.44
2001	–4.81	3.36	–10.66	8.36	–4.76

Trailing	Total Return%	+/– S&P 500	+/– Conv Bond Index	% Rank All	% Rank Cat	Growth of $10,000
3 Mo	8.36	–2.32	0.21	50	40	10,836
6 Mo	–3.19	2.36	–0.53	52	46	9,681
1 Yr	–4.76	7.12	1.12	51	37	9,525
3 Yr Avg	10.47	11.50	4.82	10	17	13,482
5 Yr Avg	8.45	–2.25	–0.52	27	51	14,999
10 Yr Avg	11.06	–1.87	0.16	25	35	28,549
15 Yr Avg	9.92	–3.81	–0.38	42	22	41,346

Tax Analysis	Tax-Adj Ret%	%Rank Cat	%Pretax Ret	%Rank Cat
3 Yr Avg	5.57	30	53.2	52
5 Yr Avg	4.32	56	51.2	85
10 Yr Avg	7.16	41	64.7	76

Potential Capital Gain Exposure: –15% of assets

Risk Analysis

Time Period	Load-Adj Return %	Risk %Rank[1] All	Risk %Rank[1] Cat	Morningstar Return	Morningstar Risk	Morningstar Risk-Adj Rating
1 Yr	–8.48					
3 Yr	9.96	41	21	1.12[2]	0.57	★★★★
5 Yr	8.32	45	25	0.77[2]	0.58	★★★
10 Yr	11.06	51	13	0.92	0.59	★★★★

Average Historical Rating (153 months): 3.4★s

[1] 1=low, 100=high [2] T-Bill return substituted for category avg.

Category Rating (3 Yr)

1 2 3 4 5
Worst Best

Return: Above Avg
Risk: Below Avg

Other Measures	Standard Index S&P 500	Best Fit Index Wil 4500
Alpha	9.4	6.2
Beta	0.66	0.44
R-Squared	67	82
Standard Deviation		14.88
Mean		10.47
Sharpe Ratio		0.42

Portfolio Analysis 11-30-01

Total Fixed-Income: 128	Date of Maturity	Amount $000	Value $000	% Net Assets
Tyco Int'l 0%	11-17-20	16,080	12,462	1.92
S & P 500 Dep Rec SPDR		103	11,758	1.81
Lehman Brothers Hldgs 0.25%	01-05-06	13,500	11,745	1.81
Intl Paper Cv Pfd 5.25%		223	10,248	1.58
Ubs Stamford Cv 1%	04-12-06	10,000	9,925	1.53
Cendant N/A	02-13-21	13,825	9,349	1.44
AmeriSource 5%	12-01-07	6,525	8,776	1.35
JC Penney 144A 5%	10-15-08	7,850	8,596	1.32
ALZA N/A	07-28-20	9,490	7,734	1.19
Brinker Intl 144A 0%	10-10-21	12,360	7,679	1.18
Jacor Comm Cv 0%	02-09-18	14,490	7,173	1.10
Danaher N/A	01-22-21	11,440	7,136	1.10
Laboratory Of Amer Hldgs 144a (zero Cou)	09-11-21	10,070	7,036	1.08
Bank of New York		167	6,549	1.01
Morgan Stan Dean Witter N/A	08-17-05	7,000	6,405	0.99
Agilent Tech 144A 3%	12-01-21	5,770	6,311	0.97
Union Pac Cv Pfd 6.25%		131	6,307	0.97
American Intl Grp FRN	05-15-07	6,020	6,171	0.95
Verizon Global 144A 0%	05-15-21	10,860	5,919	0.91
SPX N/A	02-06-21	8,510	5,691	0.88
Arrow Electronics N/A	02-21-21	12,195	5,640	0.87
Brooks Automation 4.75%	06-01-08	6,140	5,472	0.84
Lehman Brothers Hldgs 0.25%	07-08-03	6,500	5,444	0.84
Kroger		210	5,317	0.82
Boston Scientific		197	5,238	0.81

Investment Style

Avg Eff Maturity	—
Avg Credit Quality	—
Avg Wtd Coupon	3.12%
Avg Wtd Price	81.25% of par
Avg Conversion Premium	26%

Coupon Range	% of Bonds	Rel Cat
0%	17.2	1.70
0% to 7%	80.4	.99
7% to 8.5%	1.0	.13
8.5% to 10%	0.9	3.64
More than 10%	0.5	1.82

1.00 = Category Average

Special Securities % of assets 11-30-01	
Restricted/Illiquid Secs	15
Emerging-Markets Secs	Trace
Options/Futures/Warrants	No

Composition % assets 11-30-01	
Cash	9.6
Stocks	22.9
Bonds	44.4
Convertibles	20.6
Other	2.6

Credit Breakdown % bonds 03-31-99

US Govt	0	BB	9
AAA	0	B	56
AA	1	Below B	13
A	12	NR/NA	0
BBB	10		

Country Exposure % assets

NA

Sector Breakdown % bonds 11-30-01

US Treasuries	0	CMOs	0
GNMA mtgs	0	ARMs	0
FNMA mtgs	0	Other	100
FHLMC mtgs	0		

Analysis by William Harding 12-10-01

This fund won't lead the pack when stocks rally, but it's a fine option for cautious types.

Despite the many potholes in 2001's market, Mainstay Convertible Fund has offered a fairly smooth ride. The fund has lost a modest 3.8% for the year to date through Dec. 6, compared with a 7.8% loss for the average convertible fund and a 10% decline for the S&P 500 index.

The fund's relatively strong showing owes to its moderate strategy. Managers Tom Wynn and Ed Spelman invest mainly in convertibles with modest conversion premiums; such issues don't participate in all the gains of their underlying stocks, but they're a lot less volatile. That focus kept the fund clear of many equity-sensitive convertibles, such as those in the telecom sector, which have fallen hard this year. Also, the fund benefited from a stake in zero-coupon convertibles. These issues are usually favored by hedge funds, but the pair scooped some up for the downside protection they provide in a bear market.

Despite the fund's generally defensive posture, Wynn and Spelman have recently gotten a touch more aggressive. The fund has about a 17% weighting in common stocks. The bulk of that stake is devoted to companies in which they own a convert that is far out of the money (or busted). This strategy of combining a busted convert with the straight equity will allow the fund to capture more of a stock's gain while still limiting downside risk. Further, the team has cut exposure to traditionally defensive sectors like energy in favor of cyclical names, such as Tyco, which are poised to do well amid an economic recovery.

The fund's relative success in recent years is encouraging. After toiling near the bottom half of the category from 1996 to 1998, it has gained more than 11% on average for the trailing three years—a top-quartile showing. In all, this is a respectable choice for investors seeking a less-volatile convertible offering.

Address:	260 Cherry Hill Road Parsippany, NJ 07054 800–624–6782
Web Address:	www.mainstayfunds.com
Inception:	05-01-86
Advisor:	Mainstay Mgmt.
Subadvisor:	MacKay–Shields Financial
NTF Plans:	N/A

Minimum Purchase:	$500	Add: $50	IRA: $500
Min Auto Inv Plan:	$500	Add: $50	
Sales Fees:	5.00%D, 0.75%B, 0.25%S Conv. in 8 Yrs.		
Management Fee:	.72%		
Actual Fees:	Mgt: 0.72%	Dist: 1.00%	
Expense Projections:	3Yr: $973	5Yr: $1354	10Yr: $2289
Avg Brok Commission:	—	Income Distrib: Quarterly	
Total Cost (relative to category):	—		

MainStay High–Yield Corporate Bond B

Ticker	Load	NAV	Yield	SEC Yield	Total Assets	Mstar Category
MKHCX	5.00%d	$5.55	11.6%	—	$3,363.0 mil	High–Yield Bond

Prospectus Objective: Corp Bond—High Yield

MainStay High-Yield Corporate Bond Fund seeks current income; capital appreciation is a secondary consideration.

The fund invests primarily in domestic and foreign high-yield debt securities rated from BBB to B, or in those unrated but of comparable quality. It may invest up to 15% of assets in securities rated lower than B. Normally, it invests at least 65% of assets in corporate debt securities. The fund may invest more than 25% of assets in U.S. government securities for temporary defensive purposes.

Class A shares have front loads; B shares have deferred loads, higher 12b-1 fees, and conversion features; C shares have level loads.

Historical Profile

Return: Above Avg
Risk: Above Avg
Rating: ★★★★ Above Avg

Investment Style
Fixed-Income
Income Rtn %Rank Cat: 63, 7, 86, 76, 50, 10, 19, 34

Growth of Principal vs. Interest Rate Shifts
— Principal Value $000 (NAV with capital gains reinvested)
— Interest Rate % on 10 Yr Treasury
▼ Manager Change
▽ Partial Manager Change
► Mgr Unknown After
◄ Mgr Unknown Before

Performance Quartile (within Category)

Portfolio Manager(s)

Donald Morgan. Since 5-00. Other funds currently managed: MainStay High-Yield Corporate Bond A, MainStay High-Yield Corporate Bond C.

Matt Philo. Since 6-01. Other funds currently managed: MainStay High-Yield Corporate Bond A, MainStay High-Yield Corporate Bond C.

1990	1991	1992	1993	1994	1995	1996	1997	1998	1999	2000	12-01	History
5.86	6.75	7.40	7.99	7.44	7.92	8.26	8.15	7.53	7.40	6.09	5.55	NAV
–7.85	32.27	21.65	21.65	1.50	19.71	15.58	11.55	1.31	9.51	–7.20	1.71	Total Return %
–16.80	16.27	14.24	11.90	4.41	1.24	11.96	1.87	–7.37	10.34	–18.83	–6.71	+/– LB Aggregate
–1.47	–11.48	4.99	2.74	2.47	2.33	3.16	–1.08	0.73	6.23	–1.99	–4.06	+/– FB High–Yield
14.63	16.04	11.67	10.83	8.75	11.50	8.74	8.67	8.77	11.00	10.96	11.15	Income Return %
–22.48	16.23	9.98	10.82	–7.25	8.22	6.84	2.88	–7.46	–1.49	–18.15	–9.43	Capital Return %
38	68	6	18	4	10	15	77	37	12	47	56	Total Rtn % Rank Cat
1.01	0.88	0.75	0.76	0.67	0.82	0.67	0.69	0.69	0.79	0.77	0.65	Income $
0.00	0.00	0.00	0.17	0.00	0.12	0.18	0.34	0.04	0.03	0.05	0.00	Capital Gains $
2.10	2.10	1.90	1.70	1.60	1.60	1.60	1.62	1.75	1.75	1.78	—	Expense Ratio %
14.30	14.40	11.00	9.90	8.70	9.50	8.40	8.18	8.65	9.61	10.60	—	Income Ratio %
305	214	226	207	190	137	118	128	128	83	54	—	Turnover Rate %
184.7	296.4	507.7	935.5	1,122.1	1,601.2	2,439.4	3,378.9	3,309.0	3,294.4	2,609.3	2,476.9	Net Assets $mil

Performance 12-31-01

	1st Qtr	2nd Qtr	3rd Qtr	4th Qtr	Total
1997	0.57	5.55	5.00	0.09	11.55
1998	4.41	0.92	–8.41	4.97	1.31
1999	4.03	2.62	–0.52	3.12	9.51
2000	0.55	0.69	–0.60	–7.78	–7.20
2001	3.54	–2.51	–4.20	5.17	1.71

Trailing	Total Return%	+/– LB Agg	+/– FB High–Yield	% Rank All	% Rank Cat	Growth of $10,000
3 Mo	5.17	5.14	–0.47	64	63	10,517
6 Mo	0.76	–3.90	–0.68	35	49	10,076
1 Yr	1.71	–6.71	–4.06	40	56	10,171
3 Yr Avg	1.11	–5.16	–0.06	67	33	10,337
5 Yr Avg	3.16	–4.27	–0.09	84	25	11,682
10 Yr Avg	9.27	2.05	1.44	37	1	24,277
15 Yr Avg	8.27	0.15	–0.40	51	5	32,911

Tax Analysis	Tax-Adj Ret%	%Rank Cat	%Pretax Ret	%Rank Cat
3 Yr Avg	–3.21	36	—	—
5 Yr Avg	–1.04	29	—	—
10 Yr Avg	4.95	2	53.3	16

Potential Capital Gain Exposure: –40% of assets

Risk Analysis

Time Period	Load-Adj Return %	Risk %Rank[1] All	Risk %Rank[1] Cat	Morningstar Return	Morningstar Risk	Morningstar Risk-Adj Rating
1 Yr	–1.93					
3 Yr	0.63	35	31	–0.88[2]	1.80	★★
5 Yr	3.04	39	21	–0.42[2]	1.83	★★
10 Yr	9.27	41	10	1.43[2]	1.23	★★★★★

Average Historical Rating (153 months): 3.8★s

[1]1=low, 100=high [2] T–Bill return substituted for category avg.

Category Rating (3 Yr)

1 2 3 4 5
Worst Best

Return: Above Avg
Risk: Below Avg

Other Measures	Standard Index LB Agg	Best Fit Index FB HY
Alpha	–3.4	0.1
Beta	0.02	1.02
R–Squared	0	91
Standard Deviation		7.99
Mean		1.11
Sharpe Ratio		–0.55

Analysis by Christopher Davis 11-30-01

It's worth sticking with Mainstay High-Yield Corporate Bond Fund.

Don Morgan took the reins here in May 2000 after longtime manager Steve Tananbaum jumped ship to start a hedge fund. During his 11-year stint, Tananbaum guided the fund to topnotch results while keeping volatility at bay. Morgan played a role in that success—Tananbaum hired him in 1997 and he served as comanager until he took charge three years later.

Morgan hasn't altered the fund's complexion much. Like his predecessor, he keeps an eye on safety, arguing that avoiding strikeouts is more important than aiming for the fences. Thus, he tries to minimize the fund's default risk by sticking with companies that have free cash flow and asset coverage. Morgan also favors industries with high barriers to entry, which has led him to devote a chunk of the portfolio to cable and utility issuers. Further, he has continued to spread assets among 300 issues, keeping him from taking on too much company-specific risk.

Not all of Morgan's moves have been on the mark this year. He has emphasized bonds rated B or below, for instance. That stance has been a liability, however, as the slowing economy has cooled investor enthusiasm for such issues. What's more, the fund's big telecom stake earlier in the year was a liability, as the sector got battered by rising defaults. As a result, the fund lands in the high-yield category's bottom half for the year to date through Nov. 28, 2001.

Nonetheless, the fact that Morgan has helped guide the fund to category-beating returns since 1997 suggests the fund was put in good hands. That gives shareholders here reason to keep the faith, but others may want to wait until Morgan proves himself before jumping in.

Portfolio Analysis 11-30-01

Total Fixed-Income: 297	Date of Maturity	Amount $000	Value $000	% Net Assets
Medaphis 9.5%	02-15-05	65,134	58,621	1.74
Paxson Comm Pfd PIK 12.5%		61	58,216	1.73
Crescent RE Eq 7.5%	09-15-07	61,475	56,120	1.67
Millicom Intl Step 0%	06-01-06	87,038	54,834	1.63
Columbia/HCA Healthcare 7.5%	11-15-95	54,125	50,394	1.50
Comcast UK Cable Step 0%	11-15-07	60,380	42,870	1.27
Regional Indep Med N/A	07-01-08	33,125	37,792	1.12
Sovereign Bank 144A 12%		35	33,889	1.01
Charter Comm N/A	01-15-10	46,395	33,868	1.01
Octel Developments 10%	05-01-06	30,930	33,404	0.99
PSEG Energy Hldgs 10%	10-01-09	30,580	33,009	0.98
ONO Fin 14%	02-15-11	40,495	32,447	0.96
Western Resources 6.25%	08-15-03	33,360	31,556	0.94
LSI Logic Cv 4%	02-15-05	36,395	30,754	0.91
Tiverton Pwr 144A 9%	07-15-18	29,970	30,411	0.90
Great Central Mines 8.875%	04-01-08	30,897	30,279	0.90
FRI–MRD N/A	01-24-02	46,300	29,979	0.89
Pg&e Natl Energy 10.38%	05-16-11	26,275	29,891	0.89
Charter Comm N/A	05-15-11	44,460	28,454	0.85
Caithness Coso Fd 9.05%	12-15-09	26,645	27,111	0.81

Current Investment Style

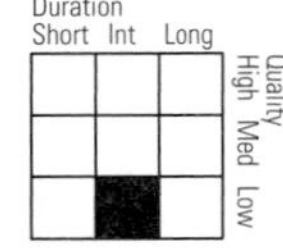

Avg Eff Duration[1]	4.1 Yrs
Avg Eff Maturity	7.9 Yrs
Avg Credit Quality	BB
Avg Wtd Coupon	8.52%
Avg Wtd Price	82.41% of par

[1]figure provided by fund

Special Securities % assets 11-30-01

Restricted/Illiquid Secs	8
Exotic Mortgage–Backed	0
Emerging–Markets Secs	Trace
Options/Futures/Warrants	Yes

Credit Analysis % bonds 09-30-01

US Govt	0	BB	24
AAA	5	B	48
AA	0	Below B	13
A	1	NR/NA	0
BBB	9		

Sector Breakdown % bonds 11-30-01

US Treasuries	0	CMOs	0
GNMA mtgs	0	ARMs	0
FNMA mtgs	0	Other	99
FHLMC mtgs	0		

Coupon Range	% of Bonds	Rel Cat
0%, PIK	8.46	1.35
0% to 9%	40.09	1.32
9% to 12%	32.84	0.62
12% to 14%	15.34	1.74
More than 14%	3.26	2.35

1.00=Category Average

Composition % assets 11-30-01

Cash	13.6	Bonds	78.6
Stocks	3.6	Other	4.3

Address:	260 Cherry Hill Road Parsippany, NJ 07054 800–624–6782
Web Address:	www.mainstayfunds.com
Inception:	05-01-86
Advisor:	Mainstay Mgmt.
Subadvisor:	MacKay–Shields Financial
NTF Plans:	N/A

Minimum Purchase:	$500	Add: $50 IRA: $500
Min Auto Inv Plan:	$500	Add: $50
Sales Fees:	5.00%D, 0.75%B, 0.25%S Conv. in 8 Yrs.	
Management Fee:	.60% mx./.55% mn.	
Actual Fees:	Mgt: 0.60%	Dist: 1.00%
Expense Projections:	3Yr: $863	5Yr: $1170 10Yr: $1906
Avg Brok Commission:	—	Income Distrib: Monthly
Total Cost (relative to category):	Average	

MainStay MAP Equity I

Ticker	Load	NAV	Yield	Total Assets	Mstar Category
MUBFX	None	$27.75	0.2%	$350.3 mil	Mid-Cap Blend

Prospectus Objective: Growth

MainStay MAP Equity Fund seeks long-term appreciation of capital; current income is a secondary concern.

The fund invests primarily in equity securities. To select specific securities, the advisor emphasizes well-managed companies that possess substantial growth potential. The advisor also seeks opportunities for capital appreciation in undervalued securities. It may hold fixed-income securities.

The fund offers A, B, C and I shares, all which differ in fee structure and availability.

Historical Profile

Return High
Risk Below Avg
Rating ★★★★★ Highest

Investment Style: Equity — Average Stock %: 99% 88% 84% 87% 96% 95% 79%

▼ Manager Change
▽ Partial Manager Change

Fund Performance vs. Category Average
■ Quarterly Fund Return +/– Category Average
— Category Baseline

Performance Quartile (within Category)

1990	1991	1992	1993	1994	1995	1996	1997	1998	1999	2000	12-01	History
15.84	19.66	20.00	18.13	16.67	19.36	20.66	22.73	24.58	26.25	27.32	27.75	NAV
–5.09	27.69	10.53	8.67	2.76	32.50	23.82	27.99	24.18	12.18	16.93	2.33	Total Return %
–1.98	–2.80	2.91	–1.38	1.44	–5.03	0.88	–5.36	–4.39	–8.85	26.03	14.20	+/– S&P 500
0.03	–22.38	–1.37	–5.26	6.35	1.59	4.64	–4.25	5.07	–2.53	–0.57	2.93	+/– S&P Mid 400
3.12	3.12	1.59	1.85	2.06	2.62	1.98	1.41	1.57	0.45	0.11	0.24	Income Return %
–8.21	24.57	8.94	6.83	0.70	29.89	21.84	26.58	22.61	11.74	16.82	2.08	Capital Return %
35	67	69	72	14	27	27	47	8	73	19	20	Total Rtn % Rank Cat
0.54	0.49	0.31	0.36	0.37	0.43	0.36	0.29	0.33	0.11	0.03	0.07	Income $
0.19	0.05	1.40	3.21	1.59	2.21	2.86	3.41	2.96	1.14	3.16	0.14	Capital Gains $
1.01	0.85	1.01	1.04	1.07	0.81	0.74	0.82	0.70	0.88	1.00	—	Expense Ratio %
3.32	2.69	2.01	1.76	2.03	2.30	1.82	1.18	1.10	0.39	0.37	—	Income Ratio %
6	9	18	20	39	39	53	58	41	32	40	—	Turnover Rate %
37.1	45.6	48.6	49.4	43.9	60.5	73.1	94.2	56.8	63.5	69.4	92.3	Net Assets $mil

Portfolio Manager(s)

Michael J. Mullarkey. Since 4-81. BA'63 Fordham U.; MBA'67 Harvard U. Other funds currently managed: MainStay MAP Equity A, MainStay MAP Equity B, MainStay MAP Equity C.

Roger M. Lob. Since 1-87. BA'82 U. of Pennsylvania; MBA'84 Columbia U. Other funds currently managed: MainStay MAP Equity A, MainStay MAP Equity B, MainStay MAP Equity C.

Chris Mullarkey. Since 10-01. Other funds currently managed: MainStay MAP Equity A, MainStay MAP Equity B, MainStay MAP Equity C.

Performance 12-31-01

	1st Qtr	2nd Qtr	3rd Qtr	4th Qtr	Total
1997	1.84	15.78	6.72	1.71	27.99
1998	13.86	–0.27	–7.65	18.43	24.18
1999	–2.69	11.63	–7.46	11.60	12.18
2000	8.72	–2.03	5.26	4.29	16.93
2001	–3.62	8.89	–14.65	14.24	2.33

Trailing	Total Return%	+/– S&P 500	+/– S&P Mid 400	% Rank All	% Rank Cat	Growth of $10,000
3 Mo	14.24	3.56	–3.74	26	67	11,424
6 Mo	–2.49	3.06	–0.94	49	42	9,751
1 Yr	2.33	14.20	2.93	39	20	10,233
3 Yr Avg	10.31	11.33	0.07	11	18	13,422
5 Yr Avg	16.36	5.66	0.25	3	10	21,334
10 Yr Avg	15.76	2.83	0.75	4	16	43,203
15 Yr Avg	15.18	1.45	–0.81	6	20	83,308

Tax Analysis	Tax-Adj Ret%	%Rank Cat	%Pretax Ret	%Rank Cat
3 Yr Avg	8.72	18	84.6	32
5 Yr Avg	13.97	7	85.4	25
10 Yr Avg	12.43	16	78.9	61

Potential Capital Gain Exposure: 16% of assets

Risk Analysis

Time Period	Load-Adj Return %	Risk %Rank[1] All	Risk %Rank[1] Cat	Morningstar Return	Morningstar Risk	Morningstar Risk-Adj Rating
1 Yr	2.33					
3 Yr	10.31	43	9	1.20[2]	0.60	★★★★
5 Yr	16.36	45	2	3.07[2]	0.59	★★★★★
10 Yr	15.76	49	1	1.99	0.56	★★★★★

Average Historical Rating (193 months): 4.0★s

[1] 1=low, 100=high [2] T-Bill return substituted for category avg.

Category Rating (3 Yr)

1 2 3 4 5 — Worst ... Best

Return Above Avg
Risk Low

Other Measures	Standard Index S&P 500	Best Fit Index SPMid400
Alpha	9.6	1.3
Beta	0.71	0.69
R-Squared	69	86

Standard Deviation	15.93
Mean	10.31
Sharpe Ratio	0.38

Analysis by Gregg Wolper 11-30-01

Mainstay MAP Equity Fund shows that an unusual approach can yield exceptional results.

Along with checking out the usual traits of companies, such as earnings-growth rates, over their many years of running this fund, managers Michael Mullarkey and Roger Lob (recently joined by Chris Mullarkey) have relied on less-common factors. In particular, they pay close attention to buying and selling by company insiders, as well as stock buybacks. They're not the only managers to note such transactions, but few peers place such emphasis on these activities.

Maybe more of them should. This fund has amassed a remarkable risk/return profile. Its five- and 10-year returns are well into the top quartile of the mid-cap blend category, and its risk scores—a measure of volatility—are in the best decile. Consistency is its hallmark. Except for 1999, when the managers' attention to valuations kept them from keeping up with more-aggressive rivals in a strong, growth-led rally, the fund has been in the top half of the category every calendar year since 1994.

The fund has followed this impressive pattern so far in 2001 as well. It has an essentially flat return through Nov. 29, which puts it in the top quartile of the mid-blend category. Michael Mullarkey says that the fund has had strong gains in the past couple of months, as the managers had scooped up shares of companies whose prices had plunged in the growth-stock collapse but that seemed attractive because of growth potential, insider buying, or both—and which have rebounded strongly. One example is Advanced Digital Information, which Mullarkey describes as a "storage merchant" supplying software and semiconductors to storage companies.

By holding up well in a rough market in 2001, this fund has demonstrated once again that it's one of the top stock offerings around.

Portfolio Analysis 10-31-01

Share change since 09-01 Total Stocks: 146	Sector	PE	YTD Ret%	% Assets
⊕ Northrop Grumman	Industrials	19.2	23.67	2.11
RadioShack	Retail	21.5	–29.20	2.03
⊕ State Street	Financials	28.6	–15.10	2.02
Kinder Morgan	Energy	32.2	7.11	1.63
⊕ Popular	Financials	14.8	13.41	1.49
Immunex	Health	89.4	–31.70	1.39
Adobe Sys	Technology	37.4	–46.50	1.29
✲ Brocade Comm Sys	Technology	—	–63.90	1.13
Mattel	Staples	31.9	19.43	1.12
Lexmark Intl	Technology	26.9	33.14	1.05
Aetna	Financials	—	–19.50	1.05
⊕ S1 I	Technology	—	208.10	1.04
Conoco Cl A	Energy	9.0	1.56	1.00
Vulcan Matls	Industrials	23.1	2.06	0.93
⊕ Harris	Technology	28.0	0.33	0.90
Archer Daniels Midland	Staples	24.7	1.91	0.88
Yahoo	Technology	—	–40.90	0.88
Sepracor	Health	—	–28.70	0.85
Wachovia	Financials	—	23.13	0.84
⊕ Advanced Digital Info	Technology	—	–30.20	0.82
PepsiCo	Staples	31.4	–0.54	0.82
⊕ Devon Energy	Energy	5.6	–36.30	0.81
Weyerhaeuser	Industrials	21.0	9.73	0.81
⊕ Centurytel	Services	13.3	–7.66	0.79
⊕ May Dept Stores	Retail	15.2	15.97	0.75

Current Investment Style

Style: Value Blnd Growth; Size: Large Med Small

	Stock Port Avg	Relative S&P 500 Current	Relative S&P 500 Hist	Rel Cat
Price/Earnings Ratio	27.5	0.89	0.83	1.01
Price/Book Ratio	4.5	0.79	0.61	1.05
Price/Cash Flow	17.7	0.98	0.73	1.02
3 Yr Earnings Growth	9.9	0.68	0.64	0.60
1 Yr Earnings Est%	0.2	—	—	0.07
Med Mkt Cap $mil	6,678	0.1	0.1	0.74

Special Securities % assets 10-31-01	
Restricted/Illiquid Secs	0
Emerging-Markets Secs	0
Options/Futures/Warrants	No

Composition % assets 10-31-01	
Cash	48.4
Stocks*	51.3
Bonds	0.3
Other	0.0
*Foreign (% stocks)	0.5

Market Cap	
Giant	7.3
Large	31.0
Medium	46.9
Small	14.1
Micro	0.7

Sector Weightings	% of Stocks	Rel S&P	5-Year High	5-Year Low
Utilities	0.4	0.1	12	0
Energy	9.2	1.3	12	1
Financials	17.3	1.0	17	8
Industrials	14.8	1.3	25	5
Durables	0.5	0.4	10	0
Staples	6.8	0.9	41	5
Services	11.4	1.1	33	8
Retail	9.1	1.3	20	4
Health	8.8	0.6	14	1
Technology	21.8	1.2	25	1

Address:	260 Cherry Hill Road Parsippany, NJ 07054 800-624-6782 / 800-624-6782
Web Address:	www.mainstayfunds.com
Inception:	01-21-71
Advisor:	Mainstay Mgmt.
Subadvisor:	Markston Intl
NTF Plans:	N/A

Minimum Purchase:	$250000	Add: $1000 IRA: None
Min Auto Inv Plan:	$100	Add: $100
Sales Fees:	No-load	
Management Fee:	.75%+(–).30%P	
Actual Fees:	Mgt: 0.75%	Dist: —
Expense Projections:	3Yr: $318	5Yr: $552 10Yr: $1225
Avg Brok Commission:	—	Income Distrib: Quarterly
Total Cost (relative to category):		Below Avg

Mairs & Power Growth

Ticker	Load	NAV	Yield	Total Assets	Mstar Category
MPGFX	None	$54.36	0.9%	$676.5 mil	Mid-Cap Blend

Prospectus Objective: Growth

Mairs & Power Growth Fund seeks long-term capital appreciation.

The fund invests primarily in common stocks; it expects to remain fully invested at all times. The advisor seeks companies with reasonably predictable earnings, above-average return on equity, market dominance, and financial strength. The fund may invest a portion of assets in cash and short-term instruments. It expects to maintain a low portfolio turnover rate relative to comparable funds. The fund may not invest in oil, gas, or other mineral leases and real-estate limited partnership interests.

Historical Profile

Return High
Risk Below Avg
Rating ★★★★★ Highest

Investment Style
Equity
Average Stock %: 96% 100% 100% 100% 100% 100%

▼ Manager Change
▽ Partial Manager Change

Fund Performance vs. Category Average
■ Quarterly Fund Return +/– Category Average
— Category Baseline

Performance Quartile (within Category)

Portfolio Manager(s)

George A. Mairs III. Since 1-80. Macalaster C.; BA'50 Yale U.

History	1990	1991	1992	1993	1994	1995	1996	1997	1998	1999	2000	12-01
NAV	12.97	17.39	17.96	19.42	19.69	28.02	34.74	43.34	46.34	46.46	53.41	54.36
Total Return %	3.51	42.09	7.87	12.83	5.66	47.70	27.76	28.67	9.36	7.17	26.47	6.48
+/– S&P 500	6.63	11.61	0.25	2.77	4.34	10.16	4.81	–4.69	–19.22	–13.87	35.57	18.35
+/– S&P Mid 400	8.63	–7.98	–4.03	–1.11	9.25	16.78	8.57	–3.58	–9.76	–7.55	8.97	7.08
Income Return %	1.64	1.51	1.15	1.20	1.68	1.43	1.34	1.44	0.83	1.01	1.18	0.96
Capital Return %	1.87	40.58	6.72	11.62	3.98	46.27	26.42	27.22	8.52	6.17	25.29	5.52
Total Rtn % Rank Cat	1	25	81	48	9	1	9	45	33	90	3	16
Income $	0.21	0.20	0.20	0.22	0.33	0.28	0.38	0.50	0.36	0.47	0.55	0.51
Capital Gains $	0.35	0.79	0.58	0.61	0.49	0.76	0.68	0.85	0.68	2.74	4.82	2.00
Expense Ratio %	1.05	1.09	1.00	0.98	0.99	0.99	0.89	0.84	0.82	0.79	0.78	—
Income Ratio %	1.65	1.18	1.19	1.15	1.74	1.00	1.18	0.98	0.97	0.83	1.06	—
Turnover Rate %	5	5	4	4	5	4	3	5	2	6	15	—
Net Assets $mil	22.5	31.4	34.4	39.1	41.9	70.5	150.2	412.6	554.7	546.8	581.7	676.5

Performance 12-31-01

	1st Qtr	2nd Qtr	3rd Qtr	4th Qtr	Total
1997	–0.26	19.05	5.86	2.36	28.67
1998	8.28	–1.01	–13.14	17.45	9.36
1999	–3.71	14.29	–4.33	1.80	7.17
2000	0.65	6.92	3.05	14.05	26.47
2001	–6.14	7.80	–5.72	11.62	6.48

Trailing	Total Return%	+/– S&P 500	+/– S&P Mid 400	% Rank All	% Rank Cat	Growth of $10,000
3 Mo	11.62	0.94	–6.36	34	76	11,162
6 Mo	5.24	10.79	6.79	3	4	10,524
1 Yr	6.48	18.35	7.08	17	16	10,648
3 Yr Avg	13.01	14.03	2.77	7	10	14,431
5 Yr Avg	15.22	4.52	–0.89	4	14	20,305
10 Yr Avg	17.29	4.36	2.28	2	6	49,269
15 Yr Avg	16.56	2.83	0.58	3	5	99,655

Tax Analysis	Tax-Adj Ret%	%Rank Cat	%Pretax Ret	%Rank Cat
3 Yr Avg	11.26	9	86.6	26
5 Yr Avg	13.82	9	90.8	13
10 Yr Avg	15.88	1	91.8	1

Potential Capital Gain Exposure: 35% of assets

Risk Analysis

Time Period	Load-Adj Return %	Risk %Rank¹ All	Risk %Rank¹ Cat	Morningstar Return	Morningstar Risk	Morningstar Risk-Adj Rating
1 Yr	6.48					
3 Yr	13.01	37	1	1.84²	0.47	★★★★★
5 Yr	15.22	46	3	2.70²	0.60	★★★★★
10 Yr	17.29	54	7	2.43	0.68	★★★★★

Average Historical Rating (193 months): 3.8★s

¹1=low, 100=high ² T-Bill return substituted for category avg.

Category Rating (3 Yr)

1 2 3 4 5
Worst Best

Return Above Avg
Risk Low

Other Measures	Standard Index S&P 500	Best Fit Index S&P 500
Alpha	10.6	10.6
Beta	0.41	0.41
R-Squared	26	26

Standard Deviation	15.10
Mean	13.01
Sharpe Ratio	0.61

Portfolio Analysis 11-30-01

Share change since 10-01 Total Stocks: 33	Sector	PE	YTD Ret%	% Assets
Target	Retail	29.8	28.05	5.07
⊕ Medtronic	Health	76.4	–14.70	4.84
⊕ Wells Fargo	Financials	22.4	–20.20	4.83
⊕ TCF Finl	Financials	18.2	10.24	4.76
⊕ Baxter Intl	Health	33.9	22.84	4.31
Graco	Industrials	18.3	43.32	4.07
General Mills	Staples	22.0	19.75	3.94
Johnson & Johnson	Health	16.6	14.01	3.82
Pfizer	Health	34.7	–12.40	3.81
Minnesota Mng & Mfg	Industrials	34.5	0.16	3.72
⊕ St. Paul	Financials	—	–16.90	3.70
⊖ St. Jude Medical	Health	42.0	26.39	3.58
Hormel Foods	Staples	20.7	46.88	3.47
⊕ Emerson Elec	Industrials	23.8	–25.60	3.44
Valspar	Industrials	35.0	25.05	3.26
⊖ Donaldson	Industrials	22.6	40.99	3.13
SuperValu	Retail	44.2	64.52	3.03
Ecolab	Industrials	25.6	–5.55	2.96
⊕ US Bancorp	Financials	13.5	–6.14	2.95
⊕ Toro	Durables	11.7	24.04	2.91
⊕ HB Fuller	Industrials	17.6	48.69	2.61
⊕ Honeywell Intl	Durables	NMF	–27.00	2.57
⊖ Bemis	Industrials	19.4	50.19	2.48
⊕ eFunds	Services	—	49.65	2.05
⊕ Ceridian	Technology	27.6	–5.96	2.01

Current Investment Style

Style: Value Blnd Growth; Size: Large Med Small

	Stock Port Avg	Relative S&P 500 Current	Relative S&P 500 Hist	Rel Cat
Price/Earnings Ratio	28.4	0.92	0.84	1.04
Price/Book Ratio	6.0	1.05	0.82	1.40
Price/Cash Flow	17.2	0.95	0.85	0.99
3 Yr Earnings Growth	12.6	0.86	0.76	0.76
1 Yr Earnings Est%	5.2	—	—	2.28
Med Mkt Cap $mil	11,082	0.2	0.2	1.23

Analysis by Catherine Hickey 11-07-01

This fund's continued strength is business as usual.

Mairs & Power Growth Fund is trouncing the competition once again. Its 3.49% gain for the year through Nov. 28, 2001, bests most of its mid-blend peers'. The portfolio's low-tech profile is coming in handy, as tech stocks have been slammed in 2001. Meanwhile, solid returns from holdings like General Mills are bolstering the fund.

To get such top-flight results, manager George Mairs and his team don't do anything fancy. They invest in firms that have strong market share and returns on equity. The portfolio usually includes about 35 companies, and management doesn't have to look far to find them, since many are based in their home state of Minnesota. Once they buy shares in a company, they tend to hold on. Turnover is usually in the single digits, though it increased last year (to a hardly sky-high 15%) when a few holdings were taken over.

In the past few months, Mairs has made characteristically few changes. He trimmed his stake in Baxter International, which he thought was getting richly valued last summer. And he added Merck because he likes its dominant position in the pharmaceutical sector.

Over time, such an uncomplicated recipe has yielded exceptionally strong results; the fund's long-term returns leave other mid-blend funds in the dust. What's more, even though Mairs runs a concentrated portfolio here, volatility has been kept quite low by his valuation-conscious style. What's more, low turnover helps keep this fund quite tax-efficient.

The one red flag with this offering is that Mairs will probably retire in the next couple of years. However, his place will most likely be taken by Bill Frels, who has worked with Mairs for years and has built a strong record at Mairs & Power Balanced. This remains a topnotch mid-cap pick.

Special Securities % assets 11-30-01	
Restricted/Illiquid Secs	0
Emerging-Markets Secs	0
Options/Futures/Warrants	No

Composition % assets 11-30-01	
Cash	0.0
Stocks*	100.0
Bonds	0.0
Other	0.0
*Foreign (% stocks)	0.0

Market Cap	
Giant	23.6
Large	28.8
Medium	32.8
Small	12.7
Micro	2.2

Sector Weightings	% of Stocks	Rel S&P	5-Year High	5-Year Low
Utilities	0.0	0.0	0	0
Energy	0.0	0.0	0	0
Financials	16.9	0.9	19	14
Industrials	30.8	2.7	33	26
Durables	5.7	3.7	7	3
Staples	7.7	1.0	8	3
Services	2.7	0.3	14	0
Retail	8.4	1.2	9	5
Health	22.9	1.5	24	16
Technology	5.0	0.3	18	5

Address: W–1420 First National Bank Bldg.
St. Paul, MN 55101
651–222–8478 / 800–304–7404
Web Address: —
Inception: 11-07-58
Advisor: Mairs & Power
Subadvisor: None
NTF Plans: N/A

Minimum Purchase: $2500 Add: $100 IRA: $1000
Min Auto Inv Plan: $2500 Add: $100
Sales Fees: No-load
Management Fee: .60%
Actual Fees: Mgt: 0.60% Dist: —
Expense Projections: 3Yr: $253 5Yr: $440 10Yr: $981
Avg Brok Commission: — Income Distrib: Semi–Ann.
Total Cost (relative to category): Below Avg

Managers Special Equity

Ticker	Load	NAV	Yield	Total Assets	Mstar Category
MGSEX	None	$70.60	0.0%	$2,312.1 mil	Small Growth

Prospectus Objective: Small Company

Managers Special Equity Fund seeks capital appreciation.

The fund invests primarily in equity securities issued by a diversified group of companies management judges to have the potential for superior growth of earnings. These companies may have small to medium market capitalizations and are in the early stages of their corporate life cycle or are not yet well recognized, or they may be more established firms experiencing accelerated earnings growth.

Prior to April 10, 1991, the fund was named Management of Managers Special Equity Fund.

Historical Profile

Return Above Avg
Risk Above Avg
Rating ★★★★ Above Avg

Investment Style
Equity
Average Stock %: 91% 91% 90% 90% 93% 90% 90%

▼ Manager Change
▽ Partial Manager Change

Fund Performance vs. Category Average
■ Quarterly Fund Return +/– Category Average
— Category Baseline

Performance Quartile (within Category)

Portfolio Manager(s)

Gary L. Pilgrim, CFA. Since 10-94.
Andrew J. Knuth, CFA. Since 12-85.
Timothy G. Ebright. Since 12-85.
Robert E. Kern. Since 9-97.
William M. Dutton. Since 12-00.
Edmund H. Nicklin Jr., CFA. Since 5-01.

1990	1991	1992	1993	1994	1995	1996	1997	1998	1999	2000	12-01	History
24.46	34.50	36.14	38.90	36.79	43.34	50.95	61.17	61.22	91.42	76.80	70.60	NAV
–15.58	49.80	16.13	17.36	–1.99	33.94	24.75	24.45	0.20	54.11	–2.56	–8.07	Total Return %
–12.47	19.31	8.51	7.30	–3.31	–3.60	1.81	–8.90	–28.37	33.07	6.54	3.80	+/– S&P 500
1.83	–1.39	8.36	4.00	0.44	2.90	13.49	11.50	–1.03	11.02	19.87	1.16	+/– Russ 2000 Grth
0.99	0.95	0.15	0.03	0.00	0.00	0.00	0.14	0.00	0.00	0.00	0.00	Income Return %
–16.57	48.85	15.98	17.32	–1.99	33.94	24.75	24.31	0.20	54.11	–2.56	–8.07	Capital Return %
82	62	26	43	48	48	26	29	64	45	44	44	Total Rtn % Rank Cat
0.32	0.23	0.05	0.01	0.00	0.00	0.00	0.07	0.00	0.00	0.00	0.00	Income $
2.56	1.74	3.70	3.37	1.34	5.66	3.07	2.07	0.07	2.82	11.77	0.00	Capital Gains $
1.19	1.30	1.29	1.26	1.37	1.44	1.43	1.35	1.34	1.31	1.26	—	Expense Ratio %
1.22	0.73	0.14	0.07	–0.06	–0.16	–0.10	0.17	–0.26	–0.47	–0.16	—	Income Ratio %
67	70	54	45	66	65	56	49	64	89	69	—	Turnover Rate %
24.4	40.9	52.9	98.9	110.0	118.3	270.6	720.0	956.5	1,544.9	2,125.3	2,312.1	Net Assets $mil

Performance 12-31-01

	1st Qtr	2nd Qtr	3rd Qtr	4th Qtr	Total
1997	–7.14	18.37	14.45	–1.07	24.45
1998	9.63	–3.44	–20.97	19.78	0.20
1999	–6.97	20.19	1.42	35.91	54.11
2000	13.59	–0.76	–2.13	–11.67	–2.56
2001	–13.50	16.23	–23.74	19.90	–8.07

Trailing	Total Return%	+/– S&P 500	+/– Russ 2000 Grth	% Rank All	% Rank Cat	Growth of $10,000
3 Mo	19.90	9.22	–6.27	14	67	11,990
6 Mo	–8.56	–3.01	0.70	80	66	9,144
1 Yr	–8.07	3.80	1.16	57	44	9,193
3 Yr Avg	11.34	12.37	11.10	9	34	13,804
5 Yr Avg	11.47	0.77	8.61	12	32	17,214
10 Yr Avg	14.41	1.48	7.22	7	6	38,418
15 Yr Avg	15.66	1.92	7.51	5	10	88,619

Tax Analysis	Tax-Adj Ret%	%Rank Cat	%Pretax Ret	%Rank Cat
3 Yr Avg	9.55	35	84.2	36
5 Yr Avg	10.18	25	88.7	18
10 Yr Avg	12.36	8	85.8	13

Potential Capital Gain Exposure: 2% of assets

Risk Analysis

Time Period	Load-Adj Return %	Risk %Rank[1] All	Risk %Rank[1] Cat	Morningstar Return	Morningstar Risk	Morningstar Risk-Adj Rating
1 Yr	–8.07					
3 Yr	11.34	85	34	1.44[2]	1.27	★★★★
5 Yr	11.47	85	24	1.59[2]	1.26	★★★
10 Yr	14.41	87	16	1.64	1.25	★★★★

Average Historical Rating (176 months): 3.6★s

[1]1=low, 100=high [2] T-Bill return substituted for category avg.

Category Rating (3 Yr)

1 2 3 4 5
Worst Best

Return Average
Risk Average

Other Measures	Standard Index S&P 500	Best Fit Index Russ 2000
Alpha	16.3	5.4
Beta	1.09	1.24
R-Squared	38	92

Standard Deviation	34.88
Mean	11.34
Sharpe Ratio	0.21

Portfolio Analysis 11-30-01

Share change since 10-01 Total Stocks: 348	Sector	PE	YTD Ret%	% Assets
ITT Educational Svcs	Services	28.6	67.59	1.29
Healthsouth	Health	28.0	–9.15	1.09
IMS Health	Technology	22.4	–27.50	0.99
Alpha Inds	Technology	NMF	–41.00	0.98
⊕ SBA Comm	Services	—	–68.20	0.95
Emmis Broadcstg Cl A	Services	—	–17.60	0.92
Allied Cap	Financials	11.6	35.33	0.88
Iron Mountain	Services	—	17.98	0.88
⊕ Anaren Microwave	Technology	42.2	–74.20	0.86
⊖ Riverstone Networks	Technology	—	—	0.81
Triad Hospitals	Health	—	–9.87	0.79
⊖ Powerwave Tech	Industrials	—	–70.40	0.74
⊖ Mobile Mini	Industrials	30.8	70.09	0.73
Ruby Tuesday	Services	21.3	35.62	0.71
⊕ Orthodontic Centers of Amer	Health	26.3	–2.40	0.69
Pittston Brink's Grp	Services	—	11.74	0.67
Hibernia	Financials	16.3	44.26	0.66
⊖ Whole Foods Market	Retail	36.0	42.53	0.65
Downey Finl	Financials	11.2	–24.30	0.65
⊕ Gene Logic	Health	—	2.53	0.63
⊖ Polycom	Technology	67.5	6.87	0.59
Farichild Semicon Intl Cl A	Technology	42.7	95.32	0.58
⊖ Krispy Kreme Doughnut	Retail	67.0	113.00	0.57
Saga Comms	Services	38.3	39.16	0.55
Synopsys	Technology	67.1	24.52	0.55

Current Investment Style

Style: Value Blnd Growth; Size: Large Med Small

	Stock Port Avg	Relative S&P 500 Current	Relative S&P 500 Hist	Rel Cat
Price/Earnings Ratio	29.5	0.95	0.94	0.92
Price/Book Ratio	4.1	0.71	0.71	0.83
Price/Cash Flow	18.9	1.05	0.99	0.86
3 Yr Earnings Growth	23.0[1]	1.57	—	0.91
1 Yr Earnings Est%	–3.5	1.96	—	–0.45
Med Mkt Cap $mil	970	0.0	0.0	0.93

[1]figure is based on 50% or less of stocks

Special Securities % assets 11-30-01	
Restricted/Illiquid Secs	0
Emerging-Markets Secs	0
Options/Futures/Warrants	No

Composition % assets 11-30-01	
Cash	9.9
Stocks*	90.1
Bonds	0.0
Other	0.0
*Foreign (% stocks)	1.4

Market Cap	
Giant	0.7
Large	1.3
Medium	31.3
Small	62.3
Micro	4.5

Sector Weightings	% of Stocks	Rel S&P	5-Year High	5-Year Low
Utilities	0.9	0.3	5	0
Energy	2.0	0.3	4	1
Financials	12.9	0.7	25	5
Industrials	11.2	1.0	13	4
Durables	2.4	1.5	5	0
Staples	0.8	0.1	5	0
Services	28.4	2.6	42	22
Retail	6.1	0.9	20	3
Health	12.9	0.9	21	7
Technology	22.5	1.2	48	8

Analysis by Peter Di Teresa 10-31-01

Managers Special Equity Fund could be a sound addition to a large-cap-focused portfolio.

While a small-cap growth fund could add variety to a portfolio, this one is more likely to fill the bill than most. That's because its assets are actually parceled out among several managers with different investment styles. The fund is a one-stop shop for supporting portfolio players.

The lead in any portfolio of stock funds ought to be a U.S. large-cap offering, but variety can help returns and provide stability. By combining six distinct strategies, this fund offers variety in spades.

Gary Pilgrim is perhaps the most aggressive manager in the group, as he is willing to pay high prices for stocks with strong earnings momentum. Micro-cap manager Bob Kern also contributes to the fund's growth bent by investing in innovative companies in fast-growing industries. On the value front, Andy Knuth invests in small- and mid-cap companies with low price multiples and high growth potential. Timothy Ebright seeks micro-caps with steady earnings and cheap prices relative to their intrinsic values.

In December 2000, the fund added another value manager to that lineup—Bill Dutton of Skyline Special Equities. Dutton focuses on small caps with low prices and strong growth prospects. He tries to exploit market inefficiencies by focusing on stocks ignored by Wall Street.

The fund's mix of styles has made it less risky than the typical small-growth fund, and its long-term returns are superior. As of November 30, 2001, its three-, five- and 10-year returns were in the category's top third or better. Cautious investors should note, however, that despite mixing strategies the fund has been riskier than most small-blend offerings.

Investors seeking variety and spice for a large-cap portfolio should consider this option.

Address:	40 Richards Avenue Norwalk, CT 06854 800–835–3879 / 203–857–5321
Web Address:	www.managersfunds.com
Inception:	06-01-84
Advisor:	Managers Funds
Subadvisor:	Goldman Sachs Asset Managment/Westport .
NTF Plans:	Fidelity , Datalynx

Minimum Purchase:	$2000	Add: $100	IRA: $500
Min Auto Inv Plan:	$100	Add: $100	
Sales Fees:	No-load		
Management Fee:	.90%, .25%A		
Actual Fees:	Mgt: 0.90%	Dist: —	
Expense Projections:	3Yr: $501	5Yr: $894	10Yr: $1995
Avg Brok Commission:	—	Income Distrib: Annually	
Total Cost (relative to category):	Average		

Marsico 21st Century

Ticker	Load	NAV	Yield	Total Assets	Mstar Category
MXXIX	12b–1 only	$7.37	0.0%	$68.6 mil	Large Growth

Prospectus Objective: Growth

Marsico 21st Century Fund seeks long-term growth of capital.

The fund primarily invests in common stocks selected for their long-term growth potential. It may invest in companies of any size, and will normally hold a core position of 35 to 50 equity securities. The fund may invest without limit in foreign securities. The advisor may invest up to 10% of total net assets in all types of fixed income securities and up to 5% of assets in high-yield bonds and mortgage and asset-backed securities. The fund may also invest up to 15% of assets in illiquid investments.

Historical Profile
Return —
Risk —
Rating Not Rated

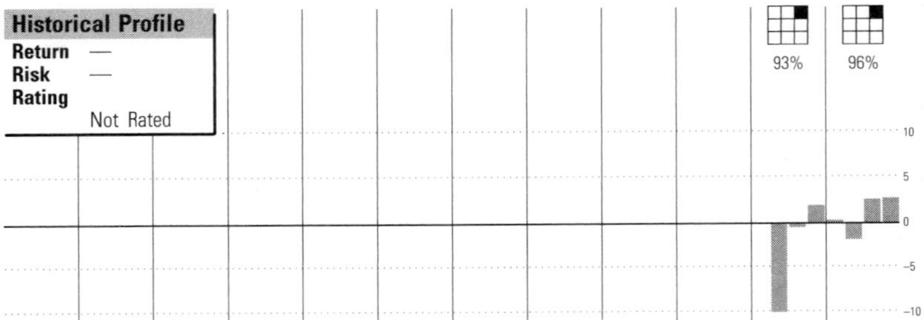

Investment Style
Equity
Average Stock %
93% 96%

▼ Manager Change
▽ Partial Manager Change

Fund Performance vs. Category Average
■ Quarterly Fund Return +/– Category Average
— Category Baseline

Performance Quartile (within Category)

Portfolio Manager(s)

James A. Hillary. Since 2-00. BS Rutgers U.; JD Fordham U.

1990	1991	1992	1993	1994	1995	1996	1997	1998	1999	2000	12–01	History
—	—	—	—	—	—	—	—	—	—	9.19	7.37	NAV
—	—	—	—	—	—	—	—	—	—	–8.10*	–19.80	Total Return %
—	—	—	—	—	—	—	—	—	—	–2.80*	–7.93	+/– S&P 500
—	—	—	—	—	—	—	—	—	—	—	0.69	+/– Russ Top 200 Grt
—	—	—	—	—	—	—	—	—	—	0.00	0.00	Income Return %
—	—	—	—	—	—	—	—	—	—	–8.10	–19.80	Capital Return %
—	—	—	—	—	—	—	—	—	—	—	39	Total Rtn % Rank Cat
—	—	—	—	—	—	—	—	—	—	0.00	0.00	Income $
—	—	—	—	—	—	—	—	—	—	0.00	0.00	Capital Gains $
—	—	—	—	—	—	—	—	—	—	1.50	—	Expense Ratio %
—	—	—	—	—	—	—	—	—	—	–0.92	—	Income Ratio %
—	—	—	—	—	—	—	—	—	—	—	—	Turnover Rate %
—	—	—	—	—	—	—	—	—	—	99.4	68.6	Net Assets $mil

Performance 12-31-01

	1st Qtr	2nd Qtr	3rd Qtr	4th Qtr	Total
1997	—	—	—	—	—
1998	—	—	—	—	—
1999	—	—	—	—	—
2000	—	–15.07	–0.18	–15.38	–8.10*
2001	–20.67	4.80	–18.06	17.73	–19.80

Trailing	Total Return%	+/– S&P 500	+/– Russ Top 200 Grth	% Rank All	% Rank Cat	Growth of $10,000
3 Mo	17.73	7.05	4.88	18	21	11,773
6 Mo	–3.53	2.02	3.45	54	10	9,647
1 Yr	–19.80	–7.93	0.69	80	39	8,020
3 Yr Avg	—	—	—	—	—	—
5 Yr Avg	—	—	—	—	—	—
10 Yr Avg	—	—	—	—	—	—
15 Yr Avg	—	—	—	—	—	—

Tax Analysis	Tax-Adj Ret%	%Rank Cat	%Pretax Ret	%Rank Cat
3 Yr Avg	—	—	—	—
5 Yr Avg	—	—	—	—
10 Yr Avg	—	—	—	—

Potential Capital Gain Exposure: –77% of assets

Risk Analysis

Time Period	Load-Adj Return %	Risk %Rank[1] All	Risk %Rank[1] Cat	Morningstar Return	Morningstar Risk	Morningstar Risk-Adj Rating
1 Yr	–19.80					
3 Yr	—	—	—	—	—	
5 Yr	—	—	—	—	—	
Incept	–14.73	—	—	—	—	

Average Historical Rating —

[1]1=low, 100=high

Category Rating (3 Yr)

Other Measures	Standard Index S&P 500	Best Fit Index
Alpha	—	—
Beta	—	—
R–Squared	—	—
Standard Deviation		—
Return — Mean		—
Risk — Sharpe Ratio		—

Portfolio Analysis 09-30-01

Share change since 07–01 Total Stocks: 40	Sector	PE	YTD Ret%	% Assets
⊕ UnitedHealth Grp	Financials	26.6	15.37	6.36
⊖ InterMune	Health	—	10.39	5.54
⊕ Citigroup	Financials	20.0	0.03	5.18
⊖ Fannie Mae	Financials	16.2	–6.95	5.11
⊖ Tenet Healthcare	Health	30.1	32.14	5.07
Federal Home Loan Bk N/A	N/A	—	—	4.99
☼ Lehman Brothers Hldgs	Financials	12.4	–0.84	4.85
⊖ Home Depot	Retail	42.9	12.07	4.54
⊖ Qualcomm	Technology	—	–38.50	3.75
⊖ BP PLC ADR	Energy	14.4	–0.90	3.35
⊖ Costco Wholesale	Retail	34.4	11.12	3.14
⊕ SkyWest	Services	27.1	–11.10	3.09
⊕ Comcast	Services	20.3	–13.70	3.05
☼ Quest Diagnostics	Health	51.2	1.00	3.01
⊕ American Intl Grp	Financials	42.0	–19.20	2.65
⊖ Tyco Intl	Industrials	27.1	6.23	2.51
⊕ Lowe's	Retail	38.7	109.00	2.42
☼ Matria Healthcare	Health	42.2	259.70	2.40
⊕ Duke Energy	Utilities	15.5	–6.04	2.40
⊖ Smith Intl	Industrials	19.3	–28.00	2.11
⊕ Amdocs	Services	NMF	–48.70	2.01
☼ Lockheed Martin	Industrials	36.8	38.98	1.71
⊖ Microsoft	Technology	57.6	52.78	1.68
☼ ExxonMobil	Energy	15.3	–7.59	1.54
☼ Starbucks	Retail	41.4	–13.90	1.53

Current Investment Style

Style: Value Blnd Growth; Size: Large Med Small

	Stock Port Avg	Relative S&P 500 Current	Relative S&P 500 Hist	Rel Cat
Price/Earnings Ratio	29.7	0.96	—	0.84
Price/Book Ratio	4.7	0.82	—	0.74
Price/Cash Flow	18.9	1.05	—	0.83
3 Yr Earnings Growth	24.4	1.67	—	1.13
1 Yr Earnings Est%	17.4	—	—	5.78
Med Mkt Cap $mil	22,101	0.4	—	0.47

Analysis by Peter Di Teresa 12-31-01

This fund adds a new dimension to its family, but it's mostly a matter of nuance.

Marsico 21st Century Fund manager Jim Hillary looks within macroeconomic themes for fast-growing firms that dominate their niches. Those are the same kinds of stocks that siblings Marsico Focus and Marsico Growth & Income target. The difference is that Hillary picks up the stocks before those mega-capitalization funds do.

So far, that style has worked pretty well. The fund had the misfortune to debut in February 2000, just in time for the bear market. It has lost money since, but less than the typical large-growth fund has. For the year to date through Dec. 28, 2001, it was down 19%, but 60% of its peers had lost more.

For much of 2001, the fund focused on firms with predictable earnings. Along with a modest, 13% tech stake, that kept losses near the group average. When prices dropped after the Sept. 11 terrorist attacks, though, Hillary snapped up tech issues such as Cisco Systems, Flextronics International, and high-tech services firm Amdocs, bringing the position up to 30% of the portfolio. As growth stocks revived in 2001's fourth quarter, this fund took off. Its 18.7% trailing three-month return through Dec. 28 ranked in the category's top quartile.

The fund also bested Focus and Growth & Income by a wide margin. Dedicating 30% of assets to mid- and small-cap issues was key, as smaller issues led the rebound. Otherwise, this fund looks very much like its siblings, even owning many of the same stocks.

Of the three funds, this one could appeal to investors who don't want to stake so much on the biggest stocks. That said, it's still very much a large-cap fund, so investors may want to accompany it with other funds that venture further down the range.

Special Securities % assets 09-30-01	
Restricted/Illiquid Secs	0
Emerging–Markets Secs	1
Options/Futures/Warrants	No

Sector Weightings	% of Stocks	Rel S&P	5-Year High	5-Year Low
Utilities	2.5	0.8	—	—
Energy	5.1	0.7	—	—
Financials	25.2	1.4	—	—
Industrials	10.6	0.9	—	—
Durables	2.0	1.3	—	—
Staples	1.6	0.2	—	—
Services	13.0	1.2	—	—
Retail	13.5	2.0	—	—
Health	17.4	1.2	—	—
Technology	9.1	0.5	—	—

Composition % assets 09-30-01	
Cash	0.1
Stocks*	94.9
Bonds	5.0
Other	0.0
*Foreign (% stocks)	6.8

Market Cap	
Giant	33.2
Large	33.0
Medium	20.0
Small	9.2
Micro	4.6

Address:	P.O. Box 3210 Milwaukee, WI 53201–3210 888–860–8686
Web Address:	www.marsicofunds.com
*Inception:	02-01-00
Advisor:	Marsico Cap. Mgmt.
Subadvisor:	None
NTF Plans:	Fidelity Inst. , Waterhouse

Minimum Purchase:	$2500	Add: $100	IRA: $1000
Min Auto Inv Plan:	$1000	Add: $50	
Sales Fees:	0.25%B		
Management Fee:	.85%, .12%A		
Actual Fees:	Mgt: 0.85%	Dist: 0.25%	
Expense Projections:	3Yr: $542	5Yr: $933	10Yr: $2030
Avg Brok Commission:	—	Income Distrib: Annually	
Total Cost (relative to category):	—		

Marsico Focus

Ticker	Load	NAV	Yield	Total Assets	Mstar Category
MFOCX	12b–1 only	$13.60	0.0%	$1,401.0 mil	Large Growth

Prospectus Objective: Growth

Marsico Focus Fund seeks long-term growth of capital.

The fund normally invests in approximately 20 to 30 common stocks management judges to have growth potential. It may also invest up to 10% of assets in fixed-income securities, and up to 5% in high-yield bonds and mortgage- and asset-backed securities. The fund may invest without limit in equity and debt securities of foreign issuers. This fund is non-diversified.

Historical Profile

Return	Average
Risk	Above Avg
Rating	★★ Below Avg

Investment Style
Equity
Average Stock %: 92% (1998), 96% (1999), 96% (2000), 96% (12-01)

▼ Manager Change
▽ Partial Manager Change

Fund Performance vs. Category Average
■ Quarterly Fund Return +/– Category Average
— Category Baseline

Performance Quartile (within Category)

Portfolio Manager(s)

Thomas F. Marsico. Since 12-97. BS'77 U. of Colorado; MBA'79 U. of Denver. Other funds currently managed: Enterprise Capital Appreciation A, Diversified Inv Equity Growth, Enterprise Capital Appreciation B.

1990	1991	1992	1993	1994	1995	1996	1997	1998	1999	2000	12-01	History
—	—	—	—	—	—	—	10.00	15.13	23.45	17.23	13.60	NAV
—	—	—	—	—	—	—	—	51.30	55.27	–17.91	–20.81	Total Return %
—	—	—	—	—	—	—	—	22.73	34.23	–8.81	–8.93	+/– S&P 500
—	—	—	—	—	—	—	—	6.20	25.59	6.61	–0.31	+/– Russ Top 200 Grt
—	—	—	—	—	—	—	—	0.00	0.00	0.00	0.00	Income Return %
—	—	—	—	—	—	—	—	51.30	55.27	–17.91	–20.81	Capital Return %
—	—	—	—	—	—	—	—	9	19	63	43	Total Rtn % Rank Cat
—	—	—	—	—	—	—	0.00	0.00	0.00	0.00	0.00	Income $
—	—	—	—	—	—	—	0.00	0.00	0.04	1.96	0.04	Capital Gains $
—	—	—	—	—	—	—	—	1.56	1.31	1.27	—	Expense Ratio %
—	—	—	—	—	—	—	—	–0.27	–0.43	–0.70	—	Income Ratio %
—	—	—	—	—	—	—	—	—	173	176	—	Turnover Rate %
—	—	—	—	—	—	—	—	1,204.4	3,256.7	2,325.2	1,401.0	Net Assets $mil

Performance 12-31-01

	1st Qtr	2nd Qtr	3rd Qtr	4th Qtr	Total
1997	—	—	—	—	—
1998	23.10	11.70	–10.11	22.41	51.30
1999	12.56	2.35	0.00	34.78	55.27
2000	0.21	–8.30	2.88	–13.17	–17.91
2001	–18.63	4.85	–16.53	11.20	–20.81

Trailing	Total Return%	+/– S&P 500	+/– Russ Top 200 Grth	% Rank All	% Rank Cat	Growth of $10,000
3 Mo	11.20	0.52	–1.65	36	76	11,120
6 Mo	–7.18	–1.63	–0.19	75	34	9,282
1 Yr	–20.81	–8.93	–0.31	82	43	7,919
3 Yr Avg	0.31	1.34	8.33	71	24	10,093
5 Yr Avg	—	—	—	—	—	—
10 Yr Avg	—	—	—	—	—	—
15 Yr Avg	—	—	—	—	—	—

Tax Analysis	Tax-Adj Ret%	%Rank Cat	%Pretax Ret	%Rank Cat
3 Yr Avg	–0.44	21	—	—
5 Yr Avg	—	—	—	—
10 Yr Avg	—	—	—	—

Potential Capital Gain Exposure: –44% of assets

Risk Analysis

Time Period	Load-Adj Return %	Risk %Rank[1] All	Risk %Rank[1] Cat	Morningstar Return	Morningstar Risk	Morningstar Risk-Adj Rating
1 Yr	–20.81					
3 Yr	0.31	86	54	–0.94[2]	1.31	★★
5 Yr	—	—	—	—	—	
Incept	11.16	—	—	—	—	

Average Historical Rating (13 months): 3.4★s

[1]1=low, 100=high [2] T-Bill return substituted for category avg.

Category Rating (3 Yr)

1 2 3 4 5
Worst — Best

Return	Above Avg
Risk	Average

Other Measures	Standard Index S&P 500	Best Fit Index Wil 4500
Alpha	3.7	–1.5
Beta	1.12	0.82
R-Squared	54	79

Standard Deviation	26.64
Mean	0.31
Sharpe Ratio	–0.20

Portfolio Analysis 09-30-01

Share change since 07-01 Total Stocks: 28	Sector	PE	YTD Ret%	% Assets
⊕ General Elec	Industrials	30.1	–15.00	6.13
Fannie Mae	Financials	16.2	–6.95	5.98
⊕ UnitedHealth Grp	Financials	26.6	15.37	5.74
⊕ Tenet Healthcare	Health	30.1	32.14	5.62
USA Educ	Financials	68.9	24.74	5.21
Citigroup	Financials	20.0	0.03	5.03
⊕ Lehman Brothers Hldgs	Financials	12.4	–0.84	4.91
⊖ General Dynamics	Industrials	17.6	3.63	4.87
⊖ Costco Wholesale	Retail	34.4	11.12	4.68
Federal Home Loan Bk N/A	N/A	—	—	4.48
⊖ Home Depot	Retail	42.9	12.07	4.42
⊖ Wal-Mart Stores	Retail	40.3	8.94	4.18
⊖ Microsoft	Technology	57.6	52.78	3.98
☼ Johnson & Johnson	Health	16.6	14.01	3.81
Tiffany	Retail	27.1	0.09	3.49
☼ PepsiCo	Staples	31.4	–0.54	3.46
⊕ Washington Mutual	Financials	10.1	–5.32	3.36
⊕ Lockheed Martin	Industrials	36.8	38.98	3.18
⊕ IBM	Technology	26.9	43.00	2.56
Four Seasons Hotels	Services	27.7	–26.40	2.40
⊖ Smith Intl	Industrials	19.3	–28.00	2.24
⊖ Southwest Air	Services	25.0	–17.20	2.23
⊖ Qualcomm	Technology	—	–38.50	2.00
⊕ Quest Diagnostics	Health	51.2	1.00	1.97
Baxter Intl	Health	33.9	22.84	1.62

Current Investment Style

Style: Value Blnd Growth; Size: Large Med Small

	Stock Port Avg	Relative S&P 500 Current	Relative S&P 500 Hist	Rel Cat
Price/Earnings Ratio	29.8	0.96	1.12	0.84
Price/Book Ratio	5.5	0.96	1.19	0.86
Price/Cash Flow	20.2	1.12	1.19	0.89
3 Yr Earnings Growth	21.0	1.44	1.31	0.98
1 Yr Earnings Est%	15.2	—	—	5.05
Med Mkt Cap $mil	29,470	0.5	1.1	0.62

Special Securities % assets 09-30-01	
Restricted/Illiquid Secs	0
Emerging-Markets Secs	0
Options/Futures/Warrants	No

Composition % assets 09-30-01	
Cash	0.0
Stocks*	95.5
Bonds	4.5
Other	0.0
*Foreign (% stocks)	3.7

Market Cap	
Giant	41.3
Large	47.1
Medium	9.2
Small	2.5
Micro	0.0

Sector Weightings	% of Stocks	Rel S&P	5-Year High	5-Year Low
Utilities	0.0	0.0	—	—
Energy	0.0	0.0	—	—
Financials	25.6	1.4	—	—
Industrials	17.2	1.5	—	—
Durables	1.2	0.7	—	—
Staples	3.6	0.5	—	—
Services	5.8	0.5	—	—
Retail	17.5	2.6	—	—
Health	19.6	1.3	—	—
Technology	9.6	0.5	—	—

Analysis by Christine Benz 11-14-01

Top-down bets are usually a dicey proposition, but you've got to hand it to Marsico Focus.

So few managers have had success with top-down strategies that most have abandoned the practice entirely. But macroeconomic factors play a distinct role in manager Tom Marsico's process. In the second half of 2000, for example, Marsico reckoned that reduced capital spending and inventory gluts would continue to weigh on technology stocks. As a result, he slashed this portfolio's technology stake from 30% of assets at midyear of 2000 to next to nothing earlier this year.

At the time, we argued that Marsico's moves had the potential to backfire badly. After all, the fund had already fallen a lot at the hands of its tech holdings in 2000, and if the sector rebounded the fund could be left behind. Yet tech stocks continued to drop like a rock for much of this year, and this fund's tech-light positioning has been a boon relative to other large-cap growth funds. The fund's trailing one-year return through mid-November is still a nasty loss, but it's good enough to land in the large-growth group's top quartile.

That's not bad for a fund that managed to ride the bull in the late 1990s, parlaying aggressive tech holdings into huge gains. In all, this fund's annualized return since its launch is 9.4%—7 percentage points better than the large-growth average. That, combined with Marsico's phenomenal run as skipper of Janus Twenty, inspires confidence that his big-picture maneuvering will be on the money more often than not.

The risk that the fund will get caught leaning the wrong way hasn't gone away—in October, for example, tech stocks staged a nice rebound, and this fund badly trailed the large-growth average. That said, we still place this offering among the large-cap growth category's elite.

Address:	P.O. Box 3210 Milwaukee, WI 53201–3210 888–860–8686
Web Address:	www.marsicofunds.com
*Inception:	12-31-97
Advisor:	Marsico Cap. Mgmt.
Subadvisor:	None
NTF Plans:	Fidelity , Fidelity Inst.

Minimum Purchase:	$2500	Add: $100 IRA: $1000
Min Auto Inv Plan:	$1000	Add: $50
Sales Fees:	0.25%B	
Management Fee:	.85%, .14%A	
Actual Fees:	Mgt: 0.85%	Dist: 0.25%
Expense Projections:	3Yr: $415	5Yr: $718 10Yr: $1579
Avg Brok Commission:	—	Income Distrib: Annually
Total Cost (relative to category):		Below Avg

Marsico International Opportunities

Ticker	Load	NAV	Yield	Total Assets	Mstar Category
MIOFX	12b–1 only	$7.86	0.1%	$19.8 mil	Foreign Stock

Prospectus Objective: Foreign Stock

Marsico International Opportunities seeks long-term growth of capital.

The fund normally invests at least 65% of assets in common stocks of foreign companies. It typically invests in issuers from at least three different countries not including the United States. The fund can invest up to 10% of assets in all types of fixed income securities and up to 5% in high-yield bonds and mortgage- and asset-backed securities. It can invest up to 15% in illiquid investments. It may also invest in options and emerging markets.

Historical Profile
Return —
Risk —
Rating
Not Rated

Investment Style
Equity
Average Stock % 77% 87%

▼ Manager Change
▽ Partial Manager Change

Fund Performance vs. Category Average
■ Quarterly Fund Return +/– Category Average
— Category Baseline

Performance Quartile (within Category)

Portfolio Manager(s)

James G. Gendelman. Since 6-00. BS Michigan State U.; MBA U. of Chicago.

1990	1991	1992	1993	1994	1995	1996	1997	1998	1999	2000	12-01	History
—	—	—	—	—	—	—	—	—	—	9.33	7.86	NAV
—	—	—	—	—	—	—	—	—	—	–3.52*	–15.65	Total Return %
—	—	—	—	—	—	—	—	—	—	5.19*	–3.78	+/– S&P 500
—	—	—	—	—	—	—	—	—	—	—	—	+/– MSCI EAFE
—	—	—	—	—	—	—	—	—	—	0.41	0.10	Income Return %
—	—	—	—	—	—	—	—	—	—	–3.93	–15.75	Capital Return %
—	—	—	—	—	—	—	—	—	—	—	16	Total Rtn % Rank Cat
—	—	—	—	—	—	—	—	—	—	0.04	0.01	Income $
—	—	—	—	—	—	—	—	—	—	0.27	0.00	Capital Gains $
—	—	—	—	—	—	—	—	—	—	1.60	—	Expense Ratio %
—	—	—	—	—	—	—	—	—	—	0.33	—	Income Ratio %
—	—	—	—	—	—	—	—	—	—	—	—	Turnover Rate %
—	—	—	—	—	—	—	—	—	—	14.0	19.8	Net Assets $mil

Performance 12-31-01

	1st Qtr	2nd Qtr	3rd Qtr	4th Qtr	Total
1997	—	—	—	—	—
1998	—	—	—	—	—
1999	—	—	—	—	—
2000	—	—	3.60	–6.87	–3.52 *
2001	–14.15	3.62	–18.31	16.07	–15.65

Trailing	Total Return%	+/– S&P 500	+/– MSCI EAFE	% Rank All	% Rank Cat	Growth of $10,000
3 Mo	16.07	5.39	—	22	7	11,607
6 Mo	–5.19	0.37	—	63	11	9,481
1 Yr	–15.65	–3.78	—	74	16	8,435
3 Yr Avg	—	—	—	—	—	—
5 Yr Avg	—	—	—	—	—	—
10 Yr Avg	—	—	—	—	—	—
15 Yr Avg	—	—	—	—	—	—

Tax Analysis	Tax-Adj Ret%	%Rank Cat	%Pretax Ret	%Rank Cat
3 Yr Avg	—	—	—	—
5 Yr Avg	—	—	—	—
10 Yr Avg	—	—	—	—

Potential Capital Gain Exposure: –23% of assets

Risk Analysis

Time Period	Load-Adj Return %	Risk %Rank[1] All	Risk %Rank[1] Cat	Morningstar Return	Morningstar Risk	Morningstar Risk-Adj Rating
1 Yr	–15.65					
3 Yr	—	—	—	—	—	
5 Yr	—	—	—	—	—	
Incept	–12.80	—	—	—	—	

Average Historical Rating —

[1]1=low, 100=high

Category Rating (3 Yr)

Other Measures	Standard Index S&P 500	Best Fit Index
Alpha	—	—
Beta	—	—
R-Squared	—	—
Standard Deviation		—
Mean		—
Sharpe Ratio		—

Return
Risk

Portfolio Analysis 09-30-01

Share change since 07-01 Total Stocks: 48	Sector	Country	% Assets
Federal Home Loan Bk N/A	N/A	N/A	4.54
⊖ Royal Bk of Scotland	Financials	United Kingdom	3.37
☼ Muenchener Rueckvers (Reg)	Financials	Germany	3.32
⊕ Glaxosmithkline	Technology	United Kingdom	3.29
⊕ Ahold	Retail	Netherlands	3.18
⊕ Unilever (Netherlands)	Staples	Netherlands	3.06
☼ UBS (Reg)	Financials	Switzerland	3.02
⊖ Northern Rock	Financials	United Kingdom	2.92
☼ Ishares Tr	N/A	N/A	2.91
⊖ Westjet Airlines	Technology	Canada	2.85
⊕ Ryanair Hldgs ADR	Services	Ireland	2.79
⊕ Mapfre	Financials	Spain	2.59
⊖ Heineken Hldg Cl A	Staples	Netherlands	2.38
☼ Diageo	Staples	United Kingdom	2.38
☼ Lafarge France	Industrials	France	2.23
☼ RWE Ag (new)	N/A	N/A	2.12
⊖ Canadian Natl Railway	Services	Canada	2.08
⊖ Total Fina Cl B	Energy	France	2.07
⊖ Karstadt	Retail	Germany	2.07
⊖ Inditex	N/A	N/A	2.07

Analysis by Gabriel Presler 12-20-01

Marsico International Opportunities has enjoyed a heady debut in a grim year.

It hasn't been an auspicious time to launch a foreign-stock fund. Weighed down by slowing global growth, trouble in the tech and telecom industries, and wilting share prices in most sectors, the average offering in the category has lost almost 22% in the trailing 12 months ending Dec. 18, 2001.

This fund has hardly been immune to trouble—in fact, it's down 17% over the same period—but its relative resilience is impressive, especially given its growth tilt. Manager Jim Gendelman emphasizes companies that are growing faster than their industry peers, such as Vodafone. But he also considers firms in flux as well as aggressive-growth companies. He's particularly focused on companies that are low-cost providers. Earlier in the year, for example, he admired AFLAC because that firm successfully targeted Japan's need for cheap, supplemental insurance. This approach—which also unearthed successful RyanAir, an Irish version of Southwest Airlines—has helped the fund outpace more than 80% of its peers since its June 2000 launch.

A lot of questions surround this offering. First of all, while Gendelman's an old hand at international investing, he has no previous retail record. What's more, while the fund has been quite agile over the past year (Gendelman dumped his tech and telecom stakes much faster than his peers), there's no telling how it will perform as its assets grow.

Still, the fund's performance—especially relative to its growth-oriented peers—has been impressive, thanks in large part to strong stock-picking and sector shifts. What's more, this is part of a strong fund family. Tom Marsico's shop has garnered attention and high marks using a similar strategy.

Current Investment Style

Style: Value Blnd Growth; Size: Large Med Small

	Stock Port Avg	Rel MSCI EAFE Current	Rel MSCI EAFE Hist	Rel Cat
Price/Earnings Ratio	26.4	1.02	—	1.03
Price/Cash Flow	14.4	1.12	—	1.00
Price/Book Ratio	5.4	1.55	—	1.38
3 Yr Earnings Growth	22.6	1.21	—	1.15
Med Mkt Cap $mil	12,436	0.4	—	0.69

Country Exposure 09-30-01	% assets
United Kingdom	17
Netherlands	12
Germany	9
Japan	6
Canada	6

Hedging History: —

Regional Exposure 09-30-01	% assets
Europe	59
Pacific Rim	1
Latin America	1
Japan	6
Other	7

Special Securities % assets 09-30-01	
Restricted/Illiquid Secs	0
Emerging-Markets Secs	3
Options/Futures/Warrants	Yes

Composition % assets 09-30-01			
Cash	2.8	Bonds	4.3
Stocks	86.0	Other	6.9

Sector Weightings	% of Stocks	Rel Cat	5-Year High	5-Year Low
Utilities	0.0	0.0	—	—
Energy	5.0	0.9	—	—
Financials	28.3	1.3	—	—
Industrials	9.5	0.7	—	—
Durables	4.7	0.7	—	—
Staples	10.5	1.5	—	—
Services	18.7	1.1	—	—
Retail	9.1	1.9	—	—
Health	3.2	0.3	—	—
Technology	11.1	1.1	—	—

Address:	P.O. Box 3210 Milwaukee, WI 53201–3210 888–860–8686
Web Address:	www.marsicofunds.com
*Inception:	06-30-00
Advisor:	Marsico Cap. Mgmt.
Subadvisor:	None
NTF Plans:	Fidelity Inst. , Waterhouse

Minimum Purchase:	$2500	Add: $100	IRA: $1000
Min Auto Inv Plan:	$1000	Add: $50	
Sales Fees:	0.25%B		
Management Fee:	.85%		
Actual Fees:	Mgt: 0.85%	Dist: 0.25%	
Expense Projections:	3Yr: $543	5Yr: —	10Yr: —
Avg Brok Commission:	—	Income Distrib: Annually	
Total Cost (relative to category):	—		

Masters' Select Value

Ticker	Load	NAV	Yield	Total Assets	Mstar Category
MSVFX	None	$11.43	0.0%	$160.2 mil	Mid-Cap Value

Prospectus Objective: Growth

The Masters' Select Value Fund seeks long-term growth of capital.

The fund engages four proven investment managers to invest in securities they believe have the potential for strong appreciation. The fund primarily invests in securities of mid and large sized U.S. companies. It may invest up to 25% of assets in the securities of small companies. The fund may also invest up to 20% of assets in foreign stock. This fund is non-diversified.

Historical Profile
Return —
Risk —
Rating Not Rated

Investment Style Equity
Average Stock % 88%

▼ Manager Change
▽ Partial Manager Change

Fund Performance vs. Category Average
■ Quarterly Fund Return +/– Category Average
— Category Baseline

Performance Quartile (within Category)

Portfolio Manager(s)

O. Mason Hawkins, CFA. Since 6-00.
William H. Miller III, CFA. Since 6-00.
William C. Nygren, CFA. Since 6-00.
G. Staley Cates, CFA. Since 6-00.
David J. Winters, CFA. Since 8-01.

1990	1991	1992	1993	1994	1995	1996	1997	1998	1999	2000	12-01	History
—	—	—	—	—	—	—	—	—	—	10.45	11.43	NAV
—	—	—	—	—	—	—	—	—	—	4.50*	9.64	Total Return %
—	—	—	—	—	—	—	—	—	—	13.21*	21.51	+/– S&P 500
—	—	—	—	—	—	—	—	—	—	—	7.30	+/– Russ Midcap Val
—	—	—	—	—	—	—	—	—	—	0.00	0.01	Income Return %
—	—	—	—	—	—	—	—	—	—	4.50	9.63	Capital Return %
—	—	—	—	—	—	—	—	—	—	—	34	Total Rtn % Rank Cat
—	—	—	—	—	—	—	—	—	—	0.00	0.00	Income $
—	—	—	—	—	—	—	—	—	—	0.00	0.03	Capital Gains $
—	—	—	—	—	—	—	—	—	—	—	—	Expense Ratio %
—	—	—	—	—	—	—	—	—	—	—	—	Income Ratio %
—	—	—	—	—	—	—	—	—	—	—	—	Turnover Rate %
—	—	—	—	—	—	—	—	—	—	56.0	160.2	Net Assets $mil

Performance 12-31-01

	1st Qtr	2nd Qtr	3rd Qtr	4th Qtr	Total
1997	—	—	—	—	—
1998	—	—	—	—	—
1999	—	—	—	—	—
2000	—	—	4.80	–0.29	4.50 *
2001	7.56	10.85	–17.42	11.34	9.64

Trailing	Total Return%	+/– S&P 500	+/– Russ Midcap Val	% Rank All	% Rank Cat	Growth of $10,000
3 Mo	11.34	0.66	–0.69	36	62	11,134
6 Mo	–8.05	–2.49	–7.14	78	98	9,195
1 Yr	9.64	21.51	7.30	6	34	10,964
3 Yr Avg	—	—	—	—	—	—
5 Yr Avg	—	—	—	—	—	—
10 Yr Avg	—	—	—	—	—	—
15 Yr Avg	—	—	—	—	—	—

Tax Analysis	Tax-Adj Ret%	%Rank Cat	%Pretax Ret	%Rank Cat
3 Yr Avg	—	—	—	—
5 Yr Avg	—	—	—	—
10 Yr Avg	—	—	—	—

Potential Capital Gain Exposure: NMF

Risk Analysis

Time Period	Load-Adj Return %	Risk %Rank[1] All	Risk %Rank[1] Cat	Morningstar Return	Morningstar Risk	Morningstar Risk-Adj Rating
1 Yr	9.64					
3 Yr	—	—	—	—	—	
5 Yr	—	—	—	—	—	
Incept	9.47	—	—	—	—	

Average Historical Rating —

[1]1=low, 100=high

Category Rating (3 Yr)

Other Measures	Standard Index S&P 500	Best Fit Index
Alpha	—	—
Beta	—	—
R-Squared	—	—

	Standard Deviation	—
Return	Mean	—
Risk	Sharpe Ratio	—

Portfolio Analysis 06-30-01

Share change since Total Stocks: 45	Sector	PE	YTD Ret%	% Assets
AT&T	Services	7.8	40.59	4.67
Cabletron Sys	Technology	—	–14.40	4.17
Washington Mutual	Financials	10.1	–5.32	3.62
Tricon Global Restaurants	Services	16.3	49.09	3.42
General Motors	Durables	NMF	–0.97	3.28
MONY Grp	Financials	50.1	–29.00	3.13
Hilton Hotels	Services	17.9	4.72	3.01
Bank One	Financials	29.1	9.13	3.00
UnumProvident	Financials	10.7	0.77	2.81
Dell Comp	Technology	61.8	55.87	2.74
Eastman Kodak	Industrials	17.8	–21.90	2.61
Republic Svcs Cl A	Services	15.6	16.19	2.43
Fairfax Finl Hldgs	Financials	—	—	2.32
Gateway Inc	Technology	—	–55.30	2.30
Waste Mgmt	Services	52.3	15.03	2.26
Telephone and Data Sys	Services	—	0.29	2.16
Mandalay Resort Grp	Services	15.3	–2.45	2.11
Lagardere	Financials	11.1	—	2.03
Federated Dept Stores	Retail	16.6	16.86	1.86
Burlington Resources	Energy	8.4	–24.60	1.76
Fedex	Services	29.3	29.83	1.74
Kroger	Retail	16.3	–22.80	1.71
Electronic Data Sys	Technology	25.7	19.83	1.70
ServiceMaster	Services	22.3	24.29	1.66
Altadis Cl A	Staples	0.2	—	1.56

Current Investment Style

Style: Value Blnd Growth; Size: Large Med Small

	Stock Port Avg	Relative S&P 500 Current	Relative S&P 500 Hist	Rel Cat
Price/Earnings Ratio	25.8	0.83	—	1.09
Price/Book Ratio	2.7	0.47	—	0.88
Price/Cash Flow	10.7	0.59	—	0.86
3 Yr Earnings Growth	16.1	1.10	—	1.36
1 Yr Earnings Est%	–15.8	8.92	—	2.57
Med Mkt Cap $mil	6,245	0.1	—	0.88

Analysis by Peter Di Teresa 10-16-01

A recent manager change shouldn't limit Masters' Select Value Fund's appeal too much.

This fund divides assets equally among four managers with differing approaches to value investing, making it a one-stop shop for value exposure. When you consider its array of impressive managers, that's a pretty compelling concept.

Given that quality of management is one of the fund's attractions, a manager change is significant. Larry Sondike, who switched roles at Mutual Series because of a shakeup at the firm, left his fund charges in late September. The good news is that his replacement is David Winters, who has worked on a number of Mutual Series funds since 1996 and is now lead manager of Sondike's old fund, Mutual Shares. As the Morningstar Take for that fund points out: "Changes at Mutual Series decrease these funds' attractiveness, but they should still be a cut above their peers."

We think that this fund also still holds appeal. The remainder of its portfolio is divvied up among Mason Hawkins and Staley Cates of Longleaf Partners, Bill Miller of Legg Mason Value Trust, and Bill Nygren of Oakmark Select. Each manager has earned an impressive record by practicing variations on value investing, and all the funds boast long-term returns in their categories' upper reaches. Combining their favorite picks makes sense: Miller's fund (which has more of a growth bent) did best in the late 1990s as the others lagged, but since 2000, those three have come to the fore.

Having been around since only mid-2000, this offering hasn't had much chance to prove its worth. That said, the fund's 3.5% return for the year to date through Oct. 12, 2001, ranks in the category's best quintile, and its 11.6% gain for the trailing 12 months is well above average.

Special Securities % assets 06-30-01	
Restricted/Illiquid Secs	0
Emerging-Markets Secs	0
Options/Futures/Warrants	No

Composition % assets 06-30-01	
Cash	11.8
Stocks*	88.2
Bonds	0.0
Other	0.0
*Foreign (% stocks)	6.7

Market Cap	
Giant	11.0
Large	26.8
Medium	61.2
Small	1.1
Micro	0.0

Sector Weightings	% of Stocks	Rel S&P	5-Year High	5-Year Low
Utilities	0.0	0.0	—	—
Energy	2.0	0.3	—	—
Financials	23.7	1.3	—	—
Industrials	4.0	0.4	—	—
Durables	9.2	5.9	—	—
Staples	3.0	0.4	—	—
Services	37.8	3.5	—	—
Retail	6.7	1.0	—	—
Health	0.0	0.0	—	—
Technology	13.6	0.7	—	—

Address:	P.O. Box 419922 Kansas City, MO 64141–6922 800–960–0188
Web Address:	www.mastersselect.com
*Inception:	06-30-00
Advisor:	Litman/Gregory Fund Adv.
Subadvisor:	None
NTF Plans:	N/A

Minimum Purchase:	$5000	Add: $250 IRA: $1000
Min Auto Inv Plan:	$2500	Add: $100
Sales Fees:	No-load, 2.00%R within 6 months	
Management Fee:	1.1%	
Actual Fees:	Mgt: 1.08%	Dist: —
Expense Projections:	3Yr: $540	5Yr: — 10Yr: —
Avg Brok Commission:	—	Income Distrib: Annually
Total Cost (relative to category):	—	

Matthews Pacific Tiger

Ticker	Load	NAV	Yield	Total Assets	Mstar Category
MAPTX	None	$8.81	0.1%	$87.3 mil	Pacific ex–Japan

Prospectus Objective: Pacific Stock

Matthews Pacific Tiger Fund seeks capital appreciation.

The fund normally invests at least 65% of assets in equity securities of Pacific Tiger economies such as Hong Kong, Singapore, South Korea, Taiwan, China and others. In selecting securities, the fund looks at management quality, competitive position, growth prospects, valuations compared to industry averages, and earnings track record. Although the assets of the fund are ordinarily invested with geographic flexibility, there is no limitation on the percentage of assets which may be invested in any one country.

Historical Profile

Return	Average
Risk	High
Rating	★★★ Neutral

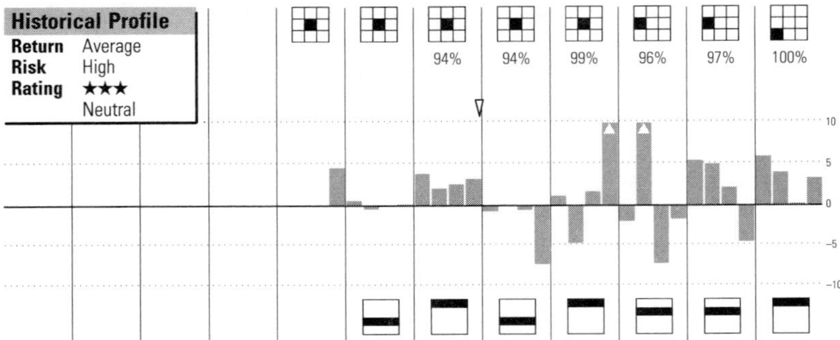

Investment Style
Equity
Average Stock %: 94% (1996), 94% (1997), 99% (1998), 96% (1999), 97% (2000), 100% (12-01)

▼ Manager Change
▽ Partial Manager Change

Fund Performance vs. Category Average
■ Quarterly Fund Return +/– Category Average
— Category Baseline

Performance Quartile (within Category)

Portfolio Manager(s)

G. Paul Matthews. Since 9-94. MA'78 Cambridge U. Other funds currently managed: Matthews Asian Growth & Income, Matthews Korea, Matthews China.

Mark W. Headley. Since 12-96. BA'83 U. of California-Santa Cruz. Other funds currently managed: Matthews Korea, Matthews China, Matthews Japan.

1990	1991	1992	1993	1994	1995	1996	1997	1998	1999	2000	12-01	History
—	—	—	—	9.47	9.76	12.12	7.15	6.84	12.32	8.20	8.81	NAV
—	—	—	—	–5.08*	3.06	24.18	–40.89	–2.86	83.01	–23.25	7.91	Total Return %
—	—	—	—	–4.29*	–34.47	1.24	–74.24	–31.44	61.97	–14.15	19.78	+/- S&P 500
—	—	—	—	—	6.59	15.95	1.18	4.30	17.77	11.74	—	+/– MSCI FE ex Jpn
—	—	—	—	0.22	0.00	0.00	0.05	0.20	2.77	4.20	0.13	Income Return %
—	—	—	—	–5.30	3.06	24.18	–40.93	–3.06	80.24	–27.45	7.78	Capital Return %
—	—	—	—	—	59	9	72	14	27	42	11	Total Rtn % Rank Cat
—	—	—	—	0.02	0.00	0.00	0.01	0.01	0.19	0.51	0.01	Income $
—	—	—	—	0.00	0.00	0.00	0.02	0.06	0.00	0.84	0.03	Capital Gains $
—	—	—	—	—	2.17	1.90	1.90	1.90	1.90	1.81	—	Expense Ratio %
—	—	—	—	—	0.36	0.32	0.27	0.30	3.35	1.56	—	Income Ratio %
—	—	—	—	—	—	125	71	73	99	52	—	Turnover Rate %
—	—	—	—	0.6	3.2	32.9	37.3	51.9	119.2	71.4	87.3	Net Assets $mil

Performance 12-31-01

	1st Qtr	2nd Qtr	3rd Qtr	4th Qtr	Total
1997	–3.38	10.82	–12.12	–37.17	–40.89
1998	6.43	–31.95	–4.51	40.45	–2.86
1999	0.29	60.23	–13.49	31.65	83.01
2000	11.44	–7.06	–11.51	–16.26	–23.25
2001	0.12	6.46	–21.62	29.17	7.91

Trailing	Total Return%	+/– S&P 500	+/– MSCI FE ex Jpn	% Rank All	% Rank Cat	Growth of $10,000
3 Mo	29.17	18.49	—	5	35	12,917
6 Mo	1.24	6.79	—	32	31	10,124
1 Yr	7.91	19.78	—	10	11	10,791
3 Yr Avg	14.87	15.89	—	5	10	15,156
5 Yr Avg	–2.74	–13.44	—	96	17	8,703
10 Yr Avg	—	—	—	—	—	—
15 Yr Avg	—	—	—	—	—	—

Tax Analysis	Tax-Adj Ret%	%Rank Cat	%Pretax Ret	%Rank Cat
3 Yr Avg	13.17	10	88.6	76
5 Yr Avg	–3.69	17	—	—
10 Yr Avg	—	—	—	—

Potential Capital Gain Exposure: –7% of assets

Risk Analysis

Time Period	Load-Adj Return %	Risk %Rank[1] All	Risk %Rank[1] Cat	Morningstar Return	Morningstar Risk	Morningstar Risk-Adj Rating
1 Yr	7.91					
3 Yr	14.87	86	35	2.31[2]	1.22	★★★★★
5 Yr	–2.74	98	62	–1.47[2]	1.63	★★
Incept	0.77	—	—	—	—	

Average Historical Rating (52 months): 2.0★s

[1] 1=low, 100=high [2] T-Bill return substituted for category avg.

Category Rating (3 Yr)

1 2 3 4 5
Worst Best

Return	Above Avg
Risk	Average

Other Measures	Standard Index S&P 500	Best Fit Index MSCIPcxIND
Alpha	22.5	14.5
Beta	1.40	1.18
R-Squared	51	67

Standard Deviation	39.76
Mean	14.87
Sharpe Ratio	0.28

Portfolio Analysis 11-30-01

Share change since 10-01 Total Stocks: 36	Sector	Country	% Assets
⊖ Hana Bk	Financials	South Korea	6.69
Giordano Intl	Retail	Hong Kong	4.83
Legend Hldgs	Technology	Hong Kong	4.59
⊕ Advanced Info Svcs	Utilities	Thailand	4.35
⊖ Samsung Electncs	Technology	South Korea	4.27
Huaneng Pwr Intl ADR	Utilities	China	4.25
Samsung Secs	Financials	South Korea	4.11
Internet Auction	N/A	N/A	3.89
Li & Fung	Retail	Hong Kong	3.74
China Mobile Hk ADR	N/A	N/A	3.69
I-cable Communications	Technology	Hong Kong	3.59
Taiwan Semicon ADR	Technology	Taiwan	3.56
Shangri-La Asia	Services	Hong Kong	3.51
Vitasoy Intl Hldgs	Staples	Hong Kong	3.36
Korea Telecom	Services	South Korea	3.07
Hite Brewery	Staples	South Korea	3.03
Venture Mfg	Technology	Singapore	2.92
⊖ Hutchison Whampoa	Financials	Hong Kong	2.84
⊕ DBS Grp Hldgs	Financials	Singapore	2.76
Via Technologies	Technology	Taiwan	2.62

Analysis by William Samuel Rocco 11-05-01

Those who still believe in the emerging Asia story should check out Matthews Pacific Tiger.

Developing Asia's markets continue to nose-dive. Indeed, after plummeting 28% in 2000, the typical Pacific/Asia ex-Japan fund has plunged another 19% for the year to date through Nov. 2, 2001. While some Chinese stocks have held up well and most Korea stocks have posted nice gains, the region's other exchanges have tanked. The Hong Kong market, which is especially popular with funds in this group, has fallen 27%, for example.

This fund has handled this prolonged slump much better than most of its peers. In fact, after suffering relatively limited losses in 2000, it has declined 8 percentage points less than its typical rival this year.

Deft moves by managers Mark Headley and Paul Matthews are behind this outperformance. For example, though they sold Samsung Fire & Marine this summer, they purchased or added to other Korea names, including Korea Telecom Freetel and the security firm S1. Thus, the fund still has 27% of its assets invested in buoyant Korea, more than twice the group norm.

Moreover, their stock selection has been excellent there and elsewhere. Top holding Hana Bank has earned strong gains, because investors like its commitment to strict loan standards and optimism about the domestic economy. And S1, which was purchased before the Sept. 11 attacks, has thrived since as interest in its home and office security products has increased.

Good stock-picking and superior results are common here. The fund also crushed the competition in the regional rallies of 1996 and 1999, so its long-term returns rank among its group's best. Therefore, we still think this fund is one of its chaotic category's best options.

Current Investment Style

	Stock Port Avg	Rel MSCI EAFE Current	Rel MSCI EAFE Hist	Rel Cat
Price/Earnings Ratio	23.2	0.90	0.76	1.19
Price/Cash Flow	12.4	0.96	0.81	0.84
Price/Book Ratio	3.5	1.00	0.75	1.06
3 Yr Earnings Growth	29.1	1.55	—	1.11
Med Mkt Cap $mil	2,213	0.1	0.0	0.29

Style: Value Blnd Growth; Size: Large Med Small

Country Exposure 11-30-01	% assets
Hong Kong	39
South Korea	26
Singapore	9
Taiwan	8
China	6

Hedging History: Never

Special Securities % assets 11-30-01	
Restricted/Illiquid Secs	0
Emerging-Markets Secs	83
Options/Futures/Warrants	No

Composition % assets 11-30-01

Cash	0.0	Bonds	0.0
Stocks	100.0	Other	0.1

Sector Weightings	% of Stocks	Rel Cat	5-Year High	5-Year Low
Utilities	9.4	2.0	11	0
Energy	0.0	0.0	2	0
Financials	23.6	0.8	53	15
Industrials	1.9	0.3	17	0
Durables	0.0	0.0	18	0
Staples	6.9	2.0	16	0
Services	17.4	0.9	25	3
Retail	9.3	2.0	16	0
Health	0.6	0.5	4	0
Technology	30.9	1.7	33	0

Address:	456 Montgomery Street Suite 1200 San Francisco, CA 94104 800–789–2742
Web Address:	www.matthewsfunds.com
*Inception:	09-13-94
Advisor:	Matthews International Cap. Mgmt
Subadvisor:	None
NTF Plans:	Fidelity , Datalynx

Minimum Purchase:	$2500	Add: $250 IRA: $500
Min Auto Inv Plan:	$2500	Add: $100
Sales Fees:	No-load, 2.00%R within 3 months	
Management Fee:	1.0%, .15%A	
Actual Fees:	Mgt: 1.00%	Dist: —
Expense Projections:	3Yr: $584	5Yr: $1010 10Yr: $2195
Avg Brok Commission:	—	Income Distrib: Annually
Total Cost (relative to category):		Below Avg

Mercury Low Duration I

Ticker	Load	NAV	Yield	SEC Yield	Total Assets	Mstar Category
MLOIX	None	$9.93	5.9%	—	$255.1 mil	Short–Term Bond

Prospectus Objective: Corp Bond—High Quality

Mercury Low Duration Fund seeks total return consistent with preservation of capital.

The fund normally invests at least 70% of assets in high-quality fixed-income securities. It may invest up to 10% of assets in debt securities rated B or BB. The average weighted maturity ranges between one and five years; the aggregate duration ranges between one and three years. The fund may invest up to 15% of assets in non-dollar-denominated securities; a total of 25% may be invested in foreign debt obligations.

Past fund names: Olympic Trust Low Duration Fund and Hotchkis & Wiley Low Duration Fund.

Historical Profile
Return Above Avg
Risk Low
Rating ★★★★★ Highest

Investment Style
Fixed-Income
Income Rtn %Rank Cat: 4, 1, 5, 8, 6, 39, 9, 12

Growth of Principal vs. Interest Rate Shifts
— Principal Value $000 (NAV with capital gains reinvested)
— Interest Rate % on 10 Yr Treasury
▼ Manager Change
▽ Partial Manager Change
► Mgr Unknown After
◄ Mgr Unknown Before

Performance Quartile (within Category)

Portfolio Manager(s)

Pat Maldari. Since 7–01.

1990	1991	1992	1993	1994	1995	1996	1997	1998	1999	2000	12–01	History
—	—	—	10.04	9.84	10.25	10.18	10.19	10.08	9.82	9.81	9.93	NAV
—	—	—	7.13*	5.25	12.75	6.22	7.60	5.65	3.17	6.98	7.41	Total Return %
—	—	—	—	8.16	–5.72	2.61	–2.09	–3.02	4.00	–4.65	–1.01	+/– LB Aggregate
—	—	—	—	4.75	2.79	0.97	0.95	–1.32	0.20	–1.20	–1.12	+/– LB 1–3 Govt
—	—	—	4.96	7.19	7.96	6.78	6.93	6.62	5.80	7.06	6.17	Income Return %
—	—	—	2.17	–1.95	4.79	–0.56	0.66	–0.97	–2.63	–0.08	1.24	Capital Return %
—	—	—	—	1	23	4	12	77	24	79	54	Total Rtn % Rank Cat
—	—	—	0.49	0.70	0.76	0.67	0.68	0.66	0.57	0.67	0.59	Income $
—	—	—	0.18	0.01	0.05	0.01	0.06	0.02	0.00	0.00	0.00	Capital Gains $
—	—	—	0.58	0.58	0.58	0.58	0.58	0.58	0.58	0.58	—	Expense Ratio %
—	—	—	6.28	7.34	7.61	7.07	6.34	6.46	5.71	6.43	—	Income Ratio %
—	—	—	—	254	71	50	202	119	201	182	—	Turnover Rate %
—	—	—	11.0	70.8	157.5	170.3	194.1	387.2	369.6	12.1	—	Net Assets $mil

Performance 12-31-01

	1st Qtr	2nd Qtr	3rd Qtr	4th Qtr	Total
1997	0.92	2.74	1.95	1.79	7.60
1998	1.44	1.82	2.38	–0.09	5.65
1999	0.47	0.37	1.35	0.94	3.17
2000	1.12	1.87	2.23	1.58	6.98
2001	2.82	1.05	2.82	0.55	7.41

Trailing	Total Return%	+/– LB Agg	+/– LB 1–3 Yr Govt	% Rank All	% Rank Cat	Growth of $10,000
3 Mo	0.55	0.51	–0.23	75	24	10,055
6 Mo	3.38	–1.27	–0.93	13	53	10,338
1 Yr	7.41	–1.01	–1.12	12	54	10,741
3 Yr Avg	5.84	–0.44	–0.69	24	51	11,855
5 Yr Avg	6.15	–1.28	–0.49	46	42	13,476
10 Yr Avg	—	—	—	—	—	—
15 Yr Avg	—	—	—	—	—	—

Tax Analysis	Tax-Adj Ret%	%Rank Cat	%Pretax Ret	%Rank Cat
3 Yr Avg	3.29	66	56.5	82
5 Yr Avg	3.49	70	56.8	88
10 Yr Avg	—	—	—	—

Potential Capital Gain Exposure: –2% of assets

Risk Analysis

Time Period	Load-Adj Return %	Risk %Rank[1] All	Risk %Rank[1] Cat	Morningstar Return	Morningstar Risk	Morningstar Risk-Adj Rating
1 Yr	7.41					
3 Yr	5.84	2	31	0.19[2]	0.26	★★★★★
5 Yr	6.15	3	23	0.25[2]	0.26	★★★★★
Incept	7.19	—	—	—	—	

Average Historical Rating (68 months): 4.8★s

[1]1=low, 100=high [2] T-Bill return substituted for category avg.

Category Rating (3 Yr)

1 2 3 4 5
Worst Best

Return Average
Risk Below Avg

Other Measures	Standard Index LB Agg	Best Fit Index LB Int
Alpha	0.4	0.3
Beta	0.34	0.43
R–Squared	53	58

Standard Deviation	1.62
Mean	5.84
Sharpe Ratio	0.64

Analysis by Catherine Hickey 07-06-01

After changing hands, Mercury Low Duration Fund's future is too murky to recommend it.

In early July 2001, Merrill Lynch announced that it planned to disband the operations of this fund's former manager, Hotchkis & Wiley. Merrill will transfer Hotchkis' fixed-income assets, which include this fund, to Merrill's Princeton, New Jersey, headquarters. Under the new regime, this fund will be managed by a team led by Pat Maldari. Maldari runs private accounts for Merrill but doesn't have a public record at a mutual fund. Meanwhile, former skippers Michael Sanchez and John Queen were recently laid off.

This is tough news for shareholders, because this offering's former managers notched consistently solid results. Much of the fund's strong record was built under former manager Roger DeBard, who retired last July. However, Sanchez had worked with DeBard since 1996, so he too could take the credit for the fund's solid record. The pair took a fairly conservative tack here, usually keeping the fund's average duration well short of the category average. This year hasn't been different; the fund's 1.6-year duration is short of the 2.3-year group norm. That short stance has been a bonus so far in 2001, as shorter-term bonds have generally performed better than longer-term securities. Indeed, the fund's 4.07% return through July 5 puts it solidly in the short-term bond group's top half.

Despite its good performance, there are too many question marks surrounding this fund to recommend it. Investors will want to hold off sending new money here.

Portfolio Analysis 09-30-01

Total Fixed-Income: 100	Date of Maturity	Amount $000	Value $000	% Net Assets
US Treasury Note 3.625%	01-15-08	18,325	20,895	7.04
US Treasury Note 3.625%	07-15-02	13,000	14,660	4.94
Federal Home Loan Bk 5.125%	01-13-03	10,900	11,222	3.78
FNMA N/A	12-05-06	9,500	9,816	3.31
Federal Farm Credit Bk N/A	03-05-04	9,280	9,644	3.25
FNMA Debenture 5.625%	05-14-04	7,500	7,889	2.66
US Treasury Note 4.75%	02-15-04	6,300	6,552	2.21
Resolution Tr 8%	06-25-26	6,341	6,321	2.13
GE Cap CMO 6.75%	02-25-11	5,984	6,110	2.06
Household Fin N/A	01-24-06	5,700	5,962	2.01
Ford Motor Credit 5.75%	02-23-04	5,750	5,868	1.98
Occidental Petro 6.4%	04-01-03	5,250	5,392	1.82
Chase Commrcl Mtg 6.025%	08-18-07	5,183	5,388	1.82
GMAC N/A	06-15-04	5,000	5,338	1.80
MCI WorldCom 7.55%	04-01-04	5,000	5,252	1.77
Qwest Cap Fdg 5.875%	08-03-04	5,000	5,106	1.72
GS Mortgage Secs 6.06%	10-18-30	4,563	4,750	1.60
Bear Stearns 6.15%	03-02-04	4,475	4,643	1.56
Ford Motor Credit N/A	08-01-05	4,400	4,638	1.56
GMAC 6.85%	06-17-04	4,000	4,192	1.41

Current Investment Style

Not Available

Avg Eff Duration	—
Avg Eff Maturity	—
Avg Credit Quality	—
Avg Wtd Coupon	2.90%
Avg Wtd Price	103.90% of par

Special Securities % assets 09-30-01	
Restricted/Illiquid Secs	2
Exotic Mortgage–Backed	0
Emerging–Markets Secs	0
Options/Futures/Warrants	No

Coupon Range	% of Bonds	Rel Cat
0%	0.00	0.00
0% to 7%	75.72	1.18
7% to 8.5%	18.57	0.65
8.5% to 10%	2.83	0.69
More than 10%	2.89	1.69

1.00=Category Average

Credit Analysis % bonds 09-30-00

US Govt	10	BB	10
AAA	22	B	0
AA	4	Below B	0
A	23	NR/NA	14
BBB	17		

Composition % assets 09-30-01

Cash	4.4	Bonds	95.3
Stocks	0.0	Other	0.4

Sector Breakdown % bonds 09-30-01

US Treasuries	0	CMOs	10
GNMA mtgs	3	ARMs	0
FNMA mtgs	10	Other	51
FHLMC mtgs	11		

Address:	Financial Data Services P.O. 44062 Jacksonville, FL 32232–4062 888–763–2260 / 888–763–2260
Web Address:	www.mercuryfunds.com
*Inception:	05-18-93
Advisor:	Mercury Adv.
Subadvisor:	None
NTF Plans:	Fidelity , Datalynx

Minimum Purchase:	$10000	Add: None IRA: —
Min Auto Inv Plan:	$10000	Add: $50
Sales Fees:	No–load	
Management Fee:	.46%	
Actual Fees:	Mgt: 0.46%	Dist: —
Expense Projections:	3Yr: $207	5Yr: $369 10Yr: $837
Avg Brok Commission:	—	Income Distrib: Monthly
Total Cost (relative to category):		Below Avg

Meridian Value

Ticker	Load	NAV	Yield	Total Assets	Mstar Category
MVALX	None	$32.42	0.1%	$1,135.0 mil	Small Blend

Prospectus Objective: Growth

Meridian Value Fund seeks long-term growth of capital; income is incidental.

The fund normally invests at least 65% of assets in equity and equity-related securities. These securities are undervalued relative to the issuer's long-term earning power or asset value because of market declines, poor economic conditions, tax-loss selling, and other factors. To select specific issues, the fund examines the issuer's growth rate relative to its price-earnings ratio, the issuer's financial strength and management, and the issuer's attractiveness relative to other investment opportunities. The balance of assets may be invested in high-yielding, low-rated debt securities. Up to 10% of assets may be invested in debt rated as low as D.

Historical Profile
Return: High
Risk: Below Avg
Rating: ★★★★★ Highest

Investment Style
Equity
Average Stock %: 100% (1995), 98% (1996), 98% (1997), 83% (1998), 96% (1999), 100% (2000), 95% (12-01)

▼ Manager Change
▽ Partial Manager Change

Fund Performance vs. Category Average
Quarterly Fund Return +/– Category Average
— Category Baseline

Performance Quartile (within Category)

Portfolio Manager(s)

Kevin C. O'Boyle. Since 6-95. Stanford U.

Richard F. Aster Jr.. Since 2-94. BA'63 U. of California-Santa Barbara; MA'65 U. of California-Santa Barbara. Other fund currently managed: Meridian Growth.

1990	1991	1992	1993	1994	1995	1996	1997	1998	1999	2000	12-01	History
—	—	—	—	9.62	11.91	14.85	15.86	18.32	22.69	29.11	32.42	NAV
—	—	—	—	–3.80*	23.81	32.29	21.37	18.94	38.28	37.14	11.70	Total Return %
—	—	—	—	–4.44*	–13.73	9.35	–11.98	–9.63	17.24	46.24	23.58	+/– S&P 500
—	—	—	—	—	–4.64	15.76	–1.00	21.50	17.02	40.16	9.21	+/– Russell 2000
—	—	—	—	0.00	0.00	4.85	2.23	0.00	3.73	4.84	0.13	Income Return %
—	—	—	—	–3.80	23.80	27.44	19.14	18.94	34.56	32.29	11.57	Capital Return %
—	—	—	—	—	59	5	83	2	10	3	31	Total Rtn % Rank Cat
—	—	—	—	0.00	0.00	0.58	0.33	0.00	0.68	1.09	0.04	Income $
—	—	—	—	0.00	0.00	0.27	1.90	0.47	1.68	0.68	0.04	Capital Gains $
—	—	—	—	—	2.78	2.55	2.51	2.16	1.63	1.41	1.10	Expense Ratio %
—	—	—	—	—	–0.58	–1.36	–1.96	–1.35	–0.65	0.39	0.60	Income Ratio %
—	—	—	—	—	77	125	144	133	124	86	76	Turnover Rate %
—	—	—	—	0.6	1.2	5.4	8.6	17.8	34.9	285.8	1,135.0	Net Assets $mil

Performance 12-31-01

	1st Qtr	2nd Qtr	3rd Qtr	4th Qtr	Total
1997	–3.30	21.17	13.30	–8.57	21.37
1998	12.86	7.82	–17.46	18.42	18.94
1999	–2.67	25.01	–0.44	14.16	38.28
2000	16.09	–1.75	5.92	13.51	37.14
2001	–2.34	8.97	–10.65	17.46	11.70

Trailing	Total Return%	+/– S&P 500	+/– Russ 2000	% Rank All	% Rank Cat	Growth of $10,000
3 Mo	17.46	6.78	–3.62	18	61	11,746
6 Mo	4.96	10.51	9.04	4	8	10,496
1 Yr	11.70	23.58	9.21	5	31	11,170
3 Yr Avg	28.43	29.45	22.01	1	2	21,182
5 Yr Avg	25.05	14.35	17.53	1	1	30,578
10 Yr Avg	—	—	—	—	—	—
15 Yr Avg	—	—	—	—	—	—

Tax Analysis	Tax-Adj Ret%	%Rank Cat	%Pretax Ret	%Rank Cat
3 Yr Avg	26.21	2	92.2	30
5 Yr Avg	22.65	1	90.4	28
10 Yr Avg	—	—	—	—

Potential Capital Gain Exposure: 10% of assets

Risk Analysis

Time Period	Load-Adj Return %	Risk %Rank[1] All	Risk %Rank[1] Cat	Morningstar Return	Morningstar Risk	Morningstar Risk-Adj Rating
1 Yr	11.70					
3 Yr	28.43	34	1	6.18[2]	0.39	★★★★★
5 Yr	25.05	46	4	6.40[2]	0.60	★★★★★
Incept	22.04	—	—	—	—	

Average Historical Rating (59 months): 4.2★s

[1] 1=low, 100=high [2] T-Bill return substituted for category avg.

Category Rating (3 Yr)
1 2 3 4 5 — Worst … Best (5)

Return: High
Risk: Low

Other Measures	Standard Index S&P 500	Best Fit Index SPMid400
Alpha	26.7	18.8
Beta	0.52	0.62
R-Squared	34	62

Standard Deviation	19.27
Mean	28.43
Sharpe Ratio	1.37

Analysis by Christopher Davis 08-02-01

Meridian Value Fund's popularity is deserved, but there's good reason to proceed with caution.

Manager Kevin O'Boyle has posted top-flight results here during his six-year tenure: The fund's record over the trailing five years through August 1, 2001, is among the best in our database. That the fund has been so successful amid vastly different markets—such as 1999 and 2000—is a testament to O'Boyle's stock-picking prowess.

The fund's strength flows from O'Boyle's distinctive strategy. Most managers steer clear of businesses that suffer disappointing operating results, but such companies are his bread and butter. He looks for downtrodden growth stocks with a catalyst in place to spark a turnaround. That often leads him to troubled sectors, as it did in early 2000, when he picked up a slug of beaten-down health-care names that had been battered by political uncertainty and increasingly stingy Medicare reimbursements. Once the government fattened Medicare payments, O'Boyle bought names such as Healthsouth and Omnicare. These stocks notched double-digit returns in 2000, helping to propel the fund to a 37% gain for the year, 24 percentage points better than the category average.

Unfortunately, the fund risks becoming a victim of its own success. Assets grew to $735 million in June 2001 (the fund began the year with just $285 million in assets). The fund's size restricts O'Boyle's ability to take larger positions in small-cap names, forcing to gravitate towards larger stocks, such as Waste Management.

Nonetheless, it's hard to argue with the fund's superb record. While its swelling asset base is cause for concern, it isn't alarming yet. Prospective investors, however, may want to see how the fund fares under its larger size before sending money here.

Portfolio Analysis 11-30-01

Share change since 10-01 Total Stocks: 75

	Sector	PE	YTD Ret%	% Assets
⊕ Waste Mgmt	Services	52.3	15.03	3.83
Healthsouth	Health	28.0	–9.15	2.41
⊖ Storage Tech	Technology	36.9	129.60	2.32
⊕ Adelphia Comms	Services	—	–39.60	2.19
Premier Parks	Services	—	–10.50	2.16
Davita	Health	18.3	42.77	2.11
⊕ Becton Dickinson	Health	22.9	–3.20	2.05
Lincare Hldgs	Health	23.7	0.41	2.01
⊕ Sprint	Services	20.5	1.18	2.00
⊕ Valassis Comms	Services	18.9	12.85	2.00
⊕ Healthcare Realty Tr	Financials	15.9	44.42	2.00
⊕ Centurytel	Services	13.3	–7.66	1.99
VF	Retail	18.1	10.38	1.96
⊕ Omnicare	Health	38.3	15.52	1.92
Albertson's	Retail	29.7	22.01	1.89
Raytheon	Industrials	—	7.27	1.81
Dial	Staples	—	57.57	1.74
⊖ Office Depot	Retail	NMF	160.20	1.70
Concurrent Comp	Technology	—	176.20	1.60
InFocus	Technology	31.5	49.29	1.57
Harris	Technology	28.0	0.33	1.57
Tommy Hilfiger	Retail	9.4	40.12	1.52
⊕ Pall	Industrials	25.3	16.26	1.50
McKesson HBOC	Health	—	4.92	1.49
⊕ Park Place Entrtnmt	Services	—	–23.10	1.48

Current Investment Style

Style: Value Blnd Growth; Size: Large Med Small

	Stock Port Avg	Relative S&P 500 Current	Relative S&P 500 Hist	Rel Cat
Price/Earnings Ratio	28.5	0.92	0.89	1.14
Price/Book Ratio	3.0	0.52	0.39	0.93
Price/Cash Flow	13.9	0.77	0.69	0.89
3 Yr Earnings Growth	1.6	0.11	0.13	0.09
1 Yr Earnings Est%	2.8	—	—	3.24
Med Mkt Cap $mil	2,871	0.1	0.0	2.93

Special Securities % assets 11-30-01	
Restricted/Illiquid Secs	0
Emerging-Markets Secs	0
Options/Futures/Warrants	No

Composition % assets 11-30-01	
Cash	10.3
Stocks*	89.7
Bonds	0.0
Other	0.0
*Foreign (% stocks)	3.1

Market Cap	
Giant	1.6
Large	17.9
Medium	51.4
Small	27.5
Micro	1.6

Sector Weightings	% of Stocks	Rel S&P	5-Year High	5-Year Low
Utilities	0.0	0.0	4	0
Energy	3.7	0.5	33	0
Financials	5.7	0.3	34	0
Industrials	8.7	0.8	23	4
Durables	0.9	0.6	19	0
Staples	3.4	0.4	9	0
Services	24.5	2.3	24	0
Retail	13.9	2.1	33	5
Health	17.8	1.2	21	0
Technology	21.4	1.2	32	0

Address:	60 E. Sir Francis Drake Blvd. #306 Larkspur, CA 94939 800–446–6662
Web Address:	—
*Inception:	02-10-94
Advisor:	Aster Cap. Mgmt.
Subadvisor:	None
NTF Plans:	N/A

Minimum Purchase:	$1000	Add: $50	IRA: $1000
Min Auto Inv Plan:	$1000	Add: $50	
Sales Fees:	No-load		
Management Fee:	1.0%		
Actual Fees:	Mgt: 1.00%	Dist: —	
Expense Projections:	3Yr: $68*	5Yr: $117*	10Yr: $251*
Avg Brok Commission:	—	Income Distrib: Annually	
Total Cost (relative to category):	—		

Merrill Lynch Basic Value A

Ticker	Load	NAV	Yield	Total Assets	Mstar Category
MABAX	5.25%	$29.28	1.2%	$8,095.3 mil	Large Value

Prospectus Objective: Growth and Income

Merrill Lynch Basic Value Fund seeks capital appreciation and secondarily, income.

The fund invests in stocks that are believed to be undervalued. It places emphasis on companies with below average price\earnings ratios but pay above average dividends. The fund focuses on companies with market caps of over $5 billion.

The fund offers A, B, C and D shares, all which differ in fee structure and availability.

Historical Profile
Return Above Avg
Risk Below Avg
Rating ★★★★ Above Avg

Investment Style
Equity
Average Stock %: 1995 82% · 1996 83% · 1997 87% · 1998 87% · 1999 93% · 2000 96% · 12-01 95%

▼ Manager Change
▽ Partial Manager Change

Fund Performance vs. Category Average
Quarterly Fund Return +/– Category Average
— Category Baseline

Performance Quartile (within Category)

Portfolio Manager(s)

Kevin Rendino. Since 7-99. BS'88 Boston C. Other funds currently managed: Merrill Lynch Focus Value A, Merrill Lynch Basic Value B, Merrill Lynch Focus Value B.

1990	1991	1992	1993	1994	1995	1996	1997	1998	1999	2000	12-01	History
16.09	19.36	20.34	23.37	22.35	28.31	31.00	37.08	38.02	38.15	32.82	29.28	NAV
–13.07	27.23	10.36	22.26	1.97	32.90	17.81	29.48	11.66	11.06	3.17	–0.51	Total Return %
–9.95	–3.25	2.74	12.20	0.65	–4.64	–5.13	–3.87	–16.91	–9.98	12.28	11.36	+/– S&P 500
–9.40	9.08	1.29	2.50	4.28	–7.14	–4.50	–6.01	–9.58	0.11	0.86	8.28	+/– Russ Top 200 Val
4.94	4.86	3.36	3.51	3.03	3.43	2.91	2.57	2.25	1.96	1.78	1.27	Income Return %
–18.01	22.37	7.00	18.75	–1.06	29.47	14.90	26.91	9.41	9.10	1.39	–1.78	Capital Return %
89	47	38	5	21	50	76	30	58	30	63	21	Total Rtn % Rank Cat
0.97	0.77	0.64	0.70	0.69	0.76	0.80	0.78	0.81	0.72	0.65	0.40	Income $
0.30	0.27	0.36	0.75	0.78	0.57	1.39	2.23	2.41	3.38	5.76	3.05	Capital Gains $
0.57	0.58	0.58	0.54	0.53	0.59	0.56	0.55	0.54	0.55	0.56	0.56	Expense Ratio %
5.05	4.76	3.52	3.48	2.76	3.19	2.88	2.54	2.14	1.95	1.68	1.60	Income Ratio %
5	20	21	21	22	12	14	13	18	16	28	38	Turnover Rate %
1,295.4	1,566.3	1,712.2	2,180.6	2,318.2	3,230.3	4,374.0	5,215.2	5,426.1	5,013.5	4,262.9	—	Net Assets $mil

Performance 12-31-01

	1st Qtr	2nd Qtr	3rd Qtr	4th Qtr	Total
1997	2.87	14.46	8.79	1.09	29.48
1998	11.52	0.48	–11.33	12.38	11.66
1999	1.39	13.36	–5.71	2.48	11.06
2000	–1.21	–1.51	6.40	–0.35	3.17
2001	–0.94	3.88	–14.11	12.57	–0.51

Trailing	Total Return%	+/– S&P 500	+/– Russ Top 200 Val	% Rank All	% Rank Cat	Growth of $10,000
3 Mo	12.57	1.89	4.25	31	13	11,257
6 Mo	–3.31	2.24	4.13	53	37	9,669
1 Yr	–0.51	11.36	7.66	43	21	9,949
3 Yr Avg	4.46	5.49	4.30	36	29	11,400
5 Yr Avg	10.51	–0.19	1.50	16	31	16,482
10 Yr Avg	13.51	0.58	0.43	11	25	35,501
15 Yr Avg	12.58	–1.16	–0.54	21	35	59,110

Tax Analysis	Tax-Adj Ret%	%Rank Cat	%Pretax Ret	%Rank Cat
3 Yr Avg	1.32	41	29.6	84
5 Yr Avg	7.62	36	72.5	58
10 Yr Avg	10.94	22	81.0	33

Potential Capital Gain Exposure: 21% of assets

Risk Analysis

Time Period	Load-Adj Return %	Risk %Rank[1] All	Risk %Rank[1] Cat	Morningstar Return	Morningstar Risk	Morningstar Risk-Adj Rating
1 Yr	–5.74					
3 Yr	2.60	48	21	–0.49[2]	0.67	★★★
5 Yr	9.32	50	17	1.02[2]	0.69	★★★
10 Yr	12.90	55	20	1.29	0.70	★★★★

Average Historical Rating (193 months): 3.6★s

[1] 1=low, 100=high [2] T-Bill return substituted for category avg.

Category Rating (3 Yr)

1 2 3 4 5
Worst Best

Return Above Avg
Risk Below Avg

Other Measures	Standard Index S&P 500	Best Fit Index S&P 500
Alpha	3.9	3.9
Beta	0.71	0.71
R-Squared	62	62

Standard Deviation	15.95
Mean	4.46
Sharpe Ratio	–0.03

Portfolio Analysis 07-31-01

Share change since 03-01 Total Stocks: 79

	Sector	PE	YTD Ret%	% Assets
⊖ Citigroup	Financials	20.0	0.03	3.49
⊕ ExxonMobil	Energy	15.3	–7.59	3.30
⊕ Wells Fargo	Financials	22.4	–20.20	3.27
⊖ IBM	Technology	26.9	43.00	2.81
American General	Financials	—	11.20	2.77
⊖ Unocal	Energy	10.9	–4.58	2.49
⊖ Bank One	Financials	29.1	9.13	2.40
⊖ First Union	Financials	21.5	16.12	2.31
⊕ Fox Entrtnmt Grp Cl A	Services	NMF	48.42	2.04
⊕ Halliburton	Energy	8.3	–63.20	1.87
⊕ Bristol-Myers Squibb	Health	20.2	–26.00	1.86
⊕ Deere	Industrials	—	–2.52	1.86
⊖ Hartford Finl Svcs Grp	Financials	23.2	–9.63	1.84
⊕ Bank of America	Financials	16.7	42.73	1.84
⊕ Philips Electrncs NV ADR	Durables	4.3	–18.70	1.80
⊖ DuPont De Nemours E.I.	Industrials	65.4	–9.14	1.77
⊖ USA Networks	Services	58.1	40.50	1.74
⊕ Diamond Offshore Drilling	Energy	25.8	–22.80	1.72
⊕ Royal Dutch Petro NY ADR	Energy	12.0	–17.10	1.61
⊖ Verizon Comms	Services	29.7	–2.52	1.56
Procter & Gamble	Staples	38.8	3.12	1.56
Georgia-Pacific	Industrials	—	–9.87	1.52
⊖ Allstate	Financials	17.1	–21.00	1.49
⊕ Gillette	Staples	56.6	–5.47	1.49
⊖ Lockheed Martin	Industrials	36.8	38.98	1.48

Current Investment Style

Style: Value Blnd Growth; Size: Large Med Small

	Stock Port Avg	Relative S&P 500 Current	Relative S&P 500 Hist	Rel Cat
Price/Earnings Ratio	26.4	0.85	0.73	1.05
Price/Book Ratio	3.8	0.66	0.54	0.92
Price/Cash Flow	12.7	0.70	0.59	0.92
3 Yr Earnings Growth	6.8	0.47	0.59	0.46
1 Yr Earnings Est%	–10.0	5.65	—	3.02
Med Mkt Cap $mil	28,289	0.5	0.7	0.89

Analysis by Gabriel Presler 10-16-01 This analysis was written for the B shares.

Merrill Lynch Basic Value Fund's recent strong performance is a step in the right direction, but we're not convinced quite yet.

As the domestic market has faltered and finally stalled in 2001, the large-value category—one of the more-stable groups at the mid-year mark—has found itself in a heap of trouble. Indeed, the average fund in the group has lost more than 10% for the year to date through Oct. 15, 2001. Against such a grim backdrop, this fund's loss of 8% over the same stretch doesn't look so bad.

The fund has been helped by a few old habits. Manager Kevin Rendino, who took over here in mid-1999, rarely trades. In fact, the fund's turnover rate is one of the lowest in the category, and performance has benefited from the apparent recoveries of a few old favorites, including behemoth IBM and Bank of America. Both have held up well, propping up returns.

Although the fund has done well in the two years since Rendino took over, its longer-term record is still relevant; after all, he worked as an analyst on this offering for nine years before being promoted. Historically, strong relative performance hasn't been the norm here. The fund's broadly diversified portfolio and its willingness to carry cash have worked to limit volatility, but they have also dragged on returns. Thus, the fund usually ends up in the category's middle reaches, and its 10-year record is just about average.

We'd like to see it do better before urging new investors to buy.

Special Securities % assets 07-31-01

Restricted/Illiquid Secs	0
Emerging-Markets Secs	0
Options/Futures/Warrants	No

Composition % assets 07-31-01

Cash	2.3
Stocks*	95.6
Bonds	2.1
Other	0.0
*Foreign (% stocks)	4.1

Market Cap

Giant	33.7
Large	43.7
Medium	21.7
Small	0.9
Micro	0.0

Sector Weightings	% of Stocks	Rel S&P	5-Year High	5-Year Low
Utilities	1.7	0.5	12	2
Energy	13.3	1.9	20	12
Financials	22.4	1.3	24	15
Industrials	16.3	1.4	29	10
Durables	5.0	3.2	11	2
Staples	7.4	0.9	8	0
Services	17.0	1.6	17	3
Retail	0.0	0.0	8	0
Health	4.2	0.3	6	0
Technology	12.8	0.7	13	6

Address:	Box 9011 Princeton, NJ 08543-9011 800-995-6526 / 609-282-2800
Web Address:	www.ml.com
Inception:	07-05-77
Advisor:	Fund Asset Mgmt.
Subadvisor:	None
NTF Plans:	N/A

Minimum Purchase:	$1000	Add: $50	IRA: $100
Min Auto Inv Plan:	$1000	Add: $50	
Sales Fees:	5.25%L		
Management Fee:	.60% mx./.40% mn.		
Actual Fees:	Mgt: 0.40%	Dist: —	
Expense Projections:	3Yr: $689	5Yr: $811	10Yr: $1167
Avg Brok Commission:	—	Income Distrib: Semi-Ann.	
Total Cost (relative to category):	—		

Merrill Lynch Global Allocation B

Ticker	Load	NAV	Yield	Total Assets	Mstar Category
MBLOX	4.00%d	$12.61	3.1%	$6,134.9 mil	International Hybrid

Prospectus Objective: Multiasset—Global

Merrill Lynch Global Allocation Fund seeks total return consistent with prudent risk.

The fund invests in domestic and foreign equities, debt, and money markets issued in at least three countries. Equity purchases are made in stocks with below-average price/earnings and price/book ratios. It may invest up to 35% of assets in debt rated below BBB. This fund is non-diversified.

The fund offers A, B, C and D shares, all which differ in fee structure and availability.

On March 1, 1996, Merrill Lynch Balanced Fund for Investment and Retirement merged into the fund.

Historical Profile
Return: High
Risk: Low
Rating: ★★★★★ Highest

Investment Style
Equity
Average Stock %

1995	1996	1997	1998	1999	2000	12-01
34%	41%	34%	40%	50%	53%	49%

▼ Manager Change
▽ Partial Manager Change

Fund Performance vs. Category Average
■ Quarterly Fund Return +/– Category Average
— Category Baseline

Performance Quartile (within Category)

Portfolio Manager(s)

Bryan N. Ison, CFA. Since 2-89. SB MIT; MBA U. of Chicago. Other funds currently managed: Merrill Lynch Global Allocation A, Merrill Lynch Global Allocation C, Merrill Lynch Global Allocation D.

Dennis W. Stattman, CFA. Since 2-89. BS U. of Virginia; MBA U. of Chicago. Other funds currently managed: Merrill Lynch Global Allocation A, Merrill Lynch Global Allocation C, Merrill Lynch Global Allocation D.

1990	1991	1992	1993	1994	1995	1996	1997	1998	1999	2000	12-01	History
9.88	11.03	11.47	13.11	12.12	13.73	14.36	13.94	12.42	13.79	12.88	12.61	NAV
0.84	27.47	11.06	19.69	–2.89	22.39	14.95	10.34	–0.42	26.46	7.83	1.01	Total Return %
17.86	9.19	16.28	–2.81	–7.97	1.67	1.48	–5.42	–24.76	1.53	21.01	—	+/– MSCI World
–10.91	12.02	6.51	7.42	–4.17	3.07	10.51	8.98	–15.74	31.54	5.49	1.81	+/– JPM World Govt
4.06	9.15	5.93	3.27	2.41	5.38	5.42	6.78	2.90	5.80	1.70	3.04	Income Return %
–3.21	18.32	5.12	16.42	–5.30	17.00	9.53	3.56	–3.32	20.66	6.13	–2.03	Capital Return %
40	16	16	37	38	33	50	58	97	14	10	23	Total Rtn % Rank Cat
0.43	0.89	0.65	0.37	0.31	0.65	0.74	0.96	0.40	0.71	0.23	0.39	Income $
0.55	0.60	0.12	0.23	0.30	0.43	0.65	0.94	1.05	1.13	1.69	0.01	Capital Gains $
2.31	2.31	2.09	1.95	1.91	1.93	1.87	1.85	1.86	1.94	1.90	—	Expense Ratio %
3.35	7.98	11.95	2.87	3.58	4.96	4.29	3.62	3.60	3.84	2.40	—	Income Ratio %
130	81	60	50	57	37	51	55	50	27	195	—	Turnover Rate %
115.1	176.4	1,117.4	4,874.2	6,155.3	7,100.7	8,964.4	9,552.4	6,178.2	4,525.7	3,563.2	2,654.6	Net Assets $mil

Performance 12-31-01

	1st Qtr	2nd Qtr	3rd Qtr	4th Qtr	Total
1997	1.39	7.14	4.18	–2.50	10.34
1998	8.11	–2.92	–13.21	9.33	–0.42
1999	6.28	12.20	–0.50	6.59	26.46
2000	1.16	1.79	1.46	3.20	7.83
2001	–0.93	4.39	–9.85	8.35	1.01

Trailing	Total Return%	+/– MSCI World	+/– JPM World Govt	% Rank All	% Rank Cat	Growth of $10,000
3 Mo	8.35	1,007.35	11.53	50	27	10,835
6 Mo	–2.33	996.67	–6.05	48	45	9,767
1 Yr	1.01	1,000.01	1.81	41	23	10,101
3 Yr Avg	11.26	1,010.26	12.49	9	10	13,774
5 Yr Avg	8.64	1,007.64	6.23	26	17	15,134
10 Yr Avg	10.64	1,009.64	5.39	28	50	27,484
15 Yr Avg	—	—	—	—	—	—

Tax Analysis	Tax-Adj Ret%	%Rank Cat	%Pretax Ret	%Rank Cat
3 Yr Avg	7.91	8	70.2	25
5 Yr Avg	5.28	20	61.1	36
10 Yr Avg	7.68	50	72.2	50

Potential Capital Gain Exposure: –15% of assets

Risk Analysis

Time Period	Load-Adj Return %	Risk %Rank[1] All	Risk %Rank[1] Cat	Morningstar Return	Morningstar Risk	Morningstar Risk-Adj Rating
1 Yr	–1.93					
3 Yr	10.99	34	13	1.36[2]	0.36	★★★★★
5 Yr	8.64	41	34	0.85[2]	0.40	★★★★★
10 Yr	10.64	46	60	1.97[2]	0.36	★★★★★

Average Historical Rating (119 months): 4.6★s

[1] 1=low, 100=high [2] T-Bill return substituted for category avg.

Category Rating (3 Yr)

1 2 3 4 5
Worst Best

Return: Above Avg
Risk: Below Avg

Other Measures	Standard Index S&P 500	Best Fit Index MSCIPcxJND
Alpha	9.0	6.5
Beta	0.49	0.40
R-Squared	58	70
Standard Deviation		11.93
Mean		11.26
Sharpe Ratio		0.60

Analysis by Dan Culloton 09-20-01

The world has changed dramatically since the Sept. 11, 2001, terrorist attacks on the World Trade Center and Pentagon, but, in response, this fund has changed little.

World stock markets reeled in the wake of the assaults that killed thousands and inflicted billions of dollars in damages. Longtime managers Bryan Ison and Dennis Stattman reacted, characteristically, by just tweaking their portfolio. They used the global sell-off to increase the fund's European equities exposure by about 2 percentage points.

That's not an enormous move, but it's consistent with Ison and Stattman's style. They prefer incremental changes to seismic ones, yet they are not afraid to go against the grain. The managers' contrarian, value bent helped them avoid the tech– and telecom–stock debacle last year. This year they've been trimming winning energy, REIT, insurance, and bank holdings and taking small bites of technology. In early August, when the Nasdaq fell nearly 11%, they bought stocks like EMC to bring the fund's tech weighting more in line with the S&P 500's. In early September they boosted their Compaq stake and bought Hewlett-Packard after the market blew raspberries at the companies' merger plans.

Despite stock-market turbulence, management has positioned the fund somewhat aggressively. In addition to a stock stake of 62% as of early September, which is above the category average, the fund has nibbled at high-yield bonds and has a 6% stake in convertible bonds. The economy will likely be weaker in the near term, but Ison and Stattman think the interest-rate cuts in U.S. and Europe and billions of dollars in promised government spending set the stage for an economic rebound later next year, which should boost the stock market.

After finishing six of the last seven years in their fund category's top half, this fund's management deserves investor confidence.

Portfolio Analysis 09-30-01

Total Stocks: 333 Share change since 03-01	Sector	PE Ratio	YTD Return %	% Net Assets
⊕ Mitsui Marine & Fire Ins	Financials	30.5	—	1.29
⊖ Security Cap Grp Cl B	Financials	11.3	26.45	1.15
☼ RWE ADR	Energy	—	—	1.04
⊖ Nasdaq Index	N/A	—	—	0.99
Yasuda Fire & Marine Ins	Financials	46.8	—	0.84
⊕ Nippon Fire & Marine Ins	Financials	37.0	—	0.77
⊕ BHP	Industrials	19.3	—	0.73
☼ La Quinta Inns	Services	—	—	0.68
Nichido Fire & Marine Ins	Financials	28.1	—	0.59
☼ Korea Telecom ADR	Services	38.3	–34.40	0.57

Total Fixed-Income: 134	Date of Maturity	Amount $000	Value $000	% Net Assets
US Treasury Note 3.375%	01-15-07	163,000	187,918	2.85
Petroliam Nasional 7.625%	10-15-26	103,314	90,529	1.38
Govt of Japan 0%	10-25-01	9,000,000	75,674	1.15
Govt of Japan 0%	11-16-01	8,240,000	69,391	1.05
Govt of Japan 0%	11-16-01	8,000,000	67,370	1.02
Govt of Japan 0%	10-18-01	8,000,000	67,232	1.02
Govt of Japan 0%	10-05-01	8,000,000	67,168	1.02
Govt of Japan 0%	11-09-01	7,500,000	63,129	0.96
Petroliam Nasional 144A 7.75%	08-15-15	60,075	59,174	0.90
Govt of Japan 0%	11-02-01	7,000,000	58,892	0.89

Equity Style
Style: Value
Size: Large-Cap

	Portfolio Avg	Rel S&P
Price/Earnings Ratio	26.8	1.04
Price/Cash Flow	12.1	0.94
Price/Book Ratio	2.6	0.73
3 Yr Earnings Growth	13.5	0.72
Med Mkt Cap $mil	6,355	0.23

Fixed-Income Style
Duration: —
Quality: —
NA

Avg Eff Duration	—
Avg Eff Maturity	—
Avg Credit Quality	—
Avg Wtd Coupon	2.74%

Special Securities % assets 09-30-01

Restricted/Illiquid Secs	2
Emerging-Markets Secs	8
Options/Futures/Warrants	No

Country Exposure 12-31-98 % of Assets

U.S.	44.7
Japan	9.4
Argentina	6.7

Composition % assets 09-30-01

Cash	25.2
U.S. Stocks	23.7
Foreign Stocks	23.0
U.S. Bonds	20.8
Foreign Bonds	3.3
Other	3.9

Address:	Box 9011 Princeton, NJ 08543–9011 800–995–6526 / 609–282–2800
Web Address:	www.ml.com
Inception:	02-03-89
Advisor:	Merrill Lynch Inv. Managers
Subadvisor:	Merrill Lynch Asset Mgmt. (UK)
NTF Plans:	N/A

Minimum Purchase:	$1000	Add: $50	IRA: $100
Min Auto Inv Plan:	$1000	Add: $50	
Sales Fees:	4.00%D, 0.75%B, 0.25%S Conv. in 8 Yrs.		
Management Fee:	.75% mx./.60% mn.		
Actual Fees:	Mgt: 0.75%	Dist: 1.00%	
Expense Projections:	3Yr: $812	5Yr: $1052	10Yr: $2081
Avg Brok Commission:	—	Income Distrib: Annually	

Total Cost (relative to category): —

Merrill Lynch Global Value D

Ticker	Load	NAV	Yield	Total Assets	Mstar Category
MDVLX	5.25%	$10.83	0.0%	$1,559.2 mil	World Stock

Prospectus Objective: World Stock

Merrill Lynch Global Value Fund seeks long-term capital appreciation.

The fund normally invests at least 65% of assets in equity securities of issuers from at least three countries, one of which may be the United States. Management seeks to purchase securities when their market prices are depressed in relation to their inherent value. This fund is non-diversified.

The fund offers A, B, C and D shares, all which differ in fee structure and availability.

Historical Profile

Return Above Avg
Risk Low
Rating ★★★★ Above Avg

Investment Style
Equity
Average Stock %

1997	1998	1999	2000	12-01
92%	94%	94%	94%	89%

▼ Manager Change
▽ Partial Manager Change

Fund Performance vs. Category Average
■ Quarterly Fund Return
+/– Category Average
— Category Baseline

Performance Quartile (within Category)

Portfolio Manager(s)

Stephen I. Silverman. Since 11-96. BA'72 Case Western Reserve U.; MBA'78 U. of Chicago. Other funds currently managed: Merrill Lynch Pacific A, Merrill Lynch Growth A, Merrill Lynch Pacific B.

1990	1991	1992	1993	1994	1995	1996	1997	1998	1999	2000	12-01	History
—	—	—	—	—	—	10.13	12.00	13.65	14.67	12.96	10.83	NAV
—	—	—	—	—	—	1.78*	23.71	26.72	10.23	0.39	−13.92	Total Return %
—	—	—	—	—	—	−3.87*	−9.64	−1.85	−10.81	9.49	−2.04	+/– S&P 500
—	—	—	—	—	—	—	7.95	2.38	−14.70	13.57	—	+/– MSCI World
—	—	—	—	—	—	0.48	5.23	2.60	0.27	2.25	0.00	Income Return %
—	—	—	—	—	—	1.30	18.47	24.12	9.96	−1.86	−13.92	Capital Return %
—	—	—	—	—	—	—	9	16	95	20	38	Total Rtn % Rank Cat
—	—	—	—	—	—	0.05	0.53	0.31	0.04	0.32	0.00	Income $
—	—	—	—	—	—	0.00	0.00	1.18	0.30	1.42	0.35	Capital Gains $
—	—	—	—	—	—	—	1.22	1.15	1.16	1.16	—	Expense Ratio %
—	—	—	—	—	—	—	1.62	1.19	0.25	0.17	—	Income Ratio %
—	—	—	—	—	—	—	78	45	71	53	—	Turnover Rate %
—	—	—	—	—	—	161.3	257.6	427.1	418.5	398.2	293.5	Net Assets $mil

Performance 12-31-01

	1st Qtr	2nd Qtr	3rd Qtr	4th Qtr	Total
1997	0.49	13.46	6.93	1.47	23.71
1998	18.58	0.79	−6.50	13.40	26.72
1999	−2.64	0.15	−5.45	19.56	10.23
2000	2.32	−0.07	3.72	−5.34	0.39
2001	−8.56	2.28	−16.62	10.40	−13.92

Trailing	Total Return%	+/– S&P 500	+/– MSCI World	% Rank All	% Rank Cat	Growth of $10,000
3 Mo	10.40	−0.29	—	41	56	11,040
6 Mo	−7.95	−2.40	—	78	58	9,205
1 Yr	−13.92	−2.04	—	70	38	8,608
3 Yr Avg	−1.61	−0.58	—	81	70	9,526
5 Yr Avg	8.35	−2.35	—	27	29	14,933
10 Yr Avg	—	—	—	—	—	—
15 Yr Avg	—	—	—	—	—	—

Tax Analysis	Tax-Adj Ret%	%Rank Cat	%Pretax Ret	%Rank Cat
3 Yr Avg	−3.32	73	—	—
5 Yr Avg	6.12	28	73.3	43
10 Yr Avg	—	—	—	—

Potential Capital Gain Exposure: 2% of assets

Risk Analysis

Time Period	Load-Adj Return %	Risk %Rank¹ All	Risk %Rank¹ Cat	Morningstar Return	Morningstar Risk	Morningstar Risk-Adj Rating
1 Yr	−18.44					
3 Yr	−3.36	58	30	−1.63²	0.76	★★★
5 Yr	7.19	55	14	0.49²	0.63	★★★★
Incept	7.31	—	—	—	—	

Average Historical Rating (27 months): 3.9★s

[1]1=low, 100=high [2] T-Bill return substituted for category avg.

Category Rating (3 Yr)

1 2 **3** 4 5
Worst — Best

Return Below Avg
Risk Below Avg

Other Measures	Standard Index S&P 500	Best Fit Index SPMid400
Alpha	−2.0	−9.6
Beta	0.74	0.69
R-Squared	66	77
Standard Deviation		15.20
Mean		−1.61
Sharpe Ratio		−0.50

Portfolio Analysis 07-31-01

Share change since 03-01 Total Stocks: 43	Sector	Country	% Assets
☆ Showpower	Services	U.S.	12.83
☆ iStar Finl	Financials	U.S.	10.52
⊖ Lattice Semicon	Technology	U.S.	9.98
⊕ El Paso	Utilities	U.S.	5.90
☆ Nestle	Staples	Switzerland	4.93
⊖ Household Intl	Financials	U.S.	4.53
⊖ Allied Irish Banks	Financials	Ireland	4.41
⊕ SPX	Durables	U.S.	4.08
⊖ AES	Utilities	U.S.	3.75
⊖ J.P. Morgan Chase & Co.	Financials	U.S.	3.58
☆ Dexia	Financials	Belgium	3.52
Danske Bk	Financials	Denmark	3.52
⊕ Johnson & Johnson	Health	U.S.	3.46
⊖ Safeway	Retail	U.S.	3.00
⊕ Bristol-Myers Squibb	Health	U.S.	2.91
Texaco	Energy	U.S.	2.85
Alltel	Services	U.S.	2.68
☆ Anadarko Petro	Energy	U.S.	2.55
☆ Kinder Morgan	Energy	U.S.	2.46
ACE	Financials	Bermuda	2.42

Current Investment Style

Style: Value Blnd Growth; Size: Large Med Small

	Stock Port Avg	Rel MSCI EAFE Current	Rel MSCI EAFE Hist	Rel Cat
Price/Earnings Ratio	20.7	0.80	0.89	0.75
Price/Cash Flow	15.3	1.19	1.16	0.93
Price/Book Ratio	2.7	0.79	0.78	0.59
3 Yr Earnings Growth	16.6	0.88	1.15	0.89
Med Mkt Cap $mil	11,406	0.4	0.5	0.48

Country Exposure 07-31-01	% assets
U.S.	81
Japan	10
Switzerland	5
Ireland	4
Belgium	4

Hedging History: —

Regional Exposure 07-31-01	% assets
Europe	22
Japan	10
Latin America	0
Pacific Rim	1
U.S.	81
Other	2

Special Securities % assets 07-31-01	
Restricted/Illiquid Secs	0
Emerging-Markets Secs	3
Options/Futures/Warrants	No

Composition % assets 07-31-01

Cash	2.1	Bonds	0.0
Stocks	97.9	Other	0.0

Sector Weightings	% of Stocks	Rel Cat	5-Year High	5-Year Low
Utilities	8.1	3.3	—	—
Energy	7.9	1.4	—	—
Financials	31.1	1.7	—	—
Industrials	2.6	0.2	—	—
Durables	5.9	1.5	—	—
Staples	6.1	0.8	—	—
Services	17.8	1.1	—	—
Retail	3.8	0.7	—	—
Health	5.4	0.4	—	—
Technology	11.2	0.8	—	—

Analysis by Dan Culloton 12-10-01

There have been better value-leaning world-stock funds this year, but Merrill Lynch Global Value is still worth a look.

The fund had lost more than 14% of its value through Dec. 7, 2001, but that was still better than 60% of the other funds in the struggling world-stock category. Global Value's tilt toward financial and services stocks has helped it hold up better than most of the group, but it has endured its share of pain—and has lagged the typical value-oriented offering in the category. Power generators El Paso and AES have hurt the fund, falling more than 37% and 70%, respectively, for the year through the first week of December. Strong gains in stocks like programmable logic chip maker Lattice Semiconductor and real-estate financial company iStar Financial have offset some of the losses.

Manager Stephen Silverman hasn't made a lot of changes to the portfolio in recent months, but he has made some tweaks. He appears to have trimmed iStar and sold computer maker Compaq when it became clear its merger with Hewlett-Packard was in peril and, on its own, Compaq was not as good as others at selling what has become a commodity. Global Value still holds mostly domestic stocks, but Silverman recently said the fund's portion of U.S. stocks had dropped to 55% of the portfolio and its cash stake had increased to 7%. He would not say specifically what he sold to raise the cash.

The fund's limited number of holdings (around 40) and tendency to load a lot of its assets in its top holdings leave it susceptible to some rough spots. Silverman, however, has proved to be an adept picker of undervalued stocks. The fund has finished three of the last four years in the top quarter of its category.

This is still a decent option for those looking for a value fund that can trot the globe.

Address:	Box 9011, Princeton, NJ 08543-9011, 609-282-2800
Web Address:	www.ml.com
*Inception:	11-01-96
Advisor:	Merrill Lynch Inv. Managers
Subadvisor:	None
NTF Plans:	N/A

Minimum Purchase:	$1000	Add: $50	IRA: $100
Min Auto Inv Plan:	$1000	Add: $50	
Sales Fees:	5.25%L, 0.25%S		
Management Fee:	.75%		
Actual Fees:	Mgt: 0.75%	Dist: 0.25%	
Expense Projections:	3Yr: $874	5Yr: $1130	10Yr: $1860
Avg Brok Commission:	—	Income Distrib: Annually	
Total Cost (relative to category):	Below Avg		

Merrill Lynch Pacific B

Ticker	Load	NAV	Yield	Total Assets	Mstar Category
MBPCX	4.00%d	$15.60	2.8%	$790.9 mil	Div Pacific Stock

Prospectus Objective: Pacific Stock

Merrill Lynch Pacific Fund seeks long-term capital appreciation.

The fund normally invests at least 80% of assets in equities issued by companies domiciled in Far Eastern or western Pacific countries. It may purchase ADRs, EDRs, GDRs, and debt of any credit quality. The fund may engage in hedging strategies against investment, interest-rate, and currency risks.

The fund offers A, B, C and D shares, all which differ in fee structure and availability.

Historical Profile

Return	Average
Risk	Above Avg
Rating	★★★ Neutral

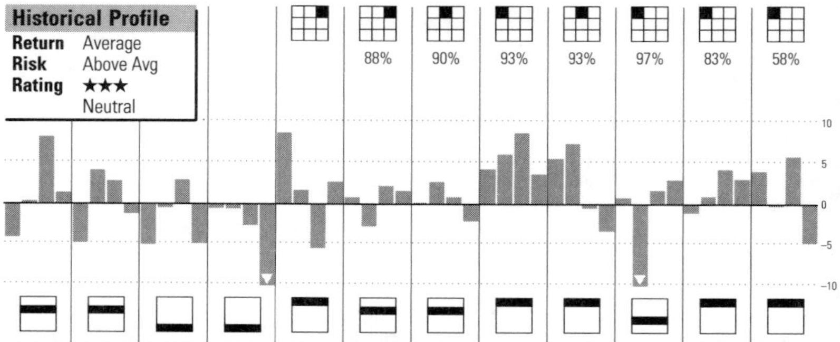

Investment Style
Equity
Average Stock %: 88% 90% 93% 93% 97% 83% 58%

▼ Manager Change
▽ Partial Manager Change

Fund Performance vs. Category Average
■ Quarterly Fund Return +/– Category Average
— Category Baseline

Performance Quartile (within Category)

Portfolio Manager(s)

Stephen I. Silverman. Since 10-88. BA'72 Case Western Reserve U.; MBA'78 U. of Chicago. Other funds currently managed: Merrill Lynch Pacific A, Merrill Lynch Growth A, Merrill Lynch Growth B.

1990	1991	1992	1993	1994	1995	1996	1997	1998	1999	2000	12-01	**History**
16.16	17.95	15.35	20.42	20.27	21.22	20.59	16.11	16.74	31.12	18.79	15.60	NAV
–10.47	16.48	–9.37	33.03	1.93	7.20	5.08	–7.31	7.29	85.90	–29.03	–14.57	Total Return %
–7.35	–14.00	–16.99	22.97	0.61	–30.34	–17.86	–40.66	–21.28	64.86	–19.93	–2.69	+/– S&P 500
23.95	5.18	9.03	–2.67	–10.90	4.42	13.66	18.19	4.85	28.27	–3.25	—	+/– MSCI Pacific
0.01	0.00	0.00	0.00	0.31	0.09	0.08	3.55	3.37	0.00	0.95	2.36	Income Return %
–10.48	16.48	–9.37	33.03	1.62	7.11	5.00	–10.85	3.92	85.90	–29.98	–16.93	Capital Return %
33	37	80	92	18	26	32	9	10	59	22	13	Total Rtn % Rank Cat
0.00	0.00	0.00	0.00	0.06	0.02	0.02	0.73	0.54	0.00	0.30	0.44	Income $
2.32	0.84	0.95	0.00	0.47	0.48	1.67	2.22	0.00	0.00	2.93	0.00	Capital Gains $
2.10	2.04	2.00	1.92	1.94	1.96	1.90	1.90	1.92	1.88	1.84	—	Expense Ratio %
–0.05	–0.60	–0.61	–0.56	–0.56	–0.50	–0.56	–0.66	–0.50	–0.76	–0.86	—	Income Ratio %
31	6	8	13	24	27	11	20	12	29	35	—	Turnover Rate %
58.0	105.7	165.0	507.3	915.4	1,041.8	1,217.5	775.1	489.0	888.7	442.3	245.7	Net Assets $mil

Performance 12-31-01

	1st Qtr	2nd Qtr	3rd Qtr	4th Qtr	Total
1997	0.00	17.68	–2.77	–18.99	–7.31
1998	7.82	–8.46	–9.12	19.62	7.29
1999	10.16	12.36	10.28	36.19	85.90
2000	–1.77	–11.29	–7.71	–11.76	–29.03
2001	–5.53	0.62	–14.17	4.72	–14.57

Trailing	Total Return%	+/– S&P 500	+/– MSCI Pacific	% Rank All	% Rank Cat	Growth of $10,000
3 Mo	4.72	–5.97	—	65	82	10,472
6 Mo	–10.12	–4.56	—	86	29	8,988
1 Yr	–14.57	–2.69	—	71	13	8,543
3 Yr Avg	4.07	5.10	—	40	22	11,272
5 Yr Avg	2.31	–8.39	—	87	6	11,210
10 Yr Avg	4.49	–8.44	—	95	10	15,518
15 Yr Avg	—	—	—	—	—	—

Tax Analysis	Tax-Adj Ret%	%Rank Cat	%Pretax Ret	%Rank Cat
3 Yr Avg	1.68	22	41.2	76
5 Yr Avg	–0.15	9	—	—
10 Yr Avg	2.61	10	58.0	66

Potential Capital Gain Exposure: –2% of assets

Risk Analysis

Time Period	Load-Adj Return %	Risk %Rank[1] All	Risk %Rank[1] Cat	Morningstar Return	Morningstar Risk	Morningstar Risk-Adj Rating
1 Yr	–17.06					
3 Yr	3.78	72	7	–0.24[2]	0.93	★★★★
5 Yr	2.31	82	10	–0.57[2]	0.97	★★★
10 Yr	4.49	89	12	–0.06[2]	1.02	★★

Average Historical Rating (123 months): 2.9★s

[1]1=low, 100=high [2] T-Bill return substituted for category avg.

Category Rating (3 Yr)

1 Worst — 5 Best (rating: 4)

Return: Above Avg
Risk: Low

Other Measures	Standard Index S&P 500	Best Fit Index MSCIPacNdD
Alpha	5.1	8.3
Beta	0.82	0.91
R-Squared	43	77

Standard Deviation	22.33
Mean	4.07
Sharpe Ratio	–0.05

Portfolio Analysis 07-31-01

Share change since 03-01 Total Stocks: 50	Sector	Country	% Assets
☼ Lonrho Africa ADR	Durables	United Kingdom	16.07
☼ Genesee B	Staples	U.S.	12.01
⊖ Mitsui Marine & Fire Ins	Financials	Japan	3.61
⊖ Nichido Fire & Marine Ins	Financials	Japan	3.53
⊕ Guinness Peat Grp	Financials	United Kingdom	2.90
Hutchison Whampoa	Financials	Hong Kong	2.79
Tokio Marine & Fire Ins	Financials	Japan	2.68
Lend Lease	Financials	Australia	2.67
⊖ Ito-Yokado	Retail	Japan	2.64
⊖ Toyoda Automatic Loom Works	Durables	Japan	2.53
⊖ Rohm	Technology	Japan	2.52
⊖ Shin-Etsu Chemical	Industrials	Japan	2.41
HSBC Hldgs (HK)	Financials	Hong Kong	2.39
⊖ Kansai Elec Pwr	Utilities	Japan	2.36
⊖ Canon	Industrials	Japan	2.31
⊖ Tokyo Elec Pwr	Utilities	Japan	2.29
Dai-Tokyo Fire & Marine Ins	Financials	Japan	2.29
Murata Mfg	Technology	Japan	2.28
East Japan Railway	Services	Japan	2.11
Chubu Elec Pwr	Utilities	Japan	2.07

Current Investment Style

Style: Value Blnd Growth; Size: Large Med Small

	Stock Port Avg	Rel MSCI EAFE Current	Rel MSCI EAFE Hist	Rel Cat
Price/Earnings Ratio	30.5	1.18	1.06	1.13
Price/Cash Flow	18.7	1.45	1.04	1.30
Price/Book Ratio	1.8	0.51	0.52	0.61
3 Yr Earnings Growth	12.5	0.67	0.54	0.68
Med Mkt Cap $mil	6,845	0.2	0.5	0.75

Country Exposure 07-31-01	% assets
Japan	51
United Kingdom	19
U.S.	12
Hong Kong	6
Australia	4

Hedging History: —

Special Securities % assets 07-31-01	
Restricted/Illiquid Secs	1
Emerging-Markets Secs	12
Options/Futures/Warrants	Yes

Composition % assets 07-31-01			
Cash	17.6	Bonds	0.0
Stocks	66.7	Other	15.7

Sector Weightings	% of Stocks	Rel Cat	5-Year High	5-Year Low
Utilities	6.8	1.8	11	0
Energy	0.0	0.0	1	0
Financials	27.5	1.2	43	21
Industrials	9.8	0.8	32	10
Durables	24.5	1.9	25	4
Staples	13.1	2.4	13	1
Services	4.6	0.3	12	0
Retail	4.0	0.8	9	3
Health	1.0	0.2	8	1
Technology	8.6	0.6	28	2

Analysis by Gabriel Presler 11-13-01

We think Merrill Lynch Pacific Fund is one of the best options available, quirks and all.

This fund, among the oldest in the diversified Pacific Asia category, has always looked a bit different from its rivals. Manager Steve Silverman doesn't strive for regional diversification. Instead, he favors Japan and in recent months, he has built the portfolio's exposure to that market to 72% of assets, almost 30 percentage points more than the category norm. Remaining assets are generally used in the category's larger markets, such as Hong Kong, so the fund doesn't have much exposure to emerging Asia. Big country bets aren't Silverman's only quirk, though. He's willing to commit to industries, so the fund's sector exposure is pretty unusual. In 2001, for example, he has built the portfolio's stake in big industrial firms like Toyoda Automatic Loom Works to virtually a fourth of assets. Finally, Silverman's a patient investor and trades about half as much as his rivals.

This unusual approach hasn't helped performance lately. Asian markets have been brutalized by slowing global growth and investors' dwindling optimism about much-touted reforms. What's more, some of the region's developed markets, including Japan, have suffered more then their neighbors, and this offering has shed more than 20% of its value for the year to date through Nov. 12, 2001.

Still, the fund's 2001 losses look benign when compared with the rest of the category. That's no surprise, given manager Steve Silverman's record of success. Silverman, who is in his 19th year at the helm here, has put together the best 10-year record in this group, and his moderate strategy has given investors a relatively smooth ride. In a rough category, it's hard to do better than this fund.

Address:	Box 9011 Princeton, NJ 08543-9011 800-995-6526 / 609-282-2800
Web Address:	www.ml.com
Inception:	10-21-88
Advisor:	Merrill Lynch Inv. Managers
Subadvisor:	Merrill Lynch Asset Mgmt. (UK)
NTF Plans:	N/A

Minimum Purchase:	$1000	Add: $50	IRA: $100
Min Auto Inv Plan:	$1000	Add: $50	
Sales Fees:	4.00%D, 0.75%B, 0.25%S Conv. in 8 Yrs.		
Management Fee:	.60%		
Actual Fees:	Mgt: 0.60%	Dist: 1.00%	
Expense Projections:	3Yr: $791	5Yr: $1016	10Yr: $2005
Avg Brok Commission:	—	Income Distrib: Annually	
Total Cost (relative to category):		Below Avg	

Merrill Lynch Premier Growth B

Ticker	Load	NAV	Yield	Total Assets	Mstar Category
MBPGX	4.00%d	$2.95	0.0%	$74.3 mil	Mid-Cap Growth

Prospectus Objective: Growth

Merrill Lynch Premier Growth seeks long-term capital appreciation.

The fund generally invests at least 65% of assets in equity securities. It may invest in companies of any size but emphasizes companies with medium to large size market capitalizations in the $1 to 5 billion range or greater. The fund may invest in investment-grade non-convertible debt and United States government securities. It may invest up to 10% of assets in foreign equity securities.

The fund offers A, B, C and D shares, all which differ in fee structure and availability.

Historical Profile
Return —
Risk —
Rating Not Rated

Investment Style
Equity
Average Stock %: 88% (2000), 91% (12-01)

▼ Manager Change
▽ Partial Manager Change

Fund Performance vs. Category Average
Quarterly Fund Return +/- Category Average
— Category Baseline

Performance Quartile (within Category)

Portfolio Manager(s)

Michael S. Hahn, CFA. Since 11-01. BS Pennsylvania State U.; MS U. of Maryland. Other funds currently managed: Merrill Lynch Focus Twenty A, Merrill Lynch Focus Twenty B, Merrill Lynch Focus Twenty C.

1990	1991	1992	1993	1994	1995	1996	1997	1998	1999	2000	12-01	History
—	—	—	—	—	—	—	—	—	—	6.27	2.95	NAV
—	—	—	—	—	—	—	—	—	—	-37.30*	-52.95	Total Return %
—	—	—	—	—	—	—	—	—	—	-31.89*	-41.07	+/- S&P 500
—	—	—	—	—	—	—	—	—	—	—	-32.79	+/- Russ Midcap Grth
—	—	—	—	—	—	—	—	—	—	0.00	0.00	Income Return %
—	—	—	—	—	—	—	—	—	—	-37.30	-52.95	Capital Return %
—	—	—	—	—	—	—	—	—	—	—	100	Total Rtn % Rank Cat
—	—	—	—	—	—	—	—	—	—	0.00	0.00	Income $
—	—	—	—	—	—	—	—	—	—	0.00	0.00	Capital Gains $
—	—	—	—	—	—	—	—	—	—	—	—	Expense Ratio %
—	—	—	—	—	—	—	—	—	—	—	—	Income Ratio %
—	—	—	—	—	—	—	—	—	—	—	—	Turnover Rate %
—	—	—	—	—	—	—	—	—	—	118.4	—	Net Assets $mil

Performance 12-31-01

	1st Qtr	2nd Qtr	3rd Qtr	4th Qtr	Total
1997	—	—	—	—	—
1998	—	—	—	—	—
1999	—	—	—	—	—
2000	—	-2.68	9.66	-34.28	-37.30*
2001	-43.70	14.16	-42.18	26.61	-52.95

Trailing	Total Return%	+/- S&P 500	+/- Russ Midcap Grth	% Rank All	% Rank Cat	Growth of $10,000
3 Mo	26.61	15.92	-0.45	6	12	12,661
6 Mo	-26.80	-21.24	-18.54	100	100	7,320
1 Yr	-52.95	-41.07	-32.79	100	100	4,705
3 Yr Avg	—	—	—	—	—	—
5 Yr Avg	—	—	—	—	—	—
10 Yr Avg	—	—	—	—	—	—
15 Yr Avg	—	—	—	—	—	—

Tax Analysis	Tax-Adj Ret%	%Rank Cat	%Pretax Ret	%Rank Cat
3 Yr Avg	—	—	—	—
5 Yr Avg	—	—	—	—
10 Yr Avg	—	—	—	—

Potential Capital Gain Exposure: NMF

Risk Analysis

Time Period	Load-Adj Return %	Risk %Rank[1] All	Risk %Rank[1] Cat	Morningstar Return	Morningstar Risk	Morningstar Risk-Adj Rating
1 Yr	-54.36					
3 Yr	—	—	—	—	—	
5 Yr	—	—	—	—	—	
Incept	-49.52	—	—	—	—	

Average Historical Rating —

[1]1=low, 100=high

Category Rating (3 Yr)

Other Measures	Standard Index S&P 500	Best Fit Index
Alpha	—	—
Beta	—	—
R-Squared	—	—
Standard Deviation		—
Mean		—
Sharpe Ratio		—

Return
Risk

Portfolio Analysis 07-31-01

Share change since 03-01 Total Stocks: 53	Sector	PE	YTD Ret%	% Assets
⊖ Harley-Davidson	Durables	40.2	36.97	4.71
⊕ Sonus Networks	Technology	—	-81.70	3.94
Enzon	Health	NMF	-9.32	3.71
⊖ S & P 500 Dep Rec SPDR		—	—	3.38
⊕ IDEC Pharmaceuticals	Health	NMF	9.09	3.37
⊕ Pfizer	Health	34.7	-12.40	3.17
⊕ Protein Design Labs	Health	NMF	-24.10	2.89
⊖ Nasdaq Index	N/A	—	—	2.81
⊖ Flextronics Intl	Technology	—	-15.80	2.61
Amdocs	Services	NMF	-48.70	2.60
TMP Worldwide	Services	71.5	-22.00	2.59
Veritas Software	Technology	—	-48.70	2.56
⊖ ONI Sys	Technology	—	-84.10	2.45
Enron	Energy	1.6	-99.00	2.40
⊕ Washington Mutual	Financials	10.1	-5.32	2.33
⊖ BEA Sys	Technology	—	-77.10	2.22
⊕ Extreme Networks	Technology	—	-67.00	2.15
⊕ Ivax	Health	17.5	-34.20	2.12
CIENA	Technology	NMF	-82.30	2.07
☼ Celestica	Technology	79.2	-25.50	1.85
⊕ Cisco Sys	Technology	—	-52.60	1.84
☼ AOL Time Warner	Technology	—	-7.76	1.75
☼ L-3 Comms Hldgs	Technology	33.0	16.88	1.73
☼ Paychex	Services	49.4	-27.10	1.70
⊕ Millennium Pharma	Health	—	-60.30	1.66

Current Investment Style

Style: Value Blnd Growth; Size: Large Med Small

	Stock Port Avg	Relative S&P 500 Current	Relative S&P 500 Hist	Rel Cat
Price/Earnings Ratio	45.2	1.46	—	1.30
Price/Book Ratio	6.6	1.15	—	1.16
Price/Cash Flow	30.4	1.69	—	1.31
3 Yr Earnings Growth	26.3[1]	1.79	—	1.12
1 Yr Earnings Est%	22.1	—	—	2.36
Med Mkt Cap $mil	6,656	0.1	—	1.18

[1]figure is based on 50% or less of stocks

Analysis by Dan Culloton 11-26-01

Merrill Lynch Premier Growth's short, abysmal life offers little to recommend it.

So far this fund, and its more-concentrated cousin Merrill Lynch Focus Twenty, offer case studies in the perils of investing with superstar managers when they're riding high. Merrill Lynch rolled out Premier Growth in 2000 for then-recently hired Jim McCall, a high-profile, high-octane stock-slinger. McCall had gained renown during the late, great bull market of the 1990s at the helm of PBHG Large Cap 20. Unfortunately, this fund made its debut just as the Nasdaq Composite fell off a cliff and McCall's momentum-driven investing style moved from the penthouse to the doghouse.

The tech-stock-loving fund had lost, as of Nov. 12, more than 72% of its value since inception, thanks to plummeting issues such as Sonus Networks. Over the last year, this offering has been one of the worst funds in one of the worst-performing categories: mid-cap growth.

The tech and telecom-related stocks that have been staples of this fund's heretofore-disastrous diet will rebound, someday. As technology stocks rallied in the month ending Nov. 16, the fund advanced more than 11%, better than 92% of its rivals. Still, this fund is staring at a long, volatile road back, and the manager many shareholders had hoped would lead them over that path is gone.

New manager Michael Hahn says he will practice the same brand of aggressive momentum investing McCall did, and Hahn's no novice. He has shadowed McCall for much of his career and has comanaged funds for PBHG and Merrill Lynch. But this is his first tour of duty as a solo fund manager.

Given the fund's dismal past and uncertain future, investors should avoid it.

Special Securities % assets 07-31-01	
Restricted/Illiquid Secs	0
Emerging-Markets Secs	1
Options/Futures/Warrants	No

Sector Weightings	% of Stocks	Rel S&P	5-Year High	5-Year Low
Utilities	1.0	0.3	—	—
Energy	3.9	0.6	—	—
Financials	2.8	0.2	—	—
Industrials	0.0	0.0	—	—
Durables	5.6	3.6	—	—
Staples	0.0	0.0	—	—
Services	8.8	0.8	—	—
Retail	1.2	0.2	—	—
Health	25.2	1.7	—	—
Technology	51.6	2.8	—	—

Composition % assets 07-31-01	
Cash	8.8
Stocks*	90.2
Bonds	1.0
Other	0.0
*Foreign (% stocks)	3.0

Market Cap	
Giant	10.2
Large	25.9
Medium	59.2
Small	4.7
Micro	0.0

Address:	Box 9011 Princeton, NJ 08543-9011 609-282-2800 / 800-995-6526
Web Address:	www.ml.com
*Inception:	03-03-00
Advisor:	Merrill Lynch Inv. Managers
Subadvisor:	None
NTF Plans:	N/A

Minimum Purchase:	$1000	Add: None IRA: $100
Min Auto Inv Plan:	$100	Add: $50
Sales Fees:	4.00%D, 0.75%B, 0.25%S Conv. in 8 Yrs.	
Management Fee:	.50%	
Actual Fees:	Mgt: 0.50%	Dist: 1.00%
Expense Projections:	3Yr: $882	5Yr: $1169 10Yr: $2323
Avg Brok Commission:	—	Income Distrib: Annually
Total Cost (relative to category):	—	

Metropolitan West AlphaTrak 500

Ticker	Load	NAV	Yield	Total Assets	Mstar Category
MWATX	12b–1 only	$8.12	5.9%	$66.8 mil	Large Blend

Prospectus Objective: Growth

Metropolitan West AlphaTrak 500 Fund seeks a total return that exceeds the total return of the S&P 500 index.

The fund primarily invests in equity derivative instruments. These investments may include S&P 500 index futures contracts, Mini S&P 500 futures contracts, options on S&P 500 derivatives, and swap agreements involving the S&P 500. The fund may at times invest all assets directly in common stocks that comprise the index. It may also invest in fixed-income securities, and up to 25% of assets in money market mutual funds.

Historical Profile

Return Average
Risk Average
Rating ★★★ Neutral

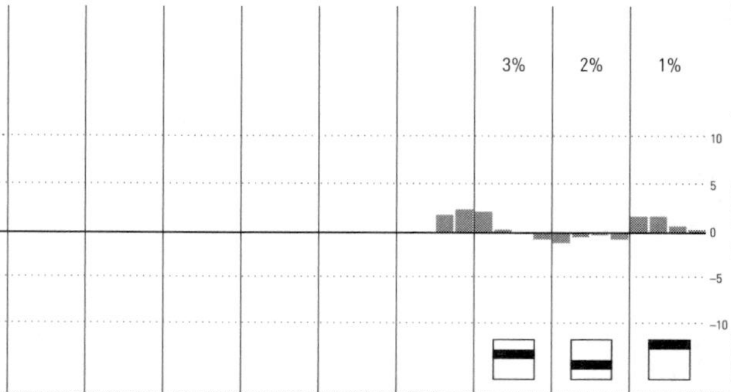

Investment Style
Equity
Average Stock %: 3% (1999), 2% (2000), 1% (12–01)

▼ Manager Change
▽ Partial Manager Change

Fund Performance vs. Category Average
■ Quarterly Fund Return +/– Category Average
— Category Baseline

Performance Quartile (within Category)

Portfolio Manager(s)

Stephen Kane. Since 6-98. BS'85 U. of California, Berkeley; MBA'90 U. of Chicago. Other funds currently managed: PaineWebber Pace Interm Fix-Inc P, Metropolitan West Low Duration Bond M, Metropolitan West Total Return Bond.

Laird Landmann. Since 6-98. BA'86 Dartmouth C.; MBA'90 U. of Chicago. Other funds currently managed: PaineWebber Pace Interm Fix-Inc P, Metropolitan West Low Duration Bond M, Metropolitan West Total Return Bond.

Tad Rivelle. Since 6-98. MS'87 U. of Southern California; MBA'90 U. of California-Los Angeles. Other funds currently managed: Managers Intermediate Bond, PaineWebber Pace Interm Fix-Inc P, Metropolitan West Low Duration Bond M.

History

1990	1991	1992	1993	1994	1995	1996	1997	1998	1999	2000	12–01	History
—	—	—	—	—	—	—	—	10.77	11.55	9.50	8.12	NAV
—	—	—	—	—	—	—	—	10.80*	22.54	–8.95	–9.36	Total Return %
—	—	—	—	—	—	—	—	1.88*	1.50	0.16	2.51	+/– S&P 500
—	—	—	—	—	—	—	—	—	0.71	2.01	3.40	+/– Wilshire Top 750
—	—	—	—	—	—	—	—	3.10	6.80	6.63	5.18	Income Return %
—	—	—	—	—	—	—	—	7.70	15.74	–15.57	–14.54	Capital Return %
—	—	—	—	—	—	—	—	—	35	53	16	Total Rtn % Rank Cat
—	—	—	—	—	—	—	—	0.26	0.70	0.74	0.48	Income $
—	—	—	—	—	—	—	—	0.00	0.86	0.33	0.00	Capital Gains $
—	—	—	—	—	—	—	—	—	—	0.66	0.63	Expense Ratio %
—	—	—	—	—	—	—	—	—	—	6.49	7.56	Income Ratio %
—	—	—	—	—	—	—	—	—	—	280	82	Turnover Rate %
—	—	—	—	—	—	—	—	7.0	12.0	31.4	66.8	Net Assets $mil

Performance 12-31-01

	1st Qtr	2nd Qtr	3rd Qtr	4th Qtr	Total
1997	—	—	—	—	—
1998	—	—	–9.54	22.97	10.80 *
1999	5.85	7.09	–6.07	15.09	22.54
2000	3.03	–3.22	–0.27	–8.44	–8.95
2001	–10.84	7.00	–14.53	11.16	–9.36

Trailing	Total Return%	+/– S&P 500	+/– Wil Top 750	% Rank All	% Rank Cat	Growth of $10,000
3 Mo	11.16	0.47	–0.16	37	40	11,116
6 Mo	–4.99	0.56	0.80	62	27	9,501
1 Yr	–9.36	2.51	3.40	59	16	9,064
3 Yr Avg	0.38	1.40	2.20	71	32	10,113
5 Yr Avg	—	—	—	—	—	—
10 Yr Avg	—	—	—	—	—	—
15 Yr Avg	—	—	—	—	—	—

Tax Analysis	Tax-Adj Ret%	%Rank Cat	%Pretax Ret	%Rank Cat
3 Yr Avg	–3.02	64	—	—
5 Yr Avg	—	—	—	—
10 Yr Avg	—	—	—	—

Potential Capital Gain Exposure: –13% of assets

Risk Analysis

Time Period	Load-Adj Return %	Risk %Rank[1] All	Risk %Rank[1] Cat	Morningstar Return	Morningstar Risk	Morningstar Risk-Adj Rating
1 Yr	–9.36					
3 Yr	0.38	66	44	–0.93[2]	0.92	★★★
5 Yr	—	—	—	—	—	
Incept	3.30	—	—	—	—	

Average Historical Rating (7 months): 3.0★s

[1]1=low, 100=high [2] T-Bill return substituted for category avg.

Category Rating (3 Yr)

1 2 3 4 5 (Worst … Best)

Return: Above Avg
Risk: Average

Other Measures	Standard Index S&P 500	Best Fit Index S&P 500
Alpha	1.6	1.6
Beta	1.03	1.03
R-Squared	99	99
Standard Deviation	17.62	
Mean	0.38	
Sharpe Ratio	–0.30	

Analysis by Heather Haynos 12-04-01

Move over PIMCO and Vanguard, Metropolitan West AlphaTrak 500 is proving to be tough competition.

This young and little-followed offering has been showing up both its like-minded peers and pure index options lately. Much like larger rival PIMCO StocksPlus, the fund uses a combination of S&P 500 futures contracts backed by the collateral of a short-term bond portfolio. To beat the index, managers Stephen Kane, Laird Landmann, and Tad Rivelle must generate a return on the bond portfolio that exceeds the cost of financing the futures contracts, otherwise known as LIBOR (the London Interbank Offered Rate).

So far, the trio's efforts have been spot on. As of Nov. 30, 2001, the fund's three-year trailing return beat the index's by 126 basis points, which is considerably better than that of PIMCO StocksPlus and Vanguard 500 Index over the same period. What's more, despite recent volatility in the corporate bond market, the team has managed to stay ahead by focusing on hard-asset companies, or, those that could easily sell assets to meet their debt obligations if necessary.

Although the fund's super-low duration helps curb tracking error versus the S&P 500, the team isn't afraid to spice things up in other ways. For instance, the bond portfolio currently holds a 60% stake in corporate bonds, including about one fourth of those in junk bonds. Still, the trio is particularly bullish on the corporate sector and believes that the potential for outperformance is greater there than it has been for years.That the team has done exceptionally well with the firm's short- and intermediate-term bond offerings is another good reason to give this fund a look. And while its expenses aren't as low as Vanguard's, they are cheaper than those at PIMCO and, more importantly, are tied to the fund's performance versus the index.

Portfolio Analysis 09-30-01

Share change since 03–00 Total Stocks: 2	Sector	PE	YTD Ret%	% Assets
Capital One Bk FRN	N/A	—	—	4.18
Keystone Home Improve 7.94%	N/A	—	—	3.22
Sempra Energy 6.8%	N/A	—	—	2.80
Corporate Ppty Inv 7.05%	N/A	—	—	2.80
Chyps CBO 6.72%	N/A	—	—	2.70
IMPAC CMB Tr 7.77%	N/A	—	—	2.42
Goodyear Tire & Rubber 8.125%	N/A	—	—	2.40
Conseco Financing 5.538%	N/A	—	—	2.28
Ios Cap 9.75%	N/A	—	—	2.22
Bear Stearns FRN	N/A	—	—	2.17
BankBoston Hm Eq Ln 6.14%	N/A	—	—	1.86
GS Escrow FRN	N/A	—	—	1.86
Green Tree Finl 7.24%	N/A	—	—	1.83
Enterprise Cap Tr FRN	N/A	—	—	1.80
Green Tree Finl 7.7%	N/A	—	—	1.80
Kansas Gas & Elec 6.76%	N/A	—	—	1.74
Countrywide CMO 6.75%	N/A	—	—	1.67
Magnus Fdg FRN	N/A	—	—	1.62
Zermatt Cbo FRN	N/A	—	—	1.58
Trizec Fin 10.875%	N/A	—	—	1.57
WCG 8.25%	N/A	—	—	1.28
America West Air 6.86%	N/A	—	—	1.23
Societe Generale FRN	N/A	—	—	1.20
United Dominion Rlty Tr 8.625%	N/A	—	—	1.13
Rouse 8.5%	N/A	—	—	1.12

Current Investment Style

Not Available

	Stock Port Avg	Relative S&P 500 Current	Relative S&P 500 Hist	Rel Cat
Price/Earnings Ratio	—	—	—	—
Price/Book Ratio	—	—	—	—
Price/Cash Flow	—	—	—	—
3 Yr Earnings Growth	—	—	—	—
1 Yr Earnings Est%	—	—	—	—
Med Mkt Cap $mil	—	—	—	—

Special Securities % assets 09-30-01	
Restricted/Illiquid Secs	Trace
Emerging-Markets Secs	0
Options/Futures/Warrants	Yes

Composition % assets 09-30-01	
Cash	34.0
Stocks*	0.9
Bonds	65.1
Other	0.0
*Foreign (% stocks)	0.0

Market Cap	
Giant	—
Large	—
Medium	—
Small	—
Micro	—

Sector Weightings	% of Stocks	Rel S&P	5-Year High	5-Year Low
Utilities	—	—	—	—
Energy	—	—	—	—
Financials	—	—	—	—
Industrials	—	—	—	—
Durables	—	—	—	—
Staples	—	—	—	—
Services	—	—	—	—
Retail	—	—	—	—
Health	—	—	—	—
Technology	—	—	—	—

Address: 11766 Wilshire Blvd Ste 1580, Los Angeles, CA 90025, 800–241–4671
Web Address: www.mwamllc.com
*Inception: 06-29-98
Advisor: Metropolitan West Asset Mgmt.
Subadvisor: None
NTF Plans: N/A

Minimum Purchase: $5000 Add: None IRA: $1000
Min Auto Inv Plan: — Add: —
Sales Fees: 0.25%S
Management Fee: .35%+(–).35%P
Actual Fees: Mgt: 0.35% Dist: 0.00%
Expense Projections: 3Yr: $18* 5Yr: — 10Yr: —
Avg Brok Commission: — Income Distrib: Quarterly
Total Cost (relative to category): —

Metropolitan West Low Duration Bond M

Ticker	Load	NAV	Yield	SEC Yield	Total Assets	Mstar Category
MWLDX	12b–1 only	$9.98	6.7%	5.91%	$598.0 mil	Short–Term Bond

Prospectus Objective: Corp Bond—General

Metropolitan West Low Duration Bond Fund seeks current income, consistent with preservation of capital.

The fund invests primarily in fixed-income securities of varying maturities. The average portfolio duration typically ranges between one and three years; the dollar-weighted average maturity usually ranges between one and five years. The fund normally invests at least 70% of assets in fixed-income securities rated at least A. Up to 20% may be invested in debt rated as low as BBB, and up to 10% may be rated as low as B.

Historical Profile
Return: High
Risk: Low
Rating: ★★★★★ Highest

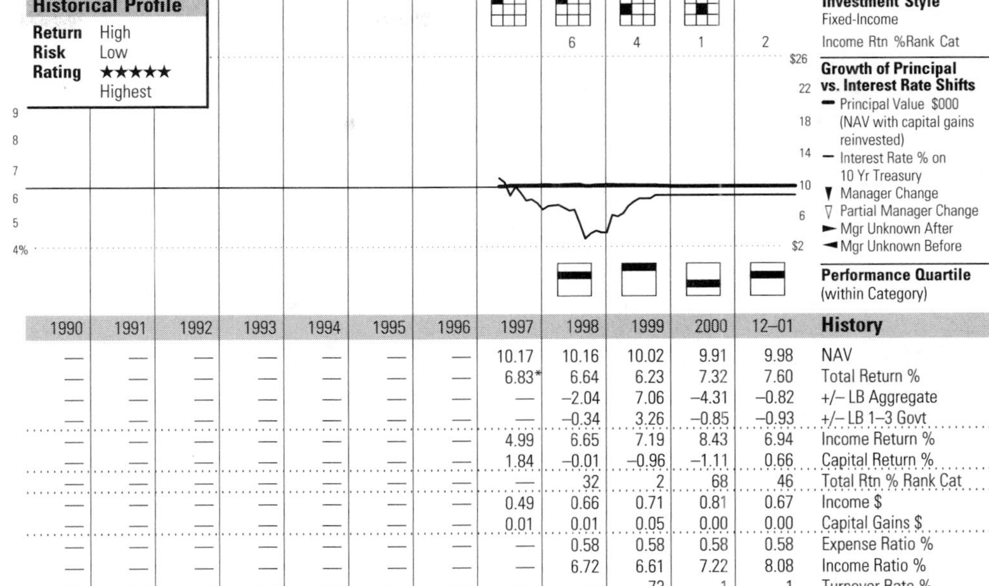

Investment Style
Fixed-Income
Income Rtn %Rank Cat

Growth of Principal vs. Interest Rate Shifts
— Principal Value $000 (NAV with capital gains reinvested)
— Interest Rate % on 10 Yr Treasury
▼ Manager Change
▽ Partial Manager Change
► Mgr Unknown After
◄ Mgr Unknown Before

Performance Quartile (within Category)

1990	1991	1992	1993	1994	1995	1996	1997	1998	1999	2000	12–01	History
—	—	—	—	—	—	—	10.17	10.16	10.02	9.91	9.98	NAV
—	—	—	—	—	—	—	6.83*	6.64	6.23	7.32	7.60	Total Return %
—	—	—	—	—	—	—	—	–2.04	7.06	–4.31	–0.82	+/– LB Aggregate
—	—	—	—	—	—	—	—	–0.34	3.26	–0.85	–0.93	+/– LB 1–3 Govt
—	—	—	—	—	—	—	4.99	6.65	7.19	8.43	6.94	Income Return %
—	—	—	—	—	—	—	1.84	–0.01	–0.96	–1.11	0.66	Capital Return %
—	—	—	—	—	—	—	—	32	2	68	46	Total Rtn % Rank Cat
—	—	—	—	—	—	—	0.49	0.66	0.71	0.81	0.67	Income $
—	—	—	—	—	—	—	0.01	0.01	0.05	0.00	0.00	Capital Gains $
—	—	—	—	—	—	—	—	0.58	0.58	0.58	0.58	Expense Ratio %
—	—	—	—	—	—	—	—	6.72	6.61	7.22	8.08	Income Ratio %
—	—	—	—	—	—	—	—	—	73	1	1	Turnover Rate %
—	—	—	—	—	—	—	78.0	210.0	337.6	139.6	333.5	Net Assets $mil

Portfolio Manager(s)

Tad Rivelle. Since 3-97. MS'87 U. of Southern California; MBA'90 U. of California-Los Angeles. Other funds currently managed: Managers Intermediate Bond, PaineWebber Pace Interm Fix-Inc P, Metropolitan West Total Return Bond.

Laird Landmann. Since 3-97. BA'86 Dartmouth C.; MBA'90 U. of Chicago. Other funds currently managed: PaineWebber Pace Interm Fix-Inc P, Metropolitan West Total Return Bond, Metropolitan West AlphaTrak 500.

Stephen Kane. Since 3-97. BS'85 U. of California, Berkeley; MBA'90 U. of Chicago. Other funds currently managed: PaineWebber Pace Interm Fix-Inc P, Metropolitan West Total Return Bond, Metropolitan West AlphaTrak 500.

Performance 12-31-01

	1st Qtr	2nd Qtr	3rd Qtr	4th Qtr	Total
1997	—	2.43	2.39	1.86	6.83 *
1998	1.76	1.97	0.28	2.48	6.64
1999	1.62	1.68	1.47	1.32	6.23
2000	1.61	1.42	2.30	1.80	7.32
2001	3.07	1.76	2.17	0.41	7.60

Trailing	Total Return%	+/– LB Agg	+/– LB 1–3 Yr Govt	% Rank All	% Rank Cat	Growth of $10,000
3 Mo	0.41	0.38	–0.36	75	36	10,041
6 Mo	2.59	–2.06	–1.72	18	84	10,259
1 Yr	7.60	–0.82	–0.93	11	46	10,760
3 Yr Avg	7.05	0.77	0.52	17	6	12,267
5 Yr Avg	—	—	—	—	—	—
10 Yr Avg	—	—	—	—	—	—
15 Yr Avg	—	—	—	—	—	—

Tax Analysis	Tax-Adj Ret%	%Rank Cat	%Pretax Ret	%Rank Cat
3 Yr Avg	4.00	13	56.8	80
5 Yr Avg	—	—	—	—
10 Yr Avg	—	—	—	—

Potential Capital Gain Exposure: 0% of assets

Risk Analysis

Time Period	Load-Adj Return %	Risk %Rank[1] All	Risk %Rank[1] Cat	Morningstar Return	Morningstar Risk	Morningstar Risk-Adj Rating
1 Yr	7.60					
3 Yr	7.05	1	5	0.45[2]	0.17	★★★★★
5 Yr	—	—	—	—	—	
Incept	7.29	—	—	—	—	

Average Historical Rating (22 months): 5.0★s

[1]1=low, 100=high [2] T-Bill return substituted for category avg.

Category Rating (3 Yr)

1 2 3 4 5
Worst Best

Return: High
Risk: Low

Other Measures	Standard Index LB Agg	Best Fit Index LB Corp
Alpha	1.7	1.8
Beta	0.24	0.22
R–Squared	30	36

Standard Deviation	1.59
Mean	7.05
Sharpe Ratio	1.56

Analysis by Scott Berry 11-16-01

Metropolitan West Low Duration looks to be hitting its way out of a recent slump.

This fund has made up some ground on its average short-term peer over the last month. Its short duration (a measure of interest-rate risk) and its stash of economically sensitive lower-quality bonds cost it some ground in the weeks following the September terrorist attacks. But in recent weeks, the fund's short duration has been an advantage, as a jump in retail sales has dimmed the prospect of future interest-rate cuts and has pushed short-term interest rates higher. The fund's 7.4% gain for the year to date through Nov. 15, 2001, still lags that of its average peer, but only by a fractional amount.

Despite the fund's middling year-to-date return, we consider it to be one of the best in its category. Indeed, since its inception in 1997, it has been one the group's top performers. Plus, its returns have typically come with far less volatility than those of its average peer. The fund's impressive total returns are largely a result of the strong performance of its investment-grade corporate bonds, while the fund's muted volatility stems from its low duration.

The fund's solid returns and low volatility should appeal to most investors, as should its attractive yield and reasonable expense ratio. Its added credit risk may be a concern for conservative investors, but we think the fund's returns have more than compensated for its increased risk.

As evidenced by its recent performance, this fund is a bit more susceptible to an economic downturn than its average peer. However, we think long-term investors will do well here, and it remains one of our Morningstar Analyst Picks.

Portfolio Analysis 09-30-01

Total Fixed-Income: 179	Date of Maturity	Amount $000	Value $000	% Net Assets
US Treasury Note 7%	07-15-06	15,260	17,291	2.94
US Treasury Note 5.625%	05-15-08	11,700	12,592	2.14
Empire Fdg Hm Eq 9%	05-25-30	11,000	11,886	2.02
FHLMC 2.85%	10-04-01	11,575	11,572	1.97
Daimler–Benz 6.46%	12-07-01	10,950	11,009	1.87
PHH Grp 8.125%	02-03-03	10,000	10,421	1.77
Conseco Financing 10%	11-15-29	9,400	10,043	1.71
Bear Stearns Cap Reset 7%	01-15-27	9,670	9,738	1.66
Lehman Struct Secs 7.995%	06-25-26	9,469	9,519	1.62
Pegasus Aviation FRN	03-25-30	8,806	9,157	1.56
Entergy Gulf States 4.826%	09-01-04	8,900	8,908	1.51
Ford Credit Australia 3.666%	06-06-03	8,500	8,618	1.47
Ford Motor Credit 6.875%	02-01-06	8,100	8,349	1.42
Oakwood Mtg Invest 5.135%	10-15-12	8,013	8,120	1.38
TMI Hm Ln Tr 7.56%	05-25-18	7,212	7,735	1.31
MBNA Amer Bk FRN	06-10-04	7,500	7,457	1.27
Xerox Equip N/A 5.801%	02-15-08	7,157	7,233	1.23
Capital One Bk 8.25%	06-15-05	6,850	7,141	1.21
New Plan Realty Tr 6.8%	05-15-02	7,000	7,123	1.21
Green Tree Finl 7.33%	11-15-29	6,750	6,940	1.18

Current Investment Style

Not Available

Avg Eff Duration[1]	1.7 Yrs
Avg Eff Maturity	2.3 Yrs
Avg Credit Quality	—
Avg Wtd Coupon	7.02%
Avg Wtd Price	99.13% of par

[1]figure provided by fund

Special Securities % assets 09-30-01	
Restricted/Illiquid Secs	5
Exotic Mortgage–Backed	Trace
Emerging–Markets Secs	0
Options/Futures/Warrants	No

Coupon Range	% of Bonds	Rel Cat
0%	0.00	0.00
0% to 7%	36.19	0.56
7% to 8.5%	52.23	1.82
8.5% to 10%	8.18	2.00
More than 10%	3.40	1.99

1.00=Category Average

Credit Analysis % bonds 03-31-01			
US Govt	10	BB	4
AAA	15	B	3
AA	23	Below B	2
A	33	NR/NA	0
BBB	10		

Composition % assets 09-30-01			
Cash	8.2	Bonds	91.8
Stocks	0.0	Other	0.0

Sector Breakdown % bonds 09-30-01			
US Treasuries	0	CMOs	9
GNMA mtgs	0	ARMs	0
FNMA mtgs	3	Other	78
FHLMC mtgs	3		

Address:	11766 Wilshire Blvd Ste 1580 Los Angeles, CA 90025 800–241–4671
Web Address:	www.mwamllc.com
*Inception:	03-31-97
Advisor:	Metropolitan West Asset Mgmt.
Subadvisor:	None
NTF Plans:	Datalynx , Fidelity Inst.

Minimum Purchase:	$5000	Add: None	IRA: $1000
Min Auto Inv Plan:	—	Add: —	
Sales Fees:	0.25%B		
Management Fee:	.48%		
Actual Fees:	Mgt: 0.48%	Dist: 0.00%	
Expense Projections:	3Yr: $19*	5Yr: —	10Yr: —
Avg Brok Commission:	—	Income Distrib: Monthly	
Total Cost (relative to category):	—		

Metropolitan West Total Return Bond

Ticker	Load	NAV	Yield	SEC Yield	Total Assets	Mstar Category
MWTRX	12b–1 only	$10.15	7.4%	6.62%	$1,588.8 mil	Interm–Term Bond

Prospectus Objective: Corp Bond—General

Metropolitan West Total Return Bond Fund seeks long-term total return.

The fund invests primarily in fixed-income securities of varying maturities. It normally invests at least 80% of assets in investment-grade debt; up to 20% may be in securities rated as low as B. The average portfolio duration typically ranges between two and eight years; the dollar-weighted average maturity usually ranges between two and 15 years. Portfolio holdings may be concentrated in areas of the bond market (based on quality, sector, coupon, or maturity) that the advisor believes to be relatively undervalued.

Historical Profile

Return High
Risk Below Avg
Rating ★★★★ Above Avg

Investment Style
Fixed-Income
Income Rtn %Rank Cat: 4 (1997), 1 (1998), 1 (1999), 2 (2000)

Growth of Principal vs. Interest Rate Shifts
— Principal Value $000 (NAV with capital gains reinvested)
— Interest Rate % on 10 Yr Treasury
▼ Manager Change
▽ Partial Manager Change
► Mgr Unknown After
◄ Mgr Unknown Before

Performance Quartile (within Category)

History

1990	1991	1992	1993	1994	1995	1996	1997	1998	1999	2000	12-01	History
—	—	—	—	—	—	—	10.51	10.65	10.05	10.11	10.15	NAV
—	—	—	—	—	—	—	11.87*	9.96	1.72	10.18	9.18	Total Return %
—	—	—	—	—	—	—	—	1.28	2.55	–1.45	0.75	+/– LB Aggregate
—	—	—	—	—	—	—	—	1.54	1.33	0.08	0.20	+/– LB Int Govt/Corp
—	—	—	—	—	—	—	5.60	7.10	7.42	9.48	7.81	Income Return %
—	—	—	—	—	—	—	6.27	2.86	–5.71	0.70	1.36	Capital Return %
—	—	—	—	—	—	—	—	3	4	47	11	Total Rtn % Rank Cat
—	—	—	—	—	—	—	0.54	0.72	0.76	0.91	0.76	Income $
—	—	—	—	—	—	—	0.11	0.15	0.01	0.00	0.10	Capital Gains $
—	—	—	—	—	—	—	—	0.65	0.65	0.65	0.65	Expense Ratio %
—	—	—	—	—	—	—	—	7.39	6.92	7.68	9.10	Income Ratio %
—	—	—	—	—	—	—	—	—	136	128	205	Turnover Rate %
—	—	—	—	—	—	—	15.1	83.3	186.7	278.1	621.0	Net Assets $mil

Portfolio Manager(s)

Stephen Kane. Since 3-97. BS'85 U. of California, Berkeley; MBA'90 U. of Chicago. Other funds currently managed: PaineWebber Pace Interm Fix-Inc P, Metropolitan West Low Duration Bond M, Metropolitan West AlphaTrak 500.

Laird Landmann. Since 3-97. BA'86 Dartmouth C.; MBA'90 U. of Chicago. Other funds currently managed: PaineWebber Pace Interm Fix-Inc P, Metropolitan West Low Duration Bond M, Metropolitan West AlphaTrak 500.

Tad Rivelle. Since 3-97. MS'87 U. of Southern California; MBA'90 U. of California-Los Angeles. Other funds currently managed: Managers Intermediate Bond, PaineWebber Pace Interm Fix-Inc P, Metropolitan West Low Duration Bond M.

Performance 12-31-01

	1st Qtr	2nd Qtr	3rd Qtr	4th Qtr	Total
1997	—	3.91	3.71	3.81	11.87 *
1998	1.64	2.59	2.28	3.10	9.96
1999	0.63	–0.29	0.99	0.38	1.72
2000	2.29	1.16	3.89	2.50	10.18
2001	4.37	0.79	4.01	–0.22	9.18

Trailing	Total Return%	+/– LB Agg	+/– LB ITGvt/Corp	% Rank All	% Rank Cat	Growth of $10,000
3 Mo	–0.22	–0.26	–0.31	81	60	9,978
6 Mo	3.78	–0.87	–0.92	11	61	10,378
1 Yr	9.18	0.75	0.20	7	11	10,918
3 Yr Avg	6.96	0.68	0.56	17	3	12,236
5 Yr Avg	—	—	—	—	—	—
10 Yr Avg	—	—	—	—	—	—
15 Yr Avg	—	—	—	—	—	—

Tax Analysis	Tax-Adj Ret%	%Rank Cat	%Pretax Ret	%Rank Cat
3 Yr Avg	3.52	21	50.6	66
5 Yr Avg	—	—	—	—
10 Yr Avg	—	—	—	—

Potential Capital Gain Exposure: 0% of assets

Risk Analysis

Time Period	Load-Adj Return %	Risk %Rank[1] All	Risk %Rank[1] Cat	Morningstar Return	Morningstar Risk	Morningstar Risk-Adj Rating
1 Yr	9.18					
3 Yr	6.96	10	15	0.44[2]	0.59	★★★★
5 Yr	—	—	—	—	—	
Incept	8.98	—	—	—	—	

Average Historical Rating (22 months): 5.0★s

[1]1=low, 100=high [2] T-Bill return substituted for category avg.

Category Rating (3 Yr)

1 2 3 4 5
Worst Best

Return High
Risk Below Avg

Other Measures	Standard Index LB Agg	Best Fit Index LB Corp
Alpha	0.8	1.3
Beta	0.89	0.76
R–Squared	70	73

Standard Deviation	3.76
Mean	6.96
Sharpe Ratio	0.63

Analysis by Scott Berry 12-20-01

Metropolitan West Total Return hasn't stood out in recent months, but it was due for a little breather.

After racking up impressive gains through the first nine months of 2001, this fund stalled in November, as an improving economic outlook pushed interest rates higher and bond prices lower. But while the fund has underperformed its average peer by a fractional amount over the last few months, it has delivered a solid 8.6% gain for the year to date through Dec. 20, 2001. That compares quite favorably with the 6.9% gain of its average intermediate-term bond peer.

The fund's long-term returns are equally impressive. The fund's three-year trailing return of 6.8% ranks near the very top of the category's performance chart and towers over the category's average of 4.9%. The fund's long-term returns have been bolstered by the added yield provided by its corporate holdings and by timely adjustments to the fund's sector and yield-curve positioning. For example, the fund bulked up on asset-backed bonds in 1999, which fared relatively well in that year's rough bond market.

As it has for the last two years, the fund continues to take on more credit risk than its average peer. However, management has done well to avoid most of the market's recent blowups, and the fund has shown few ill effects from the September terrorist attacks, which had a decidedly negative effect on lower-quality corporate bonds. The fund has also avoided wide performance swings in 2001 by keeping its duration within a narrow range of the Lehman Brothers Aggregate Bond index's.

This fund has a lot going for it. Its impressive returns, solid management, and below-average expense ratio make it tough to beat.

Portfolio Analysis 09-30-01

Total Fixed-Income: 255	Date of Maturity	Amount $000	Value $000	% Net Assets
US Treasury Bond 5.25%	02-15-29	90,461	87,319	6.13
FHLMC N/A		51,847	53,906	3.79
Calpine Canada Energy 8.50%		31,600	30,894	2.17
Wcg 8.25%		25,350	25,898	1.82
FMAC Rcvbl Tr 6.729%	12-15-19	25,000	24,591	1.73
FHLMC 5.625%		22,500	23,088	1.62
Beckman Coulter 7.5%		22,250	20,126	1.41
Resident Fdg Hm Eq Ln N/A		19,200	19,721	1.39
United Dominion Rlty Tr 8.625%	03-15-03	18,420	19,399	1.36
Delta Air Lines N/A		19,130	19,253	1.35
Ford Motor Credit N/A		18,000	19,019	1.34
Bear Stearns Cap Reset 7%	01-15-27	18,500	18,631	1.31
GMAC FRN		18,400	18,188	1.28
Skandinavinska Enskilda FRN		17,000	17,417	1.22
LB UBS Commrcl Mtg Tr 7.37%		15,155	16,735	1.18
Ford Motor Credit N/A		15,740	16,107	1.13
Capital One Finl 7.25%	05-01-06	16,000	15,939	1.12
Bank of America 7.8%	02-15-10	14,235	15,887	1.12
Ios Cap 9.75%		15,000	15,483	1.09
Polaris N/A		20,800	15,298	1.07

Current Investment Style

Not Available

Avg Eff Duration[1]	4.0 Yrs
Avg Eff Maturity	8.1 Yrs
Avg Credit Quality	—
Avg Wtd Coupon	7.24%
Avg Wtd Price	97.14% of par

[1]figure provided by fund

Special Securities % assets 09-30-01	
Restricted/Illiquid Secs	3
Exotic Mortgage–Backed	Trace
Emerging–Markets Secs	0
Options/Futures/Warrants	No

Credit Analysis % bonds 03-31-01			
US Govt	23	BB	4
AAA	6	B	3
AA	18	Below B	5
A	22	NR/NA	0
BBB	19		

Sector Breakdown % bonds 09-30-01			
US Treasuries	8	CMOs	8
GNMA mtgs	1	ARMs	1
FNMA mtgs	1	Other	74
FHLMC mtgs	7		

Coupon Range	% of Bonds	Rel Cat
0%	1.69	1.35
0% to 7%	34.36	0.64
7% to 8.5%	49.29	1.41
8.5% to 10%	13.42	1.87
More than 10%	1.25	0.46

1.00=Category Average

Composition % assets 09-30-01			
Cash	10.0	Bonds	90.0
Stocks	0.0	Other	0.0

Address:	11766 Wilshire Blvd Ste 1580 Los Angeles, CA 90025 800–241–4671
Web Address:	www.mwamllc.com
*Inception:	03-31-97
Advisor:	Metropolitan West Asset Mgmt.
Subadvisor:	None
NTF Plans:	Datalynx , Fidelity Inst.

Minimum Purchase:	$5000	Add: None IRA: $1000
Min Auto Inv Plan:	—	Add: —
Sales Fees:	0.25%B	
Management Fee:	.55%	
Actual Fees:	Mgt: 0.55%	Dist: 0.00%
Expense Projections:	3Yr: $21*	5Yr: $37* 10Yr: $84*
Avg Brok Commission:	—	Income Distrib: Monthly
Total Cost (relative to category):		—

MFS Capital Opportunities A

Ticker	Load	NAV	Yield	Total Assets	Mstar Category
MCOFX	5.75%w	$13.43	0.0%	$4,490.0 mil	Large Blend

Prospectus Objective: Growth

MFS Capital Opportunities Fund seeks capital appreciation.

The fund invests primarily in common stocks. It may also hold fixed-income securities, but it may not invest more than 25% of assets in debt rated below BBB. The fund may invest up to 50% of assets in foreign securities that are not traded on a U.S. exchange, including emerging-markets issues; it may also invest in ADRs.

Class A shares have front loads and lower 12b-1 fees; B shares have deferred loads and conversion features; C shares have level loads; I shares are for institutional investors.

Historical Profile

Return Above Avg
Risk Above Avg
Rating ★★★
Neutral

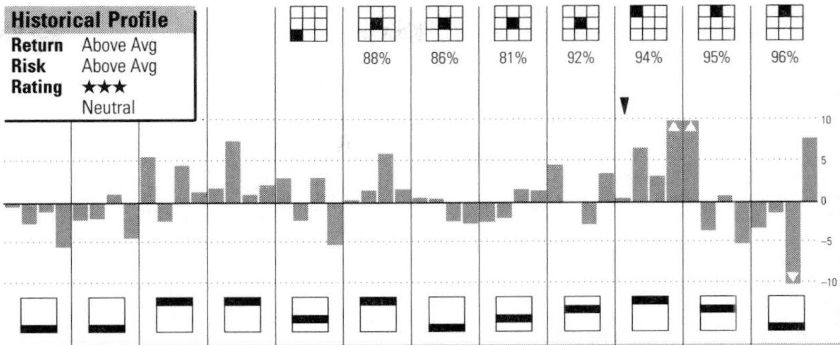

Investment Style
Equity
Average Stock %: 88% 86% 81% 92% 94% 95% 96%

▼ Manager Change
▽ Partial Manager Change

Fund Performance vs. Category Average
■ Quarterly Fund Return +/– Category Average
— Category Baseline

Performance Quartile (within Category)

Portfolio Manager(s)

Maura A. Shaughnessy, CFA. Since 2-99. BS'83 Colby C.; MBA'87 Dartmouth C. Other funds currently managed: MFS Utilities A, MFS Capital Opportunities B, MFS Utilities C.

1990	1991	1992	1993	1994	1995	1996	1997	1998	1999	2000	12-01	History
7.62	8.83	9.08	9.74	8.80	11.54	12.30	13.89	16.68	21.01	17.89	13.43	NAV
–11.84	23.95	17.99	25.31	–2.48	44.23	16.67	26.49	27.11	47.72	–5.30	–24.93	Total Return %
–8.72	–6.54	10.38	15.25	–3.79	6.69	–6.27	–6.86	–1.47	26.68	3.81	–13.05	+/– S&P 500
–7.81	–8.50	10.34	15.47	–2.93	6.62	–5.49	–6.54	–1.53	25.89	5.66	–12.17	+/– Wilshire Top 750
2.14	0.97	0.00	0.31	0.00	0.00	0.25	0.21	0.00	0.00	0.00	0.00	Income Return %
–13.98	22.97	17.99	25.00	–2.48	44.23	16.42	26.28	27.11	47.72	–5.30	–24.93	Capital Return %
93	87	5	4	71	2	84	64	36	2	34	97	Total Rtn % Rank Cat
0.19	0.07	0.00	0.03	0.00	0.00	0.03	0.03	0.00	0.00	0.00	0.00	Income $
0.13	0.52	1.33	1.60	0.70	1.15	1.12	1.58	0.92	3.32	2.02	0.00	Capital Gains $
1.51	1.50	1.53	1.42	1.37	1.35	1.32	1.29	1.23	1.18	1.11	—	Expense Ratio %
2.30	1.65	0.00	0.09	–0.05	0.06	0.43	0.49	–0.06	–0.33	–0.31	—	Income Ratio %
36	132	111	95	91	109	112	144	123	155	117	—	Turnover Rate %
102.7	111.3	115.0	138.5	142.8	232.1	435.0	623.6	1,020.5	2,048.8	3,147.2	—	Net Assets $mil

Performance 12-31-01

	1st Qtr	2nd Qtr	3rd Qtr	4th Qtr	Total
1997	–1.54	13.63	10.10	2.69	26.49
1998	17.13	1.83	–14.09	24.04	27.11
1999	4.08	13.48	–2.79	28.67	47.72
2000	15.18	–6.28	0.71	–12.88	–5.30
2001	–15.76	3.98	–27.82	18.74	–24.93

Trailing	Total Return%	+/– S&P 500	+/– Wil Top 750	% Rank All	% Rank Cat	Growth of $10,000
3 Mo	18.74	8.06	7.42	16	3	11,874
6 Mo	–14.29	–8.74	–8.50	94	98	8,571
1 Yr	–24.93	–13.05	–12.17	88	97	7,507
3 Yr Avg	1.65	2.67	3.47	64	22	10,502
5 Yr Avg	11.05	0.35	0.93	14	20	16,885
10 Yr Avg	15.15	2.22	2.70	5	2	40,971
15 Yr Avg	13.96	0.23	0.59	11	16	71,009

Tax Analysis	Tax-Adj Ret%	%Rank Cat	%Pretax Ret	%Rank Cat
3 Yr Avg	–0.97	33	—	—
5 Yr Avg	8.19	40	74.1	71
10 Yr Avg	11.67	13	77.0	68

Potential Capital Gain Exposure: –36% of assets

Risk Analysis

Time Period	Load-Adj Return %	Risk %Rank[1] All	Risk %Rank[1] Cat	Morningstar Return	Morningstar Risk	Morningstar Risk-Adj Rating
1 Yr	–29.25					
3 Yr	–0.34	84	95	–1.07[2]	1.26	★★
5 Yr	9.74	79	94	1.13[2]	1.10	★★★
10 Yr	14.47	80	88	1.65	1.07	★★★★

Average Historical Rating (187 months): 3.2★s

[1]1=low, 100=high [2] T-Bill return substituted for category avg.

Category Rating (3 Yr)

1 2 3 4 5
Worst Best

Return Above Avg
Risk High

Other Measures	Standard Index S&P 500	Best Fit Index Wil 4500
Alpha	6.1	0.1
Beta	1.29	0.86
R-Squared	70	84
Standard Deviation		27.43
Mean		1.65
Sharpe Ratio		–0.14

Portfolio Analysis 10-31-01

Share change since 09-01 Total Stocks: 110

	Sector	PE	YTD Ret%	% Assets
Tyco Intl	Industrials	27.1	6.23	3.31
⊖ Pfizer	Health	34.7	–12.40	2.83
⊕ AOL Time Warner	Technology	—	–7.76	2.38
⊕ Citigroup	Financials	20.0	0.03	2.22
General Elec	Industrials	30.1	–15.00	1.99
Applera Corporation	Industrials	38.1	–58.00	1.83
Pharmacia	Health	36.5	–29.30	1.81
⊖ Microsoft	Technology	57.6	52.78	1.74
⊖ American Intl Grp	Financials	42.0	–19.20	1.55
Flextronics Intl	Technology	—	–15.80	1.44
Santa Fe Intl	Energy	31.0	–11.00	1.44
⊕ AT&T Wireless Grp	Services	—	–17.00	1.44
⊕ Global Marine	Energy	—	–43.20	1.43
Clear Channel Comms	Services	—	5.10	1.42
⊕ EchoStar Comms	Technology	—	20.75	1.41
American Home Products	Health	—	–1.91	1.40
Danaher	Industrials	25.3	–11.60	1.37
Praxair	Industrials	28.6	26.22	1.37
⊖ Calpine	Utilities	8.9	–62.70	1.32
⊖ Cigna	Financials	13.2	–29.00	1.27
⊕ Charter Comms	Services	—	–27.50	1.27
✲ Hartford Finl Svcs Grp	Financials	23.2	–9.63	1.26
Grant Prideco	Energy	—	–47.50	1.24
Lamar Advertising Cl A	Services	—	9.71	1.18
⊖ El Paso	Utilities	NMF	–36.70	1.16

Current Investment Style

Style: Value Blnd Growth; Size: Large Med Small

	Stock Port Avg	Relative S&P 500 Current	Relative S&P 500 Hist	Rel Cat
Price/Earnings Ratio	30.3	0.98	1.08	1.00
Price/Book Ratio	4.3	0.75	0.79	0.78
Price/Cash Flow	19.0	1.06	1.11	1.03
3 Yr Earnings Growth	21.4	1.46	1.22	1.20
1 Yr Earnings Est%	–5.2	2.95	—	58.11
Med Mkt Cap $mil	18,906	0.3	0.3	0.36

[1]figure is based on 50% or less of stocks

Analysis by Gabriel Presler 10-29-01

MFS Capital Opportunities Fund's recent performance makes it hard to keep the faith, but who said loyalty is easy?

This fund posted an astonishing 47% gain in the heady days of 1999, outpacing more than 95% of its large-blend rivals. When the market turned sour in 2000, the fund fell with it, but it managed to retain its place in the top half of the category, thanks in large part to Shaughnessy's move into oil-services and natural-gas stocks.

In 2001, though, this fund's performance has taken an ugly turn. Believing that falling interest rates would precede an economic recovery, Shaughnessy added to positions in advertising-related stocks such as Viacom, some of which have continued to struggle. She also held on to some old energy favorites, particularly natural-gas-related Santa Fe and Noble Drilling. Finally, longtime financials holdings and a few battered-growth companies have hurt the fund, and its loss of more than 29% for the year to date through Oct. 26, 2001, lags 98% of its peers.

But investors shouldn't head for the exits just yet. Shaughnessy's record indicates that this fund could recover. Although she's fairly new to this fund, her nine-year tenure at MFS Utilities has resulted in a top-decile record. What's more, the fund has always been well-diversified across sectors, and Shaughnessy rarely buys stocks at top-shelf prices. Finally, the fund avoids large individual positions and is more diversified among its top picks than its peers. These characteristics, combined with the fund's strong record, call for shareholder patience.

Special Securities % assets 10-31-01	
Restricted/Illiquid Secs	0
Emerging-Markets Secs	3
Options/Futures/Warrants	No

Composition % assets 10-31-01	
Cash	3.9
Stocks*	96.1
Bonds	0.0
Other	0.0
*Foreign (% stocks)	7.5

Market Cap	
Giant	33.0
Large	36.8
Medium	26.9
Small	2.5
Micro	0.8

Sector Weightings	% of Stocks	Rel S&P	5-Year High	5-Year Low
Utilities	3.8	1.2	7	0
Energy	8.6	1.2	15	1
Financials	21.7	1.2	24	6
Industrials	17.6	1.5	25	10
Durables	0.0	0.0	11	0
Staples	0.0	0.0	9	0
Services	14.0	1.3	38	6
Retail	3.7	0.5	17	3
Health	8.2	0.6	15	2
Technology	22.4	1.2	31	2

Address:	P.O. Box 2281 Boston, MA 02107–9906 800–637–2929 / 617–954–5000
Web Address:	www.mfs.com
Inception:	06-13-83
Advisor:	MFS Inv. Mgmt.
Subadvisor:	None
NTF Plans:	Datalynx , Fidelity Inst.

Minimum Purchase:	$1000	Add: $50	IRA: $250
Min Auto Inv Plan:	$50	Add: $50	
Sales Fees:	5.75%L (W), 0.10%B, 0.25%S		
Management Fee:	.75%, .02%A		
Actual Fees:	Mgt: 0.71%	Dist: 0.25%	
Expense Projections:	3Yr: $928	5Yr: $1187	10Yr: $1924
Avg Brok Commission:	—	Income Distrib: Annually	
Total Cost (relative to category):		Average	

MFS Global Equity B

Ticker	Load	NAV	Yield	Total Assets	Mstar Category
MWEBX	4.00%d	$18.51	0.0%	$632.1 mil	World Stock

Prospectus Objective: World Stock

MFS Global Equity Fund seeks capital appreciation.

The fund invests in equities issued by foreign and domestic companies. It may invest up to 50% of assets in securities of U.S. or Canadian issuers. The fund may also invest in emerging markets. It may invest, to a limited extent, in fixed-income securities rated below BB. The fund may engage in options on securities and stock indexes.

Class A shares have front loads and no 12b-1 fees; B shares have deferred loads and conversion features; C shares have level loads; I shares are for institutional investors. Past names: MFS Lifetime Global Equity Trust, MFS Lifetime Worldwide Equity Fund, and MFS World Equity Fund.

Historical Profile
Return Above Avg
Risk Below Avg
Rating ★★★★ Above Avg

Investment Style
Equity
Average Stock %: 93% 92% 91% 82% 90% 95%

▼ Manager Change
▽ Partial Manager Change

Fund Performance vs. Category Average
■ Quarterly Fund Return +/– Category Average
— Category Baseline

Performance Quartile (within Category)

Portfolio Manager(s)

David R. Mannheim. Since 4-92. BA'82 Amherst C.; MSM'88 Sloan School of Management, MIT. Other funds currently managed: MFS Global Equity A, MFS Global Equity C, MFS Instl International Equity.

1990	1991	1992	1993	1994	1995	1996	1997	1998	1999	2000	12-01	History
12.54	13.44	13.50	16.71	14.54	16.35	17.75	19.43	21.58	24.04	20.77	18.51	NAV
–4.80	7.43	1.55	29.06	6.57	17.33	19.51	15.47	16.44	20.08	–8.03	–10.88	Total Return %
–1.69	–23.06	–6.07	19.00	5.25	–20.20	–3.44	–17.88	–12.14	–0.96	1.08	1.00	+/– S&P 500
12.21	–10.86	6.78	6.56	1.49	–3.39	6.03	–0.29	–7.90	–4.85	5.15	—	+/– MSCI World
0.31	0.00	0.00	0.11	0.00	0.00	0.00	0.00	0.00	0.00	0.00	0.00	Income Return %
–5.11	7.43	1.55	28.95	6.57	17.33	19.51	15.47	16.44	20.08	–8.03	–10.88	Capital Return %
14	96	54	66	7	51	27	35	43	81	43	25	Total Rtn % Rank Cat
0.04	0.00	0.00	0.01	0.00	0.00	0.00	0.00	0.00	0.00	0.00	0.00	Income $
0.30	0.03	0.15	0.70	3.09	0.71	1.78	1.04	0.99	1.75	1.33	0.00	Capital Gains $
2.93	2.88	2.91	2.66	2.58	2.55	2.45	2.39	2.35	2.34	2.30	—	Expense Ratio %
1.07	1.35	–0.31	–0.71	–1.01	–0.35	–0.44	–0.36	–0.51	–0.76	–0.46	—	Income Ratio %
173	160	110	70	99	73	83	65	64	92	84	—	Turnover Rate %
78.1	93.0	103.9	157.0	163.7	159.2	200.8	259.1	293.5	333.0	292.8	221.0	Net Assets $mil

Performance 12-31-01

	1st Qtr	2nd Qtr	3rd Qtr	4th Qtr	Total
1997	0.11	13.67	4.16	–2.59	15.47
1998	13.84	–0.36	–13.70	18.95	16.44
1999	–2.55	5.61	–1.89	18.93	20.08
2000	2.41	–1.99	–5.51	–3.03	–8.03
2001	–10.74	3.45	–11.26	8.75	–10.88

Trailing	Total Return%	+/– S&P 500	+/– MSCI World	% Rank All	% Rank Cat	Growth of $10,000
3 Mo	8.75	–1.93	—	48	72	10,875
6 Mo	–3.49	2.06	—	53	15	9,651
1 Yr	–10.88	1.00	—	62	25	8,912
3 Yr Avg	–0.53	0.50	—	75	61	9,843
5 Yr Avg	5.76	–4.94	—	51	50	13,234
10 Yr Avg	9.99	–2.94	—	32	30	25,918
15 Yr Avg	10.57	–3.17	—	38	25	45,121

Tax Analysis	Tax-Adj Ret%	%Rank Cat	%Pretax Ret	%Rank Cat
3 Yr Avg	–1.75	60	—	—
5 Yr Avg	4.50	43	78.1	35
10 Yr Avg	7.99	30	79.9	34

Potential Capital Gain Exposure: –2% of assets

Risk Analysis

Time Period	Load-Adj Return %	Risk %Rank[1] All	Risk %Rank[1] Cat	Morningstar Return	Morningstar Risk	Morningstar Risk-Adj Rating
1 Yr	–14.45					
3 Yr	–1.40	55	24	–1.27[2]	0.71	★★★
5 Yr	5.60	58	22	0.13[2]	0.66	★★★★
10 Yr	9.99	63	16	1.71[2]	0.64	★★★★

Average Historical Rating (145 months): 3.8★s

[1]1=low, 100=high [2] T-Bill return substituted for category avg.

Category Rating (3 Yr)

1 2 3 4 5
Worst Best

Return Average
Risk Below Avg

Other Measures	Standard Index S&P 500	Best Fit Index MSCIACWrldFree
Alpha	–1.2	2.2
Beta	0.71	0.83
R-Squared	71	84
Standard Deviation		14.19
Mean		–0.53
Sharpe Ratio		–0.45

Portfolio Analysis 10-31-01

Share change since 09-01 Total Stocks: 93	Sector	Country	% Assets
Syngenta	Technology	Switzerland	3.61
Akzo Nobel NV	Industrials	Netherlands	3.10
Diageo	Staples	United Kingdom	2.76
Praxair	Industrials	U.S.	2.05
Vodafone Airtouch	Services	United Kingdom	2.04
Eli Lilly	Health	U.S.	1.75
Sanofi-Synthelabo	Health	France	1.68
⊖ St. Paul	Financials	U.S.	1.68
Safeway	Retail	U.S.	1.66
⊖ Canon	Industrials	Japan	1.65
Elsevier (Cert)	Services	Netherlands	1.63
Reckitt Benckiser	Staples	United Kingdom	1.59
L'Air Liquide	Industrials	France	1.55
⊕ Samsung Electncs	Technology	South Korea	1.52
Royal Bk of Scotland	Financials	United Kingdom	1.47
⊕ Unilever (Cert)	Staples	United Kingdom	1.46
Total Fina Cl B	Energy	France	1.45
Cigna	Financials	U.S.	1.45
Saab Cl B	Industrials	Sweden	1.43
Conoco Cl A	Energy	U.S.	1.42

Current Investment Style

Style: Value Blnd Growth; Size: Large Med Small

	Stock Port Avg	Rel MSCI EAFE Current	Rel MSCI EAFE Hist	Rel Cat
Price/Earnings Ratio	23.2	0.90	0.96	0.84
Price/Cash Flow	13.8	1.07	1.11	0.84
Price/Book Ratio	4.7	1.34	1.09	1.02
3 Yr Earnings Growth	16.1	0.86	1.11	0.86
Med Mkt Cap $mil	13,034	0.5	0.5	0.54

Country Exposure 10-31-01	% assets
U.S.	33
United Kingdom	14
France	9
Japan	9
Netherlands	6

Hedging History: Rare

Special Securities % assets 10-31-01	
Restricted/Illiquid Secs	0
Emerging-Markets Secs	3
Options/Futures/Warrants	No

Composition % assets 10-31-01			
Cash	4.1	Bonds	0.0
Stocks	95.9	Other	0.0

Regional Exposure 10-31-01	% assets
Europe	41
Japan	9
Latin America	0
Pacific Rim	3
U.S.	33
Other	3

Sector Weightings	% of Stocks	Rel Cat	5-Year High	5-Year Low
Utilities	2.5	1.0	11	0
Energy	6.2	1.1	11	0
Financials	15.0	0.8	30	5
Industrials	17.2	1.5	22	4
Durables	2.1	0.5	18	1
Staples	7.8	1.0	21	3
Services	17.5	1.0	32	9
Retail	6.4	1.2	27	4
Health	12.7	1.0	17	6
Technology	12.5	0.8	19	4

Analysis by Gabriel Presler 11-26-01

There's not a lot of excitement about MFS Global Equity, but it gets the job done.

This fund looks a lot like its peers in the world-stock category. Manager David Mannheim devotes between 35% and 45% of assets to U.S. companies and prefers developed markets when investing abroad. What's more, he favors moderate growers, seeking the most reasonably priced misize companies in each industry. For example, Mannheim likes the cheap prices of Japan's pharmaceutical and health-care firms, so the fund's exposure to that market is a bit broader than category norms. The portfolio's valuations are a bit lower than the group average and the fund's median market cap is about half the world-stock average.

Mannheim's caution and wariness of high price tags have been helpful in 2001, as global markets have continued to punish aggressive investors. Longtime positions in a few industrial firms, such as Air Products and Chemicals, have propped up performance. And some of the fund's top consumer-related picks, such as Canon, have remained relatively flat throughout the year, an accomplishment in this volatile market. The fund hasn't completely sidestepped losses—it's down about 12% for the year to date through Nov. 23, 2001—but it looks better than 75% of its peers.

Strong relative performance isn't uncommon here. The fund avoided the worst of 2000's tech sell-off because Mannheim avoided expensive software, semiconductor, and networking firms. Generally, though, this offering bounces around the category's middle and its 10-year record is just about average. Steady performance like this might not turn heads, but it's combined with fairly low volatility, making the fund a solid—if unexciting—choice.

Address:	P.O. Box 2281 Boston, MA 02107-9906 800-637-2929 / 617-954-5000
Web Address:	www.mfs.com
Inception:	12-29-86
Advisor:	MFS Inv. Mgmt.
Subadvisor:	None
NTF Plans:	N/A

Minimum Purchase:	$1000	Add: $50 IRA: $250
Min Auto Inv Plan:	$50	Add: $50
Sales Fees:	4.00%D, 0.75%B, 0.25%S Conv. in 8 Yrs.	
Management Fee:	1.0% mx./.85% mn., .02%A	
Actual Fees:	Mgt: 1.00%	Dist: 1.00%
Expense Projections:	3Yr: $1018	5Yr: $1430 10Yr: $2448
Avg Brok Commission:	—	Income Distrib: Annually
Total Cost (relative to category):	Average	

MFS Global Total Return A

Ticker	Load	NAV	Yield	Total Assets	Mstar Category
MFWTX	4.75%w	$11.76	1.4%	$341.5 mil	International Hybrid

Prospectus Objective: Multiasset—Global

MFS Global Total Return Fund seeks total return.

The fund invests in foreign and domestic equity and fixed-income securities. It typically invests between 40% and 75% of assets in equity securities, and at least 25% of assets in fixed-income securities. It normally invests in at least three countries, including the United States. This fund is non-diversified.

Class A shares have front loads and lower 12b-1 fees; B shares have deferred loads and conversion features; C shares have level loads. Past names: MFS Worldwide Total Return Trust and MFS World Total Return Fund.

Historical Profile
Return Above Avg
Risk Low
Rating ★★★★ Above Avg

Investment Style
Equity
Average Stock %

	1994	1995	1996	1997	1998	1999	2000	12-01
Average Stock %			61%	55%	49%	52%	55%	57%

▼ Manager Change
▽ Partial Manager Change (2000)

Fund Performance vs. Category Average
■ Quarterly Fund Return +/– Category Average
— Category Baseline

Performance Quartile (within Category)

Portfolio Manager(s)

Frederick J. Simmons, CFA. Since 1-91. BA'59 Tufts U.; MBA'66 Dartmouth C. Other funds currently managed: MFS Global Total Return B, MFS Global Total Return C, MFS International Investors A.

Steven R. Gorham. Since 7-00. Other funds currently managed: MFS Global Total Return B, MFS Global Total Return C, MFS International Investors A.

Stephen C. Bryant. Since 7-00. Wesleyan U. Other funds currently managed: MFS Global Total Return B, MFS Global Total Return C, MFS Global Total Return I.

1990	1991	1992	1993	1994	1995	1996	1997	1998	1999	2000	12-01	History
8.71	10.03	9.80	11.08	10.18	11.69	12.62	13.20	14.19	13.94	12.79	11.76	NAV
3.21*	20.91	5.03	21.50	–2.93	20.29	15.34	10.16	18.00	7.58	1.42	–6.82	Total Return %
–0.27*	2.63	10.26	–1.00	–8.00	–0.43	1.86	–5.61	–6.33	–17.36	14.60	10.0	+/– MSCI World
—	5.46	0.48	9.23	–4.20	0.98	10.90	8.79	2.69	12.66	–0.92	–6.03	+/– JPM World Govt
1.10	2.71	4.64	4.29	1.82	5.36	2.09	1.46	2.71	1.59	3.66	1.25	Income Return %
2.11	18.20	0.39	17.21	–4.75	14.93	13.25	8.70	15.29	5.99	–2.24	–8.07	Capital Return %
—	50	83	12	46	58	38	66	10	88	22	32	Total Rtn % Rank Cat
0.09	0.23	0.46	0.41	0.20	0.54	0.24	0.18	0.36	0.23	0.51	0.16	Income $
0.00	0.23	0.27	0.38	0.38	0.01	0.60	0.51	0.99	1.05	0.82	0.00	Capital Gains $
1.57	2.18	1.84	1.92	1.76	1.77	1.63	1.59	1.51	1.48	1.51	—	Expense Ratio %
3.14	4.05	3.65	2.96	2.81	3.06	2.79	2.35	1.99	1.74	2.62	—	Income Ratio %
—	134	72	112	118	160	167	143	183	109	91	—	Turnover Rate %
18.0	33.9	46.8	75.6	95.4	115.8	135.4	155.2	187.9	197.5	179.4	197.5	Net Assets $mil

Performance 12-31-01

	1st Qtr	2nd Qtr	3rd Qtr	4th Qtr	Total
1997	–0.63	8.73	5.11	–3.00	10.16
1998	8.26	2.58	–3.38	9.98	18.00
1999	–2.89	1.97	–0.07	8.71	7.58
2000	1.15	0.86	–1.92	1.36	1.42
2001	–6.49	1.46	–4.50	2.83	–6.82

Trailing	Total Return%	+/– MSCI World	+/– JPM World Govt	% Rank All	% Rank Cat	Growth of $10,000
3 Mo	2.83	1,001.83	6.01	70	88	10,283
6 Mo	–1.79	997.21	–5.52	46	31	9,821
1 Yr	–6.82	992.18	–6.03	55	32	9,318
3 Yr Avg	0.55	999.55	1.78	70	62	10,167
5 Yr Avg	5.73	1,004.73	3.33	52	46	13,215
10 Yr Avg	8.55	1,007.55	3.30	41	66	22,713
15 Yr Avg	—	—	—	—	—	—

Tax Analysis	Tax-Adj Ret%	%Rank Cat	%Pretax Ret	%Rank Cat
3 Yr Avg	–1.20	58	—	—
5 Yr Avg	3.78	33	65.9	21
10 Yr Avg	6.41	66	75.0	33

Potential Capital Gain Exposure: –1% of assets

Risk Analysis

Time Period	Load-Adj Return %	Risk %Rank[1] All	Risk %Rank[1] Cat	Morningstar Return	Morningstar Risk	Morningstar Risk-Adj Rating
1 Yr	–11.25					
3 Yr	–1.07	36	25	–1.20[2]	0.43	★★★
5 Yr	4.71	40	19	–0.07[2]	0.38	★★★★
10 Yr	8.02	47	80	0.98[2]	0.39	★★★★

Average Historical Rating (101 months): 3.8★s

[1] 1=low, 100=high [2] T-Bill return substituted for category avg.

Category Rating (3 Yr)

1 2 **3** 4 5
Worst Best

Return Below Avg
Risk Below Avg

Other Measures	Standard Index S&P 500	Best Fit Index MSCIWdxUSN
Alpha	–2.3	0.0
Beta	0.37	0.48
R-Squared	59	85
Standard Deviation		8.13
Mean		0.55
Sharpe Ratio		–0.63

Portfolio Analysis 10-31-01

Total Stocks: 150 Share change since 09-01	Sector	PE Ratio	YTD Return %	% Net Assets
⊕ Philip Morris	Staples	12.1	9.12	1.43
⊕ Eli Lilly	Health	28.9	–14.40	1.31
⊕ Diageo	Staples	21.7	—	1.30
⊕ Total Fina Elf ADR	Energy	15.5	–1.76	1.21
⊕ Akzo Nobel NV	Industrials	18.5	—	1.19
⊕ Anheuser-Busch	Staples	24.6	1.01	1.06
⊕ Canadian Natl Railway	Services	18.8	64.61	1.06
⊕ Iberdrola	Utilities	19.5	—	1.03
⊕ Vodafone Airtouch	Services	—	—	0.96
⊕ IBM	Technology	26.9	43.00	0.96

Total Fixed-Income: 19	Date of Maturity	Amount $000	Value $000	% Net Assets
US Treasury Note 6.125%	08-15-07	41,188	46,086	13.49
Republic of Germany 4.5%	07-04-09	24,487	22,270	6.52
US Treasury Bond 6.25%	08-15-23	11,111	12,788	3.74
US Treasury Note 5.75%	08-15-10	11,479	12,744	3.73
United Kingdom Treasury 6.75%	11-26-04	7,506	11,640	3.41
Govt of Japan 0.%		500,000	5,738	1.68
US Treasury Note 4.625%	05-15-06	4,792	5,012	1.47
Intl Bk Reconstr/Dev 5%	03-28-06	4,319	4,510	1.32
Republic of Germany 4.75%	07-04-08	4,222	3,911	1.15
Republic of Italy 5%	05-01-08	3,578	3,346	0.98

Equity Style
Style: Growth
Size: Large-Cap

	Portfolio Avg	Rel S&P
Price/Earnings Ratio	24.6	0.95
Price/Cash Flow	14.0	1.09
Price/Book Ratio	4.9	1.41
3 Yr Earnings Growth	16.1	0.86
Med Mkt Cap $mil	31,362	1.12

Fixed-Income Style
Duration: —
Quality: —
NA

Avg Eff Duration	—
Avg Eff Maturity	—
Avg Credit Quality	—
Avg Wtd Coupon	5.47%

Special Securities % assets 10-31-01

Restricted/Illiquid Secs	Trace
Emerging-Markets Secs	1
Options/Futures/Warrants	No

Country Exposure 02-28-99

	% of Assets
U.S.	19.9
United Kingdom	7.4
France	5.2

Composition % assets 10-31-01

Cash	6.0
U.S. Stocks	24.6
Foreign Stocks	28.3
U.S. Bonds	33.0
Foreign Bonds	7.6
Other	0.5

Analysis by Gabriel Presler 09-28-01

More often than not, MFS Global Total Return's slow and steady pace wins the race.

Although its performance stands out in the international-hybrid group, this fund doesn't look that unusual—at least not at first glance. Its asset allocation, for example, tends to be around category norms, with about 55% of the portfolio committed to equities and 35% devoted to bonds. And like its rivals, the fund generally favors foreign companies in its stock portfolio, usually devoting a little more than half its equity stake to big international firms, such as Diageo and ING Groep.

But the similarities end there. A decided value bent means that this fund looks a lot different. For example, the fund historically devotes three times as much as its average peer to large consumer-staples firms, such as Anheuser-Busch and Spain's Altadis, and virtually ignores smaller, high-priced growth-oriented firms. Its tech weight, for example, has always been about 4% to 5% of assets—a tiny stake by any standard. Thus the fund's price multiples tend to be lower and its median market cap higher than the group average. And on the bond side, the fund limits exposure to corporate debt and low-quality paper, choosing sovereign debt from developed countries.

Such cautious positioning can hold the fund back at times—in 1999's growth rally, for example, this offering wound up in the category's basement—but it has helped since global markets turned sour in 2001. Large positions in staples stocks such as Philip Morris have helped the fund sidestep some losses suffered by its rivals. In fact, its loss of more than 10% for the year to date through Sept. 27, 2001, looks better than two thirds of its peers'.

Over time, the fund has been less volatile than its peers, and its performance has been admirable. It continues to be a solid choice for conservative investors.

Address:	P.O. Box 2281 Boston, MA 02107–9906 800–637–2929 / 617–954–5000
Web Address:	www.mfs.com
*Inception:	09-04-90
Advisor:	MFS Inv. Mgmt.
Subadvisor:	None
NTF Plans:	Datalynx, Fidelity Inst.

Minimum Purchase:	$1000	Add: $50 IRA: $250
Min Auto Inv Plan:	$50	Add: $50
Sales Fees:	4.75%L (W), 0.10%B, 0.25%S	
Management Fee:	.81%, .02%A	
Actual Fees:	Mgt: 0.85%	Dist: 0.35%
Expense Projections:	3Yr: $930	5Yr: $1260 10Yr: $2191
Avg Brok Commission:	—	Income Distrib: Semi-Ann.
Total Cost (relative to category):		Average

MFS Massachusetts Investors A

Ticker	Load	NAV	Yield	Total Assets	Mstar Category
MITTX	5.75%w	$16.58	1.2%	$10,170.8 mil	Large Blend

Prospectus Objective: Growth and Income

MFS Massachusetts Investors Trust seeks reasonable current income and long-term growth of capital and income.

The fund invests primarily in common stocks and convertibles, emphasizing securities that management considers to be of high or improving quality. It may invest up to 20% of assets in foreign securities; this limit does not apply to ADRs. The fund may invest a portion of the assets in cash equivalents.

Class A shares have front loads; B shares have deferred loads, higher 12b-1 fees, and conversion features; C shares have level loads; I shares are for institutional investors. Past name: Massachusetts Investors Trust

Historical Profile
Return Average
Risk Average
Rating ★★★ Neutral

Investment Style
Equity
Average Stock %: 94% 95% 96% 94% 97% 96% 96%

▼ Manager Change
▽ Partial Manager Change

Fund Performance vs. Category Average
■ Quarterly Fund Return +/– Category Average
— Category Baseline

Performance Quartile (within Category)

Portfolio Manager(s)

Mitchell D. Dynan, CFA. Since 3-95.
John D. Laupheimer Jr., CFA. Since 2-93.
Liehat Moy. Since 1-01.
Brooks Taylor. Since 1-01.

1990	1991	1992	1993	1994	1995	1996	1997	1998	1999	2000	12–01	History
12.28	13.87	12.31	11.50	10.07	12.71	14.46	17.52	20.25	20.95	20.02	16.58	NAV
–0.10	27.67	7.38	10.03	–1.02	39.34	25.90	31.69	22.95	6.95	–0.34	–16.24	Total Return %
3.02	–2.82	–0.23	–0.03	–2.33	1.81	2.95	–1.66	–5.62	–14.09	8.76	–4.36	+/– S&P 500
3.93	–4.77	–0.27	0.19	–1.47	1.74	3.74	–1.33	–5.68	–14.87	10.62	–3.47	+/– Wilshire Top 750
3.17	3.19	2.47	3.17	2.16	2.51	1.61	1.26	0.91	0.49	0.17	0.97	Income Return %
–3.27	24.48	4.91	6.86	–3.17	36.83	24.29	30.43	22.04	6.47	–0.51	–17.21	Capital Return %
28	78	48	45	57	5	12	33	56	94	17	74	Total Rtn % Rank Cat
0.43	0.39	0.34	0.39	0.25	0.25	0.20	0.18	0.16	0.10	0.04	0.19	Income $
0.82	1.35	2.23	1.67	1.07	1.03	1.32	1.27	1.05	0.58	0.82	0.00	Capital Gains $
0.47	0.62	0.62	0.68	0.71	0.70	0.74	0.74	0.73	0.88	0.87	—	Expense Ratio %
3.28	2.73	2.30	3.04	2.20	2.13	1.51	1.09	0.86	0.55	0.38	—	Income Ratio %
26	44	46	41	87	54	47	44	54	62	68	—	Turnover Rate %
1,265.7	1,530.3	1,546.4	1,626.1	1,535.2	2,074.4	2,680.9	4,296.1	7,141.8	8,530.3	7,644.1	—	Net Assets $mil

Performance 12-31-01

	1st Qtr	2nd Qtr	3rd Qtr	4th Qtr	Total
1997	1.31	17.38	6.20	4.27	31.69
1998	13.51	2.55	–10.90	18.55	22.95
1999	0.67	5.00	–8.81	10.96	6.95
2000	1.90	–1.21	1.88	–2.83	–0.34
2001	–12.71	2.71	–13.65	8.20	–16.24

Trailing	Total Return%	+/– S&P 500	+/–Wil Top 750	% Rank All	% Rank Cat	Growth of $10,000
3 Mo	8.20	–2.49	–3.12	51	88	10,820
6 Mo	–6.57	–1.02	–0.78	72	65	9,343
1 Yr	–16.24	–4.36	–3.47	75	74	8,376
3 Yr Avg	–3.71	–2.68	–1.89	89	83	8,928
5 Yr Avg	7.65	–3.05	–2.47	31	71	14,456
10 Yr Avg	11.48	–1.44	–0.97	22	55	29,658
15 Yr Avg	12.82	–0.91	–0.55	18	41	61,079

Tax Analysis	Tax-Adj Ret%	%Rank Cat	%Pretax Ret	%Rank Cat
3 Yr Avg	–4.37	78	—	—
5 Yr Avg	6.44	63	84.3	38
10 Yr Avg	8.71	61	75.9	71

Potential Capital Gain Exposure: 3% of assets

Risk Analysis

Time Period	Load-Adj Return %	Risk %Rank[1] All	Risk %Rank[1] Cat	Morningstar Return	Morningstar Risk	Morningstar Risk-Adj Rating
1 Yr	–21.06					
3 Yr	–5.59	59	20	–2.02[2]	0.82	★★
5 Yr	6.38	59	20	0.30[2]	0.82	★★★
10 Yr	10.83	63	16	0.88	0.82	★★★

Average Historical Rating (193 months): 3.4★s

[1] 1=low, 100=high [2] T-Bill return substituted for category avg.

Category Rating (3 Yr)

1 2 3 4 5
Worst Best

Return Below Avg
Risk Below Avg

Other Measures	Standard Index S&P 500	Best Fit Index S&P 500
Alpha	–4.0	–4.0
Beta	0.79	0.79
R–Squared	91	91

Standard Deviation	13.67
Mean	–3.71
Sharpe Ratio	–0.74

Analysis by Gabriel Presler 09-20-01

It may be tempting to seek flashier fare, but investors shouldn't dismiss MFS Massachusetts Investors Fund.

This fund has suffered some nasty jolts lately. Its reluctance to buy richly valued tech stocks doomed it to the large-blend category's basement in growth-dominated 1999. Although its caution boosted relative returns when equity markets turned sour in 2000, the fund wasn't able to eke its way into positive territory for the year.

Like most of its peers, the fund has suffered on many fronts in 2001. Large positions in financials firms—so helpful in 2000—have faltered in 2001. Top-25 holdings Cigna, Citigroup, and American International Group, for example, have posted significant losses. Similarly, many of the fund's favorite health-care and industrial picks, including Eli Lilly and Tyco International, have dropped sharply this year. Thus, the fund has suffered right along with its rivals in 2001, losing more than 23% of its value for the year to date through Sept. 20, 2001—a little bit more than the category average.

Obviously, unimpressive performance isn't unheard of here, but the fund rarely suffers dramatic drops. It generally hovers around the middle third of the group, and its 12% annualized gain over the last 10 years is solidly average. That may sound like faint praise, but the fund's incredibly low volatility and its consistent record lead us to regard this offering favorably. Cautious shareholders are likely to be well-served here.

Portfolio Analysis 10-31-01

Share change since 09–01 Total Stocks: 189	Sector	PE	YTD Ret%	% Assets
ExxonMobil	Energy	15.3	–7.59	3.35
Freddie Mac	Financials	14.0	–3.87	3.34
Pfizer	Health	34.7	–12.40	3.11
⊖ General Elec	Industrials	30.1	–15.00	3.01
IBM	Technology	26.9	43.00	2.51
⊖ Safeway	Retail	18.1	–33.20	2.30
Eli Lilly	Health	28.9	–14.40	2.24
⊖ Microsoft	Technology	57.6	52.78	2.17
American Home Products	Health	—	–1.91	1.85
⊕ Citigroup	Financials	20.0	0.03	1.68
⊕ Johnson & Johnson	Health	16.6	14.01	1.68
⊖ Philip Morris	Staples	12.1	9.12	1.42
Viacom Cl B	Services	—	—	1.40
⊕ Tyco Intl	Industrials	27.1	6.23	1.36
First Data	Technology	38.1	49.08	1.28
Fannie Mae	Financials	16.2	–6.95	1.27
Novartis (Reg)	Health	21.8	—	1.22
Procter & Gamble	Staples	38.8	3.12	1.22
Wal–Mart Stores	Retail	40.3	8.94	1.22
Pharmacia	Health	36.5	–29.30	1.19
⊖ State Street	Financials	28.6	–15.10	1.14
St. Paul	Financials	—	–16.90	1.14
⊕ Bank of America	Financials	16.7	42.73	1.13
⊖ Verizon Comms	Services	29.7	–2.52	1.12
⊖ Wells Fargo	Financials	22.4	–20.20	1.08

Current Investment Style

Style: Value Blnd Growth; Size: Large Med Small

	Stock Port Avg	Relative S&P 500 Current	Relative S&P 500 Hist	Rel Cat
Price/Earnings Ratio	26.5	0.86	0.93	0.87
Price/Book Ratio	6.0	1.05	0.96	1.09
Price/Cash Flow	16.8	0.93	0.96	0.91
3 Yr Earnings Growth	18.5	1.26	1.00	1.04
1 Yr Earnings Est%	2.5	—	—	–27.89
Med Mkt Cap $mil	57,072	0.9	1.2	1.09

Special Securities % assets 10-31-01	
Restricted/Illiquid Secs	0
Emerging–Markets Secs	Trace
Options/Futures/Warrants	No

Composition % assets 10-31-01	
Cash	1.5
Stocks*	98.5
Bonds	0.0
Other	0.0
*Foreign (% stocks)	8.5

Market Cap	
Giant	56.1
Large	37.4
Medium	6.5
Small	0.0
Micro	0.0

Sector Weightings	% of Stocks	Rel S&P	5-Year High	5-Year Low
Utilities	3.8	1.2	8	0
Energy	7.6	1.1	12	5
Financials	19.0	1.1	28	12
Industrials	11.1	1.0	23	9
Durables	0.1	0.1	9	0
Staples	8.0	1.0	19	4
Services	11.2	1.0	18	7
Retail	6.2	0.9	11	4
Health	17.5	1.2	23	4
Technology	15.6	0.9	28	4

Address:	P.O. Box 2281 Boston, MA 02107–9906 800–637–2929 / 617–954–5000
Web Address:	www.mfs.com
Inception:	07-15-24
Advisor:	MFS Inv. Mgmt.
Subadvisor:	None
NTF Plans:	Datalynx , Fidelity Inst.

Minimum Purchase:	$1000	Add: $50 IRA: $250
Min Auto Inv Plan:	$1000	Add: $50
Sales Fees:	5.75%L (W), 0.10%B, 0.25%S	
Management Fee:	.33%, .02%A	
Actual Fees:	Mgt: 0.33%	Dist: 0.35%
Expense Projections:	3Yr: $837	5Yr: $1029 10Yr: $1586
Avg Brok Commission:	—	Income Distrib: Annually
Total Cost (relative to category):		Average

MFS Massachusetts Investors Gr Stk A

Ticker	Load	NAV	Yield	Total Assets	Mstar Category
MIGFX	5.75%w	$12.89	0.0%	$12,882.9 mil	Large Blend

Prospectus Objective: Growth

MFS Massachusetts Investors Growth Stock Fund seeks long-term growth of capital and future income, rather than current income.

The fund invests primarily in common stocks or convertibles issued by companies exhibiting above-average prospects for long-term growth. It may invest up to 35% of assets in foreign securities. It may also invest in securities issued in emerging markets.

Class A shares have front loads; B shares have deferred loads, higher 12b-1 fees, and conversion features; C shares have level loads; I shares are for institutions. Past name: Massachusetts Investors Growth Stock Fund.

Historical Profile

Return Above Avg
Risk Above Avg
Rating ★★★ Neutral

Investment Style
Equity
Average Stock %

93% 95% 88% 95% 94% 95%

▼ Manager Change
▽ Partial Manager Change

Fund Performance vs. Category Average
■ Quarterly Fund Return +/– Category Average
— Category Baseline

Performance Quartile (within Category)

Portfolio Manager(s)

Stephen Pesek, CFA. Since 2-99. BA'82 U. of Pennsylvania; MBA'87 Columbia U. Other funds currently managed: MFS Massachusetts Investors Gr Stk B, MFS Massachusetts Investors Gr Stk C, MFS Massachusetts Investors Gr Stk I.

1990	1991	1992	1993	1994	1995	1996	1997	1998	1999	2000	12-01	History
8.45	11.69	11.71	11.40	9.55	10.63	9.98	12.42	15.91	20.33	17.14	12.89	NAV
–4.74	47.72	6.44	14.46	–6.73	28.34	22.84	48.15	40.00	38.76	–7.22	–24.80	Total Return %
–1.62	17.23	–1.18	4.41	–8.04	–9.19	–0.10	14.80	11.42	17.72	1.88	–12.92	+/– S&P 500
–0.71	15.28	–1.21	4.63	–7.18	–9.26	0.68	15.13	11.36	16.93	3.73	–12.03	+/– Wilshire Top 750
0.54	0.00	0.00	0.00	0.00	0.00	0.00	0.07	0.05	0.00	0.00	0.00	Income Return %
–5.28	47.72	6.44	14.46	–6.73	28.34	22.84	48.09	39.95	38.76	–7.22	–24.80	Capital Return %
67	5	63	24	92	82	26	1	1	8	43	96	Total Rtn % Rank Cat
0.05	0.00	0.00	0.00	0.00	0.00	0.00	0.01	0.01	0.00	0.00	0.00	Income $
0.52	0.76	0.72	1.99	1.08	1.61	3.10	2.26	1.39	1.62	1.72	0.00	Capital Gains $
0.53	0.63	0.67	0.71	0.72	0.73	0.72	0.71	0.79	0.87	0.85	—	Expense Ratio %
0.55	0.14	–0.24	–0.19	–0.06	–0.08	–0.05	0.05	0.15	–0.08	–0.15	—	Income Ratio %
44	39	16	52	56	46	107	93	62	174	261	—	Turnover Rate %
780.8	1,075.3	1,080.2	1,133.0	965.9	1,122.7	1,240.9	1,750.5	3,312.0	7,963.8	9,694.8	—	Net Assets $mil

Performance 12-31-01

	1st Qtr	2nd Qtr	3rd Qtr	4th Qtr	Total
1997	2.81	22.81	13.02	3.83	48.15
1998	19.81	3.56	–10.12	25.54	40.00
1999	4.53	7.34	–3.53	28.20	38.76
2000	9.35	–5.31	3.75	–13.64	–7.22
2001	–21.00	5.54	–21.62	15.09	–24.80

Trailing	Total Return%	+/– S&P 500	+/– Wil Top 750	% Rank All	% Rank Cat	Growth of $10,000
3 Mo	15.09	4.40	3.77	24	9	11,509
6 Mo	–9.80	–4.24	–4.00	84	91	9,020
1 Yr	–24.80	–12.92	–12.03	88	96	7,520
3 Yr Avg	–1.07	–0.05	0.75	78	48	9,681
5 Yr Avg	14.96	4.26	4.84	4	4	20,080
10 Yr Avg	13.66	0.73	1.21	10	14	35,975
15 Yr Avg	14.45	0.72	1.08	8	12	75,719

Tax Analysis	Tax-Adj Ret%	%Rank Cat	%Pretax Ret	%Rank Cat
3 Yr Avg	–2.62	60	—	—
5 Yr Avg	12.29	4	82.2	46
10 Yr Avg	10.05	45	73.6	79

Potential Capital Gain Exposure: –31% of assets

Risk Analysis

Time Period	Load-Adj Return %	Risk %Rank[1] All	Risk %Rank[1] Cat	Morningstar Return	Morningstar Risk	Morningstar Risk-Adj Rating
1 Yr	–29.12					
3 Yr	–3.01	80	92	–1.56[2]	1.14	★★
5 Yr	13.61	77	88	2.21[2]	1.05	★★★★
10 Yr	12.99	85	98	1.31	1.20	★★★

Average Historical Rating (193 months): 2.7★s

[1] 1=low, 100=high [2] T-Bill return substituted for category avg.

Category Rating (3 Yr)

1 2 3 4 5
Worst Best

Return Average
Risk High

Other Measures	Standard Index S&P 500	Best Fit Index Wil 4500
Alpha	1.8	–3.4
Beta	1.16	0.74
R-Squared	74	82
Standard Deviation		23.12
Mean		–1.07
Sharpe Ratio		–0.30

Portfolio Analysis 10-31-01

Share change since 09-01 Total Stocks: 122	Sector	PE	YTD Ret%	% Assets
⊖ Tyco Intl	Industrials	27.1	6.23	3.32
⊕ Citigroup	Financials	20.0	0.03	3.03
⊕ Pfizer	Health	34.7	–12.40	2.92
⊕ Viacom Cl B	Services	—	—	2.59
⊖ American Intl Grp	Financials	42.0	–19.20	2.58
⊕ Freddie Mac	Financials	14.0	–3.87	2.57
⊕ Abbott Labs	Health	51.6	17.08	2.26
⊖ Microsoft	Technology	57.6	52.78	2.15
⊕ Minnesota Mng & Mfg	Industrials	34.5	0.16	2.12
⊕ Johnson & Johnson	Health	16.6	14.01	2.06
⊖ Lowe's	Retail	38.7	109.00	1.69
⊖ Qualcomm	Technology	—	–38.50	1.69
⊕ Goldman Sachs Grp	Financials	20.7	–12.80	1.62
⊖ General Elec	Industrials	30.1	–15.00	1.48
⊕ First Data	Technology	38.1	49.08	1.47
⊖ Gillette	Staples	56.6	–5.47	1.45
⊖ American Home Products	Health	—	–1.91	1.43
⊕ Linear Tech	Technology	34.9	–15.30	1.37
⊕ Danaher	Industrials	25.3	–11.60	1.36
⊕ Vodafone Airtouch	Services	—	—	1.34
⊖ Eli Lilly	Health	28.9	–14.40	1.32
⊖ Baxter Intl	Health	33.9	22.84	1.29
⊖ Oracle	Technology	32.1	–52.40	1.28
⊖ AOL Time Warner	Technology	—	–7.76	1.26
⊕ Texas Instruments	Technology	87.5	–40.70	1.26

Current Investment Style

Style: Value Blnd Growth
Size: Large Med Small

	Stock Port Avg	Relative S&P 500 Current	Relative S&P 500 Hist	Rel Cat
Price/Earnings Ratio	32.9	1.06	1.15	1.08
Price/Book Ratio	6.5	1.14	1.09	1.18
Price/Cash Flow	23.2	1.29	1.20	1.26
3 Yr Earnings Growth	21.9	1.50	1.26	1.23
1 Yr Earnings Est%	–1.1	0.62	—	12.22
Med Mkt Cap $mil	43,002	0.7	0.5	0.82

Analysis by Gabriel Presler 10-05-01

Since its return to old stomping grounds, this fund couldn't look worse, but investors shouldn't dismiss it just yet.

Massachusetts Investors Growth Stock Fund has always bounced around Morningstar's style box. Manager Stephen Pesek's search for companies with fast earnings growth and dominant market share pulled the fund from large-blend into large-growth territory in 1999. More recently, he has made some defensive moves in a jittery market, purchasing consumer-related companies, such as Quaker and Philip Morris, and beaten-down communications stocks. As a result, the portfolio's valuations have come down significantly, and the fund has returned to its old large-blend peer group.

That means this fund's relative performance looks downright wretched. The fund's loss of more than 32% for the year to date through Oct. 5, 2001, lags 96% of its more-conservative rivals.

Despite these nasty numbers, we're advising investors to shut their eyes, hold their noses, and be patient—at least for now. First of all, the fund's long-term performance continues to be strong, relative to both peer groups. What's more, Pesek's record at his previous charge, MFS Large Cap Growth [MCGAX], and his admirable direction of MFS Core Growth indicate that he's an able manager. Well-timed sector shifts, including trimming energy and oil stocks early in 2001, propped up returns for the fund this year. And his stock-picking has been fairly successful, too; for example, a position in Lowe's, which he chose over Home Depot in 2000, has recovered nicely this year.

Shareholders here have enjoyed an annualized return of more than 13% over the past 10 years—solid performance by any measure. It's too early to throw in the towel.

Special Securities % assets 10-31-01	
Restricted/Illiquid Secs	0
Emerging-Markets Secs	Trace
Options/Futures/Warrants	No

Composition % assets 10-31-01	
Cash	5.5
Stocks*	94.5
Bonds	0.0
Other	0.0
*Foreign (% stocks)	8.5

Market Cap	
Giant	51.6
Large	40.0
Medium	8.4
Small	0.0
Micro	0.0

Sector Weightings	% of Stocks	Rel S&P	5-Year High	5-Year Low
Utilities	1.4	0.4	7	0
Energy	0.9	0.1	8	0
Financials	20.0	1.1	20	0
Industrials	11.8	1.0	13	0
Durables	0.7	0.4	4	0
Staples	5.6	0.7	9	0
Services	10.3	1.0	54	10
Retail	5.9	0.9	25	4
Health	17.6	1.2	20	2
Technology	26.1	1.4	46	17

Address:	P.O. Box 2281 Boston, MA 02107–9906 800–637–2929 / 617–954–5000
Web Address:	www.mfs.com
Inception:	01-01-35
Advisor:	MFS Inv. Mgmt.
Subadvisor:	None
NTF Plans:	Datalynx, Fidelity Inst.

Minimum Purchase:	$1000	Add: $50 IRA: $250
Min Auto Inv Plan:	$50	Add: $50
Sales Fees:	5.75%L (W), 0.10%B, 0.25%S	
Management Fee:	.33%, .02%A	
Actual Fees:	Mgt: 0.33%	Dist: 0.35%
Expense Projections:	3Yr: $837	5Yr: $1029 10Yr: $1586
Avg Brok Commission:	—	Income Distrib: Annually
Total Cost (relative to category):		Average

MFS Total Return A

Ticker	Load	NAV	Yield	Total Assets	Mstar Category
MSFRX	4.75%w	$14.48	3.2%	$7,520.5 mil	Domestic Hybrid

Prospectus Objective: Balanced

MFS Total Return Fund seeks above-average income; growth of capital and income is secondary.

The fund generally maintains 40% to 75% of assets in equity securities. It typically invests the balance in debt securities, including up to 20% of assets in debt rated below BB. The fund may invest in foreign securities, including Brady Bonds.

Class A shares have front loads; B shares have deferred loads, higher 12b-1 fees, and conversion features; C shares have level loads. Prior to March 31, 1986, the fund was named Massachusetts Income Development. From that date until Aug. 3, 1992, it was named Massachusetts Financial Total Return Trust.

Historical Profile
Return: Average
Risk: Low
Rating: ★★★★ Above Avg

Investment Style
Equity
Average Stock %: 47% 51% 51% 50% 56% 58% 56%

▼ Manager Change
▽ Partial Manager Change

Fund Performance vs. Category Average
■ Quarterly Fund Return +/– Category Average
— Category Baseline

Performance Quartile (within Category)

Portfolio Manager(s)

David H. Calabro. Since 7-95.
Lisa B. Nurme. Since 7-95.
Constantinos G. Mokas. Since 4-98.
Kenneth J. Enright, CFA. Since 1-99.
David S. Kennedy. Since 9-00.

1990	1991	1992	1993	1994	1995	1996	1997	1998	1999	2000	12-01	History
10.62	12.06	12.28	13.34	12.44	14.41	14.79	15.82	14.96	13.88	15.41	14.48	NAV
–2.33	21.62	10.06	15.15	–2.64	26.91	14.61	20.67	11.88	2.31	19.00	–0.63	Total Return %
0.79	–8.86	2.44	5.09	–3.96	–10.62	–8.34	–12.68	–16.69	–18.73	28.10	11.25	+/– S&P 500
–11.28	5.62	2.66	5.40	0.28	8.44	10.99	10.99	3.21	3.14	7.37	–9.05	+/– LB Aggregate
5.88	5.77	5.04	4.76	4.13	5.21	4.38	4.10	3.85	3.25	3.46	3.13	Income Return %
–8.21	15.85	5.02	10.39	–6.77	21.70	10.22	16.57	8.03	–0.94	15.54	–3.76	Capital Return %
71	62	28	22	54	34	37	33	53	81	4	26	Total Rtn % Rank Cat
0.67	0.60	0.60	0.57	0.54	0.63	0.62	0.59	0.59	0.48	0.47	0.48	Income $
0.01	0.20	0.37	0.21	0.01	0.66	1.06	1.37	2.07	0.94	0.55	0.35	Capital Gains $
0.85	0.87	0.84	0.84	0.85	0.87	0.91	0.93	0.90	0.89	0.90	—	Expense Ratio %
5.71	5.89	5.40	4.51	4.26	4.82	4.35	3.84	3.44	3.45	3.36	—	Income Ratio %
50	74	84	95	91	102	140	143	126	151	112	—	Turnover Rate %
745.5	998.7	1,269.1	1,735.2	1,825.1	2,356.2	2,707.0	3,263.0	3,810.8	3,629.1	3,794.8	—	Net Assets $mil

Performance 12-31-01

	1st Qtr	2nd Qtr	3rd Qtr	4th Qtr	Total
1997	1.31	9.30	6.24	2.57	20.67
1998	6.86	1.53	–3.89	7.30	11.88
1999	–0.41	5.02	–4.60	2.54	2.31
2000	1.96	2.27	7.61	6.05	19.00
2001	–2.93	2.55	–5.39	5.51	–0.63

Trailing	Total Return%	+/– S&P 500	+/– LB Agg	% Rank All	% Rank Cat	Growth of $10,000
3 Mo	5.51	–5.17	5.48	63	65	10,551
6 Mo	–0.17	5.38	–4.83	40	25	9,983
1 Yr	–0.63	11.25	–9.05	43	26	9,937
3 Yr Avg	6.56	7.58	0.28	19	9	12,099
5 Yr Avg	10.31	–0.39	2.88	17	12	16,334
10 Yr Avg	11.35	–1.57	4.12	23	14	29,312
15 Yr Avg	11.48	–2.25	3.36	30	14	51,075

Tax Analysis	Tax-Adj Ret%	%Rank Cat	%Pretax Ret	%Rank Cat
3 Yr Avg	4.12	10	62.8	31
5 Yr Avg	7.08	18	68.6	49
10 Yr Avg	8.29	19	73.0	44

Potential Capital Gain Exposure: 5% of assets

Risk Analysis

Time Period	Load-Adj Return %	Risk %Rank[1] All	Risk %Rank[1] Cat	Morningstar Return	Morningstar Risk	Morningstar Risk-Adj Rating
1 Yr	–5.35					
3 Yr	4.84	34	16	–0.02[2]	0.38	★★★★
5 Yr	9.24	38	15	1.00[2]	0.39	★★★★
10 Yr	10.81	44	14	0.88	0.43	★★★★

Average Historical Rating (193 months): 3.6★s

[1] 1=low, 100=high [2] T-Bill return substituted for category avg.

Category Rating (3 Yr)

1 2 3 4 5
Worst Best

Return: High
Risk: Below Avg

Other Measures	Standard Index S&P 500	Best Fit Index S&P 500
Alpha	3.6	3.6
Beta	0.36	0.36
R-Squared	48	48

Standard Deviation	9.41
Mean	6.56
Sharpe Ratio	0.20

Portfolio Analysis 10-31-01

Total Stocks: 201 Share change since 09-01	Sector	PE Ratio	YTD Return %	% Net Assets
⊕ Viacom Cl B	Services	—	—	1.33
Akzo Nobel NV	Industrials	18.5	—	1.10
⊕ Sears Roebuck	Retail	23.4	40.12	1.06
⊕ Citigroup	Financials	20.0	0.03	1.05
⊕ ExxonMobil	Energy	15.3	–7.59	1.05
⊕ Devon Energy	Energy	5.6	–36.30	1.00
⊖ Sprint	Services	20.5	1.18	1.00
⊖ Freddie Mac	Financials	14.0	–3.87	0.94
⊕ Bank of America	Financials	16.7	42.73	0.92
Deere	Industrials	—	–2.52	0.87

Total Fixed-Income: 563	Date of Maturity	Amount $000	Value $000	% Net Assets
FNMA 6.5%	09-01-31	199,725	204,662	2.72
US Treasury Bond 5.375%	02-15-31	110,832	119,110	1.58
US Treasury Note 4.625%	05-15-06	96,605	101,043	1.34
US Treasury Note 3.625%	08-31-03	95,272	97,386	1.29
US Treasury Note 6.875%	05-15-06	68,205	77,668	1.03
US Treasury Note 5.75%	08-15-10	52,111	57,852	0.77
FNMA 6.5%	02-01-16	52,226	54,328	0.72
FNMA 6%	04-01-31	44,353	44,929	0.60
GNMA 7.5%	12-15-27	43,473	41,919	0.56
FNMA Debenture 6.625%	11-15-10	25,950	29,311	0.39

Equity Style
Style: Value
Size: Large-Cap

	Portfolio Avg	Rel S&P
Price/Earnings Ratio	23.6	0.76
Price/Book Ratio	3.9	0.68
Price/Cash Flow	12.6	0.70
3 Yr Earnings Growth	10.8	0.74
1 Yr Earnings Est%	–7.0	3.93
Debt % Total Cap	37.3	1.21
Med Mkt Cap $mil	20,553	0.34

Fixed-Income Style
Duration: Intermediate
Quality: Low

Avg Eff Duration	—
Avg Eff Maturity	8.0 Yrs
Avg Credit Quality	BB
Avg Wtd Coupon	6.59%

Special Securities % assets 10-31-01	
Restricted/Illiquid Secs	4
Emerging-Markets Secs	Trace
Options/Futures/Warrants	Yes

Composition % of assets 10-31-01	
Cash	3.7
Stocks*	55.7
Bonds	38.3
Other	2.2
*Foreign (% of stocks)	9.7

Market Cap	
Giant	30.1
Large	46.2
Medium	22.2
Small	1.4
Micro	0.0

Sector Weightings	% of Stocks	Rel S&P	5-Year High	5-Year Low
Utilities	7.1	2.2	16	7
Energy	13.1	1.9	20	10
Financials	21.9	1.2	28	12
Industrials	13.8	1.2	25	13
Durables	1.1	0.7	9	1
Staples	7.5	0.9	11	3
Services	16.2	1.5	18	5
Retail	3.7	0.6	7	2
Health	7.4	0.5	10	2
Technology	8.2	0.5	8	1

Analysis by Gabriel Presler 09-27-01

Staid MFS Total Return Fund's time has arrived.

In the past, this fund has often looked a bit peaked relative to its MFS siblings, a family with a decided taste for growth. The offering has also occasionally dawdled compared with its more-aggressive rivals in the domestic-hybrid category. In 1999, for example, the fund returned a paltry 2.3%, lagging more than 80% of its rivals.

Lead manager David Calabro's conservative approach may have dragged on the fund's relative returns during growth rallies, but his moderate strategy has been a boon recently. While the fund's allocation mix—which hovers around 50% stocks and 35% bonds—looks a lot like the category average, its equity stake is quite modest, featuring old-time behemoths such as Freddie Mac and AT&T. Meanwhile, the fund has always eschewed the pricey, high-growth names that dropped sharply in 2000's sell-off, which means valuations tend to be considerably lower than group norms. Calabro runs a diverse portfolio, with more than 700 positions—three times the category average. In 2001's volatile market, this cautious positioning has helped the fund limit its losses. Though down more than 7% for the year to date through Sept. 26, 2001, it has outpaced more than two thirds of its peers.

Solid relative performance isn't unusual here. With few exceptions, the fund generally winds up in the top half of the category, and its long-term record outpaces more than 85% of its peers. What's more, it has been considerably less volatile than its rivals in the category. Finally, Calabro's willingness to overweight corporate bonds and lower credit quality issues in the fixed-income portfolio has made for a nice yield. Cautious investors interested in a little income would be well-served here.

Address:	P.O. Box 2281 Boston, MA 02107–9906 800–637–2929 / 617–954–5000
Web Address:	www.mfs.com
Inception:	10-06-70
Advisor:	MFS Inv. Mgmt.
Subadvisor:	None
NTF Plans:	Datalynx , Fidelity Inst.

Minimum Purchase:	$1000	Add: $50	IRA: $250
Min Auto Inv Plan:	$50	Add: $50	
Sales Fees:	4.75%L (W), 0.10%B, 0.25%S		
Management Fee:	.25% mx./.21% mn., .02%A		
Actual Fees:	Mgt: 0.35%	Dist: 0.35%	
Expense Projections:	3Yr: $748	5Yr: $950	10Yr: $1530
Avg Brok Commission:	—	Income Distrib: Monthly	
Total Cost (relative to category):		Average	

MFS Utilities A

Ticker	Load	NAV	Yield	Total Assets	Mstar Category
MMUFX	4.75%w	$8.72	2.4%	$2,047.6 mil	Spec Utilities

Prospectus Objective: Specialty—Utilities

MFS Utilities Fund seeks capital growth and current income.

The fund normally invests at least 65% of assets in equity and debt securities issued by domestic- and foreign-utility companies. It may invest the balance of assets in equity and debt securities of issuers in other industries. At least 80% of the debt securities held by the fund must be investment-grade. The fund typically does not invest more than 35% of assets in foreign securities; it may also invest in ADRs. This fund is non-diversified.

Class A shares have front loads; B shares have deferred loads, 12b-1 fees, and conversion features; C shares have level loads; I shares are for institutional investors.

Historical Profile
Return: Average
Risk: Below Avg
Rating: ★★★ Neutral

Investment Style
Equity
Average Stock %: 79% 79% 75% 82% 79% 76%

▼ Manager Change
▽ Partial Manager Change

Fund Performance vs. Category Average
■ Quarterly Fund Return +/– Category Average
— Category Baseline

Performance Quartile (within Category)

Portfolio Manager(s)

Maura A. Shaughnessy, CFA. Since 2-92. BS'83 Colby C.; MBA'87 Dartmouth C. Other funds currently managed: MFS Capital Opportunities A, MFS Capital Opportunities B, MFS Utilities C.

1990	1991	1992	1993	1994	1995	1996	1997	1998	1999	2000	12-01	History
—	—	6.81	7.54	6.84	8.48	8.98	9.99	10.81	12.76	11.87	8.72	NAV
—	—	11.79*	19.54	−5.34	32.48	20.06	31.55	17.79	31.79	7.10	−25.02	Total Return %
—	—	3.11*	9.48	−6.65	−5.06	−2.88	−1.80	−10.79	10.76	16.21	−13.14	+/– S&P 500
—	—	—	−0.22	−3.02	−7.56	−2.25	−3.94	−3.45	20.84	4.79	−16.23	+/– Russ Top 200 Val
—	—	3.39	5.53	4.07	4.64	4.31	3.52	2.98	2.29	3.95	1.75	Income Return %
—	—	8.40	14.00	−9.41	27.83	15.76	28.03	14.81	29.50	3.16	−26.77	Capital Return %
—	—	—	13	12	18	8	6	53	23	52	79	Total Rtn % Rank Cat
—	—	0.21	0.37	0.30	0.31	0.35	0.31	0.29	0.24	0.49	0.21	Income $
—	—	0.03	0.21	0.00	0.21	0.79	1.39	0.61	1.09	1.22	0.00	Capital Gains $
—	—	0.65	0.65	0.65	0.83	1.08	1.10	1.05	1.05	0.98	—	Expense Ratio %
—	—	5.44	4.57	4.58	4.30	4.37	3.27	2.60	1.88	4.11	—	Income Ratio %
—	—	—	119	115	152	137	153	124	137	113	—	Turnover Rate %
—	—	15.7	44.9	40.6	52.3	64.9	110.3	379.4	524.9	921.3	—	Net Assets $mil

Performance 12-31-01

	1st Qtr	2nd Qtr	3rd Qtr	4th Qtr	Total
1997	0.27	11.91	8.11	8.45	31.55
1998	11.28	−0.15	−3.61	9.98	17.79
1999	−0.62	10.73	−1.84	22.00	31.79
2000	10.91	−6.21	5.75	−2.63	7.10
2001	−5.23	−5.37	−17.19	0.97	−25.02

Trailing	Total Return%	+/– S&P 500	+/– Russ Top 200 Val	% Rank All	% Rank Cat	Growth of $10,000
3 Mo	0.97	−9.72	−4.55	73	27	10,097
6 Mo	−16.39	−10.83	−10.61	96	76	8,361
1 Yr	−25.02	−13.14	−16.23	88	79	7,498
3 Yr Avg	1.91	2.94	0.75	63	32	10,584
5 Yr Avg	10.40	−0.30	−0.81	17	24	16,400
10 Yr Avg	—	—	—	—	—	—
15 Yr Avg	—	—	—	—	—	—

Tax Analysis	Tax-Adj Ret%	%Rank Cat	%Pretax Ret	%Rank Cat
3 Yr Avg	−1.25	33	—	—
5 Yr Avg	6.51	39	62.6	71
10 Yr Avg	—	—	—	—

Potential Capital Gain Exposure: −32% of assets

Risk Analysis

Time Period	Load-Adj Return %	Risk %Rank¹ All	Risk %Rank¹ Cat	Morningstar Return	Morningstar Risk	Morningstar Risk-Adj Rating
1 Yr	−28.58					
3 Yr	0.27	52	29	−0.95²	0.73	★★★
5 Yr	9.33	50	26	1.02²	0.68	★★★
Incept	12.28	—	—	—	—	

Average Historical Rating (83 months): 3.9★s

¹1=low, 100=high ² T-Bill return substituted for category avg.

Category Rating (3 Yr)

1 2 3 4 5
Worst Best

Return: Average
Risk: Below Avg

Other Measures	Standard Index S&P 500	Best Fit Index Wil 4500
Alpha	0.8	−1.8
Beta	0.58	0.43
R-Squared	42	61
Standard Deviation		15.60
Mean		1.91
Sharpe Ratio		−0.23

Portfolio Analysis 10-31-01

Share chng since 09-01 Total Stocks: 65

	Subsector	PE	YTD Ret%	% Assets
⊖ El Paso	Utilities	NMF	−36.70	3.29
⊕ Williams Companies	Utilities	17.9	−29.10	2.65
⊖ FirstEnergy	Electric	12.8	16.42	2.38
☼ AT&T Wireless Grp	Services	—	−17.00	2.35
FNMA Debenture 6.625%	N/A	—	—	2.32
⊕ Keyspan	Energy	20.2	−14.10	2.25
⊖ Calpine	Utilities	8.9	−62.70	2.22
⊕ Dynegy	Energy	12.8	−54.20	2.20
⊖ Pinnacle West Cap	Electric	12.5	−9.06	2.20
Vodafone Airtouch	Wireless	—	—	2.18
⊕ Charter Comms	Services	—	−27.50	2.14
⊕ Qwest Comms Intl	Phone Equip.	—	−65.40	2.10
⊖ Entergy	Electric	11.7	−4.50	2.05
US Treasury Note 4.625%	N/A	—	—	1.99
Kinder Morgan LLC	Energy	—	—	1.96
⊕ TXU	Electric	13.7	12.17	1.73
Kinder Morgan	Energy	32.2	7.11	1.71
⊕ Telefonica ADR	Phone Services	22.4	−16.60	1.71
⊕ Viacom Cl B	Media	—	—	1.67
AT&T	Phone Services	7.8	40.59	1.64
⊕ Enron	Energy	1.6	−99.00	1.58
⊕ PPL	Electric	8.2	−20.90	1.53
⊖ NRG Energy	Utilities	—	−43.80	1.39
ADT Operations Cv 0%	N/A	—	—	1.38
⊕ AES	Electric	24.8	−70.40	1.37

Current Investment Style

Style: Value Blnd Growth; Size: Large Med Small

	Stock Port Avg	Relative S&P 500 Current	Relative S&P 500 Hist	Rel Cat
Price/Earnings Ratio	18.6	0.60	0.78	0.97
Price/Book Ratio	1.9	0.34	0.46	0.82
Price/Cash Flow	8.6	0.48	0.64	0.94
3 Yr Earnings Growth	21.5	1.47	0.63	1.36
1 Yr Earnings Est%	12.4	—	—	1.54
Med Mkt Cap $mil	8,422	0.1	0.2	0.69

Special Securities % assets 10-31-01	
Restricted/Illiquid Secs	2
Emerging-Markets Secs	3
Options/Futures/Warrants	No

Composition % assets 10-31-01	
Cash	6.2
Stocks*	75.0
Bonds	13.8
Other	5.0
*Foreign (% stocks)	16.1

Market Cap	
Giant	14.7
Large	33.6
Medium	44.2
Small	3.6
Micro	3.9

Subsector Weightings	% of Stocks	Rel Cat
Electric	26.7	0.6
Gas	2.5	0.7
Phone Services	10.2	0.5
Phone Equip.	3.0	1.8
Energy	8.6	1.7
Energy Services	0.0	0.0
Water	0.0	0.0
Other	49.0	1.8

Analysis by Catherine Hickey 12-12-01

Despite a tough year here, we still like a lot about this fund.

One of the more appealing things about MFS Utilities Fund is that it gives investors fairly broad exposure to the utilities arena. Manager Maura Shaughnessy spreads her bets among gas, water, and electric utilities, and telecom issues also take up a fair amount of assets. However, Shaughnessy isn't afraid to buy companies in sectors that sport fairly high growth rates. Indeed, the portfolio is populated by high-growth energy-related names, along with Qwest on the telecom front.

Unfortunately, many of these faster-growing utility issues have crashed in 2001. Consequently, the fund is posting a loss that lands in the category's bottom quartile through Dec. 11. Enron, for example, filed for bankruptcy protection recently amid questions about its accounting practices. Other independent power producers such as Dynegy and Calpine have been tarred with Enron's brush this year, as investors question whether those firms can sustain their strong growth rates.

Nevertheless, we think investors would do well to hang on here. Shaughnessy has built one of the strongest—and most consistent—records in the utilities category here. Because some utilities funds lean heavily toward either energy or telecom issues, they tend to have dramatic performance highs and lows. However, Shaughnessy spreads her bets across these areas, so the fund hasn't been overly volatile over time. A bond stake also provides cushion and helps bolster the fund's yield.

Super-conservative investors may prefer a more cautious fund, such as Vanguard Utilities Income. However, those who can tolerate a bit more risk would do well to give this fund a look.

Address:	P.O. Box 2281 Boston, MA 02107-9906 800-637-2929 / 617-954-5000
Web Address:	www.mfs.com
*Inception:	02-14-92
Advisor:	MFS Inv. Mgmt.
Subadvisor:	None
NTF Plans:	Datalynx , Fidelity Inst.

Minimum Purchase:	$1000	Add: $50	IRA: $250
Min Auto Inv Plan:	$50	Add: $50	
Sales Fees:	4.75%L (W), 0.10%B, 0.25%S		
Management Fee:	.38%, .02%A		
Actual Fees:	Mgt: 0.68%	Dist: 0.25%	
Expense Projections:	3Yr: $809	5Yr: $1066	10Yr: $1802
Avg Brok Commission:	—	Income Distrib: Monthly	
Total Cost (relative to category):	Below Avg		

Montgomery Short Duration Govt Bond R

Ticker	Load	NAV	Yield	SEC Yield	Total Assets	Mstar Category
MNSGX	None	$10.20	4.8%	4.59%	$360.8 mil	Short–Term Govt

Prospectus Objective: Government General

Montgomery Short Duration Government Bond Fund seeks total return consistent with capital preservation.

The fund normally invests at least 65% of assets in U.S. government obligations. These obligations may include U.S Treasury bills, notes, and bonds; GNMAs; Federal Home Loan Banks obligations; FNMAs; Student Loan Marketing Association obligations, etc. The average portfolio duration is equal to or less than that of three year Treasury notes. It may invest the balance of assets in commerical paper and high-quality debt.

Class R shares are no-loads; P shares have 12b-1 fees. The fund has gone through several name changes.

Historical Profile

Return: Above Avg
Risk: Low
Rating: ★★★★★ Highest

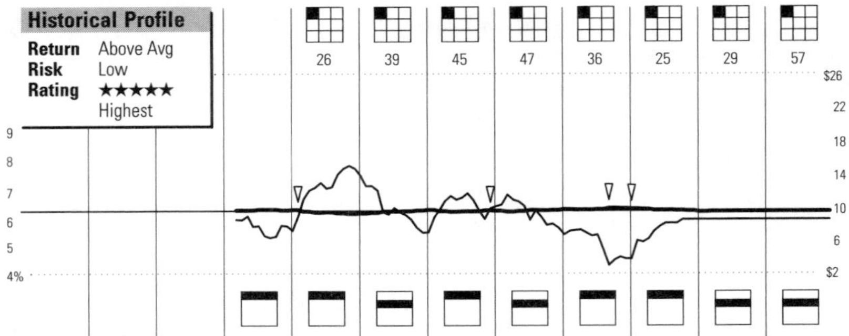

Investment Style
Fixed-Income

	1993	1994	1995	1996	1997	1998	1999	2000	12-01
Income Rtn %Rank Cat	26	39	45	47	36	25	29	57	

Growth of Principal vs. Interest Rate Shifts
— Principal Value $000 (NAV with capital gains reinvested)
— Interest Rate % on 10 Yr Treasury
▼ Manager Change
▽ Partial Manager Change
► Mgr Unknown After
◄ Mgr Unknown Before

Performance Quartile (within Category)

Portfolio Manager(s)

Marie Chandoha. Since 1-99. BA Harvard U. Other funds currently managed: Montgomery Balanced R, Montgomery Balanced P, Montgomery Short Duration Govt Bond P.

William C. Stevens. Since 12-92. BA Wesleyan U.; MBA Harvard U. Other funds currently managed: Montgomery CA Tax-Free Interm Bond R, Montgomery Balanced R, Montgomery Balanced P.

1990	1991	1992	1993	1994	1995	1996	1997	1998	1999	2000	12-01	History
—	—	10.02	10.10	9.63	10.08	10.00	10.10	10.21	9.91	10.09	10.20	NAV
—	—	0.43*	8.09	1.13	11.51	5.14	6.97	7.37	2.57	8.11	7.38	Total Return %
—	—	—	–1.66	4.05	–6.96	1.53	–2.72	–1.31	3.40	–3.53	–1.04	+/– LB Aggregate
—	—	—	2.68	0.63	1.55	–0.11	0.32	0.39	–0.39	–0.07	–1.15	+/– LB 1–3 Govt
—	—	0.23	6.63	5.90	6.59	5.92	5.92	5.72	5.58	6.19	5.03	Income Return %
—	—	0.20	1.46	–4.77	4.91	–0.77	1.05	1.64	–3.01	1.92	2.36	Capital Return %
—	—	—	12	9	44	17	28	17	24	42	35	Total Rtn % Rank Cat
—	—	0.02	0.64	0.58	0.62	0.58	0.58	0.56	0.56	0.60	0.50	Income $
—	—	0.00	0.07	0.00	0.01	0.00	0.00	0.05	0.00	0.00	0.13	Capital Gains $
—	—	—	0.22	0.71	1.38	1.55	0.60	0.28	0.62	0.63	0.60	Expense Ratio %
—	—	—	6.02	5.93	6.41	5.88	5.87	5.83	5.21	5.84	5.70	Income Ratio %
—	—	—	—	603	284	350	451	502	199	188	245	Turnover Rate %
—	—	—	24.0	19.0	17.9	39.0	53.4	134.2	165.4	198.0	355.6	Net Assets $mil

Performance 12-31-01

	1st Qtr	2nd Qtr	3rd Qtr	4th Qtr	Total
1997	0.45	2.40	2.14	1.81	6.97
1998	1.57	1.84	3.21	0.58	7.37
1999	0.62	0.35	1.01	0.57	2.57
2000	1.17	1.74	2.35	2.62	8.11
2001	2.69	1.14	3.50	–0.11	7.38

Trailing	Total Return%	+/– LB Agg	+/– LB 1–3 Yr Govt	% Rank All	% Rank Cat	Growth of $10,000
3 Mo	–0.11	–0.15	–0.89	80	64	9,989
6 Mo	3.38	–1.27	–0.93	13	68	10,338
1 Yr	7.38	–1.04	–1.15	12	35	10,738
3 Yr Avg	5.99	–0.28	–0.54	22	20	11,907
5 Yr Avg	6.46	–0.97	–0.18	42	16	13,675
10 Yr Avg	—	—	—	—	—	—
15 Yr Avg	—	—	—	—	—	—

Tax Analysis	Tax-Adj Ret%	%Rank Cat	%Pretax Ret	%Rank Cat
3 Yr Avg	3.58	32	59.8	62
5 Yr Avg	4.03	20	62.4	40
10 Yr Avg	—	—	—	—

Potential Capital Gain Exposure: 67% of assets

Risk Analysis

Time Period	Load-Adj Return %	Risk %Rank[1] All	Risk %Rank[1] Cat	Morningstar Return	Morningstar Risk	Morningstar Risk-Adj Rating
1 Yr	7.38					
3 Yr	5.99	3	32	0.22[2]	0.27	★★★★★
5 Yr	6.46	3	32	0.32[2]	0.28	★★★★★
Incept	6.45	—	—	—	—	

Average Historical Rating (73 months): 4.7★s

[1] 1=low, 100=high [2] T-Bill return substituted for category avg.

Category Rating (3 Yr)

1 Worst — 2 — 3 — 4 — 5 Best

Return: Above Avg
Risk: Below Avg

Other Measures	Standard Index LB Agg	Best Fit Index LB Int
Alpha	0.4	0.3
Beta	0.46	0.60
R-Squared	77	87

Standard Deviation	1.86
Mean	5.99
Sharpe Ratio	0.67

Portfolio Analysis 06-30-01

Total Fixed-Income: 119	Date of Maturity	Amount $000	Value $000	% Net Assets
US Treasury Note 4.25%	11-15-03	29,620	29,491	10.91
FNMA CMO N/A	12-25-20	22,933	23,161	8.57
Freddie Mac N/A	02-15-23	8,700	8,669	3.21
FNMA N/A	01-01-16	8,294	8,638	3.20
GNMA N/A	12-15-10	7,217	7,466	2.76
GNMA N/A	09-15-11	6,549	6,743	2.50
Premier Auto Tr 5.82%	10-08-03	6,225	6,319	2.34
FHLMC N/A	01-01-31	6,103	6,233	2.31
Citibank CC Master Tr 5.5%	02-15-06	6,026	6,076	2.25
FHLMC CMO N/A	04-15-08	5,717	5,766	2.13
Homeq N/A	04-15-19	4,675	4,701	1.74
Residential Asset CMO N/A	09-25-20	4,610	4,665	1.73
Onyx Accept Grantor Tr 7%	11-15-04	4,300	4,429	1.64
FNMA CMO N/A	04-25-07	4,144	4,136	1.53
FHLMC CMO TAC 10%	07-15-14	3,755	4,019	1.49
FNMA 6%	07-15-49	4,010	3,950	1.46
FNMA 8%	07-15-16	3,671	3,862	1.43
FNMA CMO N/A	09-25-05	3,596	3,676	1.36
Ford Credit Auto Tr 6.16%	08-15-03	3,600	3,665	1.36
GNMA 7%	12-15-08	3,300	3,398	1.26

Current Investment Style

Duration: Short Int Long — Quality: High Med Low

Avg Eff Duration[1]	1.7 Yrs
Avg Eff Maturity	4.2 Yrs
Avg Credit Quality	AAA
Avg Wtd Coupon	0.00%
Avg Wtd Price	101.46% of par

[1] figure provided by fund

Analysis by Eric Jacobson 10-30-01

Montgomery Short Duration Government Bond Fund is pretty close to a free lunch.

The idea behind this fund is to avoid taking on too much risk. As such, its interest-rate sensitivity is tied very closely to a short-term index. And while comanagers Marie Chandoha and William Stevens buy a fairly wide mix of securities, the pair stick to extremely high-quality sectors. The fund often holds collateralized mortgage obligations (CMOs) and asset-backed securities (ABS), for example, but will typically only buy their highest-quality tranches, and those that don't harbor major structural risks. (Their CMOs, for example, are all backed by government-linked mortgages.)

On the other hand, that mix of securities is the root of the fund's solid record of excess returns. By doing in-depth research to look for issues that appear cheap, and by rotating in and out of various sectors when they get particularly cheap or expensive, Chandoha and Stevens have been able to add incremental returns and pick up more income than would be available from a pure Treasury or government-security portfolio. During the first half of 2001, for example, the team boosted its ABS weighting to 21%, focusing mostly on the higher-quality credit-card and auto-backed subsectors. It then more than doubled the portfolio's stake in PAC CMOs (which have very predictable prepayment characteristics) to 33% by the end of the third quarter after the September attacks caused them to cheapen.

The main risk with a portfolio like this is that it could underperform more-conventional government-focused funds under some circumstances. Overall, however, the extra risk incurred by very-high-quality securities this portfolio holds is fairly small. We think this fund—which also sports a moderate expense ratio—makes a solid choice for the short-term portion of a portfolio.

Special Securities % assets 06-30-01	
Restricted/Illiquid Secs	0
Exotic Mortgage–Backed	0
Emerging–Markets Secs	0
Options/Futures/Warrants	No

Credit Analysis % bonds 09-30-01

US Govt	79	BB	0
AAA	21	B	0
AA	0	Below B	0
A	0	NR/NA	0
BBB	0		

Coupon Range	% of Bonds	Rel Cat
0%	0.00	0.00
0% to 7%	76.41	1.07
7% to 8.5%	14.88	0.74
8.5% to 10%	5.71	1.86
More than 10%	3.00	0.69

1.00=Category Average

Composition % assets 06-30-01

Cash	2.0	Bonds	98.0
Stocks	0.0	Other	0.0

Address:	101 California Street San Francisco, CA 94111 415–248–6000 / 800–572–3863
Web Address:	www.montgomeryfunds.com
*Inception:	12-18-92
Advisor:	Montgomery Asset Mgmt.
Subadvisor:	None
NTF Plans:	Fidelity , Datalynx

Minimum Purchase:	$1000	Add: $100	IRA: $1000
Min Auto Inv Plan:	$1000	Add: $100	
Sales Fees:	No–load		
Management Fee:	.50% mx./.40% mn.		
Actual Fees:	Mgt: 0.50%	Dist: —	
Expense Projections:	3Yr: $443	5Yr: $840	10Yr: $1948
Avg Brok Commission:	—	Income Distrib: Monthly	
Total Cost (relative to category):	—		

Morgan Stanley American Opp B

Ticker	Load	NAV	Yield	Total Assets	Mstar Category
AMOBX	5.00%d	$23.56	0.0%	$7,156.3 mil	Large Growth

Prospectus Objective: Growth

Morgan Stanley Dean Witter American Opportunities Fund seeks long-term capital growth consistent with low volatility.

The fund normally invests at least 65% of assets in common stocks. It may invest up to 35% in the following: foreign securities, companies in non-classified industries, convertibles, and debt.

Class A shares have front loads; B shares have deferred loads, higher 12b-1 fees, and conversion features; C shares have level loads; D shares are for institutional investors. The fund has gone through several name changes. On March 12, 1999, MSDW Capital Appreciation Fund merged into the fund.

Historical Profile

Return Average
Risk Above Avg
Rating ★★★ Neutral

Investment Style
Equity
Average Stock %: 82% 99% 96% 88% 85% 89% 74%

▼ Manager Change
▽ Partial Manager Change

Fund Performance vs. Category Average
■ Quarterly Fund Return +/– Category Average
— Category Baseline

Performance Quartile (within Category)

Portfolio Manager(s)

Anita Kolleeny. Since 4-87. BA U. of Texas; MBA New York U. Other funds currently managed: Morgan Stanley American Opp A, Morgan Stanley American Opp C, Morgan Stanley American Opp D.

1990	1991	1992	1993	1994	1995	1996	1997	1998	1999	2000	12-01	History
14.39	20.66	20.93	23.10	21.21	27.16	27.01	29.51	32.85	42.63	32.94	23.56	NAV
–0.90	56.26	3.84	18.70	–6.75	42.20	10.53	31.55	31.07	46.12	–9.94	–27.30	Total Return %
2.22	25.77	–3.78	8.65	–8.06	4.67	–12.41	–1.81	2.50	25.08	–0.83	–15.43	+/– S&P 500
–2.27	16.85	–0.05	18.78	–11.60	3.55	–14.99	–2.20	–14.03	16.44	14.59	–6.80	+/– Russ Top 200 Grt
1.90	0.21	0.14	0.04	0.00	0.01	0.04	0.00	0.00	0.00	0.00	0.00	Income Return %
–2.80	56.05	3.70	18.67	–6.75	42.19	10.49	31.55	31.07	46.12	–9.93	–27.30	Capital Return %
38	24	72	16	88	9	94	21	53	31	29	69	Total Rtn % Rank Cat
0.28	0.03	0.03	0.01	0.00	0.00	0.01	0.00	0.00	0.00	0.00	0.00	Income $
0.00	1.65	0.44	1.67	0.32	2.93	2.92	5.74	5.29	4.71	5.34	0.42	Capital Gains $
1.70	1.58	1.72	1.61	1.71	1.61	1.53	1.46	1.39	1.33	1.28	—	Expense Ratio %
1.67	0.29	0.18	–0.59	0.01	0.06	–0.33	–0.34	–0.10	–0.24	–0.11	—	Income Ratio %
234	264	305	276	295	256	279	275	321	378	425	—	Turnover Rate %
89.2	220.0	458.1	1,216.8	1,490.1	2,383.2	3,099.5	4,076.5	5,748.7	10,385.3	10,153.9	6,197.5	Net Assets $mil

Performance 12-31-01

	1st Qtr	2nd Qtr	3rd Qtr	4th Qtr	Total
1997	–0.89	13.95	16.12	0.31	31.55
1998	13.15	5.93	–7.26	17.92	31.07
1999	8.74	2.96	–3.28	34.93	46.12
2000	1.60	–5.96	7.33	–12.17	–9.94
2001	–20.28	–1.03	–12.67	5.51	–27.30

Trailing	Total Return%	+/– S&P 500	+/– Russ Top 200 Grth	% Rank All	% Rank Cat	Growth of $10,000
3 Mo	5.51	–5.18	–7.35	63	98	10,551
6 Mo	–7.86	–2.31	–0.87	77	40	9,214
1 Yr	–27.30	–15.43	–6.80	91	69	7,270
3 Yr Avg	–1.46	–0.44	6.56	80	40	9,567
5 Yr Avg	10.53	–0.17	1.94	16	31	16,496
10 Yr Avg	11.54	–1.39	0.46	22	27	29,802
15 Yr Avg	13.40	–0.33	0.03	15	27	65,961

Tax Analysis	Tax-Adj Ret%	%Rank Cat	%Pretax Ret	%Rank Cat
3 Yr Avg	–4.36	52	—	—
5 Yr Avg	6.21	52	59.0	82
10 Yr Avg	8.13	48	70.5	71

Potential Capital Gain Exposure: –31% of assets

Risk Analysis

Time Period	Load-Adj Return %	Risk %Rank[1] All	Risk %Rank[1] Cat	Morningstar Return	Morningstar Risk	Morningstar Risk-Adj Rating
1 Yr	–30.16					
3 Yr	–1.96	79	27	–1.37[2]	1.14	★★
5 Yr	10.41	77	21	1.30[2]	1.05	★★★
10 Yr	11.54	84	36	1.01	1.17	★★★

Average Historical Rating (193 months): 3.5★s

[1] 1=low, 100=high [2] T-Bill return substituted for category avg.

Category Rating (3 Yr)

Worst 1 2 **3** 4 5 Best

Return: Average
Risk: Below Avg

Other Measures	Standard Index S&P 500	Best Fit Index Wil 4500
Alpha	–0.6	–3.9
Beta	0.74	0.64
R-Squared	31	64
Standard Deviation		22.64
Mean		–1.46
Sharpe Ratio		–0.33

Portfolio Analysis 09-30-01

Share change since 06-01 Total Stocks: 116	Sector	PE	YTD Ret%	% Assets
US Treasury Bond 6.125%	N/A	—	—	3.56
⊕ Wal-Mart Stores	Retail	40.3	8.94	2.40
US Treasury Bond 3.875%	N/A	—	—	2.26
⊕ Pfizer	Health	34.7	–12.40	2.22
⊕ American Home Products	Health	—	–1.91	2.17
US Treasury Note 5%	N/A	—	—	2.14
⊖ Microsoft	Technology	57.6	52.78	2.13
⊕ Tenet Healthcare	Health	30.1	32.14	1.95
⊖ Baxter Intl	Health	33.9	22.84	1.88
Fifth Third Bancorp	Financials	38.3	4.53	1.78
US Treasury Bond 5.25%	N/A	—	—	1.67
⊕ HCA – The Healthcare Company	Health	24.1	–12.20	1.47
⊖ Freddie Mac	Financials	14.0	–3.87	1.46
⊕ PepsiCo	Staples	31.4	–0.54	1.43
⊕ Anheuser-Busch	Staples	24.6	1.01	1.41
⊖ Fannie Mae	Financials	16.2	–6.95	1.33
⊕ Abbott Labs	Health	51.6	17.08	1.33
☼ Sprint (PCS Group)	Services	—	19.43	1.28
⊕ General Dynamics	Industrials	17.6	3.63	1.19
⊕ Amgen	Health	52.8	–11.70	1.18
⊕ Lockheed Martin	Industrials	36.8	38.98	1.17
⊖ Citigroup	Financials	20.0	0.03	1.16
Cardinal Health	Health	35.1	–2.51	1.12
☼ SBC Comms	Services	18.4	–16.00	1.11
⊕ McDonald's	Services	19.2	–21.50	1.01

Current Investment Style

Style: Value Blnd Growth; Size: Large Med Small

	Stock Port Avg	Relative S&P 500 Current	Relative S&P 500 Hist	Rel Cat
Price/Earnings Ratio	34.3	1.11	1.21	0.96
Price/Book Ratio	7.7	1.35	1.26	1.20
Price/Cash Flow	22.2	1.23	1.24	0.98
3 Yr Earnings Growth	16.7	1.14	1.12	0.77
1 Yr Earnings Est%	12.3	—	—	4.11
Med Mkt Cap $mil	34,734	0.6	0.6	0.73

Special Securities % assets 09-30-01	
Restricted/Illiquid Secs	0
Emerging-Markets Secs	1
Options/Futures/Warrants	No

Composition % assets 09-30-01	
Cash	21.4
Stocks*	69.0
Bonds	9.6
Other	0.0
*Foreign (% stocks)	4.0

Market Cap	
Giant	41.5
Large	47.2
Medium	11.4
Small	0.0
Micro	0.0

Sector Weightings	% of Stocks	Rel S&P	5-Year High	5-Year Low
Utilities	0.0	0.0	6	0
Energy	2.2	0.3	11	0
Financials	15.1	0.8	28	2
Industrials	6.1	0.5	20	0
Durables	0.7	0.4	13	0
Staples	11.2	1.4	15	0
Services	13.5	1.2	31	3
Retail	5.9	0.9	22	1
Health	33.2	2.2	36	4
Technology	12.2	0.7	43	5

Analysis by Alan Papier 11-13-01

Morgan Stanley American Opportunities Fund can take shareholders on a wild ride.

Manager Anita Kolleeny uses a top-down approach to tilt the portfolio toward specific industries. And she isn't shy about boldly backing up her conviction, so the fund is left vulnerable when her forecasts are wide of the mark. For example, the fund's health-care stake recently consumed one third of its assets, so it could struggle if such stocks—especially pharmaceutical makers and facilities operators—hit the skids.

To be sure, some of the fund's bets have held it back in 2001. It lost 28.4% for the year to date through Nov. 12, which trailed more than 60% of its large-growth peers. The fund was positioned defensively coming into the year—a tactic that helped limit losses in 2000—but it hasn't been able to make up the ground it lost in January and April, when technology stocks staged brief rallies. (The portfolio has been considerably underweight in that sector relative to its peers since late last year.) The fund was also hamstrung by its exposure to financials, which centered on insurance companies. Allstate had been among the fund's top holdings throughout the first half of the year, for instance, but the position was sold after the stock plummeted during the third quarter.

That said, the fund has adequately compensated investors for its inherent risks, and Kolleeny has proven able to execute her strategy over time. The fund's trailing 10-year return ranks in the category's top quartile, and its volatility is below average.

Investors who believe in the potential of active management should find this fund appealing. Unlike many large-cap-oriented offerings, this one isn't worried about hewing close to a benchmark. But it is best suited for a tax-sheltered account, as the fund's frequent repositionings and subsequent high turnover often lead to sizable capital-gains distributions.

Address:	P.O. Box 2798 Boston, MA 02208-2798 800-869-6397 / 212-392-2550
Web Address:	www.deanwitter.com
Inception:	03-27-80
Advisor:	Morgan Stanley Dean Witter Adv.
Subadvisor:	None
NTF Plans:	N/A

Minimum Purchase:	$1000	Add: $100	IRA: $1000
Min Auto Inv Plan:	$1000	Add: $100	
Sales Fees:	5.00%D, 0.75%B, 0.25%S Conv. in 10 Yrs.		
Management Fee:	.63% mx./.43% mn.		
Actual Fees:	Mgt: 0.45%	Dist: 0.73%	
Expense Projections:	3Yr: $740	5Yr: $902	10Yr: $1545
Avg Brok Commission:	—	Income Distrib: Semi-Ann.	
Total Cost (relative to category):	Below Avg		

Morgan Stan Inst High–Yield Invmt

Ticker	Load	NAV	Yield	SEC Yield	Total Assets	Mstar Category
MPHIX	None	$5.64	13.7%	—	$655.0 mil	High–Yield Bond

Prospectus Objective: Corp Bond—High Yield

Morgan Stanley Institutional High-Yield Invmt Fund seeks above-average total return over a market cycle of three to five years, consistent with reasonable risk.

The fund normally invests at least 65% of assets in high-yielding corporate fixed-income securities. These may include bonds, preferred stocks, and convertibles rated BB through D. The average- weighted maturity typically exceeds five years.

The fund is designed for institutional investors.

Prior to Dec. 23, 1994, the fund went through several name changes.

Historical Profile

Return: Below Avg
Risk: High
Rating: ★ Lowest

Investment Style
Fixed-Income

Income Rtn %Rank Cat: 67 (1997), 70 (1998), 36 (1999), 6 (2000), 19 (12-01)

Growth of Principal vs. Interest Rate Shifts
— Principal Value $000 (NAV with capital gains reinvested)
— Interest Rate % on 10 Yr Treasury
▼ Manager Change
▽ Partial Manager Change
► Mgr Unknown After
◄ Mgr Unknown Before

Performance Quartile (within Category)

Portfolio Manager(s)

Robert E. Angevine. Since 12-96.
Stephen F. Esser, CFA. Since 1-97.
Gordon W. Loery. Since 4-99.
Deanna L. Loughnane. Since 2-00.

1990	1991	1992	1993	1994	1995	1996	1997	1998	1999	2000	12-01	History
—	—	—	—	—	—	9.21	9.57	8.87	8.69	6.81	5.64	NAV
—	—	—	—	—	—	9.88*	15.73	2.94	7.73	–10.66	–5.91	Total Return %
—	—	—	—	—	—	—	6.05	–5.74	8.56	–22.29	–14.33	+/– LB Aggregate
—	—	—	—	—	—	—	3.11	2.36	4.45	–5.45	–11.68	+/– FB High–Yield
—	—	—	—	—	—	8.22	8.85	8.40	9.89	12.14	11.92	Income Return %
—	—	—	—	—	—	1.66	6.88	–5.47	–2.16	–22.80	–17.82	Capital Return %
—	—	—	—	—	—	—	11	24	20	76	93	Total Rtn % Rank Cat
—	—	—	—	—	—	0.71	0.79	0.78	0.85	1.01	0.78	Income $
—	—	—	—	—	—	0.00	0.26	0.19	0.00	0.00	0.00	Capital Gains $
—	—	—	—	—	—	0.61	0.69	0.63	0.64	0.70	—	Expense Ratio %
—	—	—	—	—	—	11.06	8.84	8.58	9.50	10.43	—	Income Ratio %
—	—	—	—	—	—	—	96	75	45	55	—	Turnover Rate %
—	—	—	—	—	—	7.5	10.7	9.4	7.6	9.2	—	Net Assets $mil

Performance 12-31-01

	1st Qtr	2nd Qtr	3rd Qtr	4th Qtr	Total
1997	0.76	7.48	6.02	0.80	15.73
1998	4.60	–0.11	–6.35	5.20	2.94
1999	3.49	0.40	–0.58	4.29	7.73
2000	–1.04	–0.78	–2.73	–6.46	–10.66
2001	3.23	–4.74	–9.14	5.31	–5.91

Trailing	Total Return%	+/– LB Agg	+/– FB High–Yield	% Rank All	% Rank Cat	Growth of $10,000
3 Mo	5.31	5.27	–0.34	64	58	10,531
6 Mo	–4.31	–8.97	–5.75	58	93	9,569
1 Yr	–5.91	–14.33	–11.68	53	93	9,409
3 Yr Avg	–3.25	–9.52	–4.42	87	80	9,057
5 Yr Avg	1.53	–5.90	–1.71	89	52	10,789
10 Yr Avg	—	—	—	—	—	—
15 Yr Avg	—	—	—	—	—	—

Tax Analysis	Tax-Adj Ret%	%Rank Cat	%Pretax Ret	%Rank Cat
3 Yr Avg	–7.60	84	—	—
5 Yr Avg	–2.73	59	—	—
10 Yr Avg	—	—	—	—

Potential Capital Gain Exposure: –46% of assets

Risk Analysis

Time Period	Load-Adj Return %	Risk %Rank[1] All	Risk %Rank[1] Cat	Morningstar Return	Morningstar Risk	Morningstar Risk-Adj Rating
1 Yr	–5.91					
3 Yr	–3.25	42	80	–1.61[2]	2.52	★
5 Yr	1.53	43	72	–0.72[2]	2.40	★
Incept	3.08	—	—	—	—	

Average Historical Rating (32 months): 2.5★s

[1] 1=low, 100=high [2] T-Bill return substituted for category avg.

Category Rating (3 Yr)

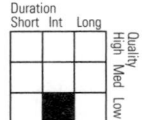

(1) (2) (3) (4) (5) — Worst … Best

Return: Below Avg
Risk: Above Avg

Other Measures	Standard Index LB Agg	Best Fit Index FB HY
Alpha	–7.6	–2.8
Beta	0.22	1.38
R–Squared	0	91

Standard Deviation	10.39
Mean	–3.25
Sharpe Ratio	–0.92

Analysis by Alan Papier 01-09-02 This analysis was written for another institutional share class.

Morgan Stanley Institutional High–Yield Fund's recent slide is a concern, but we don't think shareholders should bail out now.

This fund suffered its worst relative showing ever in 2001. Its loss of 5.8% for the year ranked in the bottom decile of the high–yield bond category. Meanwhile, its average peer eked out a 1.5% gain.

Management's willingness to load up in specific sectors was the source of its trouble. The fund has been heavy on telecom bonds for much of its life. But as the economy weakened, spending on telecommunications gear and infrastructure slowed dramatically, putting pressure on those companies' abilities to repay their debts. As a result, funds with outsized exposure to the sector struggled.

The fund's aggressive tendencies have served it well over time, however. Not only is lead manager Stephen Esser willing to sock away assets in his team's favorite sectors, but unlike many of his peers, the fund also invests in foreign and emerging–market bonds. (Management hedges all such holdings, though, to avoid foreign–currency risk.) The fund's telecom stake gave it a lift in 1998 and 1999, while its above–average emerging–markets exposure was a boon in 1996 and 1999. The fund's 10–year return through December 31, 2001, ranked in the top quartile of the category.

Despite those compelling results, the fund isn't a good choice for relatively conservative investors seeking broad high–yield exposure. Esser doesn't hesitate to focus on specific sectors or buy risky foreign securities, so the fund can take shareholders on a wild ride at times. In fact, the fund has been among the most volatile in the group.

That said, we think income–seeking investors or more–aggressive types looking for a long–term high–yield allocation will be fine here.

Address:	P.O. Box 2798 Boston, MA 02208–2798 800–548–7786 / 800–548–7786
Web Address:	www.morganstanley.com/im
*Inception:	05-21-96
Advisor:	Miller Anderson & Sherrerd
Subadvisor:	None
NTF Plans:	N/A

Minimum Purchase:	$1000000	Add: $1000 IRA: —
Min Auto Inv Plan:	—	Add: —
Sales Fees:	No–load	
Management Fee:	.38%, .08%A	
Actual Fees:	Mgt: 0.38%	Dist: —
Expense Projections:	3Yr: $16*	5Yr: $28* 10Yr: $63*
Avg Brok Commission:	—	Income Distrib: Quarterly
Total Cost (relative to category):	—	

Portfolio Analysis 03-31-01

Total Fixed-Income: 183	Date of Maturity	Amount $000	Value $000	% Net Assets
US Treasury Note (Fut)		0	33,985	3.50
United Kingdom (Fut)		0	21,366	2.20
Tenet Healthcare 8.125%	12-01-08	14,540	14,940	1.54
Musicland Grp 9.875%	03-15-08	13,950	14,578	1.50
Charter Comm 10.25%	01-15-10	13,245	13,775	1.42
Adelphia Comm 7.75%	01-15-09	15,000	13,688	1.41
Harrahs Operating 144A 8%	02-01-11	12,765	13,067	1.35
Broadwing Cmnty Cl B		13	12,802	1.32
Owens–Illinois 7.5%	05-15-10	17,500	12,775	1.32
Smithfield Foods 7.625%	02-15-08	13,000	12,675	1.31
Global Crossing 144A 8.7%	08-01-07	13,770	12,600	1.30
Dobson Comm PIK 13%		129	12,264	1.26
Husky Oil 8.9%	08-15-28	11,905	12,262	1.26
NTL Step 0%	04-01-08	14,645	12,054	1.24
Pacifica Papers 10%	03-15-09	10,890	11,598	1.20
Horseshoe Gaming 8.625%	05-15-09	11,520	11,434	1.18
Allied Waste Inds 144A 8.875%	04-01-08	10,750	11,019	1.14
GS Escrow 7.125%	08-01-05	11,050	10,811	1.11
Telewest Step 0%	04-15-09	13,730	10,619	1.09
Metromedia Fiber 10%	12-15-09	12,410	10,300	1.06

Current Investment Style

Duration: Short Int Long — Quality: High Med Low

Avg Eff Duration[1]	4.1 Yrs
Avg Eff Maturity	7.0 Yrs
Avg Credit Quality	BB
Avg Wtd Coupon	8.38%
Avg Wtd Price	87.33% of par

[1] figure provided by fund

Special Securities % assets 03-31-01	
Restricted/Illiquid Secs	14
Exotic Mortgage–Backed	Trace
Emerging–Markets Secs	4
Options/Futures/Warrants	Yes

Coupon Range	% of Bonds	Rel Cat
0%, PIK	10.84	1.73
0% to 9%	46.79	1.54
9% to 12%	32.20	0.60
12% to 14%	7.02	0.80
More than 14%	3.14	2.26

1.00=Category Average

Credit Analysis % bonds 09-30-01			
US Govt	11	BB	31
AAA	0	B	38
AA	0	Below B	7
A	0	NR/NA	2
BBB	11		

Composition % assets 03-31-01			
Cash	3.6	Bonds	86.6
Stocks	0.2	Other	9.6

Sector Breakdown % bonds 03-31-01			
US Treasuries	0	CMOs	0
GNMA mtgs	1	ARMs	0
FNMA mtgs	0	Other	95
FHLMC mtgs	0		

Morgan Stan Inst International Eq A

Ticker	Load	NAV	Yield	Total Assets	Mstar Category
MSIQX	Closed	$15.59	2.1%	$4,543.4 mil	Foreign Stock

Prospectus Objective: Foreign Stock

Morgan Stanley Institutional International Equity Portfolio seeks long-term capital appreciation.

The fund normally invests at least 65% of assets in non-U.S. equities. The advisor selects stocks it judges to be undervalued relative to the issuer's assets, cash flow, earnings, and revenues. Using a dividend-discount model, it then evaluates the future value of these stocks. Holdings are regularly reviewed and are subjected to fundamental analysis. The fund diversifies among many countries to reduce currency risk.

Shares are for institutions. Past fund names: Morgan Stanley Institutional International Equity Portfolio and Morgan Stanley Dean Witter Institutional International Equity Fund.

Historical Profile
Return: High
Risk: Low
Rating: ★★★★★ Highest

Investment Style — Equity — Average Stock %

1994	1995	1996	1997	1998	1999	2000	12-01
∇						∇	
	89%	91%	86%	91%	92%	95%	94%

▼ Manager Change
∇ Partial Manager Change

Fund Performance vs. Category Average
■ Quarterly Fund Return +/– Category Average
— Category Baseline

Performance Quartile (within Category)

Portfolio Manager(s)

Dominic Caldecott. Since 8-89.
Peter Wright. Since 7-00.
William Lock. Since 7-00.
Walter Riddell. Since 7-00.

History	1990	1991	1992	1993	1994	1995	1996	1997	1998	1999	2000	12-01
NAV	9.64	10.28	9.98	14.10	15.34	15.14	16.94	17.16	18.25	19.63	17.88	15.59
Total Return %	–5.73	8.92	–2.92	46.60	12.31	11.69	19.65	13.98	18.30	16.97	9.23	–9.74
+/– S&P 500	–2.61	–21.56	–10.54	36.55	11.00	–25.84	–3.30	–19.37	–10.28	–4.07	18.34	2.13
+/– MSCI EAFE	17.72	–3.21	9.26	14.04	4.54	0.49	13.60	12.20	–1.70	–9.99	23.40	—
Income Return %	1.43	1.76	0.00	1.38	1.26	0.42	2.37	2.84	2.19	1.00	0.19	1.89
Capital Return %	–7.16	7.16	–2.92	45.22	11.05	11.27	17.27	11.15	16.11	15.97	9.04	–11.63
Total Rtn % Rank Cat	17	78	40	15	1	34	17	15	24	96	2	5
Income $	0.15	0.17	0.00	0.14	0.18	0.06	0.36	0.48	0.38	0.18	0.04	0.34
Capital Gains $	0.08	0.05	0.00	0.27	0.27	1.84	0.80	1.62	1.66	1.49	3.39	0.20
Expense Ratio %	1.03	1.00	1.00	1.00	1.00	1.00	1.00	1.00	1.00	1.00	1.00	—
Income Ratio %	3.51	2.27	1.46	1.25	1.12	1.38	1.64	1.49	1.33	1.28	1.45	—
Turnover Rate %	38	22	12	23	16	27	18	33	33	37	53	—
Net Assets $mil	114.9	316.1	510.7	948.9	1,304.8	1,587.9	2,248.7	2,796.6	3,395.6	4,633.6	4,779.3	4,502.9

Performance 12-31-01

	1st Qtr	2nd Qtr	3rd Qtr	4th Qtr	Total
1997	4.55	10.56	3.63	–4.84	13.98
1998	16.49	1.45	–12.92	14.95	18.30
1999	1.26	5.41	3.25	6.13	16.97
2000	–0.15	8.11	–5.62	7.21	9.23
2001	–10.07	2.80	–7.50	5.54	–9.74

Trailing	Total Return%	+/– S&P 500	+/– MSCI EAFE	% Rank All	% Rank Cat	Growth of $10,000
3 Mo	5.54	–5.14	—	63	80	10,554
6 Mo	–2.37	3.18	—	49	3	9,763
1 Yr	–9.74	2.13	—	60	5	9,026
3 Yr Avg	4.87	5.89	—	32	13	11,532
5 Yr Avg	9.23	–1.47	—	23	8	15,549
10 Yr Avg	12.76	–0.17	—	14	1	33,217
15 Yr Avg	—	—	—	—	—	—

Tax Analysis	Tax-Adj Ret%	%Rank Cat	%Pretax Ret	%Rank Cat
3 Yr Avg	2.35	15	48.4	79
5 Yr Avg	6.45	10	69.9	36
10 Yr Avg	10.44	2	81.9	20

Potential Capital Gain Exposure: –3% of assets

Risk Analysis

Time Period	Load-Adj Return %	Risk %Rank[1] All	Risk %Rank[1] Cat	Morningstar Return	Morningstar Risk	Morningstar Risk-Adj Rating
1 Yr	–9.74					
3 Yr	4.87	41	1	–0.02[2]	0.51	★★★★
5 Yr	9.23	46	1	0.99[2]	0.50	★★★★★
10 Yr	12.76	57	1	2.95[2]	0.58	★★★★★

Average Historical Rating (113 months): 4.4★s

[1]1=low, 100=high [2] T-Bill return substituted for category avg.

Category Rating (3 Yr)

1 Worst — 2 — 3 — 4 — 5 Best

Return: Above Avg
Risk: Low

Other Measures	Standard Index S&P 500	Best Fit Index MSCIWdxUSN
Alpha	2.8	6.0
Beta	0.48	0.63
R-Squared	46	68

Standard Deviation	12.46
Mean	4.87
Sharpe Ratio	–0.01

Portfolio Analysis 06-30-01

Share change since 05-01 Total Stocks: 110	Sector	Country	% Assets
⊕ Nestle (Reg)	Staples	Switzerland	2.85
⊕ Cadbury Schweppes	Staples	United Kingdom	2.84
⊕ Royal Dutch Petro	Energy	Netherlands	2.56
⊖ Aventis Cl A	Health	France	2.21
⊕ Sankyo	Health	Japan	2.03
⊕ Nippon Telegraph & Tele	Services	Japan	1.92
Imperial Tobacco Grp	Staples	United Kingdom	1.84
⊕ Allied Domecq	Staples	United Kingdom	1.83
⊕ Diageo	Staples	United Kingdom	1.72
Canon	Industrials	Japan	1.61
Groupe Danone	Staples	France	1.60
⊕ Vodafone Airtouch	Services	United Kingdom	1.57
⊕ Yamanouchi Pharma	Health	Japan	1.52
⊕ Lloyds TSB Grp	Financials	United Kingdom	1.51
⊕ Muenchener Rueckvers (Reg)	Financials	Germany	1.47
⊕ Rentokil Initial	Services	United Kingdom	1.42
J Sainsbury	Retail	United Kingdom	1.40
⊕ BAE Sys	Technology	United Kingdom	1.39
⊕ CLP Hldgs	Utilities	Hong Kong	1.37
⊕ Daiwa Secs Grp	Financials	Japan	1.30

Analysis by Gabriel Presler 08-09-01

Morgan Stanley Institutional International Equity's record shows that managers don't need a lot of frills to excel in foreign markets.

Global volatility may come and go, but manager Dominic Caldecott is betting that people won't ever abandon the staples. Thus, he tends to stock up on consumer-related firms, such as Nestle and Imperial Tobacco. In fact, the portfolio's 19% stake in staples firm is significantly greater than the foreign-stock category average.

Substantial sector bets like these aren't unusual here. Under Caldecott's watch, the fund has been a bit of a maverick relative to its value-oriented peers. Caldecott has underweighted the traditional value fare that his rivals favor, for example, avoiding the housing, auto, and financials sectors. Meanwhile, he has built the fund's exposure to the Japanese market, which many of his peers eschew. He likes the country's health-care firms, which have lower valuations than their global counterparts. What's more, he's optimistic about the industry's pipeline growth. Most of the fund's unusual positioning has helped performance in 2001. Tobacco firms propped up results, and although the fund has lost 10% of its value in 2001, it has done better than 90% of its peers, including its average value-oriented rival.

The fund won't always shine during growth rallies—its relative performance in 1999, for example, was pretty miserable—but admirable performance is hardly new here. In fact, the fund's unusual approach has made for a top-quintile five-year record while providing one of the least-volatile rides in the category. It's one of the best options in the foreign-stock group.

Current Investment Style

Style: Value Blnd Growth; Size: Large Med Small

	Stock Port Avg	Rel MSCI EAFE Current	Rel MSCI EAFE Hist	Rel Cat
Price/Earnings Ratio	22.8	0.88	0.82	0.89
Price/Cash Flow	12.1	0.94	0.80	0.84
Price/Book Ratio	3.0	0.87	0.73	0.77
3 Yr Earnings Growth	13.7	0.73	0.63	0.69
Med Mkt Cap $mil	12,360	0.4	0.4	0.69

Country Exposure 06-30-01	% assets
United Kingdom	32
Japan	22
Netherlands	8
France	7
Switzerland	6

Hedging History: Rare

Regional Exposure 06-30-01	% assets
Europe	64
Japan	22
Latin America	0
Pacific Rim	7
Other	2

Special Securities % assets 06-30-01	
Restricted/Illiquid Secs	1
Emerging-Markets Secs	4
Options/Futures/Warrants	No

Composition % assets 06-30-01			
Cash	4.5	Bonds	0.0
Stocks	94.7	Other	0.8

Sector Weightings	% of Stocks	Rel Cat	5-Year High	5-Year Low
Utilities	5.1	1.8	8	0
Energy	6.4	1.1	9	1
Financials	17.7	0.8	24	13
Industrials	14.7	1.1	33	15
Durables	4.3	0.6	17	4
Staples	21.1	3.0	21	0
Services	12.7	0.7	19	5
Retail	3.9	0.8	13	2
Health	10.6	1.1	11	3
Technology	3.6	0.4	13	1

Address:	P.O. Box 2798 Boston, MA 02208–2798 800–548–7786
Web Address:	www.morganstanley.com/im
Inception:	08-04-89
Advisor:	Morgan Stanley Dean Witter Asset Mgmt
Subadvisor:	None
NTF Plans:	N/A

Minimum Purchase:	Closed	Add: $1000 IRA: —
Min Auto Inv Plan:	—	Add: —
Sales Fees:	No-load	
Management Fee:	.80%, .15%A	
Actual Fees:	Mgt: 0.80%	Dist: —
Expense Projections:	3Yr: $318	5Yr: $552 10Yr: $1225
Avg Brok Commission:	—	Income Distrib: Annually
Total Cost (relative to category):	Below Avg	

Morgan Stan Inst Mid Cap Growth

Ticker	Load	NAV	Yield	Total Assets	Mstar Category
MPEGX	None	$17.45	0.0%	$1,847.7 mil	Mid-Cap Growth

Prospectus Objective: Growth

Morgan Stanley Institutional Mid Cap Growth Portfolio seeks long-term capital growth.

The fund invests primarily in common stocks issued by companies with market capitalizations between $500 million and $6 billion. The advisor selects stocks that it judges to be a growth-oriented investment. The fund may invest in convertible securities at favorable prices relative to common stock.

The fund is available to institutional investors. The fund has gone through several name changes.

Historical Profile
Return: Above Avg
Risk: High
Rating: ★★★ Neutral

Investment Style
Equity
Average Stock %: 100% (1991), 94% (1993), 93% (1994), 95% (1995), 95% (1996), 96% (1997), 96% (1998)

▼ Manager Change
▽ Partial Manager Change

Fund Performance vs. Category Average
■ Quarterly Fund Return +/– Category Average
— Category Baseline

Performance Quartile (within Category)

Portfolio Manager(s)

Arden C. Armstrong, CFA. Since 3-90. BA'82 Brown U.; MBA'86 U. of Pennsylvania. Other funds currently managed: Morgan Stanley Developing Gr Secs B, Morgan Stanley Inst Equity, Morgan Stanley Inst Mid Cap Growth Ad.

David Pao-Kang Chu, CFA. Since 3-98. BS'82 U. of Michigan; MBA'86 U. of Pennsylvania-Wharton. Other funds currently managed: Morgan Stanley Inst Mid Cap Growth Ad, Morgan Stanley Inst Sm Cap Growth, Van Kampen Mid Cap Growth A.

Steve Chulik. Since 6-99. BS Columbia U.; MBA'97 U. of Pennsylvania, Wharton. Other funds currently managed: Morgan Stanley Inst Mid Cap Growth Ad, Morgan Stanley Inst Sm Cap Growth, Van Kampen Mid Cap Growth A.

History

1990	1991	1992	1993	1994	1995	1996	1997	1998	1999	2000	12-01	History
10.94	16.49	16.20	17.38	14.38	16.79	16.57	18.44	21.34	31.26	24.79	17.45	NAV
9.68*	59.51	2.87	18.23	–5.39	36.25	18.79	33.14	37.36	68.18	–7.34	–29.61	Total Return %
9.80*	29.02	–4.75	8.17	–6.70	–1.28	–4.15	–0.22	8.78	47.14	1.76	–17.73	+/- S&P 500
—	12.48	–5.84	7.04	–3.23	2.28	1.31	10.59	19.49	16.87	4.41	–9.45	+/- Russ Midcap Grth
0.28	0.33	0.00	0.06	0.17	0.21	0.00	0.00	0.00	0.00	0.00	0.00	Income Return %
9.40	59.18	2.87	18.17	–5.56	36.05	18.79	33.13	37.36	68.18	–7.34	–29.61	Capital Return %
—	34	77	33	77	40	38	4	5	36	55	74	Total Rtn % Rank Cat
0.03	0.04	0.00	0.01	0.03	0.03	0.00	0.00	0.00	0.00	0.00	0.00	Income $
0.00	0.83	0.76	1.70	1.90	2.75	3.43	3.43	3.49	4.27	3.86	0.00	Capital Gains $
0.64	0.60	0.60	0.59	0.60	0.61	0.60	0.61	0.60	0.62	0.61	—	Expense Ratio %
0.34	0.29	0.05	0.07	0.12	0.21	0.04	–0.07	–0.13	–0.07	–0.21	—	Income Ratio %
—	46	39	69	55	129	141	134	172	208	169	—	Turnover Rate %
118.1	184.4	242.6	331.4	293.7	377.8	407.0	435.8	566.3	1,304.4	1,729.3	—	Net Assets $mil

Performance 12-31-01

	1st Qtr	2nd Qtr	3rd Qtr	4th Qtr	Total
1997	–9.29	20.63	20.41	1.06	33.14
1998	20.72	3.50	–19.14	35.95	37.36
1999	6.47	13.38	0.08	39.21	68.18
2000	13.34	–6.80	6.45	–17.60	–7.34
2001	–24.69	9.53	–27.63	17.91	–29.61

Trailing	Total Return%	+/– S&P 500	+/– Russ Midcap Grth	% Rank All	% Rank Cat	Growth of $10,000
3 Mo	17.91	7.22	–9.16	17	57	11,791
6 Mo	–14.67	–9.11	–6.41	95	77	8,533
1 Yr	–29.61	–17.73	–9.45	93	74	7,039
3 Yr Avg	3.13	4.16	0.97	53	63	10,969
5 Yr Avg	14.94	4.24	5.92	4	13	20,059
10 Yr Avg	14.09	1.16	2.98	8	13	37,359
15 Yr Avg	—	—	—	—	—	—

Tax Analysis	Tax-Adj Ret%	%Rank Cat	%Pretax Ret	%Rank Cat
3 Yr Avg	–0.12	64	—	—
5 Yr Avg	11.16	19	74.7	52
10 Yr Avg	10.24	23	72.7	57

Potential Capital Gain Exposure: –18% of assets

Risk Analysis

Time Period	Load-Adj Return %	Risk %Rank[1] All	Risk %Rank[1] Cat	Morningstar Return	Morningstar Risk	Morningstar Risk-Adj Rating
1 Yr	–29.61					
3 Yr	3.13	92	59	–0.38[2]	1.53	★★★
5 Yr	14.94	90	51	2.61[2]	1.48	★★★★
10 Yr	14.09	94	61	1.56	1.62	★★★

Average Historical Rating (106 months): 3.3★s

[1] 1=low, 100=high [2] T-Bill return substituted for category avg.

Category Rating (3 Yr)

1 2 **3** 4 5 — Worst … Best

Return: Average
Risk: Average

Other Measures	Standard Index S&P 500	Best Fit Index Wil 4500
Alpha	10.2	3.3
Beta	1.42	1.12
R-Squared	55	93
Standard Deviation		35.44
Mean		3.13
Sharpe Ratio		–0.06

Portfolio Analysis 09-30-01

Share change since 03-01 Total Stocks: 92	Sector	PE	YTD Ret%	% Assets
⊕ Polycom	Technology	67.5	6.87	2.88
⊕ Express Scripts	Health	33.6	–8.54	2.57
⊕ Lincare Hldgs	Health	23.7	0.41	2.03
☼ VeriSign	Technology	—	–48.70	2.00
⊕ Western Wireless Cl A	Services	—	–27.90	1.95
⊖ Electronic Arts	Technology	90.8	40.65	1.83
⊕ Lamar Advertising Cl A	Services	—	9.71	1.73
⊖ St. Jude Medical	Health	42.0	26.39	1.72
⊖ Biovail Corporation Intl	Health	NMF	44.82	1.71
⊖ Tenet Healthcare	Health	30.1	32.14	1.63
⊖ Apollo Grp Cl A	Services	—	—	1.62
☼ Genzyme Corporation General Di	Health	—	33.11	1.61
☼ Caremark Rx	Health	46.6	20.25	1.61
⊖ Health Mgmt Assoc	Health	24.2	–11.30	1.60
⊖ RJ Reynolds Tobacco Hldgs	Staples	3.1	22.37	1.58
⊖ Concord EFS	Financials	86.3	49.21	1.57
⊕ Fiserv	Services	40.7	33.82	1.47
⊕ BMC Software	Technology	—	16.93	1.46
⊖ Intl Game Tech	Durables	24.4	42.29	1.45
⊖ Everest Re Grp	Financials	17.6	–1.29	1.41
⊕ Quest Diagnostics	Health	51.2	1.00	1.40
⊖ Forest Labs	Health	52.2	23.35	1.30
☼ Lockheed Martin	Industrials	36.8	38.98	1.29
⊕ Peregrine Sys	Technology	—	–24.90	1.28
⊕ J.C. Penney	Retail	—	154.60	1.28

Current Investment Style

Style: Value Blnd Growth; Size: Large Med Small

	Stock Port Avg	Relative S&P 500 Current	Relative S&P 500 Hist	Rel Cat
Price/Earnings Ratio	36.6	1.18	1.28	1.06
Price/Book Ratio	5.8	1.02	1.17	1.03
Price/Cash Flow	23.5	1.30	1.25	1.01
3 Yr Earnings Growth	26.6[1]	1.82	0.98	1.13
1 Yr Earnings Est%	15.5	—	—	1.66
Med Mkt Cap $mil	5,000	0.1	0.1	0.89

[1] figure is based on 50% or less of stocks

Special Securities % assets 09-30-01	
Restricted/Illiquid Secs	0
Emerging-Markets Secs	0
Options/Futures/Warrants	Yes

Composition % assets 09-30-01	
Cash	3.8
Stocks*	96.2
Bonds	0.0
Other	0.0
*Foreign (% stocks)	4.0

Market Cap	
Giant	0.0
Large	16.8
Medium	81.6
Small	1.6
Micro	0.0

Sector Weightings	% of Stocks	Rel S&P	5-Year High	5-Year Low
Utilities	3.0	0.9	4	0
Energy	2.7	0.4	7	0
Financials	6.6	0.4	12	1
Industrials	7.2	0.6	12	2
Durables	1.5	1.0	6	0
Staples	3.8	0.5	8	0
Services	19.9	1.8	52	20
Retail	7.5	1.1	15	1
Health	21.6	1.5	23	6
Technology	26.2	1.4	53	9

Analysis by Paul Herbert 12-09-01

This fund hasn't made the grade in 2001, but its poor showing isn't grounds for expulsion.

It's hard to be happy with Morgan Stanley Inst Mid Cap Growth Fund's performance so far in 2001. For the year to date through Dec. 10, the fund (which was known as MAS Mid Cap Growth before August) has lost 30.5%, placing behind 73% of its mid-growth peers.

The fund's loss is upsetting, given that its measured strategy should help it to avoid the category's bottom reaches. Instead of betting the ranch on aggressive-growth stocks, lead manager Arden Armstrong and her team balance racy picks with those sporting lower, more sustainable, growth rates. They'll tilt the fund toward one of these camps based on their outlook for corporate earnings growth and other economic factors. Unfortunately, the team has been caught leaning the wrong way at times this year. For example, the managers ramped up their stakes in growth sectors in summer, only to lag their typical rival when the market shunned these areas in the third quarter. Such missteps overshadow fine stock picks such as video-conferencing leader Polycom, which the managers picked up well before it rallied following the Sept. 11 attacks.

This disappointing campaign takes little away from the fund's stellar longer-term record, though. Even after its rough 2001, the fund sports a top-decile 10-year return, and all of that record can be attributed to Armstrong, its boss since 1990. And this record is not the result of one or two strong years—the fund has outpaced at least 60% of its peers in six of the past 10 years. It has also shown the ability to follow down years, such as 1992 and 1994, with strong showings.

Given the fund's sizable absolute loss, cautious investors may want to steer clear. The less risk-averse will find few better mid-growth offerings. The fund is available at lower minimums through discount brokers.

Address:	P.O. Box 2798, Boston, MA 02208-2798, 800-548-7786 / 800-548-7786
Web Address:	www.morganstanley.com/im
*Inception:	03-30-90
Advisor:	Miller Anderson & Sherrerd
Subadvisor:	None
NTF Plans:	N/A

Minimum Purchase:	$5.00 mil	Add: $1000 IRA: —
Min Auto Inv Plan:	—	Add: —
Sales Fees:	No-load	
Management Fee:	.50%, .08%A	
Actual Fees:	Mgt: 0.50%	Dist: —
Expense Projections:	3Yr: $199	5Yr: $346 10Yr: $774
Avg Brok Commission:	—	Income Distrib: Annually
Total Cost (relative to category):	—	

Morgan Stan Inst Mid Cap Value

Ticker	Load	NAV	Yield	Total Assets	Mstar Category
MPMVX	None	$20.31	0.1%	$1,301.7 mil	Mid-Cap Blend

Prospectus Objective: Growth and Income

Morgan Stanley Institutional Mid Cap Value Fund seeks total return consistent with reasonable risk.

The fund normally invests at least 65% of assets in equities of companies that are undervalued and fall in the range of the S&P MidCap 400 index. The fund aims to achieve a lower P/E ratio than the S&P 400. It may invest up to 5% of assets in foreign securities, excluding ADRs. The fund may also invest in preferred stocks, convertibles, corporate debt, and U.S. government obligations.

The fund offers Adviser, Institutional, and Investment shares. On July 17, 1998, Morgan Stanley Institutional Small Cap Value Fund merged into the fund.

Historical Profile
Return: High
Risk: Average
Rating: ★★★★★ Highest

Investment Style
Equity
Average Stock %: 100% 97% 96% 92% 91% 88% 95%

▼ Manager Change
▽ Partial Manager Change

Fund Performance vs. Category Average
■ Quarterly Fund Return +/– Category Average
— Category Baseline

Performance Quartile (within Category)

Portfolio Manager(s)

William B. Gerlach, CFA. Since 12-94. BA Other funds currently managed: Morgan Stanley Inst Small Cap Value, Morgan Stanley Inst Mid Cap Value Inv, Morgan Stanley Inst Mid Cap Value Adv.

Gary G. Schlarbaum, CFA. Since 12-94. BA'65 Coe C.; PhD'71 U. of Pennsylvania. Other funds currently managed: Morgan Stanley Inst Balanced, Morgan Stanley Inst Equity, Morgan Stanley Inst Small Cap Value.

Bradley S. Daniels, CFA. Since 1-97. BA'83 U. of Pennsylvania; MBA'89 U. of Pennsylvania. Other funds currently managed: Morgan Stanley Inst Small Cap Value, Morgan Stanley Inst Mid Cap Value Inv, Morgan Stanley Inst Mid Cap Value Adv.

1990	1991	1992	1993	1994	1995	1996	1997	1998	1999	2000	12-01	History
—	—	—	—	10.00	11.69	15.34	19.12	20.70	21.95	21.04	20.31	NAV
—	—	—	—	—	32.71	40.78	39.59	16.05	19.82	11.94	–3.38	Total Return %
—	—	—	—	—	–4.83	17.83	6.23	–12.52	–1.21	21.04	8.50	+/– S&P 500
—	—	—	—	—	1.79	21.59	7.34	–3.06	5.11	–5.56	–2.78	+/– S&P Mid 400
—	—	—	—	0.00	5.50	0.86	0.26	0.31	0.37	0.38	0.09	Income Return %
—	—	—	—	0.00	27.21	39.92	39.32	15.74	19.45	11.56	–3.47	Capital Return %
—	—	—	—	—	26	1	2	19	49	33	44	Total Rtn % Rank Cat
—	—	—	—	0.00	0.55	0.10	0.04	0.06	0.08	0.08	0.02	Income $
—	—	—	—	0.00	1.04	1.01	2.19	1.31	2.57	3.22	0.00	Capital Gains $
—	—	—	—	—	0.93	0.88	0.88	0.88	0.87	0.85	—	Expense Ratio %
—	—	—	—	—	10.13	1.61	0.28	0.40	0.57	0.28	—	Income Ratio %
—	—	—	—	—	639	377	184	213	244	226	—	Turnover Rate %
—	—	—	—	1.3	5.6	99.5	256.3	543.0	958.5	1,258.1	—	Net Assets $mil

Performance 12-31-01

	1st Qtr	2nd Qtr	3rd Qtr	4th Qtr	Total
1997	0.26	17.56	20.58	–1.78	39.59
1998	12.08	–1.91	–13.80	22.46	16.05
1999	–3.72	17.76	–6.73	13.31	19.82
2000	9.20	–2.54	7.32	–1.99	11.94
2001	–8.56	10.65	–20.62	20.29	–3.38

Trailing	Total Return%	+/– S&P 500	+/– S&P Mid 400	% Rank All	% Rank Cat	Growth of $10,000
3 Mo	20.29	9.61	2.31	13	17	12,029
6 Mo	–4.51	1.04	–2.96	59	60	9,549
1 Yr	–3.38	8.50	–2.78	48	44	9,662
3 Yr Avg	9.03	10.05	–1.21	13	29	12,960
5 Yr Avg	15.99	5.29	–0.12	3	11	20,995
10 Yr Avg	—	—	—	—	—	—
15 Yr Avg	—	—	—	—	—	—

Tax Analysis	Tax-Adj Ret%	%Rank Cat	%Pretax Ret	%Rank Cat
3 Yr Avg	5.30	40	58.7	77
5 Yr Avg	12.62	14	78.9	42
10 Yr Avg	—	—	—	—

Potential Capital Gain Exposure: –5% of assets

Risk Analysis

Time Period	Load-Adj Return %	Risk %Rank[1] All	Risk %Rank[1] Cat	Morningstar Return	Morningstar Risk	Morningstar Risk-Adj Rating
1 Yr	–3.38					
3 Yr	9.03	64	48	0.90[2]	0.90	★★★★
5 Yr	15.99	69	35	2.95[2]	0.93	★★★★★
Incept	21.53	—	—	—	—	

Average Historical Rating (49 months): 4.7★s

[1]1=low, 100=high [2] T-Bill return substituted for category avg.

Category Rating (3 Yr)

1 2 **3** 4 5
Worst Best

Return: Above Avg
Risk: Average

Other Measures	Standard Index S&P 500	Best Fit Index SPMid400
Alpha	10.6	–0.9
Beta	0.94	1.01
R-Squared	59	91
Standard Deviation		22.61
Mean		9.03
Sharpe Ratio		0.21

Portfolio Analysis 03-31-01

Share change since 12-00 Total Stocks: 222	Sector	PE	YTD Ret%	% Assets
⊕ Valassis Comms	Services	18.9	12.85	2.44
⊕ PG & E	Utilities	—	–3.80	1.87
⊕ Bally Total Fitness Hldg	Services	8.4	–36.30	1.82
⊖ Titan	Technology	—	53.54	1.62
⊕ Mellon Finl	Financials	23.8	–21.90	1.53
⊕ El Paso	Utilities	NMF	–36.70	1.52
⊕ Royal Caribbean Cruises	Services	9.6	–38.00	1.45
⊖ Affiliated Comp Svcs A	Services	39.9	74.88	1.34
⊕ Kinder Morgan	Energy	32.2	7.11	1.30
⊕ ACE	Financials	17.4	–5.39	1.29
⊕ Waters	Industrials	32.0	–53.50	1.24
⊖ Republic Svcs Cl A	Services	15.6	16.19	1.21
BF Goodrich	Industrials	6.7	–24.30	1.18
⊕ Dime Bancorp	Financials	13.0	23.63	1.12
⊖ Tenet Healthcare	Health	30.1	32.14	1.09
⊖ RJ Reynolds Tobacco Hldgs	Staples	3.1	22.37	1.08
⊖ St. Jude Medical	Health	42.0	26.39	1.08
⊖ John Hancock Finl Svcs	Financials	—	10.66	1.07
⊖ Health Net	Health	35.7	–16.80	1.05
☼ Duke Energy	Utilities	15.5	–6.04	1.02
⊕ News ADR Pfd	Services	—	—	1.01
⊖ S & P Midcap 400 SPDR		—	—	1.01
Golden State Bancorp	Financials	9.6	–15.60	1.00
⊖ SunGard Data Sys	Technology	33.3	22.78	0.99
☼ Intuit	Technology	—	8.42	0.98

Current Investment Style

Style: Value Blnd Growth; Size: Large Med Small

	Stock Port Avg	Relative S&P 500 Current	Relative S&P 500 Hist	Rel Cat
Price/Earnings Ratio	25.6	0.83	0.85	0.94
Price/Book Ratio	3.6	0.63	0.63	0.84
Price/Cash Flow	15.7	0.87	0.85	0.91
3 Yr Earnings Growth	14.4	0.98	0.99	0.87
1 Yr Earnings Est%	2.0	—	—	0.90
Med Mkt Cap $mil	4,437	0.1	0.1	0.49

[1]figure is based on 50% or less of stocks

Analysis by Paul Herbert 11-30-01

Morgan Stanley Institutional Mid Cap Value Fund isn't having its finest campaign in 2001, but it remains a solid mid-cap choice.

This fund, which was known as MAS Mid Cap Value until Aug. 1, 2001, isn't having a banner year, losing more than 7% for the year to date through Nov. 30, which ranks it just ahead of the mid-blend category's average. The fund lost significant ground to the group in the third quarter, thanks to slides from holdings such as Bally Total Fitness, which lost nearly 30% during the three-month stretch. Faltering power producers such as NRG Energy also haven't helped in 2001.

It isn't difficult to understand the fund's ho-hum performance if you leave out the value part of its name. Its managers target mid-caps that appear undervalued on the basis of metrics such as P/E ratios, as is usual for a value fund. However, they also use momentum tools to find companies with rising earnings estimates and require holdings to offer above-average earnings growth. Managers who use momentum screens have suffered this year, at least until recently, as it's been difficult to spot companies whose earnings estimates are rising in this difficult environment. Over the fund's lifetime, however, it has generally prospered in both growth and value rallies, leading it to one of the best five-year records in the category.

Fine performance isn't the fund's only likeable attribute. Management spreads its bets among more than 200 names and doesn't make large sector bets versus the S&P Midcap 400 index. As a result, the fund hasn't been much more volatile, in terms of standard deviation, than its typical peer. It also boasts long-tenured management and low expenses.

Investors in the market for a fund that offers core mid-cap exposure should give this one a long, hard look. Given its high turnover, however, it's not suitable for taxable accounts. The fund is available at lower minimums through fund supermarkets.

Special Securities % assets 03-31-01	
Restricted/Illiquid Secs	0
Emerging-Markets Secs	Trace
Options/Futures/Warrants	No

Composition % assets 03-31-01	
Cash	4.1
Stocks*	94.9
Bonds	0.0
Other	1.0
*Foreign (% stocks)	4.3

Market Cap	
Giant	0.2
Large	15.3
Medium	73.6
Small	10.3
Micro	0.6

Sector Weightings	% of Stocks	Rel S&P	5-Year High	5-Year Low
Utilities	11.0	3.5	11	3
Energy	7.5	1.1	15	1
Financials	17.1	1.0	27	9
Industrials	8.3	0.7	23	4
Durables	4.7	3.0	7	2
Staples	2.7	0.3	7	0
Services	18.7	1.7	22	8
Retail	2.5	0.4	13	2
Health	11.6	0.8	16	5
Technology	16.0	0.9	35	10

Address: P.O. Box 2798, Boston, MA 02208-2798, 800-548-7786 / 800-548-7786
Web Address: www.morganstanley.com/im
*Inception: 12-30-94
Advisor: Miller Anderson & Sherrerd
Subadvisor: None
NTF Plans: N/A

Minimum Purchase: $5.00 mil — Add: $1000 — IRA: —
Min Auto Inv Plan: — — Add: —
Sales Fees: No-load
Management Fee: .75%, .08%A
Actual Fees: Mgt: 0.75% — Dist: —
Expense Projections: 3Yr: $288 — 5Yr: $500 — 10Yr: $1111
Avg Brok Commission: — — Income Distrib: Annually
Total Cost (relative to category): —

Morgan Stan Inst Small Cap Growth

Ticker	Load	NAV	Yield	Total Assets	Mstar Category
MSCGX	None	$29.59	0.0%	$213.8 mil	Small Growth

Prospectus Objective: Small Company

Morgan Stanley Institutional Small Cap Growth Fund seeks long-term capital growth.

The fund generally invests at least 65% of assets in common stocks of small companies (capitalization range: generally $250 million to $2.5 billion). The advisor focuses on companies that demonstrate one or more of the following characteristics: high earnings growth rates; growth stability; rising profitability; and ability to produce earnings that beat market expectations.

The fund currently offers Institutional and Advisor classes, both of which differ in fee structure and availability. Prior to August 1, 2001, the fund was named MAS Small Cap Growth.

Historical Profile
Return High
Risk High
Rating ★★★★★ Highest

Investment Style
Equity
Average Stock %: 1999 90%, 2000 97%, 12-01 98%

▼ Manager Change
▽ Partial Manager Change

Fund Performance vs. Category Average
Quarterly Fund Return +/– Category Average
– Category Baseline

Performance Quartile (within Category)

Portfolio Manager(s)

Arden C. Armstrong, CFA. Since 6-98. BA'82 Brown U.; MBA'86 U. of Pennsylvania. Other funds currently managed: Morgan Stanley Developing Gr Secs B, Morgan Stanley Inst Mid Cap Growth, Morgan Stanley Inst Equity.

David Pao-Kang Chu, CFA. Since 6-98. BS'82 U. of Michigan; MBA'86 U. of Pennsylvania-Wharton. Other funds currently managed: Morgan Stanley Inst Mid Cap Growth, Morgan Stanley Inst Mid Cap Growth Ad, Van Kampen Mid Cap Growth A.

Steve Chulik. Since 8-99. BS Columbia U.; MBA'97 U. of Pennsylvania, Wharton. Other funds currently managed: Morgan Stanley Inst Mid Cap Growth, Morgan Stanley Inst Mid Cap Growth Ad, Van Kampen Mid Cap Growth A.

1990	1991	1992	1993	1994	1995	1996	1997	1998	1999	2000	12-01	History
—	—	—	—	—	—	—	—	13.22	49.79	37.25	29.59	NAV
—	—	—	—	—	—	—	—	32.20*	313.91	–18.96	–20.56	Total Return %
—	—	—	—	—	—	—	—	22.96*	292.87	–9.86	–8.69	+/– S&P 500
—	—	—	—	—	—	—	—	—	270.82	3.47	–11.33	+/– Russ 2000 Grth
—	—	—	—	—	—	—	—	0.00	0.00	0.00	0.00	Income Return %
—	—	—	—	—	—	—	—	32.20	313.91	–18.96	–20.56	Capital Return %
—	—	—	—	—	—	—	—	—	1	87	81	Total Rtn % Rank Cat
—	—	—	—	—	—	—	—	0.00	0.00	0.00	0.00	Income $
—	—	—	—	—	—	—	—	0.00	4.40	2.79	0.00	Capital Gains $
—	—	—	—	—	—	—	—	1.15	1.18	1.14	—	Expense Ratio %
—	—	—	—	—	—	—	—	–0.46	–0.50	–0.77	—	Income Ratio %
—	—	—	—	—	—	—	—	—	300	206	—	Turnover Rate %
—	—	—	—	—	—	—	—	5.5	284.7	300.1	—	Net Assets $mil

Performance 12-31-01

	1st Qtr	2nd Qtr	3rd Qtr	4th Qtr	Total
1997	—	—	—	—	—
1998	—	—	–14.30	54.26	32.20 *
1999	53.78	39.65	13.67	69.57	313.91
2000	12.75	–7.68	2.18	–23.81	–18.96
2001	–21.29	11.49	–26.46	23.09	–20.56

Trailing	Total Return%	+/– S&P 500	+/– Russ 2000 Grth	% Rank All	% Rank Cat	Growth of $10,000
3 Mo	23.09	12.40	–3.09	10	52	12,309
6 Mo	–9.48	–3.93	–0.22	83	71	9,052
1 Yr	–20.56	–8.69	–11.33	81	81	7,944
3 Yr Avg	38.63	39.66	38.39	1	2	26,644
5 Yr Avg	—	—	—	—	—	—
10 Yr Avg	—	—	—	—	—	—
15 Yr Avg	—	—	—	—	—	—

Tax Analysis	Tax-Adj Ret%	%Rank Cat	%Pretax Ret	%Rank Cat
3 Yr Avg	35.62	1	92.2	19
5 Yr Avg	—	—	—	—
10 Yr Avg	—	—	—	—

Potential Capital Gain Exposure: 3% of assets

Risk Analysis

Time Period	Load-Adj Return %	Risk %Rank[1] All	Risk %Rank[1] Cat	Morningstar Return	Morningstar Risk	Morningstar Risk-Adj Rating
1 Yr	–20.56					
3 Yr	38.63	94	65	9.68[2]	1.62	★★★★★
5 Yr	—	—	—	—	—	
Incept	43.20	—	—	—	—	

Average Historical Rating (7 months): 5.0★s

[1]1=low, 100=high [2] T-Bill return substituted for category avg.

Category Rating (3 Yr)

1 2 3 4 5 — Worst ... Best

Return: High
Risk: Average

Other Measures	Standard Index S&P 500	Best Fit Index Wil 4500
Alpha	56.3	45.0
Beta	1.69	1.45
R-Squared	40	81

Standard Deviation	68.13
Mean	38.63
Sharpe Ratio	0.55

Analysis by Paul Herbert 10-28-01

Morgan Stanley Institutional Small Cap Growth Fund simply isn't an all-weather vehicle.

This fund, which was known as MAS Small Cap Growth until Aug. 1, 2001, hasn't been impressive lately. For the year to date through Oct. 30, it has shed more than 30% of its value, which ranks in the small-growth category's bottom quartile. This showing follows on the heels of the fund's 19% drop in 2000, which also placed near the back of the small-growth pack.

These losses are somewhat unexpected given the fund's measured strategy. Its managers look for companies offering high rates of top-line growth and upward earnings estimate revisions, like most aggressive-growth managers do. However, they also pay attention to valuations, limit sector bets versus the S&P Midcap 400 index, and hold a slug of stable-growth stocks in an attempt to balance their faster-growing picks.

Unfortunately these risk-control measures haven't done much good of late. For instance, the fund's stable growers didn't prevent it from losing more than its typical category peer in this year's first and third quarters, and its bolder picks didn't help it to gain more than the category average in the second quarter.

The fund's struggles of late are also surprising given management's fine track record. Sibling Morgan Stanley Institutional Mid Cap Growth owns one of the mid-cap growth category's best 10-year returns, and this fund rocketed to a 314% gain in 1999. Each fund has been less impressive in 2000 and 2001, however, highlighting the risks that growth managers take by investing in pricey, high-growth stocks.

The fund's record earns it the benefit of the doubt, but given its struggles of late, it bears mentioning that the fund is best as a minor holding in investors' portfolios.

Portfolio Analysis 03-31-01

Share change since 02-01 Total Stocks: 88	Sector	PE	YTD Ret%	% Assets
ViaSat	Technology	38.1	18.86	2.68
⊕ AirGate PCS	Services	—	28.31	2.44
⊖ Lincare Hldgs	Health	23.7	0.41	2.07
⊕ Take-Two Interact Software	Technology	37.6	40.61	2.00
⊕ Insituform Tech A	Industrials	18.3	–35.80	1.92
⊕ C & D Tech	Industrials	12.8	–47.00	1.88
⊕ Duane Reade	Retail	25.3	–0.70	1.84
⊕ RenaissanceRe Hldgs	Financials	14.7	23.16	1.79
Ubiquitel	Services	—	35.45	1.72
⊕ Ultimate Electncs	Retail	23.3	36.75	1.71
⊖ Charles River Labs	Health	—	22.30	1.70
⊕ MIPS Tech Cl B	Technology	—	—	1.68
⊕ Mediacom Comms	Services	—	6.24	1.68
⊕ Orion Pwr Hldgs	Utilities	—	5.99	1.63
⊕ Community Health Sys	Health	—	–27.10	1.61
⊕ Spinnaker Explor	Energy	13.6	–3.15	1.52
⊖ Oxford Health Plans	Health	11.5	–23.70	1.50
⊖ AmeriSource Health Cl A	Health	30.3	25.90	1.50
⊕ Grey Wolf	Energy	8.3	–49.40	1.49
⊕ Precision Castparts	Industrials	12.4	–32.60	1.47
⊖ Province Healthcare	Health	37.6	–21.60	1.44
⊕ Mettler-Toledo Intl	Industrials	34.1	–4.64	1.44
⊕ BE Aerospace	Industrials	14.3	–42.60	1.43
Crown Media Hldgs A	Services	—	–44.40	1.42
⊕ Ticketmaster Online-City B	Services	—	95.70	1.41

Current Investment Style

Style: Value Blnd Growth; Size: Large Med Small

	Stock Port Avg	Relative S&P 500 Current	Relative S&P 500 Hist	Rel Cat
Price/Earnings Ratio	27.3	0.88	—	0.85
Price/Book Ratio	4.8	0.84	—	0.99
Price/Cash Flow	19.7	1.09	—	0.89
3 Yr Earnings Growth	14.1[1]	0.97	—	0.56
1 Yr Earnings Est%	16.5	—	—	2.12
Med Mkt Cap $mil	1,042	0.0	—	1.00

[1]figure is based on 50% or less of stocks

Special Securities % assets 03-31-01	
Restricted/Illiquid Secs	0
Emerging-Markets Secs	0
Options/Futures/Warrants	No

Composition % assets 03-31-01	
Cash	2.0
Stocks*	98.0
Bonds	0.0
Other	0.0
*Foreign (% stocks)	4.1

Market Cap	
Giant	0.0
Large	0.0
Medium	36.6
Small	60.8
Micro	2.6

Sector Weightings	% of Stocks	Rel S&P	5-Year High	5-Year Low
Utilities	2.4	0.7	—	—
Energy	7.5	1.1	—	—
Financials	2.8	0.2	—	—
Industrials	12.3	1.1	—	—
Durables	1.4	0.9	—	—
Staples	2.8	0.4	—	—
Services	21.3	2.0	—	—
Retail	6.6	1.0	—	—
Health	20.5	1.4	—	—
Technology	22.4	1.2	—	—

Address:	P.O. Box 2798, Boston, MA 02208-2798, 800-548-7786 / 800-548-7786
Web Address:	www.morganstanley.com/im
*Inception:	06-30-98
Advisor:	Miller Anderson & Sherrerd
Subadvisor:	None
NTF Plans:	N/A

Minimum Purchase:	$5.00 mil	Add: $1000 IRA: —
Min Auto Inv Plan:	—	Add: —
Sales Fees:	No-load	
Management Fee:	1.0%, .08%A	
Actual Fees:	Mgt: 1.00%	Dist: —
Expense Projections:	3Yr: $1453*	5Yr: — 10Yr: —
Avg Brok Commission:	—	Income Distrib: Annually
Total Cost (relative to category):	—	

Morgan Stan Inst U.S. Real Estate A

Ticker	Load	NAV	Yield	Total Assets	Mstar Category
MSUSX	None	$14.63	3.8%	$682.0 mil	Spec Real Estate

Prospectus Objective: Specialty—Real Estate

Morgan Stanley Institutional U.S. Real Estate Portfolio seeks current income and long-term capital appreciation.

The fund normally invests at least 65% of assets in income-producing equities of companies mainly engaged in the U.S. real-estate industry. It may invest the balance in debt issued or guaranteed by real-estate companies or secured by real-estate assets, as well as in investment-grade corporate debt. It attempts to provide a dividend yield that exceeds the composite dividend yield of the securities in the S&P 500. This fund is non-diversified.

Class A and B shares are for institutions. Past name: Morgan Stanley Institutional Funds U.S. Real Estate Portfolio and Morgan Stanley Dean Witter Institutional U.S. Real Estate Portfolio.

Historical Profile
Return Average
Risk Below Avg
Rating ★★★★ Above Avg

Investment Style
Equity
Average Stock %: 96% 92% 92% 96% 97% 99% 97%

▼ Manager Change
▽ Partial Manager Change

Fund Performance vs. Category Average
■ Quarterly Fund Return +/– Category Average
— Category Baseline

Performance Quartile (within Category)

Portfolio Manager(s)

Theodore R. Bigman. Since 2-95. BA'83 Brandeis U.; MBA'87 Harvard U. Other funds currently managed: Van Kampen Real Estate Secs A, Van Kampen Real Estate Secs B, Van Kampen Real Estate Secs C.

Douglas A. Funke. Since 1-99. BA U. of Chicago. Other funds currently managed: Van Kampen Real Estate Secs A, Van Kampen Real Estate Secs B, Van Kampen Real Estate Secs C.

1990	1991	1992	1993	1994	1995	1996	1997	1998	1999	2000	12-01	History
—	—	—	—	—	11.42	14.41	15.38	12.71	11.84	14.50	14.63	NAV
—	—	—	—	—	21.07*	39.56	27.62	–12.29	–1.48	29.65	9.27	Total Return %
—	—	—	—	—	–9.28*	16.61	–5.73	–40.87	–22.52	38.75	21.14	+/– S&P 500
—	—	—	—	—	—	2.52	7.94	4.71	1.10	–1.40	–3.09	+/– Wilshire REIT
—	—	—	—	—	2.27	3.44	3.04	3.26	5.28	4.83	4.04	Income Return %
—	—	—	—	—	18.79	36.11	24.57	–15.55	–6.75	24.82	5.22	Capital Return %
—	—	—	—	—	—	15	11	15	28	32	37	Total Rtn % Rank Cat
—	—	—	—	—	0.24	0.39	0.43	0.49	0.66	0.56	0.57	Income $
—	—	—	—	—	0.43	1.01	2.42	0.33	0.04	0.23	0.61	Capital Gains $
—	—	—	—	—	1.00	1.00	1.00	1.00	1.00	1.00	—	Expense Ratio %
—	—	—	—	—	4.04	3.08	2.72	3.33	6.52	4.13	—	Income Ratio %
—	—	—	—	—	—	171	135	117	47	31	—	Turnover Rate %
—	—	—	—	—	69.5	210.4	361.4	258.7	311.0	584.6	—	Net Assets $mil

Performance 12-31-01

	1st Qtr	2nd Qtr	3rd Qtr	4th Qtr	Total
1997	4.37	6.79	12.05	2.18	27.62
1998	–1.24	–4.05	–9.45	2.21	–12.29
1999	–2.83	12.21	–8.96	–0.75	–1.48
2000	2.11	12.29	9.34	3.41	29.65
2001	–1.59	9.10	–3.32	5.27	9.27

Trailing	Total Return%	+/– S&P 500	+/– Wil REIT	% Rank All	% Rank Cat	Growth of $10,000
3 Mo	5.27	–5.42	0.38	64	23	10,527
6 Mo	1.77	7.32	–0.60	26	45	10,177
1 Yr	9.27	21.14	–3.09	7	37	10,927
3 Yr Avg	11.75	12.78	–1.03	8	23	13,957
5 Yr Avg	9.33	–1.37	1.99	22	7	15,622
10 Yr Avg	—	—	—	—	—	—
15 Yr Avg	—	—	—	—	—	—

Tax Analysis	Tax-Adj Ret%	%Rank Cat	%Pretax Ret	%Rank Cat
3 Yr Avg	9.29	29	79.1	58
5 Yr Avg	6.15	11	65.9	51
10 Yr Avg	—	—	—	—

Potential Capital Gain Exposure: 9% of assets

Risk Analysis

Time Period	Load-Adj Return %	Risk %Rank[1] All	Risk %Rank[1] Cat	Morningstar Return	Morningstar Risk	Morningstar Risk-Adj Rating
1 Yr	9.27					
3 Yr	11.75	38	14	1.54[2]	0.51	★★★★★
5 Yr	9.33	47	6	1.02[2]	0.63	★★★★
Incept	15.23	—	—	—	—	

Average Historical Rating (47 months): 3.2★s

[1] 1=low, 100=high [2] T-Bill return substituted for category avg.

Category Rating (3 Yr)

1 Worst ... 5 Best (rating: 4)

Return: Above Avg
Risk: Below Avg

Other Measures	Standard Index S&P 500	Best Fit Index Wil REIT
Alpha	8.0	–0.6
Beta	0.12	0.96
R-Squared	2	97
Standard Deviation		14.49
Mean		11.75
Sharpe Ratio		0.54

Portfolio Analysis 06-30-01

Share chng since 05-01 Total Stocks: 58	Subsector	PE	YTD Ret%	% Assets
Equity Office Properties Tr	Industrial/Office	18.7	–1.76	6.55
⊕ AvalonBay Communities	Apartment	15.9	–0.38	6.03
Spieker Properties	Industrial/Office	—	21.14	5.18
⊕ Public Storage	Self Storage	22.6	44.92	4.91
Starwood Hotels & Resorts	Hotel	18.7	–12.90	4.40
⊕ Equity Residential Properties	Apartment	22.1	10.14	4.20
Arden Realty Grp	Industrial/Office	16.6	13.90	4.17
Brookfield Properties	Diversified	22.9	–0.80	4.00
Boston Properties	Industrial/Office	17.8	–7.37	3.97
Archstone Communities Tr	Apartment	14.8	9.11	3.70
⊕ Simon Ppty Grp	Retail	27.9	31.72	3.57
⊕ Charles E Smith Resdntl Rlty	Apartment	—	4.75	3.45
Essex Ppty Tr	Apartment	20.9	–4.44	3.39
Vornado Realty Tr	Retail	17.6	16.25	2.86
⊖ TrizecHahn	Diversified	28.0	5.92	2.82
CarrAmerica Realty	Industrial/Office	21.5	2.32	2.58
⊖ Prologis Tr	Industrial/Office	20.3	3.19	2.56
Taubman Centers	Retail	—	46.42	2.18
⊕ Federal Realty Invest Tr	Retail	15.7	32.27	2.16
⊖ Apartment Invest & Mgmt	Apartment	NMF	–1.80	1.62
⊖ Chateau Communities	Dvlp./Man. Home	23.2	5.51	1.62
⊕ AMB Ppty	Industrial/Office	17.8	7.27	1.61
AMLI Residential Properties	Apartment	9.2	10.84	1.58
Host Marriott	Hotel	6.2	–24.80	1.47
⊖ Great Lakes REIT	Industrial/Office	9.7	1.02	1.46

Current Investment Style

Style: Value Blnd Growth; Size: Large Med Small

	Stock Port Avg	Relative S&P 500 Current	Relative S&P 500 Hist	Rel Cat
Price/Earnings Ratio	20.5	0.66	0.69	1.04
Price/Book Ratio	1.7	0.29	0.23	0.95
Price/Cash Flow	—	—	—	—
3 Yr Earnings Growth	25.3	1.73	1.28	1.24
1 Yr Earnings Est%	58.7	—	—	0.97
Med Mkt Cap $mil	2,891	0.1	0.1	1.26

Special Securities % assets 06-30-01	
Restricted/Illiquid Secs	0
Emerging-Markets Secs	0
Options/Futures/Warrants	Yes

Composition % assets 06-30-01	
Cash	2.4
Stocks*	97.4
Bonds	0.0
Other	0.2
*Foreign (% stocks)	7.0

Market Cap	
Giant	0.0
Large	6.8
Medium	65.2
Small	24.7
Micro	3.2

Subsector Weightings	% of Stocks	Rel Cat
Diversified	9.6	1.0
Health Care	0.0	0.0
Industrial/Office	32.5	1.0
Mortgage Backed	0.0	0.0
Apartment	26.5	1.4
Retail	13.7	0.7
Dvlp./Man. Home	3.1	1.4
Self Storage	7.1	2.1
Hotel	6.8	1.5
Other	0.7	0.1

Analysis by Alan Papier 12-31-01

Morgan Stanley Institutional U.S. Real Estate Portfolio is the real deal.

It's easy to see why this fund remains one of our favorites in the specialty-real estate category. Its 2001 return will likely be its poorest relative calendar-year showing since inception, but it still ranks well within the group's top half. Indeed, the fund's gain of 9.5% for the year to date through Dec. 28, 2001, topped 63% of its peers'. That fact underscores just how strong and consistent the fund's performance has been over time. Its annualized five-year return of 9.7% ranks near the top of the performance charts, and the fund has been among the least volatile in the group over that span.

That excellent record is a function of management's unique approach. Most real-estate funds use an industry-specific measure of earnings called Funds From Operations (FFO) to make investment decisions. But here, comanagers Ted Bigman and Douglas Funke try to determine a company's net asset value based on their estimates of the company's recurring cash flows. They seek to buy those companies trading at a discount to their calculation of intrinsic value. For example, the team snatched up Post Properties after the stock price dipped in spring 2001, but sold the position after it quickly rebounded for a 12% gain.

While the approach has proved effective over time, the fund is not without its risks. For one thing, management often makes big subsector bets where it finds the most value. Thus, it could really struggle if a favored area, such as urban offices, were to hit the skids. Also, the fund tends to focus on the largest REITs, so it generally lags its peers when smaller caps rally, as was the case during the first half of 2001.

That said, we think this fund is among the best pure real-estate funds available.

Address:	P.O. Box 2798 Boston, MA 02208–2798 800–548–7786
Web Address:	www.morganstanley.com/im
*Inception:	02-27-95
Advisor:	Morgan Stanley Dean Witter Asset Mgmt
Subadvisor:	None
NTF Plans:	N/A

Minimum Purchase:	$500000	Add: $1000 IRA: —
Min Auto Inv Plan:	—	Add: —
Sales Fees:	No-load	
Management Fee:	.80%, .15%A	
Actual Fees:	Mgt: 0.80%	Dist: —
Expense Projections:	3Yr: $325	5Yr: $563 10Yr: $1248
Avg Brok Commission:	—	Income Distrib: Quarterly
Total Cost (relative to category):	Low	

Morgan Stanley Strategist B

Ticker	Load	NAV	Yield	Total Assets	Mstar Category
SRTBX	5.00%d	$15.81	1.7%	$1,839.3 mil	Domestic Hybrid

Prospectus Objective: Asset Allocation

Morgan Stanley Strategist Fund seeks total return.

The fund allocates assets among equities, debt, and money markets. The relative holdings in each category depend on economic conditions. The debt portion consists of investment-grade debt securities with varying maturities. This fund is non-diversified.

Class A, B, C, and D shares are offered by the fund. The fund has gone through several name changes.

Historical Profile
Return: Average
Risk: Below Avg
Rating: ★★★ Neutral

Investment Style
Equity
Average Stock %: 64% (1996), 63% (1997), 69% (1998), 69% (1999), 57% (2000), 52% (12-01)

▼ Manager Change
▽ Partial Manager Change

Fund Performance vs. Category Average
■ Quarterly Fund Return +/– Category Average
— Category Baseline

Performance Quartile (within Category)

Portfolio Manager(s)

Mark Bavoso. Since 10-88. BA'83 U. of California. Other funds currently managed: Morgan Stanley Strategist A, Morgan Stanley Strategist C, Morgan Stanley Strategist D.

History

1990	1991	1992	1993	1994	1995	1996	1997	1998	1999	2000	12-01	History
10.92	14.17	14.35	14.80	13.75	15.48	16.09	17.80	18.67	20.75	18.09	15.81	NAV
2.58	32.20	7.43	7.96	–1.93	24.32	15.29	15.78	15.37	21.97	1.44	–11.06	Total Return %
5.69	1.71	–0.19	–2.09	–3.25	–13.21	–7.66	–17.58	–13.20	0.93	10.55	0.81	+/– S&P 500
–6.38	16.19	0.03	–1.79	0.99	5.85	11.67	6.09	6.70	22.80	–10.19	–19.49	+/– LB Aggregate
2.30	2.21	2.13	1.82	1.99	2.36	2.30	1.93	1.45	0.82	1.55	1.53	Income Return %
0.27	29.98	5.30	6.14	–3.92	21.96	12.99	13.84	13.92	21.15	–0.11	–12.59	Capital Return %
26	12	54	85	40	59	33	72	34	7	47	89	Total Rtn % Rank Cat
0.25	0.24	0.30	0.26	0.29	0.32	0.35	0.31	0.26	0.15	0.32	0.28	Income $
0.07	0.00	0.56	0.42	0.47	1.26	1.40	0.51	1.53	1.75	2.60	0.00	Capital Gains $
1.53	1.59	1.63	1.62	1.62	1.63	1.58	1.56	1.54	1.58	1.53	1.63	Expense Ratio %
2.39	2.37	2.19	1.90	2.03	2.35	1.88	2.29	1.24	0.96	1.41	1.63	Income Ratio %
101	140	79	98	90	179	174	158	92	121	187	136	Turnover Rate %
181.8	300.0	548.4	821.4	766.0	1,262.7	1,370.5	1,489.6	1,704.7	2,011.2	2,068.5	1,637.6	Net Assets $mil

Performance 12-31-01

	1st Qtr	2nd Qtr	3rd Qtr	4th Qtr	Total
1997	0.40	9.76	6.42	–1.27	15.78
1998	10.22	5.08	–8.84	9.26	15.37
1999	4.34	5.35	–1.32	12.44	21.97
2000	6.98	–6.15	3.24	–2.13	1.44
2001	–11.33	3.88	–7.11	3.94	–11.07

Trailing	Total Return%	+/– S&P 500	+/– LB Agg	% Rank All	% Rank Cat	Growth of $10,000
3 Mo	3.94	–6.75	3.90	68	81	10,394
6 Mo	–3.45	2.10	–8.11	53	77	9,655
1 Yr	–11.06	0.81	–19.49	63	89	8,894
3 Yr Avg	3.24	4.27	–3.03	51	36	11,004
5 Yr Avg	8.01	–2.69	0.58	29	38	14,698
10 Yr Avg	9.13	–3.80	1.90	38	53	23,963
15 Yr Avg	—	—	—	—	—	—

Tax Analysis	Tax-Adj Ret%	%Rank Cat	%Pretax Ret	%Rank Cat
3 Yr Avg	1.15	38	35.6	77
5 Yr Avg	5.98	33	74.7	27
10 Yr Avg	6.89	47	75.4	32

Potential Capital Gain Exposure: 7% of assets

Risk Analysis

Time Period	Load-Adj Return %	Risk %Rank[1] All	Risk %Rank[1] Cat	Morningstar Return	Morningstar Risk	Morningstar Risk-Adj Rating
1 Yr	–14.56					
3 Yr	2.71	44	69	–0.46[2]	0.61	★★★
5 Yr	7.86	47	74	0.65[2]	0.63	★★★
10 Yr	9.13	53	79	0.59	0.67	★★★

Average Historical Rating (123 months): 3.1★s

[1]1=low, 100=high [2] T-Bill return substituted for category avg.

Category Rating (3 Yr)

1 2 3 4 5 — Worst … Best (rating: 3)

Return: Average
Risk: Above Avg

Other Measures	Standard Index S&P 500	Best Fit Index Wil 4500
Alpha	1.4	–0.9
Beta	0.51	0.41
R-Squared	46	79
Standard Deviation		13.14
Mean		3.24
Sharpe Ratio		–0.15

Analysis by Gabriel Presler 08-24-01

Morgan Stanley Strategist Fund's aggressiveness has caught up with it in 2001, but it isn't a bad choice overall.

In some ways, this fund is one of the boldest in the domestic-hybrid category, sometimes devoting as much as 70% of its portfolio to equities. Manager Mark Bavoso also makes significant sector bets. Recently, for example, he built the fund's stake in health-care firms to virtually 20% of assets, 8 percentage points higher than the group norm. What's more, he trades twice as much as his rivals.

Bavoso doesn't play fast and loose with the rest of the portfolio though. In fact, this fund's bond exposure is generally quite conservative, consisting mostly of Treasury bonds. While Bavoso sometimes takes on a bit more interest-rate risk than his peers, he avoids most corporate issues. Moreover, the fund generally holds between 20% and 30% of assets in cash.

This mixed approach hasn't helped performance in 2001. The fund's equity stake—which stands at about 50% of assets—faltered as some of its top health-care picks, including Oxford Health Plans, struggled. And although the fund adopted a slightly long position in Treasuries in April and May of this year, their strong performance hasn't been enough to balance losses in the rest of the portfolio. Thus the fund's 10% loss for the year to date through August 23, 2001, trails 90% of its rivals'.

Poor performance like this isn't unheard of here, but the fund winds up in the top half of the category more often than not, so its long-term record is about average for the group. Bavoso's frequent trading means that asset allocation isn't dependable, so the fund's simply not right for investors seeking to supplement their portfolio with consistent and predictable exposure to stocks and bonds.

Address:	P.O. Box 2798 Boston, MA 02208–2798 800–869–3863 / 212–392–2550
Web Address:	www.deanwitter.com
Inception:	10-31-88
Advisor:	Morgan Stanley Dean Witter Adv.
Subadvisor:	None
NTF Plans:	N/A

Minimum Purchase:	$1000 Add: $100 IRA: $1000
Min Auto Inv Plan:	$1000 Add: $100
Sales Fees:	5.00%D, 0.75%B, 0.25%S Conv. in 10 Yrs.
Management Fee:	.60% mx./.45% mn.
Actual Fees:	Mgt: 0.54% Dist: 0.88%
Expense Projections:	3Yr: $79* 5Yr: $104* 10Yr: $183*
Avg Brok Commission:	— Income Distrib: Quarterly
Total Cost (relative to category):	—

Portfolio Analysis 09-30-01

Total Stocks: 46 Share change since 06-01	Sector	PE Ratio	YTD Return %	% Net Assets
⊖ Dean Foods	Staples	40.4	127.20	2.14
⊖ Baxter Intl	Health	33.9	22.84	1.94
⊕ Newmont Mng	Industrials	—	12.69	1.91
⊕ Raytheon	Industrials	—	7.27	1.87
⊕ Placer Dome	Industrials	—	14.47	1.83
☼ RJ Reynolds Tobacco Hldgs	Staples	3.1	22.37	1.62
⊖ Oxford Health Plans	Health	11.5	–23.70	1.54
Lockheed Martin	Industrials	36.8	38.98	1.46
Phillips Petro	Energy	7.1	8.56	1.45
⊕ Barrick Gold	Industrials	—	–1.28	1.45

Total Fixed-Income: 147	Date of Maturity	Amount $000	Value $000	% Net Assets
FNMA 8% TBA		48,300	50,594	2.73
FNMA 7%	12-01-30	46,496	48,022	2.59
FNMA 6.5%	05-01-31	31,035	31,529	1.70
FHLMC 7%	05-01-31	29,401	30,412	1.64
FNMA 7.5%	12-01-30	22,970	23,853	1.28
FNMA 6% TBA		23,000	22,899	1.23
FNMA 8% TBA	10-01-31	20,100	21,055	1.13
FNMA 6%	10-01-31	15,000	14,934	0.80
FNMA Debenture 6.625%	11-15-10	13,320	14,665	0.79
FHLMC Debenture 5.125%	10-15-08	10,000	10,106	0.54

Equity Style
Style: Blend
Size: Large–Cap

Fixed-Income Style
Duration: —
Quality: —
NA

	Portfolio Avg	Rel S&P
Price/Earnings Ratio	29.5	0.95
Price/Book Ratio	5.4	0.95
Price/Cash Flow	16.4	0.91
3 Yr Earnings Growth	13.8	0.94
1 Yr Earnings Est%	3.9	—
Debt % Total Cap	40.1	1.30
Med Mkt Cap $mil	13,107	0.22

Avg Eff Duration	—
Avg Eff Maturity	—
Avg Credit Quality	—
Avg Wtd Coupon	7.04%

Special Securities % assets 09-30-01	
Restricted/Illiquid Secs	2
Emerging–Markets Secs	Trace
Options/Futures/Warrants	No

Composition % of assets 09-30-01	
Cash	28.3
Stocks*	43.5
Bonds	28.2
Other	0.0
*Foreign (% of stocks)	10.9

Market Cap	
Giant	14.7
Large	43.9
Medium	39.9
Small	1.5
Micro	0.0

Sector Weightings	% of Stocks	Rel S&P	5-Year High	5-Year Low
Utilities	2.7	0.8	5	0
Energy	5.1	0.7	14	4
Financials	11.6	0.7	27	5
Industrials	21.9	1.9	28	12
Durables	0.0	0.0	11	0
Staples	14.0	1.8	22	3
Services	9.7	0.9	15	2
Retail	4.2	0.6	13	4
Health	23.2	1.6	23	6
Technology	7.6	0.4	39	0

Muhlenkamp

Ticker	Load	NAV	Yield	Total Assets	Mstar Category
MUHLX	None	$53.56	0.0%	$538.9 mil	Mid–Cap Value

Prospectus Objective: Growth and Income

Muhlenkamp Fund seeks total return, consistent with reasonable risk.

The fund normally invests primarily in common stocks. It may hold some high-quality fixed-income securities when market conditions warrant. When selecting issues, the advisor favors low price/earnings and price/book ratios and high returns on capital. The fund places emphasis on current conditions; it does not apply historical evaluation methods directly to today's market. It may invest no more than 5% of assets in debt rated below A. The fund primarily purchases issues listed on major exchanges.

Historical Profile
Return High
Risk Average
Rating ★★★★★ Highest

Investment Style
Equity
Average Stock %: 92% 96% 82% 86% 98% 95% 94%

▼ Manager Change
▽ Partial Manager Change

Fund Performance vs. Category Average
■ Quarterly Fund Return +/– Category Average
— Category Baseline

Performance Quartile (within Category)

Portfolio Manager(s)

Ronald H. Muhlenkamp, CFA. Since 11-88. BS'66 MIT; MBA'68 Harvard U.

1990	1991	1992	1993	1994	1995	1996	1997	1998	1999	2000	12-01	History
9.21	13.25	15.20	17.86	16.23	21.26	27.52	36.55	37.65	41.11	48.98	53.56	NAV
–14.90	45.39	15.80	18.13	–7.19	32.96	29.98	33.30	3.22	11.40	25.30	9.35	Total Return %
–11.78	14.90	8.19	8.08	–8.50	–4.57	7.04	–0.05	–25.36	–9.64	34.40	21.23	+/– S&P 500
1.18	7.46	–5.88	2.51	–5.06	–1.97	9.73	–1.06	–1.87	11.50	6.12	7.01	+/– Russ Midcap Val
1.68	1.52	1.09	0.63	0.39	1.23	0.53	0.47	0.21	0.00	0.00	0.00	Income Return %
–16.58	43.87	14.72	17.50	–7.58	31.73	29.46	32.83	3.01	11.40	25.30	9.35	Capital Return %
82	4	40	58	84	32	8	17	53	39	26	35	Total Rtn % Rank Cat
0.19	0.14	0.14	0.10	0.07	0.20	0.11	0.13	0.08	0.00	0.00	0.00	Income $
0.00	0.00	0.00	0.00	0.28	0.12	0.00	0.00	0.00	0.80	2.33	0.00	Capital Gains $
1.76	1.71	1.41	1.30	1.57	1.35	1.56	1.33	1.32	1.38	1.28	—	Expense Ratio %
1.95	1.17	1.44	0.70	0.70	1.10	0.58	0.53	0.21	–0.26	–0.20	—	Income Ratio %
47	53	20	14	26	23	17	14	27	15	32	—	Turnover Rate %
1.2	2.0	4.7	12.1	16.6	23.6	41.6	125.1	195.0	176.7	266.0	538.9	Net Assets $mil

Performance 12-31-01

	1st Qtr	2nd Qtr	3rd Qtr	4th Qtr	Total
1997	2.03	14.53	14.37	–0.26	33.30
1998	12.37	3.70	–21.25	12.48	3.22
1999	–2.95	19.65	–11.51	8.40	11.40
2000	13.16	–0.24	6.70	4.02	25.30
2001	–3.06	13.94	–20.43	24.41	9.35

Trailing	Total Return%	+/– S&P 500	+/– Russ Midcap Val	% Rank All	% Rank Cat	Growth of $10,000
3 Mo	24.41	13.73	12.38	8	6	12,441
6 Mo	–1.00	4.56	–0.09	42	49	9,900
1 Yr	9.35	21.23	7.01	6	35	10,935
3 Yr Avg	15.14	16.16	8.33	5	21	15,263
5 Yr Avg	16.00	5.30	4.53	3	19	21,001
10 Yr Avg	16.51	3.58	2.09	3	17	46,083
15 Yr Avg	—	—	—	—	—	—

Tax Analysis	Tax-Adj Ret%	%Rank Cat	%Pretax Ret	%Rank Cat
3 Yr Avg	14.61	14	96.5	9
5 Yr Avg	15.62	7	97.7	1
10 Yr Avg	16.11	2	97.6	1

Potential Capital Gain Exposure: 22% of assets

Risk Analysis

Time Period	Load-Adj Return %	Risk %Rank[1] All	Risk %Rank[1] Cat	Morningstar Return	Morningstar Risk	Morningstar Risk-Adj Rating
1 Yr	9.35					
3 Yr	15.14	67	93	2.38[2]	0.93	★★★★★
5 Yr	16.00	71	88	2.95[2]	0.97	★★★★★
10 Yr	16.51	74	86	2.20	0.96	★★★★★

Average Historical Rating (122 months): 3.5★s

[1]1=low, 100=high [2] T-Bill return substituted for category avg.

Category Rating (3 Yr)

1 2 3 4 5
Worst Best

Return Above Avg
Risk High

Other Measures	Standard Index S&P 500	Best Fit Index SPMid400
Alpha	18.2	4.9
Beta	1.05	1.08
R-Squared	55	77

Standard Deviation	27.94
Mean	15.14
Sharpe Ratio	0.41

Analysis by Brian Portnoy 11-16-01

Muhlenkamp Fund has earned its place among the mid-cap value elite.

This fund has long marched to the beat of its own drummer. Manager Ron Muhlenkamp's analysis of macroeconomic and market data takes priority in shaping how exposed the fund is toward economically sensitive fare. In early 2000, for example, he reasoned that rising interest rates would hurt higher-priced growth stocks and buoy defensive fare in financials and energy. And as interest rates began to fall in early 2001, he maintained his financials stake and bought more consumer cyclicals. Meanwhile, when the signs point to an overvalued market, Muhlenkamp puts on the brakes: In mid-1998, he boosted the fund's cash stake to 20%.

This top-down approach, combined with a focus on firms with healthy returns on equity that trade cheaply, has produced one of the mid-value category's finest long-term records. Over the past decade, the fund's 15.4% annualized gain ranks in the group's top quintile and paces the S&P 500 index by 2.6 points per year. The fund is also superbly managed for tax efficiency: On an aftertax basis, the fund's 10-year return is nearly at the top of the category.

Because the fund isn't shy about making macro calls and sizable industry bets, it's more volatile than most of its rivals. In 2001, for example, the fund's tilt toward an economic turnaround was at least premature, as market-leveraged financials such as Merrill Lynch have stung badly. However, the fund's bet on homebuilders has been spot on, and that helped the fund to a breakeven return for the year to date through Nov. 15, which is a tad better than average.

A somewhat unconventional approach might scare away index huggers, but all others seeking an all-cap, tax-efficient value option with a proven track record should take a closer look.

Address:	3000 Stonewood Dr. Ste 310 Wexford, PA 15090–0598 724–935–5520 / 800–860–3863
Web Address:	www.muhlenkamp.com
Inception:	11-17-88
Advisor:	Muhlenkamp & Co.
Subadvisor:	None
NTF Plans:	Fidelity , Fidelity Inst.

Minimum Purchase:	$1500	Add: $50	IRA: $1500
Min Auto Inv Plan:	$200	Add: $50	
Sales Fees:	No–load		
Management Fee:	1.0%		
Actual Fees:	Mgt: 1.00%	Dist: —	
Expense Projections:	3Yr: $431	5Yr: $745	10Yr: $1635
Avg Brok Commission:	—	Income Distrib: Annually	
Total Cost (relative to category):		Below Avg	

Portfolio Analysis 09-30-01

Share change since 06-01 Total Stocks: 74	Sector	PE	YTD Ret%	% Assets
⊕ Fidelity Natl Finl	Financials	8.5	–25.00	5.89
⊕ Calpine	Utilities	8.9	–62.70	4.51
NVR	Industrials	9.4	65.05	4.44
Citigroup	Financials	20.0	0.03	3.69
Conoco Cl A	Energy	9.0	1.56	3.35
⊕ El Paso	Utilities	NMF	–36.70	3.27
⊕ Whirlpool	Durables	71.9	57.27	3.19
⊕ Polaris Inds	Durables	15.6	48.57	3.01
⊕ Cemex (Part) ADR	Industrials	—	—	2.94
⊕ Arkansas Best	Services	13.2	57.37	2.91
Orthodontic Centers of Amer	Health	26.3	–2.40	2.75
⊕ Cendant	Services	20.4	103.70	2.49
Superior Inds Intl	Durables	17.0	29.10	2.42
Morgan Stanley/Dean Witter	Financials	16.6	–28.20	2.38
D & K Healthcare Resources	Health	28.2	321.30	2.36
Meritage	Industrials	6.3	38.65	2.30
Beazer Homes USA	Industrials	9.0	82.93	2.19
Merrill Lynch	Financials	18.2	–22.70	2.10
⊕ Dal–Tile Intl	Industrials	16.0	63.87	1.98
⊕ Conseco	Financials	—	–66.10	1.95
Stanley Furniture	Durables	13.3	–1.47	1.90
⊕ Anadarko Petro	Energy	11.1	–19.70	1.89
IBM	Technology	26.9	43.00	1.87
Centex	Industrials	10.2	52.56	1.79
Citrix Sys	Technology	44.4	0.71	1.60

Current Investment Style

Style: Value Blnd Growth; Size: Large Med Small

	Stock Port Avg	Relative S&P 500 Current	Relative S&P 500 Hist	Rel Cat
Price/Earnings Ratio	22.0	0.71	0.61	0.93
Price/Book Ratio	3.1	0.55	0.49	1.03
Price/Cash Flow	11.0	0.61	0.70	0.89
3 Yr Earnings Growth	29.8	2.03	1.48	2.51
1 Yr Earnings Est%	8.4	—	—	–1.37
Med Mkt Cap $mil	2,182	0.0	0.1	0.31

Special Securities % assets 09-30-01	
Restricted/Illiquid Secs	0
Emerging–Markets Secs	3
Options/Futures/Warrants	No

Composition % assets 09-30-01	
Cash	0.0
Stocks*	99.5
Bonds	0.5
Other	0.0
*Foreign (% stocks)	3.1

Market Cap	
Giant	10.1
Large	18.2
Medium	30.4
Small	32.4
Micro	9.0

Sector Weightings	% of Stocks	Rel S&P	5-Year High	5-Year Low
Utilities	7.8	2.4	8	0
Energy	9.3	1.3	10	0
Financials	20.7	1.2	61	20
Industrials	22.9	2.0	34	10
Durables	18.8	12.0	19	3
Staples	0.3	0.0	9	0
Services	7.6	0.7	14	2
Retail	1.2	0.2	1	0
Health	5.3	0.4	8	0
Technology	6.3	0.3	29	0

Mutual Beacon Z

Ticker	Load	NAV	Yield	Total Assets	Mstar Category
BEGRX	Closed	$13.05	1.4%	$4,616.4 mil	Mid–Cap Value

Prospectus Objective: Growth and Income

Mutual Beacon Fund seeks capital appreciation; income is secondary.

The fund invests in common and preferred stocks and corporate debt of any credit quality. It may also invest up to 50% of assets in companies involved in mergers, consolidations, liquidations, and reorganizations.

Class A shares have front loads; B shares have deferred loads; C shares have level loads; Z shares are only available to certain qualified registered investment advisors.

Historical Profile

Return High
Risk Low
Rating ★★★★★ Highest

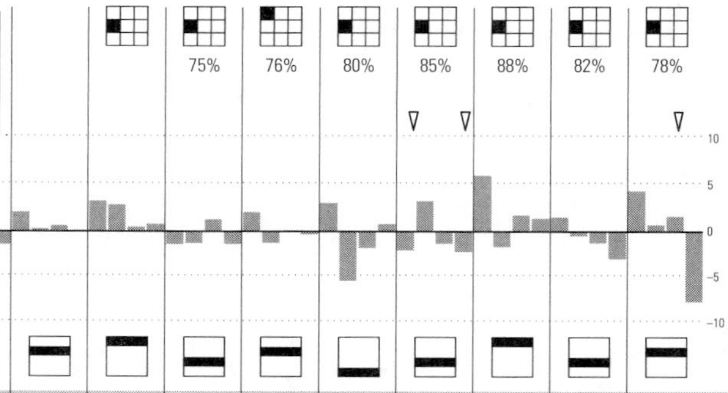

Investment Style: Equity — Average Stock %: 75%, 76%, 80%, 85%, 88%, 82%, 78%

▼ Manager Change
▽ Partial Manager Change

Fund Performance vs. Category Average
■ Quarterly Fund Return +/– Category Average
– Category Baseline

Performance Quartile (within Category)

Portfolio Manager(s)

David J. Winters, CFA. Since 3-98. BA Cornell U. Other funds currently managed: Mutual Discovery Z, Mutual Shares Z, Mutual European Z.

Matthew T. Haynes, CFA. Since 8-01. BA William Peterson U. Other funds currently managed: Morgan Stanley Global Div Gr Secs B, Mutual European Z, Mutual Beacon A.

History

1990	1991	1992	1993	1994	1995	1996	1997	1998	1999	2000	12–01	History
6.93	7.79	9.03	10.36	10.34	11.98	12.98	14.12	13.12	13.84	13.38	13.05	NAV
–8.22	17.71	22.82	22.94	5.61	25.93	21.15	23.03	2.37	16.79	14.33	6.11	Total Return %
–5.10	–12.77	15.20	12.88	4.30	–11.60	–1.79	–10.33	–26.21	–4.25	23.43	17.99	+/– S&P 500
7.87	–20.21	1.14	7.31	7.74	–9.00	0.89	–11.34	–2.72	16.90	–4.86	3.78	+/– Russ Midcap Val
4.52	3.59	2.00	1.38	1.42	2.74	3.04	4.22	3.23	2.06	3.27	1.49	Income Return %
–12.74	14.12	20.83	21.56	4.19	23.19	18.12	18.80	–0.87	14.74	11.06	4.62	Capital Return %
43	88	10	26	10	72	41	76	55	18	62	43	Total Rtn % Rank Cat
0.36	0.25	0.15	0.12	0.15	0.28	0.35	0.54	0.45	0.27	0.44	0.20	Income $
0.09	0.11	0.37	0.61	0.45	0.74	1.14	1.26	0.87	1.19	1.86	0.94	Capital Gains $
0.85	0.85	0.81	0.73	0.75	0.72	0.73	0.74	0.76	0.78	0.80	—	Expense Ratio %
4.59	3.07	1.90	1.53	1.96	2.89	3.21	1.92	2.28	1.52	1.55	—	Income Ratio %
58	57	58	53	71	73	67	55	65	68	62	—	Turnover Rate %
387.5	399.0	533.2	1,060.8	2,056.4	3,566.7	4,950.8	5,684.6	4,039.5	3,218.7	3,043.0	3,091.5	Net Assets $mil

Performance 12-31-01

	1st Qtr	2nd Qtr	3rd Qtr	4th Qtr	Total
1997	4.24	7.76	9.59	–0.06	23.03
1998	9.28	0.91	–17.54	12.58	2.37
1999	5.26	11.89	–8.06	7.85	16.79
2000	4.26	–1.10	7.04	3.59	14.33
2001	2.84	8.46	–10.20	5.94	6.11

Trailing	Total Return%	+/– S&P 500	+/– Russ Midcap Val	% Rank All	% Rank Cat	Growth of $10,000
3 Mo	5.94	–4.74	–6.09	61	94	10,594
6 Mo	–4.86	0.69	–3.95	61	87	9,514
1 Yr	6.11	17.99	3.78	18	43	10,611
3 Yr Avg	12.32	13.34	5.51	8	35	14,169
5 Yr Avg	12.28	1.58	0.82	9	43	17,844
10 Yr Avg	15.81	2.89	1.40	4	21	43,414
15 Yr Avg	14.88	1.15	1.41	7	8	80,116

Tax Analysis	Tax-Adj Ret%	%Rank Cat	%Pretax Ret	%Rank Cat
3 Yr Avg	8.92	42	72.4	73
5 Yr Avg	8.99	50	73.2	78
10 Yr Avg	12.66	28	80.1	58

Potential Capital Gain Exposure: 18% of assets

Risk Analysis

Time Period	Load-Adj Return %	Risk %Rank[1] All	Risk %Rank[1] Cat	Morningstar Return	Morningstar Risk	Morningstar Risk-Adj Rating
1 Yr	6.11					
3 Yr	12.32	36	1	1.68[2]	0.46	★★★★★
5 Yr	12.28	43	3	1.82[2]	0.54	★★★★
10 Yr	15.81	48	1	2.00	0.53	★★★★★

Average Historical Rating (193 months): 4.5★s

[1]1=low, 100=high [2] T-Bill return substituted for category avg.

Category Rating (3 Yr)

1 2 3 4 5 — Worst … Best

Return Average
Risk Low

Other Measures	Standard Index S&P 500	Best Fit Index S&P 500
Alpha	10.6	10.6
Beta	0.56	0.56
R–Squared	59	59

Standard Deviation	13.84
Mean	12.32
Sharpe Ratio	0.61

Portfolio Analysis 06-30-01

Share change since 12–00 Total Stocks: 154	Sector	PE	YTD Ret%	% Assets
⊕ Telephone and Data Sys	Services	—	0.29	2.83
⊖ Federated Dept Stores	Retail	16.6	16.86	2.47
⊖ Canary Wharf Grp	Financials	69.9	—	2.31
⊕ Lagardere	Financials	11.1	—	1.82
⊖ AT & T Liberty Media Cl A	Services	—	3.22	1.61
☼ AT&T	Services	7.8	40.59	1.58
Washington Post	Services	20.0	–13.20	1.56
⊖ EW Scripps Cl A	Services	29.9	5.94	1.55
⊖ White Mountains Ins Grp	Financials	—	9.45	1.20
☼ Tyco Intl	Industrials	27.1	6.23	1.20
⊖ Bear Stearns	Financials	12.9	16.96	1.17
⊖ Delphi Automotive Sys	Durables	—	23.78	1.17
⊕ Florida East Coast Inds	Services	62.6	–35.20	1.09
⊖ Heller Finl	Financials	—	73.46	1.09
⊕ General Motors Cl H	Technology	42.9	–32.80	1.08
⊕ Sprint	Services	20.5	1.18	1.07
Commrcl Federal	Financials	25.3	22.54	1.03
⊕ Altadis Cl A	Staples	0.2	—	1.02
Intl Paper	Industrials	—	1.43	1.02
⊕ Berkshire Hathaway Cl B	Financials	64.8	7.26	0.95
Berkshire Hathaway Cl A	Financials	—	—	0.90
⊕ USA Networks	Services	58.1	40.50	0.90
⊕ Abitibi–Consolid	Industrials	—	–17.50	0.90
⊕ Metris	Financials	11.4	–2.13	0.89
⊕ Park Place Entrtnmt	Services	—	–23.10	0.86

Current Investment Style

Style: Value Blnd Growth; Size: Large Med Small

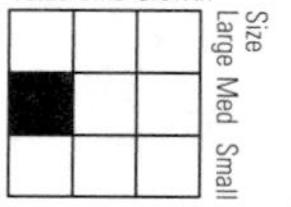

	Stock Port Avg	Relative S&P 500 Current	Relative S&P 500 Hist	Rel Cat
Price/Earnings Ratio	23.4	0.76	0.70	0.99
Price/Book Ratio	2.3	0.41	0.39	0.77
Price/Cash Flow	13.4	0.74	0.64	1.08
3 Yr Earnings Growth	12.2[1]	0.84	0.72	1.03
1 Yr Earnings Est%	–18.6[1]	10.52	—	3.03
Med Mkt Cap $mil	6,222	0.1	0.1	0.87

[1]figure is based on 50% or less of stocks

Analysis by Christopher Traulsen 12-02-01

Mutual Beacon Fund isn't quite as strong a choice as it once was, but it still holds appeal.

On the surface, this fund is having a solid year. It's up 3.7% for the year to date through Nov. 30, 2001. Although it has been held back a bit by its large European stake—a typical feature of this fund—that's still a top-half showing in the mid-value category. That kind of performance is the norm here. The fund doesn't often outleg its peers by wide margins, but it has posted strong returns over time, with much less volatility than its average rival.

But much has changed here. Although he remains at the firm, Larry Sondike stepped down as comanager of the fund in late summer. Around the same time, there was an exodus of talent at the Mutual Series complex as a whole. Mutual Qualified manager and lead financials analyst Ray Garea left the firm, as did European analyst Rob Friedman, and distressed debt analyst Jeff Altman.

That kind of talent drain is cause for substantial concern. Nevertheless, this fund is far from rudderless. Comanager David Winters, a 17-year veteran of Mutual Series, remains at the helm. In addition, foreign-stock specialist Matt Haynes has been brought on board to comanage Mutual European and this offering.

The pair has no intention of changing the fund's signature style and will continue to seek out dirt-cheap equities and distressed credits and make merger-arbitrage plays. Further, they and the rest of the Mutual Series team will continue the shop's activist approach to investing. It's also worth noting that the firm has hired another distressed-debt analyst, and has two financials specialists in Josh Ross and Jeff Diamond to offset the loss of Garea.

We think there's little reason for shareholders here to sell now. The fund's proven style and long-term success, and the continuing presence of experienced hands like Winters, still make it a reasonable, if diminished, choice.

Special Securities % assets 06-30-01	
Restricted/Illiquid Secs	0
Emerging–Markets Secs	Trace
Options/Futures/Warrants	Yes

Composition % assets 06-30-01	
Cash	13.3
Stocks*	77.8
Bonds	8.4
Other	0.5
*Foreign (% stocks)	27.9

Market Cap	
Giant	11.0
Large	23.4
Medium	58.6
Small	6.3
Micro	0.5

Sector Weightings	% of Stocks	Rel S&P	5-Year High	5-Year Low
Utilities	1.9	0.6	2	0
Energy	1.3	0.2	14	1
Financials	26.9	1.5	40	17
Industrials	13.0	1.1	19	7
Durables	3.7	2.4	12	1
Staples	8.3	1.1	13	5
Services	31.6	2.9	32	10
Retail	6.9	1.0	12	1
Health	3.0	0.2	13	1
Technology	3.3	0.2	5	0

Address:	51 John F. Kennedy Parkway Short Hills, NJ 07078 415–312–2000 / 800–342–5236
Web Address:	www.franklintempleton.com
Inception:	08-01-61
Advisor:	Franklin Mutual Advisers
Subadvisor:	None
NTF Plans:	N/A

Minimum Purchase:	Closed	Add: $50	IRA: —
Min Auto Inv Plan:	Closed	Add: $50	
Sales Fees:	No-load		
Management Fee:	.60%, .15%A		
Actual Fees:	Mgt: 0.60%	Dist: —	
Expense Projections:	3Yr: $265	5Yr: $460	10Yr: $1025
Avg Brok Commission:	—	Income Distrib: Semi–Ann.	
Total Cost (relative to category):		Low	

Mutual Discovery Z

Ticker	Load	NAV	Yield	Total Assets	Mstar Category
MDISX	Closed	$18.19	1.8%	$3,448.3 mil	World Stock

Prospectus Objective: World Stock

Mutual Discovery Fund seeks long-term capital appreciation.

The fund invests primarily in small companies. It may purchase common and preferred stocks, convertibles, and bonds of any quality. The advisor seeks securities that are undervalued. It may invest up to 50% in companies involved in mergers, consolidations, liquidations, and reorganizations.

Class A shares have front loads; B shares have deferred loads; C shares have level loads; Z shares are only available to certain qualified registered investment advisors.

Historical Profile

Return High
Risk Low
Rating ★★★★★ Highest

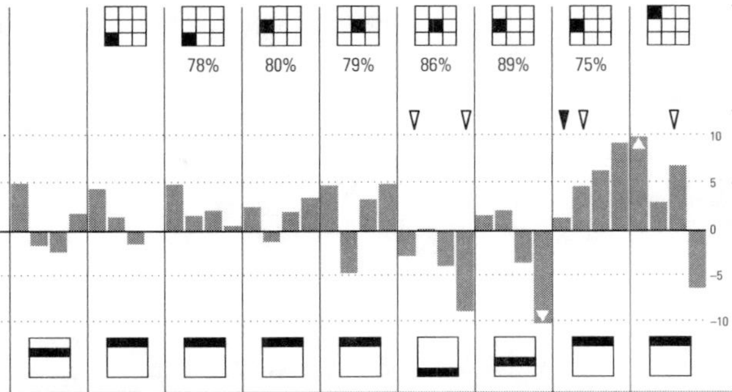

Investment Style
Equity
Average Stock %: 78% 80% 79% 86% 89% 75%

▼ Manager Change
▽ Partial Manager Change

Fund Performance vs. Category Average
Quarterly Fund Return +/– Category Average
— Category Baseline

Performance Quartile (within Category)

Portfolio Manager(s)

David J. Winters, CFA. Since 2-00. BA Cornell U. Other funds currently managed: Mutual Beacon Z, Mutual Shares Z, Mutual European Z.

Timothy Rankin. Since 7-01. Other funds currently managed: Diversified Inv High Yield Bond, Mutual Discovery A, Mutual Discovery C.

1990	1991	1992	1993	1994	1995	1996	1997	1998	1999	2000	12-01	History
—	—	10.00	13.05	12.55	15.16	17.18	18.89	17.27	21.10	18.93	18.19	NAV
—	—	—	35.85	3.62	28.63	24.93	22.94	−1.90	26.80	12.59	1.26	Total Return %
—	—	—	25.79	2.31	−8.91	1.98	−10.41	−30.48	5.76	21.70	13.14	+/– S&P 500
—	—	—	13.35	−1.46	7.91	11.45	7.18	−26.24	1.87	25.77	—	+/– MSCI World
—	—	—	0.90	1.24	1.13	2.94	4.78	2.59	2.46	3.07	1.85	Income Return %
—	—	—	34.95	2.38	27.50	21.98	18.16	−4.49	24.34	9.52	−0.59	Capital Return %
—	—	—	35	9	12	5	12	90	65	3	2	Total Rtn % Rank Cat
—	—	0.00	0.09	0.16	0.14	0.44	0.81	0.48	0.42	0.63	0.35	Income $
—	—	0.00	0.44	0.81	0.82	1.27	1.36	0.81	0.32	4.04	0.62	Capital Gains $
—	—	—	1.07	0.99	0.99	0.96	0.98	1.00	1.03	1.02	—	Expense Ratio %
—	—	—	1.17	1.64	2.00	2.24	1.82	1.81	1.33	1.64	—	Income Ratio %
—	—	—	90	73	73	80	58	84	88	75	—	Turnover Rate %
—	—	—	546.8	725.8	1,368.3	2,974.4	3,878.0	2,523.9	2,038.8	2,011.6	1,932.6	Net Assets $mil

Performance 12-31-01

	1st Qtr	2nd Qtr	3rd Qtr	4th Qtr	Total
1997	5.82	7.65	8.56	−0.58	22.94
1998	11.22	0.67	−19.44	8.76	−1.90
1999	4.11	10.58	−3.58	14.23	26.80
2000	7.20	−0.25	3.23	1.99	12.59
2001	0.00	6.51	−9.60	5.17	1.27

Trailing	Total Return%	+/– S&P 500	+/– MSCI World	% Rank All	% Rank Cat	Growth of $10,000
3 Mo	5.17	−5.51	—	64	96	10,517
6 Mo	−4.93	0.63	—	61	23	9,507
1 Yr	1.26	13.14	—	40	2	10,126
3 Yr Avg	13.07	14.10	—	7	7	14,457
5 Yr Avg	11.76	1.06	—	11	11	17,437
10 Yr Avg	—	—	—	—	—	—
15 Yr Avg	—	—	—	—	—	—

Tax Analysis	Tax-Adj Ret%	%Rank Cat	%Pretax Ret	%Rank Cat
3 Yr Avg	9.68	10	74.0	46
5 Yr Avg	8.66	14	73.6	42
10 Yr Avg	—	—	—	—

Potential Capital Gain Exposure: 11% of assets

Risk Analysis

Time Period	Load-Adj Return %	Risk %Rank[1] All	Risk %Rank[1] Cat	Morningstar Return	Morningstar Risk	Morningstar Risk-Adj Rating
1 Yr	1.26					
3 Yr	13.07	32	1	1.86[2]	0.29	★★★★★
5 Yr	11.76	40	1	1.67[2]	0.38	★★★★★
Incept	16.46	—	—	—	—	

Average Historical Rating (73 months): 4.9★s

[1] 1=low, 100=high [2] T-Bill return substituted for category avg.

Category Rating (3 Yr)

1 2 3 4 5 — Worst / Best

Return High
Risk Low

Other Measures	Standard Index S&P 500	Best Fit Index SPMid400
Alpha	10.4	5.2
Beta	0.44	0.43
R-Squared	55	71

Standard Deviation	11.09
Mean	13.07
Sharpe Ratio	0.84

Analysis by William Samuel Rocco 08-31-01

The recent personnel changes at Mutual Series shouldn't have much impact on this fine fund.

Mutual Discovery Fund won't be directly affected by the rush of manager departures that its parent firm announced in July. Ray Garea and a few other Mutual Series managers are leaving soon, but David Winters, who has run this fund for the past 18 months and has worked on it for years, will remain on board here.

Winters is taking on more responsibilities at the firm in the wake of the departures, including a comanager role on Mutual European. However, Mutual Series brought in Matt Haynes, formerly of MDSW Global Dividend Growth Securities, to comanage that fund. And it has promoted Tim Rankin, who has been working as an analyst at the firm for years, to assistant manager on this fund. The moves reduce the likelihood that Winters will get stretched too thin on the international side of the firm.

Meanwhile, the fund has thrived this year. It has benefited from its deep-value and smaller-cap biases. Further, Winters has kept a significant portion of the portfolio in cash and made several good calls. He has maintained sizable positions in Spanish construction company Acciona and French builder Vinci, and both have prospered. And though he normally fully hedges the fund's foreign currency exposure, he thought the euro had gotten too cheap this summer and unhedged 30% of the fund's exposure. That move has paid off as the euro has strengthened in recent weeks. Thus, the fund is up 5% and leads 98% of its peers for the year to date through August 30.The fund has also handily outgained its rivals over time and kept volatility low with its smaller-cap deep-value discipline.

Portfolio Analysis 12-31-00

Share change since 06-00 Total Stocks: 177

	Sector	Country	% Assets
⊖ Lagardere	Financials	France	2.31
⊖ Suez Lyon Eaux	Industrials	France	2.19
⊖ Canary Wharf Grp	Financials	United Kingdom	1.87
⊖ Railtrack Grp	Services	United Kingdom	1.87
⊕ Irish Life & Permanent	Financials	Ireland	1.55
⊕ Vinci	Industrials	France	1.49
⊕ Berkshire Hathaway Cl A	Financials	U.S.	1.47
⊕ Sulzer (Reg)	Industrials	Switzerland	1.45
⊖ Investor Cl B	Durables	Sweden	1.20
⊕ Washington Post	Services	U.S.	1.16
⊕ Brown-Forman Cl B	Staples	U.S.	1.12
⊕ Federated Dept Stores	Retail	U.S.	1.10
⊕ EW Scripps Cl A	Services	U.S.	1.01
Invik Cl B	Financials	Sweden	1.01
⊕ Telephone and Data Sys	Services	U.S.	0.95
⊕ Kinnevik Cl B	Industrials	Sweden	0.92
⊖ Investor Cl A	Durables	Sweden	0.88
☼ GIB Hldgs (Part)	Retail	Belgium	0.87
☼ AT & T Liberty Media Cl A	Services	U.S.	0.87
⊕ Acciona	Industrials	Spain	0.83

Current Investment Style

Style: Value Blnd Growth; Size: Large Med Small

	Stock Port Avg	Rel MSCI EAFE Current	Rel MSCI EAFE Hist	Rel Cat
Price/Earnings Ratio	22.2	0.86	0.76	0.80
Price/Cash Flow	13.0	1.01	0.89	0.79
Price/Book Ratio	2.3	0.67	0.65	0.51
3 Yr Earnings Growth	14.7	0.79	—	0.79
Med Mkt Cap $mil	4,864	0.2	0.1	0.20

Country Exposure 12-31-00	% assets
U.S.	29
France	8
United Kingdom	8
Sweden	6
Switzerland	4

Hedging History: Always

Regional Exposure 12-31-00	% assets
Europe	35
Japan	2
Latin America	0
Pacific Rim	1
U.S.	29
Other	3

Special Securities % assets 12-31-00	
Restricted/Illiquid Secs	0
Emerging-Markets Secs	1
Options/Futures/Warrants	No

Composition % assets 12-31-00			
Cash	23.5	Bonds	4.5
Stocks	72.0	Other	0.0

Sector Weightings	% of Stocks	Rel Cat	5-Year High	5-Year Low
Utilities	1.5	0.6	2	0
Energy	3.4	0.6	9	2
Financials	26.6	1.5	35	17
Industrials	20.3	1.8	26	9
Durables	5.3	1.3	12	1
Staples	13.0	1.6	15	4
Services	23.9	1.4	27	11
Retail	3.7	0.7	13	1
Health	1.4	0.1	14	0
Technology	1.0	0.1	4	1

Address:	51 John F. Kennedy Parkway Short Hills, NJ 07078 415-312-2000 / 800-342-5236
Web Address:	www.franklintempleton.com
*Inception:	12-31-92
Advisor:	Franklin Mutual Advisers
Subadvisor:	None
NTF Plans:	N/A

Minimum Purchase:	Closed	Add: $50	IRA: —
Min Auto Inv Plan:	Closed	Add: $50	
Sales Fees:	No-load		
Management Fee:	.80%, .15%A		
Actual Fees:	Mgt: 0.80%	Dist: —	
Expense Projections:	3Yr: $353	5Yr: $612	10Yr: $1352
Avg Brok Commission:	—	Income Distrib: Semi-Ann.	
Total Cost (relative to category):	Below Avg		

Mutual Qualified Z

Ticker	Load	NAV	Yield	Total Assets	Mstar Category
MQIFX	Closed	$16.49	1.1%	$3,779.5 mil	Mid-Cap Value

Prospectus Objective: Growth and Income

Mutual Qualified Fund seeks capital appreciation; income is secondary.

The fund invests primarily in common and preferred stocks, and debt of any credit quality. It may also invest up to 50% of assets in companies involved in prospective mergers, consolidations, liquidations, reorganizations, or other special situations.

Class A shares have front loads; B shares have deferred loads; C shares have level loads; Z shares are only available to certain qualified registered investment advisors.

Historical Profile

Return High
Risk Low
Rating ★★★★★ Highest

Investment Style: Equity — Average Stock %: 78% 74% 79% 85% 88% 81%

▼ Manager Change
▽ Partial Manager Change

Fund Performance vs. Category Average
Quarterly Fund Return +/– Category Average
— Category Baseline

Performance Quartile (within Category)

Portfolio Manager(s)

Jeff Diamond. Since 8-01. BS Cornell U.; MBA Columbia U. Other funds currently managed: Mutual Qualified A, Mutual Qualified C, Mutual Financial Services Z.

Susan Potto. Since 8-01. Other funds currently managed: Mutual Qualified A, Mutual Qualified C, Mutual Qualified B.

History

1990	1991	1992	1993	1994	1995	1996	1997	1998	1999	2000	12-01	History
9.19	10.59	12.22	13.50	13.34	14.87	16.24	18.18	16.46	16.91	16.61	16.49	NAV
–10.12	21.06	22.75	22.66	5.77	26.55	21.22	24.88	0.50	13.64	14.25	8.21	Total Return %
–7.00	–9.42	15.13	12.60	4.45	–10.99	–1.73	–8.47	–28.07	–7.40	23.35	20.09	+/– S&P 500
5.97	–16.86	1.07	7.03	7.90	–8.39	0.96	–9.48	–4.59	13.74	–4.93	5.87	+/– Russ Midcap Val
5.59	3.67	2.34	1.53	1.60	2.49	3.01	4.00	2.51	1.82	3.39	1.21	Income Return %
–15.71	17.39	20.40	21.13	4.16	24.05	18.21	20.88	–2.01	11.82	10.86	7.00	Capital Return %
58	79	12	30	9	67	40	64	61	29	64	38	Total Rtn % Rank Cat
0.62	0.34	0.25	0.19	0.22	0.33	0.44	0.64	0.45	0.29	0.55	0.20	Income $
0.19	0.19	0.51	1.28	0.72	1.64	1.29	1.40	1.33	1.48	1.98	1.27	Capital Gains $
0.89	0.87	0.82	0.78	0.73	0.72	0.75	0.75	0.76	0.77	0.78	—	Expense Ratio %
5.40	3.09	2.10	1.65	1.91	2.71	3.06	1.85	2.05	1.31	1.43	—	Income Ratio %
46	52	47	56	68	76	65	53	67	60	55	—	Turnover Rate %
1,074.8	1,111.4	1,251.9	1,539.8	1,788.8	2,999.4	4,999.1	5,239.7	3,962.3	3,153.3	2,921.3	3,022.4	Net Assets $mil

Performance 12-31-01

	1st Qtr	2nd Qtr	3rd Qtr	4th Qtr	Total
1997	4.13	9.23	9.55	0.23	24.88
1998	9.41	–0.91	–17.70	12.63	0.50
1999	2.92	13.41	–8.64	6.56	13.64
2000	2.90	0.67	7.92	2.20	14.25
2001	2.89	10.18	–10.47	6.62	8.21

Trailing	Total Return%	+/– S&P 500	+/– Russ Midcap Val	% Rank All	% Rank Cat	Growth of $10,000
3 Mo	6.62	–4.06	–5.41	58	91	10,662
6 Mo	–4.55	1.01	–3.64	59	84	9,545
1 Yr	8.21	20.09	5.87	9	38	10,821
3 Yr Avg	12.00	13.03	5.19	8	37	14,049
5 Yr Avg	12.01	1.31	0.55	10	46	17,632
10 Yr Avg	15.72	2.79	1.31	4	28	43,070
15 Yr Avg	14.41	0.67	0.94	9	20	75,300

Tax Analysis	Tax-Adj Ret%	%Rank Cat	%Pretax Ret	%Rank Cat
3 Yr Avg	8.91	42	74.3	68
5 Yr Avg	8.97	52	74.7	71
10 Yr Avg	12.47	34	79.3	65

Potential Capital Gain Exposure: 21% of assets

Risk Analysis

Time Period	Load-Adj Return %	Risk %Rank[1] All	Risk %Rank[1] Cat	Morningstar Return	Morningstar Risk	Morningstar Risk-Adj Rating
1 Yr	8.21					
3 Yr	12.00	38	8	1.60[2]	0.49	★★★★★
5 Yr	12.01	44	5	1.74[2]	0.57	★★★★
10 Yr	15.72	49	3	1.98	0.56	★★★★★

Average Historical Rating (193 months): 4.6★s

[1]1=low, 100=high [2] T-Bill return substituted for category avg.

Category Rating (3 Yr)

1 2 3 4 5 — Worst … Best

Return Average
Risk Low

Other Measures	Standard Index S&P 500	Best Fit Index SPMid400
Alpha	10.4	4.1
Beta	0.57	0.51
R-Squared	51	53
Standard Deviation		14.99
Mean		12.00
Sharpe Ratio		0.54

Portfolio Analysis 12-31-00

Share change since 06-00 Total Stocks: 159

	Sector	PE	YTD Ret%	% Assets
⊖ Canary Wharf Grp	Financials	69.9	—	2.94
⊕ Federated Dept Stores	Retail	16.6	16.86	2.23
EW Scripps Cl A	Services	29.9	5.94	1.87
⊕ Telephone and Data Sys	Services	—	0.29	1.85
⊕ AT & T Liberty Media Cl A	Services	—	3.22	1.58
Household Intl	Financials	14.7	6.89	1.52
⊖ Heller Finl	Financials	—	73.46	1.46
⊕ Republic Svcs Cl A	Services	15.6	16.19	1.34
⊖ TCF Finl	Financials	18.2	10.24	1.27
White Mountains Ins Grp	Financials	—	9.45	1.26
⊕ Florida East Coast Inds	Services	62.6	–35.20	1.17
⊕ Mead	Industrials	NMF	0.82	1.15
⊕ CIT Grp Cl A	Financials	—	98.67	1.14
⊕ J.P. Morgan Chase & Co.	Financials	27.8	–17.40	1.07
Commrcl Federal	Financials	25.3	22.54	1.04
⊖ GreenPoint Finl	Financials	13.9	–10.30	1.03
⊕ Intl Paper	Industrials	—	1.43	0.99
⊖ Metris	Financials	11.4	–2.13	0.97
⊖ MBIA	Financials	14.6	9.88	0.97
⊖ Railtrack Grp	Services	—	—	0.90
⊕ Washington Post	Services	20.0	–13.20	0.89
⊕ Sears Roebuck	Retail	23.4	40.12	0.88
⊕ M & T Bk	Financials	20.8	8.63	0.87
⊖ Total Fina Cl B	Energy	14.3	—	0.86
⊖ XL Cap Cl A	Financials	22.8	5.82	0.86

Current Investment Style

Style: Value Blnd Growth; Size: Large Med Small

	Stock Port Avg	Relative S&P 500 Current	Relative S&P 500 Hist	Rel Cat
Price/Earnings Ratio	24.4	0.79	0.73	1.03
Price/Book Ratio	2.4	0.41	0.42	0.78
Price/Cash Flow	13.8	0.77	0.55	1.12
3 Yr Earnings Growth	9.6[1]	0.65	0.65	0.81
1 Yr Earnings Est%	–13.5[1]	7.65	—	2.20
Med Mkt Cap $mil	4,628	0.1	0.1	0.65

[1]figure is based on 50% or less of stocks

Special Securities % assets 12-31-00	
Restricted/Illiquid Secs	0
Emerging-Markets Secs	Trace
Options/Futures/Warrants	No

Composition % assets 12-31-00	
Cash	17.2
Stocks*	77.2
Bonds	5.6
Other	0.0
*Foreign (% stocks)	20.4

Market Cap	
Giant	4.8
Large	21.4
Medium	60.0
Small	11.3
Micro	2.4

Sector Weightings	% of Stocks	Rel S&P	5-Year High	5-Year Low
Utilities	0.3	0.1	4	0
Energy	2.3	0.3	10	1
Financials	34.5	1.9	41	17
Industrials	13.1	1.1	15	7
Durables	4.0	2.6	18	0
Staples	6.1	0.8	14	5
Services	25.8	2.4	34	12
Retail	6.6	1.0	12	1
Health	3.5	0.2	13	1
Technology	3.8	0.2	5	0

Analysis by Christopher Traulsen 12-01-01

Even with added uncertainty, Mutual Qualified Fund is still probably a cut above many of its peers.

This fund's advisor recently saw a lot of talent walk out the door. Ray Garea stepped down here at the end of July, with Susan Potto and Jeff Diamond replacing him. A number of other investment professionals also left, including European specialist Rob Friedman and distressed debt analyst Jeff Altman.

Such a substantial exodus of talent is never a good sign. However, a few factors lead us to retain confidence in the fund. First, its unique style is intact. This and the other Mutual Series funds have long used a deep-value, activist style of investing that includes buying cheap equities and distressed debt and making merger-arbitrage plays. At their best, the funds have excelled at finding gems among securities others have left for dead, and—when necessary—browbeating the management of holdings into focusing on creating shareholder value. The resulting portfolios tend to be much less volatile than other mid-value funds and have delivered sturdy returns over time.

Potto and Diamond are not changing that line of attack. Diamond had been an assistant manager here for some time, and Potto has been with Mutual Series since the 1980s and runs an offshore portfolio in the same style. When the market cracked in September, the pair did just what their predecessor would have: started buying. Among their targets were insurers such as Berkshire Hathaway and Ace Limited—well-capitalized names that the managers figure will benefit from improving premiums in the wake of the terrorist attacks.

It's too soon to tell if Potto and Diamond can continue this fund's strong record, but we see no reason for shareholders here to walk now. The proven success of this fund's style and the experience of Potto and Diamond still give it a fair amount of appeal, if somewhat less than it had.

Address:	51 John F. Kennedy Parkway Short Hills, NJ 07078 415-312-2000 / 800-342-5236
Web Address:	www.franklintempleton.com
Inception:	09-16-80
Advisor:	Franklin Mutual Advisers
Subadvisor:	None
NTF Plans:	N/A

Minimum Purchase:	Closed	Add: $50	IRA: —
Min Auto Inv Plan:	Closed	Add: $50	
Sales Fees:	No-load		
Management Fee:	.60%, .15%A		
Actual Fees:	Mgt: 0.60%	Dist: —	
Expense Projections:	3Yr: $271	5Yr: $471	10Yr: $1049
Avg Brok Commission:	—	Income Distrib: Semi-Ann.	
Total Cost (relative to category):		Low	

Mutual Shares Z

Ticker	Load	NAV	Yield	Total Assets	Mstar Category
MUTHX	Closed	$19.44	1.2%	$8,055.1 mil	Mid–Cap Value

Prospectus Objective: Growth and Income

Mutual Shares Fund - Class Z seeks capital appreciation; income is a secondary consideration.

The fund typically invests in equity securities believed by the advisor to be trading at prices below their intrinsic value. It may invest in companies with medium to large market capitalizations.The fund may also invest a significant portion of its assets in smaller companies. It may invest in debt securities. The fund may invest up to 35% of assets in foreign securities. It hedges against foreign currency risk by using forward foreign currency exchange contracts.

Class A shares have front loads; B shares charge deferred loads; C shares have level loads. Prior to Jan. 1, 1999, Class A and C shares were called Class I and II shares.

Historical Profile
Return: High
Risk: Low
Rating: ★★★★★ Highest

Investment Style
Equity
Average Stock %: 1995 81%, 1996 77%, 1997 76%, 1998 80%, 1999 83%, 2000 81%, 12-01 77%

▼ Manager Change
▽ Partial Manager Change

Fund Performance vs. Category Average
■ Quarterly Fund Return +/– Category Average
— Category Baseline

Performance Quartile (within Category)

Portfolio Manager(s)

David J. Winters, CFA et al.Since 8-01. BA Cornell U.

1990	1991	1992	1993	1994	1995	1996	1997	1998	1999	2000	12-01	History
11.28	12.90	14.67	16.19	15.74	17.29	18.57	21.29	19.54	20.43	19.79	19.44	NAV
–9.79	20.99	21.29	20.99	4.57	29.09	20.76	26.38	0.45	15.00	13.83	6.32	Total Return %
–6.68	–9.50	13.67	10.94	3.26	–8.45	–2.19	–6.97	–28.13	–6.03	22.93	18.20	+/– S&P 500
6.29	–16.94	–0.39	5.37	6.70	–5.85	0.50	–7.98	–4.64	15.11	–5.35	3.98	+/– Russ Midcap Val
5.02	3.57	2.50	1.90	1.67	2.52	2.96	2.94	2.52	2.18	3.57	1.26	Income Return %
–14.81	17.41	18.79	19.10	2.91	26.57	17.80	23.44	–2.08	12.83	10.26	5.06	Capital Return %
53	81	14	46	12	46	46	51	61	22	66	42	Total Rtn % Rank Cat
0.67	0.40	0.32	0.28	0.27	0.39	0.50	0.54	0.53	0.42	0.70	0.24	Income $
0.18	0.33	0.63	1.26	0.91	2.56	1.74	1.58	1.29	1.58	2.51	1.35	Capital Gains $
0.85	0.82	0.78	0.74	0.72	0.69	0.70	0.72	0.73	0.75	0.76	—	Expense Ratio %
4.88	3.08	2.18	1.90	1.80	2.47	3.02	1.92	2.15	1.58	1.69	—	Income Ratio %
43	48	41	49	67	79	58	50	69	66	63	—	Turnover Rate %
2,514.1	2,642.9	2,915.3	3,527.1	3,745.3	5,224.9	6,107.5	7,917.6	6,289.6	5,573.4	5,360.3	5,465.2	Net Assets $mil

Performance 12-31-01

	1st Qtr	2nd Qtr	3rd Qtr	4th Qtr	Total
1997	4.20	9.15	9.61	1.38	26.38
1998	8.55	–1.69	–16.96	13.34	0.45
1999	4.91	11.37	–8.92	8.07	15.00
2000	2.35	–1.56	7.88	4.73	13.83
2001	3.28	8.34	–10.93	6.68	6.32

Trailing	Total Return%	+/– S&P 500	+/– Russ Midcap Val	% Rank All	% Rank Cat	Growth of $10,000
3 Mo	6.68	–4.01	–5.35	58	90	10,668
6 Mo	–4.98	0.57	–4.07	62	89	9,502
1 Yr	6.32	18.20	3.98	17	42	10,632
3 Yr Avg	11.65	12.68	4.84	8	40	13,919
5 Yr Avg	12.06	1.36	0.60	10	45	17,669
10 Yr Avg	15.51	2.58	1.09	4	32	42,268
15 Yr Avg	14.24	0.51	0.78	9	29	73,703

Tax Analysis	Tax-Adj Ret%	%Rank Cat	%Pretax Ret	%Rank Cat
3 Yr Avg	8.41	45	72.2	74
5 Yr Avg	8.99	49	74.6	71
10 Yr Avg	12.12	36	78.1	78

Potential Capital Gain Exposure: 20% of assets

Risk Analysis

Time Period	Load-Adj Return %	Risk %Rank[1] All	Risk %Rank[1] Cat	Morningstar Return	Morningstar Risk	Morningstar Risk-Adj Rating
1 Yr	6.32					
3 Yr	11.65	38	9	1.52[2]	0.51	★★★★★
5 Yr	12.06	44	6	1.76[2]	0.57	★★★★
10 Yr	15.51	50	5	1.92	0.58	★★★★★

Average Historical Rating (193 months): 4.6★s

[1] 1=low, 100=high [2] T-Bill return substituted for category avg.

Category Rating (3 Yr)

1 2 **3** 4 5
Worst — Best

Return: Average
Risk: Low

Other Measures	Standard Index S&P 500	Best Fit Index S&P 500
Alpha	10.2	10.2
Beta	0.59	0.59
R–Squared	58	58
Standard Deviation		14.60
Mean		11.65
Sharpe Ratio		0.53

Analysis by Christopher Traulsen 12-02-01

Mutual Shares Fund is diminished, but far from undone.

Since the management shakeup that rocked Mutual Series over the summer, this fund has continued to go about its business as usual. "New" manager David Winters—a 14-year Mutual Series veteran—took the helm here after Larry Sondike stepped down this fall. He has made it clear that he intends to run the fund in the style for which Mutual Series has long been known: ferreting out cheap equities, distressed credits, and making merger-arbitrage plays. When the market sold off sharply in September, he waded in and bought well-capitalized insurers, such as Berkshire Hathaway, and beaten-down travel-stocks, such as hotelier Starwood Resorts.

Over time, that style has served the fund well. It's up 3.4% for the year to date through Nov. 30, 2001. While that isn't a chart-topping performance, it ranks in the top half of the mid-value category. Considering the fund's sizable cash stake, dearth of exposure to small caps, and big European allocation, that's pretty good (small caps have generally outperformed larger names this year, and European equities have been sluggish). It also fits with the fund's record. This offering rarely outperforms its peers by a huge margin, but it has delivered sturdy long-term returns with much less volatility than its typical rival.

Only time will tell if the fund can continue that record of success. In addition to Sondike, the firm lost veteran managers and analysts such as Ray Garea, Rob Friedman, and Jeff Altman this fall. Still, a number of longtime hands remain, Winters among them, and the firm has brought in talent to fill the gaps. Despite the exodus of talent, we think the presence of veterans such as Winters and the commitment by them to adhere to the fund's time-tested style still give it a bit more appeal than many of its peers.

Portfolio Analysis 06-30-01

Share change since 12-00 Total Stocks: 139

Share change	Stock	Sector	PE	YTD Ret%	% Assets
⊖	Federated Dept Stores	Retail	16.6	16.86	2.86
⊕	Telephone and Data Sys	Services	—	0.29	2.76
⊖	Canary Wharf Grp	Financials	69.9	—	1.87
	Washington Post	Services	20.0	–13.20	1.82
⊕	Lagardere	Financials	11.1	—	1.78
⊖	White Mountains Ins Grp	Financials	—	9.45	1.78
☼	AT&T	Services	7.8	40.59	1.74
⊖	AT & T Liberty Media Cl A	Services	—	3.22	1.70
⊖	EW Scripps Cl A	Services	29.9	5.94	1.63
⊖	Delphi Automotive Sys	Durables	—	23.78	1.47
⊖	Bear Stearns	Financials	12.9	16.96	1.44
☼	Tyco Intl	Industrials	27.1	6.23	1.38
⊕	PMI Grp	Financials	10.4	–0.76	1.32
⊕	General Motors Cl H	Technology	42.9	–32.80	1.17
	Intl Paper	Industrials	—	1.43	1.16
⊖	Republic Svcs Cl A	Services	15.6	16.19	1.13
⊕	Sprint	Services	20.5	1.18	1.13
⊕	Berkshire Hathaway Cl B	Financials	64.8	7.26	1.12
⊕	BellSouth	Services	24.9	–5.09	1.04
⊕	Altadis Cl A	Staples	0.2	—	1.02
⊕	Sovereign Bancorp	Financials	76.5	52.19	1.00
⊕	Florida East Coast Inds	Services	62.6	–35.20	0.98
☼	Reader's Digest Assn A	Services	22.2	–40.50	0.95
⊕	Abitibi–Consolid	Industrials	—	–17.50	0.92
⊕	USA Networks	Services	58.1	40.50	0.90

Current Investment Style

Style: Value Blnd Growth; Size: Large Med Small

	Stock Port Avg	Relative S&P 500 Current	Relative S&P 500 Hist	Rel Cat
Price/Earnings Ratio	24.3	0.79	0.69	1.03
Price/Book Ratio	2.5	0.43	0.40	0.81
Price/Cash Flow	13.4	0.74	0.64	1.08
3 Yr Earnings Growth	11.8[1]	0.81	0.67	1.00
1 Yr Earnings Est%	–17.5[1]	9.86	—	2.84
Med Mkt Cap $mil	6,563	0.1	0.1	0.92

[1] figure is based on 50% or less of stocks

Special Securities % assets 06-30-01	
Restricted/Illiquid Secs	0
Emerging–Markets Secs	Trace
Options/Futures/Warrants	No

Composition % assets 06-30-01	
Cash	14.2
Stocks*	77.3
Bonds	8.1
Other	0.5
*Foreign (% stocks)	19.3

Market Cap	
Giant	12.1
Large	24.2
Medium	60.2
Small	3.1
Micro	0.5

Sector Weightings	% of Stocks	Rel S&P	5-Year High	5-Year Low
Utilities	1.9	0.6	6	0
Energy	1.5	0.2	12	1
Financials	26.5	1.5	42	20
Industrials	13.0	1.1	17	8
Durables	4.2	2.7	17	0
Staples	7.9	1.0	11	4
Services	32.8	3.0	33	11
Retail	6.7	1.0	10	1
Health	2.5	0.2	13	1
Technology	3.1	0.2	6	0

Address:	51 John F. Kennedy Parkway Short Hills, NJ 07078 415–312–2000 / 800–553–3014
Web Address:	www.franklintempleton.com
Inception:	07-01-49
Advisor:	Franklin Mutual Advisers
Subadvisor:	None
NTF Plans:	N/A

Minimum Purchase:	Closed	Add: $50	IRA: —
Min Auto Inv Plan:	Closed	Add: $50	
Sales Fees:	No–load		
Management Fee:	.60%, .15%A		
Actual Fees:	Mgt: 0.60%	Dist: —	
Expense Projections:	3Yr: $259	5Yr: $450	10Yr: $1002
Avg Brok Commission:	—	Income Distrib: Semi–Ann.	
Total Cost (relative to category):	Low		

Nations Blue Chip Inv A

Ticker	Load	NAV	Yield	Total Assets	Mstar Category
PHBCX	5.75%	$25.85	0.0%	$551.7 mil	Large Blend

Prospectus Objective: Growth

Nations Blue Chip Fund seeks long-term capital appreciation.

The fund ordinarily invests at least 80% of assets in blue chip stocks. It may invest the remainder of assets in cash equivalents. The fund typically limits its investments to securities included in either the Dow Jones Industrial Average or the Standard & Poor's 500 index. The fund usually holds up to 100 stocks chosen from these indices.

Class A, B, and C shares are offered by the fund, all of which differ in fee structure and availability. Prior to May 21, 1999, the fund was named Pacific Horizon Blue Chip Fund.

Historical Profile
Return Average
Risk Average
Rating ★★★ Neutral

Investment Style
Equity
Average Stock %: 99% 96% 98% 99% 99% 96% 98%

▼ Manager Change
▽ Partial Manager Change

Fund Performance vs. Category Average
■ Quarterly Fund Return +/– Category Average
— Category Baseline

Performance Quartile (within Category)

Portfolio Manager(s)

James D. Miller, CFA. Since 5-95. BS'64 Lehigh U.; MBA'67 Lehigh U. Other funds currently managed: Nations Asset Allocation Inv A, Nations Blue Chip Inv C, Nations Asset Allocation Inv C.

1990	1991	1992	1993	1994	1995	1996	1997	1998	1999	2000	12-01	History
—	—	—	—	14.82	19.59	23.45	27.54	33.20	36.55	30.72	25.85	NAV
—	—	—	—	0.93*	35.78	23.76	32.70	27.86	21.16	–9.28	–15.85	Total Return %
—	—	—	—	0.90*	–1.75	0.82	–0.66	–0.72	0.13	–0.18	–3.98	+/– S&P 500
—	—	—	—	—	–1.82	1.60	–0.33	–0.78	–0.66	1.68	–3.09	+/– Wilshire Top 750
—	—	—	—	1.86	1.91	1.15	0.67	0.39	0.00	0.01	0.00	Income Return %
—	—	—	—	–0.94	33.88	22.61	32.03	27.46	21.16	–9.29	–15.85	Capital Return %
—	—	—	—	—	32	18	23	31	40	58	72	Total Rtn % Rank Cat
—	—	—	—	0.27	0.28	0.22	0.15	0.11	0.00	0.00	0.00	Income $
—	—	—	—	0.00	0.22	0.53	3.24	1.72	3.35	2.62	0.00	Capital Gains $
—	—	—	—	0.00	0.00	0.83	1.28	1.18	1.20	1.20	1.21	Expense Ratio %
—	—	—	—	2.92	2.46	1.63	0.99	0.63	–0.08	–0.08	–0.02	Income Ratio %
—	—	—	—	—	44	108	91	67	57	—	59	Turnover Rate %
—	—	—	—	5.1	52.5	130.0	253.0	400.1	401.9	720.3	551.7	Net Assets $mil

Performance 12-31-01

	1st Qtr	2nd Qtr	3rd Qtr	4th Qtr	Total
1997	2.51	17.95	7.74	1.86	32.70
1998	14.10	3.14	–12.18	23.71	27.86
1999	4.91	6.03	–6.50	16.50	21.16
2000	1.92	–1.62	0.00	–9.52	–9.28
2001	–13.83	5.29	–15.14	9.30	–15.85

Trailing	Total Return%	+/– S&P 500	+/–Wil Top 750	% Rank All	% Rank Cat	Growth of $10,000
3 Mo	9.30	–1.38	–2.02	46	78	10,930
6 Mo	–7.25	–1.69	–1.46	75	74	9,275
1 Yr	–15.85	–3.98	–3.09	74	72	8,415
3 Yr Avg	–2.57	–1.54	–0.74	85	73	9,249
5 Yr Avg	9.43	–1.27	–0.69	22	50	15,693
10 Yr Avg	—	—	—	—	—	—
15 Yr Avg	—	—	—	—	—	—

Tax Analysis	Tax-Adj Ret%	%Rank Cat	%Pretax Ret	%Rank Cat
3 Yr Avg	–3.71	72	—	—
5 Yr Avg	7.74	48	82.0	47
10 Yr Avg	—	—	—	—

Potential Capital Gain Exposure: 5% of assets

Risk Analysis

Time Period	Load-Adj Return %	Risk %Rank[1] All	Risk %Rank[1] Cat	Morningstar Return	Morningstar Risk	Morningstar Risk-Adj Rating
1 Yr	–20.69					
3 Yr	–4.47	70	62	–1.82[2]	0.96	★★
5 Yr	8.14	69	62	0.72[2]	0.94	★★★
Incept	12.23	—	—	—	—	

Average Historical Rating (60 months): 4.0★s

[1] 1=low, 100=high [2] T-Bill return substituted for category avg.

Category Rating (3 Yr)

1 2 3 4 5 — Worst / Best

Return: Below Avg
Risk: Average

Other Measures	Standard Index S&P 500	Best Fit Index S&P 500
Alpha	–1.3	–1.3
Beta	1.03	1.03
R-Squared	98	98

Standard Deviation	17.35
Mean	–2.57
Sharpe Ratio	–0.50

Portfolio Analysis 09-30-01

Share change since 06-01 Total Stocks: 203	Sector	PE	YTD Ret%	% Assets
⊕ General Elec	Industrials	30.1	–15.00	3.88
⊕ Pfizer	Health	34.7	–12.40	3.38
⊕ Microsoft	Technology	57.6	52.78	3.01
⊕ ExxonMobil	Energy	15.3	–7.59	2.50
⊖ Citigroup	Financials	20.0	0.03	2.42
⊕ American Intl Grp	Financials	42.0	–19.20	2.39
⊕ Johnson & Johnson	Health	16.6	14.01	2.20
⊕ IBM	Technology	26.9	43.00	2.08
⊕ SBC Comms	Services	18.4	–16.00	2.08
⊕ Wal-Mart Stores	Retail	40.3	8.94	2.00
⊕ Verizon Comms	Services	29.7	–2.52	1.96
⊕ AOL Time Warner	Technology	—	–7.76	1.78
⊕ PepsiCo	Staples	31.4	–0.54	1.67
⊕ Intel	Technology	73.1	4.89	1.62
⊖ Tyco Intl	Industrials	27.1	6.23	1.53
⊕ Bristol-Myers Squibb	Health	20.2	–26.00	1.49
⊕ Philip Morris	Staples	12.1	9.12	1.33
⊖ Merck	Health	19.1	–35.90	1.15
⊕ Home Depot	Retail	42.9	12.07	1.14
⊕ Chevron	Energy	10.3	9.29	1.13
⊕ Procter & Gamble	Staples	38.8	3.12	1.13
⊕ Washington Mutual	Financials	10.1	–5.32	1.06
☼ Royal Dutch Petro NY ADR	Energy	12.0	–17.10	1.01
☼ Wachovia	Financials	—	23.13	0.90
⊖ Cardinal Health	Health	35.1	–2.51	0.89

Current Investment Style

Style: Value Blnd Growth; Size: Large Med Small

	Stock Port Avg	Relative S&P 500 Current	Relative S&P 500 Hist	Rel Cat
Price/Earnings Ratio	28.6	0.93	0.98	0.94
Price/Book Ratio	5.5	0.96	1.05	1.00
Price/Cash Flow	17.6	0.98	1.02	0.96
3 Yr Earnings Growth	18.0	1.23	1.18	1.01
1 Yr Earnings Est%	2.6	—	—	—
Med Mkt Cap $mil	66,572	1.1	0.9	1.27

Analysis by Emily Hall 10-19-01

Nations Blue Chip Fund remains a decent, if sometimes unexciting, choice.

This offering doesn't take investors out on many limbs. Its management team, led by James Miller, keeps the fund's sector and industry weightings, as well as its market capitalization, in very close proximity to its bogy, the S&P 500 index. Miller and his team then try to add value by selecting what they think are the index's better stocks, aiming to create a portfolio that, overall, is a tad cheaper than the benchmark but that is growing faster.

The result is an offering that looks and behaves a lot like an index fund. During the trailing three and five years the fund has lagged its benchmark by a narrow margin—about the same amount as it costs to run the fund. And there have been times, such as in 1996, when this offering has managed to edge past its bogy.

That determination to stick close to the index has served the fund fairly well over the long term. Over the trailing five years through Oct. 18, 2001, the fund's returns land slightly above the large-blend category average. Moreover, the fund's volatility over the same period has also stayed in close line with the group norm.

The one exception to such steady results has been during the past 18 months, when the fund has struggled to stay dry amid the market's rough waters. For the trailing year, the fund is lagging its bogy by 4.9%—a showing weak enough to land it in the bottom half of its category. The managers have responded to the recent volatility by adding to the number of names in the portfolio, but so far that hasn't offered much downside protection.

The fund's record gives reason to believe that its current rough patch is an aberration. Over the long term, this fund probably won't be the star of its category, but it shouldn't serve up too many nasty surprises either.

Special Securities % assets 09-30-01	
Restricted/Illiquid Secs	0
Emerging-Markets Secs	0
Options/Futures/Warrants	No

Composition % assets 09-30-01	
Cash	0.2
Stocks*	99.8
Bonds	0.0
Other	0.0
*Foreign (% stocks)	1.8

Market Cap	
Giant	56.3
Large	32.9
Medium	10.8
Small	0.0
Micro	0.0

Sector Weightings	% of Stocks	Rel S&P	5-Year High	5-Year Low
Utilities	3.3	1.0	4	2
Energy	7.2	1.0	9	6
Financials	18.0	1.0	18	13
Industrials	12.0	1.1	22	12
Durables	1.4	0.9	6	1
Staples	7.9	1.0	13	4
Services	11.3	1.0	15	10
Retail	6.7	1.0	9	5
Health	15.6	1.1	16	7
Technology	16.6	0.9	34	11

Address:	One Bank of America Plaza 33rd Floor Charlotte, NC 28255 800-321-7854
Web Address:	www.bankofamerica.com/nationsfunds
*Inception:	01-13-94
Advisor:	Banc of America Adv., Inc
Subadvisor:	Chicago Equity Partners, Corp
NTF Plans:	Fidelity Inst.

Minimum Purchase:	$1000	Add: $100 IRA: $500
Min Auto Inv Plan:	$1000	Add: $50
Sales Fees:	5.75%L, 0.25%S	
Management Fee:	.65%, .23%A	
Actual Fees:	Mgt: 0.65%	Dist: 0.25%
Expense Projections:	3Yr: $943	5Yr: $1214 10Yr: $1988
Avg Brok Commission:	—	Income Distrib: Quarterly
Total Cost (relative to category):		Average

Neuberger Berman Genesis Inv

Ticker	Load	NAV	Yield	Total Assets	Mstar Category
NBGNX	None	$20.33	0.0%	$3,414.6 mil	Small Blend

Prospectus Objective: Small Company

Neuberger Berman Genesis seeks capital appreciation.

The fund invests primarily in common stocks of companies with market capitalizations less than $1.5 billion at the time of purchase. Management seeks securities it believes to be undervalued and that are issued by companies that have above-average returns, an established market niche, the ability to finance their own growth and sound future business prospects.

The fund currently offers Investor, Institutional, Trust and Advisor Shares. Prior to December 19, 2000, the fund was named Neuberger Berman Genesis Assets Fund.

Historical Profile

Return: High
Risk: Below Avg
Rating: ★★★★★ Highest

Investment Style
Equity
Average Stock %: 96% (1996), 93% (1997), 90% (1998), 92% (1999), 94% (2000), 93% (12-01)

▼ Manager Change
▽ Partial Manager Change

Fund Performance vs. Category Average
■ Quarterly Fund Return +/– Category Average
— Category Baseline

Performance Quartile (within Category)

Portfolio Manager(s)

Judith M. Vale, CFA. Since 2-94. BA'74 Yale U. Other funds currently managed: Neuberger Berman Genesis Tr, Neuberger Berman Genesis Adv, Neuberger Berman Genesis Instl.

Robert W. D'Alelio. Since 8-97. BA'79 U. of Massachusetts. Other funds currently managed: Neuberger Berman Genesis Tr, Neuberger Berman Genesis Adv, Neuberger Berman Genesis Instl.

History

1990	1991	1992	1993	1994	1995	1996	1997	1998	1999	2000	12-01	History
4.91	6.85	7.92	8.26	7.80	9.38	12.03	16.03	14.44	14.94	18.67	20.33	NAV
–16.24	41.55	15.62	13.89	–1.82	27.31	29.86	34.89	–6.95	4.05	32.51	12.11	Total Return %
–13.13	11.06	8.00	3.83	–3.13	–10.23	6.92	1.54	–35.53	–16.99	41.61	23.99	+/– S&P 500
3.26	–4.50	–2.79	–5.02	0.01	–1.13	13.32	12.52	–4.40	–17.22	35.53	9.63	+/– Russell 2000
0.68	0.20	0.00	0.13	0.00	0.00	0.00	0.00	0.75	0.55	0.00	0.00	Income Return %
–16.92	41.34	15.62	13.76	–1.82	27.31	29.86	34.89	–7.70	3.49	32.51	12.11	Capital Return %
62	48	42	67	63	42	9	14	66	70	8	30	Total Rtn % Rank Cat
0.04	0.01	0.00	0.01	0.00	0.00	0.00	0.00	0.12	0.08	0.00	0.00	Income $
0.00	0.09	0.00	0.75	0.31	0.55	0.15	0.19	0.34	0.00	1.04	0.58	Capital Gains $
2.00	2.00	2.00	1.65	1.36	1.35	1.28	1.16	1.11	1.17	1.21	—	Expense Ratio %
0.41	0.60	–0.14	0.15	–0.20	–0.16	–0.18	–0.08	0.72	0.61	–0.02	—	Income Ratio %
37	46	23	54	63	37	21	18	18	33	38	—	Turnover Rate %
17.5	42.8	87.4	124.9	108.0	118.6	298.7	1,246.4	1,194.9	735.9	840.5	1,060.7	Net Assets $mil

Performance 12-31-01

	1st Qtr	2nd Qtr	3rd Qtr	4th Qtr	Total
1997	–1.66	18.77	20.07	–3.81	34.89
1998	4.74	–5.36	–16.43	12.32	–6.95
1999	–9.42	14.07	–6.97	8.24	4.05
2000	10.17	4.19	4.72	10.22	32.51
2001	–0.86	10.32	–11.17	15.39	12.11

Trailing	Total Return%	+/– S&P 500	+/– Russ 2000	% Rank All	% Rank Cat	Growth of $10,000
3 Mo	15.39	4.70	–5.69	23	78	11,539
6 Mo	2.51	8.06	6.59	18	20	10,251
1 Yr	12.11	23.99	9.63	5	30	11,211
3 Yr Avg	15.62	16.65	9.20	4	18	15,456
5 Yr Avg	14.17	3.47	6.65	5	19	19,400
10 Yr Avg	15.28	2.36	3.77	5	18	41,465
15 Yr Avg	—	—	—	—	—	—

Tax Analysis	Tax-Adj Ret%	%Rank Cat	%Pretax Ret	%Rank Cat
3 Yr Avg	14.50	16	92.9	26
5 Yr Avg	13.25	14	93.5	11
10 Yr Avg	14.14	3	92.5	3

Potential Capital Gain Exposure: 29% of assets

Risk Analysis

Time Period	Load-Adj Return %	Risk %Rank[1] All	Risk %Rank[1] Cat	Morningstar Return	Morningstar Risk	Morningstar Risk-Adj Rating
1 Yr	12.11					
3 Yr	15.62	41	7	2.50[2]	0.55	★★★★★
5 Yr	14.17	54	17	2.38[2]	0.75	★★★★★
10 Yr	15.28	61	16	1.86	0.80	★★★★★

Average Historical Rating (124 months): 3.2★s

[1]1=low, 100=high [2] T-Bill return substituted for category avg.

Category Rating (3 Yr)

1 2 3 4 5
Worst Best

Return: Above Avg
Risk: Low

Other Measures	Standard Index S&P 500	Best Fit Index SPMid400
Alpha	14.0	6.5
Beta	0.52	0.66
R-Squared	36	75
Standard Deviation		16.95
Mean		15.62
Sharpe Ratio		0.72

Analysis by Kelli Stebel 10-26-01

This fund has been a solid performer, but its large asset base is a cause for concern.

There's little doubt that Neuberger Berman Genesis has turned in some impressive results. Since Judy Vale came on board in February 1994, the fund has consistently put up topnotch numbers without a lot of volatility. During her seven-year tenure, this offering's annualized return has outpaced its average small-blend rival's by more than 4 percentage points. And the fund hasn't missed a beat in this year's difficult market, either. Its 3% gain is better than 84% of its peers' for the year to date through Oct. 25, 2001.

Such strong performance owes to the strength of Vale and comanager Robert D'Alelio's stock-picking ability. The duo keeps a keen eye on quality, looking for firms with solid fundamentals such as strong cash flow. That approach has kept the fund insulated during market downdrafts like 2000's, as more-speculative firms imploded. Good picks such as Newport News Shipbuilding helped the fund rack up a 33% gain that year, twice that of its average peer. (Vale said that she recently sold Newport.)

These days, Vale reports that she and D'Alelio aren't making any enormous moves, but they took advantage of the market volatility following the Sept. 11 attacks, nibbling on insurance companies such as PartnerRe. Though these firms dropped precipitously in the week following the attacks, Vale thinks their long-term earnings prospects remain strong.

While this fund will certainly draw attention for its good record, investors should note that its asset base has grown to more than $3 billion. That makes it increasingly difficult for the pair to maneuver in the often-illiquid small-cap market. Provided Neuberger Berman closes it soon, this offering makes a fine choice for one-stop small-cap shopping.

Address:	605 Third Avenue 2nd Floor New York, NY 10158–0006 800–877–9700 / 212–476–8800
Web Address:	www.nbfunds.com
Inception:	09-27-88
Advisor:	Neuberger Berman Mgmt., Inc.
Subadvisor:	Neuberger Berman, LLC
NTF Plans:	Schwab

Minimum Purchase:	$1000	Add: $100 IRA: $250
Min Auto Inv Plan:	$100	Add: $100
Sales Fees:	No-load	
Management Fee:	.85% mx./.65% mn., .26%A	
Actual Fees:	Mgt: 0.98%	Dist: —
Expense Projections:	3Yr: $372	5Yr: $644 10Yr: $1420
Avg Brok Commission:	—	Income Distrib: Annually
Total Cost (relative to category):	Below Avg	

Portfolio Analysis 11-30-01

Share change since 10-01 Total Stocks: 122

	Sector	PE	YTD Ret%	% Assets
⊕ AptarGroup	Industrials	19.9	20.11	2.96
⊕ Zebra Tech	Technology	27.0	36.12	2.02
⊕ Dentsply Intl	Health	22.2	29.13	1.95
Patterson Dental	Health	33.0	20.83	1.94
⊕ Church & Dwight	Staples	21.0	21.11	1.79
⊕ Fair Isaac	Technology	31.5	85.59	1.71
⊕ Electronics for Imaging	Technology	58.7	60.07	1.65
⊕ Mentor	Health	19.0	47.15	1.62
Trigon Healthcare	Health	27.5	–10.70	1.57
M & T Bk	Financials	20.8	8.63	1.54
⊕ Alberto–Culver Cl A	Staples	—	—	1.52
⊕ Wallace Comp Svc	Industrials	16.1	15.92	1.50
⊕ Henry Schein	Health	22.0	6.95	1.49
Banknorth Grp	Financials	13.3	15.81	1.44
Haemonetics	Health	24.9	9.86	1.41
Alliant Techsystems	Industrials	28.6	73.48	1.41
⊕ CEC Entrtnmt	Services	19.8	27.15	1.38
⊕ Black Box	Technology	16.3	9.45	1.28
PartnerRe	Financials	22.4	–10.50	1.28
⊕ Aon	Financials	46.1	6.32	1.27
⊕ Astoria Finl	Financials	11.7	–0.45	1.25
Idexx Labs	Health	25.9	29.59	1.22
⊕ Roper Inds	Industrials	29.0	50.94	1.22
⊕ Xto Energy	N/A	—	—	1.22
⊕ Simpson Mfg	Industrials	18.0	12.35	1.18

Current Investment Style

Style: Value Blnd Growth; Size: Large Med Small

	Stock Port Avg	Relative S&P 500 Current	Relative S&P 500 Hist	Rel Cat
Price/Earnings Ratio	25.1	0.81	0.67	1.01
Price/Book Ratio	3.2	0.56	0.39	0.99
Price/Cash Flow	16.3	0.91	0.71	1.05
3 Yr Earnings Growth	12.1	0.83	0.92	0.72
1 Yr Earnings Est%	–0.1	0.05	—	–0.09
Med Mkt Cap $mil	1,348	0.0	0.0	1.37

Special Securities % assets 11-30-01	
Restricted/Illiquid Secs	0
Emerging–Markets Secs	0
Options/Futures/Warrants	No

Composition % assets 11-30-01	
Cash	6.9
Stocks*	93.1
Bonds	0.0
Other	0.0
*Foreign (% stocks)	2.2

Market Cap	
Giant	0.0
Large	1.4
Medium	46.3
Small	51.3
Micro	1.0

Sector Weightings	% of Stocks	Rel S&P	5-Year High	5-Year Low
Utilities	0.2	0.1	17	0
Energy	6.5	0.9	22	1
Financials	20.3	1.1	25	3
Industrials	19.8	1.7	48	20
Durables	2.7	1.7	14	0
Staples	4.0	0.5	11	0
Services	10.3	1.0	21	5
Retail	5.6	0.8	19	1
Health	14.8	1.0	15	0
Technology	15.9	0.9	25	2

Neuberger Berman Partners Inv

Ticker	Load	NAV	Yield	Total Assets	Mstar Category
NPRTX	None	$20.79	0.4%	$2,162.7 mil	Large Value

Prospectus Objective: Growth

Neuberger Berman Partners Fund seeks capital growth.

The fund invests primarily in common stocks of established companies. Management focuses on securities that it believes are undervalued based on low P/E ratios, consistent cash flow, and support from asset values. The fund may invest in preferred stocks, convertible securities, and debt securities. It may invest up to 10% of assets directly in foreign securities; it may also invest in ADRs.

Fund shares are sold to individuals; Trust shares are available only through pension plans and certain financial-service providers. Past fund names: Partners Fund and Neuberger Berman Partners Fund.

Historical Profile
Return: Above Avg
Risk: Average
Rating: ★★★★ Above Avg

Investment Style
Equity
Average Stock %

			95%	94%	95%	93%	95%	97%

▼ Manager Change
▽ Partial Manager Change

Fund Performance vs. Category Average
Quarterly Fund Return +/– Category Average
– Category Baseline

Performance Quartile (within Category)

1990	1991	1992	1993	1994	1995	1996	1997	1998	1999	2000	12-01	History
16.02	18.44	19.69	20.62	18.52	22.14	25.19	26.30	25.50	24.00	21.93	20.79	NAV
–5.11	22.36	17.52	16.46	–1.89	35.21	26.49	29.23	6.28	7.80	0.57	–3.02	Total Return %
–1.99	–8.12	9.90	6.40	–3.21	–2.33	3.54	–4.12	–22.30	–13.24	9.68	8.85	+/– S&P 500
–1.44	4.21	8.45	–3.31	0.42	–4.83	4.18	–6.26	–14.96	–3.15	–1.74	5.77	+/– Russ Top 200 Val
4.18	2.17	1.03	0.56	0.53	1.08	0.99	0.75	0.00	1.14	0.71	0.36	Income Return %
–9.29	20.20	16.49	15.90	–2.42	34.13	25.49	28.48	6.28	6.66	–0.13	–3.39	Capital Return %
43	82	10	27	70	30	11	32	85	43	75	33	Total Rtn % Rank Cat
0.74	0.34	0.19	0.11	0.11	0.20	0.22	0.19	0.00	0.29	0.17	0.08	Income $
0.34	0.78	1.79	2.20	1.60	2.70	2.61	5.84	2.41	3.10	1.93	0.38	Capital Gains $
0.91	0.88	0.86	0.86	0.81	0.83	0.84	0.81	0.80	0.82	0.84	—	Expense Ratio %
4.53	2.84	1.23	0.83	0.48	0.83	0.93	0.72	0.79	0.94	0.60	—	Income Ratio %
136	161	97	82	75	98	96	77	109	132	95	—	Turnover Rate %
727.2	889.0	974.6	1,127.7	1,246.6	1,656.9	2,218.3	3,230.3	3,249.6	2,667.5	1,990.5	1,665.8	Net Assets $mil

Portfolio Manager(s)

S. Basu Mullick. Since 12-98. MA Rutgers U. Other funds currently managed: Neuberger Berman Partners Tr, Neuberger Berman Partners Adv, ASAF Neuberger Berman Mid-Cap Value A.

Performance 12-31-01

	1st Qtr	2nd Qtr	3rd Qtr	4th Qtr	Total
1997	1.79	14.04	12.79	–1.29	29.23
1998	11.48	–3.92	–14.73	16.37	6.28
1999	2.16	10.63	–12.60	9.13	7.80
2000	0.38	–1.08	0.76	0.53	0.57
2001	–6.52	6.20	–15.94	16.21	–3.02

Trailing	Total Return%	+/– S&P 500	+/– Russ Top 200 Val	% Rank All	% Rank Cat	Growth of $10,000
3 Mo	16.21	5.53	10.70	21	5	11,621
6 Mo	–2.31	3.24	3.47	48	25	9,769
1 Yr	–3.02	8.85	5.77	47	33	9,698
3 Yr Avg	1.68	2.71	0.52	64	53	10,514
5 Yr Avg	7.63	–3.07	–3.58	31	64	14,441
10 Yr Avg	12.74	–0.19	–1.29	14	38	33,158
15 Yr Avg	12.29	–1.44	–1.21	24	41	56,935

Tax Analysis	Tax-Adj Ret%	%Rank Cat	%Pretax Ret	%Rank Cat
3 Yr Avg	–0.22	59	—	—
5 Yr Avg	4.90	71	64.2	78
10 Yr Avg	9.60	41	75.4	61

Potential Capital Gain Exposure: 4% of assets

Risk Analysis

Time Period	Load-Adj Return %	Risk %Rank[1] All	Risk %Rank[1] Cat	Morningstar Return	Morningstar Risk	Morningstar Risk-Adj Rating
1 Yr	–3.02					
3 Yr	1.68	62	84	–0.67[2]	0.87	★★★
5 Yr	7.63	64	84	0.60[2]	0.88	★★★
10 Yr	12.74	70	87	1.26	0.90	★★★★

Average Historical Rating (193 months): 4.1★s

[1] 1=low, 100=high [2] T-Bill return substituted for category avg.

Category Rating (3 Yr)

1 2 3 4 5
Worst Best

Return: Average
Risk: Above Avg

Other Measures	Standard Index S&P 500	Best Fit Index S&P 500
Alpha	2.1	2.1
Beta	0.87	0.87
R-Squared	79	79
Standard Deviation		16.84
Mean		1.68
Sharpe Ratio		–0.22

Portfolio Analysis 11-30-01

Share change since 10-01 Total Stocks: 71	Sector	PE	YTD Ret%	% Assets
⊕ Cigna	Financials	13.2	–29.00	3.49
⊕ Computer Sciences	Technology	57.6	–18.50	3.05
Berkshire Hathaway Cl B	Financials	64.8	7.26	2.67
⊖ IBM	Technology	26.9	43.00	2.66
Scientific-Atlanta	Technology	15.5	–26.30	2.56
Carnival	Services	16.4	–7.54	2.36
XL Cap Cl A	Financials	22.8	5.82	2.29
Citigroup	Financials	20.0	0.03	2.20
Masco	Industrials	98.0	–2.43	2.06
⊕ Cendant	Services	20.4	103.70	2.00
J.P. Morgan Chase & Co.	Financials	27.8	–17.40	1.93
⊖ Morgan Stanley/Dean Witter	Financials	16.6	–28.20	1.89
Merck	Health	19.1	–35.90	1.86
⊕ General Motors Cl H	Technology	42.9	–32.80	1.82
Lexmark Intl	Technology	26.9	33.14	1.81
St. Paul	Financials	—	–16.90	1.79
Sabre Hldgs Cl A	Services	73.0	–1.80	1.78
Schering-Plough	Health	22.2	–35.90	1.73
Celestica	Technology	79.2	–25.50	1.72
El Paso	Utilities	NMF	–36.70	1.72
⊖ Exelon	Utilities	14.0	–29.50	1.70
Waters	Industrials	32.0	–53.50	1.68
Cadence Design Sys	Technology	5.3	–20.20	1.66
⊖ Boston Scientific	Health	—	76.21	1.63
⊕ Williams Companies	Utilities	17.9	–29.10	1.62

Current Investment Style

Style: Value Blnd Growth; Size: Large Med Small

	Stock Port Avg	Relative S&P 500 Current	Relative S&P 500 Hist	Rel Cat
Price/Earnings Ratio	28.4	0.92	0.81	1.13
Price/Book Ratio	3.6	0.63	0.61	0.87
Price/Cash Flow	14.8	0.82	0.79	1.07
3 Yr Earnings Growth	12.2	0.83	0.79	0.82
1 Yr Earnings Est%	–2.1	1.18	—	0.63
Med Mkt Cap $mil	12,891	0.2	0.3	0.41

Analysis by Kelli Stebel 10-17-01

Current investors don't have enough reason to bail, but others can find more fetching options than Neuberger Berman Partners Fund.

This fund isn't horrible. Since current manager Basu Mullick joined in late 1998, its returns fall just outside the large-value category's top half. And so far in 2001, the fund has lost about 10% for the year to date through Oct. 16, but that's on par with its average peer.

Such uninspiring performance makes it difficult to endorse this fund over more-proven peers. While some health-care picks, such as Boston Scientific, have posted strong gains this year, the fund has suffered from double-digit losses among financial holdings like Morgan Stanley Dean Witter. Mullick said that he sold struggling stocks like Providian Financial, but he generally takes a long-term approach and isn't ruffled by a few weak quarters.

Mullick has been taking advantage of the recent market volatility to add new holdings. He reports that he's interested in travel-related stocks these days, such as Carnival and Hilton Hotels. Most travel stocks slumped right after the Sept. 11 attacks, but Mullick thinks that the long-term fundamentals of these firms are solid, given their strong brand names and clean balance sheets.

With Mullick's focus on busted growth stocks with decent fundamentals, the fund rarely falls to the bottom of the pack during downturns, and its performance doesn't swing wildly. Thus, investors certainly could have done worse than this during the past few years. That said, plenty of better-performing funds with similar risk profiles are available in this category. Until this fund creeps into its category's top half consistently, not much reason exists to send money here.

Special Securities % assets 11-30-01	
Restricted/Illiquid Secs	0
Emerging-Markets Secs	0
Options/Futures/Warrants	No

Composition % assets 11-30-01	
Cash	1.1
Stocks*	98.9
Bonds	0.0
Other	0.0
*Foreign (% stocks)	4.8

Market Cap	
Giant	19.8
Large	50.3
Medium	29.8
Small	0.0
Micro	0.0

Sector Weightings	% of Stocks	Rel S&P	5-Year High	5-Year Low
Utilities	6.1	1.9	9	0
Energy	4.7	0.7	12	3
Financials	27.7	1.5	37	12
Industrials	12.5	1.1	31	7
Durables	4.5	2.9	8	0
Staples	0.0	0.0	8	0
Services	13.5	1.2	27	10
Retail	7.6	1.1	15	2
Health	5.4	0.4	14	3
Technology	18.1	1.0	23	3

Address:	605 Third Avenue 2nd Floor New York, NY 10158-0006 800-877-9700 / 212-476-8800
Web Address:	www.nbfunds.com
Inception:	07-16-68
Advisor:	Neuberger Berman Mgmt., Inc.
Subadvisor:	Neuberger Berman, LLC
NTF Plans:	Schwab

Minimum Purchase:	$1000	Add: $100	IRA: $250
Min Auto Inv Plan:	$100	Add: $100	
Sales Fees:	No-load		
Management Fee:	.55% mx./.43% mn., .26%A		
Actual Fees:	Mgt: 0.71%	Dist: —	
Expense Projections:	3Yr: $262	5Yr: $455	10Yr: $1014
Avg Brok Commission:	—	Income Distrib: Annually	
Total Cost (relative to category):		Below Avg	

Neuberger Berman Regency Inv

Ticker	Load	NAV	Yield	Total Assets	Mstar Category
NBRVX	None	$11.55	0.1%	$37.5 mil	Mid–Cap Value

Prospectus Objective: Growth

Neuberger Berman Regency Fund seeks capital appreciation.

The fund principally invests in mid-capitalization companies. It may invest in foreign securities. The fund may also engage in borrowing and securities lending as well as invest in futures, options, and other derivative agreements.

Prior to December 18, 2000, the fund was named Neuberger Berman Regency Fund.

Historical Profile
Return —
Risk —
Rating Not Rated

Investment Style
Equity
Average Stock %: 92% | 93% | 96%

▼ Manager Change
▽ Partial Manager Change

Fund Performance vs. Category Average
■ Quarterly Fund Return +/– Category Average
— Category Baseline

Performance Quartile (within Category)

Portfolio Manager(s)

Robert I. Gendelman. Since 6-99. JD'84 U. of Chicago; MBA'84 U. of Chicago. Other funds currently managed: SunAmStySel Multi-Cap Value A, SunAmStySel Multi-Cap Value B, SunAmStySel Multi-Cap Value II.

1990	1991	1992	1993	1994	1995	1996	1997	1998	1999	2000	12-01	History
—	—	—	—	—	—	—	—	—	10.76	13.37	11.55	NAV
—	—	—	—	—	—	—	—	—	9.52*	31.24	–2.35	Total Return %
—	—	—	—	—	—	—	—	—	–4.83*	40.34	9.53	+/– S&P 500
—	—	—	—	—	—	—	—	—	—	12.05	–4.69	+/– Russ Midcap Val
—	—	—	—	—	—	—	—	—	0.20	0.00	0.07	Income Return %
—	—	—	—	—	—	—	—	—	9.32	31.24	–2.42	Capital Return %
—	—	—	—	—	—	—	—	—	—	14	83	Total Rtn % Rank Cat
—	—	—	—	—	—	—	—	—	0.02	0.00	0.01	Income $
—	—	—	—	—	—	—	—	—	0.16	0.70	1.44	Capital Gains $
—	—	—	—	—	—	—	—	—	1.51	1.50	—	Expense Ratio %
—	—	—	—	—	—	—	—	—	0.66	—	—	Income Ratio %
—	—	—	—	—	—	—	—	—	—	200	—	Turnover Rate %
—	—	—	—	—	—	—	—	—	7.3	15.9	15.8	Net Assets $mil

Performance 12-31-01

	1st Qtr	2nd Qtr	3rd Qtr	4th Qtr	Total
1997	—	—	—	—	—
1998	—	—	—	—	—
1999	—	—	–11.50	15.64	9.52 *
2000	10.41	–1.94	14.08	6.25	31.24
2001	–7.26	6.69	–10.96	10.83	–2.35

Trailing	Total Return%	+/– S&P 500	+/– Russ Midcap Val	% Rank All	% Rank Cat	Growth of $10,000
3 Mo	10.83	0.15	–1.20	38	71	11,083
6 Mo	–1.31	4.24	–0.41	44	54	9,869
1 Yr	–2.35	9.53	–4.69	46	83	9,765
3 Yr Avg	—	—	—	—	—	—
5 Yr Avg	—	—	—	—	—	—
10 Yr Avg	—	—	—	—	—	—
15 Yr Avg	—	—	—	—	—	—

Tax Analysis	Tax-Adj Ret%	%Rank Cat	%Pretax Ret	%Rank Cat
3 Yr Avg	—	—	—	—
5 Yr Avg	—	—	—	—
10 Yr Avg	—	—	—	—

Potential Capital Gain Exposure: 1% of assets

Risk Analysis

Time Period	Load-Adj Return %	Risk %Rank¹ All	Risk %Rank¹ Cat	Morningstar Return	Morningstar Risk	Morningstar Risk-Adj Rating
1 Yr	–2.35					
3 Yr	—	—	—	—	—	
5 Yr	—	—	—	—	—	
Incept	14.00	—	—	—	—	

Average Historical Rating —

¹1=low, 100=high

Category Rating (3 Yr)

Other Measures	Standard Index S&P 500	Best Fit Index
Alpha	—	—
Beta	—	—
R-Squared	—	—
Standard Deviation		—
Return — Mean		—
Risk — Sharpe Ratio		—

Portfolio Analysis 11-30-01

Share change since 10-01 Total Stocks: 77

	Sector	PE	YTD Ret%	% Assets
⊖ S & P Midcap 400 SPDR		—	—	4.43
⊕ Cigna	Financials	13.2	–29.00	2.25
⊕ Archer Daniels Midland	Staples	24.7	1.91	2.21
⊕ Pitney Bowes	Industrials	17.2	19.80	2.07
⊕ Sherwin–Williams	Industrials	—	7.12	2.01
⊕ Omnicare	Health	38.3	15.52	1.94
⊕ GTech Hldgs	Services	17.2	120.20	1.93
⊕ Valassis Comms	Services	18.9	12.85	1.89
⊕ Teekay Shipping	Energy	3.3	–7.24	1.78
AvalonBay Communities	Financials	15.9	–0.38	1.76
⊖ Waste Mgmt	Services	52.3	15.03	1.73
⊕ Lear	Durables	16.8	53.71	1.71
⊕ Viad	Services	36.4	4.48	1.70
⊕ Radian Grp	Financials	11.6	14.64	1.68
⊕ May Dept Stores	Retail	15.2	15.97	1.67
⊕ Beckman Coulter	Health	21.1	6.51	1.62
⊕ Becton Dickinson	Health	22.9	–3.20	1.55
⊕ Payless Shoesource	Retail	13.7	–20.60	1.55
⊕ Cablevision Sys A	Services	5.6	–34.20	1.53
Archstone Communities Tr	Financials	14.8	9.11	1.52
⊕ Equitable Resources	Energy	14.8	3.98	1.46
USX–Marathon Grp	Energy	9.6	11.58	1.46
⊖ Ambac Finl Grp	Financials	15.2	–0.16	1.44
Knight Ridder	Services	59.0	16.13	1.43
⊕ Sierra Pacific Resources	Utilities	—	–2.25	1.36

Current Investment Style

Style: Value Blnd Growth; Size: Large Med Small

	Stock Port Avg	Relative S&P 500 Current	Relative S&P 500 Hist	Rel Cat
Price/Earnings Ratio	22.8	0.74	—	0.97
Price/Book Ratio	2.8	0.49	—	0.93
Price/Cash Flow	12.4	0.69	—	1.00
3 Yr Earnings Growth	10.2	0.70	—	0.86
1 Yr Earnings Est%	1.5	—	—	–0.24
Med Mkt Cap $mil	4,393	0.1	—	0.62

Special Securities % assets 11-30-01

Restricted/Illiquid Secs	0
Emerging–Markets Secs	2
Options/Futures/Warrants	No

Composition % assets 11-30-01

Cash	2.3
Stocks*	97.7
Bonds	0.0
Other	0.0
*Foreign (% stocks)	6.3

Market Cap

Giant	0.0
Large	24.3
Medium	68.2
Small	7.5
Micro	0.0

Sector Weightings	% of Stocks	Rel S&P	5-Year High	5-Year Low
Utilities	7.2	2.3	—	—
Energy	9.2	1.3	—	—
Financials	27.0	1.5	—	—
Industrials	8.6	0.8	—	—
Durables	3.3	2.1	—	—
Staples	3.9	0.5	—	—
Services	24.7	2.3	—	—
Retail	3.6	0.5	—	—
Health	7.0	0.5	—	—
Technology	5.5	0.3	—	—

Analysis by Kelli Stebel 12-12-01

This fund's mixed record shouldn't scare investors away.

Neuberger Berman Regency launched during an inauspicious time for value funds. Back in June 1999, growth funds made all the headlines, with tech stocks, in particular, sporting spectacular returns. This fund sought to fill a gap in the Neuberger Berman lineup, though. Its predecessor, Neuberger Berman Partners, had grown too large to effectively invest in mid-cap stocks, whereas this is a dedicated mid-value fund.

Manager Bob Gendelman employs the same strategy he used to good effect at Partners during his six-year tenure there, but his brief record on this fund has been up and down. He is a die-hard value investor, buying beaten-down companies that have some catalyst for a turnaround. Last year, for example, Gendelman picked up shares of Nabisco when it was trading cheaply. When Philip Morris announced a takeover of Nabisco, the fund benefited nicely. Thanks to some good individual stock picks and strong-performing energy names, the fund finished 2000 with a 31% return, which placed in its category's top quintile.

Things haven't gone the fund's way in 2001, though. Part of the problem has been its complement of energy stocks, such as top-20 holding Teekay Shipping, which is posting a double-digit loss through Dec. 11. In addition, the fund's financials stocks, which could have been a source of strength, have been disappointing. Shares of Cigna have limped through the year.

Investors shouldn't panic, though. Gendelman has shown that his approach worked during his six-year stint at Partners. Although the mid-value category boasts lots of terrific funds, we still think this is a solid option.

Address:	605 Third Avenue 2nd Floor New York, NY 10158–0006 800–877–9700
Web Address:	www.nbfunds.com
*Inception:	06-01-99
Advisor:	Neuberger Berman Mgmt., Inc.
Subadvisor:	Neuberger Berman, LLC
NTF Plans:	Schwab

Minimum Purchase:	$1000	Add: $100	IRA: $250
Min Auto Inv Plan:	$100	Add: $100	
Sales Fees:	No–load		
Management Fee:	.55% mx./.43% mn.		
Actual Fees:	Mgt: 0.81%	Dist: —	
Expense Projections:	3Yr: $474	5Yr: —	10Yr: —
Avg Brok Commission:	—	Income Distrib: Annually	
Total Cost (relative to category):	—		

Nicholas II

Ticker	Load	NAV	Yield	Total Assets	Mstar Category
NCTWX	None	$20.09	0.0%	$512.0 mil	Mid-Cap Growth

Prospectus Objective: Small Company

Nicholas II seeks long-term growth; current income is secondary.

The fund invests primarily in common stocks of companies with potential for consistent growth in earnings and sales. These stocks are frequently small- or mid-cap issues with newer, more-innovative products. It may invest up to 5% of assets in companies with fewer than three years of operating history. Although common stocks make up the bulk of assets, the fund does not maintain minimums or maximums for relative holdings; debt and preferred stocks may also be purchased.

Historical Profile

Return: Average
Risk: Average
Rating: ★★★ Neutral

Investment Style
Equity
Average Stock %: 99% | 99% | 99% | 100% | 100% | 99%

▼ Manager Change
▽ Partial Manager Change

Fund Performance vs. Category Average
■ Quarterly Fund Return +/– Category Average
— Category Baseline

Performance Quartile (within Category)

Portfolio Manager(s)

David O. Nicholas, CFA. Since 3-93. BBA'83 U. of Wisconsin; MS'87 U. of Wisconsin. Other funds currently managed: Nicholas Limited Edition, Nicholas.

1990	1991	1992	1993	1994	1995	1996	1997	1998	1999	2000	12-01	History
18.42	25.02	26.32	26.32	24.46	28.73	30.99	36.94	36.03	35.96	21.34	20.09	NAV
–6.21	39.56	9.38	6.40	1.03	28.55	19.38	37.01	9.24	1.17	–2.09	–3.11	Total Return %
–3.09	9.08	1.76	–3.66	–0.28	–8.98	–3.57	3.66	–19.34	–19.87	7.01	8.76	+/– S&P 500
–1.07	–7.47	0.67	–4.79	3.20	–5.43	1.90	14.47	–8.63	–50.14	9.65	17.04	+/– Russ Midcap Grth
1.70	1.33	0.94	0.76	0.78	1.11	0.77	0.22	0.36	0.03	0.00	0.00	Income Return %
–7.90	38.23	8.44	5.64	0.25	27.44	18.61	36.79	8.88	1.14	–2.09	–3.11	Capital Return %
48	78	44	88	34	75	33	2	68	99	43	9	Total Rtn % Rank Cat
0.34	0.24	0.24	0.20	0.21	0.27	0.22	0.07	0.13	0.01	0.00	0.00	Income $
0.14	0.40	0.80	1.47	1.89	2.40	3.02	5.24	4.00	0.47	13.12	0.58	Capital Gains $
0.71	0.70	0.66	0.67	0.67	0.66	0.62	0.61	0.59	0.61	0.62	—	Expense Ratio %
1.78	1.24	1.01	0.79	0.72	0.68	0.29	0.23	0.33	0.03	0.02	—	Income Ratio %
19	12	11	27	17	20	24	30	20	21	65	—	Turnover Rate %
355.4	557.4	742.3	703.7	603.9	693.3	784.3	1,025.0	1,109.5	940.9	690.2	—	Net Assets $mil

Performance 12-31-01

	1st Qtr	2nd Qtr	3rd Qtr	4th Qtr	Total
1997	0.90	14.61	13.42	4.45	37.01
1998	13.89	–2.02	–15.62	16.02	9.24
1999	–4.33	3.71	–10.97	14.51	1.17
2000	–1.11	2.45	0.41	–3.75	–2.09
2001	–13.31	14.70	–17.34	17.88	–3.11

Trailing	Total Return%	+/– S&P 500	+/– Russ Midcap Grth	% Rank All	% Rank Cat	Growth of $10,000
3 Mo	17.88	7.19	–9.19	17	57	11,788
6 Mo	–2.57	2.99	5.69	50	13	9,743
1 Yr	–3.11	8.76	17.04	47	9	9,689
3 Yr Avg	–1.36	–0.34	–3.52	79	78	9,596
5 Yr Avg	7.51	–3.19	–1.51	32	61	14,363
10 Yr Avg	9.99	–2.94	–1.11	32	54	25,916
15 Yr Avg	11.39	–2.34	–1.42	30	51	50,456

Tax Analysis	Tax-Adj Ret%	%Rank Cat	%Pretax Ret	%Rank Cat
3 Yr Avg	–4.29	79	—	—
5 Yr Avg	4.48	62	59.6	78
10 Yr Avg	7.28	54	72.8	55

Potential Capital Gain Exposure: –11% of assets

Risk Analysis

Time Period	Load-Adj Return %	Risk %Rank[1] All	Risk %Rank[1] Cat	Morningstar Return	Morningstar Risk	Morningstar Risk-Adj Rating
1 Yr	–3.11					
3 Yr	–1.36	73	20	–1.26[2]	1.01	★★
5 Yr	7.51	71	7	0.57[2]	0.97	★★★
10 Yr	9.99	76	4	0.73	1.00	★★★

Average Historical Rating (183 months): 3.2★s

[1] 1=low, 100=high [2] T-Bill return substituted for category avg.

Category Rating (3 Yr)

1 2 3 4 5 — Worst … Best

Return: Below Avg
Risk: Below Avg

Other Measures	Standard Index S&P 500	Best Fit Index S&P 500
Alpha	–0.1	–0.1
Beta	0.97	0.97
R-Squared	74	74
Standard Deviation		19.18
Mean		–1.36
Sharpe Ratio		–0.38

Portfolio Analysis 11-30-01

Share change since 10-01 Total Stocks: 58	Sector	PE	YTD Ret%	% Assets
USA Networks	Services	58.1	40.50	3.90
Guidant	Health	42.6	–7.67	3.40
Intl Speedway Cl A	Services	27.3	3.04	3.39
Renal Care Grp	Health	22.8	17.13	3.24
Plantronics	Technology	28.2	–45.40	3.22
Boston Scientific	Health	—	76.21	3.18
Apache	Energy	8.0	–21.20	3.11
Clear Channel Comms	Services	—	5.10	3.00
Natl Commerce	Financials	32.4	3.99	2.89
⊖ Apogent Tech	Health	29.0	25.85	2.58
Sprint (PCS Group)	Services	—	19.43	2.56
Robert Half Intl	Services	31.1	0.75	2.41
O'Reilly Automotive	Retail	33.8	36.34	2.40
⊕ Qwest Comms Intl	Services	—	–65.40	2.36
⊖ Fifth Third Bancorp	Financials	38.3	4.53	2.28
⊖ Choicepoint	Services	70.4	15.97	2.25
Keane	Technology	64.4	84.92	2.15
Fiserv	Services	40.7	33.82	2.15
Protective Life	Financials	13.7	–8.65	2.04
Shire Pharma Grp	Health	—	–20.50	2.00
Harris	Technology	28.0	0.33	1.97
Outback Steakhouse	Services	20.4	32.37	1.92
Biogen	Health	30.5	–4.52	1.88
⊖ Andrew	Technology	28.8	0.64	1.87
Zebra Tech	Technology	27.0	36.12	1.84

Current Investment Style

Style: Value Blnd Growth; Size: Large Med Small

	Stock Port Avg	Relative S&P 500 Current	Relative S&P 500 Hist	Rel Cat
Price/Earnings Ratio	33.3	1.08	1.00	0.96
Price/Book Ratio	5.3	0.94	0.69	0.94
Price/Cash Flow	22.2	1.23	1.09	0.96
3 Yr Earnings Growth	19.0	1.30	1.23	0.81
1 Yr Earnings Est%	2.6	—	—	0.28
Med Mkt Cap $mil	4,997	0.1	0.1	0.89

Analysis by Laura Pavlenko Lutton 12-10-01

Nicholas II Fund is a decent choice for investors seeking a conservative-leaning growth fund.

After poor showings in 1999 and early 2000, this fund has turned things around. Granted, it's down 4.78% for the year to date through Dec. 7, 2001, but the fund is outperforming more than 90% of its peers in the mid-growth category for the period.

The fund's recent success owes to manager David Nicholas' cautious, bargain-hunting approach to growth investing. He favors steadier growers over flashier fare and wants his picks to have low prices relative to their growth rates. For example, Nicholas often favors health-care and media firms for their predictable growth patterns. He recently added to top holding USA Networks, the cable TV and entertainment firm. The stock sold off in the wake of the Sept. 11 terrorist attacks because investors were leery about the health of the company's travel business, but Nicholas thinks the firm's long-term growth prospects are still strong.

Traditionally Nicholas has avoided most technology firms because they're more cyclical and often come with big price tags. That helps limit the fund's volatility and has worked well in 2001 while value stocks have been in favor. However, it also badly hurt the fund when expensive tech stocks drove growth-fund returns in 1999 and early 2000, and investors should expect the fund to continue to lag in tech-led rallies.Because of its poor performance in 1999, the fund's three-year return is poor. However, it has fared reasonably well over the longer term and has been much less volatile than its typical peer. It also boasts low expenses. For investors seeking a moderate approach to mid-growth investing, it's worth a look. For investors who can stomach additional risk, however, other funds have offered much better returns over time.

Special Securities % assets 11-30-01	
Restricted/Illiquid Secs	0
Emerging-Markets Secs	0
Options/Futures/Warrants	No

Composition % assets 11-30-01	
Cash	0.0
Stocks*	100.0
Bonds	0.0
Other	0.0
*Foreign (% stocks)	3.1

Market Cap	
Giant	0.0
Large	29.2
Medium	65.3
Small	5.5
Micro	0.0

Sector Weightings	% of Stocks	Rel S&P	5-Year High	5-Year Low
Utilities	0.0	0.0	1	0
Energy	5.5	0.8	5	0
Financials	10.8	0.6	31	8
Industrials	2.7	0.2	17	0
Durables	0.7	0.4	6	0
Staples	0.0	0.0	13	0
Services	32.3	3.0	34	8
Retail	5.8	0.9	18	5
Health	21.9	1.5	40	11
Technology	20.3	1.1	32	2

Address: 700 N. Water Street Suite 1010
Milwaukee, WI 53202
414-272-6133 / 800-227-5987
Web Address: www.nicholasfunds.com
Inception: 10-17-83
Advisor: Nicholas
Subadvisor: None
NTF Plans: N/A

Minimum Purchase: $500 — Add: $100 — IRA: $500
Min Auto Inv Plan: $500 — Add: $50
Sales Fees: No-load
Management Fee: .75% mx./.50% mn.
Actual Fees: Mgt: 0.52% — Dist: —
Expense Projections: 3Yr: $195 — 5Yr: $340 — 10Yr: $762
Avg Brok Commission: — — Income Distrib: Annually
Total Cost (relative to category): Low

Northeast Investors

Ticker	Load	NAV	Yield	SEC Yield	Total Assets	Mstar Category
NTHEX	None	$7.43	11.7%	—	$1,172.1 mil	High–Yield Bond

Prospectus Objective: Corp Bond—High Yield

Northeast Investors Trust seeks income; capital appreciation is secondary.

The fund invests primarily in securities of established companies, including bonds, preferred stocks, dividend-paying common stocks, convertibles, and warrants. Because the fund does not impose any particular ratings standards, its portfolio has generally included debt securities rated below investment-grade. Many holdings are unrated. The fund may borrow money (up to 25% of assets) to make additional investment purchases.

Historical Profile

Return	Above Avg
Risk	Above Avg
Rating	★★★ Neutral

Investment Style
Fixed-Income
Income Rtn %Rank Cat: 19, 25, 16, 64, 47, 17, 13, 37

Growth of Principal vs. Interest Rate Shifts
- Principal Value $000 (NAV with capital gains reinvested)
- Interest Rate % on 10 Yr Treasury
- ▼ Manager Change
- ▽ Partial Manager Change
- ► Mgr Unknown After
- ◄ Mgr Unknown Before

Performance Quartile (within Category)

Portfolio Manager(s)

Ernest E. Monrad. Since 6-60. BA'51 Harvard U.; LLB'56 U. of Virginia.

Bruce H. Monrad, CFA. Since 1-93. BA'84 Harvard U.; MBA'89 Harvard U.

1990	1991	1992	1993	1994	1995	1996	1997	1998	1999	2000	12–01	History
8.14	8.83	9.21	10.29	9.55	10.16	11.12	11.65	10.47	9.77	8.17	7.43	NAV
–9.17	26.38	17.49	23.60	2.20	17.27	20.16	13.89	–0.25	3.50	–6.05	1.33	Total Return %
–18.13	10.38	10.08	13.85	5.12	–1.20	16.54	4.21	–8.92	4.33	–17.68	–7.10	+/– LB Aggregate
–2.79	–17.37	0.83	4.69	3.18	–0.12	7.74	1.27	–0.83	0.22	–0.84	–4.45	+/– FB High–Yield
14.19	16.96	13.16	11.29	9.87	10.76	10.20	8.91	8.86	10.56	11.32	11.08	Income Return %
–23.36	9.42	4.33	12.31	–7.66	6.51	9.95	4.98	–9.11	–7.06	–17.37	–9.75	Capital Return %
44	87	39	7	3	47	5	29	55	60	37	59	Total Rtn % Rank Cat
1.40	1.30	1.11	1.00	0.98	0.99	1.00	0.96	1.00	1.07	1.06	0.87	Income $
0.00	0.00	0.00	0.00	0.00	0.00	0.00	0.00	0.18	0.00	0.00	0.00	Capital Gains $
1.47	1.89	1.44	1.21	1.06	1.02	0.66	0.64	0.61	0.61	0.61	—	Expense Ratio %
14.35	15.38	12.36	10.53	9.37	9.77	9.41	8.65	8.73	9.99	10.84	—	Income Ratio %
21	34	59	76	73	41	32	33	64	27	4	—	Turnover Rate %
243.2	304.6	399.1	548.6	554.6	805.2	1,354.8	2,161.0	2,313.5	1,854.0	1,318.5	—	Net Assets $mil

Performance 12-31-01

	1st Qtr	2nd Qtr	3rd Qtr	4th Qtr	Total
1997	2.69	4.52	5.20	0.86	13.89
1998	5.10	0.99	–10.45	4.94	–0.25
1999	2.81	1.97	–1.84	0.58	3.50
2000	–1.53	0.24	1.92	–6.61	–6.05
2001	6.12	–0.47	–7.03	3.19	1.33

Trailing	Total Return%	+/– LB Agg	+/– FB High–Yield	% Rank All	% Rank Cat	Growth of $10,000
3 Mo	3.19	3.16	–2.45	70	93	10,319
6 Mo	–4.06	–8.72	–5.50	56	92	9,594
1 Yr	1.33	–7.10	–4.45	40	59	10,133
3 Yr Avg	–0.49	–6.77	–1.66	75	49	9,853
5 Yr Avg	2.28	–5.14	–0.96	87	34	11,194
10 Yr Avg	8.88	1.65	1.04	39	2	23,409
15 Yr Avg	7.77	–0.35	–0.90	56	21	30,713

Tax Analysis	Tax-Adj Ret%	%Rank Cat	%Pretax Ret	%Rank Cat
3 Yr Avg	–4.66	53	—	—
5 Yr Avg	–1.71	37	—	—
10 Yr Avg	4.73	4	53.3	14

Potential Capital Gain Exposure: –59% of assets

Risk Analysis

Time Period	Load-Adj Return %	Risk %Rank[1] All	Risk %Rank[1] Cat	Morningstar Return	Morningstar Risk	Morningstar Risk-Adj Rating
1 Yr	1.33					
3 Yr	–0.49	35	32	–1.09[2]	1.80	★★
5 Yr	2.28	39	21	–0.57[2]	1.86	★★
10 Yr	8.88	43	22	1.28[2]	1.38	★★★★

Average Historical Rating (193 months): 4.2★s

[1]1=low, 100=high [2] T-Bill return substituted for category avg.

Category Rating (3 Yr)

1 2 **3** 4 5
Worst Best

Return	Average
Risk	Below Avg

Other Measures	Standard Index LB Agg	Best Fit Index FB HY
Alpha	–4.6	–2.1
Beta	–0.28	0.86
R–Squared	2	73
Standard Deviation		7.41
Mean		–0.49
Sharpe Ratio		–0.85

Portfolio Analysis 09-30-01

Total Fixed-Income: 121	Date of Maturity	Amount $000	Value $000	% Net Assets
Trump Atlantic City Fdg 11.25%	05-01-06	90,530	56,129	4.79
Stone Container 12.58%	08-01-16	43,100	45,686	3.90
Advantica Restrnt 11.25%	01-15-08	58,769	38,200	3.26
Pathmark Stores		1,600	38,089	3.25
Kaiser Alum/Chem 12.75%	02-01-03	46,230	33,286	2.84
Venetian Casino 12.25%	11-15-04	34,000	30,940	2.64
Republic of Brazil 14.5%	10-15-09	26,366	24,942	2.13
Boyd Gaming 9.5%	07-15-07	25,000	23,250	1.98
Chubb		300	21,423	1.83
Husky Oil 8.9%	08-15-28	20,000	20,400	1.74
Fleming 10.5%	12-01-04	20,000	20,000	1.71
Univ Compression Step 0%	02-15-08	22,500	19,800	1.69
Motors & Gears 10.75%	11-15-06	22,410	19,273	1.64
Sterling Chem 12.375%	07-15-06	23,990	18,712	1.60
Fleming 10.625%	07-31-07	18,000	17,820	1.52
Republic of Argentina 12%	06-19-31	32,311	17,206	1.47
Key Energy Grp 14%	01-15-09	13,951	15,904	1.36
Coast Hotels & Casino 9.5%	04-01-09	15,000	14,550	1.24
Comstock Res 11.25%	05-01-07	14,500	14,210	1.21
Riviera Hldgs 10%	08-15-04	17,000	13,770	1.17

Current Investment Style

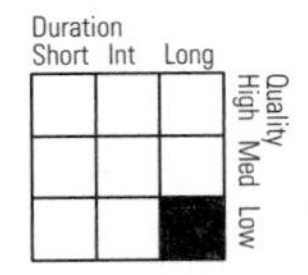

Avg Eff Duration[1]	6.2 Yrs
Avg Eff Maturity	—
Avg Credit Quality	B
Avg Wtd Coupon	10.46%
Avg Wtd Price	79.31% of par

[1]figure provided by fund

Special Securities % assets 09-30-01

Restricted/Illiquid Secs	4
Exotic Mortgage–Backed	0
Emerging–Markets Secs	0
Options/Futures/Warrants	Yes

Credit Analysis % bonds 06-30-01

US Govt	0	BB	12
AAA	0	B	60
AA	0	Below B	17
A	0	NR/NA	11
BBB	0		

Sector Breakdown % bonds 09-30-01

US Treasuries	0	CMOs	0
GNMA mtgs	0	ARMs	0
FNMA mtgs	0	Other	100
FHLMC mtgs	0		

Coupon Range	% of Bonds	Rel Cat
0%, PIK	3.23	0.52
0% to 9%	10.74	0.35
9% to 12%	59.53	1.12
12% to 14%	21.17	2.40
More than 14%	5.33	3.83

1.00=Category Average

Composition % assets 09-30-01

Cash	3.4	Bonds	85.3
Stocks	11.0	Other	0.3

Analysis by Scott Berry 07-12-01

Northeast Investors Trust is showing why it's a Morningstar Fund Analyst Pick.

This fund, along with many other high-yield offerings, got off to a flying start in January 2001. But while most of its peers struggled to hold on to their gains when the high-yield market slumped in March and April, this fund held fast and delivered a 5.6% gain for the year to date through June 10, 2001. By contrast, its average peer gained just 1.6%.

The fund's success in the first half of 2001 had more to do with what it didn't own than what it did. The telecommunications sector, which has been the bane of the high-yield market for the last few years, slumped in mid-2001 and weighed on the returns of most high-yield offerings. Fortunately, this fund had no exposure to that sector. Comanager Bruce Monrad remains open to the idea of investing in telecom issues, but with most telecoms still bleeding cash, he argues that there are more-attractive opportunities elsewhere.

Monrad's distaste for telecom is nothing new. In fact, the fund has been underweight in telecom for years. This positioning held the fund back a bit in 1998 and 1999, but the fund has more than made up any ground it lost with its recent performance. Indeed, its five- and 10-year trailing returns rank near the top of high-yield performance charts.

This fund has a lot going for it. In addition to delivering strong long-term returns with less volatility than its average peer, it sports a below-average expense ratio that checks in at a 25% discount to that of its average no-load high-yield peer. Throw in Monrad's skillful management, and this fund is tough to beat.

Address:	50 Congress Street Boston, MA 02109–4096 800–225–6704 / 617–523–3588
Web Address:	www.northeastinvestors.com
Inception:	08-01-50
Advisor:	Northeast Investors Trustees
Subadvisor:	None
NTF Plans:	N/A

Minimum Purchase:	$1000	Add: None IRA: $500
Min Auto Inv Plan:	$1000	Add: $50
Sales Fees:	No–load	
Management Fee:	.50%	
Actual Fees:	Mgt: 0.50%	Dist: —
Expense Projections:	3Yr: $19*	5Yr: $33* 10Yr: $74*
Avg Brok Commission:	—	Income Distrib: Quarterly
Total Cost (relative to category):	—	

Northern Institutional Mid Cap Gr A

Ticker	Load	NAV	Yield	Total Assets	Mstar Category
BMGRX	None	$9.33	0.0%	$36.2 mil	Mid-Cap Growth

Prospectus Objective: Growth

Northern Institutional Mid Cap Growth seeks to provide long-term capital appreciation.

The fund normally invests at least 65% of assets in the equity securities of companies with market capitalization, at the time of purchase, between $100 million and $11 billion. It may also invest significantly in initial public offerings ("IPOs"). Although the Portfolio primarily invests in the stocks of U S companies, it may invest to a limited extent in the securities of foreign issuers. The investment management team may engage in active trading, and will not consider portfolio turnover a limiting factor in making decisions for the portfolio.

Historical Profile
Return —
Risk —
Rating Not Rated

Investment Style
Equity
Average Stock % 100%

▼ Manager Change
▽ Partial Manager Change

Fund Performance vs. Category Average
■ Quarterly Fund Return +/– Category Average
— Category Baseline

Performance Quartile (within Category)

Portfolio Manager(s)

Ken Turek, CFA. Since 12-99. BA U. of Wisconsin-Madison; MBA DePaul U. Other funds currently managed: Northern Institutional Focused Grow A, Northern Institutional Focused Grow D, Northern Institutional Focused Grow C.

1990	1991	1992	1993	1994	1995	1996	1997	1998	1999	2000	12-01	History
—	—	—	—	—	—	—	—	—	10.00	11.29	9.33	NAV
—	—	—	—	—	—	—	—	—	—	12.90	–17.36	Total Return %
—	—	—	—	—	—	—	—	—	—	22.00	–5.48	+/– S&P 500
—	—	—	—	—	—	—	—	—	—	24.65	2.80	+/– Russ Midcap Grth
—	—	—	—	—	—	—	—	—	—	0.00	0.00	Income Return %
—	—	—	—	—	—	—	—	—	—	12.90	–17.36	Capital Return %
—	—	—	—	—	—	—	—	—	—	16	37	Total Rtn % Rank Cat
—	—	—	—	—	—	—	—	—	0.00	0.00	0.00	Income $
—	—	—	—	—	—	—	—	—	0.00	0.00	0.00	Capital Gains $
—	—	—	—	—	—	—	—	—	—	0.93	—	Expense Ratio %
—	—	—	—	—	—	—	—	—	—	–1.41	—	Income Ratio %
—	—	—	—	—	—	—	—	—	—	208	—	Turnover Rate %
—	—	—	—	—	—	—	—	—	—	40.1	35.2	Net Assets $mil

Performance 12-31-01

	1st Qtr	2nd Qtr	3rd Qtr	4th Qtr	Total
1997	—	—	—	—	—
1998	—	—	—	—	—
1999	—	—	—	—	—
2000	23.90	–0.48	8.68	–15.75	12.90
2001	–19.04	9.74	–19.24	15.19	–17.36

Trailing	Total Return%	+/– S&P 500	+/– Russ Midcap Grth	% Rank All	% Rank Cat	Growth of $10,000
3 Mo	15.19	4.50	—	23	72	11,519
6 Mo	–6.98	–1.42	—	74	35	9,302
1 Yr	–17.36	–5.48	—	76	37	8,264
3 Yr Avg	—	—	—	—	—	—
5 Yr Avg	—	—	—	—	—	—
10 Yr Avg	—	—	—	—	—	—
15 Yr Avg	—	—	—	—	—	—

Tax Analysis	Tax-Adj Ret%	%Rank Cat	%Pretax Ret	%Rank Cat
3 Yr Avg	—	—	—	—
5 Yr Avg	—	—	—	—
10 Yr Avg	—	—	—	—

Potential Capital Gain Exposure: NMF

Risk Analysis

Time Period	Load-Adj Return %	Risk %Rank[1] All	Risk %Rank[1] Cat	Morningstar Return	Morningstar Risk	Morningstar Risk-Adj Rating
1 Yr	–17.36					
3 Yr	—	—	—	—	—	
5 Yr	—	—	—	—	—	
Incept	–3.40	—	—	—	—	

Average Historical Rating —

[1]1=low, 100=high

Category Rating (3 Yr)

Other Measures	Standard Index S&P 500	Best Fit Index
Alpha	—	—
Beta	—	—
R-Squared	—	—

	Standard Deviation	—
Return	Mean	—
Risk	Sharpe Ratio	—

Portfolio Analysis 09-30-01

Share change since 06-01 Total Stocks: 96	Sector	PE	YTD Ret%	% Assets
Caremark Rx	Health	46.6	20.25	2.18
⊖ Tenet Healthcare	Health	30.1	32.14	1.97
Quest Diagnostics	Health	51.2	1.00	1.89
Scholastic	Services	NMF	13.58	1.88
⊕ Arthur J. Gallagher & Co.	Financials	26.3	10.31	1.77
UST, Inc.	Staples	12.3	32.23	1.76
Countrywide Credit Ind	Financials	10.6	–17.70	1.74
Andrx	Health	66.4	21.66	1.72
⊕ Everest Re Grp	Financials	17.6	–1.29	1.71
Performance Food Grp	Staples	33.5	37.25	1.67
Lincare Hldgs	Health	23.7	0.41	1.58
Heller Finl	Financials	—	73.46	1.57
⊕ King Pharmaceuticals	Health	45.8	8.68	1.55
Forest Labs	Health	52.2	23.35	1.52
XTO Energy	N/A	—	—	1.51
Affiliated Comp Svcs A	Services	39.9	74.88	1.50
☼ M & T Bk	Financials	20.8	8.63	1.47
⊕ Blockbuster Cl A	Retail	—	202.10	1.45
⊕ Packaging Corporation	Industrials	11.9	12.56	1.43
☼ Amerisourcebergen	N/A	—	—	1.40
Varian Medical Sys	Technology	34.3	4.89	1.38
⊕ Allied Cap	Financials	11.6	35.33	1.36
☼ Suiza Foods	Staples	—	25.44	1.36
⊕ Career Educ	Services	47.6	75.23	1.33
⊕ Biomet	Health	40.7	17.13	1.33

Current Investment Style

Style: Value Blnd Growth; Size: Large Med Small

	Stock Port Avg	Relative S&P 500 Current	Relative S&P 500 Hist	Rel Cat
Price/Earnings Ratio	35.1	1.13	—	1.01
Price/Book Ratio	5.8	1.02	—	1.02
Price/Cash Flow	21.4	1.19	—	0.92
3 Yr Earnings Growth	22.0	1.51	—	0.94
1 Yr Earnings Est%	15.9	—	—	1.70
Med Mkt Cap $mil	4,359	0.1	—	0.77

[1]figure is based on 50% or less of stocks

Analysis by Brian Portnoy 09-06-01

Northern Institutional Mid Cap Growth is emerging as a good fund for tough times.

Manager Ken Turek takes a somewhat-moderate approach to growth investing here. He likes companies with consistent, though not necessarily accelerating, revenue and earnings growth, as well as those that generate strong free cash flows. When possible, Turek will snap up stocks on the cheap. For example, he recently bought mortgage insurer Radian Group when its price dropped on news of new industry regulations that Turek considers relatively innocuous to the company's business prospects.

Over his limited tenure here, this approach has produced presentable results. In 2000, he avoided major blowups by eschewing pricey Internet and biotech stocks. At the same time, he earned strong returns through a big slug of energy stocks as well as some winners in technology including graphics chipmaker NVIDIA. And though the fund's performance thus far in 2001 pales when compared with last year's 12.8% gain, it's ahead of the pack again. Indeed, for the year to date through September 5, 2001, the fund's 19.5% loss outpaces two thirds of the mid-growth competition. Of course, woes in the tech sector have hurt the fund, but a large, diversified stake in health care, including Tenet Healthcare THC, has helped to mitigate loss.

Investors should keep an eye on this fund.

Special Securities % assets 09-30-01	
Restricted/Illiquid Secs	0
Emerging-Markets Secs	0
Options/Futures/Warrants	No

Composition % assets 09-30-01	
Cash	0.0
Stocks*	100.0
Bonds	0.0
Other	0.0
*Foreign (% stocks)	1.6

Market Cap	
Giant	0.0
Large	22.0
Medium	72.3
Small	5.7
Micro	0.0

Sector Weightings	% of Stocks	Rel S&P	5-Year High	5-Year Low
Utilities	1.5	0.5	—	—
Energy	2.6	0.4	—	—
Financials	17.3	1.0	—	—
Industrials	12.0	1.1	—	—
Durables	1.6	1.0	—	—
Staples	5.8	0.7	—	—
Services	15.0	1.4	—	—
Retail	5.6	0.8	—	—
Health	26.7	1.8	—	—
Technology	11.8	0.6	—	—

Address: 50 South LaSalle Street, Chicago, IL 60607, 800–637–1380 / 312–655–4400
Web Address: www.northerntrust.com
*Inception: 12-31-99
Advisor: Northern Trust
Subadvisor: None
NTF Plans: N/A

Minimum Purchase: $5.00 mil — Add: None — IRA: —
Min Auto Inv Plan: — — Add: —
Sales Fees: No-load
Management Fee: 1.1%, .10%A
Actual Fees: Mgt: 0.80% — Dist: —
Expense Projections: 3Yr: $530 — 5Yr: — — 10Yr: —
Avg Brok Commission: — — Income Distrib: Annually
Total Cost (relative to category): —

Northern Technology

Ticker	Load	NAV	Yield	Total Assets	Mstar Category
NTCHX	None	$12.47	0.0%	$608.8 mil	Spec Technology

Prospectus Objective: Specialty—Technology

Northern Technology Fund seeks long-term capital appreciation.

The fund invests primarily in equities issued by domestic and foreign companies that develop, produce, or distribute products and services related to advances in technology; it normally invests at least 65% in companies principally engaged in technology business activities. The advisor emphasizes stocks that may have the potential to out perform the market over the next one- to two-year period. Security selection is based on an issuer's financial condition, market share, product leadership or market niches, earnings-growth rates in relation to relevant competitors, comparative-market valuation, improving relative price trend, and other factors.

Historical Profile
Return Above Avg
Risk High
Rating ★★★ Neutral

Investment Style
Equity
Average Stock %: 98% 99% 96% 98% 94% 98%

▼ Manager Change
▽ Partial Manager Change

Fund Performance vs. Category Average
■ Quarterly Fund Return +/– Category Average
— Category Baseline

Performance Quartile (within Category)

Portfolio Manager(s)

John B. Leo, CFA. Since 4-96. BS Northern Illinois U.; MBA U. of Chicago. Other fund currently managed: Northern Global Communications.

George J. Gilbert. Since 9-97. BA U. of St. Thomas; MS Illinois Institute of Tech.

1990	1991	1992	1993	1994	1995	1996	1997	1998	1999	2000	12-01	History
—	—	—	—	—	—	13.11	14.35	25.58	51.76	19.03	12.47	NAV
—	—	—	—	—	—	32.53*	16.68	83.02	134.48	–38.43	–34.47	Total Return %
—	—	—	—	—	—	17.32*	–16.67	54.45	113.44	–29.33	–22.60	+/– S&P 500
—	—	—	—	—	—	—	–3.29	28.42	18.08	–22.21	–18.88	+/– PSE Tech 100
—	—	—	—	—	—	0.00	0.00	0.00	0.00	0.00	0.00	Income Return %
—	—	—	—	—	—	32.53	16.68	83.02	134.48	–38.43	–34.47	Capital Return %
—	—	—	—	—	—	—	17	11	46	77	37	Total Rtn % Rank Cat
—	—	—	—	—	—	0.00	0.00	0.00	0.00	0.00	0.00	Income $
—	—	—	—	—	—	0.15	0.90	0.67	5.74	12.51	0.00	Capital Gains $
—	—	—	—	—	—	—	1.25	1.25	1.23	1.25	1.25	Expense Ratio %
—	—	—	—	—	—	—	–0.75	–0.96	–0.87	–1.05	–0.74	Income Ratio %
—	—	—	—	—	—	—	—	75	61	156	180	Turnover Rate %
—	—	—	—	—	—	34.3	80.9	227.8	1,809.9	1,195.1	608.8	Net Assets $mil

Performance 12-31-01

	1st Qtr	2nd Qtr	3rd Qtr	4th Qtr	Total
1997	–8.85	22.18	20.75	–13.23	16.68
1998	19.23	9.29	–6.47	50.17	83.02
1999	17.24	13.40	6.79	65.15	134.48
2000	27.14	–14.44	0.67	–43.78	–38.43
2001	–31.58	9.91	–33.75	31.54	–34.47

Trailing	Total Return%	+/– S&P 500	+/– PSE Tech 100	% Rank All	% Rank Cat	Growth of $10,000
3 Mo	31.54	20.86	–1.37	4	70	13,154
6 Mo	–12.86	–7.30	–7.58	91	22	8,714
1 Yr	–34.47	–22.60	–18.88	96	37	6,553
3 Yr Avg	–1.83	–0.81	–17.07	82	48	9,460
5 Yr Avg	15.10	4.40	–8.10	4	17	20,203
10 Yr Avg	—	—	—	—	—	—
15 Yr Avg	—	—	—	—	—	—

Tax Analysis	Tax-Adj Ret%	%Rank Cat	%Pretax Ret	%Rank Cat
3 Yr Avg	–6.97	70	—	—
5 Yr Avg	10.85	21	71.8	83
10 Yr Avg	—	—	—	—

Potential Capital Gain Exposure: –95% of assets

Risk Analysis

Time Period	Load-Adj Return %	Risk %Rank[1] All	Risk %Rank[1] Cat	Morningstar Return	Morningstar Risk	Morningstar Risk-Adj Rating
1 Yr	–34.47					
3 Yr	–1.83	99	63	–1.35[2]	2.39	★
5 Yr	15.10	99	57	2.67[2]	2.13	★★★★
Incept	18.67	—	—	—	—	

Average Historical Rating (34 months): 4.7★s

[1]1=low, 100=high [2] T-Bill return substituted for category avg.

Category Rating (3 Yr)

1 2 **3** 4 5
Worst Best

Return Average
Risk Average

Other Measures	Standard Index S&P 500	Best Fit Index Wil 4500
Alpha	17.4	6.9
Beta	2.06	1.72
R-Squared	44	83
Standard Deviation		61.75
Mean		–1.83
Sharpe Ratio		–0.13

Portfolio Analysis 09-30-01

Share chng since 06-01 Total Stocks: 56	Subsector	PE	YTD Ret%	% Assets
⊖ Electronic Arts	Software	90.8	40.65	6.30
Electronic Data Sys	Computer Svs	25.7	19.83	5.63
Microsoft	Software	57.6	52.78	5.51
AOL Time Warner	Computer Svs	—	–7.76	4.63
⊕ Dell Comp	Computers	61.8	55.87	4.35
Computer Assoc Intl	Software	—	77.28	4.33
IBM	Computers	26.9	43.00	3.97
☼ Motorola	Telecom	—	–25.00	3.43
Intuit	Software	—	8.42	3.26
Texas Instruments	Semiconductors	87.5	–40.70	3.14
⊖ First Data	Computer Svs	38.1	49.08	2.91
⊕ Intel	Semiconductors	73.1	4.89	2.80
⊖ Oracle	Software	32.1	–52.40	2.46
Concord EFS	Computer Svs	86.3	49.21	2.39
Applied Matls	Semi Equipment	66.8	5.01	2.23
⊕ Micron Tech	Semiconductors	—	–12.60	2.14
⊕ Xilinx	Semiconductors	—	–15.30	1.84
⊕ Automatic Data Processing	Services	39.8	–6.27	1.84
Solectron	Technology	—	–66.70	1.82
PeopleSoft	Software	73.1	8.10	1.76
⊖ Sun Microsystems	Computers	NMF	–55.80	1.54
☼ Affiliated Comp Svcs A	Computer Svs	39.9	74.88	1.43
⊖ Cisco Sys	Networking	—	–52.60	1.43
⊕ Hewlett-Packard	Computers	97.8	–33.90	1.32
STMicroelectronics (NY)	Semiconductors	29.1	–25.90	1.26

Current Investment Style

Style: Value Blnd Growth; Size: Large Med Small

	Stock Port Avg	Relative S&P 500 Current	Relative S&P 500 Hist	Rel Cat
Price/Earnings Ratio	47.5	1.53	1.42	1.03
Price/Book Ratio	6.3	1.11	1.58	1.02
Price/Cash Flow	24.3	1.35	1.39	0.94
3 Yr Earnings Growth	27.7	1.90	1.60	0.93
1 Yr Earnings Est%	–13.5	7.63	—	0.81
Med Mkt Cap $mil	29,388	0.5	0.4	1.85

[1]figure is based on 50% or less of stocks

Analysis by Scott Cooley 09-14-01

Northern Technology Fund's defensive mien has protected its solid longer-term record.

Like other specialty-technology funds, this one has gotten pummeled so far in 2001, but it has at least held up better than most of its rivals. That's particularly remarkable given that a slug of faltering communications-equipment stocks weighed on the fund's returns early this year. But during the first quarter and thereafter, management increasingly tilted the portfolio toward defensive and consumer-oriented stocks, including First Data and Electronic Arts, respectively. That has paid off, as slow-growing, moderately priced tech firms have proven resilient, and consumer spending has remained fairly strong. For the year to date through Sept. 10, 2001, the fund had suffered a breathtaking 42% loss, but that's still better than two thirds of its peers'.

Comanager John Leo said he and his colleagues were still playing defense with the portfolio. Stable-growth companies such as Electronic Data Systems continue to be favorites, while management has sold off what Leo calls high-expectation stocks, including BEA Systems and Veritas. Both of those stocks have gotten hit hard, but Leo thinks they'll still find it difficult to meet profit expectations. Meanwhile, Leo and company are increasingly attracted to smaller caps, which frequently offer greater earnings visibility, according to management, and stocks such as RF Micro Devices, which would stand to benefit from any upturn in the hard-hit wireless area.

Despite the fund's large absolute loss over the past year, its long-term record remains solid. Indeed, over the past five years the fund has beaten more than 80% of its peers, thanks to strong picks in past years in areas like optical networking and semiconductors. Given management's record and the fund's moderate costs, this offering still looks like one of the category's most-attractive options.

Special Securities % assets 09-30-01	
Restricted/Illiquid Secs	0
Emerging-Markets Secs	Trace
Options/Futures/Warrants	No

Composition % assets 09-30-01	
Cash	0.0
Stocks*	100.0
Bonds	0.0
Other	0.0
*Foreign (% stocks)	3.3

Market Cap	
Giant	31.8
Large	48.9
Medium	17.9
Small	1.4
Micro	0.0

Subsector Weightings	% of Stocks	Rel Cat
Computers	12.6	2.3
Semiconductors	14.3	1.3
Semi Equipment	2.7	0.7
Networking	1.6	0.4
Periph/Hardware	0.3	0.2
Software	31.3	2.4
Computer Svs	19.3	3.2
Telecom	8.3	1.0
Health Care	0.0	0.0
Other	9.9	0.3

Address:	50 South LaSalle Street Chicago, IL 60607 800-595-9111 / 800-595-9111
Web Address:	www.northernfunds.com
*Inception:	04-01-96
Advisor:	Northern Trust
Subadvisor:	None
NTF Plans:	Fidelity Inst. , Waterhouse

Minimum Purchase:	$2500	Add: $50	IRA: $500
Min Auto Inv Plan:	$2500	Add: $50	
Sales Fees:	No-load		
Management Fee:	1.2%, .15%A		
Actual Fees:	Mgt: 1.00%	Dist: —	
Expense Projections:	3Yr: $40*	5Yr: $69*	10Yr: $152*
Avg Brok Commission:	—	Income Distrib: Annually	
Total Cost (relative to category):	—		

Nuveen Interm Duration Muni Bond R

Ticker	Load	NAV	Yield	SEC Yield	Total Assets	Mstar Category
NUVBX	Closed	$9.25	5.1%	—	$2,779.6 mil	Muni Natl Interm–Term

Prospectus Objective: Muni Bond—National

Nuveen Interm Duration Muni Bond Fund seeks current income exempt from federal taxes, consistent with capital preservation.

The fund normally invests at least 80% of assets in investment-grade municipal bonds. It may invest in unrated securities deemed to be of comparable quality. The fund may invest a portion of assets in AMT-subject securities. The average weighted maturity typically ranges between 15 and 30 years.

The fund offers A, B, C and R shares, all which differ in fee structure and availability.

Historical Profile
Return: Above Avg
Risk: Below Avg
Rating: ★★★★ Above Avg

Investment Style
Fixed-Income
Income Rtn %Rank Cat: 16, 9, 11, 10, 14, 10, 11, 9

Growth of Principal vs. Interest Rate Shifts
— Principal Value $000 (NAV with capital gains reinvested)
— Interest Rate % on 10 Yr Treasury
▼ Manager Change
▽ Partial Manager Change
► Mgr Unknown After
◄ Mgr Unknown Before

Performance Quartile (within Category)

Portfolio Manager(s)

Thomas C. Spalding, CFA. Since 8-78. BA'73 U. of Michigan; MBA'75 U. of Michigan. Other funds currently managed: Nuveen Interm Duration Muni Bond A, Nuveen Interm Duration Muni Bond C, Nuveen Balanced Municipal and Stock R.

History

1990	1991	1992	1993	1994	1995	1996	1997	1998	1999	2000	12-01	History
8.77	9.11	9.25	9.41	8.65	9.40	9.25	9.55	9.63	8.86	9.28	9.25	NAV
5.69	10.72	8.49	8.60	−1.85	15.29	4.30	9.08	6.15	−3.12	10.44	4.98	Total Return %
−3.26	−5.28	1.09	−1.15	1.06	−3.18	0.69	−0.60	−2.53	−2.29	−1.19	−3.44	+/– LB Aggregate
−1.61	−1.42	−0.33	−3.68	3.29	−2.18	−0.13	−0.12	−0.33	−1.05	−1.25	−0.10	+/– LB Muni
6.34	6.27	6.27	5.76	5.57	6.11	5.37	5.37	5.01	4.97	5.42	5.21	Income Return %
−0.65	4.46	2.22	2.83	−7.42	9.18	−1.06	3.72	1.14	−8.09	5.02	−0.22	Capital Return %
88	57	40	87	16	21	25	9	16	80	20	23	Total Rtn % Rank Cat
0.55	0.53	0.55	0.52	0.51	0.51	0.49	0.48	0.47	0.47	0.47	0.47	Income $
0.04	0.04	0.05	0.10	0.08	0.03	0.05	0.03	0.03	0.01	0.01	0.01	Capital Gains $
0.62	0.60	0.62	0.61	0.62	0.59	0.59	0.57	0.60	0.57	0.59	0.59	Expense Ratio %
6.78	6.48	6.24	5.95	5.49	5.79	5.53	5.33	5.04	4.90	5.22	5.11	Income Ratio %
8	10	15	14	15	17	17	12	10	12	13	9	Turnover Rate %
1,399.5	1,754.0	2,216.4	2,683.0	2,590.8	2,917.5	2,836.3	2,965.4	3,009.0	2,549.3	2,564.3	—	Net Assets $mil

Performance 12-31-01

	1st Qtr	2nd Qtr	3rd Qtr	4th Qtr	Total
1997	−0.42	3.56	3.04	2.67	9.08
1998	1.23	1.44	2.81	0.55	6.15
1999	0.70	−1.50	−1.33	−1.01	−3.12
2000	3.04	1.20	2.19	3.64	10.44
2001	1.93	0.96	2.46	−0.43	4.98

Trailing	Total Return%	+/– LB Agg	+/– LB Muni	% Rank All	% Rank Cat	Growth of $10,000
3 Mo	−0.43	−0.47	0.23	83	11	9,957
6 Mo	2.02	−2.64	−0.10	22	17	10,202
1 Yr	4.98	−3.44	−0.10	23	23	10,498
3 Yr Avg	3.95	−2.32	−0.80	41	41	11,233
5 Yr Avg	5.40	−2.03	−0.58	57	16	13,007
10 Yr Avg	6.10	−1.12	−0.53	68	27	18,086
15 Yr Avg	6.70	−1.42	−0.49	72	24	26,444

Tax Analysis	Tax-Adj Ret%	%Rank Cat	%Pretax Ret	%Rank Cat
3 Yr Avg	3.92	38	99.2	65
5 Yr Avg	5.35	14	99.1	49
10 Yr Avg	5.98	24	98.0	54

Potential Capital Gain Exposure: 4% of assets

Risk Analysis

Time Period	Load-Adj Return %	Risk %Rank[1] All	Risk %Rank[1] Cat	Morningstar Return	Morningstar Risk	Morningstar Risk-Adj Rating
1 Yr	4.98					
3 Yr	3.95	9	43	0.55[2]	0.81	★★★★
5 Yr	5.40	10	49	0.92[2]	0.83	★★★★
10 Yr	6.10	8	28	1.06	0.75	★★★★

Average Historical Rating (193 months): 4.4★s

[1]1=low, 100=high [2] T-Bill return substituted for category avg.

Category Rating (3 Yr)

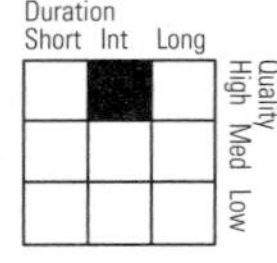

Return: Above Avg
Risk: Average

Other Measures	Standard Index LB Agg	Best Fit Index LB Muni
Alpha	−1.8	−0.8
Beta	0.68	0.88
R–Squared	46	94
Standard Deviation		3.48
Mean		3.95
Sharpe Ratio		−0.34

Portfolio Analysis 09-30-00

Total Fixed-Income: 212	Date of Maturity	Amount $000	Value $000	% Net Assets
NC East Muni Pwr Sys 6.25%	01-01-12	69,150	70,223	2.65
IL Hlth Fac Northwestern Meml Hosp 6%	08-15-24	57,600	57,722	2.18
IL Chicago O'Hare Intl Arpt 5%	01-01-16	61,250	56,474	2.13
MI Hosp Fin Detroit M/C 5.5%	08-15-23	69,575	52,675	1.99
IN Hlth Fac Fin Daughters Charity 5.75%	11-15-22	49,600	52,050	1.96
WA Pub Pwr Sply Sys Proj #3 5.375%	07-01-15	51,070	50,148	1.89
TX San Antonio Elec/Gas Sys 5%	02-01-17	53,280	49,586	1.87
IL Metro Pier/Expo McCormick Expsn 6.5%	06-15-27	43,180	46,060	1.74
VA Hsg Dev Mtg 7.15%	01-01-33	39,630	40,837	1.54
CA COP Cmnty Dev St Joseph Hlth 5.5%	07-01-23	38,795	37,593	1.42
KY Carroll Poll Cntrl Util 7.45%	09-15-16	34,500	36,589	1.38
FL Hillsborough Indl Dev Poll Cntrl 8%	05-01-22	32,000	34,286	1.29
CA Los Angeles Transp Com Tax 6.625%	07-01-19	31,360	33,354	1.26
IL Hlth Fac Rush Presbyterian M/C 5.5%	11-15-25	34,120	32,405	1.22
WI Hlth/Educ Fac Aurora Med Grp 5.75%	11-15-25	32,000	31,641	1.19

Current Investment Style

Duration: Short Int Long; Quality: High Med Low

Avg Duration	—
Avg Nominal Maturity	19.6 Yrs
Avg Credit Quality	—
Avg Wtd Coupon	5.89%
Avg Wtd Price	99.22% of par
Pricing Service	J.J. Kenny

Credit Analysis % bonds 06-30-00			
US Govt	0	BB	0
AAA	45	B	0
AA	33	Below B	0
A	12	NR/NA	0
BBB	10		

Special Securities % assets 09-30-00	
Restricted/Illiquid Secs	0
Inverse Floaters	0
Options/Futures/Warrants	No

Bond Type % assets 12-31-98	
Alternative Minimum Tax (AMT)	0.0
Insured	—
Prerefunded	10.5

Top 5 States % bonds			
IL	19.9	WA	6.7
CA	13.4	NY	5.7
MI	7.5		

Composition % assets 09-30-00			
Cash	0.0	Bonds	100.0
Stocks	0.0	Other	0.0

Sector Weightings	% of Bonds	Rel Cat
General Obligation	10.1	0.4
Utilities	16.2	1.9
Health	19.2	1.6
Water/Waste	9.9	1.6
Housing	13.5	1.9
Education	1.5	0.2
Transportation	12.9	1.1
COP/Lease	3.7	1.7
Industrial	8.6	1.1
Misc Revenue	4.5	0.9
Demand	0.0	0.0

Analysis by Scott Cooley 12-06-01

Nuveen Intermediate Duration Municipal Bond Fund is still getting the job done.

As one would expect of a good municipal fund, this one doesn't take a lot of chances. Manager Tom Spalding doesn't make big interest-rate bets—he keeps its duration within a range of five to seven years—and sticks to higher-quality credits. He seeks to add value with superior individual-issue selection and by emphasizing certain geographical areas. For example, he has stashed 20% of assets in Illinois bonds because the state doesn't exempt munis for income taxes, and 5% in Texas because it lacks an income-based levy. Therefore, both states must offer higher yields to attract muni investors.

In his 25 years at the fund, Spalding has executed this conservative strategy quite capably. Helped also by its reasonable costs, the fund boasts a top-quartile 10-year return. It has also put up respectable numbers so far in 2001. For the year to date through Dec. 5, the fund has gained 5.4%, placing in the group's top third. In large measure, the fund's solid showing owes to Spalding's avoidance of several potential minefields. For example, the fund has little or no exposure to paper, metal, or airport issues—all of which have registered weak returns in 2001.

Spalding keeps turnover to a minimum, but, anticipating an economic recovery, he says he may shift assets into more-economically sensitive issues. In particular, Spalding says he might pick up more Illinois bonds if it appears the state's revenue picture is relatively bright. Conversely, Spalding says he has no interest in adding to the fund's relatively strong-performing health-care stake, which is economically insensitive.

Spalding doesn't plan to make dramatic changes, though, and that's in keeping with how he has run the fund for more than two decades. His record suggests muni investors will find a comfortable home here.

Address:	333 W. Wacker Drive Chicago, IL 60606 312–917–7844 / 800–621–7227
Web Address:	www.nuveen.com
Inception:	11-29-76
Advisor:	Nuveen Advisory
Subadvisor:	None
NTF Plans:	N/A

Minimum Purchase:	Closed	Add: $50	IRA: —
Min Auto Inv Plan:	Closed	Add: $50	
Sales Fees:	No–load		
Management Fee:	.50% mx./.43% mn.		
Actual Fees:	Mgt: 0.45%	Dist: —	
Expense Projections:	3Yr: $183	5Yr: $317	10Yr: $714
Avg Brok Commission:	—	Income Distrib: Monthly	
Total Cost (relative to category):		Low	

Oak Value

Ticker	Load	NAV	Yield	Total Assets	Mstar Category
OAKVX	None	$29.08	0.0%	$320.1 mil	Mid–Cap Blend

Prospectus Objective: Growth

Oak Value Fund seeks capital appreciation.

The fund invests primarily in common stocks, preferred stocks, and convertible securities. The advisor selects securities based on a value approach to investing. Factors that influence investment selection include indications of shareholder-oriented management, evidence of financial strength, expected future earnings improvement, limited institutional recognition, pricing flexibility, and cash flow generation. The fund may invest in foreign securities. It may also purchase U.S. government obligations subject to repurchase agreements.

Historical Profile

Return	Above Avg
Risk	Average
Rating	★★★★ Above Avg

Investment Style
Equity
Average Stock %: 89% 91% 89% 89% 95% 95% 98%

▼ Manager Change
▽ Partial Manager Change

Fund Performance vs. Category Average
■ Quarterly Fund Return +/– Category Average
— Category Baseline

Performance Quartile (within Category)

Portfolio Manager(s)

David R. Carr Jr.. Since 1-93. BS'82 U. of North Carolina; JD'86 U. of North Carolina.

George W. Brumley III. Since 1-93. BA'82 Emory U.; MBA'86 Duke U.

1990	1991	1992	1993	1994	1995	1996	1997	1998	1999	2000	12-01	History
—	—	—	11.99	10.99	14.06	17.49	23.19	27.29	25.52	29.49	29.08	NAV
—	—	—	22.05*	−1.51	28.84	28.99	37.70	18.93	−3.12	18.17	−0.47	Total Return %
—	—	—	12.28*	−2.83	−8.70	6.04	4.35	−9.65	−24.16	27.27	11.41	+/– S&P 500
—	—	—	—	2.08	−2.08	9.80	5.46	−0.19	−17.84	0.68	0.13	+/– S&P Mid 400
—	—	—	0.00	0.00	0.00	0.00	0.00	0.41	0.29	0.11	0.00	Income Return %
—	—	—	22.05	−1.51	28.84	28.99	37.70	18.52	−3.42	18.06	−0.47	Capital Return %
—	—	—	—	40	49	6	6	13	98	15	28	Total Rtn % Rank Cat
—	—	—	0.00	0.00	0.00	0.00	0.00	0.09	0.08	0.03	0.00	Income $
—	—	—	0.22	0.81	0.10	0.63	0.81	0.19	0.91	0.55	0.27	Capital Gains $
—	—	—	2.19	1.89	1.89	1.90	1.59	1.22	1.10	1.13	—	Expense Ratio %
—	—	—	−0.81	−0.58	−0.53	−0.43	−0.16	0.41	0.27	0.28	—	Income Ratio %
—	—	—	—	91	104	58	22	15	38	22	—	Turnover Rate %
—	—	—	4.1	7.9	13.2	28.5	139.9	560.8	469.9	329.4	320.1	Net Assets $mil

Performance 12-31-01

	1st Qtr	2nd Qtr	3rd Qtr	4th Qtr	Total
1997	0.34	19.83	7.46	6.57	37.70
1998	13.63	3.40	−18.64	24.41	18.93
1999	1.50	3.95	−16.34	9.76	−3.12
2000	−3.33	3.76	5.33	11.85	18.17
2001	−2.95	7.86	−17.86	15.76	−0.47

Trailing	Total Return%	+/– S&P 500	+/– S&P Mid 400	% Rank All	% Rank Cat	Growth of $10,000
3 Mo	15.76	5.07	−2.22	22	56	11,576
6 Mo	−4.92	0.64	−3.36	61	67	9,508
1 Yr	−0.47	11.41	0.13	43	28	9,953
3 Yr Avg	4.45	5.47	−5.80	36	58	11,394
5 Yr Avg	13.29	2.59	−2.83	7	26	18,659
10 Yr Avg	—	—	—	—	—	—
15 Yr Avg	—	—	—	—	—	—

Tax Analysis	Tax-Adj Ret%	%Rank Cat	%Pretax Ret	%Rank Cat
3 Yr Avg	3.88	51	87.2	23
5 Yr Avg	12.67	13	95.4	1
10 Yr Avg	—	—	—	—

Potential Capital Gain Exposure: 21% of assets

Risk Analysis

Time Period	Load-Adj Return %	Risk %Rank[1] All	Risk %Rank[1] Cat	Morningstar Return	Morningstar Risk	Morningstar Risk-Adj Rating
1 Yr	−0.47					
3 Yr	4.45	56	25	−0.11[2]	0.78	★★★
5 Yr	13.29	58	17	2.11[2]	0.80	★★★★
Incept	15.82	—	—	—	—	

Average Historical Rating (72 months): 4.2★s

[1]1=low, 100=high [2] T-Bill return substituted for category avg.

Category Rating (3 Yr)

1 2 **3** 4 5
Worst Best

Return	Average
Risk	Below Avg

Other Measures	Standard Index S&P 500	Best Fit Index S&P 500
Alpha	4.6	4.6
Beta	0.74	0.74
R-Squared	46	46
Standard Deviation		19.49
Mean		4.45
Sharpe Ratio		−0.03

Portfolio Analysis 09-30-01

Share change since 06-01 Total Stocks: 32

	Sector	PE	YTD Ret%	% Assets
⊖ Berkshire Hathaway Cl B	Financials	64.8	7.26	9.75
Ambac Finl Grp	Financials	15.2	−0.16	7.08
⊖ Intl Flavors & Fragrances	Staples	32.3	49.78	5.89
Comcast	Services	20.3	−13.70	5.72
⊖ EW Scripps Cl A	Services	29.9	5.94	5.48
⊕ XL Cap Cl A	Financials	22.8	5.82	5.32
Republic Svcs Cl A	Services	15.6	16.19	4.89
⊖ Washington Post	Services	20.0	−13.20	4.83
⊕ Charter Comms	Services	—	−27.50	4.70
⊕ USA Networks	Services	58.1	40.50	4.31
⊕ Walt Disney	Services	—	−27.70	4.16
⊖ Household Intl	Financials	14.7	6.89	3.88
Lexmark Intl	Technology	26.9	33.14	3.72
⊕ Cendant	Services	20.4	103.70	3.43
PartnerRe	Financials	22.4	−10.50	3.06
⊕ Corning	Industrials	—	−83.00	2.55
☼ AOL Time Warner	Technology	—	−7.76	2.49
⊖ Sabre Hldgs Cl A	Services	73.0	−1.80	2.29
⊕ J.P. Morgan Chase & Co.	Financials	27.8	−17.40	2.22
☼ Tellabs	Technology	41.6	−73.50	2.03
AFLAC	Financials	19.3	−31.40	1.96
⊖ Valassis Comms	Services	18.9	12.85	1.81
☼ Waters	Industrials	32.0	−53.50	1.66
☼ Interpublic Grp	Services	—	−29.80	1.34
☼ Goldman Sachs Grp	Financials	20.7	−12.80	1.31

Current Investment Style

Style: Value Blnd Growth; Size: Large Med Small

	Stock Port Avg	Relative S&P 500 Current	Relative S&P 500 Hist	Rel Cat
Price/Earnings Ratio	30.3	0.98	0.83	1.11
Price/Book Ratio	2.9	0.51	0.71	0.68
Price/Cash Flow	15.8	0.88	0.89	0.91
3 Yr Earnings Growth	5.0	0.34	0.82	0.30
1 Yr Earnings Est%	−30.1	16.99	—	−13.25
Med Mkt Cap $mil	8,349	0.1	0.1	0.93

[1]figure is based on 50% or less of stocks

Special Securities % assets 09-30-01	
Restricted/Illiquid Secs	0
Emerging–Markets Secs	0
Options/Futures/Warrants	No

Composition % assets 09-30-01	
Cash	0.4
Stocks*	99.6
Bonds	0.0
Other	0.0
*Foreign (% stocks)	8.4

Market Cap	
Giant	14.6
Large	28.4
Medium	56.3
Small	0.7
Micro	0.0

Sector Weightings	% of Stocks	Rel S&P	5-Year High	5-Year Low
Utilities	0.0	0.0	0	0
Energy	0.0	0.0	0	0
Financials	35.8	2.0	51	28
Industrials	4.2	0.4	19	0
Durables	0.0	0.0	8	0
Staples	5.9	0.8	23	4
Services	43.2	4.0	49	17
Retail	0.4	0.1	10	0
Health	0.0	0.0	21	0
Technology	10.4	0.6	10	0

Analysis by Dan McNeela 10-19-01

Oak Value Fund has what it takes to get the job done.

Without any Wall Street experience, the duo of George Brumley and David Carr set out to beat the market by employing the investing principles of just one man. Fortunately for investors, that one man is none other than Warren Buffett—who is widely acclaimed as the world's most successful investor.

But saying is one thing, doing is another. In that regard, this fund's investors have not been let down. Its 11.9% annualized return over the five-year period ending Oct. 18, 2001, ranks in the top quartile of the mid-blend category.

The fund's long-term record has been strong enough to make up for a poor showing in 1999, when it trailed the category average by a whopping 28 percentage points. What didn't happen that year is more important than what did. Carr and Brumley refused to jump on the tech bandwagon and stuck to their philosophy of investing in companies with enduring competitive advantages selling below their intrinsic values. By staying the course, the fund snapped back in fine fashion.

While preservation of capital has been a strength of the fund in the long run, the fund's concentrated nature does expose it to additional risk at times. The fund dropped 12.9% in September 2001, as many of its travel-related companies, namely Sabre Holdings, Cendant, and Walt Disney, were beaten down after the attack on the World Trade Center. Similarly, management's current belief in the attractiveness of broadband has influenced the recent purchases of Corning, AOL Time Warner, and Scientific Atlanta, which all dovetail with an ongoing investment in cable companies.

The fund's boatload of financials and services stocks doesn't offer the diversification that some require, but it has proven itself a fine supporting player among mid-blend funds.

Address:	3435 Stelzer Road Columbus, OH 43219 800–622–2474
Web Address:	—
*Inception:	01-18-93
Advisor:	Oak Value Cap. Mgmt.
Subadvisor:	None
NTF Plans:	Fidelity , Fidelity Inst.

Minimum Purchase:	$2500	Add: $100	IRA: $1000
Min Auto Inv Plan:	$2500	Add: $100	
Sales Fees:	No–load		
Management Fee:	.90%, .10%A		
Actual Fees:	Mgt: 0.90%	Dist: —	
Expense Projections:	3Yr: $38*	5Yr: $67*	10Yr: $147*
Avg Brok Commission:	—	Income Distrib: Semi–Ann.	
Total Cost (relative to category):	—		

Oakmark I

Ticker	Load	NAV	Yield	Total Assets	Mstar Category
OAKMX	None	$35.27	0.6%	$3,182.9 mil	Mid-Cap Value

Prospectus Objective: Growth

Oakmark Fund seeks long-term capital appreciation.

The fund principally invests in United States securities. It may invest up to 25% of assets in foreign securities. The fund will normally not invest greater than 5% of assets in the securities of issuers based in emerging markets.

The fund currently offers Class I and II shares. Class II shares are offered only to certain 401(k) and other tax-qualified plans.

Historical Profile
Return High
Risk Average
Rating ★★★★★ Highest

Investment Style
Equity
Average Stock %: 1996 93%, 1997 88%, 1998 90%, 1999 93%, 2000 92%, 12-01 92%

▼ Manager Change
▽ Partial Manager Change

Fund Performance vs. Category Average
Quarterly Fund Return +/– Category Average
— Category Baseline

Performance Quartile (within Category)

Portfolio Manager(s)

William C. Nygren, CFA. Since 3-00. BS'80 U. of Minnesota; MS'81 U. of Wisconsin. Other funds currently managed: Oakmark Select I, Oakmark II, Oakmark Select II.

Kevin Grant, CFA. Since 3-00. BS'87 U. of Wisconsin-Madison. Other funds currently managed: CDC Nvest Star Advisers A, CDC Nvest Star Advisers B, CDC Nvest Star Advisers C.

1990	1991	1992	1993	1994	1995	1996	1997	1998	1999	2000	12–01	History
—	13.02	19.13	23.93	22.97	29.75	32.35	40.41	35.82	27.20	29.99	35.27	NAV
—	30.20*	48.90	30.50	3.32	34.42	16.21	32.59	3.73	–10.47	11.78	18.29	Total Return %
—	20.32*	41.28	20.45	2.00	–3.12	–6.74	–0.77	–24.85	–31.51	20.89	30.16	+/– S&P 500
—	—	27.22	14.88	5.45	–0.52	–4.05	–1.77	–1.36	–10.36	–7.40	15.95	+/– Russ Midcap Val
—	0.00	0.31	1.20	0.97	1.24	1.16	1.24	1.21	0.73	1.42	0.66	Income Return %
—	30.20	48.59	29.30	2.35	33.18	15.05	31.35	2.52	–11.20	10.36	17.63	Capital Return %
—	—	1	8	20	28	75	19	50	96	74	12	Total Rtn % Rank Cat
—	0.00	0.04	0.23	0.23	0.28	0.34	0.40	0.44	0.26	0.39	0.20	Income $
—	0.00	0.21	0.77	1.47	0.84	1.87	1.98	5.63	4.73	0.00	0.00	Capital Gains $
—	2.50	1.70	1.32	1.22	1.17	1.18	1.08	1.08	1.11	1.21	—	Expense Ratio %
—	–0.66	–0.24	0.94	1.19	1.27	1.13	1.19	1.22	1.02	1.42	—	Income Ratio %
—	—	34	18	29	18	24	—	43	13	50	—	Turnover Rate %
—	8.3	328.8	1,214.1	1,626.9	3,301.6	4,195.0	7,301.4	7,667.9	3,817.8	2,205.6	—	Net Assets $mil

Performance 12-31-01

	1st Qtr	2nd Qtr	3rd Qtr	4th Qtr	Total
1997	3.99	15.22	6.32	4.08	32.59
1998	9.95	–2.70	–13.83	12.53	3.73
1999	–0.47	11.53	–13.56	–6.69	–10.47
2000	–8.97	2.58	6.10	12.82	11.78
2001	7.37	9.25	–9.01	10.82	18.29

Trailing	Total Return%	+/– S&P 500	+/– Russ Midcap Val	% Rank All	% Rank Cat	Growth of $10,000
3 Mo	10.82	0.14	–1.21	38	72	11,082
6 Mo	0.84	6.39	1.75	35	36	10,084
1 Yr	18.29	30.16	15.95	2	12	11,829
3 Yr Avg	5.79	6.81	–1.02	24	77	11,838
5 Yr Avg	10.24	–0.46	–1.22	18	66	16,281
10 Yr Avg	17.71	4.78	3.29	2	8	51,054
15 Yr Avg	—	—	—	—	—	—

Tax Analysis	Tax-Adj Ret%	%Rank Cat	%Pretax Ret	%Rank Cat
3 Yr Avg	4.21	75	72.7	71
5 Yr Avg	8.16	61	79.7	43
10 Yr Avg	15.72	6	88.8	8

Potential Capital Gain Exposure: 11% of assets

Risk Analysis

Time Period	Load-Adj Return %	Risk %Rank[1] All	Risk %Rank[1] Cat	Morningstar Return	Morningstar Risk	Morningstar Risk-Adj Rating
1 Yr	18.29					
3 Yr	5.79	55	74	0.18[2]	0.77	★★★★
5 Yr	10.24	58	60	1.26[2]	0.80	★★★★
10 Yr	17.71	58	42	2.56	0.75	★★★★★

Average Historical Rating (89 months): 3.9★s

[1]1=low, 100=high [2] T-Bill return substituted for category avg.

Category Rating (3 Yr)

1 2 3 4 5
Worst Best

Return Below Avg
Risk Above Avg

Other Measures	Standard Index S&P 500	Best Fit Index S&P 500
Alpha	4.8	4.8
Beta	0.53	0.53
R-Squared	25	25

Standard Deviation	19.07
Mean	5.79
Sharpe Ratio	0.05

Analysis by Scott Cooley 11-01-01

Oakmark Fund is looking more and more like a solid core holding.

When manager Bill Nygren took over the fund in March 2000, he said he'd improve the fund's issue diversification and gradually move it more into large-cap territory. He has done both. At year-end 1999, the fund held fewer than 25 stocks, but as of Sept. 30, 2001, it owned 59. And Nygren has focused his recent purchases on large-cap stocks. Large-cap firms he added to the portfolio in 2001's third quarter include Fannie Mae, American Express, Gap Stores, Honeywell International, and Safeway.

Aside from being large caps, Nygren's recent buys have something else in common: Most were once growth managers' favorites that have since stumbled. For example, Gap has tanked because of an overly aggressive expansion strategy and poor merchandising decisions. Nygren likes the stock, however, because of its cheap valuation and his belief that CEO Mickey drexler will improve the firm's merchandise mix. American Express, a historically fast-growing firm, has suffered this year because of the declining stock market, lower travel-related revenues, and some bungled bond investments. But Nygren thinks the company has a good business model and trades at less than 12 times Oakmark's estimate of its 2003 earnings.

Although Nygren has moved to diversify the portfolio, the fund has still ridden the value rally to solid gains. Stocks such as J.C. Penney and H & R Block have propelled the fund to a solid 7% gain. And over the trailing year, it has returned 15.2%, beating its typical mid-value rival by 16 percentage points.

The fund's tax position is still solid, too, though Nygren reports that its tax-loss carryforward is smaller than it was at mid-year. Thus, he says it's unlikely the fund will have to make a capital-gains distribution for at least one more year, making this a particularly strong choice for taxable accounts.

Portfolio Analysis 10-31-01

Share change since 06-01 Total Stocks: 60	Sector	PE	YTD Ret%	% Assets
⊕ Washington Mutual	Financials	10.1	–5.32	3.58
⊕ H & R Block	Services	25.5	120.00	2.65
Kroger	Retail	16.3	–22.80	2.65
⊕ Electronic Data Sys	Technology	25.7	19.83	2.46
⊕ First Data	Technology	38.1	49.08	2.42
⊕ Newell Rubbermaid	Durables	25.5	25.20	2.34
⊖ Fortune Brands	Staples	—	35.68	2.28
⊕ AT&T	Services	7.8	40.59	2.19
⊖ Heinz HJ	Staples	29.6	–9.86	2.15
⊕ US Bancorp	Financials	13.5	–6.14	2.12
⊖ J.C. Penney	Retail	—	154.60	2.10
⊖ Tricon Global Restaurants	Services	16.3	49.09	2.07
⊕ Mattel	Staples	31.9	19.43	2.04
⊕ SunGard Data Sys	Technology	33.3	22.78	2.00
⊕ TXU	Utilities	13.7	12.17	1.97
⊕ Guidant	Health	42.6	–7.67	1.96
⊕ MGIC Invest	Financials	10.9	–8.33	1.94
Knight Ridder	Services	59.0	16.13	1.88
⊕ AT & T Liberty Media Cl A	Services	—	3.22	1.87
⊕ Toys "R" Us	Retail	28.8	24.28	1.87
⊕ Chiron	Health	—	–1.48	1.82
⊕ Conoco Cl A	Energy	9.0	1.56	1.82
⊕ Burlington Resources	Energy	8.4	–24.60	1.81
⊕ Motorola	Technology	—	–25.00	1.81
⊕ Black & Decker	Durables	17.6	–2.67	1.79

Current Investment Style

Style: Value Blnd Growth; Size: Large Med Small

	Stock Port Avg	Relative S&P 500 Current	Relative S&P 500 Hist	Rel Cat
Price/Earnings Ratio	25.3	0.82	0.58	1.07
Price/Book Ratio	4.0	0.70	0.40	1.32
Price/Cash Flow	13.7	0.76	0.54	1.11
3 Yr Earnings Growth	16.4	1.12	0.61	1.38
1 Yr Earnings Est%	–9.5	5.38	—	1.55
Med Mkt Cap $mil	13,353	0.2	0.1	1.88

Special Securities % assets 10-31-01	
Restricted/Illiquid Secs	0
Emerging-Markets Secs	0
Options/Futures/Warrants	No

Composition % assets 10-31-01	
Cash	9.1
Stocks*	90.9
Bonds	0.0
Other	0.0
*Foreign (% stocks)	0.0

Market Cap	
Giant	5.9
Large	53.6
Medium	40.5
Small	0.0
Micro	0.0

Sector Weightings	% of Stocks	Rel S&P	5-Year High	5-Year Low
Utilities	2.1	0.7	5	0
Energy	5.8	0.8	10	0
Financials	10.3	0.6	29	6
Industrials	5.5	0.5	30	5
Durables	9.1	5.8	18	2
Staples	11.6	1.5	35	5
Services	23.8	2.2	33	7
Retail	11.5	1.7	11	0
Health	5.6	0.4	20	0
Technology	14.7	0.8	15	0

Address:	Two N. LaSalle Street Chicago, IL 60602–3790 800–625–6275
Web Address:	www.oakmark.com
*Inception:	08-05-91
Advisor:	Harris Assoc.
Subadvisor:	None
NTF Plans:	Fidelity , Fidelity Inst.

Minimum Purchase:	$1000	Add: $100 IRA: $1000
Min Auto Inv Plan:	$500	Add: $100
Sales Fees:	No-load	
Management Fee:	1.0% mx./.85% mn.	
Actual Fees:	Mgt: 0.96%	Dist: —
Expense Projections:	3Yr: $350	5Yr: $610 10Yr: $1350
Avg Brok Commission:	—	Income Distrib: Annually
Total Cost (relative to category):		Below Avg

Oakmark Global I

Ticker	Load	NAV	Yield	Total Assets	Mstar Category
OAKGX	None	$13.26	0.0%	$52.8 mil	World Stock

Prospectus Objective: World Stock

Oakmark Global Fund seeks long-term capital appreciation.

The fund primarily invests in equity securities of companies located in at least three countries. It invests in approximately 40-50 stocks, with 40-80% of total assets invested in the securities of foreign companies and 20-60% in U.S. companies. The fund normally invests in mid-sized companies with market capitalizations between $1-8 billion. It does not usually invest greater than 15% of assets in securities of issuers based in emerging markets.

Class I shares are available to the general public. Class II shares are offered to certain 401(k) and other tax-qualified plans.

Historical Profile
Return —
Risk —
Rating Not Rated

Investment Style
Equity
Average Stock %: 97% (1999), 94% (2000), 94% (12-01)

▼ Manager Change
▽ Partial Manager Change

Fund Performance vs. Category Average
■ Quarterly Fund Return +/– Category Average
— Category Baseline

Performance Quartile (within Category)

Portfolio Manager(s)

Michael J. Welsh, CFA. Since 8-99. BS'85 U. of Kansas; MM'93 Northwestern U. Other funds currently managed: Oakmark International I, Oakmark International Small Cap I, CDC Nvest Star Worldwide A.

Gregory L. Jackson. Since 8-99. BS U. of Utah; MBA U. of Chicago. Other fund currently managed: Oakmark Global II.

History	1990	1991	1992	1993	1994	1995	1996	1997	1998	1999	2000	12-01
NAV	—	—	—	—	—	—	—	—	—	9.97	11.31	13.26
Total Return %	—	—	—	—	—	—	—	—	—	–0.19*	15.84	20.05
+/– S&P 500	—	—	—	—	—	—	—	—	—	–13.36*	24.95	31.93
+/– MSCI World	—	—	—	—	—	—	—	—	—	—	29.02	—
Income Return %	—	—	—	—	—	—	—	—	—	0.11	1.75	0.02
Capital Return %	—	—	—	—	—	—	—	—	—	–0.30	14.10	20.03
Total Rtn % Rank Cat	—	—	—	—	—	—	—	—	—	—	2	1
Income $	—	—	—	—	—	—	—	—	—	0.01	0.17	0.00
Capital Gains $	—	—	—	—	—	—	—	—	—	0.00	0.05	0.29
Expense Ratio %	—	—	—	—	—	—	—	—	—	1.75	1.75	—
Income Ratio %	—	—	—	—	—	—	—	—	—	0.98	0.54	—
Turnover Rate %	—	—	—	—	—	—	—	—	—	—	147	—
Net Assets $mil	—	—	—	—	—	—	—	—	—	31.3	28.1	—

Performance 12-31-01

	1st Qtr	2nd Qtr	3rd Qtr	4th Qtr	Total
1997	—	—	—	—	—
1998	—	—	—	—	—
1999	—	—	—	8.72	–0.19*
2000	0.80	3.18	5.21	5.86	15.84
2001	–0.71	15.76	–16.69	25.37	20.05

Trailing	Total Return%	+/– S&P 500	+/– MSCI World	% Rank All	% Rank Cat	Growth of $10,000
3 Mo	25.37	14.69	—	7	4	12,537
6 Mo	4.44	10.00	—	6	1	10,444
1 Yr	20.05	31.93	—	2	1	12,005
3 Yr Avg	—	—	—	—	—	—
5 Yr Avg	—	—	—	—	—	—
10 Yr Avg	—	—	—	—	—	—
15 Yr Avg	—	—	—	—	—	—

Tax Analysis	Tax-Adj Ret%	%Rank Cat	%Pretax Ret	%Rank Cat
3 Yr Avg	—	—	—	—
5 Yr Avg	—	—	—	—
10 Yr Avg	—	—	—	—

Potential Capital Gain Exposure: 21% of assets

Risk Analysis

Time Period	Load-Adj Return %	Risk %Rank[1] All	Risk %Rank[1] Cat	Morningstar Return	Morningstar Risk	Morningstar Risk-Adj Rating
1 Yr	20.05					
3 Yr	—	—	—	—	—	
5 Yr	—	—	—	—	—	
Incept	14.57	—	—	—	—	

Average Historical Rating —

[1]1=low, 100=high

Category Rating (3 Yr)

Return
Risk

Other Measures	Standard Index S&P 500	Best Fit Index
Alpha	—	—
Beta	—	—
R-Squared	—	—
Standard Deviation		—
Mean		—
Sharpe Ratio		—

Portfolio Analysis 10-31-01

Share change since 09-01 Total Stocks: 31

	Sector	Country	% Assets
⊕ ITT Educational Svcs	Services	U.S.	6.49
⊕ Synopsys	Technology	U.S.	5.79
⊕ Michael Page Grp	Services	United Kingdom	5.02
⊕ Ducati Motor Hldgs	Durables	Italy	4.55
⊕ Somerfield	Retail	United Kingdom	4.51
⊕ Ceridian	Technology	U.S.	4.22
⊖ Novell	Technology	U.S.	4.03
Valassis Comms	Services	U.S.	3.84
Reynolds & Reynolds	Services	U.S.	3.83
⊕ Interpublic Grp	Services	U.S.	3.62
☼ Cordiant Comm	Services	United Kingdom	3.58
⊕ Hunter Douglas	Industrials	Netherlands	3.53
⊖ Grupo Televisa (Part) ADR	Services	Mexico	3.32
Learning Tree Intl	Services	U.S.	3.19
Lotte Chilsung Beverage	Staples	South Korea	3.02
⊕ Lectra Systemes	Technology	France	2.98
Equifax	Services	U.S.	2.97
Meitec	Services	Japan	2.73
Hite Brewery	Staples	South Korea	2.45
⊕ Ichiyoshi Secs	Financials	Japan	2.36

Current Investment Style

Style: Value Blnd Growth; Size: Large Med Small

	Stock Port Avg	Rel MSCI EAFE Current	Rel MSCI EAFE Hist	Rel Cat
Price/Earnings Ratio	26.3	1.02	—	0.95
Price/Cash Flow	12.1	0.94	—	0.74
Price/Book Ratio	4.2	1.20	—	0.91
3 Yr Earnings Growth	21.9	1.17	—	1.17
Med Mkt Cap $mil	1,212	0.0	—	0.05

Country Exposure 10-31-01	% assets
U.S.	45
United Kingdom	17
South Korea	7
France	5
Japan	5

Hedging History: —

Regional Exposure 10-31-01	% assets
Europe	30
Pacific Rim	9
Latin America	3
Japan	5
U.S.	45
Other	0

Special Securities % assets 10-31-01	
Restricted/Illiquid Secs	0
Emerging-Markets Secs	11
Options/Futures/Warrants	No

Composition % assets 10-31-01

Cash	6.1	Bonds	0.0
Stocks	93.9	Other	0.0

Sector Weightings	% of Stocks	Rel Cat	5-Year High	5-Year Low
Utilities	0.0	0.0	—	—
Energy	0.0	0.0	—	—
Financials	4.2	0.2	—	—
Industrials	6.1	0.6	—	—
Durables	7.2	1.8	—	—
Staples	7.8	1.0	—	—
Services	45.2	2.7	—	—
Retail	7.0	1.3	—	—
Health	2.1	0.2	—	—
Technology	20.4	1.4	—	—

Analysis by William Samuel Rocco 11-16-01

This youngster continues to impress.

Oakmark Global Fund, which opened in September 1999, really came through in its first full calendar year. While many of its peers were being punished for their exposure to high-multiple telecom and tech issues, this fund was being rewarded for its lower-multiple selections in a variety of sectors. The winning picks of managers Greg Jackson and Michael Welsh ranged from the large-cap thrift Washington Mutual to the mid-cap data processor Ceridian. Overall, the fund gained 16% in 2000, while its typical rival lost 10%.

The fund is well on its way to a similarly superior performance this year, as the managers' stock selection has remained first-rate. Indeed, ITT Educational Services, which was 6% of assets at the start of 2001, doubled in the first half of the year (and was promptly pared way back). H&R Block, Hite Brewery, and several other holdings also thrived in the first part of 2001.

What's more, Jackson and Welsh have continued to make good choices over the past several months. They built up a sizable stake in the British placement firm Michael Page International this summer, and they've added to it, as well as the advertisers Interpublic Group and Cordiant, this fall. All three of these economically sensitive issues have soared the past couple of months. And so has ITT Educational, which they moved back into this summer. Thus, the fund has gained 10% for the year to date through Nov. 15, 2001, whereas its average rival has declined 19%. Of course, this value-oriented fund can't always post top-notch results—it did lag during its first few months as racy growth stocks led the way—but there's more than an excellent start to be excited about here. Jackson and Welsh are quite tax-conscious.

Address:	Two N. LaSalle Street Chicago, IL 60602–3790 800–625–6275
Web Address:	www.oakmark.com
*Inception:	08-04-99
Advisor:	Harris Assoc.
Subadvisor:	None
NTF Plans:	Waterhouse , Schwab

Minimum Purchase:	$1000	Add: $100 IRA: $1000
Min Auto Inv Plan:	$500	Add: $100
Sales Fees:	No-load, 2.00%R within 3 months	
Management Fee:	1.0%	
Actual Fees:	Mgt: 1.00%	Dist: —
Expense Projections:	3Yr: $550	5Yr: $950 10Yr: $2070
Avg Brok Commission:	—	Income Distrib: Annually

Total Cost (relative to category): —

Oakmark Select I

Ticker	Load	NAV	Yield	Total Assets	Mstar Category
OAKLX	Closed	$27.24	0.2%	$4,253.8 mil	Mid–Cap Value

Prospectus Objective: Growth

Oakmark Select Fund seeks long-term capital appreciation.

The fund invests primarily in domestic-equity securities. It may invest up to 25% of assets in securities of non-U.S. issuers, including foreign government obligations and foreign equity and debt securities traded over-the-counter or on foreign exchanges; it may invest no more than 5% in securities of issuers in emerging markets. This fund is non-diversified.

Prior to Jan. 4, 1999, the fund had no share class designation.

Historical Profile
Return High
Risk Below Avg
Rating ★★★★★ Highest

Investment Style
Equity
Average Stock %: 94% (1997), 91% (1998), 96% (1999), 95% (2000), 92% (12-01)

▼ Manager Change
▽ Partial Manager Change

Fund Performance vs. Category Average
■ Quarterly Fund Return +/– Category Average
— Category Baseline

Performance Quartile (within Category)

Portfolio Manager(s)

William C. Nygren, CFA. Since 11-96. BS'80 U. of Minnesota; MS'81 U. of Wisconsin. Other funds currently managed: 'Oakmark I, Oakmark II, Oakmark Select II.

Henry Berghoef, CFA. Since 3-00. BA'71 Calvin C.; MA'74 Johns Hopkins U. Other fund currently managed: Oakmark Select II.

1990	1991	1992	1993	1994	1995	1996	1997	1998	1999	2000	12-01	History
—	—	—	—	—	—	11.42	17.52	19.54	18.42	21.65	27.24	NAV
—	—	—	—	—	—	14.20*	55.02	16.21	14.49	25.81	26.06	Total Return %
—	—	—	—	—	—	8.55*	21.67	–12.36	–6.55	34.91	37.93	+/– S&P 500
—	—	—	—	—	—	—	20.66	11.12	14.59	6.62	23.72	+/– Russ Midcap Val
—	—	—	—	—	—	0.00	0.00	0.28	1.01	0.47	0.23	Income Return %
—	—	—	—	—	—	14.20	55.02	15.93	13.48	25.34	25.83	Capital Return %
—	—	—	—	—	—	—	1	11	24	24	3	Total Rtn % Rank Cat
—	—	—	—	—	—	0.00	0.00	0.05	0.20	0.09	0.05	Income $
—	—	—	—	—	—	0.00	0.17	0.71	3.72	1.36	0.00	Capital Gains $
—	—	—	—	—	—	—	1.12	1.22	1.16	1.17	—	Expense Ratio %
—	—	—	—	—	—	—	–0.11	0.17	0.98	0.76	—	Income Ratio %
—	—	—	—	—	—	—	—	56	67	69	—	Turnover Rate %
—	—	—	—	—	—	50.3	981.6	1,297.7	1,581.0	2,101.8	—	Net Assets $mil

Performance 12-31-01

	1st Qtr	2nd Qtr	3rd Qtr	4th Qtr	Total
1997	6.30	16.80	15.23	8.34	55.02
1998	13.41	1.91	–17.23	21.48	16.21
1999	10.64	7.54	–10.02	6.94	14.49
2000	8.96	–5.23	12.78	8.04	25.81
2001	10.76	9.26	–3.82	8.30	26.06

Trailing	Total Return%	+/– S&P 500	+/– Russ Midcap Val	% Rank All	% Rank Cat	Growth of $10,000
3 Mo	8.30	–2.39	–3.73	50	85	10,830
6 Mo	4.17	9.72	5.07	8	23	10,417
1 Yr	26.06	37.93	23.72	1	3	12,606
3 Yr Avg	22.00	23.02	15.19	2	3	18,157
5 Yr Avg	26.75	16.05	15.29	1	1	32,711
10 Yr Avg	—	—	—	—	—	—
15 Yr Avg	—	—	—	—	—	—

Tax Analysis	Tax-Adj Ret%	%Rank Cat	%Pretax Ret	%Rank Cat
3 Yr Avg	19.74	3	89.7	22
5 Yr Avg	25.01	1	93.5	3
10 Yr Avg	—	—	—	—

Potential Capital Gain Exposure: 25% of assets

Risk Analysis

Time Period	Load-Adj Return %	Risk %Rank[1] All	Risk %Rank[1] Cat	Morningstar Return	Morningstar Risk	Morningstar Risk-Adj Rating
1 Yr	26.06					
3 Yr	22.00	39	14	4.24[2]	0.52	★★★★★
5 Yr	26.75	50	26	7.16[2]	0.69	★★★★★
Incept	29.05	—	—	—	—	

Average Historical Rating (27 months): 4.4★s

[1]1=low, 100=high [2] T-Bill return substituted for category avg.

Category Rating (3 Yr)

Worst 1 2 3 4 **5** Best

Return High
Risk Below Avg

Other Measures	Standard Index S&P 500	Best Fit Index S&P 500
Alpha	21.1	21.1
Beta	0.62	0.62
R–Squared	39	39
Standard Deviation		20.26
Mean		22.00
Sharpe Ratio		0.95

Portfolio Analysis 09-30-01

Share change since 06–01 Total Stocks: 21	Sector	PE	YTD Ret%	% Assets
⊕ Washington Mutual	Financials	10.1	–5.32	16.16
⊕ H & R Block	Services	25.5	120.00	7.49
⊕ Toys "R" Us	Retail	28.8	24.28	5.05
⊕ AT&T	Services	7.8	40.59	4.75
⊕ Electronic Data Sys	Technology	25.7	19.83	4.49
Sprint	Services	20.5	1.18	4.15
⊕ First Data	Technology	38.1	49.08	4.14
⊕ Kroger	Retail	16.3	–22.80	4.13
⊕ Burlington Resources	Energy	8.4	–24.60	4.12
Office Depot	Retail	NMF	160.20	4.09
⊕ Chiron	Health	—	–1.48	3.80
⊕ Mattel	Staples	31.9	19.43	3.78
⊕ Tricon Global Restaurants	Services	16.3	49.09	3.77
Moody's	Services	33.5	56.04	3.67
Knight Ridder	Services	59.0	16.13	3.49
⊕ Dun & Bradstreet	Services	41.1	36.43	3.31
⊖ Reynolds & Reynolds	Services	18.2	22.02	2.84
⊕ Energizer Hldgs	Durables	—	–10.80	2.39
⊕ Liz Claiborne	Durables	13.7	20.58	2.32
Ceridian	Technology	27.6	–5.96	2.03
⊕ Visteon	Durables	—	32.88	1.89

Analysis by Scott Cooley 10-31-01

If he keeps this up, Bill Nygren may end up sending a lot of his rivals into counseling.

If Nygren's competitors have growing inferiority complexes, it would be easy to see why. For the year to date through Oct. 30, Oakmark Select has posted a 15.6% gain, leading its mid-value peers by more than 20 percentage points. Top holding Washington Mutual has stumbled over the past few weeks, on fears that the housing market will slow, but H & R Block, Tricon Global Restaurants, and Office Depot have been stellar performers for the fund. This type of success is no recent phenomenon: Since the fund's late-1996 inception, its annualized return tops its typical rival's by 17 percentage points.

When a manager is on a roll like this, even the dark clouds have a silver lining. For example, Nygren admitted defeat earlier this year and sold off two formerly large holdings, USG and U.S. Industries. Largely because of the losses realized on those two holdings, the tax-conscious Nygren said the fund would not make a capital-gains distribution in 2001.

Over the past few months, Nygren has done little trading here. Although some managers added to their stakes in troubled tech stocks during the third quarter, Nygren made no additions in that area, arguing that better values were available elsewhere. He's sticking with a huge stake in Washington Mutual, which he likes for its modest valuation, West Coast location, and strong operations. And he still has large positions in favorites such as Toys "R" Us and H & R Block, even though they are well above their lows, because he considers them significantly undervalued.

Given Nygren's concentration in individual issues and sectors, he's virtually certain to have a bad year at some point. But he's clearly proven himself a terrific stock-picker. Investors who bought in before the fund closed should consider themselves lucky.

Current Investment Style	Stock Port Avg	Relative S&P 500 Current	Relative S&P 500 Hist	Rel Cat
Price/Earnings Ratio	24.2	0.78	0.62	1.03
Price/Book Ratio	3.5	0.62	0.43	1.16
Price/Cash Flow	15.4	0.86	0.67	1.24
3 Yr Earnings Growth	14.0	0.96	1.22	1.18
1 Yr Earnings Est%	11.0	—	—	–1.79
Med Mkt Cap $mil	8,487	0.1	0.1	1.19

Style: Value Blnd Growth; Size: Large Med Small

Special Securities % assets 09-30-01	
Restricted/Illiquid Secs	0
Emerging–Markets Secs	0
Options/Futures/Warrants	No

Composition % assets 09-30-01	
Cash	8.2
Stocks*	91.8
Bonds	0.0
Other	0.0
*Foreign (% stocks)	0.0

Market Cap	
Giant	5.2
Large	36.0
Medium	58.8
Small	0.0
Micro	0.0

Sector Weightings	% of Stocks	Rel S&P	5-Year High	5-Year Low
Utilities	0.0	0.0	—	—
Energy	4.5	0.6	—	—
Financials	17.6	1.0	—	—
Industrials	0.0	0.0	—	—
Durables	7.2	4.6	—	—
Staples	4.1	0.5	—	—
Services	36.4	3.4	—	—
Retail	14.5	2.1	—	—
Health	4.1	0.3	—	—
Technology	11.6	0.6	—	—

Address:	Two N. LaSalle Street Chicago, IL 60602–3790 800–625–6275
Web Address:	www.oakmark.com
*Inception:	11-01-96
Advisor:	Harris Assoc.
Subadvisor:	None
NTF Plans:	Fidelity , Fidelity Inst.

Minimum Purchase:	Closed	Add: $100 IRA: —
Min Auto Inv Plan:	Closed	Add: $100
Sales Fees:	No–load, 2.00%R within 3 months	
Management Fee:	1.0%	
Actual Fees:	Mgt: 0.97%	Dist: —
Expense Projections:	3Yr: $370	5Yr: $640 10Yr: $1410
Avg Brok Commission:	—	Income Distrib: Annually
Total Cost (relative to category):	Below Avg	

Oakmark Small Cap I

Ticker	Load	NAV	Yield	Total Assets	Mstar Category
OAKSX	None	$17.29	0.0%	$275.9 mil	Small Value

Prospectus Objective: Small Company

Oakmark Small Cap Fund seeks long-term capital appreciation.

The fund invests primarily in equity securities. It normally invests at least 65% of assets in securities issued by companies with market capitalizations not exceeding $1 billion. To select investments, the advisor focuses on securities it judges to be undervalued, and then evaluates them based on quality of management, position within the industry, and degree of pricing power. The fund may invest up to 25% of assets in foreign securities. It may invest up to 25% of assets in debt rated below BBB.

The fund also offers I, II shares.

Historical Profile

Return Average
Risk Average
Rating ★★★ Neutral

Investment Style
Equity
Average Stock %

92% 94% 94% 96% 94% 93%

▼ Manager Change
▽ Partial Manager Change

Fund Performance vs. Category Average
Quarterly Fund Return +/– Category Average
— Category Baseline

Performance Quartile (within Category)

Portfolio Manager(s)

James P. Benson, CFA. Since 11-99. BA Westminster C.; MM Northwestern U. Other funds currently managed: CDC Nvest Star Small Cap A, CDC Nvest Star Small Cap B, CDC Nvest Star Small Cap C.

Clyde S. McGregor, CFA. Since 7-00. BA'74 Oberlin C.; MBA'77 U. of Wisconsin. Other funds currently managed: Oakmark Equity & Income I, CDC Nvest Star Small Cap A, CDC Nvest Star Small Cap B.

1990	1991	1992	1993	1994	1995	1996	1997	1998	1999	2000	12-01	History
—	—	—	—	—	10.33	14.44	19.42	14.77	13.60	13.69	17.29	NAV
—	—	—	—	—	3.30*	39.79	40.51	–13.16	–7.92	4.39	26.30	Total Return %
—	—	—	—	—	–2.60*	16.84	7.16	–41.73	–28.96	13.50	38.17	+/– S&P 500
—	—	—	—	—	—	18.42	8.82	–6.73	–6.44	–18.42	12.28	+/– Russell 2000 V
—	—	—	—	—	0.00	0.00	0.00	0.00	0.00	0.00	0.00	Income Return %
—	—	—	—	—	3.30	39.79	40.51	–13.16	–7.92	4.39	26.30	Capital Return %
—	—	—	—	—	—	6	13	83	91	90	14	Total Rtn % Rank Cat
—	—	—	—	—	0.00	0.00	0.00	0.00	0.00	0.00	0.00	Income $
—	—	—	—	—	0.00	0.00	0.84	2.11	0.00	0.51	0.00	Capital Gains $
—	—	—	—	—	—	1.61	1.37	1.45	1.48	1.50	1.27	Expense Ratio %
—	—	—	—	—	—	–0.29	–0.25	–0.40	–0.44	–0.41	–0.28	Income Ratio %
—	—	—	—	—	—	23	—	34	68	28	47	Turnover Rate %
—	—	—	—	—	25.8	316.5	1,492.2	684.2	375.0	207.2	—	Net Assets $mil

Performance 12-31-01

	1st Qtr	2nd Qtr	3rd Qtr	4th Qtr	Total
1997	5.40	16.03	15.18	–0.25	40.51
1998	7.11	–5.82	–26.83	17.65	–13.16
1999	–8.80	13.29	–9.04	–2.02	–7.92
2000	–1.54	–0.30	13.11	–5.98	4.39
2001	5.19	19.10	–15.04	18.67	26.30

Trailing	Total Return%	+/– S&P 500	+/– Russ 2000V	% Rank All	% Rank Cat	Growth of $10,000
3 Mo	18.67	7.98	1.95	16	37	11,867
6 Mo	0.82	6.37	–0.34	35	61	10,082
1 Yr	26.30	38.17	12.28	1	14	12,630
3 Yr Avg	6.68	7.70	–4.64	18	82	12,140
5 Yr Avg	8.18	–2.52	–3.02	28	77	14,814
10 Yr Avg	—	—	—	—	—	—
15 Yr Avg	—	—	—	—	—	—

Tax Analysis	Tax-Adj Ret%	%Rank Cat	%Pretax Ret	%Rank Cat
3 Yr Avg	6.42	79	96.2	28
5 Yr Avg	7.19	72	87.9	40
10 Yr Avg	—	—	—	—

Potential Capital Gain Exposure: 32% of assets

Risk Analysis

Time Period	Load-Adj Return %	Risk %Rank[1] All	Risk %Rank[1] Cat	Morningstar Return	Morningstar Risk	Morningstar Risk-Adj Rating
1 Yr	26.30					
3 Yr	6.68	56	72	0.37[2]	0.78	★★★★
5 Yr	8.18	69	74	0.73[2]	0.94	★★★
Incept	13.12	—	—	—	—	

Average Historical Rating (39 months): 2.0★s

[1] 1=low, 100=high [2] T-Bill return substituted for category avg.

Category Rating (3 Yr)

1 2 3 4 5
Worst Best

Return Below Avg
Risk Above Avg

Other Measures	Standard Index S&P 500	Best Fit Index SPMid400
Alpha	5.4	–1.2
Beta	0.51	0.62
R-Squared	27	51

Standard Deviation	17.90
Mean	6.68
Sharpe Ratio	0.11

Portfolio Analysis 11-30-01

Share change since 10-01 Total Stocks: 48	Sector	PE	YTD Ret%	% Assets
ITT Educational Svcs	Services	28.6	67.59	5.13
⊖ Catellus Dev	Financials	21.2	5.14	4.55
PMI Grp	Financials	10.4	–0.76	4.34
Ralcorp Hldgs	Staples	17.1	38.63	4.07
Mentor Graphics	Technology	27.1	–14.10	4.05
Idexx Labs	Health	25.9	29.59	3.99
Checkpoint Sys	Technology	39.4	80.16	3.31
Msc.Software	Technology	21.4	98.73	3.01
ShopKo Stores	Retail	—	90.00	3.00
Prime Hosptlty	Services	10.7	–4.95	2.97
Del Monte Foods	Staples	65.5	17.38	2.96
BankAtlantic Bancorp Cl A	Financials	16.4	149.70	2.82
InFocus	Technology	31.5	49.29	2.77
NCO Grp	Services	20.5	–24.60	2.69
Teekay Shipping	Energy	3.3	–7.24	2.60
CIBER	Technology	NMF	93.85	2.53
People's Bk	Financials	11.7	–13.00	2.38
Dept 56	Durables	6.6	–25.20	2.34
Hanger Orthopedic Grp	Health	—	356.90	2.01
Conmed	Health	21.2	74.83	1.99
St. Mary Land & Explor	Energy	10.9	–36.00	1.98
Elan ADR	Health	41.0	–3.74	1.75
Trammel Crow	Financials	29.3	–13.30	1.69
Sybron Dental Tech	Health	—	27.88	1.65
Golden State Bancorp	Financials	9.6	–15.60	1.62

Current Investment Style

Style: Value Blnd Growth; Size: Large Med Small

	Stock Port Avg	Relative S&P 500 Current	Relative S&P 500 Hist	Rel Cat
Price/Earnings Ratio	23.3	0.75	0.54	1.08
Price/Book Ratio	3.3	0.59	0.37	1.38
Price/Cash Flow	11.9	0.66	0.49	0.93
3 Yr Earnings Growth	13.1	0.89	0.49	1.13
1 Yr Earnings Est%	–1.1	0.60	—	0.27
Med Mkt Cap $mil	643	0.0	0.0	0.74

[1] figure is based on 50% or less of stocks

Analysis by Scott Cooley 11-25-01

Although we can't yet give Oakmark Small Cap Fund a wholehearted endorsement, there are definite signs of improvement.

This was once the classic hot fund turned cold. Under former manager Steve Reid, the fund posted breathtaking gains in 1996 and 1997, and its asset base swelled to more than $1.5 billion. Reid's deep-value bias, combined with some weak stock picks, subsequently hurt the fund, and shareholders fled in droves. Those massive redemptions, which sliced the fund's asset base by more than 80% from its peak, undoubtedly further pressured the selling prices of its already beaten-down holdings.

Things have stabilized a bit since Jim Benson, who was later joined by Clyde McGregor, took over here. Although the fund posted another subpar return in 2000, it has flourished so far in 2001, thanks to solid picks such as ITT Educational Services and BankAtlantic Bancorp. For the year to date through Nov. 23, the fund has gained 14.9%, beating more than three fourths of its rivals.

With the markets' heightened turbulence in recent months, several more stocks have fallen to levels that management considers attractive. Benson says the fund picked up ad agency Grey Global during the third quarter. Fears about a slowing economy had pummeled its shares, but Benson says the stock is extremely cheap in comparison with estimated 2003 earnings (which assume an economic recovery). Similarly, Benson again bought Mentor Graphics—a stock on which he had earlier taken profits—because it took a big tumble during the third quarter, and he expects demand for its software to remain strong.

Such opportunistic purchases have given the fund a lift in 2001, and we count Benson's and McGregor's decades of investment experience in the fund's favor. We can't yet recommend this fund over the group's proven options, but it's worth keeping an eye on.

Special Securities % assets 11-30-01

Restricted/Illiquid Secs	0
Emerging-Markets Secs	3
Options/Futures/Warrants	No

Sector Weightings	% of Stocks	Rel S&P	5-Year High	5-Year Low
Utilities	0.0	0.0	0	0
Energy	7.9	1.1	9	0
Financials	19.6	1.1	35	18
Industrials	5.3	0.5	34	5
Durables	3.1	2.0	20	2
Staples	9.1	1.1	19	5
Services	15.7	1.5	24	5
Retail	3.2	0.5	11	1
Health	14.8	1.0	15	0
Technology	21.5	1.2	21	0

Composition % assets 11-30-01	
Cash	5.5
Stocks*	94.5
Bonds	0.0
Other	0.0
*Foreign (% stocks)	5.8

Market Cap	
Giant	0.0
Large	1.9
Medium	16.1
Small	65.9
Micro	16.2

Address:	Two N. LaSalle Street Chicago, IL 60602–3790 800–625–6275
Web Address:	www.oakmark.com
*Inception:	11-01-95
Advisor:	Harris Assoc.
Subadvisor:	None
NTF Plans:	Fidelity , Fidelity Inst.

Minimum Purchase:	$1000	Add: $100	IRA: $1000
Min Auto Inv Plan:	$500	Add: $100	
Sales Fees:	No-load		
Management Fee:	1.3% mx./1.0% mn.		
Actual Fees:	Mgt: 1.27%	Dist: —	
Expense Projections:	3Yr: $470	5Yr: $810	10Yr: $1780
Avg Brok Commission:	—	Income Distrib: Annually	
Total Cost (relative to category):	Below Avg		

One Group Large Cap Growth A

Ticker	Load	NAV	Yield	Total Assets	Mstar Category
OLGAX	5.25%	$15.99	0.0%	$2,941.2 mil	Large Growth

Prospectus Objective: Growth

One Group Large Cap Growth Fund seeks long-term capital appreciation and growth of income.

The fund normally invests at least 65% of assets in equity securities; it may invest the balance in investment-grade debt. The fund may also invest in foreign securities.

Class A shares have front loads; B shares have deferred loads, higher 12b-1 fees, and conversion features; C shares have level loads; I shares are only available to institutional investors. The fund has gone through several name changes. One Group Blue Chip Equity Fund merged into this fund on Sept. 6, 1995. On March 22, 1999, Pegasus Growth Fund.

Historical Profile

Return	Below Avg
Risk	Above Avg
Rating	★★ Below Avg

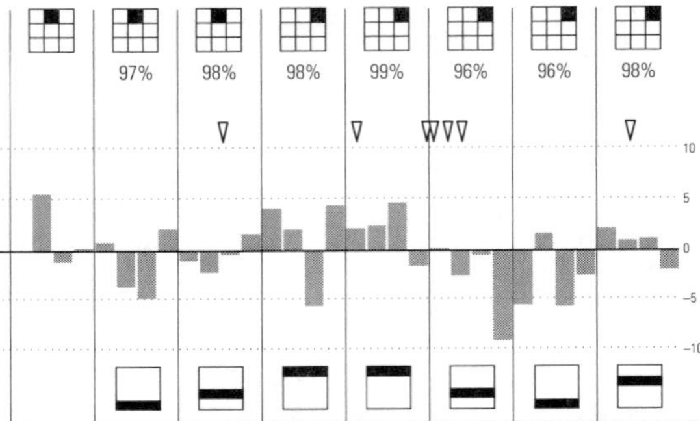

Investment Style
Equity
Average Stock %

1994	1995	1996	1997	1998	1999	2000	12-01
	97%	98%	98%	99%	96%	96%	98%

▼ Manager Change
▽ Partial Manager Change

Fund Performance vs. Category Average
Quarterly Fund Return +/– Category Average
— Category Baseline

Performance Quartile (within Category)

Portfolio Manager(s)

Management Team

1990	1991	1992	1993	1994	1995	1996	1997	1998	1999	2000	12-01	**History**
—	—	—	—	12.01	14.83	16.41	18.75	24.27	27.47	20.13	15.99	NAV
—	—	—	—	2.62*	26.44	16.87	32.31	44.33	27.49	–24.20	–20.57	Total Return %
—	—	—	—	2.52*	–11.10	–6.07	–1.05	15.75	6.45	–15.10	–8.69	+/– S&P 500
—	—	—	—	—	–12.22	–8.65	–1.44	–0.77	–2.19	0.32	–0.07	+/– Russ Top 200 Grt
—	—	—	—	1.02	1.43	0.76	0.17	0.00	0.00	0.00	0.00	Income Return %
—	—	—	—	1.60	25.01	16.11	32.14	44.33	27.49	–24.20	–20.57	Capital Return %
—	—	—	—	—	82	65	16	14	72	85	42	Total Rtn % Rank Cat
—	—	—	—	0.12	0.17	0.11	0.03	0.00	0.00	0.00	0.00	Income $
—	—	—	—	0.09	0.17	0.80	2.88	2.36	3.34	0.90	0.00	Capital Gains $
—	—	—	—	1.25	1.26	1.21	1.24	1.24	1.21	1.19	1.18	Expense Ratio %
—	—	—	—	1.78	1.49	0.95	0.44	–0.04	–0.43	–0.38	–0.63	Income Ratio %
—	—	—	—	—	14	36	57	117	86	123	73	Turnover Rate %
—	—	—	0.6	2.4	50.5	91.7	152.6	260.4	596.4	504.6	364.9	Net Assets $mil

Performance 12-31-01

	1st Qtr	2nd Qtr	3rd Qtr	4th Qtr	Total
1997	2.23	18.88	5.62	3.08	32.31
1998	16.53	6.73	–6.70	24.37	44.33
1999	7.91	2.56	–3.69	19.60	27.49
2000	3.49	–3.55	–5.32	–19.80	–24.20
2001	–18.83	7.53	–19.52	13.08	–20.57

Trailing	Total Return%	+/– S&P 500	+/– Russ Top 200 Grth	% Rank All	% Rank Cat	Growth of $10,000
3 Mo	13.08	2.40	—	29	57	11,308
6 Mo	–8.99	–3.44	—	82	50	9,101
1 Yr	–20.57	–8.69	—	81	42	7,943
3 Yr Avg	–8.44	–7.41	—	97	84	7,676
5 Yr Avg	7.95	–2.75	—	29	56	14,658
10 Yr Avg	—	—	—	—	—	—
15 Yr Avg	—	—	—	—	—	—

Tax Analysis	Tax-Adj Ret%	%Rank Cat	%Pretax Ret	%Rank Cat
3 Yr Avg	–9.36	81	—	—
5 Yr Avg	6.08	53	76.6	54
10 Yr Avg	—	—	—	—

Potential Capital Gain Exposure: 0% of assets

Risk Analysis

Time Period	Load-Adj Return %	Risk %Rank[1] All	Risk %Rank[1] Cat	Morningstar Return	Morningstar Risk	Morningstar Risk-Adj Rating
1 Yr	–24.74					
3 Yr	–10.07	90	66	–2.75[2]	1.39	★
5 Yr	6.79	84	51	0.40[2]	1.21	★★
Incept	9.94	—	—	—	—	

Average Historical Rating (59 months): 3.6★s

[1] 1=low, 100=high [2] T-Bill return substituted for category avg.

Category Rating (3 Yr)

1 2 3 4 5
Worst Best

Return	Below Avg
Risk	Average

Other Measures	Standard Index S&P 500	Best Fit Index S&P 500
Alpha	–4.9	–4.9
Beta	1.31	1.31
R-Squared	88	88
Standard Deviation		22.35
Mean		–8.44
Sharpe Ratio		–0.71

Analysis by Heather Haynos 12-10-01

Investors could do worse than buying One Group Large Cap Growth Fund, but they could also do better.

This mega-cap growth offering aims to beat its bogy, the Russell 1000 Growth index, by anywhere from 5 to 15 basis points. Its sector bets are therefore fairly modest and rarely differ from the benchmark's weightings by more than 5 percentage points. In selecting stocks, the management team looks for positive earnings revisions, price momentum, and attractive catalysts—such as new management.

Since its inception, the fund has fallen marginally short of its goal. From March 1994 through the end of October 2001, its annualized return trailed its bogy by 184 basis points and its typical large-cap peer by 13 basis points. While this performance is far from dismal, it's not exactly awe-inspiring, either. The fund's bottom-third ranking in 1999 was particularly disappointing. The fund lagged its peers by 14 percentage points that year and its bogy by a decent margin, too.

Thus far in 2001, however, the fund is holding its own. For the year to date through Dec. 7, its 19% loss placed it in the large-growth category's top half. Top-five picks Microsoft and Intel have held up fairly well, and retailers such as Wal-Mart and Home Depot have been steady as well. Day-to-day manager Dan Kapusta says the team has been favoring retail stocks lately, because it believes they will benefit from the increase in mortgage refinancings and the extra cash those will leave in consumers' pockets.

This fund provides a decent way to get exposure to large-cap growth stocks, but given the competitive nature of this group, investors can do better.

Portfolio Analysis 09-30-01

Share change since 06-01 Total Stocks: 122	Sector	PE	YTD Ret%	% Assets
⊕ General Elec	Industrials	30.1	–15.00	7.17
⊕ Pfizer	Health	34.7	–12.40	5.29
⊕ Microsoft	Technology	57.6	52.78	4.48
⊕ AOL Time Warner	Technology	—	–7.76	3.07
⊕ Intel	Technology	73.1	4.89	2.75
⊕ American Intl Grp	Financials	42.0	–19.20	2.70
⊕ Wal-Mart Stores	Retail	40.3	8.94	2.59
⊖ Home Depot	Retail	42.9	12.07	2.43
⊕ Coca-Cola	Staples	35.5	–21.40	2.17
⊖ IBM	Technology	26.9	43.00	2.16
⊕ American Home Products	Health	—	–1.91	1.81
⊕ Bristol-Myers Squibb	Health	20.2	–26.00	1.80
⊕ Johnson & Johnson	Health	16.6	14.01	1.75
⊕ Amgen	Health	52.8	–11.70	1.67
⊕ Philip Morris	Staples	12.1	9.12	1.58
⊕ Cisco Sys	Technology	—	–52.60	1.51
⊕ Merck	Health	19.1	–35.90	1.38
⊕ Pharmacia	Health	36.5	–29.30	1.38
⊕ Freddie Mac	Financials	14.0	–3.87	1.35
⊖ Medtronic	Health	76.4	–14.70	1.35
⊕ Eli Lilly	Health	28.9	–14.40	1.21
⊕ PepsiCo	Staples	31.4	–0.54	0.99
⊕ Baxter Intl	Health	33.9	22.84	0.98
⊕ Texas Instruments	Technology	87.5	–40.70	0.98
⊕ Bed Bath & Beyond	Retail	53.0	51.51	0.95

Current Investment Style

Style: Value Blnd Growth; Size: Large Med Small

	Stock Port Avg	Relative S&P 500 Current	Relative S&P 500 Hist	Rel Cat
Price/Earnings Ratio	37.5	1.21	1.28	1.05
Price/Book Ratio	7.8	1.38	1.48	1.23
Price/Cash Flow	23.2	1.29	1.29	1.02
3 Yr Earnings Growth	18.6	1.27	1.35	0.86
1 Yr Earnings Est%	4.8	—	—	1.60
Med Mkt Cap $mil	100,169	1.7	1.6	2.12

Special Securities % assets 09-30-01	
Restricted/Illiquid Secs	0
Emerging-Markets Secs	0
Options/Futures/Warrants	No

Composition % assets 09-30-01	
Cash	3.0
Stocks*	97.0
Bonds	0.0
Other	0.0
*Foreign (% stocks)	0.0

Market Cap	
Giant	68.2
Large	22.1
Medium	9.7
Small	0.0
Micro	0.0

Sector Weightings	% of Stocks	Rel S&P	5-Year High	5-Year Low
Utilities	1.6	0.5	2	0
Energy	0.9	0.1	10	0
Financials	8.1	0.5	11	1
Industrials	9.8	0.9	28	9
Durables	0.7	0.4	4	0
Staples	6.8	0.9	20	2
Services	6.8	0.6	19	7
Retail	9.9	1.5	10	4
Health	27.8	1.9	28	10
Technology	27.7	1.5	54	10

Address:	3435 Stelzer Road Columbus, OH 43219 800-480-4111
Web Address:	www.onegroup.com
*Inception:	02-22-94
Advisor:	Banc One Inv. Adv.
Subadvisor:	None
NTF Plans:	Datalynx , Fidelity Inst.

Minimum Purchase:	$1000	Add: $25	IRA: $1000
Min Auto Inv Plan:	$1000	Add: $25	
Sales Fees:	5.25%L, 0.10%B, 0.25%S		
Management Fee:	.74% mx./.65% mn., .20%A		
Actual Fees:	Mgt: 0.69%	Dist: 0.35%	
Expense Projections:	3Yr: $903	5Yr: $1186	10Yr: $1991
Avg Brok Commission:	—	Income Distrib: Quarterly	
Total Cost (relative to category):	Average		

Oppenheimer Capital Income A

Ticker	Load	NAV	Yield	Total Assets	Mstar Category
OPPEX	5.75%	$11.89	3.9%	$2,915.8 mil	Domestic Hybrid

Prospectus Objective: Equity–Income

Oppenheimer Capital Income Fund seeks current income compatible with prudent investment.

The fund normally invests at least 65% of assets in income-producing equities. The fund can typically invest no more than 25% of assets in junk bonds, and no more than 10% of assets in junk bonds that aren't convertible. It can usually invest no more than 35% of assets in foreign securities.

Class A shares have front loads; B shares have deferred loads, higher 12b-1 fees, and conversion features; C shares have level loads; N shares are available to retirement plans only.

The fund has experienced several mergers and name changes.

Historical Profile

Return Average
Risk Below Avg
Rating ★★★ Neutral

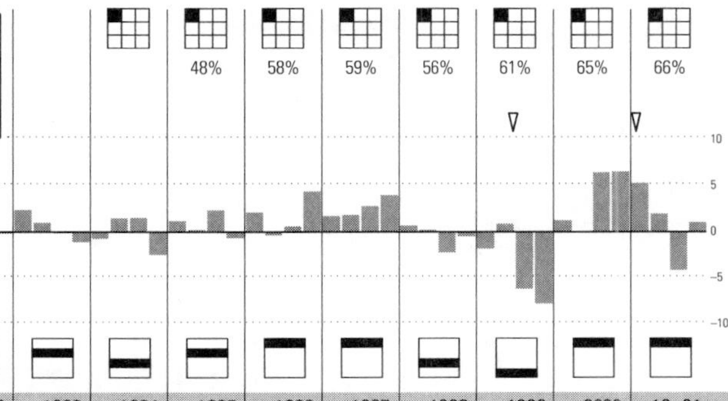

Investment Style
Equity
Average Stock %: 1995 48% · 1996 58% · 1997 59% · 1998 56% · 1999 61% · 2000 65% · 12-01 66%

▼ Manager Change
▽ Partial Manager Change

Fund Performance vs. Category Average
■ Quarterly Fund Return +/– Category Average
— Category Baseline

Performance Quartile (within Category)

Portfolio Manager(s)

Michael S. Levine. Since 6-99. U. of Pennsylvania. Other funds currently managed: Oppenheimer Multiple Strategies A, Oppenheimer Capital Income B, Oppenheimer Multiple Strategies C.

History

1990	1991	1992	1993	1994	1995	1996	1997	1998	1999	2000	12-01	History
8.49	9.32	9.33	10.02	9.14	10.92	12.18	14.45	14.25	11.81	12.74	11.89	NAV
–1.37	17.27	6.83	14.57	–2.79	27.92	20.06	29.68	10.32	–6.25	16.82	–0.19	Total Return %
1.75	–13.22	–0.79	4.51	–4.10	–9.62	–2.88	–3.67	–18.25	–27.28	25.93	11.69	+/– S&P 500
–10.32	1.26	–0.57	4.82	0.13	9.45	16.45	20.00	1.65	–5.42	5.19	–8.61	+/– LB Aggregate
5.30	5.83	5.02	5.24	4.88	5.35	4.47	4.12	3.44	3.46	4.13	3.82	Income Return %
–6.67	11.44	1.81	9.33	–7.67	22.57	15.60	25.56	6.88	–9.70	12.70	–4.01	Capital Return %
64	85	61	28	56	26	6	2	65	96	5	24	Total Rtn % Rank Cat
0.48	0.49	0.46	0.48	0.48	0.48	0.48	0.49	0.49	0.49	0.48	0.48	Income $
0.15	0.12	0.15	0.17	0.13	0.24	0.40	0.79	1.17	1.07	0.51	0.33	Capital Gains $
0.79	0.79	0.82	0.79	0.90	0.96	0.89	0.88	0.87	0.89	0.93	0.91	Expense Ratio %
5.10	5.31	5.33	5.12	4.72	5.15	4.51	3.97	3.47	3.51	3.78	3.21	Income Ratio %
122	64	37	59	30	46	43	24	18	40	37	74	Turnover Rate %
1,266.4	1,587.9	1,647.7	1,860.9	1,713.6	2,074.2	2,352.9	2,988.2	3,259.8	2,619.3	2,426.6	2,376.6	Net Assets $mil

Performance 12-31-01

	1st Qtr	2nd Qtr	3rd Qtr	4th Qtr	Total
1997	1.78	11.30	9.30	4.73	29.68
1998	7.75	1.31	–7.93	9.77	10.32
1999	–0.85	4.64	–9.58	–0.06	–6.25
2000	3.93	–0.94	8.24	4.83	16.82
2001	–0.07	5.09	–11.36	7.23	–0.19

Trailing	Total Return%	+/– S&P 500	+/– LB Agg	% Rank All	% Rank Cat	Growth of $10,000
3 Mo	7.23	–3.46	7.19	55	32	10,723
6 Mo	–4.96	0.60	–9.61	62	92	9,504
1 Yr	–0.19	11.69	–8.61	43	24	9,981
3 Yr Avg	3.02	4.04	–3.26	54	39	10,932
5 Yr Avg	9.36	–1.34	1.93	22	22	15,640
10 Yr Avg	11.07	–1.86	3.84	25	16	28,579
15 Yr Avg	11.15	–2.58	3.03	32	19	48,824

Tax Analysis	Tax-Adj Ret%	%Rank Cat	%Pretax Ret	%Rank Cat
3 Yr Avg	0.44	50	14.7	95
5 Yr Avg	6.57	25	70.2	41
10 Yr Avg	8.37	16	75.6	28

Potential Capital Gain Exposure: 15% of assets

Risk Analysis

Time Period	Load-Adj Return %	Risk %Rank[1] All	Risk %Rank[1] Cat	Morningstar Return	Morningstar Risk	Morningstar Risk-Adj Rating
1 Yr	–5.93					
3 Yr	1.00	45	73	–0.81[2]	0.63	★★★
5 Yr	8.07	47	74	0.70[2]	0.63	★★★
10 Yr	10.42	52	77	0.80	0.64	★★★

Average Historical Rating (193 months): 3.3★s

[1]1=low, 100=high [2] T-Bill return substituted for category avg.

Category Rating (3 Yr)

1 2 **3** 4 5
Worst Best

Return Average
Risk Above Avg

Other Measures	Standard Index S&P 500	Best Fit Index SPMid400
Alpha	1.2	–4.3
Beta	0.51	0.49
R-Squared	46	55
Standard Deviation		13.21
Mean		3.02
Sharpe Ratio		–0.17

Portfolio Analysis 07-31-01

Total Stocks: 116 Share change since 03-01	Sector	PE Ratio	YTD Return %	% Net Assets
⊕ Citigroup	Financials	20.0	0.03	3.60
⊕ Philip Morris	Staples	12.1	9.12	3.52
⊖ Bank of America	Financials	16.7	42.73	2.57
⊕ Tyco Intl	Industrials	27.1	6.23	2.36
FleetBoston Finl	Financials	16.2	0.55	2.32
Dynegy	Energy	12.8	–54.20	1.83
⊕ Washington Mutual	Financials	10.1	–5.32	1.76
⊕ J.P. Morgan Chase & Co.	Financials	27.8	–17.40	1.75
☼ Kinder Morgan	Energy	32.2	7.11	1.56
⊖ Clear Channel Comms	Services	—	5.10	1.47

Total Fixed-Income: 88	Date of Maturity	Amount $000	Value $000	% Net Assets
FNMA 6%		126,000	123,244	3.98
US Treasury Strip 0%	02-15-15	230,000	108,175	3.49
US Treasury Note 5%	02-15-11	50,000	49,871	1.61
Adelphia Comm Cv Pfd 5.5%		375	44,438	1.43
Sovereign Bancorp 7.5%	11-15-29	460	31,050	1.00
Adelphia Comm 6%	02-15-06	32,500	29,575	0.95
FNMA 6.5%		25,000	24,992	0.81
Ace Cv 8.25%	05-16-03	288	20,729	0.67
Rite Aid Cv 5.25%	09-15-02	20,000	19,000	0.61
Six Flags 7.25%		715	18,662	0.60

Equity Style
Style: Value
Size: Large-Cap

	Portfolio Avg	Rel S&P
Price/Earnings Ratio	18.9	0.61
Price/Book Ratio	3.2	0.55
Price/Cash Flow	12.0[1]	0.66
3 Yr Earnings Growth	15.0	1.03
1 Yr Earnings Est%	8.7	—
Debt % Total Cap	46.9[1]	1.52
Med Mkt Cap $mil	20,238	0.33

[1]figure is based on 50% or less of stocks

Fixed-Income Style NA
Duration: —
Quality: —

Avg Eff Duration[1]	2.9 Yrs
Avg Eff Maturity	4.5 Yrs
Avg Credit Quality	—
Avg Wtd Coupon	5.61%

[1]figure provided by fund as of 06-30-01

Special Securities % assets 07-31-01	
Restricted/Illiquid Secs	4
Emerging–Markets Secs	1
Options/Futures/Warrants	No

Composition % of assets 07-31-01	
Cash	2.2
Stocks*	67.8
Bonds	20.5
Other	9.4
*Foreign (% of stocks)	1.5

Market Cap	
Giant	32.7
Large	39.7
Medium	26.0
Small	0.9
Micro	0.7

Sector Weightings	% of Stocks	Rel S&P	5-Year High	5-Year Low
Utilities	6.1	1.9	20	4
Energy	18.4	2.6	18	5
Financials	43.7	2.4	58	12
Industrials	8.2	0.7	19	7
Durables	0.9	0.6	7	1
Staples	5.5	0.7	9	2
Services	8.1	0.7	26	1
Retail	3.6	0.5	5	1
Health	3.6	0.2	13	1
Technology	1.9	0.1	5	0

Analysis by William Harding 09-27-01

A management change isn't reason to sell this fund.

The recent management change at Oppenheimer Capital Income Fund doesn't seem to be having adverse effects. Mike Levine, who comanaged the fund since 1999, assumed the lead role when John Doney retired at the beginning of 2001. It's far too early to pass judgment on Levine's abilities, but the fund has continued to perform fairly well on his watch. Its 9% loss for the year to date ended Sept. 24, 2001, lands in the domestic-hybrid category's top third.

That showing is even better considering that the fund tends to have an aggressive asset mix—about 65% of assets are devoted to stocks—which has been a detriment as equities have headed south in 2001. However, as Doney did, Levine has emphasized cheap stocks that pay dividends, which have held up better than high-P/E names in 2001's rough environment for equities.

Although the fund still tilts toward equities, it will likely be a more even-keeled offering under Levine. Doney maintained big bets on financials, cash and junk bonds at times, which led to uneven performance. Levine, on the other hand, is less likely to move into cash and aims to broaden the fund's sector mix. To the latter end, he scooped up some health-care names and tech convertibles early in the year. (Convertibles offer upside potential if stocks appreciate, while providing income and limiting downside risk.) The fund still has a hefty financials stake, but Levine has hedged that bet a bit by selling call options on a portion of its position in that sector. Selling call options protects against a stock's decline while providing income from the premium.

Levine needs more time to prove himself before we can heartily endorse this offering, but current investors have little reason to sell now.

Address:	P.O. Box 5270 Denver, CO 80217–5270 800–525–7048 / 303–671–3200
Web Address:	www.oppenheimerfunds.com
Inception:	12-01-70
Advisor:	OppenheimerFunds
Subadvisor:	None
NTF Plans:	Datalynx , Fidelity Inst.

Minimum Purchase:	$1000	Add: $25	IRA: $250
Min Auto Inv Plan:	$25	Add: $25	
Sales Fees:	5.75%L, 0.25%S		
Management Fee:	.75% mx./.50% mn.		
Actual Fees:	Mgt: 0.52%	Dist: 0.25%	
Expense Projections:	3Yr: $843	5Yr: $1040	10Yr: $1608
Avg Brok Commission:	—	Income Distrib: Quarterly	
Total Cost (relative to category):	Average		

Oppenheimer Global Growth & Income A

Ticker	Load	NAV	Yield	Total Assets	Mstar Category
OPGIX	5.75%	$22.59	0.1%	$2,608.7 mil	World Stock

Prospectus Objective: Multiasset—Global

Oppenheimer Global Growth and Income Fund seeks capital appreciation consistent with preservation of principal.

The fund may emphasize investment in common stocks and convertibles, fixed-income securities, or a combination of both types of investments. It may invest without limit in foreign securities, and normally maintains investments in at least three foreign countries. The fund may invest up to 25% of assets in bonds rated below investment-grade.

This fund offers multiple shareclasses, all of which differ in fee structure and availability.

Historical Profile
Return: High
Risk: Average
Rating: ★★★★★ Highest

Investment Style
Equity
Average Stock %: 60% 74% 66% 73% 74% 85% 91%

▼ Manager Change
▽ Partial Manager Change

Fund Performance vs. Category Average
■ Quarterly Fund Return +/– Category Average
— Category Baseline

Performance Quartile (within Category)

Portfolio Manager(s)

Frank V. Jennings. Since 10-95. BA'75 Emory U.; PhD'80 U. of Geneva. Other funds currently managed: Oppenheimer Global Growth & Income C, Oppenheimer Global Growth & Income B, Oppenheimer Global Growth & Income N.

History

1990	1991	1992	1993	1994	1995	1996	1997	1998	1999	2000	12-01	History
11.41	12.73	11.61	15.47	13.53	14.60	15.00	17.44	16.64	29.12	27.04	22.59	NAV
0.57*	14.99	–6.18	39.49	–4.70	17.37	15.32	28.25	12.83	86.57	–4.23	–16.32	Total Return %
–5.38*	–15.49	–13.80	29.43	–6.01	–20.16	–7.63	–5.10	–15.75	65.53	4.88	–4.44	+/– S&P 500
—	–3.29	–0.95	16.98	–9.77	–3.35	1.84	12.49	–11.51	61.63	8.95	—	+/– MSCI World
0.74	3.01	1.84	1.73	2.61	2.99	2.77	4.36	2.31	2.30	0.18	0.07	Income Return %
–0.18	11.98	–8.02	37.75	–7.31	14.39	12.55	23.89	10.52	84.26	–4.41	–16.38	Capital Return %
—	67	93	16	78	49	64	3	51	5	29	48	Total Rtn % Rank Cat
0.08	0.34	0.23	0.20	0.40	0.40	0.40	0.65	0.40	0.38	0.05	0.02	Income $
0.00	0.03	0.11	0.48	0.82	0.83	1.38	1.07	2.56	1.32	0.81	0.02	Capital Gains $
—	1.94	1.74	1.56	1.49	1.63	1.52	1.43	1.36	1.33	1.20	—	Expense Ratio %
—	4.05	2.41	2.68	2.44	3.09	2.65	2.47	1.62	2.51	0.72	—	Income Ratio %
—	—	51	91	87	135	208	91	117	98	48	—	Turnover Rate %
12.8	31.5	50.7	112.5	124.5	108.8	123.5	187.3	256.7	788.6	1,540.1	1,352.8	Net Assets $mil

Performance 12-31-01

	1st Qtr	2nd Qtr	3rd Qtr	4th Qtr	Total
1997	6.80	8.56	13.31	–2.38	28.25
1998	10.97	2.08	–17.49	20.73	12.83
1999	4.52	24.39	8.34	32.45	86.57
2000	16.28	–3.66	–7.97	–7.10	–4.23
2001	–14.72	3.82	–24.98	25.99	–16.32

Trailing	Total Return%	+/– S&P 500	+/– MSCI World	% Rank All	% Rank Cat	Growth of $10,000
3 Mo	25.99	15.31	—	7	2	12,599
6 Mo	–5.48	0.08	—	64	31	9,452
1 Yr	–16.32	–4.44	—	75	48	8,368
3 Yr Avg	14.35	15.38	—	6	4	14,953
5 Yr Avg	16.69	5.99	—	3	1	21,638
10 Yr Avg	13.83	0.90	—	9	1	36,526
15 Yr Avg	—	—	—	—	—	—

Tax Analysis	Tax-Adj Ret%	%Rank Cat	%Pretax Ret	%Rank Cat
3 Yr Avg	13.27	3	92.5	16
5 Yr Avg	14.13	1	84.7	21
10 Yr Avg	11.21	3	81.0	28

Potential Capital Gain Exposure: –17% of assets

Risk Analysis

Time Period	Load-Adj Return %	Risk %Rank[1] All	Risk %Rank[1] Cat	Morningstar Return	Morningstar Risk	Morningstar Risk-Adj Rating
1 Yr	–21.13					
3 Yr	12.12	81	72	1.63[2]	1.10	★★★★★
5 Yr	15.32	79	63	2.74[2]	0.92	★★★★★
10 Yr	13.16	80	50	3.15[2]	0.83	★★★★★

Average Historical Rating (99 months): 4.0★s

[1]1=low, 100=high [2] T-Bill return substituted for category avg.

Category Rating (3 Yr)

1 2 3 4 5 — Worst ... Best (5)

Return: High
Risk: Above Avg

Other Measures	Standard Index S&P 500	Best Fit Index Russ 2000
Alpha	18.4	8.5
Beta	0.95	1.11
R–Squared	30	80

Standard Deviation	34.44
Mean	14.35
Sharpe Ratio	0.31

Analysis by William Harding 08-30-01

We think this offering makes a fine choice for investors looking for broad overseas exposure.

Oppenheimer Global Growth & Income has certainly not been immune to the recent downturn in stocks across the globe. The fund has lost about 17% for the year to date ended August 28, 2001, which is right in line with the world-stock category average. The fund has been hindered this year by some racy tech picks that have retreated quite a bit. But it has also had a few winners. Top holding National Semiconductor has risen 60% this year. And the fund has also found success in tamer areas of the market. For instance, German hair-care firm Wella has chipped in with a 25% gain.

Flexible security selection is the norm here. Indeed, manager Frank Jennings readily invests in value as well as growth stocks, and he's not averse to buying bonds. In recent years the fund has taken a more bullish stance on equities (the fund's average stock weighting over the past three years is more than 80%), prompting a switch to the world-stock category from international-hybrid. What hasn't changed, however, is the fund's impressive long-term record. Its trailing five-year return bests all of its world-stock rivals'.

Investors should note, however, that Jennings is apt to move in and out of bonds on occasion, so it may not always have 90% of assets devoted to stocks like it does now. Indeed, Jennings' knack for finding opportunities in various asset classes is a major selling point here. In 1997, for instance, he loaded up on U.S. Treasuries and slashed the fund's equity stake to 50% of assets.

Investors who are anxious about their fund's asset mix, or what style box it calls home, probably won't be happy here. This fund should be thought of as a flexible, go-anywhere global offering. In that regard, we think investors will be hard-pressed to find a manager more capable than Jennings.

Address:	P.O. Box 5270 Denver, CO 80217–5270 800–525–7048 / 303–671–3200
Web Address:	www.oppenheimerfunds.com
*Inception:	10-22-90
Advisor:	OppenheimerFunds
Subadvisor:	None
NTF Plans:	Datalynx , Fidelity Inst.

Minimum Purchase:	$1000	Add: $25	IRA: $250
Min Auto Inv Plan:	$25	Add: $25	
Sales Fees:	5.75%L, 0.25%S		
Management Fee:	.80% mx./.67% mn.		
Actual Fees:	Mgt: 0.78%	Dist: 0.24%	
Expense Projections:	3Yr: $972	5Yr: $1262	10Yr: $2084
Avg Brok Commission:	—	Income Distrib: Annually	
Total Cost (relative to category):	Average		

Portfolio Analysis 09-30-01

Share change since 07-01 Total Stocks: 50	Sector	Country	% Assets
Natl Semicon	Technology	U.S.	10.55
France OAT	N/A	N/A	5.41
Coherent	Health	U.S.	5.31
Wella	Staples	Germany	4.89
Eurotunnel (Paris)	Industrials	France	4.80
Sybase	Technology	U.S.	4.66
Inhale Theraptc Sys	Health	U.S.	4.22
Porsche Pfd	N/A	N/A	4.15
SanDisk	Technology	U.S.	3.97
Boots	Retail	United Kingdom	3.87
Toshiba	Technology	Japan	3.71
Six Continents	N/A	N/A	3.10
Reed Intl	Services	United Kingdom	2.98
Reckitt Benckiser	Staples	United Kingdom	2.94
⊕ Three–Five Sys	Technology	U.S.	2.94
Allied Domecq	Staples	United Kingdom	2.84
Circuit City Grp	Retail	U.S.	2.83
John Wiley & Sons A	Services	U.S.	2.73
Wolters Kluwer	Services	Netherlands	2.68
XM Satellite Radio Hldgs	Services	U.S.	2.67

Current Investment Style

Style: Value Blnd Growth; Size: Large Med Small

	Stock Port Avg	Rel MSCI EAFE Current	Rel MSCI EAFE Hist	Rel Cat
Price/Earnings Ratio	28.3	1.09	0.97	1.02
Price/Cash Flow	15.8	1.23	0.83	0.96
Price/Book Ratio	3.1	0.90	0.72	0.68
3 Yr Earnings Growth	19.0[1]	1.01	0.76	1.02
Med Mkt Cap $mil	2,851	0.1	0.1	0.12

[1]figure is based on 50% or less of stocks

Country Exposure 09-30-01	% assets
U.S.	53
United Kingdom	17
Japan	16
Germany	10
France	6

Hedging History: Frequent

Regional Exposure 09-30-01	% assets
Europe	39
Japan	16
Latin America	0
Pacific Rim	0
U.S.	53
Other	1

Special Securities % assets 09-30-01	
Restricted/Illiquid Secs	1
Emerging–Markets Secs	1
Options/Futures/Warrants	Yes

Composition % assets 09-30-01

Cash	3.5	Foreign Bonds	0.0
Stocks	92.7		
Bonds	0.3	Other	3.0
Other	3.5		

Sector Weightings	% of Stocks	Rel Cat	5–Year High	5–Year Low
Utilities	0.0	0.0	12	0
Energy	0.0	0.0	10	0
Financials	4.2	0.2	26	0
Industrials	8.0	0.7	40	0
Durables	3.9	1.0	23	0
Staples	14.1	1.8	25	1
Services	13.4	0.8	25	1
Retail	10.4	2.0	10	0
Health	14.8	1.1	42	4
Technology	31.4	2.1	45	3

Oppenheimer Main St Growth & Income A

Ticker	Load	NAV	Yield	Total Assets	Mstar Category
MSIGX	5.75%	$32.50	0.2%	$14,294.4 mil	Large Blend

Prospectus Objective: Growth and Income

Oppenheimer Main Street Growth & Income Fund seeks total return.

The fund invests in common stocks, preferreds, convertibles, bonds, debentures, and notes. The fund may invest without limit in foreign equity and debt securities. It may invest up to 25% of assets in nonconvertible debt securities rated below BBB.

This fund offers multiple shareclasses, all of which differ in fee structure and availability.

Past names: Main Street Income and Growth Fund and Oppenheimer Main Street Income & Growth Fund.

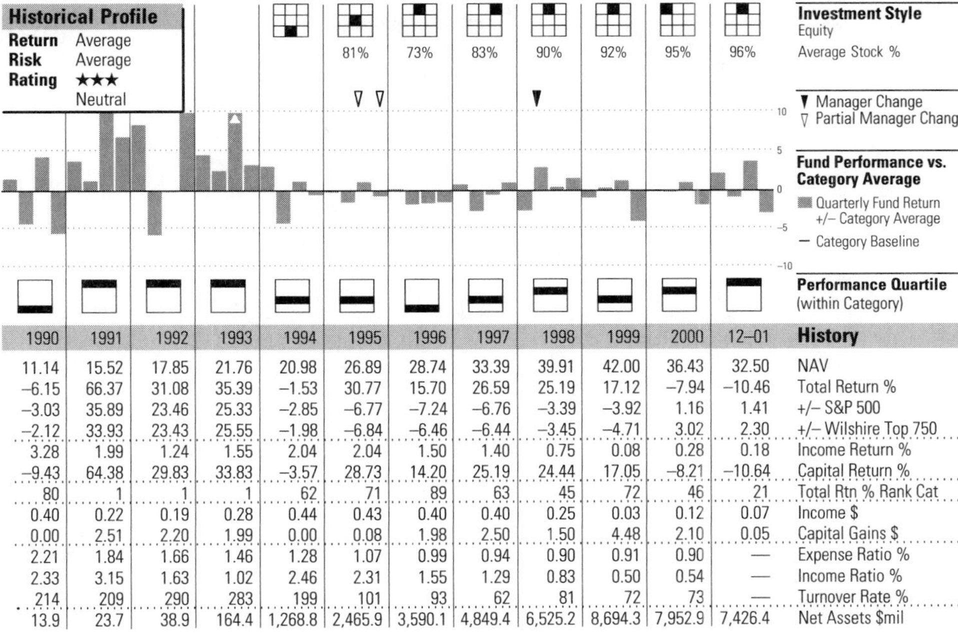

Portfolio Manager(s)

Charles E. Albers, CFA. Since 4-98. BA'62 Kenyon C.; MBA'67 Columbia U. Other funds currently managed: Oppenheimer Small Cap Value A, Oppenheimer Small Cap Value B, Oppenheimer Small Cap Value C.

Nikolaos Monoyios, CFA. Since 4-98. BA Princeton U.; MA'74 Princeton. Other funds currently managed: Oppenheimer Main St Growth & Income C, Oppenheimer Main St Growth & Income B, Oppenheimer Main St Growth & Income Y.

1990	1991	1992	1993	1994	1995	1996	1997	1998	1999	2000	12-01	History
11.14	15.52	17.85	21.76	20.98	26.89	28.74	33.39	39.91	42.00	36.43	32.50	NAV
–6.15	66.37	31.08	35.39	–1.53	30.77	15.70	26.59	25.19	17.12	–7.94	–10.46	Total Return %
–3.03	35.89	23.46	25.33	–2.85	–6.77	–7.24	–6.76	–3.39	–3.92	1.16	1.41	+/– S&P 500
–2.12	33.93	23.43	25.55	–1.98	–6.84	–6.46	–6.44	–3.45	–4.71	3.02	2.30	+/– Wilshire Top 750
3.28	1.99	1.24	1.55	2.04	2.04	1.50	1.40	0.75	0.08	0.28	0.18	Income Return %
–9.43	64.38	29.83	33.83	–3.57	28.73	14.20	25.19	24.44	17.05	–8.21	–10.64	Capital Return %
80	1	1	1	62	71	89	63	45	72	46	21	Total Rtn % Rank Cat
0.40	0.22	0.19	0.28	0.44	0.43	0.40	0.40	0.25	0.03	0.12	0.07	Income $
0.00	2.51	2.20	1.99	0.00	0.08	1.98	2.50	1.50	4.48	2.10	0.05	Capital Gains $
2.21	1.84	1.66	1.46	1.28	1.07	0.99	0.94	0.90	0.91	0.90	—	Expense Ratio %
2.33	3.15	1.63	1.02	2.46	2.31	1.55	1.29	0.83	0.50	0.54	—	Income Ratio %
214	209	290	283	199	101	93	62	81	72	73	—	Turnover Rate %
13.9	23.7	38.9	164.4	1,268.8	2,465.9	3,590.1	4,849.4	6,525.2	8,694.3	7,952.9	7,426.4	Net Assets $mil

Performance 12-31-01

	1st Qtr	2nd Qtr	3rd Qtr	4th Qtr	Total
1997	1.54	12.86	8.02	2.27	26.59
1998	10.01	4.79	–11.03	22.06	25.19
1999	2.73	7.08	–4.76	11.80	17.12
2000	4.00	–2.95	0.94	–9.64	–7.94
2001	–10.38	4.50	–11.49	8.01	–10.46

Trailing	Total Return%	+/– S&P 500	+/– Wil Top 750	% Rank All	% Rank Cat	Growth of $10,000
3 Mo	8.01	–2.68	–3.31	52	90	10,801
6 Mo	–4.40	1.16	1.39	58	21	9,560
1 Yr	–10.46	1.41	2.30	61	21	8,954
3 Yr Avg	–1.17	–0.14	0.66	78	49	9,654
5 Yr Avg	8.88	–1.82	–1.24	24	57	15,300
10 Yr Avg	15.00	2.07	2.55	5	4	40,451
15 Yr Avg	—	—	—	—	—	—

Tax Analysis	Tax-Adj Ret%	%Rank Cat	%Pretax Ret	%Rank Cat
3 Yr Avg	–2.35	55	—	—
5 Yr Avg	7.44	51	83.9	40
10 Yr Avg	12.88	4	85.9	29

Potential Capital Gain Exposure: 1% of assets

Risk Analysis

Time Period	Load-Adj Return %	Risk %Rank[1] All	Risk %Rank[1] Cat	Morningstar Return	Morningstar Risk	Morningstar Risk-Adj Rating
1 Yr	–15.61					
3 Yr	–3.10	61	24	–1.58[2]	0.86	★★
5 Yr	7.60	62	26	0.59[2]	0.85	★★★
10 Yr	14.32	70	48	1.62	0.90	★★★★

Average Historical Rating (131 months): 4.4★s

[1]1=low, 100=high [2] T-Bill return substituted for category avg.

Category Rating (3 Yr)

1 2 **3** 4 5

Worst Best

Return Average

Risk Below Avg

Other Measures	Standard Index S&P 500	Best Fit Index S&P 500
Alpha	–0.6	–0.6
Beta	0.92	0.92
R-Squared	94	94
Standard Deviation		15.95
Mean		–1.17
Sharpe Ratio		–0.44

Analysis by William Harding 10-26-01

Oppenheimer Main St. Growth & Income is a suitable core holding for most investors.

The stock market's fall this year has taken a toll on most mutual funds, and this offering is no exception—it lost 14% for the year to date ended Oct. 23, 2001. It's hard to get excited about a fund that's in the red, but at least it has held up well relative to the competition. The fund's year-to-date return outpaces 85% of its large-blend rivals and tops the S&P 500 by 250 basis points.

Managers Chuck Albers and Nikolaos Monoyios' quantitative models have helped the fund sidestep some landmines. Beginning in the middle of the year, the models favored more-defensive groups, such as financials and consumer staples, which haven't slid as far as other sectors of the market. Further, the models have signaled this year that mid-cap stocks are more attractive than mega-cap fare. The fund commits 75% of assets to large-cap names, but its median market capitalization is 30% lower than the category average. That has been a boon as smaller stocks have generally outperformed larger fare this year.

A common misconception with quant funds is that once the models are created, the managers have little work to do. Albers and Monoyios, however, continuously refine their process. This September, for example, they added factors to the models that judge the quality of a firm's earnings. Such tweaks have helped the pair add value over the years. In fact, since they came on board here in April 1998, the fund's return trounces that of Albers' former charge, Guardian Park Avenue, which still used the models he developed after he left.

The fund's large asset base and moderate approach—management rarely makes large sector bets and spreads its picks across 500 names—means it probably won't post huge gains as it did in the early 1990s. Nonetheless, the fund has performed fairly well compared with its peers.

Portfolio Analysis 09-30-01

Share change since 07-01 Total Stocks: 492	Sector	PE	YTD Ret%	% Assets
⊖ General Elec	Industrials	30.1	–15.00	3.17
Microsoft	Technology	57.6	52.78	2.68
⊕ ExxonMobil	Energy	15.3	–7.59	2.52
⊕ American Intl Grp	Financials	42.0	–19.20	2.06
Wal-Mart Stores	Retail	40.3	8.94	1.84
Merck	Health	19.1	–35.90	1.72
IBM	Technology	26.9	43.00	1.70
⊕ Johnson & Johnson	Health	16.6	14.01	1.67
⊖ Citigroup	Financials	20.0	0.03	1.63
⊕ Philip Morris	Staples	12.1	9.12	1.36
⊕ Bristol-Myers Squibb	Health	20.2	–26.00	1.31
⊕ Procter & Gamble	Staples	38.8	3.12	1.19
⊖ Coca-Cola	Staples	35.5	–21.40	1.17
⊕ Bank of America	Financials	16.7	42.73	1.16
⊕ Fannie Mae	Financials	16.2	–6.95	1.14
Royal Dutch Petro NY ADR	Energy	12.0	–17.10	1.12
⊖ Intel	Technology	73.1	4.89	1.05
⊖ AOL Time Warner	Technology	—	–7.76	1.05
Verizon Comms	Services	29.7	–2.52	1.01
Eli Lilly	Health	28.9	–14.40	1.00
⊖ Home Depot	Retail	42.9	12.07	0.99
Texaco	Energy	—	6.76	0.81
Amgen	Health	52.8	–11.70	0.77
Chevron	Energy	10.3	9.29	0.77
⊖ HCA – The Healthcare Company	Health	24.1	–12.20	0.76

Current Investment Style

Style: Value Blnd Growth; Size: Large Med Small

	Stock Port Avg	Relative S&P 500 Current	Relative S&P 500 Hist	Rel Cat
Price/Earnings Ratio	25.7	0.83	0.92	0.85
Price/Book Ratio	5.0	0.88	0.91	0.91
Price/Cash Flow	15.4	0.86	0.92	0.84
3 Yr Earnings Growth	17.6	1.20	1.05	0.98
1 Yr Earnings Est%	4.8	—	—	—
Med Mkt Cap $mil	35,342	0.6	0.7	0.68

Special Securities % assets 09-30-01	
Restricted/Illiquid Secs	0
Emerging-Markets Secs	Trace
Options/Futures/Warrants	Yes

Composition % assets 09-30-01	
Cash	5.0
Stocks*	95.0
Bonds	0.0
Other	0.0
*Foreign (% stocks)	4.0

Market Cap	
Giant	45.1
Large	35.8
Medium	16.3
Small	2.7
Micro	0.1

Sector Weightings	% of Stocks	Rel S&P	5-Year High	5-Year Low
Utilities	6.2	2.0	17	0
Energy	12.6	1.8	17	2
Financials	20.7	1.2	25	4
Industrials	9.1	0.8	19	5
Durables	1.6	1.0	8	0
Staples	9.3	1.2	13	0
Services	9.4	0.9	23	8
Retail	7.2	1.1	13	4
Health	13.4	0.9	19	6
Technology	10.6	0.6	34	11

Address:	P.O. Box 5270 Denver, CO 80217-5270 800-525-7048
Web Address:	www.oppenheimerfunds.com
Inception:	02-03-88
Advisor:	OppenheimerFunds
Subadvisor:	None
NTF Plans:	Datalynx , Fidelity Inst.

Minimum Purchase:	$1000	Add: $25	IRA: $250
Min Auto Inv Plan:	$25	Add: $25	
Sales Fees:	5.75%L, 0.25%S		
Management Fee:	.65% mx./.45% mn.		
Actual Fees:	Mgt: 0.45%	Dist: 0.25%	
Expense Projections:	3Yr: $848	5Yr: $1050	10Yr: $1630
Avg Brok Commission:	—	Income Distrib: Annually	
Total Cost (relative to category):		Average	

Oppenheimer Main St Small Cap A

Ticker	Load	NAV	Yield	Total Assets	Mstar Category
OPMSX	5.75%	$15.08	0.0%	$728.6 mil	Small Growth

Prospectus Objective: Growth

Oppenheimer Main St Small Cap Fund seeks capital appreciation.

The fund normally invests 65% of assets in common stocks and other equity securities of "growth" and /or "value" companies having a small market capitalization of up to $2.5 billion. It can invest in small, unseasoned companies (companies that have been in operation less than 10 years). However it does not intend to invest more than 20% of assets in such companies.

This fund offers multiple shareclasses, all of which differ in fee structure and availability.

Historical Profile
Return —
Risk —
Rating
Not Rated

Investment Style: Equity — Average Stock %: 97% (2000), 97% (12-01)

▼ Manager Change
▽ Partial Manager Change

Fund Performance vs. Category Average
■ Quarterly Fund Return +/– Category Average
— Category Baseline

Performance Quartile (within Category)

Portfolio Manager(s)

Charles E. Albers, CFA. Since 8-99. BA'62 Kenyon C.; MBA'67 Columbia U. Other funds currently managed: Oppenheimer Main St Growth & Income A, Oppenheimer Small Cap Value A, Oppenheimer Small Cap Value B.

Mark Zavanelli, CFA. Since 8-99. Other funds currently managed: Oppenheimer Small Cap Value A, Oppenheimer Small Cap Value B, Oppenheimer Small Cap Value C.

1990	1991	1992	1993	1994	1995	1996	1997	1998	1999	2000	12-01	History
—	—	—	—	—	—	—	—	—	12.84	13.36	15.08	NAV
—	—	—	—	—	—	—	—	—	28.64*	10.15	12.93	Total Return %
—	—	—	—	—	—	—	—	—	17.41*	19.26	24.80	+/– S&P 500
—	—	—	—	—	—	—	—	—	—	32.59	22.16	+/– Russ 2000 Grth
—	—	—	—	—	—	—	—	—	0.00	0.00	0.00	Income Return %
—	—	—	—	—	—	—	—	—	28.64	10.15	12.93	Capital Return %
—	—	—	—	—	—	—	—	—	—	19	6	Total Rtn % Rank Cat
—	—	—	—	—	—	—	—	—	0.00	0.00	0.00	Income $
—	—	—	—	—	—	—	—	—	0.02	0.79	0.01	Capital Gains $
—	—	—	—	—	—	—	—	—	—	1.50	—	Expense Ratio %
—	—	—	—	—	—	—	—	—	—	–0.82	—	Income Ratio %
—	—	—	—	—	—	—	—	—	—	—	—	Turnover Rate %
—	—	—	—	—	—	—	—	—	74.1	205.2	381.4	Net Assets $mil

Performance 12-31-01

	1st Qtr	2nd Qtr	3rd Qtr	4th Qtr	Total
1997	—	—	—	—	—
1998	—	—	—	—	—
1999	—	—	—	26.87	28.64*
2000	7.17	7.34	4.74	–8.57	10.15
2001	–3.29	16.25	–15.05	18.24	12.93

Trailing	Total Return%	+/– S&P 500	+/– Russ 2000 Grth	% Rank All	% Rank Cat	Growth of $10,000
3 Mo	18.24	7.55	–7.93	17	78	11,824
6 Mo	0.45	6.00	9.71	37	13	10,045
1 Yr	12.93	24.80	22.16	4	6	11,293
3 Yr Avg	—	—	—	—	—	—
5 Yr Avg	—	—	—	—	—	—
10 Yr Avg	—	—	—	—	—	—
15 Yr Avg	—	—	—	—	—	—

Tax Analysis	Tax-Adj Ret%	%Rank Cat	%Pretax Ret	%Rank Cat
3 Yr Avg	—	—	—	—
5 Yr Avg	—	—	—	—
10 Yr Avg	—	—	—	—

Potential Capital Gain Exposure: 10% of assets

Risk Analysis

Time Period	Load-Adj Return %	Risk %Rank¹ All	Risk %Rank¹ Cat	Morningstar Return	Morningstar Risk	Morningstar Risk-Adj Rating
1 Yr	6.43					
3 Yr	—	—	—	—	—	
5 Yr	—	—	—	—	—	
Incept	18.54	—	—	—	—	

Average Historical Rating —

¹1=low, 100=high

Category Rating (3 Yr)

Return
Risk

Other Measures	Standard Index S&P 500	Best Fit Index
Alpha	—	—
Beta	—	—
R-Squared	—	—
Standard Deviation		—
Mean		—
Sharpe Ratio		—

Portfolio Analysis 07-31-01

Share change since 06-01 Total Stocks: 644	Sector	PE	YTD Ret%	% Assets
Western Gas Resources	Energy	12.1	–3.42	0.44
Covance	Health	34.9	111.10	0.42
Velvet Exploration	Technology	12.8	—	0.41
Direct Focus	Services	23.3	109.10	0.38
Bei Tech	Technology	21.5	50.31	0.38
Pactiv	Industrials	18.3	43.43	0.38
Ryland Grp	Industrials	8.8	80.25	0.37
Tommy Hilfiger	Retail	9.4	40.12	0.37
Woodward Governor	Industrials	14.4	32.20	0.36
Global Payments	Services	—	—	0.36
Gentiva Health Svcs	Health	11.6	64.11	0.36
Reebok Intl	Staples	16.0	–3.07	0.35
Sylvan Learning Sys	Services	39.4	48.99	0.34
York Intl	Industrials	23.5	26.51	0.32
⊕ Ensign Res Svc Grp	Energy	8.1	—	0.32
MAF Bancorp	Financials	12.6	5.47	0.32
Galileo Intl	Services	—	4.62	0.32
O'Reilly Automotive	Retail	33.8	36.34	0.32
Cooper	Health	20.5	25.61	0.31
Natl Processing	Services	37.8	91.18	0.30
⊕ Beverly Enterprises (New)	Health	—	—	0.30
Sovereign Bancorp	Financials	76.5	52.19	0.30
⊖ Perrigo	Health	29.6	42.74	0.30
American Italian Pasta	Staples	29.0	56.75	0.30
Doral Finl	Financials	12.1	30.92	0.30

Current Investment Style

Style: Value Blnd Growth; Size: Large Med Small

	Stock Port Avg	Relative S&P 500 Current	Relative S&P 500 Hist	Rel Cat
Price/Earnings Ratio	22.6	0.73	—	0.70
Price/Book Ratio	3.5	0.61	—	0.72
Price/Cash Flow	16.0	0.89	—	0.73
3 Yr Earnings Growth	21.1	1.44	—	0.84
1 Yr Earnings Est%	17.0	—	—	2.18
Med Mkt Cap $mil	680	0.0	—	0.65

Analysis by William Harding 10-31-01

This fund may be a little wet behind the ears, but it deserves a serious look from investors.

Oppenheimer Main Street Small Cap is off to a strong start during tough market conditions. The fund's return since its August 1999 inception trounces the average small-blend and small-growth funds (the portfolio's valuation measures tend to toe the line between the two categories) and bests the Russell 2000 index by a huge margin. The fund has also performed well this year, gaining a modest 1.4% for the year through Oct. 29, 2001.

The fund's success this year, and since its inception, owes in large part to its quantitative models. Managers Chuck Albers and Mark Zavanelli employ top-down and bottom-up models to search for stocks that are attractive based on valuation and momentum factors. The top-down models worked well this year by favoring more-defensive issues in lieu of speculative technology and biotech stocks that have been hit especially hard.

The managers' attention to diversification across issues also deserves credit. The portfolio is spread out across more than 600 names, and the top holding accounts for less than 50 basis points. It thus takes more than a few missteps to significantly dent the fund's returns. And given the fund's strength relative to its rivals since its inception, the models appear to do a solid job of stock selection. The large number of holdings also helps temper liquidity risk.

The fund is still fairly young, and this is Zavanelli's first stint managing a fund, but it has good lineage. Albers has been fine-tuning his quantitative models for more than 30 years and earned respectable records at Guardian Park Avenue and Oppenheimer Main St Growth & Income. All told, this fund has the hallmarks of a solid choice for investors seeking a fairly moderate small-cap vehicle.

Special Securities % assets 07-31-01	
Restricted/Illiquid Secs	0
Emerging-Markets Secs	Trace
Options/Futures/Warrants	No

Composition % assets 07-31-01	
Cash	3.7
Stocks*	96.3
Bonds	0.0
Other	0.0
*Foreign (% stocks)	4.5

Market Cap	
Giant	0.0
Large	0.0
Medium	21.2
Small	69.2
Micro	9.7

Sector Weightings	% of Stocks	Rel S&P	5-Year High	5-Year Low
Utilities	0.5	0.2	—	—
Energy	7.6	1.1	—	—
Financials	19.7	1.1	—	—
Industrials	16.7	1.5	—	—
Durables	5.0	3.2	—	—
Staples	3.3	0.4	—	—
Services	18.5	1.7	—	—
Retail	6.3	0.9	—	—
Health	14.0	0.9	—	—
Technology	8.5	0.5	—	—

Address:	P.O. Box 5270 Denver, CO 80217-5270 212-323-0214 / 800-525-7048
Web Address:	www.oppenheimerfunds.com
*Inception:	08-02-99
Advisor:	OppenheimerFunds
Subadvisor:	None
NTF Plans:	Datalynx , Fidelity Inst.

Minimum Purchase:	$1000	Add: $25	IRA: $250
Min Auto Inv Plan:	$25	Add: $25	
Sales Fees:	5.75%L, 0.25%B		
Management Fee:	.75% mx./.60% mn.		
Actual Fees:	Mgt: 0.75%	Dist: 0.25%	
Expense Projections:	3Yr: $1036	5Yr: —	10Yr: —
Avg Brok Commission:	—	Income Distrib: Annually	
Total Cost (relative to category):	—		

Oppenheimer Quest Global Value A

Ticker	Load	NAV	Yield	Total Assets	Mstar Category
QVGLX	5.75%	$14.91	0.0%	$375.6 mil	World Stock

Prospectus Objective: World Stock

Oppenheimer Quest Global Value Fund - Class A seeks long-term capital appreciation.

The fund normally invests at least 65% of assets in equity securities issued in at least three countries. It may invest the balance of assets in domestic- or foreign-debt obligations with remaining maturities of one or more years. The fund may invest no more than 5% of assets in debt rated below investment-grade.

Class A shares have front loads; B shares have deferred loads, higher 12b-1 fees, and conversion features; C shares have level loads; N shares are available to retirement plans only.

Historical Profile

Return Above Avg
Risk Low
Rating ★★★★ Above Avg

Investment Style
Equity
Average Stock %: 90% 87% 92% 97% 95% 97%

▼ Manager Change
▽ Partial Manager Change

Fund Performance vs. Category Average
■ Quarterly Fund Return
+/– Category Average
— Category Baseline

Performance Quartile (within Category)

Portfolio Manager(s)

Richard J. Glasebrook II, CFA. Since 9-91. BA'70 Kenyon C.; MBA'72 Harvard U. Other funds currently managed: Oppenheimer Quest Opportunity Value A, Oppenheimer Quest Opportunity Value B, Oppenheimer Quest Opportunity Value C.

Elisa Mazen. Since 3-00. BA'83 Rutgers U. Other funds currently managed: Oppenheimer Quest Global Value B, Oppenheimer Quest Global Value C, Oppenheimer Quest Global Value N.

1990	1991	1992	1993	1994	1995	1996	1997	1998	1999	2000	12–01	History
10.48	12.13	11.45	13.74	12.98	14.30	16.06	17.62	18.52	18.55	17.35	14.91	NAV
–12.05*	15.84	1.79	25.42	3.41	20.74	16.29	14.61	12.31	24.99	2.22	–14.06	Total Return %
–5.63*	–14.65	–5.83	15.36	2.10	–16.79	–6.65	–18.74	–16.26	3.95	11.32	–2.19	+/– S&P 500
—	–2.45	7.01	2.91	–1.66	0.02	2.81	–1.15	–12.03	0.05	15.39	—	+/– MSCI World
0.98	0.08	0.81	0.24	0.00	1.01	0.04	0.16	0.49	1.18	0.00	0.00	Income Return %
–13.03	15.76	0.98	25.18	3.41	19.73	16.25	14.45	11.82	23.81	2.21	–14.06	Capital Return %
—	64	51	76	11	30	51	39	55	69	17	39	Total Rtn % Rank Cat
0.12	0.01	0.09	0.03	0.00	0.13	0.01	0.03	0.09	0.22	0.00	0.00	Income $
0.00	0.00	0.81	0.58	1.23	1.24	0.55	0.76	1.11	4.24	1.57	0.00	Capital Gains $
2.11	2.09	1.76	1.76	1.95	1.88	1.88	1.73	1.76	1.75	1.70	—	Expense Ratio %
0.92	–0.27	0.72	0.04	–0.23	0.77	0.19	0.17	0.09	–0.11	0.47	—	Income Ratio %
—	41	62	46	1	76	48	32	59	78	104	—	Turnover Rate %
58.0	140.7	108.7	142.8	147.1	161.2	194.5	266.4	299.3	358.5	300.0	241.0	Net Assets $mil

Performance 12-31-01

	1st Qtr	2nd Qtr	3rd Qtr	4th Qtr	Total
1997	2.37	11.86	4.89	–4.58	14.61
1998	12.32	1.72	–14.36	14.79	12.31
1999	3.46	7.88	–0.44	12.48	24.99
2000	–2.86	1.00	–2.64	7.00	2.22
2001	–9.11	1.08	–9.91	3.83	–14.06

Trailing	Total Return%	+/– S&P 500	+/– MSCI World	% Rank All	% Rank Cat	Growth of $10,000
3 Mo	3.83	–6.85	—	68	98	10,383
6 Mo	–6.46	–0.91	—	71	48	9,354
1 Yr	–14.06	–2.19	—	70	39	8,594
3 Yr Avg	3.16	4.19	—	52	35	10,979
5 Yr Avg	7.16	–3.54	—	34	37	14,132
10 Yr Avg	10.11	–2.82	—	32	27	26,197
15 Yr Avg	—	—	—	—	—	—

Tax Analysis	Tax-Adj Ret%	%Rank Cat	%Pretax Ret	%Rank Cat
3 Yr Avg	0.67	36	21.0	94
5 Yr Avg	5.12	39	71.5	46
10 Yr Avg	7.98	33	78.9	37

Potential Capital Gain Exposure: –2% of assets

Risk Analysis

Time Period	Load-Adj Return %	Risk %Rank[1] All	Risk %Rank[1] Cat	Morningstar Return	Morningstar Risk	Morningstar Risk-Adj Rating
1 Yr	–19.81					
3 Yr	1.15	43	8	–0.78[2]	0.56	★★★★
5 Yr	5.90	48	7	0.19[2]	0.55	★★★★
10 Yr	9.46	54	1	1.50[2]	0.53	★★★★

Average Historical Rating (103 months): 3.8★s

[1]1=low, 100=high [2] T-Bill return substituted for category avg.

Category Rating (3 Yr)

1 2 3 4 5
Worst Best

Return Average
Risk Low

Other Measures	Standard Index S&P 500	Best Fit Index MSCIACWrdFre
Alpha	1.6	4.1
Beta	0.56	0.62
R-Squared	59	64

Standard Deviation	12.76
Mean	3.16
Sharpe Ratio	–0.16

Portfolio Analysis 09-30-01

Share change since 07–01 Total Stocks: 105	Sector	Country	% Assets
Freddie Mac	Financials	U.S.	5.21
Federal Home Loan Bk 3.58%	N/A	N/A	4.83
Wells Fargo	Financials	U.S.	3.52
McDonald's	Services	U.S.	2.92
Boots	Retail	United Kingdom	2.68
Texaco	Energy	U.S.	2.45
Kroger	Retail	U.S.	2.26
WorldCom	Services	U.S.	2.23
Technip	Industrials	France	2.19
M & T Bk	Financials	U.S.	2.17
Sprint	Services	U.S.	2.09
Hong Kong Elec Hldgs	Utilities	Hong Kong	2.02
Great Universal Stores	Retail	United Kingdom	1.99
Citigroup	Financials	U.S.	1.94
Boeing	Industrials	U.S.	1.92
Lloyds TSB Grp	Financials	United Kingdom	1.85
SBC Comms	Services	U.S.	1.76
Tokyo Gas	Utilities	Japan	1.74
Household Intl	Financials	U.S.	1.70
☼ Novartis (Reg)	Health	Switzerland	1.69

Current Investment Style	Stock Port Avg	Rel MSCI EAFE Current	Rel MSCI EAFE Hist	Rel Cat
Price/Earnings Ratio	22.8	0.88	0.84	0.83
Price/Cash Flow	12.2	0.95	1.00	0.74
Price/Book Ratio	3.8	1.08	0.95	0.82
3 Yr Earnings Growth	15.5	0.83	1.02	0.83
Med Mkt Cap $mil	15,428	0.6	0.8	0.64

Style: Value Blnd Growth; Size: Large Med Small

Country Exposure 09-30-01	% assets
U.S.	51
Japan	12
United Kingdom	12
France	8
Canada	4

Hedging History: Rare

Regional Exposure 09-30-01	% assets
Europe	28
Japan	12
Latin America	0
Pacific Rim	5
U.S.	51
Other	4

Special Securities % assets 09-30-01	
Restricted/Illiquid Secs	0
Emerging–Markets Secs	6
Options/Futures/Warrants	No

Composition % assets 09-30-01			
Cash	0.0	Bonds	4.4
Stocks	95.5	Other	0.0

Sector Weightings	% of Stocks	Rel Cat	5-Year High	5-Year Low
Utilities	6.1	2.5	6	0
Energy	6.6	1.2	7	0
Financials	24.7	1.3	34	13
Industrials	14.2	1.3	39	13
Durables	5.7	1.4	10	2
Staples	4.7	0.6	13	0
Services	15.5	0.9	28	4
Retail	8.9	1.7	17	0
Health	9.8	0.8	12	3
Technology	3.9	0.3	13	2

Analysis by William Harding 12-07-01

This fund holds appeal for investors seeking a moderate take on global equities.

Oppenheimer Quest Global Value's measured approach has shown its virtues this year. Managers Dick Glasebrook and Elisa Mazen invest in well-managed firms with high returns on capital that they believe are trading at compelling valuations. This line of attack generally leads the fund to favor value-oriented stocks such as financials picks like Freddie Mac and M&T Bank, and to tread lightly in high-P/E tech and telecom names.

That value bias has been a hindrance over the last three months as growth stocks have rebounded swiftly. That said, it has generally helped during much of 2001. The fund has lost 13% for the year to date ended Dec. 6, compared with a 16.5% decline for the world-stock category average. In addition, the fund didn't fall nearly as far as its typical rival in the troubling first and third quarters of the year.

Glasebrook and Mazen let their bottom-up investment process guide the fund's regional and country allocation, though they have found greater opportunities in the U.S. (The fund's domestic stake has increased to 55% of assets from 50% at the start of the year.) In particular, domestic skipper Glasebrook scooped up shares of fallen tech angels earlier in the year, including EMC and Cisco, because they were trading at attractive discounts to their net present values (based on discounted cash flows). On the international front, Mazen, who runs the foreign portion, has liked consumer names like Great Universal Stores and spirit maker Pernod Ricard.

The fund's attention to risk control may hold it back at times, but its long-term record is appealing. Its return since inception bests its average peer's over the same period, and its risks are considerably lower. All told, this is a good pick for cautious world investors.

Address:	P.O. Box 5270 Denver, CO 80217–5270 212–323–0214 / 800–525–7048
Web Address:	www.oppenheimerfunds.com
*Inception:	07-02-90
Advisor:	OppenheimerFunds
Subadvisor:	OpCap Adv.
NTF Plans:	Datalynx , Fidelity Inst.

Minimum Purchase:	$1000	Add: $25	IRA: $250
Min Auto Inv Plan:	$1000	Add: $25	
Sales Fees:	5.75%L, 0.25%B, 0.25%S, 1.00%R		
Management Fee:	.75% mx./.65% mn., .25%A		
Actual Fees:	Mgt: 0.74%	Dist: 0.50%	
Expense Projections:	3Yr: $1097	5Yr: $1474	10Yr: $2529
Avg Brok Commission:	—	Income Distrib: Annually	

Total Cost (relative to category): —

Pax World Balanced

Ticker	Load	NAV	Yield	Total Assets	Mstar Category
PAXWX	12b–1 only	$19.91	2.4%	$1,162.0 mil	Domestic Hybrid

Prospectus Objective: Balanced

Pax World Balanced Fund primarily seeks income and capital preservation; long-term capital growth is secondary.

The fund normally invests approximately 60% of assets in common stocks, preferred stocks, and convertible securities; it may invest the balance in bonds and debentures. Management seeks companies that produce goods and services that improve the quality of life. Companies engaged in manufacturing defense or weapons-related products or those engaged in the liquor, tobacco, and gambling industries are excluded from the portfolio.

Prior to August 7, 2000, the fund was named Pax World Fund.

Historical Profile

Return Average
Risk Low
Rating ★★★★ Above Avg

Investment Style Equity — Average Stock %

▼ Manager Change
▽ Partial Manager Change

Fund Performance vs. Category Average
■ Quarterly Fund Return +/– Category Average
— Category Baseline

Performance Quartile (within Category)

Portfolio Manager(s)

Christopher H. Brown. Since 4-98. BA Boston U.; Robert P. Colin, CFA. Since 4-98. BA Rutgers U.; MBA New York U. Other fund currently managed: Pax World Growth.

1990	1991	1992	1993	1994	1995	1996	1997	1998	1999	2000	12–01	History
						60%	53%	58%	62%	63%	56%	Average Stock %
13.98	14.99	14.27	13.55	13.39	16.33	16.56	18.52	21.64	23.40	22.41	19.91	NAV
10.53	20.71	0.63	–1.06	2.65	29.19	10.36	25.12	24.63	17.23	5.66	–9.09	Total Return %
13.65	–9.77	–6.99	–11.11	1.33	–8.34	–12.59	–8.23	–3.95	–3.81	14.76	2.79	+/– S&P 500
1.57	4.71	–6.77	–10.80	5.57	10.72	6.74	15.43	15.95	18.06	–5.97	–17.51	+/– LB Aggregate
4.41	5.56	4.52	3.54	3.73	5.97	3.40	3.06	2.54	2.13	2.26	2.12	Income Return %
6.12	15.15	–3.89	–4.59	–1.08	23.22	6.96	22.06	22.08	15.10	3.41	–11.21	Capital Return %
1	73	95	100	8	15	78	7	6	14	27	82	Total Rtn % Rank Cat
0.61	0.77	0.67	0.50	0.50	0.79	0.55	0.50	0.47	0.46	0.53	0.47	Income $
0.84	1.04	0.13	0.07	0.00	0.14	0.89	1.65	0.88	1.41	1.75	0.00	Capital Gains $
1.20	1.20	1.00	0.94	0.98	0.97	0.89	0.91	0.95	0.89	0.96	—	Expense Ratio %
5.40	5.10	3.70	3.63	3.66	3.44	3.24	2.67	2.33	2.05	2.14	—	Income Ratio %
39	26	17	22	25	28	35	14	29	21	26	—	Turnover Rate %
119.9	270.5	468.6	464.4	388.3	477.0	518.5	628.8	837.6	1,070.1	1,228.1	1,162.0	Net Assets $mil

Performance 12-31-01

	1st Qtr	2nd Qtr	3rd Qtr	4th Qtr	Total
1997	1.21	11.34	5.57	5.17	25.12
1998	7.72	3.51	–2.12	14.19	24.63
1999	3.93	4.40	–0.86	8.98	17.23
2000	4.96	–3.30	5.68	–1.49	5.66
2001	–5.85	0.71	–7.81	3.99	–9.09

Trailing	Total Return%	+/– S&P 500	+/– LB Agg	% Rank All	% Rank Cat	Growth of $10,000
3 Mo	3.99	–6.69	3.96	68	80	10,399
6 Mo	–4.13	1.43	–8.78	57	84	9,587
1 Yr	–9.09	2.79	–17.51	59	82	9,091
3 Yr Avg	4.04	5.06	–2.24	40	28	11,261
5 Yr Avg	11.92	1.22	4.49	10	5	17,559
10 Yr Avg	9.85	–3.08	2.62	33	38	25,586
15 Yr Avg	11.14	–2.59	3.02	32	21	48,774

Tax Analysis	Tax-Adj Ret%	%Rank Cat	%Pretax Ret	%Rank Cat
3 Yr Avg	2.25	29	55.7	46
5 Yr Avg	9.74	4	81.7	11
10 Yr Avg	7.73	28	78.4	19

Potential Capital Gain Exposure: 11% of assets

Risk Analysis

Time Period	Load-Adj Return %	Risk %Rank[1] All	Risk %Rank[1] Cat	Morningstar Return	Morningstar Risk	Morningstar Risk-Adj Rating
1 Yr	–9.09					
3 Yr	4.04	36	28	–0.19[2]	0.45	★★★★
5 Yr	11.92	39	19	1.72[2]	0.43	★★★★
10 Yr	9.85	48	32	0.71	0.52	★★★

Average Historical Rating (193 months): 3.4★s

[1] 1=low, 100=high [2] T–Bill return substituted for category avg.

Category Rating (3 Yr)

1 2 3 4 5
Worst Best

Return Above Avg
Risk Below Avg

Other Measures	Standard Index S&P 500	Best Fit Index MSCIACWdFr
Alpha	1.4	3.2
Beta	0.42	0.46
R–Squared	65	68
Standard Deviation		9.18
Mean		4.04
Sharpe Ratio		–0.11

Portfolio Analysis 11-30-01

Total Stocks: 76 Share change since 10–01	Sector	PE Ratio	YTD Return %	% Net Assets
Amgen	Health	52.8	–11.70	2.29
Peoples Energy	Utilities	13.8	–10.70	1.98
Baxter Intl	Health	33.9	22.84	1.79
Vodafone Airtouch PLC ADR	Services	—	–27.70	1.64
American Intl Grp	Financials	42.0	–19.20	1.63
Johnson & Johnson	Health	16.6	14.01	1.49
USA Educ	Financials	68.9	24.74	1.46
Keyspan	Energy	20.2	–14.10	1.43
BellSouth	Services	24.9	–5.09	1.33
SBC Comms	Services	18.4	–16.00	1.29

Total Fixed-Income: 47	Date of Maturity	Amount $000	Value $000	% Net Assets
Federal Home Ln Bk N/A	01-23-06	15,000	15,469	1.33
Federal Home Loan Bk 5.905%	12-23-02	14,000	14,462	1.24
Federal Home Ln Bk N/A	05-16-05	10,000	10,722	0.92
Federal Home Ln Bk N/A	09-19-05	10,000	10,675	0.92
Masco 6.75%	03-15-06	10,000	10,446	0.90
FNMA 6.92%	11-08-05	10,000	10,428	0.90
TCI Comms 6.875%	02-15-06	9,960	10,366	0.89
FNMA 5.875%	02-06-06	10,000	10,325	0.89
Federal Home Ln Bk N/A	07-25-06	10,000	10,316	0.89
FNMA 7.4%	06-27-05	10,000	10,298	0.89

Equity Style
Style: Growth
Size: Large–Cap

	Portfolio Avg	Rel S&P
Price/Earnings Ratio	33.6	1.09
Price/Book Ratio	5.4	0.95
Price/Cash Flow	18.7	1.04
3 Yr Earnings Growth	13.0	0.89
1 Yr Earnings Est%	2.2	—
Debt % Total Cap	31.2	1.01
Med Mkt Cap $mil	16,473	0.27

Fixed-Income Style
Duration: Short
Quality: High

Avg Eff Duration[1]	3.1 Yrs
Avg Eff Maturity	—
Avg Credit Quality	AA
Avg Wtd Coupon	6.17%

[1] figure provided by fund as of 06-30-01

Special Securities % assets 11-30-01	
Restricted/Illiquid Secs	0
Emerging–Markets Secs	1
Options/Futures/Warrants	No

Composition % of assets 11-30-01	
Cash	12.1
Stocks*	56.0
Bonds	30.3
Other	1.6
*Foreign (% of stocks)	11.4

Market Cap	
Giant	31.9
Large	33.0
Medium	32.0
Small	3.0
Micro	0.0

Sector Weightings	% of Stocks	Rel S&P	5-Year High	5-Year Low
Utilities	8.6	2.7	49	4
Energy	7.2	1.0	18	0
Financials	7.1	0.4	8	0
Industrials	2.8	0.2	16	1
Durables	4.3	2.7	11	0
Staples	1.7	0.2	36	0
Services	27.3	2.5	32	0
Retail	8.0	1.2	23	6
Health	22.3	1.5	32	2
Technology	10.9	0.6	16	0

Analysis by William Samuel Rocco 10-18-01

If you're looking for a domestic-hybrid fund with a little extra oomph, this is still a good choice.

Pax World Balanced Fund continues to sport a relatively zesty asset allocation and stock mix. Managers Chris Brown and Bob Colin have gradually reduced their stock stake this year—it's now about 54% of assets—but the fund remains slightly overweighted in equities. Meanwhile, Brown and Colin are still growth fans—they've added to selected media and health-care stocks in recent months—and the fund's social criteria push them away from many cyclical and other value industries. Thus, the fund remains skewed toward growth sectors; its services and health weightings are currently about twice the group averages.

The fund's taste for growth stocks has backfired this year. Bonds have fared much better than equites, and value stocks have outperformed growth issues. Moreover, some of Brown and Colin's picks have really struggled. Vodafone is down 34%, while Medtronic is down 27%. Thus, while the typical domestic-hybrid offering has lost 7% for the year to date through Oct. 17, 2001, this fund has declined 11%.

That's better than most of the domestic-hybrid group's growth aficionados have done, though. Moreover, the fund prospered during Brown and Colin's first three years at the helm. It earned top-third returns in last year's sell-off, as many of its health and natural-gas stocks thrived. (A lot of natural-gas firms pass the fund's screens because they're much more environmentally friendly than other energy companies.) And the fund soared in the growth rallies of 1998 and 1999.

In light of this strong overall record, we think this offering is a first-rate option for those seeking a bolder domestic-hybrid offering.

Address:	224 State Street Portsmouth, NH 03801 800–767–1729 / 603–431–8022
Web Address:	www.paxfund.com
Inception:	11-30-71
Advisor:	Pax World Mgmt.
Subadvisor:	None
NTF Plans:	Fidelity , Fidelity Inst.

Minimum Purchase:	$250	Add: $50	IRA: $250
Min Auto Inv Plan:	$250	Add: $50	
Sales Fees:	0.25%B		
Management Fee:	.75% mx./.50% mn.		
Actual Fees:	Mgt: 0.51%	Dist: 0.19%	
Expense Projections:	3Yr: $297	5Yr: $515	10Yr: $1141
Avg Brok Commission:	—	Income Distrib: Semi–Ann.	
Total Cost (relative to category):	—		

Pilgrim GNMA Income A

Ticker	Load	NAV	Yield	SEC Yield	Total Assets	Mstar Category
LEXNX	4.75%	$8.64	5.8%	—	$619.4 mil	Intermediate Govt

Prospectus Objective: Government Mortgage

Pilgrim GNMA Income Fund seeks current income consistent with liquidity and safety of principal.

The fund normally invests at least 80% of assets in Government National Mortgage Association (GNMA) certificates. It may invest the balance of assets in other securities issued or guaranteed by the U.S. government. The fund may invest in debt securities of any maturity, although the portfolio manager expects to invest in long-term debt instruments.

The fund currently offers Class A, B, C, M, Q and T shares, all of which differ in fee structure and availability.

Prior to August 7, 2000, the fund was named Lexington GNMA Income.

Historical Profile

Return Average
Risk Below Avg
Rating ★★★★ Above Avg

Investment Style: Fixed-Income — Income Rtn %Rank Cat: 25, 6, 34, 26, 46, 21, 48, 15

Growth of Principal vs. Interest Rate Shifts
- Principal Value $000 (NAV with capital gains reinvested)
- Interest Rate % on 10 Yr Treasury
- ▼ Manager Change
- ▽ Partial Manager Change
- ► Mgr Unknown After
- ◄ Mgr Unknown Before

Performance Quartile (within Category)

Portfolio Manager(s)

Denis P. Jamison, CFA. Since 10-73. BA'69 City C. of New York. Other funds currently managed: Pilgrim GNMA Income B, Pilgrim GNMA Income C, Pilgrim GNMA Income M.

Roseann G. McCarthy. Since 5-99. BBA Hofstra U.; MBA Seton Hall U. Other funds currently managed: Pilgrim GNMA Income B, Pilgrim GNMA Income C, Pilgrim GNMA Income M.

History

1990	1991	1992	1993	1994	1995	1996	1997	1998	1999	2000	12-01	History
7.90	8.45	8.26	8.32	7.60	8.19	8.12	8.40	8.53	8.08	8.41	8.64	NAV
9.23	15.75	5.19	8.06	−2.08	15.92	5.64	10.20	7.52	0.58	10.36	8.85	Total Return %
0.27	−0.25	−2.22	−1.69	0.84	−2.55	2.02	0.52	−1.15	1.41	−1.27	0.42	+/– LB Aggregate
0.51	0.43	−2.04	−2.59	1.30	−2.42	2.87	0.63	−2.33	2.83	−2.88	1.61	+/– LB Government
8.76	8.39	7.44	7.37	6.79	7.96	6.46	6.59	5.92	6.03	6.06	6.09	Income Return %
0.47	7.36	−2.26	0.69	−8.87	7.95	−0.82	3.61	1.60	−5.45	4.29	2.76	Capital Return %
49	25	91	42	23	51	1	3	43	18	63	4	Total Rtn % Rank Cat
0.66	0.64	0.61	0.59	0.55	0.58	0.51	0.52	0.48	0.50	0.48	0.50	Income $
0.00	0.00	0.00	0.00	0.00	0.00	0.00	0.00	0.00	0.00	0.00	0.00	Capital Gains $
1.04	1.02	1.01	1.02	0.98	1.01	1.05	1.01	1.01	0.99	1.06	—	Expense Ratio %
8.43	7.97	7.31	6.96	6.90	7.10	6.56	6.28	5.85	6.04	6.54	—	Income Ratio %
113	139	180	52	37	31	129	134	54	25	65	—	Turnover Rate %
97.9	122.2	132.0	150.0	132.4	130.7	133.7	157.6	273.1	376.7	361.9	503.0	Net Assets $mil

Performance 12-31-01

	1st Qtr	2nd Qtr	3rd Qtr	4th Qtr	Total
1997	−0.41	3.72	4.14	2.44	10.20
1998	1.75	1.46	2.74	1.36	7.52
1999	0.86	−0.05	0.55	−0.77	0.58
2000	1.95	1.86	2.98	3.19	10.36
2001	4.28	0.61	4.72	−0.93	8.85

Trailing	Total Return%	+/– LB Agg	+/– LB Govt	% Rank All	% Rank Cat	Growth of $10,000
3 Mo	−0.93	−0.96	−0.34	92	84	9,907
6 Mo	3.75	−0.91	−1.10	11	72	10,375
1 Yr	8.85	0.42	1.61	7	4	10,885
3 Yr Avg	6.51	0.23	0.63	19	6	12,082
5 Yr Avg	7.44	0.01	0.04	33	2	14,316
10 Yr Avg	6.91	−0.32	−0.22	51	8	19,513
15 Yr Avg	7.83	−0.29	−0.05	54	8	30,975

Tax Analysis	Tax-Adj Ret%	%Rank Cat	%Pretax Ret	%Rank Cat
3 Yr Avg	4.07	5	62.6	10
5 Yr Avg	4.95	2	66.6	7
10 Yr Avg	4.29	8	62.0	15

Potential Capital Gain Exposure: 2% of assets

Risk Analysis

Time Period	Load-Adj Return %	Risk %Rank[1] All	Risk %Rank[1] Cat	Morningstar Return	Morningstar Risk	Morningstar Risk-Adj Rating
1 Yr	3.68					
3 Yr	4.79	10	39	−0.03[2]	0.59	★★★
5 Yr	6.40	12	31	0.31[2]	0.56	★★★★
10 Yr	6.39	13	21	0.46[2]	0.72	★★★★

Average Historical Rating (193 months): 3.2★s

[1]1=low, 100=high [2] T-Bill return substituted for category avg.

Category Rating (3 Yr)

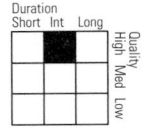

1 2 3 4 5 — Worst … Best (rating: 4)

Return High
Risk Average

Other Measures	Standard Index LB Agg	Best Fit Index LB Agg
Alpha	0.4	0.4
Beta	0.87	0.87
R-Squared	79	79

Standard Deviation	3.48
Mean	6.51
Sharpe Ratio	0.53

Analysis by Dan McNeela 12-12-01

Pilgrim GNMA Income Fund may have trouble living up to its glorious past.

It's time for lead manager Denis Jamison to take a bow. Earlier this year he reached his 20-year anniversary in managing this fund, and the results have been nothing short of spectacular. The fund's long-term returns rank near the top decile of the intermediate-term government category. Even among a more select group of GNMA-focused funds, its performance has been outstanding.

The single biggest factor in producing those results was Jamison's decision to invest heavily in multi-family GNMA mortgages. Such issues have lockout periods, which in most cases prevent borrowers from prepaying their mortgages for 10 years. That feature makes them much more valuable during periods of falling interest rates.

Multi-family GNMA mortgages have again played a starring role in 2001. The fund's 9% year-to-date return through Dec. 5 ranks in the top 5% of the category. It's true that the Fed has lowered interest rates throughout the year, which has encouraged many homeowners to refinance. But because the fund is largely shielded from such events, it has been able to more fully enjoy the benefits of falling rates.

Going forward, however, the outlook is not as rosy. Jamison is concerned that he may have to find a new game plan in future years, because he believes that the long-running trend of lower interest rates may be coming to an end. If rates creep back up, the fund's higher-than-average interest-rate sensitivity will turn against it. The fund's expense ratio of 1.06% is also a negative factor, as plenty of cheaper options are available.

We think investors should stay with this fund because of Jamison's experience and his proven track record. But those hoping this fund will dominate as it has would be wise to temper their expectations.

Address:	7337 E. Doubletree Ranch Rd Scottsdale, AZ 85258 800–334–3444 / 800–334–3444
Web Address:	www.pilgrimfunds.com
Inception:	10-10-73
Advisor:	ING Pilgrim Inv.s, LLC
Subadvisor:	None
NTF Plans:	Fidelity , Datalynx

Minimum Purchase:	$1000	Add: $100	IRA: $250
Min Auto Inv Plan:	$1000	Add: $100	
Sales Fees:	4.75%L, 0.25%S		
Management Fee:	.60% mx./.40% mn.		
Actual Fees:	Mgt: 0.54%	Dist: 0.25%	
Expense Projections:	3Yr: $829	5Yr: $1088	10Yr: $1828
Avg Brok Commission:	—	Income Distrib: Monthly	
Total Cost (relative to category):	Average		

Portfolio Analysis 11-30-01

Total Fixed-Income: 235	Date of Maturity	Amount $000	Value $000	% Net Assets
GNMA 6%	08-20-31	46,297	45,755	7.39
US Treasury Bond 6%	02-15-26	36,500	38,545	6.22
GNMA 6.5%	09-15-31	27,508	27,833	4.49
GNMA 6%	10-15-28	24,187	24,062	3.88
GNMA 7.5%	12-15-30	21,145	22,056	3.56
GNMA 7.45%	03-15-29	18,539	19,388	3.13
GNMA 6.5%	12-15-33	14,171	14,615	2.36
GNMA 6.84%	12-15-31	9,995	10,339	1.67
US Treasury Bond 5.5%	08-15-28	10,300	10,252	1.66
GNMA 7.625%	07-15-38	9,549	10,207	1.65
US Treasury Note 2.75%	10-31-03	10,000	10,003	1.62
GNMA 7.125%	09-15-39	9,053	9,617	1.55
GNMA 6.625%	12-15-39	9,278	9,574	1.55
GNMA 7%	09-15-31	8,170	8,465	1.37
GNMA 6.5%	07-20-29	8,187	8,330	1.34
GNMA 7.5%	05-15-31	7,466	7,814	1.26
FHLMC 6.5%	06-01-16	7,471	7,699	1.24
GNMA 8.5%	10-15-31	6,991	7,474	1.21
GNMA 6.5%	08-15-28	6,604	6,714	1.08
GNMA 6.6875%	07-15-40	6,273	6,447	1.04

Current Investment Style

Duration: Short Int Long — Quality: High Med Low

Avg Eff Duration[1]	4.6 Yrs
Avg Eff Maturity	—
Avg Credit Quality	AAA
Avg Wtd Coupon	6.86%
Avg Wtd Price	103.74% of par

[1]figure provided by fund

Special Securities % assets 11-30-01	
Restricted/Illiquid Secs	0
Exotic Mortgage–Backed	0
Emerging–Markets Secs	0
Options/Futures/Warrants	No

Coupon Range	% of Bonds	Rel Cat
0%	0.00	0.00
0% to 7%	55.18	0.97
7% to 8.5%	38.86	1.16
8.5% to 10%	4.35	1.07
More than 10%	1.61	0.41

1.00=Category Average

Credit Analysis % bonds 06-30-01			
US Govt	100	BB	0
AAA	0	B	0
AA	0	Below B	0
A	0	NR/NA	0
BBB	0		

Composition % assets 11-30-01			
Cash	5.8	Bonds	94.2
Stocks	0.0	Other	0.0

Sector Breakdown % bonds 11-30-01			
US Treasuries	8	CMOs	0
GNMA mtgs	82	ARMs	1
FNMA mtgs	2	Other	0
FHLMC mtgs	3		

PIMCO Foreign Bond Instl

Ticker	Load	NAV	Yield	SEC Yield	Total Assets	Mstar Category
PFORX	None	$10.46	4.8%	4.39%	$761.4 mil	International Bond

Prospectus Objective: World Bond

PIMCO Foreign Bond Fund seeks total return.

The fund normally invests at least 85% of assets in fixed-income securities issued in at least three foreign countries. A portion of these securities may be represented by options and futures contracts. The portfolio may include government and corporate debt, and mortgage- and asset-backed securities. The fund may invest up to 10% of assets in debt rated below BBB, but not lower than B. Portfolio duration varies from three to six years. "This fund is non-diversified."

The fund offers Class A, B, C, D, Administrative, and Institutional shares. Prior to Jan. 1, 1997 the fund was named PIMCO Foreign Fund.

Historical Profile
Return: High
Risk: Average
Rating: ★★★★★ Highest

Investment Style
Fixed-Income
Income Rtn %Rank Cat: 30, 93, 91, 57, 23, 32, 39, 26

Growth of Principal vs. Interest Rate Shifts
— Principal Value $000 (NAV with capital gains reinvested)
— Interest Rate % on 10 Yr Treasury
▼ Manager Change
▽ Partial Manager Change
► Mgr Unknown After
◄ Mgr Unknown Before

Performance Quartile (within Category)

Portfolio Manager(s)

Sudi Mariappa. Since 11-00. Other funds currently managed: PIMCO Global Bond Instl, PIMCO Global Bond Admin, PIMCO Foreign Bond Admin.

1990	1991	1992	1993	1994	1995	1996	1997	1998	1999	2000	12–01	History
—	—	10.12	10.78	9.41	10.43	10.40	10.53	10.57	9.97	10.10	10.46	NAV
—	—	1.23*	16.41	−7.30	21.23	18.91	9.61	10.03	1.57	9.86	8.96	Total Return %
—	—	—	6.66	−4.38	2.76	15.30	−0.08	1.36	2.40	−1.77	0.54	+/− LB Aggregate
—	—	—	1.29	−13.29	1.68	14.83	13.87	−7.76	6.64	12.49	12.51	+/− SB World Govt
—	—	0.34	5.32	5.62	5.44	4.37	5.31	6.26	5.91	6.23	5.09	Income Return %
—	—	0.90	11.09	−12.92	15.79	14.54	4.29	3.77	−4.34	3.63	3.87	Capital Return %
—	—	—	34	73	18	7	12	47	19	9	6	Total Rtn % Rank Cat
—	—	0.03	0.52	0.59	0.49	0.44	0.54	0.64	0.61	0.60	0.50	Income $
—	—	0.00	0.43	0.00	0.41	1.50	0.31	0.35	0.15	0.21	0.02	Capital Gains $
—	—	—	0.65	0.54	0.47	0.52	0.50	0.50	0.50	0.50	0.54	Expense Ratio %
—	—	—	4.97	5.12	6.44	5.83	7.88	6.32	5.39	6.20	5.78	Income Ratio %
—	—	—	—	260	299	1,234	984	280	376	330	417	Turnover Rate %
—	—	108.7	541.8	258.1	251.7	189.8	339.3	475.1	418.6	460.5	517.7	Net Assets $mil

Performance 12-31-01

	1st Qtr	2nd Qtr	3rd Qtr	4th Qtr	Total
1997	0.88	3.51	3.26	1.65	9.61
1998	3.68	1.72	3.11	1.19	10.03
1999	1.68	−1.50	−0.13	1.54	1.57
2000	2.08	1.73	2.07	3.65	9.86
2001	3.45	−0.41	4.00	1.70	8.96

Trailing	Total Return%	+/− LB Agg	+/− SB World	% Rank All	% Rank Cat	Growth of $10,000
3 Mo	1.70	1.66	5.67	72	10	10,170
6 Mo	5.77	1.11	2.29	2	14	10,577
1 Yr	8.96	0.54	12.51	7	6	10,896
3 Yr Avg	6.73	0.46	10.49	18	6	12,159
5 Yr Avg	7.96	0.53	7.85	29	7	14,664
10 Yr Avg	—	—	—	—	—	—
15 Yr Avg	—	—	—	—	—	—

Tax Analysis	Tax-Adj Ret%	%Rank Cat	%Pretax Ret	%Rank Cat
3 Yr Avg	3.89	4	57.7	16
5 Yr Avg	4.80	2	60.3	10
10 Yr Avg	—	—	—	—

Potential Capital Gain Exposure: 1% of assets

Risk Analysis

Time Period	Load-Adj Return %	Risk %Rank[1] All	Risk %Rank[1] Cat	Morningstar Return	Morningstar Risk	Morningstar Risk-Adj Rating
1 Yr	8.96					
3 Yr	6.73	9	12	0.39[2]	0.55	★★★★
5 Yr	7.96	17	21	0.68[2]	0.64	★★★★★
Incept	9.65	—	—	—	—	

Average Historical Rating (73 months): 5.0★s

[1] 1=low, 100=high [2] T-Bill return substituted for category avg.

Category Rating (3 Yr)

1 2 3 4 **5**
Worst — Best

Return: High
Risk: Below Avg

Other Measures	Standard Index LB Agg	Best Fit Index LB Agg
Alpha	0.8	0.8
Beta	0.76	0.76
R-Squared	57	57

Standard Deviation	3.54
Mean	6.73
Sharpe Ratio	0.58

Portfolio Analysis 11-30-01

Total Fixed-Income: 230	Date of Maturity	Value $000	% Net Assets
FNMA 5.5%		184,164	13.64
FNMA 6%		82,975	6.15
Republic of Italy 4.5%	05-01-09	61,727	4.57
Govt of France 0%	04-25-08	44,229	3.28
Govt of France 0%	10-25-09	39,784	2.95
Govt of Canada	09-01-05	35,540	2.63
US Treasury Bond 6.25%	08-15-23	34,293	2.54
Kingdom of Spain 5.15%	07-30-09	26,257	1.94
Republic of Germany 6.5%	07-04-27	26,228	1.94
Govt of Canada 7.25%	06-01-07	24,641	1.83
British Telecom FRN	12-15-03	20,598	1.53
Bear Stearns N/A	10-30-31	16,334	1.21
PRGT 144A 6.84%	03-15-07	13,308	0.99
Govt of France 5.5%	04-25-10	13,274	0.98
Republic of Germany 0%	01-04-31	13,168	0.98
US Treasury Note (Fut)	12-19-01	12,983	0.96
Municipal Bond Index (Fut)	12-21-01	12,909	0.96
Capital One Bk 4.415%	07-28-03	11,880	0.88
Kingdom of Belgium 7.5%	07-29-08	10,981	0.81
FNMA Debenture 5.375%	03-08-04	10,194	0.76

Current Investment Style

Duration: Short Int Long — Quality: High Med Low

Avg Eff Duration[1]	5.0 Yrs
Avg Eff Maturity	—
Avg Credit Quality	AA
Avg Wtd Coupon	4.69%
Avg Wtd Price	95.16% of par

[1] figure provided by fund

Special Securities 11-30-01	% assets
Restricted/Illiquid Secs	4
Exotic Mortgage–Backed	Trace
Emerging–Markets Secs	1
Options/Futures/Warrants	Yes

Country Exposure % assets

Not Available

Composition % assets 11-30-01

Cash	11.3	Bonds	73.9
Stocks	0.0	Other	14.7

Analysis by Gabriel Presler 12-14-01

A complicated but cautious approach helps PIMCO Foreign Bond keep up with the times.

The international bond category is known more for its variety than for strong performances. Managers in this group tend to make dramatic regional, currency, and sector commitments, and these funds range from aggressive, foreign-only offerings to staid funds investing primarily in U.S. Treasuries. This fund hugs the middle ground, sticking close to the JP Morgan Global Government Bond index and hedging its currency exposure into the dollar. But the managers here aren't idle: They make small but constant adjustments to the fund's country and duration exposure. They also use futures and then invest the cash backing those futures in shorter-term bonds, hoping to pick up an edge over time. All this activity has made for a turnover rate that is significantly higher than average.

It has also helped the fund outpace its rivals in 2001. The managers' unwillingness to take on a lot of interest-rate risk didn't affect its relative position much, despite falling interest rates, because many of its peers were similarly positioned. And the dollar has remained strong against the euro and yen, helping the fund outpace its unhedged rivals. This offering's gain of almost 10% for the year to date through Dec. 13, 2001, outpaces more than 90% of its peers.

The fund will struggle when the dollar lags, as it did in the third and fourth quarters of 1998. But over time, it has been a strong offering on an absolute basis. Its long-term record is one of the best in the category and has been achieved without undue volatility. That said, investors should be aware that this fund offers little currency diversification and won't help balance a U.S.-heavy portfolio as much as some of its rivals.

Address:	2187 Atlantic Street Stamford, CT 06902 800–927–4648
Web Address:	www.pimcofunds.com
*Inception:	12-03-92
Advisor:	Pacific Inv. Mgmt.
Subadvisor:	None
NTF Plans:	N/A

Minimum Purchase:	$5.00 mil	Add: None IRA: $5.00 mil
Min Auto Inv Plan:	—	Add: —
Sales Fees:	No–load	
Management Fee:	.25%, .25%A	
Actual Fees:	Mgt: 0.25%	Dist: —
Expense Projections:	3Yr: $16*	5Yr: $28* 10Yr: $63*
Avg Brok Commission:	—	Income Distrib: Monthly
Total Cost (relative to category):	—	

PIMCO High Yield A

Ticker	Load	NAV	Yield	SEC Yield	Total Assets	Mstar Category
PHDAX	4.50%	$9.36	8.4%	8.30%	$3,505.3 mil	High–Yield Bond

Prospectus Objective: Corp Bond—High Yield

PIMCO High Yield Fund seeks maximum total return consistent with preservation of capital.

The fund normally invests at least 65% of assets in a portfolio of fixed-income securities rated B or BB. It may invest the balance in investment-grade fixed-income securities. The portfolio may include government obligations, corporate debt, mortgage- and asset-backed securities, and bank instruments. It may also invest in dollar-denominated foreign securities. Portfolio duration varies between two and six years.

The fund offers Class A, B, C, D, Adminstrative, and Institutional Shares.

Historical Profile

Return	Below Avg
Risk	Above Avg
Rating	★★ Below Avg

Investment Style
Fixed-Income
Income Rtn %Rank Cat: 75 (1998), 81 (1999), 85 (2000), 91 (12-01)

Growth of Principal vs. Interest Rate Shifts
- Principal Value $000 (NAV with capital gains reinvested)
- Interest Rate % on 10 Yr Treasury
- ▼ Manager Change
- ▽ Partial Manager Change
- ► Mgr Unknown After
- ◄ Mgr Unknown Before

Performance Quartile (within Category)

Portfolio Manager(s)

Benjamin Trosky, CFA. Since 1-97. BBA'82 Drexel U. Other funds currently managed: PIMCO High Yield Instl, PIMCO High Yield Admin, PIMCO High Yield B.

History

	1990	1991	1992	1993	1994	1995	1996	1997	1998	1999	2000	12-01
NAV	—	—	—	—	—	—	—	11.54	11.31	10.68	9.71	9.36
Total Return %	—	—	—	—	—	—	—	12.67*	6.12	2.39	−0.84	4.59
+/– LB Aggregate	—	—	—	—	—	—	—	—	−2.56	3.22	−12.47	−3.83
+/– FB High–Yield	—	—	—	—	—	—	—	—	5.54	−0.89	4.37	−1.18
Income Return %	—	—	—	—	—	—	—	8.61	8.20	8.16	8.57	8.44
Capital Return %	—	—	—	—	—	—	—	4.06	−2.08	−5.78	−9.41	−3.85
Total Rtn % Rank Cat	—	—	—	—	—	—	—	—	4	75	11	33
Income $	—	—	—	—	—	—	—	0.91	0.91	0.89	0.88	0.79
Capital Gains $	—	—	—	—	—	—	—	0.09	0.00	0.00	0.00	0.00
Expense Ratio %	—	—	—	—	—	—	—	0.92	0.90	0.90	—	0.90
Income Ratio %	—	—	—	—	—	—	—	8.28	8.02	7.94	—	8.62
Turnover Rate %	—	—	—	—	—	—	—	67	37	39	39	53
Net Assets $mil	—	—	—	—	—	—	—	65.5	113.5	203.0	184.9	417.0

Performance 12-31-01

	1st Qtr	2nd Qtr	3rd Qtr	4th Qtr	Total
1997	—	4.80	4.17	2.11	—
1998	2.97	1.42	−1.86	3.54	6.12
1999	1.21	−0.38	−0.14	1.70	2.39
2000	−2.28	1.54	1.85	−1.87	−0.84
2001	3.90	−1.27	−1.77	3.79	4.59

Trailing	Total Return%	+/– LB Agg	+/– FB High–Yield	% Rank All	% Rank Cat	Growth of $10,000
3 Mo	3.79	3.75	—	68	88	10,379
6 Mo	1.95	−2.70	—	23	26	10,195
1 Yr	4.59	−3.83	—	26	33	10,459
3 Yr Avg	2.02	−4.25	—	62	21	10,619
5 Yr Avg	—	—	—	—	—	—
10 Yr Avg	—	—	—	—	—	—
15 Yr Avg	—	—	—	—	—	—

Tax Analysis	Tax-Adj Ret%	%Rank Cat	%Pretax Ret	%Rank Cat
3 Yr Avg	−1.26	15	—	—
5 Yr Avg	—	—	—	—
10 Yr Avg	—	—	—	—

Potential Capital Gain Exposure: −14% of assets

Risk Analysis

Time Period	Load-Adj Return %	Risk %Rank[1] All	Risk %Rank[1] Cat	Morningstar Return	Morningstar Risk	Morningstar Risk-Adj Rating
1 Yr	−1.04					
3 Yr	0.21	31	5	−0.91[2]	1.31	★★
5 Yr	—	—	—	—	—	
Incept	3.79	—	—	—	—	

Average Historical Rating (24 months): 2.1★s

[1]1=low, 100=high [2] T-Bill return substituted for category avg.

Category Rating (3 Yr)

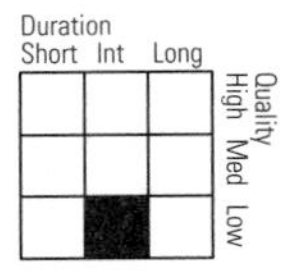

Return	Above Avg
Risk	Low

Other Measures	Standard Index LB Agg	Best Fit Index FB HY
Alpha	−3.2	−0.3
Beta	0.44	0.69
R–Squared	7	90
Standard Deviation		5.44
Mean		2.02
Sharpe Ratio		−0.62

Analysis by Eric Jacobson 12-12-01 This analysis was written for the Instl shares.

PIMCO High Yield could have done better, but not by much.

Comanager Ben Trosky has always run this fund with a careful eye on total return (rather than by chasing high yields). In that pursuit, he's been willing to buy lower-yielding high-quality bonds when they've offered compelling risk/reward tradeoffs, for example, and to forgo the fat gains garnered by loading up on hot individual issues or sectors.

Not surprisingly, then, the fund had a few stretches of weak performance over the course of the 1990s. The junk-bond market favored aggressive offerings during 1996 and 1999, for example, leaving this conservative portfolio behind. Owing to its higher-quality bent, meanwhile, the fund also proved more sensitive to rising rates a few times, as well.

The fund's recent success is therefore a bit of a moral victory. Beginning roughly 18 months ago, Trosky and his team began reassessing the valuations and risks of both the market and the portfolio. They took particular note of the tight yield spread between investment-grade BBB issues and their BB junk-bond cousins, and decided to upgrade the portfolio. The team also worried that the market's junkiest issues were too dangerous, but that there were good values in the single B arena. The net result is a portfolio with a distinct credit 'barbell' consisting of a hefty overweighting in investment-grade bonds, and a complete lack of bonds rated below B.

That stance proved invaluable both in 2000 and this year. The fund held few of the market's most troubled telecom and cyclical issues, and even among sectors that caused pain, had limited its stakes to modest levels.

Trosky believes the eventual recovery will be slow, so a big rebound is likely to leave this fund trailing. For investors who can live without the fattest yield, however, this fund would make a terrific choice.

Portfolio Analysis 11-30-01

Total Fixed-Income: 476	Date of Maturity	Amount $000	Value $000	% Net Assets
GNMA 6%		60,000	59,344	1.74
FNMA 6%		52,000	52,634	1.55
CSC Hldgs 7.625%	04-01-11	52,025	52,372	1.54
Fresenius Medical Care 9%	12-01-06	37	38,062	1.12
Rogers Cantel Mobile 9.375%	06-01-08	30,724	31,108	0.91
Fresenius Medical Care 7.875%	02-01-08	28	28,446	0.84
MGM Grand 6.95%	02-01-05	27,393	27,583	0.81
Harrahs Operating 7.875%	12-15-05	26,006	27,436	0.81
Gemstone Inv 144A 7.71%	10-31-04	27,350	27,295	0.80
CS First Boston 6.398%	10-25-39	25,000	26,039	0.76
Tritel PCS 10.375%	01-15-11	20,780	24,313	0.71
HEALTHSOUTH 144A 8.375%	10-01-11	21,800	23,108	0.68
Allied Waste 7.875%	01-01-09	23,310	22,960	0.67
British Sky Brdcstg 8.2%	07-15-09	21,949	22,738	0.67
Quebecor Prntg Cap 11.125%	07-15-11	20,900	22,677	0.67
Charter Comm 8.15%	03-31-08	23,000	22,563	0.66
Intl Game Tech 8.375%	05-15-09	20,976	22,392	0.66
Adelphia Comm 10.25%	11-01-06	21,443	22,247	0.65
EchoStar DBS 9.25%	02-01-06	20,827	21,660	0.64
Price Comm Wireless 9.125%	12-15-06	20,417	21,540	0.63

Current Investment Style

Duration: Short Int Long; Quality: High Med Low

Avg Eff Duration[1]	3.8 Yrs
Avg Eff Maturity	—
Avg Credit Quality	BB
Avg Wtd Coupon	8.08%
Avg Wtd Price	97.91% of par

[1]figure provided by fund

Special Securities % assets 11-30-01	
Restricted/Illiquid Secs	16
Exotic Mortgage–Backed	Trace
Emerging–Markets Secs	Trace
Options/Futures/Warrants	Yes

Credit Analysis % bonds 09-30-01			
US Govt	0	BB	44
AAA	11	B	22
AA	1	Below B	1
A	1	NR/NA	0
BBB	20		

Sector Breakdown % bonds 11-30-01			
US Treasuries	0	CMOs	0
GNMA mtgs	2	ARMs	0
FNMA mtgs	2	Other	96
FHLMC mtgs	0		

Coupon Range	% of Bonds	Rel Cat
0%, PIK	2.75	0.44
0% to 9%	61.86	2.04
9% to 12%	34.03	0.64
12% to 14%	1.08	0.12
More than 14%	0.28	0.20

1.00=Category Average

Composition % assets 11-30-01			
Cash	9.7	Bonds	75.4
Stocks	0.0	Other	15.0

Address:	2187 Atlantic Street Stamford, CT 06902 888–877–4626 / 888–877–4626
Web Address:	www.pimcofunds.com
*Inception:	01-13-97
Advisor:	Pacific Inv. Mgmt.
Subadvisor:	None
NTF Plans:	N/A

Minimum Purchase:	$2500	Add: $100 IRA: $1000
Min Auto Inv Plan:	$1000	Add: $50
Sales Fees:	4.50%L, 1.00%D, 0.25%S	
Management Fee:	.25%, .40%A	
Actual Fees:	Mgt: 0.25%	Dist: 0.25%
Expense Projections:	3Yr: $72*	5Yr: $93* 10Yr: $151*
Avg Brok Commission:	—	Income Distrib: Monthly
Total Cost (relative to category):	—	

PIMCO Low Duration Instl

Ticker	Load	NAV	Yield	SEC Yield	Total Assets	Mstar Category
PTLDX	None	$10.07	5.9%	4.39%	$5,667.8 mil	Short–Term Bond

Prospectus Objective: Corp Bond—General

PIMCO Low Duration Fund seeks total return.

The fund normally invests in a diversified portfolio of fixed-income securities with an average duration between one and three years. The advisor utilizes interest-rate anticipation, credit- and call-risk analysis, and foreign exchange-rate forecasting. It may invest up to 10% of assets in debt rated below investment-grade but rated B or higher. It may invest up to 20% of assets in foreign securities. The fund may invest all assets in derivative securities.

The fund offers Class A, B, C, Institutional, and Administrative shares.

Historical Profile

Return: Above Avg
Risk: Low
Rating: ★★★★★ Highest

Investment Style
Fixed-Income
Income Rtn %Rank Cat: 18, 9, 6, 20, 4, 11, 11, 13

Growth of Principal vs. Interest Rate Shifts
— Principal Value $000 (NAV with capital gains reinvested)
— Interest Rate % on 10 Yr Treasury
▼ Manager Change
▽ Partial Manager Change
► Mgr Unknown After
◄ Mgr Unknown Before

Performance Quartile (within Category)

Portfolio Manager(s)

William H. Gross, CFA. Since 5-87. BA'66 Duke U.; MBA'71 U. of California-Los Angeles. Other funds currently managed: Harbor Bond, PIMCO Total Return II Instl, PIMCO Low Duration II Instl.

History

1990	1991	1992	1993	1994	1995	1996	1997	1998	1999	2000	12-01	History
9.97	10.32	10.19	10.22	9.67	10.11	10.05	10.19	10.17	9.84	9.90	10.07	NAV
9.01	13.46	7.72	7.78	0.63	11.93	6.14	8.24	7.16	2.97	7.70	8.01	Total Return %
0.06	–2.54	0.32	–1.97	3.54	–6.54	2.53	–1.45	–1.51	3.80	–3.93	–0.41	+/– LB Aggregate
–0.77	1.79	1.46	2.37	0.13	1.97	0.89	1.59	0.19	0.01	–0.47	–0.52	+/– LB 1-3 Govt
9.14	8.88	7.69	6.50	6.15	7.02	6.68	6.50	6.73	6.30	7.03	6.15	Income Return %
–0.12	4.58	0.03	1.28	–5.53	4.91	–0.54	1.74	0.43	–3.33	0.67	1.86	Capital Return %
26	48	4	31	22	34	6	5	11	31	53	27	Total Rtn % Rank Cat
0.88	0.85	0.77	0.64	0.61	0.66	0.66	0.63	0.67	0.62	0.67	0.59	Income $
0.00	0.08	0.13	0.10	0.00	0.02	0.00	0.03	0.06	0.00	0.00	0.01	Capital Gains $
0.60	0.57	0.50	0.45	0.43	0.41	0.42	0.43	0.43	0.43	0.43	0.43	Expense Ratio %
8.83	8.97	8.08	7.21	6.05	6.46	6.88	6.46	6.39	6.36	6.40	6.86	Income Ratio %
162	44	37	68	43	77	209	240	309	245	82	348	Turnover Rate %
473.2	776.6	1,206.6	2,127.0	2,215.6	2,497.3	2,813.8	2,782.6	3,136.6	3,744.3	3,684.3	4,189.5	Net Assets $mil

Performance 12-31-01

	1st Qtr	2nd Qtr	3rd Qtr	4th Qtr	Total
1997	0.84	2.88	2.46	1.82	8.24
1998	1.55	1.44	2.93	1.06	7.16
1999	0.78	0.27	0.84	1.05	2.97
2000	1.35	1.75	2.25	2.14	7.70
2001	3.00	1.38	3.36	0.08	8.01

Trailing	Total Return%	+/– LB Agg	+/– LB 1–3 Yr Govt	% Rank All	% Rank Cat	Growth of $10,000
3 Mo	0.08	0.04	–0.70	78	55	10,008
6 Mo	3.44	–1.21	–0.87	13	51	10,344
1 Yr	8.01	–0.41	–0.52	9	27	10,801
3 Yr Avg	6.20	–0.07	–0.32	21	25	11,979
5 Yr Avg	6.80	–0.63	0.16	38	6	13,894
10 Yr Avg	6.79	–0.44	0.75	52	4	19,283
15 Yr Avg	—	—	—	—	—	—

Tax Analysis	Tax-Adj Ret%	%Rank Cat	%Pretax Ret	%Rank Cat
3 Yr Avg	3.58	48	57.7	74
5 Yr Avg	4.10	12	60.2	62
10 Yr Avg	4.05	4	59.7	31

Potential Capital Gain Exposure: 0% of assets

Risk Analysis

Time Period	Load-Adj Return %	Risk %Rank[1] All	Risk %Rank[1] Cat	Morningstar Return	Morningstar Risk	Morningstar Risk-Adj Rating
1 Yr	8.01					
3 Yr	6.20	3	45	0.27[2]	0.31	★★★★★
5 Yr	6.80	3	37	0.40[2]	0.30	★★★★★
10 Yr	6.79	3	23	0.58[2]	0.37	★★★★★

Average Historical Rating (140 months): 4.7★s

[1] 1=low, 100=high [2] T-Bill return substituted for category avg.

Category Rating (3 Yr)

1 2 3 4 5
Worst Best

Return: Above Avg
Risk: Average

Other Measures	Standard Index LB Agg	Best Fit Index LB Agg
Alpha	0.5	0.5
Beta	0.54	0.54
R-Squared	82	82

Standard Deviation	2.10
Mean	6.20
Sharpe Ratio	0.70

Portfolio Analysis 11-30-01

Total Fixed-Income: 1894	Date of Maturity	Amount $000	Value $000	% Net Assets
GNMA 7.5%		1,018,800	1,061,497	14.15
GNMA 8%		805,000	847,747	11.30
FNMA 8%		325,000	342,774	4.57
GNMA 7%		287,000	295,763	3.94
FNMA 5.5%		247,000	245,612	3.27
GNMA 6.5%		232,000	235,408	3.14
FNMA 6%	11-01-16	198,198	200,850	2.68
GNMA 7.5%	12-15-29	174,431	182,582	2.43
GNMA 8%	11-20-30	153,021	160,665	2.14
US Treasury Note 3.375%	01-15-07	114,673	116,267	1.55
US Treasury Note 3.625%	01-15-08	108,761	111,157	1.48
GMAC FRN	08-04-03	98,420	96,950	1.29
Wells Fargo 7%	02-25-16	84,662	87,474	1.17
GNMA 8.5%	12-15-30	80,610	85,647	1.14
British Telecommun 7.625%	12-15-05	73,400	79,537	1.06
US Treasury Note 3.875%	01-15-09	65,523	67,734	0.90
Merrill Lynch FRN	05-21-04	67,290	67,354	0.90
TTX 144A 7.82%	07-21-03	61,000	64,881	0.87
IMPAC Sec Assets Tr 8%	07-25-30	62,062	64,316	0.86
Cclt 4.62%	10-20-27	59,483	59,483	0.79

Current Investment Style

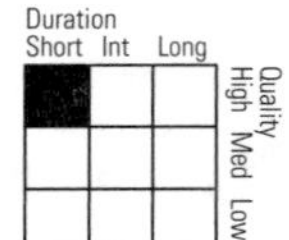

Avg Eff Duration[1]	1.5 Yrs
Avg Eff Maturity	2.2 Yrs
Avg Credit Quality	AA
Avg Wtd Coupon	6.89%
Avg Wtd Price	102.47% of par

[1] figure provided by fund

Special Securities % assets 11-30-01	
Restricted/Illiquid Secs	4
Exotic Mortgage–Backed	Trace
Emerging–Markets Secs	1
Options/Futures/Warrants	Yes

Credit Analysis % bonds 09-30-01

US Govt	0	BB	3
AAA	61	B	0
AA	4	Below B	1
A	18	NR/NA	0
BBB	13		

Coupon Range	% of Bonds	Rel Cat
0%	0.00	0.00
0% to 7%	35.95	0.56
7% to 8.5%	60.58	2.11
8.5% to 10%	3.35	0.82
More than 10%	0.14	0.08

1.00=Category Average

Composition % assets 11-30-01

Cash	9.2	Bonds	90.0
Stocks	0.0	Other	0.8

Analysis by Eric Jacobson 11-30-01

The value of PIMCO Low Duration Fund may depend a lot on who you are.

On its surface, this fund offers much appeal. It maintains very low interest-rate sensitivity, even when compared with most funds in the short-term bond category. Moreover, the fund benefits from the skills of legendary manager Bill Gross, and PIMCO's numerous sector specialists. And like many other PIMCO funds, this one uses various securities and trading tools to add increments of income and return, without taking on much added portfolio risk. For example, the portfolio invests heavily in the market for mortgage-backed securities, an activity that's driven by PIMCO's extensive analytical capabilities.

That mix has worked terrifically for the fund's institutional share class. With the exception of 2000, when the fund dipped down into the category's bottom half for the first time in years, it had a nearly unbroken record of top-half annual showings within the category. Matched up with the portfolio's extremely modest volatility, the fund's institutional shares' overall record looks excellent.

There are probably few starker illustrations, however, of how important expenses are in returns. The same fund's A share class charges 90 basis points, more than twice as much for the same services on an annual basis, and its record over the trailing three years is significantly more modest.

To be sure, one can argue that good management is worthy of high compensation, and retail share classes are clearly more expensive to operate than institutional classes with large investors. A 90-basis-point expense ratio is no bargain for any short-term bond fund, though, even one managed by Bill Gross. Investors who can't access this fund's institutional shares through a 401(k), or who can't meet its $5 million minimum investment, will probably prefer a less expensive option.

Address:	2187 Atlantic Street Stamford, CT 06902 800–927–4648
Web Address:	www.pimcofunds.com
Inception:	05-11-87
Advisor:	Pacific Inv. Mgmt.
Subadvisor:	None
NTF Plans:	N/A

Minimum Purchase:	$5.00 mil	Add: —	IRA: $5.00 mil
Min Auto Inv Plan:	—	Add: —	
Sales Fees:	No–load		
Management Fee:	.25%, .18%A		
Actual Fees:	Mgt: 0.25%	Dist: —	
Expense Projections:	3Yr: $14*	5Yr: $24*	10Yr: $54*
Avg Brok Commission:	—	Income Distrib: Monthly	
Total Cost (relative to category):	—		

PIMCO Total Return Instl

Ticker	Load	NAV	Yield	SEC Yield	Total Assets	Mstar Category
PTTRX	None	$10.46	5.5%	5.06%	$49,061.7 mil	Interm–Term Bond

Prospectus Objective: Corp Bond—General

PIMCO Total Return Fund - Institutional Shares seeks total return consistent with preservation of capital.

The fund invests at least 65% of assets in debt securities, including U.S. government securities, corporate bonds, and mortgage-related securities. It may invest up to 20% of assets in securities denominated in foreign currencies. The portfolio duration generally ranges from three to six years.

Institutional and Administrative shares are both designed for institutional investors; Administrative shares have shareholder service fees. Prior to March 31, 1992, the fund was named PIMIT Total Return Portfolio.

Historical Profile

Return High
Risk Average
Rating ★★★★★ Highest

Investment Style
Fixed-Income
Income Rtn %Rank Cat: 77, 21, 16, 36, 22, 36, 22, 42

Growth of Principal vs. Interest Rate Shifts
- Principal Value $000 (NAV with capital gains reinvested)
- Interest Rate % on 10 Yr Treasury
- ▼ Manager Change
- ▽ Partial Manager Change
- ► Mgr Unknown After
- ◄ Mgr Unknown Before

Performance Quartile (within Category)

Portfolio Manager(s)

William H. Gross, CFA. Since 5-87. BA'66 Duke U.; MBA'71 U. of California-Los Angeles. Other funds currently managed: Harbor Bond, PIMCO Total Return II Instl, PIMCO Low Duration II Instl.

1990	1991	1992	1993	1994	1995	1996	1997	1998	1999	2000	12-01	History
10.03	10.69	10.60	10.64	9.69	10.72	10.50	10.60	10.54	9.90	10.39	10.46	NAV
8.05	19.56	9.75	12.52	–3.58	19.79	4.69	10.17	9.77	–0.28	12.09	9.49	Total Return %
–0.91	3.55	2.34	2.77	–0.66	1.32	1.08	0.48	1.10	0.55	0.46	1.06	+/– LB Aggregate
–1.12	4.93	2.57	3.74	–1.65	4.48	0.64	2.30	1.36	–0.67	1.98	0.51	+/– LB Int Govt/Corp
8.85	9.46	7.58	6.89	5.53	7.54	6.65	6.48	6.29	5.94	6.89	5.88	Income Return %
–0.80	10.09	2.17	5.63	–9.10	12.25	–1.96	3.69	3.48	–6.22	5.20	3.61	Capital Return %
38	10	7	19	47	19	14	13	3	19	7	7	Total Rtn % Rank Cat
0.86	0.91	0.78	0.71	0.57	0.71	0.69	0.66	0.65	0.61	0.66	0.59	Income $
0.00	0.30	0.31	0.55	0.00	0.12	0.00	0.27	0.42	0.00	0.00	0.30	Capital Gains $
0.60	0.49	0.46	0.43	0.41	0.41	0.42	0.43	0.43	0.43	0.43	0.43	Expense Ratio %
8.60	9.10	8.18	7.07	6.27	6.72	6.85	6.60	6.06	5.91	6.25	6.57	Income Ratio %
110	99	110	90	177	98	221	173	206	154	223	450	Turnover Rate %
910.3	1,510.7	2,743.9	4,575.9	6,554.8	10,035.3	12,237.2	14,790.5	20,125.7	23,379.9	29,500.1	33,260.4	Net Assets $mil

Performance 12-31-01

	1st Qtr	2nd Qtr	3rd Qtr	4th Qtr	Total
1997	–0.62	4.06	3.56	2.86	10.17
1998	1.61	2.56	4.99	0.33	9.77
1999	–0.40	–0.75	0.82	0.06	–0.28
2000	2.21	1.82	2.87	4.69	12.09
2001	2.86	–0.27	6.49	0.22	9.49

Trailing	Total Return%	+/– LB Agg	+/– LB ITGvt/Corp	% Rank All	% Rank Cat	Growth of $10,000
3 Mo	0.22	0.19	0.13	77	27	10,022
6 Mo	6.73	2.07	2.03	2	1	10,673
1 Yr	9.49	1.06	0.51	6	7	10,949
3 Yr Avg	6.96	0.69	0.56	17	3	12,237
5 Yr Avg	8.15	0.73	1.06	28	2	14,799
10 Yr Avg	8.25	1.02	1.44	42	1	22,098
15 Yr Avg	—	—	—	—	—	—

Tax Analysis	Tax-Adj Ret%	%Rank Cat	%Pretax Ret	%Rank Cat
3 Yr Avg	4.12	4	59.1	18
5 Yr Avg	4.99	2	61.2	47
10 Yr Avg	5.04	2	61.1	30

Potential Capital Gain Exposure: 0% of assets

Risk Analysis

Time Period	Load-Adj Return %	Risk %Rank[1] All	Risk %Rank[1] Cat	Morningstar Return	Morningstar Risk	Morningstar Risk-Adj Rating
1 Yr	9.49					
3 Yr	6.96	12	22	0.43[2]	0.62	★★★★
5 Yr	8.15	16	19	0.72[2]	0.63	★★★★★
10 Yr	8.25	22	24	1.06[2]	0.85	★★★★★

Average Historical Rating (140 months): 4.7★s

[1]1=low, 100=high [2] T-Bill return substituted for category avg.

Category Rating (3 Yr)

1 2 3 4 5
Worst Best

Return High
Risk Below Avg

Other Measures	Standard Index LB Agg	Best Fit Index LB Agg
Alpha	0.5	0.5
Beta	1.12	1.12
R–Squared	95	95
Standard Deviation		4.08
Mean		6.96
Sharpe Ratio		0.58

Portfolio Analysis 11-30-01

Total Fixed-Income: 8417	Date of Maturity	Amount $000	Value $000	% Net Assets
GNMA 6.5%		10,628,500	10,784,272	16.59
US Treasury Bond (Fut)	12-23-01	2,273,000	2,381,678	3.66
FNMA 6%		1,505,348	1,521,066	2.34
GNMA 6%	11-15-29	1,424,784	1,416,787	2.18
GNMA 8%		1,281,000	1,349,014	2.08
US Treasury Note 5.625%	05-15-08	1,200,000	1,310,813	2.02
GNMA 7%		1,244,100	1,280,866	1.97
GNMA 7.5%	12-15-30	1,042,049	1,086,883	1.67
GNMA 7.5%		850,750	886,643	1.36
US Treasury Note 3.625%	01-15-08	865,090	884,150	1.36
GNMA 6%		801,500	795,737	1.22
FNMA 6%	12-01-16	696,247	705,598	1.09
US Treasury Bond 5.25%	11-15-28	636,480	613,557	0.94
US Treasury Note 3.875%	01-15-09	549,138	567,672	0.87
GNMA 6%	12-20-28	558,179	554,946	0.85
Bear Stearns N/A	10-30-31	506,900	517,493	0.80
GNMA 7.5%	12-15-29	430,897	451,063	0.69
US Treasury Note 4.625%	05-15-06	425,900	437,063	0.67
Morgan Stanley FRN	09-15-11	400,365	434,885	0.67
US Treasury Bond 12%	08-15-13	295,200	418,538	0.64

Current Investment Style

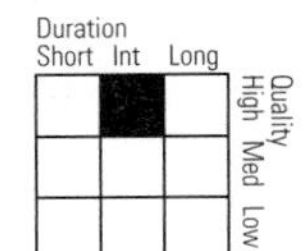

Avg Eff Duration[1]	4.4 Yrs
Avg Eff Maturity	—
Avg Credit Quality	AA
Avg Wtd Coupon	6.38%
Avg Wtd Price	102.21% of par

[1]figure provided by fund

Special Securities % assets 11-30-01	
Restricted/Illiquid Secs	5
Exotic Mortgage–Backed	2
Emerging–Markets Secs	1
Options/Futures/Warrants	Yes

Coupon Range	% of Bonds	Rel Cat
0%	0.45	0.36
0% to 7%	69.43	1.29
7% to 8.5%	27.25	0.78
8.5% to 10%	1.63	0.23
More than 10%	1.24	0.46

1.00=Category Average

Credit Analysis % bonds 09-30-01

US Govt	0	BB	2
AAA	65	B	0
AA	5	Below B	0
A	20	NR/NA	0
BBB	8		

Composition % assets 11-30-01

Cash	10.0	Bonds	84.2
Stocks	0.2	Other	5.5

Sector Breakdown % bonds 11-30-01

US Treasuries	8	CMOs	8
GNMA mtgs	33	ARMs	2
FNMA mtgs	6	Other	34
FHLMC mtgs	3		

Analysis by Eric Jacobson 12-31-01

Ho-hum. Another year, another victory.

Any buzzards circling this fund in mid-2001 probably should have known better. Skipper Bill Gross has a long history of turning lead into gold, and he's done it again. Gross has favored mortgages over the past couple of years, singing the praises of their high quality and income production. After several short-term rate cuts, however, refinancings rose, and mortgages lagged other sectors during the first half of 2001; the fund followed suit, badly trailing its peers. But while Gross held tight to the mortgage stake—a sector that continued to lag—he dramatically boosted the fund's sensitivity to interest rates at the end of June, in anticipation of falling rates. That move proved prescient, and the fund bested the Lehman Brothers Aggregate index by nearly 2 percentage points in the year's third quarter. As a result, the fund's 2001 return placed in the intermediate-term bond category's best decile.

The future should be equally interesting. After eschewing credit risk for a long time, Gross' distaste seems to be softening. He views 2002 as the year for 'spread' sectors, and he's been adding to the fund's stake in corporates and emerging-markets bonds (13% and 2%, respectively, at the end of November). He's even expressed a willingness to pick up high-yield issues when cheap. The fund has also been positioned to take advantage of falling rates, with a duration more than half a year longer than its bogy.

Based on its recent duration shifts and sector leanings, investors in this fund should clearly be prepared for a bit more volatility than usual. It's impossible to overstate how successful Gross has been in executing his bets over the years, though, a fact made clear by the fund's stellar relative performance rankings. The bottom line is that investors with strong confidence in the value of active management will find few comparable options.

Address:	2187 Atlantic Street Stamford, CT 06902 800–927–4648
Web Address:	www.pimcofunds.com
Inception:	05-11-87
Advisor:	Pacific Inv. Mgmt.
Subadvisor:	None
NTF Plans:	N/A

Minimum Purchase:	$5.00 mil	Add: —IRA: $5.00 mil
Min Auto Inv Plan:	—	Add: —
Sales Fees:	No–load	
Management Fee:	.25%, .18%A	
Actual Fees:	Mgt: 0.25%	Dist: —
Expense Projections:	3Yr: $14*	5Yr: $24* 10Yr: $54*
Avg Brok Commission:	—	Income Distrib: Monthly
Total Cost (relative to category):	—	

Pioneer A

Ticker	Load	NAV	Yield	Total Assets	Mstar Category
PIODX	5.75%	$38.91	0.4%	$7,212.4 mil	Large Value

Prospectus Objective: Growth and Income

Pioneer Fund seeks current income and capital appreciation.

The fund invests primarily in common stocks and other equities, including preferred stocks and securities convertible into common stocks. It may also invest in debt securities and cash equivalents. It usually invests a large portion of assets in securities that have paid dividends within the preceding 12 months, but it may hold some non-income-producing securities as well. The fund may also invest in foreign securities.

Class A shares have front loads; B shares have deferred loads, higher 12b-1 fees, and conversion features; C shares have level loads; Y shares are for institutional investors.

Historical Profile

Return	Above Avg
Risk	Below Avg
Rating	★★★★ Above Avg

Investment Style
Equity
Average Stock %: 97% 99% 99% 99% 99% 100% 100%

▼ Manager Change
▽ Partial Manager Change

Fund Performance vs. Category Average
■ Quarterly Fund Return +/– Category Average
— Category Baseline

Performance Quartile (within Category)

Portfolio Manager(s)

John A. Carey, CFA. Since 7-86. AM'72 Harvard U.; PhD'79 Harvard U. Other funds currently managed: Pioneer Equity-Income A, Pioneer Equity-Income B, Pioneer Equity-Income C.

1990	1991	1992	1993	1994	1995	1996	1997	1998	1999	2000	12–01	History
18.79	20.24	21.51	23.25	21.32	24.36	26.89	34.95	43.33	47.60	44.26	38.91	NAV
–10.49	22.75	13.80	14.23	–0.58	26.64	19.70	38.47	29.09	15.54	0.12	–11.04	Total Return %
–7.37	–7.73	6.18	4.17	–1.89	–10.89	–3.25	5.12	0.51	–5.50	9.22	0.84	+/– S&P 500
–6.82	4.60	4.73	–5.54	1.74	–13.39	–2.61	2.98	7.85	4.59	–2.19	–2.25	+/– Russ Top 200 Val
2.91	3.28	2.49	2.20	2.12	2.30	1.54	1.15	0.59	0.40	0.26	0.37	Income Return %
–13.40	19.47	11.31	12.02	–2.70	24.35	18.16	37.32	28.50	15.14	–0.14	–11.40	Capital Return %
78	79	19	45	51	88	56	1	3	17	78	82	Total Rtn % Rank Cat
0.67	0.61	0.50	0.47	0.49	0.49	0.37	0.31	0.20	0.17	0.12	0.16	Income $
1.39	2.04	0.99	0.83	1.30	2.09	1.82	1.89	1.49	2.22	3.24	0.30	Capital Gains $
0.78	0.87	0.98	0.95	0.94	0.94	0.99	1.03	1.08	1.09	1.11	—	Expense Ratio %
3.15	2.87	2.33	2.04	2.13	2.02	1.42	0.93	0.53	0.40	0.31	—	Income Ratio %
17	22	13	12	20	31	25	17	9	10	20	—	Turnover Rate %
1,390.0	1,615.0	1,786.0	2,042.0	2,010.9	2,446.2	2,895.9	3,991.7	5,395.2	6,637.3	6,643.6	6,146.5	Net Assets $mil

Performance 12-31-01

	1st Qtr	2nd Qtr	3rd Qtr	4th Qtr	Total
1997	2.44	18.25	9.48	4.41	38.47
1998	13.36	1.77	–8.54	22.33	29.09
1999	1.55	8.69	–5.95	11.30	15.54
2000	2.50	1.29	–1.03	–2.56	0.12
2001	–9.01	3.80	–13.95	9.46	–11.04

Trailing	Total Return%	+/– S&P 500	+/– Russ Top 200 Val	% Rank All	% Rank Cat	Growth of $10,000
3 Mo	9.46	–1.23	3.94	45	43	10,946
6 Mo	–5.81	–0.25	–0.03	67	76	9,419
1 Yr	–11.04	0.84	–2.25	62	82	8,896
3 Yr Avg	0.96	1.99	–0.20	68	62	10,291
5 Yr Avg	12.96	2.26	1.76	8	11	18,395
10 Yr Avg	13.68	0.75	–0.35	10	21	36,038
15 Yr Avg	12.76	–0.97	–0.74	19	28	60,597

Tax Analysis	Tax-Adj Ret%	%Rank Cat	%Pretax Ret	%Rank Cat
3 Yr Avg	–0.03	57	—	—
5 Yr Avg	11.75	5	90.6	7
10 Yr Avg	11.75	10	85.9	14

Potential Capital Gain Exposure: 31% of assets

Risk Analysis

Time Period	Load-Adj Return %	Risk %Rank[1] All	Risk %Rank[1] Cat	Morningstar Return	Morningstar Risk	Morningstar Risk-Adj Rating
1 Yr	–16.15					
3 Yr	–1.01	52	41	–1.19[2]	0.73	★★★
5 Yr	11.63	54	32	1.64[2]	0.74	★★★★
10 Yr	13.01	56	27	1.32	0.73	★★★★

Average Historical Rating (193 months): 3.0★s

[1] 1=low, 100=high [2] T-Bill return substituted for category avg.

Category Rating (3 Yr)

1 2 **3** 4 5
Worst Best

Return	Average
Risk	Average

Other Measures	Standard Index S&P 500	Best Fit Index S&P 500
Alpha	0.8	0.8
Beta	0.82	0.82
R-Squared	93	93

Standard Deviation	14.46
Mean	0.96
Sharpe Ratio	–0.32

Analysis by Kelli Stebel 08-29-01

Over the long haul, this fund remains a solid core holding.

Pioneer Fund isn't walking in any victory parades lately. While large-value funds have been among the better performers in this year's rough market, this offering has gotten whacked. For the year to date through August 28, the fund has dropped about 8%, placing in the large-value category's bottom quintile. And that's coming on the heels of a disappointing showing last year, too, when the fund gained a measly 12 basis points.

Longtime manager John Carey follows a growth-at-a-reasonable-price approach here, and that means the fund is a bit more aggressive than some of its peers. Indeed, the fund's price multiples are typically well-above its peer group's norm. That's been the main driver of the fund's relatively poor recent performance. Its stake in sagging health-care stocks such as Schering-Plough has been a particular culprit.

A buy-and-hold investor, Carey has been adding to the fund's health-care holdings on the dips, thinking that firms such as Merck and Pfizer have superior long-term earnings growth. Carey has also been picking up shares of PC makers like Dell and Sun Microsystems, mostly because he thinks they are solid growers trading at cheap valuations. That approach is quintessential Carey, as he has typically bought blue-chip companies when they are down on their luck.

In fact, Carey has shown a knack for buying out-of-favor firms poised for a rebound, which has led to superior returns over the years here. The fund's three-, five-, and 10-year annualized returns still land easily in its category's top half. So while this fund's penchant for pricey stocks won't please value purists, it can make a fine core holding.

Portfolio Analysis 11-30-01

Share change since 10–01 Total Stocks: 143	Sector	PE	YTD Ret%	% Assets
IBM	Technology	26.9	43.00	2.71
✲ ChevronTexaco	Energy	10.3	9.29	2.70
Schering–Plough	Health	22.2	–35.90	2.55
SBC Comms	Services	18.4	–16.00	2.35
Verizon Comms	Services	29.7	–2.52	2.19
ExxonMobil	Energy	15.3	–7.59	1.58
Johnson & Johnson	Health	16.6	14.01	1.55
BellSouth	Services	24.9	–5.09	1.54
Intel	Technology	73.1	4.89	1.48
Target	Retail	29.8	28.05	1.45
Microsoft	Technology	57.6	52.78	1.39
Bank of New York	Financials	21.9	–24.80	1.35
Merck	Health	19.1	–35.90	1.33
Walgreen	Retail	39.1	–19.20	1.32
Bristol–Myers Squibb	Health	20.2	–26.00	1.30
Texas Instruments	Technology	87.5	–40.70	1.29
McGraw–Hill	Services	24.7	5.70	1.27
State Street	Financials	28.6	–15.10	1.18
BP PLC ADR	Energy	14.4	–0.90	1.17
Chubb I	Financials	48.3	–18.60	1.15
John Wiley & Sons A	Services	23.3	8.01	1.14
Kohl's	Retail	54.2	15.48	1.13
Natl City	Financials	13.3	6.00	1.12
Colgate–Palmolive	Staples	31.1	–9.45	1.11
Marsh & McLennan	Financials	27.9	–6.30	1.09

Current Investment Style

Style: Value Blnd Growth; Size: Large Med Small

	Stock Port Avg	Relative S&P 500 Current	Relative S&P 500 Hist	Rel Cat
Price/Earnings Ratio	29.4	0.95	0.88	1.17
Price/Book Ratio	5.6	0.98	0.90	1.36
Price/Cash Flow	16.0	0.89	0.87	1.16
3 Yr Earnings Growth	15.4	1.06	0.94	1.04
1 Yr Earnings Est%	–7.3	4.12	—	2.21
Med Mkt Cap $mil	31,352	0.5	0.5	0.99

Special Securities % assets 11-30-01	
Restricted/Illiquid Secs	0
Emerging-Markets Secs	Trace
Options/Futures/Warrants	No

Composition % assets 11-30-01	
Cash	0.0
Stocks*	100.0
Bonds	0.0
Other	0.0
*Foreign (% stocks)	6.6

Market Cap	
Giant	39.2
Large	44.3
Medium	15.8
Small	0.7
Micro	0.0

Sector Weightings	% of Stocks	Rel S&P	5-Year High	5-Year Low
Utilities	2.0	0.6	8	1
Energy	7.9	1.1	13	2
Financials	13.9	0.8	24	10
Industrials	12.3	1.1	29	6
Durables	2.3	1.5	8	2
Staples	6.9	0.9	12	5
Services	18.0	1.7	23	15
Retail	7.2	1.1	10	5
Health	12.0	0.8	18	3
Technology	17.5	1.0	23	1

Address:	60 State Street Boston, MA 02109–1820 800–225–6292 / 617–742–7825
Web Address:	www.pioneerfunds.com
Inception:	02-10-28
Advisor:	Pioneer Inv. Mgmt.
Subadvisor:	None
NTF Plans:	Datalynx , Fidelity Inst.

Minimum Purchase:	$50	Add: $50	IRA: $50
Min Auto Inv Plan:	$50	Add: $50	
Sales Fees:	5.75%L, 0.25%S		
Management Fee:	.70%+(–).10%P		
Actual Fees:	Mgt: 0.67%	Dist: 0.25%	
Expense Projections:	3Yr: $905	5Yr: $1146	10Yr: $1838
Avg Brok Commission:	—	Income Distrib: Quarterly	
Total Cost (relative to category):		Average	

Pioneer Emerging Markets A

Ticker	Load	NAV	Yield	Total Assets	Mstar Category
PEMFX	5.75%	$10.24	0.0%	$180.6 mil	Div Emerging Mkts

Prospectus Objective: Diversified Emg Markets—Stock

Pioneer Emerging Markets Fund seeks long-term growth of capital.

The fund normally invests at least 65% of assets in emerging-markets securities. These include securities issued by companies domiciled in, or primarily doing business in, emerging-market countries, as well as debt issued by governments of these countries. The fund typically maintains investments in at least six emerging-markets.

Class A shares have front loads and lower 12b-1 fees; B shares have deferred loads and conversion features; C shares have level loads; Y shares are available to institutional investors.

Historical Profile

Return	Average
Risk	Above Avg
Rating	★★ Below Avg

Investment Style
Equity
Average Stock %

1995	1996	1997	1998	1999	2000	12-01
85%	86%	80%	84%	90%	97%	96%

▼ Manager Change
▽ Partial Manager Change

Fund Performance vs. Category Average
■ Quarterly Fund Return +/– Category Average
— Category Baseline

Performance Quartile (within Category)

Portfolio Manager(s)

Mark H. Madden, CFA. Since 6-94. BS'79 Trinity C.; MBA'83 U. of Virginia. Other funds currently managed: Pioneer Indo-Asia A, Pioneer Emerging Markets B, Pioneer Indo-Asia B.

1990	1991	1992	1993	1994	1995	1996	1997	1998	1999	2000	12-01	History
—	—	—	—	11.68	11.92	13.24	13.18	8.82	16.85	11.17	10.24	NAV
—	—	—	—	–5.48*	2.47	17.78	9.87	–32.14	91.04	–33.71	–8.33	Total Return %
—	—	—	—	–9.34*	–35.07	–5.16	–23.48	–60.71	70.01	–24.61	3.55	+/– S&P 500
—	—	—	—	—	13.22	13.64	24.99	–6.84	24.86	–3.71	—	+/– MSCI Emerging
—	—	—	—	0.45	0.00	0.00	0.00	0.00	0.00	0.00	0.00	Income Return %
—	—	—	—	–5.93	2.47	17.78	9.87	–32.14	91.04	–33.71	–8.33	Capital Return %
—	—	—	—	—	20	21	14	77	15	65	83	Total Rtn % Rank Cat
—	—	—	—	0.06	0.00	0.00	0.00	0.00	0.00	0.00	0.00	Income $
—	—	—	—	0.08	0.05	0.77	1.35	0.15	0.00	0.00	0.00	Capital Gains $
—	—	—	—	2.25	2.25	2.25	2.23	2.25	2.44	2.19	—	Expense Ratio %
—	—	—	—	1.85	0.27	–0.58	–0.40	0.08	–0.73	–1.10	—	Income Ratio %
—	—	—	—	259	247	143	140	195	180	139	—	Turnover Rate %
—	—	—	—	14.9	16.0	59.8	90.5	73.7	121.9	104.0	82.9	Net Assets $mil

Performance 12-31-01

	1st Qtr	2nd Qtr	3rd Qtr	4th Qtr	Total
1997	7.55	17.01	0.85	–13.43	9.87
1998	9.10	–23.48	–29.12	14.69	–32.14
1999	9.98	24.74	–10.33	55.30	91.04
2000	15.49	–17.32	–17.15	–16.20	–33.71
2001	–9.04	4.33	–15.75	14.67	–8.33

Trailing	Total Return%	+/– S&P 500	+/– MSCI Emerging	% Rank All	% Rank Cat	Growth of $10,000
3 Mo	14.67	3.98	—	25	97	11,467
6 Mo	–3.40	2.16	—	53	56	9,660
1 Yr	–8.33	3.55	—	57	83	9,167
3 Yr Avg	5.10	6.13	—	31	37	11,610
5 Yr Avg	–2.84	–13.54	—	96	22	8,656
10 Yr Avg	—	—	—	—	—	—
15 Yr Avg	—	—	—	—	—	—

Tax Analysis	Tax-Adj Ret%	%Rank Cat	%Pretax Ret	%Rank Cat
3 Yr Avg	5.10	35	100.0	1
5 Yr Avg	–3.55	27	—	—
10 Yr Avg	—	—	—	—

Potential Capital Gain Exposure: –53% of assets

Risk Analysis

Time Period	Load-Adj Return %	Risk %Rank[1] All	Risk %Rank[1] Cat	Morningstar Return	Morningstar Risk	Morningstar Risk-Adj Rating
1 Yr	–13.60					
3 Yr	3.05	89	83	–0.40[2]	1.28	★★★
5 Yr	–3.99	94	62	–1.66[2]	1.42	★★
Incept	–0.95	—	—	—	—	

Average Historical Rating (55 months): 2.2★s

[1] 1=low, 100=high [2] T-Bill return substituted for category avg.

Category Rating (3 Yr)

① ② ❸ ④ ⑤
Worst Best

Return Average
Risk Above Avg

Other Measures	Standard Index S&P 500	Best Fit Index Wil 4500
Alpha	10.5	4.8
Beta	1.17	0.95
R-Squared	40	72
Standard Deviation		34.47
Mean		5.10
Sharpe Ratio		0.01

Portfolio Analysis 11-30-01

Share change since 09-01 Total Stocks: 182	Sector	Country	% Assets
⊕ Anglogold	Industrials	South Africa	2.12
⊕ Korea Elec Pwr	Utilities	South Korea	2.00
⊕ Grupo Modelo Cl C	Staples	Mexico	2.00
⊖ SK Telecom ADR	Services	South Korea	1.47
⊕ Korea Telecom ADR	Services	South Korea	1.44
⊕ Kookmin Bk	Financials	South Korea	1.36
⊕ Telekom Malaysia	Services	Malaysia	1.29
⊕ Eletrobras Cl B ADR Pfd	Utilities	Brazil	1.27
⊕ Freeport-McMoRan Cop/Gold B	Industrials	U.S.	1.26
⊕ Lukoil ADR	Energy	Russia	1.20
⊕ Tubos de Acero de Mex ADR	Industrials	Mexico	1.14
☼ Korea Tobacco & Ginseng	Staples	South Korea	1.13
⊕ Cathay Life Ins	Financials	Taiwan	1.09
⊕ DBS Grp Hldgs	Financials	Singapore	1.09
Freeport-McMoRan 144A 8.25%	N/A	N/A	1.06
☼ Telefonos de Mexico ADR L	Services	Mexico	1.04
⊕ Teva Pharma Inds ADR	Health	Israel	1.03
⊖ China Telecom HK	Services	Hong Kong	1.03
☼ Petrobras ADR	Energy	Brazil	1.02
⊕ ITC GDR	Staples	India	0.98

Current Investment Style

Style: Value Blnd Growth; Size: Large Med Small

	Stock Port Avg	Rel MSCI EAFE Current	Rel MSCI EAFE Hist	Rel Cat
Price/Earnings Ratio	18.8	0.73	0.82	1.09
Price/Cash Flow	9.2	0.71	0.88	0.92
Price/Book Ratio	2.6	0.74	0.83	0.80
3 Yr Earnings Growth	17.7	0.95	—	0.68
Med Mkt Cap $mil	2,348	0.1	0.2	0.56

Country Exposure 11-30-01	% assets
South Korea	13
India	8
Taiwan	7
South Africa	7
Malaysia	7

Hedging History: Never

Regional Exposure 11-30-01	% assets
Europe	6
Africa/Mid East	11
Pacific/Asia	49
Latin America	15
Other	3

Special Securities % assets 11-30-01	
Restricted/Illiquid Secs	2
Emerging-Markets Secs	80
Options/Futures/Warrants	No

Composition % assets 11-30-01

Cash	0.0	Bonds	1.7
Stocks	94.0	Other	4.3

Sector Weightings	% of Stocks	Rel Cat	5-Year High	5-Year Low
Utilities	7.6	1.2	9	0
Energy	7.6	1.1	8	0
Financials	25.3	1.3	37	10
Industrials	18.9	1.1	22	2
Durables	4.7	1.5	14	1
Staples	10.4	1.4	11	1
Services	19.5	1.1	41	14
Retail	2.5	0.8	6	1
Health	2.0	0.5	6	0
Technology	1.4	0.1	37	1

Analysis by William Samuel Rocco 10-23-01

Pioneer Emerging Markets Fund has handled a mix of challenges well this year.

This fund lagged markedly in the first half of 2001. Manager Mark Madden has kept the fund light in Mexico all year—due to worries about the lofty value of its currency and other fears— which stung. His taste for telecom stocks also hurt, as did his emphasis on financials, consumer, and other domestic plays. And the fund's limited exposure to tech stocks smarted when those issue rallied in the spring. Thus, the fund fell 5% in the first six months of 2001, while its average peer dropped 1%.

But Madden's relatively defensive stance has helped since. The fund's small tech stake has been beneficial. Many of Madden's domestic plays have held up well in recent months, and a few of his telecom plays, including SK Telecom, have posted strong gains. Thus, the fund has lost significantly less than the average peer over the past three months and now leads 64% of its rivals for the year to date through Oct. 22, 2001.

Meanwhile, this fund recently absorbed Pioneer Indo-Asia. Such mergers can cause portfolio and tax problems, but this one should not cause either. Madden helped run that fund, and nearly all of its stocks were already in this portfolio. Further, he sold all the names in that fund that he didn't want to own here and raised cash to 65% of assets before the merger. And that fund had only $15 million in assets, while this one had $180 million. For all these reasons, plus the fact that both funds had similar and good tax positions, there shouldn't be tax problems for this fund's shareholders.

This fund is no parvenu. It has often outmaneuvered its peers in the past. Thus, while it has been more volatile than most of its rivals, it remains one of the best options in its wild group.

Address:	60 State Street Boston, MA 02109–1820 800–225–6292 / 617–742–7825
Web Address:	www.pioneerfunds.com
*Inception:	06-23-94
Advisor:	Pioneering Mgmt.
Subadvisor:	None
NTF Plans:	Fidelity Inst.

Minimum Purchase:	$1000	Add: $100 IRA: $250
Min Auto Inv Plan:	$1000	Add: $50
Sales Fees:	5.75%L, 0.25%S	
Management Fee:	1.3%	
Actual Fees:	Mgt: 1.25%	Dist: 0.25%
Expense Projections:	3Yr: $1244	5Yr: $1720 10Yr: $3030
Avg Brok Commission:	—	Income Distrib: Annually
Total Cost (relative to category):	—	

T. Rowe Price Balanced

Ticker	Load	NAV	Yield	Total Assets	Mstar Category
RPBAX	None	$17.49	2.9%	$1,726.8 mil	Domestic Hybrid

Prospectus Objective: Balanced

T. Rowe Price Balanced Fund seeks capital appreciation and current income consistent with preservation of capital.

The fund normally invests approximately 60% of assets in common stocks and maintains at least 25% of assets in senior fixed-income securities. The fund may invest up to 25% of assets in foreign securities, and up to 20% in mortgage-backed securities. It may also invest up to 10% of assets in debt rated below investment-grade.

Prior to Aug. 31, 1992, this fund was named USF&G Axe-Houghton Fund. On Aug. 31, 1992, the original T. Rowe Price Balanced Fund merged into this fund.

Historical Profile
Return Average
Risk Low
Rating ★★★ Neutral

Investment Style
Equity
Average Stock %: 53% 56% 59% 59% 61% 62% 60%

▼ Manager Change
▽ Partial Manager Change

Fund Performance vs. Category Average
■ Quarterly Fund Return +/– Category Average
— Category Baseline

Performance Quartile (within Category)

Portfolio Manager(s)

Richard T. Whitney, CFA et al.Since 3-91. MS'81 Rice U.; MBA'85 U. of Chicago.

1990	1991	1992	1993	1994	1995	1996	1997	1998	1999	2000	12-01	History
10.37	11.42	11.07	12.02	11.14	13.22	14.48	16.54	18.59	19.69	19.17	17.49	NAV
7.25	21.96	7.70	13.35	–2.05	24.88	14.57	18.97	15.97	10.27	2.09	–3.98	Total Return %
10.36	–8.52	0.09	3.29	–3.37	–12.65	–8.37	–14.38	–12.61	–10.77	11.19	7.90	+/– S&P 500
–1.71	5.96	0.30	3.60	0.86	6.41	10.96	9.28	7.30	11.10	–9.54	–12.40	+/– LB Aggregate
6.55	6.02	3.57	3.59	3.63	4.30	3.84	3.71	3.18	2.94	2.72	2.79	Income Return %
0.69	15.94	4.13	9.76	–5.68	20.58	10.73	15.25	12.79	7.33	–0.64	–6.76	Capital Return %
9	61	51	41	42	54	37	47	31	46	44	48	Total Rtn % Rank Cat
0.66	0.61	0.40	0.39	0.43	0.47	0.50	0.53	0.52	0.54	0.53	0.52	Income $
0.00	0.57	0.78	0.11	0.20	0.17	0.13	0.12	0.04	0.23	0.40	0.38	Capital Gains $
0.94	1.10	1.00	1.00	1.00	0.95	0.87	0.81	0.78	0.79	0.79	—	Expense Ratio %
6.82	5.61	3.85	3.45	3.72	3.87	3.70	3.36	3.04	2.80	2.75	—	Income Ratio %
127	240	58	9	33	13	22	16	13	21	17	—	Turnover Rate %
162.4	174.0	250.0	340.8	392.0	608.1	876.0	1,219.2	1,649.8	2,090.7	1,895.7	—	Net Assets $mil

Performance 12-31-01

	1st Qtr	2nd Qtr	3rd Qtr	4th Qtr	Total
1997	0.67	10.32	5.83	1.22	18.97
1998	8.59	1.80	–6.51	12.22	15.97
1999	1.93	3.57	–3.46	8.19	10.27
2000	2.54	–1.00	1.22	–0.66	2.09
2001	–5.05	2.60	–6.87	5.83	–3.98

Trailing	Total Return%	+/– S&P 500	+/– LB Agg	% Rank All	% Rank Cat	Growth of $10,000
3 Mo	5.83	–4.85	5.80	62	61	10,583
6 Mo	–1.44	4.12	–6.09	44	45	9,856
1 Yr	–3.98	7.90	–12.40	49	48	9,602
3 Yr Avg	2.63	3.65	–3.65	58	44	10,809
5 Yr Avg	8.32	–2.38	0.89	28	34	14,912
10 Yr Avg	9.82	–3.11	2.59	34	39	25,513
15 Yr Avg	10.10	–3.63	1.98	40	42	42,354

Tax Analysis	Tax-Adj Ret%	%Rank Cat	%Pretax Ret	%Rank Cat
3 Yr Avg	1.13	39	43.0	65
5 Yr Avg	6.80	21	81.7	11
10 Yr Avg	7.94	24	80.9	14

Potential Capital Gain Exposure: 22% of assets

Risk Analysis

Time Period	Load-Adj Return %	Risk %Rank[1] All	Risk %Rank[1] Cat	Morningstar Return	Morningstar Risk	Morningstar Risk-Adj Rating
1 Yr	–3.98					
3 Yr	2.63	37	36	–0.48[2]	0.49	★★★
5 Yr	8.32	41	33	0.77[2]	0.50	★★★
10 Yr	9.82	47	31	0.70	0.52	★★★

Average Historical Rating (193 months): 3.5★s

[1]1=low, 100=high [2] T-Bill return substituted for category avg.

Category Rating (3 Yr)

1 Worst, 2, 3, 4, 5 Best

Return Average
Risk Average

Other Measures	Standard Index S&P 500	Best Fit Index S&P 500
Alpha	0.5	0.5
Beta	0.52	0.52
R-Squared	95	95

Standard Deviation	9.23
Mean	2.63
Sharpe Ratio	–0.29

Portfolio Analysis 09-30-01

Total Stocks: 452 Share change since 06-01	Sector	PE Ratio	YTD Return %	% Net Assets
General Elec	Industrials	30.1	–15.00	1.68
Pfizer	Health	34.7	–12.40	1.54
⊕ ExxonMobil	Energy	15.3	–7.59	1.32
⊕ American Intl Grp	Financials	42.0	–19.20	1.18
⊕ Citigroup	Financials	20.0	0.03	1.13
SBC Comms	Services	18.4	–16.00	1.07
Verizon Comms	Services	29.7	–2.52	0.82
Wal-Mart Stores	Retail	40.3	8.94	0.82
⊕ PepsiCo	Staples	31.4	–0.54	0.78
Glaxo Wellcome PLC ADR	Health	24.2	–9.77	0.72

Total Fixed-Income: 591	Date of Maturity	Amount $000	Value $000	% Net Assets
US Treasury Bond 6.5%	11-15-26	41,750	47,538	2.80
US Treasury Note 5.88%	11-15-04	22,180	23,772	1.40
US Treasury Note 6.625%	05-15-07	18,000	20,265	1.20
US Treasury Note 6.25%	02-15-03	14,350	15,049	0.89
US Treasury Bond 7.25%	05-15-16	12,000	14,431	0.85
FNMA 5.8%	12-10-03	13,000	13,764	0.81
GNMA 6.5%	04-15-29	13,024	13,330	0.79
US Treasury Bond 7.125%	02-15-23	10,500	12,701	0.75
FNMA 5.75%	06-15-05	11,500	12,207	0.72
FNMA 7.13%	02-15-05	10,000	11,065	0.65

Equity Style
Style: Blend
Size: Large-Cap

Fixed-Income Style
Duration: —
Quality: —
NA

	Portfolio Avg	Rel S&P
Price/Earnings Ratio	27.9	0.90
Price/Book Ratio	5.2	0.91
Price/Cash Flow	15.7	0.87
3 Yr Earnings Growth	17.6	1.21
1 Yr Earnings Est%	–1.8	0.99
Debt % Total Cap	30.6	0.99
Med Mkt Cap $mil	42,071	0.69

Avg Eff Duration	—
Avg Eff Maturity	—
Avg Credit Quality	—
Avg Wtd Coupon	7.27%

Special Securities % assets 09-30-01	
Restricted/Illiquid Secs	1
Emerging-Markets Secs	1
Options/Futures/Warrants	Yes

Composition % of assets 09-30-01	
Cash	1.0
Stocks*	59.1
Bonds	39.6
Other	0.3
*Foreign (% of stocks)	21.1

Market Cap	
Giant	47.8
Large	36.6
Medium	14.5
Small	1.1
Micro	0.0

Sector Weightings	% of Stocks	Rel S&P	5-Year High	5-Year Low
Utilities	3.3	1.0	9	0
Energy	7.6	1.1	10	0
Financials	18.8	1.1	20	0
Industrials	13.5	1.2	21	4
Durables	4.0	2.6	8	0
Staples	5.9	0.7	30	5
Services	13.9	1.3	25	9
Retail	6.1	0.9	24	5
Health	14.7	1.0	31	5
Technology	12.1	0.7	20	0

Analysis by Catherine Hickey 10-02-01

This slow-going fund may not be exciting, but it gets the job done.

T. Rowe Price Balanced Fund looks a bit bolder than the typical domestic-hybrid fund these days. The stock portions of some hybrid funds has dipped to around 50% of assets as a result of depreciation and trimming by portfolio managers. However, this offering has steadfastly maintained its 60/40 split between equities and bonds. In addition, unlike some of its peers, this fund doesn't run with more than a minimal cash cushion.

However, although these traits may make the fund look somewhat aggressive, it's generally pretty staid. The fund aims for steadiness over flash, and holds a diversified stock portfolio with an emphasis on blue chips over deep-value or rapidly growing fare. Historically, the fund's performance swings have been fairly moderate, and it's a rare year when its annual return doesn't land in the hybrid group's top half.

The fund's moderate traits have held it in reasonably good stead in 2001. Its bond stake isn't huge, but bond manager Ned Notzon has kept the bulk of it in Treasuries, high-quality corporates and mortgages instead of riskier high-yield issues. Also, stock manager Rich Whitney has kept the fund light in technology relative to its peers, and that positioning has paid off well as tech has continued to falter. Thus, although the fund's stock stake is bigger than the norm at the moment, the fund's loss in 2001 is about average for the group.

This fund isn't likely to surprise you on the upside, but its relative performance is about as consistent as they come. It remains a solid core holding for cautious investors, and a viable way to get one-stop exposure to stocks and bonds.

Address:	100 E. Pratt Street Baltimore, MD 21202 800-638-5660 / 410-547-2308
Web Address:	www.troweprice.com
Inception:	05-01-38
Advisor:	T. Rowe Price Assoc.
Subadvisor:	None
NTF Plans:	N/A

Minimum Purchase:	$2500	Add: $100	IRA: $1000
Min Auto Inv Plan:	$100	Add: $100	
Sales Fees:	No-load		
Management Fee:	.15%+.48% mx./.30% mn.(G)		
Actual Fees:	Mgt: 0.47%	Dist: —	
Expense Projections:	3Yr: $252	5Yr: $439	10Yr: $978
Avg Brok Commission:	—	Income Distrib: Quarterly	
Total Cost (relative to category):	Low		

T. Rowe Price Blue Chip Growth

Ticker	Load	NAV	Yield	Total Assets	Mstar Category
TRBCX	None	$28.97	0.0%	$6,105.7 mil	Large Blend

Prospectus Objective: Growth

T. Rowe Price Blue Chip Growth Fund seeks long-term growth of capital; current income is secondary.

The fund normally invests at least 65% of assets in common stocks of mid- and large-capitalization, well-established blue-chip companies. Management looks for companies that have some or all of the following characteristics: rapid earnings growth relative to their peers, high profit margins, strong cash flows, relatively low debt, and high returns on equity with low dividend-payout ratios. The fund may invest up to 20% of assets in foreign securities.

The fund offers two different share classes, both of which differ in fee structure and availability.

Historical Profile
Return: Above Avg
Risk: Average
Rating: ★★★★ Above Avg

Investment Style
Equity
Average Stock %: 82% 89% 91% 95% 96% 98% 99%

▼ Manager Change
▽ Partial Manager Change

Fund Performance vs. Category Average
■ Quarterly Fund Return +/– Category Average
— Category Baseline

Performance Quartile (within Category)

Portfolio Manager(s)

Larry Puglia, CFA. Since 6-93. BA U. of Notre Dame; MBA U. of Virginia. Other funds currently managed: Vantagepoint Growth & Income, T. Rowe Price Blue Chip Growth Adv.

1990	1991	1992	1993	1994	1995	1996	1997	1998	1999	2000	12-01	History
—	—	—	11.24	11.11	15.09	19.06	24.17	30.60	36.34	33.85	28.97	NAV
—	—	—	14.32*	0.80	37.90	27.75	27.56	28.84	20.00	–2.53	–14.42	Total Return %
—	—	—	9.37*	–0.51	0.36	4.81	–5.79	0.27	–1.04	6.57	–2.54	+/– S&P 500
—	—	—	—	0.35	0.29	5.59	–5.47	0.21	–1.83	8.43	–1.65	+/– Wilshire Top 750
—	—	—	0.47	0.98	1.35	0.93	0.63	0.46	0.10	0.00	0.00	Income Return %
—	—	—	13.86	–0.18	36.55	26.83	26.93	28.38	19.90	–2.53	–14.42	Capital Return %
—	—	—	—	31	8	6	60	17	55	25	63	Total Rtn % Rank Cat
—	—	—	0.05	0.11	0.15	0.14	0.12	0.11	0.03	0.00	0.00	Income $
—	—	—	0.14	0.11	0.08	0.08	0.02	0.39	0.33	1.62	0.00	Capital Gains $
—	—	—	1.25	1.25	1.25	1.12	0.95	0.91	0.91	0.91	—	Expense Ratio %
—	—	—	0.80	1.05	1.27	0.87	0.86	0.43	0.10	–0.09	—	Income Ratio %
—	—	—	89	75	38	26	24	35	41	51	—	Turnover Rate %
—	—	—	24.5	39.0	146.5	539.7	2,344.6	4,330.1	6,709.0	7,836.7	—	Net Assets $mil

Performance 12-31-01

	1st Qtr	2nd Qtr	3rd Qtr	4th Qtr	Total
1997	0.16	15.30	7.27	2.98	27.56
1998	13.98	3.05	–12.05	24.71	28.84
1999	3.86	5.76	–6.25	16.53	20.00
2000	6.30	0.54	1.00	–9.71	–2.53
2001	–17.19	8.10	–15.84	13.61	–14.42

Trailing	Total Return%	+/– S&P 500	+/– Wil Top 750	% Rank All	% Rank Cat	Growth of $10,000
3 Mo	13.61	2.92	2.28	27	17	11,361
6 Mo	–4.39	1.17	1.40	58	21	9,561
1 Yr	–14.42	–2.54	–1.65	71	63	8,558
3 Yr Avg	0.03	1.06	1.86	73	36	10,010
5 Yr Avg	10.47	–0.23	0.35	16	28	16,452
10 Yr Avg	—	—	—	—	—	—
15 Yr Avg	—	—	—	—	—	—

Tax Analysis	Tax-Adj Ret%	%Rank Cat	%Pretax Ret	%Rank Cat
3 Yr Avg	–0.35	27	—	—
5 Yr Avg	10.07	14	96.2	5
10 Yr Avg	—	—	—	—

Potential Capital Gain Exposure: –18% of assets

Risk Analysis

Time Period	Load-Adj Return %	Risk %Rank[1] All	Risk %Rank[1] Cat	Morningstar Return	Morningstar Risk	Morningstar Risk-Adj Rating
1 Yr	–14.42					
3 Yr	0.03	70	63	–0.99[2]	0.97	★★★
5 Yr	10.47	69	59	1.32[2]	0.93	★★★★
Incept	15.23	—	—	—	—	

Average Historical Rating (67 months): 4.8★s

[1] 1=low, 100=high [2] T-Bill return substituted for category avg.

Category Rating (3 Yr)

1 2 **3** 4 5
Worst — Best

Return: Average
Risk: Average

Other Measures	Standard Index S&P 500	Best Fit Index S&P 500
Alpha	1.7	1.7
Beta	1.07	1.07
R-Squared	93	93

Standard Deviation	18.87
Mean	0.03
Sharpe Ratio	–0.30

Analysis by Catherine Hickey 11-30-01

This fund is still a worthy alternative to an S&P 500 index fund.

By the standards of its firm, T. Rowe Price Blue Chip Growth Fund is a bit of a swinger. The Baltimore-based fund company is known for funds that emphasize growth at a very reasonable price; the firm is so risk-conscious that few of its funds fall into the growth column of the style box.

However, this offering's manager, Larry Puglia, isn't afraid to pay up for financially healthy companies that have cornered strong market share in their industries. It's not that he has loaded up on the most aggressive growth stocks in the large-cap patch; in fact, to Puglia's credit, he avoided betting big on the tech sector. That said, Puglia made a misstep early this year by holding individual names such as Cisco Systems, Corning, Oracle, and Nortel Networks. Although he sold down some of them, they still took a toll, and the fund lost 4.7 percentage points more than its typical peer in the first quarter.

Strong picks such as Concord EFS and First Data have helped the fund outperform its typical peer since then, but its 15% year-to-date loss is still a bit worse than the large-blend norm. Still, such missteps have been relatively rare for Puglia. Even with its subpar showing this year, the fund's since-inception return handily beats its average peer's and the S&P 500 index's returns over the same period.

In addition to that strong performance, the fund's moderate expenses and the backing of T. Rowe's vast research staff add to its appeal. This offering won't appeal to conservative investors, but for those seeking a large-cap fund that offers growth exposure without throwing caution to the wind, it's well worth a look.

Portfolio Analysis 09-30-01

Share change since 06-01 Total Stocks: 120	Sector	PE	YTD Ret%	% Assets
⊕ Pfizer	Health	34.7	–12.40	4.65
⊕ Citigroup	Financials	20.0	0.03	3.90
⊕ Freddie Mac	Financials	14.0	–3.87	3.88
⊖ General Elec	Industrials	30.1	–15.00	3.34
⊕ UnitedHealth Grp	Financials	26.6	15.37	2.59
⊕ Microsoft	Technology	57.6	52.78	2.53
⊕ AOL Time Warner	Technology	—	–7.76	2.40
⊕ American Home Products	Health	—	–1.91	2.33
Johnson & Johnson	Health	16.6	14.01	2.31
Philip Morris	Staples	12.1	9.12	2.19
⊕ ExxonMobil	Energy	15.3	–7.59	2.16
⊖ First Data	Technology	38.1	49.08	1.99
⊕ American Intl Grp	Financials	42.0	–19.20	1.83
⊖ Fannie Mae	Financials	16.2	–6.95	1.77
⊕ PepsiCo	Staples	31.4	–0.54	1.74
Chevron	Energy	10.3	9.29	1.66
⊕ Sprint (PCS Group)	Services	—	19.43	1.66
⊕ Viacom Cl B	Services	—	—	1.65
⊕ Vodafone Airtouch PLC ADR	Services	—	–27.70	1.40
⊕ WellPoint Health Networks	Health	19.4	1.39	1.39
⊕ Concord EFS	Financials	86.3	49.21	1.36
⊖ Wal-Mart Stores	Retail	40.3	8.94	1.31
⊕ Coca-Cola	Staples	35.5	–21.40	1.28
⊖ Baxter Intl	Health	33.9	22.84	1.25
⊕ Tyco Intl	Industrials	27.1	6.23	1.24

Current Investment Style

Style: Value Blnd Growth; Size: Large Med Small

	Stock Port Avg	Relative S&P 500 Current	Relative S&P 500 Hist	Rel Cat
Price/Earnings Ratio	30.9	1.00	1.07	1.02
Price/Book Ratio	6.7	1.17	1.05	1.21
Price/Cash Flow	21.9	1.22	1.16	1.19
3 Yr Earnings Growth	19.6	1.34	1.15	1.10
1 Yr Earnings Est%	8.1	—	—	—
Med Mkt Cap $mil	55,398	0.9	0.8	1.06

Special Securities % assets 09-30-01	
Restricted/Illiquid Secs	0
Emerging-Markets Secs	0
Options/Futures/Warrants	No

Composition % assets 09-30-01	
Cash	0.3
Stocks*	99.7
Bonds	0.0
Other	0.0
*Foreign (% stocks)	3.0

Market Cap	
Giant	55.3
Large	38.9
Medium	5.9
Small	0.0
Micro	0.0

Sector Weightings	% of Stocks	Rel S&P	5-Year High	5-Year Low
Utilities	0.5	0.2	1	0
Energy	5.7	0.8	7	2
Financials	25.7	1.4	27	18
Industrials	6.0	0.5	23	6
Durables	0.2	0.1	7	0
Staples	5.7	0.7	11	2
Services	11.3	1.0	21	9
Retail	5.6	0.8	11	5
Health	23.9	1.6	24	8
Technology	15.3	0.8	34	4

Address:	100 E. Pratt Street Baltimore, MD 21202 800-638-5660
Web Address:	www.troweprice.com
*Inception:	06-30-93
Advisor:	T. Rowe Price Assoc.
Subadvisor:	None
NTF Plans:	N/A

Minimum Purchase:	$2500	Add: $100	IRA: $1000
Min Auto Inv Plan:	$100	Add: $100	
Sales Fees:	No-load		
Management Fee:	.30%+.33% mx./.30% mn.(G)		
Actual Fees:	Mgt: 0.62%	Dist: —	
Expense Projections:	3Yr: $290	5Yr: $504	10Yr: $1120
Avg Brok Commission:	—	Income Distrib: Annually	
Total Cost (relative to category):		Below Avg	

T. Rowe Price Developing Tech

Ticker	Load	NAV	Yield	Total Assets	Mstar Category
PRDTX	None	$4.95	0.0%	$18.9 mil	Spec Technology

Prospectus Objective: Specialty—Technology

T. Rowe Price Developing Technologies Fund seeks long-term capital growth.

The fund primarily invests at least 65% of total net assets in common stocks it expects to generate a majority of their revenues from the advancement and use of developing technologies. Its primary emphasis will be on emerging countries that are developing new technologies and services with attractive long-term growth prospectus. The fund may invest up to 30% of its total net assets in foreign stocks (established and developing countries), futures, and options.

Historical Profile
Return —
Risk —
Rating Not Rated

Investment Style
Equity
Average Stock %: 92% (2000), 94% (12-01)

▼ Manager Change
▽ Partial Manager Change

Fund Performance vs. Category Average
■ Quarterly Fund Return +/– Category Average
— Category Baseline

Performance Quartile (within Category)

Portfolio Manager(s)

Michael F. Sola. Since 8-00. BS William and Mary C.; MBA U. of Chicago.

History

1990	1991	1992	1993	1994	1995	1996	1997	1998	1999	2000	12-01	History
—	—	—	—	—	—	—	—	—	—	7.13	4.95	NAV
—	—	—	—	—	—	—	—	—	—	–27.89*	–30.58	Total Return %
—	—	—	—	—	—	—	—	—	—	–15.21*	–18.70	+/– S&P 500
—	—	—	—	—	—	—	—	—	—	—	–14.98	+/– PSE Tech 100
—	—	—	—	—	—	—	—	—	—	0.00	0.00	Income Return %
—	—	—	—	—	—	—	—	—	—	–27.89	–30.58	Capital Return %
—	—	—	—	—	—	—	—	—	—	—	27	Total Rtn % Rank Cat
—	—	—	—	—	—	—	—	—	—	0.00	0.00	Income $
—	—	—	—	—	—	—	—	—	—	0.09	0.00	Capital Gains $
—	—	—	—	—	—	—	—	—	—	—	—	Expense Ratio %
—	—	—	—	—	—	—	—	—	—	—	—	Income Ratio %
—	—	—	—	—	—	—	—	—	—	—	—	Turnover Rate %
—	—	—	—	—	—	—	—	—	—	18.2	—	Net Assets $mil

Performance 12-31-01

	1st Qtr	2nd Qtr	3rd Qtr	4th Qtr	Total
1997	—	—	—	—	—
1998	—	—	—	—	—
1999	—	—	—	—	—
2000	—	—	—	–27.24	–27.89*
2001	–41.94	31.16	–43.83	62.30	–30.58

Trailing	Total Return%	+/– S&P 500	+/– PSE Tech 100	% Rank All	% Rank Cat	Growth of $10,000
3 Mo	62.30	51.61	29.38	1	2	16,230
6 Mo	–8.84	–3.28	–3.56	81	11	9,116
1 Yr	–30.58	–18.70	–14.98	94	27	6,943
3 Yr Avg	—	—	—	—	—	—
5 Yr Avg	—	—	—	—	—	—
10 Yr Avg	—	—	—	—	—	—
15 Yr Avg	—	—	—	—	—	—

Tax Analysis	Tax-Adj Ret%	%Rank Cat	%Pretax Ret	%Rank Cat
3 Yr Avg	—	—	—	—
5 Yr Avg	—	—	—	—
10 Yr Avg	—	—	—	—

Potential Capital Gain Exposure: NMF

Risk Analysis

Time Period	Load-Adj Return %	Risk %Rank[1] All	Risk %Rank[1] Cat	Morningstar Return	Morningstar Risk	Morningstar Risk-Adj Rating
1 Yr	–30.58					
3 Yr	—	—	—	—	—	
5 Yr	—	—	—	—	—	
Incept	–40.46	—	—	—	—	

Average Historical Rating —

[1]1=low, 100=high

Category Rating (3 Yr)

Other Measures	Standard Index S&P 500	Best Fit Index
Alpha	—	—
Beta	—	—
R-Squared	—	—
Standard Deviation		—
Mean		—
Sharpe Ratio		—

Return
Risk

Portfolio Analysis 09-30-01

Share chng since 06-01 Total Stocks: 44	Subsector	PE	YTD Ret%	% Assets
⊕ VeriSign	Technology	—	–48.70	9.51
NetIQ	Technology	—	–59.60	8.07
⊕ Electronic Arts	Software	90.8	40.65	5.51
⊕ Maxim Integrated Products	Semiconductors	68.2	9.82	4.45
⊕ Cabot Microelect	Industrials	—	52.59	4.11
Lattice Semicon	Semiconductors	—	11.95	2.77
⊖ Bisys Grp	Services	42.7	22.76	2.63
Analog Devices	Periph/Hardware	47.7	–13.20	2.32
⊕ Applied Micro Circuits	Technology	—	–84.90	2.23
⊕ Internet Sec Sys	Technology	—	–59.10	2.19
Cisco Sys	Networking	—	–52.60	2.16
☼ Flextronics Intl	Technology	—	–15.80	2.11
⊕ Precise Software Solutions	Technology	—	–16.50	2.06
Qualcomm	Telecom	—	–38.50	2.02
⊕ Veritas Software	Software	—	–48.70	1.83
Cognex	Software	46.6	15.75	1.81
⊕ Openwave Sys	Technology	—	–79.50	1.81
⊕ Siebel Sys	Software	54.9	–58.60	1.75
⊕ Wind River Sys	Software	—	–47.50	1.70
⊕ Informatica	Technology	—	–63.30	1.70
⊖ Micrel	Technology	84.6	–22.10	1.70
⊕ Xilinx	Semiconductors	—	–15.30	1.67
⊕ Altera	Semiconductors	44.2	–19.30	1.63
⊕ Adobe Sys	Software	37.4	–46.50	1.53
⊕ Mercury Interactive	Software	70.8	–62.30	1.35

Current Investment Style

Style: Value Blnd Growth; Size: Large Med Small

	Stock Port Avg	Relative S&P 500 Current	Relative S&P 500 Hist	Rel Cat
Price/Earnings Ratio	52.4[1]	1.69	—	1.14
Price/Book Ratio	4.8	0.84	—	0.77
Price/Cash Flow	31.9	1.77	—	1.23
3 Yr Earnings Growth	—	—	—	—
1 Yr Earnings Est%	–47.5[1]	26.86	—	2.86
Med Mkt Cap $mil	4,316	0.1	—	0.27

[1]figure is based on 50% or less of stocks

Special Securities % assets 09-30-01	
Restricted/Illiquid Secs	0
Emerging-Markets Secs	1
Options/Futures/Warrants	No

Composition % assets 09-30-01	
Cash	3.3
Stocks*	96.7
Bonds	0.0
Other	0.0
*Foreign (% stocks)	2.0

Market Cap	
Giant	2.5
Large	18.2
Medium	60.0
Small	19.0
Micro	0.4

Subsector Weightings	% of Stocks	Rel Cat
Computers	0.0	0.0
Semiconductors	12.9	1.2
Semi Equipment	2.1	0.5
Networking	3.6	1.0
Periph/Hardware	2.6	1.7
Software	17.5	1.3
Computer Svs	0.0	0.0
Telecom	3.5	0.4
Health Care	0.0	0.0
Other	57.9	1.6

Analysis by Christine Benz 09-12-01

T. Rowe Price Developing Technologies Fund has a few notable drawbacks, but we think it's a reasonable way to bet on the resurgence in technology stocks.

If you think all T. Rowe Price funds are mild-mannered and risk-averse, think again. As if investing a substantial share of its assets in smaller-cap technology firms wasn't enough of a recipe for volatility, this fund also builds fairly sizable top positions. Its top-two holdings at the end of June, for example, soaked up nearly 15% of assets.

In addition to being far too volatile for all but a small piece of an aggressive investor's portfolio, the fund also has a lot of overlap with other T. Rowe Price funds—New Horizons and Science & Technology, in particular. That makes this fund redundant for investors in either of those two offerings. It also raises the question of whether manager Mike Sola might confront the same liquidity issues that face those two, much larger funds. For example, although this small fund owns only a tiny percentage of the shares of Electronic Arts, its two siblings own about 6% of the video-game maker.

Despite these caveats, we've been impressed with this fund's ability to get while the getting's good. Although it was launched at an extremely inauspicious time, it has managed to lose less than 83% of its peers since its start a year ago. Its strong relative showing doesn't owe to any particular defensive prowess, but rather to the fund's explosive returns on those few days when tech stocks have performed well. In April 2001, for example, the fund gained nearly 33% (amid overall strength for small caps), versus a 20% return for the typical technology fund. That bodes well for management's ability to deliver the goods when tech stocks finally snap back. In all, we think this is an intriguing choice for investors looking to bet a small portion of their portfolios on a beaten-down sector.

Address:	100 E. Pratt Street Baltimore, MD 21202 800–638–5660 / 410–547–2308
Web Address:	www.troweprice.com
*Inception:	08-31-00
Advisor:	T. Rowe Price Assoc.
Subadvisor:	None
NTF Plans:	N/A

Minimum Purchase:	$2500	Add: $100	IRA: $1000
Min Auto Inv Plan:	$50	Add: $50	
Sales Fees:	No-load, 1.00%R within 12 months		
Management Fee:	.60%+.33% mx./.30% mn.(G)		
Actual Fees:	Mgt: 0.92%	Dist: —	
Expense Projections:	3Yr: $477	5Yr: —	10Yr: —
Avg Brok Commission:	—	Income Distrib: Annually	
Total Cost (relative to category):	—		

T. Rowe Price Dividend Growth

Ticker	Load	NAV	Yield	Total Assets	Mstar Category
PRDGX	None	$20.79	1.3%	$647.2 mil	Large Value

Prospectus Objective: Growth and Income

T. Rowe Price Dividend Growth Fund seeks income and capital appreciation.

The fund normally invests at least 65% of assets in dividend-paying common stocks that demonstrate increasing dividend payments and long-term capital growth. The advisor seeks issuers with a record of, or potential for, above-average earnings and dividend growth, competitive dividend yields, sound balance sheets and solid cash flows, a leading market position, and attractive valuations. The fund may invest up to 25% of assets in foreign securities.

Historical Profile

Return	Average
Risk	Below Avg
Rating	★★★ Neutral

Investment Style
Equity
Average Stock %: 75% 81% 83% 83% 85% 90% 91%

▼ Manager Change
▽ Partial Manager Change

Fund Performance vs. Category Average
■ Quarterly Fund Return +/– Category Average
— Category Baseline

Performance Quartile (within Category)

Portfolio Manager(s)

Thomas J. Huber, CFA. Since 3-00. Other funds currently managed: IDEX T. Rowe Price Dividend Growth A, IDEX T. Rowe Price Dividend Growth B, IDEX T. Rowe Price Dividend Growth M.

1990	1991	1992	1993	1994	1995	1996	1997	1998	1999	2000	12-01	History
—	—	10.00	11.48	11.04	13.81	16.37	20.13	22.01	20.21	21.88	20.79	NAV
—	—	—	19.41	2.16	31.75	25.36	30.77	15.04	–2.82	10.06	–3.64	Total Return %
—	—	—	9.35	0.85	–5.79	2.42	–2.58	–13.54	–23.86	19.16	8.24	+/- S&P 500
—	—	—	–0.36	4.48	–8.28	3.05	–4.72	–6.20	–13.77	7.75	5.15	+/– Russ Top 200 Val
—	—	—	2.93	3.00	3.30	2.66	2.73	2.33	2.07	1.45	1.29	Income Return %
—	—	—	16.48	–0.84	28.45	22.70	28.04	12.71	–4.89	8.61	–4.93	Capital Return %
—	—	—	11	19	61	16	22	39	89	33	36	Total Rtn % Rank Cat
—	—	0.00	0.29	0.34	0.36	0.36	0.44	0.46	0.45	0.29	0.28	Income $
—	—	0.00	0.15	0.34	0.33	0.51	0.75	0.63	0.72	0.05	0.00	Capital Gains $
—	—	—	1.00	1.00	1.10	1.10	0.80	0.77	0.77	0.81	—	Expense Ratio %
—	—	—	2.60	3.11	2.92	2.53	2.42	2.26	2.01	1.43	—	Income Ratio %
—	—	—	51	71	56	43	39	37	38	36	—	Turnover Rate %
—	—	—	40.7	53.6	84.5	209.5	746.9	1,337.7	1,028.0	750.9	—	Net Assets $mil

Performance 12-31-01

	1st Qtr	2nd Qtr	3rd Qtr	4th Qtr	Total
1997	2.77	12.13	7.79	5.29	30.77
1998	10.19	–0.59	–7.11	13.05	15.04
1999	–2.92	8.08	–8.34	1.04	–2.82
2000	–0.69	3.15	3.32	3.98	10.06
2001	–6.58	4.13	–9.59	9.57	–3.64

Trailing	Total Return%	+/– S&P 500	+/– Russ Top 200 Val	% Rank All	% Rank Cat	Growth of $10,000
3 Mo	9.57	–1.12	4.05	45	41	10,957
6 Mo	–0.94	4.61	4.84	42	13	9,906
1 Yr	–3.64	8.24	5.15	48	36	9,636
3 Yr Avg	1.01	2.04	–0.16	68	62	10,306
5 Yr Avg	9.17	–1.53	–2.04	23	46	15,504
10 Yr Avg	—	—	—	—	—	—
15 Yr Avg	—	—	—	—	—	—

Tax Analysis	Tax-Adj Ret%	%Rank Cat	%Pretax Ret	%Rank Cat
3 Yr Avg	0.08	55	7.7	97
5 Yr Avg	7.79	34	85.0	17
10 Yr Avg	—	—	—	—

Potential Capital Gain Exposure: 22% of assets

Risk Analysis

Time Period	Load-Adj Return %	Risk %Rank[1] All	Risk %Rank[1] Cat	Morningstar Return	Morningstar Risk	Morningstar Risk-Adj Rating
1 Yr	–3.64					
3 Yr	1.01	46	11	–0.80[2]	0.63	★★★
5 Yr	9.17	47	7	0.98[2]	0.63	★★★
Incept	13.48	—	—	—	—	

Average Historical Rating (73 months): 4.3★s

[1] 1=low, 100=high [2] T-Bill return substituted for category avg.

Category Rating (3 Yr)

1 2 **3** 4 5 (Worst ... Best)

Return	Average
Risk	Below Avg

Other Measures	Standard Index S&P 500	Best Fit Index S&P 500
Alpha	–0.6	–0.6
Beta	0.55	0.55
R-Squared	56	56
Standard Deviation		12.52
Mean		1.01
Sharpe Ratio		–0.36

Portfolio Analysis 09-30-01

Share change since 06-01 Total Stocks: 97	Sector	PE	YTD Ret%	% Assets
Pfizer	Health	34.7	–12.40	2.97
⊕ Citigroup	Financials	20.0	0.03	2.68
⊖ Freddie Mac	Financials	14.0	–3.87	2.58
⊕ American Home Products	Health	—	–1.91	2.36
⊕ ExxonMobil	Energy	15.3	–7.59	2.27
⊕ PepsiCo	Staples	31.4	–0.54	1.85
⊕ Philip Morris	Staples	12.1	9.12	1.84
⊖ XL Cap Cl A	Financials	22.8	5.82	1.72
US Treasury Note 6%	N/A	—	—	1.72
⊖ Waddell & Reed Finl Cl A	Financials	23.3	–13.40	1.62
⊖ Family Dollar Stores	Retail	27.3	41.11	1.61
⊕ General Elec	Industrials	30.1	–15.00	1.42
⊕ Target	Retail	29.8	28.05	1.41
☼ American Intl Grp	Financials	42.0	–19.20	1.40
Chevron	Energy	10.3	9.29	1.32
⊕ First Data	Technology	38.1	49.08	1.32
Liberty Media 4%	N/A	—	—	1.31
⊕ Abbott Labs	Health	51.6	17.08	1.29
⊕ Vodafone Airtouch PLC ADR	Services	—	–27.70	1.27
Royal Dutch Petro NY ADR	Energy	12.0	–17.10	1.25
⊕ Cigna	Financials	13.2	–29.00	1.23
⊖ Verizon Comms	Services	29.7	–2.52	1.22
⊕ Omnicom Grp	Services	34.5	8.83	1.21
FleetBoston Finl	Financials	16.2	0.55	1.20
⊖ SBC Comms	Services	18.4	–16.00	1.18

Current Investment Style

Style: Value Blnd Growth; Size: Large Med Small

	Stock Port Avg	Relative S&P 500 Current	Relative S&P 500 Hist	Rel Cat
Price/Earnings Ratio	26.3	0.85	0.81	1.05
Price/Book Ratio	6.1	1.07	0.80	1.49
Price/Cash Flow	16.7	0.93	0.81	1.21
3 Yr Earnings Growth	18.4	1.26	0.85	1.24
1 Yr Earnings Est%	–0.3	0.15	—	0.08
Med Mkt Cap $mil	36,974	0.6	0.5	1.16

Special Securities % assets 09-30-01	
Restricted/Illiquid Secs	0
Emerging-Markets Secs	0
Options/Futures/Warrants	No

Composition % assets 09-30-01	
Cash	2.7
Stocks*	92.6
Bonds	4.8
Other	0.0
*Foreign (% stocks)	7.4

Market Cap	
Giant	45.6
Large	32.3
Medium	20.4
Small	1.7
Micro	0.0

Sector Weightings	% of Stocks	Rel S&P	5-Year High	5-Year Low
Utilities	1.7	0.5	6	0
Energy	9.9	1.4	10	4
Financials	30.1	1.7	33	22
Industrials	8.0	0.7	23	8
Durables	1.2	0.8	9	1
Staples	7.5	1.0	16	5
Services	16.2	1.5	21	12
Retail	5.2	0.8	6	0
Health	12.9	0.9	13	5
Technology	7.3	0.4	9	1

Analysis by William Samuel Rocco 11-15-01

Manager Tom Huber seems to have a knack for executing T. Rowe Price Dividend Growth Fund's conservative strategy.

Huber, who took charge of this offering in March 2000, has maintained his usual moderate stock selection and measured pace in recent months. He added to American Home Products and some other drug holdings on weakness this summer. He increased his exposure to PepsiCo, Philip Morris and some of his telecom picks at the same time. Meanwhile, he boosted his stakes in Target, Home Depot and some other retail stocks this fall.

Not all of Huber's recent or early-year decisions have paid off, but many have. PepsiCo and Philip Morris have posted nice gains this year, and Target and some of his other retail picks have earned even bigger returns. Meawhile, First Data is up 40%. Therefore, though the fund has lost 5% for the year to date through Nov. 14, 2001, it has outperformed two thirds of its peers.

Huber also came through during his first nine months at the helm. Indeed, the fund gained 11% over the final three quarters of 2000—nearly 5 percentage points more than the typical large-value offering—as Huber made a plethora of good financials and health-care picks.

What's more, investors have more than Huber's strong start to be encouraged by here. The fund has a low expense ratio. It has been one of the least-volatile members of its group over the long term, due to its issue diversification and emphasis on dividends. And thanks to the latter, it pays out an above-average yield. For all these reasons, we think this fund is a good choice for risk-averse investors who want some income.

Address:	100 E. Pratt Street Baltimore, MD 21202 800-638-5660 / 410-547-2308
Web Address:	www.troweprice.com
*Inception:	12-31-92
Advisor:	T. Rowe Price Assoc.
Subadvisor:	None
NTF Plans:	N/A

Minimum Purchase:	$2500	Add: $100 IRA: $1000
Min Auto Inv Plan:	$100	Add: $100
Sales Fees:	No-load	
Management Fee:	.20%+.48% mx./.30% mn.(G)	
Actual Fees:	Mgt: 0.52%	Dist: —
Expense Projections:	3Yr: $246	5Yr: $428 10Yr: $954
Avg Brok Commission:	—	Income Distrib: Quarterly
Total Cost (relative to category):	Low	

T. Rowe Price Emerging Markets Bond

Ticker	Load	NAV	Yield	SEC Yield	Total Assets	Mstar Category
PREMX	None	$10.32	11.2%	10.65%	$150.3 mil	Emerging Markets

Prospectus Objective: World Bond

T. Rowe Price Emerging Markets Bond Fund seeks high income and capital appreciation.

The fund invests at least 65% of assets in government and corporate debt securities of emerging-markets issuers. These securities are typically rated below investment-grade. The fund may invest in bonds of the lowest rating, including those in default. It maintains no restrictions on maturity, though the average weighted maturity normally ranges between five and 10 years. It may invest a substantial percentage of holdings in U.S. dollars.

Historical Profile
Return Above Avg
Risk High
Rating ★★★ Neutral

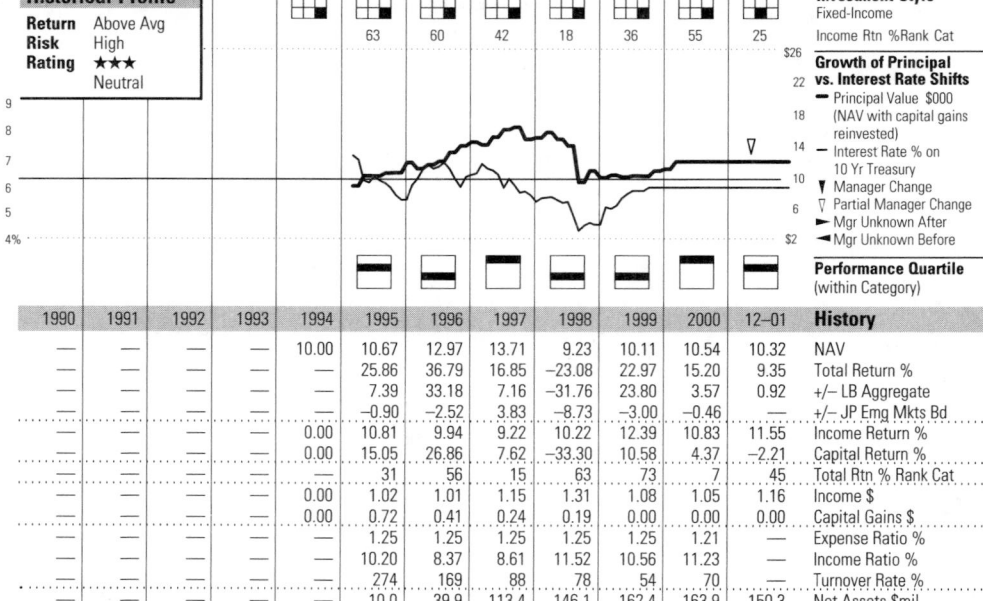

Investment Style Fixed-Income — Income Rtn %Rank Cat: 63, 60, 42, 18, 36, 55, 25

Growth of Principal vs. Interest Rate Shifts
— Principal Value $000 (NAV with capital gains reinvested)
— Interest Rate % on 10 Yr Treasury
▼ Manager Change
▽ Partial Manager Change
► Mgr Unknown After
◄ Mgr Unknown Before

Performance Quartile (within Category)

Portfolio Manager(s)

Chris Rothery. Since 12-94. Other funds currently managed: T. Rowe Price International Bond, T. Rowe Price International Bond Adv.

Mike Conelius. Since 12-94. Other funds currently managed: T. Rowe Price International Bond, T. Rowe Price International Bond Adv.

Ian Kelson. Since 5-01. BA'77 Cambridge U.; MSc'81 London School of Economics.

History

1990	1991	1992	1993	1994	1995	1996	1997	1998	1999	2000	12-01	History
—	—	—	—	10.00	10.67	12.97	13.71	9.23	10.11	10.54	10.32	NAV
—	—	—	—	—	25.86	36.79	16.85	–23.08	22.97	15.20	9.35	Total Return %
—	—	—	—	—	7.39	33.18	7.16	–31.76	23.80	3.57	0.92	+/– LB Aggregate
—	—	—	—	—	–0.90	–2.52	3.83	–8.73	–3.00	–0.46	—	+/– JP Emg Mkts Bd
—	—	—	—	0.00	10.81	9.94	9.22	10.22	12.39	10.83	11.55	Income Return %
—	—	—	—	0.00	15.05	26.86	7.62	–33.30	10.58	4.37	–2.21	Capital Return %
—	—	—	—	—	31	56	15	63	73	7	45	Total Rtn % Rank Cat
—	—	—	—	0.00	1.02	1.01	1.15	1.31	1.08	1.05	1.16	Income $
—	—	—	—	0.00	0.72	0.41	0.24	0.19	0.00	0.00	0.00	Capital Gains $
—	—	—	—	—	1.25	1.25	1.25	1.25	1.25	1.21	—	Expense Ratio %
—	—	—	—	—	10.20	8.37	8.61	11.52	10.56	11.23	—	Income Ratio %
—	—	—	—	—	274	169	88	78	54	70	—	Turnover Rate %
—	—	—	—	—	10.0	39.9	113.4	146.1	162.4	163.9	150.3	Net Assets $mil

Performance 12-31-01

	1st Qtr	2nd Qtr	3rd Qtr	4th Qtr	Total
1997	2.06	11.61	7.49	–4.58	16.85
1998	5.64	–7.65	–30.20	12.95	–23.08
1999	2.89	4.81	0.12	13.90	22.97
2000	8.61	–0.64	5.04	1.64	15.20
2001	3.19	4.06	–3.84	5.90	9.35

Trailing	Total Return%	+/– LB Agg	+/– JP Emg Mkts Bd	% Rank All	% Rank Cat	Growth of $10,000
3 Mo	5.90	5.86	—	61	68	10,590
6 Mo	1.83	–2.82	—	25	45	10,183
1 Yr	9.35	0.92	—	7	45	10,935
3 Yr Avg	15.71	9.43	—	4	47	15,490
5 Yr Avg	6.84	–0.59	—	37	30	13,922
10 Yr Avg	—	—	—	—	—	—
15 Yr Avg	—	—	—	—	—	—

Tax Analysis	Tax-Adj Ret%	%Rank Cat	%Pretax Ret	%Rank Cat
3 Yr Avg	10.87	50	69.2	74
5 Yr Avg	2.32	30	34.0	80
10 Yr Avg	—	—	—	—

Potential Capital Gain Exposure: –18% of assets

Risk Analysis

Time Period	Load-Adj Return %	Risk %Rank[1] All	Risk %Rank[1] Cat	Morningstar Return	Morningstar Risk	Morningstar Risk-Adj Rating
1 Yr	9.35					
3 Yr	15.71	35	25	2.52[2]	1.82	★★★★★
5 Yr	6.84	58	20	0.41[2]	3.62	★
Incept	13.29	—	—	—	—	

Average Historical Rating (49 months): 2.1★s

[1]1=low, 100=high [2] T-Bill return substituted for category avg.

Category Rating (3 Yr)

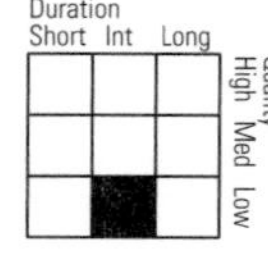

Return Average
Risk Below Avg

Other Measures	Standard Index LB Agg	Best Fit Index Wil 4500
Alpha	10.1	10.9
Beta	0.60	0.26
R-Squared	3	46

Standard Deviation	12.41
Mean	15.71
Sharpe Ratio	0.99

Analysis by Gabriel Presler 12-11-01

T. Rowe Price Emerging Market Bond Fund's recent stumble shouldn't worry investors.

A legacy of small, sound decisions boosted this fund to the top of its category in 2000. An emphasis on dollar-denominated bonds worked nicely as the greenback appreciated against most foreign currencies. Its exposure to many smaller markets, especially in Africa, also helped returns. In 2001, though, the fund hasn't been so flashy. It has gained just 8% for the year to date through Dec. 10, 2001, about average for the group.

Still, strong performances aren't uncommon here, thanks to manager Mike Conelius' moderate approach. He runs one of the more diversified portfolios in the group, staking less than 20% of assets in the universe's most popular markets, such as Mexico, and dipping into smaller, less-liquid countries, such as Nigeria and the Ivory Coast. He prefers dollar-denominated Brady bonds to local currency issues and limits the fund's exposure to corporate debt to 10% of assets.

Although caution has protected the fund from much of the volatility that plagues this asset class from time to time, 2001 has been a perfect example of how it can hurt relative performance. For example, like many of his rivals, Conelius reduced his exposure to the developing world's problem child, Argentina, throughout 2001. But unlike other funds, Conelius rarely exits countries that are included in the J.P. Morgan index. The country's finance minister, Domingo Cavallo, negotiated a debt swap in late fall, rendering part of the country's bonds inadmissable to the index. As a result, this fund was stuck with a larger-than-average slug of Argentinian bonds that no one else wanted.

The occasional mediocre year doesn't dampen our enthusiasm here. Thanks to its strong long-term record, regionally diverse portfolio, and low volatility, we consider it one of the stronger offerings in the category.

Address:	100 E. Pratt Street, Baltimore, MD 21202, 800–638–5660 / 410–547–2308
Web Address:	www.troweprice.com
*Inception:	12-30-94
Advisor:	Rowe Price–Fleming International
Subadvisor:	None
NTF Plans:	N/A

Minimum Purchase:	$2500	Add: $100 IRA: $1000
Min Auto Inv Plan:	$100	Add: $100
Sales Fees:	No-load	
Management Fee:	.60%+.33% mx./.30% mn.(G)	
Actual Fees:	Mgt: 0.77%	Dist: —
Expense Projections:	3Yr: $397	5Yr: $686 10Yr: $1511
Avg Brok Commission:	—	Income Distrib: Monthly
Total Cost (relative to category):		Below Avg

Portfolio Analysis 09-30-01

Total Fixed-Income: 49	Date of Maturity	Value $000	% Net Assets
Govt of Russia 5%	03-31-30	12,239	8.27
Republic of Brazil 8%	04-15-14	10,285	6.95
Banco Nacl de Des Econ 9.375%	06-16-08	6,440	4.35
Republic of Brazil 11%	08-17-40	5,683	3.84
Russian Federation 8.25%	03-31-10	5,362	3.62
Republic Bulgaria Reset 2.5%	07-28-12	5,220	3.53
United Mexican States 6.25%	12-31-19	5,012	3.39
Republic of Argentina FRN	03-31-05	4,721	3.19
Republic of Brazil FRN	04-15-12	4,710	3.18
Republic of Turkey 11.875%	01-15-30	4,075	2.75
Petroleos Mexicano 9.5%	09-15-27	3,923	2.65
Republic of Venezuela FRN	12-18-07	3,816	2.58
United Mexican States 11.5%	05-15-26	3,813	2.58
Republic of Bulgaria FRN	07-28-11	3,764	2.54
Republic of Panama Reset 4.25%	07-17-14	3,468	2.34
Republic of Bulgaria FRN	07-28-24	3,336	2.25
United Mexican States 8.125%	12-30-19	3,215	2.17
Republic of Brazil Reset 5.5%	04-15-24	3,043	2.06
BBVA Bancomer 10.5%	02-16-11	2,725	1.84
Republic Of Ecuador 12%	11-15-12	2,635	1.78

Current Investment Style

Duration: Short Int Long — Quality: High Med Low

Avg Eff Duration[1]	5.4 Yrs
Avg Eff Maturity	—
Avg Credit Quality	BB
Avg Wtd Coupon	7.88%
Avg Wtd Price	75.60% of par

[1]figure provided by fund

Special Securities % of assets 09-30-01	
Restricted/Illiquid Secs	Trace
Exotic Mortgage-Backed	0
Emerging-Markets Secs	52
Options/Futures/Warrants	No

Country Exposure % of assets

Not Available

Composition % assets 09-30-01

Cash	3.0	Bonds	97.0
Stocks	0.0	Other	0.0

T. Rowe Price Equity–Income

Ticker	Load	NAV	Yield	Total Assets	Mstar Category
PRFDX	None	$23.65	1.5%	$9,488.4 mil	Large Value

Prospectus Objective: Equity–Income

T. Rowe Price Equity-Income Fund seeks dividend income; potential for capital appreciation is also considered.

The fund invests at least 65% of assets in income-producing common stocks. In evaluating a security, the advisor considers the yield and prospects for earnings and dividend growth, the relative valuation of the security, and the overall competitive and financial strength of the company. The fund may invest up to 25% of assets in foreign securities.

The fund offers two different share classes, both of which differ in fee structure and availability. On Feb. 7, 1992, Bell Atlantic Equity Portfolio merged into this fund.

Historical Profile

Return Above Avg
Risk Below Avg
Rating ★★★★★ Highest

Investment Style
Equity
Average Stock %: 79% 85% 87% 92% 95% 95% 96%

▼ Manager Change
▽ Partial Manager Change

Fund Performance vs. Category Average
Quarterly Fund Return +/– Category Average
— Category Baseline

Performance Quartile (within Category)

Portfolio Manager(s)

Brian C. Rogers, CFA. Since 10-85. BA'77 Harvard U.; MBA'82 Harvard U. Other funds currently managed: T. Rowe Price Value, Vantagepoint Equity Income, T. Rowe Price Equity-Income Adv.

1990	1991	1992	1993	1994	1995	1996	1997	1998	1999	2000	12–01	History
12.27	14.62	15.63	16.65	15.98	20.01	22.54	26.07	26.32	24.81	24.67	23.65	NAV
–6.79	25.28	14.13	14.84	4.53	33.35	20.40	28.82	9.23	3.83	13.12	1.64	Total Return %
–3.67	–5.20	6.51	4.79	3.21	–4.18	–2.55	–4.53	–19.35	–17.21	22.22	13.51	+/– S&P 500
–3.12	7.13	5.06	–4.92	6.84	–6.68	–1.91	–6.67	–12.01	–7.13	10.81	10.43	+/– Russ Top 200 Val
4.71	5.05	4.38	3.52	3.61	4.15	3.30	2.99	2.40	2.04	2.12	1.49	Income Return %
–11.50	20.23	9.75	11.32	0.92	29.20	17.10	25.83	6.83	1.78	11.00	0.15	Capital Return %
58	63	17	42	7	46	49	35	73	60	20	13	Total Rtn % Rank Cat
0.65	0.61	0.63	0.54	0.59	0.65	0.65	0.66	0.61	0.53	0.51	0.36	Income $
0.19	0.10	0.39	0.72	0.81	0.54	0.84	2.14	1.49	1.97	2.64	1.01	Capital Gains $
1.13	1.05	0.97	0.91	0.88	0.85	0.81	0.79	0.77	0.77	0.78	—	Expense Ratio %
5.09	4.44	3.95	3.23	3.63	3.69	3.08	2.67	2.26	1.95	2.01	—	Income Ratio %
24	34	30	31	36	21	25	24	23	22	22	—	Turnover Rate %
862.1	1,335.4	2,091.5	2,848.5	3,203.9	5,214.8	7,818.1	12,771.2	13,495.1	12,321.2	10,245.6	—	Net Assets $mil

Performance 12-31-01

	1st Qtr	2nd Qtr	3rd Qtr	4th Qtr	Total
1997	2.90	11.43	7.89	4.13	28.82
1998	8.83	–2.35	–7.49	11.10	9.23
1999	–0.63	13.26	–8.52	0.85	3.83
2000	–2.92	0.16	6.88	8.85	13.12
2001	–2.81	5.76	–8.28	7.81	1.64

Trailing	Total Return%	+/– S&P 500	+/– Russ Top 200 Val	% Rank All	% Rank Cat	Growth of $10,000
3 Mo	7.81	–2.88	2.29	53	66	10,781
6 Mo	–1.12	4.44	4.66	43	14	9,888
1 Yr	1.64	13.51	10.43	40	13	10,164
3 Yr Avg	6.08	7.10	4.91	22	19	11,937
5 Yr Avg	10.93	0.23	–0.28	14	28	16,796
10 Yr Avg	13.96	1.03	–0.07	9	18	36,946
15 Yr Avg	13.28	–0.46	–0.22	15	22	64,880

Tax Analysis	Tax-Adj Ret%	%Rank Cat	%Pretax Ret	%Rank Cat
3 Yr Avg	3.64	25	60.0	61
5 Yr Avg	8.25	29	75.5	50
10 Yr Avg	11.26	15	80.7	34

Potential Capital Gain Exposure: 19% of assets

Risk Analysis

Time Period	Load-Adj Return %	Risk %Rank[1] All	Risk %Rank[1] Cat	Morningstar Return	Morningstar Risk	Morningstar Risk-Adj Rating
1 Yr	1.64					
3 Yr	6.08	46	13	0.24[2]	0.64	★★★★
5 Yr	10.93	48	10	1.44[2]	0.65	★★★★
10 Yr	13.96	51	6	1.53	0.61	★★★★★

Average Historical Rating (159 months): 4.1★s

[1]1=low, 100=high [2] T-Bill return substituted for category avg.

Category Rating (3 Yr)

1 2 3 4 5
Worst Best

Return Above Avg
Risk Below Avg

Other Measures	Standard Index S&P 500	Best Fit Index S&P 500
Alpha	4.6	4.6
Beta	0.53	0.53
R-Squared	36	36
Standard Deviation		15.76
Mean		6.08
Sharpe Ratio		0.08

Portfolio Analysis 09-30-01

Share change since 06–01 Total Stocks: 118	Sector	PE	YTD Ret%	% Assets
⊕ ExxonMobil	Energy	15.3	–7.59	2.50
BP PLC ADR	Energy	14.4	–0.90	1.99
Verizon Comms	Services	29.7	–2.52	1.78
Texaco	Energy	—	6.76	1.71
SBC Comms	Services	18.4	–16.00	1.71
⊖ Lockheed Martin	Industrials	36.8	38.98	1.68
⊖ American Home Products	Health	—	–1.91	1.64
FleetBoston Finl	Financials	16.2	0.55	1.60
⊕ Honeywell Intl	Durables	NMF	–27.00	1.55
Union Pacific	Services	17.1	13.96	1.55
Chevron	Energy	10.3	9.29	1.46
⊖ Mellon Finl	Financials	23.8	–21.90	1.33
Intl Paper	Industrials	—	1.43	1.33
⊕ Minnesota Mng & Mfg	Industrials	34.5	0.16	1.30
✲ American Intl Grp	Financials	42.0	–19.20	1.30
Alltel	Services	17.7	1.14	1.30
Waste Mgmt	Services	52.3	15.03	1.29
⊕ Walt Disney	Services	—	–27.70	1.28
⊖ Fannie Mae	Financials	16.2	–6.95	1.27
⊕ Bank One	Financials	29.1	9.13	1.27
⊖ UST, Inc.	Staples	12.3	32.23	1.27
✲ Chubb	Technology	—	—	1.21
⊖ Hershey Foods	Staples	25.4	7.12	1.18
DuPont De Nemours E.I.	Industrials	65.4	–9.14	1.14
Knight Ridder	Services	59.0	16.13	1.14

Current Investment Style

Style: Value Blnd Growth; Size: Large Med Small

	Stock Port Avg	Relative S&P 500 Current	Relative S&P 500 Hist	Rel Cat
Price/Earnings Ratio	26.1	0.84	0.72	1.03
Price/Book Ratio	4.6	0.81	0.60	1.12
Price/Cash Flow	12.4	0.69	0.60	0.90
3 Yr Earnings Growth	11.6	0.79	0.42	0.78
1 Yr Earnings Est%	–6.4	3.60	—	1.92
Med Mkt Cap $mil	21,639	0.4	0.3	0.68

Analysis by Catherine Hickey 10-09-01

This old-fashioned value fund continues to impress.

T. Rowe Price Equity-Income Fund is one offering that has never wavered from its emphasis on dividend-paying stocks. Thus, the fund has never owned much in the way of technology, because few tech companies pay dividends. Though the fund missed out on the tech sector's gains in 1999, it has benefited hugely from underweighting the foundering sector in 2000 and 2001. Indeed, the fund's slim 4.7% loss for the year to date through Oct. 8, 2001, makes it one of the large-value category's top performers in 2001.

Manager Brian Rogers has recently made the fund just a touch more aggressive by taking money out of defensive areas and putting it into some of the growthier sectors that were hardest hit after the terrorist attacks. He has trimmed names such as General Mills and has added to stakes in Starwood Hotels and Disney, because he thinks the latter two companies will rebound from the post-attack malaise for leisure stocks. Rogers isn't jumping into tech stocks just yet, though. He still feels that a stable recovery in that sector may not take place for a while, and that any uptick the sector makes may be brief.

If the past is any indicator, Rogers' recent buys could bode well for the fund: He has added considerable value over the years by picking up financially healthy names at depressed prices. Indeed, the fund's five-year return ranks in the category's top quartile. And despite Rogers' recent shifts, the fund's turnover is usually minuscule. That has helped make it fairly tax-efficient relative to its peers over the years. It also has helped Rogers keep a lid on volatility, though the fund's dividend focus plays a part in toning down risk, too.

Investors searching for a low-cost, conservative core holding will find this an appealing choice.

Special Securities % assets 09-30-01	
Restricted/Illiquid Secs	0
Emerging–Markets Secs	0
Options/Futures/Warrants	No

Sector Weightings	% of Stocks	Rel S&P	5-Year High	5-Year Low
Utilities	3.0	0.9	14	3
Energy	12.3	1.7	19	9
Financials	19.2	1.1	23	10
Industrials	15.2	1.3	23	11
Durables	4.8	3.0	11	1
Staples	13.0	1.6	15	3
Services	19.5	1.8	22	9
Retail	2.2	0.3	6	1
Health	6.6	0.4	17	1
Technology	4.6	0.3	6	0

Composition % assets 09-30-01	
Cash	4.2
Stocks*	95.8
Bonds	0.0
Other	0.0
*Foreign (% stocks)	4.5

Market Cap	
Giant	36.5
Large	30.5
Medium	32.0
Small	0.9
Micro	0.0

Address:	100 E. Pratt Street Baltimore, MD 21202 800–638–5660 / 410–547–2308
Web Address:	www.troweprice.com
Inception:	10-31-85
Advisor:	T. Rowe Price Assoc.
Subadvisor:	None
NTF Plans:	N/A

Minimum Purchase:	$2500	Add: $100	IRA: $1000
Min Auto Inv Plan:	$100	Add: $100	
Sales Fees:	No–load		
Management Fee:	.32%+.33% mx./.30% mn.(G)		
Actual Fees:	Mgt: 0.57%	Dist: —	
Expense Projections:	3Yr: $246	5Yr: $428	10Yr: $954
Avg Brok Commission:	—	Income Distrib: Quarterly	
Total Cost (relative to category):		Low	

T. Rowe Price European Stock

Ticker	Load	NAV	Yield	Total Assets	Mstar Category
PRESX	None	$16.01	2.2%	$814.0 mil	Europe Stock

Prospectus Objective: Europe Stock

T. Rowe Price European Stock Fund seeks long-term capital appreciation. Income is secondary.

The fund intends to invest in equity securities of issuers of any western or eastern European country. It maintains at least 65% of assets in European equities and usually invests in a minimum of five countries. Management intends to take advantage of opportunities arising from trends in privatization, reduction of trade barriers, and potential growth of eastern European countries.

On Aug. 31, 1992, USF&G European Emerging Companies Fund merged into this fund.

Historical Profile
Return Above Avg
Risk Below Avg
Rating ★★★★ Above Avg

Investment Style
Equity
Average Stock %: 95% 97% 94% 96% 97% 96% 99%

▼ Manager Change
▽ Partial Manager Change

Fund Performance vs. Category Average
Quarterly Fund Return +/– Category Average
– Category Baseline

Performance Quartile (within Category)

Portfolio Manager(s)

John R. Ford, CFA. Since 2-90. MA'79 Oxford U. Other funds currently managed: T. Rowe Price New Asia, T. Rowe Price Foreign Equity, T. Rowe Price International Discovery.

James B.M. Seddon. Since 2-90. BA'86 Oxford U. Other funds currently managed: T. Rowe Price Foreign Equity, T. Rowe Price International Stock, Lutheran Brotherhood World Grow A.

Robert Revel-Chion. Since 1-98. BA'87 U. of Manchester.

1990	1991	1992	1993	1994	1995	1996	1997	1998	1999	2000	12–01	History
9.48	10.09	9.36	11.86	12.17	14.37	17.62	19.36	21.77	23.86	20.64	16.01	NAV
–3.17*	7.31	–5.56	27.24	4.06	21.86	25.87	17.01	25.82	19.70	–6.66	–20.65	Total Return %
–5.70*	–23.18	–13.18	17.19	2.75	–15.67	2.93	–16.34	–2.76	–1.33	2.44	–8.78	+/– S&P 500
—	–5.81	–0.85	–2.04	1.78	0.24	4.79	–6.79	–2.71	3.81	1.73	—	+/– MSCI Europe
2.03	0.84	1.68	0.43	1.01	1.73	1.81	1.42	1.45	0.64	0.67	1.74	Income Return %
–5.20	6.46	–7.25	26.82	3.05	20.14	24.06	15.59	24.37	19.06	–7.33	–22.40	Capital Return %
—	41	52	55	41	8	36	61	31	70	44	30	Total Rtn % Rank Cat
0.20	0.08	0.17	0.04	0.12	0.21	0.26	0.25	0.28	0.14	0.16	0.36	Income $
0.00	0.00	0.00	0.01	0.05	0.25	0.20	1.01	2.18	1.90	1.42	0.00	Capital Gains $
1.75	1.71	1.48	1.35	1.25	1.20	1.12	1.06	1.05	1.05	1.02	—	Expense Ratio %
2.30	1.04	1.23	1.79	1.19	1.75	1.81	1.41	1.39	0.97	0.71	—	Income Ratio %
—	58	52	21	25	17	14	18	27	16	25	—	Turnover Rate %
99.4	104.0	173.8	289.5	366.5	531.6	765.1	1,020.8	1,548.6	1,587.4	1,231.6	—	Net Assets $mil

Performance 12-31-01

	1st Qtr	2nd Qtr	3rd Qtr	4th Qtr	Total
1997	2.50	8.42	5.16	0.13	17.01
1998	17.87	5.39	–14.01	17.79	25.82
1999	–1.70	–0.19	1.26	20.48	19.70
2000	–0.21	–1.39	–6.86	1.84	–6.66
2001	–17.05	–1.23	–12.54	10.73	–20.65

Trailing	Total Return%	+/– S&P 500	+/– MSCI Europe	% Rank All	% Rank Cat	Growth of $10,000
3 Mo	10.73	0.05	—	38	30	11,073
6 Mo	–3.15	2.41	—	52	25	9,685
1 Yr	–20.65	–8.78	—	81	30	7,935
3 Yr Avg	–3.93	–2.91	—	89	55	8,866
5 Yr Avg	5.47	–5.23	—	56	43	13,052
10 Yr Avg	9.61	–3.32	—	35	42	25,036
15 Yr Avg	—	—	—	—	—	—

Tax Analysis	Tax-Adj Ret%	%Rank Cat	%Pretax Ret	%Rank Cat
3 Yr Avg	–5.45	58	—	—
5 Yr Avg	3.58	40	65.5	43
10 Yr Avg	8.28	36	86.2	10

Potential Capital Gain Exposure: 10% of assets

Risk Analysis

Time Period	Load-Adj Return %	Risk %Rank[1] All	Risk %Rank[1] Cat	Morningstar Return	Morningstar Risk	Morningstar Risk-Adj Rating
1 Yr	–20.65					
3 Yr	–3.93	64	29	–1.73[2]	0.83	★★★
5 Yr	5.47	61	24	0.10[2]	0.70	★★★★
10 Yr	9.61	71	12	1.56[2]	0.71	★★★★

Average Historical Rating (107 months): 3.9★s

[1]1=low, 100=high [2] T-Bill return substituted for category avg.

Category Rating (3 Yr)

1 2 **3** 4 5
Worst Best

Return Average
Risk Below Avg

Other Measures	Standard Index S&P 500	Best Fit Index MSCIEurND
Alpha	–4.4	1.9
Beta	0.67	1.04
R-Squared	46	96
Standard Deviation		16.15
Mean		–3.93
Sharpe Ratio		–0.64

Portfolio Analysis 09-30-01

Share change since 06-01 Total Stocks: 127	Sector	Country	% Assets
⊖ Glaxosmithkline	Technology	United Kingdom	5.68
⊖ Royal Bk of Scotland	Financials	United Kingdom	4.14
⊖ Total Fina Cl B	Energy	France	3.60
⊖ Vodafone Airtouch	Services	United Kingdom	3.07
⊖ Shell Transp & Trad	Energy	United Kingdom	2.69
⊕ Ing Groepnv	N/A	N/A	2.49
⊕ Reed Intl	Services	United Kingdom	2.47
⊖ Astrazeneca	Health	United Kingdom	2.35
⊖ Sanofi-Synthelabo	Health	France	2.19
⊖ Nestle	Staples	Switzerland	2.11
⊖ Diageo	Staples	United Kingdom	2.08
⊕ Compass Grp	Services	United Kingdom	1.76
⊖ Vivendi	Services	France	1.61
☼ Philips Electncs (NV)	Durables	Netherlands	1.56
⊖ TIM	Services	Italy	1.55
⊖ Nokia	Technology	Finland	1.41
⊖ Nordic Baltic Hldg	Financials	Sweden	1.37
⊖ Unilever	Staples	United Kingdom	1.35
⊖ Alleanza Assicurazioni	Financials	Italy	1.34
⊖ Roche Hldgs (Br)	Health	Switzerland	1.33

Current Investment Style

Style: Value Blnd Growth; Size: Large Med Small

	Stock Port Avg	Rel MSCI EAFE Current	Rel MSCI EAFE Hist	Rel Cat
Price/Earnings Ratio	25.0	0.97	0.97	1.05
Price/Cash Flow	15.9	1.24	1.16	1.13
Price/Book Ratio	5.2	1.49	1.44	1.17
3 Yr Earnings Growth	21.1	1.13	1.35	0.88
Med Mkt Cap $mil	40,125	1.4	1.2	1.48

Country Exposure 09-30-01	% assets
United Kingdom	36
France	17
Italy	7
Switzerland	7
Netherlands	6

Hedging History: Rare

Special Securities % assets 09-30-01	
Restricted/Illiquid Secs	0
Emerging-Markets Secs	1
Options/Futures/Warrants	No

Sector Weightings	% of Stocks	Rel Cat	5-Year High	5-Year Low
Utilities	3.0	1.3	13	1
Energy	10.7	1.3	12	2
Financials	21.6	0.9	27	11
Industrials	5.8	0.5	27	6
Durables	3.0	0.7	8	3
Staples	8.6	1.2	19	5
Services	22.8	1.3	29	10
Retail	3.0	0.6	11	3
Health	10.1	1.0	18	5
Technology	11.5	1.4	15	0

Composition % assets 09-30-01

Cash	0.8	Bonds	0.0
Stocks	98.7	Other	0.6

Analysis by William Samuel Rocco 11-16-01

T. Rowe Price European Stock Fund continues to quietly deliver.

This fund has long been wary of dramatic portfolio moves—turnover is normally just 15% to 25% per annum here—and it has stayed that way as Europe's markets have gotten choppier in recent months. Its managers bought Hellenic Telecom this summer for its modest but steady growth and strong competitive position. They also purchased the U.K. advertiser WPP Group, because it was cheap and they think its 2002 earnings growth will be better than projected. And they've taken profits in select issues, including GlaxoSmithKline and Royal Bank of Scotland. But they have not made many other significant changes.

The fund hasn't been hurt by their restraint thus far in 2001. In fact, an array of its holdings have held up well. The food-and-drinks conglomerate Diageo has posted a small gain this year, for example,while many other longtime holdings havesuffered relatively small losses. And Hellenic Telecom has posted strong returns since purchase. As a result, though it's down a painful 22% for the year to date through Nov. 15, 2001, the fund has outpaced two thirds of its peers.

The fund has also outperformed the majority of its rivals over time and has been far less volatile than the typical Europe offering. And its expense ratio is relatively low. For all these reasons, we believe this fund is a good option for those who want to bet on Europe without assuming too much risk.

Address:	100 E. Pratt Street Baltimore, MD 21202 800-638-5660 / 410-547-2308
Web Address:	www.troweprice.com
*Inception:	02-28-90
Advisor:	T. Rowe Price Assoc.
Subadvisor:	None
NTF Plans:	N/A

Minimum Purchase:	$2500	Add: $100 IRA: $1000
Min Auto Inv Plan:	$50	Add: $50
Sales Fees:	No-load	
Management Fee:	.50%+.33% mx./.30% mn.(G)	
Actual Fees:	Mgt: 0.82%	Dist: —
Expense Projections:	3Yr: $334	5Yr: $579 10Yr: $1283
Avg Brok Commission:	—	Income Distrib: Annually
Total Cost (relative to category):		Low

T. Rowe Price Growth Stock

Ticker	Load	NAV	Yield	Total Assets	Mstar Category
PRGFX	None	$24.18	0.3%	$4,292.0 mil	Large Blend

Prospectus Objective: Growth

T. Rowe Price Growth Stock Fund seeks long-term growth of capital; income is secondary.

The fund invests primarily in dividend-paying common stocks of well-established growth companies. Management seeks companies with above-average growth rates, or that can maintain earnings momentum during economic downturns, or that occupy a lucrative market niche. In addition, dividends should rise in line with long-term earnings growth. The fund may invest up to 30% of assets in foreign securities. It may also write covered call options on up to 25% of assets.

Historical Profile
Return: Above Avg
Risk: Average
Rating: ★★★★ Above Avg

Investment Style: Equity — Average Stock %: 92% 94% 92% 93% 96% 95% 96%

▼ Manager Change
▽ Partial Manager Change

Fund Performance vs. Category Average
■ Quarterly Fund Return +/– Category Average
— Category Baseline

Performance Quartile (within Category)

Portfolio Manager(s)

Robert W. Smith. Since 5-97. BS U. of Delaware; MBA U. of Virginia. Other funds currently managed: T. Rowe Price Global Stock, SunAmerica International Equity A, SunAmerica International Equity B.

1990	1991	1992	1993	1994	1995	1996	1997	1998	1999	2000	12-01	History
14.71	18.75	18.66	20.42	18.75	23.35	26.18	28.99	32.07	33.27	27.20	24.18	NAV
-4.30	33.80	5.99	15.56	0.89	30.97	21.70	26.57	27.41	22.15	0.27	-9.79	Total Return %
-1.18	3.31	-1.62	5.50	-0.43	-6.57	-1.24	-6.78	-1.17	1.11	9.37	2.08	+/- S&P 500
-0.27	1.36	-1.66	5.72	0.44	-6.64	-0.46	-6.46	-1.23	0.32	11.23	2.97	+/- Wilshire Top 750
2.64	1.70	0.96	0.75	0.88	1.23	0.81	0.76	0.86	0.31	0.21	0.29	Income Return %
-6.94	32.10	5.03	14.81	0.00	29.74	20.89	25.81	26.55	21.84	0.06	-10.09	Capital Return %
61	35	70	20	28	69	46	63	34	36	16	18	Total Rtn % Rank Cat
0.43	0.25	0.18	0.14	0.18	0.23	0.19	0.20	0.25	0.10	0.07	0.08	Income $
0.43	0.62	1.03	0.99	1.66	0.97	2.06	3.87	4.27	5.42	6.28	0.27	Capital Gains $
0.76	0.85	0.83	0.82	0.81	0.80	0.77	0.75	0.74	0.74	0.73	—	Expense Ratio %
2.31	1.40	0.94	0.86	0.91	1.09	0.74	0.75	0.67	0.31	0.20	—	Income Ratio %
30	32	27	35	54	43	49	41	55	56	74	—	Turnover Rate %
1,396.5	1,846.0	1,946.2	2,050.6	2,067.5	2,761.8	3,430.8	3,988.4	5,041.2	5,672.3	5,428.3	—	Net Assets $mil

Performance 12-31-01

	1st Qtr	2nd Qtr	3rd Qtr	4th Qtr	Total
1997	-0.99	15.97	7.05	2.97	26.57
1998	15.01	1.56	-11.40	23.12	27.41
1999	2.40	6.00	-5.75	19.39	22.15
2000	8.60	-0.42	1.08	-8.28	0.27
2001	-14.96	8.86	-14.81	14.39	-9.79

Trailing	Total Return%	+/- S&P 500	+/-Wil Top 750	% Rank All	% Rank Cat	Growth of $10,000
3 Mo	14.39	3.71	3.07	25	11	11,439
6 Mo	-2.55	3.00	3.24	49	8	9,745
1 Yr	-9.79	2.08	2.97	60	18	9,021
3 Yr Avg	3.38	4.41	5.20	50	14	11,049
5 Yr Avg	12.25	1.55	2.13	9	10	17,817
10 Yr Avg	13.38	0.45	0.93	11	17	35,092
15 Yr Avg	12.93	-0.80	-0.44	17	35	61,985

Tax Analysis	Tax-Adj Ret%	%Rank Cat	%Pretax Ret	%Rank Cat
3 Yr Avg	0.54	20	16.1	90
5 Yr Avg	9.08	27	74.2	71
10 Yr Avg	10.68	32	79.8	53

Potential Capital Gain Exposure: 18% of assets

Risk Analysis

Time Period	Load-Adj Return %	Risk %Rank[1] All	Risk %Rank[1] Cat	Morningstar Return	Morningstar Risk	Morningstar Risk-Adj Rating
1 Yr	-9.79					
3 Yr	3.38	69	56	-0.33[2]	0.94	★★★
5 Yr	12.25	68	56	1.81[2]	0.92	★★★★
10 Yr	13.38	69	44	1.40	0.89	★★★★

Average Historical Rating (193 months): 3.3★s

[1]1=low, 100=high [2] T-Bill return substituted for category avg.

Category Rating (3 Yr)
1 2 3 4 5 — Worst … Best
Return: Above Avg
Risk: Average

Other Measures	Standard Index S&P 500	Best Fit Index MSCIACWdFr
Alpha	5.1	9.6
Beta	1.06	1.13
R-Squared	90	90

Standard Deviation	19.65
Mean	3.38
Sharpe Ratio	-0.09

Portfolio Analysis 09-30-01

Share change since 06-01 Total Stocks: 102	Sector	PE	YTD Ret%	% Assets
⊕ Pfizer	Health	34.7	-12.40	3.87
⊕ Freddie Mac	Financials	14.0	-3.87	3.81
⊕ Citigroup	Financials	20.0	0.03	3.66
⊖ General Elec	Industrials	30.1	-15.00	2.54
⊖ UnitedHealth Grp	Financials	26.6	15.37	2.53
⊖ First Data	Technology	38.1	49.08	2.42
⊕ Philip Morris	Staples	12.1	9.12	2.37
⊕ American Home Products	Health	—	-1.91	2.27
⊖ Johnson & Johnson	Health	16.6	14.01	2.10
⊕ Vodafone Airtouch	Services	—	—	1.85
⊖ Sprint (PCS Group)	Services	—	19.43	1.68
⊕ Home Depot	Retail	42.9	12.07	1.58
Microsoft	Technology	57.6	52.78	1.56
⊖ AOL Time Warner	Technology	—	-7.76	1.53
⊕ Concord EFS	Financials	86.3	49.21	1.52
⊕ Fannie Mae	Financials	16.2	-6.95	1.51
⊕ Viacom Cl B	Services	—	—	1.49
⊕ Target	Retail	29.8	28.05	1.47
⊖ WellPoint Health Networks	Health	19.4	1.39	1.47
⊕ American Intl Grp	Financials	42.0	-19.20	1.43
⊕ Tyco Intl	Industrials	27.1	6.23	1.32
☼ Liberty Livewire	Services	—	—	1.29
⊖ Chevron	Energy	10.3	9.29	1.23
⊕ ExxonMobil	Energy	15.3	-7.59	1.22
⊕ Hartford Finl Svcs Grp	Financials	23.2	-9.63	1.14

Current Investment Style

Style: Value Blnd Growth; Size: Large Med Small

	Stock Port Avg	Relative S&P 500 Current	Relative S&P 500 Hist	Rel Cat
Price/Earnings Ratio	30.3	0.98	1.04	1.00
Price/Book Ratio	6.5	1.14	1.00	1.18
Price/Cash Flow	20.9	1.16	1.12	1.13
3 Yr Earnings Growth	19.8	1.35	1.14	1.11
1 Yr Earnings Est%	7.2	—	—	—
Med Mkt Cap $mil	46,665	0.8	0.7	0.89

Analysis by Catherine Hickey 10-31-01

This fund continues to prove to be a worthy alternative to an S&P 500 index fund.

T. Rowe Price Growth Stock Fund is in an accustomed spot: the top of the large-blend chart. Its 18% loss through Oct. 31, 2001, is strong enough to land it just inside the group's top quartile. Manager Bob Smith cut the fund's technology weighting earlier this year as his concerns grew about a slowdown in capital spending. He wisely eliminated Corning and a couple of semiconductor names from the portfolio early in the year. Remaining tech names, like First Data, have been strong.

Though a number of tech names have been beaten down recently, Smith said he wasn't biting. Many of the companies are still overvalued, he said, and he doesn't think we're in for a strong enough economic recovery to bolster a lot of tech firms. So instead of tech, Smith has been buying brokers like Merrill Lynch and media companies like WPP. He thinks both of those firms are strong growth companies that were pushed down too far in the recent sell-off.

The fund's above-average foreign stake means this is no index-hugging offering. Smith has managed both domestic and international funds over the years, so he does look for companies overseas that exhibit the same kind of earnings growth and valuation characteristics he can find in the U.S. The foreign stake is usually in the double digits, so investors who already have all the foreign exposure they want should look elsewhere.

Those looking for a strong-performing large-blend fund ought to give it a look, though. Over time, Smith's picks have been on much more often than not. This knack for stock-picking is reflected in the fund's strong long-term returns; since Smith came aboard in 1997, the fund has steadily outpaced the S&P 500 index.

Special Securities % assets 09-30-01	
Restricted/Illiquid Secs	0
Emerging-Markets Secs	2
Options/Futures/Warrants	No

Composition % assets 09-30-01	
Cash	2.2
Stocks*	97.8
Bonds	0.0
Other	0.0
*Foreign (% stocks)	9.4

Market Cap	
Giant	51.3
Large	40.3
Medium	8.2
Small	0.3
Micro	0.0

Sector Weightings	% of Stocks	Rel S&P	5-Year High	5-Year Low
Utilities	0.6	0.2	3	0
Energy	4.4	0.6	5	2
Financials	23.8	1.3	27	14
Industrials	5.0	0.4	17	5
Durables	1.8	1.1	10	1
Staples	6.2	0.8	8	1
Services	16.4	1.5	28	12
Retail	8.1	1.2	9	2
Health	20.9	1.4	21	9
Technology	12.8	0.7	33	7

Address:	100 E. Pratt Street, Baltimore, MD 21202, 800-638-5660 / 410-547-2308
Web Address:	www.troweprice.com
Inception:	04-11-50
Advisor:	T. Rowe Price Assoc.
Subadvisor:	None
NTF Plans:	N/A

Minimum Purchase:	$2500	Add: $100	IRA: $1000
Min Auto Inv Plan:	$100	Add: $100	
Sales Fees:	No-load		
Management Fee:	.25%+.48% mx./.30% mn.(G)		
Actual Fees:	Mgt: 0.57%	Dist: —	
Expense Projections:	3Yr: $237	5Yr: $411	10Yr: $918
Avg Brok Commission:	—	Income Distrib: Annually	
Total Cost (relative to category):		Below Avg	

T. Rowe Price International Bond

Ticker	Load	NAV	Yield	SEC Yield	Total Assets	Mstar Category
RPIBX	None	$7.86	4.1%	3.19%	$800.1 mil	International Bond

Prospectus Objective: World Bond

T. Rowe Price International Bond Fund seeks income and capital appreciation.

The fund invests at least 65% of assets in high-quality, non-U.S.-dollar-denominated debt securities. It may invest up to 20% of assets in below investment grade, high-risk bonds, including those in default or with the lowest rating. The advisor actively manages its maturity structure based on interest-rate trends for each country. When the advisor expects interest rates to fall, it may invest in bonds with longer maturities to seek capital appreciation and higher yields; when it expects interest rates to rise, it may invest in bonds with shorter maturities to preserve principal. "This fund is non-diversified."

The fund offers two different share classes, both of which differ in fee structure and availability.

Portfolio Manager(s)

Chris Rothery. Since 1-94. Other funds currently managed: T. Rowe Price Emerging Markets Bond, T. Rowe Price International Bond Adv.

Mike Conelius. Since 1-95. Other funds currently managed: T. Rowe Price Emerging Markets Bond, T. Rowe Price International Bond Adv.

Historical Profile

Return: Low
Risk: High
Rating: ★ Lowest

Investment Style
Fixed-Income
Income Rtn %Rank Cat: 22 62 58 63 48 79 68 52

Growth of Principal vs. Interest Rate Shifts
— Principal Value $000 (NAV with capital gains reinvested)
— Interest Rate % on 10 Yr Treasury
▼ Manager Change
▽ Partial Manager Change
► Mgr Unknown After
◄ Mgr Unknown Before

Performance Quartile (within Category)

History	1990	1991	1992	1993	1994	1995	1996	1997	1998	1999	2000	12-01
NAV	9.53	10.35	9.61	10.34	9.34	10.46	10.46	9.58	10.46	9.16	8.47	7.86
Total Return %	16.06	17.75	2.41	20.03	−1.84	20.31	7.14	−3.17	15.03	−7.86	−3.13	−3.41
+/− LB Aggregate	7.10	1.74	−4.99	10.28	1.08	1.84	3.52	−12.86	6.35	−7.03	−14.76	−11.83
+/− SB World Govt	0.76	1.53	−2.36	4.91	−7.83	0.76	3.06	1.09	−2.76	−2.79	−0.49	0.13
Income Return %	9.49	8.42	8.37	7.36	5.95	6.86	5.92	5.16	5.47	3.76	4.39	3.90
Capital Return %	6.57	9.33	−5.96	12.67	−7.79	13.45	1.21	−8.33	9.55	−11.62	−7.52	−7.31
Total Rtn % Rank Cat	33	1	55	7	28	26	60	86	14	82	86	83
Income $	0.83	0.77	0.83	0.68	0.60	0.62	0.60	0.53	0.51	0.38	0.39	0.32
Capital Gains $	0.17	0.00	0.15	0.46	0.21	0.12	0.11	0.02	0.00	0.11	0.00	0.00
Expense Ratio %	1.15	1.24	1.08	0.99	0.98	0.90	0.87	0.86	0.88	0.90	0.91	—
Income Ratio %	9.04	8.11	8.66	6.58	6.07	6.10	5.86	5.38	5.19	3.93	4.76	—
Turnover Rate %	211	296	358	396	345	237	234	156	129	95	161	—
Net Assets $mil	430.4	414.0	516.3	745.2	738.1	1,015.8	969.5	825.8	926.5	778.7	668.6	800.1

Performance 12-31-01

	1st Qtr	2nd Qtr	3rd Qtr	4th Qtr	Total
1997	−5.59	3.36	0.76	−1.51	−3.17
1998	1.76	0.99	5.55	6.04	15.03
1999	−5.03	−4.81	3.53	−1.55	−7.86
2000	−1.99	−1.30	−4.07	4.39	−3.13
2001	−4.70	−1.82	7.04	−3.55	−3.41

Trailing	Total Return%	+/− LB Agg	+/− SB World	% Rank All	% Rank Cat	Growth of $10,000
3 Mo	−3.55	−3.59	0.42	100	84	9,645
6 Mo	3.24	−1.42	−0.23	14	50	10,324
1 Yr	−3.41	−11.83	0.13	48	83	9,659
3 Yr Avg	−4.82	−11.10	−1.07	91	90	8,622
5 Yr Avg	−0.81	−8.23	−0.92	94	91	9,602
10 Yr Avg	4.09	−3.14	−0.71	96	55	14,935
15 Yr Avg	6.27	−1.85	−1.00	84	40	24,886

Tax Analysis	Tax-Adj Ret%	%Rank Cat	%Pretax Ret	%Rank Cat
3 Yr Avg	−6.46	92	—	—
5 Yr Avg	−2.66	91	—	—
10 Yr Avg	1.48	62	36.1	66

Potential Capital Gain Exposure: NMF

Risk Analysis

Time Period	Load-Adj Return %	Risk %Rank[1] All	Risk %Rank[1] Cat	Morningstar Return	Morningstar Risk	Morningstar Risk-Adj Rating
1 Yr	−3.41					
3 Yr	−4.82	40	88	−1.88[2]	2.41	★
5 Yr	−0.81	43	89	−1.14[2]	2.44	★
10 Yr	4.09	51	89	−0.16[2]	2.17	★

Average Historical Rating (148 months): 1.9★s

[1]1=low, 100=high [2] T-Bill return substituted for category avg.

Category Rating (3 Yr)

1 2 3 4 5
Worst Best

Return: Low
Risk: Above Avg

Other Measures	Standard Index LB Agg	Best Fit Index SB World
Alpha	−10.7	−1.3
Beta	1.36	0.98
R-Squared	32	95

Standard Deviation	7.54
Mean	−4.82
Sharpe Ratio	−1.52

Portfolio Analysis 09-30-01

Total Fixed-Income: 65	Date of Maturity	Value $000	% Net Assets
Govt of Japan 0.9%	12-22-08	81,413	10.08
Govt of Japan 1.3%	06-20-11	51,464	6.38
Govt of France 5%	07-12-05	33,895	4.20
Govt of Netherlands 5.75%	01-15-04	32,902	4.08
Govt of France 4.5%	07-12-03	32,368	4.01
Republic of Germany 6%	01-04-07	30,755	3.81
Kfw Intl Fin 5.5%	06-18-04	29,903	3.70
Kingdom of Belgium 7.25%	04-29-04	27,876	3.45
Republic of Italy 5.25%	12-15-05	25,635	3.18
Govt of France 4%	04-25-09	24,516	3.04
Kingdom of Spain 4%	01-31-10	20,525	2.54
Govt of Japan 2.2%	06-22-20	16,962	2.10
FHLMC 5.25%	01-15-06	16,569	2.05
Govt of Japan 0.5%	06-20-06	16,181	2.00
Republic of Poland 8.5%	02-12-06	15,313	1.90
Republic of Germany 5.25%	01-04-08	14,279	1.77
Republic of Germany 4.75%	07-04-28	13,326	1.65
Republik Oestereic 5.5%	01-15-10	12,501	1.55
Kingdom of Spain 6%	01-31-29	12,428	1.54
Govt of Canada 5%	09-01-04	12,332	1.53

Current Investment Style

Duration: Short Int Long
Quality: High Med Low

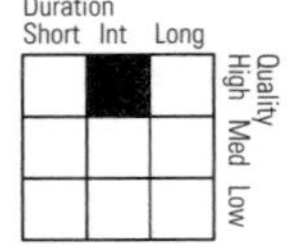

Avg Eff Duration[1]	6.0 Yrs
Avg Eff Maturity	8.0 Yrs
Avg Credit Quality	AA
Avg Wtd Coupon	4.77%
Avg Wtd Price	75.46% of par

[1]figure provided by fund

Special Securities 09-30-01	% assets
Restricted/Illiquid Secs	0
Exotic Mortgage–Backed	0
Emerging–Markets Secs	2
Options/Futures/Warrants	No

Country Exposure % assets

Not Available

Composition % assets 09-30-01			
Cash	2.6	Bonds	97.4
Stocks	0.0	Other	0.0

Analysis by Gabriel Presler 08-10-01

T. Rowe Price International Bond Fund's disappointing performance has little to do with its management changes.

This fund lost a third of its management team in December 2000 when Peter Askew left T. Rowe Price. Comanager Chris Rothery and Mike Conelius have remained behind, using the same unusual approach that has characterized this fund since 1994. The fund's main distinction is that in order to provide diversification away from the U.S., it avoids the domestic debt markets and the dollar. That's unusual in this group, where managers often devote more than a third of assets to U.S. issues and hedge much of their foreign-currency exposure into the greenback.

Their approach certainly hasn't helped performance in 2001. First of all, the dollar has remained strong against its developed-market counterparts, so the fund's foreign-currency exposure has dragged on performance. The portfolio's regional allocation wasn't helpful either; a larger-than-average position in European bonds has hurt relative returns of late. A small slug of higher-yielding European corporate paper has also been painful. Thus, although the fund has exposure to the resilient Japanese market, it's down more than 2% for the year to date through August 9, 2001.

The fund's performance often differs from its rivals, but when the dollar falters, it usually shines. In the second half of 1998 and the first quarter of 2000, for example, the fund's exposure to foreign currencies helped it outpace many of its rivals.

While the fund's dry spells and substantial volatility are hard to stomach, this hasn't been a bad bet for longtime shareholders, and its 10-year record is in the top third of the category. For those who are serious about diversification, this is a decent choice.

Address:	100 E. Pratt Street Baltimore, MD 21202 800–638–5660 / 410–547–2308
Web Address:	www.troweprice.com
Inception:	09-10-86
Advisor:	Rowe Price–Fleming International
Subadvisor:	None
NTF Plans:	N/A

Minimum Purchase:	$2500	Add: $100 IRA: $1000
Min Auto Inv Plan:	$100	Add: $100
Sales Fees:	No-load	
Management Fee:	.35%+.33% mx./.30% mn.(G)	
Actual Fees:	Mgt: 0.67%	Dist: —
Expense Projections:	3Yr: $287	5Yr: $498 10Yr: $1108
Avg Brok Commission:	—	Income Distrib: Monthly
Total Cost (relative to category):		Below Avg

T. Rowe Price International Stock

Ticker	Load	NAV	Yield	Total Assets	Mstar Category
PRITX	None	$10.99	2.7%	$6,377.4 mil	Foreign Stock

Prospectus Objective: Foreign Stock

T. Rowe Price International Stock Fund seeks long-term growth of capital.

The fund normally invests at least 65% of assets in the common stocks of established non-U.S. issuers. It may invest the balance of assets in preferred stocks, warrants, convertibles, and/or debt securities. The fund typically maintains investments in at least three foreign countries, and it may invest in both industrialized and developing countries.

The fund offers two different share classes, both of which differ in fee structure and availability. Prior to Sept. 10, 1986, the fund was named T. Rowe Price International Fund.

Historical Profile
Return: Average
Risk: Average
Rating: ★★★ Neutral

Investment Style
Equity
Average Stock %: 94% | 93% | 94% | 96% | 96% | 95% | 97%

▼ Manager Change
▽ Partial Manager Change

Fund Performance vs. Category Average
■ Quarterly Fund Return +/– Category Average
— Category Baseline

Performance Quartile (within Category)

Portfolio Manager(s)

John R. Ford, CFA. Since 1-82.
James B.M. Seddon. Since 1-87.
David J.L. Warren. Since 1-83.
Mark Bickford-Smith. Since 1-95.

1990	1991	1992	1993	1994	1995	1996	1997	1998	1999	2000	12-01	History
8.81	9.54	8.89	12.16	11.32	12.23	13.80	13.42	14.99	19.03	14.52	10.99	NAV
–8.89	15.87	–3.47	40.11	–0.76	11.39	15.99	2.70	16.14	34.60	–17.09	–22.02	Total Return %
–5.78	–14.62	–11.09	30.06	–2.07	–26.14	–6.96	–30.65	–12.44	13.56	–7.99	–10.14	+/– S&P 500
14.56	3.74	8.70	7.55	–8.54	0.19	9.94	0.92	–3.86	7.64	–2.93	—	+/– MSCI EAFE
1.56	1.70	1.68	1.01	0.99	1.59	1.47	1.45	1.64	0.87	0.47	2.07	Income Return %
–10.45	14.17	–5.15	39.10	–1.74	9.80	14.52	1.25	14.50	33.73	–17.57	–24.08	Capital Return %
34	26	46	30	64	40	34	69	31	55	54	49	Total Rtn % Rank Cat
0.16	0.15	0.16	0.09	0.12	0.18	0.18	0.20	0.22	0.13	0.09	0.30	Income $
0.36	0.49	0.16	0.20	0.62	0.20	0.20	0.55	0.35	0.91	1.18	0.03	Capital Gains $
1.09	1.10	1.05	1.01	0.96	0.91	0.88	0.85	0.85	0.85	0.84	—	Expense Ratio %
2.16	1.51	1.49	1.52	1.11	1.56	1.58	1.33	1.50	1.05	0.55	—	Income Ratio %
47	45	38	30	23	18	12	16	12	18	38	—	Turnover Rate %
1,030.8	1,476.3	1,949.6	4,290.0	5,786.9	6,703.3	9,340.8	9,720.6	10,141.8	12,674.0	9,734.6	—	Net Assets $mil

Performance 12-31-01

	1st Qtr	2nd Qtr	3rd Qtr	4th Qtr	Total
1997	0.00	11.88	–0.78	–7.49	2.70
1998	13.56	0.13	–13.70	18.34	16.14
1999	1.27	2.90	3.59	24.70	34.60
2000	0.47	–4.45	–8.10	–6.03	–17.09
2001	–15.50	–0.98	–15.14	9.83	–22.02

Trailing	Total Return%	+/– S&P 500	+/– MSCI EAFE	% Rank All	% Rank Cat	Growth of $10,000
3 Mo	9.83	–0.86	—	44	32	10,983
6 Mo	–6.81	–1.25	—	73	22	9,319
1 Yr	–22.02	–10.14	—	83	49	7,798
3 Yr Avg	–4.53	–3.50	—	91	66	8,702
5 Yr Avg	0.75	–9.95	—	91	66	10,380
10 Yr Avg	6.05	–6.87	—	69	53	18,000
15 Yr Avg	7.59	–6.15	—	58	40	29,942

Tax Analysis	Tax-Adj Ret%	%Rank Cat	%Pretax Ret	%Rank Cat
3 Yr Avg	–5.87	66	—	—
5 Yr Avg	–0.63	64	—	—
10 Yr Avg	4.73	46	78.1	42

Potential Capital Gain Exposure: –31% of assets

Risk Analysis

Time Period	Load-Adj Return %	Risk %Rank[1] All	Risk %Rank[1] Cat	Morningstar Return	Morningstar Risk	Morningstar Risk-Adj Rating
1 Yr	–22.02					
3 Yr	–4.53	75	60	–1.83[2]	0.97	★★
5 Yr	0.75	75	57	–0.86[2]	0.85	★★★
10 Yr	6.05	81	54	0.36[2]	0.85	★★★

Average Historical Rating (193 months): 3.9★s

[1] 1=low, 100=high [2] T-Bill return substituted for category avg.

Category Rating (3 Yr)
1 2 3 4 5
Worst Best
Return: Average
Risk: Average

Other Measures	Standard Index S&P 500	Best Fit Index MSCIWdxUSN
Alpha	–4.0	1.7
Beta	0.84	1.15
R-Squared	59	95
Standard Deviation		17.84
Mean		–4.53
Sharpe Ratio		–0.62

Portfolio Analysis 09-30-01

Share change since 06-01 Total Stocks: 193	Sector	Country	% Assets
☼ Glaxosmithkline	Technology	United Kingdom	5.03
Total Fina Cl B	Energy	France	2.56
⊖ Royal Bk of Scotland	Financials	United Kingdom	2.35
Reed Intl	Services	United Kingdom	2.19
⊖ Shell Transp & Trad	Energy	United Kingdom	2.07
⊕ Ing Groepnv	N/A	N/A	2.04
Vodafone Airtouch	Services	United Kingdom	2.03
⊕ Nestle	Staples	Switzerland	2.02
Aventis Cl A	Health	France	1.66
NTT DoCoMo	Services	Japan	1.60
⊖ Compass Grp	Services	United Kingdom	1.59
Sanofi-Synthelabo	Health	France	1.49
⊖ Canon	Industrials	Japan	1.46
BNP Paribus	Financials	France	1.39
Astrazeneca	Health	United Kingdom	1.37
Nokia	Technology	Finland	1.34
⊕ Securitas Cl B	Services	Sweden	1.27
⊕ Allianz (Reg)	Financials	Germany	1.23
VNU	Services	Netherlands	1.19
☼ UBS AG REG	Financials	Switzerland	1.15

Current Investment Style

Style: Value Blnd Growth; Size: Large Med Small

	Stock Port Avg	Rel MSCI EAFE Current	Rel MSCI EAFE Hist	Rel Cat
Price/Earnings Ratio	28.3	1.09	1.08	1.11
Price/Cash Flow	15.9	1.24	1.14	1.11
Price/Book Ratio	4.5	1.30	1.25	1.16
3 Yr Earnings Growth	21.9	1.17	1.07	1.11
Med Mkt Cap $mil	30,966	1.1	1.0	1.72

Country Exposure 09-30-01	% assets
United Kingdom	26
Japan	15
France	14
Italy	6
Netherlands	5

Hedging History: Never

Regional Exposure 09-30-01	% assets
Europe	69
Japan	15
Latin America	2
Pacific Rim	6
Other	1

Special Securities % assets 09-30-01	
Restricted/Illiquid Secs	0
Emerging-Markets Secs	7
Options/Futures/Warrants	No

Composition % assets 09-30-01			
Cash	1.1	Bonds	0.0
Stocks	94.8	Other	4.1

Sector Weightings	% of Stocks	Rel Cat	5-Year High	5-Year Low
Utilities	1.9	0.7	10	2
Energy	9.3	1.6	9	2
Financials	21.9	1.0	26	11
Industrials	7.4	0.6	31	7
Durables	4.2	0.6	9	4
Staples	6.7	0.9	11	4
Services	22.7	1.3	31	9
Retail	3.3	0.7	11	2
Health	13.8	1.4	14	4
Technology	9.0	0.9	21	2

Analysis by William Samuel Rocco 12-21-01

Consistency remains this fund's calling card.

While the world's markets have been awfully choppy lately, T. Rowe Price International Stock Fund's portfolio has stayed pretty steady. John Ford and his comanagers recently trimmed their stakes in Nokia, a couple of Japanese technology stocks, and a few other issues that have thrived this fall. At the same time, the managers have continued to add to their positions in the French food-services provider Sodexho and the U.K. advertising and marketing power WPP on weakness. And they've beefed up their previously small holding in Hays, the British personnel company, because they've become more optimistic about the employment business.

That's about the extent of Ford and his comanagers' portfolio moves in recent weeks. Their restraint comes as no surprise. The fund is one of the largest offerings in the foreign category, and the managers are committed to their patient growth-oriented style. Annual turnover, in fact, is normally only about one third the group average here.

This discipline has been a mixed bag in 2001. Their moderate growth bias has been helpful the past few months, as Vodafone and several of the fund's other computer- and phone-related stocks have rebounded nicely. But many of those same issues hurt earlier in 2001. Thus, the fund is right in the middle of the pack for the year to date through Dec. 20, 2001, with a 24% loss.

Respectable returns are the norm for this fund, which hasn't finished in its group's bottom third in its 20-year history. Moderate volatility and low expenses also remain attractions here. Thus, we still think it is a worthwhile option for those who are nervous about venturing overseas.

Address:	100 E. Pratt Street Baltimore, MD 21202 800-638-5660 / 410-547-2308
Web Address:	www.troweprice.com
Inception:	05-09-80
Advisor:	T. Rowe Price Assoc.
Subadvisor:	None
NTF Plans:	N/A

Minimum Purchase:	$2500	Add: $100	IRA: $1000
Min Auto Inv Plan:	$50	Add: $50	
Sales Fees:	No-load		
Management Fee:	.35%+.33% mx./.30% mn.(G)		
Actual Fees:	Mgt: 0.67%	Dist: —	
Expense Projections:	3Yr: $271	5Yr: $471	10Yr: $1049
Avg Brok Commission:	—	Income Distrib: Annually	
Total Cost (relative to category):		Low	

T. Rowe Price Mid–Cap Growth

Ticker	Load	NAV	Yield	Total Assets	Mstar Category
RPMGX	None	$39.40	0.0%	$5,833.3 mil	Mid–Cap Growth

Prospectus Objective: Growth

T. Rowe Price Mid-Cap Growth Fund seeks long-term growth of capital.

The fund normally invests at least 65% of assets in mid-cap common stocks with above-average growth potential. The advisor seeks companies that offer proven products or services; have an above-average historical record of earnings growth; have the potential for sustaining growth; operate in industries experiencing increasing demand; and/or are reasonably valued. The fund may invest up to 25% of assets in foreign securities.

The fund offers two different share classes, both of which differ in fee structure and availability.

Historical Profile
Return Above Avg
Risk Average
Rating ★★★★ Above Avg

Investment Style
Equity
Average Stock %: 91% 91% 92% 91% 91% 93% 93%

▼ Manager Change
▽ Partial Manager Change

Fund Performance vs. Category Average
■ Quarterly Fund Return +/– Category Average
— Category Baseline

Performance Quartile (within Category)

Portfolio Manager(s)

Brian W.H. Berghuis, CFA. Since 6-92. BA'81 Princeton U.; MBA'85 Harvard U. Other funds currently managed: T. Rowe Price Instl Mid-Cap Equity Gr, Maxim T. Rowe Price MidCap Growth, T. Rowe Price Mid-Cap Growth Adv.

1990	1991	1992	1993	1994	1995	1996	1997	1998	1999	2000	12-01	History
—	—	12.27	15.18	14.85	20.13	24.43	28.60	34.08	40.13	39.79	39.40	NAV
—	—	24.54*	26.24	0.29	40.95	24.84	18.33	22.00	23.78	7.43	–0.98	Total Return %
—	—	16.20*	16.18	–1.02	3.42	1.89	–15.02	–6.58	2.74	16.53	10.90	+/– S&P 500
—	—	—	15.05	2.46	6.98	7.36	–4.21	4.13	–27.53	19.17	19.18	+/– Russ Midcap Grth
—	—	0.00	0.00	0.00	0.00	0.00	0.00	0.00	0.00	0.00	0.00	Income Return %
—	—	24.54	26.24	0.29	40.95	24.84	18.33	22.00	23.78	7.43	–0.98	Capital Return %
—	—	—	10	40	24	14	45	25	85	26	5	Total Rtn % Rank Cat
—	—	0.00	0.00	0.00	0.00	0.00	0.00	0.00	0.00	0.00	0.00	Income $
—	—	0.18	0.30	0.37	0.79	0.69	0.30	0.73	1.88	3.27	0.00	Capital Gains $
—	—	1.25	1.25	1.25	1.25	1.04	0.95	0.91	0.87	0.86	—	Expense Ratio %
—	—	0.16	–0.12	0.02	–0.01	–0.11	–0.14	–0.14	–0.09	–0.09	—	Income Ratio %
—	—	52	62	49	58	38	43	47	53	54	—	Turnover Rate %
—	—	27.6	64.5	100.5	264.0	1,021.0	1,838.7	3,310.2	5,243.5	6,588.9	—	Net Assets $mil

Performance 12-31-01

	1st Qtr	2nd Qtr	3rd Qtr	4th Qtr	Total
1997	–6.55	13.67	11.45	–0.04	18.33
1998	16.12	0.42	–17.48	26.79	22.00
1999	–0.79	12.16	–7.28	19.98	23.78
2000	9.97	–3.83	5.61	–3.81	7.43
2001	–13.24	14.37	–17.71	21.27	–0.98

Trailing	Total Return%	+/– S&P 500	+/– Russ Midcap Grth	% Rank All	% Rank Cat	Growth of $10,000
3 Mo	21.27	10.58	–5.80	12	34	12,127
6 Mo	–0.20	5.35	8.06	40	4	9,980
1 Yr	–0.98	10.90	19.18	44	5	9,902
3 Yr Avg	9.60	10.63	7.45	12	27	13,167
5 Yr Avg	13.71	3.01	4.69	6	19	19,008
10 Yr Avg	—	—	—	—	—	—
15 Yr Avg	—	—	—	—	—	—

Tax Analysis	Tax-Adj Ret%	%Rank Cat	%Pretax Ret	%Rank Cat
3 Yr Avg	8.58	20	89.4	23
5 Yr Avg	12.90	11	94.1	6
10 Yr Avg	—	—	—	—

Potential Capital Gain Exposure: 22% of assets

Risk Analysis

Time Period	Load-Adj Return %	Risk %Rank[1] All	Risk %Rank[1] Cat	Morningstar Return	Morningstar Risk	Morningstar Risk-Adj Rating
1 Yr	–0.98					
3 Yr	9.60	69	13	1.03[2]	0.95	★★★★
5 Yr	13.71	73	8	2.24[2]	1.00	★★★★
Incept	19.11	—	—	—	—	

Average Historical Rating (79 months): 4.4★s

[1] 1=low, 100=high [2] T-Bill return substituted for category avg.

Category Rating (3 Yr)

Worst 1 2 3 4 5 Best

Return Above Avg
Risk Below Avg

Other Measures	Standard Index S&P 500	Best Fit Index SPMid400
Alpha	12.1	–0.4
Beta	1.09	1.04
R–Squared	73	88
Standard Deviation		23.90
Mean		9.60
Sharpe Ratio		0.22

Analysis by Catherine Hickey 08-12-01

This fund is vindicating its investors' loyalty.

T. Rowe Price Mid-Cap Growth Fund looked pretty lackluster in the late 1990s. In fact, coming into early 2000, when high-P/E stocks were still in the stratosphere, the fund's return since inception lagged that of the typical mid-growth fund. That was because manager Brian Berghuis runs a more moderate portfolio than most in the category, and stayed far away from technology stocks during the growth frenzy of 1999.

The fund has rewarded investors' patience lately, though. It has posted a modest, 6.6% loss for the 12 months ended August 16, compared with a 33% loss for the typical mid-growth fund. Curiously, even as some of his peers were slashing their tech weights this year, Berghuis increased this portfolio's stake earlier in 2001, picking through the rubble in search of companies that were unjustly tarnished by the sell-off. He soon sold some of those names, however, and swapped into health-care services and financial stocks.

Such moves are characteristic of Berghuis' steady, relatively cautious approach. Unlike other gunslinging mid-growth offerings, this one makes risk control a top priority. Thus, Berghuis keeps the portfolio well-diversified across sectors and individual names, and he steers clear of stocks with valuations that he deems to be too rich. Such an approach can mean that the fund lags its peers when go-go growth stocks rule the roost, as it did in 1999's tech-fueled bonanza. However, 1999 was an aberration; the fund regularly notches top-half performances, and its long-term returns are top-notch.

Assets have grown quite large here, and that's something we'll be keeping an eye on. However, there's no need to panic just yet, as the big asset base hasn't yet affected performance negatively. All in all, this remains a highly appealing mid-growth option.

Portfolio Analysis 09-30-01

Share change since 06-01 Total Stocks: 124

Share change	Name	Sector	PE	YTD Ret%	% Assets
	Concord EFS	Financials	86.3	49.21	2.61
	Affiliated Comp Svcs A	Services	39.9	74.88	2.60
	WellPoint Health Networks	Health	19.4	1.39	2.19
⊖	AmeriSource Health Cl A	Health	30.3	25.90	2.07
	Waddell & Reed Finl Cl A	Financials	23.3	–13.40	2.02
⊕	Western Wireless Cl A	Services	—	–27.90	1.94
	Omnicare	Health	38.3	15.52	1.83
	Gilead Sciences	Health	—	58.48	1.80
⊖	Federated Investors B	Financials	23.3	10.11	1.46
⊕	Family Dollar Stores	Retail	27.3	41.11	1.41
⊕	Robert Half Intl	Services	31.1	0.75	1.41
	Laboratory Corp of Amer	Health	21.0	–8.13	1.40
	Apogent Tech	Health	29.0	25.85	1.31
	BJ's Whlse Club	Retail	40.5	14.92	1.30
⊖	Heller Finl	Financials	—	73.46	1.29
⊕	Whole Foods Market	Retail	36.0	42.53	1.26
	Republic Svcs Cl A	Services	15.6	16.19	1.24
	Progressive	Financials	33.4	44.40	1.22
	Ocean Energy	Energy	10.6	11.58	1.19
⊕	MedImmune	Health	78.6	–2.81	1.17
	Radian Grp	Financials	11.6	14.64	1.16
⊖	King Pharmaceuticals	Health	45.8	8.68	1.15
	Lincare Hldgs	Health	23.7	0.41	1.11
	Franklin Resources	Financials	18.5	–6.78	1.11
⊕	Diamond Offshore Drilling	Energy	25.8	–22.80	1.08

Current Investment Style

Style: Value Blnd Growth; Size: Large Med Small

	Stock Port Avg	Relative S&P 500 Current	Relative S&P 500 Hist	Rel Cat
Price/Earnings Ratio	32.2	1.04	0.96	0.93
Price/Book Ratio	6.2	1.09	0.83	1.10
Price/Cash Flow	21.0	1.17	1.02	0.91
3 Yr Earnings Growth	15.9	1.09	1.27	0.68
1 Yr Earnings Est%	10.7	—	—	1.14
Med Mkt Cap $mil	4,156	0.1	0.1	0.74

Special Securities % assets 09-30-01	
Restricted/Illiquid Secs	0
Emerging–Markets Secs	2
Options/Futures/Warrants	No

Composition % assets 09-30-01	
Cash	6.3
Stocks*	93.7
Bonds	0.0
Other	0.0
*Foreign (% stocks)	4.6

Market Cap	
Giant	0.0
Large	18.0
Medium	80.2
Small	1.4
Micro	0.5

Sector Weightings	% of Stocks	Rel S&P	5-Year High	5-Year Low
Utilities	1.0	0.3	1	0
Energy	5.8	0.8	8	1
Financials	16.3	0.9	16	8
Industrials	4.2	0.4	37	3
Durables	1.6	1.0	8	0
Staples	0.5	0.1	3	0
Services	23.4	2.2	32	19
Retail	8.6	1.3	18	6
Health	24.3	1.6	24	5
Technology	14.4	0.8	27	7

Address: 100 E. Pratt Street
Baltimore, MD 21202
800–638–5660 / 410–547–2308
Web Address: www.troweprice.com
*Inception: 06-30-92
Advisor: T. Rowe Price Assoc.
Subadvisor: None
NTF Plans: N/A

Minimum Purchase: $2500 Add: $100 IRA: $1000
Min Auto Inv Plan: $50 Add: $50
Sales Fees: No–load
Management Fee: .35%+.33% mx./.30% mn.(G)
Actual Fees: Mgt: 0.67% Dist: —
Expense Projections: 3Yr: $278 5Yr: $482 10Yr: $1073
Avg Brok Commission: — Income Distrib: Annually
Total Cost (relative to category): Low

T. Rowe Price Mid–Cap Value

Ticker	Load	NAV	Yield	Total Assets	Mstar Category
TRMCX	None	$16.40	0.7%	$396.4 mil	Mid–Cap Value

Prospectus Objective: Growth

T. Rowe Price Mid-Cap Value Fund seeks long-term capital appreciation.

The fund normally invests at least 65% of assets in companies whose market capitalization falls between $300 million and $5 billion. It invests primarily in U.S. common stocks, but it may also purchase foreign stocks, convertibles, and warrants. The advisor takes a value investment approach, seeking issuers whose stock prices are low in relation to their real worth or future prospects. To select securities, the advisor evaluates criteria such as P/E, price/book, and price/cash-flow ratios; dividend yields; undervalued assets; and restructuring opportunities. The fund may also invest in futures and options.

Historical Profile
Return Above Avg
Risk Below Avg
Rating ★★★★★ Highest

Investment Style Equity
Average Stock %: 88% 89% 93% 95% 95% 91%

▼ Manager Change
▽ Partial Manager Change

Fund Performance vs. Category Average
Quarterly Fund Return +/– Category Average
– Category Baseline

Performance Quartile (within Category)

Portfolio Manager(s)

David J. Wallack. Since 12-00. BA'82 Connecticut C.; MSIA'90 Carnegie-Mellon U.

History	1990	1991	1992	1993	1994	1995	1996	1997	1998	1999	2000	12-01
NAV	—	—	—	—	—	—	11.56	14.47	13.66	13.37	15.64	16.40
Total Return %	—	—	—	—	—	—	15.96*	27.11	1.39	3.52	22.75	14.36
+/– S&P 500	—	—	—	—	—	—	4.28*	–6.24	–27.19	–17.52	31.85	26.24
+/– Russ Midcap Val	—	—	—	—	—	—	—	–7.25	–3.70	3.63	3.56	12.02
Income Return %	—	—	—	—	—	—	0.70	0.69	1.31	1.68	1.27	0.83
Capital Return %	—	—	—	—	—	—	15.25	26.41	0.07	1.84	21.48	13.53
Total Rtn % Rank Cat	—	—	—	—	—	—	—	47	59	65	31	23
Income $	—	—	—	—	—	—	0.07	0.08	0.19	0.23	0.17	0.13
Capital Gains $	—	—	—	—	—	—	0.00	0.14	0.76	0.51	0.56	1.31
Expense Ratio %	—	—	—	—	—	—	1.25	1.25	1.08	1.04	0.99	—
Income Ratio %	—	—	—	—	—	—	2.10	1.18	1.24	1.60	1.33	—
Turnover Rate %	—	—	—	—	—	—	4	16	32	27	32	—
Net Assets $mil	—	—	—	—	—	—	49.2	218.0	221.3	211.7	282.3	—

Performance 12-31-01

	1st Qtr	2nd Qtr	3rd Qtr	4th Qtr	Total
1997	–0.87	12.22	11.28	2.68	27.11
1998	9.12	–2.79	–15.90	13.64	1.39
1999	–5.12	12.81	–4.65	1.44	3.52
2000	3.74	–1.08	7.73	11.04	22.75
2001	–2.11	9.60	–9.12	17.29	14.36

Trailing	Total Return%	+/– S&P 500	+/– Russ Midcap Val	% Rank All	% Rank Cat	Growth of $10,000
3 Mo	17.29	6.60	5.26	19	26	11,729
6 Mo	6.59	12.15	7.50	2	11	10,659
1 Yr	14.36	26.24	12.02	4	23	11,436
3 Yr Avg	13.27	14.29	6.46	7	30	14,532
5 Yr Avg	13.37	2.67	1.91	7	35	18,728
10 Yr Avg	—	—	—	—	—	—
15 Yr Avg	—	—	—	—	—	—

Tax Analysis	Tax-Adj Ret%	%Rank Cat	%Pretax Ret	%Rank Cat
3 Yr Avg	11.29	28	85.1	34
5 Yr Avg	11.59	29	86.7	18
10 Yr Avg	—	—	—	—

Potential Capital Gain Exposure: 14% of assets

Risk Analysis

Time Period	Load-Adj Return %	Risk %Rank[1] All	Risk %Rank[1] Cat	Morningstar Return	Morningstar Risk	Morningstar Risk-Adj Rating
1 Yr	14.36					
3 Yr	13.27	39	12	1.91[2]	0.52	★★★★★
5 Yr	13.37	46	12	2.14[2]	0.62	★★★★★
Incept	15.12	—	—	—	—	

Average Historical Rating (31 months): 3.2★s

[1] 1=low, 100=high [2] T-Bill return substituted for category avg.

Category Rating (3 Yr)

1 2 3 4 5 (Worst – Best)

Return: Above Avg
Risk: Below Avg

Other Measures	Standard Index S&P 500	Best Fit Index SPMid400
Alpha	12.0	4.8
Beta	0.59	0.59
R–Squared	44	60
Standard Deviation		16.75
Mean		13.27
Sharpe Ratio		0.57

Portfolio Analysis 09-30-01

Share change since 06-01 Total Stocks: 111

Share change	Sector	PE	YTD Ret%	% Assets
⊕ Aetna	Financials	—	–19.50	1.67
⊕ SAFECO	Financials	—	–2.33	1.62
⊕ Meredith	Services	28.8	11.82	1.46
⊕ Guidant	Health	42.6	–7.67	1.44
⊕ Raytheon	Industrials	—	7.27	1.44
FirstEnergy	Utilities	12.8	16.42	1.42
⊕ PartnerRe	Financials	22.4	–10.50	1.41
⊕ Dover	Industrials	21.1	–7.38	1.38
⊕ Diamond Offshore Drilling	Energy	25.8	–22.80	1.36
⊕ Nucor	Industrials	24.9	35.52	1.36
⊕ Hasbro	Durables	—	54.09	1.34
☼ Compaq Comp	Technology	—	–34.50	1.34
⊕ Commerce Bancshares	Financials	14.4	–2.05	1.31
⊕ Molex Cl A	Technology	—	—	1.29
⊕ Brunswick	Industrials	15.2	35.60	1.28
⊕ CNF	Services	—	0.56	1.28
Knight Ridder	Services	59.0	16.13	1.28
⊕ Potlatch	Industrials	—	–9.40	1.26
⊕ Boston Scientific	Health	—	76.21	1.25
⊕ USX–Marathon Grp	Energy	9.6	11.58	1.24
Fortune Brands	Staples	—	35.68	1.22
⊕ Apple Comp	Technology	—	47.23	1.20
Sepracor 7%	N/A	—	—	1.19
⊕ Newell Rubbermaid	Durables	25.5	25.20	1.19
⊖ Newmont Mng	Industrials	—	12.69	1.18

Current Investment Style

Style: Value Blnd Growth; Size: Large Med Small

	Stock Port Avg	Relative S&P 500 Current	Relative S&P 500 Hist	Rel Cat
Price/Earnings Ratio	25.5	0.83	0.69	1.08
Price/Book Ratio	2.8	0.49	0.42	0.93
Price/Cash Flow	13.5	0.75	0.57	1.09
3 Yr Earnings Growth	6.9	0.47	0.59	0.58
1 Yr Earnings Est%	–16.1	9.07	—	2.61
Med Mkt Cap $mil	3,171	0.1	0.1	0.45

[1] figure is based on 50% or less of stocks

Analysis by Catherine Hickey 12-26-01

The wind may be at this offering's back right now, but shrewd portfolio maneuvering has kept this fund on top lately.

T. Rowe Price Mid-Cap Value Fund's new skipper, Dave Wallack, is closing out a very successful first year on the job. In a year when most stock funds are in the red, this offering's 13.1% return through Dec. 22, 2001, looks smashing, and it even is well above-average for the mid-value category. Solid stock picks such as Hasbro played a big role in the fund's success in 2001, though a below-average median market cap also helped.

Wallack said the fund was well-positioned for the fourth-quarter tech recovery before Sept. 11, because he had added to tech and other economically sensitive issues earlier in 2001 in anticipation of a recovery. Indeed, the fund was bolstered by Apple Computer late in the year. But during the market's post-attack sell-off in September, Wallack picked up some bargain-priced issues in the market. For instance, he added to a beaten-down position in Reader's Digest Association, a company he likes for its solid brand and vast distribution network.

This fund has been managed from the get-go in this valuation-sensitive, yet opportunistic, manner. Wallack buys stocks when they are well out of favor, but as importantly for performance, he cuts them back when they soar. For instance, he eliminated a position in Dynegy earlier this year as its valuation and market cap became inflated. That was a wise move; the stock has been battered all year.

True, Wallack has only been on board a year here, and the fund's style has been in favor for most of that time. However, it's more than just luck that has put this fund ahead of its peers under Wallack's watch.

Special Securities % assets 09-30-01	
Restricted/Illiquid Secs	0
Emerging–Markets Secs	0
Options/Futures/Warrants	No

Composition % assets 09-30-01	
Cash	6.4
Stocks*	92.1
Bonds	1.2
Other	0.2
*Foreign (% stocks)	3.8

Market Cap	
Giant	0.0
Large	15.1
Medium	71.8
Small	13.1
Micro	0.0

Sector Weightings	% of Stocks	Rel S&P	5-Year High	5-Year Low
Utilities	4.6	1.5	—	—
Energy	6.8	1.0	—	—
Financials	20.3	1.1	—	—
Industrials	25.5	2.2	—	—
Durables	3.7	2.4	—	—
Staples	5.4	0.7	—	—
Services	13.3	1.2	—	—
Retail	3.9	0.6	—	—
Health	4.4	0.3	—	—
Technology	12.1	0.7	—	—

Address:	100 E. Pratt Street Baltimore, MD 21202 800–638–5660 / 410–547–2308
Web Address:	www.troweprice.com
*Inception:	06-30-96
Advisor:	T. Rowe Price Assoc.
Subadvisor:	None
NTF Plans:	N/A

Minimum Purchase:	$2500	Add: $100 IRA: $1000
Min Auto Inv Plan:	$50	Add: $50
Sales Fees:	No–load	
Management Fee:	.35%+.33% mx./.30% mn.(G)	
Actual Fees:	Mgt: 0.67%	Dist: —
Expense Projections:	3Yr: $331	5Yr: $574 10Yr: $1271
Avg Brok Commission:	—	Income Distrib: Annually
Total Cost (relative to category):		Below Avg

T. Rowe Price New America Growth

Ticker	Load	NAV	Yield	Total Assets	Mstar Category
PRWAX	None	$30.87	0.0%	$1,053.7 mil	Large Blend

Prospectus Objective: Growth

T. Rowe Price New America Growth Fund seeks long-term capital appreciation.

The fund invests at least 65% of assets in common stocks of U.S. companies that operate in the fastest growing sectors or the sectors having the greatest growth potential. It seeks companies that are above-average performers in their fields, without regard to size. The fund may invest up to 15% of assets in foreign securities.

On Aug. 31, 1992, USF&G Axe-Houghton Growth Fund merged into this fund.

Historical Profile

Return Average
Risk Above Avg
Rating ★★ Below Avg

Investment Style: Equity — Average Stock %: 98% 96% 93% 97% 95% 95% 93%

▼ Manager Change
▽ Partial Manager Change

Fund Performance vs. Category Average
■ Quarterly Fund Return +/– Category Average
— Category Baseline

Performance Quartile (within Category)

Portfolio Manager(s)

Marc L. Baylin. Since 2-00.

1990	1991	1992	1993	1994	1995	1996	1997	1998	1999	2000	12-01	History
14.66	22.79	24.86	28.04	25.42	34.91	38.37	44.19	47.79	48.06	35.77	30.87	NAV
–12.24	61.95	9.89	17.44	–7.43	44.31	20.01	21.10	17.89	12.76	–10.53	–11.89	Total Return %
–9.13	31.47	2.27	7.38	–8.75	6.78	–2.94	–12.26	–10.68	–8.28	–1.43	–0.01	+/– S&P 500
–8.22	29.51	2.24	7.60	–7.88	6.71	–2.16	–11.93	–10.74	–9.07	0.43	0.88	+/– Wilshire Top 750
1.01	0.00	0.00	0.00	0.00	0.00	0.00	0.00	0.00	0.00	0.00	0.00	Income Return %
–13.25	61.95	9.89	17.44	–7.43	44.31	20.01	21.10	17.89	12.76	–10.53	–11.89	Capital Return %
93	2	25	14	94	2	64	86	75	84	74	33	Total Rtn % Rank Cat
0.17	0.00	0.00	0.00	0.00	0.00	0.00	0.00	0.00	0.00	0.00	0.00	Income $
0.00	0.87	0.18	1.13	0.53	1.75	3.49	2.20	3.84	5.40	7.52	0.64	Capital Gains $
1.25	1.25	1.25	1.23	1.14	1.07	1.01	0.96	0.95	0.94	0.93	—	Expense Ratio %
0.81	–0.12	–0.44	–0.39	–0.27	–0.46	–0.39	–0.34	–0.49	–0.43	–0.33	—	Income Ratio %
42	42	26	44	31	56	37	43	46	40	81	—	Turnover Rate %
95.7	231.7	480.2	618.6	646.1	1,028.2	1,440.2	1,757.9	2,064.4	1,826.0	1,518.8	—	Net Assets $mil

Performance 12-31-01

	1st Qtr	2nd Qtr	3rd Qtr	4th Qtr	Total
1997	–5.32	14.64	10.78	0.70	21.10
1998	17.27	0.00	–21.27	27.69	17.89
1999	0.61	10.27	–12.17	15.71	12.76
2000	2.23	–3.58	0.30	–9.49	–10.53
2001	–15.60	10.70	–21.78	20.57	–11.89

Trailing	Total Return%	+/– S&P 500	+/–Wil Top 750	% Rank All	% Rank Cat	Growth of $10,000
3 Mo	20.57	9.89	9.25	13	1	12,057
6 Mo	–5.69	–0.14	0.10	66	40	9,431
1 Yr	–11.89	–0.01	0.88	64	33	8,811
3 Yr Avg	–3.85	–2.82	–2.03	89	84	8,889
5 Yr Avg	4.88	–5.82	–5.24	67	91	12,690
10 Yr Avg	10.13	–2.79	–2.32	32	72	26,256
15 Yr Avg	12.10	–1.64	–1.27	25	60	55,439

Tax Analysis	Tax-Adj Ret%	%Rank Cat	%Pretax Ret	%Rank Cat
3 Yr Avg	–5.78	87	—	—
5 Yr Avg	3.02	90	61.8	88
10 Yr Avg	8.51	64	84.0	32

Potential Capital Gain Exposure: 18% of assets

Risk Analysis

Time Period	Load-Adj Return %	Risk %Rank[1] All	Risk %Rank[1] Cat	Morningstar Return	Morningstar Risk	Morningstar Risk-Adj Rating
1 Yr	–11.89					
3 Yr	–3.85	84	94	–1.71[2]	1.25	★★
5 Yr	4.88	85	98	–0.03[2]	1.24	★★
10 Yr	10.13	88	99	0.75	1.29	★★

Average Historical Rating (160 months): 3.2★s

[1] 1=low, 100=high [2] T-Bill return substituted for category avg.

Category Rating (3 Yr)

Worst 1 2 3 4 5 Best

Return Below Avg
Risk High

Other Measures	Standard Index S&P 500	Best Fit Index S&P 500
Alpha	–0.4	–0.4
Beta	1.27	1.27
R-Squared	84	84
Standard Deviation		23.08
Mean		–3.85
Sharpe Ratio		–0.44

Portfolio Analysis 09-30-01

Share change since 06-01 Total Stocks: 87

Share change / Holding	Sector	PE	YTD Ret%	% Assets
Freddie Mac	Financials	14.0	–3.87	3.37
⊖ First Data	Technology	38.1	49.08	3.34
⊖ Affiliated Comp Svcs A	Services	39.9	74.88	3.24
Concord EFS	Financials	86.3	49.21	3.03
☼ Liberty Livewire	Services	—	—	2.88
⊖ Waddell & Reed Finl Cl A	Financials	23.3	–13.40	2.78
⊖ Apollo Grp Cl A	Services	—	—	2.75
⊕ Pfizer	Health	34.7	–12.40	2.60
⊖ Family Dollar Stores	Retail	27.3	41.11	2.38
Western Wireless Cl A	Services	—	–27.90	2.38
⊕ Target	Retail	29.8	28.05	2.13
Viacom Cl B	Services	—	—	2.06
⊕ Home Depot	Retail	42.9	12.07	2.05
⊕ Crown Castle Intl	Services	—	–60.50	1.97
⊕ AOL Time Warner	Technology	—	–7.76	1.88
⊖ Clear Channel Comms	Services	—	5.10	1.80
Microsoft	Technology	57.6	52.78	1.75
⊕ Laboratory Corp of Amer	Health	21.0	–8.13	1.75
Omnicare	Health	38.3	15.52	1.74
⊕ Flextronics Intl	Technology	—	–15.80	1.62
⊕ Safeway	Retail	18.1	–33.20	1.60
Costco Wholesale	Retail	34.4	11.12	1.59
⊖ Outback Steakhouse	Services	20.4	32.37	1.55
WellPoint Health Networks	Health	19.4	1.39	1.54
⊖ Comcast	Services	20.3	–13.70	1.54

Current Investment Style

Style: Value Blnd Growth; Size: Large Med Small

	Stock Port Avg	Relative S&P 500 Current	Relative S&P 500 Hist	Rel Cat
Price/Earnings Ratio	35.9	1.16	1.00	1.18
Price/Book Ratio	6.7	1.17	0.75	1.21
Price/Cash Flow	22.8	1.27	1.06	1.24
3 Yr Earnings Growth	21.6	1.47	1.41	1.21
1 Yr Earnings Est%	10.5	—	—	—
Med Mkt Cap $mil	16,164	0.3	0.2	0.31

[1] figure is based on 50% or less of stocks

Special Securities % assets 09-30-01	
Restricted/Illiquid Secs	0
Emerging-Markets Secs	0
Options/Futures/Warrants	No

Composition % assets 09-30-01	
Cash	6.6
Stocks*	93.4
Bonds	0.0
Other	0.0
*Foreign (% stocks)	1.9

Market Cap	
Giant	26.1
Large	33.0
Medium	40.2
Small	0.7
Micro	0.0

Sector Weightings	% of Stocks	Rel S&P	5-Year High	5-Year Low
Utilities	0.0	0.0	2	0
Energy	2.6	0.4	7	1
Financials	15.5	0.9	27	11
Industrials	2.6	0.2	6	0
Durables	0.0	0.0	2	0
Staples	0.0	0.0	1	0
Services	29.3	2.7	60	28
Retail	11.5	1.7	30	10
Health	15.3	1.0	18	1
Technology	23.2	1.3	30	2

Analysis by Catherine Hickey 10-30-01

One of the growthiest options in the T. Rowe Price stable is shaping up as a solid option.

This year, T. Rowe Price New America Growth Fund is performing better than it seems. True, the fund has lost 21% for the year through Oct. 29, 2001. That showing places the fund in the large-blend category's bottom quartile, but it's probably more useful to compare the fund with the large-growth group. The fund has landed in large growth since last year, when T. Rowe gave it a growthier profile. Versus that group, performance is well above average.

Now that it's more aggressive, however, shareholders who bought it before 2000 should revisit its portfolio role. The fund has spent most of its life as a tamer growth fund that focused mainly on services stocks, and was forbidden by charter to buy much tech. However, in March of 2000, T. Rowe turned it over to Marc Baylin, who refashioned it more boldly. Though Baylin uses a valuation-sensitive style that is the norm among T. Rowe managers, his search for companies with strong earnings growth leads him to load up on tech and media issues. Thus, investors looking for a milder offering might consider the firm's large-blend funds, such as Blue Chip Growth or Capital Opportunity.

However, T. Rowe investors searching for a growth vehicle should look here. Since Baylin took over, the fund has outperformed the large-growth average through solid picks and a valuation-sensitive approach. Also, though he owns a sizable chunk of tech here, he buys companies in well-established industries, like First Data and Microsoft. This helps limit volatility. Because Baylin avoids more-speculative growth stocks, the fund probably won't top the charts when aggressive-growth investing returns to style. However, the fund probably will never burn investors, either.

Address:	100 E. Pratt Street Baltimore, MD 21202 800-638-5660 / 410-547-2308
Web Address:	www.troweprice.com
Inception:	09-30-85
Advisor:	T. Rowe Price Assoc.
Subadvisor:	None
NTF Plans:	N/A

Minimum Purchase:	$2500	Add: $100 IRA: $1000
Min Auto Inv Plan:	$50	Add: $50
Sales Fees:	No-load	
Management Fee:	.35%+.33% mx./.30% mn.(G)	
Actual Fees:	Mgt: 0.67%	Dist: —
Expense Projections:	3Yr: $300	5Yr: $520 10Yr: $1155
Avg Brok Commission:	—	Income Distrib: Annually
Total Cost (relative to category):		Below Avg

T. Rowe Price New Asia

Ticker	Load	NAV	Yield	Total Assets	Mstar Category
PRASX	None	$6.21	0.0%	$527.2 mil	Pacific ex–Japan

Prospectus Objective: Pacific Stock

T. Rowe Price New Asia Fund seeks capital appreciation.

The fund invests at least 65% of assets in the common stocks of large- and small-capitalization companies domiciled, or with primary operations, in Asia and the Pacific Basin (excluding Japan). It invests in at least five countries with primary emphasis on China, Hong Kong, Indonesia, India, Malaysia, Philippines, Singapore, South Korea, Taiwan, and Thailand.

Historical Profile
Return Below Avg
Risk Above Avg
Rating ★★ Below Avg

Investment Style
Equity
Average Stock %

1994	1995	1996	1997	1998	1999	2000	12-01
	97%	95%	92%	88%	95%	96%	93%

▼ Manager Change
▽ Partial Manager Change

Fund Performance vs. Category Average
■ Quarterly Fund Return +/– Category Average
— Category Baseline

Performance Quartile (within Category)

Portfolio Manager(s)

Mark J.T. Edwards. Since 8-96. MA Cambridge U. Other funds currently managed: T. Rowe Price International Discovery, T. Rowe Price Emerging Markets Stock, Lutheran Brotherhood World Grow A.

Frances Dydasco. Since 11-96. BA'88 Harvard U. Other funds currently managed: T. Rowe Price International Discovery, T. Rowe Price Emerging Markets Stock.

John R. Ford, CFA. Since 3-00. MA'79 Oxford U. Other funds currently managed: T. Rowe Price European Stock, T. Rowe Price Foreign Equity, T. Rowe Price International Discovery.

1990	1991	1992	1993	1994	1995	1996	1997	1998	1999	2000	12-01	History
5.04	5.91	6.34	11.10	8.01	8.22	9.26	5.74	5.01	9.97	6.90	6.21	NAV
1.60*	19.32	11.24	78.84	–19.19	3.75	13.51	–37.13	–11.11	99.88	–30.79	–10.00	Total Return %
–7.36*	–11.17	3.62	68.78	–20.50	–33.78	–9.43	–70.49	–39.69	78.84	–21.69	1.88	+/– S&P 500
—	6.21	5.05	–7.18	–10.29	7.28	5.28	4.93	–3.95	34.64	4.20	—	+/– MSCI FE ex Jpn
0.80	1.98	1.69	0.55	0.63	1.12	0.73	0.86	1.57	0.80	0.00	0.00	Income Return %
0.80	17.33	9.54	78.29	–19.82	2.63	12.78	–38.00	–12.68	99.08	–30.79	–10.00	Capital Return %
—	50	50	55	63	46	40	59	40	11	57	60	Total Rtn % Rank Cat
0.04	0.10	0.10	0.04	0.07	0.09	0.06	0.08	0.09	0.04	0.00	0.00	Income $
0.00	0.00	0.13	0.19	0.89	0.00	0.01	0.00	0.00	0.00	0.00	0.00	Capital Gains $
1.75	1.75	1.51	1.29	1.22	1.15	1.11	1.10	1.29	1.21	1.08	—	Expense Ratio %
2.10	1.75	1.64	1.02	0.85	0.97	0.66	0.76	2.33	0.87	0.41	—	Income Ratio %
—	49	36	40	63	64	42	42	68	70	52	—	Turnover Rate %
80.0	102.9	314.5	2,234.4	1,987.6	1,880.3	2,181.7	782.4	622.3	1,374.7	799.8	—	Net Assets $mil

Performance 12-31-01

	1st Qtr	2nd Qtr	3rd Qtr	4th Qtr	Total
1997	–4.00	3.94	–13.64	–27.05	–37.13
1998	4.01	–24.62	–4.22	18.38	–11.11
1999	6.99	27.99	2.77	42.04	99.88
2000	8.73	–14.11	–15.90	–11.88	–30.79
2001	–8.26	–1.58	–23.76	30.74	–10.00

Trailing	Total Return%	+/– S&P 500	+/– MSCI FE ex Jpn	% Rank All	% Rank Cat	Growth of $10,000
3 Mo	30.74	20.05	—	4	19	13,074
6 Mo	–0.32	5.23	—	40	52	9,968
1 Yr	–10.00	1.88	—	60	60	9,000
3 Yr Avg	7.58	8.60	—	16	26	12,450
5 Yr Avg	–7.00	–17.70	—	99	43	6,957
10 Yr Avg	2.79	–10.14	—	98	25	13,172
15 Yr Avg	—	—	—	—	—	—

Tax Analysis	Tax-Adj Ret%	%Rank Cat	%Pretax Ret	%Rank Cat
3 Yr Avg	7.51	26	99.2	45
5 Yr Avg	–7.27	42	—	—
10 Yr Avg	2.04	25	73.0	33

Potential Capital Gain Exposure: –32% of assets

Risk Analysis

Time Period	Load-Adj Return %	Risk %Rank[1] All	Risk %Rank[1] Cat	Morningstar Return	Morningstar Risk	Morningstar Risk-Adj Rating
1 Yr	–10.00					
3 Yr	7.58	87	37	0.57[2]	1.22	★★★★
5 Yr	–7.00	95	24	–2.09[2]	1.46	★★
10 Yr	2.79	97	34	–0.46[2]	1.43	★★

Average Historical Rating (100 months): 2.8★s

[1]1=low, 100=high [2] T-Bill return substituted for category avg.

Category Rating (3 Yr)

1 2 3 4 5
Worst Best

Return Above Avg
Risk Average

Other Measures	Standard Index S&P 500	Best Fit Index MSCIPcxJND
Alpha	13.0	6.6
Beta	1.22	1.11
R-Squared	46	70
Standard Deviation		33.97
Mean		7.58
Sharpe Ratio		0.09

Portfolio Analysis 09-30-01

Share change since 06-01 Total Stocks: 88	Sector	Country	% Assets
⊖ Hutchison Whampoa	Financials	Hong Kong	5.16
⊖ Cheung Kong Hldgs	Financials	Hong Kong	4.05
⊖ Reliance Inds	Durables	India	4.03
☼ Taiwan Semicon ADR	Technology	Taiwan	3.88
⊖ Samsung Electncs	Technology	South Korea	3.79
⊕ SK Telecom	Services	South Korea	3.60
⊖ China Telecom HK	Services	Hong Kong	2.79
☼ United Microelect ADR	Technology	Taiwan	2.53
⊖ HSBC Hldgs (HK)	Financials	Hong Kong	2.14
⊖ Hindustan Lever	Staples	India	2.06
⊖ Housing Dev Fin	Financials	India	2.02
☼ ICICI	Financials	India	1.94
⊖ HDFC Bk	Financials	India	1.88
Esprit Hldgs	Retail	Hong Kong	1.56
Great Eagle Hldgs	Financials	Hong Kong	1.53
Henderson Land Dev	Financials	Hong Kong	1.52
☼ Tenaga Nasional	Utilities	Malaysia	1.38
Samsung Fire & Marine Ins	Financials	South Korea	1.30
☼ LG Household Health	N/A	N/A	1.26
Singapore Telecom	Services	Singapore	1.23

Current Investment Style

Style: Value Blnd Growth; Size: Large Med Small

	Stock Port Avg	Rel MSCI EAFE Current	Rel MSCI EAFE Hist	Rel Cat
Price/Earnings Ratio	18.9	0.73	0.87	0.97
Price/Cash Flow	14.6	1.14	1.18	1.00
Price/Book Ratio	3.4	0.97	0.85	1.04
3 Yr Earnings Growth	26.3	1.40	0.85	1.00
Med Mkt Cap $mil	9,457	0.3	0.5	1.24

Country Exposure 09-30-01	% assets
Hong Kong	26
South Korea	17
India	15
Taiwan	13
Singapore	6

Hedging History: Never

Special Securities % assets 09-30-01	
Restricted/Illiquid Secs	0
Emerging–Markets Secs	79
Options/Futures/Warrants	No

Composition % assets 09-30-01

Cash	10.5	Bonds	0.0
Stocks	88.2	Other	1.4

Sector Weightings	% of Stocks	Rel Cat	5-Year High	5-Year Low
Utilities	2.3	0.5	18	0
Energy	0.8	0.3	6	0
Financials	41.0	1.3	52	20
Industrials	4.8	0.6	32	1
Durables	7.9	1.4	14	1
Staples	4.2	1.2	9	0
Services	15.9	0.8	31	14
Retail	3.8	0.8	4	0
Health	0.3	0.3	5	0
Technology	19.0	1.0	35	0

Analysis by William Samuel Rocco 11-08-01

Don't overreact to the fact that T. Rowe Price New Asia is on pace for the first bottom-quartile finish in its long history.

Emerging Asia's markets have been quite volatile in the 11 calendar years since this fund opened. Not only has the typical Pacific/Asia ex-Japan offering suffered four double-digit annual losses during that time, but it has also twice gained more than 75%. The fund has handled all those ups and downs with aplomb, though. Indeed, in every year but the big rally of 1999, when it soared to a top-decile finish, the fund placed in its category's middle third.

The fund's record of consistency is in serious jeopardy this year, though. Top name Heung Keung Holdings, which has been trimmed but is still more than 4% of assets, has been a poor performer, as have several of the fund's other Hong Kong property stocks. While Frances Dydasco and her comanagers have added to their stakes in Hite Brewery and some other domestic plays in Korea recent months, the fund has had less exposure to that strong market for much of 2001.

The fund's emphasis on growth stocks, particularly its taste for India software issues, has also hurt. Thus, though selected issues have done well, the fund has lost 24% and lags three fourths of its peers for the year to date through Nov. 7, 2001.

That stings, of course, but investors have ample reason to be patient with this offering. Its management remains intact, as does the moderate growth style that has generally produced solid results here. Moreover, thanks to the conservative aspects of that approach, including management's price-consciousness, the fund has been one of the least volatile members of its wild category. The fund also still boasts one of the lowest expense ratios in the group. Therefore, we think this fund is a worthwhile option for those want to make a play on emerging Asia.

Address:	100 E. Pratt Street Baltimore, MD 21202 800–638–5660 / 410–547–2308
Web Address:	www.troweprice.com
*Inception:	09-28-90
Advisor:	T. Rowe Price Assoc.
Subadvisor:	None
NTF Plans:	N/A

Minimum Purchase:	$2500	Add: $100	IRA: $1000
Min Auto Inv Plan:	$50	Add: $50	
Sales Fees:	No–load		
Management Fee:	.50%+.33% mx./.30% mn.(G)		
Actual Fees:	Mgt: 0.82%	Dist: —	
Expense Projections:	3Yr: $384	5Yr: $665	10Yr: $1466
Avg Brok Commission:	—	Income Distrib: Annually	
Total Cost (relative to category):	Low		

T. Rowe Price New Era

Ticker	Load	NAV	Yield	Total Assets	Mstar Category
PRNEX	None	$22.24	1.2%	$1,036.7 mil	Spec Natural Resources

Prospectus Objective: Specialty—Natural Resources

T. Rowe Price New Era Fund seeks long-term growth of capital; current income is not a consideration.

The fund invests primarily in common stocks of companies whose earnings and tangible assets could benefit from accelerating inflation. It typically invests in companies that own or develop natural resources, or that demonstrate the flexibility to adjust prices, or the ability to control operating costs. The fund may also invest in securities of nonresource companies, convertible securities, derivatives, and bonds. It may invest up to 50% of assets in foreign securities, including American depositary receipts.

Historical Profile

Return Average
Risk Average
Rating ★★★ Neutral

Investment Style
Equity
Average Stock %: 92% 92% 92% 96% 96% 96% 96%

▼ Manager Change
▽ Partial Manager Change

Fund Performance vs. Category Average
■ Quarterly Fund Return +/– Category Average
— Category Baseline

Performance Quartile (within Category)

Portfolio Manager(s)

Charles M. Ober, CFA. Since 3-97. BA Cornell U.; MBA Columbia U.

1990	1991	1992	1993	1994	1995	1996	1997	1998	1999	2000	12-01	History
18.48	19.86	18.88	20.35	20.15	22.65	26.06	25.95	19.78	21.80	24.30	22.24	NAV
–8.76	14.74	2.08	15.33	5.17	20.76	24.25	10.96	–9.88	21.22	20.37	–4.35	Total Return %
–5.64	–15.75	–5.54	5.28	3.86	–16.77	1.30	–22.39	–38.45	0.19	29.47	7.52	+/– S&P 500
–2.58	–19.47	–6.89	4.05	5.24	–15.68	3.05	–20.33	–33.31	–2.34	31.30	6.54	+/– Wilshire 5000
2.85	2.98	2.27	2.01	1.87	2.38	1.68	1.42	1.54	1.52	1.33	1.11	Income Return %
–11.61	11.76	–0.19	13.32	3.30	18.38	22.57	9.54	–11.42	19.71	19.04	–5.46	Capital Return %
57	12	62	82	9	56	68	26	4	72	61	22	Total Rtn % Rank Cat
0.62	0.55	0.45	0.38	0.38	0.48	0.38	0.37	0.40	0.30	0.29	0.27	Income $
0.71	0.73	0.94	1.03	0.87	1.20	1.71	2.54	3.17	1.82	1.51	0.68	Capital Gains $
0.83	0.85	0.81	0.80	0.80	0.79	0.76	0.74	0.75	0.74	0.72	—	Expense Ratio %
2.81	2.56	2.22	1.92	1.87	2.00	1.53	1.33	1.27	1.29	1.29	—	Income Ratio %
9	9	17	25	25	23	29	28	23	33	29	—	Turnover Rate %
707.5	756.8	699.6	752.6	979.5	1,090.4	1,467.7	1,492.7	996.6	1,082.3	1,194.6	—	Net Assets $mil

Performance 12-31-01

	1st Qtr	2nd Qtr	3rd Qtr	4th Qtr	Total
1997	–0.46	10.52	11.34	–9.41	10.96
1998	7.90	–4.71	–12.41	0.07	–9.88
1999	4.75	15.01	–0.25	0.87	21.22
2000	2.52	2.91	5.26	8.38	20.37
2001	–3.13	0.89	–12.21	11.47	–4.35

Trailing	Total Return%	+/– S&P 500	+/– Wil 5000	% Rank All	% Rank Cat	Growth of $10,000
3 Mo	11.47	0.79	–0.90	35	48	11,147
6 Mo	–2.14	3.42	3.35	48	12	9,786
1 Yr	–4.35	7.52	6.54	50	22	9,565
3 Yr Avg	11.75	12.78	12.40	8	59	13,956
5 Yr Avg	6.89	–3.81	–2.81	37	16	13,956
10 Yr Avg	10.00	–2.93	–2.28	32	37	25,928
15 Yr Avg	10.36	–3.38	–2.64	39	18	43,856

Tax Analysis	Tax-Adj Ret%	%Rank Cat	%Pretax Ret	%Rank Cat
3 Yr Avg	9.64	61	82.0	82
5 Yr Avg	4.30	21	62.3	80
10 Yr Avg	7.51	56	75.1	86

Potential Capital Gain Exposure: 31% of assets

Risk Analysis

Time Period	Load-Adj Return %	Risk %Rank[1] All	Risk %Rank[1] Cat	Morningstar Return	Morningstar Risk	Morningstar Risk-Adj Rating
1 Yr	–4.35					
3 Yr	11.75	56	2	1.54[2]	0.78	★★★★
5 Yr	6.89	74	1	0.42[2]	1.00	★★
10 Yr	10.00	75	1	0.73	0.97	★★★

Average Historical Rating (193 months): 2.7★s

[1]1=low, 100=high [2] T-Bill return substituted for category avg.

Category Rating (3 Yr)

1 2 **3** 4 5
Worst Best

Return Average
Risk Low

Other Measures	Standard Index S&P 500	Best Fit Index SPMid400
Alpha	11.9	3.9
Beta	0.65	0.67
R-Squared	27	39

Standard Deviation	23.53
Mean	11.75
Sharpe Ratio	0.33

Portfolio Analysis 09-30-01

Share chng since 06-01 Total Stocks: 106	Subsector	PE	YTD Ret%	% Assets
⊕ ExxonMobil	Major Oils	15.3	–7.59	4.67
⊖ Wal-Mart Stores	Retail	40.3	8.94	3.99
Royal Dutch Petro NY ADR	Major Oils	12.0	–17.10	3.17
USX–Marathon Grp	Major Oils	9.6	11.58	3.14
BP PLC ADR	Major Oils	14.4	–0.90	2.94
Total Fina Elf ADR	Major Oils	15.5	–1.76	2.39
Schlumberger	Energy Services	55.0	–30.30	2.33
Anadarko Petro	Expl. & Prod.	11.1	–19.70	2.18
⊕ Baker Hughes	Energy	45.0	–11.10	2.12
Ocean Energy	Nat. Gas Dist.	10.6	11.58	2.08
Murphy Oil	Major Oils	9.7	41.93	1.99
Chevron	Major Oils	10.3	9.29	1.82
⊖ Newmont Mng	Mining	—	12.69	1.79
⊕ Phelps Dodge	Mining	—	–40.90	1.55
Diamond Offshore Drilling	Energy Services	25.8	–22.80	1.55
⊖ Packaging Corporation	Industrials	11.9	12.56	1.49
ALCOA	Metals	21.4	7.86	1.37
⊖ Burlington Resources	Expl. & Prod.	8.4	–24.60	1.34
Unocal	Major Oils	10.9	–4.58	1.33
Rio Tinto (Reg)	Mining	15.8	—	1.28
Placer Dome	Mining	—	14.47	1.25
Dow Chemical	Chemicals	NMF	–4.43	1.24
Mitchell Energy & Dev Cl A	Expl. & Prod.	11.8	–12.10	1.18
Amerada Hess	Major Oils	4.7	–13.00	1.10
Halliburton	Energy Services	8.3	–63.20	1.08

Current Investment Style

Style: Value Blnd Growth; Size: Large Med Small

	Stock Port Avg	Relative S&P 500 Current	Relative S&P 500 Hist	Rel Cat
Price/Earnings Ratio	22.3	0.72	0.89	1.05
Price/Book Ratio	2.7	0.46	0.43	1.05
Price/Cash Flow	11.0	0.61	0.57	1.09
3 Yr Earnings Growth	16.6	1.14	0.57	1.17
1 Yr Earnings Est%	7.1	—	—	2.50
Med Mkt Cap $mil	6,646	0.1	0.1	0.61

Analysis by Dan McNeela 08-29-01

T. Rowe Price New Era Fund's dependability makes it one of our favorite ways to play the natural-resources sector.

On a relative basis, this fund fared poorly during the energy rally in 1999 and 2000, with year-end rankings in the bottom half of the specialty natural-resources category. On an absolute basis, however, it is hard to complain about 20%-plus gains in each of those years. And what we like even more about this offering is its ability to weather the cyclical downturns that are all but certain to visit the sector. A prime example was 1998. While the average natural-resources fund was down 25% that year, the fund dropped just 10%.

The fund is holding true to form this year. The sluggish economy has weakened demand for oil, thereby threatening OPEC's plan to keep prices high. Thanks to its underweighting in the most volatile energy subsectors—exploration & production and energy services—the fund has lost just 3% through August 29, 2001, versus a 10% loss for the typical fund in the category.

The fund has earned its low-volatility stripes by taking a diversified approach. While many funds have a mandate to invest solely in energy companies, this fund's holdings run the natural-resources gamut, by including chemical, mining, forestry and metals companies alongside the typical energy names. The fund also has a long-held position in Wal-Mart.

Although the fund is better diversified than many of its competitors, it's worth noting that energy companies have recently crept up to 60% of the portfolio's assets, which could lead volatility to tick up here. For now, however, we think this remains one of the category's better options.

Special Securities % assets 09-30-01	
Restricted/Illiquid Secs	0
Emerging-Markets Secs	1
Options/Futures/Warrants	No

Subsector Weightings	% of Stocks	Rel Cat
Major Oils	27.0	1.1
Energy Services	11.9	0.7
Expl. & Prod.	9.7	0.7
Nat. Gas Dist.	2.2	0.7
Chemicals	3.9	1.2
Paper/Forest	4.0	0.8
Metals	3.2	1.2
Mining	9.0	1.6
Other	29.3	1.2

Composition % assets 09-30-01	
Cash	2.3
Stocks*	97.2
Bonds	0.5
Other	0.0
*Foreign (% stocks)	19.5

Market Cap	
Giant	21.2
Large	23.5
Medium	45.3
Small	9.6
Micro	0.5

Address:	100 E. Pratt Street Baltimore, MD 21202 800–638–5660 / 410–547–2308
Web Address:	www.troweprice.com
Inception:	01-20-69
Advisor:	T. Rowe Price Assoc.
Subadvisor:	None
NTF Plans:	N/A

Minimum Purchase:	$2500	Add: $100 IRA: $1000
Min Auto Inv Plan:	$50	Add: $50
Sales Fees:	No-load	
Management Fee:	.25%+.33% mx./.30% mn.(G)	
Actual Fees:	Mgt: 0.57%	Dist: —
Expense Projections:	3Yr: $237	5Yr: $411 10Yr: $918
Avg Brok Commission:	—	Income Distrib: Annually
Total Cost (relative to category):	Low	

T. Rowe Price New Horizons

Ticker	Load	NAV	Yield	Total Assets	Mstar Category
PRNHX	Closed	$22.63	0.0%	$4,732.6 mil	Small Growth

Prospectus Objective: Small Company

T. Rowe Price New Horizons Fund seeks capital appreciation; current income is not a factor.

The fund invests primarily in common stocks of small, rapidly growing companies. Management concentrates on companies that may offer accelerating earnings growth because of new management, new products, or structural changes in the economy. The fund may invest up to 10% of assets in foreign securities, including American depositary receipts.

Historical Profile

Return Above Avg
Risk Above Avg
Rating ★★★ Neutral

Investment Style
Equity
Average Stock %: 96% | 93% | 93% | 97% | 97% | 95% | 99%

▼ Manager Change
▽ Partial Manager Change

Fund Performance vs. Category Average
■ Quarterly Fund Return +/– Category Average
— Category Baseline

Performance Quartile (within Category)

Portfolio Manager(s)

John H. Laporte, CFA. Since 9-87. BA'67 Princeton U.; MBA'69 Harvard U.

1990	1991	1992	1993	1994	1995	1996	1997	1998	1999	2000	12-01	History
10.62	15.68	15.53	16.16	14.76	20.50	21.77	23.30	23.34	27.53	23.89	22.63	NAV
–9.54	52.16	10.58	22.01	0.30	55.44	17.03	9.78	6.25	32.52	–1.86	–2.84	Total Return %
–6.42	21.68	2.96	11.95	–1.01	17.91	–5.91	–23.58	–22.33	11.48	7.24	9.04	+/– S&P 500
7.87	0.97	2.81	8.65	2.73	24.40	5.77	–3.17	5.02	–10.57	20.57	6.39	+/– Russ 2000 Grth
0.73	0.47	0.00	0.00	0.00	0.00	0.00	0.00	0.00	0.00	0.00	0.00	Income Return %
–10.27	51.69	10.58	22.01	0.30	55.44	17.03	9.77	6.25	32.52	–1.86	–2.84	Capital Return %
62	51	60	33	38	5	61	86	35	69	42	31	Total Rtn % Rank Cat
0.09	0.05	0.00	0.00	0.00	0.00	0.00	0.00	0.00	0.00	0.00	0.00	Income $
0.53	0.39	1.76	2.70	1.43	2.41	2.19	0.58	1.27	3.02	3.14	0.56	Capital Gains $
0.82	0.92	0.93	0.93	0.93	0.90	0.90	0.88	0.89	0.90	0.88	—	Expense Ratio %
0.72	0.35	–0.32	–0.50	–0.50	–0.23	–0.41	–0.57	–0.65	–0.66	–0.51	—	Income Ratio %
38	33	50	49	44	56	41	45	41	45	47	—	Turnover Rate %
855.7	1,470.4	1,547.3	1,640.4	1,648.4	2,854.5	4,363.4	5,103.7	5,228.5	6,022.0	6,122.3	—	Net Assets $mil

Performance 12-31-01

	1st Qtr	2nd Qtr	3rd Qtr	4th Qtr	Total
1997	–11.53	14.33	13.76	–4.60	9.78
1998	13.22	–4.70	–20.96	24.59	6.25
1999	–6.98	15.52	–4.03	28.50	32.52
2000	14.38	–3.37	3.32	–14.06	–1.86
2001	–16.95	20.06	–25.15	30.18	–2.84

Trailing	Total Return%	+/– S&P 500	+/– Russ 2000 Grth	% Rank All	% Rank Cat	Growth of $10,000
3 Mo	30.18	19.50	4.01	4	15	13,018
6 Mo	–2.55	3.00	6.71	49	25	9,745
1 Yr	–2.84	9.04	6.39	47	31	9,716
3 Yr Avg	8.11	9.14	7.87	14	51	12,636
5 Yr Avg	8.07	–2.63	5.20	29	55	14,738
10 Yr Avg	13.75	0.83	6.57	9	13	36,282
15 Yr Avg	13.48	–0.25	5.34	14	30	66,666

Tax Analysis	Tax-Adj Ret%	%Rank Cat	%Pretax Ret	%Rank Cat
3 Yr Avg	5.89	49	72.6	66
5 Yr Avg	6.37	51	78.9	47
10 Yr Avg	11.05	15	80.4	44

Potential Capital Gain Exposure: 26% of assets

Risk Analysis

Time Period	Load-Adj Return %	Risk %Rank[1] All	Risk %Rank[1] Cat	Morningstar Return	Morningstar Risk	Morningstar Risk-Adj Rating
1 Yr	–2.84					
3 Yr	8.11	90	49	0.69[2]	1.43	★★★★
5 Yr	8.07	90	41	0.70[2]	1.48	★★
10 Yr	13.75	92	34	1.48	1.49	★★★

Average Historical Rating (193 months): 2.3★s

[1]1=low, 100=high [2] T-Bill return substituted for category avg.

Category Rating (3 Yr)

1 2 **3** 4 5
Worst Best

Return: Average
Risk: Average

Other Measures	Standard Index S&P 500	Best Fit Index Wil 4500
Alpha	14.6	8.3
Beta	1.25	1.13
R-Squared	42	94

Standard Deviation	37.07
Mean	8.11
Sharpe Ratio	0.10

Portfolio Analysis 09-30-01

Share change since 06-01 Total Stocks: 256	Sector	PE	YTD Ret%	% Assets
Bisys Grp	Services	42.7	22.76	2.45
⊖ Affiliated Comp Svcs A	Services	39.9	74.88	2.45
⊕ Henry Schein	Health	22.0	6.95	2.10
⊖ Apollo Grp Cl A	Services	—	—	2.09
⊖ Radian Grp	Financials	11.6	14.64	1.78
⊖ Catalina Mktg	Services	37.7	–10.80	1.60
Outback Steakhouse	Services	20.4	32.37	1.54
⊖ Electronic Arts	Technology	90.8	40.65	1.53
Maxim Integrated Products	Technology	68.2	9.82	1.45
Iron Mountain	Services	—	17.98	1.44
⊖ Gilead Sciences	Health	—	58.48	1.43
Orthodontic Centers of Amer	Health	26.3	–2.40	1.42
⊖ NetIQ	Technology	—	–59.60	1.42
O'Reilly Automotive	Retail	33.8	36.34	1.32
Duane Reade	Retail	25.3	–0.70	1.28
Omnicare	Health	38.3	15.52	1.26
⊖ Cephalon	Health	—	19.38	1.24
BJ Svcs	Energy	15.5	–5.77	1.15
NPS Pharmaceuticals	Health	—	–20.20	1.05
⊖ Cabot Microelect	Industrials	—	52.59	1.04
⊖ Analog Devices	Technology	47.7	–13.20	1.02
Lamar Advertising Cl A	Services	—	9.71	0.95
Davita	Health	18.3	42.77	0.94
⊖ Lattice Semicon	Technology	—	11.95	0.90
⊖ Sonic	Services	25.7	54.42	0.88

Current Investment Style

Style: Value Blnd Growth; Size: Large Med Small

	Stock Port Avg	Relative S&P 500 Current	Relative S&P 500 Hist	Rel Cat
Price/Earnings Ratio	34.1	1.10	1.04	1.06
Price/Book Ratio	5.8	1.01	0.86	1.19
Price/Cash Flow	22.4	1.25	1.14	1.02
3 Yr Earnings Growth	23.4[1]	1.60	—	0.93
1 Yr Earnings Est%	4.6	—	—	0.60
Med Mkt Cap $mil	1,617	0.0	0.0	1.55

[1]figure is based on 50% or less of stocks

Analysis by Christine Benz 08-13-01

T. Rowe Price New Horizons Fund remains a reasonable choice for investors.

This fund can't—or in some cases chooses not to—use the tools some of its peers use to get ahead. Juicing performance with IPOs is a familiar tactic for small-growth funds, but this offering, though long closed to new investors, is too big to feel much of an impact from them. And while some aggressive small-cap funds get ahead by making sector bets or building sizable positions in their top stocks, manager Jack Laporte eschews such tactics. After all, if this fund were to build a 5% position in a true small cap such as Pegasus Communications, one of its current holdings, it would own more than a third of the company's outstanding shares.

The downside of the fund's limited arsenal is that it can have a tough time differentiating itself from the pack. Since assets ballooned in the mid-1990s, the fund hasn't touched the top quartile of the small-growth category in any calendar year. It looked particularly slow in 1999's go-go growth environment, when the market rewarded high-risk strategies. That's disappointing, because Laporte showed a talent for putting up big numbers in the fund's younger, smaller days.

But the flipside of the fund's sometimes-bland performance is that it's a lot more even-keeled than its peers; its volatility, almost any way you look at it, is below average relative to other small-growth funds. The fund has suffered a stiff loss over the past year, but it has comfortably outperformed others in its category. This is particularly impressive because the fund focuses on larger companies than its typical peer, and the past year's market has been kindest to the smallest of the small.

Investors here may want to supplement this offering with a more maneuverable fund, but we think you could do a lot worse than owning a broadly diversified, reasonably priced offering run by one of the category's most experienced skippers. It's a fund worth hanging on to.

Special Securities % assets 09-30-01	
Restricted/Illiquid Secs	0
Emerging-Markets Secs	Trace
Options/Futures/Warrants	No

Composition % assets 09-30-01	
Cash	1.1
Stocks*	98.8
Bonds	0.0
Other	0.1
*Foreign (% stocks)	1.6

Market Cap	
Giant	0.0
Large	4.5
Medium	52.3
Small	39.6
Micro	3.6

Sector Weightings	% of Stocks	Rel S&P	5-Year High	5-Year Low
Utilities	0.0	0.0	1	0
Energy	4.6	0.6	6	1
Financials	4.4	0.2	9	3
Industrials	6.4	0.6	8	2
Durables	1.5	1.0	5	1
Staples	0.3	0.0	2	0
Services	32.3	3.0	38	25
Retail	8.1	1.2	22	4
Health	22.6	1.5	23	13
Technology	19.8	1.1	37	17

Address:	100 E. Pratt Street Baltimore, MD 21202 800-638-5660 / 410-547-2308
Web Address:	www.troweprice.com
Inception:	06-03-60
Advisor:	T. Rowe Price Assoc.
Subadvisor:	None
NTF Plans:	N/A

Minimum Purchase:	Closed	Add: $100 IRA: —
Min Auto Inv Plan:	Closed	Add: $100
Sales Fees:	No-load	
Management Fee:	.35%+.48% mx./.31% mn.(G)	
Actual Fees:	Mgt: 0.67%	Dist: —
Expense Projections:	3Yr: $287	5Yr: $498 10Yr: $1108
Avg Brok Commission:	—	Income Distrib: Annually
Total Cost (relative to category):	Low	

T. Rowe Price Science & Tech

Ticker	Load	NAV	Yield	Total Assets	Mstar Category
PRSCX	None	$20.92	0.0%	$5,016.2 mil	Spec Technology

Prospectus Objective: Specialty—Technology

T. Rowe Price Science and Technology Fund seeks long-term growth of capital; current income is incidental.

The fund normally invests at least 65% of assets in companies, both foreign and domestic, that seek to develop or use scientific and technological advances. Industries include computers and peripherals, software, electronics, pharmaceuticals and medical devices, telecommunications, biotechnology, waste management, chemicals, synthetic materials, defense, and aerospace. These holdings may include both new and established companies. The fund may invest up to 30% of assets in foreign securities.

The fund offers two different share classes, both of which differ in fee structure and availability.

Historical Profile

Return: Average
Risk: High
Rating: ★★ Below Avg

Investment Style
Equity
Average Stock %: 93% 93% 92% 96% 95% 95% 92%

▼ Manager Change
▽ Partial Manager Change

Fund Performance vs. Category Average
Quarterly Fund Return +/– Category Average
— Category Baseline

Performance Quartile (within Category)

Portfolio Manager(s)

Charles A. Morris, CFA. Since 8-91. BS'85 Indiana U.; MBA'87 Stanford U. Other funds currently managed: T. Rowe Price Science & Tech Adv, SunAmerica Science & Technology A, SunAmerica Science & Technology B.

1990	1991	1992	1993	1994	1995	1996	1997	1998	1999	2000	12-01	History
10.05	15.57	17.33	18.95	21.64	29.12	29.71	27.26	37.67	63.71	35.57	20.92	NAV
–1.33	60.17	18.76	24.25	15.79	55.53	14.23	1.71	42.35	100.99	–34.19	–41.19	Total Return %
1.79	29.68	11.14	14.19	14.47	18.00	–8.72	–31.64	13.78	79.95	–25.09	–29.31	+/– S&P 500
–0.88	12.79	13.20	5.20	–5.09	7.82	–5.80	–18.26	–12.25	–15.41	–17.97	–25.60	+/– PSE Tech 100
0.88	0.00	0.00	0.00	0.00	0.00	0.00	0.00	0.00	0.00	0.00	0.00	Income Return %
–2.21	60.17	18.76	24.25	15.79	55.53	14.23	1.71	42.35	100.99	–34.19	–41.19	Capital Return %
54	9	36	58	41	10	67	91	68	73	59	54	Total Rtn % Rank Cat
0.09	0.00	0.00	0.00	0.00	0.00	0.00	0.00	0.00	0.00	0.00	0.00	Income $
0.24	0.48	1.12	2.51	0.30	4.54	3.60	2.87	0.99	10.72	7.28	0.00	Capital Gains $
1.25	1.25	1.25	1.25	1.11	1.01	0.97	0.94	0.94	0.87	0.86	—	Expense Ratio %
0.91	–0.07	–0.81	–0.68	–0.58	–0.15	–0.33	–0.44	–0.61	–0.26	–0.55	—	Income Ratio %
183	148	144	163	113	130	126	134	109	128	134	—	Turnover Rate %
61.5	166.0	281.0	500.3	915.1	2,285.3	3,291.8	3,538.5	4,695.6	12,270.6	8,891.9	—	Net Assets $mil

Performance 12-31-01

	1st Qtr	2nd Qtr	3rd Qtr	4th Qtr	Total
1997	–13.97	19.21	13.06	–12.28	1.71
1998	15.19	0.99	–17.25	47.89	42.35
1999	12.61	16.17	7.87	42.42	100.99
2000	11.57	–12.79	–0.11	–32.29	–34.19
2001	–37.76	16.85	–40.28	35.40	–41.19

Trailing	Total Return%	+/– S&P 500	+/– PSE Tech 100	% Rank All	% Rank Cat	Growth of $10,000
3 Mo	35.40	24.72	2.49	3	51	13,540
6 Mo	–19.13	–13.58	–13.85	97	56	8,087
1 Yr	–41.19	–29.31	–25.60	98	54	5,881
3 Yr Avg	–8.03	–7.00	–23.27	97	73	7,779
5 Yr Avg	2.41	–8.29	–20.79	87	78	11,264
10 Yr Avg	13.08	0.15	–9.48	12	81	34,188
15 Yr Avg	—	—	—	—	—	—

Tax Analysis	Tax-Adj Ret%	%Rank Cat	%Pretax Ret	%Rank Cat
3 Yr Avg	–10.37	75	—	—
5 Yr Avg	0.23	78	9.7	97
10 Yr Avg	10.35	81	79.1	72

Potential Capital Gain Exposure: –103% of assets

Risk Analysis

Time Period	Load-Adj Return %	Risk %Rank[1] All	Risk %Rank[1] Cat	Morningstar Return	Morningstar Risk	Morningstar Risk-Adj Rating
1 Yr	–41.19					
3 Yr	–8.03	99	57	–2.43[2]	2.36	★
5 Yr	2.41	99	61	–0.55[2]	2.20	★
10 Yr	13.08	98	80	1.33	2.07	★★

Average Historical Rating (136 months): 4.4★s

[1] 1=low, 100=high [2] T-Bill return substituted for category avg.

Category Rating (3 Yr)

1 2 3 4 5
Worst — Best

Return: Below Avg
Risk: Average

Other Measures	Standard Index S&P 500	Best Fit Index Wil 4500
Alpha	10.5	–0.9
Beta	2.38	1.58
R-Squared	66	79
Standard Deviation		53.98
Mean		–8.03
Sharpe Ratio		–0.28

Analysis by Scott Cooley 11-25-01

T. Rowe Price Science & Technology Fund has been a disappointment.

The specialty-tech group's largest fund, this offering is on its way to chalking up yet another disappointing return. For the year to date through Nov. 23, 2001, the fund has dropped 41.5%, which puts it near the midpoint of the group. That relative ranking may not sound awful, but we expected this fairly well-diversified fund to perform better in a downturn, as the category's worst performers are narrowly focused, very aggressive offerings. Manager Chip Morris' bet on VeriSign, a top holding throughout the year, has backfired. The fund's unhealthily large, early-year stake in faltering telecom-equipment and optical-fiber stocks—including JDS Uniphase, Cisco Systems, Ciena, and Corning—also took a toll on returns. So did an assortment of especially weak picks, ranging from COLT Telecom to Phone.com (now part of a merged entity called Openwave Systems).

Alas, this isn't the first disappointment the fund's shareholders have experienced. The fund has consistently appeared to be a step slow in recent years. For example, after lagging the peer group in 1999 because of Morris' reluctance to pay up for speculative fare, the fund suffered in 2000, as he used that year's sell-off to buy aggressive issues such as Ariba, which has since plummeted. For five consecutive calendar years, the fund has lagged its average rival, and its trailing 10-year return trails four fifths of the competition.

Those negatives simply outweigh the fund's considerable positives, which include a very experienced manager; a large analyst staff; a moderate expense ratio; and a string of excellent returns in the early 1990s, when the fund's asset base was much smaller. Morris would appear to have the tools to return the fund to its early-1990s glory, but at this point, we cannot recommend it to investors.

Portfolio Analysis 09-30-01

Share chng since 06-01 Total Stocks: 49	Subsector	PE	YTD Ret%	% Assets
VeriSign	Technology	—	–48.70	7.89
Electronic Arts	Software	90.8	40.65	7.53
⊖ Maxim Integrated Products	Semiconductors	68.2	9.82	4.72
Flextronics Intl	Technology	—	–15.80	3.89
⊖ Analog Devices	Periph/Hardware	47.7	–13.20	3.85
⊕ Nokia Cl A ADR	Telecom	45.8	–43.00	3.27
⊕ AOL Time Warner	Computer Svs	—	–7.76	3.08
⊖ Vodafone Airtouch PLC ADR	Telecom	—	–27.70	3.08
Cisco Sys	Networking	—	–52.60	2.87
⊖ Qualcomm	Telecom	—	–38.50	2.80
⊕ Openwave Sys	Technology	—	–79.50	2.70
⊕ EMC	Software	NMF	–79.40	2.49
☼ SAP	Software	59.9	—	2.49
☼ Concord EFS	Computer Svs	86.3	49.21	2.31
⊕ Adobe Sys	Software	37.4	–46.50	2.26
⊕ Oracle	Software	32.1	–52.40	2.22
⊕ CIENA	Telecom	NMF	–82.30	2.18
⊕ Veritas Software	Software	—	–48.70	2.17
⊖ Microsoft	Software	57.6	52.78	2.05
⊖ Xilinx	Semiconductors	—	–15.30	2.05
⊖ Agere Sys	Technology	—	—	1.94
⊖ Altera	Semiconductors	44.2	–19.30	1.93
JDS Uniphase	Technology	—	–79.00	1.79
⊕ SCI Sys	Technology	—	8.63	1.73
⊕ Siebel Sys	Software	54.9	–58.60	1.53

Current Investment Style

Style: Value Blnd Growth; Size: Large Med Small

	Stock Port Avg	Relative S&P 500 Current	Relative S&P 500 Hist	Rel Cat
Price/Earnings Ratio	53.9	1.74	1.36	1.17
Price/Book Ratio	6.1	1.07	1.23	0.99
Price/Cash Flow	30.0	1.66	1.39	1.16
3 Yr Earnings Growth	33.6[1]	2.30	1.71	1.12
1 Yr Earnings Est%	–32.9[1]	18.60	—	1.98
Med Mkt Cap $mil	12,292	0.2	0.3	0.77

[1] figure is based on 50% or less of stocks

Special Securities % assets 09-30-01	
Restricted/Illiquid Secs	0
Emerging-Markets Secs	0
Options/Futures/Warrants	No

Composition % assets 09-30-01	
Cash	3.2
Stocks*	96.8
Bonds	0.0
Other	0.0
*Foreign (% stocks)	11.7

Market Cap	
Giant	19.6
Large	34.1
Medium	42.7
Small	3.6
Micro	0.0

Subsector Weightings	% of Stocks	Rel Cat
Computers	0.0	0.0
Semiconductors	10.8	1.0
Semi Equipment	1.6	0.4
Networking	4.0	1.1
Periph/Hardware	4.2	2.8
Software	27.8	2.1
Computer Svs	7.0	1.2
Telecom	12.7	1.6
Health Care	0.0	0.0
Other	31.9	0.9

Address: 100 E. Pratt Street, Baltimore, MD 21202, 800–638–5660 / 410–547–2308
Web Address: www.troweprice.com
Inception: 09-30-87
Advisor: T. Rowe Price Assoc.
Subadvisor: None
NTF Plans: N/A

Minimum Purchase: $2500 Add: $100 IRA: $1000
Min Auto Inv Plan: $50 Add: $50
Sales Fees: No-load
Management Fee: .35%+.33% mx./.30% mn.(G)
Actual Fees: Mgt: 0.67% Dist: —
Expense Projections: 3Yr: $278 5Yr: $482 10Yr: $1073
Avg Brok Commission: — Income Distrib: Annually
Total Cost (relative to category): Low

T. Rowe Price Small–Cap Stock

Ticker	Load	NAV	Yield	Total Assets	Mstar Category
OTCFX	None	$25.34	0.4%	$2,902.0 mil	Small Blend

Prospectus Objective: Small Company

T. Rowe Price Small Cap Stock Fund seeks long-term growth of capital.

The fund normally invests at least 65% of total assets in stocks of small companies. While most assets will be invested in U.S. common stocks, other securities may also be purchased, including foreign stocks, futures, and options. Management focuses on securities of companies that it believes offer superior earnings growth or are undervalued based on various valuation measures.

The fund offers two different share classes, both of which differ in fee structure and availability. Past names include USF&G Over-The-Counter Securities Fund and T. Rowe Price Over-the-Counter Securities Fund.

Historical Profile

Return Above Avg
Risk Average
Rating ★★★★ Above Avg

Investment Style
Equity
Average Stock %: 89% 91% 89% 88% 92% 90% 91%

▼ Manager Change
▽ Partial Manager Change

Fund Performance vs. Category Average
■ Quarterly Fund Return +/– Category Average
— Category Baseline

Performance Quartile (within Category)

Portfolio Manager(s)

Gregory A. McCrickard, CFA. Since 9-92. BA U. of Virginia; MBA Dartmouth C. Other fund currently managed: T. Rowe Price Small-Cap Stock Adv.

1990	1991	1992	1993	1994	1995	1996	1997	1998	1999	2000	12-01	History
12.72	16.86	14.37	15.39	13.80	16.32	18.07	22.20	20.79	22.80	23.87	25.34	NAV
–20.47	38.60	13.91	18.40	0.08	33.85	21.05	28.81	–3.46	14.66	16.49	6.81	Total Return %
–17.35	8.12	6.29	8.35	–1.23	–3.69	–1.89	–4.54	–32.03	–6.38	25.59	18.69	+/– S&P 500
–0.96	–7.45	–4.50	–0.50	1.91	5.41	4.52	6.44	–0.90	–6.60	19.52	4.33	+/– Russell 2000
0.52	0.71	0.42	0.00	0.19	0.87	0.55	0.22	0.45	0.38	0.61	0.42	Income Return %
–21.00	37.89	13.49	18.40	–0.11	32.98	20.50	28.59	–3.91	14.28	15.88	6.39	Capital Return %
79	56	48	47	39	21	48	35	42	42	29	50	Total Rtn % Rank Cat
0.09	0.09	0.07	0.00	0.03	0.12	0.09	0.04	0.10	0.08	0.14	0.10	Income $
0.10	0.68	4.64	1.58	1.56	2.01	1.58	1.01	0.50	0.89	2.46	0.05	Capital Gains $
1.47	1.34	1.32	1.20	1.11	1.11	1.07	1.02	1.01	0.96	0.94	—	Expense Ratio %
0.73	0.48	0.03	–0.01	0.24	0.74	0.56	0.33	0.46	0.47	0.63	—	Income Ratio %
35	31	31	41	42	58	31	23	26	42	33	—	Turnover Rate %
215.4	268.1	186.8	204.6	196.7	278.6	415.6	816.4	1,152.6	1,740.3	2,255.4	—	Net Assets $mil

Performance 12-31-01

	1st Qtr	2nd Qtr	3rd Qtr	4th Qtr	Total
1997	–3.54	15.49	14.01	1.42	28.81
1998	8.56	–3.69	–19.39	14.55	–3.46
1999	–8.71	14.49	–2.49	12.50	14.66
2000	9.34	1.85	4.17	0.42	16.49
2001	–8.59	14.80	–14.69	19.31	6.81

Trailing	Total Return%	+/– S&P 500	+/– Russ 2000	% Rank All	% Rank Cat	Growth of $10,000
3 Mo	19.31	8.62	–1.77	15	45	11,931
6 Mo	1.78	7.34	5.87	26	26	10,178
1 Yr	6.81	18.69	4.33	15	50	10,681
3 Yr Avg	12.58	13.60	6.16	7	33	14,267
5 Yr Avg	12.15	1.45	4.63	10	37	17,743
10 Yr Avg	14.52	1.59	3.01	6	31	38,804
15 Yr Avg	12.25	–1.48	1.50	24	58	56,620

Tax Analysis	Tax-Adj Ret%	%Rank Cat	%Pretax Ret	%Rank Cat
3 Yr Avg	11.06	31	87.9	41
5 Yr Avg	10.78	30	88.7	30
10 Yr Avg	11.68	31	80.4	43

Potential Capital Gain Exposure: 17% of assets

Risk Analysis

Time Period	Load-Adj Return %	Risk %Rank[1] All	Risk %Rank[1] Cat	Morningstar Return	Morningstar Risk	Morningstar Risk-Adj Rating
1 Yr	6.81					
3 Yr	12.58	55	39	1.74[2]	0.76	★★★★★
5 Yr	12.15	61	29	1.78[2]	0.85	★★★★
10 Yr	14.52	69	32	1.67	0.89	★★★★

Average Historical Rating (193 months): 2.9★s

[1]1=low, 100=high [2] T-Bill return substituted for category avg.

Category Rating (3 Yr)

1 2 **3** 4 5
Worst Best

Return Average
Risk Average

Other Measures	Standard Index S&P 500	Best Fit Index Russ 2000
Alpha	12.4	5.9
Beta	0.67	0.75
R–Squared	37	88
Standard Deviation		21.09
Mean		12.58
Sharpe Ratio		0.41

Portfolio Analysis 09-30-01

Share change since 06-01 Total Stocks: 260	Sector	PE	YTD Ret%	% Assets
⊕ Brown & Brown	Financials	35.9	57.09	2.13
⊕ Harman Intl Inds	Durables	50.1	23.90	1.72
⊕ Cleco	Utilities	8.4	–16.50	1.63
⊕ Matthews Intl Cl A	Industrials	24.3	56.60	1.47
⊕ Chittenden	Financials	15.4	17.37	1.45
⊖ Downey Finl	Financials	11.2	–24.30	1.33
⊕ Westamerica Bancorp	Financials	17.2	–5.98	1.23
⊕ Citizens Bkg MI	Financials	15.4	17.64	1.21
Iron Mountain	Services	—	17.98	1.14
Valley Natl Bancorp	Financials	19.3	7.70	1.14
PartnerRe	Financials	22.4	–10.50	1.11
⊕ Horace Mann Educators	Financials	NMF	1.49	1.10
Maximus	Services	22.6	20.38	1.09
⊕ SCP Pool	Services	20.3	36.96	1.01
⊕ Casey's General Stores	Retail	24.0	0.39	0.99
Lincare Hldgs	Health	23.7	0.41	0.96
⊖ Bisys Grp	Services	42.7	22.76	0.92
⊕ WR Berkley	Financials	—	15.11	0.91
⊕ Southwest Bancorp of Texas	Financials	21.3	–29.50	0.90
⊕ Gables Residential Tr	Financials	15.8	14.43	0.83
⊕ United Stationers	Industrials	18.2	40.21	0.81
Parkway Properties	Financials	16.0	20.92	0.80
⊕ Littelfuse	Technology	41.7	–8.33	0.79
☼ Cross Timbers Oil	Energy	9.6	–5.17	0.78
⊕ FYI	Services	—	–9.15	0.77

Current Investment Style

Style: Value Blnd Growth; Size: Large Med Small

	Stock Port Avg	Relative S&P 500 Current	Relative S&P 500 Hist	Rel Cat
Price/Earnings Ratio	26.1	0.84	0.71	1.05
Price/Book Ratio	3.6	0.62	0.50	1.11
Price/Cash Flow	16.8	0.94	0.77	1.08
3 Yr Earnings Growth	11.9	0.81	1.05	0.70
1 Yr Earnings Est%	3.3	—	—	3.79
Med Mkt Cap $mil	918	0.0	0.0	0.94

[1]figure is based on 50% or less of stocks

Analysis by Catherine Hickey 11-12-01

This rock-solid small-cap fund is still worthy of attention.

T. Rowe Price Small-Cap Stock Fund has made a name for itself by being unwaveringly consistent. Year in and year out, this fund is usually found in the small-blend category's second quartile. It's thus a bit of a surprise to see this fund lagging the category average, if only by a tiny margin, in 2001. Though top holdings like Brown & Brown continue to surge, the fund is still being held back by a tough January and February, when its utility and financials holdings pulled back after strong runs in 2000.

One slightly below-average year is no reason to lose faith here, however. Manager Greg McCrickard has assembled a strong long-term record here through solid stock selection of both growth and value issues. He splits the fund into two sections; one for value stocks that are trading fairly cheaply, and one for growthier issues that still sport the sound balance sheets and management teams that T. Rowe funds always look for. The fund's balance between growth and value has helped keep volatility moderate here.

The fund's huge asset base is a potential cause for concern, as bloated assets have dampened the performance of many fine small- and mid-cap funds. However, McCrickard asserts that he and his analyst team have uncovered enough good investment ideas to invest all that money, and thus far, the fund doesn't appear to have hit any major snags. Further, its penchant for holding 200-plus small positions means that liquidity is less of an issue here than it might be for a more-concentrated offering. This small-cap fund remains a keeper.

Special Securities % assets 09-30-01	
Restricted/Illiquid Secs	0
Emerging–Markets Secs	0
Options/Futures/Warrants	No

Composition % assets 09-30-01	
Cash	8.9
Stocks*	91.1
Bonds	0.0
Other	0.0
*Foreign (% stocks)	1.7

Market Cap	
Giant	0.0
Large	0.0
Medium	29.4
Small	65.2
Micro	5.3

Sector Weightings	% of Stocks	Rel S&P	5-Year High	5-Year Low
Utilities	2.1	0.7	2	0
Energy	3.9	0.6	8	0
Financials	25.0	1.4	25	9
Industrials	16.4	1.4	22	12
Durables	5.3	3.4	7	3
Staples	1.5	0.2	8	1
Services	20.3	1.9	30	16
Retail	3.4	0.5	10	1
Health	10.8	0.7	18	6
Technology	11.5	0.6	23	10

Address: 100 E. Pratt Street, Baltimore, MD 21202, 800–638–5660 / 410–547–2308
Web Address: www.troweprice.com
Inception: 06-01-56
Advisor: T. Rowe Price Assoc.
Subadvisor: None
NTF Plans: N/A

Minimum Purchase: $2500 Add: $100 IRA: $1000
Min Auto Inv Plan: $50 Add: $50
Sales Fees: No–load
Management Fee: .45%+.33% mx./.30% mn.(G)
Actual Fees: Mgt: 0.77% Dist: —
Expense Projections: 3Yr: $306 5Yr: $531 10Yr: $1178
Avg Brok Commission: — Income Distrib: Annually
Total Cost (relative to category): Below Avg

T. Rowe Price Small–Cap Value

Ticker	Load	NAV	Yield	Total Assets	Mstar Category
PRSVX	None	$22.66	0.7%	$1,797.5 mil	Small Value

Prospectus Objective: Small Company

T. Rowe Price Small-Cap Value Fund seeks long-term capital growth.

The fund invests primarily in common stocks of companies with market capitalizations of $1 billion or less, using a value-oriented approach. The advisor identifies undervalued securities by analyzing assets, earnings, cash flows, and business franchises. The fund may invest up to 20% of assets in foreign securities, including depositary receipts.

The fund offers two share classes, both of which differ in fee structure and availability. The fund was previously known as PEMCO and was open only to partners of Peat, Marwick, & Mitchell.

Historical Profile
Return Above Avg
Risk Below Avg
Rating ★★★★★ Highest

Investment Style
Equity
Average Stock %: 77% 83% 86% 91% 93% 92% 93%

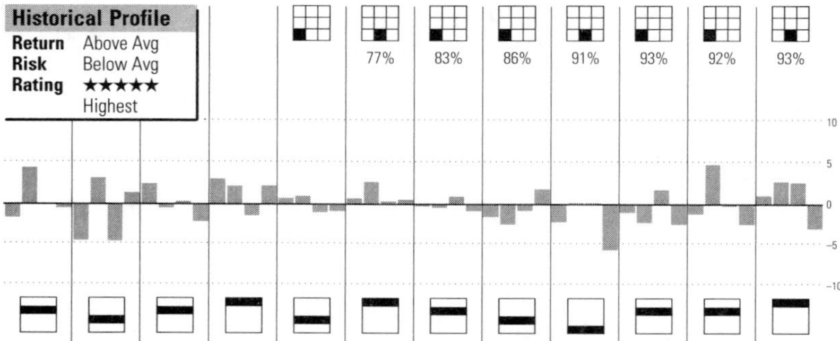

▼ Manager Change
▽ Partial Manager Change

Fund Performance vs. Category Average
■ Quarterly Fund Return +/– Category Average
— Category Baseline

Performance Quartile (within Category)

Portfolio Manager(s)

Preston Athey, CFA. Since 8-91. BA'71 Yale U.; MBA'78 Stanford U. Other fund currently managed: T. Rowe Price Small-Cap Value Adv.

History

1990	1991	1992	1993	1994	1995	1996	1997	1998	1999	2000	12-01	History
8.09	10.37	12.28	14.68	13.40	16.53	19.56	23.40	18.97	17.62	19.14	22.66	NAV
–11.27	34.18	20.87	23.30	–1.38	29.29	24.61	27.92	–12.47	1.19	19.77	21.94	Total Return %
–8.15	3.69	13.25	13.24	–2.69	–8.25	1.66	–5.43	–41.05	–19.85	28.88	33.82	+/– S&P 500
10.50	–7.53	–8.27	–0.54	0.17	3.53	3.24	–3.77	–6.04	2.67	–3.04	7.92	+/– Russell 2000 V
2.52	1.48	0.96	0.81	0.95	1.34	1.39	1.02	1.07	0.90	1.14	0.89	Income Return %
–13.79	32.69	19.90	22.49	–2.33	27.94	23.21	26.89	–13.54	0.29	18.64	21.05	Capital Return %
31	68	48	11	55	22	42	69	81	50	50	24	Total Rtn % Rank Cat
0.24	0.12	0.10	0.10	0.14	0.18	0.23	0.20	0.25	0.17	0.20	0.17	Income $
0.12	0.34	0.15	0.35	0.92	0.61	0.80	1.39	1.20	1.35	1.68	0.48	Capital Gains $
1.25	1.25	1.25	1.05	0.97	0.98	0.94	0.87	0.87	0.92	0.90	—	Expense Ratio %
2.57	1.31	0.98	0.91	0.93	1.59	1.28	1.01	1.02	0.84	1.06	—	Income Ratio %
33	31	12	12	21	18	15	15	17	7	14	—	Turnover Rate %
26.4	53.2	264.0	453.8	408.4	936.4	1,409.8	2,088.2	1,631.9	1,262.2	1,360.7	—	Net Assets $mil

Performance 12-31-01

	1st Qtr	2nd Qtr	3rd Qtr	4th Qtr	Total
1997	–0.92	12.28	14.94	0.04	27.92
1998	7.48	–4.57	–20.17	6.90	–12.47
1999	–10.54	16.68	–5.71	2.81	1.19
2000	3.46	5.92	7.04	2.10	19.77
2001	2.25	16.40	–10.67	14.69	21.94

Trailing	Total Return%	+/– S&P 500	+/– Russ 2000V	% Rank All	% Rank Cat	Growth of $10,000
3 Mo	14.69	4.00	–2.03	25	75	11,469
6 Mo	2.46	8.01	1.30	18	44	10,246
1 Yr	21.94	33.82	7.92	2	24	12,194
3 Yr Avg	13.91	14.93	2.58	6	41	14,779
5 Yr Avg	10.60	–0.10	–0.60	15	54	16,547
10 Yr Avg	14.63	1.70	–0.48	6	34	39,178
15 Yr Avg	—	—	—	—	—	—

Tax Analysis	Tax-Adj Ret%	%Rank Cat	%Pretax Ret	%Rank Cat
3 Yr Avg	12.12	39	87.1	69
5 Yr Avg	8.74	55	82.5	67
10 Yr Avg	12.90	27	88.1	13

Potential Capital Gain Exposure: 30% of assets

Risk Analysis

Time Period	Load-Adj Return %	Risk %Rank[1] All	Risk %Rank[1] Cat	Morningstar Return	Morningstar Risk	Morningstar Risk-Adj Rating
1 Yr	21.94					
3 Yr	13.91	38	15	2.07[2]	0.51	★★★★★
5 Yr	10.60	49	15	1.35[2]	0.66	★★★★
10 Yr	14.63	53	15	1.69	0.67	★★★★★

Average Historical Rating (127 months): 3.8★s

[1]1=low, 100=high [2] T-Bill return substituted for category avg.

Category Rating (3 Yr)

1 2 3 4 5
Worst Best

Return Average
Risk Below Avg

Other Measures	Standard Index S&P 500	Best Fit Index Russ 2000
Alpha	11.5	7.5
Beta	0.39	0.46
R-Squared	24	64
Standard Deviation		15.36
Mean		13.91
Sharpe Ratio		0.66

Analysis by Catherine Hickey 01-04-02

This is T. Rowe Price Small–Cap Value Fund's kind of market, but the fund is also a long–term winner.

This fund romped in 2001, not surprisingly. The market was thrilled about micro–caps last year, and this fund's $396 million median market cap situated it nicely to benefit from that sentiment. Also, the fund's overall price/earnings ratio is below average, which helped as value stocks were all the rage for most of 2001.

Those reasons account for much of the fund's top–quartile, 21.9% return last year. However, solid stock–picking was a major driver behind the fund's success, too. Insurer Brown & Brown and Community First Bankshares, two top holdings, both soared last year along with other small–cap financials stocks. Even less widely owned names such as McGrath RentCorp bolstered the fund last year.

Although the fund bested the majority of its peers in 2001, it doesn't always outperform so dramatically. Instead, its results are usually decent, but they don't crush the competition. Manager Preston Athey makes risk control a top priority, so he always searches for companies with limited downside risk, and he usually keeps the portfolio's positions relatively small. Though this approach has indeed kept volatility low, it also hasn't helped the fund break out from the pack at times. And when micro–caps underperform, this fund can really take it on the chin (as it did in 1998's bigger–is–better market).

Nevertheless, we think there is a lot to like about this offering. It sports low volatility, a talented manager in Athey, and low expenses. And years like 2001 show the kind of performance this fund is capable of when the wind is at its back. It's a sound small–value choice.

Portfolio Analysis 09-30-01

Share change since 06-01 Total Stocks: 205

Holding	Sector	PE	YTD Ret%	% Assets
⊖ Brown & Brown	Financials	35.9	57.09	4.37
☼ Cross Timbers Oil	Energy	9.6	–5.17	1.79
Allied Cap	Financials	11.6	35.33	1.66
⊕ Community First Bankshares	Financials	17.0	40.19	1.56
⊕ Analogic	Technology	NMF	–12.90	1.56
⊕ Insituform Tech A	Industrials	18.3	–35.80	1.55
⊖ FTI Consult	Services	52.9	220.00	1.52
⊖ McGrath RentCorp	Services	16.9	99.01	1.52
⊕ Electro Rent	Services	12.4	–8.74	1.51
Right Mgt Consultants	Services	18.8	147.10	1.36
⊖ Saga Comms	Services	38.3	39.16	1.20
⊕ Kilroy Realty	Financials	18.0	–1.11	1.18
⊕ Gables Residential Tr	Financials	15.8	14.43	1.17
Markel	Financials	—	–0.75	1.15
⊕ First Republic Bk	Financials	15.6	9.77	1.12
Ruby Tuesday	Services	21.3	35.62	1.11
⊖ Landauer	Services	21.2	95.24	1.10
⊕ Glenborough Realty Tr	Financials	23.7	22.37	1.09
⊕ Sun Communities	Financials	18.7	18.40	1.08
⊕ Landstar Sys	Services	13.3	30.79	1.07
⊕ Owens & Minor	Health	28.9	5.81	1.03
⊕ CSS Inds	Industrials	18.3	45.46	0.93
⊕ Bone Care Intl	Health	—	–1.06	0.91
⊕ Texas Regl Bancshares	Financials	15.9	18.42	0.89
☼ ProAssurance	N/A	—	—	0.88

Current Investment Style

Style: Value Blnd Growth; Size: Large Med Small

	Stock Port Avg	Relative S&P 500 Current	Relative S&P 500 Hist	Rel Cat
Price/Earnings Ratio	20.9	0.68	0.57	0.96
Price/Book Ratio	3.0	0.53	0.37	1.25
Price/Cash Flow	12.4	0.69	0.54	0.97
3 Yr Earnings Growth	12.1	0.82	0.93	1.04
1 Yr Earnings Est%	7.4	—	—	–1.87
Med Mkt Cap $mil	437	0.0	0.0	0.50

Special Securities % assets 09-30-01	
Restricted/Illiquid Secs	0
Emerging-Markets Secs	Trace
Options/Futures/Warrants	Yes

Composition % assets 09-30-01	
Cash	6.3
Stocks*	93.0
Bonds	0.3
Other	0.4
*Foreign (% stocks)	1.7

Market Cap	
Giant	0.0
Large	0.0
Medium	10.3
Small	68.6
Micro	21.2

Sector Weightings	% of Stocks	Rel S&P	5-Year High	5-Year Low
Utilities	3.4	1.1	5	0
Energy	5.6	0.8	10	2
Financials	26.2	1.5	27	12
Industrials	25.4	2.2	32	10
Durables	3.5	2.3	11	3
Staples	1.7	0.2	4	1
Services	20.1	1.9	38	19
Retail	3.6	0.5	8	3
Health	5.0	0.3	8	2
Technology	5.6	0.3	12	5

Address:	100 E. Pratt Street Baltimore, MD 21202 800–638–5660 / 410–547–2308
Web Address:	www.troweprice.com
Inception:	06-30-88
Advisor:	T. Rowe Price Assoc.
Subadvisor:	None
NTF Plans:	N/A

Minimum Purchase:	$2500	Add: $100 IRA: $1000
Min Auto Inv Plan:	$50	Add: $50
Sales Fees:	No-load, 1.00%R within 12 months	
Management Fee:	.35%+.33% mx./.30% mn.(G)	
Actual Fees:	Mgt: 0.67%	Dist: —
Expense Projections:	3Yr: $293	5Yr: $509 10Yr: $1131
Avg Brok Commission:	—	Income Distrib: Annually
Total Cost (relative to category):		Low

T. Rowe Price Spectrum Income

Ticker	Load	NAV	Yield	SEC Yield	Total Assets	Mstar Category
RPSIX	None	$10.59	6.0%	5.55%	$2,455.3 mil	Multisector Bond

Prospectus Objective: Multisector Bond

T. Rowe Price Spectrum Income Fund seeks current income and preservation of capital.

The fund invests in a diversified group of T. Rowe Price mutual funds that invest primarily in fixed-income securities. It may also invest in T. Rowe Price Equity-Income Fund, which invests in dividend-paying common stocks, and T. Rowe Price International Bond Fund, which invests in non-U.S. fixed-income securities. In addition, the fund may invest in T. Rowe Price's Emerging Markets Bond Fund, GNMA Fund, High-Yield Fund, New Income Fund, Summit Cash Reserves Fund, U.S. Treasury Long-Term Fund, and Short-Term Bond Fund. The fund's management fee is based on the aggregate fees of the underlying funds.

Historical Profile

Return: Above Avg
Risk: Average
Rating: ★★★★ Above Avg

Investment Style: Fixed-Income

Income Rtn %Rank Cat: 57 | 78 | 79 | 83 | 77 | 81 | 79 | 79

Growth of Principal vs. Interest Rate Shifts
- Principal Value $000 (NAV with capital gains reinvested)
- Interest Rate % on 10 Yr Treasury
- ▼ Manager Change
- ▽ Partial Manager Change
- ► Mgr Unknown After
- ◄ Mgr Unknown Before

Performance Quartile (within Category)

Portfolio Manager(s)

Ned Notzon, CFA et al.Since 12-98. PhD Stanford U.; MS Stanford U.

History

1990	1991	1992	1993	1994	1995	1996	1997	1998	1999	2000	12-01	History
9.77	10.73	10.70	11.11	10.11	11.24	11.20	11.66	11.50	10.71	10.77	10.59	NAV
2.66*	19.64	7.84	12.37	−1.93	19.42	7.65	12.19	6.58	0.26	7.41	4.50	Total Return %
—	3.64	0.44	2.62	0.99	0.95	4.03	2.51	−2.10	1.09	−4.23	−3.93	+/– LB Aggregate
—	−24.11	−8.82	−6.54	−0.96	2.03	−4.77	−0.44	6.00	−3.02	12.62	−1.28	+/– FB High-Yield
4.47	8.78	7.35	6.67	6.36	7.32	6.55	6.53	6.40	6.17	6.73	6.06	Income Return %
−1.81	10.87	0.49	5.70	−8.29	12.10	1.10	5.66	0.18	−5.91	0.67	−1.56	Capital Return %
—	62	40	82	7	28	85	8	12	70	8	49	Total Rtn % Rank Cat
0.44	0.83	0.76	0.69	0.69	0.72	0.71	0.71	0.72	0.69	0.70	0.64	Income $
0.05	0.06	0.08	0.19	0.10	0.06	0.15	0.15	0.18	0.13	0.00	0.02	Capital Gains $
0.00	0.00	0.00	0.00	0.00	0.00	0.00	0.00	0.00	0.00	0.77	—	Expense Ratio %
9.58	8.03	7.10	6.19	6.48	6.43	6.46	6.21	6.22	5.95	6.03	—	Income Ratio %
—	19	14	14	23	20	18	14	13	19	19	—	Turnover Rate %
40.1	147.9	376.4	583.8	624.9	986.7	1,356.0	2,022.2	2,574.1	2,548.4	2,471.3	2,455.3	Net Assets $mil

Performance 12-31-01

	1st Qtr	2nd Qtr	3rd Qtr	4th Qtr	Total
1997	0.04	4.98	4.06	2.65	12.19
1998	3.16	0.94	−0.74	3.12	6.58
1999	−0.38	0.62	−0.60	0.62	0.26
2000	1.37	0.72	2.04	3.10	7.41
2001	1.20	0.48	1.17	1.59	4.50

Trailing	Total Return%	+/– LB Agg	+/– FB High-Yield	% Rank All	% Rank Cat	Growth of $10,000
3 Mo	1.59	1.55	−4.06	72	71	10,159
6 Mo	2.77	−1.88	1.33	17	41	10,277
1 Yr	4.50	−3.93	−1.28	26	49	10,450
3 Yr Avg	4.01	−2.26	2.84	40	26	11,253
5 Yr Avg	6.11	−1.31	2.87	46	6	13,455
10 Yr Avg	7.47	0.24	−0.37	47	20	20,555
15 Yr Avg	—	—	—	—	—	—

Tax Analysis	Tax-Adj Ret%	%Rank Cat	%Pretax Ret	%Rank Cat
3 Yr Avg	1.40	22	34.9	41
5 Yr Avg	3.36	8	55.0	10
10 Yr Avg	4.59	15	61.5	15

Potential Capital Gain Exposure: −6% of assets

Risk Analysis

Time Period	Load-Adj Return %	Risk %Rank[1] All	Risk %Rank[1] Cat	Morningstar Return	Morningstar Risk	Morningstar Risk-Adj Rating
1 Yr	4.50					
3 Yr	4.01	26	14	−0.19[2]	0.86	★★★
5 Yr	6.11	33	11	0.25[2]	0.89	★★★
10 Yr	7.47	22	11	0.80[2]	0.85	★★★★★

Average Historical Rating (103 months): 4.3★s

[1]1=low, 100=high [2] T-Bill return substituted for category avg.

Category Rating (3 Yr)

1 2 3 4 5 — Worst … Best

Return: Above Avg
Risk: Below Avg

Other Measures	Standard Index LB Agg	Best Fit Index LB Corp
Alpha	−1.9	−1.5
Beta	0.82	0.76
R-Squared	46	56
Standard Deviation		4.15
Mean		4.01
Sharpe Ratio		−0.26

Portfolio Analysis 09-30-01

Total Fixed-Income: 0	Date of Maturity	Amount $000	Value $000	% Net Assets
T. Rowe Price New Income		69,145	609,169	25.42
T. Rowe Price High-Yield		75,207	483,578	20.18
T. Rowe Price International Bond		50,768	417,312	17.41
T. Rowe Price Equity Income Portfolio		15,076	340,274	14.20
T. Rowe Price GNMA		31,626	304,879	12.72
T. Rowe Price U.S. Treasury Long-Term		14,625	171,403	7.15
T. Rowe Price Emerging Markets Bond		7,068	70,822	2.95

Analysis by Scott Berry 07-27-01

What you see is what you get with T. Rowe Price Spectrum Income.

Unlike most multisector bond funds, which are constantly on the lookout for undervalued bonds and undervalued sectors of the bond market, this fund takes a more hands-off approach. The fund is made up of a fairly constant mix of income-oriented T. Rowe Price mutual funds, with T. Rowe Price New Income, an investment-grade bond fund, and T. Rowe Price High-Yield, a junk bond fund, accounting for nearly half of the fund's assets. T. Rowe Price Equity Income, an income-oriented stock fund, is also included in the mix, typically accounting for 15% of the fund's assets.

The fund's approach may not be flashy, but it has certainly paid off, as the fund's three-, five-, and 10-year trailing returns all rank in the multisector-bond category's top quartile.

The fund's long-term success owes much to its stake in T. Rowe Price Equity Income, which has gained an average of nearly 15% per year over the past decade.

The fund's year-to-date return through July 25, 2001, doesn't rank quite as highly as its long-term returns, but the fund still bests its average peer over the stretch. Though the fund's unhedged exposure to international bonds in T. Rowe Price International Bond cut into its recent returns due to the strength of the dollar relative to other currencies, the fund has managed to gain 2.5% for the year to date versus 2.0% for its average peer.

Investors looking for diversified bond exposure should certainly give this fund a look. It has delivered solid returns with less volatility than its average peer, and we think it's one of the better multisector-bond offerings available.

Current Investment Style

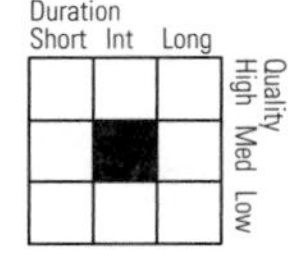

Avg Eff Duration[1]	5.3 Yrs
Avg Eff Maturity	7.9 Yrs
Avg Credit Quality	A
Avg Wtd Coupon	—
Avg Wtd Price	—

[1]figure provided by fund

Special Securities

Restricted/Illiquid Secs
Exotic Mortgage-Backed
Emerging-Markets Secs
Options/Futures/Warrants

Credit Analysis % bonds 09-30-01

US Govt	0	BB	5
AAA	51	B	14
AA	14	Below B	2
A	6	NR/NA	2
BBB	7		

Sector Breakdown % bonds 09-30-01

US Treasuries	—	CMOs	—
GNMA mtgs	—	ARMs	—
FNMA mtgs	—	Other	—
FHLMC mtgs	—		

Coupon Range	% of Bonds	Rel Cat
0%	0.00	0.00
0% to 7%	0.00	0.00
7% to 8.5%	0.00	0.00
8.5% to 10%	0.00	0.00
More than 10%	0.00	0.00

1.00=Category Average

Composition % assets 09-30-01

Cash	4.3	Bonds	80.3
Stocks	14.7	Other	0.7

Country Exp % assets

Not Available

Address:	100 E. Pratt Street Baltimore, MD 21202 800-638-5660 / 410-547-2308
Web Address:	www.troweprice.com
*Inception:	06-29-90
Advisor:	T. Rowe Price Assoc.
Subadvisor:	None
NTF Plans:	N/A

Minimum Purchase:	$2500	Add: $100	IRA: $1000
Min Auto Inv Plan:	$100	Add: $100	
Sales Fees:	No-load		
Management Fee:	None		
Actual Fees:	Mgt: 0.00%	Dist: —	
Expense Projections:	3Yr: $240	5Yr: $417	10Yr: $930
Avg Brok Commission:	—	Income Distrib: Monthly	
Total Cost (relative to category):		Low	

T. Rowe Price Tax–Free Short–Interm

Ticker	Load	NAV	Yield	SEC Yield	Total Assets	Mstar Category
PRFSX	None	$5.42	4.0%	2.86%	$442.7 mil	Muni Short–Term

Prospectus Objective: Muni Bond—National

T. Rowe Price Tax-Free Short-Intermediate Fund seeks higher yields than money-market funds with commensurate price volatility.

The fund invests primarily in short- and intermediate-term, high- and upper-medium-quality municipal securities, the interest on which is exempt from federal income tax. The average maturity typically ranges between two and five years.

Historical Profile

Return Below Avg
Risk Low
Rating ★★★★★ Highest

Investment Style
Fixed-Income
Income Rtn %Rank Cat

44 34 29 32 35 30 34 30

Growth of Principal vs. Interest Rate Shifts
— Principal Value $000 (NAV with capital gains reinvested)
— Interest Rate % on 10 Yr Treasury
▼ Manager Change
▽ Partial Manager Change
► Mgr Unknown After
◄ Mgr Unknown Before

Performance Quartile (within Category)

Portfolio Manager(s)

Charles B. Hill, et al. Since 1-95. BS'84 Guilford C.

1990	1991	1992	1993	1994	1995	1996	1997	1998	1999	2000	12–01	**History**
5.11	5.22	5.28	5.38	5.18	5.36	5.34	5.36	5.38	5.21	5.33	5.42	NAV
6.04	7.88	6.02	6.32	0.33	8.11	4.01	5.31	4.97	1.00	6.76	5.81	Total Return %
–2.91	–8.13	–1.38	–3.43	3.25	–10.36	0.39	–4.38	–3.70	1.83	–4.88	–2.61	+/– LB Aggregate
–1.26	–4.27	–2.80	–5.96	5.47	–9.36	–0.43	–3.90	–1.51	3.06	–4.94	0.73	+/– LB Muni
5.82	5.66	4.84	4.40	4.10	4.58	4.37	4.33	4.21	4.04	4.38	4.12	Income Return %
0.22	2.22	1.18	1.92	–3.77	3.52	–0.36	0.98	0.77	–3.05	2.38	1.69	Capital Return %
81	55	71	60	26	48	25	40	22	35	19	1	Total Rtn % Rank Cat
0.29	0.28	0.25	0.23	0.22	0.23	0.23	0.23	0.22	0.21	0.22	0.22	Income $
0.00	0.00	0.00	0.00	0.00	0.00	0.00	0.03	0.02	0.01	0.00	0.00	Capital Gains $
0.75	0.74	0.67	0.63	0.60	0.59	0.57	0.56	0.54	0.53	0.53	0.53	Expense Ratio %
5.93	5.67	5.34	4.61	4.18	4.19	4.39	4.30	4.23	4.06	4.07	4.27	Income Ratio %
191	190	81	39	51	93	70	84	77	40	50	41	Turnover Rate %
227.3	307.0	424.6	534.4	451.1	450.8	439.3	439.2	458.5	416.6	404.8	442.7	Net Assets $mil

Performance 12-31-01

	1st Qtr	2nd Qtr	3rd Qtr	4th Qtr	Total
1997	0.29	1.84	1.63	1.44	5.31
1998	1.03	1.04	1.78	1.03	4.97
1999	0.77	–0.70	0.83	0.10	1.00
2000	1.06	1.47	1.65	2.41	6.76
2001	2.37	1.20	1.90	0.23	5.81

Trailing	Total Return%	+/– LB Agg	+/– LB Muni	% Rank All	% Rank Cat	Growth of $10,000
3 Mo	0.23	0.19	0.89	77	27	10,023
6 Mo	2.13	–2.52	0.01	21	15	10,213
1 Yr	5.81	–2.61	0.73	19	1	10,581
3 Yr Avg	4.49	–1.78	–0.26	35	2	11,408
5 Yr Avg	4.75	–2.68	–1.22	69	13	12,611
10 Yr Avg	4.84	–2.39	–1.79	93	52	16,036
15 Yr Avg	5.08	–3.04	–2.11	96	33	21,034

Tax Analysis	Tax-Adj Ret%	%Rank Cat	%Pretax Ret	%Rank Cat
3 Yr Avg	4.48	2	99.7	67
5 Yr Avg	4.69	16	98.7	83
10 Yr Avg	4.81	52	99.4	66

Potential Capital Gain Exposure: 3% of assets

Risk Analysis

Time Period	Load-Adj Return %	Risk %Rank[1] All	Risk %Rank[1] Cat	Morningstar Return	Morningstar Risk	Morningstar Risk-Adj Rating
1 Yr	5.81					
3 Yr	4.49	2	41	0.51[2]	0.33	★★★★★
5 Yr	4.75	2	46	0.59[2]	0.37	★★★★★
10 Yr	4.84	2	45	0.57	0.32	★★★★

Average Historical Rating (181 months): 3.9★s

[1] 1=low, 100=high [2] T–Bill return substituted for category avg.

Category Rating (3 Yr)

1 2 3 4 5
Worst Best

Return Above Avg
Risk Average

Other Measures	Standard Index LB Agg	Best Fit Index LB Muni
Alpha	–0.9	–0.4
Beta	0.39	0.43
R–Squared	52	77

Standard Deviation	1.89
Mean	4.49
Sharpe Ratio	–0.28

Portfolio Analysis 09-30-01

Total Fixed-Income: 176	Date of Maturity	Amount $000	Value $000	% Net Assets
AR State Dorm 6%	08-15-03	8,070	8,559	1.96
KY Ppty/Bldg Com Proj #58 6.85%	08-01-04	7,170	7,598	1.74
PA State COP 6.2%	01-15-09	6,875	7,342	1.68
TX Houston GO 5.25%	03-01-05	6,500	6,948	1.59
GA Atlanta Arpt Fac 6.25%	01-01-05	6,220	6,810	1.56
NC State GO 5.2%	09-01-03	5,750	6,030	1.38
VA Commonwealth Transp 5.5%	10-01-04	5,500	5,939	1.36
GA De Kalb Wtr/Swr 6.25%	10-01-04	5,275	5,778	1.32
TX State GO 5%	10-01-06	5,285	5,687	1.30
NM Bernalillo Tax Receipts 5.75%	04-01-26	5,000	5,520	1.27
SC State GO 5.75%	01-01-07	4,960	5,489	1.26
LA State GO 5.5%	04-15-07	5,000	5,476	1.26
NJ Transp Cap Grant 5.5%	02-01-06	5,000	5,448	1.25
GA State GO 5.75%	07-01-04	5,000	5,398	1.24
FL Dade Aviation Miami Intl Arpt 5.75%	10-01-04	5,000	5,373	1.23

Current Investment Style

Duration: Short Int Long — Quality: High Med Low

Avg Duration[1]	2.8 Yrs
Avg Nominal Maturity	4.1 Yrs
Avg Credit Quality	AA
Avg Wtd Coupon	5.61%
Avg Wtd Price	106.19% of par
Pricing Service	J.J. Kenny

[1] figure provided by fund

Analysis by Scott Cooley 08-31-01

T. Rowe Price Tax-Free Short-Intermediate Fund is still a compelling choice.

This fund is building a streak that might have made Joe DiMaggio envious. In each of the past seven calendar years, the fund has beaten a majority of its muni-short rivals. The fund is on pace to do so again in 2001: For the year to date through August 30, this offering has beaten 90% of its category peers. Moreover, under manager Charles Hill's direction the fund has exhibited moderate volatility.

A conservative strategy and low costs have produced this enviable record. Hill doesn't make big interest-rate bets or load up on lower-yielding issues—two moves that can backfire on even talented managers. Instead of making enormous wagers, Hill makes small ones, including digging for underappreciated issues. Mainly, though, he allows the fund's below-average costs to drive its relative returns. With a 53-basis-point expense ratio, which is just more than half the category average, Hill doesn't have to do anything fancy to beat his average rival. While Hill has made some savvy moves, including making a small wager that interest rates would decline in 2000, the fund's longer-term advantage over its rivals owes primarily to its low costs. Over the past five years, the fund has beaten its average peer by an annualized 46 basis points (or 0.46%), but the fund's low costs alone give it a 38-basis-point edge over its rivals.

What's most encouraging is that the fund's advantages appear sustainable. It's a good bet the fund's expenses will still be below average a few years hence. The fund has an experienced, successful skipper. And finally, T. Rowe's muni operation is excellent; only one of the family's 14 funds in the area has a below-average five-year record, and it ranks just below its category's midpoint. In short, for investors seeking a well-run, short-term muni fund, this one should fill the bill.

Credit Analysis % bonds 09-30-01

US Govt	0	BB	2
AAA	39	B	0
AA	32	Below B	0
A	19	NR/NA	1
BBB	8		

Special Securities % assets 09-30-01

Restricted/Illiquid Secs	0
Inverse Floaters	0
Options/Futures/Warrants	No

Bond Type % assets 09-30-00

Alternative Minimum Tax (AMT)	17.4
Insured	32.8
Prerefunded	12.7

Top 5 States % bonds

VA	12.5	GA	6.2
TX	8.3	PA	6.1
NY	7.4		

Composition % assets 09-30-01

Cash	1.2	Bonds	98.8
Stocks	0.0	Other	0.0

Sector Weightings	% of Bonds	Rel Cat
General Obligation	28.9	1.0
Utilities	10.0	1.3
Health	8.3	0.7
Water/Waste	2.4	0.4
Housing	2.6	0.4
Education	6.2	1.0
Transportation	18.3	2.0
COP/Lease	2.7	0.9
Industrial	7.7	0.8
Misc Revenue	12.4	2.1
Demand	0.8	0.3

Address:	100 E. Pratt Street Baltimore, MD 21202 800–638–5660 / 410–547–2308
Web Address:	www.troweprice.com
Inception:	12-23-83
Advisor:	T. Rowe Price Assoc.
Subadvisor:	None
NTF Plans:	N/A

Minimum Purchase:	$2500	Add: $100 IRA: $1000
Min Auto Inv Plan:	$100	Add: $100
Sales Fees:	No–load	
Management Fee:	.10%+.33% mx./.30% mn.(G)	
Actual Fees:	Mgt: 0.42%	Dist: —
Expense Projections:	3Yr: $170	5Yr: $296 10Yr: $665
Avg Brok Commission:	—	Income Distrib: Monthly
Total Cost (relative to category):		Below Avg

T. Rowe Price U.S. Treasury Long–Term

Ticker	Load	NAV	Yield	SEC Yield	Total Assets	Mstar Category
PRULX	None	$11.29	5.3%	5.07%	$338.0 mil	Long Government

Prospectus Objective: Government Treasury

T. Rowe Price U.S. Treasury Long-Term Fund seeks current income consistent with maximum credit protection.

The fund normally invests at least 85% of assets in U.S. Treasury securities with the remainder in other U.S. government securities. The dollar-weighted average maturity typically ranges between 15 and 20 years, but it may range between 10 and 30 years under certain market conditions.

Historical Profile
Return High
Risk High
Rating ★★ Below Avg

Investment Style
Fixed-Income
Income Rtn %Rank Cat: 5 | 16 | 41 | 28 | 32 | 34 | 33 | 35

Growth of Principal vs. Interest Rate Shifts
— Principal Value $000 (NAV with capital gains reinvested)
— Interest Rate % on 10 Yr Treasury
▼ Manager Change
▽ Partial Manager Change
► Mgr Unknown After
◄ Mgr Unknown Before

Performance Quartile (within Category)

1990	1991	1992	1993	1994	1995	1996	1997	1998	1999	2000	12-01	History
10.01	10.78	10.36	10.71	9.41	11.36	10.43	11.27	11.98	10.22	11.50	11.29	NAV
6.67	16.28	5.83	12.93	–5.75	28.60	–2.37	14.73	12.82	–8.75	19.11	3.39	Total Return %
–2.29	0.27	–1.58	3.18	–2.83	10.13	–5.98	5.05	4.15	–7.92	7.48	–5.03	+/– LB Aggregate
0.39	–2.41	–2.26	–4.25	1.84	–2.31	–1.54	–0.39	–0.50	–0.49	–1.18	–0.95	+/– LB LT Government
8.30	8.07	6.99	6.75	6.56	7.20	5.77	6.25	5.72	5.34	6.21	5.30	Income Return %
–1.63	8.21	–1.16	6.18	–12.31	21.40	–8.14	8.48	7.10	–14.09	12.90	–1.91	Capital Return %
54	50	53	43	57	19	84	17	24	78	22	88	Total Rtn % Rank Cat
0.81	0.78	0.72	0.68	0.68	0.66	0.64	0.63	0.63	0.62	0.62	0.60	Income $
0.00	0.00	0.28	0.29	0.01	0.00	0.00	0.00	0.07	0.11	0.00	0.00	Capital Gains $
0.80	0.80	0.80	0.80	0.80	0.80	0.80	0.80	0.67	0.66	0.64	0.63	Expense Ratio %
8.23	8.01	7.66	6.75	6.17	7.05	6.05	6.22	5.71	5.30	5.89	5.51	Income Ratio %
—	159	162	165	59	99	60	68	81	74	22	31	Turnover Rate %
44.1	59.9	63.0	57.1	58.3	71.0	73.1	206.8	309.8	324.4	314.8	338.0	Net Assets $mil

Portfolio Manager(s)

William T. Reynolds, CFA. Since 11-98. BA'70 U. of North Carolina-Chapel Hill; MBA'73 American U. Other funds currently managed: T. Rowe Price New Income, T. Rowe Price U.S. Treasury Interm, T. Rowe Price Summit Municipal Income.

Jerome Clark, CFA. Since 11-98. BS U.S. Naval Academy; MS Naval Postgraduate School. Other fund currently managed: T. Rowe Price U.S. Treasury Interm.

Daniel O. Shackelford. Since 1-00. BSBA'80 U. of North Carolina-Chapel Hill; MBA'91 Duke U. Other funds currently managed: T. Rowe Price New Income, T. Rowe Price U.S. Treasury Interm.

Performance 12-31-01

	1st Qtr	2nd Qtr	3rd Qtr	4th Qtr	Total
1997	–3.13	5.34	5.61	6.46	14.73
1998	1.38	4.54	7.42	–0.90	12.82
1999	–4.12	–2.51	–0.31	–2.07	–8.75
2000	7.32	0.82	2.74	7.16	19.11
2001	0.97	–1.54	6.63	–2.46	3.39

Trailing	Total Return%	+/– LB Agg	+/– LB LT Govt	% Rank All	% Rank Cat	Growth of $10,000
3 Mo	–2.46	–2.49	–0.59	99	96	9,754
6 Mo	4.01	–0.65	–0.74	9	63	10,401
1 Yr	3.39	–5.03	–0.95	35	88	10,339
3 Yr Avg	3.97	–2.31	–0.85	41	65	11,237
5 Yr Avg	7.78	0.36	–0.70	30	19	14,546
10 Yr Avg	7.48	0.25	–1.12	46	24	20,570
15 Yr Avg	—	—	—	—	—	—

Tax Analysis	Tax-Adj Ret%	%Rank Cat	%Pretax Ret	%Rank Cat
3 Yr Avg	1.64	76	41.4	82
5 Yr Avg	5.33	19	68.5	15
10 Yr Avg	4.80	32	64.2	24

Potential Capital Gain Exposure: 3% of assets

Risk Analysis

Time Period	Load-Adj Return %	Risk %Rank[1] All	Risk %Rank[1] Cat	Morningstar Return	Morningstar Risk	Morningstar Risk-Adj Rating
1 Yr	3.39					
3 Yr	3.97	33	83	–0.21[2]	1.52	★★
5 Yr	7.78	37	84	0.63[2]	1.55	★★
10 Yr	7.48	46	79	0.80[2]	1.80	★★

Average Historical Rating (112 months): 2.1★s

[1] 1=low, 100=high [2] T-Bill return substituted for category avg.

Category Rating (3 Yr)

1 2 3 4 5
Worst Best

Return Average
Risk Above Avg

Other Measures	Standard Index LB Agg	Best Fit Index LB LTTreas
Alpha	–3.2	–0.8
Beta	1.91	0.98
R-Squared	77	99

Standard Deviation	7.51
Mean	3.97
Sharpe Ratio	–0.15

Analysis by Gabriel Presler 12-10-01

T. Rowe Price U.S. Treasury Long–Term's standard approach hasn't worked in 2001, but investors shouldn't expect a change.

Shareholders never get surprised here; this fund is one of the most orthodox offerings in the long-government category. First of all, it always favors the long end of the yield curve, which means that changes in interest rates have a large impact on its returns. And although the managers occasionally dip into mortgage-backed paper, at least 85% of the portfolio is devoted to Treasury paper.

In 2001's jittery market, this approach has been a recipe for disappointment—at least on a relative basis. Although an uncertain political environment has favored U.S. government bonds, declining interest rates have generally sent investors to the short end of the yield curve. And a couple of spikes in long-term interest rates meant that this longer-than-average fund wasn't able to fully recover relative to its peers. Its lack of agency issues has also dragged on its relative performance. Thus, while the fund's gain of just over 1% for the year to date through Dec. 10, 2001, is nothing to scoff at, it ranks in the group's lower reaches.

The fund is unlikely to do well when the interest-rate environment is uncertain—in 1999, for example, it faltered as rates soared—and it's more volatile than its peers. Still, this hasn't been a bad choice over time. In fact, its long-term record outpaces most of its like-minded rivals'. What's more, its five- and 10-year records are in the top third of the entire category. It's thus a decent choice for aggressive investors seeking interest-rate exposure.

Portfolio Analysis 09-30-01

Total Fixed-Income: 140	Date of Maturity	Amount $000	Value $000	% Net Assets
US Treasury Bond 8.875%	02-15-19	30,900	43,121	13.37
US Treasury Bond 7.25%	05-15-16	27,450	33,011	10.24
US Treasury Bond 7.125%	02-15-23	22,700	27,459	8.52
US Treasury Bond 0%	05-15-16	57,000	25,410	7.88
US Treasury Bond .01%	11-15-16	50,000	21,542	6.68
US Treasury Bond 7.625%	02-15-25	16,775	21,534	6.68
US Treasury Strip 0%	11-15-16	50,000	21,515	6.67
US Treasury Bond 8.75%	05-15-17	15,500	21,178	6.57
US Treasury Note 5.5%	02-15-08	19,500	20,882	6.48
US Treasury Bond 6.25%	08-15-23	18,500	20,343	6.31
US Treasury Strip 0%	11-15-21	64,000	20,137	6.25
GNMA 6%	12-15-13	5,834	6,005	1.86
GNMA CMO Z 6.5%	05-20-28	5,078	5,141	1.59
GNMA CMO PAC 6.35%	01-20-28	5,000	4,985	1.55
GNMA 9.5%	12-15-17	3,077	3,401	1.05
US Treasury Bond 5.375%	02-15-31	3,250	3,231	1.00
GNMA 6%	05-15-31	3,034	3,045	0.94
GNMA 6.5%	07-15-09	2,161	2,262	0.70
GNMA 6.5%	08-15-28	2,119	2,169	0.67
GNMA CMO 7%	05-16-24	2,000	2,102	0.65

Current Investment Style

Duration: Short Int Long — Quality: High Med Low

Avg Eff Duration[1]	11.2 Yrs
Avg Eff Maturity	—
Avg Credit Quality	AAA
Avg Wtd Coupon	5.34%
Avg Wtd Price	98.72% of par

[1] figure provided by fund

Special Securities % assets 09-30-01	
Restricted/Illiquid Secs	0
Exotic Mortgage–Backed	2
Emerging–Markets Secs	0
Options/Futures/Warrants	No

Coupon Range	% of Bonds	Rel Cat
0%	22.58	1.71
0% to 7%	24.08	0.47
7% to 8.5%	28.49	1.17
8.5% to 10%	24.62	2.90
More than 10%	0.23	0.10

1.00=Category Average

Credit Analysis % bonds 09-30-01			
US Govt	100	BB	0
AAA	0	B	0
AA	0	Below B	0
A	0	NR/NA	0
BBB	0		

Composition % assets 09-30-01			
Cash	0.8	Bonds	99.3
Stocks	0.0	Other	0.0

Sector Breakdown % bonds 09-30-01			
US Treasuries	81	CMOs	0
GNMA mtgs	12	ARMs	0
FNMA mtgs	0	Other	0
FHLMC mtgs	0		

Address:	100 E. Pratt Street Baltimore, MD 21202 800–638–5660 / 410–547–2308
Web Address:	www.troweprice.com
Inception:	09-29-89
Advisor:	T. Rowe Price Assoc.
Subadvisor:	None
NTF Plans:	N/A

Minimum Purchase:	$2500	Add: $100 IRA: $1000
Min Auto Inv Plan:	$100	Add: $100
Sales Fees:	No–load	
Management Fee:	.05%+.33% mx./.00% mn.(G)	
Actual Fees:	Mgt: 0.37%	Dist: —
Expense Projections:	3Yr: $211	5Yr: $368 10Yr: $822
Avg Brok Commission:	—	Income Distrib: Monthly
Total Cost (relative to category):		Below Avg

T. Rowe Price Value

Ticker	Load	NAV	Yield	Total Assets	Mstar Category
TRVLX	None	$18.88	0.9%	$1,167.0 mil	Mid-Cap Value

Prospectus Objective: Growth and Income

T. Rowe Price Value Fund seeks long-term capital appreciation; income is a secondary consideration.

The fund normally invests at least 65% of assets in equities that management believes to be undervalued. It invests primarily in large-company issues; yet it may also invest a portion of assets in smaller issues as well as convertibles and bonds, including municipals, and up to 10% of assets in noninvestment-grade debt. Management looks at price/earnings and price/book ratios, dividend yield, price/cash flow, undervalued assets, and restructuring opportunities in the selection of securities.

The fund offers two share classes, both of which differ in fee structure and availability.

Historical Profile

Return Above Avg
Risk Below Avg
Rating ★★★★ Above Avg

Investment Style
Equity
Average Stock %: 91% 92% 90% 95% 93% 95% 95%

▼ Manager Change
▽ Partial Manager Change

Fund Performance vs. Category Average
■ Quarterly Fund Return +/– Category Average
— Category Baseline

Performance Quartile (within Category)

Portfolio Manager(s)

Brian C. Rogers, CFA. Since 9-94. BA'77 Harvard U.; MBA'82 Harvard U. Other funds currently managed: T. Rowe Price Equity-Income, Vantagepoint Equity Income, T. Rowe Price Equity-Income Adv.

1990	1991	1992	1993	1994	1995	1996	1997	1998	1999	2000	12-01	History
—	—	—	—	10.24	13.21	15.76	18.24	18.31	17.50	19.15	18.88	NAV
—	—	—	—	3.10*	39.85	28.51	29.25	6.85	9.16	15.75	1.60	Total Return %
—	—	—	—	3.12*	2.32	5.56	–4.11	–21.72	–11.88	24.85	13.48	+/– S&P 500
—	—	—	—	—	4.92	8.25	–5.11	1.77	9.26	–3.44	–0.74	+/– Russ Midcap Val
—	—	—	—	0.70	2.56	2.00	1.35	1.12	1.19	1.31	0.89	Income Return %
—	—	—	—	2.40	37.29	26.51	27.90	5.73	7.97	14.43	0.72	Capital Return %
—	—	—	—	—	7	9	31	35	46	54	62	Total Rtn % Rank Cat
—	—	—	—	0.07	0.26	0.26	0.21	0.20	0.21	0.23	0.17	Income $
—	—	—	—	0.00	0.82	0.91	1.83	0.96	2.20	0.84	0.40	Capital Gains $
—	—	—	—	1.10	1.10	1.10	1.05	0.98	0.92	0.91	—	Expense Ratio %
—	—	—	—	3.16	2.03	1.71	1.26	1.06	1.14	1.38	—	Income Ratio %
—	—	—	—	31	90	68	67	72	68	56	—	Turnover Rate %
—	—	—	—	—	46.6	197.8	546.4	774.5	851.4	989.3	—	Net Assets $mil

Performance 12-31-01

	1st Qtr	2nd Qtr	3rd Qtr	4th Qtr	Total
1997	2.89	13.89	10.08	0.19	29.25
1998	12.50	–3.54	–13.40	13.70	6.85
1999	4.02	15.02	–11.13	2.66	9.16
2000	0.40	–1.20	5.82	10.27	15.75
2001	–0.57	5.72	–13.11	11.25	1.60

Trailing	Total Return%	+/– S&P 500	+/– Russ Midcap Val	% Rank All	% Rank Cat	Growth of $10,000
3 Mo	11.25	0.56	–0.78	36	66	11,125
6 Mo	–3.34	2.21	–2.43	53	74	9,666
1 Yr	1.60	13.48	–0.74	40	62	10,160
3 Yr Avg	8.68	9.71	1.87	13	60	12,837
5 Yr Avg	12.13	1.43	0.67	10	45	17,729
10 Yr Avg	—	—	—	—	—	—
15 Yr Avg	—	—	—	—	—	—

Tax Analysis	Tax-Adj Ret%	%Rank Cat	%Pretax Ret	%Rank Cat
3 Yr Avg	6.30	62	72.5	73
5 Yr Avg	9.46	45	77.9	51
10 Yr Avg	—	—	—	—

Potential Capital Gain Exposure: 3% of assets

Risk Analysis

Time Period	Load-Adj Return %	Risk %Rank[1] All	Risk %Rank[1] Cat	Morningstar Return	Morningstar Risk	Morningstar Risk-Adj Rating
1 Yr	1.60					
3 Yr	8.68	50	59	0.82[2]	0.71	★★★★
5 Yr	12.13	54	45	1.78[2]	0.75	★★★★
Incept	17.81	—	—	—	—	

Average Historical Rating (52 months): 4.0★s

[1] 1=low, 100=high [2] T-Bill return substituted for category avg.

Category Rating (3 Yr)

1 2 **3** 4 5
Worst Best

Return Average
Risk Average

Other Measures	Standard Index S&P 500	Best Fit Index S&P 500
Alpha	8.6	8.6
Beta	0.74	0.74
R-Squared	51	51

Standard Deviation	19.07
Mean	8.68
Sharpe Ratio	0.22

Portfolio Analysis 09-30-01

Share change since 06-01 Total Stocks: 103	Sector	PE	YTD Ret%	% Assets
⊕ Guidant	Health	42.6	–7.67	2.00
⊕ Schering-Plough	Health	22.2	–35.90	1.60
Bristol-Myers Squibb	Health	20.2	–26.00	1.56
⊕ ExxonMobil	Energy	15.3	–7.59	1.53
Cooper Inds	Industrials	11.5	–21.50	1.52
⊖ Lockheed Martin	Industrials	36.8	38.98	1.51
Raytheon	Industrials	—	7.27	1.50
⊕ Sprint	Services	20.5	1.18	1.45
⊕ Honeywell Intl	Durables	NMF	–27.00	1.44
⊕ McDonald's	Services	19.2	–21.50	1.41
⊕ Allstate	Financials	17.1	–21.00	1.37
⊕ Burlington Resources	Energy	8.4	–24.60	1.33
⊕ WorldCom	Services	24.3	3.12	1.30
⊕ DuPont De Nemours E.I.	Industrials	65.4	–9.14	1.30
⊕ Walt Disney	Services	—	–27.70	1.30
Becton Dickinson	Health	22.9	–3.20	1.28
Clorox	Staples	31.1	14.20	1.28
⊕ Bank One	Financials	29.1	9.13	1.28
☼ Campbell Soup	Staples	20.1	–11.20	1.27
RadioShack	Retail	21.5	–29.20	1.26
⊕ American Express	Financials	28.3	–34.40	1.26
⊕ Comcast	Services	20.3	–13.70	1.24
☼ Chubb	Technology	—	—	1.23
⊕ Ryder Sys	Services	29.2	37.06	1.21
⊕ Coca-Cola Enterprises	Staples	NMF	0.60	1.19

Current Investment Style

Style: Value Blnd Growth; Size: Large Med Small

	Stock Port Avg	Relative S&P 500 Current	Relative S&P 500 Hist	Rel Cat
Price/Earnings Ratio	27.6	0.89	0.70	1.17
Price/Book Ratio	3.3	0.58	0.44	1.08
Price/Cash Flow	12.0	0.66	0.57	0.97
3 Yr Earnings Growth	7.8	0.54	0.47	0.66
1 Yr Earnings Est%	–18.0	10.18	—	2.93
Med Mkt Cap $mil	11,400	0.2	0.1	1.60

Special Securities % assets 09-30-01

Restricted/Illiquid Secs	0
Emerging-Markets Secs	0
Options/Futures/Warrants	No

Composition % assets 09-30-01

Cash	3.2
Stocks*	96.8
Bonds	0.0
Other	0.0
*Foreign (% stocks)	4.8

Market Cap

Giant	20.1
Large	38.7
Medium	38.0
Small	3.2
Micro	0.0

Sector Weightings	% of Stocks	Rel S&P	5-Year High	5-Year Low
Utilities	0.9	0.3	5	0
Energy	8.7	1.2	10	4
Financials	17.6	1.0	30	13
Industrials	14.8	1.3	32	10
Durables	7.4	4.8	10	3
Staples	8.2	1.0	10	3
Services	22.3	2.1	24	12
Retail	4.1	0.6	10	3
Health	6.8	0.5	12	1
Technology	9.1	0.5	12	1

Analysis by Catherine Hickey 11-27-01

This remains a rock-solid value fund, and a good way to gain access to a strong stock-picker.

T. Rowe Price Value Fund can work well for investors in a couple of ways. First, many a growth-heavy portfolio could benefit from a dose of what this fund offers. Manager Brian Rogers looks for bargain-priced, financially healthy companies that he can hold on to for years. This approach leads to a portfolio with moderate volatility, and means it can diversify a growth-heavy portfolio.

This fund also offers investors access to a talented stock-picker. Rogers is a seasoned money manager who has built great records here and at his other charge, T. Rowe Price Equity-Income. This fund has had a lackluster stretch recently, partly because Rogers has had a larger-cap tilt and small caps have outperformed. Over time, however, Rogers has demonstrated a marked ability to make wise picks among some of the market's least-loved companies. He bought Lockheed Martin when it was wildly out of favor in 1999, for example, but it has come back strong since.

Shareholders in this fund should have long time horizons, though. Sometimes Rogers' picks take time to turn things around, and the fund can suffer lean periods in the meantime. However, the fund's performance is rarely subpar for long, which its five-year record bears out.

Currently, this fund is categorized as mid-cap value by Morningstar, but that may change. In order to make a bigger distinction between this fund and T. Rowe Price Mid-Cap Value, Rogers has gradually moved this offering into bigger-cap names. Indeed, the fund now hits the large-cap end of the style box. Investors who desire a pure mid-cap offering should look elsewhere.

Those looking for a stockpicker's fund run by a talented skipper, however, would do well to give this one a look.

Address:	100 E. Pratt Street Baltimore, MD 21202 800-638-5660 / 410-547-2308
Web Address:	www.troweprice.com
*Inception:	09-30-94
Advisor:	T. Rowe Price Assoc.
Subadvisor:	None
NTF Plans:	N/A

Minimum Purchase:	$2500	Add: $100 IRA: $1000
Min Auto Inv Plan:	$50	Add: $50
Sales Fees:	No-load	
Management Fee:	.67%+.33% mx./.30% mn.(G)	
Actual Fees:	Mgt: 0.67%	Dist: —
Expense Projections:	3Yr: $293	5Yr: $509 10Yr: $1131
Avg Brok Commission:	—	Income Distrib: Annually
Total Cost (relative to category):	Low	

Principal Government Securities Inc A

Ticker	Load	NAV	Yield	SEC Yield	Total Assets	Mstar Category
PRGVX	4.75%	$11.48	5.9%	5.83%	$294.5 mil	Intermediate Govt

Prospectus Objective: Government Mortgage

Principal Government Securities Income Fund seeks current income, liquidity, and safety of principal.

The fund normally invests at least 65% of assets in U.S. government obligations. Depending on market conditions, a substantial portion of assets may be invested in GNMA certificates of the modified pass-through type. The fund may also enter into repurchase agreements regarding these securities.

Class A shares have front loads; B shares have deferred loads, higher 12b-1 fees and conversion features; R shares are for certain qualified investors. Past names: BLC Government Securities Income Fund and Princor Government Securities Income Fund.

Historical Profile

Return: Average
Risk: Average
Rating: ★★★ Neutral

Investment Style
Fixed-Income

Income Rtn %Rank Cat: 51 43 40 44 21 17 33 17

Growth of Principal vs. Interest Rate Shifts
- Principal Value $000 (NAV with capital gains reinvested)
- Interest Rate % on 10 Yr Treasury
- ▼ Manager Change
- ▽ Partial Manager Change
- ► Mgr Unknown After
- ◄ Mgr Unknown Before

Performance Quartile (within Category)

Portfolio Manager(s)

Martin J. Schafer. Since 5-85. BBA'76 U. of Iowa. Other funds currently managed: Principal Tax-Exempt Bond A, Principal Investors Mtg-Backed Secs, Principal Tax-Exempt Bond B.

1990	1991	1992	1993	1994	1995	1996	1997	1998	1999	2000	12-01	History
10.79	11.62	11.31	11.48	10.24	11.45	11.16	11.52	11.62	10.93	11.40	11.48	NAV
9.52	16.83	6.13	9.16	−4.89	19.19	3.85	9.69	7.19	0.01	10.90	6.75	Total Return %
0.56	0.83	−1.28	−0.59	−1.97	0.72	0.24	0.01	−1.48	0.84	−0.74	−1.68	+/− LB Aggregate
0.80	1.51	−1.10	−1.49	−1.52	0.86	1.08	0.12	−2.66	2.26	−2.34	−0.49	+/− LB Government
8.33	8.32	7.01	6.63	6.10	7.10	6.35	6.32	6.30	6.11	6.38	6.06	Income Return %
1.19	8.51	−0.88	2.54	−10.99	12.09	−2.49	3.38	0.89	−6.10	4.52	0.69	Capital Return %
39	11	61	27	82	6	25	7	54	32	43	53	Total Rtn % Rank Cat
0.86	0.87	0.79	0.73	0.68	0.71	0.71	0.69	0.71	0.69	0.68	0.67	Income $
0.00	0.04	0.20	0.12	0.00	0.00	0.00	0.00	0.00	0.00	0.00	0.00	Capital Gains $
1.07	0.98	0.95	0.93	0.95	0.87	0.81	0.84	0.86	0.89	0.94	—	Expense Ratio %
8.15	7.80	7.04	6.38	6.35	6.57	6.31	6.19	6.07	6.04	6.14	—	Income Ratio %
22	15	54	53	25	10	26	11	17	19	7	—	Turnover Rate %
77.1	106.1	177.3	255.4	247.3	267.5	256.4	249.2	252.0	233.4	216.9	253.8	Net Assets $mil

Performance 12-31-01

	1st Qtr	2nd Qtr	3rd Qtr	4th Qtr	Total
1997	−1.06	4.71	3.48	2.32	9.69
1998	1.45	2.07	3.37	0.15	7.19
1999	0.40	−1.28	0.92	−0.01	0.01
2000	1.83	1.98	2.95	3.72	10.90
2001	2.39	0.75	3.75	−0.27	6.75

Trailing	Total Return%	+/− LB Agg	+/− LB Govt	% Rank All	% Rank Cat	Growth of $10,000
3 Mo	−0.27	−0.31	0.32	81	34	9,973
6 Mo	3.47	−1.18	−1.38	13	88	10,347
1 Yr	6.75	−1.68	−0.49	15	53	10,675
3 Yr Avg	5.79	−0.49	−0.09	24	29	11,839
5 Yr Avg	6.84	−0.59	−0.56	37	20	13,921
10 Yr Avg	6.62	−0.61	−0.52	55	17	18,986
15 Yr Avg	7.75	−0.37	−0.13	56	14	30,658

Tax Analysis	Tax-Adj Ret%	%Rank Cat	%Pretax Ret	%Rank Cat
3 Yr Avg	3.31	39	57.1	52
5 Yr Avg	4.32	21	63.2	41
10 Yr Avg	4.00	17	60.4	29

Potential Capital Gain Exposure: 1% of assets

Risk Analysis

Time Period	Load-Adj Return %	Risk %Rank[1] All	Risk %Rank[1] Cat	Morningstar Return	Morningstar Risk	Morningstar Risk-Adj Rating
1 Yr	1.68					
3 Yr	4.09	10	39	−0.18[2]	0.59	★★★
5 Yr	5.80	17	44	0.17[2]	0.63	★★★
10 Yr	6.10	33	72	0.37[2]	0.99	★★★

Average Historical Rating (164 months): 2.7★s

[1] 1=low, 100=high [2] T-Bill return substituted for category avg.

Category Rating (3 Yr)

1 2 3 4 5
Worst Best

Return: Above Avg
Risk: Average

Other Measures	Standard Index LB Agg	Best Fit Index LB Mtg
Alpha	−0.3	−1.3
Beta	0.85	1.08
R-Squared	86	95

Standard Deviation	3.27
Mean	5.79
Sharpe Ratio	0.30

Portfolio Analysis 11-30-01

Total Fixed-Income: 290	Date of Maturity	Amount $000	Value $000	% Net Assets
GNMA 6.5%	08-20-31	34,765	35,235	11.83
GNMA 7.5%	12-15-30	29,482	30,782	10.34
GNMA 7%	12-01-31	28,774	29,679	9.97
GNMA 7%	12-15-23	15,378	15,993	5.37
GNMA 7.5%	09-15-29	12,958	13,555	4.55
GNMA 6.5%	12-15-23	12,822	13,119	4.41
GNMA 7%	12-15-22	12,256	12,748	4.28
GNMA 6.5%	12-20-24	10,651	10,889	3.66
GNMA 6.5%	08-20-26	10,647	10,837	3.64
GNMA 7%	05-15-28	10,474	10,817	3.63
GNMA 6%	12-01-31	10,000	9,925	3.33
GNMA 8%	11-15-30	8,772	9,237	3.10
GNMA 6%	06-20-26	8,617	8,556	2.87
GNMA 7.5%	12-15-22	7,899	8,333	2.80
GNMA 6%	10-20-24	6,550	6,546	2.20
GNMA 7%	04-15-29	6,090	6,288	2.11
GNMA 7%	12-15-27	5,980	6,183	2.08
GNMA 6%	12-15-23	5,836	5,847	1.96
GNMA 6.5%	07-15-16	4,930	5,105	1.71
GNMA 7.5%	05-15-31	4,689	4,886	1.64

Current Investment Style

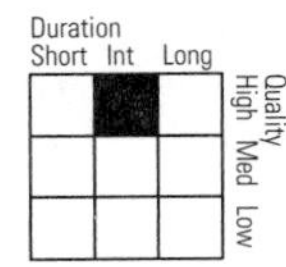

Avg Eff Duration[1]	3.7 Yrs
Avg Eff Maturity	7.6 Yrs
Avg Credit Quality	AAA
Avg Wtd Coupon	6.92%
Avg Wtd Price	103.04% of par

[1] figure provided by fund

Special Securities % assets 11-30-01	
Restricted/Illiquid Secs	0
Exotic Mortgage-Backed	0
Emerging-Markets Secs	0
Options/Futures/Warrants	No

Credit Analysis % bonds 09-30-01			
US Govt	100	BB	0
AAA	0	B	0
AA	0	Below B	0
A	0	NR/NA	0
BBB	0		

Coupon Range	% of Bonds	Rel Cat
0%	0.00	0.00
0% to 7%	40.73	0.72
7% to 8.5%	59.27	1.78
8.5% to 10%	0.00	0.00
More than 10%	0.00	0.00

1.00=Category Average

Composition % assets 11-30-01			
Cash	4.6	Bonds	95.4
Stocks	0.0	Other	0.0

Sector Breakdown % bonds 11-30-01			
US Treasuries	0	CMOs	0
GNMA mtgs	100	ARMs	0
FNMA mtgs	0	Other	0
FHLMC mtgs	0		

Analysis by Scott Cooley 08-08-01

If you hate surprises, you'll probably love Principal Government Securities Income Fund.

Since its 1985 inception, manager Marty Schafer has run this fund with a couple of guiding principles: He likes good total returns and hates principal erosion, so he has favored discount GNMAs (mortgages with relatively low interest rates). Whereas investors incur capital losses on premium mortgage-backeds when they prepay, the opposite is true with discount issues, which actually record a gain when homeowners refinance or sell (to reflect the difference between a bond's market price and its par value). Thus, while prepayment risk is a big problem for some of Schafer's rivals, it's not much of an issue here.

That has been a winning approach at this fund. Helped by a duration that was longer than average during much of the falling-rate 1990s, the fund's five- and 10-year returns handily exceed the category norm. Schafer has also beaten his average peer who focuses on mortgage-backed issues. The fund has posted continued, strong performance over the past year. For the trailing year through August 7, 2001, the fund has gained 10.7%, leaving it ahead of two thirds of its peers. Thanks to Schafer's preference for discount GNMAs, refinancing didn't hit the fund as hard as it hit some mortgage-focused rivals.

Although Schafer emphasizes consistency, it's not fair to say this fund is on autopilot. Based on his analysis of the market and economic outlook, he does vary the fund's interest-rate stance. Right now, he fears rising intermediate- to long-term interest rates, so he has brought the fund's duration roughly in line with that of its benchmark, the Lehman Brothers GNMA index. Before, Schafer frequently bet on declining rates.

This fund appears to offer nearly everything an investor would want: a good record, an experienced manager, and decent expenses. It's thus a fine option.

Address:	P.O. Box 10423 Des Moines, IA 50306 515-247-6933 / 800-451-5447
Web Address:	www.principal.com/funds/index.htm
Inception:	05-21-85
Advisor:	Principal Mgmt.
Subadvisor:	Invista Cap. Mgmt.
NTF Plans:	N/A

Minimum Purchase:	$1000	Add: $100	IRA: $500
Min Auto Inv Plan:	$1000	Add: $50	
Sales Fees:	4.75%L, 0.25%B		
Management Fee:	.50% mx./.30% mn.		
Actual Fees:	Mgt: 0.45%	Dist: 0.20%	
Expense Projections:	3Yr: $736	5Yr: $929	10Yr: $1485
Avg Brok Commission:	—	Income Distrib: Monthly	
Total Cost (relative to category):	—		

Prudential Value A

Ticker	Load	NAV	Yield	Total Assets	Mstar Category
PBEAX	5.00%	$15.95	0.6%	$1,179.1 mil	Mid–Cap Value

Prospectus Objective: Equity–Income

Prudential Value Fund seeks both current income and capital appreciation.

The fund normally invests at least 65% of assets in common stocks and convertibles that provide income returns higher than those of the S&P 500 or the NYSE Composite index. It may invest up to 35% of assets in fixed-income securities and money market instruments. The fund may invest up to 30% of assets in foreign securities; it may also invest in American Depositary Receipts.

Class A shares have front loads; B shares have deferred loads, higher 12b-1 fees, and conversion features; C shares have level loads; Z shares are for certain qualified investors. Prior to September 18, 2000, the fund was named Prudential Equity-Income Fund.

Historical Profile

Return Average
Risk Average
Rating ★★★ Neutral

Investment Style Equity — Average Stock %

	1994	1995	1996	1997	1998	1999	2000	12-01
Average Stock %		73%	88%	89%	93%	95%	97%	100%

▼ Manager Change
▽ Partial Manager Change

Fund Performance vs. Category Average
■ Quarterly Fund Return +/– Category Average
— Category Baseline

Performance Quartile (within Category)

Portfolio Manager(s)

Thomas Kolefas, CFA. Since 5-00.
Bradley T. Goldberg, CFA. Since 9-00.
Neil Kilbane, CFA. Since 2-01.
James F. Giblin, CFA. Since 2-01.

History

1990	1991	1992	1993	1994	1995	1996	1997	1998	1999	2000	12-01	History
10.18	11.98	12.14	13.76	12.81	14.39	16.28	19.79	17.75	17.14	18.12	15.95	NAV
–0.07*	26.72	9.31	21.38	0.03	21.54	21.86	36.41	–2.88	11.63	15.06	–2.89	Total Return %
–3.70*	–3.76	1.69	11.32	–1.29	–15.99	–1.09	3.06	–31.46	–9.41	24.17	8.99	+/– S&P 500
—	–11.20	–12.37	5.76	2.16	–13.39	1.60	2.05	–7.97	11.74	–4.12	–5.23	+/– Russ Midcap Val
3.80	3.68	4.07	3.46	3.08	3.64	3.46	2.82	2.19	1.90	1.64	0.56	Income Return %
–3.87	23.04	5.24	17.92	–3.06	17.91	18.40	33.59	–5.07	9.73	13.42	–3.45	Capital Return %
—	65	82	40	41	89	35	7	80	37	57	85	Total Rtn % Rank Cat
0.40	0.37	0.48	0.42	0.42	0.46	0.49	0.46	0.43	0.34	0.28	0.10	Income $
0.00	0.48	0.44	0.53	0.53	0.70	0.71	1.89	1.06	2.18	1.22	1.50	Capital Gains $
1.59	1.37	1.22	1.07	1.09	1.03	0.98	0.94	0.91	1.02	1.16	—	Expense Ratio %
3.12	3.43	3.22	3.44	2.97	3.36	3.26	2.32	2.19	1.71	1.83	—	Income Ratio %
—	64	43	57	70	74	36	36	22	17	64	—	Turnover Rate %
—	—	54.6	113.5	145.0	299.5	403.4	611.7	665.4	647.5	708.8	—	Net Assets $mil

Performance 12-31-01

	1st Qtr	2nd Qtr	3rd Qtr	4th Qtr	Total
1997	0.79	16.39	15.91	0.31	36.41
1998	11.22	–1.36	–18.36	8.43	–2.88
1999	3.29	14.08	–11.95	7.59	11.63
2000	–4.96	–0.69	11.67	9.16	15.06
2001	–3.64	4.35	–13.06	11.09	–2.89

Trailing	Total Return%	+/– S&P 500	+/– Russ Midcap Val	% Rank All	% Rank Cat	Growth of $10,000
3 Mo	11.09	0.40	–0.94	37	69	11,109
6 Mo	–3.42	2.13	–2.51	53	75	9,658
1 Yr	–2.89	8.99	–5.23	47	85	9,711
3 Yr Avg	7.65	8.67	0.84	15	64	12,474
5 Yr Avg	10.57	–0.13	–0.90	16	62	16,524
10 Yr Avg	12.50	–0.43	–1.91	15	67	32,481
15 Yr Avg	—	—	—	—	—	—

Tax Analysis	Tax-Adj Ret%	%Rank Cat	%Pretax Ret	%Rank Cat
3 Yr Avg	5.11	69	66.9	85
5 Yr Avg	7.86	65	74.4	72
10 Yr Avg	9.77	69	78.2	76

Potential Capital Gain Exposure: 5% of assets

Risk Analysis

Time Period	Load-Adj Return %	Risk %Rank[1] All	Risk %Rank[1] Cat	Morningstar Return	Morningstar Risk	Morningstar Risk-Adj Rating
1 Yr	–7.75					
3 Yr	5.82	60	87	0.19[2]	0.84	★★★★
5 Yr	9.44	67	79	1.05[2]	0.90	★★★
10 Yr	11.93	66	71	1.09	0.86	★★★

Average Historical Rating (108 months): 3.3★s

[1]1=low, 100=high [2] T-Bill return substituted for category avg.

Category Rating (3 Yr)

1 2 3 4 5 — Worst … Best

Return Average
Risk Above Avg

Other Measures	Standard Index S&P 500	Best Fit Index S&P 500
Alpha	8.6	8.6
Beta	0.86	0.86
R–Squared	54	54
Standard Deviation		21.40
Mean		7.65
Sharpe Ratio		0.14

Portfolio Analysis 09-30-01

Share change since 06–01 Total Stocks: 198

	Sector	PE	YTD Ret%	% Assets
⊕ Citigroup	Financials	20.0	0.03	2.56
⊖ Verizon Comms	Services	29.7	–2.52	1.75
⊖ Philip Morris	Staples	12.1	9.12	1.69
⊖ IBM	Technology	26.9	43.00	1.63
⊕ Lehman Brothers Hldgs	Financials	12.4	–0.84	1.50
Humana	Financials	18.1	–22.60	1.48
⊕ American Intl Grp	Financials	42.0	–19.20	1.45
⊖ PNC Finl Svcs Grp	Financials	13.5	–20.70	1.38
⊕ ExxonMobil	Energy	15.3	–7.59	1.35
⊖ Bank of America	Financials	16.7	42.73	1.33
⊕ Fannie Mae	Financials	16.2	–6.95	1.30
⊖ SBC Comms	Services	18.4	–16.00	1.27
XL Cap Cl A	Financials	22.8	5.82	1.26
⊕ Tyco Intl	Industrials	27.1	6.23	1.18
⊕ Talisman Energy	Energy	43.1	3.14	1.13
⊖ HCA – The Healthcare Company	Health	24.1	–12.20	1.13
⊕ Allstate	Financials	17.1	–21.00	1.12
⊕ Pfizer	Health	34.7	–12.40	1.08
⊕ Equity Office Properties Tr	Financials	18.7	–1.76	1.08
⊕ Household Intl	Financials	14.7	6.89	1.07
⊕ Viacom Cl B	Services	—	—	1.00
⊕ Hartford Finl Svcs Grp	Financials	23.2	–9.63	0.97
Sprint	Services	20.5	1.18	0.93
⊕ Exelon	Utilities	14.0	–29.50	0.91
⊕ Federated Dept Stores	Retail	16.6	16.86	0.89

Current Investment Style

Style: Value Blnd Growth; Size: Large Med Small

	Stock Port Avg	Relative S&P 500 Current	Relative S&P 500 Hist	Rel Cat
Price/Earnings Ratio	24.0	0.77	0.58	1.02
Price/Book Ratio	4.0	0.71	0.33	1.33
Price/Cash Flow	12.8	0.71	0.45	1.03
3 Yr Earnings Growth	14.8	1.01	0.95	1.25
1 Yr Earnings Est%	0.2	—	—	–0.03
Med Mkt Cap $mil	20,446	0.3	0.1	2.87

Analysis by Laura Pavlenko Lutton 12-03-01

Recent changes may improve Prudential Value Fund, but we'd steer clear for now.

This historically mediocre fund was recently remodeled. Longtime manager Warren Spitz was replaced in May 2000 by Thomas Kolefas of Jennison Associates. And in February 2001, James Giblin of Deutsche Asset Management and Victory Capital Management's Neil Kilbane joined as comanagers. The fund's assets are now divided into three independent parts: Kolefas manages 50%, and Giblin and Kilbane split the remainder. The trio has also shifted the fund's portfolio away from its former mid-cap bias toward large-value stocks.

Although early returns have been lackluster, the managers have fared well elsewhere. As comanager of Mainstay Value from 1991 to 1996, Kolefas turned in solid results. Now, backed by Jennison's strong research team, he is using a similar strategy for Prudential Value. Kolefas looks for stocks with low forward P/E ratios relative to the S&P 500 index and strong fundamentals. He recently added to the fund's position in Citigroup because he liked its low forward P/E ratio and its consistent double-digit earnings-growth rate.

Kilbane has also done well elsewhere. Victory Value, which he has managed since 1998, has performed respectably, although his bets on growth-leaning stocks have hurt the fund of late. Giblin's record with Deutsche isn't public, but he led AIM Value to strong results in the late 1980s and early 1990s.

While the fund's recent changes are promising, it's unclear whether the managers' portfolios will gel into a competitive large-value fund. Investors should wait for evidence of better returns before buying in, and those who bought the fund for mid-cap exposure will likely find it no longer meets their needs.

Special Securities % assets 09-30-01	
Restricted/Illiquid Secs	0
Emerging–Markets Secs	Trace
Options/Futures/Warrants	No

Composition % assets 09-30-01	
Cash	0.0
Stocks*	100.0
Bonds	0.0
Other	0.0
*Foreign (% stocks)	3.6

Market Cap	
Giant	28.7
Large	42.4
Medium	27.3
Small	1.6
Micro	0.0

Sector Weightings	% of Stocks	Rel S&P	5-Year High	5-Year Low
Utilities	7.1	2.2	17	0
Energy	9.3	1.3	23	5
Financials	29.6	1.7	39	11
Industrials	10.6	0.9	41	11
Durables	1.5	1.0	8	0
Staples	5.4	0.7	7	0
Services	15.4	1.4	16	5
Retail	3.4	0.5	9	0
Health	7.2	0.5	10	0
Technology	10.5	0.6	15	0

Address: One Seaport Plaza, New York, NY 10292, 800–225–1852
Web Address: www.prudential.com
*Inception: 01-22-90
Advisor: Prudential Inv.s Fund Mgmt.
Subadvisor: Prudential Inv./Deutsche Asset Mgmt.
NTF Plans: Fidelity Inst.

Minimum Purchase: $1000 Add: $100 IRA: None
Min Auto Inv Plan: $50 Add: $50
Sales Fees: 5.00%L, 0.05%B, 0.25%S
Management Fee: .60% mx./.45% mn.
Actual Fees: Mgt: 0.50% Dist: 0.25%
Expense Projections: 3Yr: $819 5Yr: $1056 10Yr: $1736
Avg Brok Commission: — Income Distrib: Quarterly
Total Cost (relative to category): Average

Putnam Capital Appreciation A

Ticker	Load	NAV	Yield	Total Assets	Mstar Category
PCAPX	5.75%	$16.86	0.0%	$1,498.0 mil	Large Blend

Prospectus Objective: Growth

Putnam Capital Appreciation Fund seeks capital appreciation; current income is incidental.

The fund normally invests at least 65% of assets in common stocks; it may also invest in convertibles, preferred stocks, and debt securities that offer capital-appreciation potential. To select securities, management considers an issuer's financial strength, competitive position, and projected earnings and dividends. The fund may invest in companies of any size.

Class A shares have front loads; M shares have lower front loads and higher 12b-1 fees; B shares have deferred loads, the highest 12b-1 fees, and conversion features.

Historical Profile

Return	Below Avg
Risk	Average
Rating	★★ Below Avg

Investment Style
Equity
Average Stock %

1994	1995	1996	1997	1998	1999	2000	12-01
	92%	90%	95%	95%	99%	99%	98%

▼ Manager Change
▽ Partial Manager Change

Fund Performance vs. Category Average
■ Quarterly Fund Return +/– Category Average
— Category Baseline

Performance Quartile (within Category)

Portfolio Manager(s)

Michael K. Arends, CFA. Since 2-99. BBA'75 Southern Methodist U.; MBA'77 Indiana U. Other funds currently managed: Putnam Global Equity A, Putnam Global Equity B, Putnam Capital Appreciation B.

Thomas R. Haslett, CFA. Since 2-99. BA'83 Brown U. Other funds currently managed: Putnam Capital Appreciation B, Putnam Capital Appreciation M, Putnam Emerging Markets A.

Joseph P. Joseph. Since 9-99. BA Loyola C.; MBA New York U. Other funds currently managed: Putnam Capital Appreciation B, Putnam Capital Appreciation M, Putnam International Voyager A.

History

1990	1991	1992	1993	1994	1995	1996	1997	1998	1999	2000	12-01	History
—	—	—	10.25	10.71	13.97	16.99	21.48	22.66	26.14	19.94	16.86	NAV
—	—	—	19.65*	6.00	34.50	30.12	29.77	8.69	17.86	–6.11	–15.45	Total Return %
—	—	—	14.27*	4.68	–3.03	7.17	–3.58	–19.89	–3.18	3.00	–3.57	+/– S&P 500
—	—	—	—	5.55	–3.10	7.95	–3.25	–19.95	–3.97	4.85	–2.68	+/– Wilshire Top 750
—	—	—	0.43	0.29	1.21	0.72	0.54	0.67	0.47	0.00	0.00	Income Return %
—	—	—	19.22	5.70	33.29	29.40	29.23	8.02	17.38	–6.11	–15.45	Capital Return %
—	—	—	—	3	44	5	48	95	68	37	70	Total Rtn % Rank Cat
—	—	—	0.04	0.03	0.13	0.10	0.09	0.14	0.11	0.00	0.00	Income $
—	—	—	0.09	0.12	0.29	1.08	0.46	0.50	0.45	4.68	0.00	Capital Gains $
—	—	—	—	0.95	1.13	1.29	1.20	1.03	0.93	0.96	1.00	Expense Ratio %
—	—	—	—	0.89	1.89	1.05	0.79	0.77	0.77	–0.10	0.01	Income Ratio %
—	—	—	—	—	15	77	38	31	92	188	264	Turnover Rate %
—	—	—	—	37.1	125.3	283.7	1,036.0	1,541.2	1,208.0	1,001.1	788.6	Net Assets $mil

Performance 12-31-01

	1st Qtr	2nd Qtr	3rd Qtr	4th Qtr	Total
1997	1.18	14.66	13.09	–1.09	29.77
1998	11.69	–1.58	–17.41	19.72	8.69
1999	–3.00	5.28	–6.83	23.87	17.86
2000	4.63	–5.16	4.01	–9.03	–6.11
2001	–15.50	7.66	–19.07	14.85	–15.45

Trailing	Total Return%	+/– S&P 500	+/– Wil Top 750	% Rank All	% Rank Cat	Growth of $10,000
3 Mo	14.85	4.17	3.53	24	10	11,485
6 Mo	–7.06	–1.50	–1.26	74	72	9,294
1 Yr	–15.45	–3.57	–2.68	73	70	8,455
3 Yr Avg	–2.19	–1.17	–0.37	84	68	9,357
5 Yr Avg	5.70	–4.99	–4.41	52	87	13,197
10 Yr Avg	—	—	—	—	—	—
15 Yr Avg	—	—	—	—	—	—

Tax Analysis	Tax-Adj Ret%	%Rank Cat	%Pretax Ret	%Rank Cat
3 Yr Avg	–4.06	75	—	—
5 Yr Avg	4.13	84	72.4	75
10 Yr Avg	—	—	—	—

Potential Capital Gain Exposure: –7% of assets

Risk Analysis

Time Period	Load-Adj Return %	Risk %Rank[1] All	Risk %Rank[1] Cat	Morningstar Return	Morningstar Risk	Morningstar Risk-Adj Rating
1 Yr	–20.31					
3 Yr	–4.10	79	90	–1.76[2]	1.12	★★
5 Yr	4.46	77	89	–0.12[2]	1.06	★★
Incept	12.83	—	—	—	—	

Average Historical Rating (65 months): 3.6★s

[1]1=low, 100=high [2] T-Bill return substituted for category avg.

Category Rating (3 Yr)

① ② ③ ④ ⑤
Worst Best

Return	Below Avg
Risk	High

Other Measures	Standard Index S&P 500	Best Fit Index Wil 4500
Alpha	–0.6	–4.9
Beta	0.95	0.71
R-Squared	58	89
Standard Deviation		21.08
Mean		–2.19
Sharpe Ratio		–0.39

Portfolio Analysis 05-31-01

Share change since 11-00 Total Stocks: 98

Share change	Sector	PE	YTD Ret%	% Assets
⊖ Microsoft	Technology	57.6	52.78	2.63
⊖ General Elec	Industrials	30.1	–15.00	2.51
⊕ Pfizer	Health	34.7	–12.40	2.30
⊖ Citigroup	Financials	20.0	0.03	2.02
⊖ ExxonMobil	Energy	15.3	–7.59	1.80
⊕ AT & T Liberty Media Cl A	Services	—	3.22	1.75
⊖ Merck	Health	19.1	–35.90	1.57
☼ Northrop Grumman	Industrials	19.2	23.67	1.51
☼ IBM	Technology	26.9	43.00	1.45
⊕ Philip Morris	Staples	12.1	9.12	1.35
⊖ Freddie Mac	Financials	14.0	–3.87	1.30
American Intl Grp	Financials	42.0	–19.20	1.26
⊖ Pharmacia	Health	36.5	–29.30	1.22
☼ J.P. Morgan Chase & Co.	Financials	27.8	–17.40	1.21
☼ Royal Dutch Petro NY ADR	Energy	12.0	–17.10	1.21
United Tech	Industrials	16.3	–16.70	1.17
☼ Clear Channel Comms	Services	—	5.10	1.15
⊕ Cisco Sys	Technology	—	–52.60	1.10
☼ Compaq Comp	Technology	—	–34.50	1.06
☼ Bank of America	Financials	16.7	42.73	0.98
⊖ Viacom Cl B	Services	—	—	0.98
⊖ Entergy	Utilities	11.7	–4.50	0.96
☼ Lowe's	Retail	38.7	109.00	0.94
Quaker Oats	Staples	—	–9.08	0.93
☼ Baxter Intl	Health	33.9	22.84	0.91

Current Investment Style

Style: Value Blnd Growth; Size: Large Med Small

	Stock Port Avg	Relative S&P 500 Current	Relative S&P 500 Hist	Rel Cat
Price/Earnings Ratio	29.9	0.97	1.02	0.99
Price/Book Ratio	4.9	0.86	0.99	0.90
Price/Cash Flow	18.9	1.05	0.96	1.03
3 Yr Earnings Growth	16.2	1.11	1.05	0.91
1 Yr Earnings Est%	0.6	—	—	–7.00
Med Mkt Cap $mil	44,928	0.7	1.0	0.86

Special Securities % assets 05-31-01	
Restricted/Illiquid Secs	0
Emerging-Markets Secs	0
Options/Futures/Warrants	Yes

Composition % assets 05-31-01	
Cash	2.1
Stocks*	97.9
Bonds	0.0
Other	0.0
*Foreign (% stocks)	2.7

Market Cap	
Giant	49.2
Large	36.9
Medium	13.8
Small	0.0
Micro	0.0

Sector Weightings	% of Stocks	Rel S&P	5-Year High	5-Year Low
Utilities	2.1	0.7	5	0
Energy	9.2	1.3	10	1
Financials	19.7	1.1	28	14
Industrials	10.0	0.9	20	7
Durables	0.3	0.2	9	0
Staples	7.7	1.0	9	2
Services	13.5	1.2	20	11
Retail	4.0	0.6	14	3
Health	12.1	0.8	21	6
Technology	21.3	1.2	36	8

Analysis by Kelli Stebel 08-17-01

Despite some mixed showings, investors shouldn't give up on this fund.

Since Michael Arends joined Putnam Capital Appreciation in February 1999, the fund has hit some rough spots. Though its 6% loss in 2000 and 12% loss for the year to date through August 16, 2001 are relatively decent, they've taken a toll on the fund's once-stellar long-term record. This fund uses an all-cap strategy, but recently, Arends has been concentrating his bets on large-cap stocks. (Indeed, Morningstar recently moved the fund from mid-blend to the large-blend category.) That emphasis on large caps has been the fund's Achilles' heel, particularly the fund's positions in big pharmaceuticals such as Merck and Pharmacia, which have foundered amid slowing sales growth.

Arends plans to maintain the fund's defensive positioning. Though he's trimmed Merck a bit, he says that given the uncertainty in the market, he wants to stick with large blue chips. To that end, Arends recently added IBM and Microsoft. He says these major tech players have the financial power to withstand downturns, and particularly likes the abundance of cash on each firm's balance sheet. Arends continues to favor consumer-related stocks, too. He picked up shares of Gap Stores and Reebok International, encouraged by the strong management at each company.

While the fund's recent performance is disappointing, shareholders should feel confident that this fund can deliver over the long haul. Arends is no novice to managing money, having run several strong-performing Phoenix-Engemann and Kemper funds before joining Putnam in 1997. In addition, he has Putnam's substantial resources at his disposal. So while the fund's free-ranging approach might make it a difficult fit for some investors, it continues to be a dependable core holding.

Address:	One Post Office Square Boston, MA 02109 800–225–1581 / 617–292–1000
Web Address:	www.putnaminvestments.com
*Inception:	08-05-93
Advisor:	Putnam Inv. Mgmt.
Subadvisor:	None
NTF Plans:	Fidelity Inst.

Minimum Purchase:	$500	Add: $50	IRA: $250
Min Auto Inv Plan:	$25	Add: $25	
Sales Fees:	5.75%L, 0.35%B		
Management Fee:	.65% mx./.45% mn.		
Actual Fees:	Mgt: 0.53%	Dist: 0.25%	
Expense Projections:	3Yr: $884	5Yr: $1111	10Yr: $1762
Avg Brok Commission:	—	Income Distrib: Annually	
Total Cost (relative to category):	—		

Putnam Capital Opportunities A

Ticker	Load	NAV	Yield	Total Assets	Mstar Category
PCOAX	5.75%	$10.33	0.0%	$562.5 mil	Mid-Cap Growth

Prospectus Objective: Growth

Putnam Capital Opportunities Fund seeks long-term growth of capital.

The fund primarily invests in common stocks of U.S. companies. It invests mainly in small and mid-sized companies. The fund may invest in foreign securities.

This fund offers multiple shareclasses, all of which differ in fee structure and availability. Prior to July 1, 1998, the fund was named Putnam U.S. Core II.

Historical Profile

Return	Above Avg
Risk	Above Avg
Rating	★★★★ Above Avg

Investment Style
Equity
Average Stock %: 1998 86% · 1999 98% · 2000 92% · 2001 89%

▼ Manager Change
▽ Partial Manager Change

Fund Performance vs. Category Average
■ Quarterly Fund Return +/– Category Average
— Category Baseline

Performance Quartile (within Category)

Portfolio Manager(s)

Management Team

1990	1991	1992	1993	1994	1995	1996	1997	1998	1999	2000	12-01	History
—	—	—	—	—	—	—	—	8.10	10.29	10.65	10.33	NAV
—	—	—	—	—	—	—	—	–3.47*	27.04	21.93	–2.08	Total Return %
—	—	—	—	—	—	—	—	–17.13*	6.00	31.03	9.80	+/– S&P 500
—	—	—	—	—	—	—	—	—	–24.27	33.67	18.08	+/– Russ Midcap Grth
—	—	—	—	—	—	—	—	0.33	0.00	0.00	0.00	Income Return %
—	—	—	—	—	—	—	—	–3.80	27.04	21.93	–2.08	Capital Return %
—	—	—	—	—	—	—	—	—	82	7	7	Total Rtn % Rank Cat
—	—	—	—	—	—	—	—	0.03	0.00	0.00	0.00	Income $
—	—	—	—	—	—	—	—	0.00	0.00	1.80	0.10	Capital Gains $
—	—	—	—	—	—	—	—	—	—	1.24	1.17	Expense Ratio %
—	—	—	—	—	—	—	—	—	—	–0.67	–0.40	Income Ratio %
—	—	—	—	—	—	—	—	—	—	272	221	Turnover Rate %
—	—	—	—	—	—	—	—	50.9	80.9	165.3	258.3	Net Assets $mil

Performance 12-31-01

	1st Qtr	2nd Qtr	3rd Qtr	4th Qtr	Total
1997	—	—	—	—	—
1998	—	—	–18.28	15.78	–3.47*
1999	–6.79	11.52	–6.29	30.42	27.04
2000	2.33	5.22	12.09	1.02	21.93
2001	–13.05	19.11	–24.66	25.50	–2.08

Trailing	Total Return%	+/– S&P 500	+/– Russ Midcap Grth	% Rank All	% Rank Cat	Growth of $10,000
3 Mo	25.50	14.81	—	7	17	12,550
6 Mo	–5.45	0.10	—	64	25	9,455
1 Yr	–2.08	9.80	—	46	7	9,792
3 Yr Avg	14.90	15.92	—	5	12	15,167
5 Yr Avg	—	—	—	—	—	—
10 Yr Avg	—	—	—	—	—	—
15 Yr Avg	—	—	—	—	—	—

Tax Analysis	Tax-Adj Ret%	%Rank Cat	%Pretax Ret	%Rank Cat
3 Yr Avg	12.59	11	84.5	34
5 Yr Avg	—	—	—	—
10 Yr Avg	—	—	—	—

Potential Capital Gain Exposure: 13% of assets

Risk Analysis

Time Period	Load-Adj Return %	Risk %Rank[1] All	Risk %Rank[1] Cat	Morningstar Return	Morningstar Risk	Morningstar Risk-Adj Rating
1 Yr	–7.71					
3 Yr	12.65	86	39	1.76[2]	1.31	★★★★
5 Yr	—	—	—	—	—	
Incept	9.40	—	—	—	—	

Average Historical Rating (8 months): 4.0★s

[1]1=low, 100=high [2] T-Bill return substituted for category avg.

Category Rating (3 Yr)

1 2 3 **4** 5 — Worst … Best

Return: Above Avg
Risk: Average

Other Measures	Standard Index S&P 500	Best Fit Index Russ 2000
Alpha	21.3	9.6
Beta	1.09	1.34
R-Squared	29	85

Standard Deviation	41.36
Mean	14.90
Sharpe Ratio	0.27

Portfolio Analysis 04-30-01

Share change since 10-00 Total Stocks: 95	Sector	PE	YTD Ret%	% Assets
⊕ S&P 500 Index (Fut)	N/A	—	—	4.41
⊕ Hasbro	Durables	—	54.09	3.65
⊕ Pentair	Industrials	38.0	54.40	2.87
✲ Charles River Labs	Health	—	22.30	2.60
⊕ TCF Finl	Financials	18.2	10.24	2.57
⊕ Fidelity Natl Finl	Financials	8.5	–25.00	2.47
✲ Apogent Tech	Health	29.0	25.85	2.25
⊕ Stancorp Finl Grp	Financials	15.4	–0.38	2.17
✲ Royal Caribbean Cruises	Services	9.6	–38.00	2.17
⊕ Insituform Tech A	Industrials	18.3	–35.80	2.09
✲ Premier Parks	Services	—	–10.50	2.00
✲ L-3 Comms Hldgs	Technology	33.0	16.88	1.99
✲ ServiceMaster	Services	22.3	24.29	1.97
✲ Cytec Inds	Industrials	8.1	–32.40	1.83
⊕ Multex.com	Services	—	–66.00	1.79
⊕ Trigon Healthcare	Health	27.5	–10.70	1.77
✲ Emmis Broadcstg Cl A	Services	—	–17.60	1.65
⊖ M & T Bk	Financials	20.8	8.63	1.61
⊕ Duane Reade	Retail	25.3	–0.70	1.56
✲ Rite Aid	Retail	—	113.00	1.54
✲ IPC Hldgs	Financials	17.1	40.95	1.52
✲ Mitel	Technology	—	39.53	1.44
⊕ Commerce Bancorp NJ	Financials	27.5	17.01	1.44
⊕ Cytyc	Health	49.3	25.16	1.35
✲ Avocent	Technology	—	–10.10	1.29

Current Investment Style

Style: Value Blnd Growth; Size: Large Med Small

	Stock Port Avg	Relative S&P 500 Current	Relative S&P 500 Hist	Rel Cat
Price/Earnings Ratio	24.9	0.81	—	0.72
Price/Book Ratio	3.0	0.52	—	0.52
Price/Cash Flow	17.5	0.97	—	0.76
3 Yr Earnings Growth	18.7[1]	1.28	—	0.80
1 Yr Earnings Est%	–10.4	5.88	—	–1.11
Med Mkt Cap $mil	1,427	0.0	—	0.25

[1]figure is based on 50% or less of stocks

Special Securities % assets 04-30-01	
Restricted/Illiquid Secs	Trace
Emerging-Markets Secs	0
Options/Futures/Warrants	Yes

Composition % assets 04-30-01	
Cash	7.2
Stocks*	89.0
Bonds	0.0
Other	3.8
*Foreign (% stocks)	2.7

Market Cap	
Giant	0.0
Large	0.0
Medium	50.8
Small	45.3
Micro	3.9

Sector Weightings	% of Stocks	Rel S&P	5-Year High	5-Year Low
Utilities	0.0	0.0	—	—
Energy	0.0	0.0	—	—
Financials	15.4	0.9	—	—
Industrials	16.8	1.5	—	—
Durables	5.3	3.4	—	—
Staples	1.1	0.1	—	—
Services	23.5	2.2	—	—
Retail	9.4	1.4	—	—
Health	16.0	1.1	—	—
Technology	12.5	0.7	—	—

Analysis by William Samuel Rocco 10-09-01

While it may not be readily apparent, Putnam Capital Opportunities has real merit.

This fund has fallen 20% for the year to date through Oct. 8, 2001. That stings, of course, but most other offerings in its category have suffered much more. Indeed, the typical mid-growth fund has plunged 32% this year.

The fund, which recently moved from the small-blend category, has benefited from its significant differences with its new mid-growth peers. Managers Gerald Moore, Joe Joseph, and Sandy Mehta focus on firms with market capitalizations below $3 billion. As a result, the fund's median market cap is one of its new category's smallest, which has paid off as smaller companies have held up better than larger ones this year. Meanwhile, the managers are more price-conscious than most mid-growth managers, so the fund's valuations also rank among the group's lowest, which has been helpful as value stocks have fared better than growth issues thus far in 2001.

But these stylistic differences aren't the only reasons the fund has lost 12 percentage points less than the typical mid-growth offering this year. Moore, Joseph, and Mehta's stock selection has also helped. Toy maker Hasbro and the tool and equipment manufacturer Pentair, which have been top holdings all year, are up 42% and 31%, respectively, in 2001.

This young fund hasn't always been an outperformer, but its three-year returns compare favorably with those of most smaller-cap-blend offerings as well as with those of most mid-growth funds. Moreover, it has been less volatile than most of the latter—though not the former—and its expense ratio is relatively low. Thus, we think investors seeking a moderately aggressive smaller-cap fund should keep their eyes on this one.

Address:	One Post Office Square Boston, MA 02109 800-225-1581 / 617-292-1000
Web Address:	www.putnaminvestments.com
*Inception:	06-01-98
Advisor:	Putnam Inv. Mgmt.
Subadvisor:	None
NTF Plans:	Fidelity Inst.

Minimum Purchase:	$500	Add: $50	IRA: —
Min Auto Inv Plan:	$25	Add: $25	
Sales Fees:	5.75%L, 0.10%B, 0.25%S		
Management Fee:	.65% mx./.38% mn.		
Actual Fees:	Mgt: 0.00%	Dist: 0.25%	
Expense Projections:	3Yr: $95*	5Yr: —	10Yr: —
Avg Brok Commission:	—	Income Distrib: Annually	
Total Cost (relative to category):	—		

Putnam Fund for Growth & Income A

Ticker	Load	NAV	Yield	Total Assets	Mstar Category
PGRWX	5.75%	$17.72	1.6%	$28,725.7 mil	Large Value

Prospectus Objective: Growth and Income

Putnam Fund for Growth and Income seeks capital growth and current income.

The fund invests primarily in common stocks of U.S. companies, with a focus on value stocks. It may also purchase preferreds, convertibles, and corporate debt of any credit quality. It may invest in foreign securities.

This fund offers multiple shareclasses, all of which differ in fee structure and availability; y shares are available only to institutional investors.

Historical Profile
Return Average
Risk Below Avg
Rating ★★★ Neutral

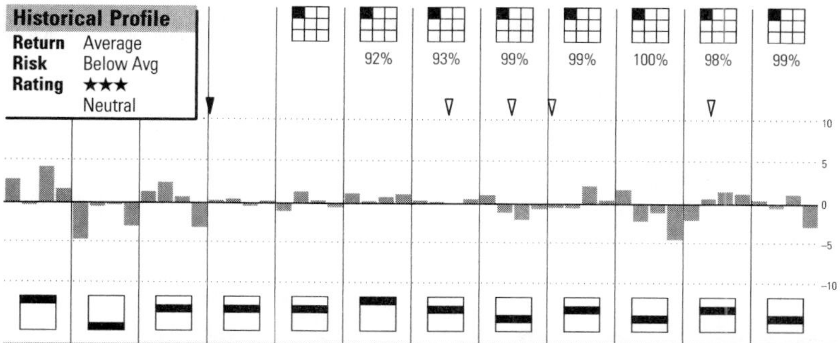

Investment Style Equity — Average Stock %: 1995 92%, 1996 93%, 1997 99%, 1998 99%, 1999 100%, 2000 98%, 12-01 99%

▼ Manager Change
▽ Partial Manager Change

Fund Performance vs. Category Average
■ Quarterly Fund Return +/– Category Average
— Category Baseline

Performance Quartile (within Category)

1990	1991	1992	1993	1994	1995	1996	1997	1998	1999	2000	12–01	**History**
11.35	12.38	12.84	13.60	12.72	16.19	18.02	19.54	20.49	18.75	19.53	17.72	NAV
2.39	19.18	11.78	14.45	–0.28	36.54	21.81	24.16	15.19	1.26	7.94	–6.37	Total Return %
5.51	–11.30	4.16	4.39	–1.59	–0.99	–1.14	–9.19	–13.39	–19.78	17.04	5.51	+/– S&P 500
6.06	1.03	2.71	–5.31	2.04	–3.49	–0.51	–11.33	–6.06	–9.69	5.63	2.42	+/– Russ Top 200 Val
5.22	5.38	4.27	4.11	2.97	3.18	2.59	2.57	1.88	1.99	1.35	1.44	Income Return %
–2.82	13.80	7.51	10.34	–3.25	33.36	19.22	21.59	13.30	–0.73	6.59	–7.81	Capital Return %
5	94	28	44	47	18	33	74	37	71	45	55	Total Rtn % Rank Cat
0.62	0.60	0.52	0.52	0.40	0.40	0.42	0.46	0.37	0.41	0.25	0.28	Income $
0.43	0.49	0.45	0.54	0.44	0.72	1.24	2.38	1.60	1.64	0.42	0.30	Capital Gains $
0.89	0.95	1.07	0.93	0.95	0.89	0.92	0.86	0.84	0.79	0.81	—	Expense Ratio %
5.01	4.45	3.72	3.18	3.18	3.20	2.59	1.95	1.27	1.32	1.38	—	Income Ratio %
81	77	67	64	49	58	41	64	79	50	52	—	Turnover Rate %
2,117.8	2,799.8	3,791.3	5,327.0	5,848.1	8,610.6	12,305.5	17,297.8	20,760.1	21,089.6	20,228.9	19,023.0	Net Assets $mil

Portfolio Manager(s)

David L. King, CFA. Since 1-93. BS'78 U. of New Hampshire; MBA'83 Harvard U. Other funds currently managed: Putnam Fund for Growth & Income B, Putnam Equity Income A, Putnam Equity Income B.

Hugh H. Mullin, CFA. Since 7-96. BA U. of Massachusetts. Other funds currently managed: Putnam Fund for Growth & Income B, Putnam Fund for Growth & Income Y, Putnam Fund for Growth & Income M.

Christopher G. Miller. Since 5-00. Other funds currently managed: Putnam Fund for Growth & Income B, Putnam Fund for Growth & Income Y, Putnam Fund for Growth & Income M.

Performance 12-31-01

	1st Qtr	2nd Qtr	3rd Qtr	4th Qtr	Total
1997	2.66	12.77	6.83	0.40	24.16
1998	10.90	–1.00	–10.06	16.65	15.19
1999	2.51	7.78	–10.26	2.13	1.26
2000	–1.76	–1.39	6.84	4.29	7.94
2001	–5.29	4.27	–10.99	6.52	–6.37

Trailing	Total Return%	+/– S&P 500	+/– Russ Top 200 Val	% Rank All	% Rank Cat	Growth of $10,000
3 Mo	6.52	–4.16	1.01	58	82	10,652
6 Mo	–5.19	0.37	0.59	63	67	9,481
1 Yr	–6.37	5.51	2.42	54	55	9,363
3 Yr Avg	0.77	1.80	–0.39	69	64	10,234
5 Yr Avg	7.92	–2.78	–3.29	30	61	14,636
10 Yr Avg	12.00	–0.93	–2.03	19	49	31,052
15 Yr Avg	12.24	–1.49	–1.26	24	44	56,556

Tax Analysis	Tax-Adj Ret%	%Rank Cat	%Pretax Ret	%Rank Cat
3 Yr Avg	–0.74	65	—	—
5 Yr Avg	5.65	62	71.4	61
10 Yr Avg	9.42	43	78.6	42

Potential Capital Gain Exposure: 8% of assets

Risk Analysis

Time Period	Load-Adj Return %	Risk %Rank[1] All	Risk %Rank[1] Cat	Morningstar Return	Morningstar Risk	Morningstar Risk-Adj Rating
1 Yr	–11.75					
3 Yr	–1.20	53	48	–1.23[2]	0.75	★★★
5 Yr	6.64	57	47	0.36[2]	0.78	★★★
10 Yr	11.34	58	36	0.97	0.75	★★★

Average Historical Rating (193 months): 3.8★s

[1] 1=low, 100=high [2] T-Bill return substituted for category avg.

Category Rating (3 Yr)

1 2 3 4 5
Worst Best

Return Average
Risk Average

Other Measures	Standard Index S&P 500	Best Fit Index S&P 500
Alpha	–0.2	–0.2
Beta	0.64	0.64
R-Squared	56	56
Standard Deviation		14.54
Mean		0.77
Sharpe Ratio		–0.33

Analysis by William Samuel Rocco 09-12-01

Putnam Fund for Growth & Income isn't exciting, but it has its charms.

This fund remains steady and staid. Its managers added to Schering-Plough and some of their other pharmaceutical holdings earlier this summer on weakness. And they adjusted their still-modest tech stake by selling or trimming issues that have done relatively well, such as Dell, and adding to others, such as Compaq, that have struggled. But they haven't made too many other moves, and the overall portfolio continues to be pretty diversifed by sector and issue, with a significant financial weight and large-cap bias.

This broad and conservative strategy has produced competitive results in 2001's sell-off. Dell and the other tech stocks that were sold or trimmed have given the fund a boost. And current top-10 names Philip Morris and IBM have posted double-digit gains for the year to date through Sept. 10, 2001, as has Bank of America. However, Citigroup and many of the fund's other financials stocks have suffered big losses, as have some health-care picks, such as Merck. Thus, the fund has lost 8.3% for the year to date through Sept. 10, 2001, while its average peer has lost 8.9%.

The fund has been a staid performer over the long term, but it is one of the few large-value offerings that provides a nice yield, and its expense ratio is low. Therefore, we think this fund remains a good choice for conservative investors who want an equity offering that provides some income.

Portfolio Analysis 04-30-01

Share change since 10–00 Total Stocks: 288	Sector	PE	YTD Ret%	% Assets
⊕ ExxonMobil	Energy	15.3	–7.59	3.70
⊕ Citigroup	Financials	20.0	0.03	3.60
⊕ IBM	Technology	26.9	43.00	2.66
⊕ Merck	Health	19.1	–35.90	2.49
⊖ Philip Morris	Staples	12.1	9.12	2.11
⊕ Johnson & Johnson	Health	16.6	14.01	2.05
⊖ SBC Comms	Services	18.4	–16.00	2.03
⊕ Royal Dutch Petro NY ADR	Energy	12.0	–17.10	1.83
⊕ Bristol–Myers Squibb	Health	20.2	–26.00	1.75
⊖ Bank of America	Financials	16.7	42.73	1.73
⊖ Verizon Comms	Services	29.7	–2.52	1.73
✲ General Elec	Industrials	30.1	–15.00	1.66
⊕ Morgan Stanley/Dean Witter	Financials	16.6	–28.20	1.56
⊕ Wells Fargo	Financials	22.4	–20.20	1.34
⊕ Tyco Intl	Industrials	27.1	6.23	1.34
⊕ J.P. Morgan Chase & Co.	Financials	27.8	–17.40	1.34
⊖ Fannie Mae	Financials	16.2	–6.95	1.22
⊖ BellSouth	Services	24.9	–5.09	1.18
⊖ Abbott Labs	Health	51.6	17.08	1.10
⊕ Chevron	Energy	10.3	9.29	1.06
⊖ American Home Products	Health	—	–1.91	1.06
⊕ US Bancorp	Financials	13.5	–6.14	0.99
⊕ Walt Disney	Services	—	–27.70	0.97
⊖ Coca–Cola	Staples	35.5	–21.40	0.95
⊖ DuPont De Nemours E.I.	Industrials	65.4	–9.14	0.94

Current Investment Style

Style: Value Blnd Growth; Size: Large Med Small

	Stock Port Avg	Relative S&P 500 Current	Relative S&P 500 Hist	Rel Cat
Price/Earnings Ratio	24.4	0.79	0.82	0.97
Price/Book Ratio	4.6	0.80	0.75	1.11
Price/Cash Flow	13.0	0.72	0.69	0.95
3 Yr Earnings Growth	14.7	1.00	0.87	0.99
1 Yr Earnings Est%	–2.8	1.56	—	0.83
Med Mkt Cap $mil	48,087	0.8	1.0	1.51

Special Securities % assets 04-30-01	
Restricted/Illiquid Secs	0
Emerging-Markets Secs	0
Options/Futures/Warrants	Yes

Composition % assets 04-30-01	
Cash	1.1
Stocks*	98.7
Bonds	0.0
Other	0.2
*Foreign (% stocks)	2.5

Market Cap	
Giant	50.0
Large	37.4
Medium	12.6
Small	0.1
Micro	0.0

Sector Weightings	% of Stocks	Rel S&P	5-Year High	5-Year Low
Utilities	4.7	1.5	10	2
Energy	11.6	1.6	16	7
Financials	26.0	1.5	27	12
Industrials	12.1	1.1	25	11
Durables	2.2	1.4	9	2
Staples	7.8	1.0	11	5
Services	12.1	1.1	21	11
Retail	3.8	0.6	7	3
Health	11.0	0.7	12	4
Technology	8.7	0.5	12	2

Address: One Post Office Square, Boston, MA 02109, 800–225–1581 / 617–292–1000
Web Address: www.putnaminvestments.com
Inception: 11-06-57
Advisor: Putnam Inv. Mgmt.
Subadvisor: None
NTF Plans: Fidelity Inst.

Minimum Purchase: $500 Add: $50 IRA: $250
Min Auto Inv Plan: $25 Add: $25
Sales Fees: 5.75%L, 0.35%B
Management Fee: .65% mx./.38% mn.
Actual Fees: Mgt: 0.42% Dist: 0.25%
Expense Projections: 3Yr: $83* 5Yr: $102* 10Yr: $157*
Avg Brok Commission: — Income Distrib: Quarterly
Total Cost (relative to category): —

George Putnam Fund of Boston A

Ticker	Load	NAV	Yield	Total Assets	Mstar Category
PGEOX	5.75%	$16.74	3.1%	$5,502.9 mil	Domestic Hybrid

Prospectus Objective: Balanced

George Putnam Fund of Boston seeks to provide a balanced investment composed of a well-diversified portfolio of stocks and bonds, which produce both capital growth and current income.

The fund invests mainly in a combination of bonds and U.S. value stocks, with a greater focus on value stocks. It normally invests at least 25% in fixed-income securities. The fund usually buys bonds of governments and private companies that are mostly investment-grade in quality with maturities of three years or longer. It invests mainly in large companies.

The fund currently offers Class A, B, C, M, and Y, all of which differ in fee structure and availability.

Historical Profile
Return: Average
Risk: Low
Rating: ★★★ Neutral

Investment Style
Equity
Average Stock %: 58% 62% 63% 59% 63% 59%

▼ Manager Change
▽ Partial Manager Change

Fund Performance vs. Category Average
■ Quarterly Fund Return +/– Category Average
— Category Baseline

Performance Quartile (within Category)

Portfolio Manager(s)

Jeanne L. Mockard, CFA. Since 4-00. BS'85 Tufts U.; MBA'90 U. of Virginia. Other funds currently managed: George Putnam Fund of Boston B, Putnam Balanced Retirement A, Putnam Equity Income A.

James M. Prusko. Since 4-98. BS MIT; MS MIT. Other funds currently managed: George Putnam Fund of Boston B, Putnam Income A, Putnam Balanced Retirement A.

Jeffrey L. Knight. Since 3-01. Other funds currently managed: George Putnam Fund of Boston B, Putnam Balanced Retirement A, Putnam Balanced Retirement B.

History

1990	1991	1992	1993	1994	1995	1996	1997	1998	1999	2000	12-01	History
12.10	13.75	13.64	13.86	12.91	15.50	16.40	17.98	18.04	16.28	17.17	16.74	NAV
–0.92	22.80	7.96	10.90	–0.38	30.12	16.26	21.02	10.60	0.12	9.28	0.51	Total Return %
2.20	–7.69	0.34	0.84	–1.69	–7.42	–6.69	–12.33	–17.98	–20.92	18.39	12.39	+/– S&P 500
–9.88	6.79	0.56	1.15	2.54	11.65	12.64	11.34	1.93	0.95	–2.35	–7.91	+/– LB Aggregate
5.15	5.73	5.04	4.70	4.18	4.54	4.30	3.64	3.38	3.37	3.55	3.07	Income Return %
–6.07	17.07	2.92	6.20	–4.55	25.58	11.95	17.38	7.22	–3.25	5.73	–2.56	Capital Return %
59	57	46	62	23	11	22	29	64	87	14	20	Total Rtn % Rank Cat
0.68	0.68	0.68	0.63	0.57	0.58	0.66	0.59	0.60	0.60	0.57	0.52	Income $
0.52	0.36	0.48	0.60	0.32	0.63	0.91	1.21	1.20	1.23	0.00	0.00	Capital Gains $
0.84	0.94	1.06	0.90	0.95	0.91	0.95	1.06	1.00	0.93	0.96	0.92	Expense Ratio %
5.52	5.42	4.62	4.34	4.15	4.58	4.07	3.51	3.11	3.10	3.32	3.11	Income Ratio %
71	65	79	89	101	103	119	135	126	128	141	333	Turnover Rate %
417.9	530.0	657.3	833.0	911.5	1,182.6	1,830.9	2,871.8	3,822.3	3,615.4	3,222.2	3,267.1	Net Assets $mil

Performance 12-31-01

	1st Qtr	2nd Qtr	3rd Qtr	4th Qtr	Total
1997	2.17	9.60	6.05	1.91	21.02
1998	8.16	–0.16	–6.14	9.13	10.60
1999	1.22	5.47	–6.95	0.79	0.12
2000	–0.75	–0.07	4.97	4.97	9.28
2001	–1.85	3.54	–5.42	4.57	0.52

Trailing	Total Return%	+/– S&P 500	+/– LB Agg	% Rank All	% Rank Cat	Growth of $10,000
3 Mo	4.57	–6.11	4.54	66	75	10,457
6 Mo	–1.09	4.47	–5.74	43	38	9,891
1 Yr	0.51	12.39	–7.91	42	20	10,051
3 Yr Avg	3.22	4.25	–3.05	51	37	10,998
5 Yr Avg	8.04	–2.66	0.61	29	37	14,720
10 Yr Avg	10.26	–2.67	3.03	31	33	26,558
15 Yr Avg	10.78	–2.95	2.66	36	27	46,437

Tax Analysis	Tax-Adj Ret%	%Rank Cat	%Pretax Ret	%Rank Cat
3 Yr Avg	1.36	37	42.4	66
5 Yr Avg	5.55	39	69.1	47
10 Yr Avg	7.44	37	72.6	48

Potential Capital Gain Exposure: 2% of assets

Risk Analysis

Time Period	Load-Adj Return %	Risk %Rank[1] All	Risk %Rank[1] Cat	Morningstar Return	Morningstar Risk	Morningstar Risk-Adj Rating
1 Yr	–5.27					
3 Yr	1.20	36	26	–0.77[2]	0.45	★★★
5 Yr	6.77	41	29	0.39[2]	0.48	★★★
10 Yr	9.61	47	27	0.67	0.51	★★★

Average Historical Rating (193 months): 3.1★s

[1] 1=low, 100=high [2] T-Bill return substituted for category avg.

Category Rating (3 Yr)

1 2 **3** 4 5
Worst — Best

Return: Average
Risk: Below Avg

Other Measures	Standard Index S&P 500	Best Fit Index S&P 500
Alpha	0.4	0.4
Beta	0.36	0.36
R-Squared	47	47

Standard Deviation	9.17
Mean	3.22
Sharpe Ratio	–0.22

Portfolio Analysis 01-31-01

Total Stocks: 181 Share change since 08–00	Sector	PE Ratio	YTD Return %	% Net Assets
⊕ ExxonMobil	Energy	15.3	–7.59	2.15
⊕ Citigroup	Financials	20.0	0.03	1.78
⊖ SBC Comms	Services	18.4	–16.00	1.65
⊖ Johnson & Johnson	Health	16.6	14.01	1.30
⊕ Royal Dutch Petro NY ADR	Energy	12.0	–17.10	1.25
⊕ Bank of America	Financials	16.7	42.73	1.22
⊖ Fannie Mae	Financials	16.2	–6.95	1.21
⊕ Philip Morris	Staples	12.1	9.12	1.19
⊕ Merck	Health	19.1	–35.90	1.04
⊖ Verizon Comms	Services	29.7	–2.52	1.03

Total Fixed-Income: 682	Date of Maturity	Amount $000	Value $000	% Net Assets
FNMA 6%		176,580	172,773	3.17
FNMA Debenture 7%	07-15-05	141,260	150,265	2.76
FNMA 7.5%	02-01-16	131,300	135,034	2.48
US Treasury Note 5.75%	08-15-10	108,260	113,047	2.07
US T–Note 5yr (Fut)		1	93,684	1.72
US Treasury Bond 6.25%	05-15-30	83,745	92,290	1.69
US Treasury Bond 6.125%	08-15-29	85,440	92,021	1.69
FNMA 7.5%	10-01-15	74,295	76,470	1.40
FNMA Cv 7%	11-01-29	50,752	51,314	0.94
GNMA 8%	12-29-26	48,355	50,097	0.92

Equity Style
Style: Value
Size: Large–Cap

	Portfolio Avg	Rel S&P
Price/Earnings Ratio	23.8	0.77
Price/Book Ratio	4.2	0.74
Price/Cash Flow	14.1	0.78
3 Yr Earnings Growth	16.1	1.10
1 Yr Earnings Est%	0.2	—
Debt % Total Cap	35.1	1.14
Med Mkt Cap $mil	38,985	0.64

Fixed-Income Style
Duration: —
Quality: —
NA

Avg Eff Duration	—
Avg Eff Maturity	—
Avg Credit Quality	—
Avg Wtd Coupon	7.11%

Special Securities % assets 01-31-01	
Restricted/Illiquid Secs	2
Emerging–Markets Secs	Trace
Options/Futures/Warrants	Yes

Composition % of assets 01-31-01	
Cash	1.4
Stocks*	59.5
Bonds	36.1
Other	3.0
*Foreign (% of stocks)	3.3

Market Cap	
Giant	43.8
Large	32.6
Medium	23.5
Small	0.2
Micro	0.0

Sector Weightings	% of Stocks	Rel S&P	5-Year High	5-Year Low
Utilities	5.7	1.8	10	2
Energy	10.1	1.4	12	7
Financials	29.6	1.7	30	8
Industrials	10.4	0.9	24	9
Durables	0.9	0.6	9	1
Staples	8.4	1.1	13	6
Services	14.1	1.3	22	10
Retail	4.0	0.6	10	2
Health	9.0	0.6	14	6
Technology	7.9	0.4	11	2

Analysis by Kelli Stebel 08-30-01

This fund is making a case for itself with its new style and new management.

Lead manager Jeanne Mockard has only run George Putnam Fund of Boston since April 2000, but her short record has been quite good. For the year to date through August 29, 2001, the fund is up about 41 basis points (or 0.41%). That might not seem like a big achievement, but the average domestic-hybrid fund has dropped more than 4% so far this year.

Like Mockard's other charge, Putnam Balanced Retirement, this offering fills its equity portfolio with value stocks. While the fund has always focused on value, Mockard put her own stamp on this fund, leaning the portfolio a bit more toward the S&P 500 than her predecessor had. And strong stock-picking, along with several savvy moves, has kept the fund a step ahead in this year's rough market. For starters, Mockard and her team began cutting the fund's energy holdings as 2001 dawned. Transocean Sedco Forex, for example, had been a source of strength last year, but with oil prices falling and softness in the drilling industry, that stock has been spiraling downward. Mockard had already trimmed several energy stocks before the second quarter, when energy began to tank. In addition, the fund has gotten a spark from its complement of financial holdings. Encouraged by falling interest rates, Mockard had added to the fund's financials in the first quarter. So with top equity holdings like Bank of America posting a solid, double-digit gain through late August, the fund has easily outpaced its peers.

Mockard reports that she hasn't been making any wholesale changes to the fund lately, preferring to keep the fund fairly defensively positioned. That kind of stance should please moderate investors. Indeed, this fund's staid makeup makes it a fine choice for investors in need of a sound sleep.

Address:	One Post Office Square Boston, MA 02109 800–225–1581 / 617–292–1000
Web Address:	www.putnaminvestments.com
Inception:	11-05-37
Advisor:	Putnam Inv. Mgmt.
Subadvisor:	None
NTF Plans:	Fidelity Inst.

Minimum Purchase:	$500	Add: $50	IRA: $250
Min Auto Inv Plan:	$25	Add: $25	
Sales Fees:	5.75%L, 0.35%B		
Management Fee:	.60% mx./.30% mn.		
Actual Fees:	Mgt: 0.48%	Dist: 0.25%	
Expense Projections:	3Yr: $854	5Yr: $1060	10Yr: $1652
Avg Brok Commission:	—	Income Distrib: Quarterly	
Total Cost (relative to category):		Average	

Putnam Global Equity A

Ticker	Load	NAV	Yield	Total Assets	Mstar Category
PDETX	5.75%	$10.82	0.2%	$994.8 mil	World Stock

Prospectus Objective: World Stock

Putnam Global Equity Trust seeks capital appreciation.

The fund normally invests at least 65% of assets in equity securities in at least three different countries worldwide including the United States. It invests mainly in mid-sized and large companies. It usually emphasizes investments in developed countries, it may also invest in companies located in emerging markets.

Class A shares have front loads; M shares have lower front loads and higher 12b-1 fees; B shares have deferred loads, the highest 12b-1 fees, and conversion features; C shares have level loads. Past name: Putnam Diversified Equity.

Historical Profile

Return Above Avg
Risk Below Avg
Rating ★★★★ Above Avg

Investment Style
Equity
Average Stock %: 93% 96% 99% 98% 98% 96% 97%

▼ Manager Change
▽ Partial Manager Change

Fund Performance vs. Category Average
■ Quarterly Fund Return +/– Category Average
— Category Baseline

Performance Quartile (within Category)

Portfolio Manager(s)

Paul Warren. Since 1-97.
Michael P. Stack, CFA. Since 6-98.
Omid Kamshad, CFA. Since 3-97.
Justin M. Scott. Since 6-98.
Michael K. Arends, CFA. Since 2-99.

1990	1991	1992	1993	1994	1995	1996	1997	1998	1999	2000	12-01	History
—	—	—	—	8.68	10.69	11.46	12.31	13.27	18.41	13.90	10.82	NAV
—	—	—	—	2.36*	28.86	16.56	23.37	17.95	59.55	–10.21	–22.01	Total Return %
—	—	—	—	–2.05*	–8.67	–6.39	–9.98	–10.62	38.51	–1.11	–10.14	+/– S&P 500
—	—	—	—	—	8.14	3.08	7.60	–6.38	34.62	2.97	—	+/– MSCI World
—	—	—	—	0.00	0.97	1.62	1.10	0.00	2.04	0.48	0.14	Income Return %
—	—	—	—	2.36	27.89	14.94	22.27	17.95	57.51	–10.69	–22.16	Capital Return %
—	—	—	—	—	11	49	10	37	23	54	67	Total Rtn % Rank Cat
—	—	—	—	0.00	0.08	0.17	0.13	0.00	0.27	0.09	0.02	Income $
—	—	—	—	0.02	0.39	0.83	1.64	1.24	2.38	2.42	0.00	Capital Gains $
—	—	—	—	—	1.12	1.56	1.43	1.37	1.26	1.20	1.17	Expense Ratio %
—	—	—	—	—	0.37	0.60	0.48	0.20	0.17	–0.14	0.93	Income Ratio %
—	—	—	—	—	47	72	82	98	241	209	199	Turnover Rate %
—	—	—	—	79.6	133.7	190.0	248.8	295.2	464.6	674.0	611.0	Net Assets $mil

Performance 12-31-01

	1st Qtr	2nd Qtr	3rd Qtr	4th Qtr	Total
1997	0.35	13.74	10.09	–1.82	23.37
1998	13.00	0.93	–14.67	21.20	17.95
1999	7.08	7.67	2.29	35.29	59.55
2000	6.84	–7.42	–4.67	–4.78	–10.21
2001	–14.96	1.02	–16.83	9.17	–22.01

Trailing	Total Return%	+/– S&P 500	+/– MSCI World	% Rank All	% Rank Cat	Growth of $10,000
3 Mo	9.17	–1.52	—	47	66	10,917
6 Mo	–9.21	–3.65	—	82	73	9,079
1 Yr	–22.01	–10.14	—	83	67	7,799
3 Yr Avg	3.77	4.79	—	44	31	11,173
5 Yr Avg	10.21	–0.49	—	18	18	16,258
10 Yr Avg	—	—	—	—	—	—
15 Yr Avg	—	—	—	—	—	—

Tax Analysis	Tax-Adj Ret%	%Rank Cat	%Pretax Ret	%Rank Cat
3 Yr Avg	0.34	37	9.1	95
5 Yr Avg	6.79	25	66.5	60
10 Yr Avg	—	—	—	—

Potential Capital Gain Exposure: –19% of assets

Risk Analysis

Time Period	Load-Adj Return %	Risk %Rank[1] All	Risk %Rank[1] Cat	Morningstar Return	Morningstar Risk	Morningstar Risk-Adj Rating
1 Yr	–26.50					
3 Yr	1.74	71	54	–0.66[2]	0.91	★★★★
5 Yr	8.91	69	41	0.91[2]	0.78	★★★★
Incept	12.09	—	—	—	—	

Average Historical Rating (55 months): 4.8★s

[1]1=low, 100=high [2] T-Bill return substituted for category avg.

Category Rating (3 Yr)

1 2 3 4 5
Worst Best

Return Above Avg
Risk Average

Other Measures	Standard Index S&P 500	Best Fit Index MSCIWdxUSN
Alpha	5.1	11.2
Beta	0.92	1.18
R-Squared	56	80
Standard Deviation		21.71
Mean		3.77
Sharpe Ratio		–0.06

Analysis by William Samuel Rocco 08-31-01

This middle-of-the-road vehicle is lagging this year, but we're not too concerned.

Putnam Global Equity Trust continues to cover the full industry spectrum. Its managers did some selective buying in the tech sector earlier this summer. They purchased Lexmark International and Compaq, for example, because they thought they were attractively priced and have good fundamentals. Thus, while the typical foreign offering has a 9% tech stake, this fund has a 12% stake in that sector. But they also initiated positions in consumer stocks like Philip Morris early this year. And they've added to their financials stake as well, so the fund now has 24% of its assets in banking, insurance, and related stocks, whereas its average peer has 22%.

The managers haven't implemented their blended approach very effectively in 2001, though. Philip Morris has posted solid gains, but the fund's tech stocks have done more harm than good. And several of the fund's financials and health-care holdings, including top-10 names Bank of New York and Pharmacia, have plunged. As a result, the fund has dropped 20.5% for the year to date through August 30, while its typical peer has fallen 17.5%.

However, the managers executed their broad-based style pretty well during the fund's first 2.5 years as a global offering. (The fund was a domestic fund until mid-1998.) Indeed, thanks largely to its late-1990s emphasis on tech and telecom stocks and its early-2000 move away from those issues and toward bank and drug stocks, the fund sports top-quartile three-year returns. Therefore, we still think this offering is worth checking out.

Portfolio Analysis 02-28-01

Share change since 08-00 Total Stocks: 106	Sector	Country	% Assets
⊖ Tyco Intl	Industrials	U.S.	2.83
⊖ Pharmacia	Health	U.S.	2.59
⊕ Total Fina Cl B	Energy	France	2.58
⊖ Pfizer	Health	U.S.	2.52
☼ SBC Comms	Services	U.S.	2.46
⊕ Shell Transp & Trad	Energy	United Kingdom	2.37
⊖ ING Groep	Financials	Netherlands	2.30
⊖ American Home Products	Health	U.S.	2.24
☼ Merck	Health	U.S.	2.21
⊕ Bank of New York	Financials	U.S.	2.21
⊖ Kimberly-Clark	Industrials	U.S.	2.19
☼ Allianz AG ADR	Financials	Germany	2.04
☼ Philip Morris	Staples	U.S.	1.90
☼ Freddie Mac	Financials	U.S.	1.81
⊕ General Elec	Industrials	U.S.	1.65
⊖ Citigroup	Financials	U.S.	1.65
☼ J.P. Morgan Chase & Co.	Financials	U.S.	1.61
☼ US Bancorp	Financials	U.S.	1.60
⊕ American General	Financials	U.S.	1.59
☼ Lowe's	Retail	U.S.	1.58

Current Investment Style

Style: Value Blnd Growth; Size: Large Med Small

	Stock Port Avg	Rel MSCI EAFE Current	Rel MSCI EAFE Hist	Rel Cat
Price/Earnings Ratio	26.4	1.02	1.13	0.95
Price/Cash Flow	15.0	1.17	1.45	0.91
Price/Book Ratio	5.1	1.46	1.44	1.10
3 Yr Earnings Growth	20.6	1.10	1.41	1.10
Med Mkt Cap $mil	55,169	2.0	1.5	2.30
Med Mkt Cap $mil	9,278	0.2	0.2	0.30

Country Exposure 02-28-01	% assets
U.S.	54
United Kingdom	9
France	8
Japan	5
Germany	4

Hedging History: —

Regional Exposure 02-28-01	% assets
Europe	32
Japan	5
Latin America	0
Pacific Rim	1
U.S.	54
Other	2

Special Securities % assets 02-28-01	
Restricted/Illiquid Secs	Trace
Emerging-Markets Secs	1
Options/Futures/Warrants	Yes

Composition % assets 02-28-01

Cash	0.8	Bonds	0.0
Stocks	97.5	Other	0.0

Sector Weightings	% of Stocks	Rel Cat	5-Year High	5-Year Low
Utilities	0.5	0.2	5	0
Energy	8.5	1.5	9	1
Financials	26.6	1.4	27	9
Industrials	9.2	0.8	17	6
Durables	2.7	0.7	8	2
Staples	6.1	0.8	8	0
Services	15.7	0.9	33	12
Retail	6.1	1.2	12	1
Health	15.8	1.2	16	2
Technology	9.0	0.6	34	9

Address: One Post Office Square, Boston, MA 02109, 800-225-1581 / 617-292-1000
Web Address: www.putnaminvestments.com

*Inception: 07-01-94
Advisor: Putnam Inv. Mgmt.
Subadvisor: None
NTF Plans: Fidelity Inst.

Minimum Purchase: $500 Add: $50 IRA: $250
Min Auto Inv Plan: $25 Add: $25
Sales Fees: 5.75%L, 0.65%B
Management Fee: .70% mx./.50% mn.
Actual Fees: Mgt: 0.68% Dist: 0.34%
Expense Projections: 3Yr: $952 5Yr: $1227 10Yr: $2010
Avg Brok Commission: — Income Distrib: Annually
Total Cost (relative to category): —

Putnam Global Growth A

Ticker	Load	NAV	Yield	Total Assets	Mstar Category
PEQUX	5.75%	$7.65	0.0%	$4,132.5 mil	World Stock

Prospectus Objective: World Stock

Putnam Global Growth Fund seeks capital appreciation.

The fund normally invests in common stocks of companies worldwide. Management employs a growth strategy to invest in medium to large sized companies, though companies of any size may be selected for the portfolio.

This fund offers multiple shareclasses, all of which differ in fee structure and availability. Prior to Aug. 1, 1990, the fund was named Putnam International Equities Fund.

Historical Profile
Return Average
Risk Average
Rating ★★★ Neutral

Investment Style
Equity
Average Stock %: 94% 95% 99% 98% 99% 96% 98%

▼ Manager Change
▽ Partial Manager Change

Fund Performance vs. Category Average
■ Quarterly Fund Return +/– Category Average
— Category Baseline

Performance Quartile (within Category)

Portfolio Manager(s)

Robert Swift, CFA. Since 1-96.
Kelly A. Morgan. Since 3-97.
Lisa H. Svensson. Since 12-97.
Manuel Weiss Herrero. Since 10-98.
Stephen Dexter. Since 6-99.

1990	1991	1992	1993	1994	1995	1996	1997	1998	1999	2000	12-01	History
6.59	7.49	7.43	9.62	9.22	9.99	10.82	9.96	12.45	18.59	10.90	7.65	NAV
–9.20	17.97	0.24	31.84	–0.85	14.81	16.62	13.40	28.80	64.54	–29.72	–29.82	Total Return %
–6.08	–12.52	–7.38	21.79	–2.17	–22.73	–6.33	–19.96	0.22	43.51	–20.62	–17.94	+/– S&P 500
7.82	–0.32	5.46	9.34	–5.93	–5.91	3.14	–2.37	4.46	39.61	–16.55	—	+/– MSCI World
1.84	1.75	0.80	0.00	0.00	1.91	2.75	2.36	0.48	0.00	0.00	0.00	Income Return %
–11.04	16.22	–0.56	31.84	–0.85	12.90	13.86	11.04	28.32	64.54	–29.72	–29.82	Capital Return %
42	46	60	52	54	67	48	46	11	15	98	93	Total Rtn % Rank Cat
0.15	0.12	0.06	0.00	0.00	0.18	0.28	0.26	0.05	0.00	0.00	0.00	Income $
0.42	0.16	0.02	0.17	0.31	0.41	0.55	1.96	0.32	1.81	2.08	0.00	Capital Gains $
1.44	1.47	1.56	1.39	1.33	1.28	1.27	1.24	1.18	1.10	1.07	—	Expense Ratio %
1.56	1.60	1.28	0.85	0.83	1.05	0.84	0.31	–0.01	–0.39	–0.63	—	Income Ratio %
95	71	62	50	17	63	73	155	162	166	157	—	Turnover Rate %
561.9	660.4	657.2	1,057.3	1,477.5	1,785.5	2,318.4	2,657.2	3,366.8	5,976.1	4,860.0	3,103.1	Net Assets $mil

Performance 12-31-01

	1st Qtr	2nd Qtr	3rd Qtr	4th Qtr	Total
1997	1.11	14.17	4.00	–5.55	13.40
1998	15.16	4.53	–12.26	21.94	28.80
1999	2.89	4.68	3.36	47.80	64.54
2000	4.46	–14.57	–5.18	–16.95	–29.72
2001	–25.05	5.39	–20.33	11.52	–29.82

Trailing	Total Return%	+/– S&P 500	+/– MSCI World	% Rank All	% Rank Cat	Growth of $10,000
3 Mo	11.52	0.83	—	35	43	11,152
6 Mo	–11.15	–5.59	—	88	88	8,885
1 Yr	–29.82	–17.94	—	93	93	7,018
3 Yr Avg	–6.72	–5.70	—	95	95	8,116
5 Yr Avg	3.46	–7.24	—	83	71	11,853
10 Yr Avg	7.59	–5.33	—	46	60	20,793
15 Yr Avg	8.16	–5.57	—	51	50	32,436

Tax Analysis	Tax-Adj Ret%	%Rank Cat	%Pretax Ret	%Rank Cat
3 Yr Avg	–8.65	95	—	—
5 Yr Avg	0.87	75	25.2	92
10 Yr Avg	5.58	60	73.5	59

Potential Capital Gain Exposure: –45% of assets

Risk Analysis

Time Period	Load-Adj Return %	Risk %Rank[1] All	Risk %Rank[1] Cat	Morningstar Return	Morningstar Risk	Morningstar Risk-Adj Rating
1 Yr	–33.85					
3 Yr	–8.55	91	96	–2.51[2]	1.34	★
5 Yr	2.24	85	88	–0.58[2]	1.06	★★★
10 Yr	6.96	86	75	0.63[2]	0.94	★★★

Average Historical Rating (193 months): 3.9★s

[1]1=low, 100=high [2] T-Bill return substituted for category avg.

Category Rating (3 Yr)

1 2 3 4 5
Worst Best

Return Low
Risk High

Other Measures	Standard Index S&P 500	Best Fit Index MSCIWdExUSND
Alpha	–2.4	4.9
Beta	1.27	1.57
R-Squared	61	79

Standard Deviation	26.91
Mean	–6.72
Sharpe Ratio	–0.51

Analysis by Brian Portnoy 12-28-01

A terrible stretch at Putnam Global Growth should put investors on alert.

There's no way to soft-pedal this fund's awful performance over the past two years. Though the management team trimmed its exposure to racy tech and telecom stocks in 2000, the fund shed 30% of its value that year, a loss which relegated it to the world-stock category's cellar. In 2001, the fund has continued to pare its riskier fare while boosting its exposure to relatively safe areas of the market, such as consumer staples and health-care stocks. For example, positions in Philip Morris and Sanofi-Synthelabo, a French drug company, have both helped mitigate losses this year. The fund hasn't become a value-vehicle, though. To mitigate risk, the managers have sought out growth stocks from traditional value sectors, such as Scottish Power and Belgian energy trader Electrabel.

Nonetheless, the fund's exposure to pricey tech and telecom fare is still substantially larger than group norms, and stakes in firms such as Cisco Systems, Vodafone Airtouch, and Matsushita Electric have stung. The fund hasn't found much traction outside those areas either. British advertising conglomerate WPP and asset-management firm Amvescap have both struggled this year, for example. All told, the fund has dropped another 30% in 2001, ranking in the category's bottom tier once again.

The fund's feast-or-famine performance over the past several years highlights its inherent volatility. While the fund gets lost when growth investing is out of favor, it certainly earned its stripes during the go-go growth market of the mid- to late-1990s. For example, it leapt 65% in 1999, well ahead of most of its peers. Still, there are better growth-oriented options in the world-stock group. While the fund has appeal as spice for a conservative portfolio, its relatively poor risk/reward profile should give investors pause.

Address:	One Post Office Square Boston, MA 02109 800–225–1581 / 617–292–1000
Web Address:	www.putnaminvestments.com
Inception:	09-01-67
Advisor:	Putnam Inv. Mgmt.
Subadvisor:	None
NTF Plans:	Fidelity Inst.

Minimum Purchase:	$500	Add: $50	IRA: $250
Min Auto Inv Plan:	$25	Add: $25	
Sales Fees:	5.75%L, 0.35%B		
Management Fee:	.80%		
Actual Fees:	Mgt: 0.64%	Dist: 0.25%	
Expense Projections:	3Yr: $928	5Yr: $1187	10Yr: $1924
Avg Brok Commission:	—	Income Distrib: Annually	

Total Cost (relative to category):

Portfolio Analysis 10-31-01

Share change since 04-01 Total Stocks: 121

	Sector	Country	% Assets
⊕ Microsoft	Technology	U.S.	3.85
⊕ Tyco Intl	Industrials	U.S.	3.46
⊖ Glaxosmithkline	Technology	United Kingdom	2.58
⊕ Schering-Plough	Health	U.S.	2.22
⊖ Sanofi-Synthelabo	Health	France	2.17
☼ Electrabel	N/A	N/A	2.03
⊖ Pfizer	Health	U.S.	2.02
☼ Kraft Foods	Staples	U.S.	1.92
⊕ Astrazeneca	Health	United Kingdom	1.74
☼ UnitedHealth Grp	Financials	U.S.	1.72
⊖ General Elec	Industrials	U.S.	1.67
⊕ Cisco Sys	Technology	U.S.	1.64
☼ Dexia	Financials	Belgium	1.59
⊖ NTT DoCoMo	Services	Japan	1.53
⊕ Samsung Electncs	Technology	South Korea	1.52
⊖ Vodafone Airtouch	Services	United Kingdom	1.50
☼ Banco Popular Espanol	Financials	Spain	1.50
⊕ Royal Dutch Petro	Energy	Netherlands	1.49
☼ KLA-Tencor	Technology	U.S.	1.31
⊕ WPP Grp	Services	United Kingdom	1.30

Current Investment Style

Style: Value Blnd Growth; Size: Large Med Small

	Stock Port Avg	Rel MSCI EAFE Current	Rel MSCI EAFE Hist	Rel Cat
Price/Earnings Ratio	29.7	1.15	1.31	1.07
Price/Cash Flow	18.6	1.45	1.79	1.13
Price/Book Ratio	5.9	1.68	1.79	1.27
3 Yr Earnings Growth	19.4	1.03	1.46	1.04
Med Mkt Cap $mil	38,514	1.4	6.2	1.60

Country Exposure 10-31-01	% assets
U.S.	53
United Kingdom	8
Japan	8
France	4
Germany	4

Hedging History: Frequent

Special Securities % assets 10-31-01	
Restricted/Illiquid Secs	Trace
Emerging-Markets Secs	4
Options/Futures/Warrants	Yes

Composition % assets 10-31-01

Cash	1.2	Bonds	0.0
Stocks	98.1	Other	0.1

Regional Exposure 10-31-01	% assets
Europe	28
Japan	8
Latin America	0
Pacific Rim	5
U.S.	53
Other	1

Sector Weightings	% of Stocks	Rel Cat	5-Year High	5-Year Low
Utilities	4.6	1.8	8	0
Energy	3.5	0.6	7	1
Financials	18.9	1.0	29	14
Industrials	8.2	0.7	31	5
Durables	4.3	1.1	13	0
Staples	7.3	0.9	11	0
Services	13.5	0.8	26	10
Retail	1.7	0.3	12	0
Health	15.0	1.1	19	3
Technology	23.1	1.5	45	3

Putnam International Growth A

Ticker	Load	NAV	Yield	Total Assets	Mstar Category
POVSX	5.75%	$19.82	0.0%	$11,466.1 mil	Foreign Stock

Prospectus Objective: Foreign Stock

Putnam International Growth Fund seeks capital appreciation.

The fund normally invests at least 65% of assets in equity securities of companies located outside of the United States. It may invest in companies of any size that it judges to be in a strong growth trend or that it believes to be undervalued. The fund may invest in both developed and emerging markets.

This fund offers multiple shareclasses, all of which differ in fee structure and availability. Past name: Putnam Overseas Growth Fund.

Historical Profile
Return: High
Risk: Below Avg
Rating: ★★★★★ Highest

Investment Style
Equity
Average Stock %: 89% 94% 100% 97% 98% 89% 91%

▼ Manager Change
▽ Partial Manager Change

Fund Performance vs. Category Average
■ Quarterly Fund Return +/– Category Average
— Category Baseline

Performance Quartile (within Category)

Portfolio Manager(s)

Justin M. Scott. Since 2-91.
Omid Kamshad, CFA. Since 11-96.
Paul Warren. Since 2-99.
Joshua Byrne. Since 1-00.
Steven Oler, CFA. Since 9-00.
Simon Davis. Since 10-00.

1990	1991	1992	1993	1994	1995	1996	1997	1998	1999	2000	12-01	History
—	8.74	8.42	11.90	11.75	13.12	15.03	16.67	19.23	29.68	24.71	19.82	NAV
—	2.86*	–3.66	43.99	0.17	13.97	16.20	17.71	18.95	60.78	–9.02	–19.79	Total Return %
—	–13.82*	–11.28	33.93	–1.15	–23.57	–6.75	–15.65	–9.63	39.74	0.08	–7.91	+/– S&P 500
—	—	8.51	11.43	–7.61	2.76	10.15	15.93	–1.05	33.81	5.14	—	+/– MSCI EAFE
—	1.59	0.00	0.00	0.00	2.21	1.15	1.66	1.27	1.76	1.32	0.00	Income Return %
—	1.27	–3.66	43.99	0.17	11.76	15.04	16.05	17.68	59.01	–10.35	–19.79	Capital Return %
—	—	48	23	53	17	34	7	21	19	23	34	Total Rtn % Rank Cat
—	0.13	0.00	0.00	0.00	0.26	0.15	0.25	0.21	0.34	0.39	0.00	Income $
—	0.00	0.00	0.22	0.17	0.01	0.06	0.79	0.36	0.79	1.81	0.00	Capital Gains $
—	—	1.98	1.80	2.17	1.61	1.74	1.59	1.36	1.27	1.14	1.13	Expense Ratio %
—	—	0.76	0.81	0.17	0.97	0.99	0.98	1.07	0.38	2.01	0.63	Income Ratio %
—	—	82	81	96	26	44	86	94	97	100	74	Turnover Rate %
—	2.3	2.4	4.4	24.2	57.9	302.4	1,102.2	2,173.1	5,014.8	7,178.8	6,561.7	Net Assets $mil

Performance 12-31-01

	1st Qtr	2nd Qtr	3rd Qtr	4th Qtr	Total
1997	3.66	12.77	6.37	–5.35	17.71
1998	16.92	2.62	–19.05	22.48	18.95
1999	5.36	6.81	5.31	35.66	60.78
2000	6.23	–5.11	–8.19	–1.70	–9.02
2001	–14.37	0.38	–13.89	8.37	–19.79

Trailing	Total Return%	+/– S&P 500	+/– MSCI EAFE	% Rank All	% Rank Cat	Growth of $10,000
3 Mo	8.37	–2.32	—	50	47	10,837
6 Mo	–6.69	–1.13	—	72	21	9,331
1 Yr	–19.79	–7.91	—	80	34	8,021
3 Yr Avg	5.47	6.49	—	27	12	11,732
5 Yr Avg	10.43	–0.26	—	16	6	16,426
10 Yr Avg	11.70	–1.23	—	21	2	30,225
15 Yr Avg	—	—	—	—	—	—

Tax Analysis	Tax-Adj Ret%	%Rank Cat	%Pretax Ret	%Rank Cat
3 Yr Avg	4.10	12	74.9	63
5 Yr Avg	8.95	6	85.8	15
10 Yr Avg	10.68	1	91.4	2

Potential Capital Gain Exposure: –15% of assets

Risk Analysis

Time Period	Load-Adj Return %	Risk %Rank[1] All	Risk %Rank[1] Cat	Morningstar Return	Morningstar Risk	Morningstar Risk-Adj Rating
1 Yr	–24.40					
3 Yr	3.41	68	36	–0.32[2]	0.87	★★★★
5 Yr	9.13	71	37	0.97[2]	0.80	★★★★★
10 Yr	11.04	77	29	2.14[2]	0.78	★★★★★

Average Historical Rating (95 months): 4.1★s

[1]1=low, 100=high [2] T-Bill return substituted for category avg.

Category Rating (3 Yr)

Worst 1 2 3 4 5 Best

Return: Above Avg
Risk: Average

Other Measures	Standard Index S&P 500	Best Fit Index
Alpha	6.2	12.7
Beta	0.81	1.17
R-Squared	49	87
Standard Deviation		20.95
Mean		5.47
Sharpe Ratio		0.03

Analysis by Brian Portnoy 12-07-01

Putnam International Growth has taken its lumps lately, but its long-term record is unassailable.

Like most foreign-stock offerings this year, this fund is deep in the red. For the year to date through Dec. 6, 2001, it has shed 18.3% of its value. As the doldrums have hit both European and Japanese markets, the fund's portfolio has had plenty of weak spots. For example, telecom-related issues, such as wireless giants Vodafone Airtouch and NTT DoCoMo, have struggled, while the fund's media exposure has been especially damaging. Advertising agency WPP has been on a long slide until very recently.

As the management team does here nearly every year, however, it manages to find a way to outperform its peers. In fact, its loss this year, though painful, is less than two thirds of its peers'. That's even more impressive than it sounds because the fund's bias toward mega-caps has been counterproductive; smaller-cap funds have paced the category this year. As always, the fund has relied on strong stock selection and a diversified portfolio to see it through. According to lead manager Omid Kamshad, a number of the fund's oil, pharmaceutical, and consumer-staples stocks, have been relatively buoyant.

The fund has been competitive in every sort of market. Throughout the late 1990s' bull run, it regularly outpaced its rivals, including a 62% gain in 1999's growth apex. Impressively, management's mid-2000 decision to back off of pricey tech and telecom issues and move into safer health and energy stocks allowed the fund's shareholders to preserve much of their bull-market gains. After playing it relatively safe through much of 2001, the fund is currently taking their bets off more-defensive fare, such as staples, and boosting the fund's telecom exposure.

Overall, this fund is a rock-solid core foreign-stock holding.

Address:	One Post Office Square Boston, MA 02109 617-292-1000 / 800-225-1581
Web Address:	www.putnaminvestments.com
*Inception:	02-28-91
Advisor:	Putnam Inv. Mgmt.
Subadvisor:	None
NTF Plans:	Fidelity Inst.

Minimum Purchase:	$500	Add: $50	IRA: $500
Min Auto Inv Plan:	$25	Add: $25	
Sales Fees:	5.75%L, 0.10%B, 0.25%S		
Management Fee:	.80%		
Actual Fees:	Mgt: 0.68%	Dist: 0.25%	
Expense Projections:	3Yr: $981	5Yr: $1277	10Yr: $2116
Avg Brok Commission:	—	Income Distrib: Annually	
Total Cost (relative to category):			

Portfolio Analysis 06-30-01

Share change since 12-00 Total Stocks: 152	Sector	Country	% Assets
☼ Total Fina Cl B	Energy	France	4.49
⊕ ING Groep	Financials	Netherlands	3.76
⊕ Shell Transp & Trad	Energy	United Kingdom	3.74
⊕ Astrazeneca	Health	United Kingdom	3.55
☼ Glaxosmithkline	Technology	United Kingdom	2.81
⊕ Vodafone Airtouch	Services	United Kingdom	2.63
⊕ Allianz (Reg)	Financials	Germany	2.10
⊖ Sanofi-Synthelabo	Health	France	2.00
⊕ NTT DoCoMo	Services	Japan	1.76
☼ Nestle 144A	Staples	Switzerland	1.75
⊖ Nikko Secs	Financials	Japan	1.59
☼ Toyota Motor	Durables	Japan	1.49
☼ Muenchener Rueckvers (Reg)	Financials	Germany	1.46
⊕ Investor Cl B	Durables	Sweden	1.44
⊕ Cheung Kong Hldgs	Financials	Hong Kong	1.41
⊕ Samsung Electrncs	Technology	South Korea	1.39
⊕ CRH	Industrials	Ireland	1.35
☼ ENI ADR	Energy	Italy	1.35
⊖ Aventis Cl A	Health	France	1.22
⊖ BMW	Durables	Germany	1.17

Current Investment Style

Style: Value Blnd Growth; Size: Large Med Small

	Stock Port Avg	Rel MSCI EAFE Current	Rel MSCI EAFE Hist	Rel Cat
Price/Earnings Ratio	24.1	0.93	0.94	0.94
Price/Cash Flow	13.7	1.07	1.11	0.96
Price/Book Ratio	4.0	1.15	1.07	1.02
3 Yr Earnings Growth	24.4	1.31	1.38	1.24
Med Mkt Cap $mil	33,639	1.2	1.3	1.86

Country Exposure 06-30-01	% assets
United Kingdom	22
Japan	13
France	13
Germany	6
Netherlands	6

Hedging History: Frequent

Regional Exposure 06-30-01	% assets
Europe	65
Japan	13
Latin America	2
Pacific Rim	8
Other	4

Special Securities % assets 06-30-01	
Restricted/Illiquid Secs	3
Emerging-Markets Secs	8
Options/Futures/Warrants	Yes

Composition % assets 06-30-01			
Cash	7.4	Bonds	0.0
Stocks	90.7	Other	0.1

Sector Weightings	% of Stocks	Rel Cat	5-Year High	5-Year Low
Utilities	2.4	0.9	5	1
Energy	12.9	2.2	15	1
Financials	24.8	1.2	38	12
Industrials	11.4	0.8	29	6
Durables	9.1	1.3	13	5
Staples	4.4	0.6	10	3
Services	18.6	1.0	32	8
Retail	1.7	0.4	6	0
Health	10.6	1.1	13	3
Technology	4.3	0.4	18	4

Putnam Investors A

Ticker	Load	NAV	Yield	Total Assets	Mstar Category
PINVX	5.75%	$11.55	0.0%	$9,146.0 mil	Large Growth

Prospectus Objective: Growth

Putnam Investors Fund seeks long-term capital appreciation; growth of income is secondary.

The fund invests primarily in common stocks. It may also invest in preferred stocks, convertibles, and debt securities. When selecting investments, management considers such factors as probable future earnings, dividends, financial strength, working assets, and competitive position. The fund may invest a portion of assets in securities of foreign issuers.

Class A shares have front loads; B shares have deferred loads, higher 12b-1 fees, and conversion features; M shares have lower front loads and higher 12b-1 fees than Class A.

Historical Profile
Return Below Avg
Risk Above Avg
Rating ★★
Below Avg

Investment Style
Equity
Average Stock %

1996	1997	1998	1999	2000	12-01
96%	99%	98%	98%	99%	96%

▼ Manager Change
▽ Partial Manager Change

Fund Performance vs. Category Average
Quarterly Fund Return +/– Category Average
— Category Baseline

Performance Quartile (within Category)

Portfolio Manager(s)

C. Beth Cotner, CFA. Since 10-95. BA'74 Ohio State U.; MBA'76 George Washington U. Other funds currently managed: Putnam Investors B, Putnam Investors C, Diversified Inv Growth & Income.

Richard B. England, CFA. Since 10-96. BS/BA U. of Florida; MBA U. of Penn-Wharton. Other funds currently managed: Putnam Health Sciences A, Putnam Health Sciences B, Putnam Investors B.

Manuel Weiss Herrero. Since 6-96. BS M. I. T.; MBA Northeastern U. Other funds currently managed: Putnam Global Growth B, Putnam Global Growth A, Putnam Investors B.

History

1990	1991	1992	1993	1994	1995	1996	1997	1998	1999	2000	12–01	History
7.59	8.70	8.13	8.16	7.14	8.61	9.21	11.24	14.82	19.15	15.36	11.55	NAV
–2.77	28.56	7.89	17.87	–3.19	37.55	21.40	34.49	35.52	30.14	–18.50	–24.80	Total Return %
0.35	–1.93	0.27	7.82	–4.51	0.01	–1.54	1.14	6.95	9.11	–9.40	–12.93	+/– S&P 500
–4.14	–10.85	4.00	17.95	–8.05	–1.11	–4.12	0.75	–9.58	0.47	6.02	–4.31	+/– Russ Top 200 Grt
2.33	2.02	1.36	0.91	0.00	1.19	0.63	0.46	0.00	0.00	0.00	0.00	Income Return %
–5.10	26.54	6.53	16.96	–3.19	36.36	20.78	34.03	35.52	30.14	–18.50	–24.80	Capital Return %
54	84	34	19	62	19	31	10	37	66	65	61	Total Rtn % Rank Cat
0.20	0.15	0.12	0.07	0.00	0.09	0.05	0.04	0.00	0.00	0.00	0.00	Income $
0.42	0.81	1.13	1.31	0.73	1.12	1.17	1.08	0.38	0.13	0.26	0.00	Capital Gains $
0.81	0.89	0.94	0.90	0.99	0.99	1.03	1.00	0.95	0.89	0.87	0.90	Expense Ratio %
2.42	1.78	1.33	0.84	0.88	1.03	0.69	0.50	0.03	–0.14	–0.25	–0.06	Income Ratio %
51	58	100	134	100	97	128	95	59	75	65	94	Turnover Rate %
643.2	756.5	735.4	829.1	766.4	1,022.2	1,323.8	1,942.6	4,218.5	7,903.1	7,310.7	5,064.1	Net Assets $mil

Performance 12-31-01

	1st Qtr	2nd Qtr	3rd Qtr	4th Qtr	Total
1997	0.43	18.49	9.40	3.31	34.49
1998	16.55	5.42	–11.95	25.27	35.52
1999	5.47	4.03	–5.10	25.00	30.14
2000	3.34	–5.66	–1.50	–15.13	–18.50
2001	–20.31	6.37	–19.66	10.42	–24.81

Trailing	Total Return%	+/– S&P 500	+/– Russ Top 200 Grth	% Rank All	% Rank Cat	Growth of $10,000
3 Mo	10.42	–0.26	–2.44	40	83	11,042
6 Mo	–11.29	–5.74	–4.30	88	72	8,871
1 Yr	–24.80	–12.93	–4.31	88	61	7,520
3 Yr Avg	–7.26	–6.24	0.76	96	79	7,976
5 Yr Avg	7.77	–2.93	–0.82	30	58	14,536
10 Yr Avg	11.57	–1.36	0.49	22	25	29,884
15 Yr Avg	12.10	–1.63	–1.27	25	48	55,503

Tax Analysis	Tax-Adj Ret%	%Rank Cat	%Pretax Ret	%Rank Cat
3 Yr Avg	–7.40	71	—	—
5 Yr Avg	7.07	44	91.0	13
10 Yr Avg	9.15	30	79.1	43

Potential Capital Gain Exposure: 25% of assets

Risk Analysis

Time Period	Load-Adj Return %	Risk %Rank[1] All	Risk %Rank[1] Cat	Morningstar Return	Morningstar Risk	Morningstar Risk-Adj Rating
1 Yr	–29.13					
3 Yr	–9.08	84	43	–2.59[2]	1.24	★
5 Yr	6.50	81	39	0.33[2]	1.15	★★
10 Yr	10.91	81	27	0.89	1.10	★★★

Average Historical Rating (193 months): 2.9★s

[1] 1=low, 100=high [2] T-Bill return substituted for category avg.

Category Rating (3 Yr)

1 2 3 4 5
Worst Best

Return Below Avg
Risk Average

Other Measures	Standard Index S&P 500	Best Fit Index MSCIACWdFr
Alpha	–4.5	0.3
Beta	1.21	1.30
R–Squared	88	90
Standard Deviation		20.74
Mean		–7.26
Sharpe Ratio		–0.69

Analysis by Kelli Stebel 11-05-01

This fund isn't horrible, but that doesn't mean investors should settle for its mediocrity.

Putnam Investors doesn't see its name in lights, and with good reason. Throughout lead manager Beth Cotner's six-year tenure, the fund has regularly landed in the middle of the large-growth category. In market rallies and downturns alike, the fund's postings have consistently matched those of its typical peer.

Even during the market's current turmoil, this offering's showing is merely average. Though the fund's 29% loss for the year to date through Nov. 2, 2001, might look startling, it's on par with its peers. Holdings like Johnson & Johnson have posted decent results, but those gains have been offset by substantial losses in top holdings such as Qwest Communications International. Comanager Richard England said that he and the team overstayed their welcome in some software plays, too, such as Siebel Systems and Adobe Systems, which were recently sold.

England said that he and the team had been trying to take advantage of the market's recent volatility. They've been adding to several brokerage shops, like Morgan Stanley Dean Witter. Though they're concerned about present fundamentals, England thinks that Morgan Stanley is the best-positioned broker, given its global focus. In addition, the team has been nibbling on tech stocks. This fund never goes whole-hog into pricey fare, so they've been adding a few shares of Automatic Data Processing and Electronic Data Systems, both of which are consistent growers, trading at historically low valuations.

There's no doubt that shareholders could have done a lot worse than the steady returns this fund has produced over the years. That said, investors can choose from a variety of better-performing funds with similar exposure.

Portfolio Analysis 09-30-01

Share change since 06–01 Total Stocks: 105	Sector	PE	YTD Ret%	% Assets
⊕ Citigroup	Financials	20.0	0.03	4.33
⊕ Pfizer	Health	34.7	–12.40	4.06
⊖ Microsoft	Technology	57.6	52.78	3.79
⊖ General Elec	Industrials	30.1	–15.00	3.69
⊖ Johnson & Johnson	Health	16.6	14.01	3.55
⊖ Tyco Intl	Industrials	27.1	6.23	3.01
⊕ Philip Morris	Staples	12.1	9.12	2.56
⊕ Fannie Mae	Financials	16.2	–6.95	2.47
⊖ American Intl Grp	Financials	42.0	–19.20	2.42
⊕ AOL Time Warner	Technology	—	–7.76	2.20
⊖ Wal–Mart Stores	Retail	40.3	8.94	2.16
⊖ Fifth Third Bancorp	Financials	38.3	4.53	1.92
⊕ Schering–Plough	Health	22.2	–35.90	1.82
⊕ ExxonMobil	Energy	15.3	–7.59	1.82
⊕ UnitedHealth Grp	Financials	26.6	15.37	1.71
⊖ Viacom Cl B	Services	—	—	1.68
⊖ American Home Products	Health	—	–1.91	1.54
⊕ IBM	Technology	26.9	43.00	1.54
⊕ MBNA	Financials	19.6	–3.66	1.47
⊖ PepsiCo	Staples	31.4	–0.54	1.43
⊖ Medtronic	Health	76.4	–14.70	1.42
⊖ Kraft Foods	Staples	—	—	1.41
⊕ Morgan Stanley/Dean Witter	Financials	16.6	–28.20	1.40
⊕ Eli Lilly	Health	28.9	–14.40	1.37
⊕ Lowe's	Retail	38.7	109.00	1.35

Current Investment Style

Style: Value Blnd Growth; Size: Large Med Small

	Stock Port Avg	Relative S&P 500 Current	Relative S&P 500 Hist	Rel Cat
Price/Earnings Ratio	30.7	0.99	1.18	0.86
Price/Book Ratio	6.6	1.15	1.24	1.03
Price/Cash Flow	21.5	1.20	1.22	0.95
3 Yr Earnings Growth	21.9	1.50	1.38	1.02
1 Yr Earnings Est%	7.0	—	—	2.34
Med Mkt Cap $mil	62,057	1.0	1.2	1.31

[1] figure is based on 50% or less of stocks

Special Securities % assets 09-30-01	
Restricted/Illiquid Secs	1
Emerging–Markets Secs	0
Options/Futures/Warrants	Yes

Composition % assets 09-30-01	
Cash	1.9
Stocks*	98.1
Bonds	0.0
Other	0.0
*Foreign (% stocks)	1.2

Market Cap	
Giant	52.9
Large	38.9
Medium	8.2
Small	0.0
Micro	0.0

Sector Weightings	% of Stocks	Rel S&P	5-Year High	5-Year Low
Utilities	0.4	0.1	5	0
Energy	3.7	0.5	14	1
Financials	22.7	1.3	23	9
Industrials	8.6	0.8	21	8
Durables	1.1	0.7	12	0
Staples	9.6	1.2	12	2
Services	8.6	0.8	21	6
Retail	7.3	1.1	16	4
Health	21.2	1.4	21	7
Technology	16.8	0.9	41	9

Address:	One Post Office Square Boston, MA 02109 800–225–1581 / 617–292–1000
Web Address:	www.putnaminvestments.com
Inception:	12-01-25
Advisor:	Putnam Inv. Mgmt.
Subadvisor:	None
NTF Plans:	Fidelity Inst.

Minimum Purchase:	$500	Add: $50	IRA: $250
Min Auto Inv Plan:	$25	Add: $25	
Sales Fees:	5.75%L, 0.10%B, 0.25%S		
Management Fee:	.70% mx./.50% mn.		
Actual Fees:	Mgt: 0.51%	Dist: 0.25%	
Expense Projections:	3Yr: $860	5Yr: $1070	10Yr: $1674
Avg Brok Commission:	—	Income Distrib: Quarterly	
Total Cost (relative to category):	—		

Putnam New Century Growth A

Ticker	Load	NAV	Yield	Total Assets	Mstar Category
PNCAX	5.75%	$12.71	0.0%	$726.5 mil	Mid–Cap Growth

Prospectus Objective: Growth

Putnam New Century Growth seeks capital appreciation.

The fund invests mainly in the common stocks of domestic companies, with a focus on growth stocks. It may invest in companies of any size. The fund may invest in preferred stocks, convertible securities, debt instruments, derivatives, and foreign securities.

Class A shares feature front-end loads; Class B shares charge deferred loads and have a conversion feature; Class C shares charge a deferred load; Class M shares charge deferred loads.

Historical Profile
Return —
Risk —
Rating
Not Rated

Investment Style
Equity
Average Stock %
95% 98%

▼ Manager Change
▽ Partial Manager Change

Fund Performance vs. Category Average
Quarterly Fund Return +/– Category Average
— Category Baseline

Performance Quartile (within Category)

Portfolio Manager(s)

Roland W. Gillis, CFA. Since 1-00. BA'72 Northeastern U.; MA'74 American School of Intl. Mgmt. Other funds currently managed: Putnam OTC Emerging Growth A, Putnam OTC Emerging Growth B, Putnam OTC Emerging Growth M.

1990	1991	1992	1993	1994	1995	1996	1997	1998	1999	2000	12-01	History
—	—	—	—	—	—	—	—	—	—	17.72	12.71	NAV
—	—	—	—	—	—	—	—	—	—	–36.24*	–28.27	Total Return %
—	—	—	—	—	—	—	—	—	—	–28.89*	–16.40	+/– S&P 500
—	—	—	—	—	—	—	—	—	—	—	–8.12	+/– Russ Midcap Grth
—	—	—	—	—	—	—	—	—	—	0.00	0.00	Income Return %
—	—	—	—	—	—	—	—	—	—	–36.24	–28.27	Capital Return %
—	—	—	—	—	—	—	—	—	—	—	71	Total Rtn % Rank Cat
—	—	—	—	—	—	—	—	—	—	0.00	0.00	Income $
—	—	—	—	—	—	—	—	—	—	0.00	0.00	Capital Gains $
—	—	—	—	—	—	—	—	—	—	1.14	1.21	Expense Ratio %
—	—	—	—	—	—	—	—	—	—	–0.72	–0.97	Income Ratio %
—	—	—	—	—	—	—	—	—	—	108	139	Turnover Rate %
—	—	—	—	—	—	—	—	—	—	564.4	360.5	Net Assets $mil

Performance 12-31-01

	1st Qtr	2nd Qtr	3rd Qtr	4th Qtr	Total
1997	—	—	—	—	—
1998	—	—	—	—	—
1999	—	—	—	—	—
2000	—	–13.07	–0.53	–28.03	–36.24*
2001	–29.40	18.31	–33.31	28.77	–28.27

Trailing	Total Return%	+/– S&P 500	+/– Russ Midcap Grth	% Rank All	% Rank Cat	Growth of $10,000
3 Mo	28.77	18.09	1.71	5	10	12,877
6 Mo	–14.12	–8.57	–5.86	94	73	8,588
1 Yr	–28.27	–16.40	–8.12	92	71	7,173
3 Yr Avg	—	—	—	—	—	—
5 Yr Avg	—	—	—	—	—	—
10 Yr Avg	—	—	—	—	—	—
15 Yr Avg	—	—	—	—	—	—

Tax Analysis	Tax-Adj Ret%	%Rank Cat	%Pretax Ret	%Rank Cat
3 Yr Avg	—	—	—	—
5 Yr Avg	—	—	—	—
10 Yr Avg	—	—	—	—

Potential Capital Gain Exposure: –82% of assets

Risk Analysis

Time Period	Load-Adj Return %	Risk %Rank[1] All	Risk %Rank[1] Cat	Morningstar Return	Morningstar Risk	Morningstar Risk-Adj Rating
1 Yr	–32.40					
3 Yr	—	—	—	—	—	
5 Yr	—	—	—	—	—	
Incept	–35.12	—	—	—	—	

Average Historical Rating —

[1]1=low, 100=high

Category Rating (3 Yr)

Return
Risk

Other Measures	Standard Index S&P 500	Best Fit Index
Alpha	—	—
Beta	—	—
R-Squared	—	—
Standard Deviation		—
Mean		—
Sharpe Ratio		—

Portfolio Analysis 06-30-01

Share change since 12-00 Total Stocks: 151

	Sector	PE	YTD Ret%	% Assets
⊕ Westwood One	Services	77.1	55.59	1.97
⊕ Qlogic	Technology	49.5	–42.10	1.85
⊖ Stryker	Health	46.0	15.38	1.77
⊖ Veritas Software	Technology	—	–48.70	1.75
⊕ Bed Bath & Beyond	Retail	53.0	51.51	1.74
⊕ Sonus Networks	Technology	—	–81.70	1.73
⊕ Emulex	Technology	—	–50.50	1.58
⊕ Cephalon	Health	—	19.38	1.57
☼ Shire Pharma Grp	Health	—	–20.50	1.54
⊕ TCF Finl	Financials	18.2	10.24	1.49
⊖ Jabil Circuit	Technology	38.5	–10.40	1.43
⊕ Lamar Advertising Cl A	Services	—	9.71	1.39
⊖ Cintas	Services	36.1	–9.33	1.34
⊕ Univision Comms A	Services	96.3	–1.17	1.34
⊕ Healthsouth	Health	28.0	–9.15	1.31
⊕ Cryolife	Health	61.2	–0.83	1.30
⊕ Invitrogen	Health	—	–28.30	1.25
⊕ Plexus	Technology	25.1	–12.50	1.23
⊕ Tiffany	Retail	27.1	0.09	1.22
☼ Forest Labs	Health	52.2	23.35	1.16
⊖ Ryanair Hldgs ADR	Services	65.8	15.11	1.15
⊖ Radio One Cl D	Services	—	—	1.13
⊖ Linear Tech	Technology	34.9	–15.30	1.10
⊖ Dollar Tree Stores	Retail	30.9	26.16	1.07
☼ Mirant	Utilities	8.3	–43.40	1.07

Current Investment Style

Style: Value Blnd Growth; Size: Large Med Small

	Stock Port Avg	Relative S&P 500 Current	Relative S&P 500 Hist	Rel Cat
Price/Earnings Ratio	40.5	1.31	—	1.17
Price/Book Ratio	5.9	1.03	—	1.03
Price/Cash Flow	27.2	1.51	—	1.17
3 Yr Earnings Growth	24.5[1]	1.68	—	1.04
1 Yr Earnings Est%	6.9	—	—	0.74
Med Mkt Cap $mil	3,146	0.1	—	0.56

[1]figure is based on 50% or less of stocks

Special Securities % assets 06-30-01	
Restricted/Illiquid Secs	0
Emerging-Markets Secs	0
Options/Futures/Warrants	No

Composition % assets 06-30-01	
Cash	2.2
Stocks*	97.8
Bonds	0.0
Other	0.0
*Foreign (% stocks)	4.7

Market Cap	
Giant	0.0
Large	17.6
Medium	59.8
Small	21.2
Micro	1.5

Sector Weightings	% of Stocks	Rel S&P	5-Year High	5-Year Low
Utilities	2.2	0.7	—	—
Energy	5.0	0.7	—	—
Financials	2.8	0.2	—	—
Industrials	0.2	0.0	—	—
Durables	0.5	0.3	—	—
Staples	0.0	0.0	—	—
Services	20.8	1.9	—	—
Retail	10.3	1.5	—	—
Health	23.5	1.6	—	—
Technology	34.9	1.9	—	—

Analysis by Kelli Stebel 12-10-01

There's little to get excited about here.

When Putnam launched Putnam New Century Growth in January 2000, we were enthusiastic. In addition to its experienced management team, the fund also uses a flexible-cap strategy, and to maintain that approach, Putnam was willing to close the fund when assets hit $1 billion. In fact, the fund briefly closed in March 2000, just two months after its launch, when assets reached that mark.

How times have changed. Comanager Chuck Swanberg was laid off as part of Putnam's downsizing effort in April 2001, leaving Roland Gillis as sole manager. More important, growth stocks have fallen off a cliff, and this fund has been hit harder than most. Since March 2000, when the recent correction began, through November 2001, its 40% loss is far worse than its average peer's 25% drop. The fund has regained some ground as growth stocks have rebounded recently, but it's still down 30% for the year to date through Dec. 7.

What went wrong? Though it's a firm known for monitoring funds and fund managers closely, Putnam took its eye off the ball here and at several other growth offerings, allowing this fund's tech weighting to get out of hand. Arguably, this fund became a tech fund in disguise throughout much of 2000, with a 62% tech stake and a hefty allocation to telecom, to boot. Gillis says that Putnam has taken steps to ensure that such excessive bets don't happen again. The fund now has additional risk controls, which evaluate the fund's bets across individual stocks, sectors, and market-cap levels. These days Gillis says they've bought a few storage stocks, like Qlogic, but aren't going to jump in with both feet.

Despite these new measures, the fund still needs to prove itself. In a growth-led market, it could strut its stuff. But until we see sustained improvement, investors should stay away.

Address:	One Post Office Square Boston, MA 02109 617-292-1000 / 800-225-1581
Web Address:	www.putnaminvestments.com
*Inception:	01-21-00
Advisor:	Putnam Inv. Mgmt.
Subadvisor:	None
NTF Plans:	N/A

Minimum Purchase:	$500	Add: $50	IRA: $250
Min Auto Inv Plan:	$25	Add: $25	
Sales Fees:	5.75%L, 0.35%B		
Management Fee:	.70%		
Actual Fees:	Mgt: 0.70%	Dist: 0.25%	
Expense Projections:	3Yr: $1088	5Yr: $1506	10Yr: $2666
Avg Brok Commission:	—	Income Distrib: Annually	
Total Cost (relative to category):	—		

Putnam OTC Emerging Growth A

Ticker	Load	NAV	Yield	Total Assets	Mstar Category
POEGX	5.75%	$7.50	0.0%	$3,283.3 mil	Mid–Cap Growth

Prospectus Objective: Small Company

Putnam OTC Emerging Growth Fund seeks capital appreciation.

The fund normally invests at least 65% of assets in stocks issued by companies that are in early stages of development and have records of profitability. It may invest up to 20% of assets in foreign securities.

This fund offers multiple shareclasses, all of which differ in fee structure and availability. Prior to Sept. 30, 1986, the fund was offered through a private distributor and was not available to the general public. The fund has gone through several name changes.

Historical Profile
Return Low
Risk High
Rating ★ Lowest

Investment Style: Equity — Average Stock %: 90% 98% 97% 98% 98% 94%

▼ Manager Change
▽ Partial Manager Change

Fund Performance vs. Category Average
Quarterly Fund Return +/– Category Average
— Category Baseline

Performance Quartile (within Category)

Portfolio Manager(s)

Steve Kirson, CFA. Since 6-96. BA U. of Miami; MBA U. of Pennsylvania. Other funds currently managed: Putnam OTC Emerging Growth B, Putnam OTC Emerging Growth M, Putnam OTC Emerging Growth Y.

Michael J. Mufson, CFA. Since 6-96. BA Vanderbilt U.; MBA Emory U. Other funds currently managed: Putnam OTC Emerging Growth B, Putnam OTC Emerging Growth M, Putnam OTC Emerging Growth Y.

Roland W. Gillis, CFA. Since 9-01. BA'72 Northeastern U.; MA'74 American School of Intl. Mgmt. Other funds currently managed: Putnam OTC Emerging Growth B, Putnam OTC Emerging Growth M, Putnam Voyager II A.

History

	1990	1991	1992	1993	1994	1995	1996	1997	1998	1999	2000	12-01
NAV	6.86	9.56	9.60	11.45	10.80	15.02	14.62	16.11	17.25	37.01	13.92	7.50
Total Return %	–9.84	40.83	12.69	32.05	2.24	55.94	4.61	10.19	11.00	126.91	–51.27	–46.12
+/– S&P 500	–6.72	10.35	5.07	21.99	0.93	18.41	–18.34	–23.16	–17.57	105.87	–42.17	–34.24
+/– Russ Midcap Grth	–4.70	–6.20	3.98	20.86	4.40	21.97	–12.87	–12.35	–6.86	75.60	–39.52	–25.96
Income Return %	0.00	0.00	0.00	0.00	0.00	0.00	0.00	0.00	0.00	0.00	0.00	0.00
Capital Return %	–9.84	40.83	12.69	32.05	2.24	55.94	4.61	10.19	11.00	126.91	–51.27	–46.12
Total Rtn % Rank Cat	70	73	23	3	30	3	97	82	63	6	100	98
Income $	0.00	0.00	0.00	0.00	0.00	0.00	0.00	0.00	0.00	0.00	0.00	0.00
Capital Gains $	0.30	0.09	1.14	1.20	0.86	1.71	1.08	0.00	0.56	1.93	4.59	0.00
Expense Ratio %	1.50	1.48	1.39	1.26	1.16	1.14	1.11	1.16	1.00	0.98	0.93	1.04
Income Ratio %	–0.47	–0.46	–0.59	–0.90	–0.97	–0.62	–0.53	–0.79	–0.70	–0.85	–0.75	–0.84
Turnover Rate %	43	54	67	108	77	116	200	113	106	140	104	99
Net Assets $mil	183.9	274.1	322.0	432.4	511.1	997.9	1,838.4	2,276.6	2,578.5	5,937.0	3,617.2	1,894.6

Performance 12-31-01

	1st Qtr	2nd Qtr	3rd Qtr	4th Qtr	Total
1997	–16.14	22.27	14.88	–6.45	10.19
1998	15.83	0.80	–26.63	29.58	11.00
1999	6.61	9.57	7.15	81.30	126.91
2000	11.27	–20.98	–6.98	–40.42	–51.27
2001	–43.18	20.35	–40.02	31.35	–46.12

Trailing	Total Return%	+/– S&P 500	+/– Russ Midcap Grth	% Rank All	% Rank Cat	Growth of $10,000
3 Mo	31.35	20.66	4.28	4	6	13,135
6 Mo	–21.22	–15.66	–12.96	99	96	7,878
1 Yr	–46.12	–34.24	–25.96	99	98	5,388
3 Yr Avg	–15.85	–14.83	–18.01	100	100	5,958
5 Yr Avg	–6.13	–16.83	–15.15	98	97	7,288
10 Yr Avg	6.11	–6.82	–5.00	68	90	18,087
15 Yr Avg	8.92	–4.81	–3.89	48	92	36,044

Tax Analysis	Tax-Adj Ret%	%Rank Cat	%Pretax Ret	%Rank Cat
3 Yr Avg	–17.89	100	—	—
5 Yr Avg	–7.64	97	—	—
10 Yr Avg	3.86	90	63.2	74

Potential Capital Gain Exposure: –50% of assets

Risk Analysis

Time Period	Load-Adj Return %	Risk %Rank[1] All	Risk %Rank[1] Cat	Morningstar Return	Morningstar Risk	Morningstar Risk-Adj Rating
1 Yr	–49.22					
3 Yr	–17.50	99	98	–3.81[2]	2.90	★
5 Yr	–7.24	99	98	–2.13[2]	2.59	★
10 Yr	5.48	99	100	0.08	2.41	★

Average Historical Rating (193 months): 2.8★s

[1]1=low, 100=high [2] T-Bill return substituted for category avg.

Category Rating (3 Yr)

1 2 3 4 5 — Worst ... Best

Return Low
Risk High

Other Measures	Standard Index S&P 500	Best Fit Index Wil 4500
Alpha	6.9	–4.1
Beta	2.37	2.03
R-Squared	46	92

Standard Deviation	63.91
Mean	–15.85
Sharpe Ratio	–0.39

Portfolio Analysis 07-31-01

Share change since 01-01 Total Stocks: 147	Sector	PE	YTD Ret%	% Assets
⊕ Marvell Tech	Technology	—	63.28	2.49
⊕ Smartforce PLC ADR	Technology	NMF	–34.10	2.29
Sonus Networks	Technology	—	–81.70	2.24
⊕ Lamar Advertising Cl A	Services	—	9.71	2.20
⊖ Manugistics Grp	Technology	—	–63.00	1.98
⊖ Peregrine Sys	Technology	—	–24.90	1.97
Univision Comms A	Services	96.3	–1.17	1.97
⊕ Invitrogen	Health	—	–28.30	1.79
⊕ Qlogic	Technology	49.5	–42.10	1.62
☼ Shire Pharma Grp	Health	—	–20.50	1.53
⊕ Alpha Inds	Technology	NMF	–41.00	1.48
⊕ Finisar	Technology	—	–64.90	1.41
⊕ Coach	Staples	—	35.58	1.35
⊕ Emulex	Technology	—	–50.50	1.32
⊕ Professional Detailing	Services	34.9	–78.80	1.29
⊕ Cytyc	Health	49.3	25.16	1.23
⊖ HomeStore.com	Services	—	–81.80	1.21
⊕ Plexus	Technology	25.1	–12.50	1.21
Time Warner Telecom Cl A	Services	—	–72.10	1.17
☼ Mirant	Utilities	8.3	–43.40	1.17
⊖ TMP Worldwide	Services	71.5	–22.00	1.17
⊖ Bed Bath & Beyond	Retail	53.0	51.51	1.17
☼ CDW Comp Centers	Retail	28.4	92.68	1.13
Dollar Tree Stores	Retail	30.9	26.16	1.12
☼ CIMA Labs	Health	39.3	–44.40	1.09

Current Investment Style

Style: Value Blnd Growth; Size: Large Med Small

	Stock Port Avg	Relative S&P 500 Current	Relative S&P 500 Hist	Rel Cat
Price/Earnings Ratio	40.3	1.30	1.23	1.16
Price/Book Ratio	5.0	0.87	1.34	0.87
Price/Cash Flow	27.8	1.54	1.46	1.20
3 Yr Earnings Growth	33.6[1]	2.29	—	1.43
1 Yr Earnings Est%	1.5[1]	—	—	0.16
Med Mkt Cap $mil	2,162	0.0	0.1	0.38

[1]figure is based on 50% or less of stocks

Special Securities % assets 07-31-01	
Restricted/Illiquid Secs	2
Emerging-Markets Secs	0
Options/Futures/Warrants	Yes

Composition % assets 07-31-01	
Cash	4.5
Stocks*	93.3
Bonds	0.0
Other	2.1
*Foreign (% stocks)	5.6

Market Cap	
Giant	0.0
Large	4.8
Medium	60.6
Small	34.5
Micro	0.1

Sector Weightings	% of Stocks	Rel S&P	5-Year High	5-Year Low
Utilities	2.7	0.9	3	0
Energy	0.0	0.0	4	0
Financials	1.9	0.1	10	0
Industrials	0.7	0.1	12	0
Durables	1.6	1.0	6	0
Staples	1.5	0.2	4	0
Services	21.2	2.0	50	12
Retail	9.0	1.3	26	1
Health	17.9	1.2	31	0
Technology	43.5	2.4	85	10

Analysis by Kelli Stebel 12-05-01

A new comanager and additional risk controls might not be enough to turn Putnam OTC Emerging Growth around.

Roland Gillis joined comanagers Mike Mufson and Steve Kirson here in September 2001. At this offering, as is the case at other Putnam funds, team management is the name of the game and the fund will be run collectively by the three managers.

Gillis reports that he and the team have continued to institute new risks controls, in hopes of avoiding the performance swings of the past few years. While the fund turned in top-flight returns in 1999, it's paid dearly for its ultra-aggressive stance during the past 20 months, posting some of the worst returns in its category. In addition to new quantitative models, Gillis says they now have a ranking system. Each stock is ranked from 1 to 5, based on a combination of quantitative measures and Putnam's analysts' sentiments. Based on these new tools and models, Gillis insists that this fund will no longer take dramatic sector bets, which in the past included an 85% stake in tech stocks.

That said, this fund is still one of Putnam's most-aggressive offerings, as the team continues to look for companies growing at a 20% to 40% clip. Gillis says that they bulked up on health care recently, particularly biotech stocks such as Invitrogen. The team hasn't abandoned tech, either. They've recently added several storage names, such as McData, which Gillis says was trading dirt-cheap.

Despite the fund's recent alterations, this fund will likely remain one of the industry's more-volatile offerings. And while Gillis is an experienced manager, his performance at his other mid-cap growth charges, Putnam New Century Growth and Putnam Voyager II, doesn't inspire much confidence, as both funds have subpar records under his watch. In short, investors can do without this hyper-aggressive fund.

Address:	One Post Office Square Boston, MA 02109 800–225–1581 / 617–292–1000
Web Address:	www.putnaminvestments.com
Inception:	11-01-82
Advisor:	Putnam Inv. Mgmt.
Subadvisor:	None
NTF Plans:	Fidelity Inst.

Minimum Purchase:	$500	Add: $50	IRA: $250
Min Auto Inv Plan:	$25	Add: $25	
Sales Fees:	5.75%L, 0.35%B		
Management Fee:	.70% mx./.50% mn.		
Actual Fees:	Mgt: 0.54%	Dist: 0.25%	
Expense Projections:	3Yr: $875	5Yr: $1096	10Yr: $1729
Avg Brok Commission:	—	Income Distrib: Annually	
Total Cost (relative to category):	—		

Putnam Small Cap Value A

Ticker	Load	NAV	Yield	Total Assets	Mstar Category
PSLAX	5.75%	$14.00	0.0%	$1,085.4 mil	Small Value

Prospectus Objective: Growth

Putnam Small Cap Value Fund seeks capital appreciation.

The fund normally invests in common stocks of small and medium-sized companies similar in size to the Russell 2000 Index. It typically invests in companies that have market capitalizations of less than $500 million. The fund may invest in foreign securities including emerging markets securities. It may also invest in preferred stocks, convertible securities, derivative instruments and fixed-income securities.

Class A shares have front loads and lower 12b-1 fees; B shares have deferred loads and full 12b-1 fees; C shares have level loads and full 12b-1 fees.

Historical Profile
Return —
Risk —
Rating
Not Rated

Investment Style
Equity
Average Stock %: 97% (1999), 99% (2000), 98% (12-01)

▼ Manager Change
▽ Partial Manager Change

Fund Performance vs. Category Average
Quarterly Fund Return +/– Category Average
— Category Baseline

Performance Quartile (within Category)

Portfolio Manager(s)

Edward T. Shadek Jr.. Since 4-99. BA Pomona C.; MBA Harvard Graduate School of Business. Other funds currently managed: Putnam Small Cap Value B, Putnam Small Cap Value C, Putnam Mid Cap Value A.

Simon Sheldon. Since 9-00. Other funds currently managed: Putnam Small Cap Value B, Putnam Small Cap Value C, Putnam Small Cap Value M.

1990	1991	1992	1993	1994	1995	1996	1997	1998	1999	2000	12-01	History
—	—	—	—	—	—	—	—	—	9.70	12.03	14.00	NAV
—	—	—	—	—	—	—	—	—	15.02*	24.43	18.95	Total Return %
—	—	—	—	—	—	—	—	—	5.14*	33.53	30.82	+/– S&P 500
—	—	—	—	—	—	—	—	—	—	1.62	4.93	+/– Russell 2000 V
—	—	—	—	—	—	—	—	—	0.42	0.00	0.00	Income Return %
—	—	—	—	—	—	—	—	—	14.60	24.43	18.95	Capital Return %
—	—	—	—	—	—	—	—	—	—	25	39	Total Rtn % Rank Cat
—	—	—	—	—	—	—	—	—	0.04	0.00	0.00	Income $
—	—	—	—	—	—	—	—	—	0.04	0.04	0.30	Capital Gains $
—	—	—	—	—	—	—	—	—	—	1.38	1.31	Expense Ratio %
—	—	—	—	—	—	—	—	—	—	–0.57	0.25	Income Ratio %
—	—	—	—	—	—	—	—	—	—	42	34	Turnover Rate %
—	—	—	—	—	—	—	—	—	66.9	209.2	540.2	Net Assets $mil

Performance 12-31-01

	1st Qtr	2nd Qtr	3rd Qtr	4th Qtr	Total
1997	—	—	—	—	—
1998	—	—	—	—	—
1999	—	—	–10.07	5.24	15.02 *
2000	7.01	–0.19	7.24	8.64	24.43
2001	1.25	15.02	–14.06	18.85	18.95

Trailing	Total Return%	+/– S&P 500	+/– Russ 2000V	% Rank All	% Rank Cat	Growth of $10,000
3 Mo	18.85	8.16	2.13	16	34	11,885
6 Mo	2.14	7.69	0.98	21	48	10,214
1 Yr	18.95	30.82	4.93	2	39	11,895
3 Yr Avg	—	—	—	—	—	—
5 Yr Avg	—	—	—	—	—	—
10 Yr Avg	—	—	—	—	—	—
15 Yr Avg	—	—	—	—	—	—

Tax Analysis	Tax-Adj Ret%	%Rank Cat	%Pretax Ret	%Rank Cat
3 Yr Avg	—	—	—	—
5 Yr Avg	—	—	—	—
10 Yr Avg	—	—	—	—

Potential Capital Gain Exposure: 14% of assets

Risk Analysis

Time Period	Load-Adj Return %	Risk %Rank[1] All	Risk %Rank[1] Cat	Morningstar Return	Morningstar Risk	Morningstar Risk-Adj Rating
1 Yr	12.11					
3 Yr	—	—	—	—	—	
5 Yr	—	—	—	—	—	
Incept	18.98	—	—	—	—	

Average Historical Rating —

[1]1=low, 100=high

Category Rating (3 Yr)

Return
Risk

Other Measures	Standard Index S&P 500	Best Fit Index
Alpha	—	—
Beta	—	—
R-Squared	—	—
Standard Deviation		—
Mean		—
Sharpe Ratio		—

Analysis by William Samuel Rocco 12-12-01

The wide-ranging value hound remains a solid offering.

Putnam Small Cap Value Fund continues to make full use of the industry spectrum while pursuing attractively priced issues with catalysts for improvement. Comanagers Sheldon Simon and Edward Shadek purchased or added to several beaten-up technology stocks earlier this fall, including Mentor Graphics and FileNet. Thus, the fund now has about 16% of its assets in software, computer distributors, and other tech stocks, while the typical small-value offering has 11% of its assets in such issues.

Meanwhile, Simon and Shadek have also been active at the other end of the industry range. They've added to several of their cyclical holdings, including Crompton and some other specialty-chemical makers, because they're optimistic that the economy will rebound in 2002. They've also added to a few of their energy stocks on weakness, so the fund continues to be overweighted in that sector.

This broad-based approach has done more good than harm this year. While most of their energy stocks have stung, several of their tech picks have come through. Computer-parts distributor Anixter International is up 44% this year, for example, while the network- equipment maker Inter-Tel is up three times that amount. Several of its industrial stocks have also earned strong gains. Thus, the fund has returned 1 percentage point more than the typical small-value fund for the year to date through Dec. 11, 2001.

The fund, which opened in April 1999, posted top-quartile results in 2000's small-value rally, and it didn't fare too badly over the latter part of 1999. Moreover, its portfolio is normally spread across more than 200 names, as well as across the industry spectrum, so volatility shouldn't be a problem here. We think this youngster is a keeper.

Portfolio Analysis 08-31-01

Share change since 02-01 Total Stocks: 225	Sector	PE	YTD Ret%	% Assets
⊕ Omnicare	Health	38.3	15.52	1.51
⊕ Sierra Pacific Resources	Utilities	—	–2.25	1.38
⊕ General Cable	Industrials	81.9	200.10	1.35
⊕ AAR	Industrials	15.3	–27.20	1.29
⊕ Anixter Intl	Technology	27.1	34.15	1.11
⊕ GenCorp	Industrials	19.1	48.08	1.07
⊕ Webster Finl	Financials	12.2	13.76	1.04
⊕ Hughes Sply	Industrials	24.7	75.09	1.02
⊕ Sovereign Bancorp	Financials	76.5	52.19	1.01
⊕ Tupperware	Industrials	20.5	–1.97	1.00
⊕ Pentair	Industrials	38.0	54.40	0.97
☼ Universal Compression	Energy	—	–21.70	0.95
⊕ PolyOne	Industrials	—	71.42	0.93
⊕ US Oncology	Health	—	19.44	0.89
⊕ Banknorth Grp	Financials	13.3	15.81	0.89
⊕ Claire's Stores	Retail	21.6	–15.00	0.85
⊕ Inter-Tel	Technology	45.8	150.90	0.84
⊕ Intl Multifoods	Staples	24.4	17.66	0.83
⊕ CBRL Grp	Services	23.7	61.98	0.82
☼ Borland Software	Technology	44.7	183.10	0.81
⊕ BE Aerospace	Industrials	14.3	–42.60	0.80
⊕ Crompton	Industrials	—	–12.40	0.80
☼ Stewart Enterprises	Services	—	214.20	0.78
⊕ Fidelity Natl Finl	Financials	8.5	–25.00	0.77
⊕ USFreightways	Services	15.9	5.74	0.76

Current Investment Style

Style: Value Blnd Growth; Size: Large Med Small

	Stock Port Avg	Relative S&P 500 Current	Relative S&P 500 Hist	Rel Cat
Price/Earnings Ratio	23.6	0.76	—	1.09
Price/Book Ratio	2.4	0.43	—	1.00
Price/Cash Flow	12.2	0.68	—	0.96
3 Yr Earnings Growth	4.9	0.33	—	0.42
1 Yr Earnings Est%	–7.6	4.32	—	1.93
Med Mkt Cap $mil	798	0.0	—	0.92

Special Securities % assets 08-31-01	
Restricted/Illiquid Secs	2
Emerging-Markets Secs	0
Options/Futures/Warrants	No

Composition % assets 08-31-01	
Cash	3.1
Stocks*	96.4
Bonds	0.0
Other	0.5
*Foreign (% stocks)	0.0

Market Cap	
Giant	0.0
Large	0.0
Medium	23.3
Small	71.0
Micro	5.7

Sector Weightings	% of Stocks	Rel S&P	5-Year High	5-Year Low
Utilities	1.8	0.6	—	—
Energy	5.9	0.8	—	—
Financials	15.7	0.9	—	—
Industrials	28.4	2.5	—	—
Durables	5.3	3.4	—	—
Staples	4.0	0.5	—	—
Services	11.6	1.1	—	—
Retail	6.4	1.0	—	—
Health	10.1	0.7	—	—
Technology	10.9	0.6	—	—

Address:	One Post Office Square Boston, MA 02109 617-292-1000 / 800-225-1581
Web Address:	www.putnaminvestments.com
*Inception:	04-13-99
Advisor:	Putnam Inv. Mgmt.
Subadvisor:	None
NTF Plans:	Fidelity Inst.

Minimum Purchase:	$500	Add: $50 IRA: —
Min Auto Inv Plan:	$25	Add: $25
Sales Fees:	5.75%L, 0.35%B	
Management Fee:	.80% mx./.53% mn.	
Actual Fees:	Mgt: 0.80%	Dist: 0.25%
Expense Projections:	3Yr: $1022	5Yr: — 10Yr: —
Avg Brok Commission:	—	Income Distrib: Annually
Total Cost (relative to category):	—	

Putnam Vista A

Ticker	Load	NAV	Yield	Total Assets	Mstar Category
PVISX	5.75%	$8.64	0.0%	$6,699.8 mil	Mid-Cap Growth

Prospectus Objective: Growth

Putnam Vista Fund - seeks capital appreciation.

The fund invests primarily in common stocks of U.S. companies, with a focus on growth stocks. The fund invests mainly in mid-sized companies. It can invest in foreign securities and options and futures.

This fund offers multiple shareclasses, all of which differ in fee structure and availability. Prior to Nov. 3, 1989, the fund was named Putnam Vista Basic Value Fund.

Historical Profile
Return Average
Risk High
Rating ★★ Below Avg

Investment Style
Equity
Average Stock %: 91% 98% 97% 98% 99% 95%

▼ Manager Change
▽ Partial Manager Change

Fund Performance vs. Category Average
▪ Quarterly Fund Return +/– Category Average
— Category Baseline

Performance Quartile (within Category)

Portfolio Manager(s)

Eric M. Wetlaufer, CFA. Since 11-97.
Margery C. Parker. Since 1-98.
Dana F. Clark. Since 1-99.
Kenneth J. Doerr. Since 5-01.

1990	1991	1992	1993	1994	1995	1996	1997	1998	1999	2000	12-01	History
5.71	7.20	6.98	7.52	7.18	9.10	10.45	11.87	13.07	17.46	13.02	8.64	NAV
–7.03	37.23	17.85	17.45	–3.86	39.37	22.35	23.23	19.53	53.21	–4.00	–33.64	Total Return %
–3.91	6.75	10.23	7.39	–5.17	1.84	–0.60	–10.12	–9.04	32.17	5.10	–21.76	+/– S&P 500
–1.89	–9.80	9.13	6.26	–1.69	5.39	4.87	0.69	1.67	1.91	7.75	–13.48	+/– Russ Midcap Grth
2.22	3.31	1.72	1.02	0.00	0.00	0.00	0.00	0.00	0.00	0.00	0.00	Income Return %
–9.24	33.92	16.13	16.43	–3.85	39.37	22.35	23.23	19.53	53.21	–4.00	–33.64	Capital Return %
56	81	12	40	62	26	24	25	32	51	47	84	Total Rtn % Rank Cat
0.15	0.19	0.12	0.07	0.00	0.00	0.00	0.00	0.00	0.00	0.00	0.00	Income $
0.26	0.40	1.34	0.58	0.05	0.86	0.67	0.96	1.03	2.29	3.82	0.00	Capital Gains $
0.92	0.99	0.96	0.96	1.09	1.07	1.10	1.04	0.98	0.94	0.87	0.89	Expense Ratio %
3.10	2.73	1.92	1.08	0.29	0.26	–0.29	–0.25	–0.38	–0.41	–0.51	–0.47	Income Ratio %
47	76	144	121	94	115	107	83	111	155	115	109	Turnover Rate %
237.2	314.2	368.4	518.7	680.9	996.3	1,677.6	2,797.2	3,437.8	5,240.3	6,318.2	4,176.2	Net Assets $mil

Performance 12-31-01

	1st Qtr	2nd Qtr	3rd Qtr	4th Qtr	Total
1997	–6.22	17.86	11.77	–0.25	23.23
1998	12.72	3.74	–17.44	23.81	19.53
1999	4.74	7.38	–4.15	42.12	53.21
2000	21.65	–4.24	4.18	–20.90	–4.00
2001	–31.18	13.17	–32.15	25.58	–33.64

Trailing	Total Return%	+/– S&P 500	+/– Russ Midcap Grth	% Rank All	% Rank Cat	Growth of $10,000
3 Mo	25.58	14.90	–1.48	7	16	12,558
6 Mo	–14.79	–9.24	–6.53	95	78	8,521
1 Yr	–33.64	–21.76	–13.48	96	84	6,636
3 Yr Avg	–0.81	0.22	–2.96	77	75	9,760
5 Yr Avg	7.53	–3.17	–1.49	32	61	14,377
10 Yr Avg	12.55	–0.38	1.45	15	26	32,624
15 Yr Avg	13.08	–0.65	0.27	16	29	63,237

Tax Analysis	Tax-Adj Ret%	%Rank Cat	%Pretax Ret	%Rank Cat
3 Yr Avg	–4.06	78	—	—
5 Yr Avg	4.66	60	61.9	75
10 Yr Avg	9.60	31	76.5	40

Potential Capital Gain Exposure: –49% of assets

Risk Analysis

Time Period	Load-Adj Return %	Risk %Rank[1] All	Risk %Rank[1] Cat	Morningstar Return	Morningstar Risk	Morningstar Risk-Adj Rating
1 Yr	–37.46					
3 Yr	–2.74	95	73	–1.51[2]	1.69	★★
5 Yr	6.27	92	63	0.28[2]	1.58	★★
10 Yr	11.89	92	42	1.08	1.47	★★

Average Historical Rating (193 months): 3.4★s

[1] 1=low, 100=high [2] T-Bill return substituted for category avg.

Category Rating (3 Yr)

1 2 3 4 5
Worst Best

Return: Below Avg
Risk: Above Avg

Other Measures	Standard Index S&P 500	Best Fit Index Wil 4500
Alpha	8.5	0.8
Beta	1.61	1.25
R-Squared	55	91

Standard Deviation	39.44
Mean	–0.81
Sharpe Ratio	–0.17

Portfolio Analysis 09-30-01

Share change since 07-01 Total Stocks: 147	Sector	PE	YTD Ret%	% Assets
⊖ Convergys	Services	41.2	–17.20	2.79
⊖ Perkinelmer	Services	29.9	–32.70	2.44
⊖ Andrx	Health	66.4	21.66	2.34
⊕ Starbucks	Retail	41.4	–13.90	2.15
⊕ Interpublic Grp	Services	—	–29.80	2.05
⊖ Ivax	Health	17.5	–34.20	2.00
☼ AmerisourceBergen	N/A	—	—	1.93
⊖ Waters	Industrials	32.0	–53.50	1.89
⊕ King Pharmaceuticals	Health	45.8	8.68	1.79
⊖ MedImmune	Health	78.6	–2.81	1.78
⊕ TJX	Retail	23.2	44.39	1.73
⊖ VeriSign	Technology	—	–48.70	1.73
⊖ Peregrine Sys	Technology	—	–24.90	1.65
⊕ Americredit	Financials	10.6	15.78	1.60
⊕ SunGard Data Sys	Technology	33.3	22.78	1.48
⊕ IDEC Pharmaceuticals	Health	NMF	9.09	1.48
⊖ Sysco	Staples	28.8	–11.70	1.46
⊖ Estee Lauder Cl A	Staples	27.2	–26.40	1.44
⊕ Genzyme Corporation General Di	Health	—	33.11	1.41
⊕ Zions Bancorp	Financials	17.2	–14.50	1.37
⊖ Smith Intl	Industrials	19.3	–28.00	1.31
⊕ Metris	Financials	11.4	–2.13	1.29
⊖ Lamar Advertising Cl A	Services	—	9.71	1.28
⊖ Family Dollar Stores	Retail	27.3	41.11	1.27
⊖ Gilead Sciences	Health	—	58.48	1.25

Current Investment Style

Style: Value Blnd Growth; Size: Large Med Small

	Stock Port Avg	Relative S&P 500 Current	Relative S&P 500 Hist	Rel Cat
Price/Earnings Ratio	32.3	1.04	1.24	0.93
Price/Book Ratio	5.8	1.01	1.09	1.01
Price/Cash Flow	25.2	1.40	1.27	1.09
3 Yr Earnings Growth	23.9[1]	1.64	1.33	1.02
1 Yr Earnings Est%	7.9	—	—	0.84
Med Mkt Cap $mil	5,565	0.1	0.1	0.99

[1] figure is based on 50% or less of stocks

Analysis by Kelli Stebel 12-10-01

Putnam Vista Fund's recent performance looks bleak, but that's not enough reason to jump ship.

This fund's returns have been absolutely horrible over the past year. From March 2000, when the Nasdaq began to teeter, through November 2001, the fund has lost 32%, compared with a 25% drop by its average mid-cap growth peer.

Plain and simple, the fund should have done better. Lead manager Eric Wetlaufer and his team follow a fairly moderate approach, which should have held it in good stead during this market downturn. Instead, the fund has been sacked by its complement of energy stocks. Holdings like National-Oilwell, which was a source of strength throughout much of last year, turned sour in 2001. (National-Oilwell is no longer in the portfolio.) And the fund missed out on the tech sector's April rally, mostly because its software names didn't pop as much as hardware companies.

Wetlaufer isn't about to throw in the towel after a few quarters of underperformance, though. Though he remains committed to software firms, he began dabbling in hardware names over the summer. For instance, he added Sonus Networks, which he likes for its growing market share and new product line. And the fund has rebounded over the past month, as technology stocks like Sonus have shown signs of life.

Although the fund's performance over the past year is disappointing, investors shouldn't panic. The fund's valuation-conscious strategy has typically insulated it during market downdrafts (though it has also limited returns during go-go growth markets like 1999's). And small individual stock positions mean the fund doesn't carry a lot of issue-specific risk. This fund remains a well-diversified, fairly moderate portfolio.

Special Securities % assets 09-30-01	
Restricted/Illiquid Secs	0
Emerging-Markets Secs	0
Options/Futures/Warrants	Yes

Sector Weightings	% of Stocks	Rel S&P	5-Year High	5-Year Low
Utilities	0.5	0.2	6	0
Energy	3.9	0.6	8	0
Financials	11.8	0.7	21	1
Industrials	6.1	0.5	19	0
Durables	3.0	2.0	10	1
Staples	3.0	0.4	11	0
Services	17.3	1.6	30	12
Retail	7.8	1.2	17	5
Health	24.5	1.7	24	6
Technology	22.1	1.2	55	5

Composition % assets 09-30-01	
Cash	1.3
Stocks*	98.7
Bonds	0.0
Other	0.0
*Foreign (% stocks)	4.6

Market Cap	
Giant	0.0
Large	21.2
Medium	73.8
Small	5.0
Micro	0.0

Address: One Post Office Square, Boston, MA 02109, 800-225-1581 / 617-292-1000
Web Address: www.putnaminvestments.com

Inception: 06-03-68
Advisor: Putnam Inv. Mgmt.
Subadvisor: None
NTF Plans: Fidelity Inst.

Minimum Purchase: $500 Add: $50 IRA: $250
Min Auto Inv Plan: $25 Add: $25
Sales Fees: 5.75%L, 0.35%B
Management Fee: .65% mx./.45% mn.
Actual Fees: Mgt: 0.49% Dist: 0.25%
Expense Projections: 3Yr: $869 5Yr: $1086 10Yr: $1707
Avg Brok Commission: — Income Distrib: Annually
Total Cost (relative to category):

Putnam Voyager A

Ticker	Load	NAV	Yield	Total Assets	Mstar Category
PVOYX	5.75%	$17.30	0.2%	$25,469.8 mil	Large Growth

Prospectus Objective: Growth

Putnam Voyager Fund seeks capital appreciation.

The fund invests primarily in common stocks. It generally invests in securities of smaller and less-seasoned companies. The fund may employ leverage. It may invest in foreign securities. The fund may also purchase stock-index futures contracts and related options, and trade for short-term profits.

Class A shares have front loads; B shares have deferred loads, the highest 12b-1 fees, and conversion features; M shares have smaller front loads. C shares also.

Historical Profile
Return Average
Risk Above Avg
Rating ★★★ Neutral

Investment Style
Equity
Average Stock %: 96% 99% 97% 99% 97% 93%

▼ Manager Change
▽ Partial Manager Change

Fund Performance vs. Category Average
■ Quarterly Fund Return +/– Category Average
— Category Baseline

Performance Quartile (within Category)

Portfolio Manager(s)

James C. Wiess, CFA. Since 11-00.
Michael P. Stack, CFA. Since 11-97.
Paul E. Marrkand. Since 11-99.
Kevin M. Divney. Since 11-00.
Paul Warren. Since 5-01.
Michael E. Nance. Since 5-01.

1990	1991	1992	1993	1994	1995	1996	1997	1998	1999	2000	12–01	History
7.07	10.07	10.52	11.99	11.52	15.25	16.12	19.05	21.92	30.96	23.30	17.30	NAV
–2.80	50.31	9.72	18.40	0.44	40.16	12.80	25.98	24.06	56.13	–16.78	–22.46	Total Return %
0.32	19.83	2.10	8.35	–0.87	2.62	–10.15	–7.37	–4.52	35.10	–7.68	–10.58	+/– S&P 500
–4.17	10.91	5.83	18.48	–4.41	1.50	–12.72	–7.76	–21.04	26.46	7.74	–1.96	+/– Russ Top 200 Grt
0.88	0.37	0.01	0.00	0.00	0.00	0.00	0.00	0.00	0.00	0.00	0.18	Income Return %
–3.68	49.94	9.71	18.40	0.44	40.15	12.80	25.98	24.06	56.13	–16.78	–22.64	Capital Return %
56	29	24	17	23	11	88	50	79	18	59	49	Total Rtn % Rank Cat
0.07	0.03	0.00	0.00	0.00	0.00	0.00	0.00	0.00	0.00	0.00	0.04	Income $
0.63	0.48	0.52	0.46	0.51	0.86	1.09	1.21	1.59	2.98	2.60	0.75	Capital Gains $
0.97	1.10	1.20	1.12	1.10	1.07	1.03	1.02	0.96	0.90	0.86	0.88	Expense Ratio %
1.10	0.29	0.27	–0.14	–0.18	0.17	–0.10	0.00	–0.20	–0.25	–0.37	0.33	Income Ratio %
62	49	44	65	58	65	58	60	60	85	77	140	Turnover Rate %
751.7	1,320.0	1,932.4	2,884.4	3,469.0	5,986.2	8,633.1	11,755.4	15,569.9	24,363.4	21,539.0	15,952.5	Net Assets $mil

Performance 12-31-01

	1st Qtr	2nd Qtr	3rd Qtr	4th Qtr	Total
1997	–5.09	17.32	11.92	1.08	25.98
1998	14.65	1.88	–16.18	26.72	24.06
1999	5.89	7.84	–2.48	40.21	56.13
2000	10.30	–8.52	–3.33	–14.69	–16.78
2001	–19.06	6.57	–18.81	10.71	–22.46

Trailing	Total Return%	+/– S&P 500	+/– Russ Top 200 Grth	% Rank All	% Rank Cat	Growth of $10,000
3 Mo	10.71	0.02	–2.15	38	79	11,071
6 Mo	–10.11	–4.56	–3.12	85	62	8,989
1 Yr	–22.46	–10.58	–1.96	84	49	7,754
3 Yr Avg	0.25	1.28	8.27	72	25	10,075
5 Yr Avg	9.50	–1.19	0.91	21	40	15,746
10 Yr Avg	12.50	–0.43	1.42	15	16	32,482
15 Yr Avg	14.79	1.05	1.42	7	10	79,152

Tax Analysis	Tax-Adj Ret%	%Rank Cat	%Pretax Ret	%Rank Cat
3 Yr Avg	–1.57	30	—	—
5 Yr Avg	7.64	38	80.4	45
10 Yr Avg	10.75	12	86.0	18

Potential Capital Gain Exposure: –4% of assets

Risk Analysis

Time Period	Load-Adj Return %	Risk %Rank[1] All	Risk %Rank[1] Cat	Morningstar Return	Morningstar Risk	Morningstar Risk-Adj Rating
1 Yr	–26.92					
3 Yr	–1.71	83	40	–1.32[2]	1.23	★★
5 Yr	8.22	83	50	0.74[2]	1.21	★★★
10 Yr	11.84	86	48	1.07	1.24	★★★

Average Historical Rating (193 months): 3.7★s

[1] 1=low, 100=high [2] T-Bill return substituted for category avg.

Category Rating (3 Yr)

1 2 3 4 5
Worst Best

Return Above Avg
Risk Average

Other Measures	Standard Index S&P 500	Best Fit Index Wil 4500
Alpha	3.9	–1.7
Beta	1.21	0.82
R–Squared	67	84

Standard Deviation	25.85
Mean	0.25
Sharpe Ratio	–0.21

Portfolio Analysis 09-30-01

Share change since 06–01 Total Stocks: 348	Sector	PE	YTD Ret%	% Assets
⊖ General Elec	Industrials	30.1	–15.00	4.52
⊖ Pfizer	Health	34.7	–12.40	4.32
⊖ Microsoft	Technology	57.6	52.78	3.78
⊕ Johnson & Johnson	Health	16.6	14.01	2.48
⊕ Philip Morris	Staples	12.1	9.12	2.24
⊕ American Intl Grp	Financials	42.0	–19.20	2.23
⊕ ExxonMobil	Energy	15.3	–7.59	2.08
⊖ Merck	Health	19.1	–35.90	1.90
⊕ Citigroup	Financials	20.0	0.03	1.89
⊖ AOL Time Warner	Technology	—	–7.76	1.77
⊖ Wal–Mart Stores	Retail	40.3	8.94	1.67
⊕ Intel	Technology	73.1	4.89	1.60
⊖ American Home Products	Health	—	–1.91	1.47
⊖ Cisco Sys	Technology	—	–52.60	1.42
⊕ Tyco Intl	Industrials	27.1	6.23	1.36
⊕ Schering–Plough	Health	22.2	–35.90	1.32
⊕ SBC Comms	Services	18.4	–16.00	1.30
⊕ Freddie Mac	Financials	14.0	–3.87	1.27
⊖ Coca–Cola	Staples	35.5	–21.40	1.27
⊖ IBM	Technology	26.9	43.00	1.26
⊖ Viacom Cl B	Services	—	—	1.19
⊕ Sprint (PCS Group)	Services	—	19.43	1.19
⊕ Motorola	Technology	—	–25.00	1.19
⊖ Medtronic	Health	76.4	–14.70	1.13
⊕ US Bancorp	Financials	13.5	–6.14	1.13

Current Investment Style

Style: Value Blnd Growth; Size: Large Med Small

	Stock Port Avg	Relative S&P 500 Current	Relative S&P 500 Hist	Rel Cat
Price/Earnings Ratio	30.5	0.99	1.21	0.86
Price/Book Ratio	6.4	1.12	1.14	1.00
Price/Cash Flow	19.5	1.08	1.22	0.86
3 Yr Earnings Growth	18.8	1.29	1.33	0.87
1 Yr Earnings Est%	1.8	—	—	0.60
Med Mkt Cap $mil	69,260	1.1	1.1	1.46

Analysis by Kelli Stebel 11-02-01

Investors should hold off sending any money here until Putnam Voyager sorts itself out.

For the third time in 2001, the fund has undergone a management change. Bob Beck and Chuck Swanberg left earlier this year, and recently, Roland Gillis stepped down, too (though he is remaining on other Putnam funds). With those changes, Putnam has effectively removed the experienced management team who built this fund's once-stellar record back in the early and mid-1990s.

Current lead manager Jim Weiss and his team have also adjusted the fund's approach. Rather than segmenting their analysis of stocks by market cap, they now aim to invest in a mix of consistent growth and riskier stocks, such as former hot-growth issues that have fallen on hard times. These days, for example, Weiss has picked up shares of J.P. Morgan Chase, which he thinks is trading well below its true value. And although Weiss said the portfolio would hold companies of any size, its asset base of about $26 billion makes establishing meaningful positions in small- and mid-cap stocks unlikely.

While these changes won't alter the fund's market-cap focus—it's been entrenched in the large-growth category—how effectively the current team can implement its approach remains to be seen. The fund has continued to put up decent numbers in recent years, and Putnam's deep research staff may also comfort investors. But there is always cause for concern when several experienced, talented managers depart. Moreover, this is yet another example of Putnam's failure to close star funds in a timely manner. Had the firm closed this fund years ago, it could have maintained its all-cap approach, which the managers had used to great effect.

Given all the question marks here, current investors should take a wait-and-see approach as the fund tries to establish a new identity.

Special Securities % assets 09-30-01	
Restricted/Illiquid Secs	1
Emerging–Markets Secs	Trace
Options/Futures/Warrants	Yes

Composition % assets 09-30-01	
Cash	1.7
Stocks*	97.0
Bonds	0.4
Other	0.9
*Foreign (% stocks)	2.0

Market Cap	
Giant	58.0
Large	31.8
Medium	9.3
Small	1.0
Micro	0.0

Sector Weightings	% of Stocks	Rel S&P	5-Year High	5-Year Low
Utilities	2.2	0.7	3	0
Energy	5.5	0.8	7	1
Financials	15.7	0.9	16	6
Industrials	8.9	0.8	13	3
Durables	0.4	0.2	4	0
Staples	8.2	1.0	8	0
Services	11.4	1.1	42	10
Retail	7.1	1.0	16	6
Health	21.5	1.5	23	6
Technology	19.2	1.1	44	11

Address:	One Post Office Square Boston, MA 02109 800–225–1581 / 617–292–1000
Web Address:	www.putnaminvestments.com
Inception:	04-01-69
Advisor:	Putnam Inv. Mgmt.
Subadvisor:	None
NTF Plans:	Fidelity Inst.

Minimum Purchase:	$500	Add: $50 IRA: $250
Min Auto Inv Plan:	$25	Add: $25
Sales Fees:	5.75%L, 0.35%B	
Management Fee:	.70% mx./.50% mn.	
Actual Fees:	Mgt: 0.48%	Dist: 0.25%
Expense Projections:	3Yr: $863	5Yr: $1075 10Yr: $1685
Avg Brok Commission:	—	Income Distrib: Annually
Total Cost (relative to category):	—	

Quaker Aggressive Growth A

Ticker	Load	NAV	Yield	Total Assets	Mstar Category
QUAGX	5.50%	$17.96	0.2%	$111.7 mil	Large Growth

Prospectus Objective: Aggressive Growth

Quaker Aggressive Growth Fund seeks long-term capital growth.

The fund invests in a limited number of equities issued by companies that the advisor judges to exhibit a high probablity of superior growth prospects. It may invest heavily in small capitalization companies. The advisor seeks to identify undervalued companies undergoing positive changes that have not been recognized by the market. The fund may also short-sell up to 25% of assets in order to enhance potential gains.

Prior to July 3, 2000, the fund was named Quaker Aggressive Growth Fund.

Historical Profile
Return High
Risk Low
Rating ★★★★★ Highest

Investment Style
Equity
Average Stock %
93% 72% 48%

▼ Manager Change
▽ Partial Manager Change

Fund Performance vs. Category Average
■ Quarterly Fund Return +/– Category Average
— Category Baseline

Performance Quartile (within Category)

Portfolio Manager(s)

Manu Daftary. Since 11-96. Other funds currently managed: Quaker Aggressive Growth B, Quaker Aggressive Growth C, Quaker Aggressive Growth I.

1990	1991	1992	1993	1994	1995	1996	1997	1998	1999	2000	12-01	History
—	—	—	—	—	—	10.33	10.48	13.04	19.50	19.58	17.96	NAV
—	—	—	—	—	—	3.43*	20.04	29.78	96.89	15.48	–8.06	Total Return %
—	—	—	—	—	—	–2.22*	–13.31	1.21	75.86	24.58	3.82	+/– S&P 500
—	—	—	—	—	—	—	–13.70	–15.32	67.22	40.01	12.44	+/– Russ Top 200 Grt
—	—	—	—	—	—	0.13	0.00	0.55	1.30	1.73	0.22	Income Return %
—	—	—	—	—	—	3.30	20.04	29.23	95.60	13.75	–8.28	Capital Return %
—	—	—	—	—	—	—	77	58	5	2	4	Total Rtn % Rank Cat
—	—	—	—	—	—	0.01	0.00	0.06	0.16	0.34	0.04	Income $
—	—	—	—	—	—	0.00	1.91	0.41	4.49	2.54	0.00	Capital Gains $
—	—	—	—	—	—	—	1.34	1.35	1.35	—	—	Expense Ratio %
—	—	—	—	—	—	—	0.64	–0.04	1.04	—	—	Income Ratio %
—	—	—	—	—	—	—	—	877	1,696	886	—	Turnover Rate %
—	—	—	—	—	—	0.3	1.3	—	8.1	22.7	101.0	Net Assets $mil

Performance 12-31-01

	1st Qtr	2nd Qtr	3rd Qtr	4th Qtr	Total
1997	1.06	7.54	16.02	–4.80	20.04
1998	13.17	1.64	–5.34	19.20	29.78
1999	19.94	10.05	9.83	35.82	96.89
2000	18.46	–2.03	2.30	–2.73	15.48
2001	–3.68	–0.90	–1.50	–2.21	–8.06

Trailing	Total Return%	+/– S&P 500	+/– Russ Top 200 Grth	% Rank All	% Rank Cat	Growth of $10,000
3 Mo	–2.21	–12.90	–15.07	99	100	9,779
6 Mo	–3.68	1.88	3.31	54	10	9,632
1 Yr	–8.06	3.82	12.44	57	4	9,194
3 Yr Avg	27.87	28.89	35.89	1	1	20,905
5 Yr Avg	26.64	15.94	18.05	1	1	32,569
10 Yr Avg	—	—	—	—	—	—
15 Yr Avg	—	—	—	—	—	—

Tax Analysis	Tax-Adj Ret%	%Rank Cat	%Pretax Ret	%Rank Cat
3 Yr Avg	21.47	1	77.0	49
5 Yr Avg	20.81	1	78.1	51
10 Yr Avg	—	—	—	—

Potential Capital Gain Exposure: –6% of assets

Risk Analysis

Time Period	Load-Adj Return %	Risk %Rank[1] All	Risk %Rank[1] Cat	Morningstar Return	Morningstar Risk	Morningstar Risk-Adj Rating
1 Yr	–13.11					
3 Yr	25.48	35	1	5.26[2]	0.43	★★★★★
5 Yr	25.21	43	1	6.47[2]	0.55	★★★★★
Incept	25.12	—	—	—	—	

Average Historical Rating (27 months): 5.0★s

[1]1=low, 100=high [2] T-Bill return substituted for category avg.

Category Rating (3 Yr)

1 2 3 4 5
Worst Best

Return High
Risk Low

Other Measures	Standard Index S&P 500	Best Fit Index Wil 4500
Alpha	26.0	24.0
Beta	0.35	0.41
R-Squared	9	33

Standard Deviation	25.20
Mean	27.87
Sharpe Ratio	1.02

Portfolio Analysis 12-31-00

Share change since 06-00 Total Stocks: 49	Sector	PE	YTD Ret%	% Assets
US Treasury Note 5.625%	N/A	—	—	14.65
☼ Fannie Mae	Financials	16.2	–6.95	2.62
☼ Comcast	Services	20.3	–13.70	2.24
☼ Nokia Cl A ADR	Technology	45.8	–43.00	2.20
☼ United Tech	Industrials	16.3	–16.70	1.89
☼ Phillips Petro	Energy	7.1	8.56	1.76
☼ St. Paul	Financials	—	–16.90	1.72
☼ Coastal	Energy	—	150.20	1.52
☼ Kerr-McGee	Energy	6.9	–15.70	1.47
☼ Dynegy	Energy	12.8	–54.20	1.41
☼ Anadarko Petro	Energy	11.1	–19.70	1.39
☼ Charter Comms	Services	—	–27.50	1.38
☼ Freddie Mac	Financials	14.0	–3.87	1.30
☼ Noble Affiliates	Energy	8.7	–22.90	1.23
☼ American Express	Financials	28.3	–34.40	1.19
☼ AT & T Liberty Media Cl A	Services	—	3.22	1.13
☼ ACE	Financials	17.4	–5.39	1.11
☼ Hartford Finl Svcs Grp	Financials	23.2	–9.63	1.07
⊕ Goldman Sachs Grp	Financials	20.7	–12.80	1.07
☼ Johnson & Johnson	Health	16.6	14.01	0.97
☼ Alberta Energy	Energy	43.9	–20.80	0.88
☼ Merrill Lynch	Financials	18.2	–22.70	0.82
⊕ Unocal	Energy	10.9	–4.58	0.77
⊕ Burlington Resources	Energy	8.4	–24.60	0.75
☼ Health Mgmt Assoc	Health	24.2	–11.30	0.73

Current Investment Style

Style: Value Blnd Growth; Size: Large Med Small

	Stock Port Avg	Relative S&P 500 Current	Relative S&P 500 Hist	Rel Cat
Price/Earnings Ratio	19.4	0.63	—	0.54
Price/Book Ratio	3.1	0.54	—	0.48
Price/Cash Flow	13.6	0.75	—	0.60
3 Yr Earnings Growth	20.4	1.39	—	0.95
1 Yr Earnings Est%	–2.9	1.64	—	–0.97
Med Mkt Cap $mil	17,557	0.3	—	0.37

Special Securities % assets 12-31-00	
Restricted/Illiquid Secs	0
Emerging-Markets Secs	0
Options/Futures/Warrants	No

Composition % assets 12-31-00	
Cash	28.5
Stocks*	55.5
Bonds	16.0
Other	0.0
*Foreign (% stocks)	12.1

Market Cap	
Giant	18.2
Large	51.9
Medium	28.4
Small	1.6
Micro	0.0

Sector Weightings	% of Stocks	Rel S&P	5-Year High	5-Year Low
Utilities	0.0	0.0	—	—
Energy	32.3	4.6	—	—
Financials	29.1	1.6	—	—
Industrials	9.9	0.9	—	—
Durables	0.4	0.2	—	—
Staples	0.0	0.0	—	—
Services	15.5	1.4	—	—
Retail	0.0	0.0	—	—
Health	6.1	0.4	—	—
Technology	6.6	0.4	—	—

Analysis by Bridget Hughes 10-23-01

Quaker Aggressive Growth Fund is cruising for a bruising.

This portfolio is hardly invested. Indeed, because 6% of assets are tied up in shorted stocks, the fund's net investments come to just 5% of assets. Said another way, the fund sports well more than 85% in cash!

To be sure, that huge cash stake has generally been a boon to returns in 2001. Through Oct. 22, the fund's 7.2% loss is much more palatable than the S&P 500 index's 16.6% drop. The fund also lands atop the large-growth category, and compared with large-value funds—which have bested their growth peers this year—it looks rather smart.

But that cash can cause problems. For example, while the S&P 500 has jumped 8.7% over the past month, the fund has lost half a percent, putting it at the bottom of the large-growth and large-value groups. Although one month is hardly enough time to condemn a fund, it highlights the risk of market-timing or aggressive asset-allocation shifts.

Manager Manu Daftary insisted, however, that he wasn't making a market-timing call, per se; rather, he said he simply couldn't find enough attractive stocks to buy. In the current weak economic climate, he's looking for stocks with positive earnings-growth rates and PEG ratios (P/E ratio divided by a stock's year-over-year earnings growth rate) of about 0.5—which is tough to find these days. He recently sold Microsoft (PEG ratio: 1.8) because he was worried about slowing PC sales. He is sticking with top holding Johnson & Johnson (PEG ratio: 2.3), whose dominant position in the coronary coated-stent arena he likes.

If Daftary's approach sounds extremely flexible, that's because it is. Over the longer haul, Daftary has executed this bold strategy well—the fund's 36% three-year return beats that of the S&P 500 index by more than 30 percentage points.

Address:	PO Box 844 Conshohocken, PA 19428–0844 800–220–8888
Web Address:	www.quakerfunds.com/
*Inception:	11-01-96
Advisor:	DG Cap. Mgmt.
Subadvisor:	None
NTF Plans:	Fidelity , Fidelity Inst.

Minimum Purchase:	$2000	Add: $1000 IRA: $1000
Min Auto Inv Plan:	$2000	Add: $100
Sales Fees:	5.50%L, 0.25%B	
Management Fee:	1.3%	
Actual Fees:	Mgt: 1.30%	Dist: 0.25%
Expense Projections:	3Yr: $1087 5Yr: —	10Yr: —
Avg Brok Commission:	—	Income Distrib: Annually
Total Cost (relative to category):	—	

Red Oak Technology Select

Ticker	Load	NAV	Yield	Total Assets	Mstar Category
ROGSX	None	$9.59	0.0%	$613.9 mil	Spec Technology

Prospectus Objective: Specialty—Technology

Red Oak Technology Select Fund seeks capital growth.

The fund primarily invests in common stocks of companies that rely in technology in their product development or operations. It may also invest in warrants and rights to purchase common stocks, debt securities, preferreds, and American Depositary Receipts. The fund may invest up to 15% of assets in various short-term investments including cash, repurchase agreement, commercial money market instruments. "This fund is non-diversified."

Historical Profile
Return: Below Avg
Risk: High
Rating: ★ Lowest

Investment Style: Equity
Average Stock %: 97% | 97% | 96%

▼ Manager Change
▽ Partial Manager Change

Fund Performance vs. Category Average
■ Quarterly Fund Return +/– Category Average
— Category Baseline

Performance Quartile (within Category)

Portfolio Manager(s)

James D. Oelschlager. Since 12-98. BA'64 Denison U.; JD'67 Northwestern U. Other funds currently managed: Pin Oak Aggressive Stock, Target Large Capitalization Growth, White Oak Growth Stock.

Douglas MacKay, CFA. Since 12-98. BS Miami U. Other funds currently managed: Pin Oak Aggressive Stock, White Oak Growth Stock.

History

	1990	1991	1992	1993	1994	1995	1996	1997	1998	1999	2000	12-01
NAV	—	—	—	—	—	—	—	—	10.00	24.34	21.78	9.59
Total Return %	—	—	—	—	—	—	—	—	—	143.40	–10.52	–55.97
+/– S&P 500	—	—	—	—	—	—	—	—	—	122.36	–1.42	–44.09
+/– PSE Tech 100	—	—	—	—	—	—	—	—	—	27.01	5.70	–40.38
Income Return %	—	—	—	—	—	—	—	—	—	0.00	0.00	0.00
Capital Return %	—	—	—	—	—	—	—	—	—	143.40	–10.52	–55.97
Total Rtn % Rank Cat	—	—	—	—	—	—	—	—	—	36	6	94
Income $	—	—	—	—	—	—	—	—	0.00	0.00	0.00	0.00
Capital Gains $	—	—	—	—	—	—	—	—	0.00	0.00	0.00	0.00
Expense Ratio %	—	—	—	—	—	—	—	—	—	1.00	—	0.99
Income Ratio %	—	—	—	—	—	—	—	—	—	–0.81	—	–0.79
Turnover Rate %	—	—	—	—	—	—	—	—	—	17	—	—
Net Assets $mil	—	—	—	—	—	—	—	—	—	361.5	1,432.9	613.9

Performance 12-31-01

	1st Qtr	2nd Qtr	3rd Qtr	4th Qtr	Total
1997	—	—	—	—	—
1998	—	—	—	—	—
1999	15.40	8.32	15.44	68.68	143.40
2000	40.80	3.47	10.97	–44.65	–10.52
2001	–46.92	9.52	–49.21	49.14	–55.97

Trailing	Total Return%	+/– S&P 500	+/– PSE Tech 100	% Rank All	% Rank Cat	Growth of $10,000
3 Mo	49.14	38.46	16.23	1	10	14,914
6 Mo	–24.25	–18.69	–18.97	99	84	7,575
1 Yr	–55.97	–44.09	–40.38	100	94	4,403
3 Yr Avg	–1.39	–0.36	–16.62	80	47	9,590
5 Yr Avg	—	—	—	—	—	—
10 Yr Avg	—	—	—	—	—	—
15 Yr Avg	—	—	—	—	—	—

Tax Analysis	Tax-Adj Ret%	%Rank Cat	%Pretax Ret	%Rank Cat
3 Yr Avg	–1.39	38	—	—
5 Yr Avg	—	—	—	—
10 Yr Avg	—	—	—	—

Potential Capital Gain Exposure: –36% of assets

Risk Analysis

Time Period	Load-Adj Return %	Risk %Rank[1] All	Risk %Rank[1] Cat	Morningstar Return	Morningstar Risk	Morningstar Risk-Adj Rating
1 Yr	–55.97					
3 Yr	–1.39	99	86	–1.26[2]	2.83	★
5 Yr	—	—	—	—	—	
Incept	–1.38	—	—	—	—	

Average Historical Rating (1 month): 1.0★s

[1]1=low, 100=high [2] T-Bill return substituted for category avg.

Category Rating (3 Yr)
1 2 **3** 4 5
Worst Best

Return: Average
Risk: Above Avg

Other Measures	Standard Index S&P 500	Best Fit Index Wil 4500
Alpha	32.1	16.5
Beta	2.79	2.06
R-Squared	52	77
Standard Deviation		86.05
Mean		–1.39
Sharpe Ratio		–0.09

Portfolio Analysis 09-30-01

Share chng since 06-01 Total Stocks: 25

Share chng	Stock	Subsector	PE	YTD Ret%	% Assets
⊖	Semtech	Semiconductors	63.7	61.76	11.02
	Cisco Sys	Networking	—	–52.60	7.36
	Applied Matls	Semi Equipment	66.8	5.01	7.33
	Integrated Device Tech	Semiconductors	8.9	–19.70	6.74
⊖	Triquint Semicon	Semiconductors	26.7	–71.90	6.21
⊖	Maxim Integrated Products	Semiconductors	68.2	9.82	6.12
⊖	Novellus Sys	Semi Equipment	25.0	9.77	6.12
	Flextronics Intl	Technology	—	–15.80	4.44
⊕	EMC	Software	NMF	–79.40	4.28
⊕	Qlogic	Semi Equipment	49.5	–42.10	3.93
⊕	JDS Uniphase	Technology	—	–79.00	3.87
⊕	Openwave Sys	Technology	—	–79.50	3.65
	Veritas Software	Software	—	–48.70	3.34
⊖	Brocade Comm Sys	Technology	—	–63.90	3.31
⊕	CIENA	Telecom	NMF	–82.30	2.72
⊕	TIBCO Software	Technology	—	–68.80	2.21
⊖	PMC Sierra	Technology	—	–72.90	2.19
	Juniper Net	Technology	NMF	–84.90	2.05
	Vitesse Semicon	Semi Equipment	—	–77.50	2.02
	Newport	Technology	—	–75.40	1.93
⊕	McDATA	Technology	—	–71.30	1.55
☼	Check Point Software Tech	Software	32.0	–55.20	1.42
⊖	JNI	Technology	—	–63.30	1.14
⊖	ONI Sys	Technology	—	–84.10	0.83
	Cacheflow	Technology	—	–84.20	0.49

Current Investment Style

Style: Value Blnd Growth; Size: Large Med Small

	Stock Port Avg	Relative S&P 500 Current	Relative S&P 500 Hist	Rel Cat
Price/Earnings Ratio	45.4	1.47	—	0.98
Price/Book Ratio	5.1	0.89	—	0.82
Price/Cash Flow	26.2	1.45	—	1.01
3 Yr Earnings Growth	53.2[1]	3.64	—	1.78
1 Yr Earnings Est%	–59.0	33.34	—	3.55
Med Mkt Cap $mil	5,940	0.1	—	0.37

[1]figure is based on 50% or less of stocks

Special Securities % assets 09-30-01	
Restricted/Illiquid Secs	0
Emerging-Markets Secs	1
Options/Futures/Warrants	No

Composition % assets 09-30-01	
Cash	3.8
Stocks*	96.2
Bonds	0.0
Other	0.0
*Foreign (% stocks)	1.5

Market Cap	
Giant	7.6
Large	27.1
Medium	59.1
Small	4.5
Micro	1.7

Subsector Weightings	% of Stocks	Rel Cat
Computers	0.0	0.0
Semiconductors	31.3	2.8
Semi Equipment	20.2	5.1
Networking	7.6	2.1
Periph/Hardware	0.0	0.0
Software	9.4	0.7
Computer Svs	0.0	0.0
Telecom	2.8	0.4
Health Care	0.0	0.0
Other	28.7	0.8

Analysis by William Harding 11-27-01

Despite the fund's lousy showing this year, there's reason for investors to stay the course.

Red Oak Technology Select Fund's brave approach will likely cause heartburn for many shareholders. This offering is one of the riskiest in an already volatile sector of the market. Managers Doug MacKay and Jim Oelschlager invest in a small number of names across only a few industries. If those areas struggle or a few stock picks implode, the blow to performance can be huge.

This year is a case in point. Many of the fund's storage and networking stocks have taken it on the chin. Further, MacKay and Oelschlager held on to and even added to positions in some firms that have been hurt by slumping sales in telecom gear, including JDS Uniphase and Ciena. As a result, the fund has shed more than half of its value for the year to date ended Nov. 26, 2001.

But the fund's difficulty this year hasn't caused management to change its stripes. MacKay and Oelschlager have kept the fund fully invested in stocks and employ a long-term approach, as evidenced by its scant turnover. Not surprisingly, there have been few changes to the portfolio of late. The pair cut Exodus and Network Appliance loose in the third quarter, but stuck with most other picks. In addition, they have added to beaten-down names that they believe are leaders in their fields, such as EMC and JDS Uniphase.

The worst step investors can take with a fund like this is to chase performance. By taking that path they are most likely to buy in near a peak that is poised for a correction or to bail out prior to a remarkable rebound. Indeed, investors who bailed out have missed the fund's 22% run over the past month—a better showing than most funds in the category.

This fund will likely lead the pack again when the outlook for tech brightens. But this is not a suitable home for investors who can't stomach steep losses along the way.

Address:	P.O. Box 219441 Kansas City, MO 64121–9441 888–462–5386
Web Address:	www.oakassociates.com
*Inception:	12-31-98
Advisor:	Oak Assoc.
Subadvisor:	None
NTF Plans:	Datalynx , Fidelity Inst.

Minimum Purchase:	$2000	Add: $50	IRA: $2000
Min Auto Inv Plan:	$2000	Add: $25	
Sales Fees:	No-load		
Management Fee:	.74%, .15%A		
Actual Fees:	Mgt: 0.54%	Dist: —	
Expense Projections:	3Yr: $381	5Yr: $660	10Yr: $1455
Avg Brok Commission:	—	Income Distrib: Annually	
Total Cost (relative to category):		Below Avg	

Royce Premier

Ticker	Load	NAV	Yield	Total Assets	Mstar Category
RYPRX	None	$10.54	0.0%	$706.0 mil	Small Blend

Prospectus Objective: Small Company

Royce Premier Fund seeks long-term growth; current income is secondary.

The fund normally invests at least 80% of assets in a limited number of common stocks and convertibles; at least 65% of these securities are income-producing and/or issued by companies with market capitalizations of less than $2 billion. To select investments, the advisor emphasizes companies with strong returns on assets, cash flows, balance sheets, or unique business strengths. It may invest the balance in securities with larger-market capitalizations, non-dividend-paying common stocks, fixed-income securities, and preferred stocks. It may also invest up to 10% of assets in foreign securities.

Historical Profile
Return: Above Avg
Risk: Below Avg
Rating: ★★★★ Above Avg

Investment Style
Equity
Average Stock %: 97% 89% 92% 91% 91% 86%

▼ Manager Change
▽ Partial Manager Change

Fund Performance vs. Category Average
▩ Quarterly Fund Return +/– Category Average
— Category Baseline

Performance Quartile (within Category)

Portfolio Manager(s)

Charles M. Royce, et al. Since 12-91. BA'61 Brown U.; MBA'63 Columbia U.

History

1990	1991	1992	1993	1994	1995	1996	1997	1998	1999	2000	12-01	History
—	5.00	5.52	6.41	6.48	7.12	7.81	8.70	9.14	9.56	9.83	10.54	NAV
—	—	15.80	19.02	3.28	17.81	18.13	18.41	6.74	11.49	17.12	9.61	Total Return %
—	—	8.18	8.97	1.96	−19.72	−4.82	−14.95	−21.84	−9.55	26.22	21.49	+/– S&P 500
—	—	−2.61	0.12	5.10	−10.63	1.59	−3.96	9.29	−9.77	20.15	7.12	+/– Russell 2000
—	—	0.40	0.36	0.78	1.42	1.40	1.13	0.57	0.11	0.31	0.00	Income Return %
—	—	15.40	18.66	2.50	16.39	16.72	17.28	6.16	11.38	16.81	9.61	Capital Return %
—	—	39	40	17	82	60	91	7	52	27	41	Total Rtn % Rank Cat
—	0.00	0.02	0.02	0.05	0.09	0.10	0.09	0.05	0.01	0.03	0.00	Income $
—	0.00	0.25	0.14	0.09	0.42	0.49	0.46	0.09	0.58	1.27	0.23	Capital Gains $
—	—	1.77	1.50	1.38	1.25	1.25	1.24	1.23	1.23	1.20	—	Expense Ratio %
—	—	0.53	0.68	1.19	1.48	1.25	1.20	0.55	0.11	0.34	—	Income Ratio %
—	—	116	85	38	39	34	18	46	48	40	—	Turnover Rate %
—	—	2.3	36.0	202.4	302.1	316.8	533.5	571.8	567.8	674.2	—	Net Assets $mil

Performance 12-31-01

	1st Qtr	2nd Qtr	3rd Qtr	4th Qtr	Total
1997	1.15	13.29	9.39	−5.54	18.41
1998	9.66	−1.05	−14.51	15.07	6.74
1999	−11.60	21.04	−6.14	11.00	11.49
2000	3.35	1.01	8.82	3.10	17.12
2001	−5.29	14.39	−14.84	18.80	9.61

Trailing	Total Return%	+/– S&P 500	+/– Russ 2000	% Rank All	% Rank Cat	Growth of $10,000
3 Mo	18.80	8.11	−2.28	16	48	11,880
6 Mo	1.17	6.73	5.26	33	30	10,117
1 Yr	9.61	21.49	7.12	6	41	10,961
3 Yr Avg	12.70	13.72	6.28	7	33	14,313
5 Yr Avg	12.59	1.89	5.06	9	34	18,089
10 Yr Avg	13.61	0.69	2.10	10	46	35,835
15 Yr Avg	—	—	—	—	—	—

Tax Analysis	Tax-Adj Ret%	%Rank Cat	%Pretax Ret	%Rank Cat
3 Yr Avg	10.78	35	84.9	48
5 Yr Avg	11.03	26	87.7	36
10 Yr Avg	12.01	21	88.2	15

Potential Capital Gain Exposure: 28% of assets

Risk Analysis

Time Period	Load-Adj Return %	Risk %Rank[1] All	Risk %Rank[1] Cat	Morningstar Return	Morningstar Risk	Morningstar Risk-Adj Rating
1 Yr	9.61					
3 Yr	12.70	50	25	1.77[2]	0.70	★★★★★
5 Yr	12.59	53	14	1.91[2]	0.73	★★★★
10 Yr	13.61	53	1	1.45	0.66	★★★★

Average Historical Rating (85 months): 3.5★s

[1]1=low, 100=high [2] T-Bill return substituted for category avg.

Category Rating (3 Yr)

1 2 3 4 5
Worst Best

Return: Average
Risk: Below Avg

Other Measures	Standard Index S&P 500	Best Fit Index SPMid400
Alpha	12.1	3.6
Beta	0.64	0.75
R-Squared	39	73

Standard Deviation	19.29
Mean	12.70
Sharpe Ratio	0.46

Portfolio Analysis 06-30-01

Share change since 03-01 Total Stocks: 50	Sector	PE	YTD Ret%	% Assets
⊖ White Mountains Ins Grp	Financials	—	9.45	3.79
Woodward Governor	Industrials	14.4	32.20	3.38
Florida Rock Inds	Industrials	15.1	41.77	2.82
⊕ Lincoln Elec Hldgs	Industrials	14.5	27.77	2.73
⊖ Arthur J. Gallagher & Co.	Financials	26.3	10.31	2.72
⊕ Big Lots	Retail	17.1	−2.02	2.71
⊕ Fair Isaac	Technology	31.5	85.59	2.64
Simpson Mfg	Industrials	18.0	12.35	2.59
⊖ Haemonetics	Health	24.9	9.86	2.43
Zenith Natl Ins	Financials	—	−1.37	2.43
⊕ Curtiss-Wright	Industrials	12.6	3.90	2.41
⊖ Pittston Brink's Grp	Services	—	11.74	2.27
⊕ Avnet	Technology	—	19.93	2.27
Aon	Financials	46.1	6.32	2.26
⊕ EGL	Services	14.2	−41.70	2.17
⊕ Erie Indemnity A	Financials	18.4	31.59	2.15
Ross Stores	Retail	17.3	91.38	2.14
Wesco Finl	Financials	23.7	12.26	2.12
⊖ Keane	Technology	64.4	84.92	2.04
⊕ Gartner Grp A	Services	—	69.42	1.91
Roper Inds	Industrials	29.0	50.94	1.87
⊕ American Mgmt Sys	Technology	26.6	−8.75	1.79
Nordson	Industrials	35.7	5.75	1.75
⊕ Tom Brown	Energy	10.8	−17.80	1.73
Wolverine World Wide	Staples	14.8	−0.25	1.73

Current Investment Style

Style: Value Blnd Growth; Size: Large Med Small

	Stock Port Avg	Relative S&P 500 Current	Relative S&P 500 Hist	Rel Cat
Price/Earnings Ratio	24.2	0.78	0.63	0.97
Price/Book Ratio	3.1	0.55	0.35	0.98
Price/Cash Flow	13.7	0.76	0.67	0.88
3 Yr Earnings Growth	15.5	1.06	0.85	0.91
1 Yr Earnings Est%	−16.2	9.14	—	−18.80
Med Mkt Cap $mil	1,156	0.0	0.0	1.18

[1]figure is based on 50% or less of stocks

Analysis by Dan McNeela 12-28-01

Royce Premier Fund has become a princely offering by sticking with companies that have few warts.

Comanagers Chuck Royce and Whitney George limit the number of holdings in this portfolio to about 50 names, but that hasn't added heaps of risk to the fund. Instead, management's stock-selection criteria and a focus on the larger stocks in the small-cap realm have made for a smooth ride. Turnaround stocks and high-flying growth stocks are usually bypassed in favor of companies with high returns on equity and solid growth prospects that are selling at reasonable valuations.

The fund's approach to the technology sector is indicative of management's style. During 2001, management increased its tech weighting from 14% to 23% of assets. But that didn't result from management's view that the market was going to return to its glory days of 1999. Royce and Whitney were finding companies that were discarded in the rush to get out of tech but still had strong fundamentals. In Avnet and Arrow Electronics, the fund owns the two largest distributors of electronic components. Those firms rise and fall with the Nasdaq, but as distributors, they don't have to worry about technological obsolescence.

Over the long term, the fund's returns rank in the top third of the small-blend category. The fund usually performs best in a value-driven market, but it has kept pace during most growth rallies too. In 2001's strong market for value stocks, the fund's 10.4% year-to-date return through Dec. 28 ranks in the top half of the category.

Royce insists that the July 2001 sale of his funds to Legg Mason will not bring any noticeable changes for investors, and we're inclined to believe that's the case from what we've seen thus far. We think this no-load fund remains a strong option in the small-cap arena.

Special Securities % assets 06-30-01	
Restricted/Illiquid Secs	0
Emerging-Markets Secs	2
Options/Futures/Warrants	No

Composition % assets 06-30-01	
Cash	13.0
Stocks*	87.0
Bonds	0.0
Other	0.0
*Foreign (% stocks)	6.3

Market Cap	
Giant	0.0
Large	0.0
Medium	43.3
Small	56.7
Micro	0.0

Sector Weightings	% of Stocks	Rel S&P	5-Year High	5-Year Low
Utilities	0.0	0.0	0	0
Energy	2.0	0.3	8	0
Financials	24.2	1.4	31	9
Industrials	23.8	2.1	37	19
Durables	2.0	1.3	14	2
Staples	0.0	0.0	5	0
Services	14.2	1.3	23	9
Retail	8.4	1.2	18	2
Health	2.8	0.2	7	1
Technology	22.5	1.2	25	2

Address:	1414 Avenue of the Americas New York, NY 10019 212-355-7311 / 800-221-4268
Web Address:	www.roycefunds.com
*Inception:	12-31-91
Advisor:	Royce & Assoc.
Subadvisor:	None
NTF Plans:	Fidelity , Datalynx

Minimum Purchase:	$2000	Add: $50	IRA: $500
Min Auto Inv Plan:	$500	Add: $50	
Sales Fees:	No-load, 1.00%R within 6 months		
Management Fee:	1.0%		
Actual Fees:	Mgt: 1.00%	Dist: —	
Expense Projections:	3Yr: $390	5Yr: $676	10Yr: $1489
Avg Brok Commission:	—	Income Distrib: Annually	
Total Cost (relative to category):		Below Avg	

Royce Total Return

Ticker	Load	NAV	Yield	Total Assets	Mstar Category
RYTRX	None	$8.59	1.2%	$429.5 mil	Small Value

Prospectus Objective: Small Company

Royce Total Return Fund seeks capital appreciation and current income.

The fund normally invests at least 65% of assets in common stocks, 90% of which are dividend-paying. It generally invests at least 65% of assets in securities of companies with market capitalizations of less than $20 billion. To select investments, the advisor uses a value-oriented approach, emphasizing various internal returns indicative of profitability, balance sheet quality, cash flows, and the relationship these factors have to the security's price. The fund may invest up to 35% in debt rated as low as BBB. It may also hold up to 10% in foreign securities.

On June 17, 1997, Royce Equity-Income Fund merged into the fund.

Historical Profile

Return Above Avg
Risk Low
Rating ★★★★ Above Avg

Investment Style
Equity
Average Stock %

1994	1995	1996	1997	1998	1999	2000	12-01
		82%	74%	80%	84%	96%	90%

▼ Manager Change
▽ Partial Manager Change (1999)

Fund Performance vs. Category Average
■ Quarterly Fund Return +/– Category Average
— Category Baseline

Performance Quartile (within Category)

Portfolio Manager(s)

Charles M. Royce, et al. Since 12-93. BA'61 Brown U.; MBA'63 Columbia U.

1990	1991	1992	1993	1994	1995	1996	1997	1998	1999	2000	12-01	History
—	—	—	5.00	5.12	5.76	6.29	7.52	7.56	7.15	7.77	8.59	NAV
—	—	—	—	5.12	26.86	25.48	23.70	4.76	1.55	19.43	14.78	Total Return %
—	—	—	–1.20*	3.81	–10.68	2.54	–9.65	–23.82	–19.49	28.53	26.65	+/– S&P 500
—	—	—	—	6.67	1.11	4.11	–7.99	11.19	3.03	–3.39	0.76	+/– Russell 2000 V
—	—	—	0.00	2.72	2.54	2.78	1.78	1.99	2.13	2.11	1.36	Income Return %
—	—	—	0.00	2.40	24.32	22.70	21.92	2.76	–0.58	17.31	13.42	Capital Return %
—	—	—	—	10	32	39	82	7	47	50	67	Total Rtn % Rank Cat
—	—	—	0.00	0.14	0.13	0.16	0.11	0.15	0.16	0.15	0.11	Income $
—	—	—	0.00	0.00	0.60	0.73	0.15	0.16	0.35	0.57	0.21	Capital Gains $
—	—	—	0.29	1.96	1.67	1.25	1.25	1.25	1.25	1.25	—	Expense Ratio %
—	—	—	–0.29	0.49	2.42	2.50	3.15	2.75	2.32	2.08	—	Income Ratio %
—	—	—	—	88	68	111	26	66	39	24	—	Turnover Rate %
—	—	—	—	—	2.5	6.2	120.6	244.2	249.0	276.9	—	Net Assets $mil

Performance 12-31-01

	1st Qtr	2nd Qtr	3rd Qtr	4th Qtr	Total
1997	2.54	9.92	8.60	1.05	23.70
1998	6.91	0.37	–10.53	9.11	4.76
1999	–9.27	12.33	–3.69	3.47	1.55
2000	1.00	2.23	10.69	4.49	19.43
2001	1.27	12.57	–12.58	15.17	14.78

Trailing	Total Return%	+/– S&P 500	+/– Russ 2000V	% Rank All	% Rank Cat	Growth of $10,000
3 Mo	15.17	4.49	–1.55	23	68	11,517
6 Mo	0.68	6.24	–0.47	36	63	10,068
1 Yr	14.78	26.65	0.76	4	67	11,478
3 Yr Avg	11.66	12.68	0.33	8	57	13,920
5 Yr Avg	12.52	1.82	1.33	9	35	18,038
10 Yr Avg	—	—	—	—	—	—
15 Yr Avg	—	—	—	—	—	—

Tax Analysis	Tax-Adj Ret%	%Rank Cat	%Pretax Ret	%Rank Cat
3 Yr Avg	9.38	65	80.5	85
5 Yr Avg	10.63	37	84.9	57
10 Yr Avg	—	—	—	—

Potential Capital Gain Exposure: 12% of assets

Risk Analysis

Time Period	Load-Adj Return %	Risk %Rank[1] All	Risk %Rank[1] Cat	Morningstar Return	Morningstar Risk	Morningstar Risk-Adj Rating
1 Yr	14.78					
3 Yr	11.66	38	12	1.52[2]	0.50	★★★★★
5 Yr	12.52	42	1	1.89[2]	0.51	★★★★
Incept	14.71	—	—	—	—	

Average Historical Rating (61 months): 4.1★s

[1]1=low, 100=high [2] T-Bill return substituted for category avg.

Category Rating (3 Yr)

1 2 3 4 5 — Worst … Best (rating: 3)

Return Average
Risk Below Avg

Other Measures	Standard Index S&P 500	Best Fit Index SPMid400
Alpha	9.3	3.5
Beta	0.41	0.54
R–Squared	29	64

Standard Deviation	14.43
Mean	11.66
Sharpe Ratio	0.53

Analysis by Dan McNeela 12-29-01

Royce Total Return Fund should hold much appeal for cautious small-cap investors.

Investors who value consistency need to take a closer look at this fund. It is one of only five small-value funds to deliver a positive return in each year since 1994. The fund has also been the least volatile offering in the category the past five years.

The fund's low-risk profile isn't accidental. To limit issue-specific risk, manager Chuck Royce seeks out companies with the financial strength to pay regular dividends, and spreads the fund's assets across more than 200 names. His criteria have another benefit: The fund's yield gives it a nice cushion in down markets. One recent addition to the fund is T. Rowe Price. Royce appreciates the value of its strong brand and its 1.9% yield.

The fund isn't without risks. Small-cap funds are inherently more volatile than large, and this offering also typically stashes 25% of its assets in less-liquid micro-cap names and piles a big chunk of assets into industrial stocks. Still, Royce's focus on financial strength and diversification across issues have made the fund far less volatile than most of its rivals.

Because of its conservative style, the fund tends to lag its peers in big rallies. In 2001, its return trailed the category average, in part because insurance holdings such as PXRE have been sluggish. Over time, however, the fund's resilience has helped it handily outpace its typical rival.

Royce is looking to set an example for the fund industry about how a no-load fund family can coexist with a parent that charges loads, but we'll be watching to make sure that Legg Mason's recent purchase of the Royce funds doesn't affect this fund's management or expenses. We think investors can count on this fund to keep impressing its shareholders.

Portfolio Analysis 06-30-01

Share change since 12-00 Total Stocks: 221	Sector	PE	YTD Ret%	% Assets
⊖ Woodward Governor	Industrials	14.4	32.20	2.02
White Mountains Ins Grp	Financials	—	9.45	1.63
☆ T Rowe Price Assoc	Financials	21.7	–16.20	1.48
⊕ Avnet	Technology	—	19.93	1.35
⊕ Franklin Elec	Industrials	18.9	21.30	1.29
⊕ ABM Inds	Services	16.2	4.57	1.23
Lincoln Elec Hldgs	Industrials	14.5	27.77	1.23
⊖ Arrow Intl	Health	19.0	6.80	1.20
John Nuveen	Financials	24.3	42.69	1.19
Florida Rock Inds	Industrials	15.1	41.77	1.14
⊖ Trenwick Grp	Financials	92.5	–59.00	1.10
⊕ Technitrol	Industrials	24.9	–32.40	1.09
Universal	Staples	8.6	7.88	1.06
Curtiss–Wright	Industrials	12.6	3.90	1.06
☆ Chelsea Ppty Grp	Financials	18.5	42.62	1.05
Charming Shoppes	Retail	18.3	–11.50	1.04
Arnold Inds	Services	—	23.38	0.95
⊕ Anglogold ADR	Industrials	11.9	27.47	0.95
☆ Perot Sys Cl A	Technology	NMF	122.20	0.93
Pittston Brink's Grp	Services	—	11.74	0.92
⊕ RLI	Financials	14.5	2.20	0.92
⊕ Erie Indemnity A	Financials	18.4	31.59	0.91
⊕ Arthur J. Gallagher & Co.	Financials	26.3	10.31	0.90
⊕ Lawson Products	Industrials	13.3	–1.47	0.89
⊕ Big Lots	Retail	17.1	–2.02	0.87

Current Investment Style

Style: Value Blnd Growth; Size: Large Med Small

	Stock Port Avg	Relative S&P 500 Current	Relative S&P 500 Hist	Rel Cat
Price/Earnings Ratio	22.4	0.72	0.54	1.03
Price/Book Ratio	2.5	0.44	0.30	1.03
Price/Cash Flow	12.2	0.68	0.51	0.96
3 Yr Earnings Growth	7.3	0.50	0.62	0.63
1 Yr Earnings Est%	–10.9	6.16	—	2.76
Med Mkt Cap $mil	662	0.0	0.0	0.76

[1]figure is based on 50% or less of stocks

Special Securities % assets 06-30-01	
Restricted/Illiquid Secs	0
Emerging–Markets Secs	1
Options/Futures/Warrants	No

Composition % assets 06-30-01	
Cash	9.5
Stocks*	89.8
Bonds	0.0
Other	0.7
*Foreign (% stocks)	3.4

Market Cap	
Giant	0.0
Large	0.9
Medium	22.9
Small	53.4
Micro	22.7

Sector Weightings	% of Stocks	Rel S&P	5-Year High	5-Year Low
Utilities	0.1	0.0	10	0
Energy	0.9	0.1	5	0
Financials	25.1	1.4	34	15
Industrials	36.2	3.2	53	4
Durables	7.8	5.0	20	7
Staples	2.2	0.3	7	0
Services	12.1	1.1	25	5
Retail	4.3	0.6	7	0
Health	4.0	0.3	4	0
Technology	7.2	0.4	17	0

Address:	1414 Avenue of the Americas New York, NY 10019 800–221–4268 / 212–355–7311
Web Address:	www.roycefunds.com
*Inception:	12-15-93
Advisor:	Royce & Assoc.
Subadvisor:	None
NTF Plans:	Fidelity , Datalynx

Minimum Purchase:	$2000	Add: $50 IRA: $500
Min Auto Inv Plan:	$500	Add: $50
Sales Fees:	No–load, 1.00%R within 6 months	
Management Fee:	1.0%	
Actual Fees:	Mgt: 1.00%	Dist: —
Expense Projections:	3Yr: $409	5Yr: $712 10Yr: $1574
Avg Brok Commission:	—	Income Distrib: Quarterly
Total Cost (relative to category):		Below Avg

RS Diversified Growth

Ticker	Load	NAV	Yield	Total Assets	Mstar Category
RSDGX	12b–1 only	$23.26	0.0%	$713.6 mil	Small Growth

Prospectus Objective: Growth

RS Diversified Growth Fund seeks long-term capital growth.

The fund invests primarily in common and preferred stocks and warrants. Management focuses on small- and mid-capitalization issuers and seeks to diversify investments over industry sectors. Although the fund typically invests in companies with capitalizations of $3 billion or less, it maintains the flexibility to invest in securities of larger issuers.

On April 12, 1999, Robertson Stephens Diversified Growth Fund merged into the fund. Past names: Robertson Stephens Diversified Growth Fund

Historical Profile
Return High
Risk High
Rating ★★★★★ Highest

Investment Style: Equity — Average Stock %: 91% (1996), 96% (1997), 97% (1998), 97% (1999), 99% (2000), 96% (12-01)

▼ Manager Change
▽ Partial Manager Change

Fund Performance vs. Category Average
■ Quarterly Fund Return +/– Category Average
— Category Baseline

Performance Quartile (within Category)

Portfolio Manager(s)

John L. Wallace. Since 8-96. BA'78 U. of Idaho; MBA'87 Pace U. Other funds currently managed: RS Value + Growth, RS MidCap Opportunities, CDC Nvest Star Small Cap A.

John H. Seabern. Since 3-98. Other funds currently managed: CDC Nvest Star Small Cap A, CDC Nvest Star Small Cap B, CDC Nvest Star Small Cap C.

History

1990	1991	1992	1993	1994	1995	1996	1997	1998	1999	2000	12-01	History
—	—	—	—	—	—	12.42	14.04	15.89	32.99	22.83	23.26	NAV
—	—	—	—	—	—	24.20*	29.45	16.28	150.21	–26.91	1.88	Total Return %
—	—	—	—	—	—	9.17*	–3.91	–12.30	129.17	–17.81	13.76	+/– S&P 500
—	—	—	—	—	—	—	16.50	15.05	107.12	–4.48	11.12	+/– Russ 2000 Grth
—	—	—	—	—	—	0.00	0.00	0.00	0.00	0.00	0.00	Income Return %
—	—	—	—	—	—	24.20	29.45	16.28	150.21	–26.91	1.88	Capital Return %
—	—	—	—	—	—	—	15	12	3	95	22	Total Rtn % Rank Cat
—	—	—	—	—	—	0.00	0.00	0.00	0.00	0.00	0.00	Income $
—	—	—	—	—	—	0.00	1.93	0.39	5.48	1.23	0.00	Capital Gains $
—	—	—	—	—	—	2.28	1.94	1.89	1.84	1.51	—	Expense Ratio %
—	—	—	—	—	—	–1.05	–1.20	–1.29	–1.40	–1.01	—	Income Ratio %
—	—	—	—	—	—	—	370	403	473	383	—	Turnover Rate %
—	—	—	—	—	—	59.6	79.6	69.1	304.7	523.0	713.6	Net Assets $mil

Performance 12-31-01

	1st Qtr	2nd Qtr	3rd Qtr	4th Qtr	Total
1997	–4.43	12.22	25.15	–3.56	29.45
1998	16.10	–7.85	–16.25	29.77	16.28
1999	12.21	29.05	6.04	62.94	150.21
2000	25.46	–19.81	–5.15	–23.41	–26.91
2001	–11.13	18.78	–29.38	36.66	1.88

Trailing	Total Return%	+/– S&P 500	+/– Russ 2000 Grth	% Rank All	% Rank Cat	Growth of $10,000
3 Mo	36.66	25.98	10.49	2	2	13,666
6 Mo	–3.49	2.07	5.78	53	33	9,651
1 Yr	1.88	13.76	11.12	39	22	10,188
3 Yr Avg	23.05	24.08	22.80	2	10	18,632
5 Yr Avg	22.90	12.20	20.04	1	4	28,044
10 Yr Avg	—	—	—	—	—	—
15 Yr Avg	—	—	—	—	—	—

Tax Analysis	Tax-Adj Ret%	%Rank Cat	%Pretax Ret	%Rank Cat
3 Yr Avg	19.43	10	84.3	35
5 Yr Avg	19.31	4	84.3	29
10 Yr Avg	—	—	—	—

Potential Capital Gain Exposure: –14% of assets

Risk Analysis

Time Period	Load-Adj Return %	Risk %Rank[1] All	Risk %Rank[1] Cat	Morningstar Return	Morningstar Risk	Morningstar Risk-Adj Rating
1 Yr	1.88					
3 Yr	23.05	95	72	4.54[2]	1.72	★★★★★
5 Yr	22.90	93	59	5.49[2]	1.62	★★★★★
Incept	25.89	—	—	—	—	

Average Historical Rating (30 months): 5.0★s

[1]1=low, 100=high [2] T-Bill return substituted for category avg.

Category Rating (3 Yr): 5 (scale 1 Worst – 5 Best)

Return High
Risk Above Avg

Other Measures	Standard Index S&P 500	Best Fit Index Wil 4500
Alpha	36.7	27.4
Beta	1.56	1.41
R-Squared	39	87

Standard Deviation	56.26
Mean	23.05
Sharpe Ratio	0.36

Portfolio Analysis 09-30-01

Share change since 06-01 Total Stocks: 128	Sector	PE	YTD Ret%	% Assets
⊕ Regeneration Tech	Health	—	–28.40	2.82
Coinstar	Industrials	—	63.93	2.39
⊕ Imanage	Technology	—	72.91	2.08
⊕ Alliant Techsystems	Industrials	28.6	73.48	1.99
Esperion Therapeutics	Health	—	–32.40	1.94
⊕ Arena Pharmaceuticals	Health	—	–22.30	1.79
⊕ Landstar Sys	Services	13.3	30.79	1.67
⊖ Novavax	Health	—	65.88	1.58
⊕ ViewPoint	Technology	—	25.23	1.57
⊖ Caremark Rx	Health	46.6	20.25	1.55
☼ Intrado	N/A	—	—	1.55
☼ Hollywood Entrtnmt	Retail	—	1,244.00	1.39
☼ Capstone Turbine	Industrials	—	–80.60	1.35
⊕ Support.com	Services	—	–69.00	1.32
☼ Saxon Cap Acquisition 144A	N/A	—	—	1.27
⊕ Oakley	Durables	20.1	20.44	1.23
⊕ Barr Labs	Health	25.0	8.80	1.18
⊕ Jacobs Engnrg Grp	Services	20.5	42.89	1.16
☼ Diebold	Technology	34.3	23.51	1.14
⊖ Earthlink	Technology	—	141.90	1.14
☼ D & K Healthcare Resources	Health	28.2	321.30	1.12
☼ Sonicwall	Technology	—	19.63	1.11
☼ Amerisourcebergen Cl A	N/A	—	—	1.10
RailAmerica	Services	16.3	84.34	1.06
⊖ Simpson Mfg	Industrials	18.0	12.35	1.04

Current Investment Style

Style: Value Blnd Growth; Size: Large Med Small

	Stock Port Avg	Relative S&P 500 Current	Relative S&P 500 Hist	Rel Cat
Price/Earnings Ratio	28.6[1]	0.92	0.89	0.89
Price/Book Ratio	5.0	0.88	0.84	1.03
Price/Cash Flow	19.5[1]	1.08	1.02	0.88
3 Yr Earnings Growth	19.8[1]	1.35	—	0.79
1 Yr Earnings Est%	15.8[1]	—	—	2.03
Med Mkt Cap $mil	464	0.0	0.0	0.44

[1]figure is based on 50% or less of stocks

Special Securities % assets 09-30-01	
Restricted/Illiquid Secs	1
Emerging-Markets Secs	1
Options/Futures/Warrants	Yes

Composition % assets 09-30-01	
Cash	5.3
Stocks*	94.3
Bonds	0.4
Other	0.0
*Foreign (% stocks)	1.5

Market Cap	
Giant	0.0
Large	0.0
Medium	14.7
Small	56.1
Micro	29.2

Sector Weightings	% of Stocks	Rel S&P	5-Year High	5-Year Low
Utilities	0.0	0.0	2	0
Energy	2.7	0.4	18	1
Financials	1.8	0.1	14	0
Industrials	14.8	1.3	21	3
Durables	4.3	2.7	7	1
Staples	1.7	0.2	5	0
Services	19.1	1.8	28	10
Retail	6.3	0.9	14	2
Health	24.5	1.7	24	5
Technology	24.8	1.4	42	19

Analysis by Christopher Traulsen 12-23-01

RS Diversified Growth remains a very good choice for aggressive investors.

This fund has reined in its bets since the go-go growth days of 1999. Coming into 2001, comanagers John Wallace and John Seabern had cut back on the pricey technology sector and added to less richly valued areas such as energy and industrials.

The fund is still far from conservative, though. It favors small firms in fast-changing, emerging areas of the economy. And although the team has cut its tech stake, the fund still has 25% of assets in the sector and owns many tech-related service companies, such as online tech-support enabler Support.com. Not surprisingly, it remains substantially more volatile than its average small-growth rival.

Within that context, however, Seabern and Wallace have deftly maneuvered the fund. They mistakenly bet on emerging telecoms in 2000, but have otherwise been on the mark. In 1999, they ramped up the fund's tech exposure sufficiently to deliver a 150% return. In 2001, they cut back on energy soon enough to avoid much of the sector's woes and homed in on solid picks in a variety of sectors, including transportation company Landstar System and Coinstar, which operates machines that exchange coins for cash.

Such moves have helped limit the fund's year-to-date loss through Dec. 21 to just 2%, a far smaller drop than the 11% plunge taken by the fund's average peer. That's no fluke: The fund's five-year return ranks in the top 5% of the small-growth category, and with the exception of 2000, it has handily beat its average rival in every calendar year since its inception. Further, Wallace built a strong record at Oppenheimer before coming to RS.

This offering is only suited for aggressive investors, but we think it's one of the best in its class. It's also sitting on a large realized loss, which should improve its tax efficiency for some time to come.

Address:	388 Market St Ste 200 San Francisco, CA 94111 800–766–3863 / 415–781–9700
Web Address:	www.rsim.com
*Inception:	08-01-96
Advisor:	RS Inv.
Subadvisor:	None
NTF Plans:	Fidelity , Datalynx

Minimum Purchase:	$5000	Add: $100 IRA: $1000
Min Auto Inv Plan:	$5000	Add: $100
Sales Fees:	0.25%B	
Management Fee:	1.0%	
Actual Fees:	Mgt: 1.00%	Dist: 0.25%
Expense Projections:	3Yr: $594	5Yr: $1020 10Yr: $2203
Avg Brok Commission:	—	Income Distrib: Annually
Total Cost (relative to category):		Average

RS Emerging Growth

Ticker	Load	NAV	Yield	Total Assets	Mstar Category
RSEGX	Closed	$32.01	0.0%	$2,497.7 mil	Mid-Cap Growth

Prospectus Objective: Small Company

RS Emerging Growth Fund seeks capital appreciation.

The fund normally invests at least 65% of assets in equity securities of emerging-growth companies. These companies usually have above-average growth potential due to superior products or services, operating characteristics, and financing capabilities. The fund usually invests in industry segments that, in the opinion of management, are also experiencing rapid growth.

Past names: RCS Emerging Growth Fund and Robertson Stephens Emerging Growth Fund. On April 12, 1999, Robertson Stephens Emerging Growth Fund merged into the fund.

Historical Profile

Return	High
Risk	High
Rating	★★★ Neutral

Investment Style
Equity
Average Stock %: 91%, 94%, 99%, 99%, 93%, 85%

▼ Manager Change
▽ Partial Manager Change

Fund Performance vs. Category Average
■ Quarterly Fund Return +/– Category Average
— Category Baseline

Performance Quartile (within Category)

Portfolio Manager(s)

James L. Callinan, CFA. Since 7-96. MBA Harvard U.; MS New York U. Other funds currently managed: SEI Instl Mgd Small Cap Growth A, SEI Instl Mgd Small Cap Growth B, RS Information Age.

1990	1991	1992	1993	1994	1995	1996	1997	1998	1999	2000	12-01	History
11.67	17.50	16.77	17.98	17.32	19.21	20.07	18.71	22.95	60.67	44.02	32.01	NAV
9.57	58.70	–2.55	7.22	7.96	20.31	21.53	18.54	28.02	182.56	–25.04	–27.28	Total Return %
12.69	28.22	–10.17	–2.84	6.65	–17.22	–1.41	–14.81	–0.55	161.52	–15.94	–15.41	+/– S&P 500
14.71	11.67	–11.26	–3.98	10.13	–13.67	4.05	–4.00	10.15	131.25	–13.29	–7.13	+/– Russ Midcap Grth
0.00	0.00	0.00	0.00	0.00	0.00	0.00	0.00	0.00	0.00	0.00	0.00	Income Return %
9.57	58.70	–2.55	7.22	7.96	20.31	21.53	18.54	28.02	182.56	–25.04	–27.28	Capital Return %
2	36	93	87	9	96	28	44	16	2	87	68	Total Rtn % Rank Cat
0.00	0.00	0.00	0.00	0.00	0.00	0.00	0.00	0.00	0.00	0.00	0.00	Income $
0.86	0.90	0.27	0.00	2.10	1.58	3.19	5.02	0.88	3.31	1.44	0.00	Capital Gains $
1.88	1.59	1.49	1.54	1.60	1.64	1.60	1.50	1.47	1.51	1.29	—	Expense Ratio %
–0.02	–0.68	–0.92	–0.61	–1.27	–0.99	–0.83	–0.68	–1.03	–1.19	–0.82	—	Income Ratio %
272	147	124	—	274	147	270	462	291	177	157	—	Turnover Rate %
22.9	141.5	277.5	169.7	176.1	158.5	210.4	248.9	394.3	3,577.1	3,868.7	2,497.7	Net Assets $mil

Performance 12-31-01

	1st Qtr	2nd Qtr	3rd Qtr	4th Qtr	Total
1997	–14.00	22.89	21.08	–7.35	18.54
1998	18.28	2.08	–23.37	38.37	28.02
1999	27.93	16.96	7.80	75.17	182.56
2000	19.40	–11.02	–4.11	–26.42	–25.04
2001	–29.69	16.70	–31.26	28.92	–27.28

Trailing	Total Return%	+/– S&P 500	+/– Russ Midcap Grth	% Rank All	% Rank Cat	Growth of $10,000
3 Mo	28.92	18.23	1.85	5	9	12,892
6 Mo	–11.38	–5.82	–3.12	89	56	8,862
1 Yr	–27.28	–15.41	–7.13	91	68	7,272
3 Yr Avg	15.49	16.51	13.33	5	12	15,402
5 Yr Avg	18.51	7.81	9.49	2	6	23,374
10 Yr Avg	14.45	1.52	3.34	7	11	38,552
15 Yr Avg	—	—	—	—	—	—

Tax Analysis	Tax-Adj Ret%	%Rank Cat	%Pretax Ret	%Rank Cat
3 Yr Avg	14.11	9	91.1	21
5 Yr Avg	15.32	7	82.8	31
10 Yr Avg	11.64	11	80.6	24

Potential Capital Gain Exposure: –34% of assets

Risk Analysis

Time Period	Load-Adj Return %	Risk %Rank[1] All	Risk %Rank[1] Cat	Morningstar Return	Morningstar Risk	Morningstar Risk-Adj Rating
1 Yr	–27.28					
3 Yr	15.49	98	93	2.47[2]	2.12	★★★★
5 Yr	18.51	98	92	3.81[2]	1.98	★★★★★
10 Yr	14.45	98	96	1.65	2.11	★★

Average Historical Rating (134 months): 3.2★s

[1] 1=low, 100=high [2] T-Bill return substituted for category avg.

Category Rating (3 Yr)

1 2 3 4 5
Worst Best

Return	Above Avg
Risk	High

Other Measures	Standard Index S&P 500	Best Fit Index Wil 4500
Alpha	34.6	23.9
Beta	1.83	1.67
R-Squared	37	84

Standard Deviation	67.75
Mean	15.49
Sharpe Ratio	0.18

Analysis by Christopher Traulsen 11-26-01

RS Emerging Growth Fund has taken some hard shots, but we still think it's a keeper.

This closed fund has incurred heavy losses in the last year and a half. In 2001, it's down 33% through Nov. 23, putting it in the mid-growth category's worst quartile for the period. Manager Jim Callinan also has a lot on his plate, as he comanages three other mutual funds and runs a hedge fund. Finally, he's running a heap of money in this style, making the fund slower-footed than smaller rivals.

That said, Callinan is an experienced manager who has put up great long-term returns. He uses a disciplined process that focuses on ferreting out rapidly growing companies with high margins and competitive advantages, and he has substantial analyst support. He also keeps position sizes small, so the fund's large asset base, while still an issue, isn't as big a handicap as it might be otherwise. Also, much of Callinan's work on his other funds flows from his efforts here, so his load isn't as heavy as it might seem.

The fund's recent losses aren't surprising. This is a high-growth vehicle that carries much industry and valuation risk. Callinan had just over 30% of the portfolio devoted to tech stocks at mid-year, with an emphasis on enterprise-software companies. He hasn't gotten much more defensive since. Indeed, on the dip in September, he added to tech names he thought had enough of a competitive edge to withstand the current downturn, such as Photon Dynamics—the dominant maker of testing equipment for flat-panel displays.

Investors have been well compensated for enduring the fund's volatility over time—its three- and five-year returns both rank in the category's best decile. It's also now sitting on a large realized loss, which it can use in future years to offset capital gains. The fund should have closed sooner, but given Callinan's past history of success and disciplined process, we think investors here should stay the course.

Portfolio Analysis 09-30-01

Share change since 06-01 Total Stocks: 157	Sector	PE	YTD Ret%	% Assets
⊖ Cytyc	Health	49.3	25.16	3.83
⊖ Sunrise Assisted Living	Services	16.2	16.44	3.24
⊕ Barr Labs	Health	25.0	8.80	2.06
⊕ Investment Tech Grp	Financials	26.6	40.37	1.69
⊕ Waddell & Reed Finl Cl A	Financials	23.3	–13.40	1.66
⊖ Power Integrations	Technology	65.3	98.61	1.59
⊕ GoTo.com	Services	—	384.40	1.49
⊖ Triton PCS Hldgs	Services	—	–13.50	1.43
☼ Natl Data	Services	38.4	54.53	1.19
⊖ Too	Retail	26.4	120.00	1.18
⊖ Four Seasons Hotels	Services	27.7	–26.40	1.14
⊕ Powerwave Tech	Industrials	—	–70.40	1.11
⊕ Silicon Labs	Technology	—	134.50	1.07
⊕ Caremark Rx	Health	46.6	20.25	1.04
⊕ Agile Software	Technology	—	–65.10	1.01
⊕ Hispanic Brdcstg Cl A	Services	85.0	0.00	0.99
⊕ Invitrogen	Health	—	–28.30	0.97
⊖ SEI Investments	Services	43.0	–19.20	0.97
⊕ Finl Federal	Financials	17.2	30.89	0.95
⊕ Expedia	Services	—	324.60	0.92
⊕ Abgenix	Health	—	–43.00	0.92
⊖ Express Scripts	Health	33.6	–8.54	0.91
⊕ Macrovision	Services	88.1	–52.40	0.91
☼ Legg Mason	Financials	23.6	–7.53	0.89
☼ School Speciality	Industrials	21.0	14.04	0.89

Current Investment Style

Style: Value Blnd Growth; Size: Large Med Small

	Stock Port Avg	Relative S&P 500 Current	Relative S&P 500 Hist	Rel Cat
Price/Earnings Ratio	39.9	1.29	1.34	1.15
Price/Book Ratio	7.1	1.25	1.52	1.26
Price/Cash Flow	28.0	1.56	1.43	1.21
3 Yr Earnings Growth	31.7[1]	2.17	—	1.35
1 Yr Earnings Est%	16.4	—	—	1.76
Med Mkt Cap $mil	1,609	0.0	0.0	0.29

[1] figure is based on 50% or less of stocks

Special Securities % assets 09-30-01	
Restricted/Illiquid Secs	0
Emerging-Markets Secs	2
Options/Futures/Warrants	No

Composition % assets 09-30-01	
Cash	12.9
Stocks*	87.1
Bonds	0.0
Other	0.0
*Foreign (% stocks)	6.7

Market Cap	
Giant	0.0
Large	0.7
Medium	51.1
Small	44.0
Micro	4.3

Sector Weightings	% of Stocks	Rel S&P	5-Year High	5-Year Low
Utilities	0.0	0.0	4	0
Energy	0.0	0.0	15	0
Financials	9.7	0.5	11	0
Industrials	4.1	0.4	6	0
Durables	0.4	0.2	3	0
Staples	0.9	0.1	3	0
Services	24.2	2.2	43	5
Retail	3.7	0.5	24	1
Health	29.3	2.0	57	2
Technology	27.8	1.5	69	10

Address:	388 Market St Ste 200 San Francisco, CA 94111 800–766–3863 / 415–781–9700
Web Address:	www.rsim.com
Inception:	11-30-87
Advisor:	RS Inv.
Subadvisor:	None
NTF Plans:	Fidelity , Datalynx

Minimum Purchase:	Closed	Add: $100 IRA: —
Min Auto Inv Plan:	Closed	Add: $100
Sales Fees:	0.25%B	
Management Fee:	1.0%	
Actual Fees:	Mgt: 1.00%	Dist: 0.25%
Expense Projections:	3Yr: $477	5Yr: $823 10Yr: $1796
Avg Brok Commission:	—	Income Distrib: Annually
Total Cost (relative to category):		Below Avg

RS Internet Age

Ticker	Load	NAV	Yield	Total Assets	Mstar Category
RIAFX	12b–1 only	$5.76	0.0%	$69.1 mil	Spec Technology

Prospectus Objective: Specialty—Technology

RS Internet Age Fund seeks capital appreciation.

The fund will generally invest at least 65% of assets in companies in any industry that may benefit as a direct or indirect result of the growth of the Internet. This may include companies that provide access, infrastructure, content, products, or services to Internet companies or Internet users. This may also include companies engaged in e-commerce, telecommunications, medical products or services, or multimedia products and services. The fund may invest in common stock, preferred stock, short sales, futures, and options.

Historical Profile
Return —
Risk —
Rating Not Rated

Investment Style
Equity
Average Stock %: 100% (1999), 98% (2000), 83% (12-01)

▼ Manager Change
▽ Partial Manager Change

Fund Performance vs. Category Average
■ Quarterly Fund Return +/– Category Average
— Category Baseline

Performance Quartile (within Category)

Portfolio Manager(s)

James L. Callinan, CFA. Since 12-99. MBA Harvard U.; MS New York U. Other funds currently managed: RS Emerging Growth, SEI Instl Mgd Small Cap Growth A, SEI Instl Mgd Small Cap Growth B.

Stephen J. Bishop. Since 2-01. BA Notre Dame; MBA Harvard Business School. Other fund currently managed: RS Information Age.

1990	1991	1992	1993	1994	1995	1996	1997	1998	1999	2000	12-01	History
—	—	—	—	—	—	—	—	—	12.18	6.53	5.76	NAV
—	—	—	—	—	—	—	—	—	21.80*	–46.39	–11.79	Total Return %
—	—	—	—	—	—	—	—	—	16.58*	–37.29	0.08	+/– S&P 500
—	—	—	—	—	—	—	—	—	—	–30.17	3.80	+/– PSE Tech 100
—	—	—	—	—	—	—	—	—	0.00	0.00	0.00	Income Return %
—	—	—	—	—	—	—	—	—	21.80	–46.39	–11.79	Capital Return %
—	—	—	—	—	—	—	—	—	—	86	6	Total Rtn % Rank Cat
—	—	—	—	—	—	—	—	—	0.00	0.00	0.00	Income $
—	—	—	—	—	—	—	—	—	0.00	0.00	0.00	Capital Gains $
—	—	—	—	—	—	—	—	—	1.76	1.78	—	Expense Ratio %
—	—	—	—	—	—	—	—	—	–1.34	–1.52	—	Income Ratio %
—	—	—	—	—	—	—	—	—	—	238	—	Turnover Rate %
—	—	—	—	—	—	—	—	—	144.7	100.3	69.1	Net Assets $mil

Performance 12-31-01

	1st Qtr	2nd Qtr	3rd Qtr	4th Qtr	Total
1997	—	—	—	—	—
1998	—	—	—	—	—
1999	—	—	—	—	21.80*
2000	17.41	–16.01	–9.91	–39.65	–46.39
2001	–26.65	24.01	–36.87	53.60	–11.79

Trailing	Total Return%	+/– S&P 500	+/– PSE Tech 100	% Rank All	% Rank Cat	Growth of $10,000
3 Mo	53.60	42.92	20.69	1	8	15,360
6 Mo	–3.03	2.52	2.25	51	4	9,697
1 Yr	–11.79	0.08	3.80	64	6	8,821
3 Yr Avg	—	—	—	—	—	—
5 Yr Avg	—	—	—	—	—	—
10 Yr Avg	—	—	—	—	—	—
15 Yr Avg	—	—	—	—	—	—

Tax Analysis	Tax-Adj Ret%	%Rank Cat	%Pretax Ret	%Rank Cat
3 Yr Avg	—	—	—	—
5 Yr Avg	—	—	—	—
10 Yr Avg	—	—	—	—

Potential Capital Gain Exposure: –147% of assets

Risk Analysis

Time Period	Load-Adj Return %	Risk %Rank¹ All	Risk %Rank¹ Cat	Morningstar Return	Morningstar Risk	Morningstar Risk-Adj Rating
1 Yr	–11.79					
3 Yr	—	—	—	—	—	
5 Yr	—	—	—	—	—	
Incept	–23.25	—	—	—	—	

Average Historical Rating —

¹1=low, 100=high

Category Rating (3 Yr)

Other Measures	Standard Index S&P 500	Best Fit Index
Alpha	—	—
Beta	—	—
R-Squared	—	—
Standard Deviation		—
Mean		—
Sharpe Ratio		—

Return
Risk

Portfolio Analysis 06-30-01

Share chng since 03-01 Total Stocks: 61

	Subsector	PE	YTD Ret%	% Assets
⊕ EBAY	Services	NMF	102.70	5.21
⊕ AOL Time Warner	Computer Svs	—	–7.76	3.51
⊕ Openwave Sys	Technology	—	–79.50	3.45
⊕ Macrovision	Services	88.1	–52.40	3.42
✲ Citrix Sys	Software	44.4	0.71	3.22
⊕ Microtune	Technology	—	41.64	2.62
Virage Logic	Technology	—	28.20	2.61
✲ Nuance Comms	Technology	—	–78.90	2.52
⊕ GoTo.com	Services	—	384.40	2.42
✲ Expedia	Services	—	324.60	2.39
✲ Vignette	Technology	—	–70.10	2.30
✲ Quest Software	Technology	—	–21.20	2.20
✲ Travelocity.com	Services	—	136.70	1.99
⊖ Oakley	Durables	20.1	20.44	1.88
⊖ Microsemi	Technology	51.2	113.50	1.76
✲ Ticketmaster Online–City B	Services	—	95.70	1.71
⊕ PLX Tech	Technology	—	51.69	1.62
⊕ Mercury Interactive	Software	70.8	–62.30	1.55
✲ Interwoven	Technology	—	–70.40	1.54
✲ Amazon.com	Retail	—	–30.40	1.49
✲ IntraNet Solutions	Technology	—	–42.00	1.48
Power Integrations	Technology	65.3	98.61	1.46
✲ Cirrus Logic	Semi Equipment	—	–29.40	1.44
NextCard	Financials	—	–93.50	1.43
⊕ O2Micro Intl	Technology	—	—	1.41

Current Investment Style

Style: Value Blnd Growth; Size: Large Med Small

	Stock Port Avg	Relative S&P 500 Current	Relative S&P 500 Hist	Rel Cat
Price/Earnings Ratio	50.1¹	1.62	—	1.09
Price/Book Ratio	5.7	0.99	—	0.92
Price/Cash Flow	32.9	1.83	—	1.27
3 Yr Earnings Growth	—	—	—	—
1 Yr Earnings Est%	19.9¹	—	—	–1.20
Med Mkt Cap $mil	1,375	0.0	—	0.09

¹figure is based on 50% or less of stocks

Special Securities % assets 06-30-01	
Restricted/Illiquid Secs	0
Emerging-Markets Secs	2
Options/Futures/Warrants	No

Composition % assets 06-30-01	
Cash	12.9
Stocks*	87.1
Bonds	0.0
Other	0.0
*Foreign (% stocks)	2.9

Market Cap	
Giant	4.2
Large	6.2
Medium	41.1
Small	44.6
Micro	4.0

Subsector Weightings	% of Stocks	Rel Cat
Computers	0.0	0.0
Semiconductors	0.0	0.0
Semi Equipment	1.7	0.4
Networking	1.1	0.3
Periph/Hardware	0.0	0.0
Software	5.6	0.4
Computer Svs	4.1	0.7
Telecom	0.9	0.1
Health Care	0.0	0.0
Other	86.6	2.3

Analysis by Christopher Traulsen 12-23-01

RS Internet Age Fund is one of the better Internet funds—just don't forget its risks.

For the year to date through Dec. 21, 2001, this fund is down 13.5%. That's poor in absolute terms, but it's a much smaller loss than the average Net-focused fund's, and handily beats the typical tech fund's 39% loss. The showing follows another strong relative performance in 2000. The fund lost a gut-wrenching 46% that year, but still bested the vast majority of its Internet-oriented rivals.

In early 2001, comanager Cathy Baker left RS for personal reasons. But new comanager Steve Bishop, who focuses on hardware picks, and growth-investing veteran Jim Callinan haven't missed a beat. The pair let cash creep up to 25% this summer, helping the fund withstand the market's downdraft far better than its rivals. They also made a number of savvy picks, including eBay, Goto.com (now called Overture Services), and travel-related sites such as Expedia.

When the market cracked in September, the pair smartly put some of that cash back to work, snapping up a basket of beaten-down hardware names such as O2 Micro, which makes power-management chips for laptop computers, and storage concern McData. Both names have rallied sharply, helping power the fund to a top-flight three-month return.

Such strong stock-picking and the presence of an experienced growth manager like Callinan put this offering among the Net-fund elite. The fund is also sitting on a realized loss of $13 a share, or more than twice its current NAV. That should help make it pretty tax-efficient for some time to come. However, we still think most investors will be better off with a broader tech fund. This fund's narrow focus makes it extremely volatile, and its emphasis on small-cap names in emerging areas exposes it to a high degree of business risk.

Address:	388 Market St Ste 200 San Francisco, CA 94111 415–781–9700 / 800–766–3863
Web Address:	www.rsim.com
*Inception:	12-01-99
Advisor:	RS Inv.
Subadvisor:	None
NTF Plans:	Fidelity Inst. , Waterhouse

Minimum Purchase:	$5000	Add: $100	IRA: $1000
Min Auto Inv Plan:	$5000	Add: $100	
Sales Fees:	0.25%B		
Management Fee:	1.3%		
Actual Fees:	Mgt: 1.25%	Dist: 0.25%	
Expense Projections:	3Yr: $572	5Yr: —	10Yr: —
Avg Brok Commission:	—	Income Distrib: Annually	
Total Cost (relative to category):	—		

SAFECO Growth Opportunities

Ticker	Load	NAV	Yield	Total Assets	Mstar Category
SAFGX	None	$27.25	0.0%	$877.5 mil	Small Blend

Prospectus Objective: Growth

SAFECO Growth Opportunities Fund seeks growth of both capital and income.

The fund normally invests virtually all assets in common stocks. To select individual equities, the fund examines the issuers' financial strength, management quality, and earnings power. The fund does not usually engage in trading for short-term profits. It may invest up to 5% of assets in each of the following: contingent value rights, warrants, and closed-end investment companies. It may invest up to 10% of assets in REITs; it may also purchase ADRs. In addition, the fund may invest in convertibles and debt securities that are linked to specific equities or equity indexes.

The fund has gone through several name changes.

Historical Profile
Return: Above Avg
Risk: Above Avg
Rating: ★★★ Neutral

Investment Style
Equity
Average Stock %: 98% 98% 94% 100% 99% 95%

▼ Manager Change
▽ Partial Manager Change

Fund Performance vs. Category Average
■ Quarterly Fund Return +/– Category Average
— Category Baseline

Performance Quartile (within Category)

Portfolio Manager(s)

Thomas M. Maguire. Since 11-89. BBA'76 U. of Washington; MBA'80 U. of Washington. Other funds currently managed: SAFECO Growth Opportunities A, SAFECO Growth Opportunities B, SAFECO Advisor Growth A {dupe 19404}.

History

1990	1991	1992	1993	1994	1995	1996	1997	1998	1999	2000	12-01	History
12.01	18.31	17.00	20.06	17.55	16.20	16.97	22.45	22.70	23.30	22.33	27.25	NAV
–14.97	62.65	–3.07	22.19	–1.62	26.10	22.90	49.97	4.37	2.64	–4.16	22.03	Total Return %
–11.85	32.16	–10.69	12.13	–2.94	–11.43	–0.04	16.61	–24.21	–18.40	4.94	33.91	+/– S&P 500
4.54	16.59	–21.48	3.29	0.20	–2.34	6.36	27.60	6.92	–18.62	–1.14	19.55	+/– Russell 2000
0.52	0.39	0.00	0.00	0.00	0.38	0.02	0.00	0.00	0.00	0.00	0.00	Income Return %
–15.49	62.26	–3.07	22.19	–1.62	25.72	22.88	49.96	4.37	2.64	–4.16	22.03	Capital Return %
54	4	96	17	60	52	35	1	12	73	88	8	Total Rtn % Rank Cat
0.09	0.05	0.00	0.00	0.00	0.07	0.00	0.00	0.00	0.00	0.00	0.00	Income $
1.88	1.15	0.62	0.70	2.15	5.67	2.66	3.00	0.73	0.00	0.00	0.00	Capital Gains $
1.01	0.90	0.91	0.91	0.95	0.98	1.02	0.85	0.77	1.07	1.05	—	Expense Ratio %
0.88	0.36	–0.10	–0.10	–0.12	0.34	–0.14	–0.17	–0.06	–0.57	–0.74	—	Income Ratio %
90	50	85	57	71	110	125	83	55	38	63	—	Turnover Rate %
65.4	172.0	171.8	163.6	150.2	183.0	196.1	638.6	1,394.2	815.6	641.5	829.1	Net Assets $mil

Performance 12-31-01

	1st Qtr	2nd Qtr	3rd Qtr	4th Qtr	Total
1997	2.00	18.95	18.46	4.34	49.97
1998	18.26	–1.05	–25.39	19.54	4.37
1999	–9.30	3.30	–6.25	16.85	2.64
2000	10.09	–10.96	6.52	–8.22	–4.16
2001	–6.18	34.46	–25.06	29.09	22.03

Trailing	Total Return%	+/– S&P 500	+/– Russ 2000	% Rank All	% Rank Cat	Growth of $10,000
3 Mo	29.09	18.40	8.01	5	7	12,909
6 Mo	–3.27	2.29	0.82	52	68	9,673
1 Yr	22.03	33.91	19.55	2	8	12,203
3 Yr Avg	6.28	7.30	–0.14	20	86	12,004
5 Yr Avg	13.44	2.74	5.92	7	28	18,788
10 Yr Avg	12.99	0.07	1.48	12	65	33,928
15 Yr Avg	14.18	0.44	3.42	10	17	73,075

Tax Analysis	Tax-Adj Ret%	%Rank Cat	%Pretax Ret	%Rank Cat
3 Yr Avg	6.28	72	100.0	1
5 Yr Avg	12.33	20	91.7	20
10 Yr Avg	10.20	68	78.5	68

Potential Capital Gain Exposure: 12% of assets

Risk Analysis

Time Period	Load-Adj Return %	Risk %Rank[1] All	Risk %Rank[1] Cat	Morningstar Return	Morningstar Risk	Morningstar Risk-Adj Rating
1 Yr	22.03					
3 Yr	6.28	83	93	0.29[2]	1.23	★★★
5 Yr	13.44	84	88	2.16[2]	1.24	★★★★
10 Yr	12.99	92	96	1.31	1.47	★★★

Average Historical Rating (193 months): 2.5★s

[1]1=low, 100=high [2] T-Bill return substituted for category avg.

Category Rating (3 Yr)

1 2 3 4 5
Worst Best

Return: Below Avg
Risk: High

Other Measures	Standard Index S&P 500	Best Fit Index Russ 2000
Alpha	9.8	0.8
Beta	1.08	0.95
R-Squared	49	72

Standard Deviation	28.50
Mean	6.28
Sharpe Ratio	0.05

Portfolio Analysis 10-31-01

Share change since 09-01 Total Stocks: 86	Sector	PE	YTD Ret%	% Assets
NCO Grp	Services	20.5	–24.60	5.15
United Stationers	Industrials	18.2	40.21	4.19
Micros Sys	Technology	NMF	37.53	3.96
⊕ Lumenis	N/A	—	—	3.68
Iron Mountain	Services	—	17.98	3.62
⊖ Endocare	Health	—	40.63	3.41
Thoratec Labs	Health	—	54.55	3.29
Serologicals	Health	30.3	42.73	3.10
Conceptus	Health	—	79.81	3.09
Polymedica	Health	7.5	–50.20	2.96
Western Wireless Cl A	Services	—	–27.90	2.94
Websense	Technology	—	121.10	2.92
Rent-Way	Services	—	34.97	2.80
☼ TMP Worldwide	Services	71.5	–22.00	2.77
Corinthian Colleges	Services	32.5	7.78	2.58
⊕ Matria Healthcare	Health	42.2	259.70	2.32
⊕ RMH Teleservices	Services	—	106.40	2.11
⊕ Plato Learning	Technology	72.2	47.03	2.10
Doral Finl	Financials	12.1	30.92	2.00
☼ Rent-A-Center	Services	14.4	–2.70	1.93
⊕ Stellent	N/A	—	—	1.82
⊕ Aspen Tech	Technology	—	–49.40	1.65
Anchor Gaming	Services	—	56.15	1.54
Res-Care	Health	26.0	96.67	1.44
Elizabeth Arden	Staples	—	26.59	1.44

Current Investment Style

Style: Value Blnd Growth; Size: Large Med Small

	Stock Port Avg	Relative S&P 500 Current	Relative S&P 500 Hist	Rel Cat
Price/Earnings Ratio	30.9[1]	1.00	0.73	1.24
Price/Book Ratio	4.9	0.87	0.55	1.54
Price/Cash Flow	16.2	0.90	0.92	1.04
3 Yr Earnings Growth	31.0[1]	2.12	1.22	1.82
1 Yr Earnings Est%	4.2[1]	—	—	4.90
Med Mkt Cap $mil	452	0.0	0.0	0.46

[1]figure is based on 50% or less of stocks

Special Securities % assets 10-31-01	
Restricted/Illiquid Secs	0
Emerging-Markets Secs	Trace
Options/Futures/Warrants	No

Composition % assets 10-31-01	
Cash	1.4
Stocks*	98.6
Bonds	0.0
Other	0.0
*Foreign (% stocks)	3.8

Market Cap	
Giant	0.5
Large	0.2
Medium	13.2
Small	61.2
Micro	25.0

Sector Weightings	% of Stocks	Rel S&P	5-Year High	5-Year Low
Utilities	0.0	0.0	9	0
Energy	0.0	0.0	12	0
Financials	3.1	0.2	19	1
Industrials	7.0	0.6	23	3
Durables	1.2	0.8	30	0
Staples	2.2	0.3	25	0
Services	33.3	3.1	44	4
Retail	0.8	0.1	19	1
Health	36.7	2.5	39	10
Technology	15.6	0.9	32	3

Analysis by Langdon Healy 11-30-01

Safeco Growth Opportunities isn't safe, but gutsy investors may find its eclectic style worth a look.

This fund is one of the riskier offerings in its category. The fund's three-, five-, and 10-year standard deviations (measures of volatility) are all among the highest in the small-blend group. Tom Maguire, the fund's iconoclastic longtime manager, almost relishes volatility and cautions investors that his style produces short-term results that can "stink."

Maguire's nebulous approach to investing will also send adherents of strict style-box fidelity scurrying. He buys companies of all sizes and types. That said, he aims for stocks with high earnings-growth potential trading at moderate prices, leading him to stick mostly to small and micro caps. Indeed, the fund's current market cap is only less than a third the size of its average peer's. That smaller-cap bent and a readiness to make big bets on the firms with which he's most enamored contribute to the fund's volatility.

The fund had a rough past couple of years, with Maguire mistakenly underweighting tech in 1999, then ramping up his exposure to the sector in 2000, just in time to get stung when the bubble burst. The fund has recovered in 2001, however, with a 10.3% return for the year to date through Nov. 29, a top-quintile showing in the category. This owes to strong stock selection, such as top holding Conceptus, a medical-device firm that has rallied strongly since he bought it in early 2000.

Since Maguire took the helm in November 1989, the fund's returns have been only slightly better than the average small-blend fund's, but much more volatile. However, his freedom to go anywhere and bet big when he finds something he likes make this an intriguing option for investors who want to shoot for the stars.

Address:	P.O. Box 34890, Seattle, WA 98124-1890, 800-426-6730 / 206-545-5530
Web Address:	www.safecofunds.com
Inception:	01-18-68
Advisor:	Safeco Asset Mgmt.
Subadvisor:	None
NTF Plans:	Fidelity , Fidelity Inst.

Minimum Purchase:	$2500	Add: $100 IRA: $1000
Min Auto Inv Plan:	$1000	Add: $100
Sales Fees:	No-load	
Management Fee:	.75% mx./.45% mn.	
Actual Fees:	Mgt: 0.66%	Dist: —
Expense Projections:	3Yr: $334	5Yr: $579 10Yr: $1283
Avg Brok Commission:	—	Income Distrib: Annually
Total Cost (relative to category):		Below Avg

Salomon Brothers Capital O

Ticker	Load	NAV	Yield	Total Assets	Mstar Category
SACPX	Closed	$25.27	1.1%	$1,073.2 mil	Mid–Cap Value

Prospectus Objective: Growth

Salomon Brothers Capital Fund seeks capital appreciation.

The fund invests primarily in common stocks and convertible securities. Management seeks companies with undervalued share prices; existing or possible changes in policies or structure; or growth potential due to technological advances; or other new developments. The fund may also invest up to 20% in foreign securities. "This fund is non-diversified."

Class A shares have front loads; B shares have deferred loads, higher 12b-1 fees, and conversion features; C shares have level loads; O shares are offered only to current Class O shareholders. Past name: Lehman Capital Fund

Historical Profile
Return High
Risk Average
Rating ★★★★★ Highest

Investment Style
Equity
Average Stock %: 88% 92% 92% 92% 90% 85%

▼ Manager Change
▽ Partial Manager Change

Fund Performance vs. Category Average
■ Quarterly Fund Return +/– Category Average
— Category Baseline

Performance Quartile (within Category)

Portfolio Manager(s)

Ross Margolies. Since 1-95. BA'80 Johns Hopkins U.; MBA'87 New York U. Other funds currently managed: Smith Barney Convertible B, Smith Barney Premium Total Return A, Smith Barney Premium Total Return B.

Robert M. Donahue, Jr.. Since 7-98. Other funds currently managed: Salomon Brothers Capital B, Salomon Brothers Capital 2, Salomon Brothers Capital A.

1990	1991	1992	1993	1994	1995	1996	1997	1998	1999	2000	12-01	History
14.86	19.06	19.67	20.80	15.62	18.67	19.88	21.23	22.98	25.43	25.60	25.27	NAV
–9.06	33.44	4.87	16.99	–14.16	34.80	33.34	26.76	23.83	23.44	19.20	2.00	Total Return %
–5.95	2.95	–2.75	6.93	–15.47	–2.73	10.39	–6.59	–4.74	2.40	28.30	13.88	+/– S&P 500
7.02	–4.49	–16.81	1.36	–12.03	–0.13	13.08	–7.60	18.74	23.54	0.01	–0.34	+/– Russ Midcap Val
1.71	2.20	0.55	0.18	0.15	0.90	0.89	0.00	1.27	0.87	0.86	1.14	Income Return %
–10.78	31.24	4.32	16.81	–14.31	33.90	32.45	26.76	22.56	22.57	18.34	0.87	Capital Return %
48	36	93	60	92	26	3	48	3	9	41	60	Total Rtn % Rank Cat
0.29	0.33	0.11	0.04	0.03	0.14	0.16	0.00	0.24	0.19	0.20	0.29	Income $
0.09	0.37	0.22	2.08	2.31	2.21	4.46	3.83	2.83	2.59	4.42	0.55	Capital Gains $
1.44	1.48	1.34	1.31	1.30	1.36	1.38	1.22	1.08	1.01	0.90	—	Expense Ratio %
1.59	1.87	0.58	0.13	0.12	0.74	0.67	0.26	0.96	0.91	0.84	—	Income Ratio %
156	94	41	104	152	217	191	159	141	126	97	—	Turnover Rate %
75.8	89.8	103.5	113.8	87.5	97.3	136.6	176.2	194.9	215.0	227.3	—	Net Assets $mil

Performance 12-31-01

	1st Qtr	2nd Qtr	3rd Qtr	4th Qtr	Total
1997	0.93	13.41	13.03	–2.03	26.76
1998	13.75	1.46	–12.41	22.50	23.83
1999	–1.31	15.37	–4.82	13.90	23.44
2000	13.04	3.92	1.40	0.07	19.20
2001	–0.60	5.81	–13.09	11.59	2.00

Trailing	Total Return%	+/– S&P 500	+/– Russ Midcap Val	% Rank All	% Rank Cat	Growth of $10,000
3 Mo	11.59	0.90	–0.44	35	58	11,159
6 Mo	–3.02	2.53	–2.11	51	73	9,698
1 Yr	2.00	13.88	–0.34	39	60	10,200
3 Yr Avg	14.49	15.52	7.69	5	24	15,009
5 Yr Avg	18.69	7.99	7.23	2	6	23,559
10 Yr Avg	16.13	3.20	1.71	3	19	44,595
15 Yr Avg	14.18	0.45	0.72	10	33	73,124

Tax Analysis	Tax-Adj Ret%	%Rank Cat	%Pretax Ret	%Rank Cat
3 Yr Avg	10.44	33	72.0	76
5 Yr Avg	14.09	17	75.4	64
10 Yr Avg	11.78	45	73.0	89

Potential Capital Gain Exposure: 8% of assets

Risk Analysis

Time Period	Load-Adj Return %	Risk %Rank[1] All	Risk %Rank[1] Cat	Morningstar Return	Morningstar Risk	Morningstar Risk-Adj Rating
1 Yr	2.00					
3 Yr	14.49	42	23	2.22[2]	0.58	★★★★★
5 Yr	18.69	48	17	3.87[2]	0.65	★★★★★
10 Yr	16.13	66	69	2.09	0.85	★★★★★

Average Historical Rating (193 months): 2.9★s

[1]1=low, 100=high [2] T-Bill return substituted for category avg.

Category Rating (3 Yr)

1 2 3 **4** 5
Worst Best

Return Above Avg
Risk Below Avg

Other Measures	Standard Index S&P 500	Best Fit Index S&P 500
Alpha	14.3	14.3
Beta	0.77	0.77
R–Squared	69	69
Standard Deviation		17.83
Mean		14.49
Sharpe Ratio		0.61

Portfolio Analysis 11-30-01

Share change since 10–01 Total Stocks: 67	Sector	PE	YTD Ret%	% Assets
Safeway	Retail	18.1	–33.20	4.60
American Intl Grp	Financials	42.0	–19.20	3.70
Costco Wholesale	Retail	34.4	11.12	2.93
Washington Mutual	Financials	10.1	–5.32	2.81
Federated Dept Stores	Retail	16.6	16.86	2.66
Novartis ADR	Health	22.3	–17.40	2.57
Sun Microsystems	Technology	NMF	–55.80	2.43
AT&T	Services	7.8	40.59	2.35
Hormel Foods	Staples	20.7	46.88	2.25
Ligand Pharmaceuticals	Health	—	27.86	2.15
XL Cap Cl A	Financials	22.8	5.82	2.09
Dell Comp	Technology	61.8	55.87	2.07
HCA – The Healthcare Company	Health	24.1	–12.20	2.05
Converse Tech	Technology	22.2	–79.40	2.02
News ADR Pfd	Services	—	—	2.00
⊕ FleetBoston Finl	Financials	16.2	0.55	1.98
Staples	Retail	77.9	58.30	1.97
⊕ AK Steel Hldg	Industrials	27.1	31.55	1.88
ConAgra	Staples	17.6	–4.73	1.85
⊕ 3Com	Technology	—	–24.90	1.81
Bank of New York	Financials	21.9	–24.80	1.76
ALCOA	Industrials	21.4	7.86	1.73
United Tech	Industrials	16.3	–16.70	1.62
Pepsi Bottling Grp	Staples	23.6	17.90	1.60
Kroger	Retail	16.3	–22.80	1.48

Current Investment Style

Style: Value Blnd Growth; Size: Large Med Small

	Stock Port Avg	Relative S&P 500 Current	Relative S&P 500 Hist	Rel Cat
Price/Earnings Ratio	28.1	0.91	0.79	1.19
Price/Book Ratio	3.6	0.63	0.55	1.19
Price/Cash Flow	14.6	0.81	0.70	1.18
3 Yr Earnings Growth	9.9	0.68	0.84	0.83
1 Yr Earnings Est%	–11.0	6.19	—	1.78
Med Mkt Cap $mil	13,752	0.2	0.2	1.93

Analysis by Gregg Wolper 11-18-01

Salomon Brothers Capital Fund is better than its recent rankings indicate, though it's shown that it's not bulletproof, either.

This fund is one of the more flexible offerings around, and thus classifying it isn't simple. It's in the mid-cap value category because with the markets getting pricey in the late 1990s, managers Ross Margolies and Rob Donahue tilted the portfolio toward the value side of the spectrum. Compared with more-strict value funds, it has performed uncharacteristically poorly over the trailing 12 months through Nov. 16, 2001. The fund's 1.8% loss over that period puts it in the bottom quartile of the category and trails the group average by 8 percentage points.

But in a sense, that's deceiving. With its broad mandate and flexible strategy, the fund can also be considered a blend offering that just chose to be more value-conscious during an extreme time. The fund looks healthier when judged that way: Its 12-month return is 7 percentage points better than the mid-blend category average. More important, its long-term performance compared with either crowd has been stellar.

In the market turmoil of recent months, the managers made significant moves. Margolies and Donahue say they sold most of what had been a large stake in hospitals when that sector rose after Sept. 11 (lately they've bought some back). They also sold some consumer-oriented holdings at that time, as investors piled into defensive stocks. In contrast, they've added to insurance and reinsurance stocks, citing a better environment for premiums.

Not every decision works out. For example, Safeway, the top holding most of the year, is down 30% in 2001. And the fund was helped by an unusually large cash stake, which is now at 12% of assets but can't be counted on to cushion losses in the future. Overall, though, this fund remains a fine choice.

Special Securities % assets 11-30-01	
Restricted/Illiquid Secs	1
Emerging–Markets Secs	Trace
Options/Futures/Warrants	No

Composition % assets 11-30-01	
Cash	0.0
Stocks*	93.6
Bonds	4.2
Other	2.3
*Foreign (% stocks)	10.0

Market Cap	
Giant	18.5
Large	34.4
Medium	30.8
Small	15.1
Micro	1.2

Sector Weightings	% of Stocks	Rel S&P	5-Year High	5-Year Low
Utilities	0.0	0.0	5	0
Energy	4.5	0.6	19	0
Financials	20.3	1.1	28	7
Industrials	9.7	0.9	32	7
Durables	0.0	0.0	25	0
Staples	6.9	0.9	22	2
Services	11.9	1.1	25	7
Retail	18.0	2.7	20	6
Health	13.8	0.9	16	0
Technology	14.8	0.8	22	0

Address: 750 Washington Blvd 11th Floor, Stamford, CT 06901, 800–725–6666 / 212–783–2081
Web Address: www.sbam.com
Inception: 12-01-76
Advisor: Salomon Brothers Asset Mgmt.
Subadvisor: None
NTF Plans: N/A

Minimum Purchase: Closed — Add: $50 — IRA: —
Min Auto Inv Plan: Closed — Add: $25
Sales Fees: No–load
Management Fee: .90%, .05%A
Actual Fees: Mgt: 0.80% — Dist: —
Expense Projections: 3Yr: $322 — 5Yr: $558 — 10Yr: $1236
Avg Brok Commission: — — Income Distrib: Annually
Total Cost (relative to category): Below Avg

Salomon Brothers Investors Value O

Ticker	Load	NAV	Yield	Total Assets	Mstar Category
SAIFX	Closed	$18.94	1.0%	$889.3 mil	Large Value

Prospectus Objective: Growth and Income

Salomon Brothers Investors Value Fund seeks long-term growth; current income is secondary.

The fund may invest without restriction in any class of security, though it invests primarily in common and preferred stocks. It generally holds a portion of assets in short-term debt instruments. It may invest up to 20% of assets in foreign securities. "This fund is non-diversified."

Class A shares have front loads; B shares have deferred loads, higher 12b-1 fees, and conversion features; 2 shares have level loads; O shares are closed to new investors. Prior to April 30, 1990, the fund was known as Lehman Investors Fund.

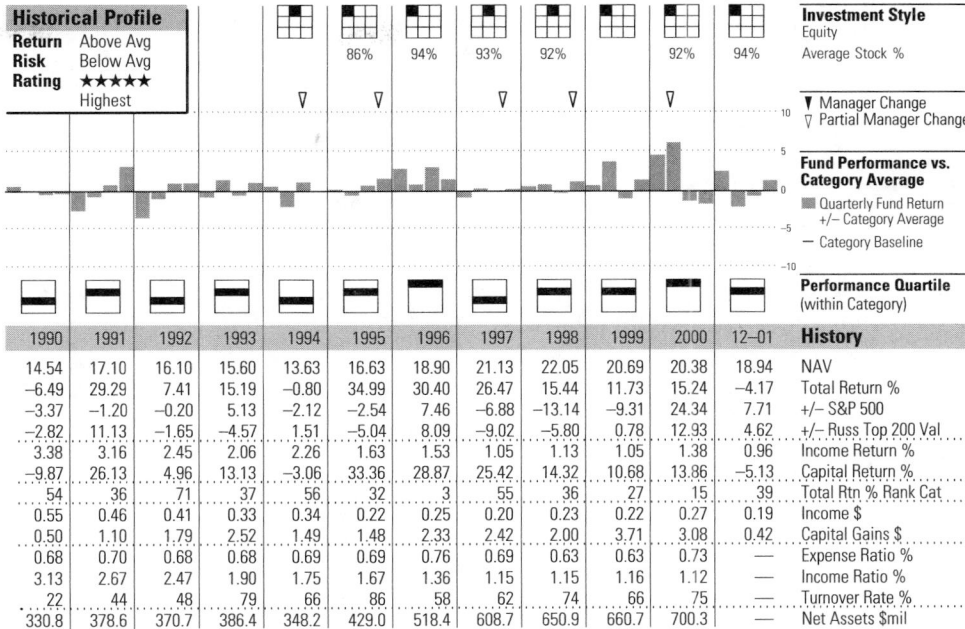

Historical Profile

Return Above Avg
Risk Below Avg
Rating ★★★★★ Highest

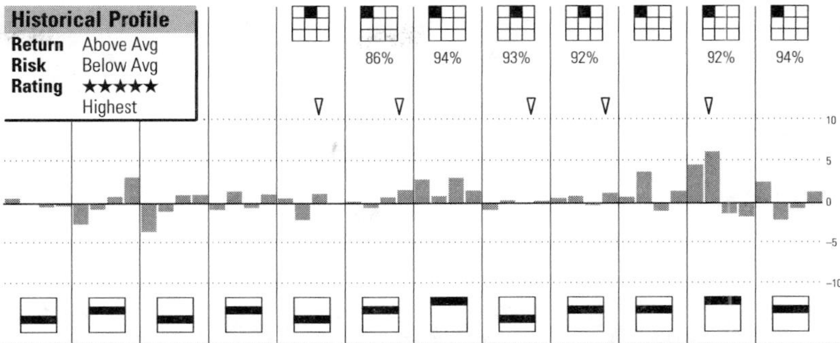

Investment Style
Equity
Average Stock %

	1994	1995	1996	1997	1998	1999	2000	12-01
Average Stock %		86%	94%	93%	92%		92%	94%

▼ Manager Change
▽ Partial Manager Change

Fund Performance vs. Category Average
■ Quarterly Fund Return +/– Category Average
— Category Baseline

Performance Quartile (within Category)

Portfolio Manager(s)

John B. Cunningham. Since 9-97. BA U. of Virginia; MBA Dartmouth C. Other funds currently managed: Salomon Brothers Investors Value A, Salomon Brothers Investors Value B, Salomon Brothers Investors Value 2.

Mark McAllister. Since 4-00. BS St. Johns U.; MBA New York U. Other funds currently managed: Salomon Brothers Investors Value A, Salomon Brothers Investors Value B, Salomon Brothers Investors Value 2.

1990	1991	1992	1993	1994	1995	1996	1997	1998	1999	2000	12–01	History
14.54	17.10	16.10	15.60	13.63	16.63	18.90	21.13	22.05	20.69	20.38	18.94	NAV
–6.49	29.29	7.41	15.19	–0.80	34.99	30.40	26.47	15.44	11.73	15.24	–4.17	Total Return %
–3.37	–1.20	–0.20	5.13	–2.12	–2.54	7.46	–6.88	–13.14	–9.31	24.34	7.71	+/– S&P 500
–2.82	11.13	–1.65	–4.57	1.51	–5.04	8.09	–9.02	–5.80	0.78	12.93	4.62	+/– Russ Top 200 Val
3.38	3.16	2.45	2.06	2.26	1.63	1.53	1.05	1.13	1.05	1.38	0.96	Income Return %
–9.87	26.13	4.96	13.13	–3.06	33.36	28.87	25.42	14.32	10.68	13.86	–5.13	Capital Return %
54	36	71	37	56	32	3	55	36	27	15	39	Total Rtn % Rank Cat
0.55	0.46	0.41	0.33	0.34	0.22	0.25	0.20	0.23	0.22	0.27	0.19	Income $
0.50	1.10	1.79	2.52	1.49	1.48	2.33	2.42	2.00	3.71	3.08	0.42	Capital Gains $
0.68	0.70	0.68	0.68	0.69	0.69	0.76	0.69	0.63	0.63	0.73	—	Expense Ratio %
3.13	2.67	2.47	1.90	1.75	1.67	1.36	1.15	1.15	1.16	1.12	—	Income Ratio %
22	44	48	79	66	86	58	62	74	66	75	—	Turnover Rate %
330.8	378.6	370.7	386.4	348.2	429.0	518.4	608.7	650.9	660.7	700.3	—	Net Assets $mil

Performance 12-31-01

	1st Qtr	2nd Qtr	3rd Qtr	4th Qtr	Total
1997	0.85	14.09	8.63	1.19	26.47
1998	11.93	0.29	–12.43	17.44	15.44
1999	1.50	13.58	–10.17	7.89	11.73
2000	4.75	4.25	4.06	1.41	15.24
2001	–3.21	2.65	–12.76	10.56	–4.17

Trailing	Total Return%	+/– S&P 500	+/– Russ Top 200 Val	% Rank All	% Rank Cat	Growth of $10,000
3 Mo	10.56	–0.13	5.04	39	30	11,056
6 Mo	–3.54	2.01	2.23	54	41	9,646
1 Yr	–4.17	7.71	4.62	49	39	9,583
3 Yr Avg	7.25	8.28	6.09	16	12	12,338
5 Yr Avg	12.49	1.79	1.29	9	13	18,013
10 Yr Avg	14.56	1.63	0.53	6	10	38,918
15 Yr Avg	13.57	–0.16	0.07	13	18	67,476

Tax Analysis	Tax-Adj Ret%	%Rank Cat	%Pretax Ret	%Rank Cat
3 Yr Avg	4.15	21	57.1	65
5 Yr Avg	9.38	19	75.1	51
10 Yr Avg	10.71	26	73.6	69

Potential Capital Gain Exposure: 18% of assets

Risk Analysis

Time Period	Load-Adj Return %	Risk %Rank[1] All	Risk %Rank[1] Cat	Morningstar Return	Morningstar Risk	Morningstar Risk-Adj Rating
1 Yr	–4.17					
3 Yr	7.25	52	38	0.50[2]	0.73	★★★★
5 Yr	12.49	55	39	1.88[2]	0.76	★★★★
10 Yr	14.56	60	49	1.68	0.78	★★★★★

Average Historical Rating (193 months): 3.5★s

[1]1=low, 100=high [2] T-Bill return substituted for category avg.

Category Rating (3 Yr)

1 2 3 4 5
Worst Best

Return Above Avg
Risk Average

Other Measures	Standard Index S&P 500	Best Fit Index S&P 500
Alpha	7.4	7.4
Beta	0.82	0.82
R-Squared	76	76

Standard Deviation	17.18
Mean	7.25
Sharpe Ratio	0.15

Portfolio Analysis 11-30-01

Share change since 10–01 Total Stocks: 74	Sector	PE	YTD Ret%	% Assets
Dell Comp	Technology	61.8	55.87	2.71
Sun Microsystems	Technology	NMF	–55.80	2.65
AT&T	Services	7.8	40.59	2.12
Safeway	Retail	18.1	–33.20	2.09
Federated Dept Stores	Retail	16.6	16.86	1.98
Kimberly–Clark	Industrials	18.5	–13.80	1.89
ALCOA	Industrials	21.4	7.86	1.88
Verizon Comms	Services	29.7	–2.52	1.84
Merrill Lynch	Financials	18.2	–22.70	1.80
FleetBoston Finl	Financials	16.2	0.55	1.79
Household Intl	Financials	14.7	6.89	1.76
Goldman Sachs Grp	Financials	20.7	–12.80	1.75
Sprint	Services	20.5	1.18	1.72
Waddell & Reed Finl Cl A	Financials	23.3	–13.40	1.72
Comverse Tech	Technology	22.2	–79.40	1.72
American Express	Financials	28.3	–34.40	1.70
Philip Morris	Staples	12.1	9.12	1.69
Bank of New York	Financials	21.9	–24.80	1.68
Washington Mutual	Financials	10.1	–5.32	1.68
Alltel	Services	17.7	1.14	1.67
US Bancorp	Financials	13.5	–6.14	1.66
El Paso	Utilities	NMF	–36.70	1.65
Novartis ADR	Health	22.3	–17.40	1.61
Intl Paper	Industrials	—	1.43	1.60
ConAgra	Staples	17.6	–4.73	1.58

Current Investment Style

Style: Value Blnd Growth; Size: Large Med Small

	Stock Port Avg	Relative S&P 500 Current	Relative S&P 500 Hist	Rel Cat
Price/Earnings Ratio	25.3	0.82	0.75	1.00
Price/Book Ratio	4.1	0.73	0.60	1.00
Price/Cash Flow	13.8	0.77	0.69	1.00
3 Yr Earnings Growth	17.8	1.21	0.96	1.20
1 Yr Earnings Est%	–10.0	5.63	—	3.01
Med Mkt Cap $mil	31,572	0.5	0.7	0.99

Analysis by Gregg Wolper 10-10-01

Salomon Brothers Investors Value Fund's dedication to its strategy costs it on occasion, but it has proven its worth over the long run.

This is a fund that isn't afraid to go against the tide—and to stick with its ideas even when the tide gets higher. Early in 2001, for example, the fund's managers decided that the long-term outlook for Sun Microsystems, whose share price was declining after management warned of slower growth, was bright enough to outweigh near-term problems. Lead manager Jack Cunningham said he and his colleagues considered it a leading technology company with a strong balance sheet and appealing new products. So they continued to buy even as its price kept sliding. With Sun down 68% for the year to date through Oct. 9, 2001, that doggedness helped drag the fund to a middling 11.6% loss so far this year. But Cunningham said that he still has confidence in Sun, as he thinks a value investor can't try to predict a stock's bottom.

Over the long term, the fund has made the right decisions much more often than not. Its trailing returns are in or near the category's top decile, and it has been less volatile than most large-value funds. And even this year, it has had successes. For example, unlike Sun, another tech pick, Dell Computer, is up 30% so far this year. Those forays into fallen tech angels don't mean the fund is contrarian just for the sake of it: Witness the decision earlier in the year to increase its stake in traditional defensive stocks, such as ConAgra and Washington Mutual, which helped cushion losses. Indeed, financials is its largest sector weighting, as it is with the typical large-value fund.

Its tech plays show that this value fund is neither conservative nor predictable. And it's certainly not immune from losses. But the fund's performance shows that it can reward patient investors quite well.

Special Securities % assets 11-30-01	
Restricted/Illiquid Secs	0
Emerging-Markets Secs	0
Options/Futures/Warrants	No

Sector Weightings	% of Stocks	Rel S&P	5-Year High	5-Year Low
Utilities	3.4	1.1	9	0
Energy	7.8	1.1	14	6
Financials	28.3	1.6	28	9
Industrials	8.1	0.7	34	6
Durables	1.5	1.0	12	1
Staples	4.8	0.6	19	2
Services	12.6	1.2	23	4
Retail	8.8	1.3	21	3
Health	6.2	0.4	16	2
Technology	18.5	1.0	21	3

Composition % assets 11-30-01	
Cash	0.0
Stocks*	98.4
Bonds	0.0
Other	1.6
*Foreign (% stocks)	9.5

Market Cap	
Giant	32.7
Large	51.6
Medium	15.4
Small	0.3
Micro	0.0

Address:	750 Washington Blvd 11th Floor Stamford, CT 06901 800–725–6666 / 212–783–1301
Web Address:	www.sbam.com
Inception:	09-01-58
Advisor:	Salomon Brothers Asset Mgmt.
Subadvisor:	None
NTF Plans:	N/A

Minimum Purchase:	Closed	Add: $50	IRA: —
Min Auto Inv Plan:	Closed	Add: $50	
Sales Fees:	No-load		
Management Fee:	.52%+(–).10%P, .05%A		
Actual Fees:	Mgt: 0.52%	Dist: —	
Expense Projections:	3Yr: $202	5Yr: $351	10Yr: $786
Avg Brok Commission:	—	Income Distrib: Quarterly	
Total Cost (relative to category):		Low	

Schwab 1000 Inv

Ticker	Load	NAV	Yield	Total Assets	Mstar Category
SNXFX	None	$31.95	0.9%	$6,216.3 mil	Large Blend

Prospectus Objective: Growth and Income

Schwab 1000 Fund seeks to match the total return of the Schwab 1000 Index, an index composed of the common stocks of the 1,000 largest publicly traded U.S. companies.

The fund normally invests at least 80% of assets in Schwab 1000 index stocks, in proportion to their weighting in the index. It may invest the balance of assets in securities not included in the index. The advisor expects the portfolio turnover rate to be low; it may not automatically buy and sell portfolio securities to reflect changes in the index. The fund may also invest a portion of assets in other investment companies.

The fund offers Investor and Select shares.

Historical Profile

Return	Above Avg
Risk	Average
Rating	★★★★ Above Avg

Investment Style Equity — Average Stock %

▼ Manager Change
▽ Partial Manager Change

Fund Performance vs. Category Average
■ Quarterly Fund Return
+/– Category Average
— Category Baseline

Performance Quartile (within Category)

Portfolio Manager(s)

Geraldine Hom. Since 5-95. BA'74 California State U. Other funds currently managed: Schwab Small Cap Index Inv, Schwab MarketTrack Growth, Schwab MarketTrack Balanced.

1990	1991	1992	1993	1994	1995	1996	1997	1998	1999	2000	12-01	History
						100%	100%	99%	100%	100%	100%	Average Stock %
—	11.26	11.96	12.85	12.57	16.94	20.34	26.56	33.51	40.28	36.73	31.95	NAV
—	14.25*	8.52	9.63	–0.11	36.61	21.58	31.92	27.16	21.00	–8.21	–12.26	Total Return %
—	1.60*	0.90	–0.43	–1.42	–0.93	–1.37	–1.43	–1.41	–0.04	0.89	–0.38	+/– S&P 500
—	—	0.87	–0.21	–0.56	–1.00	–0.59	–1.10	–1.47	–0.83	2.75	0.51	+/– Wilshire Top 750
—	1.65	2.19	2.15	2.05	1.83	1.53	1.29	0.95	0.77	0.60	0.74	Income Return %
—	12.60	6.33	7.47	–2.16	34.78	20.05	30.63	26.21	20.23	–8.81	–13.00	Capital Return %
—	—	34	55	47	25	47	31	36	42	48	40	Total Rtn % Rank Cat
—	0.15	0.25	0.26	0.26	0.23	0.26	0.26	0.25	0.26	0.24	0.27	Income $
—	0.00	0.00	0.00	0.00	0.00	0.00	0.00	0.00	0.00	0.00	0.00	Capital Gains $
—	0.00	0.35	0.45	0.51	0.54	0.49	0.47	0.46	0.46	0.47	—	Expense Ratio %
—	3.21	2.45	2.21	2.06	2.03	1.66	1.33	1.02	0.78	0.63	—	Income Ratio %
—	—	1	1	3	2	2	2	2	3	9	—	Turnover Rate %
—	192.2	371.0	529.1	554.0	1,063.4	1,908.8	2,823.1	4,184.2	5,311.2	4,730.6	4,163.2	Net Assets $mil

Performance 12-31-01

	1st Qtr	2nd Qtr	3rd Qtr	4th Qtr	Total
1997	1.43	16.72	8.43	2.77	31.92
1998	13.63	2.78	–10.70	21.93	27.16
1999	4.33	6.72	–6.67	16.45	21.00
2000	3.58	–3.76	0.35	–8.24	–8.21
2001	–12.58	6.45	–15.39	11.44	–12.26

Trailing	Total Return%	+/– S&P 500	+/–Wil Top 750	% Rank All	% Rank Cat	Growth of $10,000
3 Mo	11.44	0.76	0.12	35	35	11,144
6 Mo	–5.71	–0.15	0.08	66	41	9,429
1 Yr	–12.26	–0.38	0.51	66	40	8,774
3 Yr Avg	–0.86	0.17	0.97	77	45	9,745
5 Yr Avg	10.33	–0.37	0.21	17	32	16,348
10 Yr Avg	12.43	–0.50	–0.02	16	32	32,266
15 Yr Avg	—	—	—	—	—	—

Tax Analysis	Tax-Adj Ret%	%Rank Cat	%Pretax Ret	%Rank Cat
3 Yr Avg	–1.14	34	—	—
5 Yr Avg	9.98	14	96.7	4
10 Yr Avg	11.88	9	95.6	3

Potential Capital Gain Exposure: 30% of assets

Risk Analysis

Time Period	Load-Adj Return %	Risk %Rank[1] All	Risk %Rank[1] Cat	Morningstar Return	Morningstar Risk	Morningstar Risk-Adj Rating
1 Yr	–12.26					
3 Yr	–0.86	67	49	–1.16[2]	0.93	★★★
5 Yr	10.33	67	51	1.28[2]	0.90	★★★★
10 Yr	12.43	69	42	1.19	0.89	★★★★

Average Historical Rating (93 months): 4.0★s

[1] 1=low, 100=high [2] T-Bill return substituted for category avg.

Category Rating (3 Yr)

1 2 **3** 4 5
Worst — Best

Return	Average
Risk	Average

Other Measures	Standard Index S&P 500	Best Fit Index S&P 500
Alpha	0.3	0.3
Beta	1.01	1.01
R-Squared	99	99
Standard Deviation		17.17
Mean		–0.86
Sharpe Ratio		–0.39

Analysis by Alan Papier 09-10-01

Schwab 1000 Fund is a great choice for investors looking for a large-cap index fund with more than 500 holdings.

While most large-cap index funds follow the S&P 500 index, this one tracks a proprietary benchmark of the 1,000 largest U.S. stocks. That means the fund is tilted a bit more toward mid-caps and away from giant- and large-cap issues. Its 500 additional positions also add a bit more diversification.

So far, the fund's stable approach has generated solid results. For the 10-year period ended Aug. 31, 2001, the fund's 13% annualized gain landed in the top 30% of the crowded large-cap blend category. Plus, it was marginally less volatile than the average offering in the group. And even though index funds are generally more tax-efficient than their actively managed peers because of their lower turnover, this one has been better than most. Indeed, manager Geri Hom's primary goal is tax efficiency, and the fund hasn't yet made a capital-gains distribution. (The fund's tax-efficiency ratio is not 100%, however, because it distributes the income it receives as dividends, and those earnings are taxable.)

The fund also makes a strong case for itself relative to the S&P 500 group. Despite having to overcome its expense ratio (the index itself is not subject to management and trading costs), the fund hasn't lagged the index by more than its expense ratio on average over the past 10 years. In addition, the fund's tax-minimizing vigilance has contributed to longer-term after-tax returns that rival those of the venerable Vanguard 500 Index.

Investors should note that this fund might lag a bit when the largest, most-prominent stocks rally and that its expenses are a bit higher than those of the lowest-cost index offerings. Still, we think it is a solid core holding.

Portfolio Analysis 09-30-01

Share change since 06-01 Total Stocks: 965	Sector	PE	YTD Ret%	% Assets
⊖ General Elec	Industrials	30.1	–15.00	3.61
⊖ Microsoft	Technology	57.6	52.78	2.69
⊕ ExxonMobil	Energy	15.3	–7.59	2.66
⊖ Pfizer	Health	34.7	–12.40	2.47
⊖ Wal-Mart Stores	Retail	40.3	8.94	2.16
⊕ American Intl Grp	Financials	42.0	–19.20	2.00
⊖ Citigroup	Financials	20.0	0.03	1.99
⊖ Johnson & Johnson	Health	16.6	14.01	1.64
⊖ IBM	Technology	26.9	43.00	1.57
⊖ SBC Comms	Services	18.4	–16.00	1.55
⊖ Merck	Health	19.1	–35.90	1.49
⊖ AOL Time Warner	Technology	—	–7.76	1.43
⊖ Verizon Comms	Services	29.7	–2.52	1.43
⊖ Intel	Technology	73.1	4.89	1.34
⊖ Coca-Cola	Staples	35.5	–21.40	1.14
⊖ Bristol-Myers Squibb	Health	20.2	–26.00	1.05
⊖ Berkshire Hathaway Cl A	Financials	—	—	1.04
⊖ Philip Morris	Staples	12.1	9.12	1.04
⊖ Procter & Gamble	Staples	38.8	3.12	0.92
⊖ Bank of America	Financials	16.7	42.73	0.92
⊖ Eli Lilly	Health	28.9	–14.40	0.89
⊖ Home Depot	Retail	42.9	12.07	0.88
⊖ Cisco Sys	Technology	—	–52.60	0.87
⊕ PepsiCo	Staples	31.4	–0.54	0.84
⊖ Abbott Labs	Health	51.6	17.08	0.79

Current Investment Style

Style: Value Blnd Growth; Size: Large Med Small

	Stock Port Avg	Relative S&P 500 Current	Relative S&P 500 Hist	Rel Cat
Price/Earnings Ratio	29.8	0.96	1.00	0.98
Price/Book Ratio	5.6	0.99	1.00	1.03
Price/Cash Flow	17.9	0.99	1.01	0.97
3 Yr Earnings Growth	15.9	1.08	1.02	0.89
1 Yr Earnings Est%	–0.3	0.17	—	3.33
Med Mkt Cap $mil	49,071	0.8	0.8	0.94

Special Securities % assets 09-30-01	
Restricted/Illiquid Secs	0
Emerging-Markets Secs	0
Options/Futures/Warrants	Yes

Composition % assets 09-30-01	
Cash	0.1
Stocks*	99.9
Bonds	0.0
Other	0.0
*Foreign (% stocks)	0.0

Market Cap	
Giant	50.9
Large	30.0
Medium	18.2
Small	0.9
Micro	0.0

Sector Weightings	% of Stocks	Rel S&P	5-Year High	5-Year Low
Utilities	3.3	1.0	10	2
Energy	6.0	0.8	9	4
Financials	20.0	1.1	20	10
Industrials	10.1	0.9	17	9
Durables	1.8	1.1	5	1
Staples	7.2	0.9	14	4
Services	13.0	1.2	18	12
Retail	6.6	1.0	9	5
Health	15.6	1.1	16	8
Technology	16.5	0.9	34	6

Address:	101 Montgomery Street San Francisco, CA 94104 415-627-7000 / 800-435-4000
Web Address:	www.schwab.com
*Inception:	04-02-91
Advisor:	Charles Schwab Inv. Mgmt.
Subadvisor:	None
NTF Plans:	Schwab

Minimum Purchase:	$2500	Add: $500 IRA: $1000
Min Auto Inv Plan:	$2500	Add: $100
Sales Fees:	No-load, 0.75%R within 6 months	
Management Fee:	.30% mx./.22% mn.	
Actual Fees:	Mgt: 0.23%	Dist: —
Expense Projections:	3Yr: $156	5Yr: $276 10Yr: $624
Avg Brok Commission:	—	Income Distrib: Annually
Total Cost (relative to category):		Low

Schwab Small Cap Index Inv

Ticker	Load	NAV	Yield	Total Assets	Mstar Category
SWSMX	None	$17.50	0.5%	$1,740.7 mil	Small Blend

Prospectus Objective: Small Company

Schwab Small Cap Index Fund seeks to duplicate the price and dividend performance of a proprietary index of small-capitalization companies. This index is composed of the second 1,000 largest U.S. companies that meet certain criteria.

The fund normally invests at least 80% of assets in common stocks, preferred stocks, rights, and warrants issued by companies included on the index. It aims for a 0.95 or better correlation with the index. The fund may purchase futures contracts on stocks and stock indexes and options contracts. It may also lend securities to generate income.

The fund offers Investor and Select shares.

Historical Profile

Return Average
Risk Above Avg
Rating ★★★ Neutral

Investment Style Equity — Average Stock %: 99% 99% 99% 99% 99% 99% 100%

▼ Manager Change
▽ Partial Manager Change

Fund Performance vs. Category Average
Quarterly Fund Return +/– Category Average
— Category Baseline

Performance Quartile (within Category)

Portfolio Manager(s)

Geraldine Hom. Since 5-95. BA'74 California State U. Other funds currently managed: Schwab 1000 Inv, Schwab MarketTrack Growth, Schwab MarketTrack Balanced.

1990	1991	1992	1993	1994	1995	1996	1997	1998	1999	2000	12-01	History
—	—	—	10.14	9.77	12.41	14.27	17.87	16.25	20.14	18.36	17.50	NAV
—	—	—	1.54*	–3.08	27.65	15.49	25.69	–3.57	24.20	3.73	–0.90	Total Return %
—	—	—	1.00*	–4.39	–9.88	–7.46	–7.66	–32.15	3.16	12.84	10.98	+/– S&P 500
—	—	—	—	–1.25	–0.79	–1.05	3.33	–1.02	2.93	6.76	–3.39	+/– Russell 2000
—	—	—	0.14	0.56	0.62	0.50	0.45	0.31	0.24	0.42	0.47	Income Return %
—	—	—	1.40	–3.64	27.03	14.99	25.25	–3.88	23.95	3.32	–1.37	Capital Return %
—	—	—	—	80	38	73	47	44	22	71	90	Total Rtn % Rank Cat
—	—	—	0.01	0.06	0.06	0.06	0.06	0.06	0.04	0.08	0.09	Income $
—	—	—	0.00	0.00	0.00	0.00	0.00	0.87	0.00	2.31	0.58	Capital Gains $
—	—	—	—	0.67	0.68	0.59	0.52	0.49	0.49	0.49	—	Expense Ratio %
—	—	—	—	0.68	0.68	0.56	0.53	0.35	0.33	0.44	—	Income Ratio %
—	—	—	—	16	24	23	23	40	41	54	—	Turnover Rate %
—	—	—	44.7	70.7	138.5	232.8	410.5	548.5	551.2	807.5	930.3	Net Assets $mil

Performance 12-31-01

	1st Qtr	2nd Qtr	3rd Qtr	4th Qtr	Total
1997	–5.89	18.09	16.90	–3.26	25.69
1998	9.90	–5.40	–20.94	17.30	–3.57
1999	–6.89	15.86	–2.51	18.09	24.20
2000	5.66	–1.74	2.49	–2.51	3.73
2001	–10.29	15.85	–20.28	19.63	–0.90

Trailing	Total Return%	+/– S&P 500	+/– Russ 2000	% Rank All	% Rank Cat	Growth of $10,000
3 Mo	19.63	8.94	–1.45	14	42	11,963
6 Mo	–4.64	0.92	–0.55	60	80	9,536
1 Yr	–0.90	10.98	–3.39	44	90	9,910
3 Yr Avg	8.49	9.51	2.07	14	65	12,768
5 Yr Avg	9.12	–1.57	1.60	23	67	15,474
10 Yr Avg	—	—	—	—	—	—
15 Yr Avg	—	—	—	—	—	—

Tax Analysis	Tax-Adj Ret%	%Rank Cat	%Pretax Ret	%Rank Cat
3 Yr Avg	6.84	67	80.6	59
5 Yr Avg	7.84	65	85.9	46
10 Yr Avg	—	—	—	—

Potential Capital Gain Exposure: –2% of assets

Risk Analysis

Time Period	Load-Adj Return %	Risk %Rank[1] All	Risk %Rank[1] Cat	Morningstar Return	Morningstar Risk	Morningstar Risk-Adj Rating
1 Yr	–0.90					
3 Yr	8.49	72	74	0.78[2]	0.99	★★★★
5 Yr	9.12	79	73	0.97[2]	1.10	★★★
Incept	10.52	—	—	—	—	

Average Historical Rating (61 months): 2.1★s

[1]1=low, 100=high [2] T-Bill return substituted for category avg.

Category Rating (3 Yr)

1 2 3 4 5 (Worst — Best): 2

Return: Average
Risk: Above Avg

Other Measures	Standard Index S&P 500	Best Fit Index Russ 2000
Alpha	9.9	2.0
Beta	0.84	0.92
R-Squared	42	95

Standard Deviation	24.24
Mean	8.49
Sharpe Ratio	0.17

Portfolio Analysis 09-30-01

Share change since 06-01 Total Stocks: 953	Sector	PE	YTD Ret%	% Assets
⊕ Rite Aid	Retail	—	113.00	0.71
⊕ PanAmSat	Services	NMF	–36.90	0.66
⊕ Advance Paradigm	Health	43.2	29.01	0.57
⊕ Triad Hospitals	Health	—	–9.87	0.47
⊕ New York Community Bancorp	Financials	26.6	43.38	0.46
⊕ Homestake Mng	Industrials	—	89.70	0.46
⊕ Sicor	Health	47.5	8.60	0.36
⊕ Alliant Techsystems	Industrials	28.6	73.48	0.34
⊕ Network Assoc	Technology	—	517.20	0.33
⊕ Constellation Brands A	Staples	—	—	0.33
⊕ Service Corp Intl	Services	—	185.10	0.33
⊕ Lifepoint Hosps	Health	43.1	–32.00	0.32
⊕ 99 Cents Only Stores	Retail	43.8	108.70	0.32
⊕ Dean Foods	Staples	40.4	127.20	0.31
⊕ Brown & Brown	Financials	35.9	57.09	0.31
⊕ Perot Sys Cl A	Technology	NMF	122.20	0.30
⊕ Hearst–Argyle TV	Services	55.3	5.49	0.30
⊕ Dial	Staples	—	57.57	0.29
⊕ Copart	Services	43.8	69.16	0.29
⊕ BOK Finl	Financials	16.2	52.73	0.29
⊕ Borders Grp	Retail	53.6	69.75	0.29
⊕ AmerUs Grp	Financials	17.3	12.06	0.29
⊕ Pharmaceutical Product Dev	Services	36.3	30.05	0.28
⊕ Pentair	Industrials	38.0	54.40	0.28
⊕ Sierra Pacific Resources	Utilities	—	–2.25	0.28

Current Investment Style

Style: Value Blnd Growth; Size: Large Med Small

	Stock Port Avg	Relative S&P 500 Current	Relative S&P 500 Hist	Rel Cat
Price/Earnings Ratio	26.2	0.85	0.74	1.05
Price/Book Ratio	3.2	0.56	0.54	0.99
Price/Cash Flow	14.6	0.81	0.73	0.94
3 Yr Earnings Growth	12.0	0.82	0.87	0.71
1 Yr Earnings Est%	–3.6	2.06	—	–4.23
Med Mkt Cap $mil	841	0.0	0.0	0.86

Special Securities % assets 09-30-01	
Restricted/Illiquid Secs	0
Emerging-Markets Secs	0
Options/Futures/Warrants	No

Composition % assets 09-30-01	
Cash	0.3
Stocks*	99.8
Bonds	0.0
Other	0.0
*Foreign (% stocks)	0.0

Market Cap	
Giant	0.0
Large	0.0
Medium	18.0
Small	79.8
Micro	2.2

Sector Weightings	% of Stocks	Rel S&P	5-Year High	5-Year Low
Utilities	4.0	1.3	5	3
Energy	3.8	0.5	7	3
Financials	14.1	0.8	19	11
Industrials	19.5	1.7	21	15
Durables	3.5	2.3	5	4
Staples	4.7	0.6	5	2
Services	17.3	1.6	21	15
Retail	6.3	0.9	7	4
Health	13.3	0.9	18	9
Technology	13.4	0.7	25	13

Analysis by Alan Papier 09-12-01

Small-cap investors have a bevy of good choices, so this one only suits those committed to indexing.

Schwab Small Cap Index Fund is a unique offering among small-cap index funds. While most track the Russell 2000 index, this one follows Schwab's proprietary index of the second 1,000 largest U.S. stocks. That design means the fund excludes the third 1,000 largest U.S. companies, which can cause it to lag its peers when the market favors smaller issues, as has been the case in 2001. Indeed, for the year to date through Aug. 31, 2001, the fund lost 3.5%, while the average small-cap index offering lost just 1%.

But although the Russell-based funds provide broader size diversification, this fund's sector exposure isn't too different. Indeed, all small-cap index funds gained considerably less than the average small-blend offering as technology stocks tumbled in 2000. Actively managed funds were able to react to market events and sell their biggest losers as the economic outlook worsened last year, while the index offerings had to hold on as stock prices plummeted.

Investors should also consider the bigger picture when shopping for small-cap exposure. Whereas large-cap index funds have effectively outperformed most actively managed large-cap portfolios, the same cannot be said within the small-cap realm. In fact, the average small-blend fund has comfortably outperformed the Russell 2000 index over all time periods measured by Morningstar.

Still, this fund is a respectable choice for those who swear by passive, index strategies. It gained an average of 10.25% for the five-year period ended Aug. 31, 2001, while the average small-cap index fund gained 9.2%. Plus, the fund's expense ratio is below the group average.

Address:	101 Montgomery Street San Francisco, CA 94104 415–627–7000 / 800–435–4000
Web Address:	www.schwab.com
*Inception:	12-03-93
Advisor:	Charles Schwab Inv. Mgmt.
Subadvisor:	None
NTF Plans:	Schwab

Minimum Purchase:	$2500	Add: $500 IRA: $1000
Min Auto Inv Plan:	$2500	Add: $100
Sales Fees:	No-load, 0.75%R within 6 months	
Management Fee:	.50% mx./.45% mn.	
Actual Fees:	Mgt: 0.30%	Dist: —
Expense Projections:	3Yr: $183	5Yr: $328 10Yr: $751
Avg Brok Commission:	—	Income Distrib: Annually
Total Cost (relative to category):	Low	

Scudder Emerging Markets Income S

Ticker	Load	NAV	Yield	SEC Yield	Total Assets	Mstar Category
SCEMX	Closed	$7.74	10.7%	11.05%	$126.5 mil	Emerging Markets

Prospectus Objective: World Bond

Scudder Emerging Markets Income Fund seeks current income. Long-term capital appreciation is secondary.

The fund normally invests at least 65% of assets in high-yielding debt issued by governments and corporations in emerging market countries. It invests primarily in issuers in Latin America, but may also invest in Asia, Africa, the Middle East, and Eastern Europe. The fund does not invest more than 40% of total assets in one country. It may invest up to 35% of total assets in debt securities from developed markets and up to 20% of total assets in U.S. debt securities, including those that are not rated. "This fund is non-diversified."

Historical Profile

Return: Average
Risk: High
Rating: ★★★ Neutral

Investment Style
Fixed-Income
Income Rtn %Rank Cat: 60, 31, 24, 53, 42, 78, 42, 47

Growth of Principal vs. Interest Rate Shifts
— Principal Value $000 (NAV with capital gains reinvested)
— Interest Rate % on 10 Yr Treasury
▼ Manager Change
▽ Partial Manager Change
► Mgr Unknown After
◄ Mgr Unknown Before

Performance Quartile (within Category)

Portfolio Manager(s)

Jan Faller. Since 2-01. Other funds currently managed: Scudder Global Bond S, Scudder Emerging Markets Income AARP, Scudder Global Bond AARP.

Jack Janasiewicz. Since 3-01. Other funds currently managed: Scudder Emerging Markets Income AARP, Scudder Emerging Markets Income A, Scudder Emerging Markets Income B.

1990	1991	1992	1993	1994	1995	1996	1997	1998	1999	2000	12-01	History
—	—	—	12.00	10.27	11.00	12.28	11.26	7.03	7.88	7.79	7.74	NAV
—	—	—	—	−8.06	19.48	34.55	13.12	−30.30	23.46	10.02	10.46	Total Return %
—	—	—	—	−5.14	1.01	30.94	3.44	−38.98	24.29	−1.61	2.04	+/− LB Aggregate
—	—	—	—	10.87	−7.28	−4.76	0.10	−15.95	−2.51	−5.64	—	+/− JP Emg Mkts Bd
—	—	—	—	6.55	11.53	11.33	8.90	8.74	9.90	11.28	11.02	Income Return %
—	—	—	—	−14.61	7.95	23.22	4.22	−39.04	13.56	−1.26	−0.55	Capital Return %
—	—	—	—	1	73	60	57	66	68	68	42	Total Rtn % Rank Cat
—	—	—	0.00	0.77	1.14	1.20	1.06	0.95	0.67	0.86	0.83	Income $
—	—	—	0.00	0.00	0.00	1.18	1.50	0.00	0.04	0.00	0.00	Capital Gains $
—	—	—	—	1.50	1.50	1.44	1.49	1.56	1.75	1.71	—	Expense Ratio %
—	—	—	—	9.17	12.83	10.05	8.03	9.97	8.82	10.51	—	Income Ratio %
—	—	—	—	181	302	430	410	240	327	338	—	Turnover Rate %
—	—	—	—	89.6	188.8	323.5	345.6	208.4	184.8	142.4	120.9	Net Assets $mil

Performance 12-31-01

	1st Qtr	2nd Qtr	3rd Qtr	4th Qtr	Total
1997	3.32	7.33	4.98	−2.83	13.12
1998	6.02	−10.15	−33.73	10.40	−30.30
1999	4.57	5.08	0.55	11.75	23.46
2000	4.10	0.19	4.33	1.11	10.02
2001	2.68	3.82	−4.82	8.87	10.46

Trailing	Total Return%	+/− LB Agg	+/− JP Emg Mkts Bd	% Rank All	% Rank Cat	Growth of $10,000
3 Mo	8.87	8.84	—	48	26	10,887
6 Mo	3.62	−1.03	—	12	37	10,362
1 Yr	10.46	2.04	—	5	42	11,046
3 Yr Avg	14.48	8.21	—	5	63	15,004
5 Yr Avg	3.42	−4.01	—	83	57	11,829
10 Yr Avg	—	—	—	—	—	—
15 Yr Avg	—	—	—	—	—	—

Tax Analysis	Tax-Adj Ret%	%Rank Cat	%Pretax Ret	%Rank Cat
3 Yr Avg	10.04	63	69.4	71
5 Yr Avg	−1.00	50	—	—
10 Yr Avg	—	—	—	—

Potential Capital Gain Exposure: −86% of assets

Risk Analysis

Time Period	Load-Adj Return %	Risk %Rank[1] All	Risk %Rank[1] Cat	Morningstar Return	Morningstar Risk	Morningstar Risk-Adj Rating
1 Yr	10.46					
3 Yr	14.48	37	62	2.21[2]	2.07	★★★★★
5 Yr	3.42	64	76	−0.34[2]	3.95	★
Incept	7.23	—	—	—	—	

Average Historical Rating (61 months): 2.3★s

[1]1=low, 100=high [2] T-Bill return substituted for category avg.

Category Rating (3 Yr)

1 2 3 4 5 — Worst ... Best (rating: 3)

Return: Average
Risk: Average

Other Measures	Standard Index LB Agg	Best Fit Index Wil 4500
Alpha	9.5	9.9
Beta	0.30	0.27
R-Squared	1	40

Standard Deviation	13.64
Mean	14.48
Sharpe Ratio	0.79

Portfolio Analysis 09-30-01

Total Fixed-Income: 48	Date of Maturity	Value $000	% Net Assets
Republic of Argentina 7%	12-19-08	7,813	6.40
Govt of Russia 3%	05-14-03	7,523	6.16
Republic of Venezuela 9.25%	09-15-27	6,484	5.31
Republic of Brazil 8%	04-15-14	6,339	5.19
Pahyrs 9.37%	06-30-08	6,062	4.97
Republic of Argentina FRN	03-31-05	5,450	4.46
United Mexican States 6.25%	12-31-19	5,139	4.21
Republic Bulgaria Reset 2.5%	07-28-12	4,442	3.64
United Mexican States 8.13%	12-30-19	3,908	3.20
Republic of Peru Reset 4%	03-07-17	3,436	2.81
Hanvit Bk FRN	03-01-10	3,245	2.66
Republic Of Ecuador 4%	08-15-30	3,123	2.56
Govt of Jamaica 144A 11.75%	05-15-11	3,105	2.54
Republic of Brazil 14.5%	10-15-09	2,595	2.13
Dominican Republic 9.5%	09-27-06	2,444	2.00
Govt of Russia N/A	03-31-30	2,434	1.99
Republic of Panama Reset 4.25%	07-17-14	2,427	1.99
United Mexican States 8.38%	01-14-11	2,385	1.95
Republic of Colombia 7.625%	02-15-07	2,081	1.70
Russian Federation 7%	03-31-30	1,984	1.62

Current Investment Style

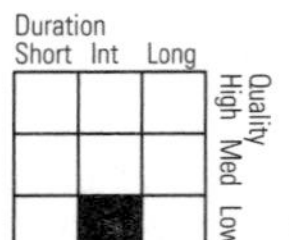

Avg Eff Duration[1]	5.4 Yrs
Avg Eff Maturity	—
Avg Credit Quality	B
Avg Wtd Coupon	7.24%
Avg Wtd Price	77.36% of par

[1]figure provided by fund

Special Securities % of assets 09-30-01

Restricted/Illiquid Secs	6
Exotic Mortgage-Backed	0
Emerging-Markets Secs	48
Options/Futures/Warrants	Yes

Country Exposure % of assets

Not Available

Composition % assets 09-30-01

Cash	6.0	Bonds	94.0
Stocks	0.0	Other	0.0

Analysis by Gregg Wolper 12-07-01

In their first year at the helm, Scudder Emerging Markets Income's new managers have shown both boldness and restraint, providing mixed results.

Jan Faller and Jack Janasiewicz took over this fund in early 2001, and in some ways, they've shown a willingness to act decisively on their convictions. For example, they say that ever since taking control, they have overweighted ever-chancy Russia, compared both with their benchmark, the JP Morgan EMBI Plus index, and their fellow emerging-markets bond funds. And when the news about Argentina's continuing financial woes became increasingly pessimistic in October, they slashed the fund's stake in that country—an important element of the emerging-markets debt universe—from 11% to 0%.

On the other hand, the managers say that in an effort to limit the chances of underperformance, they try to avoid deviating too much from the weightings of their peers at other funds. That limits their scope for taking full advantage of their insights.

The results so far are inconclusive: The fund's year-to-date return through Dec. 6 is roughly in the category's middle. The managers say overweighting Russia and some other less-common markets such as Ecuador helped early in the year, and dumping the fund's entire stake in Argentina in October has helped more recently. However, the managers erred by overweighting that beleaguered country's credits in the summer, thinking it could work through its crisis better than it has.

More time will be required to determine the managers' abilities over the long haul. Current shareholders should not be overly concerned but should be aware that the managers are still overweighting Russia, calling it one of the best fundamental stories in the emerging-debt universe.

Address:	Two International Place Boston, MA 02110 800–621–1048 / 800–621–1048
Web Address:	www.scudder.com
*Inception:	12-31-93
Advisor:	Zurich Scudder Inv.s
Subadvisor:	None
NTF Plans:	Fidelity , Datalynx

Minimum Purchase:	Closed	Add: $100 IRA: $1000
Min Auto Inv Plan:	Closed	Add: $100
Sales Fees:	No-load	
Management Fee:	1.0%	
Actual Fees:	Mgt: 1.00%	Dist: —
Expense Projections:	3Yr: $47*	5Yr: $81* 10Yr: $178*
Avg Brok Commission:	—	Income Distrib: Quarterly
Total Cost (relative to category):	—	

Scudder Global Discovery A

Ticker	Load	NAV	Yield	Total Assets	Mstar Category
KGDAX	5.75%	$23.12	0.0%	$542.8 mil	World Stock

Prospectus Objective: World Stock

Scudder Global Discovery Fund seeks long-term capital appreciation.

The fund normally invests at least 65% of assets in equity securities of small companies located in emerging or developed markets. It may invest the balance in larger companies and in investment-grade debt. The fund typically invests in issuers located in at least three countries, including the United States.

The fund offers Class A, B, C, and S shares, each of which differ in fee structure and availability. Prior to March 5, 1996, the fund was named Scudder Global Small Company Fund. From that date until April 16, 1998, the fund was named Scudder Global Discovery Fund.

Historical Profile

Return Above Avg
Risk Above Avg
Rating ★★★ Neutral

Investment Style
Equity
Average Stock %

1998	1999	2000	12-01
90%	94%	91%	92%

▼ Manager Change
▽ Partial Manager Change

Fund Performance vs. Category Average
■ Quarterly Fund Return +/– Category Average
— Category Baseline

Performance Quartile (within Category)

Portfolio Manager(s)

Gerald J. Moran, CFA. Since 4-98. BA'61 Yale U. Other funds currently managed: Scudder Global Discovery S, Scudder Global Discovery B, Scudder Global Discovery C.

Steven T. Stokes, CFA. Since 7-99. BS State U. of NY-New Paltz. Other funds currently managed: Scudder Global Discovery S, Scudder Global Discovery B, Scudder Global Discovery C.

1990	1991	1992	1993	1994	1995	1996	1997	1998	1999	2000	12-01	History
—	—	—	—	—	—	—	—	23.05	35.34	30.90	23.12	NAV
—	—	—	—	—	—	—	—	–3.88*	64.14	–5.56	–25.18	Total Return %
—	—	—	—	—	—	—	—	–15.93*	43.10	3.55	–13.30	+/– S&P 500
—	—	—	—	—	—	—	—	—	39.21	7.62	—	+/– MSCI World
—	—	—	—	—	—	—	—	0.00	0.00	0.00	0.00	Income Return %
—	—	—	—	—	—	—	—	–3.88	64.14	–5.56	–25.18	Capital Return %
—	—	—	—	—	—	—	—	—	17	32	78	Total Rtn % Rank Cat
—	—	—	—	—	—	—	—	0.00	0.00	0.00	0.00	Income $
—	—	—	—	—	—	—	—	0.00	2.38	2.41	0.00	Capital Gains $
—	—	—	—	—	—	—	—	1.95	2.01	1.99	—	Expense Ratio %
—	—	—	—	—	—	—	—	–1.00	–0.98	–1.06	—	Income Ratio %
—	—	—	—	—	—	—	—	41	64	86	—	Turnover Rate %
—	—	—	—	—	—	—	—	14.2	81.6	146.6	107.9	Net Assets $mil

Performance 12-31-01

	1st Qtr	2nd Qtr	3rd Qtr	4th Qtr	Total
1997	—	—	—	—	—
1998	—	—	–16.68	20.18	–3.88 *
1999	1.52	8.59	5.43	41.23	64.14
2000	14.94	–10.14	1.45	–9.87	–5.56
2001	–20.13	3.93	–21.83	15.31	–25.18

Trailing	Total Return%	+/– S&P 500	+/– MSCI World	% Rank All	% Rank Cat	Growth of $10,000
3 Mo	15.31	4.63	—	23	15	11,531
6 Mo	–9.86	–4.31	—	85	81	9,014
1 Yr	–25.18	–13.30	—	88	78	7,482
3 Yr Avg	5.07	6.09	—	31	25	11,599
5 Yr Avg	—	—	—	—	—	—
10 Yr Avg	—	—	—	—	—	—
15 Yr Avg	—	—	—	—	—	—

Tax Analysis	Tax-Adj Ret%	%Rank Cat	%Pretax Ret	%Rank Cat
3 Yr Avg	3.95	24	78.0	41
5 Yr Avg	—	—	—	—
10 Yr Avg	—	—	—	—

Potential Capital Gain Exposure: –6% of assets

Risk Analysis

Time Period	Load-Adj Return %	Risk %Rank¹ All	Risk %Rank¹ Cat	Morningstar Return	Morningstar Risk	Morningstar Risk-Adj Rating
1 Yr	–29.48					
3 Yr	3.01	87	88	–0.40²	1.23	★★★
5 Yr	—	—	—	—	—	
Incept	1.34	—	—	—	—	

Average Historical Rating (9 months): 3.8★s

¹1=low, 100=high ² T-Bill return substituted for category avg.

Category Rating (3 Yr)

1 2 **3** 4 5
Worst Best

Return Above Avg
Risk Above Avg

Other Measures	Standard Index S&P 500	Best Fit Index Wil 4500
Alpha	9.2	4.1
Beta	1.04	0.95
R-Squared	37	83

Standard Deviation	31.85
Mean	5.07
Sharpe Ratio	0.00

Analysis by Kunal Kapoor 07-05-01 This analysis was written for the S shares.

The next few months will tell us whether Scudder Global Discovery Fund is more than a bull-market baby.

After holding up nicely in 2000, this offering has slipped in 2001. Ironically, some of the very things that worked for the fund last year have been a burden so far this year. For example, some of the fund's energy stocks, such as top-five holding Nabors Industries, have cooled. That stock gained more than 90% in 2000 but has shed more than 35% of its value so far in 2001. Meanwhile, the fund itself has shed approximately 18% of its value for the year to date through July 4, 2001, and trails more than three fourths of its peers over the stretch.

Comanager Steve Stokes hopes the fund can climb back by being somewhat more defensively positioned. The offering's exposure to areas such as technology continues to be low because Stokes said the valuations don't reflect weak economic fundamentals just yet. That said, Stokes said the fund's management team doesn't want to miss a rally in the sector when and if it happens, so they are constantly revisiting their exposure to that area of the market. One area they aren't going to hurry back into, though, is telecom-equipment stocks, which Stokes simply calls dangerous. Conversely, the fund has sizable exposure to health-care firms, which Stokes thinks have good earnings prospects.

Overall, the offering has shown that it's capable of delivering over the long haul. (Although the fund's record looks short, it's been around since 1991, when it began under the Kemper banner.) Like other small-cap world funds, though, its key challenge is to try to smooth the up-and-down cycles.

Portfolio Analysis 09-30-01

Share change since 06-01 Total Stocks: 86	Sector	Country	% Assets
⊕ Biomet	Health	U.S.	5.81
⊕ Fiserv	Services	U.S.	4.04
Irish Life & Permanent	Financials	Ireland	4.00
⊖ Anglo Irish Bk (Ire)	Financials	Ireland	3.43
⊕ Legg Mason	Financials	U.S.	3.40
⊖ Laboratory Corp of Amer	Health	U.S.	2.99
⊕ H & R Block	Services	U.S.	2.82
Matalan	Retail	United Kingdom	2.67
Zions Bancorp	Financials	U.S.	2.67
⊖ St. Jude Medical	Health	U.S.	2.47
Serco Grp	Services	United Kingdom	2.27
⊖ Symbol Tech	Technology	U.S.	2.18
☼ Deutsche Boerse	N/A	N/A	2.08
⊕ Invitrogen	Health	U.S.	1.89
⊖ Shinko Secs	Financials	Japan	1.77
⊕ ARM Hldgs	Technology	United Kingdom	1.64
⊕ Caremark Rx	Health	U.S.	1.56
⊕ Waters	Industrials	U.S.	1.45
⊕ PizzaExpress	Services	United Kingdom	1.37
⊖ Chugai Pharma	Health	Japan	1.29

Current Investment Style

Style: Value Blnd Growth; Size: Large Med Small

	Stock Port Avg	Rel MSCI EAFE Current	Rel MSCI EAFE Hist	Rel Cat
Price/Earnings Ratio	29.4	1.14	1.35	1.06
Price/Cash Flow	21.3	1.66	1.82	1.29
Price/Book Ratio	5.7	1.65	1.99	1.25
3 Yr Earnings Growth	21.4	1.14	—	1.15
Med Mkt Cap $mil	3,119	0.1	0.1	0.13

Country Exposure 09-30-01	% assets
U.S.	49
United Kingdom	13
Ireland	9
Japan	8
France	2

Hedging History: —

Regional Exposure 09-30-01	% assets
Europe	27
Pacific Rim	3
Latin America	0
Japan	8
U.S.	49
Other	0

Special Securities % assets 09-30-01	
Restricted/Illiquid Secs	1
Emerging-Markets Secs	3
Options/Futures/Warrants	No

Composition % assets 09-30-01			
Cash	5.3	Bonds	0.0
Stocks	94.1	Other	0.6

Sector Weightings	% of Stocks	Rel Cat	5-Year High	5-Year Low
Utilities	2.3	0.9	—	—
Energy	3.7	0.7	—	—
Financials	21.3	1.2	—	—
Industrials	6.9	0.6	—	—
Durables	0.0	0.0	—	—
Staples	0.0	0.0	—	—
Services	22.8	1.4	—	—
Retail	6.2	1.2	—	—
Health	28.0	2.1	—	—
Technology	8.9	0.6	—	—

Address:	Two International Place Boston, MA 02110 800–621–1048 / 800–621–1048
Web Address:	www.scudder.com
*Inception:	04-16-98
Advisor:	Zurich Scudder Inv.s
Subadvisor:	None
NTF Plans:	Fidelity Inst.

Minimum Purchase:	$1000	Add: $100	IRA: $250
Min Auto Inv Plan:	$50	Add: $50	
Sales Fees:	5.75%L		
Management Fee:	1.1%, .25%A		
Actual Fees:	Mgt: 0.88%	Dist: —	
Expense Projections:	3Yr: $1226	5Yr: $1710	10Yr: $3038
Avg Brok Commission:	—	Income Distrib: Annually	
Total Cost (relative to category):		Above Avg	

Scudder Global S

Ticker	Load	NAV	Yield	Total Assets	Mstar Category
SCOBX	Closed	$21.71	2.1%	$1,139.3 mil	World Stock

Prospectus Objective: World Stock

Scudder Global Fund seeks long-term growth of capital; income is incidental.

The fund normally invests at least 65% of total assets in U.S. and foreign equity securities. It generally focuses on established companies in countries with developed economies. Management looks for companies that are industry leaders, have strong finances and management, and appear to make the most of local, regional and global opportunities. The fund primarily invests in companies that offer the potential for sustainable above-average earnings growth and whose market value appears reasonable in light of their business prospects.

The fund currently offers A, B, C, S and AARP shares.

Historical Profile

Return	Above Avg
Risk	Below Avg
Rating	★★★★ Above Avg

Investment Style Equity — Average Stock %: 90% 91% 81% 79% 95% 96% 93%

▼ Manager Change ▽ Partial Manager Change

Fund Performance vs. Category Average — Quarterly Fund Return +/– Category Average; — Category Baseline

Performance Quartile (within Category)

Portfolio Manager(s)

William E. Holzer. Since 7-86. U. of Lancaster; MBA New York U. Other funds currently managed: Managers International Equity, Scudder Global AARP, Scudder Global A.

Nicholas Bratt. Since 3-94. BA Oxford U.; MA Columbia U. Other funds currently managed: Scudder International S, Scudder International S, Scudder Pacific Opportunities S.

Diego Espinosa. Since 4-97. BS'83 Tufts U.; MA'87 Johns Hopkins U. Other funds currently managed: Scudder Global AARP, Scudder Global A, Scudder Global B.

History

1990	1991	1992	1993	1994	1995	1996	1997	1998	1999	2000	12-01	History
17.06	18.96	19.32	24.80	23.33	27.01	28.80	28.28	28.68	31.22	26.72	21.71	NAV
–6.40	17.07	4.55	31.10	–4.20	20.53	13.65	17.24	12.59	23.47	–3.01	–16.40	Total Return %
–3.29	–13.41	–3.07	21.05	–5.52	–17.01	–9.30	–16.11	–15.99	2.44	6.09	–4.53	+/– S&P 500
10.62	–1.21	9.77	8.60	–9.28	–0.20	0.17	1.48	–11.75	–1.46	10.17	—	+/– MSCI World
3.28	1.82	0.85	1.23	0.44	1.07	1.04	3.06	1.93	0.68	0.81	1.74	Income Return %
–9.68	15.25	3.70	29.87	–4.64	19.45	12.60	14.18	10.66	22.79	–3.82	–18.14	Capital Return %
19	53	24	54	71	32	77	28	52	73	26	48	Total Rtn % Rank Cat
0.62	0.31	0.16	0.24	0.11	0.25	0.28	0.88	0.55	0.20	0.25	0.47	Income $
0.58	0.66	0.34	0.26	0.34	0.84	1.53	4.58	2.61	3.91	3.40	0.15	Capital Gains $
1.81	1.70	1.59	1.48	1.45	1.38	1.34	1.37	1.34	1.36	1.32	—	Expense Ratio %
1.77	2.21	1.09	0.90	0.97	1.03	0.84	0.59	1.19	0.44	1.71	—	Income Ratio %
38	85	45	65	60	44	29	41	51	29	60	—	Turnover Rate %
237.6	298.8	400.5	963.0	1,117.7	1,271.9	1,409.3	1,570.5	1,613.9	1,692.1	1,403.2	990.3	Net Assets $mil

Performance 12-31-01

	1st Qtr	2nd Qtr	3rd Qtr	4th Qtr	Total
1997	2.88	13.63	3.50	–3.11	17.24
1998	12.20	2.14	–12.25	11.95	12.59
1999	–0.45	9.60	–1.76	15.20	23.47
2000	2.34	–3.82	–2.79	1.37	–3.01
2001	–12.20	4.13	–13.26	5.41	–16.41

Trailing	Total Return%	+/– S&P 500	+/– MSCI World	% Rank All	% Rank Cat	Growth of $10,000
3 Mo	5.41	–5.27	—	63	93	10,541
6 Mo	–8.57	–3.01	—	80	66	9,143
1 Yr	–16.40	–4.53	—	75	48	8,360
3 Yr Avg	0.04	1.06	—	73	56	10,011
5 Yr Avg	5.73	–4.97	—	52	50	13,215
10 Yr Avg	9.04	–3.89	—	38	48	23,767
15 Yr Avg	10.37	–3.36	—	39	31	43,942

Tax Analysis	Tax-Adj Ret%	%Rank Cat	%Pretax Ret	%Rank Cat
3 Yr Avg	–2.10	64	—	—
5 Yr Avg	3.07	56	53.5	82
10 Yr Avg	7.08	51	78.3	43

Potential Capital Gain Exposure: 3% of assets

Risk Analysis

Time Period	Load-Adj Return %	Risk %Rank[1] All	Risk %Rank[1] Cat	Morningstar Return	Morningstar Risk	Morningstar Risk-Adj Rating
1 Yr	–16.40					
3 Yr	0.04	56	27	–0.99[2]	0.73	★★★
5 Yr	5.73	56	18	0.16[2]	0.64	★★★★
10 Yr	9.04	60	7	1.34[2]	0.61	★★★★

Average Historical Rating (150 months): 4.4★s

[1] 1=low, 100=high [2] T-Bill return substituted for category avg.

Category Rating (3 Yr)

1 2 **3** 4 5 — Worst … Best

Return	Average
Risk	Below Avg

Other Measures	Standard Index S&P 500	Best Fit Index MSCIWrdExUS
Alpha	–0.6	3.4
Beta	0.70	0.86
R-Squared	63	82
Standard Deviation		14.94
Mean		0.04
Sharpe Ratio		–0.38

Portfolio Analysis 09-30-01

Share change since 06-01 Total Stocks: 110

	Sector	Country	% Assets
Bundesobligation 5%	N/A	N/A	7.15
⊖ Shell Transp & Trad	Energy	United Kingdom	1.80
⊖ Barrick Gold	Industrials	Canada	1.74
⊖ Aventis Cl A	Health	France	1.61
⊖ Rio Tinto (Reg)	Industrials	United Kingdom	1.57
⊖ Lockheed Martin	Industrials	U.S.	1.55
⊖ Conoco Cl A	Energy	U.S.	1.53
ExxonMobil	Energy	U.S.	1.53
⊖ BOC Grp	Industrials	United Kingdom	1.45
⊖ WMC	Industrials	Australia	1.43
⊖ Electronic Data Sys	Technology	U.S.	1.42
⊖ Glaxosmithkline	Technology	United Kingdom	1.41
⊖ Anadarko Petro	Energy	U.S.	1.40
⊖ Suez Lyon Eaux	Industrials	France	1.37
⊖ American Home Products	Health	U.S.	1.35
Boston Properties	Financials	U.S.	1.34
⊖ Phillips Petro	Energy	U.S.	1.34
Equity Residential Properties	Financials	U.S.	1.31
⊖ Immunex	Health	U.S.	1.30
⊖ Exelon	Utilities	U.S.	1.30

Current Investment Style

Style: Value Blnd Growth; Size: Large Med Small

	Stock Port Avg	Rel MSCI EAFE Current	Rel MSCI EAFE Hist	Rel Cat
Price/Earnings Ratio	25.9	1.00	0.98	0.93
Price/Cash Flow	11.6	0.90	1.03	0.70
Price/Book Ratio	3.4	0.96	0.97	0.73
3 Yr Earnings Growth	22.7	1.21	0.98	1.22
Med Mkt Cap $mil	12,806	0.5	0.5	0.53

Country Exposure 09-30-01	% assets
U.S.	34
United Kingdom	12
Japan	11
Germany	8
France	6

Hedging History: Frequent

Regional Exposure 09-30-01	% assets
Europe	29
Japan	11
Latin America	1
Pacific Rim	4
U.S.	34
Other	6

Special Securities % assets 09-30-01	
Restricted/Illiquid Secs	0
Emerging-Markets Secs	5
Options/Futures/Warrants	Yes

Composition % assets 09-30-01

Cash	2.7	Bonds	7.7
Stocks	89.7	Other	0.0

Sector Weightings	% of Stocks	Rel Cat	5-Year High	5-Year Low
Utilities	6.7	2.7	10	1
Energy	12.4	2.3	13	1
Financials	16.0	0.9	40	10
Industrials	26.3	2.3	34	13
Durables	2.4	0.6	12	1
Staples	0.0	0.0	6	0
Services	13.1	0.8	20	8
Retail	3.2	0.6	6	0
Health	14.0	1.1	14	2
Technology	6.0	0.4	19	4

Analysis by Langdon Healy 12-10-01

Scudder Global Fund's cautious approach may not even appeal to conservative investors.

Manager Willy Holzer makes bets, but they're usually intended to limit the fund's downside risk. This stance has resulted in one of the least volatile offerings in the world-stock category. However, Holzer's moves have limited the fund's exposure to big stock market rallies. Moreover, he has occasionally found trouble in unexpected waters. Overall, the fund's relative returns are mediocre.

Holzer and his team view the world as one big economy, emphasizing trends that transcend national boundaries. Once investment themes are identified, the team looks for moderately priced companies that are poised to take advantage of those themes. Though the themes have changed since Holzer began running it in 1986, his dedication to value has not, which is a big reason the fund has been less volatile than its peers. Another constant has been the fund's broad diversification. Holzer limits exposure to individual equities to 2% of assets and invests across sectors. These tactics limit issue specific and sector risk, which also dent volatility.

Holzer's risk controls, however, can occasionally backfire. Most importantly, he makes asset-allocation calls. For example, in 1994 he invested 15% of assets in Treasury bonds, which were hammered by rising interest rates that year. Similarly, in late 1998 he socked 27% of assets in cash. Combined with a below-average stake in tech stocks, this posture hurt relative returns in 1999, but it helped in 2000. Broad diversification and a current cash and bond stake of about 10% haven't provided substantial protection from the stock market sell-off, so its 16% loss year to date through Dec. 7, 2001, is middling.

Holzer's style has its merits, but its weaknesses considerably lessen this fund's appeal for most investors.

Address:	Two International Place Boston, MA 02110 800-621-1048 / 800-621-1048
Web Address:	www.scudder.com
Inception:	07-23-86
Advisor:	Zurich Scudder Inv.s
Subadvisor:	None
NTF Plans:	Fidelity , Datalynx

Minimum Purchase:	Closed	Add: $100 IRA: $1000
Min Auto Inv Plan:	Closed	Add: $50
Sales Fees:	No-load	
Management Fee:	1.0% mx./.90% mn.	
Actual Fees:	Mgt: 0.94%	Dist: —
Expense Projections:	3Yr: $431	5Yr: $745 10Yr: $1635
Avg Brok Commission:	—	Income Distrib: Annually
Total Cost (relative to category):		Below Avg

Scudder GNMA AARP

Ticker	Load	NAV	Yield	SEC Yield	Total Assets	Mstar Category
AGNMX	None	$15.05	6.0%	4.63%	$4,223.8 mil	Short–Term Govt

Prospectus Objective: Government General

Scudder GMNA Fund seeks current income and seeking to reduce downside risk compared to other GNMA mutual funds.

The fund invests at least 65% of net assets in mortgage-backed securities that are issued or guaranteed by the Government National Mortgage Association. It also invests in U.S. Treasury securities. In seeking to reduce downside risk, management will generally maintain a shorter duration than other GNMA funds. The fund does not invest in securities issued by tobacco-producing companies.

The fund currently offers S and AARP shares. Prior to July 17, 2000, the fund was named AARP GNMA & U.S. Treasury Fund.

Historical Profile

Return Above Avg
Risk Below Avg
Rating ★★★★ Above Avg

Investment Style: Fixed-Income

Income Rtn %Rank Cat: 23 | 26 | 19 | 7 | 7 | 10 | 9 | 5

Growth of Principal vs. Interest Rate Shifts
— Principal Value $000 (NAV with capital gains reinvested)
— Interest Rate % on 10 Yr Treasury
▼ Manager Change
▽ Partial Manager Change
► Mgr Unknown After
◄ Mgr Unknown Before

Performance Quartile (within Category)

Portfolio Manager(s)

Richard L. Vandenberg. Since 1-98. BBA'72 U. of Wisconsin; MBA'73 U. of Wisconsin. Other funds currently managed: Scudder U.S. Government Securities A, Scudder U.S. Government Securities B, Scudder U.S. Government Securities C.

Scott E. Dolan. Since 8-97. BS'89 Northeastern U.; MS'94 Boston C. Other funds currently managed: Scudder U.S. Government Securities A, Scudder U.S. Government Securities B, Scudder U.S. Government Securities C.

History

1990	1991	1992	1993	1994	1995	1996	1997	1998	1999	2000	12-01	History
15.28	16.13	15.93	15.77	14.56	15.36	15.04	15.22	15.24	14.40	14.91	15.05	NAV
9.72	14.38	6.57	5.96	–1.68	12.60	4.46	8.18	6.79	0.55	10.56	7.13	Total Return %
0.76	–1.62	–0.84	–3.79	1.24	–5.87	0.85	–1.51	–1.89	1.38	–1.07	–1.30	+/– LB Aggregate
–0.06	2.71	0.31	0.55	–2.18	2.65	–0.79	1.53	–0.19	–2.41	2.38	–1.40	+/– LB 1–3 Govt
8.89	8.51	7.80	7.07	6.16	6.97	6.54	6.91	6.66	6.22	6.82	6.20	Income Return %
0.83	5.88	–1.23	–1.11	–7.84	5.63	–2.07	1.26	0.13	–5.66	3.74	0.93	Capital Return %
20	20	20	51	65	29	37	6	33	78	4	52	Total Rtn % Rank Cat
1.30	1.25	1.21	1.09	0.94	0.98	0.97	1.01	0.98	0.92	0.95	0.90	Income $
0.00	0.00	0.00	0.00	0.00	0.00	0.00	0.00	0.00	0.00	0.00	0.00	Capital Gains $
0.79	0.74	0.72	0.70	0.66	0.67	0.64	0.65	0.61	0.65	—	—	Expense Ratio %
8.71	8.23	7.69	7.15	6.09	6.77	6.55	6.51	6.52	6.25	—	—	Income Ratio %
61	87	74	105	115	70	83	86	160	245	—	—	Turnover Rate %
2,662.6	3,736.0	5,546.9	6,629.9	5,248.9	5,257.3	4,826.1	4,539.4	4,535.2	4,014.8	3,686.4	3,816.0	Net Assets $mil

Performance 12-31-01

	1st Qtr	2nd Qtr	3rd Qtr	4th Qtr	Total
1997	0.15	3.09	2.52	2.21	8.18
1998	1.46	1.70	2.95	0.52	6.79
1999	0.43	–0.79	0.81	0.10	0.55
2000	1.88	1.81	2.71	3.77	10.56
2001	2.48	0.76	4.07	–0.32	7.13

Trailing	Total Return%	+/– LB Agg	+/– LB 1–3 Yr Govt	% Rank All	% Rank Cat	Growth of $10,000
3 Mo	–0.32	–0.35	–1.10	82	81	9,968
6 Mo	3.74	–0.91	–0.57	11	47	10,374
1 Yr	7.13	–1.30	–1.40	14	52	10,713
3 Yr Avg	6.00	–0.28	–0.53	22	19	11,909
5 Yr Avg	6.59	–0.84	–0.05	40	12	13,757
10 Yr Avg	6.03	–1.20	0.00	70	28	17,966
15 Yr Avg	7.03	–1.09	0.03	66	23	27,702

Tax Analysis	Tax-Adj Ret%	%Rank Cat	%Pretax Ret	%Rank Cat
3 Yr Avg	3.42	45	57.1	81
5 Yr Avg	3.94	26	59.9	69
10 Yr Avg	3.39	40	56.2	71

Potential Capital Gain Exposure: –7% of assets

Risk Analysis

Time Period	Load-Adj Return %	Risk %Rank[1] All	Risk %Rank[1] Cat	Morningstar Return	Morningstar Risk	Morningstar Risk-Adj Rating
1 Yr	7.13					
3 Yr	6.00	7	85	0.23[2]	0.52	★★★★
5 Yr	6.59	7	73	0.35[2]	0.47	★★★★
10 Yr	6.03	9	88	0.35[2]	0.64	★★★★

Average Historical Rating (170 months): 3.8★s

[1] 1=low, 100=high [2] T-Bill return substituted for category avg.

Category Rating (3 Yr)

2 (scale: 1 Worst – 5 Best)

Return Above Avg
Risk Above Avg

Other Measures	Standard Index LB Agg	Best Fit Index LB Mtg
Alpha	0.0	–0.9
Beta	0.78	0.99
R-Squared	88	96

Standard Deviation	2.98
Mean	6.00
Sharpe Ratio	0.42

Analysis by Eric Jacobson 12-06-01

Scudder GNMA AARP shows the elegance of simplicity.

Make no mistake, managers Dick Vandenberg and Scott Dolan know what they're doing. The pair is diligent in managing this portfolio to negotiate the shoals of the mortgage market, shifting among different maturities and coupons when it can help the fund pick up a value play or avoid prepayment trouble, for example. They also keep roughly 10% in Treasuries, and can add or subtract to that stake for some of the aforementioned reasons. The team also keeps its interest-rate plays fairly straightforward, generally keeping the fund's duration (a measure of rate sensitivity) within 10% of the Lehman Brothers 30-year GNMA index.

The fund's overall look has therefore been pretty conservative. The index's duration has been running fairly short for some time, resulting in the fund's short-term government categorization. Though it's important to note that within that very cautious group, the fund's rate sensitivity actually appears a bit high, which has hurt its Morningstar risk scores and relative rankings during rising-rate climes. Still, the fund has never lost more than about 2% in any 12-month period, and it looks a lot better when compared with mortgage funds across categories.

What sweetens the deal, however, is a combination of management skill and low expenses, which have produced a solid record of income production and returns. With credit to the fund's AARP connection, it charges a modest 0.65%, thus leaving lots of income behind for shareholders. Between that and a history of good management, the fund's three-, five- and 10-year trailing records place in the category's best quartile for each period.

There's no flash here, and as a shorter-term mortgage fund, it's not likely to show up more-aggressive rivals.

Address:	42 Longwater Drive Norwell, MA 02061–0162 800–322–2282 / 617–330–5400
Web Address:	www.aarp.scudder.com
Inception:	11-30-84
Advisor:	Zurich Scudder Inv.s
Subadvisor:	AARP Financial Services
NTF Plans:	N/A

Minimum Purchase:	$500	Add: None	IRA: $250
Min Auto Inv Plan:	$500	Add: $100	
Sales Fees:	No-load		
Management Fee:	.12%+.35% mx./.24% mn.(G)		
Actual Fees:	Mgt: 0.40%	Dist: —	
Expense Projections:	3Yr: $211	5Yr: $368	10Yr: $822
Avg Brok Commission:	—	Income Distrib: Monthly	
Total Cost (relative to category):		Below Avg	

Portfolio Analysis 09-30-01

Total Fixed-Income: 4132	Date of Maturity	Amount $000	Value $000	% Net Assets
GNMA 7%	12-15-28	613,542	638,181	14.92
GNMA 6.5%		389,400	397,980	9.30
GNMA 7.5%	12-15-28	318,979	333,611	7.80
GNMA 8%	12-15-30	297,448	313,105	7.32
GNMA 6.5%	12-15-29	279,209	286,111	6.69
GNMA 6.5%	12-15-28	203,351	208,436	4.87
GNMA 7%	07-15-31	143,392	149,105	3.49
GNMA 7.5%		133,000	138,514	3.24
GNMA 6%	09-20-31	131,831	132,005	3.09
GNMA 6%		123,000	123,371	2.88
GNMA 8%	12-15-29	116,069	122,203	2.86
US Treasury Bond 14%	11-15-11	70,000	102,058	2.39
US Treasury Bond 11.25%	02-15-15	50,000	79,860	1.87
GNMA 8.5%	12-15-30	67,002	71,145	1.66
GNMA 7.5%	12-20-27	63,926	66,971	1.57
GNMA 6%	09-15-29	61,348	61,657	1.44
GNMA 7%	12-15-29	58,930	61,278	1.43
GNMA 6.5%	08-15-31	56,820	58,224	1.36
GNMA 7.5%	07-15-31	53,104	55,363	1.29
GNMA 7%	12-15-27	49,585	51,624	1.21

Current Investment Style

Duration: Short Int Long; Quality: High Med Low

Avg Eff Duration[1]	3.0 Yrs
Avg Eff Maturity	6.1 Yrs
Avg Credit Quality	AAA
Avg Wtd Coupon	7.37%
Avg Wtd Price	105.64% of par

[1] figure provided by fund

Special Securities % assets 09-30-01	
Restricted/Illiquid Secs	0
Exotic Mortgage–Backed	0
Emerging–Markets Secs	0
Options/Futures/Warrants	No

Credit Analysis % bonds 06-30-01			
US Govt	100	BB	0
AAA	0	B	0
AA	0	Below B	0
A	0	NR/NA	0
BBB	0		

Sector Breakdown % bonds 09-30-01			
US Treasuries	7	CMOs	0
GNMA mtgs	91	ARMs	0
FNMA mtgs	0	Other	0
FHLMC mtgs	0		

Coupon Range	% of Bonds	Rel Cat
0%	0.00	0.00
0% to 7%	36.23	0.51
7% to 8.5%	54.55	2.73
8.5% to 10%	2.68	0.87
More than 10%	6.52	1.51

1.00=Category Average

Composition % assets 09-30-01			
Cash	0.0	Bonds	100.0
Stocks	0.0	Other	0.0

Scudder Greater Europe Growth S

Ticker	Load	NAV	Yield	Total Assets	Mstar Category
SCGEX	Closed	$23.00	0.3%	$711.0 mil	Europe Stock

Prospectus Objective: Europe Stock

Scudder Greater Europe Growth Fund seeks capital appreciation.

The fund normally invests at least 80% of assets in European common stocks and other equities. It may invest up to 20% of total assets in European debt securities. When selecting investments, the fund looks for companies that have effective management, competitive positioning, leading products or technologies and that appear able to make the most of local, regional and global opportunities. Other factors include significant social, economic, industrial and demographic changes, seeking stocks that may benefit from them. "This fund is non-diversified."

The fund currently offers A, B, C, S and AARP, all of which differ in fee structure and availability.

Historical Profile

Return	Above Avg
Risk	Below Avg
Rating	★★★★ Above Avg

Investment Style
Equity
Average Stock %

86% 89% 92% 88% 96% 96% 97%

▼ Manager Change
▽ Partial Manager Change

Fund Performance vs. Category Average
■ Quarterly Fund Return
+/– Category Average
— Category Baseline

Performance Quartile (within Category)

Portfolio Manager(s)

Carol L. Franklin, CFA. Since 10-94. BA'75 Smith C.; MBA'80 Columbia U. Other funds currently managed: Scudder International S, Scudder International Barrett Intl, Scudder International Growth.

Nicholas Bratt. Since 10-94. BA Oxford U.; MA Columbia U. Other funds currently managed: Scudder International S, Scudder International S, Scudder Global S.

Joseph Axtell. Since 3-01. Other funds currently managed: Scudder Greater Europe Growth AARP, Scudder Greater Europe Growth A, Scudder Greater Europe Growth B.

1990	1991	1992	1993	1994	1995	1996	1997	1998	1999	2000	12-01	History
—	—	—	—	11.50	13.97	18.08	20.58	26.53	35.52	31.05	23.00	NAV
—	—	—	—	–4.00*	23.62	30.88	24.00	29.20	34.58	–9.11	–25.69	Total Return %
—	—	—	—	–4.78*	–13.92	7.93	–9.36	0.63	13.54	–0.01	–13.82	+/– S&P 500
—	—	—	—	—	2.00	9.79	0.19	0.67	18.68	–0.72	—	+/– MSCI Europe
—	—	—	—	0.17	0.91	0.43	2.99	0.29	0.30	0.04	0.23	Income Return %
—	—	—	—	–4.17	22.70	30.45	21.01	28.91	34.27	–9.15	–25.92	Capital Return %
—	—	—	—	—	2	4	15	19	23	62	70	Total Rtn % Rank Cat
—	—	—	—	0.02	0.11	0.06	0.54	0.06	0.08	0.01	0.07	Income $
—	—	—	—	0.00	0.14	0.14	1.30	0.00	0.10	1.20	0.00	Capital Gains $
—	—	—	—	1.50	1.50	1.50	1.66	1.48	1.46	1.42	—	Expense Ratio %
—	—	—	—	2.40	1.25	0.82	0.16	0.63	0.37	0.22	—	Income Ratio %
—	—	—	—	—	28	39	89	93	83	72	—	Turnover Rate %
—	—	—	—	16.0	43.9	150.7	228.5	1,268.0	1,341.3	1,379.0	706.4	Net Assets $mil

Performance 12-31-01

	1st Qtr	2nd Qtr	3rd Qtr	4th Qtr	Total
1997	5.09	6.16	8.38	2.55	24.00
1998	25.27	8.57	–16.22	13.39	29.20
1999	–2.11	1.73	3.22	30.92	34.58
2000	5.52	–8.83	–6.82	1.40	–9.11
2001	–17.10	–1.24	–14.08	5.64	–25.69

Trailing	Total Return%	+/– S&P 500	+/– MSCI Europe	% Rank All	% Rank Cat	Growth of $10,000
3 Mo	5.64	–5.04	—	63	87	10,564
6 Mo	–9.24	–3.68	—	83	78	9,076
1 Yr	–25.69	–13.82	—	89	70	7,431
3 Yr Avg	–3.13	–2.11	—	87	48	9,089
5 Yr Avg	7.80	–2.89	—	30	26	14,561
10 Yr Avg	—	—	—	—	—	—
15 Yr Avg	—	—	—	—	—	—

Tax Analysis	Tax-Adj Ret%	%Rank Cat	%Pretax Ret	%Rank Cat
3 Yr Avg	–3.47	42	—	—
5 Yr Avg	7.10	17	91.0	2
10 Yr Avg	—	—	—	—

Potential Capital Gain Exposure: –21% of assets

Risk Analysis

Time Period	Load-Adj Return %	Risk %Rank[1] All	Risk %Rank[1] Cat	Morningstar Return	Morningstar Risk	Morningstar Risk-Adj Rating
1 Yr	–25.69					
3 Yr	–3.13	74	63	–1.59[2]	0.94	★★★
5 Yr	7.80	70	47	0.64[2]	0.79	★★★★
Incept	11.95	—	—	—	—	

Average Historical Rating (51 months): 4.8★s

[1]1=low, 100=high [2] T-Bill return substituted for category avg.

Category Rating (3 Yr)

1 2 3 4 5
Worst Best

Return	Average
Risk	Average

Other Measures	Standard Index S&P 500	Best Fit Index MSCIEurNdD
Alpha	–3.2	4.2
Beta	0.62	1.13
R-Squared	27	76
Standard Deviation		20.13
Mean		–3.13
Sharpe Ratio		–0.47

Portfolio Analysis 09-30-01

Share change since 06-01 Total Stocks: 79	Sector	Country	% Assets
⊖ Glaxosmithkline	Technology	United Kingdom	3.60
⊖ Total Fina Cl B	Energy	France	3.40
⊖ BP Amoco	Energy	United Kingdom	3.19
⊖ Sanofi–Synthelabo	Health	France	3.03
⊖ Nestle (Reg)	Staples	Switzerland	2.78
⊖ Vodafone Airtouch	Services	United Kingdom	2.70
⊖ Aventis Cl A	Health	France	2.69
⊖ Suez Lyon Eaux	Industrials	France	2.41
⊖ Banco Popular Espanol	Financials	Spain	2.40
⊖ Groupe Danone	Staples	France	1.97
⊖ Royal Dutch Petro	Energy	Netherlands	1.92
⊖ Barclays	Financials	United Kingdom	1.89
⊖ Muenchener Rueckvers (Reg)	Financials	Germany	1.85
⊖ BNP Paribus	Financials	France	1.74
⊖ Schering	Health	Germany	1.71
⊖ Assicurazioni Generali	Financials	Italy	1.58
⊖ Credit Lyonnais	Financials	France	1.44
⊖ ENI	Energy	Italy	1.43
⊖ Royal Bk of Scotland	Financials	United Kingdom	1.41
⊖ Societe Generale Cl A	Financials	France	1.40

Current Investment Style

Style: Value Blnd Growth; Size: Large Med Small

	Stock Port Avg	Rel MSCI EAFE Current	Rel MSCI EAFE Hist	Rel Cat
Price/Earnings Ratio	25.2	0.97	1.01	1.06
Price/Cash Flow	13.7	1.06	1.07	0.97
Price/Book Ratio	4.9	1.41	1.27	1.11
3 Yr Earnings Growth	27.1	1.45	1.08	1.13
Med Mkt Cap $mil	32,584	1.2	0.7	1.20

Country Exposure 09-30-01	% assets
France	26
United Kingdom	23
Germany	12
Netherlands	6
Italy	6

Hedging History: Rare

Special Securities % assets 09-30-01	
Restricted/Illiquid Secs	0
Emerging–Markets Secs	0
Options/Futures/Warrants	No

Composition % assets 09-30-01			
Cash	2.5	Bonds	0.0
Stocks	97.5	Other	0.0

Sector Weightings	% of Stocks	Rel Cat	5-Year High	5-Year Low
Utilities	1.1	0.5	5	0
Energy	12.4	1.5	13	2
Financials	22.0	0.9	36	4
Industrials	17.6	1.4	25	12
Durables	0.0	0.0	13	0
Staples	9.1	1.3	9	1
Services	12.3	0.7	35	12
Retail	5.5	1.1	16	2
Health	16.9	1.7	17	4
Technology	3.0	0.4	12	1

Analysis by Gregg Wolper 11-19-01

Scudder Greater Europe Growth Fund's underwhelming performance in 2001 is worth noting, but isn't of great concern.

From its late-1994 inception through the end of March 2000, when European stocks began to tumble, this fund rode an incredible winning streak. It's not just that its annualized return during that stretch topped the category average by 5 percentage points; the fund also finished in the category's top quartile every calendar year from 1995 through 1999.

The tide turned when growth stocks turned sour across the region. But even though it was hit very hard, the fund held its own. From April 1, 2000, through the end of August 2001, the fund's 31.4% loss was actually a bit less severe than the category average. For the year to date through Nov. 16, 2001, however, the fund is firmly in the category's bottom half.

Lead manager Carol Franklin has reacted to changing market conditions by becoming more defensive. This shift wasn't quick or substantial enough to protect the fund from absorbing large losses—Franklin said the fund's media stocks, in particular, were crushed. But by shifting toward energy and pharmaceuticals, the fund dodged worse damage. However, Franklin has reversed a move into financials, a sector that helped cushion the fund for awhile and then fell. She has sold stocks that either reached her target price or had deteriorating fundamentals.

Citing caution because of the weak economic outlook, Franklin said that drug firms Sanofi-Synthelabo, Aventis, and GlaxoSmithKline—both in the portfolio's top-five as of Sept. 30—typify what she's comfortable with now. But she said that she didn't want to be defensive forever and would shift toward firms with the potential to deliver more pop as soon as conditions warrant.

This fund's management and long-term record still inspires confidence.

Address:	Two International Place Boston, MA 02110 800–621–1048 / 800–621–1048
Web Address:	www.scudder.com
*Inception:	10-10-94
Advisor:	Zurich Scudder Inv.s
Subadvisor:	None
NTF Plans:	Fidelity , Datalynx

Minimum Purchase:	Closed	Add: $100	IRA: $1000
Min Auto Inv Plan:	Closed	Add: $50	
Sales Fees:	No–load		
Management Fee:	1.0%		
Actual Fees:	Mgt: 1.00%	Dist: —	
Expense Projections:	3Yr: $468	5Yr: $808	10Yr: $1768
Avg Brok Commission:	—	Income Distrib: Annually	
Total Cost (relative to category):	—		

Scudder Growth & Income S

Ticker	Load	NAV	Yield	Total Assets	Mstar Category
SCDGX	Closed	$21.06	0.9%	$7,279.5 mil	Large Blend

Prospectus Objective: Growth and Income

Scudder Growth & Income Fund seeks long-term growth of capital, current income, and growth of income.

The fund invests at least 65% of total assets in equities, mainly common stocks. Although the fund can invest in companies of any size and from any country, it invests primarily in large U.S. companies. The fund does not invest in securities issued by tobacco-producing companies. It may invest in dividend and non-dividend-paying stocks. Management uses bottom-up analysis, looking for companies with strong prospects for continued growth of capital and earnings.

The fund currently offers A, B, C, S and AARP shares, all of which differ in fee structure and availability.

Historical Profile
Return Average
Risk Average
Rating ★★★ Neutral

Investment Style
Equity
Average Stock %: 92% 94% 91% 94% 95% 98% 99%

▼ Manager Change
▽ Partial Manager Change

Fund Performance vs. Category Average
Quarterly Fund Return +/– Category Average
– Category Baseline

Performance Quartile (within Category)

Portfolio Manager(s)

Kathleen T. Millard, CFA. Since 10-99. BA'83 Princeton U. Other funds currently managed: Scudder Dividend & Growth S, Scudder Growth & Income AARP, Scudder Dividend & Growth AARP.

Gregory S. Adams, CFA. Since 11-99. BA'87 U. of Pennsylvania; BS'87 U. of Pennsylvania. Other funds currently managed: Scudder Growth & Income AARP, Scudder Growth & Income A, Scudder Growth & Income B.

1990	1991	1992	1993	1994	1995	1996	1997	1998	1999	2000	12-01	History
12.77	15.76	16.20	17.24	16.27	20.23	23.23	27.33	26.31	26.69	24.15	21.06	NAV
–2.33	28.16	9.57	15.59	2.60	31.18	22.18	30.31	6.07	6.15	–2.44	–12.04	Total Return %
0.79	–2.33	1.95	5.53	1.29	–6.36	–0.76	–3.04	–22.50	–14.89	6.66	–0.17	+/– S&P 500
1.70	–4.28	1.92	5.75	2.15	–6.43	0.02	–2.72	–22.56	–15.68	8.52	0.72	+/– Wilshire Top 750
4.96	4.37	3.40	2.81	2.97	3.47	2.85	2.56	2.26	1.96	0.57	0.74	Income Return %
–7.29	23.79	6.17	12.78	–0.37	27.71	19.33	27.75	3.81	4.19	–3.01	–12.78	Capital Return %
42	73	27	19	12	66	40	43	97	95	24	35	Total Rtn % Rank Cat
0.67	0.55	0.53	0.45	0.51	0.56	0.57	0.58	0.61	0.51	0.15	0.18	Income $
0.34	0.00	0.50	1.01	0.91	0.48	0.87	2.20	2.09	0.70	1.76	0.00	Capital Gains $
0.95	0.97	0.94	0.86	0.86	0.80	0.78	0.76	0.74	0.55	0.84	—	Expense Ratio %
5.03	4.03	3.60	2.93	2.98	3.10	2.77	2.31	2.20	2.01	0.64	—	Income Ratio %
65	45	28	36	42	27	27	22	41	65	55	—	Turnover Rate %
490.8	723.4	1,168.9	1,631.3	1,994.2	3,068.0	4,201.0	6,832.8	7,633.9	6,762.1	5,190.2	3,579.4	Net Assets $mil

Performance 12-31-01

	1st Qtr	2nd Qtr	3rd Qtr	4th Qtr	Total
1997	3.01	15.27	9.07	0.62	30.31
1998	12.94	–2.66	–13.39	11.41	6.07
1999	–0.24	12.42	–11.02	6.37	6.15
2000	1.32	–0.26	1.25	–4.65	–2.44
2001	–11.24	5.10	–14.71	10.55	–12.04

Trailing	Total Return%	+/– S&P 500	+/–Wil Top 750	% Rank All	% Rank Cat	Growth of $10,000
3 Mo	10.55	–0.14	5.03	40	53	11,055
6 Mo	–5.71	–0.16	0.07	66	41	9,429
1 Yr	–12.04	–0.17	–3.25	65	35	8,796
3 Yr Avg	–3.06	–2.04	–4.23	87	77	9,109
5 Yr Avg	4.72	–5.98	–6.49	70	92	12,591
10 Yr Avg	10.12	–2.81	–3.91	32	73	26,222
15 Yr Avg	11.04	–2.70	–2.46	33	69	48,080

Tax Analysis	Tax-Adj Ret%	%Rank Cat	%Pretax Ret	%Rank Cat
3 Yr Avg	–4.10	76	—	—
5 Yr Avg	3.04	90	64.4	87
10 Yr Avg	8.02	71	79.2	56

Potential Capital Gain Exposure: 12% of assets

Risk Analysis

Time Period	Load-Adj Return %	Risk %Rank[1] All	Risk %Rank[1] Cat	Morningstar Return	Morningstar Risk	Morningstar Risk-Adj Rating
1 Yr	–12.04					
3 Yr	–3.06	59	20	–1.57[2]	0.83	★★
5 Yr	4.72	60	22	–0.07[2]	0.83	★★
10 Yr	10.12	61	11	0.75	0.80	★★★

Average Historical Rating (169 months): 3.9★s

[1]1=low, 100=high [2] T-Bill return substituted for category avg.

Category Rating (3 Yr)

1 2 3 4 5 — Worst … Best (rating: 2)

Return Below Avg
Risk Below Avg

Other Measures	Standard Index S&P 500	Best Fit Index S&P 500
Alpha	–3.2	–3.2
Beta	0.79	0.79
R-Squared	78	78

Standard Deviation	14.76
Mean	–3.06
Sharpe Ratio	–0.63

Portfolio Analysis 09-30-01

Share change since 06-01 Total Stocks: 70	Sector	PE	YTD Ret%	% Assets
Bank of America	Financials	16.7	42.73	3.35
General Elec	Industrials	30.1	–15.00	3.28
⊕ Microsoft	Technology	57.6	52.78	3.22
⊕ American Home Products	Health	—	–1.91	3.16
⊖ Citigroup	Financials	20.0	0.03	3.12
⊕ ExxonMobil	Energy	15.3	–7.59	2.98
⊕ Johnson & Johnson	Health	16.6	14.01	2.89
Verizon Comms	Services	29.7	–2.52	2.50
⊖ Wal-Mart Stores	Retail	40.3	8.94	2.45
American Intl Grp	Financials	42.0	–19.20	2.18
⊖ Unilever (NY)	Staples	59.1	–6.32	1.84
Washington Mutual	Financials	10.1	–5.32	1.83
⊖ Home Depot	Retail	42.9	12.07	1.74
⊕ Abbott Labs	Health	51.6	17.08	1.70
⊕ Sprint	Services	20.5	1.18	1.69
Anheuser-Busch	Staples	24.6	1.01	1.63
Fannie Mae	Financials	16.2	–6.95	1.59
Intel	Technology	73.1	4.89	1.53
⊖ Baxter Intl	Health	33.9	22.84	1.51
Bank One	Financials	29.1	9.13	1.50
⊖ Intl Paper	Industrials	—	1.43	1.50
⊕ IBM	Technology	26.9	43.00	1.49
SBC Comms	Services	18.4	–16.00	1.44
⊖ PepsiCo	Staples	31.4	–0.54	1.44
⊖ Pfizer	Health	34.7	–12.40	1.40

Current Investment Style

Style: Value Blnd Growth; Size: Large Med Small

	Stock Port Avg	Relative S&P 500 Current	Relative S&P 500 Hist	Rel Cat
Price/Earnings Ratio	30.1	0.97	0.87	0.99
Price/Book Ratio	5.9	1.03	0.79	1.06
Price/Cash Flow	16.8	0.93	0.80	0.91
3 Yr Earnings Growth	18.4	1.25	0.82	1.03
1 Yr Earnings Est%	0.7	—	—	–8.00
Med Mkt Cap $mil	76,975	1.3	0.7	1.47

Analysis by William Harding 10-10-01

Scudder Growth & Income Fund is unexciting, but serviceable.

It's been about two years since Scudder retooled this offering. Lead manager Kathleen Millard took the helm in October 1999 and set out to make this a blend-like offering by bringing sector weightings more in line with those of the S&P 500. Prior to her arrival, the fund had tilted toward value fare, with an emphasis on high-dividend-paying stocks. That style was a drain on performance in 1998 and 1999, but the fund's makeover came at a bad time. Value stocks have held up far better than growth fare in 2000 and 2001, and this fund has badly lagged the average large-value fund in both years.

However, based on the fund's revised strategy and portfolio makeup, investors should judge it against the S&P 500 or the large-blend category. The fund's showing versus those benchmarks under this team is average, if not distinguished. Its return since October 1999 through the end of September 2001 is right in line with the average large-blend offering and outpaces the S&P 500 by less than 1 percentage point.

With the portfolio repositioned, the managers haven't made significant changes of late. Millard said that the team took some profits on utility stocks early in the year and trimmed some other winners, including Baxter and Washington Mutual. In the financials sector, the fund changed its emphasis from insurance stocks to banks, which proved a good move as insurers have come under pressure following the recent terrorist attacks.

Investors seeking a core fund that doesn't stray too far from the S&P 500 may want to stand pat here. But those who were attracted to the fund's value tilt and yield will want to look elsewhere. Offerings such as Scudder Dreman High Return Equity and Scudder Dividend & Growth may fill the bill, but plenty of good picks outside Scudder are also available.

Special Securities % assets 09-30-01	
Restricted/Illiquid Secs	0
Emerging-Markets Secs	0
Options/Futures/Warrants	No

Composition % assets 09-30-01	
Cash	0.0
Stocks*	100.0
Bonds	0.0
Other	0.0
*Foreign (% stocks)	4.6

Market Cap	
Giant	59.3
Large	35.2
Medium	5.4
Small	0.0
Micro	0.0

Sector Weightings	% of Stocks	Rel S&P	5-Year High	5-Year Low
Utilities	1.2	0.4	15	1
Energy	7.4	1.0	12	6
Financials	19.9	1.1	25	15
Industrials	8.7	0.8	27	9
Durables	1.2	0.8	11	0
Staples	7.4	0.9	13	3
Services	15.0	1.4	24	3
Retail	7.8	1.2	8	2
Health	16.6	1.1	17	3
Technology	14.9	0.8	23	2

Address:	Two International Place Boston, MA 02110 800–621–1048 / 800–621–1048
Web Address:	www.scudder.com
Inception:	12-31-84
Advisor:	Zurich Scudder Inv.s
Subadvisor:	None
NTF Plans:	Fidelity , Datalynx

Minimum Purchase:	Closed	Add: $100	IRA: $1000
Min Auto Inv Plan:	Closed	Add: $50	
Sales Fees:	No-load		
Management Fee:	.60% mx./.41% mn.		
Actual Fees:	Mgt: 0.45%	Dist: —	
Expense Projections:	3Yr: $240	5Yr: $417	10Yr: $930
Avg Brok Commission:	—	Income Distrib: Quarterly	
Total Cost (relative to category):		Below Avg	

Scudder International S

Ticker	Load	NAV	Yield	Total Assets	Mstar Category
SCINX	Closed	$36.66	0.3%	$3,124.7 mil	Foreign Stock

Prospectus Objective: Foreign Stock

Scudder International Fund seeks long-term growth of capital.

The fund normally invests at least 65% of its total assets in foreign equities. Although it can invest in companies of any size and from any country, the fund invests mainly in common stocks of established companies in countries with developed economies, other than the U.S. The fund may invest up to 20% of net assets in foreign debt securities, including convertible bonds.

The fund currently offers A, B, C, I, S, AARP and Barrett International shares, all of which differ in fee structure and availability.

Historical Profile
Return Average
Risk Average
Rating ★★★ Neutral

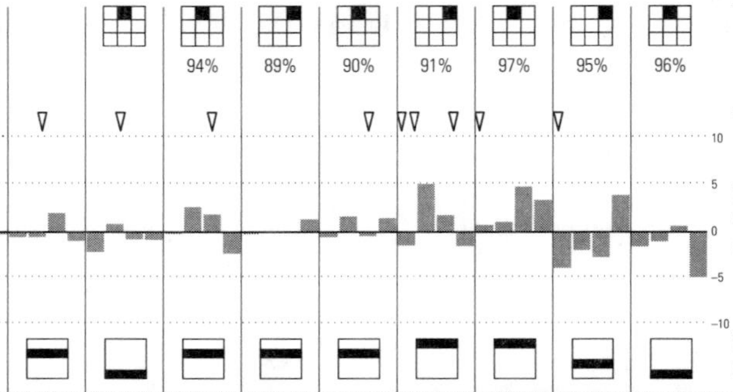

Investment Style
Equity
Average Stock %: 94% 89% 90% 91% 97% 95% 96%

▼ Manager Change
▽ Partial Manager Change

Fund Performance vs. Category Average
■ Quarterly Fund Return +/– Category Average
— Category Baseline

Performance Quartile (within Category)

Portfolio Manager(s)

Irene T. Cheng. Since 6-93.
Nicholas Bratt. Since 1-00.
Carol L. Franklin, CFA. Since 1-86.
Marc Slendebroek. Since 1-99.

1990	1991	1992	1993	1994	1995	1996	1997	1998	1999	2000	12-01	History
32.15	35.53	32.93	44.10	40.37	43.72	47.56	45.75	48.70	70.74	50.31	36.66	NAV
–8.92	11.78	–2.64	36.50	–2.99	12.22	14.55	7.98	18.62	57.89	–19.23	–26.89	Total Return %
–5.81	–18.71	–10.26	26.45	–4.31	–25.32	–8.39	–25.37	–9.95	36.85	–10.13	–15.01	+/– S&P 500
14.53	–0.35	9.54	3.94	–10.77	1.01	8.51	6.20	–1.37	30.92	–5.06	—	+/– MSCI EAFE
1.97	0.00	2.36	1.20	0.00	0.99	2.96	0.53	0.00	0.28	0.08	0.24	Income Return %
–10.89	11.78	–5.00	35.31	–2.99	11.23	11.59	7.45	18.62	57.60	–19.30	–27.12	Capital Return %
36	56	33	47	77	29	41	37	23	23	67	79	Total Rtn % Rank Cat
0.74	0.00	0.83	0.39	0.00	0.40	1.28	0.25	0.00	0.13	0.05	0.12	Income $
1.98	0.40	0.86	0.39	2.42	1.18	1.19	5.35	5.56	4.82	7.01	0.00	Capital Gains $
1.18	1.24	1.30	1.26	1.21	1.19	1.14	1.15	1.18	1.17	1.12	—	Expense Ratio %
1.33	2.22	1.25	1.13	0.75	0.48	0.86	0.64	0.83	0.92	0.25	—	Income Ratio %
49	70	50	29	40	46	45	36	56	80	83	—	Turnover Rate %
802.3	965.9	1,049.0	2,069.0	2,271.8	2,352.0	2,644.9	2,617.0	2,945.1	5,064.9	4,460.8	2,673.7	Net Assets $mil

Performance 12-31-01

	1st Qtr	2nd Qtr	3rd Qtr	4th Qtr	Total
1997	1.07	12.58	1.17	–6.20	7.98
1998	13.79	6.07	–14.41	14.82	18.62
1999	2.81	7.69	9.31	30.46	57.89
2000	–1.30	–7.72	–9.65	–1.84	–19.23
2001	–15.98	–0.80	–15.62	3.97	–26.89

Trailing	Total Return%	+/– S&P 500	+/– MSCI EAFE	% Rank All	% Rank Cat	Growth of $10,000
3 Mo	3.97	–6.72	—	68	92	10,397
6 Mo	–12.27	–6.72	—	91	84	8,773
1 Yr	–26.89	–15.01	—	90	79	7,311
3 Yr Avg	–2.31	–1.28	—	84	50	9,324
5 Yr Avg	3.62	–7.08	—	83	31	11,943
10 Yr Avg	7.07	–5.86	—	50	31	19,794
15 Yr Avg	7.76	–5.98	—	56	32	30,668

Tax Analysis	Tax-Adj Ret%	%Rank Cat	%Pretax Ret	%Rank Cat
3 Yr Avg	–3.87	50	—	—
5 Yr Avg	1.72	33	47.6	72
10 Yr Avg	5.38	33	76.1	46

Potential Capital Gain Exposure: –8% of assets

Risk Analysis

Time Period	Load-Adj Return %	Risk %Rank[1] All	Risk %Rank[1] Cat	Morningstar Return	Morningstar Risk	Morningstar Risk-Adj Rating
1 Yr	–26.89					
3 Yr	–2.31	75	58	–1.43[2]	0.96	★★★
5 Yr	3.62	73	45	–0.30[2]	0.82	★★★
10 Yr	7.07	79	36	0.67[2]	0.81	★★★

Average Historical Rating (193 months): 3.9★s

[1] 1=low, 100=high [2] T-Bill return substituted for category avg.

Category Rating (3 Yr)
1 2 3 4 5
Worst Best
Return Average
Risk Average

Other Measures	Standard Index S&P 500	Best Fit Index
Alpha	–1.7	4.6
Beta	0.79	1.19
R–Squared	47	89

Standard Deviation	19.45
Mean	–2.31
Sharpe Ratio	–0.43

Portfolio Analysis 09-30-01

Share change since 06-01 Total Stocks: 104	Sector	Country	% Assets
⊕ BP Amoco	Energy	United Kingdom	3.52
⊕ Vodafone Airtouch	Services	United Kingdom	3.24
Total Fina Cl B	Energy	France	3.19
⊕ E.ON Cl B	Services	Germany	2.87
⊕ Shell Transp & Trad	Energy	United Kingdom	2.75
⊖ Glaxosmithkline	Technology	United Kingdom	2.64
⊖ Aventis Cl A	Health	France	2.61
⊕ Suez Lyon Eaux	Industrials	France	2.47
⊕ Bayer	Health	Germany	2.22
⊖ Reed Intl	Services	United Kingdom	1.75
⊖ Nestle (Reg)	Staples	Switzerland	1.75
⊕ BNP Paribus	Financials	France	1.70
Mitsui Fudosan	Industrials	Japan	1.69
⊖ Canadian Natl Railway	Services	Canada	1.66
⊖ Mediobanca	Financials	Italy	1.55
J Sainsbury	Retail	United Kingdom	1.52
⊕ Muenchener Rueckvers (Reg)	Financials	Germany	1.43
⊖ Groupe Danone	Staples	France	1.42
⊕ Credit Lyonnais	Financials	France	1.38
⊕ Unilever (Cert)	Staples	United Kingdom	1.33

Current Investment Style

Style: Value Blnd Growth; Size: Large Med Small

	Stock Port Avg	Rel MSCI EAFE Current	Rel MSCI EAFE Hist	Rel Cat
Price/Earnings Ratio	27.0	1.04	1.10	1.06
Price/Cash Flow	13.0	1.01	1.06	0.90
Price/Book Ratio	3.5	1.02	1.02	0.91
3 Yr Earnings Growth	21.5	1.15	0.82	1.09
Med Mkt Cap $mil	27,364	1.0	0.8	1.52

Country Exposure 09-30-01	% assets
United Kingdom	21
France	19
Japan	17
Germany	12
Switzerland	6

Hedging History: Rare

Regional Exposure 09-30-01	% assets
Europe	68
Japan	17
Latin America	0
Pacific Rim	3
Other	2

Special Securities % assets 09-30-01	
Restricted/Illiquid Secs	0
Emerging–Markets Secs	1
Options/Futures/Warrants	Yes

Composition % assets 09-30-01			
Cash	1.9	Bonds	0.4
Stocks	97.8	Other	0.0

Sector Weightings	% of Stocks	Rel Cat	5-Year High	5-Year Low
Utilities	0.8	0.3	13	0
Energy	11.2	1.9	13	1
Financials	17.3	0.8	30	8
Industrials	15.8	1.2	32	12
Durables	3.0	0.4	15	3
Staples	7.6	1.1	9	1
Services	18.9	1.1	25	5
Retail	3.9	0.8	14	1
Health	15.1	1.6	15	3
Technology	6.4	0.6	26	4

Analysis by Gregg Wolper 11-05-01

It's not yet time to become alarmed over Scudder International Fund's performance, but the fund must get back on track soon if it wants to remain among the foreign-stock elite.

This offering has been one of the top choices in the international realm. Its managers try to identify demographic or economic trends that will spark long-term changes, and then pick companies that will benefit. Throughout the second half of the 1990s this strategy worked wonders. In 1999, however, the fund veered heavily toward the high-priced technology and telecom issues that were racing to remarkable heights, and though that propelled the fund to a top-quartile 57% gain that year, it sank the fund when such stocks fell to earth the following year.

It's of some concern that the fund has not recovered its stride this deep into 2001. Some other stellar funds that rode the tech and telecom wave and then were hurt to varying degrees—notably American Funds EuroPacific Growth and Artisan International—have adjusted and have top-quartile returns this year. This fund, by contrast, has a 27.9% year-to-date loss through Nov. 2, which is behind two thirds of its category rivals—right where it finished in 2000.

Lead manager Irene Cheng said the fund has made adjustments over the past 12 months, primarily becoming more defensive. Indeed, the fund's tech and services stakes are now at the category average. But other problems have stung. For example, German conglomerate Bayer has been among Cheng's favorites all year because she thinks that despite product woes and weak management, it has potential that will be realized somehow. But even after a slight boost from recent Cipro publicity, Bayer's stock has been awful this year.

This fund's strong record and management still inspire confidence. It now must show that it remains worthy of that confidence.

Address:	Two International Place Boston, MA 02110 800–621–1048 / 800–621–1048
Web Address:	www.scudder.com
Inception:	06-18-53
Advisor:	Zurich Scudder Inv.s
Subadvisor:	None
NTF Plans:	Fidelity , Datalynx

Minimum Purchase:	Closed	Add: $100	IRA: $1000
Min Auto Inv Plan:	Closed	Add: $50	
Sales Fees:	No-load		
Management Fee:	.90% mx./.70% mn.		
Actual Fees:	Mgt: 0.68%	Dist: —	
Expense Projections:	3Yr: $337	5Yr: $585	10Yr: $1294
Avg Brok Commission:	—	Income Distrib: Annually	
Total Cost (relative to category):		Below Avg	

Scudder Latin America S

Ticker	Load	NAV	Yield	Total Assets	Mstar Category
SLAFX	Closed	$19.75	1.7%	$333.9 mil	Latin America Stock

Prospectus Objective: Foreign Stock

Scudder Latin America Fund seeks long-term capital appreciation.

The fund normally invests at least 65% of assets in Latin American common stocks and other equities. Although the fund may invest in any Latin American country, it expects to invest primarily in common stocks of established companies in Argentina, Brazil, Chile, Colombia, Mexico, Panama and Peru. The fund may invest up to 35% of total assets in debt securities, 10% of which may be junk bonds. "This fund is non-diversified."

The fund currently offers A, B, C, S and AARP shares.

Historical Profile

Return Average
Risk Above Avg
Rating ★★★ Neutral

Investment Style
Equity
Average Stock %: 55% (1994), 56% (1995), 61% (1996), 64% (1997), 79% (1998), 96% (1999), 94% (2000)

▼ Manager Change
▽ Partial Manager Change

Fund Performance vs. Category Average
■ Quarterly Fund Return +/– Category Average
— Category Baseline

Performance Quartile (within Category)

Portfolio Manager(s)

Edmund B. Games Jr.. Since 12-92. BA'59 Harvard U. Other funds currently managed: Scudder Latin America AARP, Scudder Latin America A, Scudder Latin America B.

Paul Rogers. Since 3-96. BA'79 U. of Vermont; MBA'89 New York U. Other funds currently managed: Scudder Latin America AARP, Scudder Latin America A, Scudder Latin America B.

Tara C. Kenney. Since 3-96. BA'82 U. of Notre Dame; MBA'91 New York U. Other funds currently managed: Scudder Emerging Markets Growth S, Scudder International Growth, Scudder Emerging Markets Growth AARP.

History

1990	1991	1992	1993	1994	1995	1996	1997	1998	1999	2000	12-01	History
—	—	12.50	21.68	18.88	16.88	21.40	26.67	17.73	26.04	20.26	19.75	NAV
—	—	4.17*	74.32	–9.41	–9.81	28.32	31.30	–29.70	47.16	–15.64	–0.82	Total Return %
—	—	4.25*	64.26	–10.73	–47.34	5.38	–2.05	–58.28	26.12	–6.54	11.06	+/– S&P 500
—	—	—	25.24	–4.14	5.97	9.59	2.91	8.49	–14.65	0.28	—	+/– MSCI Latin Am
—	—	0.00	0.44	0.00	0.79	1.54	1.17	1.39	0.28	0.69	1.63	Income Return %
—	—	4.17	73.88	–9.41	–10.60	26.78	30.13	–31.09	46.88	–16.33	–2.45	Capital Return %
—	—	—	1	30	21	31	36	3	93	40	18	Total Rtn % Rank Cat
—	—	0.00	0.06	0.00	0.15	0.26	0.25	0.37	0.05	0.18	0.33	Income $
—	—	0.00	0.06	0.73	0.00	0.00	1.14	0.64	0.00	1.49	0.00	Capital Gains $
—	—	—	2.00	2.01	2.08	1.96	1.89	1.87	1.96	1.79	—	Expense Ratio %
—	—	—	0.44	–0.20	0.52	1.32	0.98	1.45	1.61	0.80	—	Income Ratio %
—	—	—	5	22	40	22	42	44	48	42	—	Turnover Rate %
—	—	4.2	409.1	649.6	514.9	636.9	962.4	462.3	577.2	393.8	330.8	Net Assets $mil

Performance 12-31-01

	1st Qtr	2nd Qtr	3rd Qtr	4th Qtr	Total
1997	13.60	18.68	7.70	–9.57	31.30
1998	2.81	–17.65	–22.14	6.65	–29.70
1999	11.11	10.66	–10.73	34.08	47.16
2000	1.50	–5.94	–3.94	–8.01	–15.64
2001	–2.96	10.17	–21.79	18.62	–0.82

Trailing	Total Return%	+/– S&P 500	+/– MSCI Latin Am	% Rank All	% Rank Cat	Growth of $10,000
3 Mo	18.62	7.94	—	16	86	11,862
6 Mo	–7.23	–1.67	—	75	22	9,277
1 Yr	–0.82	11.06	—	44	18	9,918
3 Yr Avg	7.18	8.21	—	16	62	12,313
5 Yr Avg	2.59	–8.11	—	86	27	11,365
10 Yr Avg	—	—	—	—	—	—
15 Yr Avg	—	—	—	—	—	—

Tax Analysis	Tax-Adj Ret%	%Rank Cat	%Pretax Ret	%Rank Cat
3 Yr Avg	6.30	59	87.7	87
5 Yr Avg	1.54	22	59.3	46
10 Yr Avg	—	—	—	—

Potential Capital Gain Exposure: –6% of assets

Risk Analysis

Time Period	Load-Adj Return %	Risk %Rank[1] All	Risk %Rank[1] Cat	Morningstar Return	Morningstar Risk	Morningstar Risk-Adj Rating
1 Yr	–0.82					
3 Yr	7.18	90	10	0.48[2]	1.30	★★★★
5 Yr	2.59	95	10	–0.51[2]	1.45	★★★
Incept	8.88	—	—	—	—	

Average Historical Rating (73 months): 2.4★s

[1] 1=low, 100=high [2] T-Bill return substituted for category avg.

Category Rating (3 Yr)

1 2 3 4 5
Worst Best

Return Average
Risk Low

Other Measures	Standard Index S&P 500	Best Fit Index MSCIPcxJND
Alpha	12.0	6.3
Beta	1.09	1.02
R-Squared	36	60

Standard Deviation	34.09
Mean	7.18
Sharpe Ratio	0.08

Portfolio Analysis 09-30-01

Share change since 06-01 Total Stocks: 35	Sector	Country	% Assets
Telefonos de Mexico ADR L	Services	Mexico	10.29
Petrobras Pfd	Energy	Brazil	10.29
⊖ Banco Itau	Financials	Brazil	5.18
Wal-Mart de Mexico Cl C	Retail	Mexico	4.90
⊖ Fomento Economico Mex	Staples	Mexico	4.25
⊖ PanAmerican Beverages	Staples	Mexico	4.10
⊖ Companhia De Bebidas Americas	Technology	Brazil	4.02
⊖ Kimberly-Clark de Mex A	Industrials	Mexico	3.90
⊖ Grupo Continental	Staples	Mexico	3.81
America Movil ADR	N/A	N/A	3.58
⊖ Cemex (Part) ADR	Industrials	Mexico	3.55
Companhia Vale do Rio Doce	Industrials	Brazil	3.26
TeleNorte Leste Part ADR	Services	Brazil	2.88
⊕ Banco Bradesco ADR	Financials	Brazil	2.82
⊖ Cervecerias Unidas ADR	Staples	Chile	2.57
Banco Latinoamer Export E	Financials	Panama	2.39
Aracruz Celulose SA ADR	Industrials	Brazil	2.24
⊕ Grupo Fin Bancomer O	Financials	Mexico	2.19
⊖ Coca-Cola FEMSA ADR	Staples	Mexico	2.07
⊖ Grupo Televisa (Part) ADR	Services	Mexico	1.87

Current Investment Style

Style: Value Blnd Growth; Size: Large Med Small

	Stock Port Avg	Rel MSCI EAFE Current	Rel MSCI EAFE Hist	Rel Cat
Price/Earnings Ratio	14.9	0.58	0.57	1.00
Price/Cash Flow	7.5	0.58	0.71	1.07
Price/Book Ratio	2.8	0.80	0.47	1.07
3 Yr Earnings Growth	26.4	1.41	0.44	1.17
Med Mkt Cap $mil	6,370	0.2	0.2	1.18

Country Exposure 09-30-01	% assets
Mexico	45
Brazil	37
Chile	4
Panama	2
Argentina	2

Hedging History: Never

Special Securities % assets 09-30-01	
Restricted/Illiquid Secs	1
Emerging-Markets Secs	91
Options/Futures/Warrants	No

Sector Weightings	% of Stocks	Rel Cat	5-Year High	5-Year Low
Utilities	1.6	0.3	16	0
Energy	14.2	1.4	23	0
Financials	15.3	1.1	18	0
Industrials	18.0	1.0	27	9
Durables	0.0	0.0	2	0
Staples	25.7	1.8	43	22
Services	20.0	0.7	36	13
Retail	5.4	0.6	11	4
Health	0.0	0.0	0	0
Technology	0.0	0.0	1	0

Composition % assets 09-30-01

Cash	3.8	Bonds	0.0
Stocks	96.2	Other	0.0

Analysis by William Samuel Rocco 09-08-01

It shouldn't be that big of a deal if Scudder Latin America Fund absorbs Argentina Fund.

Shareholders of Argentina Fund will vote on the acquisition of that closed-end offering by this fund on Oct. 16, 2001. If shareholders approve, which is likely, Argentina Fund is scheduled to merge into this offering Dec. 14, 2001. While risks exist for the acquiring fund in a merger, such as portfolio disruption and tax consequences, they seem under control here.

First, the danger of portfolio disruption seems limited. Argentina Fund does not focus exclusively on Argentina. It expanded its purview in the late 1990s and now has just 55% of its assets in Argentina. The two funds have the same lead manager and style, and that fund's Brazilian and other non-Argentine names are also holdings here. And if the merger is approved, Argentina Fund will cut its stake in Argentina so that no more than 10% of the combined assets will be invested in that nation at the time of the closing.

Any gains realized from those cuts will be distributed to Argentina Fund's shareholders just prior to the merger. That doesn't mean there aren't tax risks for this fund's shareholders. Argentina Fund's investors will be able to redeem their shares, which are currently trading at a discount, at net asset value after the merger and thus might be tempted to rush out of this fund—which could lead to distributions. But the discount has narrowed from 20% to 8% so far in 2001, and there will be a 2% redemption fee on any shares Argentina Fund investors sell within one year of the close. Thus, the potential for a rash of redemptions is not as high as it was. And this fund has negative potential capital gains exposure, which should help it handle any outflows that do occur. In any case, this fund remains one of the best options in its wild category.

Address:	Two International Place Boston, MA 02110 800-621-1048 / 800-621-1048
Web Address:	www.scudder.com
*Inception:	12-08-92
Advisor:	Zurich Scudder Inv.s
Subadvisor:	None
NTF Plans:	Fidelity , Datalynx

Minimum Purchase:	Closed	Add: $100 IRA: —
Min Auto Inv Plan:	Closed	Add: $50
Sales Fees:	No-load	
Management Fee:	1.3%	
Actual Fees:	Mgt: 1.25%	Dist: —
Expense Projections:	3Yr: $588	5Yr: $1011 10Yr: $2190
Avg Brok Commission:	—	Income Distrib: Annually

Total Cost (relative to category): —

Scudder Medium-Term Tax-Free S

Ticker	Load	NAV	Yield	SEC Yield	Total Assets	Mstar Category
SCMTX	Closed	$11.19	4.7%	3.44%	$603.2 mil	Muni Natl Interm-Term

Prospectus Objective: Muni Bond—National

Scudder Medium-Term Tax-Free Fund seeks income exempt from federal income taxes and seeks to limit principal fluctuation.

The fund invests at least 80% of assets in securities of municipalities across the U.S. and in other securities whose income is free from regular federal income tax and the AMT. It normally invests at least 65% of assets in municipal securities of the top three grades of credit quality. The fund may invest up to 35% of assets in bonds rated in the fourth credit grade, which is still considered investment-grade. The average-weighted maturity generally ranges between five and 10 years.

The fund currently offers A, B, C, S and AARP shares.

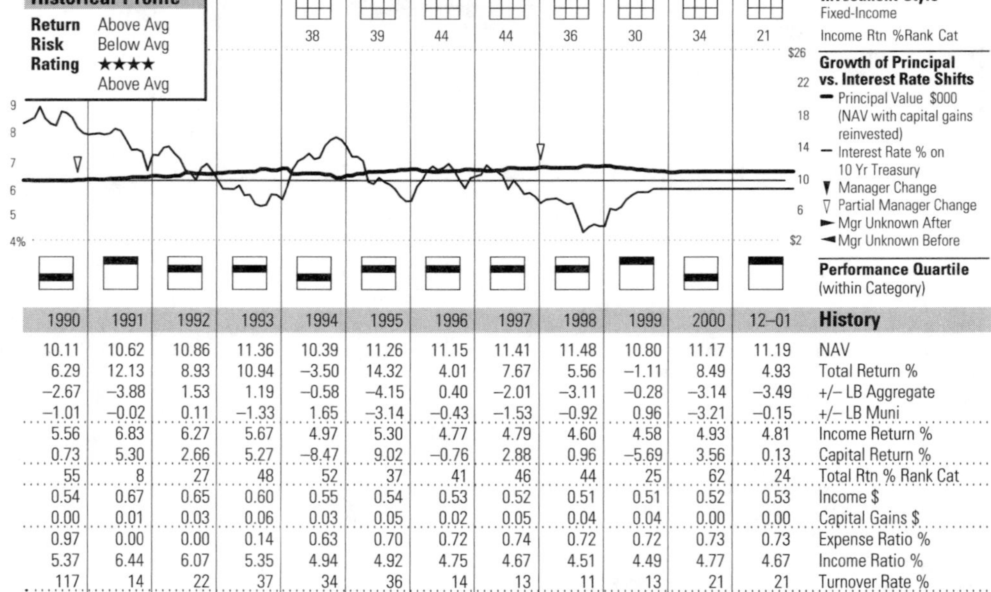

1990	1991	1992	1993	1994	1995	1996	1997	1998	1999	2000	12-01	History
10.11	10.62	10.86	11.36	10.39	11.26	11.15	11.41	11.48	10.80	11.17	11.19	NAV
6.29	12.13	8.93	10.94	-3.50	14.32	4.01	7.67	5.56	-1.11	8.49	4.93	Total Return %
-2.67	-3.88	1.53	1.19	-0.58	-4.15	0.40	-2.01	-3.11	-0.28	-3.14	-3.49	+/- LB Aggregate
-1.01	-0.02	0.11	-1.33	1.65	-3.14	-0.43	-1.53	-0.92	0.96	-3.21	-0.15	+/- LB Muni
5.56	6.83	6.27	5.67	4.97	5.30	4.77	4.79	4.60	4.58	4.93	4.81	Income Return %
0.73	5.30	2.66	5.27	-8.47	9.02	-0.76	2.88	0.96	-5.69	3.56	0.13	Capital Return %
55	8	27	48	52	37	41	46	44	25	62	24	Total Rtn % Rank Cat
0.54	0.67	0.65	0.60	0.55	0.54	0.53	0.52	0.51	0.51	0.52	0.53	Income $
0.00	0.01	0.03	0.06	0.03	0.05	0.02	0.05	0.04	0.04	0.00	0.00	Capital Gains $
0.97	0.00	0.00	0.14	0.63	0.70	0.72	0.74	0.72	0.72	0.73	0.73	Expense Ratio %
5.37	6.44	6.07	5.35	4.94	4.92	4.75	4.67	4.51	4.49	4.77	4.67	Income Ratio %
117	14	22	37	34	36	14	13	11	13	21	21	Turnover Rate %
26.2	267.1	649.5	1,012.0	703.1	710.0	649.8	654.5	676.8	559.1	600.7	572.9	Net Assets $mil

Portfolio Manager(s)

Ashton P. Goodfield, CFA. Since 11-90. BA'85 Duke U. Other funds currently managed: Scudder State Tax-Free Income NY A, Scudder Managed Municipal Bonds S, Scudder State Tax-Free Income NY B.

Philip G. Condon. Since 1-98. BA'73 U. of Massachusetts; MBA'76 U. of Massachusetts. Other funds currently managed: Scudder MA Tax-Free S, Scudder Managed Municipal Bonds S, Scudder High-Yield Tax-Free S.

Performance 12-31-01

	1st Qtr	2nd Qtr	3rd Qtr	4th Qtr	Total
1997	0.09	2.65	2.61	2.14	7.67
1998	0.92	1.14	2.91	0.50	5.56
1999	0.29	-1.70	0.54	-0.22	-1.11
2000	1.50	1.40	1.94	3.40	8.49
2001	2.42	0.61	2.90	-1.03	4.93

Trailing	Total Return%	+/- LB Agg	+/- LB Muni	% Rank All	% Rank Cat	Growth of $10,000
3 Mo	-1.03	-1.07	-0.37	93	66	9,897
6 Mo	1.83	-2.82	-0.29	25	34	10,183
1 Yr	4.93	-3.49	-0.15	23	24	10,493
3 Yr Avg	4.03	-2.25	-0.72	40	33	11,258
5 Yr Avg	5.05	-2.37	-0.92	63	35	12,796
10 Yr Avg	5.90	-1.33	-0.73	74	37	17,745
15 Yr Avg	6.13	-1.99	-1.06	87	76	24,398

Tax Analysis	Tax-Adj Ret%	%Rank Cat	%Pretax Ret	%Rank Cat
3 Yr Avg	4.00	30	99.3	57
5 Yr Avg	5.00	35	98.9	57
10 Yr Avg	5.82	35	98.5	45

Potential Capital Gain Exposure: 5% of assets

Risk Analysis

Time Period	Load-Adj Return %	Risk %Rank[1] All	Risk %Rank[1] Cat	Morningstar Return	Morningstar Risk	Morningstar Risk-Adj Rating
1 Yr	4.93					
3 Yr	4.03	6	11	0.60[2]	0.70	★★★★★
5 Yr	5.05	7	22	0.82[2]	0.75	★★★★
10 Yr	5.90	9	39	0.97	0.78	★★★★

Average Historical Rating (189 months): 4.1★s

[1]1=low, 100=high [2] T-Bill return substituted for category avg.

Category Rating (3 Yr)

1 2 3 4 5
Worst Best

Return Above Avg
Risk Below Avg

Other Measures	Standard Index LB Agg	Best Fit Index LB Muni
Alpha	-1.8	-0.7
Beta	0.71	0.79
R-Squared	60	91

Standard Deviation	3.20
Mean	4.03
Sharpe Ratio	-0.34

Portfolio Analysis 09-30-01

Total Fixed-Income: 195	Date of Maturity	Amount $000	Value $000	% Net Assets
AK North Slope GO 0%	06-30-04	19,500	17,944	2.92
NY NYC GO 6.75%	08-15-03	13,000	13,945	2.27
NY State GO 6.6%	10-01-03	9,995	10,591	1.72
IL Metro Pier/Expo McCormick Expsn 0%	06-15-04	10,500	9,677	1.57
IN Indianapolis GO Loc Pub Impr 6.75%	02-01-14	8,000	9,588	1.56
AK North Slope GO 0%	06-30-06	11,150	9,397	1.53
MA State GO 5.75%	06-01-09	8,340	9,363	1.52
TX Houston Wtr 5.5%	12-01-15	8,250	8,802	1.43
NY NYC GO 7%	08-01-04	7,650	8,447	1.37
CO Hsg Fin Sngl Fam Prog 6.125%	11-01-23	7,440	8,120	1.32
NV Clark GO Sch Dist 6.5%	06-15-07	7,000	8,022	1.30
IL Dev Fin Poll Cntrl ComEd 5.3%	01-15-04	7,500	7,898	1.28
IL State GO 5.75%	06-01-11	7,000	7,790	1.27
TX Brownsville Util Sys 6%	09-01-14	6,500	7,581	1.23
HI State GO 4.75%	11-01-08	7,050	7,460	1.21

Current Investment Style

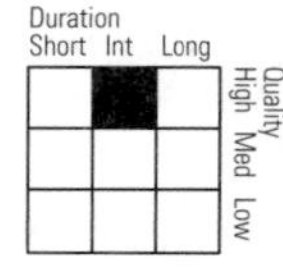

Avg Duration[1]	5.4 Yrs
Avg Nominal Maturity	6.0 Yrs
Avg Credit Quality	AA
Avg Wtd Coupon	4.63%
Avg Wtd Price	103.54% of par
Pricing Service	J.J. Kenny

[1]figure provided by fund

Analysis by Eric Jacobson 07-25-01

Those who just got here can put a smile on their faces.

As part of the Scudder/Kemper marriage, the two firms' fund families were recently combined. Most of the old Kemper funds have thus been merged into Scudder counterparts, all of which now have load share classes. (The old no-load classes are now closed to new investors.) As part of that process, Kemper Intermediate Municipal Bond Fund was merged into this portfolio.

The few shareholders who were affected by that change (the Kemper fund was very small) should be pretty happy with the result. In keeping with a successful strategy used at other funds such as Scudder Managed Muni Bonds S, comanagers Ashton Goodfield and Philip Condon prefer to keep the fund's duration roughly neutral to that of its typical peer, instead focusing mostly on picking undervalued bonds across the maturity spectrum.

Much of the fund's long-term returns, all of which place in its category's top half, can be explained by the managers' preference for noncallable bonds, which make up a huge chunk of the fund's assets. That has helped the fund's returns immensely, as noncallable bonds participate in interest-rate rallies more fully than their callable counterparts. They also react more predictably when interest rates rise, because their rate sensitivity doesn't extend dramatically (which can happen in drastic fashion to callable securities). That was the case in 1999, when the fund notched a top-quartile return. (It's worth noting, however, that the fund was a bit cautious in 2000 with regard to its maturity positioning, and it did underperform slightly.)

The fund's long-term returns have also been helped by solid issue selection.

Credit Analysis % bonds 09-30-01			
US Govt	0	BB	0
AAA	69	B	0
AA	16	Below B	0
A	11	NR/NA	1
BBB	4		

Special Securities % assets 09-30-01	
Restricted/Illiquid Secs	0
Inverse Floaters	0
Options/Futures/Warrants	No

Bond Type % assets 12-31-00	
Alternative Minimum Tax (AMT)	—
Insured	46.3
Prerefunded	4.9

Top 5 States % bonds			
TX	13.8	MI	5.3
IL	13.7	AZ	4.6
NY	10.5		

Composition % assets 09-30-01			
Cash	0.5	Bonds	99.5
Stocks	0.0	Other	0.0

Sector Weightings	% of Bonds	Rel Cat
General Obligation	45.4	1.6
Utilities	11.2	1.3
Health	10.0	0.8
Water/Waste	6.1	1.0
Housing	1.9	0.3
Education	4.5	0.6
Transportation	5.1	0.4
COP/Lease	1.2	0.6
Industrial	8.5	1.1
Misc Revenue	5.3	1.1
Demand	0.7	0.8

Address:	Two International Place Boston, MA 02110 800-621-1048 / 800-621-1048
Web Address:	www.scudder.com
Inception:	04-12-83
Advisor:	Zurich Scudder Inv.s
Subadvisor:	None
NTF Plans:	Fidelity , Datalynx

Minimum Purchase:	Closed	Add: $100	IRA: $1000
Min Auto Inv Plan:	Closed	Add: $50	
Sales Fees:	No-load		
Management Fee:	.60% mx./.50% mn.		
Actual Fees:	Mgt: 0.59%	Dist: —	
Expense Projections:	3Yr: $237	5Yr: $411	10Yr: $918
Avg Brok Commission:	—	Income Distrib: Monthly	
Total Cost (relative to category):		Below Avg	

Scudder Total Return A

Ticker	Load	NAV	Yield	Total Assets	Mstar Category
KTRAX	5.75%	$9.10	2.5%	$2,931.4 mil	Domestic Hybrid

Prospectus Objective: Balanced

Scudder Total Return Fund seeks total return consistent with reasonable risk.

The fund normally invests in both fixed-income and equity securities. The relative percentages vary according to market and economic conditions. The fund may invest up to 35% of assets in debt rated below investment-grade, and up to 25% of assets may be held in foreign securities.

Class A shares have front loads; B shares have deferred loads, higher 12b-1 fees, and conversion features; C shares have level loads; I shares are designed for institutional investors.

Prior to June 11, 2001, the fund was named Kemper Total Return Fund - Class A.

Historical Profile

Return Below Avg
Risk Below Avg
Rating ★★★ Neutral

Investment Style
Equity
Average Stock %: 60% (1995), 64% (1996), 64% (1997), 63% (1998), 65% (1999), 59% (2000), 57% (12-01)

▼ Manager Change
▽ Partial Manager Change

Fund Performance vs. Category Average
■ Quarterly Fund Return +/– Category Average
— Category Baseline

Performance Quartile (within Category)

History

1990	1991	1992	1993	1994	1995	1996	1997	1998	1999	2000	12-01	History
8.03	10.55	10.11	9.95	8.82	10.24	10.08	10.10	10.70	11.46	10.01	9.10	NAV
4.11	40.16	2.49	11.59	–9.18	25.80	16.25	19.14	15.91	14.60	–2.78	–6.79	Total Return %
7.22	9.67	–5.13	1.53	–10.49	–11.73	–6.70	–14.21	–12.66	–6.44	6.32	5.09	+/– S&P 500
–4.85	24.15	–4.91	1.84	–6.26	7.33	12.63	9.46	7.24	15.43	–14.41	–15.21	+/– LB Aggregate
6.08	4.42	2.49	1.90	2.28	3.73	2.91	3.24	2.98	2.88	2.33	2.28	Income Return %
–1.98	35.74	0.00	9.69	–11.46	22.07	13.34	15.91	12.94	11.72	–5.11	–9.06	Capital Return %
15	7	93	52	97	45	22	45	31	20	78	72	Total Rtn % Rank Cat
0.49	0.35	0.26	0.19	0.23	0.33	0.30	0.32	0.30	0.31	0.27	0.23	Income $
0.00	0.28	0.43	1.11	0.00	0.50	1.49	1.55	0.68	0.46	0.85	0.00	Capital Gains $
0.87	1.03	1.06	1.02	1.13	1.12	1.05	1.01	1.01	1.02	1.01	—	Expense Ratio %
5.87	3.96	2.23	2.94	2.34	3.00	2.76	2.92	2.75	2.71	2.29	—	Income Ratio %
157	157	150	180	121	142	85	122	80	64	95	—	Turnover Rate %
821.4	1,087.1	1,293.9	1,463.4	1,640.4	1,790.1	1,900.7	2,140.1	2,606.1	3,006.8	2,722.3	2,382.9	Net Assets $mil

Portfolio Manager(s)

Gary A. Langbaum, CFA et al.Since 1-95. BS'69 U. of Maryland; MBA'70 U. of Maryland.

Performance 12-31-01

	1st Qtr	2nd Qtr	3rd Qtr	4th Qtr	Total
1997	–0.71	13.07	5.91	0.20	19.14
1998	9.30	1.42	–6.67	12.04	15.91
1999	3.02	4.79	–4.08	10.67	14.60
2000	1.56	–1.12	1.05	–4.20	–2.78
2001	–6.23	3.11	–9.23	6.22	–6.79

Trailing	Total Return%	+/– S&P 500	+/– LB Agg	% Rank All	% Rank Cat	Growth of $10,000
3 Mo	6.22	–4.46	6.18	60	52	10,622
6 Mo	–3.58	1.97	–8.24	54	78	9,642
1 Yr	–6.79	5.09	–15.21	55	72	9,321
3 Yr Avg	1.27	2.29	–5.01	66	63	10,385
5 Yr Avg	7.48	–3.22	0.05	32	47	14,342
10 Yr Avg	8.10	–4.83	0.87	42	69	21,787
15 Yr Avg	9.76	–3.97	1.64	43	52	40,422

Tax Analysis	Tax-Adj Ret%	%Rank Cat	%Pretax Ret	%Rank Cat
3 Yr Avg	–0.57	64	—	—
5 Yr Avg	4.81	52	64.4	66
10 Yr Avg	5.20	74	64.2	81

Potential Capital Gain Exposure: 3% of assets

Risk Analysis

Time Period	Load-Adj Return %	Risk %Rank[1] All	Risk %Rank[1] Cat	Morningstar Return	Morningstar Risk	Morningstar Risk-Adj Rating
1 Yr	–12.15					
3 Yr	–0.71	43	62	–1.14[2]	0.59	★★★
5 Yr	6.21	46	70	0.26[2]	0.61	★★★
10 Yr	7.46	55	84	0.34	0.71	★★

Average Historical Rating (193 months): 2.9★s

[1]1=low, 100=high [2] T-Bill return substituted for category avg.

Category Rating (3 Yr)

1 2 **3** 4 5
Worst Best

Return Average
Risk Average

Other Measures	Standard Index S&P 500	Best Fit Index S&P 500
Alpha	–0.4	–0.4
Beta	0.59	0.59
R-Squared	94	94
Standard Deviation		10.43
Mean		1.27
Sharpe Ratio		–0.41

Portfolio Analysis 09-30-01

Total Stocks: 79 Share change since 06-01	Sector	PE Ratio	YTD Return %	% Net Assets
⊕ Pfizer	Health	34.7	–12.40	1.98
⊖ Johnson & Johnson	Health	16.6	14.01	1.93
⊖ General Elec	Industrials	30.1	–15.00	1.77
⊕ ExxonMobil	Energy	15.3	–7.59	1.72
⊕ PepsiCo	Staples	31.4	–0.54	1.54
⊕ Abbott Labs	Health	51.6	17.08	1.52
⊖ Citigroup	Financials	20.0	0.03	1.46
⊕ American Intl Grp	Financials	42.0	–19.20	1.42
⊖ Microsoft	Technology	57.6	52.78	1.38
⊖ Wal-Mart Stores	Retail	40.3	8.94	1.35

Total Fixed-Income: 89	Date of Maturity	Amount $000	Value $000	% Net Assets
US Treasury Note 6.75%	05-15-05	130,350	144,037	5.05
US Treasury Bond 9.375%	02-15-06	90,450	110,575	3.88
US Treasury Note 5.75%	08-15-10	71,925	77,893	2.73
US Treasury Bond 10.75%	08-15-05	60,000	75,075	2.63
US Treasury Note 5.75%	11-15-05	50,205	54,002	1.89
FNMA 7.5%	07-01-31	38,516	40,060	1.41
FNMA 7%		38,400	39,768	1.40
GNMA 7%	12-15-28	36,361	37,821	1.33
FNMA 6.5%	07-01-30	30,069	30,605	1.07
US Treasury Note 5.63%	11-30-02	28,830	29,830	1.05

Equity Style
Style: Growth
Size: Large-Cap

	Portfolio Avg	Rel S&P
Price/Earnings Ratio	31.4	1.02
Price/Book Ratio	6.7	1.18
Price/Cash Flow	19.4	1.08
3 Yr Earnings Growth	16.2	1.11
1 Yr Earnings Est%	2.4	—
Debt % Total Cap	30.5	0.99
Med Mkt Cap $mil	65,932	1.09

Fixed-Income Style
Duration: —
Quality: —
NA

Avg Eff Duration[1]	2.0 Yrs
Avg Eff Maturity	3.0 Yrs
Avg Credit Quality	—
Avg Wtd Coupon	7.26%

[1]figure provided by fund as of 03-31-01

Special Securities % assets 09-30-01	
Restricted/Illiquid Secs	Trace
Emerging-Markets Secs	0
Options/Futures/Warrants	Yes

Composition % of assets 09-30-01	
Cash	0.0
Stocks*	56.3
Bonds	43.7
Other	0.0
*Foreign (% of stocks)	3.5

Market Cap	
Giant	55.7
Large	36.6
Medium	7.7
Small	0.0
Micro	0.0

Sector Weightings	% of Stocks	Rel S&P	5-Year High	5-Year Low
Utilities	0.5	0.2	5	0
Energy	6.0	0.9	9	0
Financials	17.8	1.0	22	10
Industrials	11.2	1.0	22	6
Durables	0.0	0.0	8	0
Staples	9.3	1.2	16	2
Services	10.6	1.0	27	6
Retail	11.3	1.7	14	3
Health	21.1	1.4	27	5
Technology	12.2	0.7	30	6

Analysis by William Harding 07-06-01

This fund has shown some vulnerability of late, but we think that it remains a good pick.

Scudder Total Return's aggressive positioning has led to middling recent performance. Manager Gary Langbaum has typically devoted about 65% of assets to stocks, with a bias toward growth-oriented names. Consequently, the fund was more susceptible than many of its rivals to the stock market's slide over the past 15 months, and it has lost more than the average domestic-hybrid offering since growth-oriented equities began their decline in March 2000. That said, last year stands out as an anomaly: It was the first time that the fund's annual return landed in the category's bottom half since Langbaum took the helm in 1995.

Recently, Langbaum has taken some steps toward moderation. He pared the fund's equity stake to 60% of assets at the start of 2001, and he also trimmed the fund's tech weighting in the beginning of the year. Since then, however, he has added back to tech shares amid weakness, resulting in a weighting that is in line with the market's. Langbaum's price-consciousness has kept him away from many of the more-speculative tech names that were market darlings in early 2000. Instead, he has favored blue chips such as Microsoft, IBM, and AOL Time Warner. That has helped the fund sidestep weakness in some of the market's biggest disasters, such as communication-equipment stocks.

On the bond side, comanager Rob Cessine continues to walk a fairly cautious path, devoting most of the fund's bond allocation to government securities that have minimal default risk. In addition, Cessine has shortened the fund's duration recently, reducing its sensitivity to interest-rate movements.

Although the fund's current positioning is a tad more moderate than it has been historically, this fund is still better suited for more-aggressive hybrid fans.

Address:	Two International Place Boston, MA 02110 800-621-1048 / 800-621-1048
Web Address:	www.scudder.com
Inception:	03-02-64
Advisor:	Zurich Scudder Inv.s
Subadvisor:	None
NTF Plans:	Datalynx , Fidelity Inst.

Minimum Purchase:	$1000	Add: $100 IRA: $250
Min Auto Inv Plan:	$50	Add: $50
Sales Fees:	5.75%L, 0.25%B	
Management Fee:	.58% mx./.42% mn., .25%A	
Actual Fees:	Mgt: 0.53%	Dist: 0.25%
Expense Projections:	3Yr: $878	5Yr: $1101 10Yr: $1740
Avg Brok Commission:	—	Income Distrib: Quarterly
Total Cost (relative to category):		Average

Security Capital U.S. Real Estate

Ticker	Load	NAV	Yield	Total Assets	Mstar Category
SUSIX	12b–1 only	$12.16	4.6%	$159.9 mil	Spec Real Estate

Prospectus Objective: Specialty—Real Estate

Security Capital U.S. Real Estate Fund seeks total return, including current income and capital appreciation.

The fund normally invests at least 80% of assets in real-estate securities. To select investments, management integrates proprietary real-estate market research with capital markets research and modeling techniques. The fund is nondiversified.

Past fund names : Security Capital Employee REIT Fund and Security Capital U.S. Real Estate Fund - Class I.

Historical Profile

Return Above Avg
Risk Below Avg
Rating ★★★★ Above Avg

Investment Style
Equity
Average Stock %: 100% (1997), 97% (1998), 93% (1999), 95% (2000), 96% (12-01)

▼ Manager Change
▽ Partial Manager Change

Fund Performance vs. Category Average
■ Quarterly Fund Return +/– Category Average
— Category Baseline

Performance Quartile (within Category)

Portfolio Manager(s)

Anthony R. Manno Jr.. Since 12-96. BA Nortwestern U.; MBA U. of Chicago. Other fund currently managed: Security Capital European Real Estate.

Kenneth D. Statz. Since 12-96. BBA U. of Wisconsin; MBA U. of Wisconsin. Other fund currently managed: Security Capital European Real Estate.

Kevin W. Bedell. Since 12-96. BA Kenyon C.; MBA U. of Chicago. Other fund currently managed: Security Capital European Real Estate.

1990	1991	1992	1993	1994	1995	1996	1997	1998	1999	2000	12-01	History
—	—	—	—	—	—	10.38	11.95	9.82	9.37	12.14	12.16	NAV
—	—	—	—	—	—	3.80*	25.17	–11.94	0.58	35.84	7.04	Total Return %
—	—	—	—	—	—	4.71*	–8.18	–40.51	–20.46	44.94	18.92	+/– S&P 500
—	—	—	—	—	—	—	5.50	5.07	3.15	4.80	–5.32	+/– Wilshire REIT
—	—	—	—	—	—	0.00	5.08	4.02	5.33	5.75	4.78	Income Return %
—	—	—	—	—	—	3.80	20.09	–15.96	–4.74	30.10	2.26	Capital Return %
—	—	—	—	—	—	—	24	10	17	1	74	Total Rtn % Rank Cat
—	—	—	—	—	—	0.00	0.52	0.46	0.51	0.53	0.57	Income $
—	—	—	—	—	—	0.00	0.48	0.29	0.00	0.00	0.24	Capital Gains $
—	—	—	—	—	—	—	0.94	1.00	1.20	1.35	—	Expense Ratio %
—	—	—	—	—	—	—	4.08	4.75	4.18	5.02	—	Income Ratio %
—	—	—	—	—	—	—	104	109	50	91	—	Turnover Rate %
—	—	—	—	—	—	—	116.5	90.5	46.4	116.0	159.9	Net Assets $mil

Performance 12-31-01

	1st Qtr	2nd Qtr	3rd Qtr	4th Qtr	Total
1997	1.25	4.65	16.60	1.31	25.17
1998	0.42	–5.77	–10.15	3.57	–11.94
1999	–2.85	13.73	–7.81	–1.25	0.58
2000	4.66	12.40	9.80	5.17	35.84
2001	–3.93	9.18	–1.42	3.51	7.04

Trailing	Total Return%	+/– S&P 500	+/– Wil REIT	% Rank All	% Rank Cat	Growth of $10,000
3 Mo	3.51	–7.17	–1.37	69	78	10,351
6 Mo	2.05	7.60	–0.32	22	36	10,205
1 Yr	7.04	18.92	–5.32	14	74	10,704
3 Yr Avg	13.51	14.53	0.73	6	4	14,625
5 Yr Avg	10.02	–0.68	2.68	18	4	16,121
10 Yr Avg	—	—	—	—	—	—
15 Yr Avg	—	—	—	—	—	—

Tax Analysis	Tax-Adj Ret%	%Rank Cat	%Pretax Ret	%Rank Cat
3 Yr Avg	11.16	5	82.6	31
5 Yr Avg	7.35	6	73.4	16
10 Yr Avg	—	—	—	—

Potential Capital Gain Exposure: 12% of assets

Risk Analysis

Time Period	Load-Adj Return %	Risk %Rank[1] All	Risk %Rank[1] Cat	Morningstar Return	Morningstar Risk	Morningstar Risk-Adj Rating
1 Yr	7.04					
3 Yr	13.51	39	27	1.97[2]	0.53	★★★★★
5 Yr	10.02	49	26	1.20[2]	0.66	★★★★
Incept	10.77	—	—	—	—	

Average Historical Rating (25 months): 3.0★s

[1] 1=low, 100=high [2] T-Bill return substituted for category avg.

Category Rating (3 Yr)

1 2 3 4 5 — Worst … Best (5)

Return High
Risk Below Avg

Other Measures	Standard Index S&P 500	Best Fit Index Wil REIT
Alpha	9.6	0.7
Beta	0.07	1.01
R-Squared	1	91
Standard Deviation		16.03
Mean		13.51
Sharpe Ratio		0.61

Portfolio Analysis 09-30-01

Share chng since 03–01 Total Stocks: 22

	Subsector	PE	YTD Ret%	% Assets
⊕ Equity Office Properties Tr	Industrial/Office	18.7	–1.76	12.12
⊕ Mack–Cali Realty	Industrial/Office	13.3	18.32	8.23
⊕ Public Storage	Self Storage	22.6	44.92	8.10
⊕ Apartment Invest & Mgmt	Apartment	NMF	–1.80	7.82
AvalonBay Communities	Apartment	15.9	–0.38	6.67
☼ Taubman Centers	Retail	—	46.42	4.86
☼ Archstone Communities Tr	Apartment	14.8	9.11	4.62
⊕ Post Properties	Apartment	15.2	2.86	4.60
⊕ Essex Ppty Tr	Apartment	20.9	–4.44	4.47
⊖ Boston Properties	Industrial/Office	17.8	–7.37	4.24
⊕ Arden Realty Grp	Industrial/Office	16.6	13.90	4.09
⊕ Liberty Ppty Tr	Industrial/Office	13.5	13.22	4.03
Cabot Indl Tr	Industrial/Office	—	31.97	3.78
☼ Simon Ppty Grp	Retail	27.9	31.72	3.54
⊕ Prentiss Properties Tr	Industrial/Office	11.2	10.26	3.10
⊕ Equity Residential Properties	Apartment	22.1	10.14	2.73
☼ Highwoods Properties	Industrial/Office	12.2	14.30	1.88
⊖ Charles E Smith Resdntl Rlty	Apartment	—	4.75	1.82
☼ TrizecHahn	Diversified	28.0	5.92	1.52
☼ Federal Realty Invest Tr	Retail	15.7	32.27	1.18
☼ Shurgard Storage Ctrs Cl A	Self Storage	23.4	40.84	1.03
☼ Rouse	Diversified	19.3	20.91	0.11

Current Investment Style

Style: Value Blnd Growth; Size: Large Med Small

	Stock Port Avg	Relative S&P 500 Current	Relative S&P 500 Hist	Rel Cat
Price/Earnings Ratio	21.7	0.70	0.59	1.10
Price/Book Ratio	1.6	0.28	0.18	0.93
Price/Cash Flow	—	—	—	—
3 Yr Earnings Growth	23.1	1.58	0.56	1.13
1 Yr Earnings Est%	64.4	—	—	1.06
Med Mkt Cap $mil	3,098	0.1	0.0	1.35

Special Securities % assets 09-30-01	
Restricted/Illiquid Secs	0
Emerging–Markets Secs	0
Options/Futures/Warrants	No

Composition % assets 09-30-01	
Cash	4.6
Stocks*	95.4
Bonds	0.0
Other	0.0
*Foreign (% stocks)	1.6

Market Cap	
Giant	0.0
Large	15.7
Medium	64.8
Small	19.5
Micro	0.0

Subsector Weightings	% of Stocks	Rel Cat
Diversified	1.7	0.2
Health Care	0.0	0.0
Industrial/Office	43.9	1.4
Mortgage Backed	0.0	0.0
Apartment	34.6	1.8
Retail	10.1	0.5
Dvlp./Man. Home	0.0	0.0
Self Storage	9.7	2.8
Hotel	0.0	0.0
Other	0.0	0.0

Analysis by Alan Papier 11-07-01

Security Capital U.S. Real Estate Fund isn't having a banner year, but it remains one of our favorites.

After lagging the majority of its real-estate category peers for much of 2001, this fund is starting to benefit from its conviction and high-quality focus. Coming into the year, the management team was worried about the U.S. economy. They therefore placed an even greater emphasis on companies with clean balance sheets and property portfolios in markets with high barriers to entry.

That strategy didn't work so well during the first seven months of the year, as smaller-cap REITs and those with high dividend yields were the top performers. Yet the fund has held up much better than most of its peers of late, as the economy's deep-rooted weakness—crystallized in the immediate aftermath of Sept. 11's terrorist attacks—precipitated a flight to quality. Although the fund still ranked in the bottom half of the category for the year to date through Nov. 6, 2001, it had outperformed 70% of its peers for the previous three months.

Two of the fund's largest holdings, Mack-Cali Realty and Public Storage, were among the top-performing REITs during that span. And while those hefty 8%-plus positions have worked out well of late, the fund's tendency to load up on its favorite picks can contribute to uneven performance over shorter periods of time. As of Sept. 30, for example, two thirds of assets were invested in the fund's top-10 holdings. If one of those companies imploded, the fund would be hit hard. Similarly, the fund's bottom-up approach can leave it overexposed to various real-estate subsectors (and devoid of exposure in others), while more-diversified strategies may make for a smoother ride.

That said, the fund has earned an excellent risk/reward profile so far.

Address:	11 South LaSalle Street 2nd Floor Chicago, IL 60603 888–732–8748
Web Address:	www.securitycapital.com
*Inception:	12-20-96
Advisor:	Security Cap. Research & Mngt
Subadvisor:	None
NTF Plans:	Datalynx , Fidelity Inst.

Minimum Purchase:	$1000	Add: $100	IRA: $500
Min Auto Inv Plan:	$100	Add: $100	
Sales Fees:	0.25%B		
Management Fee:	.60%, .02%A		
Actual Fees:	Mgt: 0.60%	Dist: 0.25%	
Expense Projections:	3Yr: $430	5Yr: $744	10Yr: $1632
Avg Brok Commission:	—	Income Distrib: Quarterly	
Total Cost (relative to category):		Below Avg	

SEI International Equity A

Ticker	Load	NAV	Yield	Total Assets	Mstar Category
SEITX	None	$8.80	0.2%	$2,534.2 mil	Foreign Stock

Prospectus Objective: Foreign Stock

SEI International Equity Portfolio - Class A seeks long-term capital appreciation.

The fund normally invests at least 65% of assets in foreign equity securities. It also may invest up to 50% of assets in U.S. and foreign debt securities.

Class A shares are offered to institutional investors; D shares have front loads and 12b-1 fees. Prior to Feb. 16, 1995, it was named SEI International Equity Portfolio. From that date until March 25, 1996, it was called SEI Core International Trust Equity Portfolio. On March 25, 1996, both SEI International Trust European Equity Portfolio and SEI International Trust Pacific Basin Equity Portfolio merged into the fund.

Historical Profile
Return: Average
Risk: Average
Rating: ★★★ Neutral

Investment Style: Equity — Average Stock %: 94% 91% 84% 94% 95% 97%

▼ Manager Change
▽ Partial Manager Change

Fund Performance vs. Category Average
■ Quarterly Fund Return +/– Category Average
— Category Baseline

Performance Quartile (within Category)

Portfolio Manager(s)

Management Team

1990	1991	1992	1993	1994	1995	1996	1997	1998	1999	2000	12–01	History
8.70	9.28	9.01	10.54	9.93	10.02	9.88	9.31	10.53	14.31	11.39	8.80	NAV
–11.39	10.23	–2.91	22.81	–0.04	11.34	9.04	–1.86	19.29	39.63	–17.74	–22.55	Total Return %
–8.27	–20.25	–10.53	12.76	–1.35	–26.19	–13.91	–35.21	–9.29	18.59	–8.63	–10.67	+/– S&P 500
12.06	–1.90	9.26	–9.75	–7.82	0.14	2.99	–3.64	–0.71	12.66	–3.57	—	+/– MSCI EAFE
1.61	3.41	0.00	4.94	0.19	0.00	1.91	1.13	1.96	1.03	0.50	0.19	Income Return %
–13.00	6.82	–2.91	17.87	–0.23	11.34	7.12	–2.98	17.33	38.59	–18.23	–22.73	Capital Return %
60	68	39	98	57	41	72	86	19	47	58	54	Total Rtn % Rank Cat
0.16	0.30	0.00	0.44	0.02	0.00	0.19	0.11	0.18	0.11	0.07	0.02	Income $
0.00	0.00	0.00	0.00	0.59	0.99	0.82	0.27	0.35	0.23	0.31	0.00	Capital Gains $
1.10	1.10	1.10	1.10	1.10	1.19	1.25	1.28	1.21	1.28	1.28	—	Expense Ratio %
3.13	3.52	2.07	1.80	1.46	1.30	1.29	1.11	1.31	0.39	0.79	—	Income Ratio %
—	14	79	23	19	64	102	117	75	61	73	—	Turnover Rate %
28.9	72.2	162.0	444.2	387.6	311.6	478.8	707.9	1,190.1	2,360.9	2,929.1	2,534.2	Net Assets $mil

Performance 12-31-01

	1st Qtr	2nd Qtr	3rd Qtr	4th Qtr	Total
1997	–1.27	10.64	–1.59	–8.70	–1.86
1998	15.55	2.17	–15.34	19.35	19.29
1999	2.80	6.69	5.31	20.88	39.63
2000	0.49	–5.91	–8.87	–4.53	–17.74
2001	–13.70	–0.71	–15.47	6.93	–22.55

Trailing	Total Return%	+/– S&P 500	+/– MSCI EAFE	% Rank All	% Rank Cat	Growth of $10,000
3 Mo	6.93	–3.75	—	56	64	10,693
6 Mo	–9.61	–4.06	—	84	61	9,039
1 Yr	–22.55	–10.67	—	84	54	7,745
3 Yr Avg	–3.82	–2.80	—	89	60	8,896
5 Yr Avg	0.82	–9.88	—	91	65	10,415
10 Yr Avg	4.19	–8.74	—	96	81	15,071
15 Yr Avg	—	—	—	—	—	—

Tax Analysis	Tax-Adj Ret%	%Rank Cat	%Pretax Ret	%Rank Cat
3 Yr Avg	–4.33	54	—	—
5 Yr Avg	–0.06	53	—	—
10 Yr Avg	2.76	84	65.9	77

Potential Capital Gain Exposure: 42% of assets

Risk Analysis

Time Period	Load-Adj Return %	Risk %Rank[1] All	Risk %Rank[1] Cat	Morningstar Return	Morningstar Risk	Morningstar Risk-Adj Rating
1 Yr	–22.55					
3 Yr	–3.82	68	38	–1.71[2]	0.88	★★★
5 Yr	0.82	71	38	–0.85[2]	0.80	★★★
10 Yr	4.19	80	42	–0.14[2]	0.82	★★★

Average Historical Rating (109 months): 2.9★s

[1] 1=low, 100=high [2] T-Bill return substituted for category avg.

Category Rating (3 Yr): 3 (1 Worst – 5 Best)

Return: Average
Risk: Average

Other Measures	Standard Index S&P 500	Best Fit Index MSCIWdxUSN
Alpha	–3.9	1.3
Beta	0.77	1.05
R-Squared	60	96
Standard Deviation		16.24
Mean		–3.82
Sharpe Ratio		–0.63

Portfolio Analysis 09-30-01

Share change since 06–01 Total Stocks: 408	Sector	Country	% Assets
⊕ Glaxosmithkline	Technology	United Kingdom	2.58
⊕ Vodafone Airtouch	Services	United Kingdom	2.41
⊕ BAE Sys	Technology	United Kingdom	1.77
⊕ Reed Intl	Services	United Kingdom	1.75
⊕ Muenchener Rueckvers (Reg)	Financials	Germany	1.71
⊖ Novartis (Reg)	Health	Switzerland	1.46
⊖ Total Fina Cl B	Energy	France	1.46
⊕ ING Groep	Financials	Netherlands	1.35
⊕ Shell Transp & Trad	Energy	United Kingdom	1.28
⊕ Roche Hldgs (Gen)	Health	Switzerland	1.22
⊕ Unilever	Staples	United Kingdom	1.18
⊕ E.ON Cl B	Services	Germany	1.13
⊕ VNU	Services	Netherlands	1.09
⊕ Aventis Cl A	Health	France	1.05
⊕ Nokia	Technology	Finland	1.03
⊕ Akzo Nobel NV	Industrials	Netherlands	1.02
⊕ UBS (Reg)	Financials	Switzerland	0.98
⊖ ENI	Energy	Italy	0.98
⊕ Deutsche Telekom (Reg)	Services	Germany	0.97
⊕ Compass Grp	Services	United Kingdom	0.97

Current Investment Style

Style: Value Blnd Growth; Size: Large Med Small

	Stock Port Avg	Rel MSCI EAFE Current	Rel MSCI EAFE Hist	Rel Cat
Price/Earnings Ratio	26.8	1.04	0.98	1.05
Price/Cash Flow	14.9	1.16	1.05	1.04
Price/Book Ratio	3.9	1.11	1.02	0.99
3 Yr Earnings Growth	19.0	1.01	1.01	0.96
Med Mkt Cap $mil	20,019	0.7	0.9	1.11

Country Exposure 09-30-01	% assets
United Kingdom	26
Japan	21
France	9
Netherlands	8
Switzerland	7

Hedging History: Never

Regional Exposure 09-30-01	% assets
Europe	66
Japan	21
Latin America	0
Pacific Rim	8
Other	1

Special Securities % assets 09-30-01	
Restricted/Illiquid Secs	1
Emerging-Markets Secs	4
Options/Futures/Warrants	No

Composition % assets 09-30-01			
Cash	2.4	Bonds	0.1
Stocks	96.7	Other	0.8

Sector Weightings	% of Stocks	Rel Cat	5-Year High	5-Year Low
Utilities	2.7	1.0	13	2
Energy	5.4	0.9	8	1
Financials	17.7	0.8	30	16
Industrials	12.1	0.9	29	10
Durables	6.0	0.9	16	4
Staples	8.3	1.2	12	2
Services	21.4	1.2	30	6
Retail	4.9	1.0	7	2
Health	12.5	1.3	13	2
Technology	9.1	0.9	16	2

Analysis by William Samuel Rocco 07-31-01

SEI International Equity Portfolio boasts some heavy hitters in its lineup, but it still hasn't put together a high-scoring team.

This fund's management team boasts some talent. SEI divides the portfolio among six subadvisors, some of which are among the best international investors. It gives Capital Guardian Trust Company, which manages the American Funds, 20% of assets to apply its growth-at-a-reasonable-price approach to developed overseas markets. It also hired Morgan Stanley in September 2001 to run 25% of assets. Morgan Stanley uses a value style in developed markets. Both shops are outstanding. Rounding out the subadvisor crew are BlackRock (28% of assets, European growth stocks); Oechsle International Advisors (15% of assets, developed-market growth); Jardine Fleming International Management of Hong Kong (7%, Pacific Basin growth); and Martin Currie of Scotland (5%, Japan value).

There is also some active management at the advisor level. A management team at SEI attempts to control risk and mimic the style characteristics—but not the country or sector weightings—of the MSCI EAFE index. The SEI managers do so by adjusting the allocation to each subadvisor, though they say the allotments don't change much. They also hire and fire subadvisors, and the fund has had a fair amount of manager turnover as a result. In fact, once Morgan Stanley was in, Acadian Asset Management, which had the longest tenure at more than five years, was out.

Other than access to a few good managers, the fund has little else to recommend it. Over the longer haul, it has edged by its bogy but has trailed the average foreign-stock fund. And its Morningstar risk scores, which measure volatility, are only slightly better than those of its typical peer.

Although it's tough to bet against the likes of Capital Guardian and Morgan Stanley, investors can find better options elsewhere.

Address:	1 Freedom Valley Drive Oaks, PA 19456 610–254–1000 / 800–342–5734
Web Address:	www.seic.com
Inception:	12-20-89
Advisor:	SEI Inv.s Managment Corp
Subadvisor:	Acadian Asset Mgmt./Blackrock International
NTF Plans:	N/A

Minimum Purchase:	$100000	Add: $1000	IRA: —
Min Auto Inv Plan:	—	Add: —	
Sales Fees:	No-load		
Management Fee:	.51%, .45%A		
Actual Fees:	Mgt: 0.51%	Dist: —	
Expense Projections:	3Yr: $412	5Yr: $713	10Yr: $1568
Avg Brok Commission:	—	Income Distrib: Annually	
Total Cost (relative to category):		Below Avg	

Selected American

Ticker	Load	NAV	Yield	Total Assets	Mstar Category
SLASX	12b–1 only	$30.99	0.5%	$5,562.8 mil	Large Value

Prospectus Objective: Growth and Income

Selected American Fund seeks growth of capital and income.

The fund normally invests at least 65% of assets in securities of U.S. companies, including common stocks, convertibles, fixed-income securities, and short-term instruments. It invests chiefly in blue-chip firms with market capitalizations in excess of $1 billion. The fund may invest up to 30% of assets in debt rated below investment-grade.

Selected Financial Services (formerly Prescott Asset Management) managed the fund from Jan. 1, 1983, to May 1, 1993.

Historical Profile
Return: Above Avg
Risk: Average
Rating: ★★★★ Above Avg

Investment Style Equity
Average Stock %: 91% 96% 97% 93% 96% 89% 92%

▼ Manager Change
▽ Partial Manager Change

Fund Performance vs. Category Average
■ Quarterly Fund Return +/– Category Average
— Category Baseline

Performance Quartile (within Category)

Portfolio Manager(s)

Christopher C. Davis. Since 12-94. MA'87 U. of St. Andrews. Other funds currently managed: Davis NY Venture A, Davis Growth Opportunity B, Davis Financial A.

Kenneth C. Feinberg. Since 5-98. BA'79 Johns Hopkins U.; MBA'85 Columbia U. Other funds currently managed: Davis NY Venture A, Davis Growth Opportunity B, Davis Financial A.

1990	1991	1992	1993	1994	1995	1996	1997	1998	1999	2000	12–01	History
12.79	18.43	17.13	14.59	13.09	17.68	21.53	27.18	31.16	35.80	35.33	30.99	NAV
–4.50	46.90	5.80	5.42	–3.34	38.09	30.74	37.32	16.27	20.32	9.33	–11.17	Total Return %
–1.38	16.41	–1.82	–4.63	–4.65	0.56	7.79	3.97	–12.30	–0.72	18.43	0.70	+/– S&P 500
–0.83	28.74	–3.27	–14.34	–1.02	–1.94	8.42	1.83	–4.97	9.36	7.02	–2.38	+/– Russ Top 200 Val
2.56	2.44	1.03	1.58	1.38	1.69	1.03	0.97	0.55	0.48	0.38	0.41	Income Return %
–7.06	44.45	4.76	3.85	–4.71	36.40	29.70	36.35	15.72	19.83	8.95	–11.58	Capital Return %
39	3	87	94	83	10	3	2	30	7	38	82	Total Rtn % Rank Cat
0.35	0.31	0.19	0.26	0.20	0.22	0.18	0.21	0.15	0.15	0.14	0.14	Income $
0.04	0.00	2.19	3.22	0.82	0.15	1.30	2.04	0.26	1.44	3.47	0.24	Capital Gains $
1.35	1.19	1.17	1.01	1.26	1.09	1.03	0.96	0.94	0.93	0.92	—	Expense Ratio %
2.04	1.41	0.95	1.37	1.42	1.42	0.87	0.62	0.52	0.24	0.52	—	Income Ratio %
48	21	50	79	23	27	29	26	20	21	22	—	Turnover Rate %
400.6	705.6	581.9	451.9	527.9	925.0	1,378.1	2,218.1	2,905.1	3,703.2	5,703.3	5,562.8	Net Assets $mil

Performance 12-31-01

	1st Qtr	2nd Qtr	3rd Qtr	4th Qtr	Total
1997	1.83	18.15	12.44	1.50	37.32
1998	8.69	2.73	–14.78	22.19	16.27
1999	4.26	11.35	–8.23	12.93	20.32
2000	9.06	–2.21	1.23	1.26	9.33
2001	–9.71	2.91	–14.06	11.23	–11.17

Trailing	Total Return%	+/– S&P 500	+/– Russ Top 200 Val	% Rank All	% Rank Cat	Growth of $10,000
3 Mo	11.23	0.54	5.71	36	22	11,123
6 Mo	–4.41	1.15	1.37	58	56	9,559
1 Yr	–11.17	0.70	–2.38	63	82	8,883
3 Yr Avg	5.33	6.35	4.16	28	23	11,684
5 Yr Avg	13.28	2.58	2.08	7	8	18,656
10 Yr Avg	13.76	0.84	–0.27	9	20	36,312
15 Yr Avg	14.41	0.68	0.91	9	7	75,354

Tax Analysis	Tax-Adj Ret%	%Rank Cat	%Pretax Ret	%Rank Cat
3 Yr Avg	4.01	22	75.4	34
5 Yr Avg	11.88	5	89.5	9
10 Yr Avg	11.43	13	83.0	22

Potential Capital Gain Exposure: 14% of assets

Risk Analysis

Time Period	Load-Adj Return %	Risk %Rank[1] All	Risk %Rank[1] Cat	Morningstar Return	Morningstar Risk	Morningstar Risk-Adj Rating
1 Yr	–11.17					
3 Yr	5.33	51	33	0.08[2]	0.71	★★★★
5 Yr	13.28	59	60	2.11[2]	0.81	★★★★
10 Yr	13.76	69	85	1.49	0.88	★★★★

Average Historical Rating (193 months): 4.0★s

[1] 1=low, 100=high [2] T-Bill return substituted for category avg.

Category Rating (3 Yr)

1 2 3 4 5
Worst Best

Return: Above Avg
Risk: Average

Other Measures	Standard Index S&P 500	Best Fit Index S&P 500
Alpha	5.4	5.4
Beta	0.84	0.84
R-Squared	85	85
Standard Deviation		16.20
Mean		5.33
Sharpe Ratio		0.03

Portfolio Analysis 08-31-01

Share change since 07–01 Total Stocks: 70	Sector	PE	YTD Ret%	% Assets
Tyco Intl	Industrials	27.1	6.23	6.71
American Express	Financials	28.3	–34.40	5.76
Philip Morris	Staples	12.1	9.12	4.40
Household Intl	Financials	14.7	6.89	4.36
Merck	Health	19.1	–35.90	4.07
Citigroup	Financials	20.0	0.03	3.54
American Intl Grp	Financials	42.0	–19.20	3.36
Wells Fargo	Financials	22.4	–20.20	3.13
United Parcel Svc B	Services	25.0	–6.09	2.89
Costco Wholesale	Retail	34.4	11.12	2.83
Bristol-Myers Squibb	Health	20.2	–26.00	2.76
Masco	Industrials	98.0	–2.43	2.72
Eli Lilly	Health	28.9	–14.40	2.46
American Home Products	Health	—	–1.91	2.42
Berkshire Hathaway Cl A	Financials	—	—	2.24
Sealed Air	Industrials	27.4	33.84	2.11
McDonald's	Services	19.2	–21.50	2.02
Lexmark Intl	Technology	26.9	33.14	2.01
⊕ Phillips Petro	Energy	7.1	8.56	1.90
Golden West Finl	Financials	12.9	–12.40	1.86
Freddie Mac	Financials	14.0	–3.87	1.83
Hewlett-Packard	Technology	97.8	–33.90	1.70
Transatlantic Hldgs	Financials	75.8	29.55	1.57
Tellabs	Technology	41.6	–73.50	1.54
Minnesota Mng & Mfg	Industrials	34.5	0.16	1.52

Current Investment Style

Style: Value Blnd Growth; Size: Large Med Small

	Stock Port Avg	Relative S&P 500 Current	Relative S&P 500 Hist	Rel Cat
Price/Earnings Ratio	26.7	0.86	0.80	1.06
Price/Book Ratio	5.2	0.90	0.76	1.25
Price/Cash Flow	16.5	0.92	0.92	1.20
3 Yr Earnings Growth	16.9	1.16	1.06	1.15
1 Yr Earnings Est%	–2.9	1.65	—	0.88
Med Mkt Cap $mil	41,745	0.7	0.8	1.31

Analysis by Russel Kinnel 10-17-01

We expect Selected American to come back strong.

The fund's poor year-to-date performance is due to weakness in individual issues and a growing bet on pharmaceutical shares. Shares of American Express and Tellabs have taken a drubbing that far surpasses that suffered by the average stock in their industries. American Express was dealt the double blow of poor investments and a steep drop in travel following the September terrorist attacks. Tellabs, meanwhile, has lost three fourths of its value as telecom-equipment spending has plummeted.

Management's increased investment in big drug companies has also been a drag. Merck has fallen 25% because a promising new drug, Vioxx, hasn't lived up to expectations. In addition, some of the fund's other top drug stocks have fallen as much as the S&P 500, which has done significantly worse than the average large-value fund. Despite that weakness, comanagers Chris Davis and Ken Feinberg still like much about their big pharmaceutical purchases. They cited strong growth potential, "honest accounting," share buybacks, and low prices relative to owner earnings as key attractions.

Those criteria are the same as what they looked for in the past, even though the increased stake in drug stocks takes them a bit more into growth territory than before. Thus, the fund may track the S&P 500 a bit more closely than the large-value averages, but its long-term prospects are intact. All of the most important elements still remain: The Davis family has a large sum invested in its funds; management's analysis is more thorough than competitors'; and the core strategy continues to find strong companies with good growth potential whose shares trade at modest valuations.

Special Securities % assets 08-31-01	
Restricted/Illiquid Secs	0
Emerging-Markets Secs	0
Options/Futures/Warrants	No

Composition % assets 08-31-01	
Cash	2.7
Stocks*	97.3
Bonds	0.0
Other	0.0
*Foreign (% stocks)	2.6

Market Cap	
Giant	51.4
Large	24.6
Medium	21.3
Small	2.7
Micro	0.0

Sector Weightings	% of Stocks	Rel S&P	5-Year High	5-Year Low
Utilities	0.0	0.0	2	0
Energy	5.2	0.7	12	0
Financials	39.6	2.2	60	21
Industrials	15.9	1.4	16	0
Durables	0.2	0.2	4	0
Staples	6.2	0.8	36	1
Services	8.7	0.8	25	7
Retail	3.4	0.5	15	0
Health	12.3	0.8	18	4
Technology	8.5	0.5	32	0

Address: 2949 E. Elvira Rd. Ste 101, Tucson, AZ 85706, 800-243-1575 / 505-983-4335
Web Address: www.selectedfunds.com
Inception: 02-28-33
Advisor: Davis Selected Advisers
Subadvisor: None
NTF Plans: Fidelity , Datalynx

Minimum Purchase: $1000 Add: $25 IRA: $250
Min Auto Inv Plan: $1000 Add: $25
Sales Fees: 0.25%B
Management Fee: .65% mx./.50% mn.
Actual Fees: Mgt: 0.57% Dist: 0.25%
Expense Projections: 3Yr: $296 5Yr: $515 10Yr: $1143
Avg Brok Commission: — Income Distrib: Quarterly
Total Cost (relative to category): Below Avg

Sit Tax–Free Income

Ticker	Load	NAV	Yield	SEC Yield	Total Assets	Mstar Category
SNTIX	None	$9.88	4.9%	4.83%	$443.9 mil	Muni Natl Long–Term

Prospectus Objective: Muni Bond—National

Sit Tax-Free Income Fund seeks current income exempt from federal income tax, consistent with preservation of capital.

The fund ordinarily invests all assets in investment-grade municipal securities. It maintains no restrictions on portfolio maturity. The fund may invest no more than 20% of assets in taxable obligations or municipal securities subject to the Alternative Minimum Tax.

Prior to Nov. 1, 1993, the fund was named Sit "New Beginning" Tax-Free Income Fund.

Historical Profile
Return: Average
Risk: Below Avg
Rating: ★★★★★ Highest

Investment Style Fixed-Income

Income Rtn %Rank Cat: 25, 41, 19, 20, 25, 34, 33, 33

Growth of Principal vs. Interest Rate Shifts
- Principal Value $000 (NAV with capital gains reinvested)
- Interest Rate % on 10 Yr Treasury
- ▼ Manager Change
- ▽ Partial Manager Change
- ► Mgr Unknown After
- ◄ Mgr Unknown Before

Performance Quartile (within Category)

Portfolio Manager(s)

Michael C. Brilley. Since 9-88. BS'67 Millikin U. Other funds currently managed: Sit U.S. Government Securities, Sit Bond, Sit MN Tax-Free Income.

Debra A. Sit, CFA. Since 1-99. BA'82 U. of Minnesota; MBA'87 U. of Chicago. Other fund currently managed: Sit MN Tax-Free Income.

1990	1991	1992	1993	1994	1995	1996	1997	1998	1999	2000	12-01	History
9.57	9.72	9.76	10.08	9.43	10.06	10.05	10.39	10.46	9.55	9.81	9.88	NAV
7.29	9.25	7.76	10.42	–0.63	12.86	5.69	9.83	6.30	–4.09	8.27	5.76	Total Return %
–1.67	–6.75	0.36	0.67	2.29	–5.61	2.07	0.14	–2.38	–3.26	–3.36	–2.67	+/– LB Aggregate
–0.01	–2.89	–1.06	–1.86	4.52	–4.60	1.25	0.63	–0.18	–2.02	–3.43	0.68	+/– LB Muni
8.46	7.61	6.88	6.13	5.75	6.03	5.73	5.63	5.15	4.85	5.42	5.06	Income Return %
–1.17	1.64	0.88	4.29	–6.37	6.83	–0.04	4.20	1.14	–8.94	2.85	0.69	Capital Return %
8	97	87	87	1	96	4	24	9	37	79	8	Total Rtn % Rank Cat
0.79	0.70	0.65	0.58	0.56	0.55	0.56	0.55	0.52	0.50	0.50	0.49	Income $
0.00	0.00	0.04	0.09	0.02	0.00	0.00	0.07	0.05	0.00	0.00	0.00	Capital Gains $
0.80	0.80	0.80	0.80	0.77	0.79	0.80	0.79	0.76	0.71	0.70	0.74	Expense Ratio %
8.16	7.62	7.02	6.17	5.68	5.84	5.65	5.63	5.29	4.90	5.15	5.27	Income Ratio %
87	74	80	58	48	13	26	25	21	14	25	12	Turnover Rate %
47.9	133.6	278.2	340.8	243.3	281.9	305.5	452.3	800.5	666.2	494.7	443.9	Net Assets $mil

Performance 12-31-01

	1st Qtr	2nd Qtr	3rd Qtr	4th Qtr	Total
1997	0.66	3.02	3.13	2.69	9.83
1998	1.26	1.56	2.82	0.53	6.30
1999	0.50	–1.34	–1.63	–1.67	–4.09
2000	1.57	1.11	2.56	2.79	8.27
2001	2.21	0.88	2.90	–0.31	5.76

Trailing	Total Return%	+/– LB Agg	+/– LB Muni	% Rank All	% Rank Cat	Growth of $10,000
3 Mo	–0.31	–0.35	0.35	82	7	9,969
6 Mo	2.58	–2.08	0.46	18	4	10,258
1 Yr	5.76	–2.67	0.68	19	8	10,576
3 Yr Avg	3.17	–3.10	–1.58	52	45	10,982
5 Yr Avg	5.10	–2.33	–0.88	63	29	12,821
10 Yr Avg	6.10	–1.13	–0.53	68	30	18,083
15 Yr Avg	—	—	—	—	—	—

Tax Analysis	Tax-Adj Ret%	%Rank Cat	%Pretax Ret	%Rank Cat
3 Yr Avg	3.17	44	100.0	14
5 Yr Avg	5.05	27	99.1	45
10 Yr Avg	6.02	25	98.7	24

Potential Capital Gain Exposure: –7% of assets

Risk Analysis

Time Period	Load-Adj Return %	Risk %Rank[1] All	Risk %Rank[1] Cat	Morningstar Return	Morningstar Risk	Morningstar Risk-Adj Rating
1 Yr	5.76					
3 Yr	3.17	9	4	0.36[2]	0.82	★★★★
5 Yr	5.10	7	2	0.85[2]	0.73	★★★★
10 Yr	6.10	5	1	1.09	0.60	★★★★★

Average Historical Rating (124 months): 5.0★s

[1]1=low, 100=high [2] T-Bill return substituted for category avg.

Category Rating (3 Yr)

1 2 3 4 5 — Worst / Best

Return: Average
Risk: Low

Other Measures	Standard Index LB Agg	Best Fit Index LB Muni
Alpha	–2.5	–1.6
Beta	0.67	0.81
R-Squared	49	87
Standard Deviation		3.29
Mean		3.17
Sharpe Ratio		–0.63

Portfolio Analysis 10-31-01

Total Fixed-Income: 338	Date of Maturity	Amount $000	Value $000	% Net Assets
TX Nortex Hsg 6.75%	09-20-32	7,272	8,138	1.80
PA Armstrong Hosp St Francis M/C 6.25%	06-01-13	7,400	7,696	1.70
TX Dallas Hsg Fin Towne Ctr Apt 6.75%	10-20-32	6,343	7,015	1.55
TN Shelby Hlth/Educ/Hsg Fac Brd 7.75%	03-20-27	5,555	6,266	1.39
AR GO 5.375%	06-01-21	6,000	6,024	1.33
IL Dev Fin Cmnty Rehab Providers 6%	07-01-15	5,575	5,630	1.25
AR GO 4.75%	06-01-15	5,300	5,263	1.17
AK Hsg Fin 0%	12-01-17	12,505	4,908	1.09
BlackRock Insured Muni 2008		300	4,728	1.05
BlackRock Municipal Target		445	4,717	1.04
Van Kampen Merritt Municipal		300	4,695	1.04
GA Fulton Dev 7.75%	11-20-39	3,935	4,631	1.03
IL Southwestern Indl Dev 6%	04-01-10	4,505	4,534	1.00
NH Higher Educ/Hlth Fac 5.125%	07-01-18	4,525	4,448	0.98
PA Higher Educ Fac Hlth Svcs 5.875%	11-15-16	3,890	4,154	0.92

Current Investment Style

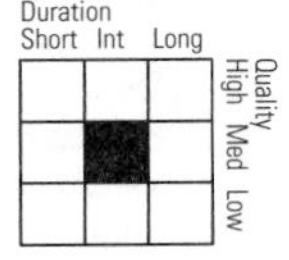

Avg Duration[1]	5.5 Yrs
Avg Nominal Maturity	17.8 Yrs
Avg Credit Quality	A
Avg Wtd Coupon	5.65%
Avg Wtd Price	99.57% of par
Pricing Service	J.J. Kenny

[1]figure provided by fund

Credit Analysis % bonds 09-30-01

US Govt	0	BB	3
AAA	29	B	0
AA	10	Below B	0
A	29	NR/NA	0
BBB	29		

Special Securities % assets 10-31-01

Restricted/Illiquid Secs	0
Inverse Floaters	Trace
Options/Futures/Warrants	No

Bond Type % assets

Alternative Minimum Tax	N/A
Insured	N/A
Prerefunded	N/A

Top 5 States % bonds

TX	15.0	IN	6.3
IL	10.5	AR	4.6
PA	8.1		

Composition % assets 10-31-01

Cash	0.8	Bonds	97.2
Stocks	0.0	Other	2.0

Sector Weightings	% of Bonds	Rel Cat
General Obligation	11.7	0.6
Utilities	0.7	0.1
Health	32.2	2.1
Water/Waste	0.7	0.1
Housing	33.2	4.7
Education	5.9	0.9
Transportation	0.5	0.0
COP/Lease	1.8	0.7
Industrial	10.9	0.9
Misc Revenue	2.5	0.5
Demand	0.0	0.0

Analysis by Eric Jacobson 12-11-01

Sit Tax-Free Income Fund appears to be getting back to its old—better—self.

This portfolio had formerly held up wonderfully in the face of rising rates, yet troubles in the health-care industry hurt it in 1999, when the fund turned in decent, but not stellar returns. Things got worse in 2000, though, and the fund's large health-care stake—and credit-sensitivity—were liabilities. It garnered reasonable returns, yet badly trailed the average muni national long-term category.

Comanagers Debra Sit and Michael Brilley didn't sit on their hands. The fund's health-care stake has fallen a bit, but the pair have sharply upgraded holdings in the sector, shifting into AAAs and As. They've also cut education and single-family housing, shifting mostly into tobacco-settlement bonds, which were cheap in early 2001. Finally, the team decided that low interest rates warranted reining in duration, which stands at 5.6 years, and could go lower.

The fund's profit taking, upgrading and duration shortening have worked well as of late. Interest rates were volatile in early 2001, and spiked up again in November. The fund's year-to-date return has thus risen to the top decile of the category.

Despite the recovery, the most important change is a strategic decision to rely less on health-care bonds. The same is true to some degree of single-family housing issues; the non-AMT variety the fund buys have become more and more scarce. The former promises to help reduce risk, while both will make it slightly (but not prohibitively) harder for the fund to keep up its historically high yield. It's not surprising, therefore, that of late management is focusing more on yield-rich callable bonds that have shown a propensity not to be called early.

Overall, management seems to be tweaking its approach but staying true to its style.

Address:	4600 Norwest Center 90 S. 7th Street Minneapolis, MN 55402–4130 800–332–5580 / 612–334–5888
Web Address:	www.sitfunds.com
Inception:	09-29-88
Advisor:	Sit Inv. Assoc.
Subadvisor:	None
NTF Plans:	Fidelity , Fidelity Inst.

Minimum Purchase:	$2000	Add: $100	IRA: None
Min Auto Inv Plan:	$2000	Add: $100	
Sales Fees:	No–load		
Management Fee:	.80%		
Actual Fees:	Mgt: 0.71%	Dist: —	
Expense Projections:	3Yr: $256	5Yr: $446	10Yr: $993
Avg Brok Commission:	—	Income Distrib: Monthly	
Total Cost (relative to category):	Below Avg		

Sit U.S. Government Securities

Ticker	Load	NAV	Yield	SEC Yield	Total Assets	Mstar Category
SNGVX	None	$10.74	5.6%	5.34%	$207.6 mil	Short–Term Govt

Prospectus Objective: Government General

Sit U.S. Government Securities Fund seeks current income and safety of principal.

The fund invests solely in debt obligations issued, guaranteed, or insured by the U.S. government, whether or not backed by the full faith and credit of the U.S. government. The average maturity may vary between two and 20 years.

Prior to Nov. 1, 1993, the fund was named Sit "New Beginning" U.S. Government Securities Fund.

Historical Profile

Return Above Avg
Risk Low
Rating ★★★★★ Highest

Investment Style
Fixed-Income
Income Rtn %Rank Cat: 22, 15, 24, 21, 52, 46, 18, 16

Growth of Principal vs. Interest Rate Shifts
— Principal Value $000 (NAV with capital gains reinvested)
— Interest Rate % on 10 Yr Treasury
▼ Manager Change
▽ Partial Manager Change
► Mgr Unknown After
◄ Mgr Unknown Before

Performance Quartile (within Category)

Portfolio Manager(s)

Michael C. Brilley. Since 6-87. BS'67 Millikin U. Other funds currently managed: Sit Tax-Free Income, Sit Bond, Sit MN Tax-Free Income.

Bryce Doty, CFA. Since 11-95. BA'88 Hamlin U.; MBA'92 U. of Minnesota. Other fund currently managed: Sit Bond.

1990	1991	1992	1993	1994	1995	1996	1997	1998	1999	2000	12-01	History
10.56	10.89	10.60	10.63	10.17	10.60	10.45	10.64	10.64	10.22	10.48	10.74	NAV
10.98	12.87	5.43	7.37	1.77	11.50	5.01	8.21	6.54	1.26	9.08	8.44	Total Return %
2.02	−3.14	−1.97	−2.38	4.69	−6.97	1.39	−1.47	−2.13	2.09	−2.55	0.02	+/– LB Aggregate
1.19	1.19	−0.82	1.96	1.27	1.55	−0.25	1.56	−0.43	−1.71	0.91	−0.09	+/– LB 1–3 Govt
7.92	7.89	6.71	6.62	6.22	7.15	6.41	6.30	5.50	5.29	6.40	5.93	Income Return %
3.05	4.98	−1.28	0.75	−4.45	4.36	−1.40	1.91	1.04	−4.03	2.68	2.52	Capital Return %
1	41	60	23	6	45	23	5	44	64	23	7	Total Rtn % Rank Cat
0.79	0.80	0.71	0.68	0.64	0.70	0.66	0.64	0.57	0.55	0.64	0.61	Income $
0.00	0.17	0.15	0.05	0.00	0.00	0.00	0.00	0.11	0.00	0.00	0.00	Capital Gains $
1.25	0.90	0.80	0.89	0.86	0.80	0.80	0.80	0.80	0.80	0.80	0.80	Expense Ratio %
8.02	7.60	7.28	6.60	5.79	6.48	6.72	6.30	5.93	5.06	5.66	6.30	Income Ratio %
126	118	134	77	74	39	51	85	51	86	98	56	Turnover Rate %
15.7	35.3	30.8	39.3	36.3	48.2	64.9	92.9	141.9	150.6	140.1	207.6	Net Assets $mil

Performance 12-31-01

	1st Qtr	2nd Qtr	3rd Qtr	4th Qtr	Total
1997	0.00	3.00	3.04	1.96	8.21
1998	1.49	1.61	2.36	0.94	6.54
1999	−0.01	−0.01	0.83	0.44	1.26
2000	1.53	1.68	2.17	3.42	9.08
2001	2.60	1.57	3.16	0.88	8.44

Trailing	Total Return%	+/– LB Agg	+/– LB 1–3 Yr Govt	% Rank All	% Rank Cat	Growth of $10,000
3 Mo	0.88	0.84	0.10	73	5	10,088
6 Mo	4.06	−0.59	−0.25	8	27	10,406
1 Yr	8.44	0.02	−0.09	8	7	10,844
3 Yr Avg	6.20	−0.07	−0.32	21	13	11,978
5 Yr Avg	6.67	−0.76	0.03	39	7	13,810
10 Yr Avg	6.42	−0.81	0.38	59	1	18,626
15 Yr Avg	—	—	—	—	—	—

Tax Analysis	Tax-Adj Ret%	%Rank Cat	%Pretax Ret	%Rank Cat
3 Yr Avg	3.84	14	62.0	39
5 Yr Avg	4.24	9	63.6	31
10 Yr Avg	3.87	5	60.3	28

Potential Capital Gain Exposure: 1% of assets

Risk Analysis

Time Period	Load-Adj Return %	Risk %Rank[1] All	Risk %Rank[1] Cat	Morningstar Return	Morningstar Risk	Morningstar Risk-Adj Rating
1 Yr	8.44					
3 Yr	6.20	3	38	0.27[2]	0.29	★★★★★
5 Yr	6.67	3	40	0.37[2]	0.31	★★★★★
10 Yr	6.42	3	27	0.47[2]	0.39	★★★★★

Average Historical Rating (139 months): 4.4★s

[1]1=low, 100=high [2] T-Bill return substituted for category avg.

Category Rating (3 Yr)

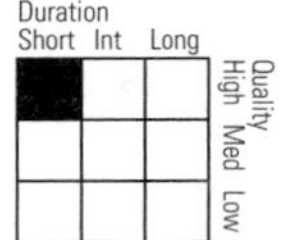

Return Above Avg
Risk Average

Other Measures	Standard Index LB Agg	Best Fit Index LB Agg
Alpha	0.5	0.5
Beta	0.51	0.51
R–Squared	86	86

Standard Deviation	1.96
Mean	6.20
Sharpe Ratio	0.76

Portfolio Analysis 11-30-01

Total Fixed-Income: 517	Date of Maturity	Amount $000	Value $000	% Net Assets
FHLMC CMO 6.25%	01-15-24	10,000	10,321	4.81
FNMA CMO 6%	08-18-28	10,000	9,899	4.62
FHLMC 6.5%	08-15-29	7,563	7,770	3.62
Vendee Mtg CMO 7.5%	05-15-24	6,775	7,262	3.39
Vendee Mtg CMO 7.5%	11-15-14	5,500	5,904	2.75
US Treasury Bond 6.375%	08-15-27	5,000	5,555	2.59
Vendee Mtg CMO 6.5%	02-15-20	5,100	5,354	2.50
FHLMC CMO 6%	02-15-27	5,127	5,194	2.42
FHLMC 6%	03-15-25	5,000	5,111	2.38
FHLMC 6.5%	09-01-31	4,985	5,091	2.37
FHLMC 7%	03-15-27	4,600	4,766	2.22
Vendee Mtg CMO 7%	02-15-18	4,427	4,481	2.09
FNMA 10%	03-01-15	3,845	4,292	2.00
GNMA 9%	08-20-17	3,891	4,272	1.99
Gnr 6.5%	09-20-30	4,038	4,124	1.92
FHLMC 9%	08-01-21	3,691	3,998	1.86
FNMA CMO Z 8.5%	09-25-21	3,203	3,483	1.62
Vendee Mtg CMO 7.5%	04-15-08	3,205	3,429	1.60
GNMA 9.5%	09-20-18	2,897	3,232	1.51
FNMA 6%	01-25-29	2,589	2,652	1.24

Current Investment Style

Duration: Short Int Long; Quality: High Med Low

Avg Eff Duration[1]	2.5 Yrs
Avg Eff Maturity	—
Avg Credit Quality	AAA
Avg Wtd Coupon	8.05%
Avg Wtd Price	107.11% of par

[1]figure provided by fund

Special Securities % assets 11-30-01	
Restricted/Illiquid Secs	0
Exotic Mortgage–Backed	3
Emerging–Markets Secs	0
Options/Futures/Warrants	No

Credit Analysis % bonds 09-30-01			
US Govt	100	BB	0
AAA	0	B	0
AA	0	Below B	0
A	0	NR/NA	0
BBB	0		

Sector Breakdown % bonds 11-30-01			
US Treasuries	3	CMOs	13
GNMA mtgs	20	ARMs	0
FNMA mtgs	27	Other	2
FHLMC mtgs	33		

Coupon Range	% of Bonds	Rel Cat
0%	0.00	0.00
0% to 7%	32.46	0.45
7% to 8.5%	14.51	0.73
8.5% to 10%	43.31	14.11
More than 10%	9.73	2.25

1.00=Category Average

Composition % assets 11-30-01			
Cash	1.6	Bonds	98.4
Stocks	0.0	Other	0.0

Analysis by Eric Jacobson 10-31-01

Sit U.S. Government Securities makes a strong case for buying government bonds through a mutual fund.

It's difficult for managers to add value in the government bond market because it's so liquid, basic, and transparent. That wisdom is much less accurate, however, when it comes to the government-agency and mortgage markets, as well as the market for collateralized mortgage obligations (CMOs). These sectors are complex—particularly owing to embedded call options and prepayment—and require sophisticated analytics. To buy them without the help of professional management would leave an investor vulnerable to getting ripped off. And while one could ignore those sectors of the market, doing so means leaving lots of extra money on the table.

Even within those sectors, though, there are pockets of securities too small for the biggest institutions to bother with. That makes ripe pickings for the likes of this fund. For example, comanagers Mike Brilley and Bryce Doty have long focused on the GNMA mobile-home subsector, and later emphasized VA Vendee mortgages. Both sectors were so small and underfollowed that they had to offer rich yields to attract buyers. As those sectors have become better known, the team has shifted its attention to low-balance, high-coupon pass-through mortgage pools, and burned-out Z-tranche CMOs, which start out complex and volatile, but become docile, plain-vanilla mortgages once borrowers refinance or pay down most of their balances.

Because of the heavy focus on premium mortgages, the fund's duration is fairly short, and its volatility correspondingly low. On the other hand, its long-term returns have been nothing short of stellar, placing in the short-term government category's best quartile. The fund has grown dramatically in recent years, but with still less than $200 million in assets, it remains a hidden gem.

Address:	4600 Norwest Center 90 S. 7th Street Minneapolis, MN 55402–4130 800–332–5580 / 612–334–5888
Web Address:	www.sitfunds.com
Inception:	06-02-87
Advisor:	Sit Inv. Assoc.
Subadvisor:	None
NTF Plans:	Fidelity , Fidelity Inst.

Minimum Purchase:	$2000	Add: $100	IRA: None
Min Auto Inv Plan:	$2000	Add: $100	
Sales Fees:	No–load		
Management Fee:	1.0%		
Actual Fees:	Mgt: 0.80%	Dist: —	
Expense Projections:	3Yr: $320	5Yr: $555	10Yr: $1229
Avg Brok Commission:	—	Income Distrib: Monthly	
Total Cost (relative to category):		Average	

Skyline Special Equities

Ticker	Load	NAV	Yield	Total Assets	Mstar Category
SKSEX	None	$22.50	0.0%	$373.7 mil	Small Value

Prospectus Objective: Small Company

Skyline Special Equities Portfolio seeks capital appreciation.

The fund normally invests at least 65% of assets in equity securities of companies with market capitalizations of less than $1 billion. These include companies with below-average price/earnings ratios but above-average revenues or earnings-growth prospects, companies with temporarily depressed stock prices but improving operations, or companies that are undervalued because of special circumstances.

Historical Profile

Return Above Avg
Risk Average
Rating ★★★★ Above Avg

Investment Style
Equity
Average Stock %: 95% 93% 93% 94% 92% 96% 95%

▼ Manager Change
▽ Partial Manager Change

Fund Performance vs. Category Average
Quarterly Fund Return +/– Category Average
— Category Baseline

Performance Quartile (within Category)

Portfolio Manager(s)

Management Team.

1990	1991	1992	1993	1994	1995	1996	1997	1998	1999	2000	12-01	History
10.32	12.67	17.12	17.83	15.64	16.79	18.16	21.66	19.78	15.90	19.75	22.50	NAV
–9.28	47.38	42.41	22.85	–1.15	13.82	30.37	35.43	–7.17	–13.29	24.21	13.92	Total Return %
–6.17	16.90	34.80	12.79	–2.46	–23.71	7.43	2.08	–35.75	–34.32	33.32	25.80	+/– S&P 500
12.49	5.68	13.28	–1.00	0.40	–11.93	9.00	3.74	–0.74	–11.81	1.40	–0.10	+/– Russell 2000 V
0.87	0.17	0.00	0.00	0.00	0.00	0.00	0.00	0.00	0.00	0.00	0.00	Income Return %
–10.15	47.21	42.41	22.84	–1.15	13.82	30.37	35.43	–7.17	–13.29	24.21	13.92	Capital Return %
27	24	3	16	51	95	14	23	54	98	26	71	Total Rtn % Rank Cat
0.10	0.02	0.00	0.00	0.00	0.00	0.00	0.00	0.00	0.00	0.00	0.00	Income $
0.00	2.39	0.91	3.14	1.93	1.00	3.61	2.89	0.32	1.23	0.00	0.00	Capital Gains $
1.59	1.55	1.51	1.48	1.49	1.51	1.51	1.48	1.47	1.48	1.51	—	Expense Ratio %
0.95	0.09	–0.19	–0.54	–0.49	0.35	–0.32	–0.41	–0.50	–0.32	–0.32	—	Income Ratio %
98	104	87	104	82	71	130	62	68	81	92	—	Turnover Rate %
22.2	37.4	168.3	227.7	202.8	175.5	218.7	466.5	445.8	222.9	286.6	373.7	Net Assets $mil

Performance 12-31-01

	1st Qtr	2nd Qtr	3rd Qtr	4th Qtr	Total
1997	2.42	19.30	15.68	–4.19	35.43
1998	11.27	–5.44	–20.49	10.96	–7.17
1999	–11.83	15.25	–12.54	–2.43	–13.29
2000	3.77	3.76	8.18	6.64	24.21
2001	–0.86	13.38	–15.77	20.32	13.92

Trailing	Total Return%	+/– S&P 500	+/– Russ 2000V	% Rank All	% Rank Cat	Growth of $10,000
3 Mo	20.32	9.64	3.60	13	26	12,032
6 Mo	1.35	6.91	0.20	31	57	10,135
1 Yr	13.92	25.80	–0.10	4	71	11,392
3 Yr Avg	7.06	8.09	–4.26	17	80	12,271
5 Yr Avg	9.06	–1.64	–2.14	24	69	15,427
10 Yr Avg	14.75	1.82	–0.36	6	31	39,589
15 Yr Avg	—	—	—	—	—	—

Tax Analysis	Tax-Adj Ret%	%Rank Cat	%Pretax Ret	%Rank Cat
3 Yr Avg	6.46	78	91.5	50
5 Yr Avg	8.07	61	89.1	30
10 Yr Avg	12.27	34	83.2	48

Potential Capital Gain Exposure: 17% of assets

Risk Analysis

Time Period	Load-Adj Return %	Risk %Rank[1] All	Risk %Rank[1] Cat	Morningstar Return	Morningstar Risk	Morningstar Risk-Adj Rating
1 Yr	13.92					
3 Yr	7.06	57	78	0.46[2]	0.80	★★★★
5 Yr	9.06	62	60	0.95[2]	0.85	★★★
10 Yr	14.75	67	71	1.72	0.87	★★★★

Average Historical Rating (141 months): 4.0★s

[1] 1=low, 100=high [2] T-Bill return substituted for category avg.

Category Rating (3 Yr)

1 2 3 4 5
Worst Best

Return Below Avg
Risk Above Avg

Other Measures	Standard Index S&P 500	Best Fit Index SPMid400
Alpha	6.6	–1.1
Beta	0.61	0.70
R-Squared	32	57
Standard Deviation		19.58
Mean		7.06
Sharpe Ratio		0.12

Portfolio Analysis 10-31-01

Share change since 09-01 Total Stocks: 67	Sector	PE	YTD Ret%	% Assets
Old Republic Intl	Financials	9.7	–10.50	2.77
⊖ Werner Enterprises	Services	24.8	43.76	2.72
Reinsurance Grp of Amer	Financials	23.6	–5.61	2.41
Monaco Coach	Durables	24.6	85.46	2.29
Polaris Inds	Durables	15.6	48.57	2.25
Aaron Rents	Services	19.6	16.19	2.10
DR Horton	Industrials	9.7	48.67	2.07
MSC Indl Direct Cl A	Retail	34.1	9.34	2.05
⊖ Kennametal	Industrials	22.0	41.03	2.04
⊖ Moore	Services	—	213.90	1.98
⊕ Ruby Tuesday	Services	21.3	35.62	1.95
HCC Ins Hldgs	Financials	81.0	3.26	1.91
United Stationers	Industrials	18.2	40.21	1.87
⊖ MCSI	Technology	18.5	9.71	1.87
Silicon Storage Tech	Technology	56.7	–18.30	1.86
Raymond James Finl	Financials	18.0	3.36	1.76
✲ iStar Finl	Financials	8.8	39.61	1.74
⊖ School Speciality	Industrials	21.0	14.04	1.72
⊖ Delphi Finl Grp	Financials	—	–12.80	1.72
⊕ Invacare	Health	16.1	–1.45	1.71
Interpool	Services	12.2	14.17	1.69
Scotts	Industrials	NMF	28.86	1.69
⊖ Landstar Sys	Services	13.3	30.79	1.68
⊖ Furniture Brands Intl	Durables	27.4	52.02	1.64
✲ Hanover Compressor	Utilities	22.4	–43.30	1.62

Current Investment Style

Style: Value Blnd Growth; Size: Large Med Small

	Stock Port Avg	Relative S&P 500 Current	Relative S&P 500 Hist	Rel Cat
Price/Earnings Ratio	22.9	0.74	0.51	1.06
Price/Book Ratio	2.6	0.45	0.32	1.07
Price/Cash Flow	13.3	0.74	0.50	1.04
3 Yr Earnings Growth	19.3	1.32	0.78	1.66
1 Yr Earnings Est%	–6.8	3.86	—	1.73
Med Mkt Cap $mil	1,019	0.0	0.0	1.17

Analysis by William Samuel Rocco 12-14-01

Skyline Special Equities' early-2000 expansion still looks like a good decision.

Right after tanking in 1999, largely due to its narrow sector range, this fund broadened its stock-selection strategy. Manager Bill Dutton began to readily consider undervalued tech, energy, real-estate, and utilities stocks, along with the cheap financial, industrial, and consumer-cyclical stocks that he had long favored. In fact, the fund, which had just 3% of its assets in tech, energy, real estate, and utilities at the end of 1999, had about 17% of its assets in such issues at the end of 2000. That was still less than the small-value norm but no longer remarkably so.

Moreover, Dutton has continued to pay attention to REITs, computer-related stocks, and other issues he once ignored. He and his comanagers—four long-term analysts were promoted this year—recently bought a few REITs. For example, they bought iStar Financial, because they thought it was cheap and are keen on its management as well as its dividend yield. And though they haven't done much tech buying since the summer, when they purchased the chipmaker Silicon Storage Technology and Kemet, the fund's tech stake remains right in line with the group norm.

The fund has posted solid results since widening its approach two years ago. It posted top-quartile returns in 2000's small-value rally, thanks to its energy as well as its industrial holdings. And though the fund was a subpar performer early in 2001, it has come on strong this fall, as its tech names and cyclical issues have thrived.

That outperformance—plus the decreased volatility that should come with the increased sector diversification—makes us optimistic about this fund.

Special Securities % assets 10-31-01	
Restricted/Illiquid Secs	0
Emerging-Markets Secs	0
Options/Futures/Warrants	No

Composition % assets 10-31-01	
Cash	3.7
Stocks*	96.3
Bonds	0.0
Other	0.0
*Foreign (% stocks)	2.1

Market Cap	
Giant	0.0
Large	0.0
Medium	28.8
Small	67.2
Micro	4.1

Sector Weightings	% of Stocks	Rel S&P	5-Year High	5-Year Low
Utilities	2.7	0.8	3	0
Energy	2.3	0.3	8	0
Financials	25.9	1.4	30	5
Industrials	18.9	1.7	37	13
Durables	9.2	5.9	15	3
Staples	1.6	0.2	11	1
Services	17.1	1.6	26	4
Retail	5.7	0.8	22	3
Health	4.2	0.3	11	1
Technology	12.4	0.7	12	0

Address:	311 S. Wacker Drive Suite 4500 Chicago, IL 60606 312-913-0900 / 800-458-5222
Web Address:	—
Inception:	04-23-87
Advisor:	Skyline Asset Mgmt.
Subadvisor:	None
NTF Plans:	Fidelity , Fidelity Inst.

Minimum Purchase:	$1000	Add: $100 IRA: $1000
Min Auto Inv Plan:	$1000	Add: $50
Sales Fees:	No-load	
Management Fee:	1.5% mx./1.4% mn.	
Actual Fees:	Mgt: 1.47%	Dist: —
Expense Projections:	3Yr: $468	5Yr: $808 10Yr: $1768
Avg Brok Commission:	—	Income Distrib: Annually
Total Cost (relative to category):	Below Avg	

Sound Shore

Ticker	Load	NAV	Yield	Total Assets	Mstar Category
SSHFX	None	$30.58	0.3%	$1,046.8 mil	Mid-Cap Value

Prospectus Objective: Growth

Sound Shore Fund seeks growth of capital; income is secondary.

The fund invests primarily in equity securities selected on the basis of fundamental value. Factors such as price, earnings expectations, earnings and price histories, balance-sheet strength, and perceived management skills play a large role in security selection. The advisor also considers changes in economic and political outlooks, as well as individual corporate developments. It may invest up to 10% of assets in the securities of other investment companies.

Historical Profile
Return High
Risk Below Avg
Rating ★★★★★ Highest

Investment Style Equity
Average Stock %: 96% 91% 89% 93% 97% 97% 94%

▼ Manager Change
▽ Partial Manager Change

Fund Performance vs. Category Average
■ Quarterly Fund Return +/– Category Average
— Category Baseline

Performance Quartile (within Category)

Portfolio Manager(s)

T. Gibbs Kane Jr., CFA. Since 5-85. BS'69 U. of Pennsylvania.

Harry Burn III, CFA. Since 5-85. BA'66 U. of Virginia; MBA'75 U. of Virginia.

1990	1991	1992	1993	1994	1995	1996	1997	1998	1999	2000	12-01	History
11.77	15.17	16.24	16.50	15.46	18.16	21.71	28.57	29.62	29.47	33.70	30.58	NAV
–10.64	32.24	21.17	11.97	0.30	29.87	33.27	36.40	4.41	0.05	20.18	–0.81	Total Return %
–7.53	1.76	13.55	1.91	–1.02	–7.66	10.33	3.05	–24.17	–20.99	29.28	11.07	+/– S&P 500
5.44	–5.68	–0.51	–3.66	2.43	–5.06	13.01	2.04	–0.68	0.15	0.99	–3.15	+/– Russ Midcap Val
3.82	2.43	1.16	0.86	1.33	1.38	0.70	0.57	0.73	0.57	0.48	0.30	Income Return %
–14.46	29.81	20.01	11.10	–1.03	28.49	32.57	35.83	3.68	–0.52	19.70	–1.11	Capital Return %
64	40	17	82	38	39	4	8	47	73	38	74	Total Rtn % Rank Cat
0.52	0.29	0.18	0.14	0.22	0.21	0.13	0.12	0.21	0.17	0.14	0.10	Income $
0.00	0.10	1.95	1.54	0.87	1.67	2.35	0.89	0.00	0.00	1.56	2.76	Capital Gains $
1.33	1.30	1.37	1.27	1.22	1.15	1.15	1.08	0.99	0.98	0.98	—	Expense Ratio %
3.55	2.10	1.10	0.88	1.32	1.41	0.70	0.62	0.77	0.50	0.44	—	Income Ratio %
105	100	88	91	76	53	69	53	44	41	98	—	Turnover Rate %
28.3	31.8	36.0	58.2	56.7	67.6	131.5	1,303.5	1,964.9	1,183.9	1,051.7	1,046.8	Net Assets $mil

Performance 12-31-01

	1st Qtr	2nd Qtr	3rd Qtr	4th Qtr	Total
1997	2.12	16.19	16.15	–1.03	36.40
1998	10.75	–5.22	–14.47	16.30	4.41
1999	–4.22	11.07	–12.35	7.30	0.05
2000	4.68	–5.71	12.81	7.92	20.18
2001	–2.05	2.75	–7.18	6.18	–0.81

Trailing	Total Return%	+/– S&P 500	+/– Russ Midcap Val	% Rank All	% Rank Cat	Growth of $10,000
3 Mo	6.18	–4.50	–5.85	60	93	10,618
6 Mo	–1.44	4.11	–0.53	44	57	9,856
1 Yr	–0.81	11.07	–3.15	44	74	9,919
3 Yr Avg	6.05	7.08	–0.76	22	75	11,927
5 Yr Avg	11.18	0.48	–0.29	13	56	16,985
10 Yr Avg	14.87	1.94	0.46	5	36	40,002
15 Yr Avg	13.52	–0.22	0.05	14	41	66,977

Tax Analysis	Tax-Adj Ret%	%Rank Cat	%Pretax Ret	%Rank Cat
3 Yr Avg	4.97	70	82.2	42
5 Yr Avg	10.26	39	91.8	6
10 Yr Avg	12.60	30	84.8	28

Potential Capital Gain Exposure: 17% of assets

Risk Analysis

Time Period	Load-Adj Return %	Risk %Rank[1] All	Risk %Rank[1] Cat	Morningstar Return	Morningstar Risk	Morningstar Risk-Adj Rating
1 Yr	–0.81					
3 Yr	6.05	47	42	0.24[2]	0.65	★★★★
5 Yr	11.18	53	42	1.51[2]	0.73	★★★★
10 Yr	14.87	55	25	1.75	0.71	★★★★★

Average Historical Rating (164 months): 3.8★s

[1] 1=low, 100=high [2] T-Bill return substituted for category avg.

Category Rating (3 Yr)

1 2 3 4 5
Worst Best

Return: Below Avg
Risk: Average

Other Measures	Standard Index S&P 500	Best Fit Index SPMid400
Alpha	4.4	–1.3
Beta	0.50	0.51
R-Squared	33	45

Standard Deviation	15.65
Mean	6.05
Sharpe Ratio	0.08

Analysis by William Harding 11-28-01

Sound Shore Fund remains a compelling pick for cautious investors.

The fund has weathered the market's storm fairly well this year, but its 2.4% loss for the year to date ended Nov. 27, 2001, lags 70% of its mid-value peers. The portfolio's median market capitalization is 70% greater than the group's average, which has been a drain on performance as smaller fare has generally outperformed this year.

Managers Harry Burn and Gibbs Kane employ a fairly typical value discipline here. The pair seeks out mid- and large-cap stocks with low absolute and relative P/E ratios that they believe will likely return to normal valuations. Finding cheap stocks is just part of the puzzle, though. Burn and Kane also plow through income and cash-flow statements and visit management to find sound companies. Names that have passed their tests lately include rural telephone firm CenturyTel and drugmaker Pharmacia.

This line of attack isn't especially unique to value managers, but the pair has executed it with aplomb over time. The fund's calendar-year returns have only trailed the mid-value category average twice over the past 10 years. Moreover, the fund has been much less volatile than its average peer. The portfolio is fairly concentrated in less than 50 names, but Burn and Kane limit individual position sizes and don't make huge sector bets.

There are a couple of additional strong points here. Burn and Kane have a lot of their own money invested in the fund. That aligns their interests with those of the fund's shareholders. The fund also has superb tax-adjusted returns relative to its peers. Burn and Kane don't manage exclusively to limit taxes, but the bulk of the gains they realize are long-term, which are taxed at lower rates than short-term gains. Finally, the fund's expenses are very reasonable.

Address:	2 Portland Square Portland, ME 04101 800-551-1980 / 800-551-1980
Web Address:	www.soundshorefund.com
Inception:	05-03-85
Advisor:	Sound Shore Mgmt.
Subadvisor:	None
NTF Plans:	Fidelity , Fidelity Inst.

Minimum Purchase:	$10000	Add: None IRA: $2000
Min Auto Inv Plan:	$10000	Add: $50
Sales Fees:	No-load	
Management Fee:	.75%, .10%A	
Actual Fees:	Mgt: 0.75%	Dist: —
Expense Projections:	3Yr: $312	5Yr: $542 10Yr: $1201
Avg Brok Commission:	—	Income Distrib: Semi-Ann.
Total Cost (relative to category):		Below Avg

Portfolio Analysis 11-30-01

Share change since 10-01 Total Stocks: 47	Sector	PE	YTD Ret%	% Assets
Centurytel	Services	13.3	–7.66	3.55
⊕ Berkshire Hathaway Cl A	Financials	—	—	3.16
⊕ Safeway	Retail	18.1	–33.20	3.14
Mylan Labs	Health	24.7	49.68	3.08
Electronic Data Sys	Technology	25.7	19.83	3.08
Aon	Financials	46.1	6.32	3.05
Fannie Mae	Financials	16.2	–6.95	2.90
Interpublic Grp	Services	—	–29.80	2.87
⊕ HCA – The Healthcare Company	Health	24.1	–12.20	2.80
⊕ Liberty Media Group A	N/A	—	—	2.72
Freddie Mac	Financials	14.0	–3.87	2.63
Republic Svcs Cl A	Services	15.6	16.19	2.62
Kimberly-Clark	Industrials	18.5	–13.80	2.50
⊖ Pharmacia	Health	36.5	–29.30	2.46
USX-Marathon Grp	Energy	9.6	11.58	2.43
⊕ Duke Energy	Utilities	15.5	–6.04	2.39
Convergys	Services	41.2	–17.20	2.30
Sprint	Services	20.5	1.18	2.18
Kinder Morgan	Energy	32.2	7.11	2.14
⊖ Guidant	Health	42.6	–7.67	2.12
Ambac Finl Grp	Financials	15.2	–0.16	2.08
Schering-Plough	Health	22.2	–35.90	2.08
⊖ TJX	Retail	23.2	44.39	2.05
MBIA	Financials	14.6	9.88	2.03
Boston Scientific	Health	—	76.21	2.01

Current Investment Style

Style: Value Blnd Growth; Size: Large Med Small

	Stock Port Avg	Relative S&P 500 Current	Relative S&P 500 Hist	Rel Cat
Price/Earnings Ratio	22.8	0.74	0.72	0.96
Price/Book Ratio	4.0	0.70	0.55	1.32
Price/Cash Flow	13.2	0.73	0.65	1.07
3 Yr Earnings Growth	13.1	0.90	0.81	1.11
1 Yr Earnings Est%	10.1	—	—	–1.65
Med Mkt Cap $mil	10,210	0.2	0.1	1.44

Special Securities % assets 11-30-01	
Restricted/Illiquid Secs	0
Emerging-Markets Secs	0
Options/Futures/Warrants	No

Composition % assets 11-30-01	
Cash	7.6
Stocks*	92.4
Bonds	0.0
Other	0.0
*Foreign (% stocks)	0.0

Market Cap	
Giant	12.7
Large	41.1
Medium	45.8
Small	0.5
Micro	0.0

Sector Weightings	% of Stocks	Rel S&P	5-Year High	5-Year Low
Utilities	4.6	1.4	13	0
Energy	7.3	1.0	14	0
Financials	23.7	1.3	36	10
Industrials	9.5	0.8	27	3
Durables	0.0	0.0	19	0
Staples	0.0	0.0	20	0
Services	23.4	2.2	25	9
Retail	7.1	1.1	17	0
Health	21.0	1.4	21	1
Technology	3.5	0.2	20	3

State Street Research Aurora A

Ticker	Load	NAV	Yield	Total Assets	Mstar Category
SSRAX	Closed	$32.35	0.0%	$2,952.6 mil	Small Value

Prospectus Objective: Small Company

State Street Research Aurora Fund seeks high total return.

The fund normally invests at least 65% of assets in small company value stocks. It invests in companies that appear to be trading below their true worth. The fund normally invests in convertible securities, warrants, common and preferred stocks. It may invest up to 5% of assets in bonds which are rated below investment grade.

The fund currently offers A, B, B1, C, and S shares, all of which differ in fee structure and availability. Prior to December 20, 1996 this fund was named State Street Research Small Cap Value.

Historical Profile
Return: High
Risk: Below Avg
Rating: ★★★★★ Highest

Investment Style
Equity
Average Stock %: 90% 98% 78% 87% 90% 86% 76%

▼ Manager Change
▽ Partial Manager Change

Fund Performance vs. Category Average
■ Quarterly Fund Return +/– Category Average
— Category Baseline

Performance Quartile (within Category)

Portfolio Manager(s)

John Burbank. Since 4-01. BA'60 Princeton U; MBA'68 U of New Hampshire. Other funds currently managed: State Street Research Aurora B, State Street Research Aurora S, State Street Research Aurora C.

1990	1991	1992	1993	1994	1995	1996	1997	1998	1999	2000	12-01	History
—	—	—	—	—	10.91	13.53	19.61	16.63	22.21	27.93	32.35	NAV
—	—	—	—	—	20.62*	56.57	46.59	–15.20	33.55	37.02	15.83	Total Return %
—	—	—	—	—	–10.31*	33.62	13.24	–43.77	12.52	46.12	27.70	+/– S&P 500
—	—	—	—	—	—	35.20	14.90	–8.77	35.03	14.21	1.81	+/– Russell 2000 V
—	—	—	—	—	0.87	0.00	0.00	0.00	0.00	0.00	0.00	Income Return %
—	—	—	—	—	19.75	56.57	46.59	–15.20	33.55	37.02	15.83	Capital Return %
—	—	—	—	—	—	2	2	87	7	4	58	Total Rtn % Rank Cat
—	—	—	—	—	0.09	0.00	0.00	0.00	0.00	0.00	0.00	Income $
—	—	—	—	—	0.50	3.48	0.22	0.00	0.00	2.31	0.00	Capital Gains $
—	—	—	—	—	1.45	1.45	1.34	1.39	1.46	1.40	—	Expense Ratio %
—	—	—	—	—	1.05	–0.56	0.17	0.09	0.30	0.42	—	Income Ratio %
—	—	—	—	—	—	125	25	68	65	77	—	Turnover Rate %
—	—	—	—	—	5.9	1.5	198.0	119.7	187.5	742.1	1,693.4	Net Assets $mil

Performance 12-31-01

	1st Qtr	2nd Qtr	3rd Qtr	4th Qtr	Total
1997	3.55	20.49	22.69	–4.23	46.59
1998	11.07	–6.93	–23.68	7.50	–15.20
1999	–4.75	22.41	–1.96	16.83	33.55
2000	10.36	7.47	10.74	4.33	37.02
2001	2.83	11.98	–17.57	22.03	15.83

Trailing	Total Return%	+/– S&P 500	+/– Russ 2000V	% Rank All	% Rank Cat	Growth of $10,000
3 Mo	22.03	11.34	5.31	11	12	12,203
6 Mo	0.59	6.15	–0.56	36	65	10,059
1 Yr	15.83	27.70	1.81	3	58	11,583
3 Yr Avg	28.45	29.48	17.13	1	3	21,196
5 Yr Avg	21.38	10.68	10.19	1	3	26,349
10 Yr Avg	—	—	—	—	—	—
15 Yr Avg	—	—	—	—	—	—

Tax Analysis	Tax-Adj Ret%	%Rank Cat	%Pretax Ret	%Rank Cat
3 Yr Avg	27.04	3	95.1	31
5 Yr Avg	20.48	2	95.8	8
10 Yr Avg	—	—	—	—

Potential Capital Gain Exposure: 16% of assets

Risk Analysis

Time Period	Load-Adj Return %	Risk %Rank[1] All	Risk %Rank[1] Cat	Morningstar Return	Morningstar Risk	Morningstar Risk-Adj Rating
1 Yr	9.17					
3 Yr	25.94	38	10	5.40[2]	0.49	★★★★★
5 Yr	19.95	51	21	4.33[2]	0.70	★★★★★
Incept	25.17	—	—	—	—	

Average Historical Rating (47 months): 4.1★s

[1] 1=low, 100=high [2] T-Bill return substituted for category avg.

Category Rating (3 Yr)

1 2 3 4 5
Worst — Best

Return: High
Risk: Low

Other Measures	Standard Index S&P 500	Best Fit Index Russ 2000
Alpha	28.1	21.1
Beta	0.63	0.73
R-Squared	32	81
Standard Deviation		24.16
Mean		28.45
Sharpe Ratio		1.09

Portfolio Analysis 06-30-01

Share change since 12-00 Total Stocks: 281	Sector	PE	YTD Ret%	% Assets
⊕ Mandalay Resort Grp	Services	15.3	–2.45	1.94
⊖ Borg Warner	Durables	19.3	32.37	1.82
⊕ Harrah's Entrtnmt	Services	—	40.32	1.70
✲ Davita	Health	18.3	42.77	1.56
⊕ Ocean Energy	Energy	10.6	11.58	1.55
Lear	Durables	16.8	53.71	1.50
⊖ Intl Game Tech	Durables	24.4	42.29	1.49
⊖ Anchor Gaming	Services	—	56.15	1.44
⊕ ACE	Financials	17.4	–5.39	1.36
⊕ HS Resources	Energy	—	51.27	1.33
✲ Proquest	N/A	—	—	1.28
⊕ PartnerRe	Financials	22.4	–10.50	1.27
⊕ Methanex	Energy	—	–13.90	1.12
⊕ Wabtec	Durables	18.1	5.00	1.10
✲ Everest Reinsurance Grp	N/A	—	—	1.10
⊕ Argosy Gaming	Services	16.5	69.48	1.09
⊕ Alliant Techsystems	Industrials	28.6	73.48	1.07
⊕ Agrium	Industrials	17.1	–27.10	1.07
⊕ Cabot Microelect	Industrials	—	52.59	0.87
⊕ Minerals Tech	Industrials	21.5	36.76	0.86
⊕ RenaissanceRe Hldgs	Financials	14.7	23.16	0.85
✲ Actel	Technology	NMF	–17.60	0.81
Western Gas Resources	Energy	12.1	–3.42	0.79
✲ Peabody Energy	Energy	—	—	0.79
Bei Tech	Technology	21.5	50.31	0.77

Current Investment Style

Style: Value Blnd Growth; Size: Large Med Small

	Stock Port Avg	Relative S&P 500 Current	Relative S&P 500 Hist	Rel Cat
Price/Earnings Ratio	23.2	0.75	0.54	1.07
Price/Book Ratio	3.4	0.59	0.41	1.40
Price/Cash Flow	12.8	0.71	0.53	1.00
3 Yr Earnings Growth	10.8	0.74	—	0.93
1 Yr Earnings Est%	–20.9	11.83	—	5.30
Med Mkt Cap $mil	1,145	0.0	0.0	1.31

Analysis by Alan Papier 12-03-01

Economic turmoil and market volatility has roiled this fund in 2001, but we think it remains a compelling choice.

Earlier this year, as State Street Research Aurora Fund was humming right along, we noted that its tendency to make industry bets could cause trouble. And although we couldn't have foreseen the terrorist attacks on Sept. 11, the fund's industry positioning wound up being a huge drag on performance in the wake of that tragedy. To be sure, the fund's biggest industry overweights—insurance, casinos, and transportation, which included a slug of regional airlines—were among the hardest hit as investors shunned economically sensitive companies. Yet the fund has rebounded since then, and its gain of 8.7% for the year to date through Nov. 30, 2001, now ranks in the middle of the small-value category.

Aside from those industry bets, however, the fund's bottom-up portfolio construction aims to minimize risk. For one thing, the fund's security selection relies on classic valuation ratios and a company's ability to generate free cash flow, so it generally avoids speculative fare that sport inflated valuation premiums and volatile prices.

As for John Burbank's transition from associate to lead portfolio manager earlier this year, we think the fund is in good hands. Not only had Burbank worked on the fund since January 1998, but also he is a veteran of the firm's research group, so he knows the people and the process. What's more, we think the recent decision to close the fund to new investments through fund supermarkets was right. Indeed, the fund's cash stake is already more manageable (at roughly 8% of assets) than it was at mid-year when it hit 24%.

Overall, we think the fund's excellent longer-term track record is an indication of the firm's research resources and disciplined approach to portfolio construction.

Special Securities % assets 06-30-01	
Restricted/Illiquid Secs	0
Emerging-Markets Secs	Trace
Options/Futures/Warrants	No

Composition % assets 06-30-01	
Cash	24.3
Stocks*	75.7
Bonds	0.0
Other	0.0
*Foreign (% stocks)	10.1

Market Cap	
Giant	0.0
Large	0.0
Medium	34.7
Small	57.3
Micro	8.0

Sector Weightings	% of Stocks	Rel S&P	5-Year High	5-Year Low
Utilities	1.9	0.6	2	0
Energy	12.8	1.8	13	1
Financials	8.3	0.5	12	4
Industrials	18.6	1.6	53	19
Durables	11.0	7.0	14	4
Staples	0.7	0.1	4	1
Services	23.0	2.1	24	13
Retail	2.5	0.4	6	2
Health	6.7	0.5	9	2
Technology	14.7	0.8	18	4

Address: One Financial Center
Boston, MA 02111
800-882-0052 / 617-357-7800
Web Address: www.ssrfunds.com
*Inception: 02-13-95
Advisor: State St. Research & Mgmt.
Subadvisor: None
NTF Plans: Datalynx , Fidelity Inst.

Minimum Purchase: Closed — Add: $Closed — IRA: —
Min Auto Inv Plan: Closed — Add: $50
Sales Fees: 5.75%L, 0.25%S
Management Fee: .85%
Actual Fees: Mgt: 0.85% — Dist: 0.25%
Expense Projections: 3Yr: $89* — 5Yr: $121* — 10Yr: $211*
Income Distrib: Annually
Total Cost (relative to category): —

Strong Advantage Inv

Ticker	Load	NAV	Yield	SEC Yield	Total Assets	Mstar Category
STADX	None	$9.75	5.7%	—	$3,807.6 mil	Ultrashort Bond

Prospectus Objective: Corp Bond—General

Strong Advantage Fund seeks current income consistent with minimum fluctuation of principal.

The fund normally invests in very short-term, corporate, and mortgage- and asset-backed bonds. To enhance its return potential, it also invests a portion of its assets in bonds that have longer maturities or are of lower-quality, though it may not invest in bonds rated below BB. The fund focuses upon high-yield bonds rated BB with positive or improving credit fundamentals. To a limited extent, the fund may also invest in foreign securities.

The fund offers Investor, Advisor and Institutional shares.

Historical Profile

Return Average
Risk Low
Rating ★★★★★ Highest

Investment Style Fixed-Income

Income Rtn %Rank Cat: 28 21 23 30 30 28 40 49

Growth of Principal vs. Interest Rate Shifts
- Principal Value $000 (NAV with capital gains reinvested)
- Interest Rate % on 10 Yr Treasury
- Manager Change
- Partial Manager Change
- Mgr Unknown After
- Mgr Unknown Before

Performance Quartile (within Category)

History

	1990	1991	1992	1993	1994	1995	1996	1997	1998	1999	2000	12-01
NAV	9.67	9.90	10.01	10.19	9.98	10.04	10.07	10.08	9.95	9.88	9.89	9.75
Total Return %	6.61	10.58	8.43	8.12	3.55	7.51	6.68	6.50	4.75	5.28	6.77	4.26
+/– LB Aggregate	−2.35	−5.42	1.03	−1.63	6.47	−10.96	3.06	−3.18	−3.93	6.11	−4.86	−4.16
+/– 6 Month CD	−1.56	4.64	4.67	4.83	−1.45	1.53	1.59	0.93	−0.62	0.13	0.45	0.78
Income Return %	8.71	8.09	7.32	6.28	5.51	6.89	6.35	6.41	6.09	6.00	6.66	5.77
Capital Return %	−2.09	2.49	1.11	1.83	−1.95	0.62	0.33	0.10	−1.35	−0.73	0.11	−1.50
Total Rtn % Rank Cat	91	1	1	1	38	53	23	50	76	28	39	53
Income $	0.83	0.75	0.70	0.61	0.55	0.67	0.62	0.63	0.60	0.58	0.64	0.56
Capital Gains $	0.00	0.00	0.00	0.00	0.02	0.00	0.00	0.00	0.00	0.00	0.00	0.00
Expense Ratio %	1.20	1.20	1.00	0.90	0.80	0.80	0.80	0.80	0.80	0.70	0.80	—
Income Ratio %	8.50	7.80	7.00	5.80	5.60	6.60	6.30	6.20	6.20	5.80	5.90	—
Turnover Rate %	274	503	316	305	221	184	—	155	110	79	48	—
Net Assets $mil	119.2	143.2	272.3	415.5	910.5	989.7	1,417.1	2,041.0	2,631.9	2,266.8	2,115.9	3,002.5

Portfolio Manager(s)

Jeffrey A. Koch, CFA. Since 7-91. BA'87 U. of Minnesota-Morris; MBA'89 Washington U. Other funds currently managed: Strong Corporate Bond Inv, Strong Balanced, Strong Advisor Short Duration Bond Z.

Thomas A. Sontag. Since 12-98. BBA'81 U. of Wisconsin; MBA'82 U. of Wisconsin. Other funds currently managed: Strong Government Securities Inv, Strong Advantage Instl, Strong Government Securities Instl.

Performance 12-31-01

	1st Qtr	2nd Qtr	3rd Qtr	4th Qtr	Total
1997	1.41	1.85	1.76	1.34	6.50
1998	1.48	1.59	0.96	0.65	4.75
1999	1.48	1.15	1.15	1.40	5.28
2000	1.34	1.72	2.06	1.48	6.77
2001	2.08	1.55	−0.03	0.61	4.27

Trailing	Total Return%	+/– LB Agg	+/– 6 Month CD	% Rank All	% Rank Cat	Growth of $10,000
3 Mo	0.61	0.58	0.13	74	55	10,061
6 Mo	0.58	−4.07	−0.68	36	80	10,058
1 Yr	4.26	−4.16	0.78	28	53	10,426
3 Yr Avg	5.43	−0.84	0.45	27	52	11,720
5 Yr Avg	5.51	−1.92	0.33	55	53	13,074
10 Yr Avg	6.17	−1.06	1.28	66	1	18,203
15 Yr Avg	—	—	—	—	—	—

Tax Analysis	Tax-Adj Ret%	%Rank Cat	%Pretax Ret	%Rank Cat
3 Yr Avg	2.98	68	54.9	82
5 Yr Avg	3.04	76	55.1	80
10 Yr Avg	3.69	6	59.8	31

Potential Capital Gain Exposure: −2% of assets

Risk Analysis

Time Period	Load-Adj Return %	Risk %Rank[1] All	Risk %Rank[1] Cat	Morningstar Return	Morningstar Risk	Morningstar Risk-Adj Rating
1 Yr	4.26					
3 Yr	5.43	1	69	0.10[2]	0.16	★★★★★
5 Yr	5.51	1	65	0.11[2]	0.17	★★★★
10 Yr	6.17	1	47	0.39[2]	0.15	★★★★★

Average Historical Rating (122 months): 4.5★s

[1] 1=low, 100=high [2] T-Bill return substituted for category avg.

Category Rating (3 Yr)

Worst 1 2 3 4 5 Best

Return Average
Risk Above Avg

Other Measures	Standard Index LB Agg	Best Fit Index FB HY
Alpha	0.4	0.8
Beta	0.06	0.10
R-Squared	3	41

Standard Deviation	1.28
Mean	5.43
Sharpe Ratio	0.48

Analysis by Scott Berry 12-11-01

Despite its middling recent returns, we're still big fans of Strong Advantage.

This fund has struggled to stand out in 2001. The fund's duration, which typically checks in a bit short of the category's average, has cost it some ground, as falling interest rates have given its longer-duration peers an added lift. In addition, the fund's stash of mid-quality bonds has held it back, as investors have favored relatively safer fixed-income alternatives, including government bonds and higher-quality corporate issues. For the year to date through Dec. 7, 2001, the fund gained 4.1%, more or less matching the gain of its average peer.

Management has bumped up the fund's average credit quality in recent weeks, but it remains one of the more economically sensitive ultrashort offerings. Indeed, the fund holds roughly 27% of its assets in bonds rated BBB and below, while its average peer holds just 16% of its assets in such issues. The added yield provided by these holdings fuels the fund's total return and helps it pay one of the category's more-generous yields. But when the economy softens or interest rates drop, these issues can prevent the fund from keeping pace with its higher-quality rivals and can even negatively affect the fund's total return. In September 2001, for example, as investors shunned risk, the fund lost 1.2% of its value.

As evidenced by its recent volatility, this fund does not behave like a money-market fund; there are certainly more-conservative ultrashort alternatives available. However, we think this fund is worth the added risk. It boasts one the best 10-year records in the group, and although its approach has been out of favor for the last couple years, it has kept pace with its average peer.

Portfolio Analysis 09-30-01

Total Fixed-Income: 354	Date of Maturity	Amount $000	Value $000	% Net Assets
FNMA ARM 7%	12-01-29	96,722	100,909	2.65
Esat Telecom Grp Step 0%	02-01-07	70,920	74,289	1.95
Rtc Sr Sub A1 9.06%	08-25-27	67,350	72,570	1.91
MetroNet Comm 12%	08-15-07	107,390	70,877	1.86
Allied Waste 7.875%	01-01-09	63,603	62,171	1.64
GS Escrow FRN	08-01-03	62,300	61,273	1.61
Rali 6.5%	04-25-31	56,058	58,143	1.53
Lilly Del Mar 0%	08-01-29	55,000	54,118	1.42
AB Spintab 144A FRN	01-30-06	50,000	50,434	1.33
FHLMC 11%	11-01-15	45,016	46,408	1.22
AMFM Operating 12.625%	10-31-06	41,229	44,733	1.18
Waste Mgmt 6.5%	12-15-02	40,410	41,315	1.09
Washington Mutual FRN	12-25-40	40,094	40,234	1.06
NY State GO 7.375%	07-01-26	39,000	39,000	1.03
Repap New Brunswick 9%	06-01-04	36,350	38,713	1.02
Halyard CBO 144A FRN	03-24-10	38,700	38,077	1.00
Sutton Bridge Fin 144A 7.125%	12-25-35	37,600	37,330	0.98
Cendant 7.75%	12-01-03	37,305	36,950	0.97
FHLMC N/A	07-01-29	35,752	36,761	0.97
Fngt 2001-t8 A2 9.5%	07-25-31	32,688	36,335	0.96

Current Investment Style

Duration: Short Int Long — Quality: High Med Low

Avg Eff Duration[1]	0.7 Yrs
Avg Eff Maturity	1.0 Yrs
Avg Credit Quality	AA
Avg Wtd Coupon	7.22%
Avg Wtd Price	96.36% of par

[1] figure provided by fund

Special Securities % assets 09-30-01	
Restricted/Illiquid Secs	22
Exotic Mortgage–Backed	1
Emerging–Markets Secs	0
Options/Futures/Warrants	Yes

Coupon Range	% of Bonds	Rel Cat
0%	6.58	0.68
0% to 7%	34.42	0.63
7% to 8.5%	26.99	1.15
8.5% to 10%	21.64	2.93
More than 10%	10.35	2.38

1.00=Category Average

Credit Analysis % bonds 09-30-01			
US Govt	18	BB	7
AAA	31	B	0
AA	6	Below B	0
A	18	NR/NA	0
BBB	20		

Composition % assets 09-30-01			
Cash	4.8	Bonds	94.8
Stocks	0.0	Other	0.4

Sector Breakdown % bonds 09-30-01			
US Treasuries	0	CMOs	9
GNMA mtgs	4	ARMs	3
FNMA mtgs	6	Other	71
FHLMC mtgs	7		

Address:	P.O. Box 2936 Milwaukee, WI 53201–2936 800–368–1030 / 414–359–1400
Web Address:	www.strongfunds.com
Inception:	11-25-88
Advisor:	Strong Cap. Mgmt.
Subadvisor:	None
NTF Plans:	Fidelity , Datalynx

Minimum Purchase:	$2500	Add: $50	IRA: $250
Min Auto Inv Plan:	$50	Add: $50	
Sales Fees:	No-load		
Management Fee:	.60%		
Actual Fees:	Mgt: 0.30%	Dist: —	
Expense Projections:	3Yr: $252	5Yr: $439	10Yr: $978
Avg Brok Commission:	—	Income Distrib: Monthly	
Total Cost (relative to category):		Average	

Strong Advisor Common Stock Z

Ticker	Load	NAV	Yield	Total Assets	Mstar Category
STCSX	Closed	$19.78	0.0%	$1,760.5 mil	Mid–Cap Blend

Prospectus Objective: Growth

Strong Advisor Common Stock Fund seeks growth of capital; current income is not a consideration.

The fund normally invests at least 80% of assets in equities. It may invest up to 20% of assets in debt obligations, including intermediate- to long-term corporate or U.S. government debt. The fund may engage in substantial short-term trading. It may also invest up to 25% of assets in foreign securities, including ADRs.

The fund closed to new investors in 1993, although the fund may continue to offer shares through certain retirement plans.

The fund also offers A, B, C, L, Z shares. Prior to November 30, 2000, the fund was named Strong Common Stock Fund.

Historical Profile
Return High
Risk Average
Rating ★★★★★ Highest

Investment Style
Equity
Average Stock %: 1996 90%, 1997 92%, 1998 89%, 1999 91%, 2000 90%, 12-01 88%

▼ Manager Change
▽ Partial Manager Change

Fund Performance vs. Category Average
■ Quarterly Fund Return +/– Category Average
— Category Baseline

Performance Quartile (within Category)

Portfolio Manager(s)

Richard T. Weiss. Since 3-91. BS'73 U. of Southern California; MBA'75 Harvard U. Other funds currently managed: Strong Opportunity Inv, Masters' Select Equity, Strong Opportunity Adv.

Ann Miletti. Since 10-01. BA'89 U of Wisconsin. Other funds currently managed: Strong Opportunity Inv, Strong Opportunity Adv, Strong Advisor Common Stock A.

1990	1991	1992	1993	1994	1995	1996	1997	1998	1999	2000	12–01	History
10.02	12.84	15.07	17.94	16.74	19.77	20.24	21.02	21.06	25.21	20.16	19.78	NAV
1.00	57.07	20.78	25.17	–0.50	32.41	20.47	24.02	6.62	40.35	–1.20	–1.70	Total Return %
4.12	26.59	13.16	15.11	–1.81	–5.12	–2.48	–9.33	–21.95	19.32	7.90	10.18	+/– S&P 500
6.12	7.01	8.88	11.24	3.09	1.50	1.28	–8.23	–12.49	25.64	–18.70	–1.10	+/– S&P Mid 400
0.81	19.24	1.75	0.26	0.25	0.71	0.59	0.20	0.03	0.00	0.21	0.00	Income Return %
0.19	37.83	19.03	24.90	–0.75	31.70	19.87	23.82	6.60	40.35	–1.41	–1.70	Capital Return %
3	1	24	8	33	29	47	64	43	10	64	34	Total Rtn % Rank Cat
0.08	1.86	0.22	0.04	0.04	0.12	0.11	0.04	0.01	0.00	0.04	0.00	Income $
0.00	0.73	0.16	0.86	1.06	2.21	3.35	3.86	1.32	4.03	4.46	0.04	Capital Gains $
2.00	2.00	1.40	1.40	1.30	1.20	1.20	1.20	1.20	1.20	1.20	—	Expense Ratio %
0.90	–0.50	0.10	0.20	0.30	0.50	0.30	0.00	0.00	–0.10	–0.10	—	Income Ratio %
291	2,461	292	81	83	92	91	117	103	80	95	—	Turnover Rate %
2.4	48.5	179.1	762.1	790.1	1,061.0	1,243.6	1,564.8	1,439.9	1,733.1	1,719.0	1,702.6	Net Assets $mil

Performance 12-31-01

	1st Qtr	2nd Qtr	3rd Qtr	4th Qtr	Total
1997	–0.11	15.05	13.26	–4.73	24.02
1998	11.49	–2.87	–16.54	17.98	6.62
1999	3.18	16.05	–6.42	25.27	40.35
2000	7.06	–6.19	3.24	–4.72	–1.20
2001	–5.26	5.97	–20.06	22.48	–1.70

Trailing	Total Return%	+/– S&P 500	+/– S&P Mid 400	% Rank All	% Rank Cat	Growth of $10,000
3 Mo	22.48	11.79	4.50	10	12	12,248
6 Mo	–2.09	3.47	–0.53	47	35	9,791
1 Yr	–1.70	10.18	–1.10	45	34	9,830
3 Yr Avg	10.88	11.90	0.63	10	13	13,631
5 Yr Avg	12.50	1.81	–3.61	9	30	18,024
10 Yr Avg	15.77	2.84	0.76	4	12	43,247
15 Yr Avg	—	—	—	—	—	—

Tax Analysis	Tax-Adj Ret%	%Rank Cat	%Pretax Ret	%Rank Cat
3 Yr Avg	7.31	25	67.2	65
5 Yr Avg	8.90	31	71.2	69
10 Yr Avg	12.34	25	78.3	64

Potential Capital Gain Exposure: NMF

Risk Analysis

Time Period	Load-Adj Return %	Risk %Rank[1] All	Risk %Rank[1] Cat	Morningstar Return	Morningstar Risk	Morningstar Risk-Adj Rating
1 Yr	–1.70					
3 Yr	10.88	64	51	1.33[2]	0.91	★★★★
5 Yr	12.50	70	41	1.88[2]	0.94	★★★★
10 Yr	15.77	73	40	1.99	0.94	★★★★★

Average Historical Rating (109 months): 4.5★s

[1]1=low, 100=high [2] T-Bill return substituted for category avg.

Category Rating (3 Yr)

1 2 3 4 5
Worst Best

Return Above Avg
Risk Average

Other Measures	Standard Index S&P 500	Best Fit Index SPMid400
Alpha	12.8	1.1
Beta	1.02	0.95
R–Squared	73	84

Standard Deviation	22.49
Mean	10.88
Sharpe Ratio	0.30

Portfolio Analysis 09-30-01

Share change since 06–01 Total Stocks: 77	Sector	PE	YTD Ret%	% Assets
⊖ WellPoint Health Networks	Health	19.4	1.39	2.03
⊕ Celgene	Health	—	–1.78	1.89
⊖ Office Depot	Retail	NMF	160.20	1.81
⊖ Tech Data	Technology	19.2	60.11	1.79
⊖ Fifth Third Bancorp	Financials	38.3	4.53	1.77
⊕ Omnicare	Health	38.3	15.52	1.69
⊕ FleetBoston Finl	Financials	16.2	0.55	1.65
⊖ Cox Comms A	Services	31.8	–9.99	1.64
⊖ Cigna	Financials	13.2	–29.00	1.63
⊕ SAFECO	Financials	—	–2.33	1.53
⊕ Jacobs Engnrg Grp	Services	20.5	42.89	1.51
⊕ AT&T Wireless Grp	Services	—	–17.00	1.50
⊖ Security Cap Grp Cl B	Financials	11.3	26.45	1.48
⊕ Vodafone Airtouch PLC ADR	Services	—	–27.70	1.46
⊕ Apache	Energy	8.0	–21.20	1.45
✲ Mentor Graphics	Technology	27.1	–14.10	1.44
✲ Liberty Media Group A	N/A	—	—	1.43
⊕ Hillenbrand Inds	Durables	22.5	9.08	1.42
⊕ Cablevision Sys A	Services	5.6	–34.20	1.39
✲ Lincoln Natl	Financials	16.5	5.48	1.39
⊕ Noble Drilling	Energy	18.3	–21.60	1.38
⊕ Broadwing	Services	—	–58.30	1.37
✲ Rockwell Intl	Industrials	10.8	2.98	1.37
⊖ Farichild Semicon Intl Cl A	Technology	42.7	95.32	1.36
⊕ Carlisle	Industrials	40.2	–11.80	1.35

Current Investment Style

Style: Value Blnd Growth; Size: Large Med Small

	Stock Port Avg	Relative S&P 500 Current	Relative S&P 500 Hist	Rel Cat
Price/Earnings Ratio	25.4	0.82	0.79	0.93
Price/Book Ratio	3.9	0.69	0.55	0.92
Price/Cash Flow	15.9	0.89	0.76	0.92
3 Yr Earnings Growth	10.6	0.73	1.04	0.64
1 Yr Earnings Est%	–2.2	1.26	—	–0.98
Med Mkt Cap $mil	4,010	0.1	0.1	0.45

[1]figure is based on 50% or less of stocks

Analysis by Paul Herbert 11-30-01

This fund has fared well since its late 2000 reopening, but investors should continue to watch its asset growth.

It looks like 2001 is going to turn out to be just another year for Strong Advisor Common Stock Fund. The typically solid-performing fund has lost about 6.2% for the year, but that's good enough to rank it in the mid-cap blend category's top half. If it finishes the year ahead of the median fund in the group, it will be the sixth time in the past eight years that it will have accomplished that feat.

Much of the fund's success owes to its exposure to smaller-cap names. While the fund's managers own stocks of different market caps, they tend to target smaller fare than their typical peer. (The fund's median market cap as of Sept. 30, 2001, was about $4 billion less than the average mid-blend fund's.) Smaller has generally been better in 2001, and smaller mid-caps such as Jacobs Engineering Group and Tech Data have helped to give the fund a leg up on its competitors in 2001.

Relying on these mighty mites will become difficult if the fund's asset base becomes too much larger, however. Strong opened the fund to load investors in November 2000, and while it hasn't had significant inflows in the year since, its ability to purchase meaningful stakes in smaller mid-cap names would be compromised if it did.

If asset growth remains modest, the fund can boast many attractive attributes. It owns a stellar 10-year record and has been less volatile, in terms of standard deviation, than its typical category rival. The fact that current comanager Dick Weiss has been at the helm for more than 10 years also gives the fund additional appeal.For the most part, the fund makes an attractive mid-cap option. Its allure would be diminished if it became unable to purchase smaller stocks, however, so investors should monitor its asset growth closely.

Special Securities % assets 09-30-01	
Restricted/Illiquid Secs	0
Emerging–Markets Secs	0
Options/Futures/Warrants	No

Composition % assets 09-30-01	
Cash	8.2
Stocks*	90.7
Bonds	1.1
Other	0.0
*Foreign (% stocks)	4.8

Market Cap	
Giant	3.5
Large	18.5
Medium	64.9
Small	12.8
Micro	0.2

Sector Weightings	% of Stocks	Rel S&P	5-Year High	5-Year Low
Utilities	0.0	0.0	3	0
Energy	10.6	1.5	16	7
Financials	17.5	1.0	17	7
Industrials	10.8	0.9	23	9
Durables	3.0	1.9	6	0
Staples	1.5	0.2	9	0
Services	23.9	2.2	30	14
Retail	5.3	0.8	18	3
Health	7.4	0.5	14	3
Technology	20.1	1.1	25	9

Address:	P.O. Box 2936 Milwaukee, WI 53201–2936 800–368–1030 / 414–359–1400
Web Address:	www.strongfunds.com
Inception:	12-29-89
Advisor:	Strong Cap. Mgmt.
Subadvisor:	None
NTF Plans:	Fidelity , Datalynx

Minimum Purchase:	Closed	Add: $50	IRA: —
Min Auto Inv Plan:	None	Add: $50	
Sales Fees:	No–load		
Management Fee:	.75%		
Actual Fees:	Mgt: 0.75%	Dist: —	
Expense Projections:	3Yr: $375	5Yr: $649	10Yr: $1432
Avg Brok Commission:	—	Income Distrib: Annually	
Total Cost (relative to category):		Below Avg	

Strong Corporate Bond Inv

Ticker	Load	NAV	Yield	SEC Yield	Total Assets	Mstar Category
STCBX	None	$10.50	7.1%	—	$1,338.9 mil	Long–Term Bond

Prospectus Objective: Corp Bond—General

Strong Corporate Bond Fund seeks total return by investing for a high level of current income with a moderate degree of share-price fluctuation.

The fund normally invests in intermediate maturity bonds issued by U.S. companies. The fund invests primarily in higher- and medium-quality bonds. To increase the income it pays out, it may also invest a small portion of its assets in lower-quality, high-yield bonds. The fund focuses primarily upon high-yield bonds rated BB with positive or improving credit fundamentals. To a limited extent, it may also invest in foreign securities.

The fund currently offers Investor, Advisor and Institutional shares.

Historical Profile
Return Above Avg
Risk Average
Rating ★★★★ Above Avg

Investment Style
Fixed-Income
Income Rtn %Rank Cat: 10, 16, 29, 17, 15, 20, 18, 14

Growth of Principal vs. Interest Rate Shifts
— Principal Value $000 (NAV with capital gains reinvested)
— Interest Rate % on 10 Yr Treasury
▼ Manager Change
▽ Partial Manager Change
► Mgr Unknown After
◄ Mgr Unknown Before

Performance Quartile (within Category)

Portfolio Manager(s)

Jeffrey A. Koch, CFA. Since 7-91.
John T. Bender, CFA. Since 12-95.
Ivor E. Schucking. Since 12-98.
Janet Rilling. Since 10-00.

1990	1991	1992	1993	1994	1995	1996	1997	1998	1999	2000	12-01	History
8.87	9.37	9.40	10.24	9.36	10.89	10.73	11.20	11.25	10.49	10.53	10.50	NAV
–6.22	14.83	9.40	16.81	–1.31	25.39	5.53	11.88	7.25	–0.23	7.89	6.83	Total Return %
–15.18	–1.18	1.99	7.07	1.61	6.92	1.92	2.20	–1.43	0.60	–3.74	–1.59	+/– LB Aggregate
–12.65	–4.70	0.86	0.65	5.79	–4.54	5.40	–2.64	–4.52	7.41	–8.27	–0.43	+/– LB LT Govt/Corp
10.52	8.94	9.05	7.67	7.47	8.49	6.85	7.30	6.81	6.72	7.44	7.32	Income Return %
–16.74	5.89	0.34	9.14	–8.78	16.90	–1.32	4.59	0.43	–6.95	0.45	–0.49	Capital Return %
93	72	15	16	2	24	27	25	49	13	69	69	Total Rtn % Rank Cat
1.06	0.76	0.82	0.70	0.74	0.77	0.72	0.76	0.74	0.73	0.75	0.75	Income $
0.00	0.00	0.00	0.00	0.00	0.00	0.00	0.00	0.00	0.00	0.00	0.00	Capital Gains $
1.40	1.50	1.30	1.10	1.10	1.00	1.00	1.00	0.90	0.80	0.90	—	Expense Ratio %
11.20	8.40	8.70	7.00	7.60	7.50	7.00	6.80	6.50	6.70	7.30	—	Income Ratio %
294	392	557	666	603	—	673	542	367	403	294	—	Turnover Rate %
92.2	92.4	102.8	123.4	123.3	259.3	305.3	560.5	844.5	837.8	954.3	1,267.9	Net Assets $mil

Performance 12-31-01

	1st Qtr	2nd Qtr	3rd Qtr	4th Qtr	Total
1997	–0.03	4.44	4.16	2.88	11.88
1998	1.83	3.17	1.62	0.45	7.25
1999	0.41	–1.53	0.34	0.57	–0.23
2000	1.65	1.30	2.75	1.97	7.89
2001	5.01	0.71	1.15	–0.13	6.83

Trailing	Total Return%	+/– LB Agg	+/– LB LTGvt/Corp	% Rank All	% Rank Cat	Growth of $10,000
3 Mo	–0.13	–0.16	–0.05	80	62	9,987
6 Mo	1.02	–3.63	–4.07	34	89	10,102
1 Yr	6.83	–1.59	–0.43	15	69	10,683
3 Yr Avg	4.77	–1.51	–0.02	33	49	11,500
5 Yr Avg	6.65	–0.78	–1.40	40	31	13,798
10 Yr Avg	8.70	1.47	0.28	40	5	23,027
15 Yr Avg	7.42	–0.70	–1.60	60	90	29,272

Tax Analysis	Tax-Adj Ret%	%Rank Cat	%Pretax Ret	%Rank Cat
3 Yr Avg	1.94	62	40.6	70
5 Yr Avg	3.80	52	57.1	66
10 Yr Avg	5.73	1	65.9	1

Potential Capital Gain Exposure: –5% of assets

Risk Analysis

Time Period	Load-Adj Return %	Risk %Rank[1] All	Risk %Rank[1] Cat	Morningstar Return	Morningstar Risk	Morningstar Risk-Adj Rating
1 Yr	6.83					
3 Yr	4.77	27	48	–0.04[2]	0.90	★★★
5 Yr	6.65	33	45	0.36[2]	0.91	★★★
10 Yr	8.70	33	23	1.22[2]	0.99	★★★★★

Average Historical Rating (157 months): 3.0★s

[1] 1=low, 100=high [2] T-Bill return substituted for category avg.

Category Rating (3 Yr)
1 2 3 4 5 — Worst … Best
Return Average
Risk Average

Other Measures	Standard Index LB Agg	Best Fit Index LB Corp
Alpha	–1.4	–1.0
Beta	1.03	1.03
R-Squared	56	81
Standard Deviation		4.77
Mean		4.77
Sharpe Ratio		–0.04

Portfolio Analysis 09-30-01

Total Fixed-Income: 195	Date of Maturity	Amount $000	Value $000	% Net Assets
GMAC 6.875%	09-15-11	23,600	23,183	1.76
DaimlerChrysler Hldg 8.5%	01-18-31	18,800	19,889	1.51
HCA–The Healthcare 7.125%	06-01-06	18,350	18,832	1.43
Lockheed Martin 8.5%	12-01-29	15,980	18,420	1.40
Cendant 144A 6.875%	08-15-06	20,000	18,088	1.37
KN Cap Tr 8.56%	04-15-27	17,500	17,562	1.33
WMX Tech 6.875%	05-15-09	16,725	17,138	1.30
AT&T Wireless 144A 8.75%	03-01-31	14,115	15,594	1.18
Pemex Proj Fdg Master Tr 144A 9.125%	10-13-10	15,000	15,263	1.16
Allied Waste Bk N/A	07-21-05	15,000	14,663	1.11
Citizens Comms Bonds 144A 9%	08-15-31	14,150	14,465	1.10
Ocean Energy Notes 7.25%	10-01-11	14,100	14,206	1.08
Raytheon 8.2%	03-01-06	13,050	14,206	1.08
El Paso Energy 7.375%	12-15-12	13,415	13,792	1.05
Calpine Canada Ener 8.5%	05-01-08	13,745	13,438	1.02
Southern Energy 7.9%	07-15-09	12,820	13,254	1.01
Wcg 144A 8.25%	03-15-04	12,840	13,118	1.00
Triton Energy 8.875%	10-01-07	12,000	13,050	0.99
Univision Net Hldg 7%	12-17-02	7,855	12,332	0.94
Humana Notes 7.25%	08-01-06	12,000	12,205	0.93

Current Investment Style

Duration: Short Int Long; Quality: High Med Low

Avg Eff Duration[1]	6.4 Yrs
Avg Eff Maturity	12.0 Yrs
Avg Credit Quality	BBB
Avg Wtd Coupon	7.36%
Avg Wtd Price	99.78% of par

[1] figure provided by fund

Special Securities % assets 09-30-01	
Restricted/Illiquid Secs	19
Exotic Mortgage–Backed	Trace
Emerging–Markets Secs	Trace
Options/Futures/Warrants	Yes

Coupon Range	% of Bonds	Rel Cat
0%	0.43	0.26
0% to 7%	24.21	0.61
7% to 8.5%	47.28	1.14
8.5% to 10%	22.73	1.58
More than 10%	5.33	1.76

1.00=Category Average

Credit Analysis % bonds 09-30-01

US Govt	0	BB	10
AAA	1	B	1
AA	1	Below B	0
A	19	NR/NA	2
BBB	67		

Composition % assets 09-30-01

Cash	1.7	Bonds	96.9
Stocks	0.0	Other	1.5

Sector Breakdown % bonds 09-30-01

US Treasuries	0	CMOs	1
GNMA mtgs	1	ARMs	0
FNMA mtgs	0	Other	98
FHLMC mtgs	0		

Analysis by Scott Berry 12-11-01

Strong Corporate Bond's recent missteps have taken a little of the shine off of its otherwise solid long-term record.

This fund has struggled in recent months, as its Enron and Global Crossing stakes have weighed heavily on its returns. The fund had roughly 1% of its assets in Enron debt, which recently filed for bankruptcy protection, and about 2% in Global Crossing, which is on the verge of bankruptcy. Though the situations differ, manager John Bender blames himself for being too slow to cut the fund's losses. In the case of Enron, Bender held out hope that a merger with Dynegy would bail out bondholders, but the merger ultimately fell through.

Over time, though, the fund's focus on mid-quality corporate bonds has paid off. Indeed, the fund's 10-year trailing return ranks in the long-term bond category's top 5%, and its five-year trailing return ranks in the group's top third. In years past, the fund was able to steer clear of the market's biggest blowups by focusing on companies and industries with stable cash flows and improving fundamentals. By staying out of harm's way, the fund benefited from the incremental yield premium provided by its lower-quality orientation.

But the fund's recent performance is evidence that it is one of the category's riskier entrants. While it may not be as sensitive to interest-rate changes as its average peer, the fund's added credit risk can sour its returns when the economy softens, as was the case in 1990 and 1991, or when individual issues run into trouble, as has been the case more recently.

Even so, the fund's long-term record shows the merits of its approach. Despite its recent slip, it remains a Morningstar Fund Analyst Pick.

Address:	P.O. Box 2936 Milwaukee, WI 53201–2936 800–368–1030 / 414–359–1400
Web Address:	www.strongfunds.com
Inception:	12-12-85
Advisor:	Strong Cap. Mgmt.
Subadvisor:	None
NTF Plans:	Fidelity , Datalynx

Minimum Purchase:	$2500	Add: $50	IRA: $250
Min Auto Inv Plan:	$50	Add: $50	
Sales Fees:	No-load		
Management Fee:	.63%		
Actual Fees:	Mgt: 0.38%	Dist: —	
Expense Projections:	3Yr: $293	5Yr: $509	10Yr: $1131
Avg Brok Commission:	—	Income Distrib: Monthly	
Total Cost (relative to category):		Average	

Strong Government Securities Inv

Ticker	Load	NAV	Yield	SEC Yield	Total Assets	Mstar Category
STVSX	None	$10.79	5.2%	—	$1,729.6 mil	Intermediate Govt

Prospectus Objective: Government General

Strong Government Securities Fund seeks total return by investing for a high level of current income with a moderate degree of share-price fluctuation.

The fund invests primarily in higher-quality bonds issued by the U.S. government or its agencies. Its dollar-weighted average maturity will normally be between five and 10 years. The fund may invest in mortgage-backed and asset-backed securities. It may invest up to 20% of its assets in foreign securities

The fund currently offers Investor, Advisor and Institutional shares.

Historical Profile
Return High
Risk Average
Rating ★★★★★ Highest

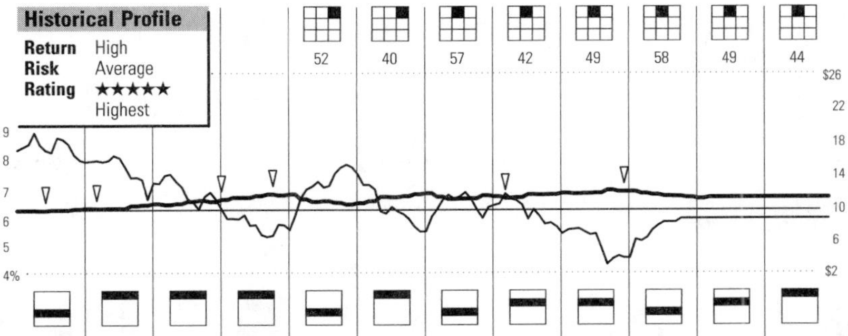

Investment Style: Fixed-Income

Income Rtn %Rank Cat: 52 40 57 42 49 58 49 44

Growth of Principal vs. Interest Rate Shifts
- Principal Value $000 (NAV with capital gains reinvested)
- Interest Rate % on 10 Yr Treasury
- Manager Change
- Partial Manager Change
- Mgr Unknown After
- Mgr Unknown Before

Performance Quartile (within Category)

Portfolio Manager(s)

Bradley C. Tank. Since 6-90. BS'80 U. of Wisconsin; MBA'82 U. of Wisconsin. Other funds currently managed: Strong Short-Term Bond Inv, Strong Balanced, Strong Advisor Short Duration Bond Z.

Thomas A. Sontag. Since 12-98. BBA'81 U. of Wisconsin; MBA'82 U. of Wisconsin. Other funds currently managed: Strong Advantage Inv, Strong Advantage Instl, Strong Government Securities Instl.

1990	1991	1992	1993	1994	1995	1996	1997	1998	1999	2000	12-01	History
10.10	10.77	10.39	10.61	9.63	10.83	10.48	10.75	10.76	10.08	10.59	10.79	NAV
8.71	16.68	9.19	12.78	−3.37	19.91	2.82	9.05	8.14	−1.09	11.32	8.92	Total Return %
−0.25	0.68	1.79	3.03	−0.45	1.44	−0.80	−0.63	−0.53	−0.26	−0.31	0.50	+/– LB Aggregate
−0.01	1.37	1.96	2.13	0.01	1.58	0.05	−0.53	−1.71	1.16	−1.92	1.68	+/– LB Government
7.46	7.90	7.97	6.62	6.07	7.12	6.00	6.34	5.88	5.38	6.04	5.50	Income Return %
1.26	8.78	1.22	6.16	−9.44	12.79	−3.18	2.71	2.27	−6.46	5.28	3.43	Capital Return %
66	13	3	3	57	3	55	28	28	51	30	4	Total Rtn % Rank Cat
0.72	0.77	0.80	0.66	0.63	0.67	0.63	0.65	0.61	0.56	0.59	0.57	Income $
0.10	0.17	0.48	0.41	0.00	0.00	0.00	0.00	0.23	0.00	0.00	0.16	Capital Gains $
1.30	0.80	0.70	0.80	0.90	0.90	0.90	0.80	0.80	0.80	0.90	—	Expense Ratio %
7.20	7.50	7.70	6.00	6.20	6.20	6.00	6.20	5.50	5.50	5.80	—	Income Ratio %
254	293	629	521	479	—	458	475	284	185	373	—	Turnover Rate %
41.1	51.9	82.2	222.0	276.8	504.9	659.9	907.4	1,326.9	1,287.8	1,336.0	1,630.2	Net Assets $mil

Performance 12-31-01

	1st Qtr	2nd Qtr	3rd Qtr	4th Qtr	Total
1997	−0.16	3.06	3.41	2.49	9.05
1998	1.49	2.39	4.16	−0.08	8.14
1999	−0.54	−0.78	0.56	−0.33	−1.09
2000	2.21	1.48	2.81	4.39	11.32
2001	3.00	0.44	5.00	0.27	8.92

Trailing	Total Return%	+/– LB Agg	+/– LB Govt	% Rank All	% Rank Cat	Growth of $10,000
3 Mo	0.27	0.23	0.86	76	5	10,027
6 Mo	5.29	0.63	0.44	3	5	10,529
1 Yr	8.92	0.50	1.68	7	4	10,892
3 Yr Avg	6.25	−0.03	0.36	21	11	11,993
5 Yr Avg	7.18	−0.25	−0.22	34	6	14,144
10 Yr Avg	7.57	0.34	0.44	46	3	20,751
15 Yr Avg	8.31	0.19	0.42	51	2	33,094

Tax Analysis	Tax-Adj Ret%	%Rank Cat	%Pretax Ret	%Rank Cat
3 Yr Avg	3.83	10	61.3	20
5 Yr Avg	4.57	8	63.7	36
10 Yr Avg	4.71	3	62.1	13

Potential Capital Gain Exposure: 1% of assets

Risk Analysis

Time Period	Load-Adj Return %	Risk %Rank[1] All	Risk %Rank[1] Cat	Morningstar Return	Morningstar Risk	Morningstar Risk-Adj Rating
1 Yr	8.92					
3 Yr	6.25	11	44	0.28[2]	0.61	★★★★
5 Yr	7.18	15	42	0.49[2]	0.61	★★★★
10 Yr	7.57	22	54	0.83[2]	0.85	★★★★★

Average Historical Rating (147 months): 4.6★s

[1] 1=low, 100=high [2] T-Bill return substituted for category avg.

Category Rating (3 Yr)

1 2 3 4 5
Worst Best

Return Above Avg
Risk Average

Other Measures	Standard Index LB Agg	Best Fit Index LB Agg
Alpha	0.0	0.0
Beta	0.99	0.99
R-Squared	98	98

Standard Deviation	3.54
Mean	6.25
Sharpe Ratio	0.43

Portfolio Analysis 09-30-01

Total Fixed-Income: 307	Date of Maturity	Amount $000	Value $000	% Net Assets
FNMA TBA 6.5%		65,250	66,368	3.91
FHLMC TBA 6%		62,000	61,913	3.64
FNMA TBA 6%		53,790	54,200	3.19
FNMA Debenture 5.25%	06-15-06	52,020	54,197	3.19
US Treasury Bond 6.25%	05-15-30	44,205	49,209	2.90
FHLMC 6%	06-15-11	36,950	38,956	2.29
US Treasury Bond 11.25%	02-15-15	23,600	37,605	2.21
US Treasury Note 4.625%	05-15-06	35,910	37,189	2.19
FNMA 5%	07-01-06	36,349	36,694	2.16
FHLMC N/A	07-01-29	35,299	36,295	2.14
SLMA FRN	04-25-06	35,320	35,289	2.08
FNMA Debenture 7%	07-15-05	30,015	33,138	1.95
US Treasury Note 4.75%	11-15-08	30,340	31,046	1.83
FNMA Debenture 5.75%	02-15-08	27,000	28,502	1.68
GNMA 9%	12-15-17	25,931	28,394	1.67
FNMA 9.5%	07-25-31	25,000	27,789	1.64
US Treasury Bond 5.5%	08-15-28	25,200	25,200	1.48
Fngt 2001–t8 A3 7.578%	05-25-30	23,535	24,234	1.43
US Treasury Note 6.625%	05-15-07	21,100	23,757	1.40
FNMA Debenture 6%	05-15-11	21,000	22,162	1.30

Current Investment Style

Duration: Short Int Long
Quality: High Med Low

Avg Eff Duration[1]	4.8 Yrs
Avg Eff Maturity	5.9 Yrs
Avg Credit Quality	AAA
Avg Wtd Coupon	6.78%
Avg Wtd Price	104.60% of par

[1] figure provided by fund

Special Securities % assets 09-30-01	
Restricted/Illiquid Secs	Trace
Exotic Mortgage–Backed	3
Emerging–Markets Secs	0
Options/Futures/Warrants	Yes

Credit Analysis % bonds 09-30-01

US Govt	87	BB	0
AAA	6	B	0
AA	1	Below B	0
A	3	NR/NA	0
BBB	3		

Sector Breakdown % bonds 09-30-01

US Treasuries	10	CMOs	4
GNMA mtgs	3	ARMs	7
FNMA mtgs	36	Other	11
FHLMC mtgs	21		

Coupon Range	% of Bonds	Rel Cat
0%	0.85	0.48
0% to 7%	55.79	0.98
7% to 8.5%	18.34	0.55
8.5% to 10%	17.44	4.27
More than 10%	7.59	1.94

1.00=Category Average

Composition % assets 09-30-01

Cash	3.2	Bonds	96.8
Stocks	0.0	Other	0.0

Analysis by Scott Berry 12-11-01

Strong Government Securities Fund is further bolstering its reputation as one of the top government bond offerings.

This fund's management has done a lot right in 2001. For one, it has kept the fund's duration (a measure of interest-rate sensitivity) about a quarter of a year longer than its benchmark for much of the year. That positioning was beneficial as falling interest rates gave longer-duration funds an added lift. Management has also scored by focusing on seasoned mortgages, which are less likely to suffer the negative effects of prepayments. For the year to date through Dec. 7, 2001, the fund gained 8.1% and outperformed roughly 95% of its intermediate-term government peers.

The fund's recent success is not surprising given its excellent long-term record. Indeed, its three-, five-, and 10-year trailing returns all rank in the category's upper echelon. Much of the fund's success owes to management's timely adjustments to the fund's sector allocations and duration. In the second half of 1999, for example, management shortened the fund's duration and cut its mortgage stake. Both moves paved the way for a top-half finish that year, which was impressive given that the fund's corporate bond holdings significantly underperformed during that period.

Corporate bonds may seem out of place in a government portfolio, but they have long been a part of this fund's strategy. Over time, the fund's corporate holdings—mainly investment-grade corporates and commerical mortgage-backed securities—have added to its yield and dampened its sensitivity to changing interest rates. And while they add a little credit risk to the portfolio, we don't think it diminishes the fund's appeal.

Purists may choose to look elsewhere, but we think most investors will be quite pleased with this solid offering.

Address:	P.O. Box 2936 Milwaukee, WI 53201–2936 800–368–1030 / 414–359–1400
Web Address:	www.strongfunds.com
Inception:	10-29-86
Advisor:	Strong Cap. Mgmt.
Subadvisor:	None
NTF Plans:	Fidelity , Datalynx

Minimum Purchase:	$2500	Add: $50	IRA: $250
Min Auto Inv Plan:	$50	Add: $50	
Sales Fees:	No–load		
Management Fee:	.60%		
Actual Fees:	Mgt: 0.35%	Dist: —	
Expense Projections:	3Yr: $255	5Yr: $444	10Yr: $990
Avg Brok Commission:	—	Income Distrib: Monthly	
Total Cost (relative to category):		Below Avg	

Strong Growth Inv

Ticker	Load	NAV	Yield	Total Assets	Mstar Category
SGROX	None	$17.68	0.0%	$2,108.9 mil	Large Growth

Prospectus Objective: Growth

Strong Growth Fund seeks capital appreciation.

The fund invests primarily in equity securities. Management typically selects companies that it believes have prospects for above-average sales and earnings growth per share; high return on invested capital; sound balance sheets, financial policies, and accounting methods; and overall financial strength. The portfolio can include stocks of any size. The fund writes put and call options. To a limited extent, the fund may also invest in foreign securities.

The fund currently offers Investor, Advisor and Institutional shares.

Historical Profile

Return	Average
Risk	Above Avg
Rating	★★★ Neutral

Investment Style Equity — Average Stock %

1995	1996	1997	1998	1999	2000	12-01
93%	93%	93%	95%	93%	93%	89%

▼ Manager Change
▽ Partial Manager Change

Fund Performance vs. Category Average
■ Quarterly Fund Return +/– Category Average
— Category Baseline

Performance Quartile (within Category)

Portfolio Manager(s)

Ronald C. Ognar, CFA. Since 12-93. BS'68 U. of Illinois. Other funds currently managed: Strong Large Cap Growth, Strong Advisor Mid Cap Growth Z, Strong Growth 20 Inv.

History

1990	1991	1992	1993	1994	1995	1996	1997	1998	1999	2000	12-01	History
—	—	—	10.00	11.61	15.88	18.50	18.31	23.25	35.66	27.05	17.68	NAV
—	—	—	—	17.27	41.00	19.52	19.05	26.98	75.06	–9.23	–34.39	Total Return %
—	—	—	—	15.95	3.47	–3.42	–14.30	–1.59	54.02	–0.13	–22.52	+/– S&P 500
—	—	—	—	12.42	2.35	–6.00	–14.69	–18.12	45.38	15.29	–13.89	+/– Russ Top 200 Grt
—	—	—	—	1.06	0.25	0.14	0.01	0.00	0.00	0.00	0.00	Income Return %
—	—	—	—	16.21	40.75	19.38	19.05	26.98	75.06	–9.23	–34.39	Capital Return %
—	—	—	—	1	10	46	80	69	9	28	89	Total Rtn % Rank Cat
—	—	—	0.00	0.11	0.03	0.02	0.00	0.00	0.00	0.00	0.00	Income $
—	—	—	0.00	0.00	0.45	0.46	3.52	0.00	4.49	5.23	0.07	Capital Gains $
—	—	—	—	1.60	1.40	1.30	1.30	1.30	1.20	1.20	—	Expense Ratio %
—	—	—	—	–0.10	–0.50	–0.20	–0.50	–0.70	–0.80	–0.60	—	Income Ratio %
—	—	—	—	386	321	295	296	249	324	366	—	Turnover Rate %
—	—	—	—	106.0	642.8	1,308.2	1,597.1	1,834.7	3,353.7	3,411.3	2,021.8	Net Assets $mil

Performance 12-31-01

	1st Qtr	2nd Qtr	3rd Qtr	4th Qtr	Total
1997	–6.83	17.70	14.13	–4.87	19.05
1998	10.76	5.03	–12.68	25.00	26.98
1999	10.37	5.00	–2.50	54.93	75.06
2000	18.96	–8.86	7.73	–22.29	–9.23
2001	–27.43	4.48	–23.16	12.61	–34.39

Trailing	Total Return%	+/– S&P 500	+/– Russ Top 200 Grth	% Rank All	% Rank Cat	Growth of $10,000
3 Mo	12.61	1.92	–0.25	31	64	11,261
6 Mo	–13.47	–7.92	–6.48	92	84	8,653
1 Yr	–34.39	–22.52	–13.89	96	89	6,561
3 Yr Avg	1.40	2.42	9.42	66	19	10,425
5 Yr Avg	9.52	–1.18	0.93	21	40	15,760
10 Yr Avg	—	—	—	—	—	—
15 Yr Avg	—	—	—	—	—	—

Tax Analysis	Tax-Adj Ret%	%Rank Cat	%Pretax Ret	%Rank Cat
3 Yr Avg	–1.55	29	—	—
5 Yr Avg	6.47	49	67.9	69
10 Yr Avg	—	—	—	—

Potential Capital Gain Exposure: –22% of assets

Risk Analysis

Time Period	Load-Adj Return %	Risk %Rank[1] All	Risk %Rank[1] Cat	Morningstar Return	Morningstar Risk	Morningstar Risk-Adj Rating
1 Yr	–34.39					
3 Yr	1.40	93	78	–0.73[2]	1.53	★★
5 Yr	9.52	89	83	1.07[2]	1.45	★★★
Incept	15.25	—	—	—	—	

Average Historical Rating (61 months): 3.5★s

[1] 1=low, 100=high [2] T-Bill return substituted for category avg.

Category Rating (3 Yr)

1 2 3 4 5 — Worst … Best

Return	Above Avg
Risk	Above Avg

Other Measures	Standard Index S&P 500	Best Fit Index Wil 4500
Alpha	8.1	2.1
Beta	1.23	1.12
R-Squared	35	79
Standard Deviation		38.14
Mean		1.40
Sharpe Ratio		–0.11

Analysis by Paul Herbert 11-11-01

Strong Growth Fund makes sense for the right kind of investor.

Despite its frequent moves in 2001, this fund is in an unenviable position. Like many growth funds, this one carried a big weighting in rapidly growing tech stocks early in the year, in the hopes that loose monetary policy would ignite a rally for the sector. A slew of earnings warnings and downward estimate revisions squashed those dreams, however, sending the group into one of its worst-ever tailspins. With the momentum out of the market, manager Ron Ognar rotated out of many of those speculative names and into PC-related stocks and mid-cap health-care and retail names. This positioning left the fund behind somewhat in the April tech rally, and it has been treading water in the months since. As a result of this rough going, the fund has lost 37.1% of its value for the year to date through Nov. 9, 2001, which places it in the large-growth category's bottom decile.

The fund's poor showing this year isn't an adequate reason to head for the exits, though. While the fund deserves criticism for the dismal showing, it managed to outpace 70% of its peers in 2000's difficult market. That performance has helped the fund to post trailing three- and five-year returns that land in the category's top half. It's also worth noting that Ognar has been the fund's steward for its entire eight-year history, and the fund's returns for that period are far above the category's average.

That said, the fund isn't for everyone. In filling the portfolio with fast-growing, market leaders, Ognar allows valuations to take a back seat, which can make for a rocky ride. He also holds a lot more mid-cap stocks than average, which can hold the fund back versus its category when these stocks are out of favor.

In all, however, the fund remains a respectable choice for aggressive investors who hold it in tax-advantaged accounts.

Portfolio Analysis 09-30-01

Share change since 06-01 Total Stocks: 110	Sector	PE	YTD Ret%	% Assets
⊖ Kohl's	Retail	54.2	15.48	2.53
☼ St. Jude Medical	Health	42.0	26.39	2.34
⊕ Johnson & Johnson	Health	16.6	14.01	2.33
⊕ Cisco Sys	Technology	—	–52.60	2.18
⊖ Microsoft	Technology	57.6	52.78	2.16
⊖ Laboratory Corp of Amer	Health	21.0	–8.13	1.95
☼ Sprint (PCS Group)	Services	—	19.43	1.94
⊕ Tenet Healthcare	Health	30.1	32.14	1.88
⊕ Lowe's	Retail	38.7	109.00	1.83
☼ Baxter Intl	Health	33.9	22.84	1.74
⊖ Home Depot	Retail	42.9	12.07	1.72
☼ Eli Lilly	Health	28.9	–14.40	1.70
⊕ Pfizer	Health	34.7	–12.40	1.58
⊕ Freddie Mac	Financials	14.0	–3.87	1.54
⊕ Harley-Davidson	Durables	40.2	36.97	1.49
Family Dollar Stores	Retail	27.3	41.11	1.45
☼ WellPoint Health Networks	Health	19.4	1.39	1.44
☼ Millipore	Industrials	63.9	–2.89	1.39
⊖ Express Scripts	Health	33.6	–8.54	1.38
⊕ Tyco Intl	Industrials	27.1	6.23	1.32
⊖ Citigroup	Financials	20.0	0.03	1.28
⊖ Abbott Labs	Health	51.6	17.08	1.23
⊖ Biomet	Health	40.7	17.13	1.22
☼ Fastenal	Retail	33.2	21.25	1.20
☼ Amerisource Bergen	N/A	—	—	1.12

Current Investment Style

Style: Value Blnd Growth; Size: Large Med Small

	Stock Port Avg	Relative S&P 500 Current	Relative S&P 500 Hist	Rel Cat
Price/Earnings Ratio	35.2	1.14	1.39	0.99
Price/Book Ratio	6.4	1.13	1.49	1.01
Price/Cash Flow	24.8	1.38	1.40	1.09
3 Yr Earnings Growth	25.6	1.75	1.45	1.19
1 Yr Earnings Est%	12.3	—	—	4.11
Med Mkt Cap $mil	13,516	0.2	0.2	0.29

Special Securities % assets 09-30-01	
Restricted/Illiquid Secs	Trace
Emerging-Markets Secs	0
Options/Futures/Warrants	No

Composition % assets 09-30-01	
Cash	8.2
Stocks*	91.8
Bonds	0.0
Other	0.0
*Foreign (% stocks)	2.0

Market Cap	
Giant	22.5
Large	36.4
Medium	39.2
Small	1.6
Micro	0.4

Sector Weightings	% of Stocks	Rel S&P	5-Year High	5-Year Low
Utilities	0.5	0.2	6	0
Energy	1.2	0.2	11	0
Financials	10.2	0.6	25	0
Industrials	10.4	0.9	18	2
Durables	1.7	1.1	6	0
Staples	0.9	0.1	5	0
Services	6.5	0.6	28	4
Retail	12.5	1.8	27	5
Health	37.7	2.5	38	3
Technology	18.5	1.0	65	15

Address:	P.O. Box 2936 Milwaukee, WI 53201–2936 800–368–1030 / 414–359–1400
Web Address:	www.strongfunds.com
*Inception:	12-31-93
Advisor:	Strong Cap. Mgmt.
Subadvisor:	None
NTF Plans:	Fidelity , Datalynx

Minimum Purchase:	$2500	Add: $50	IRA: $250
Min Auto Inv Plan:	None	Add: $50	
Sales Fees:	No-load		
Management Fee:	.75%		
Actual Fees:	Mgt: 0.75%	Dist: —	
Expense Projections:	3Yr: $393	5Yr: $681	10Yr: $1500
Avg Brok Commission:	—	Income Distrib: Annually	
Total Cost (relative to category):		Below Avg	

Strong High–Yield Bond Inv

Ticker	Load	NAV	Yield	SEC Yield	Total Assets	Mstar Category
STHYX	None	$7.94	12.4%	—	$990.1 mil	High–Yield Bond

Prospectus Objective: Corp Bond—High Yield

Strong High-Yield Bond Fund seeks total return by investing for high current income and capital growth.

The fund invests primarily in medium- and lower-quality corporate bonds. The average portfolio maturity generally ranges between five and 10 years. The fund may invest up to 20% of assets in common stocks and securities convertible into common stocks. It invests in mortgage-backed and asset-backed securities. To a limited extent, the fund may also invest in foreign securities.

The fund currently offers Investor, Advisor and Institutional classes.

Historical Profile

Return Below Avg
Risk Above Avg
Rating ★★ Below Avg

Investment Style
Fixed-Income
Income Rtn %Rank Cat: 5 (1996), 25 (1997), 27 (1998), 23 (1999), 16 (2000), 24 (12-01)

Growth of Principal vs. Interest Rate Shifts
— Principal Value $000 (NAV with capital gains reinvested)
— Interest Rate % on 10 Yr Treasury
▼ Manager Change
▽ Partial Manager Change
► Mgr Unknown After
◄ Mgr Unknown Before

Performance Quartile (within Category)

Portfolio Manager(s)

Jeffrey A. Koch, CFA. Since 12-95. BA'87 U. of Minnesota-Morris; MBA'89 Washington U. Other funds currently managed: Strong Corporate Bond Inv, Strong Advantage Inv, Strong Balanced.

Thomas M. Price. Since 5-98. BBA U. of Michigan; MM'92 Northwestern U. Other funds currently managed: Strong Short-Term High Yield Bond Inv, Strong High-Yield Bond Adv, Strong Short-Term High Yield Bond Adv.

History

1990	1991	1992	1993	1994	1995	1996	1997	1998	1999	2000	12-01	History
—	—	—	—	—	10.02	11.45	11.84	11.06	10.80	8.96	7.94	NAV
—	—	—	—	—	—	26.85	15.99	3.07	7.81	–7.08	–0.71	Total Return %
—	—	—	—	—	—	23.23	6.30	–5.61	8.64	–18.71	–9.13	+/– LB Aggregate
—	—	—	—	—	—	14.43	3.36	2.49	4.53	–1.87	–6.48	+/– FB High–Yield
—	—	—	—	—	0.00	10.68	9.51	9.31	10.29	11.11	11.59	Income Return %
—	—	—	—	—	0.00	16.17	6.47	–6.24	–2.48	–18.18	–12.30	Capital Return %
—	—	—	—	—	—	1	7	23	19	46	73	Total Rtn % Rank Cat
—	—	—	—	—	0.00	1.02	1.04	1.06	1.09	1.14	0.99	Income $
—	—	—	—	—	0.00	0.13	0.32	0.09	0.00	0.00	0.00	Capital Gains $
—	—	—	—	—	—	0.00	0.60	0.80	0.80	0.90	—	Expense Ratio %
—	—	—	—	—	—	9.60	8.90	8.80	9.80	11.00	—	Income Ratio %
—	—	—	—	—	—	—	409	224	145	104	—	Turnover Rate %
—	—	—	—	—	—	282.5	568.9	551.4	631.0	623.5	938.0	Net Assets $mil

Performance 12-31-01

	1st Qtr	2nd Qtr	3rd Qtr	4th Qtr	Total
1997	1.52	5.33	5.53	2.77	15.99
1998	4.42	1.57	–5.32	2.64	3.07
1999	3.62	0.76	–0.90	4.20	7.81
2000	–1.44	2.18	0.73	–8.40	–7.08
2001	6.65	–5.02	–7.82	6.33	–0.71

Trailing	Total Return%	+/– LB Agg	+/– FB High–Yield	% Rank All	% Rank Cat	Growth of $10,000
3 Mo	6.33	6.30	0.69	59	31	10,633
6 Mo	–1.98	–6.63	–3.42	47	82	9,802
1 Yr	–0.71	–9.13	–6.48	44	73	9,929
3 Yr Avg	–0.18	–6.45	–1.35	74	46	9,947
5 Yr Avg	3.52	–3.90	0.28	83	19	11,891
10 Yr Avg	—	—	—	—	—	—
15 Yr Avg	—	—	—	—	—	—

Tax Analysis	Tax-Adj Ret%	%Rank Cat	%Pretax Ret	%Rank Cat
3 Yr Avg	–4.35	48	—	—
5 Yr Avg	–0.75	25	—	—
10 Yr Avg	—	—	—	—

Potential Capital Gain Exposure: –30% of assets

Risk Analysis

Time Period	Load-Adj Return %	Risk %Rank¹ All	Risk %Rank¹ Cat	Morningstar Return	Morningstar Risk	Morningstar Risk-Adj Rating
1 Yr	–0.71					
3 Yr	–0.18	38	61	–1.03²	2.19	★★
5 Yr	3.52	40	41	–0.32²	2.07	★★
Incept	7.07	—	—	—	—	

Average Historical Rating (37 months): 3.4★s

¹1=low, 100=high ² T-Bill return substituted for category avg.

Category Rating (3 Yr)

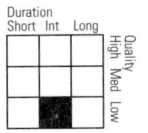

1 2 **3** 4 5
Worst Best

Return Average
Risk Average

Other Measures	Standard Index LB Agg	Best Fit Index FB HY
Alpha	–4.3	0.5
Beta	0.03	1.43
R–Squared	0	88

Standard Deviation	11.31
Mean	–0.18
Sharpe Ratio	–0.52

Portfolio Analysis 09-30-01

Total Fixed-Income: 150	Date of Maturity	Amount $000	Value $000	% Net Assets
Charter Comm 10%	04-01-09	16,050	15,528	1.83
Intermedia Pfd PIK 13.5%		14	15,195	1.79
Ameristar Casinos 10.75%	02-15-09	14,770	15,065	1.77
Telecorp PCS 10.625%	07-15-10	15,245	13,492	1.59
Allied Waste Inds 144A 8.875%	04-01-08	12,100	12,403	1.46
United Rental 144A 10.75%	04-15-08	12,305	12,243	1.44
Jostens 12.75%	05-01-10	12,010	12,010	1.41
Echostar Broadband 10.375%	10-01-07	11,295	11,464	1.35
Town Sports Intl 9.75%	10-15-04	11,650	11,301	1.33
Argosy Gaming 10.75%	06-01-09	10,500	11,235	1.32
Crown Castle Intl 9.375%	08-01-11	13,145	11,173	1.31
Adelphia Comm B Pfd 13%		124	10,550	1.24
Charter Comm 9.625%	11-15-09	11,000	10,505	1.24
Hollywood Casino 11.25%	05-01-07	10,310	10,465	1.23
Rural Cellular Pfd		13	10,409	1.22
Premier Intl Foods 12%	09-01-09	10,050	10,301	1.21
Voicestream Wireless Step 0%	11-15-09	11,935	10,085	1.19
Allied Waste Bk N/A	07-21-05	10,000	9,775	1.15
Venetian Casino 10%	11-15-05	11,200	9,576	1.13
SBA Comms 10.25%	02-01-09	11,750	9,459	1.11

Current Investment Style

Duration: Short Int Long
Quality: High Med Low

Avg Eff Duration¹	3.8 Yrs
Avg Eff Maturity	6.0 Yrs
Avg Credit Quality	B
Avg Wtd Coupon	8.71%
Avg Wtd Price	82.76% of par

¹figure provided by fund

Special Securities % assets 09-30-01	
Restricted/Illiquid Secs	15
Exotic Mortgage–Backed	Trace
Emerging–Markets Secs	0
Options/Futures/Warrants	Yes

Coupon Range	% of Bonds	Rel Cat
0%, PIK	8.54	1.36
0% to 9%	16.60	0.55
9% to 12%	59.77	1.12
12% to 14%	11.39	1.29
More than 14%	3.73	2.68

1.00=Category Average

Credit Analysis % bonds 09-30-01

US Govt	0	BB	16
AAA	5	B	56
AA	0	Below B	15
A	1	NR/NA	3
BBB	4		

Composition % assets 09-30-01

Cash	6.5	Bonds	87.2
Stocks	0.0	Other	6.3

Sector Breakdown % bonds 09-30-01

US Treasuries	0	CMOs	0
GNMA mtgs	0	ARMs	0
FNMA mtgs	0	Other	100
FHLMC mtgs	0		

Analysis by Scott Berry 07-12-01

We think Strong High-Yield Bond should be able to hit its way out of its recent slump.

The high-yield bond market had a roller-coaster ride through the first six months of 2001, and this fund felt the effects. It got out of the gate strong, gaining more than 6.5% in the first quarter, but quickly reversed course, losing more than 5% in the second quarter. The fund remained in the black for the year to date through July 9, 2001, but underperformed its average high-yield peer by a fractional amount.

The fund's troubles in the first half of 2001 stemmed largely from its below-average credit quality and above-average stash of telecom bonds. Though many of the fund's telecom holdings are big-name players, such as Global Crossing, AT&T Wireless, and Metromedia Fiber Network, even the biggest names were hit hard in recent months as earning forecasts were revised downward and defaults among smaller-cap names continued to increase. In fact, Global Crossing bonds got as low as $0.60 on the dollar before rebounding to $0.80 in early July.

Despite the sector's woes, manager Jeff Koch thinks the fund will end up benefiting from its telecom holdings and has actually added to the fund's stake in recent weeks. He argues that the sector is likely to see continued volatility, but that the yields being offered by the sector more than compensate for its added risk.

It's hard to argue with Koch given the fund's long-term success. Indeed, the fund has performed well in a variety of markets, and its five-year trailing return ranks in the category's top decile. Though Koch's current stance on telecom could add to the fund's near-term volatility, we think his solid long-term record makes this fund a worthy choice for those comfortable with its obvious risks.

Address:	P.O. Box 2936 Milwaukee, WI 53201–2936 800–368–1030 / 414–359–1400
Web Address:	www.strongfunds.com
*Inception:	12-28-95
Advisor:	Strong Cap. Mgmt.
Subadvisor:	None
NTF Plans:	Fidelity , Datalynx

Minimum Purchase:	$2500	Add: $50	IRA: $250
Min Auto Inv Plan:	$50	Add: $50	
Sales Fees:	No-load, 1.00%R within 6 months		
Management Fee:	.63%		
Actual Fees:	Mgt: 0.38%	Dist: —	
Expense Projections:	3Yr: $274	5Yr: $477	10Yr: $1061
Avg Brok Commission:	—	Income Distrib: Monthly	
Total Cost (relative to category):		Below Avg	

Strong Municipal Bond Inv

Ticker	Load	NAV	Yield	SEC Yield	Total Assets	Mstar Category
SXFIX	None	$8.63	4.7%	—	$249.2 mil	Muni Natl Long–Term

Prospectus Objective: Muni Bond—National

Strong Municipal Bond Fund seeks total return by investing for current income exempt from federal income taxes.

The fund invests primarily in long-term, higher- and medium-quality municipal bonds. The fund's manager conducts intensive research on individual issuers to uncover solid investment opportunities; especially looking for bonds whose quality is improving. The fund typically maintains an average maturity between 10 and 20 years.

The fund currently offers Investor, Advisor and Institutional shares.

Historical Profile

Return	Below Avg
Risk	Above Avg
Rating	★★ Below Avg

Investment Style
Fixed-Income

Income Rtn %Rank Cat: 33, 57, 37, 22, 14, 18, 22, 47

Growth of Principal vs. Interest Rate Shifts
— Principal Value $000 (NAV with capital gains reinvested)
— Interest Rate % on 10 Yr Treasury
▼ Manager Change
▽ Partial Manager Change
► Mgr Unknown After
◄ Mgr Unknown Before

Performance Quartile (within Category)

Portfolio Manager(s)

Lyle J. Fitterer, CFA. Since 3-00. BS'89 U. of North Dakota. Other funds currently managed: Strong Short-Term Municipal Bond Inv, Strong Municipal Advantage Inv, Strong Municipal Bond Adv.

History

	1990	1991	1992	1993	1994	1995	1996	1997	1998	1999	2000	12-01
NAV	9.22	9.76	10.00	10.25	9.23	9.52	9.24	9.82	9.95	8.83	8.63	8.63
Total Return %	4.63	13.36	12.19	11.73	–4.55	11.38	2.44	12.12	6.68	–6.48	3.32	4.69
+/– LB Aggregate	–4.33	–2.64	4.79	1.98	–1.64	–7.09	–1.18	2.43	–1.99	–5.65	–8.31	–3.73
+/– LB Muni	–2.67	1.22	3.38	–0.55	0.59	–6.08	–2.00	2.91	0.20	–4.41	–8.38	–0.39
Income Return %	7.24	7.25	6.90	6.02	5.59	5.68	5.33	5.61	5.33	5.14	5.61	4.76
Capital Return %	–2.61	6.12	5.29	5.71	–10.15	5.71	–2.89	6.50	1.35	–11.62	–2.29	–0.06
Total Rtn % Rank Cat	90	14	1	66	17	100	76	3	2	85	98	24
Income $	0.66	0.65	0.65	0.59	0.56	0.51	0.49	0.51	0.51	0.50	0.48	0.40
Capital Gains $	0.00	0.00	0.26	0.31	0.00	0.23	0.00	0.00	0.00	0.00	0.00	0.00
Expense Ratio %	0.30	0.10	0.10	0.70	0.80	0.80	0.80	0.80	0.70	0.70	0.80	—
Income Ratio %	7.20	6.90	6.40	5.60	5.80	5.40	5.40	5.40	5.20	5.10	5.60	—
Turnover Rate %	586	465	324	157	311	514	—	85	59	22	19	—
Net Assets $mil	31.6	115.2	289.8	398.9	279.8	246.7	233.8	240.9	348.7	313.5	243.4	249.2

Performance 12-31-01

	1st Qtr	2nd Qtr	3rd Qtr	4th Qtr	Total
1997	–0.06	4.39	3.79	3.54	12.12
1998	1.46	1.61	2.83	0.63	6.68
1999	1.01	–2.07	–1.93	–3.59	–6.48
2000	1.28	0.49	1.10	0.41	3.32
2001	2.42	1.08	2.09	–0.94	4.70

Trailing	Total Return%	+/– LB Agg	+/– LB Muni	% Rank All	% Rank Cat	Growth of $10,000
3 Mo	–0.94	–0.98	–0.28	92	43	9,906
6 Mo	1.12	–3.53	–1.00	33	73	10,112
1 Yr	4.69	–3.73	–0.39	25	24	10,469
3 Yr Avg	0.39	–5.89	–4.37	71	98	10,116
5 Yr Avg	3.89	–3.54	–2.09	81	84	12,100
10 Yr Avg	5.15	–2.08	–1.48	91	90	16,518
15 Yr Avg	5.46	–2.66	–1.72	95	96	22,211

Tax Analysis	Tax-Adj Ret%	%Rank Cat	%Pretax Ret	%Rank Cat
3 Yr Avg	0.39	98	100.0	14
5 Yr Avg	3.89	81	100.0	8
10 Yr Avg	4.85	93	94.2	90

Potential Capital Gain Exposure: –25% of assets

Risk Analysis

Time Period	Load-Adj Return %	Risk %Rank[1] All	Risk %Rank[1] Cat	Morningstar Return	Morningstar Risk	Morningstar Risk-Adj Rating
1 Yr	4.69					
3 Yr	0.39	29	88	–0.24[2]	1.42	★
5 Yr	3.89	30	65	0.56[2]	1.26	★★
10 Yr	5.15	29	45	0.84	1.13	★★

Average Historical Rating (147 months): 3.3★s

[1]1=low, 100=high [2] T-Bill return substituted for category avg.

Category Rating (3 Yr)

1 2 3 4 5
Worst Best

Return	Low
Risk	Above Avg

Other Measures	Standard Index LB Agg	Best Fit Index LB Muni
Alpha	–5.3	–4.2
Beta	0.83	1.02
R-Squared	41	75

Standard Deviation	4.29
Mean	0.39
Sharpe Ratio	–1.23

Portfolio Analysis 09-30-01

Total Fixed-Income: 120	Date of Maturity	Amount $000	Value $000	% Net Assets
LA Regl Transit Lease Purch 6.125%	05-01-10	13,736	14,956	5.90
LA Claiborne Law Enforcement 6.25%	03-01-19	7,500	7,688	3.03
GA Washington Wilkes Payroll Dev 0%	12-01-21	25,595	7,263	2.87
OH Toledo Hsg Mtg 7%	12-01-28	7,490	7,078	2.79
AR GO 5.23%	08-15-10	6,300	6,308	2.49
GA Rishmond Dev 0%	12-01-21	20,000	5,775	2.28
ND Richland 6.75%	05-01-29	5,090	4,791	1.89
KY Logan Wtr 5.5%	08-01-03	4,000	4,083	1.61
MS Biloxi Hsg 4.5%	09-01-05	4,000	4,040	1.59
MA Hlth 4.5%	10-01-26	3,770	3,831	1.51
TX Brazos Rvr Poll Cntrl Util 4.95%	10-20-30	3,750	3,820	1.51
OH Medina Econ Dev Multi–Fam Hsg 8.375%	10-01-23	3,800	3,710	1.46
IL Chicago Wtr 5.25%	12-01-08	3,290	3,582	1.41
OK County Fin Multi–Fam Hsg 7.125%	04-01-28	10,170	3,560	1.40
TN Johnson City Hlth/Educ Fac Brd 5.25%	07-01-26	3,475	3,527	1.39

Current Investment Style

Duration: Short Int Long; Quality: High Med Low

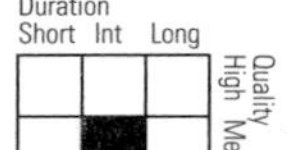

Avg Duration[1]	6.5 Yrs
Avg Nominal Maturity	16.6 Yrs
Avg Credit Quality	A
Avg Wtd Coupon	5.07%
Avg Wtd Price	92.09% of par
Pricing Service	Muller

[1]figure provided by fund

Credit Analysis % bonds 09-30-01

US Govt	0	BB	11
AAA	27	B	0
AA	15	Below B	3
A	21	NR/NA	0
BBB	24		

Special Securities % assets 09-30-01

Restricted/Illiquid Secs	0
Inverse Floaters	0
Options/Futures/Warrants	No

Bond Type % assets 09-30-01

Alternative Minimum Tax (AMT)	24.6
Insured	—
Prerefunded	—

Top 5 States % bonds

TX	10.7	IL	7.1
GA	10.5	PA	5.4
LA	10.2		

Composition % assets 09-30-01

Cash	3.0	Bonds	97.0
Stocks	0.0	Other	0.0

Sector Weightings	% of Bonds	Rel Cat
General Obligation	21.4	1.0
Utilities	3.3	0.4
Health	15.4	1.0
Water/Waste	5.2	0.9
Housing	14.0	2.0
Education	4.3	0.7
Transportation	9.2	0.7
COP/Lease	6.5	2.3
Industrial	14.7	1.2
Misc Revenue	6.1	1.2
Demand	0.0	0.0

Analysis by Scott Berry 08-03-01

Despite its recent success, potential investors may want to wait for more proof that Strong Municipal Bond is back on track.

This fund is not the same offering it was in 2000, when it lagged its average peer by a whopping 7% and ranked near the absolute bottom of the muni national long-term category. At that time, the fund was more focused on yield than total return and regularly stocked up on lower-rated issues for their added income. Now, after being remodeled by manager Lyle Fitterer, the fund is more benchmark-oriented and more focused on total return than income.

Since taking over in March 2000, Fitterer has made a number of changes to the fund's portfolio consistent with his new approach. For one, he upgraded the fund's credit quality by liquidating many of the fund's lowest-rated bonds. He also worked to increase the fund's diversification by increasing the number of holdings in the portfolio, which went to more than 125 in June 2001 from about 100 when he took over.

While the timing of the fund's quality upgrade was not ideal, as lower-rated munis rallied in the first half of 2001, the fund has posted solid gains since the first of the year. In fact, its 4.75% gain for the year to date through July 31, 2001, ranked in the muni national long-term category's top quartile. In recent months the fund has benefited from its BBB health-care stake, which got a lift from increased Medicare payments, and a dearth of California munis, which have been among this year's worst performers.

We like the changes this fund has made and think it will be a more reliable offering. However, its long-term record is in shambles. So while we think shareholders should be encouraged by its recent showing, we think potential investors will find more-proven offerings elsewhere.

Address:	P.O. Box 2936 Milwaukee, WI 53201–2936 800–368–1030 / 414–359–1400
Web Address:	www.strongfunds.com
Inception:	10-23-86
Advisor:	Strong Cap. Mgmt.
Subadvisor:	None
NTF Plans:	Fidelity , Datalynx

Minimum Purchase:	$2500	Add: $50	IRA: —
Min Auto Inv Plan:	$50	Add: $50	
Sales Fees:	No–load		
Management Fee:	.60%		
Actual Fees:	Mgt: 0.35%	Dist: —	
Expense Projections:	3Yr: $243	5Yr: $422	10Yr: $942
Avg Brok Commission:	—	Income Distrib: Monthly	
Total Cost (relative to category):		Below Avg	

Strong Opportunity Inv

Ticker	Load	NAV	Yield	Total Assets	Mstar Category
SOPFX	None	$39.29	0.2%	$3,753.2 mil	Mid-Cap Value

Prospectus Objective: Growth

Strong Opportunity Fund seeks capital appreciation.

The fund invests primarily in stocks of medium-capitalization companies that the manager believes are underpriced, yet have attractive growth prospects. Analysis is based on a company's "private market value"- the price an investor would be willing to pay for the entire company given its management, financial health, and growth potential. The manager determines a company's private market value based on a fundamental analysis of a company's cash flows, asset valuations, competitive situation, and franchise value.

The fund currently offers Investor and Advisor shares.

Historical Profile

Return: High
Risk: Average
Rating: ★★★★★ Highest

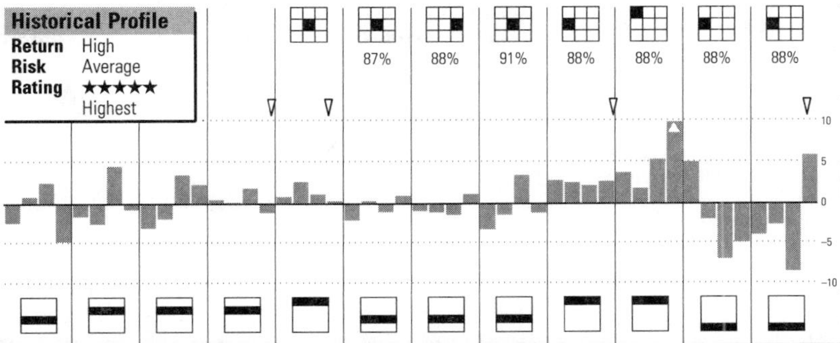

Investment Style
Equity
Average Stock %: 87% 88% 91% 88% 88% 88% 88%

▼ Manager Change
▽ Partial Manager Change

Fund Performance vs. Category Average
■ Quarterly Fund Return +/– Category Average
— Category Baseline

Performance Quartile (within Category)

Portfolio Manager(s)

Richard T. Weiss. Since 3-91. BS'73 U. of Southern California; MBA'75 Harvard U. Other funds currently managed: Strong Advisor Common Stock Z, Masters' Select Equity, Strong Opportunity Adv.

Ann Miletti. Since 10-01. BA'89 U of Wisconsin. Other funds currently managed: Strong Advisor Common Stock Z, Strong Opportunity Adv, Strong Advisor Common Stock A.

1990	1991	1992	1993	1994	1995	1996	1997	1998	1999	2000	12-01	History
16.29	21.24	24.70	28.23	27.71	33.35	35.26	37.41	38.62	44.69	42.35	39.29	NAV
–11.30	31.69	17.35	21.16	3.18	27.27	18.14	23.45	15.49	33.39	8.58	–4.80	Total Return %
–8.19	1.21	9.73	11.11	1.87	–10.26	–4.81	–9.91	–13.09	12.35	17.68	7.07	+/– S&P 500
4.78	–6.23	–4.33	5.54	5.31	–7.66	–2.12	–10.91	10.40	33.49	–10.61	–7.14	+/– Russ Midcap Val
3.93	1.17	0.27	0.25	0.48	0.78	0.77	0.30	0.14	0.22	0.43	0.17	Income Return %
–15.23	30.52	17.09	20.91	2.70	26.50	17.37	23.14	15.35	33.17	8.15	–4.98	Capital Return %
71	45	31	44	22	62	66	71	11	3	79	95	Total Rtn % Rank Cat
0.74	0.19	0.06	0.06	0.13	0.21	0.25	0.10	0.05	0.08	0.17	0.07	Income $
0.04	0.00	0.16	1.56	1.28	1.63	3.82	5.75	4.47	6.35	5.64	0.95	Capital Gains $
1.70	1.70	1.50	1.40	1.40	1.30	1.30	1.20	1.20	1.20	1.20	—	Expense Ratio %
3.30	1.10	0.30	0.20	0.50	0.70	0.60	0.30	0.20	0.20	0.50	—	Income Ratio %
275	271	139	109	59	93	103	94	86	81	87	—	Turnover Rate %
131.9	159.7	193.2	443.5	805.7	1,327.7	1,769.6	1,924.9	2,037.9	2,537.2	3,337.2	3,664.1	Net Assets $mil

Performance 12-31-01

	1st Qtr	2nd Qtr	3rd Qtr	4th Qtr	Total
1997	–1.93	11.76	14.85	–1.93	23.45
1998	14.12	0.24	–14.08	17.50	15.49
1999	3.06	15.37	–4.34	17.27	33.39
2000	7.88	–2.51	1.45	1.77	8.58
2001	–5.31	5.24	–20.09	19.56	–4.80

Trailing	Total Return%	+/– S&P 500	+/– Russ Midcap Val	% Rank All	% Rank Cat	Growth of $10,000
3 Mo	19.56	8.88	7.53	15	17	11,956
6 Mo	–4.46	1.09	–3.56	59	83	9,554
1 Yr	–4.80	7.07	–7.14	51	95	9,520
3 Yr Avg	11.30	12.32	4.49	9	41	13,787
5 Yr Avg	14.47	3.77	3.01	5	26	19,656
10 Yr Avg	15.80	2.87	1.39	4	23	43,357
15 Yr Avg	14.69	0.96	1.23	7	12	78,178

Tax Analysis	Tax-Adj Ret%	%Rank Cat	%Pretax Ret	%Rank Cat
3 Yr Avg	8.61	45	76.2	63
5 Yr Avg	11.27	33	77.9	52
10 Yr Avg	13.18	19	83.4	32

Potential Capital Gain Exposure: 10% of assets

Risk Analysis

Time Period	Load-Adj Return %	Risk %Rank[1] All	Risk %Rank[1] Cat	Morningstar Return	Morningstar Risk	Morningstar Risk-Adj Rating
1 Yr	–4.80					
3 Yr	11.30	54	70	1.43[2]	0.75	★★★★
5 Yr	14.47	57	56	2.47[2]	0.78	★★★★★
10 Yr	15.80	63	60	2.00	0.82	★★★★★

Average Historical Rating (157 months): 3.8★s

[1]1=low, 100=high [2] T-Bill return substituted for category avg.

Category Rating (3 Yr)

1 2 **3** 4 5
Worst — Best

Return: Average
Risk: Above Avg

Other Measures	Standard Index S&P 500	Best Fit Index SPMid400
Alpha	12.5	1.9
Beta	0.96	0.83
R-Squared	78	78

Standard Deviation	20.45
Mean	11.30
Sharpe Ratio	0.35

Portfolio Analysis 09-30-01

Share change since 06-01 Total Stocks: 77	Sector	PE	YTD Ret%	% Assets
⊖ Sprint (PCS Group)	Services	—	19.43	1.71
☆ Genentech	Health	NMF	–33.40	1.67
⊖ Boston Scientific	Health	—	76.21	1.65
⊖ Cox Comms A	Services	31.8	–9.99	1.60
Cigna	Financials	13.2	–29.00	1.60
⊖ Motorola	Technology	—	–25.00	1.57
⊖ Guidant	Health	42.6	–7.67	1.57
⊕ Comcast	Services	20.3	–13.70	1.56
⊕ American Intl Grp	Financials	42.0	–19.20	1.53
⊕ Phillips Petro	Energy	7.1	8.56	1.50
Praxair	Industrials	28.6	26.22	1.49
⊖ Healthsouth	Health	28.0	–9.15	1.48
Pepsi Bottling Grp	Staples	23.6	17.90	1.45
⊖ Weyerhaeuser	Industrials	21.0	9.73	1.45
⊕ Hartford Finl Svcs Grp	Financials	23.2	–9.63	1.44
⊖ EW Scripps Cl A	Services	29.9	5.94	1.42
⊕ Dover	Industrials	21.1	–7.38	1.42
⊕ Apache	Energy	8.0	–21.20	1.40
⊖ Apogent Tech	Health	29.0	25.85	1.39
⊖ HCA – The Healthcare Company	Health	24.1	–12.20	1.39
☆ Wachovia	Financials	—	23.13	1.38
⊖ Illinois Tool Works	Industrials	25.4	15.31	1.38
☆ Liberty Media Group A	N/A	—	—	1.37
⊖ PepsiAmericas	Staples	26.0	–15.50	1.37
⊕ Mellon Finl	Financials	23.8	–21.90	1.36

Current Investment Style

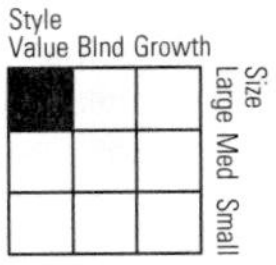

Style: Value Blnd Growth; Size: Large Med Small

	Stock Port Avg	Relative S&P 500 Current	Relative S&P 500 Hist	Rel Cat
Price/Earnings Ratio	30.5	0.99	0.87	1.29
Price/Book Ratio	3.7	0.65	0.52	1.22
Price/Cash Flow	15.1	0.84	0.80	1.21
3 Yr Earnings Growth	17.1	1.17	0.68	1.44
1 Yr Earnings Est%	–10.2	5.75	—	1.66
Med Mkt Cap $mil	10,332	0.2	0.2	1.45

Analysis by Paul Herbert 11-30-01

This fund's far-reaching style has been a burden of late, but it remains an appealing option.

This typically vibrant fund has looked lifeless for much of the past two years. Its 8.6% gain in 2000 was only good enough to rank in the revitalized mid-cap value category's bottom quintile. It has followed that showing with an 8.3% loss for the year to date through Nov. 30, 2001, which places it behind 96% of its peers for the period. These showings are quite disappointing, given that the fund's returns for the five- and 10-year periods rank in the group's top third.

Most of the fund's problems stem from its generous definitions of mid-cap and value. Like most of its category rivals, the fund's management team buys cheap stocks, which it defines as those selling at discounts to its estimates of their private-market values. Still, as the fund's above-average price multiples show, it owns more-expensive fare, on average, than its typical peer. In addition, the fund has socked more than half of its assets in giant- and large-cap stocks. These factors have combined to work against it in 2000 and 2001, as cheaper and smaller stocks have shined.

Despite the fund's lack of vigor lately, its strategy has worked over the long haul. While it hasn't paid to hold large caps or pricier stocks recently, the fund has been compensated for these biases over time. For instance, at times its sizable stakes in media and tech stocks led it to strong relative showings. Moreover, thanks to management's commitment to diversifying across holdings and sectors, it hasn't been much more volatile than its typical peer.Style purists will want to take a pass on the fund, but those looking for a solid mid- to large-cap holding will find much to like here.

Special Securities % assets 09-30-01	
Restricted/Illiquid Secs	0
Emerging–Markets Secs	0
Options/Futures/Warrants	No

Sector Weightings	% of Stocks	Rel S&P	5-Year High	5-Year Low
Utilities	1.6	0.5	6	0
Energy	10.0	1.4	17	6
Financials	14.6	0.8	19	6
Industrials	12.4	1.1	22	8
Durables	5.9	3.8	7	0
Staples	3.3	0.4	10	3
Services	18.0	1.7	29	14
Retail	5.8	0.9	17	4
Health	10.7	0.7	12	3
Technology	17.7	1.0	27	6

Composition % assets 09-30-01	
Cash	10.3
Stocks*	89.5
Bonds	0.1
Other	0.2
*Foreign (% stocks)	0.6

Market Cap	
Giant	6.0
Large	44.1
Medium	48.8
Small	1.1
Micro	0.0

Address: P.O. Box 2936, Milwaukee, WI 53201–2936, 800–368–1030 / 414–359–1400
Web Address: www.strongfunds.com

Inception: 12-31-85
Advisor: Strong Cap. Mgmt.
Subadvisor: None
NTF Plans: Fidelity , Datalynx

Minimum Purchase:	$2500	Add: $50	IRA: $250
Min Auto Inv Plan:	None	Add: $50	
Sales Fees:	No-load		
Management Fee:	.75%		
Actual Fees:	Mgt: 0.75%	Dist: —	
Expense Projections:	3Yr: $381	5Yr: $660	10Yr: $1455
Avg Brok Commission:	—	Income Distrib: Annually	
Total Cost (relative to category):		Below Avg	

Strong Short–Term Bond Inv

Ticker	Load	NAV	Yield	SEC Yield	Total Assets	Mstar Category
SSTBX	None	$9.24	6.2%	—	$1,345.6 mil	Short–Term Bond

Prospectus Objective: Corp Bond—General

Strong Short-Term Bond Fund seeks current income consistent with a low degree of share-price volatility.

The fund invests primarily in short- and intermediate-term corporate, mortgage- and asset-backed, and U.S. government bonds. It invests in higher- and medium-quality bonds. The average weighted maturity ranges from one to three years. The fund may invest a portion of its assets in lower-quality, high-yield bonds. It focuses on high-yield bonds rated BB with positive or improving credit fundamentals.

The fund currently offers Investor, Advisor and Institutional shares.

Historical Profile

Return Average
Risk Low
Rating ★★★★★ Highest

Investment Style: Fixed-Income — Income Rtn %Rank Cat: 11, 3, 2, 4, 3, 9, 12, 9

Growth of Principal vs. Interest Rate Shifts
- Principal Value $000 (NAV with capital gains reinvested)
- Interest Rate % on 10 Yr Treasury
- Manager Change
- Partial Manager Change
- Mgr Unknown After
- Mgr Unknown Before

Performance Quartile (within Category)

Portfolio Manager(s)

Bradley C. Tank. Since 6-90. BS'80 U. of Wisconsin; MBA'82 U. of Wisconsin. Other funds currently managed: Strong Balanced, Strong Government Securities Inv, Strong Advisor Short Duration Bond Z.

John T. Bender, CFA. Since 12-98. BA'88 Marquette U. Other funds currently managed: Strong Corporate Bond Inv, Strong Corporate Bond Adv, Strong Corporate Bond Instl.

1990	1991	1992	1993	1994	1995	1996	1997	1998	1999	2000	12-01	History
9.53	10.12	9.99	10.23	9.42	9.84	9.79	9.78	9.59	9.38	9.40	9.24	NAV
5.28	14.61	6.68	9.32	−1.79	12.00	6.76	6.99	4.90	4.25	7.22	4.39	Total Return %
−3.67	−1.39	−0.73	−0.43	1.13	−6.47	3.14	−2.70	−3.78	5.08	−4.42	−4.03	+/– LB Aggregate
−4.50	2.94	0.42	3.91	−2.29	2.04	1.51	0.34	−2.08	1.28	−0.96	−4.14	+/– LB 1–3 Govt
8.59	8.14	8.02	6.90	6.35	7.40	7.22	7.10	6.93	6.51	6.95	6.25	Income Return %
−3.31	6.47	−1.35	2.42	−8.14	4.60	−0.47	−0.11	−2.03	−2.26	0.26	−1.86	Capital Return %
88	16	20	9	71	33	1	27	89	7	70	98	Total Rtn % Rank Cat
0.81	0.75	0.78	0.67	0.63	0.67	0.69	0.67	0.66	0.61	0.63	0.57	Income $
0.00	0.00	0.00	0.00	0.00	0.00	0.00	0.00	0.00	0.00	0.00	0.00	Capital Gains $
1.30	1.00	0.60	0.80	0.90	0.90	0.90	0.90	0.80	0.80	0.90	—	Expense Ratio %
8.60	7.80	7.30	6.30	6.50	7.00	7.10	7.00	6.70	6.50	6.70	—	Income Ratio %
314	398	353	445	250	—	192	194	138	124	94	—	Turnover Rate %
80.1	165.0	756.9	1,531.6	1,041.1	1,105.0	1,181.0	1,320.7	1,315.1	1,224.6	1,146.2	1,281.3	Net Assets $mil

Performance 12-31-01

	1st Qtr	2nd Qtr	3rd Qtr	4th Qtr	Total
1997	1.26	2.12	2.21	1.22	6.99
1998	1.62	1.66	0.60	0.92	4.90
1999	1.45	0.80	0.78	1.16	4.25
2000	1.05	1.57	2.21	2.21	7.22
2001	3.37	1.11	0.13	−0.25	4.39

Trailing	Total Return%	+/– LB Agg	+/– LB 1–3 Yr Govt	% Rank All	% Rank Cat	Growth of $10,000
3 Mo	−0.25	−0.29	−1.03	81	70	9,975
6 Mo	−0.12	−4.78	−4.43	39	99	9,988
1 Yr	4.39	−4.03	−4.14	27	98	10,439
3 Yr Avg	5.28	−1.00	−1.25	29	78	11,668
5 Yr Avg	5.54	−1.89	−1.10	55	82	13,095
10 Yr Avg	6.01	−1.22	−0.02	70	26	17,932
15 Yr Avg	—	—	—	—	—	—

Tax Analysis	Tax-Adj Ret%	%Rank Cat	%Pretax Ret	%Rank Cat
3 Yr Avg	2.66	94	50.5	98
5 Yr Avg	2.85	95	51.4	98
10 Yr Avg	3.29	71	54.8	88

Potential Capital Gain Exposure: –10% of assets

Risk Analysis

Time Period	Load-Adj Return %	Risk %Rank[1] All	Risk %Rank[1] Cat	Morningstar Return	Morningstar Risk	Morningstar Risk-Adj Rating
1 Yr	4.39					
3 Yr	5.28	3	44	0.07[2]	0.30	★★★★
5 Yr	5.54	3	45	0.11[2]	0.31	★★★★
10 Yr	6.01	4	30	0.35[2]	0.41	★★★★★

Average Historical Rating (137 months): 4.2★s

[1] 1=low, 100=high [2] T-Bill return substituted for category avg.

Category Rating (3 Yr)

1 2 3 4 5 — Worst … Best

Return: Below Avg
Risk: Average

Other Measures	Standard Index LB Agg	Best Fit Index LB Corp
Alpha	0.0	0.1
Beta	0.27	0.30
R–Squared	30	51

Standard Deviation	1.87
Mean	5.28
Sharpe Ratio	0.22

Portfolio Analysis 09-30-01

Total Fixed-Income: 212	Date of Maturity	Amount $000	Value $000	% Net Assets
Asset Securitization 7.1%	08-13-29	29,987	32,190	2.25
Texas Utilities Hldgs 6.375%	06-15-06	30,395	31,409	2.19
Univision Net Hldg 7%	12-17-02	19,730	30,976	2.16
AB Spintab 144A FRN	01-30-06	30,000	30,260	2.11
Protective Life US Fdg 144A 5.875%	08-15-06	24,000	24,402	1.70
GMAC 6.125%	09-15-06	20,000	20,009	1.40
Railcar Leasing 144A 6.75%	07-15-06	18,133	19,197	1.34
HCA–The Healthcare 7.125%	06-01-06	18,500	18,986	1.33
MetroNet Comm 12%	08-15-07	28,375	18,728	1.31
Cendant 144A 6.875%	08-15-06	20,000	18,088	1.26
Triumph Cap CBO 0%	06-15-11	18,000	18,005	1.26
Raytheon 5.7%	11-01-03	17,595	17,911	1.25
Indosuez Hldg 144A Pfd 10.375%		699	17,511	1.22
Sprint Spectrum 11%	08-15-06	16,557	17,470	1.22
GNMA 7.5%	02-15-13	16,046	16,951	1.18
Mirant Americas 144A 7.625%	05-01-06	15,000	15,749	1.10
Monument Global Fdg 144A 6.05%	01-19-06	15,000	15,593	1.09
Wcg 144A 8.25%	03-15-04	15,000	15,324	1.07
Raytheon 6.5%	07-15-05	14,875	15,287	1.07
DaimlerChrysler Hldg 6.4%	05-15-06	15,000	15,193	1.06

Current Investment Style

Duration: Short Int Long — Quality: High Med Low

Avg Eff Duration[1]	1.9 Yrs
Avg Eff Maturity	2.4 Yrs
Avg Credit Quality	A
Avg Wtd Coupon	7.45%
Avg Wtd Price	99.14% of par

[1] figure provided by fund

Special Securities % assets 09-30-01	
Restricted/Illiquid Secs	24
Exotic Mortgage–Backed	1
Emerging–Markets Secs	Trace
Options/Futures/Warrants	No

Coupon Range	% of Bonds	Rel Cat
0%	3.52	2.93
0% to 7%	34.02	0.53
7% to 8.5%	31.63	1.10
8.5% to 10%	21.20	5.18
More than 10%	9.64	5.64

1.00=Category Average

Credit Analysis % bonds 09-30-01

US Govt	13	BB	8
AAA	18	B	0
AA	5	Below B	0
A	20	NR/NA	2
BBB	34		

Composition % assets 09-30-01

Cash	3.4	Bonds	95.4
Stocks	0.0	Other	1.2

Sector Breakdown % bonds 09-30-01

US Treasuries	0	CMOs	3
GNMA mtgs	4	ARMs	0
FNMA mtgs	7	Other	82
FHLMC mtgs	3		

Analysis by Scott Berry 12-11-01

Strong Short-Term Bond is down but not out.

No question, this fund has struggled in recent months. In fact, for the trailing three months ended Dec. 11, 2001, the fund lost 1.4%, while its average short-term peer posted a small gain of 0.76%. Enron, which recently filed for bankruptcy protection, and Global Crossing, which is on the verge of bankruptcy, have both done serious damage to the fund. Both issues now trade for pennies on the dollar, and according to management, the fund has little hope of recovering any meaningful amount. A few of the fund's other holdings have performed quite well, including Raytheon and R&B Falcon, but the damage caused by Enron and Global Crossing has dropped the fund's year-to-date return to the bottom of the barrel.

The fund's long-term record paints a somewhat brighter picture. The added yield provided by its mid-quality holdings has helped fuel the fund's long-term returns. And while the fund's recent underperformance has knocked its three- and five-year trailing returns into the category's bottom half, the fund's 10-year trailing return still ranks in the group's top third.

This fund is one of the more aggressive short-term bond offerings, and occasional bumps in the road are to be expected. The magnitude and the speed with which the fund's recent blowups have occurred are a bit unnerving, though, and should serve to warn potential investors that this fund is no money-market alternative.

That said, we think current shareholders should stay the course. Strong is known for their credit research and managers Brad Tank and John Bender have solid track records. The fund has dug a hole for itself, but if the economy gets back on track in early 2002, it should be able to make up some lost ground.

Address:	P.O. Box 2936 Milwaukee, WI 53201–2936 800–368–1030 / 414–359–1400
Web Address:	www.strongfunds.com
Inception:	08-31-87
Advisor:	Strong Cap. Mgmt.
Subadvisor:	None
NTF Plans:	Fidelity , Datalynx

Minimum Purchase:	$2500	Add: $50	IRA: $250
Min Auto Inv Plan:	$50	Add: $50	
Sales Fees:	No–load		
Management Fee:	.63%		
Actual Fees:	Mgt: 0.38%	Dist: —	
Expense Projections:	3Yr: $274	5Yr: $477	10Yr: $1061
Avg Brok Commission:	—	Income Distrib: Monthly	
Total Cost (relative to category):		Average	

Strong Short–Term Municipal Bond Inv

Ticker	Load	NAV	Yield	SEC Yield	Total Assets	Mstar Category
STSMX	None	$9.70	4.4%	—	$511.3 mil	Muni Short–Term

Prospectus Objective: Muni Bond—National

Strong Short-Term Municipal Bond Fund - Investor Class seeks income exempt from federal income tax consistent with a low degree of share-price fluctuation.

The fund invests primarily in short- and intermediate-term, higher- and medium-quality muncipal bonds. The fund's manager conducts intensive research on individual issuers to uncover solid investment opportunities; especially looking for bonds whose quality is improving. The weighted average maturity is usually three or fewer years.

The fund currently offers Investor, Advisor and Institutional shares.

Historical Profile

Return	Below Avg
Risk	Low
Rating	★★★★★ Highest

Investment Style
Fixed-Income

Income Rtn %Rank Cat: 16 | 18 | 6 | 7 | 6 | 6 | 7 | 10

Growth of Principal vs. Interest Rate Shifts
- Principal Value $000 (NAV with capital gains reinvested)
- Interest Rate % on 10 Yr Treasury
- Manager Change
- Partial Manager Change
- Mgr Unknown After
- Mgr Unknown Before

Performance Quartile (within Category)

Portfolio Manager(s)

Lyle J. Fitterer, CFA. Since 3-00. BS'89 U. of North Dakota. Other funds currently managed: Strong Municipal Bond Inv, Strong Municipal Advantage Inv, Strong Municipal Bond Adv.

1990	1991	1992	1993	1994	1995	1996	1997	1998	1999	2000	12-01	History
—	10.00	10.20	10.36	9.73	9.77	9.74	9.92	9.97	9.63	9.64	9.70	NAV
—	—	7.16	6.79	–1.49	5.37	4.87	6.93	5.55	1.17	5.15	5.17	Total Return %
—	—	–0.24	–2.96	1.42	–13.10	1.26	–2.75	–3.12	2.00	–6.48	–3.25	+/– LB Aggregate
—	—	–1.66	–5.49	3.65	–12.09	0.44	–2.27	–0.93	3.24	–6.54	0.09	+/– LB Muni
—	—	4.91	4.45	4.58	4.96	5.16	5.03	5.03	4.67	5.03	4.55	Income Return %
—	—	2.25	2.34	–6.07	0.41	–0.29	1.91	0.52	–3.51	0.12	0.62	Capital Return %
—	—	28	54	68	99	5	5	3	30	70	23	Total Rtn % Rank Cat
—	0.00	0.48	0.44	0.46	0.47	0.49	0.48	0.49	0.46	0.47	0.43	Income $
—	0.00	0.02	0.07	0.01	0.00	0.00	0.00	0.00	0.00	0.00	0.00	Capital Gains $
—	—	0.20	0.60	0.70	0.80	0.70	0.70	0.60	0.60	0.60	—	Expense Ratio %
—	—	4.90	4.20	4.50	4.80	5.10	5.00	4.80	4.70	4.80	—	Income Ratio %
—	—	140	142	273	227	—	26	16	23	49	—	Turnover Rate %
—	1.0	110.8	216.2	161.2	132.7	145.4	180.7	263.9	282.0	311.7	511.3	Net Assets $mil

Performance 12-31-01

	1st Qtr	2nd Qtr	3rd Qtr	4th Qtr	Total
1997	0.80	2.09	2.02	1.85	6.93
1998	1.21	1.24	1.94	1.06	5.55
1999	1.32	–0.77	0.55	0.07	1.17
2000	1.15	0.93	1.66	1.33	5.15
2001	1.59	1.28	1.68	0.52	5.17

Trailing	Total Return%	+/– LB Agg	+/– LB Muni	% Rank All	% Rank Cat	Growth of $10,000
3 Mo	0.52	0.49	1.19	75	14	10,052
6 Mo	2.21	–2.45	0.09	20	9	10,221
1 Yr	5.17	–3.25	0.09	22	23	10,517
3 Yr Avg	3.81	–2.46	–0.94	43	46	11,188
5 Yr Avg	4.78	–2.65	–1.20	68	9	12,628
10 Yr Avg	4.63	–2.60	–2.00	94	66	15,730
15 Yr Avg	—	—	—	—	—	—

Tax Analysis	Tax-Adj Ret%	%Rank Cat	%Pretax Ret	%Rank Cat
3 Yr Avg	3.81	45	100.0	10
5 Yr Avg	4.78	8	100.0	9
10 Yr Avg	4.59	57	99.1	76

Potential Capital Gain Exposure: –3% of assets

Risk Analysis

Time Period	Load-Adj Return %	Risk %Rank[1] All	Risk %Rank[1] Cat	Morningstar Return	Morningstar Risk	Morningstar Risk-Adj Rating
1 Yr	5.17					
3 Yr	3.81	1	29	0.45[2]	0.26	★★★★★
5 Yr	4.78	1	26	0.71[2]	0.24	★★★★★
10 Yr	4.63	2	60	0.60	0.34	★★★★

Average Historical Rating (85 months): 4.3★s

[1]1=low, 100=high [2] T-Bill return substituted for category avg.

Category Rating (3 Yr)

1 2 3 4 5 — Worst … Best

Return	Above Avg
Risk	Below Avg

Other Measures	Standard Index LB Agg	Best Fit Index LB Muni
Alpha	–1.4	–1.0
Beta	0.27	0.35
R–Squared	35	73
Standard Deviation		1.52
Mean		3.81
Sharpe Ratio		–0.85

Portfolio Analysis 09-30-01

Total Fixed-Income: 187	Date of Maturity	Amount $000	Value $000	% Net Assets
TX Harris GO 5%	10-01-09	8,375	8,930	1.86
NC East Muni Pwr Sys 6%	01-01-06	7,500	8,278	1.73
AR GO 4.75%	06-01-15	8,100	8,100	1.69
OT Northwest Trails Apt Tr Dmd	04-01-13	7,355	7,355	1.53
PA South Chester Hlth/Higher Educ 5.15%	11-01-03	7,500	7,341	1.53
AR GO 5.23%	08-15-10	7,229	7,238	1.51
NV Washoe Wtr 5.75%	03-01-36	6,500	6,638	1.38
MI GO 4.2%	08-01-27	6,500	6,541	1.36
CT Stamford Hsg 4.75%	12-01-28	6,275	6,267	1.31
KY Logan Wtr 5.5%	08-01-03	6,000	6,124	1.28
NM San 6.5%	08-01-06	5,765	5,888	1.23
OR Clackamas Hosp 5%	05-01-06	5,500	5,809	1.21
GA Atlanta Urban Resid Fin Hsg 6%	12-01-30	5,655	5,690	1.19
TN Johnson City Hlth/Educ Fac Brd 5.25%	07-01-26	5,500	5,583	1.16
TX Brazos Rvr Poll Cntrl Util 4.95%	10-20-30	5,250	5,348	1.11

Current Investment Style

Duration: Short Int Long — Quality: High Med Low

Avg Duration[1]	2.4 Yrs
Avg Nominal Maturity	2.8 Yrs
Avg Credit Quality	A
Avg Wtd Coupon	5.34%
Avg Wtd Price	101.96% of par
Pricing Service	Muller

[1]figure provided by fund

Credit Analysis % bonds 09-30-01

US Govt	0	BB	12
AAA	15	B	1
AA	18	Below B	1
A	25	NR/NA	0
BBB	29		

Special Securities % assets 09-30-01

Restricted/Illiquid Secs	0
Inverse Floaters	0
Options/Futures/Warrants	No

Bond Type % assets 09-30-01

Alternative Minimum Tax (AMT)	15.0
Insured	—
Prerefunded	—

Top 5 States % bonds

TX	12.3	MI	5.7
AR	7.1	MA	4.6
OH	5.9		

Composition % assets 09-30-01

Cash	7.7	Bonds	92.3
Stocks	0.0	Other	0.0

Sector Weightings	% of Bonds	Rel Cat
General Obligation	20.6	0.7
Utilities	7.4	1.0
Health	19.0	1.6
Water/Waste	5.6	1.0
Housing	9.8	1.3
Education	3.7	0.6
Transportation	5.5	0.6
COP/Lease	4.3	1.4
Industrial	22.1	2.2
Misc Revenue	0.5	0.1
Demand	1.5	0.5

Analysis by Scott Berry 09-27-01

Strong Short-Term Municipal Bond is a good choice for yield-starved muni investors comfortable with its added risk.

This Fund Analyst Pick has put together its fine long-term record by taking on more credit risk than its average muni short-term peer. In fact, in years past the fund has held more than 40% of its assets in nonrated bonds. And though these bonds are typically more vulnerable to an economic slowdown than higher-quality issues, a booming economy in the 1990s kept municipal-bond defaults to a minimum and allowed their added yield to fuel the fund's returns.

When Lyle Fitterer took over the fund in March 2000, he cut the fund's exposure to nonrated bonds and increased the fund's credit quality. But the fund's 40% stake in bonds rated BBB and below (including nonrateds) is still more than double its peer-group average.

After holding the fund back in 2000, these lower-quality issues have rebounded in 2001 and have helped the fund outperform its average peer fractionally for the year to date through Sept. 26, 2001. The fund's hospital bonds have done particularly well, thanks to increased Medicare reimbursements. Unfortunately, the fund's relatively short duration, which recently checked in at 2.2 years versus the category's 2.8 years, has kept the fund from standing out. With interest rates dropping, longer-term bonds have benefited more than shorter-term issues, and this fund has done well just keeping pace with its average muni short-term peer.

While this fund is not the safest short-term muni fund, we think its long-term returns more than compensate for its added credit risk and hence consider it one of the category's best.

Address:	P.O. Box 2936 Milwaukee, WI 53201–2936 800–368–1030 / 414–359–1400
Web Address:	www.strongfunds.com
*Inception:	12-31-91
Advisor:	Strong Cap. Mgmt.
Subadvisor:	None
NTF Plans:	Fidelity , Datalynx

Minimum Purchase:	$2500	Add: $50	IRA: —
Min Auto Inv Plan:	$50	Add: $50	
Sales Fees:	No–load		
Management Fee:	.50%		
Actual Fees:	Mgt: 0.25%	Dist: —	
Expense Projections:	3Yr: $192	5Yr: $335	10Yr: $750
Avg Brok Commission:	—	Income Distrib: Monthly	
Total Cost (relative to category):		Below Avg	

Strong U.S. Emerging Growth

Ticker	Load	NAV	Yield	Total Assets	Mstar Category
SEMRX	None	$15.17	0.0%	$86.3 mil	Small Growth

Prospectus Objective: Growth

Strong U.S. Emerging Growth Fund seeks capital appreciation.

The fund normally invests in the stocks of small-capitalization companies, although the fund can invests in stocks of any size. It may invest any amount in cash or cash-type securities (high quality, short-term debt securities issued by corporations, financial institutions, or the U.S. government) as a temporary defensive position. The fund may invest up to 25% of assets in foreign securities.

Historical Profile

Return	High
Risk	High
Rating	★★★★ Above Avg

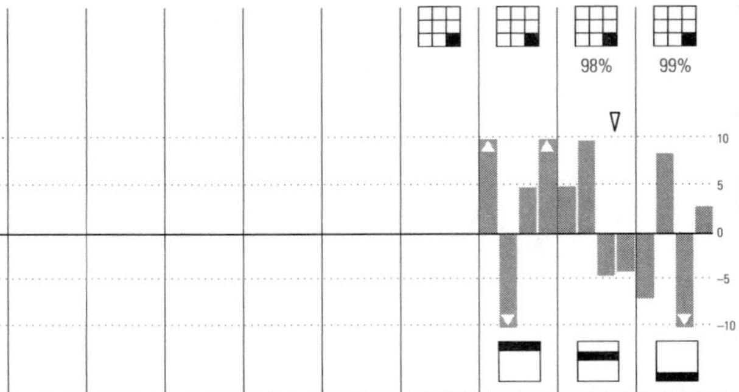

Investment Style
Equity
Average Stock %: 98% (2000), 99% (12-01)

▼ Manager Change
▽ Partial Manager Change

Fund Performance vs. Category Average
■ Quarterly Fund Return +/– Category Average
— Category Baseline

Performance Quartile (within Category)

Portfolio Manager(s)

Donald M. Longlet, CFA. Since 12-98. BA'67 U. of Minnesota.

Thomas L. Press. Since 12-98. BBA'79 U. of Minnesota; MBA St. Thomas U.

Robert E. Scott, CFA. Since 9-00. BA'90 Harvard U.

History

1990	1991	1992	1993	1994	1995	1996	1997	1998	1999	2000	12-01	History
—	—	—	—	—	—	—	—	10.00	19.59	19.17	15.17	NAV
—	—	—	—	—	—	—	—	—	98.86	0.29	–20.87	Total Return %
—	—	—	—	—	—	—	—	—	77.82	9.39	–8.99	+/– S&P 500
—	—	—	—	—	—	—	—	—	55.78	22.72	–11.63	+/– Russ 2000 Grth
—	—	—	—	—	—	—	—	—	0.00	0.00	0.00	Income Return %
—	—	—	—	—	—	—	—	—	98.86	0.29	–20.87	Capital Return %
—	—	—	—	—	—	—	—	—	17	36	82	Total Rtn % Rank Cat
—	—	—	—	—	—	—	—	0.00	0.00	0.00	0.00	Income $
—	—	—	—	—	—	—	—	0.00	0.29	0.45	0.00	Capital Gains $
—	—	—	—	—	—	—	—	—	1.80	1.40	—	Expense Ratio %
—	—	—	—	—	—	—	—	—	–1.50	–1.20	—	Income Ratio %
—	—	—	—	—	—	—	—	—	281	187	—	Turnover Rate %
—	—	—	—	—	—	—	—	—	84.4	111.6	86.3	Net Assets $mil

Performance 12-31-01

	1st Qtr	2nd Qtr	3rd Qtr	4th Qtr	Total
1997	—	—	—	—	—
1998	—	—	—	—	—
1999	20.80	2.07	5.43	52.97	98.86
2000	20.88	5.28	–3.61	–18.24	0.29
2001	–24.36	25.79	–34.16	26.31	–20.87

Trailing	Total Return%	+/– S&P 500	+/– Russ 2000 Grth	% Rank All	% Rank Cat	Growth of $10,000
3 Mo	26.31	15.63	0.14	7	29	12,631
6 Mo	–16.83	–11.28	–7.57	96	93	8,317
1 Yr	–20.87	–8.99	–11.63	82	82	7,913
3 Yr Avg	16.43	17.45	16.18	4	19	15,782
5 Yr Avg	—	—	—	—	—	—
10 Yr Avg	—	—	—	—	—	—
15 Yr Avg	—	—	—	—	—	—

Tax Analysis	Tax-Adj Ret%	%Rank Cat	%Pretax Ret	%Rank Cat
3 Yr Avg	15.94	15	97.0	10
5 Yr Avg	—	—	—	—
10 Yr Avg	—	—	—	—

Potential Capital Gain Exposure: –35% of assets

Risk Analysis

Time Period	Load-Adj Return %	Risk %Rank[1] All	Risk %Rank[1] Cat	Morningstar Return	Morningstar Risk	Morningstar Risk-Adj Rating
1 Yr	–20.87					
3 Yr	16.43	97	84	2.71[2]	1.86	★★★★
5 Yr	—	—	—	—	—	
Incept	16.41	—	—	—	—	

Average Historical Rating (1 month): 4.0★s

[1]1=low, 100=high [2] T-Bill return substituted for category avg.

Category Rating (3 Yr)

① ② ③ ④ ⑤
Worst Best

Return: Above Avg
Risk: Above Avg

Other Measures	Standard Index S&P 500	Best Fit Index Wil 4500
Alpha	31.3	22.1
Beta	1.62	1.50
R-Squared	35	83

Standard Deviation	60.01
Mean	16.43
Sharpe Ratio	0.22

Analysis by Paul Herbert 07-19-01

There's much to like about this little-known offering, and only a few things to dislike.

Strong U.S. Emerging Growth Fund has plenty of marks in its favor, not least of which is the impressive performance it has delivered over its short life. Indeed, the fund gained an annualized 29.2% from its inception on December 31, 1998, through June 30, 2001, outpacing the typical mid-cap growth fund by a big margin.

Perhaps more attractive than the fund's strong since-inception showing has been its ability to hold its ground when its strategy is out of favor. The fund's managers comb the small- and mid-cap ranks for companies offering strong revenue growth that they expect to dominate their niches. This approach paid off during 1999's growth-crazed market, and the fund delivered a 99% return. This fund's managers became uncomfortable with tech valuations in 2000, however, and replaced many positions with less-expensive health-care and financials names. As a result, the fund topped nearly two thirds of its mid-growth rivals in 2000.

While the fund's success in difficult times gives it considerable appeal, we can't give it an unqualified endorsement. For one, management consistently pays up for growth, as is shown by its high average price multiples. That can hurt the fund in downturns, such as during the period from September to November 2001, when it lost nearly 33%. In addition, a small asset base allowed the fund to profit from soaring IPOs in 1999 and to nimbly sell off tech stocks in 2000. If assets rise significantly, it may become difficult for the fund to put up the kinds of results that it has.

Overall, however, the fund is shaping up to be a strong offering for aggressive investors.

Portfolio Analysis 09-30-01

Share change since 06-01 Total Stocks: 55	Sector	PE	YTD Ret%	% Assets
⊖ CIMA Labs	Health	39.3	–44.40	4.15
⊕ Pacific Sunwear	Retail	24.9	–20.30	3.41
⊕ Advent Software	Technology	61.7	24.68	3.36
⊖ Corporate Executive Board	Services	66.7	–7.67	3.14
⊖ Investors Finl Svcs	Financials	57.1	–22.90	3.13
⊖ Advance Paradigm	Health	43.2	29.01	3.12
⊖ Cephalon	Health	—	19.38	3.08
⊖ Accredo Health	Health	53.7	18.65	2.98
⊖ P F Chang's China Bistro	Services	41.9	50.45	2.89
99 Cents Only Stores	Retail	43.8	108.70	2.79
⊕ THQ	Technology	36.2	98.85	2.79
☼ Univ of Phoenix	Services	—	—	2.51
⊕ Everest Re Grp	Financials	17.6	–1.29	2.44
⊕ Corinthian Colleges	Services	32.5	7.78	2.34
⊖ Offshore Logistics	Energy	11.1	–17.50	2.30
⊖ CH Robinson Worldwide	Services	30.1	–7.37	2.30
☼ Administaff	Services	46.5	0.77	2.15
⊖ Cytyc	Health	49.3	25.16	2.15
⊕ Retek	Technology	—	22.54	2.03
☼ Metris	Financials	11.4	–2.13	2.00
☼ Cheesecake Factory	Services	46.4	35.91	1.96
☼ Arthrocare	Health	43.7	–8.05	1.93
☼ Microsemi	Technology	51.2	113.50	1.93
⊖ Advanced Neuromodualtion	Health	NMF	73.01	1.90
⊖ SurModics	Industrials	NMF	–0.96	1.85

Current Investment Style

Style: Value Blnd Growth; Size: Large Med Small

	Stock Port Avg	Relative S&P 500 Current	Relative S&P 500 Hist	Rel Cat
Price/Earnings Ratio	41.6	1.34	—	1.29
Price/Book Ratio	6.5	1.14	—	1.34
Price/Cash Flow	27.7	1.54	—	1.26
3 Yr Earnings Growth	24.6[1]	1.68	—	0.98
1 Yr Earnings Est%	26.1	—	—	3.36
Med Mkt Cap $mil	1,029	0.0	—	0.98

[1]figure is based on 50% or less of stocks

Special Securities % assets 09-30-01	
Restricted/Illiquid Secs	0
Emerging-Markets Secs	0
Options/Futures/Warrants	No

Composition % assets 09-30-01	
Cash	0.4
Stocks*	99.6
Bonds	0.0
Other	0.0
*Foreign (% stocks)	0.0

Market Cap	
Giant	0.0
Large	0.0
Medium	37.2
Small	51.1
Micro	11.7

Sector Weightings	% of Stocks	Rel S&P	5-Year High	5-Year Low
Utilities	0.0	0.0	—	—
Energy	2.3	0.3	—	—
Financials	7.5	0.4	—	—
Industrials	2.8	0.2	—	—
Durables	0.0	0.0	—	—
Staples	0.0	0.0	—	—
Services	23.2	2.1	—	—
Retail	14.3	2.1	—	—
Health	24.4	1.7	—	—
Technology	25.4	1.4	—	—

Address:	P.O. Box 2936 Milwaukee, WI 53201–2936 414–359–1400 / 800–368–1030
Web Address:	www.strongfunds.com
*Inception:	12-31-98
Advisor:	Strong Cap. Mgmt.
Subadvisor:	Next Century Growth Investors, LLC
NTF Plans:	Datalynx , Fidelity Inst.

Minimum Purchase:	$2500	Add: $50	IRA: $250
Min Auto Inv Plan:	$50	Add: $50	
Sales Fees:	No-load		
Management Fee:	1.0%		
Actual Fees:	Mgt: 0.75%	Dist: —	
Expense Projections:	3Yr: $468	5Yr: $808	10Yr: $1768
Avg Brok Commission:	—	Income Distrib: Annually	
Total Cost (relative to category):		Below Avg	

SunAmerica Focused Growth A

Ticker	Load	NAV	Yield	Total Assets	Mstar Category
SSFAX	5.75%	$16.20	0.0%	$1,476.6 mil	Large Growth

Prospectus Objective: Growth

SunAmerica Focused Growth Fund seeks long-term growth of capital.

The fund primarily invests in equity securities. Management has selected three advisors who each invest in ten securities that represent its favorite stock-picking ideas. Each advisor may emphasize different stock-picking styles and may invest in stocks of any market capitalization. The fund is non-diversified.

Class A shares have front loads; B shares have deferred loads, higher 12b-1 fees, and conversion features; II shares have level loads. The fund also offers I shares. Prior to March 1, 2001, the fund was named Style Select Focus - Class A.

Historical Profile
Return Average
Risk Above Avg
Rating ★★★ Neutral

Investment Style
Equity
Average Stock %: 90% 91% 92%

▼ Manager Change
▽ Partial Manager Change

Fund Performance vs. Category Average
■ Quarterly Fund Return +/– Category Average
— Category Baseline

Performance Quartile (within Category)

Portfolio Manager(s)

Spiros Segalas. Since 6-98. BA'55 Princeton U. Other funds currently managed: Harbor Capital Appreciation, Scudder Focus Value+Growth A, Scudder Focus Value+Growth B.

Thomas F. Marsico. Since 6-98. BS'77 U. of Colorado; MBA'79 U. of Denver. Other funds currently managed: Enterprise Capital Appreciation A, Diversified Inv Equity Growth, Enterprise Capital Appreciation B.

Dan Chung, CFA. Since 1-00. BA'84 Stanford U.; JD'87 Harvard Law School. Other funds currently managed: Alger LargeCap Growth B, Alger Balanced B, Alger MidCap Growth B.

1990	1991	1992	1993	1994	1995	1996	1997	1998	1999	2000	12-01	History
—	—	—	—	—	—	—	—	15.24	24.06	18.90	16.20	NAV
—	—	—	—	—	—	—	—	21.93*	58.55	–19.08	–14.29	Total Return %
—	—	—	—	—	—	—	—	10.79*	37.51	–9.97	–2.41	+/– S&P 500
—	—	—	—	—	—	—	—	—	28.87	5.45	6.21	+/– Russ Top 200 Grt
—	—	—	—	—	—	—	—	0.00	0.00	0.00	0.00	Income Return %
—	—	—	—	—	—	—	—	21.93	58.55	–19.08	–14.29	Capital Return %
—	—	—	—	—	—	—	—	—	16	68	15	Total Rtn % Rank Cat
—	—	—	—	—	—	—	—	0.00	0.00	0.00	0.00	Income $
—	—	—	—	—	—	—	—	0.00	0.09	0.59	0.00	Capital Gains $
—	—	—	—	—	—	—	—	1.45	—	—	—	Expense Ratio %
—	—	—	—	—	—	—	—	–0.21	—	—	—	Income Ratio %
—	—	—	—	—	—	—	—	—	—	—	—	Turnover Rate %
—	—	—	—	—	—	—	—	51.4	255.6	367.2	326.8	Net Assets $mil

Performance 12-31-01

	1st Qtr	2nd Qtr	3rd Qtr	4th Qtr	Total
1997	—	—	—	—	—
1998	—	—	–7.49	25.96	21.93 *
1999	9.51	8.51	1.21	31.82	58.55
2000	9.27	–7.23	–4.31	–16.58	–19.08
2001	–14.23	3.76	–16.29	15.06	–14.29

Trailing	Total Return%	+/– S&P 500	+/– Russ Top 200 Grth	% Rank All	% Rank Cat	Growth of $10,000
3 Mo	15.06	4.37	2.20	24	38	11,506
6 Mo	–3.69	1.87	3.30	54	10	9,631
1 Yr	–14.29	–2.41	6.21	71	15	8,571
3 Yr Avg	3.22	4.25	11.24	51	11	10,998
5 Yr Avg	—	—	—	—	—	—
10 Yr Avg	—	—	—	—	—	—
15 Yr Avg	—	—	—	—	—	—

Tax Analysis	Tax-Adj Ret%	%Rank Cat	%Pretax Ret	%Rank Cat
3 Yr Avg	2.99	8	92.8	27
5 Yr Avg	—	—	—	—
10 Yr Avg	—	—	—	—

Potential Capital Gain Exposure: –5% of assets

Risk Analysis

Time Period	Load-Adj Return %	Risk %Rank[1] All	Risk %Rank[1] Cat	Morningstar Return	Morningstar Risk	Morningstar Risk-Adj Rating
1 Yr	–19.21					
3 Yr	1.20	81	35	–0.77[2]	1.18	★★★
5 Yr	—	—	—	—	—	
Incept	6.78	—	—	—	—	

Average Historical Rating (7 months): 3.0★s

[1]1=low, 100=high [2] T-Bill return substituted for category avg.

Category Rating (3 Yr)

1 2 3 **4** 5
Worst Best

Return Above Avg
Risk Average

Other Measures	Standard Index S&P 500	Best Fit Index Wil 4500
Alpha	6.5	1.1
Beta	1.13	0.77
R-Squared	60	76

Standard Deviation	26.02
Mean	3.22
Sharpe Ratio	–0.08

Portfolio Analysis 02-29-00

Share change since 01–00 Total Stocks: 31	Sector	PE	YTD Ret%	% Assets
⊕ Corning	Industrials	—	–83.00	6.76
⊕ Cisco Sys	Technology	—	–52.60	6.37
⊕ Vodafone Airtouch ADR	Services	—	–27.70	5.78
⊕ 3Com	Technology	—	–24.90	5.51
Flextronics Intl	Technology	—	–15.80	4.03
Sony ADR	Durables	NMF	–35.10	3.84
⊕ America Online	Technology	—	–7.76	3.70
⊕ Hewlett–Packard	Technology	97.8	–33.90	3.65
⊖ Genentech	Health	NMF	–33.40	3.61
Texas Instruments	Technology	87.5	–40.70	3.41
✷ Qwest Comms Intl	Services	—	–65.40	3.34
⊖ Citigroup	Financials	20.0	0.03	3.09
⊕ Morgan Stanley/Dean Witter	Financials	16.6	–28.20	3.08
Applied Matls	Technology	66.8	5.01	3.07
⊕ Sprint (PCS Group)	Services	—	19.43	2.92
✷ CNET	N/A	—	—	2.92
⊕ EBAY	Services	NMF	102.70	2.89
⊕ Warner–Lambert	Health	—	49.73	2.88
⊕ NTL	Services	—	–96.00	2.65
⊕ Microsoft	Technology	57.6	52.78	2.40
Halliburton	Energy	8.3	–63.20	2.31
⊖ Equant (NY)	Technology	—	–30.40	2.13
⊖ EMC/Mass	Technology	NMF	–79.40	2.09
⊖ Univision Comms A	Services	96.3	–1.17	1.92
Amgen	Health	52.8	–11.70	1.83

Current Investment Style

Style: Value Blnd Growth; Size: Large Med Small

	Stock Port Avg	Relative S&P 500 Current	Relative S&P 500 Hist	Rel Cat
Price/Earnings Ratio	47.4[1]	1.53	—	1.33
Price/Book Ratio	4.2	0.73	—	0.65
Price/Cash Flow	23.6	1.31	—	1.04
3 Yr Earnings Growth	12.4[1]	0.84	—	0.57
1 Yr Earnings Est%	–9.3[1]	5.26	—	–3.10
Med Mkt Cap $mil	32,514	0.5	—	0.69

[1]figure is based on 50% or less of stocks

Special Securities % assets 02-29-00	
Restricted/Illiquid Secs	0
Emerging–Markets Secs	0
Options/Futures/Warrants	No

Composition % assets 03-31-00	
Cash	5.6
Stocks*	94.4
Bonds	0.0
Other	0.0
*Foreign (% stocks)	13.9

Market Cap	
Giant	41.2
Large	42.1
Medium	13.7
Small	3.1
Micro	0.0

Sector Weightings	% of Stocks	Rel S&P	5-Year High	5-Year Low
Utilities	0.5	0.2	—	—
Energy	2.6	0.4	—	—
Financials	7.0	0.4	—	—
Industrials	7.7	0.7	—	—
Durables	4.4	2.8	—	—
Staples	0.0	0.0	—	—
Services	22.2	2.0	—	—
Retail	1.9	0.3	—	—
Health	9.5	0.6	—	—
Technology	44.3	2.4	—	—

Analysis by Christine Benz 12-11-01

Despite a few caveats, we think there's an awful lot to like about this offering.

This offering draws upon three growth managers, each of whom contributes his 10 "best ideas" for this portfolio. And SunAmerica certainly built a dream team in putting together its roster. The players have changed a bit since the fund's inception, but Sig Segalas, best known for the excellent Harbor Capital Appreciation, and Tom Marsico (Marsico Focus) have been aboard from the start.

The fund has certainly delivered on its promise over its three-year existence. Like other growth-oriented funds, it has racked up steep losses over the past 20 months, but its return since inception wallops the typical large-growth fund's. Curiously, its returns have also been better than those of Segalas' and Marsico's solo charges. Only 11 large-growth funds that gained more than 50% in 1999 have managed to land in the category's top quartile over the past year, and this is one of them.

Interested investors should take note of a couple of caveats, however. The esteemed growth manager David Alger, who had run a portion of this fund since early 2000, perished in the Sept. 11 World Trade Center attacks, as did many of his colleagues. SunAmerica has retained Alger's firm in the wake of the tragedy, as founder Fred Alger has returned to steer the company and has also recruited an impressive group of former managers and analysts. Still, the upheaval on Alger's portion of the fund is worth monitoring.

Another concern that won't go away any time soon is the fund's expense ratio, which is substantially higher than the levy imposed by Harbor Capital Appreciation or Marsico Focus. For investors who want to scoop up some of the best growth managers around in one neat bundle, however, this fund is hard to dismiss.

Address:	733 Third Avenue New York, NY 10017–3204 800–858–8850 / 212–551–5353
Web Address:	www.sunamerica.com
*Inception:	06-08-98
Advisor:	SunAmerica Asset Mgmt.
Subadvisor:	Bramwell Cap. Mgmt./Jennison Assoc. Cap.
NTF Plans:	Fidelity Inst.

Minimum Purchase:	$500	Add: $100	IRA: $250
Min Auto Inv Plan:	$500	Add: $25	
Sales Fees:	5.75%L, 0.10%B, 0.25%S		
Management Fee:	.85%, .22%A		
Actual Fees:	Mgt: 0.85%	Dist: 0.35%	
Expense Projections:	3Yr: $1007	5Yr: $1322	10Yr: $2210
Avg Brok Commission:	—	Income Distrib: Annually	
Total Cost (relative to category):	—		

Templeton Developing Markets A

Ticker	Load	NAV	Yield	Total Assets	Mstar Category
TEDMX	5.75%	$9.88	1.0%	$1,459.8 mil	Div Emerging Mkts

Prospectus Objective: Diversified Emg Markets—Stock

Templeton Developing Markets Trust seeks long-term capital appreciation.

The fund normally invests at least 65% of assets in equity securities of developing-markets issuers. It maintains investments in at least three developing markets. Equity investments may include common and preferred stocks, warrants or rights, and sponsored or unsponsored depositary receipts. The fund may invest up to 35% of assets in debt securities.

Class A shares have front loads; C shares have level loads; Advisor shares are designed for certain qualified investors.

Historical Profile
Return Below Avg
Risk Above Avg
Rating ★★ Below Avg

Investment Style
Equity
Average Stock %: 75% 79% 80% 83% 99% 92% 93%

▼ Manager Change
▽ Partial Manager Change

Fund Performance vs. Category Average
■ Quarterly Fund Return +/– Category Average
— Category Baseline

Performance Quartile (within Category)

Portfolio Manager(s)

J. Mark Mobius. Since 10-91. MA Boston U.; PhD'64 MIT. Other funds currently managed: Templeton Instl Emerging Markets, Templeton Developing Markets C, Templeton Developing Markets Adv.

H. Allan Lam. Since 10-91. BA Rutgers U. Other funds currently managed: Templeton Developing Markets C, Templeton Developing Markets Adv, Templeton Developing Markets B.

Tom Wu. Since 10-91. BS'83 U. of Hong Kong; MBA'85 U. of Oregon. Other funds currently managed: Templeton Developing Markets C, Templeton Developing Markets Adv, Templeton Developing Markets B.

History

1990	1991	1992	1993	1994	1995	1996	1997	1998	1999	2000	12-01	History
—	10.02	8.86	15.26	13.42	13.01	15.40	12.94	10.30	15.61	10.59	9.88	NAV
—	0.35*	–9.78	74.50	–8.58	0.36	22.51	–9.42	–18.72	51.55	–31.85	–5.76	Total Return %
—	–6.67*	–17.40	64.44	–9.90	–37.17	–0.44	–42.77	–47.29	30.52	–22.75	6.11	+/– S&P 500
—	—	–12.39	8.99	–6.17	11.12	18.37	5.70	6.59	–14.63	–1.85	—	+/– MSCI Emerging
—	0.15	0.75	0.62	0.79	1.50	1.35	1.01	1.48	0.00	0.40	0.97	Income Return %
—	0.20	–10.53	73.87	–9.37	–1.14	21.16	–10.43	–20.19	51.55	–32.25	–6.73	Capital Return %
—	—	66	50	42	38	17	78	11	91	52	67	Total Rtn % Rank Cat
—	0.02	0.08	0.06	0.12	0.20	0.18	0.16	0.19	0.00	0.06	0.10	Income $
—	0.00	0.11	0.12	0.43	0.25	0.34	0.84	0.05	0.00	0.00	0.00	Capital Gains $
—	2.25	2.25	2.20	2.11	2.10	2.03	1.96	2.11	2.02	2.09	2.09	Expense Ratio %
—	0.86	1.30	0.57	1.08	1.66	1.16	0.99	1.40	0.45	0.56	0.56	Income Ratio %
—	—	22	16	19	10	12	30	38	46	69	69	Turnover Rate %
—	22.3	179.7	1,391.5	2,000.9	2,148.2	3,306.9	3,456.6	2,182.1	2,955.2	1,540.4	1,227.8	Net Assets $mil

Performance 12-31-01

	1st Qtr	2nd Qtr	3rd Qtr	4th Qtr	Total
1997	8.46	10.77	0.38	–24.88	–9.42
1998	5.36	–21.75	–20.51	24.03	–18.72
1999	8.74	25.45	–12.17	26.50	51.55
2000	–7.16	–9.14	–11.97	–8.23	–31.85
2001	–6.36	7.89	–18.09	13.88	–5.76

Trailing	Total Return%	+/– S&P 500	+/– MSCI Emerging	% Rank All	% Rank Cat	Growth of $10,000
3 Mo	13.88	3.20	—	27	99	11,388
6 Mo	–6.72	–1.16	—	72	94	9,328
1 Yr	–5.76	6.11	—	53	67	9,424
3 Yr Avg	–0.90	0.13	—	77	94	9,733
5 Yr Avg	–6.45	–17.15	—	98	65	7,167
10 Yr Avg	2.40	–10.52	—	98	1	12,681
15 Yr Avg	—	—	—	—	—	—

Tax Analysis	Tax-Adj Ret%	%Rank Cat	%Pretax Ret	%Rank Cat
3 Yr Avg	–1.09	93	—	—
5 Yr Avg	–7.02	70	—	—
10 Yr Avg	1.60	1	66.7	1

Potential Capital Gain Exposure: –70% of assets

Risk Analysis

Time Period	Load-Adj Return %	Risk %Rank[1] All	Risk %Rank[1] Cat	Morningstar Return	Morningstar Risk	Morningstar Risk-Adj Rating
1 Yr	–11.18					
3 Yr	–2.83	87	58	–1.53[2]	1.23	★★
5 Yr	–7.55	94	65	–2.17[2]	1.42	★★
10 Yr	1.80	94	1	–0.67[2]	1.25	★★

Average Historical Rating (87 months): 2.6★s

[1]1=low, 100=high [2] T-Bill return substituted for category avg.

Category Rating (3 Yr)

1 2 3 4 5
Worst Best

Return Low
Risk Average

Other Measures	Standard Index S&P 500	Best Fit Index MSCIPcxJND
Alpha	2.4	–2.8
Beta	1.07	1.02
R-Squared	47	78

Standard Deviation	27.06
Mean	–0.90
Sharpe Ratio	–0.25

Analysis by Gabriel Presler 10-31-01

After a brief dry spell, Templeton Developing Markets is doing what it's supposed to do.

Shareholders have been bewildered by this fund's performance in recent years. It wasn't surprising that 1999's growth rally left it out in the cold. After all, manager Mark Mobius' value discipline limited the fund's stake in the wildly appreciating tech and telecom stocks that drove returns for the rest of the category. But in 2000, when developing markets dropped sharply, the fund didn't impress either. It lost 22%, more than its value-oriented rivals, partly because of its hefty stakes in struggling Korea and its lack of exposure to China.

What a difference a year can make, at least in terms of relative performance. Mobius' regional exposure has worked to his advantage in 2001, as many of his top Korean choices, particularly some beaten-down tech stocks, have rallied strongly. The fund also got a boost from Indonesian cigarette companies and a few rallying Thai stocks. Not everything has worked, of course; the fund's broad exposure to emerging Europe, particularly Poland, has hurt returns lately. Thus, while it looks better than 90% of its peers, it has dropped 15% for the year to date through Oct. 30, 2001.

There are caveats here: Except for 2000, the fund often suffers less than peers in tough markets, but overall, its gains haven't been that impressive because its value style renders it unable to maximize returns when markets rally. What's more, the fund's high expense ratio is inexcusable given its sizable asset base.

Still, the fund's annualized gain of a bit more than 1% over its lifetime isn't bad, given the volatility of its universe. Most investors can do without this asset class, but for those who really want a focused emerging-markets exposure, this is a decent—though not particularly impressive—choice.

Portfolio Analysis 06-30-01

Share change since 12-00 Total Stocks: 184	Sector	Country	% Assets
⊖ Cemex (Part)	Industrials	Mexico	5.39
Sasol	Industrials	South Africa	3.32
⊕ Cheung Kong Hldgs	Financials	Hong Kong	3.31
⊕ South African Brew	Staples	South Africa	2.81
⊖ Grupo Fin Banamex Accival	Financials	Mexico	2.42
⊕ Telefonos de Mexico ADR L	Services	Mexico	2.33
⊖ Samsung Electncs	Technology	South Korea	2.16
Telekomunikasi	Services	Indonesia	1.98
⊕ Banco Bradesco Pfd	Financials	Brazil	1.96
⊖ Barlow	Staples	South Africa	1.93
⊕ Hyundai Motor	Durables	South Korea	1.60
⊖ Akbank TAS	Financials	Turkey	1.50
⊕ Polski Koncern Nafto	Energy	Poland	1.49
⊕ Anglo American	Industrials	United Kingdom	1.49
☼ Citic Pacific	Durables	Hong Kong	1.40
Fraser & Neave	Staples	Singapore	1.39
Samsung Heavy Inds	Industrials	South Korea	1.36
⊕ Kimberly-Clark de Mex A	Industrials	Mexico	1.31
Tiger Oats	Services	South Africa	1.27
⊖ Old Mutual	Financials	United Kingdom	1.27

Current Investment Style

Style: Value Blnd Growth; Size: Large Med Small

	Stock Port Avg	Rel MSCI EAFE Current	Rel MSCI EAFE Hist	Rel Cat
Price/Earnings Ratio	12.7	0.49	0.48	0.73
Price/Cash Flow	9.6	0.75	0.63	0.96
Price/Book Ratio	1.9	0.55	0.40	0.60
3 Yr Earnings Growth	14.5	0.77	0.13	0.56
Med Mkt Cap $mil	2,916	0.1	0.1	0.69

Country Exposure 06-30-01	% assets
South Africa	14
Mexico	14
Hong Kong	9
South Korea	8
Brazil	5

Hedging History: Never

Regional Exposure 06-30-01	% assets
Europe	16
Africa/Mid East	19
Pacific/Asia	35
Latin America	22
Other	0

Special Securities % assets 06-30-01	
Restricted/Illiquid Secs	Trace
Emerging-Markets Secs	83
Options/Futures/Warrants	No

Composition % assets 06-30-01

Cash	5.8	Bonds	0.0
Stocks	93.4	Other	0.8

Sector Weightings	% of Stocks	Rel Cat	5-Year High	5-Year Low
Utilities	6.7	1.0	18	2
Energy	8.5	1.3	11	0
Financials	22.7	1.1	50	23
Industrials	21.9	1.3	24	11
Durables	5.0	1.5	16	1
Staples	13.2	1.8	13	3
Services	14.6	0.8	21	8
Retail	0.8	0.3	6	1
Health	0.9	0.3	1	0
Technology	5.5	0.4	11	1

Address:	One Franklin Parkway San Mateo, CA 94403 800-342-5236 / 650-312-3200
Web Address:	www.franklin-templeton.com
*Inception:	10-16-91
Advisor:	Templeton Asset Mgmt. Hong Kong
Subadvisor:	None
NTF Plans:	Datalynx , Fidelity Inst.

Minimum Purchase:	$1000	Add: $50	IRA: $250
Min Auto Inv Plan:	$50	Add: $50	
Sales Fees:	5.75%L, 0.35%B		
Management Fee:	1.3%, .15%A		
Actual Fees:	Mgt: 1.25%	Dist: 0.28%	
Expense Projections:	3Yr: $1172	5Yr: $1600	10Yr: $2788
Avg Brok Commission:	—	Income Distrib: Annually	
Total Cost (relative to category):		Average	

Templeton Foreign A

Ticker	Load	NAV	Yield	Total Assets	Mstar Category
TEMFX	5.75%	$9.25	2.7%	$9,748.9 mil	Foreign Stock

Prospectus Objective: Foreign Stock

Templeton Foreign Fund seeks long-term capital growth.

The fund invests primarily in stocks and debt securities of companies and governments outside of the United States. It maintains a flexible investment policy and can invest in all types of securities and in any foreign country, developed or underdeveloped. The fund generally invests up to 25% of assets in foreign debt securities.

The fund currently offers Class A, B, C, and Advisor shares, all of which differ in fee structure and availability.

Historical Profile

Return Above Avg
Risk Low
Rating ★★★★ Above Avg

	1994	1995	1996	1997	1998	1999	2000	12-01
Investment Style Equity Average Stock %		71%	71%	66%	81%	87%	86%	92%

▼ Manager Change
▽ Partial Manager Change

Fund Performance vs. Category Average
■ Quarterly Fund Return +/– Category Average
— Category Baseline

Performance Quartile (within Category)

Portfolio Manager(s)

Jeffrey A. Everett, CFA. Since 1-01. BS Pennsylvania State U. Other funds currently managed: Templeton World A, Templeton Growth A, Templeton Foreign C.

Murdo Murchison, CFA. Since 1-01. Other funds currently managed: Templeton World A, Templeton Growth A, Templeton Foreign C.

Dale A. Winner, CFA. Since 1-01. Other funds currently managed: Templeton Growth A, Templeton Foreign C, Templeton Growth C.

1990	1991	1992	1993	1994	1995	1996	1997	1998	1999	2000	12-01	History
6.99	7.63	7.10	9.43	8.82	9.18	10.36	9.95	8.39	11.22	10.34	9.25	NAV
–2.97	18.30	0.05	36.76	0.38	11.15	18.00	6.65	–4.89	39.21	–2.81	–7.92	Total Return %
0.15	–12.18	–7.57	26.71	–0.93	–26.38	–4.95	–26.70	–33.46	18.17	6.29	3.96	+/– S&P 500
20.48	6.17	12.22	4.20	–7.40	–0.06	11.95	4.87	–24.89	12.25	11.36	—	+/– MSCI EAFE
3.40	3.34	2.54	1.79	1.67	2.87	3.02	3.15	2.61	3.77	2.06	2.45	Income Return %
–6.37	14.97	–2.49	34.97	–1.29	8.29	14.97	3.50	–7.50	35.44	–4.87	–10.37	Capital Return %
2	16	17	43	49	42	25	43	98	48	10	3	Total Rtn % Rank Cat
0.26	0.23	0.19	0.13	0.16	0.25	0.28	0.32	0.26	0.31	0.23	0.25	Income $
0.30	0.39	0.33	0.14	0.52	0.36	0.18	0.85	0.77	0.09	0.30	0.00	Capital Gains $
0.77	0.80	0.94	1.12	1.14	1.15	1.12	1.08	1.12	1.13	1.15	—	Expense Ratio %
3.95	3.59	2.92	2.11	1.84	2.81	3.09	3.28	2.79	2.92	2.14	—	Income Ratio %
11	19	22	21	37	22	16	37	38	26	45	—	Turnover Rate %
934.3	1,300.6	1,709.2	3,528.8	5,305.8	7,312.5	11,081.9	14,014.3	10,861.8	13,169.7	10,742.5	8,747.5	Net Assets $mil

Performance 12-31-01

	1st Qtr	2nd Qtr	3rd Qtr	4th Qtr	Total
1997	3.47	7.46	4.51	–8.23	6.65
1998	10.75	–7.35	–17.24	12.00	–4.89
1999	6.20	15.60	–0.49	13.95	39.21
2000	–5.62	0.57	–3.94	6.60	–2.81
2001	–8.03	3.89	–13.46	11.36	–7.92

Trailing	Total Return%	+/– S&P 500	+/– MSCI EAFE	% Rank All	% Rank Cat	Growth of $10,000
3 Mo	11.36	0.67	—	36	22	11,136
6 Mo	–3.63	1.92	—	54	5	9,637
1 Yr	–7.92	3.96	—	57	3	9,208
3 Yr Avg	7.60	8.63	—	16	8	12,458
5 Yr Avg	4.79	–5.91	—	68	22	12,637
10 Yr Avg	8.57	–4.35	—	40	18	22,766
15 Yr Avg	11.60	–2.14	—	29	1	51,852

Tax Analysis	Tax-Adj Ret%	%Rank Cat	%Pretax Ret	%Rank Cat
3 Yr Avg	6.08	10	80.0	52
5 Yr Avg	2.69	25	56.2	60
10 Yr Avg	6.52	20	76.0	48

Potential Capital Gain Exposure: –2% of assets

Risk Analysis

Time Period	Load-Adj Return %	Risk %Rank[1] All	Risk %Rank[1] Cat	Morningstar Return	Morningstar Risk	Morningstar Risk-Adj Rating
1 Yr	–13.22					
3 Yr	5.50	48	4	0.12[2]	0.63	★★★★
5 Yr	3.56	59	12	–0.31[2]	0.68	★★★★
10 Yr	7.93	66	2	0.95[2]	0.66	★★★★

Average Historical Rating (193 months): 4.0★s

[1] 1=low, 100=high [2] T-Bill return substituted for category avg.

Category Rating (3 Yr)

1 2 3 4 5
Worst Best

Return High
Risk Low

Other Measures	Standard Index S&P 500	Best Fit Index MSCIPcxIND
Alpha	7.2	3.7
Beta	0.69	0.67
R-Squared	46	81

Standard Deviation	18.39
Mean	7.60
Sharpe Ratio	0.17

Portfolio Analysis 09-30-01

Share change since 06-01 Total Stocks: 129	Sector	Country	% Assets
Unilever	Staples	United Kingdom	2.40
⊕ Cheung Kong Hldgs	Financials	Hong Kong	2.35
US Treasury Bond 8.75%	N/A	N/A	2.34
⊕ E.ON Cl B	Services	Germany	2.30
Iberdrola	Utilities	Spain	1.99
HSBC Hldgs (HK)	Financials	Hong Kong	1.94
⊕ Shell Transp & Trad	Energy	United Kingdom	1.83
Hong Kong Elec Hldgs	Utilities	Hong Kong	1.70
Telefonos de Mexico ADR L	Services	Mexico	1.68
UPM-Kymmene	Industrials	Finland	1.66
⊖ Volkswagen Pfd	Durables	Germany	1.58
Banco Popular Espanol	Financials	Spain	1.54
Akzo Nobel NV	Industrials	Netherlands	1.53
CLP Hldgs	Utilities	Hong Kong	1.52
TransCanada Pipelines	Utilities	Canada	1.47
DSM	Industrials	Netherlands	1.45
⊖ ANZ Bkg Grp	Financials	Australia	1.42
BASF	Industrials	Germany	1.38
Petrobras Pfd	Energy	Brazil	1.38
Alliance & Leicester	Financials	United Kingdom	1.36

Current Investment Style

Style: Value Blnd Growth; Size: Large Med Small

	Stock Port Avg	Rel MSCI EAFE Current	Rel MSCI EAFE Hist	Rel Cat
Price/Earnings Ratio	19.6	0.76	0.64	0.77
Price/Cash Flow	10.5	0.82	0.69	0.73
Price/Book Ratio	2.3	0.65	0.44	0.58
3 Yr Earnings Growth	15.7	0.84	0.48	0.80
Med Mkt Cap $mil	12,861	0.5	1.5	0.71

Country Exposure 09-30-01	% assets
Hong Kong	14
United Kingdom	13
Japan	8
Germany	6
Netherlands	5

Hedging History: Never

Regional Exposure 09-30-01	% assets
Europe	44
Japan	8
Latin America	7
Pacific Rim	23
Other	5

Special Securities % assets 09-30-01	
Restricted/Illiquid Secs	0
Emerging-Markets Secs	26
Options/Futures/Warrants	No

Composition % assets 09-30-01			
Cash	0.0	Bonds	2.6
Stocks	95.7	Other	1.8

Sector Weightings	% of Stocks	Rel Cat	5-Year High	5-Year Low
Utilities	10.2	3.6	12	1
Energy	8.5	1.5	12	4
Financials	21.5	1.0	28	10
Industrials	22.3	1.7	36	16
Durables	6.0	0.9	17	6
Staples	3.8	0.5	6	2
Services	19.7	1.1	22	10
Retail	0.4	0.1	8	0
Health	0.9	0.1	6	1
Technology	6.8	0.7	9	0

Analysis by Gabriel Presler 01-02-02

When markets turn ugly, shareholders can depend on Templeton Foreign Fund.

This fund doesn't work miracles, but its deep-value approach often helps it sidestep nasty volatility. In 2001, a miserable year for the foreign-stock category, heavy exposure to cheap utility and industrial firms aided the fund in containing loss. To be sure, it dropped 7% of its value in 2001. Still, that loss looks better than 97% of its peers'.

The fund's performance often differs from that of its rivals, largely because manager Jeff Everett goes his own way in building the portfolio. He buys only well-established companies selling at bargain-basement prices. The portfolio's valuations tend to be among the lowest in the category, and its sell discipline is strict. In early 2001, for example, Everett abruptly cut the fund's exposure to banks and insurance firms. This proved wise, as those sectors subsequently suffered a serious sell-off.

That isn't the fund's only unusual characteristic. Everett's also willing to ignore any sector or market he considers overvalued, so the fund isn't necessarily a well-diversified option. Finally, like his Templeton colleagues, Everett dips heavily into emerging markets, where large companies—such as Petrobras—sell for extremely low prices relative to their global counterparts.

Over time, this strategy has boosted the fund's relative position, but it isn't invulnerable. In 1998, for example, when Asian markets tanked, this offering wound up in the category's basement. Still, the fund's longer-term results are some of the very best in the category—regardless of style or discipline—and the fund is one of the least volatile offerings available. Shareholders who can tolerate its quirky ways will be well-served here.

Address:	One Franklin Parkway San Mateo, CA 94403 800–342–5236 / 650–312–3200
Web Address:	www.franklin-templeton.com
Inception:	10-05-82
Advisor:	Templeton Global Adv.
Subadvisor:	None
NTF Plans:	Datalynx , Fidelity Inst.

Minimum Purchase:	$1000	Add: $50	IRA: $250
Min Auto Inv Plan:	$50	Add: $50	
Sales Fees:	5.75%L, 0.25%B		
Management Fee:	.75% mx./.60% mn., .15%A		
Actual Fees:	Mgt: 0.61%	Dist: 0.25%	
Expense Projections:	3Yr: $900	5Yr: $1232	10Yr: $2030
Avg Brok Commission:	—	Income Distrib: Annually	
Total Cost (relative to category):	Average		

Templeton Growth A

Ticker	Load	NAV	Yield	Total Assets	Mstar Category
TEPLX	5.75%	$18.00	2.2%	$13,210.5 mil	World Stock

Prospectus Objective: World Stock

Templeton Growth Fund seeks long-term capital growth.

The fund generally invests in common stocks, though it maintains a flexible investment policy that allows it to invest in all types of securities issued in any nation.

The fund currently offers Class A, B, C, and Advisor shares, all of which differ in fee structure and availability.

Historical Profile

Return: High
Risk: Low
Rating: ★★★★★ Highest

Investment Style
Equity
Average Stock %: 72% 77% 78% 81% 89% 94% 91%

▼ Manager Change
▽ Partial Manager Change

Fund Performance vs. Category Average
■ Quarterly Fund Return +/– Category Average
— Category Baseline

Performance Quartile (within Category)

Portfolio Manager(s)

Murdo Murchison, CFA. Since 1-01. Other funds currently managed: Templeton Foreign A, Templeton World A, Templeton Foreign C.

Jeffrey A. Everett, CFA. Since 1-01. BS Pennsylvania State U. Other funds currently managed: Templeton Foreign A, Templeton World A, Templeton Foreign C.

Dale A. Winner, CFA. Since 1-01. Other funds currently managed: Templeton Foreign A, Templeton Foreign C, Templeton Growth C.

1990	1991	1992	1993	1994	1995	1996	1997	1998	1999	2000	12-01	History
13.10	15.43	14.38	17.62	16.23	17.35	19.54	19.40	16.37	19.96	18.39	18.00	NAV
–9.06	31.33	4.21	32.70	0.82	19.83	20.55	16.18	–2.48	30.44	1.74	0.54	Total Return %
–5.94	0.85	–3.41	22.64	–0.50	–17.70	–2.39	–17.17	–31.05	9.40	10.84	12.42	+/– S&P 500
7.96	13.05	9.44	10.19	–4.26	–0.89	7.07	0.42	–26.82	5.50	14.92	—	+/– MSCI World
3.51	3.48	2.38	2.05	1.68	2.75	2.83	2.87	2.09	3.30	1.87	2.20	Income Return %
–12.57	27.85	1.83	30.65	–0.86	17.08	17.72	13.31	–4.57	27.14	–0.13	–1.66	Capital Return %
33	17	30	45	43	38	19	32	93	58	17	3	Total Rtn % Rank Cat
0.54	0.44	0.36	0.29	0.29	0.44	0.49	0.55	0.41	0.53	0.37	0.40	Income $
0.68	1.22	1.27	1.10	1.29	1.61	0.81	2.88	2.04	0.69	1.42	0.06	Capital Gains $
0.67	0.75	0.88	1.03	1.10	1.12	1.09	1.08	1.08	1.12	1.11	1.15	Expense Ratio %
3.70	3.09	2.62	2.10	1.76	2.40	2.87	2.81	2.53	2.60	1.83	2.11	Income Ratio %
19	30	24	29	27	35	20	42	48	32	51	24	Turnover Rate %
2,330.0	3,079.4	3,347.2	4,625.3	5,475.7	7,307.7	9,614.1	12,659.9	12,237.7	14,412.6	12,794.7	12,108.1	Net Assets $mil

Performance 12-31-01

	1st Qtr	2nd Qtr	3rd Qtr	4th Qtr	Total
1997	2.76	11.60	6.74	–5.09	16.18
1998	10.36	–5.32	–15.15	9.99	–2.48
1999	5.44	13.38	–3.63	13.21	30.44
2000	–3.51	1.04	–1.95	6.43	1.74
2001	–4.68	4.16	–9.26	11.58	0.54

Trailing	Total Return%	+/– S&P 500	+/– MSCI World	% Rank All	% Rank Cat	Growth of $10,000
3 Mo	11.58	0.90	—	35	42	11,158
6 Mo	1.26	6.81	—	32	3	10,126
1 Yr	0.54	12.42	—	42	3	10,054
3 Yr Avg	10.09	11.11	—	11	17	13,342
5 Yr Avg	8.62	–2.08	—	26	26	15,117
10 Yr Avg	11.78	–1.15	—	20	15	30,445
15 Yr Avg	12.27	–1.47	—	24	12	56,721

Tax Analysis	Tax-Adj Ret%	%Rank Cat	%Pretax Ret	%Rank Cat
3 Yr Avg	8.00	13	79.3	37
5 Yr Avg	5.81	30	67.4	58
10 Yr Avg	8.80	21	74.7	56

Potential Capital Gain Exposure: 6% of assets

Risk Analysis

Time Period	Load-Adj Return %	Risk %Rank[1] All	Risk %Rank[1] Cat	Morningstar Return	Morningstar Risk	Morningstar Risk-Adj Rating
1 Yr	–5.24					
3 Yr	7.94	41	5	0.65[2]	0.52	★★★★★
5 Yr	7.34	51	9	0.53[2]	0.58	★★★★
10 Yr	11.12	58	4	2.18[2]	0.58	★★★★★

Average Historical Rating (193 months): 3.9★s

[1]1=low, 100=high [2] T-Bill return substituted for category avg.

Category Rating (3 Yr)

1 2 3 4 5
Worst Best

Return: Above Avg
Risk: Low

Other Measures	Standard Index S&P 500	Best Fit Index MSCIPCxJND
Alpha	9.1	5.8
Beta	0.64	0.53
R-Squared	53	66

Standard Deviation	16.35
Mean	10.09
Sharpe Ratio	0.36

Portfolio Analysis 09-30-01

Share change since 06-01 Total Stocks: 130	Sector	Country	% Assets
⊕ Hsbc Hldgs (hk)	Financials	Hong Kong	2.01
⊖ Heinz Hj	Staples	U.S.	1.90
⊕ Cheung Kong Hldgs	Financials	Hong Kong	1.69
Albertson's	Retail	U.S.	1.60
Allstate	Financials	U.S.	1.53
⊕ Telefonica	Services	Spain	1.52
Abbott Labs	Health	U.S.	1.52
⊕ Nippon Telegraph & Tele	Services	Japan	1.44
⊖ Kroger	Retail	U.S.	1.43
Bae Sys	Technology	United Kingdom	1.37
E.on Cl B	Services	Germany	1.36
⊕ Akzo Nobel Nv	Industrials	Netherlands	1.36
⊕ Cable & Wireless	Services	United Kingdom	1.31
Unilever	Staples	United Kingdom	1.29
Anz Bkg Grp	Financials	Australia	1.29
⊕ Shell Transp & Trad	Energy	United Kingdom	1.25
⊕ Transcanada Pipelines	Utilities	Canada	1.24
Iberdrola	Utilities	Spain	1.22
⊕ Lloyds Tsb Grp	Financials	United Kingdom	1.20
⊖ Lockheed Martin	Industrials	U.S.	1.19

Current Investment Style

Style: Value Blnd Growth; Size: Large Med Small

	Stock Port Avg	Rel MSCI EAFE Current	Rel MSCI EAFE Hist	Rel Cat
Price/Earnings Ratio	22.3	0.86	0.70	0.81
Price/Cash Flow	10.8	0.84	0.71	0.66
Price/Book Ratio	2.8	0.82	0.53	0.62
3 Yr Earnings Growth	12.8	0.68	0.52	0.69
Med Mkt Cap $mil	16,043	0.6	0.4	0.67

Country Exposure 09-30-01	% assets
U.S.	35
United Kingdom	12
Hong Kong	7
Japan	5
Spain	5

Hedging History: Never

Regional Exposure 09-30-01	% assets
Europe	32
Japan	5
Latin America	2
Pacific Rim	15
U.S.	35
Other	4

Special Securities % assets 09-30-01	
Restricted/Illiquid Secs	0
Emerging-Markets Secs	14
Options/Futures/Warrants	No

Composition % assets 09-30-01			
Cash	2.6	Bonds	1.8
Stocks	94.7	Other	0.9

Sector Weightings	% of Stocks	Rel Cat	5-Year High	5-Year Low
Utilities	8.8	3.5	11	1
Energy	7.4	1.3	12	5
Financials	20.7	1.1	35	11
Industrials	19.0	1.7	33	17
Durables	6.8	1.7	17	5
Staples	6.3	0.8	7	1
Services	16.5	1.0	19	5
Retail	5.8	1.1	7	2
Health	3.7	0.3	5	1
Technology	5.1	0.3	7	1

Analysis by Gabriel Presler 08-31-01

Funds in the world-stock category would do well to take a page from the book of their elders.

Fifty-year old Templeton Growth Fund—the second-oldest offering in this group—is teaching its younger competitors a lesson. Since global economies faltered in mid-2000, this fund has weathered the market storms nicely, thanks to its strict value strategy and solid stock-picking. In fact, over the trailing 12-month period ending August 30, 2001, the fund has managed to post a gain of 4%, although very few of the countries in the MSCI All Country World index—this fund's universe—have been able to squeeze into the black.

Like his predecessors, manager Murdo Murchison buys mostly large, established companies selling at rock-bottom prices, and he's willing to ignore any sector or market he considers overpriced. Thus the portfolio's valuations tend to be even lower than most value-oriented funds in the group. Unlike his other bargain-hunters in the group, Murchison readily considers emerging markets, because companies like Korea Telecom and Telefonica tend to be considerably cheaper than their global competitors.

This singular approach means that the fund's performance rarely moves in lockstep with its like-minded rivals. In 1998, for example, many larger-cap conservative offerings did well, but this fund floundered, due to its exposure to tanking emerging markets. More recently, though, the fund has been successful. Murchison's horror of high prices has been a boon; early in 2001, for example, he trimmed the fund's exposure to financial stocks—often popular in value portfolios—thus sidestepping the worst of that group's subsequent selloff. The fund also got a boost form its many cyclical companies, including paper firms.

Address:	One Franklin Parkway San Mateo, CA 94403 800–342–5236 / 650–312–3200
Web Address:	www.franklin-templeton.com
Inception:	11-29-54
Advisor:	Templeton Global Adv.
Subadvisor:	None
NTF Plans:	Datalynx , Fidelity Inst.

Minimum Purchase:	$1000	Add: $50	IRA: $250
Min Auto Inv Plan:	$50	Add: $50	
Sales Fees:	5.75%L, 0.25%B		
Management Fee:	.61%		
Actual Fees:	Mgt: 0.61%	Dist: 0.25%	
Expense Projections:	3Yr: $911	5Yr: $1156	10Yr: $1860
Avg Brok Commission:	—	Income Distrib: Annually	
Total Cost (relative to category):		Below Avg	

Templeton World A

Ticker	Load	NAV	Yield	Total Assets	Mstar Category
TEMWX	5.75%	$14.86	1.8%	$7,397.1 mil	World Stock

Prospectus Objective: World Stock

Templeton World Fund - Class A seeks long-term capital growth; realized income is incidental.

The fund has a flexible policy of investing in companies and governments of any nation. It usually invests at least 65% of assets in no less than three countries, one of which may be the United States. The fund generally invests in common stocks.

Class A shares have front loads; C shares have level loads. Prior to Jan. 1, 1999, Class A shares were called Class I, and Class C shares were called Class II. On July 16, 1999, Templeton Global Infrastructure Fund - Class A merged into the fund. On July 29, 1999, Templeton Growth & Income Fund - Class A merged into the fund.

Historical Profile

Return: High
Risk: Below Avg
Rating: ★★★★★ Highest

Investment Style
Equity
Average Stock %: 81% 83% 76% 74% 82% 86% 86%

▼ Manager Change
▽ Partial Manager Change

Fund Performance vs. Category Average
■ Quarterly Fund Return +/– Category Average
— Category Baseline

Performance Quartile (within Category)

Portfolio Manager(s)

Jeffrey A. Everett, CFA. Since 6-96. BS Pennsylvania State U. Other funds currently managed: Templeton Foreign A, Templeton Growth A, Templeton Foreign C.

Murdo Murchison, CFA. Since 1-01. Other funds currently managed: Templeton Foreign A, Templeton Growth A, Templeton Foreign C.

John T. Crone. Since 12-99. Other funds currently managed: Templeton World C, Templeton World Adv, Templeton World B.

History

1990	1991	1992	1993	1994	1995	1996	1997	1998	1999	2000	12-01	History
12.41	14.27	13.06	15.71	14.17	14.91	16.55	16.82	15.93	18.69	16.48	14.86	NAV
–15.90	29.77	3.25	33.61	0.88	21.55	21.45	19.23	6.01	28.12	–2.53	–8.10	Total Return %
–12.79	–0.71	–4.37	23.55	–0.44	–15.98	–1.49	–14.12	–22.56	7.08	6.58	3.78	+/– S&P 500
1.12	11.49	8.48	11.10	–4.20	0.83	7.97	3.47	–18.33	3.18	10.65	—	+/– MSCI World
3.26	3.50	2.71	2.08	1.81	2.64	2.93	2.73	2.14	2.42	1.46	1.62	Income Return %
–19.16	26.27	0.54	31.52	–0.93	18.91	18.53	16.50	3.87	25.70	–3.99	–9.72	Capital Return %
71	21	39	42	42	28	16	23	73	63	25	14	Total Rtn % Rank Cat
0.52	0.43	0.38	0.27	0.28	0.37	0.43	0.44	0.36	0.38	0.27	0.27	Income $
0.75	1.29	1.21	1.37	1.46	1.88	1.04	2.60	1.39	1.09	1.40	0.00	Capital Gains $
0.69	0.72	0.86	1.02	1.04	1.05	1.03	1.03	1.04	1.04	1.07	1.09	Expense Ratio %
3.28	3.23	2.76	2.13	1.67	2.18	2.66	2.58	2.34	1.99	1.52	1.79	Income Ratio %
20	23	27	24	31	34	22	39	43	36	50	25	Turnover Rate %
3,667.5	4,243.9	3,981.7	4,986.1	5,020.2	5,987.9	7,160.4	8,682.0	8,723.6	9,957.2	8,448.3	7,060.1	Net Assets $mil

Performance 12-31-01

	1st Qtr	2nd Qtr	3rd Qtr	4th Qtr	Total
1997	3.81	13.21	7.97	–6.03	19.23
1998	12.19	–4.61	–14.06	15.26	6.01
1999	3.64	11.51	–3.80	15.24	28.12
2000	–1.34	–1.95	0.55	0.21	–2.53
2001	–8.68	2.59	–13.54	13.45	–8.10

Trailing	Total Return%	+/– S&P 500	+/– MSCI World	% Rank All	% Rank Cat	Growth of $10,000
3 Mo	13.45	2.76	—	28	22	11,345
6 Mo	–1.91	3.65	—	46	7	9,809
1 Yr	–8.10	3.78	—	57	14	9,190
3 Yr Avg	4.70	5.72	—	33	26	11,477
5 Yr Avg	7.72	–2.97	—	31	32	14,507
10 Yr Avg	11.54	–1.39	—	22	18	29,802
15 Yr Avg	11.22	–2.51	—	32	18	49,308

Tax Analysis	Tax-Adj Ret%	%Rank Cat	%Pretax Ret	%Rank Cat
3 Yr Avg	2.87	28	61.1	69
5 Yr Avg	5.28	38	68.3	55
10 Yr Avg	8.43	24	73.0	62

Potential Capital Gain Exposure: 11% of assets

Risk Analysis

Time Period	Load-Adj Return %	Risk %Rank[1] All	Risk %Rank[1] Cat	Morningstar Return	Morningstar Risk	Morningstar Risk-Adj Rating
1 Yr	–13.38					
3 Yr	2.65	55	25	–0.48[2]	0.72	★★★★
5 Yr	6.46	59	24	0.32[2]	0.68	★★★★
10 Yr	10.88	65	19	2.08[2]	0.66	★★★★★

Average Historical Rating (193 months): 3.8★s

[1]1=low, 100=high [2] T-Bill return substituted for category avg.

Category Rating (3 Yr)

1 2 3 4 5
Worst Best

Return: Above Avg
Risk: Below Avg

Other Measures	Standard Index S&P 500	Best Fit Index MSCIPCxJND
Alpha	4.5	0.7
Beta	0.76	0.63
R-Squared	64	82

Standard Deviation	16.83
Mean	4.70
Sharpe Ratio	–0.02

Portfolio Analysis 09-30-01

Share change since 06–01 Total Stocks: 136	Sector	Country	% Assets
⊕ Cheung Kong Hldgs	Financials	Hong Kong	3.69
Petrochina	Energy	China	2.16
E.ON Cl B	Services	Germany	2.10
⊕ XL Cap Cl A	Financials	Bermuda	2.03
HCA – The Healthcare Company	Health	U.S.	1.98
ACE	Financials	Bermuda	1.95
Kroger	Retail	U.S.	1.82
⊕ Pharmacia	Health	U.S.	1.67
Iberdrola	Utilities	Spain	1.54
⊕ American Intl Grp	Financials	U.S.	1.50
Korea Elec Pwr	Utilities	South Korea	1.39
⊕ Royal Dutch Petro	Energy	Netherlands	1.37
US Treasury Note 6.5%	N/A	N/A	1.36
⊕ WorldCom	Services	U.S.	1.35
WR Berkley	Financials	U.S.	1.34
Merrill Lynch	Financials	U.S.	1.33
US Treasury Bond 6.25%	N/A	N/A	1.33
Royal Bk of Scotland	Financials	United Kingdom	1.30
Golden West Finl	Financials	U.S.	1.25
Lockheed Martin	Industrials	U.S.	1.24

Current Investment Style

Style: Value Blnd Growth; Size: Large Med Small

	Stock Port Avg	Rel MSCI EAFE Current	Rel MSCI EAFE Hist	Rel Cat
Price/Earnings Ratio	23.6	0.91	0.73	0.85
Price/Cash Flow	13.5	1.05	0.83	0.82
Price/Book Ratio	2.8	0.80	0.61	0.60
3 Yr Earnings Growth	15.5	0.83	0.83	0.83
Med Mkt Cap $mil	15,080	0.5	0.5	0.63

Country Exposure 09-30-01	% assets
U.S.	33
Hong Kong	7
United Kingdom	7
South Korea	5
Netherlands	4

Hedging History: Never

Special Securities % assets 09-30-01	
Restricted/Illiquid Secs	1
Emerging-Markets Secs	21
Options/Futures/Warrants	No

Composition % assets 09-30-01			
Cash	2.6	Bonds	6.9
Stocks	88.8	Other	1.7

Regional Exposure 09-30-01	% assets
Europe	23
Japan	4
Latin America	4
Pacific Rim	18
U.S.	33
Other	5

Sector Weightings	% of Stocks	Rel Cat	5-Year High	5-Year Low
Utilities	5.4	2.2	12	1
Energy	8.6	1.6	11	3
Financials	29.7	1.6	40	24
Industrials	13.1	1.2	30	13
Durables	8.3	2.1	16	5
Staples	3.9	0.5	4	0
Services	11.4	0.7	19	5
Retail	4.6	0.9	7	2
Health	7.7	0.6	9	1
Technology	7.2	0.5	12	2

Analysis by Gabriel Presler 08-30-01

On the whole, no news is good news for Templeton World Fund—especially lately.

As global markets flounder, this fund—one of the most devoted value offerings in the world stock category—is staying the course. As usual, its portfolio has changed very little recently. Manager Jeff Everett buys large, established companies selling at bargain-basement prices, so this portfolio's valuations tend to be even lower than the average value-oriented rival in the group. On top of being more price-conscious than its peers, the fund is also a bit braver; Everett's not afraid of emerging markets, where large companies, such as Petrochina, sell for drastically low prices relative to their global counterparts. Finally, the fund holds its stocks for the long haul, especially when markets turn sour; thus far this year, for example, the fund's turnover rate is around 8%.

Unusual characteristics like these mean that the fund's performance often differs markedly from that of like-minded rivals. In 1999, for example, the fund posted a gain of more than 28%—significantly more than other value-oriented world-stock funds—thanks to heavy exposure in rallying Asia. Over the past year, while utility and financials companies (such as Germany's E.On) have provided a boost as global stock markets have sank, the fund's exposure to Hong Kong and a few other Asian markets has dragged on returns relative to more-conservative peers. Thus, the fund's loss of 12% over the trailing 12-month period lags most other value-oriented funds.

This lapse is fairly unusual for the fund, though. And it has some other welcome traits, including a higher-than-average yield. What's more, it hasn't been any more volatile than its comparable peers, despite its emerging-markets exposure. Thus, it's tough to argue with the fund's long-term results, which are some of the best in the category—regardless of style or discipline.

Address:	One Franklin Parkway San Mateo, CA 94403 800–342–5236 / 650–312–3200
Web Address:	www.franklin–templeton.com
Inception:	01-17-78
Advisor:	Templeton Global Adv.
Subadvisor:	None
NTF Plans:	Datalynx , Fidelity Inst.

Minimum Purchase:	$1000	Add: $50	IRA: $250
Min Auto Inv Plan:	$1000	Add: $50	
Sales Fees:	5.75%L, 0.25%B		
Management Fee:	.75% mx./.60% mn., .15%A		
Actual Fees:	Mgt: 0.61%	Dist: 0.25%	
Expense Projections:	3Yr: $890	5Yr: $1121	10Yr: $1784
Avg Brok Commission:	—	Income Distrib: Annually	
Total Cost (relative to category):	—		

Third Avenue Real Estate Value

Ticker	Load	NAV	Yield	Total Assets	Mstar Category
TAREX	None	$15.78	1.2%	$76.6 mil	Spec Real Estate

Prospectus Objective: Specialty—Real Estate

Third Avenue Real Estate Value Fund seeks long-term capital appreciation.

The fund normally invests at least 65% of assets in equity and debt securities of companies in the real-estate industry. Management seeks to acquire securities of well-financed companies at a substantial discount to the estimate of the issuing company's private market value or liquidation value. The fund is non-diversified.

Historical Profile
Return High
Risk Low
Rating ★★★★★ Highest

Investment Style
Equity
Average Stock %: 76% (1998), 100% (1999), 89% (2000), 89% (12-01)

▼ Manager Change
▽ Partial Manager Change

Fund Performance vs. Category Average
■ Quarterly Fund Return +/– Category Average
— Category Baseline

Performance Quartile (within Category)

Portfolio Manager(s)

Michael Winer. Since 9-98.

1990	1991	1992	1993	1994	1995	1996	1997	1998	1999	2000	12-01	History
—	—	—	—	—	—	—	—	10.65	10.89	13.68	15.78	NAV
—	—	—	—	—	—	—	—	7.47*	5.17	30.91	18.20	Total Return %
—	—	—	—	—	—	—	—	–13.78*	–15.86	40.01	30.08	+/– S&P 500
—	—	—	—	—	—	—	—	—	7.75	–0.13	5.84	+/– Wilshire REIT
—	—	—	—	—	—	—	—	0.97	2.37	2.49	1.37	Income Return %
—	—	—	—	—	—	—	—	6.50	2.81	28.42	16.83	Capital Return %
—	—	—	—	—	—	—	—	—	2	19	5	Total Rtn % Rank Cat
—	—	—	—	—	—	—	—	0.10	0.25	0.27	0.19	Income $
—	—	—	—	—	—	—	—	0.00	0.06	0.29	0.20	Capital Gains $
—	—	—	—	—	—	—	—	1.87	1.87	1.50	—	Expense Ratio %
—	—	—	—	—	—	—	—	3.20	3.20	3.89	—	Income Ratio %
—	—	—	—	—	—	—	—	5	5	23	—	Turnover Rate %
—	—	—	—	—	—	—	—	2.9	10.4	27.5	—	Net Assets $mil

Performance 12-31-01

	1st Qtr	2nd Qtr	3rd Qtr	4th Qtr	Total
1997	—	—	—	—	—
1998	—	—	—	7.58	7.47 *
1999	0.85	10.71	–6.73	1.00	5.17
2000	9.46	6.38	8.91	3.23	30.91
2001	5.56	8.17	–1.98	5.62	18.20

Trailing	Total Return%	+/– S&P 500	+/– Wil REIT	% Rank All	% Rank Cat	Growth of $10,000
3 Mo	5.62	–5.07	0.73	63	17	10,562
6 Mo	3.52	9.07	1.15	12	10	10,352
1 Yr	18.20	30.08	5.84	2	5	11,820
3 Yr Avg	17.62	18.65	4.84	3	1	16,274
5 Yr Avg	—	—	—	—	—	—
10 Yr Avg	—	—	—	—	—	—
15 Yr Avg	—	—	—	—	—	—

Tax Analysis	Tax-Adj Ret%	%Rank Cat	%Pretax Ret	%Rank Cat
3 Yr Avg	16.27	1	92.3	2
5 Yr Avg	—	—	—	—
10 Yr Avg	—	—	—	—

Potential Capital Gain Exposure: 14% of assets

Risk Analysis

Time Period	Load-Adj Return %	Risk %Rank[1] All	Risk %Rank[1] Cat	Morningstar Return	Morningstar Risk	Morningstar Risk-Adj Rating
1 Yr	18.20					
3 Yr	17.62	32	1	3.03[2]	0.32	★★★★★
5 Yr	—	—	—	—	—	
Incept	18.52	—	—	—	—	

Average Historical Rating (4 months): 5.0★s

[1]1=low, 100=high [2] T-Bill return substituted for category avg.

Category Rating (3 Yr)

1 2 3 4 5 — Worst … Best

Return High
Risk Low

Other Measures	Standard Index S&P 500	Best Fit Index SPMid400
Alpha	14.3	10.3
Beta	0.31	0.32
R-Squared	26	38

Standard Deviation	11.84
Mean	17.62
Sharpe Ratio	1.22

Portfolio Analysis 11-30-01

Share chng since 09-01 Total Stocks: 25	Subsector	PE	YTD Ret%	% Assets
⊕ Forest City Enterprises Cl A	Diversified	19.0	48.90	12.24
⊕ Brookfield Properties	Diversified	22.9	–0.80	9.06
⊕ Catellus Dev	Diversified	21.2	5.14	8.72
⊕ LNR Ppty	Diversified	8.5	41.97	7.62
☼ Vornado Realty Tr	Retail	17.6	16.25	6.67
⊕ Wellsford Real Properties	Diversified	36.3	22.03	6.31
Saint Joe	Diversified	25.7	26.62	6.07
⊕ Security Cap Grp Cl B	Diversified	11.3	26.45	5.99
⊕ Trammel Crow	Diversified	29.3	–13.30	3.85
Consolidated–Tomoka Land	Financials	13.2	69.40	3.60
⊕ Prime Grp Realty Tr	Industrial/Office	83.9	–30.50	3.03
☼ The St Joe	N/A	—	—	2.96
⊕ Tejon Ranch	Staples	NMF	24.27	2.91
⊕ Avatar Hldgs	Dvlp./Man. Home	43.6	11.53	2.82
Jones Lang LaSalle	Financials	—	30.09	2.60
Koger Equity	Industrial/Office	13.7	26.35	2.46
⊕ American Land Lease	N/A	—	—	1.95
Burnham Pacific Properties	Retail	—	18.30	1.84
Anthracite Cap Pfd	Mortgage Backed	8.0	60.14	1.64
First Amer	Financials	9.1	–42.20	1.35
Lodigan Cap 7%	N/A	—	—	1.27
LNR Ppty 9.375%	N/A	—	—	1.15
⊕ Anthracite Cap	N/A	—	—	0.91
⊕ Golf Tr of Amer	Financials	—	–29.90	0.75
Imperial Credit 9.75%	N/A	—	—	0.70

Current Investment Style

Style: Value Blnd Growth; Size: Large Med Small

	Stock Port Avg	Relative S&P 500 Current	Relative S&P 500 Hist	Rel Cat
Price/Earnings Ratio	23.3	0.75	—	1.18
Price/Book Ratio	2.1	0.36	—	1.18
Price/Cash Flow	—	—	—	—
3 Yr Earnings Growth	42.6[1]	2.91	—	2.08
1 Yr Earnings Est%	45.0	—	—	0.74
Med Mkt Cap $mil	1,530	0.0	—	0.67

[1]figure is based on 50% or less of stocks

Analysis by Kunal Kapoor 08-31-01

Third Avenue Real Estate Value Fund continues to build its fine reputation.

This fund continues to amaze. After hammering the competition in its first two full years of operation, the fund is again ahead of more than 95% of its peers for the year to date through August 30, 2001. In fact, this fund's 19% gain is more than double the group norm.

The fund's willingness to go its own way is the primary reason for its success. Unlike the majority of real-estate funds, this offering doesn't own the typical office and apartment companies that populate most rivals' portfolios. Instead it owns stocks such as Forest City Enterprises and Tejon Ranch that few others do. That could have been a problem in 2000, when mainstream stocks were roaring. But the offering managed to hold its own (unlike similar-minded peers—such as Longleaf Partners Realty). And the fund continues to do well in 2001, in a market more conducive to its style.

To be sure, investors should consider several factors before jumping on board here. For one, because the fund doesn't concentrate on REITs, it won't satisfy those who want income. And because it owns atypical real-estate holdings, it won't sit well with purists. Thus, investors may actually consider this fund for the small-cap value portion of their portfolios. Moreover, the fund's independent streak means that it will underperform from time to time, so investors shouldn't let their expectations get out of reach.

That said, lead manager Mike Winer deserves the credit for the fund's fast start. He is truly shaping this into one of the category's finest options.

Special Securities % assets 11-30-01	
Restricted/Illiquid Secs	1
Emerging-Markets Secs	0
Options/Futures/Warrants	No

Subsector Weightings	% of Stocks	Rel Cat
Diversified	65.8	6.7
Health Care	0.0	0.0
Industrial/Office	6.0	0.2
Mortgage Backed	1.8	2.2
Apartment	0.0	0.0
Retail	9.4	0.5
Dvlp./Man. Home	3.1	1.4
Self Storage	0.0	0.0
Hotel	0.0	0.0
Other	13.9	1.9

Composition % assets 11-30-01	
Cash	0.6
Stocks*	92.3
Bonds	5.6
Other	1.6
*Foreign (% stocks)	9.5

Market Cap	
Giant	0.0
Large	0.0
Medium	52.9
Small	24.3
Micro	22.8

Address:	767 Third Avenue Fifth Floor New York, NY 10017 212–888–2290 / 800–443–1021
Web Address:	www.mjwhitman.com/third.htm
*Inception:	09-17-98
Advisor:	EQSF Advisers
Subadvisor:	None
NTF Plans:	Fidelity Inst. , Waterhouse

Minimum Purchase:	$1000	Add: $1000 IRA: $500
Min Auto Inv Plan:	$1000	Add: $200
Sales Fees:	No-load, 1.00%R within 12 months	
Management Fee:	.90%	
Actual Fees:	Mgt: 0.90%	Dist: —
Expense Projections:	3Yr: $1007	5Yr: — 10Yr: —
Avg Brok Commission:	—	Income Distrib: Annually
Total Cost (relative to category):	—	

Third Avenue Value

Ticker	Load	NAV	Yield	Total Assets	Mstar Category
TAVFX	None	$36.43	1.7%	$2,317.2 mil	Small Value

Prospectus Objective: Growth

Third Avenue Value Fund seeks long-term capital appreciation.

The fund invests primarily in equity securities issued by companies that management believes to be undervalued and to have strong financial positions and responsible management. It may also invest in debt securities. The fund may invest a significant portion of assets in securities with relatively inactive markets. It reserves the right to invest up to one third of assets in securities of foreign issuers. The fund is non-diversified.

Prior to May 19, 1992, the fund was named Third Avenue Fund. The fund reopened to new investors in October of 1998.

Historical Profile
Return High
Risk Below Avg
Rating ★★★★★ Highest

Investment Style
Equity
Average Stock %: 61% 53% 73% 95% 76% 73%

▼ Manager Change
▽ Partial Manager Change

Fund Performance vs. Category Average
■ Quarterly Fund Return +/– Category Average
— Category Baseline

Performance Quartile (within Category)

Portfolio Manager(s)

Martin J. Whitman, CFA. Since 11-90. BS Syracuse U.; MA New School for Social Research. Other funds currently managed: SunAmStySel Small-Cap Value A, SunAmStySel Small-Cap Value B, SunAmStySel Small-Cap Value II.

1990	1991	1992	1993	1994	1995	1996	1997	1998	1999	2000	12-01	History
10.86	12.47	14.67	17.62	16.97	21.80	25.86	31.46	32.29	35.99	36.22	36.43	NAV
8.60*	34.41	21.29	23.66	–1.46	31.73	21.92	23.87	3.92	12.82	20.76	2.82	Total Return %
0.25*	3.93	13.67	13.60	–2.78	–5.80	–1.03	–9.48	–24.66	–8.21	29.86	14.70	+/– S&P 500
—	–7.29	–7.85	–0.18	0.09	5.98	0.55	–7.82	10.35	14.30	–2.06	–11.20	+/– Russell 2000 V
0.00	1.69	1.60	1.79	1.41	2.39	2.63	1.59	1.28	0.00	2.10	1.70	Income Return %
8.60	32.72	19.68	21.87	–2.88	29.34	19.29	22.28	2.64	12.82	18.66	1.12	Capital Return %
—	64	44	8	57	11	65	81	9	23	44	96	Total Rtn % Rank Cat
0.00	0.17	0.20	0.26	0.25	0.41	0.57	0.41	0.40	0.00	0.68	0.62	Income $
0.00	1.89	0.25	0.25	0.14	0.15	0.15	0.16	0.00	0.42	6.16	0.19	Capital Gains $
—	2.50	2.32	1.42	1.16	1.25	1.21	1.13	1.08	1.10	1.09	—	Expense Ratio %
—	1.71	1.71	1.45	1.85	2.24	2.67	2.10	1.44	1.27	1.41	—	Income Ratio %
—	67	31	17	5	15	14	10	24	5	30	—	Turnover Rate %
3.1	18.9	38.7	137.6	180.1	328.6	644.7	1,676.0	1,600.1	1,379.3	1,939.9	—	Net Assets $mil

Performance 12-31-01

	1st Qtr	2nd Qtr	3rd Qtr	4th Qtr	Total
1997	2.17	13.29	12.70	–5.03	23.87
1998	6.90	–2.82	–14.29	16.72	3.92
1999	–8.24	14.92	–2.79	10.06	12.82
2000	17.48	–3.30	5.34	0.91	20.76
2001	–0.28	4.26	–10.75	10.80	2.82

Trailing	Total Return%	+/– S&P 500	+/– Russ 2000V	% Rank All	% Rank Cat	Growth of $10,000
3 Mo	10.80	0.12	–5.91	38	96	11,080
6 Mo	–1.11	4.44	–2.26	43	79	9,889
1 Yr	2.82	14.70	–11.20	37	96	10,282
3 Yr Avg	11.89	12.92	0.57	8	55	14,008
5 Yr Avg	12.51	1.81	1.32	9	36	18,031
10 Yr Avg	15.65	2.72	0.54	4	20	42,798
15 Yr Avg	—	—	—	—	—	—

Tax Analysis	Tax-Adj Ret%	%Rank Cat	%Pretax Ret	%Rank Cat
3 Yr Avg	10.07	56	84.7	75
5 Yr Avg	11.17	27	89.3	28
10 Yr Avg	14.42	13	92.2	1

Potential Capital Gain Exposure: 20% of assets

Risk Analysis

Time Period	Load-Adj Return %	Risk %Rank[1] All	Risk %Rank[1] Cat	Morningstar Return	Morningstar Risk	Morningstar Risk-Adj Rating
1 Yr	2.82					
3 Yr	11.89	41	22	1.57[2]	0.57	★★★★★
5 Yr	12.51	49	16	1.89[2]	0.66	★★★★
10 Yr	15.65	52	11	1.96	0.65	★★★★★

Average Historical Rating (99 months): 4.3★s

[1]1=low, 100=high [2] T-Bill return substituted for category avg.

Category Rating (3 Yr)
1 2 3 4 5
Worst Best
Return Average
Risk Below Avg

Other Measures	Standard Index S&P 500	Best Fit Index SPMid400
Alpha	10.9	3.3
Beta	0.62	0.64
R-Squared	47	65
Standard Deviation		17.10
Mean		11.89
Sharpe Ratio		0.46

Portfolio Analysis 11-30-01

Share change since 09-01 Total Stocks: 102	Sector	PE	YTD Ret%	% Assets
AVX	Technology	14.2	45.10	5.04
MBIA	Financials	14.6	9.88	3.65
Tejon Ranch	Staples	NMF	24.27	3.39
⊕ Tokio Marine & Fire ADR	Financials	10.0	–35.40	3.06
⊕ Toyoda Automatic Loom Works	Durables	19.9	—	3.00
ASM Lithography Hldg	Technology	—	—	2.96
USG 8.5%	N/A	—	—	2.69
⊕ Kemet	Technology	8.1	17.36	2.69
⊕ Forest City Enterprises Cl A	Financials	19.0	48.90	2.58
⊕ Electro Scientific Inds	Technology	8.4	7.18	2.49
USG 9.25%	N/A	—	—	2.47
⊕ Mitsui Marine & Fire Ins	Financials	30.5	—	2.31
First Amer	Financials	9.1	–42.20	2.29
Liberty Finl	Financials	—	–24.50	2.25
Vishay Intertechnology	Technology	13.7	28.93	2.07
Home Products Intl 9.625%	N/A	—	—	2.07
Legg Mason	Financials	23.6	–7.53	1.96
Nabors Inds	Energy	15.8	–41.90	1.87
Radian Grp	Financials	11.6	14.64	1.76
Electroglas	Technology	—	–3.55	1.75
Stewart Info Svcs	Financials	9.8	–10.90	1.69
Brascan	Industrials	27.5	32.06	1.50
Raymond James Finl	Financials	18.0	3.36	1.50
GNMA 5.5%	N/A	—	—	1.37
American Pwr Conversion	Technology	23.3	16.85	1.33

Current Investment Style

Style: Value Blnd Growth; Size: Large Med Small

	Stock Port Avg	Relative S&P 500 Current	Relative S&P 500 Hist	Rel Cat
Price/Earnings Ratio	21.4	0.69	0.83	0.99
Price/Book Ratio	2.1	0.36	0.33	0.86
Price/Cash Flow	18.1	1.00	0.79	1.42
3 Yr Earnings Growth	24.2	1.65	0.94	2.08
1 Yr Earnings Est%	2.1[1]	—	—	–0.53
Med Mkt Cap $mil	2,229	0.0	0.0	2.56

[1]figure is based on 50% or less of stocks

Analysis by Christopher Traulsen 10-24-01

For Third Avenue Value Fund, the market's September slump was a golden opportunity.

This offering usually trades at a snail's pace, but it cranked it up a notch in September. Manager Marty Whitman snapped up $130 million in equities as the market skidded after reopening following the World Trade Center attack. Names he bought or added to include Forest City Enterprises, Applied Materials, American Power Conversion, Nabors Industries, and MBIA.

Such activity is unusual here, as the market rarely offers so many bargains at once. The fund had a cash position of 18% of assets at the end of June; it's now about 13% of assets. Cash can build because Whitman is very selective about the securities he buys. Many picks have poor near-term outlooks, but he wants them to be well-capitalized and trading at 50% or less of their intrinsic values. Whitman will also buy distressed debt if he can get it cheaply enough. Recently, he bought the debt of struggling web-hoster Exodus Communications.

The idea is to deliver solid long-term returns without taking a lot of chances, and the fund has done just that. Its five- and 10-year returns rank in the small-value category's best quintile, and it has been much less volatile than its peers over time. The fund does come with some caveats. For one, it's an all-cap offering, so it won't suit small-cap purists. It's also concentrated in financials and tech stocks, so its relative returns can differ markedly from its peers' in the near term. In 2001, for example, weakness among its larger financials positions and some of its tech holdings has taken a toll, leaving it with a subpar showing.

Whitman is nearing the age of retirement, but if he steps down, we think the firm has capable successors. Given the fund's terrific record and proven strategy, we think it remains a great choice for long-term investors.

Special Securities % assets 11-30-01	
Restricted/Illiquid Secs	1
Emerging-Markets Secs	1
Options/Futures/Warrants	Yes

Composition % assets 11-30-01	
Cash	1.0
Stocks*	71.4
Bonds	14.3
Other	1.8
*Foreign (% stocks)	21.7

Market Cap	
Giant	0.0
Large	7.0
Medium	56.1
Small	31.2
Micro	5.7

Sector Weightings	% of Stocks	Rel S&P	5-Year High	5-Year Low
Utilities	0.0	0.0	1	0
Energy	2.5	0.4	14	0
Financials	46.1	2.6	75	40
Industrials	5.7	0.5	26	3
Durables	5.2	3.3	6	0
Staples	5.3	0.7	9	0
Services	2.8	0.3	15	0
Retail	0.1	0.0	17	0
Health	2.3	0.2	6	0
Technology	30.2	1.6	39	0

Address: 767 Third Avenue Fifth Floor, New York, NY 10017, 212-888-2290 / 800-443-1021
Web Address: www.mjwhitman.com/third.htm
*Inception: 11-01-90
Advisor: EQSF Advisers
Subadvisor: None
NTF Plans: Fidelity, Fidelity Inst.

Minimum Purchase: $1000 Add: $1000 IRA: $500
Min Auto Inv Plan: $1000 Add: $200
Sales Fees: No-load
Management Fee: .90%
Actual Fees: Mgt: 0.90% Dist: —
Expense Projections: 3Yr: $343 5Yr: $595 10Yr: $1317
Avg Brok Commission: — Income Distrib: Annually
Total Cost (relative to category): —

Thornburg Limited–Term Muni Natl A

Ticker	Load	NAV	Yield	SEC Yield	Total Assets	Mstar Category
LTMFX	1.50%	$13.41	4.1%	3.59%	$816.3 mil	Muni Short–Term

Prospectus Objective: Muni Bond—National

Thornburg Limited-Term Municipal Fund National Portfolio - Class A seeks income exempt from federal income tax.

The fund normally invests at least 80% of assets in investment-grade municipals with an average- weighted maturity of fewer than five years. It may invest the balance in taxable bonds, some of which may be subject to the AMT.

Class A shares have front loads; C shares have level loads; Institutional shares are for institutions. The fund's B shares merged into its A shares on Sept. 28, 1995. Past name: Limited-Term Municipal Fund National Portfolio. On Sept. 5, 1997, Mackenzie Limited-Term Municipal Fund merged into the fund.

Historical Profile

Return Below Avg
Risk Low
Rating ★★★★ Above Avg

Investment Style: Fixed-Income

Income Rtn %Rank Cat: 12 | 14 | 14 | 13 | 16 | 14 | 19 | 25

Growth of Principal vs. Interest Rate Shifts
— Principal Value $000 (NAV with capital gains reinvested)
— Interest Rate % on 10 Yr Treasury
▼ Manager Change
▽ Partial Manager Change
► Mgr Unknown After
◄ Mgr Unknown Before

Performance Quartile (within Category)

Portfolio Manager(s)

Brian J. McMahon. Since 9-84. BA'77 U. of Virginia; MBA'79 Dartmouth C. Other funds currently managed: Thornburg Limited-Term Muni CA A, Thornburg Intermediate Municipal A, Thornburg NM Intermediate Municipal A.

George Strickland. Since 9-84. BA Davidson C.; MBA U. of Maryland. Other funds currently managed: Thornburg Limited-Term Muni CA A, Thornburg Intermediate Municipal A, Thornburg NM Intermediate Municipal A.

History

1990	1991	1992	1993	1994	1995	1996	1997	1998	1999	2000	12-01	History
12.76	13.01	13.25	13.75	12.92	13.55	13.45	13.55	13.59	13.05	13.33	13.41	NAV
6.48	8.61	7.74	8.81	–1.49	9.97	3.97	5.47	4.79	0.33	6.81	4.82	Total Return %
–2.47	–7.39	0.34	–0.94	1.43	–8.50	0.35	–4.21	–3.89	1.16	–4.82	–3.60	+/– LB Aggregate
–0.82	–3.53	–1.08	–3.46	3.65	–7.49	–0.47	–3.73	–1.70	2.40	–4.89	–0.26	+/– LB Muni
6.93	6.58	5.82	4.98	4.67	5.02	4.70	4.70	4.48	4.40	4.58	4.25	Income Return %
–0.45	2.04	1.92	3.83	–6.16	4.95	–0.73	0.77	0.31	–4.06	2.23	0.58	Capital Return %
56	44	19	18	66	21	29	30	35	58	17	47	Total Rtn % Rank Cat
0.86	0.81	0.74	0.65	0.63	0.63	0.62	0.62	0.59	0.59	0.59	0.56	Income $
0.00	0.00	0.00	0.00	0.00	0.00	0.00	0.00	0.00	0.00	0.00	0.00	Capital Gains $
1.11	1.07	1.04	1.01	0.95	0.97	0.97	0.96	0.97	0.96	0.96	0.99	Expense Ratio %
6.73	6.58	5.96	5.03	4.60	5.83	4.66	4.65	4.50	4.35	4.48	4.36	Income Ratio %
68	32	28	19	16	23	21	23	25	22	34	25	Turnover Rate %
236.7	384.2	719.2	911.6	1,019.2	917.4	915.3	856.2	822.0	743.1	643.8	678.7	Net Assets $mil

Performance 12-31-01

	1st Qtr	2nd Qtr	3rd Qtr	4th Qtr	Total
1997	0.35	1.92	1.75	1.36	5.47
1998	0.89	0.96	2.14	0.71	4.79
1999	0.57	–0.85	0.58	0.04	0.33
2000	1.13	1.22	1.74	2.56	6.81
2001	2.08	0.91	2.20	–0.43	4.82

Trailing	Total Return%	+/– LB Agg	+/– LB Muni	% Rank All	% Rank Cat	Growth of $10,000
3 Mo	–0.43	–0.47	0.23	83	79	9,957
6 Mo	1.75	–2.90	–0.37	26	65	10,175
1 Yr	4.82	–3.60	–0.26	24	47	10,482
3 Yr Avg	3.95	–2.32	–0.80	41	33	11,233
5 Yr Avg	4.42	–3.01	–1.55	74	30	12,415
10 Yr Avg	5.07	–2.16	–1.56	92	23	16,392
15 Yr Avg	5.70	–2.42	–1.49	93	11	22,962

Tax Analysis	Tax-Adj Ret%	%Rank Cat	%Pretax Ret	%Rank Cat
3 Yr Avg	3.95	31	100.0	5
5 Yr Avg	4.42	30	100.0	5
10 Yr Avg	5.07	23	100.0	9

Potential Capital Gain Exposure: 3% of assets

Risk Analysis

Time Period	Load-Adj Return %	Risk %Rank[1] All	Risk %Rank[1] Cat	Morningstar Return	Morningstar Risk	Morningstar Risk-Adj Rating
1 Yr	3.25					
3 Yr	3.43	3	64	0.31[2]	0.44	★★★★★
5 Yr	4.11	3	62	0.48[2]	0.45	★★★★
10 Yr	4.91	3	75	0.65	0.42	★★★★

Average Historical Rating (172 months): 4.9★s

[1]1=low, 100=high [2] T-Bill return substituted for category avg.

Category Rating (3 Yr)

1 2 3 4 5
Worst Best

Return Average
Risk Average

Other Measures	Standard Index LB Agg	Best Fit Index LB Muni
Alpha	–1.5	–0.9
Beta	0.46	0.52
R–Squared	57	89

Standard Deviation	2.15
Mean	3.95
Sharpe Ratio	–0.55

Analysis by Catherine Hickey 11-30-01

This extraordinarily consistent fund continues to dust the competition.

Thornburg Limited-Term Muni National Fund keeps delivering solid performances. For the year to date through Dec. 11, 2001, it has gained 4.5%, putting it just inside the top half of its peer group.

Manager George Strickland and his team are sticking with a decidedly unfancy approach that has delivered top-quartile long-term results. They ladder the portfolio among issues with maturities between one and 10 years. As the shorter bonds mature, they fall off the ladder, and Strickland replaces them with ones at the long end of the ladder. Management keeps credit quality fairly high: It's mostly BBB and better, with a smaller-than-average nonrated stake. Duration is the area where this fund takes on a little more risk than its average peer. At four years, the fund's interest-rate sensitivity in 2000 was greater than the muni-short-group norm, which clocks in at 2.7 years.

Of late, the fund has been in the right places. Strickland and his team have overweighted health-care bonds, and that has helped as that area has outperformed. In addition, the fund has been underexposed to New York and California, two states that have had credit blowups this year. Instead, Strickland has overweighted Texas, Illinois, and Indiana, areas that have been more economically stable.

The fund isn't without risk; its duration is often above average for the category, which means it may fare worse than its rivals in an environment of rising interest rates. However, Strickland's otherwise moderate approach and relatively low turnover have delivered fairly steady returns over time.

This fund's risk/reward profile is one of the best in the category. It remains a solid option.

Address:	119 E. Marcy Street Suite 202 Santa Fe, NM 87501 800–847–0200 / 505–984–0200
Web Address:	www.thornburg.com
Inception:	09-28-84
Advisor:	Thornburg Mgmt.
Subadvisor:	None
NTF Plans:	Datalynx , Fidelity Inst.

Minimum Purchase:	$5000	Add: $100	IRA: —
Min Auto Inv Plan:	$5000	Add: $100	
Sales Fees:	1.50%L, 0.25%S		
Management Fee:	.50% mx./.23% mn., .13%A		
Actual Fees:	Mgt: 0.45%	Dist: 0.25%	
Expense Projections:	3Yr: $55*	5Yr: $77*	10Yr: $140*
Avg Brok Commission:	—	Income Distrib: Monthly	
Total Cost (relative to category):	—		

Portfolio Analysis 09-30-01

Total Fixed-Income: 456	Date of Maturity	Amount $000	Value $000	% Net Assets
TX Harris Hosp 5.75%	02-15-11	10,000	11,022	1.38
MI Hosp Fin Assencion 5.375%	11-15-33	10,000	10,460	1.31
CA Orange Recovery 6.5%	06-01-04	7,600	8,338	1.04
LA Orleans Sch Brd 0%	02-01-08	10,000	7,369	0.92
IA Fin Coml Dev 5.75%	04-01-14	6,650	7,074	0.89
KY Econ Dev Hlth 0%	10-01-10	7,830	6,822	0.85
FL Collier Hlth 3.1%	01-01-33	6,800	6,800	0.85
KY Econ Dev Hlth 0%	10-01-09	7,400	6,451	0.81
KS Kansas City Pwr 3.9%	03-01-15	6,000	6,005	0.75
CA Orange Recovery 6.5%	06-01-05	5,200	5,842	0.73
FL Broward GO 5.375%	12-01-09	5,500	5,834	0.73
OT Municipal Tax–Exempt Tr 4.6%	08-06-08	5,600	5,749	0.72
OH Ohio Sch 5.75%	06-15-10	5,000	5,579	0.70
NE Omaha Pub Pwr Dist Elec Sys 7.5%	02-01-06	5,000	5,438	0.68
FL Lakeland Utility FRN	10-01-35	5,400	5,400	0.68

Current Investment Style

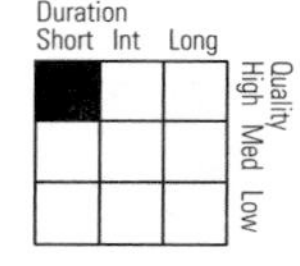

Avg Duration[1]	4.0 Yrs
Avg Nominal Maturity	4.3 Yrs
Avg Credit Quality	AA
Avg Wtd Coupon	5.22%
Avg Wtd Price	103.70% of par
Pricing Service	J.J. Kenny

[1]figure provided by fund

Credit Analysis % bonds 09-30-01

US Govt	0	BB	0
AAA	54	B	0
AA	26	Below B	0
A	12	NR/NA	2
BBB	6		

Special Securities % assets 09-30-01

Restricted/Illiquid Secs	0
Inverse Floaters	0
Options/Futures/Warrants	No

Bond Type % assets 12-31-00

Alternative Minimum Tax (AMT)	0.0
Insured	42.9
Prerefunded	14.1

Top 5 States % bonds

TX	11.5	OH	5.0
IL	11.3	CA	4.7
FL	6.2		

Composition % assets 09-30-01

Cash	2.5	Bonds	97.5
Stocks	0.0	Other	0.0

Sector Weightings	% of Bonds	Rel Cat
General Obligation	14.1	0.5
Utilities	10.3	1.3
Health	27.9	2.3
Water/Waste	2.0	0.4
Housing	7.8	1.1
Education	6.9	1.1
Transportation	3.8	0.4
COP/Lease	2.5	0.8
Industrial	11.6	1.2
Misc Revenue	10.7	1.8
Demand	2.5	0.8

Thornburg Value A

Ticker	Load	NAV	Yield	Total Assets	Mstar Category
TVAFX	4.50%	$28.73	0.4%	$2,167.2 mil	Large Blend

Prospectus Objective: Growth

Thornburg Value Fund seeks long-term capital appreciation.

The fund invests primarily in domestic equities selected on a value basis. To select securities, management concentrates on three types of companies: financially sound companies selling at low valuations, consistent growth companies, or rapidly growing companies. The fund may also purchase debt securities of any type, and it may invest up to 35% of assets in debt rated below investment-grade. The fund may also invest in foreign securities, including American depositary receipts.

Class A shares have front loads; B shares have deferred loads; C shares have level loads; I shares are for institutional investors only.

Historical Profile

Return High
Risk Below Avg
Rating ★★★★★ Highest

Investment Style
Equity
Average Stock %: 95% (1996), 93% (1997), 89% (1998), 92% (1999), 95% (2000), 95% (12-01)

▼ Manager Change
▽ Partial Manager Change

Fund Performance vs. Category Average
■ Quarterly Fund Return +/– Category Average
— Category Baseline

Performance Quartile (within Category)

Portfolio Manager(s)

William V. Fries, CFA. Since 10-95. BS'61 Pennsylvania State U.; MBA'72 Temple U. Other funds currently managed: Heritage Growth & Income A, Heritage Growth & Income C, Thornburg Value C.

1990	1991	1992	1993	1994	1995	1996	1997	1998	1999	2000	12-01	History
—	—	—	—	—	11.83	15.59	19.24	23.36	31.37	31.40	28.73	NAV
—	—	—	—	—	–0.53*	37.82	33.71	22.26	37.44	3.96	–8.11	Total Return %
—	—	—	—	—	–7.03*	14.88	0.35	–6.32	16.40	13.07	3.76	+/– S&P 500
—	—	—	—	—	—	15.66	0.68	–6.38	15.61	14.92	4.65	+/– Wilshire Top 750
—	—	—	—	—	0.39	2.43	1.18	0.77	1.06	3.26	0.40	Income Return %
—	—	—	—	—	–0.92	35.39	32.53	21.48	36.38	0.71	–8.52	Capital Return %
—	—	—	—	—	—	1	11	60	9	10	11	Total Rtn % Rank Cat
—	—	—	—	—	0.05	0.28	0.18	0.15	0.25	1.01	0.13	Income $
—	—	—	—	—	0.00	0.37	1.35	0.00	0.39	0.25	0.00	Capital Gains $
—	—	—	—	—	—	1.55	1.61	1.61	1.44	1.38	—	Expense Ratio %
—	—	—	—	—	—	2.48	1.35	0.96	0.62	2.31	—	Income Ratio %
—	—	—	—	—	—	60	79	100	63	72	—	Turnover Rate %
—	—	—	—	—	7.3	15.4	79.7	234.4	506.1	950.0	1,233.2	Net Assets $mil

Performance 12-31-01

	1st Qtr	2nd Qtr	3rd Qtr	4th Qtr	Total
1997	–0.03	14.84	15.05	1.23	33.71
1998	17.38	0.46	–13.59	19.98	22.26
1999	8.67	10.01	–5.48	21.63	37.44
2000	7.44	1.63	–1.38	–3.45	3.96
2001	–6.41	4.03	–14.45	10.33	–8.11

Trailing	Total Return%	+/– S&P 500	+/–Wil Top 750	% Rank All	% Rank Cat	Growth of $10,000
3 Mo	10.33	–0.35	–0.99	41	61	11,033
6 Mo	–5.62	–0.06	0.18	65	37	9,438
1 Yr	–8.11	3.76	4.65	57	11	9,189
3 Yr Avg	9.50	10.52	11.32	12	2	13,129
5 Yr Avg	16.50	5.80	6.38	3	1	21,461
10 Yr Avg	—	—	—	—	—	—
15 Yr Avg	—	—	—	—	—	—

Tax Analysis	Tax-Adj Ret%	%Rank Cat	%Pretax Ret	%Rank Cat
3 Yr Avg	8.72	2	91.8	10
5 Yr Avg	15.31	1	92.8	14
10 Yr Avg	—	—	—	—

Potential Capital Gain Exposure: 10% of assets

Risk Analysis

Time Period	Load-Adj Return %	Risk %Rank[1] All	Risk %Rank[1] Cat	Morningstar Return	Morningstar Risk	Morningstar Risk-Adj Rating
1 Yr	–12.25					
3 Yr	7.83	49	5	0.63[2]	0.69	★★★★
5 Yr	15.43	53	9	2.77[2]	0.74	★★★★★
Incept	17.97	—	—	—	—	

Average Historical Rating (40 months): 4.8★s

[1] 1=low, 100=high [2] T-Bill return substituted for category avg.

Category Rating (3 Yr)

1 2 3 4 5 (Worst — Best): 5

Return High
Risk Low

Other Measures	Standard Index S&P 500	Best Fit Index MSCIACWdFr
Alpha	9.6	13.4
Beta	0.82	0.90
R-Squared	77	82

Standard Deviation	17.32
Mean	9.50
Sharpe Ratio	0.30

Portfolio Analysis 11-30-01

Share change since 10-01 Total Stocks: 48	Sector	PE	YTD Ret%	% Assets
Tenet Healthcare	Health	30.1	32.14	4.15
Microsoft	Technology	57.6	52.78	3.26
PepsiCo	Staples	31.4	–0.54	3.08
Pfizer	Health	34.7	–12.40	2.98
American Home Products	Health	—	–1.91	2.97
Washington Mutual	Financials	10.1	–5.32	2.93
AOL Time Warner	Technology	—	–7.76	2.83
⊕ US Bancorp	Financials	13.5	–6.14	2.72
Verizon Comms	Services	29.7	–2.52	2.63
Unocal	Energy	10.9	–4.58	2.63
MBNA	Financials	19.6	–3.66	2.60
BP PLC ADR	Energy	14.4	–0.90	2.53
⊖ Samsung Electncs	Technology	7.0	—	2.49
Lowe's	Retail	38.7	109.00	2.48
EMC	Technology	NMF	–79.40	2.24
Alliance Cap Mgmt Hldg LP	Financials	23.8	0.95	2.23
Comcast	Services	20.3	–13.70	2.22
⊕ Anthem	Financials	—	—	2.19
Telephone and Data Sys	Services	—	0.29	2.18
☼ Merrill Lynch	Financials	18.2	–22.70	2.12
RadioShack	Retail	21.5	–29.20	2.11
Bank of New York	Financials	21.9	–24.80	2.10
Sprint	Services	20.5	1.18	2.03
⊕ Bank of Ireland	Financials	14.4	—	2.02
Fox Entrtnmt Grp Cl A	Services	NMF	48.42	1.97

Current Investment Style

Style: Value Blnd Growth; Size: Large Med Small

	Stock Port Avg	Relative S&P 500 Current	Relative S&P 500 Hist	Rel Cat
Price/Earnings Ratio	29.8	0.96	0.89	0.98
Price/Book Ratio	5.1	0.89	0.76	0.92
Price/Cash Flow	16.7	0.93	0.90	0.91
3 Yr Earnings Growth	24.0	1.64	1.08	1.34
1 Yr Earnings Est%	1.3	—	—	—
Med Mkt Cap $mil	26,153	0.4	0.3	0.50

Analysis by Catherine Hickey 08-01-01

This offering proves that index funds aren't the only viable option in the large-cap patch.

Thornburg Value Fund is a large-blend fund that has earned its keep over cheaper S&P 500 index funds. The fund's three- and five-year returns are several percentage points higher than the bogy's, and land the fund above almost all of its large-blend peers for those time periods, too. This type of performance goes to show that an S&P 500 index fund isn't the only sensible option for large-cap investing. Though index funds sport solid performance and low expenses, there are managers who earn their extra fees by producing returns that are consistently better than the index's. Bill Fries, the skipper of this offering, is one such manager.

Though the fund's near 6% loss through July 31, 2001, is hardly auspicious in absolute terms, it's still better than most of its peers', and yes, it's better than the index's. This year has been tough for large-cap funds in general, and to be sure, this portfolio holds its share of bruised fruit; for instance, Constellation Energy is off more than 34% this year as utility and power stocks continue to pull back after last year's run. Other picks have been winners, though. Tenet Health Care is doing nicely; Fries likes the prospects of health facility operator Tenet because hospitals need to increase capacity as hospital admissions trend higher.

The fund's sizable mid-cap stake and concentrated portfolio might warn off super-conservative types. However, volatility has hardly been a problem here. Fries pares back stocks when they get too pricey and doesn't take big sector bets, and that limits big performance swings. Investors looking for a talented stock-picker who continues to churn out great returns might want to take a peek here.

Special Securities % assets 11-30-01	
Restricted/Illiquid Secs	1
Emerging-Markets Secs	2
Options/Futures/Warrants	No

Composition % assets 11-30-01	
Cash	2.2
Stocks*	96.6
Bonds	0.0
Other	1.2
*Foreign (% stocks)	12.6

Market Cap	
Giant	25.9
Large	45.6
Medium	28.1
Small	0.4
Micro	0.0

Sector Weightings	% of Stocks	Rel S&P	5-Year High	5-Year Low
Utilities	2.0	0.6	10	0
Energy	5.5	0.8	13	2
Financials	26.1	1.5	42	14
Industrials	6.6	0.6	13	0
Durables	0.0	0.0	8	0
Staples	3.3	0.4	6	0
Services	14.8	1.4	34	3
Retail	6.6	1.0	10	0
Health	16.3	1.1	21	2
Technology	19.0	1.0	32	9

Address:	119 E. Marcy Street Suite 202 Santa Fe, NM 87501 800-847-0200 / 505-984-0200
Web Address:	www.thornburg.com
*Inception:	10-02-95
Advisor:	Thornburg Mgmt.
Subadvisor:	None
NTF Plans:	Datalynx , Fidelity Inst.

Minimum Purchase:	$5000	Add: $100	IRA: $2000
Min Auto Inv Plan:	$5000	Add: $100	
Sales Fees:	4.50%L, 0.25%S		
Management Fee:	.88% mx./.68% mn., .13%A		
Actual Fees:	Mgt: 0.88%	Dist: 0.25%	
Expense Projections:	3Yr: $885	5Yr: $1201	10Yr: $2097
Avg Brok Commission:	—	Income Distrib: Quarterly	
Total Cost (relative to category):		Above Avg	

TIAA–CREF Equity Index

Ticker	Load	NAV	Yield	Total Assets	Mstar Category
TCEIX	None	$8.05	0.8%	$96.7 mil	Large Blend

Prospectus Objective: Growth

TIAA-CREF Equity Index fund seeks a favorable long-term rate of return by investing in stocks of the Russell 3000 Index.

The fund uses a sampling approach to create a portfolio similar to the Russell 3000 Index. Management uses proprietary quantitative models to replicate market exposure and characteristics of the Russell 3000 Index.

The fund may also invest in futures.

Historical Profile
Return —
Risk —
Rating
Not Rated

Investment Style
Equity
Average Stock %: 99% (2000), 99% (12-01)

▼ Manager Change
▽ Partial Manager Change

Fund Performance vs. Category Average
■ Quarterly Fund Return +/– Category Average
— Category Baseline

Performance Quartile (within Category)

Portfolio Manager(s)

Management Team

History

	1990	1991	1992	1993	1994	1995	1996	1997	1998	1999	2000	12-01
NAV	—	—	—	—	—	—	—	—	—	—	9.19	8.05
Total Return %	—	—	—	—	—	—	—	—	—	—	–10.93*	–11.62
+/– S&P 500	—	—	—	—	—	—	—	—	—	—	0.65*	0.26
+/– Wilshire Top 750	—	—	—	—	—	—	—	—	—	—	—	1.15
Income Return %	—	—	—	—	—	—	—	—	—	—	0.60	0.68
Capital Return %	—	—	—	—	—	—	—	—	—	—	–11.53	–12.30
Total Rtn % Rank Cat	—	—	—	—	—	—	—	—	—	—	—	30
Income $	—	—	—	—	—	—	—	—	—	—	0.06	0.06
Capital Gains $	—	—	—	—	—	—	—	—	—	—	0.00	0.01
Expense Ratio %	—	—	—	—	—	—	—	—	—	—	—	—
Income Ratio %	—	—	—	—	—	—	—	—	—	—	—	—
Turnover Rate %	—	—	—	—	—	—	—	—	—	—	—	—
Net Assets $mil	—	—	—	—	—	—	—	—	—	—	67.1	96.7

Performance 12-31-01

	1st Qtr	2nd Qtr	3rd Qtr	4th Qtr	Total
1997	—	—	—	—	—
1998	—	—	—	—	—
1999	—	—	—	—	—
2000	—	–2.89	0.79	–9.00	–10.93 *
2001	–12.19	6.82	–15.55	11.57	–11.62

Trailing	Total Return%	+/– S&P 500	+/– Wil Top 750	% Rank All	% Rank Cat	Growth of $10,000
3 Mo	11.57	0.88	0.24	35	34	11,157
6 Mo	–5.78	–0.22	0.02	66	43	9,422
1 Yr	–11.62	0.26	1.15	64	30	8,838
3 Yr Avg	—	—	—	—	—	—
5 Yr Avg	—	—	—	—	—	—
10 Yr Avg	—	—	—	—	—	—
15 Yr Avg	—	—	—	—	—	—

Tax Analysis	Tax-Adj Ret%	%Rank Cat	%Pretax Ret	%Rank Cat
3 Yr Avg	—	—	—	—
5 Yr Avg	—	—	—	—
10 Yr Avg	—	—	—	—

Potential Capital Gain Exposure: NMF

Risk Analysis

Time Period	Load-Adj Return %	Risk %Rank¹ All	Risk %Rank¹ Cat	Morningstar Return	Morningstar Risk	Morningstar Risk-Adj Rating
1 Yr	–11.62					
3 Yr	—	—	—	—	—	
5 Yr	—	—	—	—	—	
Incept	–12.81	—	—	—	—	

Average Historical Rating —

¹1=low, 100=high

Category Rating (3 Yr)

Return
Risk

Other Measures	Standard Index S&P 500	Best Fit Index
Alpha	—	—
Beta	—	—
R–Squared	—	—
Standard Deviation		—
Mean		—
Sharpe Ratio		—

Portfolio Analysis 09-30-01

Share change since 06-01 Total Stocks: 2765

	Sector	PE	YTD Ret%	% Assets
⊕ General Elec	Industrials	30.1	–15.00	3.56
⊕ ExxonMobil	Energy	15.3	–7.59	2.62
⊕ Pfizer	Health	34.7	–12.40	2.44
⊕ Microsoft	Technology	57.6	52.78	2.15
⊕ Citigroup	Financials	20.0	0.03	2.04
⊕ American Intl Grp	Financials	42.0	–19.20	1.73
⊕ Johnson & Johnson	Health	16.6	14.01	1.63
⊕ IBM	Technology	26.9	43.00	1.55
⊕ SBC Comms	Services	18.4	–16.00	1.53
⊕ Merck	Health	19.1	–35.90	1.47
⊕ Verizon Comms	Services	29.7	–2.52	1.41
⊕ AOL Time Warner	Technology	—	–7.76	1.37
⊕ Intel	Technology	73.1	4.89	1.33
⊕ Wal-Mart Stores	Retail	40.3	8.94	1.33
⊕ Bristol-Myers Squibb	Health	20.2	–26.00	1.04
⊕ Philip Morris	Staples	12.1	9.12	1.02
⊕ Coca-Cola	Staples	35.5	–21.40	0.95
⊕ Procter & Gamble	Staples	38.8	3.12	0.91
⊕ Bank of America	Financials	16.7	42.73	0.90
⊕ Home Depot	Retail	42.9	12.07	0.86
⊕ Cisco Sys	Technology	—	–52.60	0.86
⊕ PepsiCo	Staples	31.4	–0.54	0.84
⊕ Fannie Mae	Financials	16.2	–6.95	0.79
⊕ Abbott Labs	Health	51.6	17.08	0.78
⊕ BellSouth	Services	24.9	–5.09	0.76

Current Investment Style

Style: Value Blnd Growth; Size: Large Med Small

	Stock Port Avg	Relative S&P 500 Current	Relative S&P 500 Hist	Rel Cat
Price/Earnings Ratio	29.1	0.94	—	0.96
Price/Book Ratio	5.4	0.95	—	0.99
Price/Cash Flow	17.6	0.98	—	0.95
3 Yr Earnings Growth	15.8	1.08	—	0.88
1 Yr Earnings Est%	0.5	—	—	–5.22
Med Mkt Cap $mil	42,479	0.7	—	0.81

Analysis by Christopher Davis 12-04-01

Investors in search of a solid core holding will find one right here.

TIAA-CREF Equity Index Fund, and others like it, continue to confound the critics. During the late-1990s bull market, the naysayers warned that index funds wouldn't keep pace with their actively managed rivals once stocks headed south. Active managers, they argued, could flee from falling sectors or retreat into cash, leaving index funds in the dust. The skeptics, however, were wrong. Indeed, this fund, which tracks the Russell 3000 index, bested most domestic-equity offerings and nearly two thirds of its large-blend rivals for the year through Nov. 30, 2001, with a 13% loss.

Such outperformance should continue. The fund tracks nearly the entire market, so it delivers the same pre-expense returns enjoyed by the investing public as a whole. However, because shareholders here pay a lot less in fees than most investors (just 0.26% of assets versus 1.42% for the typical domestic-equity fund), they are guaranteed above-average returns. And because the fund's low-turnover approach keeps the tax man at bay, those returns are even more attractive on an after-tax basis.

This offering is marginally more expensive than rival Vanguard Total Stock Market Index, but certain investors may find it more appealing. Although TIAA-CREF sharply raised its minimum initial investment from $500 to $1,500, that's still an easier hurdle to clear than Vanguard's $3,000 entry price. What's more, unlike Vanguard, TIAA-CREF doesn't charge a $10 annual maintenance fee on account balances below $10,000, so the fund is a cheaper option for investors with smaller accounts.

Given its broad diversification, low costs, and tax-efficient strategy, this offering is a compelling choice for a core holding.

Special Securities % assets 09-30-01	
Restricted/Illiquid Secs	0
Emerging-Markets Secs	Trace
Options/Futures/Warrants	Yes

Sector Weightings	% of Stocks	Rel S&P	5-Year High	5-Year Low
Utilities	3.6	1.1	—	—
Energy	5.8	0.8	—	—
Financials	20.5	1.1	—	—
Industrials	10.7	0.9	—	—
Durables	1.7	1.1	—	—
Staples	6.9	0.9	—	—
Services	12.9	1.2	—	—
Retail	5.7	0.9	—	—
Health	15.9	1.1	—	—
Technology	16.2	0.9	—	—

Composition % assets 09-30-01	
Cash	1.2
Stocks*	98.7
Bonds	0.0
Other	0.1
*Foreign (% stocks)	0.0

Market Cap	
Giant	48.0
Large	28.3
Medium	17.6
Small	5.5
Micro	0.6

Address:	c/o State Street Bank P.O. Box 8009 Boston, MA 02266–8009 800–223–1200
Web Address:	www.tiaa–cref.org
*Inception:	04-03-00
Advisor:	Teachers Adv., Inc.
Subadvisor:	None
NTF Plans:	N/A

Minimum Purchase:	$1500	Add: $50	IRA: $500
Min Auto Inv Plan:	$50	Add: $50	
Sales Fees:	No-load		
Management Fee:	.76%		
Actual Fees:	Mgt: 0.26%	Dist: —	
Expense Projections:	3Yr: $84	5Yr: —	10Yr: —
Avg Brok Commission:	—	Income Distrib: Annually	
Total Cost (relative to category):	—		

TIAA–CREF Growth & Income

Ticker	Load	NAV	Yield	Total Assets	Mstar Category
TIGIX	None	$12.07	0.8%	$637.5 mil	Large Blend

Prospectus Objective: Growth and Income

TIAA-CREF Growth & Income Fund seeks capital appreciation and income.

The fund normally invests at least 80% of assets in income-producing equity securities. The fund may also invest in foreign securities.

Historical Profile
Return: Average
Risk: Average
Rating: ★★★ Neutral

Investment Style
Equity
Average Stock %: 100% 99% 98% 99% 98%

▼ Manager Change
▽ Partial Manager Change

Fund Performance vs. Category Average
■ Quarterly Fund Return +/– Category Average
— Category Baseline

Performance Quartile (within Category)

Portfolio Manager(s)

Carlton Martin. Since 9-97.

1990	1991	1992	1993	1994	1995	1996	1997	1998	1999	2000	12-01	History
—	—	—	—	—	—	—	10.32	13.33	15.93	14.05	12.07	NAV
—	—	—	—	—	—	—	5.08*	30.51	24.46	–7.33	–13.37	Total Return %
—	—	—	—	—	—	—	–3.42*	1.93	3.42	1.77	–1.49	+/– S&P 500
—	—	—	—	—	—	—	—	1.87	2.63	3.62	–0.60	+/– Wilshire Top 750
—	—	—	—	—	—	—	0.41	0.98	0.84	0.70	0.72	Income Return %
—	—	—	—	—	—	—	4.67	29.52	23.62	–8.04	–14.09	Capital Return %
—	—	—	—	—	—	—	—	11	28	43	56	Total Rtn % Rank Cat
—	—	—	—	—	—	—	0.04	0.10	0.11	0.11	0.10	Income $
—	—	—	—	—	—	—	0.00	0.03	0.53	0.61	0.00	Capital Gains $
—	—	—	—	—	—	—	—	0.43	0.43	0.43	—	Expense Ratio %
—	—	—	—	—	—	—	—	0.97	0.82	0.72	—	Income Ratio %
—	—	—	—	—	—	—	—	71	39	21	—	Turnover Rate %
—	—	—	—	—	—	—	61.8	232.8	541.7	664.7	637.5	Net Assets $mil

Performance 12-31-01

	1st Qtr	2nd Qtr	3rd Qtr	4th Qtr	Total
1997	—	—	—	2.80	5.08*
1998	14.70	3.92	–10.98	22.99	30.51
1999	6.18	8.20	–7.06	16.57	24.46
2000	4.17	–2.48	–0.60	–8.23	–7.33
2001	–12.86	5.43	–14.73	10.59	–13.37

Trailing	Total Return%	+/– S&P 500	+/– Wil Top 750	% Rank All	% Rank Cat	Growth of $10,000
3 Mo	10.59	–0.10	–0.73	39	50	11,059
6 Mo	–5.71	–0.15	0.09	66	41	9,429
1 Yr	–13.37	–1.49	–0.60	69	56	8,663
3 Yr Avg	–0.03	1.00	1.80	73	36	9,992
5 Yr Avg	—	—	—	—	—	—
10 Yr Avg	—	—	—	—	—	—
15 Yr Avg	—	—	—	—	—	—

Tax Analysis	Tax-Adj Ret%	%Rank Cat	%Pretax Ret	%Rank Cat
3 Yr Avg	–0.99	33	—	—
5 Yr Avg	—	—	—	—
10 Yr Avg	—	—	—	—

Potential Capital Gain Exposure: –12% of assets

Risk Analysis

Time Period	Load-Adj Return %	Risk %Rank[1] All	Risk %Rank[1] Cat	Morningstar Return	Morningstar Risk	Morningstar Risk-Adj Rating
1 Yr	–13.37					
3 Yr	–0.03	68	51	–1.01[2]	0.93	★★★
5 Yr	—	—	—	—	—	
Incept	7.54	—	—	—	—	

Average Historical Rating (17 months): 3.4★s

[1]1=low, 100=high [2] T-Bill return substituted for category avg.

Category Rating (3 Yr)

1 2 3 4 5 — Worst … Best

Return: Average
Risk: Average

Other Measures	Standard Index S&P 500	Best Fit Index S&P 500
Alpha	1.3	1.3
Beta	1.03	1.03
R-Squared	99	99

Standard Deviation	17.71
Mean	–0.03
Sharpe Ratio	–0.33

Portfolio Analysis 09-30-01

Share change since 06-01 Total Stocks: 538

	Sector	PE	YTD Ret%	% Assets
⊖ General Elec	Industrials	30.1	–15.00	3.94
⊕ Microsoft	Technology	57.6	52.78	3.27
⊕ Pfizer	Health	34.7	–12.40	3.16
⊕ ExxonMobil	Energy	15.3	–7.59	3.08
⊕ American Intl Grp	Financials	42.0	–19.20	2.64
⊖ Wal-Mart Stores	Retail	40.3	8.94	2.39
⊕ Citigroup	Financials	20.0	0.03	2.34
⊕ Johnson & Johnson	Health	16.6	14.01	1.85
⊖ Tyco Intl	Industrials	27.1	6.23	1.73
⊕ IBM	Technology	26.9	43.00	1.70
⊖ AOL Time Warner	Technology	—	–7.76	1.63
⊕ Home Depot	Retail	42.9	12.07	1.54
⊖ Intel	Technology	73.1	4.89	1.48
⊕ Bank of America	Financials	16.7	42.73	1.43
⊕ Abbott Labs	Health	51.6	17.08	1.39
⊖ Merck	Health	19.1	–35.90	1.33
⊕ AT&T	Services	7.8	40.59	1.30
⊕ PepsiCo	Staples	31.4	–0.54	1.26
⊖ SBC Comms	Services	18.4	–16.00	1.26
⊕ Fannie Mae	Financials	16.2	–6.95	1.15
⊕ Procter & Gamble	Staples	38.8	3.12	1.12
⊕ Schering-Plough	Health	22.2	–35.90	1.08
⊕ Nokia Cl A ADR	Technology	45.8	–43.00	1.05
⊕ Amgen	Health	52.8	–11.70	0.99
⊕ FleetBoston Finl	Financials	16.2	0.55	0.92

Current Investment Style

Style: Value Blnd Growth; Size: Large Med Small

	Stock Port Avg	Relative S&P 500 Current	Relative S&P 500 Hist	Rel Cat
Price/Earnings Ratio	30.3	0.98	1.04	1.00
Price/Book Ratio	5.8	1.02	1.04	1.06
Price/Cash Flow	18.8	1.04	1.00	1.02
3 Yr Earnings Growth	17.5	1.20	1.09	0.98
1 Yr Earnings Est%	–2.4	1.33	—	—
Med Mkt Cap $mil	71,161	1.2	1.4	1.36

Special Securities % assets 09-30-01	
Restricted/Illiquid Secs	0
Emerging-Markets Secs	0
Options/Futures/Warrants	No

Composition % assets 09-30-01	
Cash	6.0
Stocks*	94.0
Bonds	0.0
Other	0.0
*Foreign (% stocks)	4.9

Market Cap	
Giant	59.0
Large	30.3
Medium	10.3
Small	0.4
Micro	0.1

Sector Weightings	% of Stocks	Rel S&P	5-Year High	5-Year Low
Utilities	2.9	0.9	—	—
Energy	7.1	1.0	—	—
Financials	19.4	1.1	—	—
Industrials	11.4	1.0	—	—
Durables	1.4	0.9	—	—
Staples	7.9	1.0	—	—
Services	10.6	1.0	—	—
Retail	6.5	1.0	—	—
Health	16.4	1.1	—	—
Technology	16.5	0.9	—	—

Analysis by Christopher Davis 10-08-01

TIAA-CREF Growth & Income Fund's recent troubles shouldn't obscure its formidable long-term strengths.

This offering had outpaced the S&P 500 index in each calendar year since its 1997 launch, but it has thus far fallen short of that mark this year. Indeed, the fund's 19.5% loss for the year to date through Oct. 3, 2001, trails the index by 1.5 percentage points and lags 53% of its large-blend rivals.

Both the active and passive components of this fund's portfolio are to blame for the lackluster showing. Manager Carlton Martin adjusts the fund's passive/active allocation if he thinks he can add value through stock-picking; the active portion can rise up to 80% of assets, though it has stood near 40% this year. That has largely left the fund's fortunes tied to its bogy, the S&P 500, which has been a sinking ship throughout most of 2001. The slumping index hasn't been the only problem, though. Although Martin hasn't made any big bets against the index, some of his moves have been off the mark. For instance, he admits he hung on to telecom picks such as Lucent for too long (though he still maintains a reduced stake in the company). And while Martin has kept the fund's tech exposure in line with its bogy, the fund's underweighting in strong-performing PC-related names like Microsoft and IBM has been a liability.

That said, the fund has lost just a touch more than the category average this year, despite that its rivals have had the flexibility to slash exposure to falling tech stocks and to shelter themselves with cash. And history suggests that shareholders have a fighting chance in besting the index here: Martin has beaten S&P 500 by 1.5% annually over the trailing three-year period. Another mark in the fund's favor is its low expenses, which gives it a significant edge over the long haul. Simply put, shareholders in search of a core holding will find this an attractive choice.

Address:	c/o State Street Bank P.O. Box 8009 Boston, MA 02266–8009 800–223–1200
Web Address:	www.tiaa–cref.org
*Inception:	09-01-97
Advisor:	Teachers Adv., Inc.
Subadvisor:	None
NTF Plans:	N/A

Minimum Purchase:	$1500	Add: $50	IRA: $500
Min Auto Inv Plan:	$50	Add: $50	
Sales Fees:	No-load		
Management Fee:	.93%		
Actual Fees:	Mgt: 0.43%	Dist: —	
Expense Projections:	3Yr: $138	5Yr: $241	10Yr: $869
Avg Brok Commission:	—	Income Distrib: Quarterly	
Total Cost (relative to category):		Below Avg	

TIAA–CREF Growth Equity

Ticker	Load	NAV	Yield	Total Assets	Mstar Category
TIGEX	None	$9.85	0.0%	$657.1 mil	Large Growth

Prospectus Objective: Growth

TIAA-CREF Growth Equity Fund seeks capital appreciation.

The fund normally invests at least 80% of assets in equities of companies that management judges to have capital appreciation potential. It may invest in companies of all sizes, including those in new and emerging areas of the economy, and those with distinctive products or promising market conditions. Management seeks issuers with the potential for strong earnings or sales growth, or that appear undervalued based on current earnings, assets, or growth prospects.

Historical Profile
Return: Low
Risk: Above Avg
Rating: ★ Lowest

Investment Style
Equity
Average Stock %: 100% (1997), 98% (1998), 98% (1999), 99% (2000), 99% (12-01)

▼ Manager Change
▽ Partial Manager Change

Fund Performance vs. Category Average
■ Quarterly Fund Return +/– Category Average
— Category Baseline

Performance Quartile (within Category)

Portfolio Manager(s)

Management Team

	1990	1991	1992	1993	1994	1995	1996	1997	1998	1999	2000	12-01	History
	—	—	—	—	—	—	—	10.12	13.65	17.19	12.87	9.85	NAV
	—	—	—	—	—	—	—	4.89*	35.97	33.00	–20.29	–23.02	Total Return %
	—	—	—	—	—	—	—	–3.61*	7.40	11.96	–11.19	–11.15	+/– S&P 500
	—	—	—	—	—	—	—	—	–9.13	3.32	4.23	–2.52	+/– Russ Top 200 Grt
	—	—	—	—	—	—	—	0.32	0.25	0.14	0.00	0.00	Income Return %
	—	—	—	—	—	—	—	4.57	35.73	32.86	–20.29	–23.02	Capital Return %
	—	—	—	—	—	—	—	—	35	59	74	51	Total Rtn % Rank Cat
	—	—	—	—	—	—	—	0.03	0.02	0.02	0.00	0.00	Income $
	—	—	—	—	—	—	—	0.16	0.08	0.93	0.85	0.06	Capital Gains $
	—	—	—	—	—	—	—	—	0.45	0.45	0.45	—	Expense Ratio %
	—	—	—	—	—	—	—	—	0.37	0.16	0.00	—	Income Ratio %
	—	—	—	—	—	—	—	—	50	70	42	—	Turnover Rate %
	—	—	—	—	—	—	—	64.5	296.6	696.3	786.2	657.1	Net Assets $mil

Performance 12-31-01

	1st Qtr	2nd Qtr	3rd Qtr	4th Qtr	Total
1997	—	—	—	2.70	4.89 *
1998	14.92	5.07	–12.28	28.36	35.97
1999	5.49	6.46	–3.59	22.83	33.00
2000	9.83	–2.60	–5.27	–21.34	–20.29
2001	–22.69	9.05	–21.11	15.74	–23.02

Trailing	Total Return%	+/– S&P 500	+/– Russ Top 200 Grth	% Rank All	% Rank Cat	Growth of $10,000
3 Mo	15.74	5.05	2.88	22	34	11,574
6 Mo	–8.69	–3.13	–1.70	81	48	9,131
1 Yr	–23.02	–11.15	–2.52	85	51	7,698
3 Yr Avg	–6.55	–5.53	1.47	95	74	8,160
5 Yr Avg	—	—	—	—	—	—
10 Yr Avg	—	—	—	—	—	—
15 Yr Avg	—	—	—	—	—	—

Tax Analysis	Tax-Adj Ret%	%Rank Cat	%Pretax Ret	%Rank Cat
3 Yr Avg	–7.33	70	—	—
5 Yr Avg	—	—	—	—
10 Yr Avg	—	—	—	—

Potential Capital Gain Exposure: –42% of assets

Risk Analysis

Time Period	Load-Adj Return %	Risk %Rank[1] All	Risk %Rank[1] Cat	Morningstar Return	Morningstar Risk	Morningstar Risk-Adj Rating
1 Yr	–23.02					
3 Yr	–6.55	90	70	–2.18[2]	1.43	★
5 Yr	—	—	—	—	—	
Incept	3.56	—	—	—	—	

Average Historical Rating (17 months): 2.4★s

[1] 1=low, 100=high [2] T-Bill return substituted for category avg.

Category Rating (3 Yr)

1 2 3 4 5 (Worst → Best)

Return: Below Avg
Risk: Above Avg

Other Measures	Standard Index S&P 500	Best Fit Index MSCIACWdFr
Alpha	–1.8	4.0
Beta	1.41	1.52
R-Squared	82	84

Standard Deviation	25.65
Mean	–6.55
Sharpe Ratio	–0.53

Analysis by Christopher Davis 10-08-01

While TIAA-CREF Growth Equity Fund may eventually bear fruit, it has been a disappointment so far.

To say that the past year was rough for this offering would be an understatement. Indeed, the fund has shed 40% of its value in the trailing 12 months through Oct. 10, 2001—a lousy showing by any measure and worse than 63% of its large-growth rivals.

The fund's woes partly stem from its aggressive bogy, the Russell 3000 Growth index. It closely tracks that index, so unlike its rivals, the fund can't build a big cash stake or flee from troubled sectors. Thus, it kept its tech weighting—which stands near 40% of assets—within spitting distance of its benchmark's, even as the sector suffered precipitous losses. Unfortunately, the fund's close ties to the index aren't the only problem. Managers Ted Wolff and Nancy Wadelton can adjust its exposure to the index if they think they can add value through stock-picking; lately, the fund's active portion has stood at 40% of assets (80% is the limit). The pair has favored data storage and software stocks, including EMC and Veritas Software, which have been hammered in the past year. In all, the fund has trailed its bogy by 2.5 percentage points in the past 12 months.

Simply put, we think the fund has yet to prove its mettle. It lagged the category average in two of the past three calendar years, and it is on pace to do so again. That bitter pill would be easier to swallow if the fund either scored big returns in favorable markets or if it held up well during rough ones, but it hasn't.

Still, we'd be mistaken to count this fund out just yet. TIAA-CREF has successfully employed its part-index, part-actively managed approach for years, and there's no reason why it can't work well here. That fact argues for keeping the faith, but current shareholders may want to consider selling if they enjoy a tax-loss benefit from doing so.

Portfolio Analysis 09-30-01

Share change since 06-01 Total Stocks: 1572	Sector	PE	YTD Ret%	% Assets
⊖ General Elec	Industrials	30.1	–15.00	7.27
⊖ Pfizer	Health	34.7	–12.40	5.78
⊖ Microsoft	Technology	57.6	52.78	4.63
⊕ AOL Time Warner	Technology	—	–7.76	3.06
⊖ Wal-Mart Stores	Retail	40.3	8.94	2.97
⊕ American Intl Grp	Financials	42.0	–19.20	2.77
⊖ Intel	Technology	73.1	4.89	2.75
⊕ Johnson & Johnson	Health	16.6	14.01	2.31
⊖ Amgen	Health	52.8	–11.70	2.27
⊕ Home Depot	Retail	42.9	12.07	2.04
⊖ Oracle	Technology	32.1	–52.40	1.83
⊕ Pharmacia	Health	36.5	–29.30	1.82
⊖ Cisco Sys	Technology	—	–52.60	1.77
⊕ Tyco Intl	Industrials	27.1	6.23	1.70
⊕ Sprint (PCS Group)	Services	—	19.43	1.58
⊕ Abbott Labs	Health	51.6	17.08	1.57
⊕ Schering-Plough	Health	22.2	–35.90	1.56
⊖ Merck	Health	19.1	–35.90	1.36
⊖ Medtronic	Health	76.4	–14.70	1.34
⊖ Cardinal Health	Health	35.1	–2.51	1.24
⊕ PepsiCo	Staples	31.4	–0.54	1.20
⊖ IBM	Technology	26.9	43.00	1.13
⊕ Citigroup	Financials	20.0	0.03	1.12
⊖ Qualcomm	Technology	—	–38.50	1.01
⊕ Gillette	Staples	56.6	–5.47	0.94

Current Investment Style

Style: Value Blnd Growth; Size: Large Med Small

	Stock Port Avg	Relative S&P 500 Current	Relative S&P 500 Hist	Rel Cat
Price/Earnings Ratio	36.8	1.19	1.25	1.03
Price/Book Ratio	7.4	1.31	1.30	1.17
Price/Cash Flow	23.2	1.29	1.23	1.02
3 Yr Earnings Growth	19.7	1.35	1.35	0.92
1 Yr Earnings Est%	3.0	—	—	1.01
Med Mkt Cap $mil	81,560	1.3	1.5	1.72

Special Securities % assets 09-30-01	
Restricted/Illiquid Secs	0
Emerging-Markets Secs	Trace
Options/Futures/Warrants	No

Composition % assets 09-30-01	
Cash	0.6
Stocks*	99.4
Bonds	0.0
Other	0.0
*Foreign (% stocks)	1.3

Market Cap	
Giant	63.3
Large	23.7
Medium	9.8
Small	2.8
Micro	0.4

Sector Weightings	% of Stocks	Rel S&P	5-Year High	5-Year Low
Utilities	0.4	0.1	—	—
Energy	2.1	0.3	—	—
Financials	8.4	0.5	—	—
Industrials	10.3	0.9	—	—
Durables	0.9	0.6	—	—
Staples	6.6	0.8	—	—
Services	7.6	0.7	—	—
Retail	8.2	1.2	—	—
Health	26.9	1.8	—	—
Technology	28.6	1.6	—	—

Address:	c/o State Street Bank P.O. Box 8009 Boston, MA 02266–8009 800–223–1200
Web Address:	www.tiaa–cref.org
*Inception:	09-01-97
Advisor:	Teachers Adv., Inc.
Subadvisor:	None
NTF Plans:	N/A

Minimum Purchase:	$1500	Add: $50	IRA: $500
Min Auto Inv Plan:	$50	Add: $50	
Sales Fees:	No-load		
Management Fee:	.95%		
Actual Fees:	Mgt: 0.45%	Dist: —	
Expense Projections:	3Yr: $144	5Yr: $252	10Yr: $893
Avg Brok Commission:	—	Income Distrib: Annually	
Total Cost (relative to category):		Low	

TIAA–CREF International Equity

Ticker	Load	NAV	Yield	Total Assets	Mstar Category
TIINX	None	$8.07	0.8%	$262.0 mil	Foreign Stock

Prospectus Objective: Foreign Stock

TIAA-CREF International Equity Fund seeks capital appreciation.

The fund normally invests at least 80% of assets in securities of issuers located in at least three foreign countries, excluding the United States. Management allocates investments to particular countries or regions based on its evaluation of the relative attractiveness of stocks in those markets.

Historical Profile

Return	Average
Risk	Average
Rating	★★★ Neutral

Investment Style
Equity
Average Stock %: 99% 95% 99% 98% 99%

▼ Manager Change
▽ Partial Manager Change

Fund Performance vs. Category Average
■ Quarterly Fund Return
+/– Category Average
— Category Baseline

Performance Quartile (within Category)

Portfolio Manager(s)

Christopher Semenuk. Since 9-97.
Sachie Makishi. Since 1–01.

1990	1991	1992	1993	1994	1995	1996	1997	1998	1999	2000	12–01	History
—	—	—	—	—	—	—	8.92	10.54	16.08	10.75	8.07	NAV
—	—	—	—	—	—	—	–2.30*	19.27	55.83	–20.00	–24.29	Total Return %
—	—	—	—	—	—	—	–10.80*	–9.31	34.79	–10.89	–12.41	+/– S&P 500
—	—	—	—	—	—	—	—	–0.73	28.87	–5.83	—	+/– MSCI EAFE
—	—	—	—	—	—	—	0.00	1.10	1.04	0.55	0.63	Income Return %
—	—	—	—	—	—	—	–2.30	18.17	54.79	–20.54	–24.92	Capital Return %
—	—	—	—	—	—	—	—	20	26	70	66	Total Rtn % Rank Cat
—	—	—	—	—	—	—	0.00	0.10	0.11	0.09	0.07	Income $
—	—	—	—	—	—	—	0.00	0.00	0.23	2.00	0.00	Capital Gains $
—	—	—	—	—	—	—	—	0.49	0.49	0.49	—	Expense Ratio %
—	—	—	—	—	—	—	—	1.23	1.03	0.49	—	Income Ratio %
—	—	—	—	—	—	—	—	27	74	138	—	Turnover Rate %
—	—	—	—	—	—	—	47.8	118.6	255.8	275.1	262.0	Net Assets $mil

Performance 12-31-01

	1st Qtr	2nd Qtr	3rd Qtr	4th Qtr	Total
1997	—	—	—	–7.56	–2.30*
1998	14.57	1.76	–16.06	21.86	19.27
1999	3.13	2.39	8.00	36.64	55.83
2000	4.85	–10.56	–8.62	–6.64	–20.00
2001	–15.35	–1.87	–14.67	6.81	–24.29

Trailing	Total Return%	+/– S&P 500	+/– MSCI EAFE	% Rank All	% Rank Cat	Growth of $10,000
3 Mo	6.81	–3.88	—	57	66	10,681
6 Mo	–8.86	–3.30	—	81	50	9,114
1 Yr	–24.29	–12.41	—	87	66	7,571
3 Yr Avg	–1.91	–0.88	—	82	45	9,439
5 Yr Avg	—	—	—	—	—	—
10 Yr Avg	—	—	—	—	—	—
15 Yr Avg	—	—	—	—	—	—

Tax Analysis	Tax-Adj Ret%	%Rank Cat	%Pretax Ret	%Rank Cat
3 Yr Avg	–3.64	48	—	—
5 Yr Avg	—	—	—	—
10 Yr Avg	—	—	—	—

Potential Capital Gain Exposure: –39% of assets

Risk Analysis

Time Period	Load-Adj Return %	Risk %Rank[1] All	Risk %Rank[1] Cat	Morningstar Return	Morningstar Risk	Morningstar Risk-Adj Rating
1 Yr	–24.29					
3 Yr	–1.91	79	74	–1.36[2]	1.05	★★★
5 Yr	—	—	—	—	—	
Incept	2.22	—	—	—	—	

Average Historical Rating (17 months): 3.5★s

[1]1=low, 100=high [2] T-Bill return substituted for category avg.

Category Rating (3 Yr)

1 2 3 4 5
Worst Best

Return	Average
Risk	Above Avg

Other Measures	Standard Index S&P 500	Best Fit Index Wil 4500
Alpha	–1.3	–4.4
Beta	0.70	0.68
R-Squared	28	71

Standard Deviation	22.45
Mean	–1.91
Sharpe Ratio	–0.35

Portfolio Analysis 06-30-01

Share change since 02–01 Total Stocks: 1036	Sector	Country	% Assets
⊕ Nokia	Technology	Finland	1.95
☆ Glaxosmithkline	Technology	United Kingdom	1.79
⊕ SAP	Technology	Germany	1.66
☆ Unilever (Netherlands)	Staples	Netherlands	1.54
⊕ Diageo	Staples	United Kingdom	1.47
⊖ Lloyds TSB Grp	Financials	United Kingdom	1.46
⊕ Asm Lithography Hldg	Technology	Netherlands	1.46
⊖ Toyota Motor	Durables	Japan	1.41
⊖ Compass Grp	Services	United Kingdom	1.27
BP Amoco	Energy	United Kingdom	1.26
⊖ IHC Caland	Industrials	Netherlands	1.22
☆ Elsevier (Cert)	Services	Netherlands	1.22
⊖ Royal Bk of Scotland	Financials	United Kingdom	1.21
⊕ HSBC Hldgs (UK) (2nd)	Financials	United Kingdom	1.18
⊖ Vodafone Grp	N/A	N/A	1.10
⊕ Royal Dutch Petro	Energy	Netherlands	1.06
⊕ Wolseley	Industrials	United Kingdom	1.04
⊖ Ahold	Retail	Netherlands	0.95
⊖ Serono	Health	Switzerland	0.95
⊕ Sony	Durables	Japan	0.92

Current Investment Style

Style: Value Blnd Growth; Size: Large Med Small

	Stock Port Avg	Rel MSCI EAFE Current	Rel MSCI EAFE Hist	Rel Cat
Price/Earnings Ratio	27.6	1.06	1.03	1.08
Price/Cash Flow	14.3	1.11	1.11	1.00
Price/Book Ratio	4.0	1.14	1.27	1.02
3 Yr Earnings Growth	16.1	0.86	1.41	0.82
Med Mkt Cap $mil	18,048	0.6	0.8	1.00

Country Exposure 06-30-01	% assets
United Kingdom	26
Japan	22
Netherlands	11
Germany	7
France	7

Hedging History: Never

Regional Exposure 06-30-01	% assets
Europe	66
Japan	22
Latin America	0
Pacific Rim	6
Other	0

Special Securities % assets 06-30-01	
Restricted/Illiquid Secs	0
Emerging–Markets Secs	2
Options/Futures/Warrants	No

Composition % assets 06-30-01

Cash	0.2	Bonds	0.0
Stocks	98.9	Other	0.9

Sector Weightings	% of Stocks	Rel Cat	5-Year High	5-Year Low
Utilities	3.5	1.3	—	—
Energy	5.8	1.0	—	—
Financials	21.4	1.0	—	—
Industrials	14.6	1.1	—	—
Durables	8.0	1.2	—	—
Staples	8.3	1.2	—	—
Services	16.2	0.9	—	—
Retail	5.6	1.2	—	—
Health	6.4	0.7	—	—
Technology	10.2	1.0	—	—

Analysis by Christopher Davis 10-10-01

If you can look past its recent performance, you'll find a lot to like in TIAA-CREF International Equity Fund.

Shareholders here will likely want to forget the past two years. The sputtering global economy and faltering profits dragged the fund to a 20% loss in 2000—a bottom-third showing in the foreign-stock group. Matters went from bad to worse in 2001, and the fund dropped 27% and lagged 55% of its rivals through Oct. 9, 2001.

Both the active and indexed components of this fund's portfolio are to blame for the lackluster showing. Managers Christopher Semenuk and Sachie Makishi adjust the fund's passive/active allocation if they think they can add value through stock-picking; the active portion can float up to 80% of assets. That approach leaves the fund's fortunes partly tied to its bogy, the MSCI EAFE index, which has been hurt by struggling European telecoms and ailing Japanese stocks. The slumping index hasn't been the only problem, though. In early 2000, Semenuk and Makishi let the fund's active component rise to 75% of assets, much of which was devoted to high-priced tech and telecom stocks. This move backfired when both sectors began to head south in March 2000. The pair has since sliced the active portion of the portfolio to 40% of assets, but they have marginally overweighted technology for much of 2001, even as the sector suffered enormous losses. And they have continued to boost their stakes in telecom names, including Nokia, which have been hit hard this year.

Nonetheless, the fund's long-term record suggests it can deliver the goods: For the trailing three-year period, it outpaces 72% of its peers. Another mark in the fund's favor is its low expenses, which gives it a significant edge over the long haul.

We think this offering remains a strong choice for a core international holding.

Address:	c/o State Street Bank P.O. Box 8009 Boston, MA 02266–8009 800–223–1200
Web Address:	www.tiaa–cref.org
*Inception:	09-01-97
Advisor:	Teachers Adv., Inc.
Subadvisor:	None
NTF Plans:	N/A

Minimum Purchase:	$1500	Add: $50	IRA: $500
Min Auto Inv Plan:	$50	Add: $50	
Sales Fees:	No–load		
Management Fee:	.99%		
Actual Fees:	Mgt: 0.49%	Dist: —	
Expense Projections:	3Yr: $157	5Yr: $274	10Yr: $941
Avg Brok Commission:	—	Income Distrib: Annually	
Total Cost (relative to category):		Low	

TIAA–CREF Managed Allocation

Ticker	Load	NAV	Yield	Total Assets	Mstar Category
TIMAX	None	$10.50	2.6%	$319.0 mil	Domestic Hybrid

Prospectus Objective: Balanced

TIAA-CREF Managed Allocation Fund seeks capital appreciation and investment income.

The fund invests primarily in other TIAA-CREF mutual funds, rather than investing directly in individual securities. It normally invests at least 60% of assets in shares of the TIAA-CREF Growth and Income, International Equity, and Growth Equity Funds. Approximately 40% of assets may be invested in shares of the TIAA-CREF Bonds Plus Fund. These percentages may fluctuate up and down by up to 15%, depending on management's analysis of market, economic, and financial conditions. The fund is non-diversified.

Historical Profile

Return Average
Risk Below Avg
Rating ★★★ Neutral

Investment Style
Equity
Average Stock %: 29% (1999), 30% (2000), 33% (12-01)

▼ Manager Change
▽ Partial Manager Change

Fund Performance vs. Category Average
■ Quarterly Fund Return
+/– Category Average
— Category Baseline

Performance Quartile (within Category)

Portfolio Manager(s)

James Fleischmann, CFA. Since 9-97. BA'67 U. of Pittsburgh; MBA'71 Pennsylvania State U.

Edward J. Grzybowski, CFA. Since 8-98. BA Hunter C.;

History

	1990	1991	1992	1993	1994	1995	1996	1997	1998	1999	2000	12–01
NAV	—	—	—	—	—	—	—	10.01	11.79	13.59	12.20	10.50
Total Return %	—	—	—	—	—	—	—	3.77*	21.24	19.20	–4.94	–8.52
+/– S&P 500	—	—	—	—	—	—	—	–4.73*	–7.33	–1.84	4.16	3.35
+/– LB Aggregate	—	—	—	—	—	—	—	—	12.57	20.03	–16.57	–16.95
Income Return %	—	—	—	—	—	—	—	1.73	3.27	3.30	3.53	2.30
Capital Return %	—	—	—	—	—	—	—	2.04	17.97	15.90	–8.47	–10.83
Total Rtn % Rank Cat	—	—	—	—	—	—	—	—	11	10	89	79
Income $	—	—	—	—	—	—	—	0.17	0.32	0.38	0.47	0.28
Capital Gains $	—	—	—	—	—	—	—	0.00	0.00	0.05	0.26	0.38
Expense Ratio %	—	—	—	—	—	—	—	—	0.00	0.00	0.00	—
Income Ratio %	—	—	—	—	—	—	—	—	2.80	5.19	2.87	—
Turnover Rate %	—	—	—	—	—	—	—	—	5	4	1	—
Net Assets $mil	—	—	—	—	—	—	—	59.1	162.9	244.4	330.8	319.0

Performance 12-31-01

	1st Qtr	2nd Qtr	3rd Qtr	4th Qtr	Total
1997	—	—	—	1.57	3.77 *
1998	9.11	3.33	–5.69	14.01	21.24
1999	3.03	3.20	–1.30	13.58	19.20
2000	4.88	–1.77	–1.27	–6.55	–4.94
2001	–9.43	3.39	–8.49	6.75	–8.53

Trailing	Total Return%	+/– S&P 500	+/– LB Agg	% Rank All	% Rank Cat	Growth of $10,000
3 Mo	6.75	–3.93	6.71	57	40	10,675
6 Mo	–2.31	3.24	–6.97	48	63	9,769
1 Yr	–8.52	3.35	–16.95	58	79	9,148
3 Yr Avg	1.20	2.23	–5.07	67	63	10,365
5 Yr Avg	—	—	—	—	—	—
10 Yr Avg	—	—	—	—	—	—
15 Yr Avg	—	—	—	—	—	—

Tax Analysis	Tax-Adj Ret%	%Rank Cat	%Pretax Ret	%Rank Cat
3 Yr Avg	–0.40	62	—	—
5 Yr Avg	—	—	—	—
10 Yr Avg	—	—	—	—

Potential Capital Gain Exposure: –12% of assets

Risk Analysis

Time Period	Load-Adj Return %	Risk %Rank[1] All	Risk %Rank[1] Cat	Morningstar Return	Morningstar Risk	Morningstar Risk-Adj Rating
1 Yr	–8.52					
3 Yr	1.20	48	83	–0.77[2]	0.67	★★★
5 Yr	—	—	—	—	—	
Incept	6.32	—	—	—	—	

Average Historical Rating (17 months): 3.5★s

[1] 1=low, 100=high [2] T-Bill return substituted for category avg.

Category Rating (3 Yr)

1 2 3 4 5 — Worst … Best

Return Average
Risk Above Avg

Other Measures	Standard Index S&P 500	Best Fit Index MSCIACWdFr
Alpha	0.0	2.9
Beta	0.66	0.73
R-Squared	81	88

Standard Deviation	12.39
Mean	1.20
Sharpe Ratio	–0.35

Portfolio Analysis 09-30-01

Total Stocks: 6

Share change since 06–01	Sector	PE Ratio	YTD Return %	% Net Assets
⊖ TIAA–CREF Bond Plus	N/A	—	—	44.10
⊕ TIAA–CREF Growth & Income	N/A	—	—	23.93
⊕ TIAA–CREF Growth Equity	N/A	—	—	21.85
☆ TIAA–CREF Intl Equity	N/A	—	—	7.78
⊕ TIAA–CREF High–Yield Bond	N/A	—	—	2.56
⊕ TIAA–CREF Money Market	N/A	—	—	0.35
⊖ TIAA–CREF International Equity	N/A	—	—	0.00

Total Fixed-Income: 0	Date of Maturity	Amount $000	Value $000	% Net Assets

Equity Style
Style: —
Size: —
NA

	Portfolio Avg	Rel S&P
Price/Earnings Ratio	30.8	1.00
Price/Book Ratio	5.5	0.97
Price/Cash Flow	18.1	1.01
3 Yr Earnings Growth	18.3	1.25
1 Yr Earnings Est%	–3.5	1.99
Debt % Total Cap	27.2	0.88
Med Mkt Cap $mil	63,049	1.04

Fixed-Income Style
Duration: —
Quality: —
NA

Avg Eff Duration	—
Avg Eff Maturity	—
Avg Credit Quality	—
Avg Wtd Coupon	—

Special Securities % assets
Restricted/Illiquid Secs
Emerging-Markets Secs
Options/Futures/Warrants

Composition % of assets 09-30-01	
Cash	13.0
Stocks*	52.7
Bonds	33.7
Other	0.6
*Foreign (% of stocks)	9.0

Market Cap	
Giant	—
Large	—
Medium	—
Small	—
Micro	—

Sector Weightings	% of Stocks	Rel S&P	5-Year High	5-Year Low
Utilities	1.0	0.3	—	—
Energy	2.7	0.4	—	—
Financials	7.5	0.4	—	—
Industrials	6.4	0.6	—	—
Durables	1.4	0.9	—	—
Staples	3.1	0.4	—	—
Services	51.9	4.8	—	—
Retail	3.4	0.5	—	—
Health	8.5	0.6	—	—
Technology	14.1	0.8	—	—

Analysis by Kunal Kapoor 07-13-01

TIAA-CREF Managed Allocation Fund is paying for its growth orientation, but we think that long-term investors will be fine here.

This fund's construction means that it hasn't been able to hide in the current market environment. Indeed, two of its underlying funds—TIAA-CREF Growth Equity and TIAA-CREF International—have had tremendous exposure to falling tech and telecom stocks, so the fund has felt their pain. Throw in the fact that TIAA-CREF Growth & Income also owns its fair share of stocks from those sectors and the picture gets even murkier. In fact, but for TIAA-CREF Bond Plus, things could have been a lot worse than the fund's 7% loss over the trailing-12 month period through July 12, 2001.

The fund looks especially bad against the rest of the domestic-hybrid set. Indeed, given that many of its rivals have greater value orientations and dip liberally into recently strong small- and mid-cap stocks, this offering has really had to fight a headwind. To be sure, just about every fund in the group with sizable large-cap growth exposure has taken a walloping, but this fund has been especially weak.

That doesn't mean the fund isn't worth owning. It has shown itself to be quite capable at handling more-favorable markets, for example. It put up fabulous returns in 1998 and 1999, for example, easily beating the majority of its competitors during that stretch. That, combined with its low expenses, means that although the fund might have to weather some ups and downs, it should be pretty competitive over the long haul.

The fund isn't a good choice for those who may want a relatively conservative hybrid fund, though. If anything, this offering should appeal to those who have long-term goals such as saving for a child's education.

Address:	c/o State Street Bank P.O. Box 8009 Boston, MA 02266–8009 800–223–1200
Web Address:	www.tiaa–cref.org
*Inception:	09-01-97
Advisor:	Teachers Adv., Inc.
Subadvisor:	None
NTF Plans:	N/A

Minimum Purchase:	$1500	Add: $50	IRA: $500
Min Auto Inv Plan:	$50	Add: $50	
Sales Fees:	No–load		
Management Fee:	.89%		
Actual Fees:	Mgt: 0.40%	Dist: —	
Expense Projections:	3Yr: $128	5Yr: $224	10Yr: $833
Avg Brok Commission:	—	Income Distrib: Quarterly	
Total Cost (relative to category):		Low	

TIAA–CREF Social Choice Equity

Ticker	Load	NAV	Yield	Total Assets	Mstar Category
TCSCX	None	$8.28	0.8%	$65.2 mil	Large Blend

Prospectus Objective: Growth

TIAA-CREF Social Choice Equity Fund seeks a favorable rate of return that reflects the performance of the U.S. stock market while giving consideration to certain social criteria.

The fund attempts to track the performance of the S & P 500 Index. The fund will not invest in companies that are engaged in the businesses of weapons, tobacco, or alcohol. The fund will also not invest in producers of nuclear energy, companies that have operations in Northern Ireland, and companies that have not adopted the MacBride Principles.

Historical Profile

Return —
Risk —
Rating Not Rated

Investment Style
Equity
Average Stock %: 98% (2000), 99% (12-01)

▼ Manager Change
▽ Partial Manager Change

Fund Performance vs. Category Average
■ Quarterly Fund Return +/– Category Average
— Category Baseline

Performance Quartile (within Category)

Portfolio Manager(s)

Management Team

1990	1991	1992	1993	1994	1995	1996	1997	1998	1999	2000	12-01	History
—	—	—	—	—	—	—	—	—	—	9.57	8.28	NAV
—	—	—	—	—	—	—	—	—	—	-9.99*	-12.75	Total Return %
—	—	—	—	—	—	—	—	—	—	1.58*	-0.87	+/– S&P 500
—	—	—	—	—	—	—	—	—	—	—	0.02	+/– Wilshire Top 750
—	—	—	—	—	—	—	—	—	—	0.61	0.67	Income Return %
—	—	—	—	—	—	—	—	—	—	-10.61	-13.42	Capital Return %
—	—	—	—	—	—	—	—	—	—	—	49	Total Rtn % Rank Cat
—	—	—	—	—	—	—	—	—	—	0.06	0.06	Income $
—	—	—	—	—	—	—	—	—	—	0.02	0.01	Capital Gains $
—	—	—	—	—	—	—	—	—	—	—	—	Expense Ratio %
—	—	—	—	—	—	—	—	—	—	—	—	Income Ratio %
—	—	—	—	—	—	—	—	—	—	—	—	Turnover Rate %
—	—	—	—	—	—	—	—	—	—	38.7	65.2	Net Assets $mil

Performance 12-31-01

	1st Qtr	2nd Qtr	3rd Qtr	4th Qtr	Total
1997	—	—	—	—	—
1998	—	—	—	—	—
1999	—	—	—	—	—
2000	—	-2.33	-1.24	-6.69	-9.99 *
2001	-12.23	4.17	-13.37	10.16	-12.75

Trailing	Total Return%	+/– S&P 500	+/– Wil Top 750	% Rank All	% Rank Cat	Growth of $10,000
3 Mo	10.16	-0.53	-1.17	42	66	11,016
6 Mo	-4.57	0.98	1.22	59	23	9,543
1 Yr	-12.75	-0.87	0.02	67	49	8,725
3 Yr Avg	—	—	—	—	—	—
5 Yr Avg	—	—	—	—	—	—
10 Yr Avg	—	—	—	—	—	—
15 Yr Avg	—	—	—	—	—	—

Tax Analysis	Tax-Adj Ret%	%Rank Cat	%Pretax Ret	%Rank Cat
3 Yr Avg	—	—	—	—
5 Yr Avg	—	—	—	—
10 Yr Avg	—	—	—	—

Potential Capital Gain Exposure: NMF

Risk Analysis

Time Period	Load-Adj Return %	Risk %Rank[1] All	Risk %Rank[1] Cat	Morningstar Return	Morningstar Risk	Morningstar Risk-Adj Rating
1 Yr	-12.75					
3 Yr	—	—	—	—	—	
5 Yr	—	—	—	—	—	
Incept	-12.93	—	—	—	—	

Average Historical Rating —

[1]1=low, 100=high

Category Rating (3 Yr)

Other Measures	Standard Index S&P 500	Best Fit Index
Alpha	—	—
Beta	—	—
R-Squared	—	—

	Standard Deviation	—
Return	Mean	—
Risk	Sharpe Ratio	—

Portfolio Analysis 09-30-01

Share change since 06-01 Total Stocks: 335	Sector	PE	YTD Ret%	% Assets
⊕ Microsoft	Technology	57.6	52.78	3.22
⊕ American Intl Grp	Financials	42.0	-19.20	2.96
⊕ Citigroup	Financials	20.0	0.03	2.79
⊕ Wal-Mart Stores	Retail	40.3	8.94	2.62
⊕ Johnson & Johnson	Health	16.6	14.01	2.52
⊕ Pfizer	Health	34.7	-12.40	2.50
⊕ Merck	Health	19.1	-35.90	2.19
⊕ IBM	Technology	26.9	43.00	2.10
⊕ SBC Comms	Services	18.4	-16.00	1.99
⊕ Verizon Comms	Services	29.7	-2.52	1.90
⊕ Intel	Technology	73.1	4.89	1.72
⊕ AOL Time Warner	Technology	—	-7.76	1.70
⊕ Coca-Cola	Staples	35.5	-21.40	1.69
⊕ Bristol-Myers Squibb	Health	20.2	-26.00	1.66
Procter & Gamble	Staples	38.8	3.12	1.57
⊕ Bank of America	Financials	16.7	42.73	1.47
⊕ Eli Lilly	Health	28.9	-14.40	1.40
⊕ PepsiCo	Staples	31.4	-0.54	1.29
Fannie Mae	Financials	16.2	-6.95	1.27
⊕ Home Depot	Retail	42.9	12.07	1.18
⊕ Wells Fargo	Financials	22.4	-20.20	1.18
⊕ J.P. Morgan Chase & Co.	Financials	27.8	-17.40	1.08
⊕ BellSouth	Services	24.9	-5.09	1.04
⊕ Cisco Sys	Technology	—	-52.60	1.02
⊕ Minnesota Mng & Mfg	Industrials	34.5	0.16	0.99

Current Investment Style

Style: Value Blnd Growth; Size: Large Med Small

	Stock Port Avg	Relative S&P 500 Current	Relative S&P 500 Hist	Rel Cat
Price/Earnings Ratio	29.9	0.97	—	0.99
Price/Book Ratio	5.7	0.99	—	1.03
Price/Cash Flow	18.5	1.03	—	1.00
3 Yr Earnings Growth	16.3	1.12	—	0.91
1 Yr Earnings Est%	0.5	—	—	-6.00
Med Mkt Cap $mil	52,928	0.9	—	1.01

Analysis by Catherine Hickey 09-19-01

It's not just rock-bottom expenses that make this young fund appealing.

TIAA-CREF Social Choice Equity Fund caught investors' attention with its low expense ratio when it launched in April 2000. These days, however, it deserves notice for its solid performance. The fund is down 23% for the year to date through Sept. 26, 2001—a stiff loss in absolute terms—but a top-half showing in the large-blend category.

The fund has managed to avoid even bigger losses in part because of its relatively well-diversified approach. Unlike some other social index funds, this one isn't overly heavy on tech stocks. Tech and telecom companies often pass screening criteria more easily than companies from other, old-economy areas of the market like energy or utilities. However, this fund's stakes in utilities and energy aren't far from the category average. Its bigger positions in these defensive areas means that this fund won't fall as hard as some peers when tech takes a drubbing (as it has so far this year).

Although the fund's exposure to such value sectors has helped in the current tough environment for growth stocks, it may make the fund inappropriate for some. Those who prefer a socially responsible fund with as little exposure to energy and utilities as possible might prefer a fund such as Citizens Core Growth, which invests very little in these areas and heavily favors tech, health care, and telecom. However, investors should expect more volatility from any offering that emphasizes such faster-growing, higher-priced areas.

On the whole, this fund should appeal to both social investors and to those looking for a well-balanced core holding. Its low expenses and low minimum investment, backed by TIAA-CREF's solid quantitative management team, make this fund an attractive option.

Special Securities % assets 09-30-01	
Restricted/Illiquid Secs	0
Emerging-Markets Secs	0
Options/Futures/Warrants	No

Composition % assets 09-30-01	
Cash	0.7
Stocks*	99.3
Bonds	0.0
Other	0.0
*Foreign (% stocks)	1.6

Market Cap	
Giant	53.7
Large	33.6
Medium	11.7
Small	1.1
Micro	0.0

Sector Weightings	% of Stocks	Rel S&P	5-Year High	5-Year Low
Utilities	3.5	1.1	—	—
Energy	5.0	0.7	—	—
Financials	23.0	1.3	—	—
Industrials	6.3	0.6	—	—
Durables	1.2	0.8	—	—
Staples	8.1	1.0	—	—
Services	13.6	1.3	—	—
Retail	6.0	0.9	—	—
Health	16.5	1.1	—	—
Technology	16.9	0.9	—	—

Address:	c/o State Street Bank P.O. Box 8009 Boston, MA 02266–8009 800–223–1200
Web Address:	www.tiaa–cref.org
*Inception:	04-03-00
Advisor:	Teachers Adv., Inc.
Subadvisor:	None
NTF Plans:	N/A

Minimum Purchase:	$1500	Add: $50	IRA: $500
Min Auto Inv Plan:	$50	Add: $50	
Sales Fees:	No-load		
Management Fee:	.77%		
Actual Fees:	Mgt: 0.27%	Dist: —	
Expense Projections:	3Yr: $87*	5Yr: —	10Yr: —
Avg Brok Commission:	—	Income Distrib: Annually	
Total Cost (relative to category):	—		

Torray

Ticker	Load	NAV	Yield	Total Assets	Mstar Category
TORYX	None	$37.53	0.5%	$1,691.8 mil	Large Value

Prospectus Objective: Growth

Torray Fund seeks capital appreciation.

The fund normally invests at least 90% of assets in common stocks. It may invest the balance of assets in U.S. Treasury bills or notes. Management seeks companies that it believes have rising sales and earnings, a strong competitive position, capable management, and a balance sheet that is appropriate to the nature of the business. It may invest in companies of any size. Management intends to invest in securities for the long-term instead of actively buying and selling stocks.

This fund also offers Instl shares.

Historical Profile
Return: High
Risk: Average
Rating: ★★★★★ Highest

Investment Style
Equity
Average Stock %: 94% 100% 99% 98% 100% 98% 100%

▼ Manager Change
▽ Partial Manager Change

Fund Performance vs. Category Average
■ Quarterly Fund Return +/– Category Average
— Category Baseline

Performance Quartile (within Category)

Portfolio Manager(s)

Douglas C. Eby. Since 1-92. BA'81 Catholic U.; MBA'82 Indiana U. Other fund currently managed: Torray Instl.

Robert E. Torray. Since 12-90. BA'59 Duke U. Other fund currently managed: Torray Instl.

1990	1991	1992	1993	1994	1995	1996	1997	1998	1999	2000	12-01	History
9.99	11.51	13.74	14.27	13.76	20.11	25.22	33.85	36.48	44.31	39.79	37.53	NAV
–0.04*	19.96	21.06	6.37	2.46	50.37	29.09	37.12	8.19	24.03	–3.38	–0.52	Total Return %
–0.39*	–10.53	13.44	–3.69	1.15	12.84	6.15	3.77	–20.39	2.99	5.73	11.36	+/– S&P 500
—	1.80	11.99	–13.39	4.78	10.34	6.78	1.63	–13.05	13.08	–5.69	8.27	+/– Russ Top 200 Val
0.06	2.35	1.57	0.89	1.50	1.56	0.93	0.52	0.41	0.20	0.58	0.47	Income Return %
–0.10	17.60	19.48	5.47	0.96	48.81	28.16	36.61	7.78	23.82	–3.96	–0.99	Capital Return %
—	92	1	92	17	1	6	2	78	5	88	21	Total Rtn % Rank Cat
0.01	0.23	0.18	0.12	0.21	0.21	0.19	0.13	0.14	0.07	0.25	0.18	Income $
0.00	0.21	0.00	0.22	0.65	0.32	0.53	0.58	0.00	0.79	2.80	1.76	Capital Gains $
0.82	1.25	1.25	1.25	1.25	1.25	1.25	1.13	1.09	1.07	1.06	—	Expense Ratio %
2.15	2.43	1.54	0.94	1.51	1.31	0.87	0.47	0.42	0.18	0.64	—	Income Ratio %
—	21	37	29	37	23	21	12	26	33	45	—	Turnover Rate %
1.0	4.4	10.3	19.7	23.4	50.7	116.6	608.5	1,460.5	1,895.6	1,821.8	1,641.1	Net Assets $mil

Performance 12-31-01

	1st Qtr	2nd Qtr	3rd Qtr	4th Qtr	Total
1997	–2.38	16.06	11.60	8.45	37.12
1998	12.22	0.99	–21.28	21.27	8.19
1999	7.23	12.37	–10.96	15.61	24.03
2000	–1.89	–5.79	7.95	–3.17	–3.38
2001	–3.02	1.81	–13.68	16.72	–0.52

Trailing	Total Return%	+/– S&P 500	+/– Russ Top 200 Val	% Rank All	% Rank Cat	Growth of $10,000
3 Mo	16.72	6.04	11.21	20	4	11,672
6 Mo	0.76	6.31	6.54	35	6	10,076
1 Yr	–0.52	11.36	8.27	43	21	9,948
3 Yr Avg	6.03	7.06	4.87	22	20	11,922
5 Yr Avg	12.08	1.38	0.87	10	16	17,686
10 Yr Avg	16.31	3.38	2.28	3	3	45,297
15 Yr Avg	—	—	—	—	—	—

Tax Analysis	Tax-Adj Ret%	%Rank Cat	%Pretax Ret	%Rank Cat
3 Yr Avg	4.92	16	81.6	20
5 Yr Avg	11.23	7	92.9	4
10 Yr Avg	15.27	1	93.6	3

Potential Capital Gain Exposure: 10% of assets

Risk Analysis

Time Period	Load-Adj Return %	Risk %Rank¹ All	Risk %Rank¹ Cat	Morningstar Return	Morningstar Risk	Morningstar Risk-Adj Rating
1 Yr	–0.52					
3 Yr	6.03	63	87	0.23²	0.88	★★★★
5 Yr	12.08	69	94	1.76²	0.93	★★★★
10 Yr	16.31	67	84	2.14	0.87	★★★★★

Average Historical Rating (97 months): 4.5★s

¹1=low, 100=high ² T-Bill return substituted for category avg.

Category Rating (3 Yr)

1 2 3 4 5 — Worst … Best (rating: 4)

Return: Above Avg
Risk: Above Avg

Other Measures	Standard Index S&P 500	Best Fit Index S&P 500
Alpha	6.9	6.9
Beta	0.89	0.89
R-Squared	66	66

Standard Deviation	19.81
Mean	6.03
Sharpe Ratio	0.06

Portfolio Analysis 11-30-01

Share change since 10-01 Total Stocks: 31	Sector	PE	YTD Ret%	% Assets
⊖ Illinois Tool Works	Industrials	25.4	15.31	5.54
General Motors Cl H	Technology	42.9	–32.80	5.23
⊖ J.P. Morgan Chase & Co.	Financials	27.8	–17.40	5.21
⊕ Bristol-Myers Squibb	Health	20.2	–26.00	4.46
Tribune	Services	NMF	–10.40	4.32
Interpublic Grp	Services	—	–29.80	4.30
Clear Channel Comms	Services	—	5.10	4.28
Boston Scientific	Health	—	76.21	4.02
Honeywell Intl	Durables	NMF	–27.00	4.00
⊖ Abbott Labs	Health	51.6	17.08	3.98
Bank of America	Financials	16.7	42.73	3.75
United Tech	Industrials	16.3	–16.70	3.25
Carnival	Services	16.4	–7.54	3.23
Kimberly-Clark	Industrials	18.5	–13.80	2.89
⊕ Markel	Financials	—	–0.75	2.85
Bank One	Financials	29.1	9.13	2.73
Procter & Gamble	Staples	38.8	3.12	2.63
Hewlett-Packard	Technology	97.8	–33.90	2.63
Automatic Data Processing	Services	39.8	–6.27	2.49
Walt Disney	Services	—	–27.70	2.48
Agilent Tech	Technology	58.2	–47.90	2.41
American Intl Grp	Financials	42.0	–19.20	2.29
Gannett	Services	20.3	8.10	2.28
American Express	Financials	28.3	–34.40	2.14
Johnson & Johnson	Health	16.6	14.01	2.13

Current Investment Style

Style: Value Blnd Growth; Size: Large Med Small

	Stock Port Avg	Relative S&P 500 Current	Relative S&P 500 Hist	Rel Cat
Price/Earnings Ratio	33.6	1.09	0.94	1.33
Price/Book Ratio	4.1	0.72	0.64	0.99
Price/Cash Flow	19.3	1.07	0.91	1.40
3 Yr Earnings Growth	9.9	0.68	0.75	0.67
1 Yr Earnings Est%	–5.7	3.20	—	1.71
Med Mkt Cap $mil	29,552	0.5	0.4	0.93

Analysis by Brian Portnoy 10-15-01

There's no ignoring Torray Fund's impressive long-term record.

This fund is among the large-value category's elite. Over the past decade, managers Bob Torray and Doug Eby have posted an annualized gain of 15%, which not only beats 96% of the competition, but also paces the S&P 500 index by 2.3 percentage points per year. Such marks stem from management's consistently well-executed strategy. It buys companies with strong long-term prospects but beaten-up stock prices and holds them for the long haul. Many of the fund's top positions have been in the portfolio for years.

Recent market volatility, however, has prompted Torray and Eby to make more changes than usual. For example, they bought AIG as the insurance bellwether has struggled throughout 2001. EMC is also new; Eby contends that the firm's dominance in the data storage market, combined with its now-cheap share price, made it compelling. The fund has also added to existing positions such as Disney and Interpublic Group. Management raised cash for these moves by selling most of its defense and auto-related stocks.

While the fund's a great choice for the long haul, investors should note that its returns are among the category's most volatile. That's because it owns only about 35 stocks and parks half of its assets in its top-10 holdings. Thus, only a few misfires can really sting, such as in 2000, when a poor showing from Hughes Electronics helped sink the fund to the category's cellar. On a relative basis, the fund has rebounded some in 2001, however. Its 10.9% loss for the year to date through Oct. 12 is near the category norm. For investors who can tolerate such swings, however, this fund is a compelling option.

Special Securities % assets 11-30-01	
Restricted/Illiquid Secs	0
Emerging-Markets Secs	0
Options/Futures/Warrants	No

Composition % assets 11-30-01	
Cash	0.0
Stocks*	100.0
Bonds	0.0
Other	0.0
*Foreign (% stocks)	0.0

Market Cap	
Giant	34.1
Large	61.6
Medium	4.3
Small	0.0
Micro	0.0

Sector Weightings	% of Stocks	Rel S&P	5-Year High	5-Year Low
Utilities	0.0	0.0	8	0
Energy	0.0	0.0	11	0
Financials	23.4	1.3	42	20
Industrials	14.1	1.2	32	6
Durables	4.2	2.7	7	0
Staples	2.8	0.4	21	1
Services	24.7	2.3	25	3
Retail	0.0	0.0	8	0
Health	15.4	1.0	24	5
Technology	15.5	0.8	26	0

Address:	6610 Rockledge Drive Bethesda, MD 20817 800-443-3036 / 301-493-4600
Web Address:	www.torray.com
*Inception:	12-18-90
Advisor:	Torray
Subadvisor:	None
NTF Plans:	N/A

Minimum Purchase:	$10000	Add: $500	IRA: $10000
Min Auto Inv Plan:	—	Add: —	
Sales Fees:	No-load		
Management Fee:	1.0%		
Actual Fees:	Mgt: 1.00%	Dist: —	
Expense Projections:	3Yr: $342	5Yr: $593	10Yr: $1310
Avg Brok Commission:	—	Income Distrib: Quarterly	
Total Cost (relative to category):		Below Avg	

Tweedy, Browne American Value

Ticker	Load	NAV	Yield	Total Assets	Mstar Category
TWEBX	None	$23.42	0.3%	$977.0 mil	Mid–Cap Value

Prospectus Objective: Growth

Tweedy, Browne American Value Fund seeks long-term growth of capital.

The fund invests primarily in undervalued equity securities issued by domestic companies of various sizes. It may invest up to 20% of assets in foreign securities. The fund may also invest a portion of assets in nonconvertible debt securities issued by governments, companies, and supranational organizations; it may invest no more than 15% of assets in debt securities rated below investment-grade.

Prior to Oct. 4, 1994, the fund was named Tweedy, Browne Value Fund.

Historical Profile

Return Above Avg
Risk Below Avg
Rating ★★★★ Above Avg

Investment Style Equity

	1994	1995	1996	1997	1998	1999	2000	12-01
Average Stock %		84%	91%	91%	88%	94%	95%	92%

▼ Manager Change
∇ Partial Manager Change

Fund Performance vs. Category Average
■ Quarterly Fund Return +/– Category Average
— Category Baseline

Performance Quartile (within Category)

Portfolio Manager(s)

Christopher H. Browne. Since 12-93. BA'69 U. of Pennsylvania. Other fund currently managed: Tweedy, Browne Global Value.

William H. Browne. Since 12-93. BA'67 Colgate U.; MBA'70 Trinity C., Dublin. Other fund currently managed: Tweedy, Browne Global Value.

John D. Spears. Since 12-93. Other fund currently managed: Tweedy, Browne Global Value.

1990	1991	1992	1993	1994	1995	1996	1997	1998	1999	2000	12–01	History
—	—	—	9.94	9.82	13.25	15.64	21.11	22.74	22.37	24.42	23.42	NAV
—	—	—	–0.60*	–0.56	36.21	22.45	38.87	9.59	2.00	14.45	–0.08	Total Return %
—	—	—	–0.83*	–1.88	–1.32	–0.50	5.52	–18.99	–19.03	23.55	11.79	+/– S&P 500
—	—	—	—	1.57	1.28	2.19	4.51	4.50	2.11	–4.74	–2.42	+/– Russ Midcap Val
—	—	—	0.00	0.64	1.08	1.29	1.07	0.67	1.21	0.46	0.33	Income Return %
—	—	—	–0.60	–1.21	35.13	21.16	37.79	8.92	0.79	13.99	–0.42	Capital Return %
—	—	—	—	46	23	31	5	28	69	61	70	Total Rtn % Rank Cat
—	—	—	0.00	0.06	0.11	0.17	0.17	0.14	0.28	0.10	0.08	Income $
—	—	—	0.00	0.00	0.02	0.42	0.43	0.25	0.53	1.08	0.90	Capital Gains $
—	—	—	—	2.26	1.74	1.39	1.39	1.39	1.39	1.37	1.36	Expense Ratio %
—	—	—	—	0.64	1.25	1.13	0.92	0.69	0.55	1.13	0.40	Income Ratio %
—	—	—	—	—	4	9	16	6	16	19	10	Turnover Rate %
—	—	—	3.1	35.7	168.0	277.6	721.3	1,160.0	1,026.0	955.6	977.0	Net Assets $mil

Performance 12-31-01

	1st Qtr	2nd Qtr	3rd Qtr	4th Qtr	Total
1997	3.71	15.66	11.25	4.07	38.87
1998	9.14	3.08	–14.61	14.07	9.59
1999	–1.50	12.28	–7.32	–0.49	2.00
2000	–2.24	0.50	11.47	4.50	14.45
2001	–1.97	6.89	–9.65	5.53	–0.08

Trailing	Total Return%	+/– S&P 500	+/– Russ Midcap Val	% Rank All	% Rank Cat	Growth of $10,000
3 Mo	5.53	–5.15	–6.50	63	96	10,553
6 Mo	–4.65	0.90	–3.74	60	86	9,535
1 Yr	–0.08	11.79	–2.42	42	70	9,992
3 Yr Avg	5.27	6.29	–1.54	29	82	11,664
5 Yr Avg	12.16	1.46	0.70	10	44	17,751
10 Yr Avg	—	—	—	—	—	—
15 Yr Avg	—	—	—	—	—	—

Tax Analysis	Tax-Adj Ret%	%Rank Cat	%Pretax Ret	%Rank Cat
3 Yr Avg	4.15	75	78.7	51
5 Yr Avg	11.13	34	91.5	7
10 Yr Avg	—	—	—	—

Potential Capital Gain Exposure: 26% of assets

Risk Analysis

Time Period	Load-Adj Return %	Risk %Rank[1] All	Risk %Rank[1] Cat	Morningstar Return	Morningstar Risk	Morningstar Risk-Adj Rating
1 Yr	–0.08					
3 Yr	5.27	40	15	0.07[2]	0.54	★★★★
5 Yr	12.16	46	11	1.79[2]	0.61	★★★★
Incept	14.23	—	—	—	—	

Average Historical Rating (61 months): 4.3★s

[1]1=low, 100=high [2] T-Bill return substituted for category avg.

Category Rating (3 Yr)

1 2 **3** 4 5
Worst Best

Return Below Avg
Risk Below Avg

Other Measures	Standard Index S&P 500	Best Fit Index SPMid400
Alpha	2.7	–1.3
Beta	0.38	0.34
R-Squared	30	32

Standard Deviation	12.38
Mean	5.27
Sharpe Ratio	0.03

Analysis by Emily Hall 11-20-01

Tweedy, Browne American Value Fund has shown its soft underbelly this year.

Unless this fund manages a dramatic turnaround in December, it is set to post its worst calendar-year showing ever. For the year to date through mid-November, the fund is down 7.4%, placing it in the bottom half of the mid-value group.

It might seem at first that the fund has suffered because of its monstrous 51% stake in financials stocks. The fund's financials have actually been a mixed bag, though: Stinkers such as Wells Fargo have been offset somewhat by solid performers such as reinsurance company Transatlantic Holdings. The primary problem actually appears to be weak stock picks across a variety of sectors. Some of the worst culprits among the portfolio's top-25 names include pharmaceutical firm Pharmacia, financial giant American Express, and railroad service firm GATX.

The fund has actually looked rather slow for a while: This is the third year in a row that it has delivered returns below the category average. As a result, the fund's long-term record has looked increasingly mediocre.

There are reasons to stick with this offering, however. For one, the managers' conservative value approach has delivered much less volatility than its typical rival over time. The fund's five-year return also remains above the category average, making for an appealing risk/reward package over the long run. Finally, the management team at Tweedy, Browne keeps turnover very low, which makes the fund's returns more appealing on an after-tax basis.

This isn't the most exciting fund around, and its recent performance is nothing to write home about, but for conservative investors willing to invest for the long haul it remains a reasonable choice.

Portfolio Analysis 09-30-01

Share change since 06–01 Total Stocks: 102

	Sector	PE	YTD Ret%	% Assets
⊕ Transatlantic Hldgs	Financials	75.8	29.55	6.73
MBIA	Financials	14.6	9.88	6.50
Household Intl	Financials	14.7	6.89	3.91
Freddie Mac	Financials	14.0	–3.87	3.87
Pharmacia	Health	36.5	–29.30	3.75
Torchmark	Financials	13.5	3.29	3.54
Schering–Plough	Health	22.2	–35.90	3.48
Federated Investors B	Financials	23.3	10.11	3.33
Proquest	N/A	—	—	2.98
☼ Bayer ADR	Health	—	—	2.94
Popular	Financials	14.8	13.41	2.78
American Express	Financials	28.3	–34.40	2.69
Comcast	Services	20.3	–13.70	2.66
PanAmerican Beverages	Staples	16.2	4.74	2.60
GATX	Services	13.0	–32.50	2.43
McDonald's	Services	19.2	–21.50	2.12
Rayonier	Industrials	22.1	30.83	2.08
Wells Fargo	Financials	22.4	–20.20	1.78
Wisconsin Central Transp	Services	—	13.39	1.62
Nestle (Reg) ADR	Staples	24.2	–5.97	1.59
⊕ ABN Amro Hldgs ADR	Financials	10.8	–25.30	1.55
Diageo ADR (New)	Staples	—	—	1.50
American Natl Ins	Financials	15.9	19.75	1.49
Glaxo Wellcome PLC ADR	Health	24.2	–9.77	1.47
Hibernia	Financials	16.3	44.26	1.32

Current Investment Style

Style: Value Blnd Growth; Size: Large Med Small

	Stock Port Avg	Relative S&P 500 Current	Relative S&P 500 Hist	Rel Cat
Price/Earnings Ratio	24.4	0.79	0.64	1.03
Price/Book Ratio	3.6	0.63	0.50	1.19
Price/Cash Flow	12.8[1]	0.71	0.53	1.03
3 Yr Earnings Growth	7.5	0.51	0.50	0.63
1 Yr Earnings Est%	–4.6	2.58	—	0.74
Med Mkt Cap $mil	6,434	0.1	0.1	0.90

[1]figure is based on 50% or less of stocks

Special Securities % assets 09-30-01	
Restricted/Illiquid Secs	0
Emerging–Markets Secs	3
Options/Futures/Warrants	Yes

Composition % assets 09-30-01	
Cash	4.0
Stocks*	95.6
Bonds	0.0
Other	0.4
*Foreign (% stocks)	19.0

Market Cap	
Giant	22.6
Large	18.2
Medium	36.5
Small	18.7
Micro	4.1

Sector Weightings	% of Stocks	Rel S&P	5-Year High	5-Year Low
Utilities	0.0	0.0	0	0
Energy	0.0	0.0	3	0
Financials	50.9	2.8	51	38
Industrials	7.1	0.6	16	5
Durables	1.6	1.0	10	1
Staples	9.3	1.2	17	9
Services	13.2	1.2	19	5
Retail	1.1	0.2	12	1
Health	15.0	1.0	15	4
Technology	1.8	0.1	4	0

Address:	350 Park Avenue New York, NY 10022 800–432–4789
Web Address:	www.tweedy.com
*Inception:	12-08-93
Advisor:	Tweedy Browne
Subadvisor:	None
NTF Plans:	N/A

Minimum Purchase:	$2500	Add: $250 IRA: $500
Min Auto Inv Plan:	$2500	Add: $250
Sales Fees:	No–load	
Management Fee:	1.3%, .09%A	
Actual Fees:	Mgt: 1.25%	Dist: 0.00%
Expense Projections:	3Yr: $434	5Yr: $750 10Yr: $1646
Avg Brok Commission:	—	Income Distrib: Annually
Total Cost (relative to category):		Below Avg

Tweedy, Browne Global Value

Ticker	Load	NAV	Yield	Total Assets	Mstar Category
TBGVX	None	$18.53	1.0%	$3,834.5 mil	Foreign Stock

Prospectus Objective: Foreign Stock

Tweedy, Browne Global Value Fund seeks long-term growth of capital.

The fund invests primarily in equity securities. It focuses on foreign issues, but may also invest in the United States. The fund generally invests in securities issued by established companies with at least three years of operations, that management judges to be undervalued relative to the company's underlying assets, earning power, or private market value. The fund may invest in government and supranational-organization debt; it may invest up to 15% of assets in debt securities rated below investment-grade.

Historical Profile

Return	High
Risk	Low
Rating	★★★★★ Highest

Investment Style
Equity
Average Stock %

1994	1995	1996	1997	1998	1999	2000	12-01
	99%	92%	89%	84%	89%	85%	84%

▼ Manager Change
▽ Partial Manager Change

Fund Performance vs. Category Average
■ Quarterly Fund Return +/– Category Average
— Category Baseline

Performance Quartile (within Category)

Portfolio Manager(s)

Christopher H. Browne. Since 6-93. BA'69 U. of Pennsylvania. Other fund currently managed: Tweedy, Browne American Value.

William H. Browne. Since 6-93. BA'67 Colgate U.; MBA'70 Trinity C., Dublin. Other fund currently managed: Tweedy, Browne American Value.

John D. Spears. Since 6-93. Other fund currently managed: Tweedy, Browne American Value.

History

1990	1991	1992	1993	1994	1995	1996	1997	1998	1999	2000	12-01	History
—	—	—	11.54	11.88	12.95	14.45	16.39	16.82	20.21	19.98	18.53	NAV
—	—	—	15.40*	4.36	10.70	20.23	22.96	10.99	25.28	12.39	–4.67	Total Return %
—	—	—	9.22*	3.05	–26.84	–2.71	–10.39	–17.58	4.24	21.49	7.21	+/– S&P 500
—	—	—	—	–3.42	–0.51	14.19	21.18	–9.00	–1.68	26.56	—	+/– MSCI EAFE
—	—	—	0.00	0.00	0.00	4.27	6.03	2.31	1.54	1.02	0.92	Income Return %
—	—	—	15.40	4.36	10.70	15.96	16.93	8.68	23.74	11.37	–5.59	Capital Return %
—	—	—	—	20	47	13	1	66	85	1	1	Total Rtn % Rank Cat
—	—	—	0.00	0.00	0.00	0.55	0.87	0.38	0.26	0.21	0.18	Income $
—	—	—	0.00	0.16	0.20	0.57	0.49	0.99	0.59	2.52	0.33	Capital Gains $
—	—	—	—	1.73	1.65	1.60	1.58	1.42	1.41	1.38	1.38	Expense Ratio %
—	—	—	—	0.00	1.08	1.15	0.73	1.05	1.26	1.10	1.06	Income Ratio %
—	—	—	—	—	16	17	20	16	23	16	12	Turnover Rate %
—	—	—	157.9	565.7	801.7	1,211.3	1,985.3	2,492.0	3,142.0	3,563.9	3,834.5	Net Assets $mil

Performance 12-31-01

	1st Qtr	2nd Qtr	3rd Qtr	4th Qtr	Total
1997	6.99	10.09	5.29	–0.85	22.96
1998	15.80	0.37	–17.85	16.24	10.99
1999	7.49	14.77	–1.25	2.84	25.28
2000	4.40	1.33	5.38	0.82	12.39
2001	–2.30	4.76	–12.62	6.59	–4.67

Trailing	Total Return%	+/– S&P 500	+/– MSCI EAFE	% Rank All	% Rank Cat	Growth of $10,000
3 Mo	6.59	–4.10	—	58	69	10,659
6 Mo	–6.86	–1.30	—	73	23	9,314
1 Yr	–4.67	7.21	—	50	1	9,533
3 Yr Avg	10.31	11.34	—	11	5	13,423
5 Yr Avg	12.87	2.17	—	8	3	18,320
10 Yr Avg	—	—	—	—	—	—
15 Yr Avg	—	—	—	—	—	—

Tax Analysis	Tax-Adj Ret%	%Rank Cat	%Pretax Ret	%Rank Cat
3 Yr Avg	8.41	6	81.6	49
5 Yr Avg	10.62	4	82.5	21
10 Yr Avg	—	—	—	—

Potential Capital Gain Exposure: 12% of assets

Risk Analysis

Time Period	Load-Adj Return %	Risk %Rank[1] All	Risk %Rank[1] Cat	Morningstar Return	Morningstar Risk	Morningstar Risk-Adj Rating
1 Yr	–4.67					
3 Yr	10.31	32	1	1.20[2]	0.31	★★★★★
5 Yr	12.87	40	1	1.99[2]	0.38	★★★★★
Incept	13.43	—	—	—	—	

Average Historical Rating (67 months): 4.7★s

[1] 1=low, 100=high [2] T-Bill return substituted for category avg.

Category Rating (3 Yr)

1 2 3 4 5 — Worst … Best (rating: 5)

Return	High
Risk	Low

Other Measures	Standard Index S&P 500	Best Fit Index MSCIPcxIND
Alpha	7.5	5.5
Beta	0.38	0.36
R–Squared	39	64

Standard Deviation	11.44
Mean	10.31
Sharpe Ratio	0.54

Portfolio Analysis 09-30-01

Share change since 05–01 Total Stocks: 192	Sector	Country	% Assets
⊕ Nestle (Reg)	Staples	Switzerland	3.38
⊕ Bayer	Health	Germany	2.89
⊕ Merck KGAA (UK)	Health	Germany	2.84
Pharmacia	Health	U.S.	2.75
⊕ Schering–Plough	Health	U.S.	2.33
⊕ ABN Amro Hldgs	Financials	Netherlands	2.29
PanAmerican Beverages	Staples	Mexico	2.19
Diageo	Staples	United Kingdom	2.12
MBIA	Financials	U.S.	2.08
⊕ Novartis (Reg)	Health	Switzerland	2.01
⊕ Axel Springer Verlag	Services	Germany	1.89
Shionogi	Health	Japan	1.83
Kone Cl B	Industrials	Finland	1.79
Telegraaf Hldgs	Services	Netherlands	1.78
⊕ Richemont Cl A (Unit)	Staples	Switzerland	1.71
⊕ Trinity Mirror	Services	United Kingdom	1.63
⊕ United Overseas Bk	Financials	Singapore	1.57
⊕ Akzo Nobel NV	Industrials	Netherlands	1.53
⊕ Huhtamaki Van Leer Cl I Free	Staples	Finland	1.21
Aiful	Financials	Japan	1.17

Current Investment Style

Style: Value Blnd Growth; Size: Large Med Small (style box: Large Value)

	Stock Port Avg	Rel MSCI EAFE Current	Rel MSCI EAFE Hist	Rel Cat
Price/Earnings Ratio	21.0	0.81	0.76	0.82
Price/Cash Flow	11.8	0.92	0.88	0.82
Price/Book Ratio	2.7	0.79	0.65	0.70
3 Yr Earnings Growth	10.9	0.58	0.32	0.56
Med Mkt Cap $mil	3,729	0.1	0.1	0.21

Country Exposure 09-30-01	% assets
United Kingdom	14
U.S.	14
Japan	13
Switzerland	10
Germany	9

Hedging History: Always

Special Securities % assets 09-30-01	
Restricted/Illiquid Secs	0
Emerging–Markets Secs	9
Options/Futures/Warrants	Yes

Composition % assets 09-30-01			
Cash	11.6	Bonds	0.0
Stocks	85.8	Other	2.6

Regional Exposure 09-30-01	% assets
Europe	50
Japan	13
Latin America	4
Pacific Rim	8
Other	15
Other	1

Sector Weightings	% of Stocks	Rel Cat	5-Year High	5-Year Low
Utilities	0.0	0.0	1	0
Energy	0.0	0.0	1	0
Financials	21.6	1.0	29	22
Industrials	15.7	1.2	30	16
Durables	3.9	0.6	11	4
Staples	21.4	3.0	21	14
Services	15.9	0.9	20	5
Retail	1.4	0.3	9	1
Health	18.7	1.9	19	2
Technology	1.6	0.2	2	0

Analysis by Emily Hall 11-27-01

Even as stock markets roil, the managers of Tweedy, Browne Global Value remain unflappable.

Many fund managers were caught by surprise when the go-go growth market came to a screeching halt in 2000, and many of them have dumped their wilting dot-com stocks for more-established fare. But there has been no need to position this offering defensively, because its managers continue to do what they've always done: Pick up a business when its stock is trading at a significant discount to the team's estimate of its intrinsic value and then hold it for the long haul.

That strategy leads Chris Browne, William Browne, and John Spears to own everything from giant European pharmaceutical stocks to small Japanese appliance makers. The result is a value-oriented all-cap portfolio filled primarily with European, Japanese, and Canadian stocks—not to mention the occasional U.S. name. The managers also fully hedge the fund's currency exposure into the U.S. dollar.

Solid stock-picking, combined with the currency policy, has given the fund one of the best records in the group, while its volatility has also been mild. Moreover, the managers' buy-and-hold approach (turnover hovers about 20% per year) has led to nice results on an after-tax basis.

The fund can't be perfect in every environment, though, and when growthier picks soar, this portfolio's lack of tech can be a hindrance. That was the case in 1999, when it trailed 85% of its peers. And the fund has looked slow during the past three months as technology and telecom stocks have enjoyed a rebound. Finally, this offering might not look as consistently strong if the dollar weakens.

Nevertheless, for many investors—especially those looking for a value-oriented offering—this remains an excellent foreign-stock choice.

Address:	350 Park Avenue New York, NY 10022 800–432–4789
Web Address:	www.tweedy.com
*Inception:	06-15-93
Advisor:	Tweedy Browne
Subadvisor:	None
NTF Plans:	N/A

Minimum Purchase:	$2500	Add: $250 IRA: $500
Min Auto Inv Plan:	$2500	Add: $250
Sales Fees:	No–load	
Management Fee:	1.3%, .09%A	
Actual Fees:	Mgt: 1.25%	Dist: —
Expense Projections:	3Yr: $45*	5Yr: $78* 10Yr: $170*
Avg Brok Commission:	—	Income Distrib: Annually
Total Cost (relative to category):	—	

UAM FMA Small Company Instl

Ticker	Load	NAV	Yield	Total Assets	Mstar Category
FMACX	None	$18.51	0.4%	$159.0 mil	Small Blend

Prospectus Objective: Small Company

UAM FMA Small Company Portfolio seeks long-term total return consistent with reasonable risk.

The fund invests at least 65% of assets in common stocks issued by U.S. companies with market capitalizations of $50 million to $1 billion. When selecting securities, the advisor looks for companies with low P/E ratios, strong cash flows, good credit lines, and improving balance sheets. The fund may invest up to 10% of assets in foreign securities.

The fund is designed for institutional investors. Prior to Oct. 31, 1995, the fund was named Regis Fund FMA Small Company Portfolio.

Historical Profile
Return Above Avg
Risk Average
Rating ★★★★ Above Avg

Investment Style
Equity
Average Stock %: 92% 95% 97% 92% 97% 94% 97%

▼ Manager Change
▽ Partial Manager Change

Fund Performance vs. Category Average
■ Quarterly Fund Return +/– Category Average
— Category Baseline

Performance Quartile (within Category)

Portfolio Manager(s)

Management Team

History

1990	1991	1992	1993	1994	1995	1996	1997	1998	1999	2000	12-01	History
—	10.90	11.50	12.00	11.22	12.17	12.66	15.89	15.48	14.04	17.77	18.51	NAV
—	9.57*	5.51	28.25	–2.89	24.25	26.20	40.39	–2.03	–8.82	27.73	4.63	Total Return %
—	0.47*	–2.11	18.19	–4.20	–13.28	3.25	7.04	–30.60	–29.86	36.83	16.51	+/– S&P 500
—	—	–12.91	9.34	–1.06	–4.19	9.66	18.03	0.52	–30.08	30.75	2.14	+/– Russell 2000
—	0.57	0.00	0.17	0.08	0.80	1.32	0.47	0.54	0.47	1.04	0.45	Income Return %
—	9.00	5.50	28.07	–2.97	23.45	24.88	39.92	–2.57	–9.29	26.68	4.18	Capital Return %
—	—	81	7	76	56	19	7	34	98	10	65	Total Rtn % Rank Cat
—	0.06	0.00	0.02	0.01	0.09	0.16	0.06	0.09	0.07	0.15	0.08	Income $
—	0.00	0.00	2.62	0.41	1.60	2.41	1.77	0.00	0.00	0.00	0.00	Capital Gains $
—	1.03	1.03	1.03	1.03	1.03	1.03	1.03	1.03	1.03	1.02	—	Expense Ratio %
—	2.14	–0.07	0.14	0.06	0.66	0.75	0.50	0.62	0.52	0.75	—	Income Ratio %
—	—	134	163	121	170	106	86	39	121	108	—	Turnover Rate %
—	17.2	20.2	18.6	19.0	22.0	26.5	56.0	217.7	130.4	127.9	158.5	Net Assets $mil

Performance 12-31-01

	1st Qtr	2nd Qtr	3rd Qtr	4th Qtr	Total
1997	0.55	14.31	13.98	7.16	40.39
1998	6.48	–4.97	–14.65	13.44	–2.03
1999	–16.41	9.05	–3.91	4.10	–8.82
2000	7.74	1.00	9.91	6.80	27.73
2001	–1.96	12.08	–15.51	12.70	4.63

Trailing	Total Return%	+/– S&P 500	+/– Russ 2000	% Rank All	% Rank Cat	Growth of $10,000
3 Mo	12.70	2.02	–8.38	30	94	11,270
6 Mo	–4.78	0.77	–0.69	61	81	9,522
1 Yr	4.63	16.51	2.14	25	65	10,463
3 Yr Avg	6.81	7.84	0.39	18	81	12,185
5 Yr Avg	10.88	0.18	3.36	14	51	16,760
10 Yr Avg	13.19	0.27	1.68	12	59	34,534
15 Yr Avg	—	—	—	—	—	—

Tax Analysis	Tax-Adj Ret%	%Rank Cat	%Pretax Ret	%Rank Cat
3 Yr Avg	6.55	69	96.1	17
5 Yr Avg	10.17	39	93.5	10
10 Yr Avg	10.82	46	82.0	37

Potential Capital Gain Exposure: 8% of assets

Risk Analysis

Time Period	Load-Adj Return %	Risk %Rank[1] All	Risk %Rank[1] Cat	Morningstar Return	Morningstar Risk	Morningstar Risk-Adj Rating
1 Yr	4.63					
3 Yr	6.81	48	22	0.40[2]	0.68	★★★★
5 Yr	10.88	53	15	1.43[2]	0.73	★★★★
10 Yr	13.19	71	36	1.36	0.92	★★★★

Average Historical Rating (90 months): 3.1★s

[1]1=low, 100=high [2] T-Bill return substituted for category avg.

Category Rating (3 Yr)

1 2 **3** 4 5
Worst Best

Return Below Avg
Risk Below Avg

Other Measures	Standard Index S&P 500	Best Fit Index SPMid400
Alpha	5.6	–1.6
Beta	0.53	0.70
R-Squared	29	68
Standard Deviation		17.72
Mean		6.81
Sharpe Ratio		0.12

Portfolio Analysis 09-30-01

Share change since 07-01 Total Stocks: 61

Share change	Sector	PE	YTD Ret%	% Assets
⊕ RehabCare Grp	Health	17.8	–42.30	3.16
⊕ Alliant Techsystems	Industrials	28.6	73.48	2.95
⊕ United Stationers	Industrials	18.2	40.21	2.38
⊕ Republic Bancorp	Financials	16.3	44.54	2.21
⊕ Jefferies Grp (New)	Financials	19.2	36.19	2.20
⊖ East West Bancorp	Financials	15.9	3.80	2.17
⊕ CBL & Assoc Properties	Financials	15.9	34.09	2.11
☼ Glenborough Realty Tr	Financials	23.7	22.37	2.10
⊕ Sonic	Services	25.7	54.42	2.08
⊕ Metris	Financials	11.4	–2.13	2.06
⊕ Finl Federal	Financials	17.2	30.89	2.06
⊕ American Cap Strategies	Financials	—	22.29	2.06
⊕ Titan	Technology	—	53.54	2.04
⊕ Duane Reade	Retail	25.3	–0.70	2.01
☼ Sierra Pacific Resources	Utilities	—	–2.25	1.91
⊕ Alberto-Culver Cl A	Staples	—	—	1.88
⊕ American Finl Hldgs	Financials	20.0	26.89	1.88
⊕ Advo	Services	17.4	–3.10	1.86
⊕ Northwestern	Utilities	10.2	–3.96	1.86
⊖ Province Healthcare	Health	37.6	–21.60	1.83
☼ The Phoenix Companies	Financials	—	—	1.82
⊕ Minerals Tech	Industrials	21.5	36.76	1.80
Brandywine Realty Tr	Financials	29.7	10.52	1.77
⊕ Home Properties of New York	Financials	16.5	22.39	1.75
⊕ eFunds	Services	—	49.65	1.73

Current Investment Style

Style: Value Blnd Growth; Size: Large Med Small

	Stock Port Avg	Relative S&P 500 Current	Relative S&P 500 Hist	Rel Cat
Price/Earnings Ratio	23.9	0.77	0.63	0.96
Price/Book Ratio	2.7	0.48	0.35	0.85
Price/Cash Flow	14.1	0.78	0.64	0.90
3 Yr Earnings Growth	13.5	0.92	0.85	0.79
1 Yr Earnings Est%	4.0	—	—	4.69
Med Mkt Cap $mil	802	0.0	0.0	0.82

[1]figure is based on 50% or less of stocks

Analysis by Brian Portnoy 10-04-01

UAM FMA Small Company ranks as a decent choice for core small-cap exposure.

This fund has held up relatively well lately. For the year to date through Oct. 3, 2001, the fund's 6% loss ranks in the small-blend category's top half. And this performance comes on the heels of 2000's impressive 27.8% gain. Thank the fund's value leanings for its good marks. Management scouts for stocks that are trading cheaply on a P/E basis but feature a catalyst for an acceleration of earnings and a stock-price turnaround. Such a focus led it to make a large, successful bet on bank and thrift-related financials last year. Meanwhile, the fund's industrials stake, including AK Steel, has generally held up well.

The fund doesn't always get it right, however. For example, part of its recent financials wager was on market-leveraged names, such as Southwest Securities and Multex.com, that have performed poorly. Furthermore, management's top-down economic analyses have been sometimes off the mark. Most notably, in early 1999 the team's expectation of a slowing economy spurred a retreat to safer havens in financials and utilities, just when the bull market kicked into overdrive. Burdened by a portfolio rife with hard-to-sell defensive stocks, the fund's 8.8% loss that year ranked in the category's cellar.

But even with the occasional wrong call, the fund's unwillingness to take large, stock-specific bets has kept volatility well below average. Management's aversion to pricey technology stocks has also kept the fund out of harm's way during the extended market slide. The fund's conservative streak doesn't bode as well for its returns when growth-oriented fare returns to style, but for now, its defensive posture has paid off.

Special Securities % assets 09-30-01	
Restricted/Illiquid Secs	0
Emerging-Markets Secs	0
Options/Futures/Warrants	No

Composition % assets 09-30-01	
Cash	2.6
Stocks*	97.4
Bonds	0.0
Other	0.0
*Foreign (% stocks)	0.0

Market Cap	
Giant	0.0
Large	0.0
Medium	20.3
Small	78.7
Micro	1.0

Sector Weightings	% of Stocks	Rel S&P	5-Year High	5-Year Low
Utilities	5.3	1.7	5	0
Energy	2.0	0.3	9	0
Financials	34.4	1.9	41	19
Industrials	18.9	1.7	36	15
Durables	3.1	2.0	11	0
Staples	3.7	0.5	13	0
Services	11.5	1.1	20	8
Retail	3.2	0.5	10	0
Health	9.6	0.7	14	0
Technology	8.4	0.5	16	0

Address:	PO Box 419081 Kansas City, MO 64141–6081 877–826–5465
Web Address:	www.uam.com
*Inception:	07-31-91
Advisor:	Fiduciary Mgmt. Assoc.
Subadvisor:	None
NTF Plans:	Fidelity , Datalynx

Minimum Purchase:	$2500	Add: $1000 IRA: —
Min Auto Inv Plan:	$2500	Add: $100
Sales Fees:	No-load	
Management Fee:	.75%, .23%A	
Actual Fees:	Mgt: 0.46%	Dist: —
Expense Projections:	3Yr: $33*	5Yr: $57* 10Yr: $126*
Avg Brok Commission:	—	Income Distrib: Quarterly
Total Cost (relative to category):	—	

UAM ICM Small Company

Ticker	Load	NAV	Yield	Total Assets	Mstar Category
ICSCX	None	$25.87	0.8%	$747.9 mil	Small Value

Prospectus Objective: Small Company

UAM ICM Small Company Portfolio seeks long-term total return, consistent with reasonable risk.

The fund invests at least 80% of assets in common stocks of companies with market capitalizations between $50 million and $700 million. To select securities, management first screens several thousand small-cap companies based on relative equity return and other financial ratios, focusing on those with recent earnings that have exceeded expectations; further evaluation is based on fundamental security analysis. The fund may invest up to 20% of assets in American depositary receipts.

The fund is designed for institutional investors. Previous name: Regis Fund ICM Small Company Portfolio.

Historical Profile
Return High
Risk Below Avg
Rating ★★★★★ Highest

Investment Style
Equity
Average Stock %: 83% 87% 87% 84% 94% 90%

▼ Manager Change
▽ Partial Manager Change

Fund Performance vs. Category Average
■ Quarterly Fund Return +/– Category Average
— Category Baseline

Performance Quartile (within Category)

Portfolio Manager(s)

Management Team

1990	1991	1992	1993	1994	1995	1996	1997	1998	1999	2000	12-01	History
8.92	12.75	15.60	16.57	16.29	18.63	21.41	26.26	24.38	20.77	22.54	25.87	NAV
–7.38	48.67	32.28	22.03	3.41	21.27	23.01	33.01	–0.51	–1.07	22.46	19.05	Total Return %
–4.26	18.18	24.66	11.97	2.10	–16.26	0.07	–0.34	–29.09	–22.11	31.56	30.93	+/– S&P 500
14.40	6.97	3.14	–1.82	4.96	–4.48	1.64	1.32	5.92	0.41	–0.35	5.03	+/– Russell 2000 V
1.53	1.58	0.71	0.45	0.54	1.11	1.35	1.03	0.91	1.16	1.46	0.89	Income Return %
–8.91	47.09	31.57	21.58	2.87	20.16	21.67	31.98	–1.42	–2.23	21.00	18.16	Capital Return %
18	12	6	19	23	69	49	38	17	58	33	38	Total Rtn % Rank Cat
0.15	0.14	0.09	0.07	0.09	0.18	0.25	0.22	0.24	0.28	0.30	0.20	Income $
0.00	0.36	1.16	2.34	0.73	0.92	1.19	1.93	1.42	2.92	2.42	0.73	Capital Gains $
1.14	1.02	0.95	0.95	0.93	0.86	0.88	0.88	0.89	0.85	0.85	—	Expense Ratio %
1.52	1.32	0.77	0.46	0.58	1.02	1.20	0.97	1.12	1.18	1.22	—	Income Ratio %
40	49	34	47	21	20	23	23	22	32	33	—	Turnover Rate %
21.7	46.7	61.8	88.3	126.4	271.0	351.0	536.4	659.5	548.2	599.4	747.9	Net Assets $mil

Performance 12-31-01

	1st Qtr	2nd Qtr	3rd Qtr	4th Qtr	Total
1997	1.59	13.46	15.05	0.30	33.01
1998	9.48	–3.03	–14.29	9.33	–0.51
1999	–13.17	22.66	–7.83	0.77	–1.07
2000	4.90	2.43	7.61	5.91	22.46
2001	3.06	12.80	–12.48	17.01	19.05

Trailing	Total Return%	+/– S&P 500	+/– Russ 2000V	% Rank All	% Rank Cat	Growth of $10,000
3 Mo	17.01	6.32	0.29	19	49	11,701
6 Mo	2.40	7.96	1.25	19	44	10,240
1 Yr	19.05	30.93	5.03	2	38	11,905
3 Yr Avg	12.98	14.01	1.66	7	48	14,423
5 Yr Avg	13.80	3.10	2.60	6	23	19,086
10 Yr Avg	16.87	3.94	1.76	3	13	47,526
15 Yr Avg	—	—	—	—	—	—

Tax Analysis	Tax-Adj Ret%	%Rank Cat	%Pretax Ret	%Rank Cat
3 Yr Avg	10.55	53	81.2	84
5 Yr Avg	11.59	24	84.0	62
10 Yr Avg	14.39	17	85.3	31

Potential Capital Gain Exposure: 21% of assets

Risk Analysis

Time Period	Load-Adj Return %	Risk %Rank[1] All	Risk %Rank[1] Cat	Morningstar Return	Morningstar Risk	Morningstar Risk-Adj Rating
1 Yr	19.05					
3 Yr	12.98	45	36	1.84[2]	0.63	★★★★★
5 Yr	13.80	50	18	2.27[2]	0.68	★★★★★
10 Yr	16.87	55	25	2.30	0.71	★★★★★

Average Historical Rating (117 months): 4.3★s

[1] 1=low, 100=high [2] T-Bill return substituted for category avg.

Category Rating (3 Yr)

1 2 3 4 5
Worst Best

Return Average
Risk Average

Other Measures	Standard Index S&P 500	Best Fit Index SPMid400
Alpha	11.7	4.3
Beta	0.52	0.67
R-Squared	28	63
Standard Deviation		18.65
Mean		12.98
Sharpe Ratio		0.49

Portfolio Analysis 09-30-01

Share change since 06-01 Total Stocks: 146	Sector	PE	YTD Ret%	% Assets
MDC Hldgs	Industrials	7.8	52.62	2.44
Granite Const	Industrials	19.3	26.58	2.05
⊕ AptarGroup	Industrials	19.9	20.11	2.03
Dentsply Intl	Health	22.2	29.13	1.84
Ryland Grp	Industrials	8.8	80.25	1.53
Toro	Durables	11.7	24.04	1.50
Omnicare	Health	38.3	15.52	1.48
⊕ Griffon	Industrials	16.3	109.50	1.45
Equitable Resources	Energy	14.8	3.98	1.44
⊕ Minerals Tech	Industrials	21.5	36.76	1.39
Radian Grp	Financials	11.6	14.64	1.23
⊕ Bio-Rad Labs Cl A	Technology	22.0	99.06	1.16
⊕ FYI	Services	—	–9.15	1.16
Penn Virginia	Energy	3.7	5.27	1.13
Hughes Sply	Industrials	24.7	75.09	1.07
Diebold	Technology	34.3	23.51	1.07
ProQuest	N/A	—	—	1.05
R. H. Donnelley	Services	13.2	19.48	1.04
⊕ Armor Hldgs	Technology	64.3	54.78	1.00
☼ Pulte	Industrials	7.6	6.36	0.99
⊕ Advanced Mktg Svcs	Services	20.3	57.66	0.98
Borg Warner	Durables	19.3	32.37	0.97
⊕ Chittenden	Financials	15.4	17.37	0.96
Liberty Ppty Tr	Financials	13.5	13.22	0.92
Quixote	Industrials	15.3	3.31	0.90

Current Investment Style

Style: Value Blnd Growth; Size: Large Med Small

	Stock Port Avg	Relative S&P 500 Current	Relative S&P 500 Hist	Rel Cat
Price/Earnings Ratio	20.4	0.66	0.52	0.94
Price/Book Ratio	2.3	0.40	0.31	0.94
Price/Cash Flow	12.9	0.72	0.50	1.02
3 Yr Earnings Growth	16.2	1.11	1.08	1.40
1 Yr Earnings Est%	0.3	—	—	–0.08
Med Mkt Cap $mil	762	0.0	0.0	0.87

Analysis by Brian Portnoy 10-02-01

UAM ICM Small Company is an exemplary small-value option.

This fund's $5 million minimum investment is geared toward institutional accounts and wealthy individuals, but ordinary investors who find this option in their 401(k) plan should consider themselves fortunate. Lead manager Bob McDorman and his team of comanagers have posted indisputably good numbers over the long haul. Over the past decade, for example, the fund's 15.8% annualized gain beats 85% of its small-value peers'.

Discipline and smart stock selection have been the keys to the fund's long-term success. McDorman, who has been at the helm since the fund's 1989 inception, has stayed focused on small caps that are cheap relative to their own histories and the market and have little debt. He's also loyal to many of the stocks in the portfolio, generating a well-below-average turnover ratio. Many of his top holdings, such as road-builder Granite Construction and homebuilder MDC Holdings, have been in the portfolio for years. Such loyalty hampered returns during the go-go growth market of the late 1990s, but it has been a boon more often than not.

Recent performance has been typically solid. For the year to date through Oct. 1, 2001, the fund's break-even return ranks in the category's top half. As usual, a number of lesser-known issues, especially industrials and financials, have kept the fund in good stead. For example, AptarGroup, Griffon, and Hughes Supply are among the fund's numerous manufacturing-related holdings that have performed well.

In sum, this offering is easy to recommend.

Special Securities % assets 09-30-01	
Restricted/Illiquid Secs	0
Emerging-Markets Secs	0
Options/Futures/Warrants	No

Composition % assets 09-30-01	
Cash	8.7
Stocks*	91.0
Bonds	0.3
Other	0.0
*Foreign (% stocks)	0.0

Market Cap	
Giant	0.0
Large	0.3
Medium	19.6
Small	68.3
Micro	11.9

Sector Weightings	% of Stocks	Rel S&P	5-Year High	5-Year Low
Utilities	0.3	0.1	3	0
Energy	7.6	1.1	9	3
Financials	21.7	1.2	23	13
Industrials	31.7	2.8	44	26
Durables	7.0	4.5	11	5
Staples	0.4	0.1	2	0
Services	9.5	0.9	15	9
Retail	5.7	0.8	12	4
Health	6.5	0.4	6	1
Technology	9.8	0.5	15	6

Address:	PO Box 419081 Kansas City, MO 64141-6081 877-826-5465
Web Address:	www.uam.com
Inception:	04-20-89
Advisor:	Inv. Counselors of Maryland
Subadvisor:	None
NTF Plans:	Fidelity Inst.

Minimum Purchase:	$5.00 mil	Add: $1000 IRA: —
Min Auto Inv Plan:	—	Add: —
Sales Fees:	No-load	
Management Fee:	.70%, .20%A	
Actual Fees:	Mgt: 0.70%	Dist: —
Expense Projections:	3Yr: $284	5Yr: $493 10Yr: $1096
Avg Brok Commission:	—	Income Distrib: Quarterly
Total Cost (relative to category):	—	

USAA Aggressive Growth

Ticker	Load	NAV	Yield	Total Assets	Mstar Category
USAUX	Closed	$28.50	0.0%	$1,037.5 mil	Mid-Cap Growth

Prospectus Objective: Aggressive Growth

USAA Aggressive Growth Fund seeks capital appreciation.

The fund invests primarily in common stocks and convertible securities issued by growth-oriented companies. It emphasizes small, less-recognized companies, but may also invest in large companies. The fund may invest up to 30% of assets in foreign securities.

Named USAA Mutual Sunbelt Era Fund prior to Feb. 13, 1989.

Historical Profile
Return: Below Avg
Risk: High
Rating: ★ Lowest

Investment Style
Equity
Average Stock %: 96% 96% 98% 98% 98% 99%

▼ Manager Change
▽ Partial Manager Change

Fund Performance vs. Category Average
Quarterly Fund Return +/– Category Average
— Category Baseline

Performance Quartile (within Category)

Portfolio Manager(s)

John K. Cabell Jr., CFA. Since 3-95. BS'76 U. of Alabama; MS'79 U. of Alabama. Other fund currently managed: USAA Small Cap Stock.

Eric Efron, CFA. Since 3-95. MA'75 U. of Michigan; MBA'80 New York U. Other fund currently managed: USAA Small Cap Stock.

1990	1991	1992	1993	1994	1995	1996	1997	1998	1999	2000	12-01	History
14.23	24.42	19.93	20.22	18.46	26.09	29.81	29.73	30.69	55.15	42.78	28.50	NAV
–11.92	71.69	–8.51	8.14	–0.81	50.42	16.47	7.56	22.22	91.09	–19.95	–33.38	Total Return %
–8.80	41.20	–16.13	–1.92	–2.13	12.88	–6.47	–25.79	–6.36	70.05	–10.85	–21.50	+/– S&P 500
–6.79	24.66	–17.23	–3.05	1.35	16.44	–1.01	–14.98	4.35	39.78	–8.21	–13.22	+/– Russ Midcap Grth
0.62	0.07	0.00	0.10	0.00	0.00	0.00	0.00	0.00	0.00	0.00	0.00	Income Return %
–12.54	71.62	–8.51	8.04	–0.81	50.42	16.47	7.56	22.22	91.09	–19.95	–33.38	Capital Return %
78	15	99	83	50	8	54	87	23	23	83	82	Total Rtn % Rank Cat
0.10	0.01	0.00	0.02	0.00	0.00	0.00	0.00	0.00	0.00	0.00	0.00	Income $
0.00	0.00	2.14	1.25	1.55	1.61	0.57	2.34	3.99	2.31	1.87	0.00	Capital Gains $
0.94	0.87	0.82	0.86	0.83	0.86	0.74	0.74	0.71	0.72	0.60	0.66	Expense Ratio %
0.68	0.17	–0.05	0.10	–0.10	–0.28	–0.42	–0.47	–0.38	–0.55	–0.42	–0.52	Income Ratio %
78	50	74	113	99	138	44	57	83	35	33	23	Turnover Rate %
135.3	271.4	290.0	288.5	283.8	442.8	716.0	732.4	833.3	1,657.8	1,587.8	1,037.5	Net Assets $mil

Performance 12-31-01

	1st Qtr	2nd Qtr	3rd Qtr	4th Qtr	Total
1997	–12.65	18.59	17.17	–11.38	7.56
1998	15.94	–1.51	–22.44	37.99	22.22
1999	7.95	14.88	1.91	51.19	91.09
2000	16.59	–8.10	3.70	–27.96	–19.95
2001	–34.20	20.85	–30.34	20.25	–33.38

Trailing	Total Return%	+/– S&P 500	+/– Russ Midcap Grth	% Rank All	% Rank Cat	Growth of $10,000
3 Mo	20.25	9.57	–6.81	13	42	12,025
6 Mo	–16.23	–10.67	–7.97	96	87	8,377
1 Yr	–33.38	–21.50	–13.22	96	82	6,662
3 Yr Avg	0.63	1.65	–1.53	70	70	10,190
5 Yr Avg	6.02	–4.68	–3.00	47	67	13,396
10 Yr Avg	8.70	–4.23	–2.41	40	70	23,029
15 Yr Avg	10.70	–3.03	–2.11	36	65	45,973

Tax Analysis	Tax-Adj Ret%	%Rank Cat	%Pretax Ret	%Rank Cat
3 Yr Avg	–0.08	63	—	—
5 Yr Avg	4.56	61	75.8	48
10 Yr Avg	6.89	55	79.1	26

Potential Capital Gain Exposure: –4% of assets

Risk Analysis

Time Period	Load-Adj Return %	Risk %Rank[1] All	Risk %Rank[1] Cat	Morningstar Return	Morningstar Risk	Morningstar Risk-Adj Rating
1 Yr	–33.38					
3 Yr	0.63	97	89	–0.88[2]	2.01	★★
5 Yr	6.02	98	90	0.22[2]	1.97	★
10 Yr	8.70	98	93	0.52	2.05	★

Average Historical Rating (193 months): 1.4★s

[1] 1=low, 100=high [2] T-Bill return substituted for category avg.

Category Rating (3 Yr)

1 2 3 4 5 — Worst … Best

Return: Below Avg
Risk: Above Avg

Other Measures	Standard Index S&P 500	Best Fit Index Wil 4500
Alpha	13.9	5.5
Beta	1.68	1.54
R-Squared	40	93

Standard Deviation	50.92
Mean	0.63
Sharpe Ratio	–0.10

Portfolio Analysis 11-30-01

Share change since 07-01 Total Stocks: 193	Sector	PE	YTD Ret%	% Assets
⊖ IDEC Pharmaceuticals	Health	NMF	9.09	4.67
MedImmune	Health	78.6	–2.81	2.65
⊖ King Pharmaceuticals	Health	45.8	8.68	2.41
99 Cents Only Stores	Retail	43.8	108.70	2.40
Biovail Corporation Intl	Health	NMF	44.82	2.17
⊕ Chico's FAS	Retail	29.2	185.20	1.73
⊖ Express Scripts	Health	33.6	–8.54	1.71
Dollar Tree Stores	Retail	30.9	26.16	1.67
Applied Micro Circuits	Technology	—	–84.90	1.61
Andrx	Health	66.4	21.66	1.54
Krispy Kreme Doughnut	Retail	67.0	113.00	1.48
⊖ Millennium Pharma	Health	—	–60.30	1.47
Flextronics Intl	Technology	—	–15.80	1.45
✲ Everest Re Grp	Financials	17.6	–1.29	1.42
⊖ Accredo Health	Health	53.7	18.65	1.41
Copart	Services	43.8	69.16	1.36
Genzyme Corporation General Di	Health	—	33.11	1.30
Suiza Foods	Staples	—	25.44	1.19
⊖ VeriSign	Technology	—	–48.70	1.17
Triquint Semicon	Technology	26.7	–71.90	1.12
⊖ Techne	Health	44.9	2.18	1.10
Waste Connections	Services	28.7	–6.27	1.07
Priority Healthcare Cl B	Health	61.7	–13.70	1.05
✲ ACE	Financials	17.4	–5.39	1.04
⊕ Atlantic Coast Air	Services	31.5	13.95	1.03

Current Investment Style

Style: Value Blnd Growth; Size: Large Med Small

	Stock Port Avg	Relative S&P 500 Current	Relative S&P 500 Hist	Rel Cat
Price/Earnings Ratio	40.4	1.31	1.31	1.17
Price/Book Ratio	6.5	1.14	1.28	1.15
Price/Cash Flow	28.4	1.58	1.39	1.23
3 Yr Earnings Growth	31.0[1]	2.12	—	1.32
1 Yr Earnings Est%	17.1	—	—	1.83
Med Mkt Cap $mil	3,214	0.1	0.0	0.57

[1] figure is based on 50% or less of stocks

Analysis by Christopher Davis 12-12-01

USAA Aggressive Growth Fund may yet end up on top, but only iron-stomached investors will want to stick around to see if it does.

Shareholders in this closed fund might just as soon forget the past two years, and we wouldn't blame them. The fund's 35% loss for the year to date through Dec. 10, 2001—a bottom-quartile showing in the mid-growth group—is tough to stomach. And in 2000, the fund's 20% drop landed it in the category's bottom quartile. Managers Eric Efron and John Cabell concentrated their picks in tech, biotech, and telecom—the sectors hardest-hit in the Nasdaq's spectacular fall—so the dismal showing isn't as surprising as it is disappointing.

Lately, though, Efron and Cabell have broadened the portfolio. They lightened the fund's still-heavy exposure to biotech and smaller-cap drugmakers and picked up a slew of energy and financials names, including regional bank Southtrust and oil driller Apache. The pair also ditched struggling tech and telecom stocks like Level 3 Communications and Ariba, opting for steadier and larger names, such as Sprint PCS and Dell. All told, the fund is more diversified and a bit less aggressive than it has been in years.

So what's to like here? The fund boasts seasoned management, and when growth stocks are in favor, as in 1999, it can post category-topping gains. The fund's slightly more-conservative posture hasn't been a liability recently, either: It outpaced the mid-growth average when the market rallied sharply in October and November 2001, with a 16% gain.

Even so, the past two years have taken a heavy toll on returns, and the fund will have to gain 120% just to recoup the losses it has suffered since its March 2000 peak. Considering that as well as the fund's extreme volatility, only aggressive types with long time horizons will want to stay the course here.

Special Securities % assets 11-30-01	
Restricted/Illiquid Secs	0
Emerging-Markets Secs	Trace
Options/Futures/Warrants	No

Sector Weightings	% of Stocks	Rel S&P	5-Year High	5-Year Low
Utilities	0.4	0.1	3	0
Energy	2.9	0.4	8	0
Financials	7.2	0.4	21	0
Industrials	2.3	0.2	22	0
Durables	0.8	0.5	11	0
Staples	2.2	0.3	5	0
Services	13.1	1.2	27	6
Retail	12.5	1.8	30	4
Health	36.4	2.5	49	11
Technology	22.3	1.2	50	11

Composition % assets 11-30-01	
Cash	2.1
Stocks*	97.9
Bonds	0.0
Other	0.0
*Foreign (% stocks)	6.4

Market Cap	
Giant	4.5
Large	21.8
Medium	51.4
Small	22.2
Micro	0.1

Address:	USAA Building San Antonio, TX 78288 800–382–8722
Web Address:	www.usaa.com
Inception:	07-29-81
Advisor:	USAA Inv. Mgmt.
Subadvisor:	None
NTF Plans:	N/A

Minimum Purchase:	Closed	Add: $50	IRA: —
Min Auto Inv Plan:	Closed	Add: $50	
Sales Fees:	No-load		
Management Fee:	.50% mx./.33% mn.		
Actual Fees:	Mgt: 0.35%	Dist: —	
Expense Projections:	3Yr: $192	5Yr: $335	10Yr: $750
Avg Brok Commission:	—	Income Distrib: Annually	
Total Cost (relative to category):		Low	

USAA Cornerstone Strategy

Ticker	Load	NAV	Yield	Total Assets	Mstar Category
USCRX	None	$23.38	4.2%	$955.0 mil	Large Value

Prospectus Objective: Multiasset—Global

USAA Cornerstone Strategy Fund seeks a positive, inflation-adjusted return while maintaining a stable share value.

The fund allocates assets among five categories: gold stocks, foreign stocks, real-estate stocks, U.S. government securities, and basic-value stocks. It may invest up to 10% of assets in gold stocks; each of the remaining sectors may receive between 22% and 30% of assets. Management rebalances the portfolio at least once each quarter to bring each category within its range.

Prior to Sept. 12, 1995, the fund was named USAA Cornerstone Fund.

Historical Profile

Return: Below Avg
Risk: Low
Rating: ★★★ Neutral

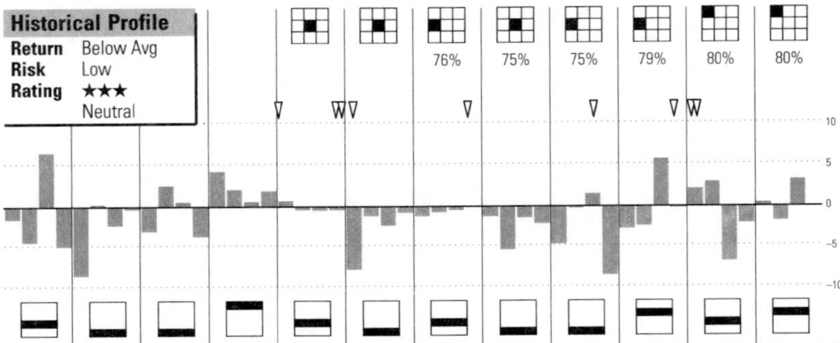

Investment Style
Equity
Average Stock %: 76% 75% 75% 79% 80% 80%

▼ Manager Change
▽ Partial Manager Change

Fund Performance vs. Category Average
■ Quarterly Fund Return +/– Category Average
— Category Baseline

Performance Quartile (within Category)

Portfolio Manager(s)

Albert C. Sebastian, CFA. Since 10-96.
R. David Ullom, CFA. Since 8-98.
Mark W. Johnson, CFA. Since 1-94.
Kevin P. Moore. Since 10-99.
Donna J. Baggerly, CFA. Since 2-00.

1990	1991	1992	1993	1994	1995	1996	1997	1998	1999	2000	12-01	History
16.98	19.12	19.69	23.46	21.24	24.03	26.59	28.06	26.33	25.98	25.53	23.38	NAV
–9.20	16.23	6.35	23.73	–1.05	18.40	17.87	15.64	2.01	8.13	2.75	–3.01	Total Return %
–6.08	–14.26	–1.27	13.67	–2.36	–19.14	–5.07	–17.71	–26.57	–12.91	11.85	8.87	+/– S&P 500
–5.53	–1.93	–2.72	3.97	1.27	–21.63	–4.44	–19.85	–19.23	–2.82	0.44	5.78	+/– Russ Top 200 Val
3.37	3.49	3.31	3.02	2.58	3.55	3.34	2.79	2.96	3.07	1.88	3.92	Income Return %
–12.57	12.73	3.04	20.71	–3.62	14.85	14.53	12.85	–0.95	5.06	0.87	–6.93	Capital Return %
73	96	81	4	60	100	75	98	93	41	66	33	Total Rtn % Rank Cat
0.65	0.59	0.63	0.59	0.58	0.74	0.78	0.72	0.81	0.78	0.48	1.00	Income $
0.00	0.00	0.00	0.29	1.38	0.33	0.84	1.90	1.53	1.67	0.71	0.35	Capital Gains $
1.21	1.18	1.18	1.18	1.11	1.13	1.15	1.06	1.01	1.05	1.09	1.07	Expense Ratio %
3.50	3.58	3.25	2.92	2.68	3.16	3.06	2.88	2.64	3.12	2.43	2.26	Income Ratio %
41	28	33	45	31	33	36	35	33	46	37	55	Turnover Rate %
551.7	603.7	578.1	762.8	841.3	949.7	1,171.3	1,413.9	1,367.0	1,193.0	1,057.5	955.0	Net Assets $mil

Performance 12-31-01

	1st Qtr	2nd Qtr	3rd Qtr	4th Qtr	Total
1997	0.41	8.50	7.37	–1.15	15.64
1998	6.74	–0.77	–10.72	7.87	2.01
1999	–1.90	7.43	–3.45	6.26	8.13
2000	2.23	0.94	–1.42	1.00	2.75
2001	–5.33	2.94	–8.88	9.23	–3.01

Trailing	Total Return%	+/– S&P 500	+/– Russ Top 200 Val	% Rank All	% Rank Cat	Growth of $10,000
3 Mo	9.23	–1.46	3.71	46	47	10,923
6 Mo	–0.47	5.08	5.30	41	11	9,953
1 Yr	–3.01	8.87	5.78	47	33	9,699
3 Yr Avg	2.52	3.55	1.36	59	46	10,776
5 Yr Avg	4.92	–5.78	–6.29	66	90	12,712
10 Yr Avg	8.73	–4.20	–5.30	40	91	23,100
15 Yr Avg	8.74	–5.00	–4.77	49	94	35,119

Tax Analysis	Tax-Adj Ret%	%Rank Cat	%Pretax Ret	%Rank Cat
3 Yr Avg	0.65	48	25.6	86
5 Yr Avg	2.66	90	54.0	91
10 Yr Avg	6.60	87	75.5	59

Potential Capital Gain Exposure: 10% of assets

Risk Analysis

Time Period	Load-Adj Return %	Risk %Rank[1] All	Risk %Rank[1] Cat	Morningstar Return	Morningstar Risk	Morningstar Risk-Adj Rating
1 Yr	–3.01					
3 Yr	2.52	38	2	–0.50[2]	0.51	★★★
5 Yr	4.92	43	2	–0.03[2]	0.54	★★
10 Yr	8.73	50	4	0.53	0.58	★★★

Average Historical Rating (173 months): 3.3★s

[1] 1=low, 100=high [2] T-Bill return substituted for category avg.

Category Rating (3 Yr)

1 2 3 4 5
Worst Best

Return: Average
Risk: Low

Other Measures	Standard Index S&P 500	Best Fit Index MSCIACWdFr
Alpha	0.5	2.7
Beta	0.52	0.56
R-Squared	75	78

Standard Deviation	10.28
Mean	2.52
Sharpe Ratio	–0.27

Analysis by Christopher Davis 10-16-01

It's tough to make a case for this unusual fund.

USAA Cornerstone Strategy Fund attempts to accomplish in a single offering what investors should do for their entire portfolio. Divided among four asset classes—U.S. and foreign stocks, government bonds, and real-estate investment trusts (REITs)—the fund acts as a one-stop shop for investors seeking a diversified core holding.

The type of investor this product targets is unclear, though. Lead manager David Ullom tends to favor cheaply priced financials and industrial stocks, and the fund typically devotes 20% of the portfolio to strait-laced government bonds, so it isn't likely to appeal to aggressive types. The fund may better suit more-conservative investors, but there's more risk here than meets the eye. For instance, it places roughly 30% of assets in international stocks. And the fund's hefty stake in REITs (usually near 15%), mostly a remnant of its former inflation-fighting guise, is far higher than that of the typical value fund.

The fund's eclectic assortment of investments has also yielded lackluster long-term results. Indeed, its trailing three-, five-, and 10-year returns lag those of its own large-value category, as well as those of the domestic-hybrid group (whose blend of stocks and bonds make it a decent, though imperfect, benchmark for this odd fund). And though it has been a bit less volatile than the typical domestic-hybrid offering, the fund has given up substantial gains to achieve such stability.

That said, management has added larger and more-growth oriented names to the portfolio in recent years, which has made the fund a better core holding. Its appeal remains limited, though, and investors can easily piece together a portfolio of funds that will meet their needs better than this one.

Portfolio Analysis 11-30-01

Share change since 10-01 Total Stocks: 292

Holding	Sector	PE	YTD Ret%	% Assets
FNMA 7%	N/A	—	—	2.02
FNMA 6.5%	N/A	—	—	1.50
FHLMC 5.25%	N/A	—	—	1.46
Equity Office Properties Tr	Financials	18.7	–1.76	1.45
Microsoft	Technology	57.6	52.78	1.43
GNMA 8%	N/A	—	—	1.35
GNMA 7.5%	N/A	—	—	1.28
General Elec	Industrials	30.1	–15.00	1.24
US Treasury Bond 5.375%	N/A	—	—	1.15
FHLMC 6.75%	N/A	—	—	1.10
Wal-Mart Stores	Retail	40.3	8.94	1.08
American Intl Grp	Financials	42.0	–19.20	1.03
Citigroup	Financials	20.0	0.03	1.01
ALCOA	Industrials	21.4	7.86	1.00
Intel	Technology	73.1	4.89	0.97
Merck	Health	19.1	–35.90	0.96
⊖ Verizon Comms	Services	29.7	–2.52	0.93
Canadian Natl Railway	Services	18.8	64.61	0.92
Bristol-Myers Squibb	Health	20.2	–26.00	0.92
GNMA 6%	N/A	—	—	0.92
FleetBoston Finl	Financials	16.2	0.55	0.89
Nokia Cl A ADR	Technology	45.8	–43.00	0.88
FNMA 6%	N/A	—	—	0.86
Simon Ppty Grp	Financials	27.9	31.72	0.86
FNMA Debenture 7.125%	N/A	—	—	0.84

Current Investment Style

Style: Value Blnd Growth; Size: Large Med Small

	Stock Port Avg	Relative S&P 500 Current	Relative S&P 500 Hist	Rel Cat
Price/Earnings Ratio	24.9	0.80	0.76	0.99
Price/Book Ratio	4.1	0.72	0.59	1.00
Price/Cash Flow	14.2	0.79	0.71	1.03
3 Yr Earnings Growth	17.9	1.22	0.97	1.21
1 Yr Earnings Est%	7.2	—	—	–2.17
Med Mkt Cap $mil	19,589	0.3	0.3	0.62

Special Securities % assets 11-30-01

Restricted/Illiquid Secs	Trace
Emerging-Markets Secs	3
Options/Futures/Warrants	No

Composition % assets 11-30-01

Cash	1.6
Stocks*	81.7
Bonds	16.5
Other	0.2
*Foreign (% stocks)	33.9

Market Cap

Giant	32.4
Large	30.7
Medium	30.7
Small	5.3
Micro	0.8

Sector Weightings	% of Stocks	Rel S&P	5-Year High	5-Year Low
Utilities	1.6	0.5	6	0
Energy	6.2	0.9	10	2
Financials	31.5	1.8	42	25
Industrials	13.5	1.2	33	11
Durables	4.0	2.6	8	2
Staples	4.2	0.5	8	1
Services	13.6	1.3	20	8
Retail	2.8	0.4	5	1
Health	8.1	0.5	10	2
Technology	14.5	0.8	18	1

Address:	USAA Building, San Antonio, TX 78288, 800-382-8722
Web Address:	www.usaa.com
Inception:	08-15-84
Advisor:	USAA Inv. Mgmt.
Subadvisor:	None
NTF Plans:	N/A

Minimum Purchase:	$3000	Add: $50	IRA: $250
Min Auto Inv Plan:	$50	Add: $50	
Sales Fees:	No-load		
Management Fee:	.75%		
Actual Fees:	Mgt: 0.75%	Dist: —	
Expense Projections:	3Yr: $347	5Yr: $601	10Yr: $1329
Avg Brok Commission:	—	Income Distrib: Annually	
Total Cost (relative to category):		Below Avg	

USAA Income

Ticker	Load	NAV	Yield	SEC Yield	Total Assets	Mstar Category
USAIX	None	$12.06	6.6%	6.00%	$1,546.7 mil	Interm–Term Bond

Prospectus Objective: Corp Bond—General

USAA Income Fund seeks current income without undue risk to principal.

The fund invests primarily in investment-grade debt securities. These securities may include U.S. government obligations, mortgage-backed securities, Eurodollar and Yankee obligations, corporate debt securities, U.S. bank obligations, and asset-backed securities. It may also purchase common stocks, convertible securities, and preferred stocks. As a temporary measure, the fund may invest up to 100% of assets in high-quality, short-term debt instruments.

Historical Profile

Return Above Avg
Risk Above Avg
Rating ★★★ Neutral

Investment Style
Fixed-Income
Income Rtn %Rank Cat

11 13 19 13 9 17 11 7

Growth of Principal vs. Interest Rate Shifts
— Principal Value $000 (NAV with capital gains reinvested)
— Interest Rate % on 10 Yr Treasury
▼ Manager Change
▽ Partial Manager Change
► Mgr Unknown After
◄ Mgr Unknown Before

Performance Quartile (within Category)

Portfolio Manager(s)

M. Didi Weinblatt, CFA. Since 2-00. PhD U. of Pennsylvania; MA U. of Pennsylvania.

1990	1991	1992	1993	1994	1995	1996	1997	1998	1999	2000	12-01	History
11.41	12.55	12.61	12.71	11.19	13.00	12.31	12.78	12.56	11.30	11.96	12.06	NAV
7.69	19.38	8.37	9.91	–5.22	24.47	1.33	11.05	8.75	–3.85	13.34	7.58	Total Return %
–1.27	3.38	0.97	0.16	–2.30	6.00	–2.29	1.37	0.08	–3.02	1.71	–0.84	+/– LB Aggregate
–1.48	4.76	1.20	1.13	–3.29	9.16	–2.73	3.19	0.34	–4.24	3.24	–1.40	+/– LB Int Govt/Corp
9.25	8.74	7.76	7.20	7.00	7.75	6.59	6.98	6.80	6.27	7.26	6.82	Income Return %
–1.57	10.64	0.61	2.71	–12.21	16.72	–5.26	4.08	1.95	–10.11	6.08	0.76	Capital Return %
45	11	20	61	85	1	95	5	17	97	1	46	Total Rtn % Rank Cat
1.03	0.96	0.94	0.88	0.86	0.84	0.83	0.83	0.84	0.76	0.79	0.79	Income $
0.00	0.01	0.00	0.25	0.00	0.00	0.00	0.00	0.46	0.03	0.00	0.00	Capital Gains $
0.53	0.47	0.42	0.41	0.41	0.41	0.40	0.39	0.38	0.38	0.42	0.41	Expense Ratio %
9.19	8.61	7.78	7.00	6.98	7.27	6.64	6.76	6.62	6.31	6.78	6.63	Income Ratio %
12	15	22	45	25	31	81	58	47	54	25	43	Turnover Rate %
481.8	1,004.3	1,452.1	1,945.8	1,611.8	1,893.2	1,928.5	1,722.0	1,768.6	1,319.1	1,338.7	1,546.7	Net Assets $mil

Performance 12-31-01

	1st Qtr	2nd Qtr	3rd Qtr	4th Qtr	Total
1997	–1.15	3.97	4.21	3.69	11.05
1998	1.42	2.93	3.17	0.98	8.75
1999	–1.04	–1.53	–0.01	–1.32	–3.85
2000	3.28	2.20	3.50	3.75	13.34
2001	3.60	1.06	4.21	–1.40	7.58

Trailing	Total Return%	+/– LB Agg	+/– LB ITGvt/Corp	% Rank All	% Rank Cat	Growth of $10,000
3 Mo	–1.40	–1.43	–1.49	97	96	9,860
6 Mo	2.75	–1.90	–1.95	17	87	10,275
1 Yr	7.58	–0.84	–1.40	11	46	10,758
3 Yr Avg	5.45	–0.83	–0.95	27	41	11,724
5 Yr Avg	7.20	–0.22	0.11	34	14	14,160
10 Yr Avg	7.26	0.03	0.45	48	17	20,162
15 Yr Avg	8.56	0.44	0.93	50	8	34,291

Tax Analysis	Tax-Adj Ret%	%Rank Cat	%Pretax Ret	%Rank Cat
3 Yr Avg	2.73	54	50.2	67
5 Yr Avg	4.19	32	58.2	69
10 Yr Avg	4.28	26	59.0	54

Potential Capital Gain Exposure: –2% of assets

Risk Analysis

Time Period	Load-Adj Return %	Risk %Rank[1] All	Risk %Rank[1] Cat	Morningstar Return	Morningstar Risk	Morningstar Risk-Adj Rating
1 Yr	7.58					
3 Yr	5.45	21	67	0.11[2]	0.76	★★★
5 Yr	7.20	24	50	0.50[2]	0.73	★★★★
10 Yr	7.26	39	90	0.73[2]	1.11	★★★

Average Historical Rating (193 months): 4.1★s

[1]1=low, 100=high [2] T-Bill return substituted for category avg.

Category Rating (3 Yr)

1 2 3 4 5
Worst Best

Return Average
Risk Average

Other Measures	Standard Index LB Agg	Best Fit Index LB Agg
Alpha	–0.9	–0.9
Beta	1.09	1.09
R-Squared	93	93
Standard Deviation		4.02
Mean		5.45
Sharpe Ratio		0.15

Analysis by Christopher Davis 11-28-01

Investors will find plenty to like in USAA Income Fund.

This offering, like many of its bond fund siblings, puts together a portfolio that pumps out heaps of income—its yield is far bigger than the intermediate-term bond group norm. In pursuit of that grail, manager Didi Weinblatt favors mid-grade corporate bonds and plain-vanilla mortgage pass-throughs, which typically sport higher yields than Treasuries. She also will devote up to 10% of assets to income-rich preferred stocks and REITs, which plump up the fund's yield. In further pursuit of income, Weinblatt has kept the fund's duration, a measure of interest-rate sensitivity, longer than the category average.

That approach has largely been a boon to returns in 2001. Interest rates have declined all year, so the fund's longer-than-average duration has been a plus. Weinblatt also pared the fund's stake in mortgages in early 2001, picking up a slew of A and BBB rated corporate issues. That move paid off handsomely: After taking a drubbing in 2000, mid-grade corporates rallied sharply in 2001. Consequently, the fund's 8.4% return for the year to date through Nov. 27, 2001, ranks in the category's top quartile. That strong showing comes on the heels of a peer-crushing 13.3% gain in 2000, Weinblatt's first year at the helm.

Another plus is the fund's rock-bottom expense ratio. Because just a few basis points can affect a bond fund's relative performance, the fund's low expense ratio is likely to help it deliver greater gains over the long haul.

Weinblatt's tendency to own longer-duration fare can lead to short-term pain when interest rates rise, though. As long-term rates ticked upward in the past month, for instance, the fund dropped 1.8%, placing it in the category's bottom decile for the period. Even so, Weinblatt's solid start and the fund's low expenses make it a solid choice.

Portfolio Analysis 11-30-01

Total Fixed-Income: 113	Date of Maturity	Amount $000	Value $000	% Net Assets
US Treasury Bond 5.25%	11-15-28	142,201	137,080	8.69
GNMA 6%	10-15-28	114,823	114,240	7.24
FNMA 6.5%	04-01-31	71,085	71,984	4.56
US Treasury Note 3.875%	01-15-09	50,006	51,694	3.28
GNMA 7.5%	07-15-26	45,062	47,323	3.00
GNMA 7%	09-15-23	38,168	39,706	2.52
GNMA 7.5%	12-15-28	28,711	30,136	1.91
Qwest Cap Fdg 144A 7%	08-03-09	30,000	29,739	1.89
General Elec Cap 7.25%	05-03-04	25,000	27,142	1.72
FNMA Debenture 6.625%	11-15-30	25,000	26,813	1.70
GNMA 7%	07-15-29	25,825	26,675	1.69
Citigroup 6.5%	01-18-11	25,000	26,145	1.66
GNMA 6.5%	12-15-23	25,435	26,031	1.65
Ford Motor Credit 7.375%	02-01-11	25,000	25,464	1.61
Household Fin 6.375%	10-15-11	25,000	25,192	1.60
Calpine Cda Energy 8.5%	05-01-08	25,000	24,917	1.58
Phillips Petro 8.75%	05-25-10	20,000	23,496	1.49
GNMA 6.5%	05-15-28	23,003	23,406	1.48
Sprint Cap 7.625%	01-30-11	20,000	20,992	1.33
Agrium 8.25%	02-15-11	20,000	20,869	1.32

Current Investment Style

Not Available

Avg Eff Duration[1]	5.1 Yrs
Avg Eff Maturity	8.8 Yrs
Avg Credit Quality	—
Avg Wtd Coupon	6.68%
Avg Wtd Price	102.71% of par

[1]figure provided by fund

Special Securities % assets 11-30-01	
Restricted/Illiquid Secs	5
Exotic Mortgage–Backed	0
Emerging–Markets Secs	0
Options/Futures/Warrants	No

Coupon Range	% of Bonds	Rel Cat
0%	0.71	0.57
0% to 7%	49.72	0.92
7% to 8.5%	42.47	1.22
8.5% to 10%	6.46	0.90
More than 10%	0.63	0.23

1.00=Category Average

Credit Analysis % bonds 03-31-01

US Govt	0	BB	0
AAA	61	B	0
AA	5	Below B	0
A	13	NR/NA	0
BBB	21		

Composition % assets 11-30-01

Cash	1.8	Bonds	90.2
Stocks	0.3	Other	7.8

Sector Breakdown % bonds 11-30-01

US Treasuries	10	CMOs	0
GNMA mtgs	28	ARMs	0
FNMA mtgs	9	Other	48
FHLMC mtgs	0		

Address:	USAA Building San Antonio, TX 78288 800–382–8722
Web Address:	www.usaa.com
Inception:	03-04-74
Advisor:	USAA Inv. Mgmt.
Subadvisor:	None
NTF Plans:	N/A

Minimum Purchase:	$3000	Add: $50	IRA: $250
Min Auto Inv Plan:	None	Add: $50	
Sales Fees:	No–load		
Management Fee:	.24%		
Actual Fees:	Mgt: 0.24%	Dist: —	
Expense Projections:	3Yr: $135	5Yr: $235	10Yr: $530
Avg Brok Commission:	—	Income Distrib: Monthly	
Total Cost (relative to category):		Low	

USAA Income Stock

Ticker	Load	NAV	Yield	Total Assets	Mstar Category
USISX	None	$16.83	2.5%	$1,869.4 mil	Large Value

Prospectus Objective: Equity–Income

USAA Income Stock Fund seeks current income consistent with potential for increasing dividend income and capital appreciation.

The fund normally invests at least 65% of assets in dividend-paying common stocks of well-established, large companies. It may invest the remaining assets in convertible securities, preferred stocks, and real-estate investment trusts. The fund is structured to provide a yield greater than the average yield of the S&P 500 index.

Historical Profile
Return Average
Risk Below Avg
Rating ★★★ Neutral

Investment Style
Equity
Average Stock %: 80% 82% 83% 89% 91% 94%

▼ Manager Change
▽ Partial Manager Change

Fund Performance vs. Category Average
■ Quarterly Fund Return +/– Category Average
— Category Baseline

Performance Quartile (within Category)

Portfolio Manager(s)

Stephan J. Klaffke, CFA. Since 9-98. BS Indiana U.; MBA Texas Christian U.

History

	1990	1991	1992	1993	1994	1995	1996	1997	1998	1999	2000	12-01
NAV	11.01	13.27	13.48	14.13	13.06	15.67	16.95	19.55	19.57	17.83	18.63	16.83
Total Return %	–1.42	27.33	7.80	11.56	–0.70	28.62	18.70	26.99	8.10	2.46	10.83	–4.18
+/– S&P 500	1.70	–3.16	0.18	1.50	–2.02	–8.91	–4.24	–6.36	–20.48	–18.58	19.93	7.70
+/– Russ Top 200 Val	2.25	9.17	–1.27	–8.21	1.61	–11.41	–3.61	–8.50	–13.14	–8.49	8.52	4.61
Income Return %	5.61	6.31	5.39	5.38	5.46	6.06	5.17	4.76	3.70	2.87	3.14	2.38
Capital Return %	–7.03	21.02	2.41	6.17	–6.16	22.56	13.54	22.23	4.40	–0.41	7.68	–6.56
Total Rtn % Rank Cat	17	45	67	65	54	78	67	51	78	67	30	39
Income $	0.65	0.68	0.70	0.71	0.75	0.77	0.78	0.78	0.70	0.55	0.55	0.44
Capital Gains $	0.00	0.00	0.09	0.19	0.22	0.27	0.74	1.02	0.73	1.66	0.51	0.55
Expense Ratio %	1.00	0.83	0.74	0.70	0.73	0.75	0.72	0.68	0.65	0.65	0.67	0.67
Income Ratio %	5.75	6.30	5.99	5.43	5.25	5.34	4.84	4.73	3.85	3.06	2.97	2.57
Turnover Rate %	49	27	16	27	25	35	32	35	22	34	13	18
Net Assets $mil	92.0	243.4	592.4	1,129.9	1,171.7	1,585.5	1,928.5	2,397.5	2,490.7	2,284.1	1,992.3	1,869.4

Performance 12-31-01

	1st Qtr	2nd Qtr	3rd Qtr	4th Qtr	Total
1997	0.34	8.62	9.95	5.98	26.99
1998	7.01	–0.77	–8.06	10.71	8.10
1999	–0.21	11.09	–7.83	0.28	2.46
2000	0.90	–0.35	4.52	5.45	10.83
2001	–3.96	2.87	–8.29	5.76	–4.18

Trailing	Total Return%	+/– S&P 500	+/– Russ Top 200 Val	% Rank All	% Rank Cat	Growth of $10,000
3 Mo	5.76	–4.93	0.24	62	90	10,576
6 Mo	–3.01	2.55	2.77	51	34	9,699
1 Yr	–4.18	7.70	4.61	50	39	9,582
3 Yr Avg	2.85	3.88	1.69	56	42	10,881
5 Yr Avg	8.36	–2.34	–2.85	27	55	14,937
10 Yr Avg	10.54	–2.39	–3.49	29	76	27,230
15 Yr Avg	—	—	—	—	—	—

Tax Analysis	Tax-Adj Ret%	%Rank Cat	%Pretax Ret	%Rank Cat
3 Yr Avg	0.66	48	23.1	87
5 Yr Avg	5.88	60	70.4	64
10 Yr Avg	7.91	77	75.1	62

Potential Capital Gain Exposure: 18% of assets

Risk Analysis

Time Period	Load-Adj Return %	Risk %Rank[1] All	Risk %Rank[1] Cat	Morningstar Return	Morningstar Risk	Morningstar Risk-Adj Rating
1 Yr	–4.18					
3 Yr	2.85	48	21	–0.43[2]	0.68	★★★
5 Yr	8.36	50	15	0.77[2]	0.68	★★★
10 Yr	10.54	55	18	0.83	0.70	★★★

Average Historical Rating (140 months): 3.7★s

[1] 1=low, 100=high [2] T-Bill return substituted for category avg.

Category Rating (3 Yr)
1 2 **3** 4 5
Worst Best

Return Average
Risk Below Avg

Other Measures	Standard Index S&P 500	Best Fit Index S&P 500
Alpha	1.5	1.5
Beta	0.58	0.58
R-Squared	49	49
Standard Deviation		14.41
Mean		2.85
Sharpe Ratio		–0.17

Analysis by Christopher Davis 09-19-01

Cautious types will find USAA Income Stock Fund an appealing option.

Even though it now has a longer leash, this offering remains the same animal. Although manager Stephan Klaffke moderated the income-above-all-else approach he inherited in 1998, the fund's yield remains nearly four times the large-value norm. To generate that plump yield, the fund has scant exposure to the dividend-poor tech sector and boasts outsized stakes in high-yielding financials, utility, and energy stocks. The result is a fairly staid, stable portfolio, where Hewlett-Packard ranks among the raciest picks.

You'd expect that calm demeanor to buoy returns this year—and to some extent, it has. Steady, dividend-paying names have fared relatively well in 2001, and the fund's perennially undersized technology stake has sheltered it from the brunt of the sector's precipitous losses. Although Klaffke's income-driven focus has undoubtedly helped, his stock-picking has largely been on the mark, too. While hefty exposure to banking and energy names could have been a big liability, top holdings like Texaco and Bank of America have given the fund a boost. In all, the fund has outpaced 79% of its large-value rivals for the year to date through Sept. 19, 2001, with a 11% loss.

Klaffke's temperate, income-oriented approach has made the fund considerably less volatile than its typical peer. What's more, he has posted solid results during this three-year tenure: The fund's annualized return over that stretch lands in the category's top half.

That said, the fund doesn't come without a couple of caveats. For one, it is likely to lag its peers when growth stocks rule the roost, as in 1999. Further, the fund's income focus reduces its tax efficiency, making it suited for tax-sheltered accounts.

Portfolio Analysis 11-30-01

Share change since 10-01 Total Stocks: 75

	Sector	PE	YTD Ret%	% Assets
☼ ChevronTexaco	Energy	10.3	9.29	4.18
Bank of America	Financials	16.7	42.73	3.35
American Home Products	Health	—	–1.91	3.28
Bristol-Myers Squibb	Health	20.2	–26.00	3.23
Citigroup	Financials	20.0	0.03	3.14
Verizon Comms	Services	29.7	–2.52	3.08
Washington Mutual	Financials	10.1	–5.32	3.08
Nicor	Services	43.8	0.90	2.98
PNC Finl Svcs Grp	Financials	13.5	–20.70	2.82
Natl Fuel Gas	Utilities	30.1	–18.20	2.81
BP PLC ADR	Energy	14.4	–0.90	2.37
TXU	Utilities	13.7	12.17	2.22
Heinz HJ	Staples	29.6	–9.86	2.08
Occidental Petro	Energy	5.7	13.49	2.05
⊕ Pharmacia	Health	36.5	–29.30	2.00
General Elec	Industrials	30.1	–15.00	1.89
Sara Lee	Staples	8.4	–6.95	1.79
Emerson Elec	Industrials	23.8	–25.60	1.77
Allegheny Energy	Utilities	10.0	–21.70	1.71
SBC Comms	Services	18.4	–16.00	1.63
Hewlett-Packard	Technology	97.8	–33.90	1.56
Ford Motor	Durables	43.7	–30.00	1.55
J.P. Morgan Chase & Co.	Financials	27.8	–17.40	1.55
FleetBoston Finl	Financials	16.2	0.55	1.51
Xcel Energy	Utilities	12.2	0.57	1.49

Current Investment Style

Style: Value Blnd Growth; Size: Large Med Small

	Stock Port Avg	Relative S&P 500 Current	Relative S&P 500 Hist	Rel Cat
Price/Earnings Ratio	23.8	0.77	0.70	0.94
Price/Book Ratio	4.1	0.72	0.63	0.99
Price/Cash Flow	12.2	0.68	0.63	0.89
3 Yr Earnings Growth	8.0	0.54	0.62	0.54
1 Yr Earnings Est%	–2.1	1.21	—	0.65
Med Mkt Cap $mil	23,857	0.4	0.6	0.75

Special Securities % assets 11-30-01	
Restricted/Illiquid Secs	0
Emerging-Markets Secs	0
Options/Futures/Warrants	No

Composition % assets 11-30-01	
Cash	3.1
Stocks*	95.7
Bonds	0.0
Other	1.2
*Foreign (% stocks)	3.4

Market Cap	
Giant	34.9
Large	41.4
Medium	21.9
Small	1.8
Micro	0.0

Sector Weightings	% of Stocks	Rel S&P	5-Year High	5-Year Low
Utilities	8.6	2.7	30	4
Energy	11.4	1.6	17	7
Financials	27.8	1.6	31	15
Industrials	13.3	1.2	18	1
Durables	2.7	1.7	14	0
Staples	8.1	1.0	12	0
Services	12.9	1.2	26	2
Retail	0.8	0.1	6	0
Health	8.9	0.6	17	5
Technology	5.4	0.3	10	0

Address: USAA Building
San Antonio, TX 78288
800–382–8722
Web Address: www.usaa.com
Inception: 05-04-87
Advisor: USAA Inv. Mgmt.
Subadvisor: None
NTF Plans: N/A

Minimum Purchase: $3000 Add: $50 IRA: $250
Min Auto Inv Plan: None Add: $50
Sales Fees: No-load
Management Fee: .50%
Actual Fees: Mgt: 0.50% Dist: —
Expense Projections: 3Yr: $214 5Yr: $373 10Yr: $835
Avg Brok Commission: — Income Distrib: Quarterly
Total Cost (relative to category): Low

USAA Tax–Exempt Intermediate–Term

Ticker	Load	NAV	Yield	SEC Yield	Total Assets	Mstar Category
USATX	None	$13.00	5.2%	4.15%	$2,397.4 mil	Muni Natl Interm–Term

Prospectus Objective: Muni Bond—National

USAA Tax-Exempt Intermediate-Term Fund seeks interest income exempt from federal income tax.

The fund invests primarily in municipal obligations. At least 80% of its annual interest income is typically exempt from regular federal income tax and the Alternative Minimum Tax. At least 50% of the municipal securities purchased by the fund are rated A or higher; the remainder may be rated no lower than BBB at the time of purchase. The average-weighted maturity typically ranges between three and 10 years.

Historical Profile

Return High
Risk Below Avg
Rating ★★★★★ Highest

Investment Style Fixed-Income

Income Rtn %Rank Cat: 21, 12, 5, 4, 4, 2, 4, 5

Growth of Principal vs. Interest Rate Shifts
- Principal Value $000 (NAV with capital gains reinvested)
- Interest Rate % on 10 Yr Treasury
- ▼ Manager Change
- ▽ Partial Manager Change
- ► Mgr Unknown After
- ◄ Mgr Unknown Before

Performance Quartile (within Category)

Portfolio Manager(s)

Clifford A. Gladson, CFA. Since 4-93. BS'85 Marquette U.-Milwaukee; MS'87 U. of Wisconsin-Milwaukee. Other funds currently managed: USAA Growth & Tax Strategy, USAA NY Bond, USAA Tax-Exempt Short-Term.

1990	1991	1992	1993	1994	1995	1996	1997	1998	1999	2000	12-01	History
11.93	12.41	12.68	13.26	12.02	13.08	12.92	13.38	13.50	12.47	12.97	13.00	NAV
6.72	11.14	8.49	11.47	–4.03	15.07	4.49	9.39	6.32	–2.56	9.83	5.55	Total Return %
–2.24	–4.87	1.09	1.72	–1.11	–3.40	0.87	–0.29	–2.35	–1.73	–1.80	–2.87	+/– LB Aggregate
–0.58	–1.01	–0.33	–0.81	1.12	–2.40	0.05	0.19	–0.16	–0.50	–1.86	0.47	+/– LB Muni
7.10	6.96	6.22	5.70	5.32	6.07	5.67	5.69	5.40	5.28	5.66	5.35	Income Return %
–0.38	4.17	2.27	5.77	–9.35	9.00	–1.18	3.70	0.92	–7.85	4.17	0.20	Capital Return %
38	42	43	40	62	26	17	6	10	71	28	6	Total Rtn % Rank Cat
0.82	0.81	0.75	0.70	0.69	0.71	0.72	0.72	0.71	0.70	0.69	0.68	Income $
0.00	0.00	0.00	0.13	0.03	0.00	0.00	0.00	0.00	0.00	0.00	0.00	Capital Gains $
0.46	0.43	0.44	0.42	0.40	0.40	0.38	0.37	0.37	0.36	0.36	0.36	Expense Ratio %
6.95	6.91	6.45	5.85	5.30	5.63	5.54	5.65	5.42	5.21	5.39	5.41	Income Ratio %
62	66	67	74	69	72	28	23	8	12	10	9	Turnover Rate %
536.9	818.3	1,205.8	1,660.9	1,416.1	1,673.1	1,711.2	1,936.0	2,252.0	2,146.8	2,230.4	2,397.4	Net Assets $mil

Performance 12-31-01

	1st Qtr	2nd Qtr	3rd Qtr	4th Qtr	Total
1997	0.23	3.07	3.08	2.73	9.39
1998	1.33	1.41	2.83	0.62	6.32
1999	0.47	–1.44	–0.84	–0.76	–2.56
2000	2.29	1.39	2.16	3.66	9.83
2001	2.27	0.78	2.65	–0.24	5.55

Trailing	Total Return%	+/– LB Agg	+/– LB Muni	% Rank All	% Rank Cat	Growth of $10,000
3 Mo	–0.24	–0.28	0.42	81	9	9,976
6 Mo	2.40	–2.25	0.28	19	5	10,240
1 Yr	5.55	–2.87	0.47	20	6	10,555
3 Yr Avg	4.14	–2.13	–0.61	39	26	11,295
5 Yr Avg	5.61	–1.82	–0.36	54	8	13,138
10 Yr Avg	6.25	–0.98	–0.38	64	16	18,333
15 Yr Avg	6.60	–1.52	–0.59	75	36	26,077

Tax Analysis	Tax-Adj Ret%	%Rank Cat	%Pretax Ret	%Rank Cat
3 Yr Avg	4.14	21	100.0	9
5 Yr Avg	5.61	5	100.0	9
10 Yr Avg	6.21	8	99.4	18

Potential Capital Gain Exposure: 3% of assets

Risk Analysis

Time Period	Load-Adj Return %	Risk %Rank[1] All	Risk %Rank[1] Cat	Morningstar Return	Morningstar Risk	Morningstar Risk-Adj Rating
1 Yr	5.55					
3 Yr	4.14	7	22	0.63[2]	0.74	★★★★★
5 Yr	5.61	7	16	1.03[2]	0.73	★★★★★
10 Yr	6.25	8	34	1.12	0.76	★★★★★

Average Historical Rating (193 months): 4.5★s

[1]1=low, 100=high [2] T-Bill return substituted for category avg.

Category Rating (3 Yr)

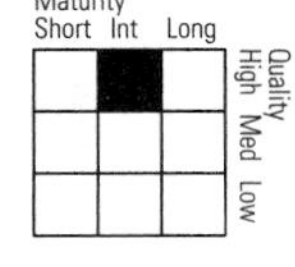

Return High
Risk Below Avg

Other Measures	Standard Index LB Agg	Best Fit Index LB Muni
Alpha	–1.6	–0.6
Beta	0.70	0.86
R-Squared	53	97
Standard Deviation		3.33
Mean		4.14
Sharpe Ratio		–0.28

Portfolio Analysis 11-30-01

Total Fixed-Income: 389	Date of Maturity	Amount $000	Value $000	% Net Assets
NY Hsg 5%	11-01-20	75,745	75,442	3.11
ME Bucksport Solid Waste Disp 6.25%	05-01-10	41,400	42,696	1.76
PA Fin Muni Cap Impr 6.6%	11-01-09	30,660	33,096	1.37
NJ Tpk 6.5%	01-01-03	31,260	32,658	1.35
TX Brazos Rvr Houston Indl 5.375%	04-01-19	32,925	31,233	1.29
DC Conv Ctr 5%	10-01-18	30,000	29,779	1.23
NY Mtg Homeownshp 5.45%	04-01-18	25,000	25,675	1.06
PR Hsg Bank/Fin FRN	12-01-06	22,200	24,901	1.03
MI Dickinson Econ Dev Solid Waste 6.55%	03-01-07	23,330	23,717	0.98
NY Metro Transp Svc Commuter Fac 5.75%	07-01-15	22,230	23,358	0.96
IL Chicago O'Hare Intl Arpt Genl 6.2%	01-01-07	21,235	22,963	0.95
NY Urban Dev Crtnl Fac 5.5%	01-01-15	21,700	22,518	0.93
NY Urban Dev Crtnl Fac 5.875%	01-01-13	20,955	21,887	0.90
CA Pleasanton Jt Pwrs Fin 6%	09-02-05	19,900	21,207	0.88
MS Mississippi Hosp 6.35%	12-01-15	19,850	20,598	0.85

Current Investment Style

Maturity: Short Int Long; Quality: High Med Low

Avg Duration[1]	4.9 Yrs
Avg Nominal Maturity	8.6 Yrs
Avg Credit Quality	AA
Avg Wtd Coupon	5.11%
Avg Wtd Price	100.82% of par
Pricing Service	J.J. Kenny

[1]figure provided by fund

Credit Analysis % bonds 09-30-01

US Govt	0	BB	0
AAA	42	B	1
AA	22	Below B	0
A	15	NR/NA	0
BBB	20		

Special Securities % assets 11-30-01

Restricted/Illiquid Secs	2
Inverse Floaters	0
Options/Futures/Warrants	No

Bond Type % assets 09-30-00

Alternative Minimum Tax (AMT)	0.0
Insured	21.2
Prerefunded	9.0

Top 5 States % bonds

NY	20.1	CA	5.3
TX	12.7	DC	4.7
IL	8.0		

Composition % assets 11-30-01

Cash	0.6	Bonds	99.4
Stocks	0.0	Other	0.0

Sector Weightings	% of Bonds	Rel Cat
General Obligation	16.6	0.6
Utilities	7.8	0.9
Health	22.1	1.8
Water/Waste	1.4	0.2
Housing	12.5	1.7
Education	6.9	0.9
Transportation	9.4	0.8
COP/Lease	1.6	0.7
Industrial	12.6	1.6
Misc Revenue	7.9	1.6
Demand	1.3	1.3

Analysis by Christopher Davis 12-12-01

Again and again, USAA Tax-Exempt Intermediate-Term Fund's yield-oriented approach produces appealing results.

Income is king at USAA's fixed-income offerings, and this one is no exception. Indeed, the fund's yield is among the highest in the muni-national intermediate group. That quest for yield has often led manager Cliff Gladson to lower-rated investment-grade bonds, particularly those rated BBB, which typically sport more-generous yields than higher-rated fare. The fund's stake in such credits, pegged at 20% of assets in June 2001, is considerably above the category norm. In pursuit of income, Gladson has also tended to keep the fund's duration, a measure of interest-rate sensitivity, longer than average for its group (it now stands a bit below the category average, though).

Despite that bolder-than-average approach, the fund hasn't been any more volatile than its typical peer. What's more, Gladson has posted peer-beating gains over the long haul: The fund's return over the trailing five years through Dec. 10, 2001, ranks in the category's top decile. More impressive is the consistency of those returns—Gladson has guided the fund to top-half category showings for seven of the past nine years, and he's on pace to do so again in 2001.

Even so, Gladson's tendency to favor longer-duration issues can hurt performance when interest rates rise, as in 1999. And though his willingness to venture down the credit-quality ladder has been a boon to returns in past years, credit troubles within the muni sector could dent returns.

Nonetheless, the fund has a lot arguing in its favor. Its expenses are among the category's lowest, giving it a significant edge. And it boasts an experienced manager, fine long-term record, and mild volatility. We'd say those traits make this offering an excellent choice.

Address:	USAA Building San Antonio, TX 78288 800–382–8722
Web Address:	www.usaa.com
Inception:	03-19-82
Advisor:	USAA Inv. Mgmt.
Subadvisor:	None
NTF Plans:	N/A

Minimum Purchase:	$3000	Add: $50	IRA: —
Min Auto Inv Plan:	$50	Add: $50	
Sales Fees:	No–load		
Management Fee:	.28%		
Actual Fees:	Mgt: 0.28%	Dist: —	
Expense Projections:	3Yr: $116	5Yr: $202	10Yr: $456
Avg Brok Commission:	—	Income Distrib: Monthly	
Total Cost (relative to category):		Low	

USAA Tax–Exempt Long–Term

Ticker	Load	NAV	Yield	SEC Yield	Total Assets	Mstar Category
USTEX	None	$13.18	5.5%	4.89%	$2,074.9 mil	Muni Natl Long–Term

Prospectus Objective: Muni Bond—National

USAA Tax-Exempt Long-Term Fund seeks interest income exempt from federal income tax.

The fund invests primarily in municipal securities. At least 80% of its annual income is ordinarily exempt from federal income tax and the Alternative Minimum Tax. At least 50% of the fund's securities are rated A or higher; the remainder may be rated no lower than BBB at the time of purchase. The average weighted maturity is typically 10 or more years.

Prior to Aug. 1, 1992, the fund was named USAA Tax-Exempt Fund

Historical Profile

Return Above Avg
Risk Average
Rating ★★★ Neutral

Investment Style: Fixed-Income — Income Rtn %Rank Cat: 28, 9, 11, 9, 6, 7, 7, 16

Growth of Principal vs. Interest Rate Shifts
- Principal Value $000 (NAV with capital gains reinvested)
- Interest Rate % on 10 Yr Treasury
- ▼ Manager Change
- ▽ Partial Manager Change
- ► Mgr Unknown After
- ◄ Mgr Unknown Before

Performance Quartile (within Category)

Portfolio Manager(s)

Robert R. Pariseau, CFA. Since 11-99. BS U.S. Naval Academy; MBA Lindenwood C. Other funds currently managed: USAA CA Bond, USAA VA Bond, USAA FL Tax-Free Income.

1990	1991	1992	1993	1994	1995	1996	1997	1998	1999	2000	12–01	History
13.09	13.73	13.90	14.18	12.22	13.63	13.42	13.99	14.04	12.60	13.33	13.18	NAV
6.56	12.38	8.62	12.51	−7.93	18.58	4.47	10.38	5.97	−5.00	12.11	4.33	Total Return %
−2.40	−3.62	1.22	2.76	−5.01	0.11	0.86	0.70	−2.70	−4.17	0.48	−4.09	+/– LB Aggregate
−0.75	0.24	−0.20	0.23	−2.78	1.12	0.03	1.18	−0.51	−2.94	0.42	−0.75	+/– LB Muni
7.40	7.28	6.71	6.30	5.64	6.77	5.94	5.96	5.62	5.58	6.06	5.53	Income Return %
−0.85	5.10	1.91	6.20	−13.57	11.81	−1.47	4.42	0.36	−10.58	6.05	−1.19	Capital Return %
35	33	62	48	80	20	17	11	21	59	21	34	Total Rtn % Rank Cat
0.95	0.92	0.89	0.84	0.78	0.80	0.79	0.78	0.77	0.76	0.74	0.72	Income $
0.00	0.00	0.08	0.56	0.09	0.00	0.00	0.00	0.00	0.00	0.00	0.00	Capital Gains $
0.43	0.40	0.40	0.39	0.38	0.38	0.37	0.37	0.36	0.36	0.36	0.36	Expense Ratio %
7.23	7.22	6.83	6.35	5.69	6.23	5.99	5.95	5.65	5.44	5.77	5.72	Income Ratio %
92	91	76	88	109	163	53	41	35	30	29	47	Turnover Rate %
1,360.2	1,637.1	1,784.3	2,014.0	1,661.2	1,910.1	1,872.7	2,002.4	2,173.0	1,910.4	2,071.0	2,074.9	Net Assets $mil

Performance 12-31-01

	1st Qtr	2nd Qtr	3rd Qtr	4th Qtr	Total
1997	−0.04	3.61	3.45	3.02	10.38
1998	1.46	1.45	3.10	−0.13	5.97
1999	0.50	−1.77	−1.80	−2.00	−5.00
2000	2.71	1.34	2.55	5.03	12.11
2001	2.00	0.24	2.60	−0.54	4.33

Trailing	Total Return%	+/– LB Agg	+/– LB Muni	% Rank All	% Rank Cat	Growth of $10,000
3 Mo	−0.54	−0.58	0.12	85	15	9,946
6 Mo	2.04	−2.61	−0.08	22	18	10,204
1 Yr	4.33	−4.09	−0.75	28	34	10,433
3 Yr Avg	3.58	−2.70	−1.18	47	31	11,112
5 Yr Avg	5.38	−2.04	−0.59	57	15	12,998
10 Yr Avg	6.12	−1.11	−0.51	67	28	18,119
15 Yr Avg	6.71	−1.41	−0.48	72	27	26,493

Tax Analysis	Tax-Adj Ret%	%Rank Cat	%Pretax Ret	%Rank Cat
3 Yr Avg	3.58	29	100.0	15
5 Yr Avg	5.38	12	100.0	9
10 Yr Avg	5.97	31	97.4	57

Potential Capital Gain Exposure: 1% of assets

Risk Analysis

Time Period	Load-Adj Return %	Risk %Rank[1] All	Risk %Rank[1] Cat	Morningstar Return	Morningstar Risk	Morningstar Risk-Adj Rating
1 Yr	4.33					
3 Yr	3.58	22	36	0.54[2]	1.11	★★★
5 Yr	5.38	21	29	1.02[2]	1.07	★★★★
10 Yr	6.12	26	35	1.16	1.09	★★★

Average Historical Rating (193 months): 3.9★s

[1]1=low, 100=high [2] T-Bill return substituted for category avg.

Category Rating (3 Yr)

Worst 1 2 3 4 5 Best

Return Above Avg
Risk Average

Other Measures	Standard Index LB Agg	Best Fit Index LB Muni
Alpha	−2.4	−1.1
Beta	0.92	1.14
R–Squared	50	92
Standard Deviation		4.52
Mean		3.58
Sharpe Ratio		−0.35

Portfolio Analysis 11-30-01

Total Fixed-Income: 223	Date of Maturity	Amount $000	Value $000	% Net Assets
CT Mashantucket West Pequot 144A 5.75%	09-01-27	62,950	60,518	2.87
NY NYC GO 7.25%	08-15-04	50,000	56,626	2.69
DC State GO 5.5%	06-01-29	52,900	54,218	2.57
NJ Tpk 5.5%	01-01-27	50,000	51,762	2.46
IL Regl Transp 6.5%	07-01-30	37,550	45,968	2.18
MI Ascension Hlth 6.125%	11-15-26	43,000	45,299	2.15
MN St Paul Hsg/Redev Healtheast 6.625%	11-01-17	45,005	38,197	1.81
ME Tpk 5.75%	07-01-28	27,750	29,455	1.40
LA Lake Charles Harbor/Term Dist 7.75%	08-15-22	25,730	27,299	1.30
IL Regl Transp 5.75%	06-01-20	23,980	26,426	1.25
RI Hsg/Mtg Fin Homeownshp 6.85%	10-01-24	25,000	26,141	1.24
NY Dorm Mental Hlth Svc Fac 6%	08-15-16	21,500	24,186	1.15
NY New York GO 5.75%	05-15-30	22,740	23,703	1.12
TX Bell Hlth Fac Dev Lutheran Hosp 6.5%	07-01-19	19,500	23,187	1.10
IN Indianapolis Arpt Spcl Fac FedEx 6.8%	04-01-17	21,750	22,778	1.08

Current Investment Style

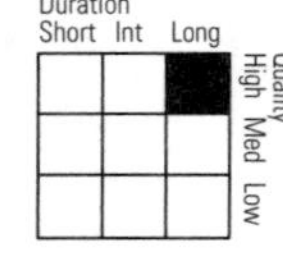

Avg Duration[1]	7.8 Yrs
Avg Nominal Maturity	20.2 Yrs
Avg Credit Quality	AA
Avg Wtd Coupon	5.74%
Avg Wtd Price	100.68% of par
Pricing Service	J.J. Kenny

[1]figure provided by fund

Credit Analysis % bonds 09-30-01

US Govt	0	BB	0
AAA	43	B	1
AA	22	Below B	0
A	17	NR/NA	0
BBB	17		

Special Securities % assets 11-30-01

Restricted/Illiquid Secs	3
Inverse Floaters	0
Options/Futures/Warrants	No

Bond Type % assets 03-31-99

Alternative Minimum Tax (AMT)	0.0
Insured	5.8
Prerefunded	25.8

Top 5 States % bonds

TX	15.4	MI	5.8
NY	12.6	DC	5.3
IL	8.0		

Composition % assets 11-30-01

Cash	0.0	Bonds	100.0
Stocks	0.0	Other	0.0

Sector Weightings	% of Bonds	Rel Cat
General Obligation	25.0	1.2
Utilities	0.3	0.0
Health	24.2	1.6
Water/Waste	5.7	0.9
Housing	2.6	0.4
Education	9.9	1.5
Transportation	14.6	1.1
COP/Lease	0.6	0.2
Industrial	9.4	0.7
Misc Revenue	6.8	1.4
Demand	1.0	1.2

Analysis by Christopher Davis 08-13-01

USAA Tax-Exempt Long-Term Fund remains as appealing as ever.

This offering, like many of its siblings, puts together a portfolio that pumps out heaps of income—its yield has long been one of the biggest in the long-term municipal bond group. In pursuit of that grail, manager Bob Pariseau has generally gravitated to lower-rated investment-grade bonds, particularly those rated BBB, which typically sport more generous yields than higher-rated fare. The fund's stake in such credits, currently pegged at 17% of assets, is considerably above the category norm. In further pursuit of income, Pariseau also tends to keep the fund's duration, a measure of interest-rate sensitivity, longer than average for its peer group. That sort of mix has made the fund a bit more volatile than its typical rival.

Pariseau has tried to temper such instability, however, by moderating the fund's income-above-all-else approach. For example, he has been less willing to venture down the credit-quality ladder than his predecessor, hiking the fund's stake in AAA and A rated bonds to 65% from 49% of assets at his November 1999 start. He has also lessened the fund's focus on longer-duration bonds, reducing its sensitivity to interest-rate swings. These moves have shrunk the fund's yield somewhat, but its income payout still remains much higher than the category average. They haven't dampened returns, however: Pariseau has outperformed his typical peer by 90 basis points a year since taking charge here.

Another mark in the fund's favor is its rock-bottom expenses. Indeed, few offerings in its group are cheaper than this one. Because just a few basis points in expenses can affect a bond fund's relative performance, the fund's low expense ratio is likely to help it deliver greater gains over the long haul.

Those in search of a long-term muni fund will find this an appealing choice.

Address:	USAA Building San Antonio, TX 78288 800–382–8722
Web Address:	www.usaa.com
Inception:	03-19-82
Advisor:	USAA Inv. Mgmt.
Subadvisor:	None
NTF Plans:	N/A

Minimum Purchase:	$3000	Add: $50	IRA: —
Min Auto Inv Plan:	$50	Add: $50	
Sales Fees:	No–load		
Management Fee:	.28%		
Actual Fees:	Mgt: 0.28%	Dist: —	
Expense Projections:	3Yr: $116	5Yr: $202	10Yr: $556
Avg Brok Commission:	—	Income Distrib: Monthly	
Total Cost (relative to category):		Low	

USAA Tax–Exempt Short–Term

Ticker	Load	NAV	Yield	SEC Yield	Total Assets	Mstar Category
USSTX	None	$10.69	4.1%	3.08%	$1,122.3 mil	Muni Short–Term

Prospectus Objective: Muni Bond—National

USAA Tax-Exempt Short-Term Fund seeks interest income exempt from federal income tax.

The fund invests primarily in municipal securities, so that at least 80% of its annual income is exempt from federal income tax and the Alternative Minimum Tax. At least 50% of the fund's securities are rated A or higher; the remainder may be rated no lower than BBB at the time of purchase. The average weighted maturity is typically three years or less.

Historical Profile

Return Below Avg
Risk Low
Rating ★★★★★ Highest

Investment Style
Fixed-Income
Income Rtn %Rank Cat: 36 | 17 | 13 | 14 | 11 | 8 | 14 | 24

Growth of Principal vs. Interest Rate Shifts
— Principal Value $000 (NAV with capital gains reinvested)
— Interest Rate % on 10 Yr Treasury
▼ Manager Change
▽ Partial Manager Change
► Mgr Unknown After
◄ Mgr Unknown Before

Performance Quartile (within Category)

Portfolio Manager(s)

Clifford A. Gladson, CFA. Since 4-94. BS'85 Marquette U.-Milwaukee; MS'87 U. of Wisconsin-Milwaukee. Other funds currently managed: USAA Tax-Exempt Intermediate-Term, USAA Growth & Tax Strategy, USAA NY Bond.

1990	1991	1992	1993	1994	1995	1996	1997	1998	1999	2000	12-01	History
10.34	10.50	10.59	10.70	10.33	10.65	10.62	10.74	10.77	10.47	10.60	10.69	NAV
5.87	7.70	5.96	5.52	0.82	8.11	4.44	5.86	5.02	1.78	6.03	5.10	Total Return %
–3.08	–8.30	–1.44	–4.23	3.74	–10.36	0.82	–3.83	–3.66	2.61	–5.60	–3.33	+/– LB Aggregate
–1.43	–4.44	–2.86	–6.76	5.97	–9.35	0.00	–3.35	–1.46	3.85	–5.66	0.01	+/– LB Muni
6.65	6.09	5.08	4.47	4.34	4.96	4.70	4.69	4.73	4.63	4.74	4.25	Income Return %
–0.77	1.61	0.88	1.05	–3.52	3.15	–0.27	1.17	0.29	–2.85	1.29	0.84	Capital Return %
87	61	76	78	14	46	13	22	21	15	43	29	Total Rtn % Rank Cat
0.67	0.61	0.52	0.46	0.46	0.50	0.49	0.49	0.50	0.49	0.49	0.44	Income $
0.00	0.00	0.00	0.00	0.00	0.00	0.00	0.00	0.00	0.00	0.00	0.00	Capital Gains $
0.52	0.50	0.48	0.43	0.43	0.42	0.42	0.41	0.39	0.38	0.38	0.38	Expense Ratio %
6.47	6.48	5.59	4.75	4.25	4.50	4.73	4.60	4.57	4.55	4.48	4.60	Income Ratio %
87	96	107	138	102	103	36	28	8	7	19	19	Turnover Rate %
360.7	602.8	840.2	954.8	810.8	776.6	785.9	937.0	1,004.6	987.7	1,003.3	1,122.3	Net Assets $mil

Performance 12-31-01

	1st Qtr	2nd Qtr	3rd Qtr	4th Qtr	Total
1997	0.66	1.75	1.81	1.52	5.86
1998	1.13	1.07	1.86	0.88	5.02
1999	0.65	–0.07	0.62	0.57	1.78
2000	1.05	1.30	1.64	1.92	6.03
2001	1.96	1.10	1.74	0.21	5.10

Trailing	Total Return%	+/– LB Agg	+/– LB Muni	% Rank All	% Rank Cat	Growth of $10,000
3 Mo	0.21	0.18	0.87	77	28	10,021
6 Mo	1.96	–2.70	–0.16	23	35	10,196
1 Yr	5.10	–3.33	0.01	22	29	10,510
3 Yr Avg	4.29	–1.99	–0.46	37	8	11,342
5 Yr Avg	4.75	–2.68	–1.23	69	14	12,609
10 Yr Avg	4.84	–2.39	–1.79	93	47	16,048
15 Yr Avg	5.21	–2.91	–1.97	96	22	21,435

Tax Analysis	Tax-Adj Ret%	%Rank Cat	%Pretax Ret	%Rank Cat
3 Yr Avg	4.29	7	100.0	11
5 Yr Avg	4.75	11	100.0	10
10 Yr Avg	4.84	47	100.0	19

Potential Capital Gain Exposure: 1% of assets

Risk Analysis

Time Period	Load-Adj Return %	Risk %Rank[1] All	Risk %Rank[1] Cat	Morningstar Return	Morningstar Risk	Morningstar Risk-Adj Rating
1 Yr	5.10					
3 Yr	4.29	1	13	0.52[2]	0.16	★★★★★
5 Yr	4.75	1	16	0.66[2]	0.18	★★★★★
10 Yr	4.84	1	20	0.62	0.19	★★★★★

Average Historical Rating (193 months): 4.5★s

[1]1=low, 100=high [2] T-Bill return substituted for category avg.

Category Rating (3 Yr)

1 2 3 4 5 — Worst … Best

Return: Above Avg
Risk: Below Avg

Other Measures	Standard Index LB Agg	Best Fit Index LB Muni
Alpha	–1.0	–0.6
Beta	0.28	0.31
R-Squared	55	82

Standard Deviation	1.32
Mean	4.29
Sharpe Ratio	–0.59

Portfolio Analysis 07-31-01

Total Fixed-Income: 235	Date of Maturity	Amount $000	Value $000	% Net Assets
TX Matagorda Navig Dist #1 Poll 4.9%	05-01-30	27,500	27,564	2.62
CA Hlth Fac Fin Meml Svcs FRN	10-01-24	25,220	25,220	2.40
KS Burlington Envir Impr Pwr/Lt 3.75%	09-01-15	24,400	24,400	2.32
LA St Charles Poll Cntrl 5.35%	10-01-29	19,860	20,368	1.94
DC Methodist Hm 6.4%	08-15-31	20,000	20,294	1.93
WA Seattle Muni Metro Swr 2.9%	01-01-32	20,000	20,000	1.90
KS Burlington Envir Impr Pwr/Lt 3.75%	09-01-15	19,800	19,800	1.88
MA New England Educ Ln Mktg 5.8%	03-01-02	17,000	17,304	1.64
NY Long Island Pwr N/A	06-01-06	20,360	17,009	1.62
TX GO 5.2%	05-01-29	16,500	16,724	1.59
AL Birmingham Spcl Care Fac Fin 6%	11-15-28	15,000	15,457	1.47
MA State GO 5.5%	06-01-08	14,000	15,336	1.46
OK Hsg Fin Sngl Fam Mtg 4.75%	12-01-02	15,000	15,047	1.43
OR Columbia Port 5.1%	12-01-14	15,000	15,000	1.43
LA Pub Fac 5%	12-01-15	14,285	14,480	1.38

Current Investment Style

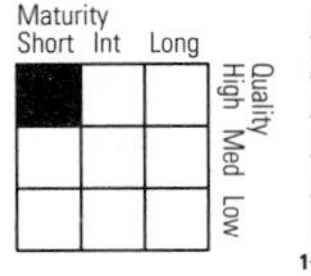

Avg Duration[1]	2.2 Yrs
Avg Nominal Maturity	2.3 Yrs
Avg Credit Quality	AA
Avg Wtd Coupon	4.61%
Avg Wtd Price	99.70% of par
Pricing Service	J.J. Kenny

[1]figure provided by fund

Analysis by Christopher Davis 09-17-01

There's a lot to like in USAA Tax-Exempt Short-Term Fund.

Manager Cliff Gladson has put together a portfolio that pumps out heaps of income—the fund's yield is among the highest in the short-term group. His quest for yield has often led him to lower-rated investment-grade bonds, particularly those rated A and BBB, which typically sport more-generous yields than higher-rated fare. The fund's stake in such credits, now pegged at 41% of assets, is considerably higher than the category norm.

Despite that bolder-than-usual approach, the fund hasn't been much more volatile than its typical peer. What's more, Gladson has posted peer-beating gains over the long haul: The fund's returns for the trailing three and five years through Sept. 19, 2001, rank in the category's top quartile. More impressive is the consistency of those returns—Gladson has guided the fund to top-half category showings in each of the past seven years.

Another mark in the fund's favor is its rock-bottom expenses. Indeed, few offerings in its group are cheaper than this one. Because just a few basis points can affect a bond fund's relative performance, the fund's low expense ratio is likely to help it deliver greater gains over the long haul.

Nonetheless, the fund has one potential chink in its armor: Even though Gladson's willingness to venture down the credit-quality ladder has been a boon to returns in past years, credit troubles within the muni sector could dent returns. Overall, however, this fund's fine record, modest volatility, and low expenses have made it a compelling choice.

Credit Analysis % bonds 09-30-01

US Govt	0	BB	0
AAA	20	B	0
AA	39	Below B	0
A	17	NR/NA	0
BBB	24		

Special Securities % assets 07-31-01

Restricted/Illiquid Secs	1
Inverse Floaters	0
Options/Futures/Warrants	No

Bond Type % assets 03-31-99

Alternative Minimum Tax (AMT)	0.0
Insured	9.5
Prerefunded	6.8

Top 5 States % bonds

TX	13.5	CA	6.4
NY	13.4	IL	5.8
LA	8.9		

Composition % assets 07-31-01

Cash	6.5	Bonds	93.5
Stocks	0.0	Other	0.0

Sector Weightings	% of Bonds	Rel Cat
General Obligation	15.0	0.5
Utilities	9.8	1.3
Health	24.4	2.0
Water/Waste	5.3	1.0
Housing	4.7	0.7
Education	3.3	0.5
Transportation	5.6	0.6
COP/Lease	4.9	1.6
Industrial	18.9	1.9
Misc Revenue	1.9	0.3
Demand	5.5	1.7

Address:	USAA Building San Antonio, TX 78288 800–382–8722
Web Address:	www.usaa.com
Inception:	03-19-82
Advisor:	USAA Inv. Mgmt.
Subadvisor:	None
NTF Plans:	N/A

Minimum Purchase:	$3000	Add: $50	IRA: —
Min Auto Inv Plan:	$50	Add: $50	
Sales Fees:	No–load		
Management Fee:	.28%		
Actual Fees:	Mgt: 0.28%	Dist: —	
Expense Projections:	3Yr: $122	5Yr: $213	10Yr: $480
Avg Brok Commission:	—	Income Distrib: Monthly	
Total Cost (relative to category):		Low	

Van Kampen Aggressive Growth A

Ticker	Load	NAV	Yield	Total Assets	Mstar Category
VAGAX	5.75%	$13.40	0.0%	$1,496.5 mil	Mid–Cap Growth

Prospectus Objective: Aggressive Growth

Van Kampen Aggressive Growth Fund seeks capital growth.

The fund normally invests at least 65% of assets in equities issued by small- and medium-capitalization companies. Using a bottom-up approach, the advisor seeks issuers that are likely to produce high future earnings through new product developments or industry and market changes. It may invest without limit in issuers involved in special situations, such as new management, mergers, or liquidations. The fund may invest up to 25% of assets in foreign securities.

Class A shares have front loads; B shares have deferred loads, higher 12b-1 fees, and conversion features; C shares have level loads. Past name: Van Kampen American Capital Aggressive Growth Fund.

Historical Profile
Return Above Avg
Risk High
Rating ★★★ Neutral

Investment Style
Equity
Average Stock %: 86% 96% 95% 97% 94% 95%

▼ Manager Change
▽ Partial Manager Change

Fund Performance vs. Category Average
■ Quarterly Fund Return +/– Category Average
— Category Baseline

Performance Quartile (within Category)

Portfolio Manager(s)

Gary M. Lewis, CFA. Since 5-96.
Dudley Brickhouse. Since 5-96.
Janet Luby. Since 5-96.
David Walker. Since 5-96.
Matthew Hart. Since 2-00.

1990	1991	1992	1993	1994	1995	1996	1997	1998	1999	2000	12-01	History
—	—	—	—	—	—	10.02	11.39	14.45	31.14	22.23	13.40	NAV
—	—	—	—	—	—	0.20*	13.67	35.40	130.59	–14.11	–39.70	Total Return %
—	—	—	—	—	—	–12.42*	–19.68	6.83	109.55	–5.01	–27.83	+/– S&P 500
—	—	—	—	—	—	—	–8.87	17.53	79.28	–2.36	–19.55	+/– Russ Midcap Grth
—	—	—	—	—	—	0.00	0.00	0.00	0.00	0.00	0.00	Income Return %
—	—	—	—	—	—	0.20	13.67	35.40	130.59	–14.11	–39.70	Capital Return %
—	—	—	—	—	—	—	68	6	5	74	93	Total Rtn % Rank Cat
—	—	—	—	—	—	0.00	0.00	0.00	0.00	0.00	0.00	Income $
—	—	—	—	—	—	0.00	0.00	0.86	1.87	4.43	0.00	Capital Gains $
—	—	—	—	—	—	1.29	1.30	1.44	1.56	1.25	1.19	Expense Ratio %
—	—	—	—	—	—	–0.50	–0.81	–1.09	–1.22	–0.86	–0.75	Income Ratio %
—	—	—	—	—	—	—	186	185	126	139	270	Turnover Rate %
—	—	—	—	—	—	83.2	102.2	149.0	896.0	1,007.2	791.2	Net Assets $mil

Performance 12-31-01

	1st Qtr	2nd Qtr	3rd Qtr	4th Qtr	Total
1997	–19.16	22.59	27.90	–10.32	13.67
1998	14.84	4.59	–15.06	32.72	35.40
1999	18.62	13.54	9.20	56.80	130.59
2000	20.20	–13.14	9.32	–24.74	–14.11
2001	–29.06	–0.19	–25.29	13.98	–39.70

Trailing	Total Return%	+/– S&P 500	+/– Russ Midcap Grth	% Rank All	% Rank Cat	Growth of $10,000
3 Mo	13.98	3.29	–13.09	26	78	11,398
6 Mo	–14.84	–9.29	–6.58	95	79	8,516
1 Yr	–39.70	–27.83	–19.55	98	93	6,030
3 Yr Avg	6.09	7.12	3.93	22	48	11,942
5 Yr Avg	12.95	2.25	3.93	8	24	18,380
10 Yr Avg	—	—	—	—	—	—
15 Yr Avg	—	—	—	—	—	—

Tax Analysis	Tax-Adj Ret%	%Rank Cat	%Pretax Ret	%Rank Cat
3 Yr Avg	3.91	44	64.1	66
5 Yr Avg	11.26	17	87.0	22
10 Yr Avg	—	—	—	—

Potential Capital Gain Exposure: –53% of assets

Risk Analysis

Time Period	Load-Adj Return %	Risk %Rank[1] All	Risk %Rank[1] Cat	Morningstar Return	Morningstar Risk	Morningstar Risk-Adj Rating
1 Yr	–43.17					
3 Yr	4.02	96	81	–0.19[2]	1.81	★★★
5 Yr	11.62	96	81	1.63[2]	1.80	★★★
Incept	10.36	—	—	—	—	

Average Historical Rating (32 months): 4.3★s

[1]1=low, 100=high [2] T-Bill return substituted for category avg.

Category Rating (3 Yr)
1 2 3 4 5
Worst Best

Return Average
Risk Above Avg

Other Measures	Standard Index S&P 500	Best Fit Index Wil 4500
Alpha	16.4	9.7
Beta	1.29	1.31
R–Squared	27	74

Standard Deviation	49.68
Mean	6.09
Sharpe Ratio	0.03

Portfolio Analysis 08-31-01

Share change since 07–01 Total Stocks: 151	Sector	PE	YTD Ret%	% Assets
Tenet Healthcare	Health	30.1	32.14	2.24
⊖ USA Educ	Financials	68.9	24.74	1.60
McKesson HBOC	Health	—	4.92	1.58
⊕ H & R Block	Services	25.5	120.00	1.57
⊕ Baker Hughes	Energy	45.0	–11.10	1.55
⊕ Genzyme Corporation General Di	Health	—	33.11	1.52
St. Jude Medical	Health	42.0	26.39	1.39
UnitedHealth Grp	Financials	26.6	15.37	1.37
Citrix Sys	Technology	44.4	0.71	1.33
KLA–Tencor	Technology	22.6	47.11	1.32
⊕ Gilead Sciences	Health	—	58.48	1.23
BJ Svcs	Energy	15.5	–5.77	1.21
Microchip Tech	Technology	53.8	76.59	1.20
⊕ Electronic Arts	Technology	90.8	40.65	1.17
King Pharmaceuticals	Health	45.8	8.68	1.16
PeopleSoft	Technology	73.1	8.10	1.16
⊕ NVIDIA	Technology	84.2	308.50	1.14
Ivax	Health	17.5	–34.20	1.13
⊕ Natl Semicon	Technology	—	52.99	1.11
Affiliated Comp Svcs A	Services	39.9	74.88	1.10
⊕ Apollo Grp Cl A	Services	—	—	1.06
⊖ Laboratory Corp of Amer	Health	21.0	–8.13	1.05
⊖ Forest Labs	Health	52.2	23.35	0.98
Healthsouth	Health	28.0	–9.15	0.97
⊖ Bed Bath & Beyond	Retail	53.0	51.51	0.97

Current Investment Style

Style: Value Blnd Growth; Size: Large Med Small

	Stock Port Avg	Relative S&P 500 Current	Relative S&P 500 Hist	Rel Cat
Price/Earnings Ratio	35.6	1.15	1.36	1.03
Price/Book Ratio	6.3	1.11	1.45	1.12
Price/Cash Flow	23.6	1.31	1.38	1.02
3 Yr Earnings Growth	19.5	1.33	1.40	0.83
1 Yr Earnings Est%	21.2	—	—	2.27
Med Mkt Cap $mil	4,932	0.1	0.0	0.88

Special Securities % assets 08-31-01

Restricted/Illiquid Secs	0
Emerging–Markets Secs	2
Options/Futures/Warrants	No

Composition % assets 08-31-01	
Cash	4.3
Stocks*	95.7
Bonds	0.0
Other	0.0
*Foreign (% stocks)	2.7

Market Cap	
Giant	0.0
Large	23.7
Medium	69.5
Small	6.8
Micro	0.0

Sector Weightings	% of Stocks	Rel S&P	5-Year High	5-Year Low
Utilities	0.0	0.0	4	0
Energy	3.7	0.5	22	0
Financials	11.7	0.7	14	0
Industrials	5.5	0.5	12	2
Durables	2.5	1.6	6	0
Staples	2.9	0.4	5	0
Services	12.8	1.2	28	2
Retail	6.7	1.0	15	1
Health	29.3	2.0	30	4
Technology	25.0	1.4	69	14

Analysis by Kelli Stebel 08-29-01

This fund gives investors a wild ride, but aggressive types will appreciate it.

Van Kampen Aggressive Growth isn't out for a Sunday drive. This fund will generally rise head and shoulders above its peers when momentum stocks dominate the market, as they did in 1999. But as investors have seen over the past year, once those stocks falter, this fund will get dinged harder than most. The fund has dropped nearly 38% for the year to date through August 29, one of the worst showings in the mid-cap growth category. Even more distressing is that the fund failed to rally in the second quarter, when many aggressive funds rebounded smartly. Part of the problem was the fund's hefty energy stake, which stood at about 20% of assets. And with oil prices on the decline, the fund's holdings such as Noble Drilling were hit hard.

With earnings growth slowing across the market, comanager Dudley Brickhouse reports that the team is fairly defensive these days. Though the fund isn't abandoning its aggressive stripes, it's hard to find firms growing at a fast rate or posting positive earnings surprises. While Brickhouse says the team is modestly adding to some of its semiconductor stocks, they're finding better opportunities in the consumer area, such as new holding Williams-Sonoma.

Despite the fund's recent downfall, there are plenty of reasons to stay the course. Although the fund's recent returns have been poor, its long-term record is still quite favorable, as its five-year annualized return still lands in its category's top quintile. In addition, this fund is led by one of the industry's most-successful managers. Lewis has guided his other charge, Van Kampen Emerging Growth, to its category's top echelon over the past 12 years. Thus, shareholders have no reason to panic, as the fund remains a solid choice for a portfolio's aggressive slot.

Address:	One Parkview Plaza Oakbrook Terrace, IL 60181 800–421–5666
Web Address:	www.vankampen.com
*Inception:	05-29-96
Advisor:	Van Kampen Inv. Adv.
Subadvisor:	None
NTF Plans:	Datalynx , Fidelity Inst.

Minimum Purchase:	$1000	Add: $25	IRA: $500
Min Auto Inv Plan:	$25	Add: $25	
Sales Fees:	5.75%L, 0.25%B		
Management Fee:	.75% mx./.65% mn.		
Actual Fees:	Mgt: 0.75%	Dist: 0.25%	
Expense Projections:	3Yr: $1039	5Yr: $1376	10Yr: $2325
Avg Brok Commission:	—	Income Distrib: Annually	
Total Cost (relative to category):		Average	

Van Kampen American Value A

Ticker	Load	NAV	Yield	Total Assets	Mstar Category
MSAVX	Closed	$18.83	0.0%	$551.9 mil	Mid-Cap Blend

Prospectus Objective: Small Company

Van Kampen American Value Fund seeks long-term total return.

The fund normally invests at least 65% of assets in equities issued by companies with capitalizations of $1 billion or less. It may invest the balance in smaller companies. Companies targeted for investment generally have above-average yields relative to companies with similar capitalizations, undervalued prices, strong balance sheets, and competitive products. The fund may invest in foreign securities.

Class A shares have front loads and lower 12b-1 fees; B shares have deferred loads and conversion features; C shares have level loads. Past name: Morgan Stanley American Value Fund.

Historical Profile
Return: Average
Risk: Above Avg
Rating: ★★★ Neutral

Investment Style
Equity
Average Stock %

1993	1994	1995	1996	1997	1998	1999	2000	12-01
	97%	98%	95%	95%	93%	96%	96%	

▼ Manager Change
▽ Partial Manager Change

Fund Performance vs. Category Average
■ Quarterly Fund Return +/– Category Average
— Category Baseline

Performance Quartile (within Category)

Portfolio Manager(s)

Gary G. Schlarbaum, CFA. Since 1-97.
James Jolinger. Since 10-01.
Bradley Daniels. Since 10-01.
Matthew Todorow. Since 10-01.

1990	1991	1992	1993	1994	1995	1996	1997	1998	1999	2000	12-01	History
—	—	—	11.97	11.71	13.51	15.11	19.41	20.03	23.53	19.37	18.83	NAV
—	—	—	0.21*	2.01	19.34	22.34	36.39	9.69	25.68	−10.80	−2.79	Total Return %
—	—	—	−0.03*	0.70	−18.20	−0.61	3.04	−18.88	4.64	−1.69	9.09	+/– S&P 500
—	—	—	—	5.60	−11.58	3.15	4.14	−9.42	10.96	−28.29	−2.19	+/– S&P Mid 400
—	—	—	0.46	2.18	2.22	2.12	0.70	0.00	0.00	0.00	0.00	Income Return %
—	—	—	−0.25	−0.17	17.12	20.22	35.69	9.69	25.68	−10.80	−2.79	Capital Return %
—	—	—	—	19	92	39	11	32	35	84	41	Total Rtn % Rank Cat
—	—	—	0.05	0.26	0.26	0.28	0.11	0.00	0.00	0.00	0.00	Income $
—	—	—	0.00	0.24	0.19	1.09	1.04	1.20	1.56	1.58	0.00	Capital Gains $
—	—	—	—	1.50	1.50	1.50	1.50	1.50	1.49	1.47	1.46	Expense Ratio %
—	—	—	—	2.14	2.29	1.90	1.25	−0.09	0.03	−0.33	−0.13	Income Ratio %
—	—	—	—	—	23	41	73	207	283	272	211	Turnover Rate %
—	—	—	—	13.1	23.9	23.1	106.9	221.1	433.6	354.3	223.0	Net Assets $mil

Performance 12-31-01

	1st Qtr	2nd Qtr	3rd Qtr	4th Qtr	Total
1997	1.95	14.67	18.85	−1.84	36.39
1998	13.24	−2.91	−15.75	18.42	9.69
1999	−3.00	21.31	−5.90	13.50	25.68
2000	10.58	−11.41	−2.04	−7.04	−10.80
2001	−11.46	13.53	−18.08	18.06	−2.79

Trailing	Total Return%	+/– S&P 500	+/– S&P Mid 400	% Rank All	% Rank Cat	Growth of $10,000
3 Mo	18.06	7.37	0.07	17	33	11,806
6 Mo	−3.29	2.27	−1.73	53	51	9,671
1 Yr	−2.79	9.09	−2.19	47	41	9,721
3 Yr Avg	2.91	3.94	−7.33	55	65	10,899
5 Yr Avg	10.27	−0.43	−5.84	17	45	16,305
10 Yr Avg	—	—	—	—	—	—
15 Yr Avg	—	—	—	—	—	—

Tax Analysis	Tax-Adj Ret%	%Rank Cat	%Pretax Ret	%Rank Cat
3 Yr Avg	0.97	63	33.4	93
5 Yr Avg	8.19	41	79.7	36
10 Yr Avg	—	—	—	—

Potential Capital Gain Exposure: 1% of assets

Risk Analysis

Time Period	Load-Adj Return %	Risk %Rank[1] All	Risk %Rank[1] Cat	Morningstar Return	Morningstar Risk	Morningstar Risk-Adj Rating
1 Yr	−8.38					
3 Yr	0.90	80	76	−0.83[2]	1.14	★★★
5 Yr	8.97	78	67	0.93[2]	1.07	★★★
Incept	10.64	—	—	—	—	

Average Historical Rating (63 months): 3.0★s

[1]1=low, 100=high [2] T-Bill return substituted for category avg.

Category Rating (3 Yr)

1 2 3 4 5
Worst Best

Return: Average
Risk: Above Avg

Other Measures	Standard Index S&P 500	Best Fit Index Russ 2000
Alpha	4.5	−3.1
Beta	0.81	0.95
R-Squared	34	90

Standard Deviation	24.77
Mean	2.91
Sharpe Ratio	−0.09

Portfolio Analysis 06-30-01

Share change since 05-01 Total Stocks: 266	Sector	PE	YTD Ret%	% Assets
NBTY	Staples	18.6	146.30	1.93
Cephalon	Health	—	19.38	1.45
Caremark Rx	Health	46.6	20.25	1.29
Allegheny Energy	Utilities	10.0	−21.70	1.19
⊕ Barnes & Noble	Retail	—	11.70	1.02
⊕ Compuware	Technology	31.0	88.64	1.01
Alliant Techsystems	Industrials	28.6	73.48	0.99
Republic Svcs Cl A	Services	15.6	16.19	0.96
Cullen/Frost Bankers	Financials	17.2	−24.20	0.96
Potomac Elec Pwr	Utilities	7.5	−3.71	0.93
⊕ Vertex Pharmaceuticals	Health	—	−65.60	0.92
Adelphia Comms	Services	—	−39.60	0.86
ITT Inds	Durables	16.2	32.06	0.86
Nationwide Finl Svcs Cl A	Financials	11.6	−11.60	0.86
⊖ Titan	Technology	—	53.54	0.80
Global Sports	Retail	—	260.60	0.79
PartnerRe	Financials	22.4	−10.50	0.78
United Rentals	Services	18.3	68.92	0.77
Martin Marietta Matls	Industrials	22.0	11.56	0.76
PPL	Utilities	8.2	−20.90	0.74
Hibernia	Financials	16.3	44.26	0.73
Conexant Sys	Technology	—	−6.60	0.72
⊕ Pactiv	Industrials	18.3	43.43	0.71
⊕ Suiza Foods	Staples	—	25.44	0.70
TXU	Utilities	13.7	12.17	0.69

Current Investment Style

Style: Value Blnd Growth; Size: Large Med Small

	Stock Port Avg	Relative S&P 500 Current	Relative S&P 500 Hist	Rel Cat
Price/Earnings Ratio	23.9	0.77	0.78	0.88
Price/Book Ratio	3.6	0.64	0.59	0.84
Price/Cash Flow	15.4	0.85	0.77	0.88
3 Yr Earnings Growth	10.1[1]	0.69	0.82	0.61
1 Yr Earnings Est%	8.8	—	—	3.89
Med Mkt Cap $mil	2,235	0.0	0.0	0.25

[1]figure is based on 50% or less of stocks

Special Securities % assets 06-30-01	
Restricted/Illiquid Secs	Trace
Emerging-Markets Secs	Trace
Options/Futures/Warrants	No

Composition % assets 06-30-01	
Cash	6.2
Stocks*	93.8
Bonds	0.0
Other	0.0
*Foreign (% stocks)	4.2

Market Cap	
Giant	0.0
Large	2.8
Medium	66.3
Small	27.4
Micro	3.5

Sector Weightings	% of Stocks	Rel S&P	5-Year High	5-Year Low
Utilities	7.5	2.3	11	1
Energy	4.3	0.6	8	1
Financials	19.2	1.1	26	12
Industrials	13.1	1.1	32	11
Durables	4.8	3.1	8	3
Staples	5.3	0.7	8	2
Services	9.6	0.9	17	8
Retail	4.7	0.7	7	2
Health	14.9	1.0	15	5
Technology	16.8	0.9	40	4

Analysis by Paul Herbert 11-30-01

A manager change isn't Van Kampen American Value Fund's biggest concern.

This fund's management team is down a man, but that shouldn't sidetrack it too much. On Oct. 1, 2001, comanager Vitaly Korchevsky left the fund's subadvisor to join a hedge fund. Korchevsky had only been on board since January 2000, most recently as the fund's technology analyst. The rest of the team—a four-person unit headed by Gary Schlarbaum, who has led Morgan Stanley Institutional Small Cap Value Fund to a topnotch long-term record—remains. Given Schlarbaum's history with that fund, this offering should be able to weather Korchevsky's departure.

What's less certain, however, is whether the fund will rebound from its recent spate of poor relative performance. It lost 10.8% in 2000, ranking it in the mid-cap blend category's bottom quintile, and has followed that disappointing showing with a 7.4% loss for the year to date through Nov. 30. Schlarbaum cites an overly aggressive posture as the cause for most of the fund's difficulties, and earlier this year he and his comanagers began reducing the fund's stake in higher-P/E stocks and limiting its sector bets versus the Russell 2500 index. These changes have yet to improve the fund's lot much, however, as the fund's results so far in 2001 are just middling.

Still, it would be unwise for investors in this closed fund to give up hope at this point. While the fund's recent slide takes some of the shine off of its fine record, its return for the trailing five-year period still ranks in the category's top half. Schlarbaum's longer record at Morgan Stanley Institutional Small Cap Value also earns the fund significant leeway. Like the Morgan Stanley offering, this fund's high turnover makes it inappropriate for taxable accounts.

Address:	One Parkview Plaza Oakbrook Terrace, IL 60181 800-421-5666
Web Address:	www.vankampen.com
*Inception:	10-18-93
Advisor:	Van Kampen Inv. Adv.
Subadvisor:	Morgan Stanley Dean Witter Inv Mgmt
NTF Plans:	Datalynx , Fidelity Inst.

Minimum Purchase:	Closed	Add: $25	IRA: —
Min Auto Inv Plan:	Closed	Add: $25	
Sales Fees:	5.75%L, 0.25%S		
Management Fee:	.85%, .25%A		
Actual Fees:	Mgt: 0.85%	Dist: 0.25%	
Expense Projections:	3Yr: $1019	5Yr: $1341	10Yr: $2252
Avg Brok Commission:	—	Income Distrib: Quarterly	
Total Cost (relative to category):		Average	

Van Kampen Comstock A

Ticker	Load	NAV	Yield	Total Assets	Mstar Category
ACSTX	5.75%	$15.68	1.4%	$5,712.4 mil	Large Value

Prospectus Objective: Growth and Income

Van Kampen Comstock Fund seeks capital growth and income.

The fund invests primarily in common stocks. It may invest up to 10% of assets in high-quality short-term debt or investment-grade corporate or government bonds. The fund may invest up to 25% of assets in foreign securities.

Class A shares have front loads; B shares have deferred loads and convert to A shares after eight years; C shares have level loads. Past fund names: American General Comstock Fund, American Capital Comstock Fund and Van Kampen American Capital Comstock Fund.

Historical Profile
Return Above Avg
Risk Below Avg
Rating ★★★★ Above Avg

Investment Style
Equity
Average Stock %: 94% 94% 90% 92% 90% 93% 90%

▼ Manager Change
▽ Partial Manager Change

Fund Performance vs. Category Average
■ Quarterly Fund Return +/– Category Average
— Category Baseline

Performance Quartile (within Category)

Portfolio Manager(s)

B. Robert Baker, Jr., CFA. Since 7-94. BA'76 Westminster C.; MBA'78 U. of Northern Texas. Other funds currently managed: Van Kampen Comstock B, Van Kampen Comstock C, Van Kampen Value Opportunities A.

Jason Leder, CFA. Since 4-95. BBA'89 U. of Texas at Austin; MBA'93 Columbia U. Other funds currently managed: Van Kampen Comstock B, Van Kampen Comstock C, Van Kampen Value Opportunities A.

Kevin C. Holt. Since 8-99. Other funds currently managed: Van Kampen Comstock B, Van Kampen Comstock C, Van Kampen Value Opportunities A.

1990	1991	1992	1993	1994	1995	1996	1997	1998	1999	2000	12-01	History
14.29	17.52	17.30	16.39	12.40	14.54	14.78	16.20	16.39	14.80	17.23	15.68	NAV
–3.36	31.95	6.53	9.10	–3.67	36.15	22.34	29.92	20.12	2.38	31.91	–1.79	Total Return %
–0.24	1.46	–1.09	–0.96	–4.98	–1.38	–0.60	–3.44	–8.46	–18.66	41.01	10.09	+/– S&P 500
0.31	13.79	–2.53	–10.67	–1.35	–3.88	0.03	–5.57	–1.12	–8.57	29.60	7.00	+/– Russ Top 200 Val
3.11	2.77	1.87	1.75	2.00	2.23	1.81	1.74	1.80	1.81	2.19	1.34	Income Return %
–6.47	29.18	4.66	7.35	–5.66	33.92	20.54	28.17	18.32	0.57	29.72	–3.12	Capital Return %
31	22	80	82	85	23	28	27	13	68	1	27	Total Rtn % Rank Cat
0.48	0.40	0.33	0.30	0.32	0.27	0.26	0.25	0.28	0.29	0.31	0.23	Income $
0.01	0.84	1.02	2.12	3.05	1.96	2.59	2.57	2.67	1.65	1.65	1.00	Capital Gains $
0.79	0.82	0.87	0.96	1.01	0.96	1.00	0.94	0.91	0.89	0.93	—	Expense Ratio %
2.99	2.32	1.84	1.82	1.93	1.82	1.71	1.71	1.59	1.73	2.10	—	Income Ratio %
30	38	36	50	136	151	176	114	102	72	89	—	Turnover Rate %
812.9	986.7	959.4	980.9	871.8	1,078.2	1,241.3	1,531.9	1,756.1	1,797.4	2,509.3	3,796.7	Net Assets $mil

Performance 12-31-01

	1st Qtr	2nd Qtr	3rd Qtr	4th Qtr	Total
1997	–0.16	12.36	12.80	2.67	29.92
1998	12.76	–1.30	–5.98	14.78	20.12
1999	–2.00	12.27	–10.14	3.56	2.38
2000	0.44	2.12	11.47	15.36	31.91
2001	–1.70	7.51	–13.50	7.44	–1.79

Trailing	Total Return%	+/– S&P 500	+/– Russ Top 200 Val	% Rank All	% Rank Cat	Growth of $10,000
3 Mo	7.44	–3.25	1.92	54	72	10,744
6 Mo	–7.07	–1.51	–1.29	74	88	9,293
1 Yr	–1.79	10.09	7.00	45	27	9,821
3 Yr Avg	9.87	10.90	8.71	11	4	13,264
5 Yr Avg	15.66	4.96	4.45	4	3	20,698
10 Yr Avg	14.46	1.53	0.43	7	11	38,602
15 Yr Avg	14.24	0.50	0.74	9	9	73,621

Tax Analysis	Tax-Adj Ret%	%Rank Cat	%Pretax Ret	%Rank Cat
3 Yr Avg	6.35	8	64.3	55
5 Yr Avg	11.11	8	71.0	63
10 Yr Avg	9.52	42	65.8	92

Potential Capital Gain Exposure: 3% of assets

Risk Analysis

Time Period	Load-Adj Return %	Risk %Rank[1] All	Risk %Rank[1] Cat	Morningstar Return	Morningstar Risk	Morningstar Risk-Adj Rating
1 Yr	–7.43					
3 Yr	7.72	48	21	0.61[2]	0.67	★★★★
5 Yr	14.30	49	13	2.42[2]	0.68	★★★★★
10 Yr	13.79	57	29	1.49	0.73	★★★★

Average Historical Rating (193 months): 3.2★s

[1] 1=low, 100=high [2] T-Bill return substituted for category avg.

Category Rating (3 Yr)

1 2 3 4 5 — Worst ... Best

Return High
Risk Below Avg

Other Measures	Standard Index S&P 500	Best Fit Index S&P 500
Alpha	9.3	9.3
Beta	0.62	0.62
R-Squared	35	35
Standard Deviation		19.53
Mean		9.87
Sharpe Ratio		0.29

Analysis by Kelli Stebel 10-17-01

If looking for a true-blue large-value fund, stop the search at Van Kampen Comstock.

The fund's name might roll off the tongue like some of this category's well-known entrants, such as American Funds Washington Mutual. But given its stellar long-term record, investors should seriously consider this fund. Lead manager Bob Baker took over in mid-1994, and since then, its returns have been hard to beat. Indeed, it's consistently put up topnotch numbers during market rallies and downturns alike, leading to an annualized return that bests its average peer's by nearly 6 percentage points during Baker's tenure. Even in this year's extremely difficult market, the fund is trumping its peers. While its 3% drop for the year to date through Oct. 16 might shock investors accustomed to double-digit gains here, that is among the best showings in the category.

Baker hasn't achieved the fund's excellent long-term record by straying from his deep-value approach either. A contrarian investor, Baker has shown a consistent knack for finding companies others have left for dead, only to see them rebound smartly. Back in 1999, Baker bought Philip Morris when many investors, fearful of ongoing tobacco litigation, wouldn't touch it. But after a difficult 1999, Philip Morris excelled in 2000, gaining more than 105% and helping the fund finish that calendar year in its category's top decile. More recently, Baker hasn't been making big adjustments to the portfolio, preferring to hold steady on current positions.

It's worth nothing that Baker's contrarian style can hit a speed bump on occasion, as its subpar performance in 1999 demonstrates. That said, Baker's keen eye for value and superb track record continues to make this an excellent choice for a portfolio's large-value slot.

Portfolio Analysis 08-31-01

Share change since 07–01 Total Stocks: 118	Sector	PE	YTD Ret%	% Assets
⊕ S&P 500 Index (Fut)	N/A	—	—	4.94
⊕ Halliburton	Energy	8.3	–63.20	4.34
⊕ Sprint	Services	20.5	1.18	3.50
⊕ BP PLC ADR	Energy	14.4	–0.90	3.17
⊕ Motorola	Technology	—	–25.00	2.78
⊕ Intl Paper	Industrials	—	1.43	2.61
⊕ Reliant Energy	Utilities	14.8	–36.00	2.57
⊕ Gap	Retail	39.8	–45.00	2.29
⊕ Conoco Cl A	Energy	9.0	1.56	2.17
⊕ Federated Dept Stores	Retail	16.6	16.86	2.12
Sara Lee	Staples	8.4	–6.95	2.04
⊕ Schlumberger	Energy	55.0	–30.30	2.01
⊕ Dow Chemical	Industrials	NMF	–4.43	1.70
AT&T	Services	7.8	40.59	1.61
⊕ Chevron	Energy	10.3	9.29	1.59
⊕ Procter & Gamble	Staples	38.8	3.12	1.54
⊕ Kroger	Retail	16.3	–22.80	1.51
⊕ DuPont De Nemours E.I.	Industrials	65.4	–9.14	1.48
⊕ Allstate	Financials	17.1	–21.00	1.32
⊕ McDonald's	Services	19.2	–21.50	1.31
⊕ Solectron	Technology	—	–66.70	1.25
⊕ TXU	Utilities	13.7	12.17	1.22
⊕ Freddie Mac	Financials	14.0	–3.87	1.21
⊕ Philip Morris	Staples	12.1	9.12	1.20
⊕ ConAgra	Staples	17.6	–4.73	1.20

Current Investment Style

Style: Value Blnd Growth; Size: Large Med Small

	Stock Port Avg	Relative S&P 500 Current	Relative S&P 500 Hist	Rel Cat
Price/Earnings Ratio	24.5	0.79	0.69	0.97
Price/Book Ratio	3.3	0.58	0.45	0.80
Price/Cash Flow	12.3	0.68	0.54	0.89
3 Yr Earnings Growth	9.6	0.66	0.54	0.65
1 Yr Earnings Est%	–8.5	4.81	—	2.57
Med Mkt Cap $mil	16,496	0.3	0.2	0.52

Special Securities % assets 08-31-01	
Restricted/Illiquid Secs	0
Emerging-Markets Secs	Trace
Options/Futures/Warrants	Yes

Composition % assets 08-31-01	
Cash	11.5
Stocks*	83.9
Bonds	0.0
Other	4.7
*Foreign (% stocks)	7.4

Market Cap	
Giant	22.2
Large	52.2
Medium	23.0
Small	2.7
Micro	0.0

Sector Weightings	% of Stocks	Rel S&P	5-Year High	5-Year Low
Utilities	9.5	3.0	25	4
Energy	16.2	2.3	18	4
Financials	12.0	0.7	24	7
Industrials	13.0	1.1	22	8
Durables	0.6	0.4	6	0
Staples	7.5	0.9	12	4
Services	13.1	1.2	26	3
Retail	8.2	1.2	9	3
Health	3.8	0.3	15	3
Technology	16.3	0.9	16	2

Address:	One Parkview Plaza Oakbrook Terrace, IL 60181 800–421–5666
Web Address:	www.vankampen.com
Inception:	10-12-68
Advisor:	Van Kampen Asset Mgmt.
Subadvisor:	None
NTF Plans:	Datalynx , Fidelity Inst.

Minimum Purchase:	$1000	Add: $25	IRA: $500
Min Auto Inv Plan:	$25	Add: $25	
Sales Fees:	5.75%L, 0.25%S		
Management Fee:	.50% mx./.35% mn.		
Actual Fees:	Mgt: 0.47%	Dist: 0.23%	
Expense Projections:	3Yr: $843	5Yr: $1040	10Yr: $1608
Avg Brok Commission:	—	Income Distrib: Quarterly	
Total Cost (relative to category):	Average		

Van Kampen Emerging Growth A

Ticker	Load	NAV	Yield	Total Assets	Mstar Category
ACEGX	5.75%	$42.32	0.0%	$10,746.8 mil	Large Growth

Prospectus Objective: Growth

Van Kampen Emerging Growth Fund seeks capital appreciation.

The fund normally invests at least 65% of assets in common stocks of small and mid-size companies in the early stages of their life cycle. It may invest up to 25% of assets in foreign securities. The fund may also invest in special situations involving new management, special products, mergers, or liquidations.

Class A shares have front loads; B shares have deferred loads, higher 12b-1 fees, and convert to A shares after six years; C shares have level loads and convert after 10 years. The fund has gone through several name changes.

Historical Profile
Return Above Avg
Risk High
Rating ★★★ Neutral

Investment Style
Equity
Average Stock %: 88% 94% 94% 94% 95% 93% 86%

▼ Manager Change
▽ Partial Manager Change

Fund Performance vs. Category Average
■ Quarterly Fund Return
+/– Category Average
— Category Baseline

Performance Quartile (within Category)

Portfolio Manager(s)

Gary M. Lewis, CFA. Since 4-89.
David Walker. Since 4-96.
Dudley Brickhouse. Since 12-98.
Matthew Hart. Since 2-01.
Janet Luby. Since 7-95.

1990	1991	1992	1993	1994	1995	1996	1997	1998	1999	2000	12-01	History
14.67	21.41	22.27	25.85	23.37	30.49	34.35	37.70	48.18	87.37	62.78	42.32	NAV
1.97	60.43	9.73	23.92	–7.13	44.63	17.91	21.34	34.73	103.72	–11.36	–32.59	Total Return %
5.09	29.95	2.11	13.86	–8.44	7.09	–5.03	–12.01	6.15	82.68	–2.26	–20.71	+/– S&P 500
0.61	21.03	5.84	23.99	–11.98	5.97	–7.61	–12.40	–10.37	74.04	13.16	–12.09	+/– Russ Top 200 Grt
0.52	0.22	0.00	0.00	0.00	0.00	0.00	0.00	0.00	0.00	0.00	0.00	Income Return %
1.45	60.21	9.73	23.92	–7.12	44.63	17.91	21.34	34.73	103.72	–11.36	–32.59	Capital Return %
22	18	23	7	89	7	55	72	41	2	35	86	Total Rtn % Rank Cat
0.08	0.03	0.00	0.00	0.00	0.00	0.00	0.00	0.00	0.00	0.00	0.00	Income $
0.37	1.91	1.16	1.66	0.62	3.19	1.55	3.75	2.31	9.30	14.86	0.00	Capital Gains $
1.15	1.14	1.04	1.10	1.18	1.14	1.10	1.05	1.00	0.97	0.87	0.93	Expense Ratio %
0.65	0.21	–0.08	–0.27	–0.30	0.19	–0.29	–0.30	–0.50	–0.45	–0.35	0.04	Income Ratio %
47	69	61	47	64	101	91	92	103	124	110	148	Turnover Rate %
212.6	345.7	391.8	582.5	677.6	1,153.6	1,623.7	2,109.3	2,989.1	7,368.4	8,605.0	6,067.1	Net Assets $mil

Performance 12-31-01

	1st Qtr	2nd Qtr	3rd Qtr	4th Qtr	Total
1997	–8.33	19.02	18.04	–5.79	21.34
1998	15.92	5.19	–12.83	26.76	34.73
1999	14.69	5.61	4.25	61.33	103.72
2000	25.79	–11.60	6.77	–25.34	–11.36
2001	–23.40	1.71	–21.06	9.61	–32.59

Trailing	Total Return%	+/– S&P 500	+/– Russ Top 200 Grth	% Rank All	% Rank Cat	Growth of $10,000
3 Mo	9.61	–1.08	–3.25	44	89	10,961
6 Mo	–13.47	–7.92	–6.49	92	84	8,653
1 Yr	–32.59	–20.71	–12.09	95	86	6,741
3 Yr Avg	6.77	7.80	14.79	18	5	12,172
5 Yr Avg	14.75	4.05	6.16	5	7	19,899
10 Yr Avg	15.66	2.74	4.58	4	2	42,853
15 Yr Avg	16.40	2.67	3.03	3	5	97,580

Tax Analysis	Tax-Adj Ret%	%Rank Cat	%Pretax Ret	%Rank Cat
3 Yr Avg	4.63	5	68.4	56
5 Yr Avg	12.65	8	85.8	30
10 Yr Avg	13.67	1	87.3	15

Potential Capital Gain Exposure: –35% of assets

Risk Analysis

Time Period	Load-Adj Return %	Risk %Rank¹ All	Risk %Rank¹ Cat	Morningstar Return	Morningstar Risk	Morningstar Risk-Adj Rating
1 Yr	–36.47					
3 Yr	4.69	93	80	–0.05²	1.57	★★★
5 Yr	13.40	91	86	2.15²	1.51	★★★★
10 Yr	14.98	94	91	1.78	1.58	★★★

Average Historical Rating (193 months): 3.2★s

¹1=low, 100=high ² T-Bill return substituted for category avg.

Category Rating (3 Yr)

1 2 3 4 5 — Worst … Best

Return: High
Risk: Above Avg

Other Measures	Standard Index S&P 500	Best Fit Index Wil 4500
Alpha	15.6	8.7
Beta	1.35	1.22
R-Squared	36	80

Standard Deviation	43.90
Mean	6.77
Sharpe Ratio	0.05

Portfolio Analysis 08-31-01

Share change since 07-01 Total Stocks: 159	Sector	PE	YTD Ret%	% Assets
Lowe's	Retail	38.7	109.00	2.32
Concord EFS	Financials	86.3	49.21	1.64
UnitedHealth Grp	Financials	26.6	15.37	1.52
Best Buy	Retail	41.2	151.90	1.32
Forest Labs	Health	52.2	23.35	1.30
Cardinal Health	Health	35.1	–2.51	1.30
⊕ Johnson & Johnson	Health	16.6	14.01	1.29
⊖ Genzyme Corporation General Di	Health	—	33.11	1.26
Tenet Healthcare	Health	30.1	32.14	1.24
HCA – The Healthcare Company	Health	24.1	–12.20	1.22
Cendant	Services	20.4	103.70	1.19
First Data	Technology	38.1	49.08	1.18
⊖ Washington Mutual	Financials	10.1	–5.32	1.17
⊖ Bed Bath & Beyond	Retail	53.0	51.51	1.16
⊖ Baxter Intl	Health	33.9	22.84	1.15
Bank of America	Financials	16.7	42.73	1.10
PeopleSoft	Technology	73.1	8.10	1.08
Electronic Data Sys	Technology	25.7	19.83	1.05
Qualcomm	Technology	—	–38.50	1.05
Electronic Arts	Technology	90.8	40.65	1.03
⊖ Baker Hughes	Energy	45.0	–11.10	1.03
⊖ EBAY	Services	NMF	102.70	1.00
King Pharmaceuticals	Health	45.8	8.68	0.97
Microchip Tech	Technology	53.8	76.59	0.96
Tyco Intl	Industrials	27.1	6.23	0.93

Current Investment Style

Style: Value Blnd Growth; Size: Large Med Small

	Stock Port Avg	Relative S&P 500 Current	Relative S&P 500 Hist	Rel Cat
Price/Earnings Ratio	35.9	1.16	1.40	1.01
Price/Book Ratio	6.1	1.07	1.55	0.95
Price/Cash Flow	23.0	1.28	1.39	1.02
3 Yr Earnings Growth	24.9	1.70	1.65	1.16
1 Yr Earnings Est%	17.2	—	—	5.74
Med Mkt Cap $mil	13,704	0.2	0.2	0.29

Special Securities % assets 08-31-01

Restricted/Illiquid Secs	0
Emerging-Markets Secs	1
Options/Futures/Warrants	No

Composition % assets 08-31-01

Cash	11.5
Stocks*	88.5
Bonds	0.0
Other	0.0
*Foreign (% stocks)	2.3

Market Cap

Giant	12.2
Large	52.9
Medium	34.9
Small	0.0
Micro	0.0

Sector Weightings	% of Stocks	Rel S&P	5-Year High	5-Year Low
Utilities	1.3	0.4	7	0
Energy	4.8	0.7	16	0
Financials	14.0	0.8	17	1
Industrials	5.9	0.5	16	2
Durables	1.9	1.2	7	0
Staples	3.5	0.4	6	0
Services	9.5	0.9	26	3
Retail	11.8	1.8	19	1
Health	25.0	1.7	25	2
Technology	22.2	1.2	78	18

Analysis by Kelli Stebel 11-13-01

Van Kampen Emerging Growth is trying to manage its enormous girth, but we're not entirely convinced it will succeed.

Longtime lead manager Gary Lewis admits that the fund's size—$11 billion—is a problem. That heft has held it back over the past 18 months, too. From March 2000, when the Nasdaq began to falter, until October 2001, the fund has lost 10 percentage points more than the average large-growth offering. The fund has, uncharacteristically, underperformed during recent growth rallies, too. Most growth funds jumpstarted their engines, albeit briefly in October 2001, but this fund barely posted a positive gain. Lewis says that given the fund's size, he and the team just couldn't move quickly enough into more-aggressive stocks.

Given those fairly dismal returns, Lewis instituted a new portfolio-building process. For starters, he has broadened the number of holdings from about 100 to 155. The majority of the top-10 holdings are liquid, household names, which Lewis can easily trade. The rest of the portfolio positions are about 1% of assets or less. With that approach, Lewis says he can easily dabble in mid-cap names again, which helped build this fund's great record. Most recently, for example, Lewis has taken advantage of the market volatility to add to some mid-cap tech names. (Van Kampen does not comment on specific stocks outside the top-10 holdings.)

There's no doubt that Lewis is an experienced manager, and his record at this offering is one of the category's best. That said, with positions hovering around 1% of assets, the fund's performance may come down to sector bets. Smaller positions will be too tiny to affect performance significantly, so Lewis might resort to sector bets to boost returns. Thus, shareholders will want to take a wait-and-see approach until Lewis secures a few victories with the fund's new structure.

Address:	One Parkview Plaza Oakbrook Terrace, IL 60181 800–421–5666
Web Address:	www.vankampen.com
Inception:	10-12-70
Advisor:	Van Kampen Asset Mgmt.
Subadvisor:	None
NTF Plans:	Datalynx , Fidelity Inst.

Minimum Purchase:	$1000	Add: $25	IRA: $500
Min Auto Inv Plan:	$25	Add: $25	
Sales Fees:	5.75%L, 0.25%S		
Management Fee:	.58% mx./.43% mn.		
Actual Fees:	Mgt: 0.44%	Dist: 0.25%	
Expense Projections:	3Yr: $866	5Yr: $1080	10Yr: $1696
Avg Brok Commission:	—	Income Distrib: Annually	
Total Cost (relative to category):		Average	

Van Kampen Global Value Equity A

Ticker	Load	NAV	Yield	Total Assets	Mstar Category
MGEAX	5.75%	$9.84	1.0%	$421.6 mil	World Stock

Prospectus Objective: World Stock

Van Kampen Global Equity Fund seeks long-term capital appreciation.

The fund normally invests at least 65% of assets in equities of issuers throughout the world, including the United States. It usually invests at least 20% of assets in U.S. securities. The remainder will be invested in issuers located throughout the world, including emerging-market countries. The sub-advisor's approach to selecting investments is oriented to individual stock selection, and is value driven.

Class A shares have front loads; B shares have deferred loads, higher 12b-1 fees, and conversion features; C shares have level loads. Past name, Morgan Stanley Global Equity Fund.

Historical Profile
Return: Average
Risk: Low
Rating: ★★★ Neutral

Investment Style
Equity
Average Stock %: 96% 96% 96% 97%

▼ Manager Change
▽ Partial Manager Change

Fund Performance vs. Category Average
■ Quarterly Fund Return +/– Category Average
— Category Baseline

Performance Quartile (within Category)

Portfolio Manager(s)

Frances Campion. Since 10-97. U. College, Dublin. Other funds currently managed: Morgan Stanley Inst Global Value Eq A, Morgan Stanley Inst Global Value Eq B, Van Kampen Global Value Equity B.

Paul Boyne. Since 10-97. Other funds currently managed: Van Kampen Global Value Equity B, Van Kampen Global Value Equity C.

1990	1991	1992	1993	1994	1995	1996	1997	1998	1999	2000	12-01	History
—	—	—	—	—	—	—	9.91	11.14	10.81	10.93	9.84	NAV
—	—	—	—	—	—	—	–0.74*	13.49	3.32	10.60	–9.04	Total Return %
—	—	—	—	—	—	—	–4.22*	–15.08	–17.72	19.70	2.83	+/– S&P 500
—	—	—	—	—	—	—	—	–10.85	–21.62	23.77	—	+/– MSCI World
—	—	—	—	—	—	—	0.16	0.91	0.00	0.00	0.90	Income Return %
—	—	—	—	—	—	—	–0.90	12.59	3.32	10.60	–9.94	Capital Return %
—	—	—	—	—	—	—	—	49	99	7	17	Total Rtn % Rank Cat
—	—	—	—	—	—	—	0.02	0.09	0.00	0.00	0.10	Income $
—	—	—	—	—	—	—	0.00	0.01	0.68	0.98	0.00	Capital Gains $
—	—	—	—	—	—	—	—	1.70	1.65	1.66	1.64	Expense Ratio %
—	—	—	—	—	—	—	—	0.88	0.44	0.53	0.60	Income Ratio %
—	—	—	—	—	—	—	—	—	40	47	33	Turnover Rate %
—	—	—	—	—	—	—	55.2	76.7	66.9	71.6	59.1	Net Assets $mil

Performance 12-31-01

	1st Qtr	2nd Qtr	3rd Qtr	4th Qtr	Total
1997	—	—	—	—	–0.74*
1998	15.24	–2.63	–12.41	15.47	13.49
1999	–4.04	7.20	–2.79	3.32	3.32
2000	–0.83	3.64	–2.16	9.98	10.60
2001	–7.32	4.24	–11.17	5.99	–9.04

Trailing	Total Return%	+/– S&P 500	+/– MSCI World	% Rank All	% Rank Cat	Growth of $10,000
3 Mo	5.99	–4.70	—	61	90	10,599
6 Mo	–5.86	–0.30	—	67	37	9,414
1 Yr	–9.04	2.83	—	59	17	9,096
3 Yr Avg	1.29	2.32	—	66	41	10,393
5 Yr Avg	—	—	—	—	—	—
10 Yr Avg	—	—	—	—	—	—
15 Yr Avg	—	—	—	—	—	—

Tax Analysis	Tax-Adj Ret%	%Rank Cat	%Pretax Ret	%Rank Cat
3 Yr Avg	0.07	40	5.3	96
5 Yr Avg	—	—	—	—
10 Yr Avg	—	—	—	—

Potential Capital Gain Exposure: –1% of assets

Risk Analysis

Time Period	Load-Adj Return %	Risk %Rank[1] All	Risk %Rank[1] Cat	Morningstar Return	Morningstar Risk	Morningstar Risk-Adj Rating
1 Yr	–14.27					
3 Yr	–0.69	43	9	–1.13[2]	0.56	★★★
5 Yr	—	—	—	—	—	
Incept	2.38	—	—	—	—	

Average Historical Rating (15 months): 3.4★s

[1]1=low, 100=high [2] T-Bill return substituted for category avg.

Category Rating (3 Yr)

1 2 **3** 4 5
Worst — Best

Return: Average
Risk: Low

Other Measures	Standard Index S&P 500	Best Fit Index MSCIACWdFree
Alpha	–0.6	1.5
Beta	0.51	0.55
R-Squared	55	56

Standard Deviation	11.84
Mean	1.29
Sharpe Ratio	–0.36

Portfolio Analysis 06-30-01

Share change since 05-01 Total Stocks: 109	Sector	Country	% Assets
Aventis Cl A	Health	France	2.71
⊖ Philip Morris	Staples	U.S.	2.50
⊖ Verizon Comms	Services	U.S.	1.90
⊖ J.P. Morgan Chase & Co.	Financials	U.S.	1.89
⊕ Nestle (Reg)	Staples	Switzerland	1.89
Total Fina Cl B	Energy	France	1.88
Cadbury Schweppes	Staples	United Kingdom	1.69
⊖ SBC Comms	Services	U.S.	1.64
NCR	Technology	U.S.	1.59
General Dynamics	Industrials	U.S.	1.54
⊕ Diageo	Staples	United Kingdom	1.51
⊖ Royal Dutch Petro NY ADR	Energy	Netherlands	1.46
⊕ Bristol-Myers Squibb	Health	U.S.	1.45
⊕ Pharmacia	Health	U.S.	1.42
⊖ Allied Domecq	Staples	United Kingdom	1.42
⊖ BAE Sys	Technology	United Kingdom	1.38
⊖ First Data	Technology	U.S.	1.38
⊖ ING Groep	Financials	Netherlands	1.34
Boise Cascade	Industrials	U.S.	1.25
Nippon Telegraph & Tele	Services	Japan	1.24

Current Investment Style

Style: Value Blnd Growth; Size: Large Med Small

	Stock Port Avg	Rel MSCI EAFE Current	Rel MSCI EAFE Hist	Rel Cat
Price/Earnings Ratio	24.4	0.94	0.78	0.88
Price/Cash Flow	12.2	0.95	0.85	0.74
Price/Book Ratio	3.6	1.03	0.84	0.77
3 Yr Earnings Growth	14.3	0.77	0.86	0.77
Med Mkt Cap $mil	19,231	0.7	0.5	0.80

Country Exposure 06-30-01	% assets
U.S.	44
United Kingdom	14
Japan	11
France	7
Netherlands	5

Hedging History: —

Regional Exposure 06-30-01	% assets
Europe	36
Pacific Rim	3
Latin America	0
Japan	11
U.S.	44
Other	2

Special Securities % assets 06-30-01	
Restricted/Illiquid Secs	Trace
Emerging-Markets Secs	1
Options/Futures/Warrants	No

Composition % assets 06-30-01			
Cash	3.1	Bonds	0.0
Stocks	96.9	Other	0.0

Sector Weightings	% of Stocks	Rel Cat	5-Year High	5-Year Low
Utilities	3.6	1.5	—	—
Energy	5.6	1.0	—	—
Financials	15.0	0.8	—	—
Industrials	16.0	1.4	—	—
Durables	3.7	0.9	—	—
Staples	14.9	1.9	—	—
Services	17.8	1.1	—	—
Retail	6.3	1.2	—	—
Health	9.7	0.7	—	—
Technology	7.5	0.5	—	—

Analysis by Gabriel Presler 11-26-01

A name change at Van Kampen Global Value Equity Fund doesn't mean much.

This fund added value to its moniker in the fall of 2001, but manager Frances Campion hasn't changed her style. In fact, since the fund's inception in 1997, Campion has scooped up large, undervalued stocks, favoring consumer-staples companies, industrial stocks and other relatively staid issues. Thus, the portfolio's valuations have always been considerably lower than group norms. That's not the only way this fund differs from its world-stock rivals, though. Campion's willing to make significant sector bets; for example, in mid-2000, she built the fund's exposure to consumer-related firms to about four times the category average. The portfolio looks much the same year in and year out, as Campion trades about a third as much as her rivals.

Her consistency has certainly helped the fund lately, partly because many of those consumer-staples firms have performed well. Large positions in tobacco-related firms, such as Philip Morris, have gained ground. And some good picks in the beaten-down telecom sector and some other areas have also helped. Top-five holding Verizon Communications has been flat this year, something of an accomplishment in a volatile market. Thus, while the fund has lost almost 10% of its value for the year to date through Nov. 23, 2001, it's ahead of more than 85% of its peers.

Campion weathers some dry spells to hang on to her favorite stocks, so this won't always be a smooth ride. In 1999's growth rally, for example, the fund's paltry 3% gain doomed it to the category's basement. Still, over the long run, this fund has been hard to beat; it's one of the least volatile funds in the group and has strong long-term returns. It's a good choice for cautious investors seeking exposure to developed markets.

Address:	One Parkview Plaza Oakbrook Terrace, IL 60181 800-421-5666
Web Address:	www.vankampen.com
*Inception:	10-24-97
Advisor:	Van Kampen Inv. Adv.
Subadvisor:	Morgan Stanley Dean Witter Asset Mgmt
NTF Plans:	Fidelity Inst.

Minimum Purchase:	$1000	Add: $25	IRA: $500
Min Auto Inv Plan:	$25	Add: $25	
Sales Fees:	5.75%L, 0.25%S		
Management Fee:	1.0%, .25%A		
Actual Fees:	Mgt: 1.00%	Dist: 0.25%	
Expense Projections:	3Yr: $1065	5Yr: $1420	10Yr: $2417
Avg Brok Commission:	—	Income Distrib: Annually	
Total Cost (relative to category):		Average	

Van Kampen Growth & Income A

Ticker	Load	NAV	Yield	Total Assets	Mstar Category
ACGIX	5.75%	$17.01	1.2%	$2,642.8 mil	Large Value

Prospectus Objective: Growth and Income

Van Kampen Growth and Income Fund seeks income and long-term growth of capital.

The fund invests primarily in income-producing equities; it may also purchase investment-grade debt. It limits investments in foreign securities to 25% of assets.

Class A shares have front loads; B shares have deferred loads and convert to A shares after six years; C shares have level loads and convert after 10 years. Past names: Fund of America, American Capital Growth and Income Fund, and Van Kampen American Capital Growth and Income Fund. Van Kampen Growth and Income Fund merged into this fund on Sept. 21, 1995.

Historical Profile
Return Above Avg
Risk Below Avg
Rating ★★★★ Above Avg

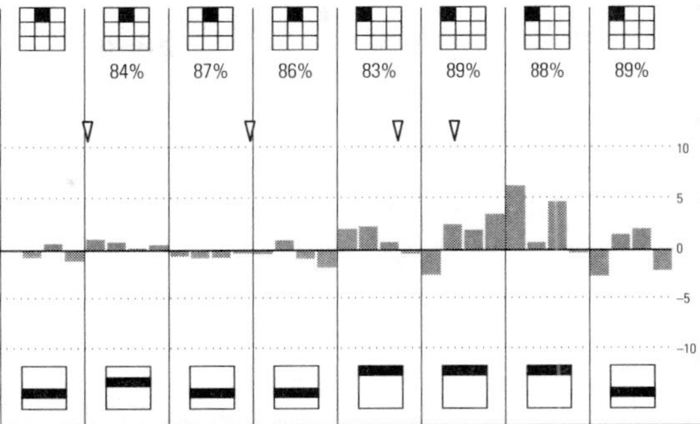

Investment Style
Equity
Average Stock %: 84% 87% 86% 83% 89% 88% 89%

▼ Manager Change
▽ Partial Manager Change

Fund Performance vs. Category Average
■ Quarterly Fund Return
+/– Category Average
— Category Baseline

Performance Quartile (within Category)

Portfolio Manager(s)

James A. Gilligan, CFA. Since 7-90. BS'80 Miami U.; MBA'81 U. of Pittsburgh. Other funds currently managed: Van Kampen Equity-Income A, Van Kampen Equity-Income B, Van Kampen Growth & Income B.

Scott Carroll. Since 12-96. BS Northern Illinois U.; MBA U. of Chicago. Other funds currently managed: Van Kampen Equity-Income A, Van Kampen Equity-Income B, Van Kampen Growth & Income B.

James O. Roeder. Since 5-99. Other funds currently managed: Van Kampen Equity-Income A, Van Kampen Equity-Income B, Van Kampen Growth & Income B.

1990	1991	1992	1993	1994	1995	1996	1997	1998	1999	2000	12-01	History
10.09	12.72	12.81	13.00	11.37	14.21	15.39	16.62	18.33	17.74	18.73	17.01	NAV
–5.24	30.24	9.52	16.33	–1.66	35.67	18.05	24.49	18.44	12.70	19.02	–6.06	Total Return %
–2.12	–0.24	1.90	6.27	–2.97	–1.86	–4.90	–8.86	–10.14	–8.34	28.12	5.82	+/– S&P 500
–1.57	12.09	0.45	–3.43	0.66	–4.36	–4.27	–11.00	–2.80	1.75	16.71	2.73	+/– Russ Top 200 Val
3.11	3.81	2.70	2.14	2.31	2.40	1.70	1.50	1.20	1.04	1.13	1.09	Income Return %
–8.35	26.43	6.82	14.19	–3.96	33.27	16.35	22.98	17.24	11.66	17.89	–7.15	Capital Return %
44	31	46	30	66	26	73	72	17	24	7	52	Total Rtn % Rank Cat
0.34	0.38	0.34	0.27	0.29	0.27	0.24	0.23	0.20	0.19	0.20	0.20	Income $
0.13	0.00	0.75	1.57	1.13	0.90	1.09	2.25	1.11	2.63	2.12	0.37	Capital Gains $
1.13	1.14	1.15	1.16	1.16	1.15	1.04	0.94	0.92	0.88	0.88	—	Expense Ratio %
3.08	3.40	2.46	2.15	2.25	2.24	1.68	1.33	1.13	1.11	1.23	—	Income Ratio %
111	89	78	134	102	108	110	94	76	93	97	—	Turnover Rate %
146.2	170.7	179.8	212.8	205.4	399.2	579.8	778.0	928.9	1,018.4	1,364.7	1,743.6	Net Assets $mil

Performance 12-31-01

	1st Qtr	2nd Qtr	3rd Qtr	4th Qtr	Total
1997	1.29	14.73	7.92	–0.74	24.49
1998	13.41	1.75	–11.45	15.91	18.44
1999	–1.65	12.33	–7.27	10.01	12.70
2000	6.53	–1.29	10.12	2.78	19.02
2001	–8.33	6.24	–10.06	7.25	–6.06

Trailing	Total Return%	+/– S&P 500	+/– Russ Top 200 Val	% Rank All	% Rank Cat	Growth of $10,000
3 Mo	7.25	–3.43	1.73	55	73	10,725
6 Mo	–3.53	2.02	2.24	54	41	9,647
1 Yr	–6.06	5.82	2.73	53	52	9,394
3 Yr Avg	8.01	9.04	6.85	15	7	12,601
5 Yr Avg	13.19	2.49	1.98	7	9	18,578
10 Yr Avg	14.06	1.14	0.03	8	16	37,278
15 Yr Avg	13.59	–0.14	0.09	13	16	67,647

Tax Analysis	Tax-Adj Ret%	%Rank Cat	%Pretax Ret	%Rank Cat
3 Yr Avg	5.44	11	67.9	48
5 Yr Avg	10.30	14	78.1	41
10 Yr Avg	10.83	25	77.0	52

Potential Capital Gain Exposure: 4% of assets

Risk Analysis

Time Period	Load-Adj Return %	Risk %Rank[1] All	Risk %Rank[1] Cat	Morningstar Return	Morningstar Risk	Morningstar Risk-Adj Rating
1 Yr	–11.46					
3 Yr	5.90	41	4	0.20[2]	0.56	★★★★
5 Yr	11.86	47	5	1.70[2]	0.63	★★★★
10 Yr	13.39	53	13	1.40	0.67	★★★★

Average Historical Rating (193 months): 3.0★s

[1]1=low, 100=high [2] T-Bill return substituted for category avg.

Category Rating (3 Yr)

1 2 3 4 5 — Worst … Best

Return High
Risk Low

Other Measures	Standard Index S&P 500	Best Fit Index SPMid400
Alpha	7.0	–0.2
Beta	0.66	0.58
R-Squared	67	69

Standard Deviation	14.70
Mean	8.01
Sharpe Ratio	0.24

Analysis by Kelli Stebel 07-26-01

This fund isn't breaking any records lately, but it remains a fine core holding.

After turning in a chart-topping 19% gain during 2000's rocky market, Van Kampen Growth & Income is having a rough go of it so far this year. For the year to date through July 25, the fund has dropped about 4%. While that showing is in line with its average large-value peer's, it's likely disappointing to shareholders who have come to expect double-digit returns here.

The fund's mediocre performance owes to a few individual blowups. Shares of Palm, for example, have been absolutely pummeled, as sales have declined sharply. Lead manager Jim Gilligan said that he was not giving up on Palm, though, contending the firm would rebound given the dominance of its operating system. In addition, the fund's complement of energy holdings, which were a boon last year, have stung performance more recently. Gilligan said that he had been trimming energy all year, thinking that investors are overly optimistic about this sector's long-term growth. He also said he added a bit to long-distance plays like AT&T and Sprint, which he thinks are trading at extremely discounted valuations. Still, Gilligan said not a lot of great bargains are available right now, so he has been making minimal changes.

Since Gilligan has made a habit of posting consistent and above-average returns here, investors shouldn't worry about the fund's minislump. Since he took the reins in July 1990, the fund's annualized total return bests its peers by two percentage points. And the fund has been less volatile than its average rival. While the fund's showing this year is in the red, it's nowhere near the category's nadir.

In short, this is the kind of fund investors can build a portfolio around.

Portfolio Analysis 08-31-01

Share change since 07-01 Total Stocks: 88

	Sector	PE	YTD Ret%	% Assets
⊕ Bank of America	Financials	16.7	42.73	3.61
⊕ First Union	Financials	21.5	16.12	2.83
S&P 500 Index (Fut)	N/A	—	—	2.58
⊕ Sprint	Services	20.5	1.18	2.51
⊕ DuPont De Nemours E.I.	Industrials	65.4	–9.14	2.45
US Bancorp	Financials	13.5	–6.14	2.29
⊖ ExxonMobil	Energy	15.3	–7.59	2.16
⊕ Minnesota Mng & Mfg	Industrials	34.5	0.16	1.94
⊖ Johnson & Johnson	Health	16.6	14.01	1.93
FleetBoston Finl	Financials	16.2	0.55	1.72
⊕ Electronic Data Sys	Technology	25.7	19.83	1.64
⊕ Micron Tech	Technology	—	–12.60	1.57
⊖ McKesson HBOC	Health	—	4.92	1.56
⊕ Ford Motor	Durables	43.7	–30.00	1.53
⊕ PepsiCo	Staples	31.4	–0.54	1.50
⊕ Procter & Gamble	Staples	38.8	3.12	1.50
⊕ Rohm and Haas	Industrials	17.9	–2.45	1.48
⊖ Goodyear Tire & Rubber	Durables	—	7.97	1.48
⊕ Raytheon	Industrials	—	7.27	1.47
⊖ Washington Mutual	Financials	10.1	–5.32	1.45
⊕ Motorola	Technology	—	–25.00	1.45
⊕ Bank One	Financials	29.1	9.13	1.39
⊕ Pharmacia	Health	36.5	–29.30	1.39
⊕ Allstate	Financials	17.1	–21.00	1.34
⊕ Johnson Controls	Industrials	15.8	58.03	1.32

Current Investment Style

Style: Value Blnd Growth; Size: Large Med Small

	Stock Port Avg	Relative S&P 500 Current	Relative S&P 500 Hist	Rel Cat
Price/Earnings Ratio	25.0	0.81	0.84	0.99
Price/Book Ratio	3.2	0.56	0.65	0.78
Price/Cash Flow	14.6	0.81	0.76	1.06
3 Yr Earnings Growth	5.5	0.37	0.70	0.37
1 Yr Earnings Est%	–10.1	5.71	—	3.05
Med Mkt Cap $mil	23,205	0.4	0.4	0.73

[1]figure is based on 50% or less of stocks

Special Securities % assets 08-31-01	
Restricted/Illiquid Secs	Trace
Emerging-Markets Secs	0
Options/Futures/Warrants	Yes

Composition % assets 08-31-01	
Cash	8.5
Stocks*	88.3
Bonds	0.4
Other	2.9
*Foreign (% stocks)	1.8

Market Cap	
Giant	26.4
Large	44.7
Medium	28.8
Small	0.0
Micro	0.0

Sector Weightings	% of Stocks	Rel S&P	5-Year High	5-Year Low
Utilities	3.6	1.1	15	2
Energy	3.9	0.6	15	4
Financials	29.2	1.6	33	10
Industrials	18.7	1.6	22	5
Durables	6.9	4.4	9	2
Staples	3.8	0.5	14	2
Services	12.1	1.1	20	5
Retail	1.9	0.3	10	0
Health	9.4	0.6	19	5
Technology	10.6	0.6	23	4

Address:	One Parkview Plaza, Oakbrook Terrace, IL 60181, 800–421–5666
Web Address:	www.vankampen.com
Inception:	08-01-46
Advisor:	Van Kampen Asset Mgmt.
Subadvisor:	None
NTF Plans:	Datalynx , Fidelity Inst.

Minimum Purchase:	$1000	Add: $25	IRA: $500
Min Auto Inv Plan:	$25	Add: $25	
Sales Fees:	5.75%L, 0.25%S		
Management Fee:	.50% mx./.35% mn.		
Actual Fees:	Mgt: 0.38%	Dist: 0.25%	
Expense Projections:	3Yr: $840	5Yr: $1035	10Yr: $1597
Avg Brok Commission:	—	Income Distrib: Quarterly	
Total Cost (relative to category):	Average		

Van Kampen High–Yield Municipal A

Ticker	Load	NAV	Yield	SEC Yield	Total Assets	Mstar Category
ACTHX	4.75%	$10.49	6.3%	0.06%	$1,889.3 mil	Muni Natl Long–Term

Prospectus Objective: Muni Bond—National

Van Kampen High-Yield Municipal Fund seeks high income exempt from federal income tax.

The fund normally invests at least 75% of assets in bonds rated BBB or lower; it may not purchase bonds rated C or lower (or unrated bonds of comparable quality). It may also normally invest up to 20% of assets in high-quality municipal bonds.

Class A shares have front loads; B shares have deferred loads and convert to A shares after six years; C shares have level loads and convert after 10 years. Fund was named American Capital Tax-Exempt Trust High-Yield Municipal Portfolio. From Aug. 28, 1998, the fund was named Van Kampen American Capital High-Yield Municipal Fund.

Historical Profile

Return: Above Avg
Risk: Low
Rating: ★★★★★ Highest

Investment Style: Fixed-Income — Income Rtn %Rank Cat: 2, 3, 1, 1, 1, 1, 3, 2

Growth of Principal vs. Interest Rate Shifts
- Principal Value $000 (NAV with capital gains reinvested)
- Interest Rate % on 10 Yr Treasury
- ▼ Manager Change
- ∇ Partial Manager Change
- ► Mgr Unknown After
- ◄ Mgr Unknown Before

Performance Quartile (within Category)

Portfolio Manager(s)

Wayne Godlin. Since 3-90. BA Union C.; MA Columbia U. Other funds currently managed: Van Kampen High-Yield Municipal B, Van Kampen High-Yield Municipal C.

1990	1991	1992	1993	1994	1995	1996	1997	1998	1999	2000	12–01	History
10.66	10.91	11.02	11.31	10.56	11.24	11.13	11.59	11.64	10.79	10.63	10.49	NAV
5.99	10.65	9.05	10.16	0.19	13.91	5.82	11.03	6.67	–1.50	4.92	4.99	Total Return %
–2.97	–5.36	1.65	0.41	3.11	–4.56	2.20	1.35	–2.00	–0.67	–6.71	–3.43	+/– LB Aggregate
–1.31	–1.50	0.23	–2.12	5.33	–3.55	1.38	1.83	0.19	0.57	–6.78	–0.09	+/– LB Muni
8.14	8.17	7.98	7.48	6.98	7.29	6.75	6.71	6.25	6.08	6.41	6.40	Income Return %
–2.15	2.48	1.07	2.67	–6.78	6.62	–0.93	4.32	0.43	–7.58	–1.49	–1.40	Capital Return %
57	88	41	90	1	92	3	5	3	1	92	17	Total Rtn % Rank Cat
0.86	0.84	0.84	0.80	0.76	0.75	0.74	0.73	0.70	0.69	0.67	0.66	Income $
0.00	0.00	0.00	0.00	0.00	0.00	0.00	0.00	0.00	0.00	0.00	0.00	Capital Gains $
0.97	1.06	1.07	1.03	1.02	0.98	1.01	0.95	0.91	0.90	0.91	—	Expense Ratio %
8.34	7.20	7.45	7.13	6.98	6.81	6.64	6.50	6.01	6.03	6.28	—	Income Ratio %
29	20	24	27	33	26	23	29	26	22	19	—	Turnover Rate %
218.1	227.9	310.9	414.8	418.1	515.9	611.3	795.4	912.2	926.1	1,003.3	1,263.3	Net Assets $mil

Performance 12-31-01

	1st Qtr	2nd Qtr	3rd Qtr	4th Qtr	Total
1997	1.12	2.83	3.32	3.36	11.03
1998	1.82	1.78	2.28	0.63	6.67
1999	1.10	–0.20	–0.72	–1.67	–1.50
2000	1.11	0.36	2.06	1.31	4.92
2001	1.78	1.40	1.93	–0.20	4.99

Trailing	Total Return%	+/– LB Agg	+/– LB Muni	% Rank All	% Rank Cat	Growth of $10,000
3 Mo	–0.20	–0.23	0.47	80	4	9,980
6 Mo	1.73	–2.92	–0.39	26	34	10,173
1 Yr	4.99	–3.43	–0.09	23	17	10,499
3 Yr Avg	2.76	–3.52	–1.99	57	62	10,850
5 Yr Avg	5.15	–2.28	–0.83	62	26	12,851
10 Yr Avg	6.43	–0.80	–0.20	59	15	18,643
15 Yr Avg	6.44	–1.68	–0.75	79	44	25,508

Tax Analysis	Tax-Adj Ret%	%Rank Cat	%Pretax Ret	%Rank Cat
3 Yr Avg	2.76	60	100.0	1
5 Yr Avg	5.15	21	100.0	1
10 Yr Avg	6.43	7	100.0	1

Potential Capital Gain Exposure: –5% of assets

Risk Analysis

Time Period	Load-Adj Return %	Risk %Rank[1] All	Risk %Rank[1] Cat	Morningstar Return	Morningstar Risk	Morningstar Risk-Adj Rating
1 Yr	0.01					
3 Yr	1.10	5	1	0.07[2]	0.61	★★★★
5 Yr	4.13	3	1	0.79[2]	0.48	★★★★★
10 Yr	5.91	3	1	1.25	0.45	★★★★★

Average Historical Rating (157 months): 4.7★s

[1]1=low, 100=high [2] T-Bill return substituted for category avg.

Category Rating (3 Yr)

1 2 3 4 5 — Worst … Best

Return: Above Avg
Risk: Low

Other Measures	Standard Index LB Agg	Best Fit Index LB Muni
Alpha	–2.6	–2.0
Beta	0.43	0.60
R–Squared	31	74

Standard Deviation	2.58
Mean	2.76
Sharpe Ratio	–0.98

Portfolio Analysis 08-31-01

Total Fixed-Income: 849	Date of Maturity	Amount $000	Value $000	% Net Assets
NY NYC Muni Wtr Fin Swr Sys 5.2%	06-15-33	15,670	15,759	0.85
IN Indianapolis Arpt Spcl Fac 6.5%	11-15-31	10,770	10,698	0.58
MA Mtg 7.1%	10-01-28	11,035	10,537	0.57
TX Houston Arpt 6.75%	07-01-29	10,000	10,006	0.54
IL State Real Estate Lease 8.8%	06-15-18	8,598	9,864	0.53
PA Allegheny Hosp 8.75%	02-01-31	8,000	8,244	0.44
IL Chicago O'Hare Intl Arpt Fac 1%	11-01-35	7,500	7,580	0.41
MA Indl Fin Newton Grp Ppty 8%	09-01-27	7,000	7,354	0.40
PA Beaver Indl Dev Poll Cntrl 7.625%	05-01-20	6,750	7,335	0.40
NY Med Care Fac Fin Mental Hlth 6.2%	04-01-31	7,130	7,273	0.39
CO Denver Spcl Fac Arpt United 6.875%	10-01-32	7,000	7,027	0.38
TX Dallas/Ft Worth Intl Arpt Fac 6.375%	05-01-35	6,540	6,672	0.36
NH Higher Educ/Hlth Fac Riverwoods 8%	07-01-31	6,315	6,329	0.34
CA Ramona COP USD 5.4%	12-01-26	6,200	6,206	0.33
IL Chicago Arpt 6.3%	05-01-16	6,000	6,170	0.33

Current Investment Style

Not Available

Avg Duration[1]	8.2 Yrs
Avg Nominal Maturity	20.5 Yrs
Avg Credit Quality	—
Avg Wtd Coupon	6.84%
Avg Wtd Price	98.83% of par
Pricing Service	Interactive Data

[1]figure provided by fund

Analysis by Eric Jacobson 09-03-01

Van Kampen High-Yield Municipal Fund delivers a potent, tasty elixir that should be consumed with care.

This fund's main goal is to deliver a healthy stream of tax-free income by taking on credit risk. On that score there have been few rivals. The portfolio's payouts have been among the highest among all muni funds, including the small subset of rivals that also invest mostly in credit-sensitive issues. And thanks to a combination of good management and a well-diversified portfolio, the fund has also managed to avoid big problems. As such, its five-year returns, in particular, place in the upper reaches of both the muni-national long-term category and the high-yield muni subset.

The key advantage here is a large credit staff of 10 analysts and managers, most of whom have several years of experience in municipal finance. The fund needs them, too. In part that's because lead manager Wayne Godlin prefers to keep roughly 60% to 80% of the fund in lower-quality bonds that carry no third-party ratings. There's also a lot of work to do because the fund has $1.8 billion in assets and roughly 800 different issues to keep track of. Like many rivals, the fund is stacked heavily with a variety of heath-care and hospital issues, as well as continuing-care retirement centers (CCRCs). Many of the former, in particular, performed badly in 1999 and 2000 amid problems with government reiumbursement allocations but have bounced back this year. Most recently, Godlin and his team have been focusing on airport infrastructure bonds that he thinks have been tainted by their airline ties, despite their lease-revenue backing.

Management has clearly done a good job of navigating the shoals of this difficult market niche and has delivered on its income promise at the price of very modest month-to-month volatility. Investors should keep the fund's risks at the forefront of their minds, though.

Address:	One Parkview Plaza Oakbrook Terrace, IL 60181 800–421–5666
Web Address:	www.vankampen.com
Inception:	01-02-86
Advisor:	Van Kampen Asset Mgmt.
Subadvisor:	Van Kampen Adv.
NTF Plans:	Datalynx , Fidelity Inst.

Minimum Purchase:	$1000	Add: $25	IRA: $500
Min Auto Inv Plan:	$25	Add: $25	
Sales Fees:	4.75%L, 0.25%S		
Management Fee:	.60% mx./.50% mn.		
Actual Fees:	Mgt: 0.53%	Dist: —	
Expense Projections:	3Yr: $748	5Yr: $950	10Yr: $1530
Avg Brok Commission:	—	Income Distrib: Monthly	
Total Cost (relative to category):		Average	

Credit Analysis % bonds 06-30-01			
US Govt	0	BB	7
AAA	4	B	1
AA	3	Below B	0
A	4	NR/NA	72
BBB	9		

Special Securities % assets 08-31-01	
Restricted/Illiquid Secs	Trace
Inverse Floaters	0
Options/Futures/Warrants	No

Bond Type % assets 06-30-99	
Alternative Minimum Tax (AMT)	—
Insured	—
Prerefunded	—

Top 5 States % bonds			
PA	10.3	NY	7.5
FL	8.1	MA	6.9
IL	7.8		

Composition % assets 08-31-01			
Cash	0.1	Bonds	99.9
Stocks	0.0	Other	0.0

Sector Weightings	% of Bonds	Rel Cat
General Obligation	2.8	0.1
Utilities	2.0	0.3
Health	34.3	2.3
Water/Waste	2.1	0.4
Housing	13.6	1.9
Education	4.2	0.7
Transportation	7.7	0.6
COP/Lease	3.6	1.3
Industrial	19.5	1.5
Misc Revenue	9.6	1.9
Demand	0.3	0.4

Van Kampen Latin American A

Ticker	Load	NAV	Yield	Total Assets	Mstar Category
MSLAX	5.75%	$11.61	0.9%	$36.7 mil	Latin America Stock

Prospectus Objective: Foreign Stock

Van Kampen Latin American Fund seeks long-term capital appreciation.

The fund normally invests at least 80% of assets in Latin American stock and sovereign debt. It invests at least 55% in equities from Argentina, Brazil, Chile, and Mexico. It may invest up to 20% in low-rated debt. It may also invest in debt-conversion programs, whereby investors may use sovereign debt to invest in local companies. It is non-diversified.

Class A shares have front loads; B shares have deferred loads and higher 12b-1 fees; C shares have level loads. Past name: Morgan Stanley Latin American Fund.

Historical Profile

Return: Average
Risk: High
Rating: ★★★ Neutral

Investment Style
Equity
Average Stock %: 59% (1995), 70% (1996), 75% (1997), 68% (1998), 86% (1999), 97% (2000), 95% (12-01)

▼ Manager Change
▽ Partial Manager Change

Fund Performance vs. Category Average
Quarterly Fund Return
+/– Category Average
— Category Baseline

Performance Quartile (within Category)

Portfolio Manager(s)

Robert L. Meyer, CFA. Since 7-94. BA Yale U.; JD Harvard U. Other funds currently managed: Morgan Stanley Inst Emerging Mkts A, Morgan Stanley Inst Latin American A, Van Kampen Emerging Markets A.

Michael Perl. Since 7-98. BS U. of New South Wales. Other funds currently managed: Morgan Stanley Inst Latin American A, Van Kampen Latin American C, SEI International Emerg Mkts A.

1990	1991	1992	1993	1994	1995	1996	1997	1998	1999	2000	12–01	History
—	—	—	—	11.86	9.42	12.15	13.48	8.48	14.26	12.07	11.61	NAV
—	—	—	—	0.48*	–20.43	47.37	39.61	–35.93	68.16	–15.36	–2.94	Total Return %
—	—	—	—	–3.94*	–57.97	24.42	6.26	–64.51	47.12	–6.26	8.94	+/– S&P 500
—	—	—	—	—	–4.66	28.64	11.22	2.26	6.35	0.56	—	+/– MSCI Latin Am
—	—	—	—	0.00	0.14	0.92	0.00	0.77	0.00	0.00	0.83	Income Return %
—	—	—	—	0.48	–20.57	46.44	39.61	–36.70	68.16	–15.36	–3.77	Capital Return %
—	—	—	—	—	57	5	9	11	25	37	27	Total Rtn % Rank Cat
—	—	—	—	0.00	0.02	0.09	0.00	0.10	0.00	0.00	0.10	Income $
—	—	—	—	0.20	0.00	1.63	3.23	0.05	0.00	0.00	0.00	Capital Gains $
—	—	—	—	—	2.46	2.11	2.24	2.25	2.20	2.17	2.18	Expense Ratio %
—	—	—	—	—	–0.44	1.18	–0.08	–0.09	0.98	0.31	0.84	Income Ratio %
—	—	—	—	—	—	131	241	249	163	78	61	Turnover Rate %
—	—	—	—	7.5	10.1	19.5	68.4	23.6	32.5	30.7	18.4	Net Assets $mil

Performance 12-31-01

	1st Qtr	2nd Qtr	3rd Qtr	4th Qtr	Total
1997	15.88	23.51	6.96	–8.81	39.61
1998	4.01	–18.54	–31.17	9.88	–35.93
1999	15.57	17.86	–11.86	40.08	68.16
2000	7.29	–6.93	–6.39	–9.45	–15.36
2001	–3.07	8.63	–24.55	22.16	–2.94

Trailing	Total Return%	+/– S&P 500	+/– MSCI Latin Am	% Rank All	% Rank Cat	Growth of $10,000
3 Mo	22.16	11.48	—	11	36	12,216
6 Mo	–7.83	–2.27	—	77	52	9,217
1 Yr	–2.94	8.94	—	47	27	9,706
3 Yr Avg	11.37	12.40	—	9	40	13,815
5 Yr Avg	4.32	–6.38	—	75	4	12,357
10 Yr Avg	—	—	—	—	—	—
15 Yr Avg	—	—	—	—	—	—

Tax Analysis	Tax-Adj Ret%	%Rank Cat	%Pretax Ret	%Rank Cat
3 Yr Avg	11.24	34	98.9	40
5 Yr Avg	2.37	4	54.7	53
10 Yr Avg	—	—	—	—

Potential Capital Gain Exposure: –56% of assets

Risk Analysis

Time Period	Load-Adj Return %	Risk %Rank[1] All	Risk %Rank[1] Cat	Morningstar Return	Morningstar Risk	Morningstar Risk-Adj Rating
1 Yr	–8.52					
3 Yr	9.20	91	29	0.94[2]	1.34	★★★★
5 Yr	3.09	97	62	–0.41[2]	1.57	★★★
Incept	4.31	—	—	—	—	

Average Historical Rating (54 months): 2.9★s

[1] 1=low, 100=high [2] T-Bill return substituted for category avg.

Category Rating (3 Yr)

1 2 3 4 5
Worst Best

Return: Average
Risk: Below Avg

Other Measures	Standard Index S&P 500	Best Fit Index Wil 4500
Alpha	18.2	11.8
Beta	1.23	0.94
R–Squared	39	61
Standard Deviation		39.30
Mean		11.37
Sharpe Ratio		0.19

Portfolio Analysis 06-30-01

Share change since 05–01 Total Stocks: 79	Sector	Country	% Assets
⊕ Telefonos de Mexico ADR L	Services	Mexico	10.32
⊕ America Movil	N/A	N/A	6.11
⊖ Grupo Fin Banamex Accival	Financials	Mexico	5.06
⊕ Petrobras ADR	Energy	Brazil	4.57
⊕ Grupo Fin Bancomer O	Financials	Mexico	3.41
⊕ Cemex (Part)	Industrials	Mexico	3.26
⊕ Kimberly–Clark de Mex A	Industrials	Mexico	3.03
⊕ Grupo Televisa (Part) ADR	Services	Mexico	2.89
⊕ Banco Itau	Financials	Brazil	2.74
☼ Wal–Mart De Mexico SA	Retail	Mexico	2.54
☼ Comp De Bebidas ADR	N/A	N/A	2.53
⊖ Fomento Economico Mex	Staples	Mexico	2.19
Wal–Mart de Mexico Cl C	Retail	Mexico	2.06
⊖ Celular Cert Part	Utilities	Brazil	1.94
⊕ Vale do Rio Doce Pfd	Industrials	Brazil	1.77
⊖ Brasil Telecom	Utilities	Brazil	1.71
⊕ TeleNorte Leste Part ADR	Services	Brazil	1.57
⊕ CANTV ADR	Services	Venezuela	1.55
⊕ Embraer ADR	Industrials	Brazil	1.52
Petrobras	Energy	Brazil	1.51

Analysis by Gabriel Presler 11-27-01

Depend on Van Kampen Latin American to find strength when there's strength to be found.

When global markets fell on hard times more than a year ago, the developing countries of Latin America were among the hardest hit. The average fund in the category gave back more than 15% of its value in 2000. The group has continued to suffer in 2001, losing about 11% for the year to date through Nov. 26, 2001. Still, there have been pockets of solid performance and funds willing to take a few risks have been able to benefit from rallies in beaten-down sectors and the strength of the Mexican market.

As usual, this fund is in the right place at the right time. In early 2001, comanagers Michael Perl and Robert Meyer broadened the fund's exposure to Mexico to virtually 50% of assets. They've been particularly interested in the country's blue-chip companies, such as Wal-mart de Mexico; the earnings of many of these firms have held up well throughout the year. What's more, the team took a chance on some beaten-up stocks in the telecom sector, adding to positions in firms such as Telmex, which posted some strong gains after a miserable 2000, and Telecommunication de Chile, which has been relatively resilient. Thus, while the fund's loss of 8% for the year to date through Nov. 26 might look ugly on an absolute basis, it has actually outpaced almost 75% of its peers.

Strong relative performance is nothing new here. The fund's aggressive country and sector bets have generally met with good results, particularly in growth rallies. Thus, its longer-term record is one of the best in the category. Still, it has been extremely volatile since its 1994 inception, and thus is suited only for very aggressive investors who need a focused Latin America offering.

Current Investment Style

Style: Value Blnd Growth
Size: Large Med Small

	Stock Port Avg	Rel MSCI EAFE Current	Rel MSCI EAFE Hist	Rel Cat
Price/Earnings Ratio	14.6	0.57	0.63	0.99
Price/Cash Flow	6.8	0.53	0.79	0.97
Price/Book Ratio	2.5	0.72	0.53	0.97
3 Yr Earnings Growth	16.7	0.89	—	0.74
Med Mkt Cap $mil	5,132	0.2	0.2	0.95

Country Exposure 06-30-01	% assets
Mexico	43
Brazil	34
Chile	6
Argentina	2
Venezuela	2

Hedging History: Rare

Special Securities % assets 06-30-01	
Restricted/Illiquid Secs	Trace
Emerging–Markets Secs	90
Options/Futures/Warrants	No

Composition % assets 06-30-01

Cash	4.9	Bonds	0.0
Stocks	95.0	Other	0.2

Sector Weightings	% of Stocks	Rel Cat	5-Year High	5-Year Low
Utilities	12.3	1.9	19	6
Energy	7.7	0.8	11	0
Financials	19.1	1.4	20	5
Industrials	20.5	1.1	21	10
Durables	0.4	1.2	3	0
Staples	9.5	0.7	22	6
Services	24.8	0.9	46	12
Retail	5.7	0.7	18	3
Health	0.0	0.0	0	0
Technology	0.1	0.1	1	0

Address:	One Parkview Plaza Oakbrook Terrace, IL 60181 800–421–5666
Web Address:	www.vankampen.com
*Inception:	07-06-94
Advisor:	Van Kampen Inv. Adv.
Subadvisor:	Morgan Stanley Dean Witter Asset Mgmt
NTF Plans:	Datalynx , Fidelity Inst.

Minimum Purchase:	$1000	Add: $25	IRA: $500
Min Auto Inv Plan:	$25	Add: $25	
Sales Fees:	5.75%L, 0.25%S		
Management Fee:	1.3%, .25%A		
Actual Fees:	Mgt: 1.25%	Dist: 0.25%	
Expense Projections:	3Yr: $1292	5Yr: $1801	10Yr: $3192
Avg Brok Commission:	—	Income Distrib: Annually	
Total Cost (relative to category):	Average		

Van Wagoner Post–Venture

Ticker	Load	NAV	Yield	Total Assets	Mstar Category
VWPVX	12b–1 only	$10.04	0.0%	$167.9 mil	Mid–Cap Growth

Prospectus Objective: Growth

Van Wagoner Post-Venture Fund seeks capital appreciation.

The fund normally invests at least 65% of assets in securities of companies that have received venture capital financing during the early stages of their existence, or as a part of a reorganization, restructuring, or recapitalization. It is anticipated that the fund will focus on investing in companies during or after they have engaged in the early stages of their public existence. The fund may invest in companies of all sizes.

Historical Profile

Return: Low
Risk: High
Rating: ★ Lowest

Investment Style
Equity
Average Stock %: 93% (1997), 84% (1998), 81% (1999), 98% (2000), 92% (12-01)

▼ Manager Change
▽ Partial Manager Change

Fund Performance vs. Category Average
■ Quarterly Fund Return +/– Category Average
— Category Baseline

Performance Quartile (within Category)

Portfolio Manager(s)

Garrett R. Van Wagoner, CFA. Since 12-96. BS'77 Bucknell U. Other funds currently managed: Van Wagoner Emerging Growth, Van Wagoner Mid-Cap Growth, Van Wagoner Technology.

Raiford Garrabrandt, CFA. Since 11-00. BS U North Carolina. Other funds currently managed: Van Wagoner Emerging Growth, Van Wagoner Mid-Cap Growth, Van Wagoner Technology.

1990	1991	1992	1993	1994	1995	1996	1997	1998	1999	2000	12-01	History
—	—	—	—	—	—	10.00	8.78	12.08	38.07	26.52	10.04	NAV
—	—	—	—	—	—	—	–12.20	37.59	237.22	–30.31	–62.14	Total Return %
—	—	—	—	—	—	—	–45.55	9.01	216.18	–21.21	–50.27	+/– S&P 500
—	—	—	—	—	—	—	–34.74	19.72	185.91	–18.57	–41.99	+/– Russ Midcap Grth
—	—	—	—	—	—	—	0.00	0.00	0.00	0.00	0.00	Income Return %
—	—	—	—	—	—	—	–12.20	37.59	237.22	–30.31	–62.14	Capital Return %
—	—	—	—	—	—	—	98	4	1	92	100	Total Rtn % Rank Cat
—	—	—	—	—	—	0.00	0.00	0.00	0.00	0.00	0.00	Income $
—	—	—	—	—	—	0.00	0.00	0.00	2.20	0.01	0.00	Capital Gains $
—	—	—	—	—	—	—	1.95	1.95	1.95	—	—	Expense Ratio %
—	—	—	—	—	—	—	–1.39	–1.39	–1.06	—	—	Income Ratio %
—	—	—	—	—	—	—	317	641	328	—	—	Turnover Rate %
—	—	—	—	—	—	0.5	20.5	19.1	391.5	485.2	167.9	Net Assets $mil

Performance 12-31-01

	1st Qtr	2nd Qtr	3rd Qtr	4th Qtr	Total
1997	–17.10	16.65	20.68	–24.76	–12.20
1998	14.69	4.87	–16.86	37.59	37.59
1999	55.30	25.27	12.55	54.01	237.22
2000	11.06	–4.97	19.89	–44.92	–30.31
2001	–60.03	29.72	–59.71	81.23	–62.14

Trailing	Total Return%	+/– S&P 500	+/– Russ Midcap Grth	% Rank All	% Rank Cat	Growth of $10,000
3 Mo	81.23	70.54	54.16	1	1	18,123
6 Mo	–26.98	–21.43	–18.72	100	100	7,302
1 Yr	–62.14	–50.27	–41.99	100	100	3,786
3 Yr Avg	–3.82	–2.80	–5.98	89	86	8,897
5 Yr Avg	1.45	–9.25	–7.57	90	87	10,747
10 Yr Avg	—	—	—	—	—	—
15 Yr Avg	—	—	—	—	—	—

Tax Analysis	Tax-Adj Ret%	%Rank Cat	%Pretax Ret	%Rank Cat
3 Yr Avg	–4.66	81	—	—
5 Yr Avg	0.92	80	63.2	74
10 Yr Avg	—	—	—	—

Potential Capital Gain Exposure: –148% of assets

Risk Analysis

Time Period	Load-Adj Return %	Risk %Rank[1] All	Risk %Rank[1] Cat	Morningstar Return	Morningstar Risk	Morningstar Risk-Adj Rating
1 Yr	–62.14					
3 Yr	–3.82	99	100	–1.71[2]	3.09	★
5 Yr	1.45	99	99	–0.73[2]	2.93	★
Incept	1.45	—	—	—	—	

Average Historical Rating (25 months): 3.7★s

[1]1=low, 100=high [2] T-Bill return substituted for category avg.

Category Rating (3 Yr)

1 2 3 4 5 (Worst – Best)

Return: Below Avg
Risk: High

Other Measures	Standard Index S&P 500	Best Fit Index Wil 4500
Alpha	38.9	21.8
Beta	2.92	2.37
R-Squared	44	78
Standard Deviation		104.94
Mean		–3.82
Sharpe Ratio		–0.10

Analysis by Christopher Traulsen 12-12-01

Van Wagoner Post Venture Fund needs to get its house in order.

This fund has had a truly awful year by any measure. It's lost 63% for the year to date through Dec. 11, 2001, and is down 72% over the trailing 12 months—returns that scrape the bottom of the mid-growth barrel.

Part of the problem is comanager Garrett Van Wagoner's aggressive style. He often loads 80% to 90% of the portfolio into the volatile tech sector and buys companies that are extremely pricey. But even given those biases, Van Wagoner made several glaring mistakes this year. Early on, he decided that software firms would be less exposed to the economic downturn than cyclical fare such as semiconductors. But software sold off much more sharply than chips, hanging this fund out to dry. He also made huge commitments to individual names that have fizzled, including Interwoven and Embarcadero Technologies.

A recent Wall Street Journal article noted that Van Wagoner had written down the value of a number of the fund's private investments. We see nothing untoward in Van Wagoner's handling of these issues, but they are an additional risk that investors here should be aware of. He carries them at cost and will write them down when fundamental changes warrant, which can exacerbate the fund's already high volatility.

This fund should excel in better times. It has in the past, and it has soared 26% over the past three months. However, we're troubled by the current makeup of its board of directors. The board has consisted of only Van Wagoner and a single independent director since mid-2000. The board's job is to safeguard the interests of shareholders, and we don't think its current composition is sufficient to the task. Until it is, we can't recommend this fund, even to the few investors who might care to brave its risks.

Portfolio Analysis 06-30-01

Share change since 12-00 Total Stocks: 84	Sector	PE	YTD Ret%	% Assets
⊕ Interwoven	Technology	—	–70.40	10.06
⊕ Embarcadero Tech	Technology	—	–46.20	5.90
⊕ StorageNetworks	Technology	—	–75.00	3.92
⊖ IntraNet Solutions	Technology	—	–42.00	3.62
⊕ Sonus Networks	Technology	—	–81.70	3.14
⊕ Netegrity	Technology	62.5	–64.40	3.03
☼ ONI Sys	Technology	—	–84.10	2.88
⊕ MatrixOne	Technology	—	–28.50	2.76
⊖ Brocade Comm Sys	Technology	—	–63.90	2.68
⊖ Emulex	Technology	—	–50.50	2.51
☼ I-many	Services	—	–22.40	2.35
⊕ Informatica	Technology	—	–63.30	2.30
☼ Interwoven (New)	N/A	—	—	2.03
☼ StorageNetworks (New)	N/A	—	—	1.90
☼ Manugistics Grp	Technology	—	–63.00	1.88
☼ Qlogic	Technology	49.5	–42.10	1.79
☼ Ourhouse	N/A	—	—	1.41
⊖ Quest Software	Technology	—	–21.20	1.38
Cardiac Pathways	Health	—	22.59	1.32
☼ Blue Pumpkin Software	N/A	—	—	1.31
☼ OPNET Tech	Technology	—	–4.34	1.25
⊕ ScreamingMedia	Services	—	–26.60	1.21
⊖ Anaren Microwave	Technology	42.2	–74.20	1.19
⊕ Micromuse	Technology	51.7	–75.10	1.17
⊕ Powerwave Tech	Industrials	—	–70.40	0.98

Current Investment Style

Style: Value Blnd Growth; Size: Large Med Small

	Stock Port Avg	Relative S&P 500 Current	Relative S&P 500 Hist	Rel Cat
Price/Earnings Ratio	—	—	—	—
Price/Book Ratio	5.3	0.92	1.22	0.93
Price/Cash Flow	37.8[1]	2.10	1.56	1.63
3 Yr Earnings Growth	—	—	—	—
1 Yr Earnings Est%	—	—	—	—
Med Mkt Cap $mil	862	0.0	0.0	0.15

[1]figure is based on 50% or less of stocks

Special Securities % assets 06-30-01	
Restricted/Illiquid Secs	Trace
Emerging–Markets Secs	1
Options/Futures/Warrants	Yes

Composition % assets 06-30-01	
Cash	6.8
Stocks*	91.9
Bonds	1.3
Other	0.1
*Foreign (% stocks)	0.8

Market Cap	
Giant	0.0
Large	5.4
Medium	13.3
Small	77.1
Micro	4.1

Sector Weightings	% of Stocks	Rel S&P	5-Year High	5-Year Low
Utilities	0.0	0.0	—	—
Energy	0.0	0.0	—	—
Financials	0.0	0.0	—	—
Industrials	1.5	0.1	—	—
Durables	0.0	0.0	—	—
Staples	0.0	0.0	—	—
Services	8.2	0.8	—	—
Retail	0.0	0.0	—	—
Health	2.0	0.1	—	—
Technology	88.3	4.8	—	—

Address:	P.O. Box 1628 Milwaukee, WI 53201–1628 800–228–2121
Web Address:	www.vanwagoner.com
*Inception:	12-31-96
Advisor:	Van Wagoner Cap. Mgmt.
Subadvisor:	None
NTF Plans:	Fidelity , Datalynx

Minimum Purchase:	$1000	Add: $50	IRA: $500
Min Auto Inv Plan:	$500	Add: $50	
Sales Fees:	0.25%B		
Management Fee:	1.5%, .18%A		
Actual Fees:	Mgt: 1.50%	Dist: 0.25%	
Expense Projections:	3Yr: $623	5Yr: $1073	10Yr: $2323
Avg Brok Commission:	—	Income Distrib: Annually	
Total Cost (relative to category):	Average		

Vanguard Asset Allocation

Ticker	Load	NAV	Yield	Total Assets	Mstar Category
VAAPX	None	$21.81	2.8%	$8,475.8 mil	Domestic Hybrid

Prospectus Objective: Asset Allocation

Vanguard Asset Allocation Fund seeks total return.

The fund allocates assets among common stocks, bonds, and money-market instruments. It varies the asset mix according to the relative attractiveness of the asset classes; there is no limitation as to the amount of assets in each class. The advisor evaluates common stocks using a dividend-discount model, a mathematical model that evaluates stocks according to the projected worth of their dividends. The bond portion consists primarily of long-term U.S. Treasuries or securities issued by other government agencies.

The fund also offers Adm shares.

Historical Profile

Return Average
Risk Below Avg
Rating ★★★★ Above Avg

Investment Style
Equity
Average Stock %: 42% 42% 39% 39% 36% 55%

▼ Manager Change
▽ Partial Manager Change

Fund Performance vs. Category Average
■ Quarterly Fund Return +/– Category Average
— Category Baseline

Performance Quartile (within Category)

Portfolio Manager(s)

William L. Fouse, CFA. Since 11-88. BA U. of Kentucky; MBA U. of Kentucky. Other fund currently managed: Vanguard Asset Allocation Adm.

Thomas F. Loeb. Since 11-88. BA Fairleigh Dickinson U.; MBA U. of Pennsylvania. Other fund currently managed: Vanguard Asset Allocation Adm.

History

1990	1991	1992	1993	1994	1995	1996	1997	1998	1999	2000	12-01	History
11.35	13.64	13.64	14.45	13.54	17.05	17.94	21.05	24.38	23.80	23.67	21.81	NAV
0.89	27.74	5.70	13.49	–2.32	35.46	15.73	27.32	25.40	5.22	4.91	–5.30	Total Return %
4.01	–2.74	–1.92	3.43	–3.63	–2.08	–7.21	–6.03	–3.18	–15.82	14.01	6.58	+/– S&P 500
–8.07	11.74	–1.70	3.74	0.60	16.99	12.12	17.64	16.72	6.05	–6.72	–13.72	+/– LB Aggregate
5.23	5.25	4.37	3.55	3.98	4.92	4.26	4.15	3.63	3.64	4.33	2.59	Income Return %
–4.34	22.49	1.33	9.94	–6.30	30.54	11.48	23.17	21.76	1.57	0.58	–7.89	Capital Return %
43	23	74	40	47	2	28	3	5	69	32	60	Total Rtn % Rank Cat
0.62	0.59	0.59	0.48	0.57	0.66	0.72	0.74	0.76	0.88	1.02	0.61	Income $
0.13	0.19	0.17	0.53	0.00	0.61	1.05	1.01	1.18	0.96	0.27	0.00	Capital Gains $
0.50	0.44	0.52	0.49	0.50	0.49	0.47	0.49	0.49	0.49	0.44	—	Expense Ratio %
5.53	5.28	4.95	4.07	3.68	4.41	4.17	3.96	3.80	3.49	4.18	—	Income Ratio %
12	44	18	31	51	34	47	10	60	11	29	—	Turnover Rate %
179.1	341.2	585.2	1,125.8	1,125.6	1,791.0	2,596.9	4,099.5	6,974.2	8,597.1	9,262.7	7,750.5	Net Assets $mil

Performance 12-31-01

	1st Qtr	2nd Qtr	3rd Qtr	4th Qtr	Total
1997	1.06	12.52	6.58	5.06	27.32
1998	10.17	4.14	–4.38	14.31	25.40
1999	1.03	2.68	–3.29	4.87	5.22
2000	5.63	–0.61	1.14	–1.20	4.91
2001	–9.29	5.20	–8.26	8.18	–5.30

Trailing	Total Return%	+/– S&P 500	+/– LB Agg	% Rank All	% Rank Cat	Growth of $10,000
3 Mo	8.18	–2.51	8.14	51	22	10,818
6 Mo	–0.76	4.80	–5.41	42	32	9,924
1 Yr	–5.30	6.58	–13.72	52	60	9,470
3 Yr Avg	1.49	2.51	–4.79	65	60	10,453
5 Yr Avg	10.79	0.09	3.36	15	10	16,689
10 Yr Avg	11.85	–1.07	4.62	20	8	30,657
15 Yr Avg	—	—	—	—	—	—

Tax Analysis	Tax-Adj Ret%	%Rank Cat	%Pretax Ret	%Rank Cat
3 Yr Avg	–0.35	61	—	—
5 Yr Avg	8.41	10	78.0	16
10 Yr Avg	9.38	8	79.1	16

Potential Capital Gain Exposure: 7% of assets

Risk Analysis

Time Period	Load-Adj Return %	Risk %Rank[1] All	Risk %Rank[1] Cat	Morningstar Return	Morningstar Risk	Morningstar Risk-Adj Rating
1 Yr	–5.30					
3 Yr	1.49	40	52	–0.71[2]	0.55	★★★
5 Yr	10.79	43	44	1.40[2]	0.53	★★★★
10 Yr	11.85	51	61	1.07	0.59	★★★★

Average Historical Rating (122 months): 4.0★s

[1]1=low, 100=high [2] T-Bill return substituted for category avg.

Category Rating (3 Yr)

1 2 3 4 5 — Worst ... Best

Return Average
Risk Average

Other Measures	Standard Index S&P 500	Best Fit Index S&P 500
Alpha	–0.1	–0.1
Beta	0.59	0.59
R-Squared	89	89
Standard Deviation		10.75
Mean		1.49
Sharpe Ratio		–0.37

Portfolio Analysis 03-31-01

Total Stocks: 502 Share change since 12-00	Sector	PE Ratio	YTD Return %	% Net Assets
⊕ General Elec	Industrials	30.1	–15.00	2.17
⊕ Microsoft	Technology	57.6	52.78	1.53
⊕ ExxonMobil	Energy	15.3	–7.59	1.48
⊕ Pfizer	Health	34.7	–12.40	1.35
⊕ Citigroup	Financials	20.0	0.03	1.18
⊕ Wal-Mart Stores	Retail	40.3	8.94	1.18
⊕ American Intl Grp	Financials	42.0	–19.20	0.98
⊕ Intel	Technology	73.1	4.89	0.93
⊕ Merck	Health	19.1	–35.90	0.92
⊕ AOL Time Warner	Technology	—	–7.76	0.91

Total Fixed-Income: 17	Date of Maturity	Amount $000	Value $000	% Net Assets
US Treasury Bond 6.875%	08-15-25	108,575	126,251	1.52
US Treasury Bond 6.375%	08-15-27	99,670	109,637	1.32
US Treasury Bond 11.75%	11-15-14	74,775	109,385	1.32
US Treasury Bond 7.25%	05-15-16	90,550	106,695	1.29
US Treasury Bond 8%	11-15-21	58,320	75,221	0.91
US Treasury Bond 8.125%	05-15-21	53,485	69,632	0.84
US Treasury Bond 5.5%	08-15-28	37,600	36,908	0.44
US Treasury Bond 7.125%	02-15-23	25,495	30,270	0.36
US Treasury Bond 5.25%	11-15-28	30,490	28,889	0.35
US Treasury Bond 6.75%	08-15-26	18,000	20,686	0.25

Equity Style
Style: Blend
Size: Large-Cap

Fixed-Income Style
Duration: —
Quality: —
NA

	Portfolio Avg	Rel S&P
Price/Earnings Ratio	30.3	0.98
Price/Book Ratio	5.4	0.95
Price/Cash Flow	17.2	0.96
3 Yr Earnings Growth	15.8	1.08
1 Yr Earnings Est%	–3.5	1.97
Debt % Total Cap	31.7	1.03
Med Mkt Cap $mil	55,530	0.91

Avg Eff Duration	—
Avg Eff Maturity	—
Avg Credit Quality	—
Avg Wtd Coupon	7.88%

Special Securities % assets 03-31-01	
Restricted/Illiquid Secs	0
Emerging-Markets Secs	0
Options/Futures/Warrants	Yes

Composition % of assets 03-31-01	
Cash	35.6
Stocks*	54.9
Bonds	9.5
Other	0.0
*Foreign (% of stocks)	2.1

Market Cap	
Giant	53.8
Large	34.3
Medium	11.3
Small	0.6
Micro	0.0

Sector Weightings	% of Stocks	Rel S&P	5-Year High	5-Year Low
Utilities	3.4	1.1	10	2
Energy	7.5	1.1	11	6
Financials	17.9	1.0	18	8
Industrials	11.4	1.0	19	10
Durables	1.9	1.2	6	2
Staples	6.7	0.9	15	5
Services	11.9	1.1	18	11
Retail	6.7	1.0	9	4
Health	13.5	0.9	14	8
Technology	19.1	1.0	33	5

Analysis by Langdon Healy 09-26-01

Vanguard Asset Allocation is down, but not for the count.

This is not a plain-vanilla balanced fund that keeps a static allocation between stocks and bonds. Rather, it embraces frequent and aggressive shifts in asset mix based on models designed to gauge the relative attractiveness (based on valuation) of stocks, bonds, and cash. Otherwise, it's pretty straightforward: Its stock portfolio tracks the S&P 500 index, and the bond segment tracks the Lehman Brothers Long Term Treasury index.

Asset-allocation bets can be risky, however, as the fund's woes this year show. As the stock market declined at the beginning of 2001, the allocation models signaled the most attractive equity market since 1986. Management thus upped the fund's equity stake to 90% of assets in March. (Part of the fund's equity exposure is in S&P 500 futures, registered as cash in our system.) The team cut the fund's equity stake to 60% in May but has since boosted it back to 80%. That has been a recipe for big losses—the stock market has continued to skid, and the fund's equity overweighting has pulled it down nearly 18% for the year to date through Sept. 21, 2001—a bottom-quartile showing in the category.

Although the fund has done a poor job of timing the markets this year, its asset calls have been good over the long haul. In 1998, for example, a large equity weighting helped it post a top-flight return. Its five- and 10-year trailing returns also rank near the category's top decile. Moreover, in the longer term, it hasn't experienced much bigger downturns than its average peer.

This fund is not suitable for investors seeking a steady balanced portfolio, but we think its strong record and ultra-low costs make it an appealing choice for others.

Address:	Vanguard Financial Ctr. P.O. Box 2600 Valley Forge, PA 19482 800-662-7447 / 610-669-1000
Web Address:	www.vanguard.com
Inception:	11-03-88
Advisor:	Mellon Cap. Mgmt.
Subadvisor:	None
NTF Plans:	N/A

Minimum Purchase:	$3000	Add: $100 IRA: $1000
Min Auto Inv Plan:	$3000	Add: $50
Sales Fees:	No-load	
Management Fee:	.20% mx./.10% mn.+(–).05%P	
Actual Fees:	Mgt: 0.47%	Dist: —
Expense Projections:	3Yr: $157	5Yr: $274 10Yr: $616
Avg Brok Commission:	—	Income Distrib: Semi-Ann.
Total Cost (relative to category):	Low	

Vanguard Balanced Index

Ticker	Load	NAV	Yield	Total Assets	Mstar Category
VBINX	None	$17.86	3.3%	$4,187.4 mil	Domestic Hybrid

Prospectus Objective: Balanced

Vanguard Balanced Index Fund seeks growth and income.

The fund normally invests 60% of assets in equities and 40% in bonds. The equity portion seeks to replicate the Wilshire 5000 Index performance; to this end, the fund invests primarily in the 500 largest companies on the index and samples the rest. The fixed-income portion seeks to replicate the Lehman Brothers Aggregate Bond Index performance; it may purchase investment-grade U.S. government obligations, corporate debt, and mortgage-backed securities to secure this goal.

The fund currently offers Investor, Institutional and Admiral shares.

Historical Profile

Return: Average
Risk: Low
Rating: ★★★★ Above Avg

Investment Style
Equity
Average Stock %: 59% 57% 58% 59% 59% 58%

▼ Manager Change
▽ Partial Manager Change

Fund Performance vs. Category Average
Quarterly Fund Return +/– Category Average
— Category Baseline

Performance Quartile (within Category)

Portfolio Manager(s)

George U. Sauter. Since 9-92. AB'76 Dartmouth C.; MBA'80 U. of Chicago. Other funds currently managed: Vanguard Small Cap Index, Vanguard Equity-Income, Vanguard European Stock Index.

Ian A. MacKinnon. Since 9-92. BA'70 Lafayette C.; MBA'74 Pennsylvania State U. Other funds currently managed: Vanguard CA Insured Long Tax-Ex, Vanguard Short-Term Treasury, Vanguard Interm-Term U.S. Treas.

Christopher W. Alwine, CFA. Since 1-98. BBA'90 Temple U.; MS'93 Drexel U. Other funds currently managed: Vanguard NJ Insured Long Tax-Ex, Vanguard OH Long-Term Tax-Exempt, Vanguard PA Insured Long Tax-Ex.

History

1990	1991	1992	1993	1994	1995	1996	1997	1998	1999	2000	12-01	History
—	—	10.31	10.91	10.34	12.77	13.92	16.29	18.48	20.22	19.08	17.86	NAV
—	—	3.90*	10.00	–1.56	28.65	13.95	22.24	17.85	13.61	–2.04	–3.02	Total Return %
—	—	–1.70*	–0.06	–2.87	–8.89	–9.00	–11.11	–10.72	–7.43	7.06	8.86	+/– S&P 500
—	—	—	0.25	1.36	10.18	10.34	12.56	9.18	14.44	–13.67	–11.44	+/– LB Aggregate
—	—	0.80	3.83	3.72	4.41	3.89	3.87	3.36	3.19	3.24	3.17	Income Return %
—	—	3.10	6.17	–5.27	24.23	10.06	18.37	14.49	10.43	–5.28	–6.19	Capital Return %
—	—	—	72	33	19	43	21	22	26	72	38	Total Rtn % Rank Cat
—	—	0.08	0.39	0.40	0.45	0.49	0.53	0.54	0.58	0.65	0.60	Income $
—	—	0.00	0.03	0.00	0.05	0.12	0.14	0.14	0.14	0.10	0.03	Capital Gains $
—	—	0.22	0.20	0.20	0.20	0.20	0.20	0.21	0.20	0.22	—	Expense Ratio %
—	—	3.76	3.53	3.86	3.85	3.69	3.56	3.29	3.18	3.30	—	Income Ratio %
—	—	—	25	16	16	37	18	25	29	28	—	Turnover Rate %
—	—	108.5	367.1	402.9	590.1	826.2	1,250.4	2,003.6	3,128.5	3,559.6	3,116.9	Net Assets $mil

Performance 12-31-01

	1st Qtr	2nd Qtr	3rd Qtr	4th Qtr	Total
1997	0.15	11.47	7.08	2.26	22.24
1998	8.47	2.11	–5.57	12.67	17.85
1999	2.09	4.25	–3.52	10.64	13.61
2000	3.30	–2.07	1.44	–4.54	–2.04
2001	–6.00	4.67	–7.82	6.92	–3.02

Trailing	Total Return%	+/– S&P 500	+/– LB Agg	% Rank All	% Rank Cat	Growth of $10,000
3 Mo	6.92	–3.76	6.89	56	36	10,692
6 Mo	–1.43	4.12	–6.09	44	44	9,857
1 Yr	–3.02	8.86	–11.44	47	38	9,698
3 Yr Avg	2.58	3.60	–3.69	59	44	10,794
5 Yr Avg	9.23	–1.47	1.80	23	24	15,550
10 Yr Avg	—	—	—	—	—	—
15 Yr Avg	—	—	—	—	—	—

Tax Analysis	Tax-Adj Ret%	%Rank Cat	%Pretax Ret	%Rank Cat
3 Yr Avg	1.17	38	45.5	61
5 Yr Avg	7.60	13	82.4	10
10 Yr Avg	—	—	—	—

Potential Capital Gain Exposure: 8% of assets

Risk Analysis

Time Period	Load-Adj Return %	Risk %Rank[1] All	Risk %Rank[1] Cat	Morningstar Return	Morningstar Risk	Morningstar Risk-Adj Rating
1 Yr	–3.02					
3 Yr	2.58	42	59	–0.49[2]	0.58	★★★
5 Yr	9.23	44	56	0.99[2]	0.57	★★★★
Incept	10.70	—	—	—	—	

Average Historical Rating (76 months): 3.4★s

[1] 1=low, 100=high [2] T-Bill return substituted for category avg.

Category Rating (3 Yr)

1 2 3 4 5 (Worst ... Best): 3

Return: Average
Risk: Average

Other Measures	Standard Index S&P 500	Best Fit Index S&P 500
Alpha	0.9	0.9
Beta	0.59	0.59
R-Squared	90	90

Standard Deviation	10.74
Mean	2.58
Sharpe Ratio	–0.25

Analysis by Scott Cooley 12-10-01

Even in a difficult environment, Vanguard Balanced Index Fund has put up solid numbers.

A couple of factors have worked against the fund this year. Management hews to a 60/40 split between stocks and bonds, so the fund has a bit more equity exposure than its typical domestic-hybrid rival, which stashes less than 55% of assets in stocks. In 2001, that has been a disadvantage, as equities have underperformed bonds. Moreover, because the fund's equity stake tracks a broad-based benchmark, the Wilshire 5000 index of regularly traded U.S. stocks, it has considerable exposure to growth issues, including Cisco Systems, that have performed poorly in 2001. By contrast, its average peer tilts more toward value.

Even so, the fund has managed to top most of its peers so far in 2001. For the year to date through Dec. 7, 2001, the fund's 3.2% loss is better than nearly 60% of its rivals'. The fund's bond portfolio has given it an advantage this year. On the bond side of the fund, comanager Ian MacKinnon tracks the Lehman Brothers Aggregate index of investment-grade issues. High-quality debt has performed better than junk issues, which some of its rivals own, giving this offering an advantage. And of course, the fund's rock-bottom expense ratio of 0.22% has continued to give it an advantage. Indeed, if this fund had average expenses, it would be in the bottom half of the category for the year to date.

The fund's low-cost, low-turnover strategy also continues to be the source of its long-term edge over its rivals. Over the trailing five years, the fund has beaten more than three fourths of the category, and it has outpaced 85% of them after taxes. For a broadly diversified fund with a terrific record and high tax efficiency, this fund is an excellent choice.

Portfolio Analysis 09-30-01

Total Stocks: 3245 Share change since 06-01	Sector	PE Ratio	YTD Return %	% Net Assets
⊕ General Elec	Industrials	30.1	–15.00	1.78
⊕ Microsoft	Technology	57.6	52.78	1.54
⊕ ExxonMobil	Energy	15.3	–7.59	1.34
⊕ Pfizer	Health	34.7	–12.40	1.31
⊕ Wal-Mart Stores	Retail	40.3	8.94	1.13
⊕ Citigroup	Financials	20.0	0.03	1.13
⊕ American Intl Grp	Financials	42.0	–19.20	1.02
⊕ IBM	Technology	26.9	43.00	0.93
⊕ Johnson & Johnson	Health	16.6	14.01	0.86
⊕ Intel	Technology	73.1	4.89	0.81

Total Fixed-Income: 1697	Date of Maturity	Amount $000	Value $000	% Net Assets
FHLMC 6.5%	08-01-29	34,358	35,431	0.92
US Treasury Bond 10.75%	02-15-03	28,350	31,435	0.81
FNMA 6.5%	11-01-29	27,297	28,120	0.73
US Treasury Bond 11.625%	11-15-02	22,250	24,432	0.63
FNMA 7.5%	12-01-30	20,796	21,811	0.56
GNMA 6.5%	08-15-29	20,305	20,987	0.54
FNMA FRN	08-01-31	19,303	19,895	0.51
US Treasury Bond 6.625%	02-15-27	15,145	18,527	0.48
US Treasury Note 6.5%	02-15-10	15,775	18,288	0.47
US Treasury Bond 7.625%	11-15-22	13,050	17,372	0.45

Equity Style
Style: Blend
Size: Large-Cap

	Portfolio Avg	Rel S&P
Price/Earnings Ratio	29.9	0.97
Price/Book Ratio	5.4	0.95
Price/Cash Flow	18.0	1.00
3 Yr Earnings Growth	15.8	1.08
1 Yr Earnings Est%	0.3	—
Debt % Total Cap	31.5	1.02
Med Mkt Cap $mil	36,764	0.61

Fixed-Income Style
Duration: —
Quality: —
NA

Avg Eff Duration	—
Avg Eff Maturity	—
Avg Credit Quality	AA
Avg Wtd Coupon	7.22%

Special Securities % assets 09-30-01	
Restricted/Illiquid Secs	1
Emerging-Markets Secs	Trace
Options/Futures/Warrants	Yes

Composition % of assets 09-30-01	
Cash	1.8
Stocks*	56.0
Bonds	42.1
Other	0.0
*Foreign (% of stocks)	0.2

Market Cap	
Giant	45.6
Large	27.4
Medium	18.6
Small	6.9
Micro	1.6

Sector Weightings	% of Stocks	Rel S&P	5-Year High	5-Year Low
Utilities	3.2	1.0	7	2
Energy	5.9	0.8	8	4
Financials	20.2	1.1	21	13
Industrials	10.1	0.9	17	9
Durables	1.7	1.1	5	2
Staples	6.9	0.9	10	4
Services	12.9	1.2	17	13
Retail	6.4	0.9	8	5
Health	14.7	1.0	15	9
Technology	18.1	1.0	35	8

Address:	Vanguard Financial Ctr. P.O. Box 2600 Valley Forge, PA 19482 800–662–7447 / 610–669–1000
Web Address:	www.vanguard.com
*Inception:	09-28-92
Advisor:	Vanguard Grp.
Subadvisor:	None
NTF Plans:	N/A

Minimum Purchase:	$3000	Add: $100 IRA: $1000
Min Auto Inv Plan:	$3000	Add: $100
Sales Fees:	No-load	
Management Fee:	.17%	
Actual Fees:	Mgt: 0.20%	Dist: —
Expense Projections:	3Yr: $71	5Yr: $124 10Yr: $280
Avg Brok Commission:	—	Income Distrib: Quarterly
Total Cost (relative to category):		Low

Vanguard Calvert Social Index

Ticker	Load	NAV	Yield	Total Assets	Mstar Category
VCSIX	None	$7.76	0.6%	$98.7 mil	Large Blend

Prospectus Objective: Growth

Vanguard Calvert Social Index Fund seeks to track the performance of the Calvert Social index.

The fund employs a passive management strategy designed to replicate the performance of the Calvert Social index. It will normally invest at least 95% of assets in the stocks of the index. The index is comprised of large and mid-cap stocks that have been screened for certain social and environmental criteria by the index sponsor, which is independent of Vanguard. The fund may invest, to a limited extent, in derivatives that are not screened based on social or environmental criteria. The fund is non-diversified.

The fund offers Investor and Institutional shares.

Historical Profile

Return —
Risk —
Rating Not Rated

Investment Style
Equity
Average Stock %: 98% (2000), 100% (12-01)

▼ Manager Change
▽ Partial Manager Change

Fund Performance vs. Category Average
Quarterly Fund Return +/– Category Average
— Category Baseline

Performance Quartile (within Category)

Portfolio Manager(s)

George U. Sauter. Since 5-00. AB'76 Dartmouth C.; MBA'80 U. of Chicago. Other funds currently managed: Vanguard Small Cap Index, Vanguard Balanced Index, Vanguard Equity-Income.

1990	1991	1992	1993	1994	1995	1996	1997	1998	1999	2000	12-01	History
—	—	—	—	—	—	—	—	—	—	9.09	7.76	NAV
—	—	—	—	—	—	—	—	—	—	–8.98*	–14.08	Total Return %
—	—	—	—	—	—	—	—	—	—	–2.41*	–2.21	+/– S&P 500
—	—	—	—	—	—	—	—	—	—	—	–1.32	+/– Wilshire Top 750
—	—	—	—	—	—	—	—	—	—	0.30	0.55	Income Return %
—	—	—	—	—	—	—	—	—	—	–9.28	–14.63	Capital Return %
—	—	—	—	—	—	—	—	—	—	—	61	Total Rtn % Rank Cat
—	—	—	—	—	—	—	—	—	—	0.03	0.05	Income $
—	—	—	—	—	—	—	—	—	—	0.01	0.00	Capital Gains $
—	—	—	—	—	—	—	—	—	—	0.25	—	Expense Ratio %
—	—	—	—	—	—	—	—	—	—	0.98	—	Income Ratio %
—	—	—	—	—	—	—	—	—	—	3	—	Turnover Rate %
—	—	—	—	—	—	—	—	—	—	72.5	98.7	Net Assets $mil

Performance 12-31-01

	1st Qtr	2nd Qtr	3rd Qtr	4th Qtr	Total
1997	—	—	—	—	—
1998	—	—	—	—	—
1999	—	—	—	—	—
2000	—	—	–1.13	–12.97	–8.98 *
2001	–14.52	7.08	–17.43	13.68	–14.08

Trailing	Total Return%	+/– S&P 500	+/– Wil Top 750	% Rank All	% Rank Cat	Growth of $10,000
3 Mo	13.68	3.00	2.36	27	16	11,368
6 Mo	–6.13	–0.58	–0.34	69	54	9,387
1 Yr	–14.08	–2.21	–1.32	70	61	8,592
3 Yr Avg	—	—	—	—	—	—
5 Yr Avg	—	—	—	—	—	—
10 Yr Avg	—	—	—	—	—	—
15 Yr Avg	—	—	—	—	—	—

Tax Analysis	Tax-Adj Ret%	%Rank Cat	%Pretax Ret	%Rank Cat
3 Yr Avg	—	—	—	—
5 Yr Avg	—	—	—	—
10 Yr Avg	—	—	—	—

Potential Capital Gain Exposure: NMF

Risk Analysis

Time Period	Load-Adj Return %	Risk %Rank[1] All	Risk %Rank[1] Cat	Morningstar Return	Morningstar Risk	Morningstar Risk-Adj Rating
1 Yr	–14.08					
3 Yr	—	—	—	—	—	
5 Yr	—	—	—	—	—	
Incept	–13.85	—	—	—	—	

Average Historical Rating —

[1]1=low, 100=high

Category Rating (3 Yr)

Other Measures	Standard Index S&P 500	Best Fit Index
Alpha	—	—
Beta	—	—
R-Squared	—	—
Standard Deviation		—
Return Mean		—
Risk Sharpe Ratio		—

Portfolio Analysis 09-30-01

Share change since 06-01 Total Stocks: 626

Stock	Sector	PE	YTD Ret%	% Assets
⊕ Microsoft	Technology	57.6	52.78	5.08
⊖ Pfizer	Health	34.7	–12.40	5.02
⊕ American Intl Grp	Financials	42.0	–19.20	3.89
⊕ IBM	Technology	26.9	43.00	3.58
⊖ Johnson & Johnson	Health	16.6	14.01	3.31
⊕ Intel	Technology	73.1	4.89	3.12
⊖ Merck	Health	19.1	–35.90	2.79
⊖ AOL Time Warner	Technology	—	–7.76	2.52
⊕ SBC Comms	Services	18.4	–16.00	2.44
⊕ Cisco Sys	Technology	—	–52.60	2.34
⊖ Bank of America	Financials	16.7	42.73	1.80
⊖ Home Depot	Retail	42.9	12.07	1.69
⊖ Fannie Mae	Financials	16.2	–6.95	1.57
⊖ J.P. Morgan Chase & Co.	Financials	27.8	–17.40	1.33
⊖ BellSouth	Services	24.9	–5.09	1.32
☼ Wells Fargo	Financials	22.4	–20.20	1.28
⊖ Amgen	Health	52.8	–11.70	1.12
⊕ Oracle	Technology	32.1	–52.40	1.10
⊕ Dell Comp	Technology	61.8	55.87	1.05
⊖ Schering-Plough	Health	22.2	–35.90	1.03
⊖ Medtronic	Health	76.4	–14.70	0.92
⊕ Texas Instruments	Technology	87.5	–40.70	0.92
⊖ Freddie Mac	Financials	14.0	–3.87	0.90
⊕ Wachovia	Financials	—	23.13	0.76
⊖ Bank One	Financials	29.1	9.13	0.73

Current Investment Style

Style: Value Blnd Growth; Size: Large Med Small

	Stock Port Avg	Relative S&P 500 Current	Relative S&P 500 Hist	Rel Cat
Price/Earnings Ratio	33.8	1.09	—	1.11
Price/Book Ratio	6.1	1.06	—	1.10
Price/Cash Flow	21.7	1.21	—	1.18
3 Yr Earnings Growth	18.1	1.24	—	1.02
1 Yr Earnings Est%	–0.6	0.33	—	6.56
Med Mkt Cap $mil	47,646	0.8	—	0.91

[1]figure is based on 50% or less of stocks

Special Securities % assets 09-30-01	
Restricted/Illiquid Secs	0
Emerging-Markets Secs	Trace
Options/Futures/Warrants	No

Composition % assets 09-30-01	
Cash	0.0
Stocks*	100.0
Bonds	0.0
Other	0.0
*Foreign (% stocks)	0.2

Market Cap	
Giant	51.1
Large	28.4
Medium	19.1
Small	1.3
Micro	0.2

Sector Weightings	% of Stocks	Rel S&P	5-Year High	5-Year Low
Utilities	0.6	0.2	—	—
Energy	0.6	0.1	—	—
Financials	25.6	1.4	—	—
Industrials	2.5	0.2	—	—
Durables	0.9	0.6	—	—
Staples	2.9	0.4	—	—
Services	10.9	1.0	—	—
Retail	5.4	0.8	—	—
Health	19.0	1.3	—	—
Technology	31.7	1.7	—	—

Analysis by Catherine Hickey 12-12-01

This low-cost social index fund is a fine option for those who can handle its risks.

Vanguard Calvert Social Index Fund is often lumped with its competitor, TIAA-CREF Social Choice Equity Fund, as one of the cheapest socially responsible funds. That's understandable: Both offerings boast expense ratios of below 30 basis points.

But, although these two funds have similar expenses, this offering is quite different than the TIAA-CREF fund. For starters, this offering has more social screens than the TIAA-CREF fund. Calvert, the firm that does the screening for the index on which this fund is based, includes workplace diversity and product safety-screens that the TIAA-CREF offering does not. Further, the Vanguard fund allocates little to energy and industrial sectors—areas where the CREF offering devotes a bit more. All of this leads the Vanguard fund to lean toward the growth end of the sector spectrum.

This fund's fairly purist take on social investing makes it a strong low-cost option for those drawn to rigorous screening criteria. But it can pay for its lack of sector diversification, as it often has since its May 2000 launch. Tech and other growth stocks have been the market's least-loved issues in the last couple of years, and because the fund favors those areas, it has lagged the TIAA-CREF fund as well as the S&P 500 index. However, investors should expect this fund to outperform when tech and other growth stocks do well.

Investors who want a more mild-mannered social fund should check out TIAA-CREF Social Choice or Domini Social Equity; both offerings are more diversified across sectors and won't blow up if tech tanks. However, low expenses and the management of Gus Sauter make this offering appealing.

Address:	Vanguard Financial Ctr. P.O. Box 2600 Valley Forge, PA 19482 610-669-1000 / 800-662-7447
Web Address:	www.vanguard.com
*Inception:	05-08-00
Advisor:	Vanguard Grp.
Subadvisor:	None
NTF Plans:	N/A

Minimum Purchase:	$3000	Add: $100 IRA: $1000
Min Auto Inv Plan:	—	Add: —
Sales Fees:	No-load	
Management Fee:	.21%	
Actual Fees:	Mgt: 0.21%	Dist: —
Expense Projections:	3Yr: $80	5Yr: $141 10Yr: $318
Avg Brok Commission:	—	Income Distrib: Annually
Total Cost (relative to category):	—	

Vanguard Capital Opportunity

Ticker	Load	NAV	Yield	Total Assets	Mstar Category
VHCOX	None	$23.61	0.3%	$5,208.8 mil	Mid-Cap Blend

Prospectus Objective: Growth

Vanguard Capital Opportunity Fund seeks long-term total return.

The fund invests primarily in equities of small and mid-cap U.S. companies. It typically concentrates investments in as few as 25 to 50 stocks. To select investments, the advisor tries to find stocks with strong industry positions, excellent prospects for growth, superior return on equity, and talented management teams. The fund may short stocks up to 10% of assets. It may invest up to 15% of assets in foreign securities. The fund may also invest up to 10% in both convertibles and high-yield bonds.

The fund offers Admiral and Investor shares.

Historical Profile
Return: High
Risk: Above Avg
Rating: ★★★★★ Highest

Investment Style Equity — Average Stock %: 1995 86% · 1996 94% · 1997 93% · 1998 87% · 1999 85% · 2000 91% · 12-01 92%

▼ Manager Change
▽ Partial Manager Change

Fund Performance vs. Category Average
■ Quarterly Fund Return +/– Category Average
— Category Baseline

Performance Quartile (within Category)

Portfolio Manager(s)

Theo A. Kolokotrones. Since 2-98. MBA Harvard U. Other funds currently managed: Vanguard Primecap, Vanguard Capital Opportunity Adm, Vanguard Primecap Adm.

Howard B. Schow. Since 2-98. BA Williams C.; MBA Harvard U. Other funds currently managed: Vanguard Primecap, Vanguard Capital Opportunity Adm, Vanguard Primecap Adm.

Joel P. Fried. Since 2-98. MBA U. of California. Other funds currently managed: Vanguard Primecap, Vanguard Capital Opportunity Adm, Vanguard Primecap Adm.

1990	1991	1992	1993	1994	1995	1996	1997	1998	1999	2000	12-01	History
—	—	—	—	—	9.82	11.13	10.20	12.49	24.02	26.22	23.61	NAV
—	—	—	—	—	–1.79*	13.41	–7.93	31.98	97.77	18.04	–9.68	Total Return %
—	—	—	—	—	–13.01*	–9.53	–41.28	3.41	76.73	27.14	2.20	+/– S&P 500
—	—	—	—	—	—	–5.77	–40.18	12.87	83.05	0.55	–9.08	+/– S&P Mid 400
—	—	—	—	—	0.30	0.07	0.40	0.15	0.28	0.67	0.27	Income Return %
—	—	—	—	—	–2.09	13.34	–8.34	31.84	97.49	17.37	–9.95	Capital Return %
—	—	—	—	—	—	89	99	1	3	16	71	Total Rtn % Rank Cat
—	—	—	—	—	0.03	0.01	0.05	0.02	0.04	0.16	0.07	Income $
—	—	—	—	—	0.00	0.00	0.00	0.90	0.59	1.92	0.00	Capital Gains $
—	—	—	—	—	0.47	0.50	0.49	0.94	0.75	0.62	—	Expense Ratio %
—	—	—	—	—	1.29	0.11	0.27	0.18	0.31	0.64	—	Income Ratio %
—	—	—	—	—	—	128	195	103	22	15	—	Turnover Rate %
—	—	—	—	—	81.0	117.4	63.4	206.5	2,366.6	5,533.8	4,845.7	Net Assets $mil

Performance 12-31-01

	1st Qtr	2nd Qtr	3rd Qtr	4th Qtr	Total
1997	–8.98	6.52	9.27	–13.09	–7.93
1998	12.84	2.61	–12.19	29.82	31.98
1999	7.29	20.97	10.73	37.61	97.77
2000	30.89	–0.54	0.80	–10.05	18.04
2001	–7.89	6.42	–23.85	21.01	–9.68

Trailing	Total Return%	+/– S&P 500	+/– S&P Mid 400	% Rank All	% Rank Cat	Growth of $10,000
3 Mo	21.01	10.33	3.03	12	15	12,101
6 Mo	–7.85	–2.30	–6.30	77	84	9,215
1 Yr	–9.68	2.20	–9.08	60	71	9,032
3 Yr Avg	28.23	29.26	17.99	1	1	21,085
5 Yr Avg	20.70	10.00	4.59	1	2	25,622
10 Yr Avg	—	—	—	—	—	—
15 Yr Avg	—	—	—	—	—	—

Tax Analysis	Tax-Adj Ret%	%Rank Cat	%Pretax Ret	%Rank Cat
3 Yr Avg	26.78	1	94.9	10
5 Yr Avg	19.27	1	93.1	7
10 Yr Avg	—	—	—	—

Potential Capital Gain Exposure: –27% of assets

Risk Analysis

Time Period	Load-Adj Return %	Risk %Rank[1] All	Risk %Rank[1] Cat	Morningstar Return	Morningstar Risk	Morningstar Risk-Adj Rating
1 Yr	–10.58					
3 Yr	27.80	70	62	5.98[2]	0.96	★★★★★
5 Yr	20.70	81	80	4.61[2]	1.15	★★★★★
Incept	17.85	—	—	—	—	

Average Historical Rating (41 months): 3.9★s

[1] 1=low, 100=high [2] T-Bill return substituted for category avg.

Category Rating (3 Yr)

1 2 3 4 5 — Worst … Best

Return: High
Risk: Average

Other Measures	Standard Index S&P 500	Best Fit Index Wil 4500
Alpha	33.3	26.6
Beta	1.16	0.87
R-Squared	51	78
Standard Deviation		35.70
Mean		28.23
Sharpe Ratio		0.73

Portfolio Analysis 09-30-01

Share change since 06-01 Total Stocks: 123

Share change	Stock	Sector	PE	YTD Ret%	% Assets
⊕	Pharmacia	Health	36.5	–29.30	5.57
	General Motors Cl H	Technology	42.9	–32.80	3.56
	Fedex	Services	29.3	29.83	3.10
⊕	Micron Tech	Technology	—	–12.60	3.01
	Motorola	Technology	—	–25.00	2.75
	Millipore	Industrials	63.9	–2.89	2.50
⊖	Sabre Hldgs Cl A	Services	73.0	–1.80	2.20
⊕	Symantec	Technology	—	98.74	2.13
	Thomas & Betts	Industrials	—	34.36	2.10
⊕	Novartis ADR	Health	22.3	–17.40	2.05
⊕	Microsoft	Technology	57.6	52.78	1.98
	MBIA	Financials	14.6	9.88	1.93
⊕	Phillips Petro	Energy	7.1	8.56	1.92
⊕	Biogen	Health	30.5	–4.52	1.90
	Murphy Oil	Energy	9.7	41.93	1.89
⊖	AMR	Services	—	–43.40	1.89
	Delta Air Lines	Services	—	–41.50	1.85
	ICOS	Health	—	10.59	1.76
⊕	Nortel Networks	Technology	—	–76.50	1.65
	Tommy Hilfiger	Retail	9.4	40.12	1.57
⊕	Concurrent Comp	Technology	—	176.20	1.53
	Atlantic Coast Air	Services	31.5	13.95	1.43
⊕	Union Pacific	Services	17.1	13.96	1.41
⊖	Best Buy	Retail	41.2	151.90	1.39
	Anadarko Petro	Energy	11.1	–19.70	1.36

Current Investment Style

Style: Value Blnd Growth; Size: Large Med Small

	Stock Port Avg	Relative S&P 500 Current	Relative S&P 500 Hist	Rel Cat
Price/Earnings Ratio	28.8	0.93	0.95	1.06
Price/Book Ratio	4.1	0.72	0.76	0.95
Price/Cash Flow	17.5	0.97	0.92	1.01
3 Yr Earnings Growth	20.3	1.39	1.18	1.22
1 Yr Earnings Est%	–5.5	3.11	—	–2.42
Med Mkt Cap $mil	6,328	0.1	0.1	0.70

Analysis by Scott Cooley 10-24-01

No one should be surprised—or alarmed—by Vanguard Capital Opportunity Fund's recent volatility.

If you're going to crush the major indexes over time, as this management team has, you have to be willing to take some chances. That's exactly what management did when it built an 11.5% stake in airlines. Unfortunately, that bet hurt the fund badly following the Sept. 11 terrorist attacks, as holdings such as AMR and Sabre Holdings declined sharply. That airline stake and the fund's above-average exposure to mostly faltering technology issues have crimped its returns in 2001. For the year to date through Oct. 23, the fund has dropped 19.8%, which lands it in the bottom quartile of the mid-cap blend group.

It's nevertheless worth keeping in mind that over time, most of management's significant wagers have paid off. Indeed, earlier this year this fund had put up solid relative returns, thanks to significant stakes in formerly out-of-favor areas such as retail. Management has made a lot of outstanding picks here during its tenure, which is reflected in a three-year annualized return of 31.7%—by far the category's best. Moreover, management has handily topped the S&P 500 over the past decade at large-blend Vanguard Primecap.

With that kind of record, it's easy to have confidence in management's recent moves. Although they have trimmed the airline stake, the managers have retained a lot of exposure to the industry, as they think several factors, including an economic recovery, could give it a boost. Tech would also gain from a recovery, they argue, and they still like the sector's long-term growth potential. And they have picked up a few energy issues, contending that the sector's recent sell-off is overdone.

Despite its recent problems, we think it would be a mistake for investors to sell this fund. This is still one of the best stock-pickers funds around.

Special Securities % assets 09-30-01	
Restricted/Illiquid Secs	0
Emerging-Markets Secs	0
Options/Futures/Warrants	No

Composition % assets 09-30-01	
Cash	10.3
Stocks*	89.8
Bonds	0.0
Other	0.0
*Foreign (% stocks)	6.2

Market Cap	
Giant	12.1
Large	32.0
Medium	35.3
Small	19.3
Micro	1.3

Sector Weightings	% of Stocks	Rel S&P	5-Year High	5-Year Low
Utilities	0.0	0.0	0	0
Energy	8.1	1.2	12	0
Financials	4.9	0.3	29	2
Industrials	10.4	0.9	16	0
Durables	0.6	0.4	8	0
Staples	0.4	0.1	8	0
Services	18.6	1.7	28	0
Retail	10.5	1.6	11	0
Health	15.3	1.0	22	3
Technology	31.3	1.7	59	27

Address:	Vanguard Financial Ctr. P.O. Box 2600 Valley Forge, PA 19482 800-662-7447 / 610-669-1000
Web Address:	www.vanguard.com
*Inception:	08-14-95
Advisor:	Primecap Mgmt.
Subadvisor:	None
NTF Plans:	N/A

Minimum Purchase:	$25000	Add: $100 IRA: $25000
Min Auto Inv Plan:	$25000	Add: $50
Sales Fees:	No-load, 1.00%R within 60 months	
Management Fee:	.50% mx./.15% mn.	
Actual Fees:	Mgt: 0.61%	Dist: —
Expense Projections:	3Yr: $312	5Yr: $346 10Yr: $774
Avg Brok Commission:	—	Income Distrib: Annually
Total Cost (relative to category):		Below Avg

Vanguard Developed Markets Index

Ticker	Load	NAV	Yield	Total Assets	Mstar Category
VDMIX	None	$6.95	1.7%	$188.6 mil	Foreign Stock

Prospectus Objective: Foreign Stock

Vanguard Developed Markets Index Fund seeks to track the performance of the MSCI EAFE index.

The fund normally invests in the Vanguard European Stock Index and Pacific Stock Index Funds. Vanguard European Stock Index Fund intends to track the MSCI Europe index while Pacific Stock Index Fund attempts to replicate the returns of the MSCI Pacific Free index; both MSCI indices comprise the MSCI EAFE index. It may invest in options, futures, and other derivative instruments.

Historical Profile
Return —
Risk —
Rating
Not Rated

Investment Style
Equity
Average Stock %: 99% (2000), 98% (12-01)

▼ Manager Change
▽ Partial Manager Change

Fund Performance vs. Category Average
▀ Quarterly Fund Return +/– Category Average
— Category Baseline

Performance Quartile (within Category)

Portfolio Manager(s)

George U. Sauter. Since 5-00. AB'76 Dartmouth C.; MBA'80 U. of Chicago. Other funds currently managed: Vanguard Small Cap Index, Vanguard Balanced Index, Vanguard Equity-Income.

1990	1991	1992	1993	1994	1995	1996	1997	1998	1999	2000	12-01	History
—	—	—	—	—	—	—	—	—	—	9.07	6.95	NAV
—	—	—	—	—	—	—	—	—	—	–7.79*	–22.05	Total Return %
—	—	—	—	—	—	—	—	—	—	–1.22*	–10.17	+/– S&P 500
—	—	—	—	—	—	—	—	—	—	—	—	+/– MSCI EAFE
—	—	—	—	—	—	—	—	—	—	1.52	1.32	Income Return %
—	—	—	—	—	—	—	—	—	—	–9.30	–23.37	Capital Return %
—	—	—	—	—	—	—	—	—	—	—	49	Total Rtn % Rank Cat
—	—	—	—	—	—	—	—	—	—	0.15	0.12	Income $
—	—	—	—	—	—	—	—	—	—	0.00	0.00	Capital Gains $
—	—	—	—	—	—	—	—	—	—	0.00	—	Expense Ratio %
—	—	—	—	—	—	—	—	—	—	1.66	—	Income Ratio %
—	—	—	—	—	—	—	—	—	—	8	—	Turnover Rate %
—	—	—	—	—	—	—	—	—	—	101.5	188.6	Net Assets $mil

Performance 12-31-01

	1st Qtr	2nd Qtr	3rd Qtr	4th Qtr	Total
1997	—	—	—	—	—
1998	—	—	—	—	—
1999	—	—	—	—	—
2000	—	—	–8.12	–2.93	–7.79*
2001	–13.78	–1.02	–13.95	6.16	–22.05

Trailing	Total Return%	+/– S&P 500	+/– MSCI EAFE	% Rank All	% Rank Cat	Growth of $10,000
3 Mo	6.16	–4.52	—	60	74	10,616
6 Mo	–8.65	–3.09	—	81	47	9,135
1 Yr	–22.05	–10.17	—	83	49	7,796
3 Yr Avg	—	—	—	—	—	—
5 Yr Avg	—	—	—	—	—	—
10 Yr Avg	—	—	—	—	—	—
15 Yr Avg	—	—	—	—	—	—

Tax Analysis	Tax-Adj Ret%	%Rank Cat	%Pretax Ret	%Rank Cat
3 Yr Avg	—	—	—	—
5 Yr Avg	—	—	—	—
10 Yr Avg	—	—	—	—

Potential Capital Gain Exposure: NMF

Risk Analysis

Time Period	Load-Adj Return %	Risk %Rank[1] All	Risk %Rank[1] Cat	Morningstar Return	Morningstar Risk	Morningstar Risk-Adj Rating
1 Yr	–22.05					
3 Yr	—	—	—	—	—	
5 Yr	—	—	—	—	—	
Incept	–18.14	—	—	—	—	

Average Historical Rating —

[1]1=low, 100=high

Category Rating (3 Yr)

Other Measures	Standard Index S&P 500	Best Fit Index
Alpha	—	—
Beta	—	—
R-Squared	—	—
Standard Deviation		—
Mean		—
Sharpe Ratio		—

Return
Risk

Portfolio Analysis 09-30-01

Share change since 06-01 Total Stocks: 2	Sector	Country	% Assets
⊕ Vanguard European Stock Index	N/A	N/A	71.30
⊕ Vanguard Pacific Stock Index	N/A	N/A	28.70

Analysis by Gabriel Presler 10-11-01

After a tumultuous infancy, Vanguard Developed Markets Index Fund is facing a few changes—from without, not within.

Like other index offerings that invest overseas, this fund is going to have to make some adjustments in the next few months. The folks who build the Morgan Stanley Composite Indices—the foreign-stock group's most popular benchmarks—are altering their methodology. They'll no longer weight stocks based on market cap; instead, they'll determine allocation according to how many shares are available on the market, thus adjusting for closely held companies and cross holdings, both of which are more prevalent abroad than in the U.S. This means the benchmark will reflect the universe that real, live investors face.

It also means that manager Gus Sauter is likely to pick up his trading pace a bit in the months before May 2002, when the change will be complete. Sauter expects the annual turnover rate to increase to approximately 20%, which is still quite low by category standards. Increased trading isn't the only change investors will see though: Because cross holding is common in Japan, the fund's stake in that country is likely to decline slightly, while its European exposure is likely to increase.

Such a change should only increase this fund's appeal. The fund's exposure to Japan has often hurt it in relation to rivals, many of which underweight that struggling market. Even with a hefty Japan stake, the fund's performance—while grim on an absolute basis—has been stronger than average. Indeed, its loss of more than 25% in the trailing 12-month period ending Oct. 9, 2001, looks better than two thirds of its foreign-stock peers. This relative resilience is due in large part to its neglect of emerging markets, which have suffered a bit more than their developed-market counterparts over the past year.

Current Investment Style	Stock Port Avg	Rel MSCI EAFE Current	Rel MSCI EAFE Hist	Rel Cat
Price/Earnings Ratio	23.5	0.91	—	0.92
Price/Cash Flow	13.6	1.06	—	0.94
Price/Book Ratio	3.6	1.02	—	0.91
3 Yr Earnings Growth	19.0	1.01	—	0.97
Med Mkt Cap $mil	38,724	1.4	—	2.15

Style: Value Blnd Growth; Size: Large Med Small

Country Exposure % assets

Hedging History: —

Regional Exposure 09-30-01	% assets
Europe	77
Pacific Rim	7
Latin America	0
Japan	23
Other	1

Special Securities % assets
Restricted/Illiquid Secs
Emerging-Markets Secs
Options/Futures/Warrants

Composition % assets 09-30-01

Cash	1.3	Bonds	0.0
Stocks	98.4	Other	0.3

Sector Weightings	% of Stocks	Rel Cat	5-Year High	5-Year Low
Utilities	4.2	1.5	—	—
Energy	7.8	1.3	—	—
Financials	23.5	1.1	—	—
Industrials	11.1	0.8	—	—
Durables	7.6	1.1	—	—
Staples	6.4	0.9	—	—
Services	15.1	0.9	—	—
Retail	4.2	0.9	—	—
Health	8.6	0.9	—	—
Technology	11.4	1.1	—	—

Address: Vanguard Financial Ctr. P.O. Box 2600, Valley Forge, PA 19482, 610–669–1000 / 800–662–7447
Web Address: www.vanguard.com
*Inception: 05-08-00
Advisor: Vanguard Grp.
Subadvisor: None
NTF Plans: N/A

Minimum Purchase: $3000 — Add: $100 — IRA: $1000
Min Auto Inv Plan: $3000 — Add: $50
Sales Fees: No-load
Management Fee: .31%
Actual Fees: Mgt: 0.00% — Dist: —
Expense Projections: 3Yr: $103 — 5Yr: $180 — 10Yr: $406
Avg Brok Commission: — — Income Distrib: Annually
Total Cost (relative to category): —

Vanguard Emerging Mkts Stock Idx

Ticker	Load	NAV	Yield	Total Assets	Mstar Category
VEIEX	None	$8.37	2.5%	$884.1 mil	Div Emerging Mkts

Prospectus Objective: Diversified Emg Markets—Stock

Vanguard Emerging Markets Stock Index Fund seeks to match the performance of the Select Emerging Markets Free Index.

The fund employs a passively managed investment approach by investing all or substantially all of its assets in a representative sample of the common stocks included in the Selected Emerging Markets Free Index. This index includes approximately 500 commons stocks of companies located in emerging markets around the world.

The fund currently offers Investor and Institutional shares. Prior to Oct. 27, 1998, the fund was named Vanguard International Equity Index Fund Emerging Markets Portfolio.

Historical Profile

Return Average
Risk Above Avg
Rating ★★★ Neutral

Investment Style
Equity
Average Stock %

1996	1997	1998	1999	2000	12-01
86%	83%	84%	91%	95%	94%

▼ Manager Change
▽ Partial Manager Change

Fund Performance vs. Category Average
■ Quarterly Fund Return +/– Category Average
— Category Baseline

Performance Quartile (within Category)

Portfolio Manager(s)

George U. Sauter. Since 5-94. AB'76 Dartmouth C.; MBA'80 U. of Chicago. Other funds currently managed: Vanguard Small Cap Index, Vanguard Balanced Index, Vanguard Equity-Income.

1990	1991	1992	1993	1994	1995	1996	1997	1998	1999	2000	12-01	History
—	—	—	—	10.87	10.75	12.28	9.98	7.91	12.50	8.84	8.37	NAV
—	—	—	—	9.81*	0.56	15.83	–16.82	–18.12	61.57	–27.56	–2.88	Total Return %
—	—	—	—	6.03*	–36.98	–7.12	–50.18	–46.70	40.53	–18.46	9.00	+/– S&P 500
—	—	—	—	—	11.31	11.69	–1.71	7.18	–4.61	2.44	—	+/– MSCI Emerging
—	—	—	—	0.69	1.66	1.58	1.87	2.61	3.41	1.75	2.38	Income Return %
—	—	—	—	9.12	–1.10	14.25	–18.70	–20.73	58.16	–29.30	–5.26	Capital Return %
—	—	—	—	—	36	29	91	9	72	26	38	Total Rtn % Rank Cat
—	—	—	—	0.07	0.18	0.17	0.23	0.26	0.27	0.22	0.21	Income $
—	—	—	—	0.04	0.00	0.00	0.00	0.00	0.00	0.00	0.00	Capital Gains $
—	—	—	—	0.60	0.60	0.60	0.57	0.61	0.58	0.59	—	Expense Ratio %
—	—	—	—	1.32	2.00	1.69	1.96	2.99	2.55	1.51	—	Income Ratio %
—	—	—	—	—	3	1	19	22	22	40	—	Turnover Rate %
—	—	—	—	83.4	234.3	637.1	680.9	577.0	1,137.6	1,019.1	801.3	Net Assets $mil

Performance 12-31-01

	1st Qtr	2nd Qtr	3rd Qtr	4th Qtr	Total
1997	4.89	6.83	–9.30	–18.16	–16.82
1998	6.61	–21.52	–17.72	18.94	–18.12
1999	10.87	19.38	–4.87	28.32	61.57
2000	–2.40	–6.97	–9.61	–11.72	–27.56
2001	–8.60	8.55	–22.03	25.55	–2.88

Trailing	Total Return%	+/– S&P 500	+/– MSCI Emerging	% Rank All	% Rank Cat	Growth of $10,000
3 Mo	25.55	14.87	—	7	37	12,555
6 Mo	–2.11	3.44	—	47	38	9,789
1 Yr	–2.88	9.00	—	47	38	9,712
3 Yr Avg	4.37	5.39	—	36	44	11,368
5 Yr Avg	–4.99	–15.69	—	97	51	7,742
10 Yr Avg	—	—	—	—	—	—
15 Yr Avg	—	—	—	—	—	—

Tax Analysis	Tax-Adj Ret%	%Rank Cat	%Pretax Ret	%Rank Cat
3 Yr Avg	3.39	55	77.7	96
5 Yr Avg	–5.93	59	—	—
10 Yr Avg	—	—	—	—

Potential Capital Gain Exposure: –45% of assets

Risk Analysis

Time Period	Load-Adj Return %	Risk %Rank[1] All	Risk %Rank[1] Cat	Morningstar Return	Morningstar Risk	Morningstar Risk-Adj Rating
1 Yr	–3.85					
3 Yr	4.02	85	41	–0.12[2]	1.18	★★★★
5 Yr	–5.18	94	61	–1.81[2]	1.41	★★
Incept	–0.26	—	—	—	—	

Average Historical Rating (56 months): 2.1★s

[1] 1=low, 100=high [2] T-Bill return substituted for category avg.

Category Rating (3 Yr)

1 2 **3** 4 5
Worst Best

Return Average
Risk Average

Other Measures	Standard Index S&P 500	Best Fit Index MSCIPcxIND
Alpha	8.4	2.4
Beta	1.16	1.02
R-Squared	54	78
Standard Deviation		28.61
Mean		4.37
Sharpe Ratio		–0.02

Portfolio Analysis 09-30-01

Share change since 06-01 Total Stocks: 388	Sector	Country	% Assets
⊕ Samsung Electncs	Technology	South Korea	5.12
⊕ Anglo Amer Coal	Industrials	South Africa	4.20
⊕ Telefonos de Mex Cl L	Services	Mexico	4.16
⊕ SK Telecom	Services	South Korea	3.67
⊕ Korea Elec Pwr	Utilities	South Korea	2.19
⊕ Wal-Mart De Mexico SA	Retail	Mexico	2.14
⊕ Petrobras Pfd	Energy	Brazil	2.05
⊕ Teva Pharma Inds	Health	Israel	1.99
⊕ Vale do Rio Doce Pfd	Industrials	Brazil	1.89
☼ America Movil Cl L	N/A	N/A	1.87
⊕ Market Amer	Services	U.S.	1.78
⊕ Grupo Modelo Cl C	Staples	Mexico	1.73
⊕ Cemex (Part)	Industrials	Mexico	1.70
⊕ Anglo Amer Platinum SA	Industrials	South Africa	1.66
⊕ Check Point Software Tech	Technology	Israel	1.61
⊕ Grupo Fin Bancomer O	Financials	Mexico	1.57
⊕ Eletrobras	Utilities	Brazil	1.39
⊕ Sasol	Industrials	South Africa	1.35
Telefonos de Mex A ADR	Services	Mexico	1.21
⊕ South African Brew	Staples	South Africa	1.13

Current Investment Style

Style: Value Blnd Growth; Size: Large Med Small

	Stock Port Avg	Rel MSCI EAFE Current	Rel MSCI EAFE Hist	Rel Cat
Price/Earnings Ratio	16.1	0.62	0.68	0.93
Price/Cash Flow	8.9	0.69	0.85	0.89
Price/Book Ratio	2.9	0.84	0.74	0.92
3 Yr Earnings Growth	31.8	1.70	1.10	1.22
Med Mkt Cap $mil	5,453	0.2	0.2	1.30

Country Exposure 09-30-01	% assets
South Korea	21
South Africa	18
Mexico	18
Brazil	14
Israel	8

Hedging History: Never

Regional Exposure 09-30-01	% assets
Europe	5
Africa/Mid East	29
Pacific/Asia	28
Latin America	32
Other	2

Special Securities % assets 09-30-01	
Restricted/Illiquid Secs	0
Emerging-Markets Secs	94
Options/Futures/Warrants	No

Composition % assets 09-30-01

Cash	5.0	Bonds	0.7
Stocks	93.9	Other	0.4

Sector Weightings	% of Stocks	Rel Cat	5-Year High	5-Year Low
Utilities	7.1	1.1	12	5
Energy	4.1	0.6	7	0
Financials	17.9	0.9	34	18
Industrials	22.4	1.3	22	14
Durables	1.8	0.5	8	2
Staples	8.6	1.2	11	7
Services	19.6	1.1	26	18
Retail	4.9	1.6	5	1
Health	2.5	0.7	3	0
Technology	11.2	0.8	16	1

Analysis by Gabriel Presler 10-11-01

A few changes won't dim Vanguard Emerging Markets Stock Index's appeal for bargain-hunting investors.

Like other index offerings that invest in emerging markets, this fund has to make some adjustments in the next few months. The folks who build the Morgan Stanley Indices—one of the group's more-popular benchmarks—are altering their methodology. They'll no longer weight stocks based on market cap; instead, they'll determine allocations according to how many shares are available on the market, thus adjusting for closely held companies and inside ownership. The benchmark will reflect the universe that real, live investors face.

Manager Gus Sauter is likely to trade more before May 2002, when the change will be complete. Sauter expects the fund's annualized turnover rate to increase to approximately 20%, which is still quite low by category standards. Increased trading isn't the only change to expect: Because cross holding is uncommon in markets such as South Africa and Korea, exposure there is likely to increase.

Such shifts aren't likely to affect the fund's performance—at least not on a relative basis. First of all, the portfolio has rarely held meaningful positions in those countries scheduled for smaller roles in the index, such as Malaysia and India. What's more, many of the fund's rivals in this category have favored large, multinational firms—such as South Africa's Anglo American Platinum and Korea's Samsung Electronics—and have generally overweighted their exposure to both countries.

Performance here is generally respectable; the fund's 21% year-to-date loss through Oct. 10, 2001, is a bit better than average, thanks largely to exposure to the group's stronger markets, such as Korea and Mexico. But with its lackluster longer-term record, the real appeal is in its unchanging bargain-basement price, which will attract those looking for a cheap ticket to the developing world.

Address:	Vanguard Financial Ctr. P.O. Box 2600 Valley Forge, PA 19482 610-669-1000 / 800-662-7447
Web Address:	www.vanguard.com
*Inception:	05-04-94
Advisor:	Vanguard Core Mgmt. Grp.
Subadvisor:	None
NTF Plans:	N/A

Minimum Purchase:	$3000	Add: $100	IRA: $1000
Min Auto Inv Plan:	$3000	Add: $100	
Sales Fees:	No-load, 1.00%R		
Management Fee:	.32%		
Actual Fees:	Mgt: 0.35%	Dist: —	
Expense Projections:	3Yr: $295	5Yr: $439	10Yr: $861
Avg Brok Commission:	—	Income Distrib: Annually	
Total Cost (relative to category):		Low	

Vanguard Energy

Ticker	Load	NAV	Yield	Total Assets	Mstar Category
VGENX	None	$25.29	1.5%	$1,336.4 mil	Spec Natural Resources

Prospectus Objective: Specialty—Natural Resources

Vanguard Energy Fund seeks long-term growth of capital.

The fund normally invests at least 80% of assets in equity securities of traditional or emerging companies engaged in energy-related activities. These companies may be involved in the production, transmission, marketing, control, or measurement of energy or energy fuels. The fund may not invest in electric-utility companies, though it may invest in natural-gas distributors and pipelines. It may invest up to 30% of assets in foreign securities.

The fund levies a 1% redemption fee within 12 months; this fee is paid to the portfolio. The fund also offers Adm shares. Prior to Oct. 27, 1998, the fund was named Vanguard Specialized Portfolios - Energy. The fund offers Admiral and Investor shares.

Historical Profile

Return Above Avg
Risk Above Avg
Rating ★★★ Neutral

Investment Style
Equity
Average Stock %: 93% 93% 95% 95% 95% 94%

▼ Manager Change
▽ Partial Manager Change

Fund Performance vs. Category Average
■ Quarterly Fund Return +/– Category Average
— Category Baseline

Performance Quartile (within Category)

Portfolio Manager(s)

Ernst H. von Metzsch, CFA. Since 5-84. MA U. of Leiden, Holland; PhD Harvard U. Other funds currently managed: Vanguard Wellington, Vanguard Wellington Adm, Vanguard Energy Adm.

History

1990	1991	1992	1993	1994	1995	1996	1997	1998	1999	2000	12-01	History
13.84	13.03	13.29	15.06	14.29	17.31	22.54	24.14	18.42	21.92	28.07	25.29	NAV
–1.37	0.28	6.18	26.42	–1.63	25.32	34.00	14.89	–20.53	20.98	36.43	–2.55	Total Return %
1.75	–30.20	–1.44	16.37	–2.94	–12.22	11.05	–18.46	–49.10	–0.06	45.54	9.33	+/– S&P 500
4.82	–33.92	–2.79	15.14	–1.56	–11.13	12.80	–16.41	–43.96	–2.58	47.37	8.34	+/– Wilshire 5000
3.01	3.07	2.77	2.18	1.60	1.96	1.39	1.43	1.45	1.93	1.64	1.43	Income Return %
–4.38	–2.79	3.41	24.24	–3.23	23.36	32.61	13.46	–21.98	19.05	34.79	–3.97	Capital Return %
14	68	37	23	38	20	42	14	47	74	32	13	Total Rtn % Rank Cat
0.46	0.42	0.36	0.29	0.24	0.28	0.24	0.32	0.35	0.36	0.36	0.40	Income $
0.88	0.42	0.18	1.38	0.29	0.30	0.40	1.33	0.42	0.00	1.38	1.54	Capital Gains $
0.38	0.35	0.30	0.21	0.17	0.30	0.48	0.39	0.38	0.38	0.47	—	Expense Ratio %
3.05	3.24	2.78	2.47	1.87	1.66	1.55	1.36	1.36	1.36	1.63	—	Income Ratio %
44	40	42	37	41	13	21	15	19	19	18	—	Turnover Rate %
119.4	116.3	155.7	269.6	445.5	506.4	847.9	1,181.4	819.9	1,018.2	1,280.8	1,281.6	Net Assets $mil

Performance 12-31-01

	1st Qtr	2nd Qtr	3rd Qtr	4th Qtr	Total
1997	–4.14	11.37	16.13	–7.32	14.89
1998	4.80	–5.59	–14.20	–6.39	–20.53
1999	8.20	15.36	–1.22	–1.88	20.98
2000	12.14	6.68	8.48	5.13	36.43
2001	–2.32	–0.29	–11.27	12.76	–2.55

Trailing	Total Return%	+/– S&P 500	+/– Wil 5000	% Rank All	% Rank Cat	Growth of $10,000
3 Mo	12.76	2.07	0.38	30	40	11,276
6 Mo	0.05	5.61	5.54	39	5	10,005
1 Yr	–2.55	9.33	8.34	46	13	9,745
3 Yr Avg	17.17	18.19	17.82	3	27	16,085
5 Yr Avg	7.99	–2.71	–1.72	29	11	14,686
10 Yr Avg	12.53	–0.40	0.25	15	6	32,566
15 Yr Avg	12.63	–1.11	–0.37	20	1	59,521

Tax Analysis	Tax-Adj Ret%	%Rank Cat	%Pretax Ret	%Rank Cat
3 Yr Avg	15.60	35	90.9	75
5 Yr Avg	6.31	9	79.0	28
10 Yr Avg	10.73	12	85.6	53

Potential Capital Gain Exposure: 27% of assets

Risk Analysis

Time Period	Load-Adj Return %	Risk %Rank[1] All	Risk %Rank[1] Cat	Morningstar Return	Morningstar Risk	Morningstar Risk-Adj Rating
1 Yr	–2.55					
3 Yr	17.17	63	16	2.91[2]	0.89	★★★★★
5 Yr	7.99	82	27	0.68[2]	1.16	★★★
10 Yr	12.53	88	40	1.21	1.28	★★★

Average Historical Rating (176 months): 2.7★s

[1]1=low, 100=high [2] T-Bill return substituted for category avg.

Category Rating (3 Yr)

Worst ① ② ③ ④ ⑤ Best

Return Above Avg
Risk Below Avg

Other Measures	Standard Index S&P 500	Best Fit Index SPMid400
Alpha	18.2	9.4
Beta	0.64	0.74
R-Squared	19	33

Standard Deviation	29.74
Mean	17.17
Sharpe Ratio	0.47

Analysis by Scott Cooley 12-28-01

Vanguard Energy Fund's stability was yet again a great asset in 2001.

Manager Ernst von Metzsch spreads his bets across energy subsectors and currently places about twice as much as his rivals in integrated oil firms. Indeed, behemoths such as BP, ChevronTexaco, and ExxonMobil occupy prominent positions in the portfolio. The integrated giants, which typically do everything from exploration to marketing gas and other products, are somewhat less affected by changes in oil prices than smaller firms.

That positioning was a plus for the fund in 2001. With the global economy slowing faster than OPEC could cut oil output, oil prices fell sharply. Natural-gas prices also took a tumble after running up dramatically last year. But although many oil-services companies posted dramatic, double-digit losses, the large, integrated firms provided considerable stability to the portfolio. Indeed, the fund's top-two holdings, ChevronTexaco and Phillips Petroleum, both posted significant gains in 2001. For the year to date through Dec. 27, 2001, the fund lost just 2.9%. Meanwhile, its average specialty-natural resources rival declined 11.3% during that period.

Von Metzsch has also steered the fund to a solid long-term gain. The fund's trailing five- and 10-year returns land comfortably within the category's top quintile. The valuation-conscious von Metzsch has made a number of well-timed, contrarian moves, including bulking up on oil-services firms in early 1999, when they were severely beaten-down. (He later tilted back toward integrated firms when he thought they offered better values.) The fund has also been fairly tax-efficient over time, as von Metzsch typically holds turnover to 20% or less.

The fund offers a solid record, a very experienced manager, and the group's lowest expense ratio. This is a great way for investors to invest in energy issues.

Portfolio Analysis 09-30-01

Share chng since 06–01 Total Stocks: 49	Subsector	PE	YTD Ret%	% Assets
ChevronTexaco	Major Oils	10.3	9.29	4.49
⊖ Phillips Petro	Major Oils	7.1	8.56	4.16
⊕ BP PLC ADR	Major Oils	14.4	–0.90	4.02
⊕ ExxonMobil	Major Oils	15.3	–7.59	3.94
Suncor Energy	Major Oils	58.1	29.23	3.68
⊕ Weatherford Intl	Energy Services	66.5	–21.10	3.42
Norsk Hydro ADR	Chemicals	23.7	–0.15	3.37
Equitable Resources	Expl. & Prod.	14.8	3.98	3.36
⊕ Noble Drilling	Energy Services	18.3	–21.60	3.35
Total Fina Elf ADR	Major Oils	15.5	–1.76	3.24
Schlumberger	Energy Services	55.0	–30.30	3.22
Unocal	Major Oils	10.9	–4.58	3.22
⊕ EOG Resources	Expl. & Prod.	8.1	–28.10	3.15
⊖ Ashland	Major Oils	7.8	31.85	2.75
Baker Hughes	Energy	45.0	–11.10	2.62
Alberta Energy	Expl. & Prod.	43.9	–20.80	2.52
⊕ Anadarko Petro	Expl. & Prod.	11.1	–19.70	2.37
Sunoco	Major Oils	5.8	13.95	2.35
⊖ Shell Transp & Trad ADR	Major Oils	13.7	–13.80	2.22
ENI ADR	Energy	18.5	–1.58	2.15
⊖ Petro–Canada (Non–resident)	Energy	53.4	–2.64	2.14
Petrobras ADR	Energy	—	—	2.11
USX–Marathon Grp	Major Oils	9.6	11.58	1.95
⊖ Occidental Petro	Major Oils	5.7	13.49	1.90
Burlington Resources	Expl. & Prod.	8.4	–24.60	1.87

Current Investment Style

Style: Value Blnd Growth; Size: Large Med Small

	Stock Port Avg	Relative S&P 500 Current	Relative S&P 500 Hist	Rel Cat
Price/Earnings Ratio	20.7	0.67	0.85	0.97
Price/Book Ratio	2.5	0.44	0.35	1.00
Price/Cash Flow	8.7	0.48	0.48	0.85
3 Yr Earnings Growth	11.7	0.80	0.53	0.83
1 Yr Earnings Est%	17.0	—	—	5.99
Med Mkt Cap $mil	8,455	0.1	0.1	0.77

Special Securities % assets 09-30-01	
Restricted/Illiquid Secs	Trace
Emerging–Markets Secs	3
Options/Futures/Warrants	No

Composition % assets 09-30-01	
Cash	7.0
Stocks*	93.1
Bonds	0.0
Other	0.0
*Foreign (% stocks)	33.3

Market Cap	
Giant	22.6
Large	21.3
Medium	53.5
Small	2.7
Micro	0.0

Subsector Weightings	% of Stocks	Rel Cat
Major Oils	46.0	1.9
Energy Services	16.9	1.0
Expl. & Prod.	17.5	1.2
Nat. Gas Dist.	0.0	0.0
Chemicals	3.4	1.1
Paper/Forest	0.0	0.0
Metals	0.0	0.0
Mining	0.0	0.0
Other	16.2	0.6

Address:	Vanguard Financial Ctr. P.O. Box 2600 Valley Forge, PA 19482 800–662–7447 / 610–669–1000
Web Address:	www.vanguard.com
Inception:	05-23-84
Advisor:	Wellington Mgmt.
Subadvisor:	None
NTF Plans:	N/A

Minimum Purchase:	$3000	Add: $100 IRA: $1000
Min Auto Inv Plan:	$3000	Add: $50
Sales Fees:	No–load, 1.00%R within 12 months	
Management Fee:	.15% mx./.05% mn.	
Actual Fees:	Mgt: 0.06%	Dist: —
Expense Projections:	3Yr: $154	5Yr: $269 10Yr: $604
Avg Brok Commission:	—	Income Distrib: Annually
Total Cost (relative to category):		Low

Vanguard Equity–Income

Ticker	Load	NAV	Yield	Total Assets	Mstar Category
VEIPX	None	$22.71	2.2%	$2,491.4 mil	Large Value

Prospectus Objective: Equity–Income

Vanguard Equity-Income Fund seeks current income; capital appreciation potential is also considered.

The fund normally invests at least 80% of assets in dividend-paying equity securities. The average income yield of the portfolio is expected to be at least 50% greater than that of the S&P 500 index. Management expects the fund to demonstrate less price volatility than the S&P 500. The fund may invest the balance of assets in cash and fixed-income securities; this portion consists primarily of higher-grade debt securities.

The fund also offers Adm shares.

Historical Profile

Return: Above Avg
Risk: Below Avg
Rating: ★★★★ Above Avg

Investment Style
Equity
Average Stock %: 91% 91% 94% 92% 92% 93%

▼ Manager Change
▽ Partial Manager Change

Fund Performance vs. Category Average
Quarterly Fund Return +/– Category Average
— Category Baseline

Performance Quartile (within Category)

Portfolio Manager(s)

Roger D. Newell. Since 3-88.
John A. Levin. Since 1-98.
George U. Sauter. Since 1-99.
Jennifer C. Newell, CFA. Since 12-93.
John R. Ryan, CFA. Since 1-00.
Daniel Theriault. Since 1-01.
Joseph A. Austin. Since 1-01.
John (Jack) W. Murphy. Since 1-01.

1990	1991	1992	1993	1994	1995	1996	1997	1998	1999	2000	12-01	History
10.54	12.40	12.92	13.66	12.77	16.69	18.32	22.39	24.73	23.17	24.44	22.71	NAV
–11.92	25.38	9.18	14.65	–1.59	37.34	17.39	31.17	17.34	–0.19	13.57	–2.34	Total Return %
–8.80	–5.10	1.56	4.59	–2.91	–0.20	–5.56	–2.18	–11.24	–21.23	22.68	9.53	+/– S&P 500
–8.25	7.23	0.11	–5.11	0.72	–2.69	–4.93	–4.32	–3.90	–11.14	11.26	6.45	+/– Russ Top 200 Val
5.79	6.29	4.84	4.80	4.32	4.77	3.89	3.70	2.89	2.65	2.66	2.10	Income Return %
–17.71	19.09	4.33	9.85	–5.91	32.57	13.50	27.47	14.45	–2.84	10.91	–4.45	Capital Return %
85	62	54	43	65	13	78	19	23	79	19	30	Total Rtn % Rank Cat
0.73	0.65	0.59	0.61	0.58	0.60	0.64	0.67	0.64	0.65	0.61	0.51	Income $
0.07	0.10	0.00	0.52	0.09	0.17	0.58	0.89	0.83	0.87	1.14	0.60	Capital Gains $
0.48	0.46	0.44	0.40	0.43	0.45	0.42	0.45	0.39	0.41	0.43	—	Expense Ratio %
5.67	5.52	4.74	4.39	4.41	4.27	3.69	3.25	2.80	2.59	2.59	—	Income Ratio %
5	9	13	15	18	31	21	22	23	18	36	—	Turnover Rate %
398.9	569.8	835.8	1,067.9	859.0	1,102.8	1,425.0	2,099.7	2,938.5	2,874.1	2,560.2	2,249.9	Net Assets $mil

Performance 12-31-01

	1st Qtr	2nd Qtr	3rd Qtr	4th Qtr	Total
1997	2.92	12.23	7.43	5.70	31.17
1998	10.90	–1.26	–5.37	13.23	17.34
1999	–1.21	9.82	–8.37	0.41	–0.19
2000	–1.54	0.12	7.37	7.30	13.57
2001	–4.97	3.68	–6.18	5.64	–2.35

Trailing	Total Return%	+/– S&P 500	+/– Russ Top 200 Val	% Rank All	% Rank Cat	Growth of $10,000
3 Mo	5.64	–5.04	0.13	63	91	10,564
6 Mo	–0.88	4.67	4.89	42	13	9,912
1 Yr	–2.34	9.53	6.45	46	30	9,766
3 Yr Avg	3.45	4.47	2.28	49	35	11,070
5 Yr Avg	11.25	0.55	0.04	13	25	17,038
10 Yr Avg	12.96	0.04	–1.07	13	33	33,835
15 Yr Avg	—	—	—	—	—	—

Tax Analysis	Tax-Adj Ret%	%Rank Cat	%Pretax Ret	%Rank Cat
3 Yr Avg	1.60	38	46.3	73
5 Yr Avg	9.15	21	81.4	27
10 Yr Avg	10.73	26	82.8	22

Potential Capital Gain Exposure: 32% of assets

Risk Analysis

Time Period	Load-Adj Return %	Risk %Rank[1] All	Risk %Rank[1] Cat	Morningstar Return	Morningstar Risk	Morningstar Risk-Adj Rating
1 Yr	–2.34					
3 Yr	3.45	46	15	–0.31[2]	0.65	★★★
5 Yr	11.25	48	9	1.53[2]	0.65	★★★★
10 Yr	12.96	53	11	1.31	0.66	★★★★

Average Historical Rating (130 months): 3.3★s

[1]1=low, 100=high [2] T-Bill return substituted for category avg.

Category Rating (3 Yr)

Worst 1 2 3 4 5 Best

Return: Average
Risk: Below Avg

Other Measures	Standard Index S&P 500	Best Fit Index S&P 500
Alpha	1.6	1.6
Beta	0.48	0.48
R–Squared	37	37
Standard Deviation		13.82
Mean		3.45
Sharpe Ratio		–0.13

Analysis by William Harding 10-16-01

Vanguard Equity-Income Fund is a solid choice for conservative investors.

A good defense has been key to this fund's strong showing of late. The fund's modest 5% loss for the year to date ended Oct. 15, 2001, bests the S&P 500 by 11 percentage points and outpaces more than 80% of its large-value peers. Management owns cheap stocks with high dividend yields, scooping up names when they are out of favor. This line of attack steers the fund clear of highfliers that are vulnerable to severe corrections and leads it to favor defensive sectors of the market that hold up well during trying times. For instance, longtime holdings in food and tobacco stocks have been among its best performers this year as investors moved into these traditionally defensive areas amid the economic slump.

Management's willingness to buy unloved names and its patience (the fund's turnover is only about 36%) have resulted in solid returns over the long haul as well. The fund will tend to lag during growth rallies, but it has returned nearly 12.9% annually over the trailing 10 years. That showing outpaces the S&P 500 index by a slight margin and lands in the large-value category's top quartile. Not surprisingly, the fund's volatility has been below average relative to the index and its peers over that time.

This attractive risk/return profile owes in large part to characteristics that can't be easily duplicated by other funds. The fund's assets are split among three veteran subadvisors who are closely monitored by Vanguard's savvy portfolio review group. This structure allows each subadvisor to take meaningful positions in their picks while still keeping the aggregate portfolio well diversified across industries and names.

With its low expenses, sturdy record, and experienced management, this fund deserves strong consideration from value investors.

Portfolio Analysis 09-30-01

Share change since 06-01 Total Stocks: 171

Holding	Sector	PE	YTD Ret%	% Assets
⊕ ExxonMobil	Energy	15.3	–7.59	3.72
⊖ Verizon Comms	Services	29.7	–2.52	3.14
☼ Total Stock Viper	N/A	—	—	2.23
⊕ ChevronTexaco	Energy	10.3	9.29	2.09
⊕ SBC Comms	Services	18.4	–16.00	1.93
⊖ BP PLC ADR	Energy	14.4	–0.90	1.79
⊕ BellSouth	Services	24.9	–5.09	1.78
⊖ Bank of America	Financials	16.7	42.73	1.74
⊖ Bristol–Myers Squibb	Health	20.2	–26.00	1.73
⊖ Philip Morris	Staples	12.1	9.12	1.54
Dow Chemical	Industrials	NMF	–4.43	1.44
⊕ J.P. Morgan Chase & Co.	Financials	27.8	–17.40	1.37
Minnesota Mng & Mfg	Industrials	34.5	0.16	1.36
⊖ Kimberly–Clark	Industrials	18.5	–13.80	1.36
⊕ Merck	Health	19.1	–35.90	1.35
⊖ American Home Products	Health	—	–1.91	1.27
Procter & Gamble	Staples	38.8	3.12	1.25
⊖ Pharmacia	Health	36.5	–29.30	1.24
⊕ General Elec	Industrials	30.1	–15.00	1.24
⊖ DuPont De Nemours E.I.	Industrials	65.4	–9.14	1.21
⊖ Washington Mutual	Financials	10.1	–5.32	1.08
⊕ XL Cap Cl A	Financials	22.8	5.82	1.08
⊕ Caterpillar	Industrials	20.0	13.72	1.03
⊖ Glaxo Wellcome PLC ADR	Health	24.2	–9.77	1.01
⊕ ACE	Financials	17.4	–5.39	0.99

Current Investment Style

Style: Value Blnd Growth; Size: Large Med Small

	Stock Port Avg	Relative S&P 500 Current	Relative S&P 500 Hist	Rel Cat
Price/Earnings Ratio	23.7	0.77	0.73	0.94
Price/Book Ratio	4.7	0.82	0.67	1.14
Price/Cash Flow	13.0	0.72	0.64	0.94
3 Yr Earnings Growth	10.6	0.72	0.49	0.71
1 Yr Earnings Est%	–7.0	3.96	—	2.12
Med Mkt Cap $mil	34,893	0.6	0.4	1.10

Special Securities % assets 09-30-01	
Restricted/Illiquid Secs	0
Emerging–Markets Secs	Trace
Options/Futures/Warrants	No

Composition % assets 09-30-01	
Cash	4.9
Stocks*	94.4
Bonds	0.4
Other	0.3
*Foreign (% stocks)	6.6

Market Cap	
Giant	44.4
Large	40.5
Medium	14.4
Small	0.8
Micro	0.0

Sector Weightings	% of Stocks	Rel S&P	5-Year High	5-Year Low
Utilities	8.3	2.6	25	6
Energy	14.0	2.0	17	10
Financials	22.6	1.3	23	11
Industrials	15.4	1.3	19	10
Durables	1.8	1.2	6	0
Staples	10.3	1.3	10	1
Services	13.0	1.2	23	8
Retail	1.9	0.3	7	0
Health	11.1	0.7	20	4
Technology	1.7	0.1	7	0

Address:	Vanguard Financial Ctr. P.O. Box 2600 Valley Forge, PA 19482 800–662–7447 / 610–669–1000
Web Address:	www.vanguard.com
Inception:	03-21-88
Advisor:	Newell Assoc./John A. Levin & Co.
Subadvisor:	None
NTF Plans:	N/A

Minimum Purchase:	$3000	Add: $100 IRA: $1000
Min Auto Inv Plan:	$3000	Add: $50
Sales Fees:	No–load	
Management Fee:	.40%	
Actual Fees:	Mgt: 0.40%	Dist: —
Expense Projections:	3Yr: $138	5Yr: $241 10Yr: $542
Avg Brok Commission:	—	Income Distrib: Quarterly
Total Cost (relative to category):		Low

Vanguard European Stock Index

Ticker	Load	NAV	Yield	Total Assets	Mstar Category
VEURX	None	$20.25	2.2%	$5,074.0 mil	Europe Stock

Prospectus Objective: Europe Stock

Vanguard European Stock Index Fund seeks results that correspond with the MSCI Europe Index.

The fund seeks to replicate the performance of the index, a market-cap-weighted index of more than 550 stocks in 15 European countries, through portfolio optimization, a statistical sampling technique. It intends to remain fully invested in common stocks.

The fund also offers Adm, Instl shares.

Historical Profile

Return	Above Avg
Risk	Below Avg
Rating	★★★★ Above Avg

Investment Style
Equity
Average Stock %: 98% 98% 98% 97% 99% 98%

▼ Manager Change
▽ Partial Manager Change

Fund Performance vs. Category Average
■ Quarterly Fund Return
+/– Category Average
— Category Baseline

Performance Quartile (within Category)

Portfolio Manager(s)

George U. Sauter. Since 6-90. AB'76 Dartmouth C.; MBA'80 U. of Chicago. Other funds currently managed: Vanguard Small Cap Index, Vanguard Balanced Index, Vanguard Equity-Income.

1990	1991	1992	1993	1994	1995	1996	1997	1998	1999	2000	12-01	History
9.06	9.92	9.33	11.88	11.76	14.02	16.57	20.13	25.28	28.83	25.99	20.25	NAV
–7.23*	12.40	–3.32	29.13	1.88	22.28	21.26	24.23	28.86	16.66	–8.21	–20.30	Total Return %
–1.71*	–18.08	–10.94	19.07	0.56	–15.25	–1.69	–9.12	0.29	–4.38	0.89	–8.43	+/– S&P 500
—	–0.71	1.39	–0.16	–0.41	0.66	0.17	0.43	0.33	0.76	0.18	—	+/– MSCI Europe
1.44	2.87	2.62	1.82	2.36	2.72	2.57	2.24	2.59	1.98	1.47	1.73	Income Return %
–8.67	9.53	–5.94	27.31	–0.49	19.56	18.68	22.00	26.27	14.68	–9.68	–22.04	Capital Return %
—	23	36	45	58	5	73	13	22	79	51	28	Total Rtn % Rank Cat
0.14	0.26	0.26	0.17	0.28	0.32	0.36	0.37	0.52	0.50	0.42	0.45	Income $
0.00	0.00	0.00	0.00	0.06	0.04	0.06	0.08	0.14	0.15	0.05	0.00	Capital Gains $
0.40	0.33	0.32	0.32	0.32	0.35	0.35	0.31	0.29	0.29	0.29	—	Expense Ratio %
3.68	3.06	3.05	2.05	2.41	2.66	2.45	2.19	1.97	1.99	1.64	—	Income Ratio %
—	15	1	4	6	2	4	3	7	7	8	—	Turnover Rate %
95.8	160.8	256.4	600.8	715.0	1,017.3	1,594.7	2,432.4	4,479.3	6,106.2	5,671.8	4,404.7	Net Assets $mil

Performance 12-31-01

	1st Qtr	2nd Qtr	3rd Qtr	4th Qtr	Total
1997	4.89	9.57	8.31	–0.20	24.23
1998	20.37	5.63	–14.41	18.42	28.86
1999	–2.14	0.28	1.09	17.59	16.66
2000	0.13	–2.74	–7.46	1.85	–8.21
2001	–15.62	–1.87	–12.09	9.48	–20.31

Trailing	Total Return%	+/– S&P 500	+/– MSCI Europe	% Rank All	% Rank Cat	Growth of $10,000
3 Mo	9.48	–1.20	—	45	46	10,948
6 Mo	–3.75	1.80	—	55	33	9,625
1 Yr	–20.30	–8.43	—	81	28	7,970
3 Yr Avg	–5.15	–4.12	—	92	63	8,534
5 Yr Avg	6.44	–4.26	—	42	29	13,662
10 Yr Avg	9.93	–3.00	—	33	36	25,763
15 Yr Avg	—	—	—	—	—	—

Tax Analysis	Tax-Adj Ret%	%Rank Cat	%Pretax Ret	%Rank Cat
3 Yr Avg	–5.89	62	—	—
5 Yr Avg	5.55	22	86.1	6
10 Yr Avg	8.98	15	90.5	1

Potential Capital Gain Exposure: 6% of assets

Risk Analysis

Time Period	Load-Adj Return %	Risk %Rank[1] All	Risk %Rank[1] Cat	Morningstar Return	Morningstar Risk	Morningstar Risk-Adj Rating
1 Yr	–20.30					
3 Yr	–5.15	64	31	–1.94[2]	0.84	★★
5 Yr	6.44	62	26	0.32[2]	0.71	★★★★
10 Yr	9.93	72	23	1.68[2]	0.72	★★★★

Average Historical Rating (103 months): 4.1★s

[1] 1=low, 100=high [2] T-Bill return substituted for category avg.

Category Rating (3 Yr)

1 2 3 4 5
Worst Best

Return	Average
Risk	Below Avg

Other Measures	Standard Index S&P 500	Best Fit Index MSCIEurND
Alpha	–5.6	0.2
Beta	0.69	1.00
R-Squared	55	100
Standard Deviation		15.12
Mean		–5.15
Sharpe Ratio		–0.78

Portfolio Analysis 09-30-01

Share change since 06-01 Total Stocks: 525	Sector	Country	% Assets
⊕ Glaxosmithkline	Technology	United Kingdom	3.60
⊕ BP Amoco	Energy	United Kingdom	3.30
⊕ Vodafone Airtouch	Services	United Kingdom	2.78
⊕ Royal Dutch Petro	Energy	Netherlands	2.32
⊕ Novartis (Br)	Health	Switzerland	2.32
⊕ Total Fina Cl B	Energy	France	2.23
⊕ HSBC Hldgs (UK) (2nd)	Financials	United Kingdom	2.19
⊕ Nokia	Technology	Finland	2.11
⊕ Nestle (Reg)	Staples	Switzerland	1.73
⊕ Astrazeneca	Health	United Kingdom	1.70
⊕ Royal Bk of Scotland	Financials	United Kingdom	1.39
⊕ UBS (Reg)	Financials	Switzerland	1.29
⊕ Aventis Cl A	Health	France	1.24
⊖ Allianz (Reg)	Financials	Germany	1.21
⊕ Lloyds TSB Grp	Financials	United Kingdom	1.20
⊕ ENI	Energy	Italy	1.08
⊕ Barclays	Financials	United Kingdom	1.08
⊕ ING Groep	Financials	Netherlands	1.05
⊕ Roche Hldgs (Br)	Health	Switzerland	1.05
⊕ Sanofi-Synthelabo	Health	France	1.04

Current Investment Style

Style: Value Blnd Growth; Size: Large Med Small

	Stock Port Avg	Rel MSCI EAFE Current	Rel MSCI EAFE Hist	Rel Cat
Price/Earnings Ratio	24.9	0.96	0.93	1.05
Price/Cash Flow	13.8	1.08	1.02	0.98
Price/Book Ratio	4.3	1.23	1.21	0.97
3 Yr Earnings Growth	22.0	1.18	1.09	0.92
Med Mkt Cap $mil	39,377	1.4	1.3	1.45

Country Exposure 09-30-01	% assets
United Kingdom	33
France	16
Germany	11
Switzerland	10
Netherlands	7

Hedging History: Rare

Special Securities % assets 09-30-01	
Restricted/Illiquid Secs	0
Emerging-Markets Secs	3
Options/Futures/Warrants	No

Sector Weightings	% of Stocks	Rel Cat	5-Year High	5-Year Low
Utilities	3.0	1.3	12	2
Energy	10.3	1.2	11	1
Financials	24.5	1.0	28	18
Industrials	8.2	0.7	21	8
Durables	4.0	0.9	9	3
Staples	7.3	1.0	16	5
Services	16.9	0.9	27	6
Retail	4.2	0.8	8	3
Health	9.6	1.0	15	5
Technology	12.1	1.5	12	1

Composition % assets 09-30-01

Cash	0.5	Bonds	0.0
Stocks	99.4	Other	0.1

Analysis by Gabriel Presler 10-11-01

The changes facing Vanguard European Stock Index Fund aren't likely to hinder its strong performance.

Like other index offerings that invest in European markets, this fund is going to have to make some adjustments in the next few months. The folks who build the MSCI indices—this category's chosen benchmark—are altering their methodology. They'll no longer weight stocks based on market cap; instead, they'll make allocation decisions according to how many shares are available on the market, thus adjusting for closely held companies and cross holdings, both of which are more prevalent abroad than in the U.S. That means the benchmark is now indicative of the universe that investors actually face.

It also means that manager Gus Sauter is likely to pick up his trading pace a bit in the months before May 2002, when the change will be completed. Sauter expects the fund's annualized turnover rate to increase to approximately 20% in most of his index portfolios, which is still quite low by category standards. Increased trading isn't the only change to expect, though: Because cross holding is common in Germany, for example, the fund's stake in that country is likely to decline slightly, while its U.K. exposure increases.

This change isn't likely to alter the fund's appeal. It could broaden the fund's portfolio. Its heavy weighting in large caps could decline, which would help performance at times. In 2000, for example, the market favored European small caps, and the fund fell into the category's lower reaches.

The fund's solid relative performance in 2001—its loss of 25% for the year to date through Oct. 10, 2001, bests two thirds of its peers—comes as no surprise to those familiar with its admirable 10-year record. A rock bottom expense ratio only adds to this fund's substantial appeal.

Address:	Vanguard Financial Ctr. P.O. Box 2600 Valley Forge, PA 19482 800-662-7447 / 610-669-1000
Web Address:	www.vanguard.com
*Inception:	06-18-90
Advisor:	Vanguard Core Mgmt. Grp.
Subadvisor:	None
NTF Plans:	N/A

Minimum Purchase:	$3000	Add: $100	IRA: $1000
Min Auto Inv Plan:	$3000	Add: $100	
Sales Fees:	No-load		
Management Fee:	.22%		
Actual Fees:	Mgt: 0.22%	Dist: —	
Expense Projections:	3Yr: $93	5Yr: $163	10Yr: $368
Avg Brok Commission:	—	Income Distrib: Annually	
Total Cost (relative to category):		Low	

Vanguard Explorer

Ticker	Load	NAV	Yield	Total Assets	Mstar Category
VEXPX	None	$60.32	0.2%	$4,753.4 mil	Small Growth

Prospectus Objective: Small Company

Vanguard Explorer Fund seeks long-term growth of capital.

The fund invests primarily in equity securities of small companies with market capitalizations less than $1 billion. It may also invest up to 20% of assets in foreign securities traded in either the United States or in foreign markets.

The fund offers Admiral and Investor shares.

Historical Profile

Return Above Avg
Risk Above Avg
Rating ★★★★ Above Avg

Investment Style
Equity
Average Stock %: 87% 87% 90% 89% 89% 89%

▼ Manager Change
▽ Partial Manager Change

Fund Performance vs. Category Average
Quarterly Fund Return +/– Category Average
— Category Baseline

Performance Quartile (within Category)

Portfolio Manager(s)

John J. Granahan, CFA. Since 2-90.
Kenneth L. Abrams. Since 2-94.
Edward N. Antoian, CFA. Since 8-97.
George U. Sauter. Since 8-97.
Chris Darnell. Since 4-00.
Robert M. Soucy. Since 4-00.

1990	1991	1992	1993	1994	1995	1996	1997	1998	1999	2000	12-01	History
25.58	39.61	43.84	45.11	42.86	49.95	53.83	55.30	56.71	68.62	60.09	60.32	NAV
–10.80	55.90	13.02	15.41	0.54	26.60	14.04	14.58	3.52	37.26	9.22	0.56	Total Return %
–7.68	25.42	5.40	5.36	–0.77	–10.94	–8.91	–18.78	–25.06	16.22	18.32	12.44	+/– S&P 500
6.61	4.71	5.25	2.05	2.97	–4.44	2.78	1.63	2.29	–5.83	31.65	9.79	+/– Russ 2000 Grth
1.17	1.02	0.33	0.32	0.38	0.56	0.54	0.46	0.36	0.41	0.36	0.17	Income Return %
–11.97	54.88	12.69	15.09	0.16	26.04	13.50	14.11	3.16	36.85	8.85	0.39	Capital Return %
68	43	48	53	36	72	69	66	45	65	23	25	Total Rtn % Rank Cat
0.34	0.26	0.13	0.14	0.17	0.24	0.27	0.25	0.20	0.23	0.25	0.11	Income $
0.00	0.00	0.78	5.17	2.26	4.00	2.83	5.85	0.30	8.03	13.91	0.00	Capital Gains $
0.67	0.56	0.69	0.73	0.70	0.68	0.63	0.62	0.62	0.74	0.71	—	Expense Ratio %
1.11	0.85	0.38	0.32	0.39	0.52	0.51	0.45	0.37	0.36	0.36	—	Income Ratio %
46	49	43	51	82	66	51	84	1	79	123	—	Turnover Rate %
237.9	429.7	620.4	847.7	1,121.6	1,647.6	2,263.7	2,541.3	2,463.6	3,136.2	4,765.0	4,648.0	Net Assets $mil

Performance 12-31-01

	1st Qtr	2nd Qtr	3rd Qtr	4th Qtr	Total
1997	–7.51	14.26	14.84	–5.59	14.58
1998	9.89	–6.30	–18.46	23.29	3.52
1999	–6.98	18.18	–3.95	29.99	37.26
2000	15.97	–1.14	1.74	–6.37	9.22
2001	–10.30	14.42	–21.73	25.18	0.56

Trailing	Total Return%	+/– S&P 500	+/– Russ 2000 Grth	% Rank All	% Rank Cat	Growth of $10,000
3 Mo	25.18	14.50	–0.99	7	37	12,518
6 Mo	–2.02	3.54	7.25	47	23	9,798
1 Yr	0.56	12.44	9.79	42	25	10,056
3 Yr Avg	14.66	15.69	14.41	5	25	15,075
5 Yr Avg	12.32	1.62	9.46	9	27	17,879
10 Yr Avg	12.97	0.04	5.78	12	20	33,853
15 Yr Avg	12.73	–1.01	4.58	19	40	60,328

Tax Analysis	Tax-Adj Ret%	%Rank Cat	%Pretax Ret	%Rank Cat
3 Yr Avg	10.97	28	74.9	61
5 Yr Avg	9.56	29	77.5	51
10 Yr Avg	10.50	22	81.0	37

Potential Capital Gain Exposure: 13% of assets

Risk Analysis

Time Period	Load-Adj Return %	Risk %Rank[1] All	Risk %Rank[1] Cat	Morningstar Return	Morningstar Risk	Morningstar Risk-Adj Rating
1 Yr	0.56					
3 Yr	14.66	79	23	2.26[2]	1.13	★★★★★
5 Yr	12.32	84	19	1.83[2]	1.22	★★★★
10 Yr	12.97	87	19	1.31	1.25	★★★

Average Historical Rating (193 months): 2.2★s

[1] 1=low, 100=high [2] T-Bill return substituted for category avg.

Category Rating (3 Yr)

1 2 3 4 5
Worst Best

Return Above Avg
Risk Below Avg

Other Measures	Standard Index S&P 500	Best Fit Index Russ 2000
Alpha	18.6	8.2
Beta	1.02	1.16
R-Squared	38	96

Standard Deviation	32.67
Mean	14.66
Sharpe Ratio	0.34

Portfolio Analysis 09-30-01

Share change since 06-01 Total Stocks: 522	Sector	PE	YTD Ret%	% Assets
⊖ Investment Tech Grp	Financials	26.6	40.37	1.11
⊖ Mettler-Toledo Intl	Industrials	34.1	–4.64	1.04
⊕ Maxtor	Technology	—	13.34	1.01
Dentsply Intl	Health	22.2	29.13	0.95
⊕ Tidewater	Energy	15.1	–22.30	0.82
Clayton Homes	Industrials	22.8	49.60	0.78
⊕ Callaway Golf	Durables	19.3	4.30	0.77
Sun Communities	Financials	18.7	18.40	0.76
⊕ Pier 1 Imports	Retail	19.5	70.54	0.71
⊕ Equity Residential Properties	Financials	22.1	10.14	0.65
⊖ Coventry Health Care	Health	16.4	–25.20	0.64
⊖ Caremark Rx	Health	46.6	20.25	0.64
⊕ Hanover Compressor	Utilities	22.4	–43.30	0.63
⊖ Corporate Executive Board	Services	66.7	–7.67	0.62
Manufactured Home Communities	Financials	21.4	14.41	0.61
⊕ Oak Tech	Technology	—	58.26	0.60
Jefferies Grp (New)	Financials	19.2	36.19	0.60
⊕ Henry Schein	Health	22.0	6.95	0.60
⊕ Mid Atlantic Medical Svcs	Health	18.8	14.57	0.57
⊖ Triad Hospitals	Health	—	–9.87	0.57
⊕ St. Mary Land & Explor	Energy	10.9	–36.00	0.55
⊕ Fleming Companies	Retail	—	57.07	0.55
Cubist Pharmaceuticals	Health	—	24.00	0.55
⊕ Polaris Inds	Durables	15.6	48.57	0.53
⊕ Insight Comm	Services	—	2.81	0.53

Current Investment Style

Style: Value Blnd Growth; Size: Large Med Small

	Stock Port Avg	Relative S&P 500 Current	Relative S&P 500 Hist	Rel Cat
Price/Earnings Ratio	28.8	0.93	0.83	0.89
Price/Book Ratio	4.3	0.76	0.67	0.89
Price/Cash Flow	19.1	1.06	0.91	0.87
3 Yr Earnings Growth	16.7[1]	1.14	1.32	0.66
1 Yr Earnings Est%	3.8	—	—	0.49
Med Mkt Cap $mil	1,090	0.0	0.0	1.04

[1] figure is based on 50% or less of stocks

Analysis by Scott Cooley 12-24-01

No, Vanguard Explorer is not just a more expensive index fund.

Investors might be forgiven for wondering if there's any active management here. With five subadvisors each running a slice of the fund's assets, the portfolio is diffuse: It contains more than 800 stocks. And its R-squared with the Russell 2000, a measure of correlation between the fund and that index, was 96 over the past three years. That correlation between the fund's and the index's returns is the group's highest.

Still, it's clear the fund's subadvisors have added some value. During the trailing three years through Dec. 21, 2001, the fund's 16.6% annualized gain handily tops those of the Russell 2000 and the small-growth group. Although the subadvisors don't use a common approach, overall they focus on issues with moderate valuations and strong earnings-growth rates. That valuation sensitivity kept the fund from loading up on the highly speculative tech issues that have crumbled since March 2000. Moreover, management has made a number of good individual picks such as Blockbuster, Clayton Homes, and Pier 1 Imports. As a result, the fund's year-to-date loss of 1.1% is much better than its average rival's 10.76% decline.

Of course, the managers' valuation-sensitive approach does have its drawbacks. The fund regularly lagged its more-aggressive rivals during the late 1990s. Thanks to its resilience in the bear market, the fund's long-term marks have improved, but they're still not outstanding. (The fund has beaten most of its rivals over the past 10 years but has lagged the category average slightly because a handful of funds recorded exceptional gains. Therefore, this fund is a decent option for investors seeking a well-diversified, growth-biased small-cap fund, but it doesn't make sense for those who want an aggressive-growth offering.

Special Securities % assets 09-30-01	
Restricted/Illiquid Secs	0
Emerging-Markets Secs	Trace
Options/Futures/Warrants	Yes

Composition % assets 09-30-01	
Cash	10.1
Stocks*	89.9
Bonds	0.0
Other	0.0
*Foreign (% stocks)	3.6

Market Cap	
Giant	0.0
Large	1.7
Medium	34.3
Small	60.4
Micro	3.6

Sector Weightings	% of Stocks	Rel S&P	5-Year High	5-Year Low
Utilities	1.0	0.3	2	0
Energy	4.3	0.6	5	0
Financials	11.4	0.6	16	5
Industrials	10.7	0.9	13	6
Durables	3.0	1.9	10	2
Staples	1.5	0.2	5	0
Services	18.2	1.7	31	17
Retail	8.1	1.2	9	3
Health	21.6	1.5	25	10
Technology	20.2	1.1	34	17

Address:	Vanguard Financial Ctr. P.O. Box 2600 Valley Forge, PA 19482 800-662-7447 / 610-669-1000
Web Address:	www.vanguard.com
Inception:	12-11-67
Advisor:	Granahan Inv. Mgmt./Wellington Mgmt.
Subadvisor:	None
NTF Plans:	N/A

Minimum Purchase:	$3000	Add: $100 IRA: $1000
Min Auto Inv Plan:	$3000	Add: $50
Sales Fees:	No-load	
Management Fee:	.55% mx./.20% mn.+(–).27%P, .40%A	
Actual Fees:	Mgt: 0.69%	Dist: —
Expense Projections:	3Yr: $227	5Yr: $395 10Yr: $883
Avg Brok Commission:	—	Income Distrib: Annually
Total Cost (relative to category):		Low

Vanguard Extended Market Idx

Ticker	Load	NAV	Yield	Total Assets	Mstar Category
VEXMX	None	$23.09	0.9%	$4,596.2 mil	Mid-Cap Blend

Prospectus Objective: Small Company

Vanguard Extended Market Index Fund seeks to match the performance of the Wilshire 4500 Index.

The fund employs a passive management strategy designed to track the performance of Wilshire 4500 Index. This index consists of more than 5,000 small- to medium-size U.S. common stocks traded on the New York Stock Exchange, the American Stock Exchange, or Nasdaq. These stocks are not included in the S&P 500 index. The fund invests all or substantially all of its assets in a representative sample of the stocks that make up the index.

The fund currently offers Investor, Institutional and Admiral shares. Previously, the fund was named Vanguard Index Trust Extended Market Portfolio.

Historical Profile
Return: Average
Risk: Above Avg
Rating: ★★ Below Avg

Investment Style
Equity
Average Stock %: 97% 97% 98% 98% 98% 99%

▼ Manager Change
▽ Partial Manager Change

Fund Performance vs. Category Average
■ Quarterly Fund Return +/– Category Average
— Category Baseline

Performance Quartile (within Category)

Portfolio Manager(s)

George U. Sauter. Since 12-87. AB'76 Dartmouth C.; MBA'80 U. of Chicago. Other funds currently managed: Vanguard Small Cap Index, Vanguard Balanced Index, Vanguard Equity-Income.

History

1990	1991	1992	1993	1994	1995	1996	1997	1998	1999	2000	12-01	History
11.48	15.82	17.35	19.43	18.52	24.07	26.20	30.75	30.63	37.07	26.62	23.09	NAV
–14.05	41.85	12.47	14.49	–1.76	33.80	17.65	26.69	8.35	36.22	–15.51	–9.17	Total Return %
–10.93	11.37	4.85	4.43	–3.08	–3.74	–5.30	–6.66	–20.22	15.18	–6.41	2.71	+/– S&P 500
–8.93	–8.22	0.57	0.56	1.83	2.88	–1.54	–5.56	–10.76	21.50	–33.01	–8.57	+/– S&P Mid 400
2.38	2.18	1.59	1.33	1.45	1.62	1.43	1.39	1.23	1.10	0.73	0.82	Income Return %
–16.43	39.67	10.88	13.16	–3.22	32.18	16.22	25.29	7.13	35.12	–16.24	–9.99	Capital Return %
60	28	63	37	47	19	77	56	40	13	89	68	Total Rtn % Rank Cat
0.33	0.25	0.25	0.23	0.28	0.30	0.34	0.36	0.37	0.32	0.26	0.21	Income $
0.16	0.20	0.18	0.20	0.29	0.40	1.72	1.91	2.17	3.64	4.43	0.81	Capital Gains $
0.23	0.19	0.20	0.20	0.20	0.25	0.25	0.23	0.23	0.25	0.25	—	Expense Ratio %
2.68	2.14	1.73	1.48	1.51	1.51	1.42	1.30	1.21	1.04	0.81	—	Income Ratio %
9	11	9	13	19	15	22	15	27	26	33	—	Turnover Rate %
178.8	372.4	583.5	927.9	967.3	1,523.2	2,098.8	2,722.8	2,937.9	—	4,068.5	3,114.9	Net Assets $mil

Performance 12-31-01

	1st Qtr	2nd Qtr	3rd Qtr	4th Qtr	Total
1997	–3.48	15.73	15.08	–1.45	26.69
1998	11.55	–2.18	–18.70	22.14	8.35
1999	–0.68	12.45	–5.88	29.58	36.22
2000	9.66	–8.66	3.79	–18.73	–15.51
2001	–15.77	14.30	–21.05	19.51	–9.17

Trailing	Total Return%	+/– S&P 500	+/– S&P Mid 400	% Rank All	% Rank Cat	Growth of $10,000
3 Mo	19.51	8.82	1.52	15	22	11,951
6 Mo	–5.65	–0.10	–4.10	65	70	9,435
1 Yr	–9.17	2.71	–8.57	59	68	9,083
3 Yr Avg	1.49	2.51	–8.75	65	73	10,453
5 Yr Avg	7.49	–3.21	–8.62	32	69	14,349
10 Yr Avg	11.07	–1.86	–3.94	25	64	28,571
15 Yr Avg	—	—	—	—	—	—

Tax Analysis	Tax-Adj Ret%	%Rank Cat	%Pretax Ret	%Rank Cat
3 Yr Avg	–1.11	75	—	—
5 Yr Avg	4.78	70	63.8	83
10 Yr Avg	9.01	61	81.4	45

Potential Capital Gain Exposure: –6% of assets

Risk Analysis

Time Period	Load-Adj Return %	Risk %Rank[1] All	Risk %Rank[1] Cat	Morningstar Return	Morningstar Risk	Morningstar Risk-Adj Rating
1 Yr	–9.17					
3 Yr	1.49	89	93	–0.71[2]	1.36	★★★
5 Yr	7.49	86	91	0.56[2]	1.29	★★
10 Yr	11.07	87	86	0.92	1.24	★★

Average Historical Rating (133 months): 2.9★s

[1] 1=low, 100=high [2] T-Bill return substituted for category avg.

Category Rating (3 Yr)

1 2 3 4 5 (Worst – Best): 2

Return: Below Avg
Risk: High

Other Measures	Standard Index S&P 500	Best Fit Index Wil 4500
Alpha	5.9	0.3
Beta	1.17	1.00
R-Squared	51	100

Standard Deviation	29.41
Mean	1.49
Sharpe Ratio	–0.14

Analysis by Scott Cooley 10-21-01

Although Vanguard Extended Market Index is a victim of the Nasdaq Composite index's collapse, it by no means is a sell candidate.

This fund is not limited to Nasdaq-listed companies, but large technology, biotech, and communications firms have often dominated its list of top holdings. The reason is simple: The fund's benchmark index tracks all regularly traded U.S. stocks that are not part of the S&P 500. The committee who picks stocks for the S&P 500 shies away from firms that lack operating earnings, even if they have huge market capitalizations. Therefore, rather large, profitless companies tend to find a home here. At times over the past few years, stocks such as BEA Systems, CMGI, and Amazon.com have occupied top positions in the portfolio.

It should therefore be no surprise that the fund has suffered mightily during the past 18 months' implosion of tech and tech-related stocks. The fund finished deep within the bottom quintile of the mid-cap blend category in 2000. This year, faltering holdings such as Gemstar-TV Guide and I2 Technologies have pushed it to a 20% loss for the year to date through Oct. 19. That puts the fund behind more the three fourths of its mid-blend peers.

Still, the fund has merit. For investors who made an S&P 500 index fund their first purchase, this offering provides considerable diversification. Moreover, over very long time periods the fund's rock-bottom expense ratio should give it an edge over costlier offerings. Finally, although sizable capital-gains distributions have sometimes been a problem here, they won't be in the near term, as manager Gus Sauter has taken advantage of the market sell-off and modest net redemptions to book net realized losses, which may be used to offset future gains.

In short, this fund still is a sensible holding for investors seeking diversification from the S&P 500.

Portfolio Analysis 09-30-01

Share change since 06-01 Total Stocks: 3026

Holding	Sector	PE	YTD Ret%	% Assets
⊖ Berkshire Hathaway Cl A	Financials	—	—	4.84
☼ AT & T Liberty Media Cl A	Services	—	3.22	1.23
⊖ Cox Comms A	Services	31.8	–9.99	0.97
⊕ United Parcel Svc B	Services	25.0	–6.09	0.70
⊖ EBAY	Services	NMF	102.70	0.64
⊖ General Motors Cl H	Technology	42.9	–32.80	0.53
⊕ Genzyme Corporation General Di	Health	—	33.11	0.49
⊖ Goldman Sachs Grp	Financials	20.7	–12.80	0.47
⊕ Kraft Foods	Staples	—	—	0.42
⊖ IDEC Pharmaceuticals	Health	NMF	9.09	0.40
⊖ Genentech	Health	NMF	–33.40	0.39
⊖ Gemstar–TV Guide Intl	Services	—	–39.90	0.37
⊖ VeriSign	Technology	—	–48.70	0.35
⊖ Juniper Net	Technology	NMF	–84.90	0.32
⊕ Equity Residential Properties	Financials	22.1	10.14	0.31
⊖ Electronic Arts	Technology	90.8	40.65	0.31
⊖ SunGard Data Sys	Technology	33.3	22.78	0.30
⊖ M & T Bk	Financials	20.8	8.63	0.28
⊖ Quest Diagnostics	Health	51.2	1.00	0.27
⊖ Marshall & Ilsley	Financials	22.0	27.06	0.27
⊖ Laboratory Corp of Amer	Health	21.0	–8.13	0.27
⊕ NVIDIA	Technology	84.2	308.50	0.27
⊖ Gilead Sciences	Health	—	58.48	0.26
⊖ USA Networks	Services	58.1	40.50	0.26
⊖ RJ Reynolds Tobacco Hldgs	Staples	3.1	22.37	0.25

Current Investment Style

Style: Value Blnd Growth; Size: Large Med Small

	Stock Port Avg	Relative S&P 500 Current	Relative S&P 500 Hist	Rel Cat
Price/Earnings Ratio	26.8	0.86	0.86	0.98
Price/Book Ratio	3.9	0.69	0.74	0.92
Price/Cash Flow	18.6	1.03	0.93	1.07
3 Yr Earnings Growth	14.9[1]	1.02	1.01	0.89
1 Yr Earnings Est%	8.3	—	—	3.67
Med Mkt Cap $mil	1,777	0.0	0.0	0.20

[1] figure is based on 50% or less of stocks

Special Securities % assets 09-30-01	
Restricted/Illiquid Secs	0
Emerging–Markets Secs	Trace
Options/Futures/Warrants	No

Composition % assets 09-30-01	
Cash	0.4
Stocks*	99.6
Bonds	0.0
Other	0.0
*Foreign (% stocks)	0.1

Market Cap	
Giant	0.7
Large	7.1
Medium	50.9
Small	33.5
Micro	7.9

Sector Weightings	% of Stocks	Rel S&P	5-Year High	5-Year Low
Utilities	3.1	1.0	12	2
Energy	4.2	0.6	6	3
Financials	25.6	1.4	27	13
Industrials	9.0	0.8	16	6
Durables	2.5	1.6	4	2
Staples	3.3	0.4	6	2
Services	18.5	1.7	22	14
Retail	4.2	0.6	7	3
Health	13.0	0.9	13	7
Technology	16.6	0.9	41	10

Address:	Vanguard Financial Ctr. P.O. Box 2600 Valley Forge, PA 19482 610–669–1000 / 800–662–7447
Web Address:	www.vanguard.com
Inception:	12-21-87
Advisor:	Vanguard Core Mgmt. Grp.
Subadvisor:	None
NTF Plans:	N/A

Minimum Purchase:	$3000	Add: $100 IRA: $1000
Min Auto Inv Plan:	$3000	Add: $50
Sales Fees:	No-load	
Management Fee:	.22%	
Actual Fees:	Mgt: 0.23%	Dist: —
Expense Projections:	3Yr: $80	5Yr: $141 10Yr: $318
Avg Brok Commission:	—	Income Distrib: Annually
Total Cost (relative to category):	Low	

Vanguard 500 Index

Ticker	Load	NAV	Yield	Total Assets	Mstar Category
VFINX	None	$105.89	1.2%	$87,013.9 mil	Large Blend

Prospectus Objective: Growth and Income

Vanguard 500 Index Fund seeks investment results that correspond with the price and yield performance of the S&P 500 Index.

The fund employs a passive management strategy designed to track the performance of the S&P 500 Index, which is dominated by the stocks of large U.S. companies. It attempts to replicate the target index by investing all or substantially all of its assets in the stocks that make up the index.

The fund currently offers Investor and Admiral shares. Prior to Dec. 21, 1987, the fund was named Vanguard Index Trust. Prior to 1980, it was named First Index Investment Trust. The fund was named Vanguard Index Trust 500 Portfolio.

Historical Profile
Return: Above Avg
Risk: Average
Rating: ★★★★ Above Avg

Investment Style
Equity
Average Stock %: 100% 98% 99% 100% 100% 100%

▼ Manager Change
▽ Partial Manager Change

Fund Performance vs. Category Average
Quarterly Fund Return +/– Category Average
— Category Baseline

Performance Quartile (within Category)

Portfolio Manager(s)

George U. Sauter. Since 10-87. AB'76 Dartmouth C.; MBA'80 U. of Chicago. Other funds currently managed: Vanguard Small Cap Index, Vanguard Balanced Index, Vanguard Equity-Income.

1990	1991	1992	1993	1994	1995	1996	1997	1998	1999	2000	12-01	History
31.24	39.32	40.97	43.83	42.97	57.60	69.17	90.07	113.95	135.33	121.86	105.89	NAV
–3.33	30.22	7.42	9.89	1.18	37.45	22.88	33.19	28.62	21.07	–9.06	–12.02	Total Return %
–0.21	–0.26	–0.20	–0.17	–0.14	–0.09	–0.07	–0.16	0.04	0.03	0.05	–0.15	+/– S&P 500
0.70	–2.22	–0.23	0.05	0.73	–0.16	0.71	0.17	–0.02	–0.76	1.90	0.74	+/– Wilshire Top 750
3.52	3.73	2.88	2.79	2.70	2.86	2.24	1.92	1.49	1.25	0.96	1.05	Income Return %
–6.85	26.50	4.55	7.11	–1.52	34.58	20.64	31.27	27.13	19.82	–10.02	–13.07	Capital Return %
51	56	47	48	21	11	26	14	20	41	54	35	Total Rtn % Rank Cat
1.17	1.15	1.12	1.13	1.17	1.22	1.28	1.32	1.33	1.41	1.30	1.28	Income $
0.10	0.12	0.10	0.03	0.20	0.13	0.25	0.59	0.42	1.00	0.00	0.00	Capital Gains $
0.22	0.20	0.19	0.19	0.19	0.20	0.20	0.19	0.18	0.18	0.18	—	Expense Ratio %
3.60	3.07	2.81	2.65	2.72	2.38	2.04	1.66	1.35	1.13	0.98	—	Income Ratio %
23	5	4	6	6	4	5	5	6	6	9	—	Turnover Rate %
2,173.0	4,345.3	6,517.7	8,272.7	9,356.4	17,371.8	30,331.9	49,357.6	74,228.5	104,652.3	90,485.8	73,150.8	Net Assets $mil

Performance 12-31-01

	1st Qtr	2nd Qtr	3rd Qtr	4th Qtr	Total
1997	2.63	17.41	7.48	2.84	33.19
1998	13.91	3.29	–9.95	21.39	28.62
1999	4.98	7.00	–6.25	14.96	21.07
2000	2.25	–2.62	–0.93	–7.81	–9.06
2001	–11.90	5.82	–14.72	10.65	–12.02

Trailing	Total Return%	+/– S&P 500	+/– Wil Top 750	% Rank All	% Rank Cat	Growth of $10,000
3 Mo	10.65	–0.03	–0.67	39	47	11,065
6 Mo	–5.63	–0.08	0.16	65	37	9,437
1 Yr	–12.02	–0.15	0.74	65	35	8,798
3 Yr Avg	–1.06	–0.03	0.77	78	47	9,687
5 Yr Avg	10.66	–0.04	0.54	15	24	16,594
10 Yr Avg	12.84	–0.09	0.39	13	22	33,473
15 Yr Avg	13.56	–0.17	0.19	13	24	67,362

Tax Analysis	Tax-Adj Ret%	%Rank Cat	%Pretax Ret	%Rank Cat
3 Yr Avg	–1.55	39	—	—
5 Yr Avg	10.01	14	94.0	11
10 Yr Avg	11.95	7	93.0	6

Potential Capital Gain Exposure: 36% of assets

Risk Analysis

Time Period	Load-Adj Return %	Risk %Rank[1] All	Risk %Rank[1] Cat	Morningstar Return	Morningstar Risk	Morningstar Risk-Adj Rating
1 Yr	–12.02					
3 Yr	–1.06	65	38	–1.20[2]	0.91	★★★
5 Yr	10.66	65	36	1.37[2]	0.89	★★★★
10 Yr	12.84	67	29	1.28	0.87	★★★★

Average Historical Rating (193 months): 4.1★s

[1] 1=low, 100=high [2] T-Bill return substituted for category avg.

Category Rating (3 Yr)

1 2 **3** 4 5
Worst Best

Return: Average
Risk: Average

Other Measures	Standard Index S&P 500	Best Fit Index S&P 500
Alpha	0.0	0.0
Beta	1.00	1.00
R-Squared	100	100
Standard Deviation		16.88
Mean		–1.06
Sharpe Ratio		–0.41

Portfolio Analysis 09-30-01

Share change since 06-01 Total Stocks: 508

	Sector	PE	YTD Ret%	% Assets
⊖ General Elec	Industrials	30.1	–15.00	3.82
⊖ Microsoft	Technology	57.6	52.78	3.30
⊕ ExxonMobil	Energy	15.3	–7.59	2.87
⊖ Pfizer	Health	34.7	–12.40	2.79
⊖ Wal-Mart Stores	Retail	40.3	8.94	2.43
⊖ Citigroup	Financials	20.0	0.03	2.42
⊕ American Intl Grp	Financials	42.0	–19.20	2.17
⊖ IBM	Technology	26.9	43.00	1.98
⊖ Johnson & Johnson	Health	16.6	14.01	1.85
⊖ Intel	Technology	73.1	4.89	1.73
⊖ Merck	Health	19.1	–35.90	1.54
⊖ AOL Time Warner	Technology	—	–7.76	1.46
⊖ Verizon Comms	Services	29.7	–2.52	1.42
⊖ SBC Comms	Services	18.4	–16.00	1.36
⊖ Cisco Sys	Technology	—	–52.60	1.31
⊖ Coca-Cola	Staples	35.5	–21.40	1.26
⊖ Royal Dutch Petro NY ADR	Energy	12.0	–17.10	1.14
⊖ Bristol-Myers Squibb	Health	20.2	–26.00	1.10
⊖ Philip Morris	Staples	12.1	9.12	1.09
⊖ Procter & Gamble	Staples	38.8	3.12	1.01
⊖ Tyco Intl	Industrials	27.1	6.23	1.00
⊖ Bank of America	Financials	16.7	42.73	1.00
⊕ ChevronTexaco	Energy	10.3	9.29	1.00
⊖ Home Depot	Retail	42.9	12.07	0.94
⊕ PepsiCo	Staples	31.4	–0.54	0.91

Current Investment Style

Style: Value Blnd Growth; Size: Large Med Small

	Stock Port Avg	Relative S&P 500 Current	Relative S&P 500 Hist	Rel Cat
Price/Earnings Ratio	30.5	0.99	1.00	1.00
Price/Book Ratio	5.7	1.00	1.00	1.04
Price/Cash Flow	17.8	0.99	1.00	0.96
3 Yr Earnings Growth	15.9	1.09	1.00	0.89
1 Yr Earnings Est%	–1.4	0.81	—	15.89
Med Mkt Cap $mil	64,049	1.1	1.0	1.23

Special Securities % assets 09-30-01	
Restricted/Illiquid Secs	0
Emerging-Markets Secs	0
Options/Futures/Warrants	No

Composition % assets 09-30-01	
Cash	0.6
Stocks*	99.4
Bonds	0.0
Other	0.0
*Foreign (% stocks)	2.0

Market Cap	
Giant	56.9
Large	31.7
Medium	11.1
Small	0.2
Micro	0.1

Sector Weightings	% of Stocks	Rel S&P	5-Year High	5-Year Low
Utilities	3.2	1.0	9	2
Energy	7.1	1.0	11	4
Financials	17.9	1.0	18	8
Industrials	11.5	1.0	19	10
Durables	1.6	1.0	6	1
Staples	7.9	1.0	15	5
Services	10.9	1.0	18	10
Retail	6.8	1.0	9	4
Health	14.9	1.0	15	8
Technology	18.4	1.0	33	5

Analysis by Scott Cooley 10-21-01

We still don't see a lot of chinks in Vanguard 500 Index Fund's armor.

Although this fund has posted a significant loss in absolute terms so far in 2001, it still stacks up pretty well against its peers. For the year to date through Oct. 19, 2001, the fund's 18% loss bests the returns of more than two thirds of its rivals. Many of the funds that trail this offering are higher-cost and less-well-managed index funds, but the fund has also beaten its actively managed peers, which have logged an average decline of 19.3%. Interestingly enough, the fund's 1.3-percentage-point edge over its actively managed rivals is roughly equal to its expense-ratio advantage versus that group.

While actively managed funds tend to hold cash, which should have given them an edge this year, they may also have more exposure to the speculative-growth stocks that have gotten creamed. The S&P committee that picks stocks for this index typically avoids companies that haven't posted a few years of operating earnings. Therefore, it avoided many faltering, large-cap biotech stocks as well as plummeting Internet issues such as Amazon.com. Some active large-blend managers cannot make the same boast. Moreover, in both 2000 and so far in 2001, the S&P 500 has held up better than a mechanically constructed index of the market's 500-largest stocks. That hypothetical index also had considerably more exposure than the S&P 500 to speculative issues.

Thanks to the fund's low costs and manager Gus Sauter's skill at adding value on the margins, the fund also sports a terrific long-term record. Over the past decade, it has beaten four fifths of its peers on a pretax basis, and even more after taxes. Furthermore, Vanguard has estimated the fund will make no capital-gains distribution this year. This is still about as fine a core holding as you'll find—especially for those in taxable accounts.

Address:	Vanguard Financial Ctr. P.O. Box 2600 Valley Forge, PA 19482 610-669-1000 / 800-662-7447
Web Address:	www.vanguard.com
Inception:	08-31-76
Advisor:	Vanguard Core Mgmt. Grp.
Subadvisor:	None
NTF Plans:	N/A

Minimum Purchase:	$3000	Add: $100 IRA: $1000
Min Auto Inv Plan:	$3000	Add: $50
Sales Fees:	No-load	
Management Fee:	.16%	
Actual Fees:	Mgt: 0.16%	Dist: —
Expense Projections:	3Yr: $58	5Yr: $101 10Yr: $230
Avg Brok Commission:	—	Income Distrib: Quarterly
Total Cost (relative to category):		Low

Vanguard GNMA

Ticker	Load	NAV	Yield	SEC Yield	Total Assets	Mstar Category
VFIIX	None	$10.38	6.3%	—	$18,981.1 mil	Intermediate Govt

Prospectus Objective: Government Mortgage

Vanguard GNMA Fund seeks current income consistent with maintenance of principal and liquidity.

The fund normally invests at least 80% of assets in Government National Mortgage Association certificates. It may invest the balance of assets in other U.S. government obligations, as well as in repurchase agreements secured by U.S. government securities. While the fund does not have specific maturity guidelines, it attempts to maintain an intermediate-term average weighted maturity.

The fund also offers Adm shares. Prior to Oct. 27, 98, the fund was named Vanguard Fixed-Income Securities GNMA Portfolio.

Historical Profile

Return High
Risk Below Avg
Rating ★★★★★ Highest

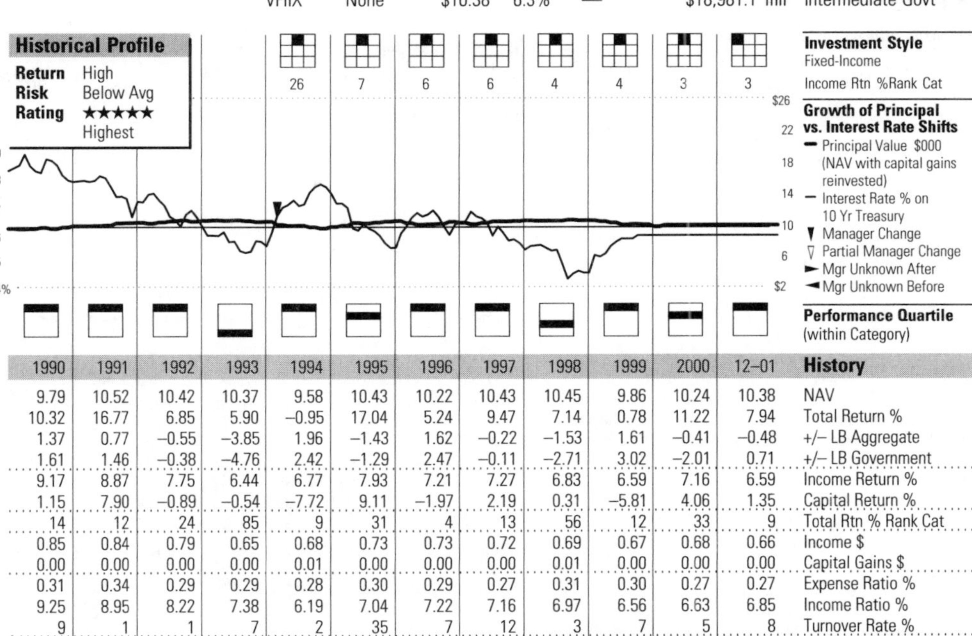

Portfolio Manager(s)

Paul D. Kaplan. Since 3-94. BA'68 Dickinson U.; MS'74 MIT. Other funds currently managed: Fortis Advantage Asset Allocation A, SEI Daily Income GNMA A, Vanguard Wellington.

1990	1991	1992	1993	1994	1995	1996	1997	1998	1999	2000	12-01	History
9.79	10.52	10.42	10.37	9.58	10.43	10.22	10.43	10.45	9.86	10.24	10.38	NAV
10.32	16.77	6.85	5.90	−0.95	17.04	5.24	9.47	7.14	0.78	11.22	7.94	Total Return %
1.37	0.77	−0.55	−3.85	1.96	−1.43	1.62	−0.22	−1.53	1.61	−0.41	−0.48	+/– LB Aggregate
1.61	1.46	−0.38	−4.76	2.42	−1.29	2.47	−0.11	−2.71	3.02	−2.01	0.71	+/– LB Government
9.17	8.87	7.75	6.44	6.77	7.93	7.21	7.27	6.83	6.59	7.16	6.59	Income Return %
1.15	7.90	−0.89	−0.54	−7.72	9.11	−1.97	2.19	0.31	−5.81	4.06	1.35	Capital Return %
14	12	24	85	9	31	4	13	56	12	33	9	Total Rtn % Rank Cat
0.85	0.84	0.79	0.65	0.68	0.73	0.73	0.72	0.69	0.67	0.68	0.66	Income $
0.00	0.00	0.00	0.00	0.01	0.00	0.00	0.00	0.01	0.00	0.00	0.00	Capital Gains $
0.31	0.34	0.29	0.29	0.28	0.30	0.29	0.27	0.31	0.30	0.27	0.27	Expense Ratio %
9.25	8.95	8.22	7.38	6.19	7.04	7.22	7.16	6.97	6.56	6.63	6.85	Income Ratio %
9	1	1	7	2	35	7	12	3	7	5	8	Turnover Rate %
2,598.0	5,297.5	6,920.6	7,073.2	5,777.8	6,907.7	7,398.8	8,725.2	10,993.1	12,548.5	14,378.3	15,531.4	Net Assets $mil

Performance 12-31-01

	1st Qtr	2nd Qtr	3rd Qtr	4th Qtr	Total
1997	−0.17	4.01	3.04	2.32	9.47
1998	1.62	1.68	2.82	0.85	7.14
1999	0.63	−1.12	1.09	0.18	0.78
2000	2.16	1.95	3.16	3.52	11.22
2001	2.75	1.03	4.03	−0.04	7.95

Trailing	Total Return%	+/– LB Agg	+/– LB Govt	% Rank All	% Rank Cat	Growth of $10,000
3 Mo	−0.04	−0.07	0.55	79	14	9,996
6 Mo	3.99	−0.67	−0.86	9	52	10,399
1 Yr	7.94	−0.48	0.71	10	9	10,794
3 Yr Avg	6.56	0.28	0.68	19	5	12,099
5 Yr Avg	7.25	−0.18	−0.15	34	5	14,190
10 Yr Avg	6.96	−0.27	−0.18	51	7	19,589
15 Yr Avg	8.11	−0.01	0.22	51	4	32,190

Tax Analysis	Tax-Adj Ret%	%Rank Cat	%Pretax Ret	%Rank Cat
3 Yr Avg	3.83	10	58.5	42
5 Yr Avg	4.46	12	61.5	67
10 Yr Avg	4.17	12	59.9	38

Potential Capital Gain Exposure: 2% of assets

Risk Analysis

Time Period	Load-Adj Return %	Risk %Rank¹ All	Risk %Rank¹ Cat	Morningstar Return	Morningstar Risk	Morningstar Risk-Adj Rating
1 Yr	7.94					
3 Yr	6.56	7	20	0.35²	0.52	★★★★
5 Yr	7.25	8	14	0.51²	0.49	★★★★★
10 Yr	6.96	11	10	0.63²	0.68	★★★★★

Average Historical Rating (193 months): 4.2★s

¹1=low, 100=high ² T-Bill return substituted for category avg.

Category Rating (3 Yr)

1 2 3 4 5
Worst Best

Return High
Risk Below Avg

Other Measures	Standard Index LB Agg	Best Fit Index LB Mtg
Alpha	0.5	−0.5
Beta	0.82	1.05
R-Squared	85	95
Standard Deviation		3.19
Mean		6.56
Sharpe Ratio		0.59

Analysis by Langdon Healy 10-30-01

Vanguard GNMA doesn't squander its advantage, making it a great choice.

Charging investors 50 basis points less than the average Ginnie Mae fund provides this offering a huge edge over its competitors coming out of the starting gate. That's because the difference between a top-performing bond fund and a laggard is sometimes a matter of only a few basis points. Ever conscious of the fund's competitive advantage, manager Paul Kaplan and the Vanguard team know that they don't need to make dazzling tactical moves to come out on top. Most importantly, Kaplan eschews interest-rate bets by keeping the fund's duration (a measure of interest-rate sensitivity) in line with the group's average.

Kaplan tries to extend his head start by looking for undervalued securities and by reducing prepayment risk. Early in 2000, for example, he concluded that interest rates had peaked and consequently purchased seasoned mortgages at what he determined were reasonable prices. (Seasoned mortgages are older issues that have survived at least one interest-rate cycle and are therefore considered less susceptible to prepayment risk than more-recently issued bonds.) He also took a stake in GNMA II bonds (which are drawn from different, more complex pools than traditional Ginnie Maes), again because he thought they were attractively priced.

Kaplan's moves have paid off as mortgage rates fell in late 2000 and 2001, and both seasoned mortgages and GNMA IIs rallied, helping the fund earn 9.0% for the year to date through Oct. 30, 2001. That's better than 71% of all intermediate-bond funds.

The fund's ultra-low expenses and moderate strategy, which have guided it to the top of the mortgage-fund group over time, should continue to hold it in good stead.

Portfolio Analysis 03-31-01

Total Fixed-Income: 23486	Date of Maturity	Amount $000	Value $000	% Net Assets
GNMA 6.5%	12-15-28	2,828,179	2,833,548	19.39
GNMA 7%	12-15-28	1,427,762	1,453,067	9.94
GNMA 7.5%	12-15-29	1,111,307	1,139,674	7.80
GNMA 8%	10-15-30	792,312	818,309	5.60
GNMA 6%	12-15-28	800,659	787,007	5.39
GNMA 7%	12-15-23	543,943	556,102	3.81
GNMA 7.5%	10-15-30	488,290	500,755	3.43
GNMA 7%	12-15-27	490,687	499,993	3.42
GNMA 7%	12-15-29	435,435	442,744	3.03
GNMA 7.5%	12-15-27	371,022	381,300	2.61
GNMA 7.5%	12-15-26	348,140	358,041	2.45
GNMA 7%	12-15-26	329,282	335,818	2.30
GNMA 6%	07-15-29	334,740	328,330	2.25
GNMA 6.5%	12-15-24	304,521	306,587	2.10
GNMA 6.5%	12-15-29	301,669	302,121	2.07
GNMA 7%	10-15-24	268,447	274,265	1.88
GNMA 7.5%	12-15-25	259,020	266,491	1.82
GNMA 7.5%	12-15-23	258,389	266,237	1.82
GNMA 6.5%	12-15-27	177,972	178,630	1.22
GNMA 6%	12-15-26	152,393	150,679	1.03

Current Investment Style

Duration: Short Int Long
Quality: High Med Low

Avg Eff Duration¹	2.2 Yrs
Avg Eff Maturity	—
Avg Credit Quality	AAA
Avg Wtd Coupon	7.01%
Avg Wtd Price	101.52% of par

¹figure provided by fund

Special Securities % assets 03-31-01	
Restricted/Illiquid Secs	0
Exotic Mortgage-Backed	0
Emerging-Markets Secs	0
Options/Futures/Warrants	No

Coupon Range	% of Bonds	Rel Cat
0%	0.00	0.00
0% to 7%	38.91	0.68
7% to 8.5%	58.72	1.76
8.5% to 10%	2.35	0.58
More than 10%	0.01	0.00

1.00=Category Average

Credit Analysis % bonds 09-30-01			
US Govt	100	BB	0
AAA	0	B	0
AA	0	Below B	0
A	0	NR/NA	0
BBB	0		

Composition % assets 03-31-01			
Cash	3.5	Bonds	96.5
Stocks	0.0	Other	0.0

Sector Breakdown % bonds 03-31-01			
US Treasuries	0	CMOs	0
GNMA mtgs	100	ARMs	0
FNMA mtgs	0	Other	0
FHLMC mtgs	0		

Address:	Vanguard Financial Ctr. P.O. Box 2600 Valley Forge, PA 19482 800-662-7447 / 610-669-1000
Web Address:	www.vanguard.com
Inception:	06-27-80
Advisor:	Wellington Mgmt.
Subadvisor:	None
NTF Plans:	N/A

Minimum Purchase:	$3000	Add: $100	IRA: $1000
Min Auto Inv Plan:	$3000	Add: $50	
Sales Fees:	No-load		
Management Fee:	.02% mx./.01% mn.		
Actual Fees:	Mgt: 0.24%	Dist: —	
Expense Projections:	3Yr: $86	5Yr: $152	10Yr: $343
Avg Brok Commission:	—	Income Distrib: Monthly	
Total Cost (relative to category):		Low	

Vanguard Growth & Income

Ticker	Load	NAV	Yield	Total Assets	Mstar Category
VQNPX	None	$28.20	1.1%	$7,525.5 mil	Large Value

Prospectus Objective: Growth and Income

Vanguard Growth and Income Fund seeks a total return greater than that of the S&P 500 index on an annual basis.

The fund invests at least 65% of assets in securities included in the S&P 500 index. It is expected that the aggregate investment characteristics of the fund will be similar to the S&P 500 index in terms of dividend yield, price/earnings ratio, return on equity, and price/book ratio. Stock selection is limited by the characteristics of the index, including the weightings of stocks and industry sectors.

The fund offers Investor and Admiral Shares. Past name: Vanguard Quantitative Portfolio. On Aug. 13, 1998, Vanguard/ Trustees' Equity Fund U.S. Portfolio merged into the fund.

Historical Profile

Return	Above Avg
Risk	Average
Rating	★★★★ Above Avg

Investment Style Equity — Average Stock %: 1995 96%, 1996 96%, 1997 95%, 1998 97%, 1999 98%, 2000 99%, 12-01 98%

▼ Manager Change ▽ Partial Manager Change

Fund Performance vs. Category Average — Quarterly Fund Return +/– Category Average; — Category Baseline

Performance Quartile (within Category)

Portfolio Manager(s)

John S. Cone, CFA. Since 7-99. BA Rice U.; MS Purdue U. Other funds currently managed: Vanguard Morgan Growth, Vanguard Morgan Growth Adm, Vanguard Growth & Income Adm.

1990	1991	1992	1993	1994	1995	1996	1997	1998	1999	2000	12-01	History
13.29	16.32	16.30	16.45	15.56	19.95	22.23	26.19	30.76	37.08	32.06	28.20	NAV
–2.44	30.29	7.01	13.83	–0.61	35.93	23.06	35.59	23.95	26.04	–8.97	–11.13	Total Return %
0.67	–0.19	–0.61	3.77	–1.93	–1.60	0.12	2.24	–4.63	5.00	0.13	0.75	+/– S&P 500
1.22	12.14	–2.06	–5.93	1.70	–4.10	0.75	0.10	2.71	15.09	–11.28	–2.34	+/– Russ Top 200 Val
3.35	3.56	2.73	2.41	2.44	2.71	2.05	1.97	1.29	1.08	0.97	0.94	Income Return %
–5.79	26.73	4.27	11.42	–3.06	33.22	21.01	33.62	22.66	24.96	–9.95	–12.07	Capital Return %
24	30	76	47	52	25	24	4	8	4	97	82	Total Rtn % Rank Cat
0.47	0.47	0.44	0.39	0.39	0.42	0.40	0.42	0.33	0.33	0.35	0.30	Income $
0.04	0.44	0.71	1.69	0.40	0.74	1.82	3.18	1.28	1.28	1.47	0.00	Capital Gains $
0.48	0.43	0.40	0.50	0.48	0.47	0.38	0.36	0.36	0.37	0.38	—	Expense Ratio %
3.34	2.95	2.67	2.22	2.50	2.25	1.97	1.74	1.27	1.04	1.02	—	Income Ratio %
81	61	51	85	71	59	75	66	47	54	65	—	Turnover Rate %
211.3	334.8	415.5	530.7	596.1	909.4	1,285.4	2,141.8	5,160.5	8,816.4	9,193.2	6,924.6	Net Assets $mil

Performance 12-31-01

	1st Qtr	2nd Qtr	3rd Qtr	4th Qtr	Total
1997	1.82	16.88	12.00	1.73	35.59
1998	13.75	3.83	–13.01	20.63	23.95
1999	4.58	8.63	–4.97	16.75	26.04
2000	0.92	–2.91	1.62	–8.58	–8.97
2001	–12.51	7.49	–15.00	11.18	–11.13

Trailing	Total Return%	+/– S&P 500	+/– Russ Top 200 Val	% Rank All	% Rank Cat	Growth of $10,000
3 Mo	11.18	0.49	5.66	36	22	11,118
6 Mo	–5.50	0.06	0.28	65	73	9,450
1 Yr	–11.13	0.75	–2.34	63	82	8,887
3 Yr Avg	0.65	1.68	–0.52	70	66	10,196
5 Yr Avg	11.37	0.67	0.17	12	22	17,135
10 Yr Avg	13.25	0.32	–0.78	11	27	34,699
15 Yr Avg	13.93	0.20	0.43	11	12	70,730

Tax Analysis	Tax-Adj Ret%	%Rank Cat	%Pretax Ret	%Rank Cat
3 Yr Avg	–0.37	60	—	—
5 Yr Avg	9.01	24	79.2	35
10 Yr Avg	10.63	29	80.3	35

Potential Capital Gain Exposure: 0% of assets

Risk Analysis

Time Period	Load-Adj Return %	Risk %Rank[1] All	Risk %Rank[1] Cat	Morningstar Return	Morningstar Risk	Morningstar Risk-Adj Rating
1 Yr	–11.13					
3 Yr	0.65	64	91	–0.87[2]	0.90	★★★
5 Yr	11.37	67	89	1.56[2]	0.90	★★★★
10 Yr	13.25	70	87	1.37	0.90	★★★★

Average Historical Rating (145 months): 4.0★s

[1] 1=low, 100=high [2] T-Bill return substituted for category avg.

Category Rating (3 Yr)

1 2 3 4 5 — Worst … Best

Return	Average
Risk	High

Other Measures	Standard Index S&P 500	Best Fit Index S&P 500
Alpha	1.9	1.9
Beta	1.02	1.02
R-Squared	97	97
Standard Deviation	17.77	
Mean	0.65	
Sharpe Ratio	–0.28	

Analysis by Scott Cooley 10-15-01

Vanguard Growth & Income Fund is still doing what it's supposed to.

By design, this fund is supposed to beat the S&P 500 index. To do so, manager John Cone and his predecessor, John Nagorniak, built computerized stock-picking models that attempt to add value with individual issue selection. That is, the models avoid big bets on sectors or industries, instead seeking to pick the stocks within each area that have the best combination of valuations and earnings momentum, among other factors. The goal is to provide index-beating returns without taking on additional risk.

So far in 2001, the fund has achieved its stated goal. For the year to date through Oct. 15, 2001, the fund has lost 16.2%, which puts it more than 40 basis points (or 0.40%) ahead of the index. Although the fund has owned a few clunkers, strong-performing stocks such as Bank of America, Philip Morris, and Sears Roebuck have given it a significant lift. The fund's management and its stock-picking models have proven themselves over the long haul, too: Over all trailing periods of at least three years, the fund has beaten the S&P 500.

To be sure, the fund's recent trailing returns stack up poorly versus the large-value category. Because its sector weights are tied to the S&P 500's, the fund has considerably more exposure than its rivals to growth issues, especially in the technology sector. That has been a huge negative over the past year and a half, as such issues have imploded.

Given its S&P 500-beating longer-term returns, however, we think this fund makes sense for some. Although we cannot recommend the fund to investors in taxable accounts, as its higher-turnover approach makes it less tax-efficient than a pure index offering, this is a great core holding for investors' IRAs and 401(k)s.

Portfolio Analysis 09-30-01

Share change since 06-01 Total Stocks: 165	Sector	PE	YTD Ret%	% Assets
⊕ Pfizer	Health	34.7	–12.40	4.14
⊖ Citigroup	Financials	20.0	0.03	3.48
⊖ Johnson & Johnson	Health	16.6	14.01	3.32
⊕ American Intl Grp	Financials	42.0	–19.20	3.22
⊕ ExxonMobil	Energy	15.3	–7.59	3.18
Microsoft	Technology	57.6	52.78	3.14
⊖ Merck	Health	19.1	–35.90	2.67
⊖ General Elec	Industrials	30.1	–15.00	2.56
Tyco Intl	Industrials	27.1	6.23	2.44
⊖ AOL Time Warner	Technology	—	–7.76	2.31
⊕ Bank of America	Financials	16.7	42.73	2.20
⊕ Procter & Gamble	Staples	38.8	3.12	2.13
PepsiCo	Staples	31.4	–0.54	1.88
⊖ Verizon Comms	Services	29.7	–2.52	1.65
⊖ Freddie Mac	Financials	14.0	–3.87	1.58
IBM	Technology	26.9	43.00	1.56
⊖ Philip Morris	Staples	12.1	9.12	1.43
⊕ Forest Labs	Health	52.2	23.35	1.39
⊖ Intel	Technology	73.1	4.89	1.34
⊕ Computer Assoc Intl	Technology	—	77.28	1.32
⊕ Home Depot	Retail	42.9	12.07	1.30
⊕ Cardinal Health	Health	35.1	–2.51	1.27
⊖ Kohl's	Retail	54.2	15.48	1.23
⊖ Sears Roebuck	Retail	23.4	40.12	1.17
⊕ Boeing	Industrials	10.2	–40.40	1.16

Current Investment Style

Style: Value Blnd Growth; Size: Large Med Small

	Stock Port Avg	Relative S&P 500 Current	Relative S&P 500 Hist	Rel Cat
Price/Earnings Ratio	27.3	0.88	0.90	1.08
Price/Book Ratio	5.1	0.90	0.85	1.25
Price/Cash Flow	17.1	0.95	0.93	1.24
3 Yr Earnings Growth	18.3	1.25	1.04	1.24
1 Yr Earnings Est%	3.2	—	—	–0.95
Med Mkt Cap $mil	66,535	1.1	0.9	2.10

Special Securities % assets 09-30-01	
Restricted/Illiquid Secs	0
Emerging-Markets Secs	0
Options/Futures/Warrants	No

Composition % assets 09-30-01	
Cash	1.2
Stocks*	98.8
Bonds	0.0
Other	0.0
*Foreign (% stocks)	1.7

Market Cap	
Giant	53.1
Large	32.7
Medium	14.2
Small	0.1
Micro	0.0

Sector Weightings	% of Stocks	Rel S&P	5-Year High	5-Year Low
Utilities	2.9	0.9	11	3
Energy	7.7	1.1	12	2
Financials	19.5	1.1	23	9
Industrials	12.1	1.1	25	10
Durables	0.6	0.4	7	0
Staples	8.1	1.0	16	3
Services	8.4	0.8	18	7
Retail	7.6	1.1	10	2
Health	14.9	1.0	17	7
Technology	18.3	1.0	34	4

Address:	Vanguard Financial Ctr. P.O. Box 2600 Valley Forge, PA 19482 800–662–7447 / 610–669–1000
Web Address:	www.vanguard.com
Inception:	12-10-86
Advisor:	Franklin Port. Assoc. Trust
Subadvisor:	None
NTF Plans:	N/A

Minimum Purchase:	$3000	Add: $100 IRA: $1000
Min Auto Inv Plan:	$3000	Add: $50
Sales Fees:	No-load	
Management Fee:	.30% mx./.06% mn.+(–).30%P	
Actual Fees:	Mgt: 0.37%	Dist: —
Expense Projections:	3Yr: $125	5Yr: $219 10Yr: $493
Avg Brok Commission:	—	Income Distrib: Semi-Ann.
Total Cost (relative to category):	Low	

Vanguard Growth Equity

Ticker	Load	NAV	Yield	Total Assets	Mstar Category
VGEQX	None	$9.64	1.2%	$728.2 mil	Large Growth

Prospectus Objective: Growth

Vanguard Growth Equity Fund seeks capital appreciation.

The fund normally invests at least 65% of assets in common stocks of U.S. companies that are reasonably valued and have strong earnings potential. The advisor seeks to maintain sector concentrations that approximate those of the Russell 1000 Growth index; it also seeks to diversify the fund by spreading investments over a broad range of industries. It may also invest up to 10% of assets in American depositary receipts.

The fund has gone through several name changes.

Historical Profile
Return Average
Risk Above Avg
Rating ★★★ Neutral

Investment Style
Equity
Average Stock %: 100% 99% 99% 99% 99% 97% 99%

▼ Manager Change
▽ Partial Manager Change

Fund Performance vs. Category Average
■ Quarterly Fund Return +/– Category Average
— Category Baseline

Performance Quartile (within Category)

Portfolio Manager(s)

Robert E. Turner, CFA et al.Since 3-92. BS'77 Bradley U.; MBA'78 Bradley U.

1990	1991	1992	1993	1994	1995	1996	1997	1998	1999	2000	12-01	History
—	—	11.25	12.89	11.92	14.53	12.76	11.71	14.44	17.27	13.28	9.64	NAV
—	—	13.19*	15.38	–6.73	29.96	19.23	31.35	38.07	53.60	–23.10	–24.24	Total Return %
—	—	2.62*	5.33	–8.05	–7.57	–3.71	–2.00	9.50	32.56	–14.00	–12.36	+/– S&P 500
—	—	—	15.46	–11.59	–8.69	–6.29	–2.39	–7.03	23.92	1.42	–3.74	+/– Russ Top 200 Grt
—	—	0.69	0.77	0.79	0.79	0.04	0.00	0.00	0.00	0.00	0.90	Income Return %
—	—	12.50	14.62	–7.53	29.17	19.19	31.35	38.07	53.60	–23.10	–25.14	Capital Return %
—	—	—	26	87	62	47	23	28	20	83	56	Total Rtn % Rank Cat
—	—	0.06	0.09	0.10	0.09	0.01	0.00	0.00	0.00	0.00	0.12	Income $
—	—	0.00	0.00	0.00	0.85	4.59	4.82	1.60	4.52	0.00	0.30	Capital Gains $
—	—	1.44	1.00	0.95	0.94	1.06	1.02	1.00	0.92	—	—	Expense Ratio %
—	—	0.73	0.80	0.86	0.78	0.03	–0.25	–0.42	–0.42	—	—	Income Ratio %
—	—	—	88	165	178	—	178	250	328	—	—	Turnover Rate %
—	—	—	81.9	113.0	105.8	90.5	89.6	123.7	203.3	994.5	728.2	Net Assets $mil

Performance 12-31-01

	1st Qtr	2nd Qtr	3rd Qtr	4th Qtr	Total
1997	–2.66	17.07	14.44	0.73	31.35
1998	12.21	7.46	–8.85	25.63	38.07
1999	8.10	2.75	–1.00	39.67	53.60
2000	13.49	–3.52	–1.16	–28.95	–23.10
2001	–26.13	10.09	–23.80	22.25	–24.24

Trailing	Total Return%	+/– S&P 500	+/– Russ Top 200 Grth	% Rank All	% Rank Cat	Growth of $10,000
3 Mo	22.25	11.56	9.39	11	10	12,225
6 Mo	–6.84	–1.29	0.14	73	31	9,316
1 Yr	–24.24	–12.36	–3.74	87	56	7,576
3 Yr Avg	–3.64	–2.61	4.38	88	57	8,948
5 Yr Avg	10.17	–0.53	1.58	18	34	16,229
10 Yr Avg	—	—	—	—	—	—
15 Yr Avg	—	—	—	—	—	—

Tax Analysis	Tax-Adj Ret%	%Rank Cat	%Pretax Ret	%Rank Cat
3 Yr Avg	–6.35	62	—	—
5 Yr Avg	5.49	60	54.0	86
10 Yr Avg	—	—	—	—

Potential Capital Gain Exposure: –11% of assets

Risk Analysis

Time Period	Load-Adj Return %	Risk %Rank[1] All	Risk %Rank[1] Cat	Morningstar Return	Morningstar Risk	Morningstar Risk-Adj Rating
1 Yr	–24.24					
3 Yr	–3.64	94	82	–1.68[2]	1.59	★★
5 Yr	10.17	89	79	1.24[2]	1.41	★★★
Incept	12.08	—	—	—	—	

Average Historical Rating (82 months): 3.3★s

[1] 1=low, 100=high [2] T-Bill return substituted for category avg.

Category Rating (3 Yr)

1 2 **3** 4 5
Worst Best

Return Average
Risk Above Avg

Other Measures	Standard Index S&P 500	Best Fit Index Wil 4500
Alpha	3.2	–3.6
Beta	1.51	1.05
R-Squared	64	85

Standard Deviation	32.46
Mean	–3.64
Sharpe Ratio	–0.31

Portfolio Analysis 09-30-01

Share change since 06-01 Total Stocks: 74	Sector	PE	YTD Ret%	% Assets
⊖ Pfizer	Health	34.7	–12.40	6.98
☆ Wal-Mart Stores	Retail	40.3	8.94	5.80
☆ Intel	Technology	73.1	4.89	5.26
⊖ Cisco Sys	Technology	—	–52.60	4.54
⊖ General Elec	Industrials	30.1	–15.00	4.16
⊕ American Intl Grp	Financials	42.0	–19.20	3.48
⊖ AOL Time Warner	Technology	—	–7.76	3.36
☆ Johnson & Johnson	Health	16.6	14.01	3.29
⊖ Home Depot	Retail	42.9	12.07	2.68
⊖ Dell Comp	Technology	61.8	55.87	2.64
☆ Procter & Gamble	Staples	38.8	3.12	2.28
⊕ Texas Instruments	Technology	87.5	–40.70	2.25
⊕ PepsiCo	Staples	31.4	–0.54	2.24
⊖ Amgen	Health	52.8	–11.70	1.96
⊖ Micron Tech	Technology	—	–12.60	1.73
☆ Forest Labs	Health	52.2	23.35	1.72
⊖ Viacom Cl B	Services	—	—	1.64
⊖ Abbott Labs	Health	51.6	17.08	1.57
☆ Genentech	Health	NMF	–33.40	1.56
⊕ IDEC Pharmaceuticals	Health	NMF	9.09	1.51
⊕ Kraft Foods	Staples	—	—	1.43
⊕ King Pharmaceuticals	Health	45.8	8.68	1.41
⊕ Citigroup	Financials	20.0	0.03	1.40
⊖ Qualcomm	Technology	—	–38.50	1.39
⊕ Flextronics Intl	Technology	—	–15.80	1.36

Current Investment Style

Style: Value Blnd Growth; Size: Large Med Small

	Stock Port Avg	Relative S&P 500 Current	Relative S&P 500 Hist	Rel Cat
Price/Earnings Ratio	41.9	1.35	1.38	1.18
Price/Book Ratio	7.2	1.26	1.44	1.13
Price/Cash Flow	24.7	1.37	1.35	1.09
3 Yr Earnings Growth	22.4	1.53	1.34	1.04
1 Yr Earnings Est%	2.7	—	—	0.89
Med Mkt Cap $mil	71,014	1.2	0.8	1.50

Special Securities % assets 09-30-01

Restricted/Illiquid Secs	0
Emerging-Markets Secs	0
Options/Futures/Warrants	No

Composition % assets 09-30-01

Cash	1.2
Stocks*	98.8
Bonds	0.0
Other	0.0
*Foreign (% stocks)	1.8

Market Cap

Giant	56.6
Large	26.2
Medium	17.2
Small	0.0
Micro	0.0

Sector Weightings	% of Stocks	Rel S&P	5-Year High	5-Year Low
Utilities	0.0	0.0	7	0
Energy	1.6	0.2	11	0
Financials	8.8	0.5	12	2
Industrials	5.5	0.5	20	3
Durables	0.6	0.4	6	0
Staples	6.9	0.9	16	1
Services	6.1	0.6	17	5
Retail	11.9	1.8	16	4
Health	25.3	1.7	25	8
Technology	33.2	1.8	59	10

Analysis by Paul Herbert 10-23-01

Vanguard Growth Equity Fund may have fallen well short of most investors' expectations, but it would be premature to write it off now.

This fund has given shareholders a healthy dose of pain since joining Vanguard's lineup last June. Manager Bob Turner's aggressive-growth strategy, which produced superior returns in the late 1990s, has been at odds with the hostile environment for growth stocks that has prevailed for most of the past two years. Indeed, from June 12, 2000, the date on which the fund first donned the Vanguard name, through Oct. 22, 2001, it has shed more than 50%. And given that its assets more than doubled from the end of May 2000 to the end of September, a great many shareholders have been around only during this agonizing period.

Investors shouldn't expect things to pick up for the fund without an economic boost. To be sure, Turner has made a few changes to the fund's aggressive positioning, such as holding fewer technology stocks among its biggest positions and favoring some larger-cap, more-defensive tech stocks like Intel. For the most part, however, he has stuck with fast-growing names. For instance, he has picked up Verisign, which he expects to offer 50% year-over-year earnings growth, thanks to its ability to offer its domain-registry services overseas. Such expectations are lofty, though, as are many tech stocks' valuations. If companies such as Verisign fail to meet their aggressive targets, the fund could be in for more difficult times.

The good news about Turner's discipline is that the fund should be positioned to surge when growth stocks awaken from their slumber. Still, for most cautious investors, losses such as the fund's 50% drop since last June are too great a cost to bear. The fund's low expenses, experienced management, and ability to shine under favorable conditions continue to make it a keeper for assertive types.

Address:	Vanguard Financial Ctr. P.O. Box 2600 Valley Forge, PA 19482 610–669–1000 / 800–662–7447
Web Address:	www.vanguard.com
*Inception:	03-11-92
Advisor:	Turner Inv. Partners
Subadvisor:	None
NTF Plans:	Fidelity

Minimum Purchase:	$10000	Add: $100 IRA: $1000
Min Auto Inv Plan:	$100	Add: $100
Sales Fees:	No-load	
Management Fee:	.75%, .12%A	
Actual Fees:	Mgt: 0.62%	Dist: —
Expense Projections:	3Yr: $208	5Yr: $362 10Yr: $810
Avg Brok Commission:	—	Income Distrib: Annually
Total Cost (relative to category):		Low

Vanguard Growth Index

Ticker	Load	NAV	Yield	Total Assets	Mstar Category
VIGRX	None	$26.42	0.7%	$10,271.8 mil	Large Growth

Prospectus Objective: Growth

Vanguard Growth Index Fund seeks to match the performance of the S&P 500/Barra Growth Index.

The fund employs a passive management strategy designed to track the performance of the S&P 500/BARRA Growth Index. It attempts to replicate the target index by investing all or substantially all of its assets in the stocks that make up the Index.

The fund currently offers Investor, Institutional and Admiral shares. Prior to Oct. 27, 1998, the fund was named Vanguard Index Trust Growth Portfolio.

Historical Profile

Return Average
Risk Average
Rating ★★★ Neutral

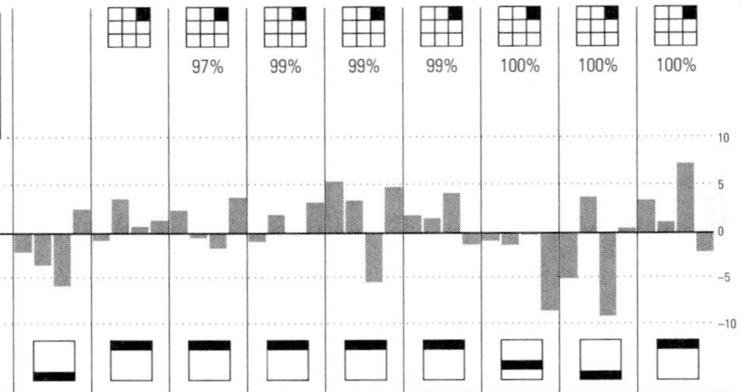

Investment Style
Equity
Average Stock %: 97% 99% 99% 99% 100% 100% 100%

▼ Manager Change
▽ Partial Manager Change

Fund Performance vs. Category Average
■ Quarterly Fund Return +/– Category Average
— Category Baseline

Performance Quartile (within Category)

Portfolio Manager(s)

George U. Sauter. Since 11-92. AB'76 Dartmouth C.; MBA'80 U. of Chicago. Other funds currently managed: Vanguard Small Cap Index, Vanguard Balanced Index, Vanguard Equity-Income.

History

1990	1991	1992	1993	1994	1995	1996	1997	1998	1999	2000	12-01	History
—	—	10.26	10.20	10.28	13.97	16.90	22.53	31.67	39.43	30.57	26.42	NAV
—	—	3.19*	1.53	2.89	38.06	23.74	36.34	42.21	28.76	−22.21	−12.93	Total Return %
—	—	−0.46*	−8.53	1.58	0.53	0.79	2.99	13.63	7.72	−13.11	−1.05	+/– S&P 500
—	—	—	1.60	−1.96	−0.59	−1.78	2.60	−2.89	−0.92	2.32	7.57	+/– Russ Top 200 Grt
—	—	0.59	2.06	2.07	1.96	1.59	1.37	0.98	0.72	0.32	0.61	Income Return %
—	—	2.60	−0.54	0.81	36.11	22.15	34.97	41.23	28.04	−22.53	−13.54	Capital Return %
—	—	—	89	11	17	13	6	19	69	78	11	Total Rtn % Rank Cat
—	—	0.06	0.21	0.21	0.20	0.22	0.23	0.22	0.23	0.13	0.19	Income $
—	—	0.00	0.00	0.00	0.00	0.14	0.25	0.12	1.04	0.00	0.00	Capital Gains $
—	—	0.00	0.20	0.20	0.20	0.20	0.20	0.22	0.22	0.22	—	Expense Ratio %
—	—	2.85	2.10	2.08	1.71	1.57	1.19	0.92	0.64	0.33	—	Income Ratio %
—	—	—	36	28	24	29	26	29	33	33	—	Turnover Rate %
—	—	15,791.5	50.6	86.2	271.0	786.9	2,365.3	6,644.3	15,232.5	11,289.6	8,444.8	Net Assets $mil

Performance 12-31-01

	1st Qtr	2nd Qtr	3rd Qtr	4th Qtr	Total
1997	3.54	20.23	5.83	3.49	36.34
1998	16.20	5.82	−7.21	24.64	42.21
1999	6.90	3.81	−3.44	20.15	28.76
2000	4.03	−1.39	−8.77	−16.88	−22.21
2001	−17.50	7.70	−13.26	12.97	−12.93

Trailing	Total Return%	+/– S&P 500	+/– Russ Top 200 Grth	% Rank All	% Rank Cat	Growth of $10,000
3 Mo	12.97	2.28	0.11	29	58	11,297
6 Mo	−2.01	3.55	4.98	47	5	9,799
1 Yr	−12.93	−1.05	7.57	68	11	8,707
3 Yr Avg	−4.46	−3.43	3.56	91	62	8,721
5 Yr Avg	11.08	0.38	2.49	14	26	16,909
10 Yr Avg	—	—	—	—	—	—
15 Yr Avg	—	—	—	—	—	—

Tax Analysis	Tax-Adj Ret%	%Rank Cat	%Pretax Ret	%Rank Cat
3 Yr Avg	−4.90	56	—	—
5 Yr Avg	10.52	15	94.9	6
10 Yr Avg	—	—	—	—

Potential Capital Gain Exposure: −18% of assets

Risk Analysis

Time Period	Load-Adj Return %	Risk %Rank[1] All	Risk %Rank[1] Cat	Morningstar Return	Morningstar Risk	Morningstar Risk-Adj Rating
1 Yr	−12.93					
3 Yr	−4.46	81	33	−1.82[2]	1.18	★★
5 Yr	11.08	77	23	1.48[2]	1.06	★★★★
Incept	13.19	—	—	—	—	

Average Historical Rating (75 months): 4.5★s

[1] 1=low, 100=high [2] T-Bill return substituted for category avg.

Category Rating (3 Yr)

1 2 **3** 4 5
Worst Best

Return Average
Risk Average

Other Measures	Standard Index S&P 500	Best Fit Index S&P 500
Alpha	−2.0	−2.0
Beta	1.17	1.17
R-Squared	88	88
Standard Deviation		20.57
Mean		−4.46
Sharpe Ratio		−0.53

Portfolio Analysis 09-30-01

Share change since 06-01 Total Stocks: 159

	Sector	PE	YTD Ret%	% Assets
⊖ General Elec	Industrials	30.1	−15.00	7.35
⊖ Microsoft	Technology	57.6	52.78	6.36
⊖ Pfizer	Health	34.7	−12.40	5.37
⊖ Wal-Mart Stores	Retail	40.3	8.94	4.67
⊖ IBM	Technology	26.9	43.00	3.81
⊖ Johnson & Johnson	Health	16.6	14.01	3.56
⊖ Intel	Technology	73.1	4.89	3.34
⊖ Merck	Health	19.1	−35.90	2.97
⊖ SBC Comms	Services	18.4	−16.00	2.61
⊖ Cisco Sys	Technology	—	−52.60	2.52
⊖ Coca-Cola	Staples	35.5	−21.40	2.42
⊖ Bristol-Myers Squibb	Health	20.2	−26.00	2.11
⊖ Philip Morris	Staples	12.1	9.12	2.09
⊖ Procter & Gamble	Staples	38.8	3.12	1.94
⊖ Tyco Intl	Industrials	27.1	6.23	1.93
⊖ Home Depot	Retail	42.9	12.07	1.81
⊕ PepsiCo	Staples	31.4	−0.54	1.75
⊖ Eli Lilly	Health	28.9	−14.40	1.75
⊖ Abbott Labs	Health	51.6	17.08	1.67
⊖ Fannie Mae	Financials	16.2	−6.95	1.65
⊖ Oracle	Technology	32.1	−52.40	1.55
⊖ American Home Products	Health	—	−1.91	1.49
⊖ Dell Comp	Technology	61.8	55.87	1.27
⊖ Amgen	Health	52.8	−11.70	1.20
⊖ Schering-Plough	Health	22.2	−35.90	1.11

Current Investment Style

Style: Value Blnd Growth; Size: Large Med Small

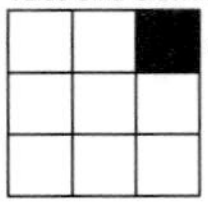

	Stock Port Avg	Relative S&P 500 Current	Relative S&P 500 Hist	Rel Cat
Price/Earnings Ratio	35.2	1.14	1.21	0.99
Price/Book Ratio	8.4	1.48	1.49	1.32
Price/Cash Flow	21.5	1.19	1.23	0.95
3 Yr Earnings Growth	17.6	1.20	1.30	0.82
1 Yr Earnings Est%	2.1	—	—	0.69
Med Mkt Cap $mil	102,899	1.7	1.8	2.17

Special Securities % assets 09-30-01	
Restricted/Illiquid Secs	0
Emerging-Markets Secs	0
Options/Futures/Warrants	No

Composition % assets 09-30-01	
Cash	0.0
Stocks*	100.0
Bonds	0.0
Other	0.0
*Foreign (% stocks)	0.6

Market Cap	
Giant	71.3
Large	23.9
Medium	4.8
Small	0.1
Micro	0.0

Sector Weightings	% of Stocks	Rel S&P	5-Year High	5-Year Low
Utilities	0.2	0.1	2	0
Energy	0.2	0.0	4	0
Financials	6.6	0.4	10	1
Industrials	11.5	1.0	20	9
Durables	0.4	0.3	2	0
Staples	13.6	1.7	23	6
Services	6.1	0.6	23	3
Retail	10.2	1.5	12	5
Health	26.5	1.8	27	13
Technology	24.8	1.4	52	7

Analysis by Scott Cooley 11-14-01

Vanguard Growth Index is defying a popular convention about indexing.

Indexing is supposed to work like this: When an asset class is in favor, the index fund that tracks it is supposed to perform extremely well. Conversely, when an asset class is out of favor, index funds in that area are supposed to underperform actively managed offerings. The theory is that because the index fund should be less subject to style drift and holds no cash, it's more fully exposed to the performance of the asset class, whether good or bad. Based on that theory, this fund should be suffering in 2001.

The fund's absolute returns aren't pretty, but they actually stack up quite well versus its peers'. For the year to date through Nov. 13, the fund has lost 13.8%, which is good enough to put it ahead of more than 90% of its large-growth rivals. Unlike many large-growth funds, this one has had little exposure to unprofitable companies with giant market caps—especially in the technology arena. While that held back the fund a bit in 1999's go-go growth market, it has allowed the fund to hold up better than its peers more recently. Moreover, the fund owns shares in some strong-performing giant-cap stocks that most of its rivals have avoided, including IBM and Philip Morris. The latter hasn't been in the portfolio the whole year, but it held up especially well in the turbulent third quarter.

Of course, the fund has considerable longer-term advantages, too. Its rock-bottom expense ratio gives it an edge over its rivals, and its buy-and-hold approach has contributed to superb historical tax efficiency. Moreover, moderate redemptions have allowed manager Gus Sauter to realize some tax losses that he can use to offset future gains, so the fund's stellar tax efficiency should stay intact.

With growth stocks more attractively valued than they were a couple of years ago, we think this fund is a particularly compelling choice.

Address:	Vanguard Financial Ctr. P.O. Box 2600, Valley Forge, PA 19482, 800-662-7447 / 610-669-1000
Web Address:	www.vanguard.com
*Inception:	11-02-92
Advisor:	Vanguard Core Mgmt. Grp.
Subadvisor:	None
NTF Plans:	N/A

Minimum Purchase:	$3000	Add: $100 IRA: $1000
Min Auto Inv Plan:	$3000	Add: $50
Sales Fees:	No-load	
Management Fee:	.20%	
Actual Fees:	Mgt: 0.20%	Dist: —
Expense Projections:	3Yr: $71	5Yr: $124 10Yr: $280
Avg Brok Commission:	—	Income Distrib: Quarterly
Total Cost (relative to category):		Low

Vanguard Health Care

Ticker	Load	NAV	Yield	Total Assets	Mstar Category
VGHCX	None	$116.84	0.8%	$17,780.3 mil	Spec Health Care

Prospectus Objective: Specialty—Health

Vanguard Health Care Fund seeks long-term growth of capital.

The fund normally invests at least 80% of assets in equities of companies engaged in the development, production, or distribution of products and services related to the treatment or prevention of diseases and other medical infirmities. This includes pharmaceutical firms, medical-supply firms, and companies that operate hospitals and other health-care facilities. It may also invest up to 30% of assets in foreign securities.

The fund levies a 1% redemption fee within 12 months; this fee is paid to the portfolio. The fund offers Admiral and Investor shares. Prior to Oct. 27, 1998, the fund was named Vanguard Specialized Portfolios - Health Care Portfolio.

Historical Profile
Return: High
Risk: Below Avg
Rating: ★★★★★ Highest

Investment Style
Equity
Average Stock %: 89% 88% 87% 90% 91% 91%

▼ Manager Change
▽ Partial Manager Change

Fund Performance vs. Category Average
■ Quarterly Fund Return +/– Category Average
— Category Baseline

Performance Quartile (within Category)

Portfolio Manager(s)

Edward P. Owens, CFA. Since 5-84. BS'68 U. of Virginia; MBA'74 Harvard U. Other fund currently managed: Vanguard Health Care Adm.

1990	1991	1992	1993	1994	1995	1996	1997	1998	1999	2000	12-01	History
25.69	36.50	34.01	35.07	35.47	49.82	58.35	71.88	96.85	95.21	132.74	116.84	NAV
16.79	46.32	–1.57	11.81	9.54	45.17	21.36	27.32	40.80	7.04	60.56	–6.87	Total Return %
19.91	15.84	–9.19	1.75	8.22	7.64	–1.59	–6.03	12.23	–14.00	69.66	5.00	+/– S&P 500
22.98	12.12	–10.54	0.52	9.61	8.73	0.16	–3.98	17.37	–16.52	71.49	4.02	+/– Wilshire 5000
2.38	2.06	1.93	2.28	1.65	1.61	1.50	1.34	1.19	1.02	1.19	0.79	Income Return %
14.42	44.26	–3.49	9.52	7.89	43.56	19.86	25.98	39.62	6.01	59.37	–7.66	Capital Return %
30	60	36	7	29	65	13	45	4	52	33	24	Total Rtn % Rank Cat
0.55	0.53	0.70	0.76	0.57	0.57	0.74	0.78	0.84	0.97	1.07	1.03	Income $
0.84	0.53	1.20	1.97	2.31	1.02	1.29	1.54	3.08	7.14	15.93	5.46	Capital Gains $
0.39	0.36	0.30	0.22	0.19	0.40	0.45	0.38	0.40	0.36	0.39	0.34	Expense Ratio %
2.34	2.54	1.98	2.06	2.37	1.58	1.57	1.41	1.28	1.13	0.92	1.03	Income Ratio %
28	17	7	15	19	25	13	7	10	11	27	21	Turnover Rate %
163.6	547.6	607.1	609.1	708.1	1,473.4	2,661.7	4,466.2	9,268.3	10,420.9	17,242.4	16,241.4	Net Assets $mil

Performance 12-31-01

	1st Qtr	2nd Qtr	3rd Qtr	4th Qtr	Total
1997	1.61	19.14	4.21	0.92	27.32
1998	15.01	5.63	–2.30	18.64	40.80
1999	1.96	3.46	–7.21	9.35	7.04
2000	14.75	16.25	9.48	9.94	60.56
2001	–12.60	5.66	–1.38	2.26	–6.87

Trailing	Total Return%	+/– S&P 500	+/– Wil 5000	% Rank All	% Rank Cat	Growth of $10,000
3 Mo	2.26	–8.42	–10.11	71	84	10,226
6 Mo	0.85	6.40	6.33	35	28	10,085
1 Yr	–6.87	5.00	4.02	55	24	9,313
3 Yr Avg	16.97	18.00	17.62	4	43	16,004
5 Yr Avg	23.47	12.77	13.76	1	3	28,690
10 Yr Avg	19.81	6.88	7.53	1	9	60,935
15 Yr Avg	21.11	7.38	8.11	1	1	176,890

Tax Analysis	Tax-Adj Ret%	%Rank Cat	%Pretax Ret	%Rank Cat
3 Yr Avg	14.38	43	84.7	79
5 Yr Avg	21.32	9	90.8	30
10 Yr Avg	17.70	9	89.4	18

Potential Capital Gain Exposure: 31% of assets

Risk Analysis

Time Period	Load-Adj Return %	Risk %Rank[1] All	Risk %Rank[1] Cat	Morningstar Return	Morningstar Risk	Morningstar Risk-Adj Rating
1 Yr	–7.81					
3 Yr	16.58	34	1	2.75[2]	0.39	★★★★★
5 Yr	23.47	40	1	5.72[2]	0.46	★★★★★
10 Yr	19.81	53	1	3.28	0.66	★★★★★

Average Historical Rating (176 months): 4.8★s

[1] 1=low, 100=high [2] T-Bill return substituted for category avg.

Category Rating (3 Yr)

1 2 3 4 5
Worst Best

Return: Average
Risk: Low

Other Measures	Standard Index S&P 500	Best Fit Index SPMid400
Alpha	13.7	10.4
Beta	0.27	0.26
R-Squared	13	16
Standard Deviation		14.64
Mean		16.97
Sharpe Ratio		0.94

Portfolio Analysis 09-30-01

Share chng since 06-01 Total Stocks: 132	Subsector	PE	YTD Ret%	% Assets
⊕ Pharmacia	Chemicals	36.5	–29.30	5.86
⊕ Pfizer	Gen Pharm/Bio	34.7	–12.40	3.34
⊕ American Home Products	Gen Pharm/Bio	—	–1.91	3.28
McKesson HBOC	Health	—	4.92	3.05
⊖ Abbott Labs	Gen Pharm/Bio	51.6	17.08	2.94
⊕ Eli Lilly	Gen Pharm/Bio	28.9	–14.40	2.85
⊖ Johnson & Johnson	Gen Pharm/Bio	16.6	14.01	2.82
⊕ Merck	Gen Pharm/Bio	19.1	–35.90	2.52
⊕ Roche Hldgs (Br)	Gen Pharm/Bio	—	—	2.39
⊖ HCA – The Healthcare Company	Hospitals	24.1	–12.20	2.30
⊖ Tenet Healthcare	Hospitals	30.1	32.14	2.05
⊖ Cardinal Health	Health	35.1	–2.51	2.01
⊖ Glaxo Wellcome PLC ADR	Gen Pharm/Bio	24.2	–9.77	2.00
⊖ Astrazeneca ADR	Gen Pharm/Bio	32.4	–8.15	1.98
Becton Dickinson	Medical Devices	22.9	–3.20	1.86
⊕ Fujisawa Pharma	Gen Pharm/Bio	39.6	—	1.86
⊖ Immunex	Gen Pharm/Bio	89.4	–31.70	1.82
⊕ CVS	Retail	16.2	–50.30	1.51
⊕ Novartis (Br)	Gen Pharm/Bio	—	—	1.47
Gilead Sciences	Emg. Pharm/Bio	—	58.48	1.47
⊕ Schering–Plough	Gen Pharm/Bio	22.2	–35.90	1.43
⊖ Genzyme Corporation General Di	Emg. Pharm/Bio	—	33.11	1.43
⊖ Astrazeneca	Gen Pharm/Bio	31.9	—	1.40
⊖ Bristol–Myers Squibb	Gen Pharm/Bio	20.2	–26.00	1.38
Allergan	Gen Pharm/Bio	48.7	–22.10	1.27

Current Investment Style

Style: Value Blnd Growth; Size: Large Med Small

	Stock Port Avg	Relative S&P 500 Current	Relative S&P 500 Hist	Rel Cat
Price/Earnings Ratio	32.6	1.05	1.12	0.81
Price/Book Ratio	7.4	1.29	1.05	0.82
Price/Cash Flow	22.3	1.24	1.12	0.78
3 Yr Earnings Growth	15.7	1.07	0.57	0.72
1 Yr Earnings Est%	16.6	—	—	0.73
Med Mkt Cap $mil	19,607	0.3	0.3	0.89

Special Securities % assets 09-30-01	
Restricted/Illiquid Secs	0
Emerging–Markets Secs	0
Options/Futures/Warrants	No

Composition % assets 09-30-01	
Cash	11.3
Stocks*	88.7
Bonds	0.0
Other	0.0
*Foreign (% stocks)	24.6

Market Cap	
Giant	40.1
Large	28.8
Medium	27.5
Small	3.5
Micro	0.1

Subsector Weightings	% of Stocks	Rel Cat
Gen Pharm/Bio	50.9	1.1
Medical Devices	6.2	1.1
Hospitals	4.9	1.7
Other Providers	0.9	0.8
HMOs/PPOs	2.9	1.4
Emg. Pharm/Bio	4.3	0.2
Diagnostics	2.0	1.4
Tech/Bus Svs	1.6	0.7
Other	26.5	1.2

Analysis by Peter Di Teresa 11-30-01

Vanguard Health Care Fund almost never shoots the lights out, but with its long-term success, so what?

Many investors seem to regard sector funds as market-timing tools, but this fund shows the appeal of buying and holding. Its 10-year return is in the category's best decile, and its 24% annualized five-year return through Nov. 29, 2001, is also top-decile. Yet the fund's calendar-year returns rarely rank so highly. At the same time, it hasn't ended a year in the category's bottom third in more than a decade, regardless of the market environment.

One key to that consistent strength has been good diversification among health-care's subsectors. Unlike many peers who seem to think that health care consists solely of drug companies and biotech firms, manager Ed Owens disperses the portfolio among a variety of subsectors. He also doesn't make big bets on single stocks or on smaller-cap issues. (The fund's enormous $17.3-billion asset base is partly responsible for that, though even when it was much smaller, Owens never really bet big on single stocks or put much into small caps.) That diverse portfolio has held up reasonably well in 2001. The fund's 6.5% year-to-date loss is less than three fourths of its peers'.

Of course, sound stock selection has also been helpful to the fund's long-term performance. While looking for companies with good long-term growth potential, Owens also pays more attention to prices than many of his peers. That value bent was particularly helpful in 2000, when he cut back on overpriced biotech stocks in favor of services stocks, which were relatively cheap and were benefiting from improved pricing power. Medical services wound up being health care's best-performing subsector for the year.

This fund remains one of our favorite health-care vehicles.

Address:	Vanguard Financial Ctr. P.O. Box 2600 Valley Forge, PA 19482 800–662–7447 / 610–669–1000
Web Address:	www.vanguard.com
Inception:	05-23-84
Advisor:	Wellington Mgmt.
Subadvisor:	None
NTF Plans:	N/A

Minimum Purchase:	$25000	Add: $100 IRA: $25000
Min Auto Inv Plan:	$25000	Add: $50
Sales Fees:	No-load, 1.00%R within 60 months	
Management Fee:	.15% mx./.05% mn.	
Actual Fees:	Mgt: 0.06%	Dist: —
Expense Projections:	3Yr: $230	5Yr: $202 10Yr: $456
Avg Brok Commission:	—	Income Distrib: Annually
Total Cost (relative to category):		Low

Vanguard High–Yield Corporate

Ticker	Load	NAV	Yield	SEC Yield	Total Assets	Mstar Category
VWEHX	None	$6.29	9.5%	—	$6,159.2 mil	High–Yield Bond

Prospectus Objective: Corp Bond—High Yield

Vanguard High-Yield Corporate Fund seeks current income.

The fund normally invests at least 80% of assets in high-yielding debt securities rated B or better. It may invest the remaining assets in convertible securities, preferred stocks, and money-market instruments. The fund may also invest in U.S. dollar-denominated foreign securities.

The fund offers Admiral and Investor shares.

Historical Profile

Return: Above Avg
Risk: Above Avg
Rating: ★★★ Neutral

Investment Style: Fixed-Income

Income Rtn %Rank Cat: 60 69 72 49 66 78 71 75

Growth of Principal vs. Interest Rate Shifts
- Principal Value $000 (NAV with capital gains reinvested)
- Interest Rate % on 10 Yr Treasury
- ▼ Manager Change
- ▽ Partial Manager Change
- ► Mgr Unknown After
- ◄ Mgr Unknown Before

Performance Quartile (within Category)

Portfolio Manager(s)

Earl E. McEvoy. Since 1-84. BA'70 Dartmouth C.; MBA'72 Columbia U. Other funds currently managed: Global Utility A, Global Utility B, Vanguard Long-Term Corporate Bond.

1990	1991	1992	1993	1994	1995	1996	1997	1998	1999	2000	12-01	History
6.22	7.16	7.41	8.02	7.20	7.85	7.87	8.08	7.83	7.39	6.69	6.29	NAV
–5.85	29.01	14.24	18.24	–1.71	19.15	9.55	11.91	5.62	2.49	–0.88	2.90	Total Return %
–14.80	13.01	6.84	8.49	1.21	0.69	5.93	2.22	–3.06	3.32	–12.51	–5.52	+/– LB Aggregate
0.54	–14.74	–2.42	–0.67	–0.74	1.77	–2.87	–0.72	5.04	–0.79	4.33	–2.87	+/– FB High–Yield
12.87	13.20	10.70	9.80	8.81	9.83	9.12	9.08	8.54	8.32	9.01	9.28	Income Return %
–18.71	15.81	3.54	8.44	–10.52	9.33	0.43	2.82	–2.93	–5.83	–9.89	–6.38	Capital Return %
26	79	83	56	32	15	99	72	5	73	12	48	Total Rtn % Rank Cat
0.92	0.78	0.73	0.70	0.68	0.68	0.69	0.69	0.66	0.63	0.64	0.60	Income $
0.00	0.00	0.00	0.00	0.00	0.00	0.00	0.00	0.03	0.00	0.00	0.00	Capital Gains $
0.38	0.40	0.34	0.34	0.32	0.34	0.34	0.29	0.28	0.29	0.28	—	Expense Ratio %
12.56	13.35	11.13	9.82	8.81	9.13	8.85	8.92	8.63	8.26	8.34	—	Income Ratio %
41	61	44	83	51	33	38	23	45	31	20	—	Turnover Rate %
693.8	1,452.2	2,021.0	2,529.8	2,120.7	2,900.0	3,563.4	4,543.9	5,380.5	5,699.2	5,882.3	5,160.3	Net Assets $mil

Performance 12-31-01

	1st Qtr	2nd Qtr	3rd Qtr	4th Qtr	Total
1997	0.23	4.97	3.85	2.42	11.91
1998	3.10	1.44	–1.54	2.57	5.62
1999	1.75	–0.81	–0.93	2.51	2.49
2000	–1.53	1.98	1.41	–2.66	–0.88
2001	4.20	–2.18	–2.71	3.77	2.90

Trailing	Total Return%	+/– LB Agg	+/– FB High–Yield	% Rank All	% Rank Cat	Growth of $10,000
3 Mo	3.77	3.73	–1.88	68	88	10,377
6 Mo	0.95	–3.70	–0.49	34	45	10,095
1 Yr	2.90	–5.52	–2.87	37	48	10,290
3 Yr Avg	1.49	–4.78	0.32	65	27	10,454
5 Yr Avg	4.32	–3.10	1.08	75	11	12,356
10 Yr Avg	7.91	0.68	0.08	44	18	21,413
15 Yr Avg	7.81	–0.31	–0.86	55	18	30,892

Tax Analysis	Tax-Adj Ret%	%Rank Cat	%Pretax Ret	%Rank Cat
3 Yr Avg	–1.95	23	—	—
5 Yr Avg	0.81	11	18.8	72
10 Yr Avg	4.28	12	54.1	8

Potential Capital Gain Exposure: –22% of assets

Risk Analysis

Time Period	Load-Adj Return %	Risk %Rank[1] All	Risk %Rank[1] Cat	Morningstar Return	Morningstar Risk	Morningstar Risk-Adj Rating
1 Yr	2.90					
3 Yr	1.49	33	11	–0.71[2]	1.51	★★
5 Yr	4.32	36	6	–0.15[2]	1.42	★★
10 Yr	7.91	40	4	0.94[2]	1.15	★★★★

Average Historical Rating (193 months): 4.0★s

[1]1=low, 100=high [2] T-Bill return substituted for category avg.

Category Rating (3 Yr)

1 2 3 4 5 — Worst / Best

Return: Above Avg
Risk: Below Avg

Other Measures	Standard Index LB Agg	Best Fit Index FB HY
Alpha	–3.6	–0.4
Beta	0.36	0.81
R–Squared	3	90
Standard Deviation		6.40
Mean		1.49
Sharpe Ratio		–0.62

Portfolio Analysis 09-30-01

Total Fixed-Income: 220	Date of Maturity	Amount $000	Value $000	% Net Assets
US Treasury Note 6.875%	05-15-06	120,000	136,542	2.36
US Treasury Note 6.5%	08-15-05	100,000	111,308	1.92
US Treasury Note 6%	08-15-04	100,000	108,294	1.87
EchoStar DBS 9.375%	02-01-09	90,000	91,575	1.58
Charter Comm 8.625%	04-01-09	92,000	87,860	1.52
British Sky Brdcstg 8.2%	07-15-09	75,000	77,458	1.34
Tenet Healthcare 8.125%	12-01-08	70,000	75,250	1.30
Us Steel 144A 10.75%	08-01-08	80,250	72,225	1.25
Lenfest Comm 8.375%	11-01-05	62,500	69,397	1.20
Dana 9%	08-15-11	75,000	65,250	1.13
WMX Tech 7.375%	08-01-10	57,000	60,762	1.05
Pioneer Natural 9.625%	04-01-10	50,000	55,000	0.95
Lyondell Petrochemical 9.625%	05-01-07	56,000	53,760	0.93
Allied Waste Inds 8.875%	04-01-08	52,000	52,780	0.91
Calpine 8.5%	02-15-11	50,000	51,684	0.89
WMX Tech 6.875%	05-15-09	50,000	51,532	0.89
Fox/Liberty Ntwks 8.875%	08-15-07	48,665	51,098	0.88
Amkor Tech 9.25%	02-15-08	60,000	51,000	0.88
American Standard 7.375%	02-01-08	50,000	50,750	0.88
MGM Grand 8.5%	09-15-10	50,000	49,912	0.86

Current Investment Style

Not Available

Avg Eff Duration[1]	4.5 Yrs
Avg Eff Maturity	—
Avg Credit Quality	BB
Avg Wtd Coupon	8.77%
Avg Wtd Price	96.95% of par

[1]figure provided by fund

Special Securities % assets 09-30-01	
Restricted/Illiquid Secs	5
Exotic Mortgage–Backed	0
Emerging–Markets Secs	0
Options/Futures/Warrants	No

Credit Analysis % bonds 09-30-01			
US Govt	6	BB	49
AAA	0	B	35
AA	0	Below B	1
A	0	NR/NA	0
BBB	10		

Sector Breakdown % bonds 09-30-01			
US Treasuries	0	CMOs	0
GNMA mtgs	0	ARMs	0
FNMA mtgs	0	Other	94
FHLMC mtgs	0		

Coupon Range	% of Bonds	Rel Cat
0%, PIK	0.00	0.00
0% to 9%	57.24	1.89
9% to 12%	40.17	0.75
12% to 14%	2.04	0.23
More than 14%	0.55	0.40

1.00=Category Average

Composition % assets 09-30-01			
Cash	0.7	Bonds	99.3
Stocks	0.0	Other	0.0

Analysis by Alan Papier 12-06-01

The nuances of this fund's conservative strategy have been highlighted in 2001.

Vanguard High-Yield Corporate Fund is among the tamest entrants in the high-yield category. That's partly because its rock-bottom expense ratio doesn't cannibalize the income stream paid to shareholders, which means longtime manager Earl McEvoy doesn't have to dig deep into lower-rated territory to produce a competitive yield. As a result, however, we expect the fund's yield to be consistently below average.

The upshot is that the fund takes on considerably less credit risk than its peers. In fact, the fund recently invested 12.5% of assets in BBB rated bonds—which are the lowest investment-grade tier—and a mere 0.6% in bonds rated below B or nonrateds. Meanwhile, the category norms were 6.5% and 13%, respectively.

That orientation means the fund will perform relatively well when the economy weakens and investors shun the risk associated with lower-quality fare. That was the case during the first nine months of 2001, a period of plummeting corporate earnings that was punctuated by the tragic events of Sept. 11. Indeed, the fund lost a modest 0.8% of its value from the first of the year through Sept. 30, while the average high-yield fund lost 3.7%.

But the flip side is that the fund tends to lag its peers during rallies, which has been perfectly illustrated during the fourth quarter of 2001. With high-yield credit spreads at historically wide levels (a general signal that the sector is attractively priced), the sector has had a nice run, rebounding off its third-quarter lows. After trailing its average peer by 80 basis points in October, the fund has continued to lag by even wider margins since.

That said, we think the fund's long-term track record speaks for itself. This is a great choice for conservative high-yield investors.

Address:	Vanguard Financial Ctr. P.O. Box 2600, Valley Forge, PA 19482, 800–662–7447 / 610–669–1000
Web Address:	www.vanguard.com
Inception:	12-27-78
Advisor:	Wellington Mgmt.
Subadvisor:	None
NTF Plans:	N/A

Minimum Purchase:	$3000	Add: $100	IRA: $1000
Min Auto Inv Plan:	$3000	Add: $100	
Sales Fees:	No–load, 1.00%R within 12 months		
Management Fee:	.06% mx./.03% mn.		
Actual Fees:	Mgt: 0.26%	Dist: —	
Expense Projections:	3Yr: $93	5Yr: $163	10Yr: $368
Avg Brok Commission:	—	Income Distrib: Monthly	
Total Cost (relative to category):		Low	

Vanguard High–Yield Tax–Exempt

Ticker	Load	NAV	Yield	SEC Yield	Total Assets	Mstar Category
VWAHX	None	$10.48	5.5%	—	$3,568.4 mil	Muni Natl Long–Term

Prospectus Objective: Muni Bond—National

Vanguard High-Yield Tax-Exempt Fund seeks income exempt from federal income tax, consistent with preservation of capital.

The fund usually invests at least 80% of assets in investment-grade municipal securities. It typically maintains an average weighted maturity between 15 and 25 years. The fund may invest up to 20% of assets in bonds subject to the Alternative Minimum Tax.

The fund offers Admiral and Investor shares.

Historical Profile
Return: High
Risk: Average
Rating: ★★★★ Above Avg

Investment Style
Fixed-Income
Income Rtn %Rank Cat: 17, 16, 23, 13, 12, 9, 11, 12

Growth of Principal vs. Interest Rate Shifts
— Principal Value $000 (NAV with capital gains reinvested)
— Interest Rate % on 10 Yr Treasury
▼ Manager Change
▽ Partial Manager Change
► Mgr Unknown After
◄ Mgr Unknown Before

Performance Quartile (within Category)

Portfolio Manager(s)

Ian A. MacKinnon. Since 11-81. BA'70 Lafayette C.; MBA'74 Pennsylvania State U. Other funds currently managed: Vanguard Balanced Index, Vanguard CA Insured Long Tax-Ex, Vanguard Short-Term Treasury.

Reid Smith, CFA. Since 9-96. BBA'81 U. of Hawaii; MBA'83 U. of Hawaii. Other funds currently managed: Vanguard FL Insured Long Tax-Ex, Vanguard Insured Long-Trm T/E, Vanguard CA Insured Interm Tax-Ex.

History

1990	1991	1992	1993	1994	1995	1996	1997	1998	1999	2000	12-01	History
9.96	10.53	10.57	11.01	9.66	10.76	10.63	10.93	10.97	10.04	10.50	10.48	NAV
5.91	14.75	9.88	12.66	−5.07	18.13	4.46	9.24	6.45	−3.38	10.73	5.34	Total Return %
−3.04	−1.25	2.48	2.91	−2.15	−0.34	0.84	−0.45	−2.22	−2.55	−0.90	−3.08	+/– LB Aggregate
−1.39	2.61	1.06	0.39	0.08	0.66	0.02	0.04	−0.03	−1.31	−0.97	0.26	+/– LB Muni
7.41	7.66	6.92	6.36	5.86	6.50	5.61	5.78	5.40	5.36	5.95	5.62	Income Return %
−1.49	7.09	2.96	6.30	−10.93	11.63	−1.15	3.46	1.05	−8.74	4.77	−0.27	Capital Return %
60	3	17	41	25	26	18	45	6	16	51	11	Total Rtn % Rank Cat
0.73	0.74	0.71	0.65	0.63	0.61	0.59	0.60	0.58	0.57	0.58	0.58	Income $
0.14	0.11	0.25	0.21	0.17	0.00	0.00	0.05	0.07	0.00	0.00	0.00	Capital Gains $
0.25	0.25	0.23	0.20	0.20	0.21	0.20	0.19	0.20	0.18	0.19	—	Expense Ratio %
7.30	7.34	6.83	6.15	5.83	6.15	5.66	5.56	5.28	5.33	5.74	—	Income Ratio %
82	58	64	34	50	33	19	27	24	22	32	—	Turnover Rate %
1,016.9	1,341.8	1,609.4	1,903.6	1,572.6	1,988.1	2,038.9	2,292.3	2,767.2	2,752.8	3,213.6	2,649.7	Net Assets $mil

Performance 12-31-01

	1st Qtr	2nd Qtr	3rd Qtr	4th Qtr	Total
1997	−0.51	3.63	3.07	2.79	9.24
1998	1.29	1.41	3.02	0.60	6.45
1999	0.82	−1.82	−1.10	−1.31	−3.38
2000	2.58	1.36	2.71	3.68	10.73
2001	2.91	1.18	1.91	−0.72	5.34

Trailing	Total Return%	+/– LB Agg	+/– LB Muni	% Rank All	% Rank Cat	Growth of $10,000
3 Mo	−0.72	−0.76	−0.06	88	28	9,928
6 Mo	1.17	−3.48	−0.95	33	71	10,117
1 Yr	5.34	−3.08	0.26	21	11	10,534
3 Yr Avg	4.07	−2.21	−0.69	40	10	11,270
5 Yr Avg	5.56	−1.87	−0.42	54	10	13,105
10 Yr Avg	6.63	−0.60	0.00	55	7	19,004
15 Yr Avg	7.29	−0.83	0.10	62	7	28,738

Tax Analysis	Tax-Adj Ret%	%Rank Cat	%Pretax Ret	%Rank Cat
3 Yr Avg	4.07	9	100.0	16
5 Yr Avg	5.51	10	99.1	46
10 Yr Avg	6.42	8	96.8	69

Potential Capital Gain Exposure: 1% of assets

Risk Analysis

Time Period	Load-Adj Return %	Risk %Rank[1] All	Risk %Rank[1] Cat	Morningstar Return	Morningstar Risk	Morningstar Risk-Adj Rating
1 Yr	5.34					
3 Yr	4.07	16	14	0.64[2]	0.98	★★★★
5 Yr	5.56	15	13	1.04[2]	0.94	★★★★
10 Yr	6.63	25	34	1.28	1.09	★★★★

Average Historical Rating (193 months): 3.9★s

[1] 1=low, 100=high [2] T-Bill return substituted for category avg.

Category Rating (3 Yr)

1 2 3 4 5
Worst Best

Return: High
Risk: Below Avg

Other Measures	Standard Index LB Agg	Best Fit Index LB Muni
Alpha	−1.8	−0.6
Beta	0.77	1.04
R–Squared	42	94

Standard Deviation	4.12
Mean	4.07
Sharpe Ratio	−0.25

Portfolio Analysis 06-30-01

Total Fixed-Income: 354	Date of Maturity	Amount $000	Value $000	% Net Assets
NJ Transp Cap Grant 5.5%	02-01-09	61,405	62,655	1.77
MA Wtr Res 6.5%	07-15-19	43,700	51,662	1.46
FL COP 5%	08-01-25	45,000	43,291	1.23
CT Dev Poll Cntrl Lt/Pwr 5.85%	09-01-28	39,975	39,810	1.13
CA State GO 5.25%	12-01-11	38,000	39,013	1.10
CA Cmnty Dev Apt 5.25%	05-15-25	37,785	36,614	1.04
MA Indl Fin Res Rec 6.3%	07-01-05	34,500	36,467	1.03
CA San Bernardino COP 6.875%	08-01-24	25,220	31,232	0.88
VA Pocahontas Pkwy Assn 5.5%	08-15-28	36,725	31,084	0.88
NJ Econ Dev Kapkowski Rd 6.375%	04-01-31	30,500	31,001	0.88
PA Delaware Indl Dev Res Rec 6.1%	01-01-31	30,500	30,721	0.87
NJ State COP 5.5%	09-15-10	28,085	30,713	0.87
AZ Maricopa Poll Cntrl 6.375%	08-01-15	30,000	30,623	0.87
AZ Univ Brd Regents 5.5%	06-01-16	26,660	30,301	0.86
MD Hlth/Higher Educ Fac 5.25%	08-15-38	32,055	30,260	0.86

Current Investment Style

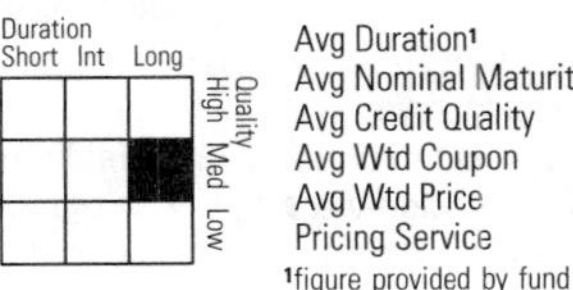

Avg Duration[1]	7.1 Yrs
Avg Nominal Maturity	12.7 Yrs
Avg Credit Quality	A
Avg Wtd Coupon	5.55%
Avg Wtd Price	100.10% of par
Pricing Service	J.J. Kenny

[1] figure provided by fund

Credit Analysis % bonds 09-30-01			
US Govt	0	BB	7
AAA	35	B	2
AA	17	Below B	0
A	9	NR/NA	9
BBB	23		

Special Securities % assets 06-30-01	
Restricted/Illiquid Secs	0
Inverse Floaters	0
Options/Futures/Warrants	No

Bond Type % assets 09-28-98	
Alternative Minimum Tax (AMT)	11.8
Insured	32.6
Prerefunded	12.5

Top 5 States % bonds			
TX	8.9	PA	7.5
CA	8.3	NJ	7.2
NY	8.3		

Composition % assets 06-30-01			
Cash	0.2	Bonds	99.9
Stocks	0.0	Other	0.0

Sector Weightings	% of Bonds	Rel Cat
General Obligation	9.0	0.4
Utilities	9.0	1.1
Health	16.5	1.1
Water/Waste	5.0	0.8
Housing	5.2	0.7
Education	3.4	0.5
Transportation	23.7	1.8
COP/Lease	4.4	1.5
Industrial	17.1	1.3
Misc Revenue	3.8	0.8
Demand	2.0	2.5

Analysis by William Harding 08-31-01

This fund will appeal to those looking for an extra shot of income but who can't stomach a lot of risk.

Looking for a fund that loads up on junk bonds to boost yield? Well, you won't find that here. But what you will get with Vanguard High-Yield Tax-Exempt Fund is even better. Management doesn't have to take on as much credit risk as its peers because the fund is blessed with extremely low expenses—only 18 basis points. Because expenses are deducted from a fund's yield, this cost advantage gives the fund a big leg up on the competition. Indeed, the fund sports a pretty fat yield of 5.38% for the trailing 12 months.

In addition to helping the fund maintain a hefty yield, its cost advantage has also led to an attractive risk/return profile. Indeed, the fund's annual returns have generally landed in the top half of the muni-national long-term category in recent years, resulting in long-term returns near the group's upper echelon.

Meanwhile, the fund's volatility has been kept in check thanks to management's mild-mannered approach. The fund holds about 25% of assets in BBB rated bonds, and almost 60% of assets are devoted to issues rated A or higher. As a result, the fund's overall credit quality is substantially higher than other tax-exempt funds that focus on high yield. Furthermore, management's interest-rate calls are typically moderate. Ian MacKinnon, Vanguard's bond strategist, has set a neutral range in recent years, which manager Reid Smith gets to work within. Smith was a little long in the range during the muni-bond market's rally in 2000, but he has since shortened it in 2001.

All told, this fund is a compelling option for investors who want juiced-up returns from their muni offering but still want to sleep at night.

Address:	Vanguard Financial Ctr. P.O. Box 2600 Valley Forge, PA 19482 800–662–7447 / 610–669–1000
Web Address:	www.vanguard.com
Inception:	12-27-78
Advisor:	Vanguard Fixed–Income Grp.
Subadvisor:	None
NTF Plans:	N/A

Minimum Purchase:	$3000	Add: $100 IRA: $1000
Min Auto Inv Plan:	$3000	Add: $50
Sales Fees:	No–load	
Management Fee:	None	
Actual Fees:	Mgt: 0.17%	Dist: —
Expense Projections:	3Yr: $61	5Yr: $107 10Yr: $243
Avg Brok Commission:	—	Income Distrib: Monthly
Total Cost (relative to category):		Low

Vanguard Inflation–Protected Secs

Ticker	Load	NAV	Yield	SEC Yield	Total Assets	Mstar Category
VIPSX	None	$10.62	4.2%	—	$772.4 mil	Short–Term Govt

Prospectus Objective: Government Treasury

Vanguard Inflation-Protected Securities Fund seeks to provide inflation protection and income consistent with investment in inflation-indexed securities.

The fund primarily invests in inflation-indexed bonds issued by the U.S. government. It may invest in bonds of any maturity, though the fund typically maintains a dollar-weighted average maturity of seven to 10 years. Up to 35% of assets may be invested in non-inflation-indexed securities, including investment-grade corporate debt and U.S. government and agency bonds. The fund may invest in options and futures agreements. It may also invest up to 15% of assets in illiquid securities.

Historical Profile

Return —
Risk —
Rating Not Rated

Investment Style
Fixed-Income
Income Rtn %Rank Cat
89

Growth of Principal vs. Interest Rate Shifts
— Principal Value $000 (NAV with capital gains reinvested)
— Interest Rate % on 10 Yr Treasury
▼ Manager Change
▽ Partial Manager Change
► Mgr Unknown After
◄ Mgr Unknown Before

Performance Quartile (within Category)

Portfolio Manager(s)

Ian A. MacKinnon. Since 6-00. BA'70 Lafayette C.; MBA'74 Pennsylvania State U. Other funds currently managed: Vanguard Balanced Index, Vanguard CA Insured Long Tax-Ex, Vanguard Short-Term Treasury.

Kenneth Volpert, CFA. Since 6-00. BS'81 U. of Illinois; MBA'85 U. of Chicago. Other funds currently managed: Vanguard Total Bond Market Index, Vanguard Interm-Term Bond Index, Vanguard Total Bond Market Index Inst.

John Hollyer, CFA. Since 6-00. BS U. of Pennsylvania. Other funds currently managed: Vanguard Short-Term Treasury, Vanguard Short-Term Federal, Vanguard Short-Term Federal Adm.

History

1990	1991	1992	1993	1994	1995	1996	1997	1998	1999	2000	12-01	History
—	—	—	—	—	—	—	—	—	—	10.34	10.62	NAV
—	—	—	—	—	—	—	—	—	—	5.92*	7.71	Total Return %
—	—	—	—	—	—	—	—	—	—	—	–0.71	+/– LB Aggregate
—	—	—	—	—	—	—	—	—	—	—	–0.82	+/– LB 1–3 Govt
—	—	—	—	—	—	—	—	—	—	2.73	4.38	Income Return %
—	—	—	—	—	—	—	—	—	—	3.19	3.34	Capital Return %
—	—	—	—	—	—	—	—	—	—	—	23	Total Rtn % Rank Cat
—	—	—	—	—	—	—	—	—	—	0.27	0.45	Income $
—	—	—	—	—	—	—	—	—	—	0.01	0.07	Capital Gains $
—	—	—	—	—	—	—	—	—	—	—	0.25	Expense Ratio %
—	—	—	—	—	—	—	—	—	—	—	6.38	Income Ratio %
—	—	—	—	—	—	—	—	—	—	—	122	Turnover Rate %
—	—	—	—	—	—	—	—	—	—	170.0	772.4	Net Assets $mil

Performance 12-31-01

	1st Qtr	2nd Qtr	3rd Qtr	4th Qtr	Total
1997	—	—	—	—	—
1998	—	—	—	—	—
1999	—	—	—	—	—
2000	—	—	1.99	3.75	5.92 *
2001	4.74	1.58	2.42	–1.14	7.72

Trailing	Total Return%	+/– LB Agg	+/– LB 1–3 Yr Govt	% Rank All	% Rank Cat	Growth of $10,000
3 Mo	–1.14	–1.18	—	95	98	9,886
6 Mo	1.25	–3.41	—	32	98	10,125
1 Yr	7.71	–0.71	—	11	23	10,771
3 Yr Avg	—	—	—	—	—	—
5 Yr Avg	—	—	—	—	—	—
10 Yr Avg	—	—	—	—	—	—
15 Yr Avg	—	—	—	—	—	—

Tax Analysis	Tax-Adj Ret%	%Rank Cat	%Pretax Ret	%Rank Cat
3 Yr Avg	—	—	—	—
5 Yr Avg	—	—	—	—
10 Yr Avg	—	—	—	—

Potential Capital Gain Exposure: NMF

Risk Analysis

Time Period	Load-Adj Return %	Risk %Rank¹ All	Risk %Rank¹ Cat	Morningstar Return	Morningstar Risk	Morningstar Risk-Adj Rating
1 Yr	7.71					
3 Yr	—	—	—	—	—	
5 Yr	—	—	—	—	—	
Incept	9.14	—	—	—	—	

Average Historical Rating —

¹1=low, 100=high

Category Rating (3 Yr)

Return
Risk

Other Measures	Standard Index LB Agg	Best Fit Index
Alpha	—	—
Beta	—	—
R–Squared	—	—
Standard Deviation		—
Mean		—
Sharpe Ratio		—

Portfolio Analysis 09-30-01

Total Fixed-Income: 8	Date of Maturity	Amount $000	Value $000	% Net Assets
US Treasury Bond 3.625%	04-15-28	194,200	228,741	36.75
US Treasury Note 3.625%	01-15-08	147,375	169,057	27.16
US Treasury Note 3.875%	01-15-09	67,950	78,037	12.54
US Treasury Note 4.25%	01-15-10	61,875	71,114	11.42
US Treasury Note 3.375%	01-15-07	48,850	56,609	9.09
US Treasury Note 3.54%	01-15-11	14,550	15,432	2.48
US Treasury Bond 3.875%	04-15-29	12,600	15,254	2.45
US Treasury Bond 3.384%	04-15-32	12,000	12,488	2.01

Analysis by Eric Jacobson 10-31-01

Don't let its short track-record fool you: Vanguard Inflation-Protected Securities is already a terrific choice.

As with the few other funds carrying a similar mandate, this one seeks to protect its investors' purchasing power against the ravages of inflation. Some rivals try to pursue that aim by holding a variety of securities. This fund has some flexibility in that department, but it is likely to stick almost exclusively with Treasury Inflation-Indexed Securities (TIPS). (As such, its long-term performance should be expected to lag that of more-adventuresome rivals.) Such issues pay a small amount of interest in similar fashion to other bonds, but they also promise a semi-annual adjustment to principal (or par) value that moves in line with the government-tracked consumer price index.

Because of the inflation protection that TIPS offer, they don't exhibit the same volatility that conventional Treasury bonds endure in response to changes in inflation expectations. Rather, inflation-indexed bond prices move more directly with the amount of yield the marketplace demands over and above the level of inflation, typically referred to as a bond's real yield. Because real yields don't shift nearly as much as inflation does, the volatility of inflation-indexed bonds is normally much lower than that of conventional issues of the same maturity.

The real clincher here, however, is Vanguard's ability to offer the fund for roughly 0.25%. In general, it's difficult to justify buying a mutual fund that holds mostly Treasury bonds because one can easily purchase them at no charge directly from the government. With this fund, however, you get the conveniences of a mutual fund along with the possibility that comanager John Hollyer will be able to sniff out the most inefficiently priced TIPS in the marketplace—and at what is likely to remain the lowest price around.

Current Investment Style

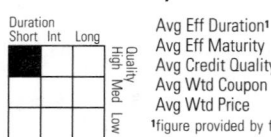

Duration: Short Int Long
Quality: High Med Low

Avg Eff Duration¹	2.0 Yrs
Avg Eff Maturity	—
Avg Credit Quality	AAA
Avg Wtd Coupon	3.70%
Avg Wtd Price	115.68% of par

¹figure provided by fund

Special Securities % assets 09-30-01	
Restricted/Illiquid Secs	0
Exotic Mortgage–Backed	0
Emerging–Markets Secs	0
Options/Futures/Warrants	No

Credit Analysis % bonds 09-30-01

US Govt	99	BB	0
AAA	2	B	0
AA	0	Below B	0
A	0	NR/NA	0
BBB	0		

Coupon Range	% of Bonds	Rel Cat
0%	0.00	0.00
0% to 7%	100.00	1.40
7% to 8.5%	0.00	0.00
8.5% to 10%	0.00	0.00
More than 10%	0.00	0.00

1.00=Category Average

Composition % assets 09-30-01

Cash	3.3	Bonds	96.7
Stocks	0.0	Other	0.0

Address: Vanguard Financial Ctr. P.O. Box 2600
Valley Forge, PA 19482
610–669–1000 / 800–662–7447
Web Address: www.vanguard.com

*Inception: 06-29-00
Advisor: Vanguard Grp.
Subadvisor: None
NTF Plans: N/A

Minimum Purchase:	$3000	Add: $100	IRA: $1000
Min Auto Inv Plan:	$3000	Add: $50	
Sales Fees:	No–load		
Management Fee:	.22%		
Actual Fees:	Mgt: 0.22%	Dist: —	
Expense Projections:	3Yr: $80	5Yr: —	10Yr: —
Avg Brok Commission:	—	Income Distrib: Quarterly	
Total Cost (relative to category):		Low	

Vanguard Insured Long–Trm T/E

Ticker	Load	NAV	Yield	SEC Yield	Total Assets	Mstar Category
VILPX	None	$12.37	5.0%	—	$2,696.5 mil	Muni Natl Long–Term

Prospectus Objective: Muni Bond—National

Vanguard Insured Long-Term Tax-Exempt Fund seeks income exempt from federal income tax.

The fund normally invests at least 80% of its assets in insured tax-free municipal securities. It may invest the balance of assets in municipal bonds rated A or higher. The average-weighted maturity generally ranges between 15 and 25 years. The overall quality of the portfolio is expected to be AAA.

The fund also offers Adm shares. Prior to Oct. 27, 1998, the fund was named Vanguard Municipal Bond Fund Insured Long-Term Portfolio.

Historical Profile

Return High
Risk Above Avg
Rating ★★★★ Above Avg

Investment Style
Fixed-Income
Income Rtn %Rank Cat: 29 33 31 23 15 15 17 31

Growth of Principal vs. Interest Rate Shifts
— Principal Value $000 (NAV with capital gains reinvested)
— Interest Rate % on 10 Yr Treasury
▼ Manager Change
▽ Partial Manager Change
► Mgr Unknown After
◄ Mgr Unknown Before

Performance Quartile (within Category)

Portfolio Manager(s)

Ian A. MacKinnon. Since 10-84. BA'70 Lafayette C.; MBA'74 Pennsylvania State U. Other funds currently managed: Vanguard Balanced Index, Vanguard CA Insured Long Tax-Ex, Vanguard Short-Term Treasury.

Reid Smith, CFA. Since 6-96. BBA'81 U. of Hawaii; MBA'83 U. of Hawaii. Other funds currently managed: Vanguard FL Insured Long Tax-Ex, Vanguard High-Yield Tax-Exempt, Vanguard CA Insured Interm Tax-Ex.

History

1990	1991	1992	1993	1994	1995	1996	1997	1998	1999	2000	12-01	History
11.50	12.03	12.14	12.81	11.23	12.60	12.34	12.62	12.65	11.65	12.54	12.37	NAV
7.04	12.49	9.17	13.09	–5.59	18.60	4.02	8.64	6.14	–2.91	13.61	4.24	Total Return %
–1.91	–3.52	1.77	3.35	–2.67	0.13	0.41	–1.04	–2.54	–2.08	1.98	–4.18	+/– LB Aggregate
–0.26	0.34	0.35	0.82	–0.45	1.13	–0.42	–0.56	–0.35	–0.85	1.92	–0.84	+/– LB Muni
7.06	6.97	6.42	5.99	5.61	6.14	5.46	5.58	5.32	5.22	5.70	5.08	Income Return %
–0.01	5.51	2.75	7.10	–11.20	12.45	–1.44	3.06	0.82	–8.13	7.91	–0.84	Capital Return %
18	28	40	29	32	19	27	68	13	8	6	38	Total Rtn % Rank Cat
0.79	0.78	0.75	0.71	0.70	0.67	0.67	0.67	0.66	0.64	0.65	0.62	Income $
0.12	0.08	0.20	0.18	0.17	0.00	0.07	0.08	0.07	0.00	0.00	0.07	Capital Gains $
0.25	0.25	0.23	0.20	0.20	0.21	0.20	0.19	0.20	0.19	0.19	—	Expense Ratio %
6.99	6.77	6.34	5.77	5.62	5.82	5.46	5.47	5.22	5.20	5.48	—	Income Ratio %
47	33	42	30	16	7	18	18	16	17	34	—	Turnover Rate %
1,250.8	1,701.6	1,997.6	2,161.7	1,738.0	2,017.3	1,949.1	2,075.3	2,268.0	2,153.0	2,496.3	1,847.0	Net Assets $mil

Performance 12-31-01

	1st Qtr	2nd Qtr	3rd Qtr	4th Qtr	Total
1997	–0.59	3.31	2.99	2.72	8.64
1998	0.90	1.32	3.40	0.41	6.14
1999	0.79	–2.15	–0.90	–0.65	–2.91
2000	3.75	1.48	2.35	5.43	13.61
2001	2.05	0.39	2.77	–0.98	4.24

Trailing	Total Return%	+/– LB Agg	+/– LB Muni	% Rank All	% Rank Cat	Growth of $10,000
3 Mo	–0.98	–1.02	–0.32	93	46	9,902
6 Mo	1.76	–2.90	–0.36	26	31	10,176
1 Yr	4.24	–4.18	–0.84	29	38	10,424
3 Yr Avg	4.76	–1.51	0.01	33	2	11,498
5 Yr Avg	5.80	–1.62	–0.17	51	5	13,259
10 Yr Avg	6.67	–0.56	0.04	54	6	19,066
15 Yr Avg	7.27	–0.85	0.09	62	10	28,672

Tax Analysis	Tax-Adj Ret%	%Rank Cat	%Pretax Ret	%Rank Cat
3 Yr Avg	4.70	2	98.7	73
5 Yr Avg	5.70	5	98.3	60
10 Yr Avg	6.45	5	96.8	67

Potential Capital Gain Exposure: 9% of assets

Risk Analysis

Time Period	Load-Adj Return %	Risk %Rank[1] All	Risk %Rank[1] Cat	Morningstar Return	Morningstar Risk	Morningstar Risk-Adj Rating
1 Yr	4.24					
3 Yr	4.76	22	36	0.71[2]	1.11	★★★★
5 Yr	5.80	24	38	1.03[2]	1.12	★★★★
10 Yr	6.67	35	72	1.22	1.23	★★★

Average Historical Rating (172 months): 3.8★s

[1]1=low, 100=high [2] T-Bill return substituted for category avg.

Category Rating (3 Yr)

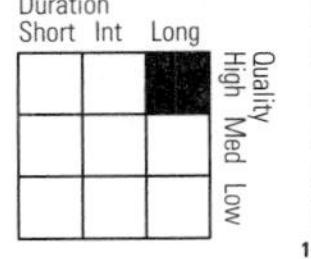

Return High
Risk Average

Other Measures	Standard Index LB Agg	Best Fit Index LB Muni
Alpha	–1.3	0.1
Beta	0.96	1.21
R-Squared	51	98
Standard Deviation		4.70
Mean		4.76
Sharpe Ratio		–0.05

Portfolio Analysis 06-30-01

Total Fixed-Income: 282	Date of Maturity	Amount $000	Value $000	% Net Assets
NJ Transp Cap Grant 5.5%	02-01-10	64,260	65,469	2.47
KY Louisville/Jefferson Metro 6%	05-15-31	51,960	55,895	2.11
IL Chicago GO 6.75%	01-01-35	40,000	47,460	1.79
AL Jefferson Swr 5.5%	02-01-40	45,000	45,285	1.71
MN Hlth 5.75%	05-01-26	37,665	39,267	1.48
VA Transp 5.5%	10-01-10	35,000	38,177	1.44
NJ Tpk 6.6%	01-01-13	30,000	35,078	1.32
NE Pub Pwr Dist Elec Sys 5%	01-01-28	34,000	32,510	1.23
MI Monroe Econ Dev Ltd Obl Edison 6.95%	09-01-22	25,000	30,810	1.16
IL Regl Transp 7.2%	11-01-20	24,000	29,706	1.12
MD Hlth/Higher Educ Fac 5.25%	08-15-38	30,000	28,320	1.07
IL Chicago Pub Bldg Com 7%	01-01-20	21,500	26,335	0.99
MA State GO 7%	07-01-09	22,250	26,013	0.98
NY Triborough Bridge/Tunl Spcl 4.75%	01-01-24	27,500	25,457	0.96
GA Smith World Congress Ctr 5.5%	07-01-20	24,740	25,101	0.95

Current Investment Style

Duration: Short Int Long; Quality: High Med Low

Avg Duration[1]	7.3 Yrs
Avg Nominal Maturity	11.6 Yrs
Avg Credit Quality	AAA
Avg Wtd Coupon	5.26%
Avg Wtd Price	102.71% of par
Pricing Service	J.J. Kenny

[1]figure provided by fund

Credit Analysis % bonds 09-30-01

US Govt	0	BB	0
AAA	93	B	0
AA	7	Below B	0
A	0	NR/NA	0
BBB	0		

Special Securities % assets 06-30-01

Restricted/Illiquid Secs	0
Inverse Floaters	0
Options/Futures/Warrants	No

Bond Type % assets 01-31-99

Alternative Minimum Tax (AMT)	3.3
Insured	96.2
Prerefunded	6.6

Top 5 States % bonds

TX	10.0	IL	6.4
NJ	8.0	FL	6.0
NY	7.0		

Composition % assets 06-30-01

Cash	0.4	Bonds	99.6
Stocks	0.0	Other	0.0

Sector Weightings	% of Bonds	Rel Cat
General Obligation	12.6	0.6
Utilities	16.0	2.0
Health	17.7	1.2
Water/Waste	13.8	2.3
Housing	1.1	0.2
Education	0.6	0.1
Transportation	23.4	1.7
COP/Lease	3.2	1.1
Industrial	6.7	0.5
Misc Revenue	3.1	0.6
Demand	2.0	2.4

Analysis by William Harding 09-04-01

This fund remains a fine option for investors who want added protection from defaults.

Vanguard Insured Long-Term Tax-Exempt Fund embodies consistency. The fund's annual returns have beaten the average muni national long fund nine times out of the past 10 years. Much of the fund's success owes to its tiny expense ratio, which is more than 90 basis points lower than its typical peer's. Low expenses are especially vital in the muni-bond world because there isn't much disparity in returns among funds.

Low expenses also help the fund maintain a hefty yield, even though it invests in lower-yielding insured bonds. The fund's insured status limits its credit risk but makes it more sensitive to interest-rate movements. That said, management's interest-rate calls have usually been fairly modest. Ian MacKinnon, Vanguard's director of fixed income, has set a neutral duration range in recent years for manager Reid Smith to work within. (Duration is a measure of interest-rate sensitivity.) Smith positioned the fund near the long end of that range in 2000, which was a boon to returns as interest rates declined, but he has shortened the fund's duration a bit this year.

The fund's increased sensitivity to interest-rate shifts has resulted in volatility slightly above the group's norm, but investors have been well compensated by above-average returns, and defaults aren't an issue here.

All told, investors who fear credit risk should consider this offering, as its low expenses will continue to provide a clear advantage over its peers.

Address:	Vanguard Financial Ctr. P.O. Box 2600 Valley Forge, PA 19482 800–662–7447 / 610–669–1000
Web Address:	www.vanguard.com
Inception:	10-01-84
Advisor:	Vanguard Fixed–Income Grp.
Subadvisor:	None
NTF Plans:	N/A

Minimum Purchase:	$3000	Add: $100 IRA: $1000
Min Auto Inv Plan:	$3000	Add: $50
Sales Fees:	No–load	
Management Fee:	None	
Actual Fees:	Mgt: 0.17%	Dist: —
Expense Projections:	3Yr: $61	5Yr: $107 10Yr: $243
Avg Brok Commission:	—	Income Distrib: Monthly
Total Cost (relative to category):		Low

Vanguard Interm–Term Tax–Ex

Ticker	Load	NAV	Yield	SEC Yield	Total Assets	Mstar Category
VWITX	None	$13.27	4.8%	—	$10,268.3 mil	Muni Natl Interm–Term

Prospectus Objective: Muni Bond—National

Vanguard Intermediate-Term Tax-Exempt Fund seeks income exempt from federal income tax, consistent with preservation of capital.

The fund normally invests at least 75% of assets in municipal securities rated A or better. It may invest up to 20% of assets in securities rated BBB, and the remaining 5% of assets in securities rated below investment-grade. The fund may also invest up to 20% of assets in securities subject to the Alternative Minimum Tax. The average weighted maturity usually ranges between seven and 12 years.

The fund also offers Adm shares. Prior to Oct. 27, 1998, the fund was named Vanguard Municipal Bond Fund Intermediate-Term Portfolio.

Historical Profile

Return Above Avg
Risk Below Avg
Rating ★★★★ Above Avg

Investment Style: Fixed-Income — Income Rtn %Rank Cat: 26 25 23 17 14 14 21 19

Growth of Principal vs. Interest Rate Shifts
— Principal Value $000 (NAV with capital gains reinvested)
— Interest Rate % on 10 Yr Treasury
▼ Manager Change
▽ Partial Manager Change
► Mgr Unknown After
◄ Mgr Unknown Before

Performance Quartile (within Category)

Portfolio Manager(s)

Ian A. MacKinnon. Since 11-81. BA'70 Lafayette C.; MBA'74 Pennsylvania State U. Other funds currently managed: Vanguard Balanced Index, Vanguard CA Insured Long Tax-Ex, Vanguard Short-Term Treasury.

Christopher M. Ryon. Since 9-97. BS Villanova U.; MBA Drexel U. Other funds currently managed: Vanguard NY Insured Long Tax-Ex, Vanguard Long-Term Tax-Exempt, Vanguard Tax-Managed Balanced.

1990	1991	1992	1993	1994	1995	1996	1997	1998	1999	2000	12-01	History
12.05	12.55	12.84	13.52	12.39	13.36	13.23	13.42	13.48	12.77	13.27	13.27	NAV
7.20	11.63	9.38	11.56	–2.12	13.64	4.20	7.06	5.76	–0.50	9.24	4.92	Total Return %
–1.76	–4.37	1.98	1.81	0.79	–4.83	0.58	–2.63	–2.91	0.33	–2.39	–3.50	+/– LB Aggregate
–0.10	–0.51	0.56	–0.72	3.02	–3.82	–0.24	–2.14	–0.72	1.56	–2.45	–0.16	+/– LB Muni
6.92	6.70	5.98	5.55	5.21	5.60	5.12	5.18	5.02	4.89	5.18	4.87	Income Return %
0.28	4.93	3.40	6.00	–7.33	8.04	–0.92	1.88	0.74	–5.40	4.06	0.06	Capital Return %
11	20	10	38	22	47	33	72	34	6	41	25	Total Rtn % Rank Cat
0.81	0.78	0.73	0.70	0.69	0.68	0.67	0.67	0.66	0.65	0.65	0.63	Income $
0.09	0.08	0.12	0.08	0.16	0.01	0.00	0.05	0.04	0.00	0.00	0.01	Capital Gains $
0.25	0.25	0.23	0.20	0.20	0.21	0.20	0.19	0.21	0.18	0.18	—	Expense Ratio %
6.83	6.49	5.91	5.41	5.15	5.35	5.09	5.07	4.93	4.83	5.03	—	Income Ratio %
54	27	32	15	18	12	14	15	14	17	17	—	Turnover Rate %
1,411.6	2,459.7	3,491.3	5,238.1	4,585.0	5,770.1	6,122.9	6,849.4	7,895.6	7,919.8	9,191.6	6,652.8	Net Assets $mil

Performance 12-31-01

	1st Qtr	2nd Qtr	3rd Qtr	4th Qtr	Total
1997	–0.04	2.68	2.25	2.01	7.06
1998	0.91	1.24	2.60	0.89	5.76
1999	0.59	–1.72	0.63	0.01	–0.50
2000	1.83	1.59	2.11	3.42	9.24
2001	2.49	0.75	2.46	–0.83	4.92

Trailing	Total Return%	+/– LB Agg	+/– LB Muni	% Rank All	% Rank Cat	Growth of $10,000
3 Mo	–0.83	–0.86	–0.16	90	45	9,917
6 Mo	1.61	–3.04	–0.51	28	53	10,161
1 Yr	4.92	–3.50	–0.16	23	25	10,492
3 Yr Avg	4.48	–1.80	–0.27	35	11	11,404
5 Yr Avg	5.25	–2.18	–0.73	60	19	12,913
10 Yr Avg	6.21	–1.02	–0.42	65	18	18,260
15 Yr Avg	6.81	–1.31	–0.38	70	12	26,875

Tax Analysis	Tax-Adj Ret%	%Rank Cat	%Pretax Ret	%Rank Cat
3 Yr Avg	4.47	10	99.8	41
5 Yr Avg	5.21	18	99.3	46
10 Yr Avg	6.09	13	98.2	48

Potential Capital Gain Exposure: –3% of assets

Risk Analysis

Time Period	Load-Adj Return %	Risk %Rank[1] All	Risk %Rank[1] Cat	Morningstar Return	Morningstar Risk	Morningstar Risk-Adj Rating
1 Yr	4.92					
3 Yr	4.48	7	19	0.63[2]	0.73	★★★★★
5 Yr	5.25	7	15	0.85[2]	0.73	★★★★
10 Yr	6.21	8	31	1.05	0.76	★★★★

Average Historical Rating (193 months): 4.0★s

[1]1=low, 100=high [2] T-Bill return substituted for category avg.

Category Rating (3 Yr)

1 2 3 4 5
Worst Best

Return High
Risk Below Avg

Other Measures	Standard Index LB Agg	Best Fit Index LB Muni
Alpha	–1.3	–0.3
Beta	0.68	0.84
R-Squared	52	95

Standard Deviation	3.33
Mean	4.48
Sharpe Ratio	–0.17

Portfolio Analysis 03-31-01

Total Fixed-Income: 1048	Date of Maturity	Amount $000	Value $000	% Net Assets
CA Cmnty Dev Apt Dmd	05-15-25	65,000	65,385	0.65
TX Brazos Rvr Poll Cntrl Util 4.95%	10-20-30	65,000	65,000	0.65
NY Triborough Bridge/Tunl Genl 6.6%	01-01-10	55,325	64,918	0.64
IL Chicago O'Hare Intl Arpt Fac 5.8%	05-01-07	63,000	63,115	0.63
TX State GO 8%	10-01-07	50,000	61,385	0.61
CA Los Angeles Transp Com Tax 6.5%	07-01-10	51,070	60,511	0.60
PA Beaver Indl Dev 4.65%	06-01-33	59,000	58,152	0.58
NJ Tpk 6.5%	01-01-09	50,000	57,789	0.57
TX Houston GO 7%	03-01-08	48,405	55,542	0.55
NE Pub Pwr Dist 5.25%	01-01-13	51,565	53,867	0.54
TX Lower Colorado Rvr 6%	05-15-07	46,565	51,551	0.51
NJ Trans Cop 5.5%	09-15-11	45,000	49,429	0.49
MA Wtr Res 6.5%	07-15-19	37,515	45,013	0.45
CT Spcl Tax Obl Infrasct 5.25%	09-01-06	42,550	44,719	0.44
UT Intermountain Pwr Sply 5.25%	07-01-09	41,240	44,053	0.44

Current Investment Style

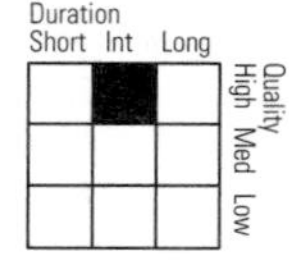

Avg Duration[1]	5.1 Yrs
Avg Nominal Maturity	6.9 Yrs
Avg Credit Quality	AA
Avg Wtd Coupon	5.62%
Avg Wtd Price	106.81% of par
Pricing Service	J.J. Kenny

[1]figure provided by fund

Analysis by William Harding 08-31-01

This fund's built-in advantage over its peers makes it easy to recommend.

Once again, Vanguard Intermediate-Term Tax-Exempt Fund is beating the majority of its peers. The fund's 6% gain for the year to date ended August 30, 2001, outpaces more than 85% of funds in the muni national intermediate category. Superior performance is nothing new here. In fact, the fund has only failed to land in the group's top half once over the past 10 years. What's the secret to the fund's success? Low costs. The fund's 0.18%-expense ratio is about 80 basis points lower than its average peer's.

That cost advantage also makes it possible for management to maintain a decent yield, without taking on a lot of risk relative to its peers. Much of the fund's bravado lies in its moderate interest-rate calls. Ian MacKinnon, head of Vanguard's fixed-income group, sets a duration range of roughly one year in which manager Christopher Ryon works. Ryon has shortened the fund's duration a bit in 2001, after being near the long end of that range in 2000, which was a boon to returns as interest rates declined sharply.

On the credit-risk side, the fund typically invests in higher-quality fare than its average peer has, as more than 90% of assets are devoted to A rated issues or better. Ryon will dabble a bit in lower-rated bonds and has about an 8% stake in BBB rated paper. And although the fund's more-conservative leaning compared with its peers has slowed it a bit when lower-quality bonds have performed well, that has hardly dampened its long-term record.

All told, investors looking for a good, middle-of-the-road muni fund will be hard-pressed to find many better candidates.

Credit Analysis % bonds 09-30-01

US Govt	0	BB	2
AAA	65	B	0
AA	25	Below B	1
A	3	NR/NA	0
BBB	6		

Special Securities % assets 03-31-01

Restricted/Illiquid Secs	0
Inverse Floaters	0
Options/Futures/Warrants	No

Bond Type % assets 12-31-98

Alternative Minimum Tax (AMT)	0.4
Insured	—
Prerefunded	—

Top 5 States % bonds

NY	11.4	CA	7.0
TX	11.2	NJ	6.9
MA	7.4		

Composition % assets 03-31-01

Cash	2.1	Bonds	97.9
Stocks	0.0	Other	0.0

Sector Weightings	% of Bonds	Rel Cat
General Obligation	28.3	1.0
Utilities	10.3	1.2
Health	6.7	0.6
Water/Waste	5.6	0.9
Housing	0.9	0.1
Education	2.8	0.3
Transportation	22.5	1.9
COP/Lease	3.8	1.7
Industrial	10.8	1.4
Misc Revenue	5.2	1.1
Demand	3.1	3.3

Address:	Vanguard Financial Ctr. P.O. Box 2600 Valley Forge, PA 19482 800–662–7447 / 610–669–1000
Web Address:	www.vanguard.com
Inception:	09-01-77
Advisor:	Vanguard Legal Department
Subadvisor:	None
NTF Plans:	N/A

Minimum Purchase:	$3000	Add: $100	IRA: $1000
Min Auto Inv Plan:	$3000	Add: $50	
Sales Fees:	No-load		
Management Fee:	None		
Actual Fees:	Mgt: 0.17%	Dist: —	
Expense Projections:	3Yr: $61	5Yr: $107	10Yr: $243
Avg Brok Commission:	—	Income Distrib: Monthly	
Total Cost (relative to category):		Low	

Vanguard International Growth

Ticker	Load	NAV	Yield	Total Assets	Mstar Category
VWIGX	None	$15.01	1.6%	$6,864.4 mil	Foreign Stock

Prospectus Objective: Foreign Stock

Vanguard International Growth Fund seeks capital appreciation.

The fund invests in a broadly diversified array of non-U.S. equity securities, primarily common stocks of seasoned companies.

The fund also offers Adm shares. This fund has gone through several name changes.

Historical Profile
Return Above Avg
Risk Below Avg
Rating ★★★ Neutral

Investment Style
Equity
Average Stock %: 97% 93% 91% 95% 92% 93%

▼ Manager Change
▽ Partial Manager Change

Fund Performance vs. Category Average
■ Quarterly Fund Return +/– Category Average
— Category Baseline

Performance Quartile (within Category)

Portfolio Manager(s)

Richard R. Foulkes. Since 9-81. BA'67 Cambridge U.; MA'68 Cambridge U. Other fund currently managed: Vanguard International Growth Adm.

History	1990	1991	1992	1993	1994	1995	1996	1997	1998	1999	2000	12-01
NAV	10.05	10.21	9.41	13.51	13.43	15.02	16.46	16.39	18.77	22.49	18.87	15.01
Total Return %	–12.05	4.74	–5.79	44.74	0.76	14.89	14.65	4.12	16.93	26.34	–8.60	–18.92
+/– S&P 500	–8.93	–25.75	–13.40	34.69	–0.56	–22.64	–8.30	–29.23	–11.65	5.30	0.50	–7.04
+/– MSCI EAFE	11.40	–7.40	6.39	12.18	–7.02	3.68	8.60	2.34	–3.07	–0.63	5.57	—
Income Return %	1.61	1.89	2.06	1.17	1.33	1.49	1.26	1.28	1.34	1.39	0.98	1.27
Capital Return %	–13.66	2.84	–7.84	43.57	–0.58	13.40	13.38	2.84	15.58	24.95	–9.58	–20.19
Total Rtn % Rank Cat	68	94	62	22	48	13	41	61	28	81	21	29
Income $	0.20	0.19	0.21	0.11	0.18	0.20	0.19	0.21	0.22	0.26	0.22	0.24
Capital Gains $	0.68	0.12	0.00	0.00	0.00	0.21	0.55	0.52	0.16	0.90	1.42	0.04
Expense Ratio %	0.68	0.67	0.58	0.59	0.46	0.58	0.56	0.57	0.59	0.58	0.53	0.61
Income Ratio %	3.01	1.80	2.04	1.27	1.37	1.53	1.35	1.26	1.39	1.42	1.26	1.19
Turnover Rate %	45	49	58	51	28	31	22	22	37	37	48	48
Net Assets $mil	733.6	869.4	880.1	2,127.3	2,927.7	3,676.4	5,568.7	6,809.0	7,723.2	9,680.6	8,898.1	6,088.0

Performance 12-31-01

	1st Qtr	2nd Qtr	3rd Qtr	4th Qtr	Total
1997	2.37	13.89	–1.35	–9.47	4.12
1998	12.81	0.87	–12.76	17.79	16.93
1999	–1.07	4.90	–0.05	21.80	26.34
2000	6.05	–3.23	–9.92	–1.13	–8.60
2001	–11.98	–2.41	–16.04	12.42	–18.92

Trailing	Total Return%	+/– S&P 500	+/– MSCI EAFE	% Rank All	% Rank Cat	Growth of $10,000
3 Mo	12.42	1.74	—	31	17	11,242
6 Mo	–5.61	–0.05	—	65	13	9,439
1 Yr	–18.92	–7.04	—	79	29	8,108
3 Yr Avg	–2.17	–1.15	—	83	48	9,363
5 Yr Avg	2.65	–8.05	—	86	39	11,399
10 Yr Avg	7.51	–5.42	—	46	23	20,629
15 Yr Avg	7.54	–6.19	—	58	44	29,765

Tax Analysis	Tax-Adj Ret%	%Rank Cat	%Pretax Ret	%Rank Cat
3 Yr Avg	–3.48	48	—	—
5 Yr Avg	1.42	37	53.6	66
10 Yr Avg	6.45	21	85.9	11

Potential Capital Gain Exposure: –5% of assets

Risk Analysis

Time Period	Load-Adj Return %	Risk %Rank[1] All	Risk %Rank[1] Cat	Morningstar Return	Morningstar Risk	Morningstar Risk-Adj Rating
1 Yr	–18.92					
3 Yr	–2.17	64	31	–1.41[2]	0.84	★★★
5 Yr	2.65	69	30	–0.50[2]	0.78	★★★
10 Yr	7.51	78	30	0.81[2]	0.79	★★★

Average Historical Rating (193 months): 3.9★s

[1] 1=low, 100=high [2] T-Bill return substituted for category avg.

Category Rating (3 Yr)

1 2 **3** 4 5
Worst Best

Return Average
Risk Below Avg

Other Measures	Standard Index S&P 500	Best Fit Index MSCIEasNdD
Alpha	–2.5	2.6
Beta	0.71	0.99
R-Squared	54	91
Standard Deviation		16.27
Mean		–2.17
Sharpe Ratio		–0.51

Analysis by Gabriel Presler 10-16-01

Despite a few missteps, Vanguard International Growth has been able to avoid the worst of the market's carnage, making it a solid choice.

Manager Richard Foulkes is quick to point out what went wrong this year. Optimistic about Japan's election of a new prime minister in the spring of 2001, he built the fund's once-undersized stake in that country to 19%—right in line with category norms—adding to positions in firms such as Yamanouchi Pharmaceuticals. To finance these purchases, he sold shares in the U.K., including pharmaceutical firms and consumer-staples companies, such as Boots.

But while U.K. food manufacturers and other consumer-related firms have held up relatively well in 2001, prime minister Koizumi's election hasn't buoyed Japan's beleaguered market. The fund has suffered accordingly, losing more than one fourth of its value for the year to date through Oct. 13, 2001, slightly better than other blend offerings in the foreign-stock category.

Mediocre performance isn't unheard of here, but Foulkes' moderate strategy has generally resulted in respectable results. Despite the fund's growth moniker, Foulkes isn't interested in the next big thing. Instead, he invests in large, well-known companies selling more cheaply than their global counterparts. That means the portfolio often looks a bit different than the group norms; Foulkes trades rarely, so the fund's turnover rate is significantly lower than the category average. What's more, the fund is often more heavily exposed to financials and industrial firms than its like-minded rivals.

While this caution can hold the fund back during growth rallies—it lagged 80% of the group in 1999, for example—it serves its purpose when global markets sour. With a low expense ratio, as well, this fund is a good bet for cautious investors.

Address:	Vanguard Financial Ctr. P.O. Box 2600 Valley Forge, PA 19482 800-662-7447 / 610-669-1000
Web Address:	www.vanguard.com
Inception:	09-30-81
Advisor:	Schroder Cap. Mgmt. Intl
Subadvisor:	None
NTF Plans:	N/A

Minimum Purchase:	$3000	Add: $100 IRA: $1000
Min Auto Inv Plan:	$3000	Add: $50
Sales Fees:	No-load	
Management Fee:	.35% mx./.13% mn.+(–).08%P	
Actual Fees:	Mgt: 0.46%	Dist: —
Expense Projections:	3Yr: $170	5Yr: $296 10Yr: $665
Avg Brok Commission:	—	Income Distrib: Annually
Total Cost (relative to category):		Low

Portfolio Analysis 09-30-01

Share change since 06-01 Total Stocks: 112

Share change	Sector	Country	% Assets
⊕ ING Groep	Financials	Netherlands	6.47
Vivendi	Services	France	3.40
Suez Canal Bank	Technology	Egypt	3.04
☼ Safari World Public	Technology	Thailand	2.94
⊖ Vodafone Airtouch	Services	United Kingdom	2.65
Astrazeneca	Health	United Kingdom	2.53
⊕ Samsung Electncs	Technology	South Korea	2.23
⊕ East Japan Railway	Services	Japan	2.19
⊖ L'Air Liquide	Industrials	France	2.15
⊕ Bank of Ireland	Financials	Ireland	1.86
⊕ Fuji Photo Film	Industrials	Japan	1.73
⊕ Yamanouchi Pharma	Health	Japan	1.71
Standard Chartered Bk	Financials	United Kingdom	1.66
Thales I	Technology	France	1.55
TNT Post Grp	Services	Netherlands	1.49
Mabuchi Motor	Industrials	Japan	1.45
⊕ Lafarge France	Industrials	France	1.44
⊖ Elan ADR	Health	Ireland	1.40
⊕ Ricoh	Technology	Japan	1.38
⊕ Syngenta	Technology	Switzerland	1.37

Current Investment Style

Style: Value Blnd Growth; Size: Large Med Small

	Stock Port Avg	Rel MSCI EAFE Current	Rel MSCI EAFE Hist	Rel Cat
Price/Earnings Ratio	23.9	0.92	0.95	0.94
Price/Cash Flow	12.6	0.98	1.01	0.88
Price/Book Ratio	3.1	0.88	0.87	0.78
3 Yr Earnings Growth	23.1	1.24	1.65	1.18
Med Mkt Cap $mil	11,379	0.4	0.7	0.63

Country Exposure 09-30-01	% assets
United Kingdom	19
Japan	18
France	14
Netherlands	11
Ireland	4

Hedging History: Rare

Regional Exposure 09-30-01	% assets
Europe	60
Japan	18
Latin America	0
Pacific Rim	11
Other	1

Special Securities % assets 09-30-01	
Restricted/Illiquid Secs	0
Emerging-Markets Secs	12
Options/Futures/Warrants	Yes

Composition % assets 09-30-01			
Cash	9.5	Bonds	0.0
Stocks	90.5	Other	0.0

Sector Weightings	% of Stocks	Rel Cat	5-Year High	5-Year Low
Utilities	0.8	0.3	12	1
Energy	0.0	0.0	8	0
Financials	22.2	1.0	30	13
Industrials	13.3	1.0	28	11
Durables	5.3	0.8	14	3
Staples	1.7	0.2	9	1
Services	21.5	1.2	26	5
Retail	5.0	1.0	15	2
Health	11.0	1.1	14	2
Technology	19.3	1.9	19	4

Vanguard LifeStrategy Conserv Growth

Ticker	Load	NAV	Yield	Total Assets	Mstar Category
VSCGX	None	$14.06	4.1%	$2,026.3 mil	Domestic Hybrid

Prospectus Objective: Asset Allocation

Vanguard LifeStrategy Funds Conservative Growth Portfolio seeks current income and low-to-moderate capital growth.

The fund typically allocates assets within the following ranges: 60% in bonds and 40% in stocks. Rather than investing directly in securities, it invests in combinations of the following Vanguard funds: Total Stock Market Portfolio, Total International Portfolio, Asset Allocation Fund, Total Bond Market Portfolio, and Fixed Income Securities Fund - Short-Term Corporate Portfolio.

Historical Profile
Return Average
Risk Low
Rating ★★★★ Above Avg

Investment Style: Equity — Average Stock %: 100% (1995), 25% (1999), 18% (2000), 32% (12-01)

▼ Manager Change
▽ Partial Manager Change

Fund Performance vs. Category Average
■ Quarterly Fund Return +/– Category Average
— Category Baseline

Performance Quartile (within Category)

Portfolio Manager(s)

Management Team

1990	1991	1992	1993	1994	1995	1996	1997	1998	1999	2000	12-01	History
—	—	—	—	9.89	11.68	12.14	13.40	14.71	15.10	14.71	14.06	NAV
—	—	—	—	0.10*	24.35	10.36	16.81	15.88	7.86	3.12	–0.08	Total Return %
—	—	—	—	0.12*	–13.19	–12.59	–16.55	–12.70	–13.18	12.22	11.79	+/– S&P 500
—	—	—	—	—	5.88	6.74	7.12	7.20	8.69	–8.52	–8.50	+/– LB Aggregate
—	—	—	—	1.40	4.82	4.61	4.69	4.47	4.35	4.74	4.01	Income Return %
—	—	—	—	–1.30	19.52	5.74	12.12	11.41	3.51	–1.62	–4.09	Capital Return %
—	—	—	—	—	58	78	64	32	59	41	23	Total Rtn % Rank Cat
—	—	—	—	0.14	0.47	0.53	0.56	0.59	0.63	0.70	0.58	Income $
—	—	—	—	0.01	0.12	0.20	0.19	0.20	0.11	0.16	0.04	Capital Gains $
—	—	—	—	0.00	0.00	0.00	0.00	0.00	0.00	0.00	—	Expense Ratio %
—	—	—	—	7.07	5.14	4.86	4.61	4.32	4.34	4.73	—	Income Ratio %
—	—	—	—	—	1	2	1	3	5	9	—	Turnover Rate %
—	—	—	—	41.3	219.3	462.5	802.9	1,415.7	1,747.7	1,969.4	2,026.3	Net Assets $mil

Performance 12-31-01

	1st Qtr	2nd Qtr	3rd Qtr	4th Qtr	Total
1997	0.23	8.53	4.94	2.32	16.81
1998	6.57	2.40	–2.44	8.84	15.88
1999	1.23	2.19	–1.47	5.83	7.86
2000	3.17	–0.51	1.33	–0.86	3.12
2001	–3.87	3.43	–4.10	4.78	–0.08

Trailing	Total Return%	+/– S&P 500	+/– LB Agg	% Rank All	% Rank Cat	Growth of $10,000
3 Mo	4.78	–5.90	4.74	65	73	10,478
6 Mo	0.49	6.05	–4.16	37	17	10,049
1 Yr	–0.08	11.79	–8.50	42	23	9,992
3 Yr Avg	3.58	4.61	–2.69	47	34	11,113
5 Yr Avg	8.51	–2.19	1.08	26	30	15,042
10 Yr Avg	—	—	—	—	—	—
15 Yr Avg	—	—	—	—	—	—

Tax Analysis	Tax-Adj Ret%	%Rank Cat	%Pretax Ret	%Rank Cat
3 Yr Avg	1.64	34	45.7	61
5 Yr Avg	6.41	27	75.3	25
10 Yr Avg	—	—	—	—

Potential Capital Gain Exposure: 5% of assets

Risk Analysis

Time Period	Load-Adj Return %	Risk %Rank[1] All	Risk %Rank[1] Cat	Morningstar Return	Morningstar Risk	Morningstar Risk-Adj Rating
1 Yr	–0.08					
3 Yr	3.58	33	15	–0.29[2]	0.37	★★★★
5 Yr	8.51	38	10	0.81[2]	0.37	★★★★
Incept	10.52	—	—	—	—	

Average Historical Rating (52 months): 3.1★s

[1]1=low, 100=high [2] T-Bill return substituted for category avg.

Category Rating (3 Yr)

1 2 3 4 5 — Worst ... Best (rating: 4)

Return Average
Risk Below Avg

Other Measures	Standard Index S&P 500	Best Fit Index S&P 500
Alpha	0.6	0.6
Beta	0.38	0.38
R-Squared	88	88

Standard Deviation	7.06
Mean	3.58
Sharpe Ratio	–0.22

Portfolio Analysis 09-30-01

Total Stocks: 5 Share change since 06-01	Sector	PE Ratio	YTD Return %	% Net Assets
☼ Vanguard Total Bond Market Index	N/A	—	—	31.08
⊕ Vanguard Asset Allocation	N/A	—	—	25.69
⊕ Vanguard Total Stock Mkt Idx	N/A	—	—	20.47
⊕ Vanguard Short-Term Corp	N/A	—	—	20.33
⊕ Vanguard Total Intl Stock Index	N/A	—	—	5.15
⊖ Vanguard Tot Bond Mkt Idx Is	N/A	—	—	0.00

Total Fixed-Income: 0	Date of Maturity	Amount $000	Value $000	% Net Assets

Analysis by Langdon Healy 10-01-01

Vanguard LifeStrategy Conservative Growth Fund is a good choice for the investor whose maxim is everything in moderation.

This fund of funds covers a wide swath of the investment universe by purchasing bonds as well as domestic and foreign stocks. With at least 50% of assets dedicated to bonds compared with a bond stake of just 35% for its average domestic-hybrid peer, the fund offers below-average volatility and a hefty yield. That mix has served it particularly well during the last couple of years of sour stock returns. Its 4.7% year-to-date loss through Sept. 28, 2001, is better than 78% of its competitors'. More impressively, its five year-annualized return now eclipses nearly three quarters of its peers'.

Though the fund's large bond position accounts for most of its conservative posture, the composition of its stock portfolio also dampens risk relative to the category. Its 20% stake in Vanguard Total Stock Market Index, for example, provides broad exposure to a range of market caps and industries and sharply limits issue-specific risk.

LifeStrategy Conservative Growth fund's low costs are another plus. Unlike many funds of funds, this offering doesn't tack on additional management fees. Instead, shareholders pay only the expense ratio on the underlying funds—which is now 0.28%. This is a full percentage point less than the average domestic-hybrid fund charges.

Though the fund's income bias will result in subpar returns when equities recover, we think this is an excellent holding for those nearing retirement or for conservative investors seeking limited and diverse exposure to equities markets.

Equity Style: NA
Style: —
Size: —

Fixed-Income Style: NA
Duration: —
Quality: —

	Portfolio Avg	Rel S&P
Price/Earnings Ratio	29.4[1]	0.95
Price/Book Ratio	5.1[1]	0.90
Price/Cash Flow	17.0[1]	0.95
3 Yr Earnings Growth	15.3[1]	1.04
1 Yr Earnings Est%	–3.5[1]	1.99
Debt % Total Cap	30.8[1]	1.00
Med Mkt Cap $mil	47,344[1]	0.78

[1]figure is based on 50% or less of stocks

Avg Eff Duration	—
Avg Eff Maturity	—
Avg Credit Quality	—
Avg Wtd Coupon	—

Special Securities
Restricted/Illiquid Secs
Emerging-Markets Secs
Options/Futures/Warrants

Composition % of assets 09-30-01	
Cash	10.8
Stocks*	38.5
Bonds	49.9
Other	0.9
*Foreign (% of stocks)	5.5

Market Cap	
Giant	—
Large	—
Medium	—
Small	—
Micro	—

Sector Weightings	% of Stocks	Rel S&P	5-Year High	5-Year Low
Utilities	3.4	1.1	—	—
Energy	6.8	1.0	—	—
Financials	19.3	1.1	—	—
Industrials	11.2	1.0	—	—
Durables	2.6	1.7	—	—
Staples	6.2	0.8	—	—
Services	12.9	1.2	—	—
Retail	6.2	0.9	—	—
Health	12.7	0.9	—	—
Technology	18.7	1.0	—	—

Address:	Vanguard Financial Ctr. P.O. Box 2600 Valley Forge, PA 19482 800–662–7447 / 610–669–1000
Web Address:	www.vanguard.com
*Inception:	09-30-94
Advisor:	Vanguard Grp.
Subadvisor:	None
NTF Plans:	N/A

Minimum Purchase:	$3000	Add: $100 IRA: $1000
Min Auto Inv Plan:	$3000	Add: $50
Sales Fees:	No-load	
Management Fee:	None	
Actual Fees:	Mgt: 0.00%	Dist: —
Expense Projections:	3Yr: $93	5Yr: $163 10Yr: $368
Avg Brok Commission:	—	Income Distrib: Quarterly
Total Cost (relative to category):	Low	

Vanguard LifeStrategy Growth

Ticker	Load	NAV	Yield	Total Assets	Mstar Category
VASGX	None	$17.43	2.1%	$3,725.8 mil	Large Blend

Prospectus Objective: Asset Allocation

Vanguard LifeStrategy Growth Portfolio seeks current income and growth of capital.

The fund typically allocates assets within the following ranges: 80% of assets in stocks and 20% in bonds. Rather than investing directly in securities, it invests in a combination of several underlying Vanguard funds. It invests in the following Vanguard funds: Total Bond Market Index, Asset Allocation, Short-Term Corporate, Total Stock Market Index, and Total International Stock Index. The fund is non-diversified.

Historical Profile

Return Average
Risk Below Avg
Rating ★★★ Neutral

Investment Style
Equity
Average Stock %: 100% (1995), 69% (1999), 65% (2000), 69% (12-01)

▼ Manager Change
▽ Partial Manager Change

Fund Performance vs. Category Average
■ Quarterly Fund Return +/– Category Average
— Category Baseline

Performance Quartile (within Category)

Portfolio Manager(s)

Management Team

1990	1991	1992	1993	1994	1995	1996	1997	1998	1999	2000	12-01	History
—	—	—	—	9.93	12.36	13.68	16.04	18.79	21.41	19.59	17.43	NAV
—	—	—	—	-0.10*	29.24	15.41	22.26	21.41	17.32	-5.44	-8.86	Total Return %
—	—	—	—	-0.08*	-8.30	-7.53	-11.09	-7.17	-3.72	3.66	3.02	+/– S&P 500
—	—	—	—	—	-8.37	-6.75	-10.76	-7.23	-4.51	5.52	3.91	+/– Wilshire Top 750
—	—	—	—	1.39	3.14	2.85	2.79	2.57	2.41	2.41	1.90	Income Return %
—	—	—	—	-1.49	26.10	12.56	19.47	18.84	14.91	-7.85	-10.76	Capital Return %
—	—	—	—	—	77	91	83	64	70	34	13	Total Rtn % Rank Cat
—	—	—	—	0.14	0.31	0.35	0.38	0.41	0.45	0.51	0.37	Income $
—	—	—	—	0.02	0.15	0.23	0.29	0.27	0.16	0.17	0.06	Capital Gains $
—	—	—	—	0.00	0.00	0.00	0.00	0.00	0.00	0.00	—	Expense Ratio %
—	—	—	—	7.06	3.67	3.18	2.84	2.53	2.50	4.73	—	Income Ratio %
—	—	—	—	—	1	0	1	2	1	9	—	Turnover Rate %
—	—	—	—	37.8	217.4	628.7	1,133.7	1,924.1	3,177.0	3,870.8	3,725.8	Net Assets $mil

Performance 12-31-01

	1st Qtr	2nd Qtr	3rd Qtr	4th Qtr	Total
1997	0.15	13.72	6.47	0.83	22.26
1998	11.28	2.02	-8.84	17.31	21.41
1999	2.45	5.12	-3.49	12.88	17.32
2000	3.59	-2.76	-0.52	-5.64	-5.44
2001	-10.10	5.13	-11.81	9.36	-8.86

Trailing	Total Return%	+/– S&P 500	+/– Wil Top 750	% Rank All	% Rank Cat	Growth of $10,000
3 Mo	9.36	-1.33	-1.97	46	78	10,936
6 Mo	-3.56	2.00	2.23	54	12	9,644
1 Yr	-8.86	3.02	3.91	58	13	9,114
3 Yr Avg	0.37	1.40	2.19	71	32	10,111
5 Yr Avg	8.46	-2.24	-1.66	27	62	15,009
10 Yr Avg	—	—	—	—	—	—
15 Yr Avg	—	—	—	—	—	—

Tax Analysis	Tax-Adj Ret%	%Rank Cat	%Pretax Ret	%Rank Cat
3 Yr Avg	-0.68	29	—	—
5 Yr Avg	7.19	54	85.0	34
10 Yr Avg	—	—	—	—

Potential Capital Gain Exposure: 2% of assets

Risk Analysis

Time Period	Load-Adj Return %	Risk %Rank[1] All	Risk %Rank[1] Cat	Morningstar Return	Morningstar Risk	Morningstar Risk-Adj Rating
1 Yr	-8.86					
3 Yr	0.37	54	10	-0.93[2]	0.75	★★★
5 Yr	8.46	53	8	0.80[2]	0.73	★★★
Incept	11.73	—	—	—	—	

Average Historical Rating (52 months): 3.4★s

[1] 1=low, 100=high [2] T-Bill return substituted for category avg.

Category Rating (3 Yr)

1 2 3 **4** 5 (Worst → Best)

Return: Above Avg
Risk: Low

Other Measures	Standard Index S&P 500	Best Fit Index MSCIACWdFr
Alpha	-0.1	3.0
Beta	0.77	0.83
R-Squared	93	95

Standard Deviation	13.51
Mean	0.37
Sharpe Ratio	-0.39

Portfolio Analysis 09-30-01

Share change since 06-01 Total Stocks: 4	Sector	PE	YTD Ret%	% Assets
⊕ Vanguard Total Stock Mkt Idx	N/A	—	—	52.75
⊕ Vanguard Asset Allocation	N/A	—	—	26.56
⊕ Vanguard Total Intl Stock Index	N/A	—	—	15.85
☼ Vanguard Total Bond Market Index	N/A	—	—	10.72

Analysis by Langdon Healy 10-31-01

Vanguard LifeStrategy Growth Fund is a good core holding for risk-averse investors.

This fund of funds covers a wide swath of the investment universe, including domestic and foreign stocks as well as bonds. The fund's bond weighting is nearly triple that of the average large-blend fund thanks to its holdings in Vanguard Total Bond Market Index Fund and Vanguard Asset Allocation Fund. The fund's bond allocation and broad equity exposure help keep a lid on volatility.

This conservative positioning has helped the fund's performance relative to its large-blend peers during the last couple of years of sour stock market returns. Its 13.6% loss for the year to date through Oct. 29 is better than 88% of large-blend funds'. Its bond stake also helps the fund generate much higher income than its typical peer, which also limits its volatility.

Not surprisingly, the fund's conservative posture means that it doesn't do as well as its peers when stocks soar. It landed near the bottom third of the category each year between 1995 and 1999, and its five-year annualized return is mediocre compared with its large-blend rivals'. Another shortcoming for investors contemplating using this fund as a one-stop option is the paucity of small-cap stocks in the fund's portfolio. Vanguard Total Stock Market Index Fund, accounting for 50% of assets, tracks the Wilshire 5000 index, which is heavily weighted toward large-cap stocks.

That said, with its steady demeanor and an expense ratio that's about 1 percentage point less than the average large-blend fund's, this offering is a solid choice for conservative investors.

Current Investment Style

Not Available

	Stock Port Avg	Relative S&P 500 Current	Relative S&P 500 Hist	Rel Cat
Price/Earnings Ratio	29.0	0.94	—	0.95
Price/Book Ratio	5.0	0.87	—	0.90
Price/Cash Flow	16.8	0.93	—	0.91
3 Yr Earnings Growth	18.1	1.24	—	1.02
1 Yr Earnings Est%	-5.3	2.99	—	58.78
Med Mkt Cap $mil	33,414	0.6	—	0.64

Special Securities

Restricted/Illiquid Secs
Emerging–Markets Secs
Options/Futures/Warrants

Composition % assets 09-30-01	
Cash	9.7
Stocks*	78.1
Bonds	12.1
Other	0.1
*Foreign (% stocks)	15.3

Market Cap	
Giant	—
Large	—
Medium	—
Small	—
Micro	—

Sector Weightings	% of Stocks	Rel S&P	5-Year High	5-Year Low
Utilities	3.5	1.1	—	—
Energy	6.5	0.9	—	—
Financials	20.1	1.1	—	—
Industrials	11.1	1.0	—	—
Durables	3.0	2.0	—	—
Staples	6.0	0.8	—	—
Services	13.4	1.2	—	—
Retail	6.0	0.9	—	—
Health	12.2	0.8	—	—
Technology	18.2	1.0	—	—

Address:	Vanguard Financial Ctr. P.O. Box 2600 Valley Forge, PA 19482 800–662–7447 / 610–669–1000
Web Address:	www.vanguard.com
*Inception:	09-30-94
Advisor:	Vanguard Grp.
Subadvisor:	None
NTF Plans:	N/A

Minimum Purchase:	$3000	Add: $100 IRA: $1000
Min Auto Inv Plan:	$3000	Add: $50
Sales Fees:	No–load	
Management Fee:	None	
Actual Fees:	Mgt: 0.00%	Dist: —
Expense Projections:	3Yr: $93	5Yr: $163 10Yr: $368
Avg Brok Commission:	—	Income Distrib: Semi–Ann.
Total Cost (relative to category):		Low

Vanguard LifeStrategy Income

Ticker	Load	NAV	Yield	Total Assets	Mstar Category
VASIX	None	$12.86	5.0%	$809.3 mil	Domestic Hybrid

Prospectus Objective: Asset Allocation

Vanguard LifeStrategy Funds Income Portfolio seeks current income and capital growth.

The fund allocates assets within the following parameters: 80% in bonds and 20% in stocks. Rather than investing directly in securities, the fund invests in combinations of the following Vanguard funds: Total Bond Market Portfolio, Asset Allocation Fund, Short-Term Corporate, and Total Stock Market Index. The fund is non-diversified.

Historical Profile

Return Average
Risk Low
Rating ★★★★ Above Avg

Investment Style
Equity
Average Stock %: 100% (1995), 8% (1999), 13% (2000), 14% (12-01)

▼ Manager Change
▽ Partial Manager Change

Fund Performance vs. Category Average
■ Quarterly Fund Return +/– Category Average
— Category Baseline

Performance Quartile (within Category)

Portfolio Manager(s)

Multiple Managers. Since 9-94. Other funds currently managed: Vanguard STAR, Aquinas Fixed-Income, Aquinas Value.

1990	1991	1992	1993	1994	1995	1996	1997	1998	1999	2000	12-01	History
—	—	—	—	9.88	11.54	11.55	12.43	13.22	12.82	13.01	12.86	NAV
—	—	—	—	0.20*	22.99	7.65	14.23	13.17	2.82	8.07	4.06	Total Return %
—	—	—	—	0.21*	–14.54	–15.30	–19.12	–15.40	–18.21	17.17	15.94	+/– S&P 500
—	—	—	—	—	4.52	4.03	4.54	4.50	3.65	–3.57	–4.36	+/– LB Aggregate
—	—	—	—	1.40	5.04	5.66	5.56	5.16	5.32	5.92	5.06	Income Return %
—	—	—	—	–1.20	17.95	1.99	8.66	8.01	–2.50	2.14	–0.99	Capital Return %
—	—	—	—	—	69	91	79	45	80	18	8	Total Rtn % Rank Cat
—	—	—	—	0.14	0.49	0.64	0.63	0.63	0.69	0.74	0.65	Income $
—	—	—	—	0.00	0.09	0.21	0.10	0.19	0.07	0.08	0.02	Capital Gains $
—	—	—	—	0.00	0.00	0.00	0.00	0.00	0.00	0.00	—	Expense Ratio %
—	—	—	—	7.31	5.76	5.66	5.54	5.24	5.37	5.84	—	Income Ratio %
—	—	—	—	—	4	22	6	3	11	17	—	Turnover Rate %
—	—	—	—	11.5	120.7	151.5	248.9	448.9	555.4	661.1	809.3	Net Assets $mil

Performance 12-31-01

	1st Qtr	2nd Qtr	3rd Qtr	4th Qtr	Total
1997	0.07	6.12	4.34	3.08	14.23
1998	4.27	2.65	0.84	4.85	13.17
1999	0.45	0.71	–0.54	2.19	2.82
2000	3.12	0.63	2.41	1.69	8.07
2001	–0.76	2.35	–0.13	2.60	4.07

Trailing	Total Return%	+/– S&P 500	+/– LB Agg	% Rank All	% Rank Cat	Growth of $10,000
3 Mo	2.60	–8.09	2.56	70	91	10,260
6 Mo	2.46	8.02	–2.19	18	6	10,246
1 Yr	4.06	15.94	–4.36	30	8	10,406
3 Yr Avg	4.96	5.99	–1.31	32	20	11,563
5 Yr Avg	8.37	–2.33	0.95	27	33	14,948
10 Yr Avg	—	—	—	—	—	—
15 Yr Avg	—	—	—	—	—	—

Tax Analysis	Tax-Adj Ret%	%Rank Cat	%Pretax Ret	%Rank Cat
3 Yr Avg	2.66	24	53.7	49
5 Yr Avg	5.97	33	71.3	37
10 Yr Avg	—	—	—	—

Potential Capital Gain Exposure: 3% of assets

Risk Analysis

Time Period	Load-Adj Return %	Risk %Rank[1] All	Risk %Rank[1] Cat	Morningstar Return	Morningstar Risk	Morningstar Risk-Adj Rating
1 Yr	4.06					
3 Yr	4.96	27	2	[2]	0.20	★★★★
5 Yr	8.37	33	1	0.78[2]	0.20	★★★★
Incept	9.89	—	—	—	—	

Average Historical Rating (52 months): 3.1★s

[1] 1=low, 100=high [2] T-Bill return substituted for category avg.

Category Rating (3 Yr)

1 Worst — 5 Best

Return: Above Avg
Risk: Low

Other Measures	Standard Index S&P 500	Best Fit Index S&P 500
Alpha	0.9	0.9
Beta	0.19	0.19
R-Squared	60	60
Standard Deviation		4.28
Mean		4.96
Sharpe Ratio		0.00

Portfolio Analysis 09-30-01

Total Stocks: 4 Share change since 06-01	Sector	PE Ratio	YTD Return %	% Net Assets
☼ Vanguard Total Bond Market Index	N/A	—	—	51.82
⊕ Vanguard Asset Allocation	N/A	—	—	25.78
⊕ Vanguard Short-Term Corp	N/A	—	—	20.36
⊕ Vanguard Total Stock Mkt Idx	N/A	—	—	5.30
⊖ Vanguard Tot Bond Mkt Idx Is	N/A	—	—	0.00

Total Fixed-Income: 0	Date of Maturity	Amount $000	Value $000	% Net Assets

Analysis by Langdon Healy 10-01-01

Vanguard LifeStrategy Funds Income Portfolio's conservative flavor with just a bit of spice has been a delectable concoction for income-seeking investors.

As the least aggressive offering in the Vanguard LifeStrategy series, this fund dedicates about three fourths of its assets to bonds. Not surprisingly, that gives it below-average volatility and a hefty yield relative to its domestic-hybrid rivals. Its stodginess has held it in particularly good stead during the past couple of years of sour stock returns. It has generated a top-decile return of 2.8% over the past year, and its five-year annualized return is better than three fourths of its peers.

The fund gets most of its stock exposure from Vanguard Asset Allocation. That fund's allocation to stocks and bonds can vary dramatically, and its big stock weighting this year has subtracted from this offering's performance. But its stock exposure—derived completely from the S&P 500 index—adds body to the LifeStrategy Income fund when stocks rally. For example, the Asset Allocation fund soared 25% in 1998, which helped juice returns for this offering that year.

LifeStrategy Income fund's low costs are another mark in its favor. Unlike many funds of funds, this offering doesn't tack on additional management fees, leaving shareholders to pay only the expenses on the underlying funds. While this fund's price tag amounts to 0.28%, the average domestic-hybrid fund charges a full percentage point more.

Though the fund's income bias will result in subpar returns when equities rally, we think this is an excellent holding for conservative investors.

Equity Style
Style: —
Size: —
NA

Fixed-Income Style
Duration: —
Quality: —
NA

	Portfolio Avg	Rel S&P
Price/Earnings Ratio	30.2[1]	0.98
Price/Book Ratio	5.4[1]	0.95
Price/Cash Flow	17.3[1]	0.96
3 Yr Earnings Growth	14.6[1]	1.00
1 Yr Earnings Est%	–2.8[1]	1.59
Debt % Total Cap	31.3[1]	1.01
Med Mkt Cap $mil	55,843[1]	0.92

[1] figure is based on 50% or less of stocks

Avg Eff Duration	—
Avg Eff Maturity	—
Avg Credit Quality	—
Avg Wtd Coupon	—

Special Securities
Restricted/Illiquid Secs
Emerging-Markets Secs
Options/Futures/Warrants

Composition % of assets 09-30-01	
Cash	11.4
Stocks*	18.8
Bonds	69.9
Other	0.0
*Foreign (% of stocks)	0.5

Market Cap	
Giant	—
Large	—
Medium	—
Small	—
Micro	—

Sector Weightings	% of Stocks	Rel S&P	5-Year High	5-Year Low
Utilities	3.4	1.1	—	—
Energy	7.2	1.0	—	—
Financials	18.2	1.0	—	—
Industrials	11.2	1.0	—	—
Durables	1.9	1.2	—	—
Staples	6.5	0.8	—	—
Services	12.1	1.1	—	—
Retail	6.6	1.0	—	—
Health	13.4	0.9	—	—
Technology	19.4	1.1	—	—

Address: Vanguard Financial Ctr. P.O. Box 2600, Valley Forge, PA 19482, 800-662-7447 / 610-669-1000
Web Address: www.vanguard.com
*Inception: 09-30-94
Advisor: Vanguard Grp.
Subadvisor: None
NTF Plans: N/A

Minimum Purchase: $3000 Add: $100 IRA: $1000
Min Auto Inv Plan: $3000 Add: $50
Sales Fees: No-load
Management Fee: None
Actual Fees: Mgt: 0.00% Dist: —
Expense Projections: 3Yr: $93 5Yr: $163 10Yr: $368
Avg Brok Commission: — Income Distrib: Quarterly
Total Cost (relative to category): —

Vanguard LifeStrategy Moderate Growth

Ticker	Load	NAV	Yield	Total Assets	Mstar Category
VSMGX	None	$15.93	3.1%	$4,243.3 mil	Domestic Hybrid

Prospectus Objective: Asset Allocation

Vanguard LifeStrategy Funds Moderate Growth Portfolio seeks capital growth and a reasonable level of current income.

The fund allocates assets within the following parameters: 60% in stocks and 40% in bonds. Rather than investing directly in securities, the fund invests in combinations of the following Vanguard funds: Total Stock Market Portfolio, Total International Stock Index Portfolio, Total Bond Market Portfolio, and Asset Allocation Fund. The fund is non-diversified.

Historical Profile

Return	Average
Risk	Low
Rating	★★★ Neutral

Investment Style
Equity
Average Stock %: 100% (1995), 38% (1999), 48% (2000), 55% (12-01)

▼ Manager Change
▽ Partial Manager Change

Fund Performance vs. Category Average
■ Quarterly Fund Return +/– Category Average
— Category Baseline

Performance Quartile (within Category)

Portfolio Manager(s)

Management Team

1990	1991	1992	1993	1994	1995	1996	1997	1998	1999	2000	12-01	History
—	—	—	—	9.86	12.11	12.97	14.81	16.86	18.18	17.25	15.93	NAV
—	—	—	—	–0.70*	27.94	12.71	19.77	19.03	12.01	–0.88	–4.48	Total Return %
—	—	—	—	–0.68*	–9.60	–10.24	–13.58	–9.54	–9.03	8.22	7.40	+/– S&P 500
—	—	—	—	—	9.47	9.10	10.08	10.36	12.84	–12.51	–12.90	+/– LB Aggregate
—	—	—	—	1.39	3.68	3.66	3.81	3.47	3.29	3.57	2.87	Income Return %
—	—	—	—	–2.09	24.26	9.05	15.96	15.56	8.72	–4.45	–7.35	Capital Return %
—	—	—	—	—	25	56	40	18	36	65	52	Total Rtn % Rank Cat
—	—	—	—	0.14	0.36	0.44	0.49	0.51	0.55	0.64	0.49	Income $
—	—	—	—	0.01	0.13	0.23	0.21	0.25	0.13	0.14	0.06	Capital Gains $
—	—	—	—	0.00	0.00	0.00	0.00	0.00	0.00	0.00	—	Expense Ratio %
—	—	—	—	7.10	4.42	3.98	3.72	3.43	3.47	3.59	—	Income Ratio %
—	—	—	—	—	1	3	2	5	3	12	—	Turnover Rate %
—	—	—	—	34.8	234.7	825.7	1,358.0	2,201.9	3,440.7	4,045.6	4,243.3	Net Assets $mil

Performance 12-31-01

	1st Qtr	2nd Qtr	3rd Qtr	4th Qtr	Total
1997	0.08	11.24	5.82	1.66	19.77
1998	8.91	2.30	–5.52	13.08	19.03
1999	1.66	3.54	–2.51	9.16	12.01
2000	3.46	–1.59	0.44	–3.08	–0.88
2001	–7.01	4.25	–7.91	7.00	–4.48

Trailing	Total Return%	+/– S&P 500	+/– LB Agg	% Rank All	% Rank Cat	Growth of $10,000
3 Mo	7.00	–3.69	6.96	56	35	10,700
6 Mo	–1.47	4.09	–6.12	44	46	9,854
1 Yr	–4.48	7.40	–12.90	50	52	9,552
3 Yr Avg	1.98	3.00	–4.30	63	54	10,605
5 Yr Avg	8.62	–2.08	1.19	26	29	15,119
10 Yr Avg	—	—	—	—	—	—
15 Yr Avg	—	—	—	—	—	—

Tax Analysis	Tax-Adj Ret%	%Rank Cat	%Pretax Ret	%Rank Cat
3 Yr Avg	0.52	49	26.2	88
5 Yr Avg	6.97	19	80.8	13
10 Yr Avg	—	—	—	—

Potential Capital Gain Exposure: 3% of assets

Risk Analysis

Time Period	Load-Adj Return %	Risk %Rank[1] All	Risk %Rank[1] Cat	Morningstar Return	Morningstar Risk	Morningstar Risk-Adj Rating
1 Yr	–4.48					
3 Yr	1.98	41	54	–0.61[2]	0.56	★★★
5 Yr	8.62	43	50	0.84[2]	0.55	★★★
Incept	11.23	—	—	—	—	

Average Historical Rating (52 months): 3.3★s

[1]1=low, 100=high [2] T-Bill return substituted for category avg.

Category Rating (3 Yr)

1 2 **3** 4 5
Worst Best

Return	Average
Risk	Average

Other Measures	Standard Index S&P 500	Best Fit Index MSCIACWdFr
Alpha	0.2	2.5
Beta	0.57	0.62
R–Squared	92	93
Standard Deviation		10.26
Mean		1.98
Sharpe Ratio		–0.33

Portfolio Analysis 09-30-01

Total Stocks: 4 (Share change since 06-01)	Sector	PE Ratio	YTD Return %	% Net Assets
⊕ Vanguard Total Stock Mkt Idx	N/A	—	—	37.46
☼ Vanguard Total Bond Market Index	N/A	—	—	32.92
⊕ Vanguard Asset Allocation	N/A	—	—	27.03
⊕ Vanguard Total Intl Stock Index	N/A	—	—	10.71
⊖ Vanguard Tot Bond Mkt Idx Is	N/A	—	—	0.00

Total Fixed-Income: 0	Date of Maturity	Amount $000	Value $000	% Net Assets

Analysis by Langdon Healy 10-01-01

Though in 2001 moderate growth has meant moderately large losses, we still think this fund makes a good core holding.

Vanguard LifeStrategy Moderate Growth fund is a fund of funds that covers a wide swath of the investment universe. It includes domestic and foreign stocks as well as bonds. With 30% of assets in Vanguard Total Bond Market Index and long-term Treasury exposure via Vanguard Asset Allocation, its bond stake is typically in line with that of the domestic-hybrid category average. This makes it a more aggressive offering than two of its siblings in the Vanguard LifeStrategy series, yet more conservative than the series' Growth fund.

The sour stock markets this year have resulted in a 10.7% year-to-date loss through Sept. 28, 2001, which is just below the category average. The fund's slightly overweight equity exposure (due to the Asset Allocation fund's poorly timed bet on stocks) and its large-cap bias in a market where small-fry are outperforming explain the underperformance.

Still, its attractions are considerable. First, its longer-term returns are strong. Over the trailing five years ended Sept. 28, 2001, it has posted a top-third return relative to its peers. And even though it doesn't load up on bonds, it throws off an attractive level of income for a hybrid fund. The fund's 12-month yield is higher than three quarters of its peers. Finally, it's just plain cheap. Unlike many funds of funds, this offering doesn't tack on additional management fees. Shareholders pay only the expenses on the underlying funds—currently 0.28%. This is a full percentage point less than the average domestic-hybrid fund charges.

Though the fund has suffered a bit more than its peers lately, investors seeking a balance between income and long-term capital appreciation should give it a look.

Equity Style NA
Style: —
Size: —

Fixed-Income Style NA
Duration: —
Quality: —

	Portfolio Avg	Rel S&P
Price/Earnings Ratio	29.1	0.94
Price/Book Ratio	5.0	0.88
Price/Cash Flow	16.9	0.94
3 Yr Earnings Growth	15.5	1.06
1 Yr Earnings Est%	–3.8	2.16
Debt % Total Cap	30.5	0.99
Med Mkt Cap $mil	35,734	0.59

Avg Eff Duration	—
Avg Eff Maturity	—
Avg Credit Quality	—
Avg Wtd Coupon	—

Special Securities
Restricted/Illiquid Secs
Emerging–Markets Secs
Options/Futures/Warrants

Composition (% of assets 09-30-01)	
Cash	10.3
Stocks*	58.0
Bonds	31.7
Other	0.0
*Foreign (% of stocks)	10.3

Market Cap	
Giant	—
Large	—
Medium	—
Small	—
Micro	—

Sector Weightings	% of Stocks	Rel S&P	5-Year High	5-Year Low
Utilities	3.5	1.1	—	—
Energy	6.6	0.9	—	—
Financials	19.8	1.1	—	—
Industrials	11.1	1.0	—	—
Durables	2.9	1.9	—	—
Staples	6.1	0.8	—	—
Services	13.2	1.2	—	—
Retail	6.1	0.9	—	—
Health	12.4	0.8	—	—
Technology	18.4	1.0	—	—

Address:	Vanguard Financial Ctr. P.O. Box 2600 Valley Forge, PA 19482 800–662–7447 / 610–669–1000
Web Address:	www.vanguard.com
*Inception:	09-30-94
Advisor:	Vanguard Legal Department
Subadvisor:	None
NTF Plans:	N/A

Minimum Purchase:	$3000	Add: $100	IRA: $1000
Min Auto Inv Plan:	$3000	Add: $50	
Sales Fees:	No–load		
Management Fee:	None		
Actual Fees:	Mgt: 0.00%	Dist: —	
Expense Projections:	3Yr: $93	5Yr: $163	10Yr: $368
Avg Brok Commission:	—	Income Distrib: Semi–Ann.	
Total Cost (relative to category):		Low	

Vanguard Ltd–Term Tax–Ex

Ticker	Load	NAV	Yield	SEC Yield	Total Assets	Mstar Category
VMLTX	None	$10.85	4.3%	—	$3,801.6 mil	Muni Short–Term

Prospectus Objective: Muni Bond—National

Vanguard Limited-Term Tax-Exempt Fund seeks income exempt from federal income tax, consistent with preservation of capital.

The fund invests primarily in tax-exempt municipal obligations, at least 95% of which are rated A or better. The average-weighted maturity usually ranges between two and five years; the fund typically purchases securities with effective maturities of 10 years or less. It may also invest, to a limited extent, in bond futures contracts and options.

The fund also offers Adm shares. Prior to Oct. 27, 1998, the fund was named Vanguard Municipal Bond Fund Limited-Term Portfolio.

Historical Profile

Return: Below Avg
Risk: Low
Rating: ★★★★★ Highest

Investment Style: Fixed-Income

Income Rtn %Rank Cat: 38, 23, 21, 19, 22, 16, 20, 12

Growth of Principal vs. Interest Rate Shifts
- Principal Value $000 (NAV with capital gains reinvested)
- Interest Rate % on 10 Yr Treasury
- ▼ Manager Change
- ▽ Partial Manager Change
- ► Mgr Unknown After
- ◄ Mgr Unknown Before

Performance Quartile (within Category)

Portfolio Manager(s)

Ian A. MacKinnon. Since 9-87. BA'70 Lafayette C.; MBA'74 Pennsylvania State U. Other funds currently managed: Vanguard Balanced Index, Vanguard CA Insured Long Tax-Ex, Vanguard Short-Term Treasury.

Pam Wisehaupt-Tynan. Since 1-97. BA'81 Temple U. Other funds currently managed: Vanguard Short-Term Tax-Ex, Vanguard Ltd-Term Tax-Ex Adm, Vanguard Short-Term Tax-Ex Adm.

1990	1991	1992	1993	1994	1995	1996	1997	1998	1999	2000	12-01	History
10.27	10.56	10.65	10.82	10.37	10.76	10.71	10.77	10.85	10.55	10.73	10.85	NAV
7.04	9.48	6.39	6.31	0.07	8.57	4.08	5.10	5.12	1.47	6.35	5.58	Total Return %
–1.92	–6.53	–1.01	–3.44	2.99	–9.90	0.46	–4.58	–3.56	2.30	–5.28	–2.85	+/– LB Aggregate
–0.26	–2.66	–2.43	–5.97	5.21	–8.89	–0.36	–4.10	–1.36	3.53	–5.35	0.50	+/– LB Muni
6.45	5.93	5.03	4.48	4.31	4.76	4.53	4.51	4.35	4.29	4.58	4.48	Income Return %
0.59	3.54	1.36	1.83	–4.23	3.81	–0.45	0.59	0.76	–2.83	1.77	1.10	Capital Return %
6	22	61	63	36	37	22	52	19	23	32	4	Total Rtn % Rank Cat
0.64	0.59	0.52	0.47	0.46	0.48	0.48	0.47	0.46	0.46	0.47	0.47	Income $
0.01	0.06	0.05	0.02	0.00	0.00	0.00	0.00	0.00	0.00	0.00	0.00	Capital Gains $
0.25	0.25	0.23	0.20	0.20	0.21	0.21	0.19	0.21	0.18	0.18	—	Expense Ratio %
6.31	5.91	5.08	4.50	4.24	4.51	4.51	4.46	4.27	4.25	4.45	—	Income Ratio %
55	57	37	20	21	35	27	28	35	14	32	—	Turnover Rate %
270.1	547.0	1,084.0	1,817.7	1,629.5	1,683.1	1,789.3	2,020.1	2,391.2	2,568.9	2,987.4	2,103.6	Net Assets $mil

Performance 12-31-01

	1st Qtr	2nd Qtr	3rd Qtr	4th Qtr	Total
1997	0.18	1.89	1.58	1.37	5.10
1998	1.05	1.08	1.82	1.07	5.12
1999	0.86	–0.62	0.89	0.33	1.47
2000	1.01	1.32	1.69	2.18	6.35
2001	2.41	1.18	2.02	–0.13	5.58

Trailing	Total Return%	+/– LB Agg	+/– LB Muni	% Rank All	% Rank Cat	Growth of $10,000
3 Mo	–0.13	–0.17	0.53	80	63	9,987
6 Mo	1.89	–2.77	–0.24	24	47	10,189
1 Yr	5.58	–2.85	0.50	20	4	10,558
3 Yr Avg	4.44	–1.83	–0.31	36	4	11,392
5 Yr Avg	4.71	–2.72	–1.27	70	16	12,587
10 Yr Avg	4.88	–2.35	–1.75	93	42	16,098
15 Yr Avg	—	—	—	—	—	—

Tax Analysis	Tax-Adj Ret%	%Rank Cat	%Pretax Ret	%Rank Cat
3 Yr Avg	4.44	4	100.0	12
5 Yr Avg	4.71	13	100.0	11
10 Yr Avg	4.86	42	99.6	61

Potential Capital Gain Exposure: 2% of assets

Risk Analysis

Time Period	Load-Adj Return %	Risk %Rank[1] All	Risk %Rank[1] Cat	Morningstar Return	Morningstar Risk	Morningstar Risk-Adj Rating
1 Yr	5.58					
3 Yr	4.44	2	33	0.54[2]	0.28	★★★★★
5 Yr	4.71	2	35	0.62[2]	0.31	★★★★★
10 Yr	4.88	2	35	0.61	0.29	★★★★

Average Historical Rating (137 months): 4.8★s

[1]1=low, 100=high [2] T-Bill return substituted for category avg.

Category Rating (3 Yr)

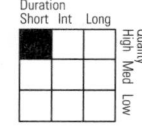

1 2 3 4 5 — Worst … Best (rating: 4)

Return: Above Avg
Risk: Average

Other Measures	Standard Index LB Agg	Best Fit Index LB Muni
Alpha	–0.9	–0.4
Beta	0.35	0.41
R-Squared	48	77

Standard Deviation	1.80
Mean	4.44
Sharpe Ratio	–0.33

Portfolio Analysis 06-30-01

Total Fixed-Income: 390	Date of Maturity	Amount $000	Value $000	% Net Assets
CO Arapahoe Cap Impr Tr Hwy 0%	08-31-26	280,005	49,827	1.51
CO Arapahoe Cap Impr Tr Hwy 0%	08-31-15	114,235	47,374	1.43
NH Busn Fin Poll Cntrl Illum 4.55%	07-01-27	36,000	35,773	1.08
OR Portland GO 4.25%	12-15-04	35,175	35,527	1.07
MT Forsyth Poll Cntrl Pwr Dmd	05-01-33	34,410	34,475	1.04
IL Metro Pier/Expo McCormick Expsn 6.5%	06-15-27	29,455	31,883	0.96
KY Tpk Econ Dev Rd 5.75%	07-01-08	26,760	29,391	0.89
CA GO 5.25%	03-01-06	26,000	27,519	0.83
TX Matagorda Navig Dist #1 Lt/Pwr 5.2%	05-01-29	27,000	27,347	0.83
NJ State COP 5.5%	09-15-08	25,000	27,262	0.82
IL Chicago GO Sch Fin 5%	06-01-03	25,190	25,995	0.79
TX Dallas/Ft Worth Intl Arpt Fac 5.95%	11-01-03	24,300	24,834	0.75
IL Chicago O'Hare Intl Arpt Fac 6.1%	11-01-35	25,000	24,829	0.75
AL Huntsville Hlth Care 4.65%	06-01-24	24,115	24,625	0.75
FL Broward Res Rec South 5.5%	12-01-08	22,980	24,490	0.74

Current Investment Style

Duration: Short Int Long; Quality: High Med Low

Avg Duration[1]	2.9 Yrs
Avg Nominal Maturity	3.3 Yrs
Avg Credit Quality	AA
Avg Wtd Coupon	5.17%
Avg Wtd Price	101.68% of par
Pricing Service	J.J. Kenny

[1]figure provided by fund

Credit Analysis % bonds 09-30-01

US Govt	0	BB	1
AAA	53	B	1
AA	31	Below B	0
A	7	NR/NA	0
BBB	8		

Special Securities % assets 06-30-01

Restricted/Illiquid Secs	0
Inverse Floaters	0
Options/Futures/Warrants	No

Bond Type % assets 10-26-98

Alternative Minimum Tax (AMT)	3.0
Insured	16.6
Prerefunded	41.0

Top 5 States % bonds

TX	13.5	MI	5.5
NY	7.3	CO	5.1
IL	7.3		

Composition % assets 06-30-01

Cash	2.2	Bonds	97.8
Stocks	0.0	Other	0.0

Sector Weightings	% of Bonds	Rel Cat
General Obligation	36.6	1.3
Utilities	3.1	0.4
Health	6.9	0.6
Water/Waste	4.5	0.8
Housing	1.4	0.2
Education	3.0	0.5
Transportation	19.6	2.1
COP/Lease	1.1	0.3
Industrial	12.9	1.3
Misc Revenue	7.2	1.2
Demand	3.9	1.2

Analysis by William Harding 08-31-01

This fund remains an easy pick for conservative-minded muni investors.

Vanguard Limited-Term Tax-Exempt Fund's annual returns have only failed to land in the top half of the muni short category three times over the past 13 years. The key to the fund's stellar long-term record is its tiny expense ratio, which is about 70 basis points lower than its typical peer's. Such a cost advantage goes a long way in the muni-bond universe because there isn't great divergence in returns among funds in the group.

The fund's low expenses also mean that management doesn't have to take on a lot of risk to maintain a competitive yield since expenses are deducted from the fund's income. Management will adjust the fund's duration (which measures sensitivity to interest-rate changes) on occasion, but the calls aren't too bold. Manager Pam Wisehaupt-Tynan has recently pegged duration at 2.85 years, which is neutral based on a range set by Vanguard's head of fixed income. Moreover, although the fund has benefited from its stake in BBB-rated paper this year, 90% of the portfolio is still dedicated to bonds rated A or higher.

Investors should note, however, that in March the fund's board approved a change that will allow it to invest in bonds with maturities greater than 10 years. This gives Wisehaupt-Tynan more flexibility in selecting securities, and for example, she invested in some bonds in the housing sector as a result. That's not to suggest that the fund's overall risk profile should change much, however, as management will maintain its current duration targets.

Investors looking for modest returns without taking on much risk will find a nice home here.

Address:	Vanguard Financial Ctr. P.O. Box 2600 Valley Forge, PA 19482 800–662–7447 / 610–669–1000
Web Address:	www.vanguard.com
Inception:	09-01-87
Advisor:	Vanguard Fixed–Income Grp.
Subadvisor:	None
NTF Plans:	N/A

Minimum Purchase:	$3000	Add: $100	IRA: $1000
Min Auto Inv Plan:	$3000	Add: $50	
Sales Fees:	No–load		
Management Fee:	None		
Actual Fees:	Mgt: 0.17%	Dist: —	
Expense Projections:	3Yr: $61	5Yr: $107	10Yr: $243
Avg Brok Commission:	—	Income Distrib: Monthly	
Total Cost (relative to category):		Low	

Vanguard Long–Term Corporate Bond

Ticker	Load	NAV	Yield	SEC Yield	Total Assets	Mstar Category
VWESX	None	$8.68	6.5%	—	$3,977.0 mil	Long–Term Bond

Prospectus Objective: Corp Bond—High Quality

Vanguard Long-Term Corporate Bond Fund seeks current income consistent with maintenance of principal and liquidity.

The fund typically invests at least 70% of assets in high-quality corporate bonds; it invests at least 80% of assets in a combination of U.S. government securities and investment-grade corporate bonds. The average weighted maturity generally ranges from 15 to 25 years.

The fund also offers Adm shares. Past names: Vanguard Fixed-Income Securities Investment Grade Bond, Vanguard Fixed-Income Securities Investment Grade Corporate Portfolio, and Vanguard Fixed-Income Long-Term Corporate Bond Fund.

Historical Profile

Return: High
Risk: Above Avg
Rating: ★★★ Neutral

Investment Style: Fixed-Income
Income Rtn %Rank Cat: 32, 22, 32, 20, 20, 32, 25, 25

Growth of Principal vs. Interest Rate Shifts
- Principal Value $000 (NAV with capital gains reinvested)
- Interest Rate % on 10 Yr Treasury
- ▼ Manager Change
- ▽ Partial Manager Change
- ► Mgr Unknown After
- ◄ Mgr Unknown Before

Performance Quartile (within Category)

Portfolio Manager(s)

Earl E. McEvoy. Since 3-94. BA'70 Dartmouth C.; MBA'72 Columbia U. Other funds currently managed: Global Utility A, Global Utility B, Vanguard High-Yield Corporate.

History

1990	1991	1992	1993	1994	1995	1996	1997	1998	1999	2000	12-01	History
7.99	8.87	8.86	9.22	8.05	9.48	8.79	9.26	9.29	8.11	8.45	8.68	NAV
6.21	20.90	9.78	14.49	–5.30	26.40	1.20	13.78	9.22	–6.23	11.76	9.57	Total Return %
–2.75	4.90	2.38	4.75	–2.38	7.93	–2.42	4.10	0.54	–5.40	0.13	1.14	+/– LB Aggregate
–0.21	1.38	1.25	–1.67	1.80	–3.53	1.06	–0.74	–2.55	1.41	–4.40	2.30	+/– LB LT Govt/Corp
9.10	9.24	7.98	7.45	6.95	8.05	6.79	7.21	6.56	6.25	7.30	6.86	Income Return %
–2.90	11.66	1.80	7.04	–12.24	18.35	–5.59	6.57	2.66	–12.48	4.46	2.71	Capital Return %
56	11	10	28	48	22	81	11	14	82	17	9	Total Rtn % Rank Cat
0.72	0.71	0.68	0.64	0.62	0.63	0.62	0.61	0.59	0.56	0.57	0.56	Income $
0.00	0.00	0.15	0.26	0.07	0.00	0.15	0.07	0.21	0.06	0.00	0.00	Capital Gains $
0.34	0.37	0.31	0.31	0.30	0.32	0.31	0.28	0.32	0.30	0.30	—	Expense Ratio %
9.07	9.16	8.46	7.68	6.71	7.37	7.03	7.06	6.87	6.26	6.59	—	Income Ratio %
70	62	72	50	77	43	49	30	33	43	7	—	Turnover Rate %
1,192.7	2,006.2	2,619.2	3,168.4	2,552.3	3,356.1	3,412.0	3,599.2	4,152.9	3,723.6	3,820.3	3,550.3	Net Assets $mil

Performance 12-31-01

	1st Qtr	2nd Qtr	3rd Qtr	4th Qtr	Total
1997	–2.23	5.28	5.56	4.72	13.78
1998	1.31	3.93	3.63	0.10	9.22
1999	–2.12	–2.95	–0.46	–0.83	–6.23
2000	2.64	0.31	3.41	4.97	11.76
2001	3.79	–0.10	4.72	0.90	9.57

Trailing	Total Return%	+/– LB Agg	+/– LB LTGvt/Corp	% Rank All	% Rank Cat	Growth of $10,000
3 Mo	0.90	0.87	0.98	73	31	10,090
6 Mo	5.67	1.01	0.58	3	7	10,567
1 Yr	9.57	1.14	2.30	6	9	10,957
3 Yr Avg	4.72	–1.56	–0.07	33	52	11,483
5 Yr Avg	7.37	–0.06	–0.68	33	7	14,269
10 Yr Avg	8.07	0.84	–0.35	43	15	21,727
15 Yr Avg	8.78	0.66	–0.24	49	20	35,320

Tax Analysis	Tax-Adj Ret%	%Rank Cat	%Pretax Ret	%Rank Cat
3 Yr Avg	1.94	61	41.2	69
5 Yr Avg	4.42	10	59.9	41
10 Yr Avg	4.92	21	61.0	26

Potential Capital Gain Exposure: 0% of assets

Risk Analysis

Time Period	Load-Adj Return %	Risk %Rank[1] All	Risk %Rank[1] Cat	Morningstar Return	Morningstar Risk	Morningstar Risk-Adj Rating
1 Yr	9.57					
3 Yr	4.72	31	69	–0.05[2]	1.20	★★★
5 Yr	7.37	36	75	0.53[2]	1.26	★★★
10 Yr	8.07	44	78	0.99[2]	1.48	★★★

Average Historical Rating (193 months): 3.5★s

[1] 1=low, 100=high [2] T–Bill return substituted for category avg.

Category Rating (3 Yr)

1 2 3 4 5
Worst Best

Return: Average
Risk: Above Avg

Other Measures	Standard Index LB Agg	Best Fit Index LB Corp
Alpha	–2.2	–1.3
Beta	1.66	1.44
R–Squared	86	92
Standard Deviation		6.20
Mean		4.72
Sharpe Ratio		–0.04

Portfolio Analysis 09-30-01

Total Fixed-Income: 128	Date of Maturity	Amount $000	Value $000	% Net Assets
Us Treasury Bond 5.5%	08-15-28	550,000	588,132	14.34
Fnma Debenture 7.125%	01-15-30	175,000	210,775	5.14
Eli Lilly 7.125%	06-01-25	50,000	55,289	1.35
Ibm 7%	10-30-25	50,000	53,844	1.31
Ge Global Ins 7%	02-15-26	50,000	53,599	1.31
Hartford Life 7.375%	03-01-31	50,000	51,615	1.26
General Elec Cap 8.125%	05-15-12	42,000	51,494	1.26
Kellogg 7.45%	04-01-31	46,750	51,288	1.25
John Hancock 144a 7.375%	02-15-24	50,000	51,179	1.25
Washington Post 5.5%	02-15-09	50,000	49,682	1.21
Liberty Mutual Ins 144a 8.5%	05-15-25	50,000	49,199	1.20
Procter & Gamble 9.36%	01-01-21	35,000	46,561	1.14
Bristol–myers Squibb 6.8%	11-15-26	40,000	44,228	1.08
Ford Motor 8.9%	01-15-32	40,000	43,922	1.07
At & T 6.5%	03-15-29	50,000	43,187	1.05
Lockheed Martin 7.65%	05-01-16	35,000	39,712	0.97
Csx 7.95%	05-01-27	35,000	39,152	0.95
Mirant Americas 9.125%	05-01-31	35,000	38,746	0.94
Norfolk Southern 7.8%	05-15-27	35,000	38,263	0.93
Indiana Bell 7.3%	08-15-26	35,000	37,918	0.92

Current Investment Style

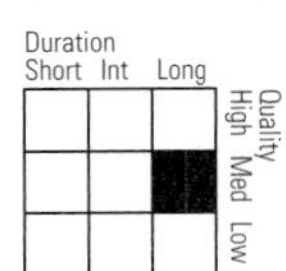

Avg Eff Duration[1]	10.2 Yrs
Avg Eff Maturity	—
Avg Credit Quality	A
Avg Wtd Coupon	7.07%
Avg Wtd Price	106.73% of par

[1] figure provided by fund

Special Securities % assets 09-30-01	
Restricted/Illiquid Secs	6
Exotic Mortgage–Backed	0
Emerging–Markets Secs	0
Options/Futures/Warrants	No

Coupon Range	% of Bonds	Rel Cat
0%	0.00	0.00
0% to 7%	44.23	1.12
7% to 8.5%	43.60	1.05
8.5% to 10%	12.16	0.85
More than 10%	0.00	0.00

1.00=Category Average

Credit Analysis % bonds 09-30-01

US Govt	19	BB	0
AAA	5	B	0
AA	20	Below B	0
A	35	NR/NA	0
BBB	21		

Composition % assets 09-30-01

Cash	3.6	Bonds	96.4
Stocks	0.0	Other	0.0

Sector Breakdown % bonds 09-30-01

US Treasuries	14	CMOs	0
GNMA mtgs	0	ARMs	0
FNMA mtgs	5	Other	80
FHLMC mtgs	0		

Analysis by Alan Papier 10-22-01

Vanguard Long-Term Corporate Bond Fund continues to deliver.

This fund's unwavering approach has it out front once again. Indeed, for the year to date through Oct. 19, 2001, the fund gained 10% and ranked ahead of 94% of its long-term bond peers. Its five- and 10-year trailing returns also rank in the group's upper echelons.

To be sure, the fund is more interest-rate sensitive than most of its peers. But manager Earl McEvoy doesn't make big interest-rate bets. Instead, he keeps the fund's duration within 20% of its benchmark's, which is typically longer than the category average to begin with. Thus, the Federal Reserve's vigilant easing of rates in 2001 has worked in the fund's favor.

Recently, though, the fund has also benefited from its high-quality focus. McEvoy hasn't invested in below-investment-grade bonds, which have substantially lagged their high-quality counterparts as the economy continues to struggle. What's more, the fund has taken full advantage of its flexibility to invest up to 20% of assets in Treasuries and other government securities, which have been the top-performing bonds since Sept. 11.

While the focus on long-term corporate bonds has produced impressive results, that posture does leave the fund vulnerable to rising interest rates and slumping corporate bonds. For example, during the first six months of 1999, the fund shed 5%, while its average peer lost only half that amount.

Even though the fund's interest-rate induced volatility has ostensibly tainted its risk scores, we think investors should look beyond those measures. For one thing, its rock-bottom expenses mean that the fund doesn't have to take on much credit risk to produce competitive yields. And for long-term, income-oriented investors able to endure intermittent turbulence, we think this fund remains a strong choice.

Address:	Vanguard Financial Ctr. P.O. Box 2600 Valley Forge, PA 19482 800–662–7447 / 610–669–1000
Web Address:	www.vanguard.com
Inception:	07-09-73
Advisor:	Vanguard Legal Department
Subadvisor:	None
NTF Plans:	N/A

Minimum Purchase:	$3000	Add: $100 IRA: $1000
Min Auto Inv Plan:	$3000	Add: $50
Sales Fees:	No–load	
Management Fee:	.04% mx./.02% mn.	
Actual Fees:	Mgt: 0.30%	Dist: —
Expense Projections:	3Yr: $78	5Yr: $135 10Yr: $306
Avg Brok Commission:	—	Income Distrib: Monthly
Total Cost (relative to category):		Low

Vanguard Long–Term Tax–Exempt

Ticker	Load	NAV	Yield	SEC Yield	Total Assets	Mstar Category
VWLTX	None	$10.98	5.1%	—	$1,909.2 mil	Muni Natl Long–Term

Prospectus Objective: Muni Bond—National

Vanguard Long-Term Tax-Exempt Fund seeks income exempt from federal income tax, consistent with preservation of capital.

The fund invests primarily in high-quality tax-exempt municipal obligations. It maintains an average-weighted maturity between 15 and 25 years. Individual maturities may vary. The fund may invest to a limited extent in bond futures contracts and options. It may invest up to 20% of assets in securities subject to the Alternative Minimum Tax.

The fund also offers Adm shares. Prior to Oct. 27, 1998, the fund was named Vanguard Municipal Bond Fund Long-Term Portfolio.

Historical Profile

Return: High
Risk: Above Avg
Rating: ★★★★ Above Avg

Investment Style
Fixed-Income
Income Rtn %Rank Cat: 33 30 33 29 17 18 18 28

Growth of Principal vs. Interest Rate Shifts
- Principal Value $000 (NAV with capital gains reinvested)
- Interest Rate % on 10 Yr Treasury
- ▼ Manager Change
- ▽ Partial Manager Change
- ► Mgr Unknown After
- ◄ Mgr Unknown Before

Performance Quartile (within Category)

Portfolio Manager(s)

Christopher M. Ryon. Since 9-96. BS Villanova U.; MBA Drexel U. Other funds currently managed: Vanguard NY Insured Long Tax-Ex, Vanguard Interm-Term Tax-Ex, Vanguard Tax-Managed Balanced.

History

1990	1991	1992	1993	1994	1995	1996	1997	1998	1999	2000	12-01	History
10.31	10.72	10.71	11.29	9.88	11.09	10.95	11.29	11.26	10.31	11.07	10.98	NAV
6.82	13.50	9.30	13.45	−5.76	18.72	4.42	9.29	6.02	−3.53	13.32	4.27	Total Return %
−2.14	−2.50	1.90	3.70	−2.84	0.25	0.80	−0.40	−2.66	−2.70	1.69	−4.16	+/– LB Aggregate
−0.49	1.36	0.49	1.18	−0.62	1.26	−0.02	0.09	−0.46	−1.46	1.63	−0.81	+/– LB Muni
7.10	7.37	6.59	5.98	5.57	6.21	5.41	5.51	5.24	5.14	5.68	5.16	Income Return %
−0.29	6.13	2.72	7.47	−11.33	12.51	−1.00	3.78	0.78	−8.67	7.64	−0.89	Capital Return %
24	10	35	18	38	18	18	43	18	21	7	37	Total Rtn % Rank Cat
0.72	0.73	0.68	0.62	0.61	0.60	0.59	0.59	0.58	0.57	0.57	0.56	Income $
0.18	0.19	0.28	0.21	0.16	0.00	0.02	0.06	0.12	0.00	0.00	0.00	Capital Gains $
0.25	0.25	0.23	0.20	0.20	0.21	0.20	0.19	0.21	0.18	0.19	—	Expense Ratio %
7.04	7.09	6.52	5.81	5.56	5.87	5.45	5.37	5.13	5.13	5.46	—	Income Ratio %
110	62	63	36	45	35	26	9	18	15	25	—	Turnover Rate %
711.5	887.8	1,012.7	1,103.9	920.3	1,114.4	1,141.8	1,281.9	1,536.7	1,486.6	1,794.2	1,186.6	Net Assets $mil

Performance 12-31-01

	1st Qtr	2nd Qtr	3rd Qtr	4th Qtr	Total
1997	−0.50	3.72	2.98	2.83	9.29
1998	1.00	1.40	3.17	0.34	6.02
1999	0.70	−2.15	−1.38	−0.73	−3.53
2000	3.46	1.57	2.30	5.42	13.32
2001	2.35	0.46	2.98	−1.52	4.27

Trailing	Total Return%	+/– LB Agg	+/– LB Muni	% Rank All	% Rank Cat	Growth of $10,000
3 Mo	−1.52	−1.56	−0.86	97	83	9,848
6 Mo	1.41	−3.24	−0.71	31	55	10,141
1 Yr	4.27	−4.16	−0.81	28	37	10,427
3 Yr Avg	4.46	−1.81	−0.29	36	4	11,399
5 Yr Avg	5.72	−1.70	−0.25	52	6	13,208
10 Yr Avg	6.70	−0.53	0.07	53	4	19,134
15 Yr Avg	7.28	−0.84	0.10	62	9	28,710

Tax Analysis	Tax-Adj Ret%	%Rank Cat	%Pretax Ret	%Rank Cat
3 Yr Avg	4.46	3	100.0	48
5 Yr Avg	5.65	5	98.7	55
10 Yr Avg	6.47	4	96.5	70

Potential Capital Gain Exposure: 6% of assets

Risk Analysis

Time Period	Load-Adj Return %	Risk %Rank[1] All	Risk %Rank[1] Cat	Morningstar Return	Morningstar Risk	Morningstar Risk-Adj Rating
1 Yr	4.27					
3 Yr	4.46	24	47	0.68[2]	1.16	★★★★
5 Yr	5.72	25	44	1.03[2]	1.15	★★★★
10 Yr	6.70	35	70	1.25	1.23	★★★

Average Historical Rating (193 months): 3.3★s

[1] 1=low, 100=high [2] T-Bill return substituted for category avg.

Category Rating (3 Yr)

1 2 3 4 5 (5 selected) — Worst … Best

Return: High
Risk: Average

Other Measures	Standard Index LB Agg	Best Fit Index LB Muni
Alpha	−1.6	−0.2
Beta	0.98	1.23
R–Squared	51	97
Standard Deviation		4.82
Mean		4.46
Sharpe Ratio		−0.12

Analysis by William Harding 08-31-01

It's easy to see why this fund is an appealing option for tax-exempt investors.

You want consistency? Look no further than Vanguard Long-Term Tax-Exempt Fund. The fund's annual returns have landed in the muni national long category's top half for 13 straight years. And 2001 has been no exception. Its 6.5% gain for the year to date ended August 29, 2001, bests more than 80% of its peers. Paramount to the fund's long-term success are its low costs, which carry a lot of weight in the muni bond world. Its expense ratio is more than 90 basis points cheaper than its average rival's.

That cost advantage also helps the fund maintain a competitive yield relative to its peer group without taking on a lot of risk. The fund will make interest-rate calls on occasion, but they tend to be fairly moderate. This year, manager Christopher Ryon has positioned the fund near the low-end of a one-year neutral duration range set by Vanguard's head of fixed-income. (Duration is a measure of interest-rate sensitivity.) Last year duration was near the long-end of the range, which boosted returns amid declining interest rates.

The fund hasn't taken on much credit risk, either, as evidenced by its large stake in AAA rated securities relative to the group average. Ryon will move down the credit-quality ladder on occasion, however. For instance, he has spied some opportunities this year in BBB rated paper, as yields have increased dramatically. Still, Ryon hasn't made big bets on lower-quality fare, so the fund's average credit quality won't likely change drastically.

The group has other quality offerings to consider. But because of this fund's low costs, none of them has as sure a chance to succeed as this one.

Portfolio Analysis 06-30-01

Total Fixed-Income: 246	Date of Maturity	Amount $000	Value $000	% Net Assets
MA Wtr Res 6.5%	07-15-19	32,000	37,830	2.00
TX Lower Colorado Rvr 5.875%	05-15-16	27,500	29,410	1.55
WA State COP 5%	04-01-16	27,820	27,278	1.44
LA De Soto Poll Cntrl SW Elec Pwr 7.6%	01-01-19	24,300	25,965	1.37
WI Clean Wtr Fd 6.875%	06-01-11	20,500	24,525	1.29
IL GO Metro Wtr Reclam Chicago 7%	01-01-11	20,000	23,832	1.26
PA Philadelphia Wtr/Wastewtr 7%	06-15-10	20,000	23,751	1.25
AR Manchester Arpt 5.625%	01-01-30	23,000	23,570	1.24
CO Trans 6%	06-15-12	20,000	22,353	1.18
CA San Bernardino COP 6.875%	08-01-24	18,000	22,291	1.18
TX Muni Pwr 0%	09-01-13	39,670	21,490	1.13
TX Texas City Indl Dev Arco 7.375%	10-01-20	17,000	21,069	1.11
GA Monroe Cmnty Dev 3.85%	01-01-20	20,615	20,615	1.09
TX Wtr Dev Brd Revolving Fd 6.4%	07-15-10	17,425	20,074	1.06
IN Office Bldg Com Cap Cmplx 6.9%	07-01-11	16,875	19,612	1.03

Current Investment Style

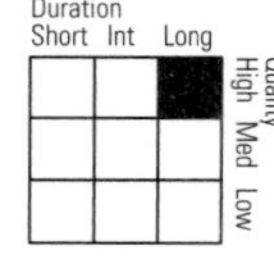

Avg Duration[1]	7.9 Yrs
Avg Nominal Maturity	12.9 Yrs
Avg Credit Quality	AA
Avg Wtd Coupon	5.37%
Avg Wtd Price	102.55% of par
Pricing Service	J.J. Kenny

[1] figure provided by fund

Credit Analysis % bonds 09-30-01

US Govt	0	BB	1
AAA	59	B	0
AA	29	Below B	0
A	6	NR/NA	0
BBB	6		

Special Securities % assets 06-30-01

Restricted/Illiquid Secs	0
Inverse Floaters	0
Options/Futures/Warrants	No

Bond Type % assets 01-31-99

Alternative Minimum Tax (AMT)	1.9
Insured	51.4
Prerefunded	7.5

Top 5 States % bonds

TX	14.9	CA	7.0
MA	8.1	IL	6.6
NY	8.0		

Composition % assets 06-30-01

Cash	0.5	Bonds	99.5
Stocks	0.0	Other	0.0

Sector Weightings	% of Bonds	Rel Cat
General Obligation	17.6	0.8
Utilities	11.9	1.5
Health	9.7	0.6
Water/Waste	12.3	2.0
Housing	1.3	0.2
Education	4.0	0.6
Transportation	18.2	1.4
COP/Lease	7.4	2.6
Industrial	8.8	0.7
Misc Revenue	6.6	1.3
Demand	2.2	2.7

Address:	Vanguard Financial Ctr. P.O. Box 2600 Valley Forge, PA 19482 800–662–7447 / 610–669–1000
Web Address:	www.vanguard.com
Inception:	09-01-77
Advisor:	Vanguard Legal Department
Subadvisor:	None
NTF Plans:	N/A

Minimum Purchase:	$3000	Add: $100	IRA: $1000
Min Auto Inv Plan:	$3000	Add: $50	
Sales Fees:	No–load		
Management Fee:	None		
Actual Fees:	Mgt: 0.17%	Dist: —	
Expense Projections:	3Yr: $61	5Yr: $107	10Yr: $243
Avg Brok Commission:	—	Income Distrib: Monthly	
Total Cost (relative to category):		Low	

Vanguard Long–Term U.S. Treasury

Ticker	Load	NAV	Yield	SEC Yield	Total Assets	Mstar Category
VUSTX	None	$10.76	5.6%	—	$1,904.0 mil	Long Government

Prospectus Objective: Government Treasury

Vanguard Long-Term U.S. Treasury Fund seeks current income consistent with maintenance of principal and liquidity.

The fund normally invests at least 85% of assets in long-term U.S. Treasury bonds and other guaranteed U.S. government obligations. It may invest the balance of assets in other U.S. government securities, including repurchase agreements on such securities.The fund typically maintains an average weighted maturity of between 15 and 30 years.

The fund also offers Adm shares. Prior names Vanguard Fixed-Income Securities Fund U.S. Treasury Bond Portfolio. The fund was named Vanguard Fixed-Income Securities Fund Long-Term U.S. Treasury Portfolio.

Historical Profile
Return High
Risk High
Rating ★★ Below Avg

Investment Style: Fixed-Income — Income Rtn %Rank Cat: 7 7 17 6 14 23 15 19

Growth of Principal vs. Interest Rate Shifts
— Principal Value $000 (NAV with capital gains reinvested)
— Interest Rate % on 10 Yr Treasury
▼ Manager Change
▽ Partial Manager Change
► Mgr Unknown After
◄ Mgr Unknown Before

Performance Quartile (within Category)

Portfolio Manager(s)

Ian A. MacKinnon. Since 5-86. BA'70 Lafayette C.; MBA'74 Pennsylvania State U. Other funds currently managed: Vanguard Balanced Index, Vanguard CA Insured Long Tax-Ex, Vanguard Short-Term Treasury.

David R. Glocke. Since 5-01. BS U. of Wisconsin. Other funds currently managed: Vanguard Short-Term Treasury, Vanguard Interm-Term U.S. Treas, Vanguard Short-Term Treasury Adm.

1990	1991	1992	1993	1994	1995	1996	1997	1998	1999	2000	12-01	History
9.70	10.54	9.82	10.57	9.05	10.79	9.96	10.64	11.36	9.67	10.90	10.76	NAV
5.78	17.43	7.41	16.79	–7.04	30.09	–1.26	13.90	13.05	–8.66	19.72	4.31	Total Return %
–3.18	1.43	—	7.04	–4.12	11.62	–4.87	4.22	4.38	–7.83	8.09	–4.12	+/– LB Aggregate
–0.51	–1.25	–0.68	–0.40	0.55	–0.81	–0.42	–1.22	–0.27	–0.40	–0.56	–0.04	+/– LB LT Government
8.09	8.20	7.34	7.25	6.50	7.66	6.25	6.67	6.10	5.57	6.61	5.67	Income Return %
–2.31	9.23	0.07	9.54	–13.54	22.43	–7.51	7.24	6.96	–14.23	13.12	–1.36	Capital Return %
81	13	23	16	73	14	80	19	20	75	17	75	Total Rtn % Rank Cat
0.78	0.77	0.74	0.69	0.66	0.67	0.65	0.64	0.63	0.61	0.62	0.60	Income $
0.00	0.00	0.70	0.18	0.12	0.23	0.01	0.00	0.00	0.12	0.00	0.00	Capital Gains $
0.28	0.30	0.26	0.27	0.26	0.28	0.27	0.25	0.27	0.27	0.28	—	Expense Ratio %
8.08	8.29	7.72	7.26	6.44	7.02	6.57	6.66	6.38	5.69	5.98	—	Income Ratio %
83	147	89	170	7	85	105	31	18	22	43	—	Turnover Rate %
698.0	892.5	856.8	823.4	644.2	917.4	918.0	1,030.2	1,415.5	1,223.5	1,365.4	1,372.8	Net Assets $mil

Performance 12-31-01

	1st Qtr	2nd Qtr	3rd Qtr	4th Qtr	Total
1997	–3.04	5.19	5.33	6.03	13.90
1998	1.29	4.65	7.72	–0.98	13.05
1999	–4.15	–2.53	–0.17	–2.06	–8.66
2000	7.52	1.16	2.71	7.17	19.72
2001	1.47	–1.62	6.64	–2.02	4.31

Trailing	Total Return%	+/– LB Agg	+/– LB LT Govt	% Rank All	% Rank Cat	Growth of $10,000
3 Mo	–2.02	–2.06	–0.15	99	83	9,798
6 Mo	4.49	–0.17	–0.26	6	33	10,449
1 Yr	4.31	–4.12	–0.04	28	75	10,431
3 Yr Avg	4.48	–1.79	–0.33	35	38	11,407
5 Yr Avg	7.99	0.57	–0.49	29	13	14,688
10 Yr Avg	8.20	0.98	–0.40	42	16	22,002
15 Yr Avg	8.53	0.41	–0.47	50	12	34,152

Tax Analysis	Tax-Adj Ret%	%Rank Cat	%Pretax Ret	%Rank Cat
3 Yr Avg	2.04	56	45.5	67
5 Yr Avg	5.45	17	68.2	20
10 Yr Avg	5.16	20	62.9	36

Potential Capital Gain Exposure: 7% of assets

Risk Analysis

Time Period	Load-Adj Return %	Risk %Rank[1] All	Risk %Rank[1] Cat	Morningstar Return	Morningstar Risk	Morningstar Risk-Adj Rating
1 Yr	4.31					
3 Yr	4.48	32	71	–0.10[2]	1.48	★★
5 Yr	7.99	37	75	0.68[2]	1.49	★★★
10 Yr	8.20	47	83	1.04[2]	1.81	★★

Average Historical Rating (152 months): 2.4★s

[1] 1=low, 100=high [2] T-Bill return substituted for category avg.

Category Rating (3 Yr)

1 2 3 4 5 — Worst … Best

Return Average
Risk Above Avg

Other Measures	Standard Index LB Agg	Best Fit Index LB LTTreas
Alpha	–2.7	–0.3
Beta	1.96	0.99
R–Squared	79	99

Standard Deviation	7.66
Mean	4.48
Sharpe Ratio	–0.07

Portfolio Analysis 09-30-01

Total Fixed-Income: 19	Date of Maturity	Amount $000	Value $000	% Net Assets
US Treasury Bond 8.125%	05-15-21	262,875	362,807	18.24
US Treasury Bond 7.875%	02-15-21	204,781	275,836	13.87
US Treasury Bond 6.75%	08-15-26	203,585	251,916	12.67
US Treasury Bond 8.875%	02-15-19	139,663	202,319	10.17
US Treasury Bond 8.125%	08-15-19	106,523	145,427	7.31
US Treasury Bond 6.375%	08-15-27	109,150	129,986	6.54
US Treasury Bond 9.25%	02-15-16	88,775	128,959	6.48
US Treasury Bond 6.125%	08-15-29	102,500	119,754	6.02
Private Export Fdg 144A 7.25%	06-15-10	64,080	74,618	3.75
US Treasury Bond 5.5%	08-15-28	60,000	64,160	3.23
US Treasury Bond 3.875%	04-15-29	50,839	61,548	3.09
US Treasury Bond 6.25%	05-15-30	39,430	47,149	2.37
US Treasury Bond 6.625%	02-15-27	35,000	42,816	2.15
US Treasury Bond 7.25%	05-15-16	31,000	38,575	1.94
US Treasury Bond 5.25%	02-15-29	32,000	33,139	1.67
Private Export Fdg 144A 6.07%	04-30-11	29,000	31,569	1.59
FHLMC Debenture 6.25%	03-15-11	28,200	29,728	1.49
Private Export Fdg 6.67%	09-15-09	17,000	19,213	0.97
Private Export Fdg 7.2%	01-15-10	7,100	8,198	0.41

Current Investment Style

Duration: Short Int Long — Quality: High Med Low

Avg Eff Duration[1]	10.1 Yrs
Avg Eff Maturity	—
Avg Credit Quality	AAA
Avg Wtd Coupon	7.39%
Avg Wtd Price	129.40% of par

[1] figure provided by fund

Special Securities % assets 09-30-01	
Restricted/Illiquid Secs	5
Exotic Mortgage–Backed	0
Emerging–Markets Secs	0
Options/Futures/Warrants	No

Coupon Range	% of Bonds	Rel Cat
0%	0.00	0.00
0% to 7%	40.18	0.78
7% to 8.5%	43.79	1.80
8.5% to 10%	16.02	1.88
More than 10%	0.00	0.00

1.00=Category Average

Credit Analysis % bonds 09-30-01			
US Govt	98	BB	0
AAA	2	B	0
AA	0	Below B	0
A	0	NR/NA	0
BBB	0		

Composition % assets 09-30-01			
Cash	0.3	Bonds	99.7
Stocks	0.0	Other	0.0

Sector Breakdown % bonds 09-30-01			
US Treasuries	92	CMOs	0
GNMA mtgs	0	ARMs	0
FNMA mtgs	0	Other	6
FHLMC mtgs	1		

Analysis by Alan Papier 10-17-01

Vanguard Long-Term U.S. Treasury Fund remains one of our favorites.

This fund hasn't knocked the cover off the ball in 2001 (as it did last year), but that isn't surprising. For the year to date through Oct. 16, the fund gained 6.8% and ranked in the middle of the long-term government bond category. That's because the portfolio holds mostly long-maturity Treasury bonds, and those bonds have generally lagged other government securities so far in 2001. Indeed, mortgage-backed securities issued by government agencies like Ginnie Mae have been slightly better performers, and short- and intermediate-maturity bonds have gotten a bigger price boost from investors seeking relative safety and security.

Still, the fund's no-frills strategy has been highly successful over time: Both its five- and 10-year annualized returns ranked in the top 15% of the long-government category. That's partly attributable to generally declining interest rates over much of the past decade, as the fund's duration (a measure of interest-rate sensitivity) is typically among the longest in the group. That positioning isn't always a good thing, however. In 1999, for example, when the Federal Reserve started hiking interest rates in an effort to head off inflation, the fund lost 8.7%, more than most of its peers' losses.

While the fund's holdings may be susceptible to shifting interest rates, credit risk isn't an issue here. Because Treasuries are backed by the U.S. government, they are considered to be the highest quality fixed-income securities. And even though management also dabbles in agency debt, those bonds are also at the top of the credit-quality spectrum.

But one of this fund's primary advantages is its rock-bottom expenses. All in all, the fund's low costs and predictable approach make it a category standout.

Address:	Vanguard Financial Ctr. P.O. Box 2600 Valley Forge, PA 19482 800–662–7447 / 610–669–1000
Web Address:	www.vanguard.com
Inception:	05-19-86
Advisor:	Vanguard Fixed–Income Grp.
Subadvisor:	None
NTF Plans:	N/A

Minimum Purchase:	$3000	Add: $100	IRA: $1000
Min Auto Inv Plan:	$3000	Add: $50	
Sales Fees:	No–load		
Management Fee:	.26%		
Actual Fees:	Mgt: 0.26%	Dist: —	
Expense Projections:	3Yr: $93	5Yr: $163	10Yr: $367
Avg Brok Commission:	—	Income Distrib: Monthly	
Total Cost (relative to category):		Low	

Vanguard Mid Capitalization Index

Ticker	Load	NAV	Yield	Total Assets	Mstar Category
VIMSX	None	$11.81	0.6%	$2,921.6 mil	Mid-Cap Blend

Prospectus Objective: Growth

Vanguard Mid Capitalization Index Fund seeks to parallel the performance of the S&P MidCap 400 index.

The fund invests substantially all assets in each stock found in the index, in approximately the same proportion as represented in the index. Management uses a passive approach when selecting securities and seeks to create a mix of securities that will match the performance of the index. The fund may also invest in stock futures and options contracts, warrants, convertible securities, and swaps.

The fund offers Admiral, Investor and Institutional shares.

Historical Profile

Return: Above Avg
Risk: Average
Rating: ★★★★ Above Avg

Investment Style
Equity
Average Stock %: 98% (1998), 99% (1999), 99% (2000), 100% (12-01)

▼ Manager Change
▽ Partial Manager Change

Fund Performance vs. Category Average
■ Quarterly Fund Return +/– Category Average
— Category Baseline

Performance Quartile (within Category)

Portfolio Manager(s)

George U. Sauter. Since 4-98. AB'76 Dartmouth C.; MBA'80 U. of Chicago. Other funds currently managed: Vanguard Small Cap Index, Vanguard Balanced Index, Vanguard Equity-Income.

History

1990	1991	1992	1993	1994	1995	1996	1997	1998	1999	2000	12-01	History
—	—	—	—	—	—	—	—	10.77	11.29	12.21	11.81	NAV
—	—	—	—	—	—	—	—	8.78*	15.43	18.20	–0.50	Total Return %
—	—	—	—	—	—	—	—	–1.86*	–5.61	27.30	11.38	+/- S&P 500
—	—	—	—	—	—	—	—	—	0.71	0.71	0.10	+/- S&P Mid 400
—	—	—	—	—	—	—	—	0.54	0.74	0.70	0.58	Income Return %
—	—	—	—	—	—	—	—	8.24	14.69	17.50	–1.08	Capital Return %
—	—	—	—	—	—	—	—	—	61	15	29	Total Rtn % Rank Cat
—	—	—	—	—	—	—	—	0.05	0.08	0.08	0.07	Income $
—	—	—	—	—	—	—	—	0.05	0.94	0.98	0.25	Capital Gains $
—	—	—	—	—	—	—	—	0.25	0.25	0.25	—	Expense Ratio %
—	—	—	—	—	—	—	—	1.19	0.99	0.90	—	Income Ratio %
—	—	—	—	—	—	—	—	44	38	51	—	Turnover Rate %
—	—	—	—	—	—	—	—	205.7	604.5	1,775.5	2,048.8	Net Assets $mil

Performance 12-31-01

	1st Qtr	2nd Qtr	3rd Qtr	4th Qtr	Total
1997	—	—	—	—	—
1998	—	—	–14.36	28.43	8.78 *
1999	–6.08	14.27	–8.30	17.29	15.43
2000	13.02	–3.17	12.12	–3.67	18.20
2001	–10.80	13.20	–16.46	17.96	–0.50

Trailing	Total Return%	+/– S&P 500	+/– S&P Mid 400	% Rank All	% Rank Cat	Growth of $10,000
3 Mo	17.96	7.27	–0.03	17	34	11,796
6 Mo	–1.46	4.10	0.10	44	26	9,854
1 Yr	–0.50	11.38	0.10	43	29	9,950
3 Yr Avg	10.73	11.75	0.49	10	16	13,576
5 Yr Avg	—	—	—	—	—	—
10 Yr Avg	—	—	—	—	—	—
15 Yr Avg	—	—	—	—	—	—

Tax Analysis	Tax-Adj Ret%	%Rank Cat	%Pretax Ret	%Rank Cat
3 Yr Avg	8.10	21	75.5	51
5 Yr Avg	—	—	—	—
10 Yr Avg	—	—	—	—

Potential Capital Gain Exposure: 6% of assets

Risk Analysis

Time Period	Load-Adj Return %	Risk %Rank[1] All	Risk %Rank[1] Cat	Morningstar Return	Morningstar Risk	Morningstar Risk-Adj Rating
1 Yr	–0.50					
3 Yr	10.73	60	35	1.30[2]	0.84	★★★★
5 Yr	—	—	—	—	—	
Incept	11.11	—	—	—	—	

Average Historical Rating (9 months): 4.9★s

[1]1=low, 100=high [2] T-Bill return substituted for category avg.

Category Rating (3 Yr)

1 Worst — 5 Best (rating: 4)

Return: Above Avg
Risk: Average

Other Measures	Standard Index S&P 500	Best Fit Index SPMid400
Alpha	12.1	0.4
Beta	0.94	1.00
R-Squared	67	100

Standard Deviation	21.66
Mean	10.73
Sharpe Ratio	0.30

Analysis by Scott Cooley 10-21-01

Plenty of reasons exist to still like Vanguard Mid Capitalization Index Fund.

Although it has posted a double-digit loss this year, this fund has continued to put up solid numbers relative to its peer group. As we have pointed out, the conservative selection criteria of the committee who picks stocks for the S&P 400 Midcap index produce a benchmark index that's less exposed to profitless companies than many of the fund's rivals. Although the fund owns some stinkers, including (profitable) Rational Software, it has nevertheless held up better than its mid-blend rivals, some of which had significant stakes in money-losing dot-coms and biotech companies. With winners such as NVIDIA and Gilead Sciences providing ballast to the portfolio, the fund has lost 12.3% for the year to date through Oct. 19, 2001. Meanwhile, the mid-blend group has shed 14.4% of its value.

Although we don't expect the fund to beat its rivals as handily as it did in 2000, when it topped them by 15 percentage points, we do think it has some sustainable advantages. For one, its expense ratio is more than 1 percentage point less than the group norm. Its management is excellent; through a variety of trading techniques, Gus Sauter and his team have managed to add value, beating the index in each calendar year of the fund's existence. Many of Sauter's strategies rely on significant cash inflows, which have been rare in 2001, but the fund is nevertheless about 10 basis points (or 0.10%) ahead of the index.

Although the fund produced a sizable capital gain last year, when it distributed 7% of NAV, shareholders need not fear the tax man this year. The market sell-off and some modest net redemptions have given Sauter an opportunity to recognize losses, meaning only a small capital-gains distribution will made this year. That's just one more reason to give this fund a close look.

Portfolio Analysis 09-30-01

Share change since 06-01 Total Stocks: 403	Sector	PE	YTD Ret%	% Assets
⊕ Genzyme Corporation General Di	Health	—	33.11	1.57
⊕ IDEC Pharmaceuticals	Health	NMF	9.09	1.27
⊕ Electronic Arts	Technology	90.8	40.65	0.97
⊕ SunGard Data Sys	Technology	33.3	22.78	0.96
⊕ M & T Bk	Financials	20.8	8.63	0.90
⊕ Quest Diagnostics	Health	51.2	1.00	0.87
⊕ Marshall & Ilsley	Financials	22.0	27.06	0.86
⊕ NVIDIA	Technology	84.2	308.50	0.85
⊕ Gilead Sciences	Health	—	58.48	0.84
⊕ RJ Reynolds Tobacco Hldgs	Staples	3.1	22.37	0.80
⊕ Millennium Pharma	Health	—	–60.30	0.79
⊕ Cadence Design Sys	Technology	5.3	–20.20	0.75
⊕ Telephone and Data Sys	Services	—	0.29	0.73
⊕ Affiliated Comp Svcs A	Services	39.9	74.88	0.73
⊕ DST Sys	Technology	26.1	–25.60	0.71
⊕ Washington Post	Services	20.0	–13.20	0.69
⊕ Health Mgmt Assoc	Health	24.2	–11.30	0.68
⊕ Apollo Grp Cl A	Services	—	—	0.67
⊕ Natl Commerce	Financials	32.4	3.99	0.66
⊕ Waters	Industrials	32.0	–53.50	0.66
⊕ Mylan Labs	Health	24.7	49.68	0.65
⊕ North Fork Bancorp	Financials	16.5	34.11	0.64
⊕ First Tennessee Natl	Financials	15.8	28.71	0.63
⊕ BJ Svcs	Energy	15.5	–5.77	0.60
⊕ Symantec	Technology	—	98.74	0.59

Current Investment Style

Style: Value Blnd Growth; Size: Large Med Small

	Stock Port Avg	Relative S&P 500 Current	Relative S&P 500 Hist	Rel Cat
Price/Earnings Ratio	26.8	0.87	0.88	0.99
Price/Book Ratio	4.0	0.70	0.65	0.93
Price/Cash Flow	17.5	0.97	0.87	1.01
3 Yr Earnings Growth	14.0	0.96	1.00	0.84
1 Yr Earnings Est%	7.3	—	—	3.20
Med Mkt Cap $mil	2,624	0.0	0.0	0.29

Special Securities % assets 09-30-01	
Restricted/Illiquid Secs	0
Emerging-Markets Secs	0
Options/Futures/Warrants	No

Composition % assets 09-30-01	
Cash	0.7
Stocks*	99.3
Bonds	0.0
Other	0.0
*Foreign (% stocks)	0.0

Market Cap	
Giant	0.0
Large	2.7
Medium	82.5
Small	14.8
Micro	0.0

Sector Weightings	% of Stocks	Rel S&P	5-Year High	5-Year Low
Utilities	6.7	2.1	—	—
Energy	6.6	0.9	—	—
Financials	18.5	1.0	—	—
Industrials	9.9	0.9	—	—
Durables	3.5	2.3	—	—
Staples	4.6	0.6	—	—
Services	13.8	1.3	—	—
Retail	4.0	0.6	—	—
Health	14.5	1.0	—	—
Technology	17.9	1.0	—	—

Address:	Vanguard Financial Ctr. P.O. Box 2600 Valley Forge, PA 19482 800-662-7447
Web Address:	www.vanguard.com
*Inception:	04-20-98
Advisor:	Vanguard Core Mgmt. Grp.
Subadvisor:	None
NTF Plans:	N/A

Minimum Purchase:	$3000	Add: $100	IRA: $1000
Min Auto Inv Plan:	$3000	Add: $50	
Sales Fees:	No-load		
Management Fee:	.22%		
Actual Fees:	Mgt: 0.22%	Dist: —	
Expense Projections:	3Yr: $80	5Yr: $141	10Yr: $318
Avg Brok Commission:	—	Income Distrib: Annually	
Total Cost (relative to category):		Low	

Vanguard Morgan Growth

Ticker	Load	NAV	Yield	Total Assets	Mstar Category
VMRGX	None	$14.63	0.5%	$3,827.9 mil	Large Blend

Prospectus Objective: Growth

Vanguard Morgan Growth Fund seeks long-term growth of capital.

The fund primarily invests in equity securities, emphasizing large- and mid-capitalization companies that have generally exhibited above-average earnings growth over an extended period. The fund may invest up to 20% of assets in foreign securities. It may also invest in derivatives and up to 15% of assets in restricted or illiquid securities.

The fund also offers Adm shares. Prior to April 24, 1990, the fund was named W.L. Morgan Growth Fund. The fund was named Vanguard/Morgan Growth Fund. Vanguard Specialized Portfolio - Service Economy.

Historical Profile
Return: Average
Risk: Above Avg
Rating: ★★★ Neutral

Investment Style: Equity — Average Stock %: 90% 91% 92% 94% 93% 91% 95%

▼ Manager Change
▽ Partial Manager Change

Fund Performance vs. Category Average
■ Quarterly Fund Return +/– Category Average
— Category Baseline

Performance Quartile (within Category)

Portfolio Manager(s)

Robert D. Rands, CFA. Since 3-94. BA'64 Yale U.; MBA'66 University of Pennsylvania. Other fund currently managed: Vanguard Morgan Growth Adm.

George U. Sauter. Since 5-93. AB'76 Dartmouth C.; MBA'80 U. of Chicago. Other funds currently managed: Vanguard Small Cap Index, Vanguard Balanced Index, Vanguard Equity-Income.

John S. Cone, CFA. Since 4-00. BA Rice U.; MS Purdue U. Other funds currently managed: Vanguard Growth & Income, Vanguard Morgan Growth Adm, Vanguard Growth & Income Adm.

1990	1991	1992	1993	1994	1995	1996	1997	1998	1999	2000	12-01	History
10.40	12.20	12.65	12.01	11.36	14.09	15.63	17.54	19.72	22.92	17.08	14.63	NAV
–1.51	29.33	9.55	7.32	–1.67	35.98	23.30	30.81	22.26	34.10	–12.51	–13.60	Total Return %
1.61	–1.15	1.93	–2.74	–2.98	–1.55	0.36	–2.54	–6.31	13.06	–3.41	–1.73	+/– S&P 500
2.52	–3.11	1.89	–2.52	–2.12	–1.62	1.14	–2.22	–6.37	12.28	–1.55	–0.84	+/– Wilshire Top 750
2.91	2.80	1.49	1.44	1.18	1.33	1.02	1.05	1.05	0.78	0.67	0.44	Income Return %
–4.42	26.53	8.05	5.88	–2.84	34.65	22.28	29.76	21.22	33.32	–13.19	–14.04	Capital Return %
34	67	27	75	64	31	22	40	60	12	85	58	Total Rtn % Rank Cat
0.34	0.29	0.18	0.18	0.14	0.15	0.14	0.16	0.18	0.15	0.15	0.08	Income $
0.80	0.86	0.52	1.35	0.31	1.16	1.53	2.52	1.43	3.08	2.95	0.05	Capital Gains $
0.55	0.46	0.48	0.49	0.50	0.48	0.51	0.48	0.44	0.42	0.40	—	Expense Ratio %
2.77	2.36	1.51	1.36	1.15	1.10	0.97	0.93	0.96	0.71	0.73	—	Income Ratio %
73	52	64	72	84	76	73	76	81	65	94	—	Turnover Rate %
696.9	956.8	1,116.3	1,135.2	1,074.8	1,471.1	2,053.8	2,795.3	3,555.2	5,066.3	5,025.7	3,493.0	Net Assets $mil

Performance 12-31-01

	1st Qtr	2nd Qtr	3rd Qtr	4th Qtr	Total
1997	–0.97	16.12	13.94	–0.17	30.81
1998	13.17	2.67	–16.41	25.88	22.26
1999	4.46	9.40	–4.66	23.09	34.10
2000	7.02	–3.57	–1.74	–13.72	–12.51
2001	–14.17	9.92	–20.86	15.70	–13.60

Trailing	Total Return%	+/– S&P 500	+/– Wil Top 750	% Rank All	% Rank Cat	Growth of $10,000
3 Mo	15.70	5.02	4.38	22	8	11,570
6 Mo	–8.43	–2.88	–2.64	80	85	9,157
1 Yr	–13.60	–1.73	–0.84	69	58	8,640
3 Yr Avg	0.45	1.48	2.28	71	31	10,136
5 Yr Avg	10.14	–0.56	0.03	18	37	16,211
10 Yr Avg	12.13	–0.80	–0.32	18	41	31,423
15 Yr Avg	13.06	–0.67	–0.31	16	32	63,078

Tax Analysis	Tax-Adj Ret%	%Rank Cat	%Pretax Ret	%Rank Cat
3 Yr Avg	–2.16	51	—	—
5 Yr Avg	6.73	60	66.3	84
10 Yr Avg	9.03	56	74.4	76

Potential Capital Gain Exposure: –5% of assets

Risk Analysis

Time Period	Load-Adj Return %	Risk %Rank[1] All	Risk %Rank[1] Cat	Morningstar Return	Morningstar Risk	Morningstar Risk-Adj Rating
1 Yr	–13.60					
3 Yr	0.45	80	92	–0.91[2]	1.15	★★★
5 Yr	10.14	79	94	1.23[2]	1.11	★★★
10 Yr	12.13	81	90	1.13	1.10	★★★

Average Historical Rating (193 months): 3.2★s

[1]1=low, 100=high [2] T-Bill return substituted for category avg.

Category Rating (3 Yr)

1 2 3 4 5 — Worst / Best (3)

Return: Above Avg
Risk: High

Other Measures	Standard Index S&P 500	Best Fit Index MSCIACWdFr
Alpha	3.7	9.1
Beta	1.24	1.34
R-Squared	87	90

Standard Deviation	23.05
Mean	0.45
Sharpe Ratio	–0.23

Portfolio Analysis 09-30-01

Share change since 06-01 Total Stocks: 326	Sector	PE	YTD Ret%	% Assets
⊕ Citigroup	Financials	20.0	0.03	3.09
⊕ AOL Time Warner	Technology	—	–7.76	2.99
☼ Total Stock Viper	N/A	—	—	2.66
⊕ Microsoft	Technology	57.6	52.78	2.59
⊕ American Intl Grp	Financials	42.0	–19.20	2.46
⊕ Pfizer	Health	34.7	–12.40	2.29
⊖ First Data	Technology	38.1	49.08	2.26
⊕ AT & T Liberty Media Cl A	Services	—	3.22	1.97
⊕ Pharmacia	Health	36.5	–29.30	1.95
⊖ Cisco Sys	Technology	—	–52.60	1.67
⊖ PepsiCo	Staples	31.4	–0.54	1.60
⊕ Home Depot	Retail	42.9	12.07	1.50
⊕ Fannie Mae	Financials	16.2	–6.95	1.45
⊕ Freddie Mac	Financials	14.0	–3.87	1.39
⊖ Viacom Cl B	Services	—	—	1.26
⊕ Dell Comp	Technology	61.8	55.87	1.26
⊕ Astrazeneca ADR	Health	32.4	–8.15	1.25
⊖ Abbott Labs	Health	51.6	17.08	1.12
⊕ WorldCom	Services	24.3	3.12	1.08
⊕ ACE	Financials	17.4	–5.39	1.05
⊖ Baxter Intl	Health	33.9	22.84	1.02
⊖ General Elec	Industrials	30.1	–15.00	1.00
⊖ VeriSign	Technology	—	–48.70	0.92
⊕ Intuit	Technology	—	8.42	0.92
⊕ Clear Channel Comms	Services	—	5.10	0.89

Current Investment Style

Style: Value Blnd Growth; Size: Large Med Small

	Stock Port Avg	Relative S&P 500 Current	Relative S&P 500 Hist	Rel Cat
Price/Earnings Ratio	32.5	1.05	1.01	1.07
Price/Book Ratio	5.1	0.90	0.91	0.93
Price/Cash Flow	21.0	1.16	1.07	1.14
3 Yr Earnings Growth	17.5	1.20	1.12	0.98
1 Yr Earnings Est%	3.3	—	—	–36.22
Med Mkt Cap $mil	27,179	0.5	0.3	0.52

Analysis by Scott Cooley 12-06-01

Vanguard Morgan Growth Fund still makes for a solid, growth-oriented core holding.

This fund's growth leanings have been a plus over the past couple of months, as tech issues have led the market higher. Although the fund's subadvisors use a variety of approaches, their overall tilt toward growth produced a well-above average, 25.7% stake in recently surging tech shares. Over the month through Dec. 5, 2001, the fund rose 7.4%, outpacing more than 90% of its large-blend rivals. Of course, the fund fell much harder than its peers earlier in the year, especially during the third-quarter technology meltdown, so its year-to-date loss of 12.1% still ranks within the group's bottom half.

Over time, the fund has put up numbers that are at least respectable. Its trailing five- and 10-year results better more than half its rivals'. The fund's low costs are the primary source of its advantage. Over the trailing five years, for example, the fund's 10.3% annualized return tops its typical peer's by 90 basis points (or 0.90%). The fund's expense ratio of 0.40% is roughly 80 basis points below the norm.

There may be reason for more optimism about the fund's prospects. Two of the subadvisors, Wellington Management and Franklin Portfolio Associates, boast stellar track records. Robert Rands, who handles Wellington's slice of the portfolio, has put up terrific numbers as a variable-annuity manager. And John Cone, who invests the Franklin-managed assets, was part of the team that has built a stellar long-term record at Vanguard Growth & Income.

Given quality of the managers here and the fund's pleasingly low expense ratio, it's worth a look. But investors should try to stash it in a tax-advantaged account, as tax-efficiency hasn't been a priority here.

Special Securities % assets 09-30-01

Restricted/Illiquid Secs	0
Emerging-Markets Secs	Trace
Options/Futures/Warrants	No

Composition % assets 09-30-01	
Cash	2.9
Stocks*	96.7
Bonds	0.0
Other	0.5
*Foreign (% stocks)	3.4

Market Cap	
Giant	37.6
Large	33.8
Medium	26.1
Small	2.1
Micro	0.5

Sector Weightings	% of Stocks	Rel S&P	5-Year High	5-Year Low
Utilities	1.0	0.3	3	0
Energy	3.6	0.5	10	2
Financials	17.2	1.0	20	9
Industrials	5.8	0.5	23	6
Durables	0.5	0.3	7	0
Staples	4.1	0.5	10	2
Services	15.1	1.4	24	10
Retail	7.0	1.0	13	5
Health	20.0	1.4	21	9
Technology	25.7	1.4	36	10

Address:	Vanguard Financial Ctr. P.O. Box 2600 Valley Forge, PA 19482 800-662-7447 / 610-669-1000
Web Address:	www.vanguard.com
Inception:	12-31-68
Advisor:	Wellington Mgmt./Franklin Port. Assoc. Trust
Subadvisor:	None
NTF Plans:	N/A

Minimum Purchase:	$3000	Add: $100 IRA: $1000
Min Auto Inv Plan:	$3000	Add: $100
Sales Fees:	No-load	
Management Fee:	.83%+(–).90%P	
Actual Fees:	Mgt: 0.40%	Dist: —
Expense Projections:	3Yr: $135	5Yr: $235 10Yr: $530
Avg Brok Commission:	—	Income Distrib: Annually
Total Cost (relative to category):	Low	

Vanguard Precious Metals

Ticker	Load	NAV	Yield	Total Assets	Mstar Category
VGPMX	None	$8.55	4.6%	$370.7 mil	Spec Precious Metals

Prospectus Objective: Specialty—Precious Metals

Vanguard Precious Metals Fund seeks long-term capital appreciation.

The fund typically invests at least 80% of assets in equity securities of companies involved in the exploration, mining, processing, or distribution of gold and other precious metals. It may also invest up to 20% of assets directly in gold, silver, or other precious-metals bullion and coins. The fund may invest a substantial portion of assets in foreign securities.

The fund levies a 1% redemption fee within 12 months; this fee is paid to the portfolio. Past fund names: Vanguard Specialized Portfolios Gold and Precious Metals Portfolio and Vanguard Gold & Precious Metals Fund.

Historical Profile

Return Average
Risk Above Avg
Rating ★★★ Neutral

Investment Style
Equity
Average Stock %: 1996 92% · 1997 89% · 1998 87% · 1999 90% · 2000 96% · 12-01 96%

▼ Manager Change
▽ Partial Manager Change

Fund Performance vs. Category Average
■ Quarterly Fund Return +/– Category Average
— Category Baseline

Performance Quartile (within Category)

Portfolio Manager(s)

Graham E. French. Since 6-96. BSC Durham U.

History

1990	1991	1992	1993	1994	1995	1996	1997	1998	1999	2000	12-01	History
9.07	9.21	7.24	13.78	12.72	11.98	11.63	6.97	6.61	8.41	7.58	8.55	NAV
–19.86	4.37	–19.41	93.36	–5.42	–4.48	–0.75	–38.92	–3.91	28.82	–7.34	18.33	Total Return %
–16.75	–26.11	–27.03	83.30	–6.74	–42.01	–23.69	–72.27	–32.49	7.79	1.77	30.21	+/– S&P 500
–13.68	–29.83	–28.38	82.08	–5.35	–40.93	–21.95	–70.21	–27.34	5.26	3.60	29.23	+/– Wilshire 5000
2.73	2.76	1.95	2.90	2.26	1.34	1.76	1.12	1.29	1.51	2.38	5.20	Income Return %
–22.59	1.62	–21.37	90.46	–7.68	–5.82	–2.51	–40.03	–5.21	27.31	–9.72	13.13	Capital Return %
37	12	62	25	22	78	79	44	20	1	3	52	Total Rtn % Rank Cat
0.32	0.25	0.18	0.21	0.31	0.17	0.21	0.13	0.09	0.10	0.20	0.39	Income $
0.00	0.00	0.00	0.00	0.00	0.00	0.07	0.00	0.00	0.00	0.00	0.00	Capital Gains $
0.45	0.42	0.35	0.36	0.26	0.25	0.60	0.50	0.62	0.77	0.77	0.65	Expense Ratio %
3.01	2.78	2.54	2.50	2.04	2.04	1.38	1.07	1.41	1.33	1.42	2.94	Income Ratio %
17	10	3	2	14	4	5	19	26	23	28	17	Turnover Rate %
129.1	170.4	173.9	609.6	639.2	549.5	496.5	293.0	311.4	381.7	307.4	370.7	Net Assets $mil

Performance 12-31-01

	1st Qtr	2nd Qtr	3rd Qtr	4th Qtr	Total
1997	–3.79	–10.29	–0.70	–28.74	–38.92
1998	11.33	–14.99	6.99	–5.11	–3.91
1999	–1.21	12.42	18.55	–2.16	28.82
2000	–19.15	0.44	2.50	11.33	–7.34
2001	–11.15	23.64	1.34	6.29	18.34

Trailing	Total Return%	+/– S&P 500	+/– Wil 5000	% Rank All	% Rank Cat	Growth of $10,000
3 Mo	6.29	–4.39	–6.08	59	2	10,629
6 Mo	7.72	13.27	13.20	1	23	10,772
1 Yr	18.33	30.21	29.23	2	52	11,833
3 Yr Avg	12.20	13.23	12.85	8	1	14,126
5 Yr Avg	–3.68	–14.38	–13.38	97	1	8,291
10 Yr Avg	1.48	–11.45	–10.80	98	6	11,584
15 Yr Avg	2.76	–10.98	–10.24	98	15	15,041

Tax Analysis	Tax-Adj Ret%	%Rank Cat	%Pretax Ret	%Rank Cat
3 Yr Avg	10.92	1	89.5	73
5 Yr Avg	–4.58	1	—	—
10 Yr Avg	0.63	18	42.6	80

Potential Capital Gain Exposure: –13% of assets

Risk Analysis

Time Period	Load-Adj Return %	Risk %Rank[1] All	Risk %Rank[1] Cat	Morningstar Return	Morningstar Risk	Morningstar Risk-Adj Rating
1 Yr	18.33					
3 Yr	12.20	80	14	1.65[2]	1.06	★★★★★
5 Yr	–3.68	96	34	–1.61[2]	1.54	★★
10 Yr	1.48	99	20	–0.73[2]	1.66	★★

Average Historical Rating (176 months): 2.2★s

[1]1=low, 100=high [2] T-Bill return substituted for category avg.

Category Rating (3 Yr)

1 2 3 4 **5** — Worst … Best

Return: High
Risk: Below Avg

Other Measures	Standard Index S&P 500	Best Fit Index JSE Gold
Alpha	13.6	9.8
Beta	0.48	0.55
R-Squared	8	53

Standard Deviation	33.19
Mean	12.20
Sharpe Ratio	0.25

Portfolio Analysis 09-30-01

Share change since 06-01 Total Stocks: 27	Sector	PE	YTD Ret%	% Assets
⊕ Newmont Mng	Industrials	—	12.69	9.74
⊕ Lihir Gold	Industrials	3.9	—	8.45
⊕ Placer Dome	Industrials	—	14.47	8.22
Impala Platinum Hldgs (ADR)	Industrials	—	—	7.99
⊕ Barrick Gold	Industrials	—	–1.28	7.76
⊕ Delta Gold	Industrials	11.7	—	7.37
⊕ Normandy Mng	Industrials	—	—	6.54
⊕ Meridian Gold	Industrials	—	50.25	6.34
⊖ Anglo Amer Platinum ADR	Industrials	—	—	6.18
⊖ Homestake Mng	Industrials	—	89.70	5.82
⊖ Aber Resources	Industrials	NMF	35.94	5.09
⊖ Franco-Nevada Mng	Industrials	34.0	—	4.74
⊕ Lonmin	Financials	9.3	—	3.99
⊕ Goldfields	Industrials	9.6	—	2.42
⊕ Ashanti Goldfields GDR	Industrials	7.1	126.60	2.11
⊕ Royal Gold	Industrials	NMF	82.60	2.01
Freeport McMoRan Cl Gold ARP	Industrials	—	—	1.00
⊖ Iluka Resources	Industrials	10.7	—	0.69
⊖ Anglogold ADR	Industrials	11.9	27.47	0.48
Aurora Gold (Australia)	Industrials	—	—	0.20
Tanami Gold	Industrials	—	—	0.08
Bougainville Copper	Industrials	4.2	—	0.04
Geomaque Explor	Industrials	—	—	0.04
Crown Resources	Industrials	—	–78.50	0.02
Star Mng	Industrials	—	—	0.00

Current Investment Style

Style: Value Blnd Growth; Size: Large Med Small

	Stock Port Avg	Relative S&P 500 Current	Relative S&P 500 Hist	Rel Cat
Price/Earnings Ratio	21.3[1]	0.82	0.81	0.99
Price/Cash Flow	13.7	1.07	0.58	0.84
Price/Book Ratio	3.4	0.99	0.36	0.99
3 Yr Earnings Growth	—	—	—	—
Med Mkt Cap $mil	1,769	0.1	0.0	0.87

[1]figure is based on 50% or less of stocks

Special Securities % assets 09-30-01	
Restricted/Illiquid Secs	0
Emerging-Markets Secs	17
Options/Futures/Warrants	No

Regional Exposure 01-31-99	% of Stocks
N. America	51.2
S. Africa	15.3
Australia	32.3
Other	1.2
Bullion	0.0

Composition % assets 09-30-01	
Cash	4.3
Stocks*	94.7
Bonds	0.0
Other	1.0
*Foreign (% stocks)	74.0

Market Cap	
Giant	0.0
Large	0.0
Medium	57.6
Small	39.6
Micro	2.8

Analysis by Christopher Davis 08-28-01

Despite its recent misfortune, Vanguard Precious Metals Fund remains among its category's most appealing options.

This fund has long been one of the most attractive offerings in an unappealing group. In a dreadful market for gold stocks, it outpaced most of its precious-metals fund rivals by a wide margin during the 1990s. In 2001, however, the fund has struggled amid one of the most hospitable markets for the yellow metal in years: Gold prices have been buoyed by a troubled economy, a rough market, and fears that inflation will rise or the mighty U.S. dollar will tumble. The fund has returned just 8% for the year to date through August 28, 2001, while its typical peer gained 14% over the same stretch.

That showing is no surprise. Manager Graham French usually devotes more than 30% of the fund's assets to non-gold plays, such as palladium and platinum. Both metals have been battered by shrinking industrial demand and a global supply glut in 2001, which has weighed on top picks like Anglo American Platinum and Impala Platinum Holdings (each soaked up about 12% of assets in June).

While the fund's diversified approach has been a liability in 2001, it has been a boon to returns more often than not during French's five-year tenure: The fund has ranked in its group's top half in four of the past five calendar years. What's more, its bargain-basement expense ratio, which is far below the lofty category average, has given the fund a significant edge.

The fund may lag its peers during gold price spikes, but with inflation at bay and a prolonged economic crisis unlikely, you've got to wonder if the gold rally can continue to sustain itself. Investors in search of pure gold exposure won't be happy here, but those who want broad precious-metals exposure would do well to consider this offering.

Address:	Vanguard Financial Ctr. P.O. Box 2600 Valley Forge, PA 19482 800–662–7447 / 610–669–1000
Web Address:	www.vanguard.com
Inception:	05-23-84
Advisor:	M&G Inv. Mgmt.
Subadvisor:	None
NTF Plans:	N/A

Minimum Purchase:	$3000	Add: $100	IRA: $1000
Min Auto Inv Plan:	$3000	Add: $50	
Sales Fees:	No-load, 1.00%R within 12 months		
Management Fee:	.30% mx./.10% mn.		
Actual Fees:	Mgt: 0.22%	Dist: —	
Expense Projections:	3Yr: $246	5Yr: $428	10Yr: $954
Avg Brok Commission:	—	Income Distrib: Annually	
Total Cost (relative to category):		Low	

Vanguard Primecap

Ticker	Load	NAV	Yield	Total Assets	Mstar Category
VPMCX	None	$51.52	0.5%	$18,887.7 mil	Large Blend

Prospectus Objective: Growth

Vanguard Primecap Fund seeks long-term growth of capital.

The fund normally invests at least 80% of assets in equity securities. The advisor selects companies on the basis of fundamental factors, including current earnings, consistency, and quality of earnings growth. The advisor then evaluates these factors in relation to the market price of each company's stock to determine which investments to make.

The fund offers Admiral and Investor shares.

Historical Profile

Return	High
Risk	Average
Rating	★★★★★ Highest

Investment Style
Equity
Average Stock %: 92% (1996), 90% (1997), 89% (1998), 90% (1999), 88% (2000), 91% (12-01)

▼ Manager Change
▽ Partial Manager Change

Fund Performance vs. Category Average
Quarterly Fund Return
+/– Category Average
— Category Baseline

Performance Quartile (within Category)

Portfolio Manager(s)

Howard B. Schow. Since 11-84. BA Williams C.; MBA Harvard U. Other funds currently managed: Vanguard Capital Opportunity, Vanguard Capital Opportunity Adm, Vanguard Primecap Adm.

Theo A. Kolokotrones. Since 6-85. MBA Harvard U. Other funds currently managed: Vanguard Capital Opportunity, Vanguard Capital Opportunity Adm, Vanguard Primecap Adm.

Joel P. Fried. Since 1-95. MBA U. of California. Other funds currently managed: Vanguard Capital Opportunity, Vanguard Capital Opportunity Adm, Vanguard Primecap Adm.

History

1990	1991	1992	1993	1994	1995	1996	1997	1998	1999	2000	12-01	History
12.21	15.36	16.19	18.42	19.98	26.23	30.08	39.57	47.66	62.07	60.38	51.52	NAV
–2.81	33.14	8.99	18.03	11.41	35.48	18.31	36.83	25.41	41.34	4.47	–13.35	Total Return %
0.31	2.66	1.38	7.97	10.10	–2.05	–4.64	3.48	–3.16	20.30	13.57	–1.47	+/– S&P 500
1.22	0.70	1.34	8.19	10.96	–2.12	–3.86	3.80	–3.22	19.52	15.43	–0.58	+/– Wilshire Top 750
1.01	1.23	0.79	0.43	0.65	1.10	0.77	0.67	0.89	0.57	0.80	0.47	Income Return %
–3.82	31.91	8.21	17.59	10.76	34.38	17.54	36.16	24.52	40.77	3.67	–13.82	Capital Return %
43	37	31	13	1	36	74	3	45	5	10	55	Total Rtn % Rank Cat
0.13	0.15	0.12	0.07	0.12	0.22	0.20	0.20	0.35	0.27	0.49	0.28	Income $
0.12	0.68	0.41	0.59	0.41	0.59	0.73	1.30	1.52	4.65	4.05	0.53	Capital Gains $
0.75	0.68	0.68	0.67	0.64	0.58	0.59	0.51	0.51	0.51	0.48	—	Expense Ratio %
1.06	1.09	0.84	0.44	0.79	0.99	0.69	0.69	0.78	0.50	0.80	—	Income Ratio %
11	24	7	16	8	7	10	13	13	19	11	—	Turnover Rate %
304.6	486.0	646.1	790.9	1,533.7	3,236.8	4,204.0	8,186.2	11,209.9	17,911.9	22,639.3	18,096.0	Net Assets $mil

Performance 12-31-01

	1st Qtr	2nd Qtr	3rd Qtr	4th Qtr	Total
1997	4.74	15.60	19.73	–5.62	36.83
1998	10.44	1.34	–13.03	28.84	25.41
1999	5.95	11.23	0.04	19.89	41.34
2000	19.54	–2.69	–3.52	–6.91	4.47
2001	–10.92	4.22	–21.68	19.17	–13.35

Trailing	Total Return%	+/– S&P 500	+/– Wil Top 750	% Rank All	% Rank Cat	Growth of $10,000
3 Mo	19.17	8.49	7.85	15	3	11,917
6 Mo	–6.66	–1.11	–0.87	72	66	9,334
1 Yr	–13.35	–1.47	–0.58	69	55	8,665
3 Yr Avg	8.56	9.59	10.39	14	3	12,795
5 Yr Avg	17.03	6.33	6.91	3	1	21,956
10 Yr Avg	17.56	4.64	5.11	2	1	50,438
15 Yr Avg	15.69	1.95	2.32	5	5	88,955

Tax Analysis	Tax-Adj Ret%	%Rank Cat	%Pretax Ret	%Rank Cat
3 Yr Avg	7.14	3	83.4	24
5 Yr Avg	15.52	1	91.1	19
10 Yr Avg	16.22	1	92.4	10

Potential Capital Gain Exposure: 26% of assets

Risk Analysis

Time Period	Load-Adj Return %	Risk %Rank[1] All	Risk %Rank[1] Cat	Morningstar Return	Morningstar Risk	Morningstar Risk-Adj Rating
1 Yr	–14.22					
3 Yr	8.20	70	60	0.71[2]	0.96	★★★★
5 Yr	17.03	69	61	3.30[2]	0.94	★★★★★
10 Yr	17.56	77	78	2.51	1.00	★★★★★

Average Historical Rating (171 months): 3.8★s

[1] 1=low, 100=high [2] T-Bill return substituted for category avg.

Category Rating (3 Yr)

1 2 3 4 5
Worst Best

Return	High
Risk	Average

Other Measures	Standard Index S&P 500	Best Fit Index
Alpha	11.2	16.6
Beta	1.07	1.20
R-Squared	65	72
Standard Deviation		24.72
Mean		8.56
Sharpe Ratio		0.17

Portfolio Analysis 09-30-01

Share change since 06-01 Total Stocks: 104	Sector	PE	YTD Ret%	% Assets
⊕ Pharmacia	Health	36.5	–29.30	5.52
Fedex	Services	29.3	29.83	4.19
Texas Instruments	Technology	87.5	–40.70	3.86
⊕ Adobe Sys	Technology	37.4	–46.50	3.22
⊕ Phillips Petro	Energy	7.1	8.56	3.05
Guidant	Health	42.6	–7.67	3.00
⊕ Microsoft	Technology	57.6	52.78	2.95
Micron Tech	Technology	—	–12.60	2.90
⊕ General Motors Cl H	Technology	42.9	–32.80	2.69
Novartis ADR	Health	22.3	–17.40	2.67
Motorola	Technology	—	–25.00	2.25
Intel	Technology	73.1	4.89	2.00
Union Pacific	Services	17.1	13.96	1.94
⊖ Sabre Hldgs Cl A	Services	73.0	–1.80	1.93
Anadarko Petro	Energy	11.1	–19.70	1.83
⊖ Southwest Air	Services	25.0	–17.20	1.71
Caterpillar	Industrials	20.0	13.72	1.66
Citrix Sys	Technology	44.4	0.71	1.55
⊖ Delta Air Lines	Services	—	–41.50	1.47
⊖ AMR	Services	—	–43.40	1.45
Robert Half Intl	Services	31.1	0.75	1.38
⊖ Sony ADR	Durables	NMF	–35.10	1.35
⊕ UtiliCorp United	Utilities	8.3	–15.60	1.30
Eastman Kodak	Industrials	17.8	–21.90	1.27
⊕ Nortel Networks	Technology	—	–76.50	1.23

Current Investment Style

Style: Value Blnd Growth; Size: Large Med Small

	Stock Port Avg	Relative S&P 500 Current	Relative S&P 500 Hist	Rel Cat
Price/Earnings Ratio	33.3	1.08	1.01	1.10
Price/Book Ratio	4.1	0.72	0.79	0.75
Price/Cash Flow	16.8	0.93	0.95	0.91
3 Yr Earnings Growth	18.0	1z.23	1.07	1.01
1 Yr Earnings Est%	–13.4	7.59	—	—
Med Mkt Cap $mil	15,935	0.3	0.2	0.30

Special Securities % assets 09-30-01	
Restricted/Illiquid Secs	0
Emerging-Markets Secs	Trace
Options/Futures/Warrants	No

Composition % assets 09-30-01	
Cash	9.7
Stocks*	90.0
Bonds	0.0
Other	0.4
*Foreign (% stocks)	8.0

Market Cap	
Giant	22.3
Large	45.3
Medium	28.6
Small	3.7
Micro	0.1

Sector Weightings	% of Stocks	Rel S&P	5-Year High	5-Year Low
Utilities	1.4	0.4	2	0
Energy	8.0	1.1	8	0
Financials	4.3	0.2	13	2
Industrials	11.3	1.0	20	5
Durables	2.5	1.6	9	2
Staples	0.1	0.0	3	0
Services	20.6	1.9	39	18
Retail	5.3	0.8	6	0
Health	14.6	1.0	22	8
Technology	32.0	1.7	49	25

Analysis by Scott Cooley 10-24-01

Our confidence in Vanguard Primecap Fund is unshaken.

There's no question that this fund has hit a rough stretch in 2001, particularly over the past few months. For the year to date through Oct. 23, 2001, the fund has dropped 22.2%, lagging 80% of its large-blend peers. The fund had put up middling numbers before the Sept. 11 terrorist attacks and fell much harder than its rivals when the stock market reopened Sept. 17. This fund and sibling Vanguard Capital Opportunity both had low-double-digit stakes in the airline industry, including large positions in AMR and Delta Air Lines. Airlines have huge fixed costs, so the reduction in demand for air travel in the wake of the attacks took a big toll on their bottom lines and share prices. Tech stocks also plunged during the month, as investors fled risky securities, so the fund's well-above average stake in the sector stung.

Investors should keep in mind, however, that there's nothing new about huge bets here. Indeed, well-timed wagers on industries ranging from biotechnology and tech to pharmaceuticals and retail have contributed to the fund's exceptional record. It's inevitable that some bets will go awry, but short-term volatility is simply the price one must pay for the stellar long-term gains management has produced.

Although the managers have trimmed the airline stake, they argue that it still could prove profitable. In the absence of additional attacks, an economic recovery could boost airlines, as well as the fund's tech firms. And in keeping with their contrarian-growth strategy, the managers are also picking up energy shares, which they believe have sold off excessively. Given how successful management has been, we wouldn't want to bet against any of these areas—or this fund—now.

Address:	Vanguard Financial Ctr. P.O. Box 2600 Valley Forge, PA 19482 610-669-1000 / 800-662-7447
Web Address:	www.vanguard.com
Inception:	11-01-84
Advisor:	Primecap Mgmt.
Subadvisor:	None
NTF Plans:	N/A

Minimum Purchase:	$25000	Add: $100 IRA: $25000
Min Auto Inv Plan:	$25000	Add: $50
Sales Fees:	No-load, 1.00%R within 60 months	
Management Fee:	.50% mx./.15% mn.	
Actual Fees:	Mgt: 0.47%	Dist: —
Expense Projections:	3Yr: $268	5Yr: $269 10Yr: $604
Avg Brok Commission:	—	Income Distrib: Annually
Total Cost (relative to category):		Low

Vanguard Short–Term Bond Index

Ticker	Load	NAV	Yield	SEC Yield	Total Assets	Mstar Category
VBISX	None	$10.19	5.5%	—	$1,953.2 mil	Short–Term Bond

Prospectus Objective: Corp Bond—General

Vanguard Short-Term Bond Index Fund seeks to replicate the performance of the Lehman Brothers 1-5 Year Government/Corporate Bond index.

The fund normally invests at least 80% of assets in securities included in the index. The index comprises U.S. government obligations and investment-grade corporate bonds with maturities between one and five years. The investment mix typically mirrors the weighting of the different bond classes in the Index. It may invest up to 20% of assets in short-term money-market instruments.

The fund offers Admiral and Investor shares.

Historical Profile

Return Above Avg
Risk Below Avg
Rating ★★★★★ Highest

Investment Style
Fixed-Income

Income Rtn %Rank Cat: 22, 42, 38, 37, 60, 42, 28

Growth of Principal vs. Interest Rate Shifts
— Principal Value $000 (NAV with capital gains reinvested)
— Interest Rate % on 10 Yr Treasury
▼ Manager Change
▽ Partial Manager Change
► Mgr Unknown After
◄ Mgr Unknown Before

Performance Quartile (within Category)

Portfolio Manager(s)

Felix B. Lim. Since 1-00. BA U. of Pennsylvania; MS U. of Pennsylvania-Wharton. Other funds currently managed: Vanguard Long-Term Bond Index, Vanguard Short-Term Bond Index Adm.

History

1990	1991	1992	1993	1994	1995	1996	1997	1998	1999	2000	12–01	History
—	—	—	—	9.50	10.07	9.92	10.00	10.10	9.73	9.97	10.19	NAV
—	—	—	—	−0.37*	12.89	4.55	7.04	7.63	2.08	8.95	8.77	Total Return %
—	—	—	—	—	−5.58	0.94	−2.65	−1.05	2.91	−2.68	0.35	+/– LB Aggregate
—	—	—	—	—	2.93	−0.70	0.39	0.66	−0.89	0.78	0.24	+/– LB 1–3 Govt
—	—	—	—	4.63	6.76	6.00	6.19	5.90	5.49	6.35	5.84	Income Return %
—	—	—	—	−5.00	6.13	−1.45	0.85	1.73	−3.41	2.60	2.93	Capital Return %
—	—	—	—	—	21	43	25	4	59	19	6	Total Rtn % Rank Cat
—	—	—	—	0.46	0.62	0.59	0.60	0.57	0.54	0.60	0.57	Income $
—	—	—	—	0.00	0.00	0.00	0.00	0.07	0.03	0.00	0.07	Capital Gains $
—	—	—	—	0.18	0.20	0.20	0.20	0.20	0.20	0.21	—	Expense Ratio %
—	—	—	—	5.77	6.28	5.93	6.03	5.68	5.48	6.16	—	Income Ratio %
—	—	—	—	—	65	65	88	112	108	74	—	Turnover Rate %
—	—	—	—	77.0	207.6	326.8	438.3	708.9	1,155.6	1,339.3	1,679.7	Net Assets $mil

Performance 12-31-01

	1st Qtr	2nd Qtr	3rd Qtr	4th Qtr	Total
1997	0.37	2.45	2.23	1.81	7.04
1998	1.50	1.66	3.67	0.61	7.63
1999	0.35	0.22	1.08	0.41	2.08
2000	1.39	1.64	2.72	2.92	8.95
2001	3.13	1.35	3.89	0.17	8.77

Trailing	Total Return%	+/– LB Agg	+/– LB 1–3 Yr Govt	% Rank All	% Rank Cat	Growth of $10,000
3 Mo	0.17	0.13	−0.61	77	51	10,017
6 Mo	4.06	−0.59	−0.25	8	16	10,406
1 Yr	8.77	0.35	0.24	7	6	10,877
3 Yr Avg	6.55	0.28	0.03	19	12	12,097
5 Yr Avg	6.86	−0.56	0.22	37	4	13,936
10 Yr Avg	—	—	—	—	—	—
15 Yr Avg	—	—	—	—	—	—

Tax Analysis	Tax-Adj Ret%	%Rank Cat	%Pretax Ret	%Rank Cat
3 Yr Avg	4.05	11	61.8	40
5 Yr Avg	4.34	4	63.3	18
10 Yr Avg	—	—	—	—

Potential Capital Gain Exposure: 2% of assets

Risk Analysis

Time Period	Load-Adj Return %	Risk %Rank[1] All	Risk %Rank[1] Cat	Morningstar Return	Morningstar Risk	Morningstar Risk-Adj Rating
1 Yr	8.77					
3 Yr	6.55	4	61	0.30[2]	0.36	★★★★★
5 Yr	6.86	4	56	0.38[2]	0.36	★★★★★
Incept	6.50	—	—	—	—	

Average Historical Rating (59 months): 4.5★s

[1] 1=low, 100=high [2] T-Bill return substituted for category avg.

Category Rating (3 Yr)

1 2 3 4 5 — Worst / Best

Return Above Avg
Risk Average

Other Measures	Standard Index LB Agg	Best Fit Index LB Int
Alpha	0.8	0.7
Beta	0.58	0.72
R–Squared	88	92

Standard Deviation	2.19
Mean	6.55
Sharpe Ratio	0.86

Portfolio Analysis 09-30-01

Total Fixed-Income: 283	Date of Maturity	Amount $000	Value $000	% Net Assets
US Treasury Bond 10.75%	02-15-03	144,925	160,694	8.52
US Treasury Note 7.875%	11-15-04	94,825	108,067	5.73
US Treasury Note 7.25%	05-15-04	76,975	85,371	4.53
US Treasury Bond 10.75%	05-15-03	65,625	74,003	3.92
US Treasury Note 7.5%	02-15-05	52,250	59,386	3.15
US Treasury Bond 11.125%	08-15-03	50,500	58,179	3.09
US Treasury Bond 10.75%	08-15-05	42,350	53,412	2.83
FHLMC Debenture 5%	01-15-04	50,500	52,767	2.80
US Treasury Note 7%	07-15-06	37,075	42,438	2.25
US Treasury Note 4.25%	11-15-03	41,000	42,433	2.25
US Treasury Bond 11.625%	11-15-02	28,450	31,240	1.66
US Treasury Note 7.25%	08-15-04	23,475	26,207	1.39
FNMA Debenture 5.5%	02-15-06	22,000	23,392	1.24
China Telecom 7.875%	11-02-04	18,500	20,331	1.08
FHLMC Debenture 6.875%	01-15-05	16,000	17,708	0.94
At&t Wireless 7.35%	03-01-06	15,000	16,017	0.85
Black & Decker 7.5%	04-01-03	14,900	15,644	0.83
FHLMC Debenture 7%	07-15-05	14,000	15,599	0.83
Cemex 8.625%	07-18-03	14,800	15,559	0.83
TCI Comms 6.375%	05-01-03	14,975	15,538	0.82

Current Investment Style

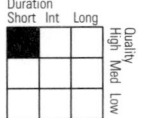

Duration: Short Int Long; Quality: High Med Low

Avg Eff Duration[1]	2.5 Yrs
Avg Eff Maturity	—
Avg Credit Quality	AA
Avg Wtd Coupon	7.74%
Avg Wtd Price	108.49% of par

[1] figure provided by fund

Special Securities % assets 09-30-01	
Restricted/Illiquid Secs	2
Exotic Mortgage–Backed	0
Emerging–Markets Secs	1
Options/Futures/Warrants	Yes

Coupon Range	% of Bonds	Rel Cat
0%	0.00	0.00
0% to 7%	36.51	0.57
7% to 8.5%	37.57	1.31
8.5% to 10%	4.09	1.00
More than 10%	21.83	12.77

1.00=Category Average

Credit Analysis % bonds 09-30-01

US Govt	48	BB	1
AAA	3	B	0
AA	6	Below B	0
A	18	NR/NA	0
BBB	23		

Composition % assets 09-30-01

Cash	2.6	Bonds	97.4
Stocks	0.0	Other	0.0

Sector Breakdown % bonds 09-30-01

US Treasuries	21	CMOs	0
GNMA mtgs	0	ARMs	0
FNMA mtgs	2	Other	51
FHLMC mtgs	7		

Analysis by Alan Papier 11-30-01

Vanguard Short-Term Bond Index Fund makes a compelling case for fixed-income indexing.

This fund seeks to replicate the returns of the Lehman Brothers 1-5 Year Government/Credit index, which is a widely diversified bogy made up of U.S. Treasury, agency, and corporate bonds. Management constructs the fund to match the cash-flow characteristics of the index, but varies its sector weightings to capture incrementally higher income streams. Thus, the portfolio's duration and yield-curve positioning, and therefore its interest-rate sensitivity, are the same as the index's, but it tends to underweight U.S. Treasuries in favor of corporates.

Over time, that strategy has allowed the fund to recover some of the ground it loses to the index vis-a-vis its expense ratio. From the fund's early 1994 inception through Oct. 31, 2001, its annualized gain was 6.78%—just 2 basis points behind its bogy.

That long-term performance places the fund among the elite in the short-term bond category. As of Nov. 29, 2001, the fund's one-, three-, and five-year annualized returns were higher than at least 85% of its peers'. And it has accomplished that feat without incurring any more volatility than the category norm.

One caveat is that the index leaves out mortgage-backed securities. So, the fund can lose ground to its peers when mortgages outperform other bond market sectors, as was the case in 1996 and 1999, when the fund generated middling returns.

That being said, the fund's demonstrated ability to outperform the majority of its peers is proving that active bond managers struggle to consistently add value relative to passive strategies. All in all, we think the fund is an excellent choice as a stable offering for investors with a one- to four-year investment horizon.

Address:	Vanguard Financial Ctr. P.O. Box 2600 Valley Forge, PA 19482 800–662–7447 / 610–669–1000
Web Address:	www.vanguard.com
*Inception:	03-01-94
Advisor:	Vanguard Fixed–Income Grp.
Subadvisor:	None
NTF Plans:	N/A

Minimum Purchase:	$3000	Add: $100 IRA: $1000
Min Auto Inv Plan:	$3000	Add: $50
Sales Fees:	No–load	
Management Fee:	.17%	
Actual Fees:	Mgt: 0.18%	Dist: —
Expense Projections:	3Yr: $68	5Yr: $118 10Yr: $268
Avg Brok Commission:	—	Income Distrib: Monthly
Total Cost (relative to category):	Low	

Vanguard Short–Term Federal

Ticker	Load	NAV	Yield	SEC Yield	Total Assets	Mstar Category
VSGBX	None	$10.48	5.2%	—	$2,136.4 mil	Short–Term Govt

Prospectus Objective: Government General

Vanguard Short-Term Federal Fund seeks current income consistent with maintenance of principal and liquidity.

The fund invests primarily in short-term U.S. government-agency securities; it also invests in U.S. Treasury obligations and repurchase agreements collateralized by government securities. The fund's average weighted maturity typically ranges between one and three years.

The fund also offers Adm shares. Prior to Oct.1991, the fund was named Vanguard Fixed-Income Securities Short-Term Government Bond. The fund was named Vanguard Fixed-Income Securities Short-Term Federal Bond Portfolio.

Historical Profile
Return: Above Avg
Risk: Below Avg
Rating: ★★★★★ Highest

Investment Style: Fixed-Income
Income Rtn %Rank Cat: 41, 51, 33, 25, 26, 21, 21, 29

Growth of Principal vs. Interest Rate Shifts
— Principal Value $000 (NAV with capital gains reinvested)
— Interest Rate % on 10 Yr Treasury
▼ Manager Change
▽ Partial Manager Change
► Mgr Unknown After
◄ Mgr Unknown Before

Performance Quartile (within Category)

Portfolio Manager(s)

Ian A. MacKinnon. Since 12-87. BA'70 Lafayette C.; MBA'74 Pennsylvania State U. Other funds currently managed: Vanguard Balanced Index, Vanguard CA Insured Long Tax-Ex, Vanguard Short-Term Treasury.

John Hollyer, CFA. Since 12-87. BS U. of Pennsylvania. Other funds currently managed: Vanguard Short-Term Treasury, Vanguard Inflation-Protected Secs, Vanguard Short-Term Federal Adm.

History

1990	1991	1992	1993	1994	1995	1996	1997	1998	1999	2000	12-01	History
10.06	10.43	10.27	10.34	9.69	10.25	10.11	10.13	10.26	9.90	10.17	10.48	NAV
9.31	12.24	6.19	7.00	–0.94	12.26	4.75	6.46	7.22	2.07	9.18	8.61	Total Return %
0.36	–3.76	–1.21	–2.75	1.97	–6.21	1.14	–3.22	–1.45	2.90	–2.45	0.18	+/– LB Aggregate
–0.47	0.57	–0.06	1.59	–1.44	2.31	–0.50	–0.19	0.25	–0.89	1.01	0.08	+/– LB 1–3 Govt
8.38	7.54	6.14	5.25	5.39	6.36	6.11	6.24	5.91	5.66	6.31	5.52	Income Return %
0.93	4.70	0.06	1.75	–6.33	5.90	–1.36	0.22	1.32	–3.59	2.87	3.09	Capital Return %
41	48	37	29	53	36	26	45	20	38	21	4	Total Rtn % Rank Cat
0.81	0.73	0.62	0.53	0.54	0.60	0.61	0.61	0.58	0.57	0.61	0.55	Income $
0.00	0.08	0.16	0.11	0.01	0.00	0.00	0.00	0.00	0.00	0.00	0.00	Capital Gains $
0.28	0.30	0.26	0.27	0.26	0.28	0.27	0.25	0.27	0.27	0.27	0.28	Expense Ratio %
8.59	8.06	6.98	5.88	4.98	5.53	5.93	6.09	6.04	5.68	5.64	6.10	Income Ratio %
133	141	111	70	49	57	74	57	94	107	93	169	Turnover Rate %
456.8	1,179.5	1,622.5	1,921.8	1,504.8	1,403.7	1,339.2	1,413.6	1,634.9	1,521.4	1,543.8	1,783.3	Net Assets $mil

Performance 12-31-01

	1st Qtr	2nd Qtr	3rd Qtr	4th Qtr	Total
1997	0.42	2.34	2.03	1.54	6.46
1998	1.53	1.57	3.35	0.61	7.22
1999	0.38	0.02	1.01	0.65	2.07
2000	1.37	1.64	2.50	3.39	9.18
2001	3.24	1.12	3.74	0.29	8.61

Trailing	Total Return%	+/– LB Agg	+/– LB 1–3 Yr Govt	% Rank All	% Rank Cat	Growth of $10,000
3 Mo	0.29	0.25	–0.49	76	44	10,029
6 Mo	4.04	–0.61	–0.27	9	30	10,404
1 Yr	8.61	0.18	0.08	8	4	10,861
3 Yr Avg	6.57	0.30	0.04	19	5	12,103
5 Yr Avg	6.68	–0.75	0.04	39	5	13,816
10 Yr Avg	6.22	–1.01	0.19	64	8	18,288
15 Yr Avg	—	—	—	—	—	—

Tax Analysis	Tax-Adj Ret%	%Rank Cat	%Pretax Ret	%Rank Cat
3 Yr Avg	4.22	5	64.3	11
5 Yr Avg	4.29	5	64.2	25
10 Yr Avg	3.81	11	61.3	22

Potential Capital Gain Exposure: 2% of assets

Risk Analysis

Time Period	Load-Adj Return %	Risk %Rank[1] All	Risk %Rank[1] Cat	Morningstar Return	Morningstar Risk	Morningstar Risk-Adj Rating
1 Yr	8.61					
3 Yr	6.57	3	37	0.35[2]	0.29	★★★★★
5 Yr	6.68	3	38	0.37[2]	0.30	★★★★★
10 Yr	6.22	4	44	0.41[2]	0.47	★★★★★

Average Historical Rating (133 months): 4.2★s

[1]1=low, 100=high [2] T-Bill return substituted for category avg.

Category Rating (3 Yr): 1 2 3 4 5 — Worst … Best

Return: High
Risk: Average

Other Measures	Standard Index LB Agg	Best Fit Index LB Int
Alpha	0.8	0.7
Beta	0.55	0.70
R–Squared	85	91

Standard Deviation	2.14
Mean	6.57
Sharpe Ratio	0.90

Portfolio Analysis 09-30-01

Total Fixed-Income: 82	Date of Maturity	Amount $000	Value $000	% Net Assets
FNMA Debenture 7%	07-15-05	397,500	442,910	22.14
Bank United 5.4%	02-02-04	128,425	134,666	6.73
FHLMC 5.25%	02-15-04	104,000	109,316	5.46
FHLMC 5.5%	04-01-16	92,494	93,895	4.69
FNMA Debenture 6.5%	08-15-04	74,000	80,435	4.02
US Treasury Note 3.875%	01-15-09	70,000	80,391	4.02
FHLMC Debenture 7%	07-15-05	68,500	76,325	3.82
FHLMC Debenture 5%	01-15-04	57,000	59,559	2.98
Private Export Fdg 144A 5.53%	04-30-06	50,000	53,426	2.67
US Treasury Note 3.54%	01-15-11	50,000	53,032	2.65
FHA 7%	12-01-11	50,000	52,360	2.62
FNMA Debenture 7.125%	02-15-05	45,000	50,093	2.50
FNMA 7%	12-01-15	45,261	47,516	2.38
US Treasury Bond 3.384%	04-15-32	40,000	41,625	2.08
FNMA ARM	09-01-16	32,401	33,667	1.68
Federal Home Ln Bk Global FRN	07-07-03	30,000	30,938	1.55
FNMA ARM	12-01-11	28,203	29,691	1.48
FHLMC 6%	08-01-05	28,726	29,526	1.48
FNMA 8%	08-01-15	27,298	28,815	1.44
FNMA 6.36%	03-02-03	26,000	27,216	1.36

Current Investment Style

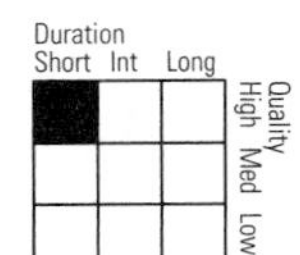

Avg Eff Duration[1]	2.2 Yrs
Avg Eff Maturity	—
Avg Credit Quality	AAA
Avg Wtd Coupon	6.16%
Avg Wtd Price	107.18% of par

[1]figure provided by fund

Special Securities % assets 09-30-01	
Restricted/Illiquid Secs	4
Exotic Mortgage–Backed	0
Emerging–Markets Secs	0
Options/Futures/Warrants	No

Credit Analysis % bonds 09-30-01			
US Govt	97	BB	0
AAA	3	B	0
AA	0	Below B	0
A	0	NR/NA	0
BBB	0		

Sector Breakdown % bonds 09-30-01			
US Treasuries	2	CMOs	2
GNMA mtgs	0	ARMs	4
FNMA mtgs	42	Other	12
FHLMC mtgs	30		

Coupon Range	% of Bonds	Rel Cat
0%	0.00	0.00
0% to 7%	52.48	0.74
7% to 8.5%	47.52	2.38
8.5% to 10%	0.00	0.00
More than 10%	0.00	0.00

1.00=Category Average

Composition % assets 09-30-01			
Cash	6.3	Bonds	93.7
Stocks	0.0	Other	0.0

Analysis by Bradley Sweeney 09-07-01

This is one of our favorite short-term government bond funds.

Vanguard Short-Term Federal hasn't had to make dramatic moves to whip the competition in 2001. As usual, the fund has relied on its enormous expense advantage to give it a leg up on its rivals—the fund's expense ratio is about 28% of its average peer's. But manager John Hollyer has also taken advantage of his flexible mandate. Unlike its sibling in the category, Vanguard Short-Term Treasury, which must keep the bulk of its assets in Treasuries, this offering faces no such restriction. That has been a huge advantage, as Hollyer has significantly underweighted Treasuries, a relatively weak segment of the government-bond market in 2001. With its low expenses and a portfolio dominated by solidly performing agency bonds, the fund has outdistanced its sibling and 92% of its other rivals for the year to date through September 6, 2001.

Although it isn't unusual for management to rotate among different segments of the government-bond market, this offering doesn't indulge in any serious interest-rate bets. That conservative approach to interest-rate sensitivity has resulted in below-average volatility. It has also helped produce a shockingly consistent record: The fund has only finished one out of the last 13 calendar years in its category's bottom half. Like its sibling, management has consistently let its expense advantage work for it. But unlike its sibling, management here has the ability to underweight Treasuries and focus on higher-yielding agency issues. Although both funds have been outstanding, that freedom has allowed this offering to outdistance its Treasury-heavy sibling over time.

While we think highly of both funds, this offering's more-flexible mandate makes it our favorite.

Address:	Vanguard Financial Ctr. P.O. Box 2600 Valley Forge, PA 19482 800–662–7447 / 610–669–1000
Web Address:	www.vanguard.com
Inception:	12-31-87
Advisor:	Vanguard Fixed–Income Grp.
Subadvisor:	None
NTF Plans:	N/A

Minimum Purchase:	$3000	Add: $100 IRA: $1000
Min Auto Inv Plan:	$3000	Add: $50
Sales Fees:	No–load	
Management Fee:	None	
Actual Fees:	Mgt: 0.27%	Dist: —
Expense Projections:	3Yr: $96	5Yr: $169 10Yr: $381
Avg Brok Commission:	—	Income Distrib: Monthly
Total Cost (relative to category):		Low

Vanguard Short–Term Treasury

Ticker	Load	NAV	Yield	SEC Yield	Total Assets	Mstar Category
VFISX	None	$10.53	4.9%	—	$2,635.7 mil	Short–Term Govt

Prospectus Objective: Government Treasury

Vanguard Short-Term U.S. Treasury Fund seeks current income consistent with maintenance of principal and liquidity.

The fund invests at least 85% of assets in U.S. Treasury bills, notes, bonds, and other guaranteed U.S. government obligations. It may invest the remaining assets in U.S. Treasury or U.S. government-agency securities, including repurchase agreements on such securities. The fund normally maintains an average weighted portfolio maturity of between one and three years.

The fund also offers Adm shares. Prior to Oct. 27, 1998, the fund was named Vanguard Fixed-Income Securities Fund Short-Term U.S. Treasury Portfolio.

Historical Profile

Return Above Avg
Risk Below Avg
Rating ★★★★★ Highest

Investment Style
Fixed-Income
Income Rtn %Rank Cat: 50, 40, 51, 33, 48, 51, 36, 44

Growth of Principal vs. Interest Rate Shifts
— Principal Value $000 (NAV with capital gains reinvested)
— Interest Rate % on 10 Yr Treasury
▼ Manager Change
▽ Partial Manager Change
► Mgr Unknown After
◄ Mgr Unknown Before

Performance Quartile (within Category)

Portfolio Manager(s)

Ian A. MacKinnon. Since 10-91. BA'70 Lafayette C.; MBA'74 Pennsylvania State U. Other funds currently managed: Vanguard Balanced Index, Vanguard CA Insured Long Tax-Ex, Vanguard Interm-Term U.S. Treas.

John Hollyer, CFA. Since 2-98. BS U. of Pennsylvania. Other funds currently managed: Vanguard Short-Term Federal, Vanguard Inflation-Protected Secs, Vanguard Short-Term Federal Adm.

David R. Glocke. Since 5-00. BS U. of Wisconsin. Other funds currently managed: Vanguard Interm-Term U.S. Treas, Vanguard Long-Term U.S. Treasury, Vanguard Short-Term Treasury Adm.

1990	1991	1992	1993	1994	1995	1996	1997	1998	1999	2000	12-01	History
—	10.21	10.31	10.38	9.79	10.32	10.17	10.21	10.37	10.01	10.27	10.53	NAV
—	3.08*	6.75	6.31	−0.48	12.11	4.39	6.51	7.36	1.85	8.83	7.80	Total Return %
—	—	−0.66	−3.44	2.44	−6.36	0.78	−3.18	−1.31	2.68	−2.80	−0.63	+/– LB Aggregate
—	—	0.49	0.89	−0.98	2.15	−0.86	−0.14	0.39	−1.12	0.66	−0.73	+/– LB 1–3 Govt
—	0.98	5.30	4.87	5.14	6.58	5.84	6.08	5.53	5.23	6.10	5.19	Income Return %
—	2.10	1.45	1.43	−5.61	5.53	−1.45	0.42	1.83	−3.38	2.73	2.61	Capital Return %
—	—	8	44	41	38	41	44	18	44	27	20	Total Rtn % Rank Cat
—	0.10	0.53	0.49	0.52	0.63	0.59	0.60	0.55	0.53	0.59	0.52	Income $
—	0.00	0.04	0.08	0.02	0.00	0.00	0.00	0.02	0.02	0.00	0.01	Capital Gains $
—	—	0.26	0.26	0.26	0.28	0.27	0.25	0.27	0.27	0.27	0.27	Expense Ratio %
—	—	5.22	5.12	4.64	5.33	6.14	5.77	5.80	5.27	5.27	5.91	Income Ratio %
—	—	—	71	86	126	93	86	83	132	124	296	Turnover Rate %
—	65.1	483.4	705.5	704.0	869.4	965.8	993.8	1,184.1	1,234.9	1,213.4	1,394.0	Net Assets $mil

Performance 12-31-01

	1st Qtr	2nd Qtr	3rd Qtr	4th Qtr	Total
1997	0.40	2.31	1.98	1.67	6.51
1998	1.38	1.65	3.82	0.35	7.36
1999	0.22	0.12	1.11	0.39	1.85
2000	1.24	1.80	2.33	3.19	8.83
2001	2.85	0.83	3.92	0.02	7.80

Trailing	Total Return%	+/– LB Agg	+/– LB 1–3 Yr Govt	% Rank All	% Rank Cat	Growth of $10,000
3 Mo	0.02	−0.01	−0.76	78	58	10,002
6 Mo	3.94	−0.71	−0.37	9	35	10,394
1 Yr	7.80	−0.63	−0.73	10	20	10,780
3 Yr Avg	6.12	−0.16	−0.41	21	15	11,949
5 Yr Avg	6.44	−0.98	−0.20	42	17	13,663
10 Yr Avg	6.09	−1.14	0.06	68	25	18,059
15 Yr Avg	—	—	—	—	—	—

Tax Analysis	Tax-Adj Ret%	%Rank Cat	%Pretax Ret	%Rank Cat
3 Yr Avg	3.88	10	63.5	22
5 Yr Avg	4.15	12	64.5	19
10 Yr Avg	3.83	8	62.9	5

Potential Capital Gain Exposure: 2% of assets

Risk Analysis

Time Period	Load-Adj Return %	Risk %Rank[1] All	Risk %Rank[1] Cat	Morningstar Return	Morningstar Risk	Morningstar Risk-Adj Rating
1 Yr	7.80					
3 Yr	6.12	3	46	0.25[2]	0.33	★★★★★
5 Yr	6.44	4	45	0.31[2]	0.34	★★★★★
10 Yr	6.09	5	53	0.37[2]	0.49	★★★★

Average Historical Rating (87 months): 4.1★s

[1] 1=low, 100=high [2] T-Bill return substituted for category avg.

Category Rating (3 Yr)

1 2 3 4 5
Worst Best

Return Above Avg
Risk Average

Other Measures	Standard Index LB Agg	Best Fit Index LB Int
Alpha	0.4	0.2
Beta	0.57	0.73
R–Squared	88	96

Standard Deviation	2.16
Mean	6.12
Sharpe Ratio	0.64

Portfolio Analysis 09-30-01

Total Fixed-Income: 60	Date of Maturity	Amount $000	Value $000	% Net Assets
US Treasury Note 7.875%	11-15-04	244,800	278,986	10.80
US Treasury Note 5.875%	11-15-04	211,000	228,502	8.85
US Treasury Note 6.25%	02-15-03	206,000	216,739	8.39
US Treasury Note 3.875%	06-30-03	136,000	139,457	5.40
Private Export Fdg 5.73%	01-15-04	124,335	131,437	5.09
US Treasury Note 5.75%	11-15-05	110,000	119,561	4.63
US Treasury Note 3.54%	01-15-11	100,000	106,064	4.11
US Treasury Note 6.5%	10-15-06	93,000	104,789	4.06
US Treasury Note 3.875%	07-31-03	95,000	97,468	3.77
US Treasury Note 4.625%	02-28-03	90,900	93,855	3.63
US Treasury Note 6.75%	05-15-05	81,000	90,432	3.50
Private Export Fdg 6.45%	09-30-04	80,000	87,031	3.37
US Treasury Note 3.875%	01-15-09	74,000	84,985	3.29
FHLMC 6%	08-01-06	64,631	66,716	2.58
Private Export Fdg 144A 7.65%	05-15-06	55,000	63,528	2.46
Federal Home Loan Bk 4.875%	06-28-04	55,000	57,257	2.22
US Treasury Note 2.75%	09-30-03	55,000	55,344	2.14
US Treasury Note 5.5%	02-28-03	52,000	54,286	2.10
US Treasury Note 3.625%	08-31-03	35,000	35,773	1.39
FNMA 7%	01-01-25	30,603	32,111	1.24

Current Investment Style

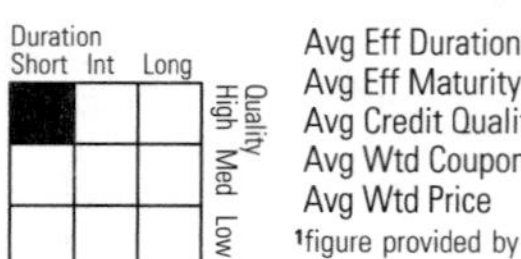

Avg Eff Duration[1]	2.3 Yrs
Avg Eff Maturity	—
Avg Credit Quality	AAA
Avg Wtd Coupon	5.76%
Avg Wtd Price	107.21% of par

[1] figure provided by fund

Special Securities % assets 09-30-01	
Restricted/Illiquid Secs	5
Exotic Mortgage–Backed	0
Emerging–Markets Secs	1
Options/Futures/Warrants	No

Credit Analysis % bonds 09-30-01

US Govt	99	BB	0
AAA	1	B	0
AA	0	Below B	0
A	0	NR/NA	0
BBB	0		

Coupon Range	% of Bonds	Rel Cat
0%	0.00	0.00
0% to 7%	81.57	1.14
7% to 8.5%	18.44	0.92
8.5% to 10%	0.00	0.00
More than 10%	0.00	0.00

1.00=Category Average

Composition % assets 09-30-01

Cash	0.4	Bonds	99.6
Stocks	0.0	Other	0.0

Analysis by Bradley Sweeney 09-05-01

Vanguard Short-Term U.S. Treasury is an excellent option for conservative-minded investors.

As we predicted a little more than a year ago, the management transition that took place here in May 2000 has been seamless. David Glocke has followed in the conservative steps of his predecessors, typically storing at least 65% of the fund's assets in Treasuries and avoiding any serious interest-rate bets. In a category where the range of absolute returns is relatively narrow, this conservative strategy has enabled the fund to take full advantage of its enormous expense advantage—its expense ratio is nearly three fourths of a percentage point less than the average short-term government–bond fund's. But that's not to say that the fund hasn't benefited from some of Glocke's modest bets. His decision to increase the portfolio's exposure to Treasury Inflation Protected Securities (TIPS), for example, has been a boon to performance, as those issues have outperformed straight Treasuries with similar maturities so far this year. Modest moves such as these and the fund's low expenses have enabled it to beat 78% of its peers for the year to date through September 4, 2001.

The fund may not be terrifically flashy, but its low costs and avoidance of large interest-rate bets have enabled it to rack up an extremely attractive long-term risk/reward profile. In addition to outdistancing 75% of its rivals over the last five years, the fund has been remarkably consistent over its life: It has finished in its category's top half in each and every full calendar year since its inception in late 1991. Interested investors who are willing to hold a short-government fund that doesn't emphasize Treasuries are likely to fare better in this offering's equally remarkable sibling, Vanguard Short-Term Federal, but those who are seeking a Treasury-heavy fund in this category would be hard-pressed to find a better offering than this one.

Address:	Vanguard Financial Ctr. P.O. Box 2600 Valley Forge, PA 19482 800–662–7447 / 610–669–1000
Web Address:	www.vanguard.com
*Inception:	10-28-91
Advisor:	Vanguard Fixed–Income Grp.
Subadvisor:	None
NTF Plans:	N/A

Minimum Purchase:	$3000	Add: $100 IRA: $1000
Min Auto Inv Plan:	$3000	Add: $50
Sales Fees:	No–load	
Management Fee:	None	
Actual Fees:	Mgt: 0.26%	Dist: —
Expense Projections:	3Yr: $93	5Yr: $163 10Yr: $368
Avg Brok Commission:	—	Income Distrib: Monthly
Total Cost (relative to category):		Low

Vanguard Small Cap Growth Index

Ticker	Load	NAV	Yield	Total Assets	Mstar Category
VISGX	None	$10.87	0.1%	$466.3 mil	Small Growth

Prospectus Objective: Small Company

Vanguard Small Capitalization Growth Index Fund seeks to track the performance of the S&P SmallCap 600/BARRA Growth Index.

The fund invests substantially all assets in each stock found in the index, in approximately the same proportion as represented in the index. The index includes stocks of the S&P SmallCap 600 index with higher than average price/earnings and price/book ratios. Management uses a passive approach when selecting securities and seeks to create a mix of securities that will match the performance of the index. It may invest in options and futures.

The fund also offers Instl shares. Previous name: Vanguard Index Small Capitalization Growth Stock Fund.

Historical Profile

Return Above Avg
Risk Above Avg
Rating ★★★ Neutral

Investment Style
Equity
Average Stock %: 98% 100% 100% 100%

▼ Manager Change
▽ Partial Manager Change

Fund Performance vs. Category Average
Quarterly Fund Return
+/– Category Average
— Category Baseline

Performance Quartile (within Category)

Portfolio Manager(s)

George U. Sauter. Since 5-98. AB'76 Dartmouth C.; MBA'80 U. of Chicago. Other funds currently managed: Vanguard Small Cap Index, Vanguard Balanced Index, Vanguard Equity-Income.

1990	1991	1992	1993	1994	1995	1996	1997	1998	1999	2000	12-01	History
—	—	—	—	—	—	—	—	9.53	11.38	10.97	10.87	NAV
—	—	—	—	—	—	—	—	–4.77*	19.80	1.59	–0.78	Total Return %
—	—	—	—	—	—	—	—	–16.20*	–1.24	10.69	11.10	+/– S&P 500
—	—	—	—	—	—	—	—	—	–23.29	24.02	8.46	+/– Russ 2000 Grth
—	—	—	—	—	—	—	—	0.31	0.37	0.03	0.14	Income Return %
—	—	—	—	—	—	—	—	–5.08	19.43	1.56	–0.91	Capital Return %
—	—	—	—	—	—	—	—	—	79	34	27	Total Rtn % Rank Cat
—	—	—	—	—	—	—	—	0.03	0.04	0.00	0.02	Income $
—	—	—	—	—	—	—	—	0.00	0.00	0.57	0.00	Capital Gains $
—	—	—	—	—	—	—	—	0.25	0.25	0.27	—	Expense Ratio %
—	—	—	—	—	—	—	—	0.63	0.33	0.03	—	Income Ratio %
—	—	—	—	—	—	—	—	—	82	136	—	Turnover Rate %
—	—	—	—	—	—	—	—	90.1	167.3	351.6	357.2	Net Assets $mil

Performance 12-31-01

	1st Qtr	2nd Qtr	3rd Qtr	4th Qtr	Total
1997	—	—	—	—	—
1998	—	—	–19.96	22.27	–4.77 *
1999	–8.29	10.87	–2.37	20.69	19.80
2000	9.14	0.32	–0.88	–6.39	1.59
2001	–13.04	14.99	–17.50	20.27	–0.78

Trailing	Total Return%	+/– S&P 500	+/– Russ 2000 Grth	% Rank All	% Rank Cat	Growth of $10,000
3 Mo	20.27	9.59	–5.90	13	66	12,027
6 Mo	–0.78	4.78	8.49	42	18	9,922
1 Yr	–0.78	11.10	8.46	44	27	9,922
3 Yr Avg	6.49	7.51	6.24	19	62	12,076
5 Yr Avg	—	—	—	—	—	—
10 Yr Avg	—	—	—	—	—	—
15 Yr Avg	—	—	—	—	—	—

Tax Analysis	Tax-Adj Ret%	%Rank Cat	%Pretax Ret	%Rank Cat
3 Yr Avg	5.91	49	91.0	21
5 Yr Avg	—	—	—	—
10 Yr Avg	—	—	—	—

Potential Capital Gain Exposure: –6% of assets

Risk Analysis

Time Period	Load-Adj Return %	Risk %Rank[1] All	Risk %Rank[1] Cat	Morningstar Return	Morningstar Risk	Morningstar Risk-Adj Rating
1 Yr	–0.78					
3 Yr	6.49	79	24	0.33[2]	1.14	★★★
5 Yr	—	—	—	—	—	
Incept	3.94	—	—	—	—	

Average Historical Rating (8 months): 3.1★s

[1]1=low, 100=high [2] T-Bill return substituted for category avg.

Category Rating (3 Yr)

1 2 **3** 4 5
Worst Best

Return Average
Risk Below Avg

Other Measures	Standard Index S&P 500	Best Fit Index Russ 2000
Alpha	8.9	0.5
Beta	0.84	1.06
R-Squared	29	90
Standard Deviation		28.82
Mean		6.49
Sharpe Ratio		0.06

Portfolio Analysis 09-30-01

Share change since 06-01 Total Stocks: 220	Sector	PE	YTD Ret%	% Assets
⊕ Cephalon	Health	—	19.38	2.05
⊕ Advance Paradigm	Health	43.2	29.01	1.67
⊕ Universal Health Svcs B	Health	12.7	–23.40	1.60
⊕ Commerce Bancorp NJ	Financials	27.5	17.01	1.55
⊕ Varian Medical Sys	Technology	34.3	4.89	1.47
⊕ XTO Energy	N/A	—	—	1.46
⊕ Cerner	Services	—	7.96	1.24
⊕ Whole Foods Market	Retail	36.0	42.53	1.23
⊕ Alliant Techsystems	Industrials	28.6	73.48	1.22
⊕ 99 Cents Only Stores	Retail	43.8	108.70	1.21
⊕ ResMed	Health	NMF	35.22	1.16
⊕ Medicis Pharma Cl A	Health	38.0	9.24	1.15
⊕ Constellation Brands A	Staples	—	—	1.14
⊕ Copart	Services	43.8	69.16	1.07
⊕ Philadelphia Suburban	Utilities	25.3	17.88	1.02
⊕ Renal Care Grp	Health	22.8	17.13	0.99
⊕ O'Reilly Automotive	Retail	33.8	36.34	0.97
⊕ OM Grp	Industrials	20.2	22.24	0.96
⊕ Zebra Tech	Technology	27.0	36.12	0.96
⊕ Cullen/Frost Bankers	Financials	17.2	–24.20	0.92
⊕ Pharmaceutical Product Dev	Services	36.3	30.05	0.91
⊕ First Midwest Bancorp	Financials	18.5	30.24	0.89
⊕ Cheesecake Factory	Services	46.4	35.91	0.88
⊕ Priority Healthcare Cl B	Health	61.7	–13.70	0.87
⊕ Roper Inds	Industrials	29.0	50.94	0.85

Current Investment Style

Style: Value Blnd Growth; Size: Large Med Small

	Stock Port Avg	Relative S&P 500 Current	Relative S&P 500 Hist	Rel Cat
Price/Earnings Ratio	30.0	0.97	0.93	0.93
Price/Book Ratio	4.9	0.87	0.77	1.02
Price/Cash Flow	20.8	1.15	1.02	0.94
3 Yr Earnings Growth	23.9	1.63	1.37	0.95
1 Yr Earnings Est%	8.6	—	—	1.11
Med Mkt Cap $mil	1,015	0.0	0.0	0.97

Special Securities % assets 09-30-01	
Restricted/Illiquid Secs	0
Emerging-Markets Secs	0
Options/Futures/Warrants	No

Composition % assets 09-30-01	
Cash	0.0
Stocks*	100.0
Bonds	0.0
Other	0.0
*Foreign (% stocks)	0.0

Market Cap	
Giant	0.0
Large	0.0
Medium	30.1
Small	68.7
Micro	1.2

Sector Weightings	% of Stocks	Rel S&P	5-Year High	5-Year Low
Utilities	1.0	0.3	—	—
Energy	2.6	0.4	—	—
Financials	7.2	0.4	—	—
Industrials	14.3	1.3	—	—
Durables	3.3	2.1	—	—
Staples	3.2	0.4	—	—
Services	18.9	1.7	—	—
Retail	7.7	1.1	—	—
Health	22.1	1.5	—	—
Technology	19.8	1.1	—	—

Analysis by William Harding 12-20-01

Investors may be able to do better with a stock-picker, but this fund isn't a shabby choice.

Vanguard Small Cap Growth Index has made up ground of late, but it's still well off the pace set by its active rivals over time. The fund has lost a modest 3% for the year to date ended Dec. 19, 2001, compared with a 10% decline for the typical small-growth offering. That said, the fund's trailing three-year return still lags its average peer's by a wide margin.

The fund's sluggishness owes in large part to the bogy it tracks, the S&P Small Cap 600/Barra Growth index. In constructing the index, the S&P committee shuns companies with limited operating histories. The fund thus often devotes less than its peers to young tech and biotech names. Such stocks led the market in 1999, and the fund's 20% annual gain paled in comparison with the 59% return posted by the average growth fund.

The case for indexing in the small-growth market also isn't as compelling as in the large-cap universe. For one, active managers may be able to add more value in the small-cap space than they can among well-followed large caps. Active managers can also benefit by holding on to their biggest winners as their market caps creep up, and by buying into IPOs—tactics unavailable to index offerings.

Still, this fund isn't without appeal. It provides the typical benefits of indexing: low costs, broad diversification, and style purity. Manager Gus Sauter is also arguably the most savvy index-fund skipper around. Finally, the S&P committee's biases have made the fund less volatile than many of its rivals. Indeed, it has held up relatively well as many racy names have imploded over the past 18 months.

Though the majority of funds in the group have bested this offering over the past three years, identifying the winners in advance is difficult. Investors who'd rather not take the chance and just want low-cost exposure to the asset class will find a decent home here.

Address:	Vanguard Financial Ctr. P.O. Box 2600 Valley Forge, PA 19482 800-662-7447
Web Address:	www.vanguard.com
*Inception:	05-21-98
Advisor:	Vanguard Core Mgmt. Grp.
Subadvisor:	None
NTF Plans:	N/A

Minimum Purchase:	$3000	Add: $100	IRA: $1000
Min Auto Inv Plan:	$3000	Add: $50	
Sales Fees:	No-load		
Management Fee:	.20%		
Actual Fees:	Mgt: 0.24%	Dist: —	
Expense Projections:	3Yr: $136	5Yr: $201	10Yr: $392
Avg Brok Commission:	—	Income Distrib: Annually	
Total Cost (relative to category):		Low	

Vanguard Small Cap Index

Ticker	Load	NAV	Yield	Total Assets	Mstar Category
NAESX	None	$19.82	1.1%	$4,676.2 mil	Small Blend

Prospectus Objective: Small Company

Vanguard Small Capitalization Index Fund seeks investment results paralleling those of the Russell 2000 Stock Index.

The fund invests in a statistically selected sample of the stocks included in the Russell 2000. Stocks are selected on the basis of industry weightings, market sensitivity, and fundamental characteristics such as capitalization, earnings variability, and financial leverage.

The fund currently offers Investor, Institutional and Admiral shares. Past names: Naess & Thomas Special Fund, Vanguard Small Capitalization Stock Fund, and Vanguard Index Trust Small Capitalization Stock Portfolio.

Historical Profile
Return: Average
Risk: Above Avg
Rating: ★★★ Neutral

Investment Style
Equity
Average Stock %: 98% 97% 96% 99% 99% 100%

▼ Manager Change
▽ Partial Manager Change

Fund Performance vs. Category Average
■ Quarterly Fund Return +/– Category Average
— Category Baseline

Performance Quartile (within Category)

Portfolio Manager(s)

George U. Sauter. Since 9-89. AB'76 Dartmouth C.; MBA'80 U. of Chicago. Other funds currently managed: Vanguard Balanced Index, Vanguard Equity-Income, Vanguard European Stock Index.

History

1990	1991	1992	1993	1994	1995	1996	1997	1998	1999	2000	12-01	History
8.74	12.19	14.07	15.67	14.99	18.61	20.23	23.75	21.20	23.60	19.44	19.82	NAV
–18.13	45.26	18.20	18.70	–0.51	28.74	18.12	24.59	–2.61	23.13	–2.67	3.10	Total Return %
–15.01	14.78	10.59	8.65	–1.82	–8.79	–4.83	–8.76	–31.19	2.10	6.44	14.98	+/– S&P 500
1.38	–0.79	–0.21	–0.20	1.32	0.30	1.58	2.22	–0.06	1.87	0.36	0.61	+/– Russell 2000
1.63	2.06	1.48	1.28	1.40	1.53	1.46	1.36	1.29	1.27	1.11	1.16	Income Return %
–19.75	43.20	16.73	17.42	–1.91	27.21	16.66	23.23	–3.90	21.86	–3.78	1.94	Capital Return %
70	36	27	45	45	36	61	55	38	23	86	74	Total Rtn % Rank Cat
0.18	0.18	0.18	0.18	0.22	0.23	0.27	0.27	0.30	0.27	0.26	0.23	Income $
0.14	0.29	0.15	0.82	0.37	0.45	1.44	1.11	1.55	2.08	3.03	0.00	Capital Gains $
0.31	0.21	0.18	0.18	0.17	0.25	0.25	0.23	0.24	0.25	0.27	—	Expense Ratio %
1.91	2.11	1.65	1.47	1.50	1.58	1.51	1.38	1.39	1.25	1.17	—	Income Ratio %
40	33	26	26	25	28	28	29	35	42	49	—	Turnover Rate %
46.1	131.1	264.2	488.9	605.4	971.2	1,713.4	2,652.4	2,768.1	3,553.1	3,718.0	3,545.4	Net Assets $mil

Performance 12-31-01

	1st Qtr	2nd Qtr	3rd Qtr	4th Qtr	Total
1997	–4.98	17.33	15.61	–3.34	24.59
1998	10.15	–5.04	–20.14	16.58	–2.61
1999	–5.61	17.04	–5.99	18.55	23.13
2000	6.87	–3.04	0.74	–6.76	–2.67
2001	–6.48	15.02	–20.71	20.88	3.10

Trailing	Total Return%	+/– S&P 500	+/– Russ 2000	% Rank All	% Rank Cat	Growth of $10,000
3 Mo	20.88	10.20	–0.19	12	24	12,088
6 Mo	–4.15	1.41	–0.06	57	75	9,585
1 Yr	3.10	14.98	0.61	36	74	10,310
3 Yr Avg	7.31	8.33	0.89	16	76	12,357
5 Yr Avg	8.44	–2.26	0.92	27	72	14,993
10 Yr Avg	12.27	–0.65	0.76	17	78	31,827
15 Yr Avg	11.10	–2.63	0.34	33	76	48,506

Tax Analysis	Tax-Adj Ret%	%Rank Cat	%Pretax Ret	%Rank Cat
3 Yr Avg	5.00	85	68.5	91
5 Yr Avg	6.24	76	74.0	83
10 Yr Avg	10.27	62	83.7	25

Potential Capital Gain Exposure: –3% of assets

Risk Analysis

Time Period	Load-Adj Return %	Risk %Rank[1] All	Risk %Rank[1] Cat	Morningstar Return	Morningstar Risk	Morningstar Risk-Adj Rating
1 Yr	3.10					
3 Yr	7.31	78	87	0.51[2]	1.09	★★★★
5 Yr	8.44	81	82	0.79[2]	1.15	★★★
10 Yr	12.27	85	84	1.16	1.19	★★★

Average Historical Rating (193 months): 1.7★s

[1]1=low, 100=high [2] T-Bill return substituted for category avg.

Category Rating (3 Yr)

1 2 3 4 5 — Worst … Best

Return: Below Avg
Risk: Above Avg

Other Measures	Standard Index S&P 500	Best Fit Index Russ 2000
Alpha	8.9	0.9
Beta	0.82	1.01
R-Squared	34	100
Standard Deviation		25.80
Mean		7.31
Sharpe Ratio		0.10

Portfolio Analysis 09-30-01

Share change since 06-01 Total Stocks: 1969	Sector	PE	YTD Ret%	% Assets
⊕ Triquint Semicon	Technology	26.7	–71.90	0.35
⊕ New York Community Bancorp	Financials	26.6	43.38	0.31
⊕ Alliant Techsystems	Industrials	28.6	73.48	0.28
⊕ Ball	Industrials	—	55.31	0.26
⊕ Michaels Stores	Retail	29.3	148.60	0.25
⊕ Fisher Scientific Intl	Health	—	–20.80	0.24
⊕ Dean Foods	Staples	40.4	127.20	0.24
⊕ Dial	Staples	—	57.57	0.24
⊕ Indymac Bancorp	Financials	15.1	–20.70	0.24
⊕ Renal Care Grp	Health	22.8	17.13	0.23
⊕ Lee Enterprises	Services	5.1	24.50	0.23
⊕ Edwards Lifesciences	Health	—	55.66	0.23
⊕ Titan	Technology	—	53.54	0.22
⊕ Andrew	Technology	28.8	0.64	0.22
⊕ STERIS	Health	NMF	13.30	0.22
⊕ Suiza Foods	Staples	—	25.44	0.22
⊕ United Dominion Realty	Financials	37.9	44.88	0.22
⊕ Independence Cmnty Bk	Financials	16.7	45.40	0.22
⊕ Sierra Pacific Resources	Utilities	—	–2.25	0.22
⊕ Colonial BancGroup	Financials	13.3	36.09	0.21
⊕ Weingarten Realty	Financials	18.8	17.56	0.21
⊕ Charles River Labs	Health	—	22.30	0.21
⊕ Coventry Health Care	Health	16.4	–25.20	0.21
⊕ Citizens Bkg MI	Financials	15.4	17.64	0.21
⊖ CBRL Grp	Services	23.7	61.98	0.21

Current Investment Style

Style: Value Blnd Growth; Size: Large Med Small

	Stock Port Avg	Relative S&P 500 Current	Relative S&P 500 Hist	Rel Cat
Price/Earnings Ratio	24.5	0.79	0.72	0.98
Price/Book Ratio	3.4	0.60	0.55	1.07
Price/Cash Flow	15.7	0.87	0.76	1.01
3 Yr Earnings Growth	13.4	0.92	0.91	0.79
1 Yr Earnings Est%	4.8	—	—	5.53
Med Mkt Cap $mil	774	0.0	0.0	0.79

[1]figure is based on 50% or less of stocks

Special Securities % assets 09-30-01	
Restricted/Illiquid Secs	0
Emerging-Markets Secs	Trace
Options/Futures/Warrants	Yes

Composition % assets 09-30-01	
Cash	0.1
Stocks*	99.9
Bonds	0.0
Other	0.0
*Foreign (% stocks)	0.1

Market Cap	
Giant	0.0
Large	0.0
Medium	13.8
Small	78.3
Micro	8.0

Sector Weightings	% of Stocks	Rel S&P	5-Year High	5-Year Low
Utilities	3.7	1.2	6	3
Energy	3.3	0.5	5	2
Financials	21.3	1.2	25	14
Industrials	15.9	1.4	21	12
Durables	2.9	1.8	6	3
Staples	3.6	0.5	4	2
Services	14.6	1.4	21	12
Retail	4.9	0.7	9	3
Health	12.9	0.9	14	8
Technology	17.0	0.9	34	10

Analysis by William Harding 12-13-01

This fund makes a lot of sense for index fans, but others may want to seek out a good stock-picker.

Chalk another year up to active managers. Vanguard Small Cap Index Fund's 0.3% return for the year to date ended Dec. 12, 2001, lags 70% of funds in the small-blend category. The fund fared even worse relative to its peers in 2000, landing in the group's bottom 15%. Active managers have benefited of late from their flexibility to park a portion of assets in cash, which has provided cushion amid stock-market declines.

The argument for indexing isn't as compelling among small caps as it is in the large-cap universe. The Russell 2000 index has been a much easier bogy for active skippers to beat compared with the S&P 500. Small-cap stocks receive less attention from Wall Street, so savvy stock-pickers have a better chance spotting inefficiently priced securities. In addition, active small-cap funds may also benefit from letting their winners run and participating in IPOs.

Of course, index proponents can counter the pro-active fund argument. First, there is a survivorship bias—funds that stink tend to go away—that may overstate the returns of the average small-blend fund over time. Further, while more than two thirds of small-blend funds have bested this offering over all trailing periods, identifying those winners in advance is difficult.

There are plenty of worthy active funds to consider, but investors who simply want low-cost exposure to small caps need look no further. Gus Sauter's ability to add value over the index through effective trading and using futures is remarkable. The fund has bested the Russell 2000 index by 44 basis points annually over the past 15 years.

Address:	Vanguard Financial Ctr. P.O. Box 2600, Valley Forge, PA 19482, 800–662–7447 / 610–669–1000
Web Address:	www.vanguard.com
Inception:	10-03-60
Advisor:	Vanguard Core Mgmt. Grp.
Subadvisor:	None
NTF Plans:	N/A

Minimum Purchase:	$3000	Add: $100	IRA: $1000
Min Auto Inv Plan:	$3000	Add: $50	
Sales Fees:	No-load		
Management Fee:	.21%		
Actual Fees:	Mgt: 0.24%	Dist: —	
Expense Projections:	3Yr: $87	5Yr: $152	10Yr: $343
Avg Brok Commission:	—	Income Distrib: Annually	
Total Cost (relative to category):		Low	

Vanguard Small Cap Value Index

Ticker	Load	NAV	Yield	Total Assets	Mstar Category
VISVX	None	$10.29	0.6%	$1,127.8 mil	Small Value

Prospectus Objective: Small Company

Vanguard Small Capitalization Value Index Fund seeks to track the performance of the S&P SmallCap 600/BARRA Value Index.

The fund invests substantially all assets in each stock found in the index, in approximately the same proportion as represented in the index. The index includes stocks of the S&P SmallCap 600 index with lower-than-average price/earnings and price/book ratios. Management uses a passive approach when selecting securities, and seeks to create a mix of securities that will match the performance of the index.

The fund also offers Instl shares. Prior to Oct. 27, 1998, the fund was named Vanguard Index Small Capitalization Value Stock Fund.

Historical Profile

Return Above Avg
Risk Below Avg
Rating ★★★★ Above Avg

Investment Style
Equity
Average Stock %: 98% (1998), 99% (1999), 100% (2000), 100% (12-01)

▼ Manager Change
▽ Partial Manager Change

Fund Performance vs. Category Average
■ Quarterly Fund Return +/– Category Average
— Category Baseline

Performance Quartile (within Category)

Portfolio Manager(s)

George U. Sauter. Since 5-98. AB'76 Dartmouth C.; MBA'80 U. of Chicago. Other funds currently managed: Vanguard Small Cap Index, Vanguard Balanced Index, Vanguard Equity-Income.

1990	1991	1992	1993	1994	1995	1996	1997	1998	1999	2000	12–01	History
—	—	—	—	—	—	—	—	8.74	8.45	9.65	10.29	NAV
—	—	—	—	—	—	—	—	–12.47*	3.35	21.88	13.55	Total Return %
—	—	—	—	—	—	—	—	–23.90*	–17.69	30.98	25.43	+/– S&P 500
—	—	—	—	—	—	—	—	—	4.83	–0.93	–0.47	+/– Russell 2000 V
—	—	—	—	—	—	—	—	0.56	0.80	1.00	0.71	Income Return %
—	—	—	—	—	—	—	—	–13.03	2.54	20.88	12.85	Capital Return %
—	—	—	—	—	—	—	—	—	43	38	73	Total Rtn % Rank Cat
—	—	—	—	—	—	—	—	0.06	0.07	0.08	0.07	Income $
—	—	—	—	—	—	—	—	0.00	0.50	0.50	0.53	Capital Gains $
—	—	—	—	—	—	—	—	0.25	0.25	0.27	—	Expense Ratio %
—	—	—	—	—	—	—	—	1.13	0.96	1.16	—	Income Ratio %
—	—	—	—	—	—	—	—	—	80	82	—	Turnover Rate %
—	—	—	—	—	—	—	—	112.6	204.4	399.4	802.5	Net Assets $mil

Performance 12-31-01

	1st Qtr	2nd Qtr	3rd Qtr	4th Qtr	Total
1997	—	—	—	—	—
1998	—	—	–21.34	13.65	–12.47 *
1999	–9.50	20.08	–7.41	2.71	3.35
2000	3.06	2.01	7.76	7.58	21.88
2001	–0.78	13.25	–16.63	21.22	13.55

Trailing	Total Return%	+/– S&P 500	+/– Russ 2000V	% Rank All	% Rank Cat	Growth of $10,000
3 Mo	21.22	10.53	4.50	12	17	12,122
6 Mo	1.05	6.61	–0.10	33	59	10,105
1 Yr	13.55	25.43	–0.47	4	73	11,355
3 Yr Avg	12.67	13.70	1.35	7	49	14,303
5 Yr Avg	—	—	—	—	—	—
10 Yr Avg	—	—	—	—	—	—
15 Yr Avg	—	—	—	—	—	—

Tax Analysis	Tax-Adj Ret%	%Rank Cat	%Pretax Ret	%Rank Cat
3 Yr Avg	10.02	58	79.1	87
5 Yr Avg	—	—	—	—
10 Yr Avg	—	—	—	—

Potential Capital Gain Exposure: 7% of assets

Risk Analysis

Time Period	Load-Adj Return %	Risk %Rank[1] All	Risk %Rank[1] Cat	Morningstar Return	Morningstar Risk	Morningstar Risk-Adj Rating
1 Yr	13.55					
3 Yr	12.67	53	63	1.69[2]	0.74	★★★★
5 Yr	—	—	—	—	—	
Incept	6.41	—	—	—	—	

Average Historical Rating (8 months): 3.9★s

[1]1=low, 100=high [2] T-Bill return substituted for category avg.

Category Rating (3 Yr)

1 2 **3** 4 5
Worst Best

Return Average
Risk Average

Other Measures	Standard Index S&P 500	Best Fit Index SPMid400
Alpha	12.7	3.4
Beta	0.70	0.82
R-Squared	39	70
Standard Deviation		21.48
Mean		12.67
Sharpe Ratio		0.41

Portfolio Analysis 09-30-01

Share change since 06–01 Total Stocks: 383	Sector	PE	YTD Ret%	% Assets
⊕ Smithfield Foods	Staples	9.5	45.00	1.45
⊕ DR Horton	Industrials	9.7	48.67	1.06
⊕ Michaels Stores	Retail	29.3	148.60	1.03
⊕ Newfield Explor	Energy	8.2	–25.10	0.98
⊕ Massey Energy Company	Industrials	—	63.97	0.95
⊕ Pogo Producing	Energy	11.7	–15.20	0.92
⊕ Raymond James Finl	Financials	18.0	3.36	0.88
⊕ Coventry Health Care	Health	16.4	–25.20	0.87
⊕ RGS Energy Grp	Utilities	16.6	21.53	0.83
⊕ Washington Federal	Financials	13.2	3.56	0.82
⊕ Commrcl Federal	Financials	25.3	22.54	0.80
⊕ Performance Food Grp	Staples	33.5	37.25	0.77
⊕ Adaptec	Technology	—	81.78	0.74
⊕ Scotts	Industrials	NMF	28.86	0.72
⊕ Toll Brothers	Industrials	7.9	7.40	0.71
⊕ United Bankshares	Financials	19.0	40.81	0.71
⊕ Alpharma Cl A	Health	16.9	–39.30	0.70
⊕ Vintage Petro	Energy	4.6	–32.20	0.69
⊕ First Amer	Financials	9.1	–42.20	0.68
⊕ La–Z–Boy	Durables	31.6	41.17	0.67
⊕ Pier 1 Imports	Retail	19.5	70.54	0.67
⊕ Corn Products Intl	Staples	21.0	22.93	0.66
⊕ Stone Energy	Energy	—	–38.80	0.65
⊕ Whitney Hldg	Financials	15.4	25.24	0.65
⊕ Southern Union	Utilities	27.7	–25.20	0.64

Current Investment Style

Style: Value Blnd Growth; Size: Large Med Small

	Stock Port Avg	Relative S&P 500 Current	Relative S&P 500 Hist	Rel Cat
Price/Earnings Ratio	21.0	0.68	0.56	0.97
Price/Book Ratio	1.8	0.32	0.24	0.75
Price/Cash Flow	12.1	0.67	0.54	0.95
3 Yr Earnings Growth	14.0	0.96	0.89	1.21
1 Yr Earnings Est%	–5.7	3.24	—	1.45
Med Mkt Cap $mil	690	0.0	0.0	0.79

Analysis by William Harding 12-13-01

This fund's a respectable choice for index fans seeking to diversify a large-cap-laden portfolio.

The small-value group has been the top-performing domestic-stock category in 2001. Vanguard Small Cap Value Index, which tracks the S&P Small Cap 600/BARRA Value index, has certainly enjoyed the ride by gaining 9.3% for the year to date ended Dec. 11. That showing, however, lands in the small-value category's worst quartile.

The fund's relative lackluster showing this year is no fault of manager Gus Sauter. He has done a fine job keeping pace with his benchmark, even beating it by a slight margin over the past year. But the S&P Small Cap 600/BARRA Value index has proven to be an easy bogy for active managers to beat. One possible explanation is that the index consists of about 380 names, whereas the Russell 2000 Value index has more than 1200 holdings. Thus, this fund likely missed out on a number of huge winners in this area of the market that active managers were able to uncover. In addition, the S&P index has scant exposure to REITs—an area that has performed well this year.

That said, this offering still makes a strong case for indexing. The fund's since-inception return is competitive with its average small-value rival's over the same period. Its low costs also give it a big edge on it peers: It's 110 basis points cheaper than the average actively managed small-cap fund. Finally, the fund offers strict adherence to its investment style.

Whether investors decide to seek out a quality stock-picker or stick with a low-cost index fund, a small-value fund is smart from a diversification standpoint. Many investors bailed on these offerings in the late 1990s as large-cap stocks led the way, but those that stood their ground have been well rewarded for maintaining a diversified portfolio.

Special Securities % assets 09-30-01

Restricted/Illiquid Secs	0
Emerging–Markets Secs	0
Options/Futures/Warrants	No

Composition % assets 09-30-01

Cash	0.0
Stocks*	100.0
Bonds	0.0
Other	0.0
*Foreign (% stocks)	0.2

Market Cap

Giant	0.0
Large	0.0
Medium	11.3
Small	81.3
Micro	7.4

Sector Weightings	% of Stocks	Rel S&P	5-Year High	5-Year Low
Utilities	6.3	2.0	—	—
Energy	6.9	1.0	—	—
Financials	15.1	0.8	—	—
Industrials	25.2	2.2	—	—
Durables	4.8	3.1	—	—
Staples	5.4	0.7	—	—
Services	12.1	1.1	—	—
Retail	8.1	1.2	—	—
Health	3.9	0.3	—	—
Technology	12.3	0.7	—	—

Address:	Vanguard Financial Ctr. P.O. Box 2600 Valley Forge, PA 19482 800–662–7447
Web Address:	www.vanguard.com
*Inception:	05-21-98
Advisor:	Vanguard Core Mgmt. Grp.
Subadvisor:	None
NTF Plans:	N/A

Minimum Purchase:	$3000	Add: $100	IRA: $1000
Min Auto Inv Plan:	$3000	Add: $50	
Sales Fees:	No–load		
Management Fee:	.20%		
Actual Fees:	Mgt: 0.21%	Dist: —	
Expense Projections:	3Yr: $136	5Yr: $201	10Yr: $392
Avg Brok Commission:	—	Income Distrib: Annually	
Total Cost (relative to category):		Low	

Vanguard STAR

Ticker	Load	NAV	Yield	Total Assets	Mstar Category
VGSTX	None	$16.44	3.2%	$8,242.1 mil	Domestic Hybrid

Prospectus Objective: Balanced

Vanguard STAR Fund seeks total return.

The fund normally allocates its assets in the following proportions: 60% to 70% of assets in equity mutual funds, 20% to 30% in bond funds, and 10% to 20% in money market funds. The equity mutual funds that it may invest in include value-oriented equity funds, namely the Vanguard/Windsor and Vanguard/Windsor II Funds, and growth-oriented funds, including Vanguard Explorer, Vanguard/Primecap, Vanguard U.S. Growth, and Vanguard/Morgan Growth. It may also invest in two fixed-income funds, Vanguard GNMA and Vanguard Long Term Corporate Bond. The money market portion consists of Vanguard Prime Portfolio. The fund is non-diversified.

Historical Profile

Return: Above Avg
Risk: Low
Rating: ★★★★ Above Avg

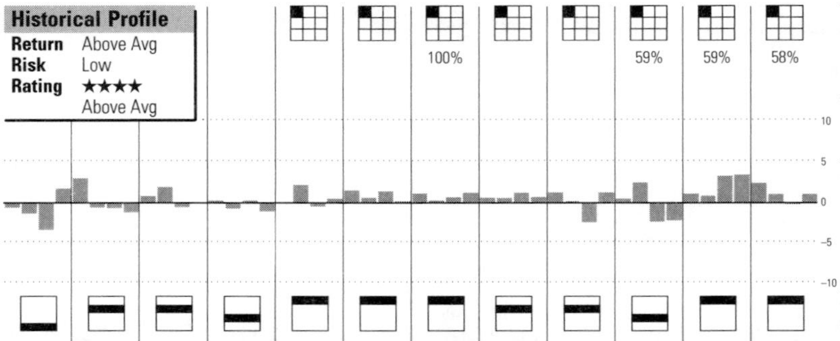

Investment Style
Equity
Average Stock %: 100% (1996), 59% (1999), 59% (2000), 58% (12-01)

▼ Manager Change
▽ Partial Manager Change

Fund Performance vs. Category Average
■ Quarterly Fund Return +/– Category Average
— Category Baseline

Performance Quartile (within Category)

Portfolio Manager(s)

Multiple Managers.

1990	1991	1992	1993	1994	1995	1996	1997	1998	1999	2000	12-01	History
10.72	12.30	12.88	13.41	12.60	15.02	15.86	17.38	17.96	18.21	17.81	16.44	NAV
–3.63	24.29	10.42	10.97	–0.29	28.65	16.19	21.15	12.38	7.13	10.96	0.50	Total Return %
–0.51	–6.19	2.81	0.91	–1.61	–8.88	–6.76	–12.20	–16.20	–13.91	20.06	12.38	+/– S&P 500
–12.59	8.29	3.02	1.22	2.63	10.18	12.57	11.47	3.70	7.96	–0.68	–7.92	+/– LB Aggregate
6.15	5.86	4.19	3.68	3.92	4.73	3.96	3.75	3.36	3.42	3.74	3.27	Income Return %
–9.78	18.43	6.23	7.29	–4.21	23.92	12.22	17.40	9.02	3.71	7.21	–2.77	Capital Return %
79	43	26	61	22	19	23	28	50	63	10	21	Total Rtn % Rank Cat
0.73	0.62	0.51	0.47	0.52	0.59	0.59	0.59	0.58	0.61	0.64	0.55	Income $
0.16	0.37	0.18	0.40	0.25	0.57	0.98	1.20	0.98	0.40	1.65	0.87	Capital Gains $
0.00	0.00	0.00	0.00	0.00	0.00	0.00	0.00	0.00	0.00	0.00	—	Expense Ratio %
6.65	5.48	4.36	3.67	4.01	4.12	3.71	3.46	3.18	3.21	3.57	—	Income Ratio %
12	11	3	3	9	13	18	15	16	10	17	—	Turnover Rate %
1,038.3	1,574.3	2,482.8	3,628.2	3,766.2	4,841.8	5,863.4	7,355.4	8,082.6	8,087.1	8,347.9	8,242.1	Net Assets $mil

Performance 12-31-01

	1st Qtr	2nd Qtr	3rd Qtr	4th Qtr	Total
1997	0.69	10.08	7.73	1.45	21.15
1998	8.34	1.28	–8.13	11.48	12.38
1999	1.39	6.29	–5.76	5.48	7.13
2000	3.80	–0.11	5.11	1.81	10.96
2001	–2.91	4.20	–7.41	7.29	0.50

Trailing	Total Return%	+/– S&P 500	+/– LB Agg	% Rank All	% Rank Cat	Growth of $10,000
3 Mo	7.29	–3.39	7.25	55	31	10,729
6 Mo	–0.66	4.89	–5.32	41	31	9,934
1 Yr	0.50	12.38	–7.92	42	21	10,050
3 Yr Avg	6.11	7.13	–0.17	22	12	11,946
5 Yr Avg	10.22	–0.48	2.79	18	14	16,265
10 Yr Avg	11.50	–1.43	4.27	22	13	29,705
15 Yr Avg	11.49	–2.24	3.37	30	12	51,112

Tax Analysis	Tax-Adj Ret%	%Rank Cat	%Pretax Ret	%Rank Cat
3 Yr Avg	3.42	16	56.0	45
5 Yr Avg	7.34	16	71.8	35
10 Yr Avg	8.76	13	76.2	25

Potential Capital Gain Exposure: 14% of assets

Risk Analysis

Time Period	Load-Adj Return %	Risk %Rank[1] All	Risk %Rank[1] Cat	Morningstar Return	Morningstar Risk	Morningstar Risk-Adj Rating
1 Yr	0.50					
3 Yr	6.11	35	25	0.25[2]	0.43	★★★★
5 Yr	10.22	41	28	1.25[2]	0.48	★★★★
10 Yr	11.50	46	22	1.01	0.50	★★★★

Average Historical Rating (166 months): 3.6★s

[1] 1=low, 100=high [2] T-Bill return substituted for category avg.

Category Rating (3 Yr)

1 Worst — 5 Best (rating: 4)

Return: Above Avg
Risk: Below Avg

Other Measures	Standard Index S&P 500	Best Fit Index S&P 500
Alpha	3.8	3.8
Beta	0.50	0.50
R-Squared	79	79
Standard Deviation		9.96
Mean		6.11
Sharpe Ratio		0.13

Portfolio Analysis 09-30-01

Total Stocks: 11 (Share change since 06-01)	Sector	PE Ratio	YTD Return %	% Net Assets
⊖ Vanguard Windsor II	N/A	—	—	26.38
⊖ Vanguard Windsor	N/A	—	—	14.55
☼ Vanguard Long-Term Corporate Bond	N/A	—	—	13.75
⊖ Vanguard GNMA	N/A	—	—	13.35
⊖ Vanguard Short-Term Corp	N/A	—	—	13.01
⊕ Vanguard Explorer	N/A	—	—	4.51
⊕ Vanguard Morgan Growth	N/A	—	—	4.44
⊕ Vanguard U.S. Growth	N/A	—	—	4.41
Vanguard Primecap	N/A	—	—	4.31
☼ Vanguard International Growth	N/A	—	—	1.62

Total Fixed-Income: 0	Date of Maturity	Amount $000	Value $000	% Net Assets

Analysis by Langdon Healy 12-11-01

Investors seeking a one-stop investment vehicle may want to hitch their fortunes to this star.

Vanguard Star is a fund-of-funds covering a wide swath of the investment universe by including domestic and foreign stocks, as well as bonds. It invests in 11 actively managed Vanguard funds, with a target asset allocation of 62% stocks, 25% intermediate- and long-term bonds, and 12% short-term bonds. Two of the 11 funds, Vanguard International Growth and International Value, were added to the fund's lineup last spring—it previously had no international exposure. While exposure to the funds will grow slowly with the addition of new cash flow, Vanguard's goal is to devote about 12% of assets to them.

With more than 40% of assets devoted to Vanguard Windsor and Windsor II, however, the fund's performance clearly depends heavily on the fortune of these two deep-value offerings. As both of these funds have done exceptionally well over the long haul, Vanguard Star shareholders have benefited from the sizable stake. This has held true in 2001, as both funds rank highly in the large-value category.

The fine performance of these two holdings combined with solid performance from small-growth fund Vanguard Explorer and the fund's fixed-income funds have produced good overall results in 2001. It lost little money this year, besting 77% of its domestic-hybrid peers. This showing is not unusual for the fund; it has landed in the category's top quartile five times over the past 10 years. Over that period, it has only dipped into the bottom half of the category twice.

The fund's strong long-term record, combined with its low expenses and the addition of international exposure, makes it a very enticing one-stop option.

Equity Style
Style: —
Size: —
NA

Fixed-Income Style
Duration: —
Quality: —
NA

	Portfolio Avg	Rel S&P
Price/Earnings Ratio	25.0	0.81
Price/Book Ratio	3.8	0.66
Price/Cash Flow	13.8	0.77
3 Yr Earnings Growth	14.2	0.97
1 Yr Earnings Est%	–0.1	0.05
Debt % Total Cap	36.0	1.16
Med Mkt Cap $mil	21,189	0.35

Avg Eff Duration	—
Avg Eff Maturity	—
Avg Credit Quality	—
Avg Wtd Coupon	—

Special Securities
Restricted/Illiquid Secs
Emerging-Markets Secs
Options/Futures/Warrants

Composition (% of assets 09-30-01)	
Cash	4.5
Stocks*	57.5
Bonds	37.5
Other	0.6
*Foreign (% of stocks)	6.2

Market Cap	
Giant	—
Large	—
Medium	—
Small	—
Micro	—

Sector Weightings	% of Stocks	Rel S&P	5-Year High	5-Year Low
Utilities	6.3	2.0	—	—
Energy	8.1	1.1	—	—
Financials	21.9	1.2	—	—
Industrials	12.0	1.0	—	—
Durables	3.6	2.3	—	—
Staples	5.6	0.7	—	—
Services	14.3	1.3	—	—
Retail	6.5	1.0	—	—
Health	9.7	0.7	—	—
Technology	12.1	0.7	—	—

Address:	Vanguard Financial Ctr. P.O. Box 2600 Valley Forge, PA 19482 800-662-7447 / 610-669-1000
Web Address:	www.vanguard.com
Inception:	03-29-85
Advisor:	Vanguard Grp.
Subadvisor:	None
NTF Plans:	N/A

Minimum Purchase:	$1000	Add: $100	IRA: $1000
Min Auto Inv Plan:	$1000	Add: $50	
Sales Fees:	No-load		
Management Fee:	None		
Actual Fees:	Mgt: 0.00%	Dist: —	
Expense Projections:	3Yr: $109	5Yr: $191	10Yr: $431
Avg Brok Commission:	—	Income Distrib: Semi-Ann.	
Total Cost (relative to category):		Low	

Vanguard Strategic Equity

Ticker	Load	NAV	Yield	Total Assets	Mstar Category
VSEQX	None	$15.23	0.9%	$879.5 mil	Mid-Cap Value

Prospectus Objective: Aggressive Growth

Vanguard Strategic Equity Fund seeks long-term total return.

The fund normally invests at least 65% of assets in equities of U.S. companies. To select investments, the advisor uses a proprietary quantitative valuation model to assess the total return potential of different market segments, categorized by two levels: market capitalization and growth versus value. The fund emphasizes small and mid-size companies, though it may invest in larger companies. Factors considered in choosing individual securities include market liquidity, valuation measures, and financial strength relative to other stocks.

Past fund names: Vanguard Aggressive Growth Fund and Vanguard Horizon Aggressive Growth Portfolio.

Historical Profile

Return Above Avg
Risk Average
Rating ★★★★ Above Avg

Investment Style Equity — Average Stock %: 99% (1995), 99% (1996), 98% (1997), 98% (1998), 97% (1999), 96% (2000), 97% (12-01)

▼ Manager Change
▽ Partial Manager Change

Fund Performance vs. Category Average
■ Quarterly Fund Return +/– Category Average
— Category Baseline

Performance Quartile (within Category)

Portfolio Manager(s)

George U. Sauter. Since 8-95. AB'76 Dartmouth C.; MBA'80 U. of Chicago. Other funds currently managed: Vanguard Small Cap Index, Vanguard Balanced Index, Vanguard Equity-Income.

1990	1991	1992	1993	1994	1995	1996	1997	1998	1999	2000	12-01	History
—	—	—	—	—	10.76	12.56	14.60	14.53	16.76	14.58	15.23	NAV
—	—	—	—	—	7.76*	25.03	26.22	0.61	19.25	7.46	5.42	Total Return %
—	—	—	—	—	–3.46*	2.08	–7.13	–27.96	–1.79	16.56	17.30	+/– S&P 500
—	—	—	—	—	—	4.77	–8.14	–4.47	19.35	–11.72	3.08	+/– Russ Midcap Val
—	—	—	—	—	0.80	1.67	1.11	1.03	1.10	1.25	0.96	Income Return %
—	—	—	—	—	6.96	23.35	25.11	–0.41	18.15	6.21	4.46	Capital Return %
—	—	—	—	—	—	17	53	60	14	82	47	Total Rtn % Rank Cat
—	—	—	—	—	0.08	0.18	0.14	0.15	0.16	0.21	0.14	Income $
—	—	—	—	—	0.00	0.71	1.08	0.00	0.37	3.03	0.00	Capital Gains $
—	—	—	—	—	0.06	0.38	0.40	0.43	0.46	0.49	—	Expense Ratio %
—	—	—	—	—	2.22	1.78	1.28	0.93	1.00	1.31	—	Income Ratio %
—	—	—	—	—	—	106	85	71	51	83	—	Turnover Rate %
—	—	—	—	—	74.6	153.2	474.1	534.5	625.6	765.0	879.5	Net Assets $mil

Performance 12-31-01

	1st Qtr	2nd Qtr	3rd Qtr	4th Qtr	Total
1997	–0.80	18.14	14.47	–5.91	26.22
1998	9.79	–4.87	–20.66	21.40	0.61
1999	–2.68	12.52	–5.22	14.90	19.25
2000	2.21	0.00	4.90	0.23	7.46
2001	–3.70	10.76	–14.02	14.96	5.42

Trailing	Total Return%	+/– S&P 500	+/– Russ Midcap Val	% Rank All	% Rank Cat	Growth of $10,000
3 Mo	14.96	4.28	2.93	24	35	11,496
6 Mo	–1.15	4.40	–0.24	43	51	9,885
1 Yr	5.42	17.30	3.08	21	47	10,542
3 Yr Avg	10.55	11.57	3.74	10	50	13,510
5 Yr Avg	11.40	0.70	–0.06	12	54	17,157
10 Yr Avg	—	—	—	—	—	—
15 Yr Avg	—	—	—	—	—	—

Tax Analysis	Tax-Adj Ret%	%Rank Cat	%Pretax Ret	%Rank Cat
3 Yr Avg	7.85	54	74.5	67
5 Yr Avg	9.13	48	80.1	41
10 Yr Avg	—	—	—	—

Potential Capital Gain Exposure: 1% of assets

Risk Analysis

Time Period	Load-Adj Return %	Risk %Rank[1] All	Risk %Rank[1] Cat	Morningstar Return	Morningstar Risk	Morningstar Risk-Adj Rating
1 Yr	5.42					
3 Yr	10.55	47	43	1.25[2]	0.65	★★★★
5 Yr	11.40	62	69	1.57[2]	0.86	★★★★
Incept	14.02	—	—	—	—	

Average Historical Rating (41 months): 2.6★s

[1] 1=low, 100=high [2] T-Bill return substituted for category avg.

Category Rating (3 Yr)

1 2 **3** 4 5 — Worst … Best

Return Average
Risk Average

Other Measures	Standard Index S&P 500	Best Fit Index SPMid400
Alpha	10.5	1.4
Beta	0.79	0.76
R-Squared	67	82

Standard Deviation	17.95
Mean	10.55
Sharpe Ratio	0.36

Portfolio Analysis 09-30-01

Share change since 06-01 Total Stocks: 185	Sector	PE	YTD Ret%	% Assets
⊖ Archer Daniels Midland	Staples	24.7	1.91	2.26
⊖ Entergy	Utilities	11.7	–4.50	2.26
⊕ FirstEnergy	Utilities	12.8	16.42	2.10
⊕ Pepsi Bottling Grp	Staples	23.6	17.90	2.07
Bear Stearns	Financials	12.9	16.96	1.98
⊕ Deluxe	Industrials	17.1	116.30	1.97
⊕ Pitney Bowes	Industrials	17.2	19.80	1.94
Apache	Energy	8.0	–21.20	1.94
⊕ Cytyc	Health	49.3	25.16	1.83
☆ Southtrust	Financials	15.9	24.18	1.68
Golden West Finl	Financials	12.9	–12.40	1.67
Whirlpool	Durables	71.9	57.27	1.60
MGIC Invest	Financials	10.9	–8.33	1.59
WellPoint Health Networks	Health	19.4	1.39	1.55
⊕ York Intl	Industrials	23.5	26.51	1.48
ESS Tech	Technology	—	329.30	1.46
⊕ Freeport-McMoRan Cop/Gold B	Industrials	—	—	1.45
TJX	Retail	23.2	44.39	1.42
Comerica	Financials	14.2	–0.47	1.38
⊕ Praxair	Industrials	28.6	26.22	1.38
Genzyme Corporation General Di	Health	—	33.11	1.29
NCR	Technology	15.5	–24.90	1.27
Noble Affiliates	Energy	8.7	–22.90	1.23
RR Donnelley & Sons	Services	26.8	13.72	1.12
PPL	Utilities	8.2	–20.90	1.09

Current Investment Style

Style: Value Blnd Growth; Size: Large Med Small

	Stock Port Avg	Relative S&P 500 Current	Relative S&P 500 Hist	Rel Cat
Price/Earnings Ratio	20.7	0.67	0.60	0.88
Price/Book Ratio	3.7	0.64	0.53	1.20
Price/Cash Flow	13.3	0.74	0.60	1.07
3 Yr Earnings Growth	22.2	1.52	0.97	1.87
1 Yr Earnings Est%	5.0	—	—	–0.81
Med Mkt Cap $mil	3,982	0.1	0.1	0.56

Special Securities % assets 09-30-01	
Restricted/Illiquid Secs	0
Emerging-Markets Secs	Trace
Options/Futures/Warrants	No

Composition % assets 09-30-01	
Cash	6.4
Stocks*	93.7
Bonds	0.0
Other	0.0
*Foreign (% stocks)	0.1

Market Cap	
Giant	0.0
Large	13.2
Medium	62.4
Small	22.8
Micro	1.6

Sector Weightings	% of Stocks	Rel S&P	5-Year High	5-Year Low
Utilities	8.1	2.5	11	6
Energy	5.7	0.8	10	3
Financials	18.9	1.1	24	12
Industrials	17.0	1.5	24	10
Durables	4.0	2.6	11	3
Staples	6.2	0.8	6	1
Services	12.6	1.2	15	9
Retail	5.3	0.8	10	3
Health	10.3	0.7	11	5
Technology	11.9	0.6	32	11

Analysis by Scott Cooley 11-29-01

Vanguard Strategic Equity Fund's returns are actually pretty good.

This fund's trailing returns versus the mid-value category are middling, but it's an awkward fit in that group. It lands in the mid-value category because, among other things, manager Gus Sauter's quantitative stock-picking models favor companies with modest valuations relative to their earnings-growth rates, giving the fund relatively low P/E and price/book ratios. But Sauter's models also keep the fund's sector weights roughly in line with its Russell 2800 benchmark's, so the fund has far more exposure to growth sectors, including tech and health care, than true value funds have. And it performs more like a mid-blend than a mid-value offering.

With that in mind, the fund's trailing returns are solid. Since its 1996 inception, it has beaten its benchmark index by 3 percentage points on an annualized basis. Because Sauter's models don't permit big industry or market-cap bets versus the index, the fund's advantage owes to stock selection. Moreover, the fund's five-year annualized return of 10.4% tops the mid-blend average by nearly 2 percentage points. So far in 2001, the fund is 10 percentage points ahead of its index, thanks to good picks such as Sensormatic and Symantec.

As we have noted before, the fund does have limitations. Like many active-quantitative strategies, this fund's approach includes relatively high turnover. It's thus unlikely this will be an especially tax-efficient fund. And it is still true that the fund is more highly correlated with the S&P 500 than most mid-cap offerings, and therefore offers less diversification away from large caps.

That said, Sauter is building an impressive record here. Shareholders shouldn't expect him to beat his index so handily every year, but this is becoming a solid holding for investors in tax-advantaged accounts.

Address:	Vanguard Financial Ctr. P.O. Box 2600 Valley Forge, PA 19482 800–662–7447 / 610–669–1000
Web Address:	www.vanguard.com
*Inception:	08-14-95
Advisor:	Vanguard Core Mgmt. Grp.
Subadvisor:	None
NTF Plans:	N/A

Minimum Purchase:	$3000	Add: $100	IRA: $1000
Min Auto Inv Plan:	$3000	Add: $100	
Sales Fees:	No-load		
Management Fee:	.42%		
Actual Fees:	Mgt: 0.47%	Dist: —	
Expense Projections:	3Yr: $271	5Yr: $274	10Yr: $616
Avg Brok Commission:	—	Income Distrib: Annually	
Total Cost (relative to category):		Low	

Vanguard Tax–Managed Capital App

Ticker	Load	NAV	Yield	Total Assets	Mstar Category
VMCAX	None	$25.73	0.7%	$2,577.8 mil	Large Growth

Prospectus Objective: Growth

Vanguard Tax-Managed Capital Appreciation Fund seeks growth of capital consistent with minimizing capital gains and dividend distributions.

The fund invests in a statistical sample of stocks included in the Russell 1000 index. To reduce taxable distributions, the fund employs techniques to minimize capital gains. It also emphasizes low-yielding stocks.

The redemption fee has a two-tier structure: 2% for redemptions within 12 months and 1% for redemptions within five years. The fund offers Admiral, Investor and Institutional shares.

Historical Profile

Return	Above Avg
Risk	Average
Rating	★★★ Neutral

Investment Style Equity

Average Stock %: 99% 100% 100% 100% 100% 100% 100%

▼ Manager Change
▽ Partial Manager Change

Fund Performance vs. Category Average
■ Quarterly Fund Return +/– Category Average
— Category Baseline

Performance Quartile (within Category)

Portfolio Manager(s)

George U. Sauter. Since 9-94. AB'76 Dartmouth C.; MBA'80 U. of Chicago. Other funds currently managed: Vanguard Small Cap Index, Vanguard Balanced Index, Vanguard Equity-Income.

1990	1991	1992	1993	1994	1995	1996	1997	1998	1999	2000	12-01	History
—	—	—	—	9.95	13.28	15.95	20.18	25.68	34.17	30.59	25.73	NAV
—	—	—	—	–0.50*	34.38	20.93	27.29	27.90	33.55	–10.13	–15.34	Total Return %
—	—	—	—	1.21*	–3.16	–2.02	–6.06	–0.67	12.51	–1.03	–3.46	+/– S&P 500
—	—	—	—	—	–4.28	–4.60	–6.45	–17.20	3.88	14.39	5.16	+/– Russ Top 200 Grt
—	—	—	—	0.40	0.90	0.83	0.75	0.64	0.48	0.35	0.56	Income Return %
—	—	—	—	–0.90	33.47	20.10	26.54	27.26	33.07	–10.48	–15.89	Capital Return %
—	—	—	—	—	34	35	41	66	58	30	20	Total Rtn % Rank Cat
—	—	—	—	0.04	0.09	0.11	0.12	0.13	0.12	0.12	0.17	Income $
—	—	—	—	0.00	0.00	0.00	0.00	0.00	0.00	0.00	0.00	Capital Gains $
—	—	—	—	0.20	0.20	0.20	0.17	0.19	0.19	0.19	—	Expense Ratio %
—	—	—	—	1.26	0.97	0.91	0.70	0.62	0.47	0.36	—	Income Ratio %
—	—	—	—	—	7	12	4	5	12	17	—	Turnover Rate %
—	—	—	—	69.7	254.2	517.4	892.5	1,478.8	2,378.3	2,817.9	1,677.8	Net Assets $mil

Performance 12-31-01

	1st Qtr	2nd Qtr	3rd Qtr	4th Qtr	Total
1997	–0.19	16.77	11.30	–1.87	27.29
1998	14.62	2.38	–13.09	25.42	27.90
1999	6.70	8.43	–5.89	22.66	33.55
2000	7.43	–4.09	–0.51	–12.34	–10.13
2001	–14.61	7.12	–18.58	13.69	–15.34

Trailing	Total Return%	+/– S&P 500	+/– Russ Top 200 Grth	% Rank All	% Rank Cat	Growth of $10,000
3 Mo	13.69	3.00	0.83	27	49	11,369
6 Mo	–7.44	–1.89	–0.45	76	35	9,256
1 Yr	–15.34	–3.46	5.16	73	20	8,466
3 Yr Avg	0.53	1.56	8.56	70	23	10,161
5 Yr Avg	10.59	–0.11	2.00	15	30	16,544
10 Yr Avg	—	—	—	—	—	—
15 Yr Avg	—	—	—	—	—	—

Tax Analysis	Tax-Adj Ret%	%Rank Cat	%Pretax Ret	%Rank Cat
3 Yr Avg	0.35	16	65.4	57
5 Yr Avg	10.37	16	97.9	4
10 Yr Avg	—	—	—	—

Potential Capital Gain Exposure: 14% of assets

Risk Analysis

Time Period	Load-Adj Return %	Risk %Rank[1] All	Risk %Rank[1] Cat	Morningstar Return	Morningstar Risk	Morningstar Risk-Adj Rating
1 Yr	–17.03					
3 Yr	–0.14	77	23	–1.03[2]	1.09	★★★
5 Yr	10.37	78	24	1.29[2]	1.07	★★★
Incept	14.22	—	—	—	—	

Average Historical Rating (52 months): 3.7★s

[1]1=low, 100=high [2] T-Bill return substituted for category avg.

Category Rating (3 Yr)

1 2 3 4 5 (Worst → Best): 4

Return	Above Avg
Risk	Below Avg

Other Measures	Standard Index S&P 500	Best Fit Index MSCIACWdFr
Alpha	3.1	8.0
Beta	1.18	1.26
R–Squared	92	93

Standard Deviation	21.14
Mean	0.53
Sharpe Ratio	–0.24

Analysis by William Harding 11-12-01

This offering is a fine core holding for growth investors to hold in taxable accounts.

Vanguard Tax-Managed Capital Appreciation Fund's growth bent has been a drain on performance lately, but not enough to limit its appeal. Manager Gus Sauter uses a sampling technique to match the attributes of the Russell 1000 index, while emphasizing the lowest-yielding stocks in the index to reduce dividend distributions. (Dividends are taxed at a higher rate than long-term capital gains.) In addition, Sauter employs various trading techniques such as offsetting gains with losses to limit capital-gains distributions.

As a result of the fund's tax biases, the portfolio is tilted more toward growth names than its bogy, the Russell 1000. For instance, the portfolio has slightly greater exposure to tech stocks than the index, and it's a little light in typically higher-yielding financial names. This growth bent was a boon to returns in 1999 and the fund's 33.6% annual gain outpaced the Russell 1000 by 13 percentage points. The fund has given some of those gains back this year and in 2000, but its return since inception is still competitive with the index's.

The fund's showing is even more impressive compared with its large-growth peers. Its diversified approach will cause the fund to lag its more-aggressive peers when go-go growth stocks rule the roost, but its long-term record is compelling nonetheless. Further, the fund does a fine job of keeping the tax man at bay. It has never paid out a capital-gains distribution, and its tax-adjusted return over the trailing five years bests 85% of funds in the large-growth category.

Investors looking for a more S&P 500-like blend offering should consider Vanguard Tax Managed Growth & Income. But this is a good choice to anchor the growth portion of an investor's taxable portfolio.

Portfolio Analysis 09-30-01

Share change since 06-01 Total Stocks: 546	Sector	PE	YTD Ret%	% Assets
⊖ General Elec	Industrials	30.1	–15.00	3.88
⊖ Pfizer	Health	34.7	–12.40	2.87
⊕ Microsoft	Technology	57.6	52.78	2.74
⊕ ExxonMobil	Energy	15.3	–7.59	2.62
⊖ Citigroup	Financials	20.0	0.03	2.55
⊖ IBM	Technology	26.9	43.00	2.05
⊕ American Intl Grp	Financials	42.0	–19.20	1.93
⊖ Intel	Technology	73.1	4.89	1.82
Johnson & Johnson	Health	16.6	14.01	1.70
⊖ Wal–Mart Stores	Retail	40.3	8.94	1.59
⊖ AOL Time Warner	Technology	—	–7.76	1.49
Merck	Health	19.1	–35.90	1.49
SBC Comms	Services	18.4	–16.00	1.12
⊕ Verizon Comms	Services	29.7	–2.52	1.12
Coca–Cola	Staples	35.5	–21.40	1.11
⊖ Cisco Sys	Technology	—	–52.60	1.06
Home Depot	Retail	42.9	12.07	0.97
Bristol–Myers Squibb	Health	20.2	–26.00	0.84
⊕ Bank of America	Financials	16.7	42.73	0.79
Philip Morris	Staples	12.1	9.12	0.77
⊕ Amgen	Health	52.8	–11.70	0.70
⊕ ChevronTexaco	Energy	10.3	9.29	0.69
Procter & Gamble	Staples	38.8	3.12	0.68
⊖ AT&T	Services	7.8	40.59	0.66
⊕ Dell Comp	Technology	61.8	55.87	0.65

Current Investment Style

Style: Value Blnd Growth; Size: Large Med Small

	Stock Port Avg	Relative S&P 500 Current	Relative S&P 500 Hist	Rel Cat
Price/Earnings Ratio	31.2	1.01	1.07	0.88
Price/Book Ratio	5.6	0.98	1.00	0.88
Price/Cash Flow	18.8	1.04	1.07	0.83
3 Yr Earnings Growth	17.7	1.21	1.16	0.82
1 Yr Earnings Est%	0.9	—	—	0.29
Med Mkt Cap $mil	39,809	0.7	0.6	0.84

Special Securities % assets 09-30-01	
Restricted/Illiquid Secs	0
Emerging–Markets Secs	Trace
Options/Futures/Warrants	No

Composition % assets 09-30-01	
Cash	0.1
Stocks*	99.9
Bonds	0.0
Other	0.0
*Foreign (% stocks)	0.1

Market Cap	
Giant	47.5
Large	23.6
Medium	27.8
Small	0.9
Micro	0.2

Sector Weightings	% of Stocks	Rel S&P	5-Year High	5-Year Low
Utilities	1.8	0.6	2	0
Energy	7.2	1.0	8	3
Financials	16.2	0.9	16	8
Industrials	9.2	0.8	16	8
Durables	2.1	1.3	6	1
Staples	4.8	0.6	9	3
Services	15.1	1.4	19	15
Retail	6.7	1.0	9	5
Health	16.4	1.1	17	9
Technology	20.6	1.1	40	17

Address:	Vanguard Financial Ctr. P.O. Box 2600 Valley Forge, PA 19482 800–662–7447 / 610–669–1000
Web Address:	www.vanguard.com
*Inception:	09-06-94
Advisor:	Vanguard Core Mgmt. Grp.
Subadvisor:	None
NTF Plans:	N/A

Minimum Purchase:	$10000	Add: $100	IRA: —
Min Auto Inv Plan:	$10000	Add: $50	
Sales Fees:	No–load, 2.00%R within 12 months		
Management Fee:	.17%		
Actual Fees:	Mgt: 0.18%	Dist: —	
Expense Projections:	3Yr: $176	5Yr: $107	10Yr: $243
Avg Brok Commission:	—	Income Distrib: Annually	
Total Cost (relative to category):		Low	

Vanguard Tax–Managed Growth & Inc

Ticker	Load	NAV	Yield	Total Assets	Mstar Category
VTGIX	None	$24.93	1.2%	$2,269.5 mil	Large Blend

Prospectus Objective: Growth and Income

Vanguard Tax-Managed Growth and Income Fund seeks growth of capital and moderate current income, consistent with minimizing capital gains.

The fund invests in substantially all of the stocks included in the S&P 500 index. To reduce taxable distributions, especially realized capital gains, an index-oriented investment approach is used. Stocks are held in approximately the same proportions as they are represented on the index.

The redemption fee has a two-tier structure: 2% for redemptions within 12 months and 1% for redemptions within five years. The fund offers Admiral, Investor and Institutional shares.

Historical Profile
Return Average
Risk Average
Rating ★★★ Neutral

Investment Style
Equity
Average Stock %: 98% 99% 100% 99% 100% 100% 99%

▼ Manager Change
▽ Partial Manager Change

Fund Performance vs. Category Average
Quarterly Fund Return +/– Category Average
— Category Baseline

Performance Quartile (within Category)

Portfolio Manager(s)

George U. Sauter. Since 9-94. AB'76 Dartmouth C.; MBA'80 U. of Chicago. Other funds currently managed: Vanguard Small Cap Index, Vanguard Balanced Index, Vanguard Equity-Income.

History

1990	1991	1992	1993	1994	1995	1996	1997	1998	1999	2000	12-01	History
—	—	—	—	9.77	13.16	15.89	20.88	26.55	31.81	28.66	24.93	NAV
—	—	—	—	–1.70*	37.53	23.03	33.31	28.67	21.12	–9.04	–11.93	Total Return %
—	—	—	—	0.01*	–0.01	0.08	–0.04	0.10	0.08	0.07	–0.05	+/– S&P 500
—	—	—	—	—	–0.08	0.86	0.29	0.04	–0.71	1.92	0.84	+/– Wilshire Top 750
—	—	—	—	0.90	2.58	2.14	1.77	1.40	1.19	0.94	1.05	Income Return %
—	—	—	—	–2.59	34.95	20.88	31.54	27.28	19.93	–9.97	–12.98	Capital Return %
—	—	—	—	—	10	25	13	19	41	54	33	Total Rtn % Rank Cat
—	—	—	—	0.09	0.25	0.28	0.28	0.29	0.31	0.30	0.30	Income $
—	—	—	—	0.00	0.00	0.00	0.00	0.00	0.00	0.00	0.00	Capital Gains $
—	—	—	—	0.20	0.20	0.20	0.17	0.19	0.19	0.19	—	Expense Ratio %
—	—	—	—	2.82	2.37	2.04	1.62	1.32	1.11	0.96	—	Income Ratio %
—	—	—	—	—	6	7	2	4	4	5	—	Turnover Rate %
—	—	—	—	31.4	98.3	234.5	579.3	1,352.4	2,240.4	2,426.9	1,606.4	Net Assets $mil

Performance 12-31-01

	1st Qtr	2nd Qtr	3rd Qtr	4th Qtr	Total
1997	2.63	17.46	7.46	2.90	33.31
1998	13.94	3.33	–9.95	21.36	28.67
1999	4.93	7.03	–6.23	15.01	21.12
2000	2.26	–2.65	–0.92	–7.78	–9.04
2001	–11.89	5.84	–14.66	10.68	–11.93

Trailing	Total Return%	+/– S&P 500	+/– Wil Top 750	% Rank All	% Rank Cat	Growth of $10,000
3 Mo	10.68	–0.01	–0.65	38	47	11,068
6 Mo	–5.55	0.00	0.24	65	35	9,445
1 Yr	–11.93	–0.05	0.84	65	33	8,807
3 Yr Avg	–1.00	0.03	0.82	78	47	9,703
5 Yr Avg	10.73	0.03	0.61	15	23	16,644
10 Yr Avg	—	—	—	—	—	—
15 Yr Avg	—	—	—	—	—	—

Tax Analysis	Tax-Adj Ret%	%Rank Cat	%Pretax Ret	%Rank Cat
3 Yr Avg	–1.42	38	—	—
5 Yr Avg	10.21	12	95.2	8
10 Yr Avg	—	—	—	—

Potential Capital Gain Exposure: 8% of assets

Risk Analysis

Time Period	Load-Adj Return %	Risk %Rank[1] All	Risk %Rank[1] Cat	Morningstar Return	Morningstar Risk	Morningstar Risk-Adj Rating
1 Yr	–13.69					
3 Yr	–1.66	65	37	–1.32[2]	0.91	★★
5 Yr	10.50	65	35	1.33[2]	0.89	★★★★
Incept	14.76	—	—	—	—	

Average Historical Rating (52 months): 4.5★s

[1] 1=low, 100=high [2] T–Bill return substituted for category avg.

Category Rating (3 Yr)

1 2 **3** 4 5
Worst Best

Return Average
Risk Average

Other Measures	Standard Index S&P 500	Best Fit Index S&P 500
Alpha	0.0	0.0
Beta	1.00	1.00
R–Squared	100	100
Standard Deviation		16.88
Mean		–1.00
Sharpe Ratio		–0.41

Portfolio Analysis 09-30-01

Share change since 06-01 Total Stocks: 504	Sector	PE	YTD Ret%	% Assets
⊖ General Elec	Industrials	30.1	–15.00	3.84
⊖ Microsoft	Technology	57.6	52.78	3.32
⊕ ExxonMobil	Energy	15.3	–7.59	2.89
⊖ Pfizer	Health	34.7	–12.40	2.81
⊖ Wal–Mart Stores	Retail	40.3	8.94	2.44
⊖ Citigroup	Financials	20.0	0.03	2.43
⊕ American Intl Grp	Financials	42.0	–19.20	2.18
⊖ IBM	Technology	26.9	43.00	1.99
⊖ Johnson & Johnson	Health	16.6	14.01	1.86
⊖ Intel	Technology	73.1	4.89	1.74
⊖ Merck	Health	19.1	–35.90	1.55
⊖ AOL Time Warner	Technology	—	–7.76	1.47
⊖ Verizon Comms	Services	29.7	–2.52	1.43
⊖ SBC Comms	Services	18.4	–16.00	1.36
⊖ Cisco Sys	Technology	—	–52.60	1.31
⊖ Coca–Cola	Staples	35.5	–21.40	1.26
⊖ Royal Dutch Petro NY ADR	Energy	12.0	–17.10	1.15
⊖ Bristol–Myers Squibb	Health	20.2	–26.00	1.10
⊖ Philip Morris	Staples	12.1	9.12	1.09
⊖ Procter & Gamble	Staples	38.8	3.12	1.01
⊖ Tyco Intl	Industrials	27.1	6.23	1.01
⊖ Bank of America	Financials	16.7	42.73	1.00
⊕ ChevronTexaco	Energy	10.3	9.29	1.00
⊖ Home Depot	Retail	42.9	12.07	0.95
⊕ PepsiCo	Staples	31.4	–0.54	0.91

Current Investment Style

Style: Value Blnd Growth; Size: Large Med Small

	Stock Port Avg	Relative S&P 500 Current	Relative S&P 500 Hist	Rel Cat
Price/Earnings Ratio	30.4	0.98	0.99	1.00
Price/Book Ratio	5.7	1.00	0.99	1.04
Price/Cash Flow	17.7	0.98	0.99	0.96
3 Yr Earnings Growth	15.9	1.09	1.00	0.89
1 Yr Earnings Est%	–1.4	0.81	—	15.89
Med Mkt Cap $mil	63,187	1.0	1.0	1.21

Analysis by William Harding 10-30-01

Investing in Vanguard Tax-Managed Growth & Income is a no-brainer for those in taxable accounts.

Mega-cap stocks that dominate the S&P 500 index, which this fund tracks, have shown that they are not invincible to steep losses. To be sure, this fund has lost 17.5% for the year to date ended Oct. 29, 2001. Though poor on an absolute basis, that showing bests two thirds of funds in the large-blend category.

The fund's relative strength addresses a main point in the active versus passive management debate. Active management proponents surmise that active managers have the ability to hold cash in down markets, which should help stem losses. While that's true, some actively managed funds are more likely to invest in speculative stocks, and most hold more-concentrated portfolios. The S&P 500 index, meanwhile, is a fairly tame benchmark. The committee that picks stocks for the index shuns companies with limited operating histories. Further, the index is well diversified across industries and names. All told, the S&P 500 has been a tough bogy for actively managed large-cap funds to beat, and this fund's cost advantage has given it a big leg up on the competition. As a result, the fund's five-year trailing return lands in the category's top quartile.

Moreover, this fund does an outstanding job of meeting its goal of maximizing after-tax returns by minimizing distributions. The fund has yet to pay a capital gains distribution since its inception, and Vanguard has estimated it will not make one this year. Further, its tax-adjusted return for the trailing five years bests more than 90% of its large-blend peers and tops Vanguard 500 Index by a slight margin.

In short, this fund is a great core holding for a taxable portfolio.

Special Securities % assets 09-30-01	
Restricted/Illiquid Secs	0
Emerging–Markets Secs	0
Options/Futures/Warrants	No

Composition % assets 09-30-01	
Cash	0.1
Stocks*	99.9
Bonds	0.0
Other	0.0
*Foreign (% stocks)	2.0

Market Cap	
Giant	56.6
Large	32.1
Medium	11.0
Small	0.2
Micro	0.1

Sector Weightings	% of Stocks	Rel S&P	5-Year High	5-Year Low
Utilities	3.2	1.0	5	2
Energy	7.2	1.0	10	6
Financials	18.2	1.0	18	11
Industrials	11.3	1.0	18	10
Durables	1.5	1.0	5	1
Staples	7.8	1.0	12	5
Services	11.1	1.0	17	11
Retail	6.7	1.0	7	4
Health	14.7	1.0	15	9
Technology	18.2	1.0	33	9

Address:	Vanguard Financial Ctr. P.O. Box 2600 Valley Forge, PA 19482 800–662–7447 / 610–669–1000
Web Address:	www.vanguard.com
*Inception:	09-06-94
Advisor:	Vanguard Core Mgmt. Grp.
Subadvisor:	None
NTF Plans:	N/A

Minimum Purchase:	$10000	Add: $100 IRA: —
Min Auto Inv Plan:	$10000	Add: $50
Sales Fees:	No–load, 2.00%R within 12 months	
Management Fee:	.15%	
Actual Fees:	Mgt: 0.17%	Dist: —
Expense Projections:	3Yr: $176	5Yr: $107 10Yr: $243
Avg Brok Commission:	—	Income Distrib: Quarterly
Total Cost (relative to category):		Low

Vanguard Tax–Managed Small Cap Ret

Ticker	Load	NAV	Yield	Total Assets	Mstar Category
VTMSX	None	$14.92	0.6%	$621.7 mil	Small Blend

Prospectus Objective: Growth

Vanguard Tax-Managed Small Cap Fund seeks a tax-efficient total return.

The fund primarily invests in stocks in the Standard & Poor's SmallCap 600 index, in approximately the same proportions as they are represented in the index. It may invest in common stocks, futures contracts, options, warrants, convertible securities, and swap agreements.

The fund also offers Instl shares.

Historical Profile

Return —
Risk —
Rating Not Rated

Investment Style
Equity
Average Stock %: 99% (1999), 100% (2000), 100% (12-01)

▼ Manager Change
▽ Partial Manager Change

Fund Performance vs. Category Average
■ Quarterly Fund Return
+/– Category Average
— Category Baseline

Performance Quartile (within Category)

Portfolio Manager(s)

George U. Sauter. Since 3-99. AB'76 Dartmouth C.; MBA'80 U. of Chicago. Other funds currently managed: Vanguard Small Cap Index, Vanguard Balanced Index, Vanguard Equity-Income.

1990	1991	1992	1993	1994	1995	1996	1997	1998	1999	2000	12-01	History
—	—	—	—	—	—	—	—	—	12.61	14.23	14.92	NAV
—	—	—	—	—	—	—	—	—	26.28*	13.44	5.44	Total Return %
—	—	—	—	—	—	—	—	—	11.18*	22.54	17.32	+/– S&P 500
—	—	—	—	—	—	—	—	—	—	16.47	2.95	+/– Russell 2000
—	—	—	—	—	—	—	—	—	0.56	0.59	0.60	Income Return %
—	—	—	—	—	—	—	—	—	25.72	12.85	4.84	Capital Return %
—	—	—	—	—	—	—	—	—	—	45	59	Total Rtn % Rank Cat
—	—	—	—	—	—	—	—	—	0.05	0.07	0.09	Income $
—	—	—	—	—	—	—	—	—	0.00	0.00	0.00	Capital Gains $
—	—	—	—	—	—	—	—	—	0.19	0.20	—	Expense Ratio %
—	—	—	—	—	—	—	—	—	0.70	0.64	—	Income Ratio %
—	—	—	—	—	—	—	—	—	27	64	—	Turnover Rate %
—	—	—	—	—	—	—	—	—	194.2	400.6	568.5	Net Assets $mil

Performance 12-31-01

	1st Qtr	2nd Qtr	3rd Qtr	4th Qtr	Total
1997	—	—	—	—	—
1998	—	—	—	—	—
1999	—	15.94	–4.41	12.49	26.28 *
2000	6.26	1.19	4.79	0.66	13.44
2001	–7.38	13.58	–16.83	20.52	5.44

Trailing	Total Return%	+/– S&P 500	+/– Russ 2000	% Rank All	% Rank Cat	Growth of $10,000
3 Mo	20.52	9.83	–0.56	13	31	12,052
6 Mo	0.23	5.78	4.32	38	38	10,023
1 Yr	5.44	17.32	2.95	21	59	10,544
3 Yr Avg	—	—	—	—	—	—
5 Yr Avg	—	—	—	—	—	—
10 Yr Avg	—	—	—	—	—	—
15 Yr Avg	—	—	—	—	—	—

Tax Analysis	Tax-Adj Ret%	%Rank Cat	%Pretax Ret	%Rank Cat
3 Yr Avg	—	—	—	—
5 Yr Avg	—	—	—	—
10 Yr Avg	—	—	—	—

Potential Capital Gain Exposure: 20% of assets

Risk Analysis

Time Period	Load-Adj Return %	Risk %Rank[1] All	Risk %Rank[1] Cat	Morningstar Return	Morningstar Risk	Morningstar Risk-Adj Rating
1 Yr	3.33					
3 Yr	—	—	—	—	—	
5 Yr	—	—	—	—	—	
Incept	15.20	—	—	—	—	

Average Historical Rating —

[1]1=low, 100=high

Category Rating (3 Yr)

Return
Risk

Other Measures	Standard Index S&P 500	Best Fit Index
Alpha	—	—
Beta	—	—
R–Squared	—	—
Standard Deviation		—
Mean		—
Sharpe Ratio		—

Portfolio Analysis 09-30-01

Share change since 06-01 Total Stocks: 599	Sector	PE	YTD Ret%	% Assets
⊕ Cephalon	Health	—	19.38	1.02
⊕ Advance Paradigm	Health	43.2	29.01	0.83
⊕ Universal Health Svcs B	Health	12.7	–23.40	0.79
⊕ Commerce Bancorp NJ	Financials	27.5	17.01	0.77
⊕ Smithfield Foods	Staples	9.5	45.00	0.76
⊕ Varian Medical Sys	Technology	34.3	4.89	0.73
⊕ XTO Energy	N/A	—	—	0.72
⊕ Cerner	Services	—	7.96	0.61
⊕ Whole Foods Market	Retail	36.0	42.53	0.61
⊕ Alliant Techsystems	Industrials	28.6	73.48	0.60
⊕ 99 Cents Only Stores	Retail	43.8	108.70	0.60
⊕ ResMed	Health	NMF	35.22	0.57
⊕ Medicis Pharma Cl A	Health	38.0	9.24	0.57
⊕ Constellation Brands A	Staples	—	—	0.56
⊕ DR Horton	Industrials	9.7	48.67	0.55
⊕ Michaels Stores	Retail	29.3	148.60	0.54
⊕ Copart	Services	43.8	69.16	0.53
⊕ Newfield Explor	Energy	8.2	–25.10	0.51
⊕ Philadelphia Suburban	Utilities	25.3	17.88	0.50
⊕ Massey Energy Company	Industrials	—	63.97	0.50
⊕ Renal Care Grp	Health	22.8	17.13	0.49
⊕ Pogo Producing	Energy	11.7	–15.20	0.48
⊕ O'Reilly Automotive	Retail	33.8	36.34	0.48
⊕ Zebra Tech	Technology	27.0	36.12	0.48
⊕ OM Grp	Industrials	20.2	22.24	0.47

Current Investment Style

Style: Value Blnd Growth; Size: Large Med Small

	Stock Port Avg	Relative S&P 500 Current	Relative S&P 500 Hist	Rel Cat
Price/Earnings Ratio	25.5	0.83	—	1.03
Price/Book Ratio	3.4	0.59	—	1.05
Price/Cash Flow	16.6	0.92	—	1.06
3 Yr Earnings Growth	18.7	1.28	—	1.10
1 Yr Earnings Est%	2.3	—	—	2.62
Med Mkt Cap $mil	839	0.0	—	0.86

Analysis by William Harding 12-21-01

This fund fills its niche admirably.

When it comes to small-cap funds that take active steps to maximize after-tax performance, investors have few options. But Vanguard Tax-Managed Small Cap is a suitable pick to fill that role. Manager Gus Sauter attempts to match the key attributes of the S&P SmallCap 600 index. To limit capital-gains distributions, he'll sell stocks at a loss to offset gains and sell highest-cost shares first.

So far, the fund's pre-tax returns during its fairly brief life have been middling relative to its small-blend peers. But the fund's after-tax picture looks a bit brighter. The fund has yet to pay out a capital-gains distribution since inception, and its after-tax performance for the trailing 12 months bests roughly 60% of funds in the small-blend category.

To be sure, investors shouldn't expect knock-your-socks-off performance here, and it's likely the fund will trail its actively managed rivals on occasion. The case for passive management among small-cap stocks isn't as compelling as it is in the large-cap universe. One reason for that is active managers can hold on to their biggest winners a while longer than an index that jettisons stocks when they creep up in market cap. Further, it's arguably easier for active managers to unearth hidden gems among small-cap stocks that receive less attention from Wall Street.

So investors looking for a tax-efficient small-cap fund have a trade-off to consider. They can search among the category's better performers for a tax-efficient offering and take the risk that the fund may be less tax-efificent in the future. On the other hand, while this offering will rarely lead the pack, it offers low-cost and dedicated exposure to small caps and is managed specifically to limit taxable distributions.

Special Securities % assets 09-30-01	
Restricted/Illiquid Secs	0
Emerging-Markets Secs	0
Options/Futures/Warrants	No

Composition % assets 09-30-01	
Cash	0.1
Stocks*	99.9
Bonds	0.0
Other	0.0
*Foreign (% stocks)	0.1

Market Cap	
Giant	0.0
Large	0.0
Medium	20.6
Small	75.3
Micro	4.1

Sector Weightings	% of Stocks	Rel S&P	5-Year High	5-Year Low
Utilities	3.7	1.2	—	—
Energy	4.9	0.7	—	—
Financials	11.3	0.6	—	—
Industrials	20.0	1.7	—	—
Durables	4.1	2.6	—	—
Staples	4.4	0.6	—	—
Services	15.5	1.4	—	—
Retail	7.9	1.2	—	—
Health	12.8	0.9	—	—
Technology	15.5	0.8	—	—

Address:	Vanguard Financial Ctr. P.O. Box 2600 Valley Forge, PA 19482 800–662–7447
Web Address:	www.vanguard.com
*Inception:	03-25-99
Advisor:	Vanguard Grp.
Subadvisor:	None
NTF Plans:	N/A

Minimum Purchase:	$10000	Add: $100 IRA: —
Min Auto Inv Plan:	$10000	Add: $50
Sales Fees:	No-load, 2.00%R within 12 months	
Management Fee:	.16%	
Actual Fees:	Mgt: 0.16%	Dist: —
Expense Projections:	3Yr: $229	5Yr: $162 10Yr: $304
Avg Brok Commission:	—	Income Distrib: Annually
Total Cost (relative to category):	—	

Vanguard Total Bond Market Index

Ticker	Load	NAV	Yield	SEC Yield	Total Assets	Mstar Category
VBMFX	None	$10.15	6.2%	—	$21,759.5 mil	Interm-Term Bond

Prospectus Objective: Corp Bond—High Quality

Vanguard Total Bond Market Index Fund seeks to replicate the total return of the Lehman Brothers Aggregate Bond index.

The fund normally invests at least 80% of assets in securities listed on the index. It attempts to keep its portfolio weightings in line with the weightings of the index.

The fund offers Admiral, Investor and Institutional shares.

Historical Profile

Return Above Avg
Risk Average
Rating ★★★★ Above Avg

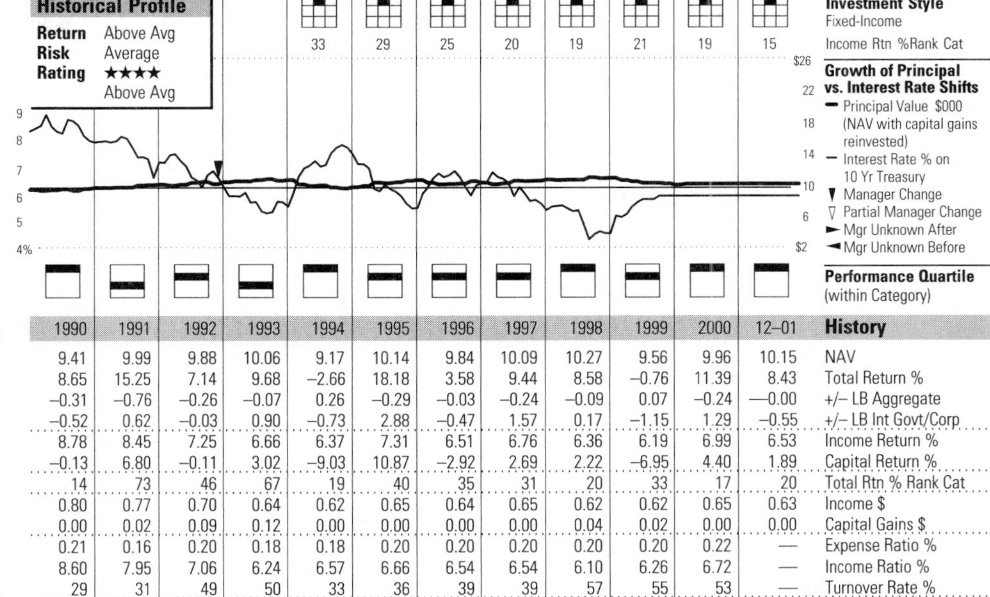

Portfolio Manager(s)

Kenneth Volpert, CFA. Since 12-92. BS'81 U. of Illinois; MBA'85 U. of Chicago. Other funds currently managed: Vanguard Interm-Term Bond Index, Vanguard Total Bond Market Index Inst, Vanguard Inflation-Protected Secs.

1990	1991	1992	1993	1994	1995	1996	1997	1998	1999	2000	12-01	History
9.41	9.99	9.88	10.06	9.17	10.14	9.84	10.09	10.27	9.56	9.96	10.15	NAV
8.65	15.25	7.14	9.68	−2.66	18.18	3.58	9.44	8.58	−0.76	11.39	8.43	Total Return %
−0.31	−0.76	−0.26	−0.07	0.26	−0.29	−0.03	−0.24	−0.09	0.07	−0.24	—0.00	+/– LB Aggregate
−0.52	0.62	−0.03	0.90	−0.73	2.88	−0.47	1.57	0.17	−1.15	1.29	−0.55	+/– LB Int Govt/Corp
8.78	8.45	7.25	6.66	6.37	7.31	6.51	6.76	6.36	6.19	6.99	6.53	Income Return %
−0.13	6.80	−0.11	3.02	−9.03	10.87	−2.92	2.69	2.22	−6.95	4.40	1.89	Capital Return %
14	73	46	67	19	40	35	31	20	33	17	20	Total Rtn % Rank Cat
0.80	0.77	0.70	0.64	0.62	0.65	0.64	0.65	0.62	0.62	0.65	0.63	Income $
0.00	0.02	0.09	0.12	0.00	0.00	0.00	0.00	0.04	0.02	0.00	0.00	Capital Gains $
0.21	0.16	0.20	0.18	0.18	0.20	0.20	0.20	0.20	0.20	0.22	—	Expense Ratio %
8.60	7.95	7.06	6.24	6.57	6.66	6.54	6.54	6.10	6.26	6.72	—	Income Ratio %
29	31	49	50	33	36	39	39	57	55	53	—	Turnover Rate %
276.7	848.8	1,059.9	1,540.2	1,730.7	2,405.0	2,952.8	5,010.0	7,764.6	9,477.2	11,642.8	14,115.7	Net Assets $mil

Performance 12-31-01

	1st Qtr	2nd Qtr	3rd Qtr	4th Qtr	Total
1997	−0.62	3.56	3.40	2.83	9.44
1998	1.55	2.36	4.13	0.31	8.58
1999	−0.43	−0.98	0.79	−0.13	−0.76
2000	2.42	1.48	3.07	3.98	11.39
2001	3.24	0.79	4.29	−0.08	8.43

Trailing	Total Return%	+/– LB Agg	+/– LB ITGvt/Corp	% Rank All	% Rank Cat	Growth of $10,000
3 Mo	−0.08	−0.12	−0.17	79	48	9,992
6 Mo	4.20	−0.45	−0.50	7	43	10,420
1 Yr	8.43	0.00	−0.55	8	20	10,843
3 Yr Avg	6.23	−0.05	−0.17	21	16	11,986
5 Yr Avg	7.33	−0.10	0.24	33	10	14,244
10 Yr Avg	7.15	−0.08	0.34	49	25	19,946
15 Yr Avg	7.82	−0.30	0.18	55	29	30,939

Tax Analysis	Tax-Adj Ret%	%Rank Cat	%Pretax Ret	%Rank Cat
3 Yr Avg	3.58	18	57.4	30
5 Yr Avg	4.65	9	63.4	22
10 Yr Avg	4.42	19	61.9	21

Potential Capital Gain Exposure: 2% of assets

Risk Analysis

Time Period	Load-Adj Return %	Risk %Rank[1] All	Risk %Rank[1] Cat	Morningstar Return	Morningstar Risk	Morningstar Risk-Adj Rating
1 Yr	8.43					
3 Yr	6.23	11	20	0.28[2]	0.61	★★★★
5 Yr	7.33	15	16	0.53[2]	0.62	★★★★
10 Yr	7.15	20	20	0.69[2]	0.84	★★★★

Average Historical Rating (145 months): 4.0★s

[1]1=low, 100=high [2] T-Bill return substituted for category avg.

Category Rating (3 Yr)

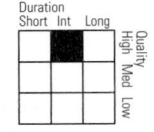

1 2 3 4 5
Worst Best

Return Above Avg
Risk Below Avg

Other Measures	Standard Index LB Agg	Best Fit Index LB Agg
Alpha	0.0	0.0
Beta	0.99	0.99
R-Squared	99	99
Standard Deviation		3.53
Mean		6.23
Sharpe Ratio		0.43

Portfolio Analysis 03-31-01

Total Fixed-Income: 4787	Date of Maturity	Amount $000	Value $000	% Net Assets
FHLMC 6.5%	08-01-29	337,610	337,461	1.93
FNMA 7.5%	12-01-30	263,248	269,139	1.54
US Treasury Bond 6.625%	02-15-27	229,140	259,515	1.48
US Treasury Bond 10.375%	11-15-09	202,850	240,393	1.37
US Treasury Bond 8.125%	08-15-21	183,175	238,824	1.37
US Treasury Bond 10.75%	02-15-03	180,925	201,634	1.15
FHLMC 6%	12-01-29	203,575	199,288	1.14
US Treasury Bond 7.625%	11-15-22	158,675	198,201	1.13
US Treasury Bond 8.125%	08-15-19	150,195	193,842	1.11
FHLMC 6.5%	12-01-28	188,163	188,389	1.08
US Treasury Bond 6.75%	08-15-26	157,575	181,085	1.04
FNMA 6.5%	12-01-29	177,642	177,423	1.01
FHLMC Debenture 7%	07-15-05	165,000	176,344	1.01
GNMA 6.5%	08-15-29	169,162	169,436	0.97
US Treasury Note 6.625%	04-30-02	154,450	158,390	0.91
US Treasury Note 5.5%	02-15-08	148,385	153,825	0.88
FHLMC 7%	12-01-28	136,765	138,938	0.79
US Treasury Note 6.625%	05-15-07	123,525	135,327	0.77
FNMA 8%	12-01-30	129,663	133,779	0.76
FHLMC 7%	10-01-29	130,751	132,573	0.76

Current Investment Style

Duration: Short Int Long — Quality: High Med Low

Avg Eff Duration[1]	4.8 Yrs
Avg Eff Maturity	—
Avg Credit Quality	AA
Avg Wtd Coupon	7.32%
Avg Wtd Price	105.17% of par

[1]figure provided by fund

Special Securities % assets 03-31-01	
Restricted/Illiquid Secs	2
Exotic Mortgage-Backed	0
Emerging-Markets Secs	1
Options/Futures/Warrants	Yes

Coupon Range	% of Bonds	Rel Cat
0%	0.00	0.00
0% to 7%	41.61	0.77
7% to 8.5%	45.93	1.32
8.5% to 10%	7.02	0.98
More than 10%	5.43	2.00

1.00=Category Average

Credit Analysis % bonds 09-30-01			
US Govt	60	BB	1
AAA	3	B	0
AA	5	Below B	0
A	14	NR/NA	0
BBB	18		

Composition % assets 03-31-01			
Cash	3.8	Bonds	96.2
Stocks	0.0	Other	0.0

Sector Breakdown % bonds 03-31-01			
US Treasuries	14	CMOs	0
GNMA mtgs	9	ARMs	0
FNMA mtgs	14	Other	39
FHLMC mtgs	20		

Analysis by Alan Papier 11-30-01

Vanguard Total Bond Market Index Fund makes a compelling case for fixed-income indexing.

Within the context of large-cap equity investing, there is a solid body of evidence suggesting that active investment managers can't consistently add value relative to passive, or indexed, strategies. In the bond world, this fund is proving much the same thing.

The fund seeks to replicate the returns of the Lehman Brothers Aggregate index, which is a widely diversified, commonly used proxy for the U.S. dollar-denominated, investment-grade bond market. But it is nearly impossible, not to mention excessively expensive, to fully replicate the index given the number of securities it holds—nearly 6,700—and the illiquidity of many old, higher-coupon issues. So manager Ken Volpert constructs the fund to match the cash-flow characteristics of the index, but varies its sector weightings to capture incrementally higher income streams. Thus, the portfolio's duration and yield-curve positioning, and therefore its interest-rate sensitivity, are the same as the index's, but it tends to underweight U.S. Treasuries in favor of short-term corporate bonds.

Over time, that strategy has allowed the fund to recover some of the ground it loses to the index vis-a-vis its expense ratio. For the 10-year period ended Oct. 31, 2001, the fund's annualized gain was 7.76%—just 10 basis points behind its bogy.

That long-term performance places the fund in select company in the intermediate-term bond category. As of Nov. 29, 2001, the fund's one-, three-, five-, and 10-year annualized returns were higher than at least 70% of its peers'. What's more, it has done so with below-average volatility. The fund's demonstrated ability to outperform the majority of its peers makes it an excellent choice as a core bond holding.

Address:	Vanguard Financial Ctr. P.O. Box 2600 Valley Forge, PA 19482 800-662-7447 / 610-669-1000
Web Address:	www.vanguard.com
Inception:	12-11-86
Advisor:	Vanguard Fixed-Income Grp.
Subadvisor:	None
NTF Plans:	N/A

Minimum Purchase:	$3000	Add: $100	IRA: $1000
Min Auto Inv Plan:	$3000	Add: $50	
Sales Fees:	No-load		
Management Fee:	.17%		
Actual Fees:	Mgt: 0.19%	Dist: —	
Expense Projections:	3Yr: $71	5Yr: $124	10Yr: $280
Avg Brok Commission:	—	Income Distrib: Monthly	
Total Cost (relative to category):		Low	

Vanguard Total Intl Stock Index

Ticker	Load	NAV	Yield	Total Assets	Mstar Category
VGTSX	None	$9.28	1.8%	$2,899.8 mil	Foreign Stock

Prospectus Objective: Foreign Stock

Vanguard Total International Stock Index Fund seeks to match the performance of the MSCI—EAFE + Select EMF index.

The fund invests substantially all assets in a combination of the European, Pacific, and Emerging Markets Portfolios, based on each market segment's contribution to the market capitalization of the index. Currently, the European and Pacific markets each contribute 45% and the Emerging Markets adds 10% to the index's market cap. Each underlying fund invests at least 80% of assets in stocks included in its respective index.

Past name: Vanguard Star Fund Total International Portfolio.

Historical Profile

Return: Average
Risk: Average
Rating: ★★★ Neutral

Investment Style
Equity
Average Stock %: 97% (1999), 49% (2000), 97% (12-01)

▼ Manager Change
▽ Partial Manager Change

Fund Performance vs. Category Average
Quarterly Fund Return +/– Category Average
— Category Baseline

Performance Quartile (within Category)

Portfolio Manager(s)

George U. Sauter. Since 4-96. AB'76 Dartmouth C.; MBA'80 U. of Chicago. Other funds currently managed: Vanguard Small Cap Index, Vanguard Balanced Index, Vanguard Equity-Income.

1990	1991	1992	1993	1994	1995	1996	1997	1998	1999	2000	12-01	History
—	—	—	—	—	—	10.14	9.87	11.19	14.31	11.83	9.28	NAV
—	—	—	—	—	—	0.55*	–0.78	15.60	29.92	–15.61	–20.15	Total Return %
—	—	—	—	—	—	–14.59*	–34.13	–12.97	8.88	–6.51	–8.28	+/– S&P 500
—	—	—	—	—	—	—	–2.55	–4.39	2.96	–1.45	—	+/– MSCI EAFE
—	—	—	—	—	—	1.58	1.68	2.13	1.88	1.40	1.39	Income Return %
—	—	—	—	—	—	–1.02	–2.45	13.48	28.04	–17.02	–21.55	Capital Return %
—	—	—	—	—	—	—	85	35	68	46	36	Total Rtn % Rank Cat
—	—	—	—	—	—	0.16	0.17	0.21	0.21	0.20	0.17	Income $
—	—	—	—	—	—	0.02	0.02	0.01	0.01	0.05	0.00	Capital Gains $
—	—	—	—	—	—	0.00	0.00	0.00	0.00	0.00	—	Expense Ratio %
—	—	—	—	—	—	1.51	2.19	2.18	2.04	1.68	—	Income Ratio %
—	—	—	—	—	—	—	6	2	1	3	—	Turnover Rate %
—	—	—	—	—	—	280.4	969.4	2,445.4	2,569.6	3,003.1	2,899.8	Net Assets $mil

Performance 12-31-01

	1st Qtr	2nd Qtr	3rd Qtr	4th Qtr	Total
1997	–0.69	12.51	–2.03	–9.36	–0.78
1998	13.68	–1.25	–14.53	20.49	15.60
1999	2.06	4.21	3.45	18.09	29.92
2000	–0.21	–4.00	–8.34	–3.89	–15.61
2001	–13.27	0.10	–14.90	8.08	–20.15

Trailing	Total Return%	+/– S&P 500	+/– MSCI EAFE	% Rank All	% Rank Cat	Growth of $10,000
3 Mo	8.08	–2.61	—	51	50	10,808
6 Mo	–8.02	–2.47	—	78	38	9,198
1 Yr	–20.15	–8.28	—	81	36	7,985
3 Yr Avg	–4.34	–3.31	—	90	64	8,754
5 Yr Avg	0.08	–10.62	—	92	73	10,041
10 Yr Avg	—	—	—	—	—	—
15 Yr Avg	—	—	—	—	—	—

Tax Analysis	Tax-Adj Ret%	%Rank Cat	%Pretax Ret	%Rank Cat
3 Yr Avg	–4.99	58	—	—
5 Yr Avg	–0.63	63	—	—
10 Yr Avg	—	—	—	—

Potential Capital Gain Exposure: –22% of assets

Risk Analysis

Time Period	Load-Adj Return %	Risk %Rank[1] All	Risk %Rank[1] Cat	Morningstar Return	Morningstar Risk	Morningstar Risk-Adj Rating
1 Yr	–20.15					
3 Yr	–4.34	69	40	–1.80[2]	0.89	★★
5 Yr	0.08	73	47	–0.99[2]	0.83	★★★
Incept	0.17	—	—	—	—	

Average Historical Rating (33 months): 3.0★s

[1]1=low, 100=high [2] T-Bill return substituted for category avg.

Category Rating (3 Yr)

1 2 **3** 4 5
Worst — Best

Return: Average
Risk: Average

Other Measures	Standard Index S&P 500	Best Fit Index MSCIWsxUSN
Alpha	–4.4	0.6
Beta	0.78	1.04
R-Squared	66	99

Standard Deviation	15.69
Mean	–4.34
Sharpe Ratio	–0.69

Portfolio Analysis 09-30-01

Share change since 06-01 Total Stocks: 3	Sector	Country	% Assets
⊕ Vanguard European Stock Index	N/A	N/A	66.27
⊕ Vanguard Pacific Stock Index	N/A	N/A	26.63
⊕ Vanguard Emerging Mkts Stock Idx	N/A	N/A	10.57

Analysis by Gabriel Presler 12-11-01

It's worth it to look beyond Vanguard Total International Stock Index Fund's short record and unexciting relative returns.

This fund of funds isn't a category killer. In jittery markets, its indexed approach keeps it in the middle third of the foreign-stock group, thanks to its broadly diversified portfolio. But its lack of flexibility renders it unable to sidestep troubled countries and industries—particularly in Japan, which plays a huge part in the index. Thus, its returns have been respectable, not impressive: It posted a decent gain in 1999, for example, but lagged its peers. In 2001's nasty market, the fund has held up relatively well. Its 20% loss for the year through Dec. 10, 2001, is a bit better than average.

Despite this innocuous performance, the fund has some solid attractions. First, like most Vanguard funds, it features rock-bottom expenses. What's more, despite its slight growth bias, it has been less volatile than most of its rivals over the last three years.

More significant, though, are the changes being made to the fund's underlying indices, the MSCI European, Pacific, and Emerging Market benchmarks. Companies in these indices will no longer be weighted based on market cap. Instead, allocation decisions will be made according to how many of a firm's shares are available on the market. Thus, Gus Sauter will pare the fund's stake in volatile Japan, where cross-holding is common, while increasing its exposure to Europe.

This change is likely to benefit investors: The fund's huge Japan exposure has generally dragged on returns, and the fund will likely start to look a bit more like its peers. These changes, combined with its diverse portfolio, low expenses, and low volatility, make the fund a decent choice for cautious investors.

Current Investment Style	Stock Port Avg	Rel MSCI EAFE Current	Rel MSCI EAFE Hist	Rel Cat
Price/Earnings Ratio	22.7	0.88	—	0.89
Price/Cash Flow	13.2	1.03	—	0.92
Price/Book Ratio	3.5	0.99	—	0.88
3 Yr Earnings Growth	20.3	1.09	—	1.04
Med Mkt Cap $mil	38,724	1.4	—	2.15

Style: Value Blnd Growth; Size: Large Med Small

Country Exposure % assets

Hedging History: —

Regional Exposure 09-30-01	% assets
Europe	67
Pacific Rim	9
Latin America	3
Japan	20
Other	1

Special Securities % assets

Restricted/Illiquid Secs
Emerging–Markets Secs
Options/Futures/Warrants

Composition % assets 09-30-01

Cash	1.3	Bonds	0.1
Stocks	98.3	Other	0.3

Sector Weightings	% of Stocks	Rel Cat	5-Year High	5-Year Low
Utilities	4.4	1.6	—	—
Energy	7.4	1.3	—	—
Financials	23.3	1.1	—	—
Industrials	12.2	0.9	—	—
Durables	7.1	1.0	—	—
Staples	6.6	0.9	—	—
Services	15.5	0.9	—	—
Retail	4.3	0.9	—	—
Health	7.9	0.8	—	—
Technology	11.4	1.1	—	—

Address:	Vanguard Financial Ctr. P.O. Box 2600 Valley Forge, PA 19482 800–662–7447 / 610–669–1000
Web Address:	www.vanguard.com
*Inception:	04-29-96
Advisor:	Vanguard Core Mgmt. Grp.
Subadvisor:	None
NTF Plans:	N/A

Minimum Purchase:	$3000	Add: $100	IRA: $1000
Min Auto Inv Plan:	$3000	Add: $100	
Sales Fees:	No-load		
Management Fee:	None		
Actual Fees:	Mgt: 0.00%	Dist: —	
Expense Projections:	3Yr: $109	5Yr: $191	10Yr: $431
Avg Brok Commission:	—	Income Distrib: Annually	
Total Cost (relative to category):	Low		

Vanguard Total Stock Mkt Idx

Ticker	Load	NAV	Yield	Total Assets	Mstar Category
VTSMX	None	$25.74	1.2%	$25,440.3 mil	Large Blend

Prospectus Objective: Growth and Income

Vanguard Total Stock Market Index Fund seeks to replicate the aggregate price and yield of the Wilshire 5000 Total Market Index.

The fund employs a passive management strategy designed to track the performance of the Wilshire 5000 Index, which consists of all the U.S. common stocks traded regularly on the NYSE, AMEX, or OTC markets. It invests all or substantially all of its assets in a representative sample of the stocks that make up the index.

The fund currently offers Institutional and Admiral shares.The fund also offers Ins, Instpls shares. Prior to Oct. 27, 1998, the fund was named Vanguard Index Trust Total Stock Market Portfolio.

Historical Profile
Return Average
Risk Average
Rating ★★★ Neutral

Investment Style
Equity
Average Stock %

	1994	1995	1996	1997	1998	1999	2000	12-01
Average Stock %		97%	97%	95%	95%	98%	98%	100%

▼ Manager Change
▽ Partial Manager Change

Fund Performance vs. Category Average
■ Quarterly Fund Return +/– Category Average
— Category Baseline

Performance Quartile (within Category)

Portfolio Manager(s)

George U. Sauter. Since 4-92. AB'76 Dartmouth C.; MBA'80 U. of Chicago. Other funds currently managed: Vanguard Small Cap Index, Vanguard Balanced Index, Vanguard Equity-Income.

History

1990	1991	1992	1993	1994	1995	1996	1997	1998	1999	2000	12-01	History
—	—	10.84	11.69	11.37	15.04	17.77	22.64	27.42	33.22	29.26	25.74	NAV
—	—	10.41*	10.62	–0.17	35.79	20.96	30.99	23.26	23.81	–10.58	–10.97	Total Return %
—	—	1.29*	0.57	–1.48	–1.75	–1.98	–2.36	–5.31	2.78	–1.47	0.91	+/– S&P 500
—	—	—	0.79	–0.62	–1.82	–1.20	–2.03	–5.37	1.99	0.38	1.80	+/– Wilshire Top 750
—	—	2.33	2.42	2.33	2.48	1.94	1.83	1.46	1.21	1.02	1.02	Income Return %
—	—	8.08	8.20	–2.50	33.30	19.02	29.17	21.80	22.60	–11.59	–11.99	Capital Return %
—	—	—	42	48	32	55	38	54	30	75	25	Total Rtn % Rank Cat
—	—	0.23	0.26	0.27	0.28	0.29	0.32	0.33	0.33	0.34	0.30	Income $
—	—	0.00	0.03	0.03	0.09	0.11	0.27	0.13	0.32	0.14	0.00	Capital Gains $
—	—	0.21	0.20	0.20	0.25	0.22	0.20	0.20	0.20	0.20	—	Expense Ratio %
—	—	2.42	2.31	2.35	2.14	1.86	1.65	1.44	1.15	1.04	—	Income Ratio %
—	—	—	1	2	3	3	2	3	3	7	—	Turnover Rate %
—	—	275.4	512.3	785.7	1,570.9	3,530.9	5,092.7	9,307.8	18,133.1	17,531.6	15,781.5	Net Assets $mil

Performance 12-31-01

	1st Qtr	2nd Qtr	3rd Qtr	4th Qtr	Total
1997	0.65	16.81	9.75	1.52	30.99
1998	13.28	1.84	–12.07	21.51	23.26
1999	3.71	7.88	–6.42	18.26	23.81
2000	3.84	–4.39	0.27	–10.17	–10.58
2001	–12.27	7.47	–15.93	12.32	–10.97

Trailing	Total Return%	+/– S&P 500	+/– Wil Top 750	% Rank All	% Rank Cat	Growth of $10,000
3 Mo	12.32	1.63	0.99	32	26	11,232
6 Mo	–5.57	–0.02	0.22	65	35	9,443
1 Yr	–10.97	0.91	1.80	62	25	8,903
3 Yr Avg	–0.48	0.55	1.35	75	41	9,858
5 Yr Avg	9.74	–0.96	–0.38	20	45	15,917
10 Yr Avg	—	—	—	—	—	—
15 Yr Avg	—	—	—	—	—	—

Tax Analysis	Tax-Adj Ret%	%Rank Cat	%Pretax Ret	%Rank Cat
3 Yr Avg	–1.05	33	—	—
5 Yr Avg	8.99	29	92.3	16
10 Yr Avg	—	—	—	—

Potential Capital Gain Exposure: 5% of assets

Risk Analysis

Time Period	Load-Adj Return %	Risk %Rank[1] All	Risk %Rank[1] Cat	Morningstar Return	Morningstar Risk	Morningstar Risk-Adj Rating
1 Yr	–10.97					
3 Yr	–0.48	71	64	–1.09[2]	0.97	★★★
5 Yr	9.74	70	64	1.13[2]	0.95	★★★
Incept	12.72	—	—	—	—	

Average Historical Rating (81 months): 3.9★s

[1] 1=low, 100=high [2] T–Bill return substituted for category avg.

Category Rating (3 Yr)

1 2 3 4 5
Worst Best

Return Average
Risk Average

Other Measures	Standard Index S&P 500	Best Fit Index S&P 500
Alpha	0.8	0.8
Beta	1.01	1.01
R–Squared	93	93
Standard Deviation		17.87
Mean		–0.48
Sharpe Ratio		–0.35

Analysis by Scott Cooley 10-23-01

Despite its recent travails, it's still pretty easy to make a strong case for Vanguard Total Stock Market Index Fund.

Nearly all large-blend funds have fallen on hard times over the past couple of months, but this one has tumbled more than most. In the wake of the Sept. 11 terrorist attacks, there was a flight to quality in the stock market, with giant-cap issues handily outperforming smaller fare. Indeed, the S&P 500 fell "just" 8.1% during the month, while the Wilshire 4500, which includes all publicly traded stocks not in the S&P 500, declined 12.9%. With considerable exposure to the Wilshire 4500's mostly small- and mid-cap issues, this fund took a tumble during the month. And for the trailing three months through Oct. 22, 2001, the fund lags nearly two thirds of its peers.

Still, one should not overlook this fund's considerable advantages. Thanks to its paltry expense ratio, the fund's annualized return since its April 1992 inception beats its average rival's by nearly a percentage point. The fund's buy-and-hold strategy has proven tax-efficient over time. And because the fund has experienced limited net redemptions in a down market, manager Gus Sauter has booked some tax-loss carryforwards. As a result, the fund will not make a capital-gains distribution in 2001, and may not for some time thereafter.

Moreover, the fund has actually put up decent numbers on a year-to-date basis. While the portfolio's smaller-cap holdings have hurt it recently, they gave the fund a boost early in the year, when giant caps fell especially hard. Thus, for the year to date through Oct. 22, 2001, the fund's 16.7% loss is better than two thirds of its peers' returns.

Over the years, the fund has proven itself an outstanding core holding, especially for those in taxable accounts. We heartily recommend it to investors.

Portfolio Analysis 06-30-01

Share change since 03–01 Total Stocks: 3437	Sector	PE	YTD Ret%	% Assets
⊕ General Elec	Industrials	30.1	–15.00	3.57
⊕ Microsoft	Technology	57.6	52.78	2.90
⊕ ExxonMobil	Energy	15.3	–7.59	2.23
⊕ Citigroup	Financials	20.0	0.03	1.96
⊕ Pfizer	Health	34.7	–12.40	1.86
⊕ AOL Time Warner	Technology	—	–7.76	1.73
⊕ Wal–Mart Stores	Retail	40.3	8.94	1.61
⊕ American Intl Grp	Financials	42.0	–19.20	1.48
⊕ IBM	Technology	26.9	43.00	1.46
⊕ Intel	Technology	73.1	4.89	1.45
⊕ Johnson & Johnson	Health	16.6	14.01	1.12
⊕ Merck	Health	19.1	–35.90	1.08
⊕ Verizon Comms	Services	29.7	–2.52	1.07
⊕ SBC Comms	Services	18.4	–16.00	1.00
⊕ Cisco Sys	Technology	—	–52.60	0.98
⊕ Philip Morris	Staples	12.1	9.12	0.83
⊕ Coca–Cola	Staples	35.5	–21.40	0.83
⊕ Home Depot	Retail	42.9	12.07	0.80
⊕ Oracle	Technology	32.1	–52.40	0.79
⊕ Berkshire Hathaway Cl A	Financials	—	—	0.77
⊕ Bristol–Myers Squibb	Health	20.2	–26.00	0.75
⊕ Bank of America	Financials	16.7	42.73	0.72
⊕ Viacom Cl B	Services	—	—	0.68
⊕ J.P. Morgan Chase & Co.	Financials	27.8	–17.40	0.65
⊕ Fannie Mae	Financials	16.2	–6.95	0.63

Current Investment Style

Style: Value Blnd Growth; Size: Large Med Small

	Stock Port Avg	Relative S&P 500 Current	Relative S&P 500 Hist	Rel Cat
Price/Earnings Ratio	30.3	0.98	0.97	1.00
Price/Book Ratio	5.2	0.91	0.96	0.94
Price/Cash Flow	17.8	0.99	0.99	0.97
3 Yr Earnings Growth	15.8	1.08	1.02	0.89
1 Yr Earnings Est%	–1.9	1.08	—	21.22
Med Mkt Cap $mil	32,817	0.5	0.6	0.63

Special Securities % assets 06-30-01	
Restricted/Illiquid Secs	0
Emerging–Markets Secs	0
Options/Futures/Warrants	No

Composition % assets 06-30-01	
Cash	0.4
Stocks*	99.7
Bonds	0.0
Other	0.0
*Foreign (% stocks)	0.0

Market Cap	
Giant	43.5
Large	28.0
Medium	19.2
Small	7.3
Micro	2.0

Sector Weightings	% of Stocks	Rel S&P	5-Year High	5-Year Low
Utilities	3.2	1.0	7	2
Energy	5.8	0.8	9	4
Financials	19.8	1.1	20	12
Industrials	10.5	0.9	17	9
Durables	1.9	1.2	5	1
Staples	5.7	0.7	12	4
Services	13.4	1.2	17	13
Retail	6.1	0.9	8	5
Health	12.8	0.9	14	9
Technology	20.9	1.1	35	7

Address:	Vanguard Financial Ctr. P.O. Box 2600 Valley Forge, PA 19482 800–662–7447 / 610–669–1000
Web Address:	www.vanguard.com
*Inception:	04-27-92
Advisor:	Vanguard Core Mgmt. Grp.
Subadvisor:	None
NTF Plans:	N/A

Minimum Purchase:	$3000	Add: $100	IRA: $1000
Min Auto Inv Plan:	$3000	Add: $50	
Sales Fees:	No–load		
Management Fee:	.18%		
Actual Fees:	Mgt: 0.13%	Dist: —	
Expense Projections:	3Yr: $64	5Yr: $113	10Yr: $255
Avg Brok Commission:	—	Income Distrib: Quarterly	
Total Cost (relative to category):		Low	

Vanguard U.S. Growth

Ticker	Load	NAV	Yield	Total Assets	Mstar Category
VWUSX	None	$18.85	0.2%	$10,028.3 mil	Large Growth

Prospectus Objective: Growth

Vanguard U.S. Growth Fund seeks long-term growth of capital.

The fund invests primarily in common stocks and convertible securities issued by established U.S. companies. In selecting investments, the advisor emphasizes companies that it believes to have exceptional growth records, strong market positions, reasonable financial strength, and relatively low sensitivity to changing economic conditions.

The fund also offers Adm shares. On Sept. 30, 1985, the Ivest Fund divided into this fund and Vanguard World International Growth Fund. May 3, 1993, the fund was named Vanguard World Fund U.S. Growth Portfolio.

Historical Profile

Return Below Avg
Risk Above Avg
Rating ★★ Below Avg

Investment Style
Equity
Average Stock %: 95% 97% 96% 98% 98% 96%

▼ Manager Change
▽ Partial Manager Change

Fund Performance vs. Category Average
■ Quarterly Fund Return
+/– Category Average
— Category Baseline

Performance Quartile (within Category)

Portfolio Manager(s)

Christopher Toub. Since 6-01. Other funds currently managed: HSBC Investor Equity A, HSBC Investor Equity Y, HSBC Investor Equity B.

John L. Blundin. Since 6-01. Other funds currently managed: Alliance A, Alliance B, Alliance C.

History

1990	1991	1992	1993	1994	1995	1996	1997	1998	1999	2000	12-01	History
10.49	15.20	15.36	14.93	15.33	20.35	23.74	28.70	37.49	43.53	27.65	18.85	NAV
4.60	46.76	2.76	–1.45	3.88	38.44	26.05	25.93	39.98	22.28	–20.17	–31.70	Total Return %
7.72	16.27	–4.86	–11.50	2.57	0.91	3.10	–7.42	11.41	1.24	–11.06	–19.82	+/– S&P 500
3.24	7.35	–1.14	–1.37	–0.97	–0.21	0.53	–7.81	–5.12	–7.40	4.36	–11.20	+/– Russ Top 200 Grt
1.86	1.81	1.18	1.37	1.21	1.89	1.28	1.14	0.66	0.56	0.11	0.13	Income Return %
2.74	44.94	1.57	–2.81	2.68	36.55	24.77	24.79	39.32	21.72	–20.28	–31.83	Capital Return %
7	36	77	97	8	16	7	50	23	85	74	83	Total Rtn % Rank Cat
0.19	0.19	0.18	0.21	0.18	0.29	0.26	0.27	0.19	0.21	0.05	0.04	Income $
0.00	0.00	0.08	0.00	0.00	0.57	1.62	0.89	2.31	2.02	7.45	0.00	Capital Gains $
0.74	0.56	0.49	0.49	0.52	0.44	0.43	0.42	0.41	0.39	0.36	0.44	Expense Ratio %
1.77	1.82	1.52	1.50	1.30	1.59	1.32	1.13	0.69	0.59	0.24	0.13	Income Ratio %
49	30	24	37	47	32	44	35	48	49	76	135	Turnover Rate %
355.9	978.1	1,813.9	1,847.2	2,109.3	3,624.1	5,532.0	8,054.6	13,623.6	19,068.0	16,831.4	9,180.0	Net Assets $mil

Performance 12-31-01

	1st Qtr	2nd Qtr	3rd Qtr	4th Qtr	Total
1997	0.59	16.71	3.12	4.02	25.93
1998	15.51	7.27	–9.42	24.73	39.98
1999	3.81	2.95	–4.79	20.16	22.28
2000	5.17	0.15	1.03	–24.97	–20.17
2001	–31.03	7.45	–23.04	19.76	–31.70

Trailing	Total Return%	+/– S&P 500	+/– Russ Top 200 Grth	% Rank All	% Rank Cat	Growth of $10,000
3 Mo	19.76	9.07	6.90	14	15	11,976
6 Mo	–7.83	–2.28	–0.84	77	40	9,217
1 Yr	–31.70	–19.82	–11.20	95	83	6,830
3 Yr Avg	–12.64	–11.61	–4.62	99	95	6,668
5 Yr Avg	3.28	–7.42	–5.31	84	86	11,753
10 Yr Avg	7.99	–4.93	–3.09	43	82	21,577
15 Yr Avg	10.80	–2.93	–2.57	36	75	46,593

Tax Analysis	Tax-Adj Ret%	%Rank Cat	%Pretax Ret	%Rank Cat
3 Yr Avg	–14.19	95	—	—
5 Yr Avg	1.63	82	49.5	88
10 Yr Avg	6.56	72	82.1	35

Potential Capital Gain Exposure: –55% of assets

Risk Analysis

Time Period	Load-Adj Return %	Risk %Rank[1] All	Risk %Rank[1] Cat	Morningstar Return	Morningstar Risk	Morningstar Risk-Adj Rating
1 Yr	–31.70					
3 Yr	–12.64	94	83	–3.14[2]	1.60	★
5 Yr	3.28	87	71	–0.37[2]	1.36	★
10 Yr	7.99	87	52	0.41	1.25	★★

Average Historical Rating (193 months): 3.4★s

[1]1=low, 100=high [2] T-Bill return substituted for category avg.

Category Rating (3 Yr)

1 2 3 4 5
Worst Best

Return Low
Risk Above Avg

Other Measures	Standard Index S&P 500	Best Fit Index S&P 500
Alpha	–6.8	–6.8
Beta	1.57	1.57
R-Squared	85	85

Standard Deviation	26.70
Mean	–12.64
Sharpe Ratio	–0.78

Portfolio Analysis 09-30-01

Share change since 06-01 Total Stocks: 51	Sector	PE	YTD Ret%	% Assets
⊕ General Elec	Industrials	30.1	–15.00	7.35
⊖ Pfizer	Health	34.7	–12.40	7.32
⊕ Citigroup	Financials	20.0	0.03	5.28
Tyco Intl	Industrials	27.1	6.23	5.00
⊕ Microsoft	Technology	57.6	52.78	4.94
⊖ American Intl Grp	Financials	42.0	–19.20	4.93
⊕ AOL Time Warner	Technology	—	–7.76	4.46
⊕ Home Depot	Retail	42.9	12.07	3.77
⊖ Johnson & Johnson	Health	16.6	14.01	3.50
⊕ AT & T Liberty Media Cl A	Services	—	3.22	3.25
⊕ Cardinal Health	Health	35.1	–2.51	2.97
⊕ Nokia Cl A ADR	Technology	45.8	–43.00	2.95
⊕ AT&T Wireless Grp	Services	—	–17.00	2.91
⊕ Cisco Sys	Technology	—	–52.60	2.71
⊖ Schering-Plough	Health	22.2	–35.90	2.48
⊖ Comcast	Services	20.3	–13.70	2.36
⊕ Kohl's	Retail	54.2	15.48	2.29
⊕ J.P. Morgan Chase & Co.	Financials	27.8	–17.40	2.14
⊕ Electronic Data Sys	Technology	25.7	19.83	2.06
⊕ Dell Comp	Technology	61.8	55.87	2.04
⊕ Micron Tech	Technology	—	–12.60	1.99
⊖ Walgreen	Retail	39.1	–19.20	1.83
⊕ Veritas Software	Technology	—	–48.70	1.80
⊕ Dynegy	Energy	12.8	–54.20	1.75
⊕ AES	Utilities	24.8	–70.40	1.60

Current Investment Style

Style: Value Blnd Growth; Size: Large Med Small

	Stock Port Avg	Relative S&P 500 Current	Relative S&P 500 Hist	Rel Cat
Price/Earnings Ratio	35.4	1.15	1.26	1.00
Price/Book Ratio	5.8	1.01	1.43	0.90
Price/Cash Flow	23.5	1.31	1.32	1.04
3 Yr Earnings Growth	23.0	1.57	1.34	1.07
1 Yr Earnings Est%	7.2	—	—	2.39
Med Mkt Cap $mil	96,793	1.6	1.4	2.04

Special Securities % assets 09-30-01	
Restricted/Illiquid Secs	0
Emerging-Markets Secs	1
Options/Futures/Warrants	No

Composition % assets 09-30-01	
Cash	1.3
Stocks*	98.7
Bonds	0.0
Other	0.0
*Foreign (% stocks)	4.8

Market Cap	
Giant	62.1
Large	33.3
Medium	4.7
Small	0.0
Micro	0.0

Sector Weightings	% of Stocks	Rel S&P	5-Year High	5-Year Low
Utilities	1.5	0.5	5	0
Energy	4.0	0.6	6	0
Financials	15.5	0.9	24	5
Industrials	11.6	1.0	19	7
Durables	0.0	0.0	3	0
Staples	0.4	0.1	27	0
Services	10.8	1.0	20	4
Retail	7.4	1.1	20	3
Health	18.4	1.2	27	8
Technology	30.4	1.7	56	0

Analysis by Christopher Traulsen 11-14-01

Vanguard U.S. Growth Fund's new team is showing its opportunistic side.

When they took the helm here back in mid-June, John Blundin and Christopher Toub of Alliance Capital stepped into a tough situation. The fund had lagged the large-growth average badly in 1999's bull market, then suffered huge losses in 2000 and the first half of 2001 as a more aggressive stance and poor stock-picking by former advisor Lincoln Capital took its toll. As a result, the fund's once strong long-term record is still in tatters.

Blundin and Toub use a fairly measured approach. They generally steer clear of money-losing concerns in favor of firms that already have strong earnings, and do pay attention to valuations. When they arrived, they cut the fund's tech stake to about 20% of assets, and upped its financials stake, as they thought the latter area offered better earnings visibility and more-attractive prices.

More recently, they've shown a flexibility that has helped the fund to profit from a suddenly buoyant market. As tech stocks cracked in the late summer and fall, they added to names such as Nokia, Cisco Systems, and Juniper Networks. As equity markets tumbled after Sept. 11, they added to some of those same names, as well as to AT&T Wireless, AOL Time Warner, and General Electric. In the near term, the move proved correct—the fund has a top-decile return for the three months ended Nov. 13, 2001.

We think current shareholders have reason to stay the course here. Blundin and Toub appear to have corrected at least some of the problems that plagued the fund over the last two years. They have also run institutional money in this style for about a decade, and Vanguard exercises great care in its selection of advisors. Given the plethora of quality choices in the large-growth category, however, new investors will want to give the team more time to prove itself before signing on here.

Address:	Vanguard Financial Ctr. P.O. Box 2600 Valley Forge, PA 19482 800-662-7447 / 610-669-1000
Web Address:	www.vanguard.com
Inception:	01-06-59
Advisor:	Alliance Cap. Mgmt. (Bernstein)
Subadvisor:	None
NTF Plans:	N/A

Minimum Purchase:	$3000	Add: $100 IRA: $1000
Min Auto Inv Plan:	$3000	Add: $50
Sales Fees:	No-load	
Management Fee:	.40% mx./.10% mn.	
Actual Fees:	Mgt: 0.36%	Dist: —
Expense Projections:	3Yr: $122	5Yr: $213 10Yr: $480
Avg Brok Commission:	—	Income Distrib: Annually
Total Cost (relative to category):	Low	

Vanguard U.S. Value

Ticker	Load	NAV	Yield	Total Assets	Mstar Category
VUVLX	None	$11.47	0.9%	$435.8 mil	Large Value

Prospectus Objective: Growth and Income

Vanguard U.S. Value Fund seeks long-term growth of capital and income.

The fund invests primarily in U.S. common stocks, with a focus on value stocks. It invests in stocks of small, medium and large companies by using a computerized model to identify stocks that are trading at lower prices below the fundamental value of the underlying companies. The fund may invest up to 15% of its assets in restricted securities with limited marketability or other illiquid securities. It may also invest, to a limited extent, in stock futures and options contracts.

Historical Profile
Return —
Risk —
Rating Not Rated

Investment Style Equity
Average Stock % 97% (2000) 94% (12-01)

▼ Manager Change
▽ Partial Manager Change

Fund Performance vs. Category Average
Quarterly Fund Return +/– Category Average
— Category Baseline

Performance Quartile (within Category)

Portfolio Manager(s)

Chris Darnell. Since 6-00. Other funds currently managed: Vanguard Explorer, GMO Intl Intrinsic Value III, GMO U.S. Core III.

Robert M. Soucy. Since 6-00. BS U. of Massachusetts. Other funds currently managed: Vanguard Explorer, Vanguard Explorer Adm.

1990	1991	1992	1993	1994	1995	1996	1997	1998	1999	2000	12-01	History
—	—	—	—	—	—	—	—	—	—	11.24	11.47	NAV
—	—	—	—	—	—	—	—	—	—	12.97*	2.94	Total Return %
—	—	—	—	—	—	—	—	—	—	20.85*	14.81	+/– S&P 500
—	—	—	—	—	—	—	—	—	—	—	11.73	+/– Russ Top 200 Val
—	—	—	—	—	—	—	—	—	—	0.80	0.89	Income Return %
—	—	—	—	—	—	—	—	—	—	12.18	2.05	Capital Return %
—	—	—	—	—	—	—	—	—	—	—	9	Total Rtn % Rank Cat
—	—	—	—	—	—	—	—	—	—	0.08	0.10	Income $
—	—	—	—	—	—	—	—	—	—	0.00	0.00	Capital Gains $
—	—	—	—	—	—	—	—	—	—	0.58	—	Expense Ratio %
—	—	—	—	—	—	—	—	—	—	2.08	—	Income Ratio %
—	—	—	—	—	—	—	—	—	—	18	—	Turnover Rate %
—	—	—	—	—	—	—	—	—	—	121.2	435.8	Net Assets $mil

Performance 12-31-01

	1st Qtr	2nd Qtr	3rd Qtr	4th Qtr	Total
1997	—	—	—	—	—
1998	—	—	—	—	—
1999	—	—	—	—	—
2000	—	—	10.27	4.43	12.97 *
2001	–2.14	6.64	–10.83	10.61	2.94

Trailing	Total Return%	+/– S&P 500	+/– Russ Top 200 Val	% Rank All	% Rank Cat	Growth of $10,000
3 Mo	10.61	–0.07	5.10	39	29	11,061
6 Mo	–1.36	4.19	4.42	44	15	9,864
1 Yr	2.94	14.81	11.73	37	9	10,294
3 Yr Avg	—	—	—	—	—	—
5 Yr Avg	—	—	—	—	—	—
10 Yr Avg	—	—	—	—	—	—
15 Yr Avg	—	—	—	—	—	—

Tax Analysis	Tax-Adj Ret%	%Rank Cat	%Pretax Ret	%Rank Cat
3 Yr Avg	—	—	—	—
5 Yr Avg	—	—	—	—
10 Yr Avg	—	—	—	—

Potential Capital Gain Exposure: NMF

Risk Analysis

Time Period	Load-Adj Return %	Risk %Rank[1] All	Risk %Rank[1] Cat	Morningstar Return	Morningstar Risk	Morningstar Risk-Adj Rating
1 Yr	2.94					
3 Yr	—	—	—	—	—	
5 Yr	—	—	—	—	—	
Incept	10.54	—	—	—	—	

Average Historical Rating —

[1]1=low, 100=high

Category Rating (3 Yr)

Other Measures	Standard Index S&P 500	Best Fit Index
Alpha	—	—
Beta	—	—
R-Squared	—	—

	Standard Deviation	—
Return	Mean	—
Risk	Sharpe Ratio	—

Portfolio Analysis 09-30-01

Share change since 06-01 Total Stocks: 403

	Sector	PE	YTD Ret%	% Assets
⊕ AT&T	Services	7.8	40.59	3.50
⊕ Philip Morris	Staples	12.1	9.12	2.84
⊕ Bank of America	Financials	16.7	42.73	2.62
⊕ Fannie Mae	Financials	16.2	–6.95	2.48
⊕ Merck	Health	19.1	–35.90	1.86
⊕ General Motors	Durables	NMF	–0.97	1.47
⊕ Verizon Comms	Services	29.7	–2.52	1.39
⊕ Schering-Plough	Health	22.2	–35.90	1.38
⊕ Intel	Technology	73.1	4.89	1.29
⊕ Wachovia	Financials	—	23.13	1.22
⊕ WorldCom	Services	24.3	3.12	1.16
⊕ Sears Roebuck	Retail	23.4	40.12	0.94
⊕ Cendant	Services	20.4	103.70	0.92
⊕ Loews	Financials	—	8.35	0.90
⊕ Oracle	Technology	32.1	–52.40	0.89
⊕ Ford Motor	Durables	43.7	–30.00	0.88
⊕ Conoco Cl A	Energy	9.0	1.56	0.87
⊕ Computer Assoc Intl	Technology	—	77.28	0.84
⊕ Raytheon	Industrials	—	7.27	0.81
✲ Honeywell Intl	Durables	NMF	–27.00	0.79
⊕ Caterpillar	Industrials	20.0	13.72	0.75
⊕ Freddie Mac	Financials	14.0	–3.87	0.74
⊕ Natl City	Financials	13.3	6.00	0.73
⊕ DuPont De Nemours E.I.	Industrials	65.4	–9.14	0.70
⊕ Allstate	Financials	17.1	–21.00	0.68

Current Investment Style

Style: Value Blnd Growth; Size: Large Med Small

	Stock Port Avg	Relative S&P 500 Current	Relative S&P 500 Hist	Rel Cat
Price/Earnings Ratio	23.2	0.75	—	0.92
Price/Book Ratio	2.8	0.50	—	0.69
Price/Cash Flow	10.6	0.59	—	0.77
3 Yr Earnings Growth	10.3	0.70	—	0.70
1 Yr Earnings Est%	–9.1	5.16	—	2.76
Med Mkt Cap $mil	7,167	0.1	—	0.23

Analysis by Scott Cooley 12-28-01

A fast start isn't the only thing to like about Vanguard U.S. Value Fund.

There's no question that this fund has made an auspicious debut. In the fund's first half-year ending December 2000, it registered a 15.2% gain, which handily beat its average large-value rival. And the fund has continued to prosper in 2001. For the year to date through Dec. 27, the fund posted a 3.1% gain, putting it in the top decile of the category.

An aversion to technology issues and some solid stock-picking have given the fund a boost. The fund's tech stake was recently 6% but has been as low as 3% during its young life, and that's well below the category norm. Given the sector's extreme weakness prior to late September, that light tech stake has been a plus. What's more, the fund's quantitative stock-picking models have made some good selections, with Computer Associates, Sears Roebuck, and Cendant among the holdings that have produced strong gains in 2001. Moreover, the fund has scored with some strong picks in the financials sector, including Bank of America. Finally, as of Sept. 30, the models had built a huge stake in transportation-related issues such as General Motors and Lear, which have rebounded sharply over the past three months.

As we've said before, however, our bullishness about this fund has less to do with its terrific start than the superb record of its subadvisor, GMO. The firm has put up terrific numbers at other value-oriented funds it manages, including GMO U.S. Core. And of course, the fund has a huge expense-ratio advantage over its rivals, which should give its long-term returns a lift.

Given GMO's record in the fund world and as an institutional manager, as well as the fund's low costs, this fund has a lot to recommend it. Investors looking for a value-oriented core holding are likely to find a comfortable home here.

Special Securities % assets 09-30-01

Restricted/Illiquid Secs	0
Emerging-Markets Secs	0
Options/Futures/Warrants	No

Composition % assets 09-30-01

Cash	4.6
Stocks*	95.4
Bonds	0.0
Other	0.0
*Foreign (% stocks)	0.0

Market Cap

Giant	22.5
Large	22.3
Medium	37.1
Small	17.3
Micro	0.9

Sector Weightings	% of Stocks	Rel S&P	5-Year High	5-Year Low
Utilities	4.8	1.5	—	—
Energy	2.5	0.4	—	—
Financials	24.9	1.4	—	—
Industrials	18.4	1.6	—	—
Durables	7.6	4.9	—	—
Staples	5.7	0.7	—	—
Services	17.4	1.6	—	—
Retail	7.1	1.0	—	—
Health	5.5	0.4	—	—
Technology	6.2	0.3	—	—

Address:	Vanguard Financial Ctr. P.O. Box 2600 Valley Forge, PA 19482 610-669-1000 / 800-662-7447
Web Address:	www.vanguard.com
*Inception:	06-29-00
Advisor:	Grantham Mayo Van Otterloo
Subadvisor:	None
NTF Plans:	N/A

Minimum Purchase:	$3000	Add: $100	IRA: $1000
Min Auto Inv Plan:	$3000	Add: $50	
Sales Fees:	No-load		
Management Fee:	.50%		
Actual Fees:	Mgt: 0.50%	Dist: —	
Expense Projections:	3Yr: $170	5Yr: —	10Yr: —
Avg Brok Commission:	—	Income Distrib: Annually	
Total Cost (relative to category):	—		

Vanguard Value Index

Ticker	Load	NAV	Yield	Total Assets	Mstar Category
VIVAX	None	$18.90	1.6%	$4,469.7 mil	Large Value

Prospectus Objective: Growth and Income

Vanguard Value Index Fund seeks to replicate the aggregate price and yield performance of the S&P 500/BARRA Value Index.

The fund employs a passive management strategy designed to track the performance of the S&P 500/BARRA Value Index. This index maintains a lower price/book ratio and has historically had a higher yield than the S&P 500. It attempts to replicate the target index by investing all or substantially all of its assets in the stocks that make up the index.

The fund currently offers Investor, Institutional and Admiral shares. Prior to Oct. 27, 1998, the fund was named Vanguard Index Trust Value Portfolio.

Historical Profile
Return Average
Risk Average
Rating ★★★ Neutral

Investment Style
Equity
Average Stock %

1993	1994	1995	1996	1997	1998	1999	2000	12-01
	100%	99%	99%	100%	100%	100%	100%	

▼ Manager Change
▽ Partial Manager Change

Fund Performance vs. Category Average
■ Quarterly Fund Return +/– Category Average
— Category Baseline

Performance Quartile (within Category)

Portfolio Manager(s)

George U. Sauter. Since 11-92. AB'76 Dartmouth C.; MBA'80 U. of Chicago. Other funds currently managed: Vanguard Small Cap Index, Vanguard Balanced Index, Vanguard Equity-Income.

1990	1991	1992	1993	1994	1995	1996	1997	1998	1999	2000	12-01	History
—	—	10.30	11.73	11.12	14.80	17.02	20.85	22.51	22.89	22.87	18.90	NAV
—	—	3.70*	18.25	–0.65	37.03	21.78	29.77	14.64	12.57	6.08	–11.98	Total Return %
—	—	0.04*	8.19	–1.96	–0.50	–1.16	–3.58	–13.93	–8.47	15.18	–0.10	+/– S&P 500
—	—	—	–1.51	1.67	–3.00	–0.53	–5.72	–6.60	1.62	3.77	–3.19	+/– Russ Top 200 Val
—	—	0.70	3.73	3.30	3.64	2.62	2.22	1.77	1.66	1.60	1.44	Income Return %
—	—	3.00	14.52	–3.95	33.39	19.16	27.55	12.87	10.91	4.49	–13.41	Capital Return %
—	—	—	18	53	14	33	28	41	24	52	87	Total Rtn % Rank Cat
—	—	0.07	0.38	0.38	0.40	0.38	0.37	0.36	0.36	0.36	0.32	Income $
—	—	0.00	0.06	0.16	0.00	0.57	0.75	0.99	1.96	0.98	0.96	Capital Gains $
—	—	0.00	0.20	0.20	0.20	0.20	0.20	0.22	0.22	0.22	—	Expense Ratio %
—	—	3.46	3.26	3.37	3.06	2.54	2.05	1.72	1.59	1.60	—	Income Ratio %
—	—	—	30	32	27	29	25	33	41	37	—	Turnover Rate %
—	—	—	190.1	296.9	496.3	1,015.7	1,795.5	2,420.6	3,377.8	3,629.0	3,017.6	Net Assets $mil

Performance 12-31-01

	1st Qtr	2nd Qtr	3rd Qtr	4th Qtr	Total
1997	1.68	14.47	9.12	2.18	29.77
1998	11.52	0.48	–12.92	17.50	14.64
1999	2.78	10.75	–9.24	8.96	12.57
2000	0.17	–4.28	8.80	1.70	6.08
2001	–6.58	4.41	–16.26	7.76	–11.98

Trailing	Total Return%	+/– S&P 500	+/– Russ Top 200 Val	% Rank All	% Rank Cat	Growth of $10,000
3 Mo	7.76	–2.92	2.24	53	67	10,776
6 Mo	–9.76	–4.21	–3.98	84	96	9,024
1 Yr	–11.98	–0.10	–3.19	65	87	8,802
3 Yr Avg	1.68	2.70	0.51	64	54	10,511
5 Yr Avg	9.35	–1.35	–1.85	22	44	15,637
10 Yr Avg	—	—	—	—	—	—
15 Yr Avg	—	—	—	—	—	—

Tax Analysis	Tax-Adj Ret%	%Rank Cat	%Pretax Ret	%Rank Cat
3 Yr Avg	–0.51	63	—	—
5 Yr Avg	7.18	45	76.8	46
10 Yr Avg	—	—	—	—

Potential Capital Gain Exposure: –10% of assets

Risk Analysis

Time Period	Load-Adj Return %	Risk %Rank[1] All	Risk %Rank[1] Cat	Morningstar Return	Morningstar Risk	Morningstar Risk-Adj Rating
1 Yr	–11.98					
3 Yr	1.68	58	70	–0.69[2]	0.82	★★★
5 Yr	9.35	61	73	1.01[2]	0.84	★★★
Incept	13.45	—	—	—	—	

Average Historical Rating (75 months): 3.9★s

[1]1=low, 100=high [2] T-Bill return substituted for category avg.

Category Rating (3 Yr)

1 2 **3** 4 5
Worst Best

Return Average
Risk Above Avg

Other Measures	Standard Index S&P 500	Best Fit Index S&P 500
Alpha	1.8	1.8
Beta	0.82	0.82
R-Squared	74	74
Standard Deviation		16.55
Mean		1.68
Sharpe Ratio		–0.23

Portfolio Analysis 09-30-01

Share change since 06-01 Total Stocks: 344	Sector	PE	YTD Ret%	% Assets
⊕ ExxonMobil	Energy	15.3	–7.59	5.82
⊖ Citigroup	Financials	20.0	0.03	4.90
⊕ American Intl Grp	Financials	42.0	–19.20	4.41
⊖ AOL Time Warner	Technology	—	–7.76	2.96
⊖ Verizon Comms	Services	29.7	–2.52	2.88
⊖ Royal Dutch Petro NY ADR	Energy	12.0	–17.10	2.32
⊖ Bank of America	Financials	16.7	42.73	2.02
⊕ ChevronTexaco	Energy	10.3	9.29	2.02
⊖ J.P. Morgan Chase & Co.	Financials	27.8	–17.40	1.50
⊖ BellSouth	Services	24.9	–5.09	1.48
⊖ Wells Fargo	Financials	22.4	–20.20	1.45
⊖ Viacom Cl B	Services	—	—	1.39
⊖ Morgan Stanley/Dean Witter	Financials	16.6	–28.20	1.16
⊖ AT&T	Services	7.8	40.59	1.13
⊖ Texas Instruments	Technology	87.5	–40.70	1.04
⊖ Freddie Mac	Financials	14.0	–3.87	1.00
⊖ DuPont De Nemours E.I.	Industrials	65.4	–9.14	0.89
⊕ Wachovia	Financials	—	23.13	0.86
⊖ Walt Disney	Services	—	–27.70	0.83
⊖ WorldCom	Services	24.3	3.12	0.83
⊖ Bank One	Financials	29.1	9.13	0.83
⊖ Merrill Lynch	Financials	18.2	–22.70	0.78
☼ AT&T Wireless Grp	Services	—	–17.00	0.78
⊖ Motorola	Technology	—	–25.00	0.77
⊖ FleetBoston Finl	Financials	16.2	0.55	0.76

Current Investment Style

Style: Value Blnd Growth; Size: Large Med Small

	Stock Port Avg	Relative S&P 500 Current	Relative S&P 500 Hist	Rel Cat
Price/Earnings Ratio	24.4	0.79	0.74	0.97
Price/Book Ratio	2.6	0.45	0.44	0.63
Price/Cash Flow	11.7	0.65	0.66	0.85
3 Yr Earnings Growth	13.6	0.93	0.65	0.92
1 Yr Earnings Est%	–5.6	3.18	—	1.70
Med Mkt Cap $mil	31,212	0.5	0.5	0.98

Special Securities % assets 09-30-01	
Restricted/Illiquid Secs	0
Emerging-Markets Secs	0
Options/Futures/Warrants	No

Composition % assets 09-30-01	
Cash	0.2
Stocks*	99.8
Bonds	0.0
Other	0.0
*Foreign (% stocks)	3.5

Market Cap	
Giant	39.8
Large	41.5
Medium	18.2
Small	0.3
Micro	0.2

Sector Weightings	% of Stocks	Rel S&P	5-Year High	5-Year Low
Utilities	6.5	2.0	12	4
Energy	15.0	2.1	20	12
Financials	31.1	1.7	32	17
Industrials	11.1	1.0	20	11
Durables	2.8	1.8	9	3
Staples	1.4	0.2	5	1
Services	16.8	1.6	22	10
Retail	2.8	0.4	6	3
Health	1.6	0.1	4	1
Technology	10.8	0.6	13	4

Analysis by Scott Cooley 08-09-01

Don't let a few poor months turn you away from Vanguard Value Index Fund.

To be sure, in 2001 this fund hasn't fully benefited from the market's preference for value stocks. For the year to date through August 8, the fund has lost 6.1%, putting it 3 percentage points behind its typical rival. The fund devotes an above-average percentage of assets to a few hard-hit brokerage stocks, including Merrill Lynch and Morgan Stanley. And because the fund's benchmark index includes stocks with relatively low price/book ratios, it includes a few growth-oriented firms that booked a lot of goodwill while making acquisitions at inflated prices. For example, JDS Uniphase was a roughly 1% position in the index when the year began, even though its P/E topped 100 and its stock was owned by less than 0.5% of the fund's rivals. JDS Uniphase has lost nearly 80% of its value so far in 2001.

Still, it's pretty clear that this fund mainly offers value exposure. Thanks to its value tilt, it has held up better than the S&P 500 this year, and it beat the index by 15 percentage points in value-driven 2000. For investors with growth-biased portfolios—especially those with big stakes in Vanguard Growth Index Fund—this offering provides useful diversification.

Thanks to its low costs, the fund also has a long-term edge on its large-value competition. Over the past five years, the fund 13.6% annualized gain tops its average rival's by 1.8 percentage points. More than half of the fund's edge over its peers derives from its rock-bottom expense ratio of 0.22%. And while the fund hasn't helped investors as much as most value offerings have in 2001, it registered category-beating returns in growth-driven years like 1998 and 1999. While this fund doesn't offer pure-value exposure, it does provide investors with a low-cost way to own a portfolio of mostly value-oriented stocks.

Address:	Vanguard Financial Ctr. P.O. Box 2600 Valley Forge, PA 19482 800-662-7447 / 610-669-1000
Web Address:	www.vanguard.com
*Inception:	11-02-92
Advisor:	Vanguard Core Mgmt. Grp.
Subadvisor:	None
NTF Plans:	N/A

Minimum Purchase:	$3000	Add: $100 IRA: $1000
Min Auto Inv Plan:	$3000	Add: $50
Sales Fees:	No-load	
Management Fee:	.19%	
Actual Fees:	Mgt: 0.20%	Dist: —
Expense Projections:	3Yr: $71	5Yr: $124 10Yr: $280
Avg Brok Commission:	—	Income Distrib: Quarterly
Total Cost (relative to category):		Low

Vanguard Wellesley Income

Ticker	Load	NAV	Yield	Total Assets	Mstar Category
VWINX	None	$19.91	4.8%	$7,200.8 mil	Domestic Hybrid

Prospectus Objective: Balanced

Vanguard Wellesley Income Fund seeks current income consistent with reasonable risk.

The fund normally invests at least 65% of assets in income-producing securities, including fixed-income securities and dividend-paying common stocks. Fixed-income securities usually account for approximately 60% of assets and may include government and corporate bonds, and preferred stocks. Bond holdings are usually rated no lower than BBB.

The fund also offers Adm shares. Prior to May 3, 1993, the fund was named Wellesley Income Fund. From that date until Oct. 27, 1998, the fund was named Vanguard/Wellesley Income Fund.

Historical Profile
Return Average
Risk Low
Rating ★★★★ Above Avg

Investment Style
Equity
Average Stock %: 38% 37% 37% 39% 38% 37%

▼ Manager Change
▽ Partial Manager Change

Fund Performance vs. Category Average
■ Quarterly Fund Return +/– Category Average
— Category Baseline

Performance Quartile (within Category)

1990	1991	1992	1993	1994	1995	1996	1997	1998	1999	2000	12–01	History
16.02	18.08	18.16	19.24	17.05	20.44	20.51	21.86	22.12	18.85	20.34	19.91	NAV
3.76	21.57	8.67	14.65	–4.44	28.91	9.42	20.19	11.84	–4.14	16.17	7.39	Total Return %
6.87	–8.92	1.06	4.59	–5.75	–8.62	–13.53	–13.16	–16.73	–25.17	25.27	19.26	+/– S&P 500
–5.20	5.56	1.27	4.90	–1.52	10.44	5.80	10.51	3.17	–3.31	4.54	–1.04	+/– LB Aggregate
7.99	8.15	6.87	6.42	5.92	6.84	5.82	6.01	5.31	5.20	5.74	5.06	Income Return %
–4.24	13.41	1.80	8.23	–10.35	22.07	3.60	14.18	6.53	–9.33	10.43	2.32	Capital Return %
18	66	41	27	76	17	82	36	53	95	6	4	Total Rtn % Rank Cat
1.30	1.27	1.21	1.14	1.11	1.14	1.16	1.20	1.13	1.12	1.06	1.01	Income $
0.08	0.00	0.21	0.40	0.24	0.28	0.60	1.44	1.14	1.25	0.40	0.86	Capital Gains $
0.45	0.40	0.35	0.33	0.34	0.34	0.31	0.31	0.31	0.30	0.31	—	Expense Ratio %
7.77	7.08	6.50	5.79	6.16	5.96	5.74	5.47	5.05	5.22	5.39	—	Income Ratio %
19	29	21	21	31	30	26	36	32	20	28	—	Turnover Rate %
1,021.9	1,934.1	3,177.7	6,011.5	5,680.6	7,180.7	7,012.7	7,645.9	8,497.8	6,976.4	6,595.4	6,494.7	Net Assets $mil

Portfolio Manager(s)

Earl E. McEvoy. Since 10-82. BA'70 Dartmouth C.; MBA'72 Columbia U. Other funds currently managed: Global Utility A, Global Utility B, Vanguard High-Yield Corporate.

John R. Ryan, CFA. Since 1-86. BS'71 Lehigh U.; MBA'81 U. of Virginia. Other funds currently managed: Vanguard Equity-Income, SunAmStySel Large-Cap Val A, SunAmStySel Large-Cap Val B.

Performance 12-31-01

	1st Qtr	2nd Qtr	3rd Qtr	4th Qtr	Total
1997	–0.61	7.17	7.39	5.07	20.19
1998	4.62	1.93	1.65	3.18	11.84
1999	–2.61	2.44	–3.10	–0.84	–4.14
2000	1.41	0.79	6.85	6.37	16.17
2001	1.40	2.73	1.91	1.15	7.39

Trailing	Total Return%	+/– S&P 500	+/– LB Agg	% Rank All	% Rank Cat	Growth of $10,000
3 Mo	1.15	–9.53	1.11	73	95	10,115
6 Mo	3.08	8.64	–1.57	15	4	10,308
1 Yr	7.39	19.26	–1.04	12	4	10,739
3 Yr Avg	6.15	7.17	–0.13	21	11	11,959
5 Yr Avg	9.96	–0.74	2.53	19	16	16,076
10 Yr Avg	10.44	–2.49	3.21	30	29	26,999
15 Yr Avg	10.69	–3.04	2.57	37	31	45,893

Tax Analysis	Tax-Adj Ret%	%Rank Cat	%Pretax Ret	%Rank Cat
3 Yr Avg	3.05	19	49.6	56
5 Yr Avg	6.43	26	64.6	66
10 Yr Avg	7.15	43	68.5	64

Potential Capital Gain Exposure: 7% of assets

Risk Analysis

Time Period	Load-Adj Return %	Risk %Rank[1] All	Risk %Rank[1] Cat	Morningstar Return	Morningstar Risk	Morningstar Risk-Adj Rating
1 Yr	7.39					
3 Yr	6.15	30	3	0.26[2]	0.24	★★★★
5 Yr	9.96	35	3	1.18[2]	0.25	★★★★
10 Yr	10.44	42	6	0.81	0.35	★★★★

Average Historical Rating (193 months): 4.0★s

[1] 1=low, 100=high [2] T–Bill return substituted for category avg.

Category Rating (3 Yr)

1 2 3 4 5
Worst Best

Return Above Avg
Risk Low

Other Measures	Standard Index S&P 500	Best Fit Index SPMid400
Alpha	1.8	0.5
Beta	0.11	0.12
R–Squared	10	15
Standard Deviation	6.24	
Mean	6.15	
Sharpe Ratio	0.22	

Portfolio Analysis 09-30-01

Total Stocks: 62 Share change since 06–01	Sector	PE Ratio	YTD Return %	% Net Assets
⊕ ExxonMobil	Energy	15.3	–7.59	1.97
⊕ BellSouth	Services	24.9	–5.09	1.38
⊕ SBC Comms	Services	18.4	–16.00	1.31
⊕ Verizon Comms	Services	29.7	–2.52	1.21
✲ XL Cap Cl A	Financials	22.8	5.82	1.11
⊕ Weyerhaeuser	Industrials	21.0	9.73	1.10
Philip Morris	Staples	12.1	9.12	1.08
⊕ Southern	Utilities	14.0	33.19	1.02
Natl City	Financials	13.3	6.00	0.96
⊕ Caterpillar	Industrials	20.0	13.72	0.94

Total Fixed-Income: 367	Date of Maturity	Amount $000	Value $000	% Net Assets
US Treasury Bond 5.5%	08-15-28	275,000	294,066	4.12
GNMA 6%	12-15-28	173,259	176,187	2.47
US Treasury Note 6.875%	05-15-06	125,000	142,231	1.99
US Treasury Note 5.75%	08-15-10	100,000	110,906	1.55
FNMA Debenture 7.125%	01-15-30	75,000	90,332	1.27
FNMA Debenture 5.75%	06-15-05	75,000	80,474	1.13
GNMA 6%	08-15-29	68,889	70,057	0.98
General Elec Cap 7.25%	02-01-05	50,000	54,726	0.77
Alcoa 6.5%	06-01-11	50,000	53,388	0.75
Coca–Cola 5.75%	03-15-11	50,000	51,358	0.72

Equity Style
Style: Value
Size: Large–Cap

Fixed-Income Style
Duration: —
Quality: —
NA

	Portfolio Avg	Rel S&P
Price/Earnings Ratio	21.6	0.70
Price/Book Ratio	3.1	0.55
Price/Cash Flow	9.7	0.54
3 Yr Earnings Growth	9.9	0.68
1 Yr Earnings Est%	–11.7	6.59
Debt % Total Cap	39.6	1.28
Med Mkt Cap $mil	20,203	0.33

Avg Eff Duration[1]	5.9 Yrs
Avg Eff Maturity	—
Avg Credit Quality	AA
Avg Wtd Coupon	6.66%

[1] figure provided by fund as of 03-31-01

Special Securities % assets 09-30-01	
Restricted/Illiquid Secs	2
Emerging–Markets Secs	Trace
Options/Futures/Warrants	No

Composition % of assets 09-30-01	
Cash	3.5
Stocks*	36.1
Bonds	60.5
Other	0.0
*Foreign (% of stocks)	7.2

Market Cap	
Giant	33.4
Large	44.3
Medium	20.3
Small	2.0
Micro	0.0

Sector Weightings	% of Stocks	Rel S&P	5-Year High	5-Year Low
Utilities	16.9	5.3	41	10
Energy	14.1	2.0	28	11
Financials	21.1	1.2	34	8
Industrials	22.8	2.0	27	9
Durables	1.0	0.6	7	0
Staples	7.5	1.0	9	0
Services	14.3	1.3	23	3
Retail	2.4	0.4	8	0
Health	0.0	0.0	10	0
Technology	0.0	0.0	4	0

Analysis by Scott Cooley 11-25-01

Vanguard Wellesley Income Fund's strengths and weaknesses have been on display this year, but we give more weight to the former.

This portfolio certainly doesn't look much like its domestic-hybrid peers'. On the stock side, comanager Jack Ryan focuses on dividend-paying issues, so the fund typically has a lot of exposure to value areas such as utilities, but small or nonexistent stakes in some growth sectors, including technology. Meanwhile, with the fund's bond holdings, which typically represent a well-above-average 60% of assets, comanager Earl McEvoy sticks to high-quality fare.

Those biases explain a lot about the fund's relative returns this year. In general, Ryan's dividend-paying stocks have held up well in a turbulent market, with Philip Morris, Baxter International, and utility Southern all posting double-digit gains for the year to date through Nov. 23, 2001. A complete absence of tech shares has overall been a plus, as has the fund's huge stash of high-quality bonds. However, over the past month or so, those pluses have turned into negatives, as the stock market—led by the tech sector—has posted a large gain. Thus, although the fund's year-to-date return leads more than 90% of its rivals', it has trailed nearly all of its peers over the past four weeks.

As usual, Ryan isn't chasing recently hot performers. He says few tech firms meet his yield hurdle, and those that do have weak operations. He has bought utilities that resell power, arguing that a surplus of generating capacity will allow them to buy at attractive prices. He also picked up some insurance stocks after the Sept. 11 terrorist attacks, in the belief they will be able to hike rates.

As evidenced by the fund's strong long-term returns, Ryan and McEvoy have done a good job here.

Address:	Vanguard Financial Ctr. P.O. Box 2600 Valley Forge, PA 19482 800–662–7447 / 610–669–1000
Web Address:	www.vanguard.com
Inception:	07-01-70
Advisor:	Wellington Mgmt.
Subadvisor:	None
NTF Plans:	N/A

Minimum Purchase:	$3000	Add: $100	IRA: $1000
Min Auto Inv Plan:	$3000	Add: $100	
Sales Fees:	No-load		
Management Fee:	.10% mx./.03% mn.		
Actual Fees:	Mgt: 0.33%	Dist: —	
Expense Projections:	3Yr: $113	5Yr: $197	10Yr: $443
Avg Brok Commission:	—	Income Distrib: Quarterly	
Total Cost (relative to category):	Low		

Vanguard Wellington

Ticker	Load	NAV	Yield	Total Assets	Mstar Category
VWELX	None	$27.26	3.5%	$24,293.0 mil	Domestic Hybrid

Prospectus Objective: Balanced

Vanguard Wellington Fund seeks conservation of capital and reasonable income.

The fund normally invests 60% to 70% of assets in common stocks and convertible securities. It typically invests the balance of assets in investment-grade corporate debt and U.S. government obligations. The fund may invest up to 10% of assets in foreign securities.

The performance fee is contingent on the preceding 36 months' performance; the fund must outperform the index (65% S&P 500, 35% Salomon Brothers High Grade index) by at least 6%.

The fund also offers Adm shares. Prior to May 3, 1993, the fund was named Wellington Fund. From that date until Oct. 27, 1998, the fund was named Vanguard/Wellington Fund.

Historical Profile

Return: Average
Risk: Low
Rating: ★★★★ Above Avg

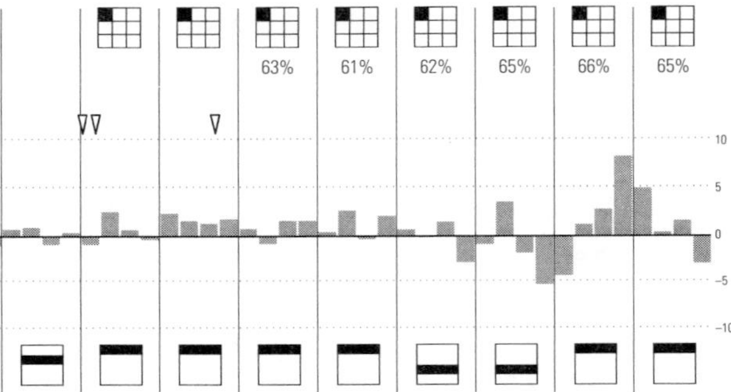

Investment Style
Equity
Average Stock %: 63% | 61% | 62% | 65% | 66% | 65%

▼ Manager Change
▽ Partial Manager Change

Fund Performance vs. Category Average
Quarterly Fund Return +/– Category Average
— Category Baseline

Performance Quartile (within Category)

History

1990	1991	1992	1993	1994	1995	1996	1997	1998	1999	2000	12–01	History
16.26	18.81	19.16	20.40	19.39	24.43	26.15	29.45	29.35	27.96	28.21	27.26	NAV
–2.81	23.65	7.93	13.52	–0.49	32.92	16.19	23.23	12.06	4.41	10.40	0.67	Total Return %
0.31	–6.84	0.31	3.46	–1.80	–4.61	–6.76	–10.12	–16.52	–16.63	19.50	12.54	+/– S&P 500
–11.76	7.65	0.52	3.77	2.43	14.45	12.57	13.55	3.38	5.24	–1.23	–7.76	+/– LB Aggregate
5.81	6.02	5.09	4.88	4.38	5.08	4.40	4.34	3.89	3.94	3.88	3.41	Income Return %
–8.61	17.63	2.84	8.63	–4.87	27.84	11.78	18.89	8.17	0.47	6.52	–2.74	Capital Return %
73	51	47	39	24	3	23	16	52	73	11	19	Total Rtn % Rank Cat
1.01	0.96	0.94	0.92	0.88	0.97	1.06	1.12	1.13	1.14	1.07	0.95	Income $
0.00	0.23	0.16	0.38	0.03	0.28	1.11	1.57	2.44	1.50	1.48	0.16	Capital Gains $
0.43	0.35	0.33	0.34	0.35	0.33	0.31	0.29	0.31	0.30	0.31	—	Expense Ratio %
5.99	5.39	4.98	4.55	4.35	4.37	4.08	3.97	3.68	3.74	3.77	—	Income Ratio %
33	35	24	34	32	24	30	27	29	22	33	—	Turnover Rate %
2,449.2	3,818.4	5,559.2	8,075.8	8,809.4	12,656.0	16,189.7	21,811.8	25,760.9	25,528.5	23,400.9	21,724.0	Net Assets $mil

Portfolio Manager(s)

Ernst H. von Metzsch, CFA. Since 9-95. MA U. of Leiden, Holland; PhD Harvard U. Other funds currently managed: Vanguard Energy, Vanguard Wellington Adm, Vanguard Energy Adm.

Paul D. Kaplan. Since 1-94. BA'68 Dickinson U.; MS'74 MIT. Other funds currently managed: Fortis Advantage Asset Allocation A, SEI Daily Income GNMA A, Vanguard GNMA.

Performance 12-31-01

	1st Qtr	2nd Qtr	3rd Qtr	4th Qtr	Total
1997	0.47	12.19	6.27	2.88	23.23
1998	7.81	1.01	–4.24	7.45	12.06
1999	0.07	7.44	–5.25	2.50	4.41
2000	–1.45	0.25	4.66	6.77	10.40
2001	–0.26	3.55	–5.68	3.35	0.67

Trailing	Total Return%	+/– S&P 500	+/– LB Agg	% Rank All	% Rank Cat	Growth of $10,000
3 Mo	3.35	–7.33	3.31	69	87	10,335
6 Mo	–2.52	3.03	–7.18	49	66	9,748
1 Yr	0.67	12.54	–7.76	41	19	10,067
3 Yr Avg	5.08	6.11	–1.19	31	20	11,604
5 Yr Avg	9.89	–0.81	2.46	19	16	16,024
10 Yr Avg	11.68	–1.25	4.45	21	11	30,171
15 Yr Avg	11.67	–2.06	3.55	29	11	52,359

Tax Analysis	Tax-Adj Ret%	%Rank Cat	%Pretax Ret	%Rank Cat
3 Yr Avg	2.72	23	53.6	49
5 Yr Avg	7.15	17	72.3	33
10 Yr Avg	9.10	9	78.0	19

Potential Capital Gain Exposure: 19% of assets

Risk Analysis

Time Period	Load-Adj Return %	Risk %Rank[1] All	Risk %Rank[1] Cat	Morningstar Return	Morningstar Risk	Morningstar Risk-Adj Rating
1 Yr	0.67					
3 Yr	5.08	37	31	0.03[2]	0.47	★★★★
5 Yr	9.89	41	30	1.17[2]	0.49	★★★★
10 Yr	11.68	48	39	1.04	0.54	★★★★

Average Historical Rating (193 months): 3.9★s

[1] 1=low, 100=high [2] T-Bill return substituted for category avg.

Category Rating (3 Yr)

1 2 3 4 5
Worst Best

Return: Above Avg
Risk: Below Avg

Other Measures	Standard Index S&P 500	Best Fit Index S&P 500
Alpha	2.5	2.5
Beta	0.42	0.42
R-Squared	48	48

Standard Deviation	10.64
Mean	5.08
Sharpe Ratio	0.01

Portfolio Analysis 09-30-01

Total Stocks: 108 Share change since 06–01	Sector	PE Ratio	YTD Return %	% Net Assets
IBM	Technology	26.9	43.00	1.91
ALCOA	Industrials	21.4	7.86	1.85
⊕ Citigroup	Financials	20.0	0.03	1.78
Verizon Comms	Services	29.7	–2.52	1.35
Abbott Labs	Health	51.6	17.08	1.29
Union Pacific	Services	17.1	13.96	1.26
Pharmacia	Health	36.5	–29.30	1.25
⊕ ACE	Financials	17.4	–5.39	1.24
Northrop Grumman	Industrials	19.2	23.67	1.22
⊕ Royal Dutch Petro NY ADR	Energy	12.0	–17.10	1.09

Total Fixed-Income: 214	Date of Maturity	Amount $000	Value $000	% Net Assets
US Treasury Note 4.625%	05-15-06	250,000	261,265	1.15
FNMA ARM N/A	07-01-09	118,612	124,240	0.55
Procter & Gamble 9.36%	01-01-21	60,945	81,075	0.36
FNMA 6.79%	07-01-09	62,212	66,489	0.29
American General Fin 7.45%	01-15-05	55,000	60,103	0.27
SunTrust Bk Atlanta 7.25%	09-15-06	54,000	59,816	0.26
Ford Motor Credit 6.875%	02-01-06	55,000	56,295	0.25
Phillips Petro 8.5%	05-25-05	50,000	55,874	0.25
FNMA FRN	02-01-11	51,861	55,587	0.25
MBNA CC Master Tr 6.9%	01-15-08	50,000	55,470	0.24

Equity Style
Style: Value
Size: Large–Cap

	Portfolio Avg	Rel S&P
Price/Earnings Ratio	25.8	0.83
Price/Book Ratio	4.0	0.70
Price/Cash Flow	12.7	0.71
3 Yr Earnings Growth	11.7	0.80
1 Yr Earnings Est%	–9.7	5.48
Debt % Total Cap	37.9	1.23
Med Mkt Cap $mil	26,114	0.43

Fixed-Income Style
Duration: —
Quality: —
NA

Avg Eff Duration[1]	5.6 Yrs
Avg Eff Maturity	—
Avg Credit Quality	A
Avg Wtd Coupon	7.02%

[1] figure provided by fund as of 03-31-01

Special Securities % assets 09-30-01	
Restricted/Illiquid Secs	3
Emerging–Markets Secs	0
Options/Futures/Warrants	No

Composition % of assets 09-30-01	
Cash	1.4
Stocks*	65.9
Bonds	32.7
Other	0.0
*Foreign (% of stocks)	11.0

Market Cap	
Giant	30.6
Large	50.3
Medium	19.1
Small	0.0
Micro	0.0

Sector Weightings	% of Stocks	Rel S&P	5-Year High	5-Year Low
Utilities	5.9	1.9	7	0
Energy	10.2	1.4	18	8
Financials	19.9	1.1	24	14
Industrials	21.2	1.9	35	21
Durables	4.3	2.8	8	1
Staples	4.8	0.6	6	0
Services	13.0	1.2	15	6
Retail	3.3	0.5	10	2
Health	8.4	0.6	16	8
Technology	9.1	0.5	9	0

Analysis by Scott Cooley 11-26-01

Even with a more-aggressive tilt, Vanguard Wellington Fund has much to like.

Lead manager Ernst von Metzsch is a contrarian at heart, and he certainly has swum against the current in recent months. When stocks sold off in the wake of the September attacks, von Metzsch started buying, gradually hiking the fund's equity exposure to 67% from 61%. He added to insurance stocks, which he thought were attractively priced in relation to their improved pricing environment. He boosted the fund's stake in Merrill Lynch, which he believed had gotten too cheap. And although the fund historically hasn't had a lot of tech exposure, he picked up shares of Apple Computer and EMC on weakness. Von Metzsch says the latter company offered not only an attractive valuation, but also the prospect of improved profitability as its high-margin services business grows as a percentage of overall sales.

Von Metzsch's moves were on the money. The stock market, led by tech, has staged a strong recovery, at least temporarily validating his decision to hike the fund's equity weight. That has allowed the fund to build on its solid performance of early 2001, when stocks such as IBM and Alcoa buoyed it. Moreover, bond-side manager Paul Kaplan's affinity for high-quality fare has been a big plus in a year when junk issues have posted weak returns. For the year to date through Nov. 23, the fund has returned 3%, putting it ahead of 90% of its domestic-hybrid peers.

Although the fund performed poorly in 1999's growth-driven market, it has earned terrific long-term marks. Thanks to Vanguard's trademark low costs and von Metzsch's solid stock-picking, the fund's 10-year return tops more than 90% of its rivals'. This fund will have a tough time posting competitive returns when growth stocks again rule the roost, but you'd be hard-pressed to find a better value-oriented domestic-hybrid offering.

Address:	Vanguard Financial Ctr. P.O. Box 2600 Valley Forge, PA 19482 800–662–7447 / 610–669–1000
Web Address:	www.vanguard.com
Inception:	07-01-29
Advisor:	Wellington Mgmt.
Subadvisor:	None
NTF Plans:	N/A

Minimum Purchase:	$3000	Add: $100	IRA: $1000
Min Auto Inv Plan:	$3000	Add: $100	
Sales Fees:	No–load		
Management Fee:	.10% mx./.03% mn.+(–).30%P		
Actual Fees:	Mgt: 0.33%	Dist: —	
Expense Projections:	3Yr: $100	5Yr: $174	10Yr: $393
Avg Brok Commission:	—	Income Distrib: Quarterly	
Total Cost (relative to category):	Low		

Vanguard Windsor

Ticker	Load	NAV	Yield	Total Assets	Mstar Category
VWNDX	None	$15.64	1.2%	$17,729.8 mil	Large Value

Prospectus Objective: Growth and Income

Vanguard Windsor Fund seeks long-term growth of capital and income; current income is a secondary consideration.

The fund invests primarily in common stocks. Management typically selects securities that it believes have relatively low P/E ratios and meaningful income yields. The fund may also invest in preferred stocks, fixed-income securities, convertible securities, and money-market instruments.This fund is non-diversified.

The fund offers Amiral and Investor shares.

Historical Profile
Return: Above Avg
Risk: Average
Rating: ★★★★ Above Avg

Investment Style
Equity
Average Stock %: 87% 96% 95% 96% 97% 97%

▼ Manager Change
▽ Partial Manager Change

Fund Performance vs. Category Average
Quarterly Fund Return +/– Category Average
— Category Baseline

Performance Quartile (within Category)

Portfolio Manager(s)

Charles T. Freeman, et al. Since 12-95. BS'66 U. of Pennsylvania; MBA'69 U. of Pennsylvania-Wharton.

1990	1991	1992	1993	1994	1995	1996	1997	1998	1999	2000	12-01	History
10.30	11.72	12.74	13.91	12.59	14.53	16.59	16.98	15.57	15.17	15.29	15.64	NAV
–15.50	28.55	16.50	19.37	–0.15	30.15	26.36	21.97	0.81	11.57	15.89	5.72	Total Return %
–12.38	–1.93	8.88	9.31	–1.46	–7.39	3.42	–11.38	–27.76	–9.47	24.99	17.60	+/– S&P 500
–11.83	10.40	7.43	–0.39	2.17	–9.89	4.05	–13.52	–20.43	0.62	13.58	14.52	+/– Russ Top 200 Val
5.60	5.60	4.22	2.92	3.19	3.68	2.84	1.94	1.48	1.74	1.79	1.31	Income Return %
–21.10	22.95	12.28	16.44	–3.34	26.46	23.52	20.04	–0.67	9.83	14.10	4.42	Capital Return %
95	40	11	12	45	70	12	84	94	28	13	5	Total Rtn % Rank Cat
0.74	0.57	0.49	0.37	0.44	0.46	0.41	0.32	0.25	0.27	0.27	0.20	Income $
0.32	0.84	0.38	0.89	0.86	1.38	1.33	2.88	1.23	1.90	1.85	0.31	Capital Gains $
0.37	0.30	0.26	0.40	0.45	0.43	0.29	0.27	0.27	0.28	0.31	—	Expense Ratio %
5.82	4.84	3.89	2.68	3.11	3.01	2.75	1.89	1.31	1.56	1.75	—	Income Ratio %
21	36	32	25	34	32	34	61	48	56	41	—	Turnover Rate %
6,523.8	7,822.3	8,832.6	10,610.8	10,672.9	13,646.3	16,738.1	20,914.6	18,187.7	16,699.8	16,777.0	16,026.7	Net Assets $mil

Performance 12-31-01

	1st Qtr	2nd Qtr	3rd Qtr	4th Qtr	Total
1997	3.50	11.11	9.80	–3.39	21.97
1998	12.84	–2.24	–19.45	13.46	0.81
1999	3.15	13.84	–10.35	5.98	11.57
2000	–0.40	–0.54	7.85	8.46	15.89
2001	–0.52	6.52	–12.74	14.35	5.72

Trailing	Total Return%	+/– S&P 500	+/– Russ Top 200 Val	% Rank All	% Rank Cat	Growth of $10,000
3 Mo	14.35	3.66	8.83	25	7	11,435
6 Mo	–0.22	5.33	5.56	40	10	9,978
1 Yr	5.72	17.60	14.52	20	5	10,572
3 Yr Avg	10.98	12.01	9.82	9	3	13,670
5 Yr Avg	10.95	0.25	–0.26	14	28	16,809
10 Yr Avg	14.40	1.47	0.37	7	11	38,384
15 Yr Avg	12.99	–0.74	–0.51	17	25	62,479

Tax Analysis	Tax-Adj Ret%	%Rank Cat	%Pretax Ret	%Rank Cat
3 Yr Avg	8.28	3	75.4	34
5 Yr Avg	7.77	35	71.0	63
10 Yr Avg	11.07	18	76.9	53

Potential Capital Gain Exposure: 14% of assets

Risk Analysis

Time Period	Load-Adj Return %	Risk %Rank[1] All	Risk %Rank[1] Cat	Morningstar Return	Morningstar Risk	Morningstar Risk-Adj Rating
1 Yr	5.72					
3 Yr	10.98	50	31	1.36[2]	0.70	★★★★
5 Yr	10.95	60	65	1.45[2]	0.83	★★★★
10 Yr	14.40	65	75	1.64	0.84	★★★★

Average Historical Rating (193 months): 3.8★s

[1] 1=low, 100=high [2] T-Bill return substituted for category avg.

Category Rating (3 Yr)

1 2 3 4 5
Worst Best

Return: High
Risk: Below Avg

Other Measures	Standard Index S&P 500	Best Fit Index S&P 500
Alpha	11.2	11.2
Beta	0.78	0.78
R-Squared	54	54
Standard Deviation		20.12
Mean		10.98
Sharpe Ratio		0.34

Portfolio Analysis 09-30-01

Share change since 06-01 Total Stocks: 171	Sector	PE	YTD Ret%	% Assets
Citigroup	Financials	20.0	0.03	5.93
ALCOA	Industrials	21.4	7.86	4.54
⊕ WorldCom	Services	24.3	3.12	3.31
⊖ TJX	Retail	23.2	44.39	3.28
⊕ Pharmacia	Health	36.5	–29.30	2.77
Washington Mutual	Financials	10.1	–5.32	2.75
⊕ IBM	Technology	26.9	43.00	2.64
Cigna	Financials	13.2	–29.00	2.00
⊖ Air Products and Chemicals	Industrials	22.1	16.61	1.93
Engelhard	Industrials	22.3	37.94	1.93
Eaton	Industrials	22.8	17.90	1.70
⊕ Arrow Electncs	Technology	NMF	4.45	1.66
⊖ Ross Stores	Retail	17.3	91.38	1.65
Staples	Retail	77.9	58.30	1.59
⊕ Health Net	Health	35.7	–16.80	1.53
☼ Total Stock Viper	N/A	—	—	1.45
Canadian Natl Railway	Services	18.8	64.61	1.45
⊕ Adelphia Comms	Services	—	–39.60	1.41
Cox Comms A	Services	31.8	–9.99	1.41
⊕ Golden West Finl	Financials	12.9	–12.40	1.31
⊕ Petrobras ADR	Energy	—	—	1.25
⊕ ExxonMobil	Energy	15.3	–7.59	1.13
Republic Svcs Cl A	Services	15.6	16.19	1.11
⊕ Schering-Plough	Health	22.2	–35.90	1.03
☼ Hartford Finl Svcs Grp	Financials	23.2	–9.63	1.00

Current Investment Style

Style: Value Blnd Growth; Size: Large Med Small

	Stock Port Avg	Relative S&P 500 Current	Relative S&P 500 Hist	Rel Cat
Price/Earnings Ratio	22.7	0.73	0.65	0.90
Price/Book Ratio	3.2	0.56	0.36	0.77
Price/Cash Flow	12.1	0.67	0.58	0.88
3 Yr Earnings Growth	13.8	0.94	0.80	0.93
1 Yr Earnings Est%	–10.2	5.75	—	3.07
Med Mkt Cap $mil	10,783	0.2	0.2	0.34

Analysis by William Samuel Rocco 12-26-01

Vanguard Windsor Fund continues to find more than its share of good bargains.

Manager Chuck Freeman, who's a pretty selective investor, found several attractively priced opportunities this fall. He bought or added to RenaissanceRe Holdings, Hartford, ACE, and IPC Holdings shortly after the September attacks; he thought that these insurers were cheap, that their losses were quantifiable and manageable, and that premiums would rise.

Freeman also purchased Weatherford International, Cooper Cameron, and a few other energy-services firms after they slipped in late summer. And he bought or added to a handful of drug stocks—including Merck, Aventis, American Home Products, and Pharmacia—earlier in the fourth quarter.

This value discipline has paid off lately. RenaissanceRe and Freeman's other insurance picks have rebounded sharply this fall. Ace, in fact, is up 63% over the past three months. Weatherford International and Cooper Cameron have also posted strong gains. And though some of his pharmaceutical selections have been sluggish, Pharmacia, which is the fund's fifth-largest holding at present, has posted a double-digit return in the fourth quarter. Thus, the fund has returned 16% in the three months ending Dec. 24, 2001, while its average peer has gained 12%. The fund also outperformed earlier in the year, and it's ahead of 94% of its rivals for the year to date.

The fund hasn't always prospered during Freeman's six-year reign, but it usually has, so the fund's long-term returns are also good. Thus, though the fund is a bit more volatile than many of its peers, it's a good option for those who want a hard-core value offering—especially if they're concerned about costs. The fund also boasts an incredibly low expense ratio for an actively managed offering.

Special Securities % assets 09-30-01	
Restricted/Illiquid Secs	0
Emerging-Markets Secs	2
Options/Futures/Warrants	Yes

Composition % assets 09-30-01	
Cash	1.6
Stocks*	98.4
Bonds	0.0
Other	0.0
*Foreign (% stocks)	9.0

Market Cap	
Giant	21.6
Large	33.2
Medium	42.2
Small	2.9
Micro	0.1

Sector Weightings	% of Stocks	Rel S&P	5-Year High	5-Year Low
Utilities	1.7	0.5	9	0
Energy	8.0	1.1	27	8
Financials	26.1	1.5	47	18
Industrials	20.9	1.8	32	11
Durables	2.0	1.3	15	0
Staples	1.5	0.2	2	0
Services	15.4	1.4	17	1
Retail	8.1	1.2	8	0
Health	7.4	0.5	14	0
Technology	9.0	0.5	14	0

Address: Vanguard Financial Ctr. P.O. Box 2600, Valley Forge, PA 19482, 800-662-7447 / 610-669-1000
Web Address: www.vanguard.com
Inception: 10-23-58
Advisor: Wellington Mgmt./Sanford C. Bernstein & Co.
Subadvisor: None
NTF Plans: N/A

Minimum Purchase: $3000 Add: $100 IRA: $1000
Min Auto Inv Plan: $3000 Add: $50
Sales Fees: No-load
Management Fee: .13% mx./.10% mn.+(–).90%P
Actual Fees: Mgt: 0.12% Dist: —
Expense Projections: 3Yr: $90 5Yr: $157 10Yr: $356
Avg Brok Commission: — Income Distrib: Semi-Ann.
Total Cost (relative to category): Low

Vanguard Windsor II

Ticker	Load	NAV	Yield	Total Assets	Mstar Category
VWNFX	None	$25.59	2.1%	$24,918.6 mil	Large Value

Prospectus Objective: Growth and Income

Vanguard Windsor II Fund seeks long-term growth of capital; current income is secondary.

The fund invests primarily in undervalued stocks of medium and large companies, characterized by above-average dividend yields and below-average price/earnings ratios relative to the stock market. Barrow, Hanley, Mewhinney & Strauss supervises approximately 67% of assets, Equinox and Tukman each supervise approximately 10%, and Vanguard supervises the remainder.

The fund also offers Adm shares. Prior to May 17, 1993, the fund was named Windsor II. From that date until Oct. 27, 1998, it was named Vanguard/Windsor II Fund. Equinox and Tukman replaced Invesco.

Historical Profile
Return Above Avg
Risk Below Avg
Rating ★★★★ Above Avg

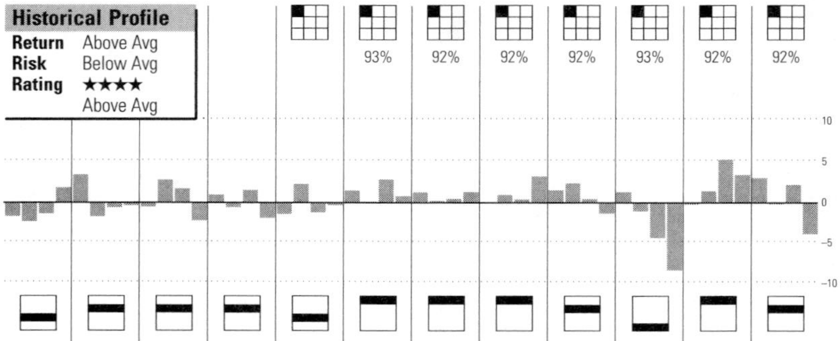

Investment Style
Equity
Average Stock %: 93% 92% 92% 92% 93% 92% 92%

▼ Manager Change
▽ Partial Manager Change

Fund Performance vs. Category Average
Quarterly Fund Return
+/– Category Average
— Category Baseline

Performance Quartile (within Category)

Portfolio Manager(s)

James P. Barrow, et al. Since 6-85. BS'62 U. of South Carolina.

1990	1991	1992	1993	1994	1995	1996	1997	1998	1999	2000	12-01	History
12.46	14.89	15.91	17.04	15.82	20.66	23.83	28.62	29.85	24.97	27.20	25.59	NAV
–9.99	28.70	11.99	13.60	–1.17	38.83	24.18	32.37	16.36	–5.81	16.86	–3.40	Total Return %
–6.87	–1.79	4.37	3.55	–2.48	1.30	1.24	–0.98	–12.22	–26.85	25.96	8.48	+/– S&P 500
–6.32	10.54	2.92	–6.16	1.15	–1.20	1.87	–3.12	–4.88	–16.76	14.55	5.39	+/– Russ Top 200 Val
4.93	4.94	3.52	3.23	3.25	3.69	3.07	2.78	2.25	2.29	2.46	2.01	Income Return %
–14.92	23.75	8.47	10.37	–4.42	35.14	21.12	29.59	14.11	–8.10	14.40	–5.41	Capital Return %
75	40	26	48	62	8	21	14	29	96	11	35	Total Rtn % Rank Cat
0.73	0.61	0.52	0.51	0.55	0.58	0.63	0.66	0.64	0.68	0.61	0.55	Income $
0.28	0.44	0.22	0.50	0.47	0.69	1.16	2.19	2.67	2.50	1.24	0.15	Capital Gains $
0.52	0.48	0.41	0.39	0.39	0.39	0.39	0.37	0.41	0.37	0.37	—	Expense Ratio %
4.93	4.51	3.72	3.11	3.26	3.27	2.92	2.49	2.16	2.08	2.36	—	Income Ratio %
20	41	23	26	24	30	32	30	31	26	26	—	Turnover Rate %
2,334.5	3,626.6	5,407.4	7,616.3	7,959.0	11,013.0	15,700.0	24,376.5	31,538.2	26,901.8	25,304.1	22,428.6	Net Assets $mil

Performance 12-31-01

	1st Qtr	2nd Qtr	3rd Qtr	4th Qtr	Total
1997	1.59	14.70	9.07	4.15	32.37
1998	12.79	1.80	–11.82	14.92	16.36
1999	2.08	8.79	–13.55	–1.88	–5.81
2000	–0.04	–0.62	10.56	6.40	16.86
2001	–2.72	4.58	–9.96	5.45	–3.40

Trailing	Total Return%	+/– S&P 500	+/– Russ Top 200 Val	% Rank All	% Rank Cat	Growth of $10,000
3 Mo	5.45	–5.23	–0.06	63	93	10,545
6 Mo	–5.05	0.50	0.73	62	66	9,495
1 Yr	–3.40	8.48	5.39	48	35	9,660
3 Yr Avg	2.07	3.09	0.90	62	50	10,633
5 Yr Avg	10.37	–0.33	–0.83	17	32	16,379
10 Yr Avg	13.51	0.58	–0.52	11	24	35,507
15 Yr Avg	13.19	–0.54	–0.31	16	23	64,177

Tax Analysis	Tax-Adj Ret%	%Rank Cat	%Pretax Ret	%Rank Cat
3 Yr Avg	0.12	55	5.9	98
5 Yr Avg	7.89	33	76.1	47
10 Yr Avg	11.10	18	82.2	27

Potential Capital Gain Exposure: 18% of assets

Risk Analysis

Time Period	Load-Adj Return %	Risk %Rank[1] All	Risk %Rank[1] Cat	Morningstar Return	Morningstar Risk	Morningstar Risk-Adj Rating
1 Yr	–3.40					
3 Yr	2.07	54	50	–0.59[2]	0.75	★★★
5 Yr	10.37	55	40	1.29[2]	0.77	★★★★
10 Yr	13.51	59	43	1.43	0.77	★★★★

Average Historical Rating (163 months): 3.9★s

[1] 1=low, 100=high [2] T-Bill return substituted for category avg.

Category Rating (3 Yr)

1 2 **3** 4 5
Worst Best

Return Average
Risk Average

Other Measures	Standard Index S&P 500	Best Fit Index S&P 500
Alpha	0.8	0.8
Beta	0.54	0.54
R-Squared	36	36

Standard Deviation	15.68
Mean	2.07
Sharpe Ratio	–0.21

Portfolio Analysis 09-30-01

Share change since 06-01 Total Stocks: 310	Sector	PE	YTD Ret%	% Assets
⊖ Philip Morris	Staples	12.1	9.12	3.31
⊕ Citigroup	Financials	20.0	0.03	2.78
Entergy	Utilities	11.7	–4.50	2.67
⊕ Bank of America	Financials	16.7	42.73	2.53
⊕ J.P. Morgan Chase & Co.	Financials	27.8	–17.40	2.40
⊕ Allstate	Financials	17.1	–21.00	2.39
American Elec Pwr	Utilities	20.2	–1.28	2.34
Sears Roebuck	Retail	23.4	40.12	2.25
Occidental Petro	Energy	5.7	13.49	2.17
⊕ Verizon Comms	Services	29.7	–2.52	2.17
⊕ SBC Comms	Services	18.4	–16.00	1.94
⊕ Reliant Energy	Utilities	14.8	–36.00	1.91
ITT Inds	Durables	16.2	32.06	1.84
⊕ Public Svc Entpr	Utilities	11.3	–8.99	1.83
⊕ Cendant	Services	20.4	103.70	1.75
⊕ Newell Rubbermaid	Durables	25.5	25.20	1.68
⊕ Boeing	Industrials	10.2	–40.40	1.62
⊕ Bristol-Myers Squibb	Health	20.2	–26.00	1.60
⊖ Phillips Petro	Energy	7.1	8.56	1.59
Imperial Tobacco Grp ADR	Staples	18.2	34.20	1.57
⊖ Waste Mgmt	Services	52.3	15.03	1.53
⊕ Procter & Gamble	Staples	38.8	3.12	1.52
⊕ Watson Pharmaceuticals	Health	51.5	–38.60	1.49
Fannie Mae	Financials	16.2	–6.95	1.44
⊕ USA Educ	Financials	68.9	24.74	1.43

Current Investment Style

Style: Value Blnd Growth; Size: Large Med Small

	Stock Port Avg	Relative S&P 500 Current	Relative S&P 500 Hist	Rel Cat
Price/Earnings Ratio	22.9	0.74	0.71	0.91
Price/Book Ratio	3.6	0.63	0.52	0.87
Price/Cash Flow	11.4	0.63	0.63	0.82
3 Yr Earnings Growth	12.6	0.86	0.52	0.85
1 Yr Earnings Est%	2.9	—	—	–0.86
Med Mkt Cap $mil	23,587	0.4	0.4	0.74

Analysis by William Samuel Rocco 12-24-01

Despite some cloudiness of late, the big picture remains bright here.

Vanguard Windsor II Fund hasn't enjoyed the fall recovery nearly as much as most of its peers. It ended the summer with more than twice the large-value norm of 5% in utilities stocks, and manager Jim Barrow has stuck with his holdings in that area. He didn't own any Enron, but several of his utilities holdings have been sluggish or worse lately. And a few that have exposure to the independent-power-production business, such as American Electric Power, have fallen significantly.

Meanwhile, a few of Barrow's other favorites, including top-10 holdings Philip Morris and Allstate, have been uninspiring performers in recent months. Thus, though he has made some good calls recently—such as adding to Cendant and Boeing right before their fall rebounds—the fund has gained less than 93% of its peers in the three months ending Dec. 21, 2001.

There's no reason to be concerned about this short-term underperformance, though. The fund has outpaced nearly two thirds of its large-value rivals in 2001, as many of Barrow's picks have posted strong results over the past 12 months. Indeed, despite its recent listlessness, Philip Morris is up 9% in 2001, and Bank of America and Sears Roebuck, which are also top-five holdings, have returned much more.

What's more, though it hasn't prospered every year, the fund has handily outpaced most of its peers over the long term. It has suffered only average volatility along the way and has low expenses and a solid yield to boot. For all these reasons, we remain big fans of this offering.

Special Securities % assets 09-30-01	
Restricted/Illiquid Secs	0
Emerging-Markets Secs	0
Options/Futures/Warrants	No

Sector Weightings	% of Stocks	Rel S&P	5-Year High	5-Year Low
Utilities	12.9	4.0	16	2
Energy	10.9	1.5	22	7
Financials	26.4	1.5	30	17
Industrials	8.2	0.7	17	5
Durables	5.2	3.3	9	1
Staples	10.8	1.4	15	6
Services	12.0	1.1	17	6
Retail	5.5	0.8	13	2
Health	4.7	0.3	13	1
Technology	3.4	0.2	7	2

Composition % assets 09-30-01	
Cash	5.9
Stocks*	94.1
Bonds	0.0
Other	0.0
*Foreign (% stocks)	3.6

Market Cap	
Giant	34.3
Large	44.1
Medium	20.9
Small	0.5
Micro	0.2

Address:	Vanguard Financial Ctr. P.O. Box 2600 Valley Forge, PA 19482 800-662-7447 / 610-669-1000
Web Address:	www.vanguard.com
Inception:	06-24-85
Advisor:	Barrow/Vanguard Core Mgmt. Grp.
Subadvisor:	None
NTF Plans:	N/A

Minimum Purchase:	$3000	Add: $100 IRA: $1000
Min Auto Inv Plan:	$3000	Add: $50
Sales Fees:	No-load	
Management Fee:	None	
Actual Fees:	Mgt: 0.35%	Dist: —
Expense Projections:	3Yr: $119	5Yr: $208 10Yr: $468
Avg Brok Commission:	—	Income Distrib: Semi-Ann.
Total Cost (relative to category):		Low

Wachovia Special Values A

Ticker	Load	NAV	Yield	Total Assets	Mstar Category
BTSVX	5.75%	$19.75	0.5%	$288.4 mil	Small Value

Prospectus Objective: Small Company

Wachovia Special Values Fund seeks capital growth.

The fund usually invests at least 65% of assets in equities of companies with market capitalizations of $1 billion or less. It may invest up to 20% of assets in ADRs and other foreign securities traded on U.S. exchanges; it may hold up to 10% directly in foreign securities. Stocks acquired by the fund typically have low P/E ratios, are out of favor in the market, are selling significantly below their book value, or are undergoing a reorganization or some other special situation that may result in price appreciation.

The fund offer A, B, C & Y shares, all which differ in fee structure and availability.

Past names: South Carolina Municipal Bond Fund and Biltmore South Carolina Municipal Bond Fund.

Historical Profile

Return: Above Avg
Risk: Low
Rating: ★★★★ Above Avg

Investment Style
Equity
Average Stock %: 91% (1995), 96% (1996), 85% (1997), 90% (1998), 81% (1999), 81% (2000), 74% (12-01)

▼ Manager Change
▽ Partial Manager Change

Fund Performance vs. Category Average
■ Quarterly Fund Return +/– Category Average
— Category Baseline

Performance Quartile (within Category)

Portfolio Manager(s)

Roger L. Glenski. Since 6-97. BS'90 U. of Missouri - Kansas City; MBA'96 U. of Chicago. Other funds currently managed: Wachovia Special Values Y, Wachovia Special Values B, Wachovia Special Values II.

James M. Tringas, CFA. Since 1-00. BA U. of Florida; MBA U. of Florida. Other funds currently managed: Wachovia Special Values Y, Wachovia Special Values B, Wachovia Special Values II.

1990	1991	1992	1993	1994	1995	1996	1997	1998	1999	2000	12–01	History
—	—	—	10.32	9.85	11.81	14.46	16.80	15.60	15.77	17.77	19.75	NAV
—	—	—	6.33*	–3.32	30.27	36.98	29.08	–1.51	6.39	15.14	18.13	Total Return %
—	—	—	–1.10*	–4.64	–7.27	14.04	–4.28	–30.09	–14.65	24.25	30.01	+/– S&P 500
—	—	—	—	–1.77	4.51	15.61	–2.62	4.92	7.87	–7.67	4.12	+/– Russell 2000 V
—	—	—	0.00	0.64	0.81	0.68	0.83	0.96	1.79	1.51	0.56	Income Return %
—	—	—	6.33	–3.96	29.45	36.30	28.25	–2.48	4.60	13.63	17.58	Capital Return %
—	—	—	—	65	15	9	64	22	32	69	42	Total Rtn % Rank Cat
—	—	—	0.00	0.07	0.08	0.08	0.12	0.16	0.28	0.24	0.10	Income $
—	—	—	0.28	0.06	0.91	1.61	1.71	0.75	0.52	0.13	1.14	Capital Gains $
—	—	—	1.25	1.26	1.29	1.21	1.35	1.25	1.23	1.21	—	Expense Ratio %
—	—	—	–0.03	1.09	0.80	0.47	0.74	0.98	1.61	1.38	—	Income Ratio %
—	—	—	—	62	57	38	46	20	44	42	—	Turnover Rate %
—	—	—	12.5	17.9	25.6	8.0	43.1	61.6	65.7	67.9	80.4	Net Assets $mil

Performance 12-31-01

	1st Qtr	2nd Qtr	3rd Qtr	4th Qtr	Total
1997	3.18	12.33	14.08	–2.38	29.08
1998	8.99	–0.49	–18.00	10.75	–1.51
1999	–6.35	16.56	–4.87	2.45	6.39
2000	2.22	1.12	5.09	6.00	15.14
2001	1.80	11.66	–8.91	14.09	18.13

Trailing	Total Return%	+/– S&P 500	+/– Russ 2000V	% Rank All	% Rank Cat	Growth of $10,000
3 Mo	14.09	3.40	–2.63	26	81	11,409
6 Mo	3.92	9.48	2.77	10	33	10,392
1 Yr	18.13	30.01	4.12	2	42	11,813
3 Yr Avg	13.11	14.14	1.79	7	47	14,471
5 Yr Avg	12.97	2.27	1.77	8	27	18,396
10 Yr Avg	—	—	—	—	—	—
15 Yr Avg	—	—	—	—	—	—

Tax Analysis	Tax-Adj Ret%	%Rank Cat	%Pretax Ret	%Rank Cat
3 Yr Avg	11.43	45	87.2	68
5 Yr Avg	10.94	33	84.4	59
10 Yr Avg	—	—	—	—

Potential Capital Gain Exposure: 24% of assets

Risk Analysis

Time Period	Load-Adj Return %	Risk %Rank[1] All	Risk %Rank[1] Cat	Morningstar Return	Morningstar Risk	Morningstar Risk-Adj Rating
1 Yr	11.34					
3 Yr	10.90	35	2	1.34[2]	0.43	★★★★
5 Yr	11.64	44	4	1.64[2]	0.56	★★★★
Incept	14.31	—	—	—	—	

Average Historical Rating (68 months): 3.8★s

[1] 1=low, 100=high [2] T-Bill return substituted for category avg.

Category Rating (3 Yr)

1 2 3 4 5
Worst Best

Return: Average
Risk: Low

Other Measures	Standard Index S&P 500	Best Fit Index SPMid400
Alpha	10.6	5.0
Beta	0.41	0.49
R-Squared	32	62

Standard Deviation	13.67
Mean	13.11
Sharpe Ratio	0.68

Portfolio Analysis 09-30-01

Share change since 06–01 Total Stocks: 111	Sector	PE	YTD Ret%	% Assets
⊕ Russell 2000 Index (Fut)	N/A	—	—	8.64
⊕ John Nuveen	Financials	24.3	42.69	2.70
⊖ Radian Grp	Financials	11.6	14.64	2.49
⊖ Lafarge	Industrials	12.9	61.92	2.15
⊕ Liberty	Services	37.1	3.36	2.10
Forest City Enterprises Cl A	Financials	19.0	48.90	2.05
⊖ Emcor Grp	Industrials	13.8	78.04	1.97
⊕ Universal	Staples	8.6	7.88	1.97
⊕ Briggs & Stratton	Industrials	25.3	–0.78	1.96
⊕ Stewart Info Svcs	Financials	9.8	–10.90	1.70
⊕ Centex Const Prods	Industrials	18.1	18.15	1.61
⊕ AO Smith	Industrials	55.7	17.77	1.51
⊖ Butler Mfg	Industrials	13.0	13.30	1.46
⊖ Superior Inds Intl	Durables	17.0	29.10	1.43
⊖ White Mountains Ins Grp	Financials	—	9.45	1.42
⊖ Granite Const	Industrials	19.3	26.58	1.38
⊕ Texas Inds	Industrials	NMF	24.18	1.35
ACLN	Services	3.2	–60.30	1.30
⊕ Forest Oil	Energy	7.4	–23.50	1.14
⊕ Berry Petro	Energy	12.6	20.64	1.13
⊖ Lands' End	Retail	28.5	99.68	1.04
⊕ West Pharma Svc	Industrials	NMF	11.55	1.02
Charter Municipal Mtg Acc	Financials	13.3	30.14	1.00
⊖ USFreightways	Services	15.9	5.74	1.00
⊖ Equity Residential Properties	Financials	22.1	10.14	0.98

Current Investment Style

Style: Value Blnd Growth; Size: Large Med Small

	Stock Port Avg	Relative S&P 500 Current	Relative S&P 500 Hist	Rel Cat
Price/Earnings Ratio	22.6	0.73	0.56	1.04
Price/Book Ratio	2.4	0.43	0.28	1.00
Price/Cash Flow	10.2	0.56	0.47	0.80
3 Yr Earnings Growth	7.4	0.51	0.66	0.64
1 Yr Earnings Est%	1.1	—	—	–0.28
Med Mkt Cap $mil	814	0.0	0.0	0.93

[1] figure is based on 50% or less of stocks

Special Securities % assets 09-30-01	
Restricted/Illiquid Secs	0
Emerging-Markets Secs	1
Options/Futures/Warrants	Yes

Composition % assets 09-30-01	
Cash	19.2
Stocks*	71.7
Bonds	0.2
Other	8.9
*Foreign (% stocks)	3.7

Market Cap	
Giant	0.0
Large	0.4
Medium	29.2
Small	56.5
Micro	14.0

Sector Weightings	% of Stocks	Rel S&P	5-Year High	5-Year Low
Utilities	1.2	0.4	2	0
Energy	5.7	0.8	21	3
Financials	25.8	1.4	38	17
Industrials	31.1	2.7	37	24
Durables	4.1	2.6	13	2
Staples	3.3	0.4	6	1
Services	15.3	1.4	17	5
Retail	3.0	0.4	7	0
Health	1.4	0.1	8	1
Technology	9.3	0.5	16	1

Analysis by Catherine Hickey 08-12-01

This cheapskate may not post flashy returns, but its steadiness makes it worth a look.

Even in the frugal small-cap value category, Wachovia Special Values Fund stands out from the crowd for its penny-pinching ways. Manager Roger Glenski looks for companies that are trading cheaply relative to their earnings or cash flows. Using this strategy, he tends to load up on beaten-down industrials and financials, which are areas that were left behind in the growth-dominated market of the late 1990s.

Such an unflinching emphasis on value has led to some ups and downs here, to be sure. As the market continues to bid up small-value stocks in 2001, Glenski says he's finding fewer bargains in the market these days. Thus, he has let cash drift up to around 18% of assets, and this has been a big drag on performance this year (though the fund is posting a healthy gain in absolute terms). Last year held similar results for this offering. Though its 2000 return was strong in absolute terms, some struggling industrial picks held it back from notching the even bigger gains posted by most small-value funds that year.

Despite a couple of relatively ho-hum years, the fund's long-term returns are strong. It notched solid numbers in 1998 and 1999, through both good stock selection and some timely sector moves. For example, Glenski dumped the fund's oil-services shares in late 1997 and picked up some tech shares in 1998 that went on to perform well. Solid performance isn't the fund's only strength, however; another draw for this fund is its moderate volatility. Glenski's attention to valuations has helped keep a lid on big performance swings.

This fund will probably never knock the lights out. But those looking for a small-value fund that won't blow up may find it a good option.

Address:	Federated Investors Tower Pittsburgh, PA 15222–3779 800–994–4414
Web Address:	www.wachovia.com/investment/html/funds.html
*Inception:	05-10-93
Advisor:	Wachovia Asset Mgmt.
Subadvisor:	None
NTF Plans:	N/A

Minimum Purchase:	$250	Add: $50	IRA: $250
Min Auto Inv Plan:	$250	Add: $25	
Sales Fees:	5.75%L		
Management Fee:	.80%, .10%A		
Actual Fees:	Mgt: 0.80%	Dist: —	
Expense Projections:	3Yr: $937	5Yr: $1202	10Yr: $1957
Avg Brok Commission:	—	Income Distrib: Annually	
Total Cost (relative to category):		Average	

Waddell & Reed Adv International Gr A

Ticker	Load	NAV	Yield	Total Assets	Mstar Category
UNCGX	5.75%	$6.14	0.8%	$1,048.4 mil	Foreign Stock

Prospectus Objective: Foreign Stock

Waddell & Reed Advisor International Growth Fund seeks long-term capital appreciation; income is secondary.

The fund normally invests at least 80% of assets in common stocks, preferred stocks, and debt securities of foreign issuers. It ordinarily maintains investments in at least three foreign countries. The fund may invest in debt of any credit quality.

Class A shares have front loads and 12b-1 fees; Y shares are designed for institutional investors. Past fund names : United Continental Growth Fund and United International Growth Fund

Historical Profile
Return Above Avg
Risk Average
Rating ★★★★ Above Avg

Investment Style
Equity
Average Stock %: 88% (1996), 82% (1997), 74% (1998), 86% (1999), 84% (2000), 69% (12-01)

▼ Manager Change
▽ Partial Manager Change

Fund Performance vs. Category Average
■ Quarterly Fund Return +/– Category Average
— Category Baseline

Performance Quartile (within Category)

Portfolio Manager(s)

Thomas A. Mengel. Since 5-96. U. of Berlin. Other funds currently managed: W&R International Growth C, Waddell & Reed Adv International Gr Y, W&R International Growth Y.

History

1990	1991	1992	1993	1994	1995	1996	1997	1998	1999	2000	12-01	History
5.77	6.75	6.56	9.04	8.24	8.23	9.38	9.14	9.85	13.81	7.97	6.14	NAV
–13.71	18.74	–1.12	46.49	1.81	8.09	18.22	17.31	21.42	57.04	–24.94	–22.36	Total Return %
–10.59	–11.74	–8.73	36.43	0.49	–29.45	–4.72	–16.04	–7.15	36.00	–15.83	–10.48	+/– S&P 500
9.74	6.61	11.06	13.93	–5.97	–3.12	12.18	15.53	1.43	30.07	–10.77	—	+/– MSCI EAFE
2.20	1.53	1.04	0.64	0.45	0.73	0.97	0.63	0.77	0.39	0.07	0.61	Income Return %
–15.91	17.21	–2.15	45.85	1.36	7.36	17.25	16.68	20.66	56.65	–25.00	–22.97	Capital Return %
82	12	23	16	38	67	25	8	13	24	85	52	Total Rtn % Rank Cat
0.15	0.09	0.07	0.04	0.04	0.06	0.08	0.06	0.07	0.04	0.01	0.05	Income $
0.00	0.01	0.05	0.50	0.93	0.60	0.26	1.78	1.15	1.44	2.36	0.00	Capital Gains $
1.17	1.20	1.18	1.18	1.20	1.25	1.25	1.28	1.23	1.30	1.41	1.44	Expense Ratio %
1.81	1.89	1.17	1.07	0.57	0.86	0.89	0.78	0.67	0.52	–0.32	0.71	Income Ratio %
196	118	113	94	84	57	59	110	114	149	113	118	Turnover Rate %
252.4	296.9	308.6	491.8	638.5	701.5	847.8	1,013.0	1,215.7	1,857.1	1,386.6	1,006.8	Net Assets $mil

Performance 12-31-01

	1st Qtr	2nd Qtr	3rd Qtr	4th Qtr	Total
1997	3.30	9.91	6.69	–3.16	17.31
1998	19.80	8.60	–17.30	12.85	21.42
1999	0.10	1.27	5.62	46.67	57.04
2000	1.16	–11.02	–9.09	–8.26	–24.94
2001	–12.80	–2.02	–11.63	2.84	–22.36

Trailing	Total Return%	+/– S&P 500	+/– MSCI EAFE	% Rank All	% Rank Cat	Growth of $10,000
3 Mo	2.84	–7.85	—	70	97	10,284
6 Mo	–9.13	–3.57	—	82	54	9,087
1 Yr	–22.36	–10.48	—	84	52	7,764
3 Yr Avg	–2.91	–1.88	—	86	54	9,153
5 Yr Avg	5.45	–5.25	—	56	18	13,037
10 Yr Avg	9.41	–3.52	—	36	11	24,569
15 Yr Avg	9.07	–4.66	—	46	16	36,791

Tax Analysis	Tax-Adj Ret%	%Rank Cat	%Pretax Ret	%Rank Cat
3 Yr Avg	–6.21	70	—	—
5 Yr Avg	1.51	35	27.8	83
10 Yr Avg	6.35	23	67.5	68

Potential Capital Gain Exposure: –18% of assets

Risk Analysis

Time Period	Load-Adj Return %	Risk %Rank[1] All	Risk %Rank[1] Cat	Morningstar Return	Morningstar Risk	Morningstar Risk-Adj Rating
1 Yr	–26.82					
3 Yr	–4.81	77	64	–1.88[2]	1.00	★★
5 Yr	4.21	76	61	–0.18[2]	0.86	★★★★
10 Yr	8.76	84	76	1.24[2]	0.91	★★★★

Average Historical Rating (193 months): 3.7★s

[1]1=low, 100=high [2] T-Bill return substituted for category avg.

Category Rating (3 Yr)
1 2 3 4 5
Worst Best
Return Average
Risk Average

Other Measures	Standard Index S&P 500	Best Fit Index Wil 4500
Alpha	–2.6	–5.5
Beta	0.67	0.61
R-Squared	27	63
Standard Deviation	21.34	
Mean	–2.91	
Sharpe Ratio	–0.43	

Portfolio Analysis 09-30-01

Share change since 06-01 Total Stocks: 65	Sector	Country	% Assets
Suez Lyon Eaux	Industrials	France	3.58
⊕ Muenchener Rueckvers (Reg)	Financials	Germany	2.80
⊕ Fortis NV	Financials	Netherlands	2.08
⊖ Lloyds TSB Grp	Financials	United Kingdom	1.87
⊕ Assicurazioni Generali	Financials	Italy	1.86
⊕ UBS (Reg)	Financials	Switzerland	1.74
⊕ Aventis Cl A	Health	France	1.62
⊕ Pharmacia	Health	U.S.	1.47
⊕ Unilever (Cert)	Staples	United Kingdom	1.46
☼ Allianz (Reg)	Financials	Germany	1.45
⊕ Reckitt Benckiser	Staples	United Kingdom	1.41
Takeda Chem Inds	Health	Japan	1.38
⊕ British Amer Tobacco	Staples	United Kingdom	1.30
Nestle (Reg)	Staples	Switzerland	1.30
⊕ ING Groep	Financials	Netherlands	1.18
AGF	Financials	France	1.18
☼ Acom	Financials	Japan	1.18
⊕ Vivendi	Services	France	1.13
⊕ Shire Pharma Grp	Health	United Kingdom	1.13
KAO	Staples	Japan	1.12

Current Investment Style

Style: Value Blnd Growth; Size: Large Med Small

	Stock Port Avg	Rel MSCI EAFE Current	Rel MSCI EAFE Hist	Rel Cat
Price/Earnings Ratio	24.9	0.96	1.15	0.98
Price/Cash Flow	13.8	1.08	1.24	0.96
Price/Book Ratio	4.0	1.16	1.50	1.03
3 Yr Earnings Growth	21.4	1.15	1.45	1.09
Med Mkt Cap $mil	24,691	0.9	1.0	1.37

Country Exposure 09-30-01	% assets
United Kingdom	13
France	11
Germany	8
Japan	8
Switzerland	6

Hedging History: Rare

Regional Exposure 09-30-01	% assets
Europe	53
Japan	8
Latin America	0
Pacific Rim	1
Other	3

Special Securities % assets 09-30-01	
Restricted/Illiquid Secs	1
Emerging-Markets Secs	1
Options/Futures/Warrants	Yes

Composition % assets 09-30-01			
Cash	30.0	Bonds	0.0
Stocks	61.6	Other	8.4

Sector Weightings	% of Stocks	Rel Cat	5-Year High	5-Year Low
Utilities	4.3	1.5	14	0
Energy	2.2	0.4	9	0
Financials	36.1	1.7	39	10
Industrials	13.2	1.0	42	7
Durables	1.5	0.2	15	1
Staples	13.5	1.9	14	0
Services	12.9	0.7	38	5
Retail	2.7	0.6	23	1
Health	12.9	1.3	24	2
Technology	0.7	0.1	20	0

Analysis by Gregg Wolper 12-08-01

Waddell & Reed Advisor International Growth Fund doesn't look as shiny as it once did, but don't give up on it yet.

This fund's year-to-date loss of 22.1% through Dec. 7, 2001, isn't just painful in the absolute sense, it also lands a bit below the category midpoint for that stretch. Coming on the heels of a bottom-quartile performance in 2000, it might seem as if this fund, which had put together an impressive stretch of four consecutive top-quartile calendar years prior to 2000, has lost its touch.

However, while its more-ordinary performance in the past two years shouldn't be overlooked, it still should be considered a respectable choice. Indeed, its year-to-date performance was much better until very recently. Manager Thomas Mengel said in the summer that he was having a hard time finding enough companies with decent growth prospects at reasonable prices, so he had an unusually large cash stake. It kept growing, and by the end of September, one third of assets was in cash.

That cash hoard helped the fund for most of the year; indeed, even after a strong October rally hurt the fund's relative ranking, its year-to-date standing was better than 70% of its foreign-stock peers—quite commendable for a growth-leaning fund. However, as the rally continued, the fund has paid the price, accounting for its current middling rank for the year. While Mengel can be justly criticized for missing out on a rally, his caution in the face of his (accurate, as it turned out) expectation of very weak economic conditions around the world is understandable.

Fortunately, Mengel doesn't make a habit of market-timing; this was more a case of him sticking with his discipline and, unusually, not finding nearly enough stocks to buy. His overall record of success offers good reason to continue to have faith in this fund.

Address:	6300 Lamar Avenue P.O. Box 29217 Shawnee Mission, KS 66201–9217 800–366–5465 / 913–236–2000
Web Address:	www.waddell.com
Inception:	06-16-70
Advisor:	Waddell & Reed Inv. Mgmt.
Subadvisor:	None
NTF Plans:	N/A

Minimum Purchase:	$500	Add: None IRA: $50
Min Auto Inv Plan:	$50	Add: $25
Sales Fees:	5.75%L, 0.25%S	
Management Fee:	.85% mx./.76% mn.+.51% mx./.36% mn.(G)	
Actual Fees:	Mgt: 0.84%	Dist: 0.25%
Expense Projections:	3Yr: $998	5Yr: $1307 10Yr: $2179
Avg Brok Commission:	—	Income Distrib: Semi-Ann.
Total Cost (relative to category):		Average

Waddell & Reed Adv Muni High–Inc A

Ticker	Load	NAV	Yield	SEC Yield	Total Assets	Mstar Category
UMUHX	4.25%	$4.88	5.5%	5.03%	$425.2 mil	Muni Natl Long–Term

Prospectus Objective: Muni Bond—National

Waddell & Reed Advisor Municipal High-Income Fund seeks income exempt from federal taxation.

The fund normally invests at least 75% of assets in medium- and lower-rated municipal bonds. It may, however, invest more than 25% of assets in higher-quality municipal bonds at times when yield spreads are narrow or when there is a lack of medium- and lower-rated security candidates from which to choose.

Class A shares have front loads and 12b-1 fees; Y shares are designed for institutional investors. Prior to June 30, 2000, the fund was named United Muni High Income Fund.

Historical Profile

Return	Average
Risk	Below Avg
Rating	★★★★ Above Avg

Investment Style
Fixed-Income

Income Rtn %Rank Cat: 7 4 3 3 2 6 5 12

Growth of Principal vs. Interest Rate Shifts
- Principal Value $000 (NAV with capital gains reinvested)
- Interest Rate % on 10 Yr Treasury
- ▼ Manager Change
- ▽ Partial Manager Change
- ► Mgr Unknown After
- ◄ Mgr Unknown Before

Performance Quartile (within Category)

Portfolio Manager(s)

Mark Otterstrom. Since 6-00. Other funds currently managed: Waddell & Reed Adv Muni High-Inc Y, Waddell & Reed Adv Muni High-Inc B, Waddell & Reed Adv Muni High-Inc C.

1990	1991	1992	1993	1994	1995	1996	1997	1998	1999	2000	12-01	History
4.92	5.11	5.21	5.46	4.93	5.39	5.39	5.60	5.52	4.94	4.90	4.88	NAV
7.20	11.90	10.15	13.20	–3.12	16.74	6.90	11.77	6.82	–5.22	5.39	5.17	Total Return %
–1.76	–4.10	2.75	3.45	–0.20	–1.73	3.29	2.09	–1.85	–4.39	–6.24	–3.25	+/– LB Aggregate
–0.11	–0.24	1.33	0.92	2.02	–0.73	2.46	2.57	0.34	–3.16	–6.31	0.09	+/– LB Muni
8.17	7.85	7.25	6.81	6.40	7.19	6.53	6.36	5.87	5.59	6.19	5.63	Income Return %
–0.98	4.05	2.90	6.38	–9.52	9.55	0.37	5.41	0.95	–10.81	–0.80	–0.46	Capital Return %
12	52	11	27	10	52	1	4	1	64	90	14	Total Rtn % Rank Cat
0.39	0.37	0.36	0.34	0.34	0.34	0.34	0.33	0.32	0.30	0.30	0.27	Income $
0.00	0.00	0.04	0.07	0.02	0.00	0.01	0.07	0.13	0.00	0.00	0.00	Capital Gains $
0.75	0.77	0.72	0.70	0.76	0.76	0.81	0.78	0.82	0.87	0.94	—	Expense Ratio %
7.97	7.63	7.08	6.49	6.39	6.75	6.41	6.19	5.72	5.59	6.08	—	Income Ratio %
27	61	54	26	26	19	27	19	35	27	22	—	Turnover Rate %
200.7	233.3	269.2	337.2	339.5	392.4	409.6	482.5	512.9	464.3	307.3	418.1	Net Assets $mil

Performance 12-31-01

	1st Qtr	2nd Qtr	3rd Qtr	4th Qtr	Total
1997	0.74	3.27	3.56	3.74	11.77
1998	1.53	1.94	2.34	0.85	6.82
1999	0.91	–1.37	–1.62	–3.21	–5.22
2000	1.44	0.94	1.74	1.17	5.39
2001	1.73	1.42	2.16	–0.22	5.17

Trailing	Total Return%	+/– LB Agg	+/– LB Muni	% Rank All	% Rank Cat	Growth of $10,000
3 Mo	–0.22	–0.26	0.44	81	4	9,978
6 Mo	1.94	–2.72	–0.19	23	23	10,194
1 Yr	5.17	–3.25	0.09	22	14	10,517
3 Yr Avg	1.66	–4.62	–3.10	64	87	10,505
5 Yr Avg	4.63	–2.79	–1.34	71	53	12,542
10 Yr Avg	6.58	–0.65	–0.05	56	9	18,907
15 Yr Avg	7.01	–1.11	–0.18	66	16	27,640

Tax Analysis	Tax-Adj Ret%	%Rank Cat	%Pretax Ret	%Rank Cat
3 Yr Avg	1.65	86	99.7	59
5 Yr Avg	4.48	56	96.7	74
10 Yr Avg	6.41	10	97.4	58

Potential Capital Gain Exposure: –7% of assets

Risk Analysis

Time Period	Load-Adj Return %	Risk %Rank[1] All	Risk %Rank[1] Cat	Morningstar Return	Morningstar Risk	Morningstar Risk-Adj Rating
1 Yr	0.70					
3 Yr	0.19	18	19	–0.20[2]	1.02	★★
5 Yr	3.73	12	9	0.62[2]	0.86	★★★
10 Yr	6.11	7	6	1.22	0.73	★★★★★

Average Historical Rating (156 months): 4.9★s

[1] 1=low, 100=high [2] T-Bill return substituted for category avg.

Category Rating (3 Yr)

1 2 3 4 5 — Worst ... Best

Return	Below Avg
Risk	Below Avg

Other Measures	Standard Index LB Agg	Best Fit Index LB Muni
Alpha	–3.9	–3.0
Beta	0.65	0.87
R-Squared	36	76
Standard Deviation		3.66
Mean		1.66
Sharpe Ratio		–1.04

Portfolio Analysis 09-30-01

Total Fixed-Income: 148	Date of Maturity	Amount $000	Value $000	% Net Assets
PA Allegheny Hosp Dev 9.25%	11-15-22	13,000	13,845	3.26
MA State GO 7.1%	10-01-28	10,660	10,354	2.44
AR GO 6.375%	05-15-28	8,750	9,286	2.19
UT Tooele Union Pacific 5.7%	11-01-26	9,000	8,584	2.02
TX Lubbock Hlth Fac Dev 6.5%	07-01-19	8,000	7,420	1.75
NY NYC Muni Wtr Fin Swr Sys 5.21%	06-15-12	5,500	5,713	1.34
NH Tpk 0%	02-01-24	5,600	5,481	1.29
OH Wtr Dev Solid Waste Disp 5.875%	09-01-20	6,000	5,243	1.23
IA Creston Indl Dev CF Processing 8%	08-01-26	5,000	5,163	1.22
CT East Res Rec Solid Waste 5.5%	01-01-14	5,250	5,158	1.21
GA Coffee Hosp Regl M/C 6.75%	12-01-16	5,000	5,144	1.21
ME Hlth/Higher Educ Fac 7.55%	01-01-29	5,000	5,025	1.18
CA Azusa Multi–Fam Hsg Dmd	07-15-15	5,000	5,000	1.18
WA Hlth Care Fac Hutchinson Cancer Dmd	01-01-18	4,900	4,900	1.15
MA Indl Fin Res Rec SEMASS 9.25%	07-01-15	4,700	4,885	1.15

Current Investment Style

Not Available

Avg Duration[1]	8.5 Yrs
Avg Nominal Maturity	15.0 Yrs
Avg Credit Quality	—
Avg Wtd Coupon	6.62%
Avg Wtd Price	97.49% of par
Pricing Service	Muller

[1] figure provided by fund

Credit Analysis % bonds 09-30-01

US Govt	0	BB	2
AAA	7	B	4
AA	2	Below B	0
A	7	NR/NA	58
BBB	21		

Special Securities % assets 09-30-01

Restricted/Illiquid Secs	0
Inverse Floaters	1
Options/Futures/Warrants	No

Bond Type % assets 06-30-99

Alternative Minimum Tax (AMT)	27.4
Insured	—
Prerefunded	—

Top 5 States % bonds

TX	7.9	AR	5.9
PA	7.7	MA	5.5
MO	6.6		

Composition % assets 09-30-01

Cash	1.5	Bonds	98.5
Stocks	0.0	Other	0.0

Sector Weightings	% of Bonds	Rel Cat
General Obligation	14.8	0.7
Utilities	1.9	0.2
Health	29.5	1.9
Water/Waste	2.5	0.4
Housing	10.6	1.5
Education	0.3	0.0
Transportation	9.9	0.7
COP/Lease	4.0	1.4
Industrial	18.8	1.5
Misc Revenue	5.1	1.0
Demand	2.6	3.2

Analysis by Langdon Healy 12-06-01

Despite this fund's weak showing in recent years, adventurous shareholders needn't throw in the towel.

Waddell & Reed Advisor Municipal High-Income Fund's three-year annualized returns lag the average long-term municipal bond fund's by 120 basis points. That's a country mile in muni-bond land, placing the fund in the bottom fifth of the category. Even more disconcerting is that much of the relative weakness occurred since Mark Otterstrom took the fund's reins in June of 2000.

The fund's recent problems owe to the fund's daring approach. Otterstrom, like his predecessor and longtime mentor John Holliday, takes on considerable credit risk here, often entrusting more than 80% of the portfolio to BBB rated and nonrated bonds. Otterstrom is also continuing Holliday's practice of making large sector bets, currently devoting about a third of assets to the health-care sector.

In 1999, the fund's large stake in health-care bonds and longer-than-average duration (a measure of interest-rate sensitivity) hurt it as the government announced changes in Medicare policy and the Fed raised interest rates. Then in 2000 the fund, along with its high-yield peers, didn't benefit from declining long-term interest rates as much as the broader category because the weakening economy threatened the creditworthiness of the portfolio. This year, however, the fund is doing better: A 5.6% return for the year to date through Dec. 5, 2001, ranks in the category's top quintile. Its health-care exposure has benefited the fund this year, as has scant exposure to airline-related bonds.

Even though the fund has done poorly over the past three years, its longer-term record is impressive. Its aggressive style, therefore, has appeal for risk-tolerant investors.

Address:	6300 Lamar Avenue P.O. Box 29217 Shawnee Mission, KS 66201–9217 800–366–5465 / 913–236–2000
Web Address:	www.waddell.com
Inception:	01-21-86
Advisor:	Waddell & Reed Inv. Mgmt.
Subadvisor:	None
NTF Plans:	N/A

Minimum Purchase:	$500	Add: None IRA: —
Min Auto Inv Plan:	$500	Add: $50
Sales Fees:	4.25%L, 0.25%B	
Management Fee:	.53% mx./.50% mn.+.51% mx./.36% mn.(G)	
Actual Fees:	Mgt: 0.53%	Dist: 0.24%
Expense Projections:	3Yr: $718	5Yr: $933 10Yr: $1553
Avg Brok Commission:	—	Income Distrib: Monthly
Total Cost (relative to category):		Average

Wasatch Core Growth

Ticker	Load	NAV	Yield	Total Assets	Mstar Category
WGROX	None	$34.60	0.0%	$1,243.8 mil	Small Blend

Prospectus Objective: Growth

Wasatch Core Growth Fund seeks long-term growth of capital. Income is a secondary consideration.

The fund will normally invest at least 65% of assets in common stocks of growth companies that are believed by the advisor to have significantly better prospects than most companies for long-term capital appreciation based on historical and projected rates of earnings growth or on development of new products and services. It may also invest in preferred stocks and convertibles or bonds with attached warrants. The fund may invest up to 15% of assets in foreign securities and up to 5% of assets in special situations, such as mergers or reorganizations.

The fund is closed to new investors as of March 16, 2001.

Historical Profile
Return High
Risk Average
Rating ★★★★★ Highest

Investment Style
Equity
Average Stock %: 93% 95% 94% 92% 98% 91% 94%

▼ Manager Change
▽ Partial Manager Change

Fund Performance vs. Category Average
■ Quarterly Fund Return +/– Category Average
— Category Baseline

Performance Quartile (within Category)

Portfolio Manager(s)

Samuel S. Stewart Jr., CFA. Since 12-86. MBA'69 Stanford U.; PhD'70 Stanford U.

J.B. Taylor. Since 1-99. BS Stanford U.

1990	1991	1992	1993	1994	1995	1996	1997	1998	1999	2000	12-01	History
11.20	14.87	14.90	15.14	11.61	15.96	17.19	20.22	19.57	22.80	28.71	34.60	NAV
10.32	40.80	4.72	11.12	2.68	40.42	16.54	27.55	1.56	19.35	37.39	28.82	Total Return %
13.44	10.32	–2.90	1.07	1.36	2.89	–6.40	–5.80	–27.01	–1.69	46.49	40.70	+/– S&P 500
29.83	–5.25	–13.69	–7.78	4.50	11.98	0.00	5.18	4.12	–1.92	40.42	26.33	+/– Russell 2000
7.23	5.45	0.00	0.00	0.00	0.43	0.44	0.17	0.00	0.00	0.00	0.00	Income Return %
3.09	35.36	4.72	11.12	2.68	39.99	16.10	27.38	1.56	19.35	37.39	28.82	Capital Return %
1	52	90	82	23	9	69	39	17	30	2	6	Total Rtn % Rank Cat
0.80	0.61	0.00	0.00	0.00	0.05	0.07	0.03	0.00	0.00	0.00	0.00	Income $
0.16	0.29	0.67	1.37	3.94	0.29	1.31	1.62	0.72	0.48	2.32	2.14	Capital Gains $
1.87	1.51	1.49	1.50	1.50	1.50	1.50	1.50	1.44	1.44	1.38	1.32	Expense Ratio %
1.45	0.51	0.15	–0.55	–0.51	0.29	0.40	0.44	–0.50	–1.07	–0.86	–0.66	Income Ratio %
69	37	40	104	163	88	62	81	63	79	75	51	Turnover Rate %
5.4	13.2	16.5	16.2	8.5	61.7	89.9	146.7	179.9	211.3	408.1	1,243.8	Net Assets $mil

Performance 12-31-01

	1st Qtr	2nd Qtr	3rd Qtr	4th Qtr	Total
1997	–1.40	17.11	12.54	–1.86	27.55
1998	10.39	–0.58	–23.39	20.80	1.56
1999	–5.52	15.63	–3.55	13.27	19.35
2000	–1.54	10.02	13.68	11.56	37.39
2001	0.84	30.74	–16.62	17.19	28.82

Trailing	Total Return%	+/– S&P 500	+/– Russ 2000	% Rank All	% Rank Cat	Growth of $10,000
3 Mo	17.19	6.50	–3.89	19	63	11,719
6 Mo	–2.29	3.27	1.80	48	64	9,771
1 Yr	28.82	40.70	26.33	1	6	12,882
3 Yr Avg	28.31	29.33	21.89	1	3	21,123
5 Yr Avg	22.30	11.60	14.78	1	2	27,363
10 Yr Avg	18.26	5.33	6.75	1	1	53,504
15 Yr Avg	16.79	3.05	6.03	2	5	102,552

Tax Analysis	Tax-Adj Ret%	%Rank Cat	%Pretax Ret	%Rank Cat
3 Yr Avg	26.60	2	94.0	23
5 Yr Avg	20.50	1	91.9	19
10 Yr Avg	15.51	1	84.9	18

Potential Capital Gain Exposure: 17% of assets

Risk Analysis

Time Period	Load-Adj Return %	Risk %Rank[1] All	Risk %Rank[1] Cat	Morningstar Return	Morningstar Risk	Morningstar Risk-Adj Rating
1 Yr	28.82					
3 Yr	28.31	52	35	6.14[2]	0.73	★★★★★
5 Yr	22.30	60	25	5.24[2]	0.82	★★★★★
10 Yr	18.26	75	45	2.74	0.97	★★★★★

Average Historical Rating (145 months): 3.4★s

[1]1=low, 100=high [2] T-Bill return substituted for category avg.

Category Rating (3 Yr)

1 2 3 4 5
Worst Best

Return High
Risk Average

Other Measures	Standard Index S&P 500	Best Fit Index SPMid400
Alpha	30.2	18.5
Beta	0.89	0.83
R-Squared	46	52
Standard Deviation		28.64
Mean		28.31
Sharpe Ratio		0.91

Portfolio Analysis 03-31-01

Share change since 12-00 Total Stocks: 49	Sector	PE	YTD Ret%	% Assets
⊕ Rent-A-Center	Services	14.4	–2.70	8.13
⊕ Americredit	Financials	10.6	15.78	8.05
⊕ Orthodontic Centers of Amer	Health	26.3	–2.40	6.90
⊕ United Rentals	Services	18.3	68.92	5.98
⊕ Microchip Tech	Technology	53.8	76.59	4.44
⊕ O'Reilly Automotive	Retail	33.8	36.34	4.20
⊕ Lincare Hldgs	Health	23.7	0.41	3.98
⊕ Pediatrix Medical Grp	Health	28.0	40.96	3.68
⊕ Metris	Financials	11.4	–2.13	3.48
⊕ Renal Care Grp	Health	22.8	17.13	3.48
⊕ Men's Wearhouse	Retail	11.2	–24.20	3.36
⊕ Express Scripts	Health	33.6	–8.54	3.19
⊕ CSG Sys Intl	Technology	20.3	–13.80	3.19
⊕ Copart	Services	43.8	69.16	3.06
⊕ First Health Grp	Health	25.8	6.26	2.77
⊕ ICU Medical	Health	29.3	47.72	2.35
⊕ SCP Pool	Services	20.3	36.96	2.11
⊕ FYI	Services	—	–9.15	2.07
⊕ Amkor Tech	Technology	—	3.42	2.05
⊕ Integrated Circuit Sys	Technology	—	36.39	1.61
⊕ Fidelity Natl Finl	Financials	8.5	–25.00	1.35
⊕ Resources Connection	Services	—	38.58	1.27
⊕ Expeditors Intl of WA	Services	32.7	6.46	1.08
⊕ Forward Air	Services	34.6	–9.09	1.07
⊕ Cabot Microelect	Industrials	—	52.59	1.01

Current Investment Style

Style: Value Blnd Growth; Size: Large Med Small

	Stock Port Avg	Relative S&P 500 Current	Relative S&P 500 Hist	Rel Cat
Price/Earnings Ratio	24.6	0.80	0.59	0.99
Price/Book Ratio	4.2	0.74	0.45	1.31
Price/Cash Flow	21.4	1.19	0.82	1.37
3 Yr Earnings Growth	31.1	2.13	1.46	1.84
1 Yr Earnings Est%	10.3	—	—	12.00
Med Mkt Cap $mil	1,685	0.0	0.0	1.72

Analysis by Peter Di Teresa 12-28-01

Someone forgot to tell Wasatch Core Growth Fund about the bear market.

For the year to date through Dec. 27, 2001, this fund was up 29%. That comes on top of a 37% gain in 2000. In both years, the fund crushed all but a handful of its small-blend peers.

The key to that strength has been the fund's longstanding emphasis on health-care stocks. Managers Sam Stewart and J.B. Taylor seek companies with earnings growth of at least 15% per year, favoring consistent growers over those that advance in fits and starts. As a result, the fund has tended to be underweight in technology versus its peers, while putting greater emphasis on health stocks. During 2000 and 2001, the fund was largely protected from the tech meltdown, while an assortment of health-care service companies helped to power returns.

Being light on tech has held the fund back a bit lately. As the market has perked up in the fourth quarter, tech has been particularly strong, and this offering lags 70% of its peers for the trailing three months. Given its strength over the course of the year, however, shareholders don't have much to complain about.

The fund's long-term numbers are nothing to sneeze at, either. Its 17.9% annualized 10-year return bests those of all other small-blend funds, and the fund beats almost all competitors for the past three and five years, too.

Our only caveat about this fund is that it's a bit riskier than its historical numbers might make it appear. Management has devoted as much as one third of assets to a single sector and often parks more than half of assets in the top-10 holdings. Stewart and Taylor have made good use of those focused bets, but the fund is definitely vulnerable to a misstep.

All told, though, this fund remains one of our favorite small-cap investments.

Special Securities % assets 03-31-01	
Restricted/Illiquid Secs	0
Emerging-Markets Secs	0
Options/Futures/Warrants	No

Sector Weightings	% of Stocks	Rel S&P	5-Year High	5-Year Low
Utilities	0.0	0.0	6	0
Energy	0.0	0.0	2	0
Financials	15.6	0.9	38	10
Industrials	1.3	0.1	15	0
Durables	0.0	0.0	10	0
Staples	0.0	0.0	5	0
Services	31.7	2.9	37	11
Retail	10.2	1.5	29	9
Health	28.4	1.9	35	5
Technology	12.8	0.7	30	0

Composition % assets 03-31-01	
Cash	5.9
Stocks*	94.1
Bonds	0.0
Other	0.0
*Foreign (% stocks)	0.0

Market Cap	
Giant	0.0
Large	0.9
Medium	39.4
Small	58.4
Micro	1.3

Address: 150 Social Hall Ave Fl 4, Salt Lake City, UT 84111, 800–551–1700 / 801–533–0777
Web Address: www.wasatchfunds.com
Inception: 12-06-86
Advisor: Wasatch Adv.
Subadvisor: None
NTF Plans: Fidelity , Fidelity Inst.

Minimum Purchase: $2000 Add: $100 IRA: $1000
Min Auto Inv Plan: $2000 Add: $50
Sales Fees: No-load, 2.00%R
Management Fee: 1.0%, .28%A
Actual Fees: Mgt: 1.00% Dist: —
Expense Projections: 3Yr: $437 5Yr: $755 10Yr: $1657
Avg Brok Commission: — Income Distrib: Annually
Total Cost (relative to category): Average

Weitz Partners Value

Ticker	Load	NAV	Yield	Total Assets	Mstar Category
WPVLX	None	$20.87	1.0%	$7,380.0 mil	Mid–Cap Value

Prospectus Objective: Growth

Weitz Partners Value Fund seeks capital appreciation.

The fund invests primarily in undervalued equity securities with low price to earnings, price to cash flow, and price to book ratios. Investments may include common stocks, preferred stocks, convertibles, rights, and warrants. The fund may also acquire U.S. government obligations, corporate debt securities, mortgage-related securities, and short-term investments. It may invest up to 25% of assets in foreign debt. "This fund is non-diversified."

Historical Profile

Return High
Risk Below Avg
Rating ★★★★★ Highest

Investment Style
Equity
Average Stock %: 88% 89% 80% 68% 81% 69%

▼ Manager Change
▽ Partial Manager Change

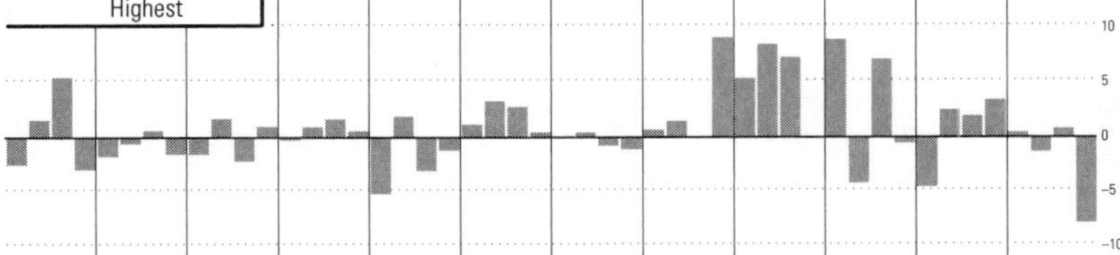

Fund Performance vs. Category Average
■ Quarterly Fund Return +/– Category Average
— Category Baseline

Performance Quartile (within Category)

Portfolio Manager(s)

Wallace R. Weitz, CFA. Since 12-93. BA'70 Carleton C. Other funds currently managed: Weitz Value, Weitz Fixed-Income.

1990	1991	1992	1993	1994	1995	1996	1997	1998	1999	2000	12–01	History
7.22	8.17	8.95	10.00	8.28	10.39	11.52	15.45	17.68	20.02	21.51	20.87	NAV
–6.35	28.00	15.14	23.03	–8.97	38.66	19.04	40.64	29.13	22.02	21.08	–0.86	Total Return %
–3.24	–2.48	7.52	12.97	–10.28	1.12	–3.90	7.29	0.55	0.98	30.18	11.02	+/– S&P 500
9.73	–9.92	–6.54	7.41	–6.84	3.72	–1.22	6.28	24.04	22.13	1.89	–3.19	+/– Russ Midcap Val
1.91	2.50	1.35	0.00	0.00	2.86	0.55	0.00	1.08	0.28	2.63	0.98	Income Return %
–8.26	25.51	13.80	23.03	–8.97	35.80	18.49	40.64	28.04	21.74	18.45	–1.84	Capital Return %
33	50	42	24	86	11	62	2	1	11	36	74	Total Rtn % Rank Cat
0.15	0.18	0.11	0.00	0.00	0.24	0.06	0.00	0.17	0.05	0.50	0.21	Income $
0.00	0.89	0.35	1.01	0.82	0.85	0.79	0.53	1.67	1.23	1.88	0.26	Capital Gains $
—	—	—	—	1.29	1.27	1.23	1.24	1.25	1.24	1.19	1.13	Expense Ratio %
—	—	—	—	0.67	0.82	0.51	1.11	0.34	1.57	1.77	1.77	Income Ratio %
—	—	—	—	33	51	37	30	36	29	5	29	Turnover Rate %
—	—	—	—	51.3	73.8	94.8	133.7	292.3	1,143.4	1,947.7	7,380.0	Net Assets $mil

Performance 12-31-01

	1st Qtr	2nd Qtr	3rd Qtr	4th Qtr	Total
1997	1.82	14.52	11.40	8.27	40.64
1998	16.62	6.15	–9.03	14.66	29.13
1999	8.14	9.40	–2.68	5.98	22.02
2000	–1.76	1.78	10.18	9.91	21.08
2001	–1.12	6.50	–11.03	5.81	–0.86

Trailing	Total Return%	+/– S&P 500	+/– Russ Midcap Val	% Rank All	% Rank Cat	Growth of $10,000
3 Mo	5.81	–4.87	–6.22	62	94	10,581
6 Mo	–5.85	–0.30	–4.95	67	95	9,415
1 Yr	–0.86	11.02	–3.19	44	74	9,914
3 Yr Avg	13.57	14.59	6.76	6	27	14,647
5 Yr Avg	21.61	10.91	10.15	1	3	26,600
10 Yr Avg	18.93	6.00	4.52	1	1	56,617
15 Yr Avg	16.42	2.68	2.95	3	1	97,775

Tax Analysis	Tax-Adj Ret%	%Rank Cat	%Pretax Ret	%Rank Cat
3 Yr Avg	11.56	25	85.2	33
5 Yr Avg	19.39	1	89.7	12
10 Yr Avg	16.45	1	86.9	17

Potential Capital Gain Exposure: 9% of assets

Risk Analysis

Time Period	Load-Adj Return %	Risk %Rank[1] All	Risk %Rank[1] Cat	Morningstar Return	Morningstar Risk	Morningstar Risk-Adj Rating
1 Yr	–0.86					
3 Yr	13.57	37	7	1.98[2]	0.48	★★★★★
5 Yr	21.61	41	1	4.97[2]	0.49	★★★★★
10 Yr	18.93	51	9	2.96	0.59	★★★★★

Average Historical Rating (188 months): 4.6★s

[1] 1=low, 100=high [2] T-Bill return substituted for category avg.

Category Rating (3 Yr)

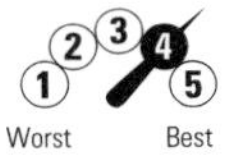

1 2 3 4 5 (4 selected)
Worst — Best

Return: Above Avg
Risk: Low

Other Measures	Standard Index S&P 500	Best Fit Index S&P 500
Alpha	11.9	11.9
Beta	0.52	0.52
R-Squared	40	40
Standard Deviation		15.90
Mean		13.57
Sharpe Ratio		0.62

Analysis by Peter Di Teresa 11-20-01

Investors might try thinking like this fund's manager and consider this a buying opportunity.

Weitz Partners Value Fund has been struggling a bit lately. For the year to date through Nov. 19, 2001, it's down 4.8% and lagging four fifths of its mid-value peers. The last three months have been especially tough—the fund is down 8.5% for the period, one of the worst losses in its category.

Blame that on manager Wally Weitz's bargain-hunting. He had a sizable stake in cheap travel-related stocks such as Park Place Entertainment, Hilton, and Host Marriott, which have all sunk in the wake of September's terrorist attacks. The fund probably suffered more than it might have—Weitz bought more shares of many of those stocks as they became even bigger bargains. Weitz also added beleaguered issues such as Qwest Communications International and cable TV firm Adelphia Communications during the third quarter.

It's hard to argue with Weitz's calls, though. He has always focused on stocks he thinks look cheap based on their discounted free cash flows and that are in fairly predictable businesses. And when a stock he likes starts going down, he buys more. That style has produced excellent results over time. The fund's three-year return is in the category's best 20% despite its recent weakness, and its five- and 10-year returns are among the category's very best. At the same time, the fund's volatility as measured by standard deviation has been modest. Its standard deviations for the trailing three, five, and 10 years are all substantially below the category averages.

We think this fund remains one of the best mid-value options around. Investors in taxable accounts should also note that this fund pays greater attention to taxes than does sibling Weitz Value.

Portfolio Analysis 09-30-01

Share change since 06–01 Total Stocks: 51	Sector	PE	YTD Ret%	% Assets
☼ Liberty Media	N/A	—	—	5.72
AT&T	Services	7.8	40.59	3.74
⊕ Citizens Comms	Services	—	–18.70	3.50
Telephone and Data Sys	Services	—	0.29	3.48
⊕ Park Place Entrtnmt	Services	—	–23.10	3.39
⊕ Washington Mutual	Financials	10.1	–5.32	3.24
Alltel	Services	17.7	1.14	3.06
Golden State Bancorp	Financials	9.6	–15.60	3.02
⊕ Berkshire Hathaway Cl B	Financials	64.8	7.26	2.82
☼ Qwest Comms Intl	Services	—	–65.40	2.75
⊕ Host Marriott	Financials	6.2	–24.80	2.72
⊕ Hilton Hotels	Services	17.9	4.72	2.51
⊕ Countrywide Credit Ind	Financials	10.6	–17.70	2.39
⊕ Adelphia Comms	Services	—	–39.60	2.38
⊕ Berkshire Hathaway Cl A	Financials	—	—	2.36
GreenPoint Finl	Financials	13.9	–10.30	2.29
☼ Washington Post	Services	20.0	–13.20	2.10
⊕ Western Resources	Utilities	—	–26.40	1.86
⊖ North Fork Bancorp	Financials	16.5	34.11	1.79
⊕ Premier Parks	Services	—	–10.50	1.77
US Bancorp	Financials	13.5	–6.14	1.72
Catellus Dev	Financials	21.2	5.14	1.55
☼ Berkshire Bancorp	Financials	7.2	–2.58	1.42
Valassis Comms	Services	18.9	12.85	1.35
⊕ Insight Comm	Services	—	2.81	1.14

Current Investment Style

Style: Value Blnd Growth; Size: Large Med Small

	Stock Port Avg	Relative S&P 500 Current	Relative S&P 500 Hist	Rel Cat
Price/Earnings Ratio	16.8	0.54	0.63	0.71
Price/Book Ratio	1.7	0.30	0.35	0.57
Price/Cash Flow	8.3	0.46	0.75	0.67
3 Yr Earnings Growth	19.0[1]	1.30	0.92	1.61
1 Yr Earnings Est%	8.8[1]	—	—	–1.43
Med Mkt Cap $mil	4,536	0.1	0.1	0.64

[1] figure is based on 50% or less of stocks

Special Securities % assets 09-30-01	
Restricted/Illiquid Secs	0
Emerging–Markets Secs	0
Options/Futures/Warrants	No

Composition % assets 09-30-01	
Cash	27.5
Stocks*	72.3
Bonds	0.2
Other	0.0
*Foreign (% stocks)	0.0

Market Cap	
Giant	13.0
Large	17.8
Medium	58.6
Small	7.4
Micro	3.3

Sector Weightings	% of Stocks	Rel S&P	5-Year High	5-Year Low
Utilities	2.8	0.9	8	0
Energy	0.0	0.0	5	0
Financials	41.8	2.3	67	39
Industrials	0.1	0.0	3	0
Durables	0.0	0.0	1	0
Staples	0.0	0.0	3	0
Services	54.5	5.0	59	29
Retail	0.9	0.1	2	0
Health	0.0	0.0	3	0
Technology	0.0	0.0	7	0

Address:	One Pacific Place 1125 S. 103 Street Omaha, NE 68124–6008 800–232–4161 / 402–391–1980
Web Address:	www.weitzfunds.com
Inception:	05-31-83
Advisor:	Wallace R. Weitz & Co.
Subadvisor:	None
NTF Plans:	Fidelity Inst. , Schwab

Minimum Purchase:	$25000	Add: $5000 IRA: $25000
Min Auto Inv Plan:	$25000	Add: $5000
Sales Fees:	No–load	
Management Fee:	1.0%, .15%A	
Actual Fees:	Mgt: 1.00%	Dist: —
Expense Projections:	3Yr: $378	5Yr: $655 10Yr: $1445
Avg Brok Commission:	—	Income Distrib: Annually
Total Cost (relative to category):		Below Avg

Weitz Hickory

Ticker	Load	NAV	Yield	Total Assets	Mstar Category
WEHIX	Closed	$26.26	0.0%	$339.3 mil	Mid-Cap Value

Prospectus Objective: Growth

Weitz Hickory Portfolio seeks capital appreciation; income is secondary.

The fund invests primarily in equity securities. Investments may include common and preferred stocks, convertible securities, rights, and warrants. Other securities the fund may acquire include U.S. government obligations, investment-grade corporate debt, and mortgage-related securities. The fund may invest up to 25% of assets in foreign securities either directly or in the form of American depositary receipts. It may also write covered call options to enhance income. The fund is non-diversified.

The fund closed to new investors on Aug. 18, 1998.

Historical Profile

Return: Above Avg
Risk: Average
Rating: ★★★★ Above Avg

Investment Style Equity
Average Stock %: 93% 92% 83% 92% 98% 98%

▼ Manager Change
▽ Partial Manager Change

Fund Performance vs. Category Average
■ Quarterly Fund Return +/– Category Average
— Category Baseline

Performance Quartile (within Category)

Portfolio Manager(s)

Richard F. Lawson, CFA. Since 4-93. MS'80 Rice U.; MBA'84 Harvard U.

1990	1991	1992	1993	1994	1995	1996	1997	1998	1999	2000	12-01	History
—	—	—	13.36	10.61	14.66	18.80	23.70	30.98	39.65	27.55	26.26	NAV
—	—	—	20.28*	–17.34	40.49	35.36	39.17	33.01	36.67	–17.24	–4.65	Total Return %
—	—	—	14.50*	–18.66	2.96	12.42	5.82	4.43	15.64	–8.14	7.23	+/– S&P 500
—	—	—	—	–15.21	5.56	15.10	4.81	27.92	36.78	–36.42	–6.98	+/– Russ Midcap Val
—	—	—	0.00	0.00	1.28	0.00	0.40	0.41	0.04	0.00	0.00	Income Return %
—	—	—	20.28	–17.34	39.21	35.36	38.77	32.59	36.64	–17.24	–4.65	Capital Return %
—	—	—	—	96	4	2	4	1	1	100	94	Total Rtn % Rank Cat
—	—	—	0.00	0.00	0.14	0.00	0.07	0.10	0.01	0.00	0.00	Income $
—	—	—	0.05	0.45	0.07	1.04	1.91	0.45	2.56	5.29	0.01	Capital Gains $
—	—	—	1.20	1.50	1.50	1.50	1.50	1.46	1.30	1.23	—	Expense Ratio %
—	—	—	–0.70	–2.90	–0.20	0.33	0.33	–0.13	0.48	–0.44	—	Income Ratio %
—	—	—	—	29	20	28	28	29	40	46	—	Turnover Rate %
—	—	—	2.5	3.2	5.4	10.2	21.6	538.8	913.0	466.1	339.3	Net Assets $mil

Performance 12-31-01

	1st Qtr	2nd Qtr	3rd Qtr	4th Qtr	Total
1997	0.53	16.23	12.31	6.04	39.17
1998	24.09	9.61	–15.58	15.83	33.01
1999	9.55	12.86	–3.73	14.82	36.67
2000	–13.44	–6.09	–0.11	1.92	–17.24
2001	–7.84	10.56	–24.55	24.03	–4.65

Trailing	Total Return%	+/– S&P 500	+/– Russ Midcap Val	% Rank All	% Rank Cat	Growth of $10,000
3 Mo	24.03	13.35	12.00	9	6	12,403
6 Mo	–6.41	–0.86	–5.50	71	97	9,359
1 Yr	–4.65	7.23	–6.98	50	94	9,535
3 Yr Avg	2.55	3.58	–4.25	59	92	10,786
5 Yr Avg	14.83	4.13	3.37	5	23	19,965
10 Yr Avg	—	—	—	—	—	—
15 Yr Avg	—	—	—	—	—	—

Tax Analysis	Tax-Adj Ret%	%Rank Cat	%Pretax Ret	%Rank Cat
3 Yr Avg	0.96	94	37.7	98
5 Yr Avg	13.04	21	87.9	15
10 Yr Avg	—	—	—	—

Potential Capital Gain Exposure: –33% of assets

Risk Analysis

Time Period	Load-Adj Return %	Risk %Rank[1] All	Risk %Rank[1] Cat	Morningstar Return	Morningstar Risk	Morningstar Risk-Adj Rating
1 Yr	–4.65					
3 Yr	2.55	79	98	–0.50[2]	1.12	★★★
5 Yr	14.83	74	95	2.58[2]	1.01	★★★★★
Incept	16.38	—	—	—	—	

Average Historical Rating (70 months): 4.3★s

[1] 1=low, 100=high [2] T-Bill return substituted for category avg.

Category Rating (3 Yr)

1 2 3 4 5 (Worst – Best)

Return: Low
Risk: High

Other Measures	Standard Index S&P 500	Best Fit Index MSCIACWdFr
Alpha	5.8	10.7
Beta	1.07	1.18
R-Squared	51	54

Standard Deviation	26.78
Mean	2.55
Sharpe Ratio	–0.10

Analysis by Peter Di Teresa 11-30-01

Weitz Hickory Fund's performance since 2000 may be painful, but we think it is worth hanging on to.

This fund jumped the tracks in 2000, losing 17% and falling into its category's depths. So far, 2001 has been a downer, too—the fund's 13% loss for the year to date through Nov. 29 puts it behind 98% of its peers.

That may be a shock to shareholders who were entranced by the fund's run of annual returns of 33% or more from 1995 through 1999. But it isn't unprecedented—witness 1994—and such risk was always inherent in this fund's style. Manager Rick Lawson invests in out-of-favor stocks and is willing to buy even somewhat troubled companies if they're especially cheap. Lawson only holds about 30 stocks and typically parks more than half of the fund's assets in the top 10. When an out-of-favor stock falls even further out of favor, it can hurt a lot.

In 2001, the problem has mostly been communications stocks. Lawson likes companies with sizable free cash flows, so he tends to invest a lot in telecom and cable issues. A stake in Winstar hurt early in the year, though it's long since out of the portfolio, and number-two holding Adelphia Communications is down 55% for the year to date.

That said, even though 2000 and 2001 have sapped some of the fund's vitality, its 13.9% five-year annualized return is excellent. It ranks in the mid-value category's best 23%, though the better comparison may be the small-blend group, which the fund left recently. (That wasn't a change of style—Lawson has always had substantial stakes in both small- and mid-cap stocks.) It stacks up even better versus those funds.

Shareholders in this closed offering need to be prepared for ugly patches like this one to reap its long-term rewards.

Address:	One Pacific Place 1125 S. 103 Street Omaha, NE 68124–6008 800–232–4161 / 402–391–1980
Web Address:	www.weitzfunds.com
*Inception:	04-01-93
Advisor:	Wallace R. Weitz & Co.
Subadvisor:	None
NTF Plans:	Schwab

Minimum Purchase:	Closed	Add: $5000 IRA: —
Min Auto Inv Plan:	Closed	Add: $5000
Sales Fees:	No-load	
Management Fee:	1.0%, .23%A	
Actual Fees:	Mgt: 1.00%	Dist: —
Expense Projections:	3Yr: $390	5Yr: $676 10Yr: $1489
Avg Brok Commission:	—	Income Distrib: Semi-Ann.
Total Cost (relative to category):		Below Avg

Portfolio Analysis 03-31-01

Share change since 12-00 Total Stocks: 32	Sector	PE	YTD Ret%	% Assets
⊖ Adelphia Comms	Services	—	–39.60	8.18
Capital One Finl	Financials	19.8	–17.80	6.66
Telephone and Data Sys	Services	—	0.29	6.61
⊖ Americredit	Financials	10.6	15.78	6.22
American Classic Voyages	Services	—	–96.70	5.75
⊖ Harrah's Entrtnmt	Services	—	40.32	5.26
Mail-Well	Services	—	–4.94	5.21
⊖ Six Flags	Services	—	—	5.11
⊖ Consolid Stores	Retail	17.1	–2.02	4.98
Quanex	Industrials	13.7	44.56	4.79
Valassis Comms	Services	18.9	12.85	4.25
Labor Ready	Services	21.3	54.24	3.88
⊖ Orbital Sciences	Industrials	—	0.12	3.70
Insurance Auto Auctions	Retail	—	20.92	3.33
⊖ Lincare Hldgs	Health	23.7	0.41	2.82
Fortress Invest	Financials	—	—	2.70
☼ Rural Cellular Cl A	Services	—	–24.80	2.30
Centennial Comm	Services	6.4	–45.30	2.27
⊕ Level 3 Comms	Services	—	–84.70	2.19
Berkshire Hathaway Cl A	Financials	—	—	1.89
Novastar Cl B	N/A	—	—	1.43
⊖ Loral Space & Comms	Technology	—	–6.21	1.39
Lynch Interactive	Services	NMF	58.62	1.18
Redwood Tr	Financials	8.8	52.26	1.04
⊖ Resource Bancshares Mtg Grp	Financials	—	71.30	0.98

Current Investment Style

Style: Value Blnd Growth; Size: Large Med Small

	Stock Port Avg	Relative S&P 500 Current	Relative S&P 500 Hist	Rel Cat
Price/Earnings Ratio	17.4[1]	0.56	0.62	0.74
Price/Book Ratio	2.4	0.42	0.48	0.80
Price/Cash Flow	8.7	0.48	0.62	0.70
3 Yr Earnings Growth	—	—	—	—
1 Yr Earnings Est%	12.3[1]	—	—	–2.00
Med Mkt Cap $mil	1,806	0.0	0.0	0.25

[1] figure is based on 50% or less of stocks

Special Securities % assets 03-31-01	
Restricted/Illiquid Secs	0
Emerging-Markets Secs	0
Options/Futures/Warrants	No

Composition % assets 03-31-01	
Cash	1.8
Stocks*	98.2
Bonds	0.0
Other	0.0
*Foreign (% stocks)	0.0

Market Cap	
Giant	0.0
Large	7.8
Medium	41.4
Small	35.4
Micro	15.5

Sector Weightings	% of Stocks	Rel S&P	5-Year High	5-Year Low
Utilities	0.0	0.0	0	0
Energy	0.0	0.0	3	0
Financials	22.8	1.3	68	23
Industrials	9.2	0.8	10	0
Durables	0.0	0.0	0	0
Staples	0.0	0.0	0	0
Services	55.0	5.1	62	27
Retail	8.7	1.3	10	0
Health	2.9	0.2	5	0
Technology	1.5	0.1	9	0

Weitz Value

Ticker	Load	NAV	Yield	Total Assets	Mstar Category
WVALX	None	$34.29	1.0%	$4,150.2 mil	Mid–Cap Value

Prospectus Objective: Growth

Weitz Series Fund Value Portfolio seeks capital appreciation; current income is secondary.

The fund invests primarily in equity securities. The advisor seeks securities trading at prices lower than their intrinsic values. Little weight is given to technical stock-market analysis. Any convertible securities the fund holds carry a rating of investment-grade. The fund may invest in foreign securities and securities that are not readily marketable. It may also write covered call options.

Historical Profile

Return High
Risk Low
Rating ★★★★★ Highest

Investment Style
Equity
Average Stock %: 86% 87% 70% 72% 85% 73%

▼ Manager Change
▽ Partial Manager Change

Fund Performance vs. Category Average
■ Quarterly Fund Return +/– Category Average
— Category Baseline

Performance Quartile (within Category)

Portfolio Manager(s)

Wallace R. Weitz, CFA. Since 5-86. BA'70 Carleton C. Other funds currently managed: Weitz Fixed-Income, Weitz Partners Value.

1990	1991	1992	1993	1994	1995	1996	1997	1998	1999	2000	12-01	History
11.22	13.58	14.54	16.80	14.43	18.38	20.59	25.15	29.07	33.08	35.22	34.29	NAV
–5.16	27.62	13.60	20.01	–9.82	38.37	18.70	38.93	28.95	20.97	19.62	0.24	Total Return %
–2.05	–2.86	5.98	9.96	–11.13	0.84	–4.25	5.58	0.37	–0.07	28.73	12.11	+/– S&P 500
10.92	–10.30	–8.08	4.39	–7.69	3.44	–1.56	4.57	23.86	21.07	0.44	–2.10	+/– Russ Midcap Val
3.12	2.90	2.09	0.16	0.00	2.93	0.68	1.59	0.73	1.30	1.56	1.06	Income Return %
–8.28	24.73	11.50	19.85	–9.82	35.44	18.02	37.34	28.22	19.67	18.06	–0.82	Capital Return %
20	54	53	52	87	12	64	5	2	12	40	69	Total Rtn % Rank Cat
0.38	0.32	0.28	0.02	0.00	0.42	0.13	0.31	0.17	0.37	0.49	0.37	Income $
0.07	0.40	0.55	0.59	0.73	1.08	1.10	2.61	3.02	1.67	3.42	0.67	Capital Gains $
1.46	1.49	1.40	1.35	1.41	1.42	1.35	1.29	1.27	1.26	1.19	—	Expense Ratio %
3.71	2.71	2.75	1.66	0.64	1.06	0.91	0.93	0.87	1.35	1.39	—	Income Ratio %
49	29	35	23	23	28	40	39	39	36	31	—	Turnover Rate %
23.5	32.3	49.5	106.7	107.7	149.4	260.7	366.0	1,196.6	2,679.8	3,316.5	4,150.2	Net Assets $mil

Performance 12-31-01

	1st Qtr	2nd Qtr	3rd Qtr	4th Qtr	Total
1997	1.94	14.12	10.97	7.62	38.93
1998	16.54	6.20	–7.31	12.40	28.95
1999	6.71	9.23	–2.87	6.84	20.97
2000	–3.23	1.80	10.34	10.06	19.62
2001	–1.39	6.80	–11.08	7.04	0.24

Trailing	Total Return%	+/– S&P 500	+/– Russ Midcap Val	% Rank All	% Rank Cat	Growth of $10,000
3 Mo	7.04	–3.65	–4.99	56	89	10,704
6 Mo	–4.82	0.73	–3.91	61	87	9,518
1 Yr	0.24	12.11	–2.10	42	69	10,024
3 Yr Avg	13.20	14.22	6.39	7	31	14,505
5 Yr Avg	21.04	10.35	9.58	1	5	25,985
10 Yr Avg	18.03	5.10	3.62	2	4	52,473
15 Yr Avg	15.75	2.02	2.28	5	4	89,719

Tax Analysis	Tax-Adj Ret%	%Rank Cat	%Pretax Ret	%Rank Cat
3 Yr Avg	11.26	28	85.3	32
5 Yr Avg	18.40	2	87.4	16
10 Yr Avg	15.73	4	87.3	13

Potential Capital Gain Exposure: 14% of assets

Risk Analysis

Time Period	Load-Adj Return %	Risk %Rank[1] All	Risk %Rank[1] Cat	Morningstar Return	Morningstar Risk	Morningstar Risk-Adj Rating
1 Yr	0.24					
3 Yr	13.20	38	10	1.89[2]	0.51	★★★★★
5 Yr	21.04	41	1	4.75[2]	0.50	★★★★★
10 Yr	18.03	51	7	2.66	0.58	★★★★★

Average Historical Rating (152 months): 4.3★s

[1] 1=low, 100=high [2] T-Bill return substituted for category avg.

Category Rating (3 Yr)

① ② ③ ❹ ⑤
Worst Best

Return Above Avg
Risk Low

Other Measures	Standard Index S&P 500	Best Fit Index S&P 500
Alpha	11.6	11.6
Beta	0.54	0.54
R–Squared	40	40

Standard Deviation	16.37
Mean	13.20
Sharpe Ratio	0.58

Analysis by Peter Di Teresa 11-20-01

Investors might try thinking like this fund's manager and consider this a buying opportunity.

Weitz Value Fund has been struggling a bit lately. For the year to date through Nov. 19, 2001, it's down 4.2% and lagging three fourths of its mid-value peers. The last three months have been especially tough—the fund is down 8.2% for the period, one of the worst losses in its category.

Blame that on manager Wally Weitz's bargain-hunting style. He had a sizable stake in downtrodden travel-related stocks such as Park Place Entertainment, Hilton, and Host Marriott, which have all suffered significant losses in the wake of September's terrorist attacks. The fund probably suffered more than it might have—Weitz bought more shares of many of those stocks as they became even bigger bargains. Weitz also added beleaguered issues such as Qwest Communications International and cable TV firm Adelphia Communications during the third quarter.

It's hard to argue with Weitz's calls, though. He has always focused on stocks he thinks look cheap based on their discounted free cash flows that are in relatively predictable businesses. And when a stock he likes starts going down, he buys more. That style has produced excellent results over time. The fund's three-year return is in the category's best third despite its recent weakness, and its five- and 10-year returns are among the category's very best. At the same time, the fund's volatility as measured by standard deviation has been modest. Its 10-year standard deviation of 14, for example, is 14% below the category average.

We think this fund remains one of the best mid-value options around—its current distress (relatively speaking) could appeal to opportunistic investors.

Portfolio Analysis 09-30-01

Share change since 06-01 Total Stocks: 57	Sector	PE	YTD Ret%	% Assets
☼ Liberty Media	N/A	—	—	5.29
Berkshire Hathaway Cl B	Financials	64.8	7.26	3.55
AT&T	Services	7.8	40.59	3.50
Telephone and Data Sys	Services	—	0.29	3.29
⊕ Park Place Entrtnmt	Services	—	–23.10	3.18
⊕ Citizens Comms	Services	—	–18.70	3.16
⊕ Washington Mutual	Financials	10.1	–5.32	3.04
⊖ Golden State Bancorp	Financials	9.6	–15.60	2.94
☼ Alltel	Services	17.7	1.14	2.78
☼ Qwest Comms Intl	Services	—	–65.40	2.54
⊕ Host Marriott	Financials	6.2	–24.80	2.52
⊖ Countrywide Credit Ind	Financials	10.6	–17.70	2.43
⊕ Hilton Hotels	Services	17.9	4.72	2.33
GreenPoint Finl	Financials	13.9	–10.30	2.33
☼ Adelphia Comms	Services	—	–39.60	2.22
☼ Washington Post	Services	20.0	–13.20	1.93
⊕ Premier Parks	Services	—	–10.50	1.66
Valassis Comms	Services	18.9	12.85	1.58
Catellus Dev	Financials	21.2	5.14	1.51
Archstone Communities Tr	Financials	14.8	9.11	1.40
⊕ Berkshire Hathaway Cl A	Financials	—	—	1.30
⊕ Western Resources	Utilities	—	–26.40	1.29
⊕ Insight Comm	Services	—	2.81	1.06
Sprint	Services	20.5	1.18	0.90
☼ AT&T Wireless Grp	Services	—	–17.00	0.87

Current Investment Style

Style: Value Blnd Growth; Size: Large Med Small

	Stock Port Avg	Relative S&P 500 Current	Relative S&P 500 Hist	Rel Cat
Price/Earnings Ratio	17.8	0.58	0.66	0.76
Price/Book Ratio	1.7	0.30	0.36	0.56
Price/Cash Flow	8.5	0.47	0.73	0.68
3 Yr Earnings Growth	19.5[1]	1.33	0.93	1.64
1 Yr Earnings Est%	11.8[1]	—	—	–1.92
Med Mkt Cap $mil	4,290	0.1	0.1	0.60

[1] figure is based on 50% or less of stocks

Special Securities % assets 09-30-01	
Restricted/Illiquid Secs	0
Emerging–Markets Secs	0
Options/Futures/Warrants	No

Composition % assets 09-30-01	
Cash	24.0
Stocks*	74.9
Bonds	1.2
Other	0.0
*Foreign (% stocks)	0.0

Market Cap	
Giant	12.7
Large	17.2
Medium	57.9
Small	9.2
Micro	3.1

Sector Weightings	% of Stocks	Rel S&P	5-Year High	5-Year Low
Utilities	2.0	0.6	8	0
Energy	0.0	0.0	7	0
Financials	44.1	2.5	70	36
Industrials	0.0	0.0	3	0
Durables	0.0	0.0	3	0
Staples	0.0	0.0	5	0
Services	52.5	4.8	60	18
Retail	1.3	0.2	2	0
Health	0.0	0.0	6	0
Technology	0.0	0.0	22	0

Address:	One Pacific Place 1125 S. 103 Street Omaha, NE 68124–6008 800–232–4161 / 402–391–1980
Web Address:	www.weitzfunds.com
Inception:	05-09-86
Advisor:	Wallace R. Weitz & Co.
Subadvisor:	None
NTF Plans:	Fidelity Inst. , Waterhouse

Minimum Purchase:	$25000	Add: $5000 IRA: $25000
Min Auto Inv Plan:	$25000	Add: $5000
Sales Fees:	No–load	
Management Fee:	1.0%, .23%A	
Actual Fees:	Mgt: 1.00%	Dist: —
Expense Projections:	3Yr: $378	5Yr: $654 10Yr: $1443
Avg Brok Commission:	—	Income Distrib: Semi–Ann.
Total Cost (relative to category):	Below Avg	

Westcore International Frontier

Ticker	Load	NAV	Yield	Total Assets	Mstar Category
WTIFX	None	$7.71	0.0%	$18.7 mil	Foreign Stock

Prospectus Objective: Growth

Westcore International Frontier Fund seeks long-term growth of capital.

The fund invests primarily in small-cap equity securities of international companies that appear to have above average revenue and earnings growth potential. It invests in securities with market capitalizations of $1.5 billion or less at the time of purchase. Normally the fund invests at least 65% of assets in stocks of foreign companies in at least five different developed countries. However, it may invest in fewer than five developed countries or even a single developed country.

Historical Profile
Return —
Risk —
Rating Not Rated

Investment Style: Equity — Average Stock %: 82% (2000), 81% (12-01)

▼ Manager Change
▽ Partial Manager Change

Fund Performance vs. Category Average
■ Quarterly Fund Return +/– Category Average
— Category Baseline

Performance Quartile (within Category)

Portfolio Manager(s)

Michael W. Gerding, CFA. Since 12-99. BBA'84 Texas Christian U.; MBA'86 Texas Christian U. Other funds currently managed: CDC Nvest Star Worldwide A, CDC Nvest Star Worldwide B, CDC Nvest Star Worldwide C.

1990	1991	1992	1993	1994	1995	1996	1997	1998	1999	2000	12-01	History
—	—	—	—	—	—	—	—	—	10.33	9.75	7.71	NAV
—	—	—	—	—	—	—	—	—	3.40*	–2.44	–20.92	Total Return %
—	—	—	—	—	—	—	—	—	–0.66*	6.67	–9.05	+/– S&P 500
—	—	—	—	—	—	—	—	—	—	11.73	—	+/– MSCI EAFE
—	—	—	—	—	—	—	—	—	0.10	0.14	0.00	Income Return %
—	—	—	—	—	—	—	—	—	3.30	–2.58	–20.92	Capital Return %
—	—	—	—	—	—	—	—	—	—	9	40	Total Rtn % Rank Cat
—	—	—	—	—	—	—	—	—	0.01	0.01	0.00	Income $
—	—	—	—	—	—	—	—	—	0.00	0.31	0.00	Capital Gains $
—	—	—	—	—	—	—	—	—	—	1.50	—	Expense Ratio %
—	—	—	—	—	—	—	—	—	—	0.39	—	Income Ratio %
—	—	—	—	—	—	—	—	—	—	93	—	Turnover Rate %
—	—	—	—	—	—	—	—	—	16.2	33.4	18.7	Net Assets $mil

Performance 12-31-01

	1st Qtr	2nd Qtr	3rd Qtr	4th Qtr	Total
1997	—	—	—	—	—
1998	—	—	—	—	—
1999	—	—	—	—	3.40 *
2000	30.49	–6.45	–3.25	–17.39	–2.44
2001	–14.77	0.12	–19.59	15.25	–20.92

Trailing	Total Return%	+/– S&P 500	+/– MSCI EAFE	% Rank All	% Rank Cat	Growth of $10,000
3 Mo	15.25	4.56	—	23	8	11,525
6 Mo	–7.33	–1.78	—	75	29	9,267
1 Yr	–20.92	–9.05	—	82	40	7,908
3 Yr Avg	—	—	—	—	—	—
5 Yr Avg	—	—	—	—	—	—
10 Yr Avg	—	—	—	—	—	—
15 Yr Avg	—	—	—	—	—	—

Tax Analysis	Tax-Adj Ret%	%Rank Cat	%Pretax Ret	%Rank Cat
3 Yr Avg	—	—	—	—
5 Yr Avg	—	—	—	—
10 Yr Avg	—	—	—	—

Potential Capital Gain Exposure: –36% of assets

Risk Analysis

Time Period	Load-Adj Return %	Risk %Rank¹ All	Risk %Rank¹ Cat	Morningstar Return	Morningstar Risk	Morningstar Risk-Adj Rating
1 Yr	–20.92					
3 Yr	—	—	—	—	—	
5 Yr	—	—	—	—	—	
Incept	–10.45	—	—	—	—	

Average Historical Rating —

¹1=low, 100=high

Category Rating (3 Yr)

Other Measures	Standard Index S&P 500	Best Fit Index
Alpha	—	—
Beta	—	—
R-Squared	—	—
Standard Deviation		—
Mean		—
Sharpe Ratio		—

Return
Risk

Portfolio Analysis 10-31-01

Share change since 09-01 Total Stocks: 53	Sector	Country	% Assets
Puma	Durables	Germany	4.79
Matsumotokiyoshi	Retail	Japan	3.88
JD Wetherspoon	Retail	United Kingdom	3.26
Electronics Boutique	Retail	United Kingdom	3.25
Grupo Dragados	Industrials	Spain	3.21
Cairn Energy	Energy	United Kingdom	3.11
PizzaExpress	Services	United Kingdom	3.08
Kose	Technology	Japan	3.05
Park24	Services	Japan	2.64
Riverdeep Grp PLC	Retail	Ireland	2.34
IHC Caland	Industrials	Netherlands	2.32
Angiotech Pharmaceuticals	Technology	Canada	2.09
Toei Animation	N/A	N/A	2.02
Eidos	Technology	United Kingdom	1.86
Alliance Atlantis Comm Cl B	Services	Canada	1.85
Lumenis	N/A	N/A	1.83
Soco Intl PLC	Energy	United Kingdom	1.82
Van Der Mollen Hldg	Financials	Netherlands	1.71
Hornbach Hldg	Industrials	Germany	1.67
Dorel Inds Cl B	Durables	Canada	1.65

Analysis by Gregg Wolper 12-28-01

Despite its manager's fine pedigree and its decent performance so far, the jury's still out on Westcore International Frontier Fund.

This fund's manager, Michael Gerding, started this offering in late 1999 after many years running an international small-cap fund for Founders, generally with success. In one sense, this fund did not start at a great time: Gerding uses a growth-oriented strategy, and three months after the fund began, the collapse of the remarkable growth rally had begun. Yet the past couple of years have also seen small caps outperform large caps, so this small-cap offering did come to the market at the right time in that sense.

This mixed picture is reflected in the fund's returns. After holding up well in 2000, it has posted middling returns in 2001; its 22.6% loss through Dec. 27, 2001, is just above the midpoint of the broad foreign-stock category. One reason the fund hasn't held up even better is Gerding's taste for technology stocks. At the end of September 2001, about a fourth of the fund was in the technology sector—a rough place to be for most of 2001. However, such stocks have rebounded in recent months, helping push this fund's three-month return into the top quartile of the category. Its year-to-date showing is now on par with the most highly regarded small- to mid-growth foreign funds, such as Liberty Acorn International and American Century International Discovery.

The limited extent of that subgroup is one reason it's premature to judge this fund definitively. Another, more important reason is its brief record—which, moreover, has occurred during a very unusual market climate. So more time is needed to determine whether the fund is worth owning. Given its manager's background and its performance so far, current shareholders should stick with this fund, but others should give it time to prove itself.

Current Investment Style

Style: Value Blnd Growth; Size: Large Med Small

	Stock Port Avg	Rel MSCI EAFE Current	Rel MSCI EAFE Hist	Rel Cat
Price/Earnings Ratio	24.1	0.93	—	0.95
Price/Cash Flow	14.4	1.12	—	1.00
Price/Book Ratio	3.7	1.07	—	0.96
3 Yr Earnings Growth	20.4	1.09	—	1.04
Med Mkt Cap $mil	615	0.0	—	0.03

Country Exposure 10-31-01	% assets
United Kingdom	24
Japan	10
Germany	9
France	9
Canada	8

Hedging History: —

Regional Exposure 10-31-01	% assets
Europe	61
Pacific Rim	0
Latin America	1
Japan	10
Other	9

Special Securities % assets 10-31-01	
Restricted/Illiquid Secs	0
Emerging-Markets Secs	1
Options/Futures/Warrants	No

Composition % assets 10-31-01			
Cash	15.5	Bonds	0.0
Stocks	84.5	Other	0.0

Sector Weightings	% of Stocks	Rel Cat	5-Year High	5-Year Low
Utilities	0.7	0.3	—	—
Energy	7.0	1.2	—	—
Financials	2.4	0.1	—	—
Industrials	19.3	1.4	—	—
Durables	11.0	1.6	—	—
Staples	4.1	0.6	—	—
Services	17.5	1.0	—	—
Retail	20.3	4.2	—	—
Health	8.9	0.9	—	—
Technology	8.9	0.9	—	—

Address:	370 Seventeenth Street Suite 2700 Denver, CO 80202 303–623–2577 / 800–392–2673
Web Address:	www.westcore.com
*Inception:	12-15-99
Advisor:	Denver Inv. Adv.
Subadvisor:	None
NTF Plans:	Datalynx , Fidelity Inst.

Minimum Purchase:	$2500	Add: $100	IRA: $1000
Min Auto Inv Plan:	$1000	Add: $100	
Sales Fees:	No-load		
Management Fee:	1.2%		
Actual Fees:	Mgt: 1.20%	Dist: —	
Expense Projections:	3Yr: $1189	5Yr: —	10Yr: —
Avg Brok Commission:	—	Income Distrib: Annually	
Total Cost (relative to category):	—		

Westport Small Cap R

Ticker	Load	NAV	Yield	Total Assets	Mstar Category
WPSRX	None	$19.45	0.0%	$668.3 mil	Small Blend

Prospectus Objective: Small Company

Westport Small Cap Fund seeks capital appreciation.

The fund normally invests at least 65% of assets in common stocks of small companies with market capitalizations of $1 billion or less. It may invest to a limited degree in companies with larger market capitalizations. The fund may also invest in securities convertible into common stocks, preferred stocks, and debt. It may invest in foreign securities through American depositary receipts.

Class R shares are for individual investors; I shares are designed for institutional investors.

Historical Profile
Return: High
Risk: Below Avg
Rating: ★★★★★ Highest

Investment Style
Equity
Average Stock %: 80% (1998), 86% (1999), 81% (2000), 83% (12-01)

▼ Manager Change
▽ Partial Manager Change

Fund Performance vs. Category Average
■ Quarterly Fund Return +/– Category Average
— Category Baseline

Performance Quartile (within Category)

Portfolio Manager(s)

Andrew J. Knuth, CFA. Since 12-97. BA Dickinson U.; MBA New York U. Other funds currently managed: Managers Special Equity, Diversified Inv Special Equity, Westport Small Cap I.

Edmund H. Nicklin Jr., CFA. Since 12-97. MS'70 Rensselaer Polytechnic Institute; PhD'74 Rensselaer Polytechnic. Other funds currently managed: Managers Special Equity, Westport Small Cap I, Westport I.

History

1990	1991	1992	1993	1994	1995	1996	1997	1998	1999	2000	12–01	History
—	—	—	—	—	—	—	10.00	11.54	16.47	18.23	19.45	NAV
—	—	—	—	—	—	—	—	15.40	42.72	13.60	8.22	Total Return %
—	—	—	—	—	—	—	—	–13.18	21.68	22.70	20.09	+/– S&P 500
—	—	—	—	—	—	—	—	17.95	21.46	16.63	5.73	+/– Russell 2000
—	—	—	—	—	—	—	—	0.00	0.00	0.20	0.00	Income Return %
—	—	—	—	—	—	—	—	15.40	42.72	13.40	8.22	Capital Return %
—	—	—	—	—	—	—	—	4	6	44	43	Total Rtn % Rank Cat
—	—	—	—	—	—	—	0.00	0.00	0.00	0.03	0.00	Income $
—	—	—	—	—	—	—	0.00	0.00	0.00	0.45	0.28	Capital Gains $
—	—	—	—	—	—	—	—	1.50	1.43	1.27	—	Expense Ratio %
—	—	—	—	—	—	—	—	–0.39	–0.33	0.13	—	Income Ratio %
—	—	—	—	—	—	—	—	19	10	15	—	Turnover Rate %
—	—	—	—	—	—	—	—	20.6	79.7	109.5	—	Net Assets $mil

Performance 12-31-01

	1st Qtr	2nd Qtr	3rd Qtr	4th Qtr	Total
1997	—	—	—	—	—
1998	17.30	–4.69	–19.14	27.65	15.40
1999	2.51	21.39	–2.30	17.39	42.72
2000	8.93	–1.73	1.76	4.29	13.60
2001	–4.06	12.06	–15.92	19.71	8.22

Trailing	Total Return%	+/– S&P 500	+/– Russ 2000	% Rank All	% Rank Cat	Growth of $10,000
3 Mo	19.71	9.02	–1.37	14	41	11,971
6 Mo	0.65	6.21	4.74	36	34	10,065
1 Yr	8.22	20.09	5.73	9	43	10,822
3 Yr Avg	20.61	21.64	14.19	2	10	17,545
5 Yr Avg	—	—	—	—	—	—
10 Yr Avg	—	—	—	—	—	—
15 Yr Avg	—	—	—	—	—	—

Tax Analysis	Tax-Adj Ret%	%Rank Cat	%Pretax Ret	%Rank Cat
3 Yr Avg	20.14	9	97.7	10
5 Yr Avg	—	—	—	—
10 Yr Avg	—	—	—	—

Potential Capital Gain Exposure: 25% of assets

Risk Analysis

Time Period	Load-Adj Return %	Risk %Rank[1] All	Risk %Rank[1] Cat	Morningstar Return	Morningstar Risk	Morningstar Risk-Adj Rating
1 Yr	8.22					
3 Yr	20.61	50	27	3.84[2]	0.70	★★★★★
5 Yr	—	—	—	—	—	
Incept	19.27	—	—	—	—	

Average Historical Rating (13 months): 5.0★s

[1]1=low, 100=high [2] T-Bill return substituted for category avg.

Category Rating (3 Yr)

1 2 3 4 **5** — Worst … Best

Return: High
Risk: Below Avg

Other Measures	Standard Index S&P 500	Best Fit Index Russ 2000
Alpha	21.0	13.5
Beta	0.78	0.73
R-Squared	49	84
Standard Deviation		22.40
Mean		20.61
Sharpe Ratio		0.79

Portfolio Analysis 11-30-01

Share change since 10–01 Total Stocks: 72	Sector	PE	YTD Ret%	% Assets
⊕ Russell 2000 Index	N/A	—	—	6.44
Hilb Rogal & Hamilton	Financials	28.7	42.84	3.95
Universal Health Svcs B	Health	12.7	–23.40	3.86
Computer Assoc Intl	Technology	—	77.28	3.44
IMS Health	Technology	22.4	–27.50	3.25
Cox Radio Cl A	Services	—	12.93	2.75
Priority Healthcare Cl B	Health	61.7	–13.70	2.61
Synopsys	Technology	67.1	24.52	2.60
Ruby Tuesday	Services	21.3	35.62	2.56
⊕ Insight Comm	Services	—	2.81	2.51
JD Edwards	Technology	—	–7.65	2.34
Tyco Intl	Industrials	27.1	6.23	2.33
American Mgmt Sys	Technology	26.6	–8.75	2.31
⊕ El Paso Elec	Utilities	11.4	9.85	2.11
ITT Educational Svcs	Services	28.6	67.59	2.06
⊕ Emmis Broadcstg Cl A	Services	—	–17.60	1.91
Precision Castparts	Industrials	12.4	–32.60	1.89
⊕ Pogo Producing	Energy	11.7	–15.20	1.83
Ceridian	Technology	27.6	–5.96	1.78
First Essex Bancorp	Financials	13.3	45.30	1.76
Dupont Photomasks	Industrials	NMF	–17.70	1.75
Conexant Sys	Technology	—	–6.60	1.70
Perot Sys Cl A	Technology	NMF	122.20	1.62
Pure Res		—	—	1.54
Houston Explor	Energy	6.9	–11.90	1.41

Current Investment Style

Style: Value Blnd Growth; Size: Large Med Small

	Stock Port Avg	Relative S&P 500 Current	Relative S&P 500 Hist	Rel Cat
Price/Earnings Ratio	28.4	0.92	0.85	1.14
Price/Book Ratio	4.2	0.74	0.61	1.32
Price/Cash Flow	17.2	0.96	0.85	1.11
3 Yr Earnings Growth	16.9	1.16	0.84	1.00
1 Yr Earnings Est%	–3.7	2.08	—	–4.28
Med Mkt Cap $mil	1,208	0.0	0.0	1.23

[1]figure is based on 50% or less of stocks

Special Securities % assets 11-30-01	
Restricted/Illiquid Secs	0
Emerging–Markets Secs	Trace
Options/Futures/Warrants	No

Composition % assets 11-30-01	
Cash	17.5
Stocks*	82.5
Bonds	0.0
Other	0.0
*Foreign (% stocks)	0.0

Market Cap	
Giant	3.8
Large	4.4
Medium	32.4
Small	54.5
Micro	4.9

Sector Weightings	% of Stocks	Rel S&P	5-Year High	5-Year Low
Utilities	2.4	0.7	—	—
Energy	6.0	0.9	—	—
Financials	12.4	0.7	—	—
Industrials	8.9	0.8	—	—
Durables	0.0	0.0	—	—
Staples	1.4	0.2	—	—
Services	22.0	2.0	—	—
Retail	4.5	0.7	—	—
Health	10.0	0.7	—	—
Technology	32.5	1.8	—	—

Analysis by Kelli Stebel 08-16-01

Despite middling performance this year, this is still one of the best small-cap funds around.

Westport Small Cap hasn't been breaking any records lately. The fund turned in a respectable 13% gain last year, and its 4% return for the year to date through August 14, 2001, is just slightly less than the average small-blend fund's 5% gain. Though the fund's recent showings are just decent, they come on the heels of two top-decile showings in 1998 and 1999.

The fund has a large tech weight, but that's not the reason for its recently middling returns. In fact, some of its technology holdings, such as IT-service provider Perot Systems, have turned in healthy gains this year. Instead, the fund's energy holdings, such as Pogo Producing, have taken a bite out of returns. Nicklin reports that the managers are still bullish on energy stocks, and have added to positions like Pogo, which they consider to have superb overseas operations.

Even with this fund's slight blip of average performance, investors have nothing to worry about here. Nicklin and Knuth's buy-and-hold strategy is a proven winner. While this fund has only been around for about four years, the duo has decades of combined management experience. Between October 1986 and August 1997, Nicklin led Evergreen Growth and Income to an above-average record. And Knuth has been running money for Westport for nearly 20 years, serving as comanager of the strong-performing Managers Special Equity since 1985.

Given that fine pedigree, investors should continue to have confidence in this fund. While Knuth and Nicklin will occasionally hold on to a stock once it grows beyond small-cap land, this fund's moderate strategy makes it a good choice for one-stop small-cap shopping.

Address:	253 Riverside Avenue Westport, CT 06880 888–593–7878
Web Address:	www.westportfunds.com
*Inception:	12-31-97
Advisor:	Westport Advisers
Subadvisor:	None
NTF Plans:	Fidelity Inst. , Waterhouse

Minimum Purchase:	$5000	Add: None IRA: $2000
Min Auto Inv Plan:	$1000	Add: $100
Sales Fees:	No–load	
Management Fee:	1.0%, .13%A	
Actual Fees:	Mgt: 1.00%	Dist: —
Expense Projections:	3Yr: $491	5Yr: $853 10Yr: $1872
Avg Brok Commission:	—	Income Distrib: Annually
Total Cost (relative to category):	Average	

White Oak Growth Stock

Ticker	Load	NAV	Yield	Total Assets	Mstar Category
WOGSX	None	$38.44	0.0%	$3,487.1 mil	Large Growth

Prospectus Objective: Growth

White Oak Growth Stock Fund seeks long-term growth of capital.

The fund normally invests at least 65% of assets in common stocks. It invests primarily in companies with market capitalizations of greater than $5 billion. The advisor selects securities that it believes to have strong earnings potential and reasonable market valuations relative to the market in general and to other companies in the same industry. The fund may invest in American depositary receipts.

Historical Profile

Return Average
Risk High
Rating ★★★ Neutral

Investment Style
Equity
Average Stock %

1993	1994	1995	1996	1997	1998	1999	2000	12-01
	93%	94%	94%	97%	97%	98%	98%	

▼ Manager Change
▽ Partial Manager Change

Fund Performance vs. Category Average
Quarterly Fund Return
+/– Category Average
— Category Baseline

Performance Quartile (within Category)

Portfolio Manager(s)

James D. Oelschlager, et al. Since 8-92. BA'64 Denison U.; JD'67 Northwestern U.

1990	1991	1992	1993	1994	1995	1996	1997	1998	1999	2000	12–01	History
—	—	11.17	11.08	11.75	17.90	23.55	29.18	40.71	61.12	63.07	38.44	NAV
—	—	11.95*	–0.26	6.29	52.70	32.28	24.30	39.51	50.14	3.60	–39.05	Total Return %
—	—	8.08*	–10.32	4.98	15.17	9.33	–9.06	10.94	29.10	12.70	–27.18	+/– S&P 500
—	—	—	–0.19	1.44	14.05	6.76	–9.45	–5.59	20.46	28.12	–18.55	+/– Russ Top 200 Grt
—	—	0.25	0.53	0.23	0.30	0.28	0.09	0.00	0.00	0.00	0.00	Income Return %
—	—	11.70	–0.79	6.06	52.40	31.99	24.20	39.51	50.14	3.60	–39.05	Capital Return %
—	—	—	93	3	2	3	57	24	25	4	95	Total Rtn % Rank Cat
—	—	0.02	0.06	0.03	0.04	0.05	0.02	0.00	0.00	0.00	0.00	Income $
—	—	0.00	0.00	0.00	0.00	0.07	0.06	0.00	0.00	0.28	0.00	Capital Gains $
—	—	1.00	0.97	0.97	0.97	0.95	0.98	1.00	1.00	0.96	—	Expense Ratio %
—	—	0.74	0.54	0.19	0.29	0.23	0.06	–0.22	–0.34	–0.38	—	Income Ratio %
—	—	—	27	37	22	8	8	6	6	14	—	Turnover Rate %
—	—	—	6.3	5.8	10.9	40.4	391.9	1,092.3	2,725.3	5,502.8	3,487.1	Net Assets $mil

Performance 12-31-01

	1st Qtr	2nd Qtr	3rd Qtr	4th Qtr	Total
1997	–2.86	22.07	14.02	–8.06	24.30
1998	17.31	6.84	–19.06	37.53	39.51
1999	13.90	6.17	–2.07	26.78	50.14
2000	20.12	8.00	1.00	–20.93	3.60
2001	–33.28	3.59	–29.04	24.28	–39.05

Trailing	Total Return%	+/– S&P 500	+/– Russ Top 200 Grth	% Rank All	% Rank Cat	Growth of $10,000
3 Mo	24.28	13.60	11.42	9	8	12,428
6 Mo	–11.81	–6.26	–4.83	90	76	8,819
1 Yr	–39.05	–27.18	–18.55	98	95	6,095
3 Yr Avg	–1.77	–0.74	6.26	82	43	9,480
5 Yr Avg	10.45	–0.25	1.86	16	32	16,439
10 Yr Avg	—	—	—	—	—	—
15 Yr Avg	—	—	—	—	—	—

Tax Analysis	Tax-Adj Ret%	%Rank Cat	%Pretax Ret	%Rank Cat
3 Yr Avg	–1.79	32	—	—
5 Yr Avg	10.42	15	99.7	2
10 Yr Avg	—	—	—	—

Potential Capital Gain Exposure: –45% of assets

Risk Analysis

Time Period	Load-Adj Return %	Risk %Rank[1] All	Risk %Rank[1] Cat	Morningstar Return	Morningstar Risk	Morningstar Risk-Adj Rating
1 Yr	–39.05					
3 Yr	–1.77	95	88	–1.33[2]	1.66	★★
5 Yr	10.45	92	93	1.31[2]	1.58	★★★
Incept	15.68	—	—	—	—	

Average Historical Rating (78 months): 4.6★s

[1]1=low, 100=high [2] T–Bill return substituted for category avg.

Category Rating (3 Yr)

1 2 **3** 4 5
Worst Best

Return Average
Risk Above Avg

Other Measures	Standard Index S&P 500	Best Fit Index S&P 500
Alpha	7.3	7.3
Beta	1.74	1.74
R–Squared	73	73
Standard Deviation		36.14
Mean		–1.77
Sharpe Ratio		–0.22

Analysis by William Harding 11-07-01

This fund looks awful right now, but we still think it holds appeal.

It has been the worst of times for White Oak Growth Stock. The fund has been pummeled in 2001, shedding 40% of its value for the year to date through Nov. 6. To be sure, it's been a dreadful year for large-growth offerings, but this fund has lagged 93% of its peers. The fund's misfortunes can be explained by its aggressive stance. Manager Jim Oelschlager invests in only about 25 stocks, many of which court high P/E ratios, across three sectors of the market (technology, financials and health care). Consequently, the fund tends to outpace its peers on the upside and fares a lot worse in down markets.

Could Oelschlager have sidestepped some of the problems this year? Sure, he could have parked some assets in cash or cut the fund's tech weighting. But that would be at odds with the investment strategy he has practiced over the last 30 years. Oelschlager doesn't believe in market or sector timing and is very patient, as is evident from the fund's very low turnover. Instead, he used the recent downturn to add to many of his tech holdings. He reckons that these companies will be winners over the long haul and the best time to buy them is when they are down in the dumps.

This approach has proven worthwhile for Oelschlager and his team over time. The fund's return since its 1992 inception still bests the average large-growth offering by 3 percentage points on an annualized basis. Further, we feel confident that this offering will lead the pack when the market rebounds. When the fund has slipped in the past, its recoveries have usually been quite strong. Indeed, the fund had a big bounce over the past month.

Investors who can't stomach steep losses over a short time period should look elsewhere. But those who accept the risks here in hopes of superior long-term performance should sit tight.

Portfolio Analysis 09-30-01

Share change since 06–01 Total Stocks: 24	Sector	PE	YTD Ret%	% Assets
⊖ Eli Lilly	Health	28.9	–14.40	8.90
Medtronic	Health	76.4	–14.70	8.23
American Intl Grp	Financials	42.0	–19.20	8.10
⊖ Pfizer	Health	34.7	–12.40	8.08
⊖ Merck	Health	19.1	–35.90	8.03
⊖ Citigroup	Financials	20.0	0.03	6.92
⊖ MBNA	Financials	19.6	–3.66	5.68
⊖ Applied Matls	Technology	66.8	5.01	5.66
⊖ Morgan Stanley/Dean Witter	Financials	16.6	–28.20	5.34
⊖ Microsoft	Technology	57.6	52.78	4.55
Linear Tech	Technology	34.9	–15.30	4.40
⊕ Cisco Sys	Technology	—	–52.60	4.00
⊕ EMC	Technology	NMF	–79.40	3.21
Charles Schwab	Financials	61.9	–45.30	2.66
⊕ Brocade Comm Sys	Technology	—	–63.90	2.62
⊖ Intel	Technology	73.1	4.89	2.39
⊕ Veritas Software	Technology	—	–48.70	2.35
JDS Uniphase	Technology	—	–79.00	1.92
PMC Sierra	Technology	—	–72.90	1.45
Corning	Industrials	—	–83.00	1.44
Juniper Net	Technology	NMF	–84.90	1.32
CIENA	Technology	NMF	–82.30	1.17
⊖ Sun Microsystems	Technology	NMF	–55.80	1.13
First Data	Technology	38.1	49.08	0.37

Current Investment Style

Style: Value Blnd Growth; Size: Large Med Small

	Stock Port Avg	Relative S&P 500 Current	Relative S&P 500 Hist	Rel Cat
Price/Earnings Ratio	38.8	1.25	1.24	1.09
Price/Book Ratio	7.1	1.24	1.40	1.11
Price/Cash Flow	25.4	1.41	1.37	1.12
3 Yr Earnings Growth	22.8	1.56	1.33	1.06
1 Yr Earnings Est%	–11.2	6.32	—	–3.73
Med Mkt Cap $mil	81,179	1.3	1.1	1.72

[1]figure is based on 50% or less of stocks

Special Securities % assets 09-30-01	
Restricted/Illiquid Secs	0
Emerging–Markets Secs	0
Options/Futures/Warrants	No

Composition % assets 09-30-01	
Cash	0.1
Stocks*	100.0
Bonds	0.0
Other	0.0
*Foreign (% stocks)	0.0

Market Cap	
Giant	64.6
Large	26.5
Medium	8.9
Small	0.0
Micro	0.0

Sector Weightings	% of Stocks	Rel S&P	5-Year High	5-Year Low
Utilities	0.0	0.0	0	0
Energy	0.0	0.0	0	0
Financials	28.7	1.6	36	18
Industrials	1.4	0.1	10	0
Durables	0.0	0.0	0	0
Staples	0.0	0.0	8	0
Services	0.0	0.0	10	0
Retail	0.0	0.0	5	0
Health	33.3	2.2	33	9
Technology	36.6	2.0	67	25

Address: P.O. Box 219441, Kansas City, MO 64121–9441, 888–462–5386
Web Address: www.oakassociates.com
*Inception: 08-03-92
Advisor: Oak Assoc.
Subadvisor: None
NTF Plans: Fidelity , Datalynx

Minimum Purchase: $2000 Add: $50 IRA: $2000
Min Auto Inv Plan: $2000 Add: $25
Sales Fees: No–load
Management Fee: .74%, .20%A
Actual Fees: Mgt: 0.70% Dist: —
Expense Projections: 3Yr: $323 5Yr: $561 10Yr: $1246
Avg Brok Commission: — Income Distrib: Annually
Total Cost (relative to category): —

Wilshire Target Large Co Growth Invmt

Ticker	Load	NAV	Yield	Total Assets	Mstar Category
DTLGX	12b–1 only	$30.21	0.0%	$473.1 mil	Large Growth

Prospectus Objective: Growth

Wilshire Target Large Company Growth Portfolio seeks investment results that correspond to those of the portion of the Wilshire 5000 index identified as large-cap, growth companies.

The fund invests substantially all assets in equities. Wilshire identifies from the index the 2,500 companies with the largest capitalizations, then divides that universe into two portions: 750 larger-cap companies and 1,750 smaller-cap companies. The fund then purchases stocks from the growth section of the large-cap company portion.

The fund has 12b-1 fees; an institutional shareclass is available. Previously named: Dreyfus - Wilshire Target Large Company Growth.

Historical Profile

Return Average
Risk Average
Rating ★★★ Neutral

Investment Style
Equity
Average Stock %

1994	1995	1996	1997	1998	1999	2000	12–01
	99%	100%	100%	100%	100%	100%	100%

▼ Manager Change
▽ Partial Manager Change

Fund Performance vs. Category Average
■ Quarterly Fund Return +/– Category Average
— Category Baseline

Performance Quartile (within Category)

Portfolio Manager(s)

Thomas D. Stevens, CFA. Since 10-92. BBA'74 U. of Wisconsin; MBA'76 U. of Wisconsin. Other funds currently managed: Wilshire Target Small Co Value Invmt, Wilshire Target Small Co Growth Invmt, Wilshire Target Large Co Value Invmt.

1990	1991	1992	1993	1994	1995	1996	1997	1998	1999	2000	12–01	History
—	—	13.29	12.96	13.16	17.47	19.27	24.90	32.90	43.60	36.31	30.21	NAV
—	—	7.48*	–0.75	2.29	36.65	25.74	32.22	40.72	33.95	–15.59	–16.59	Total Return %
—	—	2.46*	–10.80	0.98	–0.89	2.79	–1.13	12.14	12.91	–6.49	–4.71	+/– S&P 500
—	—	—	–0.67	–2.56	–2.01	0.22	–1.52	–4.38	4.27	8.93	3.91	+/– Russ Top 200 Grt
—	—	0.56	1.74	0.75	0.87	0.15	0.29	0.07	0.00	0.00	0.00	Income Return %
—	—	6.92	–2.48	1.54	35.77	25.59	31.93	40.64	33.95	–15.59	–16.59	Capital Return %
—	—	—	95	15	22	8	16	22	55	54	25	Total Rtn % Rank Cat
—	—	0.07	0.23	0.10	0.12	0.03	0.06	0.02	0.00	0.00	0.00	Income $
—	—	0.00	0.00	0.00	0.39	2.73	0.52	1.95	0.44	0.51	0.08	Capital Gains $
—	—	—	—	0.68	0.84	0.93	0.81	0.73	0.95	0.84	0.83	Expense Ratio %
—	—	—	—	1.18	0.94	0.39	0.20	0.16	–0.11	–0.28	–0.23	Income Ratio %
—	—	—	—	22	30	44	43	57	35	50	43	Turnover Rate %
—	—	8.5	8.4	12.4	26.8	18.9	74.6	154.8	601.2	514.0	366.1	Net Assets $mil

Performance 12-31-01

	1st Qtr	2nd Qtr	3rd Qtr	4th Qtr	Total
1997	2.28	19.33	6.76	1.47	32.22
1998	16.10	5.02	–7.91	25.32	40.72
1999	7.60	3.50	–3.14	24.17	33.95
2000	4.31	–2.95	–2.51	–14.47	–15.59
2001	–18.01	6.15	–15.03	12.80	–16.59

Trailing	Total Return%	+/– S&P 500	+/– Russ Top 200 Grth	% Rank All	% Rank Cat	Growth of $10,000
3 Mo	12.80	2.12	—	30	60	11,280
6 Mo	–4.15	1.40	—	57	13	9,585
1 Yr	–16.59	–4.71	—	75	25	8,341
3 Yr Avg	–1.93	–0.91	—	82	44	9,431
5 Yr Avg	11.90	1.20	—	10	18	17,548
10 Yr Avg	—	—	—	—	—	—
15 Yr Avg	—	—	—	—	—	—

Tax Analysis	Tax-Adj Ret%	%Rank Cat	%Pretax Ret	%Rank Cat
3 Yr Avg	–2.19	35	—	—
5 Yr Avg	11.22	12	94.3	7
10 Yr Avg	—	—	—	—

Potential Capital Gain Exposure: 2% of assets

Risk Analysis

Time Period	Load-Adj Return %	Risk %Rank[1] All	Risk %Rank[1] Cat	Morningstar Return	Morningstar Risk	Morningstar Risk-Adj Rating
1 Yr	–16.59					
3 Yr	–1.93	81	33	–1.37[2]	1.18	★★
5 Yr	11.90	78	24	1.71[2]	1.06	★★★★
Incept	13.73	—	—	—	—	

Average Historical Rating (76 months): 4.4★s

[1] 1=low, 100=high [2] T–Bill return substituted for category avg.

Category Rating (3 Yr)

1 2 **3** 4 5
Worst Best

Return Average
Risk Average

Other Measures	Standard Index S&P 500	Best Fit Index MSCIACWdFr
Alpha	1.1	6.1
Beta	1.22	1.31
R–Squared	88	88
Standard Deviation		22.10
Mean		–1.93
Sharpe Ratio		–0.36

Analysis by Heather Haynos 12-07-01

Wilshire Target Large Company Growth Fund's dose of moderation has served it well.

This fund picks its stocks from the 750 largest names in the Wilshire 5000 index. It then screens that universe for companies with attractive growth attributes, such as above-average earnings and revenue growth and high returns on equity. Management subjects the stocks that pass muster to a relative risk-return analysis, which weeds out names that are projected to increase portfolio risk without providing adequate compensation.

So far, this straightforward, quantitative approach has delivered impressive results. With a few exceptions, the fund has consistently beaten its large-growth competition by a comfortable margin. And because the Wilshire 5000 hasn't been home to some of the market's higher-flying tech stocks, it's done so without courting as much volatility as its typical peer.

The fund isn't exactly staid, however. In 2000, for example, it kept an average of almost 52% of assets in technology, which explains why the fund fell behind its average rival that year. Still, manager Thomas Stevens has done a commendable job of stemming losses thus far in 2001. For the year to date through Dec. 5, the fund's 15% loss places in the group's top third. The portfolio got a boost from top-10 holdings Microsoft and IBM. Recent additions such as Wal-Mart and Johnson & Johnson have been helpful, too. Stevens has been stockpiling consumer-product stocks lately, because he believes they've maintained attractive growth characteristics and are reasonably well-positioned to withstand the current economic downturn.

Although its large-cap bias doesn't make it an all-weather offering, this fund effectively provides broad exposure to large-growth stocks without taking on inordinate risk. A reasonable expense ratio also adds to its charms.

Address:	P.O. Box 9770 Providence, RI 02940–9770 888–200–6796
Web Address:	www.wilfunds.com
*Inception:	09-30-92
Advisor:	Wilshire Assoc.
Subadvisor:	None
NTF Plans:	Datalynx , Fidelity Inst.

Minimum Purchase:	$2500	Add: $100	IRA: $750
Min Auto Inv Plan:	$100	Add: $100	
Sales Fees:	0.25%S		
Management Fee:	.25%, .15%A		
Actual Fees:	Mgt: 0.25%	Dist: 0.25%	
Expense Projections:	3Yr: $268	5Yr: $466	10Yr: $1037
Avg Brok Commission:	—	Income Distrib: Annually	
Total Cost (relative to category):		Low	

Portfolio Analysis 04-30-01

Share change since 03–00 Total Stocks: 228	Sector	PE	YTD Ret%	% Assets
⊖ Microsoft	Technology	57.6	52.78	5.35
⊕ General Elec	Industrials	30.1	–15.00	5.31
⊕ Pfizer	Health	34.7	–12.40	4.68
⊖ Wal–Mart Stores	Retail	40.3	8.94	4.57
✲ IBM	Technology	26.9	43.00	3.94
⊖ Merck	Health	19.1	–35.90	3.44
✲ American Intl Grp	Financials	42.0	–19.20	3.32
⊕ Johnson & Johnson	Health	16.6	14.01	2.83
⊕ Cisco Sys	Technology	—	–52.60	2.29
⊕ Bristol–Myers Squibb	Health	20.2	–26.00	2.28
⊕ Home Depot	Retail	42.9	12.07	2.14
⊕ Oracle	Technology	32.1	–52.40	2.00
✲ Eli Lilly	Health	28.9	–14.40	1.75
⊖ Intel	Technology	73.1	4.89	1.73
✲ Merrill Lynch	Financials	18.2	–22.70	1.61
⊕ EMC	Technology	NMF	–79.40	1.60
⊕ Morgan Stanley/Dean Witter	Financials	16.6	–28.20	1.49
⊕ Dell Comp	Technology	61.8	55.87	1.45
⊖ Abbott Labs	Health	51.6	17.08	1.37
⊕ Amgen	Health	52.8	–11.70	1.33
⊕ American Express	Financials	28.3	–34.40	1.26
✲ Texas Instruments	Technology	87.5	–40.70	1.21
⊕ Sun Microsystems	Technology	NMF	–55.80	1.17
⊕ Schering–Plough	Health	22.2	–35.90	1.15
⊖ Procter & Gamble	Staples	38.8	3.12	1.13

Current Investment Style

Style: Value Blnd Growth; Size: Large Med Small

	Stock Port Avg	Relative S&P 500 Current	Relative S&P 500 Hist	Rel Cat
Price/Earnings Ratio	36.5	1.18	1.18	1.03
Price/Book Ratio	7.0	1.23	1.34	1.10
Price/Cash Flow	21.2	1.18	1.21	0.93
3 Yr Earnings Growth	20.6	1.41	1.30	0.95
1 Yr Earnings Est%	–6.2	3.52	—	–2.08
Med Mkt Cap $mil	70,264	1.2	1.5	1.48

Special Securities % assets 04-30-01	
Restricted/Illiquid Secs	0
Emerging–Markets Secs	0
Options/Futures/Warrants	No

Composition % assets 04-30-01	
Cash	0.0
Stocks*	100.0
Bonds	0.0
Other	0.0
*Foreign (% stocks)	0.0

Market Cap	
Giant	60.0
Large	26.7
Medium	12.7
Small	0.7
Micro	0.0

Sector Weightings	% of Stocks	Rel S&P	5-Year High	5-Year Low
Utilities	0.5	0.2	1	0
Energy	1.2	0.2	1	0
Financials	13.5	0.8	13	6
Industrials	8.3	0.7	17	8
Durables	0.9	0.6	3	1
Staples	2.2	0.3	25	1
Services	6.7	0.6	15	7
Retail	11.3	1.7	14	7
Health	23.3	1.6	23	13
Technology	32.2	1.8	52	10

WM Growth Fund of the Northwest A

Ticker	Load	NAV	Yield	Total Assets	Mstar Category
CMNWX	5.50%	$30.96	0.2%	$806.8 mil	Small Blend

Prospectus Objective: Growth

WM Growth Fund of the Northwest - Class A seeks long-term growth of capital.

The fund normally invests at least 65% of assets in common stocks issued by companies headquartered in Alaska, Idaho, Montana, Oregon, or Washington. It may also invest in stocks issued by other companies that do business in the Northwest.

Class A shares have front loads; B and S shares have deferred loads, higher 12b-1 fees, and conversion features; I shares are only available to various Portfolios. Past fund names : Composite Northwest 50 Fund - Class A, Composite Northwest Fund - Class A, and WM Northwest Fund - Class A.

Historical Profile
Return: High
Risk: Above Avg
Rating: ★★★★★ Highest

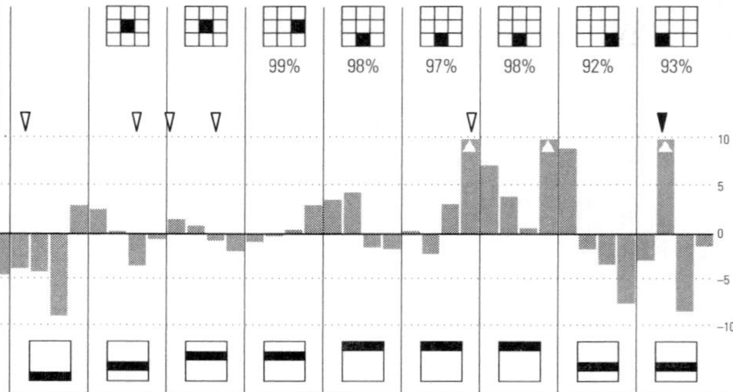

Investment Style
Equity
Average Stock %: 99% 98% 97% 98% 92% 93%

▼ Manager Change
▽ Partial Manager Change

Fund Performance vs. Category Average
Quarterly Fund Return +/– Category Average
— Category Baseline

Performance Quartile (within Category)

Portfolio Manager(s)

Management Team

1990	1991	1992	1993	1994	1995	1996	1997	1998	1999	2000	12-01	History
10.03	14.23	14.67	14.39	14.11	17.60	19.65	22.60	26.51	33.13	30.15	30.96	NAV
–1.13	43.88	3.61	2.42	–1.42	26.52	22.56	32.88	22.98	42.27	6.65	6.34	Total Return %
1.99	13.40	–4.01	–7.64	–2.73	–11.02	–0.38	–0.47	–5.59	21.23	15.75	18.22	+/– S&P 500
18.38	–2.17	–14.80	–16.48	0.41	–1.92	6.02	10.51	25.53	21.00	9.68	3.85	+/– Russell 2000
0.74	0.73	0.49	0.51	0.54	0.45	0.03	0.00	0.00	0.00	0.11	0.26	Income Return %
–1.86	43.15	3.12	1.91	–1.95	26.06	22.53	32.88	22.98	42.27	6.54	6.08	Capital Return %
20	44	93	97	58	48	39	20	1	8	63	51	Total Rtn % Rank Cat
0.08	0.07	0.07	0.08	0.08	0.06	0.01	0.00	0.00	0.00	0.03	0.08	Income $
0.00	0.11	0.00	0.55	0.00	0.18	1.88	3.60	1.17	4.13	5.07	1.02	Capital Gains $
1.45	1.21	1.11	1.09	1.09	1.10	1.08	1.05	1.10	1.15	—	—	Expense Ratio %
0.72	0.63	0.53	0.48	0.51	0.44	0.16	–0.08	–0.09	–0.21	—	—	Income Ratio %
7	8	4	8	11	11	42	37	39	41	—	—	Turnover Rate %
52.4	116.1	179.7	166.8	146.9	161.2	191.3	258.4	304.0	395.4	428.6	477.6	Net Assets $mil

Performance 12-31-01

	1st Qtr	2nd Qtr	3rd Qtr	4th Qtr	Total
1997	1.83	19.79	14.10	–4.53	32.88
1998	10.78	–6.83	–17.98	45.26	22.98
1999	–1.28	21.17	–4.10	24.02	42.27
2000	17.27	–2.19	0.89	–7.84	6.65
2001	–7.40	29.80	–25.14	18.18	6.34

Trailing	Total Return%	+/– S&P 500	+/– Russ 2000	% Rank All	% Rank Cat	Growth of $10,000
3 Mo	18.18	7.49	–2.90	17	53	11,818
6 Mo	–11.53	–5.98	–7.44	89	96	8,847
1 Yr	6.34	18.22	3.85	17	51	10,634
3 Yr Avg	17.29	18.31	10.87	3	14	16,135
5 Yr Avg	21.40	10.70	13.88	1	3	26,367
10 Yr Avg	15.64	2.71	4.13	4	12	42,771
15 Yr Avg	17.02	3.29	6.26	2	1	105,644

Tax Analysis	Tax-Adj Ret%	%Rank Cat	%Pretax Ret	%Rank Cat
3 Yr Avg	14.49	17	83.8	50
5 Yr Avg	18.66	2	87.2	37
10 Yr Avg	13.81	9	88.3	12

Potential Capital Gain Exposure: 35% of assets

Risk Analysis

Time Period	Load-Adj Return %	Risk %Rank[1] All	Risk %Rank[1] Cat	Morningstar Return	Morningstar Risk	Morningstar Risk-Adj Rating
1 Yr	0.49					
3 Yr	15.10	76	83	2.37[2]	1.05	★★★★★
5 Yr	20.03	80	76	4.36[2]	1.12	★★★★★
10 Yr	14.99	85	87	1.78	1.19	★★★★

Average Historical Rating (146 months): 3.1★s

[1]1=low, 100=high [2] T-Bill return substituted for category avg.

Category Rating (3 Yr)

1 2 3 4 5 (Worst → Best): 4

Return: Above Avg
Risk: Above Avg

Other Measures	Standard Index S&P 500	Best Fit Index Russ 2000
Alpha	21.1	10.9
Beta	1.08	0.99
R-Squared	51	83
Standard Deviation		30.60
Mean		17.29
Sharpe Ratio		0.46

Portfolio Analysis 11-30-01

Share change since 10-01 Total Stocks: 64

	Sector	PE	YTD Ret%	% Assets
Corixa	Health	—	–45.90	3.35
InFocus	Technology	31.5	49.29	3.18
Kroger	Retail	16.3	–22.80	3.13
Monaco Coach	Durables	24.6	85.46	3.04
Paccar	Industrials	27.0	36.79	2.88
Bank of America	Financials	16.7	42.73	2.75
US Bancorp	Financials	13.5	–6.14	2.74
⊕ Pixelworks	Technology	—	–28.20	2.52
SonoSite	Health	—	101.40	2.51
⊖ Hollywood Entrtnmt	Retail	—	1,244.00	2.47
Washington Federal	Financials	13.2	3.56	2.43
Advanced Digital Info	Technology	—	–30.20	2.43
Boeing	Industrials	10.2	–40.40	2.39
OraSure Tech	Health	—	47.27	2.33
FEI	Technology	29.2	38.51	2.30
Stancorp Finl Grp	Financials	15.4	–0.38	2.16
Louisiana-Pacific	Industrials	—	–14.80	2.15
Metro One Telecom	Services	28.0	81.50	2.03
Electro Scientific Inds	Technology	8.4	7.18	1.97
⊕ Plum Creek Timber	Industrials	18.4	20.75	1.85
WatchGuard Tech	Technology	—	–79.40	1.74
Wells Fargo	Financials	22.4	–20.20	1.69
Albertson's	Retail	29.7	22.01	1.64
Building Matl Hldg	Industrials	7.9	27.65	1.62
ICOS	Health	—	10.59	1.61

Current Investment Style

Style: Value Blnd Growth; Size: Large Med Small

	Stock Port Avg	Relative S&P 500 Current	Relative S&P 500 Hist	Rel Cat
Price/Earnings Ratio	23.0	0.74	0.77	0.92
Price/Book Ratio	3.3	0.57	0.60	1.02
Price/Cash Flow	16.8	0.93	0.86	1.08
3 Yr Earnings Growth	19.7	1.35	0.88	1.16
1 Yr Earnings Est%	–4.9	2.75	—	–5.66
Med Mkt Cap $mil	1,034	0.0	0.0	1.05

[1]figure is based on 50% or less of stocks

Analysis by Catherine Hickey 08-18-01

After a recent management change, there's little reason for new investors to look here.

WM Growth Fund of the Northwest just lost a great asset. David Simpson, who steered this fund to great results since 1993, left the firm for a hedge fund last April. During his tenure, the fund notched some of the best results in the small-blend category; the fund's long-term results are top-notch. Randy Yoakum, WM's chief investment officer, is Simpson's interim replacement, but Yoakum says he's actively searching for someone who will manage the fund on a permanent basis. Until that happens and the new skipper builds a track record, though, new investors should probably hold off here.

Although we generally believe investors can do without regionally focused offerings, current shareholders would probably do fine to stay for the time being, because this fund has continued to deliver solid results. For example, Hollywood Entertainment has produced eye-popping gains this year. At the other end of the flashiness spectrum, Oregon Steel Mills is also up hugely. The fund will continue to invest in both high-growth companies and value issues, Yoakum said, largely because the fund is geographically penned in to the universe of stocks offered in the Northwest.

Shareholders who remain comfortable with those limitations should hold on, but those looking for a fund with a broader perspective should seek another offering.

Special Securities % assets 11-30-01	
Restricted/Illiquid Secs	0
Emerging-Markets Secs	0
Options/Futures/Warrants	No

Composition % assets 11-30-01	
Cash	7.0
Stocks*	93.0
Bonds	0.0
Other	0.0
*Foreign (% stocks)	0.0

Market Cap	
Giant	6.8
Large	16.2
Medium	20.5
Small	41.4
Micro	15.1

Sector Weightings	% of Stocks	Rel S&P	5-Year High	5-Year Low
Utilities	0.0	0.0	5	0
Energy	0.0	0.0	1	0
Financials	17.9	1.0	20	8
Industrials	18.7	1.6	34	14
Durables	5.2	3.3	8	0
Staples	1.2	0.2	2	0
Services	6.3	0.6	14	6
Retail	9.6	1.4	25	7
Health	12.5	0.8	16	3
Technology	28.6	1.6	38	8

Address:	PO Box 9757 Providence, RI 02940-9757 509-353-3550 / 800-222-5852
Web Address:	www.wmgroupoffunds.com
Inception:	11-24-86
Advisor:	WM Adv.
Subadvisor:	None
NTF Plans:	N/A

Minimum Purchase:	$1000	Add: $50	IRA: $1000
Min Auto Inv Plan:	$50	Add: $50	
Sales Fees:	5.50%L, 0.25%B, 0.25%S		
Management Fee:	.63% mx./.38% mn.		
Actual Fees:	Mgt: 0.63%	Dist: 0.25%	
Expense Projections:	3Yr: $88*	5Yr: $113*	10Yr: $183*
Avg Brok Commission:	—	Income Distrib: Annually	
Total Cost (relative to category):	—		

Tables and Charts

This section breaks down the performance of the Morningstar Categories and lists the best- and worst-performing funds.

Performance Summary–Equity Funds

Morningstar's Open-End Fund Universe

Category	2001 Total Return % 1st Quarter	2nd Quarter	3rd Quarter	4th Quarter	2001	# of Funds	Average Annualized Total Return % 3Yr	# of Funds	5Yr	# of Funds	10Yr	# of Funds
Domestic Stock	**-13.03**	**8.60**	**-17.61**	**14.78**	**-10.89**	**5145**	**3.14**	**3633**	**9.08**	**2347**	**11.48**	**687**
Large Value	-5.73	4.72	-12.12	9.27	-5.37	808	2.31	646	8.84	473	11.88	156
Large Blend	-12.56	5.30	-15.18	10.87	-13.67	1220	-0.93	858	8.87	517	11.31	161
Large Growth	-20.97	6.57	-20.69	14.98	-23.63	988	-3.14	655	8.24	419	10.03	121
Medium Value	-1.49	7.78	-11.78	13.60	6.40	272	10.30	205	11.68	125	13.81	46
Medium Blend	-9.46	9.13	-16.87	15.96	-4.96	244	5.54	140	9.62	86	12.26	31
Medium Growth	-21.96	12.03	-24.51	19.48	-21.28	645	5.09	418	8.44	288	10.30	66
Small Value	1.23	13.65	-13.29	17.63	17.31	223	13.02	176	11.29	97	13.47	29
Small Blend	-4.59	14.67	-16.90	19.43	8.41	252	11.84	185	10.91	115	13.25	32
Small Growth	-17.42	17.31	-23.95	23.48	-9.02	493	9.32	350	8.94	227	10.89	45
International Stock	**-12.61**	**1.91**	**-16.93**	**11.54**	**-17.42**	**1690**	**0.39**	**1301**	**0.69**	**860**	**5.12**	**160**
Europe Stock	-16.14	-1.53	-13.83	9.96	-21.43	170	-1.19	112	5.30	56	8.77	19
Latin America Stock	-5.16	8.88	-24.43	22.20	-4.67	33	9.07	32	1.02	22	3.56	2
Diversified Emerging Markets	-6.96	6.52	-21.65	24.04	-3.73	175	4.45	138	-4.79	99	0.89	3
Pacific Stock	-9.54	0.79	-19.96	9.48	-20.06	63	0.18	44	-7.89	31	1.77	10
Pacific Stock ex-Japan	-5.84	2.46	-21.78	25.88	-4.72	87	5.16	76	-8.12	56	2.60	4
Japan Stock	-8.90	0.79	-21.80	-1.81	-29.97	53	-2.82	40	-4.25	21	-3.96	5
Foreign Stock	-14.44	0.18	-16.22	8.79	-21.93	804	-1.67	599	2.34	385	6.32	68
World Stock	-14.10	3.51	-16.53	11.36	-17.49	271	1.75	230	5.65	165	7.73	33
Specialty Stock	**-19.42**	**9.36**	**-21.25**	**17.94**	**-20.16**	**933**	**5.89**	**485**	**8.52**	**300**	**12.77**	**80**
Communications	-24.15	4.05	-25.46	11.30	-35.07	51	-6.63	19	10.28	14	13.39	5
Financial	-6.69	8.27	-10.86	7.32	-3.19	97	6.10	62	13.02	27	17.86	13
Health	-22.22	14.48	-10.53	10.36	-13.06	127	14.96	54	15.19	33	13.83	11
Natural Resources	-5.03	-0.11	-16.17	11.49	-11.09	70	13.76	63	3.12	42	9.16	16
Precious Metals	-4.94	19.67	2.44	1.73	18.77	34	1.71	30	-11.71	25	-3.15	16
Real Estate	-1.75	9.66	-3.19	4.76	8.93	141	10.12	109	6.19	59	9.99	6
Technology	-34.40	13.34	-38.76	36.55	-38.21	355	-1.20	95	9.41	53	18.04	11
Utilities	-6.57	-3.25	-12.88	-0.39	-21.39	92	-0.71	83	7.85	72	9.18	18
Hybrid	**-5.51**	**3.18**	**-7.61**	**6.43**	**-4.46**	**897**	**2.52**	**755**	**7.05**	**556**	**9.20**	**137**
Domestic Hybrid	-5.29	3.19	-7.26	6.26	-4.01	778	2.21	651	7.01	476	8.98	114
Convertible	-7.59	3.61	-11.74	8.96	-8.07	65	6.37	54	8.52	41	10.29	17
International Hybrid	-6.16	2.41	-7.99	5.94	-6.47	54	2.36	50	5.96	39	10.10	6
Total Equity Fund Average	**-12.86**	**6.81**	**-16.83**	**13.62**	**-12.50**	**8665**	**2.70**	**6174**	**6.99**	**4063**	**10.33**	**1064**
Total Fund Average	**-8.08**	**4.75**	**-10.94**	**9.50**	**-6.99**	**12649**	**3.06**	**9659**	**6.16**	**6868**	**8.31**	**1996**

Index Benchmarks

Category	1st Quarter	2nd Quarter	3rd Quarter	4th Quarter	2001	3Yr	5Yr	10Yr
Domestic Stock								
S&P 500	-11.85	5.85	-14.67	10.69	-11.88	-1.03	10.70	12.93
Wilshire 5000	-12.28	7.48	-15.89	12.37	-10.89	-0.65	9.71	12.28
Wilshire 4500	-15.87	14.12	-20.95	19.50	-9.31	1.16	7.16	10.66
Russell 2000	-6.50	14.28	-20.79	21.08	2.49	6.42	7.52	11.51
S&P 400	-10.77	13.15	-16.56	17.98	-0.60	10.24	16.11	15.01
International Stock								
MSCI EAFE	-14.03	-1.68	-14.31	6.85	-22.61	-6.32	-0.52	2.88
MSCI World	-13.10	2.22	-14.64	8.37	-17.83	-4.44	4.11	6.48
MSCI Europe	-15.86	-2.78	-12.41	9.94	-21.23	-6.70	4.55	7.51
MSCI Pacific	-1.18	0.15	-21.33	6.49	-17.10	-1.05	-6.00	-2.72
MSCI Latin America	-3.54	7.08	-23.96	21.85	-4.31	6.68	-0.70	4.97
MSCI Emerging Markets	-6.19	3.11	-22.14	26.26	-4.91	2.01	-7.80	0.95
Miscellaneous								
U.S. 90-Day Treasury Bill	1.29	0.97	0.85	0.51	3.67	4.94	5.03	4.73
Consumer Price Index	1.26	1.02	0.17	-0.50	1.95	2.67	2.27	2.55

Performance Summary–Fixed-Income Funds

Morningstar's Open-End Fund Universe

Category	2001 Total Return % 1st Quarter	2nd Quarter	3rd Quarter	4th Quarter	2001	# of Funds	Average Annualized Total Return % 3Yr	# of Funds	5Yr	# of Funds	10Yr	# of Funds
Specialty Bond	**2.58**	**-1.52**	**-2.06**	**3.54**	**2.30**	**655**	**0.33**	**546**	**2.36**	**345**	**5.94**	**101**
High Yield Bond	4.04	-2.32	-5.18	5.58	1.70	354	-1.01	287	1.31	149	6.56	52
Multisector Bond	1.97	-0.44	-0.19	2.49	3.82	172	2.52	140	3.58	95	6.39	20
World Bond	-0.59	-0.73	3.96	-0.63	1.91	129	0.98	119	2.76	101	4.51	29
General Bond	**2.86**	**0.58**	**3.39**	**0.09**	**7.07**	**1023**	**5.21**	**815**	**6.16**	**621**	**6.44**	**195**
Long-Term Bond	3.25	0.45	3.09	0.59	7.51	95	4.53	83	6.09	66	7.08	19
Intermediate-Term Bond	3.01	0.38	3.90	-0.06	7.36	616	5.12	496	6.29	373	6.70	115
Short-Term Bond	2.86	1.05	3.19	0.04	7.32	222	5.82	186	5.99	152	5.89	45
Ultrashort Bond	1.45	0.96	0.83	0.75	4.01	90	5.03	50	5.47	30	5.29	16
Government Bond	**2.36**	**0.29**	**4.37**	**-0.37**	**6.72**	**481**	**5.26**	**439**	**6.24**	**368**	**6.21**	**149**
Long-Term Government	1.73	-0.97	5.41	-0.78	5.31	58	4.31	54	6.80	46	7.10	25
Intermediate-Term Government	2.39	0.30	4.54	-0.49	6.84	292	5.33	263	6.33	220	6.21	89
Short-Term Government	2.55	0.82	3.51	0.08	7.09	131	5.53	122	5.81	102	5.59	35
Municipal Bond	**1.87**	**0.55**	**2.55**	**-0.83**	**4.17**	**1785**	**3.35**	**1647**	**4.75**	**1445**	**5.80**	**487**
Muni National Long-Term	1.93	0.61	2.52	-1.05	4.03	330	2.89	284	4.62	242	5.85	104
Muni National Intermed-Term	2.10	0.64	2.56	-0.91	4.39	160	3.70	137	4.85	113	5.76	37
Muni Single State Long-Term	1.83	0.57	2.57	-0.78	4.23	628	3.29	613	4.82	553	5.87	169
Muni Single State Intermed-Term	1.96	0.54	2.41	-0.68	4.29	286	3.55	266	4.67	238	5.65	61
Muni Short-Term	1.90	0.91	1.84	-0.04	4.67	108	3.69	98	4.21	82	4.81	21
NY Long-Term	1.80	0.73	2.16	-1.11	3.60	96	3.23	88	4.85	78	5.83	38
NY Intermediate	1.98	0.59	2.11	-0.94	3.75	27	3.74	26	4.92	21	5.66	8
CA Long-Term	1.36	-0.25	3.70	-1.11	3.69	117	3.50	108	5.05	96	6.08	43
CA Intermediate	1.82	0.30	3.05	-0.79	4.45	33	4.15	27	5.12	22	5.98	6
Total Fixed-Income Average	**2.30**	**0.22**	**2.16**	**0.27**	**4.98**	**3984**	**3.69**	**3485**	**4.96**	**2805**	**6.01**	**932**
Total Fund Average	**-8.08**	**4.75**	**-10.94**	**9.50**	**-6.99**	**12649**	**3.06**	**9659**	**6.16**	**6868**	**8.31**	**1996**

Index Benchmarks

Index	1st Quarter	2nd Quarter	3rd Quarter	4th Quarter	2001	3Yr	5Yr	10Yr
Government and Corporate								
Lehman Brothers Aggregate	3.03	0.56	4.62	0.04	8.42	6.27	7.43	7.23
Lehman Brothers Corporate	4.28	1.07	3.83	0.89	10.40	5.80	7.20	7.67
Lehman Brothers Government	2.52	-0.24	5.47	-0.59	7.24	5.88	7.40	7.14
Lehman Brothers Mortgage	2.73	1.01	4.22	0.07	8.22	7.01	7.49	7.10
Consumer Price Index	1.26	1.02	0.17	-0.50	1.95	2.67	2.27	2.55
Specialty Bond								
CSFB High Yield	4.93	-0.63	-3.98	5.65	5.78	1.17	3.24	7.84
Salomon Brothers World Government	-4.90	-1.97	7.75	-3.97	-3.54	-3.75	0.11	4.81
Municipal Bond								
Lehman Brothers Muni	2.23	0.66	2.80	-0.66	5.08	4.75	5.97	6.63
Lehman Brothers CA Muni	1.98	0.08	3.63	-0.59	5.15	4.82	6.14	—
Lehman Brothers NY Muni	2.20	0.82	2.24	-0.50	4.83	4.78	6.20	—
Miscellaneous								
U.S. 90-Day Treasury Bill	1.29	0.97	0.85	0.51	3.67	4.94	5.03	4.73

Performance Summary 1987–2001: Equity Funds

Morningstar's Open-End Fund Universe

Category	1987 TR%	1987 # of Funds	1988 TR%	1988 # of Funds	1989 TR%	1989 # of Funds	1990 TR%	1990 # of Funds	1991 TR%	1991 # of Funds	1992 TR%	1992 # of Funds
Domestic Stock	**1.22**	**403**	**16.40**	**474**	**25.57**	**514**	**-5.81**	**547**	**37.66**	**607**	**10.12**	**687**
Large Value	1.36	94	17.51	106	23.32	121	-6.38	128	28.35	140	10.06	156
Large Blend	3.14	92	15.37	108	27.25	118	-3.46	124	32.66	143	7.93	161
Large Growth	3.21	82	12.20	90	29.58	94	-2.47	98	44.30	107	6.25	121
Medium Value	-1.87	24	19.74	32	19.98	34	-8.93	38	31.50	43	16.25	46
Medium Blend	-0.23	20	21.97	23	25.40	23	-8.54	26	35.54	26	14.26	31
Medium Growth	0.37	41	15.49	53	29.10	56	-6.54	59	52.83	62	8.72	66
Small Value	-3.51	13	20.89	17	17.64	20	13.06	22	39.21	25	20.64	29
Small Blend	-4.37	17	22.49	18	18.85	21	12.10	23	38.99	24	14.72	32
Small Growth	-1.70	20	16.30	27	25.40	27	-6.05	29	54.42	37	11.39	45
International Stock	**16.38**	**64**	**10.98**	**73**	**23.45**	**87**	**13.15**	**98**	**12.65**	**127**	**-4.22**	**160**
Europe Stock	12.59	5	11.06	6	24.70	8	-8.03	9	6.84	17	-5.87	19
Latin America Stock	—	0	—	0	—	0	—	0	—	0	1.75	2
Diversified Emerging Markets	—	0	—	0	—	0	-5.33	1	15.05	2	-0.92	3
Pacific Stock	23.69	3	21.36	5	20.90	6	15.74	6	15.28	8	-1.97	10
Pacific Stock ex-Japan	—	0	—	0	—	0	15.14	1	22.67	2	15.64	4
Japan Stock	60.21	2	25.94	2	25.13	2	28.56	3	5.18	4	-20.66	5
Foreign Stock	8.51	25	17.62	30	22.12	35	10.09	41	13.36	50	-4.55	68
World Stock	4.55	16	14.93	17	22.44	20	11.54	21	23.39	28	1.69	33
Specialty Stock	**-0.37**	**52**	**12.30**	**56**	**29.01**	**62**	**-4.18**	**68**	**34.23**	**75**	**12.03**	**80**
Communications	9.38	4	22.90	4	46.67	4	12.98	4	31.33	5	15.48	5
Financial	-10.97	11	19.25	11	24.29	11	15.91	11	58.09	11	34.97	13
Health	0.27	8	11.64	8	38.48	9	14.76	10	63.80	10	-4.69	11
Natural Resources	9.33	11	8.98	13	30.02	14	-8.13	14	5.59	16	2.83	16
Precious Metals	39.10	13	15.84	13	27.76	16	22.49	16	-3.17	16	15.66	16
Real Estate	-9.54	2	10.06	2	16.27	2	13.96	5	29.59	5	15.87	6
Technology	3.03	10	4.53	11	20.02	11	0.75	11	50.38	11	14.96	11
Utilities	-8.69	6	15.10	7	29.55	11	-2.29	13	20.14	17	9.84	18
Hybrid	**2.04**	**70**	**12.08**	**89**	**18.04**	**106**	**-0.70**	**116**	**24.90**	**125**	**8.71**	**137**
Domestic Hybrid	3.11	60	11.97	75	18.61	87	0.02	95	23.89	103	7.97	114
Convertible	-6.40	9	12.58	12	15.03	16	-5.43	16	32.02	16	13.67	17
International Hybrid	13.78	1	13.35	2	17.70	3	0.72	5	23.23	6	8.65	6
Total Equity Fund Average	**2.82**	**589**	**14.94**	**692**	**24.57**	**769**	**-5.83**	**829**	**32.28**	**934**	**7.92**	**1064**
Total Fund Average	**1.88**	**1017**	**12.66**	**1261**	**17.72**	**1412**	**-0.64**	**1524**	**24.28**	**1717**	**8.06**	**1996**

Index benchmarks

Category	1987	1988	1989	1990	1991	1992
Domestic Stock						
S&P 500	5.26	16.61	31.68	-3.12	30.48	7.62
Wilshire 5000	2.36	17.94	29.17	-6.18	34.21	8.97
Wilshire 4500	-3.51	20.54	23.94	13.56	43.45	11.76
Russell 2000	-8.77	24.89	16.24	19.51	46.05	18.41
S&P 400	-2.03	20.87	35.54	-5.12	50.07	11.90
International Stock						
MSCI EAFE	23.18	26.66	9.22	24.71	10.19	-13.89
MSCI World	14.34	21.19	14.75	18.65	16.00	-7.14
MSCI Europe	1.43	12.73	25.40	-6.46	9.97	-7.35
MSCI Pacific	7.07	37.28	16.37	38.18	2.33	-18.74
MSCI Latin America	—	70.00	48.72	12.66	144.37	11.61
MSCI Emerging Markets	—	34.87	59.19	13.76	55.97	9.05
Miscellaneous						
U.S. 90-Day Treasury Bill	6.13	7.06	8.67	7.99	5.68	3.59
Consumer Price Index	4.43	4.42	4.65	6.11	3.06	2.90

Performance Summary 1987–2001: Equity Funds

Morningstar's Open-End Fund Universe

1993		1994		1995		1996		1997		1998		1999		2000		2001	
TR%	# of Funds	TR%	# of Funds	TR%	# of Funds	TR%	# of Funds	TR%	# of Funds	TR%	# of Funds	TR%	# of Funds	TR%	# of Funds	TR%	# of Funds
13.49	**864**	**-1.05**	**1142**	**31.95**	**1468**	**20.10**	**1803**	**25.00**	**2347**	**15.69**	**2997**	**28.80**	**3633**	**-1.57**	**4279**	**-10.89**	**5145**
13.91	198	-0.52	251	32.36	322	20.61	384	26.89	473	12.93	564	7.06	646	6.48	728	-5.37	808
11.14	204	-0.82	267	32.44	320	21.00	388	27.80	517	22.45	677	20.76	858	-6.50	1003	-13.67	1220
10.58	154	-2.23	212	32.41	279	18.71	342	25.19	419	33.28	555	41.46	655	-14.52	798	-23.63	988
19.60	49	-2.00	60	29.55	74	20.47	88	26.95	125	4.39	166	8.12	205	17.98	235	6.40	272
13.01	35	-1.44	40	28.72	56	20.99	67	26.78	86	6.92	102	23.44	140	3.80	183	-4.96	244
15.75	87	-0.77	129	35.05	167	17.91	204	17.09	288	14.82	345	61.66	418	-4.95	509	-21.28	645
15.78	36	-1.17	47	24.56	57	25.32	75	31.15	97	-6.70	137	5.43	176	18.37	200	17.31	223
16.86	39	-0.28	53	27.14	71	20.19	88	27.02	115	-4.17	162	15.62	185	11.83	205	8.41	252
15.93	62	-0.34	83	33.44	122	19.39	167	18.98	227	3.85	289	58.68	350	-4.37	418	-9.02	493
42.67	**224**	**-2.67**	**322**	**8.94**	**497**	**13.97**	**654**	**1.87**	**860**	**5.35**	**1085**	**51.57**	**1301**	**-17.00**	**1464**	**-17.42**	**1690**
28.55	20	2.14	24	16.04	37	24.54	41	18.34	56	20.01	70	29.86	112	-6.29	144	-21.43	170
57.87	5	-14.21	10	-13.34	14	28.09	19	29.13	22	-38.47	26	61.54	32	-15.47	32	-4.67	33
74.90	6	-8.81	14	-2.67	49	14.00	67	-3.45	99	-26.79	125	72.03	138	-31.02	155	-3.73	175
60.28	13	-5.60	15	5.35	22	3.65	24	-26.54	31	-4.29	38	96.70	44	-34.69	50	-20.06	63
75.58	9	-17.02	19	1.91	32	10.72	44	-33.71	56	-9.00	69	74.53	76	-27.42	80	-4.72	87
23.27	6	18.06	6	-1.80	10	-10.53	16	-13.30	21	8.99	26	121.80	40	-33.94	45	-29.97	53
36.94	107	-0.16	141	10.06	217	13.12	290	5.79	385	13.47	508	45.42	599	-15.34	681	-21.93	804
33.28	42	-1.16	75	17.85	97	16.93	129	12.60	165	13.77	198	41.88	230	-9.22	247	-17.49	271
16.98	**93**	**-1.24**	**131**	**30.57**	**184**	**21.13**	**224**	**20.86**	**300**	**11.44**	**394**	**37.35**	**485**	**9.95**	**617**	**-20.16**	**933**
27.48	6	-1.33	9	28.21	12	9.41	13	29.58	14	44.86	15	70.77	19	-32.31	23	-35.07	51
15.50	15	-2.69	15	41.82	18	28.58	18	45.78	27	6.25	45	-1.30	62	27.28	79	-3.19	97
3.03	14	2.63	17	46.17	20	13.06	22	21.03	33	18.69	46	18.16	54	55.81	73	-13.06	127
21.13	17	-1.57	21	19.96	30	33.69	35	3.77	42	-25.34	54	29.35	63	28.73	66	-11.09	70
80.97	16	-13.19	18	4.84	19	11.54	24	-41.54	25	-10.49	25	6.74	30	-16.69	30	18.77	34
21.10	6	-0.62	11	14.91	24	32.40	38	22.59	59	-16.03	82	-2.73	109	26.61	125	8.93	141
26.52	12	14.06	17	43.38	28	20.27	34	9.98	53	54.17	70	135.40	95	-31.92	165	-38.21	355
14.58	23	-8.62	41	27.67	52	11.07	64	26.30	72	19.30	82	17.52	83	8.15	86	-21.39	92
12.73	**172**	**-2.78**	**248**	**24.13**	**351**	**13.27**	**432**	**17.40**	**556**	**11.79**	**661**	**11.22**	**755**	**1.78**	**825**	**-4.46**	**897**
12.13	145	-2.56	211	24.57	299	12.93	371	17.73	476	12.53	565	8.93	651	2.21	714	-4.01	778
15.34	19	-4.70	24	22.48	28	15.92	35	18.37	41	4.72	48	31.75	54	0.02	61	-8.07	65
17.27	8	-2.93	13	20.60	24	14.59	26	12.33	39	10.23	48	18.88	50	-2.35	50	-6.47	54
18.46	**1353**	**-1.58**	**1843**	**26.17**	**2500**	**17.94**	**3113**	**18.76**	**4063**	**12.68**	**5137**	**32.12**	**6174**	**-3.34**	**7185**	**-12.50**	**8665**
15.07	**2566**	**-3.10**	**3542**	**21.43**	**4718**	**12.03**	**5625**	**14.55**	**6868**	**9.88**	**8312**	**20.08**	**9660**	**0.44**	**10890**	**-6.99**	**12649**

1993	1994	1995	1996	1997	1998	1999	2000	2001
10.06	1.32	37.53	22.95	33.35	28.58	21.04	-9.10	-11.88
11.28	-0.07	36.45	21.20	31.29	23.43	23.56	-10.94	-10.89
14.54	-2.66	33.39	17.25	25.69	8.63	35.49	-15.77	-9.31
18.91	-1.82	28.44	16.54	22.37	-2.55	21.26	-3.03	2.49
13.93	-3.59	30.92	19.18	32.25	19.11	14.72	17.49	-0.60
30.49	6.24	9.42	4.40	0.24	18.23	25.27	-15.21	-22.61
20.39	3.36	18.70	11.72	14.17	22.78	23.56	-14.05	-17.83
26.36	0.12	18.87	18.50	21.58	26.53	14.12	-9.66	-21.23
22.06	1.00	4.44	-1.16	-16.82	-8.91	43.22	-18.41	-17.10
50.67	-0.97	-15.09	18.94	28.34	-38.04	55.48	-18.39	-4.31
71.26	-8.67	-6.95	3.92	-13.41	-27.52	63.70	-31.80	-4.91
3.12	4.45	5.79	5.26	5.31	5.02	4.87	6.32	3.67
2.75	2.68	2.54	3.32	1.70	1.61	2.69	3.39	1.95

Performance Summary 1987–2001: Fixed-Income Funds

Morningstar's Open-End Fund Universe

Category	1987 TR%	1987 # of Funds	1988 TR%	1988 # of Funds	1989 TR%	1989 # of Funds	1990 TR%	1990 # of Funds	1991 TR%	1991 # of Funds	1992 TR%	1992 # of Funds
Specialty Bond	**4.23**	**46**	**11.89**	**61**	**1.41**	**69**	**-4.32**	**75**	**29.72**	**86**	**11.42**	**101**
High Yield Bond	2.41	37	12.88	45	-0.61	48	-9.84	49	36.92	52	17.22	52
Multisector Bond	0.24	4	13.12	8	5.80	11	-1.35	14	24.96	16	8.60	20
World Bond	20.91	5	5.10	8	6.30	10	14.76	12	13.13	18	2.97	29
General Bond	**2.45**	**73**	**8.15**	**103**	**11.21**	**122**	**6.81**	**140**	**15.61**	**153**	**7.00**	**195**
Long-Term Bond	3.24	10	8.14	14	12.18	15	5.80	16	17.44	18	8.15	19
Intermediate-Term Bond	1.84	48	8.44	66	11.48	79	6.52	86	16.81	92	7.34	115
Short-Term Bond	3.49	13	7.40	18	10.11	21	7.50	26	14.01	31	6.36	45
Ultrashort Bond	6.48	2	6.97	5	9.36	7	8.75	12	7.75	12	5.06	16
Government Bond	**1.17**	**80**	**7.51**	**103**	**12.69**	**118**	**8.46**	**121**	**14.41**	**126**	**6.16**	**149**
Long-Term Government	-2.21	16	9.82	17	15.39	19	6.38	21	16.22	21	6.35	25
Intermediate-Term Government	1.67	47	7.25	61	12.59	70	8.86	71	14.62	76	6.35	89
Short-Term Government	2.99	17	6.57	25	11.17	29	9.01	29	12.54	29	5.56	35
Municipal Bond	**-0.93**	**229**	**10.88**	**302**	**9.47**	**334**	**6.15**	**359**	**11.43**	**418**	**8.68**	**487**
Muni National Long-Term	-0.70	72	11.39	79	9.77	86	6.04	88	11.93	99	8.84	104
Muni National Intermed-Term	0.88	25	9.24	29	8.91	31	6.55	34	10.75	35	8.40	37
Muni Single State Long-Term	-1.68	41	11.92	82	9.69	94	6.31	103	11.67	126	8.91	169
Muni Single State Intermed-Term	-0.40	22	10.73	30	9.36	36	6.10	40	10.49	52	8.07	61
Muni Short-Term	2.51	9	6.38	15	7.36	15	6.31	16	8.57	18	6.90	21
NY Long-Term	-1.82	23	10.75	27	9.40	29	4.95	30	13.28	35	9.60	38
NY Intermediate	-1.35	2	9.19	4	8.47	4	5.79	5	11.31	6	8.74	8
CA Long-Term	-2.66	31	11.17	32	9.83	35	6.54	39	11.09	42	8.60	43
CA Intermediate	-0.75	4	9.86	4	9.21	4	6.29	4	10.58	5	8.05	6
Total Fixed-Income Average	**0.59**	**428**	**9.88**	**569**	**9.52**	**643**	**5.56**	**695**	**14.74**	**783**	**8.22**	**932**
Total Fund Average	**1.88**	**1017**	**12.66**	**1261**	**17.72**	**1412**	**-0.64**	**1524**	**24.28**	**1717**	**8.06**	**1996**

Index benchmarks	1987	1988	1989	1990	1991	1992
Government and Corporate						
Lehman Brothers Aggregate	2.76	7.89	14.53	8.96	16.00	7.40
Lehman Brothers Corporate	2.56	9.22	13.98	7.15	18.51	8.70
Lehman Brothers Government	2.20	7.03	14.23	8.72	15.32	7.23
Lehman Brothers Mortgage	4.29	8.72	15.35	10.72	15.72	6.96
Consumer Price Index	4.43	4.42	4.65	6.11	3.06	2.90
Specialty Bond						
First Boston High Yield	6.53	13.66	0.39	-6.38	43.75	16.66
Salomon Brothers World Government	35.15	2.34	-3.41	15.29	16.22	4.77
Municipal Bond						
Lehman Brothers Muni	1.50	10.16	10.79	7.30	12.14	8.82
Lehman Brothers CA Muni	—	—	—	—	—	—
Lehman Brothers NY Muni	—	—	—	—	—	—
Miscellaneous						
U.S. 90-Day Treasury Bill	6.13	7.06	8.67	7.99	5.68	3.59

Performance Summary 1987–2001: Fixed-Income Funds

Morningstar's Open-End Fund Universe

1993 TR%	# of Funds	1994 TR%	# of Funds	1995 TR%	# of Funds	1996 TR%	# of Funds	1997 TR%	# of Funds	1998 TR%	# of Funds	1999 TR%	# of Funds	2000 TR%	# of Funds	2001 TR%	# of Funds
17.22	**124**	**-4.39**	**168**	**17.13**	**228**	**11.69**	**279**	**8.99**	**345**	**2.91**	**434**	**2.72**	**546**	**-2.99**	**602**	**2.30**	**655**
19.03	58	-2.99	77	16.67	99	13.63	121	12.83	149	-0.18	204	4.84	287	-7.89	315	1.70	354
17.18	28	-5.59	40	17.87	61	10.81	76	9.28	95	1.71	117	2.74	140	1.62	164	3.82	172
14.47	38	-5.57	51	17.15	68	9.62	82	3.05	101	9.73	113	-2.40	119	3.40	123	1.91	129
9.54	**272**	**-2.95**	**365**	**15.87**	**472**	**3.76**	**528**	**8.38**	**621**	**6.94**	**716**	**-0.29**	**815**	**8.89**	**895**	**7.07**	**1023**
13.48	25	-6.07	37	21.17	50	3.88	60	10.53	66	6.36	68	-3.02	83	9.19	87	7.51	95
10.60	159	-3.89	218	17.63	279	3.25	312	8.89	373	7.51	429	-1.33	496	9.63	537	7.36	616
7.02	70	-0.74	90	11.34	116	4.43	127	6.61	152	6.17	177	2.29	186	7.76	200	7.32	222
4.46	18	3.24	20	7.37	27	6.08	29	6.33	30	5.33	42	4.97	50	6.09	71	4.01	90
8.21	**191**	**-3.32**	**245**	**15.82**	**297**	**2.93**	**332**	**8.23**	**368**	**7.38**	**413**	**-0.98**	**439**	**10.47**	**461**	**6.72**	**481**
12.61	29	-6.00	36	22.54	40	0.43	43	11.35	46	10.32	50	-5.79	54	14.85	55	5.31	58
8.04	109	-3.42	138	16.13	179	2.89	199	8.42	220	7.37	250	-1.23	263	10.71	282	6.84	292
6.14	53	-1.75	71	11.69	78	4.20	90	6.40	102	6.10	113	1.67	122	7.97	124	7.09	131
11.83	**626**	**-5.86**	**916**	**15.92**	**1202**	**3.45**	**1348**	**8.36**	**1445**	**5.40**	**1579**	**-3.77**	**1648**	**10.18**	**1709**	**4.17**	**1785**
12.24	119	-6.18	160	16.91	194	3.30	222	9.20	242	5.33	258	-4.80	284	10.05	310	4.03	330
10.93	49	-3.60	78	13.94	101	3.88	108	7.62	113	5.53	131	-2.05	138	9.03	146	4.39	160
12.56	218	-6.84	349	17.04	457	3.42	531	8.83	553	5.44	599	-4.57	613	10.84	617	4.23	628
11.02	91	-4.93	139	14.73	201	3.35	211	7.44	238	5.28	257	-2.65	266	9.40	274	4.29	286
7.03	33	-0.64	50	8.49	68	3.70	75	5.20	82	4.61	93	0.49	98	5.93	101	4.67	108
12.72	42	-7.50	51	16.85	68	3.14	75	8.98	78	5.68	86	-4.93	88	11.72	93	3.60	96
10.97	11	-4.54	12	13.66	15	3.49	17	7.71	21	5.59	24	-2.47	26	10.28	27	3.75	27
12.61	52	-7.71	63	18.80	78	3.57	88	9.18	96	5.77	106	-5.13	108	12.85	110	3.69	117
11.46	11	-5.04	14	15.42	20	4.23	21	7.62	22	5.79	25	-1.86	27	10.31	31	4.45	33
11.29	**1213**	**-4.75**	**1699**	**16.08**	**2218**	**4.71**	**2512**	**8.47**	**2805**	**5.36**	**3175**	**-1.25**	**3486**	**7.77**	**3705**	**4.98**	**3984**
15.07	**2566**	**-3.10**	**3542**	**21.43**	**4718**	**12.03**	**5625**	**14.55**	**6868**	**9.88**	**8312**	**20.08**	**9660**	**0.44**	**10890**	**-6.99**	**12649**
9.75		-2.92		18.47		3.62		9.68		8.67		-0.83		11.63		8.42	
12.17		-3.92		22.24		3.28		10.23		8.46		-1.94		9.40		10.40	
10.66		-3.37		18.33		2.77		9.58		9.85		-2.25		13.24		7.24	
6.84		-1.61		16.80		5.36		9.49		6.97		1.85		11.17		8.22	
2.75		2.68		2.54		3.32		1.70		1.61		2.69		3.39		1.95	
18.91		-0.98		17.39		12.42		12.63		0.58		3.28		-5.21		5.78	
15.12		5.99		19.55		4.08		-4.26		17.79		-5.07		-2.63		-3.54	
12.28		-5.14		17.46		4.44		9.20		6.48		-2.07		11.69		5.08	
—		-6.84		19.33		4.40		9.43		6.92		-2.80		12.67		5.15	
—		-5.52		17.22		4.73		9.85		6.88		-2.02		12.01		4.83	
3.12		4.45		5.79		5.26		5.31		5.02		4.87		6.32		3.67	

1-Year Performance

Morningstar Funds 500 Universe

Domestic Equity

Cat		1-Year Total Return %
	Highest	
SV	FPA Capital	38.13
SG	Buffalo Small Cap	31.18
SV	American Century Small Cap Value Inv	30.52
SV	Heartland Value	29.45
SB	Wasatch Core Growth	28.82
SV	Dreyfus Small Company Value	28.60
SV	Fidelity Low-Priced Stock	26.71
SV	Oakmark Small Cap I	26.30
MV	Oakmark Select I	26.06
SB	DFA U.S. Micro Cap	22.77
SB	FPA Perennial	22.73
SB	SAFECO Growth Opportunities	22.03
SV	T. Rowe Price Small-Cap Value	21.94
SV	Berger Small Cap Value Instl	20.42
SB	Liberty Acorn USA Z	19.25
SV	UAM ICM Small Company	19.05
SV	Putnam Small Cap Value A	18.95
SB	Galaxy Small Cap Value Ret A	18.29
MV	Oakmark I	18.29
SR	Third Avenue Real Estate Value	18.20
	Lowest	
MG	Van Wagoner Post-Venture	-62.14
ST	Black Oak Emerging Technology	-60.50
ST	Red Oak Technology Select	-55.97
SC	INVESCO Telecommunications Inv	-54.19
MG	Merrill Lynch Premier Growth B	-52.95
ST	Fidelity Select Network & Infrastruct	-50.25
LG	INVESCO Growth Inv	-49.07
LG	Fidelity Aggressive Growth	-47.27
MG	Putnam OTC Emerging Growth A	-46.12
ST	Calvert Social Investment Tech A	-44.34
ST	T. Rowe Price Science & Tech	-41.19
ST	Janus Global Technology	-39.96
MG	Janus Enterprise	-39.93
MG	Van Kampen Aggressive Growth A	-39.70
ST	Dresdner RCM Global Technology I	-39.31
LG	White Oak Growth Stock	-39.05
ST	Northern Technology	-34.47
LG	Strong Growth Inv	-34.39
LG	AIM Weingarten A	-34.10
ST	Enterprise Internet A	-33.94
	Average 1-Year Total Return %	**-7.09**

International Equity

Cat		1-Year Total Return %
	Highest	
WS	Oakmark Global I	20.05
SP	Vanguard Precious Metals	18.33
FS	Longleaf Partners International	10.47
IH	First Eagle SoGen Global A	10.21
PJ	Matthews Pacific Tiger	7.91
EM	Dreyfus Emerging Markets	7.70
IH	American Funds Capital Inc Builder A	4.74
WS	Mutual Discovery Z	1.26
IH	Merrill Lynch Global Allocation B	1.01
WS	Templeton Growth A	0.54
LS	Scudder Latin America S	-0.82
EM	Vanguard Emerging Mkts Stock Idx	-2.88
LS	Van Kampen Latin American A	-2.94
EM	American Funds New World A	-3.96
FS	Tweedy, Browne Global Value	-4.67
WS	American Funds Capital World Gr&Inc A	-4.96
EM	Templeton Developing Markets A	-5.76
LS	Fidelity Latin America	-6.04
WS	Fidelity Worldwide	-6.21
IH	MFS Global Total Return A	-6.82
	Lowest	
JS	Japan S	-33.63
WS	Putnam Global Growth A	-29.82
FS	Liberty Acorn Foreign Forty Z	-29.05
FS	Scudder International S	-26.89
FS	American Century Intl Growth Inv	-26.79
ES	Scudder Greater Europe Growth S	-25.69
WS	American Century Global Growth Inv	-25.65
FS	Deutsche International Equity Invm	-25.39
WS	Scudder Global Discovery A	-25.18
JS	CS Warburg Pincus Japan Growth Comm	-25.14
FS	Lazard International Equity Instl	-24.85
ES	AIM European Development A	-24.72
FS	TIAA-CREF International Equity	-24.29
WS	IDEX Janus Global A	-23.54
FS	Janus Overseas	-23.11
WS	Janus Worldwide	-22.88
FS	SEI International Equity A	-22.55
FS	Waddell & Reed Adv International Gr A	-22.36
FS	AIM International Equity A	-22.36
FS	Vanguard Developed Markets Index	-22.05
	Average 1-Year Total Return %	**-13.45**

Notes: The tables on pages 526–531 are based on Morningstar rating groups. Specialty precious-metals funds are included in the international-equity group.

1-Year Performance

Morningstar Funds 500 Universe

Taxable Bond

Cat		1-Year Total Return %
	Highest	
CI	FPA New Income	12.33
EB	Scudder Emerging Markets Income S	10.46
CI	Dodge & Cox Income	10.32
CL	Vanguard Long-Term Corporate Bond	9.57
CI	PIMCO Total Return Instl	9.49
CI	Fremont Bond	9.42
EB	T. Rowe Price Emerging Markets Bond	9.35
CI	Metropolitan West Total Return Bond	9.18
CI	Harbor Bond	9.03
IB	PIMCO Foreign Bond Instl	8.96
GI	Strong Government Securities Inv	8.92
GI	Pilgrim GNMA Income A	8.85
CS	Vanguard Short-Term Bond Index	8.77
GS	Vanguard Short-Term Federal	8.61
GS	Sit U.S. Government Securities	8.44
CI	Vanguard Total Bond Market Index	8.43
CI	ABN AMRO/Chicago Capital Bond N	8.03
CS	PIMCO Low Duration Instl	8.01
GI	Vanguard GNMA	7.94
GS	Vanguard Short-Term Treasury	7.80
	Lowest	
HY	Morgan Stan Inst High-Yield Invmt	-5.91
HY	Fidelity High-Income	-4.84
IB	T. Rowe Price International Bond	-3.41
IB	Alliance North American Govt Income B	-1.21
HY	Fidelity Advisor High-Yield T	-1.16
HY	Strong High-Yield Bond Inv	-0.71
HY	Eaton Vance Income Fund of Boston A	-0.14
HY	Northeast Investors	1.33
IB	AXP Global Bond A	1.43
IB	American Funds Capital World Bond A	1.53
HY	MainStay High-Yield Corporate Bond B	1.71
MU	Loomis Sayles Bond Instl	2.66
HY	Vanguard High-Yield Corporate	2.90
HY	Franklin AGE High Income A	2.92
GL	T. Rowe Price U.S. Treasury Long-Term	3.39
GL	American Century Long-Term Trs Inv	3.81
UB	Strong Advantage Inv	4.26
GL	Vanguard Long-Term U.S. Treasury	4.31
CS	Strong Short-Term Bond Inv	4.39
MU	T. Rowe Price Spectrum Income	4.50
	Average 1-Year Total Return %	**5.63**

Municipal-National Bond

Cat		1-Year Total Return %
	Highest	
ML	Franklin High Yield Tax-Free Inc A	5.89
MS	T. Rowe Price Tax-Free Short-Interm	5.81
ML	Sit Tax-Free Income	5.76
MS	Fidelity Spartan Short-Int Muni Inc	5.70
MS	Vanguard Ltd-Term Tax-Ex	5.58
MI	American Funds Tax-Exempt Bond Fd A	5.57
MI	USAA Tax-Exempt Intermediate-Term	5.55
MI	Fidelity Spartan Interm Muni Income	5.37
ML	Vanguard High-Yield Tax-Exempt	5.34
MS	Strong Short-Term Municipal Bond Inv	5.17
	Lowest	
ML	AXP High-Yield Tax-Exempt A	3.91
MI	Dreyfus Intermediate Municipal Bond	3.98
ML	Vanguard Insured Long-Trm T/E	4.24
ML	Vanguard Long-Term Tax-Exempt	4.27
ML	USAA Tax-Exempt Long-Term	4.33
MS	Evergreen High Income Municipal Bd B	4.42
MS	Calvert Tax-Free Reserv Limited-Trm A	4.46
ML	Franklin Insured Tax-Free Income A	4.57
ML	Franklin Federal Tax-Free Income A	4.63
ML	Alliance Muni Income National A	4.68
	Average 1-Year Total Return %	**4.96**

Notes: There are only 29 municipal-bond funds in the Morningstar Funds 500 universe.

3-Year Performance

Morningstar Funds 500 Universe

Domestic Equity

Cat		3-Year Avg Annualized Total Return %
	Highest	
SG	Morgan Stan Inst Small Cap Growth	38.63
SG	Buffalo Small Cap	33.21
SG	Brazos Micro Cap Y	31.06
SG	Fremont U.S. Micro-Cap	29.26
SV	State Street Research Aurora A	28.45
SB	Meridian Value	28.43
SB	Wasatch Core Growth	28.31
MB	Vanguard Capital Opportunity	28.23
SH	Eaton Vance Worldwide Health Sci A	28.09
LG	Quaker Aggressive Growth A	27.87
SG	John Hancock Small Cap Value B	26.42
MV	Dreyfus Midcap Value	24.10
SG	RS Diversified Growth	23.05
MV	Oakmark Select I	22.00
SV	American Century Small Cap Value Inv	21.73
SH	Fidelity Select Biotechnology	20.98
SH	Janus Global Life Sciences	20.70
SV	Berger Small Cap Value Instl	20.65
SB	Westport Small Cap R	20.61
SV	ICM/Isabelle Small Cap Value Invmt	20.57
	Lowest	
LG	INVESCO Growth Inv	-18.74
MG	Putnam OTC Emerging Growth A	-15.85
LG	Vanguard U.S. Growth	-12.64
SC	Deutsche Flag Communications A	-12.45
LG	Fidelity Destiny I	-11.47
LG	AIM Weingarten A	-10.88
LB	Fidelity Advisor Growth Opport T	-10.34
LG	One Group Large Cap Growth A	-8.44
LG	Alliance Premier Growth B	-8.35
ST	T. Rowe Price Science & Tech	-8.03
LG	Fidelity Aggressive Growth	-7.95
LG	Janus Twenty	-7.59
LG	Putnam Investors A	-7.26
LG	TIAA-CREF Growth Equity	-6.55
SC	INVESCO Telecommunications Inv	-6.48
LG	Babson Growth	-6.21
LG	AIM Summit	-5.24
SU	Fidelity Utilities	-5.09
LG	Vanguard Growth Index	-4.46
LB	T. Rowe Price New America Growth	-3.85
	Average Annualized 3-Year Total Return %	**6.42**

International Equity

Cat		3-Year Avg Annualized Total Return %
	Highest	
FS	Longleaf Partners International	20.05
PJ	Matthews Pacific Tiger	14.87
EM	Dreyfus Emerging Markets	14.51
WS	Oppenheimer Global Growth & Income A	14.35
IH	First Eagle SoGen Global A	13.08
WS	Mutual Discovery Z	13.07
SP	Vanguard Precious Metals	12.20
LS	Van Kampen Latin American A	11.37
IH	Merrill Lynch Global Allocation B	11.26
FS	Artisan International	10.90
FS	Tweedy, Browne Global Value	10.31
WS	Templeton Growth A	10.09
WS	American Century Global Growth Inv	9.25
FS	American Century Intl Discovery Inv	8.16
FS	Templeton Foreign A	7.60
PJ	T. Rowe Price New Asia	7.58
LS	Scudder Latin America S	7.18
WS	American Funds Capital World Gr&Inc A	7.04
PJ	Liberty Newport Tiger A	6.75
ES	AIM European Development A	6.65
	Lowest	
FS	Deutsche International Equity Invm	-7.65
WS	Putnam Global Growth A	-6.72
FS	Lazard International Equity Instl	-5.87
ES	Vanguard European Stock Index	-5.15
JS	CS Warburg Pincus Japan Growth Comm	-4.99
FS	T. Rowe Price International Stock	-4.53
FS	Vanguard Total Intl Stock Index	-4.34
ES	T. Rowe Price European Stock	-3.93
FS	SEI International Equity A	-3.82
FS	AIM International Equity A	-3.64
ES	Fidelity Europe	-3.25
ES	Scudder Greater Europe Growth S	-3.13
FS	Waddell & Reed Adv International Gr A	-2.91
FS	Fidelity Overseas	-2.35
FS	Scudder International S	-2.31
FS	Vanguard International Growth	-2.17
FS	TIAA-CREF International Equity	-1.91
WS	Merrill Lynch Global Value D	-1.61
EM	Templeton Developing Markets A	-0.90
WS	MFS Global Equity B	-0.53
	Average Annualized 3-Year Total Return %	**3.58**

3-Year Performance

Morningstar Funds 500 Universe

Taxable Bond

Cat		3-Year Avg Annualized Total Return %
	Highest	
EB	Fidelity New Markets Income	18.58
EB	T. Rowe Price Emerging Markets Bond	15.71
EB	Scudder Emerging Markets Income S	14.48
CI	FPA New Income	8.28
IB	Alliance North American Govt Income B	7.57
CS	Metropolitan West Low Duration Bond M	7.05
CI	PIMCO Total Return Instl	6.96
CI	Metropolitan West Total Return Bond	6.96
CI	Fremont Bond	6.81
IB	PIMCO Foreign Bond Instl	6.73
CI	Dodge & Cox Income	6.60
GS	Vanguard Short-Term Federal	6.57
CI	Harbor Bond	6.56
GI	Vanguard GNMA	6.56
CS	Vanguard Short-Term Bond Index	6.55
GI	Pilgrim GNMA Income A	6.51
GI	Fidelity Ginnie Mae	6.34
IB	BlackRock Intl Bond Svc	6.30
GI	Franklin U.S. Government Secs A	6.27
GI	Strong Government Securities Inv	6.25
	Lowest	
IB	T. Rowe Price International Bond	-4.82
HY	Fidelity High-Income	-3.84
HY	Morgan Stan Inst High-Yield Invmt	-3.25
HY	Fidelity Advisor High-Yield T	-1.69
HY	Franklin AGE High Income A	-1.42
HY	Northeast Investors	-0.49
HY	Strong High-Yield Bond Inv	-0.18
IB	AXP Global Bond A	-0.10
IB	American Funds Capital World Bond A	0.26
HY	MainStay High-Yield Corporate Bond B	1.11
HY	Eaton Vance Income Fund of Boston A	1.15
HY	Vanguard High-Yield Corporate	1.49
HY	PIMCO High Yield A	2.02
MU	John Hancock Strategic Income A	3.12
MU	Franklin Strategic Income A	3.43
MU	Loomis Sayles Bond Instl	3.84
GL	T. Rowe Price U.S. Treasury Long-Term	3.97
MU	T. Rowe Price Spectrum Income	4.01
HY	Janus High-Yield	4.18
GL	American Century Long-Term Trs Inv	4.18
	Average Annualized 3-Year Total Return %	**4.89**

Municipal-National Bond

Cat		3-Year Avg Annualized Total Return %
	Highest	
MI	Fidelity Spartan Municipal Income	4.76
ML	Vanguard Insured Long-Trm T/E	4.76
MS	T. Rowe Price Tax-Free Short-Interm	4.49
MS	Fidelity Spartan Short-Int Muni Inc	4.48
MI	Vanguard Interm-Term Tax-Ex	4.48
ML	Vanguard Long-Term Tax-Exempt	4.46
MS	Vanguard Ltd-Term Tax-Ex	4.44
MI	Fidelity Spartan Interm Muni Income	4.44
MS	USAA Tax-Exempt Short-Term	4.29
ML	Franklin Insured Tax-Free Income A	4.20
	Lowest	
ML	Strong Municipal Bond Inv	0.39
ML	Waddell & Reed Adv Muni High-Inc A	1.66
ML	Alliance Muni Income National A	2.64
ML	Franklin High Yield Tax-Free Inc A	2.75
ML	Van Kampen High-Yield Municipal A	2.76
MS	Evergreen High Income Municipal Bd B	3.10
ML	Sit Tax-Free Income	3.17
MI	Dreyfus Intermediate Municipal Bond	3.32
ML	USAA Tax-Exempt Long-Term	3.58
ML	AXP High-Yield Tax-Exempt A	3.60
	Average Annualized 3-Year Total Return %	**3.71**

Notes: There are only 29 municipal-bond funds in the Morningstar Funds 500 universe.

5-Year Performance

Morningstar Funds 500 Universe

Domestic Equity

Cat		5-Year Avg Annualized Total Return %
	Highest	
MV	Oakmark Select I	26.75
LG	Quaker Aggressive Growth A	26.64
SB	Meridian Value	25.05
ST	Dresdner RCM Global Technology I	24.67
SH	Vanguard Health Care	23.47
SH	Eaton Vance Worldwide Health Sci A	23.46
SG	RS Diversified Growth	22.90
SB	Wasatch Core Growth	22.30
SH	Fidelity Select Biotechnology	21.74
MV	Weitz Partners Value	21.61
SB	WM Growth Fund of the Northwest A	21.40
SV	State Street Research Aurora A	21.38
MV	Weitz Value	21.04
MB	Vanguard Capital Opportunity	20.70
MG	Fidelity New Millennium	20.64
SV	Berger Small Cap Value Instl	19.62
SG	John Hancock Small Cap Value B	19.57
SG	Fremont U.S. Micro-Cap	18.90
MG	Fidelity Mid-Cap Stock	18.71
MV	Salomon Brothers Capital O	18.69
	Lowest	
MG	Putnam OTC Emerging Growth A	-6.13
LG	INVESCO Growth Inv	-0.66
MG	Van Wagoner Post-Venture	1.45
ST	T. Rowe Price Science & Tech	2.41
LG	Fidelity Destiny I	2.68
LB	Fidelity Advisor Growth Opport T	2.81
LG	Vanguard U.S. Growth	3.28
LG	AIM Weingarten A	3.48
LB	Scudder Growth & Income S	4.72
SG	American Funds Smallcap World A	4.84
LB	T. Rowe Price New America Growth	4.88
LV	USAA Cornerstone Strategy	4.92
MG	AIM Aggressive Growth A	5.41
CV	Davis Convertible Securities A	5.50
LB	Putnam Capital Appreciation A	5.70
LG	AIM Constellation A	5.82
LG	Fidelity Aggressive Growth	5.95
DH	INVESCO Total Return Inv	5.99
MG	USAA Aggressive Growth	6.02
DH	Fidelity Advisor Balanced T	6.42
	Average Annualized 5-Year Total Return %	**11.73**

International Equity

Cat		5-Year Avg Annualized Total Return %
	Highest	
WS	Oppenheimer Global Growth & Income A	16.69
FS	Artisan International	13.28
FS	Tweedy, Browne Global Value	12.87
WS	American Funds New Perspective A	11.98
FS	American Century Intl Discovery Inv	11.87
WS	Mutual Discovery Z	11.76
WS	American Funds Capital World Gr&Inc A	10.96
FS	Putnam International Growth A	10.43
WS	Putnam Global Equity A	10.21
FS	Janus Overseas	9.83
WS	Janus Worldwide	9.83
IH	American Funds Capital Inc Builder A	9.57
IH	First Eagle SoGen Global A	9.37
FS	Morgan Stan Inst International Eq A	9.23
FS	Fidelity Diversified International	9.20
WS	IDEX Janus Global A	9.09
IH	Merrill Lynch Global Allocation B	8.64
WS	Templeton Growth A	8.62
WS	Merrill Lynch Global Value D	8.35
FS	American Century Intl Growth Inv	7.83
	Lowest	
PJ	T. Rowe Price New Asia	-7.00
PJ	Liberty Newport Tiger A	-6.72
EM	Templeton Developing Markets A	-6.45
EM	Vanguard Emerging Mkts Stock Idx	-4.99
SP	Vanguard Precious Metals	-3.68
EM	Pioneer Emerging Markets A	-2.84
PJ	Matthews Pacific Tiger	-2.74
JS	CS Warburg Pincus Japan Growth Comm	-2.48
LS	Fidelity Latin America	-0.32
FS	Vanguard Total Intl Stock Index	0.08
FS	T. Rowe Price International Stock	0.75
FS	SEI International Equity A	0.82
DP	Fidelity Pacific Basin	0.90
FS	AIM International Equity A	1.41
FS	Lazard International Equity Instl	1.60
FS	Deutsche International Equity Invm	2.23
DP	Merrill Lynch Pacific B	2.31
JS	Japan S	2.47
LS	Scudder Latin America S	2.59
FS	Vanguard International Growth	2.65
	Average Annualized 5-Year Total Return %	**5.02**

5-Year Performance

Morningstar Funds 500 Universe

Taxable Bond

Cat		5-Year Avg Annualized Total Return %
	Highest	
EB	Fidelity New Markets Income	8.75
IB	Alliance North American Govt Income B	8.67
CI	PIMCO Total Return Instl	8.15
CI	Fremont Bond	8.02
GL	Vanguard Long-Term U.S. Treasury	7.99
IB	BlackRock Intl Bond Svc	7.97
IB	PIMCO Foreign Bond Instl	7.96
GL	American Century Long-Term Trs Inv	7.91
GL	T. Rowe Price U.S. Treasury Long-Term	7.78
CI	Harbor Bond	7.72
CI	Dodge & Cox Income	7.57
GI	Pilgrim GNMA Income A	7.44
CI	FPA New Income	7.39
CL	Vanguard Long-Term Corporate Bond	7.37
CI	Vanguard Total Bond Market Index	7.33
GI	Vanguard GNMA	7.25
CI	USAA Income	7.20
GI	Strong Government Securities Inv	7.18
GI	Galaxy II U.S. Treasury Index Ret	6.97
GI	Franklin U.S. Government Secs A	6.97
	Lowest	
IB	T. Rowe Price International Bond	-0.81
HY	Fidelity High-Income	1.26
HY	Morgan Stan Inst High-Yield Invmt	1.53
HY	Fidelity Advisor High-Yield T	1.71
HY	Franklin AGE High Income A	1.74
IB	American Funds Capital World Bond A	2.03
IB	AXP Global Bond A	2.14
HY	Northeast Investors	2.28
HY	MainStay High-Yield Corporate Bond B	3.16
EB	Scudder Emerging Markets Income S	3.42
HY	Strong High-Yield Bond Inv	3.52
HY	Vanguard High-Yield Corporate	4.32
HY	Eaton Vance Income Fund of Boston A	4.35
MU	Franklin Strategic Income A	4.84
MU	John Hancock Strategic Income A	5.43
UB	Strong Advantage Inv	5.51
CS	Strong Short-Term Bond Inv	5.54
HY	Janus High-Yield	5.68
MU	Loomis Sayles Bond Instl	5.72
UB	DFA One-Year Fixed-Income	5.76
	Average Annualized 5-Year Total Return %	**5.87**

Municipal-National Bond

Cat		5-Year Avg Annualized Total Return %
	Highest	
MI	Fidelity Spartan Municipal Income	5.90
ML	Vanguard Insured Long-Trm T/E	5.80
ML	Vanguard Long-Term Tax-Exempt	5.72
MI	USAA Tax-Exempt Intermediate-Term	5.61
ML	Vanguard High-Yield Tax-Exempt	5.56
MI	American Funds Tax-Exempt Bond Fd A	5.51
MI	Fidelity Spartan Interm Muni Income	5.48
MI	Nuveen Interm Duration Muni Bond R	5.40
ML	USAA Tax-Exempt Long-Term	5.38
ML	Franklin Insured Tax-Free Income A	5.35
	Lowest	
ML	Strong Municipal Bond Inv	3.89
MS	Calvert Tax-Free Reserv Limited-Trm A	3.96
MS	Evergreen High Income Municipal Bd B	4.01
MS	Thornburg Limited-Term Muni Natl A	4.42
MI	Dreyfus Intermediate Municipal Bond	4.61
ML	Waddell & Reed Adv Muni High-Inc A	4.63
ML	Franklin High Yield Tax-Free Inc A	4.70
MS	Vanguard Ltd-Term Tax-Ex	4.71
MS	Fidelity Spartan Short-Int Muni Inc	4.72
MS	USAA Tax-Exempt Short-Term	4.75
	Average Annualized 5-Year Total Return %	**5.01**

Notes: There are only 29 municipal-bond funds in the Morningstar Funds 500 universe.

10-Year Performance

Morningstar Funds 500 Universe

Domestic Equity

Cat		10-Year Avg Annualized Total Return %
	Highest	
SH	Eaton Vance Worldwide Health Sci A	20.81
SH	Vanguard Health Care	19.81
SV	Berger Small Cap Value Instl	19.12
MV	Weitz Partners Value	18.93
SF	Davis Financial A	18.91
SV	FPA Capital	18.27
SB	Wasatch Core Growth	18.26
LV	Legg Mason Value Prim	18.16
ST	Fidelity Select Technology	18.15
MV	Weitz Value	18.03
SV	Fidelity Low-Priced Stock	17.90
MV	Oakmark I	17.71
MB	First Eagle Fund of America Y	17.57
LB	Vanguard Primecap	17.56
LV	Clipper	17.54
MG	Franklin CA Growth A	17.32
MV	Longleaf Partners	17.31
MB	Mairs & Power Growth	17.29
MV	Gabelli Value	17.21
SV	Heartland Value	17.15
	Lowest	
LG	INVESCO Growth Inv	5.31
MG	Putnam OTC Emerging Growth A	6.11
LG	AIM Weingarten A	6.50
DH	Fidelity Advisor Balanced T	7.67
LG	Vanguard U.S. Growth	7.99
DH	Scudder Total Return A	8.10
LG	American Century Growth Inv	8.39
MG	USAA Aggressive Growth	8.70
LV	USAA Cornerstone Strategy	8.73
MV	Evergreen Equity Income I	9.10
DH	Morgan Stanley Strategist B	9.13
LG	American Century Select Inv	9.21
DH	INVESCO Total Return Inv	9.43
DH	Franklin Income A	9.58
SG	American Funds Smallcap World A	9.63
LG	AIM Summit	9.73
DH	T. Rowe Price Balanced	9.82
SU	Fidelity Utilities	9.84
DH	Pax World Balanced	9.85
MG	Nicholas II	9.99
	Average Annualized 10-Year Total Return %	**13.24**

International Equity

Cat		10-Year Avg Annualized Total Return %
	Highest	
WS	Oppenheimer Global Growth & Income A	13.83
WS	Janus Worldwide	13.57
WS	American Funds New Perspective A	12.95
FS	Morgan Stan Inst International Eq A	12.76
WS	Templeton Growth A	11.78
FS	Putnam International Growth A	11.70
WS	Templeton World A	11.54
IH	American Funds Capital Inc Builder A	11.16
IH	First Eagle SoGen Global A	11.14
FS	Harbor International	10.88
IH	Merrill Lynch Global Allocation B	10.64
FS	American Funds EuroPacific Growth A	10.38
FS	American Century Intl Growth Inv	10.27
ES	Fidelity Europe	10.21
WS	Oppenheimer Quest Global Value A	10.11
	Lowest	
JS	Japan S	0.36
SP	Vanguard Precious Metals	1.48
EM	Templeton Developing Markets A	2.40
PJ	T. Rowe Price New Asia	2.79
DP	Fidelity Pacific Basin	3.46
FS	SEI International Equity A	4.19
DP	Merrill Lynch Pacific B	4.49
FS	Lazard International Equity Instl	5.68
FS	T. Rowe Price International Stock	6.05
FS	Fidelity Overseas	6.08
FS	Scudder International S	7.07
FS	Vanguard International Growth	7.51
WS	Putnam Global Growth A	7.59
IH	MFS Global Total Return A	8.55
FS	Templeton Foreign A	8.57
	Average Annualized 10-Year Total Return %	**8.57**

Note: Only 36 funds in the international rating group and in the Morningstar Funds 500 universe have 10-year histories.

10-Year Performance

Morningstar Funds 500 Universe

Taxable Bond

Cat		10-Year Avg Annualized Total Return %
	Highest	
MU	Loomis Sayles Bond Instl	9.92
HY	MainStay High-Yield Corporate Bond B	9.27
HY	Northeast Investors	8.88
CL	Strong Corporate Bond Inv	8.70
IB	BlackRock Intl Bond Svc	8.65
HY	Eaton Vance Income Fund of Boston A	8.37
CI	PIMCO Total Return Instl	8.25
HY	Fidelity High-Income	8.21
GL	Vanguard Long-Term U.S. Treasury	8.20
CI	FPA New Income	8.07
CL	Vanguard Long-Term Corporate Bond	8.07
HY	Fidelity Advisor High-Yield T	7.94
HY	Vanguard High-Yield Corporate	7.91
CI	Harbor Bond	7.91
CI	Dodge & Cox Income	7.65
GI	Strong Government Securities Inv	7.57
GL	T. Rowe Price U.S. Treasury Long-Term	7.48
MU	T. Rowe Price Spectrum Income	7.47
MU	John Hancock Strategic Income A	7.43
CI	USAA Income	7.26
	Lowest	
IB	T. Rowe Price International Bond	4.09
IB	American Funds Capital World Bond A	5.17
UB	DFA One-Year Fixed-Income	5.45
IB	AXP Global Bond A	5.64
CS	Fidelity Short-Term Bond	5.74
CS	Strong Short-Term Bond Inv	6.01
GS	Scudder GNMA AARP	6.03
GS	Vanguard Short-Term Treasury	6.09
UB	Strong Advantage Inv	6.17
GS	Vanguard Short-Term Federal	6.22
GS	Sit U.S. Government Securities	6.42
GI	Fidelity Ginnie Mae	6.55
GI	Principal Government Securities Inc A	6.62
GI	American Century Ginnie Mae Inv	6.66
GI	Franklin U.S. Government Secs A	6.69
GI	Galaxy II U.S. Treasury Index Ret	6.72
CS	PIMCO Low Duration Instl	6.79
GI	Pilgrim GNMA Income A	6.91
GI	Vanguard GNMA	6.96
CI	Vanguard Total Bond Market Index	7.15
	Average Annualized 10-Year Total Return %	**7.18**

Municipal-National Bond

Cat	Fund	10-Year Avg Annualized Total Return %
	Highest	
ML	Vanguard Long-Term Tax-Exempt	6.70
ML	Vanguard Insured Long-Trm T/E	6.67
ML	Vanguard High-Yield Tax-Exempt	6.63
ML	Waddell & Reed Adv Muni High-Inc A	6.58
ML	Franklin High Yield Tax-Free Inc A	6.46
ML	Van Kampen High-Yield Municipal A	6.43
MI	American Funds Tax-Exempt Bond Fd A	6.40
MI	Fidelity Spartan Municipal Income	6.30
MI	USAA Tax-Exempt Intermediate-Term	6.25
ML	Franklin Federal Tax-Free Income A	6.22
	Lowest	
MS	Calvert Tax-Free Reserv Limited-Trm A	4.08
MS	Strong Short-Term Municipal Bond Inv	4.63
MS	T. Rowe Price Tax-Free Short-Interm	4.84
MS	USAA Tax-Exempt Short-Term	4.84
MS	Vanguard Ltd-Term Tax-Ex	4.88
MS	Fidelity Spartan Short-Int Muni Inc	4.89
MS	Thornburg Limited-Term Muni Natl A	5.07
ML	Strong Municipal Bond Inv	5.15
MS	Evergreen High Income Municipal Bd B	5.22
MI	Dreyfus Intermediate Municipal Bond	5.57
	Average Annualized 10-Year Total Return %	**5.81**

Notes: There are only 29 municipal-bond funds in the Morningstar Funds 500 universe.

Equity Style-Box Performance Summary

Morningstar Funds 500 Universe

Note: See glossary page 575 for further details on how Morningstar calculates its equity style box.

Equity Style Box

Risk	Investment Style: Value	Blend	Growth	Median Market Capitalization
Low	Large-cap Value	Large-cap Blend	Large-cap Growth	Large
Moderate	Mid-cap Value	Mid-cap Blend	Mid-cap Growth	Medium
High	Small-cap Value	Small-cap Blend	Small-cap Growth	Small

Within the equity style box grid, nine possible combinations exist, ranging from large-cap value for the safest funds to small-cap growth for the riskiest.

Value
Combined relative P/E and P/B score less than 1.75

Blend
Combined relative P/E and P/B score greater than or equal to 1.75, but less than or equal to 2.25

Growth
Combined relative P/E and P/B score greater than 2.25

Large Capitalization
Largest 5% of the top 5,000 U.S. stocks

Medium Capitalization
Next largest 15% of the top 5,000 U.S. stocks

Small Capitalization
Smallest 80% of the top 5,000 U.S. stocks

2001 Quarterly Total Return %

1st Quarter

-5.53	-13.18	-20.57
-2.53	-9.44	-22.36
2.25	-3.90	-17.80

2nd Quarter

4.89	5.31	6.70
7.53	10.51	12.13
13.51	14.95	17.41

3rd Quarter

-12.50	-15.78	-20.36
-12.48	-16.71	-24.83
-13.83	-16.61	-24.12

4th Quarter

9.64	11.17	14.94
13.59	17.02	19.50
17.57	19.72	23.78

The aggregate style-box tables are based on the current style-box placement of diversified domestic open-end equity funds tracked by Morningstar. The current style box is based only on the fund's most recent portfolio. It may differ from the category, which is based on the past three years' portfolios.

The tables on pages 535 and 536 list the top-five and bottom-five-performing diversified domestic-equity funds in the *Morningstar Funds 500*, based on their average annualized three-year total returns.

Trailing Returns %*

1-Year

-5.15	-14.43	-22.61
4.02	-2.49	-21.77
17.42	9.97	-9.26

3-Year

3.02	-1.11	-3.25
10.64	8.84	3.97
12.28	12.25	9.58

5-Year

9.10	8.80	8.18
12.23	11.51	7.55
10.76	11.12	8.98

* 3- and 5-Year returns are annualized.

Cat	Ranked by 3-Year Total Return	1-Year TR%	Average Annualized TR % 3-Year	5-Year	10-Year	Morningstar 3-Year Rating Statistics Return	Risk	Star Rating	Average Star Rating	Months Rated
Large-Cap/Value										
	Highest									
LG	Quaker Aggressive Growth A	-8.06	27.87	26.64	—	High	Low	★★★★★	5.0	27
LV	Dodge & Cox Stock	9.33	15.19	15.65	16.62	High	-Avg	★★★★★	4.2	193
MV	Salomon Brothers Capital O	2.00	14.49	18.69	16.13	High	-Avg	★★★★★	2.9	193
LV	Clipper	10.26	14.07	18.21	17.54	High	Low	★★★★★	4.0	179
LV	Excelsior Value & Restructuring	-4.96	13.10	16.35	—	High	Avg	★★★★★	4.8	73
	Lowest									
LV	American Century Income & Growth Inv	-8.37	-1.12	10.66	12.91	-Avg	Avg	★★★	4.3	97
LV	Legg Mason American Leading Co Prim	-3.30	0.76	8.96	—	Avg	Avg	★★★	3.3	65
LV	Putnam Fund for Growth & Income A	-6.37	0.77	7.92	12.00	-Avg	Avg	★★★	3.8	193
LV	Fidelity Equity-Income II	-7.16	1.36	10.24	13.56	Avg	-Avg	★★★	4.3	101
LB	MFS Capital Opportunities A	-24.93	1.65	11.05	15.15	Avg	+Avg	★★	3.2	187
Large-Cap/Blend										
	Highest									
MV	Oakmark Select I	26.06	22.00	26.75	—	High	Low	★★★★★	4.4	27
LG	American Funds Growth Fund of Amer A	-12.28	11.17	18.09	15.46	+Avg	Avg	★★★★	3.6	193
LB	Thornburg Value A	-8.11	9.50	16.50	—	+Avg	-Avg	★★★★	4.8	40
LB	Vanguard Primecap	-13.35	8.56	17.03	17.56	+Avg	Avg	★★★★	3.8	171
LB	Fidelity Dividend Growth	-3.74	5.54	15.36	—	+Avg	-Avg	★★★★	4.9	69
	Lowest									
LG	Vanguard U.S. Growth	-31.70	-12.64	3.28	7.99	Low	+Avg	★	3.4	193
LG	Fidelity Destiny I	-17.29	-11.47	2.68	10.91	Low	+Avg	★	4.2	193
LB	Fidelity Advisor Growth Opport T	-15.14	-10.34	2.81	10.03	Low	+Avg	★	4.1	134
LG	Alliance Premier Growth B	-24.52	-8.35	8.51	—	Low	+Avg	★	3.8	76
LG	Janus Twenty	-29.20	-7.59	12.15	11.76	Low	High	★	3.9	165
Large-Cap/Growth										
	Highest									
MB	Mairs & Power Growth	6.48	13.01	15.22	17.29	High	Low	★★★★★	3.8	193
LG	Fidelity Growth Company	-25.31	7.89	13.70	14.28	+Avg	+Avg	★★★	4.0	192
LG	American Funds Amcap A	-5.01	7.53	16.11	13.92	+Avg	-Avg	★★★★	3.3	193
LG	Van Kampen Emerging Growth A	-32.59	6.77	14.75	15.66	Avg	+Avg	★★★	3.2	193
LB	Fidelity Contrafund II	-9.59	5.70	—	—	Avg	Avg	★★★	3.9	10
	Lowest									
LG	INVESCO Growth Inv	-49.07	-18.74	-0.66	5.31	Low	High	★	2.8	193
LG	AIM Weingarten A	-34.10	-10.88	3.48	6.50	Low	+Avg	★	3.5	193
LG	One Group Large Cap Growth A	-20.57	-8.44	7.95	—	Low	+Avg	★	3.6	59
LG	Putnam Investors A	-24.80	-7.26	7.77	11.57	Low	+Avg	★	2.9	193
LG	TIAA-CREF Growth Equity	-23.02	-6.55	—	—	Low	+Avg	★	2.4	17
Mid-Cap/Value										
	Highest									
MV	Dreyfus Midcap Value	17.10	24.10	18.57	—	High	Avg	★★★★★	3.6	40
SV	FPA Capital	38.13	15.21	12.38	18.27	High	Avg	★★★★	3.3	193
MV	Muhlenkamp	9.35	15.14	16.00	16.51	High	Avg	★★★★★	3.5	122
MV	Weitz Partners Value	-0.86	13.57	21.61	18.93	High	Low	★★★★★	4.6	188
MV	Weitz Value	0.24	13.20	21.04	18.03	High	Low	★★★★★	4.3	152
	Lowest									
MV	Weitz Hickory	-4.65	2.55	14.83	—	Avg	+Avg	★★★	4.3	70
MB	Oak Value	-0.47	4.45	13.29	—	Avg	Avg	★★★	4.2	72
MV	Tweedy, Browne American Value	-0.08	5.27	12.16	—	+Avg	Low	★★★★	4.3	61
MB	Legg Mason Special Investment Prim	2.26	6.84	12.93	13.68	+Avg	Avg	★★★★	3.2	157
MB	Gabelli Asset	0.16	7.91	15.00	14.82	+Avg	-Avg	★★★★	4.3	155
Mid-Cap/Blend										
	Highest									
SB	Meridian Value	11.70	28.43	25.05	—	High	Low	★★★★★	4.2	59
MB	Vanguard Capital Opportunity	-9.68	28.23	20.70	—	High	Avg	★★★★★	3.9	41
SB	FPA Perennial	22.73	19.21	17.16	13.93	High	Avg	★★★★★	3.1	178
MG	Fidelity Mid-Cap Stock	-12.80	17.21	18.71	—	High	Avg	★★★★★	3.8	58
MV	T. Rowe Price Mid-Cap Value	14.36	13.27	13.37	—	High	Low	★★★★★	3.2	31
	Lowest									
MB	Vanguard Extended Market Idx	-9.17	1.49	7.49	11.07	Avg	+Avg	★★★	2.9	133
MB	Janus Special Situations	-16.00	1.84	14.08	—	Avg	+Avg	★★★	4.1	25
MB	Van Kampen American Value A	-2.79	2.91	10.27	—	Avg	+Avg	★★★	3.0	63
MB	First Eagle Fund of America Y	8.25	6.77	13.78	17.57	+Avg	-Avg	★★★★	3.9	141
SV	Longleaf Partners Small-Cap	5.45	7.36	12.47	13.98	+Avg	-Avg	★★★★	3.0	121

Mid-Cap/Growth

Cat	Ranked by 3-Year Total Return	1-Year TR%	Average Annualized TR % 3-Year	5-Year	10-Year	Morningstar 3-Year Rating Statistics Return	Risk	Star Rating	Average Star Rating	Months Rated
	Highest									
MG	Fidelity New Millennium	-18.15	17.10	20.64	—	High	High	★★★★	4.7	73
MG	Liberty Acorn Twenty Z	8.00	15.97	—	—	High	-Avg	★★★★★	5.0	2
MG	Putnam Capital Opportunities A	-2.08	14.90	—	—	+Avg	+Avg	★★★★	4.0	8
MG	Franklin Small-Mid Cap Growth A	-20.53	12.21	10.34	—	+Avg	+Avg	★★★★	3.6	83
MG	Franklin CA Growth A	-23.23	11.68	12.28	17.32	+Avg	+Avg	★★★★	4.4	87
	Lowest									
MG	Putnam OTC Emerging Growth A	-46.12	-15.85	-6.13	6.11	Low	High	★	2.8	193
LG	Fidelity Aggressive Growth	-47.27	-7.95	5.95	10.54	Low	High	★	3.4	97
MG	Janus Enterprise	-39.93	-2.52	6.54	—	-Avg	High	★	3.2	77
MG	Nicholas II	-3.11	-1.36	7.51	9.99	-Avg	Avg	★★	3.2	183
MG	Putnam Vista A	-33.64	-0.81	7.53	12.55	-Avg	High	★★	3.4	193

Small-Cap/Value

Cat	Ranked by 3-Year Total Return	1-Year TR%	3-Year	5-Year	10-Year	Return	Risk	Star Rating	Average Star Rating	Months Rated
	Highest									
SV	ICM/Isabelle Small Cap Value Invmt	8.83	20.57	—	—	High	Avg	★★★★★	4.7	10
SV	Heartland Value	29.45	18.19	12.49	17.15	High	-Avg	★★★★★	3.4	169
SV	Dreyfus Small Company Value	28.60	18.01	14.20	—	High	+Avg	★★★★★	3.7	61
SV	Artisan Small Cap Value	15.04	17.07	—	—	High	Low	★★★★★	4.0	16
SB	DFA U.S. Micro Cap	22.77	15.38	11.82	15.59	High	+Avg	★★★★★	2.4	193
	Lowest									
SV	ABN AMRO/Chicago Capital Sm Cap Val N	13.70	9.69	—	—	+Avg	-Avg	★★★★	4.0	2
SV	Royce Total Return	14.78	11.66	12.52	—	+Avg	Low	★★★★★	4.1	61
SV	Franklin Balance Sheet Investment A	17.70	11.77	11.82	15.31	+Avg	Low	★★★★	4.2	106
SV	Vanguard Small Cap Value Index	13.55	12.67	—	—	+Avg	-Avg	★★★★	3.9	8
SV	Wachovia Special Values A	18.13	13.11	12.97	—	+Avg	Low	★★★★	3.8	68

Small-Cap/Blend

Cat	Ranked by 3-Year Total Return	1-Year TR%	3-Year	5-Year	10-Year	Return	Risk	Star Rating	Average Star Rating	Months Rated
	Highest									
SV	State Street Research Aurora A	15.83	28.45	21.38	—	High	Low	★★★★★	4.1	47
SV	American Century Small Cap Value Inv	30.52	21.73	—	—	High	Low	★★★★★	5.0	6
SV	Berger Small Cap Value Instl	20.42	20.65	19.62	19.12	High	-Avg	★★★★★	3.5	167
SB	Westport Small Cap R	8.22	20.61	—	—	High	-Avg	★★★★★	5.0	13
SB	WM Growth Fund of the Northwest A	6.34	17.29	21.40	15.64	High	Avg	★★★★★	3.1	146
	Lowest									
SV	Oakmark Small Cap I	26.30	6.68	8.18	—	+Avg	Avg	★★★★	2.0	39
SV	Skyline Special Equities	13.92	7.06	9.06	14.75	+Avg	Avg	★★★★	4.0	141
SB	Vanguard Small Cap Index	3.10	7.31	8.44	12.27	+Avg	+Avg	★★★★	1.7	193
SB	Schwab Small Cap Index Inv	-0.90	8.49	9.12	—	+Avg	Avg	★★★★	2.1	61
SB	Gabelli Small Cap Growth	4.65	9.98	12.66	13.81	+Avg	-Avg	★★★★	3.5	87

Small-Cap/Growth

Cat	Ranked by 3-Year Total Return	1-Year TR%	3-Year	5-Year	10-Year	Return	Risk	Star Rating	Average Star Rating	Months Rated
	Highest									
SG	Morgan Stan Inst Small Cap Growth	-20.56	38.63	—	—	High	High	★★★★★	5.0	7
SG	Buffalo Small Cap	31.18	33.21	—	—	High	-Avg	★★★★★	5.0	9
SG	Brazos Micro Cap Y	4.70	31.06	—	—	High	+Avg	★★★★★	5.0	13
SG	Fremont U.S. Micro-Cap	5.28	29.26	18.90	—	High	+Avg	★★★★★	3.8	55
SB	Wasatch Core Growth	28.82	28.31	22.30	18.26	High	-Avg	★★★★★	3.4	145
	Lowest									
MG	Van Wagoner Post-Venture	-62.14	-3.82	1.45	—	-Avg	High	★	3.7	25
SG	John Hancock Small Cap Growth B	-14.85	2.79	6.78	11.35	Avg	High	★★	3.4	135
SG	American Funds Smallcap World A	-17.35	4.10	4.84	9.63	Avg	+Avg	★★★	2.7	105
SG	Janus Venture	-11.93	4.76	9.79	10.41	Avg	High	★★	4.0	165
SB	SAFECO Growth Opportunities	22.03	6.28	13.44	12.99	+Avg	+Avg	★★★	2.5	193

Fixed-Income Style-Box Performance Summary

Morningstar Open-End Fund Universe

Fixed-Income Style Box

Note: See glossary page 575 for further details on how Morningstar calculates its fixed-income style box.

Risk	Duration: Short	Intermediate	Long	Quality
Low	Short-term High Quality	Interm-term High Quality	Long-term High Quality	High
Moderate	Short-term Medium Quality	Interm-term Medium Quality	Long-term Medium Quality	Medium
High	Short-term Low Quality	Interm-term Low Quality	Long-term Low Quality	Low

Within the fixed-income style box grid, nine possible combinations exist, ranging from short maturity or duration–high quality for the safest funds to long maturity or duration–low quality for the riskiest.

Short-Term
Average duration less than 3.5 years

Intermediate-Term
Average duration equal to or greater than 3.5 years, but less than or equal to 6 years

Long-Term
Average duration greater than 6 years

High Quality
Average credit rating greater than or equal to AA

Medium Quality
Average credit rating of A or BBB

Low Quality
Average credit rating of BB or lower

2001 Quarterly Total Return %

1st Quarter

2.61	2.73	2.29
2.84	2.96	3.08
2.93	3.49	2.45

2nd Quarter

0.96	0.28	-0.26
0.95	0.13	0.15
-1.96	-3.21	-0.31

3rd Quarter

3.13	4.23	4.80
2.53	1.87	0.96
-6.86	-5.55	-1.44

4th Quarter

0.19	-0.24	-0.33
0.21	1.10	1.88
6.00	5.19	3.20

The aggregate style-box tables are based on the current style-box placement of corporate-bond, government-bond, and multisector funds tracked by Morningstar (open-end funds only). The tables on pages 538 and 539 list the top-five and bottom-five-performing funds in the *Morningstar Funds 500*, based on their average annualized three-year total returns.

Trailing Returns %*

1-Year

7.05	7.12	6.55
6.66	6.04	6.22
-0.36	-0.33	3.89

3-Year

5.64	5.19	5.03
5.61	3.65	3.61
-0.59	-1.85	4.74

5-Year

5.96	6.33	7.06
5.83	5.31	5.14
0.00	1.21	0.00

* 3- and 5-Year returns are annualized.

Cat	Ranked by 3-Year Total Return	1-Year TR%	Average Annualized TR % 3-Year	5-Year	10-Year	Morningstar 3-Year Rating Statistics Return	Risk	Star Rating	Average Star Rating	Months Rated

High Quality/Short Maturity

Cat	Ranked by 3-Year Total Return	1-Year TR%	3-Year	5-Year	10-Year	Return	Risk	Star Rating	Average Star Rating	Months Rated
	Highest									
CS	PIMCO Low Duration Instl	8.01	6.20	6.80	6.79	+Avg	-Avg	★★★★★	4.7	140
UB	DFA One-Year Fixed-Income	5.76	5.69	5.76	5.45	+Avg	Low	★★★★★	4.6	186
UB	Strong Advantage Inv	4.26	5.43	5.51	6.17	+Avg	Low	★★★★★	4.5	122
	Lowest									
UB	Strong Advantage Inv	4.26	5.43	5.51	6.17	+Avg	Low	★★★★★	4.5	122
UB	DFA One-Year Fixed-Income	5.76	5.69	5.76	5.45	+Avg	Low	★★★★★	4.6	186
CS	PIMCO Low Duration Instl	8.01	6.20	6.80	6.79	+Avg	-Avg	★★★★★	4.7	140

High Quality/Interm Maturity

Cat	Ranked by 3-Year Total Return	1-Year TR%	3-Year	5-Year	10-Year	Return	Risk	Star Rating	Average Star Rating	Months Rated
	Highest									
CI	Fremont Bond	9.42	6.81	8.02	—	High	Avg	★★★★	4.1	69
CI	Harbor Bond	9.03	6.56	7.72	7.91	High	Avg	★★★★	4.5	133
GI	Strong Government Securities Inv	8.92	6.25	7.18	7.57	+Avg	-Avg	★★★★	4.6	147
GS	Scudder GNMA AARP	7.13	6.00	6.59	6.03	+Avg	-Avg	★★★★	3.8	170
GS	Montgomery Short Duration Govt Bond R	7.38	5.99	6.46	—	+Avg	Low	★★★★★	4.7	73
	Lowest									
GI	Galaxy II U.S. Treasury Index Ret	6.28	5.31	6.97	6.72	+Avg	Avg	★★★	3.1	91
GI	Principal Government Securities Inc A	6.75	5.79	6.84	6.62	Avg	-Avg	★★★	2.7	164
GS	Montgomery Short Duration Govt Bond R	7.38	5.99	6.46	—	+Avg	Low	★★★★★	4.7	73
GS	Scudder GNMA AARP	7.13	6.00	6.59	6.03	+Avg	-Avg	★★★★	3.8	170
GI	Strong Government Securities Inv	8.92	6.25	7.18	7.57	+Avg	-Avg	★★★★	4.6	147

High Quality/Long Maturity

Cat	Ranked by 3-Year Total Return	1-Year TR%	3-Year	5-Year	10-Year	Return	Risk	Star Rating	Average Star Rating	Months Rated
	Highest									
GL	American Century Long-Term Trs Inv	3.81	4.18	7.91	—	Avg	+Avg	★★	1.9	76
GL	T. Rowe Price U.S. Treasury Long-Term	3.39	3.97	7.78	7.48	Avg	+Avg	★★	2.1	112
	Lowest									
GL	T. Rowe Price U.S. Treasury Long-Term	3.39	3.97	7.78	7.48	Avg	+Avg	★★	2.1	112
GL	American Century Long-Term Trs Inv	3.81	4.18	7.91	—	Avg	+Avg	★★	1.9	76

Medium Quality/Short Maturity

Cat	Ranked by 3-Year Total Return	1-Year TR%	3-Year	5-Year	10-Year	Return	Risk	Star Rating	Average Star Rating	Months Rated
	Highest									
CS	Strong Short-Term Bond Inv	4.39	5.28	5.54	6.01	+Avg	Low	★★★★	4.2	137
	Lowest									
CS	Strong Short-Term Bond Inv	4.39	5.28	5.54	6.01	+Avg	Low	★★★★	4.2	137

Medium Quality/Interm Maturity

Cat	Ranked by 3-Year Total Return	1-Year TR%	3-Year	5-Year	10-Year	Return	Risk	Star Rating	Average Star Rating	Months Rated
	Highest									
MU	T. Rowe Price Spectrum Income	4.50	4.01	6.11	7.47	Avg	Avg	★★★	4.3	103
MU	John Hancock Strategic Income A	4.92	3.12	5.43	7.43	-Avg	+Avg	★★	2.7	148
	Lowest									
MU	John Hancock Strategic Income A	4.92	3.12	5.43	7.43	-Avg	+Avg	★★	2.7	148
MU	T. Rowe Price Spectrum Income	4.50	4.01	6.11	7.47	Avg	Avg	★★★	4.3	103

Cat	Ranked by 3-Year Total Return	1-Year TR%	Average Annualized TR % 3-Year	5-Year	10-Year	Morningstar 3-Year Rating Statistics Return	Risk	Star Rating	Average Star Rating	Months Rated
Medium Quality/Long Maturity										
	Highest									
CL	Strong Corporate Bond Inv	6.83	4.77	6.65	8.70	Avg	Avg	★★★	3.0	157
MU	Loomis Sayles Bond Instl	2.66	3.84	5.72	9.92	Avg	+Avg	★★	4.3	92
	Lowest									
MU	Loomis Sayles Bond Instl	2.66	3.84	5.72	9.92	Avg	+Avg	★★	4.3	92
CL	Strong Corporate Bond Inv	6.83	4.77	6.65	8.70	Avg	Avg	★★★	3.0	157
Low Quality/Short Maturity										
	Highest									
	None									
	Lowest									
	None									
Low Quality/Interm Maturity										
	Highest									
HY	Janus High-Yield	4.52	4.18	5.68	—	Avg	+Avg	★★	3.1	37
HY	MainStay High-Yield Corporate Bond B	1.71	1.11	3.16	9.27	-Avg	+Avg	★★	3.8	153
HY	Strong High-Yield Bond Inv	-0.71	-0.18	3.52	—	-Avg	High	★★	3.4	37
HY	Franklin AGE High Income A	2.92	-1.42	1.74	7.15	Low	High	★	2.8	193
HY	Fidelity Advisor High-Yield T	-1.16	-1.69	1.71	7.94	Low	High	★	4.1	144
	Lowest									
HY	Morgan Stan Inst High-Yield Invmt	-5.91	-3.25	1.53	—	Low	High	★	2.5	32
HY	Fidelity Advisor High-Yield T	-1.16	-1.69	1.71	7.94	Low	High	★	4.1	144
HY	Franklin AGE High Income A	2.92	-1.42	1.74	7.15	Low	High	★	2.8	193
HY	Strong High-Yield Bond Inv	-0.71	-0.18	3.52	—	-Avg	High	★★	3.4	37
HY	MainStay High-Yield Corporate Bond B	1.71	1.11	3.16	9.27	-Avg	+Avg	★★	3.8	153
Low Quality/Long Maturity										
	Highest									
	None									
	Lowest									
	None									

Benchmark Averages

Morningstar Open-End Fund Universe

	P/E Ratio	P/B Ratio	Market Capital ($mil)	Cash %	Turn-over %	Yield %	Exp %	Potential Cap Gains Exposure %	MPT Statistics Alpha	Beta	R^2	Morningstar Rating Statistics Return	Risk	Rating
Domestic Stock	**30.0**	**5.0**	**27828**	**5.6**	**111**	**0.3**	**1.42**	**-9.8**	**5.7**	**0.98**	**62**	—	—	—
Large Value	25.2	4.1	31658	5.4	77	0.6	1.41	4.0	1.8	0.71	62	0.12	0.78	★★★
Large Blend	30.3	5.5	52342	5.2	96	0.4	1.24	-5.8	0.1	0.95	88	-0.40	0.95	★★★
Large Growth	35.5	6.4	47378	5.1	137	0.1	1.45	-27.2	1.1	1.24	70	-0.60	1.30	★★
Mid-cap Value	23.6	3.0	7112	6.2	107	0.5	1.43	7.3	10.0	0.69	48	1.45	0.72	★★★★
Mid-cap Blend	27.2	4.3	9003	6.6	94	0.3	1.40	-2.1	7.1	0.92	59	0.52	0.98	★★★
Mid-cap Growth	34.6	5.7	5721	5.0	147	0.0	1.55	-30.2	12.5	1.30	46	0.51	1.47	★★★
Small Value	21.7	2.4	871	5.9	74	0.3	1.52	12.3	12.4	0.59	31	1.84	0.75	★★★★
Small Blend	24.9	3.2	980	7.8	111	0.2	1.43	7.1	12.5	0.73	37	1.66	0.90	★★★★
Small Growth	32.1	4.9	1042	6.7	137	0.0	1.62	-14.4	16.6	1.19	36	1.25	1.47	★★★
International Stock	**24.6**	**3.9**	**17100**	**5.4**	**100**	**0.5**	**1.81**	**-40.8**	**2.1**	**0.87**	**48**	—	—	—
Europe Stock	23.8	4.4	27178	4.2	99	0.3	1.90	-27.6	-0.5	0.71	38	-0.61	0.88	★★★
Latin America Stock	14.8	2.6	5408	6.7	72	1.1	2.12	-80.0	15.8	1.23	39	0.01	1.48	★★★
Diversified Emerging Markets	17.3	3.2	4187	5.0	112	0.4	2.08	-63.7	9.0	1.17	50	-0.80	1.27	★★★
Pacific Stock	27.1	2.9	9105	4.4	139	0.6	2.13	-74.6	3.3	1.02	45	-1.23	1.23	★★
Pacific Stock ex-Japan	19.5	3.3	7656	5.3	104	0.3	2.21	-78.8	10.6	1.18	43	-0.82	1.40	★★★
Japan Stock	32.2	2.6	7486	5.0	75	0.9	1.72	-99.7	0.5	0.91	32	-1.51	1.34	★★
Foreign Stock	25.5	3.9	18043	5.4	97	0.5	1.65	-33.0	-1.1	0.77	48	-0.92	0.91	★★★
World Stock	27.7	4.6	24005	6.4	99	0.3	1.82	-18.7	3.0	0.86	57	-0.18	0.87	★★★★
Specialty Stock	**33.0**	**4.9**	**14971**	**6.0**	**150**	**1.0**	**1.71**	**-43.0**	**9.0**	**0.79**	**25**	—	—	—
Communications	30.9	4.5	27059	11.1	172	0.0	1.57	-87.1	-0.6	1.35	56	-0.57	1.49	★★
Financial	21.3	3.0	22040	6.5	143	0.6	1.71	6.1	6.4	0.68	33	0.80	0.93	★★★★
Health	39.8	9.0	21989	7.5	176	0.0	1.70	4.2	16.7	0.40	7	2.69	1.04	★★★★
Natural Resources	21.2	2.5	10978	4.5	256	0.9	1.73	-13.1	16.2	0.73	23	0.91	1.20	★★★
Precious Metals	22.2	3.5	2045	8.2	65	1.2	2.07	-91.9	1.5	0.23	3	-1.40	1.50	★★
Real Estate	19.7	1.8	2295	3.1	56	4.0	1.69	-5.0	6.6	0.15	4	0.83	0.62	★★★★
Technology	46.1	6.2	15915	8.6	198	0.0	1.78	-117.1	18.5	2.19	53	-0.16	2.26	★★
Utilities	19.2	2.3	12195	4.7	109	2.1	1.44	-12.5	-2.2	0.47	29	-0.20	0.79	★★★
Hybrid	**28.0**	**4.8**	**34838**	**9.2**	**102**	**2.3**	**1.34**	**-13.6**	**0.2**	**0.48**	**68**	—	—	—
Domestic Hybrid	28.4	4.9	37299	9.5	102	2.4	1.30	-10.3	0.2	0.49	71	-0.10	0.56	★★★
Convertible	29.5	4.2	20287	4.0	146	3.8	1.45	-23.7	6.5	0.73	51	0.48	0.77	★★★
International Hybrid	24.8	4.0	21835	6.2	129	2.1	1.45	-11.4	0.4	0.51	62	-0.19	0.52	★★★★

Category	Avg Mat	Avg Wtd Price	Avg Wtd Coupon	Cash %	Turn-over %	Yield %	Exp %	Potential Cap Gains Exposure %	MPT Statistics Alpha	Beta	R^2	Morningstar Rating Statistics Return	Risk	Rating
Specialty Bond	**7.5**	**89.72**	**7.77**	**6.9**	**128**	**8.7**	**1.34**	**-37.6**	**-4.8**	**0.50**	**17**	—	—	—
High-Yield Bond	6.4	89.67	8.80	7.7	100	11.0	1.30	-49.4	-5.6	0.21	2	-0.93	2.06	★★
Multisector Bond	9.1	93.31	7.21	3.8	129	7.5	1.42	-25.9	-3.1	0.69	26	-0.44	1.33	★★
International Bond	8.1	85.39	5.68	8.4	198	3.9	1.32	-23.0	-4.8	0.98	42	-0.52	1.49	★★
Emerging Markets Bond	17.7	80.83	6.64	4.5	338	10.6	1.62	-48.5	10.6	0.43	2	1.59	2.79	★★★
General Bond	**6.7**	**102.72**	**6.46**	**6.3**	**170**	**5.5**	**0.96**	**-5.2**	**-0.8**	**0.84**	**79**	—	—	—
Long-Term Bond	11.5	101.37	7.14	3.3	141	6.1	1.06	-5.7	-1.8	1.17	76	0.06	1.04	★★★
Intermediate-Term Bond	7.6	103.14	6.69	4.9	184	5.5	0.99	-5.9	-1.1	0.99	86	0.13	0.76	★★★
Short-Term Bond	2.8	103.06	5.94	7.9	147	5.2	0.87	-3.6	0.2	0.52	74	0.19	0.38	★★★★
Ultrashort Bond	2.6	100.34	5.34	16.8	174	5.7	0.85	-4.5	0.0	0.04	25	0.03	0.17	★★★★
Government Bond	**6.5**	**104.16**	**6.23**	**4.3**	**201**	**5.0**	**1.12**	**-9.2**	**-0.8**	**0.89**	**84**	—	—	—
Long-Term Government	13.7	99.29	5.90	5.3	313	4.8	1.14	-3.8	-2.3	1.47	83	0.18	1.31	★★
Intermediate-Term Government	6.2	105.10	6.47	3.7	190	5.1	1.16	-10.7	-0.8	0.93	88	0.14	0.70	★★★
Short-Term Government	3.4	104.31	5.85	5.1	177	4.9	1.03	-8.0	-0.1	0.53	74	0.11	0.40	★★★★
Municipal Bond	**14.9**	**103.17**	**5.54**	**1.9**	**45**	**4.4**	**1.07**	**1.2**	**-2.5**	**0.81**	**50**	—	—	—
Muni National Long	16.9	101.94	5.70	1.5	58	4.7	1.17	-1.6	-3.0	0.86	48	0.44	1.18	★★
Muni National Intermediate	10.0	105.17	5.52	2.5	61	4.2	0.92	1.3	-2.1	0.72	54	0.50	0.86	★★★
Muni NY Long	17.2	103.93	5.60	1.7	70	4.5	1.15	0.0	-2.7	0.89	47	0.65	1.15	★★★
Muni NY Intermediate	10.0	103.36	5.44	1.5	34	4.1	1.00	2.5	-2.1	0.75	49	0.64	0.90	★★★★
Muni CA Long	18.9	101.84	5.37	1.4	47	4.5	1.10	2.4	-2.5	0.99	48	0.81	1.16	★★★
Muni CA Intermediate	9.9	105.50	5.44	3.8	56	4.1	0.79	2.4	-1.7	0.78	51	0.77	0.81	★★★★
Muni Single State Long	18.0	102.64	5.57	1.7	41	4.6	1.11	2.0	-2.6	0.86	50	0.57	1.06	★★★
Muni Single State Intermed	10.7	104.29	5.50	2.2	22	4.2	1.03	2.3	-2.2	0.73	54	0.54	0.87	★★★
Muni Short-Term	4.7	103.59	5.29	3.5	47	3.8	0.87	1.2	-1.7	0.37	49	0.38	0.39	★★★★

Highest Yield

Morningstar Funds 500 Universe

Domestic Equity

Cat		Yield %
	Highest	
DH	Franklin Income A	8.2
LB	Metropolitan West AlphaTrak 500	5.9
SU	AXP Utilities Income A	5.7
DH	Vanguard LifeStrategy Income	5.0
DH	American Funds Income Fund of Amer A	5.0
DH	Vanguard Wellesley Income	4.8
CV	Fidelity Convertible Securities	4.7
SR	Security Capital U.S. Real Estate	4.6
SR	Columbia Real Estate Equity	4.4
LV	USAA Cornerstone Strategy	4.2
DH	Fidelity Asset Manager	4.2
DH	Vanguard LifeStrategy Conserv Growth	4.1
MV	Evergreen Equity Income I	3.9
DH	Oppenheimer Capital Income A	3.9
SR	Morgan Stan Inst U.S. Real Estate A	3.8
CV	Davis Convertible Securities A	3.7
DH	American Funds American Balanced A	3.5
DH	Vanguard Wellington	3.5
DH	Vanguard Balanced Index	3.3
DH	Fidelity Puritan	3.3
	Average Yield	**0.8**

Taxable Bond

Cat		Yield %
	Highest	
HY	Morgan Stan Inst High-Yield Invmt	13.7
HY	Eaton Vance Income Fund of Boston A	13.0
HY	Strong High-Yield Bond Inv	12.4
HY	Northeast Investors	11.7
HY	MainStay High-Yield Corporate Bond B	11.6
HY	Franklin AGE High Income A	11.6
EB	T. Rowe Price Emerging Markets Bond	11.2
EB	Fidelity New Markets Income	11.1
HY	Fidelity High-Income	11.0
EB	Scudder Emerging Markets Income S	10.7
HY	Fidelity Advisor High-Yield T	9.7
IB	Alliance North American Govt Income B	9.6
HY	Vanguard High-Yield Corporate	9.5
MU	Loomis Sayles Bond Instl	8.6
MU	Franklin Strategic Income A	8.5
HY	PIMCO High Yield A	8.4
MU	John Hancock Strategic Income A	8.3
CI	Metropolitan West Total Return Bond	7.4
CL	Strong Corporate Bond Inv	7.1
CS	Metropolitan West Low Duration Bond M	6.7
	Average Yield	**7.0**

International Equity

Cat		Yield %
	Highest	
IH	American Funds Capital Inc Builder A	4.7
SP	Vanguard Precious Metals	4.6
FS	Bernstein International Value II	3.1
IH	Merrill Lynch Global Allocation B	3.1
DP	Merrill Lynch Pacific B	2.8
FS	Templeton Foreign A	2.7
FS	T. Rowe Price International Stock	2.7
EM	American Funds New World A	2.6
IH	First Eagle SoGen Global A	2.6
EM	Vanguard Emerging Mkts Stock Idx	2.5
FS	American Funds EuroPacific Growth A	2.4
ES	T. Rowe Price European Stock	2.2
WS	Templeton Growth A	2.2
ES	Vanguard European Stock Index	2.2
FS	Morgan Stan Inst International Eq A	2.1
WS	Scudder Global S	2.1
LS	Fidelity Latin America	2.1
WS	American Funds Capital World Gr&Inc A	2.0
WS	Mutual Discovery Z	1.8
FS	Bernstein Tax-Managed Intl Value	1.8
	Average Yield	**1.0**

Municipal-National Bond

Cat		Yield %
	Highest	
ML	Van Kampen High-Yield Municipal A	6.3
ML	AXP High-Yield Tax-Exempt A	5.8
ML	Franklin High Yield Tax-Free Inc A	5.6
ML	Waddell & Reed Adv Muni High-Inc A	5.5
ML	Vanguard High-Yield Tax-Exempt	5.5
ML	USAA Tax-Exempt Long-Term	5.5
ML	Franklin Federal Tax-Free Income A	5.4
ML	Alliance Muni Income National A	5.3
MI	USAA Tax-Exempt Intermediate-Term	5.2
MI	Nuveen Interm Duration Muni Bond R	5.1
ML	Vanguard Long-Term Tax-Exempt	5.1
ML	Franklin Insured Tax-Free Income A	5.0
ML	Vanguard Insured Long-Trm T/E	5.0
ML	Sit Tax-Free Income	4.9
MI	Dreyfus Intermediate Municipal Bond	4.9
MI	American Funds Tax-Exempt Bond Fd A	4.9
MI	Fidelity Spartan Municipal Income	4.8
MI	Vanguard Interm-Term Tax-Ex	4.8
MI	Scudder Medium-Term Tax-Free S	4.7
MI	Fidelity Spartan Interm Muni Income	4.7
	Average Yield	**4.9**

Notes: The tables on pages 541–547 are based on Morningstar rating groups.
Specialty precious metals funds are therefore included in the international-equity group.

Highest/Lowest Assets

Morningstar Funds 500 Universe

Domestic Equity

Cat		Assets ($mil)
	Highest	
LB	Fidelity Magellan	79515.2
LB	Vanguard 500 Index	73150.8
LV	American Funds Investment Co Amer A	54008.1
LV	American Funds Washington Mutual A	48135.1
LG	American Funds Growth Fund of Amer A	35402.0
LB	Fidelity Growth & Income	34255.1
LB	Fidelity Contrafund	32320.9
LG	Janus	25621.8
LG	Fidelity Growth Company	22741.6
LV	Vanguard Windsor II	22428.6
LG	Fidelity Blue Chip Growth	21958.6
LV	Fidelity Equity-Income	21831.5
DH	Vanguard Wellington	21724.0
DH	Fidelity Puritan	20314.8
DH	American Funds Income Fund of Amer A	19745.6
LV	American Funds Fundamental Invs A	19099.6
LV	Putnam Fund for Growth & Income A	19023.0
LB	Vanguard Primecap	18096.0
SH	Vanguard Health Care	16241.4
LV	Vanguard Windsor	16026.7
	Lowest	
ST	Calvert Social Investment Tech A	2.8
MV	Neuberger Berman Regency Inv	15.8
ST	T. Rowe Price Developing Tech	18.9
SH	Evergreen Health Care A	32.3
MG	Northern Institutional Mid Cap Gr A	35.2
SV	ABN AMRO/Chicago Capital Sm Cap Val N	40.7
LV	Gabelli Blue Chip Value AAA	42.5
MV	Delphi Value Retail	44.8
ST	Enterprise Internet A	49.1
MG	Merrill Lynch Premier Growth B	51.2
SB	FPA Perennial	51.9
LV	American Century Tax Managed Val Inv	53.1
LV	ICAP Select Equity	53.7
LB	TIAA-CREF Social Choice Equity	65.2
LB	Metropolitan West AlphaTrak 500	66.8
SG	Bogle Small Cap Growth Inv	68.6
LG	Marsico 21st Century	68.6
ST	RS Internet Age	69.1
MG	Liberty Acorn Twenty Z	69.4
SV	ICM/Isabelle Small Cap Value Invmt	75.2
	Average Assets ($mil)	**4281.5**

International Equity

Cat		Assets ($mil)
	Highest	
WS	American Funds New Perspective A	27393.8
FS	American Funds EuroPacific Growth A	26819.2
WS	Janus Worldwide	21678.6
WS	Templeton Growth A	12108.1
WS	American Funds Capital World Gr&Inc A	10345.8
FS	Templeton Foreign A	8747.5
IH	American Funds Capital Inc Builder A	8234.4
WS	Templeton World A	7060.1
FS	Putnam International Growth A	6561.7
FS	Fidelity Diversified International	6378.9
FS	T. Rowe Price International Stock	6370.5
FS	Vanguard International Growth	6088.0
FS	Janus Overseas	5278.5
FS	Artisan International	4700.0
FS	Morgan Stan Inst International Eq A	4502.9
ES	Vanguard European Stock Index	4404.7
FS	Tweedy, Browne Global Value	3834.5
FS	Harbor International	3655.5
FS	Fidelity Overseas	3481.2
FS	American Century Intl Growth Inv	3311.0
	Lowest	
LS	Van Kampen Latin American A	18.4
FS	Westcore International Frontier	18.7
FS	Marsico International Opportunities	19.8
FS	Liberty Acorn Foreign Forty Z	37.1
JS	CS Warburg Pincus Japan Growth Comm	52.5
WS	Oakmark Global I	52.8
WS	Van Kampen Global Value Equity A	59.1
EM	Pioneer Emerging Markets A	82.9
PJ	Matthews Pacific Tiger	87.3
WS	Scudder Global Discovery A	107.9
ES	AIM European Development A	157.9
PJ	Liberty Newport Tiger A	187.5
FS	Vanguard Developed Markets Index	188.6
IH	MFS Global Total Return A	197.5
LS	Fidelity Latin America	209.6
WS	MFS Global Equity B	221.0
DP	Merrill Lynch Pacific B	225.7
WS	Oppenheimer Quest Global Value A	241.0
WS	Hartford Global Leaders A	247.1
FS	TIAA-CREF International Equity	262.0
	Average Assets ($mil)	**3022.7**

Highest/Lowest Assets

Morningstar Funds 500 Universe

Taxable Bond

Cat		Assets ($mil)
	Highest	
CI	PIMCO Total Return Instl	33260.4
GI	Vanguard GNMA	15531.4
CI	Vanguard Total Bond Market Index	14115.7
GI	Franklin U.S. Government Secs A	7159.8
HY	Vanguard High-Yield Corporate	5160.3
CS	PIMCO Low Duration Instl	4189.5
GI	Fidelity Ginnie Mae	3901.4
GS	Scudder GNMA AARP	3816.0
CL	Vanguard Long-Term Corporate Bond	3550.3
CS	Fidelity Short-Term Bond	3338.6
UB	Strong Advantage Inv	3002.5
HY	MainStay High-Yield Corporate Bond B	2476.9
MU	T. Rowe Price Spectrum Income	2455.3
HY	Franklin AGE High Income A	2029.4
GS	Vanguard Short-Term Federal	1783.3
CS	Vanguard Short-Term Bond Index	1679.7
GI	American Century Ginnie Mae Inv	1646.4
GI	Strong Government Securities Inv	1630.2
HY	Fidelity High-Income	1551.1
CI	USAA Income	1546.7
	Lowest	
HY	Morgan Stan Inst High-Yield Invmt	9.7
IB	BlackRock Intl Bond Svc	12.0
GL	American Century Long-Term Trs Inv	119.0
EB	Scudder Emerging Markets Income S	120.9
EB	T. Rowe Price Emerging Markets Bond	150.3
GI	Galaxy II U.S. Treasury Index Ret	163.0
CS	Mercury Low Duration I	200.2
GS	Sit U.S. Government Securities	207.6
MU	Franklin Strategic Income A	250.4
GI	Principal Government Securities Inc A	253.8
EB	Fidelity New Markets Income	293.2
CS	Metropolitan West Low Duration Bond M	333.5
GL	T. Rowe Price U.S. Treasury Long-Term	338.0
IB	AXP Global Bond A	339.8
GS	Montgomery Short Duration Govt Bond R	355.6
CI	ABN AMRO/Chicago Capital Bond N	358.4
IB	American Funds Capital World Bond A	392.1
HY	PIMCO High Yield A	417.0
HY	Janus High-Yield	433.1
GI	Pilgrim GNMA Income A	503.0
	Average Assets ($mil)	**2313.6**

Municipal-National Bond

Cat		Assets ($mil)
	Highest	
MI	Vanguard Interm-Term Tax-Ex	6652.8
ML	Franklin Federal Tax-Free Income A	6576.4
ML	AXP High-Yield Tax-Exempt A	4625.8
ML	Franklin High Yield Tax-Free Inc A	4604.9
MI	Fidelity Spartan Municipal Income	4513.9
ML	Vanguard High-Yield Tax-Exempt	2649.7
MI	Nuveen Interm Duration Muni Bond R	2548.4
MI	USAA Tax-Exempt Intermediate-Term	2397.4
MI	American Funds Tax-Exempt Bond Fd A	2260.2
MS	Vanguard Ltd-Term Tax-Ex	2103.6
ML	USAA Tax-Exempt Long-Term	2074.9
ML	Vanguard Insured Long-Trm T/E	1847.0
	Lowest	
MS	Evergreen High Income Municipal Bd B	205.3
ML	Strong Municipal Bond Inv	249.2
ML	Waddell & Reed Adv Muni High-Inc A	418.1
ML	Alliance Muni Income National A	421.3
MS	T. Rowe Price Tax-Free Short-Interm	442.7
ML	Sit Tax-Free Income	443.9
MS	Strong Short-Term Municipal Bond Inv	511.3
MI	Scudder Medium-Term Tax-Free S	572.9
MS	Calvert Tax-Free Reserv Limited-Trm A	668.5
MS	Thornburg Limited-Term Muni Natl A	678.7
MI	Dreyfus Intermediate Municipal Bond	1056.8
	Average Assets ($mil)	**1941.1**

Notes: There are only 29 municipal-bond funds in the Morningstar Mutual Fund 500 universe.

Highest/Lowest Expense Ratio

Morningstar Funds 500 Universe

Domestic Equity

Cat		Expense Ratio %
	Highest	
SG	John Hancock Small Cap Growth B	2.16
LG	Alliance Premier Growth B	2.13
SG	John Hancock Small Cap Value B	2.05
LV	Gabelli Blue Chip Value AAA	2.00
CV	MainStay Convertible B	1.99
MB	Legg Mason Opportunity Prim	1.98
MG	Van Wagoner Post-Venture	1.95
LV	Legg Mason American Leading Co Prim	1.90
ST	Enterprise Internet A	1.86
SV	ICM/Isabelle Small Cap Value Invmt	1.82
MB	Legg Mason Special Investment Prim	1.79
ST	RS Internet Age	1.78
MV	Delphi Value Retail	1.75
SH	Evergreen Health Care A	1.75
SH	Eaton Vance Worldwide Health Sci A	1.71
LV	Legg Mason Value Prim	1.69
SG	Forward Hoover Small Cap Equity	1.64
DH	Morgan Stanley Strategist B	1.63
SG	Fremont U.S. Micro-Cap	1.57
SG	Fidelity Advisor Small Cap T	1.53
	Lowest	
LB	Vanguard 500 Index	0.18
LG	Vanguard Tax-Managed Capital App	0.19
LB	Vanguard Tax-Managed Growth & Inc	0.19
SB	Vanguard Tax-Managed Small Cap Ret	0.20
LB	Vanguard Total Stock Mkt Idx	0.20
LV	Vanguard Value Index	0.22
LG	Vanguard Growth Index	0.22
DH	Vanguard Balanced Index	0.22
MB	Vanguard Mid Capitalization Index	0.25
LB	Vanguard Calvert Social Index	0.25
MB	Vanguard Extended Market Idx	0.25
LG	Fidelity Destiny I	0.25
SG	Vanguard Small Cap Growth Index	0.27
SV	Vanguard Small Cap Value Index	0.27
SB	Vanguard Small Cap Index	0.27
LV	Vanguard Windsor	0.31
DH	Vanguard Wellington	0.31
DH	Vanguard Wellesley Income	0.31
SH	Vanguard Health Care	0.34
LV	Vanguard Windsor II	0.37
	Average Expense Ratio %	**0.98**

International Equity

Cat		Expense Ratio %
	Highest	
WS	MFS Global Equity B	2.30
EM	Pioneer Emerging Markets A	2.19
LS	Van Kampen Latin American A	2.18
EM	Templeton Developing Markets A	2.09
WS	Scudder Global Discovery A	1.99
IH	Merrill Lynch Global Allocation B	1.90
EM	Dreyfus Emerging Markets	1.85
DP	Merrill Lynch Pacific B	1.84
PJ	Matthews Pacific Tiger	1.81
LS	Scudder Latin America S	1.79
FS	Longleaf Partners International	1.79
WS	Oakmark Global I	1.75
PJ	Liberty Newport Tiger A	1.71
WS	Oppenheimer Quest Global Value A	1.70
ES	AIM European Development A	1.69
WS	IDEX Janus Global A	1.64
WS	Van Kampen Global Value Equity A	1.64
FS	Marsico International Opportunities	1.60
WS	Hartford Global Leaders A	1.57
IH	MFS Global Total Return A	1.51
	Lowest	
ES	Vanguard European Stock Index	0.29
FS	TIAA-CREF International Equity	0.49
EM	Vanguard Emerging Mkts Stock Idx	0.59
FS	Vanguard International Growth	0.61
SP	Vanguard Precious Metals	0.65
IH	American Funds Capital Inc Builder A	0.67
WS	American Funds New Perspective A	0.79
WS	American Funds Capital World Gr&Inc A	0.79
FS	Liberty Acorn Foreign Forty Z	0.83
FS	T. Rowe Price International Stock	0.84
FS	American Funds EuroPacific Growth A	0.84
WS	Janus Worldwide	0.86
FS	Janus Overseas	0.88
FS	Lazard International Equity Instl	0.88
FS	Harbor International	0.92
FS	Morgan Stan Inst International Eq A	1.00
ES	T. Rowe Price European Stock	1.02
WS	Mutual Discovery Z	1.02
WS	Fidelity Worldwide	1.04
ES	Fidelity Europe	1.05
	Average Expense Ratio %	**1.28**

Highest/Lowest Expense Ratio

Morningstar Funds 500 Universe

Taxable Bond

Cat		Expense Ratio %
	Highest	
IB	Alliance North American Govt Income B	2.03
HY	MainStay High-Yield Corporate Bond B	1.78
EB	Scudder Emerging Markets Income S	1.71
IB	AXP Global Bond A	1.30
IB	BlackRock Intl Bond Svc	1.22
EB	T. Rowe Price Emerging Markets Bond	1.21
IB	American Funds Capital World Bond A	1.12
GI	Pilgrim GNMA Income A	1.06
HY	Eaton Vance Income Fund of Boston A	1.04
HY	Fidelity Advisor High-Yield T	1.03
HY	Janus High-Yield	1.00
EB	Fidelity New Markets Income	0.99
GI	Principal Government Securities Inc A	0.94
MU	John Hancock Strategic Income A	0.93
IB	T. Rowe Price International Bond	0.91
HY	Strong High-Yield Bond Inv	0.90
GI	Strong Government Securities Inv	0.90
CL	Strong Corporate Bond Inv	0.90
CS	Strong Short-Term Bond Inv	0.90
HY	PIMCO High Yield A	0.90
	Lowest	
UB	DFA One-Year Fixed-Income	0.20
CS	Vanguard Short-Term Bond Index	0.21
CI	Vanguard Total Bond Market Index	0.22
GS	Vanguard Inflation-Protected Secs	0.25
GS	Vanguard Short-Term Treasury	0.27
GI	Vanguard GNMA	0.27
GL	Vanguard Long-Term U.S. Treasury	0.28
GS	Vanguard Short-Term Federal	0.28
HY	Vanguard High-Yield Corporate	0.28
CL	Vanguard Long-Term Corporate Bond	0.30
CI	USAA Income	0.41
GI	Galaxy II U.S. Treasury Index Ret	0.41
CI	PIMCO Total Return Instl	0.43
CS	PIMCO Low Duration Instl	0.43
CI	Dodge & Cox Income	0.46
GL	American Century Long-Term Trs Inv	0.51
IB	PIMCO Foreign Bond Instl	0.54
CS	Metropolitan West Low Duration Bond M	0.58
CS	Mercury Low Duration I	0.58
CS	Fidelity Short-Term Bond	0.58
	Average Expense Ratio %	**0.73**

Municipal-National Bond

Cat		Expense Ratio %
	Highest	
MS	Evergreen High Income Municipal Bd B	1.79
MS	Thornburg Limited-Term Muni Natl A	0.99
ML	Waddell & Reed Adv Muni High-Inc A	0.94
ML	Van Kampen High-Yield Municipal A	0.91
ML	Strong Municipal Bond Inv	0.80
ML	Strong Municipal Bond Inv	0.80
ML	AXP High-Yield Tax-Exempt A	0.79
MI	Dreyfus Intermediate Municipal Bond	0.75
ML	Sit Tax-Free Income	0.74
MI	Scudder Medium-Term Tax-Free S	0.73
	Lowest	
MI	Vanguard Interm-Term Tax-Ex	0.18
MS	Vanguard Ltd-Term Tax-Ex	0.18
ML	Vanguard Long-Term Tax-Exempt	0.19
ML	Vanguard High-Yield Tax-Exempt	0.19
ML	Vanguard Insured Long-Trm T/E	0.19
MI	USAA Tax-Exempt Intermediate-Term	0.36
ML	USAA Tax-Exempt Long-Term	0.36
MS	USAA Tax-Exempt Short-Term	0.38
MI	Fidelity Spartan Municipal Income	0.42
MS	Fidelity Spartan Short-Int Muni Inc	0.45
	Average Expense Ratio %	**0.61**

Notes: There are only 29 municipal-bond funds in the Morningstar Mutual Fund 500 universe.

Highest/Lowest Turnover Rate

Morningstar Funds 500 Universe

Domestic Equity

Cat		Turnover Rate %
	Highest	
DH	George Putnam Fund of Boston A	333
MG	Brandywine	284
MG	Van Kampen Aggressive Growth A	270
LB	Putnam Capital Appreciation A	264
MG	Putnam Capital Opportunities A	221
LG	Fidelity OTC	219
MG	Fidelity Mid-Cap Stock	218
LB	Fidelity	217
MB	Van Kampen American Value A	211
MV	Dreyfus Midcap Value	192
ST	Northern Technology	180
MV	American Century Equity Income Inv	169
LB	Fidelity Contrafund II	168
MV	American Century Value Inv	150
LG	Van Kampen Emerging Growth A	148
SV	American Century Small Cap Value Inv	144
LG	Putnam Voyager A	140
MG	Putnam New Century Growth A	139
DH	Morgan Stanley Strategist B	136
LG	Vanguard U.S. Growth	135
	Lowest	
LV	Ameristock	6
DH	Deutsche Flag Value Builder A	8
LG	Wayne Hummer Growth	9
MV	Tweedy, Browne American Value	10
LV	Davis NY Venture A	15
LV	USAA Income Stock	18
LB	Domini Social Equity	19
SH	Vanguard Health Care	21
MG	USAA Aggressive Growth	23
SH	Eaton Vance Worldwide Health Sci A	24
LB	Fidelity Magellan	24
LV	Fidelity Equity-Income	25
LV	American Funds Washington Mutual A	25
LV	Legg Mason Value Prim	27
MG	Franklin Small-Mid Cap Growth A	27
LB	AXP New Dimensions A	29
MV	Weitz Partners Value	29
LV	American Funds American Mutual A	29
SG	Buffalo Small Cap	31
SV	Putnam Small Cap Value A	34
	Average Turnover Rate %	**89**

International Equity

Cat		Turnover Rate %
	Highest	
WS	Putnam Global Equity A	199
FS	Waddell & Reed Adv International Gr A	118
FS	Putnam International Growth A	74
FS	Artisan International	72
EM	Templeton Developing Markets A	69
FS	Westcore International Frontier	61
LS	Van Kampen Latin American A	61
FS	Vanguard International Growth	48
FS	American Funds EuroPacific Growth A	37
WS	Van Kampen Global Value Equity A	33
WS	Templeton World A	25
WS	Templeton Growth A	24
SP	Vanguard Precious Metals	17
FS	Tweedy, Browne Global Value	12
	Lowest	
FS	Tweedy, Browne Global Value	12
SP	Vanguard Precious Metals	17
WS	Templeton Growth A	24
WS	Templeton World A	25
WS	Van Kampen Global Value Equity A	33
FS	American Funds EuroPacific Growth A	37
FS	Vanguard International Growth	48
LS	Van Kampen Latin American A	61
FS	Westcore International Frontier	61
EM	Templeton Developing Markets A	69
FS	Artisan International	72
FS	Putnam International Growth A	74
FS	Waddell & Reed Adv International Gr A	118
WS	Putnam Global Equity A	199
	Average Turnover Rate %	**61**

Highest/Lowest Turnover Rate

Morningstar Funds 500 Universe

Taxable Bond

Cat		Turnover Rate %
	Highest	
CI	PIMCO Total Return Instl	450
IB	PIMCO Foreign Bond Instl	417
CS	PIMCO Low Duration Instl	348
GS	Vanguard Short-Term Treasury	296
GS	Montgomery Short Duration Govt Bond R	245
CI	Metropolitan West Total Return Bond	205
GS	Vanguard Short-Term Federal	169
GI	American Century Ginnie Mae Inv	143
GS	Vanguard Inflation-Protected Secs	122
GI	Fidelity Ginnie Mae	120
GL	American Century Long-Term Trs Inv	107
CS	Fidelity Short-Term Bond	84
HY	Fidelity High-Income	68
GS	Sit U.S. Government Securities	56
HY	PIMCO High Yield A	53
MU	John Hancock Strategic Income A	48
CI	USAA Income	43
MU	Franklin Strategic Income A	36
GL	T. Rowe Price U.S. Treasury Long-Term	31
HY	Franklin AGE High Income A	21
	Lowest	
CS	Metropolitan West Low Duration Bond M	1
GI	Vanguard GNMA	8
HY	Franklin AGE High Income A	21
GL	T. Rowe Price U.S. Treasury Long-Term	31
MU	Franklin Strategic Income A	36
CI	USAA Income	43
MU	John Hancock Strategic Income A	48
HY	PIMCO High Yield A	53
GS	Sit U.S. Government Securities	56
HY	Fidelity High-Income	68
CS	Fidelity Short-Term Bond	84
GL	American Century Long-Term Trs Inv	107
GI	Fidelity Ginnie Mae	120
GS	Vanguard Inflation-Protected Secs	122
GI	American Century Ginnie Mae Inv	143
GS	Vanguard Short-Term Federal	169
CI	Metropolitan West Total Return Bond	205
GS	Montgomery Short Duration Govt Bond R	245
GS	Vanguard Short-Term Treasury	296
CS	PIMCO Low Duration Instl	348
	Average Turnover Rate %	**140**

Municipal-National Bond

Cat		Turnover Rate %
	Highest	
ML	USAA Tax-Exempt Long-Term	47
MS	T. Rowe Price Tax-Free Short-Interm	41
MS	Thornburg Limited-Term Muni Natl A	25
MI	Scudder Medium-Term Tax-Free S	21
MS	USAA Tax-Exempt Short-Term	19
ML	Sit Tax-Free Income	12
ML	Franklin High Yield Tax-Free Inc A	11
ML	Franklin Insured Tax-Free Income A	10
MI	USAA Tax-Exempt Intermediate-Term	9
MI	Nuveen Interm Duration Muni Bond R	9
	Lowest	
MI	Nuveen Interm Duration Muni Bond R	9
MI	USAA Tax-Exempt Intermediate-Term	9
ML	Franklin Insured Tax-Free Income A	10
ML	Franklin High Yield Tax-Free Inc A	11
ML	Sit Tax-Free Income	12
MS	USAA Tax-Exempt Short-Term	19
MI	Scudder Medium-Term Tax-Free S	21
MS	Thornburg Limited-Term Muni Natl A	25
MS	T. Rowe Price Tax-Free Short-Interm	41
ML	USAA Tax-Exempt Long-Term	47
	Average Turnover Rate %	**21**

Notes: There are only 29 municipal-bond funds in the Morningstar Mutual Fund 500 universe.

Manager Changes

Morningstar Funds 500 Universe

	Previous Manager/Team	Current Manager/Team	Date of Change
ABN AMRO/Chicago Capital Sm Cap Val N	Patricia A. Falkowski	Philip Tasho	04/05/2001
American Century Government Bond Inv	David W. Schroeder	Jeremy Fletcher	11/19/2001
American Century Select Inv	Crawford/Sullivan	Goodwin/Crawford/Reynolds	08/06/2001
AXP High-Yield Tax-Exempt A	Kurt Larson	Terrence M. Fettig	01/01/2001
Enterprise Internet A	David D. Alger	Dan Chung/Fred Alger	09/13/2001
Evergreen Equity Income I	O'Neill/Foreman	Sujatha Avutu	11/16/2001
Fidelity Convertible Securities	Peter Saperstone	Lawrence Rakers	06/12/2001
Fidelity Diversified International	Gregory Fraser	William Bower	04/01/2001
Fidelity Latin America	Patti Satterthwaite	Margaret Reynolds	06/01/2001
Fidelity Mid-Cap Stock	David Felman	Beso Sikharulidze	06/12/2001
Fidelity Select Technology	Lawrence Rakers	Christopher F. Zepf	06/12/2001
Fidelity Small Cap Independence	Timothy A. Krochuk	James M. Harmon	04/21/2001
Fidelity Worldwide	Penelope A. Dobkin	Chase/Mace, Jr.	04/01/2001
Fremont U.S. Micro-Cap	Finger/Kern/Weaver/Houde/Kern	Kern/Weaver/Houde/Kern	03/01/2001
Harbor Large Cap Value	Tierney/DePrince	Jeff Shaw	09/20/2001
INVESCO Balanced Inv	Paul/Mayer/Lovell	Charles P. Mayer/Peter Lovell	2001
Japan S	Allan/Kwak	Sean Lenihan/Seung Kwak	05/01/2001
Legg Mason Special Investment Prim	William H. Miller III	Lisa O. Rapuano	2001
Liberty Acorn Foreign Forty Z	Marcel Houtzager/Roger Edgley	Management Team	09/01/2001
Liberty Acorn International Z	Forster/Zell	Leah Zell	2001
Masters' Select Value	Sondike/Cates/Hawkins/Nygren/Miller III	Winters/Cates/Hawkins/Nygren/Miller III	08/01/2001
Mercury Low Duration I	John Queen/Michael Sanchez	Pat Maldari	08/01/2001
MFS Massachusetts Investors Gr Stk A	Barrett/Pesek	Stephen Pesek	2001
Mutual Beacon Z	Lawrence N. Sondike	Winters/Haynes	08/01/2001
Mutual Qualified Z	Raymond Garea	Jeff Diamond/Susan Potto	08/01/2001
Mutual Shares Z	Lawrence N. Sondike	Winters/Turner/Rankin	08/01/2001
One Group Large Cap Growth A	Creech/Spytek/Patel/Kapusta/Johnson-Grunst et al.	Patel/Kapusta/Johnson-Grunst et al.	2001
Oppenheimer Capital Income A	Doney/Levine	Michael S. Levine	2001
T. Rowe Price Emerging Markets Bond	Askew/Rothery/Conelius	Rothery/Kelson/Conelius	05/01/2001
T. Rowe Price International Bond	Askew/Rothery/Conelius	Chris Rothery/Mike Conelius	2001
Principal Government Securities Inc A	Alexander/Schafer	Martin J.Schafer	2001
George Putnam Fund of Boston A	King/Prusko/Mockard	Prusko/Mockard/Knight	03/12/2001
Putnam New Century Growth A	Swanberg/Gillis	Roland W. Gillis	2001
Putnam Vista A	Santosus/Clark/Wetlaufer/Parker	Clark/Wetlaufer/Doerr/Parker	05/14/2001
Putnam Voyager A	Swanberg/Beck/Gillis/Divney/Wiess/Marrkand/Stack	Wiess/Divney/Nance/Stack/Warren/Marrkand/Beck	05/14/2001
RS Internet Age	Cathy Baker	Callinan/Bishop	02/05/2001
Scudder Emerging Markets Income S	Isabel Saltzman/Susan E. Dahl	Jack Janasiewicz/Jan Faller	03/01/2001
Scudder Greater Europe Growth S	Gregory/Franklin/Bratt	Franklin/Axtell/Bratt	03/01/2001
Skyline Special Equities	William M. Dutton	Management Team	03/01/2001
State Street Research Aurora A	Rudolph Kluiber	John Burbank	04/27/2001

Manager Changes

Morningstar Funds 500 Universe

	Previous Manager/Team	Current Manager/Team	Date of Change
SunAmerica Focused Growth A	Alger/Segalas/Marsico	Chung/Segalas/Marsico	2001
Templeton Foreign A	Mark G. Holowesko	Winner/Everett/Murchison	01/01/2001
Templeton Growth A	Maura/Holowesko/Farrington	Winner/Everett/Murchison	01/22/2001
Third Avenue Real Estate Value	Whitman/Winer	Michael Winer	2001
UAM ICM Small Company	Neuhauser/McDorman Jr	McAree/McDorman Jr./Wooten/Heaphy	09/01/2001
Van Kampen American Value A	Korchevsky/Gerlach/Schlarbaum	Daniels/Schlarbaum/Jolinger/Todorow/Korchevsky et al.	10/26/2001
Van Kampen Latin American A	Skov/Perl/Meyer	Michael Perl/Robert L. Meyer	2001
Vanguard Long-Term U.S. Treasury	Auwaerter/MacKinnon	Glocke/MacKinnon	05/29/2001
Vanguard U.S. Growth	Fowler/Hall III/Cole	Toub/Blundin	06/22/2001
WM Growth Fund of the Northwest A	David W. Simpson	Randall L. Yoakum	04/24/2001

Fund Name Changes
Morningstar Funds 500 Universe

Previous Name	Current Name	Date of Change
Alleghany/Chicago Trust Bond N	ABN AMRO/Chicago Capital Bond N	09/24/2001
Alleghany/Chicago Trust Sm Cap Value N	ABN AMRO/Chicago Capital Sm Cap Val N	09/24/2001
Alleghany/Montag & Caldwell Growth N	ABN AMRO/Montag & Caldwell Growth N	09/24/2001
American Century GNMA Inv	American Century Ginnie Mae Inv	08/01/2001
American Century L/T Treasury Inv	American Century Government Bond Inv	12/03/2001
Brazos Micro Cap Growth	Brazos Micro Cap Y	01/02/2001
CSWP Japan Growth Comm	Credit Suisse Warburg Pincus Japan Growth Comm	04/10/2001
Evergreen Equity Income Y	Evergreen Equity Income I	05/11/2001
Fidelity Retirement Growth	Fidelity Independence	01/29/2001
Fidelity Small Cap Selector	Fidelity Small Cap Independence	07/13/2001
Flag Investors Communications A	Deutsche Flag Communications A	05/07/2001
Flag Investors Value Builder A	Deutsche Flag Value Builder A	05/07/2001
Franklin Small Cap Growth I A	Franklin Small-Mid Cap Growth A	09/01/2001
Harbor Value	Harbor Large Cap Value	09/20/2001
IDEX JCC Global A	IDEX Janus Global A	03/01/2001
Kemper Global Discovery A	Scudder Global Discovery A	05/29/2001
Kemper Total Return A	Scudder Total Return A	06/11/2001
MAS High-Yield Invmt	Morgan Stan Inst High-Yield Invmt	08/01/2001
MAS Mid Cap Growth Instl	Morgan Stan Inst Mid Cap Growth	08/01/2001
MAS Mid Cap Value Instl	Morgan Stan Inst Mid Cap Value	08/01/2001
MAS Small Cap Growth Instl	Morgan Stan Inst Small Cap Growth	08/01/2001
MSDW American Opportunity B	Morgan Stanley American Opp B	06/18/2001
MSDW Instl International Equity A	Morgan Stan Inst International Eq A	05/21/2001
MSDW Instl U.S. Real Estate A	Morgan Stan Inst U.S. Real Estate A	05/21/2001
MSDW Strategist B	Morgan Stanley Strategist B	06/18/2001
Style Select Focus A	SunAmerica Focused Growth A	03/01/2001
Van Kampen Global Equity A	Van Kampen Global Value Equity A	08/28/2001

Summary Pages

This section offers the essential risk and return data for all 500 funds in a table format, allowing you to make quick camparisons across funds.

Stock Funds—U.S. Equity

	Cat	Style Box	NAV	Total Return % through 12-31-01 1Yr	Annualized 3Yr	Annualized 5Yr	Annualized 10Yr	Trailing 12 Mo Yield %	Morningstar Risk 1.00=U.S. Equity Avg 3Yr	Morningstar Risk 5Yr	Morningstar Risk 10Yr	Rtn % Rank Cat 3Yr	Rtn % Rank Cat 5Yr	Rtn % Rank Cat 10Yr	Star Rating	Avg Star Rating
S&P 500				**-11.88**	**-1.03**	**10.70**	**12.93**									
ABN AMRO/Chicago Capital Sm Cap Val N	SV		12.34	13.70	9.69	—	—	0.1	0.58	—	—	70	—	—	★★★★	4.0
ABN AMRO/Montag & Caldwell Growth N	LG		24.12	-13.33	-0.55	11.32	—	0.0	0.86	0.89	—	31	24	—	★★★★	4.5
AIM Aggressive Growth A	MG		9.45	-26.00	3.39	5.41	14.73	0.0	1.44	1.56	1.64	62	70	8	★★	2.7
AIM Constellation A	LG		22.10	-23.61	-0.38	5.82	11.07	0.0	1.38	1.38	1.46	30	73	34	★★	3.3
AIM Summit	LG		10.30	-33.80	-5.24	7.28	9.73	0.0	1.54	1.40	1.40	66	63	65	★★	2.6
AIM Value A	LB		10.87	-12.99	-1.30	9.61	13.30	0.0	1.03	0.99	0.98	52	47	17	★★★	4.1
AIM Weingarten A	LG		13.49	-34.10	-10.88	3.48	6.50	0.0	1.47	1.30	1.32	92	85	87	★	3.5
Alliance Premier Growth B	LG		18.84	-24.52	-8.35	8.51	—	0.0	1.38	1.29	—	83	50	—	★★	3.8
American Century Equity Growth Inv	LB		19.24	-11.01	-2.08	9.89	12.26	0.7	0.93	0.92	0.90	67	42	37	★★★	4.2
American Century Equity Income Inv	MV		7.14	11.33	10.65	14.44	—	2.4	0.46	0.50	—	49	27	—	★★★★★	4.2
American Century Growth Inv	LG		19.52	-18.67	-2.24	10.57	8.39	0.0	1.18	1.12	1.30	48	30	79	★★	3.2
American Century Income & Growth Inv	LV		27.35	-8.37	-1.12	10.66	12.91	1.1	0.89	0.87	0.84	81	30	33	★★★★	4.3
American Century Select Inv	LG		37.00	-18.16	-2.98	10.38	9.21	0.2	0.92	0.89	1.01	53	32	72	★★★	3.4
American Century Small Cap Value Inv	SV		8.02	30.52	21.73	—	—	0.5	0.46	—	—	11	—	—	★★★★★	5.0
American Century Value Inv	MV		7.00	12.86	9.81	11.86	—	1.2	0.70	0.76	—	55	48	—	★★★★	3.6
American Funds Amcap A	LG		16.12	-5.01	7.53	16.11	13.92	0.5	0.67	0.69	0.80	3	3	8	★★★★	3.3
American Funds American Balanced A	DH		15.85	8.19	9.05	11.77	11.86	3.5	0.34	0.38	0.41	4	6	8	★★★★	3.5
American Funds American Mutual A	LV		24.05	6.67	5.15	11.02	12.28	2.9	0.55	0.55	0.58	25	26	47	★★★★	3.7
American Funds Fundamental Invs A	LV		27.45	-9.55	5.52	11.68	13.95	1.4	0.69	0.71	0.72	22	19	18	★★★★	3.9
American Funds Growth Fund of Amer A	LG		23.71	-12.28	11.17	18.09	15.46	0.2	0.89	0.88	0.95	2	2	3	★★★★	3.6
American Funds Income Fund of Amer A	DH		15.82	5.41	5.23	9.28	11.18	5.0	0.36	0.39	0.40	18	23	15	★★★★	3.7
American Funds Investment Co Amer A	LV		28.53	-4.59	4.91	13.00	13.14	1.8	0.59	0.63	0.67	26	11	29	★★★★	4.0
American Funds New Economy A	LB		18.30	-17.34	0.35	10.90	12.72	0.0	1.13	1.03	1.03	33	21	23	★★★	3.5
American Funds Smallcap World A	SG		22.92	-17.35	4.10	4.84	9.63	0.2	1.34	1.29	1.23	74	74	71	★★	2.7
American Funds Washington Mutual A	LV		28.25	1.51	3.85	12.25	14.12	1.9	0.69	0.69	0.70	33	14	15	★★★★	3.9
Ameristock	LV		40.40	1.25	7.88	17.09	—	0.7	0.67	0.67	—	8	1	—	★★★★★	4.6
Ariel Appreciation	MB		37.02	16.23	9.94	16.99	14.19	0.2	0.60	0.64	0.73	21	5	32	★★★★	3.0
Artisan Small Cap Value	SV		12.68	15.04	17.07	—	—	0.1	0.41	—	—	20	—	—	★★★★★	4.0
AXP New Dimensions A	LB		24.49	-15.50	0.45	10.14	12.28	0.0	0.99	0.98	1.02	31	37	37	★★★	4.3
AXP Utilities Income A	SU		7.54	-20.10	0.55	9.99	10.73	5.7	0.75	0.70	0.72	39	30	16	★★★	3.3
Babson Growth	LG		11.07	-20.47	-6.21	6.90	10.34	0.0	1.30	1.17	1.07	72	66	53	★★	3.0
Baron Asset	MG		44.46	-10.12	1.60	7.93	13.82	0.0	1.23	1.26	1.25	67	57	14	★★★	3.2
Baron Growth	SG		30.67	12.67	15.87	15.34	—	0.0	0.92	1.05	—	21	18	—	★★★★★	3.4
Baron Small Cap	SG		15.21	5.19	14.00	—	—	0.0	1.08	—	—	26	—	—	★★★★★	3.8
Berger Small Cap Value Instl	SV		28.15	20.42	20.65	19.62	19.12	0.8	0.61	0.70	0.78	13	7	1	★★★★★	3.5
Brandywine	MG		23.35	-20.55	9.31	7.77	13.33	0.0	0.93	1.10	1.23	28	58	19	★★★	3.8
Brazos Micro Cap Y	SG		19.62	4.70	31.06	—	—	0.0	1.08	—	—	5	—	—	★★★★★	5.0
Buffalo Small Cap	SG		19.96	31.18	33.21	—	—	0.0	0.73	—	—	4	—	—	★★★★★	5.0
Calamos Convertible A	CV	—	18.56	-4.14	11.53	13.28	12.71	3.3	0.53	0.55	0.64	10	7	17	★★★★	2.7
Clipper	LV		83.53	10.26	14.07	18.21	17.54	1.2	0.37	0.41	0.58	2	1	1	★★★★★	4.0
Columbia Balanced	DH		20.67	-7.40	1.71	8.45	10.02	2.8	0.60	0.54	0.54	58	31	36	★★★	3.5
Columbia Growth	LG		31.35	-21.40	-3.03	8.47	11.73	0.0	1.33	1.19	1.17	53	51	24	★★★	3.8
Columbia Real Estate Equity	SR		18.04	5.41	10.23	8.25	—	4.4	0.57	0.67	—	59	14	—	★★★	3.3
Columbia Small Cap	SG		22.20	-14.19	13.11	15.23	—	0.0	1.32	1.37	—	29	18	—	★★★★	4.0
Davis Convertible Securities A	CV	—	21.36	-7.56	1.13	5.50	—	3.7	0.71	0.69	—	86	75	—	★★	2.9
Davis Financial A	SF		32.98	-9.13	5.99	14.46	18.91	0.0	0.97	0.96	0.96	46	25	30	★★★★	4.4
Davis Growth Opportunity A	MB		16.81	-8.06	10.45	11.98	—	0.0	0.95	1.17	—	17	32	—	★★★	2.2
Davis NY Venture A	LV		25.43	-11.41	4.62	11.92	14.84	0.1	0.75	0.82	0.90	28	18	8	★★★★	4.6
Delaware Trend A	MG		17.73	-14.88	10.77	13.02	14.65	0.0	1.47	1.47	1.53	22	23	10	★★★	2.8
Delphi Value Retail	MV		13.18	1.90	9.98	—	—	0.0	0.66	—	—	55	—	—	★★★★	4.0
Deutsche Flag Communications A	SC		18.58	-29.54	-12.45	11.30	12.36	0.0	1.61	1.39	1.31	73	42	40	★★★	4.3
Deutsche Flag Value Builder A	DH		22.36	3.20	5.34	11.19	—	1.7	0.72	0.70	—	17	9	—	★★★★	3.7
DFA U.S. Micro Cap	SB		10.01	22.77	15.38	11.82	15.59	0.4	1.19	1.26	1.26	21	41	15	★★★★	2.4
Dodge & Cox Stock	LV		100.51	9.33	15.19	15.65	16.62	1.7	0.54	0.64	0.70	2	3	2	★★★★★	4.2
Dodge & Cox Balanced	DH		65.42	10.05	12.39	12.92	13.43	3.2	0.34	0.41	0.46	2	3	3	★★★★★	4.0

Bold numbers indicate *highest* return for the listed time period in each category.

Stock Funds—U.S. Equity

	Cat	Style Box	NAV	Total Return % through 12-31-01 1Yr	Annualized 3Yr	5Yr	10Yr	Trailing 12 Mo Yield %	Morningstar Risk 1.00=U.S. Equity Avg 3Yr	5Yr	10Yr	Rtn % Rank Cat 3Yr	5Yr	10Yr	Star Rating	Avg Star Rating
S&P 500				**-11.88**	**-1.03**	**10.70**	**12.93**									
Domini Social Equity	LB		27.37	-12.76	-3.14	10.45	12.41	0.2	0.99	0.95	0.92	78	28	32	★★★	4.0
Dresdner RCM Global Technology I	ST		30.54	-39.31	13.73	24.67	—	0.0	2.13	1.89	—	8	2	—	★★★★★	5.0
Dreyfus Disciplined Stock	LB		31.97	-13.31	-2.39	9.22	12.20	0.3	0.96	0.95	0.91	71	53	38	★★★	4.3
Dreyfus Emerging Leaders	SG		34.77	-9.91	10.90	14.67	—	0.0	0.95	1.03	—	35	19	—	★★★★★	4.3
Dreyfus Midcap Value	MV		26.29	17.10	24.10	18.57	—	0.0	0.96	1.08	—	2	8	—	★★★★★	3.6
Dreyfus Small Company Value	SV		20.80	28.60	18.01	14.20	—	0.0	1.16	1.22	—	17	17	—	★★★★	3.7
Eaton Vance Worldwide Health Sci A	SH		10.33	-6.63	28.09	23.46	**20.81**	0.0	0.71	0.88	1.03	4	6	1	★★★★★	3.4
Evergreen Equity Income I	MV		20.35	-5.37	5.67	8.01	9.10	3.9	0.56	0.63	0.66	80	80	91	★★★	3.2
Excelsior Value & Restructuring	LV		32.06	-4.96	13.10	16.35	—	0.3	0.87	0.91	—	2	2	—	★★★★★	4.8
FAM Value	SV		36.17	15.09	9.29	14.03	13.14	0.5	0.61	0.64	0.71	73	20	48	★★★★	3.8
Fidelity Advisor Balanced T	DH		15.53	-1.91	-1.13	6.42	7.67	2.5	0.63	0.62	0.63	86	65	78	★★★	3.4
Fidelity Advisor Equity Growth T	LG		48.69	-18.19	-0.44	11.15	—	0.0	1.15	1.09	—	30	26	—	★★★	3.7
Fidelity Advisor Growth Opport T	LB		28.76	-15.14	-10.34	2.81	10.03	0.7	1.09	0.97	0.90	97	96	73	★★	4.1
Fidelity Advisor Small Cap T	SG		18.00	-3.90	10.11	—	—	0.0	1.26	—	—	40	—	—	★★★★	4.0
Fidelity Advisor Value Strat T	SB		26.88	12.11	13.99	13.48	12.79	0.0	0.93	1.03	1.02	27	27	68	★★★★	3.1
Fidelity Aggressive Growth	LG		19.02	-47.27	-7.95	5.95	10.54	0.0	2.31	1.96	1.92	81	72	48	★	3.4
Fidelity Asset Manager	DH		15.50	-3.93	3.77	9.66	10.62	4.2	0.53	0.54	0.55	31	18	23	★★★	3.9
Fidelity Asset Manager: Growth	LB		14.34	-7.22	0.66	8.78	11.67	2.9	0.74	0.72	0.75	29	59	50	★★★	3.0
Fidelity Balanced	DH		14.90	2.25	5.44	11.71	10.30	3.0	0.44	0.46	0.51	16	6	31	★★★★	3.7
Fidelity Blue Chip Growth	LG		42.94	-16.55	-2.47	9.69	13.07	0.1	1.08	1.01	0.99	49	37	14	★★★	4.8
Fidelity Capital Appreciation	LB		20.55	-7.56	3.36	10.32	13.52	0.0	1.28	1.23	1.11	14	33	16	★★★★	3.2
Fidelity Contrafund	LB		42.77	-12.59	0.62	10.51	14.32	0.5	0.81	0.81	0.83	29	26	8	★★★★	4.2
Fidelity Contrafund II	LB		10.35	-9.59	5.70	—	—	0.4	1.00	—	—	7	—	—	★★★	3.9
Fidelity Convertible Securities	CV	—	19.90	0.50	15.79	15.62	14.89	4.7	0.88	0.87	0.83	4	4	5	★★★★★	4.4
Fidelity Destiny I	LG		12.74	-17.29	-11.47	2.68	10.91	0.9	1.13	0.99	0.92	93	90	39	★★	4.2
Fidelity Destiny II	LB		10.93	-9.35	-0.66	10.24	14.84	0.9	1.01	0.94	0.88	43	35	5	★★★	4.3
Fidelity Dividend Growth	LB		28.33	-3.74	5.54	15.36	—	0.5	0.71	0.71	—	7	2	—	★★★★★	4.9
Fidelity Equity-Income	LV		48.77	-5.02	3.37	10.07	13.65	1.5	0.72	0.76	0.74	36	36	22	★★★★	4.0
Fidelity Equity-Income II	LV		21.03	-7.16	1.36	10.24	13.56	1.5	0.72	0.75	0.73	58	34	24	★★★★	4.3
Fidelity	LB		28.88	-11.22	-0.61	11.18	13.54	0.7	1.02	0.94	0.90	42	18	15	★★★★	3.8
Fidelity Growth & Income	LB		37.38	-9.35	-0.63	10.38	13.76	1.0	0.69	0.72	0.69	43	30	12	★★★★	4.7
Fidelity Growth & Income II	LB		9.23	-9.15	-1.91	—	—	1.0	0.74	—	—	64	—	—	★★★	3.0
Fidelity Growth Company	LG		53.22	-25.31	7.89	13.70	14.28	0.0	1.46	1.34	1.31	3	11	5	★★★	4.0
Fidelity Independence	LG		15.77	-27.22	2.86	11.88	12.30	1.3	1.50	1.36	1.25	12	18	19	★★★	3.8
Fidelity Low-Priced Stock	SV		27.42	26.71	16.52	15.05	17.90	0.6	0.44	0.54	0.58	23	14	6	★★★★★	4.5
Fidelity Magellan	LB		104.22	-11.65	-0.20	10.95	12.90	0.4	0.95	0.92	0.94	38	20	21	★★★	4.6
Fidelity Mid-Cap Stock	MG		22.57	-12.80	17.21	18.71	—	0.7	0.93	0.97	—	7	6	—	★★★★★	3.8
Fidelity New Millennium	MG		27.63	-18.15	17.10	20.64	—	0.0	1.74	1.65	—	7	4	—	★★★★★	4.7
Fidelity OTC	LG		31.17	-24.07	-1.39	8.15	11.86	0.0	1.79	1.68	1.54	39	54	21	★★	4.0
Fidelity Puritan	DH		17.67	-1.05	3.13	9.37	12.06	3.3	0.43	0.47	0.50	38	22	5	★★★★	4.3
Fidelity Select Biotechnology	SH		65.12	-24.98	20.98	21.74	12.01	0.0	1.80	1.60	1.86	25	12	63	★★★★	3.3
Fidelity Select Health Care	SH		127.26	-15.01	4.10	15.88	13.70	0.1	0.71	0.70	0.96	86	51	45	★★★★	4.2
Fidelity Select Technology	ST		60.60	-31.70	2.22	15.48	18.15	0.0	2.33	2.10	2.06	31	16	36	★★★★	2.5
Fidelity Small Cap Independence	SB		16.80	6.29	8.65	8.61	—	0.0	0.86	0.96	—	63	70	—	★★★	1.7
Fidelity Small Cap Stock	SG		14.36	6.44	19.31	—	—	0.1	0.81	—	—	13	—	—	★★★★★	4.7
Fidelity Tax-Managed Stock	LB		10.60	-12.40	-1.45	—	—	0.3	0.91	—	—	55	—	—	★★	2.0
Fidelity Utilities	SU		13.49	-15.19	-5.09	7.66	9.84	1.2	1.00	0.88	0.87	84	59	38	★★★	3.8
Fidelity Value	MV		51.51	12.25	9.62	9.83	14.30	1.0	0.75	0.83	0.79	56	68	52	★★★★	3.2
First Eagle Fund of America Y	MB		21.58	8.25	6.77	13.78	17.57	0.0	0.57	0.66	0.74	48	23	3	★★★★★	3.9
Forward Hoover Small Cap Equity	SG		14.78	4.27	9.57	—	—	0.0	1.05	—	—	43	—	—	★★★★	3.8
FPA Capital	SV		28.26	**38.13**	15.21	12.38	18.27	0.1	1.03	1.03	1.11	29	40	3	★★★★★	3.3
FPA Perennial	SB		23.15	22.73	19.21	17.16	13.93	0.0	0.81	0.86	0.81	11	10	40	★★★★★	3.1
Franklin Balance Sheet Investment A	SV		40.02	17.70	11.77	11.82	15.31	1.7	0.51	0.57	0.57	56	46	24	★★★★★	4.2
Franklin CA Growth A	MG		31.76	-23.23	11.68	12.28	17.32	0.0	1.44	1.36	1.30	18	27	2	★★★★	4.4
Franklin DynaTech A	LG		20.38	-13.11	1.51	8.83	11.31	1.5	0.96	0.92	0.97	18	46	31	★★★	2.7

Bold numbers indicate *highest* return for the listed time period in each category.

Stock Funds—U.S. Equity

	Cat	Style Box	NAV	Total Return % through 12-31-01 1Yr	Annualized 3Yr	5Yr	10Yr	Trailing 12 Mo Yield %	Morningstar Risk 1.00=U.S. Equity Avg 3Yr	5Yr	10Yr	Rtn % Rank Cat 3Yr	5Yr	10Yr	Star Rating	Avg Star Rating
S&P 500				**-11.88**	**-1.03**	**10.70**	**12.93**									
Franklin Growth A	LB		31.51	-9.47	2.98	8.95	10.90	0.5	0.65	0.60	0.69	16	56	64	★★★	3.3
Franklin Income A	DH		2.18	0.65	6.40	7.28	9.58	8.2	0.32	0.38	0.41	10	50	43	★★★	3.6
Franklin Small-Mid Cap Growth A	MG		31.17	-20.53	12.21	10.34	—	0.3	1.60	1.60	—	17	40	—	★★★	3.6
Fremont U.S. Micro-Cap	SG		28.29	5.28	29.26	18.90	—	0.0	1.44	1.62	—	5	9	—	★★★★★	3.8
Gabelli Asset	MB		32.97	0.16	7.91	15.00	14.82	0.0	0.58	0.62	0.66	42	18	22	★★★★★	4.3
Gabelli Global Telecommunications	SC		13.96	-20.73	2.75	14.03	—	0.0	1.08	0.99	—	15	21	—	★★★★	3.8
Gabelli Growth	LB		28.68	-24.10	-0.24	12.94	12.58	0.0	1.13	1.07	1.07	38	7	27	★★★	4.1
Gabelli Small Cap Growth	SB		19.21	4.65	9.98	12.66	13.81	0.1	0.61	0.66	0.73	52	33	43	★★★★	3.5
Gabelli Value	MV		16.43	5.36	8.60	18.53	17.21	0.3	0.63	0.64	0.81	60	9	13	★★★★★	3.6
Gabelli Westwood Balanced Ret	DH		10.99	-3.26	5.14	9.67	11.93	2.2	0.41	0.44	0.47	19	18	7	★★★★	4.2
Galaxy Small Cap Value Ret A	SB		14.33	18.29	15.07	13.53	—	0.1	0.50	0.68	—	24	27	—	★★★★	3.3
John Hancock Financial Industries A	SF		16.52	-17.86	1.95	8.90	—	0.0	1.04	1.04	—	75	85	—	★★★	2.6
John Hancock Small Cap Growth B	SG		8.77	-14.85	2.79	6.78	11.35	0.0	1.76	1.75	1.78	77	62	42	★★	3.4
John Hancock Small Cap Value B	SG		19.90	10.20	26.42	19.57	—	0.0	1.30	1.31	—	5	6	—	★★★★★	3.1
Harbor Capital Appreciation	LG		29.23	-17.74	-0.15	12.35	14.19	0.1	1.29	1.22	1.28	28	15	5	★★★★	4.2
Harbor Large Cap Value	LV		14.39	4.10	6.27	11.47	12.61	1.4	0.76	0.80	0.82	18	20	40	★★★★	3.0
Heartland Value	SV		37.25	29.45	18.19	12.49	17.15	0.0	0.65	0.81	0.84	16	37	10	★★★★★	3.4
Homestead Value	MV		25.50	5.90	3.97	9.05	12.71	1.2	0.73	0.72	0.73	88	72	63	★★★★	3.7
Wayne Hummer Growth	LG		36.56	-6.78	7.40	13.66	11.58	0.2	0.77	0.76	0.78	4	11	24	★★★★	3.3
ICAP Equity	LV		43.01	-0.61	7.62	12.39	—	0.9	0.63	0.71	—	10	13	—	★★★★	4.1
ICAP Select Equity	LV		28.50	-1.66	11.04	—	—	0.5	0.64	—	—	3	—	—	★★★★	4.5
ICM/Isabelle Small Cap Value Invmt	SV		11.83	8.83	20.57	—	—	0.0	0.76	—	—	14	—	—	★★★★★	4.7
INVESCO Balanced Inv	DH		14.63	-11.54	0.48	7.31	—	2.0	0.72	0.65	—	73	50	—	★★★	4.0
INVESCO Dynamics Inv	MG		15.93	-32.89	2.07	10.29	13.09	0.0	1.73	1.57	1.52	66	41	20	★★★	2.9
INVESCO Financial Services Inv	SF		27.27	-10.17	4.66	13.49	17.10	0.4	1.02	1.04	1.04	57	40	61	★★★★	4.5
INVESCO Growth Inv	LG		2.60	-49.07	-18.74	-0.66	5.31	0.0	2.33	1.90	1.71	100	96	95	★	2.8
INVESCO Small Company Growth Inv	SG		12.14	-20.91	8.05	11.39	14.03	0.0	1.68	1.64	1.69	52	34	8	★★★	2.7
INVESCO Telecommunications Inv	SC		16.62	-54.19	-6.48	8.48	—	0.0	2.25	1.92	—	36	64	—	★★	4.3
INVESCO Total Return Inv	DH		25.01	-0.93	-1.99	5.99	9.43	1.7	0.61	0.58	0.57	92	72	48	★★★	3.7
Janus	LG		24.60	-26.10	-2.56	9.53	11.09	0.0	1.33	1.18	1.09	50	39	34	★★★	4.5
Janus Balanced	DH		19.63	-5.04	4.69	12.89	—	2.7	0.55	0.54	—	23	3	—	★★★★★	4.1
Janus Enterprise	MG		32.00	-39.93	-2.52	6.54	—	0.0	1.97	1.76	—	82	66	—	★★	3.2
Janus Global Life Sciences	SH		17.57	-18.09	20.70	—	—	0.0	1.24	—	—	26	—	—	★★★★★	5.0
Janus Global Technology	ST		12.14	-39.96	7.68	—	—	0.0	2.10	—	—	17	—	—	★★★	3.0
Janus Growth & Income	LG		29.97	-14.36	4.67	15.81	14.36	1.0	0.94	0.92	1.00	8	4	4	★★★★	3.9
Janus Mercury	LG		20.79	-29.78	2.10	13.54	—	0.2	1.45	1.35	—	16	11	—	★★★★	4.2
Janus Olympus	LG		27.85	-32.05	2.14	16.21	—	0.4	1.59	1.43	—	16	3	—	★★★★	4.8
Janus Special Situations	MB		14.85	-16.00	1.84	14.08	—	0.1	1.22	1.12	—	68	21	—	★★★★	4.1
Janus Twenty	LG		38.46	-29.20	-7.59	12.15	11.76	0.9	1.63	1.40	1.43	80	17	22	★★	3.9
Janus Venture	SG		43.98	-11.93	4.76	9.79	10.41	0.0	2.14	1.88	1.72	72	42	57	★★	4.0
Legg Mason American Leading Co Prim	LV		18.49	-3.30	0.76	8.96	—	0.0	0.86	0.87	—	64	49	—	★★★	3.3
Legg Mason Special Investment Prim	MB		33.73	2.26	6.84	12.93	13.68	0.0	1.02	1.11	1.24	47	28	38	★★★★	3.2
Legg Mason Value Prim	LV		50.06	-9.29	2.20	16.71	18.16	0.0	0.98	0.95	0.97	48	1	1	★★★★★	3.6
Liberty Acorn Z	SG		17.88	6.14	15.93	15.60	16.61	0.2	0.69	0.80	0.88	21	16	2	★★★★★	4.2
Liberty Acorn Twenty Z	MG		15.23	8.00	15.97	—	—	0.0	0.71	—	—	10	—	—	★★★★★	5.0
Liberty Acorn USA Z	SB		17.52	19.25	10.12	13.32	—	0.0	0.82	0.87	—	50	29	—	★★★★	3.0
LKCM Small Cap Equity	SB		17.29	7.50	11.83	10.04	—	0.4	0.60	0.78	—	38	58	—	★★★★	2.9
Longleaf Partners	MV		24.51	10.34	10.79	14.79	17.31	0.8	0.69	0.72	0.69	48	24	10	★★★★★	4.3
Longleaf Partners Small-Cap	SV		21.68	5.45	7.36	12.47	13.98	1.0	0.64	0.60	0.67	79	39	37	★★★★★	3.0
Lord Abbett Affiliated A	LV		13.69	-7.94	7.43	12.17	14.03	1.7	0.66	0.72	0.72	11	15	17	★★★★	3.3
Lord Abbett Growth Opportunities A	MG		18.22	-12.53	9.95	14.55	—	0.0	1.09	1.04	—	25	15	—	★★★★	4.3
MainStay Convertible B	CV	—	11.59	-4.76	10.47	8.45	11.06	2.4	0.57	0.58	0.59	17	51	35	★★★★	3.4
MainStay MAP Equity I	MB		27.75	2.33	10.31	16.36	15.76	0.2	0.60	0.59	0.56	18	10	16	★★★★★	4.0
Mairs & Power Growth	MB		54.36	6.48	13.01	15.22	17.29	0.9	0.47	0.60	0.68	10	14	6	★★★★★	3.8
Managers Special Equity	SG		70.60	-8.07	11.34	11.47	14.41	0.0	1.27	1.26	1.25	34	32	6	★★★★	3.6

Bold numbers indicate *highest* return for the listed time period in each category.

Stock Funds—U.S. Equity

	Cat	Style Box	NAV	Total Return % through 12-31-01 1Yr	Annualized 3Yr	Annualized 5Yr	Annualized 10Yr	Trailing 12 Mo Yield %	Morningstar Risk 1.00=U.S. Equity Avg 3Yr	Morningstar Risk 5Yr	Morningstar Risk 10Yr	Rtn % Rank Cat 3Yr	Rtn % Rank Cat 5Yr	Rtn % Rank Cat 10Yr	Star Rating	Avg Star Rating
S&P 500				**-11.88**	**-1.03**	**10.70**	**12.93**									
Marsico Focus	LG		13.60	-20.81	0.31	—	—	0.0	1.31	—	—	24	—	—	★★	3.4
Meridian Value	SB		32.42	11.70	28.43	25.05	—	0.1	0.39	0.60	—	2	1	—	★★★★★	4.2
Merrill Lynch Basic Value A	LV		29.28	-0.51	4.46	10.51	13.51	1.2	0.67	0.69	0.70	29	31	25	★★★★	3.6
Metropolitan West AlphaTrak 500	LB	—	8.12	-9.36	0.38	—	—	5.9	0.92	—	—	32	—	—	★★★	3.0
MFS Capital Opportunities A	LB		13.43	-24.93	1.65	11.05	15.15	0.0	1.26	1.10	1.07	22	20	2	★★★	3.2
MFS Massachusetts Investors A	LB		16.58	-16.24	-3.71	7.65	11.48	1.2	0.82	0.82	0.82	83	71	55	★★★	3.4
MFS Massachusetts Investors Gr Stk A	LB		12.89	-24.80	-1.07	14.96	13.66	0.0	1.14	1.05	1.20	48	4	14	★★★	2.7
MFS Total Return A	DH		14.48	-0.63	6.56	10.31	11.35	3.2	0.38	0.39	0.43	9	12	14	★★★★	3.6
MFS Utilities A	SU		8.72	-25.02	1.91	10.40	—	2.4	0.73	0.68	—	32	24	—	★★★	3.9
Morgan Stanley American Opp B	LG		23.56	-27.30	-1.46	10.53	11.54	0.0	1.14	1.05	1.17	40	31	27	★★★	3.5
Morgan Stan Inst Mid Cap Growth	MG		17.45	-29.61	3.13	14.94	14.09	0.0	1.53	1.48	1.62	63	13	13	★★★	3.3
Morgan Stan Inst Mid Cap Value	MB		20.31	-3.38	9.03	15.99	—	0.1	0.90	0.93	—	29	11	—	★★★★★	4.7
Morgan Stan Inst Small Cap Growth	SG		29.59	-20.56	**38.63**	—	—	0.0	1.62	—	—	2	—	—	★★★★★	5.0
Morgan Stan Inst U.S. Real Estate A	SR		14.63	9.27	11.75	9.33	—	3.8	0.51	0.63	—	23	7	—	★★★★	3.2
Morgan Stanley Strategist B	DH		15.81	-11.06	3.24	8.01	9.13	1.7	0.61	0.63	0.67	36	38	53	★★★	3.1
Muhlenkamp	MV		53.56	9.35	15.14	16.00	16.51	0.0	0.93	0.97	0.96	21	19	17	★★★★★	3.5
Mutual Beacon Z	MV		13.05	6.11	12.32	12.28	15.81	1.4	0.46	0.54	0.53	35	43	21	★★★★★	4.5
Mutual Qualified Z	MV		16.49	8.21	12.00	12.01	15.72	1.1	0.49	0.57	0.56	37	46	28	★★★★★	4.6
Mutual Shares Z	MV		19.44	6.32	11.65	12.06	15.51	1.2	0.51	0.57	0.58	40	45	32	★★★★★	4.6
Nations Blue Chip Inv A	LB		25.85	-15.85	-2.57	9.43	—	0.0	0.96	0.94	—	73	50	—	★★★	4.0
Neuberger Berman Genesis Inv	SB		20.33	12.11	15.62	14.17	15.28	0.0	0.55	0.75	0.80	18	19	18	★★★★★	3.2
Neuberger Berman Partners Inv	LV		20.79	-3.02	1.68	7.63	12.74	0.4	0.87	0.88	0.90	53	64	38	★★★★	4.1
Nicholas II	MG		20.09	-3.11	-1.36	7.51	9.99	0.0	1.01	0.97	1.00	78	61	54	★★★	3.2
Northern Technology	ST		12.47	-34.47	-1.83	15.10	—	0.0	2.39	2.13	—	48	17	—	★★★	4.7
Oak Value	MB		29.08	-0.47	4.45	13.29	—	0.0	0.78	0.80	—	58	26	—	★★★★	4.2
Oakmark I	MV		35.27	18.29	5.79	10.24	17.71	0.6	0.77	0.80	0.75	77	66	8	★★★★★	3.9
Oakmark Select I	MV		27.24	26.06	22.00	**26.75**	—	0.2	0.52	0.69	—	3	1	—	★★★★★	4.4
Oakmark Small Cap I	SV		17.29	26.30	6.68	8.18	—	0.0	0.78	0.94	—	82	77	—	★★★	2.0
One Group Large Cap Growth A	LG		15.99	-20.57	-8.44	7.95	—	0.0	1.39	1.21	—	84	56	—	★★	3.6
Oppenheimer Capital Income A	DH		11.89	-0.19	3.02	9.36	11.07	3.9	0.63	0.63	0.64	39	22	16	★★★	3.3
Oppenheimer Main St Growth & Income A	LB		32.50	-10.46	-1.17	8.88	15.00	0.2	0.86	0.85	0.90	49	57	4	★★★	4.4
Pax World Balanced	DH		19.91	-9.09	4.04	11.92	9.85	2.4	0.45	0.43	0.52	28	5	38	★★★★	3.4
Pioneer A	LV		38.91	-11.04	0.96	12.96	13.68	0.4	0.73	0.74	0.73	62	11	21	★★★★	3.0
T. Rowe Price Balanced	DH		17.49	-3.98	2.63	8.32	9.82	2.9	0.49	0.50	0.52	44	34	39	★★★	3.5
T. Rowe Price Blue Chip Growth	LB		28.97	-14.42	0.03	10.47	—	0.0	0.97	0.93	—	36	28	—	★★★★	4.8
T. Rowe Price Dividend Growth	LV		20.79	-3.64	1.01	9.17	—	1.3	0.63	0.63	—	62	46	—	★★★	4.3
T. Rowe Price Equity-Income	LV		23.65	1.64	6.08	10.93	13.96	1.5	0.64	0.65	0.61	19	28	18	★★★★★	4.1
T. Rowe Price Growth Stock	LB		24.18	-9.79	3.38	12.25	13.38	0.3	0.94	0.92	0.89	14	10	17	★★★★	3.3
T. Rowe Price Mid-Cap Growth	MG		39.40	-0.98	9.60	13.71	—	0.0	0.95	1.00	—	27	19	—	★★★★	4.4
T. Rowe Price Mid-Cap Value	MV		16.40	14.36	13.27	13.37	—	0.7	0.52	0.62	—	30	35	—	★★★★★	3.2
T. Rowe Price New America Growth	LB		30.87	-11.89	-3.85	4.88	10.13	0.0	1.25	1.24	1.29	84	91	72	★★	3.2
T. Rowe Price New Era	SN		22.24	-4.35	11.75	6.89	10.00	1.2	0.78	1.00	0.97	59	16	37	★★★	2.7
T. Rowe Price New Horizons	SG		22.63	-2.84	8.11	8.07	13.75	0.0	1.43	1.48	1.49	51	55	13	★★★	2.3
T. Rowe Price Science & Tech	ST		20.92	-41.19	-8.03	2.41	13.08	0.0	2.36	2.20	2.07	73	78	81	★★	4.4
T. Rowe Price Small-Cap Stock	SB		25.34	6.81	12.58	12.15	14.52	0.4	0.76	0.85	0.89	33	37	31	★★★★	2.9
T. Rowe Price Small-Cap Value	SV		22.66	21.94	13.91	10.60	14.63	0.7	0.51	0.66	0.67	41	54	34	★★★★★	3.8
T. Rowe Price Value	MV		18.88	1.60	8.68	12.13	—	0.9	0.71	0.75	—	60	45	—	★★★★	4.0
Prudential Value A	MV		15.95	-2.89	7.65	10.57	12.50	0.6	0.84	0.90	0.86	64	62	67	★★★	3.3
Putnam Capital Appreciation A	LB		16.86	-15.45	-2.19	5.70	—	0.0	1.12	1.06	—	68	87	—	★★	3.6
Putnam Capital Opportunities A	MG		10.33	-2.08	14.90	—	—	0.0	1.31	—	—	12	—	—	★★★★	4.0
Putnam Fund for Growth & Income A	LV		17.72	-6.37	0.77	7.92	12.00	1.6	0.75	0.78	0.75	64	61	49	★★★	3.8
George Putnam Fund of Boston A	DH		16.74	0.51	3.22	8.04	10.26	3.1	0.45	0.48	0.51	37	37	33	★★★	3.1
Putnam Investors A	LG		11.55	-24.80	-7.26	7.77	11.57	0.0	1.24	1.15	1.10	79	58	25	★★	2.9
Putnam OTC Emerging Growth A	MG		7.50	-46.12	-15.85	-6.13	6.11	0.0	2.90	2.59	2.41	100	97	90	★	2.8
Putnam Vista A	MG		8.64	-33.64	-0.81	7.53	12.55	0.0	1.69	1.58	1.47	75	61	26	★★	3.4

Bold numbers indicate *highest* return for the listed time period in each category.

Stock Funds—U.S. Equity

	Cat	Style Box	NAV	Total Return % through 12-31-01 1Yr	Annualized 3Yr	5Yr	10Yr	Trailing 12 Mo Yield %	Morningstar Risk 1.00=U.S. Equity Avg 3Yr	5Yr	10Yr	Rtn % Rank Cat 3Yr	5Yr	10Yr	Star Rating	Avg Star Rating
S&P 500				**-11.88**	**-1.03**	**10.70**	**12.93**									
Putnam Voyager A	LG		17.30	-22.46	0.25	9.50	12.50	0.2	1.23	1.21	1.24	25	40	16	★★★	3.7
Quaker Aggressive Growth A	LG		17.96	-8.06	27.87	26.64	—	0.2	0.43	0.55	—	1	1	—	★★★★★	5.0
Red Oak Technology Select	ST		9.59	-55.97	-1.39	—	—	0.0	2.83	—	—	47	—	—	★	1.0
Royce Premier	SB		10.54	9.61	12.70	12.59	13.61	0.0	0.70	0.73	0.66	33	34	46	★★★★	3.5
Royce Total Return	SV		8.59	14.78	11.66	12.52	—	1.2	0.50	0.51	—	57	35	—	★★★★	4.1
RS Diversified Growth	SG		23.26	1.88	23.05	22.90	—	0.0	1.72	1.62	—	10	4	—	★★★★★	5.0
RS Emerging Growth	MG		32.01	-27.28	15.49	18.51	14.45	0.0	2.12	1.98	2.11	12	6	11	★★★	3.2
SAFECO Growth Opportunities	SB		27.25	22.03	6.28	13.44	12.99	0.0	1.23	1.24	1.47	86	28	65	★★★	2.5
Salomon Brothers Capital O	MV		25.27	2.00	14.49	18.69	16.13	1.1	0.58	0.65	0.85	24	6	19	★★★★★	2.9
Salomon Brothers Investors Value O	LV		18.94	-4.17	7.25	12.49	14.56	1.0	0.73	0.76	0.78	12	13	10	★★★★★	3.5
Schwab 1000 Inv	LB		31.95	-12.26	-0.86	10.33	12.43	0.9	0.93	0.90	0.89	45	32	32	★★★★	4.0
Schwab Small Cap Index Inv	SB		17.50	-0.90	8.49	9.12	—	0.5	0.99	1.10	—	65	67	—	★★★	2.1
Scudder Growth & Income S	LB		21.06	-12.04	-3.06	4.72	10.12	0.9	0.83	0.83	0.80	77	92	73	★★★	3.9
Scudder Total Return A	DH		9.10	-6.79	1.27	7.48	8.10	2.5	0.59	0.61	0.71	63	47	69	★★★	2.9
Security Capital U.S. Real Estate	SR		12.16	7.04	13.51	10.02	—	4.6	0.53	0.66	—	4	4	—	★★★★	3.0
Selected American	LV		30.99	-11.17	5.33	13.28	13.76	0.5	0.71	0.81	0.88	23	8	20	★★★★	4.0
Skyline Special Equities	SV		22.50	13.92	7.06	9.06	14.75	0.0	0.80	0.85	0.87	80	69	31	★★★★	4.0
Sound Shore	MV		30.58	-0.81	6.05	11.18	14.87	0.3	0.65	0.73	0.71	75	56	36	★★★★★	3.8
State Street Research Aurora A	SV		32.35	15.83	28.45	21.38	—	0.0	0.49	0.70	—	3	3	—	★★★★★	4.1
Strong Advisor Common Stock Z	MB		19.78	-1.70	10.88	12.50	15.77	0.0	0.91	0.94	0.94	13	30	12	★★★★★	4.5
Strong Growth Inv	LG		17.68	-34.39	1.40	9.52	—	0.0	1.53	1.45	—	19	40	—	★★★	3.5
Strong Opportunity Inv	MV		39.29	-4.80	11.30	14.47	15.80	0.2	0.75	0.78	0.82	41	26	23	★★★★★	3.8
Strong U.S. Emerging Growth	SG		15.17	-20.87	16.43	—	—	0.0	1.86	—	—	19	—	—	★★★★	4.0
SunAmerica Focus Growth A	LG		16.20	-14.29	3.22	—	—	0.0	1.18	—	—	11	—	—	★★★	3.0
Third Avenue Real Estate Value	SR		15.78	18.20	17.62	—	—	1.2	0.32	—	—	1	—	—	★★★★★	5.0
Third Avenue Value	SV		36.43	2.82	11.89	12.51	15.65	1.7	0.57	0.66	0.65	55	36	20	★★★★★	4.3
Thornburg Value A	LB		28.73	-8.11	9.50	16.50	—	0.4	0.69	0.74	—	2	1	—	★★★★★	4.8
TIAA-CREF Growth & Income	LB		12.07	-13.37	-0.03	—	—	0.8	0.93	—	—	36	—	—	★★★	3.4
TIAA-CREF Growth Equity	LG		9.85	-23.02	-6.55	—	—	0.0	1.43	—	—	74	—	—	★	2.4
TIAA-CREF Managed Allocation	DH	—	10.50	-8.52	1.20	—	—	2.6	0.67	—	—	63	—	—	★★★	3.5
Torray	LV		37.53	-0.52	6.03	12.08	16.31	0.5	0.88	0.93	0.87	20	16	3	★★★★★	4.5
Tweedy, Browne American Value	MV		23.42	-0.08	5.27	12.16	—	0.3	0.54	0.61	—	82	44	—	★★★★	4.3
UAM FMA Small Company Instl	SB		18.51	4.63	6.81	10.88	13.19	0.4	0.68	0.73	0.92	81	51	59	★★★★	3.1
UAM ICM Small Company	SV		25.87	19.05	12.98	13.80	16.87	0.8	0.63	0.68	0.71	48	23	13	★★★★★	4.3
USAA Aggressive Growth	MG		28.50	-33.38	0.63	6.02	8.70	0.0	2.01	1.97	2.05	70	67	70	★	1.4
USAA Cornerstone Strategy	LV		23.38	-3.01	2.52	4.92	8.73	4.2	0.51	0.54	0.58	46	90	91	★★★	3.3
USAA Income Stock	LV		16.83	-4.18	2.85	8.36	10.54	2.5	0.68	0.68	0.70	42	55	76	★★★	3.7
Van Kampen Aggressive Growth A	MG		13.40	-39.70	6.09	12.95	—	0.0	1.81	1.80	—	48	24	—	★★★	4.3
Van Kampen American Value A	MB		18.83	-2.79	2.91	10.27	—	0.0	1.14	1.07	—	65	45	—	★★★	3.0
Van Kampen Comstock A	LV		15.68	-1.79	9.87	15.66	14.46	1.4	0.67	0.68	0.73	4	3	11	★★★★	3.2
Van Kampen Emerging Growth A	LG		42.32	-32.59	6.77	14.75	15.66	0.0	1.57	1.51	1.58	5	7	2	★★★	3.2
Van Kampen Growth & Income A	LV		17.01	-6.06	8.01	13.19	14.06	1.2	0.56	0.63	0.67	7	9	16	★★★★	3.0
Van Wagoner Post-Venture	MG		10.04	-62.14	-3.82	1.45	—	0.0	3.09	2.93	—	86	87	—	★	3.7
Vanguard Asset Allocation	DH		21.81	-5.30	1.49	10.79	11.85	2.8	0.55	0.53	0.59	60	10	8	★★★★	4.0
Vanguard Balanced Index	DH		17.86	-3.02	2.58	9.23	—	3.3	0.58	0.57	—	44	24	—	★★★★	3.4
Vanguard Capital Opportunity	MB		23.61	-9.68	28.23	20.70	—	0.3	0.96	1.15	—	1	2	—	★★★★★	3.9
Vanguard Energy	SN		25.29	-2.55	17.17	7.99	12.53	1.5	0.89	1.16	1.28	27	11	6	★★★	2.7
Vanguard Equity-Income	LV		22.71	-2.34	3.45	11.25	12.96	2.2	0.65	0.65	0.66	35	25	33	★★★★	3.3
Vanguard Explorer	SG		60.32	0.56	14.66	12.32	12.97	0.2	1.13	1.22	1.25	25	27	20	★★★★	2.2
Vanguard Extended Market Idx	MB		23.09	-9.17	1.49	7.49	11.07	0.9	1.36	1.29	1.24	73	69	64	★★	2.9
Vanguard 500 Index	LB		105.89	-12.02	-1.06	10.66	12.84	1.2	0.91	0.89	0.87	47	24	22	★★★★	4.1
Vanguard Growth & Income	LV		28.20	-11.13	0.65	11.37	13.25	1.1	0.90	0.90	0.90	66	22	27	★★★★	4.0
Vanguard Growth Equity	LG		9.64	-24.24	-3.64	10.17	—	1.2	1.59	1.41	—	57	34	—	★★★	3.3
Vanguard Growth Index	LG		26.42	-12.93	-4.46	11.08	—	0.7	1.18	1.06	—	62	26	—	★★★	4.5
Vanguard Health Care	SH		116.84	-6.87	16.97	23.47	19.81	0.8	0.39	0.46	0.66	43	3	9	★★★★★	4.8

Bold numbers indicate *highest* return for the listed time period in each category.

Stock Funds—U.S. Equity

	Cat	Style Box	NAV	Total Return % through 12-31-01 1Yr	Annualized 3Yr	5Yr	10Yr	Trailing 12 Mo Yield %	Morningstar Risk 1.00=U.S. Equity Avg 3Yr	5Yr	10Yr	Rtn % Rank Cat 3Yr	5Yr	10Yr	Star Rating	Avg Star Rating
S&P 500				**-11.88**	**-1.03**	**10.70**	**12.93**									
Vanguard LifeStrategy Conserv Growth	DH	—	14.06	-0.08	3.58	8.51	—	4.1	0.37	0.37	—	34	30	—	★★★★	3.1
Vanguard LifeStrategy Growth	LB	—	17.43	-8.86	0.37	8.46	—	2.1	0.75	0.73	—	32	62	—	★★★	3.4
Vanguard LifeStrategy Income	DH	—	12.86	4.06	4.96	8.37	—	5.0	0.20	0.20	—	20	33	—	★★★★	3.1
Vanguard LifeStrategy Moderate Growth	DH	—	15.93	-4.48	1.98	8.62	—	3.1	0.56	0.55	—	54	29	—	★★★	3.3
Vanguard Mid Capitalization Index	MB		11.81	-0.50	10.73	—	—	0.6	0.84	—	—	16	—	—	★★★★	4.9
Vanguard Morgan Growth	LB		14.63	-13.60	0.45	10.14	12.13	0.5	1.15	1.11	1.10	31	37	41	★★★	3.2
Vanguard Precious Metals	SP		8.55	18.33	12.20	-3.68	1.48	4.6	1.06	1.54	1.66	1	1	6	★★★	2.2
Vanguard Primecap	LB		51.52	-13.35	8.56	17.03	17.56	0.5	0.96	0.94	1.00	3	1	1	★★★★★	3.8
Vanguard Small Cap Growth Index	SG		10.87	-0.78	6.49	—	—	0.1	1.14	—	—	62	—	—	★★★	3.1
Vanguard Small Cap Index	SB		19.82	3.10	7.31	8.44	12.27	1.1	1.09	1.15	1.19	76	72	78	★★★	1.7
Vanguard Small Cap Value Index	SV		10.29	13.55	12.67	—	—	0.6	0.74	—	—	49	—	—	★★★★	3.9
Vanguard STAR	DH	—	16.44	0.50	6.11	10.22	11.50	3.2	0.43	0.48	0.50	12	14	13	★★★★	3.6
Vanguard Strategic Equity	MV		15.23	5.42	10.55	11.40	—	0.9	0.65	0.86	—	50	54	—	★★★★	2.6
Vanguard Tax-Managed Capital App	LG		25.73	-15.34	0.53	10.59	—	0.7	1.09	1.07	—	23	30	—	★★★	3.7
Vanguard Tax-Managed Growth & Inc	LB		24.93	-11.93	-1.00	10.73	—	1.2	0.91	0.89	—	47	23	—	★★★	4.5
Vanguard Total Stock Mkt Idx	LB		25.74	-10.97	-0.48	9.74	—	1.2	0.97	0.95	—	41	45	—	★★★	3.9
Vanguard U.S. Growth	LG		18.85	-31.70	-12.64	3.28	7.99	0.2	1.60	1.36	1.25	95	86	82	★★	3.4
Vanguard Value Index	LV		18.90	-11.98	1.68	9.35	—	1.6	0.82	0.84	—	54	44	—	★★★	3.9
Vanguard Wellesley Income	DH		19.91	7.39	6.15	9.96	10.44	4.8	0.24	0.25	0.35	11	16	29	★★★★	4.0
Vanguard Wellington	DH		27.26	0.67	5.08	9.89	11.68	3.5	0.47	0.49	0.54	20	16	11	★★★★	3.9
Vanguard Windsor	LV		15.64	5.72	10.98	10.95	14.40	1.2	0.70	0.83	0.84	3	28	11	★★★★	3.8
Vanguard Windsor II	LV		25.59	-3.40	2.07	10.37	13.51	2.1	0.75	0.77	0.77	50	32	24	★★★★	3.9
Wachovia Special Values A	SV		19.75	18.13	13.11	12.97	—	0.5	0.43	0.56	—	47	27	—	★★★★	3.8
Wasatch Core Growth	SB		34.60	28.82	28.31	22.30	18.26	0.0	0.73	0.82	0.97	3	2	1	★★★★★	3.4
Weitz Partners Value	MV		20.87	-0.86	13.57	21.61	18.93	1.0	0.48	0.49	0.59	27	3	1	★★★★★	4.6
Weitz Hickory	MV		26.26	-4.65	2.55	14.83	—	0.0	1.12	1.01	—	92	23	—	★★★★	4.3
Weitz Value	MV		34.29	0.24	13.20	21.04	18.03	1.0	0.51	0.50	0.58	31	5	4	★★★★★	4.3
Westport Small Cap R	SB		19.45	8.22	20.61	—	—	0.0	0.70	—	—	10	—	—	★★★★★	5.0
White Oak Growth Stock	LG		38.44	-39.05	-1.77	10.45	—	0.0	1.66	1.58	—	43	32	—	★★★	4.6
Wilshire Target Large Co Growth Invmt	LG		30.21	-16.59	-1.93	11.90	—	0.0	1.18	1.06	—	44	18	—	★★★	4.4
WM Growth Fund of the Northwest A	SB		30.96	6.34	17.29	21.40	15.64	0.2	1.05	1.12	1.19	14	3	12	★★★★★	3.1

Stock Funds—International

	Cat	Style Box	NAV	Total Return % through 12-31-01 1Yr	Annualized 3Yr	5Yr	10Yr	Trailing 12 Mo Yield %	Morningstar Risk 1.00=U.S. Equity Avg 3Yr	5Yr	10Yr	Rtn % Rank Cat 3Yr	5Yr	10Yr	Star Rating	Avg Star Rating
MSCI EAFE				**-22.61**	**-6.32**	**-0.52**	**2.88**									
AIM European Development A	ES		17.30	-24.72	6.65	—	—	0.0	1.08	—	—	10	—	—	★★★★	4.3
AIM International Equity A	FS		14.90	-22.36	-3.64	1.41	—	0.0	1.08	0.92	—	59	57	—	★★★	3.6
American Century Global Growth Inv	WS		6.32	-25.65	9.25	—	—	0.0	0.97	—	—	18	—	—	★★★★	4.5
American Century Intl Discovery Inv	FS		10.24	-21.77	8.16	11.87	—	0.0	1.13	0.97	—	8	5	—	★★★★★	5.0
American Century Intl Growth Inv	FS		7.97	-26.79	0.77	7.83	10.27	0.4	1.03	0.90	0.85	26	11	6	★★★★	4.1
American Funds Capital Inc Builder A	IH		43.59	4.74	4.65	9.57	11.16	4.7	0.33	0.33	0.35	20	7	16	★★★★★	3.7
American Funds Capital World Gr&Inc A	WS		24.50	-4.96	7.04	10.96	—	2.0	0.54	0.52	—	20	14	—	★★★★★	4.7
American Funds EuroPacific Growth A	FS		26.87	-12.18	4.24	7.40	10.38	2.4	0.77	0.70	0.68	14	12	5	★★★★	4.2
American Funds New Perspective A	WS		21.69	-8.30	6.01	11.98	12.95	1.7	0.72	0.64	0.62	21	10	6	★★★★★	4.1
Artisan International	FS		18.36	-15.86	10.90	13.28	—	0.4	0.87	0.85	—	5	3	—	★★★★★	5.0
Bernstein Tax-Managed Intl Value	FS		15.90	-12.52	0.64	4.33	—	1.8	0.61	0.62	—	27	24	—	★★★★	3.6
CS Warburg Pincus Japan Growth Comm	JS		5.21	-25.14	-4.99	-2.48	—	0.0	2.24	1.77	—	62	28	—	★★	3.3
Deutsche International Equity Invm	FS		18.87	-25.39	-7.65	2.23	—	0.1	1.04	0.88	—	90	44	—	★★★	4.5
Dreyfus Emerging Markets	EM		11.34	7.70	14.51	3.92	—	1.4	0.87	1.10	—	3	4	—	★★★★	2.9
Fidelity Diversified International	FS		19.08	-12.99	6.07	9.20	10.10	0.1	0.72	0.65	0.73	12	9	8	★★★★	4.3

Bold numbers indicate *highest* return for the listed time period in each category.

Stock Funds—International

	Cat	Style Box	NAV	Total Return % through 12-31-01 1Yr	Annualized 3Yr	5Yr	10Yr	Trailing 12 Mo Yield %	Morningstar Risk 1.00=U.S. Equity Avg 3Yr	5Yr	10Yr	Rtn % Rank Cat 3Yr	5Yr	10Yr	Star Rating	Avg Star Rating
MSCI EAFE			—	—	—	—	—									
Fidelity Europe	ES		24.76	-16.03	-3.25	6.09	10.21	1.0	0.98	0.81	0.78	49	34	26	★★★★	3.7
Fidelity Latin America	LS		12.01	-6.04	6.30	-0.32	—	2.1	1.41	1.58	—	65	72	—	★★★	1.9
Fidelity Overseas	FS		27.42	-20.22	-2.35	3.11	6.08	0.0	0.94	0.82	0.86	50	36	52	★★★	3.4
Fidelity Pacific Basin	DP		13.85	-19.90	4.40	0.90	3.46	0.0	1.15	1.15	1.20	20	12	20	★★★	2.3
Fidelity Worldwide	WS		14.66	-6.21	4.11	6.27	9.92	0.0	0.71	0.73	0.69	29	46	36	★★★★	4.0
First Eagle SoGen Global A	IH		23.82	10.21	13.08	9.37	11.14	2.6	0.29	0.35	0.32	2	12	33	★★★★★	4.2
Harbor International	FS		29.63	-12.25	1.09	5.66	10.88	0.9	0.68	0.70	0.73	24	17	3	★★★★	4.7
Hartford Global Leaders A	WS		14.00	-17.33	4.22	—	—	0.0	0.90	—	—	28	—	—	★★★★	4.0
IDEX Janus Global A	WS		25.73	-23.54	0.91	9.09	—	0.0	1.12	0.90	—	45	23	—	★★★★	4.8
Janus Overseas	FS		20.30	-23.11	5.23	9.83	—	0.5	1.19	0.99	—	12	7	—	★★★★★	4.9
Janus Worldwide	WS		43.84	-22.88	1.76	9.83	13.57	0.0	1.10	0.89	0.80	39	20	3	★★★★★	5.0
Japan S	JS		6.63	-33.63	2.00	2.47	0.36	0.0	1.21	1.17	1.43	10	4	1	★★★	3.2
Lazard International Equity Instl	FS		10.01	-24.85	-5.87	1.60	5.68	0.0	0.79	0.74	0.80	78	55	56	★★★	3.4
Liberty Acorn Foreign Forty Z	FS		12.09	-29.05	3.74	—	—	0.1	1.20	—	—	16	—	—	★★★★	4.0
Liberty Acorn International Z	FS		18.47	-21.15	4.18	5.51	—	0.0	1.02	0.88	—	14	17	—	★★★★	4.0
Liberty Newport Tiger A	PJ		9.38	-16.55	6.75	-6.72	—	0.9	1.16	1.61	—	35	42	—	★★	1.6
Longleaf Partners International	FS		12.34	**10.47**	**20.05**	—	—	1.0	0.41	—	—	2	—	—	★★★★★	5.0
Matthews Pacific Tiger	PJ		8.81	7.91	14.87	-2.74	—	0.1	1.22	1.63	—	10	17	—	★★★	2.0
Merrill Lynch Global Allocation B	IH		12.61	1.01	11.26	8.64	10.64	3.1	0.36	0.40	0.36	10	17	50	★★★★★	4.6
Merrill Lynch Global Value D	WS		10.83	-13.92	-1.61	8.35	—	0.0	0.76	0.63	—	70	29	—	★★★★	3.9
Merrill Lynch Pacific B	DP		15.60	-14.57	4.07	2.31	4.49	2.8	0.93	0.97	1.02	22	6	10	★★★	2.9
MFS Global Equity B	WS		18.51	-10.88	-0.53	5.76	9.99	0.0	0.71	0.66	0.64	61	50	30	★★★★	3.8
MFS Global Total Return A	IH		11.76	-6.82	0.55	5.73	8.55	1.4	0.43	0.38	0.39	62	46	66	★★★★	3.8
Morgan Stan Inst International Eq A	FS		15.59	-9.74	4.87	9.23	12.76	2.1	0.51	0.50	0.58	13	8	1	★★★★★	4.4
Mutual Discovery Z	WS		18.19	1.26	13.07	11.76	—	1.8	0.29	0.38	—	7	11	—	★★★★★	4.9
Oppenheimer Global Growth & Income A	WS		22.59	-16.32	14.35	**16.69**	**13.83**	0.1	1.10	0.92	0.83	4	1	1	★★★★★	4.0
Oppenheimer Quest Global Value A	WS		14.91	-14.06	3.16	7.16	10.11	0.0	0.56	0.55	0.53	35	37	27	★★★★	3.8
Pioneer Emerging Markets A	EM		10.24	-8.33	5.10	-2.84	—	0.0	1.28	1.42	—	37	22	—	★★	2.2
T. Rowe Price European Stock	ES		16.01	-20.65	-3.93	5.47	9.61	2.2	0.83	0.70	0.71	55	43	42	★★★★	3.9
T. Rowe Price International Stock	FS		10.99	-22.02	-4.53	0.75	6.05	2.7	0.97	0.85	0.85	66	66	53	★★★	3.9
T. Rowe Price New Asia	PJ		6.21	-10.00	7.58	-7.00	2.79	0.0	1.22	1.46	1.43	26	43	25	★★	2.8
Putnam Global Equity A	WS		10.82	-22.01	3.77	10.21	—	0.2	0.91	0.78	—	31	18	—	★★★★	4.8
Putnam Global Growth A	WS		7.65	-29.82	-6.72	3.46	7.59	0.0	1.34	1.06	0.94	95	71	60	★★★	3.9
Putnam International Growth A	FS		19.82	-19.79	5.47	10.43	11.70	0.0	0.87	0.80	0.78	12	6	2	★★★★★	4.1
Scudder Global Discovery A	WS		23.12	-25.18	5.07	—	—	0.0	1.23	—	—	25	—	—	★★★	3.8
Scudder Global S	WS		21.71	-16.40	0.04	5.73	9.04	2.1	0.73	0.64	0.61	56	50	48	★★★★	4.4
Scudder Greater Europe Growth S	ES		23.00	-25.69	-3.13	7.80	—	0.3	0.94	0.79	—	48	26	—	★★★★	4.8
Scudder International S	FS		36.66	-26.89	-2.31	3.62	7.07	0.3	0.96	0.82	0.81	50	31	31	★★★	3.9
Scudder Latin America S	LS		19.75	-0.82	7.18	2.59	—	1.7	1.30	1.45	—	62	27	—	★★★	2.4
SEI International Equity A	FS		8.80	-22.55	-3.82	0.82	4.19	0.2	0.88	0.80	0.82	60	65	81	★★★	2.9
Templeton Developing Markets A	EM		9.88	-5.76	-0.90	-6.45	2.40	1.0	1.23	1.42	1.25	94	65	1	★★	2.6
Templeton Foreign A	FS		9.25	-7.92	7.60	4.79	8.57	2.7	0.63	0.68	0.66	8	22	18	★★★★	4.0
Templeton Growth A	WS		18.00	0.54	10.09	8.62	11.78	2.2	0.52	0.58	0.58	17	26	15	★★★★★	3.9
Templeton World A	WS		14.86	-8.10	4.70	7.72	11.54	1.8	0.72	0.68	0.66	26	32	18	★★★★★	3.8
TIAA-CREF International Equity	FS		8.07	-24.29	-1.91	—	—	0.8	1.05	—	—	45	—	—	★★★	3.5
Tweedy, Browne Global Value	FS		18.53	-4.67	10.31	12.87	—	1.0	0.31	0.38	—	5	3	—	★★★★★	4.7
Van Kampen Global Value Equity A	WS		9.84	-9.04	1.29	—	—	1.0	0.56	—	—	41	—	—	★★★	3.4
Van Kampen Latin American A	LS		11.61	-2.94	11.37	4.32	—	0.9	1.34	1.57	—	40	4	—	★★★	2.9
Vanguard Emerging Mkts Stock Idx	EM		8.37	-2.88	4.37	-4.99	—	2.5	1.18	1.41	—	44	51	—	★★★	2.1
Vanguard European Stock Index	ES		20.25	-20.30	-5.15	6.44	9.93	2.2	0.84	0.71	0.72	63	29	36	★★★★	4.1
Vanguard International Growth	FS		15.01	-18.92	-2.17	2.65	7.51	1.6	0.84	0.78	0.79	48	39	23	★★★	3.9
Vanguard Total Intl Stock Index	FS		9.28	-20.15	-4.34	0.08	—	1.8	0.89	0.83	—	64	73	—	★★★	3.0
Waddell & Reed Adv International Gr A	FS		6.14	-22.36	-2.91	5.45	9.41	0.8	1.00	0.86	0.91	54	18	11	★★★★	3.7

Bold numbers indicate *highest* return for the listed time period in each category.

Fixed-Income Funds

	Cat	Style Box	NAV	Total Return % through 12-31-01 1Yr	Annualized 3Yr	5Yr	10Yr	Trailing 12 Mo Yield %	Morningstar Risk 1.00=U.S. Equity Avg 3Yr	5Yr	10Yr	Rtn % Rank Cat 3Yr	5Yr	10Yr	Star Rating	Avg Star Rating
Lehman Bros. Aggregate Bond Index				**8.42**	**6.27**	**7.43**	**7.23**									
ABN AMRO/Chicago Capital Bond N	CI	—	10.03	8.03	6.04	6.95	—	6.5	0.58	0.59	—	21	22	—	★★★★	3.9
Alliance Muni Income National A	ML	—	10.12	4.68	2.64	4.78	6.18	5.3	1.11	1.07	1.18	65	44	26	★★	3.6
Alliance North American Govt Income B	IB		6.98	-1.21	7.57	8.67	—	9.6	1.64	1.97	—	5	2	—	★★	2.4
American Century Ginnie Mae Inv	GI		10.62	7.43	6.18	6.73	6.66	6.0	0.49	0.45	0.64	13	31	16	★★★★	4.3
American Century Government Bond Inv	GL		10.27	3.81	4.18	7.91	—	5.2	1.48	1.50	—	54	15	—	★★	1.9
American Funds Capital World Bond A	IB		14.53	1.53	0.26	2.03	5.17	2.2	1.52	1.48	1.41	52	53	31	★★	2.1
American Funds Tax-Exempt Bond Fd A	MI		12.01	5.57	4.19	5.51	6.40	4.9	0.80	0.80	0.86	21	10	5	★★★★	2.9
AXP Global Bond A	IB		5.57	1.43	-0.10	2.14	5.64	3.4	1.68	1.69	1.61	55	51	27	★★	2.3
AXP High-Yield Tax-Exempt A	ML		4.35	3.91	3.60	5.07	5.76	5.8	0.88	0.83	0.86	29	30	57	★★★	4.1
BlackRock Intl Bond Svc	IB		10.43	7.68	6.30	7.97	8.65	5.2	0.52	0.45	0.59	11	6	3	★★★★★	4.8
Calvert Tax-Free Reserv Limited-Trm A	MS		10.69	4.46	3.95	3.96	4.08	4.1	0.03	0.04	0.03	34	75	90	★★★★★	4.5
DFA One-Year Fixed-Income	UB		10.27	5.76	5.69	5.76	5.45	4.5	0.07	0.08	0.13	44	46	50	★★★★★	4.6
Dodge & Cox Income	CI		12.20	10.32	6.60	7.57	7.65	6.0	0.58	0.62	0.92	8	5	9	★★★★★	4.0
Dreyfus Intermediate Municipal Bond	MI		13.34	3.98	3.32	4.61	5.57	4.9	0.74	0.76	0.82	75	68	62	★★★★	4.2
Eaton Vance Income Fund of Boston A	HY		6.08	-0.14	1.15	4.35	8.37	13.0	2.12	2.06	1.46	32	11	6	★★★	3.9
Evergreen High Income Municipal Bd B	MS		8.62	4.42	3.10	4.01	5.22	4.2	0.75	0.65	0.40	83	71	19	★★★★	4.6
Fidelity Advisor High-Yield T	HY		8.37	-1.16	-1.69	1.71	7.94	9.7	2.54	2.54	1.75	61	45	16	★★	4.1
Fidelity Ginnie Mae	GI	—	10.86	7.24	6.34	6.82	6.55	5.8	0.48	0.47	0.65	10	22	22	★★★★	3.9
Fidelity High-Income	HY	—	8.13	-4.84	-3.84	1.26	8.21	11.0	2.61	2.52	1.68	85	56	12	★★	4.5
Fidelity New Markets Income	EB	—	10.91	6.64	**18.58**	**8.75**	—	11.1	1.96	3.67	—	21	3	—	★★★	2.2
Fidelity Short-Term Bond	CS		8.80	7.63	6.24	6.21	5.74	5.3	0.25	0.26	0.43	21	34	53	★★★★★	3.9
Fidelity Spartan Interm Muni Income	MI	—	9.84	5.37	4.44	5.48	6.11	4.7	0.68	0.69	0.79	12	11	24	★★★★★	4.0
Fidelity Spartan Municipal Income	MI	—	12.68	5.00	4.76	5.90	6.30	4.8	0.94	0.96	1.02	8	5	10	★★★★	4.2
Fidelity Spartan Short-Int Muni Inc	MS	—	10.27	5.70	4.48	4.72	4.89	3.8	0.27	0.31	0.31	3	15	38	★★★★★	4.5
FPA New Income	CI	—	10.93	**12.33**	8.28	7.39	8.07	5.8	0.36	0.40	0.41	1	8	2	★★★★★	4.3
Franklin AGE High Income A	HY		1.92	2.92	-1.42	1.74	7.15	11.6	2.18	2.10	1.47	58	44	37	★★	2.8
Franklin Federal Tax-Free Income A	ML		11.76	4.63	3.86	5.28	6.22	5.4	0.81	0.74	0.71	17	20	24	★★★★★	4.4
Franklin High Yield Tax-Free Inc A	ML		10.49	5.89	2.75	4.70	6.46	5.6	0.83	0.77	0.64	62	48	13	★★★★	4.9
Franklin Insured Tax-Free Income A	ML		11.91	4.57	4.20	5.35	6.10	5.0	0.93	0.87	0.81	7	16	32	★★★★	3.5
Franklin Strategic Income A	MU		9.36	5.40	3.43	4.84	—	8.5	1.40	1.59	—	41	32	—	★★	3.3
Franklin U.S. Government Secs A	GI		6.83	7.67	6.27	6.97	6.69	6.4	0.49	0.46	0.65	11	14	14	★★★★	3.5
Fremont Bond	CI		10.10	9.42	6.81	8.02	—	5.2	0.70	0.69	—	4	2	—	★★★★★	4.1
Galaxy II U.S. Treasury Index Ret	GI		10.64	6.28	5.31	6.97	6.72	5.6	0.78	0.77	1.00	52	13	13	★★★	3.1
John Hancock Strategic Income A	MU		6.51	4.92	3.12	5.43	7.43	8.3	1.05	1.12	0.97	46	23	25	★★★	2.7
Harbor Bond	CI		11.42	9.03	6.56	7.72	7.91	4.6	0.64	0.65	0.86	9	4	6	★★★★★	4.5
Janus High-Yield	HY		9.37	4.52	4.18	5.68	—	8.0	1.33	1.46	—	7	5	—	★★	3.1
Loomis Sayles Bond Instl	MU		10.44	2.66	3.84	5.72	**9.92**	8.6	1.60	1.74	1.53	31	13	1	★★★★	4.3
MainStay High-Yield Corporate Bond B	HY		5.55	1.71	1.11	3.16	9.27	11.6	1.80	1.83	1.23	33	25	1	★★★★	3.8
Mercury Low Duration I	CS	—	9.93	7.41	5.84	6.15	—	5.9	0.26	0.26	—	51	42	—	★★★★★	4.8
Metropolitan West Low Duration Bond M	CS	—	9.98	7.60	7.05	—	—	6.7	0.17	—	—	6	—	—	★★★★★	5.0
Metropolitan West Total Return Bond	CI	—	10.15	9.18	6.96	—	—	7.4	0.59	—	—	3	—	—	★★★★	5.0
Montgomery Short Duration Govt Bond R	GS		10.20	7.38	5.99	6.46	—	4.8	0.27	0.28	—	20	16	—	★★★★★	4.7
Morgan Stan Inst High-Yield Invmt	HY		5.64	-5.91	-3.25	1.53	—	13.7	2.52	2.40	—	80	52	—	★	2.5
Northeast Investors	HY		7.43	1.33	-0.49	2.28	8.88	11.7	1.80	1.86	1.38	49	34	2	★★★	4.2
Nuveen Interm Duration Muni Bond R	MI		9.25	4.98	3.95	5.40	6.10	5.1	0.81	0.83	0.75	41	16	27	★★★★	4.4
Pilgrim GNMA Income A	GI		8.64	8.85	6.51	7.44	6.91	5.8	0.59	0.56	0.72	6	2	8	★★★★	3.2
PIMCO Foreign Bond Instl	IB		10.46	8.96	6.73	7.96	—	4.8	0.55	0.64	—	6	7	—	★★★★★	5.0
PIMCO High Yield A	HY		9.36	4.59	2.02	—	—	8.4	1.31	—	—	21	—	—	★★	2.1
PIMCO Low Duration Instl	CS		10.07	8.01	6.20	6.80	6.79	5.9	0.31	0.30	0.37	25	6	4	★★★★★	4.7
PIMCO Total Return Instl	CI		10.46	9.49	6.96	8.15	8.25	5.5	0.62	0.63	0.85	3	2	1	★★★★★	4.7

Bold numbers indicate *highest* return for the listed time period in each category.

Fixed-Income Funds

	Cat	Style Box	NAV	Total Return % through 12-31-01 1Yr	Annualized 3Yr	5Yr	10Yr	Trailing 12 Mo Yield %	Morningstar Risk 1.00=U.S. Equity Avg 3Yr	5Yr	10Yr	Rtn % Rank Cat 3Yr	5Yr	10Yr	Star Rating	Avg Star Rating
Lehman Bros. Aggregate Bond Index				**8.42**	**6.27**	**7.43**	**7.23**									
T. Rowe Price Emerging Markets Bond	EB		10.32	9.35	15.71	6.84	—	11.2	1.82	3.62	—	47	30	—	★★★	2.1
T. Rowe Price International Bond	IB		7.86	-3.41	-4.82	-0.81	4.09	4.1	2.41	2.44	2.17	90	91	55	★	1.9
T. Rowe Price Spectrum Income	MU		10.59	4.50	4.01	6.11	7.47	6.0	0.86	0.89	0.85	26	6	20	★★★★	4.3
T. Rowe Price Tax-Free Short-Interm	MS		5.42	5.81	4.49	4.75	4.84	4.0	0.33	0.37	0.32	2	13	52	★★★★★	3.9
T. Rowe Price U.S. Treasury Long-Term	GL		11.29	3.39	3.97	7.78	7.48	5.3	1.52	1.55	1.80	65	19	24	★★	2.1
Principal Government Securities Inc A	GI		11.48	6.75	5.79	6.84	6.62	5.9	0.59	0.63	0.99	29	20	17	★★★	2.7
Scudder Emerging Markets Income S	EB		7.74	10.46	14.48	3.42	—	10.7	2.07	3.95	—	63	57	—	★★★	2.3
Scudder GNMA AARP	GS		15.05	7.13	6.00	6.59	6.03	6.0	0.52	0.47	0.64	19	12	28	★★★★	3.8
Scudder Medium-Term Tax-Free S	MI		11.19	4.93	4.03	5.05	5.90	4.7	0.70	0.75	0.78	33	35	37	★★★★	4.1
Sit Tax-Free Income	ML		9.88	5.76	3.17	5.10	6.10	4.9	0.82	0.73	0.60	45	29	30	★★★★★	5.0
Sit U.S. Government Securities	GS		10.74	8.44	6.20	6.67	6.42	5.6	0.29	0.31	0.39	13	7	1	★★★★★	4.4
Strong Advantage Inv	UB		9.75	4.26	5.43	5.51	6.17	5.7	0.16	0.17	0.15	52	53	1	★★★★★	4.5
Strong Corporate Bond Inv	CL		10.50	6.83	4.77	6.65	8.70	7.1	0.90	0.91	0.99	49	31	5	★★★★	3.0
Strong Government Securities Inv	GI		10.79	8.92	6.25	7.18	7.57	5.2	0.61	0.61	0.85	11	6	3	★★★★★	4.6
Strong High-Yield Bond Inv	HY		7.94	-0.71	-0.18	3.52	—	12.4	2.19	2.07	—	46	19	—	★★	3.4
Strong Municipal Bond Inv	ML		8.63	4.69	0.39	3.89	5.15	4.7	1.42	1.26	1.13	98	84	90	★★	3.3
Strong Short-Term Bond Inv	CS		9.24	4.39	5.28	5.54	6.01	6.2	0.30	0.31	0.41	78	82	26	★★★★★	4.2
Strong Short-Term Municipal Bond Inv	MS		9.70	5.17	3.81	4.78	4.63	4.4	0.26	0.24	0.34	46	9	66	★★★★★	4.3
Thornburg Limited-Term Muni Natl A	MS		13.41	4.82	3.95	4.42	5.07	4.1	0.44	0.45	0.42	33	30	23	★★★★	4.9
USAA Income	CI	—	12.06	7.58	5.45	7.20	7.26	6.6	0.76	0.73	1.11	41	14	17	★★★	4.1
USAA Tax-Exempt Intermediate-Term	MI		13.00	5.55	4.14	5.61	6.25	5.2	0.74	0.73	0.76	26	8	16	★★★★★	4.5
USAA Tax-Exempt Long-Term	ML		13.18	4.33	3.58	5.38	6.12	5.5	1.11	1.07	1.09	31	15	28	★★★	3.9
USAA Tax-Exempt Short-Term	MS		10.69	5.10	4.29	4.75	4.84	4.1	0.16	0.18	0.19	8	14	47	★★★★★	4.5
Van Kampen High-Yield Municipal A	ML	—	10.49	4.99	2.76	5.15	6.43	6.3	0.61	0.48	0.45	62	26	15	★★★★★	4.7
Vanguard GNMA	GI		10.38	7.94	6.56	7.25	6.96	6.3	0.52	0.49	0.68	5	5	7	★★★★★	4.2
Vanguard High-Yield Corporate	HY	—	6.29	2.90	1.49	4.32	7.91	9.5	1.51	1.42	1.15	27	11	18	★★★	4.0
Vanguard High-Yield Tax-Exempt	ML		10.48	5.34	4.07	5.56	6.63	5.5	0.98	0.94	1.09	10	10	7	★★★★	3.9
Vanguard Insured Long-Trm T/E	ML		12.37	4.24	4.76	5.80	6.67	5.0	1.11	1.12	1.23	2	5	6	★★★★	3.8
Vanguard Interm-Term Tax-Ex	MI		13.27	4.92	4.48	5.25	6.21	4.8	0.73	0.73	0.76	11	19	18	★★★★	4.0
Vanguard Ltd-Term Tax-Ex	MS		10.85	5.58	4.44	4.71	4.88	4.3	0.28	0.31	0.29	4	16	42	★★★★★	4.8
Vanguard Long-Term Corporate Bond	CL		8.68	9.57	4.72	7.37	8.07	6.5	1.20	1.26	1.48	52	7	15	★★★	3.5
Vanguard Long-Term Tax-Exempt	ML		10.98	4.27	4.46	5.72	6.70	5.1	1.16	1.15	1.23	4	6	4	★★★★	3.3
Vanguard Long-Term U.S. Treasury	GL		10.76	4.31	4.48	7.99	8.20	5.6	1.48	1.49	1.81	38	13	16	★★	2.4
Vanguard Short-Term Bond Index	CS		10.19	8.77	6.55	6.86	—	5.5	0.36	0.36	—	12	4	—	★★★★★	4.5
Vanguard Short-Term Federal	GS		10.48	8.61	6.57	6.68	6.22	5.2	0.29	0.30	0.47	5	5	8	★★★★★	4.2
Vanguard Short-Term Treasury	GS		10.53	7.80	6.12	6.44	6.09	4.9	0.33	0.34	0.49	15	17	25	★★★★★	4.1
Vanguard Total Bond Market Index	CI		10.15	8.43	6.23	7.33	7.15	6.2	0.61	0.62	0.84	16	10	25	★★★★	4.0
Waddell & Reed Adv Muni High-Inc A	ML	—	4.88	5.17	1.66	4.63	6.58	5.5	1.02	0.86	0.73	87	53	9	★★★★	4.9

Bold numbers indicate *highest* return for the listed time period in each category.

Rookie Funds

	Cat	Style Box	NAV	Total Return % through 12-31-01 Since Inception	3Mo	6Mo	1Yr	Inception Date
American Century Tax Managed Val Inv	LV		5.80	6.92	8.77	-1.80	6.78	03/31/1999
American Century Veedot Inv	MG		4.66	-3.32	6.39	-9.86	-20.21	11/30/1999
American Funds New World A	EM		20.58	-3.27	15.38	-5.76	-3.96	06/17/1999
Bernstein International Value II	FS		14.53	-2.63	5.77	-9.50	-12.92	05/03/1999
Black Oak Emerging Technology	ST		3.95	-60.30	59.27	-35.77	-60.50	12/29/2000
Bogle Small Cap Growth Inv	SG		20.10	27.63	14.27	-1.08	5.07	09/30/1999
Calvert Social Investment Tech A	ST		5.56	-57.27	42.56	-21.36	-44.34	10/31/2000
Enterprise Internet A	ST		10.22	1.44	29.04	-24.35	-33.94	07/01/1999
Evergreen Health Care A	SH		16.21	52.25	14.40	4.24	2.14	12/22/1999
Fidelity Four-in-One Index	LB	—	21.93	-2.92	9.72	-4.42	-10.04	06/29/1999
Fidelity Freedom 2040	LB	—	7.39	-18.63	12.51	-6.52	-13.50	09/06/2000
Fidelity Leveraged Company Stock	MB		10.18	**220.79**	22.00	-3.75	3.23	12/19/2000
Fidelity Select Network & Infrastruct	ST		2.95	-61.56	46.77	-17.60	-50.25	09/21/2000
Gabelli Blue Chip Value AAA	LV		10.71	6.30	9.13	-12.77	-11.77	08/26/1999
Janus 2	LG		7.45	-25.38	11.69	-19.11	-25.50	12/29/2000
Janus Orion	MG		5.98	-28.81	22.79	**4.55**	-14.69	06/30/2000
Janus Strategic Value	LV		9.26	-2.69	16.94	-9.15	-11.74	02/29/2000
Legg Mason Opportunity Prim	MB		9.80	0.11	22.81	-13.40	1.94	12/30/1999
Marsico 21st Century	LG		7.37	-14.73	17.73	-3.53	-19.80	02/01/2000
Marsico International Opportunities	FS		7.86	-12.80	16.07	-5.19	-15.65	06/30/2000
Masters' Select Value	MV		11.43	9.47	11.34	-8.05	9.64	06/30/2000
Merrill Lynch Premier Growth B	MG		2.95	-48.68	26.61	-26.80	-52.95	03/03/2000
Neuberger Berman Regency Inv	MV		11.55	14.00	10.83	-1.31	-2.35	06/01/1999
Northern Institutional Mid Cap Gr A	MG		9.33	-3.40	15.19	-6.98	-17.36	12/31/1999
Oakmark Global I	WS		13.26	14.57	25.37	4.44	**20.05**	08/04/1999
Oppenheimer Main St Small Cap A	SG		15.08	21.48	18.24	0.45	12.93	08/02/1999
T. Rowe Price Developing Tech	ST		4.95	-40.46	**62.30**	-8.84	-30.58	08/31/2000
Putnam New Century Growth A	MG		12.71	-33.11	28.77	-14.12	-28.27	01/21/2000
Putnam Small Cap Value A	SV		14.00	21.60	18.85	2.14	18.95	04/13/1999
RS Internet Age	ST		5.76	-23.25	53.60	-3.03	-11.79	12/01/1999
TIAA-CREF Equity Index	LB		8.05	-12.81	11.57	-5.78	-11.62	04/03/2000
TIAA-CREF Social Choice Equity	LB		8.28	-12.93	10.16	-4.57	-12.75	04/03/2000
Vanguard Calvert Social Index	LB		7.76	-13.85	13.68	-6.13	-14.08	05/08/2000
Vanguard Developed Markets Index	FS		6.95	-18.14	6.16	-8.65	-22.05	05/08/2000
Vanguard Inflation-Protected Secs	GS		10.62	9.14	-1.14	1.25	7.71	06/29/2000
Vanguard Tax-Managed Small Cap Ret	SB		14.92	16.04	20.52	0.23	5.44	03/25/1999
Vanguard U.S. Value	LV		11.47	10.54	10.61	-1.36	2.94	06/29/2000
Westcore International Frontier	FS		7.71	-10.45	15.25	-7.33	-20.92	12/15/1999

Bold numbers indicate *highest* return for the listed time period in each category.

User's Guide

User's Guide

The following is a complete, alphabetical listing of the terms and features found in the pages of Morningstar Funds 500.

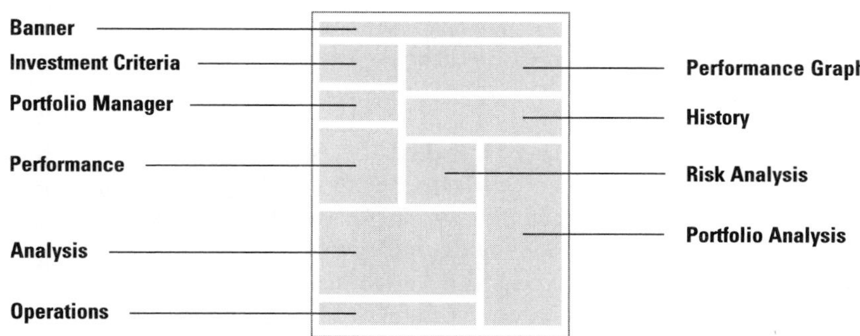

Above is a map of a fund-report page. We've broken the page into 10 main sections. These are the sections referred to by the location designations at the end of each glossary entry. Unless page type is specified, the term is located on all pages.

A

Actual Fees
see Expenses and Fees

Address
Usually the location of the fund's distributor, this address is where to write to receive a prospectus.
Location: Operations section.

Advisor
This is the company that takes primary responsibility for managing the fund.
Location: Operations section.

Alpha
see Modern Portfolio Theory Statistics

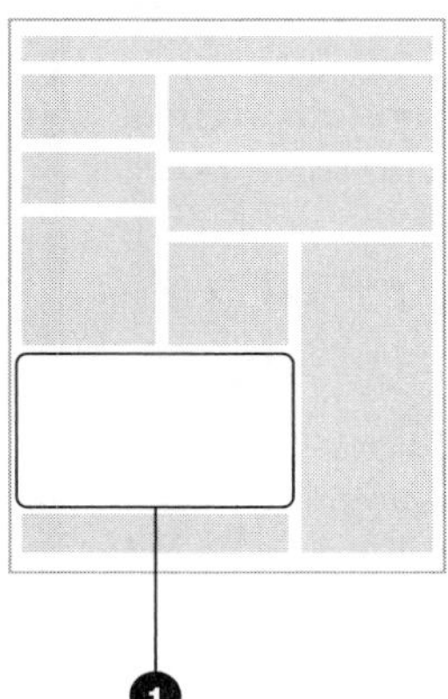

1 Analysis

Analysis by Bridget B. Hughes 01-22-99

Federated Growth Strategies Trust's disciplined strategy yields anything but a stagnant portfolio.

This fund is a stickler for growth. Like most of their Federated colleagues, comanagers James Grefenstette and Salvatore Esposito use a computer-driven model to identify attractive stocks. Each model employed at Federated is fund-specific; this offering's system puts the greatest emphasis on historic earnings growth and historic earnings revisions. Looking backward to find good prospects might seem strange, but it seems to have worked in this case: Although this portfolio's one-year earnings estimate is lower than its three-year earnings growth rate, both numbers are greater than those of the average mid-cap growth fund. Grefenstette and Esposito also apply fundamental analysis, looking for convincing reasons not to own stocks the model has ranked highly.

That computer-assisted strategy has led to a rather fluid portfolio. Since Grefenstette came on board in late 1994, the portfolio has moved around Morningstar's style box. The fund's value orientation at the end of 1994 can be partially explained by Grefenstette's move into financials. Lately, the model has suggested a heavier weighting in both mid-cap fare and technology names. At 31% of the portfolio, the fund's tech stake is at a five-year high. (It's also close to the fund's unofficial limit; the managers must keep the portfolio's sector weightings between 50% and 200% of those of the S&P 500 index.)

Overall, the fund's de facto flexibility has produced strong results. During Grefenstette's tenure, the offering's total return has surpassed that of the mid-cap growth category by more than six percentage points annually. The fund has also enjoyed limited volatility.

That the fund lagged its peers in 1998 shows the strategy isn't infallible, but it nonetheless deserves investors' attention.

The analysis interprets and enhances the numerical data that appear on the page. To accomplish this, a Morningstar analyst scrutinizes past shareholder reports, puts historical performance into the perspective of market trends, and whenever possible, interviews the fund manager or another fund official. Although many people are involved in producing the Morningstar page, the analyst is ultimately responsible for its content.
Location: Analysis section.

Average Brokerage Commission
see Expenses and Fees

Average Credit Quality
see also Credit Analysis
Average credit quality gives a snapshot of the portfolio's overall credit quality. It is an average of each bond's credit rating, adjusted for its relative weighting in the portfolio. For the purposes of Morningstar's calculations, U.S. government securities are considered AAA bonds, nonrated municipal bonds generally are classified as BB, and other nonrated bonds generally are considered B.
Location: Portfolio Analysis section of bond, convertible, and domestic-hybrid pages.

Average Effective Duration
Average effective duration provides a measure of a fund's interest-rate sensitivity. The longer a fund's duration, the more sensitive the fund is to shifts in interest rates. The relationship between funds with different durations is straightforward: A fund with a duration of 10 years is expected to be twice as volatile as a fund with a five-year duration. Duration also gives an indication of how a fund's NAV will change as interest rates change. A fund with a five-year duration would be expected to lose 5% from its NAV if interest rates rose by one percentage point or gain 5% if interest rates fell by one percentage point. Morningstar surveys fund companies for this information.
Location: Portfolio Analysis section of bond and domestic-hybrid pages.

Average Effective Maturity
see also Average Nominal Maturity
Average effective maturity is a weighted average of all the maturities of the bonds in a portfolio, computed by weighting each bond's effective maturity by the market value of the security. Average effective maturity takes into consideration all mortgage prepayments, puts, and adjustable coupons. (Because Morningstar uses fund-company calculations for this figure and because different companies use different interest-rate assumptions in determining call likelihood and timing, we ask that companies not adjust for call provisions.)

Longer-maturity funds are generally considered more interest-rate sensitive than their shorter counterparts.
Location: Portfolio Analysis section of taxable-bond, convertible, and domestic-hybrid pages.

Average Historical Rating
see Risk Analysis

Average Nominal Maturity
see also Average Effective Maturity
Listed only for municipal-bond funds, this figure is computed by weighting the nominal maturity of each security in the portfolio by the market value of the security, then averaging these weighted figures. Unlike a fund's effective maturity figure, it does not take into account prepayments, puts, or adjustable coupons.
Location: Portfolio Analysis section of municipal-bond pages.

Average Stock Percentage
see also Composition
For stock-oriented funds, we provide a yearly average stock position calculated by averaging all reported composition numbers for the year. These averages provide a valuable complement to the current composition numbers; investors can compare a fund's current level of market participation with its historical averages.
Location: Performance Graph section of stock pages.

Average Weighted Coupon
see also Coupon Range
Average weighted coupon is computed by averaging each bond's coupon rate adjusted for its relative weighting in the portfolio. This figure indicates whether the fund is opting for a high- or low-coupon strategy, and may serve as an indicator of interest-rate sensitivity, particularly for mortgage-backed funds or other funds with callable bonds. A high coupon frequently indicates less sensitivity to interest rates; a low coupon, the opposite.
Location: Portfolio Analysis section of bond pages.

Average Weighted Price
Average weighted price is computed for most bond funds by weighting the price of each bond by its relative size in the portfolio. This number reveals whether the fund favors bonds selling at prices above or below face value (premium or discount securities, respectively) and can also serve as an indicator of interest-rate sensitivity. This statistic is expressed as a percentage of par (face) value. This statistic is not calculated for international-bond funds, because their holdings are often expressed in terms of foreign currencies.
Location: Portfolio Analysis section of bond pages.

B

+/– Benchmark Index
see Indexes

Best Fit Index
see also Indexes; Modern Portfolio Theory Statistics
The Best Fit Index is the market index whose monthly returns have correlated the most closely with a given fund's in the most recent 36 consecutive months. Morningstar regresses the fund's monthly excess returns against monthly excess returns of several well-known market indexes. Best Fit signifies the index that provides the highest R-squared.

To identify the Best Fit Index, the following indexes are regressed against each stock fund: JSE Gold, MSCI Pacific, MSCI Pacific ex Japan, MSCI World ex U.S., MSCI EASEA, MSCI Europe, MSCI All Country, Russell 2000, S&P MidCap 400, Wilshire 4500, Wilshire REIT, S&P 500, LB Long-Term Treasury, and LB High-Yield.

The following indexes are regressed against each bond fund: LB Long-Term Treasury, SB World Government, LB Corporate, LB Municipal, LB Government, FB High-Yield, LB Aggregate, LB Intermediate-Term Treasury, LB Mortgage-Backed, Russell 2000, MSCI All Country, Wilshire 4500, and S&P 500. Descriptions of these indexes are listed under Indexes.
Location: Risk Analysis section.

Beta
see Modern Portfolio Theory Statistics

Bond Type
Listed for municipal-bond funds, this section details the percentage of a fund's assets that fall under the following categories.
Location: Portfolio Analysis section of municipal-bond pages.

Alternative Minimum Tax (AMT)
This figure shows the percentage of a fund's securities that are subject to the Alternative Minimum Tax. Although income from municipal bonds is usually exempt from federal taxes, some investors must pay taxes on those bonds subject to AMT. Only certain muni bonds are AMT-subject. In general, these bonds are issued to finance private economic activity.

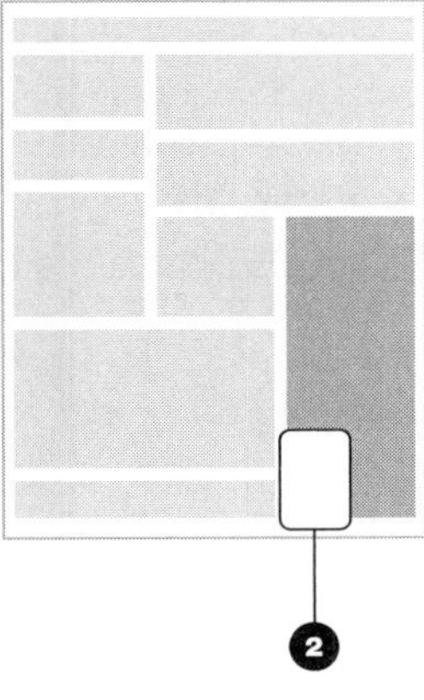

Insured
This figure shows the percentage of a fund's bonds that are insured. A muni-bond issuer or a bondholder can purchase insurance on the bond's principal amount. This automatically gives the bond the credit rating of the insurer (typically AAA).

Prerefunded
This is the percentage of a fund's bonds that are prerefunded. Muni-bond issuers will occasionally prerefund a bond if they want to refinance before the bond's first call date. When an issue is prerefunded, the municipality issues a new bond to replace the first one. They then purchase enough U.S. Treasury bonds to pay interest and principal on the first bond and store these Treasuries in an escrow account. Interest on the prerefunded bond is guaranteed until the call date, when bondholders receive their principal. Prerefunded bonds also carry an implied AAA rating because of their Treasury backing.

C

Capital Gains $
Capital gains are the profits received and distributed from the sale of securities within the portfolio. This line shows a summary of the fund's annual capital-gains distributions expressed in per-share dollar amounts. Both short- and long-term gains are included, as are options premiums and distributions from paid-in capital.
Location: History section.

Capital Return %
see also Income Return % and Total Return
Morningstar provides the portion of a fund's total returns that was generated by realized and unrealized increases in the value of securities in the portfolio. Frequently, a stock fund's returns will be derived entirely from capital return. By looking at capital return and income return, an investor can see whether the fund's returns come from capital, from income, or from a combination of both. Adding capital and income return will produce the fund's total return.
Location: History section.

Category
see Morningstar Category

Category Rating
see Morningstar Category Rating

❷ Composition
see also Average Stock Percentage

Composition % of assets 09-30-98	
Cash	3.3
Stocks*	96.7
Bonds	0.0
Other	0.0
*Foreign (% of stocks)	2.9

The composition percentages provide a simple breakdown of the fund's portfolio holdings, as of the date listed, into general investment classes. Cash encompasses both the actual cash and the cash equivalents (fixed-income securities with maturities of one year or less) held by the portfolio. Negative percentages of cash indicate that the portfolio is leveraged, meaning it has borrowed against its own assets to buy more securities or that it has used other techniques to gain additional exposure to the market. The percentage listed as Stocks incorporates only the portfolio's straight common stocks. Bonds include every fixed-income security with a maturity of more than one year, from government notes to high-yield corporate bonds. Other includes preferred stocks (equity securities that pay dividends at a specified rate), as well as convertible bonds and convertible preferreds, which are corporate securities that are exchangeable for a set amount of another form of security (usually shares of common stock) at a prestated price. Other also includes all those not-so-neatly categorized securities, such as warrants and options.
Location: Portfolio Analysis section.

Country Exposure
For each international portfolio, the country exposure information displays the countries in which the fund is invested in most heavily. This information is gathered directly from the portfolios or from fund companies.
Location: Portfolio Analysis section of international-stock, and international-bond pages.

Coupon Range
see also Average Weighted Coupon
Taxable-bond funds feature a table listing the breakdown of each portfolio's bond coupons, or rates of interest payments. The coupon range is designed to help an investor complete the picture suggested by the average weighted coupon statistic.

These ranges differ according to Morningstar Category and, due to changing interest rates, are subject to alteration over time. Whatever the breakdown may be, the first number is always exclusive and the second number is always inclusive. A range of 8% to 9%, for example, would exclude bonds that have a weighted coupon rate of exactly 8% but would include bonds with a weighted coupon rate of 9%. High-yield bond funds include PIKs in their coupon breakdown, which are payment-in-kind issues that make interest payments in the form of additional securities rather than cash.

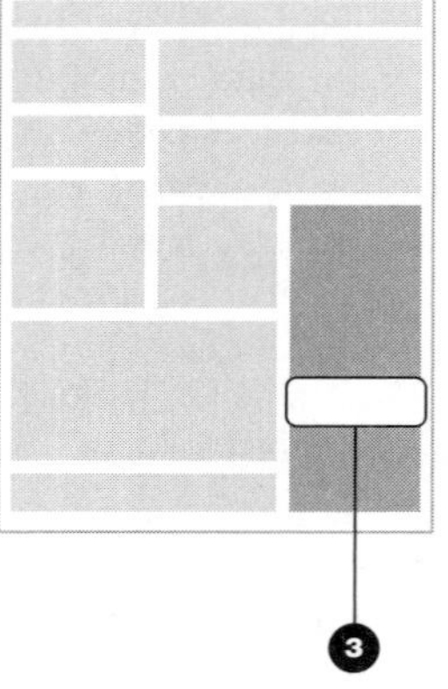

The final group in the coupon range is Not Applicable, which covers any holding without a stated coupon rate, variable or adjustable-rate securities, or certain mortgage derivatives, for example.

The overall percentage of bond assets that fall within each coupon range is noted in the % of Bonds column. The Rel Cat column compares a fund with others in its Morningstar Category. The category average is set at 1.0.

Location: Portfolio Analysis section of taxable-bond pages.

Credit Analysis

This section depicts the quality of bonds in a bond fund's portfolio. The credit analysis shows the percentage of fixed-income securities that fall within each credit-quality rating as assigned by Standard & Poor's or Moody's.

At the top of the ratings are U.S. government bonds. Bonds issued and backed by the government, as well as those backed by government-linked organizations such as FNMA and FHLMO, are of extremely high quality and thus are considered equivalent to bonds rated AAA, which is the highest possible rating a corporate issue can receive. Morningstar gives U.S. government bonds a credit rating separate from AAA securities to allow for a more accurate credit analysis of a portfolio's holdings. Bonds with a BBB rating are the lowest grade that are still considered to be investment-grade. Bonds that are rated BB or lower (often called junk bonds or high-yield bonds) are considered to be speculative. Any bonds that appear in the NR/NA category are either not rated by Standard & Poor's or Moody's, or did not have a rating available at the time of publication. Like the style box, the credit analysis can help investors determine whether a fund's portfolio meets a desired standard of quality. It can also shed light on the management strategy of the fund. If the fund holds a large percentage of assets in lower-quality issues, the fund follows a more aggressive style and is probably more concerned with yield than credit quality.

Location: Portfolio Analysis section of taxable-bond (excluding government-bond funds) and municipal-bond pages.

Currency Exposure

see also Hedging Status

In the Hedging History line, Not Allowed indicates that a fund's prospectus bars hedging; Never indicates that a fund has not chosen to engage in hedging; Rare indicates that a fund has hedged less than approximately one fourth of the time; Frequent indicates that a fund has typically hedged one half to three fourths of the time, or that a fund hedges almost all the time, but with less than 25% of its assets; and Always refers to funds that hedge most of their assets almost all the time.

Location: Portfolio Analysis section of international-stock and international-bond pages.

❸ Current Investment Style

see also Investment Style Box and listings of terms in table.

Current Investment Style	Stock Port Avg	Relative S&P 500 Current	Relative S&P 500 Hist	Rel Cat
Price/Earnings Ratio	42.4	1.29	1.28	1.11
Price/Book Ratio	11.8	1.52	1.35	1.49
Price/Cash Flow	31.7	1.38	1.38	1.11
3 Yr Earnings Growth	32.0	1.71	1.64	1.18
1 Yr Earnings Est%	28.9	2.83	—	1.13
Debt % Total Cap	26.8[1]	0.86	0.82	0.97
Med Mkt Cap $mil	5,108	0.1	0.2	0.92

Style: Value Blnd Growth; Size: Large Med Small

[1]figure is based on 50% or less of stocks

This section lists a fund portfolio's current averages for various portfolio statistics. For stock portfolios, we compare a portfolio's current and historical average with the S&P 500's (Relative S&P 500 Current/Hist). The historical average is based on the trailing three years. We also compare the averages with the fund's category (Rel Cat). The S&P 500 and category averages are always set equal to 1.00. Thus, if a fund's current P/E ratio is 0.70 relative to the S&P 500, the fund's P/E is 30% lower than the S&P 500's.

Location: Portfolio Analysis section.

D

Dollar-cost Averaging

see Minimum Automatic Investment Plan

Duration

see Average Effective Duration

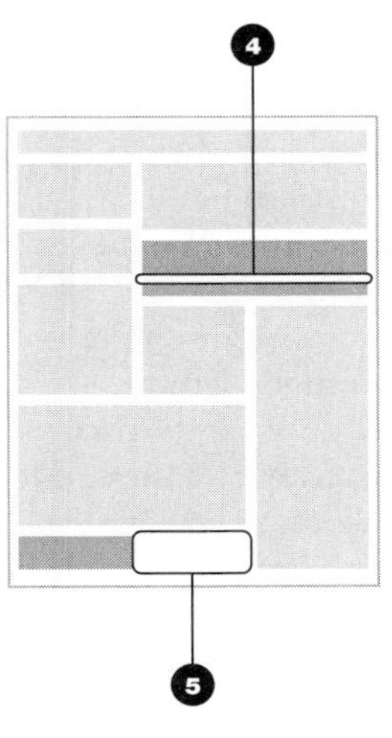

E

Emerging-Markets Securities
see Special Securities

Equity Style
see Investment Style Box

Exotic Mortgage-Backed Securities
see Special Securities

Expense Projections
see Expenses and Fees

4 Expense Ratio %
see also Expenses and Fees

93	0.92	0.97	0.99	0.98	1.18	—	Expense Ratio %

The annual expense ratio, taken from the fund's annual report, expresses the percentage of assets deducted each fiscal year for fund expenses, including 12b-1 fees, management fees, administrative fees, operating costs, and all other asset-based costs incurred by the fund. Portfolio transaction fees, or brokerage costs, as well as initial or deferred sales charges are not included in the expense ratio.

The expense ratio, which is deducted from the fund's average net assets, is accrued on a daily basis. If the fund's assets, listed in the lower part of the History section, are small, the expense ratio can be quite high because the fund must meet its expenses from a restricted asset base. Conversely, as the net assets of the fund grow, the expense percentage should ideally diminish as expenses are spread across the wider base.

Location: History section.

5 Expenses and Fees

Minimum Purchase:	$500	Add: $100	IRA: $50
Min Auto Inv Plan:	$500	Systematic Inv: $100	
Sales Fees:	5.50%L		
Management Fee:	0.75%, 0.15%A		
Actual Fees:	Mgt: 0.75%	Dist: —	
Expense Projections:	3Yr: $89	5Yr: $114	10Yr: $186
Avg Brok Commission:	—	Income Distrib:	Quarterly
Total Cost (relative to category):		Average	

Morningstar distinguishes among the myriad fees and expenses encountered with mutual funds. The different expenses and their characteristics are listed below.

Location: Operations section.

Sales Fees

Also known as loads, sales fees list the maximum level of initial (front-end) and deferred (back-end) sales charges imposed by a fund. The scales of minimum and maximum charges are taken from a fund's prospectus. Because fees change frequently and are sometimes waived, it is wise to examine the fund's prospectus carefully for specific information before investing.

B (12b-1)

The 12b-1 fee represents the maximum annual charge deducted from fund assets to pay for distribution and marketing costs. This fee is expressed as a percentage. Some funds may be permitted to impose 12b-1 fees but are currently waiving all or a portion of the fees. Total 12b-1 fees, excluding loads, are capped at 1% of average net assets annually. Of this, the distribution and marketing portion of the fee may account for up to 0.75%. The other portion of the overall 12b-1 fee, the service fee(s), is listed separately and may account for up to 0.25%. Often, funds charging a 12b-1 fee will allow shareholders to convert into a share class without the fee after a certain number of years. When this is the case, we note the conversion feature and the number of years after which it applies. Investors should check the fund's prospectus for full details.

D (Deferred Load)

Also called a contingent deferred sales charge or back-end load, a deferred load is an alternative to the traditional front-end sales charge, as it is only deducted at the time of sale of fund shares. The deferred load structure commonly decreases to zero over a period of time. A typical deferred load's structure might have a 5% charge if shares are redeemed within the first year of ownership, and decline by a percentage point each year thereafter. These loads are normally applied to the lesser of original share price or current market value. It is important to note that although the deferred load declines each year, the accumulated annual distribution and services charges (the total 12b-1 fee) usually offset this decline.

L (Front-End Load)

The initial sales charge or front-end load is a deduction made from each investment in the fund. The amount is generally based on the amount of the investment. Larger investments, both initial and cumulative, generally receive percentage discounts based on the dollar value invested. A typical front-end load might have a 4% charge for purchases less than $50,000, which decreases as the amount of the investment increases.

No-Load
This label denotes the fund as a true no-load fund, charging no sales or 12b-1 fees.

R (Redemption Fee)
The redemption fee is an amount charged when money is withdrawn from the fund. This fee does not go back into the pockets of the fund company, but rather into the fund itself and thus does not represent a net cost to shareholders. Also, unlike contingent deferred sales charges, redemption fees typically operate only in short, specific time clauses, commonly 30, 180, or 365 days. However, some redemption fees exist for up to five years. Charges are not imposed after the stated time has passed. These fees are typically imposed to discourage market timers, whose quick movements into and out of funds can be disruptive. The charge is normally imposed on the ending share value, appreciated or depreciated from the original value.

S (Service Fee)
The service fee is part of the total 12b-1 fee, but listed separately on the page. Capped at a maximum 0.25%, the service fee is designed to compensate financial planners or brokers for ongoing shareholder-liaison services, which may include responding to customer inquiries and providing information on investments. An integral component of level-load and deferred-load funds, the fees were previously known as a trail commission. Only service fees adopted pursuant to Rule 12b-1 are tracked. Despite the implication of its name, service fees do not act as compensation for transfer agency or custodial services.

W (Waived)
This indicates that the fund is waiving sales fees at the time of publication. A fund may do this to attract new shareholders. Call the fund's distributor to ensure that the waiver is still active at the time of investment.

Management Fee
The management fee is the maximum percentage deducted from a fund's average net assets to pay an advisor or subadvisor. Often, as the fund's net assets grow, the percentage deducted for management fees decreases. Alternatively, the fund may compute the fee as a flat percentage of average net assets. A portion of the management fee may also be charged in the form of a group fee (G). To determine the group fee, the fund family creates a sliding scale for the family's total net assets and determines a percentage applied to each fund's asset base. The management fee might also be amended by or be primarily composed of a performance fee (P), which raises or lowers the management fee based on the fund's returns relative to an established index (we list the maximum by which the fee can increase or decrease). It might also be composed of a gross income fee (I), a percentage based on the total amount of income generated by the investment portfolio.

The letter (a) denotes an administrative fee, which is the fund's maximum allowable charge for its management-fee structure, excluding advisor fees. Costs associated with SEC compliance may also be included under this label. Administrative fees often operate on a sliding scale and include the costs of basic fund operations, such as leasing office space. Investors should note that there is not necessarily a total expense differential between funds with disclosed administrative fees and funds without. Most funds roll administrative costs into their management fees; other funds, especially those with out-of-house administration, prefer to break them out. For this reason, we include administrative fees in the Management Fee area.

Actual Fees
Taken from the fund's prospectus, this area qualifies the management and 12b-1 distribution and service fees. Actual Fees most commonly represents the costs shareholders paid for management and distribution services over the fund's prior fiscal year. If fee levels have changed since the end of the most recent fiscal year, the actual fees will most commonly be presented as a recalculation based on the prior year's average monthly net assets using the new, current expenses. Although contract-type management and distribution costs are listed in a fund's prospectus, these are maximum amounts and funds may waive a portion, or possibly all, of those fees. Actual Fees thus represent a close approximation of the true costs to shareholders.

Expense Projections (three-, five-, and 10-Year)
The SEC mandates that each fund list its expense projections. Found in the fund's prospectus, these figures show how much an investor would expect to pay in expenses, sales charges (loads), and fees over the next three, five, and 10 years, assuming a $10,000 investment that grows by 5%

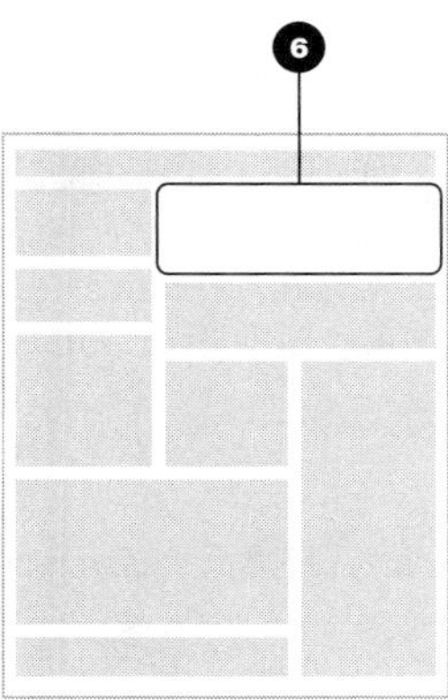

per year with redemption at the end of each time period. Expense projections are commonly based on the past year's incurred fees or an estimate of the current fiscal year's fees, should a portion of the overall fee structure change as of the printing of the fund's most current prospectus. Newer funds are only required to print expense projections for one- and three-year time periods since longer-term projections may not be possible to estimate.

Average Brokerage Commission
The average brokerage commission is the dollar amount charged per share traded in the previous fiscal 12-month period. This information is reported in each fund's annual report, with the exception of bond funds.

It is important to remember that brokerage fees are not calculated into a fund's expense ratio. However, the average brokerage commission can be added to the expense ratio found in the History section to get a better estimate of a fund's full costs. Some trading costs are omitted, however, such as those of non-exchange-listed stocks, for which higher trading costs are built into the bid-ask spread. Accordingly, the true trading costs of some international and small-company funds are understated. Because trading costs for bonds are incorporated into bond prices, we do not calculate brokerage costs for bond funds.

Total Cost
Total Cost is a relative ranking of expenses within each Morningstar Category. Total Cost is based on the expense projections. Morningstar takes these figures directly from the prospectus and plots each fund's expense projection on a bell curve. The funds in each category are then divided into five groups based on their expense projections. The least expensive 10% are designated as Low, the next 22.5% are Below Avg., the middle 35% are Average, the next 22.5% are Above Avg., and the most expensive 10% are High.

F

Five-Year High/Low
see Sector Weightings

Fixed-Income Style
see Investment Style Box

6 Fund Performance vs. Category Average Graph

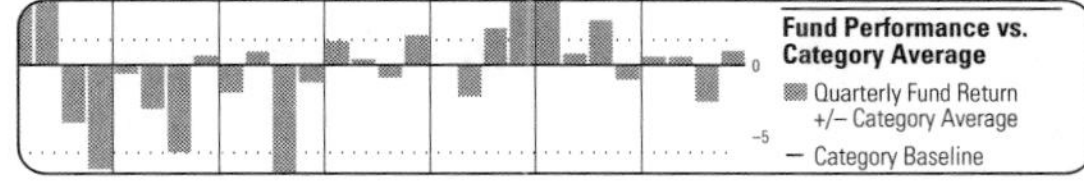

Shown near the top of each stock-fund page, this performance graph shows by what percentage the fund's total returns have beaten or trailed the average total returns of a fund in its Morningstar Category each quarter. Investors can see at a glance whether a fund's quarterly returns are consistently near the category baseline, or whether they tend to fall well above or below the category average. A fund displaying consistent performance relative to its category would be a good choice for those investors intent on avoiding surprises. A fund showing bigger ups and downs might be more appropriate for investors with a high tolerance for volatility.

Location: Performance Graph section of stock pages.

G

Growth
see also Investment Style Box and Value
Often contrasted with a value approach to investing, the term growth is used to describe an investment style that looks for equity securities with high rates of revenue growth. A company's per-share price is generally not emphasized as much as it is in value-style investing.

Growth of $10,000
see Performance

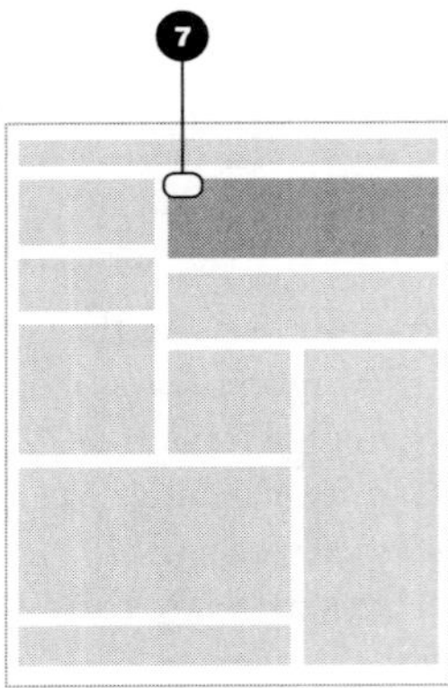

H

Hedging History

see Currency Exposure

7 Historical Profile

see also Risk Analysis

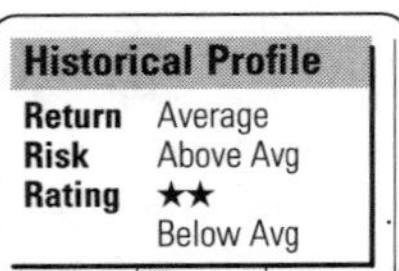

Historical Profile
Return Average
Risk Above Avg
Rating ★★
Below Avg

The Historical Profile provides Morningstar's overall assessment of a fund's historical returns and risk, and the fund's overall risk-adjusted star rating.

Location: Performance Graph section.

Return and Risk

The return and risk assessments are based on a fund's historical performance relative to other funds in one of four broad asset classes: domestic stock, international stock, taxable bond, or municipal bond. For the actual calculation of the Morningstar Return and Morningstar Risk scores, see Risk Analysis. It's important to realize that information in the Historical Profile is purely quantitative. The assessments do not reflect Morningstar's opinion of the future potential of the fund. They only give a quick summary of how a fund has performed historically relative to its peers.

A fund's overall return and risk profiles stem from a weighted average of three time periods. The 10-year statistics account for 50% of the overall score, the five-year figures for 30%, and the three-year numbers for 20%. If only five years of history are available, the five-year period is weighted 60% and the three-year period 40%. If only three years of data are available, the three-year figures alone are used. A bell curve is then used to determine the risk and return summations that appear in the box. Return scores that fall into the top 10% of the fund's broad investment category are labeled High; the next 22.5% are considered Above Average; the middle 35% are Average; the next 22.5% are labeled Below Average; and the bottom 10% are Low. For a fund's historical risk assessment, the same terms and percentages are used, ranging from High for the 10% of funds posting the largest monthly losses to Low for the 10% posting the lowest monthly losses.

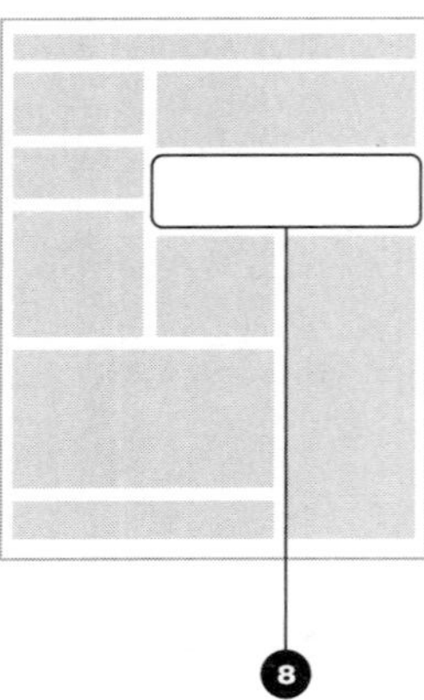

Star Rating and Overall Assessment

see also Risk Analysis

The star rating displayed in the Historical Profile section is a fund's overall risk-adjusted star rating. (For the calculation of the star rating, see Risk Analysis.) The star ratings for the three time periods in the Risk Analysis section are combined here using the same time-period weightings as discussed above. In ascending order, these categories are Lowest (1 star), Below Average (2 stars), Neutral (3 stars), Above Average (4 stars), and Highest (5 stars). Funds less than three years old are listed as Not Rated.

8 History

see also individual listings of terms in History section

1992	1993	1994	1995	1996	1997	12–98	History
13.48	13.72	12.32	13.61	13.15	13.46	13.24	NAV
6.74	12.66	–4.50	18.54	3.41	8.66	6.11	Total Return %
–0.66	2.92	–1.58	0.08	–0.20	–1.02	–2.57	+/– LB Aggregate
–0.43	3.88	–2.57	3.24	–0.65	0.79	–2.31	+/– LB Int Govt/Corp
6.93	6.65	5.67	7.15	6.09	6.15	5.96	Income Return %
–0.19	6.02	–10.17	11.39	–2.68	2.51	0.14	Capital Return %
63	14	71	30	36	54	85	Total Rtn % Rank Cat
0.93	0.87	0.76	0.86	0.81	0.79	0.79	Income $
0.40	0.57	0.02	0.09	0.09	0.01	0.24	Capital Gains $
0.93	0.92	0.97	0.99	0.98	1.18	—	Expense Ratio %
7.05	6.32	6.43	6.35	6.01	6.00	—	Income Ratio %
121	131	60	128	67	62	—	Turnover Rate %
456.2	508.9	464.1	579.4	580.4	695.6	802.9	Net Assets $mil

The History section is a table of annual information providing performance and expense statistics along with relative comparisons on a yearly basis.

Location: History section.

I

Inception

The date of inception gives the date on which the fund commenced operations. If an asterisk appears next to the date, returns for that partial year appear in the History section of the page. (Those returns are also marked with an asterisk.)

Location: Operations section.

Income $

The dividends and interest generated by a fund's holdings. This area shows a fund's yearly income distribution expressed in per-share dollar amounts.

Location: History section.

Income Distribution

Income distribution represents the number of times per year that a fund intends to make income payments (from either dividends or interest). A fund generally makes distributions monthly, quarterly, semiannually, or annually.

Location: Operations section.

Income Ratio %

The fund's income ratio reveals the percentage of current income earned per share. It is calculated by dividing the fund's net investment income by its average net assets. (Net investment income is the total income of the fund, less expenses.) An income ratio can be negative if a fund's expenses exceed its income, which can occur with funds that tend to emphasize capital gains rather than income. Because the income ratio is based on a fund's fiscal year and is taken directly from the fund's annual shareholder report, it may not exactly correspond with other calendar-year information on the page.
Location: History section.

Income Return %

see also Capital Return % and Total Return
Income return is that portion of a fund's total returns that was derived from income distributions. Income return will often be higher than capital return for bond funds, and typically lower for stock funds. Adding the income return and the capital return together will produce the fund's total return.
Location: History section.

Income Return Percentile Rank

This ranking shows how a fund's income distributions have stacked up against other funds in its category. Each calendar year features a ranking, with 1 being the highest percentile and 100 the lowest. We use the income-return figures printed in the History section to determine the rankings. This ranking is calculated off a trailing 12-month figure.
Location: Performance Graph section of bond and convertible-bond pages.

Indexes

Benchmark Index
A benchmark index gives the investor a point of reference for evaluating a fund's performance. In all cases where such comparisons are made, Morningstar uses the S&P 500 index as the basic benchmark for stock-oriented funds, including domestic-hybrid, international-hybrid, convertible-bond funds. The Lehman Brothers Aggregate Bond index is used as the benchmark index for all bond funds.

We also provide a comparison with a secondary, specialized benchmark. Because the S&P 500 index is composed almost entirely of large-cap domestic stocks, it is a good performance measure for large-cap domestic-stock funds and the overall market, but other comparisons are less useful. Comparing a foreign-stock fund with the S&P 500 index, for example, does not tell the reader how the fund has done relative to foreign stock markets. Therefore, a fund's total return in the History and Performance sections is compared with that of one of the following indexes:

FB H-Y Bond (First Boston High-Yield Bond index)
This index tracks the returns of all new publicly offered debt of more than $75 million rated below BBB.

JP EMG Mkts Bd (JPM Emerging Markets Bond index)
This index consists of debt instruments from 13 emerging markets: Argentina, Brazil, Bulgaria, Chile, Ecuador, Morocco, Nigeria, Panama, Peru, the Philippines, Poland, Russia, and Venezuela.

LB Agg (Lehman Brothers Aggregate Bond index)
This index is combination of the Lehman Brothers Government, Corporate, Mortgage-Backed, and Asset-Backed Securities indexes.

LB Corp (Lehman Brothers Corporate Bond index)
This index tracks the returns of all publicly issued, fixed-rate, nonconvertible, dollar-denominated, SEC-registered, investment-grade corporate debt.

LB Govt (Lehman Brothers Government Bond index)
This index tracks the returns of U.S. Treasuries, agency bonds, and one- to three-year U.S. government obligations.

LB Int (Lehman Brothers Intermediate-Term Treasury index)
This index tracks the performance of U.S. Treasury Bonds with maturities up to 10 years.

LB L-T (Lehman Brothers Long-Term Treasury index)
This index measures the returns of U.S. Treasury Bonds with maturities greater than 10 years.

LB Mtg (Lehman Brothers Mortgage-Backed Securities index)
This index includes 15- and 30-year fixed-rate securities backed by mortgage pools issued by GNMA, FNMA, and FHLMC.

LB Muni (Lehman Brothers Municipal Bond index)
This index serves as a benchmark for the performance of long-term, investment-grade, tax-exempt municipal bonds.

MSCI EAFE (Morgan Stanley Capital International Europe, Australasia, and Far East index)
This index is widely accepted as a benchmark for international-stock performance. The MSCI EAFE index is a market-weighted aggregate of 21 individual country indexes that collectively represent many of the world's major markets outside the U.S. and Canada: Australia, Austria, Belgium, Denmark, Finland, France, Germany, Hong Kong, Ireland, Italy, Japan, Malaysia, the Netherlands, New Zealand, Norway, Portugal, Singapore, Spain, Sweden, Switzerland, and the United Kingdom.

MSCI Emerging (Morgan Stanley Capital International Emerging Markets index)
This index is composed of 26 of the world's emerging markets: Argentina, Brazil, Chile, Colombia, China, the Czech Republic, Greece, Hungary, India, Indonesia, Israel, Jordan, Korea, Malaysia, Mexico, Pakistan, Peru, the Philippines, Poland, Russia, South Africa, Sri Lanka, Taiwan, Thailand, Turkey, and Venezuela.

MSCI Europe (Morgan Stanley Capital International Europe index)
This index measures the performance of stock markets in Austria, Belgium, Denmark, Finland, France, Germany, Ireland, Italy, the Netherlands, Norway, Portugal, Spain, Sweden, Switzerland, and the United Kingdom.

MSCI Japan (Morgan Stanley Capital International Japan index)
This index measures the performance of Japan's stock market.

MSCI Latin Am (Morgan Stanley Capital International Latin America index)
This index tracks the performance of stock markets in Argentina, Brazil, Chile, Colombia, Mexico, Peru, and Venezuela.

MSCI Pacific (Morgan Stanley Capital International Pacific index)
This index follows the performance of stock markets in Australia, Hong Kong, Japan, Malaysia, New Zealand, and Singapore.

MSCI World (Morgan Stanley Capital International World index)
This index measures the performance of stock markets in 23 nations: Australia, Austria, Belgium, Canada, Denmark, Finland, France, Germany, Hong Kong, Ireland, Italy, Japan, Malaysia, the Netherlands, New Zealand, Norway, Portugal, Singapore, Spain, Sweden, Switzerland, the United Kingdom, and the United States.

MSPacxJp (Morgan Stanley Capital International Pacific index ex Japan)
This index follows the performance of stock markets in Australia, Hong Kong, Malaysia, New Zealand, and Singapore.

Russell 2000
This commonly cited small-cap index tracks the returns of the smallest 2,000 firms in the Russell 3000 index, which is composed of the 3,000 largest companies in the United States, as measured by market capitalization.

S&P 500 (Standard and Poor's 500 index)
Often considered a surrogate for the overall market, this index is composed of the stocks of 500 of the largest companies listed on U.S. exchanges. The S&P 500 index is value-weighted, which means that the importance of individual stocks in the index depends upon the stock's market value. Therefore, a percentage change in the market value of a large company has a greater impact than an identical percentage change in a smaller company.

S&P MidCap 400 (Standard and Poor's Mid-Cap 400 index)
This index includes approximately 10% of the capitalization of U.S. equity securities. These are composed of stocks in the middle capitalization range. Any mid-cap stocks already included in the S&P 500 are excluded from this index.

Wil 4500 (Wilshire 4500 index)
This value-weighted index includes all issues in the Wilshire 5000 index, excluding those found in the S&P 500 index.

Wil 5000 (Wilshire 5000 index)
This is a value-weighted index of the most-active U.S. stocks. The Wilshire 5000 measures the performance of the broad domestic market.

Wil REIT (Wilshire Real-Estate Investment Trust index)
This is an index of real-estate investment trusts.

Investment Style Box

see also Current Investment Style, Investment Style History, and Morningstar Category

To help investors cut through the confusion and profusion of fund types, Morningstar has designed the style box, a visual tool for better understanding a fund's true investment strategy. Based on an analysis of a fund's portfolio, the Morningstar Style Box is a snapshot of the types of securities currently held by the fund. The style box is calculated with methodology similar to that used to assign the Morningstar Categories.

Location: Portfolio Analysis section.

Domestic-Stock Style Box

The stock style box is a nine-box matrix that displays both the fund's investment approach and the size of the companies in which it invests. Combining these two variables offers a broad view of a fund's holdings and risk.

Along the vertical axis of the stock style box, we categorize funds by their median market capitalizations. Along the horizontal axis of the style box are the three types of investment styles. Morningstar categorizes a fund's style as being growth, value, or a blend of the two. Generally speaking, a growth portfolio will mostly contain companies that its portfolio manager believes have the potential to increase earnings faster than the rest of the market. A value orientation, on the other hand, focuses on stocks that the manager thinks are currently undervalued in price and believes will eventually see their worth recognized by the market. A blend fund will mix the two philosophies: The portfolio may contain growth stocks and value stocks, or it may contain stocks that exhibit both characteristics.

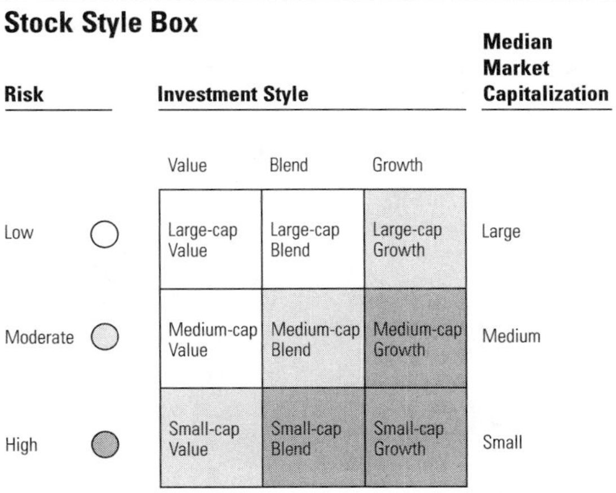

Stock Style Box

Risk		Investment Style: Value	Blend	Growth	Median Market Capitalization
Low	○	Large-cap Value	Large-cap Blend	Large-cap Growth	Large
Moderate	○	Medium-cap Value	Medium-cap Blend	Medium-cap Growth	Medium
High	●	Small-cap Value	Small-cap Blend	Small-cap Growth	Small

Within the stock style box grid, nine possible combinations exist, ranging from large-cap value for the safest funds to small-cap growth for the riskiest.

To determine a stock fund's style box, we begin by grouping the fund's stocks into market-cap classes: large, medium, or small. To determine a stock's market-cap group, we take the largest 5,000 U.S. stocks and classify the top 5% as large caps, the next 15% medium caps, and the remaining 80% small caps. We update these market-cap boundaries monthly to stay in step with the market fluctuations. We then rank each stock within each market-cap group by the stock's price/earnings and price/book ratios and determine the market-cap-weighted P/E and P/B of each market-cap group. We then create a relative valuation score (the sum of its P/E and P/B scores) for each stock. If a stock's score is 12.5% below the market-cap-weighted median, the stock is value; 12.5% above the median, it is growth. If the score falls in between, it is blend.

After classifying each stock's market cap and valuations, we tackle the fund. We call a fund large, medium, or small based on its portfolio's weighted median market cap. To classify the fund's investment style, we rank the fund's stocks by their relative valuation scores. The fund's dollar-weighted median determines its investment style. If the median stock is growth, we classify the fund as growth. If it's value, the fund is value.

In essence, we are going to the center of a fund's portfolio; a few extreme stocks on either end won't throw off our calculation.

International-Stock Style Box

These style boxes are similar to the domestic-stock style boxes described above, although the methodology is different.

On the vertical axis, international-stock funds are grouped as small, medium, or large. Funds with median market capitalizations of less than $1 billion are grouped in the small-cap box. Funds with median market caps equal to or greater than $1 billion but less than or equal to $5 billion are labeled as medium-cap offerings. Funds with median market caps exceeding $5 billion are large cap.

On the horizontal axis, international-stock funds, like their domestic counterparts, are separated into value, blend, or growth funds. We take the stock portfolio's average price/cash-flow ratio relative to the MSCI EAFE index and add it to the portfolio's average price/book figure relative to the MSCI EAFE index. (The MSCI EAFE average in each case is set equal to 1.00.) If the sum of the relative

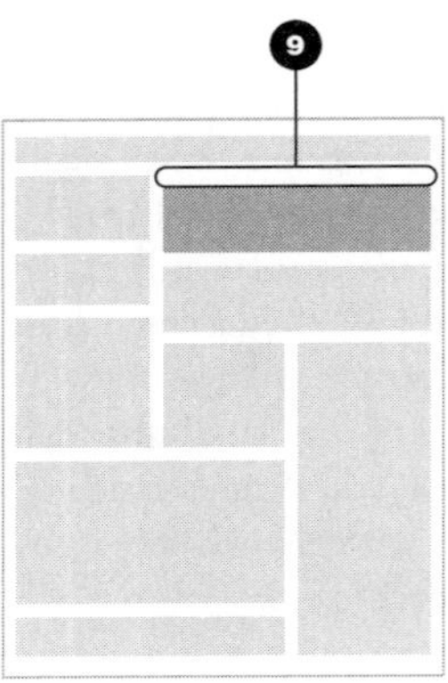

price/cash flow and the relative price/book is less than 1.75, the fund is defined as a value offering; if the sum lands from 1.75 to 2.25, the fund is classified as a blend vehicle; if the sum is greater than 2.25, the fund falls into the growth column.

Bond Style Box

Domestic- and international-bond funds feature their own Morningstar Style Box, which focuses on two pillars of bond performance: interest-rate sensitivity and credit quality. Morningstar splits bond funds into three groups of rate sensitivity as determined by duration (short, intermediate, and long) and three credit-quality groups (high, medium, and low). These groupings graphically display a portfolio's average effective duration and credit quality. As with stock funds, nine possible combinations exist, ranging from short duration/high quality for the safest funds to long duration/low quality for the more volatile.

Along the horizontal axis of the style box lies the interest-rate sensitivity of a fund's bond portfolio based on average effective duration. This figure, which is calculated by the fund companies, weights each bond's duration by its relative size within the portfolio. Duration provides a more accurate description of a bond's true interest-rate sensitivity than does maturity because it takes into consideration all mortgage prepayments, puts and call options, and adjustable coupons. Funds with an average effective duration of less than 3.5 years

Bond Style Box

Risk	Duration: Short	Intermediate	Long	Quality
Low	Short-term High Quality	Interm-term High Quality	Long-term High Quality	High
Moderate	Short-term Medium Quality	Interm-term Medium Quality	Long-term Medium Quality	Medium
High	Short-term Low Quality	Interm-term Low Quality	Long-Term Low Quality	Low

Within the bond box grid, nine possible combinations exist, ranging from short duration or maturity/high quality for the safest funds to long duration or maturity/low quality for the riskiest.

qualify as short term. Funds with an average effective duration of greater than or equal to 3.5 years and less than or equal to six years are classified as intermediate. Funds with an average effective duration of greater than six years are considered long term. (The duration ranges are slightly different for municipal-bond funds: Less than 4.5 years is short term; 4.5 to seven years is intermediate; greater than seven years is long term.)

If duration data are not available, Morningstar will use average effective maturity figures to calculate the fund's style box. Although duration is the more accurate measurement, maturity can also be used to gauge the amount of interest-rate risk in a fund's portfolio. Funds with an average effective maturity of less than four years qualify as short term. Funds with bonds that have an average effective maturity greater than or equal to four years but less than or equal to 10 years are categorized as intermediate, and those with maturity that exceeds 10 years are long term.

Along the vertical axis of a bond style box lies the average credit-quality rating of a bond portfolio. Funds that have an average credit rating of AAA or AA are categorized as high quality. Bond portfolios with average ratings of A or BBB are medium quality, and those rated BB and below are categorized as low quality. For the purposes of Morningstar's calculations, U.S. government securities are considered AAA bonds, nonrated municipal bonds generally are classified as BB, and all other nonrated bonds generally are considered B.

For hybrid categories, both stock and bond style boxes appear on the page.

9 Investment Style History

see also Investment Style Box

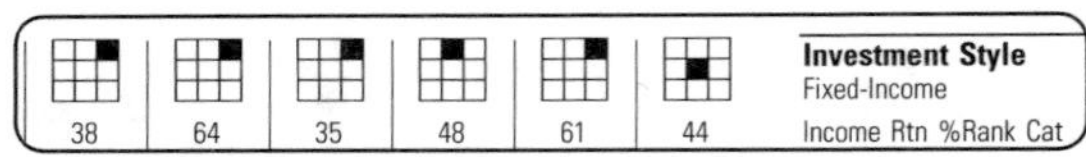

A fund's Morningstar Style Box can change over time, perhaps because of a manager or strategy change, or because market forces affect a portfolio's price ratios. To give investors an idea of how a fund's investment style has varied, a row of style boxes is included above the Performance Graph section. Each style box shows where a fund placed at the beginning of the calendar year. This feature chronicles such aspects as consistency in investment style, or it may help explain why a fund did especially well or poorly during growth- or value-driven periods or in periods when lower-quality issues were in favor.

Location: Performance Graph section.

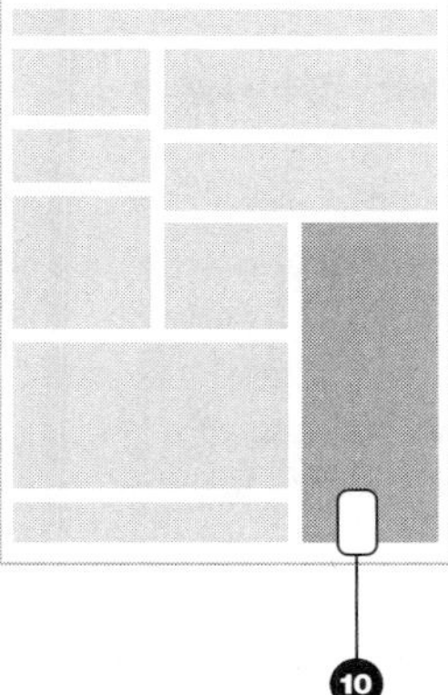

10

IRA Purchase
see Minimum Purchase

L

Load
see also Expenses and Fees
Load denotes either a fund's maximum initial or deferred sales charge. For initial, or front-end, loads, this figure is expressed as a percentage of the initial investment and is incurred upon purchase of fund shares. For deferred sales charges (also known as back-end loads or contingent deferred sales charges), the amount charged is based on the lesser of the initial or final value of the shares sold. If the fund does not have a load and remains open to investors, None appears. We list 12b-1 only in this space if the fund has no sales fees, but does have a 12b-1 fee. If the fund no longer offers shares to new investors, Closed is listed here. A percentage followed by a w indicates that, at the time of publication, the fund is waiving its load for the general public.
Location: Banner section.

Load-Adjusted Return %
For this statistic, total returns are adjusted downward to account for sales charges and are listed for the trailing one-, three-, five-, and 10-year periods. For funds with front-end loads, the full amount of the load is deducted. For deferred, or back-end loads, the percentage charged often declines the longer shares are held. This charge, often coupled with a 12b-1 fee, usually disappears entirely after several years. Morningstar adjusts the deferred load accordingly when making this calculation. For funds that lack a 10-year history, an annualized load-adjusted return figure for the period since the fund's inception is provided.
Location: Risk Analysis section.

M

Management Fee
see Expenses and Fees

Manager
see Portfolio Manager

Manager Change
see also Portfolio Manager
It is important for investors to know how much of a fund's performance can be attributed to current management. We track manager changes by using four symbols, which indicate a fund's managerial history, including partial and total manager changes, along with periods of incomplete data. The symbol (▼) marks a total manager change, when an entirely new manager or team of comanagers assumed fund leadership. The symbol (▽) indicates a partial change, when at least one manager remains with the fund while another joins or leaves. The symbol (►) marks the point at which a fund switched to a team-managed designation and stopped disclosing the names of specific individuals working on the fund. Conversely, the symbol (◄) marks the point at which a fund began to disclose the names of its managers. This symbol is also used when Morningstar has incomplete historical information about the management of the fund.
Location: Performance Graph section.

10 Market Cap
see also Median Market Capitalization

Market Cap	
Giant	17.0
Large	24.3
Medium	46.9
Small	11.9
Micro	0.0

Shown for domestic-stock funds, this section gives investors a view of the different sizes of companies in a fund's portfolio. Every month, we break down a stock portfolio into five different sizes of companies by their market capitalization and show what percentage of a fund's stock assets is devoted to each. Instead of using stationary market-cap cutoffs, we base our boundaries on percentiles: We call the largest 1% of U.S. companies Giant, the next 4% Large, the next 15% Medium, the next 30% Small, and the bottom 50% Micro. The Market Cap section is designed to help investors complete the picture suggested by the median market cap statistic. While median market cap pinpoints the size of the average holding (half the holdings are larger and half are smaller), this section allows investors to see the whole range of companies held by the fund.
Location: Portfolio Analysis section of domestic-stock pages.

Maturity
see Average Effective Maturity and Average Nominal Maturity

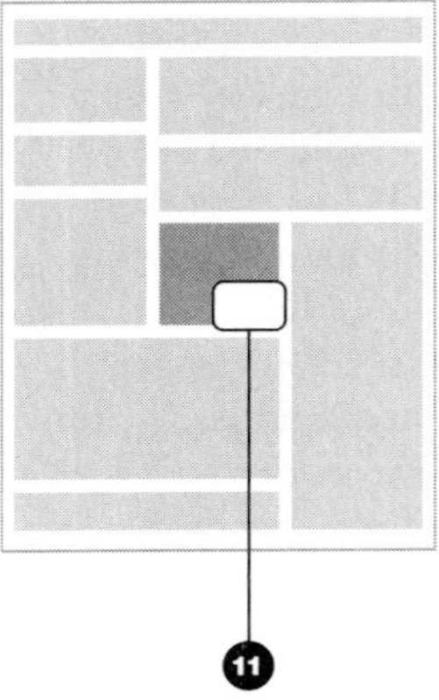

Mean

see Standard Deviation

Median Market Capitalization (Med Mkt Cap)

see also Market Cap and Relative Comparisons

The median market capitalization of a stock portfolio gives the reader a measure of the size of the companies in which the fund invests. (Market capitalization is calculated by multiplying the number of a company's shares outstanding by its price per share.) We use a trimmed mean to calculate a fund's median market cap. First, we rank the common stocks (domestic and international) in a fund's portfolio from highest to lowest based on their market capitalization. Next, we identify the stocks that fall into the middle quintile of the portfolio. We then calculate the average-weighted market cap of the stocks in this middle quintile. The result is the fund's median market cap. The advantage of a median over an average is that the median is not disproportionately affected by one or two giant-cap or micro-cap holdings. For example, a small-cap fund that holds a small position in General Electric for liquidity purposes won't have its market cap unduly skewed by that company's market cap, unless it has a substantial portion of its assets in that stock.

Location: Portfolio Analysis section of stock pages.

Minimum Automatic Investment Plan (Min Auto Inv Plan)

This indicates the smallest amount with which an investor may enter a fund's automatic-investment plan— an arrangement where the fund takes money on a monthly, quarterly, semiannual, or annual basis from the shareholder's checking account. Often, the normal minimum initial purchase requirements are waived in lieu of this systematic investment plan. Studies indicate that regular automatic investment (also known as dollar-cost averaging) can be a very successful investment plan for long-term investors.

Location: Operations section.

Minimum Purchase

Minimum purchase indicates the smallest investment amount a fund will accept to establish a new account. Also noted is the smallest additional purchase a fund will accept in an existing account (this figure follows the designation Add). None indicates initial or additional investments can be of any amount. In addition, we include the smallest permissible initial investment a fund will accept in an individual retirement account (IRA). If the fund does not offer an IRA program, N/A will appear.

Location: Operations section.

⓫ Modern Portfolio Theory Statistics

Other Measures	Standard Index S&P 500	Best Fit Index Wil 4500
Alpha	-8.7	3.7
Beta	1.26	1.12
R-Squared	80	91

Alpha, beta, and R-squared are components of Modern Portfolio Theory (MPT), which is a standard financial and academic method for assessing the performance of a fund, relative to a benchmark. To understand how to use MPT stats, readers unfamiliar with them may want to begin with the explanation of R-squared (below), then move to beta, and finally to alpha. The three statistics should be used in combination with each other.

Morningstar bases alpha, beta, and R-squared on a least-squares regression of the fund's excess return over Treasury bills compared with the excess returns of the fund's benchmark index (the S&P 500 for stock-oriented funds and the Lehman Brothers Aggregate Bond index for bond funds). These calculations are computed for the trailing 36-month period.

Morningstar also shows additional alpha, beta, and R-squared statistics based on a regression against the Best Fit Index. The Best Fit Index for each fund is selected based on the highest R-squared result from separate regressions on a number of indexes. (See also Best Fit Index for descriptions.) If the standard index already has the highest R-squared, it will be shown again as the Best Fit Index. For example, many high-yield funds show low R-squared results and thus a low degree of correlation when regressed against the standard bond index, the Lehman Brothers Aggregate. These low R-squared results indicate that the index does not explain well the behavior of most high-yield funds. Most high-yield funds, however, show significantly higher R-squared results when regressed against the CSFB High-Yield index.

Both the standard and best-fit results can be useful to investors. The standard index R-squared statistics can help investors plan the diversification of their portfolio of funds. For example, an investor who wishes to diversify and already owns a fund with a very high correlation (and thus high R-squared) with the S&P 500 might choose not to buy another fund that correlates closely to that index. In addition, the Best Fit Index can be used to compare the betas and alphas of similar funds that show the same Best Fit Index.

Location: Risk Analysis section.

Alpha

Alpha measures the difference between a fund's actual returns and its expected performance, given its level of risk (as measured by beta). A positive alpha figure indicates the fund has performed better than its beta would predict. In contrast, a negative alpha indicates a fund has underperformed, given the expectations established by the fund's beta. Many investors see alpha as a measurement of the value added or subtracted by a fund's manager.

There are limitations to alpha's ability to accurately depict a fund's added or subtracted value. In some cases, a negative alpha can result from the expenses that are present in the fund figures but are not present in the figures of the comparison index. Alpha is completely dependent on the accuracy of beta: If the investor accepts beta as a conclusive definition of risk, a positive alpha would be a conclusive indicator of good fund performance.

Beta

Beta is a measure of a fund's sensitivity to market movements. It measures the relationship between a fund's excess return over T-bills and the excess return of the benchmark index. Morningstar calculates beta using the same regression equation as the one used for alpha, which regresses excess return for the fund against excess return for the index. This approach differs slightly from other methodologies that rely on a regression of raw returns.

By definition, the beta of the benchmark (in this case, an index) is 1.00. Accordingly, a fund with a 1.10 beta has performed 10% better than its benchmark index after deducting the T-bill rate than the index in up markets and 10% worse in down markets, assuming all other factors remain constant. Conversely, a beta of 0.85 indicates that the fund has performed 15% worse than the index in up markets and 15% better in down markets. A low beta does not imply that the fund has a low level of volatility, though; rather, a low beta means only that the fund's market-related risk is low. A specialty fund that invests primarily in gold, for example, will usually have a low beta (and a low R-squared), as its performance is tied more closely to the price of gold and gold-mining stocks than to the overall stock market. Thus, though the specialty fund might fluctuate wildly because of rapid changes in gold prices, its beta will remain low.

R-squared

R-squared ranges from 0 to 100 and reflects the percentage of a fund's movements that are explained by movements in its benchmark index. An R-squared of 100 means that all movements of a fund are completely correlated with movements in the index. Thus, index funds that invest only in S&P 500 stocks will have an R-squared very close to 100. Conversely, a low R-squared indicates that very few of the fund's movements are explained by movements in its benchmark index. An R-squared measure of 35, for example, means that only 35% of the fund's movements can be explained by movements in its benchmark index. Therefore, R-squared can be used to ascertain the significance of a particular beta or alpha. Generally, a high R-squared will indicate a more reliable beta figure. If the R-squared is low, then the beta explains less of the fund's performance.

12 Morningstar Category

see also Investment Style Box

Mstar Category
Mid–Cap Growth

While the investment objective stated in a fund's prospectus may or may not reflect how the fund actually invests, the Morningstar Category is assigned based on the underlying securities in each portfolio. We assign categories based on three years of portfolio statistics.

The Morningstar Category helps investors make meaningful comparisons among funds. The categories make it easier to build well-diversified portfolios, assess potential risk, and identify the top-performing funds.

The following is a list and explanation of the categories. We place funds in a given category based on their portfolio statistics and compositions over the past three years. If the fund is new and has no portfolio history, we estimate where it will fall before giving it a more permanent category assignment. When necessary, we may change a category assignment based on recent changes to the portfolio.

Location: Banner section.

Stock Funds

Domestic-Stock Funds

Funds with at least 70% of assets in domestic stocks are categorized based on the style and size of the stocks they typically own. The style and size divisions reflect those used in the investment style box: value, blend, or growth style and small, medium, or large median market capitalization. Based on their investment style over the past three years, diversified domestic-stock funds are placed in one of the nine categories shown below:

Large Growth	Medium Growth	Small Growth
Large Blend	Medium Blend	Small Blend
Large Value	Medium Value	Small Value

These categories are based on the same parameters used for the domestic-stock style box. The portfolio's stocks are grouped by market cap. We then rank stocks in each market-cap group by their price/earnings and price/book ratios, and give valuation scores relative to each market-cap group's median P/E and P/B.

Growth: stocks with valuation scores at least 12.5% higher than the median for their market-cap group.

Blend: stocks with valuation scores up to but not including 12.5% higher or 12.5% lower than the median.

Value: stocks with valuation scores at least 12.5% lower than the median.

Large: portfolio's weighted median market cap within the top 5% of the 5,000 largest U.S. stocks.

Medium: portfolio's weighted median market cap within the next 15% of the 5,000 largest U.S. stocks.

Small: portfolio's weighted median market cap within the remaining 80% of the 5,000 largest U.S. stocks.

Morningstar also includes several other domestic-stock categories:

Communications, Financials, Heath Care, Natural Resources, Precious Metals, Real Estate, Technology, Utilities, Convertible Bond (convertible-bond funds have at least 50% of their assets invested in convertible securities), and Domestic Hybrid (domestic-hybrid funds have at least 20% but less than 70% of their assets invested in stocks; they must also invest at least 10% of assets in bonds).

International-Stock Funds

Stock funds that have invested 40% or more of their equity holdings in foreign stocks (on average over the past three years) are placed in an international-stock category, based on the following parameters:

Europe: at least 75% of stocks invested in Europe.

Latin America: at least 75% of stocks invested in Latin America.

Diversified Emerging Markets: at least 50% of stocks invested in emerging markets.

Diversified Asia/Pacific: at least 65% of stocks invested in Pacific countries, with at least an additional 10% of stocks invested in Japan.

Asia/Pacific ex-Japan: at least 75% of stocks in Pacific countries, with less than 10% of stocks invested in Japan.

Japan: at least 75% of stocks invested in Japan.

Foreign: an international fund having no more than 10% of stocks invested in the United States.

World: an international fund having more than 10% of stocks invested in the United States.

International Hybrid: used for funds with stock holdings of greater than 20% but less than 70% of the portfolio where 40% of the stocks and bonds are foreign. Also must have at least 10% of assets invested in bonds

Bond Funds

Funds with 80% or more of their assets invested in bonds are classified as bond funds. Bond funds are divided into two main groups: taxable bond and municipal bond. Note: For all bond funds, maturity figures are used only when duration figures are unavailable.

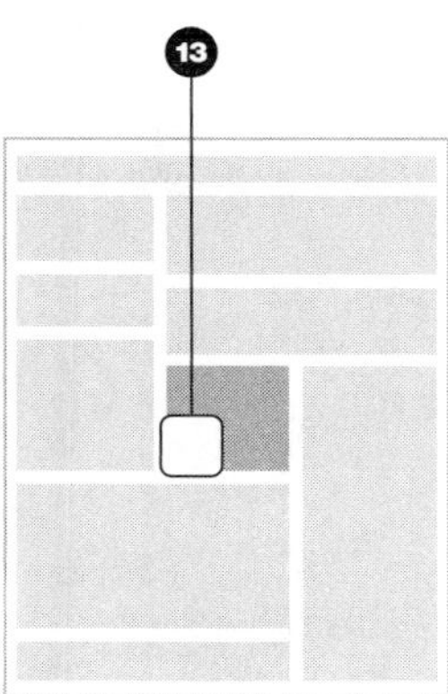

Taxable-Bond Funds

Long-Term Government: at least 90% of bond portfolio invested in government issues with a duration of greater than or equal to six years, or an average effective maturity of greater than or equal to 10 years.

Intermediate-Term Government: at least 90% of bond portfolio invested in government issues with a duration of greater than or equal to 3.5 years and less than six years, or an average effective maturity of greater than or equal to four years and less than 10 years.

Short-Term Government: at least 90% of bond portfolio invested in government issues with a duration of greater than or equal to one year and less than 3.5 years, or an average effective maturity of greater than or equal to one year and less than four years.

Long-Term Bond: focuses on corporate and other investment-grade issues with an average duration of more than six years, or an average effective maturity of more than 10 years.

Intermediate-Term Bond: focuses on corporate and other investment-grade issues with an average duration of greater than or equal to 3.5 years but less than or equal to six years, or an average effective maturity of more than four but less than 10 years.

Short-Term Bond: focuses on corporate and other investment-grade issues with an average duration of greater than or equal to one but less than 3.5 years, or an average effective maturity of more than one but less than four years.

Ultrashort Bond: used for funds with an average duration or an average effective maturity of less than one year. This category includes general corporate and government bond funds, and excludes any international, convertible, multisector and high-yield bond funds.

High-Yield Bond: at least 65% of assets in bonds rated below BBB.

Multisector Bond: seeks income by diversifying assets among several fixed-income sectors, usually U.S. government obligations, foreign bonds, and high-yield domestic debt securities.

International Bond: at least 40% of bonds invested in foreign markets.

Emerging-Markets Bond: at least 65% assets in emerging-market bonds.

Municipal-Bond Funds

Muni National Long-Term: a national fund with an average duration of more than seven years or an average maturity of more than 12 years.

Muni National Intermediate-Term: a national fund with an average duration of between 4.5 years and seven years, or an average maturity of between five years and 12 years.

Muni New York Long-Term: a fund with at least 80% of assets in New York municipal debt, with average duration of more than seven years or an average maturity of more than 12.

Muni New York Intermediate: a fund with at least 80% of assets in New York municipal debt, with average duration of between 4.5 years and seven years.

Muni California Long-Term: a fund with at least 80% of assets in California municipal debt, with average duration of more than seven years or an average maturity of more than 12.

Muni California Intermediate: a fund with at least 80% of assets in California municipal debt, with average duration of between 4.5 years and seven years.

Muni Single-State Long-Term: a single-state fund with an average duration of more than seven years or an average maturity of more than 12 years.

Muni Single-State Intermediate-Term: a single-state fund with an average duration of between 4.5 years and seven years, or an average maturity of between five years and 12 years.

Muni Bond Short-Term (national and single state): focuses on municipal debt/bonds with an average duration of less than 4.5 years or an average maturity of less than five years.

13 Morningstar Category Rating

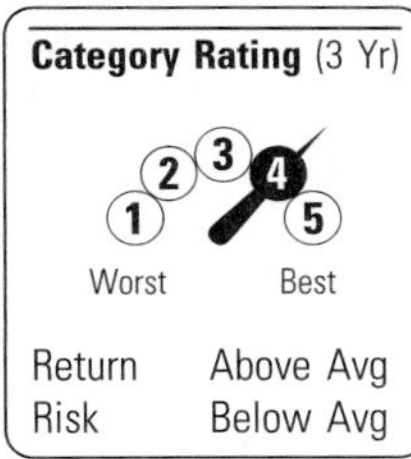

The Morningstar Category Rating shows how well a fund has balanced risk and return over the past three years, relative to other funds in its Morningstar Category. The category rating uses similar methodology for measuring risk and return as the Morningstar Risk-Adjusted Rating (the star rating). As with the star rating, 5 is the best rating, and 1 is the worst. There are, however, a few significant differences between the two rating systems. Unlike the star rating, the category rating does not reflect any front- or back-end loads. Other expenses, such as the 12b-1 fee, are included. In addition, the category rating measures risk-adjusted return over the trailing three-year period only, while the star rating is calculated for the trailing five- and 10-year periods as well. See Risk Analysis for a full description of the methodology used to calculate the star and category ratings.

Location: Risk Analysis section.

Morningstar Return

see Risk Analysis

Morningstar Risk
see Risk Analysis

Morningstar Risk-Adjusted Rating
see Risk Analysis

Morningstar Style Box
see Investment Style Box

N

NAV
see Net Asset Value

Net Assets
see also Total Assets
This figure gives the fund's asset base, net of fees and expenses, at year-end of past calendar years and at month-end for the current year.
Location: History section.

Net Asset Value
A fund's net asset value (NAV) represents its per-share price. A fund's NAV is derived by dividing the total net assets of the fund by the number of shares outstanding.
Location: Banner and History sections.

No-Load
see also Expenses and Fees
This label denotes the fund as a true no-load fund, charging no sales or 12b-1 fees.

NTF Plans
This indicates which No Transaction Fee programs offer the fund. Wrap programs are not included in this section.
Location: Operations section.

Objective
see Prospectus Objective

One-Year Earnings Estimate
This figure is an average of the estimated short-term earnings growth for the U.S. companies in the portfolio. We first obtain Wall Street's consensus earnings estimates from Zacks Investment Research, Inc. for each stock's next-reported fiscal year. We then compare that earnings estimate with the stock's most recently reported actual earnings to form a one-year estimated growth rate. Morningstar computes this rate for each stock and then calculates the weighted average for the whole portfolio of stocks. We recalculate this figure every month based on month-end stock share prices.
Location: Portfolio Analysis section of stock pages.

Options/Futures/Warrants
see Special Securities

Other Measures
see Modern Portfolio Theory Statistics, Standard Deviation, Sharpe Ratio

---

Partial Manager Change
see Manager Change

P/E
see P/E entry in Portfolio Analysis. See also Price/Earnings Ratio.

Percent Assets
see Portfolio Analysis

Percentage Pretax Return
see Tax Analysis

Percentile Rank (% Rank)
see also Performance
Located in the Performance, History, and Risk Analysis sections, these rankings allow investors to compare a fund's total returns and Morningstar Risk score with those of other funds.

In the Performance section, we list two total-return percentile rankings for each fund for various time periods. The first compares a fund with all funds in the Morningstar database (% Rank All), while the second compares the fund's total return for that period against the same Morningstar Category (% Rank Cat). In the History section, we compare a fund's calendar-year total returns to its category's (Total Rtn % Rank Cat). In both sections, a fund's total returns are ranked on a scale from 1 to 100 where 1 represents the highest-returning 1% of funds and 100 represents the lowest-returning funds. Thus, in the Performance section, a percentile rank of 15 under the % Rank Cat column for the trailing three-month period indicates that the fund's three-month return placed in the top 15% of all funds in its category for that time period.

In the Risk Analysis section, we use the per-

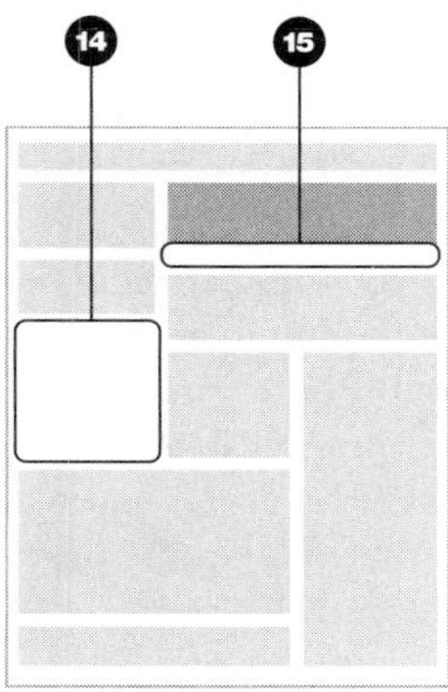

centile rank to compare a fund's Morningstar Risk score against all funds and its category (Risk % Rank All/Cat). On a scale from 1 to 100, 1 represents the lowest-risk percentile and 100 represents the highest risk.

Location: Performance, History, and Risk Analysis sections.

⓮ Performance

see also Total Return and Tax Analysis

Performance 12-31-98

	1st Qtr	2nd Qtr	3rd Qtr	4th Qtr	Total	
1994	–5.82	–5.46	0.53	–1.53	–11.87	
1995	8.49	10.58	11.96	4.25	40.02	
1996	6.25	4.23	5.28	5.77	23.33	
1997	–1.63	16.69	17.64	–5.91	27.06	
1998	13.40	1.14	–20.30	27.28	16.34	
Trailing	Total Return%	+/– S&P 500	+/– Wil MC Grth	% Rank All	% Rank Cat	Growth of $10,000
3 Mo	27.28	6.00	5.42	7	45	12,728
6 Mo	1.44	–7.80	5.55	65	65	10,144
1 Yr	16.34	–12.23	17.42	23	56	11,634
3 Yr Avg	22.16	–6.06	11.30	12	12	18,232
5 Yr Avg	17.61	–6.44	3.78	18	30	22,498
10 Yr Avg	15.77	–3.43	0.61	20	49	43,243
15 Yr Avg	—	—	—	—	—	—

The tables in this section display the fund's total return figures for various time periods. The trailing total returns are as of the date listed in the section heading above. The trailing total returns are accompanied by relative statistics that allow readers to compare the returns with appropriate indexes and category averages.

Location: Performance section.

Quarterly Returns

The first section provides the fund's quarterly and year-end total returns for the past five years. The quarterly returns are compounded to obtain the year-end total return shown on the right. (Calculating the sum of the four quarterly returns will not produce the year-end total return because simple addition does not take into account the effects of compounding.)

Total Return %

This figure is calculated by taking the change in net asset value, reinvesting all income and capital-gains distributions during the period, and dividing by the starting net asset value.

See also Total Return for more information about the calculation.

+/–S&P 500

This statistic measures the difference between a stock fund's total return and the total return of the S&P 500 index. A negative number indicates that the fund underperformed the index by the given amount, while a positive number indicates that the fund outperformed the index by the given amount. For example, a listing of -2.0 indicates that the fund underperformed the index by two percentage points. The difference between each stock fund's performance and the S&P 500 index is listed. Bond funds are compared with the Lehman Brothers Aggregate Bond index. The next column shows the same performance figure relative to another more specialized benchmark index.

See also Indexes for a complete list of the indexes and their abbreviations.

% Rank All/Cat

Morningstar lists two total return percentile rankings for each fund for various time periods. The first compares a fund with all funds in the Morningstar database (% Rank All), while the second compares the fund's total return for that period against the funds in the same Morningstar Category (% Rank Cat). In both cases 1 is the highest or best percentile ranking and 100 is the lowest, or worst.

See also Percentile Rank.

Growth of $10,000

This column shows the current value of a $10,000 investment made at the beginning of each of the time periods listed. These calculations are not load- or tax-adjusted.

⓯ Performance Quartile Graph

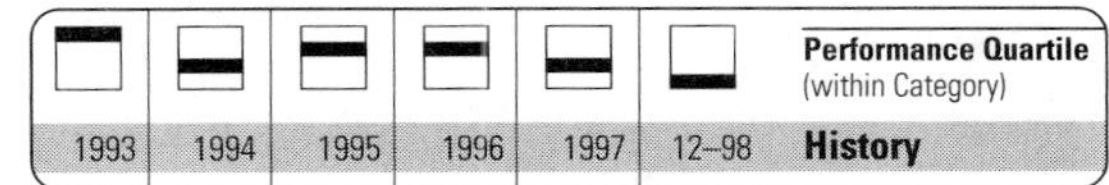

The Performance Quartile graph is a representation of the fund's calendar-year total-return percentile rank among funds in the same category. This information is presented numerically in the History section (Total Rtn % Rank Cat). The black bar on the graph represents the quartile in which the fund's performance ranking falls. If the top quarter of the graph is shaded, for example, the fund performed among the top 25% of its category that year.

Location: Performance Graph section.

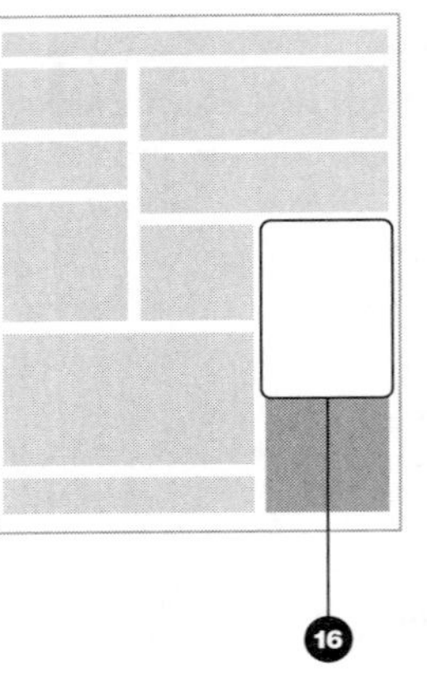

16

16 Portfolio Analysis

Portfolio Analysis 12-31-98

Share change since 09-98 Total Stocks: 120	Sector	PE	1998 Ret%	% Assets
⊕ America Online	Services	NMF	587.30	2.35
⊖ EMC/Mass	Technology	63.9	209.70	1.79
⊕ MCI WorldCom	Services	—	137.10	1.72
⊕ Safeway	Retail	40.1	92.69	1.62
☼ E Trade Group	Technology	NMF	103.40	1.58
⊕ MBNA	Financials	27.4	37.80	1.56
⊕ Abercrombie & Fitch Cl A	Retail	NMF	126.40	1.54
⊕ Providian Financial	Financials	—	—	1.42
⊖ Cisco Systems	Technology	98.7	149.70	1.37
⊕ Mastech	Technology	48.9	80.31	1.31
⊕ Compuware	Technology	59.6	144.10	1.29
⊖ Home Depot	Retail	61.5	108.40	1.27
⊖ Microsoft	Technology	68.0	114.60	1.24
⊖ TJX	Retail	24.5	69.61	1.23
⊕ Lexmark International Cl A	Technology	33.3	164.40	1.21
⊖ Lucent Technologies	Technology	NMF	175.90	1.16
⊖ Merck	Health	35.5	41.32	1.10
⊖ Citrix Systems	Technology	NMF	91.57	1.10
⊖ Clorox	Staples	40.1	49.42	1.10
⊖ Eli Lilly	Health	49.9	29.08	1.09
⊖ Intl Network Services	Services	NMF	187.50	1.07
☼ Sun Microsystems	Technology	43.9	114.70	1.07
⊕ Tele-Comm Liberty Media Cl A	Services	—	—	1.07
⊖ Pfizer	Health	50.2	68.93	1.04
⊖ Watson Pharmaceuticals	Health	53.3	93.83	1.04

Occupying much of the right side of the page is the Portfolio Analysis section. Prominent in this section are the fund's most recently reported top securities (excluding cash and cash equivalents for all but short-term bond funds), ranked in descending order by the percentage of the portfolio's net assets they occupy. With this information, investors can more clearly identify what drives the fund's performance.

Morningstar makes every effort to gather the most up-to-date portfolio information from a fund. By law, however, funds need only report this information two times during a calendar year, and they have two months after the report date to actually release the shareholder report and portfolio. Therefore, it is possible that a fund's portfolio could be up to eight months old at the time of publication. We print the date the portfolio was reported. Older portfolios should not be disregarded, however; although the list may not represent the exact current holdings of the fund, it may still provide a good picture of the overall nature of the fund's management style.
Location: Portfolio Analysis section.

Items that pertain to the fund's portfolio are detailed below:

Total Stocks/Total Fixed-Income
Total Stocks indicates the total number of stock securities in a fund's portfolio, and Total Fixed-Income denotes the number of bond securities a fund holds. These do not simply refer to the stocks or bonds listed on the page; rather, they represent all stocks and bonds in the portfolio. These listings can be quite useful for gaining greater insight into the portfolio's diversification.

Share Change
Applied only to common stocks, the share change entry indicates the change in the number of shares of each stock from the previously reported portfolio. The share change column is dated and represents the change from the portfolio received just prior to the current one on the page. For stock funds, we indicate whether a fund has enlarged, reduced, or initiated new positions with the following symbols: (⊕) for purchases, (⊖) for sales, and (☼) for new holdings.

Security
This column lists the names of the stock or bond securities held as of the portfolio date. For stock holdings, this line typically displays just the name of the issuing company. Other stock labels are included where appropriate, such as ADR, which distinguishes an American Depository Receipt. Bond holdings, however, will usually include more information to differentiate among the many types of bonds available. For most bonds, the coupon rate is listed as a percentage figure after the name of the bond. Adjustable-rate mortgages and floating-rate notes will have ARM or FRN (or IFRN for inverse-floating rate notes) listed after the name of the bond to indicate that the coupon rate is variable. Some adjustable-rate bond listings will include the formula by which the coupon rate is calculated, which is usually a fixed percentage plus some benchmark value. Securities followed by the abbreviation IO are interest-only securities, or those that consist only of the interest portion of a security, not the principal portion. PO indicates a principal-only security that sells at a discount to par and carries a coupon rate of zero.

Sector
The industry sector of each stock holding is reported in this column. This gives investors greater insight into where a fund's top holdings are concentrated and where its vulnerabilities lie. For specialty funds, we list each stock's subsector.

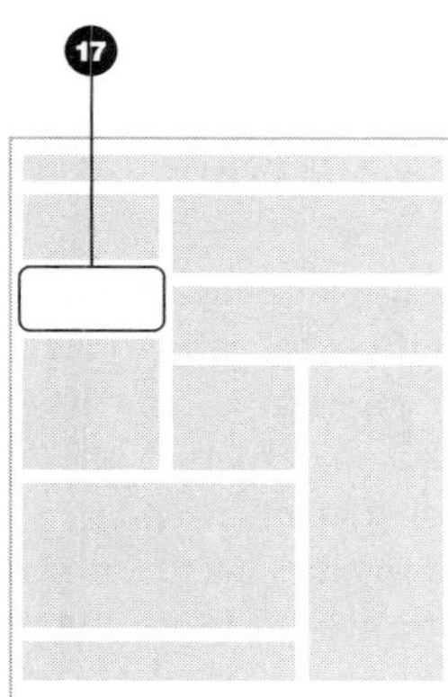

P/E
To add depth to the average P/E number for the entire portfolio (listed under Current Investment Style), the P/E ratio for each stock is reported here. NMF means the stock's P/E is 100 or more. A minus sign means the company has no earnings or the figure is not available.
See also Price/Earnings Ratio.

YTD Return %
The year-to-date stock returns show whether one or two big winners (or losers) are driving fund performance, or a lot of little successes. In some cases, losses in top holdings can suggest a bargain-hunting strategy if a position in a losing stock is new or expanded.

% Assets
The % Assets column indicates what percentage of the portfolio's net assets a given security constitutes. Morningstar calculates the percentage of net assets figure by dividing the market value of the security by the fund's total net assets. If a given security makes up a large percentage of the fund's net assets, the fund uses a concentrated portfolio strategy, at least with respect to the security in question. If, however, the percentage figures are low, then the manager is either maintaining per-issue diversification or is simply not willing to bet heavily on a particular security.

Date of Maturity
Maturity, located in the portfolio section for bond funds only, indicates the date on which a bond or note comes due. This information can be used in determining the portfolio's basic fixed-income strategy. For example, if most of these dates are a year or two away, the fund is taking a conservative, short-term approach. The maturity dates listed here, however, are not adjusted for calls (rights an issuer may have to redeem outstanding bonds before their scheduled maturity) or for the likelihood of mortgage prepayments. Thus, they might not accurately state the actual time to repayment of a bond, and might overstate a portfolio's sensitivity to interest-rate changes.
See Average Effective Duration for a better measure of interest-rate sensitivity.

Amount
The amount column refers to the size of the portfolio's investment in a given security as of the portfolio date listed above. The size is enumerated in thousands. For stocks, this figure gives the number of shares of a particular stock currently held by the fund. For bonds, this figure reflects the principal value of the security in thousands of dollars. Funds that hold both stocks and bonds will list share amounts and principal value (both in thousands), respectively, in the amount column.

Value
Value simply gives the market value of a particular security in thousands of dollars as of the portfolio date. The value column allows investors to gauge whether a fixed-income security is selling at a premium or a discount to its face value, as reflected in the amount column.

17 Portfolio Manager(s)

Portfolio Manager(s)

Stephen A. Wohler, CFA. Since 1-98. BS'71 Naval Academy; MBA'79 U. of California-Berkeley. Wohler is a managing director with Scudder Kemper Investments, Inc., his employer since 1979.

Robert S. Cessine, CFA. Since 1-98. MS'77 U. of Maryland; MBA'82 U. of Wisconsin. Cessine is a managing director at Scudder Kemper Investments Inc.

Kelly D. Babson. Since 1-98. BA'81 Georgetown; MBA'86 New York U. Babson is a vice president at Scudder Kemper Investments, Inc., her employer since 1994.

The portfolio manager is the individual or individuals responsible for the overall fund strategy, as well as the buying and selling decisions of the securities in a fund's portfolio. To help investors know who is running a fund, we detail management with a brief biography. If a fund provides a list of several manager names, Morningstar will list them as space permits. Management teams may consist of many people, but if one manager is considered a central figure or lead manager, that individual's name will be printed. We note the year in which the manager began running the fund. This information is useful for determining how much of a fund's performance is attributable to its current management. We also include a listing of other funds managed currently or in the past by each manager.
Location: Portfolio Manager section.

Potential Capital Gain Exposure
see Tax Analysis

Price/Book Ratio
see also Relative Comparisons
The price/book ratio of a fund is the weighted average of the price/book ratios of all the stocks in a fund's portfolio. Book value is the total assets of a company, less total liabilities. A company's P/B ratio is calculated by dividing the market price of its outstanding stock by the company's book

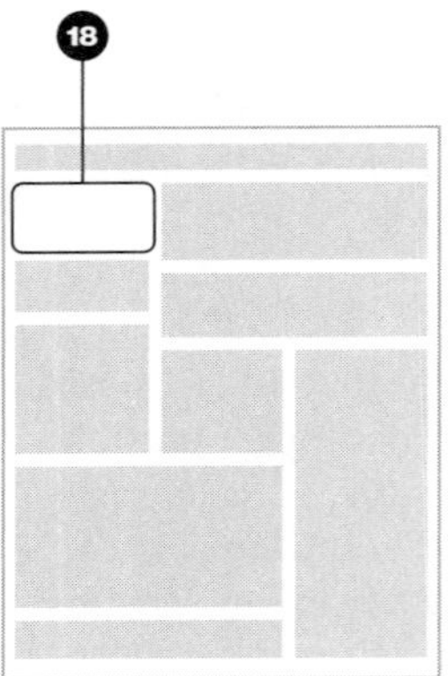

value, and then adjusting for the number of shares outstanding. (Stocks with negative book values are excluded from this calculation.) In computing a fund's average P/B ratio, Morningstar weights each portfolio holding by the percentage of equity assets it represents; larger positions thus have proportionately greater influence on the final P/B. A low P/B may indicate that the stocks are bargains, priced below what the companies assets could be worth if liquidated.
Location: Portfolio Analysis section of stock pages.

Price/Cash Flow

see also Relative Comparisons
Price/cash flow is a weighted average of the price/cash-flow ratios of the stocks in a fund's portfolio. Price/cash flow represents the amount of money an investor is willing to pay for a dollar of cash generated from a particular company's operations. Price/cash flow shows the ability of a business to generate cash and can be an effective gauge of liquidity and solvency. Because accounting conventions differ among nations, reported earnings (and thus P/B ratios) may not be comparable across national boundaries. Price/cash flow attempts to provide an internationally standardized measure of a firm's stock price relative to its financial performance.
Location: Portfolio Analysis section of stock pages.

Price/Earnings Ratio

see also Relative Comparisons
The price/earnings ratio of a fund is the weighted average of the price/earnings ratios of the stocks in a fund's portfolio. The P/E ratio of a company, which is a comparison of the price of the company's stock and its trailing 12 months earnings per share, is calculated by dividing these two figures. In computing the average, Morningstar weights each portfolio holding by the percentage of stock assets it represents; larger positions thus have proportionately greater influence on the fund's final P/E. A high P/E usually indicates that the market will pay more to obtain the company's earnings because it believes in the firm's ability to increase its earnings. (P/E can also be artificially inflated if a company has very weak trailing earnings, and thus a very small number in this equation's denominator.) A low P/E indicates the market has less confidence that the company's earnings will increase; however, a fund manager with a value investing approach may believe such stocks have been overlooked or undervalued and have potential for appreciation.
Location: Portfolio Analysis section of stock pages.

Pricing Service

Because the municipal-bond market contains a very large number of issues, many of which are small and obscure, it is common for muni funds to hold bonds that are rarely traded. In fact, some muni funds will buy up the whole supply of a municipal bond when it is issued and hold it to maturity, ensuring that the bond never trades at all. If a bond isn't traded, it has no current market price. Yet, mutual funds must calculate their net asset values at the end of every day. Most funds thus rely on an independent pricing service to estimate the prices of these bonds based on each day's market activity. Here we name the pricing service a fund uses, the most common of which are J.J. Kenny, Muller, and Interactive Data. A few funds simply estimate bond prices internally, in which case we designate those accordingly.
Location: Portfolio Analysis section of municipal-bond pages.

18 Prospectus Objective/Investment Criteria

see also Morningstar Category

Prospectus Objective: Growth

Federated Growth Strategies Trust - Class A seeks capital appreciation.

The fund invests primarily in equities of companies that have above-average earnings potential and dividend growth. It may also invest in convertibles, corporate debt, and ADRs.

Class A shares have front loads; B shares have deferred loads, higher 12b-1 fees, and conversion features; C shares have level loads. Past name: Federated Growth Trust. On Aug. 16, 1996, Capital Growth Fund - Class A merged into the fund. On Dec. 13, 1996, State Bond Common Stock Fund merged into the fund.

The prospectus objective indicates the stated investment goals of a particular fund, based on the wording in the prospectus issued by the fund's advisor. Underneath the prospectus objective is the fund's investment criteria, a description of the investment policies and objectives of the mutual fund. This section describes the objectives and strategies found in the fund's prospectus. In appropriate cases, the criteria section also clarifies the fee structures of funds that have multiple share classes or have unusual fees. Also, this section details changes in the fund's name or ownership. Because the investment criteria presents only a small portion of the information in a fund's prospectus, we recommend that investors read a fund's prospectus before investing.
Location: Investment Criteria section.

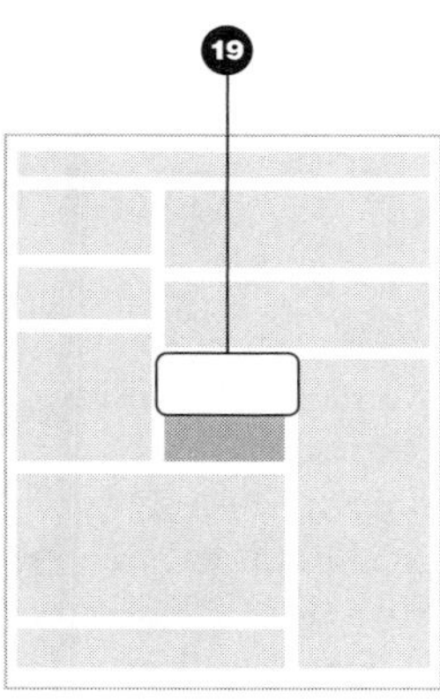

R

Rank
see Percentile Rank

Regional Exposure
All international-stock funds, as well as precious-metals funds, feature a regional exposure listing. For all but the precious-metals funds, this table displays the percentage of the fund's total net assets invested in the United States, Europe, Japan, Pacific/Asia (excluding Japan), Latin America, Africa/Middle East, and Other, which includes Canada. For precious-metals funds, the table shows the percentage of assets invested in stocks from issuers in North America, South Africa, Australia, and in other regions, or in bullion. The information in this section is gathered from portfolios and is the most recent data available.
Location: Portfolio Analysis section of international-stock and precious-metals pages.

Relative Comparisons
At various places in the Portfolio Analysis section, Morningstar shows how an individual fund compares with the average of all funds within its category (Rel Cat) or a benchmark index (Relative S&P 500). The category (or index) is always set equal to 1.00. For example, a municipal-bond fund with a utilities weighting of 1.50 relative to its category has 50% more in utilities issues than its average peer.

Stock statistics are displayed in comparison with the S&P 500 index. In this case, 1.00 represents the market average. A relative P/B ratio of 0.43, for example, indicates that the fund's P/B is 57% lower than that of the market average.
Location: Portfolio Analysis section.

Restricted/Illiquid Securities
see Special Securities

Return
see Risk Analysis and Total Return

Risk
see Risk Analysis, Standard Deviation, and Modern Portfolio Theory Statistics

19 Risk Analysis
see also Historical Profile

Risk Analysis

Time Period	Load-Adj Return %	Risk %Rank[1] All	Risk %Rank[1] Cat	Morningstar Return	Morningstar Risk	Morningstar Risk-Adj Rating
1 Yr	6.11					
3 Yr	6.04	35	48	0.17[2]	0.91	★★★
5 Yr	6.18	34	70	0.22[2]	1.04	★★★
10 Yr	8.81	32	52	0.88[2]	0.93	★★★★
Average Historical Rating (157 months):						3.6★s

[1] 1=low, 100=high [2] T-Bill return substituted for category avg.

In this section, Morningstar includes load-adjusted returns and several risk measures and proprietary statistics.
Location: Risk Analysis section.

Morningstar Risk
The Morningstar Risk statistic evaluates the fund's downside volatility relative to that of other funds in its broad asset class (domestic stock, international stock, taxable bond, or municipal bond). Morningstar uses a proprietary risk measure that operates differently from traditional risk measures, such as beta and standard deviation, which see both greater- and less-than-expected returns as added volatility. Morningstar believes that most investors' greatest fear is losing money, defined as underperforming the risk-free rate of return an investor can earn from the 90-day Treasury bill. Thus, our risk measure focuses only on that downside risk.

To calculate the Morningstar Risk score, we plot monthly fund returns in relation to T-bill returns. We add up the amounts by which the fund trails the T-bill return each month and divide that total by the period's total number of months. This number, the average monthly underperformance statistic, is then compared with those of other funds in the same broad asset class to assign our risk scores. The resulting risk score expresses how risky the fund is relative to the average fund in its asset class. The average risk score for the group is set equal to 1.00; a Morningstar Risk score of 1.35 for a taxable-bond fund, for example, means that the fund has been 35% riskier than the average taxable-bond fund for the period considered. Note that Morningstar does not rate any fund that has less than three years of performance data.

Risk % Rank All/Cat
The risk percentile rank column lists the fund's Morningstar Risk rating relative to two groups. In the column headed by All, a fund's risk is ranked against the risk scores for all funds tracked by Morningstar; the Cat column makes the same comparison within the fund's Morningstar Category. The most favorable ranking is 1, and the least favorable is 100.
See also Percentile Rank.

Morningstar Return
The Morningstar Return figure rates a fund's performance relative to other funds in its asset class. After adjusting for maximum front-end loads, applicable deferred loads, and applicable redemption fees, Morningstar calculates the excess return for each fund, defined as the fund's load-adjusted return minus the return for 90-day T-bills over the same period. The use of excess instead of raw returns reflects our belief that mutual funds should be rated highly for only those returns earned beyond those of a T-bill, which is essentially a risk-free investment. The excess returns are then compared with the higher of the average excess return of the fund's broad asset class (domestic stock, international stock, taxable bond, or municipal bond) or the 90-day T-bill return. This last adjustment prevents distortions caused by having low or negative average excess returns in the equation's denominator, as might occur during a protracted down market. The equation is:

$$\frac{\text{Return on Fund}^{*} - \text{T-bill}}{\text{Higher of (Asset Class Average}^{*} - \text{T-bill) or T-bill}}$$

* Fund returns are adjusted for loads. Asset class average is based on load-adjusted returns.

The resulting figure is the fund's Morningstar Return. A footnote indicates when the T-bill comparison is used. If the Morningstar Return figure is compared with the broad investment class, 1.00 represents the asset-class average. An international-stock fund that has a Morningstar Return figure of 1.10, for example, means that the fund outperformed the international-stock average by 10 percent, while 0.90 means that the fund underperformed by 10 percent. For T-bill comparisons, the same concept is true, but 1.00 occurs when a fund's load-adjusted excess return equals the T-bill. Therefore, a score of 0.90 with a T-bill footnote indicates that the fund's excess return has been 10% lower than the T-bill. In periods of low returns, a fund's raw returns could hypothetically underperform T-bill returns, in which case the figure would be a negative number, such as -0.35, meaning that fund's raw returns were 35% less than the T-bill's.

Morningstar Risk-Adjusted Rating
The Morningstar Risk-Adjusted Rating, commonly called the star rating, brings both returns and risk together into one evaluation. To determine a fund's star rating for a given period (three, five, or 10 years), the fund's Morningstar Risk score is subtracted from its Morningstar Return score. The resulting number is plotted along a bell curve to determine the fund's rating for each time period: If the fund scores in the top 10% of its broad asset class (domestic stock, international stock, taxable bond, or municipal bond), it receives 5 stars (High); if it falls in the next 22.5%, it receives 4 stars (Above Average); a place in the middle 35% earns it 3 stars (Neutral or Average); those in the next 22.5% receive 2 stars (Below Average); and the bottom 10% get 1 star (Low). The star ratings are recalculated monthly.
See also Historical Profile.

Average Historical Rating
The fund's average historical rating is simply the mean of the fund's Morningstar Risk-Adjusted Ratings (as they appear in the Historical Profile) for all of the months in which a fund received a rating. This statistic provides a broader context in which to evaluate a fund's current rating. A 5-star fund that also posts an average historical rating between 4 and 5 stars has consistently been highly rated in Morningstar's system. Alternatively, a 5-star fund that carries an average historical rating of only 3.2 stars has likely fluctuated among various star ratings over the time it has been rated.

To a certain extent, this statistic also reflects fund performance in time periods that may have temporarily fallen out of consideration for the current star rating. Funds that are more than five but less than 10 years old, for example, have only their most-recent five-year performance in the overall star rating. That portion of its history beyond five years will not re-enter the equation until the fund is 10 years old, because the overall star rating is a weighted average of the fund's three-, five-, and 10-year histories.

The average historical rating is followed by the number of months for which the fund has been rated. This statistic provides additional context for the star rating. If, for example, a fund with a 5.0 average star rating has been rated for only six months, the conclusions an investor can draw about the fund's resilience in various market climates are limited. On the other hand, an investor can be fairly confident that a 4-star fund with a 3.6 average rating over 90 months historically has been able to manage risk effectively in a variety of markets.

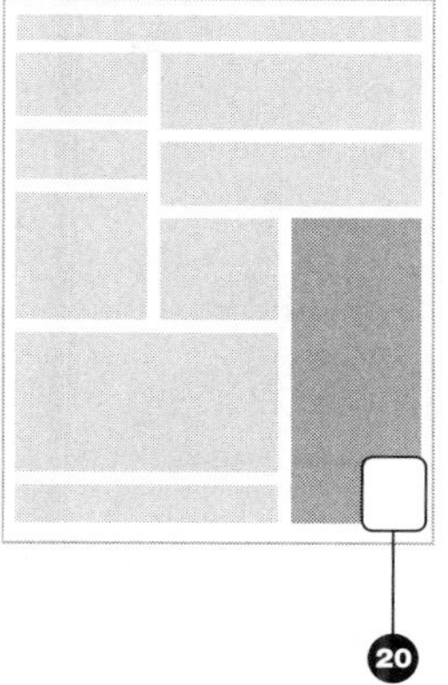

20

Risk % Rank
see Risk Analysis

R-squared
see Modern Portfolio Theory Statistics

S

Sales Fees
see Expenses and Fees

Sector Analysis
This table indicates the percentage of bond assets held in various types of bonds, including Treasuries, mortgage pass-throughs, adjustable-rate mortgages, and collateralized mortgage obligations. Because the government-bond market has become a virtual alphabet soup of acronyms, we've listed some definitions below.
Location: Portfolio Analysis section of bond pages.

ARMs
These adjustable-rate mortgage bonds are backed by loans that reset periodically based on movements in market interest rates.

CMOs (collateralized mortgage obligations)
These derivative securities are created by chopping up mortgage pass-throughs or whole loans into various slices to redistribute the cash flows (both principal and interest payments) from the underlying bonds. The CMO category found on all government-bond pages except the adjustable-rate mortgage funds includes PACs (planned amortization class bonds), floating- and inverse floating-rate CMOs, and accrual or Z-tranche bonds, among other varieties.

FHLMC mortgages
These are mortgage pass-through securities issued by the Federal Home Loan Mortgage Corporation. Like FNMA issues, FHLMC pass-throughs are implicitly, but not explicitly, guaranteed by the U.S. Government.

FNMA mortgages
These are mortgage pass-through securities issued by the Federal National Mortgage Association. FNMA mortgage pass-throughs are implicitly, but not explicitly, backed by the U.S. government.

GNMA mortgages
These are mortgage pass-through securities issued by the Government National Mortgage Association. These bonds are backed by the full faith and credit of the U.S. government.

Other
This category includes holdings that don't fall into one of the six major categories (U.S. Treasuries, GNMA, FNMA, or FHLMC mortgages, CMOs, or ARMs). Typically, corporates and agency debentures compose the holdings in Other. The latter are bonds issued by FNMA and FHLMC to finance their activities and are not backed by pools of mortgages. For ARM funds, Other includes primarily U.S. Treasuries.

US Treasuries
This category includes any bond or note issued by the U.S. Treasury.

20 Sector Weightings
see also Subsector Weightings

Sector Weightings	% of Stocks	Rel S&P	5-Year High	Low
Utilities	0.7	0.2	6	0
Energy	3.1	0.4	15	0
Financials	9.5	0.6	23	0
Industrials	9.2	0.7	49	6
Durables	1.4	0.5	7	0
Staples	3.6	0.4	20	3
Services	18.2	1.3	26	3
Retail	7.9	1.2	17	0
Health	15.8	1.3	30	8
Technology	30.7	2.0	31	0

Sector weightings are calculated for all stock and municipal-bond funds based on the securities in the fund's most recent portfolio. For domestic-stock funds, this statistic shows the percentage of the fund's stock assets invested in each of 10 major industry classifications (% of stocks) and how this weighting compares with the S&P 500 index's current weighting of the same sector (Rel S&P 500). For municipal-bond funds and international-stock funds, we compare the portfolio average with other funds in the same category (Rel Cat), not with the S&P 500. The weightings of the S&P 500 and the category are always set equal to 1.00. For example, a large-value fund with a financials weighting of 1.50 relative to its category has 50% more financials issues than its average peer.

For domestic- and international-stock funds, the table shows the high and low weightings for each sector as a percentage of the fund's stock holdings over the past five years (5-Year High/Low). These figures will provide a glimpse of how the fund's sector exposure has changed over time and where its current weightings land historically. Funds without a five-year history will have no information displayed in this section. Sector weightings appear only if 25% or more of a fund's holdings can be categorized into sectors.

Sector weighting statistics are useful because they reveal the areas a fund is favoring and the areas it's avoiding. Sector weightings are also a valuable tool for explaining why certain funds have bettered the market while others have lagged behind.

Because the individual funds may vary in how they categorize a particular security, Morningstar calculates the sector weightings in-house, using uniform categorizations that allow an investor to make meaningful sector-weighting comparisons between funds. Sectors are listed on the page beginning with the value-based, lowest-risk sectors and progressing to those sectors that typically have the highest growth rates and the most volatility.

Location: Portfolio Analysis section of stock and municipal-bond pages.

The sectors with their major inclusive industries are as follows:

Utilities
Mostly the basic gas and electric utilities firms.

Energy
The bulk of this sector is oil and gas services: drillers, refiners, distributors, pipelines, gas stations.

Financials
Not just banks, thrifts, and insurance. Also currency exchanges, high-interest lenders, brokers, accountants, REITS, and money managers.

Industrials
Stuff to make other stuff: textiles, lumber, paper, chemicals, stone, precious metals, industrial machinery, airplanes, trucks. Also, construction and contracting. They're called cyclical because they're sensitive to the ups and downs of the economy.

Consumer Durables
Household names. They make appliances, tires, lawn mowers, cars and auto parts, watches, shoes, stereos, furniture. Some apparel makers.

Consumer Staples
Makers of the things most people need to live: food, beverages, detergents, toothpaste, coffee. Also cigarettes.

Services
A grab bag of companies in often very different business environments. Some consumer-oriented subsectors: airlines, media, hotels, and phone companies. Some industrial: environmental service, barges and railroads, and temporary staffing.

Retail
Where you buy consumer staples and consumer durables. Apparel and restaurants, too.

Health
This diverse sector mimics the larger stock universe. There are services (HMOs, hospitals), staples (pharmaceuticals, medical supplies), some retailers (pharmacies), and technology (biotech and medical devices).

Technology
Computer parts, tools that build computer parts, and the computers themselves. Also, cell phones and other high-tech devices, software, Internet services, networking equipment, and various computer services.

Sector weightings are also calculated in-house for municipal-bond funds. Although they are generally listed in order of descending credit risk, the categories are not as neatly divided as the stock sector weightings. General obligation bonds, which garner income from the municipality's tax revenues, are listed first (though some perceive these as risky if the issuing municipality is shaky). Revenue-based municipal-bond sectors follow. Near the bottom of the list are lease-backed and industrial-activity bonds, which are generally considered more risky for investors to hold. Demand notes, however, are unrelated to the other types of municipal bonds and hold little credit risk due to their short durations.

The municipal-bond classifications are as follows:

General Obligation
General obligation bonds, which are repaid from general revenue and borrowings rather than from the revenue of a specific project or facility.

Utilities
Electricity, gas, nuclear power, dams, telephones.

Health
Hospitals, nursing homes, retirement facilities.

Water/Waste
Water, sewers, sanitation, irrigation, drainage.

Housing
Single-family and multi-family housing.

Education
Colleges and universities, independent and unified school districts, student loans, tuition.

Transportation
Transportation by air, water, road, or railroad.

COP/Lease
Certificates of participation and lease bonds, used to finance a variety of public endeavors.

Industrial
Economic and industrial development, pollution control, resource recovery, conventions, expositions, stadiums, hotels (typically backed by a business or corporation rather than by a municipality).

Misc Revenue
Miscellaneous revenue bonds.

Demand
Short-term municipal securities.

SEC Yield

see also Yield

SEC yield is a standardized figure that the Securities and Exchange Commission requires funds to use to calculate rates of income return on a fund's capital investment.

SEC yield is an annualized calculation that is based on a trailing 30-day period. This figure will often differ significantly from Morningstar's other yield figure, which reflects trailing 12-month distributed yield, because of differing time periods as well as differing accounting policies. For example, sec yield is based on a bond's yield to maturity, which takes into account amortization of premiums and discounts, while Morningstar's distributed yield is based on what funds actually pay out.

Location: Banner section.

Share Change

see Portfolio Analysis

Sharpe Ratio

The Sharpe ratio is a risk-adjusted measure developed by Nobel Laureate William Sharpe. It is calculated using standard deviation and excess return to determine reward per unit of risk. First, the average monthly return of the 90-day Treasury bill (over a 36-month period) is subtracted from the fund's average monthly return. The difference in total return represents the fund's excess return beyond that of the 90-day Treasury bill, a risk-free investment. An arithmetic annualized excess return is then calculated by multiplying this monthly return by 12. To show a relationship between excess return and risk, this number is then divided by the standard deviation of the fund's annualized excess returns. The higher the Sharpe ratio, the better the fund's historical risk-adjusted performance.

Location: Risk Analysis section.

Short Sales

Short sales are bets that a stock will fall. To sell short, a mutual fund borrows shares from one party and then sells them to another on the open market. The fund's managers hope the stock drops, because they would be able to buy the shares back at a lower price and then return them to the lender. The difference between the original price and the price management pays to buy the shares back is the profit or loss. Short sales can slow returns in a rising market, but reduce losses or even produce gains in a falling market. One of the risks of short sales is that the maximum gain is 100%, but potential losses are unlimited.

21 Special Securities

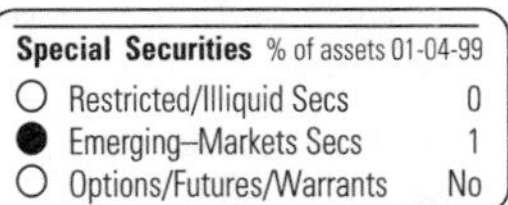

Special Securities % of assets 01-04-99	
○ Restricted/Illiquid Secs	0
● Emerging–Markets Secs	1
○ Options/Futures/Warrants	No

This section shows a fund's exposure to a variety of complex or illiquid securities, including derivatives. If a fund is allowed by charter to hold any of the categories in the special securities box and currently does hold them, a (●) is used. If a fund is allowed to hold such securities, but does not have any as of the date listed, then this is marked with a (○). Finally, a (—) indicates that a fund is prohibited by charter to hold such securities. The percentage of total net assets represented by each type of security is listed to the right of each group. Some securities may fall under more than one type. Information is compiled from the portfolio listed in a fund's most recent prospectus.

Location: Portfolio Analysis section.

Restricted/Illiquid Securities
Restricted and illiquid securities are issues that may be hard to accurately price and difficult to sell because an investor may be unable to find a buyer quickly. Private placement issues and 144(a) securities are both included here. Both types have varying degrees of liquidity and are exempt from some of the cumbersome registration and disclosure requirements that public offerings usually face.

Emerging-Markets Securities
Debt or equity securities from emerging markets are listed here. These figures are calculated from the most recently available portfolio. Anything aside from the following developed markets is considered emerging: Australia, Austria, Belgium, Canada, Denmark, Finland, France, Germany, Ireland, Italy, Japan, the Netherlands, New Zealand, Norway, Singapore, Spain, Sweden, Switzerland, the United Kingdom, and the United States. This list is subject to changes as markets become more developed or vice versa.

Exotic Mortgage-Backed Securities
This section indicates how much of a fund's net assets are held in unusual mortgage-backed derivatives. Specifically, we delineate those securities that see their price changes magnified when interest rates or mortgage-prepayment speeds change. Because not all mortgage-backed derivatives have these traits, we include the following: interest-only (IOs) and principal-only paper (POs), inverse floating-rate securities (IFRNs), and Z-tranche collateralized mortgage obligation issues, all of which are fairly clearly labeled in a fund's shareholder reports. Kitchen-sink bonds, a complex mix of interest-only, principal-only bonds, and cast-off CMO tranches, are also tallied here. For stock funds, which rarely hold mortgage-backed issues of any kind, we combine exotic mortgage-backed securities with structured notes. Municipal-bond funds do not have an exotic mortgage-backed section in the Special Securities box.

Inverse Floaters
These are fixed-income securities that are structured so that their coupons rise as interest rates fall and fall as interest rates rise. The coupon usually floats relative to a short-term index, such as LIBOR (London InterBank Offered Rate). Inverse floaters are derivatives and about twice as sensitive to interest rates as other bonds.

Options/Futures/Warrants
Options and futures may be used speculatively, to leverage a portfolio, or cautiously, as a hedge against risk. We don't show the percentage of assets devoted to options or futures because it is difficult to determine from shareholder reports how much of a portfolio is affected by an options or futures contract. We also include forward contracts and warrants in this area.

Structured Notes
These are derivatives that may be linked to any number of determinants, such as interest rates, commodity prices, foreign exchange rates, or any combination thereof. We exclude the more common types of structured notes, such as Treasury strips, convertible bonds, callable bonds, straight floating-rate notes, or payment-in-kind bonds because these have fairly predictable cash flows. Although some structured notes are highly leveraged, others are designed to reduce risk. Still, we believe investors should be aware of such holdings in a mutual fund.

Standard Deviation
Standard deviation is a statistical measure of the range of a fund's performance. When a fund has a high standard deviation, its range of performance has been very wide, indicating that there is a greater potential for volatility. The standard deviation figure provided here is an annualized statistic based on 36 monthly returns. By definition, approximately 68% of the time, the total returns of any given fund are expected to differ from its mean total return by no more than plus or minus the standard deviation figure. Ninety-five percent of the time, a fund's total returns should be within a range of plus or minus two times the standard deviation from its mean. These ranges assume that a fund's returns fall in a typical bell-shaped distribution. In any case, the greater the standard deviation, the greater the fund's volatility has been.

For example, an investor can compare two funds with the same average monthly return of 5%, but with different standard deviations. The first fund has a standard deviation of 2, which means that its range of returns for the past 36 months has typically remained between 1% and 9%. On the other hand, assume that the second fund has a standard deviation of 4 for the same period. This higher deviation indicates that this fund has experienced returns fluctuating between -3% and 13%. With the second fund, an investor can expect greater volatility.
Location: Risk Analysis section.

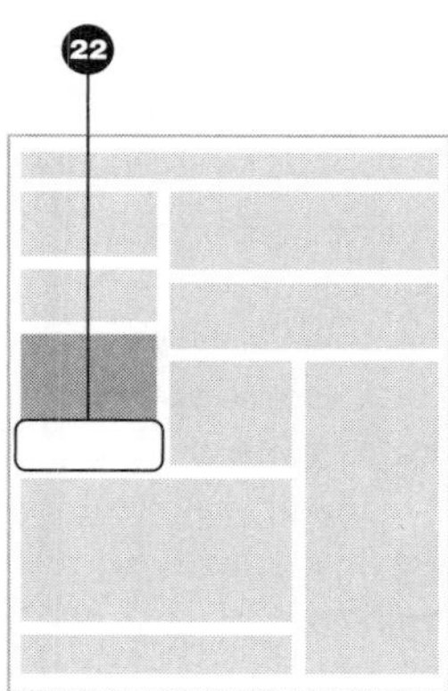

Mean
The mean represents the annualized average monthly return from which the standard deviation is calculated. The mean will be the same as the annualized trailing three-year return figure for the same time period.

Star Rating
see Historical Profile and Risk Analysis

Structured Notes
see Special Securities

Style Box
see Investment Style Box

Subadvisor
In some cases, a fund's advisor employs another company, called a subadvisor, to handle the fund's day-to-day management. If the fund employs a subadvisor, the portfolio manager probably works for the fund's subadvisor, not the fund's advisor.

Systematic Investment $
see Minimum Automatic Investment Plan

T

Tax-Adjusted Return %
see Tax Analysis

22 Tax Analysis

Tax Analysis	Tax-Adj Ret%	%Rank Cat	%Pretax Ret	%Rank Cat
3 Yr Avg	3.31	80	54.8	86
5 Yr Avg	3.47	73	56.1	81
10 Yr Avg	5.85	37	66.5	38
Potential Capital Gain Exposure: 0% of assets				

The information provided in the Tax Analysis section can be used to evaluate a fund's aftertax returns and its efficiency in achieving them. Additionally, the potential capital-gain exposure figure can provide a glimpse at a shareholder's vulnerability to taxation. All these figures can help an investor judge which funds have used tax-friendly strategies. They can also aid in deciding which funds are best suited to tax-deferred accounts and which serve better as taxable investments.
Location: Performance section.

Tax-Adjusted Return
The Tax-Adj Ret % column shows a fund's annualized aftertax total return for the three-, five-, and 10-year periods, excluding any capital-gains effects that would result from selling the fund at the end of the period. To determine this figure, all income and short-term (less than one year) capital-gain distributions are taxed at the maximum federal rate of 39.6% at the time of distribution. Long-term (more than one year) capital gains are taxed at a 20% rate. The aftertax portion is then reinvested in the fund. State and local taxes are ignored, and only the capital gains are adjusted for tax-exempt funds, because the income from these funds is nontaxable.

The category percentile rank (% Rank Cat) for each fund's tax-adjusted return is also listed. This ranking helps investors compare a fund's aftertax performance with other funds' in the category.

Pretax Return
The % Pretax Ret column provides a contrast to tax-adjusted historical return. While the latter measures the bottom-line aftertax results of a fund, without regard to pretax performance, the percentage pretax return statistic measures tax efficiency. This statistic (which excludes additional gains, taxes, or tax losses incurred upon selling the fund) is derived by dividing aftertax returns by pretax returns. The highest possible score would be 100%, which would apply to a fund that had no taxable distributions (such as many municipal-bond funds). It may seem that the lowest possible score would be 100% minus the average tax rate (roughly 60%) supposing all of a fund's total returns were paid out in distributions. But funds that pay out high income at the expense of capital can score even lower, because their taxable income distributions actually exceed total returns.

The category percentile rank (% Rank Cat) for each fund's percentage pretax return is also listed. This ranking helps investors compare a fund's tax efficiency with other funds' within the same category; 1 is the best percentile, 100 the worst.

Potential Capital Gain Exposure
Morningstar calculates potential capital-gain exposure to give investors some idea of the potential tax consequences of their investment in a fund. We cannot predict what a fund's taxable distributions might be, but we can offer some clues based on a fund's liquidation liability. The figure shows whether a fund has consistently distributed taxable gains or has been relatively tax-efficient.

A mutual fund's assets are composed of paid-in (investment) capital, appreciation or depreciation of this capital, and any undistributed net income. Paid-in capital is simply the monies investors have put into the fund (which can decrease should shareholders decide to redeem their shares). Any appreciation of this capital may eventually be taxed. Our potential capital-gain exposure figure shows what percentage of a fund's total assets represent unrealized (or at least undistributed) capital appreciation. Capital appreciation can be either unrealized or realized. In the first case, the fund's holdings have increased in value, but the fund has not yet sold these holdings; taxes are not due until the fund does so. Realized net appreciation (commonly called realized gains) represents actual gains achieved by the sale of holdings; taxes must be paid on these realized capital gains, which the fund must distribute each year if it can't offset them with realized losses. Unrealized appreciation may turn into realized gains at any time, should the fund's management decide to sell the profitable holdings. Thus, our formula includes unrealized appreciation as part of the potential capital gain exposure. A negative potential capital-gain exposure figure means that the fund has greater net losses than it has gains. This likely indicates that the fund has or will have a tax-loss carry forward, which would mean that some amount of future gains could be offset by past losses. To keep our calculation current, we update the information between shareholder reports by accounting for a fund's market losses or gains, the sale or redemption of shares, and the payment of capital gains. This updated figure is not quite as precise as the one stated in the shareholder report, but it is more current and therefore more relevant to the investor.

Telephone Numbers
These are the local and toll-free (if available) numbers that an investor may use to contact the fund, call for a prospectus, or get marketing information.
Location: Operations section.

Three-Year Earnings-Growth %
The three-year earnings-growth rate is a measure of the trailing three-year annualized earnings-growth record of the stocks currently in the fund's portfolio. This number is weighted such that larger positions in the portfolio count proportionately more than lesser positions. Stocks that lack a three-year track record are excluded from this calculation. Growth-oriented managers are more likely than are value managers to pay for stocks with high historical earnings-growth rates.
Location: Portfolio Analysis section of stock pages.

Ticker
A ticker is the symbol assigned to the fund by the Nasdaq system. The ticker is commonly used to locate a fund on electronic price-quoting systems.
Location: Banner section.

Top Five States
We display the five states or U.S. territories in which a municipal-bond fund invests most heavily and the percentage of the portfolio each state or territory represents. This information reflects the holdings of the portfolio on the page.
Location: Portfolio Analysis section of municipal-bond pages.

Total Assets
see also Net Assets
This figure is the total assets of all the fund's share classes at the end of the most recently reported month.
Location: Banner section.

Total Cost
see Expenses and Fees

Total Rtn % Rank Cat
see Percentile Rank and Performance

Total Return
All references to total return represent a fund's gains over a specified period of time. Total return includes both income (in the form of dividends or interest payments) and capital gains or losses (the increase or decrease in the value of a security). Morningstar calculates total return by taking the change in a fund's NAV, assuming the reinvestment of all income and capital-gains distributions (on the actual reinvestment date used by the fund) during the period, and then dividing by the initial NAV.

Unless marked as load-adjusted total returns, Morningstar does not adjust total return for sales charges or for redemption fees. (Morningstar Return and Morningstar Risk-Adjusted Ratings do

incorporate those fees.) Total returns do account for management, administrative, and 12b-1 fees and other costs automatically deducted from fund assets. The quarterly returns, listed in the Performance section, express the fund's return for each individual quarter; the total shown on the right is the compounded return for the four quarters of that year. An asterisk next to the total return number indicates that the return is calculated for a partial quarter or partial year because the fund began operations during that time period.
Location: History and Performance sections.

Total Stocks/Total Fixed-Income
see Portfolio Analysis

Turnover Rate %
The turnover rate provides a rough measure of the fund's level of trading activity. This publicly reported figure is calculated by the funds in accordance with SEC regulations, and Morningstar gathers the information from fund shareholder reports. A fund divides the lesser of purchases or sales (expressed in dollars and excluding all securities with maturities of less than one year) by the fund's average monthly assets. The resulting percentage can be loosely interpreted to represent the percentage of the portfolio's holdings that have changed over the past year. The turnover ratio is most accurate, however, when a fund's asset base remains stable. A low turnover figure (typically less than 30%) might indicate that the manager is following a buy-and-hold strategy. High turnover (more than 100%) could be an indication of an investment strategy involving considerable buying and selling of securities.
Location: History section.

Value $000
see Portfolio Analysis

Value
see also Growth and Investment Style Box
The investment style commonly referred to as a value approach focuses on stocks that an investor or fund manager thinks are currently undervalued in price and will eventually have their worth recognized by the market. It is often contrasted with a growth-style approach to investing.

Web Address
This is the Internet address for the fund company. Investors may go online to find information about their funds or download prospectuses and shareholder reports.
Location: Operations section.

Yield
see also SEC Yield
Yield, expressed as a percentage, represents a fund's income return on capital investment for the past 12 months. This figure refers only to interest distributions from fixed-income securities and dividends from stocks. Monies generated from the sale of securities, from options and futures transactions, and from currency transactions are considered capital gains, not income. Return of capital is also not considered income. NMF (No Meaningful Figure) appears in this space for those funds that do not properly label their distributions. We list N/A if a fund is less than one year old, in which case we cannot calculate yield. Morningstar computes yield by dividing the sum of the fund's income distributions for the past 12 months by the previous month's NAV (adjusted upward for any capital gains distributed over the same period).
Location: Banner section.

Indexes

Thornburg Value A

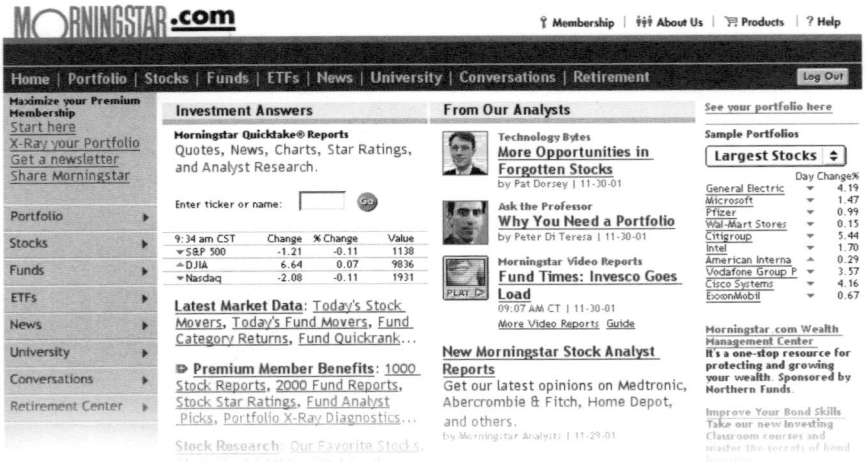